NATIONAL GUIDE TO FUNDING IN HEALTH

NATIONAL GUIDE TO FUNDING IN HEALTH
Third Edition

Edited by
Stan Olson & Ruth Kovacs

Zoe Waldron
Project Coordinator

The Foundation Center

CONTRIBUTING STAFF

Vice President for Publications	Rick Schoff
Director of Information Systems	Margaret Derrickson
Production Assistant	Cheryl L. Loe
Information Control Coordinator	Ted Murphy
Editorial Associates	Dan Havlik Margaret B. Jung Cara J. Letofsky Elizabeth H. Rich
Programmer/Analyst	Virginia Higgins
Database Analyst	M. Lara Brock Steen
Search Analyst	Althea Ashman

The editors gratefully acknowledge the many other Foundation Center staff who contributed support, encouragement, and information which was indispensible to the preparation of this volume. Special mention should be made to the staff members of the New York, Washington, DC, Cleveland, and San Francisco libraries who assisted in tracking changes in foundation information. We would like to express our appreciation as well to the many foundations which cooperated fully in updating information prior to the compilation of this volume.

CONTENTS

INTRODUCTION
Foundation and Corporate Support for Health

In 1991, the more than 33,000 active private and community foundations in America awarded over $9 billion in grants to nonprofit organizations across the country and abroad. Corporate contributions, including company-sponsored foundations and direct corporate giving programs, amounted to approximately $6.1 billion. Although foundation and corporate donations represent but a small fraction or total philanthropic giving in the U.S., they are still a key source of support for many programs.

The *National Guide to Funding in Health* is intended as a starting point for grantseekers looking for foundation and corporate support for medical or health-related organizations. It contains entries for 3,019 grantmaking foundations and 324 direct corporate giving programs that have shown a substantial interest in health-related programs, either as part of their stated purpose or through the actual grants of $10,000 or more reported to the Foundation Center in the latest year of record.[1] Health-related grants are listed for 614 of the foundations in this volume. These 9,315 grants represent over $1 billion in support for a variety of health-related programs, including hospitals, medical research, family planning, nursing and medical education, alcohol and drug abuse, mental health, national health associations, and rehabilitation.

The grantmakers listed in this *Guide* do not represent all the potential foundations or corporate funding sources available to nonprofit groups active in the health field, nor does inclusion in the *Guide* imply that these grantmakers will consider all health-related programs. Some foundations and corporate giving programs support health because of their interest in improving the overall quality of medical care and services in a specific community. Others may do so because the program relates to another highly specific subject interest of the foundation or corporation, such as family planning, drug and alcohol abuse,

or medical research projects for a particular disease or condition. Still others are interested in building the capacity of nonprofit institutions by providing specific types of support such as capital support or challenge grants.

Grantseekers are therefore urged to read each foundation and corporate giving program description carefully to determine the nature of the grantmaker's interests and to note any restrictions on giving that would prevent the foundation from considering their proposal. Readers should also refer to the next section of this introduction, "Researching Foundations and Grantseeking from Corporations," for information on identifying other potential funding sources.

WHAT IS A FOUNDATION?

The Center defines a foundation as a nongovernmental, nonprofit organization with its own funds (usually from a single source, either an individual, family, or corporation) and program managed by its own trustees and directors, which was established to maintain or aid educational, social, charitable, religious, or other activities serving the common welfare, primarily by making grants to other nonprofit organizations. All of the grantmakers in this guide fall into one of five categories:

Independent Foundation: A fund or endowment designated by the Internal Revenue Service as a private foundation under the law, the primary function of which is the making of grants. The assets of most independent foundations are derived from the gift of an individual or family. Some function under the direction of family members and are known as "family foundations." Depending on their range of giving, independent foundations may also be known as "general purpose" or "special purpose" foundations.

Company-Sponsored Foundation: A private foundation under the tax law deriving its funds from a profit-making company or corporation but independently constituted, the purpose of which is to make grants, usually on a broad basis although not without regard for the business interests of the corporation. Company-sponsored founda-

---

[1] In addition, the *Guide* contains an entry describing the Howard Hughes Medical Institute, classified by the IRS as a Medical Research Organization rather than a private foundation. The Hughes Institute closely resembles a private foundation in that it has its own funds from a single source, does not make appeals to the public for donations, and aids charitable purposes through grantmaking in accordance with an IRS payout requirement.

tions, also known as "corporate foundations", are legally distinct from contributions programs administered within the corporation directly from corporate funds.

Direct Corporate Giving: All other giving of a company, that is, money not turned over to a foundation to administer. Direct giving programs are unregulated and restricted only by the limit of taxable earnings allowable as charitable deductions. In addition to cash contributions, corporate giving includes "in- kind," i.e., non-cash, gifts of goods and services. Donations of company products, supplies, and equipment—from computers to food—is the most common form of in-kind giving. Other types of support include staff time, technical assistance, and use of office space. Direct corporate giving programs and company foundations often share the same staff, although some companies keep these functions administratively separate.

Operating Foundation: A fund or endowment designated under the tax law by the Internal Revenue Service as a private operating foundation, the primary purpose of which is to operate research, social welfare, or other programs determined by its governing body or charter. Operating foundations that award grants to outside organizations appear in this *Guide.*

Community Foundation: A publicly supported 501(c)(3) organization that makes grants in a specific community or region. In its general charitable purposes, a community foundation is much like a private foundation; however, its funds are derived from many donors rather than a single source as is usually the case with private foundations. Further, community foundations are usually classified under the tax law as public charities and are therefore subject to different rules and regulations than those which govern private foundations.

There are a number of other types of organizations that use the word "foundation" in their names but do not operate, and are not classified under tax laws, as private foundations. These groups are often nonprofit organizations that raise funds from the public to support research or education, operate various institutions, or maintain a host of other charitable activities. Some government agencies use the name "foundation" (such as the National Science Foundation), but their operating funds are drawn from tax dollars rather than private endowments. An increasing number of for-profit businesses have also adopted the name "foundation" to promote their activities. While there are no legal restrictions on the use of the word "foundation," it is important for grantseekers to understand that many of these groups do not make grants and are not governed by the same rules and regulations as private foundations are.

SOURCES OF INFORMATION

Foundation Center publications examine giving interests in two broad ways: what the grantmaker states as its purpose and what can be observed from a listing of its actual grants. In preparing the third edition of the *National Guide to Funding in Health*, we drew on three important tools to identify grantmakers with a specific interest in health and those that make contributions for health-related projects as part of a broader giving program:

1. *The Foundation Directory* provides descriptions of the nation's largest foundations (those with assets of $2 million or more or annual giving of at least $200,000). The statements of purpose for each foundation listed in the *Directory* are drawn from the descriptions provided by foundations in their annual reports, informational brochures or other publications, responses to our annual questionnaire mailings, and a broad analysis of the foundation's grantmaking program over the last three years. Although some of these statements provide very specific information about the foundation's giving interests, many were developed to last for substantial time periods and left purposely broad to allow for future shifts in emphasis.

2. The *National Directory of Corporate Giving* is the source of information on corporate grantmakers. The second edition of this directory, published in 1991, profiles 1,791 companies making contributions to nonprofit organizations. It includes entries describing 598 direct corporate giving programs and 1,494 corporate foundations. The most comprehensive directory on corporate giving available, it lists only corporations that provided information to the Center or for which public documents on giving were available.

3. The Center's *Grants Index* database, which records the actual grants of $10,000 and over reported to the Center by approximately 850 major foundations, provides a more detailed picture of foundation giving interests. Each grant record includes the name and location of the organization receiving the grant, the amount of money awarded, and a brief description of the purpose for which the grant was made. Center staff analyze and index each grant by subject focus, type of organization receiving the grant, the type of support provided, and the special population group, if any, to be served by the program.

These three sources provide all the information on foundations, corporate giving, and grants included in this *Guide.*

Researching Foundations and Grantseeking from Corporations

RESEARCHING FOUNDATIONS

Foundations receive many thousands of worthy requests each year. Most of these requests are declined because there are not enough funds to go around or because the application clearly falls outside the foundation's fields of interest. Some of the applications denied are poorly prepared and do not reflect a careful analysis of the applicant organization's needs, its credibility, or its capacity to carry out the proposed project. Sometimes the qualifications of the organization's staff are not well established. The budget or the means of evaluating the project may not be presented convincingly. The organization may not have asked itself if it is especially suited to make a contribution to the solution of the problem or to provide the service proposed or if others are not already effectively engaged in the same activity.

The first step in researching foundation funding support is to analyze your own program and organization to determine the need you plan to address, the audience you will serve, and the amount and type of support you need. Become familiar with the basic facts about foundations in general and how they operate. Consider other sources of funding, such as individual contributors, government grants, earned income possibilities, and so on. Although foundations are an important source of support for non-profit organizations, their giving represents a relatively small percentage of the total philanthropic dollars contributed annually, and an even smaller percentage of the total when government grants and earned income are included. If you are new to grantseeking, we strongly urge you to visit one of the Foundation Center's many cooperating libraries. They provide free access to all Foundation Center publications, as well as other materials on funding sources, program planning, and fundraising.

Once you have determined the amount and type of support you need and the reasons why you are seeking foundation support, this Guide can help you to develop an initial list of foundations that might be interested in funding your project. In determining whether or not it is appropriate to approach a particular foundation with a grant request, keep in mind the following questions:

1. Does the foundation's interest in health include the specific type of service or program you are proposing?
2. Does it seem likely that the foundation will make a grant in your geographic area?
3. Does the amount of money you are requesting fit within the foundation's grant range?
4. Does the foundation have any policy prohibiting grants for the type of support you are requesting?
5. Does the foundation prefer to make grants that cover the full cost of a project or do they favor projects where other foundations or funding sources share the cost?
6. What types of organizations does the foundation tend to support?
7. Does the foundation have specific application deadlines and procedures or does it review proposals continuously?

Some of these questions can be answered from the information provided in this Guide, but grantseekers will almost always want to consult a few additional resources before submitting a request for funding. If the foundation issues an annual report, application guidelines, or other printed materials describing its program, it is advisable to obtain copies and study them carefully before preparing your proposal. The foundation's annual information return (Form 990-PF) includes a list of all grants paid by the foundation, as well as basic data about its finances, officers, and giving policies. Copies of these returns are available for examination at most of the Foundation Center's cooperating libraries.

DON'T STOP HERE

The foundations listed in this Guide by no means represent all of the possible foundation funding sources for programs related to health. There are a number of foundations, including over 250 community foundations across the country that support a wide variety of programs within a specific community or region. Grantseekers should learn as much as possible about the foundations in their own area, particularly when they are seeking relatively small grants of funds for projects with purely local impact. Be sure to check any local or state directories of which the Foundation Center is currently aware. Copies of these directories are almost always available for use at the local Foundation Center cooperating library.

The Foundation Center publishes annually several national directories. *The Foundation Directory* describes foundations with assets of $2 million or more or annual giving of at least $200,000. *The Foundation Directory Part 2* provides information on the second tier of foundations, those with assets of less than $2 million and annual grant-making between $50,000 and $200,000. *Directory Part 2* entries also include a list of sample grants whenever available, to provide a concrete indication of a foundation's giving interests. The *Directory* and *Directory Part 2* are arranged by state and include a geographic index to help you identify foundations located or interested in your specific community. The Foundation Center also publishes the *Guide to U.S. Foundations and Their Trustees, Officers and Donors*, which provides basic address and financial information on all of the over 33,000 active grantmaking foundations in the United States. The *Guide to U.S. Foundations* is arranged alphabetically by state, and within states foundations are listed in descending order by annual giving amount.

For those who wish more detailed information on how to identify appropriate foundation funding sources, the Center has also published the basic guidebook, *Foundation Fundamentals*. This guide takes you step-by-step through the research process developed and taught by the Foundation Center and describes how to gather the facts you need to best approach those foundations for funding. All Foundation Center publications are available for free use at Foundation Center libraries.

We hope this *Guide* will help to begin a successful search for funds to support your programs, and we welcome your comments for future editions.

GRANTSEEKING FROM CORPORATIONS

The research process for corporate funding is similar to other institutional grantseeking: identifying companies that might be interested in the organization's mission and program, learning as much as possible about those companies, determining the best method of approach, and articulating program objectives so as to be in line with the company's giving rationale. It is different from research on other institutional funders, however, in that it is often more difficult to uncover the needed information. There is great diversity in methods and style of giving among corporations and companies are often looking for a quid pro quo for their giving. Corporate philanthropy is often called an oxymoron because many corporations see their giving not as altruism but a responsibility or good business. Soliciting support from corporations, therefore, often requires a shift in perspective from appealing to benevolence to promoting a company's self-interest.

Identifying companies to approach is accomplished in several ways. Directories, such as the *National Directory of Corporate Giving*, describe companies with known corporate giving programs. These guides help identify companies' subject interests, geographical giving, or benefits the company hopes to derive that match a nonprofit organization's program goals. General business directories aid in the search, as do the books and guides listed in the bibliography. Staff members, your organization's board, and volunteers often know or work for companies that may ultimately be able to provide funds. The telephone book is another good resource for tracking down local businesses.

After a list of likely prospects is compiled, efforts should continue to locate more information about the company, its primary and secondary business activities, its officers, giving history, and any details helpful in understanding the company's giving rationale. Understanding why a company gives is essential because it may point to a match of the grantseeker's programmatic goals and the corporation's giving goals. Although determining the specific reasons a company makes contributions can be difficult, it can be accomplished through careful research, including studying the annual reports and materials of other organizations the company has supported, and by speaking directly with company officials whenever possible.

This research usually indicates the best method of approaching a company with a request for support. Companies with formal giving programs may have guidelines and application procedures and require a written proposal, while companies with informal giving programs may be better approached through personal contacts made by board members or volunteers. Once the approach is determined, however, a written or oral presentation should be prepared which articulates how the organization's programs fit into the company's giving rationale.

Ultimately, the more you know about a company the better the chance of obtaining support. A company should not be approached without some knowledge of its business activities or past giving history as that may jeopardize your chances of receiving funding. This does not mean that companies without a record of grantmaking should not be approached. Creative fundraisers have found ways of encouraging companies of all sizes, from small businesses to large corporations, to assist in their activities. Success in acquiring such support, however, is usually the result of good research and good contacts. The job of the corporate fundraiser is to be imaginative and thorough, calling on all the knowledge, people, and ideas available. It means learning where to ask, how to ask, and what to ask for.

HOW TO USE *THE NATIONAL GUIDE TO FUNDING IN HEALTH*

When using the *Guide* to identify potential funding sources, grantseekers are urged to read each foundation description carefully to determine the nature of the grant-maker's interests and to note any restrictions on giving that would prevent the foundation from considering their proposal. Many foundations limit their giving to a particular subject field or geographic area; others are unable to provide certain types of support, such as funds for buildings and equipment or for general operating budgets. Even when a foundation has not provided an explicit limitations statement, restrictions on giving may exist. This is often the case with entries updated from public records. Further research into the giving patterns of these foundations is necessary before applying for funds.

ARRANGEMENT

The *Guide* is arranged alphabetically by state and, within states, by foundation name. Each descriptive entry is assigned a sequence number, and references in the indexes are to these entry numbers.

WHAT'S IN AN ENTRY?

There are 32 basic data elements that could be included in a descriptive entry. The content of entries varies widely due to differences in the size and nature of foundation programs and the availability of information from foundations. Specific data elements that could be included are:

1. The full legal **name of the foundation.**
2. The **former name** of the foundation.
3. **Street address, city, and zip code** of the foundation's principal office.
4. **Telephone number** of the foundation.
5. Any **additional address** (such as a separate application address) supplied by the foundation.
6. **Establishment data,** including the legal form (usually a trust or corporation) and the year and state in which the foundation was established.
7. The **donor(s)** or principal contributor(s) to the foundation, including individuals, families, and corporations. If a donor is deceased, the symbol ‡ follows the name.
8. **Foundation type:** community, company-sponsored, independent, or operating.
9. The **year-end date** of the foundation's accounting period for which financial data is supplied.
10. **Assets:** the total value of the foundation's investments at the end of the accounting period. In a few instances, foundations that act as "pass-throughs" for annual corporate or individual gifts report zero assets.
11. **Asset type:** generally, assets are reported at market value (M) or ledger value (L).
12. **Gifts received:** the total amount of new capital received by the foundation in the year of record.
13. The total amount of **qualifying distributions** made by the foundation in the year of record. This figure includes all grants paid, qualifying administrative expenses, loans and program-related investments, set-asides, and amounts paid to acquire assets used directly in carrying out charitable purposes.
14. **Expenditures:** total disbursements of the foundation, including overhead expenses (salaries; investment, legal, and other professional fees; interest; rent; etc.) and federal excise taxes, as well as the total amount paid for grants, scholarships, and matching gifts.
15. The dollar value and number of **grants paid** during the year, with the largest grant paid **(high)** and smallest grant paid **(low)**. When supplied by the foundation, the average range of grant payments is also indicated. Grant figures do not include commitments for future payment or amounts spent for grants to individuals, employee matching gifts, loans, or foundation-administered programs.
16. The total dollar value of **set-asides** made by the foundation during the year. Set-asides count as qualifying distributions toward the foundation's annual payout requirement, but they are distinct from any amounts listed as grants paid.

17. The total amount and number of **grants made directly to or on behalf of individuals,** including scholarships, fellowships, awards, and medical payments. When supplied by the foundation, high, low, and average range are also indicated.

18. The dollar amount and number of **employee matching gifts** awarded, generally by company-sponsored foundations.

19. The total dollars expended for **programs administered by the foundation** and the number of foundation-administered programs. These programs can include museums or other institutions supported exclusively by the foundation, research programs administered by the foundation, etc.

20 The dollar amount and number of **loans** or **program-related investments** made to nonprofit organizations by the foundation. When supplied by the foundation, high, low, and average range are also indicated.

21. The number of **loans to individuals** and the total amount loaned. When supplied by the foundation, high, low, and average range are also indicated.

22. The monetary value and number of **in-kind gifts.**

23. The **purpose and activities,** in general terms, of the foundation. This statement reflects funding interests as expressed by the foundation or, if no foundation statement is available, an analysis of the actual grants awarded by the foundation during the most recent two-year period for which public records exist.

24. The primary **fields of interest** reflected in the foundation's giving program.

25. The **types of support** (such as endowment funds, support for buildings and equipment, fellowships, etc.) offered by the foundation. Definitions of the terms used to describe the forms of support available are provided at the beginning of the Types of Support Index at the back of this volume.

26. Any stated **limitations** on the foundation's giving program, including geographic preferences, restrictions by subject focus or type of recipient, and specific types of support the foundation cannot provide.

27. **Publications** or other printed materials distributed by the foundation which describe its activities and giving program. These can include annual or multi-year reports, newsletters, corporate giving reports, informational brochures, grant lists, etc. It is also noted if a foundation will send copies of its IRS information return (Form 990-PF) on request.

28. **Application information,** including the name of the contact person, the preferred form of application, the number of copies of proposals requested, application deadlines, frequency and dates of board meetings, and the general amount of time the foundation requires to notify applicants of the board's

decision. Some foundations have indicated that applications are not accepted or that their funds are currently committed to ongoing projects.

29. The names and titles of **officers, principal administrators, trustees, or directors,** and members of other governing bodies. An asterisk following the individual's name indicates an officer who is also a trustee or director.

30. The number of professional and support **staff** employed by the foundation, and an indication of part-time or full-time status of these employees, as reported by the foundation.

31. **EIN:** the Employer Identification Number assigned to the foundation by the Internal Revenue Service for tax purposes. This number can be useful when ordering microfilm or paper copies of the foundation's annual information return, Form 990-PF.

32. **Recent health grants** lists grants awarded in 1990-1991. Entries include the name and location of the recipient, the grant amount and year awarded and, where available, text which describes the purpose of the grant.

INDEXES

Six indexes to the descriptive entries are provided at the back of the book to assist grantseekers and other users of this *Guide:*

1. The **Index to Donors, Officers, Trustees** is an alphabetical list of individual and corporate donors, officers, and members of governing boards whose names appear in the descriptive entries. Many grantseekers find this index helpful to learn whether current or prospective members of their own governing boards, alumni of their schools, or current contributors are affiliated with any foundations.

2. The **Geographic Index** references foundation entries by the state and city in which the foundation maintains its principal offices. The index includes "see-also" references at the end of each state section to indicate foundations that have made substantial grants in that state but are located elsewhere. Foundations that award grants on a national, regional, or international basis are indicated in bold type. The remaining foundations generally limit their giving to the state or city in which they are located.

3. The **Types of Support Index** provides access to foundation entries by the specific types of support the foundation awards. A glossary of the forms of support listed appears at the beginning of the index. Under each type of support term, entry numbers are listed by the state location and abbreviated name of the foundation. Foundations that award grants on a

national, regional, or international basis are indicated in bold type. When using this index, grantseekers should focus on foundations located in their own state that offer the specific type of support needed, or on foundations listed in bold type if their program has national impact.

4. The **Index to Foundations and Corporate Giving Programs by Subject** allows users to identify foundations by their broad giving interests. A list of subject terms is provided at the beginning of the index. As in the Types of Support Index, entry references are arranged under each term by the state in which the foundation is located, and foundations that award grants on a national, regional, or international basis are indicated in bold type. Again,

grantseekers should focus on foundations located in their own state that have indicated an interest in their subject field, as well as foundations listed in bold type that are located in other states.

5. The **Index to Grants by Subject** provides access to the individual grants included in this *Guide*. For each subject term, grants are listed first by foundation entry number, then by grant number within the foundation entry.

6. The **Index of Foundations and Corporate Giving Programs** is an alphabetical list of all foundations and giving programs appearing in this *Guide*. Former names of foundations appear with "see" references to the appropriate entry numbers.

GLOSSARY

The following list includes important terms used by grant-makers and grantseekers. A number of sources have been consulted in compiling this glossary, including *The Handbook on Private Foundations,* by David F. Freeman and the Council on Foundations (New York: The Foundation Center, 1991); *The Law of Tax-Exempt Organizations,* 6th Edition, by Bruce R. Hopkins (New York: John Wiley & Sons, 1992); and the *Glossary of Fund-Raising Terms,* (Alexandria, Va.: National Society of Fund Raising Executives Institute, 1986).

Annual Report: A *voluntary* report issued by a foundation or corporation which provides financial data and descriptions of grantmaking activities. Annual reports vary in format from simple typewritten documents listing the year's grants to detailed publications which provide substantial information about the grantmaking program.

Assets: The amount of capital or principal—money, stocks, bonds, real estate, or other resources of the foundation or corporate giving program. Generally, assets are invested and the income is used to make grants.

Beneficiary: In philanthropic terms, the donee or grantee receiving funds from a foundation or corporate giving program is the beneficiary, though society benefits as well. Foundations whose legal terms of establishment restrict their giving to one or more named beneficiaries are not included in this *Guide.*

Bricks and Mortar: An informal term for grants for buildings or construction projects.

Capital Support: Funds provided for endowment purposes, buildings, construction, or equipment and including, for example, grants for "bricks and mortar."

Challenge Grant: A grant awarded that will be paid only if the donee organization is able to raise additional funds from another source(s). Challenge grants are often used to stimulate giving from other donors. (*See also* **Matching Grant**)

Community Foundation: A 501(c)(3) organization which makes grants for charitable purposes in a specific community or region. Funds are usually derived from many donors and held in an endowment independently administered; income earned by the endowment is then used to make grants. Although a few community foundations may be classified by the IRS as private foundations, most are classified as public charities eligible for maximum income tax-deductible contributions from the general public. (*See also* **501(c)(3); Public Charity**)

Community Fund: An organized community program which makes annual appeals to the general public for funds which are usually not retained in an endowment but are used for the ongoing operational support of local social and health service agencies. (*See also* **Federated Giving Program**)

Company-Sponsored Foundation (also referred to as Corporate Foundation): A private foundation whose grant funds are derived primarily from the contributions of a profit-making business organization. The company-sponsored foundation may maintain close ties with the donor company, but it is an independent organization with its own endowment and is subject to the same rules and regulations as other private foundations. (*See also* **Private Foundation**)

Cooperative Venture: A joint effort between or among two or more grantmakers (including foundations, corporations, and government agencies). Partners may share in funding responsibilities or contribute information and technical resources.

Corporate Giving Program: A grantmaking program established and administered within a profit-making company. Corporate giving programs do not have a separate endowment and their annual grant totals are generally more directly related to current profits. They are not subject to the same reporting requirements as private foundations. Some companies make charitable contributions through both a corporate giving program and a company-sponsored foundation.

Distribution Committee: The board responsible for making grant decisions. For community foundations, it is intended to be broadly representative of the community served by the foundation.

Donee: The recipient of a grant. (Also known as the grantee or the beneficiary.)

Donor: The individual or organization which makes a grant or contribution. (Also known as the grantor.)

Employee Matching Gift: A contribution to a charitable organization by a company employee which is matched by a similar contribution from the employer. Many corporations have employee matching gift programs in higher education that stimulate their employees to give to the college or university of their choice.

Endowment: Funds intended to be kept permanently and invested to provide income for continued support of an organization.

Expenditure Responsibility: In general, when a private foundation makes a grant to an organization which is not classified by the IRS as a "public charity," the foundation is required by law to provide some assurance that the funds will be used for the intended charitable purposes. Special reports on such grants must be filed with the IRS. Most grantee organizations are public charities and many foundations do not make "expenditure responsibility" grants.

Family Foundation: An independent private foundation whose funds are derived from members of a single family. Family members often serve as officers or board members of the foundation and have a significant role in grantmaking decisions. (*See also* **Operating Foundation; Private Foundation; Public Charity**)

Federated Giving Program: A joint fundraising effort usually administered by a nonprofit "umbrella" organization which in turn distributes contributed funds to several nonprofit agencies. United Way and community chests or funds, United Jewish Appeal and other religious appeals, the United Negro College Fund, and joint arts councils are examples of federated giving programs. (*See also* **Community Fund**)

501(c)(3): The section of the Internal Revenue Code which defines nonprofit, charitable (as broadly defined), tax-exempt organizations. 501(c)(3) organizations are further defined as public charities, private operating foundations, and private non-operating foundations. (*See also* **Operating Foundation; Private Foundation; Public Charity**)

Form 990-PF: The annual information return that all private foundations must submit to the IRS each year and which is also filed with appropriate state officials. The form requires information on the foundation's assets, income, operating expenses, contributions and grants, paid staff and salaries, program funding areas, grantmaking guidelines and restrictions, and grant application procedures. Foundation Center libraries maintain files of 990-PFs for public inspection.

General Purpose Foundation: An independent private foundation which awards grants in many different fields of interest. (*See also* **Special Purpose Foundation**)

General Purpose Grant: A grant made to further the general purpose or work of an organization, rather than for a specific purpose or project. (*See also* **Operating Support Grant**)

Grantee Financial Report: A report detailing how grant funds were used by an organization. Many corporations require this kind of report from grantees. A financial report generally includes a listing of all expenditures from grant funds as well as an overall organizational financial report covering revenue and expenses, assets and liabilities.

Grassroots Fundraising: Efforts to raise money from individuals or groups from the local community on a broad basis. Usually an organization's own constituents—people who live in the neighborhood served or clients of the agency's services—are the sources of these funds. Grassroots fundraising activities include membership drives, raffles, auctions, benefits, and a range of other activities.

Independent Foundation: A grantmaking organization usually classified by the IRS as a private foundation. Independent foundations may also be known as family foundations, general purpose foundations, special purpose foundations, or private non-operating foundations. The Foundation Center defines independent foundations and company-sponsored foundations separately; however, federal law normally classifies both as private, non-operating foundations subject to the same rules and requirements. (*See also* **Private Foundation**)

In-Kind Contributions: Contributions of equipment, supplies, or other property as distinguished from monetary grants. Some organizations may also donate space or staff time as an in-kind contribution.

Matching Grant: A grant which is made to match funds provided by another donor. (*See also* **Challenge Grant; Employee Matching Gift**)

Operating Foundation: A 501(C)(3) organization classified by the IRS as a private foundation whose primary purpose is to conduct research, social welfare, or other programs determined by its governing body or establishment charter. Some grants may be made, but the sum is generally small relative to the funds used for the foundation's own programs. (*See also* **501(c)(3)**)

Operating Support Grant: A grant to cover the regular personnel, administrative, and other expenses of an existing program or project. (*See also* **General Purpose Grant**)

Payout Requirement: The minimum amount that private foundations are required to expend for charitable purposes (includes grants and, within certain limits, the administrative cost of making grants). In general, a private foundation must meet or exceed and annual payout requirement of five percent of the average market value of the foundation's assets.

Private Foundation: A nongovernmental, nonprofit organization with funds (usually from a single source, such as an individual, family, or corporation) and program managed by its own trustees or directors which was established to maintain or aid social, educational, religious or other charitable activities serving the common welfare, primarily through the making of grants. "Private foundation" also means an organization that is tax-exempt under Code section 501(C)(3) and is classified by the IRS as a private foundation as defined in the code. The code definition usually, but not always, identifies a foundation with the characteristics first described. (See also **501(c)(3); Public Charity**)

Program Amount: Funds which are expended to support a particular program administered internally by the foundation or corporate giving program.

Program Officer: A staff member of a foundation who reviews grant proposals and processes applications for the board of trustees. Only a small percentage of foundations have program officers.

Program-Related Investment (PRI): A loan or other investment (as distinguished from a grant) made by a foundation or corporate giving program to another organization for a project related to the grantmaker's stated charitable purpose and interests. Program-related investments are often made from a revolving fund; the foundation generally expects to receive its money back with interest or some other form of return at less than current market rates, which becomes available for further program-related investments.

Proposal: A written application often with supporting documents submitted to a foundation or corporate giving program in requesting a grant. Preferred procedures and formats vary. Consult published guidelines.

Public Charity: In general, an organization which is tax-exempt under Code section 501(C)(3) and is classified by the IRS as a public charity and not a private foundation. Public charities generally derive their funding or support primarily from the general public in carrying out their social, educational, religious, or other charitable activities serving the common welfare. Some public charities engage in grantmaking activities, though most engage in direct service or other tax-exempt activities. Public charities are eligible for maximum income tax-deductible contributions from the public and are not subject to the same rules and restrictions as private foundations. Some are also referred to as "public foundations" or "publicly supported organizations" and may use the term "foundation" in their names. (See also **501(c)(3); Private Foundation**)

Qualifying Distributions: Expenditures of private foundations used to satisfy payout requirement. These can include grants, reasonable administrative expenses, set-asides, loans and program-related investments, and amounts paid to acquire assets used directly in carrying out exempt purposes.

Query Letter: A brief letter outlining an organization's activities and its request for funding sent to a foundation or corporation to determine whether it would be appropriate to submit a full grant proposal. Many grantmakers prefer to be contacted in this way before receiving a full proposal.

RFP: Request For Proposal. When the government issues a new contract or grant program, it sends out RFPs to agencies that might be qualified to participate. The RFP lists project specifications and application procedures. A few foundations occasionally use RFPs in specific fields, but most prefer to consider proposals that are initiated by applicants.

Seed Money: A grant or contribution used to start a new project or organization. Seed grants may cover salaries and other operating expenses of a new project.

Set-Asides: Funds set aside by a foundation for a specific purpose or project which are counted as qualifying distributions toward the foundation's annual payout requirement. Amounts for the project must be paid within five years of the first set-aside.

Special Purpose Foundation: A private foundation which focuses its grantmaking activities in one or a few special areas of interest. For example, a foundation may only award grants in the area of cancer research or child development. (See also **General Purpose Foundation**)

Technical Assistance: Operational or management assistance given to nonprofit organizations. It can include fundraising assistance, budgeting and financial planning, program planning, legal advice, marketing, and other aids to management. Assistance may be offered directly by a foundation or corporate staff member or in the form of a grant to pay for the services of an outside consultant. (See also **In-Kind Contributions**)

Trustee: A member of a governing board. A foundation's board of trustees meets to review grant proposals and make decisions. Often also referred to as a "director" or "board member."

BIBLIOGRAPHY OF FUNDING FOR HEALTH

This selected bibliography is compiled from the Foundation Center's bibliographic database. Many of the items are available for free reference use in the Foundation Center's New York City, Washington, D.C., Cleveland, and San Francisco libraries and in many of its cooperating libraries throughout the United States. For further references on such topics as fundraising and proposal development, see *The Literature of the Nonprofit Sector: A Bibliography with Abstracts.* Vols. 1-4. New York: Foundation Center, 1989-1992.

AIDS/HIV Public Policy Casebook. New York: Funders Concerned About AIDS, 1992.

Bailey, Anne Lowrey. "David Rogers: Challenging Foundations to Take Action on AIDS." *Chronicle of Philanthropy* 3 (8 October 1991): 7-8.

Bailey, Anne Lowrey. "Non-Profits in Politics: Three Large Health Charities Attacked for Advocacy Activities and How They Use Donations." *Chronicle of Philanthropy* 2 (10 July 1990): 30-2.

Bailey, Willard. "501(c)(3) Hospitals: An Endangered Species?" *Fund Raising Management* 19 (January 1989): 60, 62, 78.

Bennett, James T. *Health Research Charities: Image and Reality.* Studies in Philanthropy, no. 6. Washington: Capital Research Center, 1990.

Bloom, Jane E. *Finding Funds for AIDS Projects in New York City.* Albany, N.Y.: Welfare Research, Inc., 1990.

Bush, Gerald W. "The National Head Injury Foundation: Eight Years of Challenge and Growth." *Journal of Head Trauma Rehabilitation* 3 (December 1988): 73-7.

Chambre, Susan Maizel. "The Volunteer Response to the AIDS Epidemic in New York City: Implications for Research on Voluntarism." *Nonprofit and Voluntary Sector Quarterly* 20 (Fall 1991): 267-87.

"Corporate-Foundation Hospital Support." *Health Funds Development Letter* 13 (June 1990): 2.

Costa, Nick G. "Planning to Reach Your Full Potential." *Fund Raising Management* 23 (April 1992): 23-8, 44.

Council on Foundations. *Bill: A Special Story.* [Video recording]. Washington: Council on Foundations, 1988.

Diehl, Richard J., and Christine D. Weger, comps. *Alcoholism Funding Service: A Directory of Federal, State and Foundation Grants for Alcohol Education, Prevention and Treatment Services.* Honolulu, Hawaii: Program Information Associates, 1987.

Diehl, Richard J., and Christine D. Weger. *Drug Abuse Funding Service: A Directory of Federal, State and Foundation Grants for Drug Abuse Education, Prevention and Treatment Services.* Honolulu, Hawaii: Program Information Associates, 1987.

Directory of Biomedical and Health Care Grants. 7th ed. Phoenix, Ariz.: Oryx Press, 1992.

Eckstein, Richard M., ed. *Handicapped Funding Directory: A Guide to Sources of Funding in the United States for Programs and Services for the Disabled.* 7th ed. Loxahatchee, Fla.: Research Grant Guides, 1990.

Feldman, Penny Hollander, Susan Putnam, and Margaret Gerteis. "The Impact of Foundation-Funded Commissions on Health Policy." *Health Affairs* 11 (Winter 1992): 207-25. Financial Aid for Minorities in Health Fields. Garrett Park, Md.: Garrett Park Press, 1991.

Funding Database Handbook. Arlington, Va.: Funding Research Institute, 1991.

Ginzberg, Eli, and Anna B. Dutka. *The Financing of Biomedical Research.* Baltimore, Md.: Johns Hopkins University Press, 1989.

Goss, Kristin A. "Breast-Cancer Prevention: Socialite Takes Field by Storm." *Chronicle of Philanthropy* 2 (12 December 1989): 1, 10-1.

Grants for Hospitals, Medical Care and Medical Research. Grant Guide, no. 14. New York: Foundation Center, 1992/93.

Grants for Medical and Professional Health Education. Grant Guide, no. 18. New York: Foundation Center, 1992/93.

Grants for Mental Health, Addictions and Crisis Services. Grant Guide, no. 19. New York: Foundation Center, 1992/93.

Grants for Public Health and Diseases. Grant Guide, no. 22. New York: Foundation Center, 1992/93.

Graveline, Denise. "A New AIDS Issue for Grant Makers." *Chronicle of Philanthropy* 4 (5 November 1991): 40-1.

Greenberg, Linda G. "Foundation Funding for Health Promotion and Disease Prevention." *Health Affairs* 9 (Summer 1990): 209-14.

Greene, Elizabeth. "Drug and Alcohol Abuse: Foundations Grope for Ways to Deal with the Issue, But Say Solutions Are Hard to Find." *Chronicle of Philanthropy* 2 (3 April 1990): 1, 8-9.

Greene, Elizabeth. "Woman Fund Raisers for Hospitals Found to Earn Less Than Their Male Counterparts." *Chronicle of Philanthropy* 2 (26 June 1990): 19, 22.

Iglehart, John K., ed. *Private Foundations and Health Policy.* Milkwood, Va.: Project HOPE, 1990.

"Improving the Health of Native Americans." *Health Funds Development Letter* 13 (October 1990): 5-6.

"Independent Foundations Favor Hospitals, Health Care." *Health Funds Development Letter* 12 (August 1989): 1-2.

Institute for Health Policy Studies. University of California, San Francisco. *The HIV Epidemic: New and Continuing Challenges for the Public and Private Sectors.* Health Care Policy Issues. Washington: Council on Foundations, 1990.

Jenkins, Robert K., ed. *The Health Funds Grants Resources Yearbook.* 6th ed. Wall Township, N.J.: Health Resources Publishing, 1993.

Kim, D. "Foundation Funding and Psychiatric Research." *American Journal of Psychiatry* 145 (July 1988): 830-5.

Lev, Michael. "Success Comes to a Start-Up Charity." *New York Times* (6 November 1990)

Lewis, David. "Ten Points to More Effective Anti-Drug Funding: Private Donors Can Outperform Government." *Philanthropy Monthly* 19 (Fall 1991): 15-6.

Mai, Charles F. "A Psychiatrist Looks at Fund Raising." *Fund Raising Management* 22 (June 1991): 59.

Montague, William. "Many Nonprofit Hospitals Successful in Raising Funds to Help Poor Patients Who Have No Health Insurance." *Chronicle of Philanthropy* 2 (28 November 1989): 21.

Murphy, C. Edward, ed. *AIDS Funding: A Guide to Giving by Foundations and Charitable Organizations.* 2nd ed. New York: Foundation Center, 1991.

National League for Nursing. *Scholarships and Loans for Nursing Education.* New York: National League for Nursing, 1992/93.

Pavoni, M.M. "Obtaining a Grant: A Collaborative Effort." *Journal of American Medical Record Association* 58 (July 1987): 18-20.

Renz, Loren. *Alcohol and Drug Abuse Funding: An Analysis of Foundation Grants.* New York: Foundation Center, 1989.

Renz, Loren. "Private Foundations and the Crisis of Alcohol and Drug Abuse." *Health Affairs* 9 (Summer 1990): 193-201.

Seltzer, Michael, ed. *AID$ Fundraising.* New York: Foundation Center, 1991.

Seltzer, Michael, and Katherine M. Galvin. "Organized Philanthropy's Response to AIDS." *Nonprofit and Voluntary Sector Quarterly* 20 (Fall 1991): 249-66.

Stehle, Vince. "Charities' Soaring Health-Insurance Costs." *Chronicle of Philanthropy* 4 (2 June 1992): 33-4.

Sulima, John P., ed. *Funding for Drug and Alcohol Programs: A Guide to Public and Private Sources.* Providence, R.I.: Manisses Communications Group, 1988.

Williams, Roger M. "To Lead or Lag?" *Foundation News* 33 (January- February 1992): 19-25.

PUBLICATIONS AND SERVICES OF THE FOUNDATION CENTER

The Foundation Center is a national service organization founded and supported by foundations to provide a single authoritative source of information on foundation and corporate giving. The Center's programs are designed to help grantseekers as they begin to select those funders which may be most interested in their projects from the over 34,000 active U.S. foundations. Among its primary activities toward this end are publishing reference books on foundation and corporate philanthropy, and disseminating information on grantmaking through a nationwide public service program.

Publications of the Foundation Center are the primary working tools of every serious grantseeker. They are also used by grantmakers, scholars, journalists, and legislators, in short, by everyone seeking any type of factual information on philanthropy. All private foundations and a significant number of corporate grantmakers actively engaged in grantmaking, regardless of size or geographic location, are included in one or more of the Center's publications. The publications are of three kinds: directories which describe specific funders, characterizing their program interests and providing fiscal and personnel data; grants indexes which list and classify by subject recent foundation and corporate awards; and guides, monographs, and bibliographies which introduce the reader to funding research, elements of proposal writing, and nonprofit management issues.

Foundation Center publications may be ordered from the Foundation Center, 79 Fifth Avenue, New York, NY 10003-3076. For more information about any aspect of the Center's program or for the name of the Center's library collection nearest you, call toll-free (800) 424-9836.

GENERAL RESEARCH DIRECTORIES

THE FOUNDATION DIRECTORY, 1993 Edition

The Foundation Directory has been widely known and respected in the field for over 30 years. It includes the latest information on all foundations whose assets exceed $2 million or whose annual grants total $200,000 or more. The new 1993 Edition includes more than 6,300 of these foundations, over 400 of which are new to this edition. *Directory* foundations hold $151 billion in assets and award $8 billion in grants annually, accounting for 90% of all U.S. foundation dollars awarded in 1991.

Each *Directory* entry contains precise information on application procedures, giving limitations, types of support awarded, the publications of each foundation, and foundation staff. In addition, each entry features such vital data as the grantmakers' giving interests, financial data, grant amounts, addresses and telephone numbers. The Foundation Center works closely with foundations to ensure the accuracy and timeliness of the information provided.

The *Directory* includes indexes by foundation name; subject areas of interest; names of donors, trustees, and officers; geographic location; and the types of support awarded. Also included are analyses of the foundation community by geography, asset and grant size, and the different foundation types.

March 1993.
Softbound: ISBN 0-87954-449-6 / $160
Hardbound: ISBN 0-87954-484-8 / $185
Published annually.

THE FOUNDATION DIRECTORY SUPPLEMENT

The Foundation Directory Supplement provides the latest-breaking information on *Foundation Directory* grantmakers six months after the *Directory* is published. Each year, thousands of policy and staff changes occur at these foundations. Fundraisers need to know about these crucial changes as rapidly as possible because they may affect the way they prepare grant proposals. The *Supplement* insures that users of the *Directory* always have the latest new addresses, contacts, policy statements, application guidelines, and financial data for the foundations they're approaching for funding.

September 1993 / ISBN 0-87954-500-3 / $110

THE FOUNDATION DIRECTORY PART 2: A Guide to Grant Programs $50,000–$200,000, 1993 (2nd) Edition

Following in the tradition of *The Foundation Directory*, *The Foundation Directory Part 2* brings you the same thorough coverage for the next largest set of foundations, those with grant programs between $50,000 and $200,000. It includes *Directory*-level information on mid-sized foundations, an important group of grantmakers responsible for millions of dollars in funding annually. Essential data on 4,327 foundations is included along with over 30,000 recently awarded foundation grants, which provide an excellent view of the foundations' giving interests. Immediate access to foundation entries is facilitated by five indexes organized by: city and state; donors, officers, and trustees; types of support; foundation names; and over 200 specific subject areas.

March 1993 / ISBN 0-87954-489-9 / $160
Published biennially.

GUIDE TO U.S. FOUNDATIONS, THEIR TRUSTEES, OFFICERS, AND DONORS

This powerful new fundraising reference tool, which has replaced the *National Data Book of Foundations,* provides fundraisers with current, accurate information on all 34,000+ active grantmaking foundations in the U.S. The two-volume set also includes a master list of the names of the people who establish, oversee, and manage those institutions. With access to this information, fundraisers can facilitate their funding prospect research by discovering the philanthropic connections of their current donors, board members, volunteers, and prominent families in their geographic area. As it provides a comprehensive list of U.S. foundations and the people who govern them, the book also helps fundraisers follow up on any giving leads they encounter. Each entry includes asset and giving amounts as well as geographic limitations, so fundraisers can quickly determine whether or not to pursue a particular grant source.

U.S. Foundations is the only source of published data on thousands of local foundations. (It includes over 20,000 grantmakers not covered in other Foundation Center publications.) Each entry also tells you if you can find more extensive information on the grantmaker in another Foundation Center reference work.

March 1993 / 0-87954-488-0 / $195

THE FOUNDATION 1000

Nonprofit fundraisers and other researchers now have access to annually published, comprehensive reports on the 1,000 largest foundations in the country. *The Foundation 1000* (formerly *Source Book Profiles*) provides access to extensive and accurate information on this set of powerful funders, a group of grantmakers responsible for distributing over 60% of all foundation grant dollars. *Foundation 1000* grantmakers hold over $100 billion in assets and each year award nearly $6 billion, more than 189,000 grants, to nonprofit organizations nationwide.

The Foundation 1000 provides the most thorough analyses available of the 1,000 largest foundations and their extensive grant programs, including all the data fundraisers need most when applying for grants from these top-level foundations. Each multi-page foundation profile features a full foundation portrait, a detailed breakdown of the foundation's grant program, and many examples of recently awarded foundation grants.

Five indexes give fundraisers the opportunity to target potential funders in a variety of ways: by foundation name, subject field, type of support, and geographic location. A special new index lets fundraisers locate grantmakers by the names of officers, donors, and trustees.

October 1992 / ISBN 0-87954-445-7 / $195
Published annually.

NATIONAL DIRECTORY OF CORPORATE GIVING, 2nd Edition

Each year, corporations donate billions of dollars to nonprofit organizations. To help fundraisers tap into this vital source of funding, the 2nd Edition of the *National Directory of Corporate Giving* offers authoritative information on over 2,000 corporate foundations and direct giving programs.

Fundraisers that want access to current, accurate fundraising facts on corporate philanthropies will benefit from the full range of data in this volume. The *National Directory* features detailed portraits of 1,500 corporate foundations plus an additional 600 direct giving programs. Fundraisers will find essential information on these corporate grantmakers including application information, key personnel, types of support generally awarded, giving limitations, financial data, and purpose and activities statements. Many entries in the 2nd Edition also include a special section, "Current Giving," which lists recent grant recipients by subject areas. These listings give you the best indication of a grantmaker's funding priorities by pointing out the nonprofits it has already funded. The volume also provides data on the corporations that sponsor foundations and direct giving programs—essential background information for corporate grant searches. Each entry gives the company's name and address, a review of the types of business, financial data complete with Forbes and Fortune ratings, all plants and subsidiaries, and a charitable giving statement.

The *National Directory* also features an extensive bibliography to guide you to further research on corporate funding. Six essential indexes help you target funding prospects by geographic region; types of support funded; subject area; officers, donors, and trustees; types of business; and names of the corporation, its foundation, and direct giving program.

October 1991 / ISBN 0-87954-400-7 / $195

CORPORATE FOUNDATION PROFILES, 7th Edition

This newly updated volume includes comprehensive information on 247 of the largest corporate foundations in the U.S., grantmakers who each give at least $1.25 million annually. Each profile covers foundation giving interests, application guidelines, recently awarded grants, information on the sponsoring company, and many other essential fundraising facts. A section on financial data provides a summary of the size and grantmaking capacity of each foundation and contains a list of assets, gifts or contributions, grants paid, operating programs, expenditures, scholarships, and loans. A quick-scan appendix lists core financial data on over 1,000 additional corporate foundations, all of which hold assets of $1 million or give at least $100,000 in grants every year. Three indexes help grantseekers search for prospective funders by subject area, geographic region, and types of support preferred by the foundation.

March 1992 / ISBN 0-87954-437-6 / $135
Published biennially.

NEW YORK STATE FOUNDATIONS: A Comprehensive Directory, 3rd Edition

New York State Foundations offers fundraisers complete coverage of independent, corporate and community foundations throughout New York State in one comprehensive source. This information-packed volume will help fundraisers to identify the giving interests and funding policies of over 5,300 foundations in New York State. Fundraisers will find carefully researched data on every known New York foundation, small and large, with funding policies that cover a broad range of program areas. Every foundation entry in this directory has been drawn from the most current sources of information available, including IRS 990-PF foundation tax returns and, in many cases, the foundations themselves. Many entries include descriptions of recently awarded grants, the best indication of a grantmaker's giving interests. A separate section covers several out-of-state grantmakers that fund nonprofits in New York State. Five time-saving indexes offer quick-access to foundations according to their fields of interest; types of support awarded; city and county; names of donors, officers, and trustees; and foundation names.

June 1993 / ISBN 0-87954-501-1/ $165.
Published biennially.

FOUNDATION GRANTS TO INDIVIDUALS, 8th Edition

The only publication devoted entirely to foundation grant opportunities for qualified individual applicants, the 8th Edition of this volume provides full descriptions of the programs of over 2,300 foundations, all of which award grants to individuals. Entries include foundation addresses and telephone numbers, financial data, giving limitations, and application guidelines. This edition—the largest ever published with over 300 entirely new grantmakers featured—will save individual grantseekers countless hours of research.

April 1993 / ISBN 0-87954-493-7 / $55

SUBJECT DIRECTORIES

AIDS FUNDING: A Guide to Giving by Foundations and Charitable Organizations, 2nd Edition

This volume covers over 500 foundations, corporate giving programs and public charities that support AIDS-related programs and services. Fundraisers seeking information on organizations awarding grants in this area will find a wealth of information on the specific interests of these grantmakers, that have recently awarded over $97 million for AIDS- and HIV-related nonprofit organizations involved in direct relief, medical research, legal aid, preventative education, and other programs to empower persons with AIDS and AIDS-related diseases. Grants lists accompany over half of the entries, to show the types of projects funded by the grantmaker.

July 1991 / ISBN 0-87954-382-5 / $60

GUIDE TO FUNDING FOR INTERNATIONAL AND FOREIGN PROGRAMS

The 1st Edition of the *Guide to Funding for International and Foreign Programs* thoroughly prepares grantseekers for an informed grant search. With hundreds of foundations and corporate direct giving programs included, the volume offers fundraisers in the field an excellent opportunity to increase their funding base. Many of the foundation entries include lists of grants recently awarded by grantmakers to projects with an international focus, both within the U.S. and abroad: international relief, conferences, disaster assistance, human rights, civil liberties, community development, education, and much more. The *Guide* provides all the facts fundraisers need to bolster their target list of funding prospects: foundation addresses, financial data, giving priorities, application procedures, contact names, and key officials; sample grants; and a range of helpful indexes that help fundraisers target funders by specific program areas funded and geographic preferences.

March 1992 / ISBN 0-87954-441-4 / $75

NATIONAL GUIDE TO FUNDING IN AGING, 3rd Edition

Carefully researched, up-to-date, and truly comprehensive, the *National Guide to Funding in Aging* is the only funding tool to cover the many public and private sources of funding support and technical assistance for programs for the aging. The new 3rd Edition of this volume provides essential facts on over 1,000 grantmakers, including federal funding programs; state government funding programs (with up-to-date listings for all 50 states and U.S. territories); foundations that have demonstrated or expressed an interest in the field (many foundation entries include lists of actual recently awarded grants); plus other academic, religious, and service agencies that provide funding and technical aid to aging-related nonprofits.

Each year the grantmakers featured in this volume award millions of grant dollars for senior citizen programs and institutions such as hospitals, community centers, nursing homes, and continuing education facilities, as well as organizations that concentrate on legal rights, housing, employment, health, veterans, cultural affairs, nutrition, and much more.

December 1992 / ISBN 0-87954-444-9 / $80

NATIONAL GUIDE TO FUNDING IN ARTS AND CULTURE, 2nd Edition

Designed specifically to meet the needs of development professionals in the field of arts and culture, the 2nd Edition of this subject guide prepares fundraisers for an informed grant search. The Foundation Center's expert staff has performed the first crucial stage of fundraising research, by including in the 2nd Edition only those foundations and corporate giving programs that have already demonstrated a commitment to funding art-colonies, dance companies, museums, theaters, and many other types of arts and culture projects and institutions. With over 4,200 grantmakers listed, six indexes, and a special bibliography, the volume facilitates rapid and accurate research. The 2nd Edition also lists thousands of actual grants recently awarded by many foundations, to show the kinds of projects currently receiving support from grantmakers.

May 1992 / ISBN 0-87954-442-2 / $125

NATIONAL GUIDE TO FUNDING FOR CHILDREN, YOUTH, AND FAMILIES, 2nd Edition

The *National Guide to Funding for Children, Youth, and Families* caters to nonprofit organizations that serve the needs of these specific population groups. The new 2nd Edition provides access to essential facts on nearly 3,000 foundations and corporate direct giving programs that together award millions of dollars each year to organizations committed to causes involving children, youth, and families. Each entry includes the grantmaker's address and contact name, purpose statement, and application guidelines. Grantseekers will also find useful the descriptions of over 8,000 sample grants recently awarded by many of these foundations, a feature that offers unique insight into a funders' giving interests. Six indexes help grantmakers target appropriate sources of funding and a bibliography facilitates further research in the field.

April 1993 / ISBN 0-87954-491-0 / $135

NATIONAL GUIDE TO FUNDING FOR THE ECONOMICALLY DISADVANTAGED

The new 1st Edition of this volume provides essential facts on over 1,000 foundations and corporate direct giving programs, each with a history of awarding grant dollars to projects and institutions that aid the economically disadvantaged. Each year the grantmakers featured in this volume award millions of grant dollars for the economically disadvantaged, employment programs, homeless shelters, hunger relief, welfare initiatives, and hundreds of other subject categories. Fundraisers can cut hours off their research time by having, in one convenient volume, a list of grantmakers already interested in their specific subject field.

The *National Guide* features information-packed grantmaker portraits that include the grantmaker's address, financial data, giving priorities statement, application procedures, contact names, and key officials. Many entries include descriptions of actual grants recently awarded by the foundation or corporate giver, the best indication of a grantmaker's particular funding interests. The volume includes over 2,000 sample grants.

April 1993 / ISBN 0-87954-494-5 / $85

NATIONAL GUIDE TO FUNDING FOR ELEMENTARY AND SECONDARY EDUCATION, 2nd Edition

With the publication of this all-new 2nd Edition, fundraisers for elementary and secondary education have access to current, accurate information on funding options in the field. *Funding for Elementary and Secondary Education* provides full profiles for over 1,600 foundations and corporate direct giving programs committed to funding nursery schools, bilingual education initiatives, gifted programs, remedial reading/math, drop-out prevention services, educational testing programs and many other nonprofit organizations and activities. The volume also includes over 4,500 descriptions of recently awarded grants, the best indication of a grantmaker's funding interests.

April 1993 / ISBN 0-87954-495-3 / $135

NATIONAL GUIDE TO FUNDING FOR THE ENVIRONMENT AND ANIMAL WELFARE

The 1st Edition of this guide thoroughly prepares grant-seekers for an informed grant search. With hundreds of foundations and corporate direct giving programs included, the volume offers fundraisers in the field an excellent opportunity to increase their funding base. Many of the foundation entries include lists of environmental grants recently awarded to projects and organizations involved in international conservation, ecological research, litigation and advocacy, waste reduction, animal welfare, and much more. Each year the grantmakers featured in this volume award millions of dollars to environment-related nonprofit institutions and projects. The *National Guide* provides all the facts fundraisers need to bolster their target list of funding prospects: foundation addresses, financial data, giving priorities, application procedures, contact names, and key officials; sample grants; and a range of helpful indexes that help fundraisers target funders by specific program areas and geographic preferences.

March 1992 / ISBN 0-87954-440-6 / $75

NATIONAL GUIDE TO FUNDING IN HEALTH, 3rd Edition

With the publication of the completely revised 3rd Edition of this volume, fundraisers have access to up-to-date information on the top health funders in the nation, all in one convenient source. The 3rd Edition contains essential facts on more than 3,000 foundations and corporate direct giving programs, all of which have a documented or stated interest in funding hospitals, universities, research institutes, community-based agencies, national health associations, and a broad range of other health-related programs and services. This comprehensive source of fundraising data includes facts on grantmakers' program interests, contact persons, application guidelines, listings of board members, and much more. Many entries include descriptions of recently awarded grants—the volume features over 8,000 sample grants in all—the best indication of a grantmaker's giving interests. Six indexes help fundraisers quickly target prospective grant sources. A useful bibliography of publications on health issues and philan-

thropic initiatives in the field is included as a guide to further study.

March 1993 / ISBN 0-87954-490-2 / $135

NATIONAL GUIDE TO FUNDING IN HIGHER EDUCATION, 2nd Edition

The 2nd Edition of the *National Guide to Funding in Higher Education* provides current data on over 3,650 foundations and corporate giving programs, all with a proven history of awarding grants to colleges, universities, graduate programs, and research institutes. Each entry gives a thorough portrait of the grantmaker, including the address, name of the contact person, financial data, purpose statement, types of support preferred, and geographic limitations. And, to show the type of projects that have already received funding from the grantmakers featured, the book includes over 13,400 descriptions of recently awarded grants. The 2nd Edition also includes a selected bibliography to direct further research on higher education and philanthropy.

April 1992 / ISBN 0-87954-443-0 / $125

NATIONAL GUIDE TO FUNDING FOR LIBRARIES AND INFORMATION SERVICES, 2nd Edition

Fundraisers for libraries and information services will benefit from the new 2nd Edition of this volume, which features a broad list of grantmakers that support such facilities. This directory provides essential data on over 400 foundations and corporate direct giving programs. Each entry includes crucial grantmaker facts such as the address, name of the contact person, financial data, purpose statement, types of support preferred, and geographic limitations. The *National Guide* also features over 800 descriptions of recently awarded grants, the best indication of a grantmaker's giving interests. This volume affords immediate access to data on the funders of a wide range of organizations and projects, from the smallest public libraries to major research institutions, as well as academic/research libraries, art, law, and medical libraries, and other specialized information centers.

May 1993 / ISBN 0-87954-497-X / $85

NATIONAL GUIDE TO FUNDING IN RELIGION, 2nd Edition

With the new 2nd Edition of this volume, fundraisers who work for nonprofits affiliated with religious organizations have access to current, accurate information on grantmakers in their field. The 2nd Edition brings together a group of over 3,000 foundations and corporate direct giving programs, all of which have demonstrated or stated an interest in funding churches, missionary societies, religious welfare and religious education programs. The *National Guide* features information-packed grantmaker portraits that include the grantmaker's address, financial data, giving priorities statement, application procedures, contact names, and key officials. Many entries include descriptions of actual grants recently awarded by the foundation or corporate giver, the best indication of a grantmaker's particular funding interests. The volume includes over 3,600 sample grants.

May 1993 / ISBN 0-87954-496-1 / $135

NATIONAL GUIDE TO FUNDING FOR WOMEN AND GIRLS, 2nd Edition

With the new 2nd Edition of this volume, fundraisers have access to current, accurate information on grantmakers in their field. The 2nd Edition brings together a group of over 800 foundations and corporate direct giving programs, all of which have demonstrated or stated an interest in funding such projects as education scholarships, shelters for abused women, girls' clubs, health clinics, employment centers, and other diverse programs. The *National Guide* features information-packed grantmaker portraits that include the grantmaker's address, financial data, giving priorities statement, application procedures, contact names, and key officials. Many entries include descriptions of actual grants recently awarded by the foundation or corporate giver, the best indication of a grantmaker's particular funding interests. The volume includes over 3,000 sample grants.

May 1993 / ISBN 0-87954-498-8 / $105

GRANT DIRECTORIES

GRANT GUIDES

Designed for fundraisers who work within defined fields of nonprofit development, this series of grant guides (formerly known as COMSEARCH) lists actual foundation grants in 30 key areas of grantmaking. These valuable research tools show thousands of grants of $10,000 or more, all of them recently awarded by many of the top funders in each field. These unique publications offer fundraisers an effective way to significantly reduce research by providing a pre-selected set of recently awarded foundation grants within particular fields of nonprofit activity.

Each volume affords immediate access to the names, addresses, and giving limitations of all foundations listed. The grant descriptions provide fundraisers with the grant recipient's name and location, the grant amount, and date it was authorized; and a description of the grant's intended use.

Plus, each *Grant Guide* provides three indexes that help fundraisers target possible sources of funding by the type of organization generally funded by the grantmaker, the subject focus of the foundation's grants, and the geographic area in which the foundation has already funded projects.

Each of the volumes also includes a concise overview of the foundation spending patterns within the specified field. The introduction uses a series of statistical tables to document such important findings as (1) the 25 top funders in your area of interest (by total dollar amount of grants), (2) the 15 largest grants reported, (3) the total dollar amount and number of grants awarded for specific types of support, recipient organization type, and population group, and (4) total grant dollars received in each U.S. state and many foreign countries.

The *Grant Guide* series gives fundraisers the data they need to target foundations making grants in their field, network with organizations that share their goals, and tailor their grant applications to the specific concerns of grantmakers, as expressed by the grants they have already made.

Series published annually in September / 1992/1993 Editions / $60 each

THE FOUNDATION GRANTS INDEX ANNUAL, 1993 Edition

A foundation's recently awarded grants offer the best indication of its future funding priorities. The all-new 1993 (21st) Edition of *The Foundation Grants Index*—the volume fundraisers have relied upon since 1970—is the most current and accurate source of information on recent grantmaker awards. The *Grants Index* has steadily expanded its coverage since the 1st Edition: it now covers the grantmaking programs of over 840 of the largest independent, corporate, and community foundations in the U.S. and includes over 58,000 grant descriptions in all.

The new 1993 Edition of the *Grants Index* is designed for fast and easy grants-based research. Grant descriptions are divided into 28 broad subject areas such as health, higher education, and arts and culture. Within each of these broad fields, the grant descriptions are listed geographically by state and alphabetically by the name of the foundation. This arrangement helps fundraisers find prospective funders that share their program interests *and* fund projects within their geographic region, determined by the grants they have already made.

The 58,000+ grant descriptions provide fundraisers with the grant recipient's name and location, the grant amount, and date it was authorized; and a description of the grant's intended use.

December 1992 / ISBN 0-87954-449-X / $125

THE FOUNDATION GRANTS INDEX QUARTERLY

This unique subscription service gives fundraisers the most up-to-date information available, providing important new information on foundation funding every three months. Each issue of the *Quarterly* delivers descriptions of over 5,000 recent foundation grants, arranged by state and indexed by subjects and recipients. This enables fundraisers to zero in on grants made in their subject area and within their geographic region. The *Quarterly* contains helpful updates on grantmakers that note changes in foundation address, personnel, program interests, and application procedures. Also included is a list of grantmakers' recent publications such as annual reports, information brochures, grants lists, and newsletters.

Annual subscription $85 / 4 issues ISSN 0735-2522

WHO GETS GRANTS / WHO GIVES GRANTS: Nonprofit Organizations and the Foundation Grants They Received

With the publication of this new directory, fundraisers can easily answer a crucial question: from which foundations do other nonprofits receive their funding? *Who Gets Grants* provides direct access to grant recipient information, an excellent way to find out who is awarding grants to organizations like yours and in your geographic region. It features over 16,000 nonprofit organizations and more than 48,000 grants.

Who Gets Grants helps fundraisers conduct their research by allowing them to target the funders of specific nonprofits, which are all listed conveniently in the front of the book.

Because the book is divided into 19 different subject headings, fundraisers can also scan through grants recently awarded within their field to generate lists of grant prospects. Within each subject area the grant recipients are listed by geographic area, an arrangement that helps fundraisers discover which foundations favor their state.

The grant recipient entries feature grant descriptions that include the grant amount, its duration and use, and the name of the grantmaker. An index provides a list of all the grants made by each foundation covered, which gives a sense of a grantmaker's larger funding priorities. An appendix lists foundation addresses and funding limitations to give fundraisers a head start on grantmaker research.

March 1993 / ISBN 0-87954-487-2 / $95

GUIDEBOOKS

FOUNDATION FUNDAMENTALS: A Guide for Grantseekers, 4th Edition
Edited by Judith B. Margolin

This comprehensive, easy-to-read guidebook presents the facts you need to understand the world of foundations, and to identify foundation funding sources for your organization. Illustrations take you step-by-step through the funding research process, and worksheets and check lists are provided to help you get started in your search for funding. Comprehensive bibliographies and detailed research examples are also supplied.

March 1991 / ISBN 0-87954-392-2 / $19.95

THE FOUNDATION CENTER'S USER-FRIENDLY GUIDE: Grantseeker's Guide to Resources
Edited by Judith B. Margolin

This helpful book answers the most commonly asked questions about grantseeking in an upbeat, easy-to-read style. Specifically designed for novice grantseekers, the *User-Friendly Guide* leads the reader through the maze of unfamiliar jargon and the wide range of research guides used successfully by professional fundraisers every day. Whether a grantseeker needs $100 or $100,000 for their project or organization, this guide offers an excellent first step in the fundraising process.

February 1992 / ISBN 0-87954-452-X / $12.95

FOUNDATION GIVING: Yearbook of Facts and Figures on Private, Corporate and Community Foundations, 1992 Edition

Foundation Giving includes data on more than 34,000 grantmaking foundations in the country. Using a range of statistical tables to chart foundation giving by subject area and type of support, to categorize foundations by asset and giving amount, and to document other noteworthy data such as the breakdown of grants awarded by the 100 largest foundations, the study offers a comprehensive review of foundation activity collected and analyzed over the past year. It is essential reading for anyone conducting research on foundations.

July 1992 / ISBN 0-87954-446-5 / $19.95

THE FOUNDATION CENTER'S GUIDE TO PROPOSAL WRITING

The Foundation Center now offers its own comprehensive guide to the strategic thinking and mechanics of proposal writing. The *Guide to Proposal Writing* guides fundraisers through each step of the process, from pre-proposal planning to the writing itself to the essential post-grant follow-up. The book features many extracts from actual grant proposals and also includes candid advice from the grantmakers themselves on the "do's and don't's" of proposal writing. Anyone who takes part in the fundraising process at a nonprofit organization will benefit from *The Foundation Center's Guide to Proposal Writing.* Written by professional fundraisers who have themselves been creating successful proposals for more than 15 years, this book offers the kind of valuable tips and in-depth, practical instruction that no other source provides

April 1993 / ISBN 0-87954-492-9 / $ 29.95

BENCHMARK STUDIES

ARTS FUNDING: A Report on Foundation and Corporate Grantmaking Trends

This comprehensive report, commissioned by Grantmakers in the Arts, documents notable shifts in arts and culture funding patterns through the 1980s. The study covers funding for the performing and visual arts, museums, ethnic arts, media, journalism, historic preservation, and arts-related humanities. Of great interest to fundraisers in the field, *Arts Funding* features profiles of over 60 top foundation and corporate grantmakers that identify their current funding priorities. The study incorporates findings from a landmark 1992 survey in which grantmakers predict funding directions within the field for the 1990s. *Arts Funding* also features case studies of grantmakers that have undergone dynamic change in their arts funding policy over the last two years.

March 1993 / ISBN 0-87954-448-1 / $40

AGING: The Burden Study on Foundation Grantmaking Trends

This in-depth analysis of foundation funding for programs that benefit the elderly covers private, corporate, and community grantmakers and considers such pertinent topics as: the availability of support for care-givers, the frail elderly, and Alzheimer's patients; a renewed interest in support services and institutional long-term care; and inter-generational programs.

September 1991 / ISBN 0-87954-389-2 / $40

ALCOHOL AND DRUG ABUSE FUNDING: An Analysis of Foundation Grants 1983-1987

This report provides an authoritative study of independent, corporate, and community foundation grants awarded between 1983-1987 for drug and alcohol abuse programs. The study presents the complete picture of pri-

vate funding, as it examines the historical background, present status, and future directions of grantmaking in this critical field. Designed for foundation policy-makers, grantseekers, and researchers in the fields of health care and prevention, education, and social service.

August 1989 / ISBN 0-87954-286-1 / $45

CRIME AND JUSTICE: The Burden Study on Foundation Grantmaking Trends

This comprehensive work examines foundation funding for programs involved with crime prevention, juvenile justice, law enforcement, correction facilities, rehabilitation, and victim assistance. *Crime and Justice* looks at significant developments in the criminal justice field, changing public perceptions of crime, and cuts in governmental expenditures. It also documents the remarkable growth of funding for programs combatting spouse and child abuse, and those assisting victims of violence.

April 1991 / ISBN 0-87954-381-7 / $35

BIBLIOGRAPHIES

THE LITERATURE OF THE NONPROFIT SECTOR: A Bibliography with Abstracts, Volumes I-IV

This bibliographical series helps fundraisers and other researchers tap into the vast and growing body of literature on philanthropy and voluntarism and covers the best references on fundraising, foundations, corporate giving, nonprofit management, and much more. Designed to help fundraisers access the books and articles they need quickly and easily, the entries are divided into twelve broad subject fields and each volume includes subject, title, and author indexes to speed research. Plus, to make thorough research even easier, nearly one-third of the entries in the first volume and well over two-thirds in the second are abstracted to give a clear idea of the material covered in each work. Whether readers are searching for a manual that outlines development strategies for museums, an article that considers philanthropic responses to rural poverty in the 1970s, or a book that tackles the interplay of federal tax policy and charitable giving, *The Literature of the Nonprofit Sector* will help direct research. The new 4th volume expands coverage to over 8,500 titles.

Volume IV, September 1992 / ISBN 0-87954-447-3 / $45
Volume III, September 1991 / ISBN 0-87954-386-8 / $45
Volume II, July 1990 / ISBN 0-87954-343-4 / $45
Volume I, August 1989 / ISBN 0-87954-287-X / $55
Volumes I-IV Set / $145

OTHER PUBLICATIONS

AN AGILE SERVANT: Community Leadership by Community Foundations

Editor Richard Magat celebrates the 75th anniversary of the founding of the first community foundation with the publication of *An Agile Servant,* a book that explores the far-reaching impact of this important branch of philanthropy. *An Agile Servant* collects essays from some of the most distinguished men and women in the field, each approaching the unique institution of the community foundation from a different perspective. Drawing on their own experience and research, the authors investigate its origins, historical development, and changing role in society and its ability to combat social ills and encourage progressive change, a point illustrated through sixteen case studies. Richard Magat has organized a study that will fascinate anyone interested in successful philanthropic efforts.

December 1989
Paperbound: ISBN 0-87954-332-9 / $15.95
Hardbound: ISBN 0-87954-330-2 / $24.95

AMERICA'S NONPROFIT SECTOR: A Primer

In this fascinating and informative book, Lester M. Salamon counteracts "the widespread lack of knowledge about America's nonprofit sector and the role it plays in our social welfare system." The author provides a basic and easy-to-understand handbook for government officials, journalists, and students, in short, for anyone who wants to comprehend the makeup of America's nonprofit sector. The book also offers a resource for officials in Eastern Europe and other parts of the world who increasingly are seeking to learn from America's mixed system of social welfare. Salamon uses many charts and tables to clearly illustrate various aspects of the nonprofit world. Anyone who works in the nonprofit or the government sector should not miss his insights.

August 1992 / ISBN 0-87954-451-1 / $14.95

AMERICA'S VOLUNTARY SPIRIT: A Book of Readings

In this thoughtful collection, Brian O'Connell, President of INDEPENDENT SECTOR, brings together 45 selections which celebrate and examine the richness and variety of America's unique voluntary sector. O'Connell researched nearly 1,000 selections spanning over 300 years of writing to identify those speeches, articles, chapters, and papers which best define and characterize the roles that philanthropy and voluntary action play in our society. Contributors as diverse as de Tocqueville and John D. Rockefeller, Thoreau and Max Lerner, Erma Bombeck and Vernon Jordan are unified in a common examination of this unique dimension of American life. The anthology includes a bibliography of over 500 important writings and a detailed subject index.

October 1983 / ISBN 0-87954-079-6 / $19.95

THE BOARD MEMBER'S BOOK

by Brian O'Connell, President, INDEPENDENT SECTOR

Based on his extensive experience working with and on the boards of voluntary organizations, Brian O'Connell has developed this practical guide to the essential functions of voluntary boards. O'Connell offers practical advice on how to be a more effective board member and how board members can help their organizations make a difference. This is an invaluable instructional and inspirational tool for anyone who works on or with a voluntary board. Includes an extensive reading list.

May 1985 / ISBN 0-87954-133-4 / $21.95

CAREERS FOR DREAMERS AND DOERS: A Guide to Management Careers in the Nonprofit Sector

Co-authors Lilly Cohen and Dennis Young have written a comprehensive career guide for the nonprofit world. *Careers for Dreamers and Doers* shows how to build a professional career on a foundation of idealism, offering practical advice for starting a job search and strategies tested by successful managers throughout the voluntary sector. The first work of its kind, this informative guide draws on the experience of 27 established professionals, offering profiles of nonprofit C.E.O.s, development officers, and consultants of the "third sector." For those looking for a job in the voluntary sector, a field that the authors predict will become increasingly exciting and remunerative, this book provides an excellent opportunity to learn both the fundamentals and the finer points of the market.

November 1989 / ISBN 0-87954-294-2 / $24.95

THE CHARITABLE IMPULSE: Wealth and Social Conscience in Communities and Cultures Outside the United States

by James A. Joseph

The Charitable Impulse is the product of author James Joseph's life-long interest in how compassionate values are developed, nurtured, and activated. In his quest to identify the motives and personal attributes that lead to a caring society, he has traveled around the world from South America to South Africa, to England, India, and the Middle East interviewing men and women who contribute to the public good. *The Charitable Impulse* adds a much-needed international dimension to the growing body of literature on philanthropy and voluntarism.

September 1989
Paperbound: ISBN 0-87954-301-9 / $19.95
Hardbound: ISBN 0-87954-300-0 / $24.95

FOUNDATION TRUSTEESHIP: Service in the Public Interest

by John W. Nason

Changing public expectations of foundations and new challenges for foundation board members necessitate a fresh approach and an expert guide through the complexities of foundation trusteeship. John Nason, calling upon his years of experience as a trustee, has identified the problem areas and provides insight into many topics of interest to foundations and their board members. Dr. Nason includes chapters covering the roles of foundations and their trustees as well as the changing programs in today's changing society.

March 1989 / ISBN 0-87954-285-3 / $19.95

HANDBOOK ON PRIVATE FOUNDATIONS

by David F. Freeman and the Council on Foundations

This publication, a completely revised edition of the classic *Handbook* published ten years ago, provides a thorough and up-to-date look at all of the issues facing the staff and boards of private foundations in the U.S. In this new edition, sponsored by the Council on Foundations, author David F. Freeman offers sound advice on establishing, staffing, and governing foundations and provides insights into legal and tax guidelines as well. Each chapter concludes with a useful annotated bibliography. The *Handbook* is an excellent "how-to" guide for those who work in private foundations or serve on their boards.

September 1991
Paperbound: ISBN 0-87954-404-X / $29.95
Hardbound: ISBN 0-87954-403-1 / $39.95

HISPANICS AND THE NONPROFIT SECTOR

by Herman E. Gallegos and Michael O'Neill

In this study, the authors explore the growing influence of the Hispanic community on the nonprofit sector. The study looks at economic development groups, legal rights and advocacy organizations, unions, cultural and educational programs, and other types of nonprofits that address the needs of the increasingly large and diverse group of Spanish-speaking U.S. citizens and immigrants. This book traces the historical roots of Hispanic nonprofit organizations to the mutualistas of the 19th century and considers such modern responses as the National Council of La

Raza and the Mexican American Legal Defense and Educational Fund. The authors have written a ground-breaking work on a sub-group of nonprofits that is destined to become even more important in the future.

March 1991 / ISBN 0-87954-398-1 / $24.95

MANAGING FOR PROFIT IN THE NONPROFIT WORLD

by Paul B. Firstenberg

How can service-oriented nonprofits expand their revenue bases? In this title in our series on nonprofit management, author Paul B. Firstenberg shares his view that a vital nonprofit is an entrepreneurial nonprofit. Drawing upon his 14 years of experience as a professional in the nonprofit sector at the Ford Foundation, Princeton, Tulane, and Yale Universities, and Children's Television Workshop as well as his extensive for-profit experience, Firstenberg outlines innovative ways in which nonprofit managers can utilize state-of-the-art management techniques developed by the most successful for-profit enterprises.

September 1986 / ISBN 0-87954-159-8 / $19.95

MANAGING FOUNDATION ASSETS: An Analysis of Foundation Investment and Payout Procedures and Performance

by Lester M. Salamon and Kenneth P. Voytek

In their study, Salamon and Voytek address critical questions on foundation investing and payout procedures, including: how do foundations manage the immense wealth in their control?, how does the payout requirement affect foundation investment operations?, what impact has the change in the payout requirement of 1981 had on both the investment and payout performance of foundations? After addressing these questions, Salamon offers insight into key topics: the process foundations use to make their payout decisions and manage their investments, the rate of return they have achieved and the payout rates foundations have adopted.

March 1989 / ISBN 0-87954-283-7 / $19.95

MAPPING THE THIRD SECTOR: Voluntarism in a Changing Social Economy

by Jon Van Til

Over 700,000 nonprofit organizations. Over 15 million volunteers. What impact do they have on society today? Professor Jon Van Til, Editor of the *Nonprofit Voluntary Sector Quarterly*, raises this compelling question in his scholarly new work as he sets the stage for a coherent view of the voluntary sector. His review of historical and contemporary models of voluntary action paves the way for one that stresses the need for a new conception of how to preserve, extend, and experience community within the interactive web of modern society.

March 1988 / ISBN 0-87954-240-3 / $24.95

THE NONPROFIT ENTREPRENEUR: Creating Ventures to Earn Income

Edited by Edward Skloot

Nonprofit consultant and entrepreneur Edward Skloot, in a well-organized topic-by-topic analytical approach to nonprofit venturing, demonstrates how nonprofits can launch successful earned income enterprises without compromising their missions. Skloot has compiled a collection of writings by the nation's top practitioners and advisors in nonprofit enterprise. Topics covered include legal issues, marketing techniques, business planning, avoiding the pitfalls of venturing for smaller nonprofits, and a special section on museums and their retail operations.

September 1988 / ISBN 0-87954-239-X / $19.95

A NONPROFIT ORGANIZATION OPERATING MANUAL: Planning for Survival and Growth

by Arnold J. Olenick and Philip R. Olenick

This straightforward, all-inclusive desk manual for nonprofit executives covers all aspects of starting and managing a nonprofit. The authors discuss legal problems, obtaining tax exemption, organizational planning and development, board relations; operational, proposal, cash, and capital budgeting; marketing, grant proposals, fundraising, and for-profit ventures; accounting, computerization, tax planning and compliance.

March 1991 / ISBN 0-87954-293-4 / $29.95

PROMOTING ISSUES AND IDEAS: A Guide to Public Relations for Nonprofit Organizations

by Public Interest, Public Relations, Inc. (PIPR)

PIPR, specialists in promoting the issues and ideas of nonprofit groups, presents proven strategies which will put your organization on the map and attract the interest of the people you wish to influence and inform. Included are the "nuts-and-bolts" of advertising, publicity, speech-making, lobbying, and special events; how to write and produce informational literature that leaps off the page; public relations on a shoe-string budget; how to plan and evaluate "pr" efforts, and the use of new communication technologies.

March 1987 / ISBN 0-87954-192-X / $24.95

RAISE MORE MONEY FOR YOUR NONPROFIT ORGANIZATION: A Guide to Evaluating and Improving Your Fundraising

by Anne L. New

In *Raise More Money,* Anne New sets guidelines for a fundraising program that will benefit the incipient as well as the established nonprofit organization. The author divides this new guidebook into three sections: "The Basics," which delineates the necessary steps a nonprofit must take before launching a development campaign; "Fundraising Methods," which encourages organizational self-analysis and points the way to an effective program involving many sources of funding; and "Fundraising Resources," a 20-page bibliography that highlights the most useful research and funding directories available.

January 1991 / ISBN 0-87954-388-4 / $14.95

THE SHADOW STATE: Government and Voluntary Sector in Transition

In this fascinating analysis, Jennifer Wolch explains the dynamics of the unfolding relationship between the voluntary sector and government. The author uses the term "shadow state" to describe a sector of society composed of technically independent voluntary organizations, a sector that, Wolch contends, is increasingly controlled by the government. *The Shadow State* is a timely and informative piece of scholarship, offering sound advice to voluntary groups that seek to accomplish significant social change: to avoid the compromising power of state control.

March 1990 / ISBN 0-87954-231-0 / $24.95

SECURING YOUR ORGANIZATION'S FUTURE: A Complete Guide to Fundraising Strategies

by Michael Seltzer

Michael Seltzer acts as your personal fundraising consultant. Beginners get bottom-line facts and easy-to-follow work-sheets to organize financial planning. Veteran fundraisers receive a complete review of the basics plus new money-making ideas.

Seltzer's work is supplemented with an extensive bibliography of selected readings and resource organizations. Highly recommended for use as a text in nonprofit management programs at colleges and universities.

February 1987 / ISBN 0-87954-190-3 / $24.95

SUCCEEDING WITH CONSULTANTS: Self-Assessment for the Changing Nonprofit

Succeeding with Consultants provides practical advice for nonprofit executives eager to improve their organization's performance. This inspirational book, written by Barbara

Kibbe and Fred Setterberg and supported by the David and Lucile Packard Foundation, guides nonprofits through the process of selecting and utilizing consultants to strengthen their organization's operations. *Succeeding with Consultants* identifies the areas that could benefit from a consultant's advice and suggests ways to find, select, and hire the right consultant. The book emphasizes self-assessment tools and covers six different areas in which a nonprofit organization might benefit from a consultant's advice: governance, planning, fund development, financial management, public relations and marketing, and quality assurance.

February 1992 / ISBN 0-87954-450-3 / $19.95

VOLUNTEERS IN ACTION

In *Volunteers in Action,* authors Brian O'Connell and Ann Brown O'Connell illustrate the impact of ordinary citizens and how their dedication to voluntary action enriches their lives and changes their communities, the country, and the world. Using interviews and anecdotes, the authors provide unique insight into the true character of the voluntary sector. The book also serves as a call to action, encouraging citizens to involve themselves in this rewarding form of participatory democracy. The authors conclude by commending efforts to foster the ethic of volunteerism in young people, suggesting that the betterment of society ultimately depends on the idealism of the young.

September 1989
Paperbound: ISBN 0-87954-292-6 / $19.95
Hardbound: ISBN 0-87954-291-8 / $24.95

MEMBERSHIP PROGRAM

ASSOCIATES PROGRAM
Direct Line to Fundraising Information

The Associates Program puts important facts and figures on your desk through a toll-free telephone reference service helping you to:

- identify potential sources of foundation funding for your organization,
- gather important information to target and present your proposals most effectively.

Your annual membership in the Associates Program gives you vital information on a timely basis, saving you hundreds of hours of research time.

- Membership in the Associates Program delivers important funding information to you, including information from:
  - —foundation and corporate annual reports, brochures, press releases, grants lists, and other annoucements
  - —IRS 990-PF information returns for all 34,000 U.S. foundations—often the only source of information on small foundations
  - —books and periodicals on the grantmaking field, including regulation and nonprofit management
- The Associates Program places this vital information at your fingertips via a *toll-free telephone number.* The Annual fee of $495 for the Associates Program entitles you to *10 free calls of 15 minutes each, or 2½ hours worth of answers per month.*
- Membership in the Associates Program allows you to request *custom searches of the Foundation Center's computerized databases* which contain information on *all 34,000* active U.S. foundations and corporate givers. There is an additional cost for this service.
- Associate Program members may request photocopies of key documents. Important information from 990-PFs, Annual Reports, Application Guidelines and other resources, can be copied and either mailed or faxed to your office. The fee for this service, available only to Associate Members, is $2.00 for the first page of material and $1 for each additional page. Fax service is available at an additional charge.
- All Associate Program members receive the Associates Program quarterly newsletter. It provides news and information about new foundations, changes in boards of directors, new programs and new publications from both the Foundation Center and other publishers in the field.

Thousands of professional fundraisers find it extremely cost effective to rely on the Center's Associates Program. Put our staff of experts to work for your fundraising program. For more information call TOLL-FREE 800-424-9836.

FOUNDATION CENTER DATABASES

Foundation and Grants Information Online

As the only nonprofit organization whose sole purpose is to provide information on grantmaking and grantseeking activity, the Foundation Center offers two important databases online. Perhaps the most flexible way to take advantage of the Foundation Center's vast resources, computer access lets you design your own search for the foundations and corporate givers most likely to support your nonprofit organization. Online retrieval provides vital information on funding sources, philanthropic giving, grant application guidelines, and the financial status of foundations to: nonprofit organizations seeking funds, grantmaking institutions, corporate contributors, researchers, journalists, and legislators.

Searches of the Center's databases can provide comprehensive and timely answers to your questions, such as . . .

- Which New York foundations support urban projects? Who are their officers and trustees?
- What are the program interest of the ten largest corporate foundations? Which ones publish annual reports?
- Which foundations gave in excess of $100,000 in the past two years for continuing education for women?
- Which are the ten largest foundations in Philadelphia by annual grants amount?
- What are the names and addresses of smaller foundations in the 441 zip code range?

The Center's up-to-date and authoritative data is available online through DIALOG Information Services, and through many online utilities. For further information on accessing the Center's databases directly through DIALOG, contact DIALOG at 415-858-2700.

DIALOG User Manual and Thesaurus

To facilitate your foundation and corporate giving research in these powerful and flexible databases, the Center now offers the new *User Manual and Thesaurus.* This comprehensive book will help you to retrieve essential facts quickly and easily on who's funding what projects in your subject or geographic area.

FOUNDATION CENTER COOPERATING COLLECTIONS
Free Funding Information Centers

The Foundation Center is an independent national service organization established by foundations to provide an authoritative source of information on private philanthropic giving. The New York, Washington (DC), Cleveland, and San Francisco reference collections operated by the Foundation Center offer a wide variety of services and comprehensive collections of information on foundations and grants. Cooperating Collections are libraries, community foundations and other nonprofit agencies that provide a core collection of Foundation Center publications and a variety of supplementary materials and services in areas useful to grantseekers. The core collection consists of :

Foundation Center's Guide to Proposal Writing	Foundation Grants Index	Literature of the Nonprofit Sector
Foundation Directory 1 and 2, and Supplement	Foundation Grants Index Quarterly	National Directory of Corporate Giving
Foundation 1000	Foundation Grants to Individuals	Selected Grant Guides
Foundation Fundamentals	Guide to U.S. Foundations, Their Trustees,	User-Friendly Guide
Foundation Giving	Officers, and Donors	

Many of the network members have sets of private foundation information returns (IRS Form 990-PF) for their state or region which are available for public use. A complete set of U.S. foundation returns can be found at the New York and Washington (DC) offices of the Foundation Center. The Cleveland and San Francisco offices contain IRS Form 990-PF returns for the midwestern and western states, respectively. Those Cooperating Collections marked with a bullet (●) have sets of private foundation information returns for their state or region.

Because the collections vary in their hours, materials and services, IT IS RECOMMENDED THAT YOU CALL EACH COLLECTION IN ADVANCE. To check on new locations or current information, call toll-free 1-800-424-9836.

Reference Collections Operated by the Foundation Center

The Foundation Center
8th Floor
79 Fifth Avenue
New York, NY 10003
212-620-4230

The Foundation Center
312 Sutter St., Rm. 312
San Francisco, CA 94108
(415) 397-0902

The Foundation Center
1001 Connecticut Ave.,NW
Washington, DC 20036
(202) 331-1400

The Foundation Center
Kent H. Smith Library
1422 Euclid, Suite 1356
Cleveland, OH 44115
(216) 861-1933

ALABAMA

● Birmingham Public Library
Government Documents
2100 Park Place
Birmingham 35203
(205) 226-3600

Huntsville Public Library
915 Monroe St.
Huntsville 35801
(205) 532-5940

University of South Alabama
Library Building
Mobile 36688
(205) 460-7025

● Auburn University at Montgomery
Library
7300 University Drive
Montgomery 36117-3596
(205) 244-3653

ALASKA

● University of Alaska at Anchorage
Library
3211 Providence Drive
Anchorage 99508
(907) 786-1848

Juneau Public Library
292 Marine Way
Juneau 99801
(907) 586-5267

ARIZONA

● Phoenix Public Library
Business & Sciences Unit
12 E. McDowell Rd.
Phoenix 85004
(602) 262-4436

● Tucson Pima Library
101 N. Stone Ave.
Tucson 87501
(602) 791-4010

ARKANSAS

● Westark Community
College—Borham Library
5210 Grand Avenue
Ft. Smith 72913
(501) 785-7133

Central Arkansas Library System
700 Louisiana
Little Rock 72201
(501) 370-5952

Pine Bluff-Jefferson County Library
System
200 E. Eighth
Pine Bluff 71601
(501) 534-2159

CALIFORNIA

● Ventura County Community
Foundation
Funding and Information
Resource Center
1355 Del Norte Rd.
Camarillo 93010
(805) 988-0196

● California Community Foundation
Funding Information Center
606 S. Olive St., Suite 2400
Los Angeles 90014-1526
(213) 413-4042

Community Foundation for
Monterey County
177 Van Buren
Monterey 93940
(408) 375-9712

Grant & Resource Center of
Northern California
Building C, Suite A
2280 Benton Dr.
Redding 96003
(916) 244-1219

Riverside City & County Public
Library
3581 Seventh St.
Riverside 92502
(714) 782-5201

California State Library
Information & Reference Center
914 Capitol Mall-Room 301
Sacramento 95814
(916) 654-0261

Nonprofit Resource Center
Sacramento Public Library
828 I Street, 2nd Floor
Sacramento 95812-2036
(916) 552-8817

● San Diego Community Foundation
Funding Information Center
101 West Broadway, Suite 1120
San Diego 92101
(619) 239-8815

● Nonprofit Development Center
Library
1762 Technology Dr., #225
San Jose 95110
(408) 452-8181

● Peninsula Community Foundation
Funding Information Library
1700 S. El Camino Real, R301
San Mateo 94402-3049
(415) 358-9392

Volunteer Center of Greater Orange
County
Nonprofit Management
Assistance Center
1000 E. Santa Ana Blvd., Ste. 200
Santa Ana 92701
(714) 953-1655

● Santa Barbara Public Library
40 E. Anapamu St.
Santa Barbara 93101
(805) 962-7653

Santa Monica Public Library
1343 Sixth St.
Santa Monica 90401-1603
(310) 458-8600

COLORADO

Pikes Peak Library District
20 N. Cascade
Colorado Springs 80901
(719) 473-2080

● Denver Public Library
Social Sciences & Genealogy
1357 Broadway
Denver 80203
(303) 640-8870

CONNECTICUT

Danbury Public Library
170 Main St.
Danbury 06810
(203) 797-4527

● Hartford Public Library
500 Main St.
Hartford 06103
(203) 293-6000

D.A.T.A.
70 Audubon St.
New Haven 06510
(203) 772-1345

DELAWARE

● University of Delaware
Hugh Morris Library
Newark 19717-5267
(302) 451-2432

FLORIDA

Volusia County Library Center
City Island
Daytona Beach 32014-4484
(904) 255-3765

● Nova University
Einstein Library
3301 College Ave.
Fort Lauderdale 33314
(305) 475-7050

Indian River Community College
Charles S. Miley Learning
  Resource Center
3209 Virginia Ave.
Fort Pierce 34981-5599
(407) 468-4757

- Jacksonville Public Libraries
  Business, Science & Documents
  122 N. Ocean St.
  Jacksonville 32202
  (904) 630-2665

- Miami-Dade Public Library
  Humanities/Social Science
  101 W. Flagler St.
  Miami 33130
  (305) 375-5575

- Orlando Public Library
  Social Sciences Department
  101 E. Central Blvd.
  Orlando 32801
  (407) 425-4694

  Selby Public Library
  1001 Blvd. of the Arts
  Sarasota 34236
  (813) 951-5501

- Tampa-Hillsborough County
    Public Library
  900 N. Ashley Drive
  Tampa 33602
  (813) 223-8865

  Community Foundation of Palm
    Beach & Martin Counties
  324 Datura St., Suite 340
  West Palm Beach 33401
  (407) 659-6800

GEORGIA

- Atlanta-Fulton Public Library
  Foundation Collection—Ivan
    Allen Department
  1 Margaret Mitchell Square
  Atlanta 30303-1089
  (404) 730-1900

  Dalton Regional Library
  310 Cappes St.
  Dalton 30720
  (706) 278-4507

HAWAII

- University of Hawaii
  Hamilton Library
  2550 The Mall
  Honolulu 96822
  (808) 956-7214

- Hawaii Community Foundation
  Hawaii Resource Center
  222 Merchant St., Second Floor
  Honolulu 96813
  (808) 537-6333

IDAHO

- Boise Public Library
  715 S. Capitol Blvd.
  Boise 83702
  (208) 384-4024

- Caldwell Public Library
  1010 Dearborn St.
  Caldwell 83605
  (208) 459-3242

ILLINOIS

- Donors Forum of Chicago
  53 W. Jackson Blvd., Suite 430
  Chicago 60604-3608
  (312) 431-0265

- Evanston Public Library
  1703 Orrington Ave.
  Evanston 60201
  (708) 866-0305

  Rock Island Public Library
  401 - 19th St.
  Rock Island 61201
  (309) 788-7627

- Sangamon State University
  Library
  Shepherd Road
  Springfield 62794-9243
  (217) 786-6633

INDIANA

- Allen County Public Library
  900 Webster St.
  Ft. Wayne 46802
  (219) 424-0544

  Indiana University Northwest Library
  3400 Broadway
  Gary 46408
  (219) 980-6582

- Indianapolis-Marion County
    Public Library
  Social Sciences
  40 W. St. Clair
  Indianapolis 46206
  (317) 269-1733

IOWA

- Cedar Rapids Public Library
  Foundation Center Collection
  500 First St., SE
  Cedar Rapids 52401
  (319) 398-5123

- Southwestern Community College
  Learning Resource Center
  1501 W. Townline Rd.
  Creston 50801
  (515) 782-7081

- Public Library of Des Moines
  100 Locust
  Des Moines 50309-1791
  (515) 283-4152

KANSAS

- Topeka and Shawnee County
    Public Library
  1515 W. 10th St.
  Topeka 66604
  (913) 233-2040

- Wichita Public Library
  223 S. Main St.
  Wichita 67202
  (316) 262-0611

KENTUCKY

  Western Kentucky University
  Helm-Cravens Library
  Bowling Green 42101-3576
  (502) 745-6125

- Louisville Free Public Library
  301 York Street
  Louisville 40203
  (502) 561-8617

LOUISIANA

- East Baton Rouge Parish Library
  Centroplex Branch Grants
    Collection
  120 St. Louis
  Baton Rouge 70802
  (504) 389-4960

  Beauregard Parish Library
  1201 West First Street
  De Ridder 70634
  (318) 463-6217

- New Orleans Public Library
  Business & Science Division
  219 Loyola Ave.
  New Orleans 70140
  (504) 596-2580

- Shreve Memorial Library
  424 Texas St.
  Shreveport 71120-1523
  (318) 226-5894

MAINE

- University of Southern Maine
  Office of Sponsored Research
  246 Deering Ave., Rm. 628
  Portland 04103
  (207) 780-4871

MARYLAND

- Enoch Pratt Free Library
  Social Science & History
  400 Cathedral St.
  Baltimore 21201
  (301) 396-5430

MASSACHUSETTS

- Associated Grantmakers of
    Massachusetts
  294 Washington St., Suite 840
  Boston 02108
  (617) 426-2606

- Boston Public Library
  Humanities Reference
  666 Boylston St
  Boston 02117
  (617) 536-5400

  Western Massachusetts Funding
    Resource Center
  65 Elliot St.
  Springfield 01101-1730
  (413) 732-3175

- Worcester Public Library
  Grants Resource Center
  Salem Square
  Worcester 01608
  (508) 799-1655

MICHIGAN

- Alpena County Library
  211 N. First St.
  Alpena 49707
  (517) 356-6188

- University of Michigan-Ann Arbor
  Graduate Library
  Reference & Research Services
    Department
  Ann Arbor 48109-1205
  (313)664-9373

- Battle Creek Community
    Foundation
  Southwest Michigan Funding
    Resource Center
  2 Riverwalk Centre
  34 W. Jackson St.
  Battle Creek 49017-3505
  (616) 962-2181

- Henry Ford Centennial Library
  Adult Services
  16301 Michigan Ave.
  Dearborn 48126
  (313) 943-2330

- Wayne State University
  Purdy/Kresge Library
  5265 Cass Avenue
  Detroit 48202
  (313) 577-6424

- Michigan State University Libraries
  Social Sciences/Humanities
  Main Library
  East Lansing 48824-1048
  (517) 353-8818

- Farmington Community Library
  32737 West 12 Mile Rd.
  Farmington Hills 48018
  (313) 553-0300

- University of Michigan—Flint
  Library
  Flint 48502-2186
  (313) 762-3408

- Grand Rapids Public Library
  Business Dept.—3rd Floor
  60 Library Plaza NE
  Grand Rapids 49503-3093
  (616) 456-3600

- Michigan Technological University
  Van Pelt Library
  1400 Townsend Dr.
  Houghton 49931
  (906) 487-2507

- Sault Ste. Marie Area Public
    Schools
  Office of Compensatory Education
  460 W. Spruce St.
  Sault Ste. Marie 49783-1874
  (906) 635-6619

- Northwestern Michigan College
  Mark & Helen Osterin Library
  1701 E. Front St.
  Traverse City 49684
  (616)922-1060

MINNESOTA

- Duluth Public Library
  520 W. Superior St.
  Duluth 55802
  (218) 723-3802

  Southwest State University
  University Library
  Marshall 56258
  (507) 537-6176

- Minneapolis Public Library
  Sociology Department
  300 Nicollet Mall
  Minneapolis 55401
  (612) 372-6555

  Rochester Public Library
  11 First St. SE
  Rochester 55904-3777
  (507) 285-8002

St. Paul Public Library
90 W. Fourth St.
St. Paul 55102
(612) 292-6307

MISSISSIPPI

Jackson/Hinds Library System
300 N. State St.
Jackson 39201
(601) 968-5803

MISSOURI

- Clearinghouse for Midcontinent
Foundations
University of Missouri
5110 Cherry St.
Kansas City 64113-0680
(816) 235-1176

- Kansas City Public Library
311 E. 12th St.
Kansas City 64111
(816) 221-9650

- Metropolitan Association for
Philanthropy, Inc.
5615 Pershing Avenue, Suite 20
St. Louis 63112
(314) 361-3900

- Springfield-Greene County Library
397 E. Central
Springfield 65802
(417) 869-9400

MONTANA

- Eastern Montana College Library
Special Collections—Grants
1500 North 30th St.
Billings 59101-0298
(406) 657-1662

Bozeman Public Library
220 E. Lamme
Bozeman 59715
(406) 586-4787

- Montana State Library
Library Services
1515 E. 6th Ave.
Helena 59620
(406) 444-3004

NEBRASKA

- University of Nebraska—Lincoln
Love Library
14th & R Streets
Lincoln 68588-0410
(402) 472-2848

- W. Dale Clark Library
Social Sciences Department
215 S. 15th St.
Omaha 68102
(402) 444-4826

NEVADA

- Las Vegas-Clark County Library
District
833 Las Vegas Blvd. North
Las Vegas 89101
(702) 382-5280

- Washoe County Library
301 S. Center St.
Reno 89501
(702) 785-4010

NEW HAMPSHIRE

- New Hampshire Charitable Fund
One South St.
Concord 03302-1335
(603) 225-6641

- Plymouth State College
Herbert H. Lamson Library
Plymouth 03264
(603) 535-2258

NEW JERSEY

Cumberland County Library
New Jersey Room
800 E. Commerce St.
Bridgeton 08302
(609) 453-2210

Free Public Library of Elizabeth
11 S. Broad St.
Elizabeth 07202
(908)354-6060

County College of Morris
Learning Resource Center
214 Center Grove Rd.
Randolph 07869
(201) 328-5296

- New Jersey State Library
Governmental Reference Services
185 West State St.
Trenton 08625-0520
(609) 292-6220

NEW MEXICO

Albuquerque Community Foundation
3301 Menual NE, Ste. 16
Albuquerque 87176-6960
(505) 883-6240

- New Mexico State Library
Information Services
325 Don Gaspar
Santa Fe 87503
(505) 827-3824

NEW YORK

- New York State Library
Humanities Reference
Cultural Education Center
Empire State Plaza
Albany 12230
(518) 474-5355

Suffolk Cooperative Library System
627 N. Sunrise Service Rd.
Bellport 11713
(516) 286-1600

New York Public Library
Fordham Branch
2556 Bainbridge Ave.
Bronx 10458
(212) 220-6575

Brooklyn-In-Touch Information
Center, Inc.
One Hanson Place—Room 2504
Brooklyn 11243
(718) 230-3200

- Buffalo & Erie County Public
Library
History Department
Lafayette Square
Buffalo 14203
(716) 858-7103

Huntington Public Library
338 Main St.
Huntington 11743
(516) 427-5165

Queens Borough Public Library
Social Sciences Division
89-11 Merrick Blvd.
Jamaica 11432
(718) 990-0700

- Levittown Public Library
1 Bluegrass Lane
Levittown 11756
(516) 731-5728

New York Public Library
Countee Cullen Branch Library
104 W. 136th St.
New York 10030
(212) 491-2070

SUNY at Old Westbury
Library
223 Store Hill Rd.
Old Westbury 11568
(516) 876-3156

Adriance Memorial Library
Special Services Department
93 Market St.
Poughkeepsie 12601
(914) 485-3445

- Rochester Public Library
Business, Economics & Law
115 South Avenue
Rochester 14604
(716) 428-7328

- Onondaga County Public Library
447 S. Salina St.
Syracuse 13202-2494
(315) 448-4636

Utica Public Library
303 Genesee St.
Utica 13501
(315)735-2279

- White Plains Public Library
100 Martine Ave.
White Plains 10601
(914) 422-1480

NORTH CAROLINA

- Asheville-Buncombe Technical
Community College
Learning Resources Center
340 Victoria Rd.
Asheville 28801
(704) 254-4960

- The Duke Endowment
200 S. Tryon St., Suite 1100
Charlotte 28202
(704) 376-0291

Durham County Public Library
301 North Roxboro
Durham 27702
(919) 560-0110

- State Library of North Carolina
Government and Business
Services
Archives Bldg., 109 E. Jones St.
Raleigh 27601
(919) 733-3270

- Winston-Salem Foundation
310 W. 4th St., Suite 229
Winston-Salem 27101-2889
(919) 725-2382

NORTH DAKOTA

- North Dakota State University
Library
Fargo 58105
(701) 237-8886

OHIO

Stark County District Library
Humanities
715 Market Ave. N.
Canton 44702
(216) 452-0665

- Public Library of Cincinnati &
Hamilton County
Grants Resource Center
800 Vine St.—Library Square
Cincinnati 45202-2071
(513) 369-6940

Columbus Metropolitan Library
Business and Technology
96 S. Grant Ave.
Columbus 43215
(614) 645-2590

- Dayton & Montgomery County
Public Library
First Floor, East Side
215 E. Third St.
Dayton 45402
(513) 227-9500 x211

- Toledo-Lucas County Public
Library
Social Sciences Department
325 Michigan St.
Toledo 43624-1614
(419) 259-5245

Ohio University—Zanesville
Community Education
Department
1425 Newark Rd.
Zanesville 43701
(614) 453-0762

OKLAHOMA

- Oklahoma City University
Dulaney Browne Library
2501 N. Blackwelder
Oklahoma City 73106
(405) 521-5072

- Tulsa City-County Library
400 Civic Center
Tulsa 74103
(918) 596-7944

OREGON

Oregon Institute of Technology
Library
3201 Campus Dr.
Klamath Falls 97601-8801
(503) 885-1773

- Pacific Non-Profit Network
Grantsmanship Resource Library
33 N. Central, Suite 211
Medford 97501
(503) 779-6044

- Multnomah County Library
Government Documents
801 SW Tenth Ave.
Portland 97205
(503) 248-5123

Oregon State Library
State Library Building
Salem 97310
(503) 378-4277

PENNSYLVANIA

Northampton Community College
Learning Resources Center
3835 Green Pond Rd.
Bethlehem 18017
(215) 861-5360

Erie County Library System
27 South Park Row
Erie 16501
(814) 451-6927

Dauphin County Library System
Central Library
101 Walnut St.
Harrisburg 17101
(717) 234-4961

Lancaster County Public Library
125 N. Duke St.
Lancaster 17602
(717) 394-2651

● Free Library of Philadelphia
Regional Foundation Center
Logan Square
Philadelphia 19103
(215) 686-5423

● Carnegie Library of Pittsburgh
Foundation Collection
4400 Forbes Ave.
Pittsburgh 15213-4080
(412) 622-3114

Pocono Northeast Development
Fund
James Pettinger Memorial Library
1151 Oak St.
Pittston 18640-3755
(717) 655-5581

Reading Public Library
100 South Fifth St.
Reading 19602
(215) 478-6355

RHODE ISLAND

● Providence Public Library
150 Empire St.
Providence 02906
(401) 521-7722

SOUTH CAROLINA

● Charleston County Library
404 King St.
Charleston 29403
(803) 723-1645

● South Carolina State Library
1500 Senate St.
Columbia 29211
(803) 734-8666

SOUTH DAKOTA

Nonprofit Grants Assistance Center
Business & Education Institute
Washington Street, East Hall
Dakota State University
Madison 57042
(605) 256-5555

● South Dakota State Library
800 Governors Drive
Pierre 57501-2294
(605) 773-5070
(800) 592-1841 (SD residents)

Sioux Falls Area Foundation
141 N. Main Ave., Suite 500
Sioux Falls 57102-1134
(605) 336-7055

TENNESSEE

● Knox County Public Library
500 W. Church Ave.
Knoxville 37902
(615) 544-5700

● Memphis & Shelby County Public
Library
1850 Peabody Ave.
Memphis 38104
(901) 725-8877

Nashville Public Library
Business Information Division
8th Ave. N. & Union
Nashville 37203
(615) 862-5843

TEXAS

● Community Foundation of Abilene
Funding Information Library
500 N. Chestnut, Suite 1509
Abilene 79604
(915) 676-3883

● Amarillo Area Foundation
700 First National Place
801 S. Fillmore
Amarillo 79101
(806) 376-4521

● Hogg Foundation for Mental
Health
Will C. Hogg Bldg., Room 301
Inner Campus Dr.
University of Texas
Austin 78713
(512) 471-5041

● Corpus Christi State University
Library
Reference Dept.
6300 Ocean Dr.
Corpus Christi 78412
(512) 994-2608

● Dallas Public Library
Urban Information
1515 Young St.
Dallas 75201
(214) 670-1487

● El Paso Community Foundation
1616 Texas Commerce Building
El Paso 79901
(915) 533-4020

● Funding Information Center of Fort
Worth
Texas Christian University Library
2800 S. University Dr.
Ft. Worth 76129
(817) 921-7664

● Houston Public Library
Bibliographic Information Center
500 McKinney
Houston 77002
(713) 236-1313

Longview Public Library
222 W. Cotton St.
Longview 75601
(903) 237-1352

Lubbock Area Foundation, Inc
502 Texas Commerce Bank
Building
Lubbock 79401
(806) 762-8061

● Funding Information Center
530 McCullough, Suite 600
San Antonio 78212-8270
(210) 227-4333

North Texas Center for Nonprofit
Management
624 Indiana, Suite 307
Witchita Falls 76301
(817) 322-4961

UTAH

● Salt Lake City Public Library
209 East 500 South
Salt Lake City 84111
(801) 524-8200

VERMONT

● Vermont Dept. of Libraries
Reference & Law Info. Services
109 State St.
Montpelier 05609
(802) 828-3268

VIRGINIA

● Hampton Public Library
4207 Victoria Blvd.
Hampton 23669
(804) 727-1312

● Richmond Public Library
Business, Science & Technology
101 East Franklin St.
Richmond 23219
(804) 780-8223

● Roanoke City Public Library
System
Central Library
706 S. Jefferson St.
Roanoke 24016
(703) 981-2477

WASHINGTON

Mid-Columbia Library
405 South Dayton
Kennewick 99336
(509) 586-3156

● Seattle Public Library
Science, Social Science
1000 Fourth Ave.
Seattle 98104
(206) 386-4620

● Spokane Public Library
Funding Information Center
West 811 Main Ave.
Spokane 99201
(509) 838-3364

Greater Wenatchee Community
Foundation at the Wenatchee
Public Library
310 Douglas St.
Wenatchee 98807
(509) 662-5021

WEST VIRGINIA

● Kanawha County Public Library
123 Capitol St.
Charleston 25304
(304) 343-4646

WISCONSIN

● University of Wisconsin-Madison
Memorial Library
728 State St.
Madison 53706
(608) 262-3242

● Marquette University Memorial
Library
Foundation Collection
1415 W. Wisconsin Ave.
Milwaukee 53233
(414) 288-1515

WYOMING

● Natrona County Public Library
307 E. 2nd St.
Casper 82601-2598
(307) 237-4935

● Laramie County Community
College
Instructional Resource Center
1400 E. College Dr.
Cheyenne 82007-3299
(307) 778-1206

Teton County Library
320 S. King St.
Jackson 83001
(307) 733-2164

Rock Springs Library
400 C St.
Rock Springs 82901
(307) 362-6212

PUERTO RICO

University of Puerto Rico
Ponce Technological College
Library
Box 7186
Ponce 00732
809-844-8181

Universidad del Sagrado Corazon
M.M.T. Guevara Library
Santurce 00914
809-728-1515 x 357

Participants in the Cooperating Collections Network are libraries or nonprofit information centers that provide fundraising information or other funding-related technical assistance in their communities. Cooperating Collections agree to provide free public access to a basic collection of Foundation Center publications during a regular schedule of hours, offering free funding research guidance to all visitors. Many also provide a variety of special services for local nonprofit organizations, using staff or volunteers to prepare special materials, organize workshops, or conduct orientations.

The Foundation Center welcomes inquiries from libraries or information centers in the U.S.A. interested in providing this type of public information service. If you are interested in establishing a funding information library for the use of nonprofit organizations in your area, or in learning more about the program, please write to: Judith Margolin, Vice President for Public Services, The Foundation Center, 79 Fifth Avenue, New York, NY 10003-3076.

DESCRIPTIVE DIRECTORY

DESCRIPTIVE DIRECTORY

ALABAMA

1
Alabama Power Foundation, Inc. ▼
600 North 18th St., 17th Fl.
Birmingham 35291   (205) 250-2393

Established in 1989 in AL.
Donor(s): Alabama Power Co.
Foundation type: Company-sponsored
Financial data (yr. ended 12/31/90): Assets,
$43,413,240 (M); gifts received, $2,500,000;
expenditures, $1,370,933; qualifying
distributions, $1,265,045, including $1,265,045
for 102 grants (high: $183,700; low: $300;
average: $5,000-$25,000).
Purpose and activities: Giving primarily for the
United Way and higher education; support also
for the arts, health associations and hospitals, and
social and family services, including youth groups.
Fields of interest: Community funds, higher
education, arts, health associations, hospitals,
social services, family services, youth.
Types of support: Scholarship funds, capital
campaigns, operating budgets.
Limitations: Giving limited to AL. No support for
religious organizations. No grants to individuals,
or for operating funds that duplicate United Way
support.
Application information:
 Initial approach: Letter
 Deadline(s): None
 Write: Mrs. Jera G. Stribling, Exec. Dir.
Officers: Travis J. Bowden, Pres.; Robert Holmes,
Jr., V.P.; William L. McDonough, V.P.; Art P.
Beattie, Secy.-Treas.; Jera G. Stribling, Exec. Dir.
Directors: T. Harold Jones, Homer H. Turner,
William E. Zales, Jr.
EIN: 570901832
Recent health grants:
1-1 Childrens Hospital of Alabama, Birmingham,
 AL, $40,000. For capital support. 1990.
1-2 Glenwood Mental Health Services,
 Birmingham, AL, $12,500. For capital support.
 1990.
1-3 Southern Research Institute, Birmingham, AL,
 $37,500. For capital support. 1990.

2
Andalusia Health Services, Inc.
P.O. Box 667
Andalusia 36420   (205) 222-5830

Established in 1981 in AL.
Foundation type: Independent
Financial data (yr. ended 06/30/91): Assets,
$2,324,621 (M); expenditures, $185,184;
qualifying distributions, $176,551, including
$124,965 for 5 grants (high: $72,500; low:
$1,100) and $43,864 for 64 grants to individuals
(high: $1,500; low: $1).
Purpose and activities: Giving primarily for
community health services; support also for
scholarships in a health-related field, such as
nursing, medicine, and medical or laboratory
technology.
Fields of interest: Health services, nursing,
medical education, medical sciences.
Types of support: Equipment, operating budgets,
student aid.
Limitations: Giving primarily in Andalusia, AL,
and the surrounding area; scholarships only to
residents of Covington County. No grants to
individuals (except scholarships); no
program-related investments.
Application information: Contributes only to
pre-selected organizations; accepts applications
only from individuals seeking scholarships;
application form required.
 Deadline(s): Apr. 15 for scholarships
 Write: Carolyn Davis
Officers and Directors:* George H. Proctor,*
Pres.; Hugh King,* V.P.; Eiland E. Anthony,*
Secy.-Treas.; J. Dige Bishop, Ray Latimer, W.B.
McDonald, John S. Merrill, Catherine D. Roland.
Number of staff: None.
EIN: 630793474

3
George W. Barber, Jr. Foundation
36 Barber Court
Birmingham 35209

Established in 1986 in AL.
Donor(s): George W. Barber, Jr.
Foundation type: Independent
Financial data (yr. ended 12/31/90): Assets,
$2,934,155 (M); expenditures, $170,875;
qualifying distributions, $164,579, including
$164,579 for 29 grants (high: $44,500; low:
$100).
Fields of interest: Ecology, wildlife, animal
welfare, social services, youth, child welfare,
medical research, health associations.

Limitations: Giving primarily in AL. No grants to
individuals.
Application information: Contributes only to
pre-selected organizations. Applications not
accepted.
Officers: George W. Barber, Chair. and Pres.;
Russell M. Cunningham III, Secy.; B. Austin
Cunningham, Treas.
EIN: 630941684

4
The BE&K Foundation
2000 International Park Dr.
Birmingham 35243-4220   (205) 969-3600
Application address: P.O. Box 2332,
Birmingham, AL 35201

Established in 1988 in AL.
Donor(s): BE&K, Inc.
Foundation type: Company-sponsored
Financial data (yr. ended 03/31/91): Assets,
$3,511 (M); gifts received, $266,319;
expenditures, $277,025; qualifying distributions,
$277,025, including $277,025 for 85 grants
(high: $50,000; low: $35).
Fields of interest: Education, higher education,
engineering, elementary education, child
development, drug abuse.
Types of support: Employee-related scholarships,
endowment funds.
Limitations: Giving primarily in Birmingham, AL.
Application information: Application form
required.
 Copies of proposal: 1
 Deadline(s): Dec.
 Board meeting date(s): Feb.
 Final notification: 2 months
 Write: T. Michael Goodrich, Trustee
Trustees: T. Michael Goodrich, Boyd E. Jordan,
Theodore Kennedy.
Number of staff: None.
EIN: 630979638

5
Herman & Emmie Bolden Foundation
P.O. Box 360028
Birmingham 35236   (205) 988-8989

Established in 1982 in AL.
Donor(s): Herman D. Bolden, Southern Coach
Manufacturing Co., Inc.
Foundation type: Independent
Financial data (yr. ended 06/30/91): Assets,
·$2,647,813 (M); gifts received, $500,000;
expenditures, $368,925; qualifying distributions,

$364,823, including $364,823 for 34 grants (high: $135,000; low: $200).
Fields of interest: Cancer, health associations, Protestant giving, social services.
Application information:
  Deadline(s): None
  Write: Herman D. Bolden, V.P.
Officers: Emmie C. Bolden, Pres.; Herman D. Bolden, V.P.; Stanley C. Bolden, Secy.
EIN: 630828670

6
The Joseph S. Bruno Charitable Foundation
P.O. Box 530441
Birmingham 35253-0441

Established in 1985.
Foundation type: Independent
Financial data (yr. ended 11/30/91): Assets, $6,989,535 (M); expenditures, $44,270; qualifying distributions, $42,500, including $42,500 for 4 grants (high: $25,000; low: $2,500).
Fields of interest: Arts, Catholic giving, community development, civic affairs, education—building funds, cancer.
Types of support: Annual campaigns, scholarship funds, building funds, endowment funds, special projects.
Limitations: Giving primarily in AL. No grants to individuals.
Application information: Contributes only to pre-selected organizations. Applications not accepted.
  Board meeting date(s): Nov.
  Write: Benny M. LaRussa, Jr., Treas.
Officers: Joseph S. Bruno, Pres.; Robert A. Sprain, Jr., V.P. and Secy.; Benny M. LaRussa, Jr., V.P. and Treas.
EIN: 630936234

7
Lee Bruno Foundation
1641 Panorama Dr.
Birmingham 35216

Established in 1985 in AL.
Donor(s): Lee J. Bruno.
Foundation type: Independent
Financial data (yr. ended 11/30/90): Assets, $4,191,751 (M); gifts received, $663,263; expenditures, $130,552; qualifying distributions, $129,965, including $129,000 for 38 grants (high: $30,000; low: $100).
Purpose and activities: Giving primarily for churches and Catholic welfare organizations; support also for social services and health.
Fields of interest: Catholic giving, Catholic welfare, social services, health.
Limitations: Giving primarily in AL. No grants to individuals.
Application information: Contributes only to pre-selected organizations. Applications not accepted.
Officers: Lee J. Bruno, Pres.; Vincent Bruno, V.P.; Carol Rumore, V.P.
EIN: 630819300

8
Central Bank Foundation
701 South 20th St.
Birmingham 35233   (205) 933-3466

Established in 1981 in AL.
Donor(s): Central Bank of the South.
Foundation type: Company-sponsored
Financial data (yr. ended 12/31/91): Assets, $440,415 (M); gifts received, $525,000; expenditures, $424,513; qualifying distributions, $422,294, including $422,294 for 424 grants (high: $25,000; low: $6).
Purpose and activities: Giving primarily for community funds, business and business education, health, social service and youth agencies, education, civic affairs, and arts and cultural programs.
Fields of interest: Community funds, youth, civic affairs, education, arts, business, business education, health.
Types of support: General purposes, annual campaigns, building funds, employee-related scholarships.
Limitations: Giving generally limited to AL-based organizations or those with significant AL connections. No support for religious organizations. No grants to individuals.
Application information:
  Copies of proposal: 1
  Deadline(s): None
  Write: DeWayne Cuthbertson, Pres.
Officers: DeWayne Cuthbertson, Pres.; Jerry W. Powell, Secy.; Michael A. Bean, Treas.
Trustee: D. Paul Jones, Jr.
EIN: 630823545

9
The Comer Foundation
P.O. Box 302
Sylacauga 35150   (205) 249-2962

Incorporated in 1945 in AL.
Donor(s): Avondale Mills, Comer-Avondale Mills, Inc., Cowikee Mills.
Foundation type: Independent
Financial data (yr. ended 12/31/91): Assets, $10,606,841 (M); expenditures, $677,673; qualifying distributions, $608,446, including $552,370 for 39 grants (high: $100,000; low: $250).
Purpose and activities: Emphasis on higher and other education; support also for health, recreation, human services, and cultural programs.
Fields of interest: Higher education, education, health, recreation, social services, cultural programs.
Limitations: Giving primarily in AL. No grants to individuals.
Application information:
  Initial approach: Letter
  Deadline(s): None
  Write: R. Larry Edmunds, Secy.-Treas.
Officers and Trustees: * Richard J. Comer,* Chair.; William Bew White,* Vice-Chair.; R. Larry Edmunds, Secy.-Treas.; Jane S. Crockard, Hugh Comers Nabers, Jr., Jane B. Selfe.
Number of staff: 1 full-time professional.
EIN: 636004424

10
The Daniel Foundation of Alabama
200 Office Park Dr., Suite 100
Birmingham 35223   (205) 879-0902

Established in 1978 in AL as partial successor to The Daniel Foundation.
Donor(s): Charles W. Daniel,‡ R. Hugh Daniel.‡
Foundation type: Independent
Financial data (yr. ended 12/31/90): Assets, $20,940,566 (M); expenditures, $1,704,972; qualifying distributions, $1,665,586, including $1,535,500 for 52 grants (high: $250,000; low: $1,000; average: $2,000-$50,000).
Purpose and activities: Emphasis on health and higher education; support also for cultural programs, social service and youth agencies, and civic affairs.
Fields of interest: Health, higher education, cultural programs, social services, youth, civic affairs.
Limitations: Giving primarily in the southeastern states, especially AL.
Application information: Application form not required.
  Initial approach: Letter
  Deadline(s): None
  Board meeting date(s): Apr. and Oct.
  Final notification: Varies
  Write: S. Garry Smith, Secy.-Treas.
Officers and Directors: * M.C. Daniel,* Chair.; Harry B. Brock, Jr.,* Pres.; Charles W. Daniel,* V.P.; S. Garry Smith,* Secy.-Treas. and Mgr.; Frances Daniel Branum.
Number of staff: 1 part-time professional.
EIN: 630736444

11
The Solon & Martha Dixon Foundation
P.O. Drawer 990
Andalusia 36420   (205) 222-3138

Established in 1981 in AL.
Donor(s): Solon Dixon.
Foundation type: Independent
Financial data (yr. ended 06/30/92): Assets, $11,830,890 (M); expenditures, $604,811; qualifying distributions, $578,562, including $520,282 for 7 grants (high: $241,209; low: $633).
Fields of interest: Education—building funds, education, higher education, religion, libraries, computer sciences, community development, crime and law enforcement, wildlife, health services, mental health, medical research.
Types of support: Building funds, special projects, equipment, research.
Limitations: Giving primarily in AL, with emphasis on the city of Andalusia and Covington County. No grants to individuals.
Application information: Contributes only to pre-selected organizations. Applications not accepted.
  Write: Gordon S. Jones, Treas.
Officers: Martha B. Dixon, Pres.; Thomas G. Mancuso, V.P. and Secy.; Gordon S. Jones, Treas.
Number of staff: 1 part-time professional.
EIN: 630812726

12
Dravo Corporate Giving Program
P.O. Box 2068
Mobile 36633   (205) 438-3531

Purpose and activities: Supports education, social services, health care and culture and the arts.
Fields of interest: Education, community funds, health, cultural programs, arts.
Types of support: Matching funds, building funds, employee matching gifts, scholarship funds.
Limitations: Giving limited to headquarters city and operating locations.
Application information:
   Initial approach: Letter to nearest company facility or headquarters
   Final notification: 6-8 weeks
   Write: Sidney G. Weinacker, Dir., Planning and Dev.

13
E. L. Gibson Foundation
P.O. Box 159
Enterprise 36331   (205) 393-4553
Application address: Office for Development, Enterprise State Junior College, Enterprise, AL 36330

Established in 1944.
Foundation type: Independent
Financial data (yr. ended 12/31/89): Assets, $2,356,818 (M); expenditures, $114,002; qualifying distributions, $86,743, including $83,309 for grants (high: $20,000; low: $1,000; average: $1,000-$20,000).
Purpose and activities: Giving for medical and nursing education and scholarships; support also for health agencies and civic affairs.
Fields of interest: Medical education, nursing, health services, civic affairs.
Types of support: Student aid, conferences and seminars, equipment, lectureships, special projects.
Limitations: Giving limited to Coffee County, AL, and contiguous counties.
Application information: Application form not required.
   Initial approach: Letter
   Copies of proposal: 1
   Deadline(s): None
   Board meeting date(s): Quarterly
   Write: J.B. Brunson, Mgr.
Officers and Trustees:* Herbert Gibson,* Chair.; J.B. Brunson,* Mgr.; Frank Bynum, Robert Foy, Joe Herod, William Mitchell, Raymond Pappas, J.E. Pittman, Horace Sanders, Roger Williams.
Directors: Whit Armstrong, Ben Henderson, Joe Pittman, Moultrie Sessions.
Number of staff: 1 part-time support.
EIN: 630383929

14
Hill Crest Foundation, Inc.
310 North 19th St.
Bessemer 35020   (205) 425-5800

Established in 1967 in AL.
Foundation type: Independent
Financial data (yr. ended 06/30/91): Assets, $22,816,755 (M); expenditures, $803,657; qualifying distributions, $628,507, including

$565,700 for 36 grants (high: $100,000; low: $1,500).
Purpose and activities: Priorities given to psychiatry and the field of mental health. Giving primarily for higher education, especially the psychiatry department of a university, and health, including mental and other health services, pharmacology, and hospitals; support also for the aged, arts and culture, a community fund, community development, and a youth organization.
Fields of interest: Higher education, psychiatry, mental health, hospitals, health, health services, aged, arts, community funds, community development, youth.
Types of support: Endowment funds, capital campaigns, special projects, research, scholarship funds, publications, equipment, building funds, professorships, renovation projects, matching funds, technical assistance, seed money.
Limitations: Giving limited to AL. No grants to individuals.
Publications: 990-PF.
Application information: Application form not required.
   Initial approach: Letter
   Copies of proposal: 8
   Deadline(s): None
   Board meeting date(s): Quarterly
   Write: Jack G. Paden, Chair.
Officers and Trustees:* Jack G. Paden,* Chair.; Charles R. Terry, Sr.,* Vice-Chair.; F. Brooks Yielding III,* Secy.; Hugh W. Agricola, Peter G. Cowin, Stanley E. Graham, Willard L. Hurley.
Number of staff: 2 full-time professional.
EIN: 630516927

15
Lowder Family Foundation
2000 Interstate Park Dr.
Montgomery 36109   (205) 270-6510

Established in 1990 in AL.
Donor(s): Catherine K. Lowder.
Foundation type: Independent
Financial data (yr. ended 12/31/90): Assets, $500 (M); gifts received, $214,828; expenditures, $214,328; qualifying distributions, $214,328, including $200,933 for 10 grants (high: $100,000; low: $250).
Purpose and activities: Giving primarily for higher education and cancer research; support also for a community fund and a Presbyterian church.
Fields of interest: Higher education, cancer, community funds, Protestant giving.
Types of support: Professorships, building funds, general purposes, research.
Limitations: Giving primarily in Montgomery, AL. No grants to individuals.
Application information: Applications not accepted.
   Write: James K. Lowder, Secy.
Officers and Directors:* Robert E. Lowder,* Pres.; Thomas H. Lowder,* V.P.; James K. Lowder,* Secy.
EIN: 631024272

16
The Ben May Charitable Trust
P.O. Drawer 1467
Mobile 36621
Application address: P.O. Box 123, Mobile, AL 36601

Established in 1971 in AL.
Foundation type: Independent
Financial data (yr. ended 12/31/90): Assets, $8,114,794 (M); expenditures, $251,048; qualifying distributions, $169,696, including $140,500 for 2 grants (high: $139,500; low: $1,000).
Fields of interest: Higher education, cancer.
Limitations: Giving primarily in AL. No grants to individuals.
Application information: Application form not required.
   Deadline(s): None
   Write: Mr. Vivian G. Johnston, Jr., Chair., Distrib. Comm.
Distribution Committee: Vivian G. Johnston, Jr., Chair.; W. Brevard Hand, Martin Perlman, M.D.
Trustee: AmSouth Bank, N.A.
EIN: 237145009

17
D. W. McMillan Foundation
329 Belleville Ave.
Brewton 36426   (205) 867-4881
Application address: P.O. Box 867, Brewton, AL 36427

Trust established in 1956 in AL.
Donor(s): D.W. McMillan Trust.
Foundation type: Independent
Financial data (yr. ended 12/31/90): Assets, $10,905,415 (M); expenditures, $709,887; qualifying distributions, $608,528, including $591,000 for 24 grants (high: $120,000; low: $1,000).
Purpose and activities: Aid to poor and needy people, including welfare and medical aid, through grants to local health and welfare organizations; limited to programs giving direct aid.
Fields of interest: Welfare, homeless, child welfare, hospitals, health, health services, mental health, handicapped, general charitable giving.
Types of support: Emergency funds.
Limitations: Giving limited to Escambia County, AL, and Escambia County, FL. No support for education or medical research.
Application information: Applications accepted only from Escambia County, AL, and Escambia County, FL. Application form not required.
   Initial approach: Letter
   Copies of proposal: 1
   Deadline(s): Dec. 1
   Board meeting date(s): Dec. 1
   Final notification: Dec. 31
   Write: Ed Leigh McMillan II, Managing Trustee
Trustees: Ed Leigh McMillan II, Managing Trustee; John David Finlay, Jr., M.N. Hoke, Jr., Allison R. Sinrod.
Number of staff: 1 part-time support.
EIN: 636044830

18
Robert R. Meyer Foundation ▼
c/o AmSouth Bank, N.A., Trust Dept.
P.O. Box 11426
Birmingham 35202   (205) 326-5396

Trust established in 1942 in AL.
Donor(s): Robert R. Meyer,‡ John E. Meyer.‡
Foundation type: Independent
Financial data (yr. ended 12/31/90): Assets,
$20,405,174 (M); expenditures, $1,557,237;
qualifying distributions, $1,473,375, including
$1,446,500 for 39 grants (high: $200,000; low:
$2,500; average: $5,000-$25,000).
Purpose and activities: Aid largely to local health
and welfare organizations, educational
institutions, and cultural organizations selected by
an advisory committee.
Fields of interest: Health, hospitals, welfare,
education.
Types of support: Building funds, equipment,
land acquisition, research, scholarship funds.
Limitations: Giving limited to the Birmingham,
AL, metropolitan area. No grants to individuals,
or for endowment funds or operating budgets.
Publications: Application guidelines.
Application information: Application form not
required.
   Initial approach: Proposal
   Copies of proposal: 7
   Deadline(s): Apr. 15 and Oct. 15
   Board meeting date(s): June and Dec.
   Final notification: 4 weeks
   Write: Leah Scalise, Trust Officer, AmSouth
      Bank, N.A.
Grants Committee: Seybourn H. Lynne, William
J. Rushton III, William M. Spencer III, Louis J.
Willie.
Trustee: AmSouth Bank, N.A.
Number of staff: None.
EIN: 636019645
Recent health grants:
18-1 Alcohol and Drug Abuse Council,
   Birmingham, AL, $15,000. 1990.
18-2 American Lung Association of Alabama,
   Birmingham, AL, $25,000. 1990.
18-3 Childrens Hospital of Alabama,
   Birmingham, AL, $50,000. 1990.
18-4 Childrens Oncology Services of Alabama,
   Birmingham, AL, $50,000. 1990.
18-5 Eye Foundation, Birmingham, AL, $25,000.
   1990.
18-6 Fairfield Community Health Center,
   Fairfield, AL, $20,000. 1990.
18-7 Glenwood Mental Health Services,
   Birmingham, AL, $10,000. 1990.
18-8 Methodist Home for the Aging,
   Birmingham, AL, $30,000. 1990.
18-9 Southern Research Institute, Birmingham,
   AL, $80,000. 1990.

19
The Mitchell Foundation, Inc.
2405 First National Bank Bldg.
P.O. Box 1126
Mobile 36633   (205) 432-1711

Incorporated in 1957 in AL.
Donor(s): A.S. Mitchell,‡ Mrs. A.S. Mitchell.
Foundation type: Independent
Financial data (yr. ended 01/31/91): Assets,
$12,703,365 (M); expenditures, $978,864;

qualifying distributions, $842,004, including
$798,500 for 48 grants (high: $130,000; low:
$3,000).
Purpose and activities: Emphasis on secondary
and higher education; support also for social
service programs, including religious welfare
agencies, aid to the handicapped, youth agencies,
hospitals and health associations, and Protestant
church support.
Fields of interest: Higher education, secondary
education, Protestant giving, religion,
handicapped, youth, hospitals, health
associations, social services.
Limitations: Giving primarily in AL. No grants to
individuals.
Application information:
   Initial approach: Letter
   Deadline(s): None
   Board meeting date(s): Quarterly
   Write: M.L. Screven, Jr., Secy.-Treas.
Officers and Directors:* Augustine Meaher, Jr.,*
Pres.; Frank B. Vinson, Jr.,* V.P.; M.L. Screven, Jr.,*
Secy.-Treas.; William Brevard Hand, Augustine
Meaher III.
EIN: 630368954

20
The Mobile Community Foundation
100 St. Joseph St., Suite 416
Mobile 36602   (205) 438-5591
Application address: P.O. Box 990, Mobile, AL
36601-0990

Incorporated in 1976 in AL.
Foundation type: Community
Financial data (yr. ended 09/30/91): Assets,
$12,622,051 (M); gifts received, $1,586,153;
expenditures, $1,105,306; qualifying
distributions, $903,636, including $903,636 for
175 grants (high: $180,200; low: $100; average:
$1,000-$5,000).
Fields of interest: Health, social services,
education, civic affairs, cultural programs, arts.
Types of support: Capital campaigns, endowment
funds, general purposes, operating budgets,
scholarship funds, special projects.
Limitations: Giving primarily in the Mobile, AL,
metropolitan area and surrounding communities.
No grants to individuals.
Publications: Annual report, informational
brochure (including application guidelines),
newsletter, 990-PF.
Application information: Application form
required.
   Initial approach: Letter
   Copies of proposal: 8
   Deadline(s): Oct. 1
   Board meeting date(s): Quarterly
   Final notification: Dec. 1
   Write: Thomas H. Davis, Jr., Exec. Dir.
Officers and Directors:* Ann W. Delchamps,*
Pres.; M. Palmer Belsole, Jr.,* V.P.; Walter A. Bell,*
Secy.; Murray E. Cape,* Treas.; Thomas H. Davis,
Jr., Exec. Dir.; and 18 additional directors.
Number of staff: 1 full-time professional; 1
full-time support; 1 part-time support.
EIN: 630695166

21
Benjamin and Roberta Russell Educational and Charitable Foundation, Inc.
P.O. Box 272
Alexander City 35010

Incorporated in 1944 in AL.
Donor(s): Benjamin Russell.
Foundation type: Independent
Financial data (yr. ended 12/31/90): Assets,
$23,930,440 (M); expenditures, $989,246;
qualifying distributions, $918,183, including
$918,183 for grants (high: $150,000).
Purpose and activities: Giving for higher and
public education, youth programs, and a hospital.
Fields of interest: Higher education, education,
youth, hospitals.
Types of support: Scholarship funds, general
purposes.
Limitations: Giving limited to AL; scholarship
funds limited to Tallapoosa and Coosa counties.
No grants to individuals.
Application information: Contributes only to
pre-selected organizations. Applications not
accepted.
   Write: James D. Nabors, Secy.-Treas.
Officers and Directors:* Nancy R. Gwaltney,*
Pres.; Benjamin Russell,* V.P.; James D. Nabors,*
Secy.-Treas.; Roberta A. Baumgardner, James W.
Brown, Jr., Ann R. Caceres, Julia G. Fuller, Edith L.
Russell, Julia W. Russell.
EIN: 630393126

22
Barbara Ingalls Shook Foundation
206 Hart Fell Crescent
Birmingham 35223-2905   (205) 870-0299

Established in 1980.
Donor(s): Robert I. Ingalls Testamentary Trust II.
Foundation type: Independent
Financial data (yr. ended 08/31/91): Assets,
$5,305,552 (M); expenditures, $395,955;
qualifying distributions, $243,667, including
$208,168 for 37 grants (high: $60,000; low: $10).
Purpose and activities: Emphasis on hospitals and
medical research; support also for higher and
secondary education and cultural programs.
Fields of interest: Hospitals, medical research,
higher education, secondary education, cultural
programs.
Types of support: Research.
Limitations: Giving primarily in AL and CO. No
grants to individuals.
Application information: Application form
required.
   Initial approach: Proposal
   Copies of proposal: 1
   Deadline(s): None
   Final notification: Within 6 months
   Write: Barbara Ingalls Shook, Chair.
Officers and Trustees:* Barbara Ingalls Shook,*
Chair. and Treas.; Robert P. Shook,* Pres. and
Secy.; Adele Shook Merck, Elesabeth Ridgely
Shook, Ellen Gregg Shook, William Bew White.
EIN: 630792812

23
The Sonat Foundation Inc. ▼
1900 Fifth Ave. North
P.O. Box 2563
Birmingham 35202   (205) 325-7460

Established in 1982 in AL.
Donor(s): Sonat Inc.
Foundation type: Company-sponsored
Financial data (yr. ended 12/31/90): Assets, $5,089,984 (M); gifts received, $3,553; expenditures, $1,533,984; qualifying distributions, $1,524,457, including $1,411,934 for 292 grants (high: $245,859; low: $1,000; average: $5,000-$25,000) and $91,357 for 38 grants to individuals (high: $3,750; low: $1,250; average: $2,500).
Purpose and activities: Giving mainly for higher education, including employee-related scholarships, and community funds; some support also for social service and youth agencies, including programs for the aged, women, and minorities; health associations and services, including AIDS and other medical research and alcohol abuse programs; community development and civic affairs; the environment; and cultural programs, including the performing arts, historic preservation, and the humanities.
Fields of interest: Higher education, education, community funds, social services, minorities, women, child welfare, aged, health, AIDS, alcoholism, community development, environment, cultural programs, humanities.
Types of support: Matching funds, employee-related scholarships, general purposes, operating budgets, building funds, research, employee matching gifts, annual campaigns, capital campaigns, emergency funds, endowment funds, land acquisition, renovation projects, program-related investments, seed money, special projects, technical assistance, lectureships, professorships, in-kind gifts, scholarship funds.
Limitations: Giving primarily in AL, CT, and TX. No grants to individuals (except for employee-related scholarships).
Publications: Application guidelines.
Application information: Application form required.
  Initial approach: Letter
  Copies of proposal: 1
  Deadline(s): None
  Board meeting date(s): As necessary
  Final notification: Normally within 2 weeks
  Write: J. Lisa Burge, Secy.
Officers and Directors:* J. Robert Doody,* Pres.; Beverley Krannich,* V.P.; William E. Matthews IV,* V.P.; Sarrah W. Rankin,* V.P.; William A.

Smith,* V.P.; J. Lisa Burge, Secy.; Don J. DeMetz, Jr.,* Treas.
Number of staff: 1 full-time professional.
EIN: 630830299
Recent health grants:
23-1 Childrens Hospital of Alabama, Birmingham, AL, $25,500. For capital campaign. 1990.
23-2 Eye Foundation, Birmingham, AL, $10,000. For general support. 1990.
23-3 Richland Regional Medical Center Foundation, Columbia, SC, $15,000. For general support. 1990.
23-4 Southern Research Institute, Birmingham, AL, $20,000. For capital campaign. 1990.
23-5 University of Alabama Medical and Education Foundation, Birmingham, AL, $202,500. For general support and capital campaign. 1990.

24
The William H. and Kate F. Stockham Foundation, Inc.
c/o Stockham Valves & Fittings, Inc.
4000 North Tenth Ave., P.O. Box 10326
Birmingham 35202
Application address: c/o Kathryn W. Miree, AmSouth Bank Trust Dept., P.O. Box 11426, Birmingham, AL 35202; Tel.: (205) 326-5387

Incorporated in 1948 in AL.
Donor(s): Stockham Valves and Fittings, Inc.
Foundation type: Company-sponsored
Financial data (yr. ended 12/31/90): Assets, $3,466,793 (M); expenditures, $391,297; qualifying distributions, $368,081, including $306,788 for 53 grants (high: $65,000; low: $100) and $57,293 for 29 grants to individuals (high: $25,000; low: $273).
Purpose and activities: Emphasis on educational purposes, including higher education and public affairs groups; human services, including community funds and hospitals; Christian religious education and church support; and assistance to employees and former employees of the donor, including scholarships, fellowships, and welfare assistance.
Fields of interest: Community funds, hospitals, higher education, education, religion—Christian, Protestant giving, public affairs, social services, welfare—indigent individuals.
Types of support: Employee-related scholarships, grants to individuals.
Limitations: Giving primarily in AL and the Southeast. No grants to individuals (except for employee-related grants, including scholarships).

Application information: Application form not required.
  Initial approach: Letter
  Copies of proposal: 1
  Deadline(s): None
  Board meeting date(s): Feb., May, Aug., and Nov.
Officer and Trustees:* Herbert C. Stockham,* Chair.; Larry W. Kinderman, Virginia Ladd, Charles Stockham, Kate Stockham, Richard J. Stockham, Jr.
EIN: 636049787

25
Vulcan Materials Company Foundation ▼
P.O. Box 530187
Birmingham 35253-0497   (205) 877-3229

Established in 1987 in AL.
Donor(s): Vulcan Materials Co.
Foundation type: Company-sponsored
Financial data (yr. ended 11/30/90): Assets, $2,665,690 (M); gifts received, $3,000,000; expenditures, $1,792,271; qualifying distributions, $1,792,271, including $1,791,783 for 493 grants (high: $133,334; low: $35; average: $100-$20,000).
Purpose and activities: Support for health care and welfare agencies, hospitals, youth and recreational organizations, educational institutions, arts organizations, environmental organizations, justice and law organizations, and women's causes.
Fields of interest: Health associations, welfare, hospitals, youth, recreation, education, adult education, education—minorities, arts, environment, law and justice, women, child welfare, community development, drug abuse.
Types of support: Annual campaigns, general purposes, scholarship funds, continuing support, seed money, endowment funds, research.
Limitations: Giving primarily in regions where major company facilities are located. No support for religious organizations for religious purposes. No grants to individuals.
Publications: Newsletter, occasional report.
Application information:
  Board meeting date(s): Quarterly
  Write: Mary S. Russom, Secy.-Treas.
Officers and Trustees:* Herbert A. Sklener,* Chair.; E.S. Sydnor,* Pres.; Peter J. Clemens III,* V.P.; R.M. Lord,* V.P.; M.S. Russom, Secy.-Treas.
Number of staff: 1 full-time professional; 1 part-time support.
EIN: 630971859

ARIZONA

26
A.P.S. Foundation, Inc.
P.O. Box 53999, Station 8532
Phoenix 85072-3999

Established in 1981 in AZ.
Donor(s): Arizona Public Service Co.
Foundation type: Company-sponsored
Financial data (yr. ended 12/31/90): Assets,
$5,969,532 (M); expenditures, $759,172;
qualifying distributions, $757,634, including
$707,221 for 54 grants (high: $25,000; low:
$250) and $50,350 for 157 employee matching
gifts.
Fields of interest: Education, cultural programs,
hospitals, youth.
Types of support: Operating budgets, matching
funds, capital campaigns.
Limitations: Giving primarily in AZ, with
emphasis on Phoenix. No grants to individuals.
Application information: Contributes only to
pre-selected organizations. Applications not
accepted.
Officers and Directors:* O. Mark De Michele,*
Pres.; Jaron B. Norberg, Jr.,* V.P.; William J. Post,*
V.P.; Nancy C. Loftin,* Secy.; William J. Hemelt,*
Treas.; Shirley A. Richard.
EIN: 953735903

27
Arizona Community Foundation
2122 East Highland Ave., Suite 400
Phoenix 85016   (602) 381-1400

Incorporated in 1978 in AZ.
Donor(s): L. Dilatush, R. Kieckhefer, Bert A. Getz,
Newton Rosenzweig, G.R. Herberger.
Foundation type: Community
Financial data (yr. ended 12/31/91): Assets,
$32,944,987 (L); gifts received, $3,072,727;
expenditures, $2,405,864; qualifying
distributions, $1,740,518, including $1,740,518
for grants (average: $1,000-$10,000).
Purpose and activities: Support for children's
mental health, youth agencies, health agencies,
organizations for the handicapped, and other
human services programs, community-based
economic development, education, conservation,
performing arts, and cultural programs.
Fields of interest: Health, AIDS, mental health,
youth, social services, community development,
education, education—early childhood,
conservation, cultural programs.
Types of support: Seed money, emergency funds,
equipment, technical assistance, special projects,
operating budgets, continuing support, building
funds, matching funds, scholarship funds, special
projects, general purposes, publications,
renovation projects, research, program-related
investments.
Limitations: Giving limited to AZ. No support for
sectarian religious purposes. No grants to
individuals, or for deficit financing, annual
campaigns, land acquisition, endowment funds,

travel to or support of conferences, consulting
services, or capital grants; no loans.
Publications: Annual report, program policy
statement, application guidelines, newsletter,
financial statement, informational brochure.
Application information: Application form
required.
  Initial approach: Letter
  Copies of proposal: 15
  Deadline(s): Feb. 1, June 1, and Oct.1
  Board meeting date(s): Semiannually
  Final notification: 60 days
  Write: Stephen D. Mittenthal, Pres.
Officers and Directors:* Richard H. Whitney,*
Chair.; Barbara J. Polk,* Vice-Chair.; Stephen D.
Mittenthal,* Pres. and Exec. Dir.; Neal Kurn,*
Secy.; F. Lee Jacquette,* Treas.; and 20 additional
directors.
Number of staff: 6 full-time professional; 1
part-time professional; 1 full-time support.
EIN: 860348306

28
Bank of America Arizona Corporate Giving Program
(Formerly Western Savings and Loan
Corporation)
P.O. Box 16290
Phoenix 85011   (602) 468-4600

Purpose and activities: Supports arts and culture,
hospitals, education, including literacy, business
and minority education and research, and civic
affairs programs.
Fields of interest: Education, civic affairs, arts,
cultural programs, business education,
community development, educational research,
homeless, literacy, education—minorities, fine
arts, higher education, hospitals, minorities.
Types of support: General purposes, capital
campaigns, annual campaigns, operating budgets.
Limitations: Giving primarily in AZ.
Publications: Application guidelines.
Application information: Handling of
contributions split between Marketing and
Executive offices. Application form not required.
  Initial approach: Written proposal; send to
    headquarters
  Copies of proposal: 1
  Deadline(s): On-going
  Board meeting date(s): As needed
  Write: Gary Miller, V.P.
Administrators: David Hanna, Chair.; David
Berry, Pres.; Gary Miller, V.P.
Number of staff: None.

29
First Interstate Bank of Arizona, N.A. Charitable Foundation
P.O. Box 29743
Phoenix 85038-9743   (602) 229-4544

Established in 1976 in AZ.
Donor(s): First Interstate Bank of Arizona, N.A.
Foundation type: Company-sponsored
Financial data (yr. ended 12/31/91): Assets,
$3,714,490 (M); gifts received, $100,000;
expenditures, $1,049,686; qualifying
distributions, $1,048,702, including $1,048,702
for 270 grants (high: $250,000; low: $100;
average: $500-$10,000).

Purpose and activities: Giving primarily for the
arts, health organizations, higher education,
social services, and youth programs.
Fields of interest: Arts, cultural programs,
museums, performing arts, theater, higher
education, libraries, literacy, secondary
education, adult education,
education—minorities, health, AIDS, drug abuse,
social services, welfare, homeless, aged, youth,
community development, civic affairs, law and
justice, community funds.
Types of support: Annual campaigns, building
funds, continuing support, emergency funds,
equipment, general purposes, scholarship funds,
seed money, capital campaigns, renovation
projects, operating budgets, special projects.
Limitations: Giving limited to AZ-based
organizations or national organizations which
fund programs in AZ. No support for solely
religious purposes. No grants to individuals, or for
endowment funds or travel; no multi-year grants;
no loans.
Publications: Application guidelines.
Application information: Application form
required.
  Initial approach: Letter
  Copies of proposal: 1
  Deadline(s): Submit proposals Jan. through
    June, Sept., and Oct.
  Board meeting date(s): Once a month
  Final notification: 2 months
  Write: Dianne Stephens, Secy.
Officers and Trustees:* Webb Todd, Chair.;
Dianne E. Stephens,* Secy.; Jack Roulier, Charles
Williamson.
Number of staff: 2 part-time professional; 1
part-time support.
EIN: 510204372

30
The Flinn Foundation ▼
3300 North Central Ave., Suite 2300
Phoenix 85012   (602) 274-9000

Trust established in 1965 in AZ.
Donor(s): Irene Flinn,‡ Robert S. Flinn, M.D.‡
Foundation type: Independent
Financial data (yr. ended 12/31/91): Assets,
$108,699,000 (M); expenditures, $3,869,000;
qualifying distributions, $3,869,000, including
$1,962,648 for 57 grants (high: $285,000; low:
$550; average: $20,000-$100,000).
Purpose and activities: The foundation's
grantmaking interests, limited to Arizona, involve
three objectives: 1) to strengthen the capabilities
of Arizona's institutions in the fields of health,
education, and the cultural arts; 2) to develop
future leaders in health and education through
research fellowship programs in the biological
sciences and programs for promising students at
the high school and college levels; and 3) to
increase the availability of basic health care
services for the frail elderly, pregnant and
parenting teenagers, young children, and persons
with AIDS.
Fields of interest: Health, medical research,
biological sciences, health services, heart disease,
education, education—minorities, higher
education, medical education, arts, public policy.
Types of support: Special projects, research, seed
money.

Limitations: Giving limited to AZ. No grants to individuals, or for building projects (capital campaigns), purchase of equipment, endowment projects, annual fundraising campaigns, ongoing operating expenses or deficit needs; requests to support conferences and workshops, publications, or the production of films and video are considered only when these activities are an integral component of a larger foundation initiative.

Publications: Application guidelines, newsletter, occasional report, biennial report.

Application information: Application form not required.

Initial approach: Letter or telephone
Copies of proposal: 2
Deadline(s): None
Board meeting date(s): 5 times a year
Final notification: Within 12 weeks
Write: John W. Murphy, Exec. Dir.

Officers and Directors: Donald K. Buffmire, M.D.,* Chair. and Pres.; David R. Frazer,* V.P. and Treas.; Merlin W. Kampfer, M.D.,* V.P., Admin.; Jay S. Ruffner,* Secy.; John W. Murphy, Exec. Dir.; Robert A. Brooks, David J. Gullen, M.D., Edward V. O'Malley, Jr., A.J. Pfister.

Number of staff: 6 full-time professional; 2 part-time professional; 3 full-time support.

EIN: 860421476

Recent health grants:

30-1 Arizona State University, School of Health Administration and Policy, Tempe, AZ, $173,000. To develop state-level physician and graduate medical education information system for use by Council of Graduate Medical Education, voluntary association of physicians assigned to study and review graduate medical education issues in Arizona. 1991.

30-2 Grantmakers in Health, NYC, NY, $30,000. For seminar program series. 1991.

30-3 Marana Unified School District, Marana, AZ, $337,314. For school-centered and community-linked health and social service programs to meet needs of pregnant and parenting teenagers. 1991.

30-4 Tuba City Unified School District No. 15, Tuba City, AZ, $229,723. For school-centered and community-linked health and social service programs to meet needs of pregnant and parenting teenagers. 1991.

30-5 University of Arizona, College of Medicine, Tucson, AZ, $25,315. For continued support for evaluation of two Flinn Foundation-funded projects: Prenatal and Infant Care Demonstration Program; and Hospital-Based Coordinated Care Program for Frail Elderly. 1991.

30-6 Yuma Union High School District, Yuma, AZ, $449,550. For school-centered and community-linked health and social service programs to meet needs of pregnant and parenting teenagers. 1991.

31
Globe Foundation

3634 Civic Ctr. Plaza
Scottsdale 85251

Established in 1958 in IL.
Donor(s): Bert A. Getz, George F. Getz, Jr.
Foundation type: Independent

Financial data (yr. ended 12/31/91): Assets, $12,489,885 (M); gifts received, $511,950; expenditures, $676,367; qualifying distributions, $650,413, including $650,395 for 70 grants (high: $290,000; low: $25).

Purpose and activities: Giving primarily for publicly supported community organizations and institutions, with emphasis on youth, cultural organizations, and hospitals.

Fields of interest: Community development, youth, cultural programs, museums, hospitals.

Types of support: General purposes.

Limitations: Giving primarily in AZ and IL. No support for privately supported groups. No grants to individuals, or for general operating expenses.

Application information: Contributes only to pre-selected organizations. Applications not accepted.

Officers and Directors: George F. Getz, Jr.,* Pres.; C.L. Lux,* V.P. and Treas.; Bert A. Getz,* Secy.; James W. Ashley, Lynn Getz Polite.

EIN: 366054050

32
Harold & Jean Grossman Foundation

c/o Forgals Financial, Inc.
5080 North 40th St., Suite 375
Phoenix 85018   (602) 954-6955

Established in 1990 in AZ as successor to Harold & Jean Grossman Foundation.
Donor(s): Harold I. Grossman.
Foundation type: Independent

Financial data (yr. ended 12/31/91): Assets, $4,974,513 (M); expenditures, $385,964; qualifying distributions, $385,965, including $368,166 for 195 grants (high: $230,000; low: $10).

Purpose and activities: Primary areas of interest include child welfare, family services, cancer, museums, and Jewish organizations.

Fields of interest: Child welfare, family services, cancer, health, Jewish giving, museums, general charitable giving.

Limitations: Giving primarily in AZ. No grants to individuals.

Application information:

Initial approach: Letter
Deadline(s): None
Write: Jean Grossman, V.P.

Officers and Directors: Harold I. Grossman,* Pres. and Treas.; Ryna Jean Grossman,* V.P. and Secy.; Judy Johnson.

EIN: 860649389

33
The Hankins Foundation

5101 North Casa Blanca, No. 309
Scottsdale 85253   (602) 994-8556

Trust established in 1952 in OH.
Donor(s): Edward R. Hankins,‡ Ann H. Long,‡ Jane H. Lockwood,‡ Ruth L. Hankins.
Foundation type: Independent

Financial data (yr. ended 12/31/90): Assets, $3,348,137 (M); expenditures, $199,149; qualifying distributions, $177,476, including $171,780 for 87 grants (high: $15,000; low: $100).

Fields of interest: Higher education, community funds, hospitals, health services, cultural programs, social services, youth.

Limitations: Giving primarily in OH, with emphasis on Cleveland. No grants to individuals; no loans.

Application information: Application form not required.

Initial approach: Proposal
Copies of proposal: 1
Deadline(s): None
Board meeting date(s): As required
Write: Edward G. Lockwood, Trustee

Trustees: Ruth L. Hankins, Richard R. Hollington, Jr., Edward G. Lockwood, Gordon G. Long, Janet L. Tarwater.

Number of staff: 1 full-time professional; 4 part-time support.

EIN: 346565426

34
The Hermundslie Foundation

3762 North Harrison Rd.
Tucson 85749-9178   (602) 749-2982

Established in 1968 in AZ.
Foundation type: Independent

Financial data (yr. ended 12/31/90): Assets, $2,615,918 (M); expenditures, $90,605; qualifying distributions, $88,000, including $88,000 for grants.

Fields of interest: Health, medical research.

Types of support: Research.

Application information: Application form not required.

Deadline(s): None
Write: Elaine Hermundslie, V.P.

Officers: Gerold Hermundslie, Pres.; Elaine Hermundslie, V.P.; G.D. Engdahl, Treas.

EIN: 237001359

35
J. W. Kieckhefer Foundation

116 East Gurley St.
P.O. Box 750
Prescott 86302   (602) 445-4010

Trust established in 1953 in AZ.
Donor(s): John W. Kieckhefer.‡
Foundation type: Independent

Financial data (yr. ended 12/31/91): Assets, $13,115,969 (M); expenditures, $519,510; qualifying distributions, $534,550, including $518,775 for 46 grants (high: $75,000; low: $750; average: $1,000-$25,000) and $15,775 for 1 in-kind gift.

Purpose and activities: Emphasis on medical research, hospices and health agencies; family planning and services, the handicapped, and other social services; education, including medical and other higher education; youth and child welfare agencies; ecology and conservation; community funds; and cultural programs.

Fields of interest: Medical research, health, child welfare, youth, family services, social services, ecology, public policy, higher education, cultural programs.

Types of support: Operating budgets, continuing support, annual campaigns, emergency funds, building funds, equipment, land acquisition, endowment funds, matching funds, research,

publications, conferences and seminars, special projects.
Limitations: No grants to individuals, or for seed money, deficit financing, scholarships, fellowships, or demonstration projects; no loans.
Publications: 990-PF.
Application information: Application form not required.
  Initial approach: Letter
  Copies of proposal: 1
  Deadline(s): Submit proposal preferably between May and Nov.
  Board meeting date(s): Nov., Dec., and as required
  Final notification: 6 months
  Write: Eugene P. Polk, Trustee
Trustees: John I. Kieckhefer, Robert H. Kieckhefer, Eugene P. Polk.
Number of staff: None.
EIN: 866022877

36
Marshall Foundation
P.O. Box 3306
Tucson 85722   (602) 622-8613

Incorporated in 1930 in AZ.
Donor(s): Louise F. Marshall.‡
Foundation type: Independent
Financial data (yr. ended 12/31/90): Assets, $7,579,512 (M); expenditures, $1,030,239; qualifying distributions, $355,755, including $352,030 for 34 grants (high: $109,832; average: $5,000-$50,000).
Purpose and activities: Giving primarily for higher education and medical research; support also for secondary and other education, health, and social services.
Fields of interest: Higher education, secondary education, medical research, health services, social services.
Limitations: Giving limited to the Tucson, AZ, area. No grants to individuals.
Publications: 990-PF.
Application information: Application form not required.
  Initial approach: Letter
  Deadline(s): None
  Board meeting date(s): Monthly
  Write: The Directors
Directors: Reuben Carranza, Charles Jackson, John F. Molloy.
Number of staff: 2 full-time professional; 2 full-time support; 1 part-time support.
EIN: 860102198

37
Margaret T. Morris Foundation ▼
P.O. Box 592
Prescott 86302   (602) 445-4010

Established in 1967.
Donor(s): Margaret T. Morris.‡
Foundation type: Independent
Financial data (yr. ended 12/31/91): Assets, $23,884,968 (M); expenditures, $630,457; qualifying distributions, $558,618, including $545,850 for 40 grants (high: $75,000; low: $500; average: $1,000-$25,000).
Purpose and activities: Support for the performing arts and other cultural programs, education, with

emphasis on higher education, youth and child welfare, a community foundation, population control, medical research and education, the environment and animal welfare, and social services, primarily those benefiting the handicapped.
Fields of interest: Performing arts, arts, cultural programs, music, education, higher education, youth, child welfare, medical research, medical education, environment, animal welfare, social services, family planning, welfare, homeless, handicapped, disadvantaged, mental health, marine sciences.
Types of support: Land acquisition, general purposes, building funds, scholarship funds, deficit financing, endowment funds, operating budgets, special projects.
Limitations: Giving primarily in AZ. No support for religious organizations or their agencies. No grants to individuals; no loans.
Publications: 990-PF.
Application information: Application form not required.
  Initial approach: Proposal or letter
  Copies of proposal: 1
  Deadline(s): Submit proposal preferably in May through Nov.
  Board meeting date(s): Aug. and Dec.
  Final notification: After board meetings
  Write: Eugene P. Polk, Trustee
Trustees: Richard L. Menschel, Eugene P. Polk.
Number of staff: None.
EIN: 866057798

38
Phelps Dodge Foundation
2600 North Central Ave.
Phoenix 85004-3014   (602) 234-8100

Incorporated in 1953 in NY.
Donor(s): Phelps Dodge Corp., and subsidiaries.
Foundation type: Company-sponsored
Financial data (yr. ended 12/31/90): Assets, $11,844,695 (M); expenditures, $1,056,048; qualifying distributions, $1,055,694, including $789,880 for 118 grants (high: $95,000; low: $100) and $265,814 for employee matching gifts.
Fields of interest: Higher education, community funds, health, welfare, civic affairs, cultural programs.
Types of support: Continuing support, annual campaigns, endowment funds, employee matching gifts, scholarship funds, fellowships.
Limitations: Giving primarily in areas of operations of Phelps Dodge Corp. and its subsidiaries. No grants to individuals, or for operating budgets, seed money, emergency funds, deficit financing, research, special projects, publications, or conferences; no loans.
Application information: Application form not required.
  Initial approach: Letter or proposal
  Copies of proposal: 1
  Deadline(s): Oct. to Nov.; budgeting process occurs in Dec.
  Board meeting date(s): Apr.
  Final notification: 3 to 4 months
  Write: William C. Tubman, Pres.
Officers: William C. Tubman, Pres.; Frank J. Longto, V.P. and Treas.; Mary K. Sterling, Secy.

Directors: Cleveland E. Dodge, Jr., George B. Munroe, Edward L. Palmer, John P. Schroeder, D.C. Yearley.
Number of staff: 2 part-time professional; 1 part-time support.
EIN: 136077350

39
Raymond Educational Foundation, Inc.
P.O. Box 1423
Flagstaff 86002   (602) 779-6263

Incorporated in 1951 in AZ.
Donor(s): R.O. Raymond.‡
Foundation type: Independent
Financial data (yr. ended 04/30/91): Assets, $2,387,350 (M); expenditures, $191,200; qualifying distributions, $166,600, including $166,600 for 10 grants (high: $100,600; low: $1,000).
Purpose and activities: Grants limited to institutions within Coconino County, AZ, principally for scholarship funds; some support for museums and other cultural programs and health services, including hospitals and medical education.
Fields of interest: Education, cultural programs, health, medical education, museums, hospitals.
Types of support: Scholarship funds, capital campaigns, continuing support.
Limitations: Giving limited to Coconino County, AZ.
Publications: Program policy statement.
Application information:
  Initial approach: Proposal not exceeding 2 pages
  Copies of proposal: 9
  Deadline(s): Mar. 1
  Board meeting date(s): As required
  Final notification: May 1
  Write: Dr. Eldon D. Bills, Pres.
Officers and Directors:* Eldon Bills,* Pres.; Ralph Wheeler,* Exec. V.P.; Robert E. Gaylord, Secy.; John Stilley,* Treas.; Catherine Adel, Valeen T. Avery, Platt C. Cline, Henry L. Giclas, Wilfred Killip, Joyce Leamon.
Number of staff: None.
EIN: 866050920

40
Southern Arizona Foundation, Inc.
(Formerly Dialysis Foundation of Southern Arizona, Inc.)
P.O. Box 13047
Tucson 85732-3047   (602) 886-5495

Established in 1988 in AZ.
Foundation type: Independent
Financial data (yr. ended 06/30/91): Assets, $3,558,521 (M); gifts received, $104; expenditures, $205,725; qualifying distributions, $128,978, including $126,978 for 13 grants (high: $26,814; low: $500).
Purpose and activities: Giving limited to kidney research.
Fields of interest: Medical research.
Limitations: Giving primarily in AZ. No grants to individuals.
Application information: Application form not required.
  Deadline(s): None

Write: Dr. Mary Fried, Pres.
Officers and Directors:* Mary Fried,* Pres.; Frederick Bondell,* V.P.; George Evanhoff,* V.P.; Robert Donfeld,* Secy.-Treas.; David Ben-Asher.
EIN: 510157715

41
Tucson Osteopathic Medical Foundation
(Formerly Tucson Osteopathic Foundation)
4280 North Campbell Ave., Suite 200
Tucson 85718   (602) 299-4545

Incorporated in 1986 in AZ with proceeds from the sale of Tucson General Hospital.
Donor(s): Tucson Hospital Liquidating Corp.
Foundation type: Operating
Financial data (yr. ended 06/30/92): Assets, $9,517,230 (M); gifts received, $149,733; expenditures, $716,443; qualifying distributions, $490,459, including $13,750 for 6 grants (high: $10,000; low: $100; average: $100-$10,000), $40,000 for 6 grants to individuals (high: $8,000; low: $2,000; average: $2,000-$10,000) and $416,709 for 6 foundation-administered programs.
Purpose and activities: The three-fold mission of the foundation is: 1) to expand and improve the quality and scope of postgraduate osteopathic medical education; 2) to improve the public's understanding of osteopathic medicine; and 3) to improve through education the health and well-being of the community.
Fields of interest: Community development, health, medical education, higher education.
Types of support: Student aid, student loans.
Limitations: Giving limited to AZ, especially southern AZ for loan recipients.
Publications: Annual report, newsletter.
Application information: Requires an interview. Application form required.
   Initial approach: Letter
   Deadline(s): Dec. 1 for scholarships

Board meeting date(s): Mar.
Final notification: By Apr. 30
Write: Lew Riggs, Exec. Dir.
Officers and Trustees:* John Q. Harris, D.O.,* Chair.; Issa Y. Hallaq, D.O.,* Vice-Chair.; Thomas Vigorito, D.O.,* Secy.-Treas.; Lew Riggs, Exec. Dir.; David W. Buechel, D.O., John Manfredonia, D.O., Harmon L. Myers, D.O., Kenneth S. Snow, D.O.
Number of staff: 4 full-time professional; 2 full-time support.
EIN: 742449503

42
Nellie Kellogg Van Schaick Scholarship Fund
c/o Valley National Bank of Arizona, Trust Dept.
P.O. Box 13779
Tucson 85732   (602) 792-7130

Established in 1975 in AZ.
Donor(s): Nellie Kellogg Van Schaick.‡
Foundation type: Independent
Financial data (yr. ended 05/31/92): Assets, $4,140,083 (M); expenditures, $256,419; qualifying distributions, $226,945, including $223,807 for 8 grants (high: $84,328; low: $2,283).
Purpose and activities: Grants limited to undergraduate and graduate scholarship programs in medicine, dentistry, or public health at nonprofit hospitals and universities.
Fields of interest: Medical education, Philippines, dentistry.
Types of support: Scholarship funds.
Limitations: Giving limited to residents and citizens of the Philippines.
Application information: Application form not required.
   Initial approach: Proposal
   Copies of proposal: 1
   Deadline(s): May 1

Write: Mason W. Borgman, V.P., Valley National Bank of Arizona
Trustee: Valley National Bank of Arizona.
Number of staff: None.
EIN: 866090500

43
Del E. Webb Foundation ▼
2023 West Wickenburg Way
P.O. Box 20519
Wickenburg 85358   (602) 684-7223

Incorporated in 1960 in AZ.
Donor(s): Del E. Webb.‡
Foundation type: Independent
Financial data (yr. ended 12/31/90): Assets, $42,766,770 (M); expenditures, $2,379,377; qualifying distributions, $2,025,588, including $1,840,000 for 25 grants (high: $500,000; low: $5,000; average: $10,000-$50,000).
Purpose and activities: Giving primarily for medical research and health care.
Fields of interest: Medical research, health.
Limitations: Giving primarily in AZ, NV, and CA. No support for government agencies, sectarian or religious organizations, or pass-through organizations. No grants to individuals, or for deficit financing or indirect costs.
Application information: Application form required.
   Initial approach: Letter
   Copies of proposal: 4
   Deadline(s): Mar. 31 and Oct. 31
   Board meeting date(s): May and Dec.
   Final notification: Following each meeting
   Write: Marjorie Klinefelter, Secy.
Officers: Robert H. Johnson, Pres.; Owens F. Childress, V.P.; Marjorie Klinefelter, Secy.; Del V. Werderman, Treas.
Director: W.D. Milliken.
Number of staff: 1
EIN: 866052737

ARKANSAS

44
Arkansas Community Foundation, Inc.
700 South Rock
Little Rock 72202   (501) 372-1116

Established in 1976 in AR.
Foundation type: Community
Financial data (yr. ended 07/31/91): Assets,
$8,787,624 (M); gifts received, $2,640,717;
expenditures, $2,154,468; qualifying
distributions, $1,931,666, including $1,850,807
for 167 grants (high: $145,347; low: $100) and
$80,859 for 151 grants to individuals (high:
$2,500; low: $100).
Fields of interest: Welfare, social services, cultural
programs, health, education, environment,
community development.
Types of support: Scholarship funds, general
purposes, research, seed money, special projects,
student loans, student aid.
Limitations: Giving primarily in AR.
Publications: Annual report (including application
guidelines), financial statement, newsletter,
informational brochure, grants list, application
guidelines.
Application information: Many funds are
donor-restricted. Application form required.
   Initial approach: Letter or telephone
   Copies of proposal: 7
   Deadline(s): Jan. 15 and July 15
   Board meeting date(s): Feb., May, Aug, and
      Nov.
   Final notification: End of Feb. and Aug.
   Write: Martha Ann Jones, Pres., Suzy Hubbell,
      Prog. Dir., or Linda Patterson, Asst. Dir.
Officers and Directors:* William B. Fisher,*
Chair.; Bronson Van Wyck,* 1st Vice-Chair.; Julia
Mobley, 2nd Vice-Chair.; Martha Ann Jones,*
Pres.; Herman Davenport,* Secy.; John Rush,*
Treas.; and 19 additional directors.
Number of staff: 6 full-time professional; 1
full-time support.
EIN: 521055743

45
**Arkansas Power and Light Company
   Contributions Program**
P.O. Box 551
Little Rock 72203   (501) 377-3540

Financial data (yr. ended 12/31/90): Total giving,
$100,000.
Purpose and activities: Support for social services,
civic and economic development, education, arts,
and health.
Fields of interest: Social services, civic affairs,
education, arts, health, community development.
Limitations: Giving limited to AR.
Application information: Include description of
organization, amount requested, purpose for
which funds are sought, audited financial
statement, and proof of 501(c)(3) status.
   Initial approach: Letter or proposal
   Deadline(s): None
   Write: Kay Arnold, Chair., Contribs. Comm.

Officers and Directors: Jerry L. Maulden, Chair.
and C.E.O.; Robert Drake Keith, Pres. and C.O.O.

46
Arkla Corporate Giving Program
400 E. Capitol Ave.
P.O. Box 751
Little Rock 72203   (501) 377-4610

Purpose and activities: Support for a wide variety
of programs, including health services, mental
health, AIDS, child welfare, drug abuse, rural
development, leadership development,
volunteerism, media and communications,
literacy, libraries, education including secondary
education, and the performing and fine arts.
Fields of interest: Education, literacy, health,
hospitals, youth, arts, performing arts, media and
communications, civic affairs, mental health,
museums, rural development, secondary
education, social services, theater, volunteerism,
AIDS, business education, child welfare,
community development, conservation, crime
and law enforcement, cultural programs, dance,
disadvantaged, drug abuse, fine arts, general
charitable giving, health services, historic
preservation, homeless, hospitals—building
funds, humanities, leadership development,
libraries.
Types of support: Annual campaigns, building
funds, conferences and seminars, deficit
financing, employee matching gifts, equipment.
Limitations: Giving primarily in major operating
areas; states served include AR, CA, KS, MN, NE,
TX, OK and MS. No grants to individuals.
Publications: Corporate report, informational
brochure.
Application information: Application form not
required.
   Initial approach: Letter of inquiry; include
      constituency
   Copies of proposal: 1
   Deadline(s): None
   Write: James L. Rutherford, III, Sr. V.P. for Little
      Rock, AR, area; or Hugh H. McCastlain for
      Shreveport, LA, area
Administrators: James L. Rutherford III, Sr. V.P.;
Hugh H. McCastlain, Exec. V.P.

47
**The Harvey and Bernice Jones Charitable
   Trust ▼**
P.O. Box 233
Springdale 72765   (501) 756-0611

Established in 1989 in AR.
Foundation type: Independent
Financial data (yr. ended 11/30/91): Assets,
$71,526,538 (M); expenditures, $5,715,205;
qualifying distributions, $5,672,472, including
$5,672,472 for 27 grants (high: $750,000; low:
$2,000; average: $100,000-$500,000).
Purpose and activities: Support for colleges and
universities, hospitals, and a Baptist convention.
Fields of interest: Higher education, hospitals,
religion—Christian.
Limitations: Giving primarily in AR.
Application information:
   Initial approach: Letter or proposal
   Deadline(s): None
   Write: Bernice Jones, Dir.

Directors: H.G. Frost, Jr., Bernice Jones.
EIN: 716135580
Recent health grants:
47-1 Arkansas Childrens Hospital, Little Rock,
   AR, $500,000. 1991.
47-2 Arkansas Childrens Hospital, Little Rock,
   AR, $500,000. 1991.
47-3 Springdale Memorial Hospital, Springdale,
   AR, $100,000. 1991.
47-4 Springdale Memorial Hospital, Springdale,
   AR, $100,000. 1991.
47-5 University of Arkansas for Medical Sciences
   Foundation, Eye Clinic, Little Rock, AR,
   $185,750. 1991.
47-6 University of Arkansas for Medical Sciences
   Foundation, Eye Clinic, Little Rock, AR,
   $90,000. 1991.

48
The Harvey and Bernice Jones Foundation
P.O. Box 233
Springdale 72765   (501) 756-0611

Trust established in 1956 in AR.
Donor(s): Harvey Jones,‡ Mrs. Harvey Jones,‡
and their related companies.
Foundation type: Independent
Financial data (yr. ended 11/30/91): Assets,
$7,805,155 (M); expenditures, $834,026;
qualifying distributions, $798,917, including
$774,582 for 66 grants (high: $18,100; low:
$100; average: $500-$50,000) and $24,335 for
29 grants to individuals (high: $1,800; low: $300).
Purpose and activities: Giving primarily for
Protestant church support, hospitals, and
education; scholarships restricted to students in
the fields of health care and religion.
Fields of interest: Protestant giving, hospitals,
education, theological education, nursing,
medical education.
Types of support: Student aid.
Limitations: Giving primarily in Springdale, AR.
Application information: Application form
required.
   Initial approach: Letter
   Deadline(s): None
   Board meeting date(s): Nov. 30
   Write: H.G. Frost, Jr., Dir.
Officers and Directors:* Bernice Jones,* Chair.
and Pres.; H.G. Frost, Jr.,* V.P. and Secy.; Hugh
Means, Gene Thompson, William Walker.
Number of staff: 3
EIN: 716057141

49
McKesson Service Merchandising
P.O. Box 790
Harrison 72601   (501) 741-3425

Purpose and activities: Emphasis on general
charitable giving including support for adult
education and literacy, community development,
health and hospitals, youth, the handicapped, and
United Way; also support through employee
volunteer groups and in-kind gifts.
Fields of interest: Adult education, community
development, handicapped, hospitals—building
funds, literacy, youth.
Types of support: Annual campaigns, matching
funds, employee matching gifts, employee-related
scholarships, in-kind gifts.

Application information:
Write: John Berry, Sr. V.P., Human Resources
Administrators: John Berry, Sr. V.P., Human Resources; Sheri Marks, Commmuns. Training Mgr.
Number of staff: None.

50

Ottenheimer Brothers Foundation
1400 Union National Bank Bldg.
Little Rock 72201

Established in 1965 in AR.
Foundation type: Independent
Financial data (yr. ended 04/30/91): Assets, $4,001,183 (M); expenditures, $267,094; qualifying distributions, $236,029, including $227,522 for 8 grants (high: $100,000; low: $500).
Fields of interest: Higher education, cancer, medical research, hospitals, libraries.
Limitations: Giving primarily in AR.
Directors: Steve Bauman, Noland Blass, Jr., Ec Eichenbaum, Judy Grundfest, Edward M. Penick, Louis Rosen, Fred Selz, Sam Strauss, Jr., E. Grainger Williams.
EIN: 716059988

51

Riggs Benevolent Fund
c/o Worthen Bank and Trust Co., N.A., Trust Dept.
P.O. Box 1681
Little Rock 72203-1681   (501) 378-1231

Trust established in 1959 in AR.
Donor(s): Members of the Riggs family, Robert G. Cress, J.A. Riggs Tractor Co., Inc.
Foundation type: Independent
Financial data (yr. ended 12/31/91): Assets, $4,345,756 (M); gifts received, $215,500; expenditures, $292,534; qualifying distributions, $269,550, including $269,550 for 55 grants (high: $50,000; low: $500).
Purpose and activities: Emphasis on higher education and Protestant church support and church-related organizations; support also for youth agencies, hospitals, and community funds.
Fields of interest: Higher education, Protestant giving, youth, hospitals, community funds.
Limitations: Giving primarily in Little Rock, AR. No grants to individuals.
Application information: Unsolicited applications rarely produce a response.
Initial approach: Proposal
Deadline(s): None
Write: Anne Roark

Trustees: Robert G. Cress, John A. Riggs III, Worthen Bank and Trust Co., N.A.
Number of staff: None.
EIN: 716050130

52

The Roy and Christine Sturgis Charitable and Educational Trust
P.O. Box 92
Malvern 72104   (501) 332-3899

Trust established about 1979.
Donor(s): Roy Sturgis,‡ Christine Sturgis.
Foundation type: Independent
Financial data (yr. ended 12/31/91): Assets, $13,180,874 (M); expenditures, $661,935; qualifying distributions, $600,239, including $530,624 for 36 grants (high: $100,000; low: $1,200).
Purpose and activities: Giving primarily for higher and secondary education, and church support; some support for hospitals and general charitable giving.
Fields of interest: Higher education, secondary education, religion—Christian, hospitals, general charitable giving.
Limitations: Giving primarily in AR. No grants to individuals.
Application information: Application form not required.
Initial approach: Proposal
Deadline(s): None
Write: Katie Speer or Barry Findley, Trustees
Trustees: Barry B. Findley, Katie Speer.
EIN: 710495345

53

W. P. Sturgis Foundation
P.O. Box 394
Arkadelphia 71923-0394   (501) 246-4563

Established in 1958 in AR.
Foundation type: Independent
Financial data (yr. ended 12/31/90): Assets, $2,948,953 (M); expenditures, $167,845; qualifying distributions, $135,876, including $53,362 for 2 grants of $26,681 each and $82,514 for grants to individuals.
Purpose and activities: Giving primarily for scholarships for higher education; support also for hospitals and child welfare programs.
Fields of interest: Hospitals, child welfare.
Types of support: Student aid.
Limitations: Giving primarily in AR.
Application information: Completion of application form required for scholarships.
Initial approach: Letter

Deadline(s): None
Write: June Anthony, Secy.-Treas.
Officers and Directors:* Curtis E. Echols,* Pres.; J. Hugh Lookadoo,* V.P.; June Anthony,* Secy.-Treas.; Harold Echols, Bill Fowler, Odus Pennington.
Trustee: Commercial National Bank.
EIN: 716057063

54

Wal-Mart Foundation ▼
702 S.W. Eighth St.
Bentonville 72716-8071   (501) 273-6504

Established in 1979 in AR.
Donor(s): Wal-Mart Stores, Inc.
Foundation type: Company-sponsored
Financial data (yr. ended 01/31/91): Assets, $11,155,098 (M); gifts received, $12,602,723; expenditures, $11,278,978; qualifying distributions, $11,273,984, including $9,799,033 for 5,958 grants (high: $15,363; low: $200; average: $1,000-$2,000) and $1,467,000 for 458 grants to individuals (high: $47,000; low: $1,000).
Purpose and activities: Giving for health and welfare, higher education, community funds, and youth. Foundation administers two scholarship programs: (1)to high school seniors graduating from schools in towns that patronize a Wal-Mart store, and (2)to associates of Wal-Mart or their children.
Fields of interest: Health, drug abuse, alcoholism, youth, child welfare, aged, hunger, minorities, community development, education, higher education, literacy, environment, safety, community funds.
Types of support: Student aid, matching funds, scholarship funds.
Limitations: Giving primarily in areas of company operations.
Publications: Informational brochure.
Application information: Application forms for community scholarships available at high schools, and from local store managers for associate scholarships.
Deadline(s): Mar. 1 for associate scholarship program, Mar. 20 for community scholarship program
Board meeting date(s): Mar., May, Aug., and Nov.
Write: Ginger Cowherd, Asst. Dir.
Trustees: David D. Glass, Don Soderquist, S. Robson Walton.
Number of staff: 1 full-time professional; 4 full-time support.
EIN: 716107283

CALIFORNIA

55
Advanced Micro Devices Corporate Contributions Program
901 Thompson Place
P.O. Box 3453, MS 42
Sunnyvale 94088   (408) 732-2400

Purpose and activities: Support for health and welfare, education, and civic affairs.
Fields of interest: Health, welfare, education, civic affairs.
Types of support: Special projects.
Limitations: Giving limited to San Jose, Santa Clara, and Sunnyvale, CA, and Austin and San Antonio, TX. No support for political, religious or fraternal organizations, or cultural programs. Generally only considers specific project requests; no grants to individuals, or for capital or endowment fund-raising drives, or research.
Publications: Corporate giving report.
Application information: Application form not required.
  Initial approach: Letter of intent
  Deadline(s): None
  Write: Theresa Wilson, Corp. Contribs. Mgr.
Administrators: Theresa Williams, Corp. Contribs. Mgr.; Tammy Bigelow, Corp. Contribs. Asst.

56
The Aerospace Corporate Contributions Program
2350 East El Segundo Blvd., M.S. MI-448
El Segundo 90245   (213) 336-6515
Special address for applications: P.O. Box 92957, Los Angeles, CA 90278

Financial data (yr. ended 09/30/90): Total giving, $379,000, including $101,000 for grants and $278,000 for employee matching gifts.
Purpose and activities: Supports education including public colleges; and federated campaigns including the United Way; also supports human services, including alcohol rehabilitation, child welfare and health care; also culture, including music, museums, and performing arts. Matching gifts used for education only.
Fields of interest: Education, higher education, science and technology, alcoholism, child welfare, civic affairs, cultural programs, drug abuse, health, heart disease, hospices, military personnel, museums, music, performing arts, public affairs, volunteerism, youth.
Types of support: General purposes, annual campaigns, employee matching gifts.
Limitations: Giving primarily in communities where company employees live and work, in Greater Los Angeles, CA, area.
Publications: Informational brochure.
Application information: Public Affairs Department handles giving. Application form not required.
  Initial approach: Letter; send requests to headquarters
  Board meeting date(s): Upon receipt of request

Write: Janet M. Antrim, Coord., Community Support
Administrators: Earl D. Flick, Dir., Public Affairs; Janet M. Antrim, Coord., Community Support.
Number of staff: 1 full-time professional.

57
The Ahmanson Foundation ▼
9215 Wilshire Blvd.
Beverly Hills 90210   (310) 278-0770

Incorporated in 1952 in CA.
Donor(s): Howard F. Ahmanson,‡ Dorothy G. Sullivan,‡ William H. Ahmanson, Robert H. Ahmanson.
Foundation type: Independent
Financial data (yr. ended 10/31/91): Assets, $445,873,000 (M); gifts received, $16,000; expenditures, $20,124,614; qualifying distributions, $19,443,539, including $19,441,614 for 395 grants (high: $2,000,000; low: $500; average: $10,000-$25,000) and $1,925 for 1 in-kind gift.
Purpose and activities: Emphasis on higher and other education, the arts and humanities, medicine and health, and a broad range of human service programs, including youth organizations.
Fields of interest: Arts, humanities, museums, fine arts, education, higher education, secondary education, elementary education, education—building funds, literacy, libraries, health, health services, medical sciences, social services, youth, homeless, disadvantaged.
Types of support: Building funds, equipment, land acquisition, endowment funds, matching funds, scholarship funds, special projects, renovation projects, capital campaigns.
Limitations: Giving primarily in Southern CA, with emphasis on the Los Angeles area. No grants to individuals, or for continuing support, annual campaigns, deficit financing, professorships, internships, fellowships, film production, underwriting, exchange programs; or loans.
Publications: Application guidelines, grants list, annual report, application guidelines.
Application information: Application form not required.
  Initial approach: Letter of inquiry or proposal
  Copies of proposal: 1
  Deadline(s): None
  Board meeting date(s): 4 times annually
  Final notification: 30 to 60 days
  Write: Lee E. Walcott, V.P. and Managing Dir.
Officers and Trustees:* Robert H. Ahmanson,* Pres.; Lee E. Walcott, V.P. and Managing Dir.; William H. Ahmanson,* V.P.; Karen A. Hoffman, Secy.; Donald B. Stark, Treas.; Howard F. Ahmanson, Jr., Daniel N. Belin, Lloyd E. Cotsen, Robert M. DeKruif, Robert F. Erburu, Franklin D. Murphy, M.D.
Number of staff: 7 full-time professional; 1 part-time professional.
EIN: 956089998
Recent health grants:
57-1 Alcoholism Center for Women, Los Angeles, CA, $15,000. Toward furnishing residential care facility. 1991.
57-2 Alisa Ann Ruch Burn Foundation, Canoga Park, CA, $10,000. Toward printing and distribution of materials for Hispanic Burn Prevention Education Program. 1991.

57-3 All Saints Episcopal Church, Pasadena, CA, $35,000. For general support for Young and Healthy Project. 1991.
57-4 Alzheimers Disease and Related Disorders Association, Los Angeles, CA, $15,000. Toward publication and dissemination of Alzheimer's Disease Resource Directory. 1991.
57-5 American Friends of the Hebrew University, Beverly Hills, CA, $50,000. Toward endowment fund for research in tumor immunology at Lautenberg Center. 1991.
57-6 Betty Clooney Foundation for the Brain Injured, Los Angeles, CA, $25,000. Toward renovation and furnishing of Long Beach facility. 1991.
57-7 Casa de las Amigas, Pasadena, CA, $35,000. Toward debt retirement on property for parking. 1991.
57-8 Cedars-Sinai Medical Center, Los Angeles, CA, $50,000. Toward additional laboratory and technician expenses incurred with research project, Long-Term Patency of Aortocoronary Bypass Grafts. 1991.
57-9 Childrens Hospital of Los Angeles, Los Angeles, CA, $500,000. Toward construction and outfitting of new six-story Outpatient Tower. 1991.
57-10 Concern Foundation, Beverly Hills, CA, $50,000. Toward endowment fund for research in tumor immunology at Lautenberg Center. 1991.
57-11 Concern Foundation, Beverly Hills, CA, $10,000. For general support. 1991.
57-12 Crittenton Center for Young Women and Infants, Los Angeles, CA, $10,000. For additional support toward remodeling and renovation of nursery. 1991.
57-13 Didi Hirsch Community Mental Health Center, Culver City, CA, $20,000. Toward completion of new 15-bed crisis treatment center for mentally ill. 1991.
57-14 Estelle Doheny Eye Institute, Los Angeles, CA, $100,000. For general support. 1991.
57-15 Florence Crittenton Services of Orange County, Fullerton, CA, $25,000. Toward furnishings for remodeled kitchen and dining room. 1991.
57-16 Grandview Foundation, Los Angeles, CA, $18,500. Toward renovation of two bathrooms at Grandview House. 1991.
57-17 Hathaway Childrens Services, Pacoima, CA, $50,000. Toward renovation of Highland Park Facility for use as Family Resource Center. 1991.
57-18 Henry Mayo Newhall Memorial Health Foundation, Valencia, CA, $25,000. For general support. 1991.
57-19 Henry Mayo Newhall Memorial Health Foundation, Valencia, CA, $15,000. For general support. 1991.
57-20 Hope for Hearing Research Foundation, Los Angeles, CA, $10,000. For general support. 1991.
57-21 Hospital of the Good Samaritan, Los Angeles, CA, $25,000. Toward Perinatal Center. 1991.
57-22 Impact Drug and Alcohol Treatment Center, Pasadena, CA, $15,200. Toward purchase of passenger vans. 1991.
57-23 Los Angeles Educational Partnership, Los Angeles, CA, $25,000. Toward technical assistance for new structure providing

comprehensive and coordinated health services within LAUSD. 1991.

57-24 Los Angeles Free Clinic, Los Angeles, CA, $18,000. Toward equipment and supplies for new Ear, Nose and Throat Clinic. 1991.

57-25 Make-A-Wish Foundation, Los Angeles, CA, $10,000. Toward fund in memory of Gene Roddenberry. 1991.

57-26 Marianne Frostig Center of Educational Therapy, Pasadena, CA, $50,000. Toward earthquake repair and renovation. 1991.

57-27 Marianne Frostig Center of Educational Therapy, Pasadena, CA, $25,000. For general support. 1991.

57-28 Mayo Foundation for Medical Education and Research, Rochester, MN, $45,000. Toward purchase of additional equipment for Optical Spectroscopy Laboratory. 1991.

57-29 Medical Resource Foundation, Ventura, CA, $10,000. Toward Campaign for Children. 1991.

57-30 Mental Health Advocacy Services, Los Angeles, CA, $15,000. Toward assisting with placement of mentally and developmentally disabled children under Dependency Court jursidiction. 1991.

57-31 National Health Foundation, Los Angeles, CA, $30,000. Toward Prenatal and Obstetrical Access Project for low-income women in Los Angeles County. 1991.

57-32 National Multiple Sclerosis Society, Glendale, CA, $15,000. For general support. 1991.

57-33 NorthEast Valley Health Corporation, Pacoima, CA, $15,000. Toward parenting education for Hispanic women in perinatal program. 1991.

57-34 Pacific Clinics, Pasadena, CA, $20,000. Toward Creative Sociomedics software program. 1991.

57-35 Pasadena Childrens Training Society, Altadena, CA, $35,000. Toward renovation of Hunter Cottage. 1991.

57-36 Planned Parenthood-World Population Los Angeles, Los Angeles, CA, $200,000. Toward pregnancy testing and prenatal services. 1991.

57-37 Queen of Angels-Hollywood Presbyterian Foundation, Los Angeles, CA, $250,000. Toward renovation and expansion of Prenatal and Obstetric Center. 1991.

57-38 Saint Annes Maternity Home, Los Angeles, CA, $500,000. Toward construction of new facilities for housing and treatment of pregnant adolescent women. 1991.

57-39 Saint Francis Medical Center Foundation, Lynwood, CA, $250,000. Toward construction of and equipment for Pediatric Emergency Treatment Area in new Health Services Pavilion. 1991.

57-40 Saint Vincent Medical Center, Los Angeles, CA, $50,000. Toward construction, renovation and equipment of new Bone Marrow Transplant Unit. 1991.

57-41 San Fernando Valley Child Guidance Clinic, Northridge, CA, $25,000. Toward purchase of computer hardware and software for administrative and clinical purposes. 1991.

57-42 Scripps Clinic and Research Foundation, La Jolla, CA, $44,600. Toward purchase of automated cell culture bioassy system for Drug Discovery Unit of Green Cancer Center. 1991.

57-43 Southern California Counseling Center, Los Angeles, CA, $15,000. Toward Abuse Prevention Program. 1991.

57-44 University of California at Los Angeles Foundation, School of Medicine, Los Angeles, CA, $50,000. Toward Medical History Program. 1991.

57-45 University of Southern California, School of Dentistry, Los Angeles, CA, $10,000. Toward Dental Microbiology Testing Laboratory in Peridontal Research and Service Laboratory. 1991.

57-46 Valley Community Clinic, North Hollywood, CA, $25,000. Toward renovation and expansion of clinic. 1991.

57-47 Westside Womens Health Center, Santa Monica, CA, $20,000. Toward acquisition of six computers, printer and two software programs. 1991.

58
Phil N. Allen Charitable Trust
c/o Wells Fargo Bank, Tax Dept.
P.O. Box 63954, Attn: C.K. Guttas
San Francisco 94163

Established in 1981 in CA.
Donor(s): Phil N. Allen.‡
Foundation type: Independent
Financial data (yr. ended 06/30/91): Assets, $3,840,520 (M); expenditures, $694,557; qualifying distributions, $492,678, including $480,500 for 4 grants (high: $445,000; low: $1,000).
Purpose and activities: Grants primarily for multiple sclerosis research.
Fields of interest: Medical research.
Types of support: Research.
Limitations: Giving primarily in CA and CT. No grants to individuals.
Application information: Contributes only to pre-selected organizations. Applications not accepted.
Trustees: Mayeta V. Allen, Marvin Siegel, Wells Fargo Bank, N.A.
EIN: 956766982

59
The Herb Alpert Foundation
c/o Kip Cohen
1416 North La Brea Ave.
Los Angeles 90028

Established in 1988 in CA.
Donor(s): Herb Alpert.
Foundation type: Independent
Financial data (yr. ended 12/31/91): Assets, $19,810,522 (M); expenditures, $1,341,580; qualifying distributions, $1,100,758, including $1,100,758 for 46 grants (high: $207,500; low: $1,000).
Purpose and activities: Support primarily for music, including music education, higher and other education, and public policy organizations, including a multi-denominational conference; support also for wildlife and environmental preservation, and for AIDS research.
Fields of interest: Music, arts, dance, performing arts, elementary education, secondary education, higher education, education—building funds, education—minorities, health, AIDS, environment, wildlife.
Limitations: Giving primarily in Los Angeles, CA. No grants to individuals.
Publications: Newsletter.
Application information: Contributes only to pre-selected organizations. Applications not accepted.
Officers: Herb Alpert, Chair.; Lani Hall Alpert, Vice-Chair. and V.P.; Kip Cohen, Pres.; Werner Wolfen, Secy.; Jack M. Ostrow, C.F.O.
EIN: 954191227

60
American Honda Foundation
P.O. Box 2205
Torrance 90509-2205   (310) 781-4090
Address for Federal Express applications: 700 Van Ness Ave., Torrance, CA 90501

Established in 1984 in CA.
Donor(s): American Honda Motor Co., Inc.
Foundation type: Company-sponsored
Financial data (yr. ended 06/30/92): Assets, $15,501,074 (M); expenditures, $1,613,160; qualifying distributions, $1,509,288, including $1,315,799 for 25 grants (high: $100,000; low: $15,000; average: $10,000-$100,000).
Purpose and activities: Support for national organizations working in the areas of youth and scientific education, including private elementary and secondary schools, public and private colleges and universities, scholarship and fellowship programs, and scientific and educational organizations. "Scientific education" encompasses both the physical and life sciences and mathematics.
Fields of interest: Science and technology, youth, physical sciences, AIDS, secondary education, higher education, social sciences, language and literature, disadvantaged.
Types of support: Scholarship funds, fellowships, special projects, operating budgets, continuing support, seed money, annual campaigns, internships, matching funds, general purposes.
Limitations: No support for religious, veterans', or fraternal organizations, labor groups, or beauty and talent contests. No grants to individuals, or for trips or hospital operating funds.
Publications: Grants list, newsletter, informational brochure (including application guidelines), program policy statement, application guidelines, 990-PF.
Application information: Proposals submitted by FAX not accepted. Application form required.
  Initial approach: Letter or telephone
  Copies of proposal: 1
  Deadline(s): Nov. 1, Feb. 1, May 1, and Aug. 1
  Board meeting date(s): Jan., Apr., July, and Oct.
  Final notification: 2 months
  Write: Kathryn A. Carey, Mgr.
Officers and Directors:* S. Iizuka,* Pres.; John Petas,* V.P.; S. Cameron,* Treas.; Kathryn A. Carey, Mgr.; M. Dopp, O. Iida, R. Thomas.
Number of staff: 2 full-time professional; 1 full-time support.
EIN: 953924667

Honda Motor Company Giving Program

1919 Torrance Blvd.
Torrance 90501   (213) 781-4090

Purpose and activities: Funding to local, community support and support for service agencies is channelled through the Community Relations Department at American Honda Motor Co., Inc.
Fields of interest: Education, health, welfare, civic affairs, arts.
Types of support: General purposes, internships, matching funds, special projects.
Limitations: No support for religious, political, veterans', fraternal, labor groups or for hospital operating funds, beauty and talent contests, fund-raising events, trips, or tours. No grants to individuals.
Application information: Application form not required.
  Initial approach: Letter; Send to headquarters
  Deadline(s): Applications accepted throughout the year
  Write: Corp. Commun. Rels. Div.

62
Apple Computer, Inc. Corporate Giving Program

20525 Mariani Ave., MS:38J
Cupertino 95014   (408) 974-2974

Financial data (yr. ended 09/30/90): Total giving, $9,298,000, including $678,000 for grants and $8,620,000 for in-kind gifts.
Purpose and activities: The Nonprofit Grants program gives computer grants to support collaborative efforts that involve between 20 and 100 agencies. Proposals are submitted by a lead agency, which is a national or regional 501(c)3 nonprofit that commits to support the computer-related activities of the group and that also has a history of working with the intended participants of the project. Nonprofit grants encourage collaborations and build bridges among nonprofits working on a common issue. They are intended to solve problems that cannot be approached as effective individually and that address community problems in new ways with technology. The Education Grants Program supports educational projects that use microcomputers to create new ways of learning and teaching, with a particular interest in K-12 programs for at-risk youth. The goal is to create examples of how microcomputer technology can be used to enhance instruction in ways that are difficult to do with traditional media. Collaborations between preschool through high school grades in public and private schools across the United States, colleges, universities, or nonprofit organizations will be considered. Recipients are tying computer technology to teaching and learning in the major curriculum areas—mathematics, science, writing, social studies, and the arts—with some incorporating interdisciplinary approaches to teaching traditional subjects. Several projects are designed to enhance the learning experience for students with special needs. Overall, the goal of the Education Grants program is to support teachers who integrate computers into the educational

process in creative ways. Current giving reflects grants made between Jan. 1 and June 30.
Fields of interest: Environment, aged, youth, arts, performing arts, social sciences, handicapped, education, health, science and technology, AIDS, social services.
Types of support: In-kind gifts, donated equipment, employee volunteer services.
Limitations: No support for political or religious uses. No grants to individuals, or for auctions or raffles.
Publications: Corporate giving report, informational brochure, application guidelines, newsletter.
Application information: Application form required.
  Initial approach: Call for application and guidelines
  Deadline(s): Call to find out latest deadlines
  Final notification: 8-10 weeks after complete application is submitted
  Write: Fred Silverman, Mgr., Community Affairs
Administrators: Fred Silverman, Mgr., Community Affairs; Donna Mar, Grants Coord.
Number of staff: 4 full-time professional; 4 full-time support.

63
Arata Brothers Trust

c/o Renato R. Parenti
P.O. Box 430
Sacramento 95802

Trust established in 1976 in CA.
Foundation type: Independent
Financial data (yr. ended 12/31/91): Assets, $3,549,807 (M); expenditures, $529,028; qualifying distributions, $508,112, including $489,362 for 49 grants (high: $42,979; low: $2,000).
Fields of interest: Catholic giving, religious schools, hospitals, social services, child welfare, health associations, cultural programs.
Types of support: General purposes.
Limitations: Giving primarily in CA. No grants to individuals.
Application information:
  Initial approach: Letter
  Deadline(s): None
Trustees: Francis B. Dillon, Nellie Lavezzo, Renato R. Parenti.
EIN: 237204615

64
Ben H. and Gladys Arkelian Foundation

P.O. Box 1825
Bakersfield 93303   (805) 324-9801

Established in 1959 in CA.
Foundation type: Independent
Financial data (yr. ended 12/31/91): Assets, $2,215,462 (L); expenditures, $161,133; qualifying distributions, $128,401, including $124,765 for 32 grants (high: $35,840; low: $100).
Fields of interest: Libraries, social services, health, higher education, general charitable giving.
Limitations: Giving limited to Kern County, CA. No grants to individuals.
Application information:
  Initial approach: Letter

Deadline(s): None
Board meeting date(s): 1st Thursday of each month
Write: Frank I. Ford, Jr., Secy.
Officers and Directors:* Henry C. Mack,* Pres.; Henry C. Mack, Jr.,* V.P.; Frank I. Ford, Jr., Secy.; D. Bianco, Harvey H. Means.
EIN: 956103223

65
AT&T Pebble Beach National Pro-Am Youth Fund

(Formerly Bing Crosby Youth Fund, Inc.)
490 Calle Principal
Monterey 93940   (408) 375-3151
Mailing address: P.O. Box 112, Monterey, CA 93942

Established in 1963 in CA.
Donor(s): Bing Crosby.‡
Foundation type: Independent
Financial data (yr. ended 06/30/91): Assets, $440,104 (M); gifts received, $436,374; expenditures, $370,805; qualifying distributions, $370,805, including $353,259 for 105 grants (high: $10,000; low: $450).
Purpose and activities: Giving primarily for youth agencies, social and family services, and higher and secondary education; support also for health services, hospices, and cultural organizations, including the fine arts.
Fields of interest: Youth, social services, family services, higher education, secondary education, health services, health, hospices, cultural programs, fine arts.
Types of support: Building funds, equipment, scholarship funds, consulting services, matching funds.
Limitations: Giving primarily in Monterey and Santa Cruz counties, CA. No grants to individuals.
Application information: Application form not required.
  Initial approach: Letter
  Copies of proposal: 1
  Deadline(s): None
  Board meeting date(s): July, Aug., Sept., Oct., and Dec.
  Write: Carmel Martin, Jr., Secy.
Officers: Ted Durein, Pres.; Carmel C. Martin, Jr., Secy.; John Burns, Treas.
Trustees: Marsha Searle Brown, Peter J. Coniglio, Leon E. Edner, Warner Keeley, Frank Thacker, Murray C. Vout.
Number of staff: 2 part-time support.
EIN: 946050251

66
Atkinson Foundation

Ten West Orange Ave.
South San Francisco 94080   (415) 876-1559

Incorporated in 1939 in CA.
Donor(s): George H. Atkinson,‡ Mildred M. Atkinson.‡
Foundation type: Independent
Financial data (yr. ended 12/31/91): Assets, $10,981,205 (M); gifts received, $46,439; expenditures, $614,409; qualifying distributions, $551,775, including $465,800 for 87 grants (high: $50,000; low: $500; average: $2,000-$10,000).

Purpose and activities: Primary areas of interest include the disadvantaged and the homeless, child welfare, family planning, and the handicapped. Broad purposes are to help people reach their highest potential in their spiritual and economic life and to reach self-sufficiency; giving for social services, including youth and the aged; education; AIDS programs; the United Methodist Church and other church activities; and international development and relief programs.
Fields of interest: Disadvantaged, child welfare, family services, family planning, homeless, handicapped, education—minorities, secondary education, higher education, AIDS, international development, international relief, Protestant giving.
Types of support: Seed money, operating budgets, scholarship funds, continuing support, general purposes, technical assistance, student aid, special projects.
Limitations: Giving primarily in San Mateo County, CA, for social welfare, secondary schools, and colleges; United Methodist churches and church activities in northern CA; and international grantmaking primarily in Latin America and Sub-Saharan and Central Africa for technical assistance, relief, and population issues. No support for doctoral study or elementary schools. No grants to individuals, or for research or fundraising events; no loans.
Publications: Annual report (including application guidelines), informational brochure (including application guidelines), application guidelines.
Application information: Application form not required.
  Initial approach: Telephone, or letter
  Copies of proposal: 1
  Deadline(s): Mar. 31 and Aug. 31 for international grants; no set deadline for other grants
  Board meeting date(s): Feb. or Mar., May or June, Sept., and Dec.
  Final notification: Within 3 months
  Write: Elizabeth H. Curtis, Treas.
Officers and Directors:* Duane E. Atkinson,* Pres.; Ray N. Atkinson,* V.P.; Thomas J. Henderson,* V.P.; James C. Ingwersen,* Secy.; Elizabeth H. Curtis,* Treas.; Lavina M. Atkinson, Lawrence A. Wright.
Number of staff: 1 part-time professional.
EIN: 946075613

67
The R. C. Baker Foundation ▼
P.O. Box 6150
Orange 92613-6150   (714) 750-8981

Trust established in 1952 in CA.
Donor(s): R.C. Baker, Sr.‡
Foundation type: Independent
Financial data (yr. ended 12/31/91): Assets, $21,816,689 (M); gifts received, $500,000; expenditures, $1,409,176; qualifying distributions, $1,314,358, including $1,241,867 for 202 grants (high: $142,000; low: $60; average: $100-$77,500).
Purpose and activities: Emphasis on higher education, including scholarships administered by selected colleges and universities; some support for hospitals and health agencies, cultural programs, and social service and youth agencies.

Fields of interest: Education, higher education, education—building funds, educational associations, health services, hospitals, hospitals—building funds, medical research, mental health, cultural programs, fine arts, museums, performing arts, social services, youth, leadership development, handicapped, hunger.
Types of support: Emergency funds, building funds, equipment, research, operating budgets, scholarship funds, fellowships, general purposes, continuing support, annual campaigns, capital campaigns, renovation projects, special projects.
Limitations: No grants to individuals, or for endowment funds; no loans.
Application information: Application form not required.
  Initial approach: Cover letter with proposal
  Copies of proposal: 1
  Deadline(s): Submit proposal preferably in Apr. or Sept.; deadline May 1 and Oct. 1
  Board meeting date(s): June and Nov.
  Write: Frank L. Scott, Chair.
Officer and Trustees:* Frank L. Scott,* Chair.; Kenny Dale, James H. Hickey, Joe Shelton, Ronald Turner, Robert N. Water, Bank of America.
Number of staff: 3
EIN: 951742283

68
The Solomon R. and Rebecca D. Baker Foundation, Inc.
1900 Ave. of the Stars, Suite 630
Los Angeles 90067   (213) 552-9822

Incorporated in 1952 in DE.
Donor(s): Solomon R. Baker.
Foundation type: Independent
Financial data (yr. ended 04/30/91): Assets, $2,832,990 (M); expenditures, $131,806; qualifying distributions, $129,637, including $129,500 for 5 grants (high: $125,000; low: $500).
Purpose and activities: Giving for medical research in autism and related fields and the care and therapy of autistic individuals; support also for education of the disadvantaged, Jewish welfare agencies, and animal welfare.
Fields of interest: Medical research, mental health, animal welfare, disadvantaged, Jewish welfare.
Limitations: Giving primarily in CA. No grants to individuals.
Application information:
  Initial approach: Letter
  Deadline(s): None
  Write: Solomon R. Baker, Pres.
Officers and Trustees:* Solomon R. Baker,* Pres.; Rebecca D. Baker,* V.P. and Treas.; Robert J. Plourde,* Secy.; Richard H. Barker, Al Marsella.
EIN: 237152503

69
Bank of America - Giannini Foundation
Bank of America Ctr., Dept. 3246
P.O. Box 37000
San Francisco 94137   (415) 953-0932

Incorporated in 1945 in CA.
Donor(s): A.P. Giannini,‡ Fred B. Fancher Trust.
Foundation type: Independent

Financial data (yr. ended 12/31/90): Assets, $10,189,997 (M); gifts received, $37,053; expenditures, $603,005; qualifying distributions, $575,505, including $239,292 for 25 grants (high: $50,000; low: $1,000) and $290,300 for 17 grants to individuals (high: $20,000; low: $150).
Purpose and activities: Medical research fellowships for advanced applicants sponsored by accredited medical schools. Limited number of grants made to support charitable or other educational endeavors, or those pertaining to the advancement of human health and the eradication of disease.
Fields of interest: Medical research, higher education, health, child welfare, youth.
Types of support: Fellowships, research.
Limitations: Giving limited to CA. No grants to individuals (except for research fellowships), or for endowment funds or matching gifts; no loans.
Publications: Application guidelines, annual report, 990-PF.
Application information: Application form required for fellowships only.
  Initial approach: Letter, telephone, or proposal
  Copies of proposal: 1
  Deadline(s): Aug. 1 for grants; Dec. 1 for fellowships
  Board meeting date(s): Apr. and Nov.
  Write: Caroline O. Boitano, Administrator
Officers and Directors:* Kyhl S. Smeby,* Chair.; Claire Giannini Hoffman,* Vice-Chair.; Cheryl Knowles-Sorokin,* Secy.; Janet Nishioka,* Treas.; Caroline O. Boitano, George E. Cherrie, Jr., James C. Deane, James P. Miscoll, D.A. Mullane, A.T. Paioni, H. Clyde Von Essen.
Number of staff: 1 shared staff
EIN: 946089512

70
BankAmerica Foundation ▼
Bank of America Ctr.
Dept. 3246, P.O. Box 37000
San Francisco 94137   (415) 953-3175

Incorporated in 1968 in CA.
Donor(s): BankAmerica Corp., and subsidiaries.
Foundation type: Company-sponsored
Financial data (yr. ended 12/31/90): Assets, $2,302,316 (M); gifts received, $7,973,533; expenditures, $8,220,225; qualifying distributions, $8,201,685, including $7,172,877 for 363 grants (high: $1,300,000; low: $15; average: $1,000-$20,000) and $1,028,808 for employee matching gifts.
Purpose and activities: To fund private, nonprofit, tax-exempt organizations providing services to communities locally, nationally, and internationally in areas where the company operates. Support both through grants and loans in 5 major funding areas: health, human resources, community and economic development, education, and culture and the arts; support also for special programs developed by the foundation to use its resources most effectively.
Fields of interest: Higher education, community development, health services, hospitals, community funds, social services, youth, arts, cultural programs.
Types of support: Annual campaigns, building funds, special projects, scholarship funds, employee-related scholarships, matching funds,

general purposes, continuing support, capital campaigns, emergency funds.
Limitations: Giving limited to areas of major company operations, including communities in CA, metropolitan areas nationwide, and foreign countries. No support for religious organizations for sectarian purposes, athletic events and programs, organizations where funding would primarily benefit membership, agencies receiving support from United Way, or government-funded programs. No grants to individuals, or for fundraising events, advertising memorial campaigns, or endowment funds. Generally, no grants for research, conferences or seminars, publications, or operating support.
Publications: Program policy statement, application guidelines, 990-PF.
Application information: The employee matching gift program has been discontinued.
Initial approach: Letter
Copies of proposal: 1
Deadline(s): For capital/major campaigns, July 31; all others, none
Board meeting date(s): Annually and as necessary
Final notification: Varies
Write: Caroline O. Boitano, Pres. and Exec. Dir.
Officers and Trustees:* Donald A. Mullane,* Chair.; Caroline O. Boitano,* Pres. and Exec. Dir.; Joanne El-Gohary, V.P.; James S. Wagele, V.P.; Janet Nishioka, Treas.; Linda Fischer-Werk, Financial Officer; Judy Granucci, Financial Officer; Robert N. Beck, Thomas E. Peterson, Richard Rosenberg, John S. Stephan.
Number of staff: 1 full-time professional; 1 full-time support.
EIN: 941670382
Recent health grants:
70-1 Davies Medical Center, San Francisco, CA, $25,000. 1990.
70-2 Easter Seal Society of Santa Cruz, Santa Cruz, CA, $10,000. 1990.
70-3 Edgewood Childrens Center, San Francisco, CA, $25,000. 1990.
70-4 Irwin Memorial Blood Bank, San Francisco, CA, $15,000. 1990.
70-5 Marin General Hospital Foundation, Greenbrae, CA, $20,000. 1990.
70-6 Mount Diablo Hospital, Concord, CA, $10,000. 1990.
70-7 Presbyterian Intercommunity Hospital Foundation, Whittier, CA, $20,000. 1990.
70-8 Saint Johns Hospital and Health Center, Santa Monica, CA, $12,000. 1990.
70-9 Saint Jude Memorial Foundation, Fullerton, CA, $15,000. 1990.
70-10 San Francisco AIDS Foundation, San Francisco, CA, $10,000. 1990.
70-11 Scripps Clinic and Research Foundation, La Jolla, CA, $25,000. 1990.
70-12 Southern California Building Fund, Los Angeles, CA, $40,000. 1990.
70-13 Torrance Memorial Hospital, Torrance, CA, $10,000. 1990.
70-14 Tulare Hospital Foundation, Tulare, CA, $10,000. 1990.
70-15 Watsonville Community Hospital, Watsonville, CA, $10,000. 1990.

71
The Donald R. Barker Foundation
11661 San Vicente Blvd., No. 300
Los Angeles 90049
Application address: P.O. Box 936, Rancho Mirage, CA 92270; Tel.: (619) 324-2656

Established in 1977 in OR.
Donor(s): Donald R. Barker.
Foundation type: Independent
Financial data (yr. ended 11/30/91): Assets, $4,264,838 (M); expenditures, $278,894; qualifying distributions, $278,894, including $194,827 for 39 grants (high: $18,000; low: $1,000).
Fields of interest: Higher education, secondary education, hospitals, health, handicapped, youth, community funds.
Types of support: Operating budgets, scholarship funds, building funds, equipment, special projects.
Limitations: Giving primarily in CA and OR. No support for sectarian religious purposes, or for agencies that rely on federal or tax dollars for their principal support. No grants to individuals, or for endowment funds, conferences, or operational deficits.
Publications: Application guidelines.
Application information: Application form required.
Initial approach: Letter
Copies of proposal: 1
Deadline(s): Mar. 1 and Aug. 1
Board meeting date(s): May and Oct.
Final notification: Promptly after decision
Trustees: John R. Lamb, Coeta Barker McGowan, J.R. McGowan, Joseph A. Moore.
EIN: 930698411

72
The Donald E. and Delia B. Baxter Foundation
201 South Lake Ave., Suite 602
Pasadena 91101-3091

Incorporated in 1959 in CA.
Donor(s): Delia B. Baxter.
Foundation type: Independent
Financial data (yr. ended 12/31/91): Assets, $20,221,355 (M); expenditures, $1,023,438; qualifying distributions, $846,860, including $831,500 for 3 grants (high: $349,500; low: $182,000).
Purpose and activities: Support for educational and scientific institutions for research and development of medicine, instruments, and fluids for alleviating pain and protecting and prolonging human life.
Fields of interest: Medical research.
Types of support: Research, building funds, professorships, fellowships, scholarship funds.
Limitations: Giving primarily in CA. No grants to individuals.
Application information: Grants initiated by the foundation's board. Applications not accepted.
Officers: Richard N. Mackay, Pres.; Richard H. Haake, V.P. and C.F.O.; Donald B. Haake, Secy.
Director: Martha B. Haake.
EIN: 956029555

73
The Bay View Federal Savings Charitable Trust
c/o Charitable Trust Comm.
2121 South El Camino Real, Suite 800, Bldg. C200
San Mateo 94403   (415) 573-7300

Financial data (yr. ended 12/31/90): Total giving, $40,000 for grants.
Purpose and activities: "To administer a program on behalf of the corporation, to support various civic and community organizations in market areas served by Bay View Federal Bank." Supports cultural, recreational, vocational, medical and eductional programs.
Fields of interest: Cultural programs, recreation, vocational education, health, education.
Types of support: General purposes.
Limitations: Giving limited to the San Francisco Bay Area counties, CA. No support for religious or political organizations.
Publications: Application guidelines.
Application information: Contributions are handled by the Marketing Dept. Application form not required.
Initial approach: Letter; Send to headquarters
Final notification: Notification of approved proposals only
Write: Donna Strout, Mktg. Coord.
Number of staff: 4

74
Beaver Foundation
190 Cypress Point Way
Moraga 94556

Established in 1969 in CA.
Donor(s): Wallace W. Knox.‡
Foundation type: Independent
Financial data (yr. ended 12/31/91): Assets, $7,304,435 (M); expenditures, $372,195; qualifying distributions, $324,504, including $289,500 for 6 grants (high: $100,000; low: $7,500).
Purpose and activities: Giving primarily for a family planning agency and youth clubs.
Fields of interest: Family planning, youth.
Types of support: Building funds, general purposes, continuing support.
Limitations: Giving limited to Alameda County, CA, excluding Livermore Valley. No grants to individuals.
Application information: Contributes only to pre-selected organizations. Applications not accepted.
Write: Marjorie J. Beard, Secy.-Treas.
Officers: Philbrick Bowhay, V.P.; John C. Ricksen, V.P.; William C. Robbins III, V.P.; Marjorie J. Beard, Secy.-Treas.
EIN: 941682883

75
Bechtel Foundation ▼
50 Beale St.
San Francisco 94105   (415) 768-5974

Incorporated in 1953 in CA.
Donor(s): Bechtel Power Corp.
Foundation type: Company-sponsored

Financial data (yr. ended 12/31/90): Assets, $19,358,352 (M); expenditures, $1,776,990; qualifying distributions, $1,556,894, including $1,410,555 for 274 grants (high: $260,000; low: $25; average: $1,000-$20,000) and $146,339 for employee matching gifts.
Purpose and activities: Grants for higher education and community funds, and to organizations related to some aspect of the engineering business and construction. Support also for cultural programs, public interest, health organizations, and social services.
Fields of interest: Higher education, community funds, engineering, cultural programs, public policy, social services, health.
Types of support: Employee matching gifts, general purposes.
Limitations: No support for religious organizations. No grants to individuals, or for endowment funds or special projects.
Application information:
   Initial approach: Letter or proposal
   Deadline(s): None
   Board meeting date(s): Annually
   Final notification: Varies
   Write: K.M. Bandarrae, Asst. Secy.
Officers and Directors:* R.P. Bechtel,* Chair.; C.W. Hull,* Vice-Chair.; John Neerhout, Jr.,* Vice-Chair.; D.M. Slavich,* Pres. and Treas.; W.L. Friend,* Exec. V.P.; D.J. Gunther,* Exec. V.P.; L.G. Hinkelman, Exec. V.P.; J.D. Carter,* Sr. V.P. and Secy.; T.G. Flynn, Sr. V.P.
Number of staff: 1 full-time professional; 1 part-time professional; 1 full-time support; 1 part-time support.
EIN: 946078120

76
Arnold and Mabel Beckman Foundation ▼
c/o Hopper Kaufman & Co.
5140 Campus Dr., Suite 100
Newport Beach 92660   (714) 851-0500

Incorporated in 1977 in CA.
Donor(s): Arnold O. Beckman, Mabel M. Beckman.‡
Foundation type: Independent
Financial data (yr. ended 08/31/90): Assets, $149,134,434 (M); expenditures, $11,474,535; qualifying distributions, $11,244,781, including $11,244,781 for 7 grants (high: $5,755,074; low: $4,000; average: $10,000-$2,000,000).
Purpose and activities: Support for higher education and scientific and medical research; emphasis on research in genetics, biochemistry, chemistry, and human and artificial intelligence.
Fields of interest: Higher education, medical research, science and technology, biochemistry, chemistry.
Types of support: Annual campaigns, conferences and seminars, endowment funds, equipment, matching funds, professorships, research, seed money, building funds.
Limitations: Giving primarily in CA. No grants to individuals; no loans.
Application information: Contributes only to pre-selected organizations. Applications not accepted.
   Board meeting date(s): Nov. and July
   Write: Arnold O. Beckman, Pres.

Officers and Trustees:* Arnold O. Beckman,* Pres.; Donald A. Strauss, V.P. and Secy.; Harold Brown, Maurice H. Stans.
Number of staff: 1 part-time support.
EIN: 953169713
Recent health grants:
76-1 Beckman Laser Institute and Medical Clinic, Irvine, CA, $5,755,074. For endowment fund. Grant made in the form of 140,000 shares of SKB stock. 1990.
76-2 Rockefeller University, NYC, NY, $1,750,707. For Arnold and Mabel Beckman Fund for Biomedical Research. 1990.

77
Milo W. Bekins Foundation
c/o Wells Fargo Bank, N.A., MAC 0103-179
P.O. Box 63954, Trust Tax Dept.
San Francisco 94163

Trust established in 1953 in CA.
Donor(s): Milo W. Bekins, The Bekins Co.
Foundation type: Independent
Financial data (yr. ended 12/31/91): Assets, $4,615,460 (M); expenditures, $261,502; qualifying distributions, $207,039, including $191,000 for 35 grants (high: $16,000; low: $2,000).
Fields of interest: Higher education, hospitals, youth, social services, community funds.
Limitations: Giving primarily in CA. No grants to individuals.
Application information: Contributes only to pre-selected organizations. Applications not accepted.
Trustees: Jacqueline Bekins, Michael Bekins, Milo W. Bekins, Jr., Virginia Bekins Daum.
Agent: Wells Fargo Bank, N.A.
EIN: 956039745

78
Bellini Foundation
400 Estudillo Ave., Suite 200
San Leandro 94577

Established in 1981 in CA.
Donor(s): J. Bellini.‡
Foundation type: Independent
Financial data (yr. ended 06/30/91): Assets, $4,109,423 (M); gifts received, $3,000; expenditures, $227,274; qualifying distributions, $167,000, including $167,000 for 32 grants (high: $15,000; low: $500).
Fields of interest: Hospitals, medical research, handicapped, secondary education, youth, social services.
Limitations: Giving primarily in CA. No grants to individuals.
Application information: Contributes only to pre-selected organizations. Applications not accepted.
Officers: Patrick W. Bellini, Pres.; Michael J. Bellini, V.P.; B.K. Jayswal, Secy.-Treas.
EIN: 942768903

79
Legler Benbough Foundation
2550 Fifth Ave., Suite 132
San Diego 92103-6622   (619) 235-8099

Established in 1985 in CA.
Donor(s): Legler Benbough.
Foundation type: Independent
Financial data (yr. ended 12/31/91): Assets $4,803,153 (M); expenditures, $240,4 qualifying distributions, $226,825, including $215,250 for 19 grants (high: $85,000; low: $50).
Purpose and activities: Giving primarily for health associations and health care, museums, and the arts; some support for community development and education.
Fields of interest: Health associations, health, museums, arts, community development, education.
Types of support: General purposes.
Limitations: Giving primarily in the San Diego, CA, area.
Application information:
   Initial approach: Letter
   Deadline(s): None
   Write: Legler Benbough, Pres.
Officers: Legler Benbough, Pres.; Winifred Deming, V.P.; Peter K. Ellsworth, Secy.; Thomas Cisco, Treas.
EIN: 330105049

80
H. N. and Frances C. Berger Foundation ▼
P.O. Box 3064
Arcadia 91006-0966   (818) 447-3351

Incorporated in 1961 in CA.
Donor(s): Frances C. Berger, H.N. Berger.
Foundation type: Independent
Financial data (yr. ended 12/31/90): Assets, $229,500,573 (M); gifts received, $62,862,521; expenditures, $9,857,855; qualifying distributions, $7,811,220, including $7,708,561 for 56 grants (high: $1,040,000; low: $1,000; average: $5,000-$100,000).
Purpose and activities: Emphasis on higher education, cultural programs, public health organizations, and hospitals. Committed to long-term support of present donees.
Fields of interest: Higher education, cultural programs, health, hospitals.
Limitations: Giving primarily in CA. No grants to individuals.
Application information:
   Initial approach: Letter
   Deadline(s): None
   Board meeting date(s): Semiannually and as required
   Write: Ron Auen, Pres.
Officers and Directors:* Lewis Webb, Jr.,* C.E.O. and V.P.; Ronald Auen,* Pres.; Shirley Allen,* V.P.; Joan Auen, Robert M. Barton, John N. Berger, Harry F. Booth, Jr., Christopher McGuire, Douglas Vance.
EIN: 956048939
Recent health grants:
80-1 Alzheimers Disease and Related Disorders Association, Los Angeles, CA, $100,000. For In Home Respite Program and Adult Day Care. 1990.
80-2 American Cancer Society, San Gabriel/Pomona Units, Pasadena, CA, $100,000. For transportation program. 1990.
80-3 Arcadia Methodist Hospital, Arcadia, CA, $500,000. For nursing scholarships and equipment purchases. 1990.

80-4 Childrens Hospital of Los Angeles, Los Angeles, CA, $110,100. For child abuse evaluation project and cystic fibrosis research. 1990.

80-5 Make-A-Wish Foundation, Los Angeles, CA, $100,000. To provide special wishes to children with life threatening diseases. 1990.

80-6 Psoriasis Research Institute, Department of Dermatology, Palo Alto, CA, $20,000. For one-year fellowship and one full-time investigator for psoriasis. 1990.

80-7 Salk Institute for Biological Studies, La Jolla, CA, $1,000,000. For building fund. 1990.

80-8 Salk Institute for Biological Studies, La Jolla, CA, $100,000. For research. 1990.

80-9 Southern California Childrens Cancer Services, Los Angeles, CA, $100,000. For building fund. 1990.

81
The Kathryne Beynon Foundation
199 South Los Robles Ave., Suite 711
Pasadena 91101-2460

Established in 1967 in CA.
Donor(s): Kathryne Beynon.‡
Foundation type: Independent
Financial data (yr. ended 10/31/90): Assets, $5,047,396 (M); expenditures, $321,673; qualifying distributions, $224,774, including $192,500 for 19 grants (high: $37,000; low: $1,000).
Purpose and activities: Emphasis on a drug abuse and alcoholism program, hospitals, youth agencies, child welfare, Catholic church support, and higher education.
Fields of interest: Drug abuse, alcoholism, hospitals, youth, child welfare, Catholic giving, higher education.
Types of support: Building funds, endowment funds, scholarship funds, general purposes.
Limitations: Giving primarily in Southern CA.
Application information: Application form not required.
   Deadline(s): None
   Write: Robert D. Bannon, Trustee
Trustee: Robert D. Bannon.
EIN: 956197328

82
The Bireley Foundation
130 North Brand Blvd., 4th Fl.
Glendale 91203   (818) 500-7755

Incorporated in 1960 in CA.
Donor(s): Frank W. Bireley.‡
Foundation type: Independent
Financial data (yr. ended 12/31/90): Assets, $5,914,669 (M); expenditures, $544,303; qualifying distributions, $500,949, including $477,100 for 65 grants (high: $50,000; low: $500).
Purpose and activities: Grants mainly to a local medical school and children's hospital for research and treatment of adolescent skin diseases. Support also for local higher education, hospitals, and health agencies.
Fields of interest: Medical education, dermatology, medical research, cancer, education, higher education, hospitals, health services, health associations.

Limitations: Giving primarily in CA, FL, and UT. No grants to individuals.
Application information: Application form not required.
   Initial approach: Letter or proposal
   Copies of proposal: 2
   Deadline(s): Submit proposal preferably between Jan. and June; no set deadline
   Board meeting date(s): 6 times a year
   Write: Christine Harriet Bireley, Pres.
Officers: Christine Harriet Bireley, Pres.; Ernest R. Baldwin, V.P. and Secy.; Frank W. Bireley, V.P.; William Robert Bireley, V.P.; Christine Bireley Oliver, V.P.; Leroy M. Gire, Treas.
Number of staff: None.
EIN: 956029475

83
Otis Booth Foundation
c/o Otis Booth, Jr.
1100 Glendon Ave., Suite 2017
Los Angeles 90024

Established in 1967 in CA.
Donor(s): Berkshire Hathaway, Inc.
Foundation type: Independent
Financial data (yr. ended 11/30/91): Assets, $2,383,700 (M); gifts received, $17,779; expenditures, $124,636; qualifying distributions, $121,216, including $121,216 for 20 grants (high: $25,000; low: $500).
Fields of interest: Medical sciences, hospitals, education, arts, museums, social services, Protestant giving.
Limitations: Giving primarily in CA. No grants to individuals.
Application information: Contributes only to pre-selected organizations. Applications not accepted.
Officers and Trustees:* Otis Booth, Jr.,* Pres.; Charles T. Munger,* V.P. and Treas.; Richard D. Esbenshade,* Secy.
EIN: 956140019

84
Albert & Elaine Borchard Foundation
22055 Clarendon St., Suite 210
Woodland Hills 91367

Established in 1978 in CA.
Foundation type: Independent
Financial data (yr. ended 07/31/91): Assets, $12,560,636 (M); expenditures, $1,167,972; qualifying distributions, $633,241, including $570,110 for 50 grants (high: $85,000; low: $1,000).
Fields of interest: Higher education, social services, youth, community development, hospitals, health services.
Types of support: Scholarship funds.
Limitations: Giving primarily in CA, UT, and MN. No grants to individuals.
Application information:
   Initial approach: Letter
   Deadline(s): None
Officers and Directors:* Willard A. Beling,* Chair.; Edward D. Spurgeon,* Pres.; Heide Galke, Secy.-Treas.; Betty Beling, Carol Spurgeon.
EIN: 953294377

85
The James G. Boswell Foundation ▼
4600 Security Pacific Plaza
333 South Hope St.
Los Angeles 90071   (213) 485-1717

Incorporated in 1947 in CA.
Donor(s): James G. Boswell.‡
Foundation type: Independent
Financial data (yr. ended 12/31/90): Assets, $57,847,606 (M); expenditures, $1,781,110; qualifying distributions, $1,716,704, including $1,652,466 for 37 grants (high: $500,000; low: $500; average: $1,000-$50,000).
Purpose and activities: Giving primarily for education, health, youth development, agricultural education, and the environment.
Fields of interest: Education, higher education, hospitals, health, environment, youth, agriculture.
Types of support: General purposes, annual campaigns, scholarship funds, continuing support.
Limitations: Giving primarily in CA.
Application information:
   Initial approach: Letter
   Deadline(s): None
   Board meeting date(s): Feb. and as required
   Final notification: Varies
   Write: Greer J. Fearon, Exec. Secy.
Trustees: James G. Boswell II, Rosalind M. Boswell, Susan W. Dulin.
Number of staff: None.
EIN: 956047326
Recent health grants:
85-1 Bridgeport Hospital, Bridgeport, CT, $10,000. For Dexter Lenci Memorial Fund medical education lectures. 1990.
85-2 Huntington Medical Research Institutes, Pasadena, CA, $50,000. For Project Stroke Research. 1990.
85-3 Palo Alto Medical Foundation, Palo Alto, CA, $333,000. For President's Discretionary Fund. 1990.

86
The Bothin Foundation
873 Sutter St., Suite B
San Francisco 94109   (415) 771-4300

Incorporated in 1917 in CA.
Donor(s): Henry E. Bothin,‡ Ellen Chabot Bothin,‡ Genevieve Bothin de Limur.‡
Foundation type: Independent
Financial data (yr. ended 12/31/91): Assets, $19,757,680 (M); expenditures, $622,207; qualifying distributions, $622,207, including $462,992 for 64 grants (high: $25,000; low: $1,000; average: $700-$25,000).
Purpose and activities: Giving primarily for youth, the elderly, disabled, including the learning disabled, health care, community human services and the environment; grants to arts groups are limited to those serving youth or with heavy emphasis on youth participation. The foundation prefers to make grants for capital or building and equipment needs.
Fields of interest: Youth, aged, handicapped, health, community development, environment.
Types of support: Building funds, equipment, capital campaigns.
Limitations: Giving primarily in CA, with emphasis on San Francisco, Marin, Sonoma, San Mateo, and Santa Barbara counties. No support

for religious organizations, medical research, educational institutions (except those directly aiding the developmentally disabled), or for production or distribution of films or other documentary presentations. No grants to individuals, or for general operating funds, endowment funds, scholarships, fellowships, or conferences; no loans.
Publications: Biennial report (including application guidelines).
Application information: Application form not required.
  Initial approach: Letter containing a brief outline of the project
  Copies of proposal: 1
  Deadline(s): 10 weeks prior to meeting
  Board meeting date(s): Early to mid-Feb., June, and Oct.
  Final notification: 2 to 3 months
  Write: Lyman H. Casey, Exec. Dir.
Officers and Directors:* Genevieve Di San Faustino,* Pres.; Edmona Lyman Mansell,* 1st V.P.; Benjamin J. Henley, Jr.,* 2nd V.P.; A. Michael Casey, Corp. Secy.; William W. Budge, William F. Geisler, Stephanie P. MacColl, Rhoda W. Schultz.
Number of staff: None.
EIN: 941196182

87
The Mervyn L. Brenner Foundation, Inc.
c/o KPMG Peat Marwick
Three Embarcadero Ctr., Suite 2100
San Francisco 94111   (415) 951-0100

Incorporated in 1961 in CA.
Donor(s): Mervyn L. Brenner.‡
Foundation type: Independent
Financial data (yr. ended 08/31/91): Assets, $3,546,673 (M); expenditures, $151,513; qualifying distributions, $130,783, including $129,270 for 55 grants (high: $18,100; low: $250).
Fields of interest: Hospitals, health services, youth, social services, Jewish welfare, higher education, accounting.
Types of support: Annual campaigns, operating budgets.
Limitations: Giving primarily in CA. No grants to individuals.
Application information:
  Initial approach: Proposal
  Deadline(s): None
  Write: John R. Gentry, Pres.
Officers: John R. Gentry, Pres. and Treas.; John T. Seigle, V.P.; Jane P. Tepperman, V.P.; Marc H. Monheimer, Secy.
Number of staff: None.
EIN: 946088679

88
Bright Family Foundation
1620 North Carpenter Rd., Suite B1
Modesto 95354   (209) 577-4181
Application address: 121 Downey, No. 102, Modesto, CA 95354

Established in 1986 in CA.
Donor(s): Calvin E. Bright, Marjorie H. Bright.
Foundation type: Independent
Financial data (yr. ended 12/31/90): Assets, $2,389,547 (M); gifts received, $370,000;

expenditures, $96,125; qualifying distributions, $89,982, including $87,129 for 18 grants (high: $15,529; low: $300; average: $300-$15,529).
Fields of interest: Education, higher education, business education, health, medical sciences, Native Americans, youth, religion, homeless, general charitable giving.
Types of support: Operating budgets, renovation projects, in-kind gifts, scholarship funds, building funds.
Limitations: Giving primarily in Stanislaus County, CA. No grants to individuals.
Application information: Contributes only to pre-selected organizations. Applications not accepted.
  Board meeting date(s): Dec.
  Write: Marjorie H. Bright, V.P.
Officers and Directors:* Calvin E. Bright,* Pres.; Marjorie H. Bright,* V.P.; Lyn E. Bright,* Secy.-Treas.
Number of staff: None.
EIN: 770126942

89
Dana & Albert R. Broccoli Charitable Foundation
2121 Ave. of the Stars, Suite 1240
Los Angeles 90067

Established in 1980 in CA.
Donor(s): Albert R. Broccoli, Dana Broccoli.
Foundation type: Independent
Financial data (yr. ended 12/31/90): Assets, $2,744,939 (M); expenditures, $257,545; qualifying distributions, $252,045, including $252,000 for 24 grants (high: $100,000; low: $1,000).
Fields of interest: Higher education, cultural programs, hospitals, health services, youth, family services, child welfare.
Types of support: General purposes.
Limitations: No grants to individuals.
Application information: Contributes only to pre-selected organizations. Applications not accepted.
Officers and Directors:* Albert R. Broccoli,* Pres.; Dana Broccoli,* V.P.; Michael G. Wilson,* C.F.O.
EIN: 953502889

90
Brotman Foundation of California
c/o Robert D. Hartford
433 North Camden Dr., No. 600
Beverly Hills 90210   (213) 271-2910

Established in 1964.
Foundation type: Independent
Financial data (yr. ended 12/31/90): Assets, $7,313,518 (M); expenditures, $420,776; qualifying distributions, $377,153, including $266,000 for 37 grants (high: $35,000; low: $1,000).
Purpose and activities: Giving mainly for children, health and medical research; some support for arts, education, and environmental organizations.
Fields of interest: Child welfare, health, medical research, AIDS, arts, education, environment.
Limitations: Giving primarily in Southern CA.
Application information:

Initial approach: Letter
Deadline(s): None
Officers and Directors:* Michael B. Sherman,* Pres.; Lowell Marks,* Secy.; Robert D. Hartford,* Treas.; Toni Brotman.
EIN: 956094639

91
Dionigi Brunetti Trust
c/o Wells Fargo Bank, N.A., Trust Tax Dept.
P.O. Box 63954
San Francisco 94163

Established in 1990.
Foundation type: Independent
Financial data (yr. ended 12/31/90): Assets, $4,555,451 (M); expenditures, $214,373; qualifying distributions, $207,291, including $206,090 for 5 grants (high: $81,636; low: $6,123).
Fields of interest: Heart disease, cancer, hospitals.
Limitations: Giving limited to CA. No grants to individuals.
Application information: Contributes only to pre-selected organizations. Applications not accepted.
Trustees: S.J. Cuttitta, Wells Fargo Bank, N.A.
EIN: 956785907

92
The Henry W. Bull Foundation
c/o Santa Barbara Bank & Trust
P.O. Box 2340
Santa Barbara 93120-2340   (805) 564-6211

Trust established in 1960 in CA.
Donor(s): Maud L. Bull.‡
Foundation type: Independent
Financial data (yr. ended 12/31/90): Assets, $5,446,205 (M); expenditures, $267,768; qualifying distributions, $244,990, including $241,875 for 73 grants (high: $25,000; low: $375; average: $1,000-$2,500).
Fields of interest: Higher education, religion—Christian, handicapped, health, music.
Limitations: No grants to individuals, or for building or endowment funds.
Application information: Applications not accepted.
  Board meeting date(s): Monthly
  Write: Gary Newman, Asst. V.P., Santa Barbara Bank & Trust
Trustees: Frederic Astaire, Jr., Frank Patty, Peter Potter, Santa Barbara Bank & Trust.
EIN: 956062058

93
The Alphonse A. Burnand Medical and Educational Foundation
P.O. Box 59
593 Palm Canyon Dr.
Borrego Springs 92004   (714) 767-5314

Incorporated in 1957 in CA.
Foundation type: Independent
Financial data (yr. ended 12/31/90): Assets, $2,726,404 (M); expenditures, $72,133; qualifying distributions, $56,160, including $56,150 for 16 grants (high: $10,000; low: $1,000).

...erest: Hospitals, handicapped, higher
..., youth.
...ons: Giving primarily in Borrego Springs
an... an Diego County, CA. No grants to
individuals, or for endowment funds.
Application information: Application form not
required.
Initial approach: Letter
Copies of proposal: 1
Deadline(s): Submit proposal in Oct.
Board meeting date(s): As required, at least
semiannually
Write: A.A. Burnand III, Pres.
Officers: A.A. Burnand III, Pres.; A.G. Hansen,
Secy.; G.J. Kuhrts III, Treas.
Number of staff: 1 part-time support.
EIN: 956083677

94
Burnham Foundation
610 West Ash St., Suite 2001
San Diego 92101

Established in 1980 in CA.
Donor(s): Malin Burnham.
Foundation type: Independent
Financial data (yr. ended 12/31/91): Assets,
$5,787,959 (M); expenditures, $598,177;
qualifying distributions, $505,445, including
$505,445 for 69 grants (high: $250,000; low:
$30).
Purpose and activities: Primary giving to higher
education and cancer research; some support for
social services, sports, and cultural programs.
Fields of interest: Higher education, cancer,
social services, recreation, cultural programs.
Limitations: Giving primarily in CA. No grants to
individuals.
Application information: Contributes only to
pre-selected organizations. Applications not
accepted.
Officers: Malin Burnham, Pres.; Roberta
Burnham, V.P.; Nina Galloway, Secy.; Louis J.
Garday, Treas.
Trustees: Robert Brettbard, Pauline des Granges,
Philip M. Klauber.
EIN: 953565278

95
Fritz B. Burns Foundation ▼
4001 West Alameda Ave., Suite 201
Burbank 91505   (818) 840-8802

Incorporated in 1955 in CA.
Donor(s): Fritz B. Burns.‡
Foundation type: Independent
Financial data (yr. ended 09/30/90): Assets,
$150,300,726 (M); expenditures, $9,363,651;
qualifying distributions, $7,827,535, including
$7,689,868 for 102 grants (high: $1,700,000;
low: $1,500; average: $2,500-$100,000).
Purpose and activities: Grants primarily for
education, hospitals and medical research
organizations; support also for Roman Catholic
religious associations and schools, social welfare
agencies, and church support.
Fields of interest: Education, higher education,
hospitals, medical research, Catholic giving,
Catholic welfare, social services.

Limitations: Giving primarily in the Los Angeles,
CA, areas. No support for private foundations. No
grants to individuals.
Application information:
Initial approach: Letter
Deadline(s): None
Board meeting date(s): Feb., May, Aug., and
Nov.
Write: Joseph E. Rawlinson, Pres.
Officers and Directors:* William Herbert
Hannon,* Chair.; Joseph E. Rawlinson,* Pres.;
W.K. Skinner,* Exec. V.P. and Secy.-Treas.; Richard
Dunn, Don Freeburg, Edward F. Slattery, J. Robert
Vaughan.
Number of staff: None.
EIN: 956064403
Recent health grants:
95-1 Childrens Hospital of Los Angeles, Los
Angeles, CA, $100,000. 1990.
95-2 Daniel Freeman Memorial Hospital,
Inglewood, CA, $115,000. 1990.
95-3 Holy Cross Medical Center, Mission Hills,
CA, $100,000. 1990.
95-4 Hospital of the Good Samaritan, Los
Angeles, CA, $100,000. 1990.
95-5 La Cuna Pregnancy Clinic, Wilmington, CA,
$10,000. 1990.
95-6 Little Company of Mary Hospital, Torrance,
CA, $100,000. 1990.
95-7 Queen of Angels-Hollywood Presbyterian
Medical Center, Los Angeles, CA, $100,000.
1990.
95-8 Saint Annes Maternity Home, Los Angeles,
CA, $300,000. 1990.
95-9 Saint Elizabeths Toluca Lake Convalescent
Hospital, North Hollywood, CA, $25,000.
1990.
95-10 Saint John of God Nursing Hospital and
Residence, Los Angeles, CA, $100,000. 1990.
95-11 Saint Josephs Medical Center, Burbank,
CA, $100,000. 1990.
95-12 Salk Institute for Biological Studies, La
Jolla, CA, $205,000. 1990.
95-13 Santa Marta Hospital and Clinic, Los
Angeles, CA, $100,000. 1990.
95-14 Valley Presbyterian Hospital Foundation,
Van Nuys, CA, $100,000. 1990.

96
California Community Foundation ▼
606 South Olive St., Suite 2400
Los Angeles 90014   (213) 413-4042

Established in 1915 in CA by bank resolution.
Foundation type: Community
Financial data (yr. ended 06/30/91): Assets,
$100,778,048 (M); gifts received, $13,658,370;
expenditures, $14,610,227; qualifying
distributions, $12,697,917, including
$11,442,526 for grants (average: $5,000-$25,000)
and $1,255,391 for 68 grants to individuals (high:
$15,000; low: $100; average: $500-$15,000).
Purpose and activities: Giving in the areas of arts
and culture, civic affairs, education, health and
medicine, and human services, with emphasis on
children and youth and community development.
Fields of interest: Disadvantaged, housing, social
services, aged, youth, child welfare,
handicapped, education, arts, community
development, civic affairs, environment, health
services, AIDS, public affairs, intercultural
relations.

Types of support: Matching funds, technical
assistance, emergency funds, program-related
investments, seed money, special projects.
Limitations: Giving limited to the greater Los
Angeles County, CA, area. No support for
sectarian purposes. No grants for building funds,
annual campaigns, equipment, endowment
funds, debt reduction, operating budgets,
scholarships, fellowships, films, conferences,
dinners, or special events; no loans.
Publications: Annual report (including application
guidelines), application guidelines, informational
brochure, newsletter.
Application information: Application form not
required.
Initial approach: Proposal
Copies of proposal: 1
Deadline(s): None
Board meeting date(s): Quarterly
Final notification: 3 months after board meets
Write: Jack Shakely, Pres.
Officers: Jack Shakely, Pres.; Linda Shestock, V.P.,
Finance and Administration; Terri Jones, V.P.,
Progs.; Joe Lumarda, V.P., Development.
Board of Governors: Stephen D. Gavin, Chair.;
Caroline L. Ahmanson, Bruce C. Corwin, Susanne
Donnelly, Claudia H. Hampton, Nini Moore
Horn, Arturo Madrid, Donn B. Miller, William G.
Ouchi, David Peters, William F. Podlich, Bruce
M. Ramer, Virgil Roberts, Ann Shaw, Jean French
Smith, Robert H. Smith, Daniel Villanueva, Esther
Wachtell, Ruth K. Watanabe, Peggy Fouke Wortz.
Trustees: Bank of America, City National Bank,
First Interstate Bank, Trust Services of America,
Wells Fargo Bank, N.A.
Number of staff: 16 full-time professional; 1
part-time professional; 9 full-time support.
EIN: 953510055
Recent health grants:
96-1 AltaMed Health Services, Los Angeles, CA,
$39,325. Toward seed funding to hire staff for
newly established La Clinica Familiar Del
Barrio Foundation. 1991.
96-2 Antelope Valley Rehabilitation Centers,
Acton, CA, $30,000. Toward training of other
rehab centers in Los Angeles County to
provide literacy services to recovering
alcoholics and drug addicts. 1991.
96-3 California School of Professional
Psychology, Los Angeles, CA, $26,020. To
initiate delivery of counseling services via
existing human service agencies in South
Central Los Angeles. 1991.
96-4 Childrens Clinic, Long Beach, CA, $36,298.
To stabilize cost reimbursement and billing
mechanisms and improve patient scheduling
and tracking procedures, by bringing these
computer-based functions in house. 1991.
96-5 Hathaway Childrens Services, Sylmar, CA,
$30,000. Toward seed money to open Family
Resource Center to serve residents of Northeast
Los Angeles with wide range of family support
programs. 1991.
96-6 Hollywood-Sunset Community Clinic, Los
Angeles, CA, $20,877. For first year's salary of
development director to broaden and stabilize
organization's funding base. 1991.
96-7 Los Angeles Educational Partnership, Los
Angeles, CA, $25,000. Toward technical
assistance for planning and implementation of
new structure to provide coordinated health
care services to children in Los Angeles
Unified School District. 1991.

96-8 Martin Luther King Legacy Association, Los Angeles, CA, $40,800. For seed funding of first year of Wings of Hope, education and training program to equip South Los Angeles churches to join battle against substance abuse in their communities. 1991.

96-9 National Health Foundation, Los Angeles, CA, $45,000. For demonstration project aimed at improving perinatal outcomes of high-risk, low-income women in Los Angeles County. 1991.

96-10 Operation U.S.A., Los Angeles, CA, $10,000. To purchase small building for street clinic in Calcutta, India. 1991.

96-11 Planned Parenthood-World Population Los Angeles, Los Angeles, CA, $40,000. Toward start-up of educational and medical outreach program to Hispanic women in Los Angeles County. 1991.

96-12 San Fernando Valley Child Guidance Clinic, Northridge, CA, $13,784. Toward seed funding for neighborhood-based system of social services for underserved Hispanic immigrants and at-risk children in area surrounding Langdon Avenue Elementary School in Sepulveda. 1991.

96-13 Santa Clarita Valley Special Childrens Center, Newhall, CA, $23,160. To expand predelinquency intervention program for preschool children and their parents. 1991.

96-14 South Bay Free Clinic, Manhattan Beach, CA, $17,350. Toward salary and benefits of half-time legal assistance program coordinator. 1991.

96-15 University of Southern California, School of Dentistry, Los Angeles, CA, $112,600. To provide preventive and maintenance dental care to 5,000 disadvantaged youth while conducting three-year longitudinal study comparing effectiveness of two sealant methods. 1991.

96-16 Valley Womens Center, Woodland Hills, CA, $38,000. To start outpatient eating disorder program for women who have no insurance. 1991.

96-17 Weingart Center Association, Los Angeles, CA, $15,000. For Recuperative Care Program for homeless people after they are released from hospital. 1991.

97
The Callison Foundation
1319 Rosita Rd.
Pacifica 94044 (415) 359-2105

Established in 1965 in CA.
Donor(s): Fred W. Callison.
Foundation type: Independent
Financial data (yr. ended 12/31/91): Assets, $5,253,385 (M); expenditures, $377,195; qualifying distributions, $320,725, including $311,000 for 29 grants (high: $25,000; low: $5,000).
Fields of interest: Catholic giving, youth, welfare, cultural programs, hospitals, handicapped, aged.
Types of support: General purposes.
Limitations: Giving primarily in San Francisco, CA. No grants to individuals.
Application information:
Initial approach: Proposal
Deadline(s): None
Write: Mrs. Dorothy J. Sola, Secy.

Officers and Directors:* Peter O'Hara,* C.E.O.; Ward Ingersoll,* Pres.; Gerald Hing,* V.P.; Dorothy J. Sola,* Secy.; Frances M. Smith.
EIN: 946127962

98
Frank A. Campini Foundation
220 Montgomery St., Suite 1000
San Francisco 94104-3419 (415) 421-4171

Established in 1960 in CA.
Donor(s): Frank A. Campini.‡
Foundation type: Independent
Financial data (yr. ended 12/31/90): Assets, $9,764,625 (M); gifts received, $314,399; expenditures, $563,722; qualifying distributions, $525,210, including $510,960 for 61 grants (high: $151,400; low: $300).
Fields of interest: Social services, education, performing arts, museums, medical research, AIDS, cancer.
Limitations: Giving primarily in CA. No grants to individuals.
Application information: Application form not required.
Initial approach: Letter
Deadline(s): None
Board meeting date(s): Dec.
Write: Paul J. Ruby, Pres.
Officers and Directors:* Paul J. Ruby,* Pres.; M. Alan Neys,* V.P.; Patricia M. Neys, Secy.-Treas.
EIN: 946107956

99
Capital Fund Foundation ▼
(Formerly The Milken Family Foundation)
15250 Ventura Blvd., 2nd Fl.
Sherman Oaks 91403 (818) 784-9224

Established in 1982 in CA.
Donor(s): Michael R. Milken, Lowell J. Milken, Lori A. Milken.
Foundation type: Independent
Financial data (yr. ended 11/30/90): Assets, $173,644,340 (M); expenditures, $15,612,121; qualifying distributions, $15,477,545, including $14,150,572 for 229 grants (high: $1,000,000; low: $50; average: $1,000-$250,000).
Purpose and activities: Grants primarily for community services, education, health care and medical research, and human welfare programs.
Fields of interest: Social services, education, health, medical research, welfare.
Limitations: No grants to individuals.
Application information:
Initial approach: Letter or proposal
Write: J. Lesner, Exec. V.P.
Officers and Directors:* Lowell J. Milken, Pres.; J. Lesner,* Exec. V.P.; C. Cohen, Secy.; Ralph Finerman, Mariano Guzman, Lori A. Milken, S. Milken, Richard Riordan, E. Sandler, H. Silbert, P. Ueberoth, Edward G. Victor.
EIN: 953727913
Recent health grants:
99-1 Betty Clooney Foundation for the Brain Injured, Los Angeles, CA, $10,000. 1990.
99-2 Drug Abuse Resistance Education (DARE), Los Angeles, CA, $405,666. 1990.
99-3 Julia Ann Singer Pre-School Psychiatric Center, Los Angeles, CA, $76,000. 1990.

99-4 Leukemia Society of America, Los Angeles, CA, $40,000. 1990.
99-5 Los Angeles Center for Therapy and Education, Van Nuys, CA, $14,600. 1990.
99-6 Planned Parenthood of Los Angeles, Los Angeles, CA, $25,000. 1990.

100
The Carsey Family Foundation
c/o Capell, Coyne & Co.
2121 Ave. of the Stars, Suite 1240
Los Angeles 90067

Established in 1988 in CA.
Donor(s): Marcia L. Carsey, John J. Carsey.
Foundation type: Independent
Financial data (yr. ended 09/30/91): Assets, $762,335 (M); expenditures, $352,733; qualifying distributions, $350,753, including $349,318 for 8 grants (high: $138,638; low: $880).
Fields of interest: Cancer, education, fine arts, media and communications, performing arts.
Types of support: Annual campaigns, general purposes, research, special projects.
Limitations: No grants to individuals.
Application information: Contributes only to pre-selected organizations. Applications not accepted.
Officers: Marcia L. Carsey, Pres.; John J. Carsey, V.P.; Frederick Richman, Secy.-Treas.
Number of staff: None.
EIN: 954135538

101
Cedars-Sinai Medical Center Section D Fund
8700 Beverly Blvd.
Los Angeles 90048

Established in 1984 in CA.
Donor(s): Mark Goodson.
Foundation type: Independent
Financial data (yr. ended 12/31/91): Assets, $3,331,332 (M); expenditures, $61,987; qualifying distributions, $42,305, including $42,305 for 24 grants (high: $5,000; low: $450).
Purpose and activities: Grants to Jewish organizations and welfare funds, hospitals and health associations, and film associations.
Fields of interest: Jewish giving, Jewish welfare, hospitals, health associations, film.
Limitations: Giving primarily in New York, NY, and Los Angeles, CA. No grants to individuals.
Application information: Contributes only to pre-selected organizations. Applications not accepted.
Trustee: Cedars-Sinai Medical Center.
EIN: 953918393

102
Hugh Stuart Center Charitable Trust
152 North Third St., Suite 400
San Jose 95115-0024

Trust established in 1977 in CA.
Donor(s): Hugh Stuart Center.‡
Foundation type: Independent
Financial data (yr. ended 12/31/91): Assets, $8,204,482 (M); expenditures, $583,570;

qualifying distributions, $526,073, including $474,898 for 195 grants (high: $25,000; low: $10).

Fields of interest: Child welfare, education, higher education, hospitals, cultural programs.
Limitations: Giving primarily in San Jose, CA. No grants to individuals.
Application information: Contributes only to pre-selected organizations. Applications not accepted.
Trustees: Arthur K. Lund, Louis O'Neal.
EIN: 942455308

103
Chevron Corporate Giving Program
575 Market St.
P.O. Box 7753
San Francisco 94120-7753   (415) 894-4193
Arts Support: c/o R.C. Wooten, Corporate Advertising and Arts Liaison, 575 Market St., P.O. Box 7753, San Francisco, CA 94120-7753

Financial data (yr. ended 12/31/89): Total giving, $25,604,025, including $22,968,057 for grants (high: $2,900,000), $1,713,594 for employee matching gifts and $922,374 for in-kind gifts.
Purpose and activities: Contributions are intended to strengthen the economic vitality of communities where company operations exist to ensure continued success, through support for programs involving the environment, education, health and social services, the arts, and international relations. Support generally for operating expenses and special projects and employee matching gifts program for culture and education. Also, in the U.S. and Canada, 37 Chevron Employee Involvement Funds award small grants to local nonprofits where employees volunteer.
Fields of interest: Health, arts, environment, international development, conservation, science and technology, secondary education, international relief, Africa, Latin America, Canada, AIDS, higher education.
Types of support: General purposes, employee matching gifts, research, scholarship funds, continuing support, program-related investments, in-kind gifts.
Limitations: Giving primarily in AL, AZ, AK, AR, CA, CO, CT, DC, FL, GA, HI, LA, MD, NJ, NM, MS, MT, NM, NV, OR, OK, PA, TX, UT and in more than 80 countries. No support for religious, veterans', labor, fraternal, athletic, or political organizations, or endowment funds, United Way-supported agencies, fund-raisers, national health, medical, and human service organizations, or courtesy advertising. No grants to individuals.
Publications: Corporate giving report, application guidelines.
Application information: Local community organizations should direct grant applications and requests to the Chevron Public Affairs Manager nearest their area; call to find out where. National and international organizations should send proposals to headquarters in San Francisco. Chevron has a staff that only handles contributions. Application form not required.
Initial approach: One or two-page letter to J.W. (Skip) Rhodes, Jr., for national and international organizations; community organizations should direct grant

applications to a local Chevron public affairs representative
Copies of proposal: 1
Final notification: 6-8 weeks
Write: J.W. Rhodes, Jr., Mgr., Corp. Contribs.
Officer: J.W. (Skip) Rhodes, Jr., Mgr., Corp. Contribs.
Number of staff: 6 full-time professional; 3 full-time support.

104
City of Hope Section E Foundation
208 West 8th St., Suite 1300
Los Angeles 90014

Established in 1989 in CA.
Donor(s): Mann Family Foundation.
Foundation type: Independent
Financial data (yr. ended 12/31/90): Assets, $2,211,416 (M); expenditures, $112,711; qualifying distributions, $107,888, including $103,916 for 11 grants (high: $33,000; low: $1,000).
Purpose and activities: Support primarily for specific disease research; some support also for child welfare, including programs aiding mentally handicapped youth and terminally ill children.
Fields of interest: Medical research, health associations, hospitals, child welfare.
Types of support: Research.
Limitations: Giving primarily in Southern CA. No grants to individuals.
Application information: Contributes only to pre-selected organizations. Applications not accepted.
Trustees: Kathy A. Marcario, Sanford M. Shapero, Karen M. Warren, Tonny van der Leeden.
EIN: 956898197

105
Clorox Company Corporate Giving Program
1221 Broadway
Oakland 94612   (415) 271-7000
Application address: P.O. Box 24305, Oakland, CA 94623

Financial data (yr. ended 12/31/90): Total giving, $960,712 for grants.
Purpose and activities: Support for youth, education, employment training, social welfare, community funds, arts and culture, civic affairs, health, and economic development; in addition, employees donate their time to charities, through the Clorox Employee Volunteer program. Current giving reflects combined foundation and corporate giving.
Fields of interest: Youth, education, employment, vocational education, social services, welfare, community funds, cultural programs, civic affairs, health, economics, arts.
Types of support: Employee volunteer services.
Limitations: Giving primarily in general operating areas in CA, FL, IL, KY, MO, NY, WA, and WI. No support for religious organizations, national conventions (meetings), athletic leagues, benefit advertising, veteran and political party organizations, and fund dinners out of the Bay area. No grants to individuals, travel, and television production.

Application information: Application form required.
Initial approach: Telephone
Write: Carmella Johnson, Contribs. Mgr.
Administrators: J.J. Calderini, V.P., Human Resources; Carmella Johnson, Contribs. Mgr.

106
The Clorox Company Foundation ▼
1221 Broadway
Oakland 94612   (415) 271-7747
Mailing address: P.O. Box 24305, Oakland, CA 94623

Incorporated in 1980 in CA.
Donor(s): Clorox Co.
Foundation type: Company-sponsored
Financial data (yr. ended 06/30/91): Assets, $2,878,185 (M); gifts received, $1,598,044; expenditures, $1,780,772; qualifying distributions, $1,837,838, including $1,693,028 for 274 grants (high: $125,000; low: $100; average: $1,000-$10,000) and $53,797 for employee matching gifts.
Purpose and activities: Giving primarily for youth, education, social welfare, civic affairs, arts and culture, and health; some support also for economic development and employment training; also makes emergency product donations.
Fields of interest: Youth, education, higher education, civic affairs, community development, cultural programs, arts, social services, handicapped, health associations, hospitals, community funds, employment, volunteerism.
Types of support: Building funds, operating budgets, general purposes, employee matching gifts, capital campaigns, matching funds, employee-related scholarships, special projects, technical assistance, scholarship funds, employee volunteer services.
Limitations: Giving primarily in Oakland, CA, and other areas of company operations. No support for sectarian religious purposes, or for veterans', fraternal, or labor organizations. No grants to individuals, or for goodwill advertising.
Publications: Corporate giving report (including application guidelines), program policy statement, application guidelines.
Application information: Application form required.
Initial approach: Letter requesting application
Copies of proposal: 1
Deadline(s): By 15th of month prior to board meetings
Board meeting date(s): July, Sept.-Nov., Jan., Mar., and May
Final notification: Varies
Write: Carmella Johnson, Contrib. Mgr.
Officers and Trustees:* Patricia J. Marino,* Pres.; David L. Goodman,* V.P.; Elizabeth A. Harvey, Secy.; Priscilla Thilmony,* Treas.; Jack J. Calderini, Rita A. Bunch, Roderic A. Lorimer, Ignacio R. Martinez, Patrick M. Meehan, Richard C. Soublet.
Number of staff: 1 full-time professional; 1 part-time professional; 1 full-time support.
EIN: 942674980
Recent health grants:
106-1 Oakland Community Counseling, Oakland, CA, $20,000. For Castlemont Corridor Project. 1991.

106-2 Providence Hospital Foundation, Oakland, CA, $40,000. For endowment fund. 1991.

106-3 Urban Indian Health Board, Oakland, CA, $25,000. To renovate building. 1991.

106-4 West Oakland Health Center, Oakland, CA, $25,000. To construct new health clinic in Oakland. 1991.

107
The Richard M. Cohen Foundation
601 North Faring Rd.
Los Angeles 90077

Established in 1989 in CA.
Donor(s): Richard M. Cohen.
Foundation type: Independent
Financial data (yr. ended 12/31/91): Assets, $450,078 (M); gifts received, $300,000; expenditures, $231,338; qualifying distributions, $231,338, including $230,857 for 91 grants (high: $25,000; low: $25).
Fields of interest: AIDS, family services, social services, health associations, homeless.
Limitations: Giving primarily in CA.
Application information: Applications not accepted.
Officer: Richard M. Cohen, Mgr.
EIN: 954245546

108
Coldwell Banker Real Estate Group Giving Program
533 South Fremont Ave.
Los Angeles 90071   (213) 613-3123

Financial data (yr. ended 12/31/90): Total giving, $328,144.
Fields of interest: Health, social services, education, cultural programs, civic affairs, community funds.
Limitations: No support for fraternal, religious, and political campaigns. No grants to individuals.
Application information:
   Write: Bill Hinckley, Dir., Corp. Communs.

109
Columbia Savings Charitable Foundation
145 South Fairfax Ave., No. 303
Los Angeles 90036

Established in 1985 in CA.
Foundation type: Independent
Financial data (yr. ended 12/31/90): Assets, $12,294,806 (M); expenditures, $1,707,959; qualifying distributions, $1,605,823, including $1,545,800 for 27 grants (high: $400,000; low: $500).
Purpose and activities: Giving primarily for Jewish organizations; contributions also for higher education and medical research.
Fields of interest: Jewish giving, higher education, medical research.
Limitations: Giving primarily in CA. No grants to individuals.
Application information:
   Initial approach: Letter
   Write: Thomas Spiegel, Pres.
Officers: Abraham Spiegel, Chair.; Thomas Spiegel, Pres.

EIN: 954002331

110
Compton Foundation, Inc. ▼
525 Middlefield Rd., Suite 115
Menlo Park 94025   (415) 328-0101

Incorporated in 1972 in NY as successor to The Compton Trust.
Donor(s): Members of the Compton family.
Foundation type: Independent
Financial data (yr. ended 12/31/90): Assets, $67,026,820 (M); gifts received, $2,161,835; expenditures, $3,831,015; qualifying distributions, $3,347,065, including $3,202,314 for 366 grants (high: $199,000; low: $50; average: $500-$5,000).
Purpose and activities: To coordinate the family giving to community, national, and international programs in areas of its special interests, including higher education, peace and world order, population control, the arts, conservation, race relations, and welfare.
Fields of interest: Higher education, international studies, family planning, race relations, welfare, arts, peace, education—minorities, arms control, conservation, AIDS.
Types of support: Endowment funds, fellowships, general purposes, matching funds, scholarship funds, operating budgets, continuing support, annual campaigns, seed money, special projects, consulting services.
Limitations: No grants to individuals, or for capital or building funds; no loans.
Publications: Biennial report.
Application information: Application form required.
   Initial approach: Letter
   Deadline(s): None
   Board meeting date(s): May and Nov.
   Final notification: 6 months, favorable replies only
   Write: James R. Compton, Pres.
Officers and Directors:* James R. Compton,* Pres.; Ann C. Stephens,* V.P. and Secy.; Arthur L. Bowen,* Treas. and Counsel; Jan H. Lewis, Kenneth W. Thompson, Michael P. Todaro.
Board Members: Susan A. Stephens, W. Danforth Compton.
Number of staff: 1 part-time support.
EIN: 237262706
Recent health grants:

110-1 Alan Guttmacher Institute, NYC, NY, $20,000. For general support. 1990.

110-2 Association for Voluntary Surgical Contraception, NYC, NY, $25,000. For general operating support. 1990.

110-3 Center for Development and Population Activities, DC, $26,430. To survey Mexican community to study and document linkages between population growth and environmental degradation at community level. 1990.

110-4 Center for Population Options, DC, $25,000. For project, International Clearinghouse on Adolescent Fertility, which seeks to reduce too early pregnancy and childbearing in developing countries. 1990.

110-5 International Womens Health Coalition, NYC, NY, $30,000. To promote reproductive and health rights in Latin America. 1990.

110-6 Meharry Medical College, Nashville, TN, $70,000. For operating budget. 1990.

110-7 National Toxics Campaign Fund, Boston, MA, $20,000. For Citizen's Environmental Laboratory. 1990.

110-8 Pathfinder International, Watertown, MA, $30,000. For development and implementation of family planning programs throughout developing world. 1990.

110-9 Physicians for Social Responsibility, DC, $25,000. To increase citizen awareness and participation in upcoming debates on restart, modernization and cleanup of nuclear weapons production facilities. 1990.

110-10 Planned Parenthood Association of Metropolitan Washington, DC, $35,000. For Latino outreach and education program to expand family planning and reproductive health services to rapidly growing Latino population. 1990.

110-11 Planned Parenthood Association of San Mateo County, San Mateo, CA, $15,000. For general support. 1990.

110-12 Planned Parenthood Association of Santa Clara County, San Jose, CA, $50,000. For general support. 1990.

110-13 Planned Parenthood Federation of America, International Division, San Francisco, CA, $12,000. For clinic in Bogota, Colombia. 1990.

110-14 Planned Parenthood of Alameda/San Francisco, San Francisco, CA, $50,000. For general support. 1990.

110-15 Planned Parenthood of Marin and Sonoma, San Rafael, CA, $10,000. For educational programs in community and in four clinics. 1990.

110-16 Planned Parenthood of New York City, NYC, NY, $50,000. For general support. 1990.

110-17 Population Council, NYC, NY, $50,000. For research focusing on population policy in developing countries, and for Council's highly respected international journal, Population and Development Policy. 1990.

110-18 Population Crisis Committee, DC, $40,000. For general support. 1990.

110-19 Population Crisis Committee, DC, $10,000. For Policymaker's Chartbook, new tool for educating national and international political leaders on world population issues. 1990.

110-20 Program for Appropriate Technology in Health, Seattle, WA, $40,000. For general support. 1990.

110-21 Sex Information and Education Council of the United States (SIECUS), NYC, NY, $10,000. For general support. 1990.

111
Computer Sciences Corporate Giving Program
2100 East Grand Ave.
El Segundo 90245   (213) 615-0311

Purpose and activities: Company primarily supports health and welfare organizations. Also supports education, civic affairs and the arts.
Fields of interest: Health, welfare, education, civic affairs, arts.
Types of support: General purposes, building funds.

Limitations: Giving primarily in major operating areas.
Application information:
Initial approach: Letter of inquiry
Deadline(s): Applications accepted throughout the year
Final notification: 4-6 weeks
Write: Linda Johnson, Sr. Staff Admin., Corp. Communs.

112
Confidence Foundation ▼
1260 Huntington Dr., Suite 204
South Pasadena 91030-4561   (213) 259-0484

Established in 1980 in CA.
Donor(s): Paul N. Whittier.‡
Foundation type: Independent
Financial data (yr. ended 12/31/90): Assets, $10,544,240 (M); gifts received, $2,122,860; expenditures, $1,871,216; qualifying distributions, $1,798,039, including $1,770,415 for 105 grants (high: $250,000; low: $150; average: $5,000-$10,000).
Purpose and activities: Giving primarily for education, social services and medical research.
Fields of interest: Education, education—early childhood, education—minorities, secondary education, health, medical sciences, medical research, science and technology, welfare, social services, disadvantaged, family planning, family services, youth, leadership development, community development, citizenship, public policy.
Types of support: Fellowships, matching funds, seed money, endowment funds, renovation projects, special projects, student aid.
Limitations: No grants to individuals; no loans.
Application information: Contributes only to pre-selected organizations. Applications not accepted.
Write: Linda J. Blinkenberg, Secy.
Officers: Arlo G. Sorensen, Pres.; Michael J. Casey, V.P.; Linda J. Blinkenberg, Secy.; Robert D. Sellers, Treas.
Number of staff: 4 shared staff
EIN: 953500483

113
Michael J. Connell Foundation
224 South Lake Ave., Suite 271
Pasadena 91101

Incorporated in 1931 in CA.
Donor(s): Michael J. Connell.‡
Foundation type: Independent
Financial data (yr. ended 06/30/91): Assets, $9,726,850 (M); expenditures, $930,878; qualifying distributions, $817,176, including $785,164 for 22 grants (high: $250,000; low: $1,000; average: $15,000-$50,000).
Purpose and activities: Giving generally restricted to programs initiated by the foundation in social, cultural, educational, and medical fields.
Fields of interest: Cultural programs, social services, education, medical sciences, hospitals, community funds, media and communications.
Types of support: Internships, fellowships, special projects.

Limitations: Giving primarily in Southern CA, with emphasis on Los Angeles. No grants to individuals, or for building funds; no loans.
Publications: Financial statement.
Application information: Application form not required.
Initial approach: Letter
Copies of proposal: 1
Deadline(s): None
Board meeting date(s): Quarterly
Final notification: 3 months
Write: Michael J. Connell, Pres.
Officers and Directors:* Michael J. Connell,* Pres.; Richard A. Wilson,* V.P.; Ruth E. Dodd, Secy.; Mary C. Bayless, Richard Grant.
Number of staff: 1 full-time professional; 1 part-time professional.
EIN: 956000904

114
James S. Copley Foundation ▼
7776 Ivanhoe Ave.
P.O. Box 1530
La Jolla 92038-1530   (619) 454-0411

Incorporated in 1953 in CA.
Donor(s): The Copley Press, Inc.
Foundation type: Company-sponsored
Financial data (yr. ended 12/31/91): Assets, $22,627,257 (M); gifts received, $23,628; expenditures, $1,618,976; qualifying distributions, $1,579,812, including $1,538,589 for grants (high: $300,000; low: $100; average: $500-$10,000) and $41,054 for 167 employee matching gifts.
Purpose and activities: Support for higher and secondary education, including an employee matching gift program, performing arts groups and other cultural programs, a community fund, journalism, social services, hospices and hospitals, the aged, and youth and child development.
Fields of interest: Education, higher education, secondary education, elementary education, literacy, libraries, cultural programs, arts, performing arts, journalism, social services, homeless, youth, child development, aged, recreation, health, hospitals, hospices, drug abuse.
Types of support: Annual campaigns, emergency funds, building funds, equipment, land acquisition, scholarship funds, employee matching gifts, capital campaigns.
Limitations: Giving primarily in circulation areas of company newspapers: San Diego, Torrance, San Pedro, and Santa Monica in CA; and Aurora, Elgin, Wheaton, Joliet, Springfield, Lincoln, Naperville, and Waukegan in IL. No support for religious, fraternal, or athletic organizations, local chapters of national organizations, or public elementary or secondary schools. No grants to individuals, or for endowment funds, research, publications, conferences, unrestricted purposes, operating budgets, or large campaigns; no loans.
Publications: Informational brochure (including application guidelines).
Application information: Application form not required.
Initial approach: Letter
Copies of proposal: 1
Deadline(s): Jan. 2 for Feb. meeting
Board meeting date(s): Feb. and as required
Final notification: 2 to 3 weeks

Write: Anita A. Baumgardner, Secy.
Officers and Directors:* Helen K. Copley,* Chair.; David C. Copley,* Pres.; Alex De Bakcsy,* V.P.; Hubert L. Kaltenbach,* V.P.; Anita A. Baumgardner,* Secy.; Charles F. Patrick,* Treas.
Number of staff: None.
EIN: 956051770

115
The Mary A. Crocker Trust
233 Post St., 2nd Fl.
San Francisco 94108   (415) 982-0138

Trust established in 1889 in CA.
Donor(s): Mary A. Crocker.‡
Foundation type: Independent
Financial data (yr. ended 12/31/90): Assets, $12,909,150 (M); expenditures, $597,909; qualifying distributions, $515,667, including $515,667 for 42 grants (high: $30,000; low: $1,000; average: $10,000-$20,000).
Purpose and activities: Primary interest in precollegiate education, the environment, and community relations; support also for youth and leadership development.
Fields of interest: Education, secondary education, elementary education, environment, agriculture, community development, volunteerism, leadership development, youth, family planning.
Types of support: Seed money, matching funds, special projects, general purposes.
Limitations: Giving primarily in the San Francisco Bay Area, CA. No support for sectarian purposes. No grants to individuals, or for operating budgets, continuing support, annual campaigns, deficit financing, building or endowment funds, land acquisition, fellowships, or conferences; no loans.
Publications: Application guidelines, program policy statement, grants list.
Application information: Application form required.
Initial approach: Letter
Copies of proposal: 1
Deadline(s): None
Board meeting date(s): 2 to 3 times a year
Final notification: 3 months
Write: Barbaree Jernigan, Administrator
Officer and Trustees:* Tania W. Stepanian,* Chair.; Elizabeth Atcheson, Lucy Blake, Charles Crocker, Frederick W. Whitridge.
Number of staff: 1 full-time professional; 1 part-time support.
EIN: 946051917

116
Roy E. Crummer Foundation
11911 San Vicente Blvd., Suite 310-B
Los Angeles 90049-6902

Established in 1964 in NV.
Foundation type: Independent
Financial data (yr. ended 12/31/90): Assets, $7,472,489 (M); expenditures, $285,922; qualifying distributions, $257,000, including $257,000 for 34 grants (high: $30,000; low: $200).
Fields of interest: Hospitals, media and communications, wildlife, higher education, social services.

Limitations: Giving primarily in CA. No grants to individuals.
Application information: Contributes only to pre-selected organizations. Applications not accepted.
Officers: Jean Crummer Coburn, Pres.; Milton Coburn, V.P.; Margarite Brown, Secy.-Treas.
Directors: Ian Gow, Lee D. Strom.
EIN: 886004422

117
Willametta K. Day Foundation
865 South Figueroa St., No. 1500
Los Angeles 90017 (213) 891-6300
Mailing address: P.O. Box 71289, Los Angeles, CA 90071

Trust established in 1954 in CA.
Donor(s): Willametta K. Day.‡
Foundation type: Independent
Financial data (yr. ended 12/31/91): Assets, $9,390,895 (M); expenditures, $617,168; qualifying distributions, $555,490, including $550,225 for grants (high: $120,000; low: $150; average: $1,000-$5,000).
Fields of interest: Higher education, secondary education, hospitals, religion, cultural programs, museums.
Types of support: General purposes.
Limitations: Giving primarily in CA. No grants to individuals.
Publications: 990-PF, financial statement.
Application information: Application form not required.
   Initial approach: Letter
   Copies of proposal: 1
   Deadline(s): Nov.
   Board meeting date(s): Annually
   Write: Javier G. Rodriguez, C.F.O.
Officers and Trustees:* Jerry W. Carlton,* Chair. and Pres.; Steven D. Holzman,* Secy.; Javier G. Rodriguez, C.F.O. and Treas.; Howard M. Day, Robert A. Day, Jr., Tammis M. Day, Theodore J. Day.
EIN: 956092476

118
Marie C. de Dampierre Memorial Foundation
(Formerly Christian de Guigne Memorial Foundation)
c/o O'Donnell, Waiss, Wall and Meschke
100 Broadway, Third Fl.
San Francisco 94111 (415) 434-3323

Established in 1960 in CA.
Foundation type: Independent
Financial data (yr. ended 12/31/91): Assets, $4,695,566 (M); expenditures, $265,840; qualifying distributions, $211,906, including $208,895 for 9 grants (high: $75,000; low: $10,000; average: $10,000-$25,000).
Purpose and activities: Support for higher and secondary education, hospitals, and health agencies; support also for a French medical institution.
Fields of interest: Higher education, secondary education, hospitals, health services.
Types of support: Equipment, general purposes, research.

Limitations: Giving limited to the San Francisco Bay Area, CA. No grants to individuals, or for building or endowment funds, fellowships, matching gifts, or special projects; no loans.
Application information: Application form not required.
   Initial approach: Letter
   Copies of proposal: 3
   Deadline(s): Submit proposal any time except Nov. or Dec.; deadline Oct. 31
   Board meeting date(s): Nov. or Dec.
   Final notification: 1 month
   Write: John A. Meschke, Secy.-Treas.
Officers and Directors:* France de Sugny Bark,* Pres.; Nicole de Sugny MacDonald,* V.P.; John A. Meschke,* Secy.-Treas.
Number of staff: None.
EIN: 946076503

119
The Deutsch Foundation
c/o The Deutsch Co.
2444 Wilshire Blvd., Suite 600
Santa Monica 90403-5813 (213) 453-0055

Incorporated in 1947 in CA.
Donor(s): The Deutsch Co.
Foundation type: Company-sponsored
Financial data (yr. ended 08/31/91): Assets, $4,318,276 (M); expenditures, $582,284; qualifying distributions, $575,460, including $575,460 for 138 grants (high: $250,000; low: $80).
Purpose and activities: Emphasis on Jewish welfare funds; support also for hospitals, higher education, social welfare, and scientific research.
Fields of interest: Jewish welfare, Jewish giving, hospitals, higher education, social services, science and technology.
Limitations: Giving primarily in CA. No grants to individuals.
Application information:
   Initial approach: Letter
   Deadline(s): None
   Write: William Holler
Officers and Directors:* Alex Deutsch,* Pres.; Carl Deutsch,* V.P.; Lester Deutsch,* Secy.-Treas.
EIN: 956027369

120
The Walt Disney Company Foundation ▼
(Formerly Disney Foundation)
500 South Buena Vista St.
Burbank 91521 (818) 840-1000

Incorporated in 1951 in CA.
Donor(s): Walt Disney Productions, and its associated companies.
Foundation type: Company-sponsored
Financial data (yr. ended 09/30/90): Assets, $362,039 (M); gifts received, $1,877,000; expenditures, $1,652,620; qualifying distributions, $1,652,620, including $1,427,869 for 83 grants (high: $500,000; low: $200; average: $1,000-$20,000) and $214,391 for 50 grants to individuals.
Purpose and activities: Emphasis on youth and child welfare agencies, health, higher education, including an arts institute, cultural programs, and community funds; scholarships for the children of employees.

Fields of interest: Health, hospitals, higher education, youth, child welfare, arts, cultural programs, community funds, social services.
Types of support: Annual campaigns, continuing support, operating budgets, special projects, scholarship funds, employee-related scholarships, general purposes, capital campaigns.
Limitations: Giving primarily in areas where the company's businesses are located, including central FL, and Los Angeles and Orange County, CA. No grants to individuals (except for scholarships to children of company employees), or for endowment funds.
Publications: Application guidelines.
Application information: Application form required.
   Initial approach: Letter, proposal, or telephone
   Copies of proposal: 1
   Deadline(s): Oct. 1 for scholarships
   Board meeting date(s): Annually between Jan. and May
   Final notification: 20 to 30 days
   Write: Doris A. Smith, Secy.
Officers and Trustees:* Michael D. Eisner,* Pres.; Roy E. Disney,* V.P.; Jack B. Lindquist,* V.P.; Doris A. Smith, Secy.; Frank G. Wells, Treas.
Number of staff: None.
EIN: 956037079

121
Carrie Estelle Doheny Foundation ▼
911 Wilshire Blvd., Suite 1750
Los Angeles 90017 (213) 488-1122

Trust established in 1949 in CA.
Donor(s): Mrs. Edward L. Doheny.‡
Foundation type: Independent
Financial data (yr. ended 12/31/90): Assets, $82,303,770 (M); expenditures, $2,887,005; qualifying distributions, $2,154,289, including $2,154,289 for 104 grants (high: $300,000; low: $750; average: $5,000-$50,000).
Purpose and activities: The foundation was established for the "advancement of education, medicine, religion, science; the improvement of the health and welfare of infants, children, adults, families, and the aged; the help and care of the sick, aged, and incapacitated; and the aid of the needy."
Fields of interest: Medical research, hospitals, ophthalmology, higher education, religious schools, religion, Catholic giving, child welfare, family services, aged, handicapped.
Types of support: General purposes.
Limitations: Giving primarily in the Los Angeles, CA, area. No support for tax-supported organizations or radio or television programs. No grants to individuals, or for endowment funds, publications, travel, advertising, or scholarships.
Publications: Annual report (including application guidelines).
Application information: Application form not required.
   Initial approach: Letter
   Copies of proposal: 1
   Deadline(s): None
   Board meeting date(s): Monthly
   Final notification: 1 to 2 months
   Write: Robert A. Smith III, Pres., Carrie Estelle Doheny Foundation Corp.
Trustee: Carrie Estelle Doheny Foundation Corp.

Officers and Directors:* Robert A. Smith III,* Pres.; Arthur E. Thunell, Secy.-Treas.; Sister Magdalen Coughlin, Robert F. Erburu, Austin F. Gavin, George Gibbs, Joseph Nally, Rev. Francis D. Pansini, C.M.

Number of staff: 1 full-time professional; 1 part-time support.

EIN: 952051633

Recent health grants:

121-1 Hospitaller Foundation of California, Los Angeles, CA, $25,000. 1990.

121-2 House Ear Institute, Los Angeles, CA, $14,000. 1990.

121-3 La Cuna Pregnancy Clinic, Lynwood, CA, $10,000. 1990.

121-4 Los Angeles Heart Institute, Los Angeles, CA, $15,000. 1990.

121-5 Saint Annes Maternity Home, Los Angeles, CA, $127,500. 1990.

121-6 Saint Joseph Convalescent Hospital, Ojai, CA, $17,500. 1990.

121-7 Saint Vincent Medical Center, Los Angeles, CA, $150,000. 1990.

122
Dr. Seuss Foundation

7301 Encelia Dr.
La Jolla 92037   (619) 454-7384

Incorporated in 1958 in CA.

Donor(s): Theodor S. Geisel.‡

Foundation type: Independent

Financial data (yr. ended 12/31/91): Assets, $2,029,871 (M); expenditures, $244,805; qualifying distributions, $213,272, including $207,922 for 113 grants (high: $20,600; low: $50).

Fields of interest: Arts, cultural programs, medical research, health associations, higher education, youth, social services.

Limitations: Giving primarily in CA. No grants to individuals.

Application information: Application form not required.

  Deadline(s): None

Officers: Audrey Geisel,* Pres.; Robert L. Bernstein,* V.P.; Karl Zobell,* Secy.

Director: Edward Lathem.

EIN: 956029752

123
Joseph Drown Foundation ▼

1999 Ave. of the Stars, No. 1930
Los Angeles 90067   (213) 277-4488

Established in 1953 in CA.

Donor(s): Joseph W. Drown.‡

Foundation type: Independent

Financial data (yr. ended 03/31/91): Assets, $64,018,010 (M); expenditures, $5,044,138; qualifying distributions, $4,124,661, including $3,775,487 for 161 grants (high: $175,000; low: $5,000; average: $5,000-$25,000).

Purpose and activities: Grants primarily for education and health services.

Fields of interest: Health services, drug abuse, education, elementary education, education—minorities, disadvantaged.

Types of support: Scholarship funds, general purposes, matching funds, seed money, operating budgets, special projects.

Limitations: Giving primarily in CA. No support for religious purposes. No grants to individuals, or for endowments, building funds, or seminars or conferences.

Publications: Informational brochure (including application guidelines).

Application information: Application form not required.

  Initial approach: Propsal and letter
  Copies of proposal: 1
  Deadline(s): Jan. 15, Apr. 15, July 15, and Oct. 15
  Board meeting date(s): Quarterly
  Final notification: Immediately after board meeting
  Write: Wendy Wachtell Schine, V.P. and Prog. Dir.

Officers and Directors:* Milton F. Fillius, Jr.,* Chair.; Norman C. Obrow,* Pres.; Wendy Wachtell Schine, V.P. and Prog. Dir.; Thomas C. Marshall,* V.P.; Philip S. Magaram,* Secy.-Treas.; Harry C. Cogen, Benton C. Coit, Elaine Mahoney.

Number of staff: 3 full-time professional.

EIN: 956093178

Recent health grants:

123-1 AIDS Health Care Foundation, Hollywood, CA, $10,000. For general support. 1991.

123-2 AIDS Interfaith Council of Southern California, Los Angeles, CA, $40,000. For Executive Director's salary. 1991.

123-3 AIDS Project Los Angeles, Los Angeles, CA, $30,000. For Insurance Assistance Program. 1991.

123-4 American Diabetes Association, Los Angeles, CA, $25,000. For research. 1991.

123-5 American Lung Association of Los Angeles County, Los Angeles, CA, $15,000. For tuberculosis education and prevention program. 1991.

123-6 California State University, Cancer and Developmental Biology Department, Northridge, CA, $30,000. For research in cell adhesion. Grant made through Northridge Trust Fund. 1991.

123-7 Cedars-Sinai Medical Center, Teen Line, Los Angeles, CA, $10,000. For general support. 1991.

123-8 Childrens Hospital of Los Angeles Foundation, Los Angeles, CA, $40,000. For research in childhood leukemia. 1991.

123-9 Clare Foundation, Santa Monica, CA, $10,000. For general support. 1991.

123-10 Coalition for the Prevention of Sudden Cardiac Death, Los Angeles, CA, $50,000. For general support. Grant shared with University of Rochester. 1991.

123-11 Crittenton Center for Young Women and Infants, Los Angeles, CA, $25,000. For general support. 1991.

123-12 Delancey Street Foundation, Santa Monica, CA, $10,000. For general support for Los Angeles facility. 1991.

123-13 Discovery Fund for Eye Research, Los Angeles, CA, $20,000. For post-doctoral research fellowship. 1991.

123-14 Estelle Doheny Eye Institute, Los Angeles, CA, $10,000. For general support of Los Angeles branch. 1991.

123-15 Harbor-UCLA Medical Center Research and Education Institute, Division of Rheumatology, Torrance, CA, $17,000. For institutional support. 1991.

123-16 Jenesse Center, Los Angeles, CA, $15,000. For general support. 1991.

123-17 Julia Ann Singer Pre-School Psychiatric Center, Los Angeles, CA, $25,000. For School Consultation Project. 1991.

123-18 Los Angeles Center for Therapy and Education, H.E.L.P. Group, Van Nuys, CA, $25,000. For therapeutic services for adult residential facilities. 1991.

123-19 Los Angeles County-USC Medical Center Auxiliary, Professional Staff Association, Los Angeles, CA, $15,000. For Teen Pregnancy Prevention Project. 1991.

123-20 Los Angeles Unified School District, School Based Health Clinics, Reseda, CA, $50,000. For general support. 1991.

123-21 Maple Center, Beverly Hills, CA, $10,000. For general support. 1991.

123-22 New Start, Santa Monica, CA, $10,000. For general support. 1991.

123-23 Olive View Medical Center Foundation, Sylmar, CA, $15,000. For Earthquake Preparedness Anniversary events. 1991.

123-24 Parents Anonymous of California, Los Angeles, CA, $30,000. For Hotline Expansion Project. 1991.

123-25 Planned Parenthood of Los Angeles, Los Angeles, CA, $50,000. For Nurse Practitioner Education Program. 1991.

123-26 Psychological Trauma Center, Los Angeles, CA, $25,000. For general support. 1991.

123-27 Saint Annes Maternity Home, Los Angeles, CA, $20,000. For Outreach Prevention Program. 1991.

123-28 Salk Institute for Biological Studies, La Jolla, CA, $25,000. For Computational Neurobiology Laboratory. 1991.

123-29 San Francisco Hearing and Speech Center, San Francisco, CA, $25,000. For general support. 1991.

123-30 Santa Monica Hospital Medical Center Foundation, Rape Treatment Center, Santa Monica, CA, $20,000. For Stuart House. 1991.

123-31 Southern California Counseling Center, Los Angeles, CA, $10,000. For general support. 1991.

123-32 University of California, Diabetes Teaching Center, San Francisco, CA, $25,000. For Diabetes Center. 1991.

123-33 University of California, Neuropsychiatric Institute, Los Angeles, CA, $28,640. For Documentary of Obsessive-Compulsive Disorder. 1991.

123-34 University of California, School of Medicine/Center for Health Sciences, Los Angeles, CA, $100,000. For Frontiers of Medical Science Program. 1991.

123-35 University of California, School of Medicine/Department of Orthopaedic Surgery, San Francisco, CA, $93,920. For Pathophysiology, Biochemistry and Anatomy of Different Limb Preservation Methods. 1991.

123-36 University of California, School of Medicine/Division of Rheumatology, Los Angeles, CA, $30,000. For institutional support. 1991.

123-37 University of Southern California, Division of Rheumatology and Immunology, Los Angeles, CA, $30,000. For institutional support. 1991.

123-38 Venice Family Clinic, Venice, CA, $35,156. For Diabetes Program. 1991.

123-39 Vital Options, Studio City, CA, $12,000. For general support. 1991.

123-40 Wellness Community-National, Santa Monica, CA, $50,000. For general support. 1991.

124

Margaret E. Early Medical Research Trust

c/o Harrington, Foxx, Dubrow, & Canter
611 West Sixth St., 30th Fl.
Los Angeles 90017   (213) 489-3222

Established in 1982.
Foundation type: Independent
Financial data (yr. ended 12/31/90): Assets, $5,343,331 (M); expenditures, $433,235; qualifying distributions, $394,951, including $350,000 for 7 grants of $50,000 each.
Fields of interest: Cancer.
Types of support: Research.
Limitations: Giving limited to Southern CA.
Application information:
  Initial approach: Proposal
  Deadline(s): Established annually
  Write: Eli B. Dubrow, Trustee
Trustee: Eli B. Dubrow.
EIN: 953740506

125

The East Bay Community Foundation

501 Wickson Ave.
Oakland 94610   (510) 836-3223
FAX: (510) 836-3287

Established in 1928 in CA as The Alameda County Community Foundation by resolution and declaration of trust; revised in 1972.
Foundation type: Community
Financial data (yr. ended 12/31/90): Assets, $14,768,797 (M); gifts received, $1,520,499; expenditures, $1,714,555; qualifying distributions, $1,193,283, including $1,193,283 for grants.
Fields of interest: Community development, health, education, cultural programs, arts, youth, aged, women.
Limitations: Giving limited to Alameda and Contra Costa counties, CA. No support for sectarian religious causes, educational or hospital foundations, public or private educational institutions, or drug and/or alcohol abuse detoxification programs. No grants to individuals, or for building and endowment funds, equipment, annual fund drives, teachers' salaries, capital improvements, scholarships, deficit financing, media production, research projects, matching gifts, travel, or conferences; no loans.
Publications: Annual report, program policy statement, application guidelines, newsletter.
Application information: Application form not required.
  Initial approach: Letter or proposal
  Copies of proposal: 1
  Deadline(s): Jan. 1, May 1, and Sept. 1
  Board meeting date(s): Feb., June, and Oct.
  Write: Virginia Hooper, Interim Exec. Dir.
Officer: Sandra L. Pyer, Exec. Dir.
Governing Board: Montague Upshaw,* Chair.; R. Kenneth Coit, Paul J. Cortese, Lois De Domenico, Margaret Stuart Graupner, Edwin A. Heafey, Jr., Lucile Lansing Levin, Cornell C. Maier, Benjamin

Major, M.D., Neil W. McDaniel, H.E. Mikkelsen, Charles J. Patterson, S. Donley Ritchey, Robert A.D. Schwartz, Peter W. Snyder, D.D. van Loben Sels, Wendy W. Webster.
Number of staff: 1 full-time professional; 1 part-time professional; 1 full-time support.
EIN: 946070996
Recent health grants:
125-1 Alameda-Contra Costa Medical Association Auxiliaries, Oakland, CA, $14,000. For special projects and scholarships. 1990.
125-2 Easter Seal Society of Alameda County, Oakland, CA, $101,035. For general support. 1990.
125-3 General Foundation for Medicine, San Francisco, CA, $101,035. For AIDS research. 1990.
125-4 Planned Parenthood of Alameda/San Francisco, San Francisco, CA, $50,518. For general support. 1990.

126

Ben B. and Joyce E. Eisenberg Foundation

11999 San Vincente Blvd., Suite 300
Los Angeles 90049   (213) 471-4220

Established in 1986 in CA.
Foundation type: Independent
Financial data (yr. ended 05/31/91): Assets, $58,777,069 (M); expenditures, $6,239,227; qualifying distributions, $3,406,600, including $3,406,600 for 55 grants (high: $2,003,100; low: $200).
Purpose and activities: Support primarily for Jewish education and Jewish giving; support also for medical research and care facilities and civic affairs.
Fields of interest: Higher education, Jewish giving, medical research, health, civic affairs, Israel.
Types of support: Annual campaigns, continuing support, research.
Limitations: Giving primarily in the U.S. and Israel.
Application information: Applications not accepted.
  Write: David J. Cohen, V.P.
Officers: Joyce E. Eisenberg-Keefer, Pres.; Richard A. Bender, Secy.-Treas.
Number of staff: 3 full-time support.
EIN: 990246427

127

The Essick Foundation, Inc.

P.O. Box 61030
Pasadena 91116-7030   (213) 626-6658

Incorporated in 1947 in CA.
Donor(s): Jeanette Marie Essick,‡ Bryant Essick, Essick Investment Co.
Foundation type: Independent
Financial data (yr. ended 12/31/90): Assets, $3,601,479 (M); expenditures, $177,954; qualifying distributions, $167,320, including $158,303 for 66 grants (high: $27,000; low: $50).
Purpose and activities: Giving mainly to local organizations in which the donors are interested, with emphasis on higher education, hospitals, and a community fund.

Fields of interest: Hospitals, higher education, community funds.
Limitations: Giving primarily in Southern CA. No grants to individuals.
Application information:
  Initial approach: Letter
  Deadline(s): None
  Write: Bryant Essick, Pres.
Officers and Directors:* Bryant Essick,* Pres.; James H. Essick,* V.P.; Robert N. Essick,* V.P.
EIN: 956048985

128

Max Factor Family Foundation

9777 Wilshire Blvd., Suite 1015
Beverly Hills 90212   (213) 274-8193

Trust established in 1941 in CA.
Donor(s): Members of the Factor family.
Foundation type: Independent
Financial data (yr. ended 12/31/90): Assets, $10,754,263 (M); expenditures, $935,134; qualifying distributions, $868,061, including $868,061 for 29 grants (high: $150,000; low: $1,000; average: $1,000-$50,000).
Fields of interest: Jewish welfare, hospitals, medical research, aged, family services.
Types of support: Research, scholarship funds, general purposes, continuing support, operating budgets, building funds.
Limitations: Giving primarily in Southern CA. No grants to individuals.
Application information: Contributes only to pre-selected organizations. Applications not accepted.
  Board meeting date(s): Monthly
  Write: Barbara Factor Bentley, Trustee
Trustees: Barbara Factor Bentley, Gerald Factor, Max Factor III.
Number of staff: 3 part-time professional.
EIN: 956030779

129

Freeman E. Fairfield Foundation

3610 Long Beach Blvd.
P.O. Box 7798
Long Beach 90807   (213) 427-7219

Established in 1969 in CA.
Donor(s): Freeman E. Fairfield.‡
Foundation type: Independent
Financial data (yr. ended 12/31/90): Assets, $4,821,818 (M); expenditures, $452,968; qualifying distributions, $412,043, including $377,945 for 23 grants (high: $100,000; low: $1,500).
Fields of interest: Hospitals, health services, psychiatry, handicapped, social services, aged, youth, child development, welfare, Catholic welfare.
Types of support: Matching funds, equipment, operating budgets, renovation projects, special projects.
Limitations: Giving limited to Long Beach and Signal Hill, CA. No support for religious purposes. No grants to individuals, or for endowment funds, unrestricted operating costs, deficit financing, intermediary funding agencies, or general fundraising drives.
Publications: Program policy statement, application guidelines.

Application information: Application form required.

Initial approach: Proposal
Copies of proposal: 3
Deadline(s): May 1
Board meeting date(s): As required
Final notification: July 1
Write: Edna E. Sellers, Trustee

Trustees: Pierre E. Auw, Glenn J. Conway, Edna E. Sellers.
Number of staff: 1 part-time support.
EIN: 237055338

130
Zalec Familian Foundation
P.O. Box 5149
Compton 90224

Established in 1958 in CA.
Donor(s): Zalec Familian,‡ Albert Levinson.
Foundation type: Independent
Financial data (yr. ended 03/31/91): Assets, $2,528,996 (M); gifts received, $557,118; expenditures, $156,093; qualifying distributions, $144,204, including $141,000 for 16 grants (high: $55,000; low: $1,000).
Fields of interest: Higher education, social services, museums, medical research.
Types of support: General purposes, scholarship funds.
Limitations: Giving primarily in CA.
Application information: Budget for grants considered late in the calendar year. Application form not required.

Initial approach: Proposal
Write: Rey Javier, Secy.-Treas.

Officers and Directors:* Albert Levinson,* Pres.; Albert J. Galen,* V.P.; Ann Parker,* V.P.; Rey Javier,* Secy.-Treas.; Sandra Mabritto.
EIN: 956099164

131
Anne & Jason Farber Foundation, Inc.
c/o Blanding Boyer & Rockwell
1660 Olympic Blvd., Suite 301
Walnut Creek 94596

Established in 1981.
Foundation type: Independent
Financial data (yr. ended 11/30/91): Assets, $2,581,746 (M); expenditures, $147,401; qualifying distributions, $122,935, including $99,300 for 6 grants (high: $50,000; low: $300).
Purpose and activities: Support primarily for research projects involving brain tumors.
Fields of interest: Medical sciences, cancer, medical research.
Limitations: No grants to individuals.
Application information: Contributes only to pre-selected organizations. Applications not accepted.
Officers and Directors:* James A. Farber,* Pres.; Connie Farber,* V.P.; Randall E. Kessler,* Secy.; Ted A. Farber, Cheryl Pirozzoli, Ward Pynn.
EIN: 942778778

132
Farmers Group Corporate Contributions
4680 Wilshire Blvd.
Los Angeles 90010   (213) 932-3508

Financial data (yr. ended 12/31/90): Total giving, $1,247,930 for grants.
Purpose and activities: Main support for civic affairs, higher education, insurance education, urban development, and minorities; also considers the arts, heart disease, and alcoholism. Under the Aid to Education Program, the company gives to the colleges and universities attended by employees.
Fields of interest: Education, higher education, civic affairs, urban development, minorities, heart disease, alcoholism, insurance education, arts.
Types of support: General purposes, annual campaigns, employee volunteer services, scholarship funds.
Limitations: Giving limited to 28 midwest and western states where operations are located, AK and the east coast excluded.
Application information: Public Relations handles giving.

Initial approach: Letter to headquarters which must be addressed to a specific officer
Deadline(s): None
Board meeting date(s): Two to three months after receiving request
Write: Jeffrey C. Beyer, Chair., Contribs. Comm. and V.P., Public Rels.

Administrators: Jeffrey C. Beyer, Chair., Corp. Contribs. Comm.; Jerald G. Clemans, Secy., Corp. Contribs. Comm.
Number of staff: 2 part-time support.

133
Femino Foundation
P.O. Box 567
West Covina 91793

Donor(s): James J. Femino, Sue Femino, Dominic Femino.
Foundation type: Independent
Financial data (yr. ended 09/30/90): Assets, $2,268,382 (M); gifts received, $225,000; expenditures, $93,407; qualifying distributions, $87,350, including $87,350 for 22 grants (high: $50,000; low: $250).
Purpose and activities: Support primarily for hospitals, health organizations, and institutions of medical research and education; support also for higher and other education.
Fields of interest: Health associations, medical research, medical education, science and technology, education, higher education.
Types of support: Scholarship funds, research.
Application information: Contributes only to pre-selected organizations; unsolicited requests for grants not considered. Applications not accepted.
Officers: James J. Femino, Pres.; Sue Femino, V.P.; Robert L. Bacon, Secy.; Frank P. Uehle, Treas.
EIN: 237423792

134
Fireman's Fund Foundation ▼
(Formerly Fireman's Fund Insurance Company Foundation)
777 San Marin Dr.
P.O. Box 777
Novato 94998   (415) 899-2757

Incorporated in 1953 in CA.

Donor(s): Fireman's Fund Insurance Co., and subsidiaries.
Foundation type: Company-sponsored
Financial data (yr. ended 12/31/91): Assets, $54,996 (M); gifts received, $1,000,000; expenditures, $1,036,022; qualifying distributions, $1,033,171, including $602,136 for 168 grants (high: $51,860; low: $25; average: $2,500) and $427,654 for 1,641 employee matching gifts.
Purpose and activities: Giving primarily to human service agencies, including the aged, the disabled, substance abuse programs, rehabilitation, and youth groups; and civic and cultural activities. Grants also for United Way campaigns nationwide in cities where principal company offices are located. Giving for education is done via the employee gift matching program only.
Fields of interest: Higher education, secondary education, elementary education, education—minorities, libraries, aged, handicapped, rehabilitation, drug abuse, child development, youth, child welfare, arts.
Types of support: Annual campaigns, equipment, technical assistance, continuing support, employee matching gifts, matching funds, donated equipment, in-kind gifts.
Limitations: Giving primarily in the counties of San Francisco, Marin, and Sonoma, CA. No support for religious organizations for religious purposes, fraternal, veterans', sectarian, health, or national organizations, or other grantmaking bodies. No grants to individuals, or for capital campaigns, endowment funds, medical research, travel, benefit events, video or film production, or operating expenses; no loans.
Publications: Application guidelines.
Application information: Application form not required.

Initial approach: Letter
Copies of proposal: 1
Deadline(s): None
Board meeting date(s): Mar. and Dec.; distribution committee meets 4 times a year
Final notification: 3 months
Write: Barbara B. Friede, Dir.

Officers and Directors:* John Meyer,* Chair.; Gary E. Black,* Pres.; Barbara B. Friede,* Secy.; Harold Marsh, Treas.; Raymond Barrette, Timothy Koo, Thomas E. Rowe, Joe Stinnette, Thomas A. Swanson.
Number of staff: 1 full-time professional; 1 full-time support.
EIN: 946078025

135
First Interstate Bank of California Foundation ▼
707 Wilshire Blvd., W35-12
Los Angeles 90017   (213) 614-3068
Additional tel.: (213) 614-3090

Established in 1978 in CA.
Donor(s): First Interstate Bank of California.
Foundation type: Company-sponsored
Financial data (yr. ended 12/31/91): Assets, $17,351,000 (M); expenditures, $2,310,336; qualifying distributions, $2,285,663, including $2,128,901 for 285 grants (high: $680,853; low: $500; average: $1,000-$25,000) and $156,762 for 799 employee matching gifts.

Purpose and activities: Giving primarily for community funds, education, the performing arts and cultural programs, hospitals, urban and civic affairs, and social service and youth agencies; employee-related scholarships made through the Citizens' Scholarship Foundation of America.
Fields of interest: Education, performing arts, cultural programs, hospitals, urban affairs, civic affairs, youth, community funds, social services.
Types of support: Building funds, land acquisition, endowment funds, matching funds, technical assistance, scholarship funds, employee-related scholarships, special projects, employee matching gifts, annual campaigns, operating budgets, continuing support, capital campaigns, general purposes.
Limitations: Giving limited to CA. No support for religious organizations for religious purposes, agencies supported by the United Way, or private foundations. No grants to individuals, or for research, conferences, or equipment for hospitals; no loans.
Publications: Informational brochure (including application guidelines).
Application information: Application form required.
Initial approach: Letter or proposal
Copies of proposal: 1
Deadline(s): July 1 for capital campaigns; none for other programs
Board meeting date(s): Quarterly
Final notification: 6 weeks to 3 months after board meeting
Write: Ruth Jones-Saxey, Secy.-Treas.
Officers and Directors:* Bruce Willison,* Chair.; Ruth Jones-Saxey, Secy.-Treas.; Roger Molvar,* C.F.O.; Daniel Eitingon, Edward Garlock, David Holman, John Popovich, William Sudmann.
Number of staff: 2 full-time professional.
EIN: 953288932

136
First Nationwide Bank Corporate Giving Program
700 Market St.
San Francisco 94102   (415) 772-1400

Financial data (yr. ended 01/31/90): Total giving, $400,000, including $300,000 for grants and $100,000 for employee matching gifts.
Purpose and activities: Supports community, social, and health services, public and civic affairs, community development, business, crime and law enforcement programs, minorities, women, youth, education, cultural organizations and the arts, and housing.
Fields of interest: Social services, health, cultural programs, arts, aged, AIDS, alcoholism, business, cancer, child development, child welfare, civic affairs, civil rights, community development, crime and law enforcement, dance, delinquency, disadvantaged, drug abuse, general charitable giving, health, health services, higher education, homeless, housing, journalism, literacy, minorities, museums, music, theater, women, youth, housing.
Types of support: Capital campaigns, emergency funds, operating budgets, scholarship funds, technical assistance.
Limitations: Giving primarily in major operating areas. No support for religious groups and groups that discriminate. No grants to individuals.

Publications: Corporate giving report, application guidelines.
Application information: Application form not required.
Copies of proposal: 1
Board meeting date(s): Bi-monthly
Final notification: Soon after each board meeting
Write: Stephen L. Johnson, Sr. V.P. and Dir., Public Affairs
Administrators: Stephen L. Johnson, Gerri Romero.

137
The Fluor Foundation
3333 Michelson Dr.
Irvine 92730   (714) 975-6797

Incorporated in 1952 in CA.
Donor(s): Fluor Corp.
Foundation type: Company-sponsored
Financial data (yr. ended 10/31/90): Assets, $427,457 (M); gifts received, $1,308,854; expenditures, $1,144,379; qualifying distributions, $1,144,222, including $1,144,222 for grants (average: $100-$40,000).
Purpose and activities: Support for higher education, culture and the arts, public and civic affairs, and health and welfare organizations, especially the United Way; scholarships for children of company employees are administered by an independent scholarship corporation.
Fields of interest: Higher education, education, educational associations, cultural programs, arts, performing arts, public policy, civic affairs, social services, community funds, engineering, science and technology, volunteerism.
Types of support: Annual campaigns, building funds, employee matching gifts, operating budgets, technical assistance, employee-related scholarships, general purposes, endowment funds, scholarship funds.
Limitations: Giving primarily in areas where the corporation has permanent offices, with some emphasis on Orange County, CA; Houston, TX; Chicago, IL; Greenville, SC; and Marlton, NJ. No support for medical research, guilds, and sports organizations. No grants to individuals (except for employee-related scholarships).
Publications: Informational brochure (including application guidelines).
Application information: Application form not required.
Initial approach: Letter
Copies of proposal: 1
Deadline(s): None
Board meeting date(s): Oct.
Final notification: 3 to 4 months
Write: Suzanne H. Esber, Dir., Comm. Affairs
Officers and Trustees:* Leslie G. McCraw,* Chair.; J. Robert Fluor II,* Pres.; Larry N. Fisher, Secy.; Andy Schwartz, Treas.; Alan Boeckmann, Hugh K. Coble, Vince L. Kontny, Emil J. Parente, Nad A. Peterson.
Number of staff: 1 full-time professional; 1 full-time support.
EIN: 510196032
Recent health grants:
137-1 Childrens Hospital Foundation of Orange County, Orange, CA, $25,000. For capital campaign. 1991.

137-2 National Foundation for Depressive Illness, NYC, NY, $25,000. For fundraising dinner. 1991.
137-3 Southern California Building Fund, Los Angeles, CA, $10,000. For distribution to nonprofit institutions for their capital projects in 1992. 1991.
137-4 Susan G. Komen Foundation, Dallas, TX, $10,000. For Race for the Cure event. 1991.

138
Forest Lawn Foundation
1712 South Glendale Ave.
Glendale 91205

Incorporated in 1951 in CA.
Donor(s): Forest Lawn Co., Hubert Eaton Estate Trust.
Foundation type: Independent
Financial data (yr. ended 12/31/91): Assets, $36,075,391 (M); gifts received, $613,584; expenditures, $1,190,930; qualifying distributions, $1,050,478, including $1,040,425 for 49 grants (high: $300,000; low: $175).
Fields of interest: Youth, hospitals, handicapped, social services, welfare.
Limitations: Giving primarily in CA. No grants to individuals, or for endowment funds or special projects.
Application information: Grants generally initiated by the foundation. Applications not accepted.
Board meeting date(s): Quarterly
Write: John Llewellyn, V.P.
Officers and Trustees:* Frederick Llewellyn,* Chair. and Pres.; John Llewellyn,* V.P. and Secy.-Treas.; Thomas E. Stephenson, C.F.O.; Timothy Applegate, General Counsel; Myron E. Smith.
EIN: 956030792

139
Georges and Germaine Fusenot Charity Foundation
7060 Hollywood Blvd., Suite 912
Hollywood 90028
Application address: 522 North Rossmore Ave., Apt. No. 302, Los Angeles, CA 90004; Tel.: (213) 462-7702

Trust established in 1967 in CA.
Donor(s): Germaine Fusenot.‡
Foundation type: Independent
Financial data (yr. ended 07/31/91): Assets, $5,338,694 (M); expenditures, $361,478; qualifying distributions, $304,721, including $272,100 for 79 grants (high: $15,000; low: $500).
Fields of interest: Hospitals, handicapped, child welfare.
Types of support: Operating budgets, continuing support, annual campaigns, seed money, building funds, equipment, land acquisition, research, general purposes, capital campaigns, special projects.
Limitations: Giving limited to CA. No grants to individuals, or for emergency or endowment funds, deficit financing, demonstration projects, publications, conferences, scholarships, or fellowships; no loans.

Application information: Application form not required.
Initial approach: Letter
Copies of proposal: 1
Deadline(s): Sept. 30 for consideration in the same year
Board meeting date(s): Oct.
Final notification: Jan.
Write: Richard G. Herlihy, Mgr.
Officer: Richard G. Herlihy, Mgr.
Trustees: Katherine S. Burns, Mrs. Marvin Chesebro, Elizabeth Herlihy, Michael J. Herlihy, Fred W. Hoar, Virginia Markel, Guy Arnold Stone, Patricia H. Stone, Troy E. Stone, Viveca Ann Stone.
Number of staff: 1 full-time professional.
EIN: 956207831

140
The Julio R. Gallo Foundation
P.O. Box 1130
Modesto 95353   (209) 579-3373

Incorporated in 1955 in CA.
Donor(s): Julio R. Gallo, Robert J. Gallo.
Foundation type: Independent
Financial data (yr. ended 10/31/91): Assets, $6,423,297 (M); gifts received, $350,000; expenditures, $504,207; qualifying distributions, $500,000, including $500,000 for 25 grants (high: $201,000; low: $500).
Fields of interest: Catholic giving, higher education, secondary education, medical research, social services.
Limitations: Giving primarily in CA. No grants to individuals.
Application information:
Initial approach: Letter
Deadline(s): None
Write: Robert J. Gallo, V.P.
Officers and Directors:* Julio R. Gallo,* Pres.; Robert J. Gallo,* V.P.; James E. Coleman,* Secy.; James B. Owens, Treas.
EIN: 946061539

141
Gamble Foundation
90 New Montgomery St., 11th Fl.
San Francisco 94105   (415) 957-9999

Established in 1968 in CA.
Donor(s): Launce E. Gamble, Mary S. Gamble, George F. Gamble.
Foundation type: Independent
Financial data (yr. ended 12/31/91): Assets, $2,498,634 (M); gifts received, $36,000; expenditures, $137,533; qualifying distributions, $135,928, including $130,000 for 59 grants (high: $8,000; low: $250).
Purpose and activities: Support for local San Francisco Bay Area community charitable projects focusing on education, science/medical issues, performing arts, social rehabilitation, and wildlife and the environment.
Fields of interest: Environment, wildlife, community development, hospitals, music, museums.
Types of support: Annual campaigns, continuing support, seed money, operating budgets, renovation projects, special projects, equipment.

Limitations: Giving primarily in northern CA, including the San Francisco Bay Area. No grants to individuals.
Application information: Due to funding limitations, trustees initiate grants; unsolicited applications not accepted. Application form not required.
Initial approach: 1-page letter
Copies of proposal: 1
Deadline(s): No later than the 3rd quarter of each year
Board meeting date(s): End of 3rd quarter
Final notification: 4th quarter, only if funded
Write: Launce E. Gamble, Pres.
Officers: Launce E. Gamble, Pres.; George F. Gamble, V.P. and Secy.-Treas.; Mary S. Gamble, V.P.
Number of staff: None.
EIN: 941680503

142
The Gap Foundation
One Harrison St.
San Francisco 94105   (415) 291-2757

Established in 1977 in CA.
Donor(s): The Gap, Inc.
Foundation type: Company-sponsored
Financial data (yr. ended 01/31/92): Assets, $25,000 (M); gifts received, $1,713,719; expenditures, $1,933,439; qualifying distributions, $1,684,949, including $850,945 for grants (high: $50,000; low: $500; average: $500-$50,000), $131,000 for employee matching gifts and $703,000 for in-kind gifts.
Purpose and activities: Support primarily for the arts, environment, and youth and child development; giving also for higher and other education, civic affairs, and health, including AIDS programs.
Fields of interest: Arts, environment, child development, youth, higher education, education, civic affairs, health, AIDS.
Types of support: Employee matching gifts, capital campaigns, general purposes, operating budgets, in-kind gifts, special projects.
Limitations: Giving primarily in San Francisco and San Mateo, CA; limited giving in Baltimore, MD, New York, NY, Ventura, CA, and Evianger, KY. No support for religious or political purposes. No grants to individuals.
Publications: Annual report, 990-PF, application guidelines.
Application information: Application form not required.
Initial approach: Letter
Copies of proposal: 1
Deadline(s): Quarterly, 1st of month before month of next board meeting
Board meeting date(s): Quarterly
Final notification: Within 2 weeks of board meeting
Write: Molly White, Dir.
Officers: Donald G. Fisher, Chair. and C.E.O.; Millard S. Drexler, Pres.; Robert J. Fisher, V.P.; Doris F. Fisher, Treas.
Number of staff: 1 full-time professional; 1 full-time support.
EIN: 942474426
Recent health grants:
142-1 Gay Mens Health Crisis (GMHC), NYC, NY, $15,000. For public policy, education and

prevention programs for high-risk populations. 1992.
142-2 Pacific Medical Center, Jerry De Chant Pediatric Fund, San Francisco, CA, $15,000. To create Family Resource Center in Pediatric Unit. 1992.
142-3 Teens Kick Off, San Francisco, CA, $10,000. For theater-based peer drug intervention (recovery and prevention) program in secondary schools. 1992.

143
Silvio and Mary Garaventa Family Foundation
4080 Mallard Dr.
Concord 94520

Established in 1986 in CA.
Donor(s): Silvio Garaventa, Mary Garaventa, SEG Trucking, Contra Costa Waste, Inc.
Foundation type: Independent
Financial data (yr. ended 03/31/91): Assets, $1,116,259 (M); gifts received, $838,000; expenditures, $459,566; qualifying distributions, $457,100, including $457,100 for 10 grants (high: $255,000; low: $500).
Fields of interest: Catholic giving, religious schools, health, medical research, education, higher education.
Limitations: Giving primarily in CA. No grants to individuals.
Application information: Contributes only to pre-selected organizations. Applications not accepted.
Officer: Silvio Garaventa, Mgr.
Trustees: Marie Adler, Louisa Binswanger, Linda Colvis.
EIN: 680100302

144
John Jewett & H. Chandler Garland Foundation ▼
P.O. Box 550
Pasadena 91102-0550

Trust established in 1959 in CA.
Donor(s): Members of the Garland family.
Foundation type: Independent
Financial data (yr. ended 12/31/90): Assets, $167,819 (M); gifts received, $1,661,614; expenditures, $1,684,715; qualifying distributions, $1,684,715, including $1,628,311 for 33 grants (high: $1,100,000; low: $500; average: $5,000-$20,000).
Purpose and activities: Support primarily for cultural and historical programs, secondary and higher education, social services, especially for the elderly, youth agencies, hospitals, and health services.
Fields of interest: Cultural programs, historic preservation, education, social services, youth, homeless, aged, health services, hospitals.
Limitations: Giving primarily in CA, with emphasis on Southern CA. No grants for seed money.
Application information: Application form not required.
Initial approach: Letter
Copies of proposal: 1
Deadline(s): None
Board meeting date(s): 3 times per year

Final notification: After each meeting
Officer and Trustees:* G.E. Morrow,* Mgr.; Ann Kelsey Babcock, Gwendolyn Garland Babcock, John Carlile Babcock, Sarah Garland Babcock, Susan Hinman Babcock.
Number of staff: None.
EIN: 956023587
Recent health grants:
144-1 National Scoliosis Foundation, Belmont, MA, $10,000. 1990.
144-2 Saint John of God Nursing Hospital and Residence Foundation, Los Angeles, CA, $15,000. 1990.
144-3 Santa Marta Foundation, Los Angeles, CA, $10,000. 1990.

145
Audette S. Garnier Trust
c/o Wells Fargo Bank, N.A., Trust Tax Dept.
P.O. Box 63954
San Francisco 94163

Foundation type: Independent
Financial data (yr. ended 12/31/90): Assets, $3,148,044 (M); expenditures, $211,726; qualifying distributions, $183,511, including $173,617 for 2 grants (high: $118,962; low: $54,655).
Fields of interest: Medical research, health associations.
Limitations: Giving limited to Los Angeles, CA. No grants to individuals.
Application information: Contributes only to pre-selected organizations. Applications not accepted.
Trustee: Wells Fargo Bank, N.A.
EIN: 956598449

146
Peter A. & Vernice H. Gasser Foundation
1834 Soscol Ave., Suite B
Napa 94559-1314

Established in 1982 in CA.
Foundation type: Independent
Financial data (yr. ended 12/31/91): Assets, $18,951,224 (M); expenditures, $1,469,168; qualifying distributions, $933,895, including $908,427 for grants (high: $255,000).
Fields of interest: Secondary education, housing, hospitals, youth, social services.
Limitations: Giving primarily in CA. No grants to individuals.
Application information: Contributes only to pre-selected organizations. Applications not accepted.
Officers: Clifford G. Hartle, Pres.; Julian N. Stern, Secy.; Amelia Scaruffi, Treas. and C.F.O.
Directors: Alvin Johnson, Joseph G. Peatman.
EIN: 942816159

147
The David Geffen Foundation
c/o Breslaver, Jacobson, Rutman, & Sherman
10345 Olympic Blvd.
Los Angeles 90064

Incorporated in 1986 in CA.
Donor(s): David Geffen.
Foundation type: Independent

Financial data (yr. ended 12/31/90): Assets, $10,087,875 (M); gifts received, $152,293; expenditures, $473,660; qualifying distributions, $473,025, including $473,025 for 135 grants (high: $100,300; low: $50).
Fields of interest: Medical research, AIDS, human rights, education, Jewish giving, film, media and communications, gays and lesbians.
Limitations: Giving primarily in Los Angeles, CA, and New York, NY.
Application information: Application form not required.
Deadline(s): None
Write: David Geffen, Trustee
Trustees: Eric Eisner, David Geffen, Richard Sherman.
EIN: 954085811

148
The Carl Gellert Foundation
2222 19th Ave.
San Francisco 94116   (415) 566-4420

Incorporated in 1958 in CA.
Donor(s): Carl Gellert,‡ Atlas Realty Co., Pacific Coast Construction Co., Gertrude E. Gellert.‡
Foundation type: Independent
Financial data (yr. ended 11/30/91): Assets, $7,936,169 (M); expenditures, $690,862; qualifying distributions, $661,836, including $628,800 for 102 grants (high: $100,000; low: $1,000; average: $1,000-$10,000).
Purpose and activities: Support for the aged, medical research, drug abuse programs, and hospitals; grants also for Roman Catholic church support; higher, secondary, and elementary education, including engineering and scholarship funds; and to community development programs and social service agencies, including family planning.
Fields of interest: Aged, medical research, drug abuse, hospitals, Catholic giving, higher education, secondary education, elementary education, education, social services.
Types of support: Operating budgets, continuing support, annual campaigns, deficit financing, building funds, equipment, endowment funds, scholarship funds, research, publications, special projects, renovation projects, capital campaigns, general purposes.
Limitations: Giving primarily in the San Francisco Bay Area, CA. No grants to individuals, or for seed money, emergency funds, land acquisition, matching gifts, or conferences; no loans.
Publications: 990-PF, program policy statement, application guidelines.
Application information: Application form not required.
Initial approach: Proposal
Copies of proposal: 5
Deadline(s): Submit proposal preferably in Aug.; deadline Oct. 1st
Board meeting date(s): Apr. and Nov.
Final notification: Nov. 30, for recipients only
Write: Peter J. Brusati, Secy.
Officers and Directors:* Fred R. Bahrt,* Pres.; Robert L. Pauly,* V.P.; Peter J. Brusati,* Secy.; Marie Simpson,* Treas.; Celia Berta Gellert.
Number of staff: None.
EIN: 946062858

149
Celia Berta Gellert Foundation
2222 19th Ave.
San Francisco 94116-1896   (415) 566-4420

Established in 1970.
Donor(s): Celia Berta Gellert.
Foundation type: Independent
Financial data (yr. ended 11/30/91): Assets, $2,449,239 (M); gifts received, $350,000; expenditures, $213,471; qualifying distributions, $208,198, including $200,000 for 41 grants (high: $16,500; low: $1,000; average: $2,500-$5,000).
Purpose and activities: Giving primarily for homes for the aged, Catholic churches, hospitals and education, especially secondary education; support also for medical research, community development, elementary education, and social services.
Fields of interest: Aged, Catholic giving, hospitals, education, secondary education, medical research, community development, elementary education, social services, drug abuse.
Types of support: Scholarship funds, general purposes, operating budgets, building funds, renovation projects, endowment funds, annual campaigns, capital campaigns, continuing support, equipment, publications, research, special projects.
Limitations: Giving primarily in the San Francisco Bay Area, CA. No grants to individuals; no loans.
Publications: 990-PF, program policy statement, application guidelines.
Application information: Application form not required.
Initial approach: Proposal
Copies of proposal: 5
Deadline(s): Oct. 1
Board meeting date(s): Nov.
Final notification: Nov. 30 for positive responses
Write: Peter J. Brusati, Secy.
Officers and Directors:* Robert L. Pauly,* Chair.; Fred R. Bahrt,* Vice-Chair.; Peter J. Brusati,* Secy. and Mgr.; Andrew A. Cresci,* Treas.; Celia Berta Gellert.
Number of staff: None.
EIN: 237083733

150
The Fred Gellert Foundation
One Embarcadero Ctr., Suite 2480
San Francisco 94111-5994   (415) 433-6174
Environmental funding inquiries: contact Jacqueline Young, Charitable Contribs. Consultant; Tel.: (415) 668-1119

Established in 1958 in CA.
Donor(s): Fred Gellert, Sr.‡
Foundation type: Independent
Financial data (yr. ended 11/30/91): Assets, $10,177,702 (M); expenditures, $696,051; qualifying distributions, $615,781, including $607,009 for grants (average: $1,000-$5,000).
Purpose and activities: "Support for programs in the following categories: health care, disabled, social services, community services, education, arts, youth and senior services. The trustees have allocated one quarter of 1992 funds for local and national groups organized to find solutions for a healthy planet. Of particular interest are environmental organizations working to balance

human numbers with the earth's resources and organizations forming coalitions to make environmental quality a national priority."

Fields of interest: Disadvantaged, handicapped, education, social services, health services, hospitals, aged, cultural programs, environment, ecology, youth, community development.

Types of support: Operating budgets, continuing support, building funds, equipment, research, special projects, general purposes, endowment funds.

Limitations: Giving primarily in San Francisco and San Mateo counties, CA. No grants to individuals, or for annual campaigns; no loans.

Publications: Application guidelines, financial statement, grants list.

Application information: Telephone inquiries regarding status of request are discouraged. Application form not required.

> *Initial approach:* Letter or full proposal prefaced by 1-page summary
> *Copies of proposal:* 4
> *Deadline(s):* Mar. 1 and Sept. 1 for environmental grants; Sept. 1 for all other grants
> *Board meeting date(s):* Apr. and Nov.
> *Final notification:* Nov. 30
> *Write:* Fred Gellert, Jr., Chair.

Officers and Directors:* Fred Gellert, Jr.,* Chair.; John D. Howard,* Secy.-Treas.; Annette Gellert, Marche H. Yoshioka.

Number of staff: 1 part-time professional.

EIN: 946062859

151
Genentech Foundation for Biomedical Sciences

(Formerly Genentech Research Foundation)
460 Point San Bruno Blvd.
South San Francisco 94080-499(415) 225-3202

Established in 1988 in CA.
Donor(s): Genentech, Inc.
Foundation type: Company-sponsored
Financial data (yr. ended 12/31/90): Assets, $140,179 (M); gifts received, $264,593; expenditures, $245,113; qualifying distributions, $245,000, including $245,000 for 6 grants (high: $75,000; low: $20,000).
Purpose and activities: Support for education and research in the biomedical sciences, including programs fostering the participation of under-represented minorities and underprivileged groups. Eligible institutions include primary schools, junior high and high schools, school districts, colleges and universities, and research organizations.
Fields of interest: Biological sciences, medical sciences, medical education.
Types of support: Scholarship funds, equipment, research, fellowships.
Limitations: Giving limited to northern CA. No support for private foundations. No grants to individuals.
Publications: Program policy statement, application guidelines.
Application information: Application form required.

> *Initial approach:* Proposal
> *Deadline(s):* Apr. 15
> *Write:* Marty Glick, C.F.O. and Secy.

Officer: Marty Glick, C.F.O. and Secy.

Directors: Bruce Alberts, Ph.D, Herbert W. Boyer, Ph.D., Edward Harris, M.D., Lloyd Smith, M.D., Robert A. Swanson.

EIN: 943083018

152
Gerard Family Trust B

P.O. Box 8267
Orange 92664

Established in 1969 in CA.
Donor(s): Leona B. Gerard,‡ Ralph W. Gerard.‡
Foundation type: Independent
Financial data (yr. ended 12/31/91): Assets, $2,042,111 (M); gifts received, $3,093; expenditures, $146,275; qualifying distributions, $94,300, including $91,000 for 7 grants (high: $25,000; low: $3,000).
Fields of interest: Higher education, hospitals, family services, biological sciences, biology, women.
Types of support: General purposes, research.
Limitations: Giving primarily in Orange County, CA. No grants to individuals.
Publications: 990-PF, financial statement.
Application information: Contributes only to pre-selected organizations. Applications not accepted.

> *Write:* Patricia Foster, Trustee

Trustee: Patricia Foster.
Number of staff: None.
EIN: 956497394

153
Wallace Alexander Gerbode Foundation ▼

470 Columbus Ave., Suite 209
San Francisco 94133   (415) 391-0911

Incorporated in 1953 in CA.
Donor(s): Members of the Gerbode family.
Foundation type: Independent
Financial data (yr. ended 12/31/90): Assets, $39,786,703 (M); expenditures, $2,316,247; qualifying distributions, $2,107,834, including $1,907,834 for 124 grants (high: $60,000; low: $500; average: $5,000-$25,000) and $200,000 for program-related investments.
Purpose and activities: Support for innovative, positive programs in the arts, education, environment, health, urban affairs, and community development.
Fields of interest: Arts, education, environment, health, urban affairs, community development, civil rights.
Types of support: Consulting services, technical assistance, program-related investments, loans, special projects.
Limitations: Giving primarily to programs directly affecting residents of Alameda, Contra Costa, Marin, San Francisco, and San Mateo counties in CA, and HI. No support for religious purposes. No grants to individuals, or for general or continuing support, direct services, operating budgets, capital or endowment funds, fundraising or annual campaigns, emergency funds, matching gifts, scholarships, fellowships, publications, deficit financing, building funds, equipment or materials, land acquisition, or renovation projects.
Publications: Grants list, annual report (including application guidelines).

Application information: The foundation does not accept applications or unsolicited materials via facsimile machine. Application form not required.

> *Initial approach:* Letter
> *Copies of proposal:* 1
> *Deadline(s):* None
> *Board meeting date(s):* 4 times a year
> *Final notification:* 2 to 3 months
> *Write:* Thomas C. Layton, Exec. Dir.

Officers and Directors:* Maryanna G. Shaw,* Chair. and Pres.; Frank A. Gerbode, M.D.,* Vice-Chair. and V.P.; Joan Richardson,* Secy.; Charles M. Stockholm,* Treas.; Thomas C. Layton.

Number of staff: 1 full-time professional; 1 full-time support.

EIN: 946065226

Recent health grants:

153-1 Birth Control Trust, London, England, $20,000. For renewed support of RU 486 Project. 1991.

153-2 Communications Consortium, Media Center, DC, $20,000. For Reproductive Health Strategies Project, working with women of color. 1991.

153-3 Ms. Foundation for Women, NYC, NY, $10,000. For renewed support of Women's Reproductive Rights Coalition Fund. 1991.

153-4 Students Organizing Students, NYC, NY, $20,000. For abortion rights work. 1991.

153-5 Tides Foundation, San Francisco, CA, $15,000. For organizational development of Restoring the Earth. 1991.

154
The William G. Gilmore Foundation

120 Montgomery St., Suite 1880
San Francisco 94104   (415) 546-1400

Incorporated in 1953 in CA.
Donor(s): William G. Gilmore,‡ Mrs. William G. Gilmore.‡
Foundation type: Independent
Financial data (yr. ended 12/31/90): Assets, $12,226,996 (M); expenditures, $957,362; qualifying distributions, $906,734, including $852,680 for 157 grants (high: $40,000; low: $380; average: $500-$5,000).
Purpose and activities: Grants largely for community-based organizations, including development and urban affairs, family and social services, the elderly, child welfare and development, health services, medical education, AIDS programs, conservation, and the arts.
Fields of interest: Community development, health services, AIDS, education, youth, family services, social services, aged, arts, conservation.
Types of support: Annual campaigns, continuing support, emergency funds, general purposes, operating budgets, scholarship funds.
Limitations: Giving primarily in northern CA and OR. No grants to individuals.
Application information: Application form not required.

> *Initial approach:* Letter of intent
> *Copies of proposal:* 1
> *Deadline(s):* May 1 and Nov. 1
> *Board meeting date(s):* June and Dec.
> *Final notification:* 2 months
> *Write:* Faye Wilson, Secy.

Officers and Trustees:* Robert C. Harris,* Pres.; Lee Emerson,* V.P., and Treas.; William R.

Mackey,* V.P.; Faye Wilson, Secy.; Thomas B. Boklund.
Number of staff: 1 part-time support.
EIN: 946079493

155
Gold Family Charitable Foundation
4444 Lakeside Dr., 2nd Fl.
Burbank 91505   (818) 845-4444

Established in 1986 in CA.
Donor(s): Stanley P. Gold, Ilene C. Gold.
Foundation type: Independent
Financial data (yr. ended 07/31/91): Assets, $5,135 (M); gifts received, $199,000; expenditures, $335,828; qualifying distributions, $335,828, including $333,928 for 48 grants (high: $65,045; low: $50).
Purpose and activities: Support primarily for Jewish organizations, including education, a welfare fund, and religious support; support also for cultural and educational advancement, and for health and social services.
Fields of interest: Jewish giving, Jewish welfare, education, higher education, cultural programs, health, social services.
Limitations: Giving primarily in CA. No grants to individuals.
Application information: Application form not required.
  Deadline(s): None
  Write: Ilene C. Gold, Pres., or Stanley P. Gold, V.P.
Officers: Ilene C. Gold, Pres.; Stanley P. Gold, V.P. and Secy.-Treas.
EIN: 954076113

156
Richard and Rhoda Goldman Fund
One Lombard St., Suite 303
San Francisco 94111   (415) 788-1090
FAX: (415) 788-7890

Incorporated in 1951 in CA.
Donor(s): Rhoda H. Goldman, Richard N. Goldman.
Foundation type: Independent
Financial data (yr. ended 10/31/90): Assets, $5,800,430 (M); gifts received, $1,000,100; expenditures, $1,061,118; qualifying distributions, $932,518, including $814,749 for 93 grants (high: $100,000; low: $300; average: $7,500-$25,000).
Fields of interest: Aged, child welfare, youth, environment, civic affairs, health, literacy.
Types of support: Seed money, special projects.
Limitations: Giving primarily in the San Francisco Bay Area, CA. No grants to individuals, or for deficit budgets, building or endowment funds, general fundraising campaigns, conferences, research, scholarships, fellowships, or matching gifts; no loans.
Publications: Annual report (including application guidelines).
Application information: Application form not required.
  Initial approach: Letter
  Copies of proposal: 1
  Deadline(s): None
  Board meeting date(s): Jan., Apr., July, and Oct.
  Write: Duane Silverstein, Exec. Dir.

Officers and Directors:* Richard N. Goldman,* Pres.; Rhoda H. Goldman,* Secy.-Treas.; Duane Silverstein,* Exec. Dir.; Michael C. Gelman, Susan R. Gelman, Douglas E. Goldman, John D. Goldman, Marcia L. Goldman, Susan S. Goldman.
Number of staff: 2 full-time professional; 1 part-time professional; 1 full-time support.
EIN: 946064502
Recent health grants:
156-1 KARA, Palo Alto, CA, $10,000. For videotape on grief counseling services. 1991.
156-2 San Francisco Adult Day Health Network, San Francisco, CA, $20,000. For On Lok Day Services. 1991.
156-3 Trauma Foundation, San Francisco, CA, $30,000. For Teens on Target, gun violence prevention project for Oakland Youth. 1991.
156-4 Volunteers to San Francisco General Hospital Medical Center, San Francisco, CA, $10,000. For Play Therapy Program on pediatric ward. 1991.
156-5 Youth Advocates, San Francisco, CA, $30,000. For teen HIV education. 1991.
156-6 Youth Law Center, San Francisco, CA, $30,000. For project to ensure preventive health screenings for foster children. 1991.

157
Goldsmith Family Foundation
400 North Roxbury Dr.
Beverly Hills 90210   (213) 550-5711

Established in 1980 in CA.
Donor(s): Mrs. Bram Goldsmith, Bram Goldsmith.
Foundation type: Independent
Financial data (yr. ended 09/30/91): Assets, $2,964,168 (M); gifts received, $58,200; expenditures, $283,916; qualifying distributions, $276,795, including $274,385 for 54 grants (high: $55,000; low: $25).
Fields of interest: Higher education, education, Jewish giving, Jewish welfare, arts, hospices, hospitals, medical research, drug abuse, crime and law enforcement.
Types of support: Annual campaigns, building funds, continuing support, endowment funds.
Limitations: Giving primarily in the Southern CA area. No grants to individuals.
Application information: Contributes only to pre-selected organizations. Applications not accepted.
  Write: Bram Goldsmith, Pres.
Officers: Bram Goldsmith, Pres.; Elaine Goldsmith, V.P. and Secy.-Treas.
Directors: Bruce L. Goldsmith, Russell Goldsmith.
Number of staff: 1 part-time support.
EIN: 953545880

158
The Samuel Goldwyn Foundation
10203 Santa Monica Blvd., Suite 500
Los Angeles 90067   (213) 552-2255

Established in 1947 in CA.
Donor(s): Samuel Goldwyn,‡ Frances H. Goldwyn.‡
Foundation type: Independent
Financial data (yr. ended 12/31/90): Assets, $19,968,981 (M); expenditures, $1,851,859; qualifying distributions, $1,120,696, including $982,439 for 52 grants (high: $482,067; low:

$25; average: $1,000-$10,000) and $7,770 for 31 employee matching gifts.
Purpose and activities: To promote community-related activities: grants primarily for a library, higher and other education, cultural programs, youth, child development, medical research and health, and innovative social service programs.
Fields of interest: Education, higher education, education—early childhood, education—minorities, cultural programs, youth, child development, medical research, health, social services.
Types of support: Annual campaigns, seed money, scholarship funds, research, special projects.
Limitations: Giving limited to the Los Angeles, CA, metropolitan area. No grants to individuals, or for building funds.
Application information: Application form not required.
  Initial approach: Proposal
  Copies of proposal: 1
  Deadline(s): Mar. 31 for June grants; Sept. 30 for Dec. grants
  Board meeting date(s): Quarterly
  Final notification: June and Dec.
Officers and Directors:* Samuel Goldwyn, Jr.,* Pres.; Peggy E. Goldwyn,* V.P.; Meyer Gottlieb,* Treas.; Anthony Goldwyn, Francis Goldwyn, John Goldwyn.
Number of staff: 1 full-time professional.
EIN: 956006859

159
I. H. and Anna Grancell Foundation
1469 Carla Ridge
Beverly Hills 90210   (213) 272-7091

Incorporated in 1957 in CA.
Donor(s): Anna Grancell, Anna Grancell Charitable Trust.
Foundation type: Independent
Financial data (yr. ended 07/31/91): Assets, $121,253 (M); expenditures, $286,449; qualifying distributions, $278,718, including $277,203 for 20 grants (high: $94,266; low: $180).
Fields of interest: Hospitals, Jewish giving, Jewish welfare, higher education, cultural programs.
Types of support: Endowment funds, building funds, scholarship funds.
Limitations: Giving primarily in CA. No grants to individuals.
Application information: Application form not required.
  Initial approach: Letter
  Deadline(s): None
  Write: Sherman Grancell, Treas.
Officers: Paul Grancell, Pres.; Morton Bauman, Secy.; Sherman Grancell, Treas.
EIN: 956027429

160
Great Western Financial Corporation Giving Program
8484 Wilshire Blvd., 9th Flr.
Beverly Hills 90211   (213) 852-3406

Financial data (yr. ended 12/31/90): Total giving, $1,441,323 for grants.

Purpose and activities: Company primarily supports housing and community affairs and development; support also for education.
Fields of interest: Housing, community development, higher education, performing arts, civic affairs, public affairs, business education, health, social services.
Types of support: General purposes, matching funds, student loans.
Limitations: Giving primarily in CA, FL, WA, and AR. No support for fraternal, political, or religious organizations. No grants to individuals.
Publications: Corporate report, application guidelines.
Application information:
  Initial approach: Letter or proposal
  Copies of proposal: 1
  Deadline(s): Early in the calender year
  Write: Sharon Butler, V.P. and Dir., Community Development
Administators: Sharon Butler, V.P. and Dir., Community Development; Josephine Hanson-Ristau, Mgr., Charitable Contribs.
Number of staff: 1 full-time professional; 1 full-time support.

161
Stella B. Gross Charitable Trust
c/o Bank of the West
P.O. Box 1121
San Jose 95108 (408) 998-6856

Trust established in 1966 in CA.
Donor(s): Stella B. Gross.‡
Foundation type: Independent
Financial data (yr. ended 06/30/91): Assets, $5,532,695 (M); expenditures, $315,031; qualifying distributions, $226,884, including $226,884 for 42 grants (high: $23,000; low: $1,000; average: $1,000-$10,000).
Fields of interest: Youth, higher education, handicapped, health, hospitals.
Types of support: Continuing support, general purposes, seed money, special projects.
Limitations: Giving limited to Santa Clara County, CA. No grants to individuals.
Publications: Annual report, 990-PF.
Application information: Contributes only to pre-selected organizations. Applications not accepted.
  Board meeting date(s): June and Dec.
  Write: Lori C. Stetzenmeyer, Asst. Trust Officer, Bank of the West
Trustee: Bank of the West.
Number of staff: None.
EIN: 237142181

162
Gruber Family Foundation
P.O. Box 214
Ross 94957

Established in 1987 in CA.
Donor(s): Jon D. Gruber, Linda W. Gruber.
Foundation type: Independent
Financial data (yr. ended 12/31/91): Assets, $2,515,000 (M); gifts received, $680,000; expenditures, $64,400; qualifying distributions, $64,400, including $64,400 for grants.
Purpose and activities: Primary areas of interest include education, family planning and women's

issues, museums, the homeless, and social services.
Fields of interest: Social services, museums, education, arts, welfare, women, family planning, youth, homeless.
Types of support: Annual campaigns, building funds, continuing support, capital campaigns, operating budgets.
Limitations: Giving primarily in CA. No grants to individuals.
Application information: Contributes only to pre-selected organizations. Applications not accepted.
Officers: Linda W. Gruber, Pres.; Jon D. Gruber, Secy.-Treas.
EIN: 943039716

163
Walter and Elise Haas Fund ▼
One Lombard St., Suite 305
San Francisco 94111 (415) 398-4474

Incorporated in 1952 in CA.
Donor(s): Walter A. Haas,‡ Elise S. Haas.‡
Foundation type: Independent
Financial data (yr. ended 12/31/91): Assets, $151,837,950 (M); gifts received, $81,005,000; expenditures, $8,941,626; qualifying distributions, $9,879,400, including $8,379,400 for 187 grants (high: $2,450,000; low: $500; average: $1,000-$25,000) and $1,500,000 for program-related investments.
Purpose and activities: Support for projects which demonstrate an ability to have a wide impact within their respective fields through enhancing public education and access to information, serving a central organizing role, addressing public policy, demonstrating creative approaches toward meeting human needs, supporting the work of a major institution in the field, or extending the arts and humanities into the community.
Fields of interest: Education, education—building funds, elementary education, higher education, citizenship, social services, child welfare, youth, health services, conservation, humanities, arts, museums, Jewish giving.
Types of support: Operating budgets, continuing support, seed money, emergency funds, building funds, equipment, endowment funds, matching funds, scholarship funds, professorships, fellowships, special projects, capital campaigns, land acquisition.
Limitations: Giving primarily in the San Francisco Bay Area, CA. No grants to individuals, or for deficit financing.
Publications: Multi-year report, program policy statement, application guidelines.
Application information: Application form required.
  Initial approach: Letter of inquiry
  Copies of proposal: 1
  Deadline(s): None
  Board meeting date(s): As required
  Final notification: 2 to 4 months
  Write: Bruce R. Sievers, Exec. Dir.
Officers and Directors:* Rhoda H. Goldman,* Pres.; Peter E. Haas,* V.P.; Walter A. Haas, Jr.,* V.P.; Bruce R. Sievers, Exec. Dir. and Secy.-Treas.; Douglas E. Goldman, Peter E. Haas, Jr., Walter J. Haas.

Number of staff: 2 full-time professional; 2 full-time support; 1 part-time support.
EIN: 946068564
Recent health grants:
163-1 Catholic Charities of the Archdiocese of San Francisco, San Francisco, CA, $25,000. For San Francisco Phoenix Project. 1990.
163-2 Childrens Health Council of the Mid-Peninsula, Palo Alto, CA, $15,000. For Child Care Mentor Program. 1990.
163-3 Childrens Hospital of San Francisco, San Francisco, CA, $25,000. For Maternal and Infant Center. 1990.
163-4 Hastings Center, Western Office, San Francisco, CA, $25,000. For project on curriculum and certification in Bioethics. 1990.
163-5 International Bioethics Institute, San Francisco, CA, $10,000. For Hospital Ethics Committees Project. 1990.
163-6 Pacific Graduate School of Psychology, Palo Alto, CA, $20,000. For mental health services for clients with HIV. 1990.
163-7 Planned Parenthood of Alameda/San Francisco, San Francisco, CA, $10,000. For annual grant. 1990.
163-8 San Francisco Suicide Prevention, San Francisco, CA, $15,000. For Youth Line Program. 1990.
163-9 Teens Kick Off, San Francisco, CA, $15,000. For purchase of van. 1990.
163-10 United Way of the Bay Area, San Francisco, CA, $15,000. For grant shared with San Francisco Adult Day Health Network and On Lok Senior Health Service for Day Services. 1990.
163-11 Volunteers to San Francisco General Hospital Medical Center, San Francisco, CA, $10,000. For Activity Therapy Program for children. 1990.

164
Evelyn and Walter Haas, Jr. Fund ▼
One Lombard St., Suite 305
San Francisco 94111 (415) 398-3744
FAX: (415) 986-4779

Incorporated in 1953 in CA.
Donor(s): Walter A. Haas, Jr., Evelyn D. Haas.
Foundation type: Independent
Financial data (yr. ended 12/31/90): Assets, $44,927,515 (M); expenditures, $3,065,083; qualifying distributions, $2,879,995, including $2,739,130 for 176 grants (high: $1,000,000; low: $50; average: $5,000-$25,000).
Purpose and activities: Giving primarily for alternatives to institutional care for the elderly, selected programs serving the hungry and homeless, higher and other education, the Hispanic community, corporate social responsibility and business ethics, and community development.
Fields of interest: Aged, community development, homeless, hunger, housing, education, higher education, business education, hospitals, AIDS.
Types of support: Seed money, special projects, technical assistance, general purposes.
Limitations: Giving primarily in San Francisco and Alameda counties, CA. No support for private foundations or religious organizations. No grants to individuals, or for deficit financing, workshops,

conferences, publications, capital campaigns, films, or research.
Publications: Annual report (including application guidelines).
Application information: Grants in the areas of arts and education are initiated by the trustees. Application form not required.
 Initial approach: Letter (1 or 2 pages)
 Copies of proposal: 1
 Deadline(s): None
 Board meeting date(s): 3 times a year
 Final notification: Within 90 days
 Write: Ira Hirschfield, Pres.
Officers and Trustees:* Walter A. Haas, Jr.,* Chair.; Ira S. Hirschfield, Pres.; Evelyn D. Haas,* V.P.; Walter J. Haas, Secy.-Treas.
Advisory Trustees: Dyke Brown, Elizabeth Haas Eisenhardt, James C. Gaither, Robert D. Haas, Cecil F. Poole.
Number of staff: 1 full-time professional; 1 full-time support.
EIN: 946068932
Recent health grants:
164-1 California Advocates for Nursing Home Reform, San Francisco, CA, $10,000. For final payment of two-year grant for general support. 1990.
164-2 California Law Center on Long Term Care, San Francisco, CA, $15,000. For second-year support of Residential Care Facilities for Elderly Project which trains elder advocates on legal rights of board and care consumers, publishes consumer guide to residential care facilities and provides advocacy at local and state levels on board and care issues. 1990.
164-3 Catholic Charities of the Archdiocese of San Francisco, San Francisco, CA, $20,000. Toward start-up of Phoenix Project, demonstration residential treatment program serving low-income, pregnant, drug-addicted women and their children. 1990.
164-4 Center for Elderly Suicide Prevention and Grief Related Services, San Francisco, CA, $25,000. For first payment of two-year pledge toward position of peer volunteer recruiter who will recruit and train seniors to serve as peer counselors for crisis intervention, information and referral, and emotional support and counseling. 1990.
164-5 Childrens Hospital of San Francisco, San Francisco, CA, $10,000. For final payment of three-year pledge toward capital campaign for new Maternal and Infant Center and general support. 1990.
164-6 On Lok Senior Health Services, San Francisco, CA, $50,000. For fourth payment of five-year grant toward purchase and renovation of new facility for senior housing, adult day health care and day care center for intergenerational activities. 1990.
164-7 Self Help for the Elderly Foundation, San Francisco, CA, $10,500. For joint project with California Advocates for Nursing Home Reform to develop and operate model, consumer-oriented information and referral service for individuals seeking placement in residential care facilities. 1990.
164-8 Vesper Society Group, San Leandro, CA, $15,000. For project coordinator position to plan, design and test training program for operators of residential care facilities for elderly. 1990.

165
Crescent Porter Hale Foundation
220 Bush St., Suite 1069
San Francisco 94104   (415) 986-5177

Incorporated in 1961 in CA.
Donor(s): Elwyn C. Hale,‡ M. Eugenie Hale.‡
Foundation type: Independent
Financial data (yr. ended 12/31/90): Assets, $19,664,615 (M); expenditures, $1,162,263; qualifying distributions, $962,298, including $878,250 for 74 grants (high: $75,000; low: $1,000; average: $10,000).
Fields of interest: Catholic giving, education, higher education, education—building funds, education—minorities, AIDS, aged, youth.
Types of support: Special projects, equipment, capital campaigns, operating budgets, scholarship funds.
Limitations: Giving primarily in the San Francisco Bay Area, CA. No grants to individuals, or for research.
Publications: Application guidelines, program policy statement.
Application information: Application form not required.
 Initial approach: Letter of intent
 Deadline(s): Given after letter of intent is received
 Board meeting date(s): Apr., Sept., and Dec.
 Final notification: After board meeting
 Write: Ulla Davis, Consultant
Officers: L.E. Alford, Pres.; Thomas J. Mellon, Jr., V.P.; A.L. Ballard, Secy.-Treas.
Directors: Eugene E. Bleck, M.D., Joan Withers Dinner, Rev. Charles Dullea, S.J., Ephraim P. Engleman, M.D., Elfreda Hale, E. William Swanson.
Number of staff: 1 full-time professional; 1 part-time support.
EIN: 946093385

166
William H. Hannon Foundation
8055 West Manchester Blvd., No. 400
Playa del Rey 90293-7990

Established in 1982 in CA.
Donor(s): William Herbert Hannon.
Foundation type: Independent
Financial data (yr. ended 11/30/91): Assets, $6,092,664 (M); gifts received, $1,165,000; expenditures, $308,680; qualifying distributions, $281,448, including $264,819 for 81 grants (high: $10,000; low: $9).
Purpose and activities: Giving primarily for higher education; support also for churches and medical research and hospitals.
Fields of interest: Higher education, religion—Christian, medical research, hospitals.
Limitations: Giving primarily in the Playa del Ray, CA, area. No support for private foundations. No grants to individuals.
Application information:
 Initial approach: Letter
 Deadline(s): None
 Write: William H. Hannon, Pres.
Officers and Directors:* William Herbert Hannon,* Chair. and Pres.; Joseph E. Rawlinson, V.P.; J. Robert Vaughn,* V.P.; Kathleen Aikenhead,* Secy.-Treas.; Nancy M. Cunningham, Elaine S. Ewen, Patrick H. Hannon.

EIN: 953847664

167
The Hanover Foundation
c/o Rosenfeld Meyer & Susman
9601 Wilshire Blvd., Suite 444
Beverly Hills 90210

Established in 1983.
Donor(s): Ralph J. Shapiro, Shirley Shapiro, Kihi Foundation, Knoll International Holdings, Inc.
Foundation type: Independent
Financial data (yr. ended 01/31/92): Assets, $1,597,086 (M); gifts received, $401,750; expenditures, $566,064; qualifying distributions, $565,393, including $565,095 for 98 grants (high: $435,773; low: $72).
Fields of interest: Medical research, handicapped, arts, Jewish giving, museums.
Limitations: Giving primarily in Southern, CA, and New York, NY. No grants to individuals.
Application information: Application form not required.
 Deadline(s): None
Officers: Ralph J. Shapiro, Pres.; Peter W. Shapiro, V.P.; Shirley Shapiro, Secy.
EIN: 953887151

168
Harden Foundation ▼
P.O. Box 779
Salinas 93902-0779   (408) 442-3005
Application address: 17 East Gabilan St., Salinas, CA 93901

Established in 1963 in CA.
Donor(s): Eugene E. Harden,‡ Ercia E. Harden.‡
Foundation type: Independent
Financial data (yr. ended 02/28/91): Assets, $42,550,261 (M); expenditures, $2,154,923; qualifying distributions, $2,027,566, including $1,736,200 for 56 grants (high: $100,000; low: $1,000; average: $10,000-$50,000).
Purpose and activities: Support primarily for a hospital; giving also for a college, social services, and youth organizations.
Fields of interest: Hospitals, mental health, family planning, higher education, social services, child welfare, youth, aged, legal services, agriculture, animal welfare, museums.
Types of support: Operating budgets, special projects, general purposes, building funds, capital campaigns, matching funds, seed money, equipment, technical assistance.
Limitations: Giving limited to Monterey County, with emphasis on the Salinas Valley, CA, area. No support for sectarian religious programs or non-agricultural related educational programs.
Publications: Application guidelines, annual report (including application guidelines).
Application information: Application form required.
 Initial approach: Letter
 Copies of proposal: 1
 Deadline(s): May 1 and Nov. 1
 Board meeting date(s): June and Dec.
 Write: Andrew Church, Secy.
Officers and Directors:* Ralph L. Kokjer,* Pres. and Treas.; Andrew Church,* Secy.; Thomas Merrill, Patricia Tynan-Chapman.

Number of staff: 2 part-time professional; 2 full-time support.
EIN: 946098887

169
The Reed L. Harman and Nan H. Harman Foundation
1820 Via Visalia
Palos Verdes Estates 90274

Established in 1987.
Donor(s): Nan M. Harman, Reed L. Harman.
Foundation type: Independent
Financial data (yr. ended 12/31/90): Assets, $4,382,868 (M); expenditures, $219,201; qualifying distributions, $202,121, including $202,121 for grants (high: $56,000).
Fields of interest: Higher education, secondary education, handicapped, hospitals.
Limitations: No grants to individuals.
Application information: Contributes only to pre-selected organizations. Applications not accepted.
Officers: Nan M. Harman, Pres.; Reed L. Harman, Pres.
EIN: 330271109

170
Hedco Foundation ▼
c/o Fitzgerald, Abbott & Beardsley
1221 Broadway, 21st Fl.
Oakland 94612-1837

Incorporated in 1972 in CA.
Donor(s): Herrick Corp., Catalina Assocs.
Foundation type: Independent
Financial data (yr. ended 11/30/90): Assets, $7,640,046 (M); gifts received, $1,500,000; expenditures, $1,205,918; qualifying distributions, $1,193,673, including $1,193,673 for 24 grants (high: $469,167; low: $500; average: $1,000-$100,000).
Purpose and activities: Giving predominantly to qualified educational and health service institutions; support also for social services, arts and culture, and youth organizations.
Fields of interest: Higher education, health services, medical research, social services, youth, arts, cultural programs, music, theater, libraries.
Types of support: Building funds, equipment, land acquisition, matching funds, renovation projects.
Limitations: Giving primarily in CA. No grants to individuals, or for general support, operating budgets, endowment funds, scholarships, fellowships, special projects, research, publications, or conferences; no loans.
Application information: Application form not required.
  Initial approach: Proposal
  Copies of proposal: 1
  Deadline(s): None
  Board meeting date(s): Nov.
  Final notification: 3 to 4 months
  Write: Mary A. Goriup, Fdn. Mgr.
Officers and Directors:* Ester M. Dornsife,* Pres.; David H. Dornsife,* V.P.; Dorothy Jernstedt,* Secy.; Harold W. Dornsife,* C.F.O.; Laine Ainsworth, S.G. Herrick, James S. Little, William Picard, J.G. Ross.
Foundation Manager: Mary A. Goriup.
Number of staff: None.

EIN: 237259742

171
Helms Foundation, Inc.
25765 Quilla Rd.
P.O. Box 55827
Valencia 91355

Incorporated in 1946 in CA.
Donor(s): The Helms family, Helms Bakeries.
Foundation type: Independent
Financial data (yr. ended 06/30/91): Assets, $4,223,089 (M); expenditures, $404,988; qualifying distributions, $387,606, including $355,524 for 80 grants (high: $90,500; low: $100).
Purpose and activities: Support primarily for higher and other education, including scholarship funds and religious education; support also for health agencies and hospitals, cultural organizations, and youth and social service agencies.
Fields of interest: Education, theological education, health services, hospitals, cultural programs, youth, social services.
Limitations: No support for private foundations. No grants to individuals.
Application information: Contributes only to pre-selected organizations. Applications not accepted.
Officers and Trustees:* Peggy Helms Hurtig,* Pres.; Elizabeth Helms Adams,* V.P. and Secy.-Treas.; William D. Manuel, Mgr.; Stephen Helms Bell, John B. Gostovich, John T. Hastings, Jr., Frank J. Kanne, Jr.
EIN: 956091335

172
The Herbst Foundation, Inc. ▼
Three Embarcadero Ctr., 21st Fl.
San Francisco 94111   (415) 951-7508

Incorporated in 1961 in CA.
Donor(s): Herman H. Herbst,‡ Maurice H. Herbst.‡
Foundation type: Independent
Financial data (yr. ended 07/31/91): Assets, $40,751,748 (M); gifts received, $1,000; expenditures, $4,632,484; qualifying distributions, $2,295,962, including $2,267,414 for 86 grants (high: $556,414; low: $500; average: $20,000-$500,000).
Purpose and activities: Grants within the city and county of San Francisco for bricks and mortar projects in areas of educational facilities, recreation for the handicapped, civic improvement of existing city structures owned by public tax-exempt entities, and hospitals and health-care organizations; very small budget per year for broad purposes.
Fields of interest: Education—building funds, secondary education, child development, disadvantaged, handicapped, rehabilitation, hospitals, health, civic affairs.
Types of support: Building funds, renovation projects.
Limitations: Giving limited to the City and County of San Francisco, CA. No grants to individuals, or for endowment funds, scholarships, fellowships, research, or matching gifts; no loans.
Publications: Application guidelines.

Application information: Application form not required.
  Initial approach: Letter
  Copies of proposal: 1
  Deadline(s): None
  Board meeting date(s): Usually in Sept., Nov., Feb., and May
  Final notification: 30 days after board meeting
  Write: John T. Seigle, Pres.
Officers and Directors:* John T. Seigle,* Pres.; Ralph L. Preston,* V.P.; Haskell Titchell,* V.P.; Melvyn I. Mark,* Secy.; William D. Crawford,* C.F.O.; George D. Hart, Dennis B. King.
Number of staff: 1 full-time support; 2 part-time support.
EIN: 946061680

173
The George E. Hewitt Foundation for Medical Research
137 Jasmine Creek Dr.
Corona del Mar 92625-1422   (714) 760-0554

Established in 1982 in CA.
Donor(s): George E. Hewitt.
Foundation type: Operating
Financial data (yr. ended 12/31/91): Assets, $2,307,423 (M); gifts received, $201,875; expenditures, $109,917; qualifying distributions, $103,474, including $103,474 for 8 grants to individuals (high: $25,667; low: $1,057).
Purpose and activities: A private operating foundation; grants limited to medical research.
Fields of interest: Medical research.
Types of support: Grants to individuals.
Limitations: Giving primarily in CA.
Application information:
  Initial approach: Letter and resume
  Deadline(s): None
  Write: George E. Hewitt, Pres. and C.F.O.
Officers: George E. Hewitt, Pres. and C.F.O.; Roy B. Woolsey, Secy.
EIN: 953711123

174
Hewlett-Packard Company Philanthropic Grants
3000 Hanover St.
Palo Alto 94304   (415) 857-3053
Application address: P.O. Box 10301, Palo Alto, CA 94303-0890

Financial data (yr. ended 10/31/90): Total giving, $67,300,000, including $3,200,000 for grants, $4,900,000 for employee matching gifts and $59,200,000 for in-kind gifts.
Purpose and activities: The company seeks to be an economic, intellectual, cultural, and social asset in the technical and geographical areas in which it functions. The University Grants Program is the largest and contributes Hewlett-Packard equipment to teaching and research laboratories nationally for engineering, science, medicine, and business. The HP Community College Equipment Program serves institutions in areas of company facilities. The National Contributions Program, which is run at the headquarters in Palo Alto, contributes equipment and cash to national organizations in the areas of mathematics and science literacy, health and human services, affirmative actions, and arts and culture.

Contributions Committees in locations where Hewlett-Packard has major facilities make contributions to support local human services, arts and culture, and education, with focus on science and engineering in higher education. Employee matching gift programs include the Product-Gift Program and Funds-Matching Program.

Fields of interest: Business education, computer sciences, education—minorities, engineering, environment, handicapped, health, higher education, minorities, museums, performing arts, arts, science and technology, social services, Europe, Latin America, education, health services, higher education, hospitals.

Types of support: General purposes, equipment, special projects, employee matching gifts, in-kind gifts.

Limitations: Giving primarily in major operating locations in CA, CO, ID, MA, NJ, OR, PA, UT, and WA, and to national organizations; grants outside the U.S., in Europe and Latin America; equipment grants only in countries where Hewlett-Packard installation, repair, and maintenance is available. No support for religious or sectarian groups, discriminatory organizations, or sports ventures. No grants to individuals; or for conferences, seminars, meetings, workshops, general fund drives, capital improvement campaigns, scholarships, endowments, fundraising events, or annual appeals.

Publications: Corporate giving report (including application guidelines).

Application information: For University Equipment Grants, a proposal including description of institution, department, and faculty member(s) making the request, and need, use, and impact of equipment requested; Community College Equipment Grants applicants should indicate in proposal how the equipment requested will be supported and how it meets HP objectives. Application form not required.

Initial approach: University equipment requests are through HP sponsor; national grants through National Contribs. Mgr. in Palo Alto; community grants through nearest company facility; international requests to the HP subsidiary in the country of origin
Copies of proposal: 2
Deadline(s): July 1 for university equipment program which is annual
Board meeting date(s): Annually for university grants; other committees meet quarterly
Final notification: 2-4 weeks after committee meetings for non-university grants; early Jan. for university grants
Write: Rod Carlson, Dir. of Corp. Grants
Administrators: Roderick Carlson, Dir. of Corporate Grants; Tony Napolitan, Jr., Univ. Grants Mgr.; Nancy Thomas, National Contribs. Mgr.

Number of staff: 6 full-time professional; 3 full-time support; 3 part-time support.

175
George Hoag Family Foundation ▼
(Formerly Hoag Foundation)
2029 Century Park East, Suite 4392
Los Angeles 90067   (213) 683-6500

Incorporated in 1940 in CA.

Donor(s): George Grant Hoag,‡ Grace E. Hoag, George Grant Hoag II.
Foundation type: Independent
Financial data (yr. ended 12/31/90): Assets, $32,085,157 (M); expenditures, $2,501,918; qualifying distributions, $2,264,829, including $2,212,100 for 25 grants (high: $2,000,000; low: $2,000; average: $2,000-$20,000).
Purpose and activities: Major giving to a hospital; emphasis on medical research and health; support also for youth and cultural programs.
Fields of interest: Hospitals, medical research, youth, cultural programs, denominational giving.
Types of support: Capital campaigns.
Limitations: Giving limited to CA, with emphasis on Orange County. No support for government agencies, tax-supported projects, or sectarian or religious organizations for the benefit of their own members. No grants to individuals, or for deficit financing or normal operating expenses.
Application information: Application form required.
Initial approach: Letter not exceeding 2 pages
Copies of proposal: 9
Deadline(s): Mar. 31 and Sept. 30
Board meeting date(s): Apr. and Oct.
Final notification: Following meeting at which proposal is acted upon
Write: W. Dickerson Milliken, Secy.
Officers and Directors:* George Grant Hoag II,* Pres.; Patty Hoag,* V.P.; W. Dickerson Milliken,* Secy.; Del V. Werderman,* Treas.; Albert J. Auer, John L. Curci, Jr., Gwyn P. Parry, Melinda Hoag Smith.
EIN: 956006885
Recent health grants:
175-1 City of Hope, Los Angeles, CA, $60,000. 1990.
175-2 Hoag Memorial Hospital Presbyterian Foundation, Newport Beach, CA, $2,000,000. 1990.
175-3 Hoag Memorial Hospital Presbyterian Foundation, Newport Beach, CA, $10,000. For public relations fund. 1990.

176
The H. Leslie Hoffman and Elaine S. Hoffman Foundation
225 South Lake Ave., Suite 1150
Pasadena 91101   (818) 793-0043

Trust established in 1952 in CA.
Donor(s): H. Leslie Hoffman,‡ Elaine S. Hoffman.‡
Foundation type: Independent
Financial data (yr. ended 12/31/91): Assets, $15,861,623 (M); gifts received, $600,000; expenditures, $580,218; qualifying distributions, $449,172, including $384,025 for 33 grants (high: $83,200; low: $500).
Fields of interest: Higher education, secondary education, cancer, youth, music.
Types of support: General purposes.
Limitations: Giving primarily in the Los Angeles, CA, area. No grants to individuals.
Application information: Application form not required.
Initial approach: Letter
Copies of proposal: 1
Board meeting date(s): As required
Write: Eugene P. Carver

Trustees: Eugene P. Carver, Herbert S. Hazeltine, Jane H. Popovich.
EIN: 956048600

177
The Hofmann Foundation ▼
(Formerly K. H. Hofmann Foundation)
P.O. Box 907
Concord 94522   (510) 682-4830

Established in 1963 in CA.
Donor(s): Alta Mortgage Co., Hofmann Co., New Discovery, Inc., Kenneth H. Hofmann.
Foundation type: Company-sponsored
Financial data (yr. ended 07/31/91): Assets, $16,062,375 (M); gifts received, $5,381,000; expenditures, $5,728,387; qualifying distributions, $5,449,785, including $5,449,785 for 131 grants (high: $1,000,000; low: $125; average: $500-$10,000).
Purpose and activities: Support for 1)acquisition, preservation,and conservation of wildlife lands specifically the wetland marshlands that are sanctuaries to waterfowl and related wildlife; 2)education of the community to its needs to preserve wildlife without undermining related sports and recreation; 3)local educational institutions that demonstrate a profound need to challenge and improve the hearts and minds of its students; 4)local cultural organizations, especially those which demonstrate a desire to establish and create long lasting cultural programs and facilities; and 5)to a limited degree, local organizations which address the general citizens' welfare. Some support for local medical and health agencies, as well as nationally recognized medical research agencies.
Fields of interest: Conservation, wildlife, higher education, secondary education, elementary education, arts, cultural programs, community development, social services, youth, homeless, handicapped, Jewish welfare, Protestant giving, denominational giving, Catholic giving, health, health services, medical sciences, medical research.
Types of support: Building funds, research, scholarship funds, special projects, emergency funds, endowment funds, matching funds.
Limitations: Giving primarily in northern CA, with a concentration on Bay Area organizations; limited support for national organizations. No grants for general purposes, capital funding, routine operating expenses, or repayment of indebtedness.
Publications: Annual report (including application guidelines).
Application information: Application form not required.
Initial approach: Inquiry letter of no more than 3 pages
Copies of proposal: 1
Deadline(s): None
Board meeting date(s): Quarterly
Final notification: 3-4 months
Write: Nick Rossi
Officers: Kenneth H. Hofmann, Pres.; Lisa Ann Hofmann-Sechrest, V.P.; Albert T. Shaw, Secy.; Lori Hofmann, Treas.
Number of staff: 4
EIN: 946108897
Recent health grants:

177-1 Make-A-Wish Foundation, Stockton, CA, $26,000. 1991.
177-2 Mount Diablo Hospital Foundation, Concord, CA, $200,000. 1991.
177-3 Mount Diablo Hospital Foundation, Concord, CA, $33,000. 1991.
177-4 Mount Diablo Hospital Foundation, Concord, CA, $10,000. 1991.
177-5 Rehabilitation Services of Northern California, Concord, CA, $20,000. 1991.

178
Royal Barney Hogan Foundation
P.O. Box 193809
San Francisco 94119-3809

Established in 1977 in CA.
Donor(s): Riley P. Bechtel.
Foundation type: Independent
Financial data (yr. ended 12/31/91): Assets, $3,261,177 (M); expenditures, $208,979; qualifying distributions, $201,339, including $201,324 for 19 grants (high: $30,000; low: $1,000).
Fields of interest: Education, secondary education, hospitals, health services.
Types of support: Equipment, general purposes, operating budgets.
Limitations: Giving primarily in CA. No grants to individuals.
Application information: Contributes only to pre-selected organizations. Applications not accepted.
Officers and Directors:* Riley P. Bechtel,* Pres.; S.D. Bechtel, Jr.,* V.P.; Susan Peters Bechtel,* V.P.; Theodore J. Van Bebber, Secy.-Treas.; Lauren B. Dachs, Shana B. Johnstone.
EIN: 942416417

179
The Margaret W. and Herbert Hoover, Jr. Foundation
200 South Los Robles Ave., Suite 520
Pasadena 91101-2431   (818) 796-4014

Incorporated in 1968 in CA.
Donor(s): Herbert Hoover, Jr.,‡ Margaret W. Hoover.‡
Foundation type: Independent
Financial data (yr. ended 12/31/91): Assets, $13,645,751 (M); expenditures, $1,717,241; qualifying distributions, $1,655,665, including $1,569,823 for 27 grants (high: $300,000; low: $450; average: $5,000-$150,000).
Purpose and activities: Giving for medical and scientific research, with particular emphasis on sight and hearing.
Fields of interest: Medical research, science and technology.
Types of support: Continuing support, seed money, emergency funds, matching funds, research.
Limitations: No support for performing arts. No grants to individuals, or for endowment funds, building funds, renovation projects, operating budgets, annual campaigns, deficit financing, land acquisition, scholarships, or fellowships; no loans.
Publications: Application guidelines.
Application information: Application form not required.

Initial approach: Letter
Copies of proposal: 1
Deadline(s): Submit proposal when requested by the foundation; no set deadline
Board meeting date(s): As required
Final notification: 2 to 3 months
Write: Herbert Hoover III, Pres.
Officers and Trustees:* Herbert Hoover III,* Pres.; Margaret Hoover Brigham,* V.P. and Secy.; Joan Hoover Vowles,* V.P. and Treas.; Sally K. Bond,* V.P.; Robert J. Plourde,* V.P.
Number of staff: 1 part-time professional.
EIN: 952560832

180
Lucile Horton Howe and Mitchell B. Howe Foundation
180 South Lake Ave.
Pasadena 91101-2619   (818) 792-0514
Additional tel.: (213) 684-2240

Incorporated in 1964 in CA.
Donor(s): Mitchell B. Howe.‡
Foundation type: Independent
Financial data (yr. ended 12/31/91): Assets, $2,083,806 (M); expenditures, $179,110; qualifying distributions, $169,519, including $147,287 for 38 grants (high: $76,000; low: $100).
Purpose and activities: Primary areas of interest include child welfare and medical research, including youth and family services, drug abuse rehabilitation programs, hospitals, church support, and education, with emphasis on local organizations.
Fields of interest: Medical research, hospitals, youth, family services, child welfare, drug abuse, religion, education.
Types of support: Continuing support, research, operating budgets.
Limitations: Giving limited to Prox-Pasadena and San Gabriel Valley, CA. No grants to individuals.
Application information: Application form not required.
Initial approach: 1 to 2 page letter
Copies of proposal: 1
Deadline(s): Sept. 15
Board meeting date(s): Mar. and Oct. or Nov.
Write: Mitchell B. Howe, Jr., Pres.
Officers and Directors:* Lynn Howe Myers,* Chair.; Mitchell B. Howe, Jr.,* Pres. and Treas.; Martha Taylor,* Secy.
Number of staff: None.
EIN: 956081945

181
The Humboldt Area Foundation
P.O. Box 632
Eureka 95502   (707) 442-2993

Established in 1972 in CA by declaration of trust.
Donor(s): Vera P. Vietor,‡ Lynn A. Vietor.‡
Foundation type: Community
Financial data (yr. ended 12/31/90): Assets, $11,152,327 (M); gifts received, $1,825,002; expenditures, $675,042; qualifying distributions, $585,587, including $557,442 for 140 grants (high: $50,000; low: $100; average: $3,000-$4,000) and $28,145 for 45 grants to individuals (high: $1,000; low: $100; average: $300-$500).

Fields of interest: Cultural programs, safety, social services, health, recreation, education.
Types of support: Special projects, equipment, building funds, continuing support, matching funds, renovation projects, student aid.
Limitations: Giving limited to Humboldt, Del Norte, Siskiyou, and Trinity counties, CA. No grants to individuals (except from donor-designated funds); generally no grants for endowment funds, unspecified emergency purposes, deficit financing, or operating budgets.
Publications: Annual report, application guidelines, informational brochure (including application guidelines).
Application information: Application form required.
Initial approach: Letter or telephone
Copies of proposal: 8
Deadline(s): Feb. 1, May 1, Aug. 1, and Nov. 1
Board meeting date(s): Monthly; applications reviewed quarterly near Jan. 15, Apr. 15, July 15, and Oct. 15
Write: Maureen Hilbrink, Asst. Dir.
Officers and Governors:* Willis J. Tyson,* Chair.; Sam B. Merryman, Jr.,* Vice-Chair.; Edythe "Edy" Vaissade, Secy.; Esther Smith Holmes, Edward L. Nilsen, John R. Selvage, Mildred Westfall.
Trustees: Bank of America, First Interstate Bank, Wells Fargo Bank, N.A.
Number of staff: 1 full-time professional; 1 part-time professional; 1 part-time support.
EIN: 237310660

182
Audrey & Sydney Irmas Charitable Foundation
11835 Olympic Blvd., Suite 1160
Los Angeles 90064   (310) 477-7979

Established in 1986 in CA.
Donor(s): Sydney M. Irmas.
Foundation type: Independent
Financial data (yr. ended 12/31/90): Assets, $17,523,799 (M); gifts received, $335,000; expenditures, $801,688; qualifying distributions, $677,297, including $677,297 for 26 grants (high: $255,000; low: $250).
Purpose and activities: Support primarily for a Jewish welfare fund and housing programs; support also for a hospital, higher education, the arts, and drug abuse programs.
Fields of interest: Jewish welfare, housing, hospitals, higher education, cultural programs, drug abuse.
Types of support: General purposes.
Limitations: Giving primarily in Los Angeles, CA.
Application information: Application form not required.
Initial approach: Letter
Copies of proposal: 1
Deadline(s): None
Write: Robert J. Irmas, Mgr.
Officer: Robert J. Irmas, Mgr.
Directors: Audrey M. Irmas, Sydney M. Irmas.
Number of staff: 1 shared staff
EIN: 954030813

183
The James Irvine Foundation ▼
One Market Plaza
Spear Tower, Suite 1715
San Francisco 94105   (415) 777-2244
Southern CA office: 777 South Figueroa St.,
Suite 740, Los Angeles, CA 90017-5430; Tel:
(213)236-0552

Incorporated in 1937 in CA.
Donor(s): James Irvine.‡
Foundation type: Independent
Financial data (yr. ended 12/31/91): Assets,
$608,962,435 (M); expenditures, $26,272,772;
qualifying distributions, $27,660,377, including
$22,107,625 for grants (high: $1,500,000;
average: $25,000-$150,000) and $1,500,000 for
3 program-related investments.
Purpose and activities: Giving primarily for
comunnity service, cultural arts, health, higher
education, and youth.
Fields of interest: Community development, rural
development, public policy, volunteerism,
immigration, intercultural relations, cultural
programs, fine arts, dance, music, performing arts,
theater, health, AIDS, health services, higher
education, literacy, youth, child development,
child welfare, leadership development, social
services, family planning, family services,
minorities, homeless, women, housing.
Types of support: Seed money, equipment,
special projects, renovation projects, technical
assistance, program-related investments.
Limitations: Giving limited to CA. No support for
primary or secondary schools, agencies receiving
substantial government support, or sectarian
religious activities. No grants to individuals, or for
operating budgets, continuing support, annual
campaigns, deficit financing, endowment funds,
research, scholarships, publications, films,
conferences, or debt reduction.
Publications: Annual report (including application
guidelines), informational brochure (including
application guidelines), 990-PF.
Application information: Application form not
required.
   Initial approach: Letter and/or proposal
   Copies of proposal: 1
   Deadline(s): Proposals from institutions of
     higher education are due by Apr. 1; no other
     deadlines
   Board meeting date(s): Mar., June, Sept., Oct.,
     and Dec.
   Final notification: 3 to 6 months
   Write: Luz A. Vega, Dir. of Grants Prog.
Officers: Dennis A. Collins, Pres.; Larry R. Fies,
Treas. and Corp. Secy.
Directors: Myron Du Bain, Chair.; Samuel H.
Armacost, Angela G. Blackwell, Camilla C. Frost,
James C. Gaither, Walter B. Gerken, Roger W.
Heyns, Joan F. Lane, Donn B. Miller, Forrest N.
Shumway, Kathryn L. Wheeler, Edward Zapanta,
M.D.
Number of staff: 10 full-time professional; 10
full-time support; 2 part-time support.
EIN: 941236937
Recent health grants:
183-1 AIDS Foundation, San Diego, CA,
$120,000. To hire Associate Director and
Director of Multicultural Affairs. 1991.
183-2 AIDS Health Care Foundation,
Hollywood, CA, $24,500. To complete

comprehensive strategic planning process and
to develop strategies for implementation. 1991.
183-3 AIDS Project Los Angeles, Los Angeles,
CA, $162,000. For Treatment Education
Program for underserved communities, in
collaboration with Search Institute. 1991.
183-4 AIDS Service Providers Association of the
Bay Area, San Francisco, CA, $100,000.
Toward salaries of Membership Services
Coordinator and Executive Director. 1991.
183-5 Alameda Health Consortium, Oakland,
CA, $40,000. For expansion of On-Site
Medi-Cal Eligibility Project to increase
enrollment of Medi-Cal eligible children. 1991.
183-6 American Academy of Arts and Sciences,
Irvine, CA, $15,000. Toward Medical
Education and Health Services to Poor and
Medically Underinsured conference. 1991.
183-7 American College of Obstetricians and
Gynecologists, San Francisco, CA, $58,000.
Toward third year of Perinatal Access Project
during its transition to independent status.
1991.
183-8 American Friends Service Committee,
Philadelphia, PA, $40,000. For Farm Labor
Program to provide health education and
advocacy to Central Valley farmworkers. 1991.
183-9 Big Valley Medical Center Services,
Bieber, CA, $60,000. Toward construction of
expanded clinic facility. 1991.
183-10 Butte Valley-Tulelake Rural Health
Projects, Dorris, CA, $50,000. For remodeling
of new, expanded site for clinic in Dorris.
1991.
183-11 California Advocates for Pregnant
Women, San Diego, CA, $60,000. For network
of health and social service professionals in
area of perinatal substance abuse. 1991.
183-12 California Perinatal Association,
Campbell, CA, $50,000. To organize statewide
Maternal and Child Health Network. 1991.
183-13 Center for Community Health and
Well-Being, Sacramento, CA, $200,000. To
establish prenatal care clinic for
African-American women. 1991.
183-14 Center for Third World Organizing,
Oakland, CA, $25,000. For Get the Lead Out
of Our Children, community education
campaign of People United for Better Oakland
(PUEBLO). 1991.
183-15 Childrens Clinic, Long Beach, CA,
$55,000. To complete computerization of
clinic operations. 1991.
183-16 Childrens Dental Foundation, Long
Beach, CA, $50,000. To expand satellite clinic
at Boys and Girls Club of Long Beach. 1991.
183-17 Childrens Hospital of Los Angeles, Los
Angeles, CA, $100,000. To develop
Adolescent AIDS Consortium for Los Angeles
County. 1991.
183-18 Childrens Research Institute of California,
Sacramento, CA, $100,000. Toward Child
Health Policy Board's policy analysis, public
education and advocacy activities. 1991.
183-19 Desert Hospital Foundation, Palm
Springs, CA, $52,000. To establish Well-Baby
Clinic for low-income Coachella Valley
mothers and their infants. 1991.
183-20 Doctors Medical Center Foundation,
Modesto, CA, $20,000. For feasibility study on
developing mobile prenatal clinic to reach
underserved areas of Stanislaus County. 1991.

183-21 Family Counseling Service of West San
Gabriel Valley, San Gabriel, CA, $38,000.
Toward incorporating STEP child abuse
prevention project into agency operations.
1991.
183-22 Family Planning Centers of Greater Los
Angeles, South Gate, CA, $60,000. To start-up
pediatric care at South Gate clinic. 1991.
183-23 Happy Camp Health Services, Happy
Camp, CA, $19,000. For continuation of
Klamath River Interagency Service Providers
project (KRISP) which provides outreach,
counseling, support groups and classes to
at-risk families. 1991.
183-24 Health Access Foundation, San
Francisco, CA, $200,000. Toward health
policy analysis, public education and start-up
of Development Program and Media/Public
Relations Center by statewide coalition of
organizations promoting affordable health
care. 1991.
183-25 Health Services Research Foundation of
Northern California, Fresno, CA, $20,000. To
hire coordinator for Women to Women:
Bridging the Gap, mentoring program linking
African-American volunteers with at-risk
pregnant women. 1991.
183-26 Jewish Family and Childrens Services,
San Francisco, CA, $40,000. Toward 18 month
continuation of evaluation of Schools
Partnership Project, program providing schools
with mental health specialists to assess and
refer students with behavior problems. 1991.
183-27 Kairos House, San Francisco, CA,
$12,000. To expand pilot program of on-site
trainings on caregiver issues to three additional
community-based HIV organizations. 1991.
183-28 Kairos House, San Francisco, CA,
$12,000. Toward The Gathering: Grief, Loss
and Organizational Healing, symposium for
staff of AIDS, cancer and arts organizations
affected by terminal illness in their ranks. 1991.
183-29 Los Angeles Free Clinic, Los Angeles, CA,
$140,000. For start-up of Hollywood Health
Center. 1991.
183-30 Manos, Diocese of Oakland, Oakland,
CA, $100,000. For fourth-year renewal under
Foundation's Women's Economic
Development Initiative for Manos Home Care,
home health care cooperative for low-income
minority women. 1991.
183-31 March of Dimes Birth Defects
Foundation, White Plains, NY, $32,000.
Toward California Healthy Mothers, Healthy
Babies project to increase access to perinatal
care for low-income women. 1991.
183-32 Mercy Hospital Foundation, San Diego,
CA, $97,000. To improve ability of Mercy
Clinic to provide perinatal care to low-income
women. 1991.
183-33 Paradise Valley Hospital, National City,
CA, $153,000. For Healthy Beginnings,
perinatal substance-abuse prevention and
early intervention program. 1991.
183-34 Planned Parenthood Association of Santa
Clara County, San Jose, CA, $160,000. For
Cambodian Outreach Project, in collaboration
with Asian Americans for Community
Involvement. 1991.
183-35 Planned Parenthood Association of Santa
Clara County, San Jose, CA, $37,000. To
develop Cambodian Outreach and Education
Project, in collaboration with Asian Americans

for Community Involvement and Cambodian New Life Association. 1991.

183-36 Planned Parenthood of Humboldt County, Six Rivers, Eureka, CA, $100,000. To expand Eureka clinic facility, to be matched by individual donations. 1991.

183-37 Planned Parenthood-World Population Los Angeles, Los Angeles, CA, $180,000. For start-up of Promotores Voluntarios, outreach program for Latina women in East Los Angeles. 1991.

183-38 Poverello House, Fresno, CA, $30,000. To expand Holy Cross Clinic, which provides free medical and dental care to low-income families in San Joaquin Valley. 1991.

183-39 Salud Para la Gente Community Health Clinic, Watsonville, CA, $200,000. Toward renovation of clinic serving farmworkers and other low-income residents of Pajaro Valley. 1991.

183-40 San Francisco Hearing and Speech Center, San Francisco, CA, $20,000. To purchase equipment for auditory brainstem measurements. 1991.

183-41 San Francisco Suicide Prevention, San Francisco, CA, $10,000. For additional salary support to maintain AIDS Nightline which provides nighttime emotional support by telephone to people dealing with AIDS-related crises. 1991.

183-42 Seton Medical Center, Daly City, CA, $110,000. For start-up of Comprehensive Perinatal Services Program. 1991.

183-43 South Central Family Health Center, Los Angeles, CA, $150,000. For start-up of Comprehensive Perinatal Services Program and expansion of primary care services to low-income women and their children in South Central Los Angeles. 1991.

183-44 South El Monte Health Promotion Council, South El Monte, CA, $50,000. For Community Coordinator position. 1991.

183-45 Su Salud, Stockton, CA, $71,000. For salary of administrative assistant, office and consultation on long-range planning for organization providing health education to Hispanic community. 1991.

183-46 Sutter Solano Medical Center Foundation, Vallejo, CA, $120,000. Toward Great Beginnings, comprehensive perinatal services program for low-income women, particularly teenagers. 1991.

183-47 Twin Services, Berkeley, CA, $20,000. For core support of organization serving multiple-birth families. 1991.

183-48 United Way of Humboldt County, Eureka, CA, $49,000. To continue Mobile Medical Clinic, including hiring consultant to assist with federal certification as Rural Health Clinic qualified for cost-based reimbursement. 1991.

183-49 Valley Community Clinic, North Hollywood, CA, $50,000. To renovate clinic to expand prenatal services and add pediatric care. 1991.

183-50 Valley Presbyterian Hospital, Olmsted Memorial, Van Nuys, CA, $19,000. For joint planning study with Valley Community Clinic to explore feasibility of collaborative service model of prenatal, obstetrical and pediatric care. 1991.

183-51 Ventura County Rape Crisis Center, Camarillo, CA, $10,000. For consultant to

assist in creating three-year development plan. 1991.

183-52 Woodland Memorial Hospital Foundation, Woodland, CA, $70,000. To expand Prenatal Care for Low-Income Women of Yolo County program. 1991.

184
Irvine Health Foundation
18301 Von Karman Ave., Suite 440
Irvine 92715   (714) 253-2959

Established in 1985 in CA.
Donor(s): Irvine Medical Center.
Foundation type: Independent
Financial data (yr. ended 06/30/92): Assets, $19,919,137 (M); gifts received, $114,820; expenditures, $1,407,788; qualifying distributions, $1,371,044, including $1,068,631 for 26 grants (high: $200,000; low: $1,000).
Purpose and activities: Emphasis on community health care including support for basic and applied medical research, research on health care systems and programs, health promotion programs and clinics, including a senior care center and a drug abuse program; support also for educational therapy for learning-disabled children, and for prevention of child abuse.
Fields of interest: Health, medical research, health services, medical education, medical sciences, child development, child welfare.
Limitations: Giving limited to Orange County, CA. No support for religious organizations for religious purposes. No grants to individuals.
Publications: Multi-year report (including application guidelines).
Application information: Application form not required.
   Initial approach: Letter
   Copies of proposal: 1
   Deadline(s): None
   Board meeting date(s): Regularly
   Write: Edward B. Kacic, Exec. Dir.
Officers and Directors:* David G. Sills,* Chair.; John C. Gaffney,* Secy.; Timothy L. Strader,* Treas.; Edward B. Kacic,* Exec. Dir.; Carol A. Hoffman, Gary H. Hunt, Jack W. Peltason, Ph.D., Gerald B. Sinykin, M.D.
Number of staff: 1 full-time professional; 1 part-time professional; 1 part-time support.
EIN: 330141599

185
The William G. Irwin Charity Foundation
▼
711 Russ Bldg.
235 Montgomery St.
San Francisco 94104   (415) 362-6954

Trust established in 1919 in CA.
Donor(s): Fannie M. Irwin,‡ Helene Irwin Fagan.‡
Foundation type: Independent
Financial data (yr. ended 12/31/90): Assets, $54,040,589 (M); expenditures, $3,471,923; qualifying distributions, $3,079,207, including $2,966,354 for 45 grants (high: $350,000; low: $10,000; average: $5,000-$50,000).
Purpose and activities: Support for charitable uses, including medical research and other scientific uses designed to promote or improve the physical condition of humankind; support

also for hospitals, cultural programs, education, and social service agencies.
Fields of interest: Hospitals, medical research, cultural programs, social services, education, higher education.
Types of support: Building funds, equipment, general purposes, land acquisition, research.
Limitations: Giving limited to HI and CA.
Application information:
   Initial approach: Letter or proposal
   Deadline(s): Approximately 3 weeks prior to board meeting
   Board meeting date(s): Approximately every 2 months
   Write: Michael R. Gorman, Exec. Dir.
Officers and Trustees:* Jane Fagan Olds,* Pres.; William Lee Olds, Jr.,* V.P.; Michael R. Gorman, Exec. Dir.; Fred R. Grant, Merl McHenry, Jane Olds Ritchie.
Number of staff: 2 full-time professional.
EIN: 946069873
Recent health grants:

185-1 Childrens Hospital of San Francisco Foundation, San Francisco, CA, $300,000. For new Maternal and Infant Center. 1990.

185-2 Mount Saint Joseph-Saint Elizabeth, San Francisco, CA, $100,000. For capital campaign. 1990.

185-3 National Multiple Sclerosis Society, Oakland, CA, $15,000. For respite care program. 1990.

185-4 Saint Lukes Hospital Foundation, San Francisco, CA, $350,000. For modernization of Intensive Care Unit. 1990.

186
The Itakura Operating Trust
c/o Marie R. Cannella, C.P.A.
135 South Maryland Ave., Suite 100
Glendale 91205-1026

Established in 1982.
Donor(s): Keiichi Itakura.
Foundation type: Operating
Financial data (yr. ended 12/31/90): Assets, $1,926,796 (M); gifts received, $473,132; expenditures, $651,922; qualifying distributions, $651,922, including $567,608 for 1 grant.
Fields of interest: Medical research.
Limitations: Giving primarily in Los Angeles, CA.
Trustees: Keiichi Itakura, Yasuko Itakura, Warren F. Ryan.
EIN: 953694738

187
Ann Jackson Family Foundation
P.O. Box 5580
Santa Barbara 93150   (805) 969-2258

Established in 1978.
Donor(s): Ann G. Jackson, The Ann Jackson Family Charitable Trust.
Foundation type: Independent
Financial data (yr. ended 05/31/91): Assets, $12,445,265 (M); gifts received, $350,000; expenditures, $885,159; qualifying distributions, $807,996, including $803,900 for 44 grants (high: $460,000; low: $200).
Fields of interest: Secondary education, health, hospitals, handicapped, animal welfare, child welfare.

Types of support: General purposes, building funds, capital campaigns.
Limitations: Giving primarily in Santa Barbara, CA. No grants to individuals.
Application information:
Initial approach: Letter
Deadline(s): None
Write: Palmer G. Jackson, C.F.O.
Officers and Directors:* Flora J. Ramsey,* Pres.; Peter Jackson,* V.P.; Palmer G. Jackson,* C.F.O.
EIN: 953367511

188
J. W. and Ida M. Jameson Foundation
P.O. Box 397
Sierra Madre 91025   (818) 355-6973

Incorporated in 1955 in CA.
Donor(s): J.W. Jameson Corp., Ida M. Jameson.‡
Foundation type: Independent
Financial data (yr. ended 06/30/91): Assets, $906,581 (M); gifts received, $955,000; expenditures, $998,530; qualifying distributions, $990,903, including $975,000 for 76 grants (high: $65,000; low: $2,000).
Purpose and activities: Emphasis on higher education, including theological seminaries, hospitals and medical research, cultural programs, and youth agencies; grants also for Protestant and Catholic church support.
Fields of interest: Higher education, theological education, hospitals, medical research, health services, cultural programs, youth, Protestant giving, Catholic giving.
Types of support: Research, general purposes.
Limitations: Giving primarily in CA.
Application information: Application form required.
Copies of proposal: 1
Deadline(s): Jan. 31
Board meeting date(s): 2nd Saturday in Mar.
Write: Les M. Huhn, Pres.
Officers and Directors:* Les M. Huhn,* Pres.; William M. Croxton,* V.P. and Treas.; Pauline Vetrovec,* Secy.; Bill B. Betz, Fred L. Leydorf.
Number of staff: None.
EIN: 956031465

189
Jerome Foundation
7439 La Palma, No. 153
Buena Park 90620   (714) 522-6548

Incorporated in 1956 in CA.
Donor(s): Frank Jerome, members of the Jerome family, Baker Commodities, Inc.
Foundation type: Independent
Financial data (yr. ended 12/31/91): Assets, $2,941,214 (M); expenditures, $95,645; qualifying distributions, $87,304, including $83,050 for 22 grants (high: $55,131; low: $100).
Purpose and activities: Emphasis on medical research, services for handicapped children, the blind, hospitals, youth, health agencies, and the Jerome Foundation in the Philippines.
Fields of interest: Medical research, handicapped, hospitals, youth, health services.
Limitations: Giving primarily in Southern CA. No grants to individuals.
Publications: Annual report.

Application information: Application form not required.
Deadline(s): None
Write: Pat Perry
Officers: James M. Andreoli, Pres.; Edward S. Murakami, V.P.; Mitchell Ebright, Secy.-Treas.
Directors: Frank Jerome, Richard Jerome.
EIN: 956039063

190
George Frederick Jewett Foundation
The Russ Bldg.
235 Montgomery St., Suite 612
San Francisco 94104   (415) 421-1351

Trust established in 1957 in MA.
Donor(s): George Frederick Jewett.‡
Foundation type: Independent
Financial data (yr. ended 12/31/89): Assets, $23,556,015 (M); gifts received, $6,050; expenditures, $1,219,999; qualifying distributions, $1,131,093, including $952,597 for 135 grants (high: $50,000; low: $500; average: $1,000-$15,000).
Purpose and activities: To carry on the charitable interests of the donor to stimulate, encourage, and support activities of established, voluntary, nonprofit organizations which are of importance to human welfare. Interests include social welfare; arts and humanities, including the performing arts; conservation of natural resources; higher education; population planning; health care and medical research and services; religion and religious training; and public affairs.
Fields of interest: Social services, arts, humanities, performing arts, conservation, family planning, health services, medical research, religion, theological education, international affairs, higher education, education—minorities, public policy.
Types of support: General purposes, building funds, equipment, land acquisition, research, matching funds, special projects, operating budgets, seed money, technical assistance.
Limitations: Giving primarily in the Pacific Northwest, with emphasis on northern ID and eastern WA, particularly Spokane, and in San Francisco, CA. No grants to individuals, or for scholarships or fellowships; no loans. No emergency grants, except for disaster relief.
Publications: Annual report (including application guidelines).
Application information: Application form not required.
Initial approach: Letter
Copies of proposal: 1
Deadline(s): Feb. 15, May 15, Aug. 15, and Nov. 1
Board meeting date(s): Mar., June, Sept., and Dec. (for annual distributions)
Final notification: Annually, at the end of the year
Write: Theresa A. Mullen, Prog. Dir.
Officers and Trustees:* George F. Jewett, Jr.,* Chair.; Mary Jewett Gaiser,* Secy.; Margaret Jewett Greer, William Hershey Greer, Jr., Lucille McIntyre Jewett.
Number of staff: 1 full-time professional; 1 full-time support.
EIN: 046013832
Recent health grants:
190-1 Cancer Patient Care of Spokane County, Spokane, WA, $20,000. For Home Assessment

and Outreach Program for cancer patients in need of financial or emotional assistance. 1991.
190-2 Deaconess Hospital, Spokane, WA, $15,000. For services provided by Diabetes Education Center. 1991.
190-3 Meharry Medical College, Nashville, TN, $12,500. For unrestricted grant for medical and health education for black students. 1991.
190-4 National Medical Fellowships, NYC, NY, $10,000. For national effort to provide financial aid to deserving minority students pursuing medical education. 1991.
190-5 Pathfinder Fund, Boston, MA, $20,000. For unrestricted support of family planning programs and services sponsored worldwide. 1991.
190-6 Planned Parenthood of Spokane, Spokane, WA, $13,000. For unrestricted support of community programs in family planning. 1991.
190-7 Teens Kick Off, San Francisco, CA, $10,000. For general operating support for teenage alcohol and drug intervention program. 1991.

191
Walter S. Johnson Foundation ▼
525 Middlefield Rd., Suite 110
Menlo Park 94025   (415) 326-0485

Established in 1968 in CA.
Donor(s): Walter S. Johnson.‡
Foundation type: Independent
Financial data (yr. ended 12/31/91): Assets, $56,584,912 (M); expenditures, $2,819,767; qualifying distributions, $2,819,767, including $2,540,775 for 108 grants (high: $86,750; low: $500; average: $20,000-$150,000).
Purpose and activities: Giving primarily for public schools and social service agencies concerned with the quality of public education and the social family experiences of children between kindergarten and twelfth grade.
Fields of interest: Education, education—minorities, educational research, education—early childhood, elementary education, secondary education, family services, child welfare, child development, social services, family planning, drug abuse, youth.
Types of support: Operating budgets, seed money, special projects, research, technical assistance, general purposes.
Limitations: Giving primarily in Alameda, Contra Costa, San Francisco, San Mateo, and Santa Clara counties, CA, and Washoe County, NV. No support for religious organizations for sectarian purposes or for private schools. No grants to individuals, or for continuing support, annual campaigns, deficit financing, memorial funds, capital or endowment funds, matching gifts, scholarships, fellowships, publications, or conferences; no loans.
Publications: Annual report (including application guidelines).
Application information: Application form not required.
Initial approach: Telephone or letter
Copies of proposal: 2
Deadline(s): Proposals reviewed on an ongoing basis
Board meeting date(s): Jan., Apr., July, and Oct.
Final notification: 3 to 6 months

Write: Ms. Jean D. Parmelee, Exec. Dir.
Officers and Trustees:* Gloria Eddie,* Pres.; Sandra Bruckner,* 1st V.P.; Christopher Johnson,* 2nd V.P.; Hathily J. Winston,* Secy.; Elio L. Martin, Treas.; Jean D. Parmelee, Exec. Dir.; Gloria Jeneal Eddie, Mary Lanigar.
Number of staff: 2 full-time professional; 1 full-time support.
EIN: 237003595
Recent health grants:
191-1 California Neuropsychology Services, San Rafael, CA, $175,000. To begin field testing Talking Fingers, writing program for early elementary students (grades K-3), at Downer School in Richmond, whole language magnet school. 1990.
191-2 East Bay Activity Center, Oakland, CA, $200,000. For Personal Adjustment and Life Skills (PALS), comprehensive preventive mental health services on school site to schools and families, including training and consultation with teachers and parents on issues confronting particular children and on child development and classroom issues in general. 1990.
191-3 East Bay Perinatal Council, Oakland, CA, $150,000. For Birth to School project, comprehensive, geographically-focused effort to coordinate health and early childhood development services to families living in high-poverty area of West Oakland. 1990.
191-4 Education, Training and Research (ETR) Associates, Santa Cruz, CA, $108,023. For Contemporary Health Series, which enables junior high and high school teachers to address pregnancy, sexually transmitted disease, AIDS and substance abuse. 1990.
191-5 New Perspectives of Marin, Larkspur, CA, $180,000. For Substance Abuse Prevention and Recreational Therapy for students at risk of drug and alcohol addiction in East Palo Alto. 1990.
191-6 Planned Parenthood Association of Monterey County, Monterey, CA, $77,746. For two-part program, A Talk in Time..., to enhance self-esteem and to help children learn to make confident, competent decisions relating to sexuality and relationships in 4th through 6th grade classrooms in Alisal Elementary School District. 1990.

192
The Fletcher Jones Foundation ▼
(Formerly The Jones Foundation)
One Wilshire Bldg., Suite 1210
624 South Grand Ave.
Los Angeles 90017-9843   (213) 689-9292

Established in 1969 in CA.
Donor(s): Fletcher Jones.‡
Foundation type: Independent
Financial data (yr. ended 12/31/90): Assets, $84,742,629 (M); expenditures, $5,094,986; qualifying distributions, $4,457,875, including $4,334,964 for 62 grants (high: $500,000; low: $3,000; average: $3,000-$500,000).
Purpose and activities: Support primarily for private college universities, particularly those in CA (over 90 percent of available funds); some support for cultural programs, social services, health and hospitals, and organizations promoting law and justice and citizenship.

Fields of interest: Higher education, education—building funds, education, cultural programs, social services, law and justice, hospitals, citizenship.
Types of support: Building funds, equipment, professorships, special projects, endowment funds, scholarship funds, renovation projects.
Limitations: Giving primarily in CA. No support for secondary schools. No grants to individuals, or for operating funds, deficit financing, conferences, travel exhibits, surveys, or projects supported by government agencies.
Publications: Annual report (including application guidelines), financial statement, grants list.
Application information: Application form not required.
  Initial approach: Letter
  Copies of proposal: 1
  Deadline(s): One month prior to board meetings
  Board meeting date(s): Mar., May, Sept., and Nov.
  Final notification: 3 to 6 months
  Write: John W. Smythe, Exec. Dir.
Officers and Trustees:* John P. Pollock,* Pres.; Houston Flournoy,* V.P.; Jess C. Wilson, Jr.,* V.P.; Jack Pettker, Secy.; John W. Smythe, Treas. and Exec. Dir.; Robert F. Erburu, Parker S. Kennedy, Chauncey J. Medberry III, Rudy J. Munzer, Donald E. Nickelson, Dickinson C. Ross.
Number of staff: 1 part-time professional; 1 part-time support.
EIN: 237030155
Recent health grants:
192-1 Childrens Dental Foundation, Long Beach, CA, $10,000. For computer equipment. 1990.
192-2 Hospital of the Good Samaritan, Los Angeles, CA, $15,000. For Lumbar Motion Monitor. 1990.
192-3 John Tracy Clinic, Los Angeles, CA, $25,000. For computer equipment. 1990.
192-4 John Tracy Clinic, Los Angeles, CA, $10,000. For services for deaf children. 1990.
192-5 Mercy Healthcare Sacramento, Sacramento, CA, $50,000. To expand computer system. 1990.
192-6 Mercy Healthcare Sacramento, Sacramento, CA, $40,000. For computer equipment. 1990.
192-7 National Health Foundation, Los Angeles, CA, $10,000. For Lifestyle Choice exhibit. 1990.

193
Marcellus L. Joslyn Foundation
12857 Camino Emparrado
San Diego 92128   (619) 485-7938

Trust established in 1960 in CA.
Donor(s): Marcellus L. Joslyn.‡
Foundation type: Independent
Financial data (yr. ended 09/30/91): Assets, $5,008,655 (M); expenditures, $1,241,594; qualifying distributions, $1,238,030, including $1,191,250 for 44 grants (high: $200,000; low: $2,209).
Purpose and activities: Support for hospitals, higher education, senior citizens centers, and lawn bowling clubs.
Fields of interest: Hospitals, higher education, aged, recreation.
Types of support: Scholarship funds, continuing support, operating budgets.

Limitations: Giving primarily in Southern CA.
Publications: Informational brochure.
Application information: Contributes only to pre-selected organizations. Applications not accepted.
  Board meeting date(s): Semiannually in Apr. and Oct.
  Write: Remy L. Hudson, Chair.
Trustees: Remy L. Hudson, Chair.; John MacIntosh, Jean Mill.
Number of staff: None.
EIN: 952276744

194
The Henry J. Kaiser Family Foundation ▼
Quadrus
2400 Sand Hill Rd.
Menlo Park 94025   (415) 854-9400

Trust established in 1948 in CA.
Donor(s): Bess F. Kaiser,‡ Henry J. Kaiser,‡ Henry J. Kaiser, Jr.,‡ and others.
Foundation type: Independent
Financial data (yr. ended 12/31/91): Assets, $406,117,069 (M); expenditures, $25,160,779; qualifying distributions, $20,952,529, including $16,278,930 for 202 grants (high: $4,270,000; low: $911), $127,974 for employee matching gifts and $896,742 for foundation-administered programs.
Purpose and activities: Major share of resources devoted to programs in health and medicine; primary areas of interest include the disadvantaged, minorities, government, health, public policy, and Southern Africa.
Fields of interest: Health, health services, nutrition, drug abuse, AIDS, medical education, disadvantaged, minorities, aged, youth, Southern Africa, government, public policy.
Types of support: Special projects, research, seed money, fellowships, conferences and seminars, publications, matching funds, technical assistance.
Limitations: Giving limited to CA, for the California Grants Program only; and South Africa for the international grants program; other grants nationwide. No grants to individuals, or for construction, equipment, capital funds, general operating expenses, or indirect costs.
Publications: Biennial report, informational brochure (including application guidelines).
Application information: Application form not required.
  Initial approach: Letter
  Copies of proposal: 1
  Deadline(s): None
  Board meeting date(s): Mar., June, Sept., and Dec.
  Final notification: 3 to 6 months
  Write: Barbara H. Kehrer, V.P.
Officers and Trustees:* Daniel J. Evans,* Chair.; Drew E. Altman,* Pres.; Dennis F. Beatrice, V.P.; Hugh C. Burroughs, V.P.; Barbara H. Kehrer, V.P.; Bruce W. Madding, V.P.; Mark D. Smith, V.P.; Richard P. Cooley, Daniel J. Evans, Barbara C. Jordan, Kim J. Kaiser, Philip R. Lee, M.D., June E. Osborn, M.D., Richard Ravitch, William C. Richardson, Carlyn K. Stark, Marta Tienda, Bruce C. Vladeck.
Number of staff: 19 full-time professional; 11 full-time support; 3 part-time support.
EIN: 946064808
Recent health grants:

194-1 ABT Associates, Cambridge, MA, $400,000. For evaluation of foundation-funded demonstration program aimed at providing healthier meals in four low-income school districts and testing practicality of using new federal dietary guidelines in school lunch programs. 1991.

194-2 Advocacy Institute, DC, $25,000. For background paper on reducing tobacco consumption among inner-city minority populations. 1991.

194-3 Alameda Health Consortium, Oakland, CA, $20,000. To help low-income people apply for Medi-Cal eligibility. 1991.

194-4 Alan Guttmacher Institute, NYC, NY, $35,000. For assessment of Title X Federal Family Planning program. 1991.

194-5 Alpha Center for Health Planning, DC, $20,000. For conference sponsored by Public Health Service/Health Care Financing Administration to promote common understanding of primary care in today's health system and its potential for future. 1991.

194-6 Alta Bates-Herrick Foundation, Berkeley, CA, $20,000. For new primary care clinic for low-income residents. 1991.

194-7 American Academy of Arts and Sciences, Irvine, CA, $15,000. For symposium on ways to reconcile competing financial demands encountered by teaching hospitals that provide health care for poor as well as medical education. 1991.

194-8 American Cancer Society, Atlanta, GA, $300,000. For administration of nutrition demonstration projects in four low-income school districts. 1991.

194-9 American Enterprise Institute for Public Policy Research, DC, $35,000. To design formal demonstration of health and welfare programs for disadvantaged children that make use of home health workers who share similar cultural and socioeconomic backgrounds with target populations. 1991.

194-10 American Enterprise Institute for Public Policy Research, DC, $20,000. For discussion series on public health issues under jurisdiction of Human Resources subcommittee of House Ways and Means Committee. 1991.

194-11 American Public Health Association, DC, $10,000. To follow up 1969 study of health conditions in cross-section of American communities. 1991.

194-12 American Public Welfare Association, DC, $10,000. For conference of federal and state leaders on major issues in federal-state relationships in health. 1991.

194-13 Arkansas Department of Health, Little Rock, AR, $400,000. For five rural pregnancy prevention projects that will integrate teen pregnancy prevention into state's effort to develop school-based health programs. 1991.

194-14 Association of Academic Health Centers, DC, $60,000. To examine health promotion activities that academic health centers can target to poor. 1991.

194-15 Association of American Medical Colleges, DC, $15,000. To plan first national database on minority physicians. 1991.

194-16 Brandeis University, Bigel Institute, Waltham, MA, $1,400,000. To help states find solutions to special needs of elderly, mentally ill and disabled populations that are heavily dependent on state services. Grant shared with National Academy for State Health Policy in Portland, Maine. 1991.

194-17 California Association of Public Hospitals, Berkeley, CA, $10,000. For study of Right-to-Treatment Law. 1991.

194-18 California Medical Education and Research Foundation, San Francisco, CA, $76,000. For special issue of The Western Journal of Medicine on cross-cultural medicine. 1991.

194-19 Children Now, Oakland, CA, $70,000. To develop policy ensuring health care for all children in state. 1991.

194-20 Childrens Defense Fund, DC, $20,000. For background paper on maternal and child health. 1991.

194-21 Coalition for Elders Independence, Berkeley, CA, $50,000. To develop comprehensive services for frail elders in East Oakland. 1991.

194-22 Columbia University, National Center for Children in Poverty, NYC, NY, $65,000. For development of guide for using Medicaid-funded case management and Early and Periodic Screening, Diagnosis and Treatment (EPSDT) programs to improve health services for poor children. 1991.

194-23 Corporation for Supportive Housing, NYC, NY, $50,000. For first year of Bay Area program. Organization promotes creation of affordable housing that integrates medical, mental health and social services for special needs populations—chronically mentally ill and persons suffering from medical disabilities, including AIDS. 1991.

194-24 East Bay Activity Center, Oakland, CA, $10,000. For replication of prevention and life skills program in East Oakland schools. 1991.

194-25 East Side Union High School District, San Jose, CA, $300,000. For academic and support services for minority students in Andrew Hill High School Health Professions Magnet Program. 1991.

194-26 Food Research and Action Center, DC, $250,000. For Community Childhood Hunger Identification Project. 1991.

194-27 Free the Children Corporation, Memphis, TN, $725,000. For Project ACHIEVE, to prepare minority students for college studies leading to health professions. 1991.

194-28 George Washington University, DC, $300,000. For series of National Health Policy Forum sessions that will examine changing nature of federal health policymaking. 1991.

194-29 George Washington University, Intergovernmental Health Policy Project, DC, $300,000. For publication, State Health Notes. 1991.

194-30 Harvard University, Boston, MA, $15,000. To explore potential for Global AIDS and Health Consortium that would be coordinated by International AIDS Center and Harvard AIDS Institute. 1991.

194-31 Harvard University, School of Public Health and KRC Communications, Boston, MA, $22,000. For post-election poll of Pennsylvania voters to gauge importance of health care and national health insurance as issue in special Senate election. 1991.

194-32 Health Access, San Francisco, CA, $60,000. For survey of California voters on health-policy options and public awareness activities. 1991.

194-33 Institute for Health Policy Studies, San Francisco, CA, $33,000. For preparation of monograph on Foundation's health promotion program. 1991.

194-34 Institute for the Future, Menlo Park, CA, $55,000. To forecast state trends in California health care issues. 1991.

194-35 John F. Kennedy Library Foundation, Cambridge, MA, $10,000. For John F. Kennedy Public Leadership Year in Boston, leadership development program in health for college students. 1991.

194-36 Johns Hopkins University, Baltimore, MD, $1,300,000. For development and operation of Kaiser Family Foundation National Commission on the Future of Medicaid. 1991.

194-37 Johns Hopkins University, Baltimore, MD, $200,000. For Hopkins/Dunbar Health Professions program, which prepares minority students for college studies appropriate to health professions. 1991.

194-38 Klein Walker Associates, Cambridge, MA, $15,000. To examine feasibility of best state practices program in health issues. 1991.

194-39 Lewin and Associates, DC, $150,000. To evaluate role of federal research and demonstration waivers in development of health policy. 1991.

194-40 Lewin and Associates, DC, $25,000. For planning for national Center for Addiction and Substance Abuse, to be based at Columbia University and function as national clearinghouse for collection and dissemination of information and ideas in prevention and treatment of substance abuse. 1991.

194-41 Louis Harris and Associates, NYC, NY, $150,000. For surveys to gauge how middle-class Americans feel about health issues and need for health reform, and their concerns about health coverage. 1991.

194-42 Marin Institute for the Prevention of Alcohol and Other Drug Problems, San Rafael, CA, $10,194. For background paper on alcohol policy and poverty. 1991.

194-43 Mathematica Policy Research, Princeton, NJ, $74,929. For first year of planned multi-year evaluation of Project ACHIEVE in Memphis, program to prepare minority middle-school and high-school students for health professions. 1991.

194-44 NAACP Legal Defense and Educational Fund, NYC, NY, $20,000. For paper on using litigation to improve health of underserved groups. 1991.

194-45 National Academy for State Health Policy, Center for Health Policy Department, Portland, ME, $125,000. To expand use of managed care in Medicaid. 1991.

194-46 National Academy of Sciences, Institute of Medicine, DC, $20,000. For national forum on health of children and low-income families. 1991.

194-47 National Academy of Social Insurance, DC, $85,000. To develop framework for analyzing proposals for national health care reform. 1991.

194-48 National Association of Community Health Centers, DC, $19,575. To develop and evaluate models for managed care in community health centers. 1991.

194-49 National Governors Association, DC, $400,000. To establish State Public Health Leadership Recruitment Center. 1991.

194-50 National Governors Association, DC, $25,000. For project to identify most promising actions that states can take to improve their health care systems. 1991.

194-51 National Health Policy Forum, DC, $19,351. For forum on value of polls in public health policy. 1991.

194-52 National Progressive Primary Health Care Network, Johannesburg, South Africa, $230,000. To strengthen health systems reform in South Africa. 1991.

194-53 National Progressive Primary Health Care Network, Johannesburg, South Africa, $120,000. To establish national commission on primary health care. 1991.

194-54 National Progressive Primary Health Care Network, Johannesburg, South Africa, $40,000. For national conference on health policy in South Africa. 1991.

194-55 National Public Health and Hospital Institute, DC, $15,000. To explore how existing data, such as vital statistics and health status indicators, can be used to increase understanding of what primary care is actually available in given area. 1991.

194-56 New England Medical Center, Boston, MA, $4,500,000. For continued support of Functional Outcomes Program. 1991.

194-57 New Perspectives of Marin, Larkspur, CA, $20,000. To launch alcohol/drug prevention program for youth in East Palo Alto. 1991.

194-58 On Lok Senior Health Services, San Francisco, CA, $18,431. To provide technical assistance to Coalition for Elders Independence. 1991.

194-59 People-to-People Health Foundation, Project HOPE, Chevy Chase, MD, $124,000. For special issue of health policy journal, Health Affairs, on how federal health policy works. 1991.

194-60 Pierce County Alliance, Tacoma, WA, $398,967. To conduct and evaluate delivery of family planning and obstetrical services for substance-abusing women. 1991.

194-61 Pre-School Coordinating Council, Pittsburg, CA, $25,000. For health services for low-income children. 1991.

194-62 Public/Private Ventures, Philadelphia, PA, $100,000. To develop and test Fatherhood Curriculum for Young Unwed Fathers Demonstration Project. 1991.

194-63 Self Help for the Elderly, San Francisco, CA, $20,000. To provide information to consumers about residential care facilities for elderly. 1991.

194-64 State University of New York, Albany, NY, $125,000. For Commission on American State and Local Public Service. Commission will focus on improving management of state health agencies and expanding minority leadership in health agencies. 1991.

194-65 Task Force for Child Survival, Atlanta, GA, $35,000. For national effort to increase awareness of problem of low levels of immunization in children. 1991.

194-66 United Hospital Fund of New York, NYC, NY, $24,400. For conference on Medicaid and managed care. 1991.

194-67 University of California, Davis, CA, $13,800. For background paper on violence

prevention at University's Washington Center. 1991.

194-68 University of California, Institute for Health Policy Studies, San Francisco, CA, $43,000. To design evaluation of impact of recent California state government plan that shifts responsibility to counties for most health and mental health services for medically indigent. 1991.

194-69 University of California, Institute for Health Policy Studies, San Francisco, CA, $33,000. For preparation of monograph describing foundation's five-year experience with community-based and statewide health promotion programs to underserved communities. 1991.

194-70 University of California, School of Medicine, Los Angeles, CA, $141,020. For study of coronary revascularization procedures—coronary artery bypass graft surgery or angioplasty to determine what factors influenced whether disadvantaged patients who need such operations got them. 1991.

194-71 University of Chicago, Chicago, IL, $82,000. For continued support of National Leadership Training Program in Clinical Medical Ethics. 1991.

194-72 University of Southern California, Pacific Center for Health Policy and Ethics, Los Angeles, CA, $25,000. For statewide consortium that is developing model materials to inform patients of their rights when facing grave or terminal illness. 1991.

194-73 Urban Institute, DC, $525,000. For evaluation of publicly-funded family planning programs. 1991.

194-74 Urban Strategies Council, Oakland, CA, $27,800. To examine resources committed by Oakland area public agencies to children and families served by eight Oakland public schools. 1991.

194-75 West Oakland Health Center, Mental Health Department, Oakland, CA, $15,000. To launch mental health initiative at Oakland school. 1991.

194-76 World Institute on Disability, Oakland, CA, $25,000. To explore alternative approaches to health care for disabled. 1991.

194-77 Youth Law Center, San Francisco, CA, $30,000. To develop ways to ensure health services to foster children. 1991.

195
Alice & Julius Kantor Charitable Trust
809 North Bedford Dr.
Beverly Hills 90210   (213) 550-6778
Application address: 350 South Figueroa, Los Angeles, CA 90071

Established in 1977 in CA.
Foundation type: Independent
Financial data (yr. ended 12/31/91): Assets, $2,218,118 (M); expenditures, $91,745; qualifying distributions, $85,060, including $65,950 for 28 grants (high: $7,500; low: $250).
Fields of interest: Medical research, education, community funds.
Limitations: Giving primarily in the Los Angeles, CA, area. No grants to individuals, or for scholarships or awards; no loans.
Application information:

Initial approach: Letter
Deadline(s): Oct. 31
Write: Arnold Seidel, Trustee
Trustee: Arnold Seidel.
EIN: 953218378

196
Carl N. and Margaret M. Karcher Foundation
P.O. Box 61021
Anaheim 92803

Established in 1982 in CA.
Donor(s): Carl N. Karcher, Margaret M. Karcher.
Foundation type: Independent
Financial data (yr. ended 12/31/91): Assets, $358,005 (M); gifts received, $697,410; expenditures, $307,346; qualifying distributions, $307,346, including $302,500 for 15 grants (high: $75,000; low: $1,000).
Fields of interest: Higher education, Catholic giving, Catholic welfare, health, general charitable giving.
Types of support: Renovation projects, building funds, general purposes.
Limitations: No grants to individuals.
Application information: Application form required.
Initial approach: Letter
Copies of proposal: 1
Deadline(s): None
Board meeting date(s): Annually
Write: Eric C. Inglett, Dir.
Officers: Carl N. Karcher, Pres.; Margaret M. Karcher, V.P.
Directors: Eric C. Inglett, Rev. Jerome T. Karcher, Joseph Karcher, Andrew F. Puzder, Barbara Wall.
Number of staff: None.
EIN: 953793133

197
W. M. Keck Foundation ▼
555 South Flower St., Suite 3230
Los Angeles 90071   (213) 680-3833

Established in 1954 and incorporated in 1959 in DE; sole beneficiary of W.M. Keck Trust.
Donor(s): William M. Keck.‡
Foundation type: Independent
Financial data (yr. ended 12/31/91): Assets, $821,028,234 (M); expenditures, $49,837,128; qualifying distributions, $46,612,500, including $46,612,500 for 74 grants (high: $3,000,000; low: $45,000; average: $100,000-$1,000,000).
Purpose and activities: To strengthen studies and programs in the areas of earth science, involving the development of natural resources; engineering; medical research and education; and, to some extent, other sciences, liberal arts, and law/legal administration. Eligible institutions in these fields are accredited colleges and universities, medical schools, and major independent medical research institutions. Some consideration, limited to southern CA, is given to organizations and institutions in health care, arts and culture, civic and community services, and pre-collegiate education.
Fields of interest: Medical research, engineering, science and technology, physical sciences, biological sciences.

Types of support: Building funds, seed money, equipment, special projects, research, renovation projects, fellowships, scholarship funds, endowment funds, professorships.

Limitations: Giving nationally in all categories except arts and culture, civic and community, health care, and pre-collegiate education, which is restricted to Southern CA. No support for conduit organizations or to organizations that have not received tax-exempt ruling determination from the federal government and state of CA (if state exemption is applicable). No grants to individuals, or for routine expenses, general endowments, deficit reduction, fundraising events, dinners, mass mailings, conferences, seminars, publications, films, or public policy research.

Publications: Annual report (including application guidelines), informational brochure (including application guidelines).

Application information: Only those organizations invited to submit a proposal will receive an Applicant Information Form to be submitted with proposal. Application form required.

  Initial approach: Letter of inquiry; unsolicited proposals not accepted
  Copies of proposal: 1
  Deadline(s): Mar. 15 and Sept. 15 for complete proposal; initial letters accepted year-round
  Board meeting date(s): June and Dec.
  Final notification: June and Dec.
  Write: Sandra A. Glass for sciences, engineering, and liberal arts; Joan DuBois for medical research, medical education, law and legal administration, arts and culture, health care, pre-collegiate education, and community services

Officers and Directors:* Howard B. Keck,* Chair., Pres., and C.E.O.; Gregory R. Ryan, V.P. and Secy.; Robert A. Day,* V.P.; Walter B. Gerken,* V.P.; W.M. Keck II,* V.P.; Julian O. von Kalinowski,* V.P.; Dorothy A. Harris, Treas.; Lew Allen, Jr., Norman Barker, Jr., Marsh A. Cooper, Naurice G. Cummings, Howard M. Day, Tammis M. Day, Theodore J. Day, Bob Rawls Dorsey, Thomas P. Ford, Erin A. Keck, Howard B. Keck, Jr., John E. Kolb, Max R. Lents, James P. Lower, Kerry K. Mott, Simon Ramo, Arthur M. Smith, Jr., David A. Thomas, C. William Verity, Jr., Thomas R. Wilcox.

Number of staff: 3 full-time professional; 8 full-time support.

EIN: 956092354

Recent health grants:

197-1 Duke University Medical Center, Durham, NC, $3,000,000. To create Center for Interdisciplinary Cell Science. 1991.

197-2 Five Acres, Altadena, CA, $250,000. For construction of new special education center. 1991.

197-3 John Tracy Clinic, Los Angeles, CA, $70,000. For children's hearing tests. 1991.

197-4 Johns Hopkins University, School of Medicine, Baltimore, MD, $2,000,000. To establish Center for Study of the Special Senses. 1991.

197-5 Mayo Foundation, Rochester, MN, $500,000. For program to train physicians in molecular biophysics. 1991.

197-6 Neurosciences Research Foundation, NYC, NY, $600,000. For fellowships in program of theoretical neuroscience. 1991.

197-7 University of Minnesota, Minneapolis, MN, $875,000. For Center for Magnetic Resonance Research. 1991.

197-8 Whitehead Institute for Biomedical Research, Cambridge, MA, $1,250,000. For Whitehead Institute Fellows Program. 1991.

198
William M. Keck, Jr. Foundation
12575 Beatrice St.
Los Angeles 90066-7001   (213) 578-5900

Incorporated in 1958 in DE.
Donor(s): William M. Keck, Jr.
Foundation type: Independent
Financial data (yr. ended 12/31/91): Assets, $12,507,011 (M); gifts received, $175,000; expenditures, $581,323; qualifying distributions, $535,831, including $519,500 for 14 grants (high: $125,000; low: $5,000).
Fields of interest: Higher education, secondary education, hospitals, cultural programs, religion—Christian.
Limitations: No grants to individuals.
Publications: 990-PF.
Application information: Application form not required.
  Initial approach: Proposal
  Copies of proposal: 1
  Deadline(s): Nov.
  Board meeting date(s): Mid-Dec.
  Write: Carl D. Hasting, Secy.
Officers and Directors:* William M. Keck II,* Pres.; Carl D. Hastings,* V.P. and Secy.-Treas.; Susan Quinn Keck.
Number of staff: 1 part-time professional; 10 part-time support.
EIN: 136097874

199
A. H. Kerr Foundation
15216 Burbank Blvd., Suite 200
Van Nuys 91411   (818) 909-9337

Incorporated in 1945 in CA.
Donor(s): Ruth Kerr.‡
Foundation type: Independent
Financial data (yr. ended 12/31/91): Assets, $6,790,030 (M); expenditures, $532,567; qualifying distributions, $364,703, including $364,703 for 40 grants (high: $89,221; low: $150; average: $150-$5,000).
Purpose and activities: Giving primarily for higher education in California and for church support and religious associations, including foreign missions. Support also for hospitals, health agencies, and social services.
Fields of interest: Higher education, religion, religion—missionary programs, hospitals, health services, social services.
Types of support: Operating budgets, continuing support, annual campaigns, emergency funds, building funds, equipment, land acquisition, publications, special projects, capital campaigns.
Limitations: No grants to individuals, or for seed money, deficit financing, or demonstration projects; no loans.
Publications: Program policy statement, application guidelines.
Application information: Application form not required.

  Initial approach: Proposal
  Copies of proposal: 1
  Deadline(s): None
  Board meeting date(s): Apr. and Oct.
  Final notification: Several months to 2 years
  Write: William A. Kerr, V.P.
Officers and Directors:* Alexander H. Kerr,* Pres.; William A. Kerr,* V.P. and Treas.; Ruth K. O'Dell,* Secy.
Number of staff: None.
EIN: 956085982

200
The Karl Kirchgessner Foundation
c/o Greenberg, Glusker, Fields, Claman & Machtinger
1900 Ave. of the Stars, Suite 2100
Los Angeles 90067   (213) 553-3610

Established in 1977 in CA.
Donor(s): Karl Kramer,‡ Nina Kramer.‡
Foundation type: Independent
Financial data (yr. ended 06/30/91): Assets, $10,206,013 (M); gifts received, $463,180; expenditures, $889,066; qualifying distributions, $796,629, including $744,699 for 22 grants (high: $180,000; low: $4,500; average: $10,000-$50,000).
Purpose and activities: "For the advancement of medical research and for the provision of medical and clinical services to disadvantaged persons, particularly the elderly, the young and handicapped." Applicants should be involved with research and/or clinical programs connected with eyesight, eye care, or helping the blind and partially-sighted to be more self-sufficient.
Fields of interest: Medical research, handicapped, youth, aged.
Types of support: Research, continuing support, endowment funds, equipment, general purposes, matching funds, operating budgets, professorships, publications, scholarship funds, seed money, special projects, technical assistance.
Limitations: Giving limited to the Southern CA area; geographical restriction may be broadened in the future. No grants to individuals, or for fundraising campaigns.
Publications: Informational brochure, application guidelines.
Application information: Application form not required.
  Initial approach: Brief letter of intent
  Copies of proposal: 1
  Deadline(s): Jan. 1 for preliminary applications
  Board meeting date(s): Grants made once a year, generally on or about June 30
  Final notification: Before June 30
  Write: Martin H. Webster, Pres.
Officers and Directors:* Martin H. Webster,* Pres.; Amelia Louise Mills,* V.P.; Lewis Whitney,* Secy.; Karl Kramer, Jr., C.F.O.; Rev. Patrick Cahalan, Jr.
Number of staff: None.
EIN: 953439716

201
George Konheim Family Foundation
9100 Wilshire Blvd., Suite 404
Beverly Hills 90212

Established in 1982 in CA.

Donor(s): George Konheim.
Foundation type: Independent
Financial data (yr. ended 06/30/91): Assets, $1,167,091 (M); gifts received, $254,000; expenditures, $310,876; qualifying distributions, $307,976, including $307,966 for 51 grants (high: $61,303; low: $40).
Fields of interest: Jewish welfare, Jewish giving, hospitals, health associations, family services, general charitable giving.
Limitations: No grants to individuals.
Application information: Contributes only to pre-selected organizations. Applications not accepted.
Trustees: Bruce Konheim, Eva Konheim, George Konheim, Lyn Konheim.
EIN: 953759426

202
Koret Foundation ▼
33 New Montgomery St., Suite 1090
San Francisco 94105-4509   (415) 882-7740
FAX: (415)882-7775

Established in 1966 in CA.
Donor(s): Joseph Koret,‡ Stephanie Koret.‡
Foundation type: Independent
Financial data (yr. ended 12/31/91): Assets, $192,544,674 (M); gifts received, $19,710; expenditures, $14,809,601; qualifying distributions, $14,809,601, including $13,641,282 for 350 grants (high: $2,220,000; low: $1,000).
Purpose and activities: Seeks to alleviate suffering and misfortune, build community, and enhance human life in the Jewish and general communities of the San Francisco Bay Area and of Israel.
Fields of interest: Higher education, social services, Jewish giving, aged, Israel, homeless, hunger, arts, performing arts, youth, AIDS.
Types of support: Operating budgets, continuing support, special projects, building funds, general purposes, consulting services, renovation projects, seed money.
Limitations: Giving limited to the Bay Area counties of San Francisco, Alameda, Contra Costa, Marin, Santa Clara, and San Mateo, CA, and Israel. No support for private foundations, or veterans', fraternal, military, religious, or sectarian organizations whose principal activity is for the benefit of their own membership. No grants to individuals, or for general fundraising campaigns, scholarships, endowment funds, equipment funds, deficit financing, or emergency funds; no loans.
Publications: Application guidelines, annual report (including application guidelines).
Application information: Consult guidelines for application deadlines. Application form required.
  Initial approach: Letter of inquiry
  Copies of proposal: 1
  Board meeting date(s): 5 times per year
  Final notification: 2 to 4 months
  Write: Michael A. Papo, Exec. Dir.
Officers and Directors:* Susan Koret, Chair.; Eugene L. Friend, Pres.; Michael A. Papo, C.E.O. and Exec. Dir.; Jack R. Curley, Treas.; Richard C. Blum, William K. Coblentz, Richard L. Greene, Stanley Herzstein, Melvin M. Swig, Thaddeus N. Taube.

Number of staff: 8 full-time professional; 4 full-time support; 1 part-time support.
EIN: 941624987
Recent health grants:
202-1 Alameda County Health Care Services Agency, Oakland, CA, $68,500. For housing coordinator position in Oakland homeless families program. 1990.
202-2 Catholic Charities of San Francisco County, San Francisco, CA, $50,000. For capital support of San Francisco Phoenix Project, residential rehabilitation program for pregnant, drug-dependent women. 1990.
202-3 Episcopal Community Services of San Francisco, Episcopal Sanctuary, San Francisco, CA, $50,000. For day treatment program for homeless, mentally ill women. 1990.
202-4 Jewish Vocational and Career Counseling, San Francisco, CA, $54,500. For vocational English and skills program for newly-arrived Soviet refugees in fields of engineering, accounting and health services. 1990.
202-5 Over Sixty Health Center, Coalition for Elders Independence, Oakland, CA, $27,500. For development of On Lok replication in Oakland. 1990.
202-6 San Francisco Suicide Prevention, San Francisco, CA, $15,000. For general operating support to assist start-up of Center for Elderly Suicide Prevention and Grief-Related Services. 1990.
202-7 San Jose Urban Ministry, San Jose, CA, $23,000. To hire caseworker for Julian Street Inn, emergency shelter and drop-in center for mentally ill, homeless individuals. 1990.
202-8 Youth Advocates, San Francisco, CA, $60,000. Toward expansion of Family Reunification Counseling Unit and Teen Peer HIV Program. 1990.

203
Arseny & Olga Kovshar Private Charitable Memorial Foundation
693 Sutter St., 6th Fl.
San Francisco 94102-1023

Established in 1983 in CA.
Foundation type: Independent
Financial data (yr. ended 04/30/91): Assets, $4,988,230 (M); expenditures, $598,066; qualifying distributions, $247,769, including $223,300 for 26 grants (high: $105,000; low: $5).
Fields of interest: Cancer, Jewish giving, general charitable giving.
Limitations: Giving primarily in the San Francisco Bay Area, CA. No grants to individuals.
Application information:
  Initial approach: Proposal
  Deadline(s): None
  Write: Alexander Anolik, Trustee
Trustee: Alexander Anolik.
EIN: 942947932

204
John & Maria Laffin Trust
c/o Wells Fargo Bank, N.A.
P.O. Box 63954, MAC 0103-179
San Francisco 94163

Foundation type: Independent

Financial data (yr. ended 12/31/91): Assets, $4,237,178 (M); expenditures, $357,171; qualifying distributions, $254,119, including $237,971 for grants.
Fields of interest: Medical research, higher education, animal welfare, AIDS, child welfare.
Limitations: Giving primarily in CA. No grants to individuals.
Application information: Contributes only to pre-selected organizations. Applications not accepted.
Trustee: Wells Fargo Bank, N.A.
EIN: 946609731

205
The Ruth Lane Charitable Foundation
c/o James W. Cowley, Esq.
701 B St., Suite 2100
San Diego 92101-8197

Established in 1983 in FL.
Donor(s): Ruth Lane.‡
Foundation type: Independent
Financial data (yr. ended 12/31/90): Assets, $2,955,694 (M); gifts received, $2,273,067; expenditures, $677,462; qualifying distributions, $576,318, including $60,000 for 10 grants (high: $10,000; low: $5,000).
Fields of interest: Social services, youth, handicapped, cancer, recreation.
Limitations: Giving primarily in the Southern CA, area. No grants to individuals.
Application information: Contributes only to pre-selected organizations. Applications not accepted.
Directors: James M. Cowley, David L. Mulliken.
EIN: 953850868

206
Stanley S. Langendorf Foundation
c/o Pat Grier & Assocs.
1674 University Ave.
Berkeley 94703   (415) 649-1300

Established in 1982 in CA.
Donor(s): Stanley S. Langendorf.‡
Foundation type: Independent
Financial data (yr. ended 12/31/90): Assets, $9,901,379 (M); expenditures, $637,851; qualifying distributions, $506,615, including $492,644 for 36 grants (high: $75,000; low: $1,000).
Purpose and activities: Annual grants for eight specified beneficiaries; additional support for education, youth, social service agencies, and Jewish giving.
Fields of interest: Education, youth, family services, social services, aged, disadvantaged, Jewish giving, AIDS, health services, arts.
Types of support: Special projects.
Limitations: Giving primarily in CA. No grants to individuals.
Publications: Application guidelines, 990-PF.
Application information: Application form not required.
  Initial approach: Letter
  Copies of proposal: 1
  Deadline(s): None
  Board meeting date(s): Quarterly
  Write: Patricia Grier, Mgr.

Officers and Trustees:* Richard J. Guggenhime,* Pres.; Ann Wagner,* Secy.; Charles H. Clifford,* C.F.O.; Patricia Grier,* Mgr.
EIN: 942861512

207
The Norman Lear Foundation
1999 Ave. of the Stars
Los Angeles 90067 (213) 553-3636

Established in 1986 in CA.
Donor(s): Norman Lear.
Foundation type: Independent
Financial data (yr. ended 11/30/90): Assets, $887,118 (M); expenditures, $419,849; qualifying distributions, $419,849, including $419,700 for 63 grants (high: $100,000; low: $200).
Purpose and activities: Giving primarily to promote health; support also for the arts, citizenship and public policy, business education, Jewish welfare, women, and conservation.
Fields of interest: Health, arts, citizenship, public policy, business education, Jewish welfare, women, conservation.
Limitations: No grants to individuals.
Application information: Contributes only to pre-selected organizations. Applications not accepted.
   Write: Betsy Kenny, Secy.
Officers and Trustees:* Norman Lear,* Pres.; Lyn Lear,* V.P.; Betsy Kenny,* Secy.; Murray Neidorf,* Treas.
Number of staff: 2 part-time support.
EIN: 954036197

208
Thomas and Dorothy Leavey Foundation ▼
4680 Wilshire Blvd.
Los Angeles 90010 (213) 930-4252

Trust established in 1952 in CA.
Donor(s): Thomas E. Leavey,‡ Dorothy E. Leavey.
Foundation type: Independent
Financial data (yr. ended 12/31/90): Assets, $134,056,744 (M); expenditures, $7,905,785; qualifying distributions, $7,232,040, including $6,958,168 for 67 grants (high: $1,000,000; low: $1,000; average: $5,000-$100,000) and $230,568 for 83 grants to individuals.
Purpose and activities: Giving primarily for hospitals, medical research, higher and secondary education, and Catholic church groups; provides scholarships to children of employees of Farmers Group, Inc.
Fields of interest: Hospitals, medical research, higher education, secondary education, Catholic giving.
Types of support: Employee-related scholarships, general purposes.
Limitations: Giving primarily in Southern CA.
Application information:
   Initial approach: Letter
   Copies of proposal: 1
   Deadline(s): None
   Board meeting date(s): As required
   Write: J. Thomas McCarthy, Trustee
Trustees: J. Thomas McCarthy, Chair.; L. Castruccio, Dorothy E. Leavey, Joseph James Leavey, Kathleen Leavey McCarthy, Kenneth Tyler.
Number of staff: None.

EIN: 956060162
Recent health grants:
208-1 Arthritis Foundation, Los Angeles, CA, $100,000. For research. 1990.
208-2 California Hospital Medical Center, Los Angeles, CA, $1,000,000. For health education and medical research. 1990.
208-3 Childrens Hospital of Los Angeles, Los Angeles, CA, $20,000. For unrestricted grant. 1990.
208-4 Five Acres, Altadena, CA, $10,000. For camp for disadvantaged children. 1990.
208-5 Friday Night Live, Downey, CA, $25,000. For Los Angeles school drug program. 1990.
208-6 Hospital of the Good Samaritan, Los Angeles, CA, $20,000. For physical therapy department. 1990.
208-7 Hospitaller Foundation of California, Los Angeles, CA, $25,000. For hospital care for nursing home residents. 1990.
208-8 Los Angeles Poison Center, Los Angeles, CA, $10,000. For general support. 1990.
208-9 Saint Annes Maternity Home, Los Angeles, CA, $50,000. For building campaign. 1990.
208-10 Saint Francis Medical Center, Lynwood, CA, $173,000. To train nurses' aids. 1990.
208-11 Saint Johns Hospital and Health Center, Santa Monica, CA, $20,000. For general support. 1990.
208-12 Saint Vincent Medical Center, Los Angeles, CA, $20,000. For capital campaign. 1990.
208-13 Santa Monica Hospital Medical Center, Orthopedic Department, Santa Monica, CA, $15,000. 1990.

209
Bertha Lebus Trust
c/o Trust Services of America
700 Wilshire Blvd., Suite 420
Los Angeles 90017

Foundation type: Independent
Financial data (yr. ended 12/31/90): Assets, $2,728,948 (M); expenditures, $164,607; qualifying distributions, $138,500, including $128,000 for 17 grants (high: $30,000; low: $2,000).
Purpose and activities: Grants primarily for colleges and universities; some support also for hospitals.
Fields of interest: Higher education, hospitals.
Limitations: No grants to individuals.
Application information: Contributes only to pre-selected organizations. Applications not accepted.
   Write: M.D. Blood
Trustee: Trust Services of America, Inc.
EIN: 956022085

210
The LEF Foundation
1095 Lodi Ln.
St. Helena 94574 (707) 963-9591

Established in 1985 in CA.
Donor(s): Lyda Ebert.‡
Foundation type: Independent
Financial data (yr. ended 06/30/91): Assets, $7,686,492 (M); gifts received, $1,028,064; expenditures, $438,727; qualifying distributions,

$403,945, including $297,200 for 74 grants (high: $20,000; low: $500; average: $5,000-$15,000).
Purpose and activities: Support for intersection of art and environment; giving also for AIDS community care issues.
Fields of interest: Cultural programs, architecture, arts, AIDS.
Types of support: Publications, special projects.
Limitations: Giving primarily in northern CA, New England, and proactive in other states.
Publications: Application guidelines, 990-PF, grants list, multi-year report.
Application information: Application form required.
   Initial approach: Letter or telephone
   Copies of proposal: 7
   Deadline(s): Varies; contact foundation for dates
   Board meeting date(s): Varies
   Write: Marina Drummer, Exec. Dir.
Officers: Marion E. Greene, Pres.; Dean Kuth, V.P.; Lyda Ebert Kuth, Secy. and C.F.O.
Number of staff: 1 full-time professional; 1 part-time support.
EIN: 680070194

211
Leonardt Foundation
1801 Ave. of the Stars, Suite 811
Los Angeles 90067 (213) 556-3932

Incorporated in 1953 in CA.
Donor(s): Amy L. Powell, Clara L. McGinnis.
Foundation type: Independent
Financial data (yr. ended 12/31/91): Assets, $3,195,186 (M); expenditures, $215,070; qualifying distributions, $188,716, including $188,716 for 84 grants (high: $25,000; low: $100).
Purpose and activities: Grants primarily for Roman Catholic church support and higher education; support also for secondary education, hospitals, youth, social services, and health agencies.
Fields of interest: Catholic giving, Catholic welfare, religious schools, higher education, secondary education, hospitals, youth, social services, health services.
Types of support: Building funds, general purposes.
Limitations: Giving primarily in CA. No grants to individuals.
Application information: Contributes only to pre-selected organizations. Applications not accepted.
Officers and Directors:* Felix S. McGinnis, Jr.,* Pres.; Carl L. McGinnis,* V.P. and Secy.-Treas.; Barbara J. McGinnis, J. Frank McGinnis.
EIN: 956045256

212
Levi Strauss Foundation ▼
1155 Battery St.
San Francisco 94111 (415) 544-2194

Incorporated in 1941 in CA.
Donor(s): Levi Strauss & Co.
Foundation type: Company-sponsored
Financial data (yr. ended 12/31/90): Assets, $38,781,037 (M); gifts received, $9,625,000; expenditures, $5,362,110; qualifying

distributions, $4,957,314, including $4,561,613 for 1,416 grants (high: $75,000; low: $500; average: $500-$20,000) and $144,789 for employee matching gifts.

Purpose and activities: To improve human services through direct grants and encouragement of employee volunteer activities. Focus is on enhancing the economic opportunities of the disadvantaged through job training and job creation, and on AIDS patient care and prevention activities.

Fields of interest: Community development, disadvantaged, employment, AIDS, rural development.

Types of support: Matching funds, seed money, employee-related scholarships, employee matching gifts, technical assistance, general purposes, special projects, operating budgets.

Limitations: Giving generally limited to areas of company operations in AR, CA, GA, KY, MS, TN, NV, NM, NC, TX, and VA. No support for sectarian or religious purposes. No grants to individuals, or for tickets for banquets, or courtesy advertising; research, conferences, films, videos, or publications are considered only if they are a small part of a larger effort being supported.

Publications: Annual report (including application guidelines), grants list.

Application information: Application forms required for scholarships for children of company employees; all other types of scholarships discontinued.

  Initial approach: Letter
  Copies of proposal: 1
  Deadline(s): None
  Board meeting date(s): Mar., June, Sept., and Dec.
  Final notification: 2 to 3 months
  Write: Judy Belk, Dir. of Contribs.; Myra Chow, Mgr. of Contribs. (Bay Area); Herman Davenport, Mgr. of Contribs. (Mid-South Region); Mario Griffin, Mgr. of Contribs. (Western Region); Elvira Chavaria; Mgr. of Contribs. (Rio Grande); Mary Ellen McLoughlin, Mgr. of Contribs. (Eastern Region); Rachel Sierra (Project Change: Race Relations Initiative); and Deborah Wallace (National Programs)

Officers: Robert D. Haas, Pres.; Robert H. Dunn, Exec. V.P.; Thomas W. Tusher, V.P.; Judy Belk, Secy.; Joseph Maurer, Treas.

Directors: Frances K. Geballe, Rhoda H. Goldman, Peter E. Haas, Peter E. Haas, Jr., George B. James, Madeleine H. Russell.

Number of staff: 8 full-time professional; 7 part-time support.

EIN: 946064702

Recent health grants:

212-1 Aid for AIDS of Nevada, Las Vegas, NV, $30,000. 1990.

212-2 AIDS Service Providers Association of the Bay Area, San Francisco, CA, $17,000. 1990.

212-3 American Cancer Society, El Paso Metro Unit, El Paso, TX, $10,000. 1990.

212-4 California Nurses Foundation, San Francisco, CA, $10,000. 1990.

212-5 Caracole, Cincinnati, OH, $23,000. 1990.

212-6 Collin County Rape Crisis Center, McKinney, TX, $15,000. 1990.

212-7 El Paso Rehabilitation Center, El Paso, TX, $10,000. 1990.

212-8 Planned Parenthood of Greater Dallas, Dallas, TX, $26,000. 1990.

212-9 San Angelo AIDS Foundation, San Angelo, TX, $24,000. 1990.

212-10 San Francisco AIDS Foundation, San Francisco, CA, $10,000. 1990.

212-11 San Francisco AIDS Foundation, San Francisco, CA, $10,000. 1990.

212-12 San Francisco Health Department, Friends of, San Francisco, CA, $10,000. 1990.

213
The Lincy Foundation
9333 Wilshire Blvd., Suite 301
Beverly Hills 90210

Established in 1989 in CA.
Foundation type: Independent
Financial data (yr. ended 09/30/90): Assets, $82,597,999 (M); expenditures, $5,786,577; qualifying distributions, $5,786,577, including $5,684,752 for 50 grants (high: $1,500,000; low: $475).

Purpose and activities: Support primarily for Armenian charities.

Fields of interest: International relief, religion, aged, medical research, arts.

Limitations: Giving primarily in CA. No grants to individuals.

Application information:
  Initial approach: Letter or proposal
  Deadline(s): None
  Write: James D. Aljian, Pres.

Officers: James D. Aljian, Pres.; Alex Yemenidjian, V.P.; Anthony Mandekic, Secy. and C.F.O.

EIN: 954238697

Recent health grants:

213-1 California Home for the Aged, Fresno, CA, $750,000. 1991.

213-2 Center for Research and Treatment of Anorexia Nervosa, Los Angeles, CA, $25,000. 1991.

213-3 Childrens Diabetes Foundation at Denver, Denver, CO, $25,000. 1991.

213-4 Holy Cross Medical Center, Mission Hills, CA, $50,000. 1991.

213-5 Jay N. Schapira, MD Medical Research Foundation, Los Angeles, CA, $25,000. 1991.

213-6 Medical Outreach for Armenians, Glendale, CA, $50,000. 1991.

213-7 Motion Picture and Television Fund, Woodland Hills, CA, $25,000. 1991.

213-8 National Council on the Aging, DC, $10,000. 1991.

213-9 National Kidney Foundation, NYC, NY, $100,000. 1991.

213-10 National Kidney Foundation, NYC, NY, $100,000. 1991.

213-11 New York University Medical Center, NYC, NY, $100,000. 1991.

213-12 Pediatric AIDS Foundation, Santa Monica, CA, $25,000. 1991.

213-13 Ronald McDonald House of Greater Las Vegas, Las Vegas, NV, $50,000. 1991.

213-14 Saint Rose Dominican Hospital, Henderson, NV, $100,000. 1991.

213-15 Senior Health and Peer Counseling Center, Santa Monica, CA, $25,000. 1991.

213-16 University Medical Center of Southern Nevada Foundation, Las Vegas, NV, $1,000,000. 1991.

213-17 University Medical Center of Southern Nevada Foundation, Las Vegas, NV, $100,000. 1991.

213-18 University of California, School of Medicine, Los Angeles, CA, $25,000. 1991.

214
Foundation of the Litton Industries
360 North Crescent Dr.
Beverly Hills 90210   (213) 859-5423

Incorporated in 1954 in CA.
Donor(s): Litton Industries, Inc., and its subsidiaries.
Foundation type: Company-sponsored
Financial data (yr. ended 04/30/91): Assets, $28,754,376 (M); gifts received, $218,939; expenditures, $1,430,757; qualifying distributions, $1,390,287, including $1,390,287 for 85 grants (high: $315,000; low: $1,000; average: $1,000-$10,000).

Purpose and activities: Grants largely for higher education, including scholarship funds, and community funds; support also for cultural activities; limited employee matching gift program.

Fields of interest: Education, higher education, computer sciences, science and technology, community funds, health, cultural programs, arts, humanities.

Types of support: Operating budgets, continuing support, seed money, endowment funds, employee matching gifts, scholarship funds.

Limitations: No grants to individuals, or for deficit financing, capital funds, equipment, land acquisition, renovation projects, special projects, publications, dinners, conferences, or purchased research; no loans.

Application information: Application form not required.
  Initial approach: Letter
  Copies of proposal: 1
  Deadline(s): None
  Board meeting date(s): As required
  Write: Clarence L. Price, Pres.

Officers and Directors:* Clarence L. Price,* Pres.; John L. Child, V.P.; Virginia S. Young,* V.P.; Jeanette M. Thomas, Secy.; Cynthia M. Stec, Treas.

Number of staff: None.

EIN: 956095343

215
Livingston Memorial Foundation
P.O. Box 9100
Oxnard 93031-9100   (805) 988-8346

Incorporated about 1974 in CA.
Donor(s): Ruth Daily Livingston.‡
Foundation type: Independent
Financial data (yr. ended 04/30/92): Assets, $5,302,025 (M); expenditures, $203,186; qualifying distributions, $169,840, including $125,000 for 1 grant and $44,840 for 2 loans.

Purpose and activities: Support for health and health-related activities.

Fields of interest: Hospitals, health services, health.

Types of support: Matching funds, operating budgets, continuing support.

Limitations: Giving limited to Ventura County, CA. No grants to individuals.

Publications: Application guidelines, program policy statement.
Application information: Application form required.
Initial approach: Letter
Copies of proposal: 8
Deadline(s): Submit proposal preferably in Dec. or Jan.; deadline Feb. 1
Board meeting date(s): As required
Write: Laura K. McAvoy
Officers and Directors:* Charles M. Hair, M.D.,* Pres.; W.C. Huff, M.D.,* V.P.; Walter W. Hoffman,* Secy.-Treas.; Ralph L. Cormany, James K. Mason, M.D.
Number of staff: None.
EIN: 237364623

216
Lockheed Advanced Development Company Contributions Program
2555 Hollywood Way
P.O. Box 250
Sunland 91041   (818) 847-5406

Financial data (yr. ended 12/31/90): Total giving, $752,500, including $750,000 for grants (high: $500,000; low: $200; average: $200-$500,000) and $2,500 for in-kind gifts.
Purpose and activities: Main emphasis on health, social services, secondary school programs, and youth; considers a wide variety of programs including drug abuse prevention, family, and child welfare, handicapped aid, community development, hunger, and literacy.
Fields of interest: Community development, drug abuse, family services, handicapped, hospitals—building funds, AIDS, community funds, cultural programs, health, hunger, alcoholism, civic affairs, education—minorities, health associations, child development, general charitable giving, health services, hospitals, mental health, minorities, secondary education, literacy, performing arts, welfare, youth.
Types of support: Annual campaigns, donated equipment, operating budgets, building funds, capital campaigns, continuing support, general purposes.
Limitations: Giving primarily in San Fernando Valley, Antelope Valley, Santa Clara Valley, and local headquarters area, CA.
Application information: Communications office handles giving in spare time.
Initial approach: Letter of request; send requests to headquarters
Copies of proposal: 1
Board meeting date(s): Sept.-Dec.
Final notification: Jan.-Mar.
Write: James W. Flagsdale, Dir., Communs.
Number of staff: None.

217
Lodzer Organization of California, Inc.
c/o Syd Schuldiner
6349 West 6th St.
Los Angeles 90048
Application address: 5850 Venice Blvd., Los Angeles, CA 90019

Established in 1975 in CA.
Donor(s): Martin Magnes, Nathan Shapow.
Foundation type: Independent

Financial data (yr. ended 12/31/91): Assets, $51,982 (M); gifts received, $387,050; expenditures, $401,406; qualifying distributions, $401,317, including $261,216 for 17 grants (high: $160,000; low: $100).
Fields of interest: Jewish giving, Israel, hospitals.
Application information: Application form not required.
Deadline(s): None
Write: Cesia Kingston, Pres.
Officers: Cesia Kingston, Pres.; Leon Gutowicz, 1st V.P.; I. Chorob, 2nd V.P.; Sam Jackson, Corresponding Secy.; Herbert Winter, Financial Secy.; Edith Wendel, Recording Secy.; Kal Berson, Treas.
Trustees: Harry Langer, Joe Levitt, Max Volk.
EIN: 510179577

218
The J. M. Long Foundation
(Formerly Long Foundation)
141 North Civic Dr.
Walnut Creek 94596
Application address: P.O. Box 5222, Walnut Creek, CA 94596

Established in 1966.
Donor(s): Joseph M. Long,‡ Vera M. Long.
Foundation type: Independent
Financial data (yr. ended 12/31/91): Assets, $26,101,785 (M); gifts received, $28,806,536; expenditures, $25,660; qualifying distributions, $15,000, including $15,000 for 3 grants (high: $5,400; low: $4,600).
Fields of interest: Pharmacy, higher education, business education.
Limitations: Giving limited to CA. No grants to individuals.
Application information:
Initial approach: Letter
Copies of proposal: 1
Deadline(s): None
Board meeting date(s): Varies
Officers and Trustees:* Robert M. Long,* Pres.; W.G. Combs,* V.P. and Treas.; C. Tessler, Secy.
Number of staff: None.
EIN: 941643626

219
Richard M. Lucas Cancer Foundation
Bldg. 3, Suite 210
3000 Sandhill Rd.
Menlo Park 94025

Established in 1982 in CA.
Foundation type: Independent
Financial data (yr. ended 06/30/91): Assets, $6,904,089 (M); gifts received, $11,000; expenditures, $547,710; qualifying distributions, $427,077, including $427,077 for 4 grants (high: $250,000; low: $377).
Purpose and activities: Support for specialized research into the diagnosis and treatment of prostate cancer.
Fields of interest: Medical research, cancer.
Types of support: Research.
Limitations: Giving primarily in Stanford, CA.
Directors: Donald L. Lucas, John W. Lucas, Mary G. Lucas, and 4 additional directors.
Number of staff: 1 part-time support.
EIN: 942781117

220
Louis R. Lurie Foundation
555 California St., Suite 5100
San Francisco 94104   (415) 392-2470

Incorporated in 1948 in CA.
Donor(s): Louis R. Lurie,‡ Robert A. Lurie, George S. Lurie.‡
Foundation type: Independent
Financial data (yr. ended 12/31/91): Assets, $16,057,763 (M); gifts received, $353,534; expenditures, $1,287,289; qualifying distributions, $1,255,732, including $1,211,000 for 151 grants (high: $200,000; low: $1,000; average: $5,000-$25,000).
Purpose and activities: Primary areas of interest include the arts, education, community development, and health.
Fields of interest: Cultural programs, arts, social services, civic affairs, education, higher education, secondary education, Jewish welfare, health services, hospitals, AIDS, community development, health.
Types of support: General purposes, matching funds, scholarship funds, special projects, operating budgets.
Limitations: Giving limited to the San Francisco Bay Area, CA, and the Chicago, IL, metropolitan area. No grants to individuals, or for building funds; no loans.
Publications: Application guidelines.
Application information: Application form not required.
Initial approach: Telephone call, followed by letter
Copies of proposal: 1
Deadline(s): Applicants should contact foundation for deadlines
Board meeting date(s): Once a year, or as needed
Final notification: After board meeting
Write: Robert A. Lurie, Pres.
Officers and Directors:* Robert A. Lurie,* Pres.; Eugene L. Valla,* V.P. and Controller; H. Michael Kurzman,* V.P.; Charles F. Jonas,* Secy.; Patricia R. Fay, A.R. Zipf.
Number of staff: None.
EIN: 946065488

221
The MacKenzie Foundation
c/o Sanwa Bank California
P.O. Box 439, Tax Dept.
Pasadena 91102
Application address: 400 South Hope St., Los Angeles, CA 90071; Tel.: (213) 669-6377

Established about 1978 in CA.
Donor(s): Sophia MacKenzie.‡
Foundation type: Independent
Financial data (yr. ended 12/31/90): Assets, $7,552,745 (M); expenditures, $459,010; qualifying distributions, $410,258, including $370,000 for 10 grants (high: $48,000; low: $10,500).
Purpose and activities: The principal purpose of the foundation is to make grants for the benefit of students enrolled in medical schools located in the state of CA.
Fields of interest: Medical education.
Limitations: Giving limited to CA. No grants to individuals.

Application information:
Deadline(s): None
Write: Philip D. Irwin, Trustee
Trustees: H. Vernon Blankenbaker, William G. Corey, Philip D. Irwin, Sanwa Bank California.
EIN: 956588350

222
Ted Mann Foundation ▼
10100 Santa Monica Blvd., Suite 900
Los Angeles 90067   (213) 284-8528

Established in 1984 in CA.
Donor(s): Ted Mann.
Foundation type: Independent
Financial data (yr. ended 11/30/91): Assets, $44,770,005 (M); gifts received, $1,490,000; expenditures, $2,079,861; qualifying distributions, $1,949,153, including $1,943,565 for 42 grants (high: $500,000; low: $300; average: $3,000-$25,000).
Purpose and activities: Support primarily for religious and medical purposes; giving also for education.
Fields of interest: Religion, medical research, health, education.
Types of support: Annual campaigns.
Limitations: No grants to individuals.
Application information: Contributes only to pre-selected organizations and does not accept unsolicited reqrests for funds. Applications not accepted.
Write: Ted Mann, Pres.
Officers and Directors:* Ted Mann,* Pres.; Marvin Mann,* V.P.; Esther Bergman,* Secy.-Treas.; Roberta Brenden, Victoria Simms.
Number of staff: None.
EIN: 953952657

223
Margoes Foundation
57 Post St., Suite 510
San Francisco 94104   (415) 981-2966

Established in 1984 in CA.
Donor(s): John A. Margoes.‡
Foundation type: Independent
Financial data (yr. ended 02/29/92): Assets, $3,700,056 (M); gifts received, $980,559; expenditures, $263,381; qualifying distributions, $240,173, including $206,429 for 21 grants (high: $25,000; low: $500; average: $5,000-$10,000).
Purpose and activities: Giving for cardiac research, and rehabilitation of mentally ill patients; also provides scholarships for minority medical students and fellowships for African nationals studying agriculture in the U.S.
Fields of interest: Heart disease, mental health, education—minorities, Africa, agriculture.
Types of support: Continuing support, operating budgets, research, special projects, matching funds.
Limitations: Giving primarily in the San Francisco Bay Area, CA. No grants to individuals.
Publications: Annual report.
Application information: Application form not required.
Initial approach: Preliminary letter or telephone prior to proposal submission
Deadline(s): None

Board meeting date(s): Aug./Sept.
Write: John S. Blum, Principal Mgr.
Officers and Directors:* A.R. Zipf,* Chair.; Neal L. Peterson,* Secy.; Robert H. Erwin III,* C.F.O.; Patrick L. McClung.
EIN: 942955164
Recent health grants:
223-1 Center for Independent Living, Berkeley, CA, $15,000. For operating support for peer counseling, attendant care, housing, job development and financial advocacy services for mentally disabled youth, adults and seniors. 1991.
223-2 Medical Research Institute of San Francisco, San Francisco, CA, $45,000. For postgraduate fellowship at Heart Research Institute of Medical Research Institute at Pacific Presbyterian Medical Center. 1991.
223-3 Progress Foundation, San Francisco, CA, $50,000. For Supported Independent Living Program to provide permanent affordable housing for mentally disabled. 1991.
223-4 University of Michigan, School of Medicine, Ann Arbor, MI, $17,354. For Michigan resident minority students enrolled in first year of School. 1991.

224
Marin Community Foundation
17 East Sir Francis Drake Blvd., Suite 200
Larkspur 94939   (415) 461-3333
FAX: (415) 461-3386

Incorporated in 1986 in CA; the Buck Foundation Trust, its original donor, was established in 1973 and administered by the San Francisco Foundation through 1986.
Foundation type: Community
Financial data (yr. ended 06/30/90): Assets, $482,431,000 (M); gifts received, $3,054,000; expenditures, $22,427,000; qualifying distributions, $21,545,000, including $20,325,000 for grants and $400,000 for foundation-administered programs.
Purpose and activities: The Marin Community Foundation was established in July 1986 as a nonprofit public benefit corporation to engage in, conduct, and promote charitable, religious, educational, scientific, artistic, and philanthropic activities primarily in Marin County, CA. On Jan. 1, 1987, administration of the Buck Trust, created in accordance with the 1973 will of Beryl Buck and valued at approximately $447,000,000, was transferred from the S.F. Foundation. As part of the settlement agreement, three major projects, located in Marin County but intended to be part of national and international importance, were selected by the Court. To realize its purposes, the foundation seeks advice and guidance from the community; works as a partner with organizations and individuals; and encourages the participation of volunteers. The foundation accepts applications in seven program areas: Arts and Humanities; Education; Environment; Housing and Community Development; Human Needs; Religion; and Integrative Approaches.
Fields of interest: Religion, education, arts, humanities, environment, social services, housing, community development.
Types of support: Continuing support, emergency funds, equipment, land acquisition, loans, matching funds, operating budgets,

program-related investments, renovation projects, seed money, special projects, technical assistance.
Limitations: Giving from the Buck Trust is limited to Marin County, CA. No grants to individuals, or for planning initiatives, research, or generally for capital projects (except those meeting criteria specified in the funding guidelines).
Publications: Annual report, application guidelines, newsletter, informational brochure.
Application information: Application form required.
Initial approach: Request for funding policies and application guidelines
Copies of proposal: 2
Deadline(s): Nov. 15 for environment, arts and humanities, housing and community development; Dec. 14 for development and training; Jan. 15 for human needs; Feb. 15 for religion and integrative approaches
Board meeting date(s): Monthly (except July)
Final notification: 3 months
Write: Pamela R. Lynch, Corp. Secy.
Officers: Stephen Mark Dobbs, Pres. and C.E.O.; Barbara B. Lawson, V.P., Finance and Administration; Pamela Lynch, Corp. Secy. and Asst. to V.P.
Trustees: William L. Hamilton, Chair.; Peter R. Arrigoni, Vice-Chair.; Rev. Douglas K. Huneke, Donald Linker, M.D., Shirley A. Thornton, David Werderger, M.D.
Number of staff: 13 full-time professional; 1 part-time professional; 10 full-time support; 1 part-time support.
EIN: 943007979
Recent health grants:
224-1 Braun Programs, San Rafael, CA, $25,000. To provide emergency bridge grant. 1992.
224-2 California Prostitutes Education Project (CAL-EP), San Francisco, CA, $45,000. For provision of AIDS education and prevention services to at-risk residents of Marin City area. 1992.
224-3 Center for Attitudinal Healing, Tiburon, CA, $10,000. To develop volunteer manual and expand volunteer tracking system. 1992.
224-4 Commonweal, Bolinas, CA, $100,000. For development of training institute demonstrating effectiveness of advanced diagnostic and case management skills in dealing with high-risk children, youth and young adults. 1992.
224-5 Foundation Consortium, Larkspur, CA, $220,000. For public/private partnership between State of California and Consortium, for development of school-linked health and human service programs designed to restructure and coordinate existing services to children and their families in Marin as well as other selected sites in California. 1992.
224-6 Marin AIDS Project, San Rafael, CA, $110,775. To continue support for client services and psychosocial support services for people living within entire HIV infection spectrum. 1992.
224-7 Marin AIDS Project, San Rafael, CA, $100,000. Fo collaborative staffing of Marin County sponsored HIV outpatient unit to persons testing HIV-positive who are medically indigent. 1992.
224-8 Marin AIDS Project, San Rafael, CA, $10,000. To provide emergency funds to people living with AIDS in Marin County. 1992.

224-9 Marin General Hospital, Greenbrae, CA, $18,000. To continue support of program ministering to spiritual and emotional needs of hospitalized patients, their families and staff. 1992.

224-10 New Perspectives of Marin, Larkspur, CA, $210,000. To assist at-risk students in elementary, middle and senior high schools throughout Marin. 1992.

224-11 Pacific Professional Consortium, Ukiah, CA, $28,200. To develop video production entitled Dilemmas in Pregnancy to assist men and women facing choices in cases of unwanted or problematic pregnancies. 1992.

224-12 Planned Parenthood of Marin and Sonoma, San Rafael, CA, $45,000. To expand ability to provide multi-cultural and community responsive educational programs for increasingly diverse populations it serves. 1992.

224-13 Redwoods Presbyterian Church, Larkspur, CA, $50,000. For Conscious Contact, interfaith program which increases communication and spiritual support between religious congregations and 12-step recovery fellowships in Marin County. 1992.

224-14 Threshold for Change, Novato, CA, $14,500. For evaluation of day treatment program for alcohol and drug dependent adolescents. 1992.

224-15 West Marin Health Project, Point Reyes Station, CA, $25,000. For Clinic Coordination Project, increasing medical services to underserved populations in West Marin. 1992.

224-16 Youth Advocates, San Rafael, CA, $60,000. For multi-agency collaborative effort to address AIDS education/prevention needs of most at-risk teens. 1992.

225
Maurice J. Masserini Charitable Trust
c/o Wells Fargo Bank, N.A.
101 West Broadway, Suite 400
San Diego 92101

Established in 1984 in CA.
Foundation type: Independent
Financial data (yr. ended 03/31/91): Assets, $4,097,474 (M); expenditures, $301,235; qualifying distributions, $263,361, including $259,025 for 13 grants (high: $53,650; low: $3,000).
Fields of interest: Higher education, marine sciences, medical research, community development, cultural programs, social services.
Types of support: Research, scholarship funds, special projects.
Limitations: Giving primarily in San Diego, CA. No grants to individuals.
Publications: 990-PF.
Application information: Contributes only to pre-selected organizations. Applications not accepted.
Trustee: Wells Fargo Bank, N.A.
EIN: 956812685

226
The Maxfield Foundation
12930 Saratoga Ave., Suite B-3
Saratoga 95070   (408) 253-0723

Established in 1985 in CA.
Donor(s): Robert R. Maxfield.
Foundation type: Independent
Financial data (yr. ended 12/31/91): Assets, $5,359,343 (M); expenditures, $241,105; qualifying distributions, $239,805, including $237,655 for 9 grants (high: $62,500; low: $5,000).
Purpose and activities: Support primarily for cancer research, including leukemia; secondary purpose is to give for charitable activities.
Fields of interest: Cancer, medical research.
Types of support: Research, seed money, special projects.
Publications: Annual report (including application guidelines).
Application information:
   Write: Robert R. Maxfield, Pres.
Officers: Robert R. Maxfield, Pres.; Melinda Maxfield, V.P.; Clarence J. Ferrari, Jr., Secy.
EIN: 770099366

227
MCA Foundation, Ltd. ▼
100 Universal City Plaza
Universal City 91608   (818) 777-1208

Incorporated in 1956 in CA.
Donor(s): MCA, Inc.
Foundation type: Company-sponsored
Financial data (yr. ended 12/31/90): Assets, $13,600,043 (M); gifts received, $2,132,500; expenditures, $1,154,540; qualifying distributions, $1,147,510, including $1,147,500 for 85 grants (high: $100,000; low: $2,000; average: $5,000-$10,000).
Purpose and activities: Grants largely for health and welfare, including support for minorities, cultural programs, higher and other education, child and youth agencies, and women.
Fields of interest: Health, minorities, education, higher education, cultural programs, performing arts, child welfare, youth, AIDS, women.
Types of support: Annual campaigns, general purposes, special projects, equipment.
Limitations: Giving primarily in the Los Angeles, CA, and New York City areas. No grants to individuals, or for film, video, or television projects.
Publications: Application guidelines.
Application information: Proposal of not more than 3 pages.
   Deadline(s): None
   Write: Helen D. Yatsko, Administrator
Officers and Directors:* Sidney J. Sheinberg,* Pres.; Richard Baker,* V.P. and C.F.O.; Thomas Wertheimer,* V.P.; Michael Samuel, Secy.
Number of staff: 2 full-time professional.
EIN: 136096061

228
The Harold McAlister Charitable Foundation
4801 Wilshire Blvd., Suite 232
Los Angeles 90010   (213) 937-0927

Incorporated in 1959 in CA.
Donor(s): Harold McAlister,‡ Fern Smith McAlister.
Foundation type: Independent

Financial data (yr. ended 05/31/91): Assets, $22,662,755 (M); gifts received, $50,000; expenditures, $1,146,061; qualifying distributions, $1,099,224, including $1,033,550 for 57 grants (high: $240,000; low: $200; average: $1,000-$30,000).
Fields of interest: Hospitals, health associations, heart disease, higher education, social services.
Limitations: Giving primarily in the Los Angeles, CA, area. No grants to individuals.
Application information: Applications not accepted.
   Board meeting date(s): Monthly
   Write: Virginia Gilbert
Officers and Trustees:* Hobart S. McAlister,* Pres.; Fern Smith McAlister,* V.P.; David B. Heyler, Jr., Soni McAlister.
Number of staff: 1 full-time professional.
EIN: 956050036

229
The McBean Family Foundation
(Formerly The Atholl McBean Foundation)
c/o Price Waterhouse
555 California St., Suite 3800
San Francisco 94104

Incorporated in 1955 in CA.
Donor(s): Atholl McBean,‡ Peter McBean.
Foundation type: Independent
Financial data (yr. ended 12/31/90): Assets, $4,193,630 (M); gifts received, $30,000; expenditures, $280,335; qualifying distributions, $230,000, including $229,000 for 14 grants (high: $30,000; low: $1,000).
Fields of interest: Hospitals, higher education, secondary education, cultural programs.
Limitations: Giving primarily in CA. No grants to individuals, or for endowment funds, research, scholarships, or fellowships; no loans.
Application information:
   Initial approach: Letter
   Copies of proposal: 1
   Deadline(s): None
   Board meeting date(s): Dec. and as required
   Write: Peter McBean, Pres.
Officers: Peter McBean, Pres.; Clark Nelson, C.F.O. and Secy.-Treas.
Directors: P. Folger, R. Gwen Follis, Judith McBean Hunt, Edith McBean, H. Newhall.
EIN: 946062239

230
McCarthy Family Foundation
P.O. Box 270051
San Diego 92198-2051

Established in 1988 in CA.
Donor(s): James T. McCarthy, Jane D. McCarthy.
Foundation type: Independent
Financial data (yr. ended 12/31/91): Assets, $2,403,766 (M); gifts received, $220,000; expenditures, $99,290; qualifying distributions, $74,032, including $72,000 for 4 grants (high: $40,000; low: $7,000).
Purpose and activities: Primary areas of interest include medical research, science and technology, AIDS, child welfare, the homeless, and and secondary education.
Fields of interest: AIDS, medical research, homeless, secondary education, child welfare,

science and technology, theater, performing arts, social services.

Types of support: Matching funds, seed money, special projects, research, capital campaigns.

Limitations: Giving primarily in CA. No grants to individuals.

Publications: Annual report, application guidelines.

Application information: Application form not required.

> *Initial approach:* Letter requesting application guidelines
> *Copies of proposal:* 1
> *Deadline(s):* None
> *Board meeting date(s):* Quarterly
> *Write:* Jane D. McCarthy, Pres.

Officers: Jane D. McCarthy, Pres.; James T. McCarthy, Secy.

Directors: Kristin L. McCarthy, Rachel K. McCarthy.

Number of staff: None.

EIN: 954182410

231
The McConnell Foundation ▼

(Formerly Carl R. & Leah F. McConnell Foundation)
P.O. Box 930
Redding 96099-1870   (916) 222-0696

Established in 1964 in CA.

Donor(s): Carl R. McConnell Trust III.

Foundation type: Independent

Financial data (yr. ended 12/31/90): Assets, $43,773,885 (M); expenditures, $2,875,445; qualifying distributions, $2,284,248, including $2,284,248 for 33 grants (high: $262,000; low: $2,500; average: $5,000-$100,000).

Purpose and activities: Giving primarily for community development; support also for education, arts and culture, the environment, health care, recreation, and social services.

Fields of interest: Community development, education, secondary education, higher education, arts, cultural programs, environment, health, recreation, social services, aged, family planning, youth.

Types of support: Scholarship funds, equipment, general purposes, renovation projects, special projects.

Limitations: Giving primarily in Shasta and Siskiyou counties, CA. No support for sectarian religious purposes. No grants to individuals, or for endowment funds, annual fund drives, or budget deficits.

Publications: Program policy statement, application guidelines, annual report.

Application information: Application form required.

> *Initial approach:* Letter of intent
> *Copies of proposal:* 1
> *Deadline(s):* Feb. 15
> *Board meeting date(s):* Feb., Mar., July, and Oct.
> *Final notification:* July 31
> *Write:* Lee W. Salter, Exec. Dir.

Officers and Directors:* Leonard B. Nelson,* Pres.; William B. Nystrom,* V.P.; Samuel Taylor,* V.P.; Leah F. McConnell,* Secy.-Treas.; Lee W. Salter,* Exec. Dir.; John A. Mancasola.

Number of staff: 1 full-time professional; 1 part-time professional; 3 part-time support.

EIN: 946102700

Recent health grants:

231-1 Anderson Police Department, Anderson, CA, $28,000. For D.A.R.E. Leadership Training Camp. 1991.

231-2 Dunsmuir Fire Department, Dunsmuir, CA, $58,000. For Trauma/Medical Emergency Rescue Vehicle. 1991.

231-3 Family Planning, Redding, CA, $75,000. For medical and office equipment upgrades and expansion of services. 1991.

231-4 Golden Umbrella, Redding, CA, $175,000. For adult day health care expansion project. 1990.

231-5 Kritikus Foundation, Redding, CA, $50,000. For nursing education in pulmonary care areas. 1990.

231-6 Mercy Medical Center, Redding, CA, $40,000. For pediatric pavilion remodeling. 1990.

231-7 Mercy Medical Center, Redding, CA, $34,400. For obstetrics equipment. 1991.

231-8 Shasta Primary Care Clinic, Redding, CA, $100,000. For mammography unit. 1990.

231-9 Shasta-Trinity Regional Occupational Program, Redding, CA, $25,000. For training equipment for health care occupations. 1991.

231-10 Shasta-Trinity Rural Indian Health Project, Anderson, CA, $43,500. For two vans. 1990.

232
McKesson Foundation, Inc. ▼

One Post St.
San Francisco 94104   (415) 983-8673

Incorporated in 1943 in FL.

Donor(s): McKesson Corp.

Foundation type: Company-sponsored

Financial data (yr. ended 03/31/91): Assets, $9,688,026 (M); expenditures, $2,080,256; qualifying distributions, $1,976,896, including $1,843,896 for 294 grants (high: $276,566; low: $25; average: $5,000-$25,000) and $133,000 for employee matching gifts.

Purpose and activities: Giving primarily to programs for junior high school students, and for emergency services such as food and shelter; limited support for other educational, civic, cultural, and human service programs.

Fields of interest: Secondary education, education—minorities, health, cultural programs, education, elementary education, welfare, civic affairs, youth, disadvantaged, child welfare, child development, delinquency.

Types of support: Continuing support, emergency funds, employee matching gifts, matching funds, operating budgets, seed money, employee-related scholarships, equipment.

Limitations: Giving primarily in the San Francisco Bay Area, CA, and in other cities where the company has a major presence. No support for religious organizations or political groups. No grants to individuals, or for endowment funds, advertising, film or research projects, or capital fund drives; no loans.

Publications: Annual report (including application guidelines), application guidelines.

Application information: Application form not required.

> *Initial approach:* Letter
> *Copies of proposal:* 1

> *Deadline(s):* Submit initial letter preferably between Apr. and Oct.; submit full proposal upon request
> *Board meeting date(s):* Bimonthly beginning in Apr.
> *Final notification:* 60 to 90 days
> *Write:* Marcia M. Argyris, Pres.

Officers and Trustees:* Marcia M. Argyris, Pres.; Arthur Chong, V.P.; Dena J. Goldberg, Secy.; Garrett A. Scholz,* Treas.; James S. Cohune, Jon d'Alessio, Judie Doherty, Stanley Greenblath, Marvin L. Krasnansky, Ivan D. Meyerson, Nancy Miller, Alan Seelenfreund, Tom Simone, Susan Weir, Charles Woods.

Number of staff: 1 full-time professional; 1 part-time professional; 1 full-time support; 1 part-time support.

EIN: 596144455

Recent health grants:

232-1 Arnold and Marie Schwartz College of Pharmacy and Health Science, Brooklyn, NY, $10,000. For general support. 1991.

232-2 Californians for Drug-Free Youth, Thousand Oaks, CA, $25,000. For state-wide, week-long conference for youth and their parents to plan drug-free strategies for California schools and communities. 1991.

232-3 Edgewood Childrens Center, San Francisco, CA, $12,500. To remodel cottage for emotionally disturbed children who are undergoing treatment in this San Francisco residential program. 1991.

232-4 Lincoln Child Center Foundation, Oakland, CA, $10,000. To create on-site classrooms at this Oakland residential facility for emotionally disturbed children. 1991.

232-5 Mental Health Association of Maricopa County, Phoenix, AZ, $10,000. To initiate program for families and children who are living in homeless shelters. 1991.

232-6 Ronald McDonald House, San Francisco Family Support House, San Francisco, CA, $15,000. For new facility that houses families while their children are undergoing intensive medical treatment. 1991.

232-7 Wake Forest University Medical Center, Paul Sticht Center on Aging, Winston-Salem, NC, $10,000. For general support for research. 1991.

233
The Catherine L. & Robert O. McMahan Foundation

P.O. Box 221580
Carmel 93922   (408) 625-6444

Donor(s): Robert O. McMahan.‡

Foundation type: Independent

Financial data (yr. ended 12/31/91): Assets, $4,132,389 (M); expenditures, $201,414; qualifying distributions, $172,900, including $172,900 for 43 grants (high: $50,000; low: $500).

Purpose and activities: Giving primarily for hospices, social services, education, and youth services; support also for cultural programs and general charitable purposes.

Fields of interest: Hospices, social services, education, youth, cultural programs, general charitable giving.

Limitations: Giving limited to CA, with emphasis on Monterey and Fresno counties. No grants to individuals.
Application information:
Initial approach: Letter
Deadline(s): None
Write: Neal W. McMahan, C.E.O.
Officers: Neal W. McMahan, C.E.O.; Michael L. McMahan, Secy. and C.F.O.
EIN: 946061273

234
McMicking Foundation
25 Ecker St., Suite 800
San Francisco 94105-2755   (415) 543-6464

Established in 1958.
Donor(s): Joseph R. McMicking.‡
Foundation type: Independent
Financial data (yr. ended 10/31/90): Assets, $5,550,217 (M); gifts received, $5,466,414; expenditures, $5,438; qualifying distributions, $3,585, including $2,750 for 7 grants (high: $1,000; low: $100).
Fields of interest: Health, higher education.
Limitations: Giving primarily in CA. No grants to individuals.
Application information:
Initial approach: Letter
Deadline(s): None
Write: Henry A. McMicking, Trustee
Officer: Javier J. Nepomuceno, Secy.-Treas.
Trustees: Roderick C.M. Hall, Henry A. McMicking.
EIN: 946058305

235
Mericos Foundation ▼
1260 Huntington Dr., Suite 204
South Pasadena 91030-4561   (213) 259-0484

Established in 1980 in CA.
Donor(s): Donald W. Whittier Charitable Trust.
Foundation type: Independent
Financial data (yr. ended 12/31/91): Assets, $16,600,906 (M); gifts received, $2,769,938; expenditures, $1,917,856; qualifying distributions, 1,661,139, including $1,619,105 for 36 grants (high: $287,500; low: $6,350; average: $10,000-$100,000).
Purpose and activities: Primarily local giving for cultural programs, the aged, and medical research.
Fields of interest: Cultural programs, education, higher education, aged, child development, youth, hospices, medical research.
Types of support: Building funds, fellowships, matching funds, endowment funds, special projects, equipment.
Limitations: Giving primarily in CA. No loans.
Application information: Grants generally initiated by foundation.
Deadline(s): None
Write: Linda J. Blinkenberg, Secy.
Officers: Joanne W. Blokker, Pres.; Michael J. Casey, V.P.; Linda J. Blinkenberg, Secy.; Arlo G. Sorensen, Treas.
Number of staff: 4 shared staff
EIN: 953500491

236
The Milken Family Foundation ▼
c/o Foundations of the Milken Families
15250 Ventura Blvd., 2nd Fl.
Sherman Oaks 91403

Established in 1986 in CA.
Donor(s): Lowell Milken, Michael Milken, L.A. Milken, S.E. Milken.
Foundation type: Independent
Financial data (yr. ended 11/30/90): Assets, $127,806,405 (M); expenditures, $5,070,669; qualifying distributions, $5,333,503, including $3,985,189 for 99 grants (high: $834,364; low: $500; average: $1,000-$25,000).
Purpose and activities: To build human resources through programs in 4 major areas: 1)Education - to reward educational innovators, stimulate creativity among students, involve parents and other citizens in the school system, and offer opportunities to the disadvantaged student; 2)Health Care and Medical Research - to make the benefits of both basic and highly advanced health care available to those who need them; 3)Community Services - to support programs and facilities that meet the essential needs at the neighborhood level; and 4)Human Welfare - to meet the compelling needs of the disadvantaged.
Fields of interest: Education, elementary education, secondary education, higher education, educational associations, health services, medical research, cancer, community development, child welfare, child development, youth, disadvantaged, welfare, Jewish welfare, Jewish giving.
Types of support: Research, conferences and seminars, scholarship funds, building funds, renovation projects, general purposes.
Limitations: Giving primarily in the Los Angeles, CA, area.
Publications: Annual report.
Application information:
Initial approach: Letter or proposal
Deadline(s): None
Write: Dr. Jules Lesner, Exec. Dir.
Officers and Directors:* L.J. Milken,* Pres.; Jules Lesner,* Exec. V.P., C.F.O., and Exec. Dir.; L. Solmon,* V.P.; C. Cohen, Secy.; Ralph Finerman, F. Milken, L.A. Milken, S.E. Milken, E. Sandler.
EIN: 954073646
Recent health grants:
236-1 Los Angeles Center for Therapy and Education, Van Nuys, CA, $10,000. 1990.
236-2 Variety Clubs International, NYC, NY, $25,000. 1990.

237
Milken Family Medical Foundation ▼
c/o Foundations of the Milken Families
15250 Ventura Blvd., 2nd Fl.
Sherman Oaks 91403

Established in 1986 in CA.
Donor(s): Michael R. Milken, Lori A. Milken.
Foundation type: Independent
Financial data (yr. ended 10/31/90): Assets, $61,734,848 (M); expenditures, $5,191,789; qualifying distributions, $4,939,401, including $4,626,597 for 109 grants (high: $1,318,500; low: $500; average: $1,000-$10,000).
Purpose and activities: To build human resources through programs in 4 major areas: 1)Education - to reward educational innovators, stimulate creativity among students, involve parents and other citizens in the school system, and offer opportunities to the disadvantaged student; 2)Health Care and Medical Research - to make the benefits of both basic and highly advanced health care available to those who need them; 3)Community Services - to support programs and facilities that meet the essential needs at the neighborhood level; and 4)Human Welfare - to meet the compelling needs of the disadvantaged.
Fields of interest: Education, elementary education, secondary education, higher education, educational associations, health services, medical research, cancer, AIDS, community development, welfare, youth, child welfare, child development, disadvantaged, Jewish welfare, Jewish giving.
Limitations: Giving primarily in the Los Angeles, CA, area. No grants to individuals.
Publications: Annual report.
Application information: Contributes only to pre-selected organizations. Applications not accepted.
Write: Dr. Jules Lesner, Exec. V.P.
Officers and Directors:* Lori A. Milken,* Pres.; A. Flans,* V.P. and Secy.; J. Lesner,* Exec. V.P. and C.F.O.; M. Hackel, E. Sandler.
EIN: 954078350
Recent health grants:
237-1 AltaMed Health Services, Los Angeles, CA, $10,000. 1990.
237-2 American Committee for Shaare Zedek Hospital in Jerusalem, San Francisco, CA, $25,000. 1990.
237-3 American Epilepsy Society, Hartford, CT, $1,318,500. For awards. 1990.
237-4 American Foundation for AIDS Research, NYC, NY, $50,000. 1990.
237-5 American Friends of Assaf Harofeh Hospital, Los Angeles, CA, $120,000. 1990.
237-6 American Institute for Cancer Research, DC, $10,000. 1990.
237-7 Betty Clooney Foundation for the Brain Injured, Los Angeles, CA, $10,000. 1990.
237-8 California Institute for Cancer Research, Los Angeles, CA, $10,000. 1990.
237-9 Cedars-Sinai Medical Center, Los Angeles, CA, $19,000. 1990.
237-10 Center for the Partially Sighted, Santa Monica, CA, $101,000. 1990.
237-11 Childrens Diabetes Foundation at Denver, Denver, CO, $25,000. 1990.
237-12 Childrens Health Fund, NYC, NY, $25,000. 1990.
237-13 Community Adult Day Health Services, Oakland, CA, $10,000. 1990.
237-14 Cystic Fibrosis Foundation, Los Angeles, CA, $10,000. 1990.
237-15 Devereux Foundation, Los Angeles, CA, $50,000. 1990.
237-16 Eisenhower Memorial Hospital at Eisenhower Medical Center, Rancho Mirage, CA, $10,000. 1990.
237-17 Epilepsy Foundation of America, DC, $50,000. 1990.
237-18 Friends of Tel Hashomer, Los Angeles, CA, $60,000. 1990.
237-19 Health Champions, Beverly Hills, CA, $30,000. 1990.
237-20 Helping Hand of Los Angeles, Los Angeles, CA, $10,000. 1990.

237-21 House Ear Institute, Los Angeles, CA, $15,000. 1990.

237-22 International Craniofacial Foundation, Dallas, TX, $15,000. 1990.

237-23 Interplast, Palo Alto, CA, $30,000. 1990.

237-24 Israel Cancer Research Fund, NYC, NY, $18,000. 1990.

237-25 Jewish Home for the Aging of Greater Los Angeles, Reseda, CA, $125,000. 1990.

237-26 Kingsbrook Jewish Medical Center, Brooklyn, NY, $15,000. 1990.

237-27 Life Savers Foundation of America, Covina, CA, $115,000. 1990.

237-28 Los Angeles County Epilepsy Society, Los Angeles, CA, $10,000. 1990.

237-29 Los Angeles Free Clinic, Los Angeles, CA, $51,500. 1990.

237-30 Memorial Sloan-Kettering Cancer Center, NYC, NY, $85,000. 1990.

237-31 Mount Sinai Hospital and Medical Center, NYC, NY, $25,000. 1990.

237-32 Muscular Dystrophy Association, Los Angeles, CA, $25,000. 1990.

237-33 National Brain Tumor Research Foundation, San Francisco, CA, $25,000. 1990.

237-34 National Jewish Center for Immunology and Respiratory Medicine, Denver, CO, $100,000. 1990.

237-35 National Kidney Foundation of Southern California, Los Angeles, CA, $15,000. 1990.

237-36 Pediatric AIDS Foundation, Santa Monica, CA, $25,000. 1990.

237-37 Southern California Childrens Cancer Services, Los Angeles, CA, $41,500. 1990.

237-38 Starlight Foundation, Los Angeles, CA, $163,300. 1990.

237-39 T. J. Martell Foundation for Leukemia and Cancer Research, NYC, NY, $10,000. 1990.

237-40 United Cerebral Palsy-Spastic Childrens Foundation, Van Nuys, CA, $11,000. 1990.

237-41 Venice Family Clinic, Venice, CA, $117,000. 1990.

237-42 Wellness Community-National, Santa Monica, CA, $10,000. 1990.

238

L. and S. Milken Foundation

c/o Foundations of the Milken Families
15250 Ventura Blvd., 2nd Fl.
Sherman Oaks 91403

Established in 1986 in CA.
Donor(s): L. Milken, S. Milken.
Foundation type: Independent
Financial data (yr. ended 10/31/90): Assets, $25,380,614 (M); gifts received, $4,000,000; expenditures, $555,117; qualifying distributions, $427,862, including $377,200 for 21 grants (high: $50,000; low: $800).
Purpose and activities: To build human resources through programs in 4 major areas: 1) Education - to reward educational innovators, stimulate creativity among students, involve parents and other citizens in the school system, and offer opportunities to the disadvantaged student; 2) Health Care and Medical Research - to make the benefits of both basic and highly advanced health care available to those who need them; 3) Community Services - to support programs and facilities that meet the essential needs at the neighborhood level; and 4) Human Welfare - to meet the compelling needs of the disadvantaged.

Fields of interest: Jewish giving, Jewish welfare, higher education, education, health associations, cancer, medical research.
Types of support: Research, conferences and seminars, scholarship funds, building funds, renovation projects, general purposes.
Limitations: Giving primarily in the Los Angeles, CA, area. No grants to individuals.
Publications: Annual report.
Application information: Contributes to pre-selected organizations. Applications not accepted.
  Write: J. Lesner, Exec. V.P.
Officers and Directors:* L. Milken,* Pres.; J. Lesner,* Exec. V.P.; E. Salka,* V.P.; S. Milken,* V.P., Secy., and C.F.O.; R. Sandler.
EIN: 954078354

239

Earl B. & Loraine H. Miller Foundation

P.O. Box 87
Long Beach 90801-0087
Application address: 444 West Ocean Blvd., Top Fl., Long Beach, CA 90802; Tel.: (213) 435-1191

Established in 1967 in CA.
Foundation type: Independent
Financial data (yr. ended 06/30/92): Assets, $23,165,000 (M); gifts received, $18,519,682; expenditures, $442,471; qualifying distributions, $300,863, including $300,863 for 4 grants (high: $200,000; low: $20,000).
Purpose and activities: Funding for a children's health clinic, child welfare, hospitals and hospital building funds, and higher education; support also for arts and cultural activities, including museums and fine arts.
Fields of interest: Child welfare, health, hospitals, higher education, cultural programs, museums, fine arts.
Types of support: Building funds, matching funds, seed money, capital campaigns, endowment funds, general purposes, special projects.
Limitations: Giving limited to Long Beach, CA. No grants to individuals.
Publications: Informational brochure.
Application information: Application form required.
  Initial approach: Letter
  Copies of proposal: 10
  Deadline(s): June 30
  Board meeting date(s): Quarterly; usually, Nov., Mar., May, and Aug.
  Write: Marilyn L. Reilly, Trustee
Officer: Larry A. Collins, Jr., Pres.
Trustees: Donald C. Carner, Richard C. Degolia, M.D., Walter Florie, Jr., Elsie Rash, Marilyn L. Reilly, Leon L. Wiltse, M.D.
Number of staff: None.
EIN: 952500545

240

Community Foundation for Monterey County

P.O. Box 1384
Monterey 93942   (408) 375-9712

Incorporated in 1945 in CA.
Foundation type: Community

Financial data (yr. ended 12/31/91): Assets, $12,300,000 (M); gifts received, $1,200,000; expenditures, $1,500,000; qualifying distributions, $1,200,000, including $1,200,000 for 75 grants (high: $500,000; low: $200; average: $500-$200,000).
Fields of interest: Social services, education, arts, environment, health, historic preservation, general charitable giving.
Types of support: Operating budgets, continuing support, seed money, emergency funds, building funds, equipment, land acquisition, matching funds, special projects, research, consulting services, technical assistance, program-related investments, capital campaigns, renovation projects, general purposes.
Limitations: Giving primarily in Monterey County, CA. No grants to individuals, or for annual campaigns, deficit financing, general endowments, or publications.
Publications: Annual report (including application guidelines), 990-PF, application guidelines, informational brochure, newsletter.
Application information: Application form required.
  Initial approach: Telephone or letter
  Copies of proposal: 2
  Deadline(s): Mar. 15, June 15, Sept. 15, and Dec. 15
  Board meeting date(s): 3rd Tuesday of every month
  Final notification: 1 week after each quarterly meeting
  Write: Todd Lueders, Exec. Dir.
Director: Todd Lueders, Exec. Dir.
Board of Governors: William G. Doolittle, Pres.; Basil Mills, V.P.
Number of staff: 3 full-time professional.
EIN: 941615897

241

Monterey Peninsula Golf Foundation

P.O. Box 869
Monterey 93942

Foundation type: Independent
Financial data (yr. ended 06/30/91): Assets, $1,028,385 (M); gifts received, $1,092,900; expenditures, $1,284,379; qualifying distributions, $1,227,504, including $1,000,000 for grants.
Fields of interest: Youth, social services, health, general charitable giving.
Limitations: Giving limited to the Monterey Peninsula, CA, area. No grants to individuals.
Application information:
  Initial approach: Letter
  Deadline(s): Apr. 1
  Write: Louis A. Russo, Exec. Dir.
Officers and Directors:* William F. Borland,* Pres.; John Zoller,* V.P.; Cindy Zoller, Secy.; Richard Falge, Treas.; Louis A. Russo, Exec. Dir.; and 8 additional directors.
EIN: 942541783

242

Montgomery Street Foundation ▼

235 Montgomery St., Suite 1107
San Francisco 94104   (415) 398-0600

Incorporated in 1952 in CA and originally funded by Crown Zellerbach Corp.; later became a totally separate entity from the corporation.
Foundation type: Independent
Financial data (yr. ended 12/31/91): Assets, $24,739,453 (M); expenditures, $1,405,619; qualifying distributions, $1,255,630, including $1,086,500 for 128 grants (high: $25,000; low: $2,000; average: $5,000-$20,000).
Purpose and activities: Grants made selectively to qualified organizations, primarily in the fields of higher education, international understanding, community funds, community welfare, cultural institutions, youth, health, rehabilitation, and related areas.
Fields of interest: Education, higher education, literacy, international affairs, public affairs, public policy, foreign policy, economics, population studies, community funds, volunteerism, social services, youth, child welfare, family services, family planning, cultural programs, museums, fine arts, performing arts, historic preservation, health, medical sciences, rehabilitation, drug abuse, alcoholism, handicapped.
Types of support: Annual campaigns, general purposes, operating budgets, capital campaigns.
Limitations: Giving primarily in CA; limited grants awarded nationally. No grants to individuals; no loans.
Application information: Application form not required.
  Initial approach: Concise letter request
  Copies of proposal: 1
  Deadline(s): Reviewed on ongoing basis
  Board meeting date(s): Generally 4 times per year
  Final notification: Usually within 3 months
  Write: Carol K. Elliott, Secy.-Treas.
Officers and Directors:* Charles E. Stine,* Pres.; Carol K. Elliott, Secy.-Treas.; C.S. Cullenbine, C.R. Dahl, Robert W. Roth, Richard G. Shephard.
Number of staff: 2 full-time professional.
EIN: 941270335

243
Moore Family Foundation
23965 Jabil Ln.
Los Altos Hills 94024

Established in 1986.
Donor(s): Betty I. Moore, Gordon E. Moore.
Foundation type: Independent
Financial data (yr. ended 09/30/91): Assets, $10,619,915 (M); expenditures, $947,182; qualifying distributions, $886,382, including $871,333 for 8 grants (high: $500,000; low: $3,000).
Fields of interest: Conservation, higher education, hospitals.
Types of support: Building funds, capital campaigns, special projects.
Limitations: No grants to individuals.
Application information: Contributes only to pre-selected organizations. Applications not accepted.
Trustees: Betty I. Moore, Gordon E. Moore, Kenneth G. Moore, Steven E. Moore.
EIN: 943024440

244
Muller Foundation
(Formerly Frank Muller, Sr. Foundation)
11357 Pala Loma Dr.
Valley Center 92082-3114   (213) 463-8176

Established in 1965 in CA.
Donor(s): Frank Muller.
Foundation type: Independent
Financial data (yr. ended 07/31/91): Assets, $6,233,082 (M); expenditures, $452,918; qualifying distributions, $381,161, including $364,422 for 255 grants (high: $23,727; low: $50).
Fields of interest: Higher education, secondary education, social services, hospitals, Catholic giving, cultural programs.
Limitations: Giving primarily in CA. No grants to individuals.
Application information: Contributes only to pre-selected organizations. Applications not accepted.
  Write: R.A. Vilmure, Pres.
Officers and Directors:* Richard Vilmure,* Pres.; James Muller,* V.P.; John Muller,* V.P.; Sheila Muller, V.P.; Tim Muller,* V.P.; Mary M. Thompson,* Secy.-Treas.
EIN: 956121774

245
Alfred C. Munger Foundation
c/o R.D. Esbenshade
355 South Grand Ave., 35th Fl.
Los Angeles 90071-1560

Established in 1965 in CA.
Donor(s): Charles T. Munger, Nancy B. Munger, Berkshire Hathaway, Inc.
Foundation type: Independent
Financial data (yr. ended 11/30/91): Assets, $9,071,071 (M); gifts received, $22,900; expenditures, $761,122; qualifying distributions, $754,769, including $754,769 for 34 grants (high: $258,698; low: $96).
Purpose and activities: Grants primarily for higher and secondary education, a hospital, a family planning and population control institute, and health agencies; giving also for Protestant religious organizations.
Fields of interest: Higher education, secondary education, family planning, health services, hospitals, Protestant giving.
Limitations: Giving primarily in CA. No grants to individuals.
Application information: Contributes only to pre-selected organizations. Applications not accepted.
Officers and Trustees:* Charles T. Munger,* Pres.; Richard D. Esbenshade,* V.P. and Secy.; Nancy B. Munger,* Treas.
EIN: 952462103

246
Lluella Morey Murphey Foundation
c/o Nossaman, Gunther, et al.
430 South Hill Ave.
Pasadena 91106

Established in 1967.
Donor(s): Lluella Morey Murphey.‡
Foundation type: Independent

Financial data (yr. ended 12/31/91): Assets, $3,911,075 (M); expenditures, $144,965; qualifying distributions, $131,617, including $75,200 for 22 grants (high: $5,000; low: $500; average: $1,000-$5,000).
Fields of interest: Youth, hospitals, health, cultural programs.
Types of support: General purposes, building funds, equipment, matching funds, scholarship funds, endowment funds, fellowships.
Limitations: Giving primarily in CA. No support for private foundations. No grants to individuals.
Application information: Funding limited; unsolicited requests not considered.
  Initial approach: Proposal
  Deadline(s): None
  Write: James A. Schlinger, Trustee and Mgr.
Trustees: Alfred B. Hastings, Jr., Leonard M. Marangi, James A. Schlinger.
EIN: 956152669

247
Dan Murphy Foundation ▼
800 West Sixth St., Suite 1240
Los Angeles 90017-2715   (213) 623-3120

Incorporated in 1957 in CA.
Donor(s): Bernadine Murphy Donohue.‡
Foundation type: Independent
Financial data (yr. ended 12/31/90): Assets, $163,158,014 (M); gifts received, $25; expenditures, $8,513,487; qualifying distributions, $8,249,991, including $8,174,394 for 93 grants (high: $3,980,194; low: $1,000; average: $10,000-$50,000).
Purpose and activities: Giving primarily for support of activities and charities of Roman Catholic Church Archdiocese of Los Angeles, including religious orders, colleges and schools, social service agencies, and medical institutions.
Fields of interest: Higher education, religious schools, hospitals, Catholic giving, Catholic welfare.
Types of support: Continuing support, special projects, general purposes.
Limitations: Giving primarily in Los Angeles, CA.
Publications: Informational brochure.
Application information: Grants generally initiated by the trustees.
  Initial approach: Letter (1 page)
  Copies of proposal: 1
  Board meeting date(s): As needed
  Write: Grace Robinson
Officers and Trustees:* Daniel J. Donohue,* Pres.; Oscar T. Lawler,* V.P.; Richard A. Grant, Jr.,* V.P.; Rosemary E. Donohue,* Mgr.; Edward A. Landry, Julia D. Schwartz.
Number of staff: 1
EIN: 956046963
Recent health grants:
247-1 Childrens Hospital of Los Angeles, Los Angeles, CA, $232,800. 1990.
247-2 Franciscan Health Center, Los Angeles, CA, $25,000. 1990.
247-3 Hospitaller Foundation of California, Los Angeles, CA, $15,000. 1990.
247-4 Saint Joseph Convalescent Hospital, Ojai, CA, $25,000. 1990.
247-5 Saint Vincent Medical Center, Los Angeles, CA, $20,000. 1990.
247-6 Santa Marta Foundation, Los Angeles, CA, $40,000. 1990.

248
National Medical Enterprises Corporate Giving Program
2700 Colorado Ave.
Santa Monica 90404   (213) 315-8000

Financial data (yr. ended 05/31/91): Total giving, $2,100,000.
Purpose and activities: "To identify and support national and local organizations that are attempting to improve the quality of health in Americans" in the areas of health, welfare, education, and social services; giving includes direct health care services to the indigent.
Fields of interest: Health, health services, medical education, higher education, medical research, aged, handicapped, youth, family services, women, minorities, social services, welfare, education, economics, AIDS, alcoholism, disadvantaged, homeless, welfare—indigent individuals, medical sciences, mental health, rehabilitation, literacy, hospices, hunger, education—minorities, business education, psychology, secondary education, education—early childhood, elementary education, museums, nursing, drug abuse, child welfare.
Types of support: General purposes, special projects, operating budgets, matching funds, fellowships, publications, research, employee-related scholarships, scholarship funds, employee matching gifts, in-kind gifts, donated products.
Limitations: Giving limited to communities where NME employees live and work. No support for political, fraternal, labor, veterans', religious or athletic organizations, athletic events, or travel and cultural exchange groups. No grants to individuals, or for goodwill advertising and capital improvement campaigns.
Publications: Application guidelines.
Application information: Application form required.
  Initial approach: Letter of inquiry
  Copies of proposal: 1
  Deadline(s): March 1, June 1, Sept. 1, Dec. 1
  Board meeting date(s): Apr., July, Oct. and Jan.
  Final notification: May, Aug., Nov., and Feb.
  Write: Sharon L. Melcher, Dir., Corp. Contrib.
Number of staff: 1 full-time professional; 1 full-time support.

249
National Semiconductor Corporate Giving Program
2900 Semiconductor Dr.
Santa Clara 95051   (408) 721-5000

Purpose and activities: Support for civic and urban affairs, the arts including music and theatre, primary, secondary and higher education, health care, medical research and federated campaigns.
Fields of interest: Civic affairs, urban development, arts, music, theater, elementary education, secondary education, higher education, health services, medical research, welfare, social services.
Limitations: Giving generally limited to major operating areas in CA.
Application information:
  Write: Lori Fraser, Mgr., Employee Communs. and Services

250
Nissan Motor Corporate Giving Program
P.O. Box 191
Gardena 90248-0191   (213) 532-3111

Purpose and activities: Support for health, social services, education, culture and the arts. Also, support for auto safety programs and U.S.-Japan relations programs.
Fields of interest: Health, welfare, social services, education, cultural programs, arts, Japan.
Types of support: General purposes, special projects, conferences and seminars, employee matching gifts, employee volunteer services, use of facilities, capital campaigns, continuing support, donated products.
Limitations: Giving primarily in major operating areas. No support for fraternal or veterans' organizations. No grants to individuals.
Application information: Contributions are handled by the Community Relations/Public Affairs Staff.
  Deadline(s): Applications accepted throughout the year
  Write: Julie Meyer, Community Rels. Coord.

251
Andrew Norman Foundation
10960 Wilshire Blvd., Suite 820
Los Angeles 90024   (310) 478-1213

Incorporated in 1958 in CA.
Donor(s): Andrew Norman.‡
Foundation type: Independent
Financial data (yr. ended 06/30/90): Assets, $5,200,000 (M); expenditures, $276,835; qualifying distributions, $233,720, including $119,480 for 11 grants (high: $26,000; low: $200; average: $500-$20,000) and $75,000 for loans.
Purpose and activities: Emphasis on seed money for the environment, medical education, justice and the legal system, and the arts and humanities.
Fields of interest: Humanities, environment, arts, medical education, law and justice.
Types of support: Seed money, special projects.
Limitations: Giving primarily in CA, with emphasis on the Los Angeles area. No grants to individuals, or for endowment funds, scholarships, or fellowships.
Application information: Contributes only to pre-selected organizations. Applications not accepted.
  Board meeting date(s): May and as required
  Write: Dan Olincy, Secy.
Officers and Trustees:* Virginia G. Olincy,* Pres.; Bernice G. Kranson,* V.P.; Dan Olincy,* Secy.-Treas.
Number of staff: None.
EIN: 953433781

252
Merle Norman/Nethercutt Foundation
15180 Bledsoe St.
Sylmar 91342-2797

Established in 1985 in CA.
Donor(s): Jack B. Nethercutt, Dorothy S. Nethercutt.
Foundation type: Independent
Financial data (yr. ended 12/31/91): Assets, $175,551 (M); gifts received, $595,000;

expenditures, $593,401; qualifying distributions, $593,401, including $593,220 for 3 grants (high: $500,000; low: $27,500).
Fields of interest: Hospitals—building funds.
Types of support: Building funds.
Limitations: Giving primarily in CA. No grants to individuals.
Application information: Contributes only to pre-selected organizations. Applications not accepted.
Officers and Directors:* Jack B. Nethercutt,* Pres.; Dorothy S. Nethercutt,* V.P.; Arthur O. Armstrong,* Secy.
EIN: 954007395

253
The Kenneth T. and Eileen L. Norris Foundation ▼
11 Golden Shore, Suite 450
Long Beach 90802   (310) 435-8444

Trust established in 1963 in CA.
Donor(s): Kenneth T. Norris,‡ Eileen L. Norris.‡
Foundation type: Independent
Financial data (yr. ended 11/30/91): Assets, $93,880,638 (M); expenditures, $4,187,662; qualifying distributions, $3,746,683, including $3,585,780 for 147 grants (high: $750,000; low: $1,000; average: $5,000-$25,000).
Purpose and activities: Emphasis on hospitals, health, higher and other education, medical research including cancer research, cultural programs, social services, child welfare, and the handicapped.
Fields of interest: Hospitals, health services, medical research, cancer, higher education, education, cultural programs, social services, child welfare, handicapped.
Types of support: Building funds, equipment, research, scholarship funds, continuing support, endowment funds, professorships, seed money, matching funds, special projects, general purposes.
Limitations: Giving limited to Los Angeles County, CA. No grants to individuals; no loans.
Publications: Biennial report.
Application information: Application form not required.
  Initial approach: Letter (2 pages) or telephone
  Copies of proposal: 1
  Deadline(s): None
  Board meeting date(s): As required
  Write: Ronald R. Barnes, Exec. Dir.
Officers and Trustees:* Kenneth T. Norris, Jr.,* Chair.; Ronald R. Barnes,* Exec. Dir.; William G. Corey, George M. Gordon, Harlyne J. Norris.
Number of staff: 3 part-time professional; 2 part-time support.
EIN: 956080374
Recent health grants:
253-1 American Diabetes Association, Los Angeles, CA, $25,000. 1991.
253-2 Angel Flight, Santa Monica, CA, $20,000. 1991.
253-3 Casa Colina Foundation, Pomona, CA, $25,000. For wheel chair sports. 1991.
253-4 Charles R. Drew Medical School, Los Angeles, CA, $15,000. 1991.
253-5 Childrens Clinic, Long Beach, CA, $10,000. 1991.
253-6 Childrens Dental Foundation, Long Beach, CA, $25,000. 1991.

253-7 Childrens Institute International, Los Angeles, CA, $25,000. 1991.

253-8 Crippled Childrens Society of Los Angeles County, Los Angeles, CA, $10,000. 1991.

253-9 Cystic Fibrosis Foundation, Los Angeles, CA, $32,400. 1991.

253-10 Estelle Doheny Eye Foundation, Los Angeles, CA, $250,000. 1991.

253-11 John Douglas French Foundation for Alzheimers Disease, Los Angeles, CA, $25,000. 1991.

253-12 John Tracy Clinic, Los Angeles, CA, $25,000. 1991.

253-13 Los Angeles Child Guidance Clinic, Los Angeles, CA, $10,000. 1991.

253-14 Los Angeles Heart Institute, Los Angeles, CA, $54,000. 1991.

253-15 National Council on Alcoholism, Los Angeles, CA, $10,000. 1991.

253-16 Norris Cancer Hospital, Los Angeles, CA, $750,000. 1991.

253-17 Pacific Clinics, Pasadena, CA, $50,000. 1991.

253-18 Saint Francis Medical Center Foundation, Lynwood, CA, $50,000. 1991.

253-19 Shriners Hospital for Crippled Children, Los Angeles, CA, $10,000. 1991.

253-20 South Central Family Health Center, Los Angeles, CA, $10,000. 1991.

253-21 University of California, Department of Dermatology, Davis, CA, $30,000. 1991.

253-22 University of Southern California, Division of Neurology, Los Angeles, CA, $64,000. 1991.

253-23 University of Southern California, Las Floristas, Los Angeles, CA, $100,000. 1991.

253-24 Valley Community Clinic, North Hollywood, CA, $10,000. 1991.

254
Occidental Petroleum Charitable Foundation, Inc.

10889 Wilshire Blvd.
Los Angeles 90024   (310) 208-8800

Incorporated in 1959 in NY.
Donor(s): Occidental Petroleum Corp.
Foundation type: Company-sponsored
Financial data (yr. ended 12/31/90): Assets, $1,514,815 (M); gifts received, $1,120,000; expenditures, $1,024,184; qualifying distributions, $1,022,354, including $785,000 for 34 grants (high: $100,000; low: $1,000; average: $5,000-$50,000) and $237,066 for 1,039 employee matching gifts.
Purpose and activities: Grants primarily for cultural programs and for higher education, including an employee matching gift program, hospitals, and a few national organizations for social betterment on a national basis.
Fields of interest: Higher education, hospitals, social services, cultural programs.
Types of support: Employee matching gifts, scholarship funds, general purposes, building funds, equipment, capital campaigns.
Limitations: No grants to individuals.
Publications: Application guidelines.
Application information:
  Initial approach: Proposal of no more than 4 pages
  Copies of proposal: 1

Deadline(s): Proposals accepted between Sept. 1 and Nov. 1
Board meeting date(s): Mar., June, Sept., and Dec.
Write: Evelyn S. Wong, Asst. Secy.-Treas.
Officers: Arthur Groman, Pres.; Morrie A. Moss, V.P.; Paul C. Hebner, Secy.-Treas.
Directors: Michael Hammer, Ray R. Irani, Rosemary Tomich.
EIN: 166052784
Recent health grants:
254-1 Saint Johns Hospital and Health Center, Santa Monica, CA, $15,000. For Jimmy Stewart Relay. 1990.

255
Orleton Trust Fund

c/o Jean J. Weaver
2240 Dancing Penny Way
Santa Rosa 95403
Additional office: c/o Mrs. Anne Johnston Greene, Co-Trustee, 1101 Runnymede Rd., Dayton, OH 45419

Trust established in 1944 in OH.
Donor(s): Mary E. Johnston.‡
Foundation type: Independent
Financial data (yr. ended 12/31/91): Assets, $7,399,273 (M); expenditures, $700,700; qualifying distributions, $675,748, including $675,748 for 107 grants (high: $100,000; low: $91; average: $500-$5,000).
Purpose and activities: Support primarily for secondary and higher education, cultural programs, youth and social service agencies, and community funds; grants also for Protestant churches and religious associations, health associations, and ecology and population control groups.
Fields of interest: Higher education, secondary education, cultural programs, youth, social services, community funds, Protestant giving, health associations, ecology, family planning.
Limitations: Giving primarily in Dayton, OH, and San Mateo County, CA. No grants to individuals.
Application information: Contributes only to pre-selected organizations. Applications not accepted.
  Board meeting date(s): As required
Trustees: Anne Johnston Greene, Jean J. Weaver.
EIN: 316024543

256
The Margaret E. Oser Foundation

360 Jasmine St.
Laguna Beach 92651

Established in 1986 in CA.
Donor(s): Margaret E. Oser.‡
Foundation type: Independent
Financial data (yr. ended 12/31/91): Assets, $7,055,734 (M); gifts received, $409,383; expenditures, $472,029; qualifying distributions, $472,029, including $400,000 for 28 grants (high: $25,000; low: $2,500).
Fields of interest: Health services, hospitals, education, elementary education, child welfare, religious schools, Protestant giving, civic affairs, biological sciences, medical sciences, performing arts.

Types of support: Scholarship funds, continuing support.
Limitations: Giving primarily in CA. No grants to individuals.
Application information: Contributes only to pre-selected organizations. Applications not accepted.
Officers: Leslie B. Knox, Pres.; Carl Mitchell, Secy.-Treas.
Number of staff: None.
EIN: 330210168

257
Bernard Osher Foundation ▼

220 San Bruno Ave.
San Francisco 94103-5090   (415) 861-5587

Established in 1977 in CA.
Donor(s): Bernard A. Osher.
Foundation type: Independent
Financial data (yr. ended 12/31/90): Assets, $39,538,682 (M); expenditures, $4,316,220; qualifying distributions, $4,223,503, including $4,166,825 for 127 grants (high: $2,000,000; low: $1,000; average: $2,500-$25,000).
Purpose and activities: Giving primarily for the arts and humanities, including the fine and performing arts; education, especially higher education; and prevention and education programs for at-risk youth in substance abuse, teenage pregnancy, suicide, and AIDS.
Fields of interest: Cultural programs, fine arts, performing arts, museums, dance, theater, music, humanities, education, higher education, family planning, youth, drug abuse.
Types of support: General purposes, special projects.
Limitations: Giving limited to San Francisco, Alameda, Contra Costa, Marin, and San Mateo counties, CA. No grants to individuals.
Publications: Informational brochure.
Application information: Application form not required.
  Initial approach: Letter
  Copies of proposal: 1
  Deadline(s): None
  Board meeting date(s): 6 times per year
  Write: Patricia Tracy-Nagle, Exec. Administrator
Officers and Directors:* Barbro Sachs-Osher,* Pres.; Patricia Tracy-Nagle, Exec. Admin.; David Agger, Frederick Balderston, Reeder Butterfield, Judith E. Ciani, Robert Friend, Ron Kaufman, Bernard A. Osher, Alfred Wilsey.
Number of staff: 1 full-time professional.
EIN: 942506257
Recent health grants:
257-1 Maine Childrens Cancer Program, Portland, ME, $10,000. 1990.
257-2 New Perspectives of Marin, Berkeley, CA, $20,000. 1990.
257-3 Planned Parenthood of Alameda/San Francisco, San Francisco, CA, $38,552. 1990.
257-4 San Francisco Suicide Prevention, San Francisco, CA, $15,000. 1990.
257-5 Teens Kick Off, San Francisco, CA, $15,000. 1990.
257-6 University of California, San Francisco, CA, $53,325. For neurology fellowship. 1990.
257-7 University of California, San Francisco, CA, $17,200. For Diabetes Teaching. 1990.

258
Ostern Foundation
841 Stone Canyon Rd.
Los Angeles 90077   (310) 471-8652

Established in 1989 in CA.
Donor(s): Rolf Ostern, Elina Ostern.
Foundation type: Independent
Financial data (yr. ended 12/31/90): Assets,
$1,842,414 (M); gifts received, $1,065,000;
expenditures, $317,999; qualifying distributions,
$2,317,999, including $215,000 for 3 grants
(high: $200,000; low: $5,000).
Fields of interest: Health associations, medical
research, health services.
Types of support: Matching funds, operating
budgets, conferences and seminars, research.
Limitations: No grants to individuals.
Application information:
  Initial approach: NIH Grant Format
  Copies of proposal: 3
  Deadline(s): May 1
  Board meeting date(s): July 1
  Final notification: Aug. 15
Officer and Director:* Rolf Ostern, Pres.
Number of staff: 3 shared staff
EIN: 954241196

259
Ottenstein Family Foundation, Inc.
225 Stevens Ave., Suite 207
Solana Beach 92075

Established in 1960 in MD and DC.
Donor(s): Members of the Ottenstein family.
Foundation type: Independent
Financial data (yr. ended 04/30/91): Assets,
$2,254,363 (M); gifts received, $1,700;
expenditures, $66,433; qualifying distributions,
$49,893, including $38,070 for 29 grants (high:
$7,500; low: $50).
Purpose and activities: Giving primarily for
Jewish welfare and temple support; support also
for cultural programs, social services, health, and
education.
Fields of interest: Jewish welfare, Jewish giving,
cultural programs, social services, health,
education.
Types of support: Annual campaigns, building
funds, renovation projects.
Limitations: Giving primarily in CA, particularly
San Diego. No grants to individuals.
Application information: Funds currently
committed.
Directors: J. Jacobs, Adam S. Ottenstein, Paul F.
Ottenstein, S.G. Ottenstein, V.H. Ottenstein.
Number of staff: None.
EIN: 526036064

260
Oxnard Foundation
505 Sansome St., Suite 1001
San Francisco 94111   (415) 981-3455

Established in 1973.
Donor(s): Thomas Thornton Oxnard.‡
Foundation type: Independent
Financial data (yr. ended 12/31/91): Assets,
$6,162,943 (M); expenditures, $386,333;
qualifying distributions, $328,155, including

$305,000 for 6 grants (high: $100,000; low:
$5,000).
Purpose and activities: Giving primarily for
medical research, with emphasis on cancer and
surgical research.
Fields of interest: Medical research, cancer.
Types of support: Matching funds, research.
Limitations: Giving primarily in NY, TX, NM, and
CA. No grants to individuals, or for general
support, capital funds, endowments, scholarships,
fellowships, special projects, publications, or
conferences; no loans.
Application information: Application form not
required.
  Initial approach: Letter
  Copies of proposal: 1
  Deadline(s): Feb. 15
  Board meeting date(s): Quarterly
  Final notification: 3 months
  Write: Stephen W. Veitch, Pres.
Officers and Directors:* Stephen W. Veitch,*
Pres.; Caroline Meade,* V.P. and Secy.;
Christopher Veitch,* V.P. and Treas.; Gary J.
Meade,* V.P.; Charles H. Thieriot, Jr.,* V.P.
Number of staff: 1 part-time support.
EIN: 237323007

261
Pacific Western Foundation
8344 East Florence, Suite E
Downey 90240

Successor to Western Gear Foundation,
incorporated in 1953 in CA; name changed in
1982.
Donor(s): Western Gear Corp.
Foundation type: Independent
Financial data (yr. ended 11/30/91): Assets,
$3,746,096 (M); expenditures, $290,210;
qualifying distributions, $248,000, including
$236,000 for 30 grants (high: $87,000; low:
$100).
Fields of interest: Higher education, Catholic
giving, Catholic welfare, hospitals, medical
research.
Limitations: Giving primarily in CA.
Application information:
  Initial approach: Proposal
  Deadline(s): None
  Write: Charles F. Bannan, Pres.
Officers: Charles F. Bannan, Pres.; Joseph T. Nally,
V.P.; M. Patricia Cruden, Secy.; Elmer L. Stone,
Treas.
EIN: 956097360

262
The David and Lucile Packard Foundation
▼
300 Second St., Suite 200
Los Altos 94022   (415) 948-7658

Incorporated in 1964 in CA.
Donor(s): David Packard, Lucile Packard.‡
Foundation type: Independent
Financial data (yr. ended 12/31/91): Assets,
$718,175,870 (M); gifts received, $401,647,131;
expenditures, $33,215,706; qualifying
distributions, $30,227,988, including
$29,297,988 for 365 grants (high: $8,500,000;
low: $1,000; average: $5,000-$500,000) and
$930,000 for program-related investments.

Purpose and activities: Primary areas of interest
include child development, elementary and
secondary education, the environment, family
planning, marine sciences, and population
studies. Local support also for the performing arts,
employment and job training, food and shelter,
and youth. Funding also for the special areas of
management assistance, archaeology, and
Pueblo, Colorado.
Fields of interest: Arts, performing arts,
archaeology, education, education—early
childhood, elementary education, secondary
education, education—minorities, educational
research, child welfare, child development,
youth, disadvantaged, homeless, housing,
employment, community development, urban
development, conservation, environment,
ecology, population studies, family planning,
Latin America, marine sciences.
Types of support: General purposes, building
funds, equipment, land acquisition, research,
internships, matching funds, program-related
investments, consulting services, technical
assistance, loans, operating budgets, capital
campaigns, seed money, renovation projects,
fellowships, special projects, emergency funds.
Limitations: Giving for the arts and community
development primarily in Santa Clara, San Mateo,
Santa Cruz, and Monterey counties, CA, with
some support also in the Pueblo area of CO;
national giving for child health and education;
national and international giving in Latin America
for population and the environment. No support
for religious purposes. No grants to individuals;
generally no grants for endowment funds.
Publications: Annual report (including application
guidelines), grants list, occasional report,
informational brochure (including application
guidelines).
Application information: Application form not
required.
  Initial approach: Proposal
  Copies of proposal: 1
  Deadline(s): Dec. 15, Mar. 15, June 15, and
    Sept. 15
  Board meeting date(s): Mar., June, Sept., and
    Dec.
  Final notification: Directly after board meetings
  Write: Colburn S. Wilbur, Exec. Dir.
Officers and Trustees:* David Packard,* Chair.
and Pres.; Susan Packard Orr,* V.P.; David
Woodley Packard,* V.P.; Barbara P. Wright, Secy.;
Edwin E. Van Bronkhorst,* Treas.; Colburn S.
Wilbur, Exec. Dir.; Nancy Packard Burnett, Robin
Chandler Duke, Robert Glaser, M.D., Dean O.
Morton, Julie E. Packard, Frank Roberts.
Number of staff: 12 full-time professional; 2
part-time professional; 17 full-time support; 4
part-time support.
EIN: 942278431
Recent health grants:
262-1 Alan Guttmacher Institute, NYC, NY,
    $70,000. For study to determine effect of
    parental consent laws on teenagers seeking
    abortions. 1991.
262-2 Alan Guttmacher Institute, NYC, NY,
    $70,000. For strategy to overturn federal
    abortion restrictions and support Title X. 1991.
262-3 American Civil Liberties Union
    Foundation of Northern California, San
    Francisco, CA, $20,000. For Abortion Rights
    Project. 1991.

262-4 American Civil Liberties Union Foundation, NYC, NY, $70,000. For Reproductive Freedom Project. 1991.

262-5 Better World Society, DC, $19,500. For one-hour TV documentary on new contraceptive alternatives. 1991.

262-6 Catholics for a Free Choice, DC, $30,000. For U.S. and Latin American programs. 1991.

262-7 Center for Population Options, DC, $30,000. For International Center on Adolescent Fertility programs in Latin America. 1991.

262-8 Children Now, Oakland, CA, $150,000. For continued monitoring of child health issues in California. 1991.

262-9 Childrens Health Council of the Mid-Peninsula, Palo Alto, CA, $441,130. To provide developmental training for neonatal intensive care nursery staff and families. 1991.

262-10 Childrens Hospital, Kempe Research Center, Denver, CO, $221,118. To evaluate effectiveness of parent-held medical passport for economically disadvantaged children. 1991.

262-11 Childrens Hospital and Health Center, San Diego, CA, $19,988. To improve health of children in foster care. 1991.

262-12 Coastside Infants/Toddler Center, Half Moon Bay, CA, $40,000. For building renovation and relocation. 1991.

262-13 Columbia University, NYC, NY, $30,000. For training program in Brazil and maternal mortality study in Ecuador. 1991.

262-14 Communications Consortium Media Center, DC, $15,000. For education campaign regarding federal abortion restrictions. 1991.

262-15 Community Living Centers, Chico, CA, $40,000. For start-up of Supported Employment Program for mentally disabled in San Mateo County. 1991.

262-16 Education Programs Associates, Campbell, CA, $40,000. To establish network of major California maternal and child health providers. 1991.

262-17 Family Health Education Center, Santa Cruz, CA, $30,000. To develop and implement family education and support program. 1991.

262-18 Family Planning Alternatives, Sunnyvale, CA, $25,000. For Women in Need Fund. 1991.

262-19 George Washington University, Center for Health Policy Research, DC, $70,174. To analyze role of Medicaid in publicly provided health care system for children. 1991.

262-20 Georgetown University, DC, $144,807. To mount informational forums in D.C. on expanding health insurance for children. 1991.

262-21 Grantmakers in Health, NYC, NY, $10,000. For conference entitled The Health of American Children. 1991.

262-22 Institute for Development Training, Chapel Hill, NC, $20,000. To market video program, Population and People of Faith. 1991.

262-23 InterAction: American Council for Voluntary International Action, NYC, NY, $40,000. To foster increased organizational collaboration for population/environment projects. 1991.

262-24 International Projects Assistance Services, Carrboro, NC, $30,000. To expand training and delivery in Michoacan and Mexico City. 1991.

262-25 Kaiser Foundation Hospitals, Division of Research, Oakland, CA, $19,000. To expand investigation of new born sepsis. 1991.

262-26 Kaiser Permanente Advisory Services, Division of Research, Oakland, CA, $125,921. For California study of environmental factors and pregnancy and birth outcomes. 1991.

262-27 National Abortion Federation, DC, $70,000. For Truth About Abortion campaign. 1991.

262-28 National Abortion Rights Action League (NARAL) Foundation, DC, $50,000. For information-gathering and public education programs. 1991.

262-29 National Association of the Partners of the Americas, DC, $19,800. For family planning workshop for Central America held in El Salvador. 1991.

262-30 National Bureau of Economic Research, NYC, NY, $120,066. For cost-benefit analysis of prenatal treatment for maternal substance abuse. 1991.

262-31 National Bureau of Economic Research, NYC, NY, $15,710. To study effects of low birth weight on performance of school-age children. 1991.

262-32 National Center for Clinical Infant Programs, Arlington, VA, $125,000. For study of supervision and mentorship in training of child development professionals. 1991.

262-33 National Family Planning and Reproductive Health Association, DC, $25,000. For public education and outreach campaign. 1991.

262-34 Natividad Medical Center, Salinas, CA, $10,100. To develop plan to increase access to prenatal care. 1991.

262-35 New York Academy of Medicine, NYC, NY, $10,000. For conference on pediatric poverty and health. 1991.

262-36 Parkview Episcopal Medical Center, Thatcher Learning Center, Pueblo, CO, $18,000. For addition to Center's building. 1991.

262-37 Pathfinder Fund, Watertown, MA, $50,000. For Asociacion Salud Con Prevencion Project continuation in Colombia and expansion into Peru. 1991.

262-38 Planned Parenthood Association of Monterey County, Monterey, CA, $30,000. To expand donor development program. 1991.

262-39 Planned Parenthood Association of Monterey County, Monterey, CA, $15,835. For consultant to conduct strategic planning process. 1991.

262-40 Planned Parenthood Association of San Mateo County, San Mateo, CA, $100,000. For capital campaign and program expansion. 1991.

262-41 Planned Parenthood Federation of America, NYC, NY, $75,000. For Campaign to Keep Abortion Safe and Legal. 1991.

262-42 Planned Parenthood Federation, International, Western Hemisphere Region, NYC, NY, $31,300. For teacher training and sexual education materials for Mexico City schools. 1991.

262-43 Planned Parenthood of Santa Cruz County, Santa Cruz, CA, $30,000. To expand donor development program. 1991.

262-44 Planned Parenthood of Santa Cruz County, Santa Cruz, CA, $14,000. For Teen

Success Program to prevent additional pregnancies among teenage mothers. 1991.

262-45 Population Council, NYC, NY, $40,000. For model rural family planning outreach program in Chiapas, Mexico. 1991.

262-46 Population Crisis Committee, DC, $90,000. For Report Card Project. 1991.

262-47 Population Crisis Committee, DC, $90,000. For public information programs. 1991.

262-48 Program for the Introduction and Adaptation of Contraceptive Technology (PIACT), DC, $20,000. To train Latin American clinicians in treating incomplete and septic abortions. 1991.

262-49 Program for the Introduction and Adaptation of Contraceptive Technology (PIACT), Seattle, WA, $32,500. For grants management and technical assistance program in Latin America. 1991.

262-50 Salud Para la Gente Community Health Clinic, Watsonville, CA, $126,800. To initiate comprehensive perinatal service program. 1991.

262-51 Samaritan Institute, Denver, CO, $25,000. For new ecumenical counseling center in Palo Alto, CA. 1991.

262-52 San Diego State University Foundation, San Diego, CA, $54,350. To establish child care health hotline. 1991.

262-53 Stanford University, Stanford, CA, $205,000. For perinatal community outreach program. 1991.

262-54 Stanford University, Hoover Institution on War, Revolution and Peace, Stanford, CA, $195,000. For research and writing project on current drug policy. 1991.

262-55 United Cerebral Palsy Association of Santa Clara/San Mateo County, Mountain View, CA, $40,000. For expansion, follow-up and evaluation of Passport to Services. 1991.

262-56 University of Washington, Seattle, WA, $10,500. For evaluation of group well-child care for low-income families. 1991.

262-57 University Pediatrics, Burlington, VT, $255,475. For neonatal outcomes research in Vermont-Oxford Trials Network. 1991.

262-58 World Neighbors, Oklahoma City, OK, $40,000. For reproductive health care program in Peru, Chile, Ecuador and Bolivia. 1991.

262-59 Zero Population Growth, DC, $40,000. For teacher workshops and curriculum materials on population. 1991.

263
The Parker Foundation

1200 Prospect St., Suite 575
La Jolla 92037   (619) 456-3038

Trust established in 1971 in CA; incorporated in 1975.

Donor(s): Gerald T. Parker,‡ Inez Grant Parker.‡
Foundation type: Independent
Financial data (yr. ended 09/30/91): Assets, $14,319,306 (M); expenditures, $884,578; qualifying distributions, $823,461, including $746,885 for 67 grants (high: $100,000; low: $1,600; average: $5,000-$15,000).
Purpose and activities: Equal emphasis on cultural programs, health and welfare, including medical support and research, adult services, and youth agencies; grants also for education and

community activities. Giving largely in the form of partial seed money and matching or challenge grants; generally no support that would make an organization dependent on the foundation.

Fields of interest: Cultural programs, arts, health, medical research, AIDS, welfare, youth, education, community development, community funds.

Types of support: Seed money, matching funds, operating budgets, annual campaigns, emergency funds, building funds, equipment, land acquisition, research, program-related investments, continuing support, special projects, publications, general purposes, renovation projects.

Limitations: Giving limited to San Diego County, CA. No support for sectarian religious purposes. No grants to individuals, or for endowment funds, scholarships, or fellowships; no loans.

Publications: Annual report, informational brochure (including application guidelines).

Application information: Application form not required.

Initial approach: Letter
Copies of proposal: 9
Deadline(s): None
Board meeting date(s): Monthly
Final notification: 2 months
Write: Robbin C. Powell, Asst. Secy.

Officers and Directors: Kenneth R. Rearwin,* Pres.; V. DeWitt Shuck,* V.P.; William E. Beamer,* Secy.-Treas.; Arnold LaGuardia, Judy McDonald, Sandra Pay.

Number of staff: None.

EIN: 510141231

Recent health grants:

263-1 Escondido Community Clinic, Escondido, CA, $10,000. For collaborative system analysis for computer equipment to allow resource sharing among three community clinics. 1990.

263-2 Family Stress Center, Pleasant Hill, CA, $12,000. Toward salary support for licensed full-time psychotherapist. 1990.

263-3 La Jolla Cancer Research Foundation, La Jolla, CA, $18,000. For computer hardware and software. 1990.

263-4 Planned Parenthood of San Diego and Riverside Counties, San Diego, CA, $25,000. For challenge matching grant for bridge fund. 1990.

263-5 Salk Institute for Biological Studies, La Jolla, CA, $70,000. For construction of new laboratory and office facility. 1990.

264
The Ralph M. Parsons Foundation ▼
1055 Wilshire Blvd., Suite 1701
Los Angeles 90017   (213) 482-3185

Incorporated in 1961 in CA.
Donor(s): Ralph M. Parsons.‡
Foundation type: Independent
Financial data (yr. ended 12/31/90): Assets, $156,600,728 (M); expenditures, $7,997,761; qualifying distributions, $7,271,204, including $6,602,105 for grants (high: $1,200,000; low: $1,000; average: $10,000-$75,000).
Purpose and activities: Giving for higher and pre-collegiate education, with emphasis on engineering, technology, science and medicine; and for social impact areas, including assistance to children, women, families, and seniors; grants

also for cultural and civic projects, and health services for disadvantaged populations.
Fields of interest: Education, higher education, secondary education, elementary education, education—early childhood, social services, youth, child welfare, aged, family services, disadvantaged, homeless, housing, cultural programs, arts, civic affairs, performing arts, health services, hospitals, AIDS, engineering, science and technology, legal services, computer sciences.
Types of support: Seed money, equipment, matching funds, special projects, internships, renovation projects, research, scholarship funds, fellowships, operating budgets.
Limitations: Giving limited to Los Angeles County, CA, with the exception of some grants for higher education. No support for sectarian, religious, or fraternal purposes, or for programs for which substantial support from government or other sources is readily available. No grants to individuals, or for continuing support, annual campaigns, federated fundraising appeals, emergency or endowment funds, land acquisition, workshops, exhibits, surveys, or conferences.
Publications: Annual report.
Application information: Application form not required.

Initial approach: Letter
Copies of proposal: 1
Deadline(s): None
Board meeting date(s): Bimonthly beginning in Jan.
Final notification: 6 months
Write: Christine Sisley, Exec. Dir.

Officers and Directors: Joseph G. Hurley,* Pres.; Leroy B. Houghton,* V.P. and C.F.O.; Edgar R. Jackson, V.P.; Everett B. Laybourne,* V.P.; Christine Sisley, Secy. and Exec. Dir.; Ira J. Blanco, Albert A. Dorskind, Robert F. Erburu.

Number of staff: 3 full-time professional; 3 full-time support.

EIN: 956085895

Recent health grants:

264-1 All Saints Church Service Center, Office of Creative Connections, Pasadena, CA, $15,000. For seed funding for Young and Healthy Demonstration Project, coordinating health care services through schools for children from low-income uninsured families. 1990.

264-2 Bienvenidos Childrens Center, West Covina, CA, $57,025. For In-Home Support Project for disabled and medically-fragile children. 1990.

264-3 Center for the Partially Sighted, Santa Monica, CA, $29,250. To expand Independent Living Skills Program which teaches partially-sighted how to remain living independently in community. 1990.

264-4 Childrens Clinic, Long Beach, CA, $10,000. For Children-At-Risk Program. 1990.

264-5 Community Counseling Service at United University Church, Los Angeles, CA, $10,000. For Youth-At-Risk program, providing psychological, educational and emotional support to immigrant youth and their families. 1990.

264-6 Crittenton Center for Young Women and Infants, Los Angeles, CA, $25,000. To renovate nursery to be used as parenting lab which will serve residents, foster families, and communities and community families. 1990.

264-7 Five Acres, Altadena, CA, $50,000. For Family Resource Center which focuses on prevention and early intervention services to families and children at risk of abuse and neglect. 1990.

264-8 Glendale Family Service, Glendale, CA, $22,600. For counseling services for women and children residing in Glendale YWCA battered women's shelter. 1990.

264-9 Hathaway Childrens Services, Pacoima, CA, $200,000. For seed funding for Family Resource Center to serve residents of Northeast Los Angeles with wide range of family support programs. 1990.

264-10 Jenesse Center, Los Angeles, CA, $30,000. To expand services to women and children who are victims of domestic violence. 1990.

264-11 Los Angeles Free Clinic, Los Angeles, CA, $20,000. For Volunteer Coordinator position. 1990.

264-12 Marianne Frostig Center of Educational Therapy, Pasadena, CA, $34,092. To purchase 26-passenger bus, essential for transportation of learning disabled youth for programs offered by agency. 1990.

264-13 Orthopaedic Hospital, Los Angeles, CA, $75,000. To purchase X-Ray Bone Densitometer for use in treatment of patients with metabolic bone diseases. 1990.

264-14 Penny Lane, Sepulveda, CA, $30,000. To purchase new group home facility for abused and neglected children. 1990.

264-15 Santa Teresita Hospital, Duarte, CA, $25,000. To purchase new equipment for use in Digestive Disorders Treatment Center. 1990.

264-16 Scripps Home, Altadena, CA, $75,000. To renovate kitchen facility, which provides meals for low-income elderly and for Altadena Meals on Wheels program. 1990.

264-17 Senior Health and Peer Counseling Center, Santa Monica, CA, $50,000. For capital development campaign to acquire and furnish expanded facilities. 1990.

264-18 South Bay Free Clinic, Manhattan Beach, CA, $36,400. For Prenatal Care Program serving low-income minority patients. 1990.

264-19 Westside Womens Health Center, Santa Monica, CA, $25,000. For seed funding for comprehensive prenatal care program for working poor women. 1990.

265
Pasadena Area Residential Aid A Corporation ▼
P.O. Box 984
Pasadena 91102   (213) 681-1331

Foundation established in 1948 in CA.
Foundation type: Independent
Financial data (yr. ended 07/31/91): Assets, $2,208,446 (M); gifts received, $2,862,125; expenditures, $2,905,251; qualifying distributions, $2,843,196, including $2,843,196 for 1,129 grants (high: $356,250; low: $15; average: $100-$25,000).
Purpose and activities: Grants largely for higher education, cultural programs, Christian church support, and social services; support also for youth agencies, hospitals, and community funds.

Fields of interest: Higher education, cultural programs, religion—Christian, religious welfare, youth, community funds, social services, hospitals.
Application information: Contributions initiated by donor/members only. Applications not accepted.
Board meeting date(s): Annually
Officers and Directors:* Robert R. Huffman,* Pres.; Philip V. Swan, V.P.; Thomas S. Jones III,* Secy.; James N. Gamble,* Treas.; Mary W. Johnson, Robert F. Niven, Lee G. Paul, Trude C. Taylor, Jack D. Whitehead.
Number of staff: 1 part-time professional.
EIN: 952048774
Recent health grants:
265-1 Akron City Hospital Foundation, Akron, OH, $10,000. 1990.
265-2 Cleveland Clinic Foundation, Cleveland, OH, $25,000. 1990.
265-3 House Ear Institute, Los Angeles, CA, $31,905. 1990.
265-4 Huntington Medical Research Institutes, Pasadena, CA, $48,752. 1990.
265-5 Huntington Memorial Hospital, Pasadena, CA, $26,975. 1990.
265-6 Memorial Sloan-Kettering Cancer Center, NYC, NY, $27,150. 1990.
265-7 Orion Medical Sciences Institute, Arcadia, CA, $10,000. 1990.
265-8 Pacific Clinics, Pasadena, CA, $10,447. 1990.
265-9 Pasadena Planned Parenthood Committee, Pasadena, CA, $29,880. 1990.
265-10 Pegasus Farm, Hartville, OH, $35,000. 1990.
265-11 Wellness Community, Los Angeles, CA, $49,465. 1990.

266
Pasadena Foundation
16 North Marengo Ave., Suite 302
Pasadena 91101   (818) 796-2097

Established in 1953 in CA by resolution and declaration of trust.
Donor(s): Louis A. Webb,‡ Marion L. Webb,‡ Helen B. Lockett,‡ Dorothy I. Stewart,‡ Rebecca R. Anthony,‡ Lucille Crumb.‡
Foundation type: Community
Financial data (yr. ended 12/31/91): Assets, $10,392,085 (M); gifts received, $249,254; expenditures, $1,005,020; qualifying distributions, $924,656, including $924,656 for 230 grants (high: $40,000; low: $50).
Purpose and activities: Grants for capital improvements to established local agencies, with emphasis on child welfare and development, youth agencies, and senior citizen welfare; support also for alcohol and drug abuse programs, family planning and services, the handicapped, hospitals, hospices, and health services, including mental health and medical research, and museums.
Fields of interest: Child development, aged, drug abuse, family planning, family services, hospitals, health services, mental health, medical research, museums.
Types of support: Building funds, equipment, matching funds, renovation projects, research.
Limitations: Giving limited to the Pasadena, CA, area. No grants to individuals, or for operating budgets, continuing support, annual campaigns,

emergency funds, seed money, deficit financing, land acquisition, endowment funds, special projects, publications, conferences, consulting services, scholarships, or fellowships; no loans.
Publications: Annual report, application guidelines, informational brochure, program policy statement.
Application information: Application form required.
Initial approach: Letter
Copies of proposal: 1
Deadline(s): July 1
Board meeting date(s): Apr. and Dec.
Final notification: After Dec. meeting
Write: Josephine L. Stephen, Exec. Dir.
Advisory Board: Fred H. Felberg, Chair.; James B. Boyle, Jr., Vice-Chair.; Josephine L. Stephen, Exec. Dir.; Harriman L. Cronk, James M. King, Sr., Albert C. Lowe, Joel V. Sheldon, Kyhl S. Smeby, David A. Werbelow, Marjorie Wyatt.
Trustees: Bank of America, Citizens Commercial Trust and Savings Bank, Interstate Bank, Sanwa Bank California.
Number of staff: 1 part-time professional.
EIN: 956047660

267
The Patron Saints Foundation
P.O. Box 40706
Pasadena 91114-7706   (818) 797-2303

Established in 1986 in CA.
Foundation type: Independent
Financial data (yr. ended 06/30/91): Assets, $3,135,457 (M); gifts received, $3,000; expenditures, $185,555; qualifying distributions, $163,158, including $144,475 for 19 grants (high: $18,000; low: $1,400).
Purpose and activities: Giving primarily for medical and other professional health care programs, including community health education and services, community outreach programs, hospitals, and medical research.
Fields of interest: Health, health services, health associations, mental health, family services, child welfare, drug abuse, alcoholism.
Types of support: Capital campaigns, renovation projects, equipment, research, continuing support, seed money, special projects.
Limitations: Giving limited to the San Gabriel Valley, CA, area. No grants to individuals, or for endowment funds, conferences, seminars, workshops, exhibits, travel, or surveys.
Application information: Application form required.
Copies of proposal: 10
Deadline(s): Early Mar. and early Oct.
Board meeting date(s): Mid-May and early Dec.
Final notification: May and Dec.
Write: Jacquie Fennessy, Dir.
Officers and Directors:* Richard D. Pettit, M.D.,* Pres.; Christine Sisley,* Secy.; J. Benjamin Earl,* Treas.; Paul F. Berger, Jr., Richard C. Dunn, W. Allan Edmiston, M.D., Jacquie Fennessy, Janet Fitzgerald, Nellie Garcia, Robert Gustafson, M.D., Martha Ingram, Margaret Landry, Marvin R. McClain, David K. Robinson, Dorothy Shea, Debra J. Spiegal, Melinda Winston.
Number of staff: 1 part-time professional.
EIN: 953484257

268
The PCS Foundation
c/o Ross Stores
8333 Central Ave.
Newark 94560   (415) 845-9080

Established in 1977 in CA.
Donor(s): Members of the Moldaw family.
Foundation type: Independent
Financial data (yr. ended 11/30/91): Assets, $3,009,287 (M); expenditures, $308,769; qualifying distributions, $305,530, including $303,247 for grants (high: $100,000).
Purpose and activities: Support primarily for Jewish welfare and other social service agencies; grants also for AIDS and other medical research and health associations, including associations for mental health and heart disease, public affairs, foreign policy and international studies, the arts, and race relations and education for minorities.
Fields of interest: Jewish welfare, social services, AIDS, medical research, health associations, public affairs, foreign policy, arts, race relations, education—minorities.
Limitations: Giving primarily in CA, with emphasis on San Francisco and Stanford.
Application information: Application form not required.
Deadline(s): None
Write: Susan J. Moldaw
Officers: Stuart Moldaw, Pres.; Phyllis Moldaw, V.P. and Treas.
EIN: 942450734

269
Peninsula Community Foundation
1700 South El Camino Real, No. 300
San Mateo 94402-3049   (415) 358-9369
Additional address: P.O. Box 6729, San Mateo, CA 94403; FAX: (415) 358-9817

Established as a trust in 1964 in CA; incorporated in 1981.
Foundation type: Community
Financial data (yr. ended 12/31/91): Assets, $55,827,828 (M); gifts received, $3,757,885; expenditures, $5,477,325; qualifying distributions, $3,229,719, including $3,229,719 for 508 grants (average: $500-$35,000).
Purpose and activities: To support local cultural, educational, social service, and health programs. Primary areas of interest include homelessness and housing, children and youth, the environment, arts and culture, and senior citizens and the needs of the aging; other interests include the disabled, civic concerns, and recreation; provides counseling services for local fund seekers. Giving includes grants to individuals as student aid, emergency assistance, and grants to local artists.
Fields of interest: Child development, youth, social services, homeless, housing, education, environment, aged, handicapped, health, arts, cultural programs, recreation, civic affairs.
Types of support: Operating budgets, continuing support, seed money, emergency funds, equipment, matching funds, consulting services, technical assistance, internships, scholarship funds, special projects, publications, conferences and seminars, general purposes, lectureships, student aid, renovation projects, grants to individuals.

Limitations: Giving limited to San Mateo County and northern Santa Clara County, CA. No grants for endowment funds, annual campaigns, building funds, deficit financing, land acquisition, or research.
Publications: Annual report (including application guidelines), application guidelines, informational brochure, newsletter, grants list, financial statement.
Application information: Application guidelines are available in Spanish, Tagalog, Tongan, Samoan, Japanese, Vietnamese, Portuguese, or large type. Application form not required.
  Initial approach: Letter or telephone
  Copies of proposal: 1
  Deadline(s): None
  Board meeting date(s): Distribution committee meets in Jan., Mar., May, July, Sept., and Nov.
  Final notification: 2 months
  Write: Sterling K. Speirn, Exec. Dir.
Officers and Directors:* Rosemary Young,* Chair.; Thomas M. Jenkins,* Vice-Chair.; John D. Taylor,* Pres.; Tom Bailard, Marjorie Bolton, Hugh C. Burroughs, T. Jack Foster, Jr., Albert J. Horn, Esq., Charles B. Johnson, Robert Kirkwood, John P. Renshaw, William Wilson III.
Number of staff: 5 full-time professional; 4 full-time support; 1 part-time support.
EIN: 942746687
Recent health grants:
269-1 Charles Armstrong School, Belmont, CA, $46,500. For classroom co-teachers and scholarships. 1991.
269-2 Jefferson Union High School District, Daly City, CA, $25,000. For Daly City Youth Center medical care, health education and counseling. 1991.
269-3 Peninsula Network of Mental Health Clients, San Mateo, CA, $25,000. For Miller Center. 1991.
269-4 Planned Parenthood Association of San Mateo County, San Mateo, CA, $10,000. For Male Involvement Program in San Mateo County. 1991.

270
Leon S. Peters Foundation, Inc.
4148 East Clinton Ave.
Fresno 93703-2520   (209) 227-5901

Established in 1959 in CA.
Donor(s): Leon S. Peters.‡
Foundation type: Independent
Financial data (yr. ended 11/30/91): Assets, $10,901,138 (M); expenditures, $526,310; qualifying distributions, $508,539, including $504,800 for 71 grants (high: $50,000; low: $300; average: $5,000).
Fields of interest: Community development, cultural programs, health, hospitals, higher education, religion—Christian, youth, social services.
Types of support: Scholarship funds, building funds, operating budgets.
Limitations: Giving primarily in Fresno, CA. No grants to individuals.
Application information: Contributes only to pre-selected organizations. Applications not accepted.
  Board meeting date(s): Feb., May, Aug., and Nov.

Officers and Directors:* Alice A. Peters,* Pres. and C.F.O.; Pete P. Peters,* V.P. and Secy.; Craig Apregan, George Apregan, Darrell Peters, Kenneth Peters, Ronald Peters.
Number of staff: None.
EIN: 946064669

271
Paul C. & Borghild T. Petersen Foundation
859 San Mateo Dr.
San Mateo 94401-2298

Established in 1987.
Foundation type: Independent
Financial data (yr. ended 12/31/90): Assets, $5,338,657 (M); gifts received, $2,500,000; expenditures, $1,090,807; qualifying distributions, $1,079,133, including $1,077,855 for grants.
Fields of interest: Religion—Christian, hospices, health associations.
Limitations: No grants to individuals.
Application information: Application form not required.
  Initial approach: Letter
  Deadline(s): None
  Write: Paul C. Petersen, Pres.
Officer and Directors:* Paul C. Petersen,* Pres.; D.D. Hughmanick.
EIN: 943060391

272
Gustavus and Louise Pfeiffer Research Foundation
P.O. Box 1153
Redlands 92373-0361   (714) 792-6269

Incorporated in 1942 in NY.
Donor(s): Gustavus A. Pfeiffer.‡
Foundation type: Independent
Financial data (yr. ended 12/31/90): Assets, $13,123,211 (M); expenditures, $867,101; qualifying distributions, $806,130, including $700,329 for 23 grants (high: $75,000; low: $15,000; average: $15,000-$75,000).
Purpose and activities: The improvement of public health through the advancement of medicine and pharmacy; the foundation's primary area of interest is in medical and pharmacological research.
Fields of interest: Medical research, pharmacy.
Types of support: Research, matching funds, seed money.
Limitations: No support for national fundraising organizations or publicly financed projects. No grants to individuals, or for building or endowment funds, scholarships, fellowships, travel, conferences, or general purposes; no loans.
Publications: Biennial report (including application guidelines).
Application information: Application form not required.
  Initial approach: Letter of inquiry
  Copies of proposal: 9
  Deadline(s): 1 month before board meeting
  Board meeting date(s): Twice annually, usually in the spring and fall
  Final notification: 1 week after annual board meeting
  Write: George R. Pfeiffer, Secy.-Treas.

Officers and Directors:* Matthew G. Herold, Jr.,* Pres.; Lise P. Chapman,* V.P. Finance; H. Robert Herold II,* V.P.; George R. Pfeiffer,* Secy.-Treas.; Alfredo Leonardi, M.D., Patricia Herold Nagle, Paul H. Pfeiffer, M.D., Robert H. Pfeiffer, Milton C. Rose.
Number of staff: 1 full-time professional.
EIN: 136086299
Recent health grants:
272-1 California Institute of Technology, Division of Biology, Pasadena, CA, $30,000. For three research projects. 1990.
272-2 Coriell Institute for Medical Research, Camden, NJ, $25,000. For research studies to help quantify risks associated with exposure to carcinogens benzo(a)pyrene and ethylene oxide. 1990.
272-3 Eye and Ear Institute, Pittsburgh, PA, $25,000. For research study of retinal degeneration. 1990.
272-4 Harvard University, School of Medicine, Boston, MA, $36,000. To prepare minority students for careers in academic medicine through research. 1990.
272-5 Istituto di Recerche Farmacologiche Mario Negri, Italy, $45,000. For general support of Gustavus A. Pfeiffer Memorial Libraries in Milan, Bergamo and province of Chieti, Italy. 1990.
272-6 Johns Hopkins University, School of Medicine, Department of Pharmacology and Molecular Sciences, DC, $45,000. For graduate students conducting medical research. 1990.
272-7 National Center for the Study of Wilsons Disease, Bronx, NY, $30,000. For research study on prevalence of Wilson's disease in selected populations of psychiatric inpatients. 1990.
272-8 Pennsylvania State University, University Park, PA, $37,635. For research study on ovarian tumor treatment. 1990.
272-9 Pfeiffer College, Misenheimer, NC, $25,000. To strengthen Division of Natural and Health Sciences. 1990.
272-10 Saint Christophers Hospital for Children, Philadelphia, PA, $25,000. For research study to develop optimum morphine doses for treatment of children and adolescents with painful episodes of Sickle Cell Disease. 1990.
272-11 Salk Institute for Biological Studies, La Jolla, CA, $15,000. For research study of genetic control of conversion of unspecialized embryonic cells into highly specialized information processing units which make connections with other nerve cells. 1990.
272-12 Stanford University, School of Medicine, Stanford, CA, $40,000. For minority medical students conducting research. 1990.
272-13 Tufts University, Sackler School of Graduate Biomedical Sciences, Medford, MA, $20,000. For research study of pathological changes in olfactory epithelium in Alzheimer's disease and aging. 1990.
272-14 University of Arizona, College of Medicine, Tucson, AZ, $25,000. For research in cardiac arrhythmias. 1990.
272-15 University of California, Harbor-UCLA Medical Center, Los Angeles, CA, $25,000. For research study of metabolic processes that cause significant weight loss in patients with head and neck cancer. 1990.

272-16 University of California, School of Medicine, Los Angeles, CA, $30,000. For research on pancreas islet transplantation as cure for diabetes. 1990.

272-17 University of North Carolina, Chapel Hill, NC, $19,352. For research study on regulation of cell growth by platelet-derived growth factor. 1990.

272-18 University of the Ozarks, Clarksville, AR, $75,000. For annual installment to establish Henry Robert Herold Chair of Biological Science. 1990.

272-19 University of Vermont, Department of Microbiology, Burlington, VT, $10,000. For research study in molecular biology. 1990.

272-20 Wistar Institute of Anatomy and Biology, Philadelphia, PA, $30,342. For research study to develop new method of producing monoclonal antibodies. 1990.

272-21 Worcester Foundation for Experimental Biology, Shrewsbury, MA, $27,000. To study nerve cell connections in cell development and aging. 1990.

272-22 Yale University, School of Medicine, New Haven, CT, $20,000. For research study on antigenic suppression of transplanted organs in Department of Surgery. 1990.

273
Mary Pickford Foundation

9171 Wilshire Blvd., Suite 512
Beverly Hills 90210   (310) 273-2770

Established in 1968.
Donor(s): Mary Pickford Rogers.‡
Foundation type: Independent
Financial data (yr. ended 05/31/91): Assets, $9,447,724 (M); expenditures, $845,459; qualifying distributions, $670,500, including $634,900 for 115 grants (high: $55,000; low: $250; average: $1,000-$20,000).
Purpose and activities: Grants largely for scholarship funds at colleges and universities, and for "well-established medical or community service organizations," including performing arts programs, museums, and agencies serving the elderly and other disadvantaged groups.
Fields of interest: Higher education, hospitals, health associations, community development, museums, film, theater, disadvantaged, aged.
Types of support: Scholarship funds, general purposes, endowment funds.
Limitations: Giving primarily in CA. No support for drug rehabilitation or medical research. No grants to individuals, or for building funds or land acquisition.
Application information: Application form not required.
 Initial approach: Letter or telephone
 Deadline(s): None
 Write: Edward G. Stotsenberg, Pres.
Officers and Directors:* Edward G. Stotsenberg,* Pres. and C.E.O.; Sull Lawrence, Secy.; Charles B. Rogers, Treas.
Number of staff: None.
EIN: 956093487

274
The Adele Morse Platt Foundation

110 East Ninth St., Suite C-663
Los Angeles 90079   (213) 239-9245

Established in 1983 in CA.
Donor(s): Adele Morse Platt.
Foundation type: Independent
Financial data (yr. ended 06/30/91): Assets, $103,012 (M); gifts received, $310,000; expenditures, $280,875; qualifying distributions, $280,855, including $280,265 for 32 grants (high: $150,100; low: $25).
Purpose and activities: Support primarily for Jewish welfare and a medical center; giving also for health associations and medical research, including AIDS research, the arts, and social services, including child welfare agencies and programs for the disabled.
Fields of interest: Jewish giving, Jewish welfare, hospitals, health associations, medical research, AIDS, arts, social services, child welfare, handicapped.
Types of support: Building funds, general purposes, research.
Limitations: Giving primarily in CA.
Publications: Annual report.
Application information: Application form not required.
 Write: Adele Morse Platt, Pres.
Officers and Directors:* Adele Morse Platt,* Pres.; David S. Morse,* V.P.; Majorie Roth,* V.P.; Susan Lee Morse,* Secy.; Lois Barbara Reinis,* C.F.O.
Number of staff: None.
EIN: 953885959

275
Plitt Southern Theatres, Inc. Employees Fund

1801 Century Park East, Suite 1225
Los Angeles 90067

Established in 1945 in TX.
Donor(s): Plitt Southern Theatres.
Foundation type: Company-sponsored
Financial data (yr. ended 12/31/90): Assets, $6,519,598 (M); expenditures, $780,811; qualifying distributions, $620,284, including $297,500 for 37 grants (high: $30,000; low: $500) and $322,784 for 108 grants to individuals (high: $12,083; low: $26).
Purpose and activities: Giving for medical research and hospitals, the arts, higher education, youth, and mental health; also supports an employee welfare fund, religious organizations, and Israeli defense.
Fields of interest: Medical research, hospitals, arts, higher education, youth, mental health, Israel.
Types of support: Grants to individuals, loans, general purposes.
Application information: Grants are awarded at the discretion of the trustees. Applications not accepted.
 Write: Joe S. Jackson, Pres.
Officers and Trustees:* Joe S. Jackson,* Pres.; W.R. Curtis,* V.P. and Secy.; Roy H. Aaron, Raymond C. Fox, Henry G. Plitt.
EIN: 756037855

276
The Pointer Foundation

10345 Olympic Blvd.
Los Angeles 90064

Established in 1990 in CA.
Foundation type: Independent
Financial data (yr. ended 12/31/90): Assets, $416,808 (M); gifts received, $600,000; expenditures, $200,305; qualifying distributions, $200,305, including $200,000 for 2 grants of $100,000 each.
Fields of interest: AIDS, medical research.
Limitations: Giving limited to Los Angeles, CA. No grants to individuals.
Application information: Contributes only to pre-selected organizations. Applications not accepted.
Officers: Michael Rutman, Pres., Secy. and C.F.O.; Amy Irving, V.P.
EIN: 954269110

277
Arthur P. Pratt and Jeanette Gladys Pratt Memorial Fund

c/o Union Bank
P.O. Box 109
San Diego 92112   (619) 230-4476

Established in 1973 in CA.
Donor(s): Jeanette Gladys Pratt.‡
Foundation type: Independent
Financial data (yr. ended 04/30/91): Assets, $3,224,483 (M); expenditures, $229,772; qualifying distributions, $204,721, including $198,775 for 56 grants (high: $30,000; low: $750; average: $3,269).
Purpose and activities: Support primarily for youth agencies and restoration of buildings in a park; support also for cultural programs, the handicapped, and hospices.
Fields of interest: Youth, historic preservation, cultural programs, handicapped, hospices.
Types of support: Operating budgets, continuing support, annual campaigns, emergency funds, general purposes, building funds, equipment, land acquisition, renovation projects, research, publications, matching funds, endowment funds.
Limitations: Giving limited to San Diego County, CA. No grants to individuals, or for scholarships or fellowships; no loans.
Application information: Application form not required.
 Initial approach: Proposal
 Copies of proposal: 1
 Deadline(s): Feb. 1
 Board meeting date(s): Mar.
 Final notification: Immediately after board meeting
 Write: R.A. Cameron, V.P., Union Bank
Corporate Trustee: Union Bank.
Number of staff: None.
EIN: 956464737

278
Radin Foundation

444 West Shaw Ave.
Fresno 93704   (209) 226-5711

Established in 1971.
Donor(s): Leta H. Radin.‡

Foundation type: Independent
Financial data (yr. ended 12/31/91): Assets, $6,792,151 (M); expenditures, $281,662; qualifying distributions, $275,803, including $273,661 for 24 grants (high: $59,000; low: $500).
Fields of interest: Hospitals, cultural programs.
Limitations: Giving primarily in Fresno, CA. No grants to individuals.
Application information:
  Initial approach: Proposal
  Deadline(s): None
  Write: H.M. Radin, Pres.
Officers and Directors:* H. Marcus Radin,* Pres.; Bruce Rosenblatt,* V.P.; Lawrence A. Meyer,* Secy.-Treas.
EIN: 237155525

279
Rasmussen Foundation
2360 Shasta Way
Simi Valley 93065   (818) 991-3024

Established in 1987 in CA.
Donor(s): C.A. Rasmussen, Inc.
Foundation type: Company-sponsored
Financial data (yr. ended 12/31/90): Assets, $2,147,190 (M); gifts received, $594,150; expenditures, $46,353; qualifying distributions, $39,230, including $39,230 for 15 grants (high: $10,900; low: $80).
Purpose and activities: Giving primarily for a public health foundation and medical research; support also for education and other general charitable activities.
Fields of interest: Health, medical research, education, general charitable giving.
Limitations: Giving primarily in CA. No grants to individuals.
Application information: Contributes only to pre-selected organizations. Applications not accepted.
  Write: Dean Rasmussen, Pres.
Officers and Director:* Dean Rasmussen,* Pres.; Larry Rasmussen, V.P.; Vicki Rasmussen, C.F.O.
EIN: 770166925

280
Research Fund of the American Otological Society, Inc.
c/o Richard A. Chole
Univ. CA-Davis, Otology Lab, 1159 Surge 3
Davis 95616-8647   (916) 752-8931

Incorporated in 1926 in NY.
Foundation type: Independent
Financial data (yr. ended 06/30/92): Assets, $4,917,831 (M); expenditures, $113,002; qualifying distributions, $113,002, including $113,002 for 5 grants to individuals (average: $25,000).
Purpose and activities: Awards grants to individuals for research in Otosclerosis or Meniere's Disease.
Fields of interest: Medical research.
Types of support: Research.
Limitations: Giving limited to U.S. and Canadian researchers.
Publications: Grants list, application guidelines.
Application information: Application form required.

Initial approach: Proposal
Copies of proposal: 15
Deadline(s): Jan. 31
Board meeting date(s): Mar. 28
Final notification: Around Apr. 15
Write: Irene Nelson, Admin. Asst.
Officers and Trustees:* F. Blair Simmons, M.D.,* Chair.; Robert A. Chole, M.D.,* Secy.-Treas.; Richard A. Altschuler, Ph.D., Robert A. Dobie, M.D., Joseph C. Farmer, M.D., George A. Gates, M.D., Glen K. Martin, Ph.D., Richard T. Miyamoto, M.D., Allen F. Ryan, Ph.D., Leonard P. Rybak, M.D.; Mansfield F.W. Smith, M.D.
Number of staff: None.
EIN: 136131376

281
Lloyd E. Rigler-Lawrence E. Deutsch Foundation ▼
(Formerly The Ledler Foundation)
1800 West Magnolia Blvd.
P.O. Box 828
Burbank 91503

Established in 1966 in CA.
Donor(s): Lawrence E. Deutsch,‡ Lloyd E. Rigler, Adolph's, Ltd., Adolph's Food Products Manufacturing Co.
Foundation type: Independent
Financial data (yr. ended 12/31/90): Assets, $57,236,488 (M); expenditures, $2,520,863; qualifying distributions, $2,246,351, including $2,122,468 for 142 grants (high: $657,500; low: $11; average: $5,000-$50,000).
Purpose and activities: Grants mainly for cultural programs and the performing arts; support also for AIDS and other medical research, health, family planning, and public policy and environmental conservation organizations.
Fields of interest: Arts, cultural programs, performing arts, medical research, AIDS, health, family planning, public policy, environment.
Limitations: Giving primarily in CA and New York, NY. No grants to individuals.
Application information: Application form not required.
  Initial approach: Letter
  Deadline(s): None
  Board meeting date(s): As necessary
  Final notification: Varies
  Write: Audre Estrin, Asst. Treas.
Officers and Director:* Lloyd E. Rigler,* Pres.; James Rigler, V.P.; Donald Rigler, Secy.; Morton Masure, C.F.O.
Number of staff: None.
EIN: 956155653
Recent health grants:
281-1 American Foundation for AIDS Research, Los Angeles, CA, $100,000. 1990.
281-2 American Foundation for AIDS Research, Los Angeles, CA, $13,500. 1990.
281-3 House Ear Institute, Los Angeles, CA, $15,000. 1990.

282
Rincon Foundation
595 East Colorado Blvd., Suite 323
Pasadena 91101   (818) 405-8950

Established in 1986 in CA.
Donor(s): Harriet P. Fullerton, James D. Fullerton.

Foundation type: Independent
Financial data (yr. ended 01/31/91): Assets, $185,588 (M); gifts received, $210,000; expenditures, $267,086; qualifying distributions, $262,115, including $261,300 for 73 grants (high: $12,000; low: $250).
Purpose and activities: Giving primarily for higher and other education, Christian institutions, medical research and health associations; support also for general charitable activities.
Fields of interest: Higher education, education, religion—Christian, medical research, health associations, general charitable giving.
Types of support: Operating budgets, matching funds, scholarship funds, building funds, capital campaigns, annual campaigns.
Limitations: Giving primarily in CA. No grants to individuals.
Application information: Contributes only to pre-selected organizations. Applications not accepted.
  Write: James D. Fullerton, V.P.
Officers and Trustees:* Harriet P. Fullerton,* Pres.; James D. Fullerton,* V.P.
Number of staff: None.
EIN: 954076512

283
The Roberts Foundation
873 Sutter St., Suite B
San Francisco 94109-6170   (415) 771-4300
FAX: (415) 771-4064

Established in 1985 in CA.
Donor(s): George R. Roberts.
Foundation type: Independent
Financial data (yr. ended 12/31/90): Assets, $9,928,270 (M); gifts received, $10,222,399; expenditures, $3,593,588; qualifying distributions, $2,884,862, including $2,884,862 for grants.
Purpose and activities: Giving primarily for youth, conservation and environmental issues, wildlife preservation, health care, the elderly, public broadcasting, and education; special emphasis on the learning disabled and innovative programs with an impact on the homeless.
Fields of interest: Mental health, homeless, youth, conservation, environment, wildlife, health, aged, media and communications, education.
Limitations: Giving limited to northern CA, with emphasis on San Francisco County and adjacent counties; limited funding in Marin County. No support for religious organizations. No grants to individuals, or for medical research, endowment funds, annual or year end appeals.
Publications: Biennial report.
Application information:
  Initial approach: Letter
  Deadline(s): 60 days prior to the board meeting
  Board meeting date(s): Feb., June, and Oct.
  Write: Lyman H. Casey, Exec. Dir.
Officers and Directors:* Leanne B. Roberts,* Pres. and C.E.O.; George R. Roberts, V.P., Secy.-Treas., and C.F.O.; Lyman Casey,* V.P.; Peggy Elberling, Jed Emerson, Theo Steele.
EIN: 942967074

284
Mary Stuart Rogers Foundation
c/o Stockton & Sadler
P.O. Box 3153
Modesto 95353

Established in 1985 in CA.
Foundation type: Independent
Financial data (yr. ended 12/31/90): Assets,
$5,579,951 (M); gifts received, $202,982;
expenditures, $227,491; qualifying distributions,
$210,748, including $205,000 for 20 grants
(high: $20,000; low: $5,000).
Fields of interest: Hospitals, health associations,
medical research, animal welfare.
Limitations: Giving primarily in CA.
Application information: Contributes only to
pre-selected organizations. Applications not
accepted.
   Write: Cleveland J. Stockton, V.P.
Officers: Mary Stuart Rogers, Pres.; Cleveland J.
Stockton, V.P.
EIN: 770099519

285
S.G. Foundation
P.O. Box 814
Santa Ynez 93460   (805) 688-0088

Established in 1984 in CA.
Donor(s): F. Javier Alverdo.
Foundation type: Independent
Financial data (yr. ended 12/31/90): Assets,
$5,566,597 (M); gifts received, $363,750;
expenditures, $53,191; qualifying distributions,
$0.
Purpose and activities: The foundation's purpose
is to encourage and enable individuals and
communities to partner together to help people
help themselves in the local community,
nationally, and internationally. The foundation
supports projects that are self-help in nature,
affirm individual dignity, and create incentives for
people to participate in their own
self-development. The foundation accepts
proposals for program expenses for national and
international human service relief and
development projects. Projects must demonstrate
a specific and focused community-based strategy
for economic development in the areas of hunger
relief, affordable housing, jobs, and small
business start up. The foundation also accepts
proposals for ethnic leadership development
programs, senior care, and educational programs
for youth in the areas of substance abuse
prevention, child abuse and neglect prevention,
and adolescent pregnancy prevention.
Fields of interest: Education, community
development, drug abuse, alcoholism, homeless,
housing, employment, business, leadership
development, international development.
Types of support: Annual campaigns, matching
funds, technical assistance, general purposes,
special projects.
Limitations: No support for athletics, the arts,
music, or museums. No grants to individuals, or
for building projects, staff salaries, capital
improvement, endowments, research, books,
films, or media.
Publications: Annual report, application
guidelines.

Application information: Application form not
required.
   Initial approach: Letter
   Copies of proposal: 1
   Deadline(s): None
   Write: Jeffrey L. Cotter, C.E.O.
Officers and Director:* Jeffrey L. Cotter, C.E.O.;
Stuart C. Gildred,* Pres.
EIN: 330048410

286
Sacramento Regional Foundation
1610 Arden Way, Suite 298
Sacramento 95815   (916) 927-2241
FAX: (916) 927-0110

Incorporated in 1983 in CA.
Foundation type: Community
Financial data (yr. ended 12/31/91): Assets,
$2,178,504 (M); gifts received, $1,686,923;
expenditures, $989,160; qualifying distributions,
$698,040, including $698,040 for grants.
Purpose and activities: Primary areas of interest
include the arts and humanities, education,
community development, and the disadvantaged,
including hunger programs.
Fields of interest: Arts, humanities, conservation,
education, health, disadvantaged, hunger, youth,
community development, urban development,
volunteerism.
Types of support: Student aid, conferences and
seminars, consulting services, emergency funds,
equipment, publications, renovation projects,
seed money, technical assistance, scholarship
funds.
Limitations: Giving limited to organizations
within or those offering services to Sacramento,
Yolo, Placer, and El Dorado counties, CA. No
support for sectarian purposes or private
foundations. No grants to individuals (except
scholarships), or for annual campaigns, operating
funds, capital campaigns, endowments, building
funds, continuing support, deficit financing,
foundation-managed projects, research, or land
acquisition; no loans.
Publications: Annual report (including application
guidelines), financial statement, grants list,
newsletter, application guidelines.
Application information: Grants are approved
annually. Application form required.
   Copies of proposal: 10
   Deadline(s): Dec.
   Board meeting date(s): Mar.
   Final notification: After board meeting
   Write: David F. Hess, Exec. Dir.
Officers and Directors:* Merrily F. Wong,* Pres.;
Thomas J. Hammer, Jr.,* V.P.; Jean Runyon
Graham,* Secy.; Edward L. Lammerding,* Treas.;
David F. Hess, Exec. Dir.; and 12 additional
directors.
Number of staff: 2 full-time professional; 1
full-time support.
EIN: 942891517
Recent health grants:
286-1 Pete Dexter Ungolf Tournament Fund,
   Sacramento, CA, $10,821. For project support.
   1990.
286-2 Sacramento Interdependence Project,
   Sacramento, CA, $45,306. For project support.
   1990.

287
San Diego Community Foundation ▼
Wells Fargo Bank Bldg.
101 West Broadway, Suite 1120
San Diego 92101   (619) 239-8815
FAX: (619) 239-1710

Established in 1975 in CA.
Foundation type: Community
Financial data (yr. ended 06/30/91): Assets,
$54,319,840 (M); gifts received, $5,212,184;
expenditures, $4,265,152; qualifying
distributions, $2,745,673, including $2,745,673
for 469 grants (high: $225,000; low: $62;
average: $2,000-$15,000).
Purpose and activities: Giving to social service
agencies with emphasis on children, youth, and
families, cultural activities, education, health,
civic affairs, and recreational activities.
Fields of interest: Social services, cultural
programs, theater, fine arts, dance, urban affairs,
civic affairs, recreation, higher education,
secondary education, elementary education,
education—minorities, education—early
childhood, education, health, AIDS, community
development, drug abuse, alcoholism, aged.
Types of support: Seed money, matching funds,
building funds, equipment, general purposes,
special projects, publications, renovation
projects, technical assistance, scholarship funds,
employee matching gifts.
Limitations: Giving limited to San Diego County,
CA. No support for political or religious
organizations. No grants to individuals, or for
operating support, annual or capital fund
campaigns, endowment funds, conferences,
travel, or to underwrite fundraising events and
performances; no loans.
Publications: Annual report, informational
brochure (including application guidelines),
newsletter.
Application information: Application form
required.
   Initial approach: Telephone
   Copies of proposal: 1
   Deadline(s): Quarterly; call for details
   Board meeting date(s): Bimonthly beginning in
   Jan.
   Final notification: 3 months
   Write: John F. Ramsey, Exec. Dir.
Officers and Board of Governors:* Maurice T.
Watson, Pres.; Sr. Sally Furay,* V.P., Distribs.;
Frank H. Ault,* V.P., Finance; William Nelson,
V.P., Investments; Ira R. Katz,* V.P., Marketing;
John A. McColl,* Secy.; B. James Polak, Treas.;
and 16 additional governors.
Number of staff: 4 full-time professional; 2
part-time professional; 4 full-time support; 1
part-time support.
EIN: 952942582
Recent health grants:
287-1 AIDS Assistance Fund, San Diego, CA,
   $18,000. For deposit on new building. 1991.
287-2 AIDS Foundation, San Diego, CA,
   $20,000. To facilitate merger with San Diego
   AIDS Project. 1991.
287-3 AIDS Foundation, San Diego, CA,
   $10,000. For San Diego AIDS information
   hotline. 1991.
287-4 American Cancer Society, San Diego, CA,
   $12,500. For Youth Science Fellowship
   Program. 1990.

287-5 Center for Social Services, San Diego, CA, $18,000. For counseling for HIV disease patients. 1991.

287-6 Center for Social Services, San Diego, CA, $10,000. For AIDS counseling and general operations of AIDS response program. 1991.

287-7 Crossroads Foundation, San Diego, CA, $11,955. To remodel kitchen. 1991.

287-8 Episcopal Community Services, San Diego, CA, $10,000. To establish transitional living center for homeless mentally ill. 1990.

287-9 Episcopal Community Services, San Diego, CA, $10,000. To establish transitional living center for homeless mentally ill. 1990.

287-10 Escondido Community Clinic, Escondido, CA, $16,750. For second clinic location nursing station. 1991.

287-11 Escondido Youth Encounter, Escondido, CA, $15,775. For equipment for Options for Recovery program for drug addicted mothers and children. 1990.

287-12 Mercy Hospital and Medical Center, San Diego, CA, $50,000. For Emergency Department satellite laboratory. 1991.

287-13 National Multiple Sclerosis Society, San Diego, CA, $12,500. For new equipment for equipment loan program. 1991.

287-14 Rural Family Counseling, La Mesa, CA, $14,000. For van for East County outreach. 1991.

287-15 Saint Pauls Manor, San Diego, CA, $25,000. For kitchen renovation. 1991.

287-16 San Diego AIDS, San Diego, CA, $18,000. For re-location costs. 1991.

287-17 San Diego Center for Children, San Diego, CA, $20,000. For Special Care residence. 1991.

287-18 San Diego City Schools, San Diego, CA, $10,000. For health and social services center at Hoover High School. 1990.

287-19 San Diego Grantmakers for AIDS, San Diego, CA, $10,000. For collaborative grantmaking effort. 1990.

287-20 San Diego Hospice, San Diego, CA, $14,000. For certified home health aids. 1990.

287-21 San Diego Hospice Corporation, San Diego, CA, $20,375. For skilled nursing program. 1991.

287-22 San Diego Youth and Community Services, San Diego, CA, $10,000. For general support of The Bridge, home for troubled youth. 1990.

287-23 San Diego Youth and Community Services, San Diego, CA, $10,000. For teen peer education streetwork project. 1991.

287-24 Trauma Intervention Programs, Carlsbad, CA, $12,000. For matching grant for resource development director. 1990.

287-25 United Way of San Diego County, San Diego, CA, $16,000. For AIDS in the Workplace educational video production. 1991.

287-26 University of California, San Diego, CA, $13,500. For Cancer Research Foundation. 1991.

287-27 University of California, San Diego, CA, $10,000. For Sally B. and John F. Thornton Hospital building fund. 1991.

287-28 University of California at San Diego Foundation, La Jolla, CA, $13,000. For University of California Cancer Center Foundation. 1990.

287-29 Visiting Nurse Association of San Diego County, San Diego, CA, $36,000. For AIDS outreach services to ethnic communities with bilingual nurse. 1991.

287-30 Vista Community Clinic, San Diego, CA, $10,000. For Fund for Moms: prenatal care loan fund. 1991.

288
The San Francisco Foundation ▼
685 Market St., Suite 910
San Francisco 94105-9716   (415) 495-3100
Additional tel.: (510) 436-3100

Established in 1948 in CA by resolution and declaration of trust.
Foundation type: Community
Financial data (yr. ended 06/30/91): Assets, $226,099,459 (M); gifts received, $29,130,175; expenditures, $21,380,363; qualifying distributions, $21,380,363, including $21,097,014 for 1,157 grants (high: $2,500,000; low: $100; average: $5,000-$50,000), $277,000 for 55 grants to individuals (high: $10,000; low: $1,000; average: $1,000-$10,000) and $6,349 for 84 employee matching gifts.
Purpose and activities: Grants principally in five categories: the arts and humanities, community health, education, environment, and urban affairs. Technical assistance grants also made, primarily to current recipients. On Jan. 1, 1987, the foundation transferred the entire Buck Trust, which is limited to use for charitable purposes in Marin County, CA, to a new and independent foundation, the Marin Community Foundation. The foundation continues to serve five counties of the Bay Area, and in the 12 months ending June 30, 1991, paid out $21 million (excluding Buck Trust funds) in grants to nonprofit agencies.
Fields of interest: Arts, humanities, performing arts, community development, urban affairs, health, AIDS, education, environment, child welfare, youth, homeless.
Types of support: Operating budgets, seed money, loans, technical assistance, special projects.
Limitations: Giving limited to the Bay Area, CA, counties of Alameda, Contra Costa, Marin, San Francisco, and San Mateo. No support for religious purposes. No grants for annual campaigns, general fundraising campaigns, emergency or endowment funds, deficit financing, matching gifts, scholarships (except when so designated by donor), or fellowships.
Publications: Annual report, newsletter, application guidelines, program policy statement, informational brochure.
Application information: Application form required.
Initial approach: Letter of intent (not exceeding 3 pages)
Copies of proposal: 1
Deadline(s): Letters reviewed continuously; proposal closing dates available upon request
Board meeting date(s): Monthly except Aug.; applications are reviewed 4 to 6 times each year
Final notification: 3 to 4 months
Write: Robert M. Fisher, Dir.
Director: Robert M. Fisher.
Board of Trustees: Leonard E. Kingsley, Chair.; John F. Kilmartin, Vice-Chair.; Lucille S.

Abrahamson, Herman Gallegos, Peter E. Haas, T.J. Saenger, Mary Lee Widener.
Number of staff: 11 full-time professional; 1 part-time professional; 12 full-time support; 4 part-time support.
EIN: 941101547
Recent health grants:

288-1 African Community Mental Health Services, Oakland, CA, $25,000. For mental health counseling to immigrants and refugees from Africa residing in Bay Area. 1991.

288-2 AIDS Legal Referral Panel, San Francisco, CA, $25,000. For free and low-cost legal services to people with AIDS and AIDS-related conditions. 1991.

288-3 Alameda County Health Care Services Agency, Oakland, CA, $50,000. For Homeless Families Program, community-wide comprehensive health and social services and housing assistance demonstration for 150 homeless families in Oakland. 1991.

288-4 Alta Bates-Herrick Foundation, Berkeley, CA, $30,000. For start-up funding for Primary Care Access Clinic located at Herrick Hospital and primarily serving medically uninsured and underinsured residents of Berkeley. 1991.

288-5 Alta Bates-Herrick Hospice, Berkeley, CA, $25,000. To assist Allen Temple Baptist Church in recruitment and training of African-American hospice volunteers to work with indigent cancer patients. 1991.

288-6 Alzheimers Services of the East Bay, Berkeley, CA, $25,000. To add second service site for agency serving people with Alzheimer's disease and their families in Alameda County. 1991.

288-7 American Cancer Society, San Francisco, CA, $28,300. 1991.

288-8 American Foundation for AIDS Research, Los Angeles, CA, $10,000. 1991.

288-9 Asian Perinatal Advocates, San Francisco, CA, $24,300. For bridge funding for child abuse prevention program using bilingual family visitors to serve Chinese and Southeast Asian families in San Francisco. 1991.

288-10 Battered Womens Alternatives, Concord, CA, $50,000. To expand substance abuse and violence prevention project to low-income, ethnically diverse families in eastern Contra Costa County. 1991.

288-11 Bay Area Tumor Institute, Oakland, CA, $192,000. To provide advanced cancer therapies to indigent cancer patients at Oakland's Highland General Hospital. 1991.

288-12 Berkeley Oakland Support Services, Berkeley, CA, $10,000. To meet needs of substance abusers in its Alameda County shelters for homeless individuals and families. 1991.

288-13 Berkeley, City of, Berkeley, CA, $14,000. For Mental Health Volunteer Project, to recruit and place volunteer mental health professionals in community agencies serving indigent mental health clients in Berkeley and Albany. 1991.

288-14 Bio-Integral Resource Center, Berkeley, CA, $15,000. To reduce toxic pollution and health hazards by promoting least toxic pest management alternatives. 1991.

288-15 Buenas Vidas Ranch, Livermore, CA, $25,000. For relocating group home for young men in southern Alameda County. 1991.

288-16 California Law Center on Long Term Care, San Francisco, CA, $20,000. To educate Bay Area health care professionals, consumers and caretakers about patient rights in long-term care settings. 1991.

288-17 Cancer Support Community, San Francisco, CA, $75,000. To provide free psychological and educational support services to indigent minority and elderly cancer patients and their families in San Francisco. 1991.

288-18 Casa de Las Madres, San Francisco, CA, $25,000. To provide therapeutic services to victims of domestic violence in San Francisco. 1991.

288-19 Catholic Charities of the Archdiocese of San Francisco, San Francisco, CA, $25,000. For start-up assistance for San Francisco Phoenix Project, model residential treatment program for pregnant, crack-addicted women and their children. 1991.

288-20 Center for Third World Organizing, Oakland, CA, $25,000. For community organizing to address high levels of environmental lead in Alameda County. 1991.

288-21 Childrens Center for Movement Therapy, San Francisco, CA, $12,000. To provide support for teenage girls with disabilities. 1991.

288-22 Childrens Council of San Francisco, San Francisco, CA, $24,000. To expand mental health consultation to child care centers and family day care providers serving high-risk children. 1991.

288-23 Childrens Health Council, Stanford, CA, $12,250. 1991.

288-24 Childrens Hospital Medical Center of Northern California, Oakland, CA, $80,000. For general support. 1991.

288-25 Childrens Hospital Medical Center of Northern California, Oakland, CA, $25,000. To add case management component to Sexual Abuse Management Clinic at Children's Hospital in Alameda County to serve victims of sexual abuse and assault. 1991.

288-26 Chronic Fatigue Immune Deficiency Syndrome Foundation, San Francisco, CA, $15,000. 1991.

288-27 Coalition for Alternatives in Mental Health, Berkeley, CA, $60,000. To reduce homelessness through residences run for and by people with mental disabilities in Alameda County. 1991.

288-28 Coalition for Elders Independence, Berkeley, CA, $150,000. To develop community-based system of long-term care for poor and minority elders in East Bay. 1991.

288-29 Commonweal, Bolinas, CA, $141,000. 1991.

288-30 Community Hospice Foundation of the Bay Area, San Francisco, CA, $44,000. To recruit and train volunteers to support cancer patients at new residential facility for indigent terminally ill in San Francisco and San Mateo counties. 1991.

288-31 Contra Costa County Health Services Department, Martinez, CA, $60,000. To improve indigent cancer patient care in Contra Costa County through volunteer support, chaplaincy services and computer. 1991.

288-32 Contra Costa County Health Services Department, Pleasant Hill, CA, $25,000. For Food Stamp Outreach Project to increase access to nutritional food for low-income residents of Contra Costa County. 1991.

288-33 Contra Costa Health and Recreation Association, Walnut Creek, CA, $105,000. To develop model recreational facility that fully integrates disabled and nondisabled users. 1991.

288-34 Down Syndrome League, Orinda, CA, $12,000. To strengthen capacity of organization serving families of children with Down Syndrome in five Bay Area counties. 1991.

288-35 East Bay Activity Center, Oakland, CA, $15,000. To support Center's merger with Pacific Children's Center and better serve emotionally disturbed children and their families in Alameda County. 1991.

288-36 East Bay Perinatal Council, Oakland, CA, $24,800. For continued support of Forum, grassroots advocacy and policy group dedicated to reducing black infant mortality and improving birth outcomes for black women in Alameda County. 1991.

288-37 Education Programs Associates, Campbell, CA, $20,000. For five-county organizing to improve access to maternal and child health care for underserved populations. 1991.

288-38 Family Counseling and Community Services, Walnut Creek, CA, $15,000. For organizational development to address increased demand for mental health services in Contra Costa County. 1991.

288-39 Family Stress Center, Concord, CA, $20,000. For Proud Fathers Program for young, unwed fathers in Contra Costa County. 1991.

288-40 Florence Crittenton Services, San Francisco, CA, $15,000. To advance organization's capacity to serve at-risk infants and their teen mothers. 1991.

288-41 Haight Ashbury Free Medical Clinic, San Francisco, CA, $45,000. To expand and improve medical services to low-income residents of San Francisco by increasing capacity to generate contributed income. 1991.

288-42 Hamilton Family Center, San Francisco, CA, $52,000. For Homeless Prenatal Program that links homeless pregnant women residing in San Francisco shelter with prenatal care. 1991.

288-43 Health Access, San Francisco, CA, $80,000. To advocate for health needs of low-income residents of five Bay Area counties to increase fundraising capacity. 1991.

288-44 Highland General Hospital, Oakland, CA, $162,800. To provide emergency transportation, food, lodging and volunteer support to Alameda County's indigent cancer patients at Highland General Hospital. 1991.

288-45 Judie Davis Marrow Donor Recruiting Program, Oakland, CA, $15,000. To recruit Bay Area African-Americans to participate in bone marrow registry program. 1991.

288-46 La Clinica De La Raza, Oakland, CA, $35,000. To develop facilities master plan for agency providing health services to low-income residents of Oakland. 1991.

288-47 Lucile Salter Packard Childrens Hospital, Palo Alto, CA, $140,400. To provide direct care to indigent Bay Area residents who are survivors of childhood cancer. 1991.

288-48 Lucile Salter Packard Childrens Hospital, Palo Alto, CA, $11,520. 1991.

288-49 Masonic Old Folks Home, San Francisco, CA, $10,000. For general support. 1991.

288-50 Mental Health Association of San Francisco, San Francisco, CA, $116,000. For community organizing to facilitate housing development for people with mental disabilities in San Francisco. 1991.

288-51 Mount Zion Hospital and Medical Center, San Francisco, CA, $114,000. 1991.

288-52 Mount Zion Hospital and Medical Center, San Francisco, CA, $13,000. To translate, produce and disseminate materials about cancer and its treatments for indigent Soviet emigre cancer patients in Bay Area. 1991.

288-53 National Latina Health Organization, Oakland, CA, $20,000. To help Hispanic women in Alameda, Contra Costa and San Francisco counties participate in health education program. 1991.

288-54 New Perspectives of Marin, Larkspur, CA, $12,000. For Gateway Project, providing recreational therapy for Richmond elementary and middle school students at risk of substance abuse. 1991.

288-55 NICOS Chinese Health Coalition, San Francisco, CA, $15,000. To prepare individuals and organizations in Chinatown to carry out volunteer disaster response plan. 1991.

288-56 Northern California Cancer Center, Belmont, CA, $50,000. To strengthen organizational capacity to raise unrestricted funds for prevention and control of cancer in Bay Area. 1991.

288-57 Northern California Cancer Center, Belmont, CA, $10,000. 1991.

288-58 Oakland Unified School District, Oakland, CA, $25,000. To continue psychosocial services at Fremont High School's school-based health center in Oakland. 1991.

288-59 Ombudsmen Services of Contra Costa, Concord, CA, $12,000. To help agency serving institutionalized elderly in Contra Costa become free-standing, nonprofit organization. 1991.

288-60 On Lok Senior Health Services, San Francisco, CA, $52,000. For technical assistance to develop community-based system of long-term care for East Bay poor and minority elders. 1991.

288-61 On Lok Senior Health Services, San Francisco, CA, $25,000. To develop model quality assurance program for On Lok's innovative, community-based system of caring for frail elderly in San Francisco's Chinatown. 1991.

288-62 Over Sixty Health Clinic, Berkeley, CA, $16,000. For continued support of consultation service providing case management to low-income elders in Alameda County. 1991.

288-63 Planned Parenthood Association of San Mateo County, San Mateo, CA, $25,250. 1991.

288-64 Planned Parenthood of Marin and Sonoma, San Rafael, CA, $24,000. 1991.

288-65 Saint Lukes Hospital, San Francisco, CA, $150,000. To advance minorities in nursing profession who will serve medically underserved populations. 1991.

288-66 San Francisco AIDS Foundation, San Francisco, CA, $15,000. 1991.

288-67 San Francisco State University, San Francisco, CA, $27,000. To design interdisciplinary focus in Master's Degree Program in Nursing to increase supply of Bay Area nurses trained in long-time care. 1991.

288-68 San Francisco Study Center, San Francisco, CA, $25,000. To develop and implement parent skill training and support curriculum for parents of children with serious mental illnesses in San Francisco. 1991.

288-69 San Francisco Suicide Prevention, San Francisco, CA, $20,000. To increase Youth Line's telephone counseling capacity for San Francisco youth in crisis. 1991.

288-70 Shriners Hospital of San Francisco, San Francisco, CA, $10,000. For general support. 1991.

288-71 Sunny Hills Childrens Services, San Anselmo, CA, $15,000. To strengthen fundraising capacity of organization serving children with emotional and behavioral problems. 1991.

288-72 United Way of the Bay Area, San Francisco, CA, $50,000. To help establish United Way Development Loan Fund to increase capacity of health and human services agencies in Bay Area through loans, loan guarantees and brokerage services. 1991.

288-73 United Way of the Bay Area, San Francisco, CA, $25,000. For feasibility study to acquire one or more buildings to house nonprofit health, human services and economic development organizations. 1991.

288-74 United Way of the Bay Area, Delta 2000, San Francisco, CA, $20,000. To strengthen health and human service infrastructure of east Contra Costa County. 1991.

288-75 University of California, AIDS Health Project, San Francisco, CA, $25,000. To train and supervise volunteers to facilitate support groups for people who are HIV positive in San Francisco. 1991.

288-76 Vesper Society Group, San Leandro, CA, $15,000. For training program to improve services to elders living in residential care homes in Alameda County. 1991.

288-77 Visiting Nurses and Hospice of San Francisco, San Francisco, CA, $140,000. For general support. 1991.

288-78 West Oakland Health Center, Oakland, CA, $25,000. To initiate mental health consultation project for students, teachers and parents in elementary school in Oakland. 1991.

288-79 Zen Center Hospice Volunteer Program, San Francisco, CA, $134,000. To recruit and train hospice volunteers to serve indigent cancer patients at San Francisco General Hospital, Laguna Honda Hospital and Zen Center Guest House. 1991.

289
Annunziata Sanguinetti Foundation
c/o Wells Fargo Bank, N.A.
420 Montgomery St., MAC No. 0101-056
San Francisco 94163   (415) 396-3215

Trust established in 1958 in CA.
Donor(s): Annunziata Sanguinetti.‡
Foundation type: Independent

Financial data (yr. ended 09/30/91): Assets, $3,914,274 (M); expenditures, $282,632; qualifying distributions, $245,533, including $236,000 for 35 grants (high: $15,000; low: $2,000; average: $2,000-$15,000).
Purpose and activities: Giving primarily for the benefit of sick, needy children; grants also for mental and physical health, including rehabilitation programs and speech pathology, hospitals, drug abuse programs, youth, social service and welfare agencies, the homeless, family services, and recreational activities.
Fields of interest: Child welfare, health, mental health, handicapped, rehabilitation, hospitals, youth, social services, welfare, family services.
Limitations: Giving limited to San Francisco, CA. No grants to individuals, or for building or endowment funds.
Publications: Application guidelines.
Application information: Application form not required.
   Initial approach: Letter and proposal
   Copies of proposal: 1
   Deadline(s): Submit proposal between July and Oct.; deadline Oct. 31
   Board meeting date(s): Nov. or Dec.
   Write: Eugene J. Ranghiasci
Trustee: Wells Fargo Bank, N.A.
EIN: 946073762

290
Santa Barbara Foundation ▼
15 East Carrillo St.
Santa Barbara 93101   (805) 963-1873

Incorporated in 1928 in CA.
Foundation type: Community
Financial data (yr. ended 12/31/90): Assets, $29,667,212 (M); gifts received, $556,284; expenditures, $2,525,128; qualifying distributions, $2,108,408, including $2,108,408 for 144 grants (high: $52,000; low: $500; average: $2,000-$20,000).
Purpose and activities: Giving for social services, youth, health services, cultural activities, education, and student aid loans for Santa Barbara County secondary school graduates.
Fields of interest: Social services, youth, health services, cultural programs, education, secondary education.
Types of support: Building funds, equipment, land acquisition, matching funds, student loans, renovation projects, publications, technical assistance.
Limitations: Giving limited to Santa Barbara County, CA. No support for religious organizations or schools, colleges, or universities. No grants to individuals (except for student loans for Santa Barbara County secondary school graduates), or for operating budgets, annual campaigns, seed money, deficit financing, endowment funds, scholarships, fellowships, research, publications, or conferences.
Publications: Annual report, application guidelines, newsletter, informational brochure.
Application information: The foundation considers 30 applications per quarter. Application form required.
   Initial approach: Letter or telephone
   Copies of proposal: 1
   Deadline(s): None

   Board meeting date(s): Monthly except July; decisions on grant requests made in Mar., June, Sept., and Dec.
   Final notification: 2 months
   Write: Bryan G. Gaggs, Exec. Dir.
Officers and Trustees:* B. Paul Blasingame,* Pres.; William L. Coulson,* V.P.; Warren E. Fenzi, V.P.; Marshall A. Rose,* V.P.; Jeanne Vesey,* Secy.; A. Spaulding Birss,* Treas.; Charles O. Slosser, Exec. Dir.; James J. Giusto, Mrs. Robert Grogan, John Howland, Charles H. Jarvis, Michael L. LeJeune, Craig Price, Joanne Rapp, Jean Schuyler, Frank Stoltze, Michael Towbes, Leroy A. Weller.
Fund Managers: Capital Research & Management Co., Crocker National Bank, Security Pacific Investment Mgrs.
Number of staff: 2 full-time professional; 1 part-time professional; 1 full-time support; 1 part-time support.
EIN: 951866094
Recent health grants:
290-1 American Heart Association, Santa Barbara, CA, $21,000. To purchase MicroVax. 1990.
290-2 Carrillo Community Medical Clinic, Santa Barbara, CA, $12,184. For medical and office equipment. 1990.
290-3 Central Coast Congregate Care, Santa Barbara, CA, $50,000. For down payment on property. 1990.
290-4 Goleta Valley Community Hospital, Santa Barbara, CA, $20,000. For circon camera and instruments. 1990.
290-5 Mental Health Association of Santa Barbara, Santa Barbara, CA, $20,091. To purchase van. 1990.
290-6 Planned Parenthood of Santa Barbara County, Santa Barbara, CA, $26,500. For capital improvements. 1990.
290-7 Rehabilitation Institute at Santa Barbara, Santa Barbara, CA, $50,000. To purchase equipment. 1990.
290-8 Saint Francis Hospital, Santa Barbara, CA, $17,063. For sigma piece folder for laundry. 1990.
290-9 Sansum Medical Research Foundation, Santa Barbara, CA, $15,000. To purchase lab equipment. 1990.
290-10 Santa Barbara Cottage Hospital, Santa Barbara, CA, $53,203. For child-transport vehicle. 1990.
290-11 Santa Barbara Council on Alcoholism and Drug Abuse, Santa Barbara, CA, $29,331. For computers, copiers, fax machine, office equipment and furniture. 1990.
290-12 Santa Barbara New House, Santa Barbara, CA, $50,000. For payment on recovery home. 1990.
290-13 United Cerebral Palsy Association of Santa Barbara, Santa Barbara, CA, $11,520. To purchase computer and table. 1990.
290-14 Visiting Nurse Association of Santa Barbara, Santa Barbara, CA, $21,500. For telephone system. 1990.

291
Community Foundation of Santa Clara County ▼
960 West Hedding, Suite 220
San Jose 95126-1215   (408) 241-2666

Established in 1954 in CA.

Foundation type: Community
Financial data (yr. ended 06/30/91): Assets, $19,308,439 (M); gifts received, $9,545,601; expenditures, $2,120,900; qualifying distributions, $1,680,440, including $1,680,440 for 404 grants (high: $111,160; low: $25; average: $2,500-$15,000).
Purpose and activities: Giving primarily for education, including awards in literature; health and social services, including AIDS programs, youth and child welfare, women and minorities, and employment and housing; the fine and performing arts; community development and urban affairs; and the environment.
Fields of interest: Education, language and literature, education—minorities, education—early childhood, higher education, AIDS, hospices, mental health, social services, child welfare, youth, women, minorities, Native Americans, employment, homeless, arts, community development, urban affairs, environment.
Types of support: Seed money, emergency funds, matching funds, consulting services, technical assistance, loans, scholarship funds, special projects.
Limitations: Giving primarily in Santa Clara County, CA. No support for religious organizations for sectarian purposes. No grants for deficit financing or building funds.
Publications: Annual report, newsletter, 990-PF, financial statement, informational brochure, application guidelines.
Application information: Application form not required.
Initial approach: Telephone or letter
Copies of proposal: 1
Deadline(s): 12 weeks prior to board meetings
Board meeting date(s): July 1, Oct. 1, and Jan. 1
Final notification: Within 2 weeks of meetings
Write: Winnie Chu, Prog. Officer
Directors: William F. Scandling, Chair.; Sven Simonsen, Vice-Chair.; Phillip Boyce, Secy.; Roger Smith, Finance and Investment; Peter Hero, Exec. Dir.; John Black, Marti de Benedetti, Leonard W. Ely, Charles J. Ferrari, Jr., John Freidenrich, Larry Jinks, Robert L. Joss, Tom Killefer, Clayton J. Klein, David W. Mitchell, Kathie Priebe, Ernest Renzel, Jr., James Rosse, Barbara Doyle Roupe, William E. Terry, John A. Wilson.
Number of staff: 7 full-time professional; 3 part-time professional.
EIN: 770066922
Recent health grants:
291-1 Alum Rock Counseling Center, San Jose, CA, $10,000. 1991.
291-2 Central Missouri Diabetic Camp, Columbia, MO, $25,000. 1991.
291-3 Lucile Salter Packard Childrens Hospital, Palo Alto, CA, $30,000. 1991.
291-4 Palo Alto Medical Foundation, Palo Alto, CA, $10,000. 1991.

292
Greater Santa Cruz County Community Foundation
2425 Porter St., Suite 11
Soquel 95073-2425   (408) 662-8290

Incorporated in 1982 in CA.
Foundation type: Community

Financial data (yr. ended 12/31/91): Assets, $7,098,111 (M); gifts received, $1,388,000; expenditures, $635,672; qualifying distributions, $364,000, including $347,940 for 43 grants (high: $35,000; low: $1,200; average: $5,000-$35,000), $4,000 for 7 grants to individuals (high: $1,000; low: $600; average: $600-$1,000) and $12,060 for 2 loans.
Fields of interest: Social services, health, education, cultural programs, arts, historic preservation, environment, community development.
Types of support: General purposes, seed money, operating budgets, emergency funds, equipment, special projects, conferences and seminars, technical assistance, consulting services, matching funds, building funds, continuing support, scholarship funds.
Limitations: Giving limited to Santa Cruz County, CA. No support for religious purposes. No grants to individuals (except for scholarships from designated funds), or for continuing support, annual campaigns, deficit financing, building funds, land acquisition, student loans, fellowships, or research.
Publications: Annual report (including application guidelines), application guidelines, newsletter, occasional report.
Application information: Full proposal required. Application form not required.
Initial approach: In person, telephone, or letter
Copies of proposal: 2
Deadline(s): Feb., May, Aug., and Oct.
Board meeting date(s): Jan., Apr., July, Oct., and Dec.
Final notification: Apr., July, Oct., and Dec.
Write: Grace Jepsen, Exec. Dir.
Officers and Directors:* Gloria Welsh,* Pres.; Margaret Lezin,* V.P., Nominating; Theresa Biggam,* V.P., Distribution; Bud Prindle,* V.P., Development; Nancy Driscoll,* Secy.; Rowland Rebele,* Treas.; and 15 additional directors.
Number of staff: 2 full-time professional; 1 full-time support.
EIN: 942808039
Recent health grants:
292-1 Visiting Nurse Association of Santa Cruz County, Santa Cruz, CA, $15,000. For seed money to initiate campaign to raise matching funds to offset unexpected reductions in Medicare reimbursements for clients already served by VNA. 1990.

293
The Daniel A. and Edna J. Sattler Beneficial Trust
200 East Carrillo St., Suite 400
Santa Barbara 93101

Donor(s): Edna J. Relyea.‡
Foundation type: Independent
Financial data (yr. ended 06/30/91): Assets, $2,491,008 (M); expenditures, $158,831; qualifying distributions, $130,207, including $120,000 for 8 grants (high: $23,600; low: $2,000).
Purpose and activities: Support for cancer research and other health associations, social service organizations, and a community foundation.
Fields of interest: Cancer, health associations, social services, volunteerism.

Types of support: General purposes.
Limitations: Giving primarily in the Santa Barbara, CA, area. No grants to individuals.
Application information: Contributes only to pre-selected organizations. Applications not accepted.
Trustees: H. Clarke Gaines, Robert M. Jones, Cecil I. Smith.
EIN: 237127370

294
Schlinger Foundation
830 Coachman Place
Clayton 94517

Established in 1986 in CA.
Donor(s): The William and E.G. Schlinger Trust, Warren G. Schlinger.
Foundation type: Independent
Financial data (yr. ended 12/31/91): Assets, $15,301,191 (M); gifts received, $100,000; expenditures, $732,569; qualifying distributions, $719,401, including $717,500 for 7 grants (high: $350,000; low: $2,000).
Fields of interest: Higher education, psychiatry, science and technology, educational research.
Types of support: Research, building funds, general purposes.
Limitations: Giving primarily in CA. No grants to individuals.
Application information: Contributes only to pre-selected organizations. Applications not accepted.
Officers and Directors:* Warren G. Schlinger,* Pres.; Evert I. Schlinger,* Secy. and C.F.O.
EIN: 944065303

295
The Charles Schwab Corporate Giving Program
101 Mongomery St., 27th Fl.
San Francisco 94104   (415) 627-8415

Financial data (yr. ended 12/31/90): Total giving, $304,000, including $200,000 for 100 grants (high: $15,000; low: $25; average: $250-$5,000), $100,000 for 800 employee matching gifts and $4,000 for 5 in-kind gifts.
Purpose and activities: Charles Schwab & Co., Inc., provides cash and in-kind contributions to qualifing nonprofit organizations and institutions in the communities where its employees live and work. Through the Corporate Contributions Program and Employee Matching Gift Program the Company financially supports services and programs that improve and enhance the quality of life in the communities in which it operates. Donations of excess or unusable supplies, equipment and furniture may be made to qualifying organizations when and if these items become available. Requests for other non-cash contributions and donated services will also be considered. Support for arts, education (math and computer), health and human services, AIDS programs, and youth; very limited giving for benefits, fundraisers, or luncheons. Most grants are unrestricted; very limited seed or capital grants; priority given to organizations with employee involvement.
Fields of interest: Arts, AIDS, health, education, health services.

Types of support: Donated equipment, employee matching gifts, operating budgets, in-kind gifts.
Limitations: Giving primarily in the San Francisco Bay Area, CA; limited giving where company has branch locations (130 cities nationwide); state or national organizations are considered only if they serve branch communities; grants are mostly to local organizations. No grants for advertising or for challenge grants.
Publications: Corporate report, application guidelines, informational brochure.
Application information: There is a staff that only handles contributions; prior grant does not ensure future funding unless a commitment or pledge to that effect is made by the Company. Written requests from previous or current grantees are required for each new funding year.
  Initial approach: Write to nearest branch or headquarters; send proposal
  Deadline(s): None
  Board meeting date(s): 4-6 weeks upon receipt of application
  Final notification: As soon as decision is reached in writing. Accepted grantees are called as well
  Write: Karen Ens, Coord., Corp. Contribs.
Number of staff: 1 full-time professional; 1 part-time support.

296
The Ellen Browning Scripps Foundation
c/o Union Bank, Trust Dept.
P.O. Box 109
San Diego 92112   (619) 230-4709

Trust established in 1935 in CA.
Donor(s): Ellen Browning Scripps,‡ Robert Paine Scripps.‡
Foundation type: Independent
Financial data (yr. ended 06/30/91): Assets, $14,742,608 (M); expenditures, $753,627; qualifying distributions, $693,608, including $673,600 for 38 grants (high: $60,000; low: $500).
Fields of interest: Medical research, marine sciences, higher education, conservation, recreation, child welfare, youth, arts.
Limitations: Giving primarily in San Diego County, CA. No grants to individuals.
Application information: Application form not required.
  Initial approach: Proposal
  Copies of proposal: 1
  Deadline(s): May 1
  Board meeting date(s): June
  Write: E. Douglas Dawson, V.P. and Regional Mgr., Union Bank
Trustees: Ellen Scripps Davis, Deborah Goddard, Edward S. Meanley, Paul K. Scripps.
Number of staff: None.
EIN: 951644633

297
The Seaver Institute ▼
800 West Sixth St., Suite 1410
Los Angeles 90017   (213) 688-7550

Incorporated in 1955 in CA.
Donor(s): Frank R. Seaver.‡
Foundation type: Independent

Financial data (yr. ended 06/30/91): Assets, $33,088,806 (M); gifts received, $47,256; expenditures, $2,446,386; qualifying distributions, $1,845,333, including $1,640,887 for 30 grants (high: $500,000; low: $100; average: $250-$2,000).
Purpose and activities: Emphasis on education, health, the arts, and the community.
Fields of interest: Education, health, arts, social services.
Types of support: Matching funds, special projects, research.
Limitations: Giving primarily in CA, MA, and MN. No grants to individuals, or for operating budgets, continuing support, annual campaigns, emergency or endowment funds, scholarships, fellowships, deficit financing, capital or building funds, equipment, land acquisition, publications, or conferences; no loans.
Publications: Informational brochure (including application guidelines).
Application information: Contributes only to pre-selected organizations. Applications not accepted.
  Board meeting date(s): Dec. and June
  Write: Richard Call, Pres.
Officers and Directors:* Blanche Ebert Seaver,* Chair.; Richard C. Seaver,* Vice-Chair.; Richard W. Call,* Pres.; John F. Hall, V.P. and Treas.; Christopher Seaver,* Secy.; Richard A. Archer, Camron Cooper, Myron E. Harpole, Raymond Jallow, Victoria Seaver.
Number of staff: 2 full-time professional; 3 part-time professional.
EIN: 956054764

298
Frances Seebe Trust
c/o Wells Fargo Bank, N.A.
525 Market St., 17th Fl.
San Francisco 94163

Established in 1983 in CA.
Foundation type: Independent
Financial data (yr. ended 01/31/91): Assets, $2,950,717 (M); expenditures, $237,970; qualifying distributions, $197,077, including $182,650 for 15 grants (high: $40,075; low: $2,500).
Purpose and activities: Giving primarily to wildlife research and animal protection; support also for medical research.
Fields of interest: Wildlife, animal welfare, medical research.
Limitations: Giving primarily in CA. No grants to individuals.
Application information: Contributes only to pre-selected organizations. Applications not accepted.
Trustee: Wells Fargo Bank, N.A.
EIN: 956795278

299
Barnet Segal Charitable Trust
P.O. Box S-1
Carmel 93921

Established in 1986 in CA.
Foundation type: Independent
Financial data (yr. ended 03/31/91): Assets, $13,161,748 (M); expenditures, $663,905;

qualifying distributions, $622,313, including $535,400 for 10 grants (high: $300,000; low: $3,500).
Purpose and activities: Giving primarily for a graduate school library; support also for fine and performing arts groups, housing for senior citizens and others in need, family planning, a hospice, and health education.
Fields of interest: Libraries, housing, aged, family planning, health, hospices, fine arts, performing arts.
Types of support: Building funds, operating budgets.
Limitations: Giving primarily in Monterey County, CA. No grants to individuals.
Application information: Contributes only to pre-selected organizations. Applications not accepted.
Trustee: Herbert Berman.
EIN: 776024786

300
The Setzer Foundation
2555 Third St., Suite 200
Sacramento 95818

Trust established in 1965 in CA.
Donor(s): Members of the Setzer family.
Foundation type: Independent
Financial data (yr. ended 03/31/91): Assets, $6,139,188 (M); expenditures, $235,093; qualifying distributions, $200,337, including $200,337 for grants (high: $15,000).
Fields of interest: Higher education, cultural programs, social services, child welfare, youth, hospitals.
Limitations: Giving primarily in CA. No grants to individuals.
Application information: Application form not required.
  Deadline(s): None
Trustees: G. Cal Setzer, Hardie C. Setzer, Mark Setzer.
EIN: 946115578

301
Shaklee Corporate Giving Program
c/o Shaklee Corp. Public Rels.
444 Market St.
San Francisco 94111   (415) 954-2007

Financial data (yr. ended 12/31/90): Total giving, $555,580, including $350,825 for grants (high: $94,342; low: $500), $33,813 for 7 grants to individuals, $58,442 for employee matching gifts and $112,500 for in-kind gifts.
Purpose and activities: "Shaklee Corporation is committed to improving society in the communities in which company employees live and work. The Company believes that business should share the responsibility for bettering the community and demonstrates and encourages this commitment through philanthropic activities in the areas of Health and Human Service, Art and Culture, Education, and Civic activities." Major support is in the area of Health and Human Services. In this category contributions will be allocated for health promotion, nutrition and physical fitness, including funding for annual federated drives supporting human service agencies. Funding for Education and the Arts are

equally considered. The Company's education contributions include The Shaklee Scholarship and Matching Gift Programs. Funding in the Culture and the Arts category emphasizes the performing arts. A smaller portion is allocated for Civic and Community activities. Organizations requesting grants should have an adequate staff of professional personnel, show evidence of volunteer support, and report regularly to a board of directors. Financial responsibility and operating integrity are expected of all requesting groups, including evidence of proper fundraising and control of administrative costs.

Fields of interest: Health, arts, nutrition, welfare, civic affairs, education, performing arts.

Types of support: General purposes, matching funds, scholarship funds, in-kind gifts.

Limitations: Giving primarily in major operating locations; the project should serve a broad group of people in an area where company employees and their families can derive direct benefits. No support for religious or sectarian institutions-that do not serve the general public on a nondenominational basis, or for fraternal, veterans, political, or labor groups. No grants to individuals, or for capital or building funds, research, advertising, conferences, seminars, and fund-raising events, or recipients of United Way funds.

Publications: Informational brochure (including application guidelines).

Application information: If a preliminary evaluation meets with policy and priorities, the organization will be asked to complete a formal application.

Initial approach: Letter of inquiry to headquarters, not longer than two pages including description of organization and project, amount requested, and constituency served

Deadline(s): None

Board meeting date(s): Requests reviewed on a quarterly basis

Write: Karin Topping, Public Relations Dir.

Number of staff: 1 part-time professional; 1 part-time support.

302

Sierra Health Foundation ▼

(Formerly The Sierra Foundation)
11211 Gold Country Blvd., Suite 101
Rancho Cordova 95670   (916) 635-4755

Established in 1984 in CA.

Donor(s): Foundation Health Plan of Sacramento, Americare Health Corp.

Foundation type: Independent

Financial data (yr. ended 06/30/91): Assets, $90,222,887 (M); gifts received, $100,000; expenditures, $4,587,181; qualifying distributions, $4,914,850, including $2,461,788 for 97 grants (high: $103,086; low: $500; average: $15,000-$80,000), $42,327 for employee matching gifts and $83,000 for program-related investments.

Purpose and activities: Giving for health-related programs that (a)will have a long-term impact on the general health of the population; (b)provide a positive change in health care systems; and (c)may cause a positive change in the use of health care resources. Support also for model projects that may be replicated by others. The

foundation has an ongoing significant involvement in prenatal care, AIDS, youth and the elderly.

Fields of interest: Health, hospitals, medical sciences, alcoholism, aged, family planning, family services, mental health, health associations, nutrition, cancer, drug abuse, AIDS, leprosy, health services, minorities, youth, child welfare, child development, delinquency, disadvantaged.

Types of support: Matching funds, seed money, special projects, technical assistance, employee matching gifts, consulting services, loans, program-related investments.

Limitations: Giving limited to the following CA counties: Alpine, Amador, Butte, Calaveras, Colusa, El Dorado, Glenn, Lassen, Modoc, Mono, Nevada, Placer, Plumas, Sacramento, San Joaquin, Shasta, Sierra, Siskiyou, Solano (eastern), Stanislaus, Sutter, Tehama, Trinity, Tuolumne, Yolo, and Yuba. No support for programs or organizations that are not health-related, or for lobbying activities. No grants to individuals, or for endowments or scholarships.

Publications: Grants list, newsletter, application guidelines, informational brochure (including application guidelines), occasional report.

Application information: Application form not required.

Initial approach: Letter of intent

Copies of proposal: 1

Deadline(s): None

Board meeting date(s): Quarterly

Write: Stephanie Koehn, Controller

Officers and Directors:* J. Rod Eason,* Chair.; Len McCandliss,* Pres.; Leo McAllister,* Secy.; Dorothy Beaumont, C.F.O.; Byron Demorest, M.D., George Deubel, Wendy Everett, Albert R. Jonsen, Robert Petersen, Gordon D. Schaber, James Schubert, M.D.

Number of staff: 6 full-time professional; 1 part-time professional; 5 full-time support; 1 part-time support.

EIN: 680050036

Recent health grants:

302-1 American River Hosptial, Teen Clinic, Carmichael, CA, $35,500. To relocate clinic, to add certified nurse-midwife and to provide baby-related gifts as incentives to teens. 1991.

302-2 Chapa-De Indian Health Program, Auburn, CA, $25,000. To develop prenatal incentives program and prenatal mentoring program. 1991.

302-3 Chemical Dependency Center for Women, Sacramento, CA, $60,000. To provide AIDS education program for women in county jails and to assess effect of education on women's drug use patterns and contraception practices. 1991.

302-4 Davis Community Clinic, Davis, CA, $31,570. To provide information and rapid approval of Medi-Cal for pregnant clients, one year transition funding of community outreach staff to assist clients with Medi-Cal application process and computerized systems. 1991.

302-5 Education Programs Associates, Campbell, CA, $59,327. For training and recruitment of nurses, nurse practitioners and physician assistants in EPA OB/GYN nurse practitioner program, Midwifery Education Program and Ambulatory Obstetrics Program. 1991.

302-6 Enloe Hospital Foundation, Chico, CA, $32,633. To implement Volunteer Outreach

and Mentoring Project to supplement Perinatal Substance Abuse Project. Project will be staffed by recovering alcoholics/addicts. 1991.

302-7 Eskaton Foundation, Carmichael, CA, $37,035. To expand Yolo Adult Day Health Centers program for people with Alzheimers disease and other dementing illnesses by renovating Center and developing volunteer program. 1991.

302-8 Merced Family Health Centers, Merced, CA, $45,000. To renovate West Modesto Medical Clinic to include two exam rooms and one counseling room. 1991.

302-9 Planned Parenthood of Sacramento Valley, Sacramento, CA, $169,086. To provide prenatal care for women with Medi-Cal insurance in Sacramento County. 1991.

302-10 Sacramento County Health Department, Sacramento, CA, $31,000. To expand outreach and referral efforts for pregnant women on Medi-Cal. 1991.

302-11 Saint Elizabeths Community Hospital, Red Bluff, CA, $27,491. To provide outpatient substance abuse counseling to pregnant women and training in recognition and management of perinatal substance abuse for providers. 1991.

302-12 San Joaquin General Hospital, Stockton, CA, $165,538. To expand prenatal care services at two clinics, establish two new clinics, develop patient incentives coupon book program and provide scholarship program for nurse practitioners. 1991.

302-13 Scenic General Hospital, Modesto, CA, $170,400. To relocate Scenic General Hospital Obstetric Services. 1991.

302-14 Sierra Foothills AIDS Foundation, Grass Valley, CA, $92,301. To provide AIDS case management and support services. 1991.

302-15 Siskiyou Child Care Council, Yreka, CA, $75,000. To increase access and utilization of prenatal services in Siskiyou County using Big Sisters program, incentive program and four Young Parents Conferences. 1991.

302-16 Solano County Health Department, Fairfield, CA, $11,700. To convert Interim Prenatal Clinic in Fairfield into Comprehensive Perinatal Services Program. 1991.

302-17 Stanislaus County Department of Public Health, Modesto, CA, $75,000. To establish prenatal service clinics for low-income women in Turlock and East Stanislaus county. 1991.

302-18 University of California, Davis, CA, $25,000. To provide matching funds to establish project that offers continuum of care services to pregnant substance-abusing women. 1991.

302-19 University of California, Davis, CA, $13,181. To study effect of cash incentives on motivating women to begin prenatal care early. 1991.

302-20 Visions Unlimited-South Area Mental Health Center, Sacramento, CA, $60,000. For new senior adult day mental health program for seniors previously homebound due to mental illness. 1991.

303

Jennifer Jones Simon Foundation

411 West Colorado Blvd.
Pasadena 91105   (818) 449-6840

Established in 1954 in LA.
Donor(s): Norton Simon, Norton Simon, Inc., and its subsidiaries and predecessors, Braun 1981 Charitable Annuity Trust, Norton Simon Charitable Lead Trust.
Foundation type: Independent
Financial data (yr. ended 11/30/91): Assets, $5,371,368 (M); gifts received, $288,562; expenditures, $291,526; qualifying distributions, $276,974, including $240,000 for 10 grants (high: $50,000; low: $500; average: $500-$50,000).
Fields of interest: Mental health, psychiatry, medical sciences, medical research.
Types of support: General purposes, special projects, research.
Limitations: No grants to individuals, or for building or endowment funds, research, scholarships, fellowships, or matching gifts; no loans.
Application information: Grants generally restricted to programs initiated by the foundation; no new scholarships to individuals will be awarded. Application form not required.
  Initial approach: Letter
  Deadline(s): None
  Board meeting date(s): As required
  Final notification: 1 month
  Write: Walter W. Timoshuk, V.P.
Officers and Trustees:* Jennifer Jones Simon,* Chair. and Pres.; Walter W. Timoshuk,* V.P. and Secy.-Treas.
Number of staff: None.
EIN: 953660147

304
L. J. Skaggs and Mary C. Skaggs Foundation ▼
1221 Broadway, 21st Fl.
Oakland 94612-1837   (510) 451-3300

Incorporated in 1967 in CA.
Donor(s): L.J. Skaggs,‡ Mary C. Skaggs.
Foundation type: Independent
Financial data (yr. ended 12/31/91): Assets, $6,137,979 (M); gifts received, $720,000; expenditures, $2,790,619; qualifying distributions, $1,988,580, including $1,988,580 for 157 grants (high: $250,000; low: $750; average: $5,000-$10,000).
Purpose and activities: Giving for the performing arts, specifically theater, ecology programs, and projects of historic interest.
Fields of interest: Historic preservation, theater, ecology, history, archaeology.
Types of support: Special projects, general purposes, continuing support, publications.
Limitations: Giving limited to northern CA for theater, ecology programs, and special projects; giving with national focus limited to projects of historic interest. No support for higher education, residence home programs, halfway houses, or sectarian religious purposes. No grants to individuals, or for capital funds, annual fund drives, budget deficits, scholarships, or fellowships; no loans.
Publications: Application guidelines, informational brochure (including application guidelines), grants list, annual report.
Application information: Application form not required.
  Initial approach: Letter

Copies of proposal: 1
Deadline(s): June 1 for letter of intent, Sept. 1 for invited proposal
Board meeting date(s): Nov.
Final notification: 2 to 3 weeks after board meeting
Write: Philip M. Jelley, Secy., or David G. Knight, Prog. Dir. and Office Mgr.
Officers and Directors:* Mary C. Skaggs,* Pres.; Peter H. Forsham, M.D.,* V.P.; Catherine L. O'Brien,* V.P.; Philip M. Jelley,* Secy. and Fdn. Mgr.; Donald D. Crawford,* Treas.; David Knight, Prog. Dir.
Number of staff: 2 full-time professional.
EIN: 946174113
Recent health grants:
304-1 California on Stage, Berkeley, CA, $10,000. For commission of new play which will take form of half-hour radio drama focusing on crack cocaine epidemic in Oakland, CA. 1990.
304-2 Centre for Development and Population Activities, DC, $10,000. To provide activities for adolescent girls in India and other South Asia communities which give them access to reproductive health information, literacy, training programs, family planning services and income generating skills. 1990.
304-3 Education Programs Associates, Campbell, CA, $10,000. For seed grant to create Institute for Applied Ethics in Reproductive Health, to work specifically on reproductive health dilemmas which have arisen in past two decades as result of new and sophisticated medical technology. 1990.
304-4 Family Care International, NYC, NY, $10,000. For Mexican programs of worldwide Safe Motherhood program which address problems of pregnancy-related illness and death. 1990.
304-5 La Clinica De La Raza, Oakland, CA, $20,000. For community-based primary health care center. 1990.
304-6 YWCA of Oakland, Health Clinic, Oakland, CA, $20,000. For third year support for Teens Talking To Teens, pregnancy prevention program in schools. 1990.
304-7 Zenaide Project, Winchester, MA, $10,000. For investigation into deaths, accidents and injuries related to new in-vitro fertilization programs. Human rights activists in countries all around the world, and women's rights organizations in U.S. will attempt to document all deaths from these programs and to release suppressed information on these fertilization techniques. 1990.

305
The H. Russell Smith Foundation
150 North Orange Grove Blvd.
Pasadena 91103-3596

Established in 1968 in CA.
Donor(s): H. Russell Smith, Jeanne R. Smith, Kinsmith Financial Corp.
Foundation type: Independent
Financial data (yr. ended 12/31/91): Assets, $253 (M); gifts received, $374,257; expenditures, $398,061; qualifying distributions, $397,670, including $397,110 for 16 grants (high: $67,238; low: $500).

Fields of interest: Hospitals, medical research, youth, community funds, higher education, cultural programs, media and communications.
Limitations: Giving primarily in CA. No grants to individuals.
Application information: Contributes only to pre-selected organizations. Applications not accepted.
Officers and Directors:* H. Russell Smith,* Chair.; Stewart R. Smith,* Pres.; Jeanne R. Smith,* V.P.; Micaela Norris, Secy.-Treas.; Jeanne Ellen Akins, Douglas H. Smith.
Number of staff: None.
EIN: 237423945

306
Lon V. Smith Foundation
9440 Santa Monica Blvd., Suite 303
Beverly Hills 90210-4201

Established in 1952 in CA.
Foundation type: Independent
Financial data (yr. ended 12/31/91): Assets, $20,175,737 (M); expenditures, $1,120,704; qualifying distributions, $905,711, including $806,100 for 82 grants (high: $40,000; low: $100).
Fields of interest: Health, hospitals, higher education, social services, museums, community funds.
Types of support: General purposes.
Limitations: Giving primarily in Southern CA. No grants to individuals.
Application information: Contributes only to pre-selected organizations. Applications not accepted.
Officers: Stefan A. Kantardjieff, Pres.; John L. Lahn, 1st V.P.; Alexander Rados, 2nd V.P.; Donald R. Mellert, 3rd V.P.; Marguerite M. Murphy, Secy.-Treas.
EIN: 956045384

307
Smith-Walker Foundation
1260 Coast Village Circle
Santa Barbara 93108   (805) 969-4764

Established in 1989 in CA.
Foundation type: Independent
Financial data (yr. ended 09/30/91): Assets, $3,412,247 (M); expenditures, $216,904; qualifying distributions, $196,724, including $195,801 for 43 grants (high: $33,267; low: $1,000).
Fields of interest: Hospitals, health, family planning, youth, cultural programs.
Limitations: Giving primarily in CA. No grants to individuals.
Application information: Contributes only to pre-selected organizations. Applications not accepted.
  Write: Mr. Gaeden, C.P.A.
Officers and Directors:* Gilbert M.W. Smith,* Pres.; Walker Smith, Jr.,* V.P.; Jean Goodrich,* Secy.
Number of staff: None.
EIN: 330327308

308
Richard & Mary Solari Charitable Trust
527 St. Andrews Dr.
Aptos 95003-5422

Established in 1984 in CA.
Donor(s): Richard C. Solari, Mary C. Solari.
Foundation type: Independent
Financial data (yr. ended 09/30/91): Assets,
$3,375,671 (M); gifts received, $400,000;
expenditures, $107,374; qualifying distributions,
$100,002, including $91,950 for 9 grants (high:
$25,000; low: $500).
Fields of interest: Community development,
health, social services, higher education, historic
preservation.
Limitations: Giving primarily in CA. No grants to
individuals.
Application information: Contributes only to
pre-selected organizations. Applications not
accepted.
Trustees: Mary C. Solari, Richard C. Solari.
EIN: 770069120

309
The Sonoma County Community Foundation
(Formerly The Sonoma County Foundation)
3550 Round Barn Blvd. No. 212
Santa Rosa 95403   (707) 579-4073

Incorporated in 1983 in CA.
Foundation type: Community
Financial data (yr. ended 12/31/91): Assets,
$4,100,308 (M); gifts received, $1,065,250;
expenditures, $386,318; qualifying distributions,
$590,713, including $263,538 for 80 grants
(high: $5,000; low: $100; average: $500-$5,000),
$12,437 for 5 grants to individuals (high: $1,000;
low: $500; average: $500-$1,000), $111,238 for
2 foundation-administered programs, $200,000
for loans and $3,500 for 15 in-kind gifts.
Fields of interest: Arts, cultural programs,
education, social services, environment, health.
Types of support: Student aid, grants to
individuals, renovation projects, building funds,
equipment, general purposes, matching funds,
publications, scholarship funds, seed money,
special projects, technical assistance.
Limitations: Giving limited to Sonoma County,
CA.
Publications: 990-PF, program policy statement,
financial statement, grants list, newsletter,
application guidelines.
Application information: Application form
required.
  Initial approach: Letter requesting application
    material
  Deadline(s): Telephone for deadlines
  Board meeting date(s): 1st Tuesday each month
  Write: Kay Marquet, Exec. Dir.
Officers and Trustees:* Peggy Bair,* Pres.; Lee
Chandler,* V.P.; Nancy Henshaw,* Secy.; Richard
Indermill,* Treas.; Kay Marquet, Exec. Dir.
Number of staff: 1 full-time professional; 3
full-time support.
EIN: 680003212

310
Southern California Gas Corporate Contributions Program
810 S. Flower St., M.L. 110H
Los Angeles 90017   (213) 689-2149

Purpose and activities: "We support organizations
that significantly enhance a community's social
and economic well-being through the Company's
current community outreach targets." These
organizations must be fundamentally
service-oriented or educational in nature. The
company looks at the management's experience
and expertise, fundraising practices, and for a
successful track record. In addition to the general
programs shown below, applicants should be
aware that community needs are annually
reviewed and giving priorities based on these
needs. For the current period, the following are
the target areas: 1) Workforce readiness -
programs which directly prepare youth or adults
with marketable skills, such as specific job and
technical training are preferred. 2) Environmental
quality - programs which address the needs of
Southern CA, especially in the area of air quality.
Funding is not granted for animal preservation,
recycling, or projects not directly related to the
natural gas industry. 3) Demographic change -
programs which address social and political
trends resulting from shifting demographics are
considered. Programs focusing on the arts and
cultural preservation efforts are not eligible for
funding. Programs which do not directly address
these areas will not be considered.
Fields of interest: Community development, drug
abuse, education—minorities, literacy, science
and technology, vocational education, minorities,
civic affairs, women, ecology, social services,
cultural programs, engineering, community funds,
race relations.
Types of support: Capital campaigns, general
purposes, matching funds, operating budgets,
special projects, technical assistance.
Limitations: Giving limited to organizations that
operate within the service territory which
includes nearly all of southern and central CA
(except San Diego County and the City of Long
Beach). No support for profit-making groups,
religious organizations for religious purposes, or
groups that already receive substantial support
from the United Way. No grants to individuals, or
for endowments or contributions of equipment,
furniture, appliances or salvaged material. No
support for telethons or walk-a-thons; no support
for third party scholarship programs, academic
research projects, or media projects.
Publications: Application guidelines.
Application information: Application form not
required.
  Initial approach: Proposal
  Copies of proposal: 1
  Deadline(s): Reviewed throughout the year,
    except for requests for capital grants should
    be received at least 2 months before Apr. or
    Nov.
  Board meeting date(s): Apr. and Nov. for capital
    grants
  Final notification: 6 weeks
  Write: Carolyn Williams, Contrib. Admin.
Number of staff: 1 full-time professional; 1
full-time support.

311
Southern Pacific Corporate Contributions Program
One Market Plaza
San Francisco 94105   (415) 541-1000

Purpose and activities: Support for United Way
and Junior Achievement, and other community
service programs; employee gifts matched for
education, libraries, hospitals, and arts and
culture.
Fields of interest: Libraries, hospitals.
Types of support: Employee matching gifts.
Limitations: Giving primarily in headquarters city
and major operating locations. No support for
fraternal or religious organizations or political
campaigns. No grants to individuals.
Application information: Applications not
accepted.
  Write: Nancy Hagen, Mgr., Administration

312
Caryll M. and Norman F. Sprague, Jr. Foundation
2049 Century Park East, Suite 2760
Los Angeles 90067-3202

Trust established in 1957 in CA.
Donor(s): Caryll M. Sprague, Norman F. Sprague,
Jr., M.D.
Foundation type: Independent
Financial data (yr. ended 12/31/91): Assets,
$3,889,620 (M); gifts received, $16,522;
expenditures, $153,424; qualifying distributions,
$147,740, including $147,250 for 38 grants
(high: $25,000; low: $250).
Fields of interest: Higher education, secondary
education, health associations, hospitals,
museums, general charitable giving.
Limitations: Giving primarily in CA. No grants to
individuals.
Application information: Contributes only to
pre-selected organizations. Applications not
accepted.
  Board meeting date(s): Annually and as required
Trustees: Cynthia S. Connolly, Caryll S. Mingst,
Charles T. Munger, Norman F. Sprague, Jr., M.D.,
Norman F. Sprague III, M.D.
EIN: 956021187

313
John Stauffer Charitable Trust ▼
301 North Lake Ave., 10th Fl.
Pasadena 91101   (213) 385-4345

Trust established in 1974 in CA.
Donor(s): John Stauffer.‡
Foundation type: Independent
Financial data (yr. ended 05/31/91): Assets,
$34,437,412 (M); expenditures, $1,656,872;
qualifying distributions, $1,419,332, including
$1,272,800 for 13 grants (high: $220,000; low:
$25,000; average: $30,000-$100,000).
Purpose and activities: Grants restricted to
hospitals, colleges and universities.
Fields of interest: Hospitals, hospitals—building
funds, higher education, education—building
funds.
Types of support: Building funds, endowment
funds, equipment, fellowships, general purposes,
matching funds, professorships, scholarship funds.

Limitations: Giving primarily in CA. No grants to individuals, or for research, special projects, conferences, or publications; no loans.
Publications: Application guidelines.
Application information: Application form not required.
   Initial approach: Letter
   Copies of proposal: 3
   Deadline(s): None
   Board meeting date(s): Bimonthly beginning in Feb.
   Final notification: 6 to 9 months
   Write: A. Richard Kimbrough, Chair.
Trustees: A. Richard Kimbrough, Chair.; Carl M. Franklin, Stanley C. Lagerlof.
Number of staff: 1 part-time support.
EIN: 237434707
Recent health grants:
313-1 Childrens Hospital of Los Angeles, Department of Radiology, Los Angeles, CA, $150,000. For remodeling and upgrading two diagnostic radiographic rooms. 1991.
313-2 Goleta Valley Community Hospital, Santa Barbara, CA, $42,000. For purchase of vitrectomy and phacoemulsification. 1991.
313-3 Queen of Angels-Hollywood Presbyterian Foundation, Los Angeles, CA, $75,000. For purchase of cardiac monitors for Definitial Observation Unit. 1991.
313-4 Saint Vincent Medical Center, Los Angeles, CA, $150,000. Toward purchase of Marquette Monitoring System. 1991.

314
John and Beverly Stauffer Foundation, Inc.
P.O. Box 48345
Los Angeles 90048   (213) 381-3933
Application address: P.O. Box 2246, Los Angeles, CA 90028

Incorporated in 1954 in CA.
Donor(s): John Stauffer,‡ Beverly Stauffer.‡
Foundation type: Independent
Financial data (yr. ended 12/31/90): Assets, $3,513,642 (M); expenditures, $225,037; qualifying distributions, $206,137, including $191,620 for grants.
Fields of interest: Higher education, secondary education, hospitals, medical research, cancer, child welfare, social services, alcoholism, drug abuse, homeless, arts, cultural programs, theater, religion—Christian.
Types of support: Continuing support, annual campaigns, building funds, equipment, scholarship funds, general purposes.
Limitations: Giving primarily in the Southern CA area. No grants to individuals, or for endowment funds or operating budgets.
Application information: Application form not required.
   Initial approach: Letter
   Copies of proposal: 1
   Deadline(s): None
   Board meeting date(s): 4 times a year
   Write: Jack R. Sheridan, Pres.
Officers: Jack R. Sheridan, Pres.; Laurence K. Gould, Jr., Treas.
Directors: Leslie Sheridan Bartleson, Harriette Hughes, Katherine Stauffer Sheridan, Thomas C. Towse.
EIN: 952241406

315
The Harry and Grace Steele Foundation ▼
441 Old Newport Blvd., Suite 301
Newport Beach 92663   (714) 631-9158

Incorporated in 1953 in CA.
Donor(s): Grace C. Steele.‡
Foundation type: Independent
Financial data (yr. ended 10/31/91): Assets, $50,093,052 (M); expenditures, $6,023,099; qualifying distributions, $6,023,099, including $5,925,555 for 48 grants (high: $750,000; low: $500; average: $10,000-$100,000).
Purpose and activities: Emphasis on higher and secondary education, including scholarship funds, the fine arts, population control, hospitals and clinics, and youth agencies.
Fields of interest: Higher education, secondary education, cultural programs, fine arts, family planning, hospitals, youth, child welfare.
Types of support: Building funds, endowment funds, scholarship funds, matching funds, continuing support, general purposes, special projects, equipment.
Limitations: Giving primarily in Orange County, CA. No support for tax-supported organizations or private foundations. No grants to individuals; no loans.
Publications: Annual report, program policy statement, application guidelines.
Application information: Application form not required.
   Initial approach: Letter, followed by proposal
   Copies of proposal: 1
   Deadline(s): None
   Board meeting date(s): Quarterly
   Final notification: 6 months
   Write: Marie F. Kowert, Asst. Secy.
Officers and Trustees:* Audrey Steele Burnand,* Pres.; Richard Steele,* V.P. and Treas.; Alphonse A. Burnand III,* Secy.; Marie F. Kowert, Elizabeth R. Steele, Barbara Steele Williams, Nick B. Williams.
Number of staff: 1 full-time support.
EIN: 956035879
Recent health grants:
315-1 Assessment and Treatment Service Center of Coastal Orange County, Santa Ana, CA, $32,925. For continued general support. 1991.
315-2 Center for Population Options, Los Angeles, CA, $25,000. For last payment against pledge for general support. 1991.
315-3 Florence Crittenton Services of Orange County, Fullerton, CA, $25,000. For general support. 1991.
315-4 Huntington Medical Research Institutes, Pasadena, CA, $20,000. For continued support. 1991.
315-5 Planned Parenthood Federation of America, NYC, NY, $500,000. For final payment against pledge for general support. 1991.
315-6 Planned Parenthood of Orange and San Bernardino Counties, Santa Ana, CA, $250,000. For payment against pledge for general support. 1991.
315-7 Planned Parenthood-World Population Los Angeles, Los Angeles, CA, $200,000. For payment against pledge for general support. 1991.
315-8 Population Crisis Committee, NYC, NY, $40,000. For research on RU-486 and

international population policy development. 1991.
315-9 Population Institute, DC, $166,000. For miscellaneous projects. 1991.
315-10 Salk Institute for Biological Studies, La Jolla, CA, $50,000. For capital improvements. 1991.

316
Jules and Doris Stein Foundation ▼
(Formerly Doris Jones Stein Foundation)
P.O. Box 30
Beverly Hills 90213   (213) 276-2101

Established in 1981 in CA.
Donor(s): Doris Jones Stein Family Trust.
Foundation type: Independent
Financial data (yr. ended 12/31/90): Assets, $41,728,746 (M); gifts received, $4,409,266; expenditures, $4,467,772; qualifying distributions, $4,255,308, including $4,132,617 for 209 grants (high: $1,584,349; low: $500; average: $5,000-$20,000).
Purpose and activities: Support for hospitals, health associations, and medical research; higher, medical, and other education; cultural organizations, including museums and the performing and fine arts; computer sciences; and social welfare.
Fields of interest: Cultural programs, museums, performing arts, fine arts, education, higher education, medical education, computer sciences, hospitals, health associations, medical research, social services, child welfare.
Types of support: Building funds, general purposes, continuing support, endowment funds, equipment, matching funds, research, special projects, capital campaigns, fellowships, operating budgets.
Limitations: Giving primarily in the metropolitan areas of Los Angeles, Kansas City, and New York City. No support for political advocacy groups. No grants to individuals.
Publications: Application guidelines, occasional report.
Application information: No new grant applications are being solicited until 1994. Application form required.
   Initial approach: Letter
   Deadline(s): None
   Board meeting date(s): Varies
   Write: Linda L. Valliant, Prog. Officer, or Tracey Boldemann, Prog. Officer
Officers and Directors:* Lew R. Wasserman,* Chair.; Gerald H. Oppenheimer,* Pres.; Jean Stein,* V.P.; Linda L. Valliant,* Secy.; Stephen P. Petty,* C.F.O.; Hamilton G. Oppenheimer, Andrew Shiva.
Number of staff: 2 part-time professional; 1 part-time support.
EIN: 953708961
Recent health grants:
316-1 Ackerman Institute for Family Therapy, NYC, NY, $18,000. For Womens Studies in Family Therapy. 1990.
316-2 American Foundation for AIDS Research, Los Angeles, CA, $15,000. For primary source of funds for research into causes, treatment and vaccine for AIDS. 1990.
316-3 Gay Mens Health Crisis (GMHC), AIDS Fund, NYC, NY, $12,000. For public

education and psychosocial support for AIDS victims. 1990.

316-4 Harvard University, School of Public Health, Boston, MA, $50,000. For Mary Woodward Lasker Professorship and Research Program. 1990.

316-5 Israel Cancer Association U.S.A., NYC, NY, $87,500. For development of oncology unit at Kaplan Hospital in Israel. 1990.

316-6 Johns Hopkins University, School of Medicine, Baltimore, MD, $25,000. For fellowship support. 1990.

316-7 Jules Stein Eye Institute, Los Angeles, CA, $1,584,349. For Susan Stein Shiva Memorial Fund. 1990.

316-8 Leukemia Society of America, Los Angeles, CA, $14,000. For general support for Hollywood Canteen Foundation Pledge Fund. 1990.

316-9 Martin Luther King Jr. General Hospital, Los Angeles, CA, $11,500. For Patient Development Fund and Hollywood Canteen Foundation Pledge Fund. 1990.

316-10 Midwest Bioethics Center, Kansas City, MO, $10,000. 1990.

316-11 Miller Health Care Institute, NYC, NY, $10,000. For general operating support. 1990.

316-12 Motion Picture Country Home Fund, Woodland Hills, CA, $200,000. 1990.

316-13 National Kidney Foundation of Kansas and West Mississippi, Kansas City, MO, $15,000. For programs in metropolitan Kansas City. 1990.

316-14 New York Hospital-Cornell Medical Center, NYC, NY, $10,000. For fellowships funding for AIDS research. 1990.

316-15 P.E.F. Israel Endowment Funds, NYC, NY, $47,000. For several projects, including purchase of heart catheterization machine and research in Israeli AIDS Task Force. 1990.

316-16 PKR Foundation, Kansas City, MO, $10,000. For research in polycystic kidney disease. 1990.

316-17 Planned Parenthood of Los Angeles, Los Angeles, CA, $20,000. For seed money for mobile clinic to bring education on prenatal care and family planning services to disadvantaged areas. 1990.

316-18 Research to Prevent Blindness, NYC, NY, $125,000. For general support for program. 1990.

316-19 Saint Annes Maternity Home, Los Angeles, CA, $15,000. For capital campaign for Doris Stein Patio and 95 beds for young teen pregnancy care. 1990.

316-20 University of California, School of Medicine, Los Angeles, CA, $45,000. For general support for Hollywood Canteen Foundation and Loan Program and for emergency loans. 1990.

316-21 University of Texas Medical Branch Hospitals, Galveston, TX, $15,000. For pledge-type scholarship for medical students. 1990.

316-22 Vital Options, Studio City, CA, $25,000. For support group for young adults with cancer. 1990.

317
The Charles H. Stern and Anna S. Stern Foundation
1200 Prospect St., Suite 575
La Jolla 92037

Established in 1988 in CA.
Donor(s): Anna S. Stern Trust.
Foundation type: Independent
Financial data (yr. ended 12/31/90): Assets, $3,166,293 (M); expenditures, $220,490; qualifying distributions, $139,732, including $139,732 for 3 grants (high: $50,000; low: $39,800).
Fields of interest: Medical research.
Types of support: Research.
Limitations: Giving primarily in CA and NE.
Application information: Grants generally limited to $75,000.
  Initial approach: Proposal
  Deadline(s): None
  Write: Melitta Fleck
Officers: William W. Gordon, Pres.; Frank Nielsen, Treas.
Trustees: Christopher C. Calkins, Frederick De La Vega, Barbara Durban.
EIN: 956878433

318
Sidney Stern Memorial Trust
P.O. Box 893
Pacific Palisades 90272

Trust established in 1974 in CA.
Donor(s): S. Sidney Stern.‡
Foundation type: Independent
Financial data (yr. ended 08/31/91): Assets, $20,418,989 (M); expenditures, $1,490,502; qualifying distributions, $1,337,023, including $1,272,187 for 202 grants (high: $31,000; low: $250; average: $1,000-$15,000).
Purpose and activities: Giving primarily for higher education, social service agencies, including aid to the handicapped; youth and child welfare agencies, health associations, and cultural programs.
Fields of interest: Higher education, social services, youth, child welfare, handicapped, health, cultural programs.
Types of support: Operating budgets, annual campaigns, seed money, emergency funds, deficit financing, building funds, equipment, land acquisition, endowment funds, matching funds, scholarship funds, special projects, research.
Limitations: Giving primarily in CA; all funds must be used within the U.S. No grants to individuals, or for continuing support, publications, or conferences; no loans.
Publications: Informational brochure (including application guidelines).
Application information: Application form not required.
  Initial approach: Letter or proposal
  Copies of proposal: 1
  Deadline(s): None
  Board meeting date(s): Monthly, except Aug.
  Write: Marvin Hoffenberg, Chair.
Officers and Board of Advisors:* Marvin Hoffenberg,* Chair.; Ira E. Bilson,* Secy.; Betty Hoffenberg, Peter H. Hoffenberg, Edith Lessler, Howard O. Wilson.
Number of staff: None.

EIN: 956495222
Recent health grants:
318-1 Cedars-Sinai Medical Center, Los Angeles, CA, $12,500. 1991.
318-2 Health Champions, Beverly Hills, CA, $10,000. 1991.
318-3 House Ear Institute, Los Angeles, CA, $15,000. 1991.
318-4 Julia Ann Singer Pre-School Psychiatric Center, Los Angeles, CA, $10,000. 1991.
318-5 Los Angeles Free Clinic, Los Angeles, CA, $15,000. 1991.
318-6 Los Angeles Homeless Health Care Project, Los Angeles, CA, $10,000. 1991.
318-7 Los Angeles Orthopaedic Foundation, Los Angeles, CA, $10,000. 1991.
318-8 Meharry Medical College, Nashville, TN, $12,500. 1991.
318-9 Pacific Clinics, Pasadena, CA, $10,000. 1991.
318-10 Queen of Angels-Hollywood Presbyterian Foundation, Los Angeles, CA, $10,000. 1991.
318-11 Reiss-Davis Child Study Center, Los Angeles, CA, $12,500. 1991.
318-12 Venice Family Clinic, Venice, CA, $16,000. 1991.

319
Leon Strauss Foundation
5332 Harbor St.
Commerce 90040-3997   (213) 728-5440

Established in 1976.
Donor(s): Leon Strauss.‡
Foundation type: Independent
Financial data (yr. ended 12/31/91): Assets, $6,594,752 (M); gifts received, $10,416; expenditures, $368,563; qualifying distributions, $361,474, including $333,000 for 36 grants (high: $69,000; low: $1,000).
Purpose and activities: Giving primarily for children's camps and hospitals.
Fields of interest: Youth, hospitals, social services, general charitable giving.
Limitations: Giving primarily in CA. No grants to individuals.
Application information: Application form not required.
  Initial approach: Letter
  Deadline(s): None
  Write: Robert P. Vossler, Trustee
Trustees: Charles Curley, Paul Simon, Robert P. Vossler.
EIN: 510205308

320
Elbridge and Evelyn Stuart Foundation
c/o Bank of America
P.O. Box 3189, Terminal Annex
Los Angeles 90051
Application address: c/o Bank of America, 333 South Hope St., Los Angeles, CA 90071; Tel.: (213) 613-4877

Trust established in 1961 in CA.
Foundation type: Independent
Financial data (yr. ended 12/31/90): Assets, $8,073,654 (M); expenditures, $556,848; qualifying distributions, $490,532, including

$470,000 for 29 grants (high: $150,000; low: $1,000).

Fields of interest: Higher education, business education, secondary education, hospitals, youth, religion—Christian.

Limitations: Giving primarily in CA. No grants to individuals.

Application information:
Initial approach: Letter
Deadline(s): None
Write: Bill August, V.P., Bank of America

Trustees: Charles Stuart Nelson, Clark A. Nelson, Bank of America.

EIN: 956014019

321
Stuart Foundations ▼
188 The Embarcadero, Suite 420
San Francisco 94105   (415) 495-1144

Elbridge Stuart Foundation created in 1937 in CA, Elbridge and Mary Stuart Foundation in 1941 in CA, and Mary Horner Stuart Foundation in 1941 in WA.

Donor(s): Elbridge A. Stuart,‡ Elbridge H. Stuart.‡

Foundation type: Independent

Financial data (yr. ended 12/31/90): Assets, $163,734,985 (M); expenditures, $9,300,414; qualifying distributions, $7,848,189, including $7,216,571 for 148 grants (high: $249,000; low: $2,000; average: $10,000-$50,000).

Purpose and activities: Support primarily for prevention of child abuse and neglect, strengthening the foster care system, strengthening public schools, preventing school failure, and preventing teenage pregnancy.

Fields of interest: Child welfare, family services, education—early childhood, elementary education, education, health, public policy, social services, youth.

Types of support: Seed money, operating budgets, special projects.

Limitations: Giving primarily in CA, although applications from WA will be considered. No grants to individuals, or generally for endowments, building funds, or annual campaigns.

Publications: Informational brochure (including application guidelines).

Application information: Application form not required.
Initial approach: Letter or telephone
Copies of proposal: 1
Deadline(s): 3 months prior to board meeting
Board meeting date(s): Mar., June, Sept., and Dec.
Final notification: Within 2 weeks after meeting
Write: Theodore E. Lobman, Pres.

Officer: Theodore E. Lobman, Pres.

Advisors: Dwight L. Stuart, Dwight L. Stuart, Jr., E. Hadley Stuart, Jr., Elbridge H. Stuart III.

Trustees: Seafirst Bank, Security Pacific National Bank.

Number of staff: 5 full-time professional; 3 part-time professional; 2 full-time support.

EIN: 942967682

Recent health grants:

321-1 Alameda Health Consortium, Oakland, CA, $20,420. To expand perinatal on-site Medi-Cal Eligibility Project to include adolescent and pediatric care for school-based health clinics and other clinics in Alameda County. 1991.

321-2 Aldea, Napa, CA, $34,535. For start-up of less expensive model for intensive therapeutic family foster care. 1991.

321-3 Birthing Project, Sacramento, CA, $52,372. For project which helps at-risk pregnant minority women to be more effective parents. 1991.

321-4 Cedars-Sinai Medical Center, Los Angeles, CA, $100,000. For Common Disease Risk Assessment Center to determine genetic susceptibilities of individuals to common diseases and provide early treatment. 1991.

321-5 Childrens Health Council of the Mid-Peninsula, Palo Alto, CA, $15,000. For continued support of School-Based Mental Health Program in four Whisman School District Schools. 1991.

321-6 Childrens Hospital and Health Center, San Diego, CA, $240,636. To create interagency collaborative system to address issues of families involved in domestic violence and child abuse. 1991.

321-7 Childrens Hospital Medical Center Foundation, Oakland, CA, $76,146. For continued support of model case management program in clinic for drug exposed infants and their mothers, clinic for foster children in Center of the Vulnerable Child and for outcome evaluation. 1991.

321-8 Childrens Hospital of Los Angeles, Los Angeles, CA, $40,893. For training program for foster parents of drug-addicted babies. 1991.

321-9 Childrens Research Institute of California, Sacramento, CA, $115,080. To encourage State to require that all children in California foster care system have health and education passport to facilitate provision of needed services. 1991.

321-10 Childrens Research Institute of California, Sacramento, CA, $70,000. For continued support for prenatal care access project. 1991.

321-11 Colorado State University, Fort Collins, CO, $35,000. For resident in clinical oncology, including salary, small research projects, travel, books and journals and miscellaneous staff costs. 1991.

321-12 Culver City Unified School District, Culver City, CA, $58,366. For continued support for Culver City School-Based Health Center and to implement school-based infant day care center. 1991.

321-13 Education, Training and Research (ETR) Associates, Santa Cruz, CA, $157,370. To establish and manage training system for dissemination of Reducing the Risk curriculum to prevent teen pregnancy. 1991.

321-14 Family Stress Center, Concord, CA, $36,849. For parenting support services component of this collaboration with county health department to help poor, pregnant women at-risk of substance abuse. 1991.

321-15 Five Acres, Altadena, CA, $34,000. Toward operating support of in-home services project of Family Resource Center. 1991.

321-16 Hathaway Childrens Services, Sylmar, CA, $150,000. For continued support of In-Home Services Project. 1991.

321-17 Los Angeles Free Clinic, Los Angeles, CA, $37,827. For High Risk Youth Project's Short Term Employment Program (STEP). 1991.

321-18 Los Angeles Unified School District, Los Angeles, CA, $78,500. For continued general support for three school-based health clinics. 1991.

321-19 National Association of Social Workers, California Chapter, Sacramento, CA, $50,000. To develop school-linked services training program for social, health, mental health and education workers by providing interdisciplinary conference, workshops and training handbook. 1991.

321-20 Oakland Unified School District, Comprehensive School Health Center, Oakland, CA, $65,500. For continued support of Tiger Medics Comprehensive School Health Center at Fremont High School. Grant made through Children's Hospital Medical Center Foundation. 1991.

321-21 San Jose Medical Center, San Jose, CA, $32,500. To continue funding San Jose Academy and Overfelt High School Health Centers. 1991.

321-22 Santa Monica Hospital Medical Center, Rape Treatment Center, Santa Monica, CA, $201,745. For start-up and operating expenses of Stuart House, for comprehensive assessment and treatment of sexually abused children. 1991.

321-23 Sheriffs Youth Foundation, Los Angeles, CA, $25,000. For SANE, drug abuse prevention program which includes information on gang violence. 1991.

321-24 Stanford University Medical Center, Department of Ophthalmology, Stanford, CA, $10,000. For research and development to assist patients undergoing retinal surgery. 1991.

321-25 University of California, Division of Behavioral and Developmental Pediatrics, San Francisco, CA, $25,000. For Center for the Study of Drug-Exposed Children. 1991.

321-26 University of California, Institute For Health Policy Studies, San Francisco, CA, $104,485. For technical assistance and evaluation services to eight school-based clinics in California. 1991.

321-27 University of California Medical Center, Child Protection Center, Davis, CA, $30,000. For continued support of psychological assessment service for dependent children and data collection to strengthen foster care system. 1991.

321-28 University of Washington, Graduate School of Public Affairs, Seattle, WA, $70,000. To develop integrated model of pre-service and in-service training for teachers, social workers, health and mental health professionals, administrators and policy analysts. 1991.

321-29 University of Washington, Harborview Medical Center, Seattle, WA, $35,222. For testing group Well-Child Health Care format for disadvantaged mothers using children's clinic. 1991.

321-30 University of Washington, School of Medicine, Seattle, WA, $27,970. For case management and clinical intervention with pregnant women who are at risk because of mental illness, poverty and histories of abuse as children. 1991.

321-31 Washington Alliance Concerned with School Age Parents, Seattle, WA, $59,379. For development of community-wide effort to integrate health, education and social services for pregnant and parenting teens and evaluation of systemic approach and outcomes. 1991.

322
The Morris Stulsaft Foundation ▼
100 Bush St., Suite 825
San Francisco 94104 (415) 986-7117

Incorporated in 1953 in CA; sole beneficiary of feeder trust created in 1965; assets reflect value of assets of testamentary trust.
Donor(s): The Morris Stulsaft Testamentary Trust.
Foundation type: Independent
Financial data (yr. ended 12/31/91): Assets, $19,520,853 (M); gifts received, $1,247,455; expenditures, $1,237,339; qualifying distributions, $1,070,420, including $1,070,420 for 144 grants (high: $55,000; low: $1,000; average: $2,500-$10,000).
Purpose and activities: "To aid and assist needy and deserving children;" giving for youth programs, including social service, educational, health, cultural and recreational programs.
Fields of interest: Youth, child welfare, health, child development, education, recreation, social services, cultural programs.
Types of support: Operating budgets, building funds, equipment, matching funds, renovation projects, research, special projects, seed money.
Limitations: Giving limited to the San Francisco Bay Area, CA: Alameda, Contra Costa, Marin, San Francisco, Santa Clara, and San Mateo counties. No support for sectarian religious projects or ongoing support for private schools. No grants to individuals, or for emergency funding, annual campaigns, workshops, or conferences.
Publications: Biennial report (including application guidelines).
Application information: Application form required.
Initial approach: Letter or call requesting application form
Copies of proposal: 1
Deadline(s): None
Board meeting date(s): Jan., Mar., May, July, Sept., and Nov.
Final notification: Approximately 7 months
Write: Joan Nelson Dills, Administrator
Officers and Directors:* J. Boatner Chamberlain,* Pres.; Adele Corvin,* V.P.; Raymond A. Marks,* Secy.-Treas.; Roy L. Bouque, Dorothy Corvin, Andrew C. Gaither, Edward A. Miller, Isadore Pivnick, Yori Wada.
Number of staff: 2 full-time professional.
EIN: 946064379

323
Swift Memorial Health Care Foundation
P.O. Box 7048
Oxnard 93031 (805) 385-3650

Established in 1984 in CA.
Foundation type: Independent
Financial data (yr. ended 06/30/91): Assets, $2,513,096 (L); expenditures, $213,368; qualifying distributions, $209,648, including $200,260 for 25 grants (high: $85,500; low: $500; average: $100-$20,000) and $7,000 for 8 grants to individuals (high: $1,000; low: $500; average: $500-$1,000).

Fields of interest: Health, health services, medical sciences, drug abuse, alcoholism, rehabilitation, mental health, psychology, social services.
Types of support: Internships, scholarship funds, matching funds, capital campaigns, operating budgets, research.
Limitations: Giving limited to Ventura County, CA.
Publications: Occasional report, 990-PF, informational brochure (including application guidelines).
Application information: Application form required.
Initial approach: Letter
Copies of proposal: 1
Deadline(s): Apr. 30 and Oct. 31
Board meeting date(s): Bimonthly
Final notification: 2 months
Write: Emma M. Orr, Chair. of Awards Comm.
Officers: Frank Leiblien, Pres.; Emma M. Orr, Secy.
Directors: Fred Buenger, Allen Camp, Jack Erbeck, C. Flager Horn, Lester E. Jacobson, Robert E. Jordan, M.D., R. Blinn Maxwell, Ray Swift.
Number of staff: None.
EIN: 770132512

324
Mae and Benjamin Swig Charity Foundation ▼
c/o The Swig Foundations
220 Montgomery St., 20th Fl.
San Francisco 94104

Established in 1955 in CA.
Donor(s): Melvin M. Swig.
Foundation type: Independent
Financial data (yr. ended 12/31/91): Assets, $9,176,671 (M); expenditures, $684,307; qualifying distributions, $672,868, including $672,868 for 52 grants (high: $100,000; low: $250; average: $5,000-$50,000).
Purpose and activities: Grants primarily for Jewish welfare funds, higher and other education, and the arts.
Fields of interest: Jewish welfare, education, higher education, arts, AIDS.
Limitations: Giving primarily in the San Francisco Bay Area, CA.
Application information:
Initial approach: Letter
Deadline(s): None
Board meeting date(s): Apr., Aug., and Dec.
Final notification: Immediately following board meeting
Write: Melvin M. Swig, Trustee
Trustees: Richard S. Dinner, Melvin M. Swig, Richard L. Swig.
Number of staff: 1 shared staff
EIN: 237416746

325
Swig Foundation ▼
c/o The Swig Foundations
220 Montgomery Street, 20th Fl.
San Francisco 94104 (415) 291-1131

Established in 1957 in CA.
Donor(s): Benjamin H. Swig,‡ members of the Swig family.
Foundation type: Independent

Financial data (yr. ended 12/31/91): Assets, $16,620,591 (M); expenditures, $957,780; qualifying distributions, $870,837, including $870,837 for 81 grants (high: $108,334; low: $84; average: $10,000-$50,000).
Fields of interest: Arts, cultural programs, higher education, Jewish welfare, Israel, health services, education, AIDS.
Limitations: Giving primarily in the San Francisco Bay Area, CA. No grants to individuals, or for conferences, seminars, or workshops.
Application information: Application form not required.
Initial approach: Letter
Deadline(s): None
Board meeting date(s): Apr., Aug., and Dec.
Final notification: Immediately following board meeting
Write: Melvin M. Swig, Trustee
Trustees: Richard S. Dinner, Melvin M. Swig, Richard L. Swig.
Number of staff: 1 shared staff
EIN: 946065205

326
Syntex Corporate Contributions Program
3401 Hillview Ave., A1-291
Palo Alto 94304 (415) 855-6111

Financial data (yr. ended 07/31/90): Total giving, $3,712,912, including $3,335,502 for grants (high: $150,000; low: $500; average: $2,500-$10,000), $148,499 for employee matching gifts and $228,911 for in-kind gifts.
Purpose and activities: Supports education with an emphasis on health, AIDS, medicine, science, community affairs in operating areas, environment, the handicapped, and the arts.
Fields of interest: Science and technology, arts, minorities, AIDS, environment, handicapped, Mexico, pharmacy, education—building funds, family services, Japan, Canada, community funds, education—early childhood, elementary education, homeless, chemistry, Europe, higher education, Latin America, disadvantaged, Caribbean, United Kingdom, Europe, Spain, Scotland, public policy.
Types of support: Special projects, scholarship funds, fellowships, capital campaigns, continuing support, employee matching gifts, employee-related scholarships, annual campaigns, building funds, employee volunteer services, donated products, matching funds.
Limitations: Giving primarily in Santa Clara County, CA, Des Moines, IA, Boulder, CO, and Springfield, MO; also in Mexico, Puerto Rico, Bahamas, Bermuda, Canada, U.K., France, Ireland, Japan, Panama, Scotland, and Spain. No support for religious, political, veterans' or fraternal organizations, or tax supported organizations. No grants to individuals, or for fund-raising events where the company is not involved, program ads, film, TV, or video productions, emergency loans or deficit reduction, or general support for United Way members.
Publications: Application guidelines, corporate giving report, corporate report.
Application information: Syntex has a staff that only handles contributions. Application form not required.

Initial approach: Letter of inquiry; send to nearest company facility
Copies of proposal: 1
Deadline(s): None
Board meeting date(s): Quarterly
Write: Suzanne Ward-Seidel, Dir., Community Affairs
Jennifer Sims, Dir. Comm. Affairs.
Number of staff: 2 full-time professional; 2 full-time support.

327
Teledyne Charitable Trust Foundation ▼
1901 Ave. of the Stars, Suite 1800
Los Angeles 90067-6046 (213) 277-3311

Trust established in 1966 in PA.
Donor(s): Teledyne, Inc., and its subsidiaries and divisions.
Foundation type: Company-sponsored
Financial data (yr. ended 12/31/90): Assets, $100 (M); gifts received, $1,430,580; expenditures, $1,430,580; qualifying distributions, $1,430,580, including $692,532 for 255 grants (high: $34,500; low: $50; average: $500-$5,000) and $738,048 for 440 employee matching gifts.
Purpose and activities: Support for higher and secondary education, community funds, hospitals, social services, and youth agencies.
Fields of interest: Community funds, higher education, secondary education, hospitals, youth, social services.
Types of support: Employee matching gifts, general purposes.
Limitations: No support for projects directly related to religious or political activities.
Application information:
Initial approach: Letter
Deadline(s): None
Write: G.A. Zitterbart, Treas.
Officer and Trustees:* Gilbert A. Zitterbart,* Treas.; Berkley J. Baker, Jack H. Hamilton, George A. Roberts, William Rutlage.
EIN: 256074705

328
Thagard Foundation
341 Bayside Dr., Suite 1
Newport Beach 92660 (714) 723-4940

Established in 1968 in CA.
Foundation type: Independent
Financial data (yr. ended 04/30/91): Assets, $3,132,736 (M); expenditures, $259,476; qualifying distributions, $231,000, including $217,000 for 14 grants (high: $80,000; low: $1,000).
Fields of interest: Higher education, hospitals, medical research.
Limitations: Giving primarily in CA.
Application information:
Initial approach: Letter
Deadline(s): None
Write: Richard L. O'Connor, Secy.-Treas.
Officers and Trustees:* George F. Thagard, Jr.,* Pres.; Raymond G. Thagard, Sr.,* Exec. V.P.; Belle L. Ellis,* V.P.; Roy Reynolds,* V.P.; Richard L. O'Connor,* Secy.-Treas.
Number of staff: None.
EIN: 956225425

329
Roy E. Thomas Medical Foundation
c/o Bank of America
P.O. Box 3189 Terminal Annex
Los Angeles 90051
Application address: 333 South Hope St., Los Angeles, CA 90071; Tel.: (213) 613-7141

Established in 1979.
Donor(s): Roy E. Thomas,‡ Georgia Seaver Thomas.‡
Foundation type: Independent
Financial data (yr. ended 12/31/90): Assets, $2,018,783 (M); expenditures, $137,213; qualifying distributions, $118,277, including $110,000 for 1 grant.
Purpose and activities: Giving solely for charitable purposes of a medical nature.
Fields of interest: Hospitals, medical research.
Limitations: Giving primarily in CA.
Application information:
Initial approach: Letter
Deadline(s): None
Write: Kim E. Wilkinson
Trustees: Seaver T. Page, Richard C. Seaver, Bank of America.
EIN: 953190677

330
Flora L. Thornton Foundation
c/o Edward A. Landry
4444 Lakeside Dr., Suite 300
Burbank 91505 (818) 842-1645

Established in 1983 in CA.
Donor(s): Flora L. Thornton.
Foundation type: Independent
Financial data (yr. ended 11/30/91): Assets, $4,652,471 (M); gifts received, $874,428; expenditures, $836,779; qualifying distributions, $805,500, including $805,500 for 32 grants (high: $200,000; low: $500).
Fields of interest: Cultural programs, music, higher education, elementary education, medical research, cancer.
Limitations: Giving primarily in Los Angeles and San Francisco, CA.
Application information: Application form not required.
Deadline(s): None
Write: Flora L. Thornton, Trustee
Trustees: Edward A. Landry, Glen P. McDaniel, Flora L. Thornton, William Laney Thornton.
EIN: 953855595

331
The Times Mirror Foundation ▼
Times Mirror Sq.
Los Angeles 90053 (213) 237-3945

Incorporated in 1962 in CA.
Donor(s): The Times Mirror Co.
Foundation type: Company-sponsored
Financial data (yr. ended 12/31/90): Assets, $13,591,885 (M); gifts received, $5,000,000; expenditures, $4,717,899; qualifying distributions, $4,706,000, including $4,706,000 for 192 grants (high: $655,000; low: $2,500; average: $1,000-$25,000).
Purpose and activities: Giving largely for higher education, including liberal arts, business and

communications programs, and arts and culture; support also for health, community service, and civic organizations.
Fields of interest: Higher education, education, education—early childhood, elementary education, business education, media and communications, cultural programs, dance, arts, museums, performing arts, humanities, health, AIDS, civic affairs.
Types of support: Operating budgets, annual campaigns, seed money, building funds, endowment funds, program-related investments, scholarship funds, continuing support, capital campaigns, equipment, general purposes, renovation projects, special projects.
Limitations: Giving primarily in communities served by the company's subsidiaries, with emphasis on southern CA. No support for religious organizations or fraternal purposes. No grants to individuals, or for publications, conferences, or films; no loans.
Publications: Corporate giving report (including application guidelines).
Application information: Application form not required.
Initial approach: 2-3 page letter
Copies of proposal: 1
Deadline(s): At least 8 weeks prior to board meetings: Apr. 1 and Oct. 1
Board meeting date(s): May and Nov.
Final notification: June 30 or Jan. 15
Write: Cassandra Malry, Mgr., Corp. Contribs.
Officers and Directors:* Robert F. Erburu,* Chair.; Charles R. Redmond,* Pres. and C.E.O.; Stephen C. Meier,* Secy.; Cassandra Malry, C.F.O. and Treas.; Shelby Coffey III, David L. Laventhol, Richard T. Schlosberg III, Phillip L. Williams, Donald F. Wright.
Number of staff: 1 full-time professional; 1 full-time support.
EIN: 956079651
Recent health grants:
331-1 American Foundation for AIDS Research, NYC, NY, $50,000. For research and programs relating to AIDS. 1990.
331-2 Hoag Memorial Hospital Presbyterian Foundation, Newport Beach, CA, $10,000. 1990.
331-3 Mercy Hospital and Medical Center, San Diego, CA, $40,000. 1990.
331-4 Occupational Physicians Scholarship Fund, NYC, NY, $25,000. 1990.
331-5 Planned Parenthood of Los Angeles, Los Angeles, CA, $10,000. 1990.

332
Tosco Refining Company Philanthropy Program
2300 Clayton Rd., Suite 1100
Concord 94520-2100 (415) 602-4370

Purpose and activities: Five main areas of funding: child welfare, education, law enforcement, substance abuse prevention, and "persons with special needs". Support also for community funds, environmental issues, hospitals, hunger, and arts and culture.
Fields of interest: Child welfare, drug abuse, handicapped, hospitals—building funds, community funds, elementary education, environment, hunger, civic affairs, education—minorities, higher education,

education, educational associations, hospitals, leadership development, secondary education, museums, performing arts, law and justice.
Types of support: Annual campaigns, donated equipment, employee volunteer services, use of facilities, scholarship funds, general purposes.
Limitations: Giving limited to the San Francisco Bay Area, CA only.
Application information: Application form not required.
  Initial approach: One page letter to headquarters
  Copies of proposal: 1
  Deadline(s): July 1
  Board meeting date(s): Nov.
  Write: James E. Simmons, Dir., Public Affairs
Administrator: James E. Simmons, Dir., Public Affairs.
Number of staff: 1 full-time professional; 1 part-time professional.

333
Toyota USA Foundation
c/o Corp. Tax Dept.
19001 South Western Ave.
Torrance 90501   (213) 618-4727

Established in 1987 in CA.
Foundation type: Company-sponsored
Financial data (yr. ended 06/30/91): Assets, $15,532,121 (M); expenditures, $795,224; qualifying distributions, $755,598, including $754,808 for 17 grants (high: $76,000; low: $20,000).
Fields of interest: Education, education—minorities, elementary education, secondary education, health services, AIDS, disadvantaged, youth, minorities, community development, cultural programs.
Types of support: Special projects.
Limitations: No support for religious, fraternal, veterans', or labor groups. No grants to individuals, or for trips, tours, seminars, advertising, deficit reduction, or fundraising dinners.
Publications: Annual report, informational brochure, application guidelines.
Application information: Application form not required.
  Initial approach: Letter
  Deadline(s): Feb. 15, May 15, Aug. 15, and Nov. 15
  Write: Joe Tethrow
Officers and Directors:* Yukiyasu Togo,* Pres.; Yale Gieszl,* Sr. V.P. and Secy.; T. Ishikawa, V.P.; K. Usuda, V.P.; M. Maruhashi, Treas.; Robert B. McCurry.
Number of staff: 1 full-time professional; 1 full-time support.
EIN: 953255038

334
Transamerica Foundation ▼
600 Montgomery St.
San Francisco 94111   (415) 983-4333

Established in 1987 in CA.
Donor(s): Transamerica Airlines, Inc., Transamerica Corp.
Foundation type: Company-sponsored

Financial data (yr. ended 12/31/90): Assets, $24,307,581 (M); expenditures, $1,359,265; qualifying distributions, $1,453,997, including $1,330,750 for grants (average: $250-$55,000).
Purpose and activities: Support for programs involving AIDS, drug abuse, economics, housing, and the homeless.
Fields of interest: AIDS, drug abuse, economics, homeless, housing, alcoholism, arts, fine arts.
Types of support: Annual campaigns, capital campaigns, continuing support, matching funds, endowment funds, operating budgets, employee-related scholarships, employee matching gifts.
Limitations: Giving primarily in the San Francisco Bay Area, CA. No support for religious, fraternal, or veterans' organizations. No grants to individuals; no loans.
Application information: Application form required.
  Initial approach: Letter
  Copies of proposal: 1
  Deadline(s): None
  Write: Mary Sawai, Admin. Asst.
Officers and Directors:* James R. Harvey,* Chair.; Blair C. Pascoe,* Vice-Chair.; James B. Lockhart,* Pres.; Burton E. Broome, Treas.; Frank C. Herringer, Richard N. Latzer, Richard J. Olsen, Christopher M. McLain.
Number of staff: None.
EIN: 943034825
Recent health grants:
334-1 El Camino Hospital Foundation, Mountain View, CA, $10,000. 1990.
334-2 San Francisco AIDS Foundation, San Francisco, CA, $10,125. 1990.

335
Nora Eccles Treadwell Foundation ▼
239 Joaquin Ave.
San Leandro 94577   (415) 775-2879
Mailing address: Richard A. Harrison, Chair., 400 Maryland Ave., St. Cloud, FL 32769

Established in 1962 in UT.
Donor(s): Nora Eccles Treadwell Harrison.‡
Foundation type: Independent
Financial data (yr. ended 12/31/90): Assets, $1,934,232 (M); gifts received, $2,863,334; expenditures, $2,773,313; qualifying distributions, $2,713,244, including $2,610,606 for 36 grants (high: $800,000; low: $500; average: $500-$125,000).
Purpose and activities: Grants primarily for health and cardiovascular, diabetes, and arthritis research.
Fields of interest: Health, medical research, heart disease.
Types of support: Professorships, research, general purposes, equipment.
Limitations: Giving limited to UT and CA. No grants to individuals, or for research in areas not related to the cardiovascular system, diabetes, or arthritis.
Application information: Application form not required.
  Deadline(s): None
  Write: Patricia Canepa, Pres.
Officers and Directors:* Patricia Canepa,* Pres.; Richard A. Harrison,* V.P.; Alonzo W. Watson, Jr.,* Secy.; Nicholas T. Prepouses,* Treas.; Spencer

F. Eccles, Lawrence M. Harrison, William D. Hilger.
Trustee: First Security Bank of Utah, N.A.
Number of staff: 3
EIN: 237425351
Recent health grants:
335-1 Easter Seal Society of Alameda County, Oakland, CA, $15,000. For general support. 1990.
335-2 Planned Parenthood Association of Utah, Salt Lake City, UT, $15,000. For general support. 1990.
335-3 Stanford University Medical Center, Stanford, CA, $125,000. For diabetes research. 1990.
335-4 Stanford University Medical Center, Stanford, CA, $20,000. For diabetes nutrition research. 1990.
335-5 University of California, School of Medicine, San Francisco, CA, $125,000. For arthritis research. 1990.
335-6 University of California Medical Center, Davis, CA, $20,000. For diabetes nutrition research. 1990.
335-7 University of California Medical Center, Los Angeles, CA, $125,000. For arthritis research. 1990.
335-8 University of California Medical Center, Los Angeles, CA, $125,000. For diabetes research. 1990.
335-9 University of Southern California, School of Medicine, Los Angeles, CA, $50,000. For diabetes research. 1990.
335-10 University of Utah, N.E. Harrison Cardiovascular Research and Training Institute, Salt Lake City, UT, $800,000. For cardiovascular electrophy. 1990.
335-11 University of Utah, N.E. Harrison Cardiovascular Research and Training Institute, Salt Lake City, UT, $200,000. For cardiovascular pharmacy. 1990.
335-12 University of Utah, N.E. Harrison Cardiovascular Research and Training Institute, Salt Lake City, UT, $200,000. For cardiovascular flow. 1990.
335-13 University of Utah, N.E. Harrison Cardiovascular Research and Training Institute, Salt Lake City, UT, $125,000. For cardio-electric mapping. 1990.
335-14 University of Utah, N.E. Harrison Cardiovascular Research and Training Institute, Salt Lake City, UT, $75,000. For chair in rheumatology. 1990.
335-15 University of Utah, N.E. Harrison Cardiovascular Research and Training Institute, Salt Lake City, UT, $60,000. For heart laser surgery. 1990.
335-16 University of Utah Medical Center, Salt Lake City, UT, $125,000. For arthritis research. 1990.
335-17 University of Utah Medical Center, Development Fund, Salt Lake City, UT, $124,875. For diabetes research. 1990.
335-18 University of Utah Medical Center, Development Fund, Salt Lake City, UT, $20,000. For diabetes nutrition research. 1990.
335-19 Utah State University, Development Fund, Logan, UT, $20,000. For diabetes nutrition research. 1990.

336
Alice Tweed Tuohy Foundation
205 East Carrillo St., Rm. 219
Santa Barbara 93101 (805) 962-6430
Mailing address: P.O. Box 1328, Santa Barbara,
CA 93102

Incorporated in 1956 in CA.
Donor(s): Alice Tweed Tuohy.‡
Foundation type: Independent
Financial data (yr. ended 06/30/91): Assets,
$11,298,526 (M); expenditures, $772,394;
qualifying distributions, $616,668, including
$516,152 for 33 grants (high: $66,456; low:
$500; average: $1,000-$10,000).
Purpose and activities: Grants to nonprofit
organizations serving young people, educational
institutions, selected health care and medical
organizations, and community projects;
substantial support also for the art program at the
Duluth Campus of the University of Minnesota.
Fields of interest: Youth, education, higher
education, hospitals, community development,
arts.
Types of support: Seed money, matching funds,
building funds, equipment, land acquisition,
scholarship funds, renovation projects.
Limitations: Giving limited to the Santa Barbara,
CA, area. No support for private foundations,
national campaigns, establishment of
development offices, drug prevention or
rehabilitation programs, or private K through 12
grade schools. No grants to individuals, or for
operating budgets, research, or unrestricted
purposes; no loans.
Publications: Annual report (including application
guidelines).
Application information: Application form not
required.
 Initial approach: Letter
 Copies of proposal: 5
 Deadline(s): Submit proposal between July 1
 and Sept. 15; proposals received after
 deadline may be deferred for a year
 Board meeting date(s): Apr. or May, and Nov.
 Final notification: 2 to 3 months
 Write: Harris W. Seed, Pres.
Officers and Directors:* Harris W. Seed,* Pres.
and C.E.O.; Eleanor Van Cott,* Exec. V.P. and
Secy.-Treas.; Lorenzo Dall'Armi, Jr., Paul W.
Hartloff, Jr., John R. Mackall.
Number of staff: 2 part-time professional.
EIN: 956036471
Recent health grants:
336-1 Goleta Valley Community Hospital
 Foundation, Santa Barbara, CA, $25,000. For
 endowment fund. 1991.
336-2 Rehabilitation Institute at Santa Barbara,
 Santa Barbara, CA, $48,100. For replacement
 of telemetry system, which monitors patient's
 heart rate during rehabilitation activities. 1991.
336-3 Santa Barbara Council on Alcoholism and
 Drug Abuse, Santa Barbara, CA, $10,269. For
 purchase of new telephone system and
 computer system. 1991.
336-4 Santa Barbara New House, Santa Barbara,
 CA, $25,000. Toward purchase of third
 residential facility. 1991.

337
U.S. Leasing International Giving Program
733 Front St., MS 12
San Francisco 94111 (415) 627-9710

Financial data (yr. ended 12/31/90): Total giving,
$480,000, including $440,000 for 100 grants
(high: $7,500; low: $500; average:
$1,000-$50,000) and $40,000 for employee
matching gifts.
Purpose and activities: Supports a wide range of
social services, legal services, civic and public
affairs, AIDS programs, community development,
arts and culture, employment, and elementary
education where employees have made a regular
volunteer commitment.
Fields of interest: Arts, museums, dance, music,
performing arts, child welfare, family planning,
legal education, youth, AIDS, community
development, cultural programs, elementary
education, employment, legal services.
Types of support: Matching funds, general
purposes, publications, employee matching gifts,
operating budgets, special projects.
Limitations: Giving primarily in the San Francisco
Bay Area, CA. No support for political, religious
or sectarian activities.
Application information: U.S. Leasing
International has a staff that only handles
contributions. Applications are not being
accepted for 1991. Application form not required.
 Initial approach: Letter and proposal
 Copies of proposal: 1
 Deadline(s): None
 Board meeting date(s): 6 times a year
 Final notification: Notice of denial sent
 Write: Thomas Donahoe, Contribs. Mgr.
Number of staff: 1 part-time professional.

338
Union Bank Corporate Giving Program
P.O. Box 3100
Los Angeles 90071 (213) 236-5826
Additional address: 445 South Figueroa St., Los
Angeles, CA 90071

Purpose and activities: Union Bank accepts a
responsibility as a major corporate citizen to help
meet the health and welfare, community
economic development, educational, cultural,
and civic needs of the communities in which it
does business. The bank, both through the Union
Bank foundation and direct contributions, makes
selected contributions to effective non-profit
community organizations. In making
determinations on donation requests, the bank
will place emphasis on firmly established
organizations and programs in granting
contributions, but will maintain the flexibility to
accommodate new and innovative approaches to
meeting community needs. The organizations
seeking funding must 1) be tax-exempt and
charitable; 2) be equal opportunity employers
operating their programs in a manner supportive
of equal opportunity objectives; 3) have their
objectives clearly defined and be reasonably
capable of achieving them; 4) have objectives
and programs supportive of the public and
corporate interests; 5) not needlessly duplicate
other programs; 6) have demonstrated by past
accomplishment an ability to fulfill objectives and
successfully implement programs; 7) be efficiently

and ethically managed; 8) have an active
governing board and support from the
community. Combined foundation and corporate
giving totaled $1.7 million in 1990.
Fields of interest: Cultural programs, education,
arts, medical research, higher education,
community development, elementary education,
secondary education.
Types of support: Employee volunteer services.
Limitations: Giving primarily in headquarters city
and major operating locations. No support for
political, veterans', military, fraternal, or
professional organizations, or service club
activities; generally no support for organizations
receiving the majority of their funds from the
United Way; private foundations, hospital or
other patient care institution operating funds,
educational institution operating funds, beauty or
talent contests. No grants to individuals; or for
dinner or luncheon tickets or advertising,
videotape or film production unless distribution
and screening are guaranteed.
Application information:
 Final notification: Rejection notice will be sent
 Write: John F. Harrigan, Chair. and C.E.O.

339
Union Bank Foundation
P.O. Box 3100
Los Angeles 90051 (213) 236-5826

Trust established in 1953 in CA.
Donor(s): Union Bank.
Foundation type: Company-sponsored
Financial data (yr. ended 12/31/90): Assets,
$625,105 (M); gifts received, $1,695,000;
expenditures, $1,329,803; qualifying
distributions, $1,329,115, including $1,328,373
for 221 grants (high: $235,000; low: $200).
Purpose and activities: Emphasis on community
funds and civic affairs; support also for higher
education, hospitals, cultural prorams, and social
service and youth agencies.
Fields of interest: Community funds, higher
education, hospitals, cultural programs, social
services, youth.
Types of support: General purposes, operating
budgets, continuing support, annual campaigns,
emergency funds, building funds, equipment,
employee matching gifts.
Limitations: Giving primarily in CA, particularly
in areas of company operations. No support for
religious organizations. No grants to individuals,
or for endowment funds, scholarships,
fellowships, or research; no loans.
Application information: Application form not
required.
 Initial approach: Proposal
 Copies of proposal: 1
 Deadline(s): Submit proposal preferably in Jan.;
 no set deadline
 Board meeting date(s): Monthly
 Final notification: 3 months
 Write: Christopher Houser, Pres.
Trustee: Union Bank.
Number of staff: 3
EIN: 956023551

340
The Valley Foundation ▼
333 West Santa Clara St., Suite 500
San Jose 95113   (408) 292-1124

Established in 1984 in CA.
Foundation type: Independent
Financial data (yr. ended 09/30/91): Assets,
$44,616,716 (M); expenditures, $2,439,731;
qualifying distributions, $2,211,671, including
$2,128,383 for 50 grants (high: $100,000; low:
$1,000; average: $10,000-$100,000).
Purpose and activities: Support primarily for
medical services and health care for lower
income households within Santa Clara County
and for research, social services, and higher
education. Support also for youth, the arts,
seniors, education, and general medical areas.
Fields of interest: Health services, social services,
higher education, education, youth, aged,
medical research, arts.
Types of support: Operating budgets, general
purposes, matching funds.
Limitations: Giving limited to Santa Clara County,
CA. No support for religious purposes or,
generally, for primary or secondary schools. No
grants to individuals.
Application information: Application form
required.
  Initial approach: Letter of intent
  Copies of proposal: 1
  Deadline(s): Dec. 1, Mar. 1, July 1, and Sept. 1
  Board meeting date(s): Quarterly
  Write: Ms. Ervie L. Smith, Exec. Dir.
Officers and Directors:* Philip Boyce,* Chair.;
Ralph Ross,* Vice-Chair.; Richard Sieve, M.D.,
Secy.; Sidney Resnick, Treas. and C.F.O.; Warren
Belanger, M.D., Herbert Kain, M.D., Edgar G. La
Veque, M.D., Walter Silberman, M.D.
Number of staff: 1 part-time professional.
EIN: 941584547

341
Wayne & Gladys Valley Foundation
4000 Executive Pkwy., Suite 535
San Ramon 94583   (510) 275-9330

Established in 1977 in CA.
Donor(s): F. Wayne Valley,‡ Gladys Valley.
Foundation type: Independent
Financial data (yr. ended 09/30/90): Assets,
$118,022,608 (M); gifts received, $52,460,000;
expenditures, $4,994,939; qualifying
distributions, $4,208,362, including $4,052,286
for grants.
Purpose and activities: Primary areas of interest
include higher, secondary, and other education,
medicine, hospitals, youth, religious schools, and
local Catholic welfare.
Fields of interest: Education, higher education,
secondary education, medical research, medical
sciences, hospitals, youth, religious schools,
Catholic welfare.
Types of support: Building funds, general
purposes, matching funds, renovation projects,
research, special projects, professorships.
Limitations: Giving primarily in Alameda, Contra
Costa, and Santa Clara counties, CA.
Publications: Informational brochure, application
guidelines.
Application information: Application form not
required.

Initial approach: Letter
Copies of proposal: 1
Deadline(s): None
Board meeting date(s): Feb., May, Sept., and
  Nov.
Final notification: Usually within 3 to 4 months
Write: Paul D. O'Connor, Pres. and Exec. Dir.
Officers and Directors:* Gladys Valley,* Chair.;
Paul O'Connor,* Pres. and Exec. Dir.; Richard M.
Kingsland,* Treas. and C.F.O.; Robert C. Brown,
Stephen M. Chandler, Edwin A. Heafey, Jr., John
Stock, Sonya Valley, Tamara Valley.
Number of staff: 1 part-time professional; 4
part-time support.
EIN: 953203014
Recent health grants:
341-1 Fairmont Hospital Foundation, San
  Leandro, CA, $25,000. 1991.
341-2 Salk Institute for Biological Studies, La
  Jolla, CA, $300,000. 1991.

342
Ernst D. van Loben Sels-Eleanor Slate van Loben Sels Charitable Foundation
235 Montgomery St., No. 1635
San Francisco 94104   (415) 983-1093
Application address: P.O. Box 7880, Rm. 1635,
San Francisco, CA 94120-7880

Incorporated in 1964 in CA.
Donor(s): Ernst D. van Loben Sels.‡
Foundation type: Independent
Financial data (yr. ended 12/31/90): Assets,
$8,678,851 (M); expenditures, $575,884;
qualifying distributions, $438,900, including
$438,900 for 62 grants (high: $20,000; low:
$500; average: $500-$20,000).
Purpose and activities: Priority given to
nonrecurring grants in support of projects which
will test potentially useful innovations in the area
of education, including assistance for minority
students, health, AIDS research, the handicapped,
welfare, family services and planning, child
welfare, law and justice, legal services, and
humanities; support also for chemical
dependency programs, the homeless, immigrants,
and the environment.
Fields of interest: Education, AIDS, handicapped,
welfare, family services, child welfare, legal
services, humanities, immigration, environment.
Types of support: Seed money, emergency funds,
matching funds, special projects, research,
publications, conferences and seminars, loans.
Limitations: Giving limited to northern CA. No
support for national organizations unless for a
specific local project, or to projects requiring
medical, scientific, or other technical knowledge
for evaluation. No grants to individuals, or for
operating budgets of well-established
organizations, continuing support, deficit
financing, capital or endowment funds,
scholarships, or fellowships.
Publications: Annual report, program policy
statement, application guidelines.
Application information: Application form not
required.
  Initial approach: Proposal, letter, or telephone
  Copies of proposal: 3
  Deadline(s): None
  Board meeting date(s): About every 6-8 weeks
  Final notification: 3 to 4 weeks
  Write: Claude H. Hogan, Pres.

Officers and Directors:* Claude H. Hogan,*
Pres.; Edward A. Nathan,* V.P.; Toni Rembe,*
Secy.-Treas.
Number of staff: None.
EIN: 946109309
Recent health grants:
342-1 Childrens Research Institute of California,
  Sacramento, CA, $10,000. For Health Passport
  Project to provide medical and mental health
  care services to children in foster care. 1990.

343
J. B. and Emily Van Nuys Charities
P.O. Box 33
Palos Verdes Estates 90274   (310) 373-8521

Incorporated in 1957 in CA.
Donor(s): Emily Van Nuys,‡ J. Benton Van Nuys.‡
Foundation type: Independent
Financial data (yr. ended 12/31/91): Assets,
$526,882 (M); gifts received, $692,723;
expenditures, $734,779; qualifying distributions,
$632,296, including $632,296 for 142 grants
(high: $25,000; low: $1,000; average: $5,000).
Purpose and activities: Preference is given to
organizations "whose activities are directed
toward enhancement of the social, educational,
and environmental climate of California and the
health of its citizens." Giving for hospitals and
health agencies, child welfare, and youth
agencies; support also for the handicapped, social
service agencies, education, and the environment.
Fields of interest: Hospitals, health services, child
welfare, youth, handicapped, social services,
health, education, environment.
Types of support: General purposes, special
projects, research, building funds, equipment.
Limitations: Giving primarily in Southern CA,
including the Los Angeles area. No grants to
individuals.
Application information: Application form not
required.
  Initial approach: Proposal
  Deadline(s): None
  Board meeting date(s): Quarterly to award
    grants
  Write: Franklin F. Moulton, Pres.
Officer and Trustees:* Franklin F. Moulton,* Pres.;
John M. Heidt, Robert S. Warner.
EIN: 956096134

344
I. N. & Susanna H. Van Nuys Foundation
c/o Bank of America
P.O. Box 3189, Terminal Annex
Los Angeles 90051
Application address: 444 South Flower St., Suite
2340, Los Angeles, CA 90071

Established in 1950 in CA.
Foundation type: Independent
Financial data (yr. ended 05/31/91): Assets,
$11,493,987 (M); expenditures, $876,905;
qualifying distributions, $797,854, including
$772,406 for 15 grants (high: $404,604; low:
$500).
Purpose and activities: "Support primarily in
those fields favored by the original grantor,
including a private hospital, secondary schools
and colleges, and generally related activities."

Fields of interest: Hospitals, higher education, elementary education, child welfare, museums.
Limitations: Giving primarily in CA. No grants to individuals.
Application information:
  Initial approach: Letter
  Deadline(s): None
  Write: George A. Bender, Trustee
Trustees: George A. Bender, Freeman Gates, George H. Whitney, Bank of America.
EIN: 956006019

345
Varian Associates Corporate Giving Program
3100 Hansen Way
Palo Alto 94304   (415) 424-6496

Financial data (yr. ended 12/31/89): Total giving, $380,000, including $280,000 for grants (high: $50,000; low: $500; average: $250-$1,000) and $100,000 for employee matching gifts.
Purpose and activities: Support for education in engineering, science, business, and medicine. Areas of principal activity are equipment grants, engineering and science faculty development, science and engineering-oriented Affirmative Action and student fellowship programs, and university high technology centers. Grants also to science, math, and business education programs at the secondary level; employee matching gift program for higher education. Grants generally are confined to United Way in communities where Varian has major operations; employee's contributions to such United Way contributions are matched. Interest in initiatives that involve public/private partnerships; grants have been made in such fields as environmental improvement, transportation services, and housing; grants also made occasionally to selected arts and cultural programs with emphasis on local programs which either build creative bridges between the sciences and the humanities, or promote audience development.
Fields of interest: Education, engineering, arts, business education, cultural programs, disadvantaged, family services, fine arts, handicapped, health, housing, medical sciences, museums, performing arts, science and technology, social services, urban development, welfare, youth.
Types of support: Annual campaigns, building funds, capital campaigns, matching funds, employee-related scholarships, scholarship funds, seed money, special projects, employee matching gifts.
Limitations: Giving primarily in communities where there are manufacturing operations or where a large number of employees live; limited amount of national giving in fields of communications, engineering, medicine, science, and technology. No support for fraternal or religious groups or disease-related organizations. No grants to individuals, or for research projects; advertising campaigns; conferences, seminars and meetings; film or other creative productions. Employee matching gifts limited to higher education and United Way.
Publications: Informational brochure (including application guidelines).

Application information: Contributions are handled by the Marketing department. Application form not required.
  Initial approach: Written proposal
  Copies of proposal: 1
  Deadline(s): End of Aug. for consideration in the upcoming year
  Board meeting date(s): Fall
  Final notification: Within 4 weeks
  Write: Gary Simpson, v.P., Mktg.
Number of staff: 1 part-time support.

346
W.W.W. Foundation ▼
1260 Huntington Dr., Suite 204
South Pasadena 91030-4561   (213) 259-0484

Established in 1981 in CA.
Donor(s): Helen W. Woodward.‡
Foundation type: Independent
Financial data (yr. ended 07/31/91): Assets, $9,578,324 (M); gifts received, $2,532,653; expenditures, $2,027,943; qualifying distributions, $1,913,835, including $1,881,130 for 18 grants (high: $1,450,000; low: $480; average: $5,000-$40,000).
Purpose and activities: Giving primarily for an animal care center; support also for hospitals, civic affairs, and the arts.
Fields of interest: Animal welfare, hospitals, civic affairs, education, welfare, youth, medical research.
Types of support: Operating budgets, renovation projects, building funds, matching funds, endowment funds, special projects.
Limitations: Giving primarily in CA. No grants for No loans.
Application information: Contributes only to pre-selected organizations.
  Board meeting date(s): Varies
  Write: Linda J. Blinkenberg, Secy.
Officers: Marcia W. Constance, Pres.; Winifred W. Rhodes-Bea, V.P.; Linda J. Blinkenberg, Secy.; Arlo G. Sorensen, C.F.O.
Number of staff: 4 shared staff
EIN: 953694741

347
Wasserman Foundation ▼
c/o Musick, Peeler & Garrett
One Wilshire Blvd., Suite 2000
Los Angeles 90017-3383

Incorporated in 1956 in CA.
Donor(s): Lew R. Wasserman, Edith Wasserman.
Foundation type: Independent
Financial data (yr. ended 12/31/90): Assets, $38,294,393 (M); gifts received, $4,683,020; expenditures, $1,304,851; qualifying distributions, $1,296,355, including $1,280,381 for 66 grants (high: $254,531; low: $150; average: $1,000-$15,000).
Purpose and activities: Emphasis on hospitals and medical research, Jewish welfare funds, higher education, public policy groups, and the performing arts.
Fields of interest: Hospitals, medical research, Jewish welfare, higher education, performing arts, public policy.
Types of support: Capital campaigns, endowment funds, research, scholarship funds.

Limitations: Giving primarily in CA.
Application information: Contributes only to pre-selected organizations. Applications not accepted.
  Write: William J. Bird, V.P.
Officers and Directors: Lew R. Wasserman, Pres.; Edith Wasserman, V.P., C.F.O., and Secy.; William J. Bird, V.P.; Carol Ann Leif, Casey Myers, Lynne Wasserman.
EIN: 956038762
Recent health grants:
347-1 American Foundation for AIDS Research, Los Angeles, CA, $10,000. 1990.
347-2 Betty Clooney Foundation for the Brain Injured, Los Angeles, CA, $12,500. 1990.
347-3 Childrens Diabetes Foundation at Denver, Denver, CO, $10,000. 1990.
347-4 Cystic Fibrosis Foundation, Los Angeles, CA, $25,000. 1990.
347-5 Israel Cancer Research Fund, Los Angeles, CA, $15,000. 1990.
347-6 Motion Picture and Television Fund, Woodland Hills, CA, $48,500. 1990.
347-7 Nancy Reagan Foundation, Los Angeles, CA, $25,000. 1990.
347-8 Research to Prevent Blindness, NYC, NY, $113,125. 1990.

348
Weingart Foundation ▼
1055 West Seventh St., Suite 3050
Los Angeles 90017-1984   (213) 688-7799
Mailing address: P.O. Box 17982, Los Angeles, CA 90017-0982; FAX: (213) 688-1515

Incorporated in 1951 in CA.
Donor(s): Ben Weingart,‡ Stella Weingart.‡
Foundation type: Independent
Financial data (yr. ended 06/30/91): Assets, $458,795,070 (M); gifts received, $3,210; expenditures, $23,595,468; qualifying distributions, $23,595,468, including $22,686,999 for 323 grants (high: $1,000,000; low: $500; average: $10,000-$250,000) and $206,358 for 136 employee matching gifts.
Purpose and activities: Support for community services, health and medicine, higher education, including a student loan program, and public policy, with emphasis on programs for children and youth.
Fields of interest: Social services, higher education, secondary education, elementary education, education—early childhood, education—minorities, youth, child development, child welfare, hospitals, hospitals—building funds.
Types of support: Seed money, building funds, equipment, matching funds, special projects, renovation projects, capital campaigns, student loans, employee matching gifts.
Limitations: Giving limited to Southern CA. No support for environmental or religious programs, political refugee or international concerns, or federated fundraising groups. No grants to individuals, or for endowment funds, normal operating expenses, annual campaigns, emergency funds, deficit financing, land acquisition, scholarships, fellowships, seminars, conferences, publications, workshops, travel, surveys, films, or publishing activities.
Publications: Annual report (including application guidelines), application guidelines, occasional report.

Application information: Student loan program limited to 14 private colleges and universities in southern CA. Application form required.

Initial approach: Letter
Copies of proposal: 15
Deadline(s): None
Board meeting date(s): Bimonthly, except July and Aug.
Final notification: 3 to 4 months
Write: Charles W. Jacobson, Pres.

Officers and Directors:* Harry J. Volk,* Chair. and C.E.O.; Charles W. Jacobson, Pres. and C.O.O.; Ann Van Dormolen, V.P. and Treas.; Laurence A. Wolfe, V.P.; Harvey L. Price, V.P., Grants; Susan H. Grimes, Secy.; Roy A. Anderson, Steven D. Broidy, John T. Gurash, William J. McGill, Sol Price, Dennis Stanfill.
Number of staff: 5 full-time professional; 6 full-time support.
EIN: 956054814
Recent health grants:

348-1 AIDS Project Los Angeles, Los Angeles, CA, $42,500. Toward construction and expansion of existing facility. 1990.
348-2 Centinela Hospital Medical Center Foundation, Inglewood, CA, $25,000. Toward community-wide immunization project for children in Inglewood community. 1990.
348-3 Childrens Hospital of Los Angeles, Los Angeles, CA, $3,000,000. Toward construction of Imaging and Diagnosis Center including radiographic reading space, pathological laboratories, conference rooms and classrooms. 1990.
348-4 Crittenton Center for Young Women and Infants, Los Angeles, CA, $40,000. Toward remodeling of shelter to care for medically fragile infants. 1990.
348-5 Culver City Youth Health Center, Culver City, CA, $32,000. For Positive Options Health Education program. 1990.
348-6 Hollywood Presbyterian Medical Center, Queen of Angels, Hollywood, CA, $26,000. Toward developing plan to expand existing obstetrical facility. 1990.
348-7 Hospital of the Good Samaritan, Los Angeles, CA, $500,000. Toward capital improvement project related to Weingart House residential facility. 1990.
348-8 Human Services Network, Los Angeles, CA, $30,000. Toward intensive counseling demonstration project for abused and disturbed children. 1990.
348-9 Impact Drug and Alcohol Treatment Center, Pasadena, CA, $30,000. Toward rehabilitation and reconstruction work on newly acquired facility. 1990.
348-10 Preuss Foundation, Solana Beach, CA, $25,000. For pediatric brain tumor research program. 1990.
348-11 Rand Corporation, Santa Monica, CA, $1,500,000. Toward Drug Policy Research Center. 1990.
348-12 Saint Annes Maternity Home, Los Angeles, CA, $500,000. Toward construction of new 96-bed maternity home. 1990.
348-13 Saint Mary Medical Center, Long Beach, CA, $100,000. Toward expansion of Emergency Department/Trauma Care Center. 1990.
348-14 Salk Institute for Biological Studies, La Jolla, CA, $125,000. Toward creation of new

multidisciplinary program to study basis of learning and memory. 1990.
348-15 Solheim Lutheran Home, Los Angeles, CA, $50,000. Toward construction of new 76-bed nursing facility. 1990.
348-16 United Cerebral Palsy Association of Orange County, Santa Ana, CA, $100,000. Toward construction of Infant Center building. 1990.
348-17 University of San Diego, San Diego, CA, $1,549,834. Toward Children's Advocacy program and study of California Board of Medical Quality Assurance disciplinary system. 1990.
348-18 Venice Family Clinic, Venice, CA, $200,000. Toward capital expansion program. 1990.
348-19 Westside Childrens Center, Santa Monica, CA, $75,000. Toward first year's budget for operation of Therapeutic Day Care/Family Development program. 1990.

349
The David & Sylvia Weisz Foundation
1933 South Broadway, Rm. 244
Los Angeles 90007

Established in 1980 in CA.
Foundation type: Independent
Financial data (yr. ended 10/31/91): Assets, $6,578,441 (M); expenditures, $801,698; qualifying distributions, $503,517, including $503,517 for 48 grants (high: $202,650; low: $500).
Fields of interest: Jewish welfare, cultural programs, social services, health services, hospitals.
Types of support: General purposes.
Limitations: Giving primarily in CA. No grants to individuals.
Application information: Contributes only to pre-selected organizations. Applications not accepted.
Officers and Directors:* Sylvia Weisz Hirshfield,* Pres.; Jay Grodin,* Secy.; Louis Leviton, Treas.
EIN: 953551424

350
Western Cardiac Foundation
436 North Roxbury Dr., No. 222
Beverly Hills 90210   (213) 276-2379

Established in 1964 in CA.
Donor(s): Katherine R. Vance.‡
Foundation type: Independent
Financial data (yr. ended 12/31/90): Assets, $4,318,527 (M); gifts received, $62,324; expenditures, $188,557; qualifying distributions, $158,968, including $145,000 for 3 grants (high: $115,000; low: $5,000).
Fields of interest: Medical research, medical education, hospitals, higher education.
Types of support: Fellowships, research.
Limitations: Giving primarily in Los Angeles, CA. No grants to individuals.
Application information: Application form not required.
Initial approach: Letter
Copies of proposal: 1
Deadline(s): None
Write: Rexford Kennamer, M.D., Pres.

Officers: Rexford Kennamer, M.D., Pres.; George Mercader, V.P. and Financial Officer; Gladys Bishop, Secy.
Number of staff: 1 part-time professional.
EIN: 956116853

351
L. K. Whittier Foundation ▼
(Formerly Whittier Foundation)
1260 Huntington Dr., Suite 204
South Pasadena 91030-4561   (213) 259-0484

Incorporated in 1955 in CA.
Donor(s): Leland K. Whittier,‡ and members of the Whittier family.
Foundation type: Independent
Financial data (yr. ended 04/30/91): Assets, $38,148,998 (M); gifts received, $2,553,228; expenditures, $3,406,872; qualifying distributions, $3,143,414, including $3,035,754 for 55 grants (high: $495,410; low: $200; average: $1,000-$50,000).
Purpose and activities: Emphasis on hospitals and medical research; support also for youth agencies.
Fields of interest: Hospitals, medical research, youth, education, higher education.
Types of support: Fellowships, matching funds, endowment funds, special projects.
Limitations: Giving primarily in CA. No grants to individuals; no loans.
Application information: Foundation manager prefers to initiate grants.
Initial approach: Proposal
Deadline(s): None
Board meeting date(s): Annually and as necessary
Final notification: Varies
Write: Linda J. Blinkenberg, Secy.

Officers: Laura-Lee Whittier Woods, Pres.; Arlo G. Sorensen, V.P.; Linda J. Blinkenberg, Secy. and C.F.O.
Number of staff: 4 shared staff
EIN: 956027493
Recent health grants:

351-1 Harvard University, Medical School, Boston, MA, $83,333. For graduate study in medical science. 1991.
351-2 Hope Cottage, Anchorage, AK, $15,000. For operations. 1991.
351-3 Huntington Medical Research Institutes, Pasadena, CA, $125,000. For unit for clinical magnetic resonance spectroscopy. 1991.
351-4 J. David Gladstone Foundation, San Francisco, CA, $427,971. For research in genetic mutation and blood cholesterol. 1991.
351-5 Johns Hopkins University, Mind/Brain Institute, Baltimore, MD, $301,042. For neurobiology research. 1991.
351-6 Phoenix House, Los Angeles, CA, $40,000. For operations. 1991.
351-7 Senior Health and Peer Counseling Center, Santa Monica, CA, $10,000. For volunteer care coordinator project. 1991.
351-8 University of California, Los Angeles, CA, $283,686. For Human Values and Communications in Medicine program. 1991.
351-9 University of Louisville, Department of Psychiatry/Behavioral Science, Louisville, KY, $20,000. For attitudinal and behavioral medicine program. 1991.

351-10 Whittier Institute for Diabetes and Endocrinology, La Jolla, CA, $50,000. For Pediatric Endocrine-Diabetes Unit. 1991.

352
Brayton Wilbur Foundation
320 California St., Suite 200
San Francisco 94104 (415) 772-4006

Incorporated in 1947 in CA.
Donor(s): Wilbur-Ellis Co.
Foundation type: Company-sponsored
Financial data (yr. ended 12/31/90): Assets, $3,831,535 (M); gifts received, $75,000; expenditures, $215,911; qualifying distributions, $200,214, including $200,110 for 44 grants (high: $27,500; low: $250; average: $1,000-$5,000).
Purpose and activities: Emphasis on the arts and on higher and secondary education; grants also for hospitals and conservation.
Fields of interest: Arts, higher education, secondary education, hospitals, conservation.
Types of support: Annual campaigns, building funds, capital campaigns, continuing support, endowment funds.
Limitations: Giving primarily in San Francisco, CA. No grants to individuals.
Application information: Contributes only to pre-selected organizations. Applications not accepted.
    Write: Brayton Wilbur, Jr., Pres.
Officers and Directors: Brayton Wilbur, Jr.,* Pres.; Carter P. Thacher,* V.P.; Herbert B. Tully,* Secc.-Treas.
Number of staff: None.
EIN: 946088667

353
The Wollenberg Foundation
235 Montgomery St., Suite 2700
San Francisco 94104 (415) 981-1300

Trust established in 1952 in CA.
Donor(s): H.L. Wollenberg.‡
Foundation type: Independent
Financial data (yr. ended 12/31/90): Assets, $23,805,727 (M); expenditures, $1,224,252; qualifying distributions, $1,195,272, including $1,194,000 for 27 grants (high: $600,000; low: $4,000; average: $2,000-$20,000).
Purpose and activities: Grants primarily to assist non-tax-supported colleges.
Fields of interest: Higher education, medical education.
Types of support: Endowment funds, special projects, operating budgets, general purposes.
Limitations: Giving primarily in CA and WA. No support for sectarian purposes or religious-affiliated institutions. No grants to individuals; no loans.
Application information: Contributes only to pre-selected organizations. Applications not accepted.
    Write: Marc H. Monheimer, Trustee
Trustees: Marc H. Monheimer, J. Roger Wollenberg, Richard P. Wollenberg.
Number of staff: None.
EIN: 946072264
Recent health grants:
353-1 Meharry Medical College, Nashville, TN, $70,000. For general operating funds. 1990.

353-2 National Fund for Medical Education, Boston, MA, $35,000. For unrestricted grant. 1990.

354
Wood-Claeyssens Foundation
P.O. Box 99
Santa Barbara 93102 (805) 962-0011

Established in 1980.
Donor(s): Ailene B. Claeyssens, Pierre P. Claeyssens.
Foundation type: Independent
Financial data (yr. ended 03/31/91): Assets, $8,220,431 (M); expenditures, $613,943; qualifying distributions, $585,574, including $572,700 for 69 grants (high: $50,000; low: $1,000; average: $500-$2,000).
Fields of interest: Hospitals, health services, social services, youth, theater, music.
Types of support: Annual campaigns, general purposes, operating budgets, continuing support, capital campaigns.
Limitations: Giving primarily in Santa Barbara and Ventura counties, CA. No support for educational institutions. No grants to individuals.
Publications: 990-PF.
Application information: Application form not required.
    Initial approach: Letter
    Deadline(s): Aug. 31
    Board meeting date(s): As needed
    Write: James H. Hurley, Jr., Secy.
Officers and Directors: Ailene B. Claeyssens,* Pres.; Pierre P. Claeyssens,* 1st V.P.; Cynthia S. Wood,* 2nd V.P.; James H. Hurley, Jr., Secy.; Charles C. Gray, Treas.
Number of staff: None.
EIN: 953514017

355
Wrather Family Foundation
(Formerly J. D. & Mazie Wrather Foundation)
301 North Canon Dr., Suite 210
Beverly Hills 90210

Established in 1962 as the J. D. & Mazie Wrather Foundation, Inc.
Foundation type: Independent
Financial data (yr. ended 12/31/90): Assets, $3,383,604 (M); expenditures, $139,882; qualifying distributions, $131,326, including $131,326 for 47 grants (high: $25,506; low: $100).
Fields of interest: Rehabilitation, higher education, education, social services, health associations.
Limitations: Giving primarily in CA.
Officers and Directors: Christopher C. Wrather,* Pres.; Wendy S. Lees, Secy.-Treas.; Molly W. Dolle, Linda W. Finocchiaro.
EIN: 956100110

356
Wynn Foundation
P.O. Box 14143
Orange 92613-1543

Established in 1966.
Donor(s): Bee Wynn,‡ Carl Wynn.‡

Foundation type: Independent
Financial data (yr. ended 12/31/90): Assets, $7,505,774 (M); gifts received, $318,296; expenditures, $549,145; qualifying distributions, $546,570, including $543,000 for grants.
Fields of interest: Higher education, education, health, alcoholism, medical research, drug abuse, child welfare, handicapped, disadvantaged, wildlife.
Limitations: Giving primarily in Los Angeles County, San Gabriel Valley, and Orange County, CA.
Application information: Application form required.
    Initial approach: Letter
    Copies of proposal: 1
    Deadline(s): 2nd Tuesday of Mar.
    Board meeting date(s): Mar.
    Final notification: Only approved proposals receive notice
    Write: Wesley E. Bellwood, Pres.
Officers and Trustees: Wesley E. Bellwood,* Pres.; Billie A. Fischer,* V.P.; John D. Borie,* Secy.; Dorothy L. Frey,* Treas.; William Christian.
Number of staff: None.
EIN: 956136231

357
The Zellerbach Family Fund ▼
120 Montgomery St., Suite 2125
San Francisco 94104 (415) 421-2629

Incorporated in 1956 in CA.
Donor(s): Jennie B. Zellerbach.‡
Foundation type: Independent
Financial data (yr. ended 12/31/90): Assets, $40,067,331 (M); gifts received, $110,000; expenditures, $2,410,856; qualifying distributions, $1,869,216, including $1,616,620 for grants (high: $80,000; low: $1,000; average: $5,000-$35,000) and $3,000 for 2 in-kind gifts.
Purpose and activities: Support for direct-service projects in the arts, health, mental health, and social and child welfare.
Fields of interest: Arts, cultural programs, dance, theater, health, AIDS, mental health, welfare, child welfare.
Types of support: Continuing support, technical assistance, special projects.
Limitations: Giving primarily in the San Francisco Bay Area, CA. No grants to individuals, or for capital or endowment funds, research, scholarships, or fellowships; no loans.
Publications: Annual report (including application guidelines).
Application information: Applications rarely granted; foundation develops most of its own grant proposals. The foundation is currently committed to projects underway and does not expect to make grants to new programs over the next few years. Community arts groups will continue to be funded. Application form not required.
    Initial approach: Telephone or proposal (8 copies for arts proposals)
    Deadline(s): Submit full art proposal, preferably 2 weeks prior to board meeting
    Board meeting date(s): Quarterly
    Final notification: 1 week after board meeting for art applications
    Write: Edward A. Nathan, Exec. Dir.

Officers and Directors:* William J. Zellerbach,* Pres.; Louis J. Saroni II,* V.P. and Treas.; Robert E. Sinton,* V.P.; Philip S. Ehrlich, Jr.,* Secy.; Edward A. Nathan,* Exec. Dir.; Stewart E. Adams, Nancy Z. Boschwitz, Jeanette M. Dunckel, George B. James, Verneice Thompson, John W. Zellerbach, Thomas H. Zellerbach.
Number of staff: 1 full-time professional; 2 part-time professional; 2 full-time support.
EIN: 946069482
Recent health grants:
357-1 Center for Families in Transition, San Francisco, CA, $12,500. To develop preventive interventions for children who have experienced severe family conflict. 1990.
357-2 Center for Family Counseling, Family Enrichment Network, East Oakland, CA, $58,000. For support groups and activities for parents and youth in East Oakland. 1990.
357-3 Childrens Research Institute of California, Sacramento, CA, $25,000. To improve services to foster children and to continue work of statewide Foster Care Network. 1990.
357-4 Film Arts Foundation, San Francisco, CA, $37,000. To produce video, Season of Hope, about mothers of drug-exposed infants. Grant shared with Searchlight Films. 1990.

357-5 Pregnancy to Parenthood Family Center, San Rafael, CA, $30,000. For program offering assessment, emergency and continuing services to parents and infant children, in collaboration with Marin Community Foundation and Marin Community Mental Health Services. 1990.
357-6 San Francisco Community Mental Health Services, San Francisco, CA, $15,000. To develop parent education services and to compete for major grant to improve mental health services for children in San Francisco. 1990.
357-7 San Mateo County Family Outreach Project, Redwood City, CA, $51,000. For public health/mental health/social services collaborative approach to providing outreach and in-home services to at-risk families. 1990.
357-8 Solid Foundation, Mandela House, Oakland, CA, $57,500. For family maintenance and reunification, healthy child development and community outreach program for drug-addicted mothers and their infants, in collaboration with Alameda County Drug and Alcohol Services. 1990.
357-9 University of California, School of Social Welfare, Berkeley, CA, $15,500. For Pediatric

AIDS Project of Bay Area Social Services Consortium. 1990.

358
Ruth/Allen Ziegler Foundation
7351 Crider Ave.
Pico Rivera 90660

Established in 1986 in CA.
Donor(s): Allen S. Ziegler, Ruth B. Ziegler.
Foundation type: Independent
Financial data (yr. ended 11/30/91): Assets, $6,028,450 (M); gifts received, $6,988,500; expenditures, $1,063,261; qualifying distributions, $1,060,059, including $1,056,977 for 18 grants (high: $295,313; low: $3,400).
Fields of interest: Jewish giving, Jewish welfare, hospitals, theological education.
Limitations: Giving primarily in Los Angeles, CA. No grants to individuals.
Application information: Contributes only to pre-selected organizations. Applications not accepted.
Officers: Allen S. Ziegler, Pres.; Ruth B. Ziegler, Secy.
EIN: 954113690

COLORADO

359
The Hugh Bancroft, Jr. Foundation
1700 Lincoln, Suite 4100
Denver 80203-4541   (303) 861-7000

Established in 1960 in CO.
Donor(s): Jacqueline E. Spencer.
Foundation type: Independent
Financial data (yr. ended 12/31/91): Assets,
$7,408,574 (M); gifts received, $1,000,000;
expenditures, $242,688; qualifying distributions,
$185,000, including $185,000 for grants (high:
$100,000; low: $30,000; average:
$30,000-$100,000).
Fields of interest: Arts, music, recreation, youth,
hospitals.
Types of support: Continuing support, general
purposes.
Limitations: Giving primarily in NM. No grants to
individuals.
Application information: Application form not
required.
  Initial approach: Letter
  Copies of proposal: 1
  Deadline(s): None
  Write: Paul D. Holleman, Trustee
Officers: A.N. Spencer, Mgr.; Jacqueline E.
Spencer, Mgr.
Trustees: Judson W. Detrick, Paul D. Holleman,
Thomas R. Richardson.
Number of staff: 2 part-time professional; 2
part-time support.
EIN: 846020971

360
The Bloedorn Foundation
P.O. Box 798
Fort Morgan 80701   (303) 867-5661

Established about 1961.
Donor(s): H.B. Bloedorn.‡
Foundation type: Independent
Financial data (yr. ended 12/31/90): Assets,
$2,409,588 (M); gifts received, $600;
expenditures, $119,682; qualifying distributions,
$113,407, including $111,925 for 40 grants (high:
$26,550; low: $125).
Fields of interest: Hospitals, higher education,
secondary education, Protestant giving,
community development.
Types of support: Scholarship funds.
Limitations: Giving primarily in Morgan County,
CO.
Application information:
  Initial approach: Letter
  Deadline(s): None
  Write: John Bloedorn, Jr., Secy.-Treas.
Officer and Trustees:* John H. Bloedorn, Jr.,*
Secy.-Treas.; Beverly Haley, Rosalyn Hansen, Jerry
Jones, Donald F. McClary, Robert Spencer.
EIN: 846025296

361
Boettcher Foundation ▼
600 17th St., Suite 2210 South
Denver 80202   (303) 534-1937

Incorporated in 1937 in CO.
Donor(s): C.K. Boettcher,‡ Mrs. C.K. Boettcher,‡
Charles Boettcher,‡ Fannie Boettcher,‡ Ruth
Boettcher Humphreys.‡
Foundation type: Independent
Financial data (yr. ended 12/31/90): Assets,
$110,117,677 (M); expenditures, $6,017,428;
qualifying distributions, $4,615,184, including
$3,232,486 for 120 grants (high: $500,000; low:
$500; average: $10,000-$50,000) and
$1,382,698 for 159 grants to individuals.
Purpose and activities: Grants to educational
institutions, with emphasis on scholarships and
fellowships; community and social services,
including child welfare and women, the
disadvantaged and the homeless, and urban and
rural development; health, including
rehabilitation and drug abuse; and civic and
cultural programs, including support for the fine
and performing arts.
Fields of interest: Education, higher education,
education—early childhood, welfare, child
welfare, employment, family planning, homeless,
women, rural development, community
development, urban affairs, health, rehabilitation,
drug abuse, cultural programs, fine arts, historic
preservation, performing arts, ecology.
Types of support: Scholarship funds, operating
budgets, seed money, building funds, equipment,
land acquisition, matching funds, general
purposes, annual campaigns, capital campaigns,
renovation projects.
Limitations: Giving limited to CO. No grants to
individuals (except for scholarship and fellowship
programs), or for endowment funds.
Publications: Annual report (including application
guidelines), informational brochure, application
guidelines.
Application information: Application form not
required.
  Initial approach: Letter
  Copies of proposal: 1
  Deadline(s): None
  Board meeting date(s): Monthly
  Final notification: 2 to 3 months
  Write: William A. Douglas, Pres.
Officers and Trustees:* Claudia B. Merthan,*
Chair.; Hover T. Lentz,* Vice-Chair.; William A.
Douglas, Pres. and Exec. Dir.; John C. Mitchell II,*
Secy.; George M. Wilfley,* Treas.; Mrs. Charles
Boettcher II, E. Atwill Gilman, A. Barry
Hirschfeld, Edward Lehman, Harry T. Lewis, Jr.
Number of staff: 2 full-time professional; 2
full-time support.
EIN: 840404274
Recent health grants:
361-1 Colorado Foundation of Dentistry for the
Handicapped, Denver, CO, $10,000. For
operations. 1990.
361-2 Easter Seal Society of Colorado, Empire,
CO, $20,000. For summer camperships for
handicapped children. 1990.
361-3 Hilltop Foundation, Grand Junction, CO,
$25,000. Toward construction of client
recreation complex. 1990.
361-4 Kit Carson County Memorial Hospital,
Burlington, CO, $25,000. Toward x-ray
equipment. 1990.

361-5 La Puente Home, Alamosa, CO, $10,000.
For operations. 1990.
361-6 Planned Parenthood, Rocky Mountain,
Aurora, CO, $35,000. For operations. 1990.
361-7 Rocky Mountain Center for Health
Promotion and Education, Lakewood, CO,
$50,000. Toward implementation of Shepard
Program. 1990.
361-8 Rocky Mountain Poison and Drug Center,
Denver, CO, $10,000. For operations. 1990.
361-9 Saint Vincent General Hospital, Leadville,
CO, $30,000. For expansion of Physical
Therapy Department. 1990.
361-10 Step Thirteen, Denver, CO, $10,000. For
operations. 1990.
361-11 University Hills Christian Living Center,
Denver, CO, $50,000. Toward furnishing and
equipping of new Johnson Center. 1990.
361-12 University of Colorado Health Sciences
Center, Denver, CO, $15,000. For Denver
School-Based Clinics project. 1990.
361-13 Visiting Nurse Association of the Denver
Area, Denver, CO, $15,000. Toward purchase
of equipment. 1990.
361-14 Yuma, City of, Yuma, CO, $35,000. For
facilities and equipment for Yuma Community
Wellness Program. 1990.

362
The Carroll Foundation
R.R. 1, Box 159
Franktown 80116

Established in 1978.
Donor(s): International Metals & Machines, Inc.,
Champion Pneumatic Machinery Co., Inc.,
Ludlow Industries, Inc., and other companies.
Foundation type: Company-sponsored
Financial data (yr. ended 04/30/91): Assets,
$1,684,128 (M); gifts received, $802,210;
expenditures, $3,878,872; qualifying
distributions, $3,876,094, including $3,876,094
for 103 grants (high: $2,900,000; low: $10).
Purpose and activities: Giving primarily for higher
education and hospitals; some support also for
elementary education.
Fields of interest: Higher education, hospitals,
elementary education.
Limitations: Giving primarily in MA and IL. No
grants to individuals.
Application information:
  Initial approach: Letter
  Deadline(s): None
Trustees: Barry J. Carroll, Denis H. Carroll,
Wallace E. Carroll, Jr., Lelia C. Johnson.
EIN: 840800849

363
Colorado Springs Community Trust Fund
P.O. Box 2340
Colorado Springs 80901   (719) 475-7730

Established in 1928 in CO by declaration of trust.
Foundation type: Community
Financial data (yr. ended 12/31/90): Assets,
$3,143,529 (M); gifts received, $31,981;
expenditures, $189,276; qualifying distributions,
$148,469, including $142,207 for 32 grants
(high: $19,559; low: $250; average:
$500-$24,880).

Purpose and activities: Emphasis on community funds, youth agencies, health, and child welfare.

Fields of interest: Community funds, community development, youth, child welfare, health, handicapped, rehabilitation, civic affairs, education, welfare.

Types of support: Continuing support, annual campaigns, seed money, emergency funds, building funds, equipment.

Limitations: Giving primarily in CO, with emphasis on El Paso County. No grants to individuals, or for operating budgets, deficit financing, endowment funds, matching gifts, scholarships, fellowships, research, demonstration projects, publications, or conferences; no loans.

Publications: Annual report.

Application information: Application form not required.

> *Initial approach:* Letter
> *Deadline(s):* None
> *Board meeting date(s):* 3 or 4 times a year
> *Final notification:* 3 to 4 months
> *Write:* Jack W. Foutch

Trustees: Richard G. Gillaspie, Gary Mammel, Rex Stephenson.

Director: Wilton Cogswell III.

Number of staff: 1 part-time support.

EIN: 510217708

364
The Colorado Trust ▼

The Colorado Trust Bldg.
1600 Sherman St.
Denver 80203-1604   (303) 837-1200
FAX: (303) 839-9034

Established in 1985 in CO.

Donor(s): Presbyterian/St. Lukes Health Care Corp.

Foundation type: Independent

Financial data (yr. ended 12/31/91): Assets, $226,475,533 (M); gifts received, $635,019; expenditures, $39,533,924; qualifying distributions, $39,824,022, including $37,390,669 for 59 grants (high: $30,000,000; low: $3,500); $159,892 for 115 employee matching gifts and $220,000 for program-related investments.

Purpose and activities: Support for affordable and accessible health care programs, human development, and the strengthening of families.

Types of support: Program-related investments, seed money, technical assistance.

Limitations: Giving primarily in CO. No support for religious organizations for religious purposes, private foundations, or direct subsidization of care to the medically indigent. No grants to individuals, or for endowments, deficit financing or debt retirement, building funds, real estate acquisition, medical research, fundraising drives and events, testimonial dinners, or advertising.

Publications: Annual report, application guidelines, newsletter, occasional report.

Application information: Applications are accepted following release of Requests for Proposals issued by the trust. Application form not required.

> *Initial approach:* Letter and proposal
> *Deadline(s):* Varies
> *Board meeting date(s):* Monthly
> *Final notification:* Varies
> *Write:* Jean Merrick, V.P., Programs

Officers and Trustees:* Richard F. Walker,* Chair.; Robert G. Boucher,* Vice-Chair.; John R. Moran, Jr., Pres.; Walter F. LaMendola, M.D., V.P., Research; Jean D. Merrick, V.P., Programs and Public Information; Peter A. Konrad, V.P., Admin.; William F. Beattie,* Secy.; A. Gordon Rippey,* Treas.; W.R. Alexander, Donald G. Butterfield, M.D., Rev. Kady Cone, Donald W. Fink, M.D., James G. Urban, M.D.

Number of staff: 7 full-time professional; 3 part-time professional; 7 full-time support; 3 part-time support.

EIN: 840994055

Recent health grants:

364-1 American Cancer Society, Denver, CO, $35,000. For statewide Breast Cancer Awareness Month in October. 1990.

364-2 Childrens Hospital, Denver, CO, $100,000. For Merit Award. 1990.

364-3 Colorado Action for Healthy People, Denver, CO, $862,500. For operation and evaluation of statewide program to address leading preventable causes of disease and premature death in Colorado through community activation. 1990.

364-4 Colorado Department of Education, Denver, CO, $25,000. For adolescent health education consultant to monitor implementation of comprehensive health education curricula in public schools throughout state. 1990.

364-5 Colorado Department of Health, Denver, CO, $75,000. For evaluation of Emergency Medical Services (EMS) grant program and planning activities for EMS Division. 1990.

364-6 Colorado Domestic Violence Coalition, Denver, CO, $30,000. For development and implementation of statewide medical protocol for use by health care personnel to identify and serve families coping with abuse. 1990.

364-7 Colorado Personalized Education Program for Physicians, Denver, CO, $50,000. For development of model for personalized continuing medical education for physicians who seek to improve their professional skills. 1990.

364-8 Colorado Plains Rural Health Network, Burlington, CO, $433,393. For development of consortium in northeastern Colorado representing eight rural and nine urban hospitals to provide forum to identify and address rural health care issues. 1990.

364-9 Colorado West Regional Mental Health Center, Colorado Springs, CO, $50,000. For Homebuilders Replication Project. 1990.

364-10 Denver Department of Health and Hospitals, Denver, CO, $30,000. For mammography screening program for black women in northeast Denver. 1990.

364-11 Denver Public Schools, Denver, CO, $324,246. For five-site expansion (Baker, Cole, Mann, Martin Luther King, Jr. and Merrill Middle Schools) of school-based health services and education designed to modify health-compromising behaviors of high-risk young people. Grant shared with Denver Department of Health and Hospitals. 1990.

364-12 Denver Public Schools, Denver, CO, $30,590. For study of health of Denver's school children and its impact on education. 1990.

364-13 Denver Public Schools, Denver, CO, $10,000. For Early Childhood Education Task Force to examine current and prospective early childhood health care systems in schools. Grant shared with University of Colorado at Denver. 1990.

364-14 Englewood Public Schools, Englewood, CO, $20,000. For seed funding for Early Childhood Care and Education Project, replication of The Center in Leadville, which provides comprehensive early childhood care and programs before and after school. 1990.

364-15 Garfield County Board of Commissioners, Glenwood Springs, CO, $139,665. For coalition of providers and agencies in Garfield, Eagle and Pitkin Counties which provides perinatal services to low-income women through clinic established in Glenwood Springs, and physician volunteer at clinic on rotating basis, with deliveries occurring at local hospitals. 1990.

364-16 Grantmakers in Health, NYC, NY, $12,000. For national organization of foundations specializing in health care issues. 1990.

364-17 Hilltop Community Clinic, Cripple Creek, CO, $55,000. For rural health clinic originally established through Rural Healthcare Initiative grant. 1990.

364-18 Inner City Health Center, Denver, CO, $23,862. For development of program to provide dental services to low-income, inner-city Denver residents. 1990.

364-19 Jefferson County Mental Health Center, Arvada, CO, $50,000. For Homebuilders Replication Project. 1990.

364-20 Medical Care and Research Foundation, Denver, CO, $10,000. For dental care program for elderly in Denver. 1990.

364-21 Mental Health Corporation of Denver, Denver, CO, $50,000. For Homebuilders Replication Project. 1990.

364-22 N.U.R.S.E.S. of Colorado Corporation, Denver, CO, $24,118. For statewide peer-assistance program for nurses. 1990.

364-23 Northeast Womens Center, Denver, CO, $42,454. For implementation of Natural Helper Wellness Project in Curtis Park housing project in northeast Denver. Grant shared with Northeast Denver Health Issues Coalition. 1990.

364-24 Northeast Womens Center, Denver, CO, $10,000. For health-related programs for women in northeast Denver. 1990.

364-25 Plains Medical Center, Limon, CO, $50,000. For development of regional single point of entry through medical clinic in Limon. 1990.

364-26 Planned Parenthood, Rocky Mountain, Aurora, CO, $198,126. For project to serve southeast Colorado towns of La Junta, Trinidad and Walsenburg in which bilingual case managers act as liaison among patients, physicians and social service systems. 1990.

364-27 Poudre Hospital Foundation, Fort Collins, CO, $204,752. For perinatal services provided to southern Larimer County, in which case managers provide financial services and social counseling, and local physicians participate in rotation system to serve low-income women. 1990.

364-28 Pueblo Community Health Center, Pueblo, CO, $12,000. For assessment of future facility requirements of community health clinic in Pueblo County. 1990.

364-29 Saint Vincent General Hospital, Leadville, CO, $86,097. For project in Leadville to serve low-income women from Summit, Lake and Eagle counties. 1990.

364-30 San Luis Valley Comprehensive Community Mental Health Center, Alamosa, CO, $50,000. For Homebuilders Replication Project. 1990.

364-31 Southern Ute Indian Tribe, Ignacio, CO, $50,000. For wellness program in Ignacio that involves tribal and non-Indian community members and provides education awareness activities, training for staff and volunteers and access to exercise programs. 1990.

364-32 Total Longterm Care, Denver, CO, $734,209. For project to replicate On Lok Senior Health Services model in Denver to provide comprehensive health care services to frail elderly through capitated financing. 1990.

364-33 University of Colorado, Denver, CO, $10,000. For national conference to explore restructuring of American health care system. 1990.

364-34 University of Colorado, Center for Health Ethics and Policy, Denver, CO, $25,000. For planning grant to establish Health Policy Council's mission and agenda. 1990.

364-35 University of Colorado Health Sciences Center, Denver, CO, $100,000. For school-based health clinics at East, Manual and Lincoln High Schools in Denver. 1990.

364-36 University of Colorado Health Sciences Center, Colorado Prevention Center, Denver, CO, $50,000. For planning grant to develop cardiovascular disease prevention and intervention strategy for Colorado. 1990.

364-37 University of Colorado Health Sciences Center, Task Force Office on Nursing, Denver, CO, $150,000. To develop models to implement differentiated nursing practice in Colorado so as to promote nursing recruitment and retention in workplace. 1990.

364-38 University of Colorado Health Sciences Center, Task Force Office on Nursing, Denver, CO, $16,049. For use of information technology to support nursing practice and education networks in rural Colorado. 1990.

364-39 University of Colorado Health Sciences Center, The Children's Hospital, Denver, CO, $197,289. For program to serve pregnant women younger than 19 who live in metropolitan Denver and deliver at University Hospital. 1990.

364-40 Ute Mountain Ute Tribe, Towaoc, CO, $50,000. For employee-assistance counseling program and expansion of community health and exercise program to include aerobics, running clubs, weight lifting, walking clubs, water aerobics and circuit room. 1990.

364-41 Weld County Department of Health, Greeley, CO, $173,800. For Weld County Community Health Coalition's Promoting Healthy Decisions offering case management services county-wide to low-income women. 1990.

364-42 Western Colorado Healthcare Alliance, Gunnison, CO, $413,010. For development of consortium on Colorado's western slope representing 14 rural hospitals to enhance, through joint efforts and programs, operating efficiencies, market positions and quality of services provided by members. 1990.

365
Comprecare Foundation, Inc.
P.O. Box 441170
Aurora 80044   (303) 832-1005

Established in 1986 in CO.
Foundation type: Independent
Financial data (yr. ended 12/31/91): Assets, $4,539,643 (M); expenditures, $603,861; qualifying distributions, $476,783, including $476,783 for 15 grants (high: $320,000; low: $500).
Purpose and activities: "To encourage, aid or assist specific health related programs and to support the actvities of organizations and individuals who advance and promote health care education, the delivery of health care services, and the improvement of community health and welfare."
Fields of interest: Health, hospitals, health services, mental health, alcoholism, aged, child welfare.
Types of support: Conferences and seminars, research, seed money, special projects.
Limitations: Giving primarily in CO, with emphasis on front range. No support for private foundations. No grants to individuals, or for fellowships, scholarships, operating expenses, debt reduction, land acquisition, fundraising events, or testimonial dinners or promotions.
Publications: Annual report.
Application information: Application form not required.
   Initial approach: Letter (1 to 2 pages)
   Copies of proposal: 1
   Deadline(s): Aug. 15 of each year for calendar year funding
   Board meeting date(s): Monthly
   Final notification: Following board meeting
   Write: J.R. Gilsdorf, Exec. Dir.
Officers and Directors:* Joseph P. Natale,* Chair.; Marcus B. Bond, M.D.,* Vice-Chair.; Richard F. Negri,* Secy.-Treas.; Bradford L. Darling, Raymond C. Delisle, Ellen J. Mangione, M.D., M. Eugene Sherman, M.D.
Number of staff: 1 part-time professional; 1 part-time support.
EIN: 840641406

366
Adolph Coors Corporate Contributions Program
Community Affairs Dept.
MAIL NH410
Golden 80401   (303) 277-3397

Financial data (yr. ended 12/31/90): Total giving, $4,000,000 for grants.
Purpose and activities: "At Adolph Coors Company we always believed in giving back to the community that has given so much to us." A charitable donation begins as a written request for money, product, advertising items which bear the Coors logo, obsolete equipment or in-kind services such as graphics, printing and employee volunteers contributing expertise through service on boards of directors and speaking engagements. "Our Corporate Contributions Program is a resource which helps us to identify community concerns, participate in solutions and develop close working relationships with community organizations and special interest groups. Our activities and donations are concentrated in the metro Denver area and with organizations of national scope and membership. Only in very special instances are donations outside Colorado considered. Distributors of Coors products are encouraged to be actively involved with community organizations and events scheduled within their respective market areas." Coors also gives through the employee V.I.C.E. (Volunteers in Community Enrichment) Squad and in 1989, launched the High School Internship/Scholarship program, through which high school minority students are recruited to work as summer interns and receive $2,000 scholarships. Areas of interest include Native Americans, women, and minorities, religious organizations, community sports, military programs, literacy, volunteerism, the arts and humanities, education, health, civic organizations. Special emphasis on reducing substance abuse.
Fields of interest: Civic affairs, women, health, military personnel, education, community funds, arts, minorities, Native Americans, volunteerism, literacy, education—minorities.
Types of support: General purposes, special projects, employee volunteer services, donated equipment, donated products.
Limitations: Giving limited to the metropolitan Denver area. No grants to individuals; or for telethons, walkathons, or travel; no monetary assistance for third party fundraisers or sales promotions; for these events gifts are limited to items bearing the Coors logo; no loans of company vehicles.
Publications: Corporate giving report (including application guidelines), newsletter.
Application information: Application form not required.
   Initial approach: Letter
   Copies of proposal: 1
   Deadline(s): 60 days in advance of needed funds
   Write: Mary Anne Fleet, Corp. Contribs. Mgr.
Administrator: Mary Anne Fleet, Corp. Contribs. Mgr.
Number of staff: 2 full-time professional; 2 full-time support.

367
Adolph Coors Foundation ▼
350-C Clayton St.
Denver 80206   (303) 388-1636

Incorporated in 1975 in CO.
Donor(s): Adolph Coors, Jr.,‡ Gertrude S. Coors,‡ Janet Coors.
Foundation type: Independent
Financial data (yr. ended 11/30/90): Assets, $97,350,014 (M); expenditures, $5,938,152; qualifying distributions, $4,965,806, including $4,586,500 for 130 grants (high: $200,000; low: $750; average: $5,000-$20,000) and $55,500 for 1 foundation-administered program.
Purpose and activities: Emphasis on education, public policy, civic affairs, human services, youth, and health.
Fields of interest: Education, public policy, civic affairs, social services, disadvantaged, youth, health.
Types of support: Building funds, general purposes, seed money, operating budgets, special projects.

Limitations: Giving primarily in CO; national giving is limited. No support for pre-schools, daycare centers, nursing homes or other extended care facilities, or tax-supported organizations. Generally, no grants to individuals, or for endowment funds, research, production of films or other media-related projects, capital or program needs of churches, conduit funding, deficits, debt retirement, special benefit programs, or purchase of blocks of tickets.
Publications: Annual report (including application guidelines).
Application information: Application form not required.
   Initial approach: Letter
   Copies of proposal: 1
   Deadline(s): 8 weeks prior to meetings
   Board meeting date(s): Jan., Apr., July, and Oct.
   Final notification: 3 months
   Write: Linda S. Tafoya, Exec. Dir.
Officers and Trustees:* William K. Coors,* Pres.; Peter H. Coors,* V.P.; Linda S. Tafoya, Secy. and Exec. Dir.; Jeffrey H. Coors,* Treas.; Joseph Coors, Robert G. Windsor.
Number of staff: 2 full-time professional; 2 full-time support.
EIN: 510172279
Recent health grants:
367-1 Childrens Hospital Foundation, Denver, CO, $100,000. 1990.
367-2 Cleo Wallace Center, Westminster, CO, $50,000. For academic building. 1990.
367-3 Colorado Foundation of Dentistry for the Handicapped, Denver, CO, $10,000. For Donated Dental Services Program, reduction of dental health-care costs for handicapped and elderly persons. 1990.
367-4 Colorado Optometric Center, Denver, CO, $20,000. For Optometric equipment. 1990.
367-5 Colorado, State of, Denver, CO, $50,000. For Communities for Drug-Free Colorado youth leadership training workshops. 1990.
367-6 Fort Morgan Community Hospital, Fort Morgan, CO, $25,000. For capital improvements. 1990.
367-7 Hilltop Foundation, Grand Junction, CO, $10,000. For capital and equipment needs. 1990.
367-8 Karis, Denver, CO, $10,000. For general operating support. 1990.
367-9 Qualife Wellness Community, Denver, CO, $20,000. For one to one counseling program for those newly-diagnosed with cancer and support of patient follow-up program. 1990.
367-10 Rocky Mountain Center for Health Promotion and Education, Lakewood, CO, $30,000. For rural health teacher training project. 1990.
367-11 University of Colorado, Denver, CO, $10,000. For Canadian American Conference on health. 1990.

368
Viola Vestal Coulter Foundation, Inc.
c/o Norwest Investments & Trust
1740 Broadway
Denver 80274-8698

Established in 1935.
Donor(s): Mabel Munro Coulter.‡
Foundation type: Independent

Financial data (yr. ended 12/31/90): Assets, $4,052,243 (M); gifts received, $124,900; expenditures, $226,448; qualifying distributions, $180,978, including $113,000 for 3 grants (high: $70,000; low: $8,000) and $67,000 for grants to individuals.
Purpose and activities: Support for higher education, including scholarships to students attending specifically designated colleges and universities in the western U.S. for undergraduate and graduate programs.
Fields of interest: Higher education, law and justice, engineering, nursing, medical research.
Types of support: Student aid.
Limitations: Giving primarily in CO.
Application information: Applications available at financial aid offices at pre-selected universities; unsolicited requests not accepted. Applications not accepted.
   Write: Marcy Carroll
Officers and Trustees:* Harold A. Norblom,* Pres.; William B. Kottinger III, V.P.; Bruce T. Buell, Secy.-Treas.; Priscilla Ann Barsotti, James Gutshall, Pamela L. Saxton, William W. Schley, M.E. Timmins, Judy C. Ward.
EIN: 846029641

369
The Denver Foundation ▼
455 Sherman St., Suite 220
Denver 80203   (303) 778-7587
FAX: (303) 778-0124

Established in 1925 in CO by resolution and declaration of trust.
Foundation type: Community
Financial data (yr. ended 12/31/91): Assets, $27,477,157 (M); gifts received, $2,431,375; expenditures, $1,995,270; qualifying distributions, $2,524,832, including $1,590,302 for 163 grants (high: $72,000; low: $75; average: $15,000-$20,000), $49,530 for 2 foundation-administered programs and $885,000 for 3 program-related investments.
Purpose and activities: To "assist, encourage and promote the well-being of mankind, and primarily the inhabitants of metropolitan Denver." Grants primarily for education, health, AIDS research, social services, and cultural programs.
Fields of interest: Education, health, hospitals, AIDS, social services, cultural programs, arts, civic affairs.
Types of support: Seed money, renovation projects, technical assistance, special projects, matching funds, scholarship funds, program-related investments.
Limitations: Giving limited to Adams, Denver, Douglas, Jefferson, Arapahoe, and Boulder counties, CO. No support for sectarian programs, or projects supported largely by public funds. No grants to individuals, or for debt liquidation, endowment funds, research, publications, films, travel, or conferences; no loans.
Publications: Annual report, program policy statement, newsletter, informational brochure, newsletter.
Application information: Application form not required.
   Initial approach: Letter
   Copies of proposal: 1
   Deadline(s): None

Board meeting date(s): Mar., June, Sept., and Nov.
Final notification: Within 6 months
Write: Robert E. Lee, Exec. Dir.
Officers and Distribution Committee:* John H. McLagan,* Chair.; Donald K. Bain,* Vice-Chair.; Mary Lee Anderson,* Treas.; Robert E. Lee, Exec. Dir.; Sidney Friedman, Carol Gossard, Phyllis Jennings-Byrd, C. Howard Kast, Richard Robinson, Virginia P. Rockwell, Darlene Silver, Robert S. Slosky, Bernard Valdez.
Trustee Banks: Central Bank Denver, Colorado National Bank of Denver, Colorado State Bank of Denver, First Interstate Bank of Denver, N.A., Guaranty Bank & Trust, Investment Trust Co.. Jefferson Bank and Trust, Norwest Bank.
Number of staff: 4 full-time professional; 1 part-time professional; 1 full-time support.
EIN: 846048381
Recent health grants:
369-1 Cenikor Foundation, Denver, CO, $15,000. For Knock Out Drugs Program. 1990.
369-2 Center for Creative Arts Therapy, Denver, CO, $12,500. For Clinical Consultant Staff Position. 1990.
369-3 Childrens Hospital Association, Denver, CO, $10,000. For capital support for Health Center. 1990.
369-4 Colorado Foundation of Dentistry for the Handicapped, Denver, CO, $10,000. For expansion of Donated Dental Services Program. 1990.
369-5 Colorado State University, School of Veterinary Medicine, Fort Collins, CO, $10,000. For equipment for small animal clinic. 1990.
369-6 Communities for a Drug-Free Colorado, Denver, CO, $25,000. For team training in urban communities. 1990.
369-7 Epilepsy Foundation of Colorado, Englewood, CO, $10,000. For Training and Placement Services Program support. 1990.
369-8 Make-A-Wish Foundation of Colorado, Denver, CO, $10,000. For computer system expansion and upgrade. 1990.
369-9 Miriam Hart Radiation Therapy Center, Boulder, CO, $14,135. For indigent health care. 1990.
369-10 University Hills Christian Living Center, Denver, CO, $15,000. For furnishings for Alzheimer's Assisted Care Facility. 1990.
369-11 University of Colorado Health Sciences Center, Denver, CO, $25,000. For operating support for School-Based Clinics. 1990.
369-12 University of Colorado Health Sciences Center, Denver, CO, $16,200. For continuing support of Eye Pathology Laboratory. 1990.
369-13 Visiting Nurse Association of the Denver Area, Denver, CO, $15,805. For computerization of admissions and scheduling systems. 1990.

370
John G. Duncan Trust
c/o First Interstate Bank of Denver, N.A.
P.O. Box 5825 TA
Denver 80217   (303) 293-5324

Trust established in 1955 in CO.
Donor(s): John G. Duncan.‡
Foundation type: Independent

Financial data (yr. ended 12/31/90): Assets, $3,092,079 (M); expenditures, $218,587; qualifying distributions, $182,500, including $182,500 for 37 grants (high: $10,000; low: $2,000).
Fields of interest: Hospitals, higher education, secondary education, youth, cultural programs.
Types of support: Annual campaigns, building funds, equipment, research, operating budgets, continuing support, seed money, emergency funds, special projects.
Limitations: Giving limited to CO. No grants to individuals, or for endowment funds, scholarships, or fellowships; no loans.
Publications: Application guidelines.
Application information: Application form not required.
  Initial approach: Letter or proposal
  Copies of proposal: 1
  Deadline(s): Dec. 1
  Board meeting date(s): Dec.
  Final notification: Dec. 31
  Write: Yvonne Baca, Sr. V.P., First Interstate Bank of Denver, N.A.
Trustee: First Interstate Bank of Denver, N.A.
Number of staff: None.
EIN: 846016555

371
El Pomar Foundation ▼
Ten Lake Circle
P.O. Box 158
Colorado Springs 80906   (719) 633-7733

Incorporated in 1937 in CO.
Donor(s): Spencer Penrose,‡ Mrs. Spencer Penrose.‡
Foundation type: Independent
Financial data (yr. ended 12/31/90): Assets, $252,724,960 (M); expenditures, $10,357,839; qualifying distributions, $9,387,020, including $8,479,720 for 93 grants (high: $3,150,000; low: $2,500; average: $10,000-$100,000).
Purpose and activities: Grants only to nonprofit organizations for public, educational, arts and humanities, health, and welfare purposes, including child welfare, the disadvantaged, and housing; municipalities may request funds for specific projects.
Fields of interest: Education, adult education, business education, health, hospitals, pharmacy, hospices, welfare, disadvantaged, homeless, child welfare, employment, housing, cultural programs, arts, humanities, historic preservation, performing arts, theater, civic affairs.
Types of support: Operating budgets, continuing support, emergency funds, building funds, equipment, land acquisition, scholarship funds, special projects, general purposes, capital campaigns, renovation projects.
Limitations: Giving limited to CO. No support for organizations that distribute funds to other grantees, or for camps or seasonal facilities. No grants to individuals, or for annual campaigns, travel, film or other media projects, conferences, deficit financing, endowment funds, research, matching gifts, seed money, or publications; no loans.
Publications: Annual report (including application guidelines), application guidelines, grants list.
Application information: Application form not required.

  Initial approach: Proposal
  Copies of proposal: 1
  Deadline(s): None
  Board meeting date(s): 7 to 9 times a year
  Final notification: 90 days
  Write: William J. Hybl, Chair.
Officers and Trustees:* William J. Hybl,* Chair. and C.E.O.; Karl E. Eitel, Chair., Exec. Committee; R. Thayer Tutt, Jr.,* Pres., C.O.O., and C.I.O.; Robert J. Hilbert, V.P., Administration and Secy.-Treas.; David J. Palenchar, V.P., Programs; Russell T. Tutt.
Number of staff: 6 full-time professional; 6 full-time support; 2 part-time support.
EIN: 846002373
Recent health grants:
371-1 Commerce City Community Health Services, Commerce City, CO, $25,000. For constructing and equipping new clinic building. 1990.
371-2 Community Health Center, Colorado Springs, CO, $50,000. For indigent care program. 1990.
371-3 Community Health Center, Colorado Springs, CO, $50,000. For Pharmacy Services Program. 1990.
371-4 Craig Hospital, Englewood, CO, $10,000. For Joel A.H. Webb Award for Excellence in Health Care. 1990.
371-5 Custer County Medical Foundation, Westcliffe, CO, $20,000. For purchase of medical equipment. 1990.
371-6 Health Association of the Pikes Peak Region, Colorado Springs, CO, $27,000. For specially equipped van for transporting wheelchair bound individuals. 1990.
371-7 Huerfano County Medical Center, Walsenburg, CO, $50,000. For capital needs associated with new medical center. 1990.
371-8 La Clinica Del Valle, Rocky Ford, CO, $10,000. For Joel A.H. Webb Award for Excellence in Health Care. 1990.
371-9 Lake City Area Medical Center, Lake City, CO, $10,000. For completion of new medical center. 1990.
371-10 Penrose-Saint Francis Health Care System, Colorado Springs, CO, $121,750. For support of cancer center and Webb Memorial Library. 1990.
371-11 Plains Medical Center, Limon, CO, $50,000. For capital expenses associated with new medical complex. 1990.
371-12 Prowers Medical Center, Lamar, CO, $19,500. For replacement of existing phone system. 1990.
371-13 Rocky Mountain Rehabilitation Center, Colorado Springs, CO, $25,000. For roof repairs. 1990.

372
The Frost Foundation, Ltd.
Cherry Creek Plaza II, Suite 205
650 South Cherry St.
Denver 80222   (303) 388-1687
IRS filing state: LA

Incorporated in 1959 in LA.
Donor(s): Virginia C. Frost.‡
Foundation type: Independent
Financial data (yr. ended 12/31/90): Assets, $20,961,855 (M); expenditures, $1,513,244; qualifying distributions, $1,234,369, including

$1,234,369 for 74 grants (high: $200,000; low: $1,000; average: $5,000-$15,000).
Purpose and activities: Giving primarily for education, including medical and other higher education and business administration, health associations and hospitals, social services, and women and youth organizations; grants also for denominational giving.
Fields of interest: Education, higher education, business education, medical education, health, health associations, hospitals, social services, women, youth, denominational giving.
Types of support: Seed money, equipment, matching funds, professorships, internships, fellowships, special projects, research, publications, conferences and seminars, consulting services, technical assistance.
Limitations: No grants to individuals, or for operating expenses or building funds; no loans.
Publications: Annual report, application guidelines.
Application information: Application form not required.
  Initial approach: Telephone or letter
  Copies of proposal: 5
  Deadline(s): Dec. 1 and June 1
  Board meeting date(s): Mar. and Sept.
  Final notification: 7 to 10 days
  Write: Theodore R. Kauss, Exec. Dir.
Officers and Directors:* Mary Amelia D. Whited,* Pres.; Mary Amelia Whited-Howell,* Exec. V.P.; Theodore R. Kauss, V.P. and Exec. Dir.; Claude G. Rives III,* V.P.; Mitchell R. Woodard, Treas.; Dallas P. Dickinson, J. Luther Jordan, Jr., John A. LeVan, John W. Loftus, Taylor F. Moore.
Number of staff: 1 full-time professional; 1 part-time professional; 1 full-time support.
EIN: 720520342
Recent health grants:
372-1 Baylor University Medical Center Foundation, Dallas, TX, $25,000. Toward research project to develop improved environmental control unit (ECU). 1990.
372-2 Council on Alcoholism and Drug Abuse, Shreveport, LA, $10,000. Toward establishment of Chemical Dependency Training Institute in Shreveport. 1990.
372-3 Eleanor Roosevelt Institute for Cancer Research, Denver, CO, $30,000. For recruitment program to bring distinguished scientists to assist with research in molecular biology, cell biology, cancer and human genetics. 1990.
372-4 New Mexico AIDS Services, Albuquerque, NM, $10,000. For development and maintenance of Emotional Support Services program. 1990.
372-5 Planned Parenthood, Rocky Mountain, Aurora, CO, $20,000. For educational efforts to prevent primary pregnancies in high-risk teenage population. 1990.
372-6 Porter Memorial Hospital Foundation, Denver, CO, $30,000. For establishment of third Center of Excellence, Oncology Center, at Hospital. 1990.
372-7 Saint Josephs Hospital and Medical Center, Phoenix, AZ, $20,000. Toward four-year budget for new Pediatric Cardiac Rehabilitation of hospital's Children's Health Center. 1990.
372-8 Southern University, Shreveport, LA, $10,000. For development of effective educational materials and information

programs to delay, control and reduce early mortality rate of black Americans with diabetes. 1990.

372-9 Tulane University Medical Center, New Orleans, LA, $50,000. For reconstruction of neonatal intensive care unit of Tulane University Hospital and Clinic. 1990.

372-10 University of Colorado Health Sciences Center, Denver, CO, $20,000. For 96-megabyte PIXAR computer memory expansion and 35mm color transparency recorder for anatomical imaging laboratories. 1990.

373
Gates Foundation ▼
3200 Cherry Creek South Dr., Suite 630
Denver 80209-3247   (303) 722-1881

Incorporated in 1946 in CO.
Donor(s): Charles Gates,‡ Hazel Gates,‡ John Gates.‡
Foundation type: Independent
Financial data (yr. ended 12/31/90): Assets, $95,411,627 (M); expenditures, $5,299,724; qualifying distributions, $4,165,403, including $4,165,403 for 103 grants (high: $555,000; low: $500; average: $5,000-$25,000).
Purpose and activities: To promote the health, welfare, and broad education of mankind whether by means of research, grants, publications, the foundation's own agencies and activities, or through cooperation with agencies and institutions already in existence. Grants primarily for education and youth services, including leadership development; public policy; historic preservation, humanities, and cultural affairs; health care, including cost reduction; and human services.
Fields of interest: Youth, leadership development, humanities, cultural programs, historic preservation, social services, education, civic affairs.
Types of support: Continuing support, building funds, capital campaigns, endowment funds, matching funds, renovation projects, special projects, equipment, fellowships, general purposes, land acquisition, publications.
Limitations: Giving limited to CO, especially the Denver area, except for foundation-initiated grants. No support for private foundations. No grants to individuals, or for operating budgets, annual campaigns, emergency funds, deficit financing, purchase of tickets for fundraising dinners, parties, balls, or other social fundraising events, research, or scholarships; no loans.
Publications: Annual report, informational brochure (including application guidelines), program policy statement, grants list.
Application information: Application form not required.
   Initial approach: Telephone
   Copies of proposal: 1
   Deadline(s): Jan. 15, Apr. 1, July 15, and Oct. 15
   Board meeting date(s): Approximately Apr. 1, June 15, Oct. 1, and Dec. 15
   Final notification: 2 weeks following meetings
   Write: Thomas Stokes, Exec. Dir.
Officers and Trustees:* Charles C. Gates,* Pres.; Brown W. Cannon, Jr.,* V.P.; Thomas Stokes, Secy. and Exec. Dir.; T.J. Gibson, Treas.; George B.

Beardsley, F. Charles Froelicher, William W. Grant III, Thomas C. Stokes, Diane Gates Wallach, Michael Wilfley.
Number of staff: 4 full-time professional; 2 full-time support.
EIN: 840474837
Recent health grants:
373-1 Colorado Business Coalition for Health, Denver, CO, $23,250. Toward funding of Pinpoint Study. 1990.
373-2 Colorado Business Coalition for Health, Denver, CO, $20,000. For final portion of two-year commitment toward educational programs in field of purchasing health care prudently. 1990.
373-3 Communities for a Drug-Free Colorado, Denver, CO, $25,000. For final portion of three-year commitment toward program being sponsored by Governor Roy Romer, State of Colorado. 1990.
373-4 Planned Parenthood, Rocky Mountain, Aurora, CO, $14,500. Toward purchase of equipment to train volunteers, and for community outreach materials for Educational Resource Center. 1990.
373-5 Rocky Mountain Center for Health Promotion and Education, Lakewood, CO, $15,000. For second portion of three-year commitment to continue support of elementary and middle school health education program in public schools of Colorado and for teacher training. 1990.
373-6 Wray Rehabilitation and Activities Center, Wray, CO, $27,500. Toward construction of new community recreation and wellness center. 1990.

374
General Service Foundation ▼
1445 Pearl St., Suite 201
Boulder 80302   (303) 447-9541
FAX: (303) 447-0595

Incorporated in 1946 in IL.
Donor(s): Clifton R. Musser,‡ Margaret K. Musser.‡
Foundation type: Independent
Financial data (yr. ended 12/31/91): Assets, $34,880,308 (M); expenditures, $1,752,182; qualifying distributions, $1,422,123, including $1,422,123 for 71 grants (high: $150,000; low: $700; average: $10,000-$35,000).
Purpose and activities: Major areas of interest include population, resources, and non-military aspects of international peace. Support for experimental, demonstration, or research projects on a national and international level, particularly in Latin America, Mexico, the Caribbean, and other developing areas.
Fields of interest: Population studies, conservation, environment, international studies, international affairs, public policy, leadership development, peace, rural development, human rights, family planning, Latin America, Mexico, Caribbean, Haiti.
Types of support: Special projects, research, general purposes, seed money.
Limitations: Giving primarily in the U.S., Mexico, Central America, and the Caribbean. No support for the arts (except through a small discretionary fund). No grants to individuals, or for capital funds, relief, operating budgets, endowments, scholarships, fellowships, matching gifts, or the

annual campaigns of established organizations; no loans.
Publications: Annual report (including application guidelines), grants list.
Application information: Application form required.
   Initial approach: Letter or telephone
   Copies of proposal: 1
   Deadline(s): Mar. 1 and Sept. 1
   Board meeting date(s): May and Nov.
   Final notification: 6 months
   Write: Robert W. Musser, Pres.
Officers and Directors:* Robert W. Musser,* Pres.; Marcie J. Musser,* V.P. and Treas.; Mary L. Estrin,* V.P.; Ruth C. Dingler, Secy.; Robert L. Estrin, Patricia A. King, Heidi Lloyd, Marion M. Lloyd, Elizabeth W. Musser, James P. Shannon.
Number of staff: 2 full-time support.
EIN: 366018535
Recent health grants:
374-1 Alan Guttmacher Institute, NYC, NY, $18,000. For Communications Program, to enhance ability to disseminate information concerning abortion to press, advocates, policymakers and public. 1990.
374-2 Catholics for a Free Choice, DC, $32,000. For general program support. 1990.
374-3 Center for Population Options, DC, $53,000. For Community-Based HIV/AIDS Prevention Education Programs for High-Risk Youth. 1990.
374-4 Colorado Organization on Adolescent Pregnancy and Parenting, Denver, CO, $10,000. For program to reduce adolescent pregnancies and encourage healthy lifestyles of Colorado teenagers by providing accurate information on pregnancy prevention. 1990.
374-5 Communications Consortium, Media Center, DC, $20,000. For Reproductive Health Media Strategies Project. 1990.
374-6 Education, Training and Research (ETR) Associates, Santa Cruz, CA, $15,000. For development and dissemination of photo-tabloids designed to reduce incidence of HIV/AIDS among ethnic minority youth. 1990.
374-7 International Projects Assistance Services, Chapel Hill, NC, $20,000. For continued support of project in Nicaragua training physicians in use of manual vacuum aspiration technique for treatment of abortion complications. 1990.
374-8 International Womens Health Coalition, DC, $21,000. For Latin American program seeking to reform abortion policy and improve quality of family planning services and sexuality education for health professionals. 1990.
374-9 Population Crisis Committee, DC, $15,000. For Public Education Through Media Program which helps strengthen and encourage U.S. support for population programs worldwide. 1990.
374-10 Unitarian Universalist Service Committee, Boston, MA, $19,000. For reproductive health component of program, North-South Partnership in Central America. 1990.
374-11 Women Judges Fund for Justice, DC, $20,000. For programs designed to educate judiciary on developments and trends in law regarding reproductive and bioethical issues. 1990.

375
Will E. Heginbotham Trust
P.O. Box 245
Holyoke 80734-0245   (303) 854-2497

Trust established in 1968 in CO.
Donor(s): Will E. Heginbotham.‡
Foundation type: Independent
Financial data (yr. ended 12/31/90): Assets, $4,295,759 (M); expenditures, $432,409; qualifying distributions, $421,875, including $405,325 for 19 grants (high: $100,000; low: $1,000).
Purpose and activities: Giving primarily for hospitals; support also for public schools, recreation, and community development.
Fields of interest: Hospitals, education, recreation, community development, civic affairs.
Types of support: Building funds, equipment.
Limitations: Giving limited to Phillips County, CO.
Application information: Application form not required.
  Deadline(s): None
  Write: David O. Colver, Trustee
Trustees: Theodore P. Clark, David O. Colver, Josephine McWilliams.
EIN: 846053496

376
Hewit Family Foundation
621 17th St., Suite 2555
Denver 80293

Established in 1985 in CO.
Donor(s): Members of the Hewit family.
Foundation type: Independent
Financial data (yr. ended 11/30/91): Assets, $2,160,874 (M); gifts received, $75,000; expenditures, $96,402; qualifying distributions, $91,612, including $90,000 for 13 grants (high: $10,000; low: $2,000).
Purpose and activities: Support primarily for health, youth organizations, social services, a natural history museum, and a zoo.
Fields of interest: Museums, social services, health, animal welfare, youth.
Limitations: Giving primarily in Denver, CO. No grants to individuals.
Application information: Application form not required.
  Initial approach: Letter
  Deadline(s): None
  Write: William D. Hewit, Pres.
Officers: William D. Hewit, Pres. and Treas.; Christie F. Andrews, V.P.; Betty Ruth Hewit, V.P.; William E. Hewit, V.P.
EIN: 742397040

377
Hill Foundation
c/o Kutak, Rock & Campbell
2400 Arco Tower, 707 17th St.
Denver 80202   (303) 297-2400
Additional address: First Interstate Bank of Denver, N.A., Terminal Annex, Box 5825, Denver, CO 80217

Trust established in 1955 in CO.
Donor(s): Virginia W. Hill.‡
Foundation type: Independent

Financial data (yr. ended 04/30/91): Assets, $9,386,600 (M); expenditures, $778,078; qualifying distributions, $623,532, including $623,532 for 72 grants (high: $35,000; low: $500; average: $10,000-$15,000).
Purpose and activities: Grants largely for health care for the medically indigent, higher education, services for the elderly, and cultural programs; support also for social service agencies and the disabled.
Fields of interest: Higher education, education, hospitals, health services, cultural programs, social services, aged, handicapped.
Types of support: Scholarship funds, matching funds, special projects.
Limitations: Giving primarily in CO and WY. No grants to individuals, or for capital improvements other than equipment acquisition for health care and related purposes.
Publications: Program policy statement, informational brochure.
Application information: Grants only to qualified charitable organizations from which the foundation will have first requested a proposal or which have been selected by the foundation to carry out one of its specific objectives. Applications not accepted.
  Initial approach: Trustees initiate proposals
  Deadline(s): 3rd Thursday of each month
  Write: John R. Moran, Jr., Trustee
Trustees: Francis W. Collopy, John R. Moran, Jr., First Interstate Bank of Denver, N.A.
Number of staff: None.
EIN: 846081879

378
Mabel Y. Hughes Charitable Trust
c/o First Interstate Bank of Denver, N.A.
P.O. Box 5825
Denver 80217   (303) 293-5324

Trust established in 1969 in CO.
Donor(s): Mabel Y. Hughes.‡
Foundation type: Independent
Financial data (yr. ended 08/31/91): Assets, $7,991,025 (M); expenditures, $470,360; qualifying distributions, $417,500, including $417,500 for 61 grants (high: $40,000; low: $2,500).
Fields of interest: Hospitals, education, museums, community funds.
Types of support: Operating budgets, continuing support, annual campaigns, seed money, emergency funds, building funds, equipment, endowment funds, research, special projects.
Limitations: Giving limited to CO, with emphasis on the Denver area. No grants to individuals, or for deficit financing, scholarships, or fellowships; no loans.
Publications: Application guidelines, 990-PF.
Application information: Application form not required.
  Initial approach: Letter
  Copies of proposal: 1
  Deadline(s): Dec. 1 of funding year
  Board meeting date(s): Dec.
  Write: Yvonne J. Baca, Sr. V.P., First Interstate Bank of Denver, N.A.
Trustee: First Interstate Bank of Denver, N.A.
Number of staff: None.
EIN: 846070398

379
Joslin-Needham Family Foundation
c/o Farmers State Bank
200 Clayton St.
Brush 80723   (303) 842-5101

Donor(s): Gladys Joslin.‡
Foundation type: Independent
Financial data (yr. ended 12/31/90): Assets, $3,184,868 (M); expenditures, $177,386; qualifying distributions, $156,873, including $146,900 for 16 grants (high: $36,000; low: $300).
Purpose and activities: Giving primarily for a hospital and a municipality; support also for a public library, social services and youth development organizations.
Fields of interest: Hospitals, libraries, civic affairs, social services, youth.
Types of support: General purposes, scholarship funds, equipment.
Limitations: Giving primarily in the Brush, CO, area.
Application information: Application form not required.
  Initial approach: Letter
  Deadline(s): None
  Write: Judy Gunnon
Directors: Robert U. Hansen, Robert Petteys.
Trustee: Farmers State Bank, Brush.
EIN: 846038670

380
Kitzmiller-Bales Trust
P.O. Box 96
Wray 80758   (303) 332-4824
Additional tel.: (303) 332-4406

Established in 1984 in CO.
Donor(s): Edna B. Kitzmiller.‡
Foundation type: Independent
Financial data (yr. ended 12/31/91): Assets, $5,863,434 (M); expenditures, $355,737; qualifying distributions, $341,249, including $341,249 for 14 grants (high: $318,000; low: $500).
Fields of interest: Civic affairs, community development, community funds, education, libraries, hospitals, health, health services, aged, cultural programs.
Types of support: Building funds, capital campaigns, equipment, matching funds, continuing support, special projects.
Limitations: Giving limited to projects benefiting the area of East Yuma County School District, RJ-2, CO.
Application information: Application form not required.
  Initial approach: Letter
  Copies of proposal: 1
  Deadline(s): None
  Board meeting date(s): Monthly
  Final notification: Following board meetings
  Write: Robert U. Hansen, Trustee
Trustees: Duard Fix, Robert U. Hansen, Farmers State Bank, Brush.
Number of staff: None.
EIN: 846178085

381
Susan M. Lindsay Trust
210 University Blvd., Suite 725
Denver 80206

Established in 1985 in CO.
Donor(s): Susan M. Lindsay.‡
Foundation type: Independent
Financial data (yr. ended 12/31/90): Assets,
$8,134,824 (M); expenditures, $307,534;
qualifying distributions, $215,249, including
$200,400 for 11 grants (high: $50,000; low:
$2,000).
Fields of interest: Health.
Limitations: Giving primarily in CO. No grants to
individuals.
Application information:
Initial approach: Letter
Write: James C. Seccombe, Jr., Esq., Trustee
Trustees: Bruce C. Hepp, James C. Seccombe, Jr.
EIN: 846198548

382
Lowe Foundation
Colorado Judicial Ctr.
Two East 14th Ave.
Denver 80203   (303) 837-3750

Incorporated in 1960 in CO.
Donor(s): John G. Lowe,‡ Edith Eaton Lowe.‡
Foundation type: Independent
Financial data (yr. ended 11/30/91): Assets,
$3,739,253 (M); expenditures, $150,849;
qualifying distributions, $144,500, including
$144,500 for 22 grants (average: $6,000).
Purpose and activities: Grants to organizations
involved in the treatment and teaching of the
mentally retarded and victims of cerebral palsy
and research in these areas.
Fields of interest: Handicapped, medical research.
Types of support: Building funds, equipment,
general purposes, operating budgets,
program-related investments, seed money.
Limitations: Giving primarily in CO. No grants to
individuals, or for endowment funds.
Publications: 990-PF, application guidelines,
annual report.
Application information: Application form not
required.
Initial approach: Letter
Copies of proposal: 5
Deadline(s): Submit proposal preferably in Jan.;
deadline Feb. 1
Board meeting date(s): Mar. and Nov.
Write: Justice Luis D. Rovira, Pres.
Officer and Trustees:* Luis D. Rovira,* Pres.;
Donald E. Burton, Richard I. Kaye, William
Martinez.
Number of staff: None.
EIN: 846021560

383
Manville Fund, Inc.
P.O. Box 5108
Denver 80217-0008   (303) 978-3863

Incorporated in 1952 in DE.
Donor(s): Manville Corp.
Foundation type: Company-sponsored
Financial data (yr. ended 12/31/90): Assets,
$900,000 (M); expenditures, $734,332;

qualifying distributions, $734,782, including
$389,800 for 51 grants, $228,482 for employee
matching gifts and $116,500 for
foundation-administered programs.
Purpose and activities: Giving primarily to those
nonprofit organizations for which employees
volunteer; support also for higher education and
employee matching gifts to community drives and
colleges and universities.
Fields of interest: Community development,
homeless, housing, hunger, higher education,
cultural programs, health, civic affairs,
environment, general charitable giving, cancer,
humanities, education, vocational education,
welfare—indigent individuals.
Types of support: General purposes, employee
matching gifts, employee-related scholarships,
special projects.
Limitations: Giving primarily in areas of company
operations. No support for groups that attempt to
influence legislation, including veterans'
organizations, or religious organizations. No
grants to individuals.
Publications: Corporate giving report, application
guidelines, informational brochure (including
application guidelines).
Application information: Application form
required.
Initial approach: Request copy of guidelines
Copies of proposal: 1
Deadline(s): Feb. 15, May 15, Aug. 15, and
Dec. 15 for community grants
Board meeting date(s): Jan., Apr., Aug., and Oct.
Write: Joy Fox, Secy.
Officers and Trustees:* Pamela J. Hamilton,*
Pres.; C. Van Draper, V.P. and Treas.; Donald L.
Ferguson, V.P.; Joseph A. Fullmer, V.P.; John L.
Grantham, V.P.; Betty Hite, V.P.; Al LeBrun, V.P.;
David E. Pullen, V.P.; Mary Rhinehart, V.P.
Number of staff: None.
EIN: 136034039

384
Monfort Charitable Foundation
1900 AA St.
Greeley 80631   (303) 353-2311

Established in 1970 in CO.
Foundation type: Independent
Financial data (yr. ended 12/31/91): Assets,
$35,088,683 (M); gifts received, $1,691,360;
expenditures, $1,084,693; qualifying
distributions, $979,602, including $979,602 for
33 grants (high: $315,000; low: $500).
Fields of interest: Community funds, cultural
programs, performing arts, cancer, education,
general charitable giving.
Types of support: General purposes.
Limitations: Giving limited to northern CO. No
grants to individuals.
Publications: 990-PF.
Application information: Application form not
required.
Deadline(s): None
Write: Dave Evans
Officers and Trustees:* Kaye C. Montera,* Pres.;
Kyle Futo,* V.P.; Kenneth W. Monfort,* Secy.-Treas.
Number of staff: None.
EIN: 237068253

385
The J. K. Mullen Foundation
(Formerly The John K. and Catherine S. Mullen
Benevolent Corporation)
1640 Logan St.
Denver 80203   (303) 893-3151

Incorporated in 1924 in CO.
Donor(s): John K. Mullen,‡ Catherine S. Mullen,‡
The J.K. Mullen Co.
Foundation type: Independent
Financial data (yr. ended 07/31/91): Assets,
$4,433,136 (M); expenditures, $347,920;
qualifying distributions, $315,804, including
$299,000 for 43 grants (high: $35,000; low:
$1,000).
Purpose and activities: Support primarily for
higher and secondary education, with emphasis
on Roman Catholic church-affiliated institutions;
some support also for health associations and
hospitals, Catholic welfare organizations, the
handicapped, and youth.
Fields of interest: Higher education, secondary
education, Catholic giving, religious schools,
health associations, hospitals, Catholic welfare,
handicapped, youth.
Limitations: Giving primarily in Denver, CO. No
grants to individuals.
Application information:
Initial approach: Letter
Copies of proposal: 1
Deadline(s): Sept. 1
Board meeting date(s): Annually and as required
Write: John F. Malo, Pres.
Officers and Directors:* John F. Malo,* Pres.;
John K. Weckbaugh,* V.P. and Secy.; Walter S.
Weckbaugh,* Treas.; J. Kenneth Malo, Jr., Timothy
M. O'Connor, Edith M. Roberts, Sheila Sevier,
Anne H. Weckbaugh.
EIN: 846002475

386
Carl A. Norgren Foundation
2696 South Colorado Blvd., No. 585
Denver 80222   (303) 758-8393

Incorporated in 1951 in CO.
Donor(s): Carl A. Norgren,‡ Juliet E. Norgren,‡
C.A. Norgren Co.
Foundation type: Independent
Financial data (yr. ended 12/31/91): Assets,
$2,766,389 (M); expenditures, $171,857;
qualifying distributions, $171,857, including
$145,600 for 71 grants (high: $19,000; low:
$500; average: $500-$2,000).
Purpose and activities: Support primarily limited
to activities in which the board has a direct
interest.
Fields of interest: Education, health, hospitals,
museums, community funds, social services,
youth.
Types of support: General purposes, annual
campaigns, emergency funds, building funds,
equipment, matching funds, capital campaigns.
Limitations: Giving limited to the metropolitan
Denver, CO, area. No grants to individuals, or for
endowment funds, research, scholarships, or
fellowships; no loans.
Publications: Annual report (including application
guidelines).
Application information: Application form not
required.

Initial approach: Letter
Copies of proposal: 1
Deadline(s): None
Board meeting date(s): June and Dec.
Write: Mr. Leigh H. Norgren, Pres.
Officers and Directors:* Leigh H. Norgren,* Pres.;
Gene N. Koelbel,* V.P.; Vanda N. Werner,* Secy.;
Donald K. Norgren.
Number of staff: None.
EIN: 846034195

387
The Jack Petteys Memorial Foundation
P.O. Box 324
Brush 80723   (303) 842-5101

Established about 1943 in CO.
Foundation type: Independent
Financial data (yr. ended 12/31/90): Assets,
$2,837,404 (M); expenditures, $149,478;
qualifying distributions, $147,947, including
$143,441 for 32 grants (high: $20,500; low:
$100).
Purpose and activities: Giving primarily to
undergraduate scholarship funds; support also for
hospitals and civic projects.
Fields of interest: Higher education, hospitals,
civic affairs.
Types of support: Scholarship funds, equipment.
Limitations: Giving limited to northeastern CO.
Application information:
  Initial approach: Letter
  Copies of proposal: 1
  Deadline(s): Submit proposal in Oct. and Nov.;
    deadline Dec. 1
  Board meeting date(s): Monthly
  Write: Robert Gunnon
Directors: Robert U. Hansen, Robert A. Petteys,
Helen C. Watrous.
Trustee: Farmers State Bank, Brush.
EIN: 846036239

388
The Piton Foundation
Kittredge Bldg.
511 16th St., Suite 700
Denver 80202   (303) 825-6246

Incorporated in 1976 in CO.
Donor(s): Samuel Gary, Gary Williams Co.
Foundation type: Operating
Financial data (yr. ended 11/30/91): Assets,
$3,610,036 (M); gifts received, $1,217,559;
expenditures, $1,780,903; qualifying
distributions, $1,127,332, including $677,332 for
64 grants (high: $25,000; low: $250), $350,000
for 1 foundation-administered program and
$100,000 for 1 loan.
Purpose and activities: Creates and supports
opportunities that allow children and adults to
move from poverty and dependency to
self-reliance and self-determination. Grantmaking
emphasis on strengthening and revitalizing
low-income neighborhoods and strengthening
families by focusing on affordable housing, the
health and well-being of children, improving
public education, self-help initiatives, promoting
economic opportunities, and promoting effective
citizen involvement.
Fields of interest: Child welfare, youth, family
services, education, education—early childhood,

education—minorities, social services, health,
welfare, community development.
Types of support: Operating budgets, seed money,
technical assistance, program-related investments,
student aid.
Limitations: Giving limited to the City of Denver,
CO.
Publications: Biennial report (including
application guidelines), program policy statement.
Application information: Applications not
accepted.
  Board meeting date(s): As required
  Write: Phyllis Buchele
Officer and Directors:* Samuel Gary,* Chair. and
Pres.; James E. Bye, Mary Gittings Cronin, Kathryn
Gary, Nancy Gary, Jack A. MacAllister, Federico
Pena, Adele Phelan, Ronald W. Williams.
Number of staff: 7 full-time professional; 2
part-time professional; 3 full-time support; 1
part-time support.
EIN: 840719486

389
Presbyterian/St. Luke's Community
Foundation
55 Madison, Suite 655
Denver 80206   (303) 322-3515
FAX: (303) 322-4576

Foundation type: Community
Financial data (yr. ended 12/31/90): Assets,
$6,501,316 (M); gifts received, $301,107;
expenditures, $2,695,802; qualifying
distributions, $1,055,592, including $855,473 for
15 grants (high: $169,921; low: $2,550) and
$200,119 for 4 grants to individuals (high:
$96,876; low: $7,320).
Purpose and activities: "To promote health care
services, research, and education that improve the
quality of human lives within the Rocky
Mountain region." Interests include addressing
health care and social needs of the elderly,
women, and children, organ transplant patients,
and cancer patients; support also for public and
health professions education.
Fields of interest: Health, health services, aged,
cancer, women, child development, mental
health.
Types of support: Grants to individuals.
Limitations: Giving limited to CO and the Rocky
Mountain Region.
Publications: Annual report, newsletter.
Application information:
  Write: Nancy H. Shanks, Ph.D., Exec. Dir.
Officers and Directors:* Robert B. Sawyer, M.D.,*
Chair.; Barbara C. Welles, Vice-Chair.; Alan P.
Pius,* Secy.-Treas.; Nancy H. Shanks, Exec. Dir.;
Norman O. Aarestad, M.D., Robert G. Boucher,
and 10 additional directors.
Recent health grants:
389-1 CHARG Resource Center, Denver, CO,
  $30,000. To design and implement medical
  screening and referral program for chronically
  mentally ill. 1990.
389-2 Colorado Cancer Research Program,
  Denver, CO, $24,944. For research and
  education related to cancer. 1990.
389-3 Denver Ear Institute, Denver, CO,
  $23,436. For audiology fellowship program.
  1990.
389-4 Grow Surgical Group, Denver, CO,
  $122,100. To assess efficacy of methods to

diagnose and differentiate cytomegalovirus
from organ rejection in kidney transplant
patients. 1990.
389-5 Institute for Transtracheal Oxygen Therapy,
  Denver, CO, $96,876. To study use of
  transtracheal oxygen therapy in treatment of
  patients with respiratory failure. 1990.
389-6 Lung Cancer Institute of Colorado, Denver,
  CO, $117,301. To establish educational and
  research efforts to prevent and treat lung
  cancer. 1990.
389-7 Presbyterian/Saint Lukes Medical Center,
  Presbyterian Aurora Hospital, Denver, CO,
  $169,921. To develop information and
  screening program for breast, cervical and skin
  cancer. 1990.
389-8 Presbyterian/Saint Lukes Medical Center,
  Saint Lukes Hospital, Denver, CO, $25,436. To
  complete research that examines factors
  influencing infant feeding decisions made by
  adolescent mothers. 1990.
389-9 Presbyterian/Saint Lukes Medical Center,
  Saint Lukes Hospital, Denver, CO, $12,000. To
  develop and conduct public seminars
  addressing issues and concerns of adolescents.
  1990.
389-10 S.E.T. Ministries of Colorado, Denver,
  CO, $30,705. For wellness clinics for elderly
  residing in public housing. 1990.
389-11 Safehouse for Battered Women, Denver,
  CO, $66,267. To provide health screening,
  medical treatment and health education to
  battered women and their children. 1990.
389-12 University of Denver, Denver, CO,
  $70,487. To develop practical and reliable
  neurologic assessment tools for low
  birthweight and two-week old infants. 1990.

390
Harry W. Rabb Foundation
6242 South Elmira Circle
Englewood 80111   (303) 721-0048

Established in 1960.
Donor(s): Harry W. Rabb.‡
Foundation type: Independent
Financial data (yr. ended 06/30/91): Assets,
$2,014,162 (M); expenditures, $145,919;
qualifying distributions, $132,310, including
$131,410 for 73 grants (high: $24,000; low:
$100).
Fields of interest: Hospitals, Jewish welfare, aged.
Types of support: Annual campaigns.
Limitations: Giving primarily in Denver, CO. No
grants to individuals.
Application information: Application form not
required.
  Initial approach: Letter (1 to 2 pages)
  Copies of proposal: 1
  Deadline(s): None
  Write: Richard A. Zarlengo, Secy.-Treas.
Officers and Trustees:* Jacob B. Kaufman,* Pres.;
Miles Dolan,* V.P.; Richard A. Zarlengo,*
Secy.-Treas.
Number of staff: 1 part-time professional.
EIN: 237236149

391
The Schramm Foundation
8528 West 10th Ave.
Lakewood 80215   (303) 232-1772

Established in 1956.
Foundation type: Independent
Financial data (yr. ended 06/30/91): Assets, $4,285,340 (M); expenditures, $220,846; qualifying distributions, $205,235, including $192,235 for 42 grants (high: $20,000; low: $1,000).
Fields of interest: Hospitals, cancer, higher education, social services, cultural programs, youth.
Types of support: Equipment, general purposes, scholarship funds, operating budgets.
Limitations: Giving limited to CO, with emphasis on the Denver area. No grants to individuals.
Application information:
  Initial approach: Letter
  Deadline(s): Aug. 15
  Write: Lesley E. Kring, Pres.
Officers: Lesley E. Kring, Pres.; Arnold Tietze, V.P.; Gary S. Kring, Secy.; Joseph Heit, Treas.
Number of staff: 4
EIN: 846032196

392
Sterne-Elder Memorial Trust
c/o Norwest Bank Denver, N.A.
1740 Broadway, MS8695
Denver 80274-8695

Established in 1977 in CO.
Donor(s): Charles S. Sterne.
Foundation type: Independent
Financial data (yr. ended 03/31/91): Assets, $4,258,589 (M); expenditures, $284,584; qualifying distributions, $261,468, including $255,000 for 45 grants (high: $50,000; low: $1,000).
Purpose and activities: Primary areas of interest include the performing arts and other cultural programs.
Fields of interest: Hospitals, health services, health associations, child welfare, social services, performing arts, cultural programs, community funds.
Types of support: Continuing support.
Limitations: Giving primarily in Denver, CO. No grants to individuals.
Application information: Application form not required.
  Initial approach: Letter
  Copies of proposal: 1
  Deadline(s): None
  Write: Michael J. Love, V.P., Norwest Bank Denver, N.A.
Director: Dorothy Elder Sterne.
Trustee: Norwest Bank Denver, N.A.
Number of staff: 1
EIN: 846143172

393
H. Chase Stone Trust
c/o Affiliated National Bank
P.O. Box 1699
Colorado Springs 80942   (719) 471-5000

Foundation type: Independent
Financial data (yr. ended 12/31/91): Assets, $2,558,360 (M); expenditures, $111,997; qualifying distributions, $104,241, including $99,608 for 21 grants (high: $15,000; low: $500).

Fields of interest: Education, higher education, performing arts, youth, health, general charitable giving.
Types of support: Equipment, renovation projects, general purposes.
Limitations: Giving limited to El Paso County, CO. No grants to individuals.
Application information: Application form not required.
  Initial approach: Letter
  Deadline(s): Apr. 30 and Oct. 31
Trustee: Affiliated National Bank.
EIN: 846066113

394
Stuart-James Foundation
P.O. Box 1407
Denver 80201-1407   (303) 796-8488

Established in 1985 in CO.
Foundation type: Independent
Financial data (yr. ended 11/30/90): Assets, $9,806 (M); gifts received, $11,460; expenditures, $301,926; qualifying distributions, $300,339, including $300,339 for 32 grants (high: $52,000; low: $100).
Fields of interest: Health services, medical research, social services, family services, music, arts.
Limitations: No grants to individuals.
Application information:
  Initial approach: Letter
  Deadline(s): None
  Write: C. James Padgett, Chair., or Stuart Graff, Pres.
Officers: C. James Padgett, Chair.; Stuart Graff, Pres.
EIN: 742411759

395
The Bal F. and Hilda N. Swan Foundation
c/o First Interstate Bank of Denver, N.A.
P.O. Box 5825, Terminal Annex
Denver 80217   (303) 293-5275

Established in 1976.
Donor(s): Bal F. Swan.‡
Foundation type: Independent
Financial data (yr. ended 12/31/90): Assets, $1,382,000 (M); expenditures, $528,931; qualifying distributions, $318,877, including $318,877 for 49 grants (high: $30,000; low: $500).
Fields of interest: Handicapped, medical research, child welfare, cultural programs, social services, higher education.
Types of support: Scholarship funds, fellowships, special projects, equipment, research, general purposes.
Limitations: Giving restricted to CO.
Publications: 990-PF.
Application information: Application form not required.
  Initial approach: Letter
  Copies of proposal: 1
  Deadline(s): None
  Write: Julie Dines, Trust Officer, First Interstate Bank of Denver, N.A.
Trustees: Richard Zarlengo, First Interstate Bank of Denver, N.A.
EIN: 742108775

396
The Ruth and Vernon Taylor Foundation ▼
1670 Denver Club Bldg.
Denver 80202   (303) 893-5284

Trust established in 1950 in TX.
Donor(s): Members of the Taylor family.
Foundation type: Independent
Financial data (yr. ended 06/30/91): Assets, $26,252,629 (M); expenditures, $1,425,007; qualifying distributions, $1,317,383, including $1,317,383 for 151 grants (high: $170,000; low: $50; average: $1,000-$20,000).
Purpose and activities: Support for education, the arts, health, human services and conservation.
Fields of interest: Higher education, secondary education, arts, cultural programs, social services, youth, ecology, conservation, hospitals, medical research.
Types of support: Research, endowment funds, building funds, general purposes.
Limitations: Giving primarily in TX, CO, WY, MT, IL, and the Mid-Atlantic states. No grants to individuals.
Application information: Application form not required.
  Initial approach: Proposal
  Copies of proposal: 1
  Deadline(s): Apr. 30 after June 1 and Sept. 1
  Board meeting date(s): May and Aug.
  Final notification: 30 days after June 1 and Sept. 1
  Write: Miss Friday A. Green, Trustee
Trustees: Ruth Taylor Campbell, Friday A. Green, Sara Taylor Swift, Vernon F. Taylor, Jr.
Number of staff: None.
EIN: 846021788
Recent health grants:
396-1 Araba Temple, Burned and Crippled Childrens Transportation Fund, Fort Myers, FL, $16,250. 1991.
396-2 Central Montana Medical Center, Lewiston, MT, $30,000. 1991.
396-3 Childrens Memorial Hospital, Willis J. Potts Heart Center, Chicago, IL, $14,000. 1991.
396-4 Cleo Wallace Center, Westminster, CO, $10,000. 1991.
396-5 Mayo Foundation, Rochester, MN, $10,000. For Vernon Taylor professorship. 1991.
396-6 Steadman Sports Medicine Foundation, Vail, CO, $10,000. 1991.

397
The Thatcher Foundation
P.O. Box 1401
Pueblo 81002
Scholarship application address: Bernadine Hardin, The Thatcher Foundation, Minnequa Bank of Pueblo, Pueblo, CO 81004; Tel.: (719) 545-2345

Established in 1924 in CO.
Foundation type: Independent
Financial data (yr. ended 12/31/90): Assets, $3,098,467 (M); expenditures, $285,985; qualifying distributions, $268,985, including $229,010 for 48 grants (high: $40,000; low: $100) and $36,354 for 25 grants to individuals (high: $3,000; low: $83).
Purpose and activities: Giving for higher education, including undergraduate scholarships,

a community fund, cultural programs, youth agencies, and health.

Fields of interest: Higher education, youth, health, cultural programs, community funds.

Types of support: Student aid, general purposes.

Limitations: Giving limited to organizations and residents of Pueblo County, CO.

Application information: Applications accepted only for scholarships; contributions to organizations are pre-selected.

   Deadline(s): Prior to beginning of school year in which assistance is requested

Officers and Trustees:* Mahlon T. White,* Pres.; Mrs. Mahlon T. White,* V.P.; Lester L. Ward, Jr.,* Secy.-Treas.; Adrian Comer, Mahlon T. White II.

EIN: 840581724

398
True North Foundation
4619 South Mason, No. C7
Fort Collins 80525   (503) 293-3348

Established in 1986 in CO.

Foundation type: Independent

Financial data (yr. ended 12/31/90): Assets, $6,885,110 (M); expenditures, $427,349; qualifying distributions, $410,429, including $389,000 for 28 grants (high: $50,000; low: $500).

Fields of interest: Conservation, environment, wildlife, family planning, family services, urban affairs, social services.

Types of support: Equipment, general purposes, research, seed money, special projects, conferences and seminars.

Limitations: Giving primarily in CA, particularly San Francisco, and will consider national giving on environmental issues. No support for religious purposes. No grants to individuals.

Publications: Informational brochure (including application guidelines).

Application information: Application form required.

   Initial approach: Letter
   Copies of proposal: 1
   Deadline(s): None
   Board meeting date(s): Approximately bimonthly
   Write: Ms. K. Hoffman, Pres.

Officer and Directors:* K. Hoffman,* Pres.; S. O'Hara, K.F. Stephens.

Number of staff: 2 part-time professional.

EIN: 742421528

399
United Bank of Denver Contributions
  Program
1700 Broadway
Denver 80274-0106   (303) 861-8811

Financial data (yr. ended 12/31/90): Total giving, $1,000,000 for grants.

Purpose and activities: Supports arts, culture, health, welfare, education, and civic affairs programs. Types of support include in-kind services and public affairs counsel.

Fields of interest: Arts, cultural programs, health, welfare, education, civic affairs, humanities, social services.

Types of support: Consulting services, building funds, capital campaigns, employee matching

gifts, operating budgets, special projects, in-kind gifts.

Limitations: Giving primarily in Denver, CO. No support for religious organizations. No grants to individuals.

Application information:

   Initial approach: Letter or proposal
   Deadline(s): No deadline; applications accepted throughout the year.
   Board meeting date(s): Continually
   Final notification: 2-3 months
   Write: Leslie Tweed, Mgr.

Number of staff: 2

400
US WEST Foundation ▼
(Formerly Mountain Bell Foundation)
7800 East Orchard Rd., Suite 300
Englewood 80111   (303) 793-6661
Application address: Local US WEST Public Relations Office or Community Relations Team

Established in 1985 in CO.

Donor(s): US WEST, and its family of companies.

Foundation type: Company-sponsored

Financial data (yr. ended 12/31/90): Assets, $13,853,913 (M); gifts received, $20,329,415; expenditures, $23,336,545; qualifying distributions, $23,300,270, including $17,274,167 for 2,596 grants (high: $300,000; low: $300; average: $500-$10,000) and $5,461,494 for 3,939 employee matching gifts.

Purpose and activities: Giving primarily for health and human services, including programs for minorities and youth; early childhood, elementary, secondary, higher, and other education; rural and community development; and cultural programs.

Fields of interest: Disadvantaged, leadership development, minorities, homeless, Native Americans, volunteerism, youth, AIDS, education, higher education, business education, secondary education, education—early childhood, education—minorities, elementary education, community development, rural development, cultural programs.

Types of support: Operating budgets, general purposes, employee matching gifts, special projects, continuing support, matching funds, seed money, technical assistance.

Limitations: Giving limited to the states served by the US WEST calling areas, including AZ, CO, IA, ID, MN, MT, ND, NE, NM, SD, OR, UT, WA, and WY. No support for international organizations, religious organizations for religious purposes, national health agencies, grantmaking foundations, school or fraternal organizations, or general operating budgets of United Way supported organizations or public educational institutions. No grants to individuals, or for endowment funds, deficit financing, scholarships, athletic funds, trips, tours, or goodwill advertising.

Publications: Annual report (including application guidelines), grants list.

Application information: Application form not required.

   Initial approach: Proposal
   Copies of proposal: 1
   Deadline(s): None
   Board meeting date(s): Feb., May, Aug., and Nov.

   Final notification: Most funds disbursed during 4th quarter each year
   Write: Larry J. Nash, Dir. of Administration

Officers and Directors:* Richard D. McCormick,* Pres.; Judith A. Servoss,* V.P.; George Ann Harding,* Secy.; Howard P. Doerr,* Treas.; Jane Prancan,* Exec. Dir.; Gary A. Ames, Joanne R. Crosson, Ron James, Jack A. MacAllister, James Smith, Solomon Trujillo, Bud Wonsiewicz.

Number of staff: 8 full-time professional.

EIN: 840978668

Recent health grants:

400-1 A Chance to Grow, Minneapolis, MN, $25,000. For Reading Recovery Project. 1990.

400-2 AIDS Housing of Washington, Seattle, WA, $10,000. For capital campaign. 1990.

400-3 Arizona State University Foundation, Tempe, AZ, $25,348. For Rural Speech and Hearing Program. 1990.

400-4 Arizona State University Foundation, Tempe, AZ, $25,348. For Rural Speech and Hearing Program. 1990.

400-5 Arizona State University Foundation, Tempe, AZ, $25,348. For Rural Speech and Hearing Program. 1990.

400-6 Arizona State University Foundation, Tempe, AZ, $25,348. For Rural Speech and Hearing Program. 1990.

400-7 Charles Drew Health Center, Omaha, NE, $10,000. For capital campaign. 1990.

400-8 Courage Center, Golden Valley, MN, $12,500. For psychosocial services. 1990.

400-9 Idaho State University, Pocatello, ID, $35,824. For Rural Speech and Hearing Program. 1990.

400-10 Idaho State University, Pocatello, ID, $35,824. For Rural Speech and Hearing Program. 1990.

400-11 Idaho State University, Pocatello, ID, $35,824. For Rural Speech and Hearing Consultation. 1990.

400-12 Idaho State University, Pocatello, ID, $35,824. For Rural Speech and Hearing Consultation. 1990.

400-13 Idaho State University, Pocatello, ID, $16,443. For Rural Speech and Hearing Consultation. 1990.

400-14 Idaho State University, Pocatello, ID, $16,000. For rural health fairs in Idaho. 1990.

400-15 LDS Hospital-Deseret Foundation, Salt Lake City, UT, $10,000. For Cancer Institute. 1990.

400-16 McKenzie-Willamette Memorial Hospital, Springfield, OR, $10,000. To enlarge short stay unit. 1990.

400-17 Merle West Medical Center, Klamath Falls, OR, $12,500. For cancer center. 1990.

400-18 Minneapolis Police Department, Minneapolis, MN, $12,500. For DARE (Drug Abuse Resistance Education) program. 1990.

400-19 Minneapolis Society for the Blind, Minneapolis, MN, $29,400. For community low vision screening project. 1990.

400-20 Primary Childrens Medical Center Foundation, Salt Lake City, UT, $25,000. For capital campaign. 1990.

400-21 Saint Charles Medical Center, Bend, OR, $10,000. For HealthyStart Prenatal Clinic. 1990.

400-22 Saint Lukes Foundation, Fargo, ND, $25,000. For Roger Maris Cancer Center. 1990.

400-23 Saint Paul Department of Police, Saint Paul, MN, $10,000. For DARE (Drug Abuse Resistance Education) Program. 1990.

400-24 Seattle Indian Health Board, Seattle, WA, $12,500. For fundraising for new site. 1990.

400-25 Senators Ski Cup, Park City, UT, $19,000. For fundraiser. 1990.

400-26 United Cerebral Palsy of the Sioux Empire, Sioux Falls, SD, $15,000. 1990.

400-27 University of Colorado, Boulder, CO, $31,752. For Rural Speech and Hearing Program. 1990.

400-28 University of Colorado, Boulder, CO, $31,057. For Rural Speech and Hearing Program. 1990.

400-29 University of Colorado, Boulder, CO, $31,057. For Rural Speech and Hearing Program. 1990.

400-30 University of Colorado, Boulder, CO, $31,057. For Rural Speech and Hearing Program. 1990.

400-31 University of Montana, Missoula, MT, $18,625. For Montana Rural Speech and Hearing Program. 1990.

400-32 University of Montana, Missoula, MT, $15,493. For Montana Rural Speech and Hearing Program. 1990.

400-33 University of Utah, Salt Lake City, UT, $25,000. For Obstetrics/Gynecology Department, Community Service Center, MESA/MEP Program and Museum. 1990.

400-34 University of Wyoming, Laramie, WY, $29,972. For Rural Speech and Hearing Program. 1990.

400-35 University of Wyoming, Laramie, WY, $29,177. For Rural Speech and Hearing Program. 1990.

400-36 University of Wyoming, Laramie, WY, $29,177. For Rural Speech and Hearing Program. 1990.

400-37 University of Wyoming, Laramie, WY, $29,177. For Rural Speech and Hearing Program. 1990.

400-38 Utah Advisory Group on Immunization Activities, Salt Lake City, UT, $10,000. For Immunization Action Month. 1990.

400-39 Variety Club of the Pacific Northwest, Seattle, WA, $18,500. To purchase Sunshine Coach for Childhaven. 1990.

401
Eleanore Mullen Weckbaugh Foundation
13064 Parkview Dr.
Aurora 80011   (303) 367-1545
Application address: P.O. Box 31678, Aurora, CO 80041

Established in 1975.

Donor(s): Eleanore Mullen Weckbaugh.‡
Foundation type: Independent
Financial data (yr. ended 03/31/91): Assets, $6,299,428 (M); expenditures, $454,435; qualifying distributions, $416,980, including $416,980 for 60 grants (high: $30,000; low: $1,000).
Purpose and activities: Emphasis on Roman Catholic church support, welfare funds, education, and missionary programs; grants also for higher and secondary education, libraries, museums and the performing arts, hospitals and hospices, health agencies, AIDS research, employment, Latin America, child welfare and development, and women.
Fields of interest: Catholic giving, arts, higher education, secondary education, libraries, health, AIDS, Latin America, child development, women.
Types of support: General purposes, scholarship funds.
Limitations: Giving primarily in CO. No grants to individuals.
Application information: Application form not required.
  Initial approach: Letter
  Copies of proposal: 1
  Deadline(s): None
  Board meeting date(s): Mar., June, Sept., and Dec.
  Write: Edward J. Limes, Pres.
Officers and Trustees:* Edward J. Limes,* Pres. and Treas.; Teresa Polakovic,* V.P. and Secy.; Jean Guyton, S.P. Guyton, Michael Polakovic.
Number of staff: 1 part-time professional.
EIN: 237437761

402
Paul R. and Anna Lee White Family Charitable Foundation
c/o Colorado National Bank of Denver
P.O. Box 5168 TA
Denver 80217

Established in 1985 in CO.
Foundation type: Independent
Financial data (yr. ended 12/31/90): Assets, $2,100,140 (M); expenditures, $96,694; qualifying distributions, $84,791, including $80,000 for 7 grants (high: $25,000; low: $5,000).
Fields of interest: Hospitals, health services, cancer, higher education.
Limitations: Giving primarily in CO. No grants to individuals.
Application information: Contributes only to pre-selected organizations. Applications not accepted.
Trustees: Lela Green, George E. White, Melvin P. White, Colorado National Bank of Denver.

EIN: 846191934

403
The Williams Family Foundation
317 Ensign St.
P.O. Box 597
Fort Morgan 80701   (303) 867-5621

Trust established about 1958 in CO.
Donor(s): A.F. Williams, M.D.,‡ Mrs. A.F. Williams.‡
Foundation type: Independent
Financial data (yr. ended 12/31/90): Assets, $5,826,695 (M); expenditures, $231,594; qualifying distributions, $210,000, including $207,150 for 18 grants (high: $88,350; low: $500).
Purpose and activities: Giving for higher and secondary education, including scholarships for medical-oriented study, hospitals, and civic affairs.
Fields of interest: Hospitals, secondary education, medical education, hospitals, civic affairs.
Types of support: Scholarship funds, research.
Limitations: Giving primarily in CO; scholarships for Morgan County high school graduates.
Application information: Scholarship applicants nominated by high schools.
  Deadline(s): None
  Final notification: Apr.
  Write: Edward L. Zorn, Trustee
Trustees: Catherine M. Woodward, Paul E. Woodward, Edward L. Zorn.
EIN: 846023379

404
Melvin & Elaine Wolf Foundation, Inc.
1560 Broadway, Suite 1000
Denver 80202   (303) 691-0370

Established in 1978 in CO.
Donor(s): Melvin Wolf, Elaine Wolf.
Foundation type: Independent
Financial data (yr. ended 06/30/91): Assets, $6,300,983 (M); expenditures, $324,069; qualifying distributions, $280,125, including $280,125 for 56 grants (high: $75,000; low: $100).
Fields of interest: Hospitals, health services, Jewish welfare, youth, social services.
Types of support: General purposes, equipment.
Limitations: Giving primarily in CO. No grants to individuals.
Application information: Contributes only to pre-selected organizations. Applications not accepted.
Officers and Directors:* Melvin Wolf,* Pres.; Elaine Wolf,* V.P.; Henry Reckler,* Treas.
EIN: 840797937

CONNECTICUT

405

Adler Foundation, Inc.
534 East Putnam Ave.
Greenwich 06830   (203) 622-9069

Incorporated in 1951 in NY.
Donor(s): Morton M. Adler,‡ Helen R. Adler,‡
Harry Rosenthal.‡
Foundation type: Independent
Financial data (yr. ended 09/30/91): Assets,
$5,029,922 (M); gifts received, $1,000;
expenditures, $302,833; qualifying distributions,
$250,625, including $250,625 for 22 grants
(high: $60,000; low: $15).
Purpose and activities: Grants chiefly for medical
research in diabetes, leukemia, and Alzheimer's
Disease.
Fields of interest: Medical research, cancer, aged.
Types of support: Research, seed money.
Limitations: No grants to individuals.
Application information: Application form not
required.
    Initial approach: Letter
    Copies of proposal: 2
    Deadline(s): None
    Board meeting date(s): Late Apr.
    Write: John Adler, Pres.
Officers and Trustees:* John Adler,* Pres.; Joel I.
Berson,* Secy.; Helen A. Potter,* Treas.; Katherine
A. Astrove, William C. Felch, William G. Kuhns,
Paul Leblang, Edmond V. Ledonne, Kenneth E.
Quickel, Jr., Wylie Vale.
Number of staff: None.
EIN: 136087869

406

Aetna Foundation, Inc. ▼
(Formerly Aetna Life & Casualty Foundation,
Inc.)
151 Farmington Ave.
Hartford 06156-3180   (203) 273-6382

Incorporated in 1972 in CT.
Donor(s): Aetna Life and Casualty Co.
Foundation type: Company-sponsored
Financial data (yr. ended 12/31/90): Assets,
$40,393,110 (M); gifts received, $5,007,438;
expenditures, $10,023,550; qualifying
distributions, $9,956,802, including $9,073,170
for grants (high: $1,225,000; low: $300; average:
$500-$25,000) and $868,390 for employee
matching gifts.
Purpose and activities: To help preserve a viable
society by supporting programs and organizations
that can have a real impact on solving social
problems and by providing support that will
stimulate other donors. Priority areas for giving
are problems of urban public education; minority
higher education; improving minority youth
employment opportunities; urban neighborhood
revitalization; reform of the civil justice system;
support for the arts (only in the Hartford area);
and social services, with an emphasis on AIDS.
The foundation encourages employee
participation in community affairs through
support for regional grants and FOCUS,
foundation initiatives that serve the headquarters
city, Hartford, CT, and cities where Aetna has
major field office operations, and several
international initiatives in countries where the
company operates. Other programs for
employees are the Dollars-for-Doers program and
matching gifts for higher education.
Fields of interest: Urban development, urban
affairs, community development, education,
education—minorities, higher education,
educational associations, literacy, leadership
development, youth, employment, minorities,
housing, law and justice, arts, performing arts,
disadvantaged, AIDS, international affairs,
insurance education.
Types of support: Matching funds, employee
matching gifts, employee-related scholarships,
scholarship funds, special projects, annual
campaigns, renovation projects.
Limitations: Giving limited to organizations in the
U.S. No support for religious organizations for
religious purposes, private secondary schools, or
sporting events. No grants to individuals, or for
endowment funds, medical research, capital or
building funds, or renovation projects; or annual
operating funds for colleges, universities, social
service agencies, secondary schools, museums,
hospitals, or other such institutions; no grants for
computer hardware; no loans.
Publications: Corporate giving report (including
application guidelines), program policy statement,
informational brochure (including application
guidelines).
Application information: Application form
required for FOCUS grants, Dollars for Doers, and
Matching Gifts.
    Initial approach: Letter with proposal summary
    Copies of proposal: 1
    Deadline(s): None
    Board meeting date(s): Feb., May, July, and Nov.
    Final notification: 2 months
    Write: Diana Kinosh, Management Information
    Supervisor
Officers and Directors:* William H. Donaldson,*
Chair.; Ronald E. Compton,* Pres.; Sanford Cloud,
Jr.,* V.P. and Exec. Dir.; Stephen B. Middlebrook,*
V.P.; Frederick W. Kingsley, Treas.; Robert A.
Morse,* Comptroller; Peter Arakas, Counsel;
Arthur R. Ashe, Jr., Marian W. Edelman, Barbara
Hackman Franklin, Edward K. Hamilton, James T.
Lynn, Frank R. O'Keefe.
Number of staff: 10 full-time professional; 7
full-time support.
EIN: 237241940
Recent health grants:
406-1 AIDS Council of Northeastern New York,
Albany, NY, $10,000. For AIDS grant. 1990.
406-2 AIDS Family Service of New York, NYC,
NY, $10,000. 1990.
406-3 AIDS Project/Hartford, Hartford, CT,
$25,900. 1990.
406-4 American Council on Science and Health,
NYC, NY, $10,000. 1990.
406-5 Center City Churches, Hartford, CT,
$10,000. For AIDS grant. 1990.
406-6 Charter Oak Terrace Rice Heights Health
Center, Hartford, CT, $10,000. 1990.
406-7 Community Health Center, Middletown,
CT, $40,000. 1990.
406-8 Community Health Services, Hartford, CT,
$20,000. 1990.
406-9 Community Response, Oak Park, IL,
$18,500. For AIDS grant. 1990.
406-10 Compeer, Rochester, NY, $10,000. 1990.
406-11 CONIN - Corporacion Para La Nutricion
Infantil, Santiago, Chile, $20,000. 1990.
406-12 Connecticut AIDS Residence Program,
New Haven, CT, $10,000. 1990.
406-13 Cystic Fibrosis Foundation, Atlanta, GA,
$10,000. 1990.
406-14 DYouville College, Buffalo, NY, $10,000.
For AIDS grant. 1990.
406-15 Easter Seal Rehabilitation Center of
Hartford, Hartford, CT, $10,000. 1990.
406-16 Episcopal Diocese of Connecticut, AIDS
Ministries, Hartford, CT, $19,000. 1990.
406-17 Fremont Public Association, Seattle, WA,
$10,000. For AIDS grant. 1990.
406-18 Gay Mens Health Crisis (GMHC), NYC,
NY, $10,000. 1990.
406-19 Georgetown University, Institute for
Health Policy Analysis, DC, $15,000. 1990.
406-20 Hartford Action Plan on Infant Health,
Hartford, CT, $50,000. 1990.
406-21 Hill Health Corporation, New Haven,
CT, $10,000. For AIDS grant. 1990.
406-22 James Whitcomb Riley Memorial
Association, Indianapolis, IN, $14,000. For
AIDS grant. 1990.
406-23 Minnesota AIDS Project, Minneapolis,
MN, $15,000. 1990.
406-24 National Community AIDS Partnership,
DC, $50,000. For grant shared with Cleveland
Foundation. 1990.
406-25 National Fund for Medical Education,
Boston, MA, $20,000. 1990.
406-26 National Leadership Coalition on AIDS,
DC, $25,000. 1990.
406-27 National Minority AIDS Council, DC,
$15,000. 1990.
406-28 New Beginnings, Lewiston, ME, $19,000.
For AIDS grant. 1990.
406-29 Raritan Bay Healthcare Foundation, Perth
Amboy, NJ, $10,000. For AIDS grant. 1990.
406-30 Southeastern Connecticut AIDS Project,
New London, CT, $20,000. 1990.
406-31 Stewart B. McKinney Foundation,
Fairfield, CT, $10,000. For AIDS grant. 1990.
406-32 Tri-County Alcohol Council, Rushford
Center, Middletown, CT, $43,500. 1990.
406-33 Tri-State Drug Rehabilitation and
Counseling Program, Cincinnati, OH,
$10,000. For Kids Helping Kids. 1990.
406-34 United Action for Youth, Iowa City, IA,
$17,000. For AIDS grant. 1990.
406-35 United Way of the Capital Area,
Combined Health Appeal, Hartford, CT,
$1,225,000. 1990.
406-36 Visiting Nurse Association of
Connecticut, New Britain, CT, $12,000. 1990.
406-37 Youth Advocates, San Francisco, CA,
$12,000. For AIDS grant. 1990.

407

Aetna Life & Casualty Company
Contributions Program
151 Farmington Ave., RE1B
Hartford 06156   (203) 273-3340

Financial data (yr. ended 12/31/90): Total giving,
$4,162,820, including $3,829,823 for 172 grants
(high: $859,456) and $332,997 for in-kind gifts.

Purpose and activities: "We believe that good corporate citizenship contributes to our success as a company. Our participation in addressing social issues has involved identifying and funding programs within a diverse, yet carefully focused set of priorities. For the last several years, these priorities have been education and youth employment, civil justice reform, neighborhood revitalization, civic involvement in our field office communities, and community-based AIDS services." Support also for leadership development, and the United Way. A portion of corporate giving consists of manager-referred programs in the communities where Aetna is located. National grants are those for organizations outside of Hartford or those with nationwide programs; regional grants are made primarily in Hartford or nearby. In addition to providing pro-bono services and in-kind donations, Aetna lends money for community development through the Corporate Responsibility Investment Committee. As part of its program to aid youth, Aetna designed and funds the Saturday Academy, which is run by public school teachers for students who are at risk of dropping out. The academies are in Hartford, CT, and Washington, DC. In 1991, corporate and foundation grantmaking and community investment priorities will undergo thorough examination and reassessment.
Fields of interest: Education, minorities, youth, law and justice, social services, arts, higher education, education—minorities, community development, civic affairs, urban affairs, educational associations, urban development, housing, disadvantaged, community funds, leadership development, health, hospitals.
Types of support: In-kind gifts, employee volunteer services.
Limitations: No support for religious organizations for religious purposes, private secondary schools, or non-501(c)(3) organizations, medical research, or political activities. No grants to individuals, or for capital or endowment drives, medical research, fundraising dinners or similar special events, sporting events, and conferences.
Publications: Corporate giving report.
Application information: If the staff believes a program will be more appropriately served by one of the regional or field offices, the inquiry may be referred to the nearest field office for review.
  Initial approach: Preliminary letter of inquiry
  Copies of proposal: 1
  Deadline(s): None
  Final notification: Applicant will receive an approximate schedule for the review and decision
Corporate Public Involvement Staff: Thomas Q. Callahan, Robert L. Hill, Marie F. Massaro, Marjorie R. Mlodzinski, Stephen T. Moskey, Gail B. Promboin, Glenda C. Reed, Patricia A. Sheeran, Richard J. Wackenreuter.
Corporate Public Involvement Advisory Group: John J. Dwyer, Chair., Advisory Group; Mary Ann Champlin, David Chew, Laura R. Estes, William C. Hogue, Hylan T. Hubbard, Elizabeth Krupnic, Stephen B. Middlebrook, T. Jerald Moore.

408
American Brands, Inc. Contributions Program
1700 East Putnam Avenue
Old Greenwich 06870   (203) 698-5148
Additional address: P.O. Box 811, Old Greenwich, CT 06870

Financial data (yr. ended 12/31/90): Total giving, $13,787,117, including $13,424,369 for grants (average: $500-$5,000) and $362,748 for employee matching gifts.
Purpose and activities: Supports programs concerning the following: arts and humanities, civic and public affairs, education, health, social services, women and minorities in business. Types of support include employee gift matching and in-kind services.
Fields of interest: Arts, cultural programs, civic affairs, education, education—minorities, health, hospitals, women, minorities.
Types of support: Employee matching gifts, in-kind gifts, employee volunteer services, use of facilities, capital campaigns, donated products.
Limitations: Giving primarily in operating locations. No support for fraternal organizations, member agencies of united funds, or religious organizations for sectarian purposes. No grants to individuals.
Publications: Corporate report.
Application information: Include a description of project and 501(c)(3) status letter; Public Affairs office handles giving. Application form not required.
  Initial approach: Letter of inquiry; send requests to headquarters
  Copies of proposal: 1
  Deadline(s): None
  Final notification: One month
  Write: Roger W.W. Baker, Secy., Contribs. Comm.

409
ASEA Brown Bover Corporate Giving Program
(Formerly Combustion Engineering Corporate Giving Program)
900 Long Ridge Road
P.O. Box 9308
Stamford 06904   (203) 328-7646

Purpose and activities: Supports the arts and higher education, including minority education, health organizations including hospitals, hospices, and national disease associations, community funds, employment programs, help for the disadvantaged, individuals, family planning, conservation, ecology, engineering, science and technology, and programs to benefit minorities and women and disadvantaged persons; also gives for human and civil rights.
Fields of interest: Community funds, conservation, ecology, higher education, minorities, science and technology, women, engineering, environment, education, arts, health, health associations, education—minorities, employment, civil rights, disadvantaged, family planning, human rights, Native Americans.
Types of support: Endowment funds, scholarship funds, capital campaigns, employee matching gifts, fellowships, operating budgets, research, special projects, conferences and seminars.

Limitations: Giving primarily in headquarters state and national operating locations. No support for tax-supported, political, fraternal, or veterans' organizations. No grants to individuals.
Publications: Corporate report.
Application information: Application form not required.
  Initial approach: Query letter to headquarters or nearest company facility
  Deadline(s): Best time to apply is between Aug. and Oct.
  Board meeting date(s): Within one month of receiving request
  Final notification: Within 6 weeks
  Write: Richard P. Randazzo, Contribs. and Community Affairs; Dorothy D. Arnette, Educational Contribs.; Dr. Jack Sanderson, Science and Technology Contribs.

410
The Beatrice Fox Auerbach Foundation ▼
25 Brookside Blvd.
West Hartford 06107   (203) 232-5854

Incorporated in 1941 by special Act of the CT Legislature.
Donor(s): Beatrice Fox Auerbach,‡ Fannie F. Samuels, Standard Investment Co.
Foundation type: Independent
Financial data (yr. ended 12/31/91): Assets, $33,829,777 (M); expenditures, $1,734,561; qualifying distributions, $1,513,040, including $1,464,232 for 63 grants (high: $200,000; low: $100; average: $1,000-$25,000).
Purpose and activities: Giving for social service and youth agencies, including a community fund, health and hospitals, Jewish welfare funds, higher education, and some cultural organizations.
Fields of interest: Social services, youth, community funds, health, hospitals, Jewish welfare, higher education.
Types of support: Endowment funds, general purposes.
Limitations: Giving primarily in the Hartford, CT, area. No grants to individuals.
Application information: Application form not required.
  Initial approach: Proposal
  Deadline(s): None
  Write: Dorothy A. Schiro, Treas.
Officers and Trustees:* Bernard Schiro,* Chair.; Georgette A. Koopman,* Pres.; Dorothy A. Schiro,* V.P. and Treas.; Elizabeth A. Schiro, Secy.; Rena B. Koopman.
Number of staff: 1
EIN: 066033334

411
Bank of Boston Connecticut Corporate Giving Program
81 West Main St.
Waterbury 06720   (203) 574-7522

Financial data (yr. ended 12/31/90): Total giving, $350,000, including $230,000 for grants and $120,000 for employee matching gifts.
Purpose and activities: Support for education, employment, and training, higher education, health and human services, culture and the arts, social services, civic and community affairs, memberships, benefits, and program ads; also

provides in-kind contributions of personnel, products, and facilities. In addition, the Bank matches employee pledges to United Way branches.
Fields of interest: Community funds, education, employment, vocational education, higher education, health, social services, cultural programs, arts, civic affairs, community development.
Types of support: In-kind gifts.
Limitations: Giving limited to CT. No support for religious or fraternal organizations.
Application information:
Initial approach: Letter
Write: Bill Stanley, V.P., External Affairs

412
The Barden Foundation, Inc.
200 Park Ave.
Danbury 06810 (203) 744-2211

Incorporated in 1959 in DE.
Donor(s): The Barden Corp.
Foundation type: Company-sponsored
Financial data (yr. ended 10/31/91): Assets, $5,671,787 (M); gifts received, $8,877; expenditures, $445,825; qualifying distributions, $357,070, including $343,695 for 48 grants (high: $100,000; low: $50) and $13,375 for 18 grants to individuals (high: $1,000; low: $313).
Purpose and activities: Emphasis on higher education, including an employee-related scholarship award program administered through colleges and universities; giving also for hospitals, a community fund, and the handicapped; scholarships are restricted to sons and daughters of The Division of The Barden Corp.
Fields of interest: Higher education, hospitals, community funds, handicapped.
Types of support: Employee-related scholarships, general purposes.
Limitations: Giving primarily in CT.
Publications: Informational brochure.
Application information: Application information for scholarship program available from Scholarship Committee, The Barden Corp. Application form required.
Deadline(s): Apr. 1
Officers and Trustees:* Stanley Noss,* Pres.; Eduard Baruch,* Secy.; R.D. Moore,* Treas.; R.H. Buch, T.R. Hensal, T.F. Loughman.
EIN: 066054855

413
Carl and Dorothy Bennett Foundation, Inc.
28 Windrose Way
Greenwich 06830

Established in 1963.
Donor(s): Caldor, Inc., Carl Bennett, and other members of the Bennett family.
Foundation type: Independent
Financial data (yr. ended 06/30/91): Assets, $4,744,824 (M); gifts received, $424,665; expenditures, $377,394; qualifying distributions, $362,141, including $340,803 for 27 grants (high: $100,000; low: $100).
Fields of interest: Jewish welfare, hospitals, higher education.

Limitations: Giving primarily in CT. No grants to individuals.
Application information: Contributes only to pre-selected organizations. Applications not accepted.
Write: Carl Bennett, Pres.
Officers and Directors:* Carl Bennett,* Pres.; Marc Bennett,* V.P.; Malcolm E. Martin,* Secy.; Dorothy Bennett,* Treas.; Bruce Bennett, Robin Bennett Kanarek, Harold Karun, Matthew Manes, Grace Tully.
EIN: 066051371

414
Walter J. and Lille A. Berbecker Scholarship Fund
c/o Cummings & Lockwood
P.O. Box 120
Stamford 06904 (203) 351-4294

Established in 1988 in NY.
Foundation type: Independent
Financial data (yr. ended 02/28/91): Assets, $5,073,856 (M); expenditures, $517,773; qualifying distributions, $446,681, including $425,000 for 7 grants (high: $100,000; low: $25,000).
Fields of interest: Higher education, medical education.
Types of support: Scholarship funds.
Application information:
Initial approach: Letter
Deadline(s): None
Write: Robert A. Beer, Esq., Trustee
Trustees: Robert A. Beer, Earle W. Moffitt, F. Brower Moffitt, Francis P. Schiaroli.
EIN: 222801843

415
Bodenwein Public Benevolent Foundation
c/o Shawmut Bank Connecticut, N.A.
250 State St.
New London 06320-0911 (203) 447-6133

Established in 1938 in CT.
Donor(s): The Day Trust, Theodore Bodenwein.‡
Foundation type: Independent
Financial data (yr. ended 12/31/91): Assets, $371,125 (M); gifts received, $196,929; expenditures, $237,339; qualifying distributions, $232,970, including $221,565 for 26 grants (high: $57,800; low: $327; average: $327-$57,800).
Purpose and activities: Giving to social service and health agencies, including AIDS support, the fine and performing arts and other cultural programs, youth and child welfare agencies, civic affairs and community development groups, education, and minority programs.
Fields of interest: Arts, youth, aged, women, AIDS, health, health services, family services, family planning, community development, minorities, education—early childhood, adult education, libraries, religion, transportation.
Types of support: Building funds, capital campaigns, conferences and seminars, consulting services, equipment, matching funds, publications, renovation projects, research, scholarship funds, seed money, special projects.
Limitations: Giving limited to Lyme, Old Lyme, East Lyme, Waterford, New London, Montville,

Groton, Ledyard, Stonington, North Stonington, and Salem, CT.
Publications: Informational brochure (including application guidelines), program policy statement.
Application information: An applicant is limited to submission of 1 grant application per calendar year. Application form required.
Initial approach: Telephone
Copies of proposal: 1
Deadline(s): May 15 and Nov. 15
Board meeting date(s): Jan. and July
Final notification: Feb. 1 and Aug. 1
Write: Mildred E. Devine, V.P., Shawmut Bank Connecticut, N.A.
Trustee: Shawmut Bank Connecticut, N.A.
Number of staff: None.
EIN: 066030548

416
Donald C. Brace Foundation
c/o R.A. Beer, Esq., Cummings & Lockwood
P.O. Box 120
Stamford 06904-0120
Application address: 919 Third Ave., New York, NY 10022-9998; Tel.: (212) 586-1640

Established in 1987 in CT.
Donor(s): Donna Brace Ogilvie.
Foundation type: Independent
Financial data (yr. ended 12/31/91): Assets, $4,122,078 (M); expenditures, $425,851; qualifying distributions, $397,484, including $382,500 for 7 grants (high: $300,000; low: $2,500).
Purpose and activities: Support primarily for a hospital; some support also for cultural programs.
Fields of interest: Hospitals, cultural programs.
Limitations: Giving primarily in Stamford, CT, and Westhampton, NY.
Application information:
Initial approach: Letter
Deadline(s): None
Write: Paul Gitlin, Esq., Trustee
Trustees: Katherine Butler, Paul Gitlin, John Brace Latham, Donna Brace Ogilvie, Karen Scheid.
EIN: 133442680

417
The Bridgeport Area Foundation, Inc.
280 State St.
Bridgeport 06604 (203) 334-7511

Incorporated in 1967 in CT.
Foundation type: Community
Financial data (yr. ended 12/31/91): Assets, $11,576,018 (M); gifts received, $2,436,251; expenditures, $1,048,806; qualifying distributions, $761,340, including $761,340 for 392 grants (high: $75,536; low: $16; average: $3,000-$5,000).
Purpose and activities: Grants to organizations and for projects that benefit named local communities including support for higher and other education, social service agencies, health, and culture.
Fields of interest: Education, higher education, cultural programs, social services, health, drug abuse, homeless, civic affairs, housing, AIDS, environment.
Types of support: Continuing support, seed money, emergency funds, consulting services,

technical assistance, conferences and seminars, special projects, general purposes, scholarship funds.

Limitations: Giving primarily in Bridgeport, Easton, Fairfield, Milford, Monroe, Shelton, Stratford, Trumbull, and Westport, CT. No grants to individuals, or for operating budgets, deficit financing, or major capital gifts; no loans.

Publications: Annual report (including application guidelines), newsletter, application guidelines, financial statement, informational brochure (including application guidelines).

Application information: Application form required.

> *Initial approach:* Letter
> *Copies of proposal:* 2
> *Deadline(s):* Feb. 15, May 15, and Sept. 15
> *Board meeting date(s):* Mar., July and Nov.; Distribution Committee meets in Mar., June, and Oct.
> *Final notification:* Nov.
> *Write:* Richard F. Freeman, Pres. and C.E.O.

Officers and Directors:* Richard P. Bodine, Sr.,* Chair.; David J. Sullivan, Jr.,* Vice-Chair.; Richard F. Freeman,* Pres. and C.E.O.; Robert J. Ashkins,* Secy.; Henry L. Katz,* Treas.; John P. Bassett, Anthony J. Cernera, George R. Dunbar, Frank G. Elliott, Jr., M.D., Michael H. Flynn, Norwick R.G. Goodspeed, Lois J. Hughes, John Marshall Lee, George B. Longstreth, Carmen L. Lopez, Newman M. Marsilius, Jr., John F. Menchent, Anthony V. Milano, Robert D. Scinto, Harold C. Smith, Jack C. Stawarky, Jr., Richard I. Steiber, George F. Taylor, Robert S. Tellalian, James F. Tomchik, Philip Trager, William S. Warner, Ernest A. Wiehl, Jr., Peter Wilkinson, Austin K. Wolf.

Distribution Committee: James F. Tomchik, Chair.; Carmen L. Lopez, Vice-Chair.; H. Richard Brew, Mrs. Henry B. duPont III, Geraldine W. Johnson, Mrs. Hobant C. Kneitler, Peter T. Mott, Ronald B. Noren, Meredith Baum Reuben, Reginald L. Sapp, Greta E. Solomon.

Trustees: Chase/CT, Connecticut National Bank, Lafayette Bank & Trust Co., People's Bank.

Number of staff: 3 full-time professional; 1 part-time support.

EIN: 066103832

418
The Bulkley Foundation Trust

25 Forest Rd.
Weston 06883-2307   (203) 227-8161

Established in 1989 in CT.
Foundation type: Independent
Financial data (yr. ended 12/31/90): Assets, $3,082,095 (M); expenditures, $345,910; qualifying distributions, $284,689, including $284,689 for 41 grants (high: $25,000; low: $500; average: $500-$25,000).
Purpose and activities: Primary areas of interest include welfare and family services, cancer and heart disease, and community funds.
Fields of interest: Child welfare, family services, welfare—indigent individuals, homeless, hunger, hospices, nursing, alcoholism, cancer, heart disease, volunteerism, community funds.
Types of support: Annual campaigns, scholarship funds, building funds, capital campaigns.
Limitations: Giving primarily in the greater Norwalk, CT, area.

Application information: Application form not required.

> *Copies of proposal:* 1
> *Deadline(s):* None
> *Write:* Kenneth M. Park, Trustee

Trustees: William O. Keene, Kenneth M. Park.
Number of staff: None.
EIN: 066332021

419
Champion International Corporate Contributions Program

One Champion Plaza
Stamford 06921   (203) 358-7000

Financial data (yr. ended 12/31/90): Total giving, $7,025,147, including $6,156,534 for grants (high: $750,000; low: $500; average: $2,500-$5,000), $742,684 for 3,724 employee matching gifts and $125,929 for in-kind gifts.
Purpose and activities: "In addition to our shareholders and customers, we believe we have equally important responsibilities to our employees, to the communities in which we operate, and to society at large. Champion believes that responsible corporate citizenship is good business." Support for middle school and higher education, literacy, business, technical, engineering, and minority education. Also supports the United Way, natural resources and the environment, hospital building funds, volunteerism, human services, visual and graphic arts, and national organizations.
Fields of interest: Education, environment, social services, hospitals—building funds, volunteerism, arts, fine arts, education—minorities, business education, higher education, engineering, AIDS, literacy, health, civic affairs, conservation, educational associations, hospitals, libraries, minorities, museums, science and technology, youth.
Types of support: Building funds, capital campaigns, employee matching gifts, general purposes, special projects, donated products, donated land, employee volunteer services, employee-related scholarships, endowment funds, matching funds, scholarship funds.
Limitations: Giving limited to areas of company operations. No support for political candidates or organizations, sports events, or religious, veterans' or fraternal organizations unless funds donated are used to benefit the general public. No grants to individuals, or for endowments, dinners, benefits, conferences, one-time activities, advertisements, or supplementary operating funds for United Way agencies.
Publications: Informational brochure (including application guidelines), corporate giving report, application guidelines.
Application information: Company has a staff that only handles contributions. The Contributions Committee, made up of senior executives, reviews requests six times a year. Requests can be sent to the nearest Champion facility or the headquarters. Application form not required.

> *Initial approach:* Request "Guidelines for Giving" for proper procedure
> *Copies of proposal:* 1
> *Deadline(s):* None
> *Final notification:* In 3 weeks as to whether request fits guidelines and will be reviewed

within 10 days after final review by Contributions Committee
> *Write:* Maris Vanasse, Dir., Corp. Contribs. and Community Relations

Number of staff: 3 full-time professional; 2 full-time support.

420
Frances Chapin Foundation

31 Linden Tree Rd.
Wilton 06897

Incorporated in 1966 in NJ.
Donor(s): Frances C. Crook.‡
Foundation type: Independent
Financial data (yr. ended 03/31/91): Assets, $3,586,523 (M); expenditures, $159,114; qualifying distributions, $152,926, including $148,800 for 30 grants (high: $35,000; low: $1,000).
Purpose and activities: Emphasis on hospitals, hospices and other social services, youth, higher and secondary education, and cultural programs, including art museums; support also for conservation and historic preservation.
Fields of interest: Hospitals, cultural programs, museums, social services, hospices, youth, secondary education, higher education, conservation, historic preservation.
Limitations: Giving primarily in CT, IL, and AZ. No grants to individuals.
Application information: Contributes only to pre-selected organizations. Applications not accepted.
Officer and Director:* Thomas O. Maxfield III,* Pres.
EIN: 226087456

421
Chesebrough-Pond's Corporate Giving Program

33 Benedict Place
P.O. Box 6000
Greenwich 06836   (203) 661-2000

Purpose and activities: Supports education, health, welfare, the arts, civic affairs, and an AIDS program.
Fields of interest: Education—minorities, family services, general charitable giving, education, health, welfare, cultural programs, arts, civic affairs.
Types of support: Building funds, capital campaigns, employee matching gifts, fellowships, general purposes, operating budgets, special projects, scholarship funds, research.
Limitations: Giving primarily in operating locations. No support for political or religious groups, current United Way recipients, or government-supported agencies. No grants to individuals, or for endowments or seed money; very few fellowships given.
Publications: Informational brochure.
Application information: Application form required.

> *Initial approach:* Letter
> *Copies of proposal:* 1
> *Deadline(s):* None
> *Board meeting date(s):* 4-5 times yearly
> *Final notification:* Within 1-3 1/2 months

Write: Janet Hooper, Mgr., Corp. Social Responsibility
Number of staff: 1 full-time professional; 1 full-time support.

422
The Jane Coffin Childs Memorial Fund for Medical Research ▼

333 Cedar St.
P.O. Box 3333
New Haven 06510   (203) 785-4612

Trust established in 1937 in CT.
Donor(s): Alice S. Coffin,‡ Starling W. Childs.‡
Foundation type: Independent
Financial data (yr. ended 06/30/91): Assets, $27,479,027 (M); gifts received, $108,600; expenditures, $1,917,737; qualifying distributions, $1,799,701, including $1,583,046 for 61 grants (high: $29,000; low: $2,500; average: $12,500-$24,500) and $35,892 for 1 foundation-administered program.
Purpose and activities: "Primarily for medical research into the causes, origins and treatment of cancer." Grants to institutions only for support of cancer research fellowships.
Fields of interest: Medical research, cancer.
Types of support: Fellowships, research.
Limitations: No grants to individuals, or for building or endowment funds, matching gifts, or general purposes; no loans.
Publications: Annual report, program policy statement, application guidelines.
Application information: Applicants for fellowships in general should not be more than 30 years old and not more than two years postdoctoral. They must hold either an M.D. or a Ph.D. in the field in which they propose to study. Applicants may be citizens of any country, but, for foreign nationals, awards will be made only for study in the U.S. American citizens may hold a fellowships either in the U.S. or in a foreign country. The initial appointment may be for 1 or 2 years, with the possibility of renewal for a 3rd year. Applications must be approved by the affiliated institution. Application form required.
  Initial approach: Letter or telephone
  Copies of proposal: 17
  Deadline(s): Feb. 1
  Board meeting date(s): Oct. or Nov. and Apr. or May
  Final notification: Nov. and May
  Write: Elizabeth M. Ford, Admin. Dir.
Officers and Managers:* John W. Childs, Chair.; H. Allen Mali, Vice-Chair.; William G. Gridley, Jr.,* Treas.; Joan A. Steitz, Dir.; Robert N. Schmalz, Legal Counsel; John W. Barclay, Edward C. Childs, James E. Childs, Richard S. Childs, Jr., Patrick Crossman, Edgar Koerner, Donald S. Lamm, Mrs. James F. Lawrence, Starling R. Lawrence.
Number of staff: 1 full-time professional; 1 part-time professional; 1 full-time support.
EIN: 066034840

423
Wellsford Starr and Mildred M. Clark Medical Memorial Fund

(Formerly W.S. Clark & M.M. Clark Memorial Trust Fund)
c/o Bank of Boston Connecticut, Trust Tax Dept.
P.O. Box 2210
Waterbury 06722
Application address: Waterbury Medical Assn., 30 Central Ave., Waterbury, CT 06702

Established in 1989 in CT.
Donor(s): Mildred Clark.‡
Foundation type: Independent
Financial data (yr. ended 12/31/91): Assets, $2,162,907 (M); expenditures, $204,304; qualifying distributions, $188,428, including $48,575 for 14 grants (high: $11,250; low: $87) and $137,177 for 36 grants to individuals (high: $9,150; low: $25).
Purpose and activities: Scholarships for medical students.
Fields of interest: Medical education.
Application information: Application form required.
  Deadline(s): Jan. 1 of applicant's third year of medical school
  Write: Alice J. Zeiss, Trust Admin.
Directors: Jeffrey Alter, M.D., Craig Czarsty, M.D., Joseph Renda, M.D., Richard Rostecki, M.D.
Trustee: Bank of Boston Connecticut.
EIN: 066326364

424
Connecticut Mutual Life Corporate Giving Program

140 Garden St.
Hartford 06154   (203) 727-6500

Financial data (yr. ended 12/31/90): Total giving, $18,063, including $14,063 for grants and $4,000 for in-kind gifts.
Purpose and activities: "The Connecticut Mutual Life Insurance Company has been distinguished throughout its long history by unusual commitment to high principles of corporate purpose and business ethics. That commitment has been reflected not only in the firm belief that normal business functions must be carried out with a sense of responsibility beyond that required by the marketplace, but also in the conviction that sound business practice requires Connecticut Mutual to strive for a creative leadership position in meeting its responsibilities both to its local community of Hartford and to society generally. One of the components of that commitment is a planned program of corporate contributions which benefits policyholders, employees and the general public by supporting the continued sound functioning of Connecticut Mutual and by furthering the public welfare." Most giving is through the foundation. The Community Relations Program supports local events such as benefits which the company considers to be of importance in the community, donations of surplus equipment, and use of facilities, and Social Purpose Investments. Federated drives are conducted annually in the Home Office on behalf of the Greater Hartford United Way and the Combined Health Appeal. No other federated drives or social service solicitations of employees are conducted.

Fields of interest: Community development, business, minorities, economics, disadvantaged, women, AIDS, arts, education, education—minorities, employment, health, higher education, homeless, housing, leadership development, secondary education.
Types of support: Program-related investments, loans, in-kind gifts, employee volunteer services.
Limitations: Giving primarily in the Hartford, CT, area. No support for sectarian organizations whose services benefit only members of a particular denomination, or member agencies of the United Way of the Capital Area. No grants for goodwill advertising.
Application information: Application form not required.
  Initial approach: Brief letter
  Deadline(s): None
  Write: Astrida R. Olds, Corp. Responsibility Officer
Number of staff: 2 full-time professional; 1 part-time professional; 1 full-time support.

425
The Connecticut Mutual Life Foundation, Inc. ▼

140 Garden St.
Hartford 06154   (203) 727-6500

Established in 1976.
Donor(s): Connecticut Mutual Life Insurance Co.
Foundation type: Company-sponsored
Financial data (yr. ended 12/31/90): Assets, $8,662,163 (M); gifts received, $75; expenditures, $1,488,414; qualifying distributions, $1,363,326, including $1,173,542 for 181 grants (high: $115,400; low: $300; average: $3,000-$6,000) and $189,784 for 1,016 employee matching gifts.
Purpose and activities: Giving largely for education, particularly higher education, equal opportunity and employment programs, social services, including housing, civic affairs, health agencies, and cultural programs.
Fields of interest: Higher education, elementary education, secondary education, vocational education, minorities, employment, community development, housing, health, AIDS, cultural programs.
Types of support: Operating budgets, continuing support, seed money, matching funds, employee matching gifts, technical assistance, program-related investments, scholarship funds, special projects, capital campaigns, internships, loans.
Limitations: Giving primarily in the Hartford, CT, area. No support for sectarian groups, political organizations, or federated drives outside the local area. No grants to individuals, or for endowment funds, deficit financing, emergency funds, publications, land acquisition, scholarships, fellowships, capital fund drives outside the local area, or goodwill advertising.
Publications: Corporate giving report, informational brochure (including application guidelines).
Application information: Application form not required.
  Initial approach: Letter or proposal
  Copies of proposal: 1
  Deadline(s): None
  Board meeting date(s): Mar. and Nov.
  Final notification: 3 months

Write: Astrida R. Olds, Exec. Dir.
Officers and Directors:* Myron P. Curzan,* Pres.; Walter J. Gorski,* V.P.; Katharine K. Miller, Secy.; William J. Sullivan, Treas.; Constance Clayton, William Ellis, Robert Furek, Denis F. Mullane, William C. Steere, Jr.
Number of staff: 2 full-time professional; 1 part-time professional; 1 full-time support.
EIN: 510192500
Recent health grants:

425-1 AIDS Ministries Episcopal Diocese, Hartford, CT, $10,000. For operating grant for minority outreach program. 1990.

425-2 Community Health Services, Hartford, CT, $15,000. For operating grant for neighborhood health clinic. 1990.

425-3 Hartford Action Plan on Infant Health, Hartford, CT, $90,000. For operating grant for infant mortality and teen pregnancy prevention. 1990.

425-4 Hartford Hospital, Hartford, CT, $50,000. For capital grant for expansion and renovation. 1990.

426
Charles E. Culpeper Foundation, Inc. ▼
Financial Centre
695 East Main St., Suite 404
Stamford 06901-2138   (203) 975-1240
FAX: (203) 975-1847

Incorporated in 1940 in CT; re-incorporated in 1955 in NY.
Donor(s): Charles E. Culpeper.‡
Foundation type: Independent
Financial data (yr. ended 12/31/91): Assets, $135,763,345 (M); expenditures, $7,631,388; qualifying distributions, $5,793,022, including $5,793,022 for 174 grants (high: $250,000; low: $500; average: $26,000).
Purpose and activities: Grants to organizations concerned with health, education, including higher and medical education, medical research, arts and culture, and the administration of justice.
Fields of interest: Health, medical research, medical sciences, health services, education, higher education, medical education, arts, law and justice.
Types of support: Research, general purposes, special projects, seed money.
Limitations: No grants to individuals, or conduit organizations; no loans. Rarely supports endowments, building funds, operating budgets, conferences, or travel.
Publications: Informational brochure (including application guidelines), multi-year report.
Application information:
  Initial approach: Proposal
  Copies of proposal: 1
  Deadline(s): None
  Board meeting date(s): Quarterly
  Write: Linda E. Jacobs, V.P., Programs
Officers and Directors:* Francis J. McNamara, Jr.,* Pres.; Philip M. Drake,* V.P. and Secy.-Treas.; Michael G. Ulasky, Comptroller; Colin G. Campbell, Joseph F. Fahey, Jr., Ronald P. Lynch, John Morning, John C. Rose, M.D.
Number of staff: 5 full-time professional; 1 part-time professional; 1 full-time support.
EIN: 131956297
Recent health grants:

426-1 Door - A Center of Alternatives, NYC, NY, $25,000. Toward adolescent health center. 1991.

426-2 Georgetown University, DC, $60,000. Toward career development in area of medical ethics and philosophy of medicine. 1991.

426-3 Massachusetts General Hospital, Boston, MA, $150,000. Toward research. 1991.

426-4 Memorial Sloan-Kettering Cancer Center, NYC, NY, $100,000. Toward program in cellular biochemistry and biophysics. 1991.

426-5 Norwalk Hospital, Norwalk, CT, $300,000. Toward ambulatory surgical suite. 1991.

426-6 Research Foundation of the State University of New York, Kings County Hospital Center, Brooklyn, NY, $68,800. Toward research on congenital syphilis in infants. 1991.

426-7 Saint Vincents Medical Center Foundation, College of Nursing, Bridgeport, CT, $100,000. Toward student enrichment and library services. 1991.

426-8 University of California, Los Angeles, CA, $97,200. For Medical Humanities Scholar. 1991.

426-9 University of California, San Francisco, CA, $324,000. For Medical Science Scholar. 1991.

426-10 University of Medicine and Dentistry of New Jersey, Robert Wood Johnson Medical School, Camden, NJ, $97,200. For Medical Humanities Scholar. 1991.

426-11 University of North Carolina, Chapel Hill, NC, $97,200. For Medical Humanities Scholar. 1991.

426-12 University of Washington, School of Medicine, Seattle, WA, $10,000. Toward Birth of Bioethics Conference. 1991.

426-13 Vanderbilt University, Nashville, TN, $108,000. For Medical Science Scholar. 1991.

426-14 Washington University, Saint Louis, MO, $324,000. For Medical Science Scholar. 1991.

426-15 Yale University, New Haven, CT, $324,000. For Medical Science Scholar. 1991.

427
The Daphne Seybolt Culpeper Memorial Foundation, Inc.
129 Musket Ridge Rd.
Norwalk 06850   (203) 762-3984
Application address: P.O. Box 206, Norwalk, CT 06852

Established in 1983 in DE.
Donor(s): Daphne Seybolt Culpeper.‡
Foundation type: Independent
Financial data (yr. ended 12/31/91): Assets, $11,798,274 (M); expenditures, $551,379; qualifying distributions, $511,183, including $495,500 for 125 grants (high: $35,000; low: $250).
Fields of interest: Higher education, education, welfare, child welfare, Native Americans, health, hospitals, handicapped.
Types of support: Annual campaigns, continuing support, equipment, general purposes, matching funds, scholarship funds.
Limitations: Giving primarily in CT and FL. No grants to individuals.
Publications: Application guidelines.
Application information: Application form not required.

Initial approach: Letter
Copies of proposal: 1
Deadline(s): None
Board meeting date(s): Varies
Write: Nicholas J. Nardi, Secy.-Treas.
Officers: Rodney S. Eielson, Pres.; Nicholas J. Nardi, Secy.-Treas.
Number of staff: 1 part-time professional.
EIN: 222478755

428
The Hazel Dell Foundation
c/o Carroll & Lane
P.O. Box 771
Norwalk 06852   (203) 853-6565

Incorporated in 1956 in DE.
Donor(s): Harry C. McClarity.‡
Foundation type: Independent
Financial data (yr. ended 12/31/91): Assets, $2,735,859 (M); expenditures, $185,598; qualifying distributions, $158,870, including $111,750 for 45 grants (high: $17,000; low: $100) and $12,000 for 1 grant to an individual.
Purpose and activities: Giving primarily for hospitals and medical centers; support also for higher and other education, including limited student aid, churches, and municipal police and fire departments.
Fields of interest: Hospitals, education, higher education, religion—Christian, civic affairs.
Limitations: Giving primarily in CT, NY, and NJ.
Application information: Application form not required.
  Deadline(s): None
  Write: June M. Powers, Pres.
Officers and Directors:* June M. Powers,* Pres.; Joy S. Dunlop,* Secy.; Thomas F. Ryan, Treas.; Gail A. Fallon, Diane Schroeder, William J. Sullivan.
EIN: 136161744

429
Marie G. Dennett Foundation
c/o Whitman & Ransom
Two Greenwich Plaza, P.O. Box 2250
Greenwich 06836-2250   (203) 862-2361

Incorporated in 1956 in IL.
Donor(s): Marie G. Dennett,‡ Priscilla D. Ramsey.
Foundation type: Independent
Financial data (yr. ended 08/31/91): Assets, $3,506,833 (M); expenditures, $157,992; qualifying distributions, $155,749, including $152,000 for 53 grants (high: $10,000; low: $500).
Fields of interest: Hospitals, health services, education, cultural programs, youth, conservation, wildlife.
Limitations: No grants to individuals.
Application information: Application form not required.
  Initial approach: Proposal
  Deadline(s): Sept. 30
  Board meeting date(s): Oct.
  Final notification: Dec.; notification only to applicants selected for grants
  Write: William B. Smith, Esq.
Officers and Trustees:* Priscilla D. Ramsey,* Pres.; Lyle B. Ramsey,* V.P.; Everett Fisher,* Secy.-Treas.; Peter H. Blair, James D. Farley,

Dennett W. Goodrich, John A. Goodrich, Richard L. Ramsey.
Number of staff: None.
EIN: 061060970

430
Dexter Corporation Foundation, Inc.
One Elm St.
Windsor Locks 06096   (203) 627-9051

Established in 1976.
Donor(s): The Dexter Corp.
Foundation type: Company-sponsored
Financial data (yr. ended 12/31/90): Assets, $198,348 (M); gifts received, $400,000; expenditures, $517,430; qualifying distributions, $516,502, including $421,340 for 243 grants (high: $13,860; low: $7) and $95,162 for 204 employee matching gifts.
Purpose and activities: Grants largely for higher education, including employee matching gifts, and for community funds, public policy organizations, business and professional organizations, health and youth agencies, and cultural and historic programs.
Fields of interest: Higher education, community funds, public policy, business, health, youth, cultural programs, historic preservation.
Types of support: Employee matching gifts, annual campaigns, capital campaigns, scholarship funds.
Limitations: Giving primarily in areas of business operations. No grants to individuals.
Publications: Application guidelines.
Application information:
   Initial approach: Letter
   Deadline(s): None
   Write: K. Grahame Walker, Pres.
Officers and Director:* David L. Coffin,* Chair.; K. Grahame Walker, Pres. and C.E.O.; Robert E. McGill III, V.P.; Bruce H. Beatt, Secy.; David A. Willis, Treas.
EIN: 061013754

431
Echlin Corporate Contributions Program
100 Double Beach Rd.
Branford 06405   (203) 481-5751

Purpose and activities: Support for child welfare and development, youth programs; giving also for hospices and hospitals.
Fields of interest: Child development, child welfare, education, youth, hospices, hospitals.
Types of support: Annual campaigns, capital campaigns.
Limitations: Giving primarily in communities where Echlin has facilities and employees.
Application information: Funds have been committed for future years. Applications not accepted.
   Write: Joe Onoratio, Treas.
Administrators: Milton Makoski, V.P., Human Resources; Anne Fitzgerald, Secy.; Joe Onorato.

432
The Sidney and Arthur Eder Foundation, Inc.
P.O. Box 949
New Haven 06504   (203) 934-8381

Incorporated in 1954 in CT.
Donor(s): Sidney Eder,‡ Arthur Eder, Eder Bros., Inc.
Foundation type: Independent
Financial data (yr. ended 12/31/90): Assets, $3,902,499 (M); gifts received, $133,000; expenditures, $331,663; qualifying distributions, $318,400, including $280,350 for 48 grants (high: $145,000; low: $50) and $38,050 for 16 grants to individuals (high: $6,000; low: $1,000).
Purpose and activities: Grants primarily to local Jewish welfare funds, hospitals and health services, and educational institutions; also awards scholarships for children of present or former employees of Eder Bros., Inc.
Fields of interest: Jewish welfare, hospitals, health services, education.
Types of support: Operating budgets, continuing support, annual campaigns, seed money, emergency funds, building funds, employee-related scholarships.
Limitations: Giving primarily in CT. No grants for matching gifts; no loans.
Application information: Application form required for scholarships.
   Initial approach: Letter
   Board meeting date(s): Semiannually
   Write: Richard Weiss, Trustee
Officers and Trustees:* Arthur Eder,* Chair.; Richard M. Weiss,* Secy.; Andrew J. Eder,* Treas.; Jill Paulette Weiss.
Number of staff: None.
EIN: 066035306

433
The Educational Foundation of America ▼
35 Church Ln.
Westport 06880   (203) 226-6498
Grant application office: 23161 Ventura Blvd., Suite 201, Woodland Hills, CA 91364; Tel.: (818) 999-0921

Trust established in 1959 in NY.
Donor(s): Richard P. Ettinger,‡ Elsie Ettinger,‡ Richard P. Ettinger, Jr., Elaine P. Hapgood, Paul R. Andrews,‡ Virgil P. Ettinger,‡ Barbara P. Ettinger, John G. Powers.
Foundation type: Independent
Financial data (yr. ended 12/31/90): Assets, $98,517,440 (M); gifts received, $69,414; expenditures, $5,323,260; qualifying distributions, $4,573,855, including $4,305,063 for 88 grants (high: $375,000; low: $7,362; average: $10,000-$50,000).
Purpose and activities: Grants primarily for arts, education, the environment and medical sciences; giving also for higher education, including education for American Indians, medical education, and medical research; population control, children's education, and research in gerontology.
Fields of interest: Education, secondary education, higher education, medical education, medical research, medical sciences, family planning, aged, arts, theater, fine arts, libraries, environment, energy, youth, Native Americans.
Types of support: General purposes, operating budgets, continuing support, seed money, professorships, internships, scholarship funds, matching funds, special projects, research, publications, fellowships.

Limitations: No grants to individuals, or for capital or endowment funds; no loans.
Publications: Annual report, application guidelines.
Application information: Application form not required.
   Initial approach: Letter
   Copies of proposal: 1
   Deadline(s): None
   Board meeting date(s): Mar., July, and Nov.
   Final notification: 2 to 3 months
   Write: Diane M. Allison, Exec. Dir.
Officer: Diane M. Allison, Exec. Dir.
Directors: Barbara P. Ettinger, Chair.; Jerry Babicka, Lynn P. Babicka, David W. Ehrenfeld, Richard P. Ettinger, Jr., Wendy P. Ettinger, Elaine P. Hapgood, Edward E. Harrison, Heidi Landesman, Erica Pifer, John P. Powers, Rosalind C. Whitehead, Paul Windels, Jr.
Number of staff: 1 full-time professional; 3 part-time professional; 4 part-time support.
EIN: 133424750
Recent health grants:
433-1   American Indian Graduate Center, Albuquerque, NM, $40,000. For medical and health-related scholarships and general support. 1991.
433-2   Association for Voluntary Surgical Contraception, NYC, NY, $12,400. For expanded no-scalpel vasectomy training program. 1991.
433-3   Catholics for a Free Choice, DC, $50,000. For grassroots organizing and Hispanic outreach projects. 1991.
433-4   Childhood Cancer Research Institute, Arlington, MA, $25,000. For collaborative programs on monitoring child health risks of radiation contamination. 1991.
433-5   International Projects Assistance Services, Carrboro, NC, $40,028. For introduction of Manual Vacuum Aspiration (MVA) to Mexican National Institute of Perinatology. 1991.
433-6   Interplast, Palo Alto, CA, $40,000. For Host Country Program in Cusco, Peru. 1991.
433-7   Johns Hopkins University, Baltimore, MD, $115,604. For Plasticity and Recovery of Human Brain. 1991.
433-8   National Toxics Campaign Fund, Boston, MA, $45,000. For Citizens' Environmental Laboratory. 1991.
433-9   Planned Parenthood League of Connecticut, New Haven, CT, $100,000. For Emergency Access Fund. 1991.
433-10   Planned Parenthood-World Population Los Angeles, Los Angeles, CA, $50,000. For South Bay Clinic: Meeting Family Planning and Abortion Needs in Los Angeles County. 1991.
433-11   Reproductive Health Technologies Project, DC, $30,000. For general support. 1991.

434
EIS Foundation, Inc.
19 West Walk
Clinton 06413   (203) 669-5367
Additional address (Oct. 15 to May 15): c/o 4900 Sanctuary Ln., Boca Raton, FL 33431; Tel.: (407) 368-1074

Incorporated in 1951 in CT.

Donor(s): Joseph W. Gilfix,‡ C.C. Weiss,‡ and members of the Weiss and Schwarz families.
Foundation type: Independent
Financial data (yr. ended 12/31/90): Assets, $2,485,466 (M); gifts received, $9,203; expenditures, $221,242; qualifying distributions, $210,598, including $196,164 for 73 grants (high: $30,000; low: $100).
Purpose and activities: Grants largely for welfare funds, hospitals, higher education, care of the aged and physically handicapped, temple support, and Israel.
Fields of interest: Welfare, hospitals, higher education, aged, handicapped, Jewish giving, Israel.
Types of support: Capital campaigns, continuing support, emergency funds, scholarship funds.
Limitations: Giving primarily in CT, NY, and FL. No grants to individuals.
Application information:
Initial approach: Letter
Deadline(s): None
Board meeting date(s): Quarterly
Write: Maurice L. Schwarz, Pres.
Officers and Director:* Maurice L. Schwarz,* Pres. and Treas.; Bernard M. Schwarz, V.P. and Secy.-Treas.
Number of staff: None.
EIN: 066021896

435
The Ensworth Charitable Foundation
c/o Connecticut National Bank
777 Main St. MSN 242
Hartford 06115   (203) 728-2274

Trust established in 1948 in CT.
Donor(s): Antoinette L. Ensworth.‡
Foundation type: Independent
Financial data (yr. ended 05/31/90): Assets, $10,751,453 (M); gifts received, $6,956; expenditures, $606,669; qualifying distributions, $568,446, including $528,448 for 108 grants (high: $14,250; low: $500).
Fields of interest: Health, AIDS, welfare, youth, environment, religion, arts, education.
Types of support: Continuing support, seed money, emergency funds, matching funds, conferences and seminars.
Limitations: Giving limited to Hartford, CT, and vicinity. No grants to individuals, or for operating budgets, annual campaigns, deficit financing, building or endowment funds, equipment and materials, land acquisition, renovation projects, scholarships, fellowships, research, or publications; no loans.
Publications: 990-PF, program policy statement, application guidelines.
Application information: Application form required.
Initial approach: Letter or full proposal
Copies of proposal: 5
Deadline(s): 18th of month preceding board meetings
Board meeting date(s): Feb., May, Aug., and Nov.
Final notification: 1 month
Write: Amy Lynch
Trustee: Connecticut National Bank.
Number of staff: 1 full-time professional.
EIN: 066026018

436
The Sherman Fairchild Foundation, Inc. ▼
71 Arch St.
Greenwich 06830   (203) 661-9360

Incorporated in 1955 in NY.
Donor(s): May Fairchild,‡ Sherman Fairchild.‡
Foundation type: Independent
Financial data (yr. ended 12/31/90): Assets, $195,410,048 (M); gifts received, $3,447; expenditures, $14,392,317; qualifying distributions, $12,454,573, including $12,139,583 for 50 grants (high: $1,250,000; low: $14,000; average: $100,000-$800,000).
Purpose and activities: Emphasis on higher education and fine arts and cultural institutions; some support for medical research and social welfare.
Fields of interest: Higher education, cultural programs, fine arts, medical research, social services.
Application information: Application form not required.
Initial approach: Proposal
Deadline(s): None
Write: Patricia A. Lydon, V.P.
Officers and Directors:* Walter Burke,* Pres. and Treas.; Bonnie Himmelman,* Exec. V.P.; Patricia A. Lydon, V.P.; Sandra S. Weiksner, Secy.; Walter F. Burke III, William Elfers, Robert P. Henderson, Paul D. Paganucci, Agnar Pytte.
Number of staff: 1 full-time support; 1 part-time support.
EIN: 131951698
Recent health grants:
436-1 Case Western Reserve University, Cleveland, OH, $250,000. For nursing program. 1990.
436-2 Columbia Presbyterian Medical Center, NYC, NY, $1,099,069. For Information/Communications Center. 1990.
436-3 Hospital for Special Surgery, NYC, NY, $146,460. To purchase electron microscope. 1990.
436-4 Memorial Sloan-Kettering Cancer Center, NYC, NY, $999,069. For Radiation Oncology Treatment Center. 1990.
436-5 Saint Lukes-Roosevelt Hospital Center, NYC, NY, $125,000. For master plan rebuilding program. 1990.
436-6 Stanford University, Stanford, CA, $800,000. For M.D./Ph.D. Training Program. 1990.
436-7 University of California, San Francisco, CA, $450,000. For degenerative diseases research. 1990.

437
Fox Steel Company Giving Program
312 Boston Post Rd.
Orange 06477   (203) 799-2356

Purpose and activities: Giving for education, health, arts and culture, civic affairs, and general purposes.
Fields of interest: Education, health, arts, cultural programs, civic affairs, general charitable giving.
Application information:
Write: Jay I. Vlock, Pres.

438
General Electric Company Contributions Program
Bldg. E1A
3135 Easton Turnpike
Fairfield 06431   (203) 373-3216

Financial data (yr. ended 12/31/90): Total giving, $28,326,811, including $27,975,603 for grants (high: $10,420,340; low: $100) and $351,208 for in-kind gifts.
Purpose and activities: General Electric's direct giving program is decentralized, with each plant following its own giving procedures. Support is provided for education, arts and culture, health, community development, civic affairs, and general contribution causes.
Fields of interest: Education, arts, cultural programs, health, community development, civic affairs, general charitable giving, France, Japan, Canada.
Types of support: Donated equipment, donated products, employee volunteer services.
Limitations: Giving primarily in communities where GE has a significant presence; support abroad includes France, Japan, Canada and other operating locations. No grants to individuals.
Application information: The company has a staff that only handles contributions. Application form not required.
Initial approach: Contact local GE Community Relations Manager
Copies of proposal: 1
Deadline(s): None
Board meeting date(s): Varies
Write: Clifford Smith, Fdn. Pres.
Number of staff: 7 full-time professional; 4 full-time support.

439
General Electric Foundation ▼
(also known as GE Foundation)
3135 Easton Tpke.
Fairfield 06431   (203) 373-3216

Trust established in 1952 in NY.
Donor(s): General Electric Co.
Foundation type: Company-sponsored
Financial data (yr. ended 12/31/90): Assets, $15,359,675 (M); gifts received, $563,550; expenditures, $22,270,233; qualifying distributions, $21,224,875, including $14,735,889 for 443 grants (high: $600,000; average: $5,000-$100,000) and $5,466,494 for employee matching gifts.
Purpose and activities: Institutional grants primarily in support of education, with emphasis on: 1)strengthening specific areas of work in undergraduate education; 2)graduate-level research and teaching; 3)support for disciplinary fields, including the physical sciences, engineering, computer science, mathematics, industrial management, and business administration; 4)support for minority group education programs, with emphasis on engineering and business; and 5)matching educational contributions of employees and retirees. Support also for community funds in communities where the company has a significant presence, selected public schools, arts and cultural centers, public issues research and analysis, equal opportunity, international

understanding, and other special grants. Grants are directed toward specific programs authorized by the trustees and most are approved in advance of each calendar year.

Fields of interest: Higher education, educational associations, educational research, education—minorities, business education, physical sciences, engineering, science and technology, computer sciences, mathematics, urban affairs, community funds, arts, cultural programs, public policy, intercultural relations, civil rights, AIDS.

Types of support: Annual campaigns, continuing support, employee matching gifts, fellowships, general purposes, publications, research, scholarship funds, seed money, special projects.

Limitations: Giving limited to the U.S.; grants to community funds limited to areas where the company has a significant presence. No support for religious or sectarian groups. No grants to individuals, or for capital or endowment funds, or other special purpose campaigns, scholarships, or equipment donations; no loans.

Publications: Annual report (including application guidelines), informational brochure.

Application information: Application form not required.

Initial approach: Proposal
Copies of proposal: 1
Deadline(s): None
Board meeting date(s): Quarterly
Final notification: Varies
Write: Clifford V. Smith, Jr., Pres.

Officers: Clifford V. Smith, Jr., Pres.; Michael J. Cosgrove, Treas.; Jane L. Polin, Comptroller; William J. Sheeran.

Trustees: Dennis D. Dammerman, Chair.; James P. Baughman, Frank P. Doyle, Benjamin W. Heineman, Jr., Joyce Hergenhan, Jack O. Peiffer.

Number of staff: 7 full-time professional; 4 full-time support.

EIN: 146015766

Recent health grants:

439-1 American Council on Science and Health, NYC, NY, $10,000. 1990.

439-2 Harvard University, School of Public Health, Cambridge, MA, $25,000. 1990.

439-3 Institute for Evaluating Health Policy Risks, Irvine, CA, $25,000. 1990.

439-4 Media-Advertising Partnership for a Drug-Free America, NYC, NY, $50,000. 1990.

439-5 Nancy Reagan Foundation, DC, $10,000. 1990.

439-6 National Council on the Aging, DC, $25,000. 1990.

439-7 National Leadership Coalition for Health Care Reform, DC, $25,000. 1990.

440
General Electric Foundation, Inc.
(also known as GE Foundation, Inc.)
3135 Easton Tpke.
Fairfield 06431   (203) 373-3216

Established in 1985 in CT.
Donor(s): General Electric Co.
Foundation type: Company-sponsored
Financial data (yr. ended 12/31/90): Assets, $0 (M); expenditures, $799,736; qualifying distributions, $799,353, including $737,286 for 71 grants (high: $80,000; low: $250; average: $5,000-$50,000).

Purpose and activities: Giving primarily to innovative organizations that will play a significant role internationally in advancing charitable, scientific, literary, or educational programs.

Fields of interest: Intercultural relations, international relief, international development.

Types of support: Special projects, research, employee matching gifts.

Limitations: Giving limited to foreign or domestic organizations whose funds will be spent outside the U.S. No support for religious or sectarian groups. No grants to individuals, or for capital or endowment funds, scholarships, or equipment donations; no loans.

Publications: Annual report (including application guidelines).

Application information: Ability to respond to unsolicited proposals is extremely limited. Applications for funding is largely by invitation only. Application form not required.

Initial approach: Proposal
Copies of proposal: 1
Deadline(s): None
Board meeting date(s): Quarterly
Final notification: Varies
Write: Clifford V. Smith, Jr., Pres.

Officers: Clifford V. Smith, Jr., Pres.; Michael J. Cosgrove, Treas.; Jane L. Polin, Comptroller.

Directors: Dennis D. Dammerman, Chair.; James P. Baughman, Frank P. Doyle, Benjamin W. Heineman, Joyce Hergenhan, Jack O. Peiffer, William J. Sheeran.

Number of staff: 3 part-time professional; 1 part-time support.

EIN: 222621967

Recent health grants:

440-1 American University of Beirut Hospital, Beirut, Lebanon, $10,000. 1990.

440-2 Assistance Publique-Hopitaux De Paris, Paris, France, $40,000. 1990.

440-3 Project HOPE, Cairo, Egypt, $50,000. 1990.

440-4 SEE International, Santa Barbara, CA, $10,000. 1990.

440-5 Texas Childrens Hospital, Houston, TX, $25,000. 1990.

441
General Signal Corporate Giving Program
One High Ridge Park
Box 10010
Stamford 06904   (203) 357-8800

Financial data (yr. ended 12/31/90): Total giving, $770,000 for grants.

Purpose and activities: Supports education, social services, health, civic affairs, and cultural programs; employee matching gifts for education only.

Fields of interest: Education, social services, health, civic affairs, cultural programs, health services, hospitals.

Types of support: Donated equipment, donated products, employee matching gifts, in-kind gifts, special projects, capital campaigns.

Limitations: Giving primarily in headquarters area and operating areas.

Publications: Corporate report.

Application information: Human Resources handles giving. Application form not required.

Initial approach: Write to headquarters or nearest company facility
Copies of proposal: 1
Deadline(s): None
Write: Eilene M. F. Joyce, Dir., E.E.O. and Mgr., Human Resources

442
Herbert Gilman Family Charitable Foundation
165 Orchard Rd.
West Hartford 06117

Established in 1964 in CT.
Foundation type: Independent
Financial data (yr. ended 01/31/91): Assets, $816,402 (M); expenditures, $530,403; qualifying distributions, $529,128, including $529,128 for 43 grants (high: $176,336; low: $8).

Fields of interest: Jewish welfare, higher education, hospitals, health.

Types of support: General purposes.

Limitations: Giving primarily in Hartford, CT. No grants to individuals.

Application information: Contributes only to pre-selected organizations. Applications not accepted.

Trustees: Evelyn Gilman, Randy Gilman.

EIN: 066071321

443
Bernard F. and Alva B. Gimbel Foundation, Inc.
c/o Bregman & Co.
600 Summer St.
Stamford 06901   (203) 325-4155

Incorporated in 1943 in NY.
Donor(s): Bernard F. Gimbel,‡ Alva B. Gimbel.‡
Foundation type: Independent
Financial data (yr. ended 12/31/91): Assets, $5,798,794 (M); expenditures, $458,988; qualifying distributions, $458,988, including $380,221 for 43 grants (high: $29,800; low: $221).

Fields of interest: Social services, homeless, child welfare, family services, health services, hospitals, family planning, rehabilitation, environment, arts.

Types of support: Continuing support, special projects.

Limitations: Giving primarily in NY and CT. No grants for scholarships, fellowships, or matching gifts; no loans.

Application information:
Initial approach: Letter
Copies of proposal: 1
Deadline(s): None
Board meeting date(s): Nov.
Write: Carol Lebworth, Pres., and Hope Solinger, Secy.-Treas.

Officers and Directors:* Carol G. Lebworth,* Pres.; Hope G. Solinger,* Secy.-Treas.; Glenn H. Greenberg, Lynn Stern.

EIN: 136090843

444
GTE Foundation ▼
One Stamford Forum
Stamford 06904   (203) 965-3620

Trust established in 1952 in NY as the Sylvania Foundation; renamed in 1960 as General Telephone & Electronics Foundation; renamed again in 1982.
Donor(s): GTE Corp., and subsidiaries.
Foundation type: Company-sponsored
Financial data (yr. ended 12/31/91): Assets, $27,054,123 (M); gifts received, $18,097,648; expenditures, $19,384,892; qualifying distributions, $19,317,522, including $18,054,655 for 1,468 grants.
Purpose and activities: Emphasis on higher education in mathematics, science, and technology, and retention of minority students; sponsors an employee-related scholarship program through the College Scholarship Service; support also for community funds, the performing arts, and social service agencies.
Fields of interest: Education, higher education, education—minorities, science and technology, community funds, performing arts, fine arts, museums, social services, volunteerism, hospitals.
Types of support: Emergency funds, scholarship funds, fellowships, employee matching gifts, continuing support, employee-related scholarships, lectureships, operating budgets, special projects, program-related investments.
Limitations: Giving limited to areas of company operations and national organizations deemed to be of broad benefit to GTE companies, employees, shareholders, or customers. No grants to individuals (except for scholarships to the children of GTE employees), or for research.
Publications: Annual report, application guidelines.
Application information: Application form required.
   Initial approach: Letter or proposal
   Copies of proposal: 2
   Deadline(s): Summer
   Board meeting date(s): Feb., May, Aug., Nov., and as required
   Final notification: After Dec. 15
   Write: Maureen Gorman, Fdn. V.P. and Secy. and Dir., Corp. Social Responsiblility, GTE Corp.
Officer: Maureen Gorman, V.P. and Secy.
Trustees: Charles R. Lee,* Chair.; Bruce Carswell, Edward C. MacEwen, Edward Schmults, Nicholas Trivisonno, Bankers Trust Co.
Number of staff: 5 full-time professional; 4 full-time support; 2 part-time support.
EIN: 136046680
Recent health grants:
444-1 All Childrens Hospital, Saint Petersburg, FL, $20,000. 1990.
444-2 Casa Colina Foundation, Pomona, CA, $10,000. 1990.
444-3 Downey Community Hospital, Downey, CA, $10,000. For Memorial Trust Fund. 1990.
444-4 Durhams War on Drug and Alcohol Abuse, Durham, NC, $25,000. 1990.
444-5 El Camino Hospital Foundation, Mountain View, CA, $20,000. 1990.
444-6 Irving Healthcare System, Irving, TX, $25,000. 1990.
444-7 Liberation Programs, Stamford, CT, $15,000. 1990.
444-8 Massachusetts General Hospital, Boston, MA, $15,000. 1990.
444-9 Massachusetts General Hospital, Boston, MA, $10,000. 1990.

444-10 Providence Hospital, Everett, WA, $10,000. For children's center. 1990.
444-11 Saint Francis Health Care System of Hawaii, Honolulu, HI, $10,000. 1990.
444-12 Saint Johns Regional Medical Center, Oxnard, CA, $15,000. 1990.
444-13 Saint Joseph Medical Center, Stamford, CT, $15,000. 1990.
444-14 Salem Hospital, Salem, MA, $20,000. 1990.
444-15 Salem Hospital, Salem, MA, $10,000. 1990.
444-16 Stamford Hospital, Stamford, CT, $25,000. 1990.
444-17 Torrance Memorial Hospital, Torrance, CA, $10,000. 1990.
444-18 Venice Family Clinic, Venice, CA, $13,000. 1990.
444-19 Vitam Center, Norwalk, CT, $25,000. 1990.

445
Ellen Knowles Harcourt Foundation, Inc.
c/o George Verenes
12 Aspetuck Ave.
New Milford 06776
Application address: 51 Main St., New Milford, CT 06776; Tel.: (203) 355-2631

Established in 1982 in CT.
Donor(s): Ellen Knowles Harcourt.‡
Foundation type: Independent
Financial data (yr. ended 12/31/91): Assets, $2,262,288 (M); expenditures, $98,330; qualifying distributions, $81,193, including $71,725 for 30 grants (high: $10,000; low: $100).
Fields of interest: Higher education, conservation, health, civic affairs.
Types of support: Scholarship funds, general purposes.
Limitations: Giving primarily in the New Milford, CT, area. No grants to individuals.
Application information:
   Initial approach: Letter
   Deadline(s): None
   Write: Paul Altermatt, Pres.
Officers and Directors:* Paul B. Altermatt,* Pres.; Barbara Chappus,* Secy.; R. McFarlane Tilley,* Secy.; George Verenes,* Treas.; Adele F. Ghisalbert, Alice McCallister, Leandro Pasqual.
EIN: 061068025

446
The Hartford Courant Foundation, Inc.
285 Broad St.
Hartford 06115   (203) 241-6472

Established in 1950 in CT as a corporate foundation; restructured in 1980 as a private, independent foundation.
Foundation type: Independent
Financial data (yr. ended 12/31/91): Assets, $11,353,783 (M); expenditures, $709,935; qualifying distributions, $656,804, including $623,304 for 73 grants (high: $65,000; average: $3,000-$10,000) and $33,500 for 34 grants to individuals (average: $500-$2,000).
Purpose and activities: Giving primarily for arts and cultural programs, education, health and social service agencies, and emerging community needs; support also for promotion of excellence

in secondary school scholarship; aid for Hispanic students through foundation-operated program.
Fields of interest: Arts, cultural programs, health, social services, welfare—indigent individuals, community development, education, education—minorities, secondary education, general charitable giving.
Types of support: Land acquisition, building funds, capital campaigns, equipment, general purposes, operating budgets, renovation projects, seed money, special projects, technical assistance, matching funds, publications, scholarship funds.
Limitations: Giving limited to central CT, including Tolland, Hartford, and Middlesex counties. No support for religious organizations (for sectarian purposes), veterans', fraternal, professional, or business associations, political groups, or private schools. No grants to individuals or for continuing support, endowment or emergency funds, conferences, performances, or other short-term, one-time events; no loans.
Publications: Annual report, application guidelines, informational brochure (including application guidelines).
Application information: Application form required.
   Initial approach: Telephone
   Copies of proposal: 1
   Deadline(s): Dec. 15, Mar. 15, June 15, and Sept. 15
   Board meeting date(s): Feb., May, Sept., and Nov.
   Final notification: 3 months
   Write: Alexandrina M. Sergio, Exec. Dir.
Officers and Trustees:* Elliot F. Gerson,* Pres.; Martha S. Newman,* V.P.; Alexandrina M. Sergio, Secy.; Richard H. King, Treas.; Paul Copes, Joyce Fields, Raymond A. Jansen, Jr., Linda J. Kelly, David Laventhol, Sylvia Levy, Worth Loomis, Millard H. Pryor, Jr., Richard T. Schlosberg III, George A. Scott.
Number of staff: 1 full-time professional.
EIN: 060759107
Recent health grants:
446-1 Connecticut AIDS Consortium, Hartford, CT, $15,000. For programs addressing AIDS in Central Connecticut. 1990.
446-2 Hartford Areas Rally Together, Hartford, CT, $10,000. Toward community anti-drug project. 1990.
446-3 Hartford Hospital, Hartford, CT, $20,000. For second installment of grant toward construction of Visitor Reception/Nursing Station in new cardiovascular surgical unit. 1990.
446-4 Rushford Center, Middletown, CT, $12,000. Toward renovation of new facility. 1990.
446-5 Visiting Nurse and Home Care of East Hartford, East Hartford, CT, $10,000. Toward establishing child care program. 1990.

447
Hartford Fire Insurance Corporate Giving Program
Hartford Plaza
Hartford 06115   (203) 547-4972

Financial data (yr. ended 12/31/89): Total giving, $593,688 for grants.

Purpose and activities: Giving in five major areas: Education and Equal Opportunity, Health and Human Services, Urban and Civic Affairs, Arts and Culture, and Mature Americans. Emphasis is on agencies which help people help themselves, show initiative and creativity in their fundraising efforts, and are managed effectively and prudently. Where possible The Hartford will try to leverage its funds through matching and/or challenge grants. In addition to cash grants, the company gives non-monetary support in four major areas for nonprofits: access to corporate facilities, in-kind printing, donation of corporate surplus, and through an organization of employee volunteers, "The Hartford Insurance People - helping people" or H.I.P. through which employees volunteer their time to charities. The Community Service Fund provides grants to community programs to which staff members contribute money and time. The Company matches employee gifts to education and donations employees raise by participating in walk-a-thons and other sporting events. In 1987, the Hartford developed a unique model home called the Hartford House to demonstrate how subtle home improvements can compensate for the changes people experience as they age.
Fields of interest: Education, health, social services, urban affairs, civic affairs, arts, cultural programs, aged, volunteerism.
Types of support: In-kind gifts, donated equipment, use of facilities, employee volunteer services, special projects.
Limitations: Giving limited to headquarters and company locations; a large portion of giving is in Hartford, CT. Generally support for national fund drives and research programs is limited to those efforts with a clear relationship to the company's overall interest and only on an exception basis. No support for organizations receiving United Way funding, single disease organizations, programs benefiting only members of any one religious group, or international organizations. No grants to individuals, or for endowments, conferences or seminars, courtesy advertising, testimonial or fundraising dinners, or professional memberships.
Publications: Corporate report, corporate giving report (including application guidelines), program policy statement.
Application information: Community Affairs staff handles contributions. Application form required.
    Initial approach: Write to General Manager in nearest regional office. Depending on size of the grant requested, manager may fund it or forward it to headquarters. Proposals received in Hartford from agencies outside Hartford will be referred to appropriate regional manager
    Copies of proposal: 1
    Deadline(s): None
    Board meeting date(s): Quarterly
    Write: Sandra A. Sharr, Commun. Affairs
Administrators: Sandra A. Sharr, Dir., Commun. Affairs; Sabbaye McGriff, Mgr., Commun. Affairs.
Number of staff: 2 full-time professional; 1 full-time support; 1 part-time support.

448
Hartford Foundation for Public Giving ▼
85 Gillett St.
Hartford 06105   (203) 548-1888

Established in 1925 in CT by resolution and declaration of trust.
Foundation type: Community
Financial data (yr. ended 09/30/90): Assets, $151,387,286 (M); gifts received, $19,276,818; expenditures, $10,339,795; qualifying distributions, $9,443,701, including $9,302,421 for 279 grants (high: $1,387,216; low: $48; average: $45,000-$55,000) and $141,280 for loans.
Purpose and activities: Giving for demonstration programs and capital purposes, with emphasis on community advancement, educational institutions, youth groups, hospitals, social services, including the aged, and cultural and civic endeavors.
Fields of interest: Community development, education, youth, aged, social services, cultural programs, civic affairs, hospitals, health, AIDS.
Types of support: Seed money, emergency funds, building funds, equipment, land acquisition, matching funds, scholarship funds, loans, special projects, renovation projects, technical assistance, capital campaigns.
Limitations: Giving limited to the greater Hartford, CT, area. No support for sectarian purposes or tax-supported agencies. No grants to individuals, or for operating budgets, continuing support, annual campaigns, deficit financing, endowment funds, research, publications, or conferences.
Publications: Annual report, application guidelines, program policy statement, newsletter, informational brochure.
Application information: Application form required.
    Initial approach: Telephone
    Copies of proposal: 3
    Deadline(s): Educ. & youth, Jan. 30; Family, children, & early childhood, Mar. 30; Health care, July 30; Housing & economic development, Sept. 30; Arts & culture, Nov. 30; Summer program & camperships, Jan. 15; and general grants, May 30
    Board meeting date(s): Monthly except Aug.
    Final notification: 60 to 90 days
    Write: Michael R. Bangser, Exec. Dir.
Officers and Distribution Committee:* James F. English, Jr.,* Chair.; Judith S. Wawro,* Vice-Chair.; Michael R. Bangser,* Secy. and Exec. Dir.; Brewster P. Perkins,* Treas.; Paul Copes, Alan E. Green, George Levine, Jon O. Newman, Rosaida Morales Rosario, Sue Ann Shay, Wilson Wilde.
Trustee Banks: Connecticut National Bank, Fleet Bank, N.A., Society for Savings, United Bank & Trust Co.
Number of staff: 7 full-time professional; 4 part-time professional; 6 full-time support.
EIN: 060699252
Recent health grants:
448-1 Alzheimers Disease and Related Disorders Association of the Greater Hartford Area, Bloomfield, CT, $75,000. To develop family support groups in minority communities of Hartford and to increase network of support groups in surrounding towns. 1991.
448-2 American Leadership Forum, Class V, Hartford, CT, $19,060. To increase awareness of severity of AIDS/HIV epidemic in Greater Hartford and to help organizations act accordingly. 1991.
448-3 Brainard Fund, Hartford, CT, $137,200. To 24 health care agencies to help qualified

patients meet catastrophic medical or hospital bills. 1991.
448-4 Community Health Services, Hartford, CT, $300,000. For renovation of building. 1991.
448-5 Connecticut Speech and Hearing, Hartford, CT, $45,000. For computerized communication equipment for severely disabled persons. 1991.
448-6 Hartford Community Mental Health Center, Hartford, CT, $150,000. To support families of mentally ill adults in Hartford's Northend. 1991.
448-7 Hartford Hospital, Family Friends Program, Hartford, CT, $120,000. For expansion of volunteer/family matching effort by including HIV-infected children and infants in Neonatal Intensive Care Unit. 1991.
448-8 Hartford Primary Care Consortium, Hartford, CT, $312,848. To link Hartford's at-risk children with needed primary and preventive care. 1991.
448-9 Hartford Primary Care Consortium, Hartford, CT, $50,000. For one year extension of mental health services program at Quirk Middle and Hartford Public High Schools. 1991.
448-10 Hartford, City of, Health Department, Hartford, CT, $188,832. To continue Adolescent Parenting and Development Program. 1991.
448-11 Institute of Living, Hartford, CT, $104,500. For refurbishing and equipping of three diagnostic classrooms for intensive observation of severely impaired children. 1991.
448-12 Khmer Health Advocates, West Hartford, CT, $100,455. For new program devoted to Cambodian children which will include therapy, support groups and education for parents and children. 1991.
448-13 Saint Francis Hospital and Medical Center, Hartford, CT, $250,000. For comprehensive adolescent substance abuse program. 1991.
448-14 United Cerebral Palsy Association of Greater Hartford, Hartford, CT, $100,000. To construct second floor of building. 1991.
448-15 Visiting Nurse Association Hospice, Hartford, CT, $100,000. To apply for Medicare license and to expand both quality and quantity of hospice services. 1991.

449
The Hascoe Foundation
35 Mason St.
Greenwich 06830-5383

Donor(s): Norman Hascoe.
Foundation type: Operating
Financial data (yr. ended 01/31/91): Assets, $1,618,826 (M); expenditures, $353,555; qualifying distributions, $11,202,465, including $351,500 for 3 grants (high: $250,000; low: $1,500) and $848,910 for 23 program-related investments.
Purpose and activities: Giving primarily for medical research and education; also provides loans in the form of artwork and antiques.
Fields of interest: Medical research, education, arts.
Types of support: Research.
Limitations: Giving primarily in NY.

Application information: Application form not required.
- *Deadline(s):* None
- *Write:* Norman Hascoe, Pres.

Officers and Directors:* Norman Hascoe,* Pres.; Suzanne Hascoe,* Secy.; Lloyd Hascoe,* Treas.; Andrew Hascoe, Stephanie Hascoe.
EIN: 222534970

450

The Carl J. Herzog Foundation, Inc. ▼
c/o Bentley, Lane, Mosher, and Babson
970 Summer St.
Stamford 06905   (203) 323-1414

Incorporated in 1952 in CT.
Foundation type: Independent
Financial data (yr. ended 12/31/90): Assets, $21,274,377 (M); expenditures, $1,749,086; qualifying distributions, $1,735,862, including $1,631,659 for 75 grants (high: $500,000; low: $10; average: $6,000-$50,000).
Purpose and activities: To promote medical research, particularly in the field of dermatology; general support also for hospitals, colleges and universities.
Fields of interest: Medical research, dermatology, hospitals.
Types of support: Research, general purposes.
Application information:
- *Initial approach:* Letter
- *Deadline(s):* None
- *Write:* Peter Bentley, Pres.

Officers and Directors:* Peter Bentley,* Pres.; Sidney A. Woodd-Cahusac,* V.P.; Nancy M. Alcock,* Secy.; David F. Babson, Jr.,* Treas.
EIN: 510200524
Recent health grants:
450-1 Cancer Research Institute, NYC, NY, $50,000. 1990.
450-2 Danbury Hospital, Danbury, CT, $10,000. 1990.
450-3 New Milford Hospital, New Milford, CT, $10,000. 1990.
450-4 Norwalk Hospital, Norwalk, CT, $10,000. 1990.
450-5 Prosthetics Research Foundation, Seattle, WA, $35,000. 1990.
450-6 Rockefeller University, NYC, NY, $167,600. 1990.
450-7 Saint Joseph Medical Center, Stamford, CT, $10,000. 1990.
450-8 University of Texas Medical Branch Hospitals, Galveston, TX, $101,000. 1990.

451

Heublein Foundation, Inc. ▼
P.O. Box 388
Farmington 06034-0388   (203) 231-5000
Application address: Heublein Foundation Scholarship Program, College Scholarship Service, CN 6730, Princeton, NJ 08541

Incorporated in 1960 in DE.
Donor(s): Heublein, Inc., KFC Corp.
Foundation type: Company-sponsored
Financial data (yr. ended 12/31/91): Assets, $91,280 (M); gifts received, $1,004,646; expenditures, $1,006,146; qualifying distributions, $1,004,646, including $902,750 for 75 grants (high: $101,700; low: $1,000; average:

$1,000-$50,000) and $93,270 for 394 employee matching gifts.
Purpose and activities: Emphasis on the arts, community funds, higher education, including employee-related scholarships, hospitals and health services, youth agencies, and hunger.
Fields of interest: Arts, education, higher education, literacy, health services, hospitals, community funds, youth, hunger.
Types of support: Employee matching gifts, scholarship funds, employee-related scholarships.
Limitations: Giving primarily in Farmington, CT, and areas of company operations. No grants to individuals, except employee-related scholarships, or for endowment funds.
Application information: Scholarship program for children of employees of Heublein, Inc.; send for guidelines. Application form not required.
- *Initial approach:* Letter
- *Copies of proposal:* 1
- *Deadline(s):* Dec. 30 for scholarships
- *Board meeting date(s):* As required
- *Write:* L. Eileen Hall, Treas.

Officers and Directors:* John A. Powers,* Chair.; Peter M. Seremet, Pres.; Robert C. Barker, V.P.; Robert M. Furek, V.P.; Richard E. Walton,* Secy.; Joan T. Mastrota, Treas.; Chester J. Evans.
EIN: 066051280

452

The Maximilian E. & Marion O. Hoffman Foundation, Inc.
970 Farmington Ave., Suite 203
West Hartford 06107

Established in 1986 in CT as a successor foundation of the Maximilian E. & Marion O. Hoffman Foundation.
Foundation type: Independent
Financial data (yr. ended 06/30/91): Assets, $33,710,985 (M); expenditures, $1,805,968; qualifying distributions, $1,410,531, including $1,409,720 for 27 grants (high: $650,000; low: $3,000).
Fields of interest: Hospitals, public policy, environment, education.
Types of support: Special projects, general purposes, scholarship funds.
Limitations: No grants to individuals.
Application information: Contributes only to pre-selected organizations. Applications not accepted.
Officers: Doris C. Chaho, Pres.; Bahij Chaho, Treas.
Director: Ralph Nader.
EIN: 222648036

453

The Harvey Hubbell Foundation
c/o Harry B. Rowell, Jr.
584 Derby-Milford Rd.
Orange 06477-4024

Trust established in 1959 in CT.
Donor(s): Harvey Hubbell, Inc.
Foundation type: Company-sponsored
Financial data (yr. ended 12/31/90): Assets, $2,982,995 (M); expenditures, $320,945; qualifying distributions, $320,945, including $289,100 for 143 grants (high: $40,000; low:

$100) and $26,908 for 135 employee matching gifts (high: $2,000; low: $25).
Fields of interest: Community funds, youth, social services, hospitals, health services, higher education.
Types of support: Employee matching gifts, annual campaigns, building funds, capital campaigns.
Limitations: Giving primarily in areas of company operations in CT. No grants to individuals.
Application information: Contributes only to pre-selected organizations. Applications not accepted.
Trustees: Richard W. Davies, G. Jackson Ratcliffe, Harry B. Rowell, Jr.
Number of staff: None.
EIN: 066078177

454

The Huisking Foundation, Inc.
P.O. Box 353
Botsford 06404-0353
Application address: Plumtree Rd. (R.R. No. 1), Newtown, CT 06470

Incorporated in 1946 in NY.
Donor(s): Members of the Huisking family and family-related corporations.
Foundation type: Independent
Financial data (yr. ended 12/31/90): Assets, $6,520,896 (M); gifts received, $7,796; expenditures, $336,526; qualifying distributions, $309,275, including $303,812 for 36 grants (high: $60,000; low: $100).
Purpose and activities: Giving for Catholic higher and secondary education, church support and welfare funds, hospitals, and religious associations.
Fields of interest: Catholic giving, hospitals, secondary education, higher education, Catholic welfare.
Types of support: Operating budgets, research, special projects.
Limitations: No grants to individuals.
Application information:
- *Initial approach:* Letter
- *Copies of proposal:* 1
- *Deadline(s):* Submit proposal in Feb. and Aug.
- *Board meeting date(s):* Mar. and Oct.
- *Write:* Frank R. Huisking, Treas.

Officers and Directors:* John E. Haigney,* Pres.; William W. Huisking, Jr.,* V.P.; Richard V. Huisking, Jr.,* Secy.; Frank R. Huisking,* Treas.; Helen Crawford, Evelyn F. Daly, Robert P. Daly, Claire F. Hanavan, Taylor W. Hanavan, Richard V. Huisking, Sr., Jean M. Steinschneider.
EIN: 136117501

455

ITT Hartford Insurance Group Foundation, Inc. ▼
(Formerly The Hartford Insurance Group Foundation, Inc.)
Hartford Plaza
Hartford 06115   (203) 547-4972
Additional tel.: (203) 547-5816

Incorporated in 1966 in CT.
Donor(s): Hartford Fire Insurance Co., and affiliates.
Foundation type: Company-sponsored

Financial data (yr. ended 12/31/90): Assets, $42,575 (M); gifts received, $2,000,000; expenditures, $2,064,939; qualifying distributions, $2,064,112, including $1,803,545 for grants (high: $184,756; low: $25; average: $2,000-$25,000) and $260,567 for employee matching gifts.

Purpose and activities: Giving primarily for higher education (including employee-related scholarships through the National Merit Scholarship Corp. and employee matching gifts), job training, community funds, health, urban and civic affairs, arts and culture, and the aged; also administers a community service fund that supports the efforts of its employees in community programs.

Fields of interest: Higher education, education, insurance education, education—minorities, employment, community development, community funds, urban affairs, civic affairs, arts, cultural programs, health, drug abuse, alcoholism, health services, homeless, hunger, housing, AIDS, social services, aged, volunteerism.

Types of support: Scholarship funds, employee matching gifts, employee-related scholarships, building funds, annual campaigns, special projects.

Limitations: Giving primarily in the Hartford, CT, area, and in communities where the company has a regional office. No support for political or religious purposes, disease-specific health organizations, student group trips or parades, United Way member agencies, public educational organizations (except for matching gift program), or national fund drives or research programs not having a clear relationship to overall interests of the company and only on an exceptional basis. No grants to individuals, or for endowment funds, conferences, travel, testimonial or fundraising dinners, membership in business, professional and trade associations, courtesy advertising, or capital fund drives outside the greater Hartford area.

Publications: Corporate giving report (including application guidelines), informational brochure.

Application information: Application form required.

   Initial approach: Letter
   Copies of proposal: 1
   Deadline(s): None
   Board meeting date(s): Quarterly
   Write: Sandra A. Sharr, Dir., Community Affairs

Officers and Director:* Donald R. Frahm,* Pres.; Edward L. Morgan, Jr., V.P.; Michael S. Wilder,* V.P.; Michael O'Halloran, Secy.; J. Richard Garrett, Treas.; Edward N. Bennett.

Number of staff: 1 full-time professional; 1 part-time support.

EIN: 066079761

Recent health grants:

455-1 Chamber of Commerce Foundation of Greater Hartford, Hartford, CT, $31,000. Toward Business Community Study on proposed new Newington Children's Hospital and establishment of Child Council to plan and promote health care services for Hartford children. 1990.

455-2 Charter Oak Terrace Rice Heights Health Center, Hartford, CT, $10,000. For program coordinator for Homeless Health Care Program which provides health care to homeless individuals in Hartford. 1990.

455-3 Community Health Services, Hartford, CT, $12,500. For operating support for community health center serving low-income residents of Hartford's North End. 1990.

455-4 Connecticut AIDS Consortium, Hartford, CT, $15,000. For consortium that provides funding for organizations services, including housing and drug rehabilitation assistance, to people with AIDS and their families. 1990.

455-5 Connecticut, State of, Hartford, CT, $20,000. For Connecticut Aging Awareness Project and for associated publication expenses. 1990.

455-6 Drugs Dont Work, Hartford, CT, $12,500. For first installment of two-year pledge. 1990.

455-7 Hartford Action Plan on Infant Health, Hartford, CT, $10,000. For public/private progam to reduce infant mortality and address teen pregnancy in seven target Hartford neighborhoods. 1990.

455-8 Hartford Hospital, Hartford, CT, $100,000. For continuing support toward eight-year renovation and expansion project. 1990.

455-9 National Council on the Aging, DC, $12,500. For Job Start Program, established in Hartford as adjunct to Hartford Hospital's Family Friends Progam, and to help establish programs in which young volunteers assist older home-bound adults to improve their day-to-day lives. 1990.

455-10 United Cerebral Palsy Association of Greater Hartford, Hartford, CT, $10,000. Toward renovations to bring facility up to standard and to enhance current programs and extend services to more families. 1990.

455-11 Visiting Nurse Association of Farmington Valley, Farmington, CT, $10,000. For continuing support for expansion of facility serving towns of Simsbury, Farmington and Granby. 1990.

456
The ITT Rayonier Foundation

1177 Summer St.
Stamford 06904   (203) 348-7000

Incorporated in 1952 in NY.

Donor(s): ITT Rayonier, Inc.

Foundation type: Company-sponsored

Financial data (yr. ended 12/31/90): Assets, $3,107,942 (M); gifts received, $400,000; expenditures, $414,051; qualifying distributions, $394,948, including $337,048 for 213 grants (high: $20,000; low: $25; average: $1,000-$3,000) and $57,900 for 52 grants to individuals (high: $2,000; low: $500; average: $1,000-$1,500).

Purpose and activities: Created as a medium to meet civic responsibilities in the areas of company operations and educational institutions related to ITT Rayonier recruitment or to forest industry specializations. Grants to educational associations for scholarships, hospitals for buildings and equipment, health agencies and community funds, the arts, and environmental organizations; scholarships to individuals residing in areas of company operations in Nassau County, FL, Wayne County, GA, and Clallam, Mason, and Grays Harbor counties, WA.

Fields of interest: Educational associations, hospitals—building funds, health services, community funds, education, community

development, performing arts, science and technology, conservation.

Types of support: Scholarship funds, employee-related scholarships, building funds, equipment, operating budgets, continuing support, annual campaigns, seed money, emergency funds, deficit financing, land acquisition, endowment funds, special projects, matching funds, general purposes, capital campaigns, employee matching gifts, in-kind gifts, research.

Limitations: Giving primarily in areas of company operations in FL, GA, and WA. No loans.

Application information: Application form not required.

   Initial approach: Letter or proposal
   Copies of proposal: 1
   Deadline(s): Nov. 30
   Board meeting date(s): Feb.
   Final notification: 1 month
   Write: Jerome D. Gregoire, V.P.

Officers and Directors:* Ronald M. Gross,* Chair. and Pres.; Jerome D. Gregoire,* V.P.; C.W. Peacock,* V.P.; J.B. Canning, Secy.; Gerald J. Pollack, Comptroller; W.S. Berry, W.L. Nutter.

Number of staff: None.

EIN: 136064462

457
The Cyrus W. & Amy F. Jones & Bessie D. Phelps Foundation, Inc.

c/o Tellalian & Tellalian
211 State St.
Bridgeport 06604   (203) 333-5566

Incorporated in CT.

Donor(s): Amy F. Jones.‡

Foundation type: Independent

Financial data (yr. ended 09/30/91): Assets, $2,517,277 (M); expenditures, $177,146; qualifying distributions, $154,320, including $123,100 for 32 grants (high: $13,000; low: $100).

Fields of interest: Cultural programs, religion—Christian, medical sciences, child development.

Types of support: Operating budgets, capital campaigns.

Limitations: Giving primarily in CT, with emphasis on Bridgeport. No grants to individuals.

Application information:

   Initial approach: Letter
   Deadline(s): None
   Write: Aram H. Tellalian, Jr., Esq., Pres.

Officers and Trustees:* Aram H. Tellalian, Jr.,* Chair., Pres., and Treas.; Alexander R. Nestor,* V.P.; Robert S. Tellalian,* Secy.

EIN: 060943204

458
Paul L. Jones Fund

c/o Meridan Trust & Safe Deposit Co.
P.O. Box 951
Meriden 06450   (203) 235-4456

Established in 1979 in CT.

Foundation type: Independent

Financial data (yr. ended 10/31/91): Assets, $3,461,351 (M); expenditures, $145,632; qualifying distributions, $131,350, including

$125,000 for 14 grants (high: $20,000; low: $2,000).

Purpose and activities: Giving only for scholarship programs to assist students in medical and health-related fields.

Fields of interest: Medical education, nursing.

Types of support: Scholarship funds.

Limitations: Giving limited to residents of CT. No grants to individuals.

Application information: Contributes only to pre-selected organizations. Applications not accepted.

Trustees: James D. Kircaldie, Meriden Trust & Safe Deposit Co.

EIN: 066222118

459
Charles & Mabel P. Jost Foundation, Inc.

c/o Nestor, Sarka & Co.
1140 Fairfield Ave.
Bridgeport 06605   (203) 336-0166

Incorporated about 1969.

Foundation type: Independent

Financial data (yr. ended 04/30/91): Assets, $2,857,130 (M); expenditures, $234,044; qualifying distributions, $210,010, including $186,000 for 22 grants (high: $25,000; low: $500).

Fields of interest: Handicapped, hospitals, higher education, legal education.

Types of support: Operating budgets.

Limitations: Giving primarily in CT. No grants to individuals, or for scholarships, fellowships, or prizes; no loans.

Application information: Contributes only to pre-selected organizations. Applications not accepted.

Officers and Trustees:* Alexander R. Nestor,* Chair. and Pres.; Robert S. Tellalian,* V.P.; Aram H. Tellalian, Jr.,* Secy.

EIN: 237070398

460
Kaman Corporate Giving Program

Corp. Finance Dept., 1332 Blue Hills Ave.
P.O. Box 1
Bloomfield 06002-0001   (203) 243-6307

Financial data (yr. ended 12/31/90): Total giving, $280,000 for 90 grants (high: $5,000; average: $500-$5,000).

Purpose and activities: Supports social services, rehabilitation, volunteerism, community development, education, and civic affairs. Emphasis on organizations providing services to the disabled, handicapped, and disadvantaged.

Fields of interest: Education, civic affairs, child welfare, community development, community funds, disadvantaged, employment, handicapped, literacy, social services, rehabilitation, volunteerism.

Types of support: Annual campaigns, capital campaigns, special projects, employee-related scholarships.

Limitations: Giving limited to subsidiary and corporate headquarters areas.

Application information: Contributions are handled by the Corporate Finance department. Application form not required.

Initial approach: Query letter; Send to headquarters
Copies of proposal: 1
Deadline(s): None
Final notification: 12 weeks maximum
Write: Russell H. Jones, V.P.

Administrator: Russell H. Jones, V.P.

Number of staff: 1

461
John & Evelyn Kossak Foundation, Inc.

68 Cross Hwy.
Westport 06880-2147   (203) 259-8779

Established in 1969 in CT.

Donor(s): Evelyn K. Kossak, Jeffrey Kossak, Steven M. Kossak.

Foundation type: Independent

Financial data (yr. ended 12/31/90): Assets, $2,230,790 (M); gifts received, $281,000; expenditures, $34,545; qualifying distributions, $31,045, including $31,025 for 38 grants (high: $5,000; low: $25).

Purpose and activities: Support primarily for higher education, health organizations, music, and the fine arts, including an art museum.

Fields of interest: Higher education, health, music, fine arts, museums.

Limitations: No grants to individuals.

Application information: Contributes only to pre-selected organizations. Applications not accepted.

Write: Evelyn K. Kossak, Pres.

Officers: Evelyn K. Kossak, Pres.; Jeffrey Kossak, V.P.; Steven M. Kossak, Treas.

EIN: 237045906

462
The Vernon K. Krieble Foundation, Inc.

P.O. Box 389
Marlborough 06447

Established in 1985 in CT.

Donor(s): Gladys V.K. Delmas.

Foundation type: Independent

Financial data (yr. ended 12/31/90): Assets, $9,561,195 (M); expenditures, $702,172; qualifying distributions, $553,500, including $553,500 for 52 grants (high: $50,000; low: $1,000).

Purpose and activities: Giving primarily for public policy organizations, including government, national security, and civil rights issues; support also for universities and hospitals in the U.S. and Canada.

Fields of interest: Public policy, government, public affairs, civil rights, higher education, hospitals, Canada.

Limitations: Giving primarily in the U.S.; some giving in Montreal, Canada. No grants to individuals.

Application information: Contributes only to pre-selected organizations. Applications not accepted.

Officers: Helen K. Fusscas, Pres.; Frederick B. Krieble, V.P.; Nancy B. Krieble, Secy.; J. Peter Fusscas, Treas.

EIN: 222538914

463
Marie Keese Lelash Foundation, Inc.

456 Main St.
Ridgefield 06877   (203) 431-0231

Established in 1988 in FL.

Donor(s): Marie Keese Lelash.‡

Foundation type: Independent

Financial data (yr. ended 06/30/91): Assets, $4,426,440 (M); gifts received, $2,853,087; expenditures, $169,352; qualifying distributions, $57,323, including $46,806 for 7 grants (high: $7,500; low: $1,806).

Fields of interest: Education, medical research, general charitable giving.

Types of support: Building funds, program-related investments, capital campaigns, general purposes, operating budgets, special projects.

Limitations: No grants to individuals.

Application information: Contributes only to pre-selected organizations. Applications not accepted.

Board meeting date(s): Varies
Write: Richard W. Lelash, Pres.

Officers and Trustees:* Richard Lelash,* Pres.; Ray Anderson,* V.P. and Secy.; John Harriman,* V.P. and Treas.

Number of staff: 3 part-time professional; 2 part-time support.

EIN: 650011076

464
Loctite Corporate Contributions Program

Hartford Square North
10 Columbus Blvd.
Hartford 06106   (203) 520-5000

Financial data (yr. ended 12/31/90): Total giving, $400,000 for grants.

Purpose and activities: Supports health, community arts, dance, economic education, fine arts institutes, general education, science and technology, engineering, and private colleges. Types of support include funding for equipment. Funding is also given for educational programs for inner city youths in grades K to 12.

Fields of interest: Arts, education, fine arts, economics, higher education, chemistry, engineering, health, science and technology, youth, elementary education, secondary education.

Types of support: General purposes, employee-related scholarships.

Limitations: Giving primarily in headquarters city and major operating areas. No support for religious, fraternal, and political campaigns. No grants to individuals.

Application information:

Initial approach: Proposal or letter; send to headquarters
Final notification: All requests will be answered
Write: Robert Aller, Sr. V.P.

465
George A. and Grace L. Long Foundation

c/o Connecticut National Bank
777 Main St. - MSN 242
Hartford 06115   (203) 728-4071

Trust established in 1960 in CT.

Donor(s): George A. Long,‡ Grace L. Long.‡

Foundation type: Independent
Financial data (yr. ended 12/31/91): Assets, $6,605,218 (M); expenditures, $426,741; qualifying distributions, $379,757, including $337,825 for 93 grants (high: $20,000; low: $500).
Fields of interest: Cultural programs, education, hospitals, social services, community funds.
Types of support: Scholarship funds, special projects, building funds.
Limitations: Giving primarily in the greater Hartford, CT, area. No grants to individuals, or for operating budgets or endowment funds; no loans.
Application information: Application form required.
   Initial approach: Letter
   Copies of proposal: 3
   Deadline(s): Mar. 15 and Sept. 15
   Board meeting date(s): Apr. and Oct.
   Write: Karen Estes, Trust Officer, Connecticut National Bank
Trustees: Willis Parsons, Jr., Connecticut National Bank.
EIN: 066030953

466
The Katherine Matthies Foundation
c/o Connecticut National Bank
915 Main St., MSN 252
Hartford 06103
Application address: P.O. Box 1146, Waterbury, CT 06721; Tel.: (203) 597-6788

Established in 1987 in CT.
Donor(s): Katherine Matthies.‡
Foundation type: Independent
Financial data (yr. ended 12/31/91): Assets, $11,347,368 (M); gifts received, $2,468,976; expenditures, $839,458; qualifying distributions, $786,619, including $759,175 for grants.
Fields of interest: Community development, civic affairs, Catholic welfare, hospitals, youth, family services.
Limitations: Giving limited to Seymour, Ansonia, Derby, Oxford, and Beacon Falls, CT.
Application information:
   Deadline(s): Quarterly
   Write: James Fallon
Trustee: Connecticut National Bank.
EIN: 066261860

467
The Meriden Foundation
c/o Meriden Trust & Safe Deposit Co.
P.O. Box 951
Meriden 06450   (203) 235-4456

Donor(s): A. Leo Ricci.‡
Foundation type: Community
Financial data (yr. ended 12/31/91): Assets, $7,554,781 (M); gifts received, $3,408,838; expenditures, $563,283; qualifying distributions, $529,526, including $457,818 for 54 grants (high: $37,325; low: $200) and $64,182 for 59 grants to individuals (high: $2,500; low: $300).
Fields of interest: Civic affairs, youth, hospitals, social services, community funds.
Types of support: Student aid, general purposes, annual campaigns.
Limitations: Giving limited to the Meriden-Wallingford, CT, area.

Application information:
   Initial approach: Letter for grants; application form for scholarship requests
   Deadline(s): None
   Write: Jeffrey F. Otis, Dir.
Distribution Committee: Richard S. Boynton, Chair.; James P. Rybek, Vice-Chair.; Jeffrey F. Otis, Secy.; Robert Bailey, Elsa H. Bradford, Frederick A. Flatow, John F. Peckham, Robert J. Sokolowski, Peter Vouras, Jr.
Trustee: Meriden Trust & Safe Deposit Co.
EIN: 066037849

468
Emil Mosbacher, Jr. Foundation, Inc.
c/o The Meridian Bldg.
170 Mason St.
Greenwich 06830   (203) 869-4100

Incorporated in 1974 in NY.
Donor(s): Emil Mosbacher, Jr., Emil Mosbacher III, John D. Mosbacher, R. Bruce Mosbacher.
Foundation type: Independent
Financial data (yr. ended 11/30/91): Assets, $3,028,751 (M); expenditures, $96,242; qualifying distributions, $95,957, including $95,957 for 85 grants (high: $16,667; low: $25).
Fields of interest: Higher education, medical education, hospitals, general charitable giving.
Limitations: Giving primarily in NY and CT. No grants to individuals.
Application information:
   Initial approach: Letter
   Deadline(s): None
   Write: Emil Mosbacher, Jr., Pres.
Officers and Directors:* Emil Mosbacher, Jr.,* Pres. and Treas.; Patricia Mosbacher,* V.P. and Secy.; Emil Mosbacher III,* V.P.; John D. Mosbacher,* V.P.; R. Bruce Mosbacher,* V.P.
EIN: 237454106

469
New Britain Foundation for Public Giving
29 Russell St.
New Britain 06052   (203) 229-6018

Established in 1941 in CT.
Foundation type: Community
Financial data (yr. ended 03/31/92): Assets, $3,179,095 (M); expenditures, $378,908; qualifying distributions, $324,085, including $324,085 for grants.
Purpose and activities: To meet the needs of the community through support for community services, housing, day care, employment, education, youth services, and drug and alcohol treatment.
Fields of interest: Community development, social services, health.
Types of support: Building funds, scholarship funds, capital campaigns, renovation projects, matching funds, seed money, deficit financing, operating budgets, special projects, conferences and seminars, emergency funds.
Limitations: Giving limited to New Britain and central CT.
Publications: Annual report (including application guidelines), newsletter, financial statement, application guidelines.
Application information: Application form not required.

Initial approach: Contact foundation for application format
Copies of proposal: 1
Deadline(s): Feb., May, Aug., and Nov.
Board meeting date(s): Mar., June, Sept., and Dec.
Write: Ronald Gilrain, Chair.
Officers and Directors:* Ronald F. Gilrain,* Chair.; Linda Tatarczuch,* Secy.; Charles Bauer, Connie Collins, Virginia C. Davis, Charles Glendon, Edward Januszewski, William T. Livingston, M.D., Rev. Malcolm McDowell, Jr., Hector Ortiz, Susan Rathgeber, Stanley Shepard, George Springer.
Number of staff: 1 part-time professional.
EIN: 066036461

470
The New Haven Foundation ▼
70 Audubon St.
New Haven 06510   (203) 777-2386

Established in 1928 in CT by Resolution and Declaration of Trust.
Foundation type: Community
Financial data (yr. ended 12/31/90): Assets, $93,473,155 (M); gifts received, $3,069,761; expenditures, $5,440,027; qualifying distributions, $4,443,009, including $4,443,009 for grants (high: $146,255; low: $99; average: $5,000-$30,000).
Purpose and activities: Emphasis on social service and youth agencies, hospitals and health agencies, educational institutions, community funds, and the arts.
Fields of interest: Youth, hospitals, health services, education, community funds, arts, social services, AIDS.
Types of support: Operating budgets, continuing support, seed money, emergency funds, building funds, equipment, matching funds, consulting services, technical assistance, special projects, loans, scholarship funds, endowment funds.
Limitations: Giving primarily in greater New Haven, CT, and the lower Naugatuck River Valley. No grants to individuals, or for annual campaigns, deficit financing, endowment funds, research, scholarships, or fellowships, or generally for capital projects.
Publications: Annual report, application guidelines, newsletter.
Application information: Application form required.
   Initial approach: Telephone or letter
   Copies of proposal: 14
   Deadline(s): Jan., Apr., Aug., and Oct.
   Board meeting date(s): Mar., June, Oct., and Dec.
   Final notification: Within 1 week of decision
   Write: Helmer N. Ekstrom, Dir.
Distribution Committee: Richard G. Bell, Chair.; Richard H. Bowerman, Anne Tyler Calabresi, Donald W. Celotto, Jr., F. Patrick McFadden, Jr., Mary L. Pepe, Agnes W. Timpson, Charles Twyman, Barbara Wareck.
Trustees: Bank of Boston Connecticut, Connecticut National Bank, Fleet Bank, N.A., New Haven Savings Bank, People's Bank, Union Trust Co.
Number of staff: 10 full-time professional; 2 part-time professional; 6 full-time support; 1 part-time support.

EIN: 066032106
Recent health grants:

470-1 AIDS Interfaith Network, New Haven, CT, $30,000. For housing program. 1991.

470-2 AIDS Project New Haven, New Haven, CT, $19,000. For city-wide case management team which helps people with AIDS get services they need. 1991.

470-3 Connecticut AIDS Consortium, Hartford, CT, $30,000. For AIDS prevention education. 1991.

470-4 Connecticut AIDS Residence Program, New Haven, CT, $30,000. For housing program. 1991.

470-5 Connecticut AIDS Residence Program, New Haven, CT, $25,000. 1991.

470-6 Crossroads, New Haven, CT, $25,000. 1991.

470-7 Fair Haven Community Health Clinic, New Haven, CT, $23,000. For matching grant for AIDS prevention education. 1991.

470-8 Gaylord Hospital, Wallingford, CT, $57,737. For capital campaign. 1991.

470-9 Hill Health Center, New Haven, CT, $20,000. For matching grant for AIDS prevention education for teenage drop-outs. 1991.

470-10 Infoline of South Central Connecticut, Pregnancy Healthline, New Haven, CT, $46,700. 1991.

470-11 Infoline of South Central Connecticut, Pregnancy Healthline, New Haven, CT, $32,500. 1991.

470-12 Phelps Community Project, Hamden, CT, $45,000. For access to health services project. 1991.

470-13 Special Commission on Infant Health, New Haven, CT, $142,901. 1991.

470-14 Special Commission on Infant Health, New Haven, CT, $53,275. 1991.

470-15 Special Commission on Infant Health, New Haven, CT, $12,500. 1991.

470-16 Visiting Nurse Association of South Central Connecticut, New Haven, CT, $40,000. For matching grant. 1991.

470-17 Womens Health Services, New Haven, CT, $27,000. 1991.

470-18 Womens Health Services, New Haven, CT, $25,000. 1991.

470-19 Y-Me Breast Cancer Support Program, Bradford, CT, $15,000. 1991.

470-20 Yale University, School of Medicine, Department of Pediatrics, New Haven, CT, $44,000. 1991.

470-21 Yale-New Haven Hospital, New Haven, CT, $250,000. For capital campaign. 1991.

470-22 Yale-New Haven Hospital, New Haven, CT, $40,000. 1991.

470-23 Yale-New Haven Hospital, Department of Geriatrics, New Haven, CT, $21,000. 1991.

471
Newman's Own Foundation, Inc.

246 Post Rd. East
Westport 06880-3615   (203) 222-0136

Established in 1989 in CT.
Donor(s): Paul L. Newman, Mauri Foods.
Foundation type: Company-sponsored
Financial data (yr. ended 08/31/91): Assets, $7,108 (M); gifts received, $519,911; expenditures, $527,064; qualifying distributions,

$527,064, including $527,000 for 33 grants (high: $60,000; low: $1,000).
Fields of interest: Youth, child welfare, hospitals, education, homeless, Canada, Australia, general charitable giving.
Limitations: Giving on a domestic and international basis.
Publications: Grants list.
Application information:
Initial approach: Proposal
Deadline(s): None
Write: Pamela M. Papay, Dir. of Administration
Officers and Directors:* Paul L. Newman,* Pres.; A.E. Hotchner,* V.P.; Jamie K. Gerard,* Secy.; Joanne Woodward.
EIN: 061247230

472
Northeast Utilities Corporate Giving Program

P.O. Box 270
Hartford 06141-0270   (203) 721-2751

Financial data (yr. ended 12/31/90): Total giving, $2,480,000, including $2,300,000 for 1,500 grants (high: $145,000; low: $25; average: $100-$5,000), $150,000 for 1,018 employee matching gifts and $30,000 for 130 in-kind gifts.
Purpose and activities: Supports programs concerning the following: education, specifically engineering and technology; health, including hospitals and national disease associations; social services, such as YMCA, YWCA and youth organizations; the United Way, arts, humanities and public affairs.
Fields of interest: Education, health, social services, community funds, arts, humanities, cultural programs, community development, child development, disadvantaged, family services, hospitals—building funds, AIDS, ecology, homeless.
Types of support: Capital campaigns, employee matching gifts, general purposes, equipment, operating budgets, scholarship funds, special projects, technical assistance, in-kind gifts, loaned talent, use of facilities, continuing support.
Limitations: Giving primarily in CT and western MA. No support for foundations, religious and political groups, or veterans' and fraternal organizations. No grants to individuals.
Publications: Informational brochure, program policy statement, application guidelines.
Application information: Include description of organization, services offered, beneficiaries of service, geographic area served, list of board members and donors and proof of tax-exemption; community relations office handles giving. Application form required.
Initial approach: Letter requesting application form; higher educational organizations should write to Ann Johnson of Northeast's educational grants committee
Copies of proposal: 1
Deadline(s): Aug. 1, for the following year
Write: Sara Ellison, Secy., Corporate Dues and Contributions Committee
Corp. Dues and Contribs. Comm.: Hugh C. Mackenzie, Jr., Chair.; Sara Ellison, Secy.
Number of staff: 7 part-time professional.

473
The Obernauer Foundation, Inc.

Six Stamford Forum, Suite 501
Stamford 06901-3227

Incorporated in 1966 in CT as the Marne and Joan Obernauer Foundation.
Donor(s): Marne Obernauer, Marne Obernauer, Jr.
Foundation type: Independent
Financial data (yr. ended 12/31/91): Assets, $2,432,167 (M); expenditures, $126,349; qualifying distributions, $108,564, including $101,265 for 55 grants (high: $20,000; low: $25).
Fields of interest: International affairs, Jewish giving, youth, higher education, medical research.
Types of support: Annual campaigns, endowment funds, scholarship funds.
Limitations: Giving primarily in PA and New York, NY. No grants to individuals.
Application information: Contributes only to pre-selected organizations. Applications not accepted.
Officers and Directors:* Marne Obernauer,* Pres.; Joan S. Obernauer,* V.P.; Marne Obernauer, Jr.,* V.P.; June E. Sisson, Secy.
EIN: 956149147

474
Olin Corporation Charitable Trust ▼

120 Long Ridge Rd.
Stamford 06904   (203) 356-3301

Trust established in 1945 in MO.
Donor(s): Olin Corp.
Foundation type: Company-sponsored
Financial data (yr. ended 12/31/90): Assets, $12,571,091 (M); expenditures, $1,996,108; qualifying distributions, $1,816,384, including $1,811,999 for grants (average: $500-$10,000).
Purpose and activities: Emphasis on science and engineering in higher education, business education, environmental studies, conservation programs, community funds, hospitals, youth agencies, and health associations. Support also for a wide variety of programs such as drug abuse, volunteerism, economics, and housing. The trust matches employee gifts to education and arts and culture and awards scholarships to children of employees through the National Merit Scholarship Corporation.
Fields of interest: Higher education, science and technology, engineering, economics, education—minorities, environment, conservation, wildlife, community funds, health services, hospitals, drug abuse, hospices, youth, homeless, volunteerism, women, freedom, South Pacific, safety.
Types of support: General purposes, operating budgets, continuing support, annual campaigns, seed money, emergency funds, building funds, equipment, land acquisition, special projects, research, publications, conferences and seminars, internships, scholarship funds, employee-related scholarships, fellowships, matching funds, employee matching gifts.
Limitations: Giving primarily in areas of company operations. No grants to individuals, or for endowment funds; no loans.
Application information: Application form not required.
Initial approach: Letter or proposal
Copies of proposal: 1

Deadline(s): Submit proposal preferably between Jan. and Aug.; no set deadline
Board meeting date(s): Dec.
Final notification: 2 to 3 months
Write: Carmella V. Piacentini, Admin.
Trustees: Donald W. Griffin, John W. Johnstone, Jr., Boatmen's Trust Co.
Number of staff: 1 full-time professional; 1 full-time support; 1 part-time support.
EIN: 436022750

475
The Frank Loomis Palmer Fund

c/o Shawmut Bank Connecticut, N.A.
250 State St.
New London 06320-0911   (203) 447-6133

Trust established in 1936 in CT.
Donor(s): Virginia Palmer.‡
Foundation type: Independent
Financial data (yr. ended 07/31/92): Assets, $16,929,815 (M); expenditures, $864,336; qualifying distributions, $809,218, including $764,745 for 70 grants (high: $38,268; low: $750).
Purpose and activities: Grants to encourage new projects and to provide seed money, with emphasis on child welfare and family services, youth agencies, and higher and secondary education; support also for civic groups, cultural programs, social services, churches, and hospitals.
Fields of interest: Arts, religion, family services, youth, aged, higher education, elementary education, libraries, AIDS, health.
Types of support: Seed money, special projects, capital campaigns, conferences and seminars, consulting services, equipment, matching funds, publications, research, scholarship funds, renovation projects.
Limitations: Giving limited to New London, CT. No grants to individuals, or for endowment funds.
Publications: Informational brochure (including application guidelines).
Application information: Application form required.
Initial approach: Telephone
Copies of proposal: 1
Deadline(s): May 15 and Nov. 15
Board meeting date(s): Jan. and July
Final notification: Feb. 1 and Aug. 1
Write: Mildred E. Devine, V.P., Shawmut Bank Connecticut, N.A.
Trustee: Shawmut Bank Connecticut, N.A.
Number of staff: None.
EIN: 066026043

476
Panwy Foundation, Inc.

Greenwich Office Park IX
10 Valley Dr.
Greenwich 06831   (203) 661-6616

Trust established in 1943 in NY; incorporated in 1951 in NJ; reincorporated in 1988 in CT.
Donor(s): Olga Resseguier, Henry W. Wyman, Maria Wyman, Ralph M. Wyman, Ruth L. Russell.
Foundation type: Independent
Financial data (yr. ended 12/31/90): Assets, $821,460 (M); gifts received, $92,000; expenditures, $311,042; qualifying distributions,

$298,049, including $297,842 for grants (average: $25-$35,800).
Fields of interest: Religion, higher education, hospitals, cultural programs, music.
Types of support: Operating budgets, continuing support, annual campaigns, seed money, emergency funds, endowment funds, building funds, equipment, capital campaigns, general purposes, loans, renovation projects.
Limitations: No grants to individuals, or for matching gifts.
Application information: Application form not required.
Initial approach: Letter
Copies of proposal: 1
Deadline(s): None
Board meeting date(s): As required
Final notification: 1 month
Write: Ralph M. Wyman, Pres.
Officers and Trustees:* Henry W. Wyman,* Chair.; Ralph M. Wyman,* Pres.; Harry A. Russell,* V.P.; Virginia A.W. Meyer,* Secy.-Treas.
Number of staff: None.
EIN: 136130759

477
Robert Leet Patterson & Clara Guthrie Patterson Trust

c/o Connecticut National Bank
One Landmark Sq.
Stamford 06904-1454   (203) 358-6124

Established in 1981 in CT.
Donor(s): Robert Patterson Trust No. 2, Robert Leet Patterson,‡ Clara Guthrie Patterson.‡
Foundation type: Independent
Financial data (yr. ended 01/31/91): Assets, $11,003,777 (M); expenditures, $673,383; qualifying distributions, $571,520, including $549,961 for 9 grants (high: $176,000; low: $10,000; average: $100,000).
Purpose and activities: Giving to hospitals and organizations which are devoted to the advancement of medical science and are engaged in research relating to human diseases.
Fields of interest: Medical research, hospitals.
Types of support: Equipment, matching funds, professorships, research, seed money, special projects.
Limitations: Giving limited to the continental U.S.; support primarily in CT and other eastern states. No grants to individuals, or for operating budgets, continuing support, annual campaigns, emergency funds, deficit financing, endowment funds, consulting services, technical assistance, demonstration projects, publications, or conferences and seminars; no loans.
Publications: Informational brochure (including application guidelines).
Application information: Application form required.
Initial approach: Letter or proposal
Copies of proposal: 6
Deadline(s): May 1 for June meeting and Nov. 1 for Dec. meeting
Board meeting date(s): June and Dec.
Final notification: 3 months
Write: Peter B. Guenther, V.P., Connecticut National Bank
Trustee: John H. McBride.
Corporate Trustee: Connecticut National Bank.
Number of staff: None.

EIN: 066236358

478
People's Bank Corporate Giving Program

Bridgeport Center
850 Main St.
Bridgeport 06604-4913   (203) 338-7171

Financial data (yr. ended 12/31/90): Total giving, $1,371,000, including $1,336,489 for 375 grants (high: $200,675; low: $25) and $34,511 for 167 employee matching gifts.
Purpose and activities: Main emphasis on arts, community development and education; areas of interest include the homeless, employment, housing, health services, and higher and pre-college education.
Fields of interest: Arts, community development, hospitals—building funds, community funds, cultural programs, elementary education, homeless, dance, education—minorities, employment, higher education, housing, disadvantaged, education, health services, hospitals.
Types of support: Donated equipment, employee matching gifts, equipment, operating budgets, seed money, building funds, employee volunteer services, in-kind gifts, loaned talent, use of facilities, capital campaigns, continuing support, loans, general purposes, scholarship funds, public relations services.
Limitations: Giving primarily in organizations located in 32 communities in CT in which the company operates.
Publications: Corporate report.
Application information: Corporate communications office handles giving. Application form required.
Initial approach: Letter, phone call or visit requesting application form
Copies of proposal: 1
Board meeting date(s): Rolling
Write: Lisa P. Oswald, Corp. and Community Rels. Officer
Number of staff: 5

479
The Perkin Fund

340 Country Club Rd.
New Canaan 06840   (203) 966-1920
Additional address: c/o Morris & McVeigh, 767 Third Ave., New York, NY 10017

Trust established in 1967 in NY.
Donor(s): Richard S. Perkin.‡
Foundation type: Independent
Financial data (yr. ended 12/31/90): Assets, $11,321,034 (M); expenditures, $680,863; qualifying distributions, $529,746, including $516,000 for 15 grants (high: $100,000; low: $10,000).
Purpose and activities: Support for advanced education and medical research, especially in astronomy, biomedicine, and optics.
Fields of interest: Higher education, medical sciences, medical research, physical sciences.
Limitations: No grants to individuals, or for operating budgets; no loans.
Application information:
Initial approach: Letter
Copies of proposal: 1

Deadline(s): Sept. 30
Board meeting date(s): May and Nov.
Write: Mrs. Richard S. Perkin, Chair.
Trustees: Mrs. Richard S. Perkin, Chair.; James G. Baker, Winifred P. Gray, Gladys T. Perkin, John T. Perkin, Richard T. Perkin, Robert S. Perkin, Howard Phipps, Jr., Roderic M. Scott.
EIN: 136222498

480
Norma F. Pfriem Foundation, Inc.
P.O. Box 697
Southport 06490   (203) 256-3743

Established in 1988.
Donor(s): Norma F. Pfriem.
Foundation type: Independent
Financial data (yr. ended 12/31/91): Assets, $4,689,576 (M); gifts received, $1,500,000; expenditures, $190,908; qualifying distributions, $173,582, including $173,582 for 5 grants (high: $95,000; low: $15,000).
Fields of interest: Hospitals, cancer, medical sciences, health services, nursing, mental health, handicapped, rehabilitation, arts, museums.
Limitations: Giving primarily in CT.
Application information: Application form not required.
  Initial approach: Proposal
  Deadline(s): Sept. 30
  Write: Vincent A. Griffin, Jr., Treas.
Officers and Directors:* Norma F. Pfriem,* Pres.; Christine M. Griffin,* Secy.; Vincent A. Griffin, Jr.,* Treas.
Number of staff: None.
EIN: 222940194

481
Phoenix Mutual Life Insurance Company Contributions Program
One American Row
Hartford 06115   (203) 275-5000

Financial data (yr. ended 12/31/90): Total giving, $611,943, including $505,500 for 83 grants (high: $116,000; low: $300; average: $2,000-$5,000), $81,443 for 458 employee matching gifts and $25,000 for in-kind gifts.
Purpose and activities: Supports health care, education, and housing programs.
Fields of interest: AIDS, elementary education, housing, health, education.
Types of support: Capital campaigns, general purposes, seed money, employee matching gifts, donated equipment, use of facilities, loaned talent, employee volunteer services.
Limitations: Giving limited to the Hartford and Enfield, CT, and Greenfield, MA.
Publications: Application guidelines, corporate report.
Application information: Contributions are handled by Public Affairs. Application form required.
  Initial approach: Telephone inquiry
  Deadline(s): Oct. 1
  Board meeting date(s): Dec.
  Write: Chip Geer, Public Affairs Specialist
Number of staff: 1 part-time professional.

482
Pitney Bowes Corporate Contributions Program
World Headquarters
Stamford 06926-0700   (203) 351-7751

Financial data (yr. ended 12/31/90): Total giving, $1,900,000, including $1,490,000 for grants and $410,000 for employee matching gifts.
Purpose and activities: Supports programs concerning education, human services, health, the United Way, community services and culture. Types of support include capital campaigns, employee matching gifts, and general support.
Fields of interest: Education, health, welfare, community development, cultural programs, community funds.
Types of support: Operating budgets, capital campaigns, employee matching gifts.
Limitations: Giving primarily in company operating areas of CT, NE, NY, and OH. No support for individuals, tax-supported institutions, fraternal, political, lobbying or religious organizations, sporting events, or single-disease health programs. Generally does not give company products or equipment. Does not purchase tickets or advertising space. No scholarships are given; no sponsorship or underwriting the costs associated with conferences, underwriting or advertising for television programing, or participation in auctions.
Publications: Application guidelines.
Application information: "Corporate Contributions are administered at the headquarters location on an ongoing basis. Each branch, operating unit and subsidiary has a smaller budget primarily earmarked for the United Way and other local community projects".
  Initial approach: Proposal
  Deadline(s): None
  Write: Mary M. McCaskey, Mgr., Community Rels. and Corp. Contribs.

483
The RORD Foundation
26 Deer Park Dr.
Greenwich 06830

Established in 1987 in CT.
Donor(s): Richard Dowling.
Foundation type: Operating
Financial data (yr. ended 07/31/91): Assets, $5,577,435 (M); expenditures, $592,356; qualifying distributions, $543,635, including $217,900 for 15 grants (high: $82,400; low: $1,000).
Fields of interest: Secondary education, higher education, international affairs, Catholic giving, youth, drug abuse.
Limitations: Giving primarily in CT, NY, and Washington, DC. No grants to individuals.
Application information: Contributes only to pre-selected organizations. Applications not accepted.
Trustees: Janet Dowling, Richard Dowling.
EIN: 222848972

484
The Richard and Hinda Rosenthal Foundation
Five High Ridge Park
Stamford 06905   (203) 322-9900

Trust established in 1948 in NY.
Donor(s): The Richard L. Rosenthal family, and associated interests.
Foundation type: Independent
Financial data (yr. ended 12/31/91): Assets, $13,200,000 (M); expenditures, $600,000; qualifying distributions, $600,000, including $500,000 for 160 grants (high: $100,000; low: $500).
Purpose and activities: To encourage achievement and excellence in the arts, social sciences, medical and scientific research, and clinical medicine. Conceived and annually sponsors the Rosenthal Awards for Fiction and for Painting through the American Academy and National Institute of Arts and Letters; also conceived and sponsors five national awards in clinical medicine through the American College of Physicians, American Heart Association, American Association for Cancer Research, and others. Has sponsored similar "discovery" awards in film.
Fields of interest: Social sciences, medical sciences, film, medical research, language and literature, child development, hospices, theater.
Types of support: Research, special projects, general purposes, continuing support, fellowships, matching funds, conferences and seminars.
Limitations: No grants to individuals.
Publications: Program policy statement.
Application information:
  Initial approach: Letter
  Copies of proposal: 1
  Deadline(s): Oct. 31
  Board meeting date(s): As required
  Write: Hinda Gould Rosenthal, Pres.
Officers and Trustees:* Richard L. Rosenthal,* Chair.; Hinda Gould Rosenthal,* Pres.; Richard L. Rosenthal, Jr.,* V.P.; Jamie G.R. Wolf,* V.P.
Number of staff: 2 part-time professional; 2 part-time support.
EIN: 136104817

485
The Robert and Ruth Satter Charitable Trust
339 Stanley Dr.
Glastonbury 06033   (203) 659-2498

Established in 1989 in CT.
Donor(s): Robert Satter, Ruth Satter, Helen and Milton Kimmelman Foundation.
Foundation type: Independent
Financial data (yr. ended 04/30/91): Assets, $183,552 (M); gifts received, $175,000; expenditures, $335,970; qualifying distributions, $333,350, including $333,350 for 22 grants (high: $52,550; low: $250).
Fields of interest: Performing arts, family planning, education, civil rights, conservation, delinquency, disadvantaged, crime and law enforcement, cancer, aged.
Types of support: General purposes.
Limitations: Giving primarily in CT. No grants to individuals.

Application information:
Copies of proposal: 8
Deadline(s): Mar. 1
Board meeting date(s): Mid-Apr.
Write: Robert Satter, Trustee
Trustee: Robert Satter.
Number of staff: None.
EIN: 222986191

486
The Helen M. Saunders Charitable Foundation, Inc.
One American Row
Hartford 06103-2819   (203) 251-5152

Established in 1985 in CT.
Foundation type: Independent
Financial data (yr. ended 06/30/91): Assets,
$2,987,605 (M); expenditures, $165,246;
qualifying distributions, $150,881, including
$122,481 for 47 grants (high: $17,000; low:
$200).
Purpose and activities: Giving primarily for
hospitals and performing arts groups; support also
for education, public broadcasting, and a
Protestant church.
Fields of interest: Hospitals, performing arts,
education, media and communications, cultural
programs, Protestant giving.
Types of support: Annual campaigns, general
purposes, matching funds, capital campaigns,
endowment funds.
Limitations: Giving primarily in CT, with
emphasis on Hartford. No grants to individuals.
Publications: Application guidelines.
Application information:
Initial approach: Letter
Deadline(s): None
Write: Coleman H. Casey, Trustee
Trustee: Coleman H. Casey.
EIN: 066284362

487
Martin T. Sosnoff Foundation
84 Turtleback Rd.
New Canaan 06840

Established in 1978.
Donor(s): Martin T. Sosnoff.
Foundation type: Independent
Financial data (yr. ended 11/30/91): Assets,
$1,808,699 (M); expenditures, $254,037;
qualifying distributions, $253,900, including
$253,900 for 18 grants (high: $100,000; low:
$300).
Fields of interest: Hospitals, museums, higher
education, medical education, secondary
education.
Types of support: Building funds, general
purposes.
Limitations: Giving primarily in NY and CT. No
support for private foundations. No grants to
individuals.
Application information: Contributes only to
pre-selected organizations. Applications not
accepted.
Write: Martin T. Sosnoff, Trustee
Trustees: Eugene Sosnoff, Martin T. Sosnoff, Toni
Sosnoff.
EIN: 222231640

488
The Stanley Works Foundation ▼
c/o The New Connecticut Bank & Trust Co., N.A.
P.O. Box 567
Hartford 06141-0567   (203) 225-5111

Trust established in 1967 in CT.
Donor(s): The Stanley Works.
Foundation type: Company-sponsored
Financial data (yr. ended 12/31/90): Assets,
$1,678,832 (M); gifts received, $1,000,125;
expenditures, $1,231,567; qualifying
distributions, $1,221,040, including $1,219,735
for 868 grants (high: $50,000; average:
$1,000-$5,000).
Purpose and activities: Main emphasis on
affordable housing, education, including retention
programs in elementary and secondary education
and higher education; support also for child
welfare, health, hospital building funds,
engineering, and the environment.
Fields of interest: Housing, homeless, higher
education, secondary education, elementary
education, literacy, child welfare,
hospitals—building funds, engineering,
environment.
Types of support: Continuing support, annual
campaigns, seed money, emergency funds,
special projects, research, matching funds,
employee matching gifts, building funds,
internships.
Limitations: Giving primarily in areas of company
operations in CA, CT, GA, MI, OH, OR, PA, RI,
SC, TN, and VT. No support for United Way
supported organizations. No grants to individuals,
or for endowments, operating budgets, deficit
financing, equipment, land acquisition,
renovation projects, publications, or conferences;
no loans.
Publications: Application guidelines.
Application information: Application form
required.
Initial approach: Letter
Deadline(s): Jan., Apr., July, and Oct.
Board meeting date(s): Feb., May, Aug., and
Nov.
Final notification: 1 month after board meeting
Write: Ronald F. Gilrain, V.P., Public Affairs
Trustee: The New Connecticut Bank & Trust Co.,
N.A.
Number of staff: 1 full-time professional; 1
part-time professional; 1 full-time support.
EIN: 066088099

489
The Stone Foundation, Inc.
25 Ford Rd., Suite 200
Westport 06880   (203) 227-2000

Incorporated in 1964 in OH; reincorporated in
1972 in CT.
Donor(s): Marion H. Stone,‡ Charles Lynn Stone.‡
Foundation type: Independent
Financial data (yr. ended 12/31/91): Assets,
$10,220,079 (M); expenditures, $456,580;
qualifying distributions, $216,906, including
$188,818 for 7 grants (high: $50,000; low: $700;
average: $700-$50,000).
Purpose and activities: Primary interest in seed
money for unique projects and programs in
medicine, education, and related areas.

Fields of interest: Medical education, medical
sciences.
Types of support: Seed money, general purposes,
building funds, endowment funds.
Limitations: No grants to individuals, or for
matching gifts, scholarships, fellowships, or
special projects; no loans.
Publications: Program policy statement,
application guidelines.
Application information: Funds presently
committed; grant requests only from qualified
medical schools, colleges, and universities.
Application form not required.
Initial approach: Proposal
Copies of proposal: 1
Deadline(s): Submit proposal preferably in
Sept.; deadline Oct. 15
Board meeting date(s): Nov.
Final notification: By Jan. 31
Write: Robert B. Milligan, Jr., Secy.-Treas.
Officers and Trustees:* Charles Lynn Stone, Jr.,*
Pres.; Edward E. Stone,* V.P.; Robert B. Milligan,
Jr.,* Secy.-Treas.; Paul W. Adams, Mary Stone
Payson, Sara S. Stone.
Number of staff: 1 part-time professional.
EIN: 237148468

490
The Tow Foundation, Inc.
(Formerly The Claire and Leonard Tow
Foundation, Inc.)
c/o Century Communications Corp.
50 Locust Ave.
New Canaan 06840

Established in 1988 in CT.
Donor(s): Leonard Tow, Claire Tow.
Foundation type: Independent
Financial data (yr. ended 12/31/91): Assets,
$3,983,700 (M); gifts received, $1,141,875;
expenditures, $199,337; qualifying distributions,
$197,969, including $197,969 for 85 grants
(high: $50,000; low: $50).
Purpose and activities: Giving primarily to a
hospital.
Fields of interest: Hospitals, cancer, general
charitable giving.
Types of support: Research.
Limitations: Giving primarily in NY, CT, and MA.
No grants to individuals.
Application information: Contributes only to
pre-selected organizations. Applications not
accepted.
Directors: David Rosensweig, Scott Schneider,
Claire Tow, Leonard Tow.
EIN: 061255825

491
The Travelers Companies Foundation ▼
One Tower Sq.
Hartford 06183-1060   (203) 277-2303
Additional tel.: (203) 277-4070

Established about 1984 in CT.
Donor(s): The Travelers Corp., and subsidiaries.
Foundation type: Company-sponsored
Financial data (yr. ended 12/31/90): Assets,
$5,614,421 (M); gifts received, $4,750,000;
expenditures, $4,412,686; qualifying
distributions, $4,412,686, including $3,783,672
for 143 grants (high: $250,000; low: $110;

average: $2,000-$25,000) and $629,014 for 2,729 employee matching gifts.

Purpose and activities: Support primarily for programs that benefit older Americans, youth education, and children's health. Grants also for community development, health and social services, arts and culture, and higher education; support for capital campaigns on a local level only.

Fields of interest: Aged, youth, civic affairs, public affairs, community development, community funds, social services, health services, AIDS, education, secondary education, cultural programs, arts, higher education.

Types of support: General purposes, operating budgets, special projects, research, fellowships, technical assistance, capital campaigns, employee matching gifts, seed money.

Limitations: Giving primarily in areas of company operations; giving for capital projects limited to the greater Hartford, CT, area; grants for youth education limited to programs within Hartford, CT, schools, giving for health initiatives restricted to the Hartford, CT, area. No support for political, fraternal, athletic, social, or veterans' organizations; religious sectarian activities; or for business, professional, or trade associations. No grants to individuals, or for mass mail appeals, testimonial dinners, films, conferences, annual meetings, advertising, or publication of magazines or books.

Publications: Annual report, 990-PF, application guidelines.

Application information: Application form not required.

Initial approach: Proposal
Copies of proposal: 1
Deadline(s): None
Board meeting date(s): Quarterly
Final notification: Usually within 60 days
Write: Debbie McCants, Fdn. Asst.

Officers and Directors:* F. Peter Libassi,* Chair.; Nancy Van Doren,* Pres.; Michael S. Smiley, Secy. and Counsel; William White,* Treas.; Elliot F. Gerson, Thomas Helfrich, Brooks Joslin, John Motley.

Number of staff: 1 full-time professional; 4 part-time professional; 1 full-time support; 2 part-time support.

EIN: 222535386

Recent health grants:

491-1 Alliance for Aging Research, DC, $25,000. For general support. 1990.

491-2 American Red Cross, Greater Hartford Chapter, Farmington, CT, $11,250. For one self-contained blood donor vehicle. 1990.

491-3 California State University, Ruby Gerontology Center and Research Institute, Fullerton, CA, $10,000. For research, teaching and health promotion services. 1990.

491-4 Connecticut AIDS Consortium, Hartford, CT, $15,000. For social worker to serve needs of Hartford-area pediatric AIDS patients and their families. 1990.

491-5 Connecticut Community Care, Bristol, CT, $16,010. For one-day seminars in five cities, in response to growing national interest in case management services. 1990.

491-6 Drugs Dont Work, Hartford, CT, $12,500. To train teachers in design and implementation of curricula focused on substance abuse prevention. 1990.

491-7 Hartford Action Plan on Infant Health, Hartford, CT, $20,000. For general support. 1990.

491-8 Hartford Hospital, Hartford, CT, $250,000. For capital campaign. 1990.

491-9 National Council on the Aging, DC, $60,000. For geriatric fellowship program. 1990.

491-10 National Council on the Aging, DC, $15,000. For general support. 1990.

491-11 Project HOPE, Chevy Chase, MD, $10,000. For Community Health Education-Medicaid Access Project for low-income Hispanic residents in Lower Rio Grande Valley, Texas. 1990.

491-12 University of Connecticut Foundation, Travelers Center on Aging, Storrs, CT, $250,000. For expansion of Center through establishment of Research Institute on Health Promotion and Aging. 1990.

491-13 University of Connecticut Health Center, Farmington, CT, $25,000. For program activities of Travelers Center on Aging and to stimulate interest in geriatrics and gerontology within university. 1990.

491-14 University of Hartford, West Hartford, CT, $125,000. For Hartford Early Learning Partnership, program in which University's Colleges of Education, Nursing and Health Professions work with Hartford Public Schools to implement model kindergarten curricula. 1990.

492
Union Carbide Contributions Program

39 Old Ridgebury Road
Danbury 06817-0001   (203) 794-7053

Financial data (yr. ended 12/31/89): Total giving, $3,044,000, including $2,991,000 for grants (high: $100,000; low: $100; average: $3,000-$10,000) and $53,000 for in-kind gifts.

Purpose and activities: Main interest in the restructuring of public education, primarily targeting secondary and elementary programs that stress the sciences and elementary programs that encourage at-risk youths and minorities; health, engineering, environment, law and justice, hospices and hospitals in operating areas, public policy, science and technology, and civic affairs. Minimal consideration is given to the arts. Types of support include general support, in-kind donations and volunteer recruitment.

Fields of interest: Education, health, civic affairs, education—minorities, engineering, environment, higher education, hospices, law and justice, physical sciences, public policy, science and technology.

Types of support: General purposes, equipment, emergency funds, special projects, in-kind gifts, employee volunteer services, use of facilities, donated equipment, operating budgets, fellowships, internships.

Limitations: Giving primarily in company operating areas in Danbury, CT, Taft, CA, Texas City, TX, Charleston, WV, and Buffalo and Tarrytown, NY. No support for public-supported health organizations. No grants to individuals, or for capital campaigns or advertising.

Application information: Application form not required.

Initial approach: Preferred initial contact: phone call, and letter of proposal to nearest company facility
Copies of proposal: 1
Deadline(s): Applications accepted throughout the year
Board meeting date(s): Quarterly
Final notification: 4 weeks
Write: Clyde H. Greenert, Dir. of Contribs.

Administrators: Judith A. Hlavenka, Contribs. Admin.; Patricia T. Barker, Contribs. Assoc.

Number of staff: 2 full-time professional; 2 full-time support.

493
United Technologies Corporate Contributions Program

United Technologies Bldg.
Hartford 06101   (203) 728-7943

Financial data (yr. ended 12/31/90): Total giving, $12,125,367, including $10,489,912 for grants (high: $300,000; low: $1,000; average: $5,000-$20,000) and $1,635,455 for 8,007 employee matching gifts.

Purpose and activities: Supports education, including higher education, engineering, health, human services, culture and civic affairs. Types of support include employee matching gifts for education and culture, special project funding and research/study funding. Programs of interest are: Head Start, family literacy, kindergarten to graduate school math and science, health care cost containment, family arts series, and technical education.

Fields of interest: Education, health, social services, cultural programs, civic affairs, higher education, mathematics, Italy, Mexico, Spain, Asia, Australia, Canada, France, United Kingdom, Southern Africa, South Pacific, Europe, Southeast Asia.

Types of support: Capital campaigns, employee matching gifts, matching funds, special projects, research, scholarship funds, donated equipment, employee volunteer services, in-kind gifts, use of facilities.

Limitations: Giving primarily in company operating areas which include all states except ID, ND, SD, UT, and WY, and Italy, Mexico, Spain, Asia Pacific, Latin America, Puerto Rico, Germany, Australia, Canada, France, Germany, Hong Kong, India, Netherlands, New Zealand, Singapore, South Africa, Taiwan, and the United Kingdom.

Publications: Corporate giving report (including application guidelines).

Application information: Include 501 (c)(3), organization description, project description, board list and donor list, expected results of activity. Application form not required.

Initial approach: Letter; Send requests to headquarters
Copies of proposal: 1
Deadline(s): Applications preferred in Aug.
Board meeting date(s): Jan.
Final notification: If approved
Write: Richard Creighton Cole, Dir., Public Affairs

Directors: Deborah Hanley, Sr., Contribs. Admin., Education; Jane E. Wlochowski, Contribs. Admin.

Number of staff: 4 full-time professional.

494
UST Corporate Giving Program
100 West Putnam Ave.
Greenwich 06830   (203) 622-3696

Financial data (yr. ended 12/31/90): Total giving, $4,000,000 for 350 grants (high: $500,000; low: $100; average: $1,000-$2,500).
Purpose and activities: Supports social services, education, arts and humanities, civic and public affairs, and science. Types of support include printing, meeting space, donated materials, donated company products and services, general operating expenses, capital projects, special projects, and employee matching gifts.
Fields of interest: Education, higher education, education—minorities, arts, cultural programs, humanities, civic affairs, women, health, medical research, social services, aged, international relief, ecology, homeless, hunger, alcoholism, fine arts, housing, general charitable giving, leadership development, minorities, secondary education, literacy, museums, theater, wildlife, marine sciences, performing arts, urban affairs, volunteerism, Native Americans, safety, welfare, youth.
Types of support: General purposes, capital campaigns, special projects, employee matching gifts, employee-related scholarships, operating budgets, in-kind gifts.
Limitations: Giving primarily in headquarters city and major operating locations. No support for fraternal organizations, political, lobbying groups, or religious organizations. No grants to individuals, dinners, or goodwill advertising.
Publications: Corporate report, corporate giving report.
Application information: Company has a staff that only handles contributions. Application form not required.
   Initial approach: Letter and proposal; Send requests to headquarters
   Copies of proposal: 1
   Deadline(s): None
   Board meeting date(s): Quarterly
   Write: Geraldine K. Morgan, Mgr., Corp. Contributions Committee
Administrators: Ralph L. Rossi, Chair., Corp. Contribs.; Geraldine K. Morgan, Mgr., Corp. Contribs.
Number of staff: 2 full-time professional; 1 part-time support.

495
Robert C. Vance Charitable Foundation
21 Winesap Rd.
Kensington 06037-2932   (203) 828-6037

Established in 1960 in CT.
Donor(s): Robert C. Vance.‡
Foundation type: Independent
Financial data (yr. ended 01/31/91): Assets, $6,127,411 (M); expenditures, $311,566; qualifying distributions, $292,861, including $288,193 for 20 grants (high: $60,000; low: $500).
Fields of interest: Education, youth, hospitals, civic affairs, homeless.
Limitations: Giving limited to the New Britain-Berlin, CT, area. No grants to individuals.
Publications: Application guidelines.

Application information: Application form not required.
   Deadline(s): None
   Write: Herbert E. Carlson, Jr., Pres.
Officer: Herbert E. Carlson, Jr., Pres.
Trustee Bank: Connecticut National Bank.
Number of staff: None.
EIN: 066050188

496
R. T. Vanderbilt Trust
30 Winfield St.
Norwalk 06855   (203) 853-1400

Trust established in 1951 in CT.
Foundation type: Independent
Financial data (yr. ended 12/31/90): Assets, $6,893,059 (M); expenditures, $347,373; qualifying distributions, $319,016, including $302,060 for 116 grants (high: $73,000; low: $100).
Purpose and activities: Emphasis on education and conservation; support also for hospitals, cultural programs, and historic preservation.
Fields of interest: Education, conservation, hospitals, cultural programs, historic preservation.
Types of support: Building funds, endowment funds, operating budgets, special projects.
Limitations: Giving primarily in CT and NY. No grants to individuals.
Application information: Application form not required.
   Initial approach: Proposal
   Copies of proposal: 1
   Deadline(s): Submit proposal preferably in Nov.
   Board meeting date(s): Apr., June, Sept., and Dec.
   Write: Hugh B. Vanderbilt, Chair.
Trustees: Hugh B. Vanderbilt, Chair.; Robert T. Vanderbilt, Jr.
Number of staff: 2 part-time support.
EIN: 066040981

497
The Waterbury Foundation
P.O. Box 252
Waterbury 06720   (203) 753-1315

Incorporated in 1923 by special Act of the CT Legislature.
Donor(s): Katherine Pomeroy,‡ Edith Chase.‡
Foundation type: Community
Financial data (yr. ended 12/31/91): Assets, $10,794,696 (M); gifts received, $531,258; expenditures, $592,053; qualifying distributions, $369,637, including $341,787 for 62 grants (high: $62,608) and $27,850 for 37 grants to individuals.
Purpose and activities: Current priority areas of grantmaking are teenage growth and development and arts and humanities; emphasis on providing seed money and venture capital for new projects.
Fields of interest: Social services, health services, higher education, education, youth, community funds, arts, AIDS.
Types of support: Seed money, emergency funds, building funds, equipment, matching funds, research, special projects, publications, conferences and seminars, capital campaigns, consulting services, renovation projects,

scholarship funds, technical assistance, student aid.
Limitations: Giving limited to the greater Waterbury, CT, area. No support for sectarian or religious purposes. No grants for deficit financing, continuing support, or annual campaigns; no loans.
Publications: Annual report (including application guidelines), program policy statement, newsletter, informational brochure (including application guidelines), application guidelines.
Application information: Application form required.
   Initial approach: Telephone or letter
   Copies of proposal: 30
   Deadline(s): Jan. for arts and historic preservation and designated fund requests, May for teenage growth and development and education, and Sept. for all other requests
   Board meeting date(s): Mar., June, and Nov.; Grants Committee meets twice, 6 weeks and 1 week prior to each board meeting
   Final notification: 7 weeks
   Write: Mrs. Ingrid Manning, Administrator
Officers and Trustees:* Patricia B. Sweet,* Pres.; Charles W. Henry,* V.P.; Ann Y. Smith,* V.P.; W. Scott Peterson, M.D.,* Secy.; Sean T. Egan,* Treas.; Burton Albert, Carol B. Andrews, Dirck Barhydt, Robert E. Beaudoin, Lillian H. Brown, George Frantzis, Sr., Robert W. Garthwait, Sr., Sr. Margaret Rosita Kenney, Pasquale Palumbo, Isabel Romero, Paul N. Vonckx, Jr.
Trustee Banks: Bank of Boston Connecticut, Chase Manhattan Bank of Connecticut, Connecticut National Bank.
Number of staff: 2 full-time professional; 1 full-time support.
EIN: 066038074

498
The Whitehead Charitable Foundation
P.O. Box 120033
Stamford 06912-0033

Established in 1976.
Donor(s): Edwin C. Whitehead.‡
Foundation type: Independent
Financial data (yr. ended 11/30/90): Assets, $8,141,482 (M); gifts received, $767,972; expenditures, $124,561; qualifying distributions, $50,000, including $50,000 for 1 grant.
Purpose and activities: Grants primarily for biomedical research.
Fields of interest: Medical research, biological sciences.
Types of support: Research, endowment funds.
Application information: Application form not required.
   Deadline(s): None
   Write: William F. Campbell
Officers and Directors:* John J. Whitehead,* Pres.; Peter J. Whitehead,* V.P.; Arthur W. Brill, Secy.-Treas.; Susan Whitehead.
EIN: 060956618

499
Xerox Corporate Contributions Program
P.O. Box 1600
Stamford 06904   (203) 968-3306

Financial data (yr. ended 12/31/90): Total giving, $15,400,000, including $14,400,000 for grants and $1,000,000 for employee matching gifts.
Purpose and activities: Supports community affairs, cultural affairs, national and international affairs, and education.
Fields of interest: Civic affairs, arts, humanities, health, welfare, education, community funds, law and justice, urban affairs, employment, international affairs.
Types of support: Exchange programs, research.
Limitations: No support for religious organizations, political parties. No grants to individuals, or for capital grants (except in major cities) or endowments.
Publications: Informational brochure.
Application information:
  Initial approach: Letter
  Final notification: If turned down, company will send a rejection notice
  Write: Robert H. Gudger, Mgr. of Corp. Responsibilities and V.P., The Xerox Foundation

500
The Xerox Foundation ▼
P.O. Box 1600
Stamford 06904   (203) 968-3306

Incorporated in 1978 in DE as successor to Xerox Fund.
Donor(s): Xerox Corp.
Foundation type: Company-sponsored
Financial data (yr. ended 12/31/90): Assets, $777,487 (M); gifts received, $12,500,000; expenditures, $14,787,370; qualifying distributions, $14,779,482, including $14,728,185 for 1,526 grants (high: $1,000,000; low: $25; average: $2,000-$20,000).
Purpose and activities: Broad commitment in support of higher education to prepare qualified men and women for careers in business, government, and education; advance knowledge in science and technology; commitment also to enhance learning opportunities for minorities and the disadvantaged. Also operates employee matching gift program. Support additionally for social, civic, and cultural organizations including the United Way, providing broad-based programs and services in cities where Xerox employees live and work, organizations that foster debate on major national public policy issues, and worldwide, for leadership efforts around major social problems, education, employability, and student exchange.
Fields of interest: Higher education, education—minorities, business education, education—early childhood, secondary education, science and technology, social services, rural development, drug abuse, community funds, cultural programs, public policy, international affairs, foreign policy, Southern Africa, Asia, Canada, Latin America, Caribbean, Middle East, leprosy.
Types of support: General purposes, operating budgets, annual campaigns, seed money,

emergency funds, research, conferences and seminars, scholarship funds, fellowships, professorships, internships, employee-related scholarships, exchange programs, employee matching gifts, program-related investments, consulting services, publications.
Limitations: Giving on a domestic and international basis. No support for community colleges, organizations supported by United Way, religious organizations, or governmental agencies. No grants to individuals, or for capital or endowment funds; no donations of machines or related services; no loans.
Publications: Application guidelines.
Application information: Application form not required.
  Initial approach: Brief proposal
  Copies of proposal: 1
  Deadline(s): None
  Board meeting date(s): Usually in Dec. and as required
  Final notification: 3 months
  Write: Robert H. Gudger, V.P.
Officers: Robert H. Gudger, V.P.; Martin S. Wagner, Secy.; Allan Z. Senter, Treas.
Trustees: Paul A. Allaire, David T. Kearns, Stuart B. Ross.
Number of staff: 1 full-time professional; 4 full-time support.
EIN: 060996443
Recent health grants:
500-1 Al Sigl Center for Rehabilitation Agencies, Rochester, NY, $50,000. 1990.
500-2 Center for Development and Population Activities, DC, $20,000. 1990.
500-3 Genesee Region Home Care Association, Rochester, NY, $10,000. 1990.
500-4 Hole in the Wall Gang Camp Fund, Westport, CT, $25,000. 1990.
500-5 Kingsbury Center, DC, $20,000. 1990.
500-6 Leonard Wood Memorial for the Eradication of Leprosy, Rockville, MD, $30,000. 1990.
500-7 Liberation Programs, Stamford, CT, $15,000. 1990.
500-8 Media-Advertising Partnership for a Drug-Free America, NYC, NY, $25,000. 1990.
500-9 Memorial Sloan-Kettering Cancer Center, NYC, NY, $25,000. 1990.
500-10 Occupational Physicians Scholarship Fund, NYC, NY, $10,000. 1990.
500-11 Occupational Physicians Scholarship Fund, NYC, NY, $10,000. 1990.
500-12 Project Orbis, NYC, NY, $30,000. 1990.
500-13 Ronald McDonald House of Rochester, Rochester, NY, $10,000. 1990.
500-14 Saint Vincents Medical Center Foundation, Bridgeport, CT, $10,000. 1990.

501
Robert R. Young Foundation
P.O. Box 1423
Greenwich 06830

Established about 1959.
Donor(s): Anita O'Keefe Young.‡

Foundation type: Independent
Financial data (yr. ended 12/31/91): Assets, $31,060,048 (M); expenditures, $755,152; qualifying distributions, $731,253, including $703,125 for 39 grants (high: $265,000; low: $100).
Purpose and activities: Giving primarily for higher and other education; support also for Protestant churches, youth, and health and hospitals.
Fields of interest: Higher education, education, Protestant giving, youth, health, hospitals.
Types of support: Research, general purposes.
Limitations: Giving primarily in CT, RI, MA, and New York, NY. No grants to individuals.
Application information:
  Initial approach: Letter
  Deadline(s): None
  Final notification: 3 months
  Write: David W. Wallace, Pres.
Officer and Trustees:* David W. Wallace,* Pres.; Jean W. Wallace.
EIN: 136131394

502
The E. Matilda Ziegler Foundation for the Blind, Inc.
250 Harbor Dr.
P.O. Box 10128
Stamford 06904-2128   (203) 356-9000

Incorporated in 1928 in NY.
Donor(s): Mrs. William Ziegler.‡
Foundation type: Independent
Financial data (yr. ended 12/31/90): Assets, $10,573,780 (M); gifts received, $300; expenditures, $684,987; qualifying distributions, $572,556, including $540,750 for 19 grants (high: $251,250; low: $1,000).
Purpose and activities: Giving for charitable and educational work to ameliorate the condition of the blind; support largely for the monthly publication and free distribution of the Matilda Ziegler Magazine for the Blind.
Fields of interest: Ophthalmology, handicapped.
Types of support: General purposes, continuing support, annual campaigns, research.
Limitations: Giving primarily in CT, NY, and MA. No grants to individuals, or for endowment funds, scholarships, fellowships, or matching gifts; no loans.
Application information:
  Initial approach: Proposal
  Copies of proposal: 1
  Deadline(s): None
  Write: William Ziegler III, Pres.
Officers and Directors:* William Ziegler III,* Pres.; Helen Z. Steinkraus,* Secy.; Beatrice H. Page, Treas.; Charles B. Cook, Jr., Marvin L. Sears, Eric M. Steinkraus, Cynthia Zeigler-Brighton.
EIN: 136086195

DELAWARE

503
Jack and Mimi Leviton Amsterdam Foundation

One Rodney Sq., 10th Fl.
Tenth and King Sts.
Wilmington 19801

Established in 1977 in DE.
Donor(s): Jack Amsterdam.
Foundation type: Independent
Financial data (yr. ended 12/31/91): Assets, $2,112,494 (M); gifts received, $45,000; expenditures, $122,102; qualifying distributions, $121,450, including $121,450 for 21 grants (high: $50,000; low: $100).
Fields of interest: Medical research, medical education, higher education, Jewish welfare.
Types of support: Research, general purposes.
Limitations: Giving primarily in NY and DE. No grants to individuals.
Application information: Contributes only to pre-selected organizations. Applications not accepted.
  Write: Thomas Sweeney
Officers: Jack Amsterdam, Pres.; Dasha L. Epstein, V.P.
EIN: 510220854

504
Beneficial Foundation, Inc.

P.O. Box 911
Wilmington 19899   (302) 798-0800

Incorporated in 1951 in DE.
Donor(s): Beneficial Corp., and its subsidiaries, Beneficial New Jersey.
Foundation type: Company-sponsored
Financial data (yr. ended 12/31/90): Assets, $5,345,980 (M); gifts received, $350,000; expenditures, $794,543; qualifying distributions, $782,982, including $571,000 for 35 grants (high: $175,000; low: $1,000; average: $1,000-$10,000) and $192,100 for 175 grants to individuals (high: $2,500; low: $100).
Purpose and activities: Grants primarily to educational institutions, hospitals, and medical research; giving also through a scholarship program for children of employees of Beneficial Corp. or of the Beneficial Finance System. Support also for cultural programs.
Fields of interest: Hospitals, medical research, higher education, cultural programs.
Types of support: Employee-related scholarships, research, continuing support, annual campaigns, seed money, building funds, equipment, special projects.
Limitations: Giving primarily in DE, FL, NJ, and NY. No grants for endowment funds; no loans.
Application information: Application form required for scholarship applicants.
  Initial approach: Proposal
  Copies of proposal: 1
  Deadline(s): None
  Board meeting date(s): Usually in May and Dec.
  Write: John O. Williams, Dir.

Officers and Directors:* Robert A. Tucker,* Pres.; Finn M.W. Caspersen,* V.P.; M.A. McCardle, Secy.; J.H. Gilliam, Jr., Treas.; Freda R. Caspersen, John O. Williams.
Number of staff: 2 part-time support.
EIN: 516011637

505
Bernard A. & Rebecca S. Bernard Foundation

5007 Old Capitol Trail
Wilmington 19808   (302) 996-0505

Established in 1960.
Foundation type: Independent
Financial data (yr. ended 07/31/91): Assets, $3,600,613 (M); expenditures, $427,174; qualifying distributions, $408,623, including $408,623 for 65 grants (high: $50,000; low: $20).
Fields of interest: Jewish giving, Jewish welfare, higher education, cancer.
Limitations: Giving primarily in DE, MD, and PA.
Application information: Application form not required.
  Initial approach: Letter
  Deadline(s): None
Trustees: Bernard Bernstein, Marlyn Bernstein, Estelle Soloman.
EIN: 516157356

506
Stephen and Mary Birch Foundation, Inc.
▼
501 Silverside Rd., Suite 13
Wilmington 19809

Incorporated in 1938 in DE.
Donor(s): Stephen Birch.‡
Foundation type: Independent
Financial data (yr. ended 12/31/90): Assets, $101,328,851 (M); expenditures, $3,942,172; qualifying distributions, $2,801,859, including $2,116,215 for 51 grants (high: $770,000; low: $500; average: $10,000-$100,000) and $250,000 for loans.
Purpose and activities: Emphasis on health agencies, hospitals, youth agencies, cultural programs, social services, civic organizations, and the blind.
Fields of interest: Health services, handicapped, hospitals, youth, cultural programs, social services, civic affairs.
Application information: Application form not required.
  Initial approach: Letter
  Copies of proposal: 1
  Deadline(s): None
  Board meeting date(s): Quarterly
  Write: Elfriede Looze
Officers: Patrick J. Patek, Pres.; Christopher Patek, V.P.; Rose B. Patek, Secy.-Treas.
EIN: 221713022
Recent health grants:
506-1 Epilepsy Society of San Diego County, San Diego, CA, $25,000. For nonrestricted grant. 1990.

507
Chichester duPont Foundation, Inc.

3120 Kennett Pike
Wilmington 19807-3045   (302) 658-5244

Incorporated in 1946 in DE.
Donor(s): Lydia Chichester duPont,‡ Mary Chichester duPont Clark,‡ A. Felix duPont, Jr., Alice duPont Mills.
Foundation type: Independent
Financial data (yr. ended 12/31/90): Assets, $24,494,856 (M); expenditures, $1,409,344; qualifying distributions, $1,392,477, including $1,336,500 for 37 grants (high: $290,000; low: $5,000; average: $15,000-$50,000).
Purpose and activities: Emphasis on child welfare, including support for a camp for handicapped children, education, health, and cultural programs; some support for conservation.
Fields of interest: Child welfare, handicapped, education, health, cultural programs, conservation.
Types of support: Operating budgets, building funds.
Limitations: Giving primarily in DE, MD, and PA. No grants to individuals.
Application information: Application form not required.
  Deadline(s): Oct. 1
  Board meeting date(s): Dec.
  Final notification: 2 weeks after meeting
  Write: Gregory F. Fields, Secy.
Officers: Alice duPont Mills, Pres.; Christopher T. duPont, V.P.; Gregory F. Fields, Secy.; A. Felix duPont, Jr., Treas.
Trustees: Mary Mills Abel-Smith, Caroline J. duPont, Mrs. Richard C. duPont, Jr., Phyllis Mills Wyeth.
Number of staff: None.
EIN: 516011641

508
Columbia Gas Foundation

20 Montchanin Rd.
P.O. Box 4020
Wilmington 19807-0200   (302) 429-5000

Established in 1990 in DE.
Donor(s): The Columbia Gas System, Inc., and its affiliated companies.
Foundation type: Company-sponsored
Financial data (yr. ended 12/31/91): Assets, $734,000 (M); gifts received, $1,079,000; expenditures, $1,042,000; qualifying distributions, $1,040,000, including $939,000 for 177 grants (high: $186,000; low: $25; average: $25-$186,000) and $101,000 for 203 employee matching gifts.
Fields of interest: Health, education, cultural programs, arts, civic affairs, community funds, youth.
Types of support: Annual campaigns, building funds, continuing support, employee matching gifts.
Limitations: Giving limited to areas of company operations. No support for organizations established for religious purposes or fraternal, advocacy, or labor organizations. No grants to individuals, or for printed programs, yearbooks, advertising, or tickets for benefit performances or functions.
Publications: 990-PF.

Application information: Application form required.

Initial approach: Proposal
Copies of proposal: 1
Deadline(s): Sept. 1 for renewal grants
Board meeting date(s): Nov.
Final notification: Dec.

Officers and Directors:* J.D. Croon,* Chair.; J.B. Lange, Pres.; W.L. McLaughlin, V.P.; J.K. Hayes, Secy.; D.P. Detan, Treas.; D.L. Bell, Jr., J.C. Daly, J.P. Holland, R.A. Oswald, C.R. Tilley, L.W. Wallingford.
Number of staff: None.
EIN: 510324200

509
The Columbia Gas System Corporate Contributions Program

20 Montchanin Rd.
Wilmington 19807   (302) 429-5261

Financial data (yr. ended 12/31/90): Total giving, $1,430,000, including $1,305,000 for grants and $125,000 for employee matching gifts.
Purpose and activities: Supports primarily social welfare, community development, health and hospitals, cultural and civic affairs, conservation, education, and economic education. Types of support include matching gifts and employee volunteer/loan programs.
Fields of interest: Social services, cultural programs, civic affairs, education, economics, hospitals, libraries, arts, higher education, public policy, safety, urban development, media and communications, environment, secondary education, medical research, recreation, aged, child welfare, community funds, volunteerism, business education, conservation, health associations, hospitals—building funds, music, performing arts, race relations, community development.
Types of support: Matching funds, research, building funds, capital campaigns, general purposes, operating budgets, special projects, endowment funds, employee matching gifts.
Limitations: Giving primarily in Wilmington, DE, Columbus and Toledo, OH, KY, MD, NJ, NY, PA, TX, and VA. No support for political, labor, veterans', or strictly sectarian/denominational religious organizations. No grants to organizations eligible for but not participating in United Way support. No grants to individuals; or for operating expenses of United Way agencies; or for courtesy advertising.
Publications: Informational brochure (including application guidelines).
Application information: Application form not required.

Initial approach: Letter
Copies of proposal: 1
Final notification: 8-10 weeks
Write: William Chaddock, V.P., Corp. Communs.

510
Crystal Trust ▼

1088 DuPont Bldg.
Wilmington 19898   (302) 774-8421

Trust established in 1947 in DE.
Donor(s): Irenee duPont.‡

Foundation type: Independent
Financial data (yr. ended 12/31/91): Assets, $66,113,196 (M); expenditures, $3,294,145; qualifying distributions, $3,294,145, including $3,196,700 for 48 grants (high: $320,000; low: $3,600; average: $10,000-$100,000).
Purpose and activities: Giving mainly for higher and secondary education and social and family services, including youth and child welfare agencies, family planning, and programs for the aged, the disadvantaged, and the homeless; support also for the arts and cultural programs, health and hospitals, conservation programs, and historical preservation.
Fields of interest: Education, higher education, secondary education, libraries, social services, family services, family planning, youth, child welfare, aged, disadvantaged, homeless, housing, hunger, cultural programs, arts, museums, music, health, hospitals, hospices, conservation.
Types of support: Seed money, building funds, equipment, land acquisition, program-related investments, renovation projects, capital campaigns, special projects.
Limitations: Giving primarily in DE, especially Wilmington. No grants to individuals, or for endowment funds, research, scholarships, fellowships, or matching gifts.
Publications: Application guidelines, program policy statement, informational brochure (including application guidelines).
Application information: Application form not required.

Initial approach: Proposal
Copies of proposal: 1
Deadline(s): Oct. 1
Board meeting date(s): Nov.
Final notification: Dec. 15
Write: Stephen C. Doberstein, Dir.

Director: Burt C. Pratt.
Trustees: Irenee duPont, Jr., David Greenewalt, Eleanor S. Maroney.
Number of staff: 1 part-time professional; 1 part-time support.
EIN: 516015063
Recent health grants:
510-1 Easter Seal Society of Del-Mar, Wilmington, DE, $25,000. For capital needs. 1990.
510-2 Open Door, Claymont, DE, $10,000. For relocation costs. 1990.
510-3 Peninsula United Methodist Homes and Hospitals, Seaford Manor House, Wilmington, DE, $25,000. For Alzheimer wing. 1990.
510-4 United Cerebral Palsy of Delaware, Wilmington, DE, $65,000. For renovations. 1990.

511
Delaware Community Foundation

P.O. Box 25207
Wilmington 19899   (302) 571-8004

Incorporated in 1986 in DE.
Foundation type: Community
Financial data (yr. ended 06/30/91): Assets, $11,059,319 (M); gifts received, $2,613,900; expenditures, $877,662; qualifying distributions, $630,254, including $605,254 for 90 grants (high: $30,000; low: $1,000; average: $1,000-$10,000) and $25,000 for 20 grants to

individuals (high: $5,000; low: $1,000; average: $1,000).
Fields of interest: Community development, housing, arts, environment, health, education, general charitable giving.
Types of support: Seed money, technical assistance, capital campaigns, general purposes.
Limitations: Giving limited to DE. No support for religious or sectarian purposes, or for fraternal or veterans' groups. No grants to individuals, or for annual funds.
Publications: Annual report, application guidelines, informational brochure, newsletter.
Application information: Application form not required.

Initial approach: Telephone
Deadline(s): Nov. and Feb.
Board meeting date(s): Quarterly
Final notification: After final reviews in Dec. and Mar. meetings
Write: Collis O. Townsend, Exec. Dir.

Officers and Executive Committee Members:* Jeremiah P. Sheer,* Chair.; Elisabeth S. Poole,* Vice-Chair.; Steven R. Director, Secy.; Alexander L. Searl,* Treas.; Collis O. Townsend, Exec. Dir.; Sandra V. Dull, Judith H. Hoopes, Charles F. Richards, Jr., Sherman L. Townsend.
Number of staff: 2 full-time professional; 1 full-time support; 1 part-time support.
EIN: 222804785
Recent health grants:
511-1 Delaware Theater Company, Wilmington, DE, $10,000. For statewide tour of Crossin' the Line, production on legal and moral consequences of drinking and driving. 1991.
511-2 Henrietta Johnson Medical Center, Wilmington, DE, $10,000. To reduce barriers to access to health care and to support educational programs for teens/adolescents to reduce number of low birthweight babies in Southbridge. 1991.
511-3 Peninsula United Methodist Homes and Hospitals, Wilmington, DE, $25,000. Toward construction of Alzheimer's wing at Seaford Methodist Manor House. 1991.
511-4 Turnabout Counseling Center, Georgetown, DE, $10,000. To expand in-home family treatment program for at-risk adolescents and families suffering from substance abuse, divorce, bereavement or poor parenting skills. 1991.
511-5 Volunteers for Adolescent Pregnancy Prevention, Wilmington, DE, $10,000. To expand counseling and health services at Latin American Community Center to decrease incidence of teenage pregnancy and sexually transmitted diseases. 1991.

512
Delmarva Power and Light Corporate Giving Program

P.O. Box 231
Wilmington 19899   (302) 429-3410

Financial data (yr. ended 12/31/90): Total giving, $325,000 for grants.
Purpose and activities: Support for culture, business, business education, computer sciences, economics, community development, crime and law enforcement, leadership development, employment, minorities, the handicapped, rural development, science and technology, media and

communications, volunteerism, and medical institutions.

Fields of interest: Aged, business, business education, cancer, citizenship, community development, computer sciences, conservation, crime and law enforcement, cultural programs, economics, employment, energy, leadership development, legal services, literacy, mental health, minorities, rural development, science and technology, volunteerism, hospitals.

Types of support: Annual campaigns, building funds, capital campaigns, conferences and seminars, general purposes, operating budgets, research, scholarship funds.

Limitations: Giving primarily in service territory of corporation.

Publications: Informational brochure (including application guidelines).

Application information: Application form required.

Board meeting date(s): July and as necessary
Final notification: Within 30 days of application
Write: Richard H. Evans, V.P., Corp. Communs.

513
DuPont Corporate Contributions Program

External Affairs Dept., DuPont and Co.
8065 DuPont Bldg.
Wilmington 19898   (302) 774-1000

Financial data (yr. ended 12/31/91): Total giving, $33,264,550, including $30,685,712 for grants (high: $1,500,000; low: $500; average: $500-$5,000) and $2,578,838 for in-kind gifts.

Purpose and activities: "Du Pont's Corporate Contributions Program is committed to improving the quality of life and enhancing the vitality of communities in which the Company has a major business presence. Its mission is to integrate such activities on a global scale with Du Pont's overall goals and objectives. All contributions, therefore, must serve to maintain institutions and services which impact Du Pont and its employees, the local community, and society in general." This includes programs which address special company interests or areas of expertise; organizations that provide resources and information upon which the company depends; nonprofit organizations whose functions are important to the company and society; programs which contribute to the well-being of employees as well as their community, and volunteer efforts. Main areas of support are education and the environment. In addition, Du Pont provides considerable support to the arts, health and human services organizations, and community and civic activities in communities where substantial company operations are located. The Committee on Contributions and Membership is responsible for non-higher educational monetary donations and business memberships. Individual business units with locations throughout the world, support programs relevant to their respective manufacturing, research, marketing, scientific, or community interests.

Fields of interest: Education, higher education, health, humanities, environment, civic affairs, community development, cultural programs, arts, community funds, economics, hospitals, public policy, women, minorities, housing, urban development, science and technology,

mathematics, Asia, Europe, Latin America, United Kingdom, international relief, international affairs.

Types of support: Capital campaigns, fellowships, general purposes, research, special projects, scholarship funds, donated equipment, donated products, donated land, annual campaigns, technical assistance, conferences and seminars, equipment, emergency funds, program-related investments, matching funds, research, seed money.

Limitations: Giving primarily in areas of company operations in U.S. and Mexico, Brazil, Argentina, Columbia, Venezuela, Canada, Japan, Korea, Hong Kong, Singapore, Australia, New Zealand, U.K., Belgium, Spain, France, Germany, Italy, Netherlands, Switzerland, and Indonesia; national and regional programs also supported. No support for sectarian religious groups, fraternal organizations, veterans' groups, or disease-specific organizations. No grants to individuals, or for endowments, student loans, surplus equipment, or advertising; generally no operating funds.

Publications: Application guidelines.

Application information: National organizations or programs in Wilmington, DE, write to headquarters; other projects should be addressed to nearest company site; most education grants are initiated by Du Pont, but applications are accepted. Application form not required.

Initial approach: Letter or proposal with cover letter; send request to headquarters or nearest company facility
Deadline(s): Major requests should be received by Aug.
Board meeting date(s): Corporate Committee meets in early summer and Oct.; major grants considered at annual budget review in Oct.
Final notification: For grants which are included in Du Pont's contribution budget, early Jan., other grants-shortly after committee meeting
Write: Peter C. Morrow, Mgr., Contribs. and Community Affairs

Number of staff: 5 full-time professional; 2 part-time professional; 4 full-time support.

514
Ederic Foundation, Inc.

P.O. Box 4420
Wilmington 19807

Incorporated in 1958 in DE.

Donor(s): John E. Riegel, Natalie R. Weymouth, Richard E. Riegel, Jr., Mrs. G. Burton Pearson, Jr.

Foundation type: Independent

Financial data (yr. ended 12/31/91): Assets, $7,209 (M); gifts received, $443,552; expenditures, $436,592; qualifying distributions, $436,592, including $436,535 for 97 grants (high: $55,335; low: $50).

Purpose and activities: Giving for private elementary and secondary schools, hospitals and health care, community funds, cultural institutions, and higher education; grants also for youth agencies and conservation.

Fields of interest: Elementary education, secondary education, hospitals, health services, community funds, cultural programs, higher education, youth, conservation.

Limitations: Giving primarily in DE, with emphasis on Wilmington. No grants to individuals.

Application information:
Initial approach: Letter
Deadline(s): None
Write: Harry S. Short, Secy.-Treas.

Officers and Trustees:* John E. Riegel, Pres.; Harry S. Short,* Secy.-Treas.; Robert C. McCoy, Richard E. Riegel, Jr., Philip B. Weymouth, Jr.

EIN: 516017927

515
Sumner Gerard Foundation

1209 Orange St.
Wilmington 19801

Established in 1963 in DE.

Donor(s): Sumner Gerard.‡

Foundation type: Independent

Financial data (yr. ended 04/30/91): Assets, $2,137,838 (M); expenditures, $118,588; qualifying distributions, $92,166, including $85,000 for 61 grants (high: $15,000; low: $250).

Fields of interest: Higher education, secondary education, religion—Christian, hospitals.

Limitations: No grants to individuals.

Application information: Contributes only to pre-selected organizations. Applications not accepted.

Officers: C.H. Coster Gerard, Pres.; John P. Campbell, V.P. and Secy.-Treas.; Hariet C. Gerard, V.P.; Edward Ortiz, V.P.

EIN: 136155552

516
Good Samaritan, Inc.

600 Center Mill Rd.
Wilmington 19807   (302) 654-7558

Incorporated in 1938 in DE.

Donor(s): Elias Ahuja.‡

Foundation type: Independent

Financial data (yr. ended 12/31/90): Assets, $2,000,472 (M); expenditures, $1,006,721; qualifying distributions, $995,635, including $993,620 for 11 grants (high: $250,000; low: $7,000).

Purpose and activities: Support for higher education, medicine, the study and treatment of dyslexia, improvement of the administration of justice, protection of the environment, and projects relating to Spain.

Fields of interest: Education, higher education, medical education, medical research, conservation, environment, hospitals.

Types of support: Endowment funds, operating budgets, special projects, conferences and seminars, professorships.

Limitations: Giving with special attention to projects relating to Spain. No grants to individuals, or for building funds.

Publications: Application guidelines.

Application information: Application form not required.

Initial approach: Proposal
Copies of proposal: 1
Deadline(s): None
Board meeting date(s): As required
Write: Carroll M. Carpenter, II, Secy.-Treas.

Officers and Directors:* H. Sinclair Sherrill,* Pres.; Jeffrey M. Nielsen,* V.P.; Carroll M. Carpenter,* Secy.-Treas.
Number of staff: None.
EIN: 516000401

517
ICI Americas Corporate Giving Program
Public Affairs Dept.
Concord Pike and New Murphy Rd.
Wilmington 19897   (302) 571-8004
Application Address: P.O. Box 25207, Wilmington, DE 19899

Purpose and activities: Support for the arts, environment, health care, chemistry, education, minorities, literacy, and general charitable giving.
Fields of interest: Arts, environment, health, chemistry, education, general charitable giving, minorities, literacy.
Types of support: Annual campaigns, matching funds, equipment, capital campaigns, general purposes.
Limitations: Giving primarily in areas of company operations.
Publications: Application guidelines.
Application information: Application form not required.
   Initial approach: Written request; send to nearest company facility
   Copies of proposal: 1
   Deadline(s): None
   Board meeting date(s): Quarterly
   Final notification: Written
   Write: Collis O. Townsend
Administrators: John P. Lynch, Chair., Corp. Contribs. Comm. Group; Leslie Green, Corp. Communs. Assist.; Collis O. Townsend.
Number of staff: 1 full-time support.

518
Kent-Lucas Foundation, Inc.
101 Springer Bldg.
3411 Silverside Rd.
Wilmington 19810   (302) 478-4383

Incorporated in 1968 in DE.
Donor(s): Atwater Kent Foundation, Inc.
Foundation type: Independent
Financial data (yr. ended 12/31/91): Assets, $2,852,598 (M); expenditures, $169,504; qualifying distributions, $157,075, including $155,400 for grants (average: $100-$5,000).
Purpose and activities: Grants largely for social service agencies aiding the disadvantaged; giving also for cultural programs, including historic preservation, hospitals, education, and church support.
Fields of interest: Social services, disadvantaged, cultural programs, historic preservation, hospitals, education, religion—Christian, general charitable giving.
Types of support: General purposes, operating budgets, continuing support, building funds.
Limitations: Giving primarily in the Philadelphia, PA, metropolitan area, ME, and FL. No grants to individuals, or for endowment funds.
Publications: Application guidelines.
Application information: Application form not required.
   Initial approach: Letter

Copies of proposal: 1
Deadline(s): None
Board meeting date(s): As required
Final notification: 1 to 3 months
Write: Elizabeth K. Van Alen, Pres.
Officers and Trustees:* Elizabeth K. Van Alen,* Pres. and Treas.; William L. Van Alen,* V.P.; James R. Weaver, Secy.; James L. Van Alen II, William L. Van Alen, Jr.
Number of staff: 4
EIN: 237010084

519
The Kingsley Foundation
c/o Wilmington Trust Co.
Rodney Sq. North
Wilmington 19890

Established in 1961 in CT.
Donor(s): F.G. Kingsley, Ora K. Smith.
Foundation type: Independent
Financial data (yr. ended 12/31/91): Assets, $3,897,798 (M); expenditures, $191,485; qualifying distributions, $186,297, including $185,500 for 52 grants (high: $50,000; low: $400).
Fields of interest: Hospitals, cultural programs, museums, education, social services, historic preservation, general charitable giving.
Types of support: General purposes.
Limitations: Giving primarily in NY. No grants to individuals.
Application information: Contributes only to pre-selected organizations. Applications not accepted.
Advisors: L. Heagney, Ora Rimes Kingsley, Minot K. Milliken, Roger Milliken, Ora K. Smith.
Trustee: Wilmington Trust Co.
EIN: 516163698

520
Milton and Hattie Kutz Foundation
101 Garden of Eden Rd.
Wilmington 19803   (302) 478-6200

Established in 1955 in DE.
Donor(s): Milton Kutz, Hattie Kutz.
Foundation type: Independent
Financial data (yr. ended 06/30/91): Assets, $2,334,581 (M); expenditures, $168,691; qualifying distributions, $149,618, including $102,575 for 18 grants (high: $20,000; low: $875; average: $1,000-$10,000) and $41,000 for grants to individuals (average: $1,000-$1,500).
Purpose and activities: Giving largely for social service organizations; grants also for child welfare, drug abuse programs, and higher education, including scholarships to residents of DE who will be college freshmen.
Fields of interest: Social services, child welfare, drug abuse, higher education.
Types of support: Student aid, building funds, capital campaigns, emergency funds, general purposes, operating budgets, grants to individuals, seed money, special projects.
Limitations: Giving primarily in DE.
Publications: Financial statement.
Application information: Scholarship application form required.
   Initial approach: Letter
   Copies of proposal: 1

Deadline(s): Apr. 15 for scholarships
Board meeting date(s): June and Dec.
Final notification: July and Jan.
Write: Robert N. Kerbel, Exec. Secy.
Officers and Directors:* Bennet N. Epstein,* Pres.; Rolf E. Erikson,* V.P.; Robert N. Kerbel,* Exec. Secy.; Henry Topel,* Secy.; Bernard L. Siegel,* Treas.; Steven Dombchick, Martin G. Mand, Irving Morris, Jeremiah P. Shea, William M. Topkis, Toni Young.
Number of staff: None.
EIN: 510187055

521
Laffey-McHugh Foundation ▼
1220 Market Bldg.
P.O. Box 2207
Wilmington 19899   (302) 658-9141

Incorporated in 1959 in DE.
Donor(s): Alice L. McHugh,‡ Frank A. McHugh, Jr.‡
Foundation type: Independent
Financial data (yr. ended 12/31/91): Assets, $44,877,591 (M); expenditures, $2,056,740; qualifying distributions, $1,824,489, including $1,773,640 for 81 grants (high: $165,000; low: $1,500; average: $5,000-$50,000).
Purpose and activities: Grants for Roman Catholic church support and church-related institutions, including schools, welfare agencies, religious associations, child welfare agencies, and a school for the handicapped; support also for a community fund, higher education, and hospitals.
Fields of interest: Catholic giving, Catholic welfare, higher education, secondary education, social services, youth, child welfare, hospitals, handicapped, religious schools, community funds.
Types of support: Annual campaigns, seed money, emergency funds, building funds, equipment, land acquisition, matching funds, general purposes.
Limitations: Giving primarily in DE, with emphasis on Wilmington. No grants to individuals, or for operating budgets, endowment funds, research, demonstration projects, publications, conferences, professorships, internships, consulting services, technical assistance, scholarships, or fellowships; no loans or program-related investments.
Publications: 990-PF.
Application information: Application form not required.
   Initial approach: Letter
   Copies of proposal: 1
   Deadline(s): Apr. and Oct. 15
   Board meeting date(s): May and Nov.
   Final notification: Shortly after meeting
   Write: Arthur G. Connolly, Sr., Pres.
Officers and Directors:* Arthur G. Connolly, Sr.,* Pres.; Marie Louise McHugh,* V.P.; Collins J. Seitz,* V.P.; Thomas S. Lodge, Secy.; Arthur G. Connolly, Jr.,* Treas.; Edward G. Goett.
Number of staff: None.
EIN: 516015095

522
The Lalor Foundation
Bldg. C-100F
3801 Kennett Pike
Wilmington 19807   (302) 571-1262

Incorporated in 1935 in DE.
Donor(s): Members of the Lalor family, Willard A. Lalor.‡
Foundation type: Independent
Financial data (yr. ended 09/30/91): Assets, $7,060,941 (M); expenditures, $330,387; qualifying distributions, $313,677, including $297,500 for 38 grants (high: $16,000; low: $1,000; average: $16,000-$20,000).
Purpose and activities: Support for educational and/or scientific research institutions for postdoctoral fellowship awards in the field of mammalian reproductive physiology research bearing on improved methods of contraception, abortion, and sterilization.
Fields of interest: Science and technology, biological sciences, family planning.
Types of support: Fellowships, research.
Limitations: Giving on a domestic and international basis. No grants to individuals, or for operating budgets, capital or endowment funds, continuing support, annual campaigns, seed money, emergency funds, deficit financing, or matching gifts; no loans.
Publications: Informational brochure (including application guidelines).
Application information: Application form required.
   Initial approach: Letter or telephone
   Copies of proposal: 1
   Deadline(s): Submit proposal from Oct. 1 to Jan. 15; deadline Jan. 15
   Board meeting date(s): Nov. or Dec.
   Final notification: Mar. 1 to 15
   Write: Helen L. Colvard, Asst. Secy.
Officers and Trustees:* Mrs. James T. Patterson,* Pres.; Sally H. Zeckhauser,* V.P.; Lalor Burdick,* Secy.-Treas.; Andrew G. Braun, Carol Chandler.
Number of staff: 1 part-time support.
EIN: 516000153

523
Longwood Foundation, Inc. ▼
1004 Wilmington Trust Ctr.
Wilmington 19801   (302) 654-2477

Incorporated in 1937 in DE.
Donor(s): Pierre S. duPont.‡
Foundation type: Independent
Financial data (yr. ended 09/30/91): Assets, $401,989,675 (M); expenditures, $17,288,848; qualifying distributions, $14,986,738, including $14,812,915 for 72 grants (high: $3,000,000; low: $2,400; average: $25,000-$400,000).
Purpose and activities: Primary obligation is the support, operation, and development of Longwood Gardens, which is open to the public; limited grants generally to educational institutions, to local hospitals for construction purposes, and to social service and youth agencies, and cultural programs.
Fields of interest: Education, education—building funds, hospitals, hospitals—building funds, social services, youth, cultural programs.
Types of support: Annual campaigns, building funds, equipment, land acquisition, endowment funds, research.
Limitations: Giving limited to DE, with emphasis on the greater Wilmington area; some giving in PA. No grants to individuals, or for special projects.

Application information: Application form not required.
   Initial approach: Letter
   Copies of proposal: 1
   Deadline(s): Submit proposal by Apr. 15 or Oct. 1
   Board meeting date(s): May and Oct.
   Final notification: At time of next board meeting
   Write: David D. Wakefield, Exec. Secy.
Officers and Trustees:* H. Rodney Sharp III,* Pres.; Edward B. duPont,* V.P.; Irenee duPont May,* Secy.; Henry H. Silliman, Jr.,* Treas.; Gerret van S. Copeland, David L. Craven, Pierre S. duPont IV.
Number of staff: 4 full-time professional.
EIN: 510066734
Recent health grants:
523-1 Alliance for the Mentally Ill in Delaware, Wilmington, DE, $25,000. For housing project for mentally ill. 1990.
523-2 American Cancer Society, Wilmington, DE, $150,000. For capital campaign. 1990.
523-3 Easter Seal Society of Del-Mar, Wilmington, DE, $250,000. For capital campaign. 1990.
523-4 Medical Center of Delaware, Wilmington, DE, $15,900. For annual contribution. 1990.
523-5 Nanticoke Hospital, Seaford, DE, $300,000. For capital campaign. 1990.
523-6 Southbridge Medical Advisory Council, Wilmington, DE, $10,000. For computer equipment. 1990.
523-7 Turnabout Counseling Center, Seaford, DE, $15,000. For program expenses. 1990.
523-8 Unionville Community Ambulance Service, Unionville, PA, $20,000. For equipment. 1990.

524
The Lovett Foundation, Inc.
82 Governor Printz Blvd.
Claymont 19703   (302) 798-6604

Incorporated in 1952 in DE.
Donor(s): Walter L. Morgan.
Foundation type: Independent
Financial data (yr. ended 11/30/91): Assets, $2,772,024 (M); expenditures, $196,955; qualifying distributions, $182,855, including $168,810 for 79 grants (high: $25,000; low: $100).
Purpose and activities: Emphasis on church support, hospitals, cultural programs, and historic preservation; grants also for education, health associations, and social service agencies.
Fields of interest: Religion—Christian, hospitals, cultural programs, museums, historic preservation, higher education, health associations, social services.
Types of support: General purposes, annual campaigns, operating budgets.
Limitations: Giving primarily in the Wilmington, DE, and Philadelphia, PA, metropolitan areas. No grants to individuals.
Application information:
   Initial approach: Letter
   Deadline(s): Submit proposal prior to Mar. 15; no set deadline
   Board meeting date(s): Quarterly
   Write: Michael J. Robinson III, V.P.

Officers and Trustees:* Walter L. Morgan,* Pres.; Michael J. Robinson III,* V.P.; Leanor H. Silver,* Secy.; Andrew B. Young.
EIN: 236253918

525
The Marmot Foundation
1004 Wilmington Trust Ctr.
Wilmington 19801   (302) 654-2477
Application address for FL organizations: P.O. Box 2468, Palm Beach, FL 33480

Established in 1968 in DE.
Donor(s): Margaret F. duPont Trust.
Foundation type: Independent
Financial data (yr. ended 12/31/91): Assets, $19,615,572 (M); expenditures, $817,000; qualifying distributions, $817,000, including $815,000 for 62 grants (high: $65,000; low: $1,000).
Purpose and activities: Support for hospitals, health, higher and secondary education, including libraries, community funds, cultural programs, including museums, youth agencies, social services, literacy programs, and environmental and ecological organizations.
Fields of interest: Hospitals, health, family planning, higher education, secondary education, libraries, cultural programs, youth, social services, environment.
Types of support: Building funds, equipment, research, matching funds, capital campaigns.
Limitations: Giving primarily in DE and FL. No support for religious organizations. No grants to individuals, or for operating budgets or scholarships; no loans.
Application information: Application form not required.
   Initial approach: Letter
   Copies of proposal: 1
   Deadline(s): Submit proposal preferably in Apr. and Oct.
   Board meeting date(s): May and Nov.
   Final notification: 2 weeks after board meeting
   Write: Endsley P. Fairman, Secy. (for DE organizations), or Willis H. duPont, Chair. (for FL organizations)
Officers and Trustees:* Willis H. duPont,* Chair.; Endsley P. Fairman,* Secy.; Lammot Joseph duPont, Miren deA. duPont, George S. Harrington.
Number of staff: None.
EIN: 516022487

526
The Agnes G. Milliken Foundation
c/o Wilmington Trust Co.
Rodney Sq. North
Wilmington 19890

Established in 1954 in DE.
Donor(s): Agnes M. Franchetti, Anne Milliken Franchetti, Agnes Gayley Milliken.
Foundation type: Independent
Financial data (yr. ended 12/31/91): Assets, $3,129,046 (M); expenditures, $131,971; qualifying distributions, $130,301, including $130,000 for 16 grants (high: $50,000; low: $1,000).
Fields of interest: Education, higher education, secondary education, Protestant giving, hospitals.
Types of support: General purposes.

Limitations: Giving primarily in ME, NY, and PA. No grants to individuals.
Application information: Contributes only to pre-selected organizations. Applications not accepted.
Officer: Lawrence Heagney, Treas.
Trustees: Sylvia M. Erhart, Gerrish H. Milliken, Jr., Roger Milliken.
EIN: 136103241

527
The Bernard Lee Schwartz Foundation, Inc.
1105 North Market St., Suite 1300
P.O. Box 8985
Wilmington 19899

Incorporated in 1951 in NY.
Donor(s): Bernard L. Schwartz,‡ Michael L. Schwartz, Eric A. Schwartz.
Foundation type: Independent
Financial data (yr. ended 09/30/91): Assets, $12,710,896 (M); gifts received, $100,000; expenditures, $431,706; qualifying distributions, $391,181, including $391,181 for grants (high: $295,000; average: $100-$30,000).
Purpose and activities: Support largely for higher education, cultural programs, and medical tax-exempt institutions, including hospitals and research facilities.
Fields of interest: Higher education, cultural programs, hospitals, medical research.
Types of support: Continuing support, building funds, equipment, endowment funds, internships, fellowships, research.
Limitations: No grants to individuals, or for annual campaigns, seed money, emergency funds, deficit financing, renovation projects, land acquisition, demonstration projects, publications, or conferences; no loans.
Publications: 990-PF.
Application information: Contributes only to pre-selected organizations. Applications not accepted.
Officers and Directors:* Rosalyn R. Schwartz,* Pres.; Tilda R. Orr,* Secy.; Michael L. Schwartz,* Treas.; Eric A. Schwartz.
Number of staff: None.
EIN: 136096198

528
Ruby R. Vale Foundation
c/o Bank of Delaware
300 Delaware Ave.
Wilmington 19899

Established in 1960 in DE.
Donor(s): Ruby R. Vale.‡
Foundation type: Independent
Financial data (yr. ended 12/31/91): Assets, $3,060,644 (M); expenditures, $204,005; qualifying distributions, $176,500, including $176,500 for 10 grants (high: $40,000; low: $5,000).
Fields of interest: Higher education, secondary education, museums, cancer.
Types of support: Scholarship funds, general purposes, research.
Application information:
  Deadline(s): Sept. 1
  Write: Richard E. Menkiewicz, Sr. Trust Administrator, Bank of Delaware
Trustee: Bank of Delaware.
EIN: 516018883

529
The Weezie Foundation
c/o J.P. Morgan Services Inc.
P.O. Box 8714
Wilmington 19899-8714
Application address: c/o Morgan Guaranty Trust Co. of New York, Nine West 57th St., New York, NY 10019; Tel.: (212) 826-7607

Trust established in 1961 in NY.
Donor(s): Adelaide T. Corbett.‡
Foundation type: Independent
Financial data (yr. ended 12/31/91): Assets, $16,780,102 (M); expenditures, $922,148; qualifying distributions, $765,342, including $746,000 for 24 grants (high: $120,000; low: $5,000).
Fields of interest: Education, secondary education, hospitals, youth, social services, housing, community development.
Limitations: Giving primarily in MA and New York, NY.
Application information:
  Initial approach: Letter
  Deadline(s): None

Write: Robert Schwecherl, Trustee
Advisory Committee: D. Nelson Adams, Adelrick Benziger, Jr., Mrs. Thomas W. Carroll, James F. Dolan, Mrs. George F. Fiske, Jr., Mrs. William H. Hays III, Mrs. H.S. Graham McBride, Charles H. Theriot.
Trustees: Robert Schwecherl, Morgan Guaranty Trust Co. of New York.
EIN: 136090903

530
Welfare Foundation, Inc.
1004 Wilmington Trust Ctr.
Wilmington 19801   (302) 654-2477

Incorporated in 1930 in DE.
Donor(s): Pierre S. duPont.‡
Foundation type: Independent
Financial data (yr. ended 12/31/91): Assets, $60,334,555 (M); expenditures, $2,804,672; qualifying distributions, $2,252,799, including $2,235,000 for 61 grants (high: $125,000; low: $2,000; average: $25,000-$75,000).
Purpose and activities: Emphasis on education, hospitals, a community fund, and social service agencies.
Fields of interest: Hospitals, education, social services, community funds.
Types of support: Building funds, equipment, matching funds, annual campaigns.
Limitations: Giving limited to DE, with emphasis on the greater Wilmington area. No grants to individuals.
Publications: 990-PF.
Application information: Application form not required.
  Initial approach: Letter
  Copies of proposal: 1
  Deadline(s): Submit proposal preferably in Apr. or Oct.; deadlines Apr. 15 and Nov. 1
  Board meeting date(s): May and Dec.
  Final notification: 30 to 45 days
  Write: David D. Wakefield, Exec. Secy.
Officers and Trustees:* Robert H. Bolling, Jr.,* Pres.; J. Simpson Dean, Jr.,* V.P.; Mrs. W. Laird Stabler, Jr.,* Secy.; Edward B. duPont,* Treas.
Number of staff: 4 part-time professional.
EIN: 516015916

DISTRICT OF COLUMBIA

531
The Appleby Foundation
c/o Crestar Bank, N.A., Trust Div.
1445 New York Ave., N.W.
Washington 20005   (202) 879-6341

Trust established in 1958 in DC.
Donor(s): Scott B. Appleby.‡
Foundation type: Independent
Financial data (yr. ended 12/31/90): Assets, $7,973,007 (M); expenditures, $441,601; qualifying distributions, $376,421, including $348,340 for grants.
Purpose and activities: Grants primarily for higher education; giving also for youth agencies, music, Protestant church support, cultural programs, hospitals, and hospices.
Fields of interest: Higher education, youth, music, Protestant giving, cultural programs, hospitals, hospices.
Types of support: Scholarship funds, general purposes.
Limitations: Giving primarily in Washington, DC, FL, and GA.
Application information: Application form not required.
  Initial approach: Letter
  Copies of proposal: 1
  Deadline(s): None
  Board meeting date(s): July or Aug.
  Write: Virginia M. Herrin, V.P., Crestar Bank, N.A.
Trustees: F. Jordan Colby, Sarah P. Williams, Crestar Bank, N.A.
Number of staff: 1 part-time support.
EIN: 546026971

532
Diane & Norman Bernstein Foundation, Inc.
5301 Wisconsin Ave. N.W., Suite 600
Washington 20015   (202) 363-6301
FAX: (202) 363-6341

Established in 1965 in DC.
Foundation type: Independent
Financial data (yr. ended 09/30/91): Assets, $1,825,006 (M); gifts received, $250,000; expenditures, $316,153; qualifying distributions, $300,000, including $300,000 for 22 grants (high: $185,000; low: $2,500; average: $2,500-$40,000).
Purpose and activities: Grants primarily "for those institutions and organizations, identified by its family members, which perpetuate and nurture the educational, religious, humanitarian, health, cultural and social aspects of society"; including support for the Jewish community.
Fields of interest: Jewish welfare, Israel, social services, homeless, education, health, AIDS, cultural programs, arts, environment.
Types of support: General purposes.
Limitations: Giving primarily in Washington, DC; support for the Jewish community on a local,

national, and international basis. No grants to individuals.
Application information: Contributes only to pre-selected organizations. Applications not accepted.
  Board meeting date(s): Aug.
  Write: Diane and Norman Bernstein, Directors
Directors: Celia Ellen Bernstein, Diane Bernstein, Norman Bernstein, James R. Connell, Marianne Bernstein Kalb.
Number of staff: 1 part-time professional.
EIN: 526047356

533
Walter A. Bloedorn Foundation
c/o Reasoner, Davis & Fox
888 17th St., N.W., Suite 800
Washington 20006   (202) 463-8282

Incorporated in 1966 in DC.
Donor(s): Walter A. Bloedorn.‡
Foundation type: Independent
Financial data (yr. ended 12/31/91): Assets, $5,467,980 (M); expenditures, $322,840; qualifying distributions, $292,280, including $247,250 for 32 grants (high: $125,000; low: $250; average: $1,000-$4,000).
Purpose and activities: Support for higher and medical education, youth agencies, and medical research and hospitals; support also for civic affairs and a nature conservancy.
Fields of interest: Higher education, medical education, youth, hospitals, medical research, civic affairs, conservation.
Types of support: Continuing support, annual campaigns, endowment funds, professorships.
Limitations: Giving primarily in the Washington, DC, area. No grants to individuals.
Application information: Application form not required.
  Initial approach: Proposal
  Copies of proposal: 1
  Deadline(s): Submit proposal preferably in Jan. and Feb.; should be received by Mar. 31 for consideration at Apr. meeting
  Board meeting date(s): Apr.
  Final notification: 30 days after board meets
  Write: Philip J. Sweeny, Attorney
Officers and Directors:* F. Elwood Davis,* Chair.; Robert E. Davis,* Pres. and Treas.; Anne D. Spratt, Secy.; John H. Bloedorn, Lloyd H. Elliott.
Number of staff: None.
EIN: 520846147

534
Walter Brownley Trust
c/o Security Trust Co., N.A.
15th St. and Pennsylvania Ave., N.W.
Washington 20013   (202) 624-5744

Trust established in 1931.
Foundation type: Independent
Financial data (yr. ended 12/31/90): Assets, $2,929,958 (M); expenditures, $234,335; qualifying distributions, $213,403, including $213,333 for 12 grants (high: $48,333; low: $15,000).
Purpose and activities: Giving restricted to orphanages and public charitable hospitals in Washington, DC.
Fields of interest: Child welfare, hospitals.

Limitations: Giving limited to Washington, DC. No grants to individuals.
Application information: Contributes only to pre-selected organizations. Applications not accepted.
  Write: F. William Burke, V.P., Security Trust Co., N.A.
Trustee: Security Trust Co., N.A.
EIN: 526028605

535
The Morris and Gwendolyn Cafritz Foundation ▼
1825 K St., N.W., 14th Fl.
Washington 20006   (202) 223-3100

Incorporated in 1948 in DC.
Donor(s): Morris Cafritz,‡ Gwendolyn D. Cafritz.‡
Foundation type: Independent
Financial data (yr. ended 04/30/91): Assets, $187,803,268 (M); expenditures, $11,563,996; qualifying distributions, $10,525,966, including $9,893,780 for 230 grants (high: $1,000,000; low: $20; average: $10,000-$50,000).
Purpose and activities: Giving only for programs of direct assistance, with emphasis on community service, arts and humanities, education, and health.
Fields of interest: Arts, cultural programs, performing arts, education, education—minorities, conservation, environment, health, AIDS, drug abuse, social services, youth, disadvantaged, aged, homeless, hospices, housing, women, community development, volunteerism.
Types of support: Operating budgets, continuing support, seed money, matching funds, scholarship funds, fellowships, general purposes.
Limitations: Giving limited to the greater metropolitan Washington, DC, area. No grants to individuals, or for emergency funds, deficit financing, capital, endowment, or building funds, demonstration projects, or conferences; no loans.
Publications: Annual report, application guidelines.
Application information: Application form not required.
  Initial approach: Proposal
  Copies of proposal: 1
  Deadline(s): July 1, Nov. 1, and Mar. 1
  Write: Martin Atlas, Pres.
Officers and Directors:* Calvin Cafritz,* Chair.; Martin Atlas,* Pres., C.E.O. and Treas.; Roger A. Clark, Secy.; Anne Allen, Prog. Dir.; Daniel J. Boorstin, Warren E. Burger, William P. Rogers.
Number of staff: 3 full-time professional; 4 full-time support.
EIN: 526036989
Recent health grants:
535-1 Arts for the Aging, DC, $20,000. For art instruction for frail elderly and those with Alzheimer's disease. 1991.
535-2 Center for Child Protection and Family Support, DC, $25,000. For matching funds to work with families and their children to prevent youth involvement with gangs, substance abuse and drug trafficking. 1991.
535-3 Center for Population Options, DC, $20,000. For Teen Council, to prevent teen pregnancy and HIV infection among teenagers. 1991.

535-4 Central American Refugee Center, DC, $60,000. For three projects: pro bono legal defense and advocacy project, women and family project and La Clinica Del Pueblo. 1991.

535-5 Child Center, Rockville, MD, $30,000. To establish school-based mental health program for children and families from Central and South America. 1991.

535-6 Community Psychiatric Clinic, DC, $10,000. For five children to attend Camp Greentree, summer day treatment program for emotionally disturbed and learning disabled children. 1991.

535-7 Corporation Against Drug Abuse, DC, $150,000. For Project STAR, alcohol and drug abuse prevention program for 10-13 year old students, in 11 D.C. public schools. 1991.

535-8 Easter Seal Society for Disabled Children and Adults, DC, $42,550. For monthly medical specialty clinics for orthopedically-impaired children. 1991.

535-9 Family Place, DC, $40,000. To expand social services and health programs for low-income families. 1991.

535-10 George Washington University Medical Center, DC, $100,000. For new software technology to be used with magnetic resonance imager in treating heart patients. 1991.

535-11 Georgetown University, School of Medicine, DC, $50,000. For scholarship aid for Georgetown Experimental Medical Studies (GEMS) program for minority students. 1991.

535-12 Georgetown University Medical Center, DC, $159,000. To establish model program for treating women with HIV and AIDS, and to address their special needs. 1991.

535-13 Georgetown University Medical Center, Lombardi Cancer Information Center, DC, $124,000. To purchase two pieces of equipment: Image Analysis System and photomicroscope, to diagnose and treat breast cancer. 1991.

535-14 Green Door, DC, $100,000. To purchase vocational training equipment for kitchen, dining room and cafe units. 1991.

535-15 Hebrew Home of Greater Washington, Rockville, MD, $34,200. To purchase equipment which allows for removal of physical restraints from elderly residents. 1991.

535-16 Interfaith Conference of Metropolitan Washington, DC, $25,000. For Task Force on Drugs and Violence, AIDS Task Force, 11th annual Interfaith Concert and work on racial and ethnic polarization. 1991.

535-17 Ionia R. Whipper Home, DC, $20,000. For start-up support for Tutorial and Enrichment Program for abused, abandoned and neglected young women ages 12-20. 1991.

535-18 Kingsbury Center, DC, $20,000. To implement computer instruction for learning disabled students. 1991.

535-19 Kingsbury Center, DC, $15,000. For scholarship support. 1991.

535-20 Latin American Youth Center, DC, $20,000. Toward Substance Abuse and Delinquency Prevention Program, providing educational and recreational activities for at-risk Hispanic youth. 1991.

535-21 Luther Place Memorial Church, DC, $45,500. For outpatient mental health clinic for homeless, mentally disabled women. 1991.

535-22 Marys Center for Maternal and Child Care, DC, $30,000. To increase number of women served by opening clinic one evening a week and on weekend. 1991.

535-23 Mental Health Law Project, DC, $48,778. For collaborative program including community development corporations, nonprofit organizations and city government, to increase city's stock of affordable housing and supportive housing for mentally ill. 1991.

535-24 National Rehabilitation Hospital, DC, $100,000. For matching grant toward Care Assistance Fund for those with limited financial resources, and to help establish primary health care program for severely disabled. 1991.

535-25 National Rehabilitation Hospital, DC, $46,700. To purchase Clinitron therapeutic bed for at-home use of patients not covered by insurance and without sufficient personal resources. 1991.

535-26 New Way Recovery Program, DC, $40,000. For 24-hour drug and alcohol therapeutic center for 90 homeless men and women at CCNV Shelter, partially matching. 1991.

535-27 Oak Leaf Center, DC, $10,000. For financial aid for five abused and emotionally disturbed children ages 2 1/2-6, in nursery school's therapeutic program. 1991.

535-28 Pediatric AIDS/HIV Care, DC, $25,000. For supportive services for families with HIV-infected children. 1991.

535-29 Planned Parenthood Association of Metropolitan Washington, DC, $250,000. For community education, training programs and medical services. 1991.

535-30 Saint Anns Infant and Maternity Home, Hyattsville, MD, $20,000. For education program for pregnant adolescents and young mothers, ages 13-20. 1991.

535-31 Saint Francis Center, DC, $10,200. For Schools Training Program, to assist Washington area teachers in responding to emotional needs of their students as they encounter loss, illness and death. 1991.

535-32 Second Genesis, Bethesda, MD, $52,000. Toward matching funds for 95 District residents, to receive drug and alcohol treatment in one-year residential program and for equipment. 1991.

535-33 United Cerebral Palsy Associations, DC, $20,000. To provide respite care to Northern Virginia families who have children with developmental disabilities. 1991.

535-34 Visiting Nurse Association of Northern Virginia, Arlington, VA, $22,000. For Living with Cancer program, to provide subsidized in-home care. 1991.

535-35 Washington Area Council on Alcoholism and Drug Abuse, DC, $50,000. To expand outpatient treatment program for recovering drug and alcohol abusers. 1991.

535-36 Washington Free Clinic, DC, $40,000. To start pediatric care program and to expand prenatal clinic for low-income women who lack health insurance. 1991.

535-37 Washington Hospital Center, Washington Heart, DC, $35,000. For matching grant to purchase 2D Echocardiogram Doppler Machine. 1991.

535-38 Zacchaeus Medical Clinic, DC, $10,000. To purchase computer system to record patient files. 1991.

536
The Manny and Ruthy Cohen Foundation, Inc.

3020 Rodman St., N.W.
Washington 20008   (202) 244-8884

Established in 1986 in CT.
Donor(s): Ruth Cohen.‡
Foundation type: Independent
Financial data (yr. ended 12/31/91): Assets, $6,255,380 (M); gifts received, $601,183; expenditures, $390,631; qualifying distributions, $386,031, including $320,544 for 120 grants (high: $26,459; low: $35).
Fields of interest: Jewish giving, Jewish welfare, hospitals, higher education, performing arts.
Limitations: Giving primarily in Washington, DC, Miami, FL, NJ, and MD. No grants to individuals.
Application information: Application form not required.
  Deadline(s): None
  Write: Alvin Morgenstein, Pres.
Officers: Alvin Morgenstein, Pres.; Steve Morgan, V.P.; Melvin Morgenstein, Secy.; Gertrude Morgenstein, Treas.
EIN: 592744621

537
The Helen Pumphrey Denit Trust for Charitable and Educational Purposes

c/o Security Trust Co., N.A.
1501 Pennsylvania Ave., N.W., B2W/415
Washington 20013

Established in 1989 in DC.
Donor(s): Helen P. Denit.‡
Foundation type: Independent
Financial data (yr. ended 06/30/91): Assets, $13,634,370 (M); gifts received, $11,416,119; expenditures, $238,486; qualifying distributions, $100,377, including $100,000 for 1 grant.
Fields of interest: Heart disease.
Limitations: Giving primarily in Baltimore, MD. No grants to individuals.
Application information:
  Initial approach: Letter
  Deadline(s): None
Trustee: Security Trust Co., N.A.
EIN: 526401248

538
Fannie Mae Foundation ▼
(also known as Federal National Mortgage Association Foundation)
3900 Wisconsin Ave., N.W.
Washington 20016   (202) 752-6500

Established in 1979 in DC.
Donor(s): Fannie Mae Assn.
Foundation type: Company-sponsored
Financial data (yr. ended 12/31/91): Assets, $13,562,811 (M); gifts received, $11,250,000; expenditures, $4,111,016; qualifying distributions, $4,036,209, including $3,882,717

for 477 grants (high: $125,000; low: $259; average: $1,000-$5,000) and $104,083 for 386 employee matching gifts.

Purpose and activities: Support primarily awarded for housing and community development programs, cultural and artistic programs, media and communications, youth programs, and health and social concerns.

Fields of interest: Arts, cultural programs, AIDS, media and communications, community development, public policy, social services, homeless, housing, youth.

Types of support: Annual campaigns, building funds, conferences and seminars, employee matching gifts, endowment funds, equipment, general purposes, matching funds, operating budgets, renovation projects, research, seed money, special projects, technical assistance, scholarship funds, capital campaigns.

Limitations: No support for organizations whose fundraising costs are in excess of 20 percent of their contributed support; generally, no support for organizations that benefit from United Way support or for churches and sectarian organizations, though contributions to religious group-sponsored, nondenominational activities are considered. No grants to support charitable activities undertaken outside of the U.S. No grants to individuals; generally no grants to institutions of higher learning or secondary education for general or scholarship support.

Publications: Informational brochure (including application guidelines), grants list, annual report.

Application information: Postcard mailed to confirm receipt of proposal. Application form not required.

> *Initial approach:* Proposal
> *Copies of proposal:* 1
> *Deadline(s):* None
> *Board meeting date(s):* Twice annually
> *Write:* Harriet M. Ivey, Exec. Dir.

Officers and Directors:* James A. Johnson,* Chair.; Lawrence M. Small,* Pres.; Michael A. Smilow,* V.P.; Caryl S. Bernstein,* Secy.; Douglas M. Bibby,* Treas.; Harriet M. Ivey,* Exec. Dir.; Larry H. Dale, Judith Dedmon, William R. Maloni, Franklin D. Raines, Samuel J. Simmons, Mallory Walker, Karen Hastie Williams.

EIN: 521172718

539
First American Bankshares Corporate Contributions Program
15th and H St., N.W.
Washington 20005   (202) 383-1462

Financial data (yr. ended 12/31/90): Total giving, $1,006,500, including $975,000 for 329 grants (high: $45,000; low: $100) and $31,500 for 332 employee matching gifts.

Purpose and activities: Primarily supports the fine arts and education, including higher education, health and civic affairs.

Fields of interest: Child welfare, civic affairs, community development, cultural programs, health, hospitals, hospitals—building funds, mental health, museums, performing arts, welfare, fine arts, arts, education, higher education, education—building funds.

Types of support: Annual campaigns, building funds, capital campaigns, continuing support,

donated equipment, employee matching gifts, employee volunteer services, special projects.

Limitations: Giving limited to communities within service areas, except matching gifts to education.

Publications: Application guidelines.

Application information: Send letter to Marketing Dir. of FA affiliate in community or to FA Contributions Prog. Admin.; Corporate Relations office handles giving. Application form required.

> *Copies of proposal:* 1
> *Deadline(s):* None
> *Board meeting date(s):* Quarterly
> *Write:* Carol S. Gimmel, Asst. V.P. and Prog. Admin.

Administrator: Carol S. Gimmel, Prog. Admin.

Number of staff: 1 part-time professional; 1 full-time support.

540
The Folger Fund
2800 Woodley Rd., N.W.
Washington 20008   (202) 626-5200

Incorporated in 1955 in DC.

Donor(s): Eugenia B. Dulin,‡ Kathrine Dulin Folger, Lee Merritt Folger.

Foundation type: Independent

Financial data (yr. ended 08/31/91): Assets, $12,780,826 (M); gifts received, $72,160; expenditures $471,935; qualifying distributions, $457,447, including $453,715 for 82 grants (high: $85,300; low: $50).

Purpose and activities: Primary support for a cancer clinic and other health associations; grants also for education and the arts, including museums and historic preservation.

Fields of interest: Cancer, hospitals, health, education, arts, museums, historic preservation.

Types of support: General purposes, building funds, scholarship funds, endowment funds.

Limitations: Giving primarily in Washington, DC; Knox County, TN; and Palm Beach County, FL. No grants to individuals.

Publications: Annual report.

Application information: Application form not required.

> *Initial approach:* Proposal
> *Deadline(s):* None
> *Board meeting date(s):* Sept.
> *Final notification:* Usually within 3 months
> *Write:* Kathrine Dulin Folger, Pres.

Officers: Kathrine Dulin Folger, Pres.; John Dulin Folger, V.P.; Lee Merritt Folger, Secy.-Treas.

EIN: 520794388

541
The Foundation for the National Capital Region ▼
(Formerly The Community Foundation of Greater Washington, Inc.)
1002 Wisconsin Ave., N.W.
Washington 20007   (202) 338-8993

Incorporated in 1973 in DC.

Foundation type: Community

Financial data (yr. ended 03/31/90): Assets, $10,684,972 (M); gifts received, $8,603,964; expenditures, $9,707,883; qualifying distributions, $77,458,921, including $5,030,941 for 357 grants (high: $4,024,676; low: $25; average: $1,000-$10,000), $129,132 for grants to

individuals and $389,699 for foundation-administered programs.

Purpose and activities: Through its programs and unrestricted funds, the foundation works to establish new coalitions for delivery of public services, develop public-private partnerships of shared resources to meet public needs, catalyze efforts leading to social change, and promote self-help grassroot efforts and increase use of volunteers. Areas of interest include health care for the homeless, substance abuse, community development, newcomers, youth in philanthropy, and ecology.

Fields of interest: Public policy, social services, health services, homeless, community development, youth, disadvantaged, drug abuse, AIDS, women, conservation, ecology.

Types of support: Seed money, emergency funds, technical assistance, special projects, research, publications, general purposes, continuing support.

Limitations: Giving limited to the metropolitan Washington, DC, area. No support for religious purposes. No grants to individuals (except for designated grants), or for annual campaigns, endowment funds, equipment, land acquisition, renovation projects, scholarships, fellowships, operating budgets, or matching gifts.

Publications: Annual report (including application guidelines), informational brochure.

Application information: Application form not required.

> *Initial approach:* Letter
> *Copies of proposal:* 1
> *Deadline(s):* May and Oct.
> *Board meeting date(s):* June and Nov.
> *Final notification:* Up to 6 months
> *Write:* Deborah S. McKown, Dir. of Finance

Officers and Directors:* John V. Pollack,* Chair.; John W. Hechinger, Jr.,* Vice-Chair.; George Bohlinger,* Pres.; Stephen J. Slade,* Secy.; James B. Adler,* Treas.; Haida Sale,* Acting Dir.; and 22 additional directors.

Number of staff: 11 full-time professional; 3 full-time support.

EIN: 237343119

Recent health grants:

541-1 Corporation Against Drug Abuse, DC, $23,333. 1990.

541-2 Institute for Advanced Studies in Immunology and Aging, DC, $15,385. 1990.

541-3 Institute for Advanced Studies in Immunology and Aging, DC, $12,000. 1990.

541-4 Nancy Reagan Foundation, Los Angeles, CA, $4,024,676. 1990.

541-5 Population Crisis Committee, DC, $25,250. 1990.

541-6 Washington Metro Area Business Leadership Taskforce on AIDS, DC, $10,000. 1990.

542
The Freed Foundation
3050 K St., N.W., Suite 335
Washington 20007   (202) 337-5487

Incorporated in 1954 in DC.

Donor(s): Frances W. Freed,‡ Gerald A. Freed.‡

Foundation type: Independent

Financial data (yr. ended 05/31/91): Assets, $16,566,522 (M); gifts received, $232,397; expenditures, $653,635; qualifying distributions,

$506,539, including $394,700 for 20 grants (average: $100-$20,000).

Purpose and activities: "Support primarily for teenage and young adult health and social issues", including public education in the areas of AIDS, nutrition, and substance abuse.

Fields of interest: Ecology, environment, mental health, AIDS, nutrition.

Types of support: General purposes, special projects, annual campaigns, continuing support, equipment, land acquisition, operating budgets.

Limitations: Giving primarily in metropolitan Washington, DC, and NJ. No support for foreign organizations or international projects. No grants to individuals, or for scholarships, endowment funds, research, or conferences and meetings.

Publications: Annual report (including application guidelines).

Application information: Application form not required.

Initial approach: Letter
Copies of proposal: 1
Deadline(s): None
Board meeting date(s): Feb., May, Aug., and Nov.
Final notification: 3 months
Write: Lorraine Barnhart, Exec. Dir.

Officers and Trustees:* Elizabeth Ann Freed,* Pres. and Treas.; Lloyd J. Derrickson,* Secy.; Joan F. Kahn, Sherwood Monahan.

Number of staff: 1 part-time professional.

EIN: 526047591

543
GEICO Philanthropic Foundation

c/o GEICO Corp.
One GEICO Plaza
Washington 20076-0001   (301) 986-2055
Application address for Leo Goodwin Scholarship program: c/o Susan Johnson, Citizens Scholarship Foundation of America, P.O. Box 297, St. Peter, MN 56082; Tel.: (507) 931-1682

Established in 1980 in DC.

Donor(s): Criterion Insurance Co., Government Employees Insurance Co., Government Employees Insurance Co.

Foundation type: Company-sponsored

Financial data (yr. ended 12/31/91): Assets, $4,299,652 (M); gifts received, $773,957; expenditures, $1,043,870; qualifying distributions, $1,038,113, including $1,038,113 for 461 grants (high: $123,182; low: $15).

Purpose and activities: Grants for higher education, including a scholarship fund for business or insurance studies, community funds, health agencies, a safety association, hospitals, cultural programs, child welfare, and youth and social service agencies.

Fields of interest: Higher education, business education, insurance education, community funds, health associations, cultural programs, youth, child welfare, social services, hospitals, safety.

Types of support: Scholarship funds, general purposes.

Limitations: Giving primarily in areas of company operations. No grants to individuals directly.

Application information: Application form required for scholarship program.

Initial approach: Letter

Deadline(s): Feb. 15 for scholarship program; no set deadline for grants
Write: Carroll R. Franklin, Dir.

Officers and Directors:* Edward H. Utley,* Chair.; Donald K. Smith,* Pres.; Rosalind Ann Phillips, Secy.; Charles G. Schara,* Treas.; August P. Alegi, Carroll R. Franklin, Merrill D. Knight III, John J. Krieger, William B. Snyder, W. Alvon Sparks, Jr.

EIN: 521202740

544
Melvin and Estelle Gelman Foundation

2120 L St., N.W., Suite 800
Washington 20037   (202) 872-9070

Established in 1963 in DC.

Donor(s): Melvin Gelman.‡

Foundation type: Independent

Financial data (yr. ended 11/30/91): Assets, $2,285,498 (M); expenditures, $540,163; qualifying distributions, $524,919, including $524,919 for 101 grants (high: $100,250; low: $10).

Fields of interest: Jewish welfare, cultural programs, arts, fine arts, medical research, health associations, general charitable giving.

Types of support: Continuing support.

Limitations: Giving primarily in Washington, DC. No grants to individuals.

Application information: Applications not accepted.

Officers and Board Members:* Estelle S. Gelman,* Pres. and Treas.; Elise G. Lefkowitz,* V.P.; Elaine G. Miller,* V.P.; Martin Goldstein, Secy.

Number of staff: None.

EIN: 526042344

545
Giant Food Foundation, Inc.

P.O. Box 1804
Washington 20013

Incorporated in 1950 in DC.

Donor(s): Giant Food, Inc.

Foundation type: Company-sponsored

Financial data (yr. ended 01/31/92): Assets, $1,049,829 (M); gifts received, $750,000; expenditures, $588,526; qualifying distributions, $587,707, including $585,914 for 194 grants (high: $175,000; low: $100).

Purpose and activities: Funds largely committed for continuing support in fields of Jewish welfare, community service, community funds, education, culture, and health, including mental health.

Fields of interest: Community development, health, mental health, education, community funds, social services, Jewish welfare, cultural programs.

Types of support: General purposes, continuing support.

Limitations: Giving primarily in the Baltimore, MD, and Washington, DC, metropolitan areas; normally no grants to programs of national or international scope. No grants to individuals, or for scholarships, fellowships, or matching gifts; no loans.

Application information: Application form not required.

Initial approach: Proposal
Copies of proposal: 1

Deadline(s): None
Board meeting date(s): Monthly
Final notification: 1 month
Write: Israel Cohen, Pres.

Officers and Directors:* Israel Cohen,* Pres.; Samuel Lehrman,* V.P.; David W. Rutstein,* Secy.; David B. Sykes.

Number of staff: None.

EIN: 526045041

546
Glen Eagles Foundation

c/o Betsy K. Frampton
2000 P St., N.W., Suite 410
Washington 20036

Established in 1985 in DC.

Foundation type: Independent

Financial data (yr. ended 12/31/91): Assets, $1,001,277 (M); gifts received, $805,697; expenditures, $691,523; qualifying distributions, $691,523, including $667,085 for 56 grants (high: $30,000; low: $1,000; average: $1,000-$50,000).

Purpose and activities: Giving primarily to organizations providing AIDS prevention and education and women and child advocacy, including reproductive freedom issues; support also for the arts and education.

Fields of interest: AIDS, arts, cultural programs, education, women, child welfare.

Types of support: General purposes, matching funds, seed money, special projects.

Limitations: Giving primarily in Washington, DC. No grants to individuals.

Publications: Application guidelines.

Application information: Contributes only to pre-selected organizations. Applications not accepted.

Officers and Director:* Betsy K. Frampton, Pres.; Susan E. Kaslow,* V.P.; George T. Frampton, Jr., Secy.-Treas.

Number of staff: 1 shared staff

EIN: 521451828

547
The Gottesman Fund

1818 N St., N.W., Suite 200
Washington 20036

Established in 1965 in DC.

Donor(s): Members of the Gottesman family.

Foundation type: Independent

Financial data (yr. ended 08/31/91): Assets, $23,602,878 (M); gifts received, $3,200,351; expenditures, $1,149,987; qualifying distributions, $1,118,295, including $1,117,060 for 103 grants (high: $510,000; low: $100).

Fields of interest: Health associations, hospitals, higher education, Jewish giving, Jewish welfare, social services.

Types of support: General purposes.

Limitations: Giving primarily in NY. No grants to individuals.

Application information: Contributes only to pre-selected organizations. Applications not accepted.

Officers: David S. Gottesman, Pres.; Milton M. Gottesman, V.P. and Secy.; Esther Gottesman, V.P.; Ruth L. Gottesman, V.P.; Robert W. Gottesman, Treas.

EIN: 526061469

548
The Philip L. Graham Fund ▼
c/o The Washington Post Co.
1150 Fifteenth St., N.W.
Washington 20071   (202) 334-6640

Trust established in 1963 in DC.
Donor(s): Katharine Graham, Frederick S. Beebe,‡ The Washington Post Co., Newsweek, Inc., Post-Newsweek Stations.
Foundation type: Independent
Financial data (yr. ended 12/31/90): Assets, $51,916,838 (M); expenditures, $3,313,544; qualifying distributions, $3,307,972, including $3,286,517 for 107 grants (high: $500,000; low: $2,817; average: $10,000-$50,000).
Purpose and activities: Support for raising standards of excellence in journalism. Grants also for arts and culture, education, social welfare, with an emphasis on youth agencies, and civic and community affairs.
Fields of interest: Journalism, arts, cultural programs, welfare, youth, social services, civic affairs, education, community development.
Types of support: Seed money, building funds, equipment, endowment funds, matching funds, renovation projects, capital campaigns, special projects.
Limitations: Giving primarily in metropolitan Washington, DC. No support for national or international organizations, or for religious organizations for religious purposes. No grants to individuals, or for medical services, research, annual campaigns, operating expenses, conferences, publications, tickets, films, or courtesy advertising; no loans.
Publications: Application guidelines, program policy statement, grants list.
Application information: Application form not required.
  Initial approach: Letter, telephone, or proposal
  Copies of proposal: 1
  Deadline(s): Apr. 1, Aug. 1, and Nov. 1
  Board meeting date(s): Spring, summer, and fall
  Final notification: 6 months
  Write: Mary M. Bellor, Secy.
Officers and Trustees:* Mary M. Bellor, Secy. and Exec. Dir.; Martin Cohen,* Treas.; Donald E. Graham, Katharine Graham, Vincent E. Reed, John W. Sweeterman.
Number of staff: 2 part-time professional; 1 part-time support.
EIN: 526051781
Recent health grants:
548-1 Columbia University, School of Nursing, NYC, NY, $10,000. For Centennial Campaign. 1990.
548-2 Green Door, DC, $50,000. For additional support to Campaign for the Green Door, proceeds of which will be used to renovate and vocationally equip building to better meet needs of members who suffer from chronic mental illness. 1990.
548-3 Loudoun County Youth Shelter, Leesburg, VA, $20,000. For school-based substance abuse awareness and intervention program for teens. 1990.
548-4 Marys Center for Maternal and Child Care, DC, $10,000. For center in its early years of providing prenatal, obstetric and pediatric care

to primarily Hispanic women and children. 1990.
548-5 Rape Crisis Center, DC, $10,000. To expand rape prevention program by producing and distributing written materials to churches, community organizations, libraries, shelters and youth organizations. 1990.
548-6 Saint Lukes House, Bethesda, MD, $50,000. For capital campaign toward construction of new mental health center. 1990.
548-7 Washington Free Clinic, DC, $23,000. To replace worn out medical and laboratory equipment, to purchase photocopier machine and install ceiling and exhaust fans. 1990.
548-8 Zacchaeus Medical Clinic, DC, $10,000. To help clinic expand its ability to provide primary and preventive medical care for chronic illnesses known to be prevalent in minority and poor populations. 1990.

549
The Isadore and Bertha Gudelsky Family Foundation, Inc.
1828 L St., N.W., Suite 500
Washington 20036   (202) 296-1000

Incorporated in 1955 in MD.
Donor(s): Members of the Gudelsky family.
Foundation type: Independent
Financial data (yr. ended 04/30/92): Assets, $11,643,032 (M); expenditures, $819,690; qualifying distributions, $752,877, including $745,933 for 15 grants (high: $525,000; low: $2,500).
Purpose and activities: Emphasis on Jewish welfare funds and temple support; grants also for education, hospitals, and youth agencies.
Fields of interest: Jewish giving, hospitals, youth, education, Jewish welfare.
Limitations: Giving primarily in Washington, DC. No grants to individuals.
Application information:
  Initial approach: Letter
  Deadline(s): None
  Write: Philip N. Margolius, Secy.-Treas.
Officers and Directors:* Arlene G. Zimmerman,* Pres.; Shelley G. Mulitz,* V.P.; Philip N. Margolius, Secy.-Treas.; Paul S. Berger, Iris G. Markel.
Number of staff: 1 part-time professional.
EIN: 526036621

550
Paul and Annetta Himmelfarb Foundation, Inc.
4545 42nd St., Suite 309
Washington 20016   (202) 966-3795

Incorporated in 1947 in DE.
Donor(s): Members of the Himmelfarb family.
Foundation type: Independent
Financial data (yr. ended 12/31/90): Assets, $5,782,397 (M); expenditures, $590,187; qualifying distributions, $488,150, including $488,150 for 91 grants (high: $40,000; low: $50; average: $100-$40,000).
Purpose and activities: Primary areas of interest include educational and medical research, health, the elderly, and Israel.

Fields of interest: Health, AIDS, cancer, medical research, education, educational research, education—early childhood, Israel, Jewish welfare, aged, handicapped, homeless, environment.
Limitations: Giving primarily in the Washington, DC, area, and Israel. No grants to individuals.
Application information: Application form not required.
  Initial approach: Letter
  Copies of proposal: 1
  Deadline(s): None
  Board meeting date(s): Monthly
  Final notification: 3 to 6 months
  Write: Lillian N. Kronstadt, Treas. and Exec. Dir.
Officers and Directors:* Ada Naiman,* Pres.; Carol Himmelfarb Parker,* V.P.; Carole Preston,* Secy.; Lillian N. Kronstadt,* Treas. and Exec. Dir.; Annette Kronstadt.
Number of staff: 1 full-time professional; 1 part-time professional.
EIN: 520784206

551
The James M. Johnston Trust for Charitable and Educational Purposes ▼
1101 Vermont Ave., N.W., Suite 403
Washington 20005   (202) 289-4996

Trust established in 1968 in DC.
Donor(s): James M. Johnston.‡
Foundation type: Independent
Financial data (yr. ended 12/31/90): Assets, $56,766,981 (M); expenditures, $3,662,176; qualifying distributions, $2,703,206, including $2,511,224 for 95 grants (high: $125,000; low: $1,000; average: $5,000-$20,000).
Purpose and activities: Grants largely to higher and secondary educational institutions located in Washington, DC and NC. This includes support for scholarships and training of nurses.
Fields of interest: Higher education, secondary education, nursing.
Types of support: Scholarship funds, continuing support.
Limitations: Giving limited to NC and Washington, DC. No grants to individuals, or for building or endowment funds, or operating budgets.
Application information: Application form not required.
  Initial approach: Letter
  Copies of proposal: 1
  Deadline(s): None
  Board meeting date(s): Monthly
  Final notification: 30 days
  Write: Betty Frost Hayes, Chair., or Julie Sanders, Office Mgr.
Officer and Trustees:* Betty Frost Hayes,* Chair.; Barnum L. Colton, Jr., Wallace Dunbar Gram.
Number of staff: 1 full-time professional.
EIN: 237019796
Recent health grants:
551-1 Berea College, Berea, KY, $25,000. For nursing scholarship. 1990.
551-2 Catholic University of America, DC, $20,000. For nursing scholarship. 1990.
551-3 Childrens National Medical Center, DC, $25,000. For nursing education. 1990.
551-4 Cumberland College, Williamsburg, KY, $20,000. For nursing scholarship. 1990.

551-5 Georgetown University, School of Nursing, DC, $30,000. For nursing training programs. 1990.

551-6 Georgetown University Medical Center, DC, $15,000. For cancer research. 1990.

551-7 Hospital for Sick Children, DC, $20,000. For general support. 1990.

551-8 Howard University, College of Nursing, DC, $20,000. For nursing scholarship. 1990.

551-9 Lenoir-Rhyne College, Hickory, NC, $10,000. For nursing scholarship. 1990.

551-10 National Rehabilitation Hospital, DC, $15,000. For nurses training. 1990.

551-11 Queens College, Charlotte, NC, $15,000. For nursing scholarship. 1990.

551-12 Sibley Memorial Hospital, DC, $10,000. For Community Scholarship Fund for nurses. 1990.

551-13 Sibley Memorial Hospital, DC, $10,000. For nurses education. 1990.

551-14 University of North Carolina, Chapel Hill, NC, $260,000. For nursing scholarship. 1990.

552

The Joseph P. Kennedy, Jr. Foundation ▼
1350 New York Ave., N.W., Suite 500
Washington 20005-4709   (202) 393-1250

Incorporated in 1946 in DC.
Donor(s): Joseph P. Kennedy,‡ Mrs. Joseph P. Kennedy.
Foundation type: Independent
Financial data (yr. ended 12/31/90): Assets, $17,390,649 (M); gifts received, $57,198; expenditures, $3,071,021; qualifying distributions, $2,981,925, including $1,442,290 for 24 grants (high: $622,593; average: $10,000-$50,000) and $152,100 for 11 grants to individuals.
Purpose and activities: The foundation's main objectives are "the prevention of mental retardation by identifying its causes and improving means by which society deals with its mentally retarded citizens." Emphasis on the use of funds in areas where a multiplier effect is possible. Awards scholarships to a one week bioethics course at the Kennedy Institute of Ethics, Georgetown University; fellowships limited to two Kennedy Foundation Public Policy Leadership Fellows.
Fields of interest: Handicapped, biological sciences, family services, youth, aged, AIDS, medical research, public policy, child development, health services, education—early childhood, elementary education, secondary education, employment, drug abuse, homeless.
Types of support: Seed money, research, special projects, conferences and seminars, consulting services, general purposes, technical assistance.
Limitations: No grants for building or endowment funds, equipment, or operating budgets of schools or service organizations.
Publications: Informational brochure, application guidelines.
Application information: Funds are substantially committed to grants initiated by the foundation; however, applications considered for research projects and new models of service for persons with mental retardation and their families. Only proposals in the field of mental retardation are funded. Application form not required.

Initial approach: 2-page letter of intent
Copies of proposal: 1
Deadline(s): Submit letter of intent prior to Oct. 1; deadline for proposals, Nov. 15
Board meeting date(s): Usually Spring
Final notification: 2 weeks to 1 month
Write: Eunice Kennedy Shriver, Exec. V.P.
Officers and Trustees:* Edward M. Kennedy,* Pres.; Eunice Kennedy Shriver,* Exec. V.P.; Joseph E. Hakim, Treas.; Patricia Kennedy Lawford, Jean Kennedy Smith.
Number of staff: 3 full-time professional; 3 part-time professional; 4 full-time support.
EIN: 136083407

553

The Kiplinger Foundation ▼
1729 H St., N.W.
Washington 20006   (202) 887-6559

Incorporated in 1948 in MD.
Donor(s): Willard M. Kiplinger.‡
Foundation type: Independent
Financial data (yr. ended 12/31/91): Assets, $20,647,804 (M); gifts received, $1,000,000; expenditures, $592,271; qualifying distributions, $1,592,271, including $478,492 for 81 grants (high: $100,000; average: $1,000-$2,000), $71,651 for 99 employee matching gifts and $1,000,000 for 1 in-kind gift.
Purpose and activities: Support primarily for educational, health, welfare, civic, and cultural organizations.
Fields of interest: Education, health, welfare, civic affairs, cultural programs.
Types of support: Operating budgets, continuing support, annual campaigns, building funds, endowment funds, capital campaigns, matching funds, special projects, employee matching gifts.
Limitations: Giving primarily in the greater Washington, DC, area. No grants to individuals, or for seed money, emergency funds, deficit financing, equipment and materials, land acquisition, or renovation projects.
Publications: Application guidelines.
Application information: Application form required for matching gift program.

Initial approach: Letter
Copies of proposal: 1
Deadline(s): None
Board meeting date(s): 4 or 5 times a year
Final notification: 3 to 6 months
Write: Andrea B. Wilkes, Secy.
Officers and Trustees:* Austin H. Kiplinger,* Pres.; Andrea B. Wilkes, Secy.; David M. Daugherty, Treas.; Knight A. Kiplinger, Todd L. Kiplinger, James O. Mayo, Frances Turgeon.
Number of staff: 1 part-time professional; 1 part-time support.
EIN: 520792570

554

Jacob and Charlotte Lehrman Foundation, Inc.
4801 Massachusetts Ave., N.W., Suite 400
Washington 20016   (202) 362-9500

Incorporated in 1953 in DC.
Donor(s): Jacob J. Lehrman,‡ Charlotte F. Lehrman.‡
Foundation type: Independent

Financial data (yr. ended 10/31/91): Assets, $8,589,944 (M); expenditures, $575,105; qualifying distributions, $543,490, including $543,250 for 51 grants (high: $250,000; low: $100).
Purpose and activities: Giving to establish scholarships and fellowships at institutions of learning, and to foster research in medicine and science; grants also for Jewish welfare funds, care of the aged and sick, cancer research, the establishment of trade schools, the fostering of religious observance, museums, and aid to refugees.
Fields of interest: Education, Jewish welfare, Jewish giving, aged, health, medical research, cancer, vocational education, religion, museums, welfare.
Types of support: Scholarship funds, fellowships, research, matching funds.
Limitations: Giving primarily in metropolitan Washington, DC. No grants to individuals; no loans.
Application information: Application form not required.

Initial approach: Proposal
Copies of proposal: 1
Deadline(s): Submit proposal preferably in May or Sept.; deadline Oct. 15
Board meeting date(s): May and Sept. or Oct.
Write: Robert Lehrman, V.P.
Officers: Heidi Berry, Pres.; Fredrica Carmichael, V.P.; Robert Lehrman, V.P.; Samuel Lehrman, V.P.; Leslie Handler, Secy.; Robert Barry Wertlieb, Treas.
Number of staff: None.
EIN: 526035666

555

Marpat Foundation, Inc.
c/o Miller & Chevalier
655 15th St., N.W., Suite 900
Washington 20005   (202) 626-5832

Incorporated in 1985 in MD.
Donor(s): Marvin Breckinridge Patterson.
Foundation type: Independent
Financial data (yr. ended 12/31/91): Assets, $12,221,764 (M); expenditures, $809,930; qualifying distributions, $689,923, including $689,923 for 48 grants (high: $75,000; low: $1,800; average: $5,000-$75,000).
Purpose and activities: "It is anticipated that grants will be made primarily to established charitable organizations whose activities are personally known to the directors. Grants will be made to the following: organizations that advance peace through international understanding, especially through programs involving national and world leaders and future leaders; schools, universities, museums, and libraries for the advancement and diffusion of knowledge; organizations and schools which sponsor programs that advocate and encourage family planning, or which promote or provide health care; organizations promoting or conducting scientific programs and research projects; organizations providing services and/or education designed to preserve natural and historical resources, or advance the knowledge of mankind's history and cultural past; and organizations which promote volunteer participation in, and citizen involvement with, such organizations."

Fields of interest: Peace, international affairs, cultural programs, libraries, higher education, family planning, health, science and technology, environment.

Types of support: Building funds, equipment, special projects, publications.

Limitations: Giving primarily in the mid-Atlantic region. No support for projects or organizations for any weapons development. No grants to individuals, or for endowment funds.

Publications: Informational brochure (including application guidelines).

Application information: Request summary sheet from foundation. Application form required.

Initial approach: Letter or proposal
Copies of proposal: 5
Deadline(s): Oct. 1
Board meeting date(s): Nov. or Dec.
Final notification: After Dec. 15

Officers and Directors:* Marvin Breckinridge Patterson,* Pres.; Charles T. Akre,* V.P.; Joan F. Koven,* Secy.-Treas.; Isabella B. Dubow, Mrs. John Farr Simmons.

Number of staff: 1 part-time professional.

EIN: 521358159

556
The J. Willard Marriott Foundation ▼
c/o Kay Bodeen
One Marriott Dr.
Washington 20058

Established in 1966 in DC.

Donor(s): J. Willard Marriott,‡ Alice S. Marriott, J. Willard Marriott Charitable Annuity Trust.

Foundation type: Independent

Financial data (yr. ended 12/31/90): Assets, $38,080,134 (M); gifts received, $10,365,694; expenditures, $8,943,007; qualifying distributions, $8,741,450, including $8,741,450 for 169 grants (high: $1,000,000; low: $200; average: $5,000-$25,000).

Purpose and activities: Grants primarily to local, previously supported charities and a few general scholarship funds.

Fields of interest: Higher education, health, social services.

Types of support: Continuing support, scholarship funds.

Limitations: Giving primarily in Washington, DC. No grants to individuals.

Application information: Contributes only to pre-selected organizations. Applications not accepted.

Trustees: Sterling D. Colton, Alice S. Marriott, J. Willard Marriott, Jr., Richard E. Marriott.

Number of staff: 1 part-time support.

EIN: 526068678

Recent health grants:

556-1 Arthritis Foundation, Arlington, VA, $10,000. 1990.

556-2 Borgess Medical Center, Kalamazoo, MI, $20,000. 1990.

556-3 Childrens National Medical Center, DC, $10,000. 1990.

556-4 Elyria Memorial Hospital and Medical Center Foundation, Elyria, OH, $30,000. 1990.

556-5 Georgetown University Medical Center, DC, $100,000. 1990.

556-6 Gratiot Community Hospital, Alma, MI, $10,000. 1990.

556-7 Health Volunteers Overseas, DC, $25,000. 1990.

556-8 Johns Hopkins Health Plan, Baltimore, MD, $25,000. 1990.

556-9 Kennebec Health Trust, Augusta, ME, $10,000. 1990.

556-10 Lakewood Hospital, Lakewood, OH, $25,000. 1990.

556-11 Massachusetts General Hospital, Boston, MA, $300,000. 1990.

556-12 Mayo Foundation, Rochester, MN, $200,000. 1990.

556-13 Mercy Center for Health Care Services, Aurora, IL, $20,000. 1990.

556-14 Mount Sinai Hospital, Hartford, CT, $20,000. 1990.

556-15 Presbyterian Intercommunity Hospital Foundation, Whittier, CA, $15,000. 1990.

556-16 Primary Childrens Medical Center, Salt Lake City, UT, $50,000. 1990.

556-17 Providence Foundation, Seattle, WA, $10,000. 1990.

556-18 Redlands Community Hospital, Redlands, CA, $10,000. 1990.

556-19 Saint Francis Health System, Pittsburgh, PA, $30,000. 1990.

556-20 Saint Joseph Hospital Foundation, Townson, MD, $25,000. 1990.

556-21 Saint Louis University Medical Center, Saint Louis, MO, $75,000. 1990.

556-22 Second Genesis, Bethesda, MD, $10,000. 1990.

556-23 Stanford University, Neonatal Department, Stanford, CA, $250,000. 1990.

556-24 Tallahassee Memorial Regional Medical Center, Tallahassee, FL, $15,000. 1990.

556-25 Target, Westminister, MD, $25,000. 1990.

556-26 Touro Infirmary, New Orleans, LA, $125,000. 1990.

556-27 Vincent T. Lombardi Cancer Research Center, DC, $10,000. 1990.

556-28 Yale-New Haven Hospital, New Haven, CT, $10,000. 1990.

557
Eugene and Agnes E. Meyer Foundation ▼
1400 16th St., N.W., Suite 360
Washington 20036   (202) 483-8294

Incorporated in 1944 in NY.

Donor(s): Eugene Meyer,‡ Agnes E. Meyer.‡

Foundation type: Independent

Financial data (yr. ended 12/31/90): Assets, $55,934,614 (M); expenditures, $2,525,118; qualifying distributions, $2,100,347, including $2,100,347 for grants (average: $10,000-$25,000).

Purpose and activities: Grants principally for neighborhood development/housing, education, health and mental health, the arts and humanities, law and justice, and community service. The foundation also administers the Metropolitan Washington Community AIDS Partnership.

Fields of interest: Education, health, mental health, AIDS, law and justice, housing, community development, arts, humanities, social services.

Types of support: Seed money, matching funds, special projects, technical assistance, continuing support, operating budgets, general purposes.

Limitations: Giving limited to the metropolitan Washington, DC, area, including VA and MD. No support for sectarian purposes, or for programs that are national or international in scope. No grants to individuals, or for annual campaigns, deficit financing, building or endowment funds, equipment, land acquisition, renovations, scholarships, fellowships, research, publications, or conferences.

Publications: Annual report (including application guidelines), grants list.

Application information: For a thorough understanding of application procedures, interested parties are strongly urged to read the foundation's annual report and guidelines. Application form not required.

Initial approach: 2-page letter of inquiry
Copies of proposal: 4
Deadline(s): Apr. 1, Aug. 1, and Dec. 1
Board meeting date(s): Applications considered only at Feb., June, and Oct. meetings; board meets also in Apr. and Dec.
Final notification: 1 month after board meetings
Write: Julie L. Rogers, Pres.

Officers and Directors:* Delano E. Lewis,* Chair.; Theodore C. Lutz,* Vice-Chair.; Julie L. Rogers,* Pres.; David W. Rutstein,* Secy.-Treas.; Lucy M. Cohen, Maureen E. Dwyer, Alice Rivlin, James T. Speight, Jr., Carrie Thornhill, Ricardo M. Urbina.

Staff: Irene S. Lee, Prog. Officer; Benita Kornegay-Henry, Grants Mgr. and Prog. Assoc.; Betsy Ringel, Prog. Dir., Metro. WA Community AIDS Partnership.

Number of staff: 4 full-time professional; 1 full-time support; 1 part-time support.

EIN: 530241716

Recent health grants:

557-1 Alice Hamilton Occupational Health Center, DC, $17,325. For second-year support of D.C. Hispanic Worker Project, educating immigrant workers on health and safety issues and rights. 1991.

557-2 Alliance for the Mentally Ill of Montgomery County, Bethesda, MD, $20,000. For start-up support for thrift business to train and employ adults with long-term mental illness. 1991.

557-3 Center for Youth Services, DC, $25,000. For continued support for outpatient drug prevention and treatment program serving 100 youth. 1991.

557-4 Child Center, Rockville, MD, $25,000. For second-year support for AMIGO program, school-based mental health program for Hispanic immigrant children in Montgomery County. 1991.

557-5 D.C. Hotline, DC, $10,000. To purchase state of the art telephone system. 1991.

557-6 Emmaus Services for the Aging, DC, $10,000. To conduct study to improve home health care delivery system to low-income DC residents. 1991.

557-7 Green Door, DC, $50,000. For continued support for capital campaign. 1991.

557-8 Hebrew Home of Greater Washington, Rockville, MD, $15,792. For salary support for pilot program to recruit, train and employ two developmentally disabled adults to become transportation aides. 1991.

557-9 Homemaker Health Aide Service, DC, $22,700. For salary of additional registered nurse to assist in evaluation of potential homemaker home health aides and to prepare them for certification. 1991.

557-10 Interfaith Conference of Metropolitan Washington, DC, $10,000. For second-year support for drugs and violence network project. 1991.

557-11 La Leche League-Maryland-Delaware-DC, Baltimore, MD, $10,000. For second-year support for breast feeding peer counselor program targeting low-income mothers and infants in Montgomery County. 1991.

557-12 March of Dimes Birth Defects Foundation, Arlington, VA, $30,000. For Healthy Babies Project, to reduce low birthweight, infant mortality and morbidity rates among infants of pregnant, substance-abusing women in Ward 5. 1991.

557-13 Oxford House, Great Falls, VA, $30,000. For existing staff to develop chapter system and regional council infrastructure for 68 Oxford recovery houses in metropolitan area. 1991.

557-14 Planned Parenthood Association of Metropolitan Washington, DC, $20,000. For second-year support for Latino outreach program. 1991.

557-15 Round House Theater, Friends of the, Silver Spring, MD, $10,000. For outreach and education of Roasted Shoes, play on substance abuse to Prince Georges County schools. 1991.

557-16 Sasha Bruce Youthwork, DC, $20,000. For matching funds for substance abuse prevention services for runaway and homeless youth. 1991.

557-17 United Seniors Health Cooperative, DC, $10,000. For start-up support for community-wide service program that will help older persons remain at home. 1991.

557-18 W E T A-Greater Washington Educational Telecommunications Association, DC, $25,000. For outreach costs of Nine Months, 20-week series profiling eight pregnant women. 1991.

557-19 Zacchaeus Medical Clinic, DC, $15,000. To provide health screening and medical treatment to low-income and elderly minority individuals. 1991.

558
Pettus-Crowe Foundation, Inc.
1616 P St., N.W., Suite 100
Washington 20036   (202) 328-5186

Incorporated in 1968 in NY.
Donor(s): Irene Pettus-Crowe.‡
Foundation type: Independent
Financial data (yr. ended 12/31/90): Assets, $2,117,833 (M); expenditures, $109,198; qualifying distributions, $96,818, including $72,582 for 39 grants (high: $17,500; low: $100).
Purpose and activities: Support for ethical issues and reproductive rights.
Fields of interest: Women, family planning, AIDS.
Types of support: Conferences and seminars, continuing support, seed money, special projects.
Limitations: Giving primarily on the East Coast and in the southern U.S. No grants to individuals.
Application information: Contributes only to pre-selected organizations. Applications not accepted.
Write: Dr. Irene Crowe, Pres.

Officers and Directors:* Irene Crowe,* Pres. and Treas.; John R. Young, V.P. and Secy.; Mary Crowe,* V.P.; Phillipa Crowe Neilson,* V.P.
Number of staff: None.
EIN: 237025310

559
The Marjorie Merriweather Post Foundation
P.O. Box 96202
Washington 20090-6202

Established in 1956.
Donor(s): Marjorie Merriweather Post.‡
Foundation type: Independent
Financial data (yr. ended 12/31/90): Assets, $3,677,533 (M); expenditures, $210,772; qualifying distributions, $188,314, including $181,000 for 55 grants (high: $10,000; low: $1,000; average: $500-$5,000).
Purpose and activities: Primary areas of interest include higher and secondary education, the arts, international affairs, and social services.
Fields of interest: Higher education, secondary education, arts, international affairs, social services, health services, drug abuse.
Limitations: No grants to individuals.
Application information: Application form not required.
Initial approach: Proposal
Copies of proposal: 1
Deadline(s): Mar. 31 and Sept. 30
Board meeting date(s): Spring and fall
Final notification: Notification sent only to those organizations which are approved for grants
Write: Lois J. Shortell
Officers and Trustees:* John A. Logan, Jr.,* Chair.; Spottswood P. Dudley,* Vice-Chair.; Leonard L. Silverstein,* Treas.; Nina Craig, Henry A. Dudley, Jr., George B. Hertzog, Godfrey T. McHugh.
Number of staff: None.
EIN: 526054705

560
Marjorie Merriweather Post Foundation of D.C.
4155 Linnean Ave., N.W.
Washington 20008   (202) 686-8500

Established in 1967 in DC.
Donor(s): Marjorie Merriweather Post.‡
Foundation type: Independent
Financial data (yr. ended 12/31/90): Assets, $81,769,135 (M); gifts received, $4,348; expenditures, $4,297,708; qualifying distributions, $5,276,224, including $900,000 for 75 grants (high: $90,000; average: $5,000-$10,000), $2,851,071 for 1 foundation-administered program and $223,746 for 1 loan.
Purpose and activities: The foundation was formed to perpetuate Hillwood Museum; when an excess of funds is available, grants are utilized for other charitable purposes, including social services, education, hospitals and health associations, and cultural programs.
Fields of interest: Social services, education, hospitals, health associations, cultural programs, museums.

Types of support: Building funds, capital campaigns, conferences and seminars, continuing support, general purposes, special projects, renovation projects, research, loans, matching funds, operating budgets.
Limitations: Giving primarily in Washington, DC. No grants to individuals.
Publications: Application guidelines.
Application information: Application form not required.
Copies of proposal: 1
Deadline(s): Oct. 1
Board meeting date(s): Dec. and as required
Final notification: Varies
Write: Raymond P. Hunter, Secy.-Treas.
Officers and Directors:* Ellen MacNeille Charles,* Pres.; Nedenia Hartley,* V.P.; Raymond P. Hunter,* Secy.-Treas.; Melissa Cantacuzene, David P. Close, Nina Rumbough Craig, Antal Post de Beckessy, Nancy Young Duncan, Albert G. Perkins, Stanley Rumbough, Douglas R. Smith.
Number of staff: 1 full-time support.
EIN: 526080752

561
Public Welfare Foundation, Inc. ▼
2600 Virginia Ave., N.W., Rm. 505
Washington 20037-1977   (202) 965-1800

Incorporated in 1947 in TX; reincorporated in 1951 in DE.
Donor(s): Charles Edward Marsh.‡
Foundation type: Independent
Financial data (yr. ended 10/31/91): Assets, $250,284,699 (M); expenditures, $18,529,169; qualifying distributions, $16,750,568, including $16,750,568 for grants (high: $250,000; low: $1,000; average: $42,450).
Purpose and activities: Grants primarily to grass roots organizations in the U.S. and abroad, with emphasis on the environment, population, health, the elderly, disadvantaged youth, and criminal justice; support also for community services. Programs must serve low-income populations, with preference to short-term needs.
Fields of interest: Crime and law enforcement, disadvantaged, population studies, aged, youth, health.
Types of support: Matching funds, operating budgets, seed money, special projects.
Limitations: No support for religious purposes. No grants to individuals, or for building funds, capital improvements, endowments, scholarships, graduate work, foreign study, conferences, seminars, publications, research, workshops, consulting services, annual campaigns, or deficit financing; no loans.
Publications: Annual report (including application guidelines).
Application information: Application form not required.
Initial approach: Proposal with summary sheet
Copies of proposal: 1
Deadline(s): None
Board meeting date(s): Jan., Apr., July, and Oct.
Final notification: 3-4 months
Write: Larry Kressley, Exec. Dir.
Officers and Directors:* Donald T. Warner,* Chair.; Thomas J. Scanlon,* V.P.; Linda J. Campbell, Secy.; Veronica T. Keating,* Treas.; Antoinette M. Haskell, Robert H. Haskell, Robert

R. Nathan, Myrtis H. Powell, Thomas W. Scoville, Jerome W.D. Stokes, Murat W. Williams.

Number of staff: 10 full-time professional; 3 full-time support.

EIN: 540597601

Recent health grants:

561-1 AIDS Action Committee of Massachusetts, Boston, MA, $46,000. For general support to pilot education and referral project reaching drug-addicted individuals during hospitalizations. 1991.

561-2 AIDSFilms, NYC, NY, $80,000. For continued general support for additional AIDS education films aimed at high-risk populations and for promoting prevention of disease. 1991.

561-3 Albert Einstein College of Medicine of Yeshiva University, Bronx, NY, $170,000. For clinical and support services provided to families and children with HIV infection. 1991.

561-4 Alzheimers Disease and Related Disorders Association, Louisville, KY, $20,000. For start-up of Volunteer Interfaith Caregivers of Kentuckiana providing respite services for families of people stricken with Alzheimer's Disease or related dementia. 1991.

561-5 American Civil Liberties Union Foundation, National Prison Project, DC, $45,000. For continued support for AIDS Education Program providing inmates, correctional officers, and corrections officials with materials related specifically to corrections arena. 1991.

561-6 Associacao Brasileira Interdisciplinar de AIDS, Rio de Janeiro, Brazil, $40,000. For AIDS prevention education provided to children in Brazilian public schools. 1991.

561-7 Barnert Memorial Hospital Center Foundation, Paterson, NJ, $14,000. For outreach program to increase number of women receiving prenatal care in Paterson. 1991.

561-8 Barrier Free Living, NYC, NY, $40,500. For general support to hire social worker with expertise in counseling for substance abuse. 1991.

561-9 Boston Pediatric AIDS Project, Roxbury, MA, $57,000. For general support for efforts to prevent spread of AIDS, reduce high cost of care and increase community and home-based services for inner city mothers and babies with AIDS. 1991.

561-10 Brookdale Center on Aging, NYC, NY, $33,300. For Respite Program for Alzheimer's patients and their families to provide families who take care of chronically ill with regular intervals of relief from demands of caregiving. 1991.

561-11 California Law Center on Long Term Care, San Francisco, CA, $50,800. For In-Home Care Project to promote access to already existing programs providing assistance to those elderly desiring to remain at home. 1991.

561-12 California Rural Legal Assistance Foundation, San Francisco, CA, $50,000. For continued support for farmworker pesticide education project which provides information to farmworkers about health risks of pesticide use and will assist victims of poisoning incidents. 1991.

561-13 Catholics for a Free Choice, DC, $50,000. For general support for work to reduce incidence of abortion and to increase women's choices in child-bearing and child-rearing through advocacy of social and economic programs for women, families and children. 1991.

561-14 Center for Population Options, DC, $40,000. For continued support for advocacy initiative which encourages and supports efforts to distribute condoms through schools in hopes of preventing pregnancy and spread of HIV among adolescents. 1991.

561-15 Center for Third World Organizing, Oakland, CA, $30,000. For Campaign for Accessible Health Care promoting lead poisoning testing for children in low-income areas of Oakland, CA, and encourage action by officials to clean up sources of lead. 1991.

561-16 Central American Refugee Center, DC, $35,000. For Center's legal, medical and social services in response to increased demand occasioned by influx of Salvadoran refugees. 1991.

561-17 Centro Para Los Adolescentes de San Miguel de Allende, A.C., Guanajuato, Mexico, $27,700. For continued general support for sex education and counseling and reproductive health services for adolescents and young families. 1991.

561-18 Childrens Health Fund, NYC, NY, $250,000. For continuing general support to New York Children's Health Project which provides comprehensive pediatric care to homeless and other disadvantaged children in New York City. 1991.

561-19 Citizens Committee for New York City, NYC, NY, $75,000. For continued support to complete National Partnership Project, which is assisting six cities to develop their capacity to successfully fight drug traffic and drug abuse in targeted neighborhoods. 1991.

561-20 Coalition of Vermont Elders (COVE), Burlington, VT, $25,000. For general support to obtain affordable prescription drugs for low-income elders. 1991.

561-21 Columbia Road Health Services, DC, $25,000. For Health Care for Children Project, which provides quality health care to children for regular illnesses and complicated medical problems arising from very poor socio-economic conditions. 1991.

561-22 Comite de Apoyo, Edinburg, TX, $20,000. To provide women workers in factories along U.S.-Mexico border with information about their rights under Mexican labor law and on workplace safety. 1991.

561-23 Community Action Committee of the Lehigh Valley, Bethlehem, PA, $50,000. For start-up of medically supervised shelter for homeless people who have been discharged from hospitals but are in no condition to live independently. 1991.

561-24 Community Care, Rochester, VT, $20,000. For support for hiring of executive director to coordinate homecare services to elderly and oversee operations at Rochester Inn, shared housing facility. 1991.

561-25 Community Health Center, Ashland, OR, $32,200. To help clinic qualify as Primary Care Organization, enabling it to participate in Oregon's prospective payment system. 1991.

561-26 Community of Hope, DC, $40,000. For continued support for Maternal-Infant Support and Recovery Program, offering health and rehabilitative services to drug-abusing mothers and pregnant women, health services to drug-exposed infants and children and drug prevention education services to adolescents in community. 1991.

561-27 Correctional Association of New York, NYC, NY, $50,000. For continued support for AIDS in Prison Project, providing services to families of inmates with AIDS in New York prisons. 1991.

561-28 Crossroads, New Haven, CT, $25,000. For expansion of women's drug treatment program to include assertiveness training directed toward prevention of relapse and promotion of assertiveness in sexual relationships as deterrent to contracting HIV/AIDS. 1991.

561-29 D.C. Prisoners Legal Services Project, DC, $50,000. For Medical Delivery System Litigation Project that will seek to improve medical care provided to inmates in District of Columbia's prison system. 1991.

561-30 Development Centers, Detroit, MI, $40,000. For continued support for New Chance Program, which provides educational, vocational and life skills training for teen mothers and their children. 1991.

561-31 Diamond Street Wholistic Health Center, Philadelphia, PA, $40,000. For general support for health center which serves indigent population of Diamond Street neighborhood in north Philadelphia. 1991.

561-32 District of Columbia Womens Council on AIDS, DC, $30,500. For general operating support targeted to new AIDS prevention and support project for incarcerated women. 1991.

561-33 Drug Policy Foundation, DC, $75,000. For America's Drug Forum, weekly television series that examines complicated drug policy issues. 1991.

561-34 Easter Seal Society of New York, Albany, NY, $43,800. For Tweemill House, 39-unit residence for disabled people in Harlem, providing housing to 45 people who are deaf, blind or confined to wheelchair. 1991.

561-35 Eldercare New Mexico, Corrales, NM, $20,000. For general support to provide in-home care to individuals experiencing chronic debilitating illnesses, Alzheimer's disease and other afflictions affecting older people. 1991.

561-36 Elderly Health Screening Service, Waterbury, CT, $41,700. For general support to health screening service for early detection of physiological abnormalities in people aged sixty and over. 1991.

561-37 Environmental Health Coalition, San Diego, CA, $25,000. For Toxic-Free Neighborhoods Campaign which assists low-income, minority people in San Diego in dealing with health and safety threats in their neighborhoods posed by use of toxic materials. 1991.

561-38 Environmental Health Network, Harvey, LA, $15,000. To provide technical and other assistance to communities with health problems resulting from toxic contamination. 1991.

561-39 Esperanca, Phoenix, AZ, $26,000. For extension of family planning services from urban clinic to outlying districts. 1991.

561-40 Family Health Services, Jacksonville, FL, $40,000. For continued support for New Chance Program providing comprehensive health, education, life skills and parenting services to teen mothers and their children. 1991.

561-41 Freedom From Hunger Foundation, Davis, CA, $50,000. For continued support for Mali Institutional Development Enterprise and Nutrition Project, seeking to improve health and nutrition of villagers, especially women and children, in rural Mali, Africa. 1991.

561-42 Hanford Education Action League, Spokane, WA, $20,000. To provide research, education and advocacy on environmental health and safety issues that effect communities near Hanford Nuclear Reservation in Washington. 1991.

561-43 Hebrew Home of Greater Washington, Rockville, MD, $61,300. For support for further development, evaluation and dissemination of system to remove restraints used in nursing homes, in compliance with federal OBRA mandate. 1991.

561-44 Highbridge Community Life Center, Bronx, NY, $30,000. For general support for Highbridge/Woodcrest Center for Persons with AIDS. 1991.

561-45 Highlander Research and Education Center, New Market, TN, $60,000. For continued support for Community Environmental Health Program which offers training, technical assistance and other support services to grassroots groups across country that are dealing with serious environmental health problems in their communities. 1991.

561-46 Hospital for Special Surgery, NYC, NY, $25,000. For national replication of Lupus Line, peer counseling service for persons with systemic lupus erythematosus. 1991.

561-47 Implementing Agency for Cooperation and Training, Los Angeles, CA, $47,500. For continued support for AIDS outreach among high-risk groups in Haiti. 1991.

561-48 Ingleside Homes, Wilmington, DE, $32,300. For start-up costs for nonprofit nursing personnel service to be developed for Ingleside Homes and other Medicaid-certified agencies in area. 1991.

561-49 Institute for Southern Studies, Durham, NC, $36,500. For Healing Hands project assisting rural minorities suffering from cumulative trauma disorders as result of working in poultry industry. 1991.

561-50 Institute of Integrated Rural Development, Dhaka, Bangladesh, $40,000. For continued support for Integrated Health Program, providing health care, sanitation and nutritional services to over 43 Bangladese villages. 1991.

561-51 Instituto de Estudos Monteiro Lobato, Sao Paulo, Brazil, $59,800. For start-up of six rural health sites to care for poor families in Santo Antonio do Pinhal, near Taubate, in state of Sao Paulo, Brazil. 1991.

561-52 Integrated Health Project of Dondon, Port au Prince, Haiti, $20,000. To defray costs of giving physical therapy, orthotic devices and orthopedic surgery to handicapped Haitians, mostly children, in northern part of Haiti. 1991.

561-53 InterAction: American Council for Voluntary International Action, NYC, NY, $30,000. For project to encourage member organizations of InterAction to integrate population and environmental components into existing international development efforts. 1991.

561-54 Interfaith Program for the Elderly, Milwaukee, WI, $20,000. To establish Near South Side Interfaith Program providing homecare services to elderly and disabled in low-income, ethnically diversified area of Milwaukee. 1991.

561-55 International Projects Assistance Services, Carrboro, NC, $60,000. For work to help reduce abortion-related maternal mortality by improving women's access to safe abortion services. 1991.

561-56 International Rescue Committee, NYC, NY, $49,000. For training of Sudanese primary health supervisors. 1991.

561-57 International Womens Health Coalition, NYC, NY, $20,000. To promote reform of reproductive health issues and improve family planning services in Latin America. 1991.

561-58 Legal Aid Society, NYC, NY, $75,000. For litigation to improve health care services afforded to inmates infected with AIDS in New York State Department of Correctional Services. 1991.

561-59 Lower East Side Family Union, NYC, NY, $20,000. For continued support for case-managed services to single, women-headed households where mother is HIV-positive. 1991.

561-60 Madre, NYC, NY, $25,000. For Women's Campaign and Congress for Universal Health Care to build grassroots movements of people to inform public and to get them involved in current health care debate. Grant shared with Women's Peace Network. 1991.

561-61 Marie Stopes International, London, England, $150,000. For development of information, education and communications campaign to promote family planning in Tanzania. 1991.

561-62 Marie Stopes International, London, England, $87,500. For start-up of three new family planning clinics in Kisii, Mombasa and Kisumu, Kenya. 1991.

561-63 Marys Center for Maternal and Child Care, DC, $55,000. For general support for pediatric services to children born by teenaged Hispanic mothers receiving prenatal care at Mary's Center. 1991.

561-64 Meharry Medical College, Nashville, TN, $50,000. For Early Intervention Program offering preventive health services to children and their families. 1991.

561-65 Memorial Hospital of Martinsville, Martinsville, VA, $10,000. For hospice program. 1991.

561-66 Mental Health Association of Montgomery County, Rockville, MD, $18,000. For continued support for Springboard Program, providing stable residence and support services to homeless young mothers, primarily between the ages of 18 to 21 years old. 1991.

561-67 Mental Health Law Project, DC, $75,000. For Community Watch program to increase housing opportunities for people with mental disabilities and expand financial resources available for affordable housing and housing linked to supportive services to meet their needs. 1991.

561-68 Mercy Hospital, Devils Lake, ND, $20,000. For purchase of equipment and educational materials to help establish program to train approximately 70 emergency medical technicians. 1991.

561-69 Midtown Churches Community Association, Baltimore, MD, $30,000. For Extra Care Program serving homeless people who have been discharged from hospitals but are not well enough to live in shelters or independently. 1991.

561-70 Minnesota Senior Federation, Saint Paul, MN, $48,000. For continued support for Senior Partners Care Program assisting low-income seniors in gaining access to affordable health care. 1991.

561-71 Morgantown Health Right, Morgantown, WV, $26,200. For continuing support for Pharmacy Assistance Project. 1991.

561-72 Mount Sinai Hospital and Medical Center, Geriatrics and Adult Development, NYC, NY, $175,000. For continued support to complete creation of unified data management system to improve access of indigent, primarily minority, elderly people to medical care and social services. 1991.

561-73 National Family Planning and Reproductive Health Association, DC, $50,000. For continued general support for coordinating and improving distribution of family planning services and materials in U.S.. 1991.

561-74 National Minority AIDS Council, DC, $50,000. For general support to Project Heal, which provides direct technical support to community-based minority AIDS organizations. 1991.

561-75 National Toxics Campaign Fund, Boston, MA, $75,000. For continued support for technical assistance to help grassroots groups develop and implement toxic cleanup and pollution prevention plans. 1991.

561-76 Nuclear Safety Campaign, Seattle, WA, $25,000. For continued general support for its work with grassroots efforts around country to deal with growing public health and safety problems resulting from nation's nuclear weapons production. 1991.

561-77 Outreach Counseling Services, Charlottesville, VA, $19,800. For expansion of services to troubled youths and their families in five additional counties in southern Virginia. 1991.

561-78 Partners of the Americas, DC, $80,000. For special projects to support and stimulate Partnership programs on AIDS in Latin America and Caribbean countries. 1991.

561-79 Planned Parenthood Association of Metropolitan Washington, DC, $75,000. For continued support to provide comprehensive reproductive health care and sexuality education in national capital area. 1991.

561-80 Planned Parenthood Association of Nashville, Nashville, TN, $35,000. For Family Life Education Program which provides sexuality education and information to teens and parents. 1991.

561-81 Planned Parenthood Federation of America, NYC, NY, $100,000. For general support for training, technical assistance, supplies and funding for population programs in developing countries. 1991.

561-82 Planned Parenthood Federation of America, NYC, NY, $50,000. For continued support for project offering educational and family planning services to people in four districts of upper Guinea, Africa. 1991.

561-83 Planned Parenthood Federation of America, NYC, NY, $22,500. For continued support for clinic providing family planning services and community-based contraceptive distribution system in Veracruz, Mexico. 1991.

561-84 Planned Parenthood Federation, International, NYC, NY, $46,000. For project to begin to deliver family planning and maternal and child health services to hill tribe people in northern Thailand. 1991.

561-85 Planned Parenthood Federation, International, NYC, NY, $45,800. For youth centers providing family planning services and education to underserved adolescents in Cuajimalpa, Colima, Monterrey, Toluca, Guadalajara, and Tampico, Mexico. 1991.

561-86 Planned Parenthood Federation, International, NYC, NY, $26,000. To train volunteer family planning teams to provide information about family planning and contraceptive options to coal mining workers in Quang Nin province of Vietnam. 1991.

561-87 Planned Parenthood of Greater Charlotte, Charlotte, NC, $30,000. For start-up of third family planning clinic in greater metropolitan Charlotte. 1991.

561-88 Planned Parenthood of Maryland, Baltimore, MD, $50,000. For Teen Pregnancy Prevention Project providing intensive services to inner-city teens who receive negative pregnancy test. 1991.

561-89 Planned Parenthood of New York City, NYC, NY, $50,000. For HUB Learning Center and Street Beat, providing medical and counseling services as well as education and vocational training for at-risk teens in South Bronx. 1991.

561-90 Planned Parenthood of Orange County, Chapel Hill, NC, $45,000. For start-up of clinic in Durham, NC. 1991.

561-91 Planned Parenthood of the Blue Ridge, Roanoke, VA, $40,000. For general support and revolving loan fund to enable poor women to receive services they normally would not be able to afford. 1991.

561-92 Planned Parenthood of the Capital and Coast, Raleigh, NC, $25,000. For start-up of new clinic site in Wilmington, NC. 1991.

561-93 Population Crisis Committee, DC, $75,000. For continued support for public education and policy analysis regarding implications of rapid population growth, and development of alternative courses of action. 1991.

561-94 Population Services International, DC, $120,000. For AIDS prevention social marketing condom distribution project to combat growing AIDS epidemic in Ivory Coast, Africa. 1991.

561-95 Population Services International, DC, $80,000. For AIDS prevention social marketing condom distribution project to combat growing AIDS epidemic in Central Africa. 1991.

561-96 Population Services International, DC, $60,000. For AIDS prevention social marketing condom distribution project to combat rising AIDS epidemic in Rwanda, Africa. 1991.

561-97 Population Services International, DC, $50,000. For AIDS prevention social

marketing condom distribution project to combat growing AIDS epidemic in Benin, Africa. 1991.

561-98 Population Services International, DC, $41,000. For AIDS prevention social marketing condom distribution project aimed at young adults to combat growing AIDS epidemic in Burkina Faso, Africa. 1991.

561-99 Program for the Introduction and Adaptation of Contraceptive Technology (PIACT), Seattle, WA, $120,000. For general support for information, education and communication campaign to help prevent unsafe abortion and promote family planning in Kenya, Nigeria and Zambia. 1991.

561-100 Project Concern International, San Diego, CA, $70,200. For start-up of health care project to provide maternal and child health care and family planning in Province of Moluccas, area with highest infant mortality in Indonesia. 1991.

561-101 Respite Services, South Gibson, PA, $10,000. For general support providing respite care to handicapped youth. 1991.

561-102 S.E.T. Ministries of Colorado, Denver, CO, $25,000. To replicate model designed to provide preventive health services to elderly. 1991.

561-103 Sex Information and Education Council of the United States (SIECUS), NYC, NY, $30,000. For general support to develop, collect and disseminate information and to promote comprehensive education about sexuality. 1991.

561-104 Sioux Valley Hospital, Family Service, Sioux Falls, SD, $100,000. To establish peer counselors program, providing volunteer services and geriatric assessment to elderly. 1991.

561-105 South Central Family Health Center, Los Angeles, CA, $37,000. For expansion of program services to add perinatal care to 150 pregnant women and comprehensive health care to additional 400 families. 1991.

561-106 Stevan Greenwood Childhood Cancer Foundation, Arlington, VA, $35,000. For general support to hire full-time Executive Director. 1991.

561-107 Sunnyside Community Services, Sunnyside, NY, $10,600. To expand homecare program serving disabled, homebound elderly clients. 1991.

561-108 Unemployment Information Center, Philadelphia, PA, $35,000. For general support to work on health access for unemployed and uninsured in Philadelphia, PA. 1991.

561-109 United Seniors Health Cooperative, Cooperative Caring Network, DC, $47,500. To provide formal structure through which elderly and disabled can become informed and gain access to entitlements which enable them to stay independent longer. 1991.

561-110 University of Arizona Health Sciences Center, Tucson, AZ, $51,000. To establish Breastfeeding Intervention Project to promote breastfeeding among Navajo women at Shiprock Reservation in New Mexico. 1991.

561-111 University of Virginia, Young Women's Health Center, Charlottesville, VA, $35,000. For capital support for start-up of clinical program specializing in prenatal care and family planning service delivery for young women. 1991.

561-112 Utah AIDS Foundation, Salt Lake City, UT, $25,000. For general support to provide information and prevention education, practical advocacy and support services for people with AIDS and programs to promote behavior changes in people at risk of contracting HIV. 1991.

561-113 Vanderbilt University, Nashville, TN, $35,000. For continued support for Service Training for Environmental Progress Program providing student interns, laboratory analysis and other technical assistance to low-income communities in south dealing with environmental health problems. 1991.

561-114 Village Nursing Home, NYC, NY, $50,000. For start-up of home care program for persons with AIDS. 1991.

561-115 Vive Organization, Buffalo, NY, $22,600. For continued support for Medical Care Project, providing health screening, immunizations, tuberculosis testing, surveillance and treatment of medical conditions to refugees awaiting entry into Canada. 1991.

561-116 W G B H Educational Foundation, Boston, MA, $75,000. For general support for production of one hour drama for teens about AIDS. 1991.

561-117 Washington Free Clinic, DC, $24,000. For continued support for Teen Pregnancy Prevention Project, providing services for primary prevention of teen pregnancy as part of its clinical program. 1991.

561-118 World Vision, Monrovia, CA, $100,000. To provide AIDS education and counseling training to World Vision personnel, health workers and communities they serve in Zimbabwe and Kenya, Africa. 1991.

561-119 Zacchaeus Medical Clinic, DC, $30,000. For general support as Zacchaeus merges with another nonprofit, Bread for the City. 1991.

562
Walter G. Ross Foundation

c/o ASB Capital Management Inc.
655 15th St., N.W., Suite 800
Washington 20005

Trust established about 1964 in DC.
Foundation type: Independent
Financial data (yr. ended 12/31/91): Assets, $7,183,240 (M); expenditures, $404,941; qualifying distributions, $343,433, including $330,000 for 13 grants (high: $125,000; low: $5,000).

Purpose and activities: Giving primarily for medical research and programs for the mentally or physically handicapped; support also for higher education and the disadvantaged, including family services and child welfare and development.
Fields of interest: Medical research, health associations, hospitals, heart disease, handicapped, higher education, disadvantaged, family services, child development, hospices.
Types of support: Research, general purposes, endowment funds, matching funds.
Limitations: Giving limited to the Washington, DC, area and FL. No grants to individuals, or for scholarships or fellowships; no loans.
Publications: Application guidelines.

Application information: Application form not required.
Initial approach: Letter
Copies of proposal: 1
Deadline(s): Submit proposal preferably in Aug.; deadline Sept. 15
Board meeting date(s): Oct.
Final notification: 1 month after annual meeting
Write: Ian W. Jones, Secy.
Trustees: Lloyd H. Elliott, Chair.; Eugene L. Bernard, J. Hillman Zahn.
EIN: 526057560

563
Alexander and Margaret Stewart Trust u/w of the late Mary E. Stewart ▼
c/o First American Bank, N.A.
740 15th St., N.W. - Trust Dept.
Washington 20005   (202) 637-7887

Trust established in 1947 in DC.
Donor(s): Mary E. Stewart.‡
Foundation type: Independent
Financial data (yr. ended 12/31/90): Assets, $24,827,401 (M); expenditures, $1,314,278; qualifying distributions, $1,127,541, including $1,058,893 for 17 grants (high: $170,000; low: $1,000; average: $40,000-$80,000).
Purpose and activities: Giving for the prevention of cancer and for the care of those afflicted with cancer.
Fields of interest: Health services, cancer, hospices.
Types of support: Seed money, equipment, matching funds, continuing support, operating budgets.
Limitations: Giving primarily in the Washington, DC, area. No grants to individuals, or for endowment funds, annual campaigns, deficit financing, building funds, land acquisition, renovation projects, publications, conferences, research, scholarships, or fellowships; no loans.
Publications: Program policy statement, application guidelines.

Application information: Application form required.
Initial approach: Letter
Copies of proposal: 1
Deadline(s): None
Board meeting date(s): Apr., June, Sept., Nov., and Dec.
Final notification: Upon decision of trustees
Write: Ruth C. Shaw, Group V.P., First American Bank, N.A.
Trustees: Francis G. Addison III, George E. Hamilton III, First American Bank, N.A.
Number of staff: None.
EIN: 526020260

564
George Wasserman Foundation, Inc.
3134 Ellicott St., N.W.
Washington 20008-2025   (202) 966-3355

Established in 1948.
Donor(s): George Wasserman.‡
Foundation type: Independent
Financial data (yr. ended 12/31/90): Assets, $2,821,931 (M); expenditures, $71,645; qualifying distributions, $56,100, including $56,100 for 8 grants (high: $30,000; low: $100).
Purpose and activities: Grants primarily for Jewish welfare funds, theological studies, and temple support; giving also for social services and health.
Fields of interest: Jewish giving, Jewish welfare, theological education, health, social services, disadvantaged.
Types of support: Annual campaigns, building funds, continuing support, endowment funds, exchange programs, general purposes, research, scholarship funds, seed money, special projects, technical assistance.
Limitations: No grants to individuals.
Application information:
Initial approach: Letter
Deadline(s): None
Write: Janice W. Goldsten, Pres.

Officers and Directors:* Janice W. Goldsten,* Pres. and Treas.; Carolyn Stopak,* V.P. and Secy.; Lisa Gill,* V.P.
EIN: 526035888

565
The Westport Fund
1815 Randolph St., N.W.
Washington 20011

Established in 1943.
Donor(s): Milton McGreevy,‡ Jean McGreevy Green.
Foundation type: Independent
Financial data (yr. ended 12/31/90): Assets, $3,063,560 (M); gifts received, $5,048; expenditures, $174,563; qualifying distributions, $160,172, including $157,207 for 73 grants (high: $16,000; low: $7).
Fields of interest: Cultural programs, social services, education, higher education, family planning, peace, legal services.
Types of support: Annual campaigns, building funds, capital campaigns, continuing support, endowment funds, equipment, general purposes, lectureships, operating budgets, publications, research, scholarship funds.
Limitations: Giving primarily in Kansas City, MO. No grants to individuals, or for consulting services, deficit financing, exchange programs, internships, matching funds, land acquisition, renovation projects, seed money, or technical assistance; no loans.
Application information: Contributes only to pre-selected organizations. Applications not accepted.
Officers: Gail McGreevy Harmon, Pres.; Thomas J. McGreevy, V.P.; Jean McGreevy Green, Secy.; Ann McGreevy Heller, Treas.
Director: Barbara James McGreevy.
Number of staff: None.
EIN: 446007971

FLORIDA

566
The Abbey Foundation, Inc.
P.O. Box 140458
Coral Gables 33114

Donor(s): Nestor Martinez.
Foundation type: Independent
Financial data (yr. ended 12/31/90): Assets, $4,749,308 (M); expenditures, $572,062; qualifying distributions, $423,495, including $403,040 for 34 grants (high: $166,000; low: $200).
Fields of interest: Medical education, higher education, health associations.
Types of support: Research.
Limitations: Giving primarily in Coral Gables and Miami, FL. No grants to individuals.
Application information: Contributes only to pre-selected organizations. Applications not accepted.
Officer: Norbert Touchette, Exec. Dir.
Directors: J. Fred Danker, Nestor Martinez, Marion Roletti, Jack Widrich.
EIN: 590992098

567
Anthony R. Abraham Foundation, Inc.
6600 S.W. 57th Ave.
Miami 33143   (305) 665-2222

Established in 1978 in FL.
Donor(s): Anthony R. Abraham.
Foundation type: Independent
Financial data (yr. ended 12/31/90): Assets, $6,378,025 (M); gifts received, $100; expenditures, $126,506; qualifying distributions, $126,506, including $103,733 for 75 grants (high: $25,691; low: $25).
Purpose and activities: Giving largely to a children's hospital and youth agencies; some support for religious organizations and medical research.
Fields of interest: Hospitals, child welfare, youth, religion, medical research.
Types of support: Grants to individuals.
Application information:
  Initial approach: Letter
  Deadline(s): None
  Write: Thomas G. Abraham, Secy.
Officers and Directors:* Anthony R. Abraham,* Pres.; Thomas G. Abraham,* Secy.; Joseph Shaker,* Treas.; Robert Fried, Anthony Shaker.
EIN: 591837290

568
Arthur F. and Alice E. Adams Charitable Foundation
c/o Southeast Bank, N.A.
One Southeast Financial Ctr., MS 1153
Miami 33131   (305) 375-6839

Established in 1987 in FL.
Donor(s): Alice E. Adams.‡
Foundation type: Independent

Financial data (yr. ended 09/30/91): Assets, $15,981,339 (M); gifts received, $6,063,661; expenditures, $779,926; qualifying distributions, $737,663, including $667,410 for 18 grants (high: $305,000; low: $5,000).
Fields of interest: Music, performing arts, theater, education, higher education, hospitals.
Limitations: Giving primarily in FL and TN. No grants to individuals.
Application information:
  Initial approach: Letter
  Deadline(s): None
  Write: Richard Chapman, V.P., Southeast Bank, N.A.
Trustees: Southeast Bank, N.A., Dewey, Ballantine et al.
EIN: 656003785

569
The Amaturo Foundation, Inc.
2929 East Commercial Blvd., PH-C
Fort Lauderdale 33308   (305) 776-7815

Established in 1986 in FL.
Donor(s): Joseph C. Amaturo.
Foundation type: Independent
Financial data (yr. ended 06/30/91): Assets, $2,431,542 (M); gifts received, $1,292,139; expenditures, $46,077; qualifying distributions, $45,427, including $45,200 for 6 grants (high: $20,000; low: $100).
Purpose and activities: Giving primarily for education, child welfare, and hospitals, with emphasis on Catholic organizations.
Fields of interest: Catholic giving, Catholic welfare, education, child welfare, hospitals.
Types of support: Research.
Limitations: Giving primarily in FL.
Application information:
  Initial approach: Letter
  Deadline(s): None
  Write: Cara E. Cameron, Mgr.
Officer and Directors:* Cara E. Cameron,* Mgr.; Douglas Q. Amaturo, Joseph C. Amaturo, Lawrence V. Amaturo, Lorna J. Amaturo, Winifred Amaturo, Winifred L. Amaturo, Frances A. Arnold, Elizabeth A. Eisenstein, Joseph E. Ferguson, William Ruane.
EIN: 592718130

570
The Applebaum Foundation, Inc.
11111 Biscayne Blvd., Tower 3, Rm. 853
North Miami 33181

Incorporated in 1949 in NY.
Donor(s): Joseph Applebaum,‡ Leila Applebaum.
Foundation type: Independent
Financial data (yr. ended 02/28/90): Assets, $19,089,029 (M); gifts received, $100,188; expenditures, $1,056,925; qualifying distributions, $1,007,727, including $998,995 for 97 grants (high: $250,000; low: $25).
Purpose and activities: Emphasis on higher education, hospitals and medical research, and Jewish organizations, including welfare agencies, schools, and temple support.
Fields of interest: Hospitals, medical research, higher education, religious schools, Jewish giving, Jewish welfare.

Limitations: Giving primarily in Miami, FL, and New York, NY. No grants to individuals.
Application information: Contributes only to pre-selected organizations. Applications not accepted.
Officer: Leila Applebaum, Pres.
EIN: 591002714

571
The Appleman Foundation, Inc.
c/o Bessemer Trust Co. of Florida
222 Royal Palm Way
Palm Beach 33480-4303   (407) 655-4030

Incorporated in 1952 in DE.
Donor(s): Nathan Appleman,‡ and members of the Appleman family.
Foundation type: Independent
Financial data (yr. ended 12/31/90): Assets, $1,108,818 (M); expenditures, $658,667; qualifying distributions, $650,656, including $650,656 for grants.
Purpose and activities: Giving for Jewish welfare funds, higher education, including a Jewish theological seminary, hospitals, social services, and temple support.
Fields of interest: Jewish welfare, Jewish giving, higher education, hospitals, social services.
Types of support: Research.
Limitations: Giving primarily in NY and Palm Beach, FL.
Application information:
  Initial approach: Letter
  Deadline(s): None
Officers: Jill A. Roberts, V.P.; Susan A. Unterberg, V.P.; Michael F. Page, Secy.-Treas.
Number of staff: None.
EIN: 136154978

572
Banyan Foundation, Inc.
5300 West Cypress St., Suite 250
Tampa 33607-1712   (813) 281-0091
Mailing address: P.O. Box 24168, Tampa, FL 33623-4168

Incorporated in 1985 in FL.
Donor(s): Reese Coppage, Martha Ann Coppage.
Foundation type: Independent
Financial data (yr. ended 06/30/92): Assets, $2,343,120 (M); expenditures, $83,922; qualifying distributions, $70,050, including $65,376 for 24 grants (high: $20,000; low: $60).
Purpose and activities: Giving "to support research, education, and treatment in the areas of substance abuse, emotional problems, family counseling, trauma-related adjustment problems, stress, and other related mental health problems."
Fields of interest: Mental health, drug abuse.
Limitations: Giving primarily in central FL. No grants to individuals.
Application information: Application form not required.
  Initial approach: Letter
  Copies of proposal: 1
  Deadline(s): None
  Board meeting date(s): Monthly
  Write: Reese Coppage, Pres.
Officers and Directors:* Reese Coppage,* Pres.; Martha Ann Coppage,* Secy.-Treas.; H. Stephen Merlin.

Number of staff: None.
EIN: 592578626

573
John E. and Nellie J. Bastien Memorial Foundation
100 East Sample Rd., Suite B
Pompano Beach 33064

Trust established in 1965 in FL.
Donor(s): Nellie J. Bastien.‡
Foundation type: Independent
Financial data (yr. ended 12/31/90): Assets, $9,376,901 (M); expenditures, $636,757; qualifying distributions, $531,720, including $460,150 for 89 grants (high: $25,000; low: $150).
Fields of interest: Higher education, medical sciences, hospitals, health, youth, welfare.
Types of support: Scholarship funds.
Limitations: Giving primarily in FL.
Application information: Application form not required.
   Deadline(s): None
   Write: The Trustees
Trustees: Carol R. Kearns, Gene F. Schneider, J. Wallace Wrightson.
EIN: 596160694

574
The Frank Stanley Beveridge Foundation, Inc. ▼
301 Yamato Rd., Suite 1130
Boca Raton 33431-4929   (407) 241-8388
Additional tel.: (800) 356-9779; FAX: (407) 241-8332

Trust established in 1947 in MA; incorporated in 1956.
Donor(s): Frank Stanley Beveridge.‡
Foundation type: Independent
Financial data (yr. ended 12/31/90): Assets, $34,296,167 (M); expenditures, $2,244,904; qualifying distributions, $1,921,093, including $1,921,093 for 91 grants (high: $80,000; low: $500; average: $1,000-$25,000).
Purpose and activities: A portion of the income designated for maintenance of a local park established by the donor in Westfield, MA; the balance for general giving, with emphasis on higher and secondary education, social service and youth agencies, community development, culture, health, minorities, ecological programs, and religious organizations.
Fields of interest: Higher education, secondary education, social services, homeless, housing, youth, child development, community development, cultural programs, hospitals, hospitals—building funds, health, handicapped, mental health, hospices, minorities, ecology, religion, religion—Christian.
Types of support: Capital campaigns, seed money, equipment, building funds, renovation projects, matching funds, continuing support, special projects, technical assistance, scholarship funds, land acquisition, emergency funds.
Limitations: Giving primarily in Hampden County, MA, and Hillsborough and Palm Beach counties, FL. No support for tax-supported organizations. No grants to individuals, or for

endowment or operating funds, scholarships, or fellowships; no loans.
Publications: Informational brochure (including application guidelines), application guidelines.
Application information: Applicants outside the Hampden County, MA, area must have support of at least 1 director; such support must be solicited only by the foundation. Application form required.
   Initial approach: Telephone
   Copies of proposal: 1
   Deadline(s): Feb. 1 and Aug. 1
   Board meeting date(s): Apr. and Oct.
   Final notification: 2 weeks after meeting date
   Write: Philip Caswell, Pres.
Officers and Directors:* Philip Caswell,* Pres.; Carole S. Lenhart, Treas.; David F. Woods,* Clerk; Sarah Caswell Bartelt, William R. Cass, John Beveridge Caswell, John G. Gallup, Joseph Beveridge Palmer, Homer G. Perkins, Evelyn Beveridge Russell, Patsy Palmer Stecher, J. Thomas Touchton.
Number of staff: 1 full-time professional; 1 part-time professional.
EIN: 046032164
Recent health grants:
574-1 Pines of Sarasota, Sarasota, FL, $25,000. To remodel space for new on-site daycare center for 50 children (30 of whom are infant through preschool) for employees who staff nursing/care center for needy aged. 1990.
574-2 Project Return Florida, Tampa, FL, $15,000. For renovation of new building to house center and thrift shop, and for new van for thrift shop. 1990.
574-3 Western New England Childrens Center, Springfield, MA, $25,000. To construct Ronald McDonald House. 1990.

575
Lydia H. Bickerton Charitable Trust
32 Leeward Island
Clearwater 34630

Established in 1986 in FL.
Foundation type: Independent
Financial data (yr. ended 06/30/91): Assets, $2,012,307 (M); expenditures, $122,467; qualifying distributions, $76,700, including $76,700 for 25 grants (high: $10,000; low: $50).
Fields of interest: Religion—Christian, higher education, secondary education, hospitals, medical research.
Limitations: Giving primarily in FL.
Application information:
   Initial approach: Proposal
   Deadline(s): None
   Write: Beatrice M. Hurley, Trustee
Trustee: Beatrice M. Hurley.
EIN: 592745408

576
John Blair Foundation
c/o Northern Trust Bank of Florida/Naples, N.A.
530 Fifth Ave. South
Naples 33940   (813) 262-8800

Established in 1978 in FL.
Donor(s): E. Blake Blair, Jr. Trust.
Foundation type: Independent
Financial data (yr. ended 12/31/90): Assets, $2,485,559 (M); gifts received, $136;

expenditures, $167,649; qualifying distributions, $154,633, including $145,300 for 74 grants (high: $7,000; low: $250).
Fields of interest: Social services, family planning, population studies, health associations, health services.
Types of support: General purposes.
Limitations: Giving primarily in FL and NC. No grants to individuals.
Application information: Application form not required.
   Deadline(s): None
Trustees: Dorothy S. Blair, Robert W. Rieman, M.D., Northern Trust Bank of Florida/Naples, N.A.
EIN: 591831565

577
Blank Family Foundation, Inc.
9350 South Dixie Hwy., Suite 900
Miami 33156

Established in 1987 in FL.
Foundation type: Independent
Financial data (yr. ended 12/31/90): Assets, $7,833,343 (M); gifts received, $6,784,360; expenditures, $369,613; qualifying distributions, $327,653, including $327,653 for 70 grants (high: $75,000; low: $100).
Fields of interest: Jewish welfare, Jewish giving, hospitals.
Limitations: Giving primarily in the Miami, FL, area. No grants to individuals.
Application information:
   Initial approach: Proposal
   Deadline(s): None
   Write: Robert J. Puck, Secy.-Treas.
Officers and Directors:* Jerome Blank,* Pres.; Andrew Blank,* V.P.; Mark Blank,* V.P.; Robert J. Puck, Secy.-Treas.
EIN: 650060771

578
The Briggs Family Foundation
2325 Gordon Dr.
Naples 33940-7649   (813) 261-7625

Incorporated in 1957 in FL.
Donor(s): Stephen F. Briggs,‡ Beatrice B. Briggs.‡
Foundation type: Independent
Financial data (yr. ended 11/30/90): Assets, $4,950,843 (M); expenditures, $182,596; qualifying distributions, $182,596, including $170,100 for 20 grants (high: $75,000; low: $100; average: $100-$10,000).
Purpose and activities: Giving for a university, education, health, and conservation.
Fields of interest: Higher education, education, health, conservation, environment.
Types of support: Continuing support, annual campaigns, building funds, equipment, land acquisition, special projects, research, scholarship funds, capital campaigns.
Limitations: Giving primarily in Collier County, FL. No grants to individuals, or for endowment funds or matching gifts; no loans.
Application information: Application form not required.
   Initial approach: Letter
   Copies of proposal: 1
   Deadline(s): Submit proposal in Oct.; deadline Nov. 1

Board meeting date(s): As required
Final notification: 1 month
Write: John N. Briggs, Pres.
Officers: John N. Briggs, Pres.; Mary Jane Briggs, Secy-Treas.
Number of staff: None.
EIN: 596130222

579
The Shepard Broad Foundation, Inc.
2925 Aventura Blvd., Suite 303
North Miami Beach 33180-3104

Incorporated in 1956 in FL.
Donor(s): Shepard Broad, Ruth K. Broad, Morris N. Broad, and many others.
Foundation type: Independent
Financial data (yr. ended 12/31/90): Assets, $4,142,542 (M); expenditures, $134,823; qualifying distributions, $115,718, including $115,718 for 46 grants (high: $25,000; low: $10).
Fields of interest: Higher education, Jewish giving, Jewish welfare, education, health services, hospitals.
Limitations: Giving primarily in FL. No grants to individuals.
Application information: Funds are currently fully committed. Applications not accepted.
Write: Shepard Broad, Pres.
Officers and Directors:* Shepard Broad,* Pres.; Ann B. Bussel,* V.P. and Secy.; Morris N. Broad,* V.P. and Treas.
EIN: 590998866

580
Broward Community Foundation, Inc.
2601 East Oakland Park Blvd., Suite 202
Fort Lauderdale 33306   (305) 563-4483

Incorporated in 1984 in FL.
Foundation type: Community
Financial data (yr. ended 06/30/91): Assets, $5,007,456 (M); gifts received, $2,495,354; expenditures, $465,569; qualifying distributions, $361,605, including $361,605 for 69 grants (high: $100,000; low: $75).
Fields of interest: Education, health, environment, arts, social services.
Types of support: Equipment, matching funds, seed money, special projects.
Limitations: Giving primarily in Broward County, FL. No support for religious purposes. No grants to individuals, or for annual campaigns, building funds, consulting services, continuing support, deficit financing, endowment funds, emergency funds, land acquisition, or operating budgets; no loans.
Publications: Annual report (including application guidelines), newsletter, informational brochure.
Application information: Application form not required.
Initial approach: Letter
Copies of proposal: 1
Deadline(s): Sept. 1
Board meeting date(s): Nov.
Final notification: Nov.
Write: Elizabeth C. Deinhardt, Exec. Dir.
Officers and Directors:* Wilson B. Greaton, Jr.,* Pres.; Roy Rogers,* V.P.; Marti Huizenga,* Secy.; John B. Deinhardt, Treas.; Elizabeth C. Deinhardt, Exec. Dir.; Suzanne Y. Allen, W. George Allen,

James J. Blosser, Daniel B. Gordon, Robert J. Henninger, Jr., William D. Horvitz, Joseph E. Jack, Joe Millsaps, Chris Mobley, A. Gordon Oliver.
Number of staff: 1 full-time professional; 1 full-time support.
EIN: 592477112

581
Edyth Bush Charitable Foundation, Inc. ▼
199 East Welbourne Ave.
P.O. Box 1967
Winter Park 32790-1967   (407) 647-4322

Originally incorporated in 1966 in MN; reincorporated in 1973 in FL.
Donor(s): Edyth Bush.‡
Foundation type: Independent
Financial data (yr. ended 08/31/91): Assets, $51,600,636 (M); expenditures, $2,812,411; qualifying distributions, $2,516,433, including $1,695,306 for 47 grants (high: $100,000; low: $3,000; average: $20,000-$70,000), $116,060 for 3 foundation-administered programs and $52,679 for loans.
Purpose and activities: Support for charitable, educational, and health service organizations, with emphasis on human services and health; higher education; the elderly; youth services; the handicapped; and demonstrated nationally-recognized quality arts or cultural programs. Provides limited number of program-related investment loans for construction, land purchase, emergency or similar purposes to organizations otherwise qualified to receive grants. Active programs directly managed and/or financed for able learner education, and for management/volunteer development of nonprofits.
Fields of interest: Social services, welfare, health services, hospitals, education, higher education, aged, youth, handicapped, cultural programs.
Types of support: Seed money, emergency funds, building funds, equipment, land acquisition, loans, conferences and seminars, matching funds, consulting services, technical assistance, program-related investments, renovation projects, capital campaigns, continuing support.
Limitations: Giving primarily within a 100-mile radius of Winter Park, FL; also AZ and CA if supported by one or more family member directors (normally less than 10 percent of grants). No support for alcohol or drug abuse projects or organizations, church, denominational, sacramental, or religious facilities or functions; primarily (50 percent or more) tax-supported institutions; advocacy organizations; foreign organizations; or generally for cultural programs. No grants to individuals, or for scholarships or individual research projects, endowments, fellowships, travel, routine operating expenses for more than 1 or 2 years, annual campaigns, or deficit financing.
Publications: 990-PF, program policy statement, application guidelines, financial statement, grants list, 990-PF (including application guidelines).
Application information: Outline required for applications; see Policy Statement before applying. Application guidelines available upon request. Application form not required.
Initial approach: Telephone
Copies of proposal: 2
Deadline(s): Sept. 1 or Dec. 31

Board meeting date(s): Usually in Nov., Apr., and as required
Final notification: 2 weeks after board meetings
Write: David A. Odahowski, Pres.
Officers and Directors:* Charlotte H. Forward,* Chair.; David A. Odahowski, Pres. and C.E.O.; Herbert W. Holm,* V.P.-Finance; Michael R. Cross, Treas. and Corp. Secy.; Betty Condon, Controller; Mary Gretchen Belloff, Guy D. Colado, David R. Roberts, Vernon Swartsel, Jerrold S. Trumbower, Milton P. Woodard.
Number of staff: 3 full-time professional; 1 part-time professional; 4 full-time support.
EIN: 237318041

582
Kathleen K. Catlin Charitable Trust
c/o First Florida Bank, N.A.
P.O. Box 676
Venice 34284-0676   (813) 488-2261

Established in 1987 in FL.
Foundation type: Independent
Financial data (yr. ended 02/28/91): Assets, $5,374,806 (M); expenditures, $301,289; qualifying distributions, $277,295, including $269,794 for 30 grants (high: $177,622; low: $400).
Fields of interest: Hospitals, secondary education, social services, aged, marine sciences.
Types of support: General purposes, building funds, special projects, equipment.
Limitations: Giving primarily in Venice and Sarasota, FL. No grants to individuals.
Application information: Application form required.
Deadline(s): None
Write: Mary G. Toundas, Trust Officer, First Florida Bank, N.A.
Trustee: First Florida Bank, N.A.
EIN: 596877094

583
The Chatlos Foundation, Inc. ▼
P.O. Box 915048
Longwood 32791-5048   (407) 862-5077

Incorporated in 1953 in NY.
Donor(s): Bristol Door and Lumber Co., Inc., William F. Chatlos.‡
Foundation type: Independent
Financial data (yr. ended 12/31/90): Assets, $81,486,782 (M); expenditures, $3,525,776; qualifying distributions, $3,065,717, including $2,592,371 for 205 grants (high: $100,000; low: $200; average: $1,000-$25,000).
Purpose and activities: Grants for higher education, including religious education, and religious associations; giving also for hospitals, health agencies, social services, international relief, and child welfare.
Fields of interest: Education, higher education, religious schools, theological education, religion—Christian, hospitals, health, social services, homeless, hunger, nursing, international relief, child welfare.
Types of support: Operating budgets, emergency funds, equipment, land acquisition, matching funds, scholarship funds, special projects, publications, renovation projects, student aid.

Limitations: No support for the arts. No grants to individuals, or for seed money, deficit financing, building or endowment funds, research, or conferences; no loans.
Publications: Informational brochure (including application guidelines).
Application information: Only 1 grant to an organization within a 12-month period. Application form not required.
   Initial approach: Letter or proposal
   Copies of proposal: 1
   Deadline(s): None
   Board meeting date(s): Feb., May, Aug., and Nov.
   Final notification: 30 days after board meeting
   Write: William J. Chatlos, Pres.
Officers and Trustees:* Alice E. Chatlos, Chair. and Sr. V.P.; Kathryn A. Randle,* Vice-Chair.; William J. Chatlos, Pres. and Treas.; Joy E. D'Arata,* V.P.; Carol Leongomez,* Secy.; Charles O. Morgan, Michele C. Roach.
Number of staff: 6 full-time professional.
EIN: 136161425
Recent health grants:
583-1 Bayfront Medical Center, Saint Petersburg, FL, $10,000. For trauma center equipment project. 1990.
583-2 Baylor University Medical Center, Dallas, TX, $11,500. For community room for Twice Blessed House. 1990.
583-3 Cancer Research Council, Bethesda, MD, $25,000. For cancer therapy review for ICARE Program. 1990.
583-4 Elizabeth H. Faulk Foundation, Center for Group Counseling, Boca Raton, FL, $10,000. To permanently fund six scholarships for senior high school students for training in children at risk. 1990.
583-5 Food for the Poor, Pompano Beach, FL, $25,000. To purchase intra-aortic balloon pump. 1990.
583-6 General Hospital Center at Passaic, Passaic, NJ, $18,850. For cryo-surgical probe. 1990.
583-7 Henry H. Kessler Foundation, West Orange, NJ, $20,000. For therapeutic equipment work simulator. 1990.
583-8 Immaculata College, Sisters, Servants of the Immaculate Heart of Mary, Immaculata, PA, $25,000. For retirement fund for Camilla Nursing Home. 1990.
583-9 Interplast, Palo Alto, CA, $10,000. For medical supplies/equipment. 1990.
583-10 Manhattan Eye, Ear and Throat Hospital, NYC, NY, $10,000. For pediatric medical services. 1990.
583-11 MAP International, Brunswick, GA, $41,000. For ophthalmic sutures and ophthalmic surgical support. 1990.
583-12 Mercy Hospital Medical Center, Des Moines, IA, $26,491. For augmentative communication devices. 1990.
583-13 Mercy Medical Airlift, Manassas, VA, $20,000. For concerned contact counseling ministry. 1990.
583-14 National Foundation for Facial Reconstruction, NYC, NY, $15,000. For general support for budget relief. 1990.
583-15 National Jewish Center for Immunology and Respiratory Medicine, Denver, CO, $15,000. To purchase equipment in lung imaging center. 1990.

583-16 New York Foundling Hospital, NYC, NY, $25,000. For equipment for 160-bed skilled nursing facility. 1990.
583-17 North Broward Hospital District, Fort Lauderdale, FL, $22,500. For electroencephalograph for children's diagnostic treatment center. 1990.
583-18 Project Orbis, NYC, NY, $10,000. For general operating expenses. 1990.
583-19 RP Foundation Fighting Blindness, Baltimore, MD, $100,000. For final payment on pledge. 1990.
583-20 Saint John Hospital, Leavenworth, KS, $11,722. For fetal monitor for women's center. 1990.
583-21 Saint Joseph Hospital Foundation, Lexington, KY, $25,000. For new olympus video bronchoscope. 1990.
583-22 Saint Jude Childrens Research Hospital, NYC, NY, $25,000. For work with children with cancer. 1990.
583-23 Sentara Health System, Norfolk, VA, $13,000. For coherent laser indirect ophthalmoscope. 1990.
583-24 Society for Urology and Engineering (SUE), NYC, NY, $25,000. For second payment on three-year pledge. 1990.
583-25 Society for Urology and Engineering (SUE), NYC, NY, $18,175. For MacIntosh desktop publishing system. 1990.
583-26 Southeastern College of Osteopathic Medicine, North Miami Beach, FL, $25,000. For equipment for indigent care optometric clinics. 1990.
583-27 Temple University, Philadelphia, PA, $29,500. For blood gas analyzer. 1990.
583-28 University of Alabama, Tuscaloosa, AL, $10,000. For Introduction to Nursing summer recruitment institute for high school juniors. 1990.
583-29 University of Florida Foundation, J. Hillis Miller Health Center, College of Medicine, Gainesville, FL, $25,000. For laboratory equipment. 1990.
583-30 University of Miami, Bascom Palmer Eye Institute, Miami, FL, $51,026. For imaging fundus reflectometer. 1990.
583-31 University of Washington, School of Medicine, Seattle, WA, $21,970. For Log E Enlarger. 1990.
583-32 Valley Health Foundation, Easton, PA, $23,000. For specific equipment for laparoscopic cholecytstectomy set and camera. 1990.
583-33 Wheaton Eye Foundation, Wheaton, IL, $10,000. For Center for Visual Rehabilitation. 1990.
583-34 White Plains Hospital Medical Center, White Plains, NY, $10,000. For palliative care program. 1990.
583-35 World Radio Missionary Fellowship, Opa Locka, FL, $50,000. For charity fund for health care department. 1990.

584
The Francis and Miranda Childress Foundation, Inc.
P.O. Box 479
Jacksonville 32201-0479

Established in 1963 in FL.

Donor(s): Francis B. Childress,‡ Miranda Y. Childress.
Foundation type: Independent
Financial data (yr. ended 12/31/90): Assets, $2,504,019 (M); gifts received, $9,216; expenditures, $150,578; qualifying distributions, $129,673, including $128,000 for 12 grants (high: $27,000; low: $1,000).
Purpose and activities: Emphasis on higher and secondary education, Protestant church support, youth agencies, cultural programs, and hospitals.
Fields of interest: Higher education, secondary education, youth, Protestant giving, cultural programs, hospitals.
Limitations: Giving primarily in FL. No grants to individuals.
Application information: Contributes only to pre-selected organizations. Applications not accepted.
Officers: Miranda Y. Childress, Pres.; Francis Childress Lee, V.P. and Secy.; Lewis S. Lee, Jr., Treas.
EIN: 591051733

585
Conn Memorial Foundation, Inc.
220 East Madison St., Suite 822
P.O. Box 229
Tampa 33601   (813) 223-3838

Incorporated in 1954 in FL.
Donor(s): Fred K. Conn,‡ Edith F. Conn.‡
Foundation type: Independent
Financial data (yr. ended 07/31/91): Assets, $15,759,875 (M); expenditures, $862,174; qualifying distributions, $717,001, including $702,250 for 64 grants (high: $100,000; low: $1,000; average: $1,000-$20,000).
Fields of interest: Youth, higher education, rehabilitation, alcoholism, drug abuse.
Types of support: Building funds, equipment, matching funds, scholarship funds, seed money.
Limitations: Giving limited to the greater Tampa Bay, FL, area. No grants to individuals, or for endowment funds; no loans.
Publications: 990-PF.
Application information: Application form not required.
   Initial approach: Letter
   Copies of proposal: 5
   Deadline(s): Submit proposal preferably in Nov. or May; deadlines Nov. 30 and May 31
   Board meeting date(s): Jan. and July
   Final notification: 1 month after board meeting
   Write: David B. Frye, Pres.
Officers and Directors:* David B. Frye,* Pres. and Treas.; George W. Ericksen,* V.P.; Mary S. Boisselle,* Secy.; Paul S. Eisberry, James N. Gray, Charles C. Murphy.
Number of staff: 2 full-time professional; 1 part-time professional.
EIN: 590978713

586
The Raymond E. and Ellen F. Crane Foundation
P.O. Box 2097
Alachua 32615-2097

Trust established in 1949 in PA.
Donor(s): Raymond E. Crane,‡ Ellen F. Crane.‡

Foundation type: Independent
Financial data (yr. ended 12/31/90): Assets,
$3,509,177 (M); expenditures, $181,036;
qualifying distributions, $172,889, including
$170,750 for 58 grants (high: $5,000; low: $500).
Purpose and activities: Giving for higher
education and community funds; grants also for
cultural programs, secondary education, health,
and Protestant church support.
Fields of interest: Higher education, community
funds, cultural programs, health, Protestant giving,
secondary education.
Limitations: Giving primarily in the southeastern
states. No grants to individuals.
Application information: Contributes only to
pre-selected organizations. Applications not
accepted.
Trustees: Alpo F. Crane, David J. Crane, Jr., Robert
F. Crane, Jr., S.R. Crane.
EIN: 596139265

587
Dade Community Foundation ▼
(Formerly Dade Foundation)
200 South Biscayne Blvd., Suite 4770
Miami 33131-2343   (305) 371-2711

Established in 1967 in FL.
Foundation type: Community
Financial data (yr. ended 12/31/91): Assets,
$22,597,725 (M); gifts received, $4,691,064;
expenditures, $4,506,121; qualifying
distributions, $3,971,528, including $3,949,758
for 414 grants (high: $25,000; low: $250;
average: $250-$25,000), $10,770 for 5 loans and
$11,000 for 1 in-kind gift.
Purpose and activities: Support for projects which
provide an innovative response to a recognized
community need but which do not duplicate
other efforts; help an organization build internal
stability; promise to affect a broad segment of the
residents of Dade County; and exert a leverage or
multiplier effect in addressing community
problems to be solved. Primary areas of support
are AIDS, community development, the
disadvantaged, leadership development, and
housing; other areas of support include health,
social services, the homeless and housing, civic
affairs, education, arts and culture, and religious
organizations.
Fields of interest: Health services, AIDS, social
services, child welfare, aged, homeless, housing,
women, disadvantaged, civic affairs, community
development, citizenship, leadership
development, arts, cultural programs, education,
literacy, legal education.
Types of support: Equipment, land acquisition,
seed money, research, general purposes,
matching funds, publications, scholarship funds,
special projects, technical assistance, annual
campaigns, continuing support, endowment
funds, internships, operating budgets, renovation
projects.
Limitations: Giving limited to Dade County, FL.
No grants to individuals, or for emergency funds,
deficit financing, or conferences.
Publications: Annual report, application
guidelines, informational brochure (including
application guidelines), newsletter, grants list,
occasional report, application guidelines.
Application information: Application form not
required.

Initial approach: Letter
Copies of proposal: 1
Deadline(s): Submit proposal preferably in
Nov.; deadline Dec. 1
Board meeting date(s): Feb., May, Sept., and
Nov.
Final notification: 1st quarter of the year
Write: Ruth Shack, Pres.
Officers and Governors:* Juan P. Loumiet,*
Chair.; David Lawrence,* Vice-Chair.; Ruth Shack,
Pres.; Marilyn Holifield,* Secy.; Henry Raattam,*
Treas.; and 17 additional governors.
Trustee Banks: Barnett Banks Trust Co., N.A.,
Bessemer Trust Co. of Florida, First Union
National Bank of Florida, Northern Trust Bank of
Florida, N.A., SunBank Miami, N.A., Trust Co. of
the South.
Number of staff: 4 full-time professional; 1
full-time support; 1 part-time support.
EIN: 596183655
Recent health grants:
587-1 American Heart Association of Greater
Miami, Miami, FL, $44,762. 1990.
587-2 Camillus Health Concern, Miami, FL,
$25,000. For matching grant for
pediatric/adolescent health care component of
clinic. 1990.
587-3 Cedars Medical Center Foundation,
Miami, FL, $10,000. 1990.
587-4 Childrens Hospital of Tampa, Tampa, FL,
$11,000. 1990.
587-5 Diabetes Research Institute, Miami, FL,
$13,000. 1990.
587-6 Easter Seal Society of Dade County,
Miami, FL, $26,600. 1990.
587-7 Heart Association of Miami, Miami, FL,
$10,000. 1990.
587-8 Miami Childrens Hospital, Miami, FL,
$10,500. 1990.
587-9 Miami Heart Institute, Miami Beach, FL,
$30,000. 1990.
587-10 Mount Sinai Medical Center of Greater
Miami, Miami Beach, FL, $25,000. 1990.
587-11 YMCA of Greater Miami, Miami, FL,
$18,000. To create special exercise and health
education program for middle school youth
with health profile indicative of risk of
coronary artery disease. 1990.

588
The Tine W. Davis Family - W.D.
Charities, Inc.
4190 Belfort Rd., Suite 240
Jacksonville 32216

Incorporated in 1950 in FL.
Donor(s): Tine W. Davis, and others.
Foundation type: Independent
Financial data (yr. ended 12/31/90): Assets,
$10,113,823 (M); expenditures, $1,319,173;
qualifying distributions, $1,130,176, including
$840,382 for 140 grants (high: $100,000; low:
$200; average: $1,000-$5,000).
Fields of interest: Higher education,
religion—Christian, youth, medical research,
health services, social services, community funds,
cultural programs.
Limitations: Giving primarily in the southeastern
U.S. No grants to individuals.
Application information: Contributes only to
pre-selected organizations. Applications not
accepted.

Board meeting date(s): 2nd Tuesday in Apr.
Write: Charitable Grants Comm.
Officer: Tine Wayne Davis, Jr., Pres. and
Secy.-Treas.
Directors: Fred W. Baggett, Eunice Davis McNeil,
James D. O'Donnell.
Number of staff: None.
EIN: 590995388

589
The Leonard and Sophie Davis
Foundation, Inc. ▼
601 Clearwater Park Rd.
West Palm Beach 33401   (407) 832-6466

Incorporated in 1961 in NY.
Donor(s): Leonard Davis, Sophie Davis.
Foundation type: Independent
Financial data (yr. ended 12/31/90): Assets,
$20,259,070 (M); expenditures, $2,213,651;
qualifying distributions, $2,185,974, including
$2,179,550 for 82 grants (high: $700,000; low:
$100; average: $1,000-$25,000).
Purpose and activities: Grants primarily for Jewish
charitable, religious, and educational
organizations, and for higher education; support
also for the arts, community services, and health
agencies and hospitals; limited giving to public
interest groups.
Fields of interest: Jewish giving, Jewish welfare,
higher education, arts, dance, museums, music,
community funds, social services, aged, health
services, hospitals, AIDS, hospices, public policy.
Types of support: Annual campaigns, building
funds, conferences and seminars, continuing
support.
Limitations: Giving primarily in Palm Beach
County, FL, and New York, NY. No grants to
individuals.
Application information: Applications not
accepted.
Board meeting date(s): As required
Write: Marilyn Hoadley, Pres.
Officers: Marilyn Hoadley, Pres.; Leonard Davis,
V.P.; Sophie Davis, V.P.
Directors: Alan Davis, Michael Davis.
Number of staff: None.
EIN: 136062579
Recent health grants:
589-1 Albert Einstein College of Medicine of
Yeshiva University, Bronx, NY, $35,000. 1990.
589-2 Medical Development for Israel, NYC, NY,
$75,000. 1990.
589-3 Morse Geriatric Center, West Palm Beach,
FL, $50,850. 1990.
589-4 New York University Medical Center,
NYC, NY, $10,000. 1990.
589-5 Saint Marys Hospital, West Palm Beach,
FL, $26,000. 1990.

590
The Arthur Vining Davis Foundations ▼
645 Riverside Ave., Suite 520
Jacksonville 32204   (904) 359-0670

Three trusts established: in 1952 and 1965 in PA;
in 1965 in FL.
Donor(s): Arthur Vining Davis.‡
Foundation type: Independent
Financial data (yr. ended 12/31/90): Assets,
$111,190,000 (M); gifts received, $5,827,000;

expenditures, $5,432,000; qualifying distributions, $4,992,000, including $4,992,000 for 79 grants (high: $300,000; low: $5,000; average: $75,000-$125,000).
Purpose and activities: Support largely for private higher education, hospices, health care, public television, and graduate theological education.
Fields of interest: Higher education, theological education, hospices, medical sciences, media and communications, film.
Types of support: Building funds, continuing support, endowment funds, equipment, fellowships, internships, land acquisition, matching funds, professorships, research, capital campaigns, general purposes, lectureships, operating budgets, publications, renovation projects, special projects, technical assistance.
Limitations: Giving limited to the U.S. and its possessions and territories. No support for community chests, institutions primarily supported by government funds, and projects incurring obligations extending over many years. No grants to individuals; no loans.
Publications: Annual report (including application guidelines), informational brochure.
Application information: Application form not required.
  Initial approach: Letter
  Copies of proposal: 1
  Deadline(s): None
  Board meeting date(s): Spring, fall, and winter
  Final notification: 10 to 15 months for approvals; 8 months for rejections
  Write: Max Morris, Exec. Dir.
Officer: Max Morris, Exec. Dir.
Trustees: Nathanael V. Davis, Chair.; Holbrook R. Davis, J.H. Dow Davis, Joel P. Davis, Maynard K. Davis, Atwood Dunwody, Rev. Davis Given, Serena Davis Hall, Dorothy Davis Kee, Mrs. John L. Kee, Jr., W.R. Wright, Mellon Bank, N.A., SunBank/North Florida, N.A.
Number of staff: 3 full-time professional; 2 part-time professional; 3 full-time support.
EIN: 256018909
Recent health grants:
590-1 Barnes Hospital, Saint Louis, MO, $72,000. For research project. 1991.
590-2 Childrens Hospital of Los Angeles, Los Angeles, CA, $30,000. For video equipment. 1991.
590-3 Pennsylvania State University, College of Medicine, Hershey, PA, $90,000. For challenge grant for research project. 1991.
590-4 University of Florida, College of Health Related Professions, Gainesville, FL, $98,000. For program research. 1991.
590-5 University of Massachusetts Medical Center, Worcester, MA, $68,000. For Harbor of Hope video. 1991.

591
Donnell-Kay Foundation, Inc.
c/o Audrey K. Dines
15 Isle Ridge East
Hobe Sound 33455

Established in 1965 in FL.
Donor(s): Elizabeth D. Kay.‡
Foundation type: Independent
Financial data (yr. ended 01/31/92): Assets, $15,623,876 (M); expenditures, $604,173; qualifying distributions, $562,036, including

$558,940 for 33 grants (high: $250,000; low: $1,000; average: $1,000-$15,000).
Fields of interest: Higher education, education, family planning, population studies, ecology, economics, community funds.
Limitations: No grants to individuals.
Application information: Contributes only to pre-selected organizations; unsolicited applications not considered. Applications not accepted.
Officers and Directors: Audrey K. Dines,* Pres.; Allen Dines,* V.P. and Treas.; Sidney A. Dines,* Secy.; Lucy D. DelSol.
Number of staff: None.
EIN: 596169704

592
The Dunspaugh-Dalton Foundation, Inc.
9040 S.W. 72nd St. Suite 30
Miami 33173   (305) 596-6951

Incorporated in 1963 in FL.
Donor(s): Ann V. Dalton.‡
Foundation type: Independent
Financial data (yr. ended 12/31/90): Assets, $23,082,769 (M); expenditures, $1,578,200; qualifying distributions, $1,345,647, including $1,191,652 for 108 grants (high: $182,500; low: $500; average: $5,000-$20,000).
Fields of interest: Education, higher education, cultural programs, youth, social services, hospitals, health associations, civic affairs.
Types of support: General purposes.
Limitations: Giving primarily in Dade County, FL, and Monterey, CA; some giving also in NC. No grants to individuals; no loans.
Publications: 990-PF.
Application information: Application form not required.
  Initial approach: Letter
  Copies of proposal: 1
  Deadline(s): None
  Board meeting date(s): Monthly
  Write: William A. Lane, Jr., Pres.
Officers and Trustees: William A. Lane, Jr.,* Pres.; Sarah L. Bonner,* V.P.; Thomas H. Wakefield, Secy.-Treas.
Number of staff: 3 part-time professional; 2 part-time support.
EIN: 591055300

593
Alfred I. duPont Foundation
P.O. Box 1380
Jacksonville 32201   (904) 396-6600

Incorporated in 1936 in FL.
Donor(s): Jessie Ball duPont.‡
Foundation type: Independent
Financial data (yr. ended 12/31/90): Assets, $16,453,657 (M); expenditures, $758,226; qualifying distributions, $736,106, including $331,143 for 88 grants (high: $40,000; low: $100) and $403,092 for grants to individuals.
Purpose and activities: Giving primarily to the elderly in distressed situations requiring health, economic, or educational assistance; support also for higher education and medical research.
Fields of interest: Aged, welfare—indigent individuals, higher education, medical research.
Types of support: Grants to individuals.

Limitations: Giving primarily in the Southeast.
Application information: Application form required.
  Initial approach: Proposal
  Copies of proposal: 1
  Deadline(s): None
  Write: Rosemary C. Wills, Asst. Secy.
Officers and Directors: Braden Ball,* Pres.; J.C. Belin,* V.P. and Treas.; Lillie S. Land,* Secy.; R.E. Nedley.
EIN: 591297267

594
Jessie Ball duPont Fund ▼
(Formerly Jessie Ball duPont Religious, Charitable and Educational Fund)
225 Water St., Suite 1200
Jacksonville 32202-5176   (904) 353-0890

Trust established in 1976 in FL.
Donor(s): Jessie Ball duPont.‡
Foundation type: Independent
Financial data (yr. ended 10/31/91): Assets, $155,342,694 (M); gifts received, $161,000; expenditures, $9,306,318; qualifying distributions, $8,353,644, including $7,511,657 for 205 grants (high: $400,000; low: $1,500; average: $5,000-$100,000).
Purpose and activities: Grants limited to those institutions to which the donor contributed personally during the five-year period ending December 31, 1964. Among the 350 institutions eligible to receive funds are higher and secondary education institutions, cultural and historic preservation programs, social service organizations, hospitals, health agencies, churches and church-related organizations, and youth agencies.
Fields of interest: Education, higher education, secondary education, cultural programs, historic preservation, social services, hospitals, health services, religion, youth.
Types of support: Seed money, equipment, special projects, research, publications, professorships, scholarship funds, exchange programs, matching funds, general purposes, internships, technical assistance, renovation projects, emergency funds.
Limitations: Giving primarily in the South, especially FL, DE, and VA. No support for organizations other than those awarded gifts by the donor from 1960-1964. No grants to individuals, or, generally, for capital campaigns.
Publications: Annual report (including application guidelines), application guidelines, informational brochure, grants list, newsletter, occasional report.
Application information: Applicant must submit proof with initial application that a contribution was received from the donor between 1960 and 1964. Application form required.
  Initial approach: Brief proposal or telephone call to program staff
  Copies of proposal: 1
  Deadline(s): None
  Board meeting date(s): Bimonthly beginning in Jan.
  Final notification: Approximately 3 to 4 months
  Write: Dr. Sherry Magill, Acting Exec. Dir.
Officers and Trustees: Jean W. Ludlow,* Chair.; George C. Bedell,* Vice-Chair.; Ronald V. Gallo, Exec. Dir.; Jo Ann P. Bennett, Exec. Secy.; Mary K. Phillips, Northern Trust Bank of Florida, N.A.

Number of staff: 4 full-time professional; 2 full-time support.
EIN: 596368632
Recent health grants:

594-1 American Cancer Society, Delaware Division, New Castle, DE, $83,219. For grassroots effort for underserved at-risk population. 1990.

594-2 Baptist Memorial Hospital System, School of Vocational Nursing, San Antonio, TX, $46,400. For staff development to improve quality of training offered to aspiring Licensed Vocational Nurses. 1990.

594-3 Daniel Memorial Home for Children, Jacksonville, FL, $50,850. For software development for Independent Living Skills System for Use in Schools. 1990.

594-4 Episcopal Diocese of North Carolina, Bishop's Discretionary Fund, Raleigh, NC, $150,000. For Healing Hands Program to create educational materials and to organize infrastructure of medical and legal professionals, community advocates and counselors to establish health clinics for poultry workers. 1990.

594-5 Hathaway Childrens Services, Sylmar, CA, $98,654. For Therapeutic Foster Family Program. 1990.

594-6 Hospital for Special Surgery, Lupus Line, NYC, NY, $50,000. For curriculum development and publication of training manual. 1990.

594-7 Kilmarnock-Lancaster County Volunteer Rescue Squad, Kilmarnock, VA, $50,000. Toward purchase of new ambulances. 1990.

594-8 Medical College of Virginia, Richmond, VA, $170,152. For Community Home Health Care component of Cancer Outreach and Education program serving rural areas. 1990.

594-9 Northumberland County Rescue Squad, Reedville, VA, $10,000. To purchase diesel chassis for ambulance. 1990.

594-10 Osborne Association, EL RIO Program, NYC, NY, $50,000. For substance abuse counselor and outreach/aftercare counselor. 1990.

594-11 Riverside Hospital, Jacksonville, FL, $150,000. For start-up of Life Excellence and Aging Resource Network (LEAARN). 1990.

594-12 University of Miami, Miami, FL, $361,321. For staff salaries for pediatrician and nurse practitioner, to provide health care for homeless children, adolescents and their families. 1990.

595
The Echlin Foundation
c/o Engelberg, Cantor & Kushner, P.A.
125 Worth Ave.
Palm Beach 33480

Trust established in 1960 in CT.
Donor(s): John E. Echlin, Beryl G. Echlin.
Foundation type: Independent
Financial data (yr. ended 11/30/91): Assets, $3,106,767 (M); expenditures, $161,892; qualifying distributions, $157,000, including $157,000 for 17 grants (high: $60,000; low: $1,000).
Fields of interest: Higher education, secondary education, hospitals, health associations, heart disease.

Limitations: No grants to individuals.
Application information: Contributes only to pre-selected organizations. Applications not accepted.
Trustee: Beryl G. Echlin.
EIN: 066037282

596
Jack Eckerd Corporation Foundation
P.O. Box 4689
Clearwater 34618   (813) 398-8318

Established in 1973 in FL.
Donor(s): Jack Eckerd Corp.
Foundation type: Company-sponsored
Financial data (yr. ended 07/30/90): Assets, $2,842 (M); gifts received, $455,000; expenditures, $558,264; qualifying distributions, $558,008, including $516,506 for grants and $41,364 for 208 employee matching gifts (high: $1,000; low: $50).
Purpose and activities: Support primarily for higher education, including pharmacy scholarships, and health services, including optometry.
Fields of interest: Higher education, pharmacy, health, health services, hospitals, hospitals—building funds, hospices, community funds, cultural programs, economics.
Types of support: Operating budgets, continuing support, annual campaigns, emergency funds, building funds, employee matching gifts, scholarship funds, program-related investments, special projects, capital campaigns.
Limitations: Giving primarily in areas with company locations, in AL, DE, FL, GA, LA, MS, NJ, NC, OK, SC, TN, and TX. No grants to individuals, or for endowment funds, deficit financing, equipment, land acquisition, renovation projects, special projects, research, publications, or conferences; no loans.
Publications: Annual report.
Application information: Application form not required.
   Initial approach: Letter
   Copies of proposal: 1
   Deadline(s): None
   Board meeting date(s): Quarterly
   Final notification: 4 to 6 months
   Write: Michael Zagorac, Jr., Chair.
Officer and Trustees:* Michael Zagorac, Jr.,* Chair.; Harry W. Lambert, Ronald D. Peterson, James M. Santo.
Number of staff: 1 full-time professional; 1 part-time professional.
EIN: 237322099

597
Albert E. & Birdie W. Einstein Fund
P.O. Box 6794
Hollywood 33081
Application address: P.O. Box 6297, Hollywood, FL 33081

Established about 1967 in FL.
Donor(s): Albert E. Einstein,‡ Birdie W. Einstein.‡
Foundation type: Independent
Financial data (yr. ended 06/30/91): Assets, $7,474,723 (M); expenditures, $400,182; qualifying distributions, $358,050, including

$358,050 for 25 grants (high: $100,000; low: $500).
Purpose and activities: Giving primarily to a medical school and a performing arts fund; support also for Jewish welfare funds, youth, and medical research.
Fields of interest: Medical education, performing arts, Jewish welfare, youth, medical research.
Limitations: Giving primarily in Broward, Dade, and Palm Beach counties, FL. No grants to individuals.
Application information: Application form required.
   Deadline(s): None
   Write: Joyce Boyer, Pres.
Officers: Joyce Boyer, Pres.; R.M. Gardner, V.P.; Harold Satchell, Secy.-Treas.
EIN: 596127412

598
Ellis Foundation, Inc.
c/o S.G. Gibson, Jr.
P.O. Box 31590
Tampa 33631

Established in 1984 in FL.
Donor(s): A.L. Ellis.
Foundation type: Independent
Financial data (yr. ended 06/30/91): Assets, $1,890,158 (M); gifts received, $952,500; expenditures, $795,130; qualifying distributions, $562,326, including $537,540 for 18 grants (high: $200,000; low: $100).
Fields of interest: Higher education, Protestant giving, performing arts, hospitals.
Limitations: Giving primarily in FL. No grants to individuals.
Application information: Contributes only to pre-selected organizations. Applications not accepted.
Officers and Directors:* Stanley G. Gibson, Jr.,* Chair. and Fund Mgr.; Carol E. Martin,* Pres.; Mary L. Toth,* Secy.; A.L. Ellis, W. Franklin Ellis.
EIN: 592471638

599
The David Falk Foundation, Inc.
c/o SunBank of Tampa Bay
P.O. Box 1498
Tampa 33601   (813) 224-1877

Incorporated in 1945 in FL.
Donor(s): David A. Falk.‡
Foundation type: Independent
Financial data (yr. ended 12/31/91): Assets, $2,262,377 (M); expenditures, $167,168; qualifying distributions, $139,561, including $129,301 for 35 grants (high: $10,000; low: $30; average: $100-$12,500).
Fields of interest: Child welfare, youth, social services, handicapped, aged, higher education, hospitals, drug abuse.
Types of support: Operating budgets, seed money, emergency funds, building funds, equipment, land acquisition, matching funds, publications, general purposes, renovation projects, research, special projects.
Limitations: Giving limited to the Tampa Bay, FL, area. No support for community funds or electoral or political projects. No grants to individuals, or for continuing support, annual

campaigns, deficit financing, conferences, scholarships, or fellowships; no loans.
Publications: Program policy statement, application guidelines.
Application information: Application form required.
  Initial approach: Proposal
  Copies of proposal: 1
  Deadline(s): Submit proposal in Jan., Apr., July, or Oct.; no set deadline
  Board meeting date(s): Feb., Apr., June, Sept., Nov., and Dec.
  Final notification: 90 days after board meeting
  Write: John J. Howley, Secy.-Treas.
Officers and Directors:* Mary Irene McKay Falk,* Chair.; Herbert G. McKay,* Pres.; John C. Peters,* V.P.; John J. Howley,* Secy.-Treas.; H.D. Carrington, Jr., David G. Kerr.
Number of staff: None.
EIN: 591055570

600
J. Hugh and Earle W. Fellows Memorial Fund
c/o Beggs and Lane
P.O. Box 12950
Pensacola 32576-2950   (904) 432-2451
Loan application office: c/o Exec. V.P., Pensacola Junior College, 1000 College Blvd., Pensacola, FL 32504; Tel.: (904) 484-1706

Trust established in 1961 in FL.
Donor(s): Earle W. Fellows-Williamson.‡
Foundation type: Independent
Financial data (yr. ended 04/30/92): Assets, $3,396,185 (M); expenditures, $33,379; qualifying distributions, $1,062,780, including $912,000 for 30 program-related investments and $150,780 for 60 loans to individuals.
Purpose and activities: To provide low-interest-rate loans to students of medicine, theology, nursing, and medical technology who reside in four northwest FL counties and who agree to pursue their professions in this area for five years after graduation.
Fields of interest: Medical education, theological education, nursing, medical sciences.
Types of support: Student loans.
Limitations: Giving primarily in Escambia, Okaloosa, Santa Rosa, and Walton counties, FL.
Publications: Informational brochure (including application guidelines).
Application information: Application form required.
  Initial approach: Letter
  Copies of proposal: 1
  Deadline(s): None
  Board meeting date(s): Apr. and Dec.
  Write: Gary B. Leuchtman.
Officers and Trustees:* Rev. LeVan Davis,* Chair.; C. Roger Vinson,* Secy.; W.C. Payne, Jr., M.D., Milton Rogers, Harold N. Smith.
EIN: 596132238

601
The Bert Fish Foundation, Inc.
(Formerly Bert Fish Testamentary Trust)
P.O. Box 46
De Land 32720

Foundation type: Independent

Financial data (yr. ended 09/30/90): Assets, $7,894,453 (M); expenditures, $497,407; qualifying distributions, $366,804, including $366,804 for 5 grants (high: $231,187; low: $1,000).
Purpose and activities: Giving primarily for a hospital and health services; support also for higher education and social services.
Fields of interest: Hospitals, health, higher education, social services.
Types of support: Equipment, scholarship funds, seed money.
Limitations: No grants to individuals.
Application information: Contributes only to pre-selected organizations. Applications not accepted.
  Write: Frank G. Gillingham, Treas.
Officers and Trustees:* W. Amory Underhill,* Chair.; William W. Schildecker,* Exec. V.P.; William C. Keebler,* Secy.; Frank G. Gillingham,* Treas.; William Cox, Frank Ford, Joseph J. Master, Lowell E. Renfroe, Carl Ward.
Number of staff: 2 full-time professional.
EIN: 593020772

602
Florida Power & Light Company Contributions Program
Box 14000
Juno Beach 33408   (305) 556-4946

Financial data (yr. ended 12/31/90): Total giving, $1,840,414, including $1,694,661 for 350 grants (high: $350,000; low: $100; average: $400-$2,000) and $145,753 for in-kind gifts.
Purpose and activities: Supports programs concerning health, welfare, arts, humanities, education, and public affairs. The in-kind figure refers to community service activities such as buying tickets and helping to fund employee participation in charitable events.
Fields of interest: Health, welfare, arts, humanities, education, civic affairs.
Types of support: Capital campaigns, operating budgets.
Limitations: Giving limited to service area in FL. No support for religious or political groups. No grants to individuals.
Publications: Application guidelines.
Application information:
  Initial approach: Letter of proposal; Send requests to nearest company facility; Corporate Planning Department handles giving
  Deadline(s): Applications accepted throughout the year. The budget is completed in May and June
  Board meeting date(s): July
  Write: Jose Bestard, V.P.
Number of staff: 1 full-time professional; 5 part-time professional.

603
Jefferson Lee Ford III Memorial Foundation, Inc.
c/o SunBank, Bal Harbour
9600 Collins Ave., P.O. Box 546487
Bal Harbour 33154   (305) 868-2630
IRS filing state: MD

Incorporated in 1950 in FL.

Donor(s): Jefferson L. Ford, Jr.‡
Foundation type: Independent
Financial data (yr. ended 02/28/91): Assets, $2,200,383 (M); expenditures, $226,491; qualifying distributions, $195,808, including $194,500 for grants.
Fields of interest: Health services, medical research, hospitals, handicapped, education, religion.
Limitations: Giving primarily in FL.
Application information:
  Initial approach: Letter
  Deadline(s): None
  Write: Herbert L. Kurras, Sr., V.P., SunBank, Bal Harbour
Officer and Directors:* Doris King,* V.P.; David P. Catsman, Herbert L. Kurras, Alfonsine Palermo, Anthony Palermo.
EIN: 526037179

604
Fort Pierce Memorial Hospital Scholarship Foundation
c/o Lawnwood Medical Center
P.O. Box 188, 1700 South 23rd St.
Fort Pierce 34950   (407) 461-4000

Foundation type: Independent
Financial data (yr. ended 09/30/90): Assets, $4,088,932 (M); expenditures, $330,021; qualifying distributions, $294,510, including $116,660 for grants and $161,861 for 23 grants to individuals (high: $15,000; low: $2,500).
Purpose and activities: Awards scholarships to local area students following a course of study in the health field; payments also made to Lawnwood Medical Center for care of indigent children.
Fields of interest: Nursing, medical education, health, dentistry, welfare—indigent individuals.
Types of support: Scholarship funds, student aid, grants to individuals.
Limitations: Giving limited to St. Lucie County, FL.
Application information: Completion of application form required for scholarships; application not accepted for indigent care assistance.
  Deadline(s): Apr. 15
Officer: David Riley, Secy.
Directors: Bruce Abernathy, John Bahl, C.R. Cambron, Frank H. Fee III, Philip C. Gates, Charles Hayling, Fred Johnston, Basil King, Virginia Sines.
EIN: 590651084

605
The Fortin Foundation of Florida, Inc.
c/o First National in Palm Beach, Trust Dept.
255 South County Rd.
Palm Beach 33480-4113

Established in 1986 in FL.
Foundation type: Independent
Financial data (yr. ended 12/31/90): Assets, $11,938,049 (M); gifts received, $620,270; expenditures, $671,828; qualifying distributions, $599,357, including $594,320 for 77 grants (high: $250,000; low: $50).
Purpose and activities: Giving primarily for a college and an affiliated foundation; support also

for hospitals, social service and youth agencies, and Catholic churches and a diocese.
Fields of interest: Higher education, hospitals, social services, youth, Catholic giving.
Limitations: Giving primarily in FL and MT. No grants to individuals.
Application information:
  Initial approach: Letter
  Deadline(s): None
  Write: Mary Alice Fortin, Pres.
Officers and Directors:* Mary Alice Fortin,* Pres.; Susan Stockard Rawle,* V.P.; L. Frank Chopin,* Secy.-Treas.
EIN: 592707197

606
A. Friends' Foundation Trust
P.O. Box 3838
Orlando 32802   (407) 363-4621
Application address: P.O. Box 7217, Orlando, FL 32854

Established in 1959 in FL as the Hubbard Foundation; merged in 1985 with A. Friends' Fund, Inc., into A. Friends' Foundation Trust.
Donor(s): Frank M. Hubbard, A Friends' Fund, Inc.
Foundation type: Independent
Financial data (yr. ended 12/31/90): Assets, $6,012,820 (M); gifts received, $8,000; expenditures, $360,178; qualifying distributions, $326,900, including $310,000 for 85 grants (high: $35,000; low: $1,000; average: $3,900).
Purpose and activities: Support for private higher education, civic affairs, the arts, youth activities, religion, and health.
Fields of interest: Higher education, civic affairs, arts, youth, religion, health.
Types of support: Annual campaigns, building funds, capital campaigns, conferences and seminars, continuing support, emergency funds, equipment, general purposes, land acquisition, matching funds, operating budgets, renovation projects, special projects.
Limitations: Giving principally in central FL. No grants to individuals, or for endowment funds.
Publications: 990-PF, grants list.
Application information: Emergency funding available at all times. Application form not required.
  Initial approach: Letter
  Copies of proposal: 1
  Deadline(s): Sept.
  Board meeting date(s): Varies
  Final notification: Oct.
  Write: Frank M. Hubbard, Chair.
Officer: Frank M. Hubbard, Chair.
Board Members: L. Evans Hubbard, Ruth C.H. Miller.
Trustee: Sun Bank, N.A.
Number of staff: None.
EIN: 596125247

607
Charles A. Frueauff Foundation, Inc. ▼
307 East Seventh Ave.
Tallahassee 32303   (904) 561-3508

Incorporated in 1950 in NY.
Donor(s): Charles A. Frueauff.‡
Foundation type: Independent

Financial data (yr. ended 12/31/90): Assets, $69,410,662 (M); expenditures, $3,667,704; qualifying distributions, $3,451,573, including $3,288,440 for 152 grants (high: $50,000; low: $2,840; average: $10,000-$25,000).
Purpose and activities: Support for health, including hospitals, mental health, and other health services; welfare purposes, including services to children, the indigent, and the handicapped; and higher education, including student aid.
Fields of interest: Higher education, health, hospitals, mental health, health services, welfare, child welfare, handicapped.
Types of support: Operating budgets, annual campaigns, emergency funds, building funds, equipment, endowment funds, scholarship funds, matching funds, general purposes, continuing support, capital campaigns, renovation projects.
Limitations: Giving limited to U.S. No grants to individuals, or for research; no loans.
Publications: Program policy statement, annual report.
Application information: Application form not required.
  Initial approach: Proposal, telephone, or letter
  Copies of proposal: 1
  Deadline(s): Submit proposal between Sept. and Mar.; deadline Mar. 31
  Board meeting date(s): May
  Final notification: After annual meeting
  Write: David A. Frueauff, Secy.
Officers and Trustees:* A.C. McCully,* Pres.; Harry D. Frueauff,* V.P.; Charles T. Klein,* V.P.; David Frueauff,* Secy.; James P. Fallon, Karl P. Fanning, Margaret Perry Fanning.
Number of staff: 1 full-time support; 3 part-time support.
EIN: 135605371
Recent health grants:
607-1 Arkansas Childrens Hospital, Little Rock, AR, $25,000. For equipment purchase. 1990.
607-2 Cleo Wallace Center, Westminster, CO, $25,000. For Quadrangle Campaign support. 1990.
607-3 Cornell University Medical Center, NYC, NY, $25,000. For equipment purchase. 1990.
607-4 Craig Hospital Foundation, Englewood, CO, $10,000. For educational program support. 1990.
607-5 Deborah Hospital Foundation, Flushing, NY, $15,000. For heart and lung service programs. 1990.
607-6 Frontier Nursing Service, Wendover, KY, $10,000. For program support. 1990.
607-7 Geisinger Foundation, Danville, PA, $25,000. For hematology oncology unit. 1990.
607-8 Heart of the Rockies Regional Medical Center, Salida, CO, $25,000. For equipment purchase. 1990.
607-9 Lutheran Medical Center, Brooklyn, NY, $15,000. For Seniors in Touch Program. 1990.
607-10 Mississippi College, Clinton, MS, $20,000. For nursing library endowment. 1990.
607-11 Mountainside Hospital, Montclair, NJ, $25,000. For cardiac services program. 1990.
607-12 National Hypertension Association, NYC, NY, $15,000. For research and detection programs. 1990.
607-13 New York Foundling Hospital, NYC, NY, $25,000. For skilled nursing facility. 1990.

607-14 Northwest Mississippi Regional Medical Center, Clarksdale, MS, $25,000. For perinatal unit and expansion project. 1990.
607-15 Park County Rural Health Services, Fairplay, CO, $25,000. For nurse and physician assistant program. 1990.
607-16 Primary Childrens Medical Center, Salt Lake City, UT, $25,000. For equipment purchase for Newborn Critical Care Center. 1990.
607-17 Putnam Hospital Center, Carmel, NY, $15,000. Toward equipment purchase. 1990.
607-18 Saint Vincents Hospital and Medical Center of New York, NYC, NY, $48,000. For equipment purchase and program support. 1990.
607-19 Spalding Rehabilitation Hospital, Denver, CO, $15,000. For equipment purchase for neurological care unit. 1990.
607-20 Tallahassee Memorial Hospital Regional Medical Center Foundation, Tallahassee, FL, $50,000. For emergency medical services communication system. 1990.
607-21 Village Nursing Home, NYC, NY, $25,000. For Alzheimer's Program. 1990.
607-22 W N E T Channel 13, NYC, NY, $15,000. For Health Care Across the Boarder. 1990.
607-23 Webb Waring Lung Institute, Denver, CO, $25,000. For molecular biology laboratory. 1990.
607-24 West Virginia Wesleyan College, Buckhannon, WV, $10,000. For nursing scholarships. 1990.

608
The James G. Garner Charitable Trust
c/o Barnett Banks Trust Co., N.A.
701 Brickell Ave., 7th Fl.
Miami 33131-2801

Donor(s): James G. Garner.‡
Foundation type: Independent
Financial data (yr. ended 03/31/91): Assets, $6,088,117 (M); expenditures, $823,212; qualifying distributions, $789,440, including $764,750 for grants (high: $300,000).
Fields of interest: Education, higher education, Protestant giving, medical research, welfare.
Limitations: Giving primarily in FL and NC. No grants to individuals.
Application information:
  Initial approach: Proposal
  Write: The Trustees
Trustees: John Michael Garner, Beverly Garner Graves, Barnett Banks Trust Co., N.A.
EIN: 596824564

609
B. Milfred Gerson Trust
c/o Gary R. Gerson
666 71st St.
Miami Beach 33141-3099

Established in 1971 in FL.
Donor(s): Bertram Gerson,‡ B.M. Gerson Trust.
Foundation type: Independent
Financial data (yr. ended 12/31/90): Assets, $5,170,225 (M); expenditures, $722,528; qualifying distributions, $650,394, including $650,394 for grants.

Fields of interest: Jewish welfare, hospitals, health services, higher education.
Trustees: Irving Cyphen, Gary R. Gerson.
EIN: 596473286

610
Leo Goodwin Foundation, Inc.
c/o Borkson, Simon & Moskowitz
1500 N.W. 49th St., Suite 401
Fort Lauderdale 33309

Established in 1977 in FL.
Donor(s): Leo Goodwin, Jr.‡
Foundation type: Independent
Financial data (yr. ended 10/31/91): Assets, $7,578,604 (M); gifts received, $800,000; expenditures, $419,134; qualifying distributions, $401,299, including $370,270 for 16 grants (high: $102,770; low: $1,000).
Purpose and activities: Support primarily for child welfare and cancer research; some support also for youth groups and education.
Fields of interest: Child welfare, cancer, youth, education.
Types of support: General purposes.
Limitations: Giving primarily in FL. No grants to individuals.
Application information: Application form not required.
Initial approach: Proposal
Deadline(s): Allow sufficient time for review before end of fiscal year, Oct. 31
Write: Helen M. Furia, Secy.-Treas.
Officers: Francis B. Goodwin, Pres.; Elliot P. Borkson, V.P.; Helen M. Furia, Secy.-Treas.
EIN: 526054098

611
Grace Foundation Inc. ▼
One Town Center Rd.
Boca Raton 33486-1010   (407) 362-1487

Incorporated in 1961 in NY.
Donor(s): W.R. Grace & Co.
Foundation type: Company-sponsored
Financial data (yr. ended 12/31/91): Assets, $18,395,066 (M); gifts received, $1,200,000; expenditures, $3,242,549; qualifying distributions, $3,643,800, including $2,694,056 for 400 grants (high: $200,000; low: $100; average: $1,000-$20,000); $57,205 for 30 grants to individuals (high: $2,000; low: $970) and $336,309 for 600 employee matching gifts.
Purpose and activities: Grants primarily to organizations in communities in which the corporation does business, for education (including employee matching gifts and scholarships to children of domestic employees of W.R. Grace & Co.), urban and minority affairs, cultural programs, including performing arts, community funds, and health and hospitals.
Fields of interest: Education, higher education, civic affairs, urban affairs, minorities, handicapped, youth, social services, performing arts, cultural programs, community funds, hospitals, health, chemistry, science and technology.
Types of support: Operating budgets, continuing support, annual campaigns, building funds, equipment, matching funds, employee matching

gifts, scholarship funds, employee-related scholarships, fellowships, capital campaigns.
Limitations: No grants to individuals (except for employee-related scholarships), or for endowment funds, seed money, emergency funds, deficit financing, land acquisition, publications, demonstration projects, conferences, or specific research projects.
Application information: Application form not required.
Initial approach: Letter
Copies of proposal: 1
Deadline(s): None
Board meeting date(s): As required
Final notification: 2 to 3 months
Write: Susan Harris, Asst. Treas.
Officers and Directors:* J. Murfree Butler,* Chair.; Brian J. Smith,* Pres.; James P. Neeves,* V.P. and Treas.; Thomas M. Doyle,* V.P.; Robert B. Lamm,* Secy.; J.P. Bolduc, James W. Frick, George P. Jenkins, Paul D. Paganucci, Eben W. Pyne, John R. Young.
Number of staff: None.
EIN: 136153305

612
The Greenburg-May Foundation, Inc.
P.O. Box 54-6119
Miami Beach 33154   (305) 864-8639

Incorporated in 1947 in DE.
Donor(s): Harry Greenburg.‡
Foundation type: Independent
Financial data (yr. ended 12/31/90): Assets, $3,365,769 (M); expenditures, $182,546; qualifying distributions, $170,320, including $163,300 for 55 grants (high: $50,700; low: $100).
Purpose and activities: Grants almost entirely for medical research, primarily in cancer and heart disease; some support also for aging, hospitals, Jewish welfare funds, and temples.
Fields of interest: Medical research, hospitals, Jewish welfare, aged, cancer, heart disease, Jewish giving.
Types of support: Operating budgets, continuing support, building funds, research, endowment funds, scholarship funds.
Limitations: Giving primarily in southern FL, IL, and NY. No grants to individuals, or for conferences; generally no grants for scholarships or fellowships; no loans.
Application information: Application form not required.
Initial approach: Letter
Copies of proposal: 1
Deadline(s): None
Board meeting date(s): Jan., Apr., July, and Oct.
Final notification: 1 to 2 months
Write: Samuel D. May, Pres.
Officers and Directors:* Samuel D. May,* Pres. and Treas.; Peter May,* V.P.; Linda Sklar,* V.P.; Isabel May,* Secy.
Number of staff: 2 part-time support.
EIN: 136162935

613
Alice Busch Gronewaldt Foundation, Inc.
c/o Caldwell & Pacetti
Royal Park Bldg., 324 Royal Palm Way
Palm Beach 33480

Established in 1990 in FL.
Donor(s): Alice Busch Gronewaldt.
Foundation type: Independent
Financial data (yr. ended 12/31/90): Assets, $3,438,774 (M); gifts received, $3,862,500; expenditures, $590,426; qualifying distributions, $590,000, including $590,000 for 6 grants (high: $300,000; low: $20,000).
Fields of interest: Hospitals, animal welfare, conservation.
Types of support: General purposes, operating budgets.
Limitations: Giving primarily in Cooperstown, NY, and Palm Beach, FL. No grants to individuals.
Application information: Contributes only to pre-selected organizations. Applications not accepted.
Officers and Directors:* Alice Busch Gronewaldt,* Pres.; Louis Busch Hager, Jr.,* V.P. and Treas.; Alice Hager Holbrook,* V.P.; Mary Hager Thomas,* V.P.; Andrew W. Regan,* Secy.
EIN: 650212289

614
J. Erwin Groover Trust
c/o Barnett Banks Trust Co., N.A.
P.O. Box 40200
Jacksonville 32203-0200
Application address: c/o Florence Groover, 10155 Collins Ave., No. 407, Bal Harbour, FL 33154

Established in 1984 in FL.
Foundation type: Independent
Financial data (yr. ended 09/30/91): Assets, $2,586,507 (M); gifts received, $251,820; expenditures, $419,042; qualifying distributions, $385,146, including $378,300 for 16 grants (high: $80,000; low: $3,300).
Fields of interest: Handicapped, education, medical research, cancer, child welfare, hospitals.
Limitations: Giving primarily in FL.
Application information:
Initial approach: Letter
Deadline(s): None
Trustee: Barnett Banks Trust Co., N.A.
EIN: 596781660

615
The Hanley Family Foundation, Inc.
c/o John W. Hanley
713 S.W. Thornhill Ln.
Palm City 33490

Established in 1986 in FL.
Donor(s): John W. Hanley, Sr., John W. Hanley, Jr., Michael Hanley, Susan Hanley Myers, Mary Reel Hanley.
Foundation type: Independent
Financial data (yr. ended 05/31/91): Assets, $2,294,442 (M); gifts received, $241,250; expenditures, $81,076; qualifying distributions, $67,000, including $67,000 for 4 grants (high: $25,000; low: $5,000).

Purpose and activities: Giving limited to the diagnosis or treatment of alcoholism or chemical dependency, including related research or education.
Fields of interest: Alcoholism, drug abuse.
Limitations: No grants to individuals.
Application information: Application form not required.
Board meeting date(s): As required
Directors: John W. Hanley, Sr., Chair.; John W. Hanley, Jr., Mary Jane Hanley, Susan Jane Hanley, Douglas Tieman.
Number of staff: None.
EIN: 592745187

616
John H. & Lucile Harris Foundation, Inc.
(Formerly Harris Family Charitable Foundation)
5811 Pelican Bay Blvd., Suite 615
Naples 33963   (813) 597-8687

Donor(s): John H. Harris.
Foundation type: Independent
Financial data (yr. ended 12/31/91): Assets, $1,160,180 (M); expenditures, $715,279; qualifying distributions, $702,306, including $348,005 for 63 grants (high: $250,000; low: $10).
Fields of interest: Higher education, medical research, social services, recreation.
Limitations: No grants to individuals.
Application information:
Initial approach: Letter or proposal
Deadline(s): None
Write: John W. Hoyt, Secy.-Treas.
Officers: John H. Harris, Pres.; Lucile H. Harris, V.P.; John W. Hoyt, Secy.-Treas.
EIN: 592600172

617
The John T. and Winifred Hayward Foundation Charitable Trust
c/o First National Bank of Clearwater
P.O. Box 2918
Clearwater 34617-2918

Trust established in 1973 in FL.
Donor(s): John T. Hayward,‡ Winifred M. Hayward.‡
Foundation type: Independent
Financial data (yr. ended 12/31/90): Assets, $5,743,908 (M); expenditures, $106,995; qualifying distributions, $80,307, including $46,000 for 1 grant.
Purpose and activities: Support for medical research organizations and schools involved in the field of genetics, with emphasis on birth defects and inheritable diseases.
Fields of interest: Medical research.
Types of support: Research.
Limitations: No grants to individuals, or for building or endowment funds or operating budgets.
Application information: Contributes only to pre-selected organizations. Applications not accepted.
Write: L. Bernard Stephenson, V.P., First National Bank of Clearwater
Trustees: William R. LaRosa, M.D., Howard P. Rives, First National Bank of Clearwater.
EIN: 237363201

618
Dorothy B. Hersh Foundation, Inc.
3725 Prairie Dunes Dr.
Sarasota 34238   (813) 924-1678
Additional tel.: (201) 539-9818

Established in 1982 in NJ.
Donor(s): Dorothy B. Hersh.‡
Foundation type: Independent
Financial data (yr. ended 05/31/92): Assets, $5,791,202 (M); expenditures, $268,035; qualifying distributions, $235,562, including $220,117 for 8 grants (high: $56,800; low: $5,000).
Purpose and activities: Giving to programs aiding children and the underprivileged, including schools and hospitals.
Fields of interest: Child welfare, disadvantaged, hospitals, health associations, education—building funds.
Types of support: Building funds, equipment.
Limitations: Giving primarily in northern NJ. No grants to individuals.
Application information: Grant requests must be for capital purposes only. Application form not required.
Initial approach: Letter
Copies of proposal: 4
Deadline(s): None
Board meeting date(s): Varies
Write: Robert W. Donnelly, Sr., Administrator
Officer and Directors: * Robert Donnelly, Jr.,* Pres.; Ray Bauer, United Counties Trust Co.
Number of staff: None.
EIN: 222280011

619
J. E. & Mildred Hollingsworth Foundation, Inc.
425 Worth Ave.
Palm Beach 33480

Established in 1966 in FL.
Foundation type: Independent
Financial data (yr. ended 12/31/90): Assets, $2,098,257 (M); expenditures, $117,869; qualifying distributions, $112,087, including $102,472 for 62 grants (high: $50,021; low: $20).
Purpose and activities: Giving primarily for higher education, hospitals, and health agencies; support also for a family planning organization.
Fields of interest: Higher education, hospitals, health services, family planning.
Limitations: Giving primarily in FL, with emphasis on Palm Beach.
Directors: William B. Cudahy, Virginia Heiges, Mildred Hollingsworth, Wyckoff Myers, John Van Ryn.
EIN: 596170607

620
Jacksonville Community Foundation ▼
112 West Adams St., No. 1414
Jacksonville 32202   (904) 356-4483

Trust established in 1979 in FL.
Foundation type: Community
Financial data (yr. ended 12/31/91): Assets, $10,047,409 (M); gifts received, $4,701,953; expenditures, $2,953,208; qualifying distributions, $2,565,407, including $2,565,407

for 755 grants (high: $100,000; average: $100-$20,000).
Purpose and activities: General charitable giving.
Types of support: Consulting services, emergency funds, endowment funds, internships, loans, matching funds, program-related investments, seed money, special projects, technical assistance.
Limitations: Giving primarily in northeastern FL.
Publications: Annual report (including application guidelines), newsletter, informational brochure, application guidelines, 990-PF.
Application information: Application form not required.
Initial approach: Telphone
Copies of proposal: 1
Deadline(s): None
Board meeting date(s): Feb., April, June, Oct. and Dec.
Write: L. Andrew Bell III, Pres.
Officers and Distribution Committee: * John D. Uible,* Chair.; L. Andrew Bell III, Pres.; Ann Baker, J. Shepard Bryan, Jr., David M. Hicks, Max Michael, Jr., James F. Moseley, Jr., Willard Payne, Jr., Billy J. Walker, Courtenay Wilson.
Number of staff: 4 full-time professional; 2 part-time professional.
EIN: 596150746
Recent health grants:
620-1 Alzheimers Care and Research Center at Cypress Village, Jacksonville, FL, $20,900. 1990.
620-2 American Cancer Society, Jacksonville, FL, $37,325. 1990.
620-3 Eye Research Foundation, Jacksonville, FL, $25,000. 1990.
620-4 Hope Haven Childrens Clinic, Jacksonville, FL, $10,300. 1990.
620-5 Jacksonville Wolfson Childrens Hospital, Jacksonville, FL, $10,650. 1990.
620-6 Mayo Foundation, Jacksonville, FL, $35,000. 1990.
620-7 Saint Lukes Hospital Foundation, Jacksonville, FL, $10,000. 1990.
620-8 Saint Vincents Foundation, Jacksonville, FL, $64,501. 1990.

621
Janirve Foundation
c/o First National Bank in Palm Beach
255 South County Rd.
Palm Beach 33480
Application address: P.O. Box 2450, Asheville, NC 28802; Tel.: (704) 258-1877

Established in 1964 in FL.
Donor(s): Irving J. Reuter,‡ Jeannett M. Reuter.‡
Foundation type: Independent
Financial data (yr. ended 12/31/90): Assets, $44,160,852 (M); expenditures, $2,504,493; qualifying distributions, $2,305,742, including $2,153,272 for 92 grants (high: $100,000; low: $100; average: $25,000-$150,000).
Purpose and activities: Giving primarily for colleges and universities and human services, including child welfare, family services, and housing programs; some support also for hospitals and health associations and community development projects.
Fields of interest: Higher education, social services, child welfare, family services, housing, hospitals, health associations, community development, general charitable giving.

Types of support: General purposes.
Limitations: Giving primarily in NC. No grants to individuals, or generally for operating budgets or endowments; no loans.
Application information: Applicants should contact Asheville, NC, office for application procedures. Application form required.
  Deadline(s): None
  Board meeting date(s): At least monthly
  Final notification: Within 4 months
  Write: James H. Glenn, Chair.
Advisory Committee: James H. Glenn, Chair.; John W. Erichson, Met R. Poston, James Woolcott, Richard B. Wynne.
Trustee: First National Bank in Palm Beach.
Number of staff: 1 full-time professional.
EIN: 596147678

622
George W. Jenkins Foundation, Inc.
1936 George Jenkins Blvd.
P.O. Box 407
Lakeland 33802-0407   (813) 688-1188

Incorporated in 1967 in FL.
Donor(s): George W. Jenkins.
Foundation type: Independent
Financial data (yr. ended 12/31/90): Assets, $111,939,837 (M); gifts received, $89,820,733; expenditures, $2,592,314; qualifying distributions, $2,561,064, including $2,524,269 for 378 grants (high: $250,000; low: $100).
Fields of interest: Higher education, youth, community funds, health, social services, handicapped.
Types of support: Operating budgets, special projects.
Limitations: Giving limited to FL. No grants to individuals.
Application information: Application form not required.
  Initial approach: Proposal
  Copies of proposal: 1
  Deadline(s): None
  Board meeting date(s): Monthly
  Final notification: 2 weeks after 1st Monday of the month
  Write: Barbara O. Hart, Pres.
Officers and Directors:* Carol Jenkins Barnett,* Chair.; Barbara O. Hart, Pres.; Charles H. Jenkins, Sr., V.P.; John A. Turner, Secy.-Treas.; Hoyt Barnett, Mark C. Hollis, Charles H. Jenkins, Jr., George W. Jenkins, Howard Jenkins, Tina Johnson, William Schroter.
Number of staff: None.
EIN: 596194119

623
Alma Jennings Foundation, Inc.
2222 Ponce de Leon Blvd.
Coral Gables 33134

Established in 1966 in FL.
Foundation type: Independent
Financial data (yr. ended 12/31/90): Assets, $4,589,251 (M); expenditures, $400,743; qualifying distributions, $289,375, including $289,375 for 43 grants (high: $50,000; low: $300).
Fields of interest: Higher education, health, hospitals.

Limitations: Giving primarily in FL. No grants to individuals.
Application information: Contributes only to pre-selected organizations. Applications not accepted.
Directors: Allan T. Abess, Jr., Jeffrey M. Fine, Frank W. Guilford.
EIN: 596168955

624
Jones Intercable Tampa Trust
(Formerly Tampa Cable Television Trust)
P.O. Box 320265
Tampa 33679-3332   (813) 875-9461

Established in 1982 in FL.
Donor(s): Jones Intercable, Inc.
Foundation type: Independent
Financial data (yr. ended 12/31/91): Assets, $551,967 (M); gifts received, $250,000; expenditures, $293,306; qualifying distributions, $290,537, including $267,300 for 42 grants (high: $25,000; low: $1,250).
Purpose and activities: Giving for youth, social service agencies, cultural programs, religious organizations, and health; strong preference for matching funds.
Fields of interest: Youth, social services, cultural programs, religion, health.
Types of support: Matching funds, equipment, building funds, scholarship funds.
Limitations: Giving limited to the Tampa, FL, community. No support for organizations which limit services to members of any one religious group. No grants to individuals, or for start-up funds, deficit financing, or fundraising events.
Application information: Application form required.
  Deadline(s): Varies each year
  Write: Homer Tillery, Chair.
Officers and Trustees:* Homer Tillery,* Chair.; T. Terrell Sessums,* Secy.; Otis Anthony, Laura Blain, Nick Capitano, Robert L. Cromwell, Joseph Garcia, Rev. Laurence Higgins, Richard S. Hodes, M.D., William R. Klich, J. Leonard Levy, Rev. A. Leon Lowry, J. Benton Stewart, Gilbert E. Turner, Sandra H. Wilson.
EIN: 592273947

625
Keating Family Foundation, Inc.
4134 Gulf of Mexico Dr., Suite 10
Longboat Key 34228

Incorporated in 1967 in IL.
Donor(s): Edward Keating.
Foundation type: Independent
Financial data (yr. ended 12/31/90): Assets, $3,853,141 (M); expenditures, $189,927; qualifying distributions, $168,964, including $160,880 for 76 grants (high: $38,000; low: $30).
Fields of interest: Hospitals, health services, religion—Christian, mental health, child welfare, Jewish welfare, education, higher education, arts, performing arts, cultural programs.
Limitations: Giving primarily in IL. No grants to individuals.
Application information: Contributes only to pre-selected organizations. Applications not accepted.

Officers and Directors:* Edward Keating,* Pres.; Arthur E. Keating,* V.P.; Lee B. Keating,* V.P.; Lucie S. Keating,* V.P.; Elaine Mason,* V.P.; Alan M. Berry,* Secy.-Treas.; Robert Cottle, Joel Mogy.
EIN: 366198002

626
The Ethel & W. George Kennedy Family Foundation, Inc.
One S.E. 15th Rd., Suite 250
Miami 33129-1205   (305) 374-2455

Established in 1968 in FL.
Donor(s): W. George Kennedy.‡
Foundation type: Independent
Financial data (yr. ended 12/31/91): Assets, $12,839,492 (M); expenditures, $510,074; qualifying distributions, $418,391, including $407,215 for 43 grants (high: $59,000; low: $250).
Purpose and activities: Support primarily for organizations which 1) provide or support care, rehabilitation, and welfare for children, both physically and psychologically; 2) conduct or provide services for research, education, and medical equipment in the areas of heart, brain and eye diseases, diabetes, and cancer; and 3) conduct or provide services for the rehabilitation and education of the newly handicapped and their families.
Fields of interest: Medical research, health associations, rehabilitation, health services, medical education, heart disease, cancer, child welfare, handicapped, family services, education.
Types of support: Building funds, matching funds, capital campaigns, endowment funds, general purposes, land acquisition, renovation projects, special projects, equipment.
Limitations: Giving limited to Miami, FL. No grants to individuals.
Publications: Application guidelines.
Application information: Application form required.
  Initial approach: Letter
  Copies of proposal: 8
  Deadline(s): Feb. 1 and Aug. 1
  Board meeting date(s): Mar. and Oct.
  Final notification: Following board meetings
  Write: Wayne G. Kennedy, Pres.
Officers and Directors:* Wayne G. Kennedy,* Pres.; Kendel Kennedy Dobkin, V.P.; Karen Kennedy Herterich,* V.P.; Kimberly Kennedy,* Secy.
Number of staff: None.
EIN: 596204880

627
The Edward & Lucille Kimmel Foundation, Inc.
625 North Flagler Dr.
West Palm Beach 33401-4024

Established in 1983 in FL.
Foundation type: Independent
Financial data (yr. ended 12/31/91): Assets, $3,509,545 (M); gifts received, $111; expenditures, $116,640; qualifying distributions, $109,561, including $105,000 for 5 grants (high: $100,000; low: $1,000).
Fields of interest: Hospitals.

Limitations: Giving primarily in West Palm Beach, FL. No grants to individuals.
Application information: Contributes only to pre-selected organizations. Applications not accepted.

Write: Edward A. Kimmel, Pres.
Officer and Trustees:* Edward A. Kimmel,* Pres.; Joan K. Eigen, Alan Kimmel, Lucille Kimmel.
EIN: 592380662

628
The Thomas M. and Irene B. Kirbo Charitable Trust
112 West Adams St., Suite 1111
Jacksonville 32202   (904) 354-7212

Established in 1959 in GA.
Donor(s): Thomas M. Kirbo,‡ Irene B. Kirbo.
Foundation type: Independent
Financial data (yr. ended 09/30/91): Assets, $30,189,630 (M); expenditures, $1,427,319; qualifying distributions, $1,354,376, including $1,335,520 for 47 grants (high: $163,420; low: $3,500).
Fields of interest: Hospitals, religion—Christian, higher education, youth, libraries.
Limitations: Giving primarily in FL and GA. No grants to individuals.
Application information: Application form required.
Deadline(s): None
Write: R. Murray Jenks, Pres.
Officers and Trustees:* Charles H. Kirbo,* Chair.; R. Murray Jenks,* Pres.; John T. Jenks, Bruce W. Kirbo.
EIN: 592151720

629
John S. and James L. Knight Foundation ▼
(Formerly Knight Foundation)
One Biscayne Tower, Suite 3800
Two South Biscayne Blvd.
Miami 33131-1803   (305) 539-0009

Incorporated in 1950 in OH.
Donor(s): John S. Knight,‡ James L. Knight,‡ and their families and associates.
Foundation type: Independent
Financial data (yr. ended 12/31/91): Assets, $605,039,445 (M); gifts received, $6,629,326; expenditures, $28,479,935; qualifying distributions, $28,579,935, including $25,193,263 for 439 grants (high: $2,500,000; low: $3,000; average: $5,000-$100,000) and $833,000 for 3 program-related investments.
Purpose and activities: Four major programs: Community Initiatives (formerly Cities), Journalism, Education, and Arts and Culture. The Community Initiatives Program funds a broad spectrum of social service and civic organizations in 26 communities of foundation interest. Special areas of interest for the Community Initiatives Program are literacy, community development, homelessness, citizenship, and children. The Journalism Program is national in scope. The Education and Arts and Culture programs award grants nationally and locally. Local grants in education and arts and culture are restricted to the 26 communities of Knight Foundation interest.

Fields of interest: Journalism, education, arts, cultural programs, community development, literacy, citizenship, homeless, child welfare.
Types of support: Special projects, building funds, capital campaigns, endowment funds, general purposes, matching funds, seed money, renovation projects, program-related investments, emergency funds, professorships, fellowships.
Limitations: Giving limited to 26 communities where John S. and James L. Knight were involved in publishing newspapers for Community Initiatives Program; Journalism Program is national in scope; Education and Arts and Culture programs each have a national and local component, with local grants restricted to the above-mentioned 26 communities. No support for organizations with grantmaking activities other than community foundations; organizations whose mission is to prevent, eradicate and/or alleviate the effects of a specific disease; activity to propagate a religious faith; political candidates; international programs, except in support of a free press around the world; agencies that are supported by the United Way, except for pilot programs or capital expenditures; or activities that are the responsibility of government. No grants to individuals, or for annual fundraising campaigns or dinners; ongoing requests for general operating support; operating deficits; trips or uniforms for bands; films, videos, or television programs; honoraria; scholarly research leading to a book; group travel; memorials; medical research; or conferences.
Publications: Annual report (including application guidelines), application guidelines, grants list, newsletter.
Application information: Detailed guidelines available upon request; considers only 1 request from an organization during a 12-month period; all proposals must have endorsement of president of organization or institution requesting grant and should be clearly indicated as such on outside envelope. Application form not required.
Initial approach: Letter; proposals submitted by fax not accepted
Copies of proposal: 2
Deadline(s): Jan. 1, Apr. 1, July 1, and Oct. 1
Board meeting date(s): Mar., June, Sept., and Dec.
Final notification: 2 weeks after meeting dates
Officers and Trustees:* Lee Hills,* Chair.; W. Gerald Austen, M.D.,* Vice-Chair.; Creed C. Black,* Pres. and C.E.O.; James D. Spaniolo, V.P. and C.P.O.; Timothy Crowe, V.P. and C.F.O.; James K. Batten, Alvah H. Chapman, Jr., Jill K. Conway, C.C. Gibson, Gordon E. Heffern, Larry Jinks, Thomas Johnson, Beverly Knight Olson, Henry King Stanford, Barbara Knight Toomey.
Number of staff: 8 full-time professional; 9 full-time support.
EIN: 346519827
Recent health grants:
629-1 American Cancer Society, Florida Division, Miami, FL, $10,000. For patient suite in honor and memory of Charles Whited at the American Cancer Society Winn Dixie Hope Lodge. 1991.
629-2 Central State Hospital, Milledgeville, GA, $12,090. To build miniature golf course for mentally handicapped residents. 1991.
629-3 Childrens Hospital Foundation, Akron, OH, $150,000. For Centennial Modernization and Renovation Campaign. 1991.

629-4 Clinic Campesina/Rural Health Clinic, Lafayette, CO, $25,000. To expand and remodel medical facility. 1991.
629-5 Columbia Free Medical Clinic, Columbia, SC, $20,000. To construct new facility. 1991.
629-6 Edwin Shaw Hospital Development Foundation, Akron, OH, $15,000. To renovate and furnish residential treatment center for women addicted to cocaine. 1991.
629-7 Elizabeth H. Faulk Foundation, Boca Raton, FL, $10,000. For Seniors Counseling Program. 1991.
629-8 Florence Crittenton Services, Charlotte, NC, $25,000. For capital campaign to renovate substance abuse treatment facility for pregnant girls and their children. 1991.
629-9 Hope Haven, Charlotte, NC, $50,000. To construct halfway home for recovering alcoholic and chemically dependent men. 1991.
629-10 House of Ichtus, Pompano Beach, FL, $10,000. To purchase van for Turning Point, residential program for substance abusers. 1991.
629-11 Mariners Inn, Detroit, MI, $50,000. To renovate men's shelter and treatment center. 1991.
629-12 Memorial Medical Center Foundation, Long Beach, CA, $63,000. To renovate and endow Child Protection Center. 1991.
629-13 Mental Health Association of Dade County, Miami, FL, $25,000. For operating support for A Woman's Place, shelter for homeless women and children. 1991.
629-14 Michigan Dyslexia Institute, Detroit, MI, $20,000. To support pilot project for dyslexic students in Wayne County Juvenile Court system. 1991.
629-15 Neighborhood Housing Services of Miami-Dade, Miami, FL, $26,375. To expand substance abuse prevention program, Operation Youth Empowerment Solutions. 1991.
629-16 North Broward Hospital District, Fort Lauderdale, FL, $25,000. Toward construction of new pediatric intensive care unit at Broward General Hospital. 1991.
629-17 Planned Parenthood of Greater Miami, Miami, FL, $10,000. For trustee discretionary grant. 1991.
629-18 Poverello Center, Pompano Beach, FL, $10,000. To purchase truck needed to collect donations of food and furniture for people with AIDS. 1991.
629-19 Public Health Trust of Dade County, Miami, FL, $50,000. For construction of Breast Health Center to serve economically disadvantaged Dade residents. 1991.
629-20 Safe Harbor of Northeast Kentucky, Morehead, KY, $15,000. For child counselor. 1991.
629-21 Shepherd Care Ministries, Hollywood, FL, $25,000. For capital campaign to expand The Fold, maternity home for young women. 1991.
629-22 Southwest Detroit Community Mental Health Services, Detroit, MI, $25,000. For Phase II of capital campaign to expand and renovate facilities. 1991.
629-23 Tallahassee Memorial Hospital Regional Medical Center Foundation, Tallahassee, FL, $18,000. For providing health care to homeless. 1991.

629-24 United Hospitals Foundation, Saint Paul, MN, $50,000. For United Nineties Campaign supporting renovation, expansion and technological advancement. 1991.

629-25 University of Miami, Coral Gables, FL, $300,000. For Miami Project to Cure Paralysis to continue and expand its program of educational outreach disseminating research findings about spinal cord injury. 1991.

629-26 Variety Audio Foundation, San Jose, CA, $27,000. For endowment of Books Aloud, reading by listening program for blind and physically disabled. 1991.

629-27 Visiting Nurse Association, San Jose, CA, $25,000. For development of perinatal and pediatric home care services for high-risk mothers, fragile babies and seriously ill children. 1991.

630
The William A. Krueger Charitable Trust
2600 N.E. 21st St.
Fort Lauderdale 33305-3514   (305) 537-5359

Established in 1985 in FL.
Donor(s): William A. Krueger.
Foundation type: Independent
Financial data (yr. ended 11/30/91): Assets, $1,796,157 (M); expenditures, $933,582; qualifying distributions, $925,737, including $925,737 for 33 grants (high: $815,000; low: $24).
Fields of interest: Hospitals, health, social services, community funds, religion—Christian, higher education.
Limitations: Giving primarily in Fort Lauderdale, FL, and NC. No grants to individuals.
Application information: Contributes only to pre-selected organizations. Applications not accepted.
  Write: William A. Krueger, Trustee
Trustees: Evelyn J. Krueger, William A. Krueger.
EIN: 596872412

631
Forrest C. Lattner Foundation, Inc.
777 East Atlantic Ave., Suite 317
Delray Beach 33483-5352   (407) 278-3781

Incorporated in 1981 in FL.
Donor(s): Mrs. Forrest C. Lattner, Forrest C. Lattner,‡ Mrs. Francis H. Lattner.
Foundation type: Independent
Financial data (yr. ended 12/31/90): Assets, $58,247,654 (M); gifts received, $51,591,212; expenditures, $3,227,982; qualifying distributions, $3,109,310, including $3,041,135 for 91 grants (high: $500,000; low: $500).
Fields of interest: Religion—Christian, health associations, hospitals, arts.
Limitations: Giving primarily in Palm Beach County, FL, Wichita, KS, St. Louis, MO, and Westerly, RI.
Application information: Application form not required.
  Copies of proposal: 1
  Deadline(s): None
  Board meeting date(s): June and Dec.
  Write: Susan L. Hollenbeck, Pres., or Martha L. Connelly, Chair.

Officers and Directors:* Martha L. Connelly,* Chair.; Susan L. Hollenbeck,* Pres. and Secy.; Daniel S. Hall,* Treas.
Number of staff: 1 part-time professional; 1 part-time support.
EIN: 592147657
Recent health grants:

631-1 Alton Ochsner Medical Foundation, New Orleans, LA, $50,000. 1990.

631-2 Alzheimers Association, Boca Raton, FL, $90,000. 1990.

631-3 Alzheimers Disease and Related Disorders Association, Wichita, KS, $10,000. 1990.

631-4 Alzheimers Disease and Related Disorders Association, Saint Louis, MO, $10,000. 1990.

631-5 Alzheimers Disease and Related Disorders Association, National Chapter, Chicago, IL, $75,000. 1990.

631-6 American Paralysis Association, Saint Louis, MO, $15,000. 1990.

631-7 Arthritis Foundation, West Palm Beach, FL, $30,000. 1990.

631-8 Arthritis Foundation, Wichita, KS, $20,000. 1990.

631-9 Arthritis Foundation, Saint Louis, MO, $10,000. 1990.

631-10 Bethesda Hospital Association, Delray Beach, FL, $25,000. 1990.

631-11 Horses and the Handicapped Foundation, Delray Beach, FL, $21,450. 1990.

631-12 Independence Center, Saint Louis, MO, $35,000. 1990.

631-13 Menninger Foundation, Topeka, KS, $250,000. 1990.

631-14 Mental Health Association of South Central Kansas, Wichita, KS, $100,000. 1990.

631-15 Midwest Cancer Foundation, Wichita, KS, $25,000. 1990.

631-16 Professional Care/Saint Francis Hospital, Wichita, KS, $30,000. 1990.

631-17 Ronald McDonald House, Saint Louis, MO, $10,000. 1990.

631-18 Saint Louis Childrens Hospital, Saint Louis, MO, $250,000. 1990.

631-19 Sedgwick County Department of Mental Health, Wichita, KS, $50,000. 1990.

631-20 Westerly Hospital, Westerly, RI, $250,000. 1990.

631-21 Wichita Guidance Center, Wichita, KS, $28,000. 1990.

632
Charles A. Lauffer Trust
c/o NationsBank
P.O. Box 11388
St. Petersburg 33733-1388

Established in 1945 in FL.
Foundation type: Independent
Financial data (yr. ended 08/31/91): Assets, $2,585,067 (M); expenditures, $61,395; qualifying distributions, $134,656, including $43,563 for 25 grants (high: $5,641; low: $1,000) and $86,900 for loans to individuals.
Purpose and activities: Support primarily for youth, children, and social services; student loans awarded for the study of medicine, agriculture, and engineering.
Fields of interest: Youth, child welfare, social services, medical education, agriculture, engineering.
Types of support: Student loans, general purposes.

Limitations: Giving primarily in FL.
Application information: Contributes only to pre-selected organizations. Completion of application form required for student loans.
  Initial approach: Letter for student loans
  Deadline(s): No set deadline for student loans applications
Trustees: Richard A. Eagle, NationsBank.
EIN: 596121126

633
Robert O. Law Foundation
P.O. Box 11025
Fort Lauderdale 33339

Incorporated in 1958 in FL.
Donor(s): Robert O. Law.‡
Foundation type: Independent
Financial data (yr. ended 12/31/91): Assets, $3,726,088 (M); expenditures, $200,948; qualifying distributions, $157,835, including $117,300 for 29 grants (high: $25,000; low: $800).
Fields of interest: Youth, health services, hospitals, education.
Limitations: Giving limited to Broward County, FL. No grants to individuals.
Application information: Contributes only to pre-selected organizations. Applications not accepted.
Officers and Trustees:* Robert O. Law III,* Pres.; William J. Leonard,* Secy.-Treas.; Leslie Law Fitzgerald, Mary Jane Law.
EIN: 590914810

634
Lost Tree Charitable Foundation, Inc.
11555 Lost Tree Way
North Palm Beach 33408   (407) 622-3780

Incorporated in 1982 in FL.
Foundation type: Independent
Financial data (yr. ended 12/31/90): Assets, $1,790,582 (M); gifts received, $241,991; expenditures, $246,002; qualifying distributions, $200,015, including $200,015 for 33 grants (high: $14,546; low: $500).
Purpose and activities: Giving primarily for family and social services, including programs for rehabilitation, alcohol and drug abuse, and the disabled; support also for higher, medical, early childhood and other education, and health services.
Fields of interest: Family services, social services, rehabilitation, drug abuse, handicapped, aged, education, higher education, medical education, Catholic welfare, health services.
Types of support: General purposes, special projects, matching funds, seed money, scholarship funds, building funds, renovation projects, equipment.
Limitations: Giving limited to Palm Beach and Martin counties, FL. No grants to individuals.
Publications: Annual report, newsletter, occasional report, informational brochure.
Application information: Application form not required.
  Initial approach: Letter
  Deadline(s): None
  Write: Robert C. Porter, Pres., or Pamela M. Rue, Exec. Secy.

Officers: Robert C. Porter, Pres.; Mrs. John T. Connor, V.P.; Joseph D. Harnett, V.P.; Selim N. Tideman, Jr., V.P.; William N. Poundstone, Secy.; Robert A. Waidner, Treas.
Number of staff: 1 full-time professional.
EIN: 592104920

635
The Joe and Emily Lowe Foundation, Inc. ▼

249 Royal Palm Way
Palm Beach 33480   (407) 655-7001

Incorporated in 1949 in NY.
Donor(s): Joe Lowe,‡ Emily Lowe.‡
Foundation type: Independent
Financial data (yr. ended 12/31/91): Assets, $21,853,932 (M); expenditures, $1,229,784; qualifying distributions, $1,084,440, including $1,007,000 for 353 grants (high: $175,000; low: $100; average: $1,000-$10,000).
Purpose and activities: Emphasis on Jewish welfare funds and social and religious groups, the arts, museums, higher education, including medical education, hospitals, health services, and medical research; support also for social services, including aid to the handicapped, underprivileged children's organizations, and women's projects.
Fields of interest: Jewish welfare, Jewish giving, arts, museums, higher education, medical education, health services, hospitals, medical research, social services, handicapped, women, child welfare, disadvantaged, youth.
Types of support: Building funds, general purposes, equipment, endowment funds, matching funds, continuing support.
Limitations: Giving primarily in the New York, NY, metropolitan area, including NJ, and in FL, including Palm Beach. No grants to individuals, or for scholarships, fellowships, or prizes; no loans.
Application information: Application form not required.
    Initial approach: Letter or brief proposal
    Copies of proposal: 1
    Deadline(s): None
    Board meeting date(s): Feb. and May or June
    Final notification: 1 to 3 months
Officers and Trustees:* Bernard Stern,* Pres. and Treas.; David Fogelson,* V.P. and Secy.; Helen G. Hauben,* V.P.
Number of staff: 1 full-time professional.
EIN: 136121361
Recent health grants:
635-1 Albert Einstein College of Medicine of Yeshiva University, Bronx, NY, $12,500. For general support. 1990.
635-2 John F. Kennedy Memorial Hospital, Lake Worth, FL, $10,000. For general support. 1990.

636
Chesley G. Magruder Foundation, Inc.
c/o NationsBank
P.O. Box 8750
Winter Park 32790-8750   (407) 646-6378
Application address: P.O. Box 8751, Winter Park, FL 32790

Established in 1979 in FL.
Donor(s): Chesley G. Magruder Trust.

Foundation type: Independent
Financial data (yr. ended 06/30/92): Assets, $11,194,206 (M); expenditures, $848,884; qualifying distributions, $774,950, including $774,950 for 54 grants (high: $25,000; low: $2,000).
Fields of interest: Higher education, education, youth, social services, health.
Limitations: Giving primarily in central FL. No grants to individuals.
Application information: Application form not required.
    Initial approach: Proposal
    Copies of proposal: 7
    Deadline(s): None
    Board meeting date(s): Jan., Mar., May, July, Sept., and Nov.
    Write: Board of Trustees
Trustee: NationsBank.
EIN: 591920736

637
Lucille P. Markey Charitable Trust ▼
3250 Mary St., Suite 405
Miami 33133   (305) 445-5612

Established in 1983 in FL; set up to distribute entire estate of donor by 1997.
Donor(s): Lucille P. Markey.‡
Foundation type: Independent
Financial data (yr. ended 06/30/91): Assets, $186,577,896 (M); gifts received, $12,500,000; expenditures, $45,246,613; qualifying distributions, $43,909,388, including $33,303,618 for 77 grants (high: $3,935,800; low: $2,000; average: $80,000-$2,000,000) and $8,676,170 for 108 grants to individuals (high: $160,380; low: $7,690; average: $33,150-$118,800).
Purpose and activities: Established solely for the purpose of supporting and encouraging basic medical research.
Fields of interest: Medical research.
Types of support: Fellowships, research, matching funds.
Limitations: No grants for endowments, construction, renovation projects, or equipment (except as essential to research project).
Publications: Multi-year report, application guidelines, informational brochure, annual report.
Application information: Policies and application guidlines: Nomination information for Scholar Awards in Biomedical Science available from trust office. Nominations submitted by the college or university; nominations by individuals are not accepted. Application form not required.
    Initial approach: 2- to 3-page outline of proposal with curriculum vitaes of investigators
    Copies of proposal: 7
    Deadline(s): None
    Board meeting date(s): Quarterly
    Final notification: Shortly after trustees' decision
    Write: Nancy W. Weber, Dir., Prog. Administration
Officers and Trustees:* Louis J. Hector,* Chair.; William P. Sutter,* Pres.; John H. Dickason, V.P., Finance and Administration; Robert J. Glaser, M.D.,* Dir. for Medical Science; Nancy W. Weber, Prog. Coord.; Margaret Glass, George L. Shinn.

Number of staff: 4 full-time professional; 2 part-time professional; 4 full-time support; 2 part-time support.
EIN: 592276359
Recent health grants:
637-1 Cold Spring Harbor Laboratory, Neuroscience Center, Cold Spring Harbor, NY, $4,000,000. For start-up expenses for scientific staff, procurement of range of multi-user equipment and completion of laboratory space for research in developmental neurobiology. 1991.
637-2 Delegation for Basic Biomedical Research, Shrewsbury, MA, $25,000. For development of strategic agency for support of biomedical research with federal and private funding. 1991.
637-3 Florida State University, Institute of Molecular Biophysics, Tallahassee, FL, $4,000,000. To investigate molecular structure and dynamics of complex systems and to relate this information to biological function. 1991.
637-4 Fox Chase Cancer Center, Division of Basic Sciences, Philadelphia, PA, $4,000,000. For development of molecular oncology program. 1991.
637-5 Harvard University, School of Public Health, Laboratory of Toxicology, Boston, MA, $3,000,000. For development of research program in environmental toxicology. 1991.
637-6 Massachusetts Institute of Technology, Department of Brain and Cognitive Sciences, Cambridge, MA, $3,850,000. For program in developmental neurobiology. 1991.
637-7 Memorial Sloan-Kettering Cancer Center, NYC, NY, $2,700,000. For program in developmental biology. 1991.
637-8 New York Academy of Medicine, NYC, NY, $15,000. For symposium to examine human genome project from each of three policy perspectives: science, social and public. 1991.
637-9 New York University, Department of Pathology, Division of Immunology, NYC, NY, $2,600,000. For program in molecular vaccinology. 1991.
637-10 Rockefeller University, NYC, NY, $300,000. For research on environmental influences on mutagenesis and on theory formation and validation. 1991.
637-11 Stanford University, Stanford, CA, $196,071. For research program in history and sociology of modern immunology. 1991.
637-12 Stanford University, Stanford, CA, $83,250. For symposium entitled Beyond the Human Genome: Biological Nature and Social Opportunities. 1991.
637-13 Tufts University, Medford, MA, $100,000. To continue support of pathobiology training program for graduate students and postdoctoral fellows in basic biomedical science. 1991.
637-14 University of Alabama, Birmingham, AL, $1,500,000. For program in neural network research. 1991.
637-15 University of Colorado Health Sciences Center, Denver, CO, $5,000,000. For studies on molecular biology of cell proliferation. 1991.
637-16 University of Kentucky, Lexington, KY, $30,000. For isolation facility for infectious

disease research at Gluck Equine Research Center. 1991.

637-17 University of Rochester, School of Medicine and Dentistry, Rochester, NY, $4,000,000. For development of neuroscience institute. 1991.

637-18 University of Texas Southwestern Medical Center, Dallas, TX, $300,000. To continue support of exploratory research projects which are not fundable by conventional extramural support sources. 1991.

637-19 University of Vermont, Department of Microbiology and Molecular Genetics, Burlington, VT, $1,800,000. For development of program in molecular genetics. 1991.

637-20 Vanderbilt University, Department of Biochemistry, Nashville, TN, $5,000,000. For research on molecular mechanisms of growth regulation. 1991.

638
The Morris M. and Helen F. Messing Foundation

P.O. Box 3637
Boynton Beach 33424-3637

Incorporated in 1957 in NJ.
Donor(s): Morris M. Messing.
Foundation type: Independent
Financial data (yr. ended 12/31/91): Assets, $2,456,870 (M); expenditures, $198,935; qualifying distributions, $186,216, including $176,720 for 50 grants (high: $20,000; low: $1,000).
Purpose and activities: Grants largely for Jewish welfare funds, temple support, medical research, and higher education.
Fields of interest: Jewish welfare, Jewish giving, medical research, higher education.
Limitations: No grants to individuals.
Application information: Contributes only to pre-selected organizations. Applications not accepted.
Trustees: Sam Falcone, Madeline Levy, Andrew Messing, Gilbert Messing.
EIN: 226045391

639
The Baron de Hirsch Meyer Foundation

407 Lincoln Rd., Suite 6J
Miami Beach 33139   (305) 538-2531

Incorporated in 1940 in FL.
Donor(s): Baron de Hirsch Meyer.‡
Foundation type: Independent
Financial data (yr. ended 12/31/90): Assets, $3,220,520 (M); expenditures, $191,481; qualifying distributions, $119,787, including $119,787 for 27 grants (high: $25,000; low: $35).
Fields of interest: Hospitals, health services, cancer, child welfare, Jewish welfare, religious welfare, Catholic giving, performing arts, aged, animal welfare, general charitable giving.
Types of support: Building funds.
Limitations: Giving primarily in FL. No grants to individuals.
Publications: Informational brochure (including application guidelines).
Application information: Application form not required.

Initial approach: Proposal or letter
Copies of proposal: 1
Board meeting date(s): Feb.
Officers and Directors:* Polly de Hirsch Meyer,* Pres. and Treas.; Marie Williams,* V.P.; Martin Steedman,* Secy.
EIN: 596129646

640
Henry L. & Kathryn Mills Charitable Foundation

4950 N.W. 72nd Ave.
Miami 33166   (305) 887-6631

Established in 1984 in FL.
Donor(s): Kathryn Mills.
Foundation type: Independent
Financial data (yr. ended 06/30/91): Assets, $3,421,203 (M); expenditures, $166,628; qualifying distributions, $141,905, including $109,575 for 9 grants (high: $50,000; low: $2,000).
Fields of interest: Social services, recreation, health.
Types of support: Renovation projects, building funds, emergency funds, scholarship funds, research.
Limitations: Giving primarily in Miami, FL, and the surrounding area. No grants to individuals.
Application information: Contributes only to pre-selected organizations. Applications not accepted.
Write: Debra Mills Grimm, Trustee
Trustees: Kathryn Mills, Managing Trustee; Debra Mills Grimm, James R. Kaufman, Michael Mills, Northern Trust Bank of Florida, N.A.
EIN: 592474884

641
Henry Nias Foundation, Inc.

2760 South Ocean Blvd.
Palm Beach 33480   (407) 582-1011
Additional address: 720 Milton Rd., Rye, NY 10580; Tel.: (914) 967-9555

Incorporated in 1955 in NY.
Donor(s): Henry Nias.‡
Foundation type: Independent
Financial data (yr. ended 11/30/90): Assets, $13,686,242 (M); expenditures, $721,571; qualifying distributions, $672,332, including $608,000 for 56 grants (high: $25,000; low: $2,500; average: $5,000-$15,000).
Purpose and activities: Emphasis on medical sciences, including hospitals, aid to the handicapped, and medical school student loan funds; support also for education, cultural programs, child welfare and youth, the aged, and Jewish organizations, including welfare funds.
Fields of interest: Hospitals, handicapped, medical education, education, cultural programs, child welfare, youth, aged, Jewish giving, Jewish welfare.
Types of support: Continuing support.
Limitations: Giving limited to the New York, NY, metropolitan area.
Application information: Applications by invitation only.
Deadline(s): Aug. 31
Board meeting date(s): Sept. and Oct.
Final notification: Grants paid in Nov.

Write: Albert Rosenberg, Pres.
Officers and Directors:* Albert J. Rosenberg,* Pres.; Stanley Edelman, M.D.,* V.P.; Richard J. Edelman, Charles D. Fleischman, William F. Rosenberg.
Number of staff: None.
EIN: 136075785

642
Calvin & Flavia Oak Foundation, Inc.

P.O. Box 430
La Belle 33935

Established in 1965.
Donor(s): Flavia DeCamp Oak.‡
Foundation type: Independent
Financial data (yr. ended 11/30/91): Assets, $6,070,097 (M); gifts received, $4,237,500; expenditures, $461,757; qualifying distributions, $404,003, including $331,000 for 30 grants (high: $36,000; low: $2,000).
Purpose and activities: Support primarily for hospitals, organizations serving the blind, and medical schools; support also for an Episcopal church.
Fields of interest: Medical education, handicapped, hospitals, religion—Christian.
Limitations: Giving primarily in Miami and Coral Gables, FL. No grants to individuals.
Application information: Contributes only to pre-selected organizations. Applications not accepted.
Board meeting date(s): 2nd Friday in Mar., June, Sept., and Dec.
Write: Tully F. Dunlap, Pres.
Officers and Directors:* Tully F. Dunlap,* Pres. and Treas.; Theresa M. Moore,* V.P.; James H. Peck II, Secy.; Catherine Holloway, Emily M. Romfh.
EIN: 596192591

643
Matred Carlton Olliff Foundation

P.O. Box 995
Wauchula 33873
Application address: P.O. Box 385, Wauchula, FL 33873; Tel.: (813) 773-4131

Established in 1982 in FL.
Donor(s): Matred Carlton Olliff.‡
Foundation type: Independent
Financial data (yr. ended 08/31/91): Assets, $4,394,528 (L); gifts received, $300; expenditures, $285,560; qualifying distributions, $263,163, including $123,595 for 51 grants (high: $23,000; low: $50) and $128,591 for 196 grants to individuals (high: $4,800; low: $65).
Fields of interest: Protestant giving, hospitals, health associations.
Types of support: Student aid.
Limitations: Giving primarily in FL.
Application information: Application form not required.
Initial approach: Proposal
Deadline(s): July 1
Write: Doyle E. Carlton, Jr., Trustee
Trustees: Doyle E. Carlton, Jr., Doyle E. Carlton III, Walter S. Farr.
EIN: 592241303

644
The Community Foundation for Palm Beach and Martin Counties, Inc.

(Formerly Palm Beach County Community Foundation)
324 Datura St., Suite 340
West Palm Beach 33401-5431   (407) 659-6800

Incorporated in 1972 in FL.
Foundation type: Community
Financial data (yr. ended 06/30/92): Assets, $25,078,284 (M); gifts received, $1,614,748; expenditures, $1,782,191; qualifying distributions, $644,210, including $598,135 for grants (average: $1,000-$20,000) and $46,075 for grants to individuals (average: $500-$6,000).
Purpose and activities: Primary areas of interest include health, social services, education, arts and culture, and conservation and preservation.
Fields of interest: Community development, education, education—early childhood, elementary education, arts, cultural programs, health, social services, conservation, environment, historic preservation.
Types of support: Seed money, student aid, conferences and seminars, equipment, matching funds, special projects, technical assistance, general purposes.
Limitations: Giving primarily in Palm Beach, Martin, and Hendry counties, FL. No grants to individuals (except scholarships), or for operating funds, building campaigns, endowments, or annual campaigns.
Publications: Annual report (including application guidelines), newsletter, application guidelines, informational brochure (including application guidelines).
Application information: Application form required.
Initial approach: Telephone call followed by proposal
Copies of proposal: 5
Deadline(s): Mar. 1 and Oct. 1
Board meeting date(s): Oct., Dec., Mar., and May
Final notification: June and Dec.
Write: Shannon G. Sadler, Exec. Dir.
Officers and Directors:* Tom A. Giuffrida,* Pres.; Julian Cohen,* 1st V.P.; Winsome McIntosh,* V.P.; Arthur I. Meyer,* Secy.; Mary Jane Grant,* Treas.; Shannon G. Sadler, Exec. Dir.; and 18 additional directors.
Number of staff: 4 full-time professional; 1 full-time support.
EIN: 237181875

645
Vera Davis Parsons-W. D. Charities, Inc.

5050 Edgewood Court
Jacksonville 32205

Established in 1967 in FL.
Donor(s): Vera Davis Parsons.
Foundation type: Independent
Financial data (yr. ended 12/31/90): Assets, $24,409,162 (M); expenditures, $1,338,002; qualifying distributions, $1,271,236, including $1,219,825 for 201 grants (high: $530,338; low: $500).
Purpose and activities: Giving primarily for youth activities and education; support also for medical research and health, welfare relief, and social service agencies.
Fields of interest: Youth, education, health, medical research, social services, welfare.
Limitations: Giving primarily in FL, GA, NC, SC, and AL. No grants to individuals.
Application information: Contributes only to pre-selected organizations. Applications not accepted.
Write: H.J. Skelton, Pres.
Officers and Directors:* H.J. Skelton,* Pres.; Robert D. Davis, V.P. and Treas.; H.D. Francis, V.P.; G.P. Bishop, Jr., Secy.; R.J. Head, Charles M. Thompson.
EIN: 596180346

646
The Paulucci Family Foundation

201 West First St.
Sanford 32771   (407) 321-7004

Incorporated in 1966 in MN.
Donor(s): Jeno F. Paulucci.
Foundation type: Independent
Financial data (yr. ended 12/31/90): Assets, $2,108,684 (M); expenditures, $82,631; qualifying distributions, $68,695, including $68,695 for grants.
Purpose and activities: Emphasis on higher education, medical research, and support of Italian-American cultural and charitable activities.
Fields of interest: Higher education, medical research, recreation, Italy, cultural programs.
Limitations: Giving primarily in MN and FL. No grants to individuals.
Application information:
Initial approach: Letter
Copies of proposal: 1
Deadline(s): Oct. 1
Board meeting date(s): Annually
Write: Jeno F. Paulucci, Pres.
Officers and Directors:* Jeno F. Paulucci,* Pres.; Larry W. Nelson,* V.P. and Treas.; Donald Vanneste, Secy.; Gina J. Paulucci, Lois M. Paulucci, Michael J. Paulucci, Cynthia J. Soderstrom.
EIN: 416054004

647
The Dr. M. Lee Pearce Foundation, Inc.

11880 Bird Rd., Suite 101
Miami 33175   (305) 477-0222

Established in 1984 in FL.
Donor(s): M. Lee Pearce, M.D.
Foundation type: Independent
Financial data (yr. ended 12/31/90): Assets, $6,049,267 (M); gifts received, $18,765; expenditures, $369,699; qualifying distributions, $365,575, including $365,500 for 9 grants (high: $300,000; low: $1,000).
Purpose and activities: Giving primarily to a graduate school; some support also for health, culture, and historic preservation.
Fields of interest: Higher education, education, health, medical research, cultural programs, historic preservation.
Limitations: Giving primarily in FL, with emphasis on Miami. No grants to individuals.

Application information: Contributes only to pre-selected organizations. Applications not accepted.
Write: A.B. Wiener, V.P. and Secy.-Treas.
Officers and Directors:* M. Lee Pearce, M.D.,* Pres.; A.B. Wiener, V.P. and Secy.-Treas.; Robert L. Achor,* V.P.; Marc H. Bivins, M.D.,* V.P.; John Mudd,* V.P.
EIN: 592424272

648
A. P. Phillips Foundation, Inc.

P.O. Box 3628
Orlando 32802   (407) 422-8250

Established in 1965.
Foundation type: Independent
Financial data (yr. ended 06/30/90): Assets, $2,663,834 (M); expenditures, $95,943; qualifying distributions, $71,907, including $70,370 for 16 grants (high: $20,000; low: $100).
Purpose and activities: Support for a university journalism program; grants also for youth, drug abuse programs, and general charitable organizations.
Fields of interest: Higher education, journalism, youth, drug abuse, general charitable giving.
Types of support: Special projects, general purposes.
Limitations: Giving primarily in central FL.
Application information: Application form not required.
Initial approach: Proposal
Copies of proposal: 1
Deadline(s): None
Board meeting date(s): Requests considered in May
Final notification: June 30
Write: M.W. Wells, Jr., Pres.
Officers and Directors:* M.W. Wells, Jr.,* Pres.; D.K. Wells,* V.P.; J.W. Jordan,* Secy.; L.A. Wells.
Number of staff: 1 part-time support.
EIN: 596165157

649
Phipps Florida Foundation

P.O. Box 1351
Tallahassee 32302   (904) 222-2717

Trust established in 1959 in FL.
Foundation type: Independent
Financial data (yr. ended 11/30/91): Assets, $609,966 (M); expenditures, $588,805; qualifying distributions, $661,660, including $578,250 for 1 grant and $83,410 for 2 program-related investments.
Fields of interest: Conservation, health.
Types of support: Operating budgets, continuing support, annual campaigns, seed money, emergency funds, building funds, equipment, land acquisition, matching funds, research, publications.
Limitations: Giving primarily in FL. No grants to individuals, or for deficit financing, scholarships, or fellowships; no loans except on an emergency basis.
Application information: Application form not required.
Initial approach: Letter
Board meeting date(s): Monthly except in June, July, and Aug.

Final notification: 2 to 4 months
Write: Benjamin K. Phipps, Secy.
Officer and Trustees:* Benjamin K. Phipps,* Secy.; Colin S. Phipps, John E. Phipps.
Number of staff: None.
EIN: 596159046

650
Jeffrey M. & Barbara Picower Foundation

2000 South Ocean Blvd.
Five Sloans Curve
Palm Beach 33480

Established in 1989 in FL.
Donor(s): Jeffrey M. Picower.
Foundation type: Independent
Financial data (yr. ended 12/31/90): Assets, $15,616,872 (M); gifts received, $12,015,000; expenditures, $193,294; qualifying distributions, $191,975, including $191,852 for 57 grants (high: $25,000; low: $100).
Fields of interest: Jewish welfare, higher education, secondary education, health, performing arts, dance.
Limitations: Giving primarily in New York, NY. No grants to individuals.
Application information: Contributes only to pre-selected organizations. Applications not accepted.
Trustees: Barbara Picower, Jeffrey M. Picower.
EIN: 136927043

651
Psychists, Inc.

100 Lakeshore Dr., No. L7
North Palm Beach 33408-3660

Incorporated in 1943 in NY.
Donor(s): Richard L. Parish,‡ American Flange & Manufacturing Co., Inc.
Foundation type: Independent
Financial data (yr. ended 08/31/90): Assets, $3,143,156 (M); expenditures, $117,541; qualifying distributions, $110,181, including $106,650 for 39 grants (high: $50,000; low: $350).
Fields of interest: Health services, health associations, hospitals, higher education, secondary education.
Limitations: No grants to individuals.
Application information: Contributes only to pre-selected organizations. Applications not accepted.
Trustees: David L. McKissock, Richard L. Parish, Jr., Richard L. Parish III.
EIN: 131869530

652
Pyramid Foundation, Inc.

P.O. Box 13225
Tampa 33681-3225

Established in 1950 in NY.
Foundation type: Independent
Financial data (yr. ended 12/31/90): Assets, $2,061,519 (M); expenditures, $203,178; qualifying distributions, $194,816, including $190,530 for 52 grants (high: $100,000; low: $40).

Purpose and activities: Giving primarily for Jewish welfare and temple support; support also for social services and hospitals.
Fields of interest: Jewish welfare, Jewish giving, social services, hospitals.
Limitations: Giving primarily in NY. No grants to individuals.
Application information: Contributes only to pre-selected organizations. Applications not accepted.
Officers: Donald B. Cohen, V.P.; Michael Cohen, Treas.
EIN: 136083997

653
Leslie C. Quick, Jr. & Regina A. Quick Charitable Trust Foundation

11475 Turtle Beach Rd.
North Palm Beach 33408

Established in 1988 in FL.
Donor(s): Leslie C. Quick, Jr.
Foundation type: Independent
Financial data (yr. ended 10/31/91): Assets, $506,114 (M); gifts received, $401,250; expenditures, $362,206; qualifying distributions, $359,102, including $359,090 for 23 grants (high: $200,000; low: $100).
Purpose and activities: Support primarily for higher education, Christian churches, a mission, and a diocese; grants also for hospitals and medical research.
Fields of interest: Higher education, religion—missionary programs, religion—Christian, hospitals, medical research.
Limitations: Giving primarily in FL and NY. No grants to individuals.
Application information: Contributes only to pre-selected organizations. Applications not accepted.
Trustees: Leslie C. Quick, Jr., Regina A. Quick.
EIN: 650083436

654
Nathan Ratner Charitable Foundation

c/o S. Kohn
1688 Meridian Ave., No. 1025
Miami Beach 33139

Established in 1990 in FL.
Donor(s): Nathan Ratner.‡
Foundation type: Independent
Financial data (yr. ended 12/31/91): Assets, $2,822,690 (M); expenditures, $51,188; qualifying distributions, $50,000, including $50,000 for 5 grants (high: $15,000; low: $5,000).
Fields of interest: Hospitals, homeless, community funds, Jewish welfare.
Types of support: Research, general purposes.
Limitations: Giving primarily in Miami, FL. No grants to individuals.
Application information: Contributes only to pre-selected organizations. Applications not accepted.
Officer and Directors:* Stanley Ratner,* Pres.; Ruth Miller, Albert B. Ratner.
EIN: 650175289

655
Paul E. & Klare N. Reinhold Foundation, Inc.

(Formerly Paul E. & Ida Klare Reinhold Foundation, Inc.)
225 Water St., Suite 2175
Jacksonville 32202   (904) 354-2359
Application address: P.O. Box 299, Jacksonville, FL 32201-0299

Established in 1954.
Donor(s): Paul E. Reinhold.‡
Foundation type: Independent
Financial data (yr. ended 12/31/91): Assets, $4,246,248 (M); expenditures, $259,511; qualifying distributions, $250,480, including $250,480 for 30 grants (high: $45,360; low: $220).
Fields of interest: Higher education, education, hospitals, health associations, social services, animal welfare, arts, religion, child welfare, youth.
Types of support: Annual campaigns, building funds, capital campaigns, operating budgets.
Limitations: Giving primarily in northeastern FL. No grants to individuals.
Publications: 990-PF.
Application information: Application form required.
   Initial approach: Letter
   Copies of proposal: 1
   Deadline(s): Apr. 30 and Sept. 30
   Board meeting date(s): May and Oct.
   Write: June R. Myers, Chair.
Officers and Trustees:* June R. Myers,* Chair. and Treas.; Leah B. Giebeig, Secy.; Thomas E. Camp III, Ralph H. Martin.
Number of staff: None.
EIN: 596140495

656
Rinker Companies Foundation, Inc. ▼

1501 Belvedere Rd.
West Palm Beach 33406   (407) 833-5555

Incorporated in 1957 in FL.
Donor(s): Rinker Materials Corp.
Foundation type: Company-sponsored
Financial data (yr. ended 03/31/91): Assets, $8,886,183 (M); expenditures, $1,375,724; qualifying distributions, $1,367,970, including $1,263,700 for 50 grants (high: $500,000; low: $500; average: $2,000-$100,000) and $104,270 for 70 grants to individuals (high: $3,000; low: $500).
Purpose and activities: Grants primarily for higher education, including scholarships to individuals who are FL residents with business or construction industry-related majors; support also for the United Way, Protestant churches, and hospitals and health organizations.
Fields of interest: Higher education, Protestant giving, community funds, hospitals, health.
Types of support: General purposes, student aid.
Limitations: Giving primarily in FL.
Application information: Application form required.
   Deadline(s): Apr. 1
   Write: Frank S. LaPlaca, Administrator
Officers and Trustees: D.V. Clarke, Pres.; W.J. Payne,* V.P.; C.P. Elkington,* Secy.; K.H. Watson,* Treas.; J.P. Garrity, J.F. Jackson, M.E. Rinker, Sr., Frank S. LaPlaca, Administrator.

EIN: 596139266

657
William Rosenberg Family Foundation
6586 Patio Ln.
Boca Raton 33433   (407) 392-2189

Established in 1986 in FL.
Donor(s): Ann Rosenberg, William Rosenberg.
Foundation type: Independent
Financial data (yr. ended 12/31/90): Assets, $2,670,245 (M); expenditures, $163,821; qualifying distributions, $160,250, including $160,250 for 17 grants (high: $100,000; low: $100).
Purpose and activities: Support primarily for a cancer research institute and an umbrella organization that "enables educational institutions to obtain certification in franchising as an academic program." Support also for child development and welfare, social services, Jewish giving, the environment, and health.
Fields of interest: Cancer, medical research, educational associations, child development, social services, Jewish giving, environment, health.
Types of support: Endowment funds, general purposes, professorships, research, seed money, building funds, fellowships, special projects.
Limitations: Giving primarily in the New England area and FL. No grants to individuals.
Application information: Contributes only to pre-selected organizations. Applications not accepted.
   Board meeting date(s): 1st week in Dec.
   Write: Ann Rosenberg, Dir.
Officers and Director:* William Rosenberg, Pres. and Treas.; Ann Rosenberg,* V.P. and Secy.
Number of staff: 1 part-time professional.
EIN: 592675613

658
William J. & Tina Rosenberg Foundation
2511 Ponce de Leon Blvd.
Coral Gables 33134   (305) 444-6121

Established in 1970 in FL.
Donor(s): Tina Rosenberg.‡
Foundation type: Independent
Financial data (yr. ended 04/30/91): Assets, $3,047,792 (M); expenditures, $170,958; qualifying distributions, $145,924, including $125,350 for 21 grants (high: $20,000; low: $250; average: $250-$20,000).
Purpose and activities: Primary areas of giving include education, the environment, social services, and cultural programs, including museums.
Fields of interest: Education, environment, social services, cultural programs, museums, general charitable giving, youth, child welfare, handicapped, delinquency, disadvantaged, homeless, welfare, human rights, family planning, hospices.
Types of support: Matching funds, seed money, general purposes, operating budgets, special projects.
Limitations: Giving primarily in Dade County, FL. No grants to individuals.
Publications: Application guidelines.
Application information: Application form not required.

Initial approach: Proposal
Copies of proposal: 1
Deadline(s): None
Board meeting date(s): Varies
Write: Jack G. Admire or Ruth S. Admire, Trustees
Trustees: Jack G. Admire, John G. Admire, Ruth S. Admire, John C. Sullivan, Jr., First Union Bank.
Number of staff: None.
EIN: 237088390

659
The Community Foundation of Sarasota County, Inc.
(Formerly The Sarasota County Community Foundation, Inc.)
P.O. Box 49587
Sarasota 34230-6587   (813) 955-3000
Office address: 1800 Second St., Suite 753, Sarasota, FL 34236

Incorporated in 1979 in FL.
Foundation type: Community
Financial data (yr. ended 12/31/91): Assets, $4,005,385 (M); gifts received, $1,550,947; expenditures, $241,316; qualifying distributions, $171,843, including $122,225 for 43 grants (high: $6,600; low: $100; average: $2,500) and $49,618 for 3 foundation-administered programs.
Fields of interest: Arts, cultural programs, health, education, environment, social services.
Types of support: Emergency funds, equipment, seed money, special projects, scholarship funds.
Limitations: Giving limited to Sarasota County, FL. No support for religious or fraternal organizations.
Publications: Informational brochure, annual report, application guidelines, grants list, newsletter, program policy statement.
Application information: Contact Exec. Dir. concerning grant proposals. Application form required.
   Initial approach: Proposal
   Copies of proposal: 1
   Board meeting date(s): Jan., Mar., May, July, Sept., and Nov.
   Write: Stewart W. Stearns, Exec. Dir.
Officers and Directors:* David Steves,* Pres.; Carolyn Fitzpatrick, V.P.; Jerome A. Jannopoulo,* V.P.; Kay E. Glasser, Secy.; Ralph E. Jaret,* Treas.; Stewart W. Stearns, Exec. Dir.; Dee Anderson, Gregory M. Colby, Mrs. R.G. Donovan, Mrs. Michael Gompertz, Kent Stottlemyer, Judith Voigt, and 31 additional directors.
Number of staff: 1 full-time professional; 1 full-time support.
EIN: 591956886

660
Schultz Foundation, Inc.
c/o Schultz Bldg.
P.O. Box 1200
Jacksonville 32201   (904) 354-3603
Application address: 50 North Laura St., Suite 2725, Jacksonville, FL 32202

Established in 1964 in FL.
Donor(s): Mae W. Schultz,‡ Geneive S. Ayers,‡ Frederick H. Schultz, Nancy R. Schultz.
Foundation type: Independent

Financial data (yr. ended 12/31/90): Assets, $2,455,093 (M); expenditures, $146,597; qualifying distributions, $123,822, including $122,222 for 110 grants (high: $10,025; low: $20).
Purpose and activities: Support primarily for community funds; cultural organizations, including the fine arts, music, and dance; social services, including programs for youth and child welfare, drug abuse, and AIDS; educational institutions; and wildlife and the environment.
Fields of interest: Community funds, cultural programs, performing arts, social services, child welfare, AIDS, education, adult education, environment, religion—Christian.
Types of support: General purposes.
Limitations: Giving primarily in Jacksonville, FL, and GA. No grants to individuals.
Publications: Annual report.
Application information: Application form not required.
   Initial approach: Letter; no telephone calls
   Deadline(s): None
   Write: Clifford G. Schultz II, Pres.
Officers and Trustees:* Clifford G. Schultz II,* Pres.; John F. Reilly, Secy.-Treas.; Catherine Kelly, Frederick H. Schultz, Jr., John R. Schultz, Nancy R. Schultz.
Number of staff: None.
EIN: 591055869

661
Setzer Family Foundation, Inc.
P.O. Box 3035, Station F
Jacksonville 32206-0035

Established in 1986.
Donor(s): Sidney Setzer.
Foundation type: Independent
Financial data (yr. ended 06/30/91): Assets, $1,860,487 (L); gifts received, $300,000; expenditures, $228,962; qualifying distributions, $204,600, including $204,600 for 5 grants (high: $93,600; low: $1,000).
Fields of interest: Jewish giving, hospitals.
Limitations: Giving primarily in Jacksonville, FL. No grants to individuals.
Application information: Contributes only to pre-selected organizations. Applications not accepted.
Trustees: Debra Setzer, Leonard R. Setzer, Alan S. Trager.
EIN: 592685979

662
Sidney, Milton and Leoma Simon Foundation
2025 N.W. 29th Rd.
Boca Raton 33431

Established in 1964.
Donor(s): Milton Simon.‡
Foundation type: Independent
Financial data (yr. ended 05/31/91): Assets, $11,166,216 (M); expenditures, $670,715; qualifying distributions, $509,489, including $445,000 for 65 grants (high: $12,000; low: $2,500).
Fields of interest: Handicapped, performing arts, medical research, hospitals, health associations, Jewish welfare.

Types of support: Research.
Limitations: Giving primarily in NY.
Application information:
Initial approach: Letter or proposal
Deadline(s): None
Write: Joseph C. Warner, Trustee
Trustees: Joseph C. Warner, Meryl Warner, Alan Wechsler.
EIN: 136175218

663
Roy M. Speer Foundation
1803 U.S. Hwy. 19
Holiday 34691-5536

Established in 1986 in FL.
Foundation type: Independent
Financial data (yr. ended 06/30/91): Assets, $2,006,083 (M); expenditures, $81,126; qualifying distributions, $41,105, including $37,000 for 3 grants (high: $25,000; low: $2,000) and $3,000 for 1 grant to an individual.
Fields of interest: Higher education, hospitals, recreation.
Limitations: Giving primarily in FL and VA.
Application information:
Initial approach: Letter
Deadline(s): None
Write: Richard W. Baker, Trustee
Trustee: Richard W. Baker.
EIN: 592785945

664
The George B. Storer Foundation, Inc. ▼
P.O. Box 1207
Islamorada 33036   (305) 852-3323

Incorporated in 1955 in FL.
Foundation type: Independent
Financial data (yr. ended 12/31/90): Assets, $51,161,141 (M); expenditures, $2,818,121; qualifying distributions, $2,413,866, including $2,400,000 for 90 grants (high: $150,000; low: $1,000; average: $10,000-$100,000).
Purpose and activities: Grants for higher education, social services, particularly for the blind, youth organizations, conservation, hospitals, and cultural programs.
Fields of interest: Higher education, conservation, hospitals, social services, youth, handicapped, cultural programs.
Types of support: Research, general purposes, building funds, matching funds, endowment funds.
Limitations: Giving primarily in FL. No grants for scholarships or fellowships; no loans.
Application information:
Initial approach: Letter and proposal
Copies of proposal: 1
Deadline(s): Nov. 30
Board meeting date(s): Dec.
Write: Peter Storer, Pres.
Officers and Directors: Peter Storer,* Pres. and Treas.; William Michaels,* V.P.; James P. Storer, Secy.
EIN: 596136392
Recent health grants:
664-1 Cleveland Clinic Foundation, Cleveland, OH, $100,000. 1990.
664-2 Cleveland Sight Center, Cleveland, OH, $99,000. 1990.

664-3 Heather Hill, Chardon, OH, $75,000. 1990.
664-4 Lahey Clinic Foundation, Burlington, MA, $25,000. 1990.
664-5 Marian Medical Center, Santa Maria, CA, $10,000. 1990.
664-6 Miami Childrens Hospital Foundation, Miami, FL, $10,000. 1990.
664-7 Miami Heart Institute, Miami Beach, FL, $100,000. For unrestricted fund. 1990.
664-8 Miami Project to Cure Paralysis, Miami, FL, $30,000. 1990.
664-9 University of Miami, Miami, FL, $10,000. For Jackson Memorial Burn Center. 1990.

665
Carl S. Swisher Foundation, Inc.
P.O. Box 14790
Jacksonville 32238-1790   (904) 389-8320

Incorporated in 1949 in FL.
Donor(s): Carl S. Swisher.‡
Foundation type: Independent
Financial data (yr. ended 12/31/91): Assets, $6,793,092 (M); expenditures, $512,307; qualifying distributions, $493,489, including $484,500 for grants.
Purpose and activities: Support for higher education; grants also for youth agencies, hospitals, and social services.
Fields of interest: Higher education, youth, hospitals, social services.
Types of support: General purposes, matching funds, scholarship funds.
Limitations: Giving primarily in the Jacksonville, FL, area. No grants to individuals; no loans.
Application information:
Initial approach: Letter or proposal
Copies of proposal: 1
Deadline(s): None
Board meeting date(s): Usually quarterly
Write: E.A. Middlebrooks, Jr., Secy.-Treas.
Officers and Trustees:* George S. Coulter,* Pres.; Kenneth G. Anderson,* V.P.; Harold W. Smith,* V.P.; E.A. Middlebrooks, Jr.,* Secy.-Treas.
Number of staff: 1 part-time professional.
EIN: 590998262

666
The Community Foundation of Greater Tampa, Inc.
315 East Madison, Suite 600
Tampa 33602-9889   (813) 221-1776

Established in 1990 in FL.
Foundation type: Community
Financial data (yr. ended 06/30/92): Assets, $2,754,123 (M); gifts received, $648,863; expenditures, $407,829; qualifying distributions, $233,934, including $233,934 for 54 grants (high: $30,400; low: $100; average: $500-$5,000).
Purpose and activities: Primary areas of interest include the arts, child welfare, elementary and higher education, and homelessness.
Fields of interest: Welfare, education, elementary education, higher education, health services, medical research, arts, fine arts, performing arts, religion, child welfare, youth, environment, historic preservation, civic affairs, public affairs,

aged, community development, housing, homeless.
Types of support: Seed money, continuing support, endowment funds.
Limitations: Giving primarily in the Hillsborough County, FL, area. No grants to individuals, or for operating costs of established programs.
Publications: Annual report, informational brochure, newsletter.
Application information: Application form not required.
Board meeting date(s): Jan., May, and Oct.
Write: George J. Baxter, Pres.
Officers and Trustees:* H. Doyle Harvill,* Chair.; Gay Culverhouse,* Vice-Chair.; George J. Baxter,* Pres.; James Ferman, Jr.,* Secy.; Jerry Dingle,* Treas.; G. Robert Blanchard, Grants Committee Chair.; John A. Brabson, Jr., Development Committee Chair.; James H. Shimberg, Fund Acceptance Committee Chair.; John M. Tapley, Advisory Committee Chair.; W. Scott Trundle, Public Information Committee Chair.; and 24 additional trustees.
Number of staff: 2 full-time professional; 1 full-time support; 1 part-time support.
EIN: 593001853

667
Jack Taylor Family Foundation, Inc.
1111 Kane Concourse, Suite 619
Bay Harbor Islands 33154

Established in 1968.
Donor(s): Taylor Development Corp., Jack Taylor, Mitchell Taylor, and other members of the Taylor family.
Foundation type: Independent
Financial data (yr. ended 12/31/91): Assets, $11,340,713 (M); gifts received, $300,250; expenditures, $569,082; qualifying distributions, $544,880, including $544,880 for 30 grants (high: $200,000; low: $250).
Fields of interest: Hospitals, health, higher education, Jewish giving, social services.
Limitations: No grants to individuals.
Application information: Contributes only to pre-selected organizations. Applications not accepted.
Officers and Directors:* Mitchell Taylor,* Pres. and Treas.; Ilene B. Eefting,* V.P. and Secy.; Norman A. Arkin, Victor D. Dembrow, M.D., Saul S. Silverman, Jack Taylor.
EIN: 596205187

668
TECO Energy Corporate Contributions Program
(Formerly Tampa Electric Company Contributions Program)
Corporate Communications
P.O. Box 111
Tampa 33601   (813) 228-4111

Financial data (yr. ended 12/31/90): Total giving, $1,000,000 for grants.
Purpose and activities: Support for health and human services, arts and culture, civic, community, and education.
Fields of interest: Arts, business education, child development, higher education, community development, community funds, disadvantaged,

cultural programs, museums, music, handicapped, health, housing, fine arts, education, medical research, performing arts, youth, women, drug abuse, elementary education, environment, homeless, hunger, civic affairs, education—minorities, leadership development, minorities, education—early childhood.
Types of support: Annual campaigns, capital campaigns, operating budgets, matching funds.
Limitations: Giving limited to Hillsborough, FL; generally no support for national organizations unless local community is affected.
Application information: Application form required.
  Initial approach: Mail to Contribs. Admin. at headquarters
  Copies of proposal: 1
  Deadline(s): Sept.
  Board meeting date(s): As needed; generally once a month
  Final notification: Within 90-120 days
  Write: Julius Hobbs, Dir., Corp. Rels.
Number of staff: 2 part-time professional.

669
Harold & Patricia Toppel Foundation
21439 Linwood Ct.
Boca Raton 33433   (305) 977-2510

Established in 1970.
Foundation type: Independent
Financial data (yr. ended 12/31/90): Assets, $621,481 (M); expenditures, $245,104; qualifying distributions, $242,280, including $241,128 for 28 grants (high: $125,000; low: $50).
Fields of interest: Hospitals, cultural programs, higher education.
Limitations: Giving primarily in FL.
Application information: Application form not required.
  Initial approach: Letter
  Deadline(s): None
  Write: Harold Toppel, Pres.
Officers: Harold Toppel, Pres.; Patricia Toppel, Secy.
EIN: 237050394

670
United States Sugar Corporation Charitable Trust
c/o United States Sugar Corp.
P.O. Drawer 1207
Clewiston 33440   (813) 983-8121

Trust established in 1952 in FL.
Donor(s): United States Sugar Corp.
Foundation type: Company-sponsored
Financial data (yr. ended 10/31/91): Assets, $1,976,535 (M); expenditures, $404,979; qualifying distributions, $377,671, including $377,671 for 75 grants (high: $41,437; low: $200).
Purpose and activities: Giving for private higher education, community improvement, social service agencies, and hospitals.
Fields of interest: Higher education, hospitals, community development, social services.
Limitations: Giving primarily in FL. No grants to individuals, or for scholarships or fellowships; no loans.

Application information:
  Initial approach: Proposal
  Deadline(s): None
  Write: Atwood Dunwody, Trustee
Trustees: Fleming A. Barbour, M.D., John B. Boy, Atwood Dunwody.
EIN: 596142825

671
The Wahlstrom Foundation, Inc.
2855 Ocean Dr., Suite D-4
Vero Beach 32963   (407) 231-0373
Mailing address: P.O. Box 3276, Vero Beach, FL 32964

Incorporated in 1956 in CT.
Donor(s): Magnus Wahlstrom.‡
Foundation type: Independent
Financial data (yr. ended 12/31/91): Assets, $5,562,163 (M); expenditures, $319,268; qualifying distributions, $268,785, including $242,850 for 27 grants (high: $101,900; low: $50).
Fields of interest: Handicapped, higher education, hospitals, youth, religion, arts, humanities, disadvantaged, civic affairs.
Types of support: Continuing support, seed money, building funds, equipment, research, special projects, matching funds, capital campaigns, endowment funds.
Limitations: Giving primarily in Indian River County, FL. No grants to individuals.
Publications: Annual report (including application guidelines), application guidelines.
Application information: Application form required.
  Initial approach: Letter and proposal
  Copies of proposal: 1
  Deadline(s): Feb. and Sept.
  Board meeting date(s): June and Nov.
  Final notification: Within 6 weeks
  Write: Eleonora W. McCabe, Pres.
Officers and Directors:* Eleonora W. McCabe,* Pres.; Lois J. Hughes,* V.P.; Bruce R. Johnson,* V.P.; Charles B. Kaufman III,* Secy.; Jim D. Machen,* Treas.; Donna J. Lockhart, Agnes S. Wahlstrom.
Number of staff: 1 part-time support.
EIN: 066053378

672
The I. Waldbaum Family Foundation, Inc.
16519 Ironwood Dr.
Delray Beach 33445

Incorporated in 1961 in NY.
Donor(s): Bernice Waldbaum, Ira Waldbaum, Waldbaum, Inc.
Foundation type: Independent
Financial data (yr. ended 12/31/90): Assets, $8,568,263 (M); expenditures, $444,442; qualifying distributions, $383,902, including $377,417 for 69 grants (high: $150,000; low: $13).
Purpose and activities: Giving primarily to Jewish organizations, including welfare funds, religious schools, and temple support, and to cultural programs and hospitals.
Fields of interest: Jewish giving, Jewish welfare, cultural programs, hospitals, religious schools.

Limitations: Giving primarily in the New York, NY, metropolitan area.
Application information:
  Initial approach: Proposal
  Write: Lawrence J. Waldman
Officers: Ira Waldbaum, Pres.; Bernice Waldbaum, Treas.
Directors: Randie Malinsky, Julia Waldbaum.
EIN: 136145916

673
The Walter Foundation
(Formerly Jim Walter Corporation Foundation)
1500 North Dale Mabry Hwy.
P.O. Box 31601
Tampa 33631-3601   (813) 871-4168

Established in 1966 in FL.
Donor(s): Jim Walter Corp., and subsidiaries.
Foundation type: Company-sponsored
Financial data (yr. ended 08/31/91): Assets, $8,198,470 (M); gifts received, $375,725; expenditures, $545,065; qualifying distributions, $512,775, including $507,975 for 86 grants (high: $200,000; low: $50).
Fields of interest: Community funds, higher education, youth, social services, hospitals, arts.
Limitations: Giving primarily in FL.
Application information: Application form not required.
  Deadline(s): None
  Write: W.K. Baker, Trustee
Trustees: W.K. Baker, James W. Walter, Robert A. Walter.
EIN: 596205802

674
Watson Clinic Foundation, Inc.
1600 Lakeland Hills Blvd.
Lakeland 33805

Established in 1986 in FL.
Donor(s): William F. McKee, Jean Tanous, Intermedics, Watson Clinic, SciMed, Medtronic, Inc.
Foundation type: Operating
Financial data (yr. ended 07/31/91): Assets, $1,651,240 (M); gifts received, $239,033; expenditures, $461,805; qualifying distributions, $461,805, including $5,709 for 4 grants (high: $3,000; low: $100), $5,000 for 7 grants to individuals (high: $1,000; low: $500) and $309,950 for 2 foundation-administered programs.
Purpose and activities: A private operating foundation; awards scholarships by nomination to third-year medical students and provides cardiac pacemakers through an international cooperative project to indigent persons in the Caribbean Basin and the Gulf of Mexico perimeter countries, including El Salvador; recent recipients have also included nationals of China, the Philippines, and India.
Fields of interest: Medical education, heart disease, Latin America, Caribbean, Asia, China, Mexico, Philippines.
Types of support: Student aid, in-kind gifts.
Limitations: Giving in Latin America, the Caribbean, and Asia.
Application information: Awards by nomination only for third-year medical students attending the

Univ. of FL College of Medicine or Duke Univ. School of Medicine. Completion of application form required for cardiac pacemaker program.
Deadline(s): Sept. for medical student award nominations
Officers and Directors:* John P. Collins, M.D.,* Chair.; Angelo P. Spoto, Jr., M.D.,* Pres.; Henry D. McIntosh, M.D.,* V.P.; Glen A. Barden, M.D., Robert H. Chapman, M.D.
EIN: 591100876

675
Joseph Weintraub Family Foundation, Inc.
(Formerly Weintraub-Landfield Charity Foundation, Inc.)
200 S.E. First St., Suite 901
Miami 33131

Established in 1949 in FL.
Donor(s): Joseph Weintraub.
Foundation type: Independent
Financial data (yr. ended 10/31/90): Assets, $3,604,020 (M); expenditures, $244,199; qualifying distributions, $225,150, including $225,150 for 17 grants (high: $121,300; low: $50).
Purpose and activities: Support primarily for a university; some support also for social services and health associations and hospitals, including cancer research.
Fields of interest: Higher education, social services, health associations, hospitals, cancer.
Limitations: Giving primarily in FL. No grants to individuals.
Application information: Application form not required.
Initial approach: Letter
Deadline(s): None
Write: Michael Weintraub, Pres.
Officers: Michael Weintraub, Pres.; Hortense Weintraub, Treas.
EIN: 590975815

676
Lillian S. Wells Foundation, Inc.
600 Sagamore Rd.
Fort Lauderdale 33301
Application address: P.O. Box 14338, Fort Lauderdale, FL 33302; Tel.: (305) 462-8639

Donor(s): Barbara W. Van Fleet; Preston A. Wells, Jr.
Foundation type: Independent
Financial data (yr. ended 12/31/91): Assets, $7,016,660 (M); expenditures, $299,804; qualifying distributions, $293,023, including $293,000 for 4 grants (high: $200,000; low: $3,000).
Purpose and activities: Giving primarily for higher education; support also for medical research.
Fields of interest: Higher education, medical research.
Types of support: Endowment funds, research, scholarship funds, general purposes.
Limitations: Giving limited to Chicago, IL, Fort Lauderdale, FL, and Garden County, NE.
Application information: Application form not required.
Deadline(s): None
Write: Barbara Van Fleet, Pres.

Officers: Barbara W. Van Fleet, Pres.; Preston A. Wells, Jr., V.P.; Mary B. Moulding, Secy.; Joseph E. Malecek, Treas.
EIN: 237433827

677
Dr. Herbert A. Wertheim Foundation, Inc.
4470 S.W. 74th Ave.
Miami 33155   (305) 264-4465

Established in 1977 in FL.
Donor(s): Herbert A. Wertheim.
Foundation type: Independent
Financial data (yr. ended 09/30/90): Assets, $3,432,679 (M); expenditures, $212,445; qualifying distributions, $212,159, including $212,159 for grants (high: $100,000).
Fields of interest: Fine arts, cultural programs, medical research, general charitable giving.
Types of support: Research.
Limitations: Giving primarily in Miami, FL, and Vail, Co. No grants to individuals.
Application information:
Initial approach: Letter
Deadline(s): None
Write: Dr. Herbert A. Wertheim, Pres.
Officers: Herbert A. Wertheim, Pres.; Nicole J. Wertheim, Secy.
EIN: 591778605

678
Whitehall Foundation, Inc. ▼
251 Royal Palm Way, Suite 211
Palm Beach 33480   (407) 655-4474
FAX: (407) 659-4978

Incorporated in 1937 in NJ.
Donor(s): George M. Moffett,‡ and others.
Foundation type: Independent
Financial data (yr. ended 09/30/91): Assets, $53,556,033 (M); expenditures, $2,818,252; qualifying distributions, $2,552,471, including $2,330,519 for 156 grants (high: $250,000; low: $100; average: $1,100-$30,000) and $106,950 for 41 grants to individuals (high: $10,000; low: $600; average: $500-$5,000).
Purpose and activities: Support for scholarly research in the life sciences, with emphasis on behavioral neuroscience and invertebrate neurophysiology; innovative and imaginative projects preferred. Research grants are paid to sponsoring institutions, rather than directly to individuals. Grants-in-aid are paid to assistant and/or senior professors; research grants are available to Ph.D.s with established labs. Employee-related scholarships are awarded only through CPC International.
Fields of interest: Biological sciences, biology.
Types of support: Research, seed money, technical assistance, special projects, equipment, publications, employee-related scholarships.
Limitations: No support for investigators who already have, or expect to receive, substantial support from other quarters. No grants for the purchase of major items of permanent equipment; travel, unless to unique field areas essential to the research; salary support; living expenses while working at home; travel to conferences or for consultation; or secretarial services.
Publications: Informational brochure (including application guidelines), grants list.

Application information: Applicant must have Ph.D. before applying or assistant professor status at institution. Application form required.
Initial approach: Letter
Copies of proposal: 2
Deadline(s): Deadline date will be assigned when issuing application; no longer any set voting sessions, but there will be no fewer than 3 per year for each program
Board meeting date(s): 3 grant review sessions per year
Final notification: 4 months
Write: Laurel T. Baker, Secy.
Officers and Trustees:* George M. Moffett II,* Pres. and Treas.; J. Wright Rumbough, Jr.,* V.P.; Laurel T. Baker,* Secy.; Warren S. Adams II, Kenneth S. Beall, Jr., Helen M. Brooks, Michael Dawes, Peter G. Neff.
Number of staff: 2 part-time professional.
EIN: 135637595
Recent health grants:
678-1 Mount Sinai School of Medicine, NYC, NY, $40,800. For research project, Behavioral Role of Neuromodulation: A Simple System Approach. 1991.
678-2 New Jersey Medical School, Newark, NJ, $42,210. For research project, Neuroanatomical and Neurochemical Basis of Circadian Rhythms. 1991.
678-3 Rockefeller University, NYC, NY, $40,000. For research project, Steroid Hormone Effects on Spinal Circuitry Involved in Reproductive Behavior and Somatosensory Processing. 1991.
678-4 Rockefeller University, NYC, NY, $39,324. For research project, Hormonal Effects on Hippocampal Plasticity and Behavior. 1991.
678-5 Rockefeller University, NYC, NY, $34,000. For research project, Identifying Genes that Regulate Neuroplasticity in Canaries. 1991.
678-6 Rockefeller University, NYC, NY, $33,000. For Neuropsychology of Birdsong. 1991.

679
Winn-Dixie Stores Foundation ▼
5050 Edgewood Court
Jacksonville 32254-3699   (904) 783-5000
Application address: P.O. Box B, Jacksonville, FL 32203-0297

Incorporated in 1943 in FL.
Donor(s): Winn-Dixie Stores, Inc.
Foundation type: Company-sponsored
Financial data (yr. ended 12/31/91): Assets, $1,963,486 (M); expenditures, $1,987,567; qualifying distributions, $1,982,472, including $687,847 for 452 grants (high: $60,043; low: $15; average: $100-$5,000) and $1,294,266 for employee matching gifts.
Purpose and activities: Functions solely as a conduit through which Winn-Dixie Stores, Inc., in its thirteen-state trade area, makes contributions to local and national welfare agencies, including community funds, youth agencies, educational institutions, scholarship programs, and hospitals.
Fields of interest: Hospitals, higher education, community funds, youth, social services, civic affairs.
Types of support: Annual campaigns, building funds, equipment, matching funds, employee matching gifts, research, special projects, conferences and seminars, continuing support, scholarship funds.

Limitations: Giving primarily in the southern states, in areas of company operations. No grants to individuals.
Publications: Annual report (including application guidelines).
Application information: Application form not required.
　Initial approach: Letter
　Deadline(s): None
　Board meeting date(s): As required
　Final notification: 30 days
　Write: L. H. May, Pres.
Officers and Directors:* L.H. May, Pres.; A. Dano Davis,* V.P.; James Kufeldt, V.P.; C.H. McKellar, V.P.; W.E. Ripley, Jr., Secy.; D.H. Bragin,* Treas.
Number of staff: None.
EIN: 590995428

680
Winter Park Community Trust Fund
c/o Barnett Banks Trust Co., N.A.
P.O. Box 1000
Winter Park 32790

Trust established in 1951 in FL.
Foundation type: Community
Financial data (yr. ended 06/30/91): Assets, $2,295,814 (M); expenditures, $131,667; qualifying distributions, $114,049, including $93,679 for 42 grants (high: $20,097; low: $34) and $14,800 for 12 grants to individuals (high: $1,950; low: $400).
Purpose and activities: As 90 percent of the fund's income is pre-designated and only 10 percent is for discretionary giving, grantmaking is limited. Emphasis is on health, education, social services, and scholarships for residents of Orange and Seminole counties, FL.
Fields of interest: Health, education, social services.
Types of support: Continuing support, student aid, general purposes.
Limitations: Giving limited to Orange and Seminole counties, FL. No grants for building or endowment funds, or matching gifts; no loans.
Application information: Application form required.
　Initial approach: Letter
　Copies of proposal: 1
　Deadline(s): June 30 and Dec. 31
　Board meeting date(s): Last Thursday of Jan. and July

Final notification: 1 week
Trustee: Barnett Banks Trust Co., N.A.
Number of staff: None.
EIN: 596126473

681
The Wolfson Family Foundation, Inc.
P.O. Box 4
Jacksonville 32201　　　　(904) 731-7942

Incorporated in 1951 in FL.
Donor(s): Louis E. Wolfson, Sam W. Wolfson,‡ Saul Wolfson, Florence M. Wolfson,‡ Cecil Wolfson.
Foundation type: Independent
Financial data (yr. ended 09/30/91): Assets, $4,380,440 (M); gifts received, $200; expenditures, $184,820; qualifying distributions, $173,100, including $119,850 for 33 grants (high: $75,000; low: $100).
Fields of interest: Higher education, hospitals, education—building funds, hospitals—building funds, Jewish welfare, community funds, child welfare.
Types of support: Building funds, equipment.
Limitations: Giving primarily in FL. No grants to individuals.
Application information: Contributes only to pre-selected organizations. Applications not accepted.
Officers and Trustees:* Cecil Wolfson,* Chair.; M.C. Tomberlin,* Secy.; Robert O. Johnson, Treas.; Joe I. Degen, Sylvia W. Degen, Edith W. Edwards, Morris D. Edwards, Rabbi Sidney M. Lefkowitz, Gary L. Wolfson, Nathan Wolfson, Stephen P. Wolfson.
Number of staff: 5 part-time support.
EIN: 590995431

682
Rubin and Gladys Wollowick Foundation, Inc.
c/o Trust Co. of the South
25 West Flagler St., 4th Fl.
Miami 33130
Application address: 407 Lincoln Rd., Miami Beach, FL 33139; Tel.: (305) 534-6171

Established in 1984 in FL.
Donor(s): Gladys Wollowick.‡
Foundation type: Independent

Financial data (yr. ended 01/31/91): Assets, $8,352,294 (M); gifts received, $1,030,850; expenditures, $764,437; qualifying distributions, $580,100, including $580,100 for grants (high: $140,000).
Fields of interest: Jewish giving, Jewish welfare, Israel, hospitals, medical research, ophthalmology, education, general charitable giving.
Types of support: General purposes.
Limitations: Giving primarily in Miami, FL.
Application information:
　Initial approach: Letter
　Deadline(s): None
　Write: Edward Levinson, V.P.
Officers: Isidore Wollowick,* Pres. and Secy.; Edward Levinson, V.P. and Treas.
Directors: Nat Levy, Richard Lowe, Sandra Lowe, Rhoda Samuels, Robert Tesher, Burton Wollowick, Herbert Wollowick, Janet Amy Wollowick, Patricia Wollowick.
Number of staff: None.
EIN: 592469452

683
Yablick Charities, Inc.
c/o Jefferson National Bank of Miami
301-41st St.
Miami Beach 33140

Incorporated in 1960 in NJ.
Donor(s): Herman Yablick.‡
Foundation type: Independent
Financial data (yr. ended 12/31/90): Assets, $2,218,586 (M); expenditures, $197,924; qualifying distributions, $140,575, including $102,415 for 92 grants (high: $16,550; low: $25).
Purpose and activities: Grants largely for hospitals, Jewish organizations, and community development; some giving also for cultural programs.
Fields of interest: Hospitals, Jewish giving, community development, cultural programs.
Limitations: Giving primarily in FL and Israel.
Application information:
　Initial approach: Letter
　Deadline(s): Sept. 30
　Write: Jerrold F. Goodman, Pres.
Officers: Jerrold F. Goodman, Pres.; Ruth Cohen, V.P.; Jane Goodman, V.P.
EIN: 591411171

GEORGIA

684
Anncox Foundation, Inc.
c/o Dow Lohnes & Albertson
One Ravina Dr., Suite 1300
Atlanta 30346
Application address: 426 West Paces Ferry Rd.,
Atlanta, GA 30305

Incorporated in 1960 in GA.
Donor(s): Anne Cox Chambers.
Foundation type: Independent
Financial data (yr. ended 12/31/91): Assets,
$20,997 (M); gifts received, $361,821;
expenditures, $347,364; qualifying distributions,
$347,364, including $347,364 for 27 grants
(high: $100,000; low: $75).
Fields of interest: Higher education, museums,
cultural programs, wildlife, conservation, medical
research, health.
Limitations: Giving primarily in GA and the
greater metropolitan New York, NY, area. No
grants to individuals.
Application information:
Initial approach: Letter
Deadline(s): None
Write: Anne C. Chambers, Pres.
Officers and Directors:* Anne Cox Chambers,*
Pres. and Treas.; James Cox Chambers,* V.P. and
Secy.
EIN: 586033966

685
Arnold Fund
c/o Alston & Bird, One Atlantic Ctr.
1201 West Peachtree St.
Atlanta 30309-3424   (404) 881-7540

Established in 1952 in GA.
Donor(s): Florence Arnold,‡ Robert O. Arnold.‡
Foundation type: Independent
Financial data (yr. ended 12/31/90): Assets,
$3,166,503 (M); expenditures, $227,093;
qualifying distributions, $215,800, including
$215,800 for 20 grants (high: $48,300; low:
$1,000).
Fields of interest: Education, higher education,
music, performing arts, medical sciences, libraries.
Limitations: Giving primarily in Covington, GA.
No grants to individuals.
Application information:
Initial approach: Letter
Deadline(s): None
Board meeting date(s): Spring and fall
Write: Arthur Howell, Exec. Dir.
Officer: Arthur Howell, Exec. Dir.
Trustees: Robert Fowler III, David Newman,
Frank Turner.
Number of staff: None.
EIN: 586032079

686
Metropolitan Atlanta Community Foundation, Inc. ▼
The Hurt Bldg., Suite 449
Atlanta 30303   (404) 688-5525

Incorporated in 1977 as successor to
Metropolitan Foundation of Atlanta established in
1951 in GA by bank resolution and declaration of
trust.
Foundation type: Community
Financial data (yr. ended 06/30/91): Assets,
$91,211,040 (M); gifts received, $6,515,066;
expenditures, $10,792,918; qualifying
distributions, $9,452,894, including $9,452,894
for 490 grants (high: $1,077,243; low: $25;
average: $1,000-$20,000).
Purpose and activities: Organized for the
permanent administration of funds placed in trust
by various donors for charitable purposes. Grants,
unless designated by the donor, are confined to
the metropolitan area of Atlanta, with emphasis
on social services, arts and culture, education,
health, and civic purposes.
Fields of interest: Education, arts, cultural
programs, social services, housing, civic affairs,
health, AIDS, homeless.
Types of support: Seed money, emergency funds,
building funds, equipment, land acquisition,
technical assistance, program-related investments,
special projects, publications, capital campaigns,
matching funds, renovation projects.
Limitations: Giving limited to the metropolitan
area of Atlanta, GA, and surrounding regions. No
support for religious organizations (except
through donor-advised funds). No grants to
individuals, or for endowment funds, continuing
support, annual campaigns, deficit financing,
research, films, conferences, scholarships (except
for George & Pearl Strickland Scholarship Fund
which is limited to Atlanta University Center
schools), or fellowships; generally no grants for
operating budgets.
Publications: Annual report, program policy
statement, application guidelines, newsletter,
informational brochure.
Application information: Application form
required.
Initial approach: Letter or telephone
Copies of proposal: 1
Deadline(s): Mar. 15, July 15, and Nov. 15
Board meeting date(s): May, Sept., and Jan.
Final notification: 6 weeks
Write: Winsome Hawkins, Prog. Officer
Officers and Directors:* L.L. Gellerstedt, Jr.,*
Pres.; Alicia Philipp, Exec. Dir.; Juanita Baranco,
William A. Clement, Jr., Cecil D. Conlee, Hon.
Clarence Cooper, Marie Dodd, Susie Elson,
Edward Gould, George Johnson, D. Lurton
Massee, Jr., William McClatchey, M.D., Mebane
M. Pritchett, Raymond D. Riddle, Betty Siegel,
Don Speaks, Judith G. Taylor, Sue Wieland.
Trustees: Bank South, N.A., First American Bank,
The First National Bank of Atlanta, NationsBank,
Suntrust, Inc.
Number of staff: 5 full-time professional; 3
full-time support; 1 part-time support.
EIN: 581344646
Recent health grants:
686-1 American Cancer Society, Atlanta, GA,
$16,683. 1991.
686-2 Atlanta Speech School, Atlanta, GA,
$15,032. 1991.
686-3 Crohns and Colitis Foundation of America,
Atlanta, GA, $10,000. 1991.
686-4 Georgia Health Decisions, Atlanta, GA,
$48,373. 1991.
686-5 Georgia Nurses Foundation, Atlanta, GA,
$10,000. 1991.
686-6 National Foundation for Ileitis and Colitis,
Atlanta, GA, $11,000. 1991.
686-7 Outreach, Atlanta, GA, $12,500. 1991.
686-8 Piedmont Hospital Foundation, Atlanta,
GA, $73,106. 1991.
686-9 Scottish Rite Childrens Medical Center,
Atlanta, GA, $25,762. 1991.
686-10 Shepherd Center for Treatment of Spinal
Injuries, Atlanta, GA, $17,920. 1991.

687
Atlanta Foundation
c/o Wachovia Bank of Georgia, N.A.
191 Peachtree St., Suite 1503
Atlanta 30303   (404) 332-6677

Established in 1921 in GA by bank resolution and
declaration of trust.
Foundation type: Independent
Financial data (yr. ended 12/31/91): Assets,
$6,877,409 (M); expenditures, $380,492;
qualifying distributions, $445,865, including
$328,500 for 64 grants (high: $25,000; low:
$1,000).
Purpose and activities: Assistance to charitable
and educational institutions for promoting
education and improving local living conditions.
Primary areas of interest include education,
cultural programs, housing, and other general
charitable activities.
Fields of interest: Community funds, hospitals,
education, higher education, family services,
welfare, housing, youth, cultural programs,
performing arts, general charitable giving.
Types of support: General purposes, seed money,
emergency funds, building funds, equipment,
land acquisition, renovation projects, special
projects.
Limitations: Giving limited to Fulton and DeKalb
counties, GA. No grants to individuals, or for
scholarships or fellowships; no loans.
Publications: Application guidelines.
Application information: Application form not
required.
Initial approach: Letter
Copies of proposal: 1
Deadline(s): Dec. 1
Board meeting date(s): Jan.
Final notification: 1 week
Write: Ms. Ann Morris
Distribution Committee: McChesney H. Jeffries,
Chair.; Thomas E. Boland, Kathleen Clement,
Edward C. Harris, D. Raymond Riddle.
Trustee: Wachovia Bank of Georgia, N.A.
Number of staff: None.
EIN: 586026879

688
Bradley-Turner Foundation ▼
P.O. Box 140
Columbus 31902   (404) 571-6040

Incorporated in 1943 in GA as W.C. and Sarah H.
Bradley Foundation; in 1982 absorbed the D.A.
and Elizabeth Turner Foundation, Inc., also of GA.

Donor(s): W.C. Bradley,‡ D.A. Turner,‡ Elizabeth B. Turner.‡
Foundation type: Independent
Financial data (yr. ended 12/31/90): Assets, $66,367,463 (M); gifts received, $243,098; expenditures, $3,866,466; qualifying distributions, $3,703,456, including $3,703,456 for 68 grants (high: $575,000; low: $400; average: $1,000-$50,000).
Purpose and activities: Giving primarily for higher education, religious associations, a community fund, youth and social service agencies; support also for cultural and health-related programs.
Fields of interest: Higher education, education, youth, social services, cultural programs, health, religion.
Limitations: Giving primarily in GA, with emphasis on Columbus. No grants to individuals.
Application information: Application form not required.
   Initial approach: Letter
   Copies of proposal: 2
   Deadline(s): None
   Board meeting date(s): Quarterly
   Final notification: Varies
   Write: R. Neal Gregory, Exec. Secy.
Officers and Trustees:* Stephen T. Butler,* Chair.; Lovick P. Corn,* Vice-Chair.; R. Neal Gregory,* Exec. Secy.; William B. Turner,* Treas.; Clarence C. Butler, M.D., Sarah T. Butler, Elizabeth T. Corn, Elizabeth C. Ogie, Sue T. Turner, William B. Turner, Jr.
Number of staff: None.
EIN: 586032142
Recent health grants:
688-1 Bradley Center, Columbus, GA, $575,000. 1990.
688-2 Columbus Medical Center Foundation, Columbus, GA, $50,000. 1990.
688-3 Family Counseling Center, Columbus, GA, $20,000. 1990.
688-4 Saint Francis Hospital, Columbus, GA, $25,000. 1990.

689
Thomas C. Burke Foundation
182 Riley Ave., Suite B
Macon 31204   (912) 477-1931

Established in 1965 in GA.
Donor(s): Thomas C. Burke.‡
Foundation type: Independent
Financial data (yr. ended 09/30/90): Assets, $3,772,612 (M); gifts received, $16,550; expenditures, $283,739; qualifying distributions, $269,557, including $182,130 for grants.
Purpose and activities: "Dedicated to the needs of cancer patients in the Macon-Bibb County area." Assistance provided for medical services, including drugs, food supplement, supplies, equipment, oxygen, and limited sitter assistance.
Fields of interest: Cancer.
Limitations: Giving limited to Macon-Bibb County, GA, and/or surrounding counties for patients under the care of Macon physicians.
Application information: Must be referred by doctor. Application form not required.
   Initial approach: By telephone or in person
   Deadline(s): None
   Board meeting date(s): Bimonthly
   Write: Carolyn P. Griggers

Advisory Board Members: Mrs. John D. Comer, Donald Rhame, M.D., J. Benham Stewart, M.D.
Trustee: NationsBank.
Number of staff: 1 full-time professional; 1 part-time professional; 1 part-time support.
EIN: 586047627

690
Callaway Foundation, Inc. ▼
209 Broome St.
P.O. Box 790
La Grange 30241   (706) 884-7348

Incorporated in 1943 in GA.
Donor(s): Textile Benefit Assn., Callaway Mills, Callaway Institute, Inc.
Foundation type: Independent
Financial data (yr. ended 09/30/91): Assets, $156,059,446 (M); expenditures, $7,047,242; qualifying distributions, $6,379,265, including $6,374,765 for 98 grants (high: $1,205,000; low: $200; average: $1,000-$100,000) and $4,500 for 1 in-kind gift.
Purpose and activities: Giving for elementary, higher, and secondary education, including libraries and buildings and equipment; health and hospitals; community funds; care for the aged; community development; historic preservation; and church support.
Fields of interest: Education, elementary education, higher education, secondary education, educational associations, libraries, health, hospitals, community funds, aged, community development, historic preservation, religion—Christian, general charitable giving.
Types of support: Continuing support, annual campaigns, general purposes, building funds, equipment, land acquisition, matching funds.
Limitations: Giving primarily in GA, with emphasis on the city of LaGrange and Troup County. No grants to individuals, or for endowment funds, operating expenses, deficit financing, scholarships, or fellowships; no loans.
Publications: Annual report (including application guidelines).
Application information: Application form not required.
   Initial approach: Letter
   Copies of proposal: 1
   Deadline(s): End of month preceding board meetings
   Board meeting date(s): Jan., Apr., July, and Oct.
   Final notification: 2 months
   Write: J.T. Gresham, Pres.
Officers and Trustees:* J.T. Gresham, Pres., General Mgr., and Treas.; Charles D. Hudson,* V.P.; C.L. Pitts, Secy.; Mark Clayton Callaway, Ida Callaway Hudson, James R. Lewis, Fred L. Turner.
Number of staff: 5 shared staff
EIN: 580566147
Recent health grants:
690-1 American Cancer Society, Georgia Division, Atlanta, GA, $20,000. For computerized processing/retrieval system. 1990.
690-2 Bradley Center, Columbus, GA, $120,000. For Clergy Resource Center Project. 1990.
690-3 Crawford Center for Therapeutic Horsemanship, Atlanta, GA, $15,000. For operations. 1990.

690-4 Easter Seal Society of Georgia, Atlanta, GA, $150,000. For Camp Dream construction project. 1990.
690-5 Enoch Callaway Cancer Clinic, LaGrange, GA, $502,000. For CT Scanner Project. 1990.
690-6 LaGrange, City of, LaGrange, GA, $132,800. For Illegal Drug-Use Reduction Program. 1990.
690-7 Metro Atlanta Firefighters Burn Foundation, Atlanta, GA, $10,000. For fire safety project. 1990.
690-8 Self-Help Harbor, LaGrange, GA, $130,000. For acquisition of property. 1990.
690-9 West Georgia Medical Center, LaGrange, GA, $1,350,000. For building renovation project. 1990.

691
Fuller E. Callaway Foundation
209 Broome St.
P.O. Box 790
La Grange 30241   (706) 884-7348

Incorporated in 1917 in GA.
Donor(s): Fuller E. Callaway, Sr.,‡ and family.
Foundation type: Independent
Financial data (yr. ended 12/31/91): Assets, $32,331,958 (M); expenditures, $1,201,424; qualifying distributions, $1,251,446, including $900,316 for 29 grants (high: $455,000; low: $250; average: $250-$10,000), $264,430 for 74 grants to individuals (high: $10,000; low: $1,000; average: $1,000-$3,300) and $86,700 for 1 in-kind gift.
Purpose and activities: Grants to religious, charitable, and educational organizations; scholarships for worthy students; modest gifts toward operating expenses of community welfare agencies, including youth programs, and health organizations.
Fields of interest: Religion, higher education, education, social services, youth, health.
Types of support: Operating budgets, annual campaigns, building funds, equipment, matching funds, general purposes, student aid.
Limitations: Giving primarily in the city of LaGrange and Troup County, GA. No grants for endowment funds; no loans.
Application information: Application form required for scholarship program. Application form not required.
   Initial approach: Letter
   Copies of proposal: 1
   Deadline(s): End of the month preceding board meeting for grants; Feb. 15 for college scholarships; June 30 for law school scholarships
   Board meeting date(s): Jan., Apr., July, and Oct.
   Final notification: 60 to 90 days
   Write: J.T. Gresham, General Mgr.
Officers: J.T. Gresham, Pres., General Mgr., and Treas.; Charles D. Hudson, V.P.; C.L. Pitts, Secy.
Trustees: Mark Clayton Callaway, Ida Callaway Hudson, James R. Lewis, Fred L. Turner.
Number of staff: None.
EIN: 580566148

692
Camp Younts Foundation ▼
c/o Trust Co. Bank
P.O. Box 4655
Atlanta 30302-4655

Established in 1955 in GA.
Donor(s): Charles Younts,‡ Willie Camp Younts.‡
Foundation type: Independent
Financial data (yr. ended 12/31/90): Assets,
$26,720,840 (M); gifts received, $35,403;
expenditures, $1,616,086; qualifying
distributions, $1,546,882, including $1,469,500
for 219 grants (high: $50,000; low: $250;
average: $1,000-$25,000).
Purpose and activities: Giving primarily for
education, with emphasis on higher and
secondary educational institutions (including
colleges and universities), and social services;
support also for youth, Protestant giving, and
health associations and hospitals.
Fields of interest: Secondary education, higher
education, education, social services, youth,
Protestant giving, health associations, hospitals.
Limitations: Giving primarily in VA, GA, NC, and
FL. No grants to individuals.
Application information:
Initial approach: Letter
Deadline(s): None
Trustees: Harold S. Atkinson, John M. Camp, Jr.,
Phillip L. Humann, Paul Camp Marks, Harry W.
Walker.
Trustee Bank: Trust Co. Bank.
EIN: 586026001

693
J. Bulow Campbell Foundation ▼
1401 Trust Co. Tower
25 Park Place, N.E.
Atlanta 30303   (404) 658-9066

Trust established in 1940 in GA.
Donor(s): J. Bulow Campbell.‡
Foundation type: Independent
Financial data (yr. ended 12/31/91): Assets,
$169,130,829 (M); expenditures, $8,101,400;
qualifying distributions, $7,740,909, including
$7,476,000 for 31 grants (high: $1,000,000; low:
$50,000; average: $100,000-$300,000).
Purpose and activities: Broad purposes "including
but not limited to privately-supported education,
human welfare, youth development, the arts,
church-related agencies and agencies of the
Presbyterian Church (not congregations) operating
within the foundation's giving area. Concern for
improving quality of spiritual and intellectual life,
with priority to private agencies undertaking work
of regional importance, preferably projects of
permanent nature or for capital funds. Gives
anonymously and requests no publicity."
Fields of interest: Education, higher education,
secondary education, family services, youth, child
development, arts, Protestant giving,
religion—Christian.
Types of support: Building funds, endowment
funds, land acquisition, matching funds,
renovation projects, capital campaigns.
Limitations: Giving primarily in GA; very limited
giving in AL, FL, NC, SC, and TN. No support for
local church congregations. No grants to
individuals, or for research, scholarships,

fellowships, operating budgets, or recurring items;
no loans.
Publications: Informational brochure (including
application guidelines).
Application information: Submit 1-page
proposal, 3 copies of tax information. Application
form not required.
Initial approach: Letter or telephone
Copies of proposal: 1
Deadline(s): Jan. 15, Apr. 15, July 15, and Oct.
15
Board meeting date(s): Jan., Apr., July, and Oct.
Final notification: Within 1 week after board
meets
Write: John W. Stephenson, Exec. Dir.
Officers and Trustees:* William A. Parker, Jr.,*
Chair.; Richard W. Courts II,* Vice-Chair.; John W.
Stephenson, Exec. Dir.; John B. Ellis, Mark P.
Pentecost, Jr., M.D., Lawrence B. Teague, Robert
W. Woodson.
Number of staff: 1 full-time professional; 1
full-time support.
EIN: 580566149
Recent health grants:
693-1 Emory University, Center for Genetics and
Molecular Medicine, Atlanta, GA, $1,000,000.
For equipment. 1991.
693-2 Henrietta Egleston Hospital for Children,
Atlanta, GA, $1,000,000. For renovation and
expansion project. 1991.

694
The Dave and Bunny Center Foundation, Inc.
3400 Peachtree Rd., N.E., Suite 1701
Atlanta 30326

Established in 1968.
Donor(s): Dave Center.
Foundation type: Independent
Financial data (yr. ended 12/31/90): Assets,
$757,709 (M); gifts received, $14,600;
expenditures, $272,059; qualifying distributions,
$271,004, including $269,806 for 36 grants
(high: $202,275; low: $50).
Fields of interest: Jewish giving, medical research,
general charitable giving, hospitals, Jewish
welfare.
Limitations: Giving primarily in Atlanta, GA. No
grants to individuals.
Application information: Contributes only to
pre-selected organizations. Applications not
accepted.
Officers: Dave Center, Pres.; Arthur Long, V.P.;
Charles Center, Secy.-Treas.
EIN: 586076183

695
Ty Cobb Educational Fund
P.O. Box 725
Forest Park 30051

Trust established in 1953 in GA.
Donor(s): Tyrus R. Cobb.‡
Foundation type: Independent
Financial data (yr. ended 12/31/90): Assets,
$6,512,347 (M); expenditures, $352,429;
qualifying distributions, $316,281, including
$276,205 for 98 grants to individuals (high:
$19,500; low: $333).

Purpose and activities: Scholarship aid for needy
and deserving youth who have completed one
year in an accredited institution of higher
learning, payable to the institution; graduate
school scholarships available to law, medical, or
dental students.
Fields of interest: Medical education, legal
education, dentistry.
Types of support: Student aid.
Limitations: Giving limited to GA residents. No
grants for building or endowment funds,
operating budgets, special projects, or matching
gifts; no loans.
Publications: Application guidelines.
Application information: Application form
required.
Initial approach: Letter
Copies of proposal: 1
Deadline(s): June 15
Board meeting date(s): July and Jan.
Write: Rosie Atkins, Secy.
Officer: Rosie Atkins, Secy.
Scholarship Board: Harry S. Downs, Chair.;
Merritt E. Hoag, S. Walter Martin, Walter Murphy,
Darrell C. Roberts.
Trustee: Trust Co. Bank.
EIN: 586026003

696
The Coca-Cola Foundation, Inc. ▼
One Coca-Cola Plaza, N.W.
Atlanta 30313   (404) 676-2680
Application address: P.O. Drawer 1734, Atlanta,
GA 30301

Incorporated in 1984 in GA.
Donor(s): Coca-Cola Co.
Foundation type: Company-sponsored
Financial data (yr. ended 12/31/90): Assets,
$15,195,405 (M); gifts received, $7,190,097;
expenditures, $6,191,215; qualifying
distributions, $6,139,735, including $6,139,735
for 164 grants (high: $200,000; low: $2,500;
average: $10,000-$100,000).
Purpose and activities: Support primarily for
education.
Fields of interest: Education, elementary
education, education—minorities, minorities,
secondary education, literacy, higher education.
Types of support: Annual campaigns, scholarship
funds, fellowships, internships, endowment funds,
capital campaigns, special projects.
Limitations: No support for religious
organizations or religious endeavors, veterans'
organizations, hospitals, or local chapters of
national organizations. No grants to individuals,
or for workshops, travel costs, conferences or
seminars, building or endowment funds,
operating budgets, charitable dinners, fundraising
events and related advertising publications,
equipment, or land acquisition; generally, no
loans.
Publications: Annual report, application
guidelines, informational brochure (including
application guidelines).
Application information: Application form not
required.
Initial approach: 2-page letter of request
Copies of proposal: 1
Deadline(s): None
Board meeting date(s): Feb., May, July, and Nov.

Final notification: Notice of approval or rejection usually within four months
Write: Donald R. Greene, Pres.
Officers and Directors:* Carl Ware,* Chair.; Donald R. Greene,* Pres.; Joseph W. Jones, Secy.; Jack L. Stahl, Treas.; William W. Allison, Michelle Beale, Lawrence Cowart, R. Bruce Kirkman.
Number of staff: 6 full-time professional; 5 full-time support.
EIN: 581574705
Recent health grants:
696-1 American Friends of the Hebrew University, Beverly Hills, CA, $25,000. For D. R. Bloom Center for Pharmacy. 1990.
696-2 Arthritis Foundation, Atlanta, GA, $50,000. For Kids On The Block Program. 1990.
696-3 Baylor College of Medicine, Houston, TX, $50,000. For Houston Elementary Science Alliance. 1990.
696-4 Boy Scouts of America, Irving, TX, $50,000. For Drugs: A Deadly Game Program. 1990.
696-5 Bradley Center, Columbus, GA, $100,000. For in-service training for teachers. 1990.
696-6 Center for Rehabilitation Technology, Atlanta, GA, $20,000. For general support. 1990.
696-7 Harvard University, Department of Preventive Medicine, Boston, MA, $10,000. For technical grant. 1990.
696-8 Harvard University, Medical School, Boston, MA, $10,000. For technical grant. 1990.
696-9 Howard Schools, Atlanta, GA, $25,000. For education building. 1990.
696-10 International Life Sciences Institute-Nutrition Foundation, DC, $100,000. For Research Foundation and Research Institute. 1990.
696-11 International Life Sciences Institute-Nutrition Foundation, DC, $100,000. For annual support. 1990.
696-12 Juvenile Diabetes Foundation International, NYC, NY, $83,334. For professional and educational brochures. 1990.
696-13 Meharry Medical College, Nashville, TN, $25,000. For Title Three Program. 1990.
696-14 Morehouse School of Medicine, Atlanta, GA, $50,000. For clinical sciences faculty. 1990.
696-15 Morehouse School of Medicine, Atlanta, GA, $25,000. For land acquisition and site development project. 1990.
696-16 National Jewish Center for Immunology and Respiratory Medicine, Denver, CO, $14,000. For technical grant. 1990.
696-17 University of Iowa, Department of Pediatric Endocrinology, Iowa City, IA, $33,000. For technical grant. 1990.
696-18 University of Medicine and Dentistry of New Jersey, Occupational Health Science Institute, Newark, NJ, $10,000. For technical grant. 1990.

697

Community Enterprises, Inc.
115 East Main St.
Thomaston 30286   (404) 647-7131

Incorporated in 1944 in GA.

Donor(s): Julian T. Hightower, Thomaston Cotton Mills.
Foundation type: Independent
Financial data (yr. ended 06/30/91): Assets, $7,575,570 (M); expenditures, $399,982; qualifying distributions, $382,157, including $382,157 for 43 grants (high: $54,047; low: $300).
Fields of interest: Higher education, secondary education, community development, civic affairs, hospitals, Protestant giving.
Limitations: Giving primarily in Thomaston and Upson counties, GA.
Application information:
Initial approach: Letter or proposal
Deadline(s): Dec. 31
Write: William H. Hightower, Jr., Pres.
Officers and Trustees:* William H. Hightower, Jr.,* Pres.; George H. Hightower,* V.P.; Neil H. Hightower,* Secy.-Treas.
EIN: 586043415

698

Cox Enterprises Corporate Giving Program
1400 Lake Hearn Dr.
P.O. Box 105357
Atlanta 30348   (404) 843-5123

Purpose and activities: Supports education including private colleges, civic affairs, media and journalism programs, minority and youth programs, arts and culture, and social science and health programs. Also supports the United Way. Types of support include scholarships.
Fields of interest: Community funds, minorities, youth, higher education, education, civic affairs, arts, cultural programs, health.
Types of support: Scholarship funds, operating budgets.
Limitations: Giving primarily in the metropolitan Atlanta, GA, area.
Application information: Application form not required.
Initial approach: Written request with supporting information; send to headquarters
Copies of proposal: 1
Write: Lynda J. Stewart, Dir., Communs.

699

The Davis Foundation, Inc. ▼
One National Dr.
Atlanta 30336

Established in 1960.
Donor(s): Raleigh Linen Service, Inc., National Distributing Co., Inc., and subsidiaries, Truck Rental Co., Alfred M. Davis, ADP Rental Co., Servitex, Inc.
Foundation type: Independent
Financial data (yr. ended 07/31/90): Assets, $135,025 (M); gifts received, $1,294,100; expenditures, $1,249,872; qualifying distributions, $1,249,872, including $1,249,660 for 33 grants (high: $450,000; low: $50; average: $1,000-$50,000).
Purpose and activities: Grants primarily for Jewish welfare funds and temple support in the Atlanta area and for higher education; support also for cultural programs and health services.

Fields of interest: Jewish welfare, Jewish giving, higher education, cultural programs, hospitals, health services.
Limitations: Giving primarily in Atlanta, GA.
Application information:
Initial approach: Proposal
Deadline(s): None
Write: Alfred A. Davis, Pres.
Officers: Alfred A. Davis, Pres.; Jay M. Davis, V.P.
EIN: 586035088
Recent health grants:
699-1 Emory University, School of Medicine, Atlanta, GA, $450,000. 1990.

700

The James Glenwell and Clara May Dodson Foundation
c/o Trust Co. Bank, Trust Dept.
P.O. Box 4655
Atlanta 30302

Trust established in 1967 in GA.
Donor(s): Clara May Dodson.‡
Foundation type: Independent
Financial data (yr. ended 12/31/90): Assets, $2,622,710 (M); expenditures, $159,923; qualifying distributions, $140,683, including $131,890 for 16 grants (high: $22,890; low: $2,000).
Purpose and activities: Giving to benefit underprivileged children; grants largely for homes and hospitals, including medical research; support also for education.
Fields of interest: Child welfare, child development, disadvantaged, hospitals, health services, medical research, education.
Types of support: Building funds, capital campaigns, equipment, general purposes, special projects.
Limitations: Giving primarily in GA and SC. No grants to individuals.
Publications: Annual report.
Application information: Application form not required.
Initial approach: Typewritten letter
Copies of proposal: 1
Deadline(s): Oct. 1
Board meeting date(s): Nov.
Write: Cathy S. Nix, V.P., Trust Co. Bank
Officers: Robert F. Bryan, Mgr.; Constance G. Chapman, Mgr.; Clara May Godshall, Mgr.; Ellis Godshall, Mgr.; William Reynolds, Mgr.; Elenora Richardson, Mgr.; Edwin L. Sterne, Mgr.
Trustee: Trust Co. Bank.
EIN: 586074354

701

Robert and Polly Dunn Foundation, Inc.
c/o Trust Co. Bank
P.O. Box 4655
Atlanta 30302   (404) 588-7356

Established in 1986 in GA.
Foundation type: Independent
Financial data (yr. ended 12/31/90): Assets, $3,702,080 (M); expenditures, $235,382; qualifying distributions, $222,631, including $205,914 for 41 grants (high: $25,000; low: $500).
Fields of interest: Youth, child development, higher education, religion, health.

Types of support: Operating budgets, scholarship funds.
Limitations: Giving limited to the southeast, with emphasis of the metropolitan Atlanta, GA, area. No loans or program-related investments.
Application information:
  Initial approach: Letter
  Deadline(s): None
  Write: Brenda Rambeau
Officer and Trustees:* J.R. Perry,* Chair.; Richard B. Freeman, Preston Hays, Stanley B. Knapp, Karen C. Wilbanks, Trust Co. Bank.
EIN: 581671255

702
Nell Warren & William Simpson Elkin Memorial Foundation
c/o Trust Co. Bank
P.O. Box 4655
Atlanta 30302   (404) 588-8449

Established in 1979 in GA.
Donor(s): Josephine W. Asbury.‡
Foundation type: Independent
Financial data (yr. ended 09/30/91): Assets, $2,680,292 (M); gifts received, $15,000; expenditures, $160,817; qualifying distributions, $150,495, including $138,534 for 23 grants (high: $33,334; low: $1,000).
Fields of interest: Higher education, educational associations, cancer, religion, denominational giving.
Types of support: Scholarship funds, building funds.
Limitations: Giving primarily in GA, especially Atlanta, and FL, SC, NC, TN, KY, and AL.
Application information: Application form required.
  Initial approach: Letter and proposal
  Copies of proposal: 1
  Deadline(s): Aug. 15 and Feb. 15
  Board meeting date(s): Mar. and Sept.
  Write: Clare Ranney, Advisory Comm. Member
Advisory Committee: Edward P. Gould, Jesse C. Hall, Clare Ranney.
Trustee: Trust Co. Bank.
EIN: 581378819

703
The Florence C. and Harry L. English Memorial Fund
P.O. Box 4418, MC 041
Atlanta 30302   (404) 588-8246

Established in 1964 in GA.
Donor(s): Florence Cruft English.‡
Foundation type: Independent
Financial data (yr. ended 12/31/90): Assets, $8,299,168 (M); gifts received, $530,799; expenditures, $522,066; qualifying distributions, $470,019, including $470,019 for grants (average: $3,000-$5,000).
Purpose and activities: Grants only for education, health, general welfare, and culture, with emphasis on assisting the aged and chronically ill, the blind, and those persons generally designated as the "underprivileged."
Fields of interest: Disadvantaged, homeless, aged, handicapped, welfare, education, higher education, education—building funds, health, cultural programs, community development.

Types of support: Renovation projects, equipment, special projects, building funds.
Limitations: Giving limited to the metropolitan Atlanta, GA, area. No support for veterans' organizations or organizations which have not been operating without a deficit for at least a year. No grants to individuals; no loans.
Publications: Program policy statement, application guidelines.
Application information: Application form required.
  Initial approach: Telephone or letter
  Copies of proposal: 1
  Deadline(s): Mar. 1, June 1, Sept. 1, and Dec. 1
  Board meeting date(s): Jan., Apr., July, and Oct.
  Write: Victor A. Gregory, Secy.
Distribution Committee: Edward P. Gould, Chair.; Victor A. Gregory, Secy.; Jesse S. Hall, Robert Strickland.
Trustee: Trust Co. Bank.
Number of staff: 1 full-time professional; 2 part-time support.
EIN: 586045781

704
Equifax Foundation
c/o Equifax Inc.
1600 Peachtree St., N.W.
Atlanta 30309   (404) 885-8301
Mailing address: P.O. Box 4081, Atlanta, GA 30302

Trust established in 1978 in GA.
Donor(s): Equifax Inc.
Foundation type: Company-sponsored
Financial data (yr. ended 12/31/90): Assets, $1,144,370 (M); expenditures, $739,854; qualifying distributions, $739,854, including $699,714 for 206 grants (high: $290,000; low: $25; average: $25-$5,000) and $39,000 for 184 employee matching gifts.
Purpose and activities: Giving primarily for higher education, a community fund, and an arts alliance; support also for health and welfare organizations.
Fields of interest: Higher education, community funds, arts, health, welfare.
Types of support: Continuing support, annual campaigns, seed money, building funds, land acquisition, endowment funds, scholarship funds, special projects, research, renovation projects, capital campaigns, general purposes.
Limitations: Giving primarily in GA; increasing support for national organizations. No grants to individuals, or for deficit financing, fellowships, publications, matching gifts, or travel.
Publications: Informational brochure (including application guidelines).
Application information: Application form not required.
  Initial approach: Proposal
  Copies of proposal: 1
  Deadline(s): None
  Board meeting date(s): Quarterly
  Final notification: 60 days
  Write: Nancy Golonka Rozier, V.P., Corp. Public Affairs
Board Members: John A. Baker, C.B. Rogers, Jr., Nancy Rozier, Jeff V. White.
Number of staff: 2 full-time professional.
EIN: 581296807

705
Exposition Foundation, Inc.
520 East Paces Ferry Rd., N.E.
Atlanta 30305   (404) 233-6404

Incorporated in 1950 in GA.
Foundation type: Independent
Financial data (yr. ended 08/31/91): Assets, $3,256,058 (M); expenditures, $176,059; qualifying distributions, $156,600, including $156,600 for 42 grants (high: $20,000; low: $500).
Purpose and activities: Primary areas of interest include the fine arts and other cultural programs and education, including historic preservation, music, and higher and secondary education; support also for social services, housing, health, and AIDS research.
Fields of interest: Cultural programs, arts, fine arts, museums, historic preservation, music, education, higher education, secondary education, social services, housing, health, AIDS.
Types of support: Annual campaigns, building funds, capital campaigns, equipment, endowment funds, operating budgets, renovation projects, special projects, general purposes.
Limitations: Giving primarily in GA.
Publications: Annual report.
Application information: Application form not required.
  Copies of proposal: 1
  Board meeting date(s): Varies
  Write: Frank L. Rozelle, Jr., Secy.-Treas.
Officers and Trustees:* Frances F. Cocke,* Pres.; Jane C. Black,* V.P.; Frank L. Rozelle, Jr.,* Secy.-Treas.
Number of staff: None.
EIN: 586043273

706
Foundation for Advancement of Chiropractic Education
1001 Cambridge Sq., Suite D
Alpharetta 30201

Established in 1986 in GA.
Foundation type: Independent
Financial data (yr. ended 12/31/90): Assets, $8,425,965 (M); expenditures, $510,042; qualifying distributions, $370,133, including $355,000 for 4 grants (high: $250,000; low: $15,000).
Purpose and activities: Giving limited to chiropractic education and research.
Fields of interest: Medical education, medical research.
Types of support: Research.
Limitations: No grants to individuals.
Application information: Contributes only to pre-selected organizations. Applications not accepted.
Officer: William Harris, Pres.
EIN: 581422604

707
John and Mary Franklin Foundation, Inc.
c/o Bank South, N.A.
P.O. Box 4956
Atlanta 30302   (404) 529-4614

Incorporated in 1955 in GA.

Donor(s): John Franklin, Mary O. Franklin.‡
Foundation type: Independent
Financial data (yr. ended 12/31/90): Assets,
$17,452,355 (M); expenditures, $1,095,434;
qualifying distributions, $1,005,329, including
$952,400 for 119 grants (high: $85,000; low:
$50).
Fields of interest: Higher education, secondary
education, youth, hospitals, cultural programs.
Types of support: General purposes, scholarship
funds, building funds.
Limitations: Giving primarily in GA, with
emphasis on the metropolitan Atlanta area;
special types of grants awarded to institutions in
adjoining states. No grants to individuals.
Publications: Annual report.
Application information: Application form not
required.
  Initial approach: Letter
  Copies of proposal: 1
  Deadline(s): June and Nov.
  Board meeting date(s): Jan. and July, and as
    needed
  Final notification: Jan. and Dec.
  Write: Robert B. Rountree, Treas.
Officers and Trustees:* W. Kelly Mosely,* Chair.
and Exec. Comm. Member; Virlyn B. Moore, Jr.,*
Secy. and Exec. Comm. Member; Robert B.
Rountree,* Treas.; L. Edmund Rast,* Exec. Comm.
Member; George T. Duncan; John B. Ellis; Frank
M. Malone, Jr., Marilu H. McCarty, Alexander W.
Smith, Jr., William M. Suttles.
Number of staff: 1 part-time professional; 1
part-time support.
EIN: 586036131

708
Philip and Irene Toll Gage Foundation
c/o NationsBank
P.O. Box 4446
Atlanta 30302   (404) 607-4530

Established in 1985 in GA.
Donor(s): Betty G. Holland.
Foundation type: Independent
Financial data (yr. ended 11/30/91): Assets,
$4,501,161 (M); gifts received, $1,000;
expenditures, $265,682; qualifying distributions,
$247,478, including $229,467 for 54 grants
(high: $40,000; low: $100).
Purpose and activities: Support for education,
culture, including the arts and theater, and
hospitals and health services; grants also for
Protestant giving.
Fields of interest: Education, education—building
funds, cultural programs, theater, museums,
hospitals, health services, health, child welfare,
Protestant giving, community development.
Types of support: Annual campaigns, general
purposes, building funds.
Limitations: Giving primarily in Atlanta, GA. No
grants to individuals, or for endowment programs.
Publications: Application guidelines.
Application information: Application form not
required.
  Initial approach: Proposal
  Copies of proposal: 1
  Deadline(s): Submit proposals preferably in
    Aug. and Sept.; deadline Oct. 15
  Board meeting date(s): Nov. or Dec., annually
  Final notification: Within 1 week of annual
    meeting

Write: Larry B. Hooks, Pres., NationsBank
Officers: Betty G. Holland, Chair.; William J.
Holland, Vice-Chair.; Larry B. Hooks, Secy.
Trustee: NationsBank.
Number of staff: None.
EIN: 581727394

709
Georgia Health Foundation, Inc.
Four Executive Park Dr., Suite 2406
Atlanta 30329   (404) 636-2525

Established in 1985 in GA.
Donor(s): Georgia Medical Plan.
Foundation type: Independent
Financial data (yr. ended 12/31/90): Assets,
$6,124,984 (M); expenditures, $323,954;
qualifying distributions, $292,262, including
$259,174 for 14 grants (high: $30,000; low:
$4,000).
Fields of interest: Health, medical research,
medical education, health services, medical
sciences.
Types of support: General purposes, research,
scholarship funds, seed money, special projects.
Limitations: Giving primarily in GA.
Publications: Informational brochure (including
application guidelines).
Application information: Application form not
required.
  Initial approach: Proposal
  Copies of proposal: 6
  Deadline(s): Preferably before Aug. 1
  Board meeting date(s): 4th Monday of Feb.,
    May, Aug., and Dec.
  Final notification: Dec. 1
  Write: Louise Hewell, Secy.
Officers and Directors:* J. Rhodes Haverty,
M.D.,* Chair.; Robert Zwald,* Vice-Chair.; Louise
Hewell,* Secy.; Eugene E. Adams,* Treas.; John
Borek, Henry D. Cornelius, E.P. Coverdell,
Richard A. Elmer, M.D., Jaquelin Gotlieb, M.D.,
S. Jarvin Levison, John T. Maudlin, M.D., Frances
Posey.
Number of staff: 1 part-time professional.
EIN: 581352076
Recent health grants:
709-1 Alzheimers Disease and Related Disorders
  Association, Atlanta Chapter, Atlanta, GA,
  $40,000. To implement telephone help-line
  service for families of patients and for training
  and recruitment program to establish volunteer
  staff of counselors for families and caregivers.
  1991.
709-2 Downtown Atlanta Senior Services,
  Atlanta, GA, $10,000. For development and
  publication of training manual and materials
  for exercise and fitness program. 1991.
709-3 FCS Urban Ministries, Grant Park Family
  Health Center, Atlanta, GA, $20,000. For
  prenatal care program for low-income and
  poverty neighborhoods. 1991.
709-4 Georgia Lions Lighthouse Foundation,
  Atlanta, GA, $20,000. For vision care, eye
  surgery, prostheses and eye glasses to needy
  patients. 1991.
709-5 Georgia State University, Atlanta, GA,
  $18,927. For seminar on Adult Emotional
  Abuse for education and mental health
  professionals. 1991.

709-6 Hemophilia of Georgia, Atlanta, GA,
  $29,333. To revise, publish and distribute
  Hemophilia Handbook. 1991.
709-7 March of Dimes Birth Defects Foundation,
  Atlanta, GA, $50,000. For one-year research
  project to determine prevalence of cocaine in
  newborns in Georgia. 1991.
709-8 Morehouse School of Medicine,
  Department of Family Practice, Atlanta, GA,
  $19,739. For diagnostic and training
  equipment. 1991.
709-9 Our Lady of Perpetual Help Cancer
  Home, Atlanta, GA, $10,000. For general
  support. 1991.
709-10 Planned Parenthood Association of the
  Atlanta Area, Atlanta, GA, $28,000. For
  stipends for advanced training for two
  registered nurses and to replace medical
  equipment. 1991.

710
Georgia Power Company Corporate
Giving Program
333 Piedmont Ave., 20th Floor
Atlanta 30302   (404) 526-6784

Financial data (yr. ended 12/31/90): Total giving,
$1,414,175, including $1,360,000 for 1,052
grants (high: $758,967; low: $25; average:
$25-$758,967) and $54,175 for 330 employee
matching gifts.
Purpose and activities: Program areas of major
interest are: education, health and human
services, civic and community services, and arts
and culture. Following is a list of subjects that are
considered: conservation, dance, drug abuse,
education, museums, performing arts, fine arts,
race relations, wildlife, social services, family
services, historic preservation, literacy, medical
education and research, mental health, and
minorities.
Fields of interest: Aged, AIDS, business
education, child welfare, civic affairs, civil rights,
community funds, conservation, cultural
programs, disadvantaged, drug abuse, education,
education—early childhood, education—building
funds, education—minorities, educational
associations, educational research, elementary
education, family services, fine arts, handicapped,
health associations, health services, heart disease,
higher education, historic preservation, homeless,
hospices, hospitals, hospitals—building funds,
housing, humanities, human rights, hunger,
rehabilitation, intercultural relations, international
relief, journalism, international relief, Latin
America.
Types of support: Annual campaigns, conferences
and seminars, donated equipment, employee
matching gifts, operating budgets, seed money,
technical assistance, building funds, employee
volunteer services, loaned talent, professorships,
renovation projects, special projects, use of
facilities, capital campaigns, donated products,
continuing support, employee-related
scholarships, research, deficit financing,
emergency funds, endowment funds, general
purposes, scholarship funds.
Limitations: Giving primarily in the state of GA.
Publications: Corporate report.
Application information: Corporate Secretary's
office handles giving; grants are only for 501(c)(3)
organizations. Application form not required.

Initial approach: Letter to headquarters
Copies of proposal: 1
Deadline(s): None
Board meeting date(s): First week of each month
Final notification: After board review
Write: Judy Anderson, V.P. and Corp. Secy.
Administrator: Risa Hammonds, Coord., Investor Relations.
Number of staff: 2 part-time professional; 1 part-time support.

711
Georgia Power Foundation, Inc. ▼
333 Piedmont Ave., 20th Fl.
Atlanta 30308   (404) 526-6784

Established in 1986 in GA.
Donor(s): Georgia Power Co.
Foundation type: Company-sponsored
Financial data (yr. ended 12/31/91): Assets, $33,349,567 (M); expenditures, $2,744,776; qualifying distributions, $2,630,210, including $2,630,210 for 355 grants (high: $150,000; low: $200; average: $200-$150,000).
Purpose and activities: Primary areas of interest include social and family services, youth, civic affairs and community development, the arts, health, and education. Support also for the aged, AIDS, cancer, race relations, the homeless, rehabilitation, human rights, leadership development, legal services, libraries, medical research, museums, performing arts, theater, historic preservation, fine arts, and environmental conservation.
Fields of interest: Social services, family services, youth, women, handicapped, minorities, civic affairs, community development, arts, health, conservation, education.
Types of support: Annual campaigns, building funds, capital campaigns, conferences and seminars, endowment funds, equipment, operating budgets, renovation projects, research, scholarship funds, seed money, special projects, deficit financing.
Limitations: Giving primarily in GA. No support for private foundations. No grants to individuals.
Publications: Informational brochure (including application guidelines), 990-PF.
Application information: Application form not required.
Initial approach: Letter with proposal
Copies of proposal: 1
Deadline(s): None
Board meeting date(s): Every other month
Final notification: After board review
Write: Ms. Judy M. Anderson, Exec. Dir.
Officers and Directors:* Warren Y. Jobe,* Pres.; Judy M. Anderson,* Secy.-Treas. and Exec. Dir.; E.C. Barineau, Wayne T. Dahlke, James K. Davis, Carl L. Donaldson, Dwight H. Evans, Gene R. Hodges, Brian D. Spickard.
Number of staff: None.
EIN: 581709417

712
Georgia-Pacific Foundation, Inc. ▼
133 Peachtree St., N.E.
Atlanta 30303   (404) 521-5228

Incorporated in 1958 in OR.
Donor(s): Georgia-Pacific Corp., and subsidiaries.

Foundation type: Company-sponsored
Financial data (yr. ended 12/31/90): Assets, $87,361 (M); gifts received, $1,675,240; expenditures, $2,488,174; qualifying distributions, $2,487,316, including $1,327,255 for 320 grants (high: $184,000; low: $500; average: $1,000-$7,000) and $1,160,061 for 1,168 grants to individuals (high: $244,182; low: $417; average: $625-$1,250).
Purpose and activities: Giving for higher and other education, including employee-related scholarships to graduating seniors in areas of major company operations; support also for community funds, hospitals and health services, and social services and youth agencies.
Fields of interest: Higher education, education, community funds, hospitals, health services, youth, social services.
Types of support: Employee-related scholarships.
Limitations: Giving limited to areas of company operations, with some emphasis on the Atlanta, GA, area.
Application information:
Deadline(s): None
Board meeting date(s): As required
Write: W.I. Tamblyn, Pres. and Treas.
Officers and Trustees:* Harold L. Arlington,* Chair.; Wayne I. Tamblyn, Pres. and Treas.; Ronald P. Hogan, Exec. V.P.; Diane Durgin, Secy.; T. Marshall Hahn, Jr., Stephen K. Jackson, Robert A. Schumacher, James C. Van Meter.
Number of staff: 1 full-time support.
EIN: 936023726

713
GFF Educational Foundation, Inc.
P.O. Box 826
Norcross 30091   (404) 447-4488

Established in 1982 in GA.
Donor(s): Waffle House, Inc.
Foundation type: Independent
Financial data (yr. ended 05/31/90): Assets, $151,630 (M); gifts received, $250,000; expenditures, $243,196; qualifying distributions, $242,315, including $182,979 for 69 grants (high: $25,000; low: $30) and $59,336 for 22 grants to individuals (high: $7,704; low: $98).
Purpose and activities: Support for civic affairs and education, health and youth organizations; grants also as scholarship support to individuals.
Fields of interest: Civic affairs, education, health, youth.
Types of support: Student aid, grants to individuals.
Application information: Application form required for scholarships.
Deadline(s): None
Write: Roy Nelson, Secy.
Officers: Alice Johnson, Pres.; Don Balfour, V.P.; Roy Nelson, Secy.
EIN: 581477023

714
Lenora and Alfred Glancy Foundation, Inc.
One Atlantic Ctr., Suite 4200
1201 West Peachtree St.
Atlanta 30309-3424   (404) 881-7000

Incorporated in 1954 in GA.
Donor(s): Alfred R. Glancy, Sr.‡

Foundation type: Independent
Financial data (yr. ended 12/31/90): Assets, $5,830,320 (M); expenditures, $328,858; qualifying distributions, $272,903, including $270,000 for 47 grants (high: $30,000; low: $500; average: $1,000-$10,000).
Purpose and activities: Support for higher and secondary education; grants also for hospitals, medical research, cultural programs, and community funds.
Fields of interest: Higher education, secondary education, hospitals, medical research, cultural programs, community funds.
Types of support: Operating budgets, continuing support, annual campaigns, seed money, emergency funds, deficit financing, building funds, equipment, land acquisition, endowment funds, general purposes, capital campaigns, conferences and seminars, publications, renovation projects, research, special projects.
Limitations: Giving primarily in Atlanta, GA, and MI. No grants to individuals, or for scholarships or fellowships; no loans.
Publications: Application guidelines, 990-PF.
Application information: Application form not required.
Initial approach: Letter or proposal
Copies of proposal: 1
Board meeting date(s): Nov. or Dec.
Write: Benjamin T. White, Asst. Secy.
Officers and Directors:* Gerry Hull,* Chair.; Alfred R. Glancy III,* Vice-Chair.; Christopher Brandon,* Treas.
Number of staff: None.
EIN: 586041425

715
John H. and Wilhelmina D. Harland Charitable Foundation, Inc. ▼
Two Piedmont Ctr., Suite 106
Atlanta 30305   (404) 264-9912

Incorporated in 1972 in GA.
Donor(s): John H. Harland.‡
Foundation type: Independent
Financial data (yr. ended 12/31/91): Assets, $22,901,611 (M); gifts received, $35,000; expenditures, $1,097,670; qualifying distributions, $1,077,262, including $1,043,250 for 52 grants (high: $100,000; low: $750; average: $10,000-$25,000).
Purpose and activities: Support for youth agencies, child welfare, higher education, and community funds. Preference given to projects with little chance of gaining popular support, and which increase long-term effectiveness of the grantee.
Fields of interest: Youth, child welfare, child development, education, higher education, literacy, community funds, religion—Christian, religion, community development, arts, cultural programs, museums, music, health, health services, handicapped, homeless.
Types of support: Operating budgets, annual campaigns, building funds, equipment, endowment funds, professorships, scholarship funds, publications.
Limitations: Giving limited to GA, with emphasis on metropolitan Atlanta. No grants to individuals; no loans.
Publications: Annual report (including application guidelines).

Application information: Application form not required.

Initial approach: Letter
Copies of proposal: 1
Deadline(s): Mar. 1 and Sept. 1
Board meeting date(s): Apr. 1 and Oct. 1
Final notification: 3 to 4 weeks after board meeting
Write: John A. Conant, Secy.

Officers and Trustees:* Miriam Harland Conant,* Pres.; Margaret C. Dickson,* V.P. and Treas.; John A. Conant,* Secy.; James M. Sibley, Allison F. Williams.
Number of staff: 1 part-time professional; 1 part-time support.
EIN: 237225012
Recent health grants:

715-1 American Red Cross, Atlanta Region, Atlanta, GA, $25,000. For expansion of Blood Services Unit. 1990.

715-2 Atlanta Hospital Hospitality House, Atlanta, GA, $10,000. For endowment fund. 1990.

715-3 George West Mental Health Foundation, Atlanta, GA, $10,000. For Skyland Trail Residential Social Rehabilitation Program. 1990.

715-4 Hillside Specialty Psychiatric Hospital, Atlanta, GA, $50,000. For new 20-bed residential unit. 1990.

715-5 Howard Schools, Atlanta, GA, $50,000. For Phase II of Campaign to Grow. 1990.

715-6 Hub Counseling and Education Center, Atlanta, GA, $10,000. For new facility. 1990.

715-7 International Service Association for Health (INSA), Atlanta, GA, $35,000. To acquire and expand facility. 1990.

715-8 Northside Shepherd Center, Atlanta, GA, $15,000. For nurse-managed health care clinic. 1990.

715-9 Our Lady of Perpetual Help Cancer Home, Atlanta, GA, $10,000. For operating fund. 1990.

715-10 Sadie G. Mays Memorial Nursing Home, Atlanta, GA, $50,000. For capital improvements and equipment. 1990.

715-11 Saint Josephs Hospital Foundation, Atlanta, GA, $15,000. For Mercy Mobile Health Program which serves homeless. 1990.

715-12 Shepherd Center for Treatment of Spinal Injuries, Atlanta, GA, $35,000. For expansion program. 1990.

715-13 Village of Saint Joseph, Atlanta, GA, $25,000. For Focus on the Future Campaign. 1990.

716
Health 1st Foundation, Inc.
2070 South Park Place, N.W., Suite 330
Atlanta 30339   (404) 952-8375

Established in 1986 in GA.
Foundation type: Independent
Financial data (yr. ended 06/30/91): Assets, $4,534,835 (M); expenditures, $264,512; qualifying distributions, $194,957, including $185,000 for 1 grant.
Purpose and activities: Giving only to health care related activities.
Fields of interest: Medical education, hospitals, health, health associations.

Types of support: Continuing support, operating budgets.
Limitations: Giving limited to GA.
Application information: Application form required.

Initial approach: Letter
Copies of proposal: 3
Deadline(s): Apr. 1
Write: Joseph Barber, Exec. Dir.

Officer and Directors:* Delutha H. King, Jr., M.D.,* Chair.; Joseph Barber, Exec. Dir.; Benjamin A. Blackburn II, James Hindy, M. Gerald Hood, Mandy Schwartz, and 6 additional directors.
Number of staff: 1 part-time professional.
EIN: 581265915

717
John P. and Dorothy S. Illges Foundation, Inc.
945 Broadway
Columbus 31901
Application address: P.O. Box 1673, Columbus, GA 31902

Incorporated in 1947 in GA.
Donor(s): John P. Illges.‡
Foundation type: Independent
Financial data (yr. ended 09/30/91): Assets, $4,402,089 (M); expenditures, $212,841; qualifying distributions, $201,375, including $188,150 for 11 grants (high: $100,000; low: $150; average: $150-$100,000).
Purpose and activities: Primary areas of interest include education, the environment, civic affairs, and health.
Fields of interest: Education, libraries, social services, child welfare, welfare, civic affairs, museums, health, environment.
Types of support: Annual campaigns, building funds, capital campaigns, endowment funds, equipment, operating budgets, renovation projects, seed money, special projects.
Limitations: Giving primarily in the areas of west central and Atlanta, GA, and east central AL. No grants to individuals.
Application information: Application form not required.

Initial approach: Letter
Copies of proposal: 1
Deadline(s): Sept. 1
Board meeting date(s): Jan., May, and Sept.
Final notification: Following board meeting review
Write: John P. Illges III, Pres.

Officers and Directors:* John P. Illges III,* Pres.; Custis G. Illges,* V.P.; Mary S. Boyd, Secy.; Philip A. Badcock,* Treas.; Richard B. Illges, Susan I. Lanier, John W. Mayher, Jr.
Number of staff: 1 part-time professional.
EIN: 580691476

718
A. and M. L. Illges Memorial Foundation, Inc.
1224 Peacock Ave., Suite 103
Columbus 31902   (404) 323-5342

Incorporated in 1947 in GA.
Foundation type: Independent
Financial data (yr. ended 09/30/91): Assets, $3,965,770 (M); expenditures, $241,550;

qualifying distributions, $229,261, including $210,023 for grants.
Purpose and activities: Emphasis on higher education, including scholarship funds, hospitals, church support, and cultural programs.
Fields of interest: Higher education, hospitals, Protestant giving, cultural programs.
Types of support: Operating budgets, endowment funds, scholarship funds.
Limitations: Giving primarily in GA.
Application information: Application form not required.

Deadline(s): None
Write: J. Barnett Woodruff, V.P.

Officers and Directors:* Howell Hollis,* Pres. and Treas.; J. Barnett Woodruff,* V.P.; John P. Illges III,* Secy.; Arthur I. Chenoweth, B.M. Chenoweth, Jr., Martha H. Heinz, A. Illges, Jr.
EIN: 586033958

719
Ruth T. Jinks Foundation
P.O. Box 375
Colquitt 31737   (912) 758-5355

Established in 1955.
Donor(s): Members of the Jinks family.
Foundation type: Independent
Financial data (yr. ended 11/30/91): Assets, $12,485,978 (M); gifts received, $7,852,612; expenditures, $287,168; qualifying distributions, $281,809, including $280,355 for 35 grants (high: $61,100; low: $50).
Fields of interest: Religion—Christian, religion—missionary programs, social services, community development, urban development, rural development, cultural programs, higher education, educational associations, hospitals.
Types of support: Annual campaigns, building funds, matching funds, general purposes, special projects.
Limitations: Giving primarily in GA.
Application information: Applications not accepted.

Board meeting date(s): Annually
Write: G.C. Jinks, Jr., Pres.

Officers and Board:* G.C. Jinks, Jr.,* Pres. and Treas.; G.C. Jinks III,* V.P.; H.L. Jinks,* Secy.
Number of staff: None.
EIN: 586043856

720
The Ray M. and Mary Elizabeth Lee Foundation, Inc.
c/o NationsBank, Trust Dept.
P.O. Box 4446
Atlanta 30302-4899   (404) 607-4530

Incorporated in 1966 in GA.
Donor(s): Ray M. Lee,‡ Mary Elizabeth Lee.‡
Foundation type: Independent
Financial data (yr. ended 09/30/91): Assets, $10,035,012 (M); expenditures, $841,288; qualifying distributions, $467,275, including $429,000 for 67 grants (high: $35,000; low: $1,000; average: $6,000).
Fields of interest: Health services, hospitals, education, religion, arts, cultural programs, theater.
Types of support: Annual campaigns, building funds, capital campaigns, conferences and

seminars, consulting services, continuing support, deficit financing, emergency funds, equipment, exchange programs, fellowships, general purposes, internships, land acquisition, lectureships, matching funds, operating budgets, professorships, program-related investments, publications, renovation projects, research, seed money, special projects, technical assistance.
Limitations: Giving primarily in Atlanta, GA. No grants to individuals.
Publications: Application guidelines.
Application information: Application form not required.
  Initial approach: Proposal
  Copies of proposal: 1
  Deadline(s): Jan. 31, Apr. 30, July 31, and Oct. 31
  Board meeting date(s): Feb., May, Aug., and Nov.
  Final notification: Following board meeting
  Write: Larry B. Hooks, Admin. Mgr.
Officers and Trustees:* William B. Stark,* Pres. and Treas.; Donald D. Smith,* Secy.; Ronald W. Gann.
Number of staff: None.
EIN: 586049441

721
Blanche Lipscomb Foundation, Inc.
c/o NationsBank
P.O. Box 4446
Atlanta 30302-4446

Established in 1945 in GA.
Donor(s): William D. Ellis,‡ Southern Mills.
Foundation type: Independent
Financial data (yr. ended 12/31/91): Assets, $2,150,956 (M); gifts received, $124,030; expenditures, $115,346; qualifying distributions, $107,965, including $102,000 for 26 grants (high: $23,000; low: $1,000).
Fields of interest: Community funds, social services, literacy, higher education, arts, youth, hospitals.
Limitations: Giving limited to the metropolitan Atlanta, GA, area. No grants to individuals.
Application information:
  Initial approach: Letter
  Deadline(s): None
  Write: W. Douglas Ellis, Jr., Trustee
Trustees: William D. Ellis, Jr., Albert Nixon Parker, George D. Ray, Jr.
EIN: 586033155

722
Livingston Foundation, Inc.
55 Park Place, 5th Fl.
Atlanta 30303   (404) 577-5100

Incorporated in 1964 in GA.
Donor(s): Roy N. Livingston,‡ Mrs. Leslie Livingston Kellar,‡ Bess B. Livingston.‡
Foundation type: Independent
Financial data (yr. ended 09/30/91): Assets, $7,919,579 (M); expenditures, $624,005; qualifying distributions, $549,905, including $504,125 for 16 grants (high: $210,000; low: $750).
Fields of interest: Fine arts, arts, cultural programs, museums, historic preservation,

hospitals, medical research, community development, civic affairs, international studies.
Types of support: Operating budgets, continuing support, annual campaigns, building funds, conferences and seminars, lectureships.
Limitations: Giving primarily in the Atlanta, GA, area. No grants to individuals, or for endowment funds, scholarships, fellowships, or matching gifts; no loans.
Application information: Application form not required.
  Initial approach: Letter
  Copies of proposal: 1
  Deadline(s): None
  Board meeting date(s): Quarterly
  Final notification: 4 months
  Write: Milton W. Brannon, Pres.
Officers and Trustees:* Jonathan Golden,* Chair.; Milton Brannon,* Pres. and Treas.; C.E. Gregory III, Secy.; Ellis Arnall, Ben W. Brannon, George P. Schmidt.
Number of staff: 1 part-time support.
EIN: 586044858

723
Mattie H. Marshall Foundation
c/o Trust Co. Bank
P.O. Box 4655
Atlanta 30302-4655   (404) 588-8197

Established in 1963 in GA.
Foundation type: Independent
Financial data (yr. ended 12/31/90): Assets, $2,586,910 (M); expenditures, $127,879; qualifying distributions, $103,621, including $93,000 for 18 grants (high: $30,000; low: $1,000).
Purpose and activities: Giving primarily for higher education; support also for churches, hospitals, a clinic, a humane society, and a home for the aged.
Fields of interest: Higher education, religion—Christian, hospitals, health associations, animal welfare, aged.
Types of support: Operating budgets, annual campaigns, building funds, capital campaigns, endowment funds, general purposes, special projects.
Limitations: Giving limited to GA, especially Americus and southern GA.
Publications: Application guidelines.
Application information: Application form not required.
  Initial approach: Letter
  Copies of proposal: 1
  Deadline(s): None
  Board meeting date(s): Dec.
  Write: Mr. Kelly McCutchen, Trust Officer, Trust Co. Bank
Officer: Thomas O. Marshall, Chair. and Secy.
Director: Martha M. Dykes.
Number of staff: None.
EIN: 586042019

724
Harriet McDaniel Marshall Trust in Memory of Sanders McDaniel
c/o Trust Co. Bank
P.O. Box 4418, MC 041
Atlanta 30302   (404) 588-8246

Trust established in 1962 in GA.
Donor(s): Harriet McDaniel Marshall.‡
Foundation type: Independent
Financial data (yr. ended 12/30/91): Assets, $4,575,315 (M); expenditures, $249,037; qualifying distributions, $240,400, including $226,998 for 61 grants (high: $12,500; low: $500; average: $3,000-$5,000).
Purpose and activities: Giving primarily for higher education and building funds for educational institutions, health, and the handicapped; support also for welfare, including organizations assisting the disadvantaged, the homeless, and the elderly, community funds and development, and arts and culture.
Fields of interest: Education, higher education, education—building funds, health, handicapped, welfare, disadvantaged, homeless, aged, community development, cultural programs.
Types of support: Building funds, equipment, renovation projects, special projects.
Limitations: Giving primarily in the metropolitan Atlanta, GA, area. No grants to individuals, or for scholarships or fellowships; no loans.
Publications: Application guidelines, program policy statement.
Application information: Application form required.
  Initial approach: Letter
  Copies of proposal: 1
  Deadline(s): Mar. 1, June 1, Sept. 1, and Dec. 1
  Board meeting date(s): Jan., Apr., July, and Oct.
  Write: Victor A. Gregory, Secy.
Distribution Committee: Edward P. Gould, Chair.; Victor A. Gregory, Secy.; Jesse S. Hall, Robert Strickland.
Trustee: Trust Co. Bank.
Number of staff: 1 full-time professional; 2 part-time support.
EIN: 586089937

725
Mauldin Foundation, Inc.
c/o Trust Co. Bank
P.O. Box 4655
Atlanta 30302-4655

Established in 1988 in GA.
Donor(s): Lyman H. Mauldin.‡
Foundation type: Independent
Financial data (yr. ended 12/31/90): Assets, $997,178 (M); expenditures, $255,178; qualifying distributions, $257,587, including $255,000 for 7 grants (high: $150,000; low: $5,000).
Fields of interest: Medical research, heart disease, theological education, Protestant giving, social services.
Types of support: Operating budgets.
Limitations: Giving primarily in GA, with emphasis on Atlanta. No loans or program-related investments.
Application information:
  Initial approach: Letter
  Deadline(s): None
  Write: James S. Toney, Trust Officer, Trust Co. Bank
Officers and Trustees:* Mrs. Vance Mauldin,* Chair.; Wilton D. Looney,* Vice-Chair.; Robert E. Edge,* Secy.; J. Guy Beatty, Jr.,* Treas.; Benjamin T. White.
EIN: 581818885

726
McCamish Foundation ▼
One Buckhead Plaza
3060 Peachtree Rd., 19th Fl.
Atlanta 30305-2228

Established in 1988 in GA.
Donor(s): Henry F. McCamish, Jr.
Foundation type: Independent
Financial data (yr. ended 12/31/90): Assets,
$2,198,092 (M); gifts received, $2,000,000;
expenditures, $2,537,498; qualifying
distributions, $2,534,400, including $2,534,400
for 43 grants (high: $1,500,000; low: $500;
average: $1,000-$50,000).
Purpose and activities: Giving primarily for a
wildlife preservation group and other
conservation associations and a Methodist
church; support also for a performing arts group
and other cultural programs, international affairs,
educational associations; minor support for social
services and health, especially specific disease
associations.
Fields of interest: Wildlife, conservation,
Protestant giving, performing arts, cultural
programs, international affairs, educational
associations, social services, health associations.
Limitations: Giving primarily in GA. No grants to
individuals.
Application information: Contributes only to
pre-selected organizations. Applications not
accepted.
Officers: Margaret P. McCamish, Pres.; Henry F.
McCamish, Jr., V.P.; H. Stephen Merlin, Secy.
EIN: 581808980
Recent health grants:
726-1 American Heart Association, Atlanta, GA,
$20,000. 1990.

727
James Starr Moore Memorial Foundation, Inc.
526 East Paces Ferry Rd., N.E.
Atlanta 30305   (404) 237-6295

Incorporated in 1953 in GA.
Foundation type: Independent
Financial data (yr. ended 12/31/91): Assets,
$9,439,349 (M); gifts received, $254,254;
expenditures, $474,136; qualifying distributions,
$412,366, including $402,330 for 94 grants
(high: $35,000; low: $50).
Fields of interest: Cultural programs, arts, family
planning, AIDS, health services, educational
research, higher education, Protestant giving,
community funds, disadvantaged.
Limitations: Giving primarily in GA. No grants to
individuals.
Application information: Applications not
accepted.
   Board meeting date(s): Dec.
   Write: Bobbie J. Burnham, Secy.
Officer: Bobbie J. Burnham, Secy.
Trustees: Sara Giles Moore, Chair.; Morton S.
Hodgson, Jr., Starr Moore, Emily Redwine.
EIN: 586033190

728
Katherine John Murphy Foundation
c/o Trust Co. Bank
P.O. Box 4655
Atlanta 30302   (404) 588-7356

Trust established in 1954 in GA.
Donor(s): Katherine M. Riley.
Foundation type: Independent
Financial data (yr. ended 12/31/90): Assets,
$10,325,000 (M); gifts received, $302,891;
expenditures, $723,130; qualifying distributions,
$696,167, including $665,600 for 73 grants
(high: $75,000; low: $1,000).
Fields of interest: Hospitals, health services,
cultural programs, higher education, youth, child
welfare.
Types of support: Annual campaigns, building
funds, capital campaigns, equipment, general
purposes, renovation projects, continuing
support, operating budgets, seed money, special
projects.
Limitations: Giving primarily in Atlanta, GA. No
grants to individuals, or for research, scholarships,
fellowships, or matching gifts; no loans.
Application information:
   Initial approach: Letter
   Copies of proposal: 1
   Deadline(s): Mar. 1
   Board meeting date(s): Apr., Oct., and as
   required
   Write: Brenda Rambeau, V.P., Trust Co. Bank
Officers: A.D. Boylston, Jr., Chair.; Dameron
Black, Mgr.; Martin Gatins, Mgr.
Trustee: Trust Co. Bank.
EIN: 586026045

729
National Service Foundation
1420 Peachtree St., N.E.
Atlanta 30309

Established about 1969.
Donor(s): National Service Industries, Inc.
Foundation type: Company-sponsored
Financial data (yr. ended 08/31/91): Assets,
$272,517 (M); expenditures, $269,522;
qualifying distributions, $269,272, including
$269,223 for 119 grants (high: $20,000; low:
$50).
Purpose and activities: Support for culture,
education, community funds, and health; some
support for social services and Jewish
organizations.
Fields of interest: Cultural programs, education,
community funds, health, social services, Jewish
giving.
Limitations: Giving primarily in GA. No grants to
individuals.
Application information: Contributes only to
pre-selected organizations. Applications not
accepted.
Officer and Trustees:* J.R. Hipps,* Mgr.; Henry R.
Dressel, Jr., Sidney Kirschner, David Levy, Erwin
Zaban.
EIN: 586051102

730
Patterson-Barclay Memorial Foundation, Inc.
1020 Spring St., N.W.
Atlanta 30309   (404) 876-1022

Incorporated in 1953 in GA.
Donor(s): Frederick W. Patterson.
Foundation type: Independent
Financial data (yr. ended 12/31/90): Assets,
$7,200,898 (M); expenditures, $356,258;
qualifying distributions, $288,969, including
$271,584 for 90 grants (high: $10,000; low:
$1,000; average: $1,000-$5,000).
Purpose and activities: Giving for Christian
organizations, hospitals, and higher, secondary,
and other education; grants also for health, social
service and youth agencies, arts and culture, and
the environment.
Fields of interest: Religion, hospitals, higher
education, secondary education, health services,
social services, youth, women, arts, environment.
Types of support: Program-related investments,
annual campaigns, capital campaigns, continuing
support, endowment funds, general purposes,
building funds, scholarship funds.
Limitations: Giving limited to the Atlanta, GA,
metropolitan area. No grants to individuals.
Publications: 990-PF.
Application information: Contributes only to
pre-selected organizations. Applications not
accepted.
   Board meeting date(s): 3rd Tuesday in Apr. and
   Oct.
   Write: Mrs. Lee Barclay Patterson Allen, Pres.
Officers and Trustees:* Mrs. Lee Barclay Patterson
Allen,* Pres. and Treas.; Jack W. Allen,* V.P. and
Secy.; Ross Arnold, Robert F. Bryan.
Number of staff: None.
EIN: 580904580

731
The Rich Foundation, Inc.
10 Piedmont Ctr., Suite 802
Atlanta 30305   (404) 262-2266

Incorporated in 1942 in GA.
Donor(s): Rich's, Inc., and members of the Rich
family.
Foundation type: Independent
Financial data (yr. ended 01/31/91): Assets,
$21,215,342 (M); expenditures, $1,065,029;
qualifying distributions, $969,786, including
$937,300 for 48 grants (high: $187,500; low:
$1,000).
Purpose and activities: Giving primarily for a
community fund, the performing arts and other
cultural programs, higher education, including
private schools, social services, including
programs for the homeless and drug abuse, youth
agencies, and hospitals, including research in
heart disease.
Fields of interest: Arts, historic preservation,
theater, higher education, social services, youth,
hospitals, heart disease, drug abuse, community
funds.
Types of support: Annual campaigns, building
funds, consulting services, continuing support,
equipment, operating budgets, technical
assistance, research.

Limitations: Giving limited to Atlanta, GA, area. No grants to individuals, or for matching gifts; no loans.
Publications: Application guidelines.
Application information: Application form required.
  Initial approach: Letter
  Copies of proposal: 10
  Deadline(s): Submit proposal 6 weeks prior to meetings
  Board meeting date(s): Feb., May, Aug., and Nov.
  Final notification: 2 weeks
  Write: Anne Poland Berg, Grant Consultant
Officers and Trustees:* Joel Goldberg,* Pres.; Thomas J. Asher,* V.P.; David S. Baker, Joseph K. Heyman, Margaret S. Weiller.
Number of staff: None.
EIN: 586038037

732
William F. Shallenberger Trust Fund
c/o Alston & Bird, One Atlantic Ctr.
1201 West Peachtree St., Suite 4200
Atlanta 30309-3424   (404) 881-7000

Established in 1980 in GA.
Foundation type: Independent
Financial data (yr. ended 12/31/90): Assets, $3,221,508 (M); expenditures, $137,410; qualifying distributions, $126,526, including $123,026 for 18 grants (high: $13,026; low: $1,000; average: $1,000-$10,000).
Fields of interest: Hospitals, aged, health, social services.
Limitations: Giving primarily in Atlanta, GA.
Application information:
  Initial approach: Letter
  Deadline(s): None
  Write: Benjamin T. White, Mgr.
Officer: Benjamin T. White, Mgr.
Trustees: Mark P. Pentecost, Jr., M.D., Charles K. Wright, M.D.
Number of staff: None.
EIN: 581403009

733
The South Atlantic Foundation, Inc.
428 Bull St.
Savannah 31401   (912) 238-3288

Established in 1953 in GA; incorporated as a community foundation in 1986.
Foundation type: Community
Financial data (yr. ended 12/31/91): Assets, $2,385,805 (M); gifts received, $513,203; expenditures, $418,000; qualifying distributions, $257,904, including $257,904 for 105 grants (high: $25,000; low: $50; average: $100-$20,000).
Fields of interest: Social services, welfare, general charitable giving, religion, health, medical research, education, cultural programs.
Types of support: Annual campaigns, building funds, conferences and seminars, emergency funds, employee-related scholarships, equipment, land acquisition, professorships, program-related investments, publications, renovation projects, seed money, scholarship funds, capital campaigns, endowment funds, general purposes, operating budgets, special projects.

Limitations: Giving primarily in GA, SC, and FL. No grants to individuals, or for continuing support, deficit financing, foundation managed projects, matching or challenge grants; no program-related investments.
Publications: Annual report, informational brochure, application guidelines.
Application information: Application form required.
  Initial approach: Telephone
  Copies of proposal: 1
  Deadline(s): Before end of each quarter
  Board meeting date(s): Jan., Apr., July, and Oct.
  Write: William W. Byram, Jr., Exec. Dir.
Officers: Norton M. Melaver, Pres.; David T. Johnson, V.P.; James M. Piette, Secy.-Treas.; William W. Byram, Jr., Exec. Dir.
Number of staff: 1 full-time professional; 1 full-time support.
EIN: 586033468

734
Spalding Health Care Trust
c/o First Union National Bank of Georgia
Capitol Mgmt. Group - 9007, P.O. Box 740074
Atlanta 30374

Established in 1986 in GA.
Foundation type: Independent
Financial data (yr. ended 12/31/90): Assets, $8,081,214 (M); gifts received, $688,627; expenditures, $780,187; qualifying distributions, $757,134, including $757,134 for 1 grant.
Purpose and activities: Giving to a hospital providing care to the indigent.
Fields of interest: Hospitals.
Limitations: Giving limited to GA.
Application information: Applications not accepted.
Trustee: First Union National Bank of Georgia.
EIN: 581657005

735
Kate and Elwyn Tomlinson Foundation, Inc.
3000 Habersham Rd., N.W.
Atlanta 30305-2844   (404) 952-2277

Incorporated in 1949 in GA.
Foundation type: Independent
Financial data (yr. ended 12/31/90): Assets, $2,583,194 (M); expenditures, $325,549; qualifying distributions, $136,980, including $131,800 for 49 grants (high: $30,000; low: $300).
Fields of interest: Higher education, secondary education, hospitals, health associations, cultural programs, Protestant giving.
Limitations: Giving primarily in GA. No grants to individuals.
Application information:
  Initial approach: Letter
  Deadline(s): None
  Write: Kathryn Bridges, Chair.
Officers: Kathryn T. Bridges, Chair.; Mark P. Tomlinson, Vice-Chair.
EIN: 580634727

736
The Tull Charitable Foundation ▼
230 Peachtree St., N.E., Suite 1502
Atlanta 30303   (404) 659-7079

Trust established in 1952 in GA as The J. M. Tull Foundation; reorganized under current name in 1984 with the Tull Charitable Foundation.
Donor(s): J.M. Tull,‡ J.M. Tull Metal and Supply Co., Inc.
Foundation type: Independent
Financial data (yr. ended 12/31/91): Assets, $43,800,000 (M); expenditures, $2,528,000; qualifying distributions, $2,101,500, including $2,101,500 for 48 grants (high: $150,000; low: $2,000; average: $25,000-$75,000).
Purpose and activities: Support for higher and secondary education; grants also for health and human services, youth and child welfare agencies, and culture.
Fields of interest: Higher education, secondary education, education—building funds, health, social services, homeless, housing, youth, child welfare.
Types of support: Building funds, seed money, endowment funds, capital campaigns, professorships, scholarship funds, renovation projects.
Limitations: Giving limited to GA. No support for projects of religious organizations that primarily benefit their own adherents. No grants to individuals, or for conferences or seminars, scientific research, purchase of tickets to benefit events, operating support, or scholarships (except for scholarship endowments); no loans.
Publications: Informational brochure (including application guidelines).
Application information: Application form not required.
  Initial approach: Letter
  Copies of proposal: 1
  Deadline(s): 1st day of month of meeting
  Board meeting date(s): Jan., Apr., July, and Oct.
  Final notification: 1 week after board meeting
  Write: Barbara Cleveland, Exec. Dir.
Officers and Trustees:* George E. Smith,* Pres.; Walter J. Thomas,* Secy.-Treas.; Barbara Cleveland, Exec. Dir.; John McIntyre, Larry Prince, Franklin Skinner, John B. Zellars.
Agent: Trust Co. Bank.
Number of staff: 1 part-time professional; 1 part-time support.
EIN: 581687028

737
The UPS Foundation ▼
400 Perimeter Ctr., Terraces North
Atlanta 30346   (404) 913-6451
Additional tel.: (404) 913-6374

Incorporated in 1951 in DE.
Donor(s): UPS, Inc.
Foundation type: Company-sponsored
Financial data (yr. ended 12/31/91): Assets, $48,000,000 (M); expenditures, $10,394,579; qualifying distributions, $9,880,998, including $7,962,809 for 248 grants (high: $100,000; low: $5,000; average: $5,000-$50,000), $1,439,699 for grants to individuals (high: $6,000; low: $500) and $478,480 for 2,389 employee matching gifts.
Purpose and activities: Support for philanthropic human welfare or education projects or

organizations that are tax-exempt under 501(c)(3) and meet the guidelines of the foundation. Emphasis on programs for families and children in crisis, adult literacy, the distribution of food to hungry Americans, economic opportunity for minorities, programs for the handicapped, and support for higher education, including academic, public policy, and transportation/logistics research.

Fields of interest: Welfare, youth, child welfare, disadvantaged, welfare—indigent individuals, hunger, aged, higher education, adult education, education—minorities, AIDS, public policy, civic affairs, transportation, Canada.

Types of support: Continuing support, seed money, equipment, matching funds, employee matching gifts, professorships, internships, scholarship funds, employee-related scholarships, fellowships, special projects, research.

Limitations: No support for religious organizations or theological functions, or church-sponsored programs limited to church members. No grants to individuals (except for employee-related scholarships), or for building or endowment funds, operating funds, annual campaigns, emergency funds, deficit financing, land acquisition, or publications; no loans.

Publications: Annual report (including application guidelines).

Application information: Application form not required.

> *Initial approach:* Letter, preferably no more than 2 pages addressing programs, objectives, and cost
> *Copies of proposal:* 1
> *Deadline(s):* Submit proposal Jan. through Aug.
> *Board meeting date(s):* Oct. and Nov.
> *Final notification:* For local programs, Nov. 1; for national programs, Dec. 1
> *Write:* Clement E. Hanrahan, Exec. Dir.

Officers and Trustees:* Kent C. Nelson,* Chair.; Clement E. Hanrahan, V.P.; Calvin Tyler, Secy.

Number of staff: 2 full-time professional; 3 full-time support.

EIN: 136099176

Recent health grants:

737-1 Alcove, The, Monroe, GA, $10,000. For purchase and renovation of facility within walking distance of shelter, to serve as community and family counseling center. 1990.

737-2 American College of Cardiology, Bethesda, MD, $10,000. For unrestricted use. 1990.

737-3 Beth Israel Medical Center, NYC, NY, $10,000. For unrestricted use. 1990.

737-4 Cerebral Palsy Association of Middlesex County, Lakeview School, Edison, NJ, $10,000. To renovate for more classroom and therapy space. 1990.

737-5 Christian Rehabilitation Center, Charlotte, NC, $10,000. To provide residential rental housing for 12 women and live-in staff member. 1990.

737-6 Elderly Interest Fund, Fort Lauderdale, FL, $10,000. To replace van for Medivan Program. 1990.

737-7 Greenwich Hospital Association, Greenwich, CT, $25,000. Toward building free-standing Cancer Center which will consolidate in one building all medical and support services needed by cancer patients and their families. 1990.

737-8 Hathaway Childrens Services, Sylmar, CA, $10,000. Toward renovation of existing facility for child care and counseling for abused and disturbed underprivileged children. 1990.

737-9 Hope Cottage, Anchorage, AK, $10,000. For materials and training for Adult Vocational Program for Vocational Independence. 1990.

737-10 Indianapolis Indiana Care Campaign for Healthy Babies, Indianapolis, IN, $10,000. Toward ultrasound equipment. 1990.

737-11 M. D. Anderson Hospital and Tumor Institute, Houston, TX, $10,000. For unrestricted use. 1990.

737-12 Marian Manor Nursing Home, Pittsburgh, PA, $10,000. For initial staffing of new Child Care/Intergenerational program to benefit 30 pre-school children and 100 elderly residents. 1990.

737-13 Media-Advertising Partnership for a Drug-Free America, NYC, NY, $10,000. For fund to generate educational messages. 1990.

737-14 Meharry Hubbard Hospital, Nashville, TN, $10,000. For unrestricted use. 1990.

737-15 National Foundation for Facial Reconstruction, NYC, NY, $10,000. For unrestricted use. 1990.

737-16 New York University Medical Center, NYC, NY, $20,000. For diabetes research. 1990.

737-17 Norwalk Hospital, Norwalk, CT, $10,000. For allergy research and gastro-intestinal tract research. 1990.

737-18 Saint Marys Medical Center, Alzheimers Day Treatment Center, Knoxville, TN, $10,000. For renovation and expansion of existing space in hospital wing. 1990.

737-19 Vanderbilt University Hospital and Clinic, Nashville, TN, $10,000. For unrestricted use. 1990.

737-20 Washington University, School of Medicine, Saint Louis, MO, $35,000. For continuation of Human Islet Transplantation studies. 1990.

738

Gertrude and William C. Wardlaw Fund, Inc.

c/o Trust Co. Bank
P.O. Box 4655
Atlanta 30302

Trust established in 1936 in GA; incorporated in 1951.

Donor(s): Gertrude Wardlaw, William C. Wardlaw, Jr.‡

Foundation type: Independent

Financial data (yr. ended 12/31/90): Assets, $7,284,435 (M); expenditures, $286,592; qualifying distributions, $265,125, including $252,500 for 38 grants (high: $30,000; low: $2,000).

Purpose and activities: Emphasis on education, including higher education, youth agencies, cultural programs, a community fund, and health and hospitals.

Fields of interest: Higher education, cultural programs, youth, community funds, health, hospitals.

Types of support: Operating budgets.

Limitations: Giving primarily in Atlanta, GA. No grants to individuals.

Application information:

> *Initial approach:* Letter
> *Deadline(s):* None

Officers and Trustees:* Edna Raine Wardlaw,* Chair.; A. Pickney Straughn,* Secy.; Victor A. Gregory, William C. Wardlaw III, Trust Co. Bank.

EIN: 586026065

739

West Point-Pepperell Foundation, Inc.

400 West Tenth St.
P.O. Box 342
West Point 31833-0342   (404) 645-4000

Incorporated in 1953 in GA as West Point Foundation, Inc.; merged with Sanford Dunson Foundation, Inc. in 1965.

Donor(s): West Point-Pepperell, Inc.

Foundation type: Company-sponsored

Financial data (yr. ended 12/31/90): Assets, $1,532,047 (M); gifts received, $40,000; expenditures, $1,377,975; qualifying distributions, $1,353,111, including $1,308,995 for grants.

Purpose and activities: Support for higher and secondary education, hospitals, and health agencies; grants also for youth agencies and community funds.

Fields of interest: Higher education, secondary education, hospitals, health services, youth, community funds.

Types of support: Employee matching gifts.

Limitations: Giving primarily in areas with West Point-Pepperell, Inc. facilities in AL, FL, ME, NC, SC, and TX. No grants to individuals.

Application information: Application form not required.

> *Initial approach:* Letter
> *Copies of proposal:* 1
> *Board meeting date(s):* Varies
> *Write:* H. Hart Cobb, Jr., V.P.

Officers and Trustees:* William F. Farley,* Pres.; H. Hart Cobb, Jr.,* V.P.; Edgar E. Davis,* V.P.; John Holland,* V.P.; Paul M. O'Hara,* V.P.; Pamela L. Webber,* V.P.; Ninette Bragg, Secy.; Charles A. Lieppe.

Number of staff: 2 full-time professional; 2 part-time support.

EIN: 580801512

740

Joseph B. Whitehead Foundation ▼

50 Hurt Plaza, Suite 1200
Atlanta 30303   (404) 522-6755

Incorporated in 1937 in GA.

Donor(s): Joseph B. Whitehead, Jr.‡

Foundation type: Independent

Financial data (yr. ended 12/31/90): Assets, $353,487,542 (M); expenditures, $12,746,695; qualifying distributions, $11,714,791, including $11,621,577 for 50 grants (high: $1,500,000; low: $15,000; average: $10,000-$750,000).

Purpose and activities: Giving primarily for child care and youth programs, education, health, cultural programs, the arts, care of the aged, and civic affairs. Preference is given to one-time capital projects of established private charitable organizations.

Fields of interest: Education, youth, child welfare, child development, cultural programs, arts, health, arts, civic affairs, aged.

Types of support: Seed money, building funds, equipment, land acquisition, special projects, capital campaigns.
Limitations: Giving limited to metropolitan Atlanta, GA. No grants to individuals, or for endowment funds, research, scholarships, fellowships, or matching gifts; generally no support for operating expenses; no loans.
Publications: Application guidelines, informational brochure (including application guidelines), program policy statement.
Application information: Application form not required.
   Initial approach: Letter
   Copies of proposal: 1
   Deadline(s): 1st of Feb. and Sept.
   Board meeting date(s): Apr. and Nov.
   Final notification: 30 days after board meeting
   Write: Charles H. McTier, Pres.
Officers and Trustees:* J.W. Jones,* Chair.; James M. Sibley,* Vice-Chair.; Charles H. McTier, Pres.; P. Russell Hardin, Secy.-Treas.; Roberto C. Goizueta.
Number of staff: 9 shared staff
EIN: 586001954
Recent health grants:

740-1 American Cancer Society, Atlanta, GA, $1,036,000. Toward three-year pilot cancer control program at Grady Memorial Hospital. 1990.

740-2 American Lung Association of Atlanta, Atlanta, GA, $80,000. For renovation at agency's office. 1990.

740-3 American Lung Association of Georgia, Atlanta, GA, $20,000. For renovation at State headquarters building. 1990.

740-4 American Red Cross, Atlanta, GA, $250,000. For campaign for renovation and expansion of regional blood services center. 1990.

740-5 Arthritis Foundation, Atlanta, GA, $28,000. Toward purchase of walkers, wheelchairs, braces and other orthopedic equipment to stock seven loan closets from which needy Georgians may borrow. 1990.

740-6 Atlanta Speech School, Atlanta, GA, $300,000. To endow Joseph B. Whitehead Scholarship Fund. 1990.

740-7 Emory University, Atlanta, GA, $200,000. For campaign to renovate facility to house Emory Autism Resource Center. 1990.

740-8 Emory University, School of Medicine, Atlanta, GA, $750,000. To endow Joseph B. Whitehead Scholarship Fund. 1990.

740-9 George West Mental Health Foundation, Atlanta, GA, $100,000. Toward purchase of duplex for use as halfway house in aftercare program for mentally disturbed. 1990.

740-10 Grady Memorial Hospital, Atlanta, GA, $36,577. Toward purchase of television production equipment utilized in Hospital's health education programs. 1990.

740-11 Hillside Treatment Center, Atlanta, GA, $550,000. For campaign to construct addition to children's psychiatric hospital. 1990.

740-12 International Service Association for Health (INSA), Atlanta, GA, $300,000. For campaign to purchase and expand facilities for organization training nurses and other health workers from developing countries. 1990.

740-13 Schenck School, Atlanta, GA, $250,000. Toward construction of multipurpose building for children with learning disorders. 1990.

740-14 Village of Saint Joseph, Atlanta, GA, $150,000. For facility improvements and additions for five-day residential treatment program for children with conduct disorders. 1990.

741
Lettie Pate Whitehead Foundation, Inc. ▼
50 Hurt Plaza, Suite 1200
Atlanta 30303   (404) 522-6755

Incorporated in 1946 in GA.
Donor(s): Conkey Pate Whitehead.‡
Foundation type: Independent
Financial data (yr. ended 12/31/90): Assets, $250,359,516 (M); expenditures, $9,731,708; qualifying distributions, $9,081,173, including $9,000,000 for 202 grants (high: $350,000; low: $6,000; average: $20,000-$65,000).
Purpose and activities: Grants to institutions for scholarships for the education of poor Christian girls and institutional grants for assistance to poor aged Christian women.
Fields of interest: Aged, women, religion—Christian, higher education, medical education, nursing.
Types of support: Scholarship funds.
Limitations: Giving limited to AL, FL, GA, LA, MS, NC, SC, TN, and VA. No grants to individuals, or for building or endowment funds, or matching gifts; no loans.
Publications: Application guidelines, informational brochure.
Application information: Application form not required.
   Initial approach: Letter
   Copies of proposal: 1
   Deadline(s): Sept. 1
   Board meeting date(s): Apr. and Nov.
   Final notification: Mar. 1
   Write: Charles H. McTier, Pres.
Officers and Trustees:* Hughes Spalding, Jr.,* Chair.; Herbert A. Claiborne, Jr., M.D.,* Vice-Chair.; Charles H. McTier, Pres.; P. Russell Hardin, Secy.-Treas.; Lyons Gray.
Number of staff: 9 shared staff
EIN: 586012629
Recent health grants:

741-1 A. G. Rhodes Home, Atlanta, GA, $30,000. For care of aged women. 1990.

741-2 Auburn University Foundation, Auburn University, AL, $40,000. For nursing and pre-nursing scholarships. 1990.

741-3 Augusta College, Augusta, GA, $20,000. For scholarships in nursing, allied health and paramedical training. 1990.

741-4 Averett College, Danville, VA, $45,000. For scholarships in medical technology, nursing and special education. 1990.

741-5 Baptist Memorial Hospital, Memphis, TN, $35,000. For nursing scholarships. 1990.

741-6 Barry University, Miami, FL, $30,000. For nursing scholarships. 1990.

741-7 Bowman Gray School of Medicine, Winston-Salem, NC, $85,000. For scholarships in medicine and physician assistant programs. 1990.

741-8 Cabarrus Memorial Hospital, Concord, NC, $30,000. For nursing scholarships. 1990.

741-9 Charity Hospital, New Orleans, LA, $40,000. For nursing scholarships. 1990.

741-10 Clinch Valley College, Wise, VA, $60,000. For general nursing and allied health scholarships. 1990.

741-11 DeKalb Community College, Clarkston, GA, $20,000. For nursing and allied health scholarships. 1990.

741-12 DePaul Hospital, Norfolk, VA, $50,000. For nursing scholarships. 1990.

741-13 Dillard University, New Orleans, LA, $30,000. For nursing scholarships. 1990.

741-14 Duke University, Duke University Medical Center, Durham, NC, $32,000. For nursing scholarships. 1990.

741-15 Eastern Mennonite College, Harrisonburg, VA, $50,000. For nursing scholarships. 1990.

741-16 Emory University, Emory College, Oxford College, Atlanta, GA, $245,000. For scholarships in allied health, general nursing and nurse practitioner. 1990.

741-17 Fulton-DeKalb Hospital Authority, Grady Memorial Hospital, Atlanta, GA, $10,000. For Nephrology Center scholarships. 1990.

741-18 Fulton-DeKalb Hospital Authority, Grady Memorial Hospital, Atlanta, GA, $10,000. For allied health scholarships. 1990.

741-19 Gardner-Webb College, Boiling Springs, NC, $37,500. For scholarships in nursing and program for deaf students. 1990.

741-20 Georgetown University, DC, $45,000. For nursing scholarships. 1990.

741-21 Georgia Baptist Medical Center, Atlanta, GA, $30,000. For nursing scholarships. 1990.

741-22 Georgia College Foundation, Milledgeville, GA, $40,000. For nursing scholarships. 1990.

741-23 Georgia Southern University, Statesboro, GA, $35,000. For nursing scholarships. 1990.

741-24 Georgia State University Foundation, Atlanta, GA, $55,000. For nursing and allied health scholarships. 1990.

741-25 Hollins College, Roanoke, VA, $45,000. For scholarships in health education, psychology and nursing. 1990.

741-26 James Madison University Foundation, Harrisonburg, VA, $50,000. For nursing scholarships. 1990.

741-27 Lenoir-Rhyne College, Hickory, NC, $30,000. For nursing scholarships. 1990.

741-28 Lewis Gale Medical Foundation, Salem, VA, $45,000. For nursing scholarships. 1990.

741-29 Louisiana College, Pineville, LA, $25,000. For nursing scholarships. 1990.

741-30 Louisiana State University, Alexandria, LA, $20,000. For nursing scholarships. 1990.

741-31 Louisiana State University, Eunice, LA, $30,000. For nursing scholarships. 1990.

741-32 Louisiana State University Medical Center, New Orleans, LA, $50,000. For medical, nursing and allied health scholarships. 1990.

741-33 Louisiana Technical University, Ruston, LA, $30,000. For scholarships in nursing and health sciences. 1990.

741-34 Lynchburg College, Lynchburg, VA, $50,000. For nursing scholarships. 1990.

741-35 Marymount University, Arlington, VA, $45,000. For nursing and allied health scholarships. 1990.

741-36 Medical College of Georgia, Augusta, GA, $75,000. For nursing and allied health scholarships. 1990.

741-37 Medical College of Virginia, Richmond, VA, $80,000. For nursing and nurse practitioner scholarships. 1990.

741-38 Medical University of South Carolina, Charleston, SC, $20,000. For scholarships in nursing and health related professions. 1990.

741-39 Meharry Medical College, Nashville, TN, $50,000. For allied health scholarships. 1990.

741-40 Memorial Hospital, Danville, VA, $15,000. For nursing, laboratory and x-ray technology scholarships. 1990.

741-41 Methodist Hospital, Memphis, TN, $30,000. For nursing scholarships. 1990.

741-42 Miami-Dade Community College Foundation, Miami, FL, $30,000. For nursing scholarships. 1990.

741-43 Mississippi College, Clinton, MS, $50,000. For general and nursing scholarships. 1990.

741-44 Moravian Home, Winston-Salem, NC, $25,000. For care of aged women. 1990.

741-45 North Carolina Baptist Hospital, Winston-Salem, NC, $31,500. For scholarships in practical nursing, medical technology, nurse anesthesia and nursing. 1990.

741-46 North Georgia Presbyterian Homes, Austell, GA, $50,000. For care of aged women. 1990.

741-47 Northeast Louisiana University, Monroe, LA, $30,000. For scholarships in nursing and health sciences. 1990.

741-48 Northwestern State University, Natchitoches, LA, $20,000. For nursing scholarships. 1990.

741-49 Our Lady of Perpetual Help Cancer Home, Atlanta, GA, $150,000. For care of aged women. 1990.

741-50 Our Lady of the Lake Hospital, Baton Rouge, LA, $30,000. For nursing scholarships. 1990.

741-51 Presbyterian Hospital, Charlotte, NC, $55,000. For nursing scholarships. 1990.

741-52 Radford University, Radford, VA, $45,000. For nursing scholarships. 1990.

741-53 Radford University, Radford, VA, $20,000. For medical technology scholarships. 1990.

741-54 Randolph-Macon Womans College, Lynchburg, VA, $25,000. For scholarships in medical technology and health-related fields. 1990.

741-55 Richmond Memorial Hospital, Richmond, VA, $45,000. For nursing scholarships. 1990.

741-56 Riverside Hospital, Newport News, VA, $40,000. For nursing scholarships. 1990.

741-57 Roanoke Memorial Hospital, Roanoke, VA, $15,000. For nursing and allied health scholarships. 1990.

741-58 Saint Josephs Hospital, Memphis, TN, $30,000. For nursing scholarships. 1990.

741-59 Saint Josephs Hospital Foundation, Atlanta, GA, $40,000. For nursing scholarships. 1990.

741-60 Samford University, Birmingham, AL, $50,000. For general and nursing scholarships. 1990.

741-61 Sentara Norfolk General Hospital, Norfolk, VA, $45,000. For nursing scholarships. 1990.

741-62 Southeastern Louisiana University, Hammond, LA, $25,000. For nursing scholarships. 1990.

741-63 Southside Regional Medical Center, Petersburg, VA, $45,000. For nursing scholarships. 1990.

741-64 Tougaloo College, Tougaloo, MS, $35,000. For pre-health scholarships. 1990.

741-65 Triad United Methodist Home, Winston-Salem, NC, $125,000. For care of aged women. 1990.

741-66 Tulane University, New Orleans, LA, $60,000. For medical and master of social work scholarships. 1990.

741-67 University of Alabama, Birmingham, AL, $60,000. For nursing and allied health scholarships. 1990.

741-68 University of Miami, Coral Gables, FL, $60,000. For medicine and nursing scholarships. 1990.

741-69 University of Mississippi Medical Center, Jackson, MS, $60,000. For scholarships in nursing, health related professions, dental and medical schools. 1990.

741-70 University of North Carolina, Chapel Hill, NC, $124,000. For scholarships in medicine, medical technology, nursing, physical therapy, dental hygiene, denistry, pharmacy and public health. 1990.

741-71 University of North Carolina, Charlotte, NC, $26,000. For nursing scholarships. 1990.

741-72 University of North Carolina, Greensboro, NC, $40,000. For scholarships in nursing, medical technology and speech technology. 1990.

741-73 University of South Carolina Educational Foundation, Columbia, SC, $50,000. For scholarships in nursing, public health, audiology, speech pathology and medicine. 1990.

741-74 University of Southwestern Louisiana, Lafayette, LA, $30,000. For nursing scholarships. 1990.

741-75 University of Tennessee, Memphis, TN, $20,000. For nursing scholarships. 1990.

741-76 University of Virginia Medical School Foundation, Charlottesville, VA, $70,000. For medicine, nursing and allied health scholarships. 1990.

741-77 Vanderbilt University, Nashville, TN, $50,000. For nursing scholarships. 1990.

741-78 Washington and Lee University, Lexington, VA, $50,000. For general scholarships with priority to education in natural and premedical sciences. 1990.

741-79 Wesley Homes, Atlanta, GA, $350,000. For care of aged women in Geriatric Hospital program. 1990.

741-80 Wesley Homes, Atlanta, GA, $200,000. For care of aged women in Health Center program. 1990.

742

The Frances Wood Wilson Foundation, Inc. ▼

1501 Clairmont Rd.
Decatur 30033 (404) 634-3363
Application address: P.O. Box 33188, Decatur, GA 30033

Incorporated in 1954 in GA.
Donor(s): Fred B. Wilson,‡ Mrs. Frances W. Wilson, St. Louis - San Francisco Railroad.
Foundation type: Independent

Financial data (yr. ended 05/31/91): Assets, $32,515,549 (M); expenditures, $2,681,195; qualifying distributions, $1,683,933, including $1,630,104 for 54 grants (high: $520,000; low: $300; average: $1,000-$25,000).
Purpose and activities: Grants largely for child welfare, and religious, civic, health, and higher educational organizations; support also for college scholarship funds.
Fields of interest: Protestant giving, higher education, child welfare, health.
Types of support: Operating budgets, general purposes, continuing support, annual campaigns, seed money, emergency funds, building funds, equipment, land acquisition, scholarship funds.
Limitations: Giving limited to GA, except for programs carried on by Chestnut Hill Benevolent Association in Boston, MA. No grants to individuals, or for endowment funds; no loans.
Publications: Application guidelines, program policy statement.
Application information:
Initial approach: Proposal
Copies of proposal: 1
Deadline(s): None
Board meeting date(s): Apr. and Oct.
Write: W.T. Wingfield, Pres.
Officers and Trustees:* W.T. Wingfield,* Pres.; T. Cecil Myers,* V.P.; J.M. Pate,* V.P.
EIN: 586035441
Recent health grants:
742-1 American Cancer Society, Atlanta, GA, $20,000. 1991.
742-2 Chestnut Hill Benevolent Association, Brookline, MA, $25,000. 1991.
742-3 Henrietta Egleston Hospital for Children, Atlanta, GA, $20,000. 1991.
742-4 Our Lady of Perpetual Help Cancer Home, Atlanta, GA, $20,000. 1991.
742-5 Scottish Rite Childrens Medical Center, Atlanta, GA, $520,000. 1991.
742-6 Shepherd Center for Treatment of Spinal Injuries, Atlanta, GA, $25,000. 1991.
742-7 Wesley Homes, Atlanta, GA, $10,000. 1991.

743

Robert W. Woodruff Foundation, Inc. ▼

(Formerly Trebor Foundation, Inc.)
50 Hurt Plaza, Suite 1200
Atlanta 30303 (404) 522-6755

Incorporated in 1937 in DE.
Donor(s): Robert W. Woodruff,‡ The Acmaro Securities Corp., and others.
Foundation type: Independent
Financial data (yr. ended 12/31/90): Assets, $995,893,546 (M); gifts received, $47,736,224; expenditures, $27,380,765; qualifying distributions, $56,585,744, including $26,448,425 for 21 grants (high: $7,023,500; low: $10,000; average: $25,000-$750,000).
Purpose and activities: Interests include expansion and improvement of health and educational facilities, youth and child welfare programs, care of the aged, cultural and civic affairs, and conservation and the environment.
Fields of interest: Health, higher education, education, youth, child welfare, aged, social services, cultural programs, arts, civic affairs, public affairs, conservation, environment.

Types of support: Building funds, renovation projects, land acquisition, equipment, general purposes, scholarship funds, capital campaigns.
Limitations: Giving primarily in Atlanta, GA. No grants to individuals, or for endowment funds, research, special projects, publications, conferences and seminars, or operating budgets; no loans.
Publications: Application guidelines.
Application information: Application form not required.
  Initial approach: Letter
  Copies of proposal: 1
  Deadline(s): 1st of Feb. and Sept.
  Board meeting date(s): Apr. and Nov.
  Final notification: Within 30 days of trustees meeting
  Write: Charles H. McTier, Pres.
Officers and Trustees:* Joseph W. Jones,* Chair.; James M. Sibley,* Vice-Chair.; Charles H. McTier, Pres.; P. Russell Hardin, Secy.-Treas.; Ivan Allen, Jr., James B. Williams.
Number of staff: 1
EIN: 581695425
Recent health grants:
743-1 Bradley Center, Columbus, GA, $500,000. For capital campaign to build adolescent residential treatment center and multi-purpose activity center. 1990.

743-2 Clifton Corridor Biomedical Research Council, Decatur, GA, $100,000. For three-year budget of new organization promoting collaborative biomedical research and technological development among Georgia-based research institutions. 1990.
743-3 Emory University, Atlanta, GA, $25,000. Toward renovation and refurbishments in Health Sciences Center Administration Building. 1990.
743-4 Phoebe Putney Memorial Hospital, Albany, GA, $10,000. Toward care of indigent patients. 1990.

744
The David, Helen, and Marian Woodward Fund-Atlanta ▼
(also known as Marian W. Ottley Trust-Atlanta)
c/o Wachovia Bank of Georgia, N.A.
191 Peachtree St., MC 705
Atlanta 30303   (404) 332-6677
Application address: Ann Morris, Wachovia Bank of GA, 191 Peachtree St., MC 1540, Atlanta, GA 30303

Trust established in 1975 in GA.
Donor(s): Marian W. Ottley.‡
Foundation type: Independent

Financial data (yr. ended 05/31/92): Assets, $34,036,897 (M); expenditures, $1,475,154; qualifying distributions, $1,072,643, including $1,072,643 for 45 grants (high: $100,000; low: $10,000).
Fields of interest: Hospitals, cultural programs, social services, youth, arts, education, civic affairs.
Types of support: Building funds, equipment, special projects.
Limitations: Giving primarily in Atlanta, GA. No grants to individuals, or for scholarships or student loans.
Publications: Application guidelines.
Application information: Application form not required.
  Initial approach: Letter
  Copies of proposal: 1
  Deadline(s): May 1 and Nov. 1
  Board meeting date(s): June and Dec.
  Final notification: 10 days after meeting
  Write: Beverly Blake
Distribution Committee: William D. Ellis, Jr., Robert L. Foreman, Jr., Joseph H. Hilsman, Horace Sibley, Edward D. Smith.
Trustee: Wachovia Bank of Georgia, N.A.
Number of staff: None.
EIN: 586222004

HAWAII

745
Alexander & Baldwin Corporate Giving Program
822 Bishop St.
P.O. Box 3440
Honolulu 96801   (808) 525-6611

Purpose and activities: "The company's charitable activities are directed toward enhancing and improving the quality of life for its employees and the communities in which it does business." The contributions program provides support to various community organizations and programs through contributions of cash, land, equipment, employees' time, and in-kind services. Support goes to health and human services, arts, and education. A&B funds higher education, including a scholarship program for employees' children, and is also interested in educational programs in economics and business for young people and is involved in the Hawaii Business Roundtable's efforts to bring reform to public schools. Employees, in addition to giving their time to nonprofit organizations, also make cash gifts which are matched by the company.
Fields of interest: Arts, cultural programs, health, welfare, education, civic affairs, humanities.
Types of support: Operating budgets, capital campaigns, special projects, employee matching gifts, in-kind gifts, equipment.
Limitations: Giving primarily in headquarters city and major operating locations in HI and CA.
Application information:
   Initial approach: Query letter describing project
   Deadline(s): None
   Write: John B. Kelley, V.P., Public Relations

746
Atherton Family Foundation ▼
c/o Hawaiian Trust Co., Ltd.
P.O. Box 3170
Honolulu 96802
Application address: c/o Hawaii Community Foundation, 222 Merchant St., 2nd Fl., Honolulu, HI 96813; Tel.: (808) 537-6333 for grants; Tel.: (808) 536-8839 for scholarships; FAX: (808) 521-6286

Incorporated in 1975 in HI as successor to Juliette M. Atherton Trust established in 1915; F. C. Atherton Trust merged into the foundation in 1976.
Donor(s): Juliette M. Atherton,‡ Frank C. Atherton.‡
Foundation type: Independent
Financial data (yr. ended 12/31/90): Assets, $48,055,619 (M); expenditures, $3,054,959; qualifying distributions, $2,590,220, including $2,445,375 for 106 grants (high: $285,000; low: $1,000; average: $2,000-$10,000) and $62,550 for 56 grants to individuals (high: $3,050; low: $500; average: $500-$2,000).
Purpose and activities: Concerned with education, social welfare, culture and the arts, religion, health, and the environment.

Scholarships for the education of Protestant ministers for postgraduate education, Protestant ministers' children for undergraduate study, and for graduate theological education at a Protestant seminary.
Fields of interest: Arts, cultural programs, humanities, education, health, social services, welfare, humanities, Protestant giving, environment, theological education.
Types of support: Building funds, student aid, annual campaigns, continuing support, equipment, matching funds, renovation projects, research, seed money, special projects.
Limitations: Giving limited to HI; student aid for HI residents only. No support for private foundations or for organizations engaged in fundraising for the purpose of distributing grants to recipients of their own choosing.
Publications: Annual report, application guidelines.
Application information: Application forms required for scholarships.
   Initial approach: Telephone or proposal
   Copies of proposal: 6
   Deadline(s): 1st day of month preceding board meeting for organizations; Mar. 1 for scholarships
   Board meeting date(s): 3rd Wednesday of Feb., Apr., June, Aug., Oct., and Dec.
   Final notification: 1 to 2 months
   Write: Charlie Medeiros for grants; Doug Birdsall for scholarships
Officers and Directors:* Alexander S. Atherton,* Pres.; Judith Dawson,* V.P. and Secy.; Robert R. Midkiff,* V.P.; James F. Morgan, Jr.,* V.P.; Joan H. Rohlfing,* V.P.; Hawaiian Trust Co., Ltd., Treas.
Number of staff: 3 shared staff
EIN: 510175971

Recent health grants:
746-1 Alcoholic Rehabilitation Services of Hawaii, Hina Mauka, HI, $50,000. For capital campaign. 1990.
746-2 Ohana Hale, Waianae, HI, $10,000. For three staff positions. 1990.
746-3 Rehabilitation Hospital of the Pacific, Honolulu, HI, $12,500. For re-roofing. 1990.

747
Fred Baldwin Memorial Foundation
222 Merchant St., 2nd Fl.
Honolulu 96813   (808) 537-6333
FAX: (808) 521-6286

Established in 1910 in HI as the Fred Baldwin Memorial Home.
Donor(s): Fred Baldwin,‡ and other members of the Baldwin family.
Foundation type: Independent
Financial data (yr. ended 12/31/90): Assets, $2,686,391 (M); expenditures, $249,224; qualifying distributions, $209,698, including $135,960 for 31 grants (high: $12,000; low: $500; average: $1,000-$5,000).
Fields of interest: Social services, youth, arts, health.
Types of support: Seed money, renovation projects, special projects.
Limitations: Giving limited to HI, with emphasis on Maui County.
Publications: Annual report.
Application information: Application form not required.

Initial approach: Proposal
Copies of proposal: 1
Deadline(s): Jan. 15, May 15, and Sept. 15
Board meeting date(s): Mar., July, and Nov.
Final notification: 1 month following meeting
Write: Janis Reischmann, Grants Administrator
Officers and Trustees:* Michael H. Lyons II,* Pres.; Shaun L. McKay, V.P.; Joseph P. Cooke, Jr., Secy.-Treas.; Bennet M. Baldwin, Douglas B. Cameron, Frances B. Cameron, Henry Rice, Mary C. Sanford, Emily Young.
Number of staff: None.
EIN: 990075264

748
Bancorp Hawaii Charitable Foundation
P.O. Box 3170
Honolulu 96802

Established in 1981 in HI.
Donor(s): Bank of Hawaii.
Foundation type: Company-sponsored
Financial data (yr. ended 12/31/91): Assets, $10,200,574 (M); expenditures, $468,474; qualifying distributions, $417,760, including $409,300 for 30 grants (high: $25,000; low: $2,500).
Fields of interest: Education, secondary education, higher education, social services, cultural programs, conservation, hospitals, religion—Christian.
Types of support: General purposes, endowment funds, building funds.
Limitations: Giving limited to HI. No grants to individuals.
Application information: Contributes only to pre-selected organizations. Applications not accepted.
Officers and Directors:* H. Howard Stephenson,* Pres.; Richard J. Dahl, V.P. and Treas.; Lawrence M. Johnson,* V.P.; Ruth E. Miyashiro, Secy.; Frank J. Manaut, and 17 additional directors.
Number of staff: None.
EIN: 990210467

749
Harold K. L. Castle Foundation ▼
629 Kailua Rd., Rm. 210
Kailua 96734   (808) 262-9413

Incorporated in 1962 in HI.
Donor(s): Harold K.L. Castle,‡ Mrs. Harold K.L. Castle.‡
Foundation type: Independent
Financial data (yr. ended 12/31/90): Assets, $83,986,484 (M); expenditures, $3,720,943; qualifying distributions, $3,362,899, including $3,312,190 for 47 grants (high: $500,000; low: $1,000; average: $10,000-$100,000).
Purpose and activities: Emphasis on education; support also for youth agencies, hospitals, cultural programs, and marine research.
Fields of interest: Education, youth, hospitals, marine sciences, cultural programs.
Types of support: Annual campaigns, seed money, emergency funds, building funds, equipment, research, general purposes, continuing support, capital campaigns.
Limitations: Giving primarily in HI. No grants to individuals.

Application information: Application form not required.

Initial approach: Letter
Copies of proposal: 1
Deadline(s): Submit proposal preferably in Jan. or Feb.; deadline Mar. 31
Board meeting date(s): Apr.
Final notification: May
Write: David D. Thoma, V.P.

Officers and Directors:* James C. Castle,* Pres.; David D. Thoma, V.P. and Treas.; James C. Castle, Jr.,* V.P.; Randolph Moore, V.P.; Carol Conrad, Secy.; John C. Baldwin, James C. McIntosh, Peter E. Russell.

Number of staff: 1
EIN: 996005445
Recent health grants:

749-1 American Heart Association, Honolulu, HI, $15,000. 1990.

749-2 Castle Medical Center, Kailua, HI, $330,000. 1990.

749-3 Habilitat, Kaneohe, HI, $10,000. 1990.

749-4 Kahuku Hospital Foundation, Kahuku, HI, $50,000. 1990.

749-5 March of Dimes Birth Defects Foundation, Honolulu, HI, $25,000. 1990.

749-6 Rehabilitation Hospital of the Pacific, Honolulu, HI, $30,000. 1990.

749-7 Samaritan Counseling Center of Hawaii, Honolulu, HI, $10,000. 1990.

750
Samuel N. and Mary Castle Foundation

222 Merchant St.
Honolulu 96813   (808) 537-6333
FAX: (808) 521-6286

Incorporated in 1925 in HI; founded as Mary Castle Fund in 1898.
Donor(s): Mary Castle.‡
Foundation type: Independent
Financial data (yr. ended 12/31/90): Assets, $22,228,602 (M); expenditures, $1,054,775; qualifying distributions, $937,705, including $875,753 for 60 grants (high: $75,000; low: $353; average: $3,000-$25,000).
Purpose and activities: Emphasis on private higher and secondary education, human service organizations, community funds, and denominational giving; special fund for early childhood education programs. Most grants for direct service activities or capital projects.
Fields of interest: Education, higher education, education—early childhood, secondary education, elementary education, education—building funds, denominational giving.
Types of support: Special projects, building funds, equipment, seed money, land acquisition, renovation projects, general purposes, capital campaigns.
Limitations: Giving limited to HI. No grants to individuals, or for continuing support, endowment funds, or scholarships; generally no support for research; no loans.
Publications: Annual report.
Application information: Application form not required.

Initial approach: Telephone or proposal
Copies of proposal: 1
Deadline(s): Jan. 1, Apr. 1, July 1, and Oct. 1

Board meeting date(s): 2nd Thursday in Mar., June, Sept., and Dec.
Final notification: 3 months
Write: Susan Jones, Grants Administrator
Officers and Trustees:* W. Donald Castle,* Pres.; William E. Aull,* V.P.; Zadoc W. Brown,* V.P.; James C. Castle,* V.P.; Robert R. Midkiff,* V.P.; Alfred L. Castle,* Secy.; Hawaiian Trust Co., Ltd., Treas.
Number of staff: None.
EIN: 996003321
Recent health grants:

750-1 Bobby Benson Foundation, Honolulu, HI, $50,000. For construction of substance abuse treatment center. 1990.

750-2 Castle Medical Center, Kailua, HI, $40,000. For building construction and equipment purchase. 1990.

751
Cooke Foundation, Ltd.

c/o Hawaiian Trust Co., Ltd.
P.O. Box 3170
Honolulu 96802   (808) 537-6333
Application address: Grants Administrator, c/o Hawaii Community Foundation, 222 Merchant St., 2nd Fl., Honolulu, HI 96813

Trust established in 1920 in HI; incorporated in 1971.
Donor(s): Anna C. Cooke.‡
Foundation type: Independent
Financial data (yr. ended 06/30/90): Assets, $16,236,976 (M); expenditures, $539,972; qualifying distributions, $470,083, including $425,250 for 71 grants (high: $50,000; low: $1,000; average: $2,000-$10,000).
Fields of interest: Cultural programs, arts, social services, education, youth, health, environment, humanities, aged.
Types of support: Special projects, annual campaigns, equipment, research, publications, conferences and seminars, matching funds, operating budgets, renovation projects, seed money, capital campaigns.
Limitations: Giving limited to HI or to organizations serving the people of HI. No support for churches or religious organizations, unless the trustees' "missionary forebears" were involved with them. No grants to individuals, or for scholarships, fellowships, or endowment funds; no loans.
Publications: Program policy statement, application guidelines, annual report (including application guidelines).
Application information: Application form not required.

Initial approach: Telephone or proposal
Copies of proposal: 7
Deadline(s): 1st week of month preceding each board meeting
Board meeting date(s): 4th Wednesday in Jan., Apr., July, and Oct.
Final notification: 2 weeks after board meeting
Write: Prog. Officer, Prog. Officer
Officers and Trustees:* Samuel A. Cooke,* Pres.; Richard A. Cooke, Jr.,* V.P.; Betty P. Dunford,* V.P.; Charles C. Spalding, Jr.,* V.P.; Catherine C. Summers,* V.P.; Anna Blackwell,* Secy.; Hawaiian Trust Co., Ltd., Treas.
Number of staff: 3 shared staff
EIN: 237120804

Recent health grants:

751-1 Maui Rehabilitation Center, Wailuku, HI, $10,000. For purchase of rotary mower. 1990.

751-2 Planned Parenthood of Hawaii, Honolulu, HI, $10,000. For community affairs program. 1990.

752
Mary D. and Walter F. Frear
Eleemosynary Trust

c/o Bishop Trust Co., Ltd.
1000 Bishop St.
Honolulu 96813   (808) 523-2233
Mailing address: P.O. Box 2390, Honolulu, HI 96804-2390

Trust established in 1936 in HI.
Donor(s): Mary D. Frear,‡ Walter F. Frear.†
Foundation type: Independent
Financial data (yr. ended 12/31/90): Assets, $10,663,056 (M); expenditures, $722,652; qualifying distributions, $686,430, including $665,002 for 127 grants (high: $25,000; low: $1,000).
Purpose and activities: Giving primarily for education, welfare and social services, and child welfare and youth; support also for music and the arts and AIDS research.
Fields of interest: Education, welfare, social services, child welfare, youth, arts, music, AIDS.
Types of support: Operating budgets, seed money, building funds, equipment, matching funds, scholarship funds, special projects, conferences and seminars, capital campaigns.
Limitations: Giving limited to HI. No grants to individuals, or for endowment funds, reserve funds, travel, or deficit financing; no loans.
Publications: Annual report (including application guidelines).
Application information: Application form not required.

Initial approach: Proposal
Copies of proposal: 4
Deadline(s): Jan. 15, Apr. 15, July 15, and Oct. 15
Board meeting date(s): Distribution committee meets in Mar., June, Sept., and Dec.; scholarship requests considered at Mar. meeting, capital requests in Dec.
Final notification: 2 to 3 months
Write: Lois C. Loomis, V.P. and Corp. Secy., Bishop Trust Co., Ltd.
Distribution Committee: Sharon McPhee, Chair.; Edwin L. Carter, Howard Hamamoto.
Trustee: Bishop Trust Co., Ltd.
Number of staff: 2 shared staff
EIN: 996002270
Recent health grants:

752-1 Bobby Benson Foundation, Honolulu, HI, $10,000. For capital fund drive. 1990.

752-2 Kalihi-Palama Health Clinic, Honolulu, HI, $12,500. For programs. 1990.

752-3 Rehabilitation Hospital of the Pacific Foundation, Honolulu, HI, $15,000. Toward replacing hospital roof. 1990.

752-4 Saint Francis Medical Center, Honolulu, HI, $20,000. For capital fund drive. 1990.

752-5 Wilcox Hospital Foundation, Lihue, HI, $20,000. For capital fund drive. 1990.

753
The Hawaii Community Foundation
(Formerly The Hawaiian Foundation)
222 Merchant St.
Honolulu 96813   (808) 537-6333
FAX: (808) 521-6286

Established in 1916 in HI by trust resolution;
incorporated in 1987; reorganized in 1988.
Foundation type: Community
Financial data (yr. ended 12/31/91): Assets,
$140,141,937 (M); gifts received, $20,814,076;
expenditures, $8,298,906; qualifying
distributions, $6,748,768, including $6,220,569
for 747 grants (high: $2,583,000; low: $11;
average: $500-$50,000) and $528,199 for 748
grants to individuals (high: $5,000; low: $25;
average: $250-$10,000).
Purpose and activities: To assist charitable,
religious, and educational institutions by the
distribution of funds, many of which have been
restricted for specific purposes and in some
instances for specific institutions. General fund
priorities are problems of youth, families in crisis,
environmental concerns, cultural and historic
preservation, and community-based economic
development; also provided: one-time only
welfare assistance to needy adults or children and
partial tuition support for learning disabled
children.
Fields of interest: Youth, family services,
environment, cultural programs, historic
preservation, welfare, welfare—indigent
individuals, disadvantaged, aged, health.
Types of support: Operating budgets, seed money,
equipment, technical assistance, scholarship
funds, student aid, research, special projects,
grants to individuals, conferences and seminars,
consulting services, renovation projects.
Limitations: Giving limited to HI. No grants for
annual campaigns; no loans.
Publications: Program policy statement,
application guidelines, informational brochure,
annual report, newsletter.
Application information: Application procedures
vary with foundation's component funds.
Application form not required.
   Initial approach: Letter requesting application
      guidelines
   Copies of proposal: 1
   Deadline(s): 2 months prior to committee
      meetings
   Board meeting date(s): Monthly, except Apr.
      and Sept.
   Final notification: 2 weeks after meeting
   Write: Jane Renfro Smith, C.E.O.
Officers and Board Members:* Jane Renfro
Smith, C.E.O; Samuel A. Cooke,* Pres.; Douglas
Philpotts,* V.P.; Diane J. Plotts,* V.P.; Robert R.
Midkiff,* Secy.; Philip H. Ching,* Treas.; and 25
additional board members.
Trustees: Bishop Trust Co., Ltd., First Hawaiian
Bank, Hawaiian Trust Co., Ltd.
Number of staff: 13 full-time professional; 2
part-time professional; 10 full-time support; 1
part-time support.
EIN: 990261283

754
Hawaiian Electric Industries Charitable Foundation
P.O. Box 730
Honolulu 96808   (808) 532-5860

Established in 1984 in HI.
Donor(s): Hawaiian Electric Industries, Inc.
Foundation type: Company-sponsored
Financial data (yr. ended 12/31/91): Assets,
$3,288,000 (M); expenditures, $1,048,000;
qualifying distributions, $1,000,000, including
$973,450 for 150 grants (high: $330,000; low:
$300; average: $300-$330,000), $18,000 for 15
grants to individuals of $1,200 each and $8,550
for 40 employee matching gifts.
Purpose and activities: Support for museums and
the performing arts; education, including higher
and secondary schools, business education,
educational associations, and libraries; health
services and associations, hospitals, and cancer,
mental health, and drug abuse programs; social
services and welfare, including child
development and family services, the
disadvantaged, and housing and hunger
programs; community funds and development;
and ecology.
Fields of interest: Education, higher education,
health, welfare, youth, community funds,
environment.
Types of support: Employee matching gifts,
capital campaigns, building funds, renovation
projects, scholarship funds, matching funds,
professorships, research, annual campaigns,
employee-related scholarships, endowment
funds, special projects.
Limitations: Giving primarily in HI. No support
for religious, veterans', or fraternal organizations.
No grants for operating budgets or maintenance
activities.
Publications: Annual report, application
guidelines.
Application information: Application form not
required.
   Initial approach: Letter, with project data
   Copies of proposal: 1
   Deadline(s): Dec. 1 and June 1
   Board meeting date(s): Feb. and Aug.
   Write: Scott Shirai, Dir., Community Relations
Officers and Directors:* Robert F. Clarke,* Pres.;
E.J. Blackburn,* V.P.; Harwood D. Williamson,*
V.P.; Ben F. Kaito, Victor Li, Jeffrey Watanabe.
Number of staff: 1 full-time professional; 1
part-time support.
EIN: 990230697

755
McInerny Foundation ▼
c/o Bishop Trust Co., Ltd.
1000 Bishop St.
Honolulu 96813   (808) 523-2233
Mailing address: P.O. Box 2390, Honolulu, HI
96804-2390

Trust established in 1937 in HI.
Donor(s): William H. McInerny,‡ James D.
McInerny,‡ Ella McInerny.‡
Foundation type: Independent
Financial data (yr. ended 09/30/91): Assets,
$38,342,419 (M); expenditures, $2,391,415;
qualifying distributions, $1,853,113, including

$1,739,575 for 139 grants (high: $50,000; low:
$1,000; average: $5,000-$10,000).
Purpose and activities: Emphasis on education,
youth and social services, health and
rehabilitation, and culture and the arts.
Fields of interest: Education, youth, welfare,
health, rehabilitation, AIDS, social services,
cultural programs, arts.
Types of support: Operating budgets, continuing
support, seed money, building funds, equipment,
matching funds, scholarship funds, special
projects, capital campaigns.
Limitations: Giving limited to HI. No support for
religious institutions. No grants to individuals, or
for endowment funds, deficit financing, or
research; no loans.
Publications: Annual report (including application
guidelines).
Application information: Application form
required for capital or scholarship funds.
   Initial approach: Proposal
   Copies of proposal: 7
   Deadline(s): Jan. 15 for scholarship funds; July
      15 for capital fund drives; none for others
   Board meeting date(s): Distribution committee
      generally meets monthly
   Final notification: 2 months
   Write: Mrs. Lois C. Loomis, V.P. and Corp.
      Secy., Bishop Trust Co., Ltd.
Distribution Committee: Edwin L. Carter, Chair.;
Henry B. Clark, Jr., Vice-Chair.; Mrs. Gerry Ching.
Trustee: Bishop Trust Co., Ltd.
Number of staff: 2 shared staff
EIN: 996002356
Recent health grants:
755-1 Bobby Benson Foundation, Honolulu, HI,
   $30,000. For pledge payment for capital fund
   drive for Bobby Benson Center. 1991.
755-2 Habilitat, Kaneohe, HI, $10,000. For
   kitchen/dining area renovations. 1991.
755-3 Hina Mauka, Honolulu, HI, $50,000. For
   pledge payment toward residence for
   recovering alcoholics. 1991.
755-4 Ohana Hale, Waianae, HI, $10,000. For
   programs for recovering alcoholics. 1991.
755-5 Second Chance, Honolulu, HI, $10,000.
   For staff positions for program for recovering
   alcoholics. 1991.
755-6 Waikiki Health Center, Honolulu, HI,
   $10,000. For low-cost primary health case.
   1991.
755-7 Wilcox Hospital Foundation, Lihue, HI,
   $25,000. For pledge payment for capital fund
   drive. 1991.

756
PRI Foundation
c/o Bishop Trust Co., Ltd.
P.O. Box 2390
Honolulu 96804   (808) 547-3136
Application address: P.O. Box 3379, Honolulu,
HI 96842

Established in 1986 in HI.
Foundation type: Company-sponsored
Financial data (yr. ended 12/31/91): Assets,
$58,153 (M); gifts received, $623,012;
expenditures, $661,199; qualifying distributions,
$660,039, including $655,865 for 120 grants
(high: $50,000; low: $100).

Purpose and activities: Primary areas of interest include health, welfare, social services, and education, including secondary education.
Fields of interest: Cultural programs, arts, education, secondary education, health, social services, youth, welfare.
Types of support: Equipment, renovation projects, capital campaigns, building funds, matching funds.
Limitations: Giving primarily in HI and other areas of company operations. No support for sports. No grants to individuals, or for operating support to Aloha United Way-supported organizations, educational institutions for scholarships, or subsidization of travel.
Publications: Annual report (including application guidelines), application guidelines.
Application information: Application form not required.
 Initial approach: Proposal
 Copies of proposal: 1
 Deadline(s): 1 month prior to board meetings
 Board meeting date(s): Mar., June, Sept., and Dec.
 Write: Linda Howe, Secy.
Officers and Trustees:* Andrea L. Simpson,* Pres.; Linda M. Howe, Secy.; George E. Bates, Muriel M. Kaminaka, Fidencio M. Mares, Melvin M. Nakamura, Heidi K. Wild.
Number of staff: 1 part-time professional.
EIN: 990248628

757
M. M. Scott Scholarship Fund - Gertrude S. Straub Trust Estate

c/o Hawaiian Trust Co., Ltd.
P.O. Box 3170
Honolulu 96802
Scholarship application address: c/o Hawaii Community Foundation, 222 Merchant St., Honolulu, HI 96813; Tel.: (808) 537-6333

Established in 1966.
Donor(s): Gertrude S. Straub.‡
Foundation type: Independent
Financial data (yr. ended 03/31/91): Assets, $4,328,212 (M); expenditures, $286,510; qualifying distributions, $272,982, including $254,380 for 94 grants to individuals (high: $6,500; low: $400; average: $500-$4,000).
Purpose and activities: Scholarship grants to HI high school graduates to attend mainland colleges and major in a subject relating to the better understanding of peace and the promotion of international peace.
Fields of interest: Peace, international studies, international affairs, political science, government, economics, anthropology, social sciences, psychology, history.
Types of support: Student aid.
Limitations: Giving limited to HI.
Publications: Informational brochure (including application guidelines).
Application information: Applicants must be a graduate from a public high school in HI. Application form required.
 Initial approach: Telephone or letter of inquiry
 Copies of proposal: 1
 Deadline(s): Submit application preferably between Jan. 1 and Mar. 1; deadline Mar. 1
 Board meeting date(s): Apr.
 Final notification: May

Trustee: Hawaiian Trust Co., Ltd.
Number of staff: 3 shared staff
EIN: 996003243

758
A. & E. Vidinha Charitable Trust

c/o Bishop Trust Co., Ltd.
1000 Bishop St.
Honolulu 96813 (808) 523-2233
Mailing address: P.O. Box 2390, Honolulu, HI 96804-2390

Established in 1989 in HI.
Donor(s): Antone Vidinha,‡ Edene Vidinha.‡
Foundation type: Independent
Financial data (yr. ended 06/30/91): Assets, $4,540,437 (M); expenditures, $461,877; qualifying distributions, $430,732, including $428,500 for 36 grants (high: $30,000; low: $500).
Purpose and activities: Giving limited to hospitals and health associations benefiting Kauai residents, churches on Kauai, and scholarships to Hawaii colleges and universities for residents of the island of Kauai.
Fields of interest: Hospitals, health associations, religion, higher education.
Types of support: General purposes, operating budgets, scholarship funds, building funds, equipment.
Limitations: Giving limited to Kauai, HI. No grants to individuals.
Publications: Annual report (including application guidelines), program policy statement.
Application information: Contributes with preference to pre-selected organizations. Application form required.
 Initial approach: Proposal
 Copies of proposal: 4
 Deadline(s): Mar. 15
 Board meeting date(s): May or June
 Final notification: 2 to 3 months
 Write: Lois C. Loomis, V.P. and Corp. Secy., Bishop Trust Co., Ltd.
Distribution Committee: E.L. Carter, Chair.; Marion Espinda, Carol Mon Lee.
Trustee: Bishop Trust Co., Ltd.
Number of staff: None.
EIN: 990273993

759
G. N. Wilcox Trust

c/o Bishop Trust Co., Ltd.
1000 Bishop St.
Honolulu 96813-2390 (808) 523-2233
Mailing address: P.O. Box 2390, Honolulu, HI 96804-2390

Trust established in 1916 in HI.
Donor(s): George N. Wilcox.‡
Foundation type: Independent
Financial data (yr. ended 12/31/90): Assets, $12,654,752 (M); gifts received, $65,000; expenditures, $817,537; qualifying distributions, $735,554, including $706,393 for 122 grants (high: $50,000; low: $500; average: $1,000-$10,000).
Purpose and activities: Support primarily for education, including literacy programs, the elderly, health agencies and care of the sick, and social service agencies, including family services

and child welfare; grants also for arts and culture, hospices, AIDS services and education, community funds, delinquency and crime prevention, and Protestant church support.
Fields of interest: Education, literacy, social services, child welfare, family services, arts, health, AIDS, aged, community funds, family services, Protestant giving.
Types of support: Seed money, building funds, equipment, matching funds, scholarship funds, general purposes, continuing support, capital campaigns, special projects.
Limitations: Giving limited to HI, particularly the Island of Kauai. No support for government agencies or organizations substantially supported by government funds. No grants to individuals, or for endowment funds (except endowments for scholarships), reserve funds, research, or deficit financing; no direct student aid or scholarships; no loans.
Publications: Annual report (including application guidelines).
Application information: Scholarship requests considered at Mar. meeting; capital campaign requests considered at Dec. meeting. Application form not required.
 Initial approach: Telephone or proposal
 Copies of proposal: 5
 Deadline(s): Jan. 15, Apr. 15, July 15, and Oct. 15
 Board meeting date(s): Mar., June, Sept., and Dec.
 Final notification: 2 to 3 months
 Write: Mrs. Lois C. Loomis, V.P. and Corp. Secy., Bishop Trust Co., Ltd.
Committee on Beneficiaries: Edwin L. Carter, Chair.; Gale Fisher Carswell, Aletha Kaohi.
Trustee: Bishop Trust Co., Ltd.
Number of staff: None.
EIN: 996002445
Recent health grants:
 759-1 Bobby Benson Foundation, Honolulu, HI, $10,000. For capital fund drive. 1990.
 759-2 Kalihi-Palama Health Clinic, Honolulu, HI, $10,000. For primary health care services. 1990.
 759-3 Saint Francis Medical Center, Honolulu, HI, $15,000. For capital fund drive. 1990.
 759-4 Wilcox Hospital Foundation, Lihue, HI, $50,000. For capital fund drive. 1990.

760
S. W. Wilcox Trust

c/o Bishop Trust Co., Ltd.
1000 Bishop St.
Honolulu 96813 (808) 245-2822
Application address: P.O. Box 2096, Puhi-Rural Station, Lihue, HI 96766

Trust established in 1921 in HI.
Donor(s): Samuel Whitney Wilcox.‡
Foundation type: Independent
Financial data (yr. ended 12/31/91): Assets, $4,442,345 (M); expenditures, $247,116; qualifying distributions, $235,388, including $233,500 for 13 grants (high: $112,000; low: $5,000; average: $5,000-$25,000).
Purpose and activities: Funds presently committed to the support of local health, welfare, and educational organizations.
Fields of interest: Health, welfare, education.

Types of support: Continuing support, seed money, building funds.
Limitations: Giving limited to Kauai and Big Island, HI. No grants to individuals, or for research programs, scholarships, fellowships, or matching gifts; no loans.
Application information: Unsolicited proposals not considered. Applications not accepted.
   Board meeting date(s): Dec. and as required
   Write: David W. Pratt, Trustee
Trustees: Gale Fisher Carswell, Pam Dohrman, David W. Pratt.
Number of staff: None.
EIN: 996002547

761
The James and Juanita Wo Foundation
(Formerly C. S. Wo Foundation)
1314 South King St., No. 524
Honolulu 96814   (808) 523-5078

Established in 1960.
Donor(s): C.S. Wo & Sons, Inc., James C. Wo, Robert C. Wo.
Foundation type: Independent
Financial data (yr. ended 05/31/91): Assets, $572,786 (M); expenditures, $571,463; qualifying distributions, $565,740, including $562,098 for 14 grants (high: $532,998; low: $100).

Fields of interest: Social services, education, health, religion—Christian, community development.
Limitations: Giving primarily in HI. No grants to individuals.
Application information:
   Initial approach: Letter
   Deadline(s): None
   Write: James C. Wo, Chair.
Officers and Directors:* James C. Wo,* Chair.; Juanita C. Wo,* Vice-Chair.; Richard C. Wo,* Pres.; Julia C. Wo,* V.P.; David C. Wo,* Secy.-Treas.
EIN: 996009140

762
Hans and Clara Davis Zimmerman Foundation
c/o Hawaiian Trust Co., Ltd.
P.O. Box 3170
Honolulu 96802   (808) 537-6333
Application address: c/o Hawaii Community Foundation, 222 Merchant St., Honolulu, HI 96813

Established in 1963.
Donor(s): Hans Zimmerman,‡ Clara Zimmerman.‡

Foundation type: Independent
Financial data (yr. ended 12/31/90): Assets, $7,236,376 (M); expenditures, $424,111; qualifying distributions, $390,230, including $361,890 for 158 grants to individuals (high: $3,500; low: $150; average: $500-$3,000).
Purpose and activities: Giving for scholarships, with preference given to students majoring in medicine, nursing, or related health fields.
Fields of interest: Nursing, medical education, health, pharmacy.
Types of support: Student aid.
Limitations: Giving primarily in HI.
Publications: Informational brochure (including application guidelines).
Application information: Request application forms by Feb. 1. Application form required.
   Deadline(s): Mar. 1
   Board meeting date(s): May
Trustee: Hawaiian Trust Co., Ltd.
Scholarship Committee: Agnes Gutman, Marilyn Kim Infiesto, Leon Julian, Harold Nicolaus.
Number of staff: 3 shared staff
EIN: 996006669

IDAHO

763
Boise Cascade Corporate Giving Program
One Jefferson Sq.
Boise 83703   (208) 384-7673

Financial data (yr. ended 12/31/90): Total giving, $2,100,000 for grants.
Purpose and activities: Support for 1) Health and Human Services-United Way, hospitals, health and wellness promotion, programs to reduce health care costs, youth, senior citizens, emergency services; 2) Education-institutions conducting research in pulp and paper science, wood products manufacturing and forest management, or other fields related to the business, institutions that are sources for recruiting employees, school districts or communities where company operates, and affirmative action programs; 3) Public Issues and Economic Education-emphasis on business and teacher education and programs involving volunteers from the business sector; 4) Civic and Environmental-civic improvement, sports, recreation, parks, zoos, urban development, law and enforcement, housing and conservation, efforts supporting multiple forest management; 5) Culture-local and regional arts, museums, libraries, and public broadcasting; 6) Affirmative action-to improve the educational and employment opportunities for minorities, women, the disabled, and Vietnam era veterans in the private sector, housing rehabilitation, and social and recreational activities. In addition, the company donates products, services, inventory, equipment, and land, and employee volunteers donate their time to charities.
Fields of interest: Health, education, higher education, public policy, civic affairs, community development, environment, arts, cultural programs, business, economics.
Types of support: Capital campaigns, fellowships, general purposes, operating budgets, research, scholarship funds, special projects, employee matching gifts, in-kind gifts.
Limitations: Giving primarily in areas of company operations. No support for private foundations or for international, fraternal, social, labor, veterans, or religious organizations. No grants for political, sensitive, or controversial projects, or for projects perceived to be harmful to the company or those posing a possible conflict of interest; generally no support for local or regional chapters of national health organizations. No grants to individuals, or for courtesy ads, deficit financing, testimonials, school trips, or tours; no operating funds for United Way recipients.
Publications: Corporate giving report.
Application information: National organizations, programs that address company issues, organizations in Boise, and institutions where the company recruits employees write to headquarters, other organizations write to nearest plant. Application form required.
　Initial approach: Letter
　Write: Vicki M. Wheeler, Contribs. Mgr.
Administrators: Jean Miller, Bobbi Youmans.

764
Laura Moore Cunningham Foundation, Inc.
510 Main
Boise 83702-5932   (208) 347-7852

Incorporated in 1964 in ID.
Donor(s): Laura Moore Cunningham.‡
Foundation type: Independent
Financial data (yr. ended 08/31/91): Assets, $12,890,921 (M); expenditures, $486,518; qualifying distributions, $486,722, including $475,140 for 40 grants (high: $60,000; low: $1,000).
Purpose and activities: Emphasis on higher and other education, particularly for business scholarship funds; support also for hospitals and child welfare.
Fields of interest: Education, education—building funds, higher education, business education, hospitals, child welfare.
Types of support: Building funds, endowment funds, equipment, scholarship funds, special projects.
Limitations: Giving limited to ID. No grants to individuals.
Publications: Informational brochure (including application guidelines).
Application information: Application form required.
　Copies of proposal: 3
　Deadline(s): Feb. 28
　Board meeting date(s): Spring
　Write: Joan Davidson Carley, Secy.-Treas.
Officers and Directors:* Harry Little Bettis,* Pres.; Marjorie Moore Davidson,* V.P.; Joan Davidson Carley,* Secy.-Treas.
Number of staff: 1 part-time support.
EIN: 826008294

765
Daugherty Foundation
c/o West One Bank, Idaho, N.A.
P.O. Box 7928
Boise 83707
Application address: P.O. Box 51448, Idaho Falls, ID 83405

Established in 1965.
Donor(s): West One Bank, Idaho, N.A.
Foundation type: Independent
Financial data (yr. ended 12/31/91): Assets, $4,082,007 (M); expenditures, $753,927; qualifying distributions, $732,350, including $727,081 for 24 grants (high: $141,109; low: $1,000).
Purpose and activities: Giving for hospitals, youth organizations, child welfare, and a historical village.
Fields of interest: Hospitals, youth, child welfare, child development, historic preservation.
Types of support: Equipment, matching funds.
Limitations: Giving limited to eastern ID.
Publications: Informational brochure (including application guidelines).
Application information: Application form required.
　Initial approach: Letter
　Deadline(s): July 31
　Write: Hal Peterson, Trust Mgr., West One Bank, Idaho, N.A.
Trustee: West One Bank, Idaho, N.A.

EIN: 826010665

766
West One Bancorp Corporate Giving Program
P.O. Box 8247
Boise 83733   (208) 383-7275

Financial data (yr. ended 12/31/90): Total giving, $560,000 for grants.
Purpose and activities: Grants for the arts, education, community development, and health services.
Fields of interest: Arts, community development, business education, child welfare, handicapped, hospitals—building funds, libraries, citizenship, community funds, elementary education, homeless, literacy, dance, higher education, housing, education, health, hospitals, secondary education, museums, theater, music, rural development, volunteerism, women, safety, youth.
Types of support: Annual campaigns, capital campaigns, employee matching gifts, scholarship funds.
Limitations: Giving limited to ID, OR, UT, and WA.
Publications: Application guidelines.
Application information: There is a staff that only handles contributions. Application form required.
　Initial approach: Letter
　Copies of proposal: 1
　Board meeting date(s): Monthly
　Write: Mellodee Thornton, Mgr., Commun. Affairs
Number of staff: 1 full-time professional; 1 part-time support.

767
Macauley and Helen Dow Whiting Foundation
P.O. Box 1980
Sun Valley 83353

Incorporated in 1957 in MI.
Foundation type: Independent
Financial data (yr. ended 12/31/90): Assets, $3,846,646 (M); expenditures, $236,767; qualifying distributions, $173,072, including $162,193 for 22 grants (high: $25,000; low: $795).
Purpose and activities: Emphasis on higher and secondary education and hospitals; support also to environmental and energy conservation organizations; grants only to institutions with which trustees are familiar.
Fields of interest: Higher education, secondary education, hospitals, environment, energy, conservation.
Limitations: No grants to individuals.
Application information: Application form not required.
　Initial approach: Letter
　Copies of proposal: 1
　Deadline(s): None
　Board meeting date(s): At least twice a year
　Write: Macauley Whiting, Pres.
Officers and Trustees:* Macauley Whiting,* Pres.; Mary Macauley Whiting,* Secy.; Helen Dow Whiting,* Treas.; Sara Whiting.
EIN: 237418814

ILLINOIS

768
Abbott Laboratories Fund ▼
Dept. 379, Bldg. 6C
One Abbott Park Rd.
North Chicago 60064-3500 (708) 937-7075
Additional tel.: (708) 937-8686

Incorporated in 1951 in IL.
Donor(s): Abbott Laboratories.
Foundation type: Company-sponsored
Financial data (yr. ended 12/31/90): Assets,
$33,325,399 (M); gifts received, $513,725;
expenditures, $2,909,868; qualifying
distributions, $2,893,519, including $2,254,722
for 276 grants (high: $400,000; low: $500;
average: $10,000-$25,000) and $598,819 for
employee matching gifts.
Purpose and activities: Grants primarily to
institutions for higher education, including
medicine, pharmacy, and nursing, and for
medical research and selected health and welfare
causes; also matches contributions of company
employees and retirees to higher educational
institutions and hospitals.
Fields of interest: Higher education, hospitals,
medical education, pharmacy, nursing, medical
research, health, welfare, education.
Types of support: Operating budgets, continuing
support, scholarship funds, research, employee
matching gifts.
Limitations: Giving primarily in areas of company
operations. No support for social organizations,
religious institutions, or fundraising events. No
grants to individuals, or for deficit financing, land
acquisition, internships, employee-related
scholarships, exchange programs, fellowships, or
publications; no loans.
Publications: Program policy statement.
Application information: Application form not
required.
  Initial approach: Letter or proposal
  Copies of proposal: 1
  Deadline(s): None
  Board meeting date(s): Apr. and Dec.
  Final notification: 6 to 8 weeks
  Write: Gary P. Coughlan, President
Officers and Directors:* Gary P. Coughlan,*
Pres.; O. Ralph Edwards,* V.P.; Kenneth W.
Farmer,* V.P.; Paul E. Roge, Secy.; Barry R.
Wojtak, Treas.; Richard B. Hamilton, James A.
Hanley, Robert S. Janicki, John C. Kane, John G.
Kringel, David A. Thompson.
Number of staff: 1 full-time professional; 1
part-time professional; 1 full-time support; 1
part-time support.
EIN: 366069793

769
Alberto-Culver Company Giving Program
2525 Armitage Ave.
Melrose Park 60160 (312) 450-3000

Purpose and activities: Supports civic and
community programs, health and welfare,
education, culture, the arts and youth related

programs. Organizations in which company
employees are involved receive special
consideration as do non-sectarian groups that are
well-managed. Support is also given to women's
groups, minorities, the underprivileged and the
handicapped.
Fields of interest: Civic affairs, community
development, health, welfare, education, cultural
programs, arts, youth, women, minorities,
handicapped.
Types of support: Capital campaigns, general
purposes, matching funds, special projects.
Limitations: Giving primarily in headquarters city
and major operating areas.
Application information:
  Initial approach: Letter
  Write: Stephen Crews, V.P., Public Affairs and
  Communs.

770
Norris & Margaret Aldeen Charitable Foundation
4209 Marsh Ave.
Rockford 61111-6143

Established in 1965 in IL.
Donor(s): Norris A. Aldeen, Margaret Aldeen.
Foundation type: Independent
Financial data (yr. ended 12/31/90): Assets,
$1,323,673 (M); gifts received, $5,000;
expenditures, $452,330; qualifying distributions,
$440,500, including $440,500 for 14 grants
(high: $202,000; low: $1,000).
Purpose and activities: Support primarily for
Christian education; some support also for
churches and hospitals.
Fields of interest: Higher education,
religion—Christian, social services, hospitals,
youth.
Types of support: General purposes.
Limitations: Giving limited to the Rockford, IL,
area.
Application information: Application form not
required.
  Initial approach: Letter
  Deadline(s): None
  Write: The Trustees
Trustees: Margaret Aldeen, Norris A. Aldeen.
EIN: 366105736

771
Allen-Heath Memorial Foundation
135 South LaSalle St., Suite 1610
Chicago 60603-4391 (312) 845-5800

Incorporated in 1947 in CA.
Donor(s): Harriet A. Heath,‡ John E.S. Heath.‡
Foundation type: Independent
Financial data (yr. ended 12/31/91): Assets,
$3,490,104 (M); expenditures, $190,425;
qualifying distributions, $165,000, including
$165,000 for grants (average: $1,000-$25,000).
Purpose and activities: Grants to a limited
number of educational institutions, hospitals,
museums, air safety organizations, and other
charitable institutions.
Fields of interest: Higher education, hospitals,
museums, safety, aged, women, community
funds, community development.
Types of support: Annual campaigns, building
funds, operating budgets, special projects.

Limitations: No support for religious or foreign
organizations. No grants to individuals; no loans.
Publications: Application guidelines, annual
report.
Application information: Contributes only to
pre-selected organizations. Applications not
accepted.
  Board meeting date(s): Nov.
  Write: Paul E. Hoelschen, Jr., Secy.-Treas.
Officers and Directors:* Charles K. Heath,* Pres.;
Ruth R. Hooper,* V.P.; Paul E. Hoelschen, Jr.,
Secy.-Treas.; Nolan Baird.
Number of staff: None.
EIN: 363056910

772
The Allstate Foundation ▼
Allstate Plaza North
Northbrook 60062 (708) 402-5502

Incorporated in 1952 in IL.
Donor(s): Allstate Insurance Co.
Foundation type: Company-sponsored
Financial data (yr. ended 12/31/91): Assets,
$2,922,148 (M); expenditures, $6,054,975;
qualifying distributions, $6,054,975, including
$5,776,406 for 1,673 grants (high: $349,850;
low: $100; average: $5,000-$25,000) and
$278,569 for 1,878 employee matching gifts.
Purpose and activities: To assist deserving
organizations serving the fields of education,
including colleges and universities, urban and
civic affairs, safety, and health and welfare,
including youth agencies and community funds.
Particular interest in organizations dedicated to
principles of self-help and self-motivation.
Fields of interest: Education, higher education,
education—minorities, insurance education, civic
affairs, urban affairs, urban development, safety,
housing, rehabilitation, community development.
Types of support: Employee-related scholarships,
program-related investments, special projects.
Limitations: No support for fraternal or religious
organizations. No grants to individuals (except for
employee-related scholarships), or for annual
campaigns, deficit financing, building funds,
capital campaigns, endowment funds, fundraising
events, conferences, films, videotapes or audio
productions, or travel funds.
Publications: Informational brochure (including
application guidelines).
Application information: Application guidelines
available from the foundation. Application form
not required.
  Initial approach: Proposal
  Copies of proposal: 1
  Deadline(s): None
  Board meeting date(s): Mar., June, Sept., and
  Dec.
  Final notification: 30 to 90 days
  Write: Alan Benedeck, Exec. Dir., Allen
  Goldhamer, Mgr., or Dawn Bourgart, Admin.
  Asst.
Officers and Trustees:* Wayne E. Hedien,* Pres.;
Robert W. Pike,* V.P. and Secy.; Myron J.
Resnick,* V.P. and Treas.; John D. Callahan,* V.P.;
J.D. Choate,* V.P.; Raymond H. Kiefer,* V.P.; Rita
P. Wilson,* V.P.; Alan F. Benedeck, Exec. Dir.
Number of staff: 2 full-time professional; 1
full-time support; 1 part-time support.
EIN: 366116535
Recent health grants:

772-1 AIDS Foundation of Chicago, Chicago, IL, $10,000. 1990.

772-2 Alcoholism-Drug Dependence Institute of Illinois, Chicago, IL, $25,000. 1990.

772-3 Alivio Medical Center, Chicago, IL, $20,000. 1990.

772-4 Amyotrophic Lateral Sclerosis (ALS) Association, Prairie Village, KS, $10,000. 1990.

772-5 Cystic Fibrosis Foundation, San Francisco, CA, $15,000. 1990.

772-6 Dallas Challenge, Dallas, TX, $10,000. 1990.

772-7 Evangelical Health Systems, Bethany Hospital, Oak Brook, IL, $40,000. 1990.

772-8 Evanston Hospital, Evanston, IL, $100,000. 1990.

772-9 Good Shepherd Hospital, Barrington, IL, $26,500. For nursing education program. 1990.

772-10 Hinds Community College, Division of Associate Degree Nursing, Raymond, MS, $20,000. 1990.

772-11 Infant Welfare Society of Chicago, Chicago, IL, $14,215. 1990.

772-12 Juvenile Diabetes Foundation, Plano, TX, $10,000. 1990.

772-13 Life Savers Foundation of America, Covina, CA, $10,000. 1990.

772-14 Make-A-Wish Foundation, Bethesda, MD, $10,000. 1990.

772-15 March of Dimes Birth Defects Foundation, Costa Mesa, CA, $20,000. 1990.

772-16 March of Dimes Birth Defects Foundation, Costa Mesa, CA, $15,000. 1990.

772-17 Mental Health Association of Greater Chicago, Chicago, IL, $10,000. 1990.

772-18 Misericordia Home/Heart of Mercy Village, Chicago, IL, $15,000. 1990.

772-19 Muscular Dystrophy Association, Manhattan District Office, NYC, NY, $10,000. 1990.

772-20 National AIDS Network, DC, $65,000. 1990.

772-21 National Fitness Leaders Association, Chantilly, VA, $45,000. 1990.

772-22 National Student Nurses Association Foundation, NYC, NY, $25,000. 1990.

772-23 Partnership for a Drug Free America, NYC, NY, $15,000. 1990.

772-24 Ronald McDonald House, Kansas City, MO, $12,000. 1990.

772-25 Ronald McDonald House, Kansas City, MO, $10,936. 1990.

772-26 Rush-Presbyterian-Saint Lukes Medical Center, Chicago, IL, $50,000. 1990.

772-27 San Antonio College, School of Nursing, San Antonio, TX, $15,000. 1990.

772-28 University of Miami, School of Medicine, Miami, FL, $10,000. For Miami Project. 1990.

773

American National Bank and Trust Company of Chicago Foundation ▼
33 North LaSalle St.
Chicago 60690   (312) 661-6115

Trust established in 1955 in IL.
Donor(s): American National Bank & Trust Co. of Chicago.
Foundation type: Company-sponsored
Financial data (yr. ended 12/31/90): Assets, $1,260,684 (M); gifts received, $853,000;

---

expenditures, $1,445,603; qualifying distributions, $1,433,631, including $1,336,099 for 277 grants (high: $300,000; low: $50; average: $500-$5,000) and $53,319 for 234 employee matching gifts.
Purpose and activities: Giving for hospitals, the arts, and elementary and higher education; support also for community organizations, youth agencies, and urban affairs.
Fields of interest: Hospitals, arts, elementary education, higher education, education—minorities, community development, youth, urban affairs.
Types of support: Employee matching gifts, operating budgets, general purposes, continuing support, annual campaigns, building funds, special projects, capital campaigns.
Limitations: Giving limited to the six-county Chicago, IL, metropolitan area. No support for sectarian religious organizations. No grants to individuals, or for conferences or seminars, land acquisition, endowment funds, fellowships, lectureships, professorships, or scholarships; no loans.
Publications: Application guidelines, program policy statement.
Application information: Application form not required.
   Initial approach: Proposal; no telephone calls
   Copies of proposal: 1
   Deadline(s): None
   Board meeting date(s): Bimonthly
   Final notification: 3 months
   Write: Joan M. Klaus, Dir.
Trustees: Timothy P. Moen, Chair.; David W. Bender, Samuel Crayton, Jr., Ronald J. Grayheck, Joan M. Klaus, John F. Reuss, Robert F. Schnoes.
Number of staff: 1 full-time professional; 1 part-time support.
EIN: 366052269

774

Ameritech Foundation ▼
30 South Wacker Dr., 34th Fl.
Chicago 60606   (312) 750-5223

Established in 1984 in IL.
Donor(s): American Information Technologies.
Foundation type: Company-sponsored
Financial data (yr. ended 12/31/90): Assets, $63,242,200 (M); expenditures, $5,239,756; qualifying distributions, $5,005,656, including $4,852,918 for 137 grants (high: $250,000; low: $2,000; average: $10,000-$25,000) and $152,738 for 264 employee matching gifts.
Purpose and activities: Grants largely to multi-state organizations for economic revitalization, education, and culture in the Great Lakes region. Support also for research and programs designed to determine ways communications can contribute to the betterment of society, and selected public policy issues which are relevant to the telecommunications industry, health and human services, and to national organizations which address the foundation's stated interests.
Fields of interest: Community development, education, cultural programs, public policy, media and communications, health.
Types of support: Employee matching gifts, special projects, conferences and seminars, research.

Limitations: Giving primarily in IL, WI, IN, MI, and OH. No support for religious organizations for sectarian purposes, national or international organizations with limited relationships to local company operations, affiliates of labor organizations, local chapters of national organizations, veterans' or military organizations, discriminatory organizations, political groups, athletics, or health organizations concentrating on research and treatment in one area of human disease. No grants to individuals, or for start-up funds, advertising, or for the purchase of tickets for benefits and fundraising events.
Publications: Annual report (including application guidelines).
Application information: Application form not required.
   Initial approach: Letter
   Copies of proposal: 1
   Deadline(s): None
   Board meeting date(s): Mar., June, Sept., and Dec.
   Final notification: 3 months
   Write: Michael E. Kuhlin, Dir.
Officers and Directors:* John A. Koten,* Pres.; Robert Kolbe, V.P. and C.F.O.; Michael E. Kuhlin,* Secy.; Ronald G. Pippin, Comptroller; Hanna Holborn Gray, James R. Heidenreich, John A. Koten, Martha L. Thornton, William L. Weiss.
Number of staff: 1 full-time professional; 1 part-time support.
EIN: 363350561
Recent health grants:
774-1 Cleveland Clinic Foundation, Cleveland, OH, $25,000. For first payment of five-year pledge for new Health Science Center. 1990.
774-2 National Leadership Commission on Health Care, DC, $25,000. For comprehensive reform of American's health care system. 1990.
774-3 Rehabilitation Institute of Chicago, Chicago, IL, $25,000. For first payment of five-year pledge for rehabilitation research and engineering programs. 1990.
774-4 United Cerebral Palsy of Greater Chicago, Chicago, IL, $10,000. For annual campaign. 1990.
774-5 Washington Business Group on Health, DC, $15,000. For Quality Resource Center. 1990.

775

Amoco Foundation, Inc. ▼
200 East Randolph Dr.
Chicago 60601   (312) 856-6306

Incorporated in 1952 in IN.
Donor(s): Amoco Corp.
Foundation type: Company-sponsored
Financial data (yr. ended 12/31/91): Assets, $63,800,216 (M); gifts received, $24,709,623; expenditures, $28,001,219; qualifying distributions, $26,474,779, including $26,474,779 for grants (average: $10,000-$100,000).
Purpose and activities: Grants awarded for higher and pre-college education, primarily in science and engineering, and for community organizations, urban programs, and energy conservation, with emphasis on new initiatives; support also for independent public interest research, a limited program in culture and art, a volunteer program, and an employee educational

gift matching program. Limited contributions to foreign charitable and educational institutions.
Fields of interest: Education, higher education, science and technology, engineering, community development, urban affairs, conservation, energy, cultural programs, social services, youth, medical research.
Types of support: Operating budgets, continuing support, annual campaigns, seed money, emergency funds, building funds, equipment, scholarship funds, fellowships, special projects, general purposes, capital campaigns, employee matching gifts.
Limitations: Giving primarily in areas of company representation to assist communities. No support for primary or secondary schools or religious, fraternal, social, or athletic organizations; generally, no support for organizations already receiving operating support through the United Way. No grants to individuals, or for endowment funds, research, publications, or conferences.
Publications: Annual report (including application guidelines).
Application information: Application form not required.
   Initial approach: Letter or proposal
   Copies of proposal: 1
   Deadline(s): Sept. 1
   Board meeting date(s): Mar., June, Sept., and Dec.; contributions committee meets monthly
   Final notification: 4 to 6 weeks
   Write: Patricia D. Wright, Exec. Dir.
Officers and Directors:* Robert D. Cadieux,* Chair.; Frederick S. Addy,* Pres.; Patricia D. Wright, Secy. and Exec. Dir.; John S. Ruey, Treas.; R. Wayne Anderson, Jerry M. Brown, Richard E. Evans, Arthur R. McCaughan, George S. Spindler, Terrance R. Weaver.
Number of staff: 6 full-time professional; 5 full-time support; 2 part-time support.
EIN: 366046879

776
Amsted Industries Corporate Giving Program
205 North Michigan Ave., 44th Fl.
Chicago 60601   (312) 819-8518

Financial data (yr. ended 09/30/90): Total giving, $20,000.
Purpose and activities: Support is usually through the foundation. The Corporation makes occasional gifts, mostly in Europe and Canada. Overall contributions are for higher education and technical institutes as well as social services, and civic programs including United Way and youth related activities. Cultural programs also receive some support.
Fields of interest: Higher education, social services, health, civic affairs, community funds, youth, cultural programs, arts, Europe, Canada.
Types of support: General purposes.
Limitations: Giving primarily in headquarters city and major operating areas; no support for national organizations. No support for political, religious, or veteran's groups. No grants to individuals, or for endowments, fellowships, scholarships, or courtesy advertising. No grants on a matching basis.
Application information: Public Affairs Department handles giving. Application form not required.

   Initial approach: Brief letter; send requests to nearest company facility
   Copies of proposal: 1
   Deadline(s): Apr.
   Board meeting date(s): Meetings as required
   Final notification: 4-6 weeks
   Write: Jerry W. Gura, Dir., Public Affairs
Number of staff: 1 part-time professional; 1 part-time support.

777
Amsted Industries Foundation
205 North Michigan Ave.
Blvd. Towers South, 44th Fl.
Chicago 60601   (312) 645-1700

Trust established in 1953 in IL.
Donor(s): Amsted Industries, Inc.
Foundation type: Company-sponsored
Financial data (yr. ended 09/30/90): Assets, $3,943,655 (M); expenditures, $457,821; qualifying distributions, $437,875, including $437,875 for 297 grants (high: $30,000; low: $50).
Fields of interest: Cultural programs, civic affairs, health, health services, social services, education.
Types of support: Operating budgets, employee matching gifts, building funds, continuing support.
Limitations: Giving limited to areas of company operations; main emphasis on Chicago, IL; support also in KS, AL, MO, MD, IN, NE, DE, VA, CA, PA, DE, CT, and Washington, DC. No support for religious organizations or veterans' groups. No grants to individuals, or for endowment funds, scholarships, fellowships, or courtesy advertising; no loans.
Application information: Commencing with the 1993 fiscal period, the foundation's focus will shift to disbursements through its employee matching gift program, curtailing and restricting its present giving patterns. New requests for funding not considered. Applications not accepted.
   Board meeting date(s): Annually
   Write: Jerry W. Gura, Dir., Public Affairs
Officer and Trustees:* Arthur W. Goetschel, Mgr.; O.J. Sopranos, G.K. Walter, R.H. Wellington.
Number of staff: 1 part-time professional; 1 part-time support.
EIN: 366050609

778
Arthur Andersen Foundation
P.O. Box 6
Barrington 60010   (708) 381-8134

Incorporated in 1953 in IL.
Donor(s): Arthur A. Andersen.‡
Foundation type: Independent
Financial data (yr. ended 10/31/90): Assets, $2,283,215 (M); gifts received, $4,750; expenditures, $217,088; qualifying distributions, $189,357, including $163,000 for 12 grants (high: $50,000; low: $1,000).
Fields of interest: Higher education, youth, hospitals, music.
Limitations: Giving primarily in IL.
Application information: Application form not required.
   Deadline(s): None
   Write: Arthur Andersen III, Pres.

Officers: Arthur E. Andersen III, Pres.; Joan N. Andersen, V.P. and Treas.; John E. Hicks, Secy.
EIN: 510175922

779
The Andreas Foundation
c/o Archer-Daniels-Midland Co.
P.O. Box 1470
Decatur 62525   (217) 424-5200

Incorporated in 1945 in IA.
Donor(s): Dwayne O. Andreas, Lowell W. Andreas, Glenn A. Andreas.
Foundation type: Independent
Financial data (yr. ended 11/30/90): Assets, $3,140,519 (M); gifts received, $4,500; expenditures, $1,102,122; qualifying distributions, $1,092,186, including $1,092,186 for 104 grants (high: $230,000; low: $30; average: $500-$5,000).
Purpose and activities: Giving primarily for higher and secondary education, civil rights and economic opportunities for minority groups, and cultural programs; some support for hospitals, public policy research, churches, and youth agencies.
Fields of interest: Higher education, secondary education, civil rights, minorities, cultural programs, hospitals, youth, public policy, religion.
Types of support: Continuing support.
Limitations: No grants to individuals.
Application information: Contributes only to pre-selected organizations. Applications not accepted.
   Board meeting date(s): As required
   Write: Dwayne O. Andreas, Pres.
Officers and Trustees:* Dwayne O. Andreas,* Pres.; Lowell W. Andreas,* Exec. V.P. and Treas.; Michael D. Andreas,* V.P. and Secy.; Dorothy Inez Andreas, Terry Herbert-Burns, Sandra Andreas McMurtrie.
Number of staff: None.
EIN: 416017057

780
Aileen S. Andrew Foundation
10500 West 153rd St.
Orland Park 60462   (708) 349-3300

Incorporated in 1946 in IL.
Foundation type: Independent
Financial data (yr. ended 11/30/90): Assets, $15,032,545 (M); expenditures, $745,264; qualifying distributions, $635,384, including $349,976 for 100 grants (high: $63,440; low: $100) and $236,941 for 28 grants to individuals (high: $13,000; low: $943).
Purpose and activities: Giving for higher education, including scholarships for children of Andrew Corp. employees and graduates of a local high school; support also for civic affairs and general charitable giving locally.
Fields of interest: Higher education, civic affairs, hospitals, general charitable giving.
Types of support: Employee-related scholarships.
Limitations: Giving primarily in Orland Park, IL.
Application information: Application forms are available for scholarship program.
   Deadline(s): Apr. 1 for scholarships
   Board meeting date(s): Several times a year
   Final notification: May 1 for scholarships

Write: Robert E. Hord, Pres.
Officers and Directors:* Robert E. Hord,* Pres.;
Edward J. Andrew,* V.P.; Juanita A. Hord,* Secy.;
Richard L. Dybala, Treas.; Edith G. Andrew,
Robert E. Hord, Jr.
Number of staff: None.
EIN: 366049910

781
AON Foundation ▼
(Formerly Combined International Foundation)
123 North Wacker Dr.
Chicago 60606   (312) 701-3000

Established in 1984 in IL.
Donor(s): Aon Corp., and subsidiaries.
Foundation type: Company-sponsored
Financial data (yr. ended 12/31/90): Assets,
$999,542 (M); gifts received, $2,769,520;
expenditures, $3,212,143; qualifying
distributions, $3,212,143, including $3,160,082
for 534 grants (high: $400,000; low: $25;
average: $1,000-$10,000).
Purpose and activities: Support for higher and
other education, social services, community
funds, and hospitals and health associations.
Fields of interest: Higher education, education,
social services, youth, health associations,
hospitals, community funds.
Limitations: No support for the operation of
secondary educational institutions or vocational
schools.
Application information: Application form not
required.
  Initial approach: Letter
  Deadline(s): None
  Board meeting date(s): 4 times a year
  Final notification: Varies
  Write: Wallace J. Buya, V.P.
Officers and Directors:* Donald S. Perkins,*
Chair.; Patrick G. Ryan,* Pres.; Wallace J. Buya,
V.P., Secy., and Exec. Dir.; Harvey N. Medvin,
Treas.; Franklin A. Cole, Ronald K. Holmberg,
Andrew J. McKenna, Raymond I. Skilling.
Number of staff: 1 part-time professional.
EIN: 363337340

782
Archer-Daniels-Midland Foundation ▼
P.O. Box 1470
Decatur 62525   (217) 424-5200

Incorporated in 1953 in MN.
Donor(s): Archer-Daniels-Midland Co.
Foundation type: Company-sponsored
Financial data (yr. ended 06/30/91): Assets,
$5,694,275 (M); gifts received, $5,000,000;
expenditures, $3,285,087; qualifying
distributions, $2,728,589, including $2,728,589
for 471 grants (high: $100,000; low: $25;
average: $1,000-$10,000).
Purpose and activities: Grants largely for higher
education; support also for minority group
development, cultural activities, hospitals, youth
agencies, community funds, public policy
organizations, and for the prevention of cruelty to
animals and children.
Fields of interest: Higher education, minorities,
cultural programs, hospitals, youth, community
funds, public policy, animal welfare, child
welfare.

Application information:
  Initial approach: Letter
  Deadline(s): None
  Board meeting date(s): As needed
  Final notification: Upon acceptance; no
    notification of negative decision
  Write: Ken Struttmann, General Auditor
Officers and Directors:* John H. Daniels,* Chair.;
Lowell W. Andreas,* Pres.; Roy L. Erickson,
Secy.-Treas.; Richard E. Burket, Mgr.; Shreve
Archer.
EIN: 416023126

783
The Aurora Foundation
111 West Downer Place, Suite 312
Aurora 60506-5136   (708) 896-7800

Incorporated in 1948 in IL.
Foundation type: Community
Financial data (yr. ended 09/30/92): Assets,
$7,647,000 (M); gifts received, $745,908;
expenditures, $535,562; qualifying distributions,
$392,171, including $240,771 for grants and
$151,400 for grants to individuals (average:
$500-$2,500).
Purpose and activities: Grants for higher
education, including scholarships and colleges,
hospitals, youth activities, and community
services.
Fields of interest: Higher education, education,
health, hospitals, youth, social services, arts.
Types of support: Student aid, matching funds,
building funds, equipment, capital campaigns,
seed money.
Limitations: Giving limited to the immediate
Aurora, IL, area. No grants for operating budgets,
research, annual campaigns, or continuing
support.
Publications: Annual report, application
guidelines, newsletter.
Application information: Application form
required.
  Initial approach: Telephone
  Copies of proposal: 9
  Deadline(s): Mar. and Aug.
  Board meeting date(s): May and Nov.;
    executive committee meets as required
  Final notification: Apr. and Sept.
  Write: Sharon Stredde, Exec. Dir.
Officers and Directors:* Donald A. Schindlbeck,*
Pres.; Ruby Frank,* V.P.; Sharon Stredde, Secy.
and Exec. Dir.; Thomas S. Alexander,* Treas.; and
24 additional directors.
Number of staff: 1 full-time professional; 1
full-time support.
EIN: 366086742

784
Axia Incorporated Giving Program
122 West 22nd St.
Oak Brook 60521   (312) 571-3350

Purpose and activities: Supports arts and culture,
health and welfare, education, and civic
programs. Community service programs also
receive some support. Arts support includes
museums, public television and radio,
symphonies and chamber orchestras.

Fields of interest: Museums, arts, cultural
programs, health, welfare, education, civic affairs,
community development, education.
Types of support: Employee matching gifts,
employee-related scholarships.
Limitations: Giving primarily in home office area
and plant locations.
Publications: Informational brochure.
Application information: Application form not
required.
  Initial approach: Letter describing project
  Copies of proposal: 1
  Deadline(s): End of calendar year
  Write: Dennis W. Sheehan, Chair., Pres., and
    C.E.O.
Number of staff: 3

785
Barber-Colman Charitable Contribution
   Program
P.O. Box 7040
555 Colman Center Dr.
Rockford 61125   (815) 397-7400

Financial data (yr. ended 04/01/91): Total giving,
$130,000, including $120,000 for grants (high:
$30,000; low: $500; average: $3,000-$5,000)
and $10,000 for employee matching gifts.
Purpose and activities: Support for the arts,
community development, economics,
unemployment, health services, including
hospices, higher and secondary education, and
science and technology.
Fields of interest: Arts, community development,
economics, employment, health services, higher
education, hospices, science and technology,
secondary education, welfare.
Types of support: Building funds, capital
campaigns, equipment, seed money, technical
assistance, employee matching gifts.
Limitations: Giving primarily in communities
where company has manufacturing facilities
employing 100 or more, mainly IL. No grants to
individuals, or for deficit financing, research,
scholarships or fellowships; no loans.
Publications: Application guidelines, program
policy statement.
Application information: Application form
required.
  Initial approach: Letter
  Copies of proposal: 1
  Deadline(s): May 15 and Nov.15
  Board meeting date(s): Usually June and Dec.
  Final notification: Within 10 weeks after
    meeting
  Write: Robert M. Hammes, Secy.
Administrator: Robert M. Hammes, Secy.
Number of staff: 1 part-time professional; 1
part-time support.

786
M. R. Bauer Foundation ▼
208 South LaSalle St., Suite 1750
Chicago 60604   (312) 372-1947

Established in 1955 in IL.
Donor(s): M.R. Bauer,‡ Evelyn M. Bauer.‡
Foundation type: Independent
Financial data (yr. ended 12/31/90): Assets,
$42,360,193 (M); expenditures, $2,140,311;
qualifying distributions, $1,992,555, including

$1,900,000 for 103 grants (high: $180,000; low: $500; average: $1,000-$55,000).
Purpose and activities: Grants primarily for higher education, including medical and legal education, hospitals, cultural programs, and social service and youth agencies.
Fields of interest: Higher education, legal education, medical education, hospitals, cultural programs, social services, youth.
Types of support: Operating budgets, general purposes, professorships, research.
Limitations: Giving primarily in CA and IL. No grants to individuals.
Application information: Contributes only to pre-selected organizations. Applications not accepted.
    Board meeting date(s): Irregularly
    Write: Kent Lawrence, Pres.
Officers and Directors:* Kent Lawrence,* Pres.; James H. Ackerman,* V.P. and Secy.; Loraine E. Ackerman,* V.P.; Robert J. Lawrence,* Treas.; Lee James Ackerman, Lawrence A. Reich.
Number of staff: None.
EIN: 366052129

787
The Baxter Foundation ▼
(Formerly The Baxter Travenol Foundation)
One Baxter Pkwy.
Deerfield 60015   (708) 948-4604

Established in 1982 in IL.
Donor(s): American Hospital Supply Corp., Baxter Travenol Laboratories, Inc.
Foundation type: Company-sponsored
Financial data (yr. ended 12/31/90): Assets, $6,092,391 (M); expenditures, $4,271,625; qualifying distributions, $4,037,556, including $3,824,251 for 202 grants (high: $333,330; low: $100; average: $2,000-$20,000) and $213,305 for 1,324 employee matching gifts.
Purpose and activities: Supports health care organizations which address a broad national need. Emphasis on research and advocacy efforts that have a broad effect on increasing access to health care services and that provide resources to help hospital managers and medical personnel become more effective. Prize programs include the Foster G. McGraw Prize, the Baxter Health Services Research Award, the Baxter Fellowships for Innovation in Health Care Management, and the Baxter Foundation Episteme award. Matching gift program for hospitals and education. Scholarships for the children of company employees are paid through the Citizen's Scholarship Foundation of America. The Dollars for Doers program supports organizations in which Baxter employees are active volunteers.
Fields of interest: Health, health services, health associations, civic affairs, social services, cultural programs, education.
Types of support: Employee matching gifts, employee-related scholarships, special projects, seed money.
Limitations: Giving nationally for health care organizations which address a broad national or regional need. No support for religious organizations, disease-specific organizations, or educational institutions except where grant supports a health care goal. No grants to individuals, or for dinners and special fundraising events.

Publications: Annual report, application guidelines.
Application information: Application form not required.
    Initial approach: Letter
    Copies of proposal: 1
    Deadline(s): 1 month before meetings
    Board meeting date(s): Jan., Apr., July, Oct., and Dec.
    Write: Patricia A. Morgan, Exec. Dir.
Officers and Directors:* Wilbur H. Gantz,* Chair.; G. Marshall Abbey,* Pres.; Barbara Young Morris,* Treas.; William B. Graham, Wilfred J. Lucas, Terrence J. Mulligan.
Number of staff: 1 full-time professional; 1 full-time support.
EIN: 363159396
Recent health grants:
787-1 American Refugee Committee, Evanston, IL, $10,000. For hospital-based outreach program. 1990.
787-2 Drug Abuse Resistance Education (DARE) of Puerto Rico, Mayaguez, PR, $10,000. For drug prevention project. 1990.
787-3 Family Institute of Chicago, Chicago, IL, $10,000. For training for minority therapists. 1990.
787-4 Healthy Mothers and Babies Coalition, Chicago, IL, $10,000. For maternal and child health policy research project. 1990.
787-5 Hospital Research and Educational Trust, Chicago, IL, $641,200. For Foster G. McGaw Prize. 1990.
787-6 Metropolitan Planning Council, Chicago, IL, $20,000. For policy research on restructuring county health care system. 1990.
787-7 National Medical Fellowships, NYC, NY, $15,000. For minority medical students. 1990.
787-8 Northside Ecumenical Night Ministry, Chicago, IL, $35,000. For Health Outreach program for homeless youth. 1990.
787-9 University of Chicago, Center for Urban Research, Chicago, IL, $20,000. For 1990 Chicago Assembly, Paying for Healthcare in Illinois. 1990.
787-10 University of Chicago Medical Center, Chicago, IL, $1,000,000. For William B. Graham Fellows. 1990.

788
Baxter Healthcare Corporate Giving Program
One Baxter Pkwy.
Deerfield 60015   (708) 948-4606

Financial data (yr. ended 12/31/89): Total giving, $4,367,000, including $2,739,000 for grants (average: $50-$178,000) and $1,628,000 for in-kind gifts.
Purpose and activities: "Improving health care is central to the mission of Baxter International." Though most giving is through the Baxter Foundation, the direct giving program also emphasizes improving the quality and availability of health care for all. The goal is to donate two percent of domestic pretax net income per year. In 1989, the corporation underwrote the PBS documentary "Can't Afford to Grow Old," which called attention to the issues involved in long-term care for the elderly. Support also for social services with an emphasis on organizations in which employees are volunteers. Nonmonetary

contributions include graphic design and printing services.
Fields of interest: Health, social services.
Types of support: In-kind gifts, donated equipment, donated products, donated land, use of facilities.
Limitations: Giving primarily in areas where employees live and work. No support for religious, athletic, fraternal organizations, or organizations that have discriminatory policies. No grants to individuals.
Publications: Corporate giving report.
Application information: Community Relations handles giving.
    Write: Kristin A. Forsyth, Dir., External Affairs

789
Francis Beidler Charitable Trust
53 West Jackson Blvd., Rm. 530
Chicago 60604-3608   (312) 922-3792

Trust established in 1924 in IL.
Donor(s): Francis Beidler.‡
Foundation type: Independent
Financial data (yr. ended 12/31/91): Assets, $7,573,498 (M); expenditures, $359,214; qualifying distributions, $317,824, including $317,230 for 102 grants (high: $40,750; low: $200).
Purpose and activities: To aid public and operating charitable organizations; giving for social services, including care of the aged or crippled, family planning, youth agencies, child development and welfare, and education; support also for legal services and education, the mental and behavioral sciences, international affairs and foreign policy, arms control, and the environment. No beneficiary may receive more than one-fifth of the net income yearly.
Fields of interest: Social services, aged, disadvantaged, family planning, youth, child development, child welfare, education, legal services, international affairs.
Types of support: Continuing support, operating budgets.
Limitations: Giving primarily in IL. No grants to individuals, or for building funds, research, or matching gifts; no loans.
Application information: Application form not required.
    Initial approach: Letter
    Copies of proposal: 1
    Deadline(s): None
    Board meeting date(s): May or June
    Write: Rosemarie Smith, Trustee
Trustees: Francis Beidler III, Thomas B. Dorris, Rosemarie Smith.
Number of staff: None.
EIN: 362166969

790
Beloit Foundation, Inc.
11722 Main St.
Roscoe 61073   (815) 623-6600

Incorporated in 1959 in WI.
Donor(s): Elbert H. Neese.‡
Foundation type: Independent
Financial data (yr. ended 12/31/90): Assets, $11,991,400 (M); expenditures, $882,700; qualifying distributions, $674,100, including

$674,100 for 37 grants (high: $150,000; low: $400; average: $500-$20,000).
Purpose and activities: Giving only to local community organizations for special projects, and new program development: support for education, with emphasis on a local college; family and social services, including youth, minorities, and the homeless; hospital building funds, hospices, and health; recreation; the arts; a community fund; and community development and crime and law enforcement programs.
Fields of interest: Education, higher education, social services, family services, youth, minorities, homeless, health, hospitals—building funds, hospices, recreation, arts, community development, crime and law enforcement.
Types of support: Building funds, matching funds, seed money, special projects, capital campaigns, equipment, renovation projects.
Limitations: Giving limited to local stateline area, including Beloit, WI, and South Beloit, Rockton, and Roscoe, IL. No grants to individuals, or for endowment funds, research, direct scholarships, fellowships, or nationally organized fundraising campaigns.
Application information: Application form required.
Initial approach: Letter
Copies of proposal: 1
Deadline(s): Submit proposal in Dec. or June; no set deadline
Board meeting date(s): May and Sept.
Final notification: 3 months
Write: Gary G. Grabowski, Exec. Dir.
Officers and Directors:* Elbert H. Neese,* Pres.; Kim Kotthaus, Secy.; Gary G. Grabowski,* Treas. and Exec. Dir.; Harry C. Moore, Alonzo A. Neese, Jr., Gordon C. Neese, Laura Neese-Malik, Jane Petit-Moore.
Number of staff: 1 part-time professional; 1 part-time support.
EIN: 396068763

791
Bere Foundation, Inc.
641 South Elm St.
Hinsdale 60521   (312) 322-8510

Incorporated in 1983 in IL.
Donor(s): James F. Bere, Barbara L. Bere.
Foundation type: Independent
Financial data (yr. ended 12/31/90): Assets, $5,587,087 (M); gifts received, $165,715; expenditures, $508,676; qualifying distributions, $505,970, including $469,225 for 40 grants (high: $158,700; low: $200).
Fields of interest: Religion—Christian, theological education, hospitals, music.
Types of support: General purposes.
Limitations: Giving primarily in the greater Chicago, IL, area. No grants to individuals.
Application information: Contributes only to pre-selected organizations. Applications not accepted.
Write: James F. Bere, Pres.
Officers and Directors:* James F. Bere,* Pres.; David L. Bere,* V.P.; James F. Bere, Jr.,* V.P.; Robert P. Bere,* V.P.; Becky B. Sigfusson,* V.P.; Lynn B. Stine,* V.P.; Barbara Van Dellen Bere,* Secy.-Treas.
EIN: 363272779

792
The Bersted Foundation
c/o Continental Bank, N.A.
30 North LaSalle St.
Chicago 60697   (312) 828-8026

Established in 1972 in IL.
Donor(s): Alfred Bersted.‡
Foundation type: Independent
Financial data (yr. ended 12/31/90): Assets, $10,809,672 (M); expenditures, $569,534; qualifying distributions, $491,525, including $475,834 for 25 grants (high: $55,000; low: $5,000).
Fields of interest: Community development, social services, family services, handicapped, conservation, youth, health, mental health.
Types of support: Building funds, technical assistance, general purposes, operating budgets.
Limitations: Giving limited to Kane, DuPage, DeKalb, and McHenry counties, IL. No support for religious houses of worship or degree-conferring institutions of higher learning. No grants to individuals.
Publications: Multi-year report.
Application information: Application form not required.
Initial approach: Letter
Copies of proposal: 2
Deadline(s): None
Board meeting date(s): Generally in Feb., May, Aug., and Nov.
Write: A.W. Murray
Trustee: Continental Bank, N.A.
EIN: 366493609

793
Grace A. Bersted Foundation
c/o Continental Bank, N.A., Trust Tax
30 North LaSalle St., 6th Fl.
Chicago 60697   (312) 828-1785

Established in 1986 in IL.
Donor(s): Grace A. Bersted.‡
Foundation type: Independent
Financial data (yr. ended 12/31/90): Assets, $4,896,537 (M); expenditures, $251,432; qualifying distributions, $215,049, including $193,000 for 10 grants (high: $68,000; low: $10,000).
Fields of interest: Higher education, youth, social services, wildlife, conservation, hospitals, drug abuse.
Limitations: Giving limited to DuPage, Kane, Lake and McHenry counties, IL.
Application information:
Initial approach: Proposal
Deadline(s): None
Write: M.C. Ryan
Trustee: Continental Bank, N.A.
EIN: 366841348

794
Walter J. and Edith E. Best Foundation
c/o Harris Trust & Savings Bank
111 West Monroe St.
Chicago 60603

Established in 1986 in IL.
Donor(s): Edith Best,‡ Walter Best.‡
Foundation type: Independent

Financial data (yr. ended 11/30/90): Assets, $2,997,956 (M); gifts received, $47,284; expenditures, $279,869; qualifying distributions, $266,380, including $252,000 for 17 grants (high: $50,000; low: $1,000).
Fields of interest: Hospitals, health associations, child welfare.
Limitations: Giving primarily in IL. No grants to individuals.
Application information:
Initial approach: Proposal
Deadline(s): None
Write: Ronald F. Tuite, Jr., Asst. V.P., Harris Trust & Savings Bank
Trustees: Robert J. Kuhn, Harris Trust & Savings Bank.
EIN: 366857916

795
The Gary K. and Carlotta J. Bielfeldt Foundation
124 S.W. Adams, Suite 340
Peoria 61602

Established in 1985 in IL.
Donor(s): Gary K. Bielfeldt.
Foundation type: Independent
Financial data (yr. ended 12/31/90): Assets, $31,913,809 (M); expenditures, $1,877,196; qualifying distributions, $1,620,288, including $1,467,520 for 118 grants (high: $400,000; low: $25; average: $100-$15,000).
Fields of interest: Health, higher education, community development, general charitable giving.
Limitations: Giving primarily in Peoria, IL. No grants to individuals.
Publications: Application guidelines.
Application information: Application form required.
Initial approach: Letter
Copies of proposal: 4
Deadline(s): None
Board meeting date(s): End of Mar., June, Oct., and Dec.
Final notification: 1 week after board meetings
Write: Carlotta J. Bielfeldt, Pres.
Officer and Directors:* Carlotta J. Bielfeldt,* Pres.; David L. Bielfeldt, Gary K. Bielfeldt, Karen J. Bielfeldt, Linda S. Bielfeldt.
Number of staff: 1
EIN: 371188243

796
William Blair and Company Foundation
135 South LaSalle St.
Chicago 60603   (312) 236-1600

Established in 1980 in IL.
Donor(s): William Blair & Co.
Foundation type: Company-sponsored
Financial data (yr. ended 08/31/90): Assets, $1,096,904 (M); gifts received, $150,000; expenditures, $201,852; qualifying distributions, $201,545, including $201,545 for 118 grants (high: $5,000; low: $200).
Fields of interest: Cultural programs, hospitals, health associations, cancer, higher education, social services, youth, civic affairs, public affairs, Jewish giving, Catholic giving.

Types of support: Annual campaigns, building funds, capital campaigns, continuing support, endowment funds, fellowships, general purposes, internships, operating budgets.
Limitations: Giving primarily in the metropolitan Chicago, IL, area; the grantee should have significant, but not necessarily exclusive impact on the Chicago metropolitan area. No grants to individuals.
Application information: Application form not required.
  Initial approach: Letter
  Copies of proposal: 1
  Deadline(s): None
  Write: Stephen Campbell, Treas.
Officers: Edgar D. Jannotta, Pres.; E. David Coolidge III, V.P.; James M. McMullan, V.P.; Gregory N. Thomas, Secy.; Stephen Campbell, Treas.
Number of staff: None.
EIN: 363092291

797
The Blowitz-Ridgeway Foundation
2700 River Rd., Suite 211
Des Plaines 60018   (708) 298-2378

Status changed from public charity to private foundation in 1984.
Foundation type: Independent
Financial data (yr. ended 09/30/91): Assets, $16,117,510 (M); expenditures, $849,813; qualifying distributions, $670,974, including $532,596 for 46 grants (high: $45,000; low: $2,000).
Purpose and activities: Support for organizations devoted to improving the psychiatric and psychological health and general welfare of juveniles; appropriate research activities may also be considered.
Fields of interest: Psychiatry, youth, mental health, child welfare, social services, handicapped.
Types of support: Research, continuing support, special projects, capital campaigns.
Limitations: Giving generally limited to IL. No support for government agencies, or for organizations which subsist mainly on 3rd-party funding. No grants to individuals.
Publications: Application guidelines, annual report, grants list, informational brochure (including application guidelines).
Application information: Application form required.
  Initial approach: Letter or telephone requesting guidelines
  Copies of proposal: 5
  Deadline(s): Ongoing review
  Board meeting date(s): Monthly
  Write: Robert DiLeonardi, Administrator (preliminary information), and Max Pastin, Pres. (applications)
Officer and Trustees:* Max Pastin,* Pres.; Daniel Kline,* V.P.; Joanne Lanigan,* Secy.; Tony Dean,* Treas.; Arthur Collison, Rev. J.W. Jackson, Patricia A. MacAlister, Marvin Pitluk, Allin Proufoot, Samuel Winston.
Number of staff: 1 full-time professional; 1 part-time support.
EIN: 362488355

798
The Nathan and Emily S. Blum Foundation
c/o Harris Trust & Savings Bank
111 West Monroe St.
Chicago 60603
Grant application address: c/o Harris Trust & Savings Bank, P.O. Box 755, Chicago, IL 60690; Tel.: (312) 461-2613

Established in 1980.
Donor(s): Nathan Blum.‡
Foundation type: Independent
Financial data (yr. ended 12/31/90): Assets, $5,885,894 (M); expenditures, $350,401; qualifying distributions, $310,050, including $310,000 for 8 grants (high: $115,000; low: $4,500).
Fields of interest: Jewish welfare, hospitals, social services, community funds, general charitable giving.
Limitations: Giving primarily in Chicago, IL.
Application information: Application form not required.
  Initial approach: Proposal
  Deadline(s): None
  Write: Ellen A. Bechthold, V.P., Harris Trust & Savings Bank
Trustee: Harris Trust & Savings Bank.
EIN: 366706638

799
Blum-Kovler Foundation
919 North Michigan Ave.
Chicago 60611   (312) 664-5050

Incorporated in 1953 in IL.
Donor(s): Harry Blum,‡ Everett Kovler.
Foundation type: Independent
Financial data (yr. ended 12/31/90): Assets, $30,787,357 (M); expenditures, $1,999,241; qualifying distributions, $1,664,598, including $1,567,990 for 187 grants (high: $100,200; low: $100; average: $500-$5,000).
Purpose and activities: Emphasis on social services, Jewish welfare funds, higher education, hospitals, health services, medical research, and cultural programs; support also for youth and child welfare agencies and public interest and civic affairs groups.
Fields of interest: Higher education, Jewish welfare, hospitals, health services, medical research, social services, cultural programs, civic affairs, public policy, youth, child welfare.
Types of support: General purposes.
Limitations: Giving primarily in the Chicago, IL, area.
Application information:
  Initial approach: Written request
  Deadline(s): None
  Board meeting date(s): As required
  Final notification: Varies
  Write: H. Jonathan Kovler, Treas.
Officers and Directors: Everett Kovler, Pres.; H.H. Bregar, Secy.; H. Jonathan Kovler, Treas.
Number of staff: 1 full-time support.
EIN: 362476143

800
George W. Bock Charitable Trust
c/o First National Bank
1515 Charleston Ave.
Mattoon 61938   (217) 234-7454

Established in 1987 in IL.
Donor(s): George W. Bock.‡
Foundation type: Independent
Financial data (yr. ended 12/31/90): Assets, $2,021,616 (M); gifts received, $81,720; expenditures, $134,894; qualifying distributions, $121,047, including $110,000 for 2 grants (high: $100,000; low: $10,000).
Fields of interest: Child welfare, hospices.
Types of support: General purposes.
Limitations: Giving primarily in Columbia, SC. No grants to individuals.
Application information: Grants will not exceed $100,000 to any 1 recipient organization. Application form not required.
  Deadline(s): None
  Write: Dan Cunningham, Sr. V.P. and Trust Officer, First National Bank
Trustee: First National Bank.
EIN: 371224690

801
Charles H. and Bertha L. Boothroyd Foundation
120 West Madison St., Suite 14L
Chicago 60602   (312) 346-8333

Incorporated in 1958 in IL.
Donor(s): Mary T. Palzkill,‡ Agnes K. McAvoy Trust.
Foundation type: Independent
Financial data (yr. ended 06/30/90): Assets, $3,370,174 (M); gifts received, $1,115; expenditures, $201,308; qualifying distributions, $179,508, including $167,500 for 22 grants (high: $25,000; low: $1,000).
Purpose and activities: Grants to medical schools for research on Parkinson's disease, hospitals, higher education, social services, and cultural institutions.
Fields of interest: Medical research, higher education, medical education, hospitals, cultural programs, social services.
Types of support: Scholarship funds, research.
Limitations: Giving primarily in IL.
Application information:
  Initial approach: Letter
  Deadline(s): None
  Write: Bruce E. Brown, Pres.
Officers: Bruce E. Brown, Pres.; Donald C. Gancer, V.P.; Lorraine Marcus, Secy.
EIN: 366047045

802
Borwell Charitable Foundation ▼
c/o Naomi T. Borwell
1040 North Lake Shore Dr.
Chicago 60611

Established in 1981 in IL.
Donor(s): Robert C. Borwell, Sr., Mrs. Robert C. Borwell, Sr.
Foundation type: Independent
Financial data (yr. ended 10/31/90): Assets, $541,813 (M); gifts received, $1,087,851;

expenditures, $1,159,426; qualifying distributions, $1,111,890, including $1,102,125 for 43 grants (high: $1,010,000; low: $100; average: $500-$1,000).

Purpose and activities: Support primarily for a college; minor support also for hospitals and health associations.

Fields of interest: Higher education, hospitals, health associations, general charitable giving.

Limitations: Giving primarily in IL, with emphasis on Chicago. No grants to individuals.

Application information: Contributes only to pre-selected organizations. Applications not accepted.

Officers and Directors: Naomi T. Borwell, Pres.; Robert C. Borwell, Jr., V.P.; Herbert B. Knight, V.P.; Carolyn W. Lodge, Secy.-Treas.

Number of staff: None.
EIN: 363155489

803
The Ambrose and Gladys Bowyer Foundation
175 West Jackson Blvd., Suite 909
Chicago 60604

Incorporated in 1953 in IL.
Donor(s): Ambrose Bowyer,‡ Gladys Bowyer.‡
Foundation type: Independent
Financial data (yr. ended 12/31/90): Assets, $1,658,033 (M); expenditures, $453,421; qualifying distributions, $438,700, including $438,700 for 50 grants (high: $54,000; low: $1,000).

Fields of interest: Higher education, hospitals, welfare, social services.

Limitations: Giving primarily in IL, with emphasis on Chicago. No grants to individuals.

Application information: Contributes only to pre-selected organizations. Applications not accepted.

Write: D.T. Hutchison, Pres.
Officers and Directors:* D.T. Hutchison,* Pres.; E.V. Quinn,* V.P.; R.F. Prendergast,* Secy.-Treas.
EIN: 366091247

804
Edwin J. Brach Foundation
664 South Beverly Place
Lake Forest 60045
Application address: 560 Neapolitan Way, Naples, FL 33940; Tel.: (813) 262-8998

Incorporated in 1962 in IL.
Foundation type: Independent
Financial data (yr. ended 10/31/90): Assets, $3,179,369 (M); expenditures, $171,864; qualifying distributions, $168,000, including $166,000 for 30 grants (high: $25,000; low: $1,000).

Fields of interest: Health associations, child welfare, social services, family planning, general charitable giving.

Limitations: Giving primarily in IL. No grants to individuals.

Application information: All grants pre-determined by board members. Applications not accepted.

Write: E.H. Moore
Officers: Hazel S. Brodie, Pres. and Secy.; Bertram Z. Brodie, V.P. and Treas.

Director: George O'Callaghan.
EIN: 366073506

805
Helen Brach Foundation ▼
55 West Wacker Dr., Suite 701
Chicago 60601   (312) 372-4417

Established in 1974 in IL.
Donor(s): Helen Brach.‡
Foundation type: Independent
Financial data (yr. ended 03/31/91): Assets, $56,040,936 (M); gifts received, $2,831,333; expenditures, $2,766,983; qualifying distributions, $2,438,248, including $2,319,254 for 247 grants (high: $100,000; low: $75; average: $5,000-$25,000).

Purpose and activities: Support for the prevention of cruelty to animals; programs that test public safety; social and family services, including programs for the prevention of cruelty to children and child welfare, the homeless and housing, the aged, youth, women, and the disabled and disadvantaged; conservation of the environment; secondary, higher, and other education; the fine arts, including museums; health and hospitals; and law and justice.

Fields of interest: Animal welfare, safety, child welfare, aged, family services, handicapped, social services, disadvantaged, homeless, hunger, women, environment, higher education, secondary education, fine arts, health, law and justice, citizenship.

Types of support: Annual campaigns, building funds, equipment, general purposes, operating budgets, publications, renovation projects, research, special projects.

Limitations: No grants to individuals.
Publications: Annual report (including application guidelines), application guidelines.
Application information: Application form required.

> *Initial approach:* Letter
> *Copies of proposal:* 1
> *Deadline(s):* Dec. 31
> *Board meeting date(s):* Quarterly
> *Final notification:* Mar.
> *Write:* Raymond F. Simon, Pres.

Officers and Directors:* Charles M. Vorhees,* Chair.; Raymond F. Simon,* Pres.; James J. O'Connor,* V.P.; John J. Sheridan,* Secy.-Treas.; R. Matthew Simon, Charles A. Vorhees.

Number of staff: 1 full-time support.
EIN: 237376427

806
The Brunswick Foundation, Inc. ▼
One Brunswick Plaza
Skokie 60077   (708) 470-4646

Incorporated in 1957 in IL.
Donor(s): Brunswick Corp.
Foundation type: Company-sponsored
Financial data (yr. ended 12/31/90): Assets, $2,048,256 (M); expenditures, $1,253,239; qualifying distributions, $1,197,197, including $547,862 for 289 grants (high: $50,000; low: $100; average: $1,000-$25,000), and $282,500 for 151 grants to individuals and $366,835 for 368 employee matching gifts (high: $24,020; low: $30).

Purpose and activities: Support primarily for higher education, welfare, civic and health causes, and cultural organizations in areas where there are high concentrations of Brunswick employees, with a preference towards local (plant community) organizations in which employees are personally involved.

Fields of interest: Education, higher education, welfare, social services, health, environment.

Types of support: Employee-related scholarships, employee matching gifts, general purposes, operating budgets, special projects, continuing support.

Limitations: Giving primarily in areas of company operations in CA, FL, MD, MI, NE, OK, TX, TN, VA, WA, WI, AL, AR, AZ, CT, GA, IL, IN, KY, LA, MN, MS, NC, OH, and SC. No support for religious organizations, preschools, primary or secondary schools, fraternal orders, veterans' or labor groups, or trips, tours, tickets, or advertising for benefit purposes. No grants to individuals (except for scholarships to children of company employees), or for endowment or capital funds, or company equipment or products; no loans.

Publications: Annual report (including application guidelines).

Application information: Accepts only written requests for application form and guidelines; priority given to organizations that have already generated Brunswick Corp. employee involvement. Application form required.

> *Initial approach:* Letter
> *Copies of proposal:* 1
> *Deadline(s):* None
> *Board meeting date(s):* 3 times a year, usually Jan., May, and Oct.
> *Final notification:* Within 90 days
> *Write:* Wendy L. Fuhs, Pres.

Officers and Directors:* Wendy L. Fuhs,* Pres.; Dianne M. Yaconetti,* V.P.; Michael D. Schmitz,* Secy.; Paul Kilius,* Treas.; Jack F. Reichert, Pierre A. Rinfret.

Donations Committee: Paul F. Duvall, Jerry Hetrick, James C. Hubbard, David Kern, John Mikusa, Wayne Paulison, Christopher F. Speegle, Robert Teague, Gail Truelsen.

Number of staff: 1 full-time professional.
EIN: 366033576
Recent health grants:
806-1 Muscular Dystrophy Association, NYC, NY, $50,000. 1990.

807
The Buchanan Family Foundation ▼
222 East Wisconsin Ave.
Lake Forest 60045-1701

Established in 1967 in IL.
Donor(s): D.W. Buchanan, Sr.,‡ D.W. Buchanan, Jr.
Foundation type: Independent
Financial data (yr. ended 12/31/90): Assets, $35,875,837 (M); expenditures, $1,853,336; qualifying distributions, $1,793,336, including $1,780,000 for grants (average: $5,000-$100,000).

Purpose and activities: Emphasis on cultural programs, hospitals and health associations, education, social service agencies, community funds, and environmental associations.

Fields of interest: Health, hospitals, cultural programs, community funds, environment, social services, education.
Limitations: Giving primarily in Chicago, IL. No grants to individuals.
Application information:
  Board meeting date(s): Fall
  Write: Huntington Eldridge, Jr., Treas.
Officers: Kenneth H. Buchanan, Pres.; G.M. Walsh, V.P. and Secy.; Huntington Eldridge, Jr., Treas.
Director: Kent Chandler, Jr.
Number of staff: None.
EIN: 366160998

808
A. C. Buehler Foundation
c/o Continental Bank, N.A., Trust Tax
30 North LaSalle St., 6th Fl.
Chicago 60697   (312) 828-1785

Incorporated in 1972 in IL.
Donor(s): Albert C. Buehler.
Foundation type: Independent
Financial data (yr. ended 12/31/90): Assets, $14,502,390 (M); expenditures, $757,407; qualifying distributions, $675,661, including $668,600 for 5 grants (high: $367,500; low: $10,000).
Fields of interest: Hospitals.
Types of support: Equipment, research.
Limitations: Giving primarily in metropolitan Chicago, IL.
Application information:
  Initial approach: Letter
  Deadline(s): None
  Write: M.C. Ryan
Officers and Directors:* A.C. Buehler, Jr.,* Chair.; Rose B. Grosse,* Pres.; Carl Buehler III,* V.P.; Dale Park, Jr., Secy.; James M. Termondt,* Treas.
EIN: 237166014

809
Dean L. & Rosemarie Buntrock Foundation
3003 Butterfield Rd.
Oak Brook 60521-1107

Established in 1979.
Donor(s): Dean L. Buntrock.
Foundation type: Independent
Financial data (yr. ended 12/31/91): Assets, $4,222,480 (M); gifts received, $1,348,588; expenditures, $187,521; qualifying distributions, $183,250, including $179,473 for 71 grants (high: $50,000; low: $22).
Fields of interest: Hospitals, higher education, arts, performing arts.
Limitations: Giving primarily in Chicago, IL. No grants to individuals.
Application information: Contributes only to pre-selected organizations. Applications not accepted.
Directors: Dean L. Buntrock, Rosemarie Buntrock, Peer Pedersen.
EIN: 363001925

810
The Butz Foundation
c/o The Northern Trust Co., Tom Boyden, Admin.
50 South LaSalle St.
Chicago 60675   (312) 630-6000

Incorporated in 1951 in IL.
Donor(s): Theodore C. Butz,‡ Jean Butz James.
Foundation type: Independent
Financial data (yr. ended 12/31/90): Assets, $2,546,757 (M); expenditures, $162,354; qualifying distributions, $140,740, including $137,600 for 27 grants (high: $15,000; low: $100; average: $10,000-$15,000).
Purpose and activities: Emphasis on medical research; support for institutions of higher and secondary education, aid to the handicapped, religious associations, and hospitals.
Fields of interest: Medical research, higher education, secondary education, handicapped, religion.
Types of support: Operating budgets, continuing support, equipment, research.
Limitations: Giving primarily in IL. No grants to individuals; no loans.
Application information:
  Initial approach: Letter
  Copies of proposal: 1
  Deadline(s): Submit proposal preferably in 1st 6 months of calendar year; deadline Oct. 1
  Board meeting date(s): Quarterly
  Final notification: 6 months
  Write: Jean Butz James, Pres.
Officers and Directors:* Jean Butz James,* Pres.; Barbara Butz,* V.P. and Secy.; Theodore H. Butz,* Treas.; Elvira M. Butz, Herbert K. Butz, Thompson H. Butz.
Number of staff: None.
EIN: 366008818

811
The Charles and Marie Caestecker Foundation
c/o Frank Karaba
20 South Clark St., Suite 2310
Chicago 60603-1802
Scholarship application address: c/o Guidance Counselor, Green Lake Public High School, Green Lake, WI 54941

Established about 1967.
Donor(s): Charles E. Caestecker.‡
Foundation type: Independent
Financial data (yr. ended 04/30/91): Assets, $6,211,684 (M); expenditures, $379,716; qualifying distributions, $364,745, including $345,900 for 11 grants (high: $300,000; low: $400) and $18,845 for 4 grants to individuals (high: $5,000; low: $3,845).
Purpose and activities: Giving primarily for hospitals and higher education, including scholarships to graduates of Green Lake Public High School, WI.
Fields of interest: Secondary education, higher education, hospitals, general charitable giving.
Types of support: Student aid, operating budgets, scholarship funds, building funds.
Limitations: Giving primarily in WI.
Application information: Application form required for scholarships.
  Deadline(s): Feb. 1 of graduation year for scholarships

Trustees: Thomas E. Caestecker, Frank A. Karaba.
EIN: 363154453

812
Carylon Foundation
2500 West Arthington St.
Chicago 60612-4108

Established in 1956 in IL.
Foundation type: Independent
Financial data (yr. ended 06/30/90): Assets, $2,393,341 (M); gifts received, $313,000; expenditures, $280,902; qualifying distributions, $273,879, including $273,879 for 85 grants (high: $50,000; low: $15).
Purpose and activities: Giving primarily to Jewish welfare groups, health agencies and hospitals, and to a science institute.
Fields of interest: Jewish welfare, health associations, hospitals.
Application information:
  Initial approach: Letter
  Deadline(s): None
  Write: Mrs. Marcie Mervis, Dir.
Directors: C. Hemmelstein, Julius Hemmelstein, M. Mervis.
EIN: 366033583

813
Caterpillar Corporate Giving Program
100 N.E. Adams St.
Peoria 61629-1480

Financial data (yr. ended 12/31/90): Total giving, $449,939 for grants.
Purpose and activities: Support mainly for civic and community activities, affairs on the local, state, and national level, for trade and public policy organizations, and for international development; smaller grants for education, health and welfare, and culture.
Fields of interest: Health, welfare, education, cultural programs, civic affairs, public policy.
Types of support: Special projects, capital campaigns, operating budgets.
Limitations: Giving primarily in areas of company operations; support also for national organizations. No support for fraternal organizations, political activities or religious organizations whose services are limited to one sectarian group. No grants to individuals, or for tickets or advertising for fundraising benefits, general operations or ongoing programs of agencies funded by United Way.
Publications: Informational brochure (including application guidelines).
Application information:
  Initial approach: Letter
  Deadline(s): None
  Write: Edward W. Siebert, Mgr., Corp. Support Programs

814
Caterpillar Foundation ▼
100 N.E. Adams St.
Peoria 61629-1480

Established in 1952 in IL.
Donor(s): Caterpillar, Inc.
Foundation type: Company-sponsored

Financial data (yr. ended 12/31/90): Assets, $19,427,125 (M); gifts received, $8,209,500; expenditures, $5,306,180; qualifying distributions, $5,300,791, including $4,730,901 for grants (high: $623,146; low: $10) and $569,890 for employee matching gifts.
Purpose and activities: Giving primarily to community funds, higher education, and a youth agency; employee matching gift support for cultural and educational institutions.
Fields of interest: Community funds, higher education, cultural programs.
Types of support: Employee matching gifts, operating budgets, special projects, capital campaigns.
Limitations: Giving primarily in areas of company operations. No support for fraternal organizations, religious organizations whose services are limited to one sectarian group, or political activities. No grants to individuals, or for general operations or ongoing programs of agencies funded by the United Way, or tickets or advertising for fundraising benefits.
Publications: Corporate giving report.
Application information: Application form not required.
  Initial approach: Letter or proposal
  Deadline(s): None
  Board meeting date(s): Dec. 1
  Final notification: 1 month
  Write: Edward W. Siebert, Mgr.
Officers and Directors:* D.V. Fites,* Pres.; G.S. Flaherty,* Exec. V.P.; Edward W. Siebert, V.P. and Mgr.; B. DeHaan,* V.P.; H.W. Holling, V.P.; Len A. Kuchan, V.P.; R.R. Thornton, Secy.; R.D. Beran, Treas.
EIN: 376022314
Recent health grants:
814-1 Easter Seal Rehabilitation Center of Will-Grundy Counties, Joliet, IL, $25,000. 1990.
814-2 Health Education Center, Pittsburgh, PA, $100,000. 1990.
814-3 Occupational Physicians Scholarship Fund, Arlington Heights, IL, $20,000. 1990.
814-4 University of Illinois, College of Medicine, Peoria, IL, $50,000. 1990.

815
CBI Foundation
800 Jorie Blvd.
Oak Brook 60521

Incorporated in 1953 in IL.
Donor(s): Chicago Bridge & Iron Co.
Foundation type: Company-sponsored
Financial data (yr. ended 12/31/90): Assets, $0 (M); gifts received, $256,000; expenditures, $269,647; qualifying distributions, $269,584, including $269,584 for 69 grants (high: $79,607; low: $100; average: $100-$500).
Purpose and activities: Grants primarily for community funds, the arts, scientific and medical research, health associations and hospitals, child welfare, higher and other education, and civic affairs.
Fields of interest: Community funds, medical research, hospitals, health associations, higher education, education, civic affairs, arts, child welfare.
Types of support: Continuing support, annual campaigns, emergency funds, scholarship funds,

research, operating budgets, special projects, general purposes.
Limitations: Giving primarily in IL. No grants to individuals, or for building or endowment funds; no loans.
Application information: Application form not required.
  Initial approach: Letter or proposal
  Copies of proposal: 1
  Deadline(s): None
  Board meeting date(s): Quarterly
  Final notification: 45 days after board meets
  Write: Susan E. Marks, Sccy.
Officers and Directors:* J.J. Muth,* Pres.; C.O. Zeimer,* V.P.; S.E. Marks, Secy.; Buel T. Adams, Treas.; R.W. Dudley, John E. Jones, W.R. Robinson, George L. Schueppert.
Number of staff: None.
EIN: 366050115

816
Centel Corporate Giving Program
8725 Higgins Rd.
Chicago 60631   (312) 399-2714

Purpose and activities: The Centel Foundation has been established by Centel Corporation as the local point for its corporate social responsibility efforts. Its grants complement other Centel-sponsored activities including employee matching gifts, in-kind contributions, sponsorship of the Centel Classic and Western Open golf tournaments, which annually contribute net proceeds to charity, and employee volunteer leadership on a variety of important issues. The Foundation is governed by a Board composed of Centel executives who, in turn, are responsive to the oversight of the Public Policy committee of Centel Corporation's Board of Directors. Day-to-day management is provided by a professional staff, while grantmaking decisions are assigned to a Contributions Council composed of Centel employees representing the company's diverse business units. Periodically, Centel will contribute surplus materials, equipment or supplies to eligible not-for-profits. This is done on an "as available" basis. Requests for such support should be directed to the Foundation Administrator. The Centel Foundation coordinates contributions on behalf of several Centel business units. Each of them, however, has a small budget which they administer independently of Foundation staff. Grant requests under $2,000 should be sent directly to local business unit staff. Requests for grants in excess of $2,000 and all general inquiries may be directed to the Foundation Administrator.
Fields of interest: Civic affairs, economics, education, higher education, environment, health, minorities, music, theater, welfare, cultural programs, fine arts, arts, community funds.
Types of support: Employee matching gifts, in-kind gifts, donated products, donated equipment, employee volunteer services.
Limitations: Giving primarily in headquarters city and major operating locations.
Application information:
  Initial approach: Letter
  Write: Foundation Admin.

817
The Centel Foundation
8725 West Higgins Rd.
Chicago 60631   (312) 399-2500

Established in 1988 in IL.
Foundation type: Company-sponsored
Financial data (yr. ended 12/31/91): Assets, $103,358 (M); gifts received, $1,353,000; expenditures, $1,238,000; qualifying distributions, $1,238,000, including $1,238,000 for 208 grants (high: $120,000; low: $300).
Fields of interest: Higher education, health associations, community funds, medical research, arts, cultural programs, civic affairs, handicapped, minorities.
Limitations: Giving primarily in areas of company operations, with emphasis on Chicago, IL; giving also to organizations with national scope and impact; no support for agencies whose program emphasis is outside the U.S. No support for single-disease agencies, fraternal, veterans', labor, athletic or religious organizations serving a limited constituency. No grants to individuals, or for travel, fundraising events, benefits, or courtesy advertising.
Application information: Site visits or interviews may be scheduled.
  Initial approach: Proposal, with a 2-page maximum summary statement
  Board meeting date(s): Contributions Council meets bimonthly
  Write: Carrol J. Babcock, Pres.
Officers and Directors:* Carrol J. Babcock,* Pres.; Maxwell S. Davis, Jr., V.P.; Richard C. Pagano, Secy.; Dale I. Parker, Treas.; John P. Frazee, Jr., S.E. Leftwich.
EIN: 363616313

818
Centralia Foundation
P.O. Box 709
Centralia 62801

Established in 1943.
Donor(s): Rollen Robinson, Lecta Rae Robinson.
Foundation type: Operating
Financial data (yr. ended 12/31/90): Assets, $6,256,587 (M); gifts received, $276,500; expenditures, $188,540; qualifying distributions, $402,117, including $29,426 for 19 grants (high: $5,376; low: $548), $3,000 for 1 grant to an individual and $369,691 for 2 foundation-administered programs.
Purpose and activities: A private operating foundation; giving for civic affairs, churches, and a hospital; also awards interest-free loans for higher education to local students. The foundation operates and maintains a park system and a Carillon Bell Tower.
Fields of interest: Civic affairs, hospitals, Protestant giving.
Types of support: Student aid, general purposes.
Limitations: Giving primarily in Centralia, IL.
Application information:
  Write: Nina Buchele
Officers: Wendell Lamblin, Chair.; Verle Besant, Vice-Chair.
Trustees: Lloyd Allen, Bruce Geary, David Harris, John Lackey.
EIN: 376029269

819
Chicago Board of Trade Foundation

141 West Jackson Blvd.
Chicago 60604   (312) 435-3456

Established in 1984 in IL.
Donor(s): Chicago Board of Trade.
Foundation type: Company-sponsored
Financial data (yr. ended 06/30/91): Assets, $2,554,806 (M); gifts received, $500,000; expenditures, $128,128; qualifying distributions, $124,928, including $120,000 for 34 grants (high: $6,000; low: $1,000).
Purpose and activities: Support for hospitals, rehabilitation and the handicapped; arts and culture, including libraries and museums; education, including higher education and science and technology; youth and child development; wildlife; and media and communications.
Fields of interest: Hospitals, handicapped, arts, cultural programs, libraries, education, higher education, youth, child development, wildlife.
Types of support: General purposes.
Limitations: Giving primarily in the metropolitan Chicago, IL, area. No loans or program-related investments.
Application information: Application form not required.
Initial approach: Letter
Copies of proposal: 1
Deadline(s): None
Board meeting date(s): Feb. and Apr.
Write: George Sladoje, Exec. V.P.
Officers and Directors:* William O'Connor,* Chair.; George Sladoje, Exec. V.P.; Glen M. Johnson, Treas.; David E. Blum, Dale E. Lorenzen, Francis X. O'Donnell, Irwin N. Smith.
Number of staff: None.
EIN: 363348469

820
The Chicago Community Trust ▼

222 North LaSalle St., Suite 1400
Chicago 60601   (312) 372-3356

Established in 1915 in IL by bank resolution and declaration of trust.
Donor(s): Albert W. Harris, and members of the Harris family.
Foundation type: Community
Financial data (yr. ended 09/30/90): Assets, $295,928,031 (M); gifts received, $9,488,380; expenditures, $35,487,896; qualifying distributions, $31,651,123, including $25,408,337 for grants (high: $1,868,000; low: $100; average: $10,000-$50,000), $5,975,626 for foundation-administered programs and $267,160 for loans.
Purpose and activities: Established "for such charitable purposes as will...best make for the mental, moral, intellectual and physical improvement, assistance and relief of the inhabitants of the County of Cook, State of Illinois." Grants for both general operating support and specific programs and projects in the areas of health and social services, youth agencies, education, particularly higher education, and cultural and civic affairs; awards fellowships to individuals in leadership positions in local community service organizations.

Fields of interest: Health, AIDS, social services, aged, handicapped, leadership development, child development, women, hunger, minorities, secondary education, higher education, libraries, cultural programs, fine arts, performing arts, public policy, community development, urban affairs, environment.
Types of support: Operating budgets, continuing support, emergency funds, building funds, equipment, land acquisition, loans, research, special projects, renovation projects, capital campaigns, general purposes, technical assistance, matching funds, program-related investments, seed money.
Limitations: Giving primarily in Cook County, IL. No support for religious purposes. No grants to individuals, (except for the Community Service Fellowship Program), or for annual campaigns, deficit financing, endowment funds, publications, conferences, or scholarships; no support for the purchase of computer hardware; no general operating support for agencies or institutions whose program activities substantially duplicate those already undertaken by others.
Publications: Annual report, informational brochure, program policy statement, application guidelines, newsletter.
Application information: Application form required for various special programs.
Initial approach: Proposal
Copies of proposal: 2
Deadline(s): Proposals scheduled for next available board meeting; no set deadline
Board meeting date(s): Jan., Mar., June, and Sept.
Final notification: 4 to 6 months after submission
Write: Ms. Sandy Cheers, Asst. to the Dir. (grants to organizations) and Joan Miller Wood (Community Service Fellowship Program)
Officer: Bruce L. Newman, Exec. Dir.
Executive Committee: Edgar D. Jannotta, Chair.; Franklin A. Cole, Vice-Chair.; Judith S. Block, James J. Brice, William M. Daley, Margaret D. Hartigan, Margaret P. MacKimm, Cordell Reed, Shirley W. Ryan, Mrs. Gordon H. Smith, Rev. Dr. Kenneth B. Smith, Arthur R. Velasquez.
Trustees: American National Bank & Trust Co. of Chicago, Boulevard Bank, N.A., Chicago Title and Trust Co., Continental Illinois National Bank & Trust Co. of Chicago, First National Bank of Chicago, Harris Trust & Savings Bank, Heritage Pullman Bank, LaSalle National Bank, The Northern Trust Co.
Number of staff: 18 full-time professional; 1 part-time professional; 13 full-time support; 1 part-time support.
EIN: 362167000
Recent health grants:
820-1 Alexian Brothers Bonaventure House, Chicago, IL, $35,000. For facilities expansion component of current capital campaign. 1991.
820-2 Alexian Brothers Bonaventure House, Chicago, IL, $25,000. For general operating support. 1991.
820-3 Clarence Darrow Community Center, Chicago, IL, $150,000. For general operating support for Southwest Community Health Center. 1991.
820-4 Crisis Center for South Suburbia, Worth, IL, $50,000. For matching grant for capital campaign. 1991.

820-5 Doctor William M. Scholl College of Podiatric Medicine, Chicago, IL, $10,000. For operation of Foot Care for the Homeless Project. 1991.
820-6 Health and Medicine Policy Research Group, Chicago, IL, $150,000. For general operating support. 1991.
820-7 Healthy Mothers and Babies Coalition, Chicago, IL, $15,000. Toward Community Advocates Program. 1991.
820-8 Illinois Center for Citizen Involvement, Champaign, IL, $30,000. For salary support of Campaign for Better Health Care. 1991.
820-9 Illinois Center for Citizen Involvement, Champaign, IL, $30,000. For general operating support of Campaign for Better Health Care. 1991.
820-10 Illinois Maternal and Child Health Coalition, Chicago, IL, $10,000. For Chicago Breastfeeding Task Force/Lawndale Healthy Start breastfeeding promotion project. 1991.
820-11 Japanese American Service Committee, Chicago, IL, $70,000. For construction and initial maintenance of Keiro Nursing Home. 1991.
820-12 La Rabida Childrens Hospital and Research Center, Chicago, IL, $158,600. For general operating support of Children's Support Services Project. 1991.
820-13 LaGrange Community Nurse and Service Association, LaGrange, IL, $91,572. To replace dental equipment and remodel dental suite. 1991.
820-14 Misericordia Home/Heart of Mercy Village, Chicago, IL, $100,000. For new recreational and social center. 1991.
820-15 Polish Welfare Association, Chicago, IL, $40,500. For salary support of addictions counselor. 1991.
820-16 Polish Welfare Association, Chicago, IL, $20,250. For partial salary support of second addictions counselor. 1991.
820-17 Rape Victim Advocates, Chicago, IL, $20,000. For general operating support. 1991.
820-18 Saint Basils Health Service, Chicago, IL, $75,000. For general operating support. 1991.
820-19 Saint Leonards House, Chicago, IL, $25,000. For salary support of substance abuse counselor. 1991.
820-20 Suburban Primary Health Care Council, Hinsdale, IL, $150,000. Toward administrative costs of Access to Care Project. 1991.
820-21 Thresholds, Chicago, IL, $183,000. For expansion of Young Adult Program. 1991.
820-22 Travelers and Immigrants Aid of Chicago, Chicago, IL, $19,137. To conduct service needs assessment and prepare business plan for Health Outreach Program. 1991.
820-23 Umoja Care, Chicago, IL, $100,000. For operating costs of system of comprehensive care for frail elderly. 1991.
820-24 University of Illinois Foundation, Health Sciences Center, Chicago, IL, $229,000. For Community-Based Primary Health Care Program. 1991.
820-25 Westside Health Authority, Chicago, IL, $15,000. For organizational development. Grant made through Westside Holistic Family Center. 1991.
820-26 White Crane Wellness Center, Chicago, IL, $50,000. For general operating support. 1991.

821
Chicago Resource Center
104 South Michigan Ave., Suite 1220
Chicago 60603 (312) 759-8700

Established in 1981 in IL.
Donor(s): Thomas A. Dennis, Richard J. Dennis.
Foundation type: Independent
Financial data (yr. ended 12/31/89): Assets, $83,692 (M); gifts received, $1,205,000; expenditures, $1,239,485; qualifying distributions, $1,246,426, including $1,015,261 for 164 grants (high: $188,472; low: $500; average: $3,000-$10,000).
Purpose and activities: Support for projects dealing with violence against women and families, gay and lesbian issues, and AIDS education.
Fields of interest: Women, law and justice, civil rights, family services, social services, health, AIDS, gays and lesbians.
Types of support: Operating budgets, seed money, equipment, matching funds, continuing support.
Limitations: No grants to individuals, or for annual campaigns, deficit financing, building funds, land acquisition, endowment funds, scholarships, or fellowships; no loans.
Publications: Application guidelines, program policy statement, grants list.
Application information: Application form required.
> *Initial approach:* Proposal
> *Copies of proposal:* 1
> *Deadline(s):* Mar. 30, June 29, and Sept. 28
> *Board meeting date(s):* Jan., July, and Oct.
> *Final notification:* 4 months
> *Write:* Mary Ann Snyder, Dir.
Officers and Managers:* Richard J. Dennis,* Pres.; Thomas A. Dennis,* V.P.
Director: Mary Ann Snyder.
Number of staff: 2 full-time professional; 1 full-time support.
EIN: 363121813
Recent health grants:
821-1 AIDS Housing Association, Tacoma, WA, $10,000. For general support. 1990.
821-2 AIDS Outreach, Easton, PA, $10,000. For general support. 1990.
821-3 AIDS Treatment Registry, NYC, NY, $10,000. For general support. 1990.
821-4 AIDSLAW of Louisiana, New Orleans, LA, $10,000. For general support. 1990.
821-5 Downtown Immigrant Advocates, Los Angeles, CA, $10,000. For seropositive legalization project. 1990.
821-6 Hunter College of the City University of New York, Center for Community Action to Prevent AIDS, NYC, NY, $10,000. For community outreach. 1990.
821-7 National Community AIDS Partnership, Chicago, IL, $20,000. For participation in Partnership. 1990.
821-8 New Jersey Women and AIDS Network, New Brunswick, NJ, $10,000. For general support and for Women and AIDS Information Clearinghouse. 1990.

822
Chicago Title and Trust Company Foundation
c/o Chester R. Davis
111 West Washington St.
Chicago 60602-2703 (312) 630-2911

Trust established in 1951 in IL.
Donor(s): Chicago Title and Trust Co.
Foundation type: Company-sponsored
Financial data (yr. ended 12/31/90): Assets, $1,967,630 (M); gifts received, $600,000; expenditures, $407,715; qualifying distributions, $407,715, including $392,996 for grants.
Purpose and activities: Emphasis on community funds, social services, higher education, health, hospitals, and culture; support also for community improvement, public policy, and economic understanding and development.
Fields of interest: Cultural programs, higher education, community funds, hospitals, social services.
Types of support: Continuing support, employee matching gifts, special projects.
Limitations: Giving primarily in Chicago, IL. No support for United Way member agencies. No grants to individuals, or for operating budgets, annual campaigns, seed money, emergency funds, deficit financing, building funds, equipment, land acquisition, research, scholarships, fellowships, publications, or conferences; no loans.
Publications: Program policy statement, application guidelines.
Application information: Application form required.
> *Initial approach:* Letter
> *Copies of proposal:* 1
> *Deadline(s):* Feb. 1 for culture, May 1 for education, and Aug. 1 for health
> *Board meeting date(s):* Jan., Apr., July, and Oct.
> *Final notification:* 60 days
> *Write:* Ms. Margaret Kelly
Trustees: Alvin Behnke, Stuart Bilton, M. Leanne Lachman, Alvin Long, Richard Pollay, Richard P. Toft, Lannette Zimmerman.
Number of staff: 2 part-time professional; 1 full-time support.
EIN: 366036809

823
CLARCOR Foundation
(Formerly Clark Foundation)
2323 Sixth St.
P.O. Box 7007
Rockford 61125 (815) 962-8867

Trust established in 1954 in IL.
Donor(s): CLARCOR.
Foundation type: Company-sponsored
Financial data (yr. ended 12/31/90): Assets, $6,699,537 (M); expenditures, $951,685; qualifying distributions, $857,369, including $844,814 for grants (high: $400,000; low: $300) and $12,555 for 24 employee matching gifts.
Fields of interest: Health, hospitals, hospices, social services, youth, community funds, higher education, cultural programs, museums, theater, arts.
Types of support: Employee matching gifts, continuing support, annual campaigns, emergency funds, building funds, equipment, capital campaigns, operating budgets, renovation projects.
Limitations: Giving primarily in areas of company operations in IL, IN, MD, MI, NE, and PA. No grants to individuals, or for endowment funds, research, scholarships, or fellowships; no loans.
Publications: Program policy statement, application guidelines.
Application information: Application form required.
> *Initial approach:* Letter
> *Copies of proposal:* 1
> *Deadline(s):* None
> *Board meeting date(s):* Jan., Apr., July, and Oct.
> *Write:* W.F. Knese, Chair.
Officer and Trustees:* William F. Knese,* Chair.; Marshall C. Arne, Lawrence E. Gloyd, L.P. Harnois, Norman E. Johnson, R.A. Moreau, J.S. Waddell.
Number of staff: None.
EIN: 366032573

824
CNA Financial Corporate Giving Program
CNA Plaza
Chicago 60685 (312) 822-5318

Financial data (yr. ended 12/31/90): Total giving, $908,904 for grants.
Purpose and activities: Support for education, health and human services, and civic and cultural programs. CNA is also concerned with special projects of interest to the insurance industry, including crime, arson, violence, and fraud prevention, health maintenance, rehabilitation through improved communications for the mentally and physically handicapped, neighborhood and community revitalization, and the advancement of basic curriculum in public schools. Inkind support includes printing, equipment, and furniture. In addition, employees volunteer at local schools.
Fields of interest: Education, higher education, secondary education, arts, youth, elementary education, crime and law enforcement, rehabilitation, handicapped, community development.
Types of support: In-kind gifts, employee volunteer services.
Limitations: Giving primarily in areas of company operations; field offices give in their own areas, but most giving is in Chicago. No support for organizations that discriminate, sectarian purposes, political organizations, veterans', fraternal, or military organizations, or grant making foundations. No grants to individuals, or for capital campaigns, or good will advertising.
Publications: Application guidelines.
Application information:
> *Initial approach:* Letter
> *Board meeting date(s):* Contributions Committee meets quarterly
> *Write:* Joan E. Cacciatore, Mgr., Comm. Relations

825
The Coleman Foundation, Inc. ▼
(Formerly The Coleman/Fannie May Candies Foundation, Inc.)
575 West Madison, Suite 4605-II
Chicago 60661 (312) 902-7120

Trust established in 1953 in IL.
Donor(s): J.D. Stetson Coleman,‡ Dorothy W. Coleman.‡
Foundation type: Independent
Financial data (yr. ended 12/31/90): Assets, $58,062,754 (M); expenditures, $2,069,406; qualifying distributions, $2,069,406, including $1,741,498 for 142 grants (high: $200,000; low: $200; average: $1,000-$30,000).
Purpose and activities: Giving for elementary, secondary, entrepreneurial, self-employment awareness, and other educational organizations; cancer research, rehabilitation, and programs to aid the handicapped.
Fields of interest: Education, elementary education, secondary education, education—minorities, business, adult education, business education, cancer, rehabilitation, handicapped, disadvantaged, community development, urban development.
Types of support: Operating budgets, general purposes, seed money, special projects, research, conferences and seminars, professorships, scholarship funds, renovation projects, emergency funds, matching funds, program-related investments.
Limitations: Giving primarily in the Chicago, IL, metropolitan area; support also in the Midwest. No grants to individuals (including direct scholarships or fellowships), or for deficit financing, or ticket purchases; no loans.
Publications: Annual report (including application guidelines), financial statement, informational brochure (including application guidelines), program policy statement, application guidelines.
Application information: Submit full proposal only at the request of the foundation. Unsolicited applications not accepted. Application form not required.
  Initial approach: Concise letter describing program or institution
  Copies of proposal: 1
  Deadline(s): Sept. 30 for solicited proposals only
  Board meeting date(s): Usually in Jan., Apr., June. Aug., and Nov.
  Final notification: 3 months; no response to unsolicited proposals
  Write: Jean D. Thorne, Exec. Dir.
Officers and Directors:* John E. Hughes,* Pres.; Michael W. Hennsessy,* Exec. V.P.; C. Hugh Albers,* V.P.; R. Michael Furlong,* V.P.; Richard M. Peritz,* V.P.; Trevor C. Davies,* Treas.; Jean D. Thorne,* Exec. Dir.; James H. Jones.
Number of staff: 4 full-time professional.
EIN: 363025967

826
Commonwealth Edison Corporate Giving Program
P.O. Box 767
Chicago 60690   (312) 294-3062

Financial data (yr. ended 12/31/90): Total giving, $3,200,000 for 400 grants (average: $1,000-$5,000).
Purpose and activities: Supports organizations in the company's service areas, including higher education, hospitals, arts institutes, civil rights, and community service.
Fields of interest: Higher education, education, hospitals, community funds, civic affairs, public affairs, health.

Types of support: Building funds, capital campaigns.
Limitations: Giving primarily in northern IL and service area. No support for religious, political, or fraternal organizations. No grants to individuals, or for advertising.
Publications: Informational brochure.
Application information:
  Initial approach: Brief outline of proposal; corporate affairs department handles giving
  Deadline(s): None
  Board meeting date(s): Quarterly
  Write: Edward Peterson, Corp. Responsibility Mgr.
Number of staff: None.

827
A. G. Cox Charitable Trust
c/o First National Bank of Chicago
One First National Plaza, Suite 0111
Chicago 60670-0484   (312) 732-4280

Established in 1924 in IL.
Foundation type: Independent
Financial data (yr. ended 12/31/90): Assets, $3,871,482 (M); expenditures, $122,536; qualifying distributions, $117,349, including $117,000 for 31 grants (high: $12,000; low: $2,000).
Fields of interest: Health, health associations, social services.
Limitations: Giving primarily in Chicago, IL.
Application information: Application form not required.
  Initial approach: Letter
  Deadline(s): None
  Write: Dan Lydon
Trustee: First National Bank of Chicago.
EIN: 366011498

828
Arie and Ida Crown Memorial ▼
222 North LaSalle St., Suite 2000
Chicago 60601   (312) 236-6300

Incorporated in 1947 in IL.
Donor(s): Members of the Crown family.
Foundation type: Independent
Financial data (yr. ended 12/31/90): Assets, $77,900,185 (M); expenditures, $5,582,611; qualifying distributions, $5,160,555, including $5,141,555 for 654 grants (high: $300,000; low: $100; average: $1,000-$25,000).
Purpose and activities: Broad mandate with focus on "opportunity building"; emphasis on Jewish issues, education, arts and culture, health care, community development, youth agencies, inner city welfare, women, and assistance to the aged and the handicapped.
Fields of interest: Jewish giving, Israel, education, cultural programs, arts, dance, health, community development, urban affairs, youth, social services, homeless, women, aged, handicapped.
Types of support: Continuing support, annual campaigns, equipment, endowment funds, matching funds, professorships, research, special projects, general purposes, operating budgets, renovation projects, technical assistance.
Limitations: Giving primarily in the metropolitan Chicago, IL, area or to national organizations with local programs. No support for

government-sponsored programs. No grants to individuals, or for consulting services or conferences; no loans.
Application information: Application form not required.
  Initial approach: Letter of inquiry (1 page)
  Copies of proposal: 1
  Deadline(s): Jan. 30, May 31, and Sept. 30
  Board meeting date(s): Spring, summer, and fall
  Write: Susan Crown, Pres.
Officers and Directors:* Susan Crown,* Pres.; Lester Crown,* V.P. and Treas.; Arie Steven Crown,* V.P.; James Schine Crown,* V.P.; Charles Goodman,* V.P.; Barbara Manilow,* V.P.; Byron S. Miller,* V.P.; Barbara Brigel, Secy.
Number of staff: 1 full-time professional; 1 part-time professional; 1 full-time support.
EIN: 366076088
Recent health grants:
828-1 Alzheimers Disease and Related Disorders Association, NYC, NY, $30,000. 1990.
828-2 Alzheimers Disease and Related Disorders Association, NYC, NY, $10,000. 1990.
828-3 American Foundation for AIDS Research, NYC, NY, $12,500. 1990.
828-4 Community Response, Oak Park, IL, $10,000. 1990.
828-5 Cystic Fibrosis Foundation, Chicago, IL, $10,000. 1990.
828-6 Evanston Hospital, Evanston, IL, $220,000. 1990.
828-7 Highland Park Hospital Foundation, Highland Park, IL, $10,000. 1990.
828-8 LaRabidia Childrens Hospital and Research Center, Chicago, IL, $50,000. 1990.
828-9 Life Savers, Buffalo Grove, IL, $50,000. 1990.
828-10 Medical Education for South African Blacks, DC, $10,000. 1990.
828-11 Mercy Hospital and Medical Center, Chicago, IL, $25,000. 1990.
828-12 Mount Sinai Hospital Medical Center of Chicago, Chicago, IL, $250,000. 1990.
828-13 National Foundation for Ileitis and Colitis, NYC, NY, $50,000. 1990.
828-14 Planned Parenthood Federation of America, NYC, NY, $10,000. 1990.
828-15 Thresholds, Chicago, IL, $50,000. 1990.

829
The Cuneo Foundation
9101 Greenwood Ave., Suite 210
Niles 60648-1466

Incorporated in 1945 in IL.
Donor(s): John F. Cuneo, Milwaukee Golf Development Corp.
Foundation type: Independent
Financial data (yr. ended 12/31/90): Assets, $22,378,610 (M); expenditures, $1,055,051; qualifying distributions, $1,109,386, including $797,496 for 142 grants (high: $58,500; low: $50) and $100,000 for 1 foundation-administered program.
Purpose and activities: Emphasis on hospitals, Roman Catholic church support, church-related organizations, religious associations, and welfare funds; support also for youth agencies and higher education.
Fields of interest: Hospitals, Catholic giving, Catholic welfare, youth, higher education.

Types of support: General purposes, building funds, equipment, matching funds.
Limitations: Giving primarily in the Chicago, IL, metropolitan area. No grants to individuals, or for scholarships, fellowships, or research projects; no loans.
Application information:
Initial approach: Proposal
Copies of proposal: 1
Deadline(s): None
Board meeting date(s): May and Oct.
Final notification: 2 months
Write: John F. Cuneo, Jr., Pres.
Officers and Directors:* John F. Cuneo, Jr.,* Pres.; Charles L. McEvoy,* V.P.; Robert F. Routh, Secy.-Treas.; Herta Cuneo, Rev. Msgr. Harry C. Koenig, Consuela Cuneo McAlister, Tim McAlister, Rosemary McEvoy.
Number of staff: None.
EIN: 362261606

830
The Davee Foundation
180 East Pearson St., No. 6503
Chicago 60611-2119   (312) 664-4128

Established in 1964 in IL.
Donor(s): Ken M. Davee.
Foundation type: Independent
Financial data (yr. ended 12/31/90): Assets, $13,119,477 (M); expenditures, $203,536; qualifying distributions, $202,775, including $202,775 for grants.
Purpose and activities: Support primarily for a university; emphasis also on the arts, hospitals, higher education, social services and civil rights organizations.
Fields of interest: Higher education, arts, hospitals, social services, civil rights.
Types of support: General purposes.
Limitations: Giving primarily in IL.
Application information:
Initial approach: Letter
Deadline(s): None
Write: Ken M. Davee, Pres.
Officer: Ken M. Davee, Pres.
Directors: J.W. Dugdale, Jr., Ruth Davee.
EIN: 366124598

831
Deering Foundation
410 North Michigan Ave., Rm. 590
Chicago 60611-4252

Incorporated in 1956 in IL.
Donor(s): Barbara D. Danielson, Richard E. Danielson, Jr., Marion D. Campbell, Miami Corp.
Foundation type: Independent
Financial data (yr. ended 11/30/90): Assets, $7,398,725 (M); expenditures, $495,307; qualifying distributions, $501,582, including $480,000 for grants.
Purpose and activities: Support for other foundations, hospitals, secondary education, conservation, and museums.
Fields of interest: Hospitals, secondary education, conservation, museums.
Types of support: General purposes.
Limitations: Giving primarily in IL and MA.

Application information: Contributes only to pre-selected organizations. Applications not accepted.
Officers and Directors:* Marion D. Campbell,* Pres.; Candida D. Burnap,* V.P.; James Deering Danielson,* V.P.; Charles E. Schroeder,* Secy.-Treas.
EIN: 366051876

832
DeKalb Genetics Foundation
(Formerly The DeKalb Foundation)
3100 Sycamore Rd.
DeKalb 60115   (815) 758-3461

Incorporated in 1964 in IL.
Donor(s): DeKalb Genetics Corp.
Foundation type: Company-sponsored
Financial data (yr. ended 08/31/90): Assets, $378,286 (M); gifts received, $206,160; expenditures, $231,420; qualifying distributions, $230,795, including $177,176 for 107 grants (high: $20,000; low: $25; average: $800-$1,000) and $53,113 for 196 employee matching gifts.
Purpose and activities: Grants largely for colleges, civic affairs, social welfare and youth agencies, and community funds in areas of company operations. Educational support limited normally to privately endowed institutions not supported by public tax funds.
Fields of interest: Higher education, business education, secondary education, elementary education, civic affairs, health, social services, youth, community funds, rural development.
Types of support: Continuing support, annual campaigns, seed money, emergency funds, building funds, equipment, land acquisition, matching funds, special projects, employee matching gifts, publications, general purposes.
Limitations: Giving primarily in areas of company operations. No support for religious or labor organizations, or policemen's or firemen's ball activities. No grants to individuals, or for operating budgets, individual travel, study, or similar purposes; no loans.
Publications: Annual report, application guidelines.
Application information: Application form not required.
Initial approach: Letter
Copies of proposal: 1
Deadline(s): None
Board meeting date(s): Quarterly
Final notification: 2 months
Write: Gregory L. Olson, Secy.
Officers and Directors:* Bruce P. Bickner,* Pres.; Richard O. Ryan,* V.P.; Gregory L. Olson,* Secy.; Alan D. Skouby,* Treas.
Number of staff: None.
EIN: 366117737

833
The Dick Family Foundation
249 Market Sq.
Box 312
Lake Forest 60045

Foundation type: Independent
Financial data (yr. ended 12/31/90): Assets, $2,132,687 (M); expenditures, $122,435;

qualifying distributions, $101,610, including $91,300 for 45 grants (high: $19,950; low: $200).
Fields of interest: Hospitals, higher education, education, cultural programs, arts, conservation.
Limitations: Giving primarily in IL, especially Chicago and Lake Forest. No grants to individuals.
Application information: Contributes only to pre-selected organizations. Applications not accepted.
Officers and Directors:* John H. Dick,* Pres. and Treas.; Natalie C. Culley,* Secy.; Helen D. Bronson, Edison Dick, Letitia Ellis.
EIN: 366057056

834
Dillon Foundation
2804 West LeFevre Rd.
P.O. Box 537
Sterling 61081   (815) 626-9000

Incorporated in 1953 in IL.
Donor(s): Members of the Dillon family.
Foundation type: Independent
Financial data (yr. ended 10/31/91): Assets, $23,119,394 (M); expenditures, $1,662,375; qualifying distributions, $1,394,281, including $1,367,634 for 90 grants (high: $652,155; low: $400; average: $700-$7,500).
Purpose and activities: Support for community development and civic and urban affairs; vocational, secondary, and other education; hospitals, social services and youth; historic preservation and museums; recreation; and libraries.
Fields of interest: Community development, secondary education, education, hospitals, social services, youth, museums, recreation, libraries.
Types of support: Continuing support, annual campaigns, seed money, emergency funds, building funds, scholarship funds, general purposes, endowment funds, equipment, land acquisition, matching funds, special projects, capital campaigns.
Limitations: Giving primarily in the Sterling, IL, area. No grants to individuals; no loans.
Application information: Application form not required.
Initial approach: Letter
Copies of proposal: 1
Deadline(s): None
Board meeting date(s): Jan.; committee meets quarterly
Final notification: As soon as possible following committee meetings
Write: Peter W. Dillon, Pres.
Officers and Directors:* Peter W. Dillon,* Pres.; John P. Conway,* V.P. and Secy.; James M. Boesen,* Treas.; Margo Dillon, Gale Inglee.
Number of staff: 1 part-time professional.
EIN: 366059349
Recent health grants:
834-1 Community General Hospital Medical Center, Northern Illinois Cancer Treatment Center, Sterling, IL, $21,000. 1991.
834-2 Delnor Community Hospital, Saint Charles, IL, $10,000. 1991.

835
Gaylord and Dorothy Donnelley Foundation
350 East 22nd St.
Chicago 60616-1428 (312) 326-7255

Incorporated in 1952 in IL.
Donor(s): Gaylord Donnelley, Dorothy Ranney Donnelley.
Foundation type: Independent
Financial data (yr. ended 12/31/91): Assets, $10,294,962 (M); gifts received, $545,000; expenditures, $775,201; qualifying distributions, $696,050, including $696,050 for 147 grants (high: $91,450; low: $500; average: $1,000-$2,000).
Purpose and activities: Primary areas of interest include education, conservation and ecology, cultural organizations and museums, and social services. Support also for health, wildlife, animal health and welfare, historic preservation, general welfare institutions, including programs for the homeless, and public affairs.
Fields of interest: Higher education, education, health, ecology, conservation, animal welfare, cultural programs, historic preservation, public affairs, welfare, social services, homeless.
Types of support: General purposes, operating budgets, special projects.
Limitations: Giving primarily in the Chicago, IL, area and in SC. No support for the performing arts. No grants to individuals, or for emergency funds, pledges, benefits, conferences, meetings, fundraising events, or matching gifts; no loans or multiple year grants.
Publications: Annual report (including application guidelines), application guidelines.
Application information: Application form not required.
   Initial approach: Letter requesting guidelines; telephone requests not considered
   Copies of proposal: 1
   Deadline(s): None
   Board meeting date(s): Spring and fall
   Write: Mrs. Jane Rishel, Pres.
Officers and Directors:* Gaylord Donnelley,* Chair.; Jane Rishel,* Pres. and Treas.; Dorothy Ranney Donnelley,* V.P.; Elliott R. Donnelley,* V.P.; Strachan Donnelley,* V.P.; Laura Donnelley-Morton,* V.P.; Middleton Miller,* Secy.; Larry D. Berning, Robert T. Carter, Robert W. Carton, M.D., C. Bouton McDougal.
Number of staff: 1 full-time professional.
EIN: 366108460

836
Thomas W. Dower Foundation
c/o John M. Hartigan
9730 South Western Ave., Suite 206
Evergreen Park 60642-2814

Established in 1951.
Donor(s): Thomas W. Dower.‡
Foundation type: Independent
Financial data (yr. ended 04/30/91): Assets, $5,333,730 (M); gifts received, $1,599,972; expenditures, $343,243; qualifying distributions, $262,362, including $235,402 for 96 grants (high: $55,102; low: $400).
Fields of interest: Higher education, education, welfare, health, hospitals, religion—Christian, Catholic giving.

Limitations: Giving primarily in IL.
Officer: Daniel J. O'Shaughnessy, Exec. Dir.
Trustee: Mary Hartigan.
EIN: 366071665

837
The Richard H. Driehaus Foundation
Three First National Plaza, Suite 5315
Chicago 60602

Established in 1983 in IL.
Donor(s): Richard H. Driehaus.
Foundation type: Independent
Financial data (yr. ended 10/31/90): Assets, $9,682,713 (M); expenditures, $458,263; qualifying distributions, $362,418, including $362,418 for 21 grants (high: $100,000; low: $150).
Fields of interest: Social services, housing, alcoholism, education, handicapped.
Types of support: General purposes.
Limitations: Giving primarily in IL. No grants to individuals.
Application information: Contributes only to pre-selected organizations. Applications not accepted.
Trustees: Margaret F. Driehaus, Joni S. Taylor.
EIN: 363261347

838
The Duchossois Foundation
845 Larch Ave.
Elmhurst 60126 (312) 279-3600

Established in 1984 in IL.
Donor(s): Duchossois Industries, Inc.
Foundation type: Company-sponsored
Financial data (yr. ended 12/31/90): Assets, $344,314 (M); expenditures, $511,674; qualifying distributions, $478,400, including $478,400 for 50 grants (high: $250,000; low: $100).
Fields of interest: Social services, community funds, cancer, elementary education, cultural programs.
Types of support: General purposes, capital campaigns.
Limitations: Giving primarily in the metropolitan Chicago, IL, area.
Publications: Application guidelines.
Application information: Guidelines available upon request. Application form not required.
   Initial approach: Letter
   Copies of proposal: 1
   Deadline(s): None
   Board meeting date(s): Every 6 weeks
   Write: Kimberly Duchossois Lenczuk, Secy.
Officers and Directors:* Richard L. Duchossois,* Pres.; Craig J. Duchossois,* V.P.; R. Bruce Duchossois,* V.P.; Kimberly Duchossois Lenczuk,* Secy.
Number of staff: 1 part-time professional.
EIN: 363327987

839
The George M. Eisenberg Foundation
4100 West Fullerton Ave.
Chicago 60639-2106

Trust established in 1945 in IL.

Donor(s): George M. Eisenberg, American Decal and Manufacturing Co.
Foundation type: Independent
Financial data (yr. ended 12/31/90): Assets, $5,125,691 (M); gifts received, $491,715; expenditures, $12,948; qualifying distributions, $0.
Fields of interest: Hospitals, medical research, Jewish welfare, social services, aged, handicapped, youth.
Limitations: Giving primarily in IL. No grants to individuals.
Application information: Contributes only to pre-selected organizations. Applications not accepted.
Trustees: James L. Pollack, Charles H. Weinman.
EIN: 366091694

840
The Field Foundation of Illinois, Inc. ▼
135 South LaSalle St., Suite 1250
Chicago 60603 (312) 263-3211

Incorporated in 1960 in IL.
Donor(s): Marshall Field IV.‡
Foundation type: Independent
Financial data (yr. ended 04/30/90): Assets, $28,861,595 (M); expenditures, $2,066,921; qualifying distributions, $1,650,931, including $1,650,931 for 66 grants (high: $100,000; low: $3,000; average: $10,000-$50,000).
Purpose and activities: Giving in the fields of health, community welfare, primary and secondary education, cultural activities, conservation, and urban and community affairs.
Fields of interest: Health, health services, AIDS, rehabilitation, mental health, drug abuse, welfare, social services, disadvantaged, child welfare, youth, employment, homeless, hunger, aged, race relations, education, education—early childhood, elementary education, secondary education, literacy, cultural programs, museums, environment, conservation, urban affairs, public policy, public affairs.
Types of support: Building funds, emergency funds, equipment, special projects, land acquisition, technical assistance.
Limitations: Giving primarily in the Chicago, IL, area. No support for member agencies of community funds, national health agencies, neighborhood health clinics, small cultural groups, or for religious purposes. No grants to individuals, or for endowment funds, continuing operating support, medical research, conferences, operating support of day care centers, fundraising events, advertising, scholarships, printed materials or video equipment, or fellowships; no loans.
Publications: Annual report (including application guidelines).
Application information: Application form not required.
   Initial approach: Proposal
   Copies of proposal: 1
   Deadline(s): None
   Board meeting date(s): 3 times a year
   Write: Handy L. Lindsey, Jr., Exec. Dir.
Officers and Directors:* Arthur F. Quern,* Chair.; Gary H. Kline, Secy.; Handy L. Lindsey, Jr., Exec. Dir. and Treas.; Marshall Field, Hanna H. Gray, Philip Wayne Hummer, George A. Ranney, Jr., Arthur E. Rasmussen.

Number of staff: 4 full-time professional; 1 part-time professional; 1 part-time support.
EIN: 366059408
Recent health grants:

840-1 Healthy Mothers and Babies Coalition, Chicago, IL, $15,000. For general operating expenses. 1990.

840-2 La Rabida Childrens Hospital and Research Center, Chicago, IL, $25,000. For campaign to construct new Mechanical Plant, Children's Pavilion and Lakeside Garden Playground. 1990.

840-3 Misericordia Home/Heart of Mercy Village, Chicago, IL, $30,000. For third payment toward constructing Independent Living Apartment Complex for young adults with mild to moderate disabilities. 1990.

840-4 Mount Sinai Hospital Medical Center of Chicago, Chicago, IL, $33,333. For capital improvement of facility and acquisition of new medical equipment. 1990.

840-5 Near North Health Service Corporation, Chicago, IL, $50,000. For completing renovation of basement space in Winfield Moody Health Center to facilitate on-site operation of new clinical and supportive social service programs. 1990.

840-6 Northwestern Memorial Hospital, Chicago, IL, $33,333. For second payment toward capital campaign for expansion of Prentice Women's Hospital and Maternity Center. 1990.

840-7 Rehabilitation Institute of Chicago, Chicago, IL, $17,500. For fifth payment toward establishing new Head Injury Center. 1990.

840-8 Rush-Presbyterian-Saint Lukes Medical Center, Chicago, IL, $40,000. For fourth payment for medical care and day care components of Alzheimer's Disease Center. 1990.

840-9 Stop AIDS Chicago, Chicago, IL, $15,000. To expand outreach efforts to Chicago's south side African American community. 1990.

840-10 Thresholds, Chicago, IL, $50,000. Toward capital campaign for purchase, renovation and furnishing of new facility in which to operate and expand Young Adult Program. 1990.

840-11 Voices for Illinois Children, Chicago, IL, $30,000. For project: Policy Options in Children's Mental Health. 1990.

841
First Evergreen Foundation
c/o First National Bank of Evergreen Park
3101 West 95th St.
Evergreen Park 60642   (708) 422-6700

Established in 1985 in IL.
Donor(s): First National Bank of Evergreen Park.
Foundation type: Company-sponsored
Financial data (yr. ended 12/31/90): Assets, $3,132,310 (M); gifts received, $500,000; expenditures, $176,541; qualifying distributions, $169,000, including $169,000 for 12 grants (high: $40,000; low: $5,000).
Fields of interest: Hospitals, higher education, religion—Christian.
Limitations: Giving primarily in the southwest Chicago, IL, area. No grants to individuals.
Application information:
Initial approach: Proposal

Deadline(s): None
Write: Kenneth Ozinga, Trustee
Trustees: Alfred E. Bleeker, Jerome J. Cismoski, Kenneth J. Ozinga, Martin Ozinga, Jr.
EIN: 363456053

842
FMC Foundation ▼
200 East Randolph Dr.
Chicago 60601   (312) 861-6135

Incorporated in 1953 in CA.
Donor(s): FMC Corp.
Foundation type: Company-sponsored
Financial data (yr. ended 11/30/89): Assets, $636,203 (M); gifts received, $1,350,000; expenditures, $1,902,423; qualifying distributions, $1,816,517, including $1,557,755 for 200 grants (high: $215,900; low: $100; average: $2,000-$15,000) and $258,603 for 1,491 employee matching gifts.
Purpose and activities: Giving primarily for higher education and community improvement funds; grants also for public issues, economic education, urban affairs, health and human services, cultural institutions, civic affairs groups, and youth agencies.
Fields of interest: Education, higher education, business education, education—minorities, economics, civic affairs, public policy, urban affairs, agriculture, law and justice, public affairs, safety, environment, cultural programs, youth, social services, hospitals.
Types of support: Building funds, continuing support, employee matching gifts, scholarship funds, special projects, general purposes, employee-related scholarships, capital campaigns, equipment.
Limitations: Giving primarily in areas in which company facilities are located. No support for educational institutions below the college or university level, or state or regional associations of independent colleges, national health agencies, or United Way supported organizations. No grants to individuals, or for endowment funds or hospital operating expenses or research; no loans.
Publications: Program policy statement, application guidelines.
Application information: Application form not required.
Initial approach: Letter
Copies of proposal: 1
Deadline(s): None
Board meeting date(s): Quarterly
Final notification: 6 weeks
Write: Catherine Johnston, Exec. Dir.
Officers and Directors:* William R. Jenkins,* Pres.; William J. Kirby,* V.P.; James A. McClung,* V.P.; Daniel N. Schuchardt, Secy.-Treas.; Robert N. Burt, Robert H. Malott.
Number of staff: 1 full-time professional; 1 part-time support.
EIN: 946063032

843
The Forest Fund
Route 1, Box 32, St. Mary's Rd.
Libertyville 60048   (312) 362-2994

Incorporated in 1956 in IL.
Donor(s): Marion M. Lloyd.

Foundation type: Independent
Financial data (yr. ended 12/31/90): Assets, $2,507,790 (M); expenditures, $161,342; qualifying distributions, $153,350, including $151,100 for 160 grants (high: $12,500; low: $250; average: $500-$750).
Fields of interest: Education, adult education, health services, AIDS, child welfare, family services, drug abuse, crime and law enforcement, cultural programs, community development.
Limitations: Giving primarily in IL, with emphasis on Chicago. No grants to individuals, or for endowment funds, scholarships, or fellowships; no loans.
Application information: Application form not required.
Initial approach: Proposal
Copies of proposal: 1
Deadline(s): None
Board meeting date(s): Mar., July, Sept., and Dec.
Write: Marion M. Lloyd, Pres.
Officers: Marion M. Lloyd, Pres. and Treas.; Louise A. Baker, Secy.
Director: Marianne S. Harper.
EIN: 366047859

844
Fraida Foundation
Two North LaSalle St., Suite 2100
Chicago 60602

Donor(s): Hy Greenhill, Michael L. Greenhill, Mark A. Greenhill.
Foundation type: Independent
Financial data (yr. ended 04/30/91): Assets, $2,280,063 (M); gifts received, $302,250; expenditures, $148,636; qualifying distributions, $132,000, including $132,000 for 5 grants (high: $100,000; low: $1,000).
Purpose and activities: Giving primarily for higher education and medical development in Israel.
Fields of interest: Higher education, medical sciences, Israel.
Limitations: No grants to individuals.
Application information: Contributes only to pre-selected organizations. Applications not accepted.
Write: Marc Simon, Pres.
Officers: Hy Greenhill, Chair.; Marc S. Simon, Pres.; Mark A. Greenhill, V.P.; Michael L. Greenhill, V.P.; Leonard H. Popowcer, V.P.
EIN: 363126643

845
Zollie and Elaine Frank Fund
666 Garland Place
Des Plaines 60016

Incorporated in 1953 in IL.
Donor(s): Zollie S. Frank, Elaine S. Frank, Z. Frank, Inc., Four Wheels, Inc., Wheels, Inc.
Foundation type: Independent
Financial data (yr. ended 12/31/90): Assets, $1,712,757 (M); gifts received, $135,000; expenditures, $582,619; qualifying distributions, $577,206, including $576,976 for 195 grants (high: $252,500; low: $3).
Purpose and activities: Emphasis on Jewish welfare funds and temple support; grants also for

higher education, hospitals, youth clubs, a senior citizens' center, and organized charities.
Fields of interest: Jewish welfare, Jewish giving, higher education, hospitals, youth, aged.
Types of support: General purposes.
Limitations: Giving primarily in IL.
Application information:
  Initial approach: Letter
  Deadline(s): None
  Write: Elaine S. Frank, Pres.
Officers: Elaine S. Frank, Pres.; James S. Frank, Secy.
EIN: 366118400

846
Frankel Foundation ▼
c/o Harris Trust & Savings Bank
111 West Monroe St.
Chicago 60603
Application address: P.O. Box 755, Chicago, IL 60603

Established in 1959 in IL.
Donor(s): Gerald Frankel,‡ Gustav Frankel,‡ Julius N. Frankel.‡
Foundation type: Independent
Financial data (yr. ended 10/31/89): Assets, $26,953,124 (M); expenditures, $1,567,216; qualifying distributions, $1,462,520, including $1,399,650 for 42 grants (high: $226,550; low: $5,000; average: $10,000-$25,000).
Purpose and activities: Giving primarily for higher education, hospitals, arts and culture, and social services.
Fields of interest: Hospitals, higher education, social services, arts, cultural programs.
Limitations: Giving primarily in IL. No grants to individuals.
Application information: Application form not required.
  Initial approach: Letter
  Deadline(s): None
  Board meeting date(s): 4 or 5 times a year
  Final notification: Immediately following meetings
  Write: Ellen A. Bechtold
Trustees: Nelson O. Cornelius, John L. Georgas, Harris Trust & Savings Bank.
Number of staff: None.
EIN: 366765844

847
The Franklin Life Insurance Corporate Giving Program
Franklin Square
Springfield 62713   (217) 528-2011

Purpose and activities: Supports educational institutions, community organizations, arts centers, the theatre, performing arts and community arts programs.
Fields of interest: Education, arts, performing arts, theater, music, health.
Limitations: Giving primarily in headquarters area.
Application information: Applications not accepted.
  Write: John C. Watson, Pres.

848
Lloyd A. Fry Foundation ▼
135 South LaSalle St., Suite 1910
Chicago 60603   (312) 580-0310

Established in 1959 in IL.
Donor(s): Lloyd A. Fry.‡
Foundation type: Independent
Financial data (yr. ended 06/30/91): Assets, $76,126,166 (M); expenditures, $4,017,863; qualifying distributions, $3,358,750, including $3,358,750 for 227 grants (high: $125,000; low: $500; average: $5,000-$50,000).
Purpose and activities: Emphasis on higher and other education, civic and urban affairs, public policy, minorities and race relations, law and justice, employment, child welfare, the disadvantaged, health and social services, including AIDS programs, and cultural programs, including performing arts.
Fields of interest: Education, higher education, elementary education, secondary education, education—minorities, civic affairs, community development, public affairs, minorities, law and justice, legal services, urban affairs, employment, child welfare, social services, hospitals, health, AIDS, cultural programs, performing arts.
Types of support: Special projects, seed money, equipment, matching funds, research, publications, conferences and seminars, internships, scholarship funds.
Limitations: Giving primarily in the Chicago, IL, area. No support for governmental bodies or tax-supported educational institutions for services that fall within their responsibilities, or for fundraising benefits. No grants to individuals, or for continuing support, annual campaigns, emergency funds, general operating budgets, deficit financing, building funds, land acquisition, renovation projects, or endowment funds; no loans.
Publications: Application guidelines, annual report (including application guidelines).
Application information: Application form not required.
  Initial approach: Letter
  Copies of proposal: 1
  Deadline(s): None
  Board meeting date(s): Feb., May, Aug., and Nov.
  Final notification: 3 months
  Write: Ben Rothblatt, Exec. Dir.
Officers and Directors:* Edmund A. Stephan,* Chair.; Roger E. Anderson,* Vice-Chair.; Lloyd A. Fry, Jr.,* Pres.; M. James Termondt,* V.P. and Treas.; Howard M. McCue III,* Secy.; Ben Rothblatt, Exec. Dir.
Number of staff: 1 full-time professional; 1 part-time professional; 1 full-time support.
EIN: 366108775
Recent health grants:
848-1 AIDS Legal Council of Chicago, Chicago, IL, $10,000. For general operating support. 1991.
848-2 Alivio Medical Center, Chicago, IL, $10,000. For community health education programs. 1991.
848-3 Bonaventure House, Chicago, IL, $50,000. For expanded services for persons with AIDS. 1991.
848-4 Brain Research Foundation, Chicago, IL, $75,000. For Seed Grants Program. 1991.

848-5 Chicago House and Social Service Agency, Chicago, IL, $15,000. For intermediate care program for persons with AIDS. 1991.
848-6 Community Response, Oak Park, IL, $10,000. For start-up support for AIDS service organization. 1991.
848-7 Counseling Center of Lake View, Chicago, IL, $10,000. For Homeless Youth Substance Abuse Project. 1991.
848-8 Erie Family Health Center, Chicago, IL, $10,000. To establish Senior Wellness Program in public housing complex. 1991.
848-9 Family Institute of Chicago, Chicago, IL, $20,000. For expanded clinical services to low-income families. 1991.
848-10 Five Hospital Foundation, Chicago, IL, $10,000. For training program in home care nursing of elderly. 1991.
848-11 Gateway Foundation, Chicago, IL, $10,000. For substance abuse prevention program in Lakeview community. 1991.
848-12 Infant Welfare Society of Chicago, Chicago, IL, $25,000. To expand Visiting Nurse and Home Visitor program for young children and their families. 1991.
848-13 Mental Health Association of Greater Chicago, Chicago, IL, $10,000. For expansion of mental health curriculum in Chicago Public Schools. 1991.
848-14 Mercy Hospital and Medical Center, Chicago, IL, $17,500. For internship and mentoring program for high school students in Chicago Housing Authority residence. 1991.
848-15 Metropolitan Planning Council, Chicago, IL, $40,000. For policy research and planning for health care system for medically underserved in Cook County. 1991.
848-16 Misericordia Home/Heart of Mercy Village, Chicago, IL, $25,000. For educational program for young adults. 1991.
848-17 Peoples Reinvestment and Development Effort, Chicago, IL, $15,000. For anti-drug organizing project. 1991.
848-18 Robert Crown Center for Health Education, Hinsdale, IL, $15,000. For Family Life Education Outreach Program. 1991.
848-19 Rush-Presbyterian-Saint Lukes Medical Center, Chicago, IL, $100,000. For Rush Medical College Community Service Initiative. 1991.
848-20 Safer Foundation, Pace Institute, Chicago, IL, $30,000. For Male Counseling Program at Cook County Jail. 1991.
848-21 Saint Xavier College, Chicago, IL, $50,000. To establish Advance Option Nursing Program. 1991.
848-22 Thresholds, Chicago, IL, $15,000. For Bridge for the Homeless Program. 1991.
848-23 University of Chicago Hospitals, Chicago, IL, $50,000. To initiate Infant and Family Follow-up Program, providing comprehensive health care and social services to high-risk infants and their families. 1991.
848-24 Voices for Illinois Children, Chicago, IL, $25,000. For research and policy development on children's mental health. 1991.

849
Paul A. Funk Foundation
1001 North Main St.
P.O. Box 3488
Bloomington 61702-3488   (309) 828-6241

Established in 1967.
Foundation type: Independent
Financial data (yr. ended 12/31/90): Assets, $2,508,464 (M); expenditures, $93,201; qualifying distributions, $91,497, including $88,975 for 38 grants (high: $16,000; low: $200).
Fields of interest: Higher education, hospitals, health associations, social services.
Limitations: Giving primarily in McLean County, IL.
Application information: Applications not accepted.
Write: David Dunn
Trustees: Eugene D. Funk III, Lafayette Funk III, Richard C. Funk, Stephen McCormick, Calvin Rehtmeyer, Eugene D. Roth.
Number of staff: None.
EIN: 376075515

850
Furnas Foundation, Inc.
1000 McKee St.
Batavia 60510-1663   (312) 879-6000

Incorporated in 1960 in IL.
Donor(s): W.C. Furnas,‡ Leto M. Furnas.‡
Foundation type: Independent
Financial data (yr. ended 12/31/90): Assets, $638,278 (M); gifts received, $300,200; expenditures, $341,970; qualifying distributions, $341,021, including $329,021 for grants.
Purpose and activities: Emphasis on higher education, including a scholarship program limited to undergraduate study; support also for health and youth agencies, hospitals, and community funds.
Fields of interest: Higher education, health services, youth, hospitals, community funds, hospices.
Types of support: Annual campaigns, building funds, equipment, matching funds, student aid, capital campaigns.
Limitations: Giving primarily in IL and IA; giving limited to Batavia, IL, and Clarke County, IA, for scholarships. No support for postgraduate students. No grants to individuals (except for scholarships); no loans.
Publications: Informational brochure, program policy statement, application guidelines.
Application information: Application form required for scholarships; request form from Scholarship Committee.
Initial approach: Proposal or letter
Copies of proposal: 1
Deadline(s): Mar. 1 for scholarships
Board meeting date(s): Jan., Apr., July, and Oct.
Final notification: 2 to 3 months
Officers: Joanne B. Hansen, Pres.; Robert A. Becker, V.P.; Gilbert R. Nary, Treas.
Directors: Thomas F. Caughlin, Elizabeth Hall, Richard W. Hansen, William F. Lisman, Robert F. Peterson, Dale F. Willcox.
Scholarship Committee: Theodore Clauser, Dorothy J. Lowe, William Wood.
Number of staff: None.
EIN: 366049894

851
The Galter Foundation
215 East Chicago Ave.
Chicago 60611

Incorporated in 1943 in IL.
Donor(s): Dollie Galter, Jack Galter, Spartus Corp.
Foundation type: Independent
Financial data (yr. ended 12/31/90): Assets, $9,885,974 (M); gifts received, $10,000,000; expenditures, $2,014,449; qualifying distributions, $2,010,347, including $2,007,393 for 38 grants (high: $500,000; low: $3).
Purpose and activities: Giving for Jewish welfare funds and temple support, hospitals, and the handicapped.
Fields of interest: Jewish giving, Jewish welfare, hospitals, handicapped.
Limitations: No grants to individuals; no loans or program-related investments.
Application information: Contributes only to pre-selected organizations. Applications not accepted.
Officers: Dollie Galter, Mgr.; Jack Galter, Mgr.
EIN: 366082419

852
Robert W. Galvin Foundation
1303 East Algonquin Rd.
Schaumburg 60196   (708) 576-5300

Incorporated in 1953 in IL.
Donor(s): Robert W. Galvin.
Foundation type: Independent
Financial data (yr. ended 12/31/90): Assets, $7,704,633 (M); gifts received, $250,000; expenditures, $809,200; qualifying distributions, $807,800, including $807,745 for 35 grants (high: $456,750; low: $15).
Purpose and activities: Giving largely for higher, secondary and medical education; grants also for child welfare agencies, hospitals, and a medical rehabilitation center.
Fields of interest: Higher education, secondary education, medical education, child welfare, hospitals, rehabilitation.
Limitations: Giving primarily in IL. No grants to individuals.
Application information: Application form not required.
Initial approach: Letter
Board meeting date(s): Annually
Write: Robert W. Galvin, Pres.
Officers and Directors:* Robert W. Galvin,* Pres.; Christopher B. Galvin,* V.P.; Mary G. Galvin,* Secy.-Treas.
EIN: 366065560

853
GATX Corporate Contributions Program
120 South Riverside Plaza
Chicago 60606-3998   (312) 621-6221

Financial data (yr. ended 12/31/90): Total giving, $1,113,120, including $1,025,656 for 161 grants (high: $16,000; low: $1,000; average: $5,000), $71,657 for 475 employee matching gifts and $15,807 for 20 in-kind gifts.
Purpose and activities: "GATX Corporation is committed to the communities in which it does business, based on the recognition that its vitality

as an institution is affected by the well-being of the environment in which it operates. GATX acts as a responsible corporate citizen in many ways—one of which is through its contributions program which supports organizations that enrich the community and address critical public needs. Helping people help themselves pays dividends—by reducing the individuals social dependency, and by increasing his or her pride and sense of dignity. Because breaking the bonds of poverty and frustration can have an impact that lasts a lifetime, most of GATX's funding is for programs that aid the economically disadvantaged." The following factors are taken into consideration when evaluating proposals: involvement of GATX employees in organization, area served, impact on the community, efficiency of the organization's structure and management, cost of fund-raising activities, level of government funding, evidence of broad community support, potential of a program to become self-sustaining, and proven effectiveness of the organization in meeting community needs.
Fields of interest: Civic affairs, cultural programs, arts, social services, education, community funds, adult education, aged, AIDS, child welfare, civic affairs, community development, crime and law enforcement, dance, disadvantaged, education—minorities, elementary education, employment, health, health services, higher education, homeless, hospices, housing, hunger, law and justice, legal services, literacy, mental health, minorities, museums, music, rehabilitation, theater, women, youth, drug abuse, family services, handicapped, secondary education.
Types of support: Employee matching gifts, matching funds, general purposes, operating budgets, scholarship funds, special projects, in-kind gifts, donated equipment, seed money, employee volunteer services, use of facilities, donated products.
Limitations: Giving primarily in Chicago; some giving in other operating locations; no support for local chapters of national organizations. No support for political, labor or fraternal organizations, sectarian religious programs, or health research. No grants to individuals, or for trips or tours, advertising, tickets for benefit purposes, capital campaigns, endowments, land acquisition, deficit financing, conferences, or general operating support for United Way agencies.
Publications: Grants list, newsletter, application guidelines.
Application information: GATX employs a staff to handle contributions only; decisions are made by the contribs. comm., comprised of a chairman and five members representing various subsidiaries and depts. The board chair of the company is an ex-officio member. Application form required.
Initial approach: Letter; send to headquarters
Copies of proposal: 1
Deadline(s): 15th day of the month preceding a board meeting
Board meeting date(s): Quarterly in Feb., May, Aug. and Nov.
Final notification: 2 weeks following board meeting
Write: Christiane S. Wilczura, Mgr., Community Affairs

Number of staff: 1 full-time professional; 1 part-time support.

854

Geraldi-Norton Memorial Corporation
One First National Plaza, Suite 3148
Chicago 60603

Incorporated in 1952 in IL.
Donor(s): Grace Geraldi Norton.‡
Foundation type: Independent
Financial data (yr. ended 12/31/90): Assets, $2,329,373 (M); gifts received, $22,065; expenditures, $217,389; qualifying distributions, $216,010, including $211,700 for 89 grants (high: $25,000; low: $250).
Fields of interest: Arts, cultural programs, education, higher education, youth, medical sciences, hospitals.
Types of support: Building funds, research, general purposes.
Limitations: Giving primarily in the Chicago, IL, area. No grants to individuals.
Application information:
  Initial approach: Letter
  Deadline(s): None
  Write: Roger P. Eklund, Pres.
Officers: Roger P. Eklund, Pres. and Treas.; Dariel Ann Eklund, V.P.; Sally S. Eklund, Secy.
EIN: 366069997

855

Emma & Oscar Getz Foundation
30 North LaSalle St., Suite 2900
Chicago 60602

Established in 1966 in IL.
Donor(s): Oscar Getz,‡ Emma Getz.
Foundation type: Independent
Financial data (yr. ended 12/31/90): Assets, $2,827,744 (M); expenditures, $130,809; qualifying distributions, $118,787, including $114,750 for 34 grants (high: $15,000; low: $100).
Fields of interest: Higher education, film, theater, arts, Jewish giving, Jewish welfare, medical research.
Limitations: Giving primarily in Chicago, IL. No grants to individuals.
Application information: Contributes only to pre-selected organizations. Applications not accepted.
Officers: Emma Getz, Pres.; William Getz, V.P. and Secy.; Ralph P. Silver, Treas.
EIN: 366150787

856

Max Goldenberg Foundation
c/o Harris Trust & Savings Bank
111 West Monroe St.
Chicago 60603
Application address: Ellen A. Bechthold, c/o Harris Trust & Savings Bank, P.O. Box 755, Chicago, IL 60690; Tel.: (312) 461-2613

Trust established in 1946 in IL.
Donor(s): Max Goldenberg.‡
Foundation type: Independent
Financial data (yr. ended 12/31/90): Assets, $3,481,920 (M); expenditures, $210,908;

qualifying distributions, $182,852, including $174,000 for 36 grants (high: $15,000; low: $1,000).
Purpose and activities: Grants are awarded in three areas: hospitals and medical research in the fields of cancer, heart ailments, multiple sclerosis, eye disorders, and other medical ailments; schools, colleges, universities, and other leading institutions of learning; and social services, particularly Jewish charities.
Fields of interest: Hospitals, medical research, higher education, social services, Jewish welfare.
Limitations: Giving primarily in IL.
Publications: Annual report.
Application information:
  Initial approach: Proposal
  Copies of proposal: 3
  Deadline(s): Aug. 31
  Board meeting date(s): Oct.
Trustees: Marian Goodman, Harris Trust & Savings Bank.
EIN: 362471625

857

The Grainger Foundation, Inc. ▼
5500 West Howard St.
Skokie 60077   (708) 982-9000

Incorporated in 1967 in IL as successor to the Grainger Charitable Trust established in 1949.
Donor(s): W.W. Grainger,‡ Hally W. Grainger,‡ David W. Grainger.
Foundation type: Independent
Financial data (yr. ended 12/31/91): Assets, $71,903,595 (M); expenditures, $14,706,259; qualifying distributions, $14,579,037, including $14,579,037 for 42 grants (high: $4,805,000; low: $500; average: $5,000-$200,000).
Purpose and activities: Emphasis on endowments, capital funds, and special program funds for higher education (colleges & universities), cultural and historical institutions (the arts, symphony orchestras, and museums), hospitals, and human service organizations.
Fields of interest: Higher education, hospitals, museums, cultural programs, arts, historic preservation.
Types of support: Continuing support, building funds, equipment, endowment funds, research, general purposes, renovation projects, special projects, operating budgets.
Limitations: Giving primarily in the Chicago, IL, area. No grants to individuals, or for general operating budgets, seed money, emergency funds, deficit financing, publications, conferences, scholarships, fellowships, or matching gifts; no loans.
Publications: 990-PF.
Application information: The foundation contributes only to pre-selected charitable organizations as determined by its directors and officers. For this reason, and due to staffing constraints, grant requests received from organizations other than those first contacted by the Grainger Foundation cannot be reviewed or acknowledged.
  Board meeting date(s): Periodically
  Final notification: Favorable decisions only
  Write: Lee J. Flory, V.P.
Officers and Directors:* David W. Grainger,* Pres. and Treas.; Lee J. Flory,* V.P. and Secy.; Juli P. Grainger,* V.P.; John S. Chapman.

Number of staff: None.
EIN: 366192971

858

GSC Enterprises Foundation
737 North Michigan Ave., Suite 1200
Chicago 60611-2658

Established in 1987 in IL.
Donor(s): GSC Enterprises, Inc.
Foundation type: Company-sponsored
Financial data (yr. ended 12/31/90): Assets, $679 (M); gifts received, $46,000; expenditures, $306,510; qualifying distributions, $306,500, including $306,500 for 7 grants (high: $171,000; low: $1,000).
Fields of interest: Secondary education, Protestant giving, medical research.
Types of support: Endowment funds, research, general purposes.
Limitations: Giving primarily in IL. No grants to individuals.
Application information: Contributes only to pre-selected organizations. Applications not accepted.
Officers and Directors:* Clyde William Engle,* Pres.; Amelia R. Stroemel,* Secy.-Treas.; Gerald M. Tierney, Jr.
EIN: 363567238

859

Armand Hammer Foundation
135 South LaSalle St., Suite 1000
Chicago 60603   (312) 580-1225

Established in 1968 in CA.
Donor(s): Armand Hammer.‡
Foundation type: Operating
Financial data (yr. ended 12/31/90): Assets, $330,805 (M); gifts received, $1,390,000; expenditures, $25,597,313; qualifying distributions, $25,597,313, including $25,326,857 for 34 grants (high: $24,264,916; low: $20; average: $500-$25,000) and $268,049 for foundation-administered programs.
Purpose and activities: Giving primarily for higher education, art museums and galleries, and medical research; support also for the state of Israel.
Fields of interest: Arts, higher education, museums, medical research, Israel.
Limitations: No grants to individuals.
Application information: Application form not required.
  Initial approach: Letter
  Copies of proposal: 2
  Deadline(s): None
  Board meeting date(s): Annually and as required
  Write: David J. Creagan, Jr.
Directors: Dru Hammer, Michael A. Hammer.
Number of staff: None.
EIN: 237010813

860

Philip S. Harper Foundation
c/o Harper-Wyman Co.
930 North York Rd., Suite 204
Hinsdale 60521-2913

Incorporated in 1953 in IL.

Donor(s): Philip S. Harper, Harper-Wyman Co.
Foundation type: Independent
Financial data (yr. ended 11/30/90): Assets, $5,077,089 (M); expenditures, $292,112; qualifying distributions, $269,100, including $249,893 for grants.
Fields of interest: Higher education, Protestant giving, youth, child welfare, health services, medical research, cultural programs, social services, media and communications.
Officers: Philip S. Harper, Jr., Pres.; Lamar Harper Williams, V.P.; Charles C. Lamar, Secy.-Treas.
EIN: 366049875

861
Harris Bankcorp Corporate Giving Program
P.O. Box 755
111 West Monroe St.
Chicago 60690-7791   (312) 461-6660

Financial data (yr. ended 12/31/91): Total giving, $1,931,840 for grants.
Purpose and activities: "A program that makes use of volunteers and leaders from the community, that reaches children and their families, and that places an emphasis on self-knowledge and increased self-sufficiency, is our ideal." Support is for education, culture and the arts, social services, health, and civic programs, and also for United Way/Crusade of Mercy. Contributions (corporate and foundation combined) are targeted at 2 percent of the net profits of Harris Trust and Savings Bank. In addition to giving through contributions and employee involvement, the bank also has a Neighborhood Lending Program, which in 1988 pledged $50 million in loans and $625,000 over five years in grants to help Chicago neighborhoods. Figures represent giving by Harris Bankcorp, Harris Trust and Savings, its employees, and other subsidiaries. Current giving entries reflect the interests of Harris Bank Foundation, Harris Trust and Savings, and Harris BankCorp. Other subsidiairies may have different priorities. An annual gift is made to Chicago United Way/Crusade of Mercy by Harris Trust and Savings. The foundation gave $878,160 in 1991.
Fields of interest: Education, higher education, civic affairs, health, social services, cultural programs, arts.
Types of support: Special projects, employee matching gifts, employee-related scholarships.
Limitations: Giving primarily in areas where banks are located. The foundation and Harris Bank concentrate on metropolitan Chicago; Harris community banks give in their respective locales. No support for political activities, sectarian or religious organizations or fraternal organizations. No grants to individuals, or for testimonial dinners or benefits or advertisements, conferences or seminars.
Publications: Informational brochure.
Application information: Application form not required.
  Initial approach: Letter
  Copies of proposal: 1
  Deadline(s): One month prior to bimonthly meetings
  Board meeting date(s): Bimonthly
  Final notification: Following Board meeting
  Write: Joan Neal, Public Affairs

Number of staff: 2 full-time professional; 1 full-time support.

862
Harris Family Foundation
P.O. Box 2279
Northbrook 60065-2279   (708) 498-1261

Incorporated in 1957 in IL.
Donor(s): Neison Harris, and family.
Foundation type: Independent
Financial data (yr. ended 02/28/92): Assets, $11,854,291 (M); expenditures, $1,320,509; qualifying distributions, $1,308,182, including $1,308,182 for 121 grants (high: $326,000; low: $25).
Fields of interest: Medical research, health services, rehabilitation, social services, child development, education, education—early childhood, secondary education, higher education, Jewish giving, race relations, cultural programs.
Types of support: General purposes, building funds, annual campaigns, internships.
Limitations: Giving primarily in the Chicago, IL, area. No grants to individuals.
Application information: Application form not required.
  Initial approach: Letter
  Copies of proposal: 1
  Deadline(s): Submit proposal preferably in May; no set deadline
  Board meeting date(s): May and Nov.
  Final notification: 30 days
  Write: Neison Harris, Pres.
Officers and Directors:* Neison Harris,* Pres. and Treas.; Bette D. Harris,* V.P. and Secy.; Sidney Barrows, Katherine Harris, King W. Harris, Toni H. Paul.
Number of staff: None.
EIN: 366054378

863
The Harris Foundation ▼
Two North LaSalle St., Suite 605
Chicago 60602-3703   (312) 621-0566

Incorporated in 1945 in MN.
Donor(s): Members of the Harris family.
Foundation type: Independent
Financial data (yr. ended 12/31/90): Assets, $18,428,937 (M); gifts received, $966,428; expenditures, $2,656,737; qualifying distributions, $2,257,708, including $2,056,780 for 313 grants (high: $100,000; low: $25; average: $100-$10,000).
Purpose and activities: Interests include demonstration and research programs in prevention of family dysfunction: prevention of teenage pregnancy and infant mortality and morbidity; infant mental health and early childhood development; Jewish charities; and the arts and educational television.
Fields of interest: Child welfare, education—early childhood, child development, family services, Jewish welfare, family planning, arts.
Types of support: Annual campaigns, seed money, special projects, research, publications, conferences and seminars, general purposes, operating budgets, scholarship funds, equipment.

Limitations: No grants to individuals, or for continuing support, emergency or endowment funds, deficit financing, land acquisition, renovations, scholarships, or fellowships; no loans.
Application information: Application form not required.
  Initial approach: Letter
  Copies of proposal: 1
  Deadline(s): None
  Board meeting date(s): Semiannually
  Final notification: Following board meeting
  Write: Ruth K. Belzer, Exec. Dir.
Officers and Trustees:* Irving B. Harris,* Chair.; William W. Harris,* Vice-Chair.; Benno F. Wolff,* Secy.; Sidney Barrows, Roxanne Harris Frank, Joan W. Harris, Neison Harris, Daniel Meyer, Virginia Harris Polsky.
Staff: Ruth K. Belzer, Exec. Dir.
Number of staff: 1 full-time professional; 1 part-time professional; 1 full-time support.
EIN: 366055115

864
Hartmarx Charitable Foundation
101 North Wacker Dr.
Chicago 60606   (312) 372-6300

Incorporated in 1966 in IL.
Donor(s): Hartmarx Corp.
Foundation type: Company-sponsored
Financial data (yr. ended 11/30/90): Assets, $45,876 (M); gifts received, $885,859; expenditures, $685,610; qualifying distributions, $685,610, including $659,194 for 368 grants (high: $95,000; low: $25) and $26,096 for employee matching gifts.
Fields of interest: Community funds, higher education, cultural programs, civic affairs, health.
Types of support: Employee matching gifts, annual campaigns, building funds, capital campaigns, endowment funds, general purposes, operating budgets, professorships, scholarship funds.
Limitations: Giving primarily in GA, IL, IN, MI, NY, OR, and WA. No grants to individuals.
Publications: Application guidelines.
Application information: Application form not required.
  Initial approach: Letter
  Copies of proposal: 1
  Deadline(s): None
  Board meeting date(s): Dec., Mar., June, and Sept.
  Write: Kay C. Nalbach, Pres.
Officers and Directors:* Kay C. Nalbach,* Pres.; Jerome Dorf,* V.P.; Glenn R. Morgan,* V.P.; Carey M. Stein,* Secy.; James E. Condon,* Treas.
EIN: 366152745

865
The Grover Hermann Foundation ▼
c/o Schiff, Hardin & Waite
7200 Sears Tower, 233 South Wacker Dr.
Chicago 60606   (312) 876-1000
Application address for Monterey County, CA, programs: P.O. Box 596, Pebble Beach, CA 93953

Incorporated in 1955 in IL.
Donor(s): Grover M. Hermann.

Foundation type: Independent
Financial data (yr. ended 12/31/90): Assets, $14,126,669 (M); expenditures, $5,184,670; qualifying distributions, $5,123,639, including $5,100,168 for grants (average: $5,000-$25,000).
Purpose and activities: Grants largely for higher education, social services, community development, health, public policy organizations, and religion.
Fields of interest: Higher education, social services, health associations, health, public policy, community development, religion.
Types of support: Renovation projects, equipment, building funds, seed money, endowment funds, annual campaigns, scholarship funds, special projects, general purposes.
Limitations: Giving limited to Chicago, IL, and Monterey County, CA, for social services and community development; other programs funded nationwide. No support for fraternal, athletic, or foreign organizations, private foundations or political entities. No grants to individuals; generally no support for operating budgets, except for national health organizations.
Publications: Application guidelines.
Application information: Organizations in Monterey County, CA should write to the Pebble Beach office; all other inquiries to the Chicago, IL, office. Application form not required.
   Initial approach: Letter (telephone inquiries not considered)
   Copies of proposal: 1
   Deadline(s): None
   Board meeting date(s): Quarterly; annual meeting in May
   Final notification: From several weeks to 3 or 4 months
   Write: Paul K. Rhoads, V.P.
Officers and Directors:* Sarah T. Hermann,* Pres.; Paul K. Rhoads,* V.P.; Harriet R. Thurmond,* Treas.
Number of staff: None.
EIN: 366064489

866
The H. Earl Hoover Foundation
1801 Green Bay Rd.
P.O. Box 330
Glencoe 60022

Trust established in 1947 in IL.
Donor(s): H. Earl Hoover.
Foundation type: Independent
Financial data (yr. ended 12/31/90): Assets, $3,037,491 (M); expenditures, $221,878; qualifying distributions, $204,000, including $204,000 for 63 grants (high: $25,000; low: $500).
Purpose and activities: Giving primarily for youth clubs, Episcopal churches, and museums and other cultural programs; some support also for hospitals, social and welfare agencies, and education.
Fields of interest: Youth, Protestant giving, museums, cultural programs, hospitals, social services, welfare, education.
Limitations: Giving primarily in IL. No grants to individuals.
Application information: Application form not required.
   Initial approach: Letter

   Deadline(s): None
Trustees: Robert L. Foote, Miriam W. Hoover, Michael A. Leppen.
EIN: 366063814

867
Illinois Tool Works Foundation ▼
3600 West Lake Ave.
Glenview 60025-5811   (312) 693-3040

Incorporated in 1954 in IL.
Donor(s): Illinois Tool Works, Inc.
Foundation type: Company-sponsored
Financial data (yr. ended 02/28/90): Assets, $12,707,351 (M); expenditures, $1,648,479; qualifying distributions, $1,615,401, including $720,483 for 121 grants (high: $208,500; low: $300; average: $1,000-$20,000) and $599,518 for 1,114 employee matching gifts.
Purpose and activities: Support for education, health and hospitals, social services, including drug abuse and crime prevention programs, museums and the humanities, the United Way, and technical and public affairs programs.
Fields of interest: Education, hospitals, community funds, youth, urban affairs, alcoholism, engineering, public affairs.
Types of support: Operating budgets, continuing support, annual campaigns, seed money, building funds, employee-related scholarships, employee matching gifts, capital campaigns.
Limitations: Giving primarily in areas of company operations, particularly Chicago, IL. No grants to individuals, or for endowment funds or research; no loans.
Application information:
   Initial approach: Letter
   Copies of proposal: 1
   Deadline(s): None
   Board meeting date(s): Mar., June, Sept., and Dec.
   Final notification: Same month as board meeting
   Write: Stephen B. Smith, Dir.
Officers: Harold Byron Smith, Jr., Pres.; Arthur M. Wright, Secy.; Michael J. Robinson, Treas.
Directors: W. James Farrell, Michael H. Hudson, John D. Nichols, Stephen B. Smith.
Number of staff: 1
EIN: 366087160
Recent health grants:
867-1 Childrens Memorial Hospital, Chicago, IL, $10,000. 1990.
867-2 Lutheran General Health Care System, Parkside Alcoholic Research Foundation, Park Ridge, IL, $36,000. 1990.
867-3 Lutheran General Health Care System, Parkside Alcoholic Research Foundation, Park Ridge, IL, $12,483. 1990.
867-4 Lutheran General Hospital, Park Ridge, IL, $10,000. 1990.

868
Inland Steel-Ryerson Foundation, Inc. ▼
c/o Inland Steel Industries
30 West Monroe St.
Chicago 60603   (312) 899-3420

Incorporated in 1945 in IL as Inland Steel Foundation, Inc.

Donor(s): Inland Steel Co., its subsidiaries and divisions.
Foundation type: Company-sponsored
Financial data (yr. ended 12/31/90): Assets, $25,601 (M); gifts received, $1,402,500; expenditures, $1,383,198; qualifying distributions, $1,383,198, including $1,364,000 for 192 grants (high: $350,000; low: $250; average: $500-$20,000).
Purpose and activities: The foundation's funding priorities are as follows: 1) support for the United Way in areas where business units are located; 2) programs that encourage student, especially minority, participation in science, math, engineering, and business; 3) programs that provide scholarships to the sons and daughters of company employees; 4) funding of capital projects which will improve the physical and equipment needs of the instruction of science, math, engineering, or business at private post-secondary institutions; 5) funding of local nonprofit agencies which address a need not served by the local United Way.
Fields of interest: Social services, youth, aged, minorities, hospitals, rehabilitation, handicapped, mental health, community development, civil rights, human rights, community funds, education, higher education, secondary education, business education, education—minorities, educational associations, engineering, science and technology.
Types of support: Operating budgets, special projects, employee-related scholarships, scholarship funds, fellowships, general purposes, capital campaigns.
Limitations: Giving primarily in areas of company operations, particularly Chicago, IL, and northwest IN. Generally no grants for sectarian or religious organizations (except churches under the category of social welfare). No grants to individuals directly, or for endowment funds, capital programs, matching grants, publications, conferences, seminars, or benefit affairs. Scholarships awarded under the All Inland Scholarship Plan and the National Merit and National Achievement Scholarship programs are restricted to children of company employees. Lawndale Community Scholarships are for area high school seniors.
Publications: Application guidelines.
Application information: Application form not required.
   Initial approach: Letter or telephone
   Copies of proposal: 1
   Deadline(s): Sept. 30
   Board meeting date(s): Dec.
   Final notification: 3 to 4 months
   Write: Maria Pojeta Hibbs, Mgr., Corp. Community Affairs
Officers and Directors:* David B. Anderson,* Pres.; W. Gordon Kay,* V.P.; Earl S. Thompson,* Secy.; Jay E. Dittus,* Treas.; Paul M. Anderson, Judd R. Cool, Joseph D. Corso, Robert J. Darnall, Frederick G. Jaicks, Frank W. Luerssen, Robert E. Powell.
Number of staff: 1 part-time professional; 1 part-time support.
EIN: 366046944

869
Jewel Food Stores Corporate Giving Program
1955 West North Ave.
Melrose Park 60160   (312) 531-6000

Purpose and activities: Support for health, social services, and educational institutions and programs with job training.
Fields of interest: Health, social services, education.
Limitations: Giving primarily in areas of company operations in IL, IN, IA, and MI for local organizations. No support for fraternal and religious organizations. No grants to individuals.
Application information: Application form required.
   Initial approach: Proposal
   Write: Michael DePaola, V.P., Community Affairs
Officers: Joseph V. Bugos, Pres.; Carol Okuda, Secy.; Michael DePaola, V.P., Community Affairs.

870
A. D. Johnson Foundation
One North LaSalle St., Suite 3000
Chicago 60602   (312) 782-7320

Incorporated in 1965 in IL.
Donor(s): A.D. Johnson.‡
Foundation type: Independent
Financial data (yr. ended 12/31/90): Assets, $2,283,861 (M); expenditures, $182,017; qualifying distributions, $176,003, including $174,000 for 18 grants (high: $25,000; low: $2,000).
Fields of interest: Social services, medical research, hospitals, hospices, education, child welfare, youth, arts.
Types of support: General purposes, research, endowment funds, building funds.
Limitations: Giving primarily in IL and FL. No grants to individuals.
Application information: Application form not required.
   Deadline(s): None
   Write: Committee on Charities
Officers: Wayne J. Johnson, Pres. and Treas.; Diane T. Johnson, V.P. and Secy.
EIN: 366124270

871
Hattie Hannah Keeney Trust
c/o First National Bank of Chicago
One First National Plaza, Suite 0111
Chicago 60670-0111   (312) 732-4281

Established in 1950 in IL.
Foundation type: Independent
Financial data (yr. ended 12/31/90): Assets, $3,590,385 (M); expenditures, $139,580; qualifying distributions, $114,459, including $110,892 for 1 grant.
Purpose and activities: Support for the benefit of crippled children; grants primarily awarded to a hospital.
Fields of interest: Hospitals, handicapped, child welfare.
Limitations: Giving primarily in the Traverse City, MI, area. No grants to individuals.
Application information:

Initial approach: Letter
Deadline(s): None
Write: A. Gergets
Trustee: First National Bank of Chicago.
EIN: 366016171

872
T. Lloyd Kelly Foundation
c/o Continental Bank, N.A.
30 North LaSalle St., 6th Fl.
Chicago 60697   (312) 828-1785

Incorporated in 1951 in IL.
Donor(s): Mildred Wetten Kelly McDermott.
Foundation type: Independent
Financial data (yr. ended 12/31/90): Assets, $2,142,038 (M); expenditures, $146,968; qualifying distributions, $129,874, including $128,400 for 34 grants (high: $48,000; low: $100).
Purpose and activities: Giving primarily for family planning; support also for secondary and higher education and hospitals.
Fields of interest: Family planning, secondary education, higher education, hospitals.
Limitations: Giving primarily in IL.
Application information: Application form not required.
   Deadline(s): None
   Write: Mildred Wetten Kelly McDermott, V.P.
Officers and Directors:* Robert A. Malstrom,* Pres.; Mildred Wetten Kelly McDermott,* V.P.; H. Blair White,* Secy.; M.C. Ryan,* Treas.; Barbara Kelly Hull, Arthur L. Kelly, Sally Morris.
EIN: 366050341

873
Kemper Educational and Charitable Fund
400 North Michigan Ave., Suite 710
Chicago 60611

Incorporated in 1961 in IL.
Donor(s): James Scott Kemper.‡
Foundation type: Independent
Financial data (yr. ended 09/30/91): Assets, $9,071,291 (M); expenditures, $536,615; qualifying distributions, $476,065, including $422,708 for 34 grants (high: $100,000; low: $1,000; average: $10,000).
Purpose and activities: Giving primarily for higher and secondary education; support also for cultural programs, including music, and health.
Fields of interest: Higher education, secondary education, cultural programs, music, health.
Types of support: Continuing support, equipment, scholarship funds, research.
Limitations: Giving primarily in metropolitan Chicago, IL, area, and adjoining states. No grants to individuals, or for building or endowment funds; no loans.
Publications: Application guidelines.
Application information: Contributes only to pre-selected organizations. Applications not accepted.
   Board meeting date(s): Annually and as required
   Write: Virginia J. Heitz, Secy.-Treas.
Officers and Trustees:* Peter Van Cleave,* Vice-Chair.; Dale Park, Jr.,* Pres.; Virginia J. Heitz, Secy.-Treas.; Margaret M. Archambault, Leslie N. Christensen, Frank D. Stout, Mildred K. Terrill, John Van Cleave.

Number of staff: 1 part-time professional; 1 part-time support.
EIN: 366054499

874
Kemper National Insurance Companies Corporate Contributions
F-3
Long Grove 60049   (708) 540-2512

Financial data (yr. ended 12/31/90): Total giving, $1,500,000.
Purpose and activities: Supports health and welfare, youth, civic, cultural and education programs. Types of support include employee matching gifts for health, welfare and education, equipment funds, and in-kind donations in the form of employee volunteers.
Fields of interest: Health, welfare, youth, civic affairs, cultural programs, education, religious welfare, child welfare, crime and law enforcement, drug abuse, family services, handicapped, humanities, international relief, intercultural relations, adult education, AIDS, education—early childhood, environment, hunger, Jewish giving, education—minorities, hospitals, housing, animal welfare, civil rights, delinquency, law and justice, media and communications, peace, wildlife, volunteerism, medical sciences, science and technology, disadvantaged, secondary education, welfare—indigent individuals, urban affairs.
Types of support: Employee matching gifts, equipment, general purposes, special projects, in-kind gifts, annual campaigns, conferences and seminars, building funds, use of facilities, capital campaigns, internships, continuing support, cause-related marketing, matching funds.
Limitations: Giving primarily in headquarters city and major operating areas nationwide including CA, IL, IA, KS, NJ, NY, OH, and WI. No grants to individuals.
Publications: Corporate report, program policy statement, application guidelines.
Application information: There is a staff that only handles contributions. Application form not required.
   Initial approach: Letter to headquarters
   Copies of proposal: 1
   Deadline(s): None
   Board meeting date(s): Committee meets monthly
   Final notification: 6 weeks
   Write: Charles W. Meinhardt, Secy., Corp. Contribs. Comm.
Administrators: H.L. Knight, Chair. and Corp. Cont.; C.F. Johann, Sr. V.P., Public Affairs and Communs.; A.E. Catania, V.P., Corp. Human Resources.

875
Solomon Klein Foundation
1560 Tower Rd.
Winnetka 60093

Established in 1986 in PA.
Donor(s): Solomon Klein.
Foundation type: Independent
Financial data (yr. ended 12/31/90): Assets, $282,032 (M); gifts received, $250; expenditures,

$396,166; qualifying distributions, $394,364, including $394,233 for grants.
Fields of interest: Hospitals, health associations, Jewish giving, education, general charitable giving.
Limitations: Giving primarily in Chicago, IL, New York, NY, and Miami, FL.
Application information: Contributes only to pre-selected organizations. Applications not accepted.
Trustees: Harry Klein, Alexander Kleine, Rita L. Millner.
EIN: 363411662

876
L.C. Klenk Charitable Foundation
P.O. Box 584
Glen Ellyn 60138

Established in 1987 in TX.
Donor(s): JMK International, Inc., Lester C. Klenk.‡
Foundation type: Independent
Financial data (yr. ended 12/31/90): Assets, $2,051,802 (M); expenditures, $146,421; qualifying distributions, $146,421, including $105,246 for 14 grants (high: $16,246; low: $2,000).
Purpose and activities: Support primarily for Lutheran churches, hospitals, and medical research.
Fields of interest: Protestant giving, hospitals, medical research.
Types of support: General purposes, equipment, research.
Limitations: Giving primarily in TX, IL, and MI. No loans or program-related investments.
Application information: Application form required.
Deadline(s): None
Officers: Ardena L. Klenk, Pres.; Don L. Klenk, V.P.; Elaine Klenk Pope, V.P.; Edward J. Phillips, Secy.-Treas.
EIN: 752192617

877
Knowles Foundation
c/o John W. Hupp, Secy.
200 South Michigan Ave., Suite 1100
Chicago 60604-2404

Established in 1955 in IL.
Donor(s): Knowles Electronics, Inc.
Foundation type: Independent
Financial data (yr. ended 09/30/90): Assets, $2,245,907 (M); gifts received, $35,000; expenditures, $138,139; qualifying distributions, $122,050, including $116,000 for 10 grants (high: $28,000; low: $2,500).
Fields of interest: Medical research.
Limitations: No grants to individuals.
Application information: Contributions are made only at the discretion of the directors. Applications not accepted.
Officers: Nancy W. Knowles, V.P.; John W. Hupp, Secy.; Robert G. Roth, Treas.
EIN: 366051968

878
The Francis L. Lederer Foundation
c/o Leo H. Arnstein
120 South Riverside Plaza, No. 1200
Chicago 60606

Established in 1966 in IL.
Foundation type: Independent
Financial data (yr. ended 12/31/90): Assets, $4,285,472 (M); expenditures, $280,647; qualifying distributions, $239,292, including $236,500 for 27 grants (high: $38,000; low: $500).
Fields of interest: Higher education, education—early childhood, child welfare, medical research, health associations, Jewish welfare, arts.
Limitations: Giving primarily in Chicago, IL. No grants to individuals.
Application information:
Initial approach: Proposal
Deadline(s): None
Officers and Directors:* Francis L. Lederer II,* Pres. and Treas.; Adrienne Lederer,* V.P.; Leo H. Arnstein,* Secy.
EIN: 362594937

879
Anne P. Lederer Research Institute
c/o Rosenthal & Schanfield
55 East Monroe St., Suite 4620
Chicago 60603-5805

Established in 1980 in IL.
Donor(s): Anne P. Lederer.‡
Foundation type: Independent
Financial data (yr. ended 12/31/91): Assets, $3,817,414 (M); gifts received, $117,000; expenditures, $271,246; qualifying distributions, $230,387, including $226,000 for 8 grants (high: $75,000; low: $2,000).
Purpose and activities: Grants are restricted to applicants in a field related to psychoanalysis, psychiatry, or the field of music.
Fields of interest: Psychology, psychiatry, music, Jewish giving.
Types of support: Scholarship funds.
Limitations: Giving limited to Chicago, IL.
Application information: Application form required.
Deadline(s): None
Officers: Laurence S. Kaplan, Secy.; Paul V. Anglin, Treas.
Director: Audrey G. Ratner.
EIN: 363076805

880
Otto W. Lehmann Foundation
3240 North Lake Shore Dr., Apt. 7A
Chicago 60657   (312) 929-9851
Mailing address: P.O. Box 11194, Chicago, IL 60611

Incorporated in 1967 in IL.
Donor(s): Otto W. Lehmann.‡
Foundation type: Independent
Financial data (yr. ended 07/31/92): Assets, $2,522,793 (M); expenditures, $186,603; qualifying distributions, $167,000, including $167,000 for 67 grants (high: $10,000; low: $1,000; average: $1,000-$10,000).

Purpose and activities: Emphasis on youth agencies and child welfare, social services, aid for the handicapped, higher and other education, health agencies, medical research, rehabilitation, and cultural organizations, including museums and the performing arts.
Fields of interest: Youth, child welfare, social services, handicapped, higher education, health services, rehabilitation, museums, cultural programs.
Types of support: Annual campaigns, capital campaigns, scholarship funds.
Limitations: Giving limited to the Chicago, IL, area. No support for advocacy groups. No grants to individuals.
Application information: Application form required.
Initial approach: Letter
Copies of proposal: 1
Deadline(s): June 30
Board meeting date(s): July 2
Final notification: July 31
Write: Richard J. Peterson, Managing Trustee
Trustees: Richard J. Peterson, Managing Trustee; David W. Peterson, Lucille S. Peterson.
Number of staff: 1 part-time support.
EIN: 366160836

881
Marcus and Theresa Levie Educational Fund
c/o Jewish Federation of Metropolitan Chicago
One South Franklin St.
Chicago 60606   (312) 346-6700

Trust established in 1959 in IL.
Donor(s): Maude M. Levie,‡ Jerome M. Levie,‡ Charles M. Levie.‡
Foundation type: Independent
Financial data (yr. ended 07/31/90): Assets, $2,600,000 (M); expenditures, $200,000; qualifying distributions, $180,000, including $180,000 for 34 grants to individuals (high: $6,100; low: $4,800; average: $3,000-$6,000).
Purpose and activities: Scholarships awarded to Jewish students who are residents of Cook County and who have demonstrated career promise and have financial need to complete their professional or vocational training in the helping professions.
Fields of interest: Jewish giving, Jewish welfare, elementary education, adult education, higher education, medical education, social services, aged, child welfare, health, nursing.
Types of support: Student aid.
Limitations: Giving limited to Cook County, IL. No grants for general support, or for building or endowment funds, research, or matching gifts; no loans.
Publications: Application guidelines, program policy statement.
Application information: Application form required.
Initial approach: Letter or telephone
Copies of proposal: 2
Deadline(s): Submit scholarship application between Nov. and Feb.; deadline Mar. 1
Board meeting date(s): As required, usually in July
Final notification: July or Aug.
Trustee: Chicago Title and Trust Co.
Number of staff: 14 part-time professional; 1 full-time support; 1 part-time support.

EIN: 366010074

882
Frank J. Lewis Foundation ▼
Three First National Plaza, Suite 1950
Chicago 60602

Incorporated in 1927 in IL.
Donor(s): Frank J. Lewis.‡
Foundation type: Independent
Financial data (yr. ended 12/31/90): Assets,
$19,327,314 (M); expenditures, $1,609,114;
qualifying distributions, $1,489,195, including
$1,439,475 for 114 grants (high: $202,500; low:
$100; average: $1,000-$15,000).
Purpose and activities: To foster, preserve, and
extend the Roman Catholic faith; grants largely
for Roman Catholic educational institutions,
churches, social services, religious orders and
church-sponsored programs, and hospitals.
Fields of interest: Catholic giving, higher
education, Catholic welfare, hospitals, social
services.
Types of support: General purposes.
Limitations: No grants to individuals, or for
endowment funds.
Application information: Contributes only to
pre-selected organizations. Applications not
accepted.
  Board meeting date(s): Feb., May, Aug., and
    Nov.
Officers and Trustees:* Edward D. Lewis,* Pres.;
Philip D. Lewis,* V.P.; Victor Hedberg,* Treas.;
Diana B. Lewis, Megan Lewis.
EIN: 362441931

883
E. J. Logan Foundation
735 Normandy Ln.
Glenview 60025

Established in 1986 in IL.
Donor(s): M. Joseph Hickey, Jr.
Foundation type: Independent
Financial data (yr. ended 12/31/90): Assets,
$2,111,961 (M); gifts received, $325,000;
expenditures, $677,039; qualifying distributions,
$677,039, including $673,924 for 14 grants
(high: $350,000; low: $5,000).
Purpose and activities: Emphasis on child
welfare, health and hospitals, hospices, and
programs for people with AIDS; support also for
the handicapped and international development.
Fields of interest: Child welfare, health, hospitals,
hospices, AIDS, handicapped, international
development.
Limitations: Giving primarily in IL. No grants to
individuals.
Application information: Contributes only to
pre-selected organizations. Applications not
accepted.
Trustee: M. Joseph Hickey, Jr.
EIN: 363488565

884
The Lumpkin Foundation
7200 Sears Tower
233 South Wacker Dr.
Chicago 60606   (217) 235-3361

Application address: 121 South 17th St.,
Mattoon, IL 61938

Incorporated in 1953 in IL.
Donor(s): Besse Adamson Lumpkin,‡ Richard
Adamson Lumpkin,‡ Illinois Consolidated
Telephone Co., Richard Anthony Lumpkin.
Foundation type: Independent
Financial data (yr. ended 12/31/90): Assets,
$4,386,613 (M); expenditures, $201,124;
qualifying distributions, $154,350, including
$154,350 for 42 grants (high: $25,000; low:
$100).
Purpose and activities: Grants primarily for higher
and secondary education, hospitals, and health
agencies; support also for public libraries.
Fields of interest: Higher education, secondary
education, hospitals, health services, libraries.
Limitations: Giving primarily in central IL. No
grants to individuals.
Application information: Application form not
required.
  Initial approach: Proposal
  Copies of proposal: 1
  Deadline(s): Nov. 30
  Board meeting date(s): June, Dec., and as
    required
  Write: Richard Anthony Lumpkin, Pres.
Officers and Directors:* Richard Anthony
Lumpkin,* Pres.; Mary G. Lumpkin,* V.P.; S.L.
Grissom, Secy.-Treas.
Number of staff: None.
EIN: 237423640

885
Lurie Family Foundation
c/o R. Lurie
Two North Riverside Plaza, No. 600
Chicago 60606-2639

Established in 1986 in IL.
Donor(s): Robert Lurie.
Foundation type: Independent
Financial data (yr. ended 12/31/90): Assets,
$851,146 (M); expenditures, $1,130,416;
qualifying distributions, $1,127,783, including
$1,125,635 for 20 grants (high: $1,025,000; low:
$100).
Fields of interest: Higher education, health,
youth, child welfare.
Types of support: Endowment funds.
Limitations: Giving primarily in Chicago, IL, MI,
and IN. No grants to individuals.
Application information: Contributes only to
pre-selected organizations. Applications not
accepted.
Officers: B. Ann Lurie, Pres. and Treas.; Sheli Z.
Rosenberg, Secy.
EIN: 363486274

886
J. Roderick MacArthur Foundation ▼
9333 North Milwaukee Ave.
Niles 60714   (708) 966-0143

Established in 1976 in IL.
Donor(s): J. Roderick MacArthur,‡ Bradford
Exchange AG, Solange D. MacArthur, Bradford
Exchange, Ltd.
Foundation type: Independent
Financial data (yr. ended 01/31/91): Assets,
$27,756,321 (M); gifts received, $450,000;

expenditures, $2,666,351; qualifying
distributions, $2,579,873, including $2,203,300
for 96 grants (high: $500,000; low: $3,000;
average: $3,000-$20,000).
Purpose and activities: The foundation seeks to
"aid those who are inequitably or unjustly treated
by established institutions" by "protecting and
encouraging freedom of expression, human
rights, civil liberties, and social justice; and by
eliminating political, economic, social, religious,
and cultural oppression."
Fields of interest: Civil rights, law and justice,
international affairs, freedom, public policy,
human rights.
Types of support: Seed money, publications,
special projects.
Limitations: No support for ongoing social
services, government programs, religious,
church-based activities, university or other
educational programs, economic development or
training programs, or grassroots organizing or
demonstrations. No grants to individuals, or for
capital projects, endowments, development
campaigns, statues or memorials, annual
campaigns, conferences, continuing support,
deficit financing, land acquisition, endowments,
matching gifts, consulting services, technical
assistance, scholarships, internships, fellowships,
seminars or benefits; no pass-through grants; no
loans.
Publications: Financial statement, grants list,
informational brochure (including application
guidelines).
Application information: Application form not
required.
  Initial approach: Letter
  Copies of proposal: 1
  Deadline(s): None
  Board meeting date(s): Approximately every 2
    months
  Final notification: 1 to 2 months
  Write: Lance E. Lindblom, Pres.
Officers and Directors:* Gregoire C. MacArthur,*
Chair.; Solange D. MacArthur,* Vice-Chair.; Lance
E. Lindblom, Pres.; John R. MacArthur,*
Secy.-Treas.
Number of staff: 4 full-time professional.
EIN: 510214450
Recent health grants:
886-1 Drug Policy Foundation, DC, $20,000.
  For litigation project to constitutionally and
  legally challenge use of U.S. Armed Forces,
  National Guard and local police in U.S.
  civilian drug law enforcement. 1991.
886-2 Fundamentalists Anonymous, NYC, NY,
  $20,000. To protect their first amendment
  rights by supporting litigation and media
  expenses of their project to challenge alleged
  arbitrary actions and harassment by IRS. 1991.
886-3 Mental Health Law Project, DC, $20,000.
  For two federal class action lawsuits seeking
  alternative home and community based
  intervention systems: first suit challenges use of
  seclusion and restraint of patients in Montana
  state psychiatric hospital; and second suit
  challenges needless institutionalization of
  emotionally disturbed children in foster care
  away from their families. 1991.
886-4 Physicians for Human Rights, Somerville,
  MA, $20,000. For project to conduct medical
  fact-finding missions in Middle East, including
  Israel and Occupied Territories, to investigate

and report on medical consequences of human rights abuses in region. 1991.

886-5 Roger Baldwin Foundation of the American Civil Liberties Union, Chicago, IL, $20,000. For litigation costs of AIDS and Civil Liberties Project, to protect individual civil liberties and halt illegal discrimination on basis of AIDS or AIDS-related conditions. 1991.

887
John D. and Catherine T. MacArthur Foundation ▼

140 South Dearborn St.
Chicago 60603   (312) 726-8000

Incorporated in 1970 in IL.
Donor(s): John D. MacArthur.‡
Foundation type: Independent
Financial data (yr. ended 12/31/90): Assets, $3,077,581,000 (M); expenditures, $163,575,503; qualifying distributions, $141,838,181, including $115,675,981 for grants and $6,050,000 for program-related investments.
Purpose and activities: Seven major initiatives currently authorized: MacArthur Fellows Program, for highly talented individuals in any field of endeavor who are chosen in a foundation-initiated effort (no applications are accepted for this program); the Health Program, for research in mental health and the psychological and behavioral aspects of health and rehabilitation (including designated programs in parasitology and aging); the Community Initiatives Program for support of cultural and community development in the Chicago metropolitan area; the Program on Peace and International Cooperation, for support of initiatives which promote and strengthen international security; the World Environment and Resources Program, for support of conservation programs which protect the earth's biological diversity and work to protect tropical ecology; the Education Program, to focus on the promotion of literacy; and the Population Program, concerned with women's reproductive health, population and natural resources, communications and popular education, and leadership development. Through the General Program, the foundation makes grants for a changing array of purposes.
Fields of interest: Health, mental health, rehabilitation, biological sciences, AIDS, media and communications, cultural programs, community development, foreign policy, public policy, international affairs, government, law and justice, arms control, conservation, ecology, environment, education.
Types of support: Matching funds, general purposes, operating budgets, special projects, research, fellowships.
Limitations: No support for churches or religious programs, political activities or campaigns, or other foundations or institutions. No grants for capital or endowment funds, equipment purchases, plant construction, conferences, publications, media productions, debt retirement, development campaigns, fundraising appeals, scholarships, or fellowships (other than those sponsored by the foundation).
Publications: Annual report, program policy statement, application guidelines, informational brochure.

Application information: Direct applications for Fellows Program not accepted. Grants increasingly initiated by the board.
  Initial approach: Letter
  Copies of proposal: 1
  Deadline(s): None
  Board meeting date(s): Monthly, except Aug.
  Write: Richard Kaplan, Dir., Grants Management, Research, and Information
Officers and Directors:* Elizabeth Jane McCormack,* Chair.; Adele Simmons,* Pres.; Lawrence L. Landry, V.P. and C.F.O.; Lawrence G. Martin, V.P., Real Estate; Victor Rabinowitch, V.P. for Programs; Woodward A. Wickham, V.P. for Public Affairs; William Bevan, Senior Advisor for Health Program; Nancy B. Ewing, Secy.; Philip M. Grace, Treas.; James T. Griffin, General Counsel; John E. Corbally, Robert P. Ewing, James M. Furman, Murray Gell-Mann, Alan M. Hallene, Paul Harvey, Shirley Mount Hufstedler, Sara Lawrence Lightfoot, Margaret E. Mahoney, George A. Ranney, Jr., Jonas Salk, M.D., Jerome B. Wiesner.
Number of staff: 65
EIN: 237093598
Recent health grants:
887-1 Ahmadu Bello University, Center for Social and Economic Research, Zaria, Nigeria, $120,000. To plan and establish interdisciplinary Women and Development Program, which will emphasize research, training and demonstration projects on health and population issues particular to northern Nigeria. 1990.
887-2 Associacao Brasileira de Video Popular, Sao Paulo, Brazil, $340,000. To establish regional video libraries and train non-governmental organizations in Brazil to use video more effectively, particularly in work on health, family planning and reproductive rights. 1990.
887-3 Boston University, Boston, MA, $20,000. For publication of book on topic of emotion. 1990.
887-4 Boston Womens Health Book Collective, Somerville, MA, $25,000. For planning meeting to develop international information system on women's reproductive health. 1990.
887-5 Carter Center, Atlanta, GA, $35,000. For symposium, Families Coping With Mental Illness: Improving Public Understanding. 1990.
887-6 Case Western Reserve University, Cleveland, OH, $160,000. For research on molecular biology of parasite vectors. 1990.
887-7 Center for Population Options, International Center on Adolescent Fertility (ICAF), DC, $400,000. To diversify network of organizations ICAF reaches and to provide seed money to launch new projects aimed at reducing adolescent fertility, especially in Latin America and sub-Saharan Africa. 1990.
887-8 Centre for Development and Population Activities, DC, $393,000. To expand Options for a Better Life for Young Women program in Nigeria and India, which provides alternatives to early and frequent pregnancy through skills development and education in family planning, primary health care, environmental conservation, personal development and income generation. 1990.
887-9 Coletivo Feminista Sexualidade E Saude, Sao Paulo, Brazil, $420,000. For service delivery and advocacy for women's health and

family planning. Grant also will enable group to provide technical and financial assistance to similar organizations in Sao Paulo to strengthen reproductive health components of programs. 1990.
887-10 Colorado State University, College of Veterinary Medicine and Biomedical Sciences, Fort Collins, CO, $25,000. For summer course on vector biology. 1990.
887-11 Committee for Health in Southern Africa, Brooklyn Heights, NY, $10,000. For Fourth International Workshop on Health in Southern Africa held in Maputo, Mozambique. 1990.
887-12 Communications Consortium, Media Center, DC, $15,000. To commission poll to assess attitudes of women of color toward reproductive health issues. 1990.
887-13 Development Alternatives, New Delhi, India, $580,000. For continued support of Population Unit, which incorporates population and family planning concerns into organization's program of economic development and environmental conservation. Grant will support research on link between population and sustainable development and will fund demonstration projects aimed at lowering fertility by creating well-paying and meaningful employment opportunities for women. 1990.
887-14 Fundacao Do Desenvolvmento Da Pesquisa (FUNDEP), Belo Horizonto, Brazil, $15,000. For XVII Annual Meeting on Basic Research in Chagas' disease. 1990.
887-15 George Washington University, DC, $20,000. For computer purchase and software design consultancy for intergovernmental Health Policy Project. 1990.
887-16 Global Fund for Women, Menlo Park, CA, $400,000. For grantmaking program for women's organizations in developing countries whose work focuses on reproductive rights and women's health. 1990.
887-17 Grantmakers in Health, NYC, NY, $120,000. For general operations. 1990.
887-18 Harvard University, School of Public Health, Boston, MA, $2,500,000. For continued support of Research Network on Human Development and Criminal Behavior, long-term research program intended to identify developmental determinants of serious criminal behavior and to establish empirical foundations for effective preventive interventions. 1990.
887-19 Harvard University, School of Public Health, Boston, MA, $200,000. For international initiative to promote and facilitate health research judged essential to development goals of Third World nations. 1990.
887-20 Healthy Companies Institute, Arlington, VA, $2,225,000. For Program on Human Development and Healthy Organizations. 1990.
887-21 Healthy Mothers and Babies Coalition, Chicago, IL, $10,000. For general operations. 1990.
887-22 Hunter College of the City University of New York, Women's Studies Program, NYC, NY, $22,450. For participant travel and sessions on women's health and reproductive rights at International Interdisciplinary Congress on Women. 1990.

887-23 International Womens Rights Action Watch (IWRAW), Minneapolis, MN, $390,000. To develop leadership training program addressing women's health and reproductive rights within IWRAW's ongoing work on expanding legal protection for women's rights around world. Grant will fund intensive seminars for women leaders from developing countries and summer fellowships that would allow women to study, plan and redirect their efforts in field of women's reproductive health. 1990.

887-24 Karolinska Institute, Stockholm, Sweden, $270,000. For general operations for Swedish Twin Registry. 1990.

887-25 Martha Stuart Communications, NYC, NY, $760,000. For training in video production and communication for non-governmental organizations working in women's health and family planning in Nigeria and Bangladesh. 1990.

887-26 National Polytechnic Institute, Mexico City, Mexico, $10,000. For scientific symposium on future of parasite biology. 1990.

887-27 Parivar Seva Sanstha, New Dehli, India, $800,000. To train and supervise community workers to teach women and girls in Uttar Pradesh, India's most populous state, about health and family planning. 1990.

887-28 Pennsylvania State University, University Park, PA, $90,000. For collaboration with Swedish Twin Registry at Karolinska Institute. 1990.

887-29 Planned Parenthood Federation, International, Western Hemisphere Region, NYC, NY, $575,000. To provide small grants and technical assistance to affiliated family planning associations in Latin America, in support of activities to improve service quality. 1990.

887-30 Population and Community Development Association, Bangkok, Thailand, $930,000. To continue South-to-South Global Innovations program, which provides small grants, project-related technical assistance and training for non-governmental organizations in Asia and Africa to develop family planning communication and community development programs. Particular attention will be focused on helping organizations adapt and improve PDA's communications methods to help destigmatize discussion of contraception and AIDS among local populations. 1990.

887-31 Rehabilitation Institute of Chicago, Medical Program for Performing Artists, Chicago, IL, $30,000. For renewed support of general operations. 1990.

887-32 Seattle Biomedical Research Institute, Seattle, WA, $15,000. For workshop on molecular biology of leishmaniasis and trypanosomiases. 1990.

887-33 Self-Employed Womens Association (SEWA), Ahmedabad, India, $450,000. For training programs in health, economics and basic management skills for members who work in informal sector of economy and include street vendors, cart pullers and landless laborers. 1990.

887-34 Society for Education, Action and Research in Community Health, Gadchiroli, India, $300,000. For demonstration program of integrated health care, family planning, research on neglected health issues and community development in remote rural area of Maharashtra in central India. 1990.

887-35 SOS Corpo-Womens Health Group, Recife, Brazil, $377,000. For research and documentation center for organizations working on family planning and women's programs in northeast Brazil. 1990.

887-36 South-South Solidarity, New Delhi, India, $130,000. For development of integrated programs addressing population, health and environmental problems by non-governmental organizations in South and Southeast Asia. 1990.

887-37 University of Arizona, Tucson, AZ, $20,000. For World Health Organization-University of Arizona conference, Prospects for Malaria Control by Genetic Manipulation of its Vectors. 1990.

887-38 University of California, Berkeley, CA, $815,979. For collaborative research project on crawling and walking as organizer of psychological development during first seven to ten months of age. 1990.

887-39 University of California, San Francisco, CA, $3,423,586. For Open Door Center for Research on Conscious and Unconscious Mental Processes. 1990.

887-40 University of Chicago Press, Chicago, IL, $35,000. For publication of book, Longevity, Senescence and the Genome. 1990.

887-41 University of Colorado, Health Sciences Center, Denver, CO, $3,224,578. For continued support of Research Network on Early Childhood Transitions, long-term program focused on understanding social and emotional development in young children. 1990.

887-42 University of Michigan, Institute for Social Research, Ann Arbor, MI, $20,000. For research project, Intellectual Collaboration as Evidenced in MacArthur Mental Health Research Networks. 1990.

887-43 University of Pittsburgh, Western Psychiatric Institute and Clinic, Pittsburgh, PA, $3,893,099. For Network on the Psychobiology of Depression. 1990.

887-44 University of Virginia, School of Law, Charlottesville, VA, $5,733,750. For Research Network on Mental Health and the Law. 1990.

887-45 Westside Health Coalition, Chicago, IL, $15,000. To address critical problems related to health services on Chicago's West Side. 1990.

887-46 WomanHealth Philippines, Quezon City, Philippines, $25,000. For Sixth International Women and Health Meeting, held in Manila. 1990.

887-47 Yale University, New Haven, CT, $6,499,208. For continued support of Research Network on Health and Behavior. Grant monies will fund studies of how genetic, biologic, environmental, and psychosocial factors interact in etiology of disease, the progression of, and recovery from, illness and accomplishment of good health. 1990.

887-48 Yale University, New Haven, CT, $72,500. For supplement for activities of Research Network on Health and Behavior. 1990.

887-49 Yale University, School of Medicine, New Haven, CT, $300,000. For research on molecular biology of parasite vectors. 1990.

888
Nathan Manilow Foundation
754 North Milwaukee Ave.
Chicago 60622   (312) 829-3655

Incorporated in 1955 in IL.
Donor(s): Nathan Manilow,‡ Lewis Manilow.
Foundation type: Independent
Financial data (yr. ended 05/31/90): Assets, $4,570,111 (M); gifts received, $921; expenditures, $357,301; qualifying distributions, $316,763, including $278,700 for 58 grants (high: $75,000; low: $150).
Purpose and activities: Emphasis on Jewish welfare funds, culture, and education; grants also for temple support and child welfare.
Fields of interest: Jewish welfare, cultural programs, museums, education, Jewish giving, child welfare, hospitals.
Limitations: Giving primarily in IL. No grants to individuals.
Application information: Application form not required.
   Initial approach: Letter
   Deadline(s): None
   Write: Lewis Manilow, Pres.
Officers: Lewis Manilow, Pres. and Treas.; Susan Manilow, Secy.
Director: Norman Altman.
EIN: 366079220

889
Bert William Martin Foundation
c/o The Northern Trust Co.
50 South LaSalle St.
Chicago 60675   (312) 630-6000

Incorporated in 1946 in IL.
Donor(s): Bert W. Martin, Ada La May Martin.
Foundation type: Independent
Financial data (yr. ended 12/31/90): Assets, $3,686,339 (M); expenditures, $253,020; qualifying distributions, $235,216, including $219,001 for 22 grants (high: $100,000; low: $500).
Fields of interest: Higher education, hospitals, health services.
Limitations: Giving primarily in CA and Orlando, FL. No grants to individuals.
Application information: Contributes only to pre-selected organizations. Applications not accepted.
   Write: Bert W. Martin
Officers and Directors:* Winifred M. Warden,* Pres.; Joseph J. Regan,* V.P.; Bert M. Warden,* V.P.; James W. Fisher,* Secy.-Treas.; Winston C. Moore, J. Terrance Murray.
EIN: 366060591

890
Oscar G. and Elsa S. Mayer Charitable Trust
c/o Hugo J. Melvoin, P.C.
115 South LaSalle St., Rm. 2500
Chicago 60603   (312) 332-3682
Additional application address: c/o Karla K. Ritt, One South Pinckney St., Suite 312, Madison, WI 53703; Tel.: (608) 256-3682

Trust established in 1965 in IL.
Donor(s): Oscar G. Mayer, Sr.,‡ Elsa S. Mayer.‡

Foundation type: Independent
Financial data (yr. ended 12/31/91): Assets, $12,860,861 (M); expenditures, $669,388; qualifying distributions, $545,000, including $545,000 for 36 grants (high: $50,000; low: $5,000).
Purpose and activities: Grants limited to charitable institutions in which the donors did or their descendants do actively participate, including higher education, hospitals, music, and museums.
Fields of interest: Higher education, hospitals, music, museums.
Types of support: General purposes.
Limitations: Giving primarily in the Chicago, IL, metropolitan area and in WI. No grants to individuals.
Application information: Application form not required.
  Initial approach: Letter
  Copies of proposal: 1
  Deadline(s): None
  Board meeting date(s): As required
  Final notification: 2 weeks
  Write: Oscar G. Mayer, Managing Trustee
Trustees: Oscar G. Mayer, Managing Trustee; Allan C. Mayer, Harold F. Mayer, Harold M. Mayer.
Number of staff: 1 part-time professional; 1 part-time support.
EIN: 366134354

891
Mazza Foundation ▼
225 West Washington St., Suite 1300
Chicago 60606-3405   (312) 444-9300

Incorporated in 1957 in IL.
Donor(s): Leonard M. Lavezzorio,‡ Louise T. Mazza Trust.
Foundation type: Independent
Financial data (yr. ended 11/30/90): Assets, $41,260,225 (M); expenditures, $1,937,061; qualifying distributions, $1,876,073, including $1,825,000 for 40 grants (high: $125,000; low: $1,500; average: $25,000-$100,000).
Purpose and activities: Giving primarily for churches, religious organizations, social service agencies, hospitals, and health organizations; support also for education.
Fields of interest: Religion, religion—Christian, social services, hospitals, education.
Limitations: Giving primarily in Chicago, IL.
Application information: Application form not required.
  Deadline(s): None
  Write: Joseph O. Rubinelli, Secy.
Officers and Directors:* Tina Lavezzorio,* Pres.; Joseph O. Rubinelli,* V.P. and Secy.; Mary Jane Rubinelli, V.P. and Treas.; Joan F. Lavezzorio, V.P.
EIN: 366054751
Recent health grants:
891-1 Alzheimers Disease and Related Disorders Association, Chicago, IL, $25,000. 1990.
891-2 Arthritis Foundation, Illinois Chapter, Chicago, IL, $10,000. 1990.
891-3 Bonaventure House, Chicago, IL, $35,000. 1990.
891-4 Howard Street Health Center, Chicago, IL, $10,000. 1990.
891-5 Maryville, Glassboro, NJ, $50,000. 1990.

891-6 McDermott Foundation, Chicago, IL, $25,000. 1990.
891-7 Rehabilitation Institute of Chicago, Chicago, IL, $50,000. 1990.
891-8 Saint Benedicts Home for the Aged, Chicago, IL, $50,000. 1990.
891-9 Thresholds, Chicago, IL, $50,000. 1990.

892
Chauncey and Marion Deering
McCormick Foundation
410 North Michigan Ave., Rm. 590
Chicago 60611-4252   (312) 644-6720

Incorporated in 1957 in IL.
Donor(s): Brooks McCormick, Brooks McCormick Trust, Charles Deering McCormick Trust, Roger McCormick Trust.
Foundation type: Independent
Financial data (yr. ended 07/31/90): Assets, $15,251,387 (M); gifts received, $4,250; expenditures, $954,433; qualifying distributions, $925,925, including $695,600 for 22 grants (high: $165,000; low: $1,000).
Purpose and activities: Emphasis on higher and secondary education, hospitals, and cultural institutions, including an art museum; support also for conservation and child welfare.
Fields of interest: Higher education, secondary education, hospitals, cultural programs, museums, conservation, child welfare.
Types of support: General purposes.
Limitations: Giving primarily in Chicago, IL. No grants to individuals.
Application information: Application form not required.
Officers and Directors:* Charles Deering McCormick,* Pres.; Brooks McCormick,* V.P.; Charles E. Schroeder,* Secy.-Treas.; Charlotte McCormick Collins.
EIN: 366054815

893
Robert R. McCormick Tribune Foundation
▼
(Formerly Robert R. McCormick Charitable Trust)
435 North Michigan Ave., Suite 770
Chicago 60611   (312) 222-3512

Trust established in 1955 in IL; became a foundation in 1990.
Donor(s): Robert R. McCormick.‡
Foundation type: Independent
Financial data (yr. ended 12/31/90): Assets, $470,292,080 (M); gifts received, $1,738,239; expenditures, $24,897,432; qualifying distributions, $32,016,048, including $15,719,932 for 500 grants (high: $6,911,000; low: $883; average: $2,500-$100,000), $3,185 for employee matching gifts, $7,376,000 for 2 foundation-administered programs and $1,250,000 for loans.
Purpose and activities: Largest contributions for private higher education, health services, including AIDS research and rehabilitation for the physically and mentally handicapped, the performing arts and cultural programs, human services, including family and legal services, the elderly, the homeless, women, and youth, conservation, and journalism.

Fields of interest: Journalism, education—early childhood, education—minorities, vocational education, employment, homeless, housing, child welfare, child development, citizenship, civic affairs, community development, volunteerism.
Types of support: Operating budgets, technical assistance, matching funds, program-related investments, special projects, general purposes.
Limitations: Giving primarily in the Chicago, IL, metropolitan area. No grants to individuals, or for endowment funds, research, scholarships, fellowships, or single events.
Publications: Annual report (including application guidelines), application guidelines, informational brochure.
Application information: Application form not required.
  Initial approach: Letter
  Copies of proposal: 1
  Deadline(s): Feb. 1, May 1, Aug. 1, and Nov. 1
  Board meeting date(s): Mar., June, Sept., and Dec.
  Final notification: Within 2 weeks
  Write: Nicholas Goodban, V.P. of Philanthropy
Officers and Directors:* Stanton R. Cook,* Chair.; Neal Creighton, Pres. and C.E.O.; Richard A. Behrenhausen, V.P., C.O.O. and Secy.; Nicholas Goodban, V.P. of Philanthropy; Louis J. Marsico, Jr., Treas.; Charles T. Brumback, James C. Dowdle, Jack Fuller, John W. Madigan.
Number of staff: 6 full-time professional; 3 full-time support.
EIN: 363689171
Recent health grants:
893-1 AIDS Foundation of Chicago, Chicago, IL, $25,000. For unrestricted support. 1990.
893-2 American Indian Health Service of Chicago, Chicago, IL, $20,000. For specific program. 1990.
893-3 Austin Peoples Action Center, Chicago, IL, $35,000. For capital support for health program. 1990.
893-4 Chicago Community Programs for Clinical Research on AIDS, Chicago, IL, $15,000. For unrestricted support. 1990.
893-5 Chicago Osteopathic Health Systems, Chicago, IL, $37,500. For specific program. 1990.
893-6 Easter Seal Rehabilitation Center of Will-Grundy Counties, Joliet, IL, $15,000. For specific program. 1990.
893-7 Five Hospital Foundation, Chicago, IL, $25,000. For unrestricted support. 1990.
893-8 Harbor Home Support Services, Chicago, IL, $20,000. For unrestricted support. 1990.
893-9 Hektoen Institute for Medical Research, Chicago, IL, $15,000. For specific program. 1990.
893-10 Helping Hand Rehabilitation Center, Countryside, IL, $10,000. For specific program. 1990.
893-11 Hispanic AIDS Network, Chicago, IL, $15,000. For specific program. 1990.
893-12 Illinois Masonic Medical Center, Chicago, IL, $10,000. For specific program. 1990.
893-13 Illinois Maternal and Child Health Coalition, Chicago, IL, $10,000. For specific program. 1990.
893-14 Infant Welfare Society of Chicago, Chicago, IL, $75,000. For capital support. 1990.

893-15 Infant Welfare Society of Chicago, Chicago, IL, $10,000. For specific program. 1990.

893-16 Kupona Network, Chicago, IL, $10,000. For unrestricted support. 1990.

893-17 Lawndale Christian Health Center, Chicago, IL, $50,000. For capital support. 1990.

893-18 Lutheran Social Services of Illinois, Chicago, IL, $50,000. For capital support for alcoholic-drug dependency program. 1990.

893-19 Mental Health Association in Illinois, Elk Grove Village, IL, $25,000. For specific program. 1990.

893-20 Michael Reese Hospital and Medical Center, Chicago, IL, $25,000. For specific program. 1990.

893-21 Midwest Association for Sickle Cell Anemia, Chicago, IL, $10,000. For specific program. 1990.

893-22 Pilsen-Little Village Community Mental Health Center, Chicago, IL, $15,000. For unrestricted support. 1990.

893-23 Planned Parenthood Association of Chicago, Chicago, IL, $35,000. For unrestricted support. 1990.

893-24 Robert Crown Center for Health Education, Hinsdale, IL, $23,200. For capital support. 1990.

893-25 Saint Josephs Carondelet Child Center, Chicago, IL, $25,000. For capital support. 1990.

893-26 South Shore Hospital, Chicago, IL, $75,000. For capital support. 1990.

893-27 South Suburban Council on Alcoholism and Substance Abuse, East Hazelcrest, IL, $25,000. For capital support. 1990.

893-28 Thresholds, Chicago, IL, $50,000. For capital support. 1990.

893-29 White Crane Wellness Center, Chicago, IL, $10,000. For unrestricted support. 1990.

894
McDonald's Contributions Department
McDonald's Plaza
Oak Brook 60521   (708) 575-3000

Financial data (yr. ended 12/31/90): Total giving, $1,000,000 for grants.
Purpose and activities: Support is given in five major focus areas: education, health, arts and culture, civic affairs, and community development.
Fields of interest: Cultural programs, civic affairs, education, health, community development.
Types of support: Matching funds, seed money, special projects, in-kind gifts.
Limitations: Giving primarily in operating locations, through restaurants, and nationally through the corporation. No support for fraternal, veterans', religious, political, or sectarian programs; intermediary funding organizations; or the United Way outside of Chicago area. No grants to individuals, or for capital funds, general operating purposes, endowments, scholarship funds, loans, investment funds, advertising, unspecified funds for specific elementary or secondary schools, multi-year grants, or research.
Publications: Corporate giving report, informational brochure.
Application information: Application form not required.

Initial approach: Full proposal (submit only one proposal per year)
Copies of proposal: 1
Deadline(s): None
Board meeting date(s): Review on an on-going basis
Final notification: Within 3 months
Write: Kenneth L. Barun, Supervisor, Contribs.
Administrators: Kenneth L. Barun, Supvr., Contribs.; Jackie Meara, Admin. Secy.

895
McGraw Foundation ▼
3436 North Kennicott Dr.
Arlington Heights 60004   (708) 870-8014
Mailing address: P.O. Box 307 B, Wheeling, IL 60090

Incorporated in 1948 in IL.
Donor(s): Alfred Bersted,‡ Carol Jean Root,‡ Maxine Elrod,‡ Donald S. Elrod,‡ Max McGraw,‡ Richard F. McGraw,‡ McGraw-Edison Co., and others.
Foundation type: Independent
Financial data (yr. ended 12/31/91): Assets, $14,118,751 (M); gifts received, $5,000; expenditures, $934,902; qualifying distributions, $804,618, including $673,703 for 45 grants (average: $5,000-$25,000) and $56,000 for employee matching gifts.
Purpose and activities: Giving primarily for higher education, health, civic affairs, social services, science, culture, and the environment.
Fields of interest: Higher education, social services, science and technology, cultural programs, environment, civic affairs, health.
Types of support: Operating budgets, annual campaigns, building funds, equipment, research, matching funds, seed money, continuing support.
Limitations: Giving primarily in the Chicago, IL, area, and in adjoining states. No grants to individuals.
Publications: Program policy statement, application guidelines.
Application information: Application form not required.

Initial approach: Letter
Copies of proposal: 1
Deadline(s): Submit proposal between Dec. 1 and Feb. 1
Board meeting date(s): June; grant committee meets annually in Mar.
Final notification: 30 days to 1 year
Write: James F. Quilter, V.P.
Officers and Directors:* Bernard B. Rinella,* Pres.; James F. Quilter,* V.P., Secy.-Treas., and Exec. Dir.; J. Bradley Davis, Scott M. Elrod, Dennis W. Fitzgerald, Jean E. Fitzgerald, Raymond H. Giesecke, Jerry D. Jones, William W. Mauritz, Catherine B. Nelson, Leah K. Robson.
Number of staff: 1 full-time professional; 1 part-time support.
EIN: 362490000

896
The Meyer-Ceco Foundation
c/o Robertson-Ceco Corp.
One Tower Ln., Suite 2300
Oakbrook Terrace 60181   (312) 242-2000

Trust established in 1946 in NE.

Donor(s): M.L. Meyer Trust.
Foundation type: Independent
Financial data (yr. ended 12/31/90): Assets, $4,537,564 (M); expenditures, $262,079; qualifying distributions, $237,525, including $227,400 for 117 grants (high: $16,500; low: $25; average: $500-$1,500) and $10,125 for 38 employee matching gifts.
Fields of interest: Education, higher education, community funds, civic affairs, hospitals, health, youth, religion.
Types of support: Continuing support, program-related investments.
Limitations: Giving primarily in the Midwest and Southeast.
Publications: 990-PF.
Application information: Application form not required.

Initial approach: Letter
Copies of proposal: 1
Deadline(s): None
Board meeting date(s): Varies
Write: Ned A. Ochiltree, Jr., Trustee
Trustees: C. Foster Brown III, Heidi Hall Jones, Ned A. Ochiltree, Jr.
Number of staff: 1 part-time support.
EIN: 366053404

897
MidCon Corporate Giving Program
701 E. 22nd St.
Lombard 60148-5072   (312) 691-3000

Purpose and activities: Supports higher education, culture, health, social services, child welfare, law and justice, libraries, museums, and programs for minorities. Types of support include employee matching gifts for higher education.
Fields of interest: Child welfare, law and justice, libraries, literacy, minorities, museums, education, higher education, cultural programs, health, social services.
Types of support: Employee matching gifts, donated equipment.
Application information:

Initial approach: Written proposal
Deadline(s): None
Board meeting date(s): Proposals are continuously reviewed
Write: Suzanne Nowaczyk, Adm., Corp. Services
Number of staff: 1

898
Milbro Charitable Foundation
100 South Schelter Rd.
Lincolnshire 60069   (708) 634-5713

Established in 1985 in IL.
Donor(s): Harvey L. Miller, Jack Miller, Quill Corp.
Foundation type: Independent
Financial data (yr. ended 12/31/90): Assets, $539,760 (M); gifts received, $137,000; expenditures, $379,249; qualifying distributions, $378,679, including $378,659 for 61 grants (high: $110,000; low: $10).
Purpose and activities: Giving primarily for Jewish organizations, especially Jewish welfare funds, and health agencies with emphasis on

pediatric research; some support for social services.
Fields of interest: Jewish giving, Jewish welfare, health, youth, medical research, social services.
Limitations: Giving primarily in IL.
Application information: Application form not required.
  Initial approach: Letter or proposal
  Deadline(s): None
  Write: Arnold Miller, Treas.
Officers and Directors:* Jack Miller,* Pres.; Harvey L. Miller,* V.P. and Secy.; Arnold Miller,* V.P. and Treas.
EIN: 363390647

899
James Millikin Trust
P.O. Box 1278
Decatur 62525-1813   (217) 429-4253
Application address: 295 North Franklin, Decatur, IL 26523; Tel.: (217) 429-2391

Trust established in 1910 in IL.
Donor(s): James Millikin.‡
Foundation type: Independent
Financial data (yr. ended 12/31/90): Assets, $13,137,977 (M); expenditures, $644,789; qualifying distributions, $527,566, including $505,103 for grants.
Purpose and activities: Grants to a university and a hospital; grants also for a community fund and youth organizations.
Fields of interest: Higher education, hospitals, community funds, youth.
Types of support: Operating budgets.
Limitations: Giving primarily in Decatur, IL.
Application information: Application form not required.
  Initial approach: Proposal
  Deadline(s): None
  Board meeting date(s): 3rd Wednesday of each month
  Write: James Uhl
Officer and Trustees:* Bernard Wright,* Chair.; James W. Alling, G. William Harner, Jack Hunter, Wayne S. Martin.
Number of staff: None.
EIN: 370661226

900
Bernard & Marjorie Mitchell Family Foundation
875 North Michigan Ave., Suite 3412
Chicago 60611

Donor(s): Bernard A. Mitchell Trust, Lee H. Mitchell, Marjorie I. Mitchell.
Foundation type: Independent
Financial data (yr. ended 12/31/90): Assets, $3,054,722 (M); expenditures, $141,337; qualifying distributions, $122,300, including $122,300 for 13 grants (high: $50,000; low: $200).
Fields of interest: Jewish welfare, arts, museums, medical research.
Limitations: Giving primarily in Chicago, IL. No grants to individuals.
Application information: Contributes only to pre-selected organizations. Applications not accepted.

Trustees: Victoria C. Kohn, Lee H. Mitchell, Marjorie I. Mitchell.
EIN: 237007014

901
Moorman Company Fund
1000 North 30th St.
Quincy 62305-3115   (217) 222-7100

Incorporated in 1952 in IL.
Donor(s): Moorman Manufacturing Co.
Foundation type: Company-sponsored
Financial data (yr. ended 12/31/90): Assets, $1,092,174 (M); gifts received, $125,000; expenditures, $430,312; qualifying distributions, $426,770, including $425,405 for 115 grants (high: $69,986; low: $125).
Purpose and activities: Emphasis on land-grant universities for agricultural scholarships, and educational associations in the company's market areas; and for local colleges, community funds, youth agencies, health associations, hospitals, and welfare organizations in Adams County, IL.
Fields of interest: Higher education, agriculture, community funds, youth, welfare, health associations, hospitals, educational associations.
Types of support: Scholarship funds, operating budgets, general purposes, building funds, equipment.
Limitations: Giving limited to areas of company operations, with emphasis on Adams County, IL. No grants to individuals.
Application information: Application form not required.
  Initial approach: Letter
  Copies of proposal: 1
  Deadline(s): Jan. 1
  Board meeting date(s): 3rd Wednesday bimonthly
  Final notification: Varies
  Write: L.B. Davis, Secy.
Officers and Directors:* S.K. Adams,* Pres.; T.M. McKenna,* V.P.; L.B. Davis, Secy.; R.L. Jackson,* Treas.; M.J. Foster, W.D. George, R.A. Liebig, T.M. McKenna, T.L. Shade, R.H. Upper, H.L. Williams.
Number of staff: None.
EIN: 376026253

902
Morton International Corporate Giving Program
c/o Corporate Human Resources
100 N. Riverside Plaza
Chicago 60606   (312) 807-2000

Financial data (yr. ended 06/30/90): Total giving, $466,000 for grants.
Purpose and activities: "Morton International recognizes its responsibility to be a good citizen and a good neighbor in those communities where the company has plants or facilities. Therefore the company contributes to appropriate projects which enhance these communities and their business climate." Contributions which are principally of interest to one business unit are budgeted and administered by the unit concerned. Contributions to organizations not principally identifiable with one unit are included in the corporate budget and administered by the Corporate Contributions Committee. Each business unit submits an annual contributions

budget, as well as its unbudgeted requests, to the committee for approval. Support is given for education, including research, education building funds, and minority education, hospitals, and rehabilitation. Commitments are not made for more than one annual payment (including capital funds) unless exceptional circumstances require it.
Fields of interest: Education—building funds, educational research, chemistry, education—minorities, hospitals, museums, rehabilitation.
Types of support: Employee matching gifts, in-kind gifts.
Limitations: Giving primarily in headquarters area and areas of company operations; emphasis on areas where company is the major employer. No support for political organizations or campaigns, sectarian or denominational religious organizations unless they provide services for the general population, institutions other than hospitals or educational institutions receiving income through taxation, or generally for operating expenses of United Way members.
Publications: Corporate report, application guidelines.
Application information: Corporate Human Resources handles giving. If a grant is made, periodic reports may be requested from the recipient. Application form not required.
  Initial approach: Brief one or two page letter outlining goals, geographic area, and why Morton International funds should be used; approach must be in writing
  Final notification: Every proposal will receive a response
  Write: Richard C. Kyrouac, Secy., Contribs. Comm.
Number of staff: 1 part-time professional; 1 part-time support.

903
Motorola Foundation ▼
1303 East Algonquin Rd.
Schaumburg 60196   (708) 576-6200

Incorporated in 1953 in IL.
Donor(s): Motorola, Inc.
Foundation type: Company-sponsored
Financial data (yr. ended 12/31/90): Assets, $1,116,860 (M); gifts received, $3,200,000; expenditures, $3,274,286; qualifying distributions, $3,269,463, including $2,838,885 for 439 grants (high: $275,000; low: $100; average: $1,000-$5,000) and $430,578 for 2,931 employee matching gifts.
Purpose and activities: Giving for higher and other education, including an employee matching gift program, united funds, and hospitals; support also for cultural programs, social services, and youth agencies.
Fields of interest: Education, higher education, science and technology, community funds, hospitals, cultural programs, youth, social services.
Types of support: Operating budgets, building funds, scholarship funds, employee matching gifts, fellowships, general purposes, continuing support.
Limitations: Giving primarily in communities where the company has major facilities, with emphasis on Huntsville, AL; Mt. Pleasant, IA; Chicago, IL; Phoenix, AZ; Austin, Fort Worth, and Sequin, TX; and Fort Lauderdale and Boynton

Beach, FL. No support for strictly sectarian or denominational religious organizations; national health organizations or their local chapters; or secondary schools, trade schools, or state institutions (except through the employee matching gift program). No grants to individuals, or for university endowment funds, research, courtesy advertising, operating expenses of organizations receiving United Way funding, benefits or capital fund drives of colleges or universities; no loans.

Publications: Application guidelines.

Application information: Application form not required.

Initial approach: Letter, telephone, or proposal
Copies of proposal: 1
Deadline(s): Nov.
Board meeting date(s): Monthly and as required
Final notification: 1 to 2 months
Write: Mrs. Herta Betty Nikolai, Administrator

Officers and Directors:* George M.C. Fisher,* Pres.; Garth L. Milne, V.P. and Exec. Dir.; Donald R. Jones,* V.P.; Victor R. Kopidlansky, Secy.; William H.S. Preece, Jr., Treas.; Carl F. Koenemann.

Number of staff: 1 full-time professional; 1 full-time support.

EIN: 366109323

Recent health grants:

903-1 American Cancer Society, Chicago, IL, $10,000. 1990.

903-2 Media-Advertising Partnership for a Drug-Free America, NYC, NY, $25,000. 1990.

904
Nalco Chemical Company Giving Program
One Nalco Ctr.
Naperville 60563-1198   (708) 305-1556

Financial data (yr. ended 12/31/91): Total giving, $817,197, including $573,399 for grants and $243,798 for 527 employee matching gifts.

Purpose and activities: "The philanthropic goal of Nalco Chemical Company is to improve conditions in communities where we have facilities in order to produce a healthy environment in which to live and conduct business." The Nalco Foundation makes most charitable gifts for the company. Nalco Corporate Contributions—giving by headquarters, subsidiaries, and plants—includes employee matching gifts, United Way campaigns (company and employee giving), and contributions to numerous organizations made locally by Nalco plants and offices. The educational matching gifts program matches the contributions of Nalco employees, directors, and retirees to accredited colleges and universities at a $2 to $1 ratio with a minimum donation of $25 and maximum of $2,000. The Matching Gift Program for cultural organizations and nonprofit hospitals, is on a dollar-for-dollar basis with a minimum donation of $25 and a maximum of $500.

Fields of interest: Community funds, higher education, health, social services, youth, economics, leadership development, rehabilitation, aged, cultural programs, hospitals, arts.

Types of support: Employee matching gifts, employee volunteer services.

Limitations: Giving primarily in major operating locations.

Publications: Corporate giving report, application guidelines.

Application information: Most giving handled through the Nalco Foundation.

Initial approach: Request guidelines to be sure organization meets giving criteria
Write: Joanne C. Ford, Pres., Nalco Fdn.

Number of staff: None.

905
The Nalco Foundation ▼
One Nalco Ctr.
Naperville 60563-1198   (708) 305-1556

Incorporated in 1953 in IL.

Donor(s): Nalco Chemical Co.

Foundation type: Company-sponsored

Financial data (yr. ended 12/31/91): Assets, $1,618,572 (M); gifts received, $1,000,300; expenditures, $1,588,513; qualifying distributions, $1,588,513, including $1,588,513 for 223 grants (high: $85,000; low: $500; average: $2,000-$10,000).

Purpose and activities: Grants largely for private institutions of higher education, educational associations, hospitals, social service and youth agencies, and cultural activities.

Fields of interest: Cultural programs, social services, education, health.

Types of support: Operating budgets, continuing support, annual campaigns, seed money, building funds, equipment, land acquisition, capital campaigns, renovation projects, general purposes.

Limitations: Giving primarily in areas where company has manufacturing operations: the metropolitan Chicago area and DuPage County, IL; Carson, CA; Garyville, LA; Jonesboro, GA; Jackson, MI; Paulsboro, NJ; and Sugar Land and Freeport, TX. No support for state-supported colleges or universities, secondary or elementary schools, churches, or religious education. No grants to individuals, or for endowments, research, scholarships, fellowships, purchase of tickets for fundraising banquets, or matching gifts; no loans.

Publications: Corporate giving report (including application guidelines), application guidelines.

Application information: Application form not required.

Initial approach: Request guidelines
Copies of proposal: 1
Deadline(s): None
Board meeting date(s): Mar., June, Sept., and Dec.
Final notification: 3 to 6 months
Write: Joanne C. Ford, Pres.

Officers and Directors:* Joanne C. Ford,* Pres.; Terrence J. Taylor, V.P. and Treas.; Mary F. Carhart, Secy.; David R. Bertran, James F. Lambe.

Number of staff: 1 full-time professional; 1 full-time support.

EIN: 366065864

906
Navistar Foundation
455 North Cityfront Plaza Dr.
Chicago 60611   (312) 836-3034

Incorporated in 1944 in IL.

Donor(s): Navistar International Transportation Corp.

Foundation type: Company-sponsored

Financial data (yr. ended 10/31/90): Assets, $250,556 (M); gifts received, $306,500; expenditures, $277,571; qualifying distributions, $277,571, including $277,485 for 72 grants (high: $100,000; low: $200).

Fields of interest: Civic affairs, community development, community funds, safety, volunteerism, education, education—minorities, health, hospitals—building funds.

Limitations: Giving primarily in Chicago, IL; Springfield, OH; Fort Wayne and Indianapolis, IN; and Waukesha, WI. No support for strictly sectarian or denominational religious organizations. No grants to individuals, or for scholarships, fellowships, or matching gifts; the foundation does not contribute Navistar International Transportation Corp. equipment or provide funds for special occasions; support for hospitals generally restricted to building programs or equipment additions; no loans.

Application information:

Initial approach: Letter
Copies of proposal: 1
Deadline(s): None
Board meeting date(s): As required
Write: Brian B. Whalen, Pres.

Officers and Directors:* Brian B. Whalen,* Pres.; Patricia A. Hays, Secy.; Robert C. Lannert, Treas.; James C. Cotting, Roxanne J. Decyk, Neil A. Springer.

EIN: 366058875

907
The Neese Family Foundation, Inc.
11722 Main St.
Roscoe 61073

Incorporated in 1986 in IL.

Donor(s): Members of the Neese family.

Foundation type: Independent

Financial data (yr. ended 06/30/90): Assets, $2,061,459 (M); gifts received, $154,444; expenditures, $304,542; qualifying distributions, $303,224, including $303,125 for 6 grants (high: $100,000; low: $1,000).

Fields of interest: Hospitals, hospitals—building funds, higher education, community funds, community development, public policy.

Types of support: Capital campaigns, scholarship funds, building funds, general purposes.

Limitations: Giving limited to the Beloit, WI, stateline area. No grants to individuals.

Application information: Application form not required.

Initial approach: Letter
Deadline(s): None
Board meeting date(s): Varies
Write: Gary G. Grabowski, Treas.

Officers: Margaret K. Neese, Pres.; Elbert H. Neese, V.P and Secy.; Gary G. Grabowski, Treas. and Exec. Dir.

Number of staff: None.

EIN: 363473918

908
New Prospect Foundation
1420 Sheridan Rd., Apt. 9A
Wilmette 60091   (708) 256-3886

Established in 1969 in IL.

Donor(s): Elliot Lehman, Frances Lehman, Fel-Pro Inc.
Foundation type: Independent
Financial data (yr. ended 12/31/91): Assets, $8,431,458 (M); gifts received, $101,626; expenditures, $668,260; qualifying distributions, $626,076, including $607,682 for 180 grants (high: $45,000; low: $500; average: $1,500-$7,500).
Purpose and activities: Support for activities directed toward the improvement of housing, employment, health, welfare, and the economic viability of urban and inner-city neighborhoods. Funding priority given to organizations with modest budgets that may not qualify for traditional sources of financial assistance; also supports efforts undertaken in the public interest through legal services. Additional areas of interest: pro-choice activities, nuclear disarmament, human and civil rights, Chicago public school reform, AIDS research, Southern Africa, the Middle East, and women's organizations.
Fields of interest: Health, community development, urban affairs, legal services, family planning, elementary education, secondary education, AIDS, women, social services.
Types of support: General purposes, operating budgets, continuing support, seed money, emergency funds, special projects, matching funds.
Limitations: Giving limited to the Chicago, IL, metropolitan area. Generally no funding for the arts or higher education. No grants to individuals, or for capital or endowment funds, basic research, scholarships, or fellowships; no loans.
Publications: Informational brochure (including application guidelines).
Application information: Application form not required.
   Initial approach: Letter, proposal, or telephone
   Copies of proposal: 1
   Deadline(s): 6 weeks before board meetings
   Board meeting date(s): Mar., June, Oct., and Dec.
   Final notification: 3 months
   Write: Frances Lehman, Pres.
Officer and Directors:* Frances Lehman,* Pres.; Elliot Lehman, Kenneth Lehman, Lucy Lehman, Paul Lehman, Ronna Stamm Lehman, Kay Schlozman, Stanley Schlozman.
Number of staff: 1 part-time professional.
EIN: 237032384

909
Dellora A. & Lester J. Norris Foundation ▼
P.O. Box 1081
St. Charles 60174   (708) 377-4111

Established in 1979 in IL.
Donor(s): Dellora A. Norris,‡ Lester J. Norris.‡
Foundation type: Independent
Financial data (yr. ended 12/31/90): Assets, $20,122,948 (M); gifts received, $645,033; expenditures, $1,223,174; qualifying distributions, $1,043,330, including $1,007,144 for 71 grants (high: $100,000; low: $1,000; average: $5,000-$50,000).
Purpose and activities: Giving primarily for hospitals, higher and secondary education, and church support.
Fields of interest: Hospitals, higher education, secondary education, religion.

Application information: Support mainly for organizations started by donors and officers. Application form not required.
   Initial approach: Letter
   Deadline(s): None
   Board meeting date(s): Quarterly
   Write: Eugene Butler, Treas.
Officers and Directors:* Robert C. Norris,* Chair.; Joann N. Pace,* Pres.; Laverne N. Gaynor,* V.P.; Howard S. Tuthill,* Secy.; Eugene W. Butler,* Treas.; M. James Termondt, Linda N. Wheeler.
EIN: 363054939

910
Northern Illinois Gas Corporate Giving Program
P.O. Box 190
Aurora 60507-0190   (312) 983-8888

Financial data (yr. ended 12/31/90): Total giving, $1,300,000, including $1,261,000 for grants and $39,000 for employee matching gifts.
Purpose and activities: Support for social services, health care, arts and cultural activities, economic development, youth activities, education, civic affairs, and community development.
Fields of interest: Social services, health, cultural programs, economics, youth, education, community development, civic affairs, arts.
Types of support: Building funds.
Limitations: Giving primarily in company's service area, the northern third of IL except for Chicago and a few North Shore suburbs. No grants for organizations funded by United Ways and the Crusade of Mercy, except for approved building funds.
Application information: Division offices handle small, local contributions; major giving and building fund requests must be approved by a committee. Application form required.
   Initial approach: Telephone inquiry or written proposal directed to Office of Community Affairs; invitations for on-site visits or follow-up phone calls are not necessary unless requested
   Write: Julian E. Brown, Dir., Community Affairs

911
The Northern Trust Company Charitable Trust ▼
c/o The Northern Trust Co., Community Affairs Div.
50 South LaSalle St.
Chicago 60675   (312) 444-4059

Trust established in 1966 in IL.
Donor(s): The Northern Trust Co.
Foundation type: Company-sponsored
Financial data (yr. ended 12/31/89): Assets, $389,502 (M); gifts received, $1,600,000; expenditures, $1,546,388; qualifying distributions, $1,544,950, including $1,243,745 for 166 grants (high: $348,200; low: $500; average: $2,000-$5,000) and $294,371 for employee matching gifts.
Purpose and activities: Giving primarily for community development; education, including early childhood education, programs for minority students, and literacy programs; health services, including mental illness programs and drug treatment; cultural activities, including the

performing arts and theater; social services and welfare agencies, including aid for the disadvantaged and homeless; youth agencies and child welfare and development; and women's organizations.
Fields of interest: Community development, urban development, urban affairs, education, education—early childhood, literacy, mental health, drug abuse, health services, cultural programs, performing arts, social services, disadvantaged, housing, welfare, homeless, youth, child welfare, child development, women.
Types of support: Operating budgets, continuing support, annual campaigns, seed money, emergency funds, employee matching gifts, consulting services, technical assistance, special projects, renovation projects, matching funds, capital campaigns, general purposes.
Limitations: Giving limited to Cook County, IL, with focus on Chicago area. No support for national organizations, health organizations concentrating efforts in one area of human disease (except through matching gift program), religious organizations whose services are limited to any one sectarian group, fraternal or political groups, or operating support for United Way agencies. No grants to individuals, or for fellowships, advertising for fundraising benefits, or research; no loans.
Publications: Corporate giving report (including application guidelines), grants list, annual report.
Application information: Grants are not renewed automatically. Application form not required.
   Initial approach: Proposal
   Copies of proposal: 1
   Deadline(s): Community Revitalization - Dec. 1 and Aug. 1; Health - Feb. 1; Social Welfare - Feb. 1 and Oct. 1; Arts & Culture - June 1; Education - Apr. 1
   Board meeting date(s): Bimonthly
   Final notification: 2 months
   Write: Marjorie W. Lundy, V.P., The Northern Trust Co., or Eleanor Alcantara, Comm. Coord./ Matching Gifts Mgr.
Contributions Committee: William N. Setterstrom, Chair.; Sidney R. Bundrage, John S. Darrow, Michelle Griffin, Robert L. Head, John V.N. McClure, Maria Medria, Lorraine M. Reepmeyer, Douglas Regan.
Trustee: The Northern Trust Co.
Number of staff: 2 full-time professional; 1 full-time support; 1 part-time support.
EIN: 366147253
Recent health grants:
911-1 Childrens Memorial Medical Center, Chicago, IL, $15,000. For indigent patient care. 1990.
911-2 Erie Family Health Center, Chicago, IL, $10,000. For Teen Health Center serving Wells Academy students. 1990.
911-3 Evangelical Health Foundation, Oak Brook, IL, $10,000. For Community Center of Bethany Hospital. 1990.
911-4 Northwestern Memorial Hospital, Chicago, IL, $10,000. For Prentice Women's Hospital Developmental Evaluation Clinic. 1990.
911-5 Winfield-Moody Health Center, Chicago, IL, $10,000. For outreach and community health education services. 1990.

912
The Offield Family Foundation ▼
410 North Michigan Ave., Rm. 942
Chicago 60611

Incorporated in 1940 in IL.
Donor(s): Dorothy Wrigley Offield.
Foundation type: Independent
Financial data (yr. ended 06/30/91): Assets,
$40,932,081 (M); expenditures, $1,919,524;
qualifying distributions, $1,867,654, including
$1,768,661 for 50 grants (high: $268,761; low:
$1,000; average: $2,000-$50,000).
Purpose and activities: Emphasis on hospitals, a
population control agency, education, and
cultural programs.
Fields of interest: Hospitals, education, cultural
programs.
Limitations: Giving primarily in the Chicago, IL,
area and MI. No grants to individuals.
Application information: Contributes only to
pre-selected organizations. Applications not
accepted.
Officers and Directors:* Wrigley Offield,* Pres.;
Edna Jean Offield,* V.P.; Marie Larson,* Secy.;
Raymond H. Drymalski,* Treas.; James S. Offield,
Paxson H. Offield.
EIN: 366066240

913
The OMC Foundation
(Formerly The Ole Evinrude Foundation)
100 Sea Horse Dr.
Waukegan 60085   (708) 689-5483

Incorporated in 1945 in WI.
Donor(s): Outboard Marine Corp.
Foundation type: Company-sponsored
Financial data (yr. ended 06/30/90): Assets,
$3,942,387 (M); gifts received, $2,500,000;
expenditures, $439,996; qualifying distributions,
$403,700, including $360,200 for grants (high:
$35,930) and $42,000 for 43 grants to individuals
(high: $1,000; low: $500).
Purpose and activities: Support of private higher
education, especially business and engineering,
in states in which the company operates,
scholarship aid to children of company
employees, and capital grants to hospital and
cultural building projects in company locations;
support also for recreation and environmental
programs.
Fields of interest: Higher education, business
education, engineering, secondary education,
hospitals, cultural programs, environment,
recreation.
Types of support: Continuing support, annual
campaigns, seed money, building funds,
equipment, special projects, research, scholarship
funds, employee-related scholarships, capital
campaigns, employee matching gifts, renovation
projects.
Limitations: Giving limited to areas of company
operations in GA, IL, NC, TN, WI, SC, MI, TX, FL,
MO, OR, IN, AR, and NY. No support for
organizations participating in local combined
appeals. No grants to individuals (except for
employee-related scholarships), or for
endowment funds or operating expenses; no
loans.
Application information: Application form not
required.

Initial approach: Letter
Copies of proposal: 1
Deadline(s): Submit proposal preferably in
Aug.; deadline Sept. 30
Board meeting date(s): Dec.
Final notification: 30 days after annual meeting
Write: Mr. Laurin M. Baker, Dir., Public Affairs
Officers and Directors:* James C. Chapman,*
Chair. and Pres.; Thomas J. Beeler,* V.P.; F. James
Short,* V.P.; Laurin M. Baker,* Secy.; Michael S.
Duffy,* Treas.
Number of staff: None.
EIN: 396037139

914
OMRON Foundation, Inc.
1375 East Woodfield Rd., Suite 520
Schaumburg 60173   (708) 240-5330

Established in 1989 in IL.
Donor(s): OMRON Electronics, Inc., OMRON
Management Center of America, OMRON
Systems of America, Inc., OMRON Healthcare,
Inc., OMRON Advanced Systems, Inc., OMRON
Office Automation Products, Inc.
Foundation type: Company-sponsored
Financial data (yr. ended 03/31/90): Assets,
$9,791 (M); gifts received, $535,000;
expenditures, $535,034; qualifying distributions,
$535,000, including $535,000 for 6 grants (high:
$105,000; low: $10,000).
Purpose and activities: Primary areas of interest
include higher and other education, the
handicapped, cultural programs, the
environment, and the elderly.
Fields of interest: Education, higher education,
libraries, handicapped, rehabilitation, medical
sciences, health, cultural programs, arts,
humanities, environment, conservation, aged,
welfare, social services, youth, women, civil
rights, human rights, public policy, community
development.
Types of support: Scholarship funds, employee
matching gifts, in-kind gifts, building funds,
continuing support, employee-related
scholarships, operating budgets.
Limitations: Giving primarily in IL; national giving
also considered.
Publications: Corporate giving report (including
application guidelines), grants list, informational
brochure, program policy statement, application
guidelines.
Application information: Application form not
required.
Initial approach: Letter
Deadline(s): None
Board meeting date(s): Monthly
Write: Takuji Yamamoto, Secy.
Officers and Directors:* Yoshio Tateisi,* Pres.;
Takuji Yamamoto, Secy.; Shigeru Kobayashi,
Treas.; Gordon Boyd, Nick Hahn, Hideki Masuda,
John Roberts, Noboru Sano.
Number of staff: None.
EIN: 363644055

915
Edmond and Alice Opler Foundation
(Formerly Edmond Opler Foundation)
Two First National Plaza
Chicago 60603   (312) 845-5107

Established in 1981.
Donor(s): Edmond Opler.
Foundation type: Independent
Financial data (yr. ended 12/31/90): Assets,
$1,072,156 (M); gifts received, $1,000,000;
expenditures, $1,046,750; qualifying
distributions, $1,046,750, including $1,046,750
for grants.
Fields of interest: Hospitals, health, higher
education, Catholic giving, general charitable
giving.
Limitations: Giving primarily in IL.
Application information:
Initial approach: Letter
Deadline(s): None
Write: Lloyd S. Kupferberg
Officers: Edmond Opler, Pres.; Edmond Opler, Jr.,
V.P.; Francis J. Nudd, Secy.; Thomas F. Morris,
Treas.
EIN: 363137745

916
Frank E. Payne and Seba B. Payne
Foundation ▼
c/o Continental Bank, N.A.
30 North LaSalle St.
Chicago 60697   (312) 828-1785

Trust established in 1962 in IL.
Donor(s): Seba B. Payne.‡
Foundation type: Independent
Financial data (yr. ended 06/30/91): Assets,
$72,330,527 (M); expenditures, $3,434,245;
qualifying distributions, $3,267,462, including
$3,182,840 for 48 grants (high: $1,000,000; low:
$5,000; average: $10,000-$100,000).
Purpose and activities: Support for education,
hospitals, and cultural programs; support also for
child and animal welfare.
Fields of interest: Education, hospitals, cultural
programs, child welfare, animal welfare, AIDS.
Types of support: Equipment, operating budgets,
building funds, general purposes.
Limitations: Giving primarily in the metropolitan
Chicago, IL, area and PA. No grants to
individuals, or for endowment funds, or
fellowships; no loans.
Publications: Application guidelines.
Application information: Application form not
required.
Initial approach: Proposal
Copies of proposal: 1
Deadline(s): None
Board meeting date(s): May and Nov., and as
required
Final notification: 4 months
Write: M.C. Ryan, 2nd V.P., Continental Bank,
N.A.
Trustees: Susan Hurd Cummings, George A.
Hurd, Sr., Priscilla Payne Hurd, Charles M. Nisen,
Continental Bank, N.A.
Number of staff: None.
EIN: 237435471

917
Peoples Energy Corporate Giving Program
122 South Michigan Avenue
Chicago 60603   (312) 431-4393

Financial data (yr. ended 09/30/90): Total giving,
$859,387, including $798,706 for grants (high:

$242,000; low: $500) and $60,681 for employee matching gifts.

Purpose and activities: Supports health and welfare, civic and community affairs, education and arts and culture. Types of support include employee matching gifts for pre-collegiate and higher education, in-kind services of donations of materials and printing and technical assistance through design services and printing.

Fields of interest: Health, welfare, civic affairs, community development, education, arts, cultural programs, hospitals.

Types of support: Building funds, capital campaigns, employee matching gifts, general purposes, operating budgets, renovation projects, special projects, technical assistance, in-kind gifts.

Limitations: Giving primarily in headquarters city and service areas in northeast IL. No support for political or lobbying organizations; discriminatory organizations; government agencies; or religious groups for sectarian purposes. No grants to individuals, or for trips or tours, or advertising.

Publications: Informational brochure.

Application information: Company has a staff that handles giving only. Application form required.

Initial approach: Proposal to headquarters
Copies of proposal: 1
Deadline(s): None
Final notification: 8 weeks
Write: George E. Charles, Mgr., Corp. Contribs.

Number of staff: 1 full-time professional; 1 full-time support.

918
Peoria Area Community Foundation

Jefferson Bank Bldg.
124 S.W. Adams St., Mezzanine, Suite One
Peoria 61614 (309) 674-8730

Community foundation incorporated in 1987 in IL.

Foundation type: Community

Financial data (yr. ended 06/30/91): Assets, $729,711 (M); gifts received, $397,399; expenditures, $410,472; qualifying distributions, $326,087, including $326,087 for 34 grants (high: $13,000; low: $500).

Purpose and activities: Primary areas of interest include community development, the arts and humanities, education, and health.

Fields of interest: Community development, arts, cultural programs, humanities, health, leadership development, education, literacy, higher education, secondary education, welfare, family services, aged, environment, conservation.

Types of support: Scholarship funds, seed money, special projects, capital campaigns, operating budgets, equipment.

Limitations: Giving limited to the central IL, area. No support for sectarian religious purposes. No grants to individuals (except designated scholarship funds), or for annual campaigns or endowments; no loans.

Publications: Annual report (including application guidelines), application guidelines, newsletter, informational brochure.

Application information: Application form required.

Initial approach: Letter or telephone

Deadline(s): Feb. 1 and July 1 for preliminary application; Mar. 15 and Sept. 1 for final application

Board meeting date(s): Monthly
Final notification: Oct. and Apr.
Write: Donna Haerr, Exec. Dir.

Officers and Directors:* Duane Livingston, Pres.; Vicky Stewart,* V.P.; Jerold Horn,* Secy.; Warren Webber, Treas.; Donna Haerr, Exec. Dir.; Romaine Bayless, David Bielfeldt, Lewis Burger, David Connor, Taylor French, Edward Hoerr, Lynn Landes, Duane H. Livingston, Harriet Parkhurst, Edward Siebert, Thomas E. Spurgeon, Harriett P. Swager, William Tunis, Robert Viets, James Wogsland.

Number of staff: 1 full-time professional; 1 part-time professional.

EIN: 371185713

919
Kitty M. Perkins Foundation

208 South LaSalle St., Suite 1750
Chicago 60604 (312) 372-1947

Incorporated in 1966 in IL.

Donor(s): Kitty M. Perkins.‡

Foundation type: Independent

Financial data (yr. ended 12/31/90): Assets, $7,663,735 (M); expenditures, $364,620; qualifying distributions, $347,000, including $347,000 for 21 grants (high: $105,000; low: $1,000; average: $15,000).

Purpose and activities: Grants largely for a hospital and a law school; support also for higher education, rural libraries, medical research, and rural community hospitals.

Fields of interest: Hospitals, higher education, libraries, medical research.

Types of support: Annual campaigns, building funds, capital campaigns, continuing support, general purposes, operating budgets, professorships, research, special projects, equipment.

Limitations: Giving primarily in NE. No grants to individuals, or for matching gifts; no loans.

Application information: Contributes only to pre-selected organizations. Applications not accepted.

Board meeting date(s): As required
Write: Kent Lawrence, Treas.

Officers and Directors:* Don C. Shoemaker,* Pres.; William Shoemaker,* V.P.; George Franklin Shoemaker,* Secy.; Kent Lawrence,* Treas.; Kathryn Hertmann, Robert J. Lawrence, Honor Shoemaker, J. Richard Shoemaker, Ome C. Shoemaker.

Number of staff: None.

EIN: 366154399

920
Esper A. Petersen Foundation

1300 Skokie Hwy.
Gurnee 60031 (708) 336-0900

Incorporated in 1944 in IL.

Donor(s): Esper A. Petersen.‡

Foundation type: Independent

Financial data (yr. ended 12/31/90): Assets, $6,107,213 (M); expenditures, $420,919; qualifying distributions, $270,515, including $268,515 for 48 grants (high: $44,200; low: $75)

and $2,000 for 2 grants to individuals of $1,000 each.

Fields of interest: Handicapped, hospitals, child welfare, youth.

Types of support: General purposes, research, building funds.

Limitations: Giving primarily in IL and CA. No grants to individuals.

Publications: Application guidelines.

Application information: The foundation's scholarship program has been discontinued. Prior commitments will be paid. Application form required.

Initial approach: Letter
Deadline(s): Dec. 1
Board meeting date(s): July and Dec.
Final notification: Dec. 31
Write: Esper A. Petersen, Jr., Dir.

Directors: Daniel H. Foster, Stephen A. Malato, Ann Petersen Pam, Esper A. Petersen, Jr.

Number of staff: None.

EIN: 366125570

921
Pilot Foundation

321 North Clark St., Suite 340
Chicago 60610-4715

Established in 1964 in IL.

Donor(s): Harriet McClure Stuart,‡ Robert D. Stuart, Anne Stuart Batchelder, Margaret Stuart Hart, Harriet S. Spencer, Robert D. Stuart, Jr.

Foundation type: Independent

Financial data (yr. ended 06/30/90): Assets, $2,012,149 (M); gifts received, $516,267; expenditures, $103,391; qualifying distributions, $99,716, including $96,000 for 37 grants (high: $15,000; low: $500).

Fields of interest: Social services, family planning, community development, education, arts, history, religion, theological education, youth, international affairs.

Limitations: Giving primarily in IL. No grants to individuals.

Application information: Contributes only to pre-selected organizations. Applications not accepted.

Officers and Directors:* Robert D. Stuart, Jr.,* Pres.; Margaret Stuart Hart,* V.P. and Treas.; James J. McClure, Jr.,* Secy.

EIN: 366087653

922
Virginia G. Piper Foundation

Three First National Plaza, Suite 1950
Chicago 60602

Established in 1972 in IL.

Donor(s): Virginia G. Piper.

Foundation type: Independent

Financial data (yr. ended 12/31/90): Assets, $1,614,773 (M); expenditures, $407,400; qualifying distributions, $406,700, including $406,700 for 38 grants (high: $150,000; low: $250).

Purpose and activities: Support primarily for social services, the arts, including dance, higher education, hospitals and nursing programs; support also for Catholic churches and religious orders.

Fields of interest: Social services, arts, dance, higher education, hospitals, nursing, religion—Christian.
Limitations: Giving primarily in AZ and IL. No grants to individuals.
Application information: Contributes only to pre-selected organizations. Applications not accepted.
Officer and Directors:* Virginia G. Piper,* Pres.; Carol Critchfield, Raymond Harkrider.
EIN: 237230872

923

The Playboy Foundation
680 North Lake Dr.
Chicago 60611   (312) 751-8000

Financial data (yr. ended 06/30/90): Total giving, $372,575, including $166,275 for 32 grants (high: $5,000; low: $250; average: $3,500), $18,000 for 6 grants to individuals of $3,000 each, $8,300 for 96 employee matching gifts, $20,000 for 2 loans and $160,000 for 6 in-kind gifts.
Purpose and activities: The Playboy Foundation has two main areas of support: 1)innovative advocacy projects and organizations that are working in one of its priority categories. Current interests are in funding projects concerned with First Amendment freedoms; civil liberties and civil rights, including the rights of women, lesbians and gays; AIDS and reproductive rights. Support is earmarked for lobbying and litigating purposes for projects of national impact and scope. Grants are generally made for special projects or particular events, rather than for general operating support; most grants are under $10,000. In evaluating grants, the Foundation will take into consideration the extent to which organizations provide equality of opportunity with respect to staff employment and promotion, selection of board members, and service to clients. The Foundation also funds social change documentary film or videos in the distribution and/or post-production phase. Grants range from $500-$1,000. The $3,000 Hugh M. Hefner First Amendment Awards honor individuals who have made significant contributions in protecting and enhancing First Amendment rights. In 1990, the Foundation launched a newsletter, Perspectives, which highlights the company's public affairs. 2)The aim of the Neighborhood Relations Program is to enhance the quality of life in Chicago, Los Angeles, and New York (areas where employees reside). The Board is interested in innovative, community-based organizations that emerge from neighborhood residents' identification of needs that are inadequately addressed or recognized by conventional institutions. Support is for programs addressing the needs of traditionally disadvantaged people, including the poor, senior citizens, homeless, disabled, women, minorities, and children. Grants may be for advocacy/issue organizing around community reinvestment, municipal services, housing, education, the environment, race relations, or crime prevention; or social services concerned with employment/job training, day care, youth recreation, legal aid, food and shelter, or immigrant resettlement, or arts organizations and groups that are catalysts for positive social change. Grants do not exceed

$1,000, and preference is given to community-based organizations serving a particular neighborhood. Grants are for general operating support and specific projects. Grants for both programs are made on a year to year basis, and in special circumstances are renewable. The Foundation also provides printing services for grassroots organizations and public-service advertising.
Fields of interest: AIDS, civil rights, community development, disadvantaged, human rights, employment, family planning, minorities, women, law and justice, film, youth, gays and lesbians.
Types of support: Equipment, general purposes, loans, publications, seed money, special projects, technical assistance, operating budgets, in-kind gifts, grants to individuals.
Limitations: Giving limited to Chicago, IL, New York, NY, and Los Angeles, CA, for the Neighborhood Relations Program; civil liberties program operates on a national basis; no support for organizations concerned with issues outside the U.S. No support for religious purposes. No grants to individuals, except for First Amendment Awards, research/writing projects or individual scholarships, capital campaigns, endowments, or deficit financing; generally no support for conferences/symposia.
Publications: Corporate report, newsletter, application guidelines.
Application information: First Amendment awards by nomination only; Playboy has a staff that only handles contributions. Application form not required.
  Initial approach: Letter of inquiry; send to headquarters
  Copies of proposal: 1
  Deadline(s): Proposals accepted on an on-going basis
  Board meeting date(s): 3 times per year: spring, fall, and winter
  Write: Cleo Wilson, Exec. Dir.
Directors: Burton Joseph, Chair.; Christie Hefner, James Petersen, Robyn L. Radomski, Richard Rosenzweig, Howard Shapiro, Bruce Williamson, Steve Rechtschaffner.
Number of staff: 2 full-time professional.

924

Polk Bros. Foundation, Inc. ▼
420 North Wabash Ave., No. 204
Chicago 60611   (312) 527-4684

Incorporated in 1957 in IL.
Donor(s): David D. Polk,‡ Harry Polk,‡ Morris G. Polk,‡ Samuel H. Polk,‡ Sol Polk,‡ and members of the Polk family, Rand Realty and Development Co., Polk Bros., Inc.
Foundation type: Independent
Financial data (yr. ended 08/31/91): Assets, $141,801,505 (M); gifts received, $86,976,985; expenditures, $3,822,043; qualifying distributions, $3,540,386, including $3,165,457 for 403 grants (high: $100,000; low: $50; average: $5,000-$50,000) and $6,050 for 21 employee matching gifts.
Purpose and activities: Grants primarily for new or ongoing programs to organizations whose work is in the area of social service, education, arts and culture, and health care. Main emphasis

is support for organizations that serve populations of need in communities that are underserved.
Fields of interest: Arts, education, disadvantaged, health.
Types of support: Scholarship funds, technical assistance, equipment, student aid, continuing support, general purposes, special projects.
Limitations: Giving primarily in the Chicago, IL, area. No support for religious institutions seeking support for programs whose participants are restricted by religious affiliation; or tax generating entities (municipalities and school districts) for services within their normal responsibilities. No grants to individuals, or for medical, scientific or academic research; or purchase of dinner or raffle tickets.
Publications: Annual report, informational brochure.
Application information: Application form required.
  Initial approach: Letter
  Copies of proposal: 1
  Deadline(s): None
  Board meeting date(s): Feb., May, Aug., and Nov.
  Write: Nikki W. Stein, Exec. Dir., or Suzanne D. Kerbow, Assoc. Dir.
Officers and Directors:* Sandra P. Guthman,* Pres.; J. Ira Harris,* V.P.; Raymond F. Simon,* V.P.; Gordon Prussian,* Secy.; Sidney Epstein,* Treas.; Nikki W. Stein, Exec. Dir.; Roberta B. Lewis, Howard J. Polk.
Number of staff: 2 full-time professional; 1 full-time support.
EIN: 366108293

925

The Pontikes Family Foundation
c/o Comdisco, Inc.
6111 North River Rd.
Rosemont 60018

Established in 1986 in IL.
Donor(s): Kenneth N. Pontikes.
Foundation type: Independent
Financial data (yr. ended 06/30/90): Assets, $319,227 (M); gifts received, $583,680; expenditures, $345,874; qualifying distributions, $345,874, including $345,874 for 4 grants (high: $284,280; low: $2,369).
Fields of interest: Higher education, medical research, religion—Christian, conservation, general charitable giving.
Limitations: No grants to individuals.
Application information: Contributes only to pre-selected organizations. Applications not accepted.
Officers and Directors:* Kenneth N. Pontikes,* Pres. and Treas.; Nicholas K. Pontikes,* V.P.; Edward H. Fiedler, Jr., Secy.; Victoria Pontikes.
EIN: 363456975

926

Abra Prentice Foundation, Inc.
c/o The Northern Trust Co.
50 South LaSalle St.
Chicago 60675
Application address: c/o Alta Enterprises, 401 East Illinois, Suite 601, Chicago, IL 60611

Established in 1980 in IL.

Donor(s): Abra Prentice Wilkin.
Foundation type: Independent
Financial data (yr. ended 06/30/91): Assets, $4,864,787 (M); gifts received, $2,909; expenditures, $372,179; qualifying distributions, $341,758, including $340,000 for 7 grants (high: $250,000; low: $10,000).
Fields of interest: Secondary education, medical education.
Types of support: Building funds, general purposes.
Limitations: Giving primarily in Chicago, IL. No grants to individuals.
Application information: Application form not required.
  Deadline(s): None
Officers and Directors: Abra Prentice Wilkin,* Chair. and Pres.; William G. Demas,* Secy.-Treas.; Roy M. Adams, Jere Scott Zenko.
EIN: 363092281

927
Prince Charitable Trusts ▼
Ten South Wacker Dr., Suite 2575
Chicago 60606   (312) 454-9130

Frederick Henry Prince Trust dated July 9, 1947, Frederick Henry Prince Testamentary Trust and Abbie Norman Prince Trust established in 1947, 1947 and 1949 in IL respectively.
Foundation type: Independent
Financial data (yr. ended 12/31/91): Assets, $104,000,000 (M); expenditures, $5,000,000; qualifying distributions, $4,736,100, including $4,736,100 for 332 grants (high: $200,000; low: $230; average: $5,000-$25,000).
Purpose and activities: Support for cultural programs, public school programming, youth organizations, social services, hospitals, hospital morale, rehabilitation, and environment.
Fields of interest: Ecology, environment, arts, cultural programs, hospitals, health, education, education—minorities, elementary education, higher education, secondary education, disadvantaged, social services, housing, rehabilitation, youth, child welfare, family services.
Types of support: Capital campaigns, continuing support, general purposes, seed money, special projects, technical assistance, endowment funds.
Limitations: Giving limited to Washington, DC, Chicago, IL, and RI. No grants to individuals.
Publications: Application guidelines.
Application information: Application form not required.
  Initial approach: Letter or proposal
  Copies of proposal: 1
  Deadline(s): Determined by meeting schedule
  Board meeting date(s): Board meets a minimum of 6 times per year; schedule to be determined annually
  Write: Tracey Shafroth, Prog. Dir., or Jill Darrow, Prog. Officer
Trustees: Frederick Henry Prince IV, William Norman Wood Prince, William Wood Prince.
Number of staff: 1 full-time professional; 1 part-time professional.
Recent health grants:
927-1 Campaign for Better Health Care, Champaign, IL, $10,000. 1991.
927-2 Cook County Hospital, Chicago, IL, $30,000. 1991.

927-3 District of Columbia Institute for Mental Health, DC, $20,000. 1991.
927-4 Evanston Hospital, Evanston, IL, $58,000. 1991.
927-5 Evanston Hospital, Evanston, IL, $50,587. 1991.
927-6 Health and Medicine Policy Research Group, Chicago, IL, $10,000. 1991.
927-7 La Rabida Childrens Hospital and Research Center, Chicago, IL, $10,000. 1991.
927-8 Lawndale Christian Health Center, Chicago, IL, $25,000. 1991.
927-9 National Center for the Study of Wilsons Disease, Bronx, NY, $25,000. 1991.
927-10 Northwestern Memorial Foundation, Chicago, IL, $50,000. 1991.
927-11 Northwestern Memorial Foundation, Chicago, IL, $20,000. 1991.
927-12 Northwestern Memorial Hospital, Chicago, IL, $15,025. 1991.
927-13 Planned Parenthood Association of Chicago, Chicago, IL, $10,000. 1991.
927-14 Rehabilitation Institute of Chicago, Chicago, IL, $100,000. 1991.
927-15 Rehabilitation Institute of Chicago, Chicago, IL, $78,735. 1991.
927-16 Rehabilitation Institute of Chicago, Chicago, IL, $67,500. 1991.
927-17 Rehabilitation Institute of Chicago, Chicago, IL, $50,000. 1991.
927-18 Rehabilitation Institute of Chicago, Chicago, IL, $21,265. 1991.
927-19 Rhode Island Rape Crisis Center, Providence, RI, $10,000. 1991.
927-20 Saint Basils Health Service, Chicago, IL, $10,000. 1991.

928
Pritzker Foundation ▼
200 West Madison St., 38th Fl.
Chicago 60606   (312) 621-4200

Incorporated in 1944 in IL.
Donor(s): Members of the Pritzker family.
Foundation type: Independent
Financial data (yr. ended 12/31/90): Assets, $51,182,590 (M); gifts received, $1,913,271; expenditures, $10,289,290; qualifying distributions, $10,058,631, including $10,033,114 for 230 grants (high: $7,600,000; low: $25; average: $100-$25,000).
Purpose and activities: Grants largely for higher education, including medical education, and religious welfare funds; giving also for hospitals, temple support, and cultural programs.
Fields of interest: Higher education, medical education, religious welfare, hospitals, Jewish giving, cultural programs.
Limitations: No grants to individuals.
Application information: Contributes only to pre-selected organizations. Applications not accepted.
  Board meeting date(s): Dec. and as required
  Write: Simon Zunamon, Asst. Treas.
Officers and Directors: Robert A. Pritzker,* Chair. and V.P.; Jay A. Pritzker,* Pres.; Nicholas J. Pritzker,* V.P. and Secy.; Thomas J. Pritzker,* V.P. and Treas.; Daniel F. Pritzker,* V.P.; James N. Pritzker,* V.P.; John A. Pritzker,* V.P.; Penny F. Pritzker,* V.P.
Number of staff: None.
EIN: 366058062

929
The Quaker Oats Company Giving Program
P.O. Box 9001
Chicago 60604-9001   (312) 222-7111

Purpose and activities: Funding for education, health, and hunger. In addition to cash grants by headquarters and divisions, types of support include volunteer and "in-kind" support. Donations of food are made to selected organizations in communities in which Quaker operates and in which its employees are involved as volunteers. The majority of food products are made to Second Harvest, a network of more than 70 food banks across the country. The "loaned executive" program allows employees and retirees to donate their time to worthy nonprofit organizations.
Fields of interest: Education, health, hunger, volunteerism.
Types of support: In-kind gifts, loaned talent.
Limitations: Giving primarily in operating areas. No support for religious organizations or politics. No grants to individuals or for advertising.
Application information:
  Initial approach: Letter
  Deadline(s): None
  Write: Charles Curry, Mgr., Community Affairs and Asst. Secy.
Administrators: Charles Curry, Mgr., Community Affairs and Asst. Secy.; W. Thomas Phillips, V.P., Corp. Progs.

930
The Quaker Oats Foundation ▼
Quaker Tower
321 North Clark St.
Chicago 60610   (312) 222-7033

Incorporated in 1947 in IL.
Donor(s): The Quaker Oats Co.
Foundation type: Company-sponsored
Financial data (yr. ended 06/30/90): Assets, $4,188,320 (M); gifts received, $2,042,800; expenditures, $3,211,991; qualifying distributions, $3,173,125, including $1,694,254 for 515 grants (high: $140,000; low: $83; average: $2,000-$4,000) and $1,336,063 for 4,078 employee matching gifts.
Purpose and activities: Emphasis on higher education, including scholarships and an employee matching gift program, and guaranteeing of loans through United Student Aid Funds (USAF); civic affairs, social services, community funds, youth agencies, arts and culture, hospitals, and public policy.
Fields of interest: Social services, higher education, civic affairs, community funds, youth, hospitals, arts, cultural programs, economics, government.
Types of support: General purposes, building funds, equipment, land acquisition, internships, scholarship funds, employee-related scholarships, fellowships, employee matching gifts, operating budgets, special projects, matching funds, annual campaigns, publications, conferences and seminars, continuing support, renovation projects.
Limitations: Giving primarily in areas of company operations, particularly IL. No support for religious organizations. No grants to individuals

(except employee-related scholarships), or for advertising; no loans, except for USAF program.
Publications: Corporate giving report (including application guidelines), program policy statement.
Application information: Application form not required.
Initial approach: Letter or telephone
Copies of proposal: 1
Deadline(s): None
Board meeting date(s): Sept., Dec., Mar., and June
Final notification: 6 to 8 weeks
Write: W. Thomas Phillips, Secy.
Officers and Directors:* William D. Smithburg,* Chair.; Frank J. Morgan,* Pres.; Luther C. McKinney,* V.P.; W. Thomas Phillips, Secy.; Richard D. Jaquith, Treas.; Weston R. Christopherson, William J. Kennedy III, Donald E. Meads, Gertrude G. Michelson, William L. Weiss.
Number of staff: 2 full-time professional; 3 full-time support; 1 part-time support.
EIN: 366084548

931
R.F. Foundation
One First National Plaza, Rm. 4700
Chicago 60603

Incorporated in 1953 in IL.
Donor(s): Thomas H. Roberts, Thomas H. Roberts, Jr., Eleanor T. Roberts, Mary R. Roberts.
Foundation type: Independent
Financial data (yr. ended 12/31/90): Assets, $6,113,384 (M); expenditures, $298,009; qualifying distributions, $270,207, including $270,000 for 33 grants (high: $55,000; low: $500; average: $8,000-$50,000).
Fields of interest: Education, higher education, international development, international relief, social services, hospitals, handicapped, health services, community funds.
Types of support: Operating budgets, continuing support, annual campaigns, building funds, equipment.
Limitations: Giving limited to the Chicago and DeKalb County, IL, area. No grants to individuals, or for seed money, emergency funds, deficit financing, land acquisition, renovations, endowment funds, matching gifts, scholarships, fellowships, special projects, research, publications, or conferences; no loans.
Application information: Application form not required.
Initial approach: Proposal
Copies of proposal: 1
Deadline(s): None
Board meeting date(s): Sept. and Oct.
Final notification: By Dec. 31
Write: H. Blair White, Pres.
Officers and Directors:* H. Blair White,* Pres.; Mary R. Roberts,* V.P.; Charles S. Roberts,* Secy.-Treas.; Thomas H. Roberts, Jr.,* Treas.
Number of staff: None.
EIN: 366069098

932
James M. Ragen, Jr. Memorial Fund Trust No. 1.
c/o Michigan Avenue National Bank of Chicago
30 North Michigan Ave.
Chicago 60602-3402   (312) 641-1000

Established in 1973 in IL.
Foundation type: Independent
Financial data (yr. ended 12/31/90): Assets, $2,328,161 (M); expenditures, $176,255; qualifying distributions, $144,000, including $144,000 for 24 grants (high: $21,000; low: $2,000).
Fields of interest: Hospitals, social services, secondary education, higher education, religion—Christian, Catholic giving, disadvantaged.
Limitations: Giving primarily in CA and IL. No grants to individuals.
Application information: Application form required.
Initial approach: Letter
Copies of proposal: 1
Deadline(s): Dec. 31
Write: Donald R. Bonistalli, V.P. and Trust Officer, Michigan Avenue National Bank of Chicago
Advisory Board: Therse Ragen, Thomas Ragen, William Ragen, Patricia Schaefer, Gerald Trodell.
Trustee: Michigan Avenue National Bank of Chicago.
Number of staff: None.
EIN: 237444822

933
Redhill Foundation - Samuel & Jean Rothberg Family Charitable Trust
700 Commercial National Bank Bldg.
Peoria 61602-1641

Established in 1987 in IL.
Donor(s): Samuel Rothberg, Lee Patrick Rothberg.
Foundation type: Independent
Financial data (yr. ended 12/31/90): Assets, $1,213,392 (M); gifts received, $425,813; expenditures, $248,665; qualifying distributions, $247,081, including $246,500 for grants.
Purpose and activities: Giving primarily for higher education, including a Hebrew university; support also for Jewish giving and hospitals and medical research.
Fields of interest: Higher education, Jewish giving, hospitals, medical research.
Types of support: Scholarship funds, general purposes, research.
Limitations: Giving primarily in IL and NY.
Trustees: Kathleen M. Barnett, Heidi B. Munday, Jean C. Rothberg, Lee Patrick Rothberg, Michael Rothberg, Samuel Rothberg.
EIN: 371217165

934
The Regenstein Foundation ▼
8600 West Bryn Mawr Ave., Suite 705N
Chicago 60631   (312) 693-6464

Incorporated in 1950 in IL.
Donor(s): Joseph Regenstein,‡ Helen Regenstein.‡
Foundation type: Independent
Financial data (yr. ended 12/31/91): Assets, $97,021,828 (M); expenditures, $3,980,518; qualifying distributions, $2,480,583, including $2,480,583 for 41 grants (high: $600,000; low: $500; average: $5,000-$300,000).
Purpose and activities: Giving primarily for music, art, higher and early childhood education, and medical research.

Fields of interest: Music, arts, medical research, education—early childhood, educational research, medical education.
Types of support: Building funds, equipment, research, endowment funds, special projects, renovation projects, capital campaigns.
Limitations: Giving primarily in the Chicago, IL, metropolitan area. No grants to individuals, or for scholarships, fellowships, annual campaigns, seed money, emergency funds, deficit financing, land acquisition, publications, conferences, matching gifts, or operating support; no loans.
Publications: Program policy statement, application guidelines.
Application information: Most grants made on the initiative of the directors. Application form not required.
Initial approach: Letter
Copies of proposal: 1
Deadline(s): None
Board meeting date(s): May and as required
Final notification: 30 days
Write: Joseph Regenstein, Jr., Pres.
Officers and Directors:* Joseph Regenstein, Jr.,* Pres.; Betty R. Hartman,* V.P.; Robert A. Mecca, V.P.; John Eggum,* Secy.-Treas.
Number of staff: 3 full-time professional; 1 part-time support.
EIN: 363152531

935
Relations Foundation
927 Fischer Ln.
Winnetka 60093   (708) 446-4211

Established in 1969 in IL.
Foundation type: Independent
Financial data (yr. ended 12/31/90): Assets, $3,219,958 (M); gifts received, $100,000; expenditures, $551,992; qualifying distributions, $548,095, including $547,982 for 178 grants (high: $68,000; low: $159).
Purpose and activities: Giving primarily to Jewish welfare funds; support also for medical research and social service agencies.
Fields of interest: Jewish welfare, social services, medical research.
Types of support: Operating budgets, research.
Limitations: Giving primarily in the Chicago, IL, area. No grants to individuals, or for endowment funds; no loans.
Publications: Application guidelines.
Application information: Application form not required.
Initial approach: Letter
Copies of proposal: 1
Deadline(s): None
Board meeting date(s): Apr., July, and Nov.
Officers and Directors:* Joseph Radov,* Pres.; Dennis L. Kessler,* V.P.; Sylvia M. Radov,* V.P.; Carol Weinberg,* V.P.; Daniel C. Weinberg,* V.P.; Barbara Kessler,* Secy.; David A. Weinberg,* Treas.
EIN: 237032294

936
Luther I. Replogle Foundation
5744 South Blackstone Ave.
Chicago 60637-1824
Application address: 726 Fifth St. N.E.,
Washington, DC 20002-4320; Tel.: (202)
544-2355

Established in 1966.
Foundation type: Independent
Financial data (yr. ended 12/31/90): Assets,
$7,704,070 (M); expenditures, $387,437;
qualifying distributions, $306,447, including
$274,990 for 76 grants (high: $67,000; low:
$200; average: $500-$5,000).
Purpose and activities: The areas in which the
foundation is interested include the following: 1)
Education - particularly the special needs of the
inner-city; 2) Culture - with an emphasis on
institutions serving Chicago; 3) Religion - to
strengthen church work in disadvantaged
communities and improve theological education;
4) Health - especially institutions in the area of
Chicago; 5) U.S. Department of State - rewarding
individuals who through their managerial ability
have contributed to the effective running of the
Department and its programs; 6) Classical
Archaeology; and 7) Social Services - with an
emphasis on programs that enable individuals to
help themselves, whether needy senior citizens or
the disadvantaged young.
Fields of interest: Education, humanities, arts,
archaeology, religion—Christian, family planning,
social services.
Types of support: Scholarship funds, continuing
support, matching funds, operating budgets,
special projects.
Limitations: Giving primarily in Chicago, IL.
Generally no support for nationally-affiliated
organizations. No grants to individuals (except for
the Luther I. Replogle Award).
Publications: Program policy statement.
Application information: Luther I. Replogle Award
for Management Improvement recipients selected
by U.S. Dept. of State. Application form not
required.
  Initial approach: Letter
  Copies of proposal: 1
  Deadline(s): None
  Board meeting date(s): Spring and fall (usually
    Apr. and Oct.)
  Write: Ms. Gwenn Gebhard, Exec. Dir.
Officers: Elizabeth R. Dickie, Pres. and Treas.;
James D. Hinchliff, V.P.; William O. Petersen,
Secy.; Gwenn H.S. Gebhard, Exec. Dir.
Number of staff: 1 part-time professional.
EIN: 366141697

937
The Retirement Research Foundation ▼
8765 West Higgins Rd., Suite 401
Chicago 60631   (312) 714-8080
FAX: (312) 714-8089

Incorporated in 1950 in MI.
Donor(s): John D. MacArthur.‡
Foundation type: Independent
Financial data (yr. ended 12/31/90): Assets,
$115,079,417 (M); expenditures, $6,321,716;
qualifying distributions, $6,113,212, including
$5,593,574 for 131 grants (high: $400,000; low:
$500; average: $30,000-$35,000), $28,000 for 13

grants to individuals (high: $5,000; low: $500;
average: $500-$5,000), $91,638 for 100
employee matching gifts and $400,000 for
foundation-administered programs.
Purpose and activities: Support principally to
improve the quality of life of older persons in the
U.S. Priority interests are innovative model
projects and research designed to: 1)increase the
availability and effectiveness of community
programs to maintain older persons in
independent living environments; 2)improve the
quality of nursing home care; 3)provide volunteer
and employment opportunities for the elderly;
and 4)seek causes and solutions to significant
problems of the aged.
Fields of interest: Aged, health services, health,
mental health, medical research, public policy,
employment, social services, social sciences,
homeless.
Types of support: Seed money, matching funds,
research, special projects, employee matching
gifts, program-related investments.
Limitations: Giving limited to the Midwest (IL, IN,
IA, KY, MI, MO, WI) and FL for service projects
not having the potential of national impact. No
grants to individuals (except through National
Media Awards Program), or for construction,
general operating expenses of established
organizations, endowment or developmental
campaigns, emergency funds, deficit financing,
land acquisition, publications, conferences,
scholarships, media productions, dissertation
research, annual campaigns, or renovation
projects.
Publications: Program policy statement,
application guidelines, occasional report,
multi-year report (including application
guidelines), grants list, informational brochure
(including application guidelines), annual report.
Application information: All proposals must
relate to aged population. Application form not
required.
  Initial approach: Letter or proposal
  Copies of proposal: 3
  Deadline(s): Submit proposal preferably in Jan.,
    Apr., or July; deadlines Feb. 1, May 1, and
    Aug. 1
  Board meeting date(s): Jan., Apr., July, and Oct.
  Final notification: 4 to 6 months
  Write: Marilyn Hennessy, Sr. V.P.
Officers and Trustees:* Edward J. Kelly,* Chair.;
Joe L. Parkin,* Pres.; Marilyn Hennessy, Sr. V.P.;
Brian F. Hofland, V.P.; Robert P. Ewing,* Secy.;
Floyd Caldini, Treas.; Duane Chapman, Nathaniel
McPaland, M.D., Marvin Meyerson, John F.
Santos, Ph.D., Sister Stella Louise, C.S.F.N.,
George E. Weaver.
Number of staff: 3 full-time professional; 2
part-time professional; 3 full-time support; 1
part-time support.
EIN: 362429540
Recent health grants:
937-1 Alliance for Aging Research, DC, $25,000.
To support programs and work to advance
research on human aging process. 1991.
937-2 American Bar Association, DC, $23,873.
To develop resource guide and provide
technical support to states to improve clarity,
comprehensiveness and comparability of state
descriptions of law required under Patient Self
Determination Act concerning health care
decision-making and advance directives. 1991.

937-3 Bethel New Life, Chicago, IL, $20,000.
Toward construction of 23-unit residential
facility with adult day health care center
attached. 1991.
937-4 Better Government Association, Chicago,
IL, $75,000. To update consumers guide to
long-term care facilities annually for next three
years. 1991.
937-5 Bon Secours Hospital-Villa Maria Nursing
Center, North Miami, FL, $37,100. For
expansion of community/parish based
outreach program to low-income frail elderly.
1991.
937-6 Catholic Health Alliance of Chicago,
Chicago, IL, $14,300. For Handy Home
Helpers Handyman, home repair and
housekeeping services for seniors and disabled
individuals. 1991.
937-7 Catholic Health Association of the United
States, Saint Louis, MO, $46,260. To develop
and disseminate resources to health care
providers to assist in education of employees,
medical staff, patients/clients/residents, families
and general public regarding advance
directives. 1991.
937-8 Champaign County Health Care
Consumers, Champaign, IL, $30,127. To
support model program to educate senior
citizens about potential hazards associated
with use of prescription drugs and to mobilize
community resources around issue. 1991.
937-9 Chicago Council of Lawyers, Fund for
Justice, Chicago, IL, $24,950. To evaluate
enforcement system employed by Illinois
Department of Public Health regarding
Chicago area nursing homes. 1991.
937-10 Chicago Osteopathic Health Systems,
Chicago, IL, $25,000. For 1991 ENCORE
Award for Geri-Wheels Program. 1991.
937-11 Coalition of Advocates for the Rights of
the Infirm Elderly, Philadelphia, PA, $25,000.
For continued support of project to develop,
conduct and evaluate patient abuse prevention
training program for nursing assistants. 1991.
937-12 Community Renewal Society, Chicago,
IL, $11,500. Toward research and writing of
book on sick and poor, examination of health
care policy through eyes of the poor. 1991.
937-13 Des Plaines Valley Health Center, Argo,
IL, $25,000. For 1991 ENCORE Award for
Healthy Aging Program. 1991.
937-14 George Washington University, DC,
$23,524. To evaluate state laws that each state
is required to develop under Patient
Self-Determination Act, federal law requiring
hospitals to advise all patients on admission of
advance directives. 1991.
937-15 Georgetown University, DC, $293,653.
For research examining potential for reform of
income and health care policy toward elderly.
1991.
937-16 Hillhaven Foundation, Tacoma, WA,
$94,050. To replicate Project One-Age,
recruiting and placing older nurses in
long-term care facilities in central Illinois.
1991.
937-17 Illinois State Council of Senior Citizens
Foundation, Chicago, IL, $30,000. For
outreach campaign aimed at enrolling eligible
seniors for benefits under Illinois' underutilized
Qualified Medicare Beneficiary Program. 1991.
937-18 Little Company of Mary Hospital,
Evergreen Park, IL, $50,000. To continue

development of mobile medical care program for homebound seniors. 1991.

937-19 Loyola University Medical Center, Maywood, IL, $49,975. For research to synthesize and test series of promising chemical variants of naturally occuring substance Huperzine-A (Hup-A) as potential agents for treatment of Alzheimer's disease. 1991.

937-20 Lutheran Social Services of Illinois, Des Plaines, IL, $218,632. To develop knowledge and skills to meet demands of managed care, to initiate home health services in pilot sites, and to replicate private case management model in seven areas of Illinois. 1991.

937-21 Mental Health Law Project, DC, $75,000. For project promoting development of community-based alternatives for elderly nursing home and hospital residents and protecting elders with mental disabilities. 1991.

937-22 Mercy Hospital and Medical Center, Chicago, IL, $15,000. To develop community outreach program to provide health care services to homebound elderly. 1991.

937-23 National Chronic Care Consortium, Bloomington, MN, $285,340. For model project which will bridge gap between acute and long term care by establishing providers based managed care systems through local networks of geriatric care. 1991.

937-24 National Citizens Coalition for Nursing Home Reform, DC, $73,575. For efforts to reduce use of physical and chemical restraints on nursing home residents through expansion and improvement of information, referral and technical assistance services to public. 1991.

937-25 National Osteoporosis Foundation, DC, $297,120. To expand scope and quality of osteoporosis education nationwide through education of physicians, nurses and physical therapists. 1991.

937-26 National Senior Citizens Law Center, DC, $118,600. To examine implementation of 1987 Federal Nursing Home Reform Law and to disseminate information about strategies for successful implementation. 1991.

937-27 Northern Lakes Health Care Consortium, Duluth, MN, $66,000. For consortium of nursing homes in Northeast Minnesota to plan and implement continuous quality improvement programs in their individual facilities. 1991.

937-28 Northwestern University, Evanston, IL, $99,454. For research examining self-perceived hearing handicap, intellectual function and personality as they relate to perceived control and competence in aging adults who do and do not follow professional advice in management of hearing loss. 1991.

937-29 Rockefeller University, NYC, NY, $31,573. For research examining mechanism by which high-density lipoprotein and its major apoprotein seem to protect against heart disease in middle-aged individuals. 1991.

937-30 Umoja Care, Chicago, IL, $135,000. For year three of long term care demonstration project. 1991.

937-31 United Methodist Homes and Services, Chicago, IL, $25,000. For 1991 ENCORE Award for Community Health Center for Senior Adults. 1991.

937-32 United Seniors Health Cooperative, DC, $98,670. To develop and provide older

persons with practical, consumer-tested information about how individuals can maximize personal autonomy when they need help at home. 1991.

937-33 University of California, Berkeley, CA, $13,222. For research on grandparents raising children of crack cocaine epidemic. 1991.

937-34 University of Michigan, Ann Arbor, MI, $19,113. For research to identify attributes and characteristics of home environment that can be effectively transferred to institutional environment. 1991.

937-35 University of Notre Dame, Notre Dame, IN, $17,000. For survey about current availability and level of support for gerontological and geriatric specialization within core health and mental health professions. 1991.

937-36 University of Pittsburgh, Pittsburgh, PA, $106,402. For research to document nature and context of disruptive vocalizations of nursing home residents and to assess effectiveness of three different behavior interventions in decreasing frequency and duration of vocalizations. 1991.

937-37 University of Wisconsin, Madison, WI, $19,500. For research examining long term effects on rhesus monkeys in late life from exposure earlier in life to environmental toxin, TCDD, dioxin. 1991.

937-38 University of Wisconsin, Milwaukee, WI, $26,146. For work with ten project directors of new National Institute on Aging research initiative on nursing home special care units for people with dementia. 1991.

937-39 Washington University, Saint Louis, MO, $50,000. For training of two graduate students in clinical psychology of aging program. 1991.

937-40 White Crane Senior Health Center, Chicago, IL, $30,000. To upgrade facility to allow for program expansion and to support only full-time staff. 1991.

937-41 Wright State University, Dayton, OH, $58,990. To identify and examine actual and perceived barriers to more widespread use of less intrusive alternatives for formal legal guardianship or conservatorship for older adults with mental impairments. 1991.

937-42 Yale University, New Haven, CT, $150,000. For research investigating delirium in hospitalized elderly, occurrence, risk factors and adverse outcomes. 1991.

937-43 YMCA, Greater Lake County Family, Waukegan, IL, $25,000. For Stroke Rehabilitation Program. 1991.

938
Otto L. and Hazel T. Rhoades Fund

c/o Julius Lewis
8000 Sears Tower
Chicago 60606   (312) 876-8033

Established in 1978.
Donor(s): Otto L. Rhoades.
Foundation type: Independent
Financial data (yr. ended 12/31/90): Assets, $2,234,576 (M); expenditures, $147,470; qualifying distributions, $123,000, including $123,000 for 20 grants (high: $20,000; low: $1,000).

Fields of interest: Religion—Christian, rehabilitation, handicapped, health, social services.
Limitations: Giving primarily in IL.
Officers and Directors:* Hazel T. Rhoades, Pres.; Julius Lewis,* V.P. and Treas.; H. Allan Stark.
EIN: 362994856

939
Rice Foundation ▼

222 Waukegan Rd.
Glenview 60025   (708) 998-6666

Incorporated in 1947 in IL.
Donor(s): Daniel F. Rice,‡ Ada Rice,‡ and others.
Foundation type: Independent
Financial data (yr. ended 12/31/90): Assets, $78,670,372 (M); gifts received, $1,000; expenditures, $5,128,804; qualifying distributions, $4,620,662, including $4,209,587 for 50 grants (high: $1,501,837; low: $250; average: $5,000-$40,000).
Purpose and activities: Emphasis on higher education, including medical education, hospitals, and youth agencies.
Fields of interest: Higher education, medical education, hospitals, youth, civic affairs.
Types of support: General purposes.
Limitations: Giving primarily in IL. No grants to individuals.
Application information:
  Initial approach: Proposal
  Deadline(s): None
  Write: Arthur A. Nolan, Jr., Pres.
Officers and Directors:* Arthur A. Nolan, Jr.,* Pres.; Patricia G. Nolan,* V.P. and Treas.; James P. Doherty, Jr.,* Secy.; Marilyn Alsdorf, Donald M. Graham, David P. Winchester, Barbara M.J. Wood.
EIN: 366043160
Recent health grants:
939-1 Arthritis Foundation, Chicago, IL, $20,000. 1990.
939-2 Cystic Fibrosis Foundation, Chicago, IL, $10,000. 1990.
939-3 Five Hospital Homebound Elderly Program, Women's Board, Chicago, IL, $20,000. 1990.
939-4 Little Company of Mary Hospital, Evergreen Park, IL, $15,000. 1990.
939-5 Mercy Hospital and Medical Center, Chicago, IL, $10,000. 1990.
939-6 Rehabilitation Institute of Chicago, Chicago, IL, $100,000. 1990.
939-7 South Shore Hospital, Chicago, IL, $10,000. 1990.
939-8 University of Chicago Medical Center, Chicago, IL, $50,000. 1990.

940
Hulda B. & Maurice L. Rothschild Foundation

c/o First National Bank of Chicago
One First National Plaza, Suite 0101
Chicago 60670-0101   (312) 732-6473
FAX: (312) 732-1649

Established in 1981 in IL.
Donor(s): Hulda B. Rothschild.‡
Foundation type: Independent
Financial data (yr. ended 12/31/91): Assets, $8,320,200 (M); expenditures, $372,363;

qualifying distributions, $298,776, including $291,586 for 14 grants (high: $81,323; low: $1,100; average: $5,000-$10,000).

Purpose and activities: "Giving primarily toward improving the quality of life for older adults in the Chicago metropolitan area; the foundation is particularly interested in innovative projects which develop and/or demonstrate new approaches and creative solutions to the problems of older adults and which have the potential for significant impact."

Fields of interest: Aged, health services, medical sciences, arts, cultural programs.

Types of support: Publications, seed money, special projects, research.

Limitations: Giving primarily in the Chicago, IL, metropolitan area. No support for projects outside the U.S. No grants to individuals, or for general purposes, construction, operating budgets, endowment or development campaigns, or scholarships; no loans.

Publications: Application guidelines.

Application information: Priority given to organizations which have clear objectives, well-defined outcomes or impact, and cost effective approaches. Application form not required.

  Initial approach: Letter
  Copies of proposal: 1
  Deadline(s): None
  Final notification: 30 to 40 days
  Write: Donald A. Kress, V.P., First National Bank of Chicago

Officer and Trustees:* Robert N. Mayer,* Pres.; Beatrice Mayer, First National Bank of Chicago.

Number of staff: None.

EIN: 366752787

941
Tom Russell Charitable Foundation, Inc.
1315 West 22nd St., Suite 300
Oak Brook 60521

Incorporated in 1960 in IL.

Donor(s): Thomas C. Russell,‡ Wrap-On Co., Inc., Huron & Orleans Building Corp.

Foundation type: Independent

Financial data (yr. ended 08/31/90): Assets, $9,522,514 (M); expenditures, $589,844; qualifying distributions, $453,543, including $440,000 for 55 grants (high: $20,000; low: $1,000).

Purpose and activities: "To help people to help themselves"; emphasis on higher education; support also for hospitals, health and social service agencies, and youth programs.

Fields of interest: Higher education, education, hospitals, health associations, health services, cancer, social services, youth, Catholic welfare.

Limitations: Giving limited to the metropolitan Chicago, IL, area. No grants to individuals.

Publications: Application guidelines.

Application information: Application form not required.

  Initial approach: Proposal
  Copies of proposal: 1
  Board meeting date(s): Grants are generally made in July and Aug.
  Write: Leslie R. Bishop, Secy.

Officers and Directors:* J. Tod Meserow,* Pres.; Thomas A. Hearn,* V.P.; Leslie R. Bishop,* Secy.; John Linquist.

EIN: 366082517

942
Patrick G. & Shirley W. Ryan Foundation
123 North Wacker Dr., Suite 1190
Chicago 60606

Established in 1984 in IL.

Donor(s): Ryan Holding Corp. of Illinois, Ryan Enterprises Corp., Patrick G. Ryan, Shirley W. Ryan.

Foundation type: Independent

Financial data (yr. ended 11/30/90): Assets, $9,314 (M); gifts received, $516,500; expenditures, $516,723; qualifying distributions, $515,958, including $515,903 for 40 grants (high: $100,000; low: $141).

Fields of interest: Education, higher education, international affairs, cultural programs, social services, health.

Limitations: Giving primarily in IL. No grants to individuals.

Application information: Contributes only to pre-selected organizations. Applications not accepted.

Officers and Directors:* Shirley W. Ryan,* Pres.; Patrick G. Ryan,* V.P.; Glen E. Hess,* Secy.

EIN: 363305162

943
Alyce F. Salerno Charitable Foundation
c/o Harris Trust & Savings Bank
111 West Monroe St.
Chicago 60603
Application address: c/o Harris Trust & Savings Bank, P.O. Box 755, Chicago, IL 60690; Tel.: (312) 461-2609

Established in 1985 in IL.

Donor(s): Alyce F. Salerno Trust.

Foundation type: Independent

Financial data (yr. ended 12/31/90): Assets, $828,087 (M); expenditures, $466,722; qualifying distributions, $464,963, including $445,000 for 8 grants (high: $100,000; low: $5,000).

Purpose and activities: Grants primarily for hospitals and a college.

Fields of interest: Hospitals, arts, higher education.

Limitations: Giving primarily in IL. No support for fraternal or religious organizations. No grants to individuals.

Application information: Application form required.

  Initial approach: Letter or telephone
  Deadline(s): None
  Write: Ronald F. Tuite, Jr.

Trustees: Marian A. Hodgkinson, Maxine Hovereid, Harris Trust & Savings Bank.

EIN: 363353261

944
Salwil Foundation
400 Skokie Blvd., Suite 675
Northbrook 60062

Established in 1985 in IL.

Donor(s): William L. Searle.

Foundation type: Independent

Financial data (yr. ended 12/31/91): Assets, $2,246,496 (M); expenditures, $106,604;

---

qualifying distributions, $105,609, including $105,609 for 18 grants (high: $17,122; low: $1,000).

Fields of interest: Education, wildlife, environment, hospitals, cultural programs.

Types of support: Annual campaigns, capital campaigns, general purposes.

Limitations: No grants to individuals.

Application information: Contributes only to pre-selected organizations. Applications not accepted.

  Write: William L. Searle, Pres.

Officers: William L. Searle, Pres.; Sally B. Searle, V.P. and Secy.-Treas.

Director: Marianne L. Pohle.

EIN: 363377945

945
Elsie O. and Philip D. Sang Foundation
180 East Pearson St., Apt. 5805
Chicago 60611

Established in 1954.

Foundation type: Independent

Financial data (yr. ended 10/31/90): Assets, $2,756,264 (M); expenditures, $306,855; qualifying distributions, $305,005, including $302,000 for 37 grants (high: $150,000; low: $100).

Purpose and activities: Grants primarily for Jewish welfare funds; support also for hospitals and higher education.

Fields of interest: Jewish welfare, hospitals, higher education.

Limitations: Giving primarily in Chicago, IL. No grants to individuals.

Application information: Application form not required.

  Initial approach: Letter
  Deadline(s): None
  Board meeting date(s): As required
  Write: Elsie O. Sang, Pres.

Officers: Elsie O. Sang, Pres.; Bernard Sang, Secy.

Number of staff: None.

EIN: 366214200

946
Robert E. Schneider Foundation
150 East Ontario St.
Chicago 60611-2809

Established in 1968 in IL.

Donor(s): Phyllis Schneider, Melvin Schneider.

Foundation type: Independent

Financial data (yr. ended 12/31/90): Assets, $2,398,505 (M); expenditures, $136,406; qualifying distributions, $129,815, including $129,815 for grants.

Purpose and activities: Primary giving for cleft lip and palate research; support also for a hospital.

Fields of interest: Medical research, hospitals, higher education.

Limitations: No grants to individuals.

Application information: Contributes only to pre-selected organizations. Applications not accepted.

Officers and Directors:* Melvin Schneider,* Pres.; Phyllis Schneider,* Secy.-Treas.; Frederic Schneider, Richard Schneider.

EIN: 366212061

947
Dr. Scholl Foundation ▼
11 South LaSalle St., Suite 2100
Chicago 60603   (312) 782-5210

Incorporated in 1947 in IL.
Donor(s): William M. Scholl, M.D.‡
Foundation type: Independent
Financial data (yr. ended 12/31/90): Assets, $112,379,267 (M); expenditures, $8,991,500; qualifying distributions, $7,980,939, including $7,640,285 for 366 grants (high: $200,000; low: $1,000; average: $10,000-$50,000) and $101,250 for 23 grants to individuals (high: $4,500; low: $2,250).
Purpose and activities: Support for private education at all levels, including elementary, secondary, and post-secondary schools, colleges and universities, and medical and nursing institutions; general charitable programs, including grants to hospitals, and programs for children, the developmentally disabled, and senior citizens; and civic, cultural, social welfare, economic, and religious activities.
Fields of interest: Higher education, secondary education, elementary education, medical education, nursing, health, hospitals, youth, aged, handicapped, mental health, arts, cultural programs, community development, civic affairs, economics, science and technology, social services, disadvantaged, religion.
Types of support: Equipment, conferences and seminars, special projects, endowment funds, fellowships, renovation projects, research.
Limitations: No support for public education. No grants to individuals, or for building funds, general support, continuing support, operating budgets, deficit financing, or unrestricted purposes.
Publications: Informational brochure (including application guidelines).
Application information: The scholarship program for the children of company employees, except for renewals, has been discontinued. Application form required.
   Copies of proposal: 1
   Deadline(s): May 15
   Board meeting date(s): Feb., May, Aug., and Oct.
   Final notification: Nov.
   Write: Jack E. Scholl, Exec. Dir.
Officers and Trustees:* William H. Scholl,* Pres.; Jack E. Scholl,* V.P., Secy., and Exec. Dir.; Leonard J. Knirko, Treas.; George W. Alexander, William T. Branham, Neil Flanagin, William B. Jordan, Pamela Scholl Mahaffee, Michael L. Scholl, Douglas C. Witherspoon.
Number of staff: 2 full-time professional; 2 part-time professional; 3 full-time support.
EIN: 366068724
Recent health grants:
947-1 Action Research, United Kingdom, $25,000. Toward research project at Bath Institute. 1990.
947-2 ALSAC - Saint Jude Childrens Research Hospital, Midwestern Regional Office, Chicago, IL, $25,000. Toward exploration of childhood Acute Myeloid Leukemia. 1990.
947-3 Alzheimers Disease and Related Disorders Association, Skokie, IL, $15,000. For Respite Aide Training and Registry Program. 1990.

947-4 American Cancer Society, Illinois Division, Chicago, IL, $25,000. Toward publication and distribution of booklets. 1990.
947-5 American Fund for Dental Health, Chicago, IL, $10,000. Toward expansion of national volunteer network. 1990.
947-6 American Heart Association of Metropolitan Chicago, Chicago, IL, $15,000. For long-term heart health education program. 1990.
947-7 American Leprosy Missions, Elmwood Park, NJ, $15,000. For training programs in surgery and rehabilitation. 1990.
947-8 Arizona AIDS Project, Phoenix, AZ, $10,000. Toward implementing management system. 1990.
947-9 Arthritis Foundation, Chicago, IL, $20,000. To continue research program. 1990.
947-10 Bob Champion Cancer Trust, London, England, $57,600. For cancer research. 1990.
947-11 Boys and Girls Clubs of Chicago, Chicago, IL, $15,000. For preventive/correctional health program. 1990.
947-12 Brain Research Foundation, Chicago, IL, $50,000. To purchase equipment for neurosurgery. 1990.
947-13 Catholic Home Bureau, NYC, NY, $12,000. To assist with cost of child psychologist. 1990.
947-14 Cheshire Home for Handicapped Boys, Marrakech, Morocco, $14,000. For medical supplies. 1990.
947-15 Doctor William M. Scholl College of Podiatric Medicine, Chicago, IL, $100,000. For scholarship and museum project. 1990.
947-16 Easter Seal Rehabilitation Center of Will-Grundy Counties, Joliet, IL, $10,000. Toward expansion of outpatient therapy services. 1990.
947-17 Easter Seal Society of Metropolitan Chicago, Chicago, IL, $25,000. To provide direct medical intervention to primarily Hispanic infants. 1990.
947-18 Episcopal Home for the Aging, Southern Pines, NC, $25,000. For scholarships for low-income employees. 1990.
947-19 Esperanca, Phoenix, AZ, $30,000. For one orthopedic surgery team. 1990.
947-20 Evanston Hospital Corporation, Evanston, IL, $25,000. To purchase two IBM PC computer stations. 1990.
947-21 Family Service and Mental Health Centers of South Cook County, Matteson, IL, $35,000. Toward mental health clinic services division. 1990.
947-22 Friends of Handicapped Riders, Chicago, IL, $25,000. Toward therapeutic equestrian riding program. 1990.
947-23 Gateway Foundation, Chicago, IL, $30,000. For substance abuse education. 1990.
947-24 Georgetown University Medical Center, DC, $150,000. To endow academic professorship and support pediatric project. 1990.
947-25 Glenwood School for Boys, Glenwood, IL, $30,000. Toward salary requirements for teachers and speech therapist. 1990.
947-26 Hillary Foundation, Chicago, IL, $12,000. For educational and medical projects. 1990.
947-27 Hospice of the North Shore, Evanston, IL, $20,000. For Youth in Grief program. 1990.

947-28 Illinois Cancer Council, Chicago, IL, $25,000. For cancer control and clinical trials programs. 1990.
947-29 Illinois Society for Autistic Citizens, Lombard, IL, $25,000. Toward support of Resource Center. 1990.
947-30 Illinois Society for the Prevention of Blindness, Chicago, IL, $10,000. Toward establishing eye injury registry. 1990.
947-31 Infant Welfare Society of Chicago, Chicago, IL, $45,000. For Good Start Home Visiting Program. 1990.
947-32 Infant Welfare Society of Evanston, Evanston, IL, $11,500. For The Sooner, the Better program. 1990.
947-33 Leukemia Research Foundation, Northbrook, IL, $25,000. Toward recruiting donors for bone marrow transplants. 1990.
947-34 Leukemia Society of America, Chicago, IL, $30,000. Toward studies to examine mutations introduced into antibody genes. 1990.
947-35 Long Beach Memorial Hospital, Long Beach, NY, $25,000. Toward Multiple Sclerosis Care Center's research project. 1990.
947-36 Lupus Foundation of America, DC, $15,000. For second of two research projects. 1990.
947-37 MacMurray College, Jacksonville, IL, $15,000. Toward Nursing Department program. 1990.
947-38 Make-A-Wish Foundation, Chicago, IL, $10,000. Toward fulfilling favorite wishes of ill children. 1990.
947-39 MAP International, Brunswick, GA, $50,000. Toward cost of distributing donated medical supplies. 1990.
947-40 Marian Manor Nursing Home, Pittsburgh, PA, $10,000. Toward medical equipment. 1990.
947-41 Marianjoy Rehabilitation Center, Wheaton, IL, $20,000. Toward purchase of Powerciser. 1990.
947-42 Marklund Childrens Home, Bloomingdale, IL, $15,000. Toward purchase of 1990 Bluebird Bus. 1990.
947-43 Mayo Foundation for Medical Education and Research, Rochester, MN, $28,000. For research program. 1990.
947-44 Menninger Foundation, Topeka, KS, $10,000. For psychiatric residency training programs. 1990.
947-45 Mercy Hospital and Medical Center, Chicago, IL, $10,000. Toward transitional living program. 1990.
947-46 Mercy Residence, Olympia Fields, IL, $25,000. To continue Activity Program Development. 1990.
947-47 Michael Reese Hospital and Medical Center, Chicago, IL, $15,000. For Child Abuse/Prevention Program. 1990.
947-48 Multi-CAP, Charleston, WV, $25,000. Toward drug abuse prevention educational program. 1990.
947-49 National Commission on Human Life, Reproduction and Rhythm, Oak Park, IL, $15,000. Toward preparation of Child and Family. 1990.
947-50 National Multiple Sclerosis Society, Chicago, IL, $15,000. Toward transportation program. 1990.
947-51 National Retinitis Pigmentosa Foundation, Baltimore, MD, $72,000. For

investigators and technicians for Retinitis Pigmentosa Research Center. 1990.

947-52 National Sudden Infant Death Syndrome Foundation, Columbia, MD, $15,000. Toward high quality experience in SIDS research. 1990.

947-53 Ozanam Home for Boys, Kansas City, MO, $10,000. For scholarship program. 1990.

947-54 Plymouth Place, La Grange Park, IL, $10,000. Toward purchase of van. 1990.

947-55 Presbyterian Home, Evanston, IL, $50,000. Toward x-ray machine replacement. 1990.

947-56 Ravenswood Hospital Medical Center, Chicago, IL, $25,000. For single-room maternity care center. 1990.

947-57 Rehabilitation Institute Foundation, Chicago, IL, $25,000. For resident rehabilitation research program. 1990.

947-58 Rimland Services for Autistic Citizens, Evanston, IL, $25,000. Toward benefits and job security to individuals. 1990.

947-59 Rush-Presbyterian-Saint Lukes Medical Center, Chicago, IL, $25,000. Toward study of cause of disability among elderly. 1990.

947-60 Saint Clare Hospital, Monroe, WI, $37,000. For volunteer coordinator's program. 1990.

947-61 Saint Francis Hospital, Evanston, IL, $20,000. Toward Cosman Arc System. 1990.

947-62 Saint Joseph Health Care Foundation, Chicago, IL, $25,000. To renovate and purchase equipment. 1990.

947-63 Saint Josephs Carondelet Child Center, Chicago, IL, $20,000. Toward hiring of Learning Resource Director. 1990.

947-64 Saint Mary of Nazareth Hospital Center, Chicago, IL, $20,000. Toward problem pregnancy program. 1990.

947-65 Saint Xavier College, Chicago, IL, $15,000. For scholarships for nursing students. 1990.

947-66 Scripps Clinic and Research Foundation, La Jolla, CA, $15,000. Toward study to evaluate transfusions. 1990.

947-67 Shriners Hospital for Crippled Children, Chicago, IL, $10,000. Toward wheelchair purchases. 1990.

947-68 Thresholds, Chicago, IL, $25,000. Toward primary and secondary educational services. 1990.

947-69 United Cerebral Palsy of Greater Chicago, Chicago, IL, $36,640. For special communication devices. 1990.

947-70 United Cerebral Palsy of Will County, Joliet, IL, $12,000. For respite and family support services. 1990.

947-71 Visiting Nurse Association of Chicago, Chicago, IL, $20,000. Toward home health care to elderly. 1990.

947-72 Voices for Illinois Children, Chicago, IL, $30,000. Toward Children's Mental Health Project. 1990.

948
The Seabury Foundation

c/o The Northern Trust Co.
50 South LaSalle St.
Chicago 60675   (312) 630-6000

Trust established in 1947 in IL.
Donor(s): Charles Ward Seabury,‡ Louise Lovett Seabury.‡

Foundation type: Independent
Financial data (yr. ended 12/31/90): Assets, $17,205,039 (M); expenditures, $1,019,589; qualifying distributions, $986,675, including $972,038 for 162 grants (high: $50,000; low: $500).
Fields of interest: Higher education, hospitals, cultural programs, performing arts, handicapped, youth, child welfare, child development.
Types of support: Scholarship funds, general purposes.
Limitations: Giving primarily in the greater Chicago, IL, area. No grants to individuals; no loans.
Application information: Contributes only to pre-selected organizations. Applications not accepted.
Trustees: Clara Seabury Boone, Daniel J. Boone, Robert S. Boone, Charles B. Fisk, Elizabeth Seabury Mitchell, Louis Fisk Morris, Charlene B. Seabury, David G. Seabury, The Northern Trust Co.
EIN: 366027398

949
G. D. Searle & Company Contributions Program

c/o G.D. Searle & Co.
P.O. Box 5110
Skokie 60680   (312) 982-7000

Purpose and activities: Supports health care, medical research, preventive medicine, education, social services and welfare; loaned executive support and employee volunteerism sometimes given on a case by case basis.
Fields of interest: Health, medical research, education, social services, welfare.
Types of support: Loaned talent, employee volunteer services.
Limitations: Giving primarily in headquarters area. No support for political or religious organizations. No grants to individuals; or for United Way recipients.
Application information: Application form not required.
  Initial approach: Letter
  Deadline(s): None
  Board meeting date(s): As needed
  Write: Pat Coyle, Public Rels. Analyst

950
Sears, Roebuck and Co. Corporate Contributions

Sears, Roebuck and Co.
Dept. 903 BSC 38-23, Sears Tower
Chicago 60684   (312) 875-8337

Financial data (yr. ended 12/31/90): Total giving, $5,092,217 for grants.
Purpose and activities: "Through the decades, Sears has conscientiously demonstrated its good corporate citizenship through an active program of contributions and community relations." There are essentially three tiers of funding at Sears. The Sears-Roebuck Foundation is the philanthropic umbrella for the entire corporation and funds specific national programs related to the National Priorities (work-force readiness and volunteerism among company employees). Sears, Roebuck and Co. corporate contributions are allocated in

response to major grant requests from national organizations or for activities in Chicago, Sears' headquarters city. Community programs are supported by local units of Sears' four business groups: Sears Merchandise Group, Allstate Insurance Group (gives through the Allstate Foundation), Dean Witter Financial Services Group and Coldwells Banker Real Estate Group. To be considered national, a program or organization must serve constituents in multiple states, not limited to a specific geographic region. Each business group has its own major interests. Combined giving for Sears, Roebuck and the subsidiaries totaled $23,832,497 in 1990.
Fields of interest: Social services, health, handicapped, disadvantaged, education—early childhood, child welfare, employment, literacy, education, arts, civic affairs, community development, adult education, civic affairs, volunteerism, education.
Types of support: Annual campaigns, conferences and seminars, donated equipment, employee matching gifts, equipment, seed money, employee volunteer services, in-kind gifts, loaned talent, special projects, use of facilities, donated products, employee-related scholarships, internships, program-related investments, scholarship funds, cause-related marketing.
Limitations: Giving primarily in major operating locations in the continental U.S.A. and PR. No support for political, fraternal or religious organizations. No grants to individuals, or for advertising in books, brochures, pamphlets, or yearbooks.
Publications: Corporate giving report (including application guidelines).
Application information: The company has a staff that only handles contributions.
  Initial approach: Letter
  Board meeting date(s): Jan., and at four other times during the year in Apr., June, Sept., and Nov.
  Write: Paula A. Banks, Exec. Dir., Community Relations/Contribs.
Number of staff: 7 full-time professional; 1 part-time professional; 6 full-time support.

951
Fern Goldstein Shapiro, Morris R. Shapiro, and Charles Shapiro Foundation, Inc.

(Formerly Charles and M. R. Shapiro Foundation, Inc.)
200 North LaSalle St.
Chicago 60601-1014

Incorporated in 1958 in IL.
Donor(s): Charles Shapiro,‡ Mary Shapiro,‡ Molly Shapiro,‡ Morris R. Shapiro.‡
Foundation type: Independent
Financial data (yr. ended 07/31/91): Assets, $17,397,235 (M); expenditures, $1,201,206; qualifying distributions, $1,174,019, including $1,161,349 for 74 grants (high: $305,000; low: $10).
Purpose and activities: Emphasis on Jewish welfare funds and temple support; grants also for a hospital and social services.
Fields of interest: Jewish giving, Jewish welfare, hospitals, social services.
Limitations: Giving primarily in Chicago, IL. No grants to individuals.

Application information: Contributes only to pre-selected organizations. Applications not accepted.
Officers: Philip B. Heller, Pres. and Treas.; Joseph L. Muskal, Secy.
Number of staff: None.
EIN: 366109757

952
Walden W. & Jean Young Shaw Foundation
30 North LaSalle St., Suite 2800
Chicago 60602

Established in 1967 in IL.
Donor(s): Walden W. Shaw, Jean Young Shaw.
Foundation type: Independent
Financial data (yr. ended 06/30/90): Assets, $10,103,903 (M); gifts received, $563,751; expenditures, $518,916; qualifying distributions, $485,745, including $423,000 for 6 grants (high: $100,000; low: $15,000).
Purpose and activities: Giving limited to hospitals and other medical facilities.
Fields of interest: Hospitals, medical research.
Limitations: No grants to individuals.
Application information: Contributes only to pre-selected organizations. Applications not accepted.
Officers and Director:* Newell Carey Iler, Pres.; Robert Gordon Iler, V.P.; Walter Roth,* Secy.-Treas.
EIN: 366162196

953
John M. Simpson Foundation
33 North Dearborn St., Rm. 1300
Chicago 60602

Established in 1961.
Donor(s): Susan Cavender, Patricia O'Kieffe, Michael Simpson.
Foundation type: Independent
Financial data (yr. ended 12/31/90): Assets, $3,380,162 (M); gifts received, $569,148; expenditures, $77,788; qualifying distributions, $55,250, including $55,250 for grants.
Purpose and activities: Giving primarily for hospitals, clinics, health services, including family planning, and social services; some support also for a nature conservatory.
Fields of interest: Hospitals, health services, family planning, social services, conservation.
Limitations: No grants to individuals.
Application information: Contributes only to pre-selected organizations. Applications not accepted.
Officers: Nancy T. Simpson, Pres.; P.J. Herbert, V.P.; W.J. McDermott, V.P.; J.D. Brown, Secy.; Allison Lang, Treas.
Directors: Patricia S. O'Kieffe, Howard B. Simpson, William Simpson.
EIN: 366071621

954
The Siragusa Foundation
919 North Michigan Ave., Suite 2701
Chicago 60611   (312) 280-0833

Trust established in 1950 in IL; incorporated in 1980.

Donor(s): Ross D. Siragusa.
Foundation type: Independent
Financial data (yr. ended 12/31/91): Assets, $12,020,534 (M); expenditures, $661,923; qualifying distributions, $552,730, including $494,450 for 76 grants (average: $5,690).
Purpose and activities: Emphasis on higher education and medical research; support also for cultural activities, child development programs, education of the handicapped, and care of the elderly.
Fields of interest: Higher education, medical research, cultural programs, aged, handicapped, child development.
Types of support: Equipment, matching funds, research, special projects, general purposes, scholarship funds.
Limitations: Giving primarily in in the Midwest, with preference to the Chicago, IL, metropolitan area. No grants to individuals, or for endowment funds; no loans.
Publications: Program policy statement, application guidelines.
Application information: Submit proposal only when invited. Application form not required.
  Initial approach: Letter
  Copies of proposal: 1
  Board meeting date(s): Mar. and Dec.
  Final notification: 2 to 3 months
  Write: John R. Siragusa, V.P.
Officers and Directors:* Ross D. Siragusa,* Pres.; John R. Siragusa,* V.P. and Secy.-Treas.; Roy M. Adams, George E. Driscoll, Melvyn H. Schneider; Martha P. Siragusa, Richard D. Siragusa, Ross D. Siragusa, Jr., Sinclair C. Siragusa, James B. Wilson.
Number of staff: 1 full-time professional; 1 full-time support.
EIN: 363100492

955
Smail Family Foundation
66 West Oak St., No. 827
Chicago 60610

Established in 1965.
Foundation type: Independent
Financial data (yr. ended 06/30/91): Assets, $1,890 (M); gifts received, $237,000; expenditures, $280,050; qualifying distributions, $280,050, including $280,050 for 22 grants (high: $180,000; low: $100).
Purpose and activities: "To further the prevention and relief of human suffering;" with emphasis on a medical center, health organizations, hospitals, and social services.
Fields of interest: Hospitals, health, social services.
Types of support: General purposes.
Limitations: Giving primarily in Chicago, IL. No grants to individuals.
Application information: Contributes only to pre-selected organizations. Applications not accepted.
Trustee: Anne W. Smail.
EIN: 366136148

956
Special People In Need
500 West Madison St., Suite 3700
Chicago 60606   (312) 715-5000

Established in 1987.
Donor(s): Josephine M. Thompson, Katherine Morningstar Irrevocable Trust.
Foundation type: Independent
Financial data (yr. ended 12/31/90): Assets, $2,549,565 (M); gifts received, $200; expenditures, $112,143; qualifying distributions, $104,291, including $82,055 for 18 grants (high: $12,000; low: $4,800) and $1,550 for 1 grant to an individual.
Purpose and activities: "To provide support to financially needy and handicapped persons...and scholarships and fellowships;" grants for higher, secondary, and elementary education; and a hospital.
Fields of interest: Higher education, secondary education, elementary education, hospitals, health, handicapped, disadvantaged.
Types of support: Grants to individuals, student aid, fellowships, general purposes, scholarship funds, special projects.
Application information: Scholarship applicants must be sponsored by a college or university; other individuals must be sponsored by an organization. Only a small number of grants are available. Application form not required.
  Initial approach: Proposal
  Copies of proposal: 1
  Deadline(s): None
  Board meeting date(s): Spring and early winter, and as required
  Write: Gary H. Kline, Secy.
Officers and Directors:* Molly M. Gerbaz,* Chair.; John M. Morningstar,* Vice-Chair.; Josephine M. Thompson,* Pres.; Larry D. Gerbaz,* V.P.; Leslie H. Morningstar,* V.P.; Gary H. Kline,* Secy.; Thomas A. Polachek,* Treas.; Kent Chandler, Jr.
EIN: 581483651

957
The Otho S. A. Sprague Memorial Institute
c/o Harris Trust Savings Bank
190 South LaSalle St., 4th Fl., P.O. Box 755
Chicago 60690   (312) 461-7054

Incorporated in 1910 in IL.
Donor(s): Members of the Sprague family.
Foundation type: Independent
Financial data (yr. ended 12/31/90): Assets, $17,320,000 (M); expenditures, $823,808; qualifying distributions, $726,000, including $726,000 for 8 grants (high: $175,000; low: $25,000).
Purpose and activities: To investigate the cause of disease and the prevention and relief of human suffering caused by disease. In accordance with the wishes of the founder, support primarily to the major private, medical teaching and research universities in Chicago.
Fields of interest: Medical research, cancer, health services, hospitals, higher education.
Types of support: Research, special projects.
Limitations: Giving limited to Chicago, IL. No grants to individuals, or for building or endowment funds, general purposes, scholarships, fellowships, or matching gifts; no loans.
Publications: Annual report.
Application information: Application form not required.
  Initial approach: Letter

Copies of proposal: 4
Deadline(s): None
Board meeting date(s): Semiannually in May and Dec.
Write: Thomas E. Macior
Officers and Trustees:* Vernon Armour,* Pres.; Charles C. Hoffner III,* V.P.; Steward S. Dixon,* Secy.; Harry N. Beaty, M.D., John P. Bent, Charles F. Clark, Jr., Leo M. Henikoff, M.D., Leon O. Jacobson, M.D.
Number of staff: None.
EIN: 366068723

958
A. E. Staley, Jr. Foundation
c/o First of America Bank
236 North Water St.
Decatur 62525

Trust established in 1955 in IL.
Donor(s): Augustus Eugene Staley, Jr.
Foundation type: Independent
Financial data (yr. ended 12/31/90): Assets, $4,076,682 (M); expenditures, $333,858; qualifying distributions, $312,582, including $309,435 for 45 grants (high: $80,750; low: $125).
Fields of interest: Higher education, hospitals, health services, community funds.
Limitations: Giving primarily in IL. No grants to individuals.
Application information: Contributes only to pre-selected organizations. Applications not accepted.
Trustee: First of America Bank.
EIN: 376023961

959
State Farm Companies Foundation ▼
One State Farm Plaza
Bloomington 61710   (309) 766-2161
FAX: (309) 766-3700

Incorporated in 1963 in IL.
Donor(s): State Farm Insurance Cos.
Foundation type: Company-sponsored
Financial data (yr. ended 12/31/91): Assets, $7,005,669 (M); expenditures, $5,967,746; qualifying distributions, $5,931,561, including $4,539,527 for 342 grants (high: $1,000,000; low: $14; average: $500-$15,000), $206,000 for grants to individuals (high: $10,000; low: $2,000; average: $2,000-$10,000) and $1,186,034 for 948 employee matching gifts.
Purpose and activities: Support for higher education, including scholarships for children of employees/agents/retirees, doctoral dissertation awards in business and insurance, exceptional student fellowships for business majors, and promotion of education activities in areas related to the insurance business; ongoing grants are generally to national organizations; limited grants for capital fund drives for social service agencies, hospitals, and health and human service agencies in major State Farm employment centers and to key colleges; also support for a matching gift program to colleges and universities; also support for United Way.
Fields of interest: Higher education, insurance education, business education, education, education—minorities, community funds,

hospitals—building funds, safety, law and justice, education—building funds, social services.
Types of support: Fellowships, scholarship funds, employee-related scholarships, employee matching gifts, building funds, capital campaigns.
Limitations: Giving in Bloomington, IL, and 27 U.S. regional office sites. No support for fraternal organizations, or religious organizations for sectarian purposes. No grants to individuals (except for employee-related scholarship programs), or for dinners, special events or goodwill advertising, conferences or seminars.
Publications: Informational brochure, application guidelines.
Application information: Funds largely committed; no direct appeals accepted; scholarship and fellowship recipients must be nominated by their schools; application form is required. Application form not required.
Initial approach: Proposal
Copies of proposal: 1
Deadline(s): For scholarships, Dec. 31; for fellowships, Feb. 15; for doctoral program, Mar. 31; for grants, 3 wks. befor quarterly board meetings
Board meeting date(s): Mar., June, Sept., and Dec.
Write: David Polzin, Asst. V.P., Prog., or Donna Vincent, Asst. Secy.
Officers and Directors:* Edward B. Rust, Jr.,* Pres. and Treas.; Laura P. Sullivan,* V.P. and Secy.; Bruce Callis,* V.P., Progs.; Robert S. Eckley, Charles O. Galvin.
Number of staff: 2 full-time professional; 1 full-time support; 2 part-time support.
EIN: 366110423

960
Irvin Stern Foundation
53 West Jackson Blvd., Suite 838
Chicago 60604   (312) 786-9355

Trust established in 1957 in IL.
Donor(s): Irvin Stern.‡
Foundation type: Independent
Financial data (yr. ended 09/30/90): Assets, $7,718,686 (M); expenditures, $541,198; qualifying distributions, $474,031, including $454,682 for 42 grants (high: $110,000; low: $400; average: $3,000-$20,000).
Purpose and activities: Emphasis on meeting the needs of the Jewish community in the United States and Israel; support for efforts to combat heart disease, mental illness, and cancer; for vocational training and help for the aged; and for improving urban living conditions via neighborhood organizations.
Fields of interest: Jewish welfare, heart disease, mental health, cancer, vocational education, employment, aged, community development, urban affairs, homeless.
Types of support: Operating budgets, continuing support, seed money, emergency funds, matching funds, conferences and seminars, equipment, internships.
Limitations: Giving primarily in Chicago, IL; New York, NY; and San Diego, CA. No support for religious or political purposes, or research. No grants to individuals, or for endowment funds, deficit financing, building funds, or advertising or program books.

Publications: Application guidelines, program policy statement, 990-PF.
Application information: Application form required.
Initial approach: Letter
Deadline(s): Submit proposal preferably in Mar. or Aug.; deadlines Apr. 1 and Sept. 1
Board meeting date(s): Apr. and Oct.
Write: Jeffrey Epstein, Trustee
Officer: Rae W. Epstein, Secy.
Trustees: E. Allan Epstein, Jeffrey Epstein, Stuart Epstein, Arthur Winter, Dorothy G. Winter, Stanley Winter.
Number of staff: 1 part-time support.
EIN: 366047947

961
Jerome H. Stone Family Foundation
150 North Michigan Ave.
Chicago 60601

Established in 1963 in IL.
Donor(s): Jerome H. Stone, Cynthia Raskin.
Foundation type: Independent
Financial data (yr. ended 12/31/90): Assets, $2,010,779 (M); gifts received, $284,951; expenditures, $88,929; qualifying distributions, $84,969, including $84,914 for 86 grants (high: $16,667; low: $20).
Fields of interest: Jewish giving, arts, performing arts, education, health, social services.
Limitations: Giving primarily in IL, with emphasis in Chicago. No grants to individuals.
Application information: Contributes only to pre-selected organizations. Applications not accepted.
Officers: Jerome H. Stone, Pres.; James H. Stone, V.P.; Cynthia Raskin, Secy.
Director: Ellen Stone Belic.
EIN: 366061300

962
Stone Foundation, Inc.
150 North Michigan Ave.
Chicago 60601

Incorporated in 1944 in IL.
Donor(s): Stone Container Corp.
Foundation type: Company-sponsored
Financial data (yr. ended 12/31/90): Assets, $3,375,991 (M); gifts received, $71,667; expenditures, $958,007; qualifying distributions, $943,537, including $871,537 for 82 grants (high: $369,333; low: $100) and $72,000 for 47 grants to individuals (high: $2,000; low: $1,000).
Purpose and activities: Emphasis on Jewish welfare funds, higher education, hospitals, and cultural activities; scholarships limited to children of employees with two or more years of service.
Fields of interest: Jewish welfare, higher education, hospitals, cultural programs.
Types of support: Employee-related scholarships, general purposes.
Limitations: Giving primarily in Chicago, IL.
Application information: Application form required.
Deadline(s): Apr. 1 for scholarships
Write: Arnold Brookstone, Administrator
Officers and Directors:* Roger W. Stone,* Pres.; Jerome H. Stone,* V.P. and Secy.-Treas.; Marvin N. Stone,* V.P.

EIN: 366063761

963
Sundstrand Corporation Foundation ▼
4949 Harrison Ave.
P.O. Box 7003
Rockford 61125   (815) 226-6000

Incorporated in 1952 in IL.
Donor(s): Sundstrand Corp.
Foundation type: Company-sponsored
Financial data (yr. ended 10/31/90): Assets, $2,445,508 (M); gifts received, $2,000,000; expenditures, $1,511,022; qualifying distributions, $1,496,403, including $1,375,950 for 128 grants (high: $500,000; low: $500; average: $1,000-$25,000) and $120,453 for employee matching gifts.
Purpose and activities: Grants for community funds, education, particularly higher education, hospitals, and youth agencies; support also for the handicapped, social service and health agencies, an employee-related scholarship program and cultural programs.
Fields of interest: Community funds, higher education, hospitals, youth, cultural programs, education, social services, handicapped, health services.
Types of support: Building funds, equipment, scholarship funds, employee-related scholarships, employee matching gifts, capital campaigns.
Limitations: Giving primarily in areas of company operations. No support for projects of a religious or political nature. No grants to individuals (except for employee-related scholarships), or for operating funds.
Application information: Application form not required.
   Initial approach: Letter
   Copies of proposal: 1
   Deadline(s): None
   Board meeting date(s): Mar., June, Sept., and Dec.
   Final notification: 2 months
   Write: Carolyn J. Thomas, Secy.
Officers and Directors:* Don R. O'Hare,* Pres.; Gary J. Hedges,* V.P.; Carolyn J. Thomas, Secy.; Jim White, Treas.; Richard Schilling, Claude Vernam.
EIN: 366072477

964
Susman and Asher Foundation
c/o Norman Asher
134 North LaSalle St., Suite 1900
Chicago 60602

Incorporated in 1949 in IL.
Donor(s): Louis Susman, and members of the Asher family.
Foundation type: Independent
Financial data (yr. ended 12/31/90): Assets, $4,667,972 (M); gifts received, $45,100; expenditures, $292,285; qualifying distributions, $291,789, including $288,042 for 59 grants (high: $50,000; low: $30).
Purpose and activities: Emphasis on higher, including religious, education, and Jewish welfare funds; support also for health and hospitals.

Fields of interest: Higher education, theological education, Jewish giving, Jewish welfare, health, hospitals.
Types of support: Scholarship funds, general purposes.
Limitations: Giving primarily in IL. No grants to individuals.
Application information: Contributes only to pre-selected organizations. Applications not accepted.
Officer and Trustee:* Norman Asher,* Mgr.
EIN: 366049760

965
Lucille S. Thompson Family Foundation
c/o The Northern Trust Co.
50 South LaSalle St.
Chicago 60675
Application address: 4823 Old Kingston Pike, Suite 140, Knoxville, TN 37919

Established in 1988 in TN.
Donor(s): Lucille S. Thompson.
Foundation type: Independent
Financial data (yr. ended 02/28/91): Assets, $19,677,374 (M); expenditures, $888,929; qualifying distributions, $823,291, including $785,136 for 31 grants (high: $397,990; low: $100).
Fields of interest: Health, cancer, child welfare, cultural programs, museums.
Types of support: General purposes, equipment.
Limitations: Giving primarily in Knoxville, TN. No grants to individuals.
Application information: Application form required.
   Initial approach: Proposal
   Deadline(s): None
   Write: Lila K. Pfleger, Mgr.
Trustee: The Northern Trust Co.
Trust Committee: Archer W. Bishop, Jr., Chair.; John W. Baker, Jr., Archer W. Bishop III, Baker O'Neil Bishop, Kristen Kohlhase Bishop, Sandra K. Bishop, Thompson Alexander Bishop, Lindsey Young.
EIN: 581788548

966
The Thorson Foundation
399 Fullerton Pkwy.
Chicago 60614   (312) 327-2687

Established in 1954 in IL.
Donor(s): Robert D. Thorson,‡ Reuben Thorson,‡ Dorothy W. Thorson.
Foundation type: Independent
Financial data (yr. ended 12/31/91): Assets, $2,423,748 (M); expenditures, $107,552; qualifying distributions, $101,965, including $99,925 for 54 grants (high: $20,000; low: $100).
Purpose and activities: Primary areas of interest include higher and other education and the arts, including a zoological society, museums, and an art institute; support also for child welfare.
Fields of interest: Wildlife, animal welfare, conservation, arts, child welfare, museums, higher education, education, hospitals, general charitable giving.
Types of support: Annual campaigns, capital campaigns, continuing support, scholarship funds.

Limitations: Giving primarily in IL. No grants to individuals.
Application information: Contributes only to pre-selected organizations. Applications not accepted.
   Write: Dorothy W. Thorson, Pres.
Officers and Directors:* Dorothy W. Thorson,* Pres.; Virginia T. Goodall,* V.P. and Treas.; John C. Goodall III,* Secy.
EIN: 366051916

967
Trans Union Corporation Giving Program
555 West Adams
Chicago 60601   (312) 431-0144

Financial data (yr. ended 12/31/90): Total giving, $51,938 for 150 employee matching gifts.
Purpose and activities: Supports the arts and culture, all levels of education, medical research, civic and social services, United Way, legal advocacy, legal services, youth organizations and general charitable programs.
Fields of interest: Arts, cultural programs, fine arts, dance, education, elementary education, secondary education, higher education, medical research, civic affairs, social services, community funds, legal services, youth.
Types of support: Employee matching gifts.
Limitations: Giving primarily in headquarters city and major operating locations.
Publications: Program policy statement.
Application information: Applications not accepted.
   Write: Allen Flitcraft, Chair.

968
United Airlines Foundation ▼
(Formerly UAL Foundation)
P.O. Box 66100
Chicago 60666   (708) 952-5714

Incorporated in 1951 in IL.
Donor(s): United Air Lines, Inc.
Foundation type: Company-sponsored
Financial data (yr. ended 12/31/90): Assets, $5,387,576 (M); expenditures, $2,898,297; qualifying distributions, $2,891,503, including $2,891,342 for 218 grants (high: $500,000; low: $250; average: $5,000-$10,000).
Purpose and activities: Emphasis on programs encompassing education and educational reform, arts and culture, the United Way, and the Friendly Skies program which airlifts terminally and critically ill children to hospitals for treatment.
Fields of interest: Community funds, education, higher education, educational research, cultural programs, arts, health, educational research.
Types of support: Annual campaigns, operating budgets, research, employee-related scholarships.
Limitations: Giving limited to areas of company operations. No support for labor unions, fraternal or veterans' organizations, or for sectarian religious organizations. No grants to individuals, or for endowments, advertising campaigns, purchase of tickets or tables for fundraising dinners or similar events, club memberships, conferences, or travel; no loans.
Publications: Application guidelines.
Application information: Application form not required.

Initial approach: Proposal
Copies of proposal: 1
Deadline(s): 60 days prior to board meetings
Board meeting date(s): Mar., June, Sept., and Dec.
Final notification: 1 month
Write: Paul G. George, V.P. and Exec. Dir.
Officers and Directors:* Stephen M. Wolf,* Pres.; Paul G. George,* V.P. and Exec. Dir.; Eileen M. Younglove, Secy. and Contribs. Mgr.; James M. Guyette, Lawrence M. Nagin, Joseph R. O'Gorman, Jr., John C. Pope.
Number of staff: 2
EIN: 366109873

969
USG Foundation, Inc.
c/o Harold E. Pendexter, Jr.
P.O. Box 6721
Chicago 60680-6721　　　　(312) 606-4594

Incorporated in 1978 in IL.
Donor(s): USG Corp.
Foundation type: Company-sponsored
Financial data (yr. ended 12/31/91): Assets, $477,156 (M); expenditures, $503,026; qualifying distributions, $290,259, including $161,255 for 76 grants (high: $25,282; low: $100; average: $500-$5,000) and $129,004 for employee matching gifts.
Purpose and activities: Emphasis on higher education and community funds; support also for arts and cultural organizations, hospitals and health, welfare, youth agencies, and public interest organizations. Preference given to supporting appropriate programs in which USG employees actively participate.
Fields of interest: Higher education, community funds, cultural programs, hospitals, health, welfare, youth, public policy, arts, civic affairs.
Types of support: Continuing support, annual campaigns, building funds, equipment, research, matching funds, employee matching gifts, technical assistance, general purposes, capital campaigns, employee-related scholarships, scholarship funds, renovation projects.
Limitations: Giving primarily in areas of company operations. No support for sectarian organizations that are exclusively religious, fraternal or veterans' organizations, primary or secondary schools, or generally organizations receiving funds from united campaigns. No grants to individuals, or for courtesy advertising; no loans.
Publications: Program policy statement.
Application information: Application form not required.
Initial approach: Proposal
Copies of proposal: 1
Deadline(s): None
Board meeting date(s): Quarterly
Write: Eve Krit-Anderson, Secy. of Foundation Affairs
Officers and Directors:* Harold E. Pendexter, Jr.,* Pres.; M.P. Gonring,* V.P.; D.E. Roller,* V.P.; S.K. Torrey,* Secy.; Richard Fleming,* Treas.
Number of staff: 1 full-time professional.
EIN: 362984045

970
Walgreen Giving Program
200 Wilmot Rd.
Deerfield 60015　　　　(708) 940-2931

Financial data (yr. ended 08/31/90): Total giving, $3,200,000 for grants.
Purpose and activities: Supports a variety of programs including: social services, with giving to the United Way and programs for crime rehabilitation, underprivileged children and emotionally disturbed children, youth service, race relations and rehabilitation programs; and arts and culture, including theater and symphonies. Individuals and national organizations are considered for funding.
Fields of interest: Community funds, social services, child welfare, child development, youth, race relations, rehabilitation, arts, theater, music, literacy, cancer, mental health, Jewish giving, handicapped, pharmacy, Native Americans, business education, secondary education, community development, drug abuse, family services, heart disease, intercultural relations, adult education, AIDS, Catholic welfare, cultural programs, ecology, education—early childhood, health, homeless, hunger, alcoholism, education—minorities, higher education, hospices, aged, civil rights, minorities.
Types of support: Building funds, general purposes, equipment, capital campaigns, operating budgets, annual campaigns, special projects.
Limitations: Giving primarily in headquarters city and major operating areas. No support for international organizations.
Application information: Government and Corporate Relations office handles giving. Application form not required.
Initial approach: Letter or proposal to headquarters
Deadline(s): None
Board meeting date(s): Monthly and as needed
Final notification: 1-2 months
Write: Edward H. King, Dir., Govt. and Corp. Rels.
Number of staff: 2 full-time professional; 2 part-time professional; 1 full-time support; 1 part-time support.

971
The A. Montgomery Ward Foundation
c/o Continental Bank, N.A., Attn.: M.C. Ryan
30 North LaSalle St.
Chicago 60697　　　　(312) 828-1785

Trust established in 1959 in IL.
Donor(s): Marjorie Montgomery Ward Baker.‡
Foundation type: Independent
Financial data (yr. ended 06/30/90): Assets, $9,804,692 (M); expenditures, $640,925; qualifying distributions, $570,395, including $532,600 for 19 grants (high: $150,000; low: $5,000).
Fields of interest: Hospitals, higher education, youth, cultural programs, social services.
Types of support: Capital campaigns, scholarship funds, operating budgets.
Limitations: Giving primarily in Chicago, IL, and surrounding metropolitan areas. No grants to individuals.
Publications: Application guidelines.

Application information:
Initial approach: Letter
Copies of proposal: 2
Deadline(s): None
Board meeting date(s): May and Nov.
Trustees: Richard A. Beck, John A. Hutchings, Continental Bank, N.A.
EIN: 362417437

972
Washington Square Health Foundation, Inc.
875 North Michigan Ave., Suite 3516
Chicago 60611　　　　(312) 664-6488

Established in 1985 in IL.
Donor(s): Henrotin Hospital.
Foundation type: Independent
Financial data (yr. ended 09/30/91): Assets, $21,553,735 (M); gifts received, $18,014; expenditures, $1,235,219; qualifying distributions, $1,018,591, including $855,860 for 50 grants (high: $72,800; low: $1,000; average: $22,000) and $26,093 for program-related investments.
Purpose and activities: "To promote and maintain access to adequate health care," through grants for medical and nursing scholarships, medical research, and direct health care services.
Fields of interest: Health services, medical research, medical education, nursing.
Types of support: Research, equipment, scholarship funds, special projects.
Limitations: Giving primarily in the Chicago, IL, area. No support for general operating or administrative expenses. No grants to individuals, or for land acquisition.
Publications: Annual report, application guidelines.
Application information: Application form required.
Initial approach: Pre-application form
Copies of proposal: 4
Deadline(s): June 1 and Dec. 1
Write: Howard Nochumson, Exec. Dir.
Officers and Directors:* James Lutz,* Chair.; Angelo P. Creticos, M.D.,* Vice-Chair.; Mrs. Arthur M. Wirtz,* V.P. and Secy.; John C. York,* Treas.; Howard Nochumson, Exec. Dir.; Robert S. Bleier, M.D., William B. Friedeman, Robert S. Kirby, Howard M. McCue III, Bill G. Wiley.
Number of staff: 2 full-time professional.
EIN: 361210140

973
Waste Management Corporate Giving Program
3003 Butterfield Rd.
Oak Brook 60521　　　　(708) 572-8800

Financial data (yr. ended 12/30/90): Total giving, $7,618,000, including $5,571,000 for grants, $1,229,000 for employee matching gifts and $818,000 for in-kind gifts.
Purpose and activities: "Waste Management's social responsibility begins with our people. As our ambassadors in the communities in which they live and work, our people convert the Waste Management philosophy of corporate giving into action. The corporate contributions program is largely based upon their personal donations,

dedicated volunteerism and continued generosity. A Matching Gift program provides corporate matching funds of employees' donations to charities, educational institutions, and environmental groups. This program is supplemented by corporate grants and donations of company services to a diverse range of community groups and charities. The company places a high priority on corporate giving to students and environmentalists." Giving falls in the following categories: community and civic affairs, the United Way, culture and the arts, environmental preservation and conservation, education, and certain medical and research areas. Philanthropic efforts come from three sources: local operating companies, the corporate office, and matching gifts.
Fields of interest: Arts, cultural programs, education, health, welfare, higher education, social services, environment, conservation, community funds, child development, medical research.
Types of support: Employee matching gifts, in-kind gifts, donated equipment, use of facilities, public relations services, annual campaigns, conferences and seminars, equipment, operating budgets, seed money, building funds, employee volunteer services, special projects, capital campaigns, continuing support, research, emergency funds, endowment funds, matching funds, scholarship funds, student loans, employee-related scholarships.
Limitations: Giving primarily in areas of company operations to organizations that benefit customers and employees; some national giving. No support for veterans' groups or fraternities, or sectarian or religious organizations that don't serve the general public on a nondenominational basis. No grants to individuals; or for non-eleemosynary organizations, or organizations that discriminate on the basis of race, creed, or sex.
Publications: Corporate report, corporate giving report, program policy statement.
Application information: Grant proposals that relate to Chicago/Oak Brook area of Illinois or to institutions with a national scope should be directed to the corporate office. Programs with regional or state focus should be directed to regional offices; local impact programs should go to local granting division management.
Initial approach: Letter or proposal; no telephone proposals
Deadline(s): None
Write: Paul P. Pyrcik, Dir. of Progs.
Number of staff: 1 full-time professional; 2 full-time support.

974
W. P. and H. B. White Foundation
540 Frontage Rd., Suite 3240
Northfield 60093   (708) 446-1441

Incorporated in 1953 in IL.
Donor(s): William P. White,‡ Hazel B. White.‡
Foundation type: Independent
Financial data (yr. ended 12/31/91): Assets, $21,664,197 (M); expenditures, $1,314,327; qualifying distributions, $1,020,375, including $1,020,375 for 164 grants (high: $25,000; low: $1,000).
Purpose and activities: "Funding to organizations in the Chicago metropolitan area that contribute

to the future good of the country, primarily in the areas of education, health, and human services, with an emphasis on helping those most in need."
Fields of interest: Social services, child welfare, Catholic welfare, education, hospitals, health, urban development.
Types of support: Operating budgets, continuing support, annual campaigns, building funds, capital campaigns, general purposes, special projects.
Limitations: Giving primarily in metropolitan Chicago, IL. No grants to individuals, or for land acquisition, endowment funds, publications, conferences, deficit financing, or matching gifts; no loans.
Publications: Application guidelines.
Application information: Application form not required.
Initial approach: Letter
Copies of proposal: 1
Deadline(s): 1st day of preceding month to be considered in that quarter
Board meeting date(s): Mar., June, Sept., and Dec.
Final notification: Several weeks
Write: M. Margaret Blandford, Exec. Dir.
Officers and Directors:* Roger B. White,* Pres.; John H. McCortney,* V.P. and Treas.; Steven R. White,* Secy.; Paul E. Plunkett, Paul M. Plunkett, Robert P. White, William P. White, Jr.
Number of staff: 1 full-time professional; 1 full-time support.
EIN: 362601558

975
Whitman Corporation Foundation
3501 Algonquin Rd.
Rolling Meadows 60008   (708) 818-5014

Established in 1988 in IL.
Donor(s): Whitman Corp.
Foundation type: Company-sponsored
Financial data (yr. ended 12/31/91): Assets, $2,980,683 (M); expenditures, $9,108,568; qualifying distributions, $908,893, including $736,148 for 146 grants (high: $100,000; low: $50).
Fields of interest: Education, health, welfare, cultural programs, general charitable giving.
Application information: Application form not required.
Initial approach: Letter; telephone inquiries not accepted
Copies of proposal: 1
Write: Charles H. Connolly, Pres.
Officers and Directors:* Charles H. Connolly,* Pres.; William B. Moore, Secy.; Thomas L. Bindley, Treas.; Bruce S. Chelberg, Frank T. Westover.
EIN: 363610784

976
Winona Corporation
70 East Cedar St., Apt. 10-W
Chicago 60611-1133

Established in 1965 in IL.
Donor(s): Marjorie M. Kelly.‡
Foundation type: Independent
Financial data (yr. ended 12/31/90): Assets, $5,183,208 (M); expenditures, $396,623;

qualifying distributions, $360,000, including $360,000 for grants.
Purpose and activities: Giving for cultural programs, and higher and pre-college education; some support for hospitals and social services.
Fields of interest: Cultural programs, higher education, elementary education, social services, hospitals.
Limitations: Giving primarily in IL. No grants to individuals.
Application information: Contributes only to pre-selected organizations. Applications not accepted.
Write: Thomas A. Kelly, Secy.
Officers and Directors:* Patricia K. Healy,* Pres.; Marjorie K. Webster,* V.P. and Treas.; Thomas A. Kelly,* Secy.
EIN: 366132949

977
Woods Charitable Fund, Inc. ▼
Three First National Plaza, Suite 2010
Chicago 60602   (312) 782-2698
For applications from Nebraska: Pam Baker, P.O. Box 81309, Lincoln, NE 68501; Tel.: (402) 474-0707

Incorporated in 1941 in NE.
Donor(s): Frank H. Woods,‡ Nelle C. Woods,‡ Sahara Coal Co., Inc.
Foundation type: Independent
Financial data (yr. ended 12/31/91): Assets, $53,473,368 (M); expenditures, $3,162,105; qualifying distributions, $2,506,644, including $2,506,644 for 168 grants (high: $100,000; low: $1,000; average: $10,000-$20,000).
Purpose and activities: Grants primarily to nonprofit organizations working to build stronger communities in metropolitan Chicago and Lincoln, NE, including support of the nonprofit sector in its role to identify and promote more just, effective, and creative approaches; a particular interest is to increase opportunities for less advantaged people. In Chicago, as a modest size foundation in a major city, the fund's grantmaking emphasizes community participation in exploring policy options and seeking long-term solutions for urban challenges. In Lincoln, as a proportionately larger donor in a smaller city, the grant program is broader in outlook, supporting both direct service and policy programs that advance the fund's overall purpose.
Fields of interest: Community development, leadership development, urban development, urban affairs, public policy, government, social services, welfare, disadvantaged, women, minorities, race relations, family services, education, secondary education, higher education, arts, cultural programs, humanities, fine arts, employment, performing arts.
Types of support: Operating budgets, seed money, matching funds, special projects, research, renovation projects, continuing support, technical assistance, general purposes.
Limitations: Giving primarily in the metropolitan Chicago, IL, and Lincoln, NE, areas. No support for medical or scientific research, religious activities, national health, welfare, or educational organizations or their state or local affiliates, or college or university programs that do not involve students and/or faculty in projects of benefit to the Chicago or Lincoln areas. No support for housing

construction or rehabilitation, or business or economic development practitioners (Chicago). In Lincoln, no support for capital projects in health care institutions or for government agencies or projects; in Chicago, no support for residential care, treatment programs, clinics, recreation programs, social services, or health care institutions. No grants to individuals, or for endowments, scholarships, fellowships, fundraising benefits, program advertising, or capital campaigns and capital projects.

Publications: Annual report (including application guidelines), program policy statement, application guidelines, informational brochure (including application guidelines).

Application information: Chicago arts proposals considered only at June meeting. Application form not required.

> *Initial approach:* Telephone or letter
> *Copies of proposal:* 1
> *Deadline(s):* Apr. 15, July 15, and Oct. 15
> *Board meeting date(s):* June, Sept., and Dec.
> *Final notification:* 1 week after board meeting
> *Write:* Jean Rudd, Exec. Dir., Ken Rolling, or Daryl Woods (Chicago area); Pam Baker (Lincoln area)

Officers and Trustees:* Lucia Woods Lindley,* Pres.; George Kelm,* V.P.; Thomas C. Woods III,* V.P.; Charles N. Wheatley, Jr.,* Secy.-Treas.; Jean Rudd, Exec. Dir.; Sydney Beane, Mary Decker, Marie Fischer.

Number of staff: 4 full-time professional; 1 full-time support; 1 part-time support.

EIN: 476032847

Recent health grants:

977-1 Interchurch Ministries of Nebraska, Lincoln, NE, $10,000. For Church and Mental Illness Program. 1991.

977-2 Lincoln Lancaster Drug Projects, Lincoln, NE, $25,000. Toward general operating budget. 1991.

977-3 Lincoln Medical Education Foundation, Lincoln, NE, $23,500. For nursing coordinator salary and benefits, minority consultant expense, teenage pregnancy and adolescent parent study and one-day conference to review study with community leaders and service providers. 1991.

977-4 Nebraska AIDS Project (NAP), Omaha, NE, $40,000. For salary and associated expense of caseworker position in Lincoln to assure continuation and expansion of programs in Lincoln which serve those affected by AIDS and HIV disease. 1991.

977-5 Nebraska Urban Indian Health Coalition, Lincoln, NE, $24,000. For Lincoln Development Specialist's salary, benefits and related taxes. 1991.

977-6 Northwest Austin Council, Chicago, IL, $10,000. For operating grant for community organizing principally concerned with drug-related problems on Chicago's far west side. 1991.

977-7 Planned Parenthood of Lincoln, Lincoln, NE, $20,000. For education department. 1991.

977-8 Rape Spouse Abuse Crisis Center, Lincoln, NE, $20,000. For salary, benefits and related taxes for client advocate who provides information and support to victims of domestic violence, sexual assault and incest. 1991.

978
Woodward Governor Company Charitable Trust

c/o Woodward Governor Co.
5001 North Second St.
Rockford 61125-7001   (815) 877-7441

Trust established in 1947 in IL.

Donor(s): Woodward Governor Co.

Foundation type: Company-sponsored

Financial data (yr. ended 12/31/90): Assets, $7,840,215 (M); expenditures, $528,988; qualifying distributions, $514,506, including $510,879 for 95 grants (high: $87,000; low: $100; average: $2,000).

Purpose and activities: Support for community funds; social services, including programs for the homeless, hunger, minorities, the handicapped, and youth; hospitals; higher and other education and literacy programs; and cultural programs, including museums.

Fields of interest: Community development, health, education, literacy, cultural programs, welfare, homeless, minorities, youth, delinquency.

Types of support: Continuing support, annual campaigns, seed money, emergency funds, equipment, capital campaigns, operating budgets.

Limitations: Giving primarily in areas of company operations, including Rockford, IL; Fort Collins, CO; and Stevens Point, WI. No grants to individuals, or for endowment funds, research, scholarships, fellowships, special projects, publications, conferences, or matching gifts; no loans.

Application information: Application form not required.

> *Initial approach:* Letter
> *Copies of proposal:* 1
> *Deadline(s):* Submit proposal preferably in Mar. or July; no set deadline
> *Board meeting date(s):* As required
> *Final notification:* 8 weeks
> *Write:* Harry Tallacksen, Chair., Contrib. Comm., Woodward Governor Co.

Trustees: Edward Abegg, Duane Miller, Maurice O. Nelson, Leo Powelson, Robert E. Reuterfors, Dick Robbins.

Number of staff: None.

EIN: 846025403

979
Wm. Wrigley Jr. Company Foundation

410 North Michigan Ave.
Chicago 60611   (312) 645-3950

Established in 1986 in IL.

Donor(s): Wm. Wrigley Jr. Co.

Foundation type: Company-sponsored

Financial data (yr. ended 12/31/90): Assets, $13,166,332 (M); gifts received, $2,600,000; expenditures, $1,048,645; qualifying distributions, $1,038,500, including $1,038,500 for 70 grants (high: $81,900; low: $400).

Purpose and activities: Interest is primarily in national basic health and welfare organizations; support also for community funds, education, and youth organizations.

Fields of interest: Community funds, education, youth, health.

Limitations: No grants to individuals.

Application information:

> *Initial approach:* Proposal
> *Deadline(s):* Oct. 1 for consideration for the following year
> *Write:* William M. Piet, Pres.

Officers and Directors:* William Wrigley,* Chair.; William M. Piet,* Pres.; William Wrigley, Jr.,* V.P.; Mark Monroe, Secy.; Hollis Moyse, Treas.

EIN: 363486958

980
Pauline Yacktman Foundation

2640 Golf Rd.
Glenview 60025

Foundation type: Independent

Financial data (yr. ended 10/31/90): Assets, $2,542,910 (M); gifts received, $90,600; expenditures, $79,340; qualifying distributions, $79,340, including $75,300 for 13 grants (high: $25,000; low: $300).

Fields of interest: Arts, Protestant giving, hospitals.

Types of support: Operating budgets.

Limitations: Giving primarily in NY, IL, and FL.

Application information: Funds fully committed through 1998. Applications not accepted.

> *Write:* Pauline Yacktman Petre, Trustee

Trustee: Pauline Yacktman Petre.

EIN: 363335154

INDIANA

981
John W. Anderson Foundation ▼
402 Wall St.
Valparaiso 46383   (219) 462-4611

Trust established in 1967 in IN.
Donor(s): John W. Anderson.‡
Foundation type: Independent
Financial data (yr. ended 12/31/90): Assets, $101,271,791 (M); expenditures, $4,001,895; qualifying distributions, $3,280,197, including $3,059,129 for 169 grants (high: $708,400; low: $500; average: $5,000-$50,000).
Purpose and activities: Emphasis on youth agencies; support also for higher education, legal services, libraries, community funds, aid to the handicapped, and hospitals.
Fields of interest: Youth, education, higher education, legal services, libraries, community funds, handicapped, hospitals, nursing.
Types of support: Continuing support, special projects, employee-related scholarships, operating budgets.
Limitations: Giving primarily in Lake and Porter counties in northwest IN. No grants to individuals (except for scholarships for children of Anderson Company employees), or for endowment funds, annual campaigns, seed money, deficit financing, scholarship funds, or renovation projects; no loans.
Publications: 990-PF.
Application information: Application form not required.
>*Initial approach:* Letter
>*Copies of proposal:* 5
>*Deadline(s):* None
>*Board meeting date(s):* Feb., Apr., June, Aug., Oct., and Dec.
>*Final notification:* 1 month
>*Write:* Paul G. Wallace, Secy.

Officers and Trustees:* Richard S. Melvin,* Chair.; Wilfred G. Wilkins,* Vice-Chair.; Paul G. Wallace,* Secy.; William Vinovich, Bruce W. Wargo.
Number of staff: 2 part-time professional; 5 full-time support; 1 part-time support.
EIN: 356070695
Recent health grants:
981-1 American Fund for Dental Health, Chicago, IL, $10,000. 1990.
981-2 Caring Place, Hobart, IN, $20,000. 1990.
981-3 Cerebral Palsy of Northwest Indiana, Hobart, IN, $120,000. 1990.
981-4 Childrens Memorial Foundation, Chicago, IL, $30,000. 1990.
981-5 Indiana University, School of Medicine, Indianapolis, IN, $25,000. 1990.
981-6 Mayo Foundation, Rochester, MN, $25,000. 1990.
981-7 Planned Parenthood of Northwest Indiana, Gary, IN, $15,000. 1990.
981-8 Saint Anthony Medical Center, Crown Point, IN, $10,000. 1990.
981-9 Southlake Center for Mental Health, Merrillville, IN, $10,000. 1990.
981-10 Trade Winds Rehabilitation Center, Gary, IN, $75,000. 1990.
981-11 University of Chicago Cancer Research Foundation, Chicago, IL, $25,000. 1990.
981-12 Valparaiso University, School of Nursing, Valparaiso, IN, $20,000. 1990.
981-13 Visiting Nurse Association of Northwest Indiana, Hammond, IN, $10,000. 1990.

982
Ball Brothers Foundation ▼
222 South Mulberry St.
P.O. Box 1408
Muncie 47308   (317) 741-5500
FAX: (317) 741-5518

Incorporated in 1926 in IN.
Donor(s): Edmund B. Ball,‡ Frank C. Ball,‡ George A. Ball,‡ Lucius L. Ball, M.D.,‡ William A. Ball.‡
Foundation type: Independent
Financial data (yr. ended 12/31/90): Assets, $72,247,000 (M); expenditures, $4,100,000; qualifying distributions, $3,447,651, including $3,447,651 for 28 grants (high: $1,840,201; low: $1,000; average: $1,000-$50,000).
Purpose and activities: Support for the humanities and cultural programs, higher and other education, health and medical education, religion, and youth, family and social services.
Fields of interest: Cultural programs, humanities, museums, education, higher education, medical education, health, religion, youth, social services, family services.
Types of support: Matching funds, professorships, research, publications, conferences and seminars, special projects, annual campaigns, fellowships, internships, operating budgets, renovation projects, seed money, technical assistance, capital campaigns.
Limitations: Giving limited to IN. No grants to individuals.
Publications: 990-PF, application guidelines, occasional report, informational brochure.
Application information: Application form not required.
>*Initial approach:* Letter and proposal
>*Copies of proposal:* 1
>*Deadline(s):* Submit proposal preferably before June; no set deadline
>*Board meeting date(s):* Quarterly and as necessary
>*Final notification:* Varies
>*Write:* Douglas A. Bakken, Exec. Dir.

Officers and Directors:* Edmund F. Ball,* Chair.; John W. Fisher,* Pres.; Frank E. Ball,* V.P.; Reed D. Voran,* Secy.; Douglas J. Foy,* Treas.; Douglas A. Bakken, Exec. Dir.; William M. Bracken, Lucina B. Moxley, John J. Pruis, Richard M. Ringoen.
Number of staff: 1 full-time professional; 1 part-time professional; 1 full-time support; 1 part-time support.
EIN: 350882856
Recent health grants:
982-1 Hospital Hospitality House, Muncie, IN, $50,000. For challenge grant. 1990.

983
George and Frances Ball Foundation ▼
P.O. Box 1408
Muncie 47308   (317) 741-5500
Additional address: 222 South Mulberry St., Muncie, IN 47305

Incorporated in 1937 in IN.
Donor(s): George A. Ball.‡
Foundation type: Independent
Financial data (yr. ended 12/31/91): Assets, $68,182,000 (M); expenditures, $2,787,659; qualifying distributions, $2,600,000, including $2,600,000 for 32 grants (high: $1,031,225; low: $750; average: $10,000-$50,000).
Purpose and activities: Emphasis on higher education.
Fields of interest: Education, higher education, community development, historic preservation.
Types of support: Equipment, general purposes, renovation projects, special projects, capital campaigns.
Limitations: Giving primarily in Muncie, IN. No grants to individuals.
Application information: Application form required.
>*Initial approach:* Letter and proposal
>*Copies of proposal:* 1
>*Deadline(s):* None
>*Board meeting date(s):* Quarterly
>*Final notification:* Following board review
>*Write:* Joyce Beck, Admin. Secy.

Officers and Directors:* Frank A. Bracken,* Pres.; John J. Pruis,* Exec. V.P.; Reed D. Voran,* Secy.; Douglas J. Foy, Treas.; Stefan S. Anderson, Rosemary B. Bracken, Mary R. Sissel.
Number of staff: None.
EIN: 356033917
Recent health grants:
983-1 Ball Memorial Hospital, Muncie, IN, $40,000. For research department. 1990.
983-2 Comprehensive Mental Health Services, Muncie, IN, $100,000. For matching funds for new facility. 1990.

984
Clark Equipment Company Giving Program
100 North Michigan St.
South Bend 46624   (219) 239-0100
Mailing address: P.O. Box 7008, South Bend, IN 46634

Purpose and activities: Supports education, health, general community welfare, civic affairs programs, arts and minority programs.
Fields of interest: Education, civic affairs, welfare, minorities, higher education, economics, youth, community funds, journalism, health, arts, minorities.
Types of support: Matching funds, general purposes, special projects.
Limitations: Giving primarily in major operating areas. No grants to individuals.
Publications: Corporate report.
Application information: Include project description and budget.
>*Initial approach:* Letter
>*Deadline(s):* Oct.
>*Write:* T.C. Clark, Sr. V.P.

Staff: Marion Runyan, Office Coord.

Number of staff: 1 part-time professional; 1 part-time support.

985
The Clowes Fund, Inc.
250 East 38th St.
Indianapolis 46205   (317) 923-3264

Incorporated in 1952 in IN.
Donor(s): Edith W. Clowes,‡ George H.A. Clowes,‡ Allen W. Clowes.
Foundation type: Independent
Financial data (yr. ended 12/31/90): Assets, $43,482,176 (M); expenditures, $1,318,685; qualifying distributions, $1,243,128, including $1,202,000 for 35 grants (high: $500,000; low: $2,000; average: $5,000-$50,000).
Purpose and activities: Giving largely for higher and secondary education; the fine and performing arts, including music and maintenance of the Clowes Collection of Old Master Paintings in Clowes Pavillion, Indianapolis Museum of Art; support also for social services and marine biology.
Fields of interest: Higher education, secondary education, arts, performing arts, music, marine sciences, social services.
Types of support: Operating budgets, continuing support, building funds, endowment funds, scholarship funds, special projects, research.
Limitations: Giving primarily in Indianapolis, IN, and Boston, MA. No grants to individuals, or for publications or conferences; no loans.
Application information: Application form not required.
    Initial approach: Letter or proposal
    Copies of proposal: 2
    Deadline(s): Submit proposal between Sept. and Jan.; proposal must be received in our office by the last business day of Jan. of each year
    Board meeting date(s): Annually, between Feb. 1 and June 1
    Final notification: 1 month after board meeting
    Write: Allen W. Clowes, Pres.
Officers and Directors:* Allen W. Clowes,* Pres. and Treas.; Margaret J. Clowes,* V.P.; Margaret C. Bowles,* Secy.; Alexander W. Clowes, Jonathan J. Clowes, Thomas J. Clowes, Byron P. Hollett, Thomas M. Lofton, William H. Marshall.
Number of staff: 2 full-time professional; 1 part-time support.
EIN: 351079679
Recent health grants:
985-1 American College of Surgeons, Chicago, IL, $500,000. For FACS Memorial Research Career Development Award. 1990.
985-2 Community Hospital Foundation, Indianapolis, IN, $25,000. For Indiana Regional Cancer Center Campaign. 1990.
985-3 Fairbanks Hospital, Indianapolis, IN, $50,000. To expand and renovate facility. 1990.
985-4 Falmouth Hospital Foundation, Falmouth, MA, $50,000. For laboratory information system. 1990.

986
Olive B. Cole Foundation, Inc.
3242 Mallard Cove Ln.
Fort Wayne 46804   (219) 436-2182

Incorporated in 1954 in IN.
Donor(s): Richard R. Cole,‡ Olive B. Cole.
Foundation type: Independent
Financial data (yr. ended 03/31/91): Assets, $19,278,162 (M); expenditures, $901,098; qualifying distributions, $801,433, including $518,405 for 40 grants (high: $250,000; low: $500; average: $10,400), $140,984 for 231 grants to individuals (high: $1,000; low: $350; average: $500-$700) and $35,000 for program-related investments.
Purpose and activities: Grants largely for education, including student aid for graduates of Noble County high schools, hospitals, civic affairs, youth agencies, and cultural programs.
Fields of interest: Higher education, civic affairs, cultural programs, youth, hospitals.
Types of support: Seed money, building funds, equipment, land acquisition, student aid, matching funds, program-related investments, general purposes, continuing support.
Limitations: Giving limited to the Kendallville, Noble County, area, and to LaGrange, Steuben, and DeKalb counties, IN. No grants for endowment funds or research; no loans.
Publications: Application guidelines, program policy statement.
Application information: Scholarship applications available at all Noble County, IN, secondary schools. Application form required.
    Initial approach: Letter
    Copies of proposal: 7
    Deadline(s): None
    Board meeting date(s): Feb., May, Aug., and Nov.
    Final notification: 4 months
    Write: John E. Hogan, Jr., Exec. V.P.
Officers and Directors:* John N. Pichon, Jr., Pres.; John E. Hogan, Jr., Exec. V.P.; Maclyn T. Parker,* Secy.; Merrill B. Frick, Victor B. Porter, John W. Riemke.
Scholarship Administrator: Gwendlyn I. Tipton.
Number of staff: 1 full-time professional; 1 full-time support.
EIN: 356040491

987
Clarence E. Custer & Inez R. Custer Foundation
c/o R.H. Willmore
2624 Chestnut St.
Columbus 47201
Application address: c/o Irwin Union Bank & Trust Co., Trust Dept., 500 Washington St., Columbus, IN 47201; Tel.: (812) 376-1718

Established in 1988 in IN.
Foundation type: Independent
Financial data (yr. ended 12/31/90): Assets, $5,171,837 (M); expenditures, $321,868; qualifying distributions, $227,250, including $225,000 for 29 grants (high: $50,000; low: $500).
Fields of interest: Higher education, hospitals, health, youth, social services, community development.
Limitations: Giving primarily within a 50-mile radius of Columbus, IN. No grants to individuals.
Application information: Application form required.
    Deadline(s): None
    Write: William Helmbrecht, Treas.

Officers and Directors:* Richard H. Willmore,* Pres. and Mgr.; James W. Holland,* Secy.; William A. Heimbrecht,* Treas.; Max E. Carothers, Hildreth Cockley.
Managers: Irwin Union Bank & Trust Co., Trustcorp Bank Columbus, N.A.
EIN: 311130385

988
English-Bonter-Mitchell Foundation
900 Fort Wayne National Bank Bldg.
Fort Wayne 46802

Established in 1972 in IN.
Donor(s): Mary Tower English, Louise Bonter, and others.
Foundation type: Independent
Financial data (yr. ended 12/31/90): Assets, $40,272,392 (M); expenditures, $2,511,092; qualifying distributions, $2,363,415, including $2,293,000 for 62 grants (high: $150,000; low: $1,000; average: $5,000-$60,000).
Purpose and activities: Giving primarily for cultural programs and programs for youth; support also for higher education, hospitals, churches and religious organizations, social services, health, and community development.
Fields of interest: Cultural programs, youth, hospitals, higher education, religion—Christian, social services, health, community development.
Limitations: Giving primarily in Fort Wayne, IN. No grants to individuals.
Application information: Contributes only to pre-selected organizations. Applications not accepted.
Trustees: Mary E. Mitchell, Fort Wayne National Bank.
Number of staff: None.
EIN: 356247168
Recent health grants:
988-1 Fort Wayne Medical Society Foundation, Fort Wayne, IN, $10,000. 1990.
988-2 Harold W. McMillen Center for Health Education, Fort Wayne, IN, $10,000. 1990.
988-3 Indiana University, School of Medicine, Fort Wayne, IN, $40,000. For scholarships. 1990.
988-4 Lutheran Hospital Foundation, Fort Wayne, IN, $50,000. 1990.
988-5 Morton Plant Hospital, Clearwater, FL, $60,000. 1990.
988-6 Muhlenberg Hospital Center, Bethleham, PA, $25,000. 1990.
988-7 Parkview Foundation, Fort Wayne, IN, $50,000. 1990.
988-8 Saint Josephs Health Foundation, Fort Wayne, IN, $50,000. 1990.
988-9 Washington House, Fort Wayne, IN, $20,000. 1990.

989
Foellinger Foundation, Inc. ▼
520 East Berry St.
Fort Wayne 46802   (219) 422-2900

Incorporated in 1958 in IN.
Donor(s): Esther A. Foellinger,‡ Helene R. Foellinger.‡
Foundation type: Independent
Financial data (yr. ended 08/31/91): Assets, $118,988,418 (M); expenditures, $5,963,464;

qualifying distributions, $5,598,750, including $5,092,266 for 230 grants (high: $1,200,000; low: $90; average: $10,000-$200,000).

Purpose and activities: Giving primarily for cultural organizations, higher and other education, parks and recreation, social services, including programs for the disadvantaged and youth, a community fund, and health, including AIDS research and programs for drug abuse and alchoholism.

Fields of interest: Cultural programs, historic preservation, education, higher education, elementary education, educational associations, adult education, literacy, recreation, environment, social services, family services, youth, handicapped, leadership development, minorities, disadvantaged, community devclopment, health, AIDS, drug abuse, alcoholism, health services.

Types of support: Operating budgets, building funds, special projects, capital campaigns, conferences and seminars, consulting services, equipment, general purposes, land acquisition, matching funds, renovation projects, seed money, annual campaigns.

Limitations: Giving primarily in the Fort Wayne, IN, area. Generally, no grants for religious groups or pre-college education. No grants to individuals, or generally, for endowments.

Publications: Annual report (including application guidelines), occasional report.

Application information: Application form not required.

   Initial approach: Letter or proposal
   Copies of proposal: 1
   Deadline(s): 90 days before funds needed
   Board meeting date(s): 3rd Thursday of each month
   Final notification: Varies, depending on request
   Write: Harry V. Owen, Pres.

Officers and Directors:* Carl D. Rolfsen,* Chair; Harry V. Owen,* Pres.; Walter P. Helmke,* V.P.; Barbara Burt, Hilliard Gates.

Number of staff: 7 full-time professional; 2 full-time support.

EIN: 356027059

Recent health grants:

989-1 Alcohol Abuse Deterrent Program, Fort Wayne, IN, $50,000. For operating expenses. 1990.

989-2 American Red Cross, Fort Wayne Region, Fort Wayne, IN, $100,000. To purchase bloodmobile bus. 1990.

989-3 Benet Learning Center, Fort Wayne, IN, $50,000. For operating support for tuition assistance. 1990.

989-4 Washington House, Fort Wayne, IN, $40,000. For matching campaign with labor unions. 1990.

990
Fort Wayne Community Foundation, Inc.

709 South Clinton St.
Fort Wayne 46802   (219) 426-4083

Incorporated in 1956 in IN.
Foundation type: Community
Financial data (yr. ended 12/31/90): Assets, $7,754,336 (M); gifts received, $570,185; expenditures, $452,919; qualifying distributions, $398,369, including $380,085 for 68 grants

(high: $25,000; low: $100) and $18,284 for foundation-administered programs.

Purpose and activities: Discretionary grantmaking preference given to "projects expected to generate substantial benefits for the greater Fort Wayne area," including capital projects, demonstration projects, and projects promoting effective management, efficient use of community resources or volunteer participation. Areas of interest include social services, education, community development, health services, including AIDS research, environmental programs, and the arts.

Fields of interest: Health services, AIDS, social services, handicapped, disadvantaged, youth, community development, arts, business education, education—early childhood.

Types of support: Seed money, emergency funds, building funds, equipment, land acquisition, matching funds, consulting services, conferences and seminars, special projects, renovation projects, research, technical assistance, scholarship funds.

Limitations: Giving primarily in the Fort Wayne and Allen County, IN, area. No support for religious purposes, hospitals or medical research, or private schools. No grants to individuals, or for operating budgets, continuing support, annual campaigns, deficit financing, endowment funds, fellowships, or publications; no loans.

Publications: Application guidelines, grants list, occasional report, financial statement.

Application information: Application form not required.

   Initial approach: Proposal, letter, or telephone
   Copies of proposal: 1
   Deadline(s): None
   Board meeting date(s): Feb., May, Aug., and Nov.
   Final notification: 3 months
   Write: Mrs. Barbara Burt, Exec. Dir.

Officers and Board Members:* William A. Black,* Pres.; Richard J. Sadowski,* V.P.; William F. McNagny,* Secy.; Teri L. Whittaker,* Treas.; Barbara Burt, Exec. Dir.; Paul Clarke, Dir.-Special Projects.

Number of staff: 1 full-time professional; 1 part-time professional.

EIN: 351119450

Recent health grants:

990-1 Washington House, Fort Wayne, IN, $10,000. 1990.

991
The Froderman Foundation, Inc.

18 South Ninth St.
Terre Haute 47807

Donor(s): Harvey Froderman.‡
Foundation type: Independent
Financial data (yr. ended 06/30/91): Assets, $7,928,019 (M); expenditures, $411,006; qualifying distributions, $356,348, including $356,348 for 28 grants (high: $45,000; low: $769).

Fields of interest: Religion—Christian, religion—missionary programs, medical education, higher education, youth.

Types of support: Building funds, equipment, scholarship funds, operating budgets, publications.

Limitations: Giving primarily in IN.

Application information: Application form required.

   Initial approach: Letter
   Deadline(s): None
   Write: Esten Fuson, Secy.-Treas.

Officers: Carl M. Froderman, Pres.; Esten Fuson, Secy.-Treas.

EIN: 356025283

992
The W. C. Griffith Foundation

c/o Merchants National Bank & Trust Co.
P.O. Box 5031
Indianapolis 46255   (317) 267-7281
Application address: 340 Century Bldg., 36 South Pennsylvania St., Indianapolis, IN 46204

Trust established in 1959 in IN.
Donor(s): William C. Griffith,‡ Ruth Perry Griffith.‡
Foundation type: Independent
Financial data (yr. ended 11/30/91): Assets, $7,773,663 (M); expenditures, $377,851; qualifying distributions, $360,800, including $349,500 for 74 grants (high: $31,500; low: $500; average: $1,000-$15,000).

Purpose and activities: Support primarily for hospitals, health associations, medical and cancer research, the arts, including music and museums, community funds and development, higher, secondary, and other education, family planning services, child welfare, the homeless, the environment, libraries, and Christian religious organizations.

Fields of interest: Hospitals, health associations, arts, community funds, higher education, secondary education, child welfare, environment, libraries, religion—Christian.

Types of support: Building funds, capital campaigns, continuing support.

Limitations: Giving primarily in Indianapolis, IN. No grants to individuals, or for scholarships or fellowships.

Publications: 990-PF.

Application information: Application form not required.

   Initial approach: Letter
   Copies of proposal: 1
   Deadline(s): None
   Board meeting date(s): June and Nov.
   Write: Mike Miner, Trust Officer, Merchants National Bank & Trust Co.

Trustee: Merchants National Bank & Trust Co.
Advisors: C. Perry Griffith, Jr., Ruthelen G. Burns, W.C. Griffith, Jr., Walter S. Griffith, William C. Griffith III, Wendy G. Kortepeter.

Number of staff: 1 part-time support.

EIN: 356007742

993
Heritage Fund of Bartholomew County, Inc.

430 Second St.
P.O. Box 1547
Columbus 47202   (812) 376-7772

Incorporated in 1977 in IN.
Foundation type: Community
Financial data (yr. ended 12/31/91): Assets, $5,114,281 (M); gifts received, $39,183;

expenditures, $346,624; qualifying distributions, $244,215, including $244,215 for grants.
Fields of interest: Education, social services, health, hospitals, cultural programs, civic affairs.
Types of support: Operating budgets, continuing support, seed money, emergency funds, deficit financing, building funds, equipment, land acquisition, matching funds, consulting services, technical assistance, scholarship funds, program-related investments, special projects, research, publications, conferences and seminars, loans, capital campaigns, renovation projects.
Limitations: Giving primarily in Bartholomew County, IN. No support for sectarian religious purposes. No grants to individuals (except for scholarships and special educational programs), or for annual campaigns or endowment funds; no loans.
Publications: Annual report, program policy statement, application guidelines, 990-PF.
Application information: Scholarship payments are made to the educational institutions for the benefit of the individual recipients. Application form required.
  Initial approach: Letter of inquiry
  Deadline(s): None
  Board meeting date(s): Bimonthly
  Write: Edward F. Sullivan, Exec. Dir.
Officers and Directors:* Thomas C. Bigley, Jr.,* Chair. and Pres.; Nancy K. King,* V.P.; Raymond Boll, Jr.,* Treas.; Randall Allman, Carole S. Bonnell, W. Calvert Brand, Peter B. Hamilton, Susanna Jones, Bobbi Kroot, Christine W. Letts, Toshikazu Suzuki, Thomas Vickers, Charles H. Watson.
Number of staff: 1 full-time professional; 2 part-time support.
EIN: 351343903

994
Hook Drug Foundation
2800 Enterprise St.
Indianapolis 46219

Established in 1969 in IN.
Donor(s): Hook Drugs, Inc.
Foundation type: Company-sponsored
Financial data (yr. ended 12/31/91): Assets, $2,297,741 (M); gifts received, $175; expenditures, $149,474; qualifying distributions, $135,038, including $134,682 for 105 grants (high: $20,000; low: $10).
Purpose and activities: Giving to organizations involved in education, community, cultural, civic and health issues.
Fields of interest: Higher education, cultural programs, medical education, pharmacy, community funds, community development, handicapped.
Types of support: Scholarship funds, general purposes.
Limitations: Giving primarily in IN, IL, MO, and OH.
Application information:
  Initial approach: Varies with nature of request; information available
  Deadline(s): None
  Write: Thomas G. Dingledy, Secy.
Officers and Directors:* Gayl W. Doster,* Pres.; James A. Richter,* V.P.; Thomas G. Dingledy,* Secy.; John J. Kelly,* Treas.; Russell D. Mesalam, John R. Roesch, Mark A. Varnau.

EIN: 237046664

995
INB Corporate Giving Program
(Formerly Indiana National Corporate Giving Program)
One Indiana Square
Indianapolis 46266   (317) 266-5271

Financial data (yr. ended 12/31/90): Total giving, $1,106,000, including $1,037,375 for grants (high: $350,000; low: $100), $20,000 for 10 grants to individuals and $48,625 for employee matching gifts.
Purpose and activities: When reviewing proposals INB seeks: clear definition and recognition of the merit of the organization's objectives and programs; evidence that the organization and its leadership have accomplished previous goals; evidence that the community directly served by the Bank will benefit either directly or indirectly; evidence of a sound financial position; evidence of a plan for the financing of future programs; evidence of support from other named business interests in the community; and plans for reporting the results of program and fund-raising activities to the benefactors. Support for arts and culture, United Way, civic affairs, urban programs, health and human services, the homeless, and hunger.
Fields of interest: Business education, education—building funds, education—minorities, health associations, leadership development, mental health, conservation, dance, historic preservation, homeless, hospitals—building funds, housing, humanities, hunger, minorities, music, performing arts, urban development, volunteerism, cultural programs, libraries, community development, women, higher education, vocational education, community funds, hospitals, drug abuse, hunger, civic affairs, education—minorities, higher education, child development, health services, nursing, literacy, museums, race relations, youth.
Types of support: Annual campaigns, capital campaigns, emergency funds, employee matching gifts, equipment, general purposes, operating budgets, renovation projects, seed money, matching funds, endowment funds, building funds, special projects, publications, in-kind gifts, employee-related scholarships, donated products, technical assistance.
Limitations: Giving limited to IN; no support for national organizations. No support for political parties and candidates, religious organizations and primary or secondary educational institutions, public or private.
Publications: Informational brochure (including application guidelines), corporate giving report.
Application information: Public Relations/Community Affairs handles giving; site visits are often required. Application form not required.
  Initial approach: Prefers written request; letter of inquiry acceptable
  Copies of proposal: 1
  Deadline(s): 45 days in advance of need
  Board meeting date(s): Varies
  Write: Jean M. Smith, 1st. V.P., Public Rels. and Community Affairs
Number of staff: 1 part-time professional; 1 part-time support.

996
The Indianapolis Foundation ▼
615 North Alabama St., Rm. 119
Indianapolis 46204   (317) 634-7497

Established in 1916 in IN by resolution of trust.
Donor(s): James Proctor,‡ James E. Roberts,‡ Delavan Smith,‡ Charles N. Thompson,‡ Georgeanna Zumpfe.‡
Foundation type: Community
Financial data (yr. ended 12/31/91): Assets, $90,525,390 (M); gifts received, $9,393,087; expenditures, $3,386,313; qualifying distributions, $3,126,899, including $3,126,899 for 93 grants (high: $505,000; low: $1,000; average: $4,000-$50,000).
Purpose and activities: Support for the areas of health, welfare, education, character building, and culture through grants for services to youth and children; health, hospitals, and the handicapped; family and neighborhood services; civic and cultural programs; research and community planning; and general education.
Fields of interest: Youth, child welfare, health, health services, mental health, rehabilitation, handicapped, arts, cultural programs, welfare, housing, family planning, family services, aged, social services, civic affairs, community development, education, community funds.
Types of support: Program-related investments, seed money, general purposes, equipment, special projects, annual campaigns, emergency funds, renovation projects, capital campaigns.
Limitations: Giving limited to Indianapolis and Marion County, IN. No support for religious or sectarian purposes, elementary or secondary private schools, or sectarian preschool or day care centers. No grants to individuals, or for endowment funds; no loans.
Publications: Annual report (including application guidelines), newsletter, informational brochure.
Application information: Application form not required.
  Initial approach: Telephone or letter
  Copies of proposal: 7
  Deadline(s): Submit proposal by last day of Jan., Mar., May, July, Sept., or Nov.
  Board meeting date(s): Feb., Apr., June, Aug., Oct., and Dec.
  Final notification: Immediately following meetings
  Write: Kenneth I. Chapman, Exec. Dir.
Officers and Trustees:* Rexford C. Early,* Chair.; Daniel R. Efroymson,* Vice-Chair.; Louis S. Hensley, Jr.,* Secy.; Martha Lamkin, Charles A. Pechette, Matthew E. Welsh.
Trustee Banks: Ameritrust National Bank, Bank One, Indianapolis, N.A., Fifth Third Bank, First of America Bank, Huntington National Bank of Indiana, Indiana National Bank, Merchants National Bank & Trust Co., Peoples Bank & Trust Co.
Staff: Kenneth I. Chapman, Exec. Dir.
Number of staff: 2 full-time professional; 2 full-time support.
EIN: 350868115
Recent health grants:
996-1 Damien Center, Indianapolis, IN, $26,411. For continued support of HIV/AIDS Legal Project, which provides legal services to AIDS patients who were denied insurance benefits or other services. 1991.

996-2 Indianapolis Jewish Home, Hooverwood, IN, $100,000. To renovate and expand facility and include dementia care facility. 1991.

996-3 Orton Dyslexia Society of Indiana, Indiana Branch, Indianapolis, IN, $166,500. To expand programs for dyslexic children. 1991.

996-4 RISE Special Services, Indianapolis, IN, $14,933. To replace 11 auditory trainers used by severely hearing impaired children. 1991.

996-5 Saint Elizabeths Home, Indianapolis, IN, $118,700. For interim support as agency expands from maternity residence for un-wed mothers to include other types of service delivery emphasizing parenting skills, counseling and education. 1991.

996-6 Saint Francis Hospital Center, Beech Grove, IN, $150,000. For Building on a Vision capital campaign. 1991.

996-7 Southside Fellowship Center, Indianapolis, IN, $20,000. For new roof, plumbing and electrical improvements at meeting facility for recovering alcoholics. 1991.

996-8 Talbot House, Indianapolis, IN, $48,691. To renovate basement into useable activity space for recovering alcoholics. 1991.

996-9 Visiting Nurse Home Care Foundation, Indianapolis, IN, $25,744. For first year of reorganized development program. 1991.

997
Journal-Gazette Foundation, Inc.
701 South Clinton St.
Fort Wayne 46802   (219) 461-8202

Established in 1985 in IN.
Donor(s): Journal-Gazette Co., Richard G. Inskeep, Harriet J. Inskeep.
Foundation type: Company-sponsored
Financial data (yr. ended 12/31/91): Assets, $2,962,275 (M); gifts received, $712,000; expenditures, $465,863; qualifying distributions, $462,104, including $462,081 for 128 grants (high: $57,500; low: $30).
Fields of interest: Social services, community funds, higher education, education, hospitals, health associations, youth.
Types of support: Operating budgets, capital campaigns.
Limitations: Giving limited to northeastern IN. No grants to individuals.
Application information:
  Initial approach: Letter
  Deadline(s): None
  Write: Richard G. Inskeep, Pres.
Officers and Directors:* Richard G. Inskeep,* Pres.; Jerry D. Fox, Secy.-Treas.; Harriet J. Inskeep, Julie Inskeep Walda.
EIN: 311134237

998
Eli Lilly and Company Corporate Contributions Program
Lilly Corporate Ctr.
Indianapolis 46285   (317) 276-2000

Purpose and activities: Support for health, culture, civic affairs and higher education; also, donations of pharmaceutical products and equipment.
Fields of interest: Health, cultural programs, museums, civic affairs, higher education.

Types of support: In-kind gifts, donated products, donated equipment.
Limitations: Giving primarily in Indianapolis, IN, and other areas of company operations.
Application information:
  Initial approach: Proposal
  Copies of proposal: 1
  Deadline(s): None
  Write: Carol Edgar, Secy., Eli Lilly and Company Foundation

999
Eli Lilly and Company Foundation ▼
Lilly Corporate Ctr.
Indianapolis 46285   (317) 276-5342

Incorporated in 1968 in IN.
Donor(s): Eli Lilly and Co.
Foundation type: Company-sponsored
Financial data (yr. ended 12/31/90): Assets, $794,835 (M); gifts received, $2,000,000; expenditures, $9,418,266; qualifying distributions, $9,405,953, including $6,091,373 for 169 grants (high: $1,780,318; low: $250; average: $1,000-$100,000) and $3,314,580 for 6,390 employee matching gifts.
Purpose and activities: Giving primarily for health, civic and public affairs, cultural activities, and education, including higher education, educational programs for minorities, and schools of pharmacy.
Fields of interest: Health, civic affairs, public affairs, cultural programs, arts, education, higher education, education—minorities, pharmacy, educational associations, welfare.
Types of support: General purposes, operating budgets, building funds, land acquisition, fellowships, annual campaigns, capital campaigns, employee matching gifts, matching funds.
Limitations: Giving primarily in Indianapolis, IN, and other areas of company operations. No grants to individuals, or for endowment funds, special projects, research, publications, or conferences; no loans.
Application information: Application form not required.
  Initial approach: Proposal
  Copies of proposal: 1
  Deadline(s): None
  Board meeting date(s): Quarterly
  Final notification: 3 weeks to 3 months
  Write: Carol Edgar, Secy.
Officers: Vaughn D. Bryson,* Pres.; Michael S. Hunt, V.P. and Treas.; Carol Edgar, Secy.
Directors:* James M. Cornelius, Earl B. Herr, Jr., Mel Perelman, Eugene L. Step, Richard D. Wood.
Number of staff: 1 full-time professional; 2 full-time support.
EIN: 356202479
Recent health grants:
999-1 American College of Chest Physicians, Park Ridge, IL, $35,000. For operating expenses. 1990.
999-2 American Foundation for Pharmaceutical Education, North Plainfield, NJ, $27,500. For operating expenses. 1990.
999-3 American Psychiatric Association, DC, $35,000. For operating expenses. 1990.
999-4 Associated Patient Services, Indianapolis, IN, $25,000. For operating expenses. 1990.

999-5 Community Health Network, Indianapolis, IN, $80,000. For community programs. 1990.
999-6 Crossroads Rehabilitation Center, Indianapolis, IN, $100,000. For community programs. 1990.
999-7 Fairbanks Hospital, Indianapolis, IN, $30,000. For operating expenses. 1990.
999-8 Indianapolis Campaign for Healthy Babies, Indianapolis, IN, $100,000. For community programs. 1990.
999-9 March of Dimes Birth Defects Foundation, Indianapolis, IN, $80,000. For operating expenses. 1990.
999-10 National Medical Fellowships, NYC, NY, $18,000. For community programs. 1990.
999-11 Occupational Physicians Scholarship Fund, NYC, NY, $10,000. For operating expenses. 1990.
999-12 People-to-People Health Foundation, Millwood, VA, $50,000. For operating expenses. 1990.
999-13 Pharmaceutical Manufacturers Association Foundation, DC, $100,000. For operating expenses. 1990.
999-14 Saint Vincent Hospital Foundation, Indianapolis, IN, $50,000. For operating expenses. 1990.
999-15 Society of Critical Care Medicine, Fullerton, CA, $35,000. For community programs. 1990.

1000
The Lincoln National Life Insurance Company Giving Program
1300 South Clinton St.
P.O. Box 1110
Fort Wayne 46801   (219) 455-3901

Financial data (yr. ended 12/31/90): Total giving, $5,200,000.
Purpose and activities: "The Corporate Public Involvement (CPI) program is part of Lincoln National Corporation's commitment to contribute to the quality of life offered within its community. LNC contributes two percent of pretax earnings for charitable contributions. Additionally, $50,000 is awarded to an employees' committee which regrants the funds to not-for-profit projects." Supports services for the disadvantaged, education, arts, and culture. Special attention paid to programs which support victims of AIDS and disabled people.
Fields of interest: Disadvantaged, education, arts, cultural programs, AIDS, medical research, disadvantaged, handicapped.
Limitations: Giving primarily in headquarters city and major operating locations. No support for religious, fraternal or political organizations. No grants to individuals.
Application information: Application form required.
  Initial approach: Letter
  Board meeting date(s): Every 2 months
  Write: C. Suzanne Womack, V.P. and Secy., Lincoln National Life Foundation
Administrators: C. Suzanne Womack, V.P. and Secy., Lincoln National Life Fdn.; Kharis Roach, Asst. Secy.

1001
Magee-O'Connor Foundation, Inc.
P.O. Box 11196
Fort Wayne 46856   (219) 461-6280

Established in 1963 in IN.
Foundation type: Independent
Financial data (yr. ended 12/31/91): Assets,
$2,856,636 (M); expenditures, $81,373;
qualifying distributions, $58,356, including
$57,500 for 17 grants (high: $20,000; low: $500).
Fields of interest: Community development,
health, social services, religion—Christian, youth.
Limitations: Giving primarily in Fort Wayne, IN.
No grants to individuals.
Application information: Application form not
required.
  Deadline(s): None
  Write: Donald Perrey
Trustee: Lincoln National Bank & Trust Co.
EIN: 237087967

1002
The Martin Foundation, Inc. ▼
500 Simpson Ave.
Elkhart 46515   (219) 295-3343

Incorporated in 1953 in IN.
Donor(s): Ross Martin,‡ Esther Martin,‡ Lee
Martin, Geraldine F. Martin, NIBCO, Inc.
Foundation type: Independent
Financial data (yr. ended 06/30/91): Assets,
$25,614,382 (M); expenditures, $1,625,668;
qualifying distributions, $1,298,864, including
$1,261,364 for 99 grants (high: $100,000; low:
$250; average: $500-$25,000).
Purpose and activities: Emphasis on education
and social services, including programs for
women and youth; support also for
environmental and conservation organizations,
cultural programs, public interest programs, and
international development.
Fields of interest: Education, higher education,
education—minorities, libraries, social services,
family services, women, youth, environment,
conservation, cultural programs, museums, public
affairs, community development, population
studies, international development, international
studies, rehabilitation, animal welfare, Native
Americans.
Types of support: Capital campaigns, seed
money, continuing support, special projects,
emergency funds, equipment, general purposes,
matching funds, operating budgets, publications,
renovation projects.
Limitations: Giving primarily in IN; limited
national and international support. No grants to
individuals.
Application information: Application form not
required.
  Initial approach: Letter
  Copies of proposal: 1
  Deadline(s): None
  Board meeting date(s): As required
  Final notification: 4 to 8 weeks
  Write: Geraldine F. Martin, Pres.
Officers and Directors:* Geraldine F. Martin,*
Pres.; Elizabeth Martin,* Secy.; Jennifer Martin,*
Treas.; Casper Martin, Lee Martin.
Number of staff: None.
EIN: 351070929
Recent health grants:

1002-1 Bethel College, Mishawaka, IN, $25,000.
For continued support of Associate Degree in
Nursing/scholarship program. 1991.
1002-2 Haitian Health Foundation, Norwich, CT,
$10,000. To help provide tuition, uniforms,
books, and daily meal for poorest children in
Jeremie. 1991.
1002-3 Indiana Family Health Council,
Indianapolis, IN, $37,500. For scholarship
program at Indiana University School of
Nursing in OB/GYN Nurse Clinician Program.
1991.
1002-4 Planned Parenthood Federation of
America, NYC, NY, $12,500. For continued
support. 1991.
1002-5 Planned Parenthood of North Central
Indiana, South Bend, IN, $15,000. For
continued support for grass roots public
relations/education. 1991.
1002-6 Saint Joseph Care Foundation, South
Bend, IN, $10,000. For completion of pledge
for Chapin Street Health Center. 1991.
1002-7 San Lucas Mission, New Ulm, MN,
$10,000. For capital improvement grant to
parish clinic. 1991.
1002-8 United Cancer Society, Elkhart County
Chapter, Elkhart, IN, $10,000. For continued
operating support. 1991.
1002-9 Zero Population Growth, DC, $10,000.
For development and distribution of public
education materials. 1991.

1003
**The Metropolitan Health Council of
Indianapolis, Inc.**
(also known as The Health Foundation)
401 Marott Ctr.
342 Massachusetts Ave.
Indianapolis 46204   (317) 630-1805
FAX: (317) 630-1806

Established as a private foundation in 1986 in IN.
Foundation type: Independent
Financial data (yr. ended 11/30/91): Assets,
$22,822,959 (M); expenditures, $985,620;
qualifying distributions, $835,731, including
$698,618 for 44 grants (high: $125,000; low:
$1,000).
Purpose and activities: Primary areas of interest
include child development and youth, health
services, and AIDS education and services.
Encourages requests from community-based
organizations relating to adolescent health,
geriatrics, health education and promotion,
mental health, drug and alcohol abuse, and
dental and prenatal care.
Fields of interest: Youth, child development,
health, health services, aged, mental health,
AIDS, disadvantaged.
Types of support: Building funds, capital
campaigns, equipment, matching funds, seed
money, special projects, conferences and
seminars, scholarship funds, technical assistance.
Limitations: Giving limited to Marion County, IN,
and seven contiguous counties in IN.
Publications: Informational brochure (including
application guidelines), application guidelines,
grants list (including application guidelines).
Application information: Application form not
required.
  Initial approach: Telephone or letter
  Copies of proposal: 18

  Deadline(s): None
  Write: Betty H. Wilson, Exec. Dir.
Officers and Directors:* Lawrence M. Ryan,*
Pres.; Cynthia Holmes,* V.P.; Betty A. Conner,*
Secy.; Beverly Baker,* Treas.; Betty Wilson, Exec.
Dir,; Thomas Feeney, Buford Holt, Elmer Huse,
Terence Kahn, Phillip Love, George E. Ludwig,
Robert L. North, Mary O'Donnell, G. Scott Olive,
Jr., Martin Radecki, Robert Robinson, M.D.,
Reuben L. White.
Number of staff: 1 full-time professional; 1
full-time support.
EIN: 356203550

1004
Miles Foundation
(Formerly Miles Laboratories Foundation)
1127 Myrtle St.
P.O. Box 40
Elkhart 46515   (219) 264-8225

Trust established in 1953 in IN.
Donor(s): Miles, Inc.
Foundation type: Company-sponsored
Financial data (yr. ended 12/31/91): Assets,
$12,291,705 (M); gifts received, $1,001,500;
expenditures, $1,046,310; qualifying
distributions, $1,010,063, including $917,419 for
158 grants (high: $376,189; low: $100; average:
$4,200) and $40,000 for 32 grants to individuals
(high: $1,500; low: $500; average: $1,200).
Purpose and activities: Support for higher
education, including scholarship grants, to local
area high school students, community funds in
areas of company operations, and hospitals and
health organizations.
Fields of interest: Higher education, community
funds, hospitals, health services, youth.
Types of support: Annual campaigns, building
funds, capital campaigns, continuing support,
endowment funds, renovation projects, research,
special projects, student aid, operating budgets,
seed money.
Limitations: Giving primarily in IN, with some
support for organizations in other areas of
company operations.
Application information: Application form not
required.
  Initial approach: Letter
  Copies of proposal: 1
  Deadline(s): None
  Board meeting date(s): Periodically
  Write: Lehman F. Beardsley, Chair.
Officers and Trustees:* Lehman F. Beardsley,*
Chair.; Franklin E. Breckenridge,* Secy.; D.L.
Cutter, J.A. D'Arco, D.M. Hillenbrand, W.C.
Ostern.
Number of staff: None.
EIN: 356026510

1005
Moriah Fund ▼
445 North Pennsylvania St., Suite 550
Indianapolis 46204   (301) 951-3933
Application address: 35 Wisconsin Circle, Suite
520, Chevy Chase, MD 20815; Tel.: (301)
951-3933

Established in 1985 in IN.

Donor(s): Clarence W. Efroymson,‡ Robert A. Efroymson,‡ Gershon Ben-Ephraim Fund, Gustave Aaron Efroymson Fund.
Foundation type: Independent
Financial data (yr. ended 12/31/91): Assets, $165,676,732 (M); gifts received, $736,117; expenditures, $7,023,331; qualifying distributions, $6,761,676, including $6,489,200 for 76 grants.
Purpose and activities: Support primarily for pluralism, democracy, community development and education in Israel; for community institutions in IN; for family planning and conservation of natural resources internationally; and amelioration of poverty in the U.S., with a focus on closing the housing gap.
Fields of interest: Conservation, environment, housing, family planning, community development, leadership development, population studies, Israel, international development.
Types of support: Continuing support, matching funds, operating budgets, seed money, special projects, technical assistance, general purposes.
Limitations: Giving primarily in Indianapolis, IN, Israel, and internationally. No support for private foundations or arts organizations. No grants to individuals, or for medical research.
Publications: Annual report (including application guidelines).
Application information: Application form not required.
Initial approach: Letter
Copies of proposal: 1
Deadline(s): April 1 and Aug. 15
Board meeting date(s): May and Nov.
Write: Mary Ann Stein, Pres.
Officers and Program Board:* Mary Ann Stein,* Pres.; Daniel R. Efroymson,* V.P.; Lori Efroymson, Shirley G. Efroymson-Kahn, Judith Lichtman, Karl Mathiasen, Frank H. Newman, Harriet Rabb, Robert J. Stein.
Number of staff: 5 part-time professional; 1 full-time support; 2 part-time support.
EIN: 311129589
Recent health grants:
1005-1 Alan Guttmacher Institute, NYC, NY, $70,000. For general support. 1990.
1005-2 Center for Development and Population Activities, DC, $60,000. For general support. 1990.
1005-3 Center for Population Options, DC, $60,000. For general support. 1990.
1005-4 Center for Population Options, DC, $60,000. For general support. 1990.
1005-5 International Womens Health Coalition, NYC, NY, $50,000. For general support. 1990.
1005-6 Pathfinder Fund, Watertown, MA, $75,000. For Indonesia program and for general support. 1990.
1005-7 Planned Parenthood Federation of America, NYC, NY, $50,000. For prevention of teen pregnancy. 1990.
1005-8 Planned Parenthood Federation, International, NYC, NY, $75,000. For Profamilia's and Mexfam's Family Planning Programs for Teens. 1990.
1005-9 Planned Parenthood Federation, International, Western Hemisphere Region, NYC, NY, $75,000. For programming support and for Progamilia's Family Planning Center. 1990.

1005-10 Planned Parenthood of Central Indiana, Indianapolis, IN, $50,000. For general support. 1990.
1005-11 Population Crisis Committee, DC, $85,000. For general support and for special projects. 1990.
1005-12 Population Institute, DC, $25,000. For general support. 1990.
1005-13 Population Institute, DC, $25,000. For general support. 1990.
1005-14 Population Services International, DC, $25,000. For AIDS program and condom social marketing program in Cameroon. 1990.

1006
The Community Foundation of Muncie and Delaware County, Inc.
P.O. Box 807
Muncie 47308-0807   (317) 747-7181

Incorporated in 1985 in IN.
Foundation type: Community
Financial data (yr. ended 12/31/91): Assets, $5,776,201 (M); gifts received, $470,240; expenditures, $322,675; qualifying distributions, $242,518, including $242,518 for 35 grants (high: $60,000; low: $1,000).
Purpose and activities: Support for the improvement of the quality of life; primary areas of interest include community development, cultural programs, educational associations, the environment, and social services.
Fields of interest: Social services, community development, cultural programs, theater, health, youth, libraries, environment, minorities, economics, educational associations.
Types of support: Equipment, general purposes.
Limitations: Giving limited to Muncie and Delaware County, IN. No support for religious purposes or public agency projects. No grants to individuals, or for endowment support or budget deficits.
Publications: Annual report, application guidelines, newsletter, informational brochure.
Application information: Application form required.
Initial approach: Letter
Copies of proposal: 7
Deadline(s): 4th Friday of Jan., Apr., July, and Oct.
Board meeting date(s): 3rd Monday of each month
Final notification: 3rd Monday of Feb., May, Aug., and Nov.
Write: Roni Johnson, Exec. Dir.
Officers and Trustees:* David Sursa,* Pres.; Hamer D. Shafer,* V.P.; William L. Peterson,* Secy..; Jean Drumm,* Treas.; Roni Johnson, Exec. Dir.
Number of staff: 1 full-time professional; 1 part-time support.
EIN: 351640051

1007
Northern Indiana Public Service Company Giving Program
5265 Hohman Ave.
Hammond 46320   (219) 853-5200

Purpose and activities: Supports energy assistance funds, education, health, hospitals, hospital

building funds, mental health, cultural programs, social welfare, arts and sciences, and civic and community affairs including youth programs.
Fields of interest: Cultural programs, hospitals, hospitals—building funds, mental health, music, education, higher education, arts, youth, energy, health, social services, science and technology, civic affairs, community funds.
Types of support: Building funds, capital campaigns, general purposes, matching funds, renovation projects, research, grants to individuals, special projects.
Limitations: Giving primarily in operating areas. No support for religious organizations, religious purposes, or agencies not serving company operating locations. No grants to individuals or political candidates.
Publications: Corporate report.
Application information: Giving is to pre-selected organizations only.
Write: Mr. Gary L. Neal, Pres., and C.E.O.
Number of staff: None.

1008
Nicholas H. Noyes, Jr. Memorial Foundation, Inc.
Lilly Corporate Ctr.
Indianapolis 46285   (317) 276-3171

Incorporated in 1951 in IN.
Donor(s): Nicholas H. Noyes,‡ Marguerite Lilly Noyes.‡
Foundation type: Independent
Financial data (yr. ended 12/31/91): Assets, $26,070,545 (M); expenditures, $1,235,039; qualifying distributions, $1,181,068, including $1,170,000 for 73 grants (high: $100,000; low: $500).
Fields of interest: Higher education, secondary education, performing arts, museums, health, hospitals, social services, youth.
Types of support: Operating budgets, endowment funds, scholarship funds, matching funds.
Limitations: Giving primarily in IN. No grants to individuals, or for building funds; no loans.
Application information: Application form not required.
Initial approach: Letter
Copies of proposal: 1
Deadline(s): None
Board meeting date(s): Semiannually
Write: James M. Cornelius, Treas.
Officers and Directors:* Evan L. Noyes, Jr.,* Pres.; Robert H. Reynolds, V.P.; Frederic M. Ayres,* Secy.; James M. Cornelius, Treas.; Nancy Ayres, Janet A. Carrington, Diane C. Leslie, Nicholas S. Noyes.
EIN: 351003699

1009
Hollie & Anna Oakley Foundation, Inc.
18 South 16th St.
Terre Haute 47807   (812) 232-4437

Established in 1954 in IN.
Donor(s): Hollie N. Oakley.‡
Foundation type: Independent
Financial data (yr. ended 12/31/91): Assets, $2,424,310 (M); gifts received, $73,478; expenditures, $98,678; qualifying distributions,

$88,724, including $82,424 for 35 grants (high: $20,750; low: $100).

Fields of interest: Higher education, education, hospitals, youth, health associations, community funds.

Types of support: General purposes, scholarship funds.

Limitations: Giving primarily in the Terre Haute, IN, and Winter Park, FL, areas.

Application information:

Initial approach: Letter

Deadline(s): None

Officers and Directors:* Alice Oakley Schmidt,* Pres.; John G. Schmidt,* V.P.; Doris Kiburis,* Secy.; Eston L. Perry,* Treas.; Julie Perry Heck, Alice Ann Perry, Jeffrey J. Perry.

EIN: 237008034

1010
Oliver Memorial Trust Foundation

c/o Norwest Bank Indiana, N.A.

112 West Jefferson Blvd.

South Bend 46601   (219) 237-3475

Trust established in 1959 in IN.

Donor(s): C. Frederick Cunningham,‡ Gertrude Oliver Cunningham, Walter C. Steenburg,‡ Jane Cunningham Warriner, J. Oliver Cunningham.

Foundation type: Independent

Financial data (yr. ended 12/31/91): Assets, $6,800,796 (M); gifts received, $50,000; expenditures, $368,174; qualifying distributions, $336,725, including $328,458 for 28 grants (average: $5,000-$10,000).

Purpose and activities: Emphasis on hospitals, higher education, particularly college endowments, community funds, and youth agencies.

Fields of interest: Hospitals, higher education, community funds, youth.

Types of support: Continuing support, annual campaigns, building funds, endowment funds, matching funds, research, capital campaigns, equipment, seed money, special projects.

Limitations: Giving primarily in the South Bend, IN, area. No grants to individuals, or for land acquisition, conferences, scholarships, or fellowships; no loans.

Application information: Application form not required.

Initial approach: Letter

Deadline(s): None

Board meeting date(s): Quarterly or as required

Write: Charles F. Nelson

Trustee: Norwest Bank Indiana, N.A.

Number of staff: None.

EIN: 356013076

1011
Reilly Foundation

1510 Market Square Ctr.

151 North Delaware St.

Indianapolis 46204   (317) 638-7531

Trust established in 1962 in IN.

Donor(s): Reilly Industries, Inc.

Foundation type: Company-sponsored

Financial data (yr. ended 12/31/91): Assets, $586,854 (M); gifts received, $350,000; expenditures, $456,995; qualifying distributions, $456,995, including $421,114 for 93 grants (high: $43,200; low: $100), $18,547 for 38 grants to individuals (high: $750; low: $150) and $8,475 for 33 employee matching gifts.

Purpose and activities: Giving primarily for higher education, community funds, hospitals, and social service agencies; educational grants and scholarships limited to children of company employees.

Fields of interest: Higher education, community funds, hospitals, social services.

Types of support: Employee-related scholarships, employee matching gifts, general purposes.

Limitations: Giving limited to areas of company operations.

Application information:

Initial approach: Letter

Deadline(s): None

Write: Lorraine D. Schroeder, Trustee

Trustees: Rolla E. McAdams, Elizabeth C. Reilly, Thomas E. Reilly, Jr., Lorraine D. Schroeder, Clarke L. Wilhelm.

EIN: 352061750

1012
Clarence L. & Edith B. Schust Foundation

c/o Fort Wayne National Bank

110 West Berry St., P.O. Box 110

Fort Wayne 46801   (219) 426-0555

Established in 1983 in IN.

Foundation type: Independent

Financial data (yr. ended 04/30/91): Assets, $3,771,481 (M); expenditures, $218,626; qualifying distributions, $206,560, including $203,447 for 28 grants (high: $20,326; low: $1,000).

Fields of interest: Protestant giving, hospitals, youth, social services, community development.

Limitations: Giving primarily in IN, with emphasis on Fort Wayne. No grants to individuals.

Application information:

Initial approach: Proposal

Deadline(s): None

Trustee: Fort Wayne National Bank.

EIN: 311064803

1013
Zollner Foundation

c/o Lincoln National Bank & Trust Co.

P.O. Box 2363

Fort Wayne 46801   (219) 461-6451

Established in 1983 in IN.

Foundation type: Independent

Financial data (yr. ended 12/31/90): Assets, $6,711,395 (M); expenditures, $260,947; qualifying distributions, $243,044, including $230,415 for 19 grants (high: $50,000; low: $5,000).

Fields of interest: Higher education, hospitals, youth.

Types of support: General purposes, annual campaigns, equipment.

Limitations: Giving primarily in Allen County, IN.

Application information: Application form not required.

Initial approach: Letter

Deadline(s): None

Board meeting date(s): June and Dec.

Write: Alice Kopfer, V.P., Lincoln National Bank & Trust Co.

Trustee: Lincoln National Bank & Trust Co.

Number of staff: None.

EIN: 356381471

IOWA

1014
The Bohen Foundation ▼
1716 Locust St.
Des Moines 50336   (515) 284-2556

Incorporated in 1958 in IA.
Donor(s): Mildred M. Bohen Charitable Trust,
Edna E. Meredith Charitable Trust.
Foundation type: Independent
Financial data (yr. ended 06/30/90): Assets,
$8,484,831 (M); gifts received, $915,951;
expenditures, $1,909,034; qualifying
distributions, $1,785,765, including $1,738,700
for 52 grants (high: $330,000; low: $250;
average: $5,000-$50,000).
Purpose and activities: Emphasis on higher and
secondary education, conservation, and the
performing arts.
Fields of interest: Higher education, secondary
education, conservation, performing arts, AIDS.
Types of support: Operating budgets, building
funds, annual campaigns, special projects.
Limitations: No grants to individuals.
Application information:
Initial approach: Letter
Copies of proposal: 1
Deadline(s): None
Board meeting date(s): As required
Write: Marilyn J. Dillivan, Treas.
Officers and Directors:* Frederick B. Henry,*
Pres.; Linda C. Behr, Secy.; Marilyn J. Dillivan,
Treas.
Number of staff: None.
EIN: 426054774

1015
Roy J. Carver Charitable Trust
P.O. Box 76
Muscatine 52761   (319) 263-4010

Established in 1982 in IA.
Donor(s): Roy J. Carver, Sr.‡
Foundation type: Independent
Financial data (yr. ended 04/30/91): Assets,
$150,458,913 (M); expenditures, $6,733,262;
qualifying distributions, $6,112,135, including
$5,856,954 for 23 grants (high: $1,188,696; low:
$500; average: $20,000-$300,000).
Purpose and activities: Support primarily for
education, medical research, science and
technology, and youth programs.
Fields of interest: Medical research, science and
technology, youth, education.
Types of support: Research, seed money, special
projects, scholarship funds.
Limitations: Giving primarily in IA.
Publications: Informational brochure (including
application guidelines).
Application information: Application form not
required.
Initial approach: Letter
Deadline(s): None
Board meeting date(s): Jan., Apr., July, and Oct.
Write: Roger A. Hughes, Exec. Admin.

Officers and Trustees:* William F. Cory,* Chair.;
Roger A. Hughes,* Exec. Admin.; Willard L.
Boyd, Lucille A. Carver, Roy J. Carver, Jr., Arthur
Dahl, J. Larry Griffith, Clay LeGrand.
Number of staff: 2 full-time professional; 2
full-time support; 1 part-time support.
EIN: 421186589

1016
The Greater Cedar Rapids Foundation
(Formerly Community Welfare Foundation of
Cedar Rapids, Iowa)
101 Second St., S.E., Suite 306
Cedar Rapids 52401   (319) 366-2862

Established in 1949 in IA.
Foundation type: Community
Financial data (yr. ended 12/31/90): Assets,
$1,905,062 (M); gifts received, $706,688;
expenditures, $375,257; qualifying distributions,
$252,749, including $252,749 for 24 grants
(high: $100,000; low: $1,170).
Purpose and activities: To enhance the quality of
life in the community by supporting creative and
innovative programs, current or emerging
charitable opportunities, services not presently
offered, and occasional capital projects.
Fields of interest: Community development,
social services, arts, humanities, health,
education, historic preservation, environment.
Limitations: Giving limited to the greater Cedar
Rapids and surrounding Linn County, IA, area. No
grants for annual operating budgets; generally no
support for crisis intervention, deficit financing, or
after-the-fact funding.
Publications: Annual report (including application
guidelines), informational brochure, application
guidelines.
Application information: Applicants are
encouraged to telephone regarding preliminary
information prior to submitting an application.
Initial approach: Letter
Copies of proposal: 5
Deadline(s): Apr. 19 and Oct. 25
Board meeting date(s): June and Dec.
Final notification: June 13 and Dec. 12
Write: Malcolm L. Peel, Exec. Dir.
Officers and Directors:* Nancy G. McHugh,*
Pres.; Thomas L. Aller,* V.P.; Mimi A. Meffert,*
Secy.-Treas.; Malcolm L. Peel, Exec. Dir.; Robert
L. DeMeulenaere, Russell I. Hess, David C.
Neuhaus, Susan K. Turner.
EIN: 426053860
Recent health grants:
1016-1 Cornell College, Mount Vernon, IA,
$18,000. For enrichment and general support
of Fitness and Wellness Center program. 1990.

1017
Employers Mutual Casualty Company Corporate Giving Program
717 Mulberry St.
P.O. Box 712
Des Moines 50303   (515) 280-2587

Financial data (yr. ended 12/31/90): Total giving,
$350,000 for grants.
Purpose and activities: Support for the arts,
including museums and the performing arts,
insurance education, community development,
hospitals, and the United Way. Gifts of over

$3,000 must be approved by the contributions
committee. At times equipment may be awarded;
a loaned executive program supports United Way.
Fields of interest: Community development,
community funds, arts, hospitals, insurance
education, museums, performing arts.
Types of support: Annual campaigns, building
funds, capital campaigns, continuing support,
endowment funds, equipment, professorships,
loaned talent.
Limitations: Giving primarily in the Des Moines,
IA, area. No support for religion.
Application information:
Initial approach: Short letter
Deadline(s): None
Write: Robb B. Kelley, Chair. and C.E.O.
Number of staff: None.

1018
The Hall Foundation, Inc. ▼
115 Third St., S.E., No. 803
Cedar Rapids 52401   (319) 362-9079

Incorporated in 1953 in IA.
Donor(s): Members of the Hall family.
Foundation type: Independent
Financial data (yr. ended 12/31/91): Assets,
$51,297,946 (M); expenditures, $4,272,937;
qualifying distributions, $4,123,258, including
$4,106,015 for 52 grants (high: $500,000; low:
$500; average: $10,000-$100,000).
Purpose and activities: Primary areas of interest
include the arts, higher education, social services,
community funds, and hospitals. Support also for
cultural programs, including fine and performing
arts groups, youth agencies, and health services.
Fields of interest: Cultural programs, arts,
museums, music, theater, higher education,
libraries, social services, youth, aged, family
services, minorities, community funds, hospitals,
health services, cancer, handicapped, health,
hospitals—building funds, mental health, drug
abuse, civic affairs.
Types of support: Annual campaigns, seed
money, emergency funds, building funds,
equipment, land acquisition, special projects,
capital campaigns, scholarship funds, matching
funds.
Limitations: Giving limited to Cedar Rapids, IA,
and the immediate trade area. No grants to
individuals, or for deficit financing, endowment
funds, or fellowships; no loans.
Publications: Informational brochure (including
application guidelines).
Application information: Application form not
required.
Initial approach: Letter
Copies of proposal: 1
Deadline(s): None
Board meeting date(s): Quarterly
Final notification: 3 months
Write: John G. Lidvall, Exec. Dir.
Officers and Directors:* Irene H. Perrine,* Chair.;
William P. Whipple,* Pres.; John G. Lidvall,* V.P.
and Exec. Dir.; George C. Foerstner,* V.P.; Darrel
A. Morf,* Secy.; Joseph R. Loufek,* Treas.; Dennis
L. Boatman, E.J. Buresh, James E. Coquillette, Jack
B. Evans, Carleen Grandon, Alex Meyer.
Number of staff: 2 part-time professional.
EIN: 426057097

1019
Iowa and Illinois Gas and Electric Company Giving Program
206 E. 2nd St.
Davenport 52802   (319) 326-7038

Financial data (yr. ended 12/31/90): Total giving, $519,072, including $504,010 for 106 grants (high: $113,425; low: $10) and $15,062 for 130 employee matching gifts.
Purpose and activities: Supports community arts, fine arts, cultural institutes, humanities, libraries, music, theater, economic development, environmental issues, education, health care, child welfare, civic affairs, community development, family services, the handicapped, and mental health programs. Special uses for funding include equipment and short term projects.
Fields of interest: Arts, cultural programs, education, environment, health, theater, health services, music, higher education, child welfare, civic affairs, community development, conservation, education—building funds, educational associations, family services, fine arts, general charitable giving, handicapped, humanities, libraries, mental health, museums, performing arts, welfare.
Types of support: Program-related investments, building funds, annual campaigns, capital campaigns, continuing support, general purposes.
Limitations: Giving primarily in Davenport, Bettendorf, Cedar Rapids, Iowa City, Ottumwa, and Fort Dodge, IA; Rock Island and Moline, IL.
Application information: Contributions are handled by the finance department. Application form not required.
  Initial approach: Letter; send to headquarters
  Copies of proposal: 1
  Board meeting date(s): Jan., Apr., July, and Oct.
  Final notification: If rejected, applicant will receive notification
  Write: John C. Decker, Secy.-Treas.
Number of staff: 1

1020
Kinney-Lindstrom Foundation, Inc.
P.O. Box 520
Mason City 50401   (515) 896-3888
Application address: c/o Kinney-Lindstrom Foundation, Inc., Hanlontown, IA 50444

Incorporated in 1957 in IA.
Donor(s): Ida Lindstrom Kinney.‡
Foundation type: Independent
Financial data (yr. ended 12/31/90): Assets, $6,421,596 (M); expenditures, $533,884; qualifying distributions, $379,025, including $374,425 for 29 grants (high: $200,000; low: $170; average: $2,000-$50,000).
Purpose and activities: Grants primarily for building funds for libraries in IA towns; support also for education, historical museums and other cultural programs, social service and youth agencies, health agencies, and civic programs.
Fields of interest: Libraries, education, history, museums, cultural programs, social services, youth, health, civic affairs.
Types of support: Building funds.
Limitations: Giving primarily in IA. No grants to individuals, or for endowment funds, operating budgets, or research; no loans.

Application information: Application form not required.
  Initial approach: Letter
  Copies of proposal: 1
  Deadline(s): None
  Board meeting date(s): 10 times a year
  Final notification: 2 weeks after interview
  Write: Lowell K. Hall, Secy.
Officer: Lowell K. Hall, Secy.
Trustees: Everett J. Hermanson, Thor Jenson.
Number of staff: 1 full-time professional.
EIN: 426037351

1021
Peter H. and E. Lucille Gaass Kuyper Foundation
c/o Rolscreen Co.
Pella 50219   (515) 628-1000

Established in 1970 in IA.
Donor(s): Peter H. Kuyper, E. Lucille Gaass Kuyper, Joan Kuyper Farver.
Foundation type: Independent
Financial data (yr. ended 04/30/92): Assets, $12,324,462 (M); expenditures, $1,054,276; qualifying distributions, $1,043,362, including $1,043,362 for 110 grants (high: $300,000; low: $100; average: $5,000-$10,000).
Fields of interest: Higher education, arts, religion—Christian, hospitals, general charitable giving.
Limitations: Giving primarily in the Pella, IA, area.
Application information: Application form not required.
  Initial approach: Letter
  Copies of proposal: 1
  Deadline(s): None
  Board meeting date(s): Apr.
  Write: Joan Kuyper Farver, Pres.
Officers and Directors:* Joan Kuyper Farver,* Pres.; Suzanne Farver,* V.P.; Carol Kuyper Rosenberg,* V.P.; Thomas W. Carpenter,* Secy.; William J. Anderson,* Treas.
Number of staff: None.
EIN: 237068402

1022
Lee Foundation
215 North Main St.
Davenport 52801

Incorporated in 1962 in IA.
Donor(s): Lee Enterprises.
Foundation type: Company-sponsored
Financial data (yr. ended 09/30/90): Assets, $4,312,703 (M); expenditures, $277,120; qualifying distributions, $273,220, including $273,220 for 46 grants (high: $37,500; low: $500).
Fields of interest: Higher education, hospitals, youth, cultural programs, journalism.
Types of support: Endowment funds, building funds.
Limitations: Giving primarily in areas of company operations in IA, IL, WI, MT, ND, OR, CA, and NE. No grants to individuals.
Officers and Directors:* Lloyd G. Schermer,* Pres.; Richard D. Gottlieb,* V.P.; Ronald L. Rickman,* V.P.; Gary N. Schmedding,* V.P.; Richard P. Galligan,* Secy.; Michael J. Riley,* Treas.

EIN: 426057173

1023
Wesley Mansfield and Irene Mansfield Charitable Foundation
823 13th St.
P.O. Box 283
Belle Plaine 52208

Established in 1984 in IA.
Foundation type: Independent
Financial data (yr. ended 07/31/91): Assets, $11,695,346 (M); gifts received, $5,000; expenditures, $497,907; qualifying distributions, $437,579, including $432,492 for 18 grants (high: $100,000; low: $1,000).
Fields of interest: Medical education, higher education, community development, civic affairs.
Types of support: General purposes, building funds, scholarship funds.
Limitations: Giving primarily in IA.
Application information: Application form not required.
  Deadline(s): June 1
  Write: Larry Schlue
Trustees: M.D. Dreibelbis, Evelyn Mansfield, Leonard Taylor.
EIN: 421226535

1024
The Fred Maytag Family Foundation ▼
200 First St. South
P.O. Box 426
Newton 50208   (515) 792-1800

Trust established in 1945 in IA.
Donor(s): Fred Maytag II,‡ Members of the Maytag family.
Foundation type: Independent
Financial data (yr. ended 12/31/91): Assets, $27,733,100 (M); expenditures, $1,545,544; qualifying distributions, $1,330,303, including $1,330,303 for 88 grants (high: $250,000; low: $100; average: $1,000-$50,000).
Purpose and activities: Giving for higher and other education, arts and culture, public affairs, social services, and health, including cancer research, the handicapped, and family planning.
Fields of interest: Education, higher education, arts, cultural programs, social services, family planning, handicapped, health, cancer, public affairs.
Types of support: Operating budgets, continuing support, annual campaigns, seed money, building funds, equipment, land acquisition, matching funds, research, special projects, renovation projects.
Limitations: Giving primarily in Des Moines and Newton, IA. No grants to individuals, or for emergency funds, deficit financing, endowment funds, scholarships, fellowships, demonstration projects, publications, or conferences; no loans.
Application information: Application form not required.
  Initial approach: Letter
  Copies of proposal: 4
  Deadline(s): Submit proposal preferably in Apr. or May; deadline May 31
  Board meeting date(s): June or July
  Final notification: 30 days after meeting
  Write: Francis C. Miller, Secy.

Officer: Francis C. Miller, Secy.
Trustees: Ellen Pray Maytag Madsen, Frederick L. Maytag III, Kenneth P. Maytag.
Number of staff: 2 part-time support.
EIN: 426055654

1025
Mid-Iowa Health Foundation
550 39th St., Suite 104
Des Moines 50312   (515) 277-6411

Established in 1984 in IA.
Foundation type: Independent
Financial data (yr. ended 12/31/91): Assets, $13,588,991 (M); expenditures, $596,424; qualifying distributions, $596,424, including $517,050 for 41 grants.
Purpose and activities: Primary areas of interest include the disadvantaged, the elderly, youth, the handicapped, and health services. Support limited to health-related service projects, including the areas of drug abuse and alcoholism, mental health, nutrition and hunger, nursing, pharmacy, and hospices; giving also for child welfare, the homeless, early childhood and medical education, and capital projects.
Fields of interest: Health, health services, drug abuse, mental health, nutrition, homeless, disadvantaged, aged, youth, medical education, handicapped.
Types of support: General purposes, equipment, scholarship funds, building funds, matching funds, operating budgets, special projects.
Limitations: Giving limited to Polk County, IA, and seven surrounding counties. No support for hospital programs. No grants for research.
Publications: 990-PF, informational brochure (including application guidelines), application guidelines, grants list.
Application information: Application form required.
  Initial approach: Letter or telephone
  Copies of proposal: 1
  Deadline(s): Feb. 1, May 1, Aug. 1, and Nov. 1
  Board meeting date(s): Mar., June, Sept., and Dec.
  Final notification: 6 to 8 weeks
  Write: Kathryn Bradley
Officers and Directors:* Ivan Johnson,* Chair.; Bernard Mercer,* Vice-Chair.; Rex Burns,* Secy.-Treas.; Simon Casady, Donna Drees, Don C. Green, Dale Grunewald, T. Ward Phillips, F.F. Satterlee.
Number of staff: 1 full-time professional.
EIN: 421235348

1026
Pioneer Hi-Bred International Corporate Giving Program
400 Locust St., Suite 700
Des Moines 50309   (515) 245-3593

Financial data (yr. ended 08/31/90): Total giving, $3,451,597, including $3,304,913 for 506 grants (high: $175,000; low: $50; average: $2,500-$10,000) and $85,000 for in-kind gifts.
Purpose and activities: Supports children's welfare, civic affairs, economic development, environmental programs, fine arts, general arts, education, health care, handicapped, disabled, minority, science, senior citizens, vocational education, welfare and youth service programs. Also supports international groups, private and public colleges, as well as projects concerned with rural issues. Types of support include employee matching gifts for education and in-kind donations in the form of equipment and printing services.
Fields of interest: Youth, civic affairs, economics, environment, education, fine arts, arts, health, handicapped, higher education, Canada, international affairs, minorities, rural development, science and technology, community funds, vocational education, welfare, Asia, Europe.
Types of support: Building funds, capital campaigns, employee matching gifts, endowment funds, fellowships, general purposes, matching funds, operating budgets, scholarship funds, research, in-kind gifts, donated equipment.
Limitations: Giving primarily in headquarters city and major operating areas. No support for religious, political, or lobbying organizations. No support for health associations unless they provide direct services; athletic activities; or for touring or co-curricular activities. No grants to individuals, or for ticket sales or emergency funding.
Publications: Informational brochure.
Application information: Application form not required.
  Initial approach: Brief letter; send to nearest company facility
  Copies of proposal: 1
  Deadline(s): None
  Board meeting date(s): Requests reviewed quarterly
  Final notification: As soon as possible
  Write: Lu Jean Cole, Dir., Community Relations
Number of staff: 1 full-time professional; 1 part-time professional; 2 full-time support.

1027
The Principal Financial Group Corporate Giving Program
711 High St.
Des Moines 50392-0150   (515) 247-5209

Financial data (yr. ended 12/31/90): Total giving, $919,455, including $223,455 for 87 grants (high: $43,000; low: $100; average: $500-$2,000), $618,000 for loans and $78,000 for in-kind gifts.
Purpose and activities: Support for social services, arts and culture, health, civic and community affairs, education, and the United Way.
Fields of interest: Arts, AIDS, aged, community development, cultural programs, civic affairs, education—early childhood, education—minorities, environment, family services, fine arts, health, higher education, health services, homeless, housing, insurance education, minorities, medical education, medical research, music, performing arts, public policy, theater, urban development, business education, dance, civil rights.
Types of support: Annual campaigns, employee matching gifts, operating budgets, building funds, in-kind gifts, continuing support, general purposes, donated products, use of facilities, public relations services, employee volunteer services.

Limitations: Giving primarily in Iowa with emphasis on the Des Moines, IA, area; some support for national organizations. No support for athletic, fraternal, religious, denominational, sectarian, trade, industry, professional associations, private foundations, or veterans groups. No grants to individuals, conference or seminar attendance; festival participation, hospital/health care capital fund drives; or goodwill ads.
Publications: Application guidelines.
Application information: Giving handled by Corporate Relations. Application form not required.
  Initial approach: Written proposal; Send requests to headquarters
  Copies of proposal: 1
  Deadline(s): 4 to 6 weeks prior to contributions meeting
  Board meeting date(s): Monthly
  Final notification: 6 to 8 weeks
  Write: Debra J. Jensen, Community Rels. Mgr.
Administrators: Karen Shaff, Chair., Contribs. Comm.; Debra J. Jensen, Secy., Contribs. Comm.

1028
The Principal Financial Group Foundation, Inc. ▼
711 High St.
Des Moines 50392-0150   (515) 247-5209

Established in 1987 in IA.
Foundation type: Company-sponsored
Financial data (yr. ended 12/31/90): Assets, $22,523,917 (M); expenditures, $2,270,114; qualifying distributions, $2,225,925, including $2,004,917 for 135 grants (high: $500,000; low: $100; average: $2,500-$5,000) and $221,008 for 386 employee matching gifts.
Purpose and activities: Support for social services, arts and culture, health, education, civic and community affairs, and the United Way of Central IA.
Fields of interest: Social services, minorities, aged, family services, housing, arts, cultural programs, performing arts, health, health services, medical research, AIDS, education, education—early childhood, higher education, medical education, education—minorities, civic affairs, community development, urban development, public policy, environment.
Types of support: Annual campaigns, building funds, capital campaigns, continuing support, operating budgets, special projects, general purposes, in-kind gifts, employee matching gifts.
Limitations: Giving primarily in IA with emphasis on the Des Moines, IA, area. No support for athletic organizations, fraternal organizations, organizations redistributing funds, private foundations, sectarian, religious, or denominational organizations, social organizations, trade, industrial or professional associations, or veteran's groups. No grants to individuals, or for conference or seminar attendance, goodwill ads, endowments, festival participation, or hospital or health care capital fund drives.
Publications: Application guidelines.
Application information: Application form not required.
  Initial approach: Proposal
  Copies of proposal: 1

Deadline(s): 4 to 6 weeks prior to contributions committee meeting
Board meeting date(s): Approximately once a month
Final notification: 6 to 8 weeks
Write: Debra J. Jensen, Secy.
Officers and Directors:* G. David Hurd,* Chair.; Theodore Hutchinson,* Vice-Chair.; Thomas Gaard,* V.P.; Thomas J. Graf,* V.P.; James Van Lew,* V.P.; Karen E. Shaff,* V.P.; Debra J. Jensen, Secy.; Richard W. Waugh,* Treas.
Number of staff: None.
EIN: 421312301

1029
Quad City Osteopathic Foundation
c/o ERA Assoc. Counselors
6236 North Brady St.
Davenport 52806   (319) 386-5204

Established in 1984 in IA.
Foundation type: Independent
Financial data (yr. ended 11/30/91): Assets, $4,499,953 (M); gifts received, $1,550; expenditures, $411,371; qualifying distributions, $412,498, including $188,498 for 14 grants (high: $135,000; low: $650), $99,000 for 30 grants to individuals (high: $7,000; low: $1,000; average: $1,000-$7,000) and $125,000 for 5 loans to individuals.
Purpose and activities: Awards scholarships in the field of osteopathy; substantial support for a clinic, health, and medical education.
Fields of interest: Medical education, health, medical sciences, community funds, community development.

Types of support: Student aid.
Limitations: Giving primarily in IA and IL.
Publications: Newsletter, annual report.
Application information: Application form required.
Initial approach: Letter
Copies of proposal: 1
Deadline(s): None
Board meeting date(s): 2nd Tuesday of each month
Write: Eugene Holst, Pres.
Officers and Directors:* Patrick Irving,* Chair.; Michael Koury,* Vice-Chair.; Eugene R. Holst, Pres.; Charles Elmondorf,* Secy.; Tim Hart,* Treas.; John Cannon, C.E. Cunningham, G.H. Goettsch, Bruce McElhinney, Susan Skura.
Number of staff: 1 full-time professional.
EIN: 420666090

1030
Wahlert Foundation
c/o FDL Foods, Inc.
P.O. Box 898
Dubuque 52001   (319) 588-5400

Incorporated in 1948 in IA.
Donor(s): Dubuque Packing Co., FDL Foods, Inc., H.W. Wahlert,‡ and officers of the foundation.
Foundation type: Independent
Financial data (yr. ended 11/30/91): Assets, $4,375,613 (M); gifts received, $3,015; expenditures, $326,708; qualifying distributions, $321,500, including $321,500 for 22 grants (high: $240,000; low: $500; average: $500-$240,000).

Purpose and activities: Support primarily for higher, secondary, medical and theological education; grants also for health services and hospitals, including medical and cancer research, social service agencies, including drug abuse prevention programs and services for families, the homeless and the handicapped, child welfare programs for minorities, cultural activities, including the arts and museums, Catholic welfare organizations and schools, and agricultural programs and rural development.
Fields of interest: Higher education, secondary education, health, social services, family services, minorities, arts, religion, rural development, general charitable giving.
Types of support: Continuing support, annual campaigns, seed money, emergency funds, building funds, equipment, capital campaigns, scholarship funds, special projects.
Limitations: Giving primarily in the Dubuque, IA, metropolitan area. No grants to individuals, or for publications, conferences, or matching gifts; no loans.
Application information: Application form not required.
Initial approach: Proposal
Copies of proposal: 1
Deadline(s): Nov. 30
Board meeting date(s): Dec.
Final notification: Jan. 30
Write: R.H. Wahlert, Pres. and Treas.
Officers and Trustees:* R.H. Wahlert,* Pres. and Treas.; Alfred E. Hughes,* Secy.; Donald Strausse, David Wahlert, Donna Wahlert, James Wahlert, R.C. Wahlert, R.C. Wahlert II.
Number of staff: None.
EIN: 426051124

KANSAS

1031
Louis W. & Dolpha Baehr Foundation
c/o Miami County National Bank and Trust
Box 369
Paola 66071   (913) 294-4311

Established in 1967 in KS.
Donor(s): L.W. Baehr,‡ Dolpha Baehr.‡
Foundation type: Independent
Financial data (yr. ended 04/30/91): Assets,
$2,844,113 (M); expenditures, $181,958;
qualifying distributions, $170,695, including
$162,006 for 13 grants (high: $38,120; low:
$300).
Fields of interest: Recreation, education,
hospitals, mental health, community
development.
Types of support: Building funds, endowment
funds, equipment, matching funds, renovation
projects, research, seed money, special projects.
Limitations: Giving limited to eastern KS,
including the greater Kansas City area. No
support for sectarian or religious organizations
whose services are limited to members of any one
religious group, or for agencies operating as
chapters of a state or national organization. No
grants to individuals, or for advertising; no loans.
Publications: Application guidelines.
Application information: Application form not
required.
  Initial approach: Proposal
  Deadline(s): Dec., Mar., July, and Sept.
  Board meeting date(s): Jan., Apr., Aug., and Oct.
  Final notification: Within 12 weeks
  Write: Carl F. Gump, Chair., or Kathy Lovig,
    Secy.
Trustee: Miami County National Bank and Trust.
Number of staff: None.
EIN: 486129741

1032
Bank IV Charitable Trust
(Formerly Fourth National Bank of Wichita
Charitable Trust)
c/o Bank IV Kansas, N.A.
P.O. Box 1122
Wichita 67201   (316) 261-4361

Trust established in 1952 in KS.
Donor(s): Bank IV Kansas, N.A.
Foundation type: Company-sponsored
Financial data (yr. ended 11/30/91): Assets,
$571,157 (M); expenditures, $605,132;
qualifying distributions, $603,027, including
$601,973 for 99 grants (high: $100,000; low:
$100; average: $1,000-$10,000).
Fields of interest: Community funds, child
development, youth, higher education, health
services, hospitals, handicapped, cultural
programs.
Types of support: Building funds, equipment,
endowment funds, scholarship funds, capital
campaigns, research, operating budgets.
Limitations: Giving primarily in KS, in
communities where Bank IV has operations. No

support for political or religious organizations,
fraternal groups, or organizations which receive a
major portion of their support from government
funds. No grants to individuals, or for general
support, dinners, travel, annual campaigns, seed
money, emergency funds, deficit financing,
publications, conferences, or matching gifts; no
loans.
Publications: Application guidelines.
Application information: Application form not
required.
  Initial approach: Letter
  Copies of proposal: 1
  Deadline(s): None
  Board meeting date(s): As needed
  Final notification: Up to 3 months
  Write: Marilyn B. Pauly, Exec. V.P., Bank IV
    Kansas, N.A.
Trustee: Bank IV Kansas, N.A.
Number of staff: None.
EIN: 486103519

1033
Beech Aircraft Foundation
9709 East Central Ave.
Wichita 67201   (316) 681-8177

Incorporated in 1966 in KS.
Donor(s): Beech Aircraft Corp.
Foundation type: Company-sponsored
Financial data (yr. ended 12/31/91): Assets,
$5,795,739 (M); gifts received, $145,000;
expenditures, $539,277; qualifying distributions,
$539,338, including $491,663 for 101 grants
(high: $10,000; low: $75; average: $75-$10,000)
and $42,053 for 183 employee matching gifts.
Purpose and activities: Grants for higher
education, community funds, youth agencies, and
hospitals; some support for cultural activities,
conservation, the handicapped, and the aged.
Fields of interest: Education, higher education,
community funds, youth, hospitals, cultural
programs, conservation, handicapped, aged.
Types of support: Exchange programs,
program-related investments, publications, seed
money, employee-related scholarships, employee
matching gifts, annual campaigns, capital
campaigns, continuing support, matching funds,
renovation projects, special projects, building
funds.
Limitations: Giving primarily in communities
with company facilities, with an emphasis on KS.
No grants to individuals (except for
employee-related scholarships), or for
endowment funds, research, or matching gifts; no
loans.
Application information: Application form not
required.
  Initial approach: Letter
  Copies of proposal: 1
  Deadline(s): Dec., Mar., June, and Sept.
  Board meeting date(s): Jan., Apr., July, and Oct.
  Write: Larry E. Lawrence, Secy.-Treas.
Officers and Directors:* O.A. Beech,* Chair. and
Pres.; Wey D. Kenny,* V.P.; Larry E. Lawrence,
Secy.-Treas.; Max E. Bleck, J.A. Elliot.
Number of staff: None.
EIN: 486125881

1034
Willard J. and Mary G. Breidenthal Foundation
c/o Commercial National Bank, Trust Div.
P.O. Box 1400
Kansas City 66117   (913) 371-0035
Application address: c/o Commercial National
Bank, 601 Minnesota Ave., Kansas City, KS
66117

Trust established in 1962 in KS.
Donor(s): Willard J. Breidenthal,‡ Mary G.
Breidenthal,‡ and members of the Breidenthal
family.
Foundation type: Independent
Financial data (yr. ended 12/31/90): Assets,
$2,746,700 (M); expenditures, $180,128;
qualifying distributions, $165,141, including
$164,250 for 39 grants (high: $15,000; low:
$250; average: $3,725).
Purpose and activities: Emphasis on higher
education and hospitals; support also for
agriculture, child welfare, youth agencies, and
cultural programs.
Fields of interest: Higher education, hospitals,
agriculture, child welfare, youth, cultural
programs.
Limitations: Giving primarily in the Kansas City,
KS, and Kansas City, MO, area. No grants to
individuals.
Application information: Application form not
required.
  Initial approach: Letter
  Deadline(s): Submit proposal preferably in
    Sept. or Oct.; deadline Nov. 1
  Board meeting date(s): Nov.
  Write: Ruth B. Snyder, Trustee
Trustees: George Gray Breidenthal, Ruth B.
Snyder, Commercial National Bank.
Number of staff: None.
EIN: 486103376

1035
Cessna Foundation, Inc.
P.O. Box 7706
Wichita 67277   (316) 941-6000

Incorporated in 1952 in KS.
Donor(s): The Cessna Aircraft Co.
Foundation type: Company-sponsored
Financial data (yr. ended 12/31/90): Assets,
$7,082,260 (M); gifts received, $505,000;
expenditures, $505,904; qualifying distributions,
$495,179, including $476,587 for grants and
$18,592 for employee matching gifts.
Purpose and activities: Grants largely for the
United Way, higher education, and youth
agencies; support also for hospitals and cultural
programs, including museums.
Fields of interest: Community funds, youth,
higher education, museums, cultural programs,
hospitals, education—building funds, educational
research, engineering, education.
Types of support: Employee matching gifts,
building funds, annual campaigns, capital
campaigns, emergency funds, employee-related
scholarships, special projects.
Limitations: Giving limited to areas of company
operations, primarily Wichita, KS. No grants to
individuals.
Application information: Application form not
required.

Initial approach: Letter
Copies of proposal: 1
Deadline(s): Submit proposals preferably in Nov.
Board meeting date(s): Feb. and Dec.
Write: H.D. Humphrey, Secy.-Treas.
Officers and Trustees:* Russell W. Meyer, Jr.,* Pres.; John E. Moore,* V.P.; H.D. Humphrey,* Secy.-Treas.; Roy H. Norris, Bruce E. Peterman.
Number of staff: None.
EIN: 486108801

1036
DeVore Foundation, Inc.
P.O. Box 118
Wichita 67201 (316) 267-3211

Incorporated in 1953 in KS.
Donor(s): Floyd DeVore,‡ Richard A. DeVore, William D. DeVore, and their businesses.
Foundation type: Independent
Financial data (yr. ended 11/30/91): Assets, $2,746,625 (M); gifts received, $26,000; expenditures, $146,190; qualifying distributions, $97,301, including $95,451 for 58 grants (high: $25,000; low: $50).
Fields of interest: Youth, Protestant giving, arts, cultural programs, higher education, health, social services, community funds.
Types of support: Annual campaigns, building funds, capital campaigns, continuing support, endowment funds, equipment, general purposes, operating budgets, renovation projects, seed money, special projects.
Limitations: Giving limited to the Wichita, KS, area.
Publications: 990-PF, application guidelines, annual report.
Application information: Application form not required.
Initial approach: Letter
Copies of proposal: 1
Deadline(s): None
Write: Richard A. DeVore, Pres.
Officers: Richard A. DeVore, Pres. and Secy.; William D. DeVore, V.P. and Treas.
Number of staff: None.
EIN: 486109754

1037
Dane G. Hansen Foundation ▼
P.O. Box 187
Logan 67646 (913) 689-4832

Incorporated in 1965 in KS.
Donor(s): Dane G. Hansen.‡
Foundation type: Independent
Financial data (yr. ended 09/30/90): Assets, $29,053,279 (M); expenditures, $1,678,739; qualifying distributions, $1,403,222, including $1,130,127 for 72 grants (high: $200,000; low: $148; average: $10,000-$30,000), $121,865 for 100 grants to individuals (high: $3,500; low: $750) and $15,656 for 1 foundation-administered program.
Purpose and activities: Grants largely for higher education, including undergraduate, graduate, theological, and vocational scholarships to individuals, civic affairs and public interest groups, youth agencies, services for the handicapped, and hospitals.

Fields of interest: Higher education, vocational education, youth, hospitals, handicapped, civic affairs, public policy.
Types of support: Building funds, equipment, operating budgets, publications, general purposes, continuing support, scholarship funds, student aid.
Limitations: Giving primarily in Logan, Phillips County, and northwestern KS; scholarships limited to residents of 26 northwestern KS counties.
Application information: Scholarship seekers should call or write the foundation about eligibility requirements, application forms, and interviews.
Deadline(s): Sept. and Oct. for scholarships
Board meeting date(s): Monthly
Final notification: Within 2 weeks for grants to organizations
Write: Oscar Belin, Pres.
Officers and Trustees:* Oscar Belin,* Pres.; W.R. Lappin,* V.P.; Doyle D. Rahjes,* Secy.; Dane G. Bales, Treas.; Ross Beach, Ralph E. Reitz.
Number of staff: 7 full-time support.
EIN: 486121156

1038
David H. Koch Charitable Foundation ▼
4111 East 37th St. North
Wichita 67220 (316) 832-5227
Application address: P.O. Box 2256, Wichita, KS 67201

Established in 1982 in KS.
Donor(s): David H. Koch, Fred C. Koch Trusts for Charity.
Foundation type: Independent
Financial data (yr. ended 12/31/90): Assets, $8,162,339 (M); gifts received, $8,000,000; expenditures, $3,766,684; qualifying distributions, $3,759,002, including $3,741,354 for 46 grants (high: $500,000; low: $500; average: $10,000-$100,000).
Purpose and activities: Giving for arts, culture, education, public interest, and economic concerns.
Fields of interest: Arts, education, cultural programs, public policy, economics.
Types of support: Annual campaigns, building funds, capital campaigns, conferences and seminars, emergency funds, conferences and seminars, emergency funds, endowment funds, equipment, fellowships, general purposes, internships, lectureships, matching funds, operating budgets, program-related investments, publications, renovation projects, scholarship funds, seed money, special projects, continuing support.
Limitations: No grants to individuals, or for deficit financing, exchange programs, land acquisition, or professorships; no loans.
Application information:
Initial approach: Proposal
Deadline(s): None
Board meeting date(s): As necessary
Final notification: Varies
Write: George Pearson, Secy.
Officers: David H. Koch, Pres.; George H. Pearson, Secy.; Vonda Holliman, Treas.
Number of staff: None.
EIN: 480926946
Recent health grants:

1038-1 Drug Policy Foundation, DC, $25,000. For general support. 1990.
1038-2 Drug Policy Foundation, DC, $20,000. For economic study. 1990.
1038-3 House Ear Institute, Los Angeles, CA, $50,000. For general support. 1990.
1038-4 Memorial Sloan-Kettering Cancer Center, NYC, NY, $500,000. For general support. 1990.
1038-5 Memorial Sloan-Kettering Cancer Center, NYC, NY, $100,000. For general support. 1990.
1038-6 Rockefeller University, NYC, NY, $10,000. For general support. 1990.
1038-7 Society of the New York Hospital, NYC, NY, $100,000. For general support. 1990.

1039
The Marley Fund
1900 Shawnee Mission Pkwy.
Mission Woods 66205 (913) 362-1818
Application address: P.O. Box 2965, Shawnee, KS 66201

Incorporated in 1961 in MO.
Donor(s): The Marley Co.
Foundation type: Company-sponsored
Financial data (yr. ended 04/30/91): Assets, $183 (M); gifts received, $341,250; expenditures, $342,546; qualifying distributions, $342,464, including $266,924 for 116 grants (high: $41,250; low: $100), $64,500 for 88 grants to individuals (high: $750; low: $375; average: $750) and $11,040 for 69 employee matching gifts.
Purpose and activities: Emphasis on higher education, including scholarships and an employee matching gift program, community funds, health agencies, hospitals, youth and child welfare, and social service agencies.
Fields of interest: Higher education, community funds, health services, hospitals, youth, child welfare, social services.
Types of support: Operating budgets, continuing support, annual campaigns, building funds, equipment, employee matching gifts, employee-related scholarships.
Limitations: Giving limited to areas of company operations. No grants to individuals (except for employee-related scholarships), or for seed money, emergency funds, deficit financing, land acquisition, endowment funds, scholarships, fellowships, special projects, research, publications, or conferences; no loans.
Publications: Application guidelines, program policy statement.
Application information: Application form not required.
Initial approach: Letter
Copies of proposal: 1
Deadline(s): None
Board meeting date(s): Monthly
Final notification: 1 month
Write: Betty L. Paine, V.P.
Officers: Timothy J. Verhagen, Pres.; Betty L. Paine, V.P. and Secy.; Marc G. Naughton, Treas.
Number of staff: None.
EIN: 446012343

1040
The Julia J. Mingenback Foundation, Inc.
c/o Bank IV Kansas, N.A.
One Main Place
McPherson 67460   (316) 241-8000

Incorporated in 1959 in KS.
Donor(s): E.C. Mingenback.‡
Foundation type: Independent
Financial data (yr. ended 12/31/91): Assets,
$3,708,341 (M); expenditures, $290,132;
qualifying distributions, $188,666, including
$188,666 for 7 grants (high: $50,000; low:
$2,000).
Fields of interest: Higher education, religious
schools, aged, hospitals.
Types of support: Capital campaigns, renovation
projects, equipment, building funds.
Limitations: Giving primarily in McPherson
County, KS.
Application information:
   Initial approach: Letter
   Deadline(s): None
   Write: Don Steffes, Pres.
Officers: Don C. Steffes, Pres.; Ruth Lancaster,
Secy.-Treas.
Directors: James Ketcherside, Edwin T. Pyle.
Trustee: Bank IV Kansas, N.A.
EIN: 486109567

1041
Muchnic Foundation
107 North Sixth St., Suite 2
P.O. Box 329
Atchison 66002   (913) 367-4164
Application address: 777 Third Ave., New York,
NY 10017

Trust established in 1946 in KS.
Donor(s): Valley Co., Inc., Helen Q. Muchnic,‡
H.E. Muchnic.
Foundation type: Independent
Financial data (yr. ended 11/30/91): Assets,
$7,731,231 (M); expenditures, $234,269;
qualifying distributions, $214,099, including
$213,352 for 36 grants (high: $57,052; low:
$100).
Purpose and activities: Giving primarily for
higher education and cultural programs,
including museums, and civic affairs; support also
for health associations and medical research.
Fields of interest: Higher education, cultural
programs, museums, health associations, medical
research.
Limitations: No grants to individuals.
Application information:
   Initial approach: Proposal
   Deadline(s): Oct. 31
   Board meeting date(s): As required
   Write: Peter Powers
Trustee: Elizabeth M. Elicker.
EIN: 486102818

1042
Ethel and Raymond F. Rice Foundation
700 Massachusetts St.
Lawrence 66044   (913) 843-0420

Established about 1972.
Foundation type: Independent

Financial data (yr. ended 12/31/91): Assets,
$7,771,898 (M); expenditures, $361,511;
qualifying distributions, $341,856, including
$322,200 for 98 grants (high: $28,000; low:
$500).
Purpose and activities: Emphasis on higher
education, health, youth and social service
agencies; support also for the aid of the
handicapped.
Fields of interest: Higher education, health,
youth, social services, handicapped.
Types of support: Capital campaigns, scholarship
funds, research, building funds, equipment.
Limitations: Giving limited to the Douglas County
and Lawrence, KS, area. No grants to individuals.
Application information:
   Initial approach: Proposal
   Deadline(s): Nov. 15
   Write: Robert B. Oyler, Pres., or George M.
      Clem, Treas.
Officers: Robert B. Oyler, Pres.; James W.
Paddock, Secy.; George M. Clem, Treas.
EIN: 237156608

1043
Sarver Charitable Trust
P.O. Box 307
Smith Center 66967
Application address: P.O. Box 345, Osborne, KS
67473; Tel.: (913) 346-5445

Established in 1990 in KS.
Donor(s): Gail Sarver,‡ Sarver, Inc.
Foundation type: Independent
Financial data (yr. ended 12/31/90): Assets,
$6,628,945 (M); expenditures, $650,094;
qualifying distributions, $650,094, including
$517,812 for grants (low: $250) and $40,850 for
82 grants to individuals (high: $700; low: $250;
average: $250-$1,400).
Purpose and activities: Awards scholarships to
high school graduates in Osborne County, KS;
support also for a hospital, a hospice, cancer
research, agriculture, and religion.
Fields of interest: Hospitals, cancer, hospices,
agriculture, religion.
Types of support: Scholarship funds, general
purposes, lectureships.
Limitations: Giving limited to Osborne County,
KS.
Application information: Application form
required for scholarships.
   Copies of proposal: 1
   Deadline(s): Apr. 1 for scholarships; Dec. 31 for
      grants
   Board meeting date(s): Varies
   Write: Paul S. Gregory, Dir.
Directors: Pete Bohm, Wm C. Cady, Paul S.
Gregory, Steve Windscheffel, Melvin Wilcoxson.
Trustee: Smith County State Bank & Trust.
Number of staff: None.
EIN: 486298990

1044
Kenneth L. & Eva S. Smith Foundation
P.O. Box 25625
Overland Park 66225

Established in 1968 in KS.
Donor(s): Kenneth L. Smith.‡
Foundation type: Independent

Financial data (yr. ended 12/31/90): Assets,
$4,446,695 (M); expenditures, $256,946;
qualifying distributions, $162,289, including
$155,025 for 4 grants (high: $50,000; low:
$25,000).
Fields of interest: Hospitals.
Types of support: Continuing support.
Limitations: Giving primarily in the greater
Kansas City, MO, area. No grants to individuals.
Application information: Contributes only to
pre-selected organizations. Applications not
accepted.
   Write: Thomas K. Jones, Trustee
Trustees: Thomas K. Jones, Eva S. Smith.
Number of staff: None.
EIN: 486142517

1045
Sprint Corporate Giving Program
(Formerly United Telecommunications
Corporate Giving Program)
2330 Shawnee Mission Pkwy.
Westwood 66205   (913) 624-3343
Mailing address: P.O. Box 11315, Kansas City,
MO 64112

Financial data (yr. ended 12/31/90): Total giving,
$1,153,300, including $1,130,000 for 66 grants
(high: $139,000; low: $50) and $23,300 for 36
in-kind gifts.
Purpose and activities: Support for education,
through private colleges and universities,
minority, business, economic, continuing, and
elementary education, science/technology
education, and education associations; the arts,
primarily the performing arts, arts institutes,
museums and galleries, and public broadcasting;
urban and community affairs; health
organizations; social services, including United
Funds, youth organizations and community
service organizations. Types of support include
employee matching gifts for education and the
donation of in-kind services and loaned
employees.
Fields of interest: Education, higher education,
minorities, business education, economics,
science and technology, arts, performing arts, fine
arts, museums, urban development, community
development, health, social services, community
funds, youth, elementary education,
education—minorities.
Types of support: Capital campaigns, fellowships,
employee matching gifts, in-kind gifts, donated
equipment, public relations services, annual
campaigns, special projects, continuing support.
Limitations: Giving primarily in headquarters city
and subsidiary locations.
Application information: Contributions are
handled by the Corporate Relations department.
Application form not required.
   Initial approach: Brief letter or proposal to
      headquarters
   Copies of proposal: 1
   Deadline(s): None
   Board meeting date(s): As needed
   Write: Don G. Forsythe, V.P., Corp. Rels.
Number of staff: 1 part-time professional; 1
part-time support.

1046
Sprint Foundation
(Formerly United Telecommunications Foundation)
2330 Shawnee Mission Pkwy.
Westwood 66205　　　　(913) 624-3343
Mailing address: P.O. Box 11315, Kansas City, MO 64112

Established in 1988 in KS.
Foundation type: Company-sponsored
Financial data (yr. ended 12/31/91): Assets, $9,604,379 (M); gifts received, $968,000; expenditures, $1,530,395; qualifying distributions, $1,465,538, including $1,125,225 for 79 grants (high: $235,000; low: $225) and $340,313 for 946 employee matching gifts.
Purpose and activities: Emphasis on education, including business education, secondary education, and higher education, performing arts, and youth; support also for community development and drug abuse programs.
Fields of interest: Education, business education, education—minorities, secondary education, higher education, performing arts, youth, community development, drug abuse.
Types of support: Annual campaigns, employee matching gifts, capital campaigns, special projects, fellowships, general purposes.
Limitations: Giving primarily in headquarters city and subsidiary locations in CA, GA, KS, MO, TX, VA, and Washington, DC. No support for religious, fraternal, labor or veterans' organizations, or for hospitals or neighborhood associations. No grants to individuals, or for fundraising.
Publications: 990-PF, application guidelines.
Application information: Application form not required.
　Initial approach: Brief letter or proposal
　Copies of proposal: 1
　Deadline(s): None
　Board meeting date(s): Bimonthly
　Write: Don G. Forsythe, V.P., Corp. Relations
Directors: J.R. Devlin, Richard C. Smith, M. Jeannine Strandjord.
Number of staff: None.
EIN: 481062018

1047
Topeka Community Foundation
5100 S.W. 10th
P.O. Box 4525
Topeka 66604　　　　(913) 272-4804

Incorporated in 1983 in KS.
Foundation type: Community
Financial data (yr. ended 12/31/91): Assets, $1,230,781 (M); gifts received, $655,001; expenditures, $361,606; qualifying distributions, $326,212, including $326,212 for grants (average: $500-$5,000).
Fields of interest: Arts, education, community development, civic affairs, social services, drug abuse, family services, child welfare, environment, general charitable giving.
Types of support: Annual campaigns, building funds, matching funds, operating budgets, employee matching gifts, capital campaigns, emergency funds, general purposes, scholarship funds, seed money, special projects, student aid, in-kind gifts, continuing support.
Limitations: Giving limited to Topeka and Shawnee County, KS. No support for religion, or scientific, medical, or academic research.
Publications: Annual report, application guidelines, newsletter, informational brochure (including application guidelines), 990-PF, financial statement.
Application information: Application form required.
　Copies of proposal: 5
　Deadline(s): Feb. 15
　Board meeting date(s): Bimonthly, last Thursday of month
　Final notification: Apr. 1
　Write: Karen Welch, Exec. Dir.
Officers and Directors:* Charles Henson,* Chair.; John E. Salisbury,* Vice-Chair.; Jane Mackey,* Secy.; Robert Swett,* Treas.; Karen Welch, Exec. Dir.; Carolyn Alexander, Robert Mehlinger, James Rhodes, John H. Stauffer, and 16 additional directors.
Number of staff: 1 part-time professional; 1 part-time support.
EIN: 480972106

1048
Greater Wichita Community Foundation
Centre City Plaza
151 North Main, Suite 680
Wichita 67202　　　　(316) 264-4880
FAX: (316) 264-7592

Incorporated in 1986 in KS.
Foundation type: Community
Financial data (yr. ended 06/30/90): Assets, $2,364,374 (M); gifts received, $421,054; expenditures, $389,398; qualifying distributions, $249,005, including $249,005 for grants (high: $26,162).
Fields of interest: Education, health, social services, welfare, youth, arts, cultural programs.
Limitations: Giving limited to Harper, Kingman, Harvey, Reno, Butler, Cowley, Sedgwick, and Sumner counties, KS. No grants to individuals.
Publications: Annual report, newsletter, application guidelines, informational brochure.
Application information: Application form required.
　Initial approach: Proposal
　Copies of proposal: 4
　Deadline(s): May 30
　Board meeting date(s): 4 times per year
　Final notification: June 30
　Write: James D. Moore, Exec. Dir.
Officers and Directors:* H. Dean Ritchie,* Chair.; Fred F. Berry, Jr.,* Vice Chair.; Dorothy J. Reed,* Secy.; Daniel M. Carney,* Treas.; James D. Moore, Exec. Dir.; Reid Ashe, H. Marvin Bastian, Kenneth P. Brasted II, Charlie Chandler, Sheldon C. Coleman, Jack P. DeBoer, Thomas R. Devlin, Richard A. DeVore, Martin K. Eby, Jr., Larry D. Fleming, Gordon Greer, Alvin Marcus, R.D. Martens, Russell W. Meyer, Jr., Mary Lynn Oliver, D. Creamer Reed, M.D., Donald C. Slawson, Kenneth J. Wagnon.
Number of staff: 1 full-time professional; 1 full-time support.
EIN: 481022361
Recent health grants:
1048-1 Donald J. Allen Memorial Huntingtons Disease Clinic, Wichita, KS, $37,285. 1991.
1048-2 Sedgwick County Department of Mental Health, Wichita, KS, $50,000. 1991.

KENTUCKY

1049
The Ashland Oil Foundation, Inc. ▼
1000 Ashland Dr.
Russell 41114 (606) 329-4525
Mailing address: P.O. Box 391, Ashland, KY
41105

Incorporated in 1968 in DE.
Donor(s): Ashland Oil, Inc.
Foundation type: Company-sponsored
Financial data (yr. ended 12/31/90): Assets, $0
(M); gifts received, $4,020,000; expenditures,
$4,301,470; qualifying distributions, $4,296,413,
including $2,877,370 for 254 grants (high:
$221,500; low: $500; average: $1,000-$5,000)
and $1,419,043 for 1,963 employee matching
gifts.
Purpose and activities: Direct support primarily to
educational organizations, mainly colleges and
universities; giving also through an employee
matching gift program to higher education and
community funds.
Fields of interest: Higher education, community
funds.
Types of support: Employee matching gifts,
professorships, scholarship funds, fellowships.
Limitations: Giving primarily in KY, MN, OH, and
WV. No grants to individuals, or for building or
endowment funds.
Publications: Informational brochure (including
application guidelines).
Application information:
  Initial approach: Telephone or letter; form
    letters are ignored
  Deadline(s): None
  Board meeting date(s): Feb.
  Final notification: Varies
  Write: Judy B. Thomas, Pres.
Officers and Trustees:* Harry M. Zachem,*
Chair.; Judy B. Thomas,* Pres.; Franklin P. Justice,
Jr.,* V.P.; J. Marvin Quin,* V.P.; Frederick M.
Greenwood, Secy.; Gregory W. McKnight,*
Treas.; John A. Brothers, Rick E. Music, Walter L.
Gooch.
Members: Paul W. Chellgren, Richard W. Spears.
Number of staff: 2 full-time professional; 3
full-time support; 3 part-time support.
EIN: 616057900
Recent health grants:
1049-1 Cleveland Clinic Foundation, Cleveland,
  OH, $15,000. 1990.
1049-2 Ephraim McDowell Cancer Research
  Foundation, Lexington, KY, $50,500. 1990.
1049-3 Ephraim McDowell Community Cancer
  Network, Lexington, KY, $50,000. 1990.
1049-4 Kentucky Health Care Access
  Foundation, Lexington, KY, $12,500. 1990.
1049-5 Kings Daughters Health Foundation,
  Ashland, KY, $41,600. 1990.
1049-6 Memorial Sloan-Kettering Cancer Center,
  NYC, NY, $25,000. 1990.

1050
Bank of Louisville Charities, Inc.
P.O. Box 1101
Louisville 40201
Application address: 500 West Broadway,
Louisville, KY 40202; Tel.: (502) 589-3351

Established in 1973.
Donor(s): Bank of Louisville.
Foundation type: Company-sponsored
Financial data (yr. ended 12/31/90): Assets,
$3,502,265 (M); gifts received, $28,000;
expenditures, $318,631; qualifying distributions,
$313,133, including $313,015 for 142 grants
(high: $45,273; low: $25).
Purpose and activities: Emphasis on cultural
programs, especially in the arts; support also for
education, health, a housing corporation, civic
affairs, a community fund, and child welfare and
development.
Fields of interest: Cultural programs, arts,
education, health, media and communications,
housing, civic affairs, community funds, child
development, child welfare.
Types of support: Annual campaigns, building
funds, continuing support, emergency funds,
program-related investments, special projects.
Limitations: Giving primarily in Jefferson County,
KY.
Application information: Application form not
required.
  Initial approach: Letter
  Deadline(s): None
  Write: Beth Paxtonklein
Officer and Directors:* Bertram W. Klein,* Chair.;
Orson Oliver, Thomas L. Weber.
EIN: 237423454

1051
Albert A. Brennan Foundation
c/o Citizens Fidelity Bank & Trust Co.
Citizens Plaza
Louisville 40296

Established in 1977.
Foundation type: Independent
Financial data (yr. ended 09/30/90): Assets,
$3,611,718 (M); expenditures, $187,350;
qualifying distributions, $161,087, including
$160,597 for 2 grants (high: $80,299; low:
$80,298).
Purpose and activities: Support for a hospital and
a club.
Fields of interest: Hospitals.
Types of support: Operating budgets.
Limitations: Giving primarily in Louisville, KY. No
grants to individuals.
Application information: Contributes only to
pre-selected organizations. Applications not
accepted.
Trustee: Citizens Fidelity Bank & Trust Co.
EIN: 616094299

1052
James Graham Brown Foundation, Inc. ▼
132 East Gray St.
Louisville 40202 (502) 583-4085

Trust established in 1943 in KY; incorporated in
1954.
Donor(s): J. Graham Brown,‡ Agnes B. Duggan.‡

Foundation type: Independent
Financial data (yr. ended 12/31/90): Assets,
$196,290,920 (M); expenditures, $14,598,423;
qualifying distributions, $8,968,222, including
$8,803,053 for 70 grants (high: $500,000; low:
$100; average: $5,000-$250,000).
Purpose and activities: Support for higher
education, civic organizations, community
development, museums, and social service,
youth, and health agencies.
Fields of interest: Education, higher education,
education—building funds, educational
associations, educational research, health
services, social services, youth, employment,
handicapped, urban development, civic affairs,
community development, community funds,
museums, historic preservation, general
charitable giving, homeless.
Types of support: Annual campaigns, building
funds, capital campaigns, conferences and
seminars, emergency funds, endowment funds,
equipment, matching funds, professorships,
renovation projects, research, scholarship funds,
special projects, land acquisition.
Limitations: Giving primarily in KY, with
emphasis on Louisville. No support for private
foundations or the performing arts. No grants to
individuals.
Publications: Grants list, 990-PF, informational
brochure (including application guidelines).
Application information: Application form
required if board approves request for permission
to apply. Application form not required.
  Initial approach: Letter
  Copies of proposal: 12
  Deadline(s): None
  Board meeting date(s): Monthly
  Final notification: Grants paid Dec. 31
  Write: Mason Rummel, Grants Mgr.
Officers and Trustees:* Joe M. Rodes,* Chair.;
David E. Ferguson, Pres.; Graham B. Loper,* V.P.;
Arthur H. Keeney, M.D.,* Secy.; Mark G. Hyland,
Treas.; H. Curtis Craig, Stanley S. Dickson, Frank
B. Hower, Jr., Stanley F. Hugenberg, Jr., Ray E.
Loper, Robert L. Royer.
Number of staff: 3 full-time professional; 2
part-time professional; 2 full-time support; 2
part-time support.
EIN: 610724060
Recent health grants:
1052-1 Arthritis Foundation, Kentucky Chapter,
  Louisville, KY, $10,000. 1990.
1052-2 Come-Unity Cooperative Care,
  Louisville, KY, $75,000. 1990.
1052-3 Medical Center Hospitality House,
  Louisville, KY, $10,000. 1990.
1052-4 Spina Bifida Association of Kentucky,
  Louisville, KY, $10,000. 1990.

1053
Capital Holding Corporate Giving
Program
P.O. Box 32830
Louisville 40232 (502) 560-2536

Financial data (yr. ended 12/31/90): Total giving,
$1,096,432, including $1,054,278 for 123 grants
(high: $50,000; low: $100; average:
$100-$50,000) and $42,154 for 153 employee
matching gifts.
Purpose and activities: Primarily focuses on
education including scholarships; support also for

civic and community affairs, health and human services, culture and the arts, and subsidiary contributions. The program also matches employee gifts.
Fields of interest: AIDS, libraries, education, civic affairs, health, cultural programs, arts, volunteerism.
Types of support: Employee matching gifts, internships, matching funds, general purposes, special projects, scholarship funds, donated products, loaned talent, employee volunteer services.
Limitations: Giving primarily in the Louisville, KY, area. No support for religious or political organizations. No grants to individuals.
Publications: Corporate report.
Application information: Application form required.
   Initial approach: Letter of inquiry to headquarters
   Copies of proposal: 1
   Deadline(s): Applications accepted throughout the year
   Board meeting date(s): Bi-monthly
   Final notification: Aug. and Sept.
   Write: Christy Callahan, Asst. V.P., Community Rels.

1054
V. V. Cooke Foundation Corporation
4350 Brownsboro Rd., Suite 110
Louisville 40207-1681   (502) 893-4598

Incorporated in 1947 in KY.
Donor(s): V.V. Cooke,‡ Cooke Chevrolet Co., Cooke Pontiac Co., and others.
Foundation type: Independent
Financial data (yr. ended 08/31/91): Assets, $5,065,345 (M); expenditures, $287,086; qualifying distributions, $237,643, including $232,305 for 34 grants (high: $60,000; low: $100).
Purpose and activities: Emphasis on Baptist church and school support and higher education, including medical education.
Fields of interest: Protestant giving, higher education, medical education, religion—Christian, religious schools.
Types of support: Continuing support, annual campaigns, emergency funds, building funds, equipment, professorships, capital campaigns, general purposes, operating budgets, renovation projects, special projects.
Limitations: Giving primarily in Louisville, KY. No grants to individuals, or for general endowment funds, research, scholarships, or fellowships; no loans.
Application information: Personal interviews not granted. Application form not required.
   Initial approach: Proposal
   Copies of proposal: 1
   Deadline(s): None
   Board meeting date(s): Quarterly
   Final notification: Following board meeting
   Write: John B. Gray, Exec. Dir.
Officers and Directors:* V.V. Cooke, Jr.,* Pres.; Jane C. Cross,* V.P.; Robert L. Hook,* Secy.-Treas.; John B. Gray, Exec. Dir.; June C. Hook.
Number of staff: 1 part-time professional.
EIN: 616033714

1055
The Courier-Journal Corporate Giving Program
525 W. Broadway
Louisville 40202   (502) 582-4552

Financial data (yr. ended 12/31/90): Total giving, $30,000 for grants.
Purpose and activities: Supports programs for drug abuse, health, rehabilitation, mental health, child abuse, homelessness, housing, hunger, family services, higher and minority education, community and rural development, recreation, literacy, leadership development, legal services, speech pathology, performing arts, journalism, and media and communications.
Fields of interest: Alcoholism, business education, cancer, child development, child welfare, community development, dance, drug abuse, education, education—early childhood, education—minorities, elementary education, family services, handicapped, health, heart disease, higher education, historic preservation, homeless, housing, hunger, journalism, leadership development, legal services, libraries, literacy, media and communications, mental health, minorities, music, performing arts, recreation, rehabilitation, rural development, speech pathology, theater, urban development, volunteerism.
Types of support: Capital campaigns, consulting services, continuing support, emergency funds, employee matching gifts, equipment, seed money, special projects.
Limitations: Giving primarily in KY and southern IN.
Application information: The company decides on the grant recipients and then reports to the Gannett Foundation, which makes the actual gifts. Application form required.
   Deadline(s): Jan. 1, May 1, and Sept.1
   Final notification: 60 days after application
   Write: Donald Towles, V.P., Public Affairs
Number of staff: None.

1056
Ervin G. Houchens Foundation, Inc.
(Formerly Houchens Foundation, Inc.)
900 Church St., P.O. Box 90009
Bowling Green 42101-9009   (502) 843-3252

Incorporated in 1954 in KY.
Donor(s): Houchens Markets, Inc., B.G. Wholesale, Inc.
Foundation type: Independent
Financial data (yr. ended 12/31/90): Assets, $3,872,180 (M); gifts received, $21,418; expenditures, $78,625; qualifying distributions, $1,005,403, including $69,435 for 14 grants (high: $45,000; low: $200), $3,113 for 2 foundation-administered programs and $932,420 for 36 loans.
Purpose and activities: Support mainly in the form of loans to Baptist and Methodist churches; smaller cash contributions to churches, youth agencies, health organizations, and education.
Fields of interest: Protestant giving, youth, education, health.
Types of support: Loans, general purposes.
Limitations: Giving limited to southwest KY.
Application information:

   Initial approach: Letter with comprehensive details
   Deadline(s): None
   Write: Ervin D. Houchens, Pres.
Officers and Directors:* Ervin G. Houchens,* Pres.; Lois Lynn Martin,* Secy.; Covella H. Biggers,* Treas.; Erin Biggers, Gil E. Biggers, Gil M. Biggers, George Suel Houchens, C. Cecil Martin.
EIN: 610623087

1057
The Humana Foundation, Inc. ▼
The Humana Bldg., 500 West Main St.
P.O. Box 1438
Louisville 40201   (502) 580-3920

Incorporated in 1981 in KY.
Donor(s): Humana, Inc.
Foundation type: Company-sponsored
Financial data (yr. ended 08/31/90): Assets, $21,581,174 (M); gifts received, $10,904,694; expenditures, $5,739,057; qualifying distributions, $5,723,740, including $5,723,699 for 125 grants (high: $800,000; low: $100; average: $5,000-$25,000).
Purpose and activities: Support for the performing arts, health organizations, medical research, higher and secondary education, community and economic development, and a community center.
Fields of interest: Performing arts, health, medical research, higher education, secondary education, community development.
Limitations: Giving primarily in KY.
Application information:
   Initial approach: Letter
   Deadline(s): None
   Board meeting date(s): Every 2 months
   Final notification: Generally, 6 weeks to 2 months
   Write: Joy L. Foley, Contribution Mgr.
Officers and Directors:* David A. Jones,* Chair. and C.E.O.; Wendell Cherry,* Pres. and C.O.O.; Carl F. Pollard,* Sr. Exec. V.P.; William C. Ballard, Jr., Exec. V.P., Finance and Administration; Thomas J. Flynn, Exec. V.P. and General Counsel; W. Roger Drury, Sr. V.P., Finance; David G. Anderson,* V.P., Finance and Treas.; George G. Bavernfeind, V.P., Taxes; James W. Doucette, V.P., Investment Management; Arthur P. Hipwell, V.P.; Alice F. Newton, Secy.
Number of staff: None.
EIN: 611004763
Recent health grants:
1057-1 Alaska Arctic Medical Research, Anchorage, AK, $25,000. 1991.
1057-2 American Cancer Society, Louisville, KY, $20,000. 1991.
1057-3 American Diabetes Foundation, Kentucky Affiliate, Louisville, KY, $15,000. 1991.
1057-4 Childrens Hospital and Health Center, San Diego, CA, $10,000. 1991.
1057-5 Fund for Medical Education and Research, Los Angeles, CA, $10,000. 1991.
1057-6 Hospital Research and Educational Trust, Chicago, IL, $50,000. 1991.
1057-7 Leukemia Society of America, Kentucky Chapter, Louisville, KY, $10,000. 1991.
1057-8 Planned Parenthood of Louisville, Louisville, KY, $35,000. 1991.

1057-9 Society of Perinatal Obstetricians, DC, $10,000. 1991.

1057-10 Spina Bifida Association of Kentucky, Louisville, KY, $20,000. 1991.

1057-11 Union Memorial Hospital, Foot and Ankle Research Fund, Baltimore, MD, $10,000. 1991.

1057-12 West Virginia School of Osteopathic Medicine, Lewisburg, WV, $40,000. 1991.

1058

The Juilfs Foundation

One Riverfront Place
Newport 41071   (606) 292-7000

Established in 1962 in OH.
Foundation type: Independent
Financial data (yr. ended 12/31/91): Assets, $2,669,442 (M); expenditures, $118,217; qualifying distributions, $114,600, including $114,600 for 27 grants (high: $27,000; low: $200).
Fields of interest: Museums, arts, recreation, community development, hospitals.
Types of support: Capital campaigns, annual campaigns.
Limitations: Giving primarily in the greater Cincinnati, OH, area. No grants to individuals.
Application information:
  Initial approach: Letter
  Deadline(s): None
  Write: George C. Juilfs, Trustee
Trustees: George C. Juilfs, Howard W. Juilfs, Faye Kuluris.
EIN: 316027571

1059

Kentucky Fried Chicken Corporate Giving Program

P.O. Box 32070
Louisville 40232   (502) 456-8300

Purpose and activities: Support for arts, health services, drug rehabilitation, education, community development and funds, social services, welfare, child welfare, and minority issues; also in-kind giving.
Fields of interest: Arts, child welfare, community development, community funds, drug abuse, education, health services, minorities, social services, welfare.
Types of support: Annual campaigns, capital campaigns, employee matching gifts, special projects, in-kind gifts.
Limitations: Giving limited to Louisville, KY; no giving elsewhere.
Application information:
  Write: Shirley Topmiller, Grp. Mgr., Corp. Contribs.

1060

Harry and Maxie LaViers Foundation, Inc.

P.O. Box 332
Irvine 40336   (606) 723-5111

Established in 1977.
Donor(s): Harry LaViers.‡
Foundation type: Independent
Financial data (yr. ended 08/31/91): Assets, $2,766,785 (M); expenditures, $145,779; qualifying distributions, $145,679, including $145,525 for 1 grant.
Fields of interest: Protestant giving, higher education, medical research.
Types of support: Annual campaigns, building funds, capital campaigns, special projects.
Limitations: Giving primarily in rural eastern KY. No support for national programs. No grants to individuals, or for scholarships.
Application information:
  Deadline(s): None
  Write: Harry LaViers, Jr., Pres.
Officers and Directors:* Harry LaViers, Jr.,* Pres.; Elizabeth LaViers Owen,* V.P.; Barbara P. LaViers,* Secy.-Treas.
Number of staff: None.
EIN: 310902455

1061

Long John Silver's Inc. Giving Program

(Formerly Jerrico Corporate Giving Program)
P.O. Box 11988
Lexington 40579   (606) 263-6000

Purpose and activities: Primary interests are business education, health, civic affairs, child development and mental health; also supports conservation, adult education, aid for the handicapped, medical research, and youth.
Fields of interest: Business education, handicapped, adult education, health, civic affairs, higher education, child development, conservation, education, hospitals, mental health, medical research, social services, youth.
Types of support: Annual campaigns, conferences and seminars, general purposes, donated equipment, employee volunteer services, scholarship funds, public relations services.
Application information: Contributions are handled by Public Affairs Dept. Application form not required.
  Initial approach: Letter of inquiry; send to headquarters
  Copies of proposal: 1
  Write: Bruce C. Cotton, Sr. V.P., Public Affairs

1062

Ralph E. Mills Foundation

Drawer M
Frankfort 40601

Incorporated in 1947 in KY.
Donor(s): Ralph E. Mills.
Foundation type: Independent
Financial data (yr. ended 12/31/91): Assets, $10,018,146 (M); gifts received, $38,520; expenditures, $2,439,908; qualifying distributions, $2,414,001, including $2,412,480 for 69 grants (high: $200,000; low: $247; average: $10,000-$100,000).
Fields of interest: Higher education, religion—Christian, social services, cancer, hospitals.
Limitations: Giving primarily in KY. No grants to individuals.
Officers: Ralph E. Mills, Pres.; John E. Brown, V.P. and Treas.; Robert M. Hardy, Jr., Secy.
Directors: Travis Bush, Zack Saufley.
EIN: 610529834

1063

E. O. Robinson Mountain Fund

P.O. Box 54930
Lexington 40555-4930   (606) 233-0817

Incorporated in 1922 in KY.
Donor(s): Edward O. Robinson.‡
Foundation type: Independent
Financial data (yr. ended 06/30/91): Assets, $10,455,076 (M); expenditures, $514,015; qualifying distributions, $429,720, including $429,720 for 36 grants (high: $38,000; low: $1,520; average: $1,000-$36,000).
Purpose and activities: To help the people, particularly the youth, of the mountain region of eastern KY improve their living conditions; grants primarily to hospitals and health agencies for medical care and to higher educational institutions for scholarships.
Fields of interest: Community development, hospitals, higher education, health services.
Types of support: Scholarship funds, continuing support, equipment, matching funds, operating budgets, renovation projects.
Limitations: Giving primarily in eastern KY. No grants to individuals.
Publications: Informational brochure.
Application information: Application form not required.
  Initial approach: Letter and 3-page proposal
  Copies of proposal: 11
  Deadline(s): 3 weeks prior to meeting
  Board meeting date(s): Every 4 months
  Write: Juanita Stollings, Secy.-Treas.
Officers and Directors:* Lyman V. Ginger,* Pres.; N. Mitchell Meade,* V.P.; Juanita Stollings, Secy.-Treas.; J.C. Codell, Jr., William Engle III, Mary P. Fox, M.D., Harold H. Mullis, Burl Phillips, Jr., J. Phil Smith, Robert A. Sparks, Jr., Vinson A. Watts.
Number of staff: 1 full-time professional; 2 full-time support.
EIN: 610449642

1064

The Rosenthal Foundation, Inc.

3300 First National Tower
Louisville 40202

Established in 1989 in KY.
Donor(s): Warren W. Rosenthal.
Foundation type: Independent
Financial data (yr. ended 12/31/91): Assets, $4,575,133 (M); expenditures, $285,699; qualifying distributions, $282,249, including $278,705 for 48 grants (high: $50,000; low: $100).
Fields of interest: Higher education, museums, arts, hospitals, health, youth.
Types of support: Land acquisition, endowment funds, operating budgets, general purposes.
Limitations: Giving primarily in Lexington, KY. No grants to individuals.
Application information: Contributes only to pre-selected organizations. Applications not accepted.
Officers: Warren W. Rosenthal, Pres. and Mgr.; Betty M. Rosenthal, Secy.-Treas.
Director: Martin S. Weinberg.
EIN: 611161776

1065
Rural Kentucky Medical Scholarship Fund
301 North Hurstbourne Pkwy., Suite 200
Louisville 40222

Established in 1987 in KY.
Foundation type: Independent
Financial data (yr. ended 04/30/91): Assets, $2,645,835 (M); expenditures, $150,152; qualifying distributions, $121,971, including $35,000 for 4 grants to individuals (high: $10,000; low: $5,000) and $19,000 for 19 loans to individuals.
Purpose and activities: Awards low-interest loans to medical school students and grants to new physicians toward payment of educational debt who agree to practice medicine in a rural or critical KY county.
Fields of interest: Medical education.
Types of support: Student loans, grants to individuals.
Limitations: Giving limited to KY.
Application information: Application form required.
  Initial approach: Letter requesting application form
  Deadline(s): Apr. 12
  Write: Vicki Thorpe
Officers and Directors:* Donald R. Stephens, M.D.,* Chair.; Ray A. Gibson, M.D.,* V.P.;

William T. Applegate,* Secy.; John W. Koon,* Treas.; and 8 additional directors.
EIN: 610967967

1066
Al J. Schneider Foundation Corporation
3720 Seventh St. Rd.
Louisville 40216

Incorporated in 1957 in KY.
Donor(s): Al J. Schneider.
Foundation type: Independent
Financial data (yr. ended 02/28/91): Assets, $2,037,830 (M); gifts received, $491,000; expenditures, $279,374; qualifying distributions, $275,327, including $269,427 for 104 grants (high: $36,948; low: $25) and $5,900 for 12 grants to individuals (high: $1,000; low: $200).
Purpose and activities: Emphasis on a Baptist church and other religious associations, health, cultural programs, youth agencies, and education, particularly higher education; minor support also to religious members of the community and other individuals.
Fields of interest: Protestant giving, religion—Christian, health, cultural programs, youth, education, higher education.
Types of support: General purposes, grants to individuals.

Limitations: Giving primarily in KY.
Officers: Al J. Schneider, Pres.; Thelma E. Schneider, V.P.; Robert L. Ackerson, Secy.-Treas.
EIN: 610621591

1067
W. T. Young Family Foundation, Inc.
P.O. Box 1110
Lexington 40589-1110

Established in 1981 in KY.
Donor(s): William T. Young, William T. Young, Jr.
Foundation type: Independent
Financial data (yr. ended 12/31/91): Assets, $5,960,171 (M); gifts received, $6,477,500; expenditures, $551,195; qualifying distributions, $535,855, including $532,301 for 25 grants (high: $100,000; low: $500).
Fields of interest: Family planning, homeless, cultural programs, arts, museums, higher education, education.
Limitations: Giving primarily in Louisville and Lexington, KY. No grants to individuals.
Application information: Contributes only to pre-selected organizations. Applications not accepted.
Officers: William T. Young, Pres.; Lucy M. Young, V.P.; William T. Young, Jr., Secy.-Treas.
EIN: 311020207

LOUISIANA

1068
The Azby Fund
1311 Whitney Bank Bldg.
New Orleans 70130-2613

Established in 1969 in LA.
Donor(s): Marion W. Harvey,‡ Herbert J. Harvey, Jr.‡
Foundation type: Independent
Financial data (yr. ended 12/31/91): Assets, $10,258,865 (M); gifts received, $8,400; expenditures, $955,858; qualifying distributions, $732,665, including $690,052 for 34 grants (high: $300,000; low: $624).
Fields of interest: Catholic giving, higher education, medical sciences, conservation.
Limitations: Giving primarily in New Orleans, LA. No grants to individuals.
Application information: Contributes only to pre-selected organizations. Applications not accepted.
Officers and Directors:* Erminia Wadsworth,* Pres.; S. Stewart Farnet,* V.P.; Thomas B. Lemann,* Secy.-Treas.; Michael Liebaert,* Managing Dir.; Ann Wadsworth Fitzmorris, Rev. Earl C. Woods.
EIN: 726049781

1069
Baton Rouge Area Foundation
One American Place, Suite 610
Baton Rouge 70825   (504) 387-6126

Incorporated in 1964 in LA.
Foundation type: Community
Financial data (yr. ended 12/31/91): Assets, $10,607,672 (M); gifts received, $1,082,759; expenditures, $1,001,318; qualifying distributions, $616,526, including $616,526 for grants.
Purpose and activities: Primary areas of interest include elementary and secondary education and health. Preference given to those projects which promise to affect a broad segment of the population or which tend to help a segment of the citizenry who are not being adequately served by the community's resources.
Fields of interest: Secondary education, elementary education, health, cultural programs, social services, youth, aged, child development, women, education, environment, community development.
Types of support: Seed money, emergency funds, research, equipment, matching funds, special projects, renovation projects, endowment funds.
Limitations: Giving limited to the Baton Rouge, LA, area, including East Baton Rouge, West Baton Rouge, Livingston, Ascension, Iberville, Pointe Coupee, East Feliciana, and West Feliciana parishes. No grants to individuals, or for continuing support, annual campaigns, deficit financing, scholarships, fellowships, or operating budgets; no loans.
Publications: Annual report, application guidelines, newsletter, informational brochure.

Application information: Application form required.
Initial approach: Telephone, letter, or proposal
Copies of proposal: 1
Deadline(s): Feb. 15, May 15, Aug. 15, and Nov. 15
Board meeting date(s): Mar., June, Sept., and Dec.
Final notification: 1 week after board meeting
Write: John G. Davies, Pres.
Officers and Directors:* Dudley W. Coates,* Chair.; John G. Davies,* Pres.; Gordon A. Pugh,* V.P.; Carolyn W. Carnahan,* Secy.; John C. Gaurreau II,* Treas.; and 18 additional directors.
Trustee Banks: Hibernia National Bank, Premier Bank, N.A.
Number of staff: 3 full-time professional.
EIN: 726030391
Recent health grants:
1069-1 Cancer Radiation Center, Perkins Cancer Center, Baton Rouge, LA, $55,500. 1990.
1069-2 Pennington Biomedical Research Center Foundation, Baton Rouge, LA, $30,000. 1990.
1069-3 Stop Rape Crisis Center of Baton Rouge, Baton Rouge, LA, $16,545. For rape awareness documentary addressing issue of date rape entitled Rape by Any Name to be broadcast by Louisiana Public Broadcasting and offered for national distribution. 1990.
1069-4 Womens Community Rehabilitation Center, Baton Rouge, LA, $13,000. For purchase of five-passenger mini-van to help transport clients to their jobs and appointments. 1990.
1069-5 Womens Hospital Foundation, Baton Rouge, LA, $25,000. To purchase Acuson Computed Sonography machine. 1990.

1070
The Booth-Bricker Fund
830 Union St., Suite 200
New Orleans 70112   (504) 581-2430

Established in 1976 in LA.
Donor(s): John F. Bricker, Nina B. Bricker.‡
Foundation type: Independent
Financial data (yr. ended 12/31/90): Assets, $16,482,789 (M); gifts received, $161,709; expenditures, $1,029,992; qualifying distributions, $926,152, including $858,438 for 84 grants (high: $100,000; low: $50).
Fields of interest: Higher education, education, social services, youth, hospitals, health.
Types of support: Research, scholarship funds, capital campaigns, endowment funds, renovation projects.
Limitations: Giving primarily in New Orleans, LA. No grants to individuals.
Application information: Application form not required.
Initial approach: Letter or proposal
Deadline(s): None
Board meeting date(s): Quarterly
Write: Gray S. Parker, Trustee
Officers and Trustees:* John F. Bricker,* Chair.; Donald J. Nalty,* Secy.; Dorothy A. Boyle, Robert L. Goodwin, Henry N. Kuechler III, Gray S. Parker, N.P. Phillips, Jr., John B. Waid, H. Hunter White.
EIN: 720818077

1071
Joe W. & Dorothy Dorsett Brown Foundation
1801 Pere Marquette Bldg.
New Orleans 70112   (504) 522-4233

Established in 1959 in LA.
Donor(s): Mrs. Joe W. Brown, Dorothy Dorsett Brown.‡
Foundation type: Independent
Financial data (yr. ended 12/31/90): Assets, $4,623,404 (M); expenditures, $310,387; qualifying distributions, $279,244, including $171,410 for grants.
Purpose and activities: Giving for scholarships, hospitals, a community fund, and welfare.
Fields of interest: Welfare, higher education, hospitals.
Types of support: Operating budgets, research, student aid.
Limitations: Giving primarily in LA.
Application information:
Initial approach: Proposal
Deadline(s): None
Write: D.P. Spencer, Pres.
Officers: D.P. Spencer, Pres.; V.C. Rodriguez, V.P.; D.B. Spencer, V.P.; E.K. Hunter, Secy.; B.M. Estopinal, Treas.
EIN: 726027232

1072
Coughlin-Saunders Foundation, Inc.
c/o Adler & Pias
1412 Centre Court, Suite 202
Alexandria 71301-3406   (318) 442-9642
Application address: Rapides Bank and Trust Co., 3rd St., Alexandria, LA 71303

Incorporated in 1950 in LA.
Donor(s): Anne S. Coughlin,‡ R.R. Saunders,‡ F.H. Coughlin,‡ J.A. Adams.
Foundation type: Independent
Financial data (yr. ended 11/30/91): Assets, $9,918,972 (M); gifts received, $19,900; expenditures, $477,964; qualifying distributions, $442,774, including $442,160 for grants.
Purpose and activities: Emphasis on higher education and church support; support also for the arts, health, social services, youth, and community funds. Preference given to organizations that have received grants between 1949 and 1983.
Fields of interest: Education, higher education, Protestant giving, arts, health, youth, social services, community funds.
Types of support: Professorships, internships, scholarship funds, exchange programs, fellowships, loans, building funds, equipment, emergency funds.
Limitations: Giving primarily in central LA. No grants to individuals, or for matching gifts.
Publications: Application guidelines, program policy statement.
Application information: Application form not required.
Initial approach: Letter
Copies of proposal: 1
Deadline(s): Submit proposal preferably in Jan. or Feb.; deadline Mar. 15
Board meeting date(s): Mar. and Sept.
Final notification: Between Mar. 31 and Oct. 31
Write: Ed Crump, Dir.

Officer and Directors: Carolyn Saunders,* Pres.; John Adams, Nellie Adams, Homer Adler, Scott Brame, Sarah Cockerham, Ed Crump, Ann Maynard.
Number of staff: None.
EIN: 726027641

1073
Freeport-McMoRan Inc. Corporate Giving Program
1615 Poydras St.
New Orleans 70112   (504) 582-4000

Financial data (yr. ended 12/03/90): Total giving, $5,601,793, including $4,423,230 for 200 grants (high: $100,000; low: $1,000; average: $2,500-$7,500) and $1,178,563 for employee matching gifts.
Purpose and activities: Areas of special funding interest include education, health and welfare and social services, the arts, civic and community affairs and environmental concerns. Also support for agriculture, engineering, and business education.
Fields of interest: Education, health, welfare, social services, arts, civic affairs, environment, agriculture, business education, community development, conservation, crime and law enforcement, disadvantaged, engineering, general charitable giving, higher education, hospitals, housing, minorities, museums, music, performing arts, chemistry, computer sciences, education—minorities, child development, civil rights, health services, law and justice, secondary education, wildlife, urban development, women, Protestant giving, recreation, educational research, family services, hospitals—building funds, humanities, biology.
Types of support: Matching funds, general purposes, research, scholarship funds, annual campaigns, building funds, capital campaigns, special projects, employee matching gifts, donated equipment, operating budgets, employee volunteer services, loaned talent, use of facilities, employee-related scholarships, endowment funds, public relations services.
Limitations: Giving primarily in operating areas in FL; Baton Rouge, Belle Chase, Donaldsonville, Metairie, New Orleans, Uncle Sam, LA; and the Southeast. No support for national disease agencies or religious, political, fraternal, veterans', national, or tax-supported organizations. No grants to individuals.
Publications: Corporate report.
Application information: Contributions are handled by Public Relations. Application form not required.
Initial approach: Initial contact by phone or letter; follow with full proposal; send letter or proposal to headquarters
Copies of proposal: 1
Deadline(s): Applications accepted throughout the year.
Board meeting date(s): Feb., Apr., June, Aug., Oct., and Dec.
Final notification: Within six weeks after receipt of application
Write: Jay Handelman, Dir. Public Relations
Number of staff: 1 full-time professional.

1074
Mr. and Mrs. Jimmy Heymann Special Account
1201 Canal St.
New Orleans 70112

Incorporated in 1958 in LA.
Donor(s): Jimmy Heymann, May H. Wolf.
Foundation type: Independent
Financial data (yr. ended 12/31/91): Assets, $3,743,075 (M); expenditures, $162,382; qualifying distributions, $159,268, including $156,540 for 83 grants (high: $50,425; low: $15).
Purpose and activities: Giving primarily for an infirmary and a community foundation; some support also for a community fund, health services, and Jewish organizations.
Fields of interest: Hospitals, community development, community funds, health services, Jewish giving.
Limitations: Giving primarily in LA. No grants to individuals.
Application information: Contributes only to pre-selected organizations. Applications not accepted.
Officers: Janice Heymann, Pres.; Jerry Heymann, V.P. and Secy.-Treas.
Directors: Marion Levy Southeimer, Maurice Southeimer.
EIN: 726019367

1075
Heymann-Wolf Foundation
1201 Canal St.
New Orleans 70112-2676

Incorporated in 1947 in LA.
Donor(s): Leon Heymann,‡ Mrs. Leon Heymann,‡ Leon M. Wolf,‡ May H. Wolf, Jimmy Heymann, Mrs. Jimmy Heymann, Krauss Co., Ltd.
Foundation type: Independent
Financial data (yr. ended 12/31/90): Assets, $4,171,283 (M); expenditures, $238,734; qualifying distributions, $114,093, including $111,750 for grants.
Purpose and activities: Giving for a university, a community fund, hospitals, and cultural programs.
Fields of interest: Hospitals, cultural programs.
Limitations: Giving primarily in LA. No grants to individuals.
Application information: Contributes only to pre-selected organizations. Applications not accepted.
Officers: Jerry Heymann, Pres.; Marjorie Heymann, V.P.; Mrs. Jimmy Heymann, Treas.
EIN: 726019363

1076
Keller Family Foundation
P.O. Box 13625
New Orleans 70185-3625

Trust established in 1949 in LA.
Donor(s): Charles Keller, Jr., Rosa F. Keller.
Foundation type: Independent
Financial data (yr. ended 12/31/90): Assets, $3,736,926 (M); expenditures, $155,650; qualifying distributions, $152,000, including $152,000 for 36 grants (high: $16,000; low: $100).

Purpose and activities: Giving for public and foreign policy organizations and higher education; support also for cultural programs including music, community development, Catholic giving, hospitals, media and communications, and building funds for educational institutions.
Fields of interest: Public policy, foreign policy, higher education, cultural programs, music, community development, Catholic giving, hospitals, media and communications, education—building funds.
Types of support: Capital campaigns, operating budgets.
Limitations: Giving primarily in LA.
Application information: Application form not required.
Initial approach: Proposal
Copies of proposal: 3
Deadline(s): Nov. 1
Board meeting date(s): As needed
Write: Mary Keller Zervigon, Corresponding Secy.
Trustees: Charles Keller, Jr., Chair.; Mary K. Zervigon, Corresponding Secy.; Julie F. Breitmeyer, Rosa F. Keller, Caroline K. Loughlin.
EIN: 726027426

1077
LaNasa-Greco Foundation
3201 Ridgelake Dr.
Metairie 70002-4992   (504) 834-4226

Established in 1961 in LA.
Foundation type: Independent
Financial data (yr. ended 12/31/90): Assets, $2,116,436 (M); expenditures, $118,469; qualifying distributions, $102,500, including $102,500 for 6 grants (high: $47,500; low: $7,500).
Purpose and activities: Support primarily for higher education; contributions also for music and health.
Fields of interest: Higher education, music, health.
Types of support: Scholarship funds.
Limitations: Giving primarily in New Orleans, LA. No grants to individuals.
Application information: Contributes only to pre-selected organizations. Applications not accepted.
Write: Sarah LaNasa, Pres.
Officers: Sarah LaNasa, Pres.; C. Ellis Henican, V.P.; Sidney M. Rihner, Secy.-Treas.
EIN: 726028040

1078
Milton H. Latter Educational and Charitable Foundation
1010 Common St., Suite 1510
New Orleans 70112   (504) 524-1921

Established in 1947 in LA.
Foundation type: Independent
Financial data (yr. ended 12/31/90): Assets, $1,167,946 (M); expenditures, $423,161; qualifying distributions, $416,320, including $416,320 for 18 grants (high: $330,000; low: $200).
Purpose and activities: Giving primarily to a medical center; some support also for health

services, a community fund, Jewish organizations, and higher education.
Fields of interest: Hospitals, health services, community funds, Jewish giving, higher education.
Limitations: Giving primarily in New Orleans, LA.
Application information:
Deadline(s): None
Write: Shirley L. Kaufmann, Pres.
Officers: Shirley L. Kaufmann, Pres.; Lee H. Schlesinger, 1st V.P.; Suzanne R. Rose, V.P.; D.K. Stirton, Secy.-Treas.
EIN: 726028027

1079
Libby-Dufour Fund
321 Hibernia Bank Bldg., Suite 202
New Orleans 70112

Incorporated in 1952 in LA.
Donor(s): Edith Libby Dufour.‡
Foundation type: Independent
Financial data (yr. ended 05/31/90): Assets, $6,597,400 (M); expenditures, $476,806; qualifying distributions, $438,316, including $435,680 for 34 grants (high: $65,000; low: $400).
Purpose and activities: Emphasis on Christian charities, including support for churches, colleges and schools, and Christian welfare funds; giving also for hospitals and medical centers.
Fields of interest: Religion—Christian, religious welfare, higher education, religious schools, hospitals.
Limitations: Giving limited to the New Orleans, LA, area. No grants to individuals, or for endowment funds or operating budgets.
Application information:
Initial approach: Proposal
Copies of proposal: 1
Deadline(s): None
Board meeting date(s): Quarterly
Write: Eben Hardie, Pres.
Officers and Trustees:* Eben Hardie,* Pres.; E. James Kock, Jr.,* Secy.; M.C. Powell,* Treas.; Jackson P. Ducournau, Harry B. Kelleher, Jr., Denis McDonald.
EIN: 726027406

1080
The Lupin Foundation
3715 Prytania St., Suite 307
New Orleans 70115   (504) 897-6125
FAX: (504) 894-6640

Incorporated in 1981 in LA.
Foundation type: Independent
Financial data (yr. ended 12/31/90): Assets, $20,197,984 (M); expenditures, $1,580,524; qualifying distributions, $1,164,914, including $938,687 for 64 grants (high: $83,333; low: $500).
Fields of interest: Arts, education, educational research, community funds, civic affairs, health, medical research, handicapped, religion, environment.
Limitations: Giving primarily in LA. No grants to individuals; no loans.
Publications: Application guidelines.
Application information: Application form required.

Initial approach: Brief proposal (not exceeding 6 pages)
Copies of proposal: 1
Deadline(s): 3 weeks before board meetings
Board meeting date(s): 9 times yearly
Final notification: 2 weeks
Write: Lori Wesolowski, Coord.
Officers and Directors:* Arnold M. Lupin, M.D.,* Pres.; Samuel Lupin, M.D.,* V.P.; Louis Levy II, M.D.,* Secy.; E. Ralph Lupin, M.D.,* Treas.; Jay S. Lupin, M.D., Louis Lupin, Suzanne Lupin Stokar.
Number of staff: 1 full-time support.
EIN: 720940770

1081
J. Edgar Monroe Foundation (1976)
228 St. Charles St., Suite 1402
New Orleans 70130   (504) 529-3539

Established in 1976 in LA.
Donor(s): J. Edgar Monroe.
Foundation type: Independent
Financial data (yr. ended 12/31/90): Assets, $8,161,451 (M); expenditures, $463,526; qualifying distributions, $385,050, including $385,050 for 40 grants (high: $100,000; low: $25; average: $25-$1,000).
Fields of interest: Social services, higher education, arts, historic preservation, religion—Christian, hospices, hospitals.
Types of support: Annual campaigns, building funds, capital campaigns, emergency funds, equipment, renovation projects, research.
Limitations: Giving primarily in LA.
Application information:
Write: Robert J. Monroe, Trustee
Officers and Trustees:* J. Edgar Monroe,* Pres.; William F. Finegan,* V.P.; J. Percy Monroe, Jr.,* V.P.; Robert J. Monroe,* Secy.-Treas.
Number of staff: 1 full-time support.
EIN: 720784059

1082
The Greater New Orleans Foundation
(Formerly The Greater New Orleans Regional Foundation)
2515 Canal St., Suite 401
New Orleans 70119   (504) 822-4906

Established in 1924 in LA, as the Community Chest; became a community foundation in 1983.
Foundation type: Community
Financial data (yr. ended 12/31/90): Assets, $11,887,640 (M); gifts received, $3,037,047; expenditures, $1,096,202; qualifying distributions, $793,706, including $793,706 for 207 grants (high: $10,000; low: $59; average: $500-$10,000).
Fields of interest: Health, social services, arts, cultural programs, education.
Types of support: Emergency funds, technical assistance, seed money, special projects, matching funds, equipment.
Limitations: Giving limited to southeast LA, including the greater New Orleans area. No support for religion. No grants to individuals, or for operating budgets, annual fund campaigns, continuing support, endowment funds, building funds, or deficit financing.

Publications: Annual report, application guidelines, program policy statement, newsletter, informational brochure.
Application information: Application form required.
Initial approach: Proposal
Copies of proposal: 2
Board meeting date(s): Quarterly
Officers and Trustees:* Mrs. J. Thomas Lewis,* Chair.; David Conroy, Vice-Chair.; Mrs. Francis E. Lauricella, Secy.; Ian Arnof, Emmett W. Bashful, M.D., Harry J. Blumenthal, Jr., Mrs. Morris E. Burka, Leah Chase, Philip Claverle, Moise Dennery, Thomas J. Egan, D. Blair Favrot, William F. Finegan, Norman Francis, Mrs. Ronald French, Mrs. Robert Haspel, Wayne J. Lee, William Marks, G. Frank Purvis, Mrs. Roger T. Stone, Charles C. Teamer, Sr., Robert Young.
Number of staff: 2 full-time professional; 1 part-time professional; 2 full-time support; 1 part-time support.
EIN: 720408921
Recent health grants:
1082-1 Planned Parenthood of Louisiana, New Orleans, LA, $12,500. For Our Youth: Opportunities and Options, from Ford-MacArthur Grant for teen pregnancy prevention. 1990.
1082-2 Southern Eye Bank, New Orleans, LA, $10,000. For projects furthering eye care. 1990.

1083
Edward G. Schlieder Educational Foundation
431 Gravier St., Suite 400
New Orleans 70130   (504) 581-6179

Incorporated in 1945 in LA.
Donor(s): Edward G. Schlieder.‡
Foundation type: Independent
Financial data (yr. ended 12/31/91): Assets, $21,976,826 (M); expenditures, $1,171,177; qualifying distributions, $1,040,957, including $1,013,539 for 17 grants (high: $120,000; low: $15,000; average: $12,000-$30,000).
Purpose and activities: To aid schools, colleges, and universities; grants largely to universities for medical research.
Fields of interest: Medical research, education, higher education.
Types of support: Research, equipment, capital campaigns.
Limitations: Giving limited to educational institutions in LA. No grants to individuals, or for general purposes, building or endowment funds, scholarships, fellowships, or operating budgets; no loans.
Publications: Annual report.
Application information: Application form not required.
Initial approach: Letter
Copies of proposal: 3
Deadline(s): Submit proposal preferably in Feb.; no set deadline
Board meeting date(s): As required
Final notification: 30 to 45 days
Write: Blanc A. Parker, Exec. Consultant
Officers and Directors:* Donald J. Nalty,* Pres.; George G. Westfeldt, Jr.,* Secy.-Treas.; Blanc A. Parker, Exec. Consultant; John F. Bricker, Thomas D. Westfeldt.

Number of staff: 1 part-time professional; 1 part-time support.
EIN: 720408974

1084
The Community Foundation of Shreveport-Bossier
401 Edwards St., Suite 517
Shreveport 71101   (318) 221-0582

Incorporated in 1961 in LA.
Foundation type: Community
Financial data (yr. ended 12/31/91): Assets, $13,814,914 (M); gifts received, $1,456,437; expenditures, $1,179,314; qualifying distributions, $955,425, including $955,425 for 62 grants (high: $100,000; low: $500).
Purpose and activities: Primary areas of interest include health services, literacy, and higher education.
Fields of interest: Health, health services, welfare, homeless, handicapped, aged, youth, education, higher education, literacy, cultural programs, arts.
Types of support: Special projects, equipment, building funds, matching funds, scholarship funds, seed money, conferences and seminars, publications, renovation projects, research, capital campaigns.
Limitations: Giving limited to the Caddo and Bossier parishes, LA. No grants to individuals.
Publications: Annual report, application guidelines, informational brochure.
Application information: Application form required.
   Initial approach: Letter of inquiry prior to submitting full grant request
   Copies of proposal: 8
   Deadline(s): Feb. 15, May 15, and Aug. 15
   Board meeting date(s): Apr., July, and Oct.
   Final notification: Immediately after board meetings
   Write: Carol Emanuel, Exec. Dir.
Officers and Directors:* W.C. Rasberry, Jr.,* Chair.; Joseph L. Hargrove,* Vice-Chair.; Charles Ellis Brown,* Secy.; William C. Peatross,* Treas.; Margaret W. Kinsey, Louis Pendleton, Donald P. Weiss.
Trustee Banks: Commercial National Bank in Shreveport, Hibernia National Bank, Pioneer Bank & Trust Co., Premier Bank, N.A.
Number of staff: 1 full-time professional; 2 full-time support.
EIN: 726022365

1085
The Woldenberg Foundation
(Formerly Dorothy & Malcolm Woldenberg Foundation)
301 Magazine St., 2nd Fl.
New Orleans 70130

Incorporated in 1959 in LA as Woldenberg Charitable and Educational Foundation.

Donor(s): Malcolm Woldenberg, Magnolia Liquor Co., Inc., Sazerac Co., Inc., Great Southern Liquor Co., Inc., Duval Spirits, Inc.
Foundation type: Independent
Financial data (yr. ended 12/31/90): Assets, $2,750,176 (M); expenditures, $318,492; qualifying distributions, $309,550, including $309,550 for 36 grants (high: $190,000; low: $250).
Fields of interest: Jewish giving, Jewish welfare, higher education, secondary education, health associations, AIDS.
Limitations: Giving primarily in LA and FL. No grants to individuals.
Application information:
   Initial approach: Letter
   Deadline(s): None
   Write: Dorothy Woldenberg, Pres.
Officers: Dorothy Woldenberg, Pres.; Stephen Goldring, V.P.; C. Halpern, Secy.-Treas.
EIN: 726022665

1086
William C. Woolf Foundation
P.O. Box 21119
Shreveport 71152

Incorporated in 1959 in LA.
Donor(s): William C. Woolf,‡ Geraldine H. Woolf.‡
Foundation type: Independent
Financial data (yr. ended 02/28/91): Assets, $3,889,638 (M); expenditures, $224,368; qualifying distributions, $170,838, including $163,162 for 43 grants (high: $50,000; low: $250).
Fields of interest: Religion—Christian, higher education, youth, social services, medical research.
Limitations: Giving primarily in Shreveport, LA.
Application information: Contributes only to pre-selected organizations. Applications not accepted.
   Write: Brett B. Josey, Secy.
Officer: Brett B. Josey, Secy.
Trustees: Nicholas Hobson Wheless, Jr., Chair.; Claude G. Rives III, C. Lane Sartor.
EIN: 726020630

1087
Zemurray Foundation ▼
1436 Whitney Bldg.
228 St. Charles
New Orleans 70130   (504) 525-0091

Incorporated in 1951 in LA.
Donor(s): Sarah W. Zemurray.
Foundation type: Independent
Financial data (yr. ended 12/31/90): Assets, $43,011,030 (M); expenditures, $2,394,391; qualifying distributions, $2,165,272, including $2,090,630 for grants.
Purpose and activities: Grants primarily for education, particularly higher education, cultural programs, civic affairs, hospitals, and medical research.
Fields of interest: Education, higher education, cultural programs, hospitals, medical research, civic affairs.
Limitations: Giving primarily in New Orleans, LA, and Cambridge, MA. No grants to individuals.
Application information: Contributes only to pre-selected organizations. Applications not accepted.
   Board meeting date(s): Usually in Nov.
   Write: Walter J. Belsom, Jr., Treas.
Officers and Directors:* Doris Z. Stone,* Pres.; Samuel Z. Stone,* V.P.; Thomas B. Lemann,* Secy.; Walter J. Belsom, Jr.,* Treas.
EIN: 720539603

1088
Fred B. and Ruth B. Zigler Foundation
P.O. Box 986
Jennings 70546-0986   (318) 824-2413

Incorporated in 1956 in LA.
Donor(s): Fred B. Zigler,‡ Ruth B. Zigler.‡
Foundation type: Independent
Financial data (yr. ended 12/31/90): Assets, $6,117,882 (M); expenditures, $427,693; qualifying distributions, $290,998, including $273,369 for grants.
Purpose and activities: Emphasis on higher and secondary education, including scholarships for local students, and youth agencies; support also for a museum and drug abuse programs.
Fields of interest: Higher education, secondary education, youth, drug abuse.
Types of support: Operating budgets, building funds, general purposes, equipment, student aid, research, endowment funds, matching funds, renovation projects, special projects.
Limitations: Giving primarily in Jefferson Davis Parish, LA. No grants to individuals (except scholarships for graduates of Jefferson Davis Parish high schools).
Publications: Annual report.
Application information: Scholarship application forms available through Parish high schools.
   Initial approach: Proposal or letter
   Copies of proposal: 1
   Deadline(s): 3 weeks prior to board meetings; scholarship deadline Mar. 10
   Board meeting date(s): Bimonthly beginning in Jan.
   Write: Margaret Cormier, Secy.-Treas.
Officers: Paul E. Brummett, Pres.; Margaret Cormier, Secy.-Treas.
Trustees: Dave Elmore, John Michael Elmore, Mark Fehl, A.J.M. Oustalet, John Pipkin.
Number of staff: 1 full-time professional; 1 part-time professional.
EIN: 726019403

MAINE

1089
Casco Northern Bank Corporate Contributions

c/o Marketing Communications
One Monument Sq., P.O. Box 678
Portland 04101   (207) 774-8221

Financial data (yr. ended 12/31/90): Total giving, $325,000 for grants.
Purpose and activities: Support for United Ways, education, employment, and training, higher education, health and human services, culture and the arts, social services, civic and community affairs, memberships, benefits, and program ads; also provides in-kind services and products.
Fields of interest: Community funds, education, employment, vocational education, higher education, health, social services, cultural programs, arts, civic affairs, community development.
Types of support: Donated equipment.
Limitations: Giving limited to ME.
Application information: Decisions are made by the Contributions Committee representing the bank's board, management, and community at large. In addition, the bank's regions are given authority to make contributions within limited amounts to projects regional in scope.
  Initial approach: Letter
  Write: Charles Kennedy, Mgr., Govt. and
    Community Affairs
Administrators: Charles Kennedy, Mgr., Govt. and Community Affairs; Jackie Perna, Admin. Asst.

1090
Central Maine Power Corporate Contributions Program

c/o Public Affairs
Edison Drive
Augusta 04336   (207) 623-3521

Financial data (yr. ended 12/31/90): Total giving, $513,625, including $300,000 for grants (high: $10,000; low: $100; average: $20-$50,000), $213,000 for 12 grants to individuals (high: $70,000; low: $1,600; average: $1,600-$70,000) and $625 for 8 employee matching gifts.
Purpose and activities: Giving primarily for education and community funds, especially the United Way; some support for hospitals, health, civic affairs, humanities, capital campaigns, and youth. Giving also includes in-kind support and employee matching gifts, and scholarship and research grants.
Fields of interest: Education, community funds, hospitals, health, performing arts, youth, leadership development, humanities, public policy, women, environment, leadership development.
Types of support: Annual campaigns, capital campaigns, continuing support, building funds, in-kind gifts, donated equipment, donated products, public relations services, loaned talent, conferences and seminars, employee matching gifts, equipment, student aid, publications,

technical assistance, special projects, employee-related scholarships, research, matching funds, scholarship funds, student aid.
Limitations: Giving limited to ME with preference to southern and central regions (CMP service territory). No support for political action.
Publications: Corporate report, application guidelines.
Application information: Public Affairs handles contributions. Application form not required.
  Initial approach: Letter to headquarters
  Copies of proposal: 1
  Deadline(s): None
  Board meeting date(s): Monthly
  Final notification: Within two weeks of decision
  Write: David F. Allen, Mgr., Public Affairs
Administrator: David F. Allen, Dir., Community Relations.
Number of staff: 1 part-time professional; 1 part-time support.

1091
The Maine Community Foundation, Inc.

210 Main St.
P.O. Box 148
Ellsworth 04605   (207) 667-9735

Incorporated in 1983 in ME.
Foundation type: Community
Financial data (yr. ended 12/31/91): Assets, $7,302,228 (M); gifts received, $2,505,260; expenditures, $894,788; qualifying distributions, $671,286, including $559,926 for 250 grants (high: $116,873; low: $100; average: $500-$5,000), $27,994 for 32 grants to individuals (high: $4,000; low: $100; average: $100-$4,000), $33,366 for 3 foundation-administered programs and $50,000 for loans.
Purpose and activities: Primary areas of interest include the arts, child welfare and youth, the disadvantaged, education, and health.
Fields of interest: Education, elementary education, arts, leadership development, child welfare, youth, aged, disadvantaged, environment, health.
Types of support: Seed money, matching funds, conferences and seminars, general purposes, publications, scholarship funds, special projects, technical assistance, student aid, emergency funds.
Limitations: Giving limited to ME. No support for religious organizations for religious purposes. No grants to individuals (except from donor-designated funds), or for endowment funds, equipment, or annual campaigns for regular operations; grants rarely made for capital campaigns.
Publications: Annual report (including application guidelines), informational brochure, newsletter, program policy statement, application guidelines.
Application information: Application form required.
  Initial approach: Letter
  Copies of proposal: 1
  Deadline(s): Jan. 15, Apr. 1, July 15, and Oct. 1
  Board meeting date(s): 4 times a year
  Final notification: 2 months after deadline
  Write: Rebecca Buyers-Basso, Program Dir.
Officers and Directors:* P. Andrews Nixon,* Chair.; Marion M. Kane,* Pres.; and 23 additional directors.

Number of staff: 2 full-time professional; 1 part-time professional; 1 full-time support.
EIN: 010391479
Recent health grants:
1091-1 Maine Committee on Aging, Augusta, ME, $19,894. For pilot training program in Maine nursing homes. 1990.
1091-2 Maine Medical Assessment Foundation, Manchester, ME, $10,000. For general support. 1990.

1092
Maine Medical Assessment Foundation

P.O. Box 190
Manchester 04351

Established in 1989 in ME.
Donor(s): Department of Health and Human Services, Blue Cross & Blue Shield of Maine, University of Washington, New England Medical Center Hospital.
Foundation type: Operating
Financial data (yr. ended 12/31/91): Assets, $55,834 (M); gifts received, $533,146; expenditures, $559,894; qualifying distributions, $839,150, including $277,919 for 5 grants (high: $75,108; low: $18,128) and $561,231 for 4 foundation-administered programs.
Purpose and activities: A private operating foundation; grants for the "study of the hysterectomy decision and the assessment of outcomes."
Fields of interest: Medical research, medical sciences, heart disease.
Limitations: Giving primarily in MA and ME. No grants to individuals.
Application information:
  Initial approach: Letter
  Deadline(s): None
  Write: Robert B. Keller, M.D., Exec. Dir.
Officers and Directors:* Daniel F. Hanley, M.D.,* Chair.; Buell Miller, M.D.,* Vice-Chair.; Brinton Darlington, M.D.,* Secy.-Treas.; Robert B. Keller, M.D.,* Exec. Dir.; Mrs. Cary W. Bok, Richard Chamberlin, M.D., Gerry Hayes, M.D., Robert E. McAfee, M.D., Daniel Onion, M.D., Donald Robertson, M.D., Terrence Sheehan, M.D., John Wennberg, M.D.
Number of staff: 1 full-time professional; 1 part-time professional; 1 part-time support.
EIN: 010440180

1093
Shaw's Market Trust Fund

(Formerly Market Trust)
c/o Fleet Bank of Maine
P.O. Box 3555
Portland 04104

Trust established in 1959 in ME.
Donor(s): Brockton Public Market, Inc., George C. Shaw Co., and subsidiaries.
Foundation type: Company-sponsored
Financial data (yr. ended 07/31/91): Assets, $1,930,873 (M); gifts received, $300,000; expenditures, $345,239; qualifying distributions, $345,239, including $338,950 for 45 grants (high: $72,500; low: $750).
Fields of interest: Community funds, hospitals, youth, cultural programs, arts, museums.

Types of support: Annual campaigns, building funds, capital campaigns, emergency funds.
Limitations: Giving limited to southern ME, southern NH, and MA. No grants to individuals.
Application information: Contributes only to pre-selected organizations. Applications not accepted.
 Write: David MacNichol
Trustee: Fleet Bank of Maine, N.A.
EIN: 016008389

1094
UNUM Charitable Foundation
2211 Congress St.
Portland 04122   (207) 770-2211

Established in 1969 in ME.
Donor(s): UNUM Life Insurance Co.
Foundation type: Company-sponsored
Financial data (yr. ended 12/31/91): Assets, $3,333,961 (M); gifts received, $1,300,000;

expenditures, $1,786,447; qualifying distributions, $1,777,764, including $1,562,015 for 155 grants (high: $260,000; low: $1,000) and $51,282 for employee matching gifts.
Purpose and activities: Primary areas of interest include AIDS, aging, the diabled, economic development, economic development for the arts, education (K-12), and family issues, including United Way support.
Fields of interest: AIDS, aged, handicapped, community development, arts, education, family services, community funds.
Types of support: Employee matching gifts, capital campaigns, special projects, matching funds, seed money, in-kind gifts, employee-related scholarships.
Limitations: Giving primarily in ME; capital grants limited to the greater Portland area. No support for religious organizations, fundraising or athletic events, goodwill advertising, or United Way member agencies. No grants to individuals.

Publications: Corporate giving report (including application guidelines), informational brochure (including application guidelines), grants list.
Application information: Completion of formal application may be required after review of initial submission. Application form not required.
 Initial approach: Letter
 Copies of proposal: 1
 Deadline(s): None
 Board meeting date(s): Trustees meet quarterly; grants under $25,000 reviewed by staff on an ongoing basis
 Write: Janine M. Manning, Secy.
Officers and Trustees:* James F. Orr III,* Pres.; Donna T. Mundy,* V.P.; Kathryn Yates,* V.P.; Janine M. Manning, Secy.; Ann Beadle, Terry Cohen, Rosemary LaVoie, Melinda Loring, Richard McMurry, James S. Orser, Cheryl Stewart, Janet Whitehouse.
Number of staff: 3 full-time professional; 2 full-time support; 1 part-time support.
EIN: 237026979

MARYLAND

1095
The Abell Foundation, Inc. ▼
1116 Fidelity Bldg.
210 North Charles St.
Baltimore 21201-4013   (301) 547-1300

Incorporated in 1953 in MD.
Donor(s): A.S. Abell Co., Harry C. Black,‡ Gary Black, Sr.‡
Foundation type: Independent
Financial data (yr. ended 12/31/90): Assets, $118,383,435 (M); expenditures, $6,719,640; qualifying distributions, $6,521,994, including $5,521,575 for 172 grants (high: $324,405; low: $278; average: $1,000-$50,000), $66,950 for 60 employee matching gifts and $175,000 for 1 foundation-administered program.
Purpose and activities: Supports education with emphasis on public education, including early childhood and elementary education, educational research, and minority education; economic development; human services, including programs for child welfare and development and health and family services; the arts and culture, including arts preservation; conservation; and the homeless, including hunger issues.
Fields of interest: Higher education, education, education—early childhood, education—minorities, educational research, elementary education, economics, arts, cultural programs, historic preservation, conservation, environment, social services, hunger, health services, child welfare, disadvantaged, family services, homeless, child development.
Types of support: Endowment funds, capital campaigns, equipment, land acquisition, matching funds, renovation projects, conferences and seminars, general purposes, scholarship funds, seed money, special projects.
Limitations: Giving limited to MD, with a focus on Baltimore. Generally no support for housing or medical facilities. No grants to individuals, or for operating budgets, sponsorships, memberships, sustaining funds, or deficit financing.
Publications: Annual report (including application guidelines), application guidelines, newsletter, occasional report, program policy statement.
Application information: Detailed information about what to submit with proposal should be requested. Employee-related scholarships have been phased out; previous commitments are being honored. Application form required.
  Initial approach: Letter
  Copies of proposal: 1
  Deadline(s): Jan. 1, Mar. 1, May 1, July 1, Sept. 1, and Nov. 1
  Board meeting date(s): Bimonthly
  Final notification: Within 1 week of board meetings
  Write: Robert C. Embry, Jr., Pres.
Officers and Trustees:* Gary Black, Jr.,* Chair.; Robert C. Embry, Jr.,* Pres.; Anne La Farge Culman, V.P.; Faye V. Auchenpaugh, Secy.; Frances M. Keenan, Treas.; W. Shepherdson Abell, Jr., George L. Bunting, Jr., Robert Garrett,

William Jews, Sally Michael, Donald H. Patterson, Walter Sondheim, Jr.
Number of staff: 5 full-time professional; 2 part-time professional; 2 full-time support; 2 part-time support.
EIN: 526036106
Recent health grants:
1095-1 Center City-Inner Harbor, Baltimore, MD, $80,000. For expenses to cover legal representation for initiative designed to encourage major health administration agency to relocate its headquarters in downtown Baltimore. 1990.
1095-2 Episcopal Social Ministries, Baltimore, MD, $15,000. For program expansion of Cathedral House Reentry Program, serving drug and alcohol-addicted homeless persons who are committed to sobriety and recovery after leaving treatment centers and/or jail. 1990.
1095-3 Greater Baltimore Committee (GBC) Foundation, Baltimore, MD, $60,000. For study to determine feasibility of establishing federal narcotics research center in Baltimore. 1990.
1095-4 Health Care for the Homeless, Baltimore, MD, $50,000. Toward bridge funding of operating costs for primary health care services to uninsured homeless in Maryland. 1990.

1096
Abramson Family Foundation, Inc.
(Formerly Abramson Foundation, Inc.)
11501 Huff Court
North Bethesda 20895

Established in 1959 in MD.
Donor(s): Albert Abramson, Gary M. Abramson, Ronald D. Abramson.
Foundation type: Independent
Financial data (yr. ended 12/31/91): Assets, $3,755,464 (M); expenditures, $590,059; qualifying distributions, $582,836, including $582,601 for 58 grants (high: $250,000; low: $100).
Fields of interest: Performing arts, fine arts, higher education, medical research, Jewish giving.
Types of support: General purposes.
Limitations: Giving primarily in the greater Washington, DC, area. No grants to individuals.
Application information: Contributes only to pre-selected organizations. Applications not accepted.
Officers: Albert Abramson, Pres.; Gary M. Abramson, Secy.; Ronald D. Abramson, Treas.
EIN: 526039192

1097
Aegon USA, Inc.
1111 N. Charles St.
Baltimore 21201   (301) 685-2900

Purpose and activities: Supports education, including elementary and secondary schools and private colleges, health, through hospitals and medical research and education, urban programs, housing, and United Way. Types of support include employee gift matching for education, use of company facilities and donations of company's primary goods or services.

Fields of interest: Education, elementary education, secondary education, higher education, health, hospitals, medical research, medical education, urban development, community funds, housing.
Types of support: Employee matching gifts, annual campaigns, capital campaigns, endowment funds, general purposes, scholarship funds.
Limitations: Giving primarily in headquarters city and major operating locations.
Application information:
  Write: Larry G. Brown, Sr. V.P. and Gen. Coun.

1098
Summerfield Baldwin, Jr. Foundation
c/o Mercantile-Safe Deposit & Trust Co.
766 Old Hammonds Ferry Rd.
Linthicum 21090
Application address: Two Hopkins Plaza, Baltimore, MD 21201; Tel.: (410) 237-5653

Trust established in 1946 in MD.
Foundation type: Independent
Financial data (yr. ended 12/31/91): Assets, $3,582,048 (M); expenditures, $159,796; qualifying distributions, $143,611, including $143,530 for 15 grants (high: $50,000; low: $500).
Purpose and activities: Primary support for hospitals; giving also for Episcopal church support, including church-sponsored secondary schools, and higher education.
Fields of interest: Hospitals, Protestant giving, religious schools, higher education.
Types of support: General purposes.
Limitations: Giving primarily in MD.
Application information: Application form not required.
  Initial approach: Letter
  Deadline(s): None
  Write: J. Michael Miller, V.P., Mercantile-Safe Deposit & Trust Co.
Trustee: Mercantile-Safe Deposit & Trust Co.
EIN: 526023112

1099
The Baltimore Community Foundation
(Formerly The Community Foundation of the Greater Baltimore Area, Inc.)
The Latrobe Bldg.
Two East Read St., 9th Fl.
Baltimore 21202   (301) 332-4171

Incorporated in 1972 in MD.
Foundation type: Community
Financial data (yr. ended 12/31/90): Assets, $23,607,348 (M); gifts received, $4,617,523; expenditures, $2,455,604; qualifying distributions, $1,965,733, including $1,682,164 for 180 grants (high: $219,000; average: $1,000-$10,000), $147,000 for grants to individuals and $136,569 for 1 foundation-administered program.
Purpose and activities: Giving primarily for educational, civic, cultural, health, welfare, environmental, and other community needs. Grants primarily for pilot projects, system-wide solutions, and to increase organizational effectiveness and self-sufficiency.

Fields of interest: Civic affairs, arts, cultural programs, health, education, social services, community development, environment, aged, youth.

Types of support: General purposes, endowment funds, scholarship funds, matching funds, consulting services, technical assistance, seed money, special projects.

Limitations: Giving primarily in the Baltimore, MD, area.

Publications: Annual report, informational brochure (including application guidelines).

Application information: Application form not required.

   Initial approach: Letter
   Copies of proposal: 1
   Deadline(s): 60 days before meetings
   Board meeting date(s): 3 times a year
   Final notification: Within 2 weeks after meetings
   Write: Timothy D. Armbruster, Exec. Dir.

Officers and Trustees:* Edward K. Dunn, Jr.,* Chair.; Herbert M. Katzenberg,* Vice-Chair.; Calman J. Zamoiski, Jr.,* Vice-Chair.; Timothy D. Armbruster, Pres. and Exec. Dir.; Martha K. Johnston, Secy.; W. Wallace Lanahan, Jr.,* Treas.; and 22 additional trustees.

Number of staff: 3 full-time professional; 1 part-time professional; 2 full-time support; 1 part-time support.

EIN: 237180620

1100

Baltimore Gas and Electric Foundation, Inc. ▼
Box 1475
Baltimore 21203   (410) 234-7480

Established in 1986 in MD.
Donor(s): Baltimore Gas and Electric Co.
Foundation type: Company-sponsored
Financial data (yr. ended 12/31/90): Assets, $270,280 (M); gifts received, $1,000,697; expenditures, $2,737,635; qualifying distributions, $2,516,050, including $2,516,050 for 51 grants (high: $645,000; low: $2,000; average: $10,000-$50,000).

Purpose and activities: Support primarily for cultural programs, education, community development, health, and family services. Support also for civic and public affairs, the environment, youth and handicapped services.

Fields of interest: Arts, cultural programs, museums, higher education, education, literacy, community development, volunteerism, civic affairs, community funds, public affairs, health, hospitals, hospitals—building funds, handicapped, youth, aged, family services, homeless, environment.

Types of support: Annual campaigns, general purposes, capital campaigns.

Limitations: Giving primarily in MD, with emphasis on Baltimore area.

Application information: Contributes only to pre-selected organizations. Application form not required. Applications not accepted.

   Board meeting date(s): 4 times a year
   Write: Malinda B. Small

Officers and Directors:* George V. McGowan,* Chair.; Edward A. Crooke,* Pres.; J.A. Tiernan,* V.P.; C.W. Shivery, Secy.-Treas.; H. Furlong Baldwin, J. Owen Cole, L.B. Disharoon, K. Feeley, Jerome W. Geckle, W. Hackerman, P.G.

Miller, G.G. Radcliffe, G.L. Russell, Jr., B.C. Trueschler, H.K. Wells.
Number of staff: 3
EIN: 521452037

1101

Helen & Merrill Bank Foundation, Inc.
c/o Weil, Akman et al.
201 West Padonia Rd., Suite 600
Timonium 21093
Application address: 1200 Mercantile Bank & Trust Bldg., Two Hopkins Plaza, Baltimore, MD 21201; Tel.: (301) 385-4099

Established about 1969.
Donor(s): Helen S. Bank, Merrill L. Bank.
Foundation type: Independent
Financial data (yr. ended 06/30/91): Assets, $5,770,433 (M); gifts received, $250,863; expenditures, $216,919; qualifying distributions, $190,981, including $188,451 for 58 grants (high: $56,150; low: $2).

Fields of interest: Health, Jewish welfare, higher education, arts.

Limitations: Giving primarily in West Palm Beach and Palm Beach, FL, and Baltimore, MD.

Application information:

   Initial approach: Letter or proposal
   Deadline(s): None
   Write: Irving Cohn, Secy.

Officers: Helen S. Bank, Pres.; Merrill L. Bank, V.P. and Treas.; Irving Cohn, Secy.
EIN: 237031791

1102

The Jacob and Hilda Blaustein Foundation, Inc. ▼
Blaustein Bldg.
P.O. Box 238
Baltimore 21203

Incorporated in 1957 in MD.
Donor(s): Jacob Blaustein.‡
Foundation type: Independent
Financial data (yr. ended 12/31/90): Assets, $63,353,518 (M); gifts received, $575,000; expenditures, $3,611,270; qualifying distributions, $3,262,882, including $3,260,518 for 43 grants (high: $760,000; low: $500; average: $2,000-$60,000).

Purpose and activities: Giving primarily for Jewish welfare funds and higher education.

Fields of interest: Higher education, Jewish welfare.

Types of support: General purposes.

Limitations: Giving primarily in MD and NY.

Application information:

   Initial approach: Letter
   Deadline(s): None
   Board meeting date(s): Every 4 to 6 weeks
   Final notification: 2 to 3 months
   Write: David Hirschhorn, Pres.

Officers and Trustees:* David Hirschhorn,* Pres.; Henry A. Rosenberg, Jr., V.P.; Louis B. Thalheimer, V.P.; Frank A. Strzelczyk,* Secy.-Treas.; Mary Jane Blaustein, Barbara B. Hirschhorn, Ruth B. Rosenberg, Arthur E. Roswell, Elizabeth B. Roswell.

Number of staff: None.
EIN: 526038382
Recent health grants:

1102-1 Basic Cancer Research Foundation, Baltimore, MD, $50,000. For unrestricted support. 1990.

1102-2 Hadassah, Womens Zionist Organization of America, Hadassah University Hospital, NYC, NY, $30,000. For unrestricted support. 1990.

1102-3 Johns Hopkins Hospital, Baltimore, MD, $208,000. For unrestricted support. 1990.

1102-4 National Foundation for Ileitis and Colitis, NYC, NY, $30,000. For unrestricted support. 1990.

1103

Alex Brown and Sons Charitable Foundation, Inc.
c/o Alex Brown and Sons, Inc.
135 East Baltimore St.
Baltimore 21202   (301) 727-1700

Established in 1954 in MD.
Donor(s): Alex Brown and Sons, Inc., Alex Brown Partners, Alex Brown Investment Management, Alex Brown Management Services, Inc.
Foundation type: Company-sponsored
Financial data (yr. ended 12/31/91): Assets, $5,821,884 (M); gifts received, $338,121; expenditures, $647,293; qualifying distributions, $601,788, including $601,751 for 93 grants (high: $60,000; low: $500).

Fields of interest: Cultural programs, humanities, museums, education, higher education, hospitals, hospitals—building funds, social services, conservation.

Types of support: Annual campaigns, building funds, capital campaigns, continuing support, endowment funds, general purposes, operating budgets, scholarship funds, employee-related scholarships.

Limitations: Giving primarily in MD. No grants to individuals.

Publications: 990-PF.

Application information: Application form not required.

   Copies of proposal: 1
   Deadline(s): Fall, for next year's budget
   Board meeting date(s): Mar. of each year
   Write: Walter W. Brewster, Secy.

Officers and Trustees:* Benjamin H. Griswold IV,* Pres.; Truman T. Semans,* V.P.; Walter W. Brewster, Secy.; Alvin B. Krongard,* Treas.; F. Barton Harvey, Jr., William Rienhoff IV, Thomas Schweizer, Jr.

Number of staff: None.
EIN: 526054236

1104

Capital Gazette Foundation, Inc.
c/o Wilbert H. Sirota
300 East Lombard St., Suite 1800
Baltimore 21202-3229

Established in 1986 in MD.
Donor(s): Capital Gazette Communications, Inc., Washington Magazine, Inc., Washingtonian.
Foundation type: Operating
Financial data (yr. ended 12/31/91): Assets, $3,359 (M); gifts received, $242,000; expenditures, $338,000; qualifying distributions, $338,000, including $338,000 for 36 grants (high: $60,000; low: $500).

Fields of interest: Education, higher education, international studies, economics, child welfare, social services, hospitals.
Types of support: Matching funds, general purposes.
Limitations: Giving primarily in MD and Washington, DC. No grants to individuals.
Application information: Contributes only to pre-selected organizations. Applications not accepted.
Officers: Philip Merrill, Pres.; Wilbert H. Sirota, Secy.; Eleanor Merrill, Treas.
EIN: 521490576

1105
Eugene B. Casey Foundation ▼
800 South Frederick Ave., Suite 100
Gaithersburg 20877-4102   (301) 948-4595

Established in 1981 in MD.
Foundation type: Independent
Financial data (yr. ended 08/31/91): Assets, $77,229,672 (M); expenditures, $4,441,194; qualifying distributions, $3,366,299, including $3,364,455 for 39 grants (high: $1,000,000; low: $2,500; average: $20,000-$250,000).
Purpose and activities: Support primarily for higher education and medical research; support also for fine arts and community development.
Fields of interest: Higher education, medical research, fine arts, community development.
Types of support: General purposes.
Limitations: Giving primarily in MD, and the greater Washington, DC, area.
Application information: Application form not required.
 Initial approach: Proposal
 Deadline(s): None
 Write: Betty Brown Casey, Chair.
Officer and Trustees:* Betty Brown Casey,* Chair. and Pres.; Stephen N. Jones, Nancy Casey Kelly, Jean K. Motsinger, W. James Price.
EIN: 526220316
Recent health grants:
1105-1 Bethesda Chevy Chase Rescue Squad, Bethesda, MD, $20,000. For new emergency vehicle. 1991.
1105-2 District of Columbia Institute for Mental Health, DC, $10,000. To provide primary mental health care for D.C. residents. 1991.
1105-3 Family Service of Montgomery County, Gaithersburg, MD, $14,550. For family counseling for mentally ill or those under stress. 1991.
1105-4 Georgetown University Medical Center, Stephen N. Jones Revolving Loan Fund, DC, $100,000. For loans to medical students. 1991.
1105-5 Methodist Hospital, Baylor Infectious Diseases Unit, Houston, TX, $35,661. For salary of upper-level Research Fellow. 1991.
1105-6 Methodist Hospital, Baylor Infectious Diseases Unit, Houston, TX, $25,339. For laboratory technician, equipment and supplies for upper-level Research Fellow. 1991.
1105-7 Planned Parenthood Association of Metropolitan Washington, DC, $15,000. For counseling and assistance. 1991.
1105-8 Planned Parenthood of Westchester, White Plains, NY, $35,000. For counseling and assistance. 1991.
1105-9 Samaritan Inns, DC, $10,000. To provide shelter in structured environment to formerly

homeless men and women recovering from drug and alcohol addiction. 1991.
1105-10 Suburban Hospital, Bethesda, MD, $1,000,000. For creation of Eugene B. Casey Center for Diagnostic Cardiology. 1991.
1105-11 Washington Home, DC, $10,000. For long-term nursing and hospice care. 1991.
1105-12 Winchester Medical Center, Winchester, VA, $25,000. For establishment of heart center. 1991.

1106
Clark-Winchcole Foundation ▼
Air Rights Bldg.
4550 Montgomery Ave., Suite 345N
Bethesda 20814   (301) 654-3607

Established in 1964 in DC.
Donor(s): Dorothy C. Winchcole,‡ Elizabeth G. Clark.‡
Foundation type: Independent
Financial data (yr. ended 12/31/90): Assets, $42,272,080 (M); expenditures, $2,466,108; qualifying distributions, $2,229,194, including $2,121,000 for 122 grants (high: $550,000; low: $1,000; average: $10,000-$30,000).
Purpose and activities: Emphasis on higher education, hospitals, health agencies, cultural programs, social service and youth agencies, aid to the handicapped, and Protestant church support.
Fields of interest: Higher education, health services, hospitals, cultural programs, handicapped, social services, youth, Protestant giving.
Types of support: Operating budgets, building funds, general purposes.
Limitations: Giving primarily in the Washington, DC, area.
Application information:
 Initial approach: Letter
 Deadline(s): Generally, during first 6 months of calendar year
 Write: Laura E. Phillips, Pres.
Officers and Trustees:* Laura E. Phillips, Pres.; Vincent E. Burke, Jr.,* V.P.; Joseph H. Riley, V.P.; Grover B. Russell, V.P. and Treas.; Thomas C. Thompson, Jr.,* V.P.
EIN: 526058340
Recent health grants:
1106-1 Capitol Hill Crisis Pregnancy Center, DC, $10,000. For aid to low-income crisis pregnancies. 1990.
1106-2 Childrens Inn at NIH, DC, $10,000. For accommodations for families of seriously ill children. 1990.
1106-3 Christ House, DC, $10,000. For health care for the homeless. 1990.
1106-4 Columbia Hospital for Women, DC, $10,000. 1990.
1106-5 Columbia Road Health Services, DC, $10,000. For health care to needy. 1990.
1106-6 District of Columbia Institute of Mental Hygiene, DC, $10,000. For health services. 1990.
1106-7 Easter Seal Society for Disabled Children and Adults, DC, $20,000. For aid to disabled. 1990.
1106-8 Family Service of Montgomery County, Gaithersburg, MD, $10,000. For mental health services. 1990.

1106-9 Green Door, DC, $10,000. For training for handicapped. 1990.
1106-10 Hospice Care of the District of Columbia, DC, $10,000. For home care for terminally ill. 1990.
1106-11 Hospital for Sick Children, DC, $40,000. For health care to needy children. 1990.
1106-12 Kids, Inc., Burke, VA, $15,000. To assist gravely ill children. 1990.
1106-13 National Multiple Sclerosis Society, National Capital Chapter, DC, $20,000. For health research. 1990.
1106-14 National Rehabilitation Hospital, DC, $25,000. 1990.
1106-15 Northwest Center, DC, $10,000. For health care for needy pregnant women. 1990.
1106-16 Oak Leaf Center, Bethesda, MD, $10,000. For health services. 1990.
1106-17 Providence Hospital, DC, $30,000. For health care for needy. 1990.
1106-18 Sibley Memorial Hospital, DC, $30,000. For National Training School. 1990.
1106-19 Suburban Hospital Association, Bethesda, MD, $30,000. 1990.
1106-20 Visiting Nurse Association of Washington, D.C., DC, $20,000. For health care for needy. 1990.
1106-21 Washington Home, DC, $30,000. For nursing home for incurables. Grant shared with Hospice of Washington. 1990.

1107
Crown Books Foundation, Inc.
3300 75th Ave.
Landover 20785

Established in 1988 in MD.
Donor(s): Crown Books Corp.
Foundation type: Company-sponsored
Financial data (yr. ended 12/31/91): Assets, $3,630,116 (M); expenditures, $77,950; qualifying distributions, $77,878, including $77,855 for 28 grants (high: $17,000; low: $25).
Fields of interest: Higher education, hospitals, cultural programs, arts, general charitable giving.
Types of support: General purposes.
Limitations: Giving primarily in Washington, DC. No grants to individuals.
Application information:
 Initial approach: Letter
 Deadline(s): None
 Write: Ron Marshall, Asst. Secy.
Officers and Directors:* Herbert H. Haft, Chair.; Robert M. Haft,* Pres.; Gloria G. Haft,* V.P. and Secy.-Treas.; Linda Haft, V.P.
EIN: 521590726

1108
Dart Group Foundation, Inc.
c/o Dart Group Corp.
3300 75th Ave.
Landover 20785-1599   (301) 731-1200

Established in 1987 in MD.
Foundation type: Company-sponsored
Financial data (yr. ended 12/31/91): Assets, $2,104,147 (M); expenditures, $75,077; qualifying distributions, $75,051, including $75,035 for 30 grants (high: $11,000; low: $85).

Fields of interest: Performing arts, cultural programs, higher education, education, health associations, medical research, social services.
Types of support: General purposes.
Limitations: Giving primarily in MD and Washington, DC. No grants to individuals.
Application information:
  Initial approach: Letter
  Deadline(s): None
  Write: Ron Marshall, Asst. Secy.
Officers and Directors:* Herbert H. Haft,* Chair.; Robert M. Haft,* Pres.; Gloria G. Haft,* V.P. and Secy.-Treas.; Linda Haft, V.P.
EIN: 521497671

1109
Cora & John H. Davis Foundation, Inc.
c/o Herman Glazer
7101 Wisconsin Ave., Suite 600
Bethesda 20814-4805
Application address: 4720 Montgomery Ln., Suite 712, Bethesda, MD 20814

Established in 1983 in DC.
Foundation type: Independent
Financial data (yr. ended 12/31/91): Assets, $4,344,240 (M); expenditures, $269,707; qualifying distributions, $219,100, including $219,100 for 29 grants (high: $25,000; low: $1,000).
Purpose and activities: Giving primarily for universities; support also for social services and youth, hospitals and health associations, and secondary schools.
Fields of interest: Higher education, social services, youth, hospitals, health associations, secondary education.
Types of support: Scholarship funds, general purposes, research, building funds, equipment.
Limitations: Giving primarily in the Washington, DC, area.
Application information:
  Initial approach: Letter
  Deadline(s): None
  Write: Stuart L. Bindeman, Pres.
Officers: Stuart L. Bindeman, Pres.; Harold Zirkin, V.P.; Herman Glazer, Secy.-Treas.
EIN: 521282054

1110
Community Foundation of the Eastern Shore, Inc.
200 West Main St.
Salisbury 21801   (410) 742-9911
Additional address: P.O. Box 156, Salisbury, MD 21803

Established in 1984 in MD.
Foundation type: Community
Financial data (yr. ended 06/30/91): Assets, $4,229,638 (M); gifts received, $1,814,535; expenditures, $1,409,825; qualifying distributions, $1,300,708, including $1,300,708 for grants.
Purpose and activities: Giving primarily for human services, including youth organizations, the handicapped and homeless, community development, historic preservation, museums, hospices, and drug abuse; support also for higher and other education, including scholarship funds to institutions; and health and hospitals.

Fields of interest: Social services, youth, handicapped, homeless, community development, historic preservation, museums, higher education, elementary education, health.
Types of support: Scholarship funds, conferences and seminars, consulting services, emergency funds, equipment, matching funds, seed money, special projects.
Limitations: Giving within a 50-mile radius of Salisbury, MD. No support for sectarian or religious purposes. No grants to individuals, or for annual campaigns, building funds, continuing support, land acquisition, operating budgets, debt retirement or budget deficits; no program-related investments.
Publications: Annual report, application guidelines, financial statement, informational brochure.
Application information: Application form required.
  Initial approach: Letter or telephone
  Copies of proposal: 2
  Deadline(s): 60 days prior to board meeting
  Board meeting date(s): Feb., June, and Oct.
  Final notification: Immediately following board decision
  Write: Lucy A. Mohler, Exec. Dir.
Officers and Directors:* Herbert H. Fincher,* Pres.; W. Thomas Hershey,* V.P.; Michael G. Abercrombie,* Secy.; Flo J. Mabe,* Treas.; and 14 additional directors.
Number of staff: 1 full-time professional; 1 part-time support.
EIN: 521326014

1111
First Maryland Foundation, Inc. ▼
25 South Charles St.
Baltimore 21201   (301) 244-4907

Incorporated in 1967 in MD.
Donor(s): First Maryland Bancorp.
Foundation type: Company-sponsored
Financial data (yr. ended 12/31/90): Assets, $1,575,970 (M); gifts received, $1,320,000; expenditures, $1,375,958; qualifying distributions, $1,375,085, including $1,348,124 for 253 grants (high: $195,000; low: $25) and $26,400 for 92 employee matching gifts.
Purpose and activities: Emphasis on community funds; support also for higher education, music, youth agencies, and hospitals.
Fields of interest: Community funds, higher education, music, youth, hospitals.
Types of support: Annual campaigns, general purposes, scholarship funds, employee matching gifts.
Limitations: Giving primarily in the Baltimore, MD, area. No grants to individuals, or for endowment funds, scholarships, or fellowships; no loans.
Publications: 990-PF.
Application information: Application form not required.
  Initial approach: Letter
  Copies of proposal: 1
  Deadline(s): Mar. 31
  Board meeting date(s): Mar., June, Sept., and Dec.
  Write: Robert W. Schaefer, Secy.-Treas.

Officers and Trustees:* Jeremiah E. Casey,* Chair.; Charles W. Cole, Jr.,* Pres.; Robert W. Schaefer,* Secy.-Treas.
EIN: 526077253

1112
The Jacob and Annita France Foundation, Inc. ▼
The Exchange, Suite 118
1122 Kenilworth Dr.
Baltimore 21204   (410) 832-5700

Incorporated in 1959 in MD.
Donor(s): Jacob France,‡ Annita A. France.‡
Foundation type: Independent
Financial data (yr. ended 05/31/91): Assets, $59,483,217 (M); expenditures, $2,958,707; qualifying distributions, $2,441,402, including $2,432,620 for 92 grants (high: $265,920; low: $100; average: $2,500-$50,000).
Purpose and activities: Giving within five program areas: higher education, social services and health, historic preservation, arts and culture, and conservation and civic projects.
Fields of interest: Higher education, social services, health, historic preservation, arts, cultural programs, conservation, civic affairs.
Types of support: Special projects, general purposes.
Limitations: Giving limited to MD, with emphasis on Baltimore. No grants to individuals.
Publications: Application guidelines.
Application information: Application form not required.
  Initial approach: Letter
  Copies of proposal: 1
  Deadline(s): None
  Board meeting date(s): Quarterly
  Write: Frederick W. Lafferty, Exec. Dir.
Officers and Directors:* Anne M. Pinkard, Pres.; Walter D. Pinkard, Jr.,* V.P.; Robert M. Pinkard,* Secy.-Treas.; Frederick W. Lafferty, Exec. Dir.; Joseph H. Hall, Robert G. Merrick III, Vernon T. Pittinger.
Number of staff: 1 full-time professional; 2 full-time support; 1 part-time support.
EIN: 520794585
Recent health grants:
1112-1 Church Home and Hospital, Baltimore, MD, $18,000. 1991.
1112-2 Health Care for the Homeless, Baltimore, MD, $15,000. 1991.
1112-3 Johns Hopkins Medical Institutions, Baltimore, MD, $15,000. 1991.
1112-4 Johns Hopkins University, School of Medicine, Baltimore, MD, $50,000. For Richard Starr Ross Fund. 1991.
1112-5 Johns Hopkins University, Zanvyl Kreiger Mind/Brain Institute, Baltimore, MD, $150,000. 1991.
1112-6 Mercy Medical Center, Baltimore, MD, $30,000. 1991.
1112-7 Mount Washington Pediatric Hospital, Baltimore, MD, $15,000. 1991.
1112-8 University of Maryland Foundation, Shock Trauma Research Fund, Baltimore, MD, $12,000. 1991.

1113
Morris Goldseker Foundation of Maryland, Inc. ▼
The Latrobe Bldg.
Two East Read St., 9th Fl.
Baltimore 21202   (410) 837-5100
FAX: (410)837-4701

Incorporated in 1973 in MD.
Donor(s): Morris Goldseker.‡
Foundation type: Independent
Financial data (yr. ended 12/31/91): Assets, $49,462,944 (M); expenditures, $1,953,284; qualifying distributions, $1,953,284, including $1,462,649 for grants (high: $96,900; low: $700; average: $700-$96,900).
Purpose and activities: Grants to nonprofit institutions operating or initiating programs in community affairs, health, education, neighborhood development, and human services, primarily benefiting economically disadvantaged persons.
Fields of interest: Civic affairs, community development, education, social services, health.
Types of support: Seed money, matching funds, technical assistance, special projects.
Limitations: Giving limited to the Baltimore, MD, area. No support for advocacy or political action groups, religious purposes, arts or cultural affairs, specific diseases or disabilities, or for projects normally financed with public funds. No grants to individuals, or for building or endowment funds, equipment, land acquisition, renovation projects, deficit financing, annual campaigns, research, or publications.
Publications: Annual report, informational brochure (including application guidelines).
Application information: Submit preliminary letter as early as possible before deadlines. Application form not required.
   Initial approach: Letter
   Copies of proposal: 2
   Deadline(s): Apr. 1, Aug. 1, and Dec. 1
   Board meeting date(s): Distribution committee meets 3 times a year in Mar., June, and Oct.
   Final notification: After meetings
   Write: Timothy D. Armbruster, Pres.
Officers and Trustees:* Sheldon Goldseker,* Chair.; Simon Goldseker,* Vice-Chair.; Timothy D. Armbruster, Pres.; Harry C. Blubaugh, Secy.; Sheila L. Dodson, Treas.; Security Trust Company, N.A.
Selection Committee: Darrell Friedman, Earl Richardson, William C. Richardson.
Number of staff: 2 full-time professional; 1 full-time support.
EIN: 520983502
Recent health grants:
1113-1 National Crime Prevention Council, Baltimore, MD, $40,000. For Community Responses to Drug Abuse Prevention. Grant shared with Coalition of Peninsula Organizations. 1991.

1114
Louis H. Gross Foundation, Inc.
1314 Dulaney Valley Rd.
Baltimore 21204-1308   (301) 821-5171

Established in 1959 in MD.
Donor(s): Frank Sutland, Josephine Sutland.
Foundation type: Independent

Financial data (yr. ended 12/31/91): Assets, $2,250,556 (M); gifts received, $79,750; expenditures, $1,502,470; qualifying distributions, $1,501,558, including $1,501,558 for 7 grants (high: $1,492,958; low: $300).
Purpose and activities: Giving primarily for child welfare, including pediatric centers and programs for physically or learning disabled youth.
Fields of interest: Child welfare, hospitals, handicapped.
Limitations: Giving primarily in Baltimore, MD, and New York, NY.
Application information:
   Write: Josephine Sutland, Pres.
Officer: Josephine Sutland, Pres.
EIN: 146018307

1115
Nathan and Sophie Gumenick Foundation
c/o Robert Philipson & Co.
8601 Georgia Ave., Suite 1001
Silver Spring 20910-3440

Established in 1954 in DC.
Foundation type: Independent
Financial data (yr. ended 11/30/91): Assets, $3,030,776 (M); expenditures, $906,171; qualifying distributions, $893,360, including $893,360 for 60 grants (high: $300,560; low: $5).
Fields of interest: Higher education, medical education, medical research, hospitals, Jewish giving.
Limitations: Giving on a national basis, with some emphasis on Richmond, VA, and Miami Beach, FL.
Application information:
   Initial approach: Letter
   Deadline(s): None
   Write: Nathan S. Gumenick, Treas.
Officers: Nathan S. Gumenick, Pres. and Treas.; Sophia Gumenick, V.P.; Harry Grandis, Secy.
EIN: 546055611

1116
Hechinger Foundation ▼
(also known as Sidney L. Hechinger Foundation)
1616 McCormick Dr.
Landover 20785   (301) 341-0999
Scholarship Application address: Hechinger Foundation Scholarship Program, Citizens Scholarship Foundation of America, P.O. Box 297, St. Peter, MN 56082

Incorporated in 1955 in DC.
Donor(s): Hechinger Co., members of the Hechinger family.
Foundation type: Company-sponsored
Financial data (yr. ended 06/30/91): Assets, $1,702,092 (M); gifts received, $250,000; expenditures, $1,286,414; qualifying distributions, $1,204,690, including $1,204,210 for 519 grants (high: $220,000; low: $100; average: $500-$10,000).
Purpose and activities: Emphasis on the performing arts, music, and other cultural programs, Jewish welfare funds, higher education, United Way, and youth and social service agencies, including aid to the handicapped.
Fields of interest: Performing arts, arts, music, theater, cultural programs, higher education, community funds, youth, social services, health.

Types of support: General purposes, employee-related scholarships.
Limitations: Giving limited to areas of company operations in Washington, DC, DE, MD, NJ, NY, NC, OH, PA, SC, UT, and VA. No grants to individuals.
Publications: Application guidelines.
Application information: Application form not required.
   Initial approach: Proposal
   Copies of proposal: 1
   Deadline(s): May 31 for scholarships
   Board meeting date(s): Continuously
   Final notification: 8 to 10 weeks if approved
   Write: Richard England, Pres.
Manager and Trustees:* Richard England,* Pres.; Lois H. England, John W. Hechinger, Jr., June R. Hechinger.
Number of staff: 1 full-time professional; 1 full-time support; 1 part-time support.
EIN: 526054428

1117
Corina Higginson Trust
c/o The Accokeek Foundation, Inc.
3400 Bryan Point Rd.
Accokeek 20607   (301) 283-2113

Trust established in 1962 in DC.
Donor(s): Corina Higginson.‡
Foundation type: Independent
Financial data (yr. ended 12/31/91): Assets, $3,460,476 (M); expenditures, $150,094; qualifying distributions, $109,592, including $109,592 for 21 grants (high: $7,500; low: $300; average: $5,000).
Purpose and activities: Emphasis on education and self-help.
Fields of interest: Education, social services, AIDS.
Types of support: Operating budgets, continuing support, seed money, emergency funds, equipment, matching funds, special projects, research, publications, conferences and seminars, exchange programs, general purposes, internships, lectureships.
Limitations: Giving primarily in the Washington, DC, area, including MD and VA. No support for medical or health-related programs or organizations. No grants to individuals, or for endowment funds or scholarship funds.
Publications: Application guidelines.
Application information: Application form required.
   Initial approach: Proposal, letter, or telephone
   Copies of proposal: 5
   Deadline(s): Mar. 1 and Sept. 1
   Board meeting date(s): Apr. and Oct.
   Final notification: 2 months
   Write: Dr. Wilton C. Corkern, Jr., Trustee
Trustees: Charles C. Abeles, Wilton C. Corkern, Jr., John Perkins, Jean Sisco, Rev. John P. Whalen.
Number of staff: None.
EIN: 526055743

1118
The David and Barbara B. Hirschhorn Foundation, Inc.
Blaustein Bldg.
P.O. Box 238
Baltimore 21203-0238

Established in 1986 in MD.
Donor(s): Barbara B. Hirschhorn, David Hirschhorn.
Foundation type: Independent
Financial data (yr. ended 12/31/91): Assets, $2,030,175 (M); expenditures, $93,552; qualifying distributions, $92,081, including $92,000 for 20 grants (high: $30,000; low: $500).
Purpose and activities: Giving primarily for Jewish organizations; support also for higher education, health organizations, and social services.
Fields of interest: Jewish giving, Jewish welfare, higher education, health, social services.
Limitations: Giving primarily in NY, CT, NJ, and Baltimore, MD.
Application information:
  Initial approach: Letter
  Deadline(s): None
  Write: David Hirschhorn, Pres.
Officers and Trustees:* Barbara B. Hirschhorn,* Chair.; David Hirschhorn,* Pres.; Daniel B. Hirschhorn,* V.P.; Michael J. Hirschhorn,* V.P.; Sarah H. Shapiro,* V.P.; Deborah H. Vogelstein,* V.P.; Frank A. Strzelczyk, Secy.-Treas.
EIN: 521489400

1119
The Emmert Hobbs Foundation, Inc.
c/o Friedman & Friedman
409 Washington Ave., Suite 900
Towson 21204   (301) 494-0100

Incorporated in 1983 in MD.
Donor(s): Emmert Hobbs.‡
Foundation type: Independent
Financial data (yr. ended 07/31/91): Assets, $3,037,503 (M); expenditures, $183,883; qualifying distributions, $145,250, including $145,250 for 27 grants (high: $50,000; low: $1,000; average: $3,000).
Fields of interest: Health, handicapped, homeless, social services, education.
Types of support: General purposes, scholarship funds, building funds.
Limitations: Giving primarily in the Baltimore, MD, metropolitan area. No support for research. No grants to individuals.
Application information:
  Initial approach: Letter
  Deadline(s): None
  Write: Louis F. Friedman, Dir.
Directors: D. Sylvan Friedman, Louis F. Friedman, Phyliss C. Friedman.
EIN: 521285106

1120
The Howard Hughes Medical Institute
Office of Special Grants and Programs
4000 Jones Bridge Rd.
Chevy Chase 20815-6789   (301) 215-8500
Additional tel.: 1-800-498-4882

Incorporated in 1953 in DE.

Donor(s): Howard R. Hughes.‡
Financial data (yr. ended 08/31/92): Assets, $7,369,036,000 (M); expenditures, $324,445,000; qualifying distributions, $324,445,000, including $39,669,000 for 300 grants (high: $2,000,000; low: $5,000; average: $5,000-$2,000,000), $11,549,000 for 440 grants to individuals (high: $77,000; low: $21,700) and $273,227,000 for 1 foundation-administered program.
Purpose and activities: A nonprofit scientific and philanthropic organization whose principal purpose is the direct conduct of medical research. According to the Institute's charter: "The primary purpose and objective of the Howard Hughes Medical Institute shall be the promotion of human knowledge within the field of the basic sciences (principally the field of medical research and medical education) and the effective application thereof for the benefit of mankind." The Institute is qualified as a medical research organization, not as a private foundation, under the federal tax code. It administers a medical research program for the direct conduct of medical research and a grants program for support of science education. Through its Medical Research Program, the Institute's investigators conduct fundamental biomedical research throughout the U.S. in the fields of cell biology and regulation, genetics, immunology, neuroscience, and structural biology. Through its Office of Grants and Special Programs, the Institute awards grants to help strengthen education in biology and related sciences and supports fundamental research abroad, complementing the Institute's medical research activities. The emphasis of the grants program is on graduate, undergraduate, and precollege and public science education. Graduate support is primarily for fellowships awarded under three programs: 1) Predoctoral (Ph.D., Sc.D.) Fellowships in Biological Sciences. Deadline: early Nov.; 2) Research Training Fellowships for Medical Students. Deadline: early Dec.; and 3) Postdoctoral Research Fellowships for Physicians. Deadline: early Jan. Through the Undergraduate Biological Sciences Education Program, grant awards have been made directly to colleges and universities for 1) student research and broadening access in the sciences; 2) science faculty development; 3) curriculum and laboratory development; and 4) outreach programs in the sciences and mathematics with elementary and secondary schools, and with junior and community colleges. Deadline for invited proposals: early Dec. Support is available to general science museums and science and technology centers, children's and youth museums, natural history and natural science museums, zoos, and aquatic and botanical gardens under the 1993 Precollege Science Education Initiative for Museums. Deadline: Jan. Through a nomination and invited application process, the Institute awards grants to support the research of scientists in selected countries. The Institute continues to monitor the public and private sector and other trends in science education and science.
Fields of interest: Medical research, medical education, medical sciences, biological sciences, education.
Types of support: Research, fellowships, special projects.

Limitations: No support for the direct conduct of biomedical research in the U.S., except to scientific investigators employed by the Institute; no grants or fellowships except to individuals or institutions competing under established science education programs.
Publications: Annual report, application guidelines, occasional report, program policy statement.
Application information: Applicants should consult guidelines in the Institute's publication, "Grants for Science Education" or in specific program announcements prior to application. All fellowships and grants are awarded on the basis of a national or international competition and peer review. Proposals for the undergraduate science education and the international research program are by invitation only. In addition to the science education programs, grants are awarded to biomedical scientists in specified countries under the International Research Scholars Program. Application form required.
  Initial approach: Letter, proposal, or application, depending on program
  Deadline(s): Consult "Purpose and activities" for all other specific deadline periods
  Board meeting date(s): Feb., May, Aug., and Nov.
  Final notification: Each grants program has individual notification date; program brochures and announcements should be consulted
  Write: Dr. Joseph G. Perpich, V.P., for general inquiries; Stephen A. Barkanic, Prog. Officer, for undergraduate programs; David Davis-Van Atta for assessment programs; Dr. Barbara Filner, Prog. Officer, for graduate and international programs; and Dr. Kathi E. Hanna, Prog. Officer, for precollege and public programs
Officers: Purnell W. Choppin, M.D., Pres.; W. Maxwell Cowan, M.D., Ph.D., V.P. and Chief Scientific Officer; Graham O. Harrison, V.P. and Chief Investment Officer; Joseph G. Perpich, M.D., J.D., V.P., Grants and Special Programs; Jose E. Trias, V.P. and General Counsel; Robert C. White, V.P. and C.F.O.
Trustees: Irving S. Shapiro, Chair.; Alexander G. Bearn, M.D., Helen K. Copley, Frank William Gay, James H. Gilliam, Jr., Hanna H. Gray, Ph.D., William R. Lummis, George W. Thorn, M.D., James D. Wolfensohn.
Number of staff: 1479 full-time professional; 30 part-time professional; 537 full-time support; 85 part-time support.
EIN: 590735717

1121
Ensign C. Markland Kelly, Jr. Memorial Foundation, Inc.
1406 Fidelity Bldg.
Baltimore 21201   (301) 837-8822

Incorporated in 1946 in MD.
Donor(s): C. Markland Kelly,‡ Kelly Buick Sales Corp.
Foundation type: Independent
Financial data (yr. ended 12/31/91): Assets, $4,392,372 (M); expenditures, $293,778; qualifying distributions, $239,216, including $195,369 for 30 grants (high: $31,280; low: $322).

Fields of interest: Secondary education, youth, civic affairs, cultural programs, historic preservation, health, handicapped.
Types of support: Annual campaigns, building funds, equipment, endowment funds, special projects, matching funds, capital campaigns.
Limitations: Giving limited to the greater Baltimore, MD, metropolitan area. No grants to individuals, or for operating budgets, research, fellowships, or travel; no loans.
Publications: Informational brochure, program policy statement, application guidelines, occasional report.
Application information: Application form not required.
 Initial approach: Letter requesting guidelines
 Copies of proposal: 3
 Deadline(s): None
 Board meeting date(s): Monthly
 Final notification: 6 months
 Write: Herbert E. Witz, Pres.
Officers and Directors:* Herbert E. Witz,* Pres.; Bowen P. Weisheit,* V.P.; Carol A. Witz,* Secy.; Bowen P. Weisheit, Jr.,* Treas.
Number of staff: 1 part-time professional; 1 part-time support.
EIN: 526033330

1122
The Marion I. and Henry J. Knott Foundation, Inc.
3904 Hickory Ave.
Baltimore 21211 (410) 235-7068

Established in 1978 in MD as successor to the first Marion I. and Henry J. Knott Foundation, Inc.
Donor(s): Marion I. Knott, Henry J. Knott, Sr.
Foundation type: Independent
Financial data (yr. ended 12/31/91): Assets, $25,656,143 (M); expenditures, $1,511,050; qualifying distributions, $1,878,110, including $1,206,129 for 54 grants (high: $400,000; low: $50; average: $10,000-$30,000).
Purpose and activities: "Giving for Roman Catholic activities and other charitable, cultural, educational, and health and human service organizations." Areas of interest include the fine and performing arts; higher, secondary, elementary, early childhood, adult, and vocational education; hospitals and health services, including hospices and programs for the mentally ill; social and family services, including youth, the elderly, the handicapped, and the homeless; and community development and civic affairs.
Fields of interest: Catholic giving, religious welfare, arts, cultural programs, humanities, higher education, secondary education, health, hospitals, youth, child development, child welfare, aged, social services, disadvantaged, community development, urban development, volunteerism.
Types of support: Building funds, capital campaigns, endowment funds, equipment, general purposes, land acquisition, matching funds, operating budgets, renovation projects, seed money, special projects.
Limitations: Giving limited to the area served by the Archdiocese of Baltimore: all counties in MD except those south of Frederick, Anne Arundel, and Howard, and the Eastern Shore region. No

support for public education. No grants to individuals, or for annual giving or scholarships.
Publications: Annual report, application guidelines, financial statement, grants list.
Application information: Application guidelines available upon request. Application form not required.
 Initial approach: Telephone
 Copies of proposal: 2
 Deadline(s): Feb. 1 and Aug. 1; deadline extensions cannot be made
 Board meeting date(s): June and Dec.
 Write: Robin R. Platts, Exec. Dir.
Officers and Directors:* Henry J. Knott, Sr.,* Chair.; Marion I. Knott,* Vice-Chair.; Alice K. Voelkel,* Pres.; Patricia K. Smyth,* V.P.; John C. Smyth,* Secy.; Henry J. Knott, Jr.,* Treas.; Daniel J. Gallagher, Lindsay R. Gallagher, Mark F. Grenoble, Tracy H. Grenoble, Marty Voelkel Hanssen, Stephen A. Hanssen, E.B. Harris, Carlisle V. Hashim, Carroll D. Knott, Francis X. Knott, James F. Knott, Martin Knott, Teresa A. Knott, Susan O. Riehl, Geralynn D. Smyth, Mary M. Voelkel, Catherine K. Wies.
Number of staff: 1 full-time professional; 1 full-time support.
EIN: 521517876

1123
John J. Leidy Foundation, Inc.
217 East Redwood St., Suite 1600
Baltimore 21202 (410) 727-4136

Incorporated in 1957 in MD.
Donor(s): John J. Leidy.‡
Foundation type: Independent
Financial data (yr. ended 12/31/91): Assets, $6,649,382 (M); expenditures, $281,375; qualifying distributions, $253,379, including $226,874 for 114 grants (high: $25,000; low: $50).
Fields of interest: Child welfare, hospitals, higher education, social services, handicapped, community funds, Jewish giving.
Types of support: Scholarship funds, general purposes.
Limitations: Giving primarily in MD. No grants to individuals.
Application information:
 Initial approach: Proposal
 Deadline(s): None
 Write: Sharon Schaefer
Officers: W. Michel Pierson, Pres.; Robert Pierson, V.P.; Allan H. Fisher, Secy.; Henry E. Pear, Treas.
EIN: 526034785

1124
Life Sciences Research Foundation ▼
115 West University Pkwy.
Baltimore 21210 (410) 467-2597
Application address: c/o Lewis Thomas Laboratories, Princeton University, Princeton, NJ 08544; Tel.: (609) 258-3551

Changed status to a private foundation in 1984 in MD.
Donor(s): Various donors.
Foundation type: Independent
Financial data (yr. ended 05/31/91): Assets, $811,584 (M); gifts received, $1,225,249;

expenditures, $1,293,225; qualifying distributions, $1,293,225, including $1,264,955 for 45 grants to individuals (high: $43,750; low: $8,750; average: $8,750-$35,000).
Purpose and activities: Awards postdoctoral research fellowships to graduates of medical schools and graduate schools in the biological sciences.
Fields of interest: Biological sciences, medical research.
Types of support: Research, fellowships.
Publications: Annual report, informational brochure, application guidelines.
Application information: In the spring of each year an application notice is sent to every graduate school in biology and every medical school in the U.S. A list of these schools may be obtained from the "Graduate Programs and Admissions Manual, Volume A" put out by the Graduate Record Examination Board or by directly requesting an application form from the foundation. Application form required.
 Copies of proposal: 3
 Deadline(s): Oct. 1; supporting letters must be received by Nov. 2
 Final notification: Mar.
Officers: Donald D. Brown, Pres.; Patricia Englar, Secy.; Roger Redden, Treas.
Directors: David Baltimore, Paul Berg, Konrad Bloch, David Blotsein, Michael S. Brown, Pedro Cuatrecasas, James E. Darnell, Jr., Joseph M. Davie, Donald Frederickson, Daniel Nathans, Hamilton O. Smith, Lewis Thomas, James Watson, and 15 additional directors.
EIN: 521231801

1125
Martin Marietta Corporation Foundation ▼
6801 Rockledge Dr.
Bethesda 20817 (301) 897-6863

Trust established in 1955 in MD.
Donor(s): Martin Marietta Corp.
Foundation type: Company-sponsored
Financial data (yr. ended 12/31/90): Assets, $785,838 (M); gifts received, $5,170,000; expenditures, $5,423,331; qualifying distributions, $5,405,942, including $3,031,629 for 385 grants (high: $324,069; low: $48; average: $1,000-$10,000), $592,640 for 210 grants to individuals (high: $4,500; low: $750; average: $1,000-$3,000) and $1,779,841 for employee matching gifts.
Purpose and activities: Primary interest in higher education, particularly through support of scholarships for children of corporation employees; support also for health, cultural, and civic programs.
Fields of interest: Higher education, cultural programs, health, civic affairs.
Types of support: Employee-related scholarships, employee matching gifts, general purposes.
Limitations: Giving primarily in areas of company operations. No support for political or religious groups, or current United Way recipients. No grants to individuals (except for employee-related scholarships).
Publications: Application guidelines.
Application information: Application form not required.
 Initial approach: Proposal

Copies of proposal: 1
Deadline(s): Applications accepted throughout the year, with majority of commitments made in the fall
Board meeting date(s): As needed
Final notification: 2 to 3 months
Write: John T. de Visser, Dir., Corp. Affairs
Trustees: Wayne A. Shaner, Peter F. Warren, Jr., A. Thomas Young.
Number of staff: 1
EIN: 136161566
Recent health grants:
1125-1 Franklin Square Hospital, Baltimore, MD, $30,000. 1990.
1125-2 Georgetown University Medical Center, Lombardi Cancer Research Center, DC, $50,000. 1990.
1125-3 Grove Counseling Center, Winter Springs, FL, $10,000. 1990.
1125-4 Guardian Care, Convalescent Center, Orlando, FL, $15,000. 1990.

1126
The Morris A. Mechanic Foundation, Inc.
P.O. Box 1623
Baltimore 21203

Established in 1942 in MD.
Donor(s): Morris A. Mechanic.‡
Foundation type: Independent
Financial data (yr. ended 12/31/91): Assets, $3,259,981 (M); gifts received, $6,734; expenditures, $166,667; qualifying distributions, $142,500, including $142,500 for 29 grants (high: $15,000; low: $250).
Fields of interest: Hospitals, health associations, cultural programs, youth, higher education.
Limitations: Giving primarily in Baltimore, MD. No grants to individuals.
Application information: Maximum grant award will not exceed $50,000.
Initial approach: Letter
Deadline(s): None
Write: Clarisse B. Mechanic, Pres.
Officers: Clarisse B. Mechanic, Pres.; Blue Barron, Secy.
EIN: 526034753

1127
Robert G. and Anne M. Merrick Foundation, Inc. ▼
The Exchange
1122 Kenilworth Dr., Suite 118
Baltimore 21204   (410) 832-5700

Established in 1962.
Donor(s): Robert G. Merrick, Sr.,‡ Anne M. Merrick,‡ Homewood Holding Co.
Foundation type: Independent
Financial data (yr. ended 05/31/91): Assets, $42,156,871 (M); expenditures, $2,188,144; qualifying distributions, $1,894,948, including $1,773,779 for 68 grants (high: $305,000; low: $250; average: $10,000-$50,000).
Purpose and activities: Emphasis on arts and cultural programs, historic preservation, higher education, conservation, health, social services, and civic affairs.
Fields of interest: Arts, cultural programs, historic preservation, higher education, conservation, health, social services.

Types of support: General purposes, special projects.
Limitations: Giving primarily in Baltimore, MD. No grants to individuals.
Publications: Application guidelines.
Application information:
Initial approach: Letter
Deadline(s): None
Board meeting date(s): As needed
Write: Frederick W. Lafferty, Exec. Dir.
Officers and Directors:* Anne M. Pinkard,* Pres.; Robert M. Pinkard,* V.P. and Treas.; Walter D. Pinkard, Jr., Secy.; Frederick W. Lafferty, Exec. Dir.; Joseph S. Hall, Robert G. Merrick III, Vernon T. Pittinger.
Number of staff: None.
EIN: 526072964
Recent health grants:
1127-1 Church Home and Hospital, Baltimore, MD, $12,000. 1991.
1127-2 Health Care for the Homeless, Baltimore, MD, $10,000. 1991.
1127-3 Johns Hopkins Medical Institutions, Office of Cultural and Social Affairs, Baltimore, MD, $10,000. 1991.
1127-4 Johns Hopkins University, School of Medicine, Baltimore, MD, $50,000. For Richard Starr Ross Fund. 1991.
1127-5 Johns Hopkins University, Zanvyl Kreiger Mind/Brain Institute, Baltimore, MD, $100,000. 1991.
1127-6 Mercy Medical Center, Baltimore, MD, $20,000. 1991.
1127-7 Mount Washington Pediatric Hospital, Baltimore, MD, $10,000. 1991.

1128
MNC Financial Foundation, Inc. ▼
(Formerly The Maryland National Foundation, Inc.)
P.O. Box 987, MS250334
Baltimore 21203   (301) 547-4126

Incorporated in 1965 in MD.
Donor(s): Maryland National Bank.
Foundation type: Company-sponsored
Financial data (yr. ended 12/31/90): Assets, $3,225,423 (M); gifts received, $1,096,525; expenditures, $4,312,364; qualifying distributions, $4,291,242, including $4,074,486 for 204 grants (high: $635,000; low: $210; average: $1,000-$25,000), $143,074 for 622 employee matching gifts and $50,000 for 1 loan to an individual.
Purpose and activities: To enhance health and welfare in all the communities the foundation serves, and to support those institutions that make communities desirable places to live and work. Emphasis on community funds, education, arts and culture, environmental issues, health and hospitals, and human and community services.
Limitations: Giving limited to recipient organizations whose activities are principally conducted within the geographic areas in which MNC Financial and its subsidiaries are active, especially MD. No support for strictly sectarian, fraternal, veterans', religious, social, or athletic organizations, or organizations receiving support through the United Way or other federated drives, exclusive of capital funding needs. No grants to individuals, or for fundraising events, trips, conferences, or publications.

Application information: The foundation is currently not accepting applications.
Write: George B.P. Ward, Jr., Secy.-Treas.
Officers: H. Grant Hathaway, Pres.; George B.P. Ward, Jr., Secy.-Treas.
Number of staff: 1 part-time professional.
EIN: 526062721
Recent health grants:
1128-1 Anne Arundel General Hospital, Annapolis, MD, $18,000. 1990.
1128-2 Baltimore County General Hospital, Baltimore, MD, $10,000. 1990.
1128-3 Calvert Memorial Hospital, Prince Frederick, MD, $12,500. 1990.
1128-4 Greater Baltimore Medical Center Foundation, Baltimore, MD, $45,000. 1990.
1128-5 Harbor Hospital Center, Baltimore, MD, $33,000. 1990.
1128-6 Health Care for the Homeless, Baltimore, MD, $10,000. 1990.
1128-7 Health Education Resource Organization (HERO), Baltimore, MD, $25,000. 1990.
1128-8 Holy Cross Hospital, Silver Spring, MD, $10,000. 1990.
1128-9 Memorial Hospital at Easton Maryland, Easton, MD, $10,000. 1990.
1128-10 Mercy Medical Center, Baltimore, MD, $20,000. 1990.
1128-11 Saint Agnes Hospital, Baltimore, MD, $21,000. 1990.
1128-12 Tissue Banks International, Baltimore, MD, $14,500. For medical research. 1990.
1128-13 Union Memorial Hospital, Baltimore, MD, $10,000. 1990.
1128-14 Way Station, Frederick, MD, $10,000. 1990.

1129
The Thomas F. and Clementine L. Mullan Foundation, Inc.
2330 West Joppa Rd., Suite 210
Lutherville 21093

Incorporated in 1958 in MD.
Donor(s): Thomas F. Mullan, Sr., and his corporations.
Foundation type: Independent
Financial data (yr. ended 11/30/91): Assets, $3,802,235 (M); expenditures, $164,478; qualifying distributions, $155,898, including $150,530 for 94 grants (high: $12,000; low: $25).
Fields of interest: Hospitals, health, higher education, secondary education, Catholic giving, social services.
Limitations: Giving primarily in Baltimore, MD. No grants to individuals.
Application information: Contributes only to pre-selected organizations. Applications not accepted.
Officers: Thomas F. Mullan, Jr.,* Pres. and Treas.; Charles A. Mullan, V.P.; C. Louise Mullan, Secy.
Trustee: Thomas F. Mullan III.
EIN: 526050776

1130
Nathan Foundation, Inc.
c/o Mercantile-Safe Deposit & Trust Co.
766 Old Hammonds Ferry Rd.
Linthicum 21090
Application address: c/o Mercantile-Safe
Deposit & Trust Co., Two Hopkins Plaza,
Baltimore, MD 21201; Tel.: (410) 237-5518

Established in 1961 in MD.
Foundation type: Independent
Financial data (yr. ended 12/31/91): Assets,
$3,061,809 (M); gifts received, $7,870;
expenditures, $177,233; qualifying distributions,
$159,462, including $158,916 for 35 grants
(high: $40,000; low: $850).
Purpose and activities: Emphasis on aid to the
"mentally and physically handicapped to provide
needed care for the indigent and other charitable
purposes," including support for volunteerism,
higher education, community development, and
a hospital.
Fields of interest: Handicapped, mental health,
welfare, volunteerism, higher education,
community development, hospitals.
Limitations: Giving limited to Dorchester County,
MD. No grants to individuals.
Application information:
   Initial approach: Letter
   Deadline(s): None
   Write: Paul P. Klender, Treas.
Officers and Directors:* Edward H. Nabb,* Pres.;
Russell S. Baker, Jr.,* V.P.; T. Sewell Hubbard,*
Secy.; Paul P. Klender,* Treas.; Edward Conway,
Mrs. J. Dorsey Johnson.
EIN: 526033999

1131
PHH Foundation, Inc.
(Formerly PHH Group Foundation, Inc.)
11333 McCormick Rd.
Hunt Valley 21031   (301) 771-2733

Established in 1959 in MD.
Foundation type: Company-sponsored
Financial data (yr. ended 04/30/91): Assets,
$242,285 (M); gifts received, $289,900;
expenditures, $383,127; qualifying distributions,
$382,706, including $341,150 for 47 grants
(high: $86,300; low: $50) and $41,556 for 236
employee matching gifts.
Fields of interest: Arts, community funds, literacy,
higher education, education, health,
hospitals—building funds.
Types of support: Operating budgets, annual
campaigns, seed money, emergency funds,
building funds, equipment, employee matching
gifts.
Limitations: Giving limited to the Baltimore, MD,
area. No support for governmental or religious
organizations. No grants to individuals, or for
deficit financing, endowment funds, research,
special projects, publications, or conferences; no
loans.
Publications: Program policy statement,
application guidelines.
Application information: Application form not
required.
   Initial approach: Letter
   Copies of proposal: 1
   Deadline(s): None

Board meeting date(s): June, Sept., Dec., and
   Mar.
Final notification: 3 months
   Write: Pilar M. Page, V.P.
Officers: Robert D. Kunisch, Chair.; Eugene A.
Arbaugh, Pres.; Pilar M. Page, V.P.; S.H. Wright,
Secy.; Terry E. Kridler, Treas.
Number of staff: 12 full-time professional; 1
full-time support.
EIN: 526040911

1132
Linda Pollin Foundation
4701 Willard Ave., Suite 223
Chevy Chase 20814

Established in 1987 in MD.
Donor(s): Abe Pollin.
Foundation type: Independent
Financial data (yr. ended 12/31/91): Assets,
$1,189,407 (M); gifts received, $25,100;
expenditures, $476,591; qualifying distributions,
$465,236, including $299,154 for 8 grants (high:
$52,000; low: $10,426), $3,787 for 2 grants to
individuals (high: $2,500; low: $1,287) and
$35,511 for 1 foundation-administered program.
Purpose and activities: Awards grants to hospitals
and individuals for training in medical crisis
counseling and education; also co-sponsored a
conference on counseling chronically ill patients.
Fields of interest: Medical education, mental
health.
Types of support: Fellowships.
Limitations: Giving primarily in CA, New York,
NY, and Philadelphia, PA. No grants to
individuals.
Application information: The foundation has
discontinued making direct grants to individuals.
   Initial approach: Proposal
   Deadline(s): None
   Write: Selection Committee
Officers: Irene S. Pollin, Pres. and Treas.; Abe
Pollin, V.P. and Secy.
Board Members: James Pollin, Robert Pollin.
EIN: 521510398

1133
The Procter & Gamble/Noxell
Foundation, Inc. ▼
(Formerly The Noxell Foundation, Inc.)
11050 York Rd.
Hunt Valley 21030-2098   (410) 785-4361

Incorporated in 1951 in MD.
Donor(s): Noxell Corp.
Foundation type: Company-sponsored
Financial data (yr. ended 12/31/90): Assets,
$1,970,914 (M); gifts received, $250,000;
expenditures, $1,775,779; qualifying
distributions, $1,763,298, including $1,745,320
for 138 grants (high: $300,000; low: $100;
average: $1,000-$25,000) and $14,426 for 52
employee matching gifts.
Purpose and activities: Emphasis on colleges and
universities, health and welfare, civic affairs, the
arts, including the performing arts, music,
museums, and other cultural programs.
Fields of interest: Higher education, health,
hospitals, social services, civic affairs, arts,
cultural programs, performing arts, music,
museums, theater.

Types of support: Annual campaigns, seed
money, emergency funds, building funds,
equipment, land acquisition, employee matching
gifts, internships, capital campaigns, endowment
funds, matching funds, research, scholarship
funds.
Limitations: Giving primarily in the Baltimore,
MD, area. No grants to individuals, or for
operating budgets or deficit financing; no loans.
Application information: Application form not
required.
   Initial approach: Proposal
   Copies of proposal: 1
   Deadline(s): None
   Board meeting date(s): Quarterly
   Final notification: 3 months
   Write: Catherine A. Warburton, Administrator
Officers: John A. Saxton, V.P.; Carroll A. Bodie,
Secy.; William R. McCartin, Treas.
Number of staff: None.
EIN: 526041435

1134
The Rollins-Luetkemeyer Charitable
Foundation, Inc.
P.O. Box 10147
17 West Pennsylvania Ave.
Baltimore 21285   (301) 296-4800

Established in 1961 in MD.
Foundation type: Independent
Financial data (yr. ended 12/31/90): Assets,
$10,005,580 (M); gifts received, $1,000,000;
expenditures, $593,429; qualifying distributions,
$545,970, including $535,970 for 94 grants
(high: $334,250; low: $50).
Purpose and activities: At least 70 percent of
future giving will be for building funds for early
childhood, elementary and secondary schools;
support also for certain Methodist schools and
institutions, social service agencies, health
organizations, and historical preservation.
Fields of interest: Higher education, elementary
education, education—early childhood,
education, social services, health, hospitals,
historic preservation.
Types of support: General purposes.
Limitations: Giving primarily in the Baltimore,
MD, area. No grants to individuals.
Application information: Funds largely to
organizations in which donors have a direct
interest. Application form not required.
   Initial approach: Letter
   Deadline(s): None
   Write: John A. Luetkemeyer, Sr., Pres.
Officers and Directors:* John A. Luetkemeyer,
Sr.,* Pres.; Robert F. Wilson,* V.P. and Treas.; Anne
A. Luetkemeyer,* Secy.; John A. Luetkemeyer, Jr.,
Mary E. Rollins, Anne L. Stone.
Number of staff: 1 part-time professional; 1
part-time support.
EIN: 526041536

1135
The Henry and Ruth Blaustein Rosenberg
Foundation, Inc.
Blaustein Bldg.
P.O. Box 238
Baltimore 21203

Incorporated in 1959 in MD.

Donor(s): Ruth Blaustein Rosenberg, Henry A. Rosenberg, Jr., American Trading and Production Corp.
Foundation type: Independent
Financial data (yr. ended 12/31/90): Assets, $8,162,379 (M); gifts received, $387,500; expenditures, $1,215,030; qualifying distributions, $1,155,687, including $1,155,612 for 76 grants (high: $421,012; low: $150).
Fields of interest: Secondary education, higher education, performing arts, music, Jewish welfare, health services.
Limitations: Giving primarily in the greater Baltimore, MD, area.
Application information:
Initial approach: Letter
Deadline(s): None
Write: Henry A. Rosenberg, Jr., Pres.
Officers and Trustees:* Ruth Blaustein Rosenberg,* Chair.; Henry A. Rosenberg, Jr.,* Pres.; Frank A. Strzelczyk, Secy.-Treas.; Judith R. Hoffberger, Ruth R. Marder.
EIN: 526038384
Recent health grants:
1135-1 Johns Hopkins University, Wilmer Ophthalmological Institute, Baltimore, MD, $15,000. 1990.

1136
The Rouse Company Corporate Contributions
10275 Little Patuxent Pkwy.
Columbia 21044   (301) 992-6375

Purpose and activities: Support for arts and humanities, social services including family services, the homeless, housing, the aged, and the disadvantaged, higher education, conservation and ecology, and health and human services.
Fields of interest: Arts, family services, humanities, ecology, conservation, health, homeless, aged, disadvantaged, higher education, hospices, housing, performing arts, social services.
Types of support: Annual campaigns, operating budgets, seed money, building funds, employee volunteer services, capital campaigns, continuing support, program-related investments, endowment funds, general purposes, scholarship funds.
Limitations: Giving primarily in the Columbia, MD, area.
Publications: Informational brochure (including application guidelines).
Application information: Company has a staff that only handles contributions. Application form not required.
Initial approach: Letter or phone to headquarters
Copies of proposal: 1
Deadline(s): None
Board meeting date(s): Every 2 months
Write: Margaret Mauro, Prog. Officer
Number of staff: 1 part-time professional.

1137
Rymland Foundation, Inc.
c/o Alperstein, Stelmack & Gordon
530 East Joppa Rd.
Towson 21204

Established in 1944.

Donor(s): Murray J. Rymland.
Foundation type: Independent
Financial data (yr. ended 12/31/91): Assets, $1,892,848 (M); expenditures, $302; qualifying distributions, $0.
Fields of interest: Jewish welfare, hospitals, museums.
Limitations: Giving limited to Baltimore, MD. No grants to individuals.
Application information: Contributes only to pre-selected organizations. Applications not accepted.
Officers: Howard Rymland, Pres.; Allan C. Alperstein, V.P. and Treas.; Allan Gibbar, Secy.
EIN: 526054735

1138
The Schoeneman-Weiler Fund, Inc.
c/o Mercantile-Safe Deposit & Trust Co.
766 Old Hammonds Ferry Rd.
Linthicum 21090
Application address: c/o Andrew Nichols, Mercantile-Safe Deposit & Trust Co., Two Hopkins Plaza, Baltimore, MD 21201; Tel.: (410) 237-5177

Established in 1946.
Foundation type: Independent
Financial data (yr. ended 11/30/91): Assets, $2,166,591 (M); expenditures, $68,440; qualifying distributions, $53,802, including $52,988 for 57 grants (high: $6,700; low: $13).
Fields of interest: Health, cultural programs, Jewish giving, Jewish welfare.
Limitations: Giving primarily in the greater Baltimore, MD, area.
Application information:
Initial approach: Letter
Deadline(s): None
Write: Josepha S. Miller, Pres.
Officers and Directors:* Josepha S. Miller,* Pres.; Edward A. Halle,* Secy.-Treas.; J. Jefferson Miller.
EIN: 526038453

1139
J. B. & Maurice C. Shapiro Charitable Trust
12012 Piney Glen Ln.
Potomac 20854

Established in 1967 in MD.
Donor(s): Maurice C. Shapiro,‡ Shapiro, Inc.
Foundation type: Company-sponsored
Financial data (yr. ended 07/31/91): Assets, $11,269,957 (M); expenditures, $685,622; qualifying distributions, $643,000, including $640,000 for 12 grants (high: $300,000; low: $5,000).
Fields of interest: Hospitals, child welfare, Jewish welfare.
Types of support: General purposes.
Limitations: Giving primarily in the Washington, DC, and MD areas. No grants to individuals.
Application information: Contributes only to pre-selected organizations. Applications not accepted.
Trustees: Kathleen Carpenter Kester, Leonard S. Melrod, Gary Roggin, Perry L. Sandler.
EIN: 526073880

1140
Signet Bank/Maryland Corporate Giving
c/o Public Affairs
P.O. Box 1077
Baltimore 21203   (301) 332-5194

Financial data (yr. ended 12/31/90): Total giving, $675,750, including $645,750 for 120 grants (high: $100,000; low: $1,000; average: $1,000-$10,000) and $30,000 for 10 in-kind gifts.
Purpose and activities: Support for arts and culture, including theater, museums, and performing arts; civic and community affairs, including housing and employment; education, including business and adult education, and literacy; and health and human services, including aid for the homeless.
Fields of interest: Arts, civic affairs, cultural programs, education, education—early childhood, education—building funds, health, health associations, health services, museums, music, business education, community development, adult education, homeless, literacy, employment, housing, disadvantaged, theater, performing arts.
Types of support: Annual campaigns, building funds, continuing support, general purposes, publications, research, special projects, loaned talent, capital campaigns, cause-related marketing.
Limitations: Giving primarily in the Baltimore metropolitan area and eastern shore of MD.
Publications: Application guidelines.
Application information: Contributions are handled by Public Affairs Department. Application form not required.
Initial approach: Letter; send to headquarters
Copies of proposal: 1
Board meeting date(s): Monthly
Final notification: Monthly
Write: Patricia K. Sisley
Number of staff: 1 part-time professional; 1 part-time support.

1141
The Aaron Straus and Lillie Straus Foundation, Inc. ▼
101 West Mt. Royal Ave.
Baltimore 21201   (301) 539-8308

Incorporated in 1926 in MD.
Donor(s): Aaron Straus,‡ Lillie Straus.‡
Foundation type: Independent
Financial data (yr. ended 12/31/90): Assets, $45,587,552 (M); expenditures, $3,601,838; qualifying distributions, $3,486,483, including $3,093,883 for 60 grants (high: $1,061,500; low: $100; average: $1,000-$45,000).
Purpose and activities: Emphasis on Jewish welfare funds, family support, and child welfare. The foundation also operates a camp.
Fields of interest: Jewish welfare, family planning, family services, child welfare, child development, education—early childhood, literacy, public policy, citizenship, volunteerism.
Types of support: Seed money, special projects, loans, operating budgets.
Limitations: Giving limited to the Baltimore, MD, metropolitan area. No grants to individuals, or for endowment funds.
Publications: Application guidelines.
Application information: Application form not required.

Initial approach: Proposal
Copies of proposal: 1
Deadline(s): Feb. 1, May 1, Aug. 1, and Nov. 1
Board meeting date(s): Mar., June, Sept., and Dec.
Final notification: 7 days
Write: Jan Rivitz, Exec. Dir.
Officers and Trustees:* Richard M. Barnett,* Pres.; Henry L. Abraham,* V.P.; Alfred I. Coplan,* Secy.-Treas.; Jan Rivitz, Exec. Dir.; Darrell Friedman.
Number of staff: 1 full-time professional; 2 part-time support.
EIN: 520563083
Recent health grants:
1141-1 Georgetown Hospital, Lombardi Center, Baltimore, MD, $20,000. For general support. 1991.
1141-2 Planned Parenthood of Maryland, Baltimore, MD, $25,000. For general support. 1991.
1141-3 Volunteers for Medical Engineering (VME), Baltimore, MD, $100,000. For general support. 1991.

1142
USF&G Corporate Giving Program
100 Light St., 25th Fl.
Baltimore 21202   (301) 547-3000

Financial data (yr. ended 12/31/90): Total giving, $770,913 for grants.
Purpose and activities: Most support is through the foundation, but the company will support programs unable to be funded by its foundation. Supports health through hospitals, welfare, education, including private colleges, culture and the arts, museums, theater, civic and community programs, minority programs, youth welfare, federated campaigns, United Way, conservation and safety. Types of support include employee gift matching for education, use of company facilities, employee volunteer programs and donations of company's facilities and primary goods or services.
Fields of interest: Museums, theater, health, hospitals, welfare, education, higher education, cultural programs, arts, civic affairs, community funds, community development, minorities, youth, child welfare, conservation, safety.
Types of support: In-kind gifts, capital campaigns, renovation projects, employee matching gifts, scholarship funds, continuing support.
Limitations: Giving primarily in headquarters city and major operating locations. Giving concentrated in greater Baltimore area. No support for projects/organizations for business

reasons alone; trade and industry associations; primary or secondary schools; except for College of Insurance, no funding for educational institutions outside of MD; non-tax-exempt organizations; political organizations or candidates, religious organizations, veterans' organizations; or propaganda institutions. No grants to individuals.
Application information:
Initial approach: Letter and proposal
Copies of proposal: 1
Final notification: 3 to 4 weeks
Write: Norma P. Blake, Mgr.

1143
The USF&G Foundation, Inc. ▼
100 Light St.
Baltimore 21202   (410) 547-3000

Foundation established in 1980 in MD.
Donor(s): United States Fidelity and Guaranty Co.
Foundation type: Company-sponsored
Financial data (yr. ended 12/31/90): Assets, $15,050,235 (M); gifts received, $2,200,000; expenditures, $3,156,838; qualifying distributions, $3,127,354, including $3,127,301 for 84 grants (high: $451,171; low: $500; average: $1,000-$50,000).
Purpose and activities: Support largely for a community fund, environmental conservation, health and hospitals, child welfare, arts and cultural programs, and higher education.
Fields of interest: Arts, cultural programs, higher education, child welfare, environment, health, museums, hospitals, community funds, conservation.
Types of support: Operating budgets, continuing support, annual campaigns, building funds, equipment, scholarship funds, special projects, endowment funds, capital campaigns, renovation projects.
Limitations: Giving primarily in MD, particularly the Baltimore area. No support for trade and industry associations, political or veterans' organizations, or religious organizations for religious purposes; generally, no grants to primary or secondary schools. No grants to individuals, or for seed money, emergency funds, deficit financing, land acquisition, matching gifts, research, publications, or conferences; no loans.
Publications: Program policy statement, application guidelines.
Application information: Application form required.
Initial approach: Proposal
Copies of proposal: 1
Deadline(s): None

Board meeting date(s): As required
Final notification: 3 to 4 weeks
Write: Sue Lovell, Corp. Foundation Administrator
Officers and Trustees:* Norman P. Blake, Jr.,* Pres.; John M. Hart,* V.P.; Charles D. Zimmerman III,* V.P.; William F. Spliedt, Secy.-Treas.
Number of staff: None.
EIN: 521197155
Recent health grants:
1143-1 Sexual Assault/Domestic Violence Center, Baltimore, MD, $10,000. For sustaining funds. 1990.
1143-2 Sheppard and Enoch Pratt Hospital, Baltimore, MD, $25,000. For capital campaign. 1990.
1143-3 Target, Westminister, MD, $25,000. For endowment. 1990.
1143-4 Way Station, Frederick, MD, $25,000. For capital campaign. 1990.

1144
Thomas Wilson Sanitarium for Children of Baltimore City
c/o Alex Brown & Sons
135 East Baltimore St.
Baltimore 21202   (301) 727-1700

Trust established in 1879 in MD.
Donor(s): Thomas Wilson.‡
Foundation type: Independent
Financial data (yr. ended 01/31/91): Assets, $4,328,559 (M); expenditures, $214,982; qualifying distributions, $195,078, including $190,000 for 13 grants (high: $24,000; low: $1,300).
Purpose and activities: Emphasis on hospitals, medical and educational research, and social services, largely relating to children.
Fields of interest: Hospitals, medical research, educational research, child welfare, social services.
Limitations: Giving limited to Baltimore, MD.
Application information:
Initial approach: Letter
Deadline(s): None
Write: Charles L. Stout, Pres.
Officers and Trustees:* Charles L. Stout,* Pres.; William C. Trimble, Jr.,* Secy.-Treas.; Perry J. Bolton, Edward K. Dunn, Jr., Nina Gardner, M.D., Kenneth Schuberth, M.D., Melchijah Spragins, M.D., Francis Trimble, M.D., Frederick Whitridge, Ralph N. Willis, Kinloch N. Yellott III.
EIN: 526044885

MASSACHUSETTS

1145
The Acushnet Foundation
21 Francis St.
Fairhaven 02719   (508) 992-0820

Trust established in 1953 in MA.
Donor(s): Acushnet Co.
Foundation type: Company-sponsored
Financial data (yr. ended 06/30/91): Assets,
$6,609,772 (M); expenditures, $314,332;
qualifying distributions, $301,634, including
$293,520 for 63 grants (high: $55,000; low:
$500; average: $1,000-$5,000).
Fields of interest: Youth, higher education,
community funds, hospitals.
Types of support: Continuing support, annual
campaigns, seed money, emergency funds,
building funds, professorships, scholarship funds.
Limitations: Giving generally limited to the
greater New Bedford, MA, area. No grants to
individuals, or for endowment funds, operating
budgets, deficit financing, or matching gifts.
Application information: Application form not
required.
  Initial approach: Letter
  Copies of proposal: 1
  Deadline(s): None
  Board meeting date(s): As required
  Final notification: 4 to 6 weeks
  Write: Edward Powers, Mgr.
Trustees: William Bonner, Graeme L. Flanders,
Glen Johnson, John T. Ludes, Ed Powers, Thomas
C. Weaver, Richard B. Young.
Number of staff: 1 part-time support.
EIN: 046032197

1146
Frank W. and Carl S. Adams Memorial Fund
(also known as Charles E. & Caroline J. Adams
Trust)
c/o First National Bank of Boston
P.O. Box 1861
Boston 02105   (617) 434-5660

Trust established in 1955 in MA.
Donor(s): Charles E. Adams,‡ Caroline J. Adams.‡
Foundation type: Independent
Financial data (yr. ended 05/31/91): Assets,
$9,927,313 (M); expenditures, $510,939;
qualifying distributions, $449,853, including
$443,624 for 20 grants (high: $114,062; low:
$5,000; average: $1,000-$7,500).
Purpose and activities: One half of the net
income is distributed for general purposes, in the
fields of health, welfare, the humanities, and
education; the balance of income is designated to
assist needy and deserving students selected by
Massachusetts Institute of Technology and the
Harvard Medical School.
Fields of interest: Health, welfare, humanities,
education, higher education, medical education.
Types of support: General purposes, building
funds, operating budgets, capital campaigns, seed
money.

Limitations: Giving limited to the City of Boston,
MA. No support for national organizations. No
grants to individuals, or for conferences, film
production, scholarships, travel, research projects,
or publications; no loans.
Application information:
  Initial approach: Proposal
  Copies of proposal: 1
  Deadline(s): 1st day of month prior to board
  meetings
  Board meeting date(s): Mar., June, Sept., and
  Dec.
  Write: Miss Sharon M. Driscoll, Trust Officer,
  First National Bank of Boston
Trustee: First National Bank of Boston.
EIN: 046011995

1147
The George I. Alden Trust ▼
370 Main St., Suite 1250
Worcester 01608   (508) 798-8621

Trust established in 1912 in MA.
Donor(s): George I. Alden.‡
Foundation type: Independent
Financial data (yr. ended 12/31/90): Assets,
$85,824,919 (L); expenditures, $5,387,843;
qualifying distributions, $5,112,150, including
$4,936,500 for 161 grants (high: $800,000; low:
$1,000; average: $1,000-$25,000).
Purpose and activities: For the promotion of
education in schools, colleges, or other
educational institutions, with a preference for
industrial, vocational, or professional education;
for the promotion of the work carried on by the
Young Men's Christian Association, or its
successors, either in this country or abroad; and
for the benefit of the Worcester Trade Schools and
the Worcester Polytechnic Institute; some support
also for cultural and historic programs.
Fields of interest: Education, vocational
education, higher education, youth, cultural
programs, historic preservation.
Types of support: Seed money, emergency funds,
building funds, equipment, land acquisition,
research, publications, conferences and seminars,
scholarship funds, internships, professorships,
matching funds, renovation projects, endowment
funds.
Limitations: Giving primarily in the northeast,
with emphasis on Worcester, MA. No grants to
individuals; no loans.
Publications: Annual report, informational
brochure (including application guidelines).
Application information: Application form not
required.
  Initial approach: Proposal
  Copies of proposal: 1
  Deadline(s): None
  Board meeting date(s): Bimonthly beginning in
  Feb.
  Final notification: 2 months
  Write: Francis H. Dewey III, Chair.
Officers and Trustees:* Francis H. Dewey III,*
Chair.; Robert G. Hess,* Vice-Chair.; Warner S.
Fletcher,* Secy.; Harry G. Bayliss,* Treas.
Number of staff: None.
EIN: 046023784
Recent health grants:
1147-1 Dartmouth Medical School, Hanover,
  NH, $40,000. For new construction. 1990.

1147-2 Medical Center of Central Massachusetts
  Foundation, Worcester, MA, $10,000. For
  scholarship and operating aid. 1990.
1147-3 Meharry Medical College, Nashville, TN,
  $10,000. For scholarship and operating aid.
  1990.
1147-4 Planned Parenthood League of
  Massachusetts, Cambridge, MA, $10,000. For
  designated programmatic support. 1990.
1147-5 Tufts University, School of Veterinary
  Medicine, Grafton, MA, $100,000. For capital
  repairs and renovations. 1990.

1148
John W. Alden Trust
c/o Rackemann Sayer & Brewster
P.O. Box 351
Boston 02101
Application address: c/o William Osgood, State
Street Bank & Trust Co., 225 Franklin St.,
Boston, MA 02110; Tel.: (617) 654-3321

Established in 1986 in MA.
Donor(s): Priscilla Alden.‡
Foundation type: Independent
Financial data (yr. ended 09/30/91): Assets,
$5,819,188 (M); gifts received, $143,500;
expenditures, $283,789; qualifying distributions,
$246,704, including $220,925 for 17 grants
(high: $25,000; low: $2,000).
Purpose and activities: Grant support directed
toward "organizations providing care and
administering to the needs of children who are
blind, retarded, disabled, or who are either
mentally or physically ill...or organizations
engaged in medical and scientific research
directed toward the prevention or cure of diseases
and disabilities particularly affecting children."
Fields of interest: Child development, child
welfare, handicapped, medical research,
hospitals, higher education, elementary education.
Types of support: Research, seed money, special
projects.
Limitations: Giving primarily in MA. No grants to
individuals.
Publications: Application guidelines.
Application information: Application form not
required.
  Initial approach: Letter
  Copies of proposal: 2
  Deadline(s): None
  Board meeting date(s): Feb., May, Aug., and
  Nov.
  Final notification: Within 1 month
Trustees: William B. Tyler, State Street Bank &
Trust Co.
Number of staff: 1 part-time professional; 1
part-time support.
EIN: 222719727

1149
Mary Alice Arakelian Foundation
c/o Institution for Savings
P.O. Box 510
Newburyport 01950

Established in 1966 in MA.
Foundation type: Independent
Financial data (yr. ended 12/31/91): Assets,
$4,989,493 (M); expenditures, $239,318;
qualifying distributions, $205,968, including

$177,509 for 12 grants (high: $25,000; low: $10,000).
Fields of interest: Cultural programs, hospitals, higher education.
Limitations: Giving primarily in Newburyport, MA. No grants to individuals.
Application information: Application form not required.
  Deadline(s): Sept. 15
  Board meeting date(s): Grants are decided in Oct.
  Write: John H. Pramberg, Jr., Pres.
Officer and Trustees: John H. Pramberg, Jr.,* Pres.; Rose M. Marshal, Donald D. Mitchell, Charles P. Richmond.
EIN: 046155695

1150
Elisha V. Ashton Trust
c/o Choate Hall & Stewart
Exchange Place
Boston 02109

Established in 1884.
Foundation type: Independent
Financial data (yr. ended 10/31/91): Assets, $10,459,526 (M); expenditures, $502,452; qualifying distributions, $459,661, including $448,500 for 23 grants of $19,500 each.
Purpose and activities: Giving primarily for social services, especially organizations which aid and house the needy, indigent, aged, and women and children; support also for hospitals and animal welfare.
Fields of interest: Welfare, women, aged, child welfare, hospitals, animal welfare.
Limitations: Giving primarily in the Boston, MA, area. No grants to individuals.
Application information: Contributes only to pre-selected organizations. Applications not accepted.
Trustees: Marion R. Fremont-Smith, James R. Nichols.
EIN: 046016303

1151
The Paul and Edith Babson Foundation
c/o Nichols & Pratt
50 Congress St.
Boston 02109   (617) 523-6800

Trust established in 1957 in MA.
Donor(s): Paul T. Babson.‡
Foundation type: Independent
Financial data (yr. ended 12/31/90): Assets, $5,444,788 (M); expenditures, $268,068; qualifying distributions, $249,188, including $247,000 for 34 grants (high: $40,000; low: $1,000).
Fields of interest: Education, youth, health.
Limitations: Giving primarily in the metropolitan Boston, MA, area, with a few continuing exceptions. No grants to individuals.
Publications: Program policy statement, application guidelines.
Application information: Application form not required.
  Initial approach: Letter or telephone
  Copies of proposal: 1
  Deadline(s): Apr. 15 and Oct. 15
  Board meeting date(s): May and Nov.

Write: Elizabeth D. Nichols, Grant Administrator
Trustees: Donald P. Babson, Susan A. Babson, James R. Nichols.
Number of staff: None.
EIN: 046037891

1152
Bank of Boston Corporate Giving Program
c/o Public Affairs Dept., 01-17-04
P.O. Box 2016
Boston 02106-2016   (617) 434-2200

Financial data (yr. ended 12/31/90): Total giving, $1,800,000 for grants.
Purpose and activities: "Since its founding in 1784, Bank of Boston has considered it an essential part of its role to recognize community needs and channel its resources to most productively meet them." Bank of Boston seeks to help meet the financial needs of its communities, enhance the health and welfare of all the communities the Bank serves, improve educational programs and opportunities for all members of these communities, help those who require special assistance to assume a full role in society, and participate in major public policy issues that affect the well-being of the community. Because the communities it serves are so diverse, the subject areas of interest to Bank of Boston are broadly defined. Support for civic and community organizations, culture and the arts, education, including higher education, health and hospitals, social services, in-kind services, and United Way. The Bank also administers an employee matching gifts program and through ECHO (Employees in the Community Helping Others) donates employee time and service. Giving abroad takes place where the bank has branches. Combined contributions from Bank of Boston and the foundation totaled $6.9 million in 1990.
Fields of interest: Civic affairs, community development, community funds, higher education, education, cultural programs, arts, health, hospitals, social services, youth, international relief, international affairs.
Types of support: In-kind gifts, operating budgets, capital campaigns, endowment funds, donated equipment, use of facilities, employee volunteer services.
Limitations: Giving primarily in the Greater Boston region, and four other regions in MA: Cape Cod, Eastern, Southeastern, and Western; affiliate banks in CT, ME, RI, and VT have contributions programs in their own communities. No support for religious programs for religious purposes, or for national health organizations, including state and local chapters. No grants to individuals, or for research projects, conferences, forums, benefits, and similar events.
Application information: Application form not required.
  Initial approach: Proposal; write to nearest branch; except for in kind requests from MA which should be addressed to the Boston office
  Copies of proposal: 1
  Deadline(s): 6 weeks prior to Committee meeting
  Board meeting date(s): The Corporate Contributions Committee considers requests in Mar., June, Sept., and Dec.

Write: Karen Wilson, Dir., Corp. Contribs.
Administrators: Karen Wilson, Dir., Corp. Contribs.; Brenda Corbin, Exec. Secy.

1153
Bank of Boston Corporation Charitable Foundation ▼
c/o Bank of Boston
100 Federal St., Govt. & Community Affairs Dept.
Boston 02110   (617) 434-2171

Trust established in 1961 in MA for First National Bank of Boston Charitable Foundation; absorbed into First National Boston Corporation Foundation in 1983; present name adopted in 1983.
Donor(s): Bank of Boston.
Foundation type: Company-sponsored
Financial data (yr. ended 12/31/91): Assets, $14,531,164 (M); expenditures, $4,727,303; qualifying distributions, $4,594,061, including $4,592,080 for 944 grants (high: $674,835; low: $25; average: $1,000-$15,000).
Purpose and activities: Giving limited to community organizations with programs in education, health and hospitals, social services, arts and culture, and the civic community.
Fields of interest: Community development, education, higher education, health, AIDS, arts, cultural programs, welfare, youth, urban development, volunteerism.
Types of support: Annual campaigns, building funds, matching funds, special projects, capital campaigns, endowment funds, equipment, scholarship funds, renovation projects.
Limitations: Giving primarily in New England. No support for religious or partisan causes, fundraising events, conferences, forums, or nationally organized health programs. No grants to individuals, or for research or fellowships; no loans.
Publications: Application guidelines.
Application information:
  Initial approach: Proposal or letter
  Copies of proposal: 1
  Deadline(s): At least 6 weeks before meetings
  Board meeting date(s): 3rd week of Mar., July, Nov., and Jan.
  Final notification: 2 months
  Write: Karyn M. Wilson, Dir., Corp. Contribs.
Trustees: Charles K. Gifford, Ira Stepanian, Eliot N. Vestner, Bank of Boston.
Number of staff: 2 full-time professional; 1 full-time support.
EIN: 042748070
Recent health grants:
1153-1 AIDS Action Committee of Massachusetts, Boston, MA, $20,000. 1990.
1153-2 AIDS Action Committee of Massachusetts, Boston, MA, $10,000. 1990.
1153-3 Bridge Over Troubled Waters, Boston, MA, $20,000. 1990.
1153-4 Brigham and Womens Hospital, Boston, MA, $10,000. 1990.
1153-5 Childrens Medical Center, Boston, MA, $25,000. 1990.
1153-6 Dana-Farber Cancer Institute, Boston, MA, $30,000. 1990.
1153-7 Dartmouth-Hitchcock Medical Center, Hanover, NH, $15,000. 1990.

1153-8 Dimock Community Health Center, Roxbury, MA, $50,000. 1990.

1153-9 Falmouth Hospital, Falmouth, MA, $10,000. 1990.

1153-10 Health Care for the Homeless, Boston, MA, $25,000. 1990.

1153-11 Massachusetts General Hospital, Boston, MA, $100,000. 1990.

1153-12 Massachusetts General Hospital, Boston, MA, $30,000. 1990.

1153-13 Saint Elizabeths Hospital, Brighton, MA, $10,000. 1990.

1153-14 Saint Marys Hospital, Waterbury, CT, $20,000. For campaign. 1990.

1154
BayBanks Corporate Giving Program
175 Federal St.
Boston 02110   (617) 482-1040

Financial data (yr. ended 12/31/90): Total giving, $926,000 for grants (high: $20,000; average: $100-$25,000).

Purpose and activities: "...the BayBanks as corporate citizens accept responsibility to support those organizations and activities which directly benefit the communities in which they operate and in which their employees and shareholders live—in such ways and amounts as will strengthen the economy and enhance the quality of life." BayBanks, Inc. and its subsidiaries have two vehicles through which to consider requests for contributions from organizations in: health and welfare, education, culture and the arts, and civic activities. The majority of requests for charitable contributions are considered by the individual BayBanks. Most BayBanks have appropriated a portion of their assets to establish Clifford Trusts for charitable contributions, thus enabling those banks to maintain a consistent level of charitable support in their locales. In addition, BayBanks, Inc., has a Charitable Contributions Committee to consider requests from organizations transcending the constituencies of individual BayBanks. The Committee gives priority to solicitations from organizations which are statewide or regional in their impact and thus qualify for broad-based area support. The Committee ordinarily considers requests for capital rather than operating funds. Priority is given to organizations with which BayBanks has an on-going business relationship, and which employees serve actively. The following criteria are considered in evaluating requests: The organization should offer a high-quality program which does not overlap significantly with programs of other organizations. It should have an active and effective board, a strong administration and clear-cut management goals. The organization must be economically viable on an intermediate and long-term basis. It should have a broad base of community support, and the amount solicited from BayBanks, Inc., should be equitable in relation to other solicitations.

Fields of interest: Health, education, higher education, arts, civic affairs, welfare, community development, hospitals, hospitals—building funds, museums, child welfare.

Types of support: Capital campaigns, employee matching gifts, operating budgets.

Limitations: Giving primarily in state of MA, and parts of CT. No support for political, religious, fraternal or social, veteran, labor or directly tax-supported organizations. No grants for individual study or research, program advertising, fundraising dinners, luncheons, or benefits; generally no support for United Way supported organizations.

Publications: Corporate report, application guidelines.

Application information: Private Bank and Community Affairs handles giving. Application form not required.

   Initial approach: Letter and proposal; local organizations write to nearest branch; state or regional organizations write to headquarters

   Copies of proposal: 1

   Deadline(s): None

   Board meeting date(s): Annually, beginning in Dec.

   Final notification: Within a month of decision

   Write: Pamela S. Henrikson, Sr. V.P.

Administrators: Pamela S. Henrikson, Sr. V.P.; Thomas B. Kennedy, Sr. V.P.

Number of staff: 2 part-time professional; 2 part-time support.

1155
Adelaide Breed Bayrd Foundation
28 Pilgrim Rd.
Melrose 02176   (617) 662-7342

Incorporated in 1927 in MA.

Donor(s): Frank A. Bayrd,‡ Blanche S. Bayrd.‡

Foundation type: Independent

Financial data (yr. ended 12/31/91): Assets, $2,494,065 (M); gifts received, $345,000; expenditures, $349,908; qualifying distributions, $307,350, including $307,350 for 44 grants (high: $50,000; low: $750; average: $5,000).

Purpose and activities: To support primarily those activities in which the donor's mother took an active interest. This includes local hospitals, social welfare concerns, libraries, youth oriented programs, and cultural activities. The foundation does not grant individual scholarships but does fund ten scholarships annually through the Malden High School. All grants must in some manner benefit the citizens of Malden.

Fields of interest: Hospitals—building funds, welfare, libraries, youth, cultural programs, community development.

Types of support: Operating budgets, annual campaigns, emergency funds, building funds, equipment, endowment funds, research, special projects, scholarship funds.

Limitations: Giving primarily in the metropolitan Boston, MA, area, with emphasis on Malden. No support for national or out-of-state organizations. No grants to individuals (except for scholarships supplementary to the will of Blanche Bayrd), or for matching or challenge grants, demonstration projects, conferences, or publications; no loans.

Publications: Annual report (including application guidelines).

Application information: Application form not required.

   Initial approach: Proposal

   Copies of proposal: 1

   Deadline(s): Submit proposal preferably in Dec. or Jan.; deadline Feb. 15

   Board meeting date(s): 2nd Tuesday in Feb.; special meetings usually held in Mar. or Apr. to consider grant requests

   Final notification: Generally in Apr. or May

   Write: Russell E. Watts, M.D., Pres.

Officers and Trustees:* Russell E. Watts, M.D.,* Pres.; Susan C. Mansur,* Treas.; Florence C. Burns, C. Henry Kezer, Fred I. Lamson, William H. Marshall, Gaynor K. Rutherford, Jean H. Stearns, H. Allen Stevens.

Number of staff: 1 part-time professional; 1 part-time support.

EIN: 046051258

Recent health grants:

1155-1 Malden Home for Aged Persons, Malden, MA, $50,000. 1990.

1155-2 Middlesex Home Health Care, Malden, MA, $15,000. 1990.

1155-3 Tri-City Community Mental Health Center, Malden, MA, $25,000. 1990.

1156
Birmingham Foundation
Ten Post Office Sq., Suite 600
Boston 02109   (617) 451-5562

Established about 1954.

Donor(s): John P. Birmingham.‡

Foundation type: Independent

Financial data (yr. ended 12/31/90): Assets, $5,534,945 (M); expenditures, $480,190; qualifying distributions, $451,830, including $445,679 for 21 grants (high: $51,350; low: $1,000).

Purpose and activities: Giving for Roman Catholic welfare funds, and primary and secondary education; some support also for other social service agencies.

Fields of interest: Catholic giving, Catholic welfare, education, education—minorities, secondary education, higher education, social services, hospices.

Types of support: Scholarship funds, seed money, special projects.

Limitations: Giving primarily in Boston, MA. No grants to individuals.

Application information: Contributes only to pre-selected organizations. Applications not accepted.

   Write: Paul J. Birmingham, Trustee

Trustees: Paul J. Birmingham, Lois I. Wrightson.

EIN: 046050748

1157
Boston Edison Foundation
800 Boylston St., P203
Boston 02199   (617) 424-2235
Additional tel.: (617) 424-2272

Established in 1981 in MA.

Donor(s): Boston Edison Co.

Foundation type: Company-sponsored

Financial data (yr. ended 12/31/91): Assets, $335,064 (M); gifts received, $500,000; expenditures, $821,897; qualifying distributions, $821,397, including $758,250 for 70 grants (high: $400,000; low: $250; average: $500-$50,000) and $61,497 for 127 employee matching gifts.

Purpose and activities: Support for urban program services of special need to the people and the communities within the district served by the company. Grants awarded for higher education, health and welfare organizations, including hospitals and community funds; museums, performing arts groups, and other cultural programs; civic affairs, and community development groups.

Fields of interest: Higher education, health services, welfare, hospitals, community funds, cultural programs, arts, museums, civic affairs, community development.

Types of support: Employee matching gifts, annual campaigns, building funds, capital campaigns, continuing support, emergency funds, endowment funds, general purposes, renovation projects, research, operating budgets, scholarship funds, in-kind gifts, donated equipment.

Limitations: Giving primarily in areas of company operations, with emphasis on Boston and eastern MA. No support for programs receiving substantial support from others or third party organizations. No grants to individuals, or for capital campaigns, or for commitments beyond one year.

Publications: Application guidelines.

Application information: Application form not required.

Initial approach: Proposal
Write: Robert Palmer, Dir.

Officers: Ann L. Cardello, Administrator; Emilie F. O'Neil, Treas.; Catherine J. Keuthen, Counsel; C.S. Daisy Jao, Tax Advisor.

Trustees: Bernard W. Reznicek, Chair.; Ralph G. Bird, Theodora S. Convisser, Cameron H. Daley, Lester C. Gustin, John J. Higgins, Thomas J. May, Charles E. Peters, Jr.

Number of staff: None.

EIN: 042754285

1158

The Boston Foundation, Inc. ▼

One Boston Place, 24th Fl.
Boston 02108-4402   (617) 723-7415
FAX: (617) 589-3616

Established in 1915 in MA by agreement and declaration of trust; incorporated in 1917.

Foundation type: Community

Financial data (yr. ended 06/30/91): Assets, $256,248,834 (M); gifts received, $7,101,825; expenditures, $21,328,115; qualifying distributions, $16,980,716, including $16,980,716 for 1,101 grants (high: $250,000; low: $500; average: $20,000-$40,000).

Purpose and activities: To support local health, welfare, educational, cultural, environmental, social services and housing programs and institutions; grants for start-up expenses of new or experimental programs of both established and new institutions, as well as for capital needs and for coordination and planning projects.

Fields of interest: Community development, health, AIDS, rehabilitation, child welfare, education, elementary education, secondary education, higher education, cultural programs, environment, welfare, social services, housing, homeless, disadvantaged, minorities, race relations, civil rights, family planning, women.

Types of support: Building funds, emergency funds, equipment, land acquisition, matching funds, seed money, special projects, renovation projects, technical assistance.

Limitations: Giving limited to the Boston, MA, metropolitan area. No support for religious purposes, small arts groups, public or private schools, municipalities, or national or international programs. No grants to individuals, or for general operating funds, medical, scientific, or academic research, books or articles, films, radio, or television programs, equipment, travel, scholarships, fellowships, conferences, or capital campaigns; no loans.

Publications: Annual report, application guidelines, newsletter, occasional report, 990-PF, grants list.

Application information: Application form not required.

Initial approach: Proposal
Copies of proposal: 1
Deadline(s): 3 months prior to board meetings
Board meeting date(s): Mar., June, Sept., and Dec.
Final notification: Within 1 or 2 weeks of board meeting
Write: Anna Faith Jones, Pres.

Officers and Distribution Committee:* Dwight L. Allison, Jr.,* Chair.; Lawrence T. Perera,* Vice-Chair.; Anna Faith Jones, Pres., C.E.O., and Secy.-Treas.; Joan T. Bok, Ronald A. Homer, Frieda Garcia, Charles Ray Johnson, Martin S. Kaplan, Gael Mahony, David R. Pokross, Sr., David Rockefeller, Jr., Simon Scheff.

Trustee Banks: Bank of Boston, Boston Safe Deposit & Trust Co., Fleet Bank of Massachusetts, N.A., Shawmut Bank, N.A., State Street Bank & Trust Co.

Number of staff: 15 full-time professional; 11 full-time support; 1 part-time support.

EIN: 042104021

Recent health grants:

1158-1 Boston Area Rape Crisis Center, Cambridge, MA, $10,000. For counseling and outreach/education services. 1991.

1158-2 Boston Education Development Foundation, Boston High School-Based Health Center, Boston, MA, $22,500. For general support. 1991.

1158-3 Boston Education Development Foundation, Brighton High School-Based Health Center, Boston, MA, $22,500. For general support. 1991.

1158-4 Boston University, School of Social Work, Boston, MA, $30,000. For third and final year support of Dorchester Alcohol and Drug Abuse Prevention Project. 1991.

1158-5 Center for Public Representation, Northampton, MA, $20,000. For project providing legal representation to mentally ill persons at Bridgewater State Hospital. 1991.

1158-6 Church of United Community, United Community Advocacy Program, Boston, MA, $15,000. For staff of Treatment on Demand Program. Grant made through United Church of Christ. 1991.

1158-7 East Boston Neighborhood Health Center, East Boston, MA, $50,000. For Elder Services Program. Grant administered by East Boston Community Health Committee. 1991.

1158-8 Fenway Community Health Center, Boston Women's AIDS Information Project, Boston, MA, $15,000. For Project Coordinator. 1991.

1158-9 Haitian Multi-Service Center, Dorchester, MA, $45,000. For Sante Manman Se Sante Pitit program. Grant made through Catholic

Charitable Bureau of the Archdiocese of Boston. 1991.

1158-10 Harvard University, Law School, Cambridge, MA, $40,000. For expansion of AIDS Law Clinic. 1991.

1158-11 Harvard University, School of Public Health, Boston, MA, $40,000. For continued support of Boston AIDS Consortium. 1991.

1158-12 Health Care for All, Boston, MA, $35,000. For Public Education Campaign. 1991.

1158-13 Health Care for the Homeless, Boston, MA, $50,000. For planning and developing expanded respite care unit. Grant made through Trustees of Health and Hospitals of the City of Boston. 1991.

1158-14 Judge Baker Childrens Center, Boston, MA, $50,000. For Camille Cosby Center's program development project. 1991.

1158-15 M-Power, Boston, MA, $15,000. For organizing activities. Grant made through Empowerment Sponsoring Committee. 1991.

1158-16 Martha Eliot Health Center, Jamaica Plain, MA, $35,000. For Life Cycle Coalition. Grant administered by Childern's Hospital Corporation. 1991.

1158-17 Massachusetts Advocacy Center, Boston, MA, $30,000. For staff assistance for Healthy Start Coalition. Grant administered by Task Force on Children Out of School. 1991.

1158-18 Massachusetts League of Community Health Centers, Boston, MA, $20,000. For Physician Recruitment Program. 1991.

1158-19 Massachusetts Senior Action Council, Boston, MA, $25,000. Toward Boston Health Care Access for Elders Project. 1991.

1158-20 Medical Foundation, Boston, MA, $40,000. For Warmline component of Project Mattapan's prenatal service project. 1991.

1158-21 Odwin Learning Center, Dorchester, MA, $65,000. For health education and careers training program for under- and unemployed adults in Boston. 1991.

1158-22 Partners for Disabled Youth, Boston, MA, $25,000. To develop mentoring program which matches learning disabled youth with adults who have similar disabilities. 1991.

1158-23 Partners in Health, Cambridge, MA, $20,000. For Haitian Teens Confront AIDS programming. 1991.

1158-24 Somerville Portuguese American League, Somerville, MA, $15,000. For Recovery Program. 1991.

1158-25 Traditional Childbearing Group, Boston, MA, $50,000. Toward staff salaries and rental expenses. 1991.

1158-26 Trustees of Health and Hospitals of the City of Boston, Boston, MA, $150,000. For Healthy Child Program. 1991.

1158-27 Trustees of Health and Hospitals of the City of Boston, Boston, MA, $33,640. For Failure to Thrive Clinic. 1991.

1158-28 Tufts University, School of Medicine, Medford, MA, $40,000. For New England Health and Poverty Action Center. 1991.

1158-29 United South End Settlements, Multi-Cultural AIDS Coalition, Boston, MA, $35,000. For development and strategic planning efforts. 1991.

1158-30 Vision Foundation, Watertown, MA, $40,000. For expansion of Visually Impaired Elders Project to inner-city Boston neighborhoods and to build in-house training program for rehabilitation teachers. 1991.

1159
Boston Gas Company Giving Program
One Beacon St.
Boston 02108   (617) 742-8400
Application address: 201 Rivermore St., West Roxbury, MA 02132; Tel. (617) 323-9210

Financial data (yr. ended 12/31/88): Total giving, $186,000 for 100 grants (high: $1,500; low: $100; average: $500-$5,000).
Purpose and activities: Grants are usually restricted to capital, seed, or one-time community service projects in three categories: Civic and cultural, education, and health and welfare; major supporter of the United Way; supports business and minority education; child welfare; programs for the disadvantaged, the handicapped, and the homeless, housing, safety, community funds, intercultural relations, legal services, performing arts, and health.
Fields of interest: Aged, arts, business education, child welfare, civic affairs, community development, conservation, cultural programs, disadvantaged, education, education—minorities, employment, handicapped, health associations, higher education, homeless, housing, intercultural relations, law and justice, legal services, literacy, mental health, performing arts, race relations, urban affairs, urban development, volunteerism, women, youth, general charitable giving, hospitals, safety, health, drug abuse, community funds, education—early childhood.
Types of support: Employee matching gifts, renovation projects, general purposes, donated equipment, loaned talent, capital campaigns, seed money.
Limitations: Giving primarily in company territory of central and eastern MA. No support for political or religious organizations. No grants to individuals.
Publications: Application guidelines, newsletter, informational brochure (including application guidelines).
Application information: Public Relations and Community Affairs Departments handle giving; decisions are made by a Direct Giving Advisory Comm., comprised of employees; Project sites may be visited. Application form required.
> *Initial approach:* Proposal; elaborate, costly submissions are discouraged; if more data is needed it will be requested
> *Copies of proposal:* 1
> *Deadline(s):* Apr. 15
> *Board meeting date(s):* Late Apr.
> *Write:* S.T. Horwitz, V.P., Public Rels.
Administrators: S.T. Horwitz, V.P., Public Rels. and Advertising; Tom Netley, Dir., Community Affairs; Lauren Murphy, Secy.
Number of staff: 6 part-time professional.

1160
The Boston Globe Foundation II, Inc. ▼
135 Morrissey Blvd.
Boston 02107   (617) 929-2895

Established in 1987.
Donor(s): Affiliated Publications, Inc.
Foundation type: Company-sponsored

Financial data (yr. ended 06/30/90): Assets, $58,022 (M); gifts received, $2,781,000; expenditures, $3,142,878; qualifying distributions, $3,137,411, including $3,115,837 for 490 grants (high: $100,000; average: $5,000-$20,000).
Purpose and activities: Giving primarily for community services, with emphasis on multiservice agencies, handicapped accessibility, housing development, and race relations; support also for culture and the arts, education, science and the environment, hospitals and health care, summer camps, and media business.
Fields of interest: Social services, community funds, family services, handicapped, housing, race relations, cultural programs, arts, museums, science and technology, hospitals, health services, education, higher education, youth, media and communications, environment.
Types of support: Employee matching gifts, operating budgets, special projects, building funds, scholarship funds, employee-related scholarships, research, renovation projects, emergency funds, endowment funds, internships, publications.
Limitations: Giving primarily in the greater Boston, MA, area.
Publications: Application guidelines.
Application information:
> *Initial approach:* Proposal
> *Deadline(s):* None
> *Board meeting date(s):* Feb., Mar., June, Sept., and Nov.
> *Final notification:* 4 months after submitting proposal
Officers and Directors:* William O. Taylor,* Pres.; John P. Guiggio,* Treas.; George M. Collins, Jr., Dexter Eure, Jr., Catherine E.C. Henn, Benjamin Taylor, William D. Taylor.
EIN: 222821421
Recent health grants:
1160-1 AIDS Action Committee of Massachusetts, Boston, MA, $20,000. For All Walks of Life annual fund raiser. 1991.
1160-2 Bridge Over Troubled Waters, Boston, MA, $10,000. For operating support of existing programs and for development of new programs to deal with substance abuse and AIDS prevention. 1991.
1160-3 Carney Hospital, Boston, MA, $15,000. For capital equipment. 1991.
1160-4 Dimock Community Health Center, Roxbury, MA, $20,000. For capital campaign for revitalization of Dimock's historical physical plant and campus. 1991.
1160-5 Medical Foundation, Boston, MA, $10,000. For operating costs of Project Mattapan and for Medical Foundation. 1991.
1160-6 Trustees of Health and Hospitals of the City of Boston, Boston, MA, $21,000. To maintain Pediatric Nutrition Surveilliance program during winter. 1991.
1160-7 Tufts University, School of Nutrition, Boston, MA, $10,000. For start-up costs for new Center on Hunger, Poverty and Nutrition. 1991.

1161
The Harold Brooks Foundation
c/o South Shore Bank
1400 Hancock St.
Quincy 02169   (617) 847-3301

Established in 1984.
Donor(s): Harold Brooks.‡
Foundation type: Independent
Financial data (yr. ended 12/31/91): Assets, $6,264,380 (M); expenditures, $332,588; qualifying distributions, $294,201, including $279,032 for 40 grants (high: $18,000; low: $1,000).
Fields of interest: Community development, health, social services, general charitable giving.
Types of support: Building funds, matching funds, capital campaigns, general purposes, equipment.
Limitations: Giving only in MA, with emphasis on the South Shore area. No grants to individuals.
Publications: Application guidelines.
Application information:
> *Initial approach:* Letter requesting guidelines
> *Copies of proposal:* 1
> *Deadline(s):* Feb. 15, May 15, Aug. 15, and Nov. 15
> *Board meeting date(s):* Mar., June, Sept., and Dec.
> *Write:* Robert F. Dwyer, Sr. V.P., South Shore Bank
Trustees: Forrest R. Cook, Jr., Harry W. Healey, Rev. James Workman, South Shore Bank.
Number of staff: None.
EIN: 046043983

1162
Cabot Family Charitable Trust
c/o Cabot Corp.
75 State St.
Boston 02109-1806   (617) 345-0100

Trust established in 1942 in MA.
Donor(s): Godfrey L. Cabot.‡
Foundation type: Independent
Financial data (yr. ended 12/31/91): Assets, $10,693,266 (M); expenditures, $638,962; qualifying distributions, $632,019, including $581,779 for 42 grants (high: $25,000; low: $630; average: $5,000-$25,000).
Purpose and activities: "Program interests include problems of overpopulation in the world, environmental issues of New England, and projects that represent volunteer efforts and educational interests of family members."
Fields of interest: Education, higher education, youth, family services, family planning, cultural programs, conservation, environment.
Types of support: Annual campaigns, seed money, building funds, land acquisition, endowment funds, general purposes, continuing support, capital campaigns, research.
Limitations: No support for computer-related projects, or environmental programs outside the New England area. No grants to individuals, or for medical or scientific research, scholarships, fellowships, or matching gifts; no loans.
Publications: Annual report (including application guidelines).
Application information: Application form not required.
> *Initial approach:* Proposal (no more than 2 pages)
> *Copies of proposal:* 1
> *Deadline(s):* Mar. 1 and Oct. 1
> *Board meeting date(s):* Apr. and Nov.
> *Final notification:* 3 to 5 months
> *Write:* Ruth C. Scheer, Exec. Dir.

Trustees: Jane C. Bradley, John G.L. Cabot, Louis W. Cabot.
Number of staff: 1 part-time professional; 1 part-time support.
EIN: 046036446
Recent health grants:
1162-1 African Medical and Research Foundation, Nairobi, Kenya, $10,000. To train birth attendants in Kenya. 1991.
1162-2 Brigham and Womens Hospital, Boston, MA, $15,000. To research new contraceptive method. 1991.
1162-3 Center for Development and Population Activities, DC, $20,000. To train women managers in third world. 1991.
1162-4 International Projects Assistance Services, Carrboro, NC, $20,000. For general support. 1991.
1162-5 Mental Health Association, North Suffolk, Chelsea, MA, $15,000. For teen pregnancy prevention program for males in Chelsea. 1991.
1162-6 Planned Parenthood League of Massachusetts, Cambridge, MA, $25,000. For general support. 1991.
1162-7 Population Crisis Committee, DC, $20,000. For general support. 1991.
1162-8 Preterm, Boston, MA, $20,000. For general support. 1991.
1162-9 San Miguel Educational Foundation, San Miguel de Allende, Mexico, $25,000. For general support. 1991.
1162-10 Spaulding Rehabilitation Hospital, Boston, MA, $10,000. For Child and Adolescent Program. 1991.

1163
Cabot-Saltonstall Charitable Trust
One Financial Ctr., 38th Fl.
Boston 02111

Trust established in 1936 in MA.
Donor(s): Paul C. Cabot, Virginia C. Cabot, Charles Cabot.‡
Foundation type: Independent
Financial data (yr. ended 12/31/90): Assets, $6,482,232 (M); expenditures, $296,664; qualifying distributions, $287,750, including $287,035 for 83 grants (high: $50,000; low: $25).
Purpose and activities: Emphasis on higher and secondary education, hospitals, and a community fund.
Fields of interest: Hospitals, higher education, secondary education, community funds.
Limitations: Giving primarily in the Boston, MA, area. No grants to individuals.
Application information: Contributes only to pre-selected organizations. Applications not accepted.
Trustees: Paul C. Cabot, Paul C. Cabot, Jr., Virginia C. Cabot.
EIN: 046042037

1164
Cambridge Community Foundation
(Formerly The Cambridge Foundation)
99 Bishop Richard Allen Dr.
Cambridge 02139 (617) 876-5214

Established in 1916 in MA by declaration of trust.
Foundation type: Community

Financial data (yr. ended 12/31/90): Assets, $3,713,676 (M); expenditures, $247,758; qualifying distributions, $174,692, including $174,692 for grants (average: $1,000-$5,000).
Purpose and activities: To promote the mental, moral, and physical welfare of the inhabitants of Cambridge, MA (or elsewhere, if specified by the donor), through grants to community agencies, generally for 1) social services - child welfare and development, emergency aid, employment and job training, legal assistance, and family services; 2) education - elementary and secondary education and ESL/GED programs; 3) health - hospice and home care, mental health and counseling, and substance abuse programs; and 4) housing and shelter - home improvement and repair, housing development, and shelter and transitional housing.
Fields of interest: Health, welfare, social services, youth, mental health, education, housing, child welfare.
Types of support: Operating budgets, general purposes, special projects, seed money, building funds, equipment.
Limitations: Giving primarily in Cambridge, MA, except as specified by donors. No support for municipal, state, or federal agencies. No grants to individuals, or for scholarships, research studies, conferences, films, or capital fund drives; no loans.
Publications: Annual report, application guidelines, program policy statement.
Application information:
    Initial approach: Telephone or letter requesting guidelines
    Copies of proposal: 6
    Deadline(s): Submit proposal preferably in Feb. through Apr. and Sept. through Oct.; deadline Apr. 15 for June consideration and Oct. 15 for Dec. consideration
    Board meeting date(s): Distribution committee meets in June and Dec.
    Write: Lynn D'Ambrose, Exec. Dir.
Distribution Committee: Patricia R. Pratt, Pres.; Sallie M. Bass, Sybil C. d'Arbeloff, Marion B. Eiseman, Hon. Lawrence F. Feloney, Joan Von Mehren.
Trustees: BayBank Harvard Trust Co., Cambridge Trust Co.
EIN: 046012492

1165
Cambridge Mustard Seed Foundation
c/o Shawmut Bank, N.A.
P.O. Box 2176
Boston 02211

Established in 1985 in MA.
Donor(s): Sarah C. Doering, R & T Liquidating Trust.
Foundation type: Independent
Financial data (yr. ended 07/31/91): Assets, $4,725,267 (M); gifts received, $385; expenditures, $303,000; qualifying distributions, $282,558, including $262,500 for 7 grants (high: $72,500; low: $15,000).
Fields of interest: Secondary education, education, welfare, social services, family planning, youth.
Limitations: Giving primarily in MA. No grants to individuals.

Application information: Trustees do not encourage unsolicited applications.
    Initial approach: Letter
    Write: David Green, V.P., Shawmut Bank, N.A.
Trustees: Gerald E. Fosbroke, Shawmut Bank, N.A.
EIN: 046527529

1166
Bushrod H. Campbell and Adah F. Hall Charity Fund
c/o Palmer & Dodge
One Beacon St.
Boston 02108 (617) 573-0464

Trust established in 1956 in MA.
Donor(s): Bushrod H. Campbell,‡ Adah F. Hall.‡
Foundation type: Independent
Financial data (yr. ended 05/31/92): Assets, $11,683,283 (M); expenditures, $566,097; qualifying distributions, $506,863, including $452,459 for 92 grants (high: $48,000; low: $450; average: $2,000-$8,000).
Purpose and activities: Grants limited to organizations and/or their projects devoted to aid the elderly, population control, and health care. Medical research grants administered through the Medical Foundation. Grants made primarily for services and programs.
Fields of interest: Health associations, family planning, aged, medical research.
Types of support: Operating budgets, continuing support, seed money, equipment, research, conferences and seminars, special projects, renovation projects.
Limitations: Giving limited to the greater Boston, MA, area (within Route 128 and Boston); giving on a national basis to organizations dealing with population control. No grants to individuals, or for annual campaigns, emergency funds, deficit financing, land acquisition, publications, or general endowments; no loans.
Publications: Application guidelines, informational brochure, grants list.
Application information: Application form required.
    Initial approach: Telephone or letter
    Copies of proposal: 1
    Deadline(s): Feb. 1, May 1, Sept. 1, or Nov. 1
    Board meeting date(s): Feb., May, Sept., and Nov.
    Final notification: By mail only
    Write: Hilary M. Langille, Sr. Legal Asst.
Trustees: Donald J. Barker, Casimir de Rham, Jr., Curtis Prout.
Number of staff: 1 part-time professional.
EIN: 046013598

1167
Earle P. Charlton, Jr. Charitable Trust
c/o First National Bank of Boston
P.O. Box 1861
Boston 02105 (617) 434-5669

Trust established in 1973 in MA.
Donor(s): Earle P. Charlton, Jr.‡
Foundation type: Independent
Financial data (yr. ended 12/31/90): Assets, $4,968,716 (M); expenditures, $295,008; qualifying distributions, $242,701, including $237,356 for 3 grants (high: $100,000; low: $37,356).

Purpose and activities: Giving primarily to hospitals; some support for a community fund.
Fields of interest: Hospitals, community funds.
Limitations: Giving primarily in Boston and Fall River, MA.
Application information: Contributes only to pre-selected organizations. Applications not accepted.
 Write: S. Driscoll, Sr. V.P., First National Bank of Boston
Trustees: Earle P. Charlton II, Alfred Fuller, First National Bank of Boston.
EIN: 046334412

1168
The Alfred E. Chase Charity Foundation
c/o Fleet Bank of Massachusetts, N.A.
28 State St.
Boston 02109   (617) 573-6416

Trust established in 1956 in MA.
Donor(s): Alfred E. Chase.‡
Foundation type: Independent
Financial data (yr. ended 10/31/91): Assets, $4,375,628 (M); expenditures, $260,187; qualifying distributions, $227,695, including $211,490 for 19 grants (high: $25,000; low: $700; average: $10,000-$20,000).
Purpose and activities: Particular interest in social service and welfare organizations and programs for children and youth; support also for hospitals and health services, community development, delinquency programs, the disabled and homeless, and hunger and nutrition.
Fields of interest: Hospitals, social services, youth, child welfare, health services, community development, delinquency, disadvantaged, homeless, hunger, nutrition, welfare.
Types of support: Capital campaigns, operating budgets, building funds, renovation projects, annual campaigns, capital campaigns, equipment, general purposes, operating budgets, renovation projects, special projects.
Limitations: Giving limited to MA, primarily the greater Boston and North Shore areas. No grants to individuals, or for research, scholarships, or fellowships; no loans.
Publications: Application guidelines, 990-PF.
Application information: Application form required.
 Initial approach: Proposal
 Copies of proposal: 1
 Deadline(s): Feb. 28
 Board meeting date(s): Apr.
 Write: Kerry A. Herlihy, V.P., Fleet Bank of Massachusetts, N.A.
Trustee: Fleet Bank of Massachusetts, N.A.
Number of staff: 4 full-time professional; 1 full-time support.
EIN: 046026314

1169
Clifford Charitable Foundation, Inc.
c/o Choate, Hall & Stewart
Exchange Place
Boston 02109

Established in 1980 in MA.
Donor(s): Ellinor B. Clifford.
Foundation type: Independent

Financial data (yr. ended 12/31/91): Assets, $942,246 (M); gifts received, $377,775; expenditures, $266,995; qualifying distributions, $264,446, including $264,165 for 39 grants (high: $35,000; low: $250).
Fields of interest: Higher education, education, hospitals, child welfare, community funds, medical research.
Types of support: Annual campaigns, capital campaigns, operating budgets.
Limitations: Giving primarily in Boston, MA. No grants to individuals.
Application information: Contributes only to pre-selected organizations. Applications not accepted.
Officers: Stewart H. Clifford, Pres.; Ellinor B. Clifford, Treas.
Director: Frederic M. Clifford.
EIN: 042690883

1170
Conservation, Food and Health Foundation, Inc.
c/o Grant Management Assocs.
230 Congress St., 3rd Fl.
Boston 02110   (617) 426-7172

Established in 1985 in MA.
Foundation type: Independent
Financial data (yr. ended 06/30/90): Assets, $5,489,026 (M); expenditures, $678,550; qualifying distributions, $359,434, including $342,443 for 33 grants (high: $25,000; low: $1,000).
Fields of interest: Conservation, ecology, environment, wildlife, international relief, agriculture, health.
Types of support: Special projects, research, technical assistance.
Limitations: Giving limited to the Third World.
Publications: Annual report (including application guidelines).
Application information: Application form not required.
 Initial approach: Letter
 Copies of proposal: 5
 Deadline(s): Apr. 1 and Nov. 1
 Board meeting date(s): May and Dec.
 Final notification: Immediately after board meetings
 Write: Ann F. Wallace
Officer: Philip M. Fearnside,* Pres.
Number of staff: 1 part-time professional; 1 part-time support.
EIN: 222625024

1171
The Cove Charitable Trust
Boston Safe Deposit & Trust Co.
One Boston Place
Boston 02108   (617) 722-7340

Established in 1964 in MA.
Donor(s): Aileen Kelly Pratt,‡ Edwin H.B. Pratt.‡
Foundation type: Independent
Financial data (yr. ended 12/31/90): Assets, $2,411,350 (M); expenditures, $111,724; qualifying distributions, $91,236, including $85,500 for 14 grants (high: $28,000; low: $1,000; average: $1,000-$2,000).

Fields of interest: Hospitals, homeless, religious welfare, education.
Types of support: General purposes, special projects, operating budgets, continuing support, annual campaigns, seed money, building funds.
Limitations: Giving primarily in MA. No grants to individuals, or for scholarships, fellowships, emergency funds, deficit financing, equipment and materials, land acquisition, renovation projects, endowments, program-related investments, research, publications, or conferences and seminars; no loans.
Application information: Applications not accepted.
 Write: Sylvia Salas, Trust Officer, Boston Safe Deposit & Trust Co.
Trustees: Charlotte P. Sudduth, Boston Safe Deposit & Trust Co.
Number of staff: None.
EIN: 046118955

1172
The Lillian L. and Harry A. Cowan Foundation Corporation
20 Chapel St., Apt. 412-B
Brookline 02146   (617) 738-1461

Incorporated in 1962 in MA.
Donor(s): Harry A. Cowan.‡
Foundation type: Independent
Financial data (yr. ended 04/30/91): Assets, $3,267,951 (M); gifts received, $750; expenditures, $201,917; qualifying distributions, $165,842, including $141,694 for 34 grants (high: $10,390; low: $1,000; average: $1,000-$5,000).
Purpose and activities: Giving primarily to aid the blind and physically and emotionally handicapped children.
Fields of interest: Handicapped, child welfare, homeless, hospices, hunger, family services, adult education, elementary education, education—minorities, aged.
Types of support: Matching funds, seed money, operating budgets.
Limitations: Giving primarily in the greater Boston, MA, area. No support for umbrella agencies. No grants to individuals, or for capital or annual campaigns, or building funds.
Application information: Application form not required.
 Initial approach: Proposal
 Copies of proposal: 1
 Deadline(s): Apr. 10 and Nov. 10
 Board meeting date(s): Semiannually, usually in May and Dec.
 Write: Albert Slavin, Pres. and Treas.
Officers and Trustees:* Albert Slavin,* Pres. and Treas.; Ellen Glazer,* V.P. and Clerk; Marjorie Herson,* V.P.; Andrea Weinstein,* V.P.; Donald Glazer.
Number of staff: 1 part-time professional; 2 part-time support.
EIN: 046130077

1173
Jessie B. Cox Charitable Trust ▼
c/o Grants Management Assocs.
230 Congress St., 3rd Fl.
Boston 02110   (617) 426-7172

Charitable lead trust established in 1982 in Boston, MA.
Donor(s): Jessie B. Cox.‡
Foundation type: Independent
Financial data (yr. ended 12/31/90): Assets, $51,000,000 (M); expenditures, $3,077,976; qualifying distributions, $3,077,976, including $3,077,976 for 87 grants (high: $105,000; low: $1,000; average: $20,000-$50,000).
Purpose and activities: Grants for education, health, the protection of the environment, and the development of philanthropy. The trustees tend to favor organizations which have not received prior grants, and new approaches over those similar to previously funded projects; fixed amount of approximately $3 million to be paid out annually through the life of the trust.
Fields of interest: Education, higher education, environment, conservation, health.
Types of support: Seed money, special projects.
Limitations: Giving primarily in New England. No support for sectarian religious activities, or efforts usually supported by the general public. No grants to individuals, or for capital or building funds, equipment and materials, land acquisition, renovation projects, deficit financing, operating budgets, continuing support, annual campaigns, or general endowments; no loans.
Publications: Annual report, informational brochure (including application guidelines).
Application information: Application form not required.
Initial approach: Brief concept paper, telephone call, or full proposal
Copies of proposal: 2
Deadline(s): Jan. 15, Apr. 15, July 15, and Oct. 15
Board meeting date(s): Mar., June, Sept., and Dec.
Final notification: Within 3 months of deadline
Write: Michealle Larkins, Fdn. Asst.
Administrators: Newell Flather, Gloria Oldsman, Ala H. Reid, Ann Fowler Wallace.
Trustees: William C. Cox, Jr., Roy A. Hammer, Jane Cox MacElree, George T. Shaw.
Number of staff: 4 part-time professional; 1 full-time support.
EIN: 046478024
Recent health grants:
1173-1 Center for Public Representation, Northampton, MA, $25,000. To provide legal representation for mentally ill patients at Bridgewater State Hospital. 1990.
1173-2 Dana-Farber Cancer Institute, Boston, MA, $35,000. Toward breast cancer screening project, attempt to reduce incidence of breast cancer in very high risk groups of women, especially relatives of breast cancer patients. 1990.
1173-3 Easter Seal Society of New Hampshire and Vermont, Manchester, NH, $25,000. For Child Development Services Consortium in conjunction with William J. Moore Center and Child Health Services to demonstrate developmental assessment service for children 0-3 in Manchester, NH. 1990.
1173-4 Health Care for All, Boston, MA, $40,000. For Community Access Education Project to strengthen and expand role of consumers in developing health care policy. 1990.
1173-5 Holyoke Chicopee Area Mental Health Center, Holyoke, MA, $75,000. For Holyoke

Middle School Health Initiative, project to develop health centers in two middle schools and in Holyoke's vocational high school. 1990.
1173-6 Kennebec Valley Regional Health Agency, Waterville, ME, $25,000. To expand Teen Parenting Project in seven health centers in central and western Maine. 1990.
1173-7 Massachusetts Human Services Coalition, Boston, MA, $29,000. To establish state-wide network to help forge solutions to Massachusetts' Medicaid budget problems. 1990.
1173-8 May Institute for Autistic Children, Chatham, MA, $34,000. To provide home-based communication training for parents of children with autism or other severe handicaps. 1990.
1173-9 Mental Health Association of Kennebec Valley, Waterville, ME, $29,500. Toward Secondary Prevention Program for Child Abuse, two-year demonstration project to try to break cycle of child abuse within families. 1990.
1173-10 Nantucket Cottage Hospital, Nantucket, MA, $25,000. To build endowment. 1990.
1173-11 National Toxics Campaign Fund, Boston, MA, $26,806. Toward Boston Harbor Toxics Project, effort to reduce toxic discharges into harbor, and to promote MWRA rate structure that reflects toxic impacts of certain system users. 1990.
1173-12 New England Medical Center, Boston, MA, $31,000. Toward Nursing Case Management Program, effort to redesign way in which patient care is administered at Center, and to disseminate results to other hospitals nationwide. 1990.
1173-13 Regional Medical Center at Lubec, Lubec, ME, $15,000. To institutionalize mental health services in isolated rural area of Maine. 1990.
1173-14 Rogerson House, Boston, MA, $35,000. Toward project to plan and begin to develop skilled nursing facility for elderly, and to develop ways of serving mentally impaired elders in residential settings. 1990.
1173-15 Social Justice for Women, Boston, MA, $64,000. Toward Project Catch the Hope, program which provides intensive health and other family support services to drug-addicted mothers involved in criminal justice system in Massachusetts. 1990.
1173-16 Tufts University, School of Nutrition, Medford, MA, $50,000. For start-up support for Center on Hunger, Poverty and Nutrition Policy. 1990.
1173-17 University of Pennsylvania, School of Veterinary Medicine, Philadelphia, PA, $24,000. To initiate Molecular Genetics Laboratory. 1990.
1173-18 Vermont Childrens Forum, Montpelier, VT, $20,000. For Prenatal Care Project to improve and expand prenatal care for low-income women in Vermont. 1990.
1173-19 Yale University, School of Medicine, New Haven, CT, $50,000. For in-house research capability for Program in Geriatrics. 1990.

1174
Cox Foundation, Inc.
c/o Choate Hall & Stewart
Exchange Place
Boston 02109 (617) 227-5020

Established in 1970.
Donor(s): William C. Cox, Jr.
Foundation type: Independent
Financial data (yr. ended 12/31/91): Assets, $6,652,732 (M); gifts received, $755,145; expenditures, $266,415; qualifying distributions, $231,594, including $221,500 for 30 grants (high: $25,000; low: $1,000).
Fields of interest: Secondary education, hospitals, medical research, conservation, environment, cultural programs, museums.
Types of support: Annual campaigns, continuing support, general purposes, land acquisition, operating budgets, research, special projects, capital campaigns.
Limitations: Giving primarily in MA and FL. No grants to individuals.
Application information: Contributes only to pre-selected organizations. Applications not accepted.
Write: Robert Perkins
Officers: William C. Cox, Jr., Pres.; David E. Place, Secy.; Martha W. Cox, Treas.
EIN: 237068786

1175
Crane & Company Fund
30 South St.
Dalton 01226

Established in 1953 in MA.
Donor(s): Crane & Co., Inc., Byron-Weston Co.
Foundation type: Company-sponsored
Financial data (yr. ended 12/31/91): Assets, $44,773 (M); gifts received, $200,000; expenditures, $217,020; qualifying distributions, $216,650, including $216,650 for 52 grants (high: $60,000; low: $100).
Fields of interest: Community funds, museums, education, cultural programs, conservation, social services, health, civic affairs.
Types of support: Capital campaigns, general purposes.
Limitations: Giving primarily in MA.
Application information:
Deadline(s): None
Trustees: Thomas A. White, Stephen H. Wismer.
EIN: 046057388

1176
Cummings Properties Foundation
200 West Cummings Park
Woburn 01801 (617) 935-8000

Established in 1986 in MA.
Foundation type: Company-sponsored
Financial data (yr. ended 12/31/91): Assets, $2,479,527 (M); gifts received, $488,000; expenditures, $225,704; qualifying distributions, $204,634, including $201,289 for 14 grants (high: $191,204; low: $50).
Fields of interest: Mental health, hospitals, youth, social services.
Types of support: Scholarship funds.

Limitations: Giving primarily in Woburn and Winchester, MA. No grants to individuals.
Application information: Application form not required.
  Initial approach: Letter
  Deadline(s): None
  Write: James L. McKeown
Trustees: John A. Forsyth, Marian E. Forsyth, James L. McKeown.
EIN: 046541313

1177
The Fred Harris Daniels Foundation, Inc.
c/o The Mechanics Bank, Trust Dept.
P.O. Box 987
Worcester 01613   (508) 798-6443
Application address: c/o The Mechanics Bank, Trust Dept., 2000 Mechanics Tower, Worcester, MA 01608

Incorporated in 1949 in MA.
Donor(s): Fred H. Daniels,‡ Eleanor G. Daniels.‡
Foundation type: Independent
Financial data (yr. ended 10/31/91): Assets, $8,787,252 (M); expenditures, $476,270; qualifying distributions, $441,662, including $432,400 for 66 grants (high: $60,000; low: $700; average: $1,000-$20,000).
Purpose and activities: Grants for the advancement of the sciences, including marine and medical sciences; support also for secondary and higher education, health services and hospitals, including programs for the mentally ill, community funds, social and family services, including museums, music organizations and historical preservation, libraries, and Protestant giving.
Fields of interest: Science and technology, secondary education, higher education, health, community funds, social services, child welfare, arts, libraries, Protestant giving.
Types of support: Operating budgets, continuing support, annual campaigns, emergency funds, building funds, equipment, land acquisition, endowment funds, matching funds, professorships, internships, scholarship funds, fellowships, special projects, capital campaigns, general purposes, renovation projects.
Limitations: Giving primarily in the Worcester, MA, area. No grants to individuals, or for seed money or deficit financing; no loans.
Application information: Application form not required.
  Initial approach: Letter
  Copies of proposal: 1
  Deadline(s): Mar. 1, June 1, Sept. 1, and Dec. 1
  Board meeting date(s): Mar., June, Sept., and Dec.
  Final notification: 1 to 2 1/2 months
  Write: Bruce G. Daniels, Pres.
Officers and Directors:* Bruce G. Daniels,* Pres.; F. Turner Blake, Jr.,* Secy.; William O. Pettit, Jr.,* Treas.; Jonathan D. Blake, Fred H. Daniels II, Janet B. Daniels, Eleanor D. Hodge, Amy B. Key, Sarah D. Morse, William S. Nicholson, Meridith D. Wesby.
Number of staff: None.
EIN: 046014333

1178
Irene E. and George A. Davis Foundation
American Saw and Manufacturing Co.
301 Chestnut St.
East Longmeadow 01028   (413) 525-3961

Established in 1970 in MA.
Donor(s): American Saw and Manufacturing Co., Irene E. Davis.
Foundation type: Company-sponsored
Financial data (yr. ended 12/31/90): Assets, $22,497,679 (M); gifts received, $2,325,000; expenditures, $1,320,749; qualifying distributions, $1,305,874, including $1,240,440 for 145 grants (high: $325,000; low: $10).
Purpose and activities: Emphasis on higher education and Catholic institutions, including churches; grants also for social services, hospitals, and community funds.
Fields of interest: Higher education, Catholic giving, social services, hospitals, community funds.
Types of support: Operating budgets, continuing support, annual campaigns, seed money, emergency funds, building funds, land acquisition, general purposes.
Limitations: Giving primarily in western MA. No grants to individuals, or for deficit financing, equipment, endowment funds, matching gifts, scholarships, fellowships, research, special projects, publications, or conferences; no loans.
Application information: Application form not required.
  Initial approach: Proposal
  Copies of proposal: 1
  Board meeting date(s): As required
  Write: John H. Davis, Trustee
Trustees: John H. Davis, Mary E. Davis, Stephen A. Davis, Robert R. Lepak.
Number of staff: None.
EIN: 237102734

1179
Demoulas Foundation ▼
875 East St.
Tewksbury 01876

Trust established in 1964 in MA.
Donor(s): Demoulas Super Markets, Inc., and members of the Demoulas family.
Foundation type: Company-sponsored
Financial data (yr. ended 12/31/90): Assets, $29,046,377 (M); expenditures, $1,915,365; qualifying distributions, $1,860,840, including $1,771,218 for 157 grants (high: $250,000; low: $50; average: $1,000-$10,000).
Purpose and activities: Grants largely for the Greek Orthodox Church, higher and secondary education, youth agencies, and hospitals and health organizations.
Fields of interest: Religion, higher education, secondary education, youth, hospitals, health.
Application information:
  Initial approach: Letter
  Write: Telemachus A. Demoulas, Trustee
Trustees: A.T. Demoulas, Telemachus A. Demoulas, D. Harold Sullivan.
EIN: 042723441
Recent health grants:
1179-1 Anna Jaques Hospital, Newburyport, MA, $10,000. 1990.

1179-2 Lowell General Hospital, Lowell, MA, $250,000. For pledge. 1990.
1179-3 Lowell General Hospital, Lowell, MA, $50,000. For intensive care. 1990.
1179-4 Massachusetts General Hospital, Boston, MA, $200,000. 1990.
1179-5 Massachusetts General Hospital, Boston, MA, $25,000. For Desanctis Scholarship Fund. 1990.
1179-6 Massachusetts General Hospital, Boston, MA, $10,000. For Gastro-Endoscopy Fund. 1990.
1179-7 Saint Josephs Hospital, Lowell, MA, $150,000. 1990.
1179-8 Shriners Burns Institute, Boston, MA, $10,000. 1990.

1180
Digital Equipment Corporate Giving Program
111 Powdermill Rd.
Maynard 01754-1418   (508) 493-9210

Financial data (yr. ended 12/31/90): Total giving, $37,000,000, including $31,000,000 for grants and $6,000,000 for employee matching gifts.
Purpose and activities: "Digital's Corporate Contributions Program seeks to achieve the following goals on a worldwide basis: to improve the quality of life and encourage active employee participation in those communities in which we conduct business; to promote solutions to critical challenges facing the company and the community; to help people develop the skills needed to support industrial growth and productivity; to encourage and promote equal access for all citizens; to promote advances in technical and scientific knowledge." To achieve these goals, Digital supports a variety of programs and activities through a strategic plan that is based on priorities and available resources. Grants, in the form of cash and equipment, are awarded in five program areas: education, culture and the arts, health care, civic/environment, and programs for people with disabilities. In addition, the company has programs that support the interests of its employees, through the employee scholarship program and the matching gift program to education, the United Way and other nonprofits.
Fields of interest: Israel, higher education, arts, health, civic affairs, humanities, youth, hospitals, cultural programs, education—minorities, environment, handicapped, secondary education, Europe, Asia, AIDS, science and technology.
Types of support: Research, scholarship funds, matching funds, employee matching gifts, employee-related scholarships, donated products.
Limitations: Giving primarily in Digital operating areas worldwide, including the U.S., Europe, Asia, and Israel. No support for political activities, religious and veterans' organizations. No grants for endowments, or capital campaigns.
Publications: Informational brochure (including application guidelines).
Application information: Application form not required.
  Initial approach: Letter and proposal
  Copies of proposal: 1
  Deadline(s): None
  Final notification: 120 days
  Write: Jane Hamel, Corp. Contrib. Mgr.

Number of staff: 4 full-time professional; 1 full-time support.

1181
Harry Doehla Foundation, Inc.
c/o Singer and Lusardi
370 Main St.
Worcester 01608   (508) 756-4657

Incorporated in 1950 in DE.
Donor(s): Harry Doehla.‡
Foundation type: Independent
Financial data (yr. ended 03/31/91): Assets, $916,190 (M); expenditures, $297,073; qualifying distributions, $276,967, including $276,000 for 24 grants (high: $75,000; low: $1,000).
Fields of interest: Higher education, health, mental health.
Limitations: Giving primarily in MA. No grants to individuals.
Application information:
  Initial approach: Letter
  Deadline(s): None
  Write: Henry Lusardi, Pres.
Officers: Henry Lusardi, Pres.; Philip Straus, V.P.; Paul Singer, Secy.; Philip H. Steckler, Jr., Treas.
EIN: 026014132

1182
Eastern Bank Foundation
270 Union St.
Lynn 01901-1380

Established in 1985 in MA.
Foundation type: Independent
Financial data (yr. ended 10/31/91): Assets, $2,166,829 (M); expenditures, $104,320; qualifying distributions, $102,965, including $102,565 for 53 grants (high: $33,800; low: $25).
Purpose and activities: Support primarily for hospitals and hospital building funds, hospices, and health associations, including drug abuse and AIDS programs; support also for community funds and development, family services, business education, museums, and the performing arts.
Fields of interest: Hospitals, hospitals—building funds, hospices, drug abuse, AIDS, community funds, family services, business education, museums, performing arts.
Limitations: Giving primarily in the North Shore of MA.
Application information: The foundation currently funds numerous projects, and funds available for additional grants are restricted due to existing obligations which presently consume the income generated by the Trust.
Trustees: Douglas F. Allen, Joseph A. Jones, Stanley J. Lukowski, Francis F. Perry, Robert H. Studley.
EIN: 222623146

1183
Georgiana Goddard Eaton Memorial Fund
c/o Welch & Forbes
45 School St.
Boston 02108   (617) 523-1635

Trust established in 1917 in MA.
Donor(s): Georgiana Goddard Eaton.‡

Foundation type: Independent
Financial data (yr. ended 06/30/91): Assets, $8,078,346 (M); expenditures, $455,447; qualifying distributions, $347,834, including $278,358 for 6 grants (high: $257,358; low: $1,000) and $69,476 for 6 grants to individuals (high: $18,480; low: $6,270; average: $8,000-$12,000).
Purpose and activities: Support currently for a rehabilitation agency, including support through pensions to its former employees.
Fields of interest: Rehabilitation, employment, environment, family services, handicapped, recreation, social services, homeless, urban development, welfare.
Types of support: General purposes.
Limitations: Giving limited to Boston, MA. No grants to individuals (except former employees of Community Workshops, Inc.), or for endowment funds, or matching gifts; no loans.
Application information: Application form not required.
  Initial approach: Brief proposal
  Copies of proposal: 1
  Deadline(s): None
  Board meeting date(s): As required
  Write: Kenneth S. Safe, Jr., Trustee
Trustees: Kenneth S. Safe, Jr., Welch & Forbes.
Number of staff: None.
EIN: 046112820

1184
EG&G Foundation
c/o EG&G, Inc.
45 William St.
Wellesley 02181   (617) 237-5100

Established in 1979 in MA.
Donor(s): EG&G, Inc.
Foundation type: Company-sponsored
Financial data (yr. ended 06/30/91): Assets, $5,390,643 (M); expenditures, $420,204; qualifying distributions, $414,006, including $301,339 for 166 grants (high: $25,000; low: $25) and $112,667 for 235 employee matching gifts.
Purpose and activities: Grants primarily for higher education, including an employee matching gift program; support also for community funds, health, and welfare.
Fields of interest: Higher education, community funds, health, welfare.
Types of support: Employee matching gifts, general purposes.
Application information: Application form required.
  Deadline(s): None
  Write: Kathleen M. Russo, Trustee
Trustees: Donald M. Kerr, John M. Kucharski, Richard F. Murphy, Samuel Rubinovitz, Kathleen M. Russo.
EIN: 042683042

1185
Ruth H. and Warren A. Ellsworth Foundation
370 Main St., 12th Fl.
Worcester 01608   (508) 798-8621

Trust established in 1964 in MA.
Donor(s): Ruth H. Ellsworth.‡

Foundation type: Independent
Financial data (yr. ended 12/31/90): Assets, $11,315,888 (M); expenditures, $630,112; qualifying distributions, $569,551, including $523,500 for 41 grants (high: $60,000; low: $1,000; average: $7,500).
Purpose and activities: Emphasis on higher education, scientific research, youth agencies, and hospitals.
Fields of interest: Education, higher education, youth, welfare, science and technology, health, hospitals.
Types of support: Operating budgets, general purposes, continuing support, annual campaigns, seed money, emergency funds, deficit financing, building funds, equipment, land acquisition.
Limitations: Giving primarily in the Worcester, MA, area. No grants to individuals, or for endowment funds, scholarships, fellowships, research, publications, conferences, or matching gifts; no loans.
Application information: Application form not required.
  Initial approach: Proposal
  Copies of proposal: 1
  Deadline(s): Submit proposal preferably before June; deadline Nov. 30
  Board meeting date(s): June and Dec.
  Final notification: By Dec. 28
  Write: Sumner B. Tilton, Jr., Trustee
Trustees: David H. Ellsworth, Sumner B. Tilton, Jr., Joyce E. Wetzel.
Number of staff: 1 part-time professional.
EIN: 046113491

1186
Aubert J. Fay Charitable Fund
100 Holyrood Ave.
Lowell 01852-3804   (508) 453-8452

Established in 1965.
Foundation type: Independent
Financial data (yr. ended 12/31/91): Assets, $2,440,952 (M); expenditures, $127,172; qualifying distributions, $120,395, including $76,050 for 32 grants (high: $10,000; low: $250).
Fields of interest: Catholic giving, Catholic welfare, hospitals, youth, social services.
Limitations: Giving limited to Lowell, MA. No grants to individuals.
Application information:
  Initial approach: Letter
  Deadline(s): None
  Write: Gerald F. Donehue, Trustee
Trustees: Gerald F. Donehue, Stephen L. Gervais, Stanley J. Polak.
EIN: 510203622

1187
The Feldberg Family Foundation
P.O. Box 9175
Framingham 01701

Established in 1951 in MA.
Donor(s): Max Feldberg, Morris Feldberg.‡
Foundation type: Independent
Financial data (yr. ended 11/30/91): Assets, $4,596,793 (M); expenditures, $782,978; qualifying distributions, $780,000, including $780,000 for 9 grants (high: $350,000; low: $5,000).

Fields of interest: Jewish welfare, hospitals, higher education.
Limitations: Giving primarily in MA. No grants to individuals.
Application information: Contributes only to pre-selected organizations. Applications not accepted.
Board meeting date(s): As required
Trustees: Stanley H. Feldberg, Sumner Feldberg.
EIN: 046065393

1188
Fidelity Foundation ▼
Boston Safe Deposit & Trust Co.
82 Devonshire St., S4A
Boston 02109-3614   (617) 570-6806

Trust established in 1965 in MA.
Donor(s): Fidelity Management & Research Co. (FMR).
Foundation type: Company-sponsored
Financial data (yr. ended 12/31/90): Assets, $25,140,672 (M); expenditures, $2,049,161; qualifying distributions, $2,049,161, including $1,939,161 for grants (average: $5,000-$50,000).
Purpose and activities: Giving largely to organizations working in the fields of community development, cultural affairs, education, and health.
Fields of interest: Education, community development, health, cultural programs.
Types of support: Building funds, special projects, endowment funds, employee matching gifts, capital campaigns, technical assistance.
Limitations: Giving primarily in MA, and in other communities where Fidelity employees live and work. No grants to individuals.
Publications: Informational brochure (including application guidelines).
Application information: Application form required.
Initial approach: Request for guidelines
Copies of proposal: 1
Deadline(s): Mar. 1 and Oct. 30
Board meeting date(s): Nov.
Final notification: Immediately following board meeting
Write: Anne-Marie Soulliere, Fdn. Dir.
Trustees: Edward C. Johnson III, Caleb Loring, Jr., Ross E. Sherbrooke.
Number of staff: 1 full-time professional; 2 full-time support; 1 part-time support.
EIN: 046131201

1189
First Petroleum Corporation Charitable Trust
800 South St.
P.O. Box 9161
Waltham 02254-9161

Established in 1986 in MA.
Donor(s): Global Petroleum Corp.
Foundation type: Company-sponsored
Financial data (yr. ended 12/31/91): Assets, $189,375 (M); gifts received, $350,000; expenditures, $427,188; qualifying distributions, $427,100, including $427,100 for 41 grants (high: $231,600; low: $100).

Fields of interest: Higher education, education, social services, community funds, Jewish giving, Jewish welfare, hospitals.
Limitations: Giving primarily in MA.
Application information: Application form not required.
Deadline(s): None
Write: Richard Slifka, Trustee
Trustees: Alfred Slifka, Richard Slifka.
EIN: 046549918

1190
Florence Charitable Trust
99 Lyman Rd.
Brookline 02167

Established in 1967.
Foundation type: Independent
Financial data (yr. ended 12/31/90): Assets, $405,357 (M); expenditures, $261,026; qualifying distributions, $245,514, including $245,514 for grants.
Fields of interest: Jewish giving, health, law and justice, education, general charitable giving.
Application information: Contributes only to pre-selected organizations. Applications not accepted.
Trustee: Charlotte Florence.
EIN: 046171728

1191
Joseph F. and Clara Ford Foundation
850 Boylston St., Suite 403
Chestnut Hill 02167

Established in 1946 in MA.
Donor(s): Clara Ford,‡ Joseph F. Ford.‡
Foundation type: Independent
Financial data (yr. ended 07/31/91): Assets, $2,342,418 (M); expenditures, $398,669; qualifying distributions, $280,000, including $280,000 for 12 grants (high: $126,703; low: $5,460; average: $9,000-$15,000).
Purpose and activities: Giving primarily for colleges and universities, including medical schools and a Jewish theological seminary; support also for hospitals and Jewish organizations.
Fields of interest: Higher education, medical education, theological education, hospitals, Jewish giving.
Limitations: Giving primarily in MA. No grants to individuals.
Application information: Contributes only to pre-selected organizations. Applications not accepted.
Trustees: David Casty, Avram J. Goldberg, Joseph M. Linsey, Irving W. Rabb, Norman S. Rabb.
EIN: 046111820

1192
Fraser Family Foundation, Inc.
c/o Boyd, MacCrellish & Wheeler
75 Federal St.
Boston 02110

Established in 1988 in MA.
Donor(s): Richard M. Fraser, Richard M. & Helen T. Fraser Foundation.
Foundation type: Independent

Financial data (yr. ended 12/31/91): Assets, $378,047 (M); gifts received, $350,000; expenditures, $231,167; qualifying distributions, $231,025, including $231,000 for 12 grants (high: $61,000; low: $5,000).
Fields of interest: Museums, performing arts, hospitals, heart disease, health associations.
Limitations: Giving primarily in Boston, MA. No grants to individuals.
Application information: Contributes only to pre-selected organizations. Applications not accepted.
Officers: Richard M. Fraser, Pres.; Helen T. Fraser, Treas.
EIN: 043005593

1193
George F. and Sybil H. Fuller Foundation ▼
105 Madison St.
Worcester 01610   (508) 756-5111

Trust established in 1955 in MA.
Donor(s): George Freeman Fuller.‡
Foundation type: Independent
Financial data (yr. ended 12/31/90): Assets, $30,638,719 (M); expenditures, $3,279,646; qualifying distributions, $3,160,720, including $3,088,975 for 112 grants (high: $460,000; low: $1,000; average: $5,000-$50,000).
Purpose and activities: Emphasis on higher education, cultural institutions, historic preservation, hospitals, community funds, and youth organizations; support also for social service agencies and schools.
Fields of interest: Higher education, cultural programs, historic preservation, hospitals, community funds, youth, social services, education.
Types of support: Annual campaigns, seed money, emergency funds, general purposes, building funds, endowment funds, research, continuing support, renovation projects.
Limitations: Giving primarily in MA, with emphasis on Worcester. No grants to individuals, or for scholarships, fellowships, or matching gifts; no loans.
Application information: Application form not required.
Initial approach: Proposal
Copies of proposal: 1
Deadline(s): None
Board meeting date(s): Jan.-Mar., June-Aug., and Oct.-Dec.
Final notification: Varies
Write: Russell E. Fuller, Chair.
Officers and Trustees:* Russell E. Fuller,* Chair. and Treas.; Robert P. Hallock, Jr.,* Vice-Chair.; David P. Hallock,* Secy.; Ernest M. Fuller, Joyce I. Fuller, Mark W. Fuller.
Number of staff: 1
EIN: 046125606
Recent health grants:
1193-1 Clara Barton Camp for Diabetic Girls, North Oxford, MA, $25,000. 1990.
1193-2 Diabetes Foundation of New England, Worcester, MA, $60,000. 1990.
1193-3 Memorial Hospital Foundation, Worcester, MA, $25,000. 1990.
1193-4 Spectrum House, Westboro, MA, $40,000. 1990.

1193-5 Tufts University, Dental School, Medford, MA, $10,000. 1990.
1193-6 Tufts University, Veterinary School, Medford, MA, $35,000. 1990.
1193-7 Worcester Pastoral Counseling Center, Worcester, MA, $12,000. 1990.

1194
G. Peabody & Rose Gardner Charitable Trust
c/o Gardner & Preston Moss, Inc.
101 Federal St.
Boston 02110

Established in 1956 in MA.
Foundation type: Independent
Financial data (yr. ended 12/31/91): Assets, $2,451,481 (M); expenditures, $144,909; qualifying distributions, $121,097, including $120,000 for 47 grants (high: $12,500; low: $500).
Fields of interest: Hospitals, social services, museums, cultural programs, community funds.
Limitations: Giving primarily in MA. No grants to individuals.
Application information: Application form not required.
  Initial approach: Letter
  Deadline(s): Nov. 1
  Write: John L. Gardner, Trustee
Trustees: George P. Gardner, John L. Gardner, Robert G. Gardner.
EIN: 046018072

1195
General Cinema Corporate Giving Program
27 Boylston St.
Chestnut Hill 02167   (617) 232-8200
One copy of proposal to: Grant Management Associates, Proposal Secy., Review Staff for General Cinema, 100 Franklin St., Boston, MA 02110

Purpose and activities: Support for medical research, child and youth programs, the arts and culture, and education.
Fields of interest: Child welfare, medical research, museums, education, higher education, cultural programs, arts, youth.
Types of support: Research, capital campaigns, employee matching gifts, general purposes, matching funds.
Limitations: Giving primarily in the Greater Boston area. No support for sectarian religious activities; political and lobbying activities; projects usually supported by the general public; recent grantees; organizations whose applications have been denied within the past year; and instances where General Cinema may become the predominant source of an organization's support. No grants to individuals, or for film, operating budgets, or deficits.
Publications: Application guidelines.
Application information: Application form not required.
  Initial approach: Letter and proposal; one copy of proposal must be sent to proposal review staff at Grant Management Assocs.
  Copies of proposal: 2
  Deadline(s): Jan. 2, Apr. 1, July 1, and Oct. 1

Board meeting date(s): Feb., May, Aug., and Nov.
Final notification: After meeting
Write: Kay M. Kilpatrick, Contribs. Secy.
Corporate Contributions Committee: Richard A. Smith, Chair.; Samuel Frankenheim, J. Atwood Ives, Brian J. Knez, Robert A. Smith, Robert J. Tarr, Jr.

1196
General Cinema Corporation Charitable Foundation, Inc.
27 Boylston St.
Chestnut Hill 02167-1700   (617) 232-8200
Additional application address: c/o Grants Management Assocs., 230 Congress St., Boston, MA 02110

Established in 1989 in MA.
Donor(s): General Cinema Corp.
Foundation type: Company-sponsored
Financial data (yr. ended 10/31/90): Assets, $21,672,397 (M); expenditures, $402,118; qualifying distributions, $272,000, including $272,000 for 5 grants (high: $125,000; low: $5,000).
Purpose and activities: Support primarily for medical research, children and youth, arts, and education.
Fields of interest: Medical research, hospitals, AIDS, youth, child development, arts, education, higher education, cultural programs, homeless, minorities.
Types of support: Annual campaigns, building funds, fellowships, matching funds, seed money, capital campaigns, general purposes, special projects.
Limitations: Giving primarily in the greater Boston, MA, area. No grants to individuals.
Publications: 990-PF, application guidelines.
Application information:
  Initial approach: Letter
  Copies of proposal: 2
  Deadline(s): Jan. 2, Apr. 1, July 1, and Oct. 1
  Board meeting date(s): Quarterly
  Write: Kay M. Kilpatrick, Contribs. Administrator
Officers and Directors:* Richard A. Smith,* Chair. and Pres.; Robert J. Tarr, Jr.,* V.P.; Brian J. Knez, Robert A. Smith.
Number of staff: 1
EIN: 223026002

1197
Gerondelis Foundation, Inc.
56 Central Ave.
Lynn 01901   (617) 595-3311

Established in 1966 in MA.
Foundation type: Independent
Financial data (yr. ended 12/31/91): Assets, $5,054,595 (M); expenditures, $320,759; qualifying distributions, $312,009, including $215,300 for 30 grants (high: $6,000; low: $500) and $39,000 for 13 grants to individuals of $3,000 each.
Fields of interest: Education, higher education, child development, Greece, medical education, hospitals, civic affairs.
Types of support: Scholarship funds.
Limitations: Giving primarily in MA.

Application information: Application form not required.
  Copies of proposal: 1
  Deadline(s): None
  Board meeting date(s): 1st Wednesday in Jan., Apr., July, and Oct.
  Final notification: Following board meetings
  Write: Charles Demakis, Pres.
Officers and Board Members: Charles Demakis, Pres., Clerk, and Dir.; James C. Kaddaras, Treas. and Dir.; Gregory C. Demakis, Louis Demakes, Thomas C. Demakis, Benjamin A. Smith II, Nicholas T. Zervas, M.D.
Directors: Paul C. Demakis, Thomas L. Demakis, Michael Frangos, George J. Marcopoulos, Christopher Scangas.
Number of staff: 1 part-time professional; 1 part-time support.
EIN: 046130871

1198
The Goldberg Family Foundation
(Formerly Avram & Carol Goldberg Charitable Foundation)
Boston Safe Deposit & Trust Co.
Boston 02106

Established in 1961 in MA.
Foundation type: Independent
Financial data (yr. ended 06/30/90): Assets, $6,031,655 (M); gifts received, $529,546; expenditures, $281,773; qualifying distributions, $277,822, including $250,050 for 151 grants (high: $37,500; low: $2).
Fields of interest: Higher education, Jewish welfare, education, child welfare, family services, social services, women, health, arts, general charitable giving.
Types of support: Annual campaigns, building funds, continuing support, capital campaigns, endowment funds, general purposes.
Limitations: Giving primarily in greater Boston, MA, area and overseas. No support for advocacy groups. No grants to individuals; no loans.
Application information: Application form not required.
  Initial approach: Letter
  Deadline(s): None
  Board meeting date(s): Varies
  Write: Avram J. Goldberg, Trustee
Trustees: Avram J. Goldberg, Carol R. Goldberg, Deborah Goldberg, Joshua Goldberg.
EIN: 046039556

1199
The Nehemias Gorin Foundation
c/o William Gorin
1330 Beacon St.
Brookline 02146   (617) 738-4319

Established in 1964 in MA.
Donor(s): Nehemias Gorin.‡
Foundation type: Independent
Financial data (yr. ended 11/30/90): Assets, $2,762,000 (M); gifts received, $8,000; expenditures, $309,900; qualifying distributions, $282,400, including $282,400 for 68 grants (high: $60,000; low: $100; average: $100-$70,000).
Purpose and activities: Support for health, including hospitals and cancer research; Jewish

welfare funds and other Jewish organizations and Israel; higher education; museums and other cultural programs; community funds; and Catholic organizations.
Fields of interest: Health, hospitals, Jewish giving, Jewish welfare, education, higher education, arts, community funds, aged, Catholic giving.
Types of support: Annual campaigns.
Limitations: Giving primarily in MA.
Application information: Applications not accepted.
> *Board meeting date(s):* Oct. 14
Trustees: Bertha G. Fritz, Stephen Goldenberg, William Gorin, Ida G. Leckart.
Number of staff: None.
EIN: 046119939

1200
The Grass Foundation
77 Reservoir Rd.
Quincy 02170   (617) 773-0002

Incorporated in 1955 in MA.
Donor(s): Grass Instrument Co., Albert M. Grass, Ellen R. Grass, Cannon Manufacturing Co.
Foundation type: Independent
Financial data (yr. ended 12/31/90): Assets, $5,426,332 (M); gifts received, $217,000; expenditures, $498,201; qualifying distributions, $463,255, including $405,461 for 25 grants (high: $162,954; low: $1,000).
Purpose and activities: To encourage research in biology, physiology, neurobiology, and neurophysiology and allied fields of science and medicine; grants primarily for fellowships for summer study at a marine biological laboratory, lectureships, and for higher education.
Fields of interest: Medical research, science and technology, marine sciences, biology, biochemistry, biological sciences, medical sciences.
Types of support: Fellowships, research, lectureships.
Publications: Application guidelines, program policy statement.
Application information: Application formats and deadlines depend upon type of grant; specific information will be sent upon request.
Application form not required.
> *Board meeting date(s):* Feb. and July
> *Write:* Mary G. Grass, Secy.
Officers and Directors:* Ellen R. Grass,* Pres.; Albert M. Grass,* V.P.; Mary G. Grass,* Secy.; Richmond B. Woodward,* Treas.; George H. Acheson, M.D., Sidney R. Goldring, M.D., Bernice Grafstein, Henry J. Grass, M.D., R.R. Hoy, Donald B. Lindsley, Steven J. Zottoli, Ph.D.
Number of staff: 1 part-time professional.
EIN: 046049529

1201
Francis A. & Jacquelyn H. Harrington Foundation
370 Main St., Suite 1200
Worcester 01608   (508) 798-8621

Trust established in 1965 in MA.
Donor(s): Francis A. Harrington,‡ Jacquelyn H. Harrington.
Foundation type: Independent

Financial data (yr. ended 12/31/91): Assets, $9,648,295 (M); expenditures, $430,025; qualifying distributions, $430,025, including $405,500 for 37 grants (high: $100,000; low: $1,000; average: $8,100) and $10,000 for 1 loan.
Purpose and activities: Giving primarily for higher and secondary education, a science center, scientific and medical research, hospitals, and social services.
Fields of interest: Higher education, secondary education, science and technology, medical research, hospitals, social services.
Types of support: Capital campaigns, equipment, general purposes, special projects.
Limitations: Giving primarily in Worcester, MA. No grants to individuals, or for scholarships; no loans.
Application information: Application form not required.
> *Initial approach:* Letter
> *Copies of proposal:* 1
> *Deadline(s):* Nov. 30, preferably before June
> *Board meeting date(s):* June and Dec. 15
> *Final notification:* Dec. 31
> *Write:* Sumner B. Tilton, Jr., Trustee
Trustees: Francis A. Harrington, Jr., James H. Harrington, Sumner B. Tilton, Jr.
Number of staff: 1 part-time professional.
EIN: 046125088

1202
George Harrington Trust
c/o Choate, Hall & Stewart
Exchange Place, 53 State St.
Boston 02109   (617) 227-5020

Trust established in 1936 in MA.
Donor(s): George Harrington.‡
Foundation type: Independent
Financial data (yr. ended 08/31/91): Assets, $2,613,999 (M); expenditures, $274,546; qualifying distributions, $255,296, including $250,000 for 3 grants (high: $150,000; low: $20,000).
Purpose and activities: "To stimulate major new efforts in the understanding, prevention, and treatment of the mental disorders of adolescents and young adults through the George Harrington Professorship in Clinical and Epidemiologic Psychiatry at Harvard Medical School."
Fields of interest: Mental health, psychiatry.
Types of support: Professorships.
Limitations: Giving limited to Cambridge, MA. No grants to individuals.
Publications: 990-PF.
Application information: Application form not required.
> *Initial approach:* Proposal
> *Deadline(s):* Feb., May, Aug., and Nov.
> *Board meeting date(s):* Mar., June, Sept., and Dec.
> *Write:* John M. Cornish, Trustee
Trustees: John M. Cornish, William G. Cornish.
EIN: 046037725

1203
Henderson Foundation
P.O. Box 420
Sudbury 01776   (508) 443-4646

Trust established in 1947 in MA.

Donor(s): Ernest Henderson,‡ George B. Henderson,‡ J. Brooks Fenno,‡ Ernest Henderson III.
Foundation type: Independent
Financial data (yr. ended 12/31/90): Assets, $10,856,831 (M); expenditures, $578,600; qualifying distributions, $491,771, including $478,120 for 95 grants (high: $50,000; low: $1,000).
Purpose and activities: Support for public policy organizations in the field of foreign policy, defense, peace, and media issues, and higher and pre-college education; minor support for hospitals and health organizations, and churches.
Fields of interest: Public policy, foreign policy, peace, media and communications, higher education, elementary education, secondary education, hospitals, health associations, religion—Christian.
Types of support: Continuing support, general purposes.
Limitations: No grants to individuals, or for scholarships or fellowships.
Application information:
> *Initial approach:* Letter
> *Copies of proposal:* 1
> *Deadline(s):* None
> *Board meeting date(s):* As required
> *Write:* Ernest Henderson III, Trustee
Trustees: Barclay G.S. Henderson, Ernest Henderson III, Joseph Petrone.
EIN: 046051095

1204
Nan and Matilda Heydt Fund
c/o Baybank Valley Trust Co.
P.O. Box 3422
Burlington 01803   (617) 273-1700

Established in 1966 in MA.
Donor(s): Matilda L. Heydt.‡
Foundation type: Independent
Financial data (yr. ended 12/31/90): Assets, $3,691,709 (M); expenditures, $268,038; qualifying distributions, $244,466, including $219,779 for grants.
Purpose and activities: Grants for public charitable purposes including health, welfare, the humanities, and education; emphasis on child welfare and youth agencies, community funds, and aid to the handicapped.
Fields of interest: Health, humanities, education, child welfare, youth, community funds, handicapped.
Types of support: Capital campaigns, equipment, land acquisition, matching funds, publications, renovation projects, seed money, special projects.
Limitations: Giving limited to Hampden County, MA. No grants to individuals, or for endowment funds, scholarships, fellowships, or operating budgets; no loans.
Publications: Informational brochure (including application guidelines).
Application information: Application form not required.
> *Initial approach:* Telephone, letter, or proposal
> *Copies of proposal:* 12
> *Deadline(s):* Submit proposal preferably in Dec., Apr., or Aug.; deadline 1st Monday in Jan. and May, and 1st Tuesday in Sept.
> *Board meeting date(s):* Mar., July, and Nov.
> *Final notification:* 4 months

Write: Bernie Stephan, Trust Officer, Baybank Valley Trust Co.
Trustee: Baybank Valley Trust Co.
Number of staff: 1 part-time professional; 1 part-time support.
EIN: 046136421

1205
High Meadow Foundation, Inc.
c/o Country Curtains, Inc.
Main St.
Stockbridge 01262   (413) 298-5565

Established in 1984 in MA.
Donor(s): John H. Fitzpatrick, Jane P. Fitzpatrick, Country Curtains, Inc., Housatonic Curtain Co., Red Lion Inn, Country Curtains Retail.
Foundation type: Independent
Financial data (yr. ended 09/30/91): Assets, $952,516 (M); gifts received, $673,296; expenditures, $887,667; qualifying distributions, $888,649, including $880,919 for 301 grants (high: $103,925; low: $25).
Purpose and activities: Support primarily for the performing arts, especially theater and music, and other cultural organizations; giving also for health, social services, and higher and other education.
Fields of interest: Performing arts, theater, music, cultural programs, arts, health, social services, higher education, elementary education.
Types of support: Annual campaigns, building funds, capital campaigns, continuing support, deficit financing, emergency funds, equipment, matching funds, employee-related scholarships, special projects.
Limitations: Giving primarily in Bershire County, MA.
Application information: Application form not required.
  Initial approach: Letter
  Deadline(s): None
  Write: Robert B. Trask, Dir.
Officers and Directors:* Jane P. Fitzpatrick,* Chair. and Treas.; John H. Fitzpatrick,* Pres.; JoAnn Brown, Nancy J. Fitzpatrick, Mary Ann Snyder, Robert B. Trask.
Number of staff: 1
EIN: 222527419

1206
The Hinduja Foundation, U.S.
c/o David Donaldson, Ropes & Gray
One International Place, Rm. 250
Boston 02110-2624

Established in 1984 in MA.
Donor(s): Hinduja Trust.
Foundation type: Independent
Financial data (yr. ended 12/31/91): Assets, $640,328 (M); gifts received, $466,025; expenditures, $291,694; qualifying distributions, $259,505, including $245,839 for 13 grants (high: $125,000; low: $100).
Fields of interest: Hospitals, higher education, cultural programs, general charitable giving.
Types of support: Research, general purposes.
Limitations: Giving primarily in Boston, MA, and New York, NY. No grants to individuals.
Publications: Newsletter.

Application information: Contributes only to pre-selected organizations. Applications not accepted.
Officer: John E. Lawrence, Pres.
Trustees: G.P. Hinduja, P.P. Hinduja, Srichand P. Hinduja.
EIN: 222570780

1207
The Hoche-Scofield Foundation
c/o Shawmut Bank, N.A.
446 Main St.
Worcester 01608   (508) 793-4205

Established in 1983 in MA.
Donor(s): William B. Scofield.‡
Foundation type: Independent
Financial data (yr. ended 06/30/91): Assets, $10,312,181 (M); expenditures, $716,201; qualifying distributions, $641,026, including $601,695 for 81 grants (high: $66,529; low: $1,000; average: $1,000-$10,000).
Fields of interest: Community development, higher education, cultural programs, health, social services, women, youth, disadvantaged, child welfare.
Types of support: Capital campaigns, continuing support, seed money, special projects.
Limitations: Giving primarily in the city and county of Worcester, MA.
Publications: Application guidelines.
Application information: Application form required.
  Initial approach: Letter or telephone
  Copies of proposal: 4
  Deadline(s): Feb. 15, May 15, Aug. 15, and Nov. 15
  Board meeting date(s): Mar. 15, June 15, Sept. 15, and Dec. 15
  Final notification: Mar. 31, June 30, Sept. 30, and Dec. 30
  Write: Stephen G. Fritch, V.P., Shawmut Bank, N.A.
Trustees: Henry B. Dewey, Lois B. Green, Paul S. Morgan, Shawmut Bank, N.A.
EIN: 222519554

1208
The John Ernest Hoffman Foundation
c/o Loring, Wolcott & Coolidge Office
230 Congress St.
Boston 02110

Established in 1985 in MA.
Donor(s): Effe K.D. Hoffman.
Foundation type: Independent
Financial data (yr. ended 12/31/90): Assets, $2,514,569 (M); expenditures, $135,757; qualifying distributions, $121,653, including $119,952 for 6 grants (high: $29,952; low: $10,000).
Fields of interest: Hospitals, cancer, education, secondary education, higher education, social services, religious welfare.
Types of support: Annual campaigns, building funds, continuing support, capital campaigns, operating budgets, general purposes.
Limitations: Giving primarily in Boston, MA. No grants to individuals.
Publications: 990-PF.

Application information: Contributes only to pre-selected organizations. Applications not accepted.
Trustees: Effe K.D. Hoffman, Stephen A. Moore, Roger M. Thomas.
Number of staff: None.
EIN: 222677966

1209
Home for Aged Men in the City of Brockton
c/o Creedon & Creedon
One Centre St.
Brockton 02401

Trust established in MA.
Donor(s): Horace Howard.‡
Foundation type: Operating
Financial data (yr. ended 03/31/91): Assets, $2,682,103 (M); gifts received, $6,165; expenditures, $143,123; qualifying distributions, $113,953, including $109,415 for 11 grants (high: $73,665; low: $2,000).
Purpose and activities: A private operating foundation; awards grants for homes for the aged and hospitals to encourage development of the facilities' public assistance programs; support also for a seminary.
Fields of interest: Aged, hospitals, theological education.
Limitations: Giving primarily in MA. No grants to individuals.
Application information: Contributes only to pre-selected organizations. Applications not accepted.
Officers: John Creedon, Pres.; Anthony Froio, Treas.; Ida Cassiano, Clerk.
EIN: 042103796

1210
Charles H. Hood Foundation
95 Berkeley St., Suite 201
Boston 02116   (617) 695-9439

Fund established in 1931; incorporated in 1942 in NH.
Donor(s): Charles H. Hood.‡
Foundation type: Independent
Financial data (yr. ended 12/31/90): Assets, $21,575,343 (M); expenditures, $1,115,409; qualifying distributions, $1,006,437, including $970,824 for 13 grants (high: $275,000; low: $18,500; average: $30,000-$50,000).
Purpose and activities: Supports projects concerned with child health through its Child Health Advisory Committee; emphasis on the initiation or furtherance of medical research and related projects contributing to a reduction of the health problems and health needs of large numbers of children.
Fields of interest: Health, medical research, child welfare.
Types of support: Research.
Limitations: Giving limited to New England. No support for nutrition, public health, mental health, education, or social or general welfare. No grants to individuals, or for building or endowment funds, operating budgets, general support, publications, scholarships, fellowships, fundraising campaigns, or matching gifts; no loans.

Publications: Application guidelines.
Application information: Application form required.
  Initial approach: Letter or telephone
  Copies of proposal: 9
  Deadline(s): Submit proposal after Feb. 1 for Apr. 15 deadline, and after Aug. 1 for Oct. 15 deadline
  Board meeting date(s): Usually in June and Dec.
  Final notification: 60 to 70 days
  Write: Raymond Considine, Exec. Dir.
Officers and Members:* Charles H. Hood II,* Pres. and Treas.; Raymond Considine, Exec. Dir.; Roswell M. Boutwell III, John O. Parker, Henry M. Sanders.
Number of staff: 1 part-time professional; 1 part-time support.
EIN: 046036790
Recent health grants:
1210-1 Baystate Medical Center, Springfield, MA, $37,337. For pediatric research project, Specific Regulatory Effects of Gonadal Hormones on Growth Hormone Neuroaxis. 1990.
1210-2 Boston University Medical Center, Boston, MA, $45,000. For pediatric research project, ApoB Domain Required for LDL Assemble and Secretion. 1990.
1210-3 Childrens Hospital, Boston, MA, $43,375. For pediatric research project, Fetal Neucleated Erythrocytes (NRBC) in Maternal Blood: A Source of Fetal Cells for Prenatal Diagnosis. 1990.
1210-4 Childrens Hospital, Boston, MA, $42,606. For pediatric research project, Influences of Mechanical Forces on Gene Expression during Craniofacial Development. 1990.
1210-5 Childrens Hospital, Boston, MA, $42,575. For pediatric research project, Regulation of GATA Binding Transcription Factors in Normal and Abnormal Hematopoiesis in Children. 1990.
1210-6 Childrens Hospital, Boston, MA, $18,500. For pediatric research project, Molecular Basis of Autosomal Recessive Polycystic Kidney Disease in cpk Mouse and Man. 1990.
1210-7 Childrens Hospital, Bone Marrow Transplant Unit, Boston, MA, $250,000. 1990.
1210-8 Dana-Farber Cancer Institute, Boston, MA, $18,500. For pediatric research project, Studies on Regulation of Platelet-Derived Growth Factor Production by Endothelial Cells. 1990.
1210-9 Dartmouth Medical School, Center for Research on Families and Children with Disabilities, Hanover, NH, $275,000. 1990.
1210-10 Joslin Diabetes Center, Boston, MA, $51,602. For pediatric research project, Transgenic Approach to Analyze Putative Autoantigens in Type I Diabetes. 1990.
1210-11 University of Connecticut Health Center, Farmington, CT, $53,094. For pediatric research project, Regulation of Growth Plate Chondrocyte Maturation and Calcification by Thyroid Hormone. 1990.
1210-12 Yale University, School of Medicine, New Haven, CT, $53,235. For pediatric research project, Regulation of Gene Expression in Developing Epididymis. 1990.
1210-13 Yale University, School of Medicine, New Haven, CT, $40,000. For pediatric

research project, Identifying DNA Landmarks for Primary Hemochromatosis. 1990.

1211
The Hopedale Foundation
43 Hope St.
Hopedale 01747   (508) 473-0820

Trust established in 1946 in MA.
Donor(s): Draper Corp., Thomas H. West,‡ John D. Gannett.‡
Foundation type: Independent
Financial data (yr. ended 10/31/91): Assets, $4,594,470 (M); expenditures, $188,920; qualifying distributions, $255,570, including $179,000 for 23 grants (high: $55,000; low: $1,500) and $68,450 for 55 loans to individuals.
Purpose and activities: Emphasis on area community funds and hospitals; support also for museums and other cultural programs, health agencies, youth services, and higher education; student loans limited to local high school graduates. New grants only to organizations having direct impact on the local community.
Fields of interest: Community funds, hospitals, health services, youth, higher education, educational associations, social sciences, cultural programs, museums.
Types of support: Annual campaigns, capital campaigns, general purposes, student loans.
Limitations: Giving primarily in MA. No grants for endowment funds.
Application information: Application form not required.
  Initial approach: Letter
  Copies of proposal: 1
  Deadline(s): June 1 for student loans; no set deadline for grants
  Board meeting date(s): Feb., June, and Oct.
  Write: H. Raymond Grant, Secy.-Treas.
Officers and Trustees:* William B. Gannett,* Chair.; H. Raymond Grant, Secy.-Treas.; W. Gregory Burrill, Peter S. Ellis, Alfred H. Sparling, Jr., Thomas H. West, Jr.
Number of staff: 1 part-time professional; 1 part-time support.
EIN: 046044779

1212
Henry Hornblower Fund, Inc.
P.O. Box 2365
Boston 02107

Incorporated in 1945 in MA.
Donor(s): Hornblower & Weeks - Hemphill, Noyes.
Foundation type: Independent
Financial data (yr. ended 12/31/90): Assets, $2,631,713 (M); expenditures, $98,878; qualifying distributions, $85,600, including $81,600 for 32 grants (high: $5,000; low: $100) and $4,000 for 2 grants to individuals (high: $3,000; low: $1,000).
Purpose and activities: Emphasis on higher and secondary education, hospitals, and cultural programs; support also for needy individuals presently or formerly employed by Hornblower & Weeks.
Fields of interest: Higher education, secondary education, hospitals, cultural programs, fine arts, performing arts.

Types of support: Capital campaigns, endowment funds, emergency funds, general purposes.
Limitations: Giving primarily in Boston, MA.
Application information: Applications not accepted.
  Board meeting date(s): June and Dec.
  Write: Nathan N. Withington, Pres.
Officers and Directors:* Nathan N. Withington,* Pres.; Jack Beaty, V.P.; Karl Grace,* Treas.; Dudley H. Bradlee II.
Number of staff: 1 part-time support.
EIN: 237425285

1213
Mabel A. Horne Trust
c/o First National Bank of Boston
P.O. Box 1890
Boston 02105   (617) 434-5660

Trust established in 1964 in MA.
Donor(s): Mabel A. Horne.‡
Foundation type: Independent
Financial data (yr. ended 09/30/91): Assets, $4,507,951 (M); expenditures, $221,520; qualifying distributions, $196,838, including $185,500 for 23 grants (high: $20,000; low: $2,000; average: $1,000-$7,500).
Fields of interest: Family services, youth, aged, urban development, education, health services, health, social services.
Types of support: Capital campaigns.
Limitations: Giving limited to MA, with emphasis on Boston. No support for national organizations. No grants to individuals, or for conferences, film production, scholarships, travel, book publication, projects requiring multi-year commitment, or research projects not under the aegis of a recognized organization; no loans.
Publications: Application guidelines.
Application information: Application form required.
  Initial approach: Proposal
  Copies of proposal: 1
  Deadline(s): Submit proposal preferably in Dec., May, June, or Sept.; deadline is 1st day of month prior to meetings
  Board meeting date(s): Mar., June, Sept., and Dec.
  Write: Ms. Sharon M. Driscoll, Trust Officer, First National Bank of Boston
Trustee: First National Bank of Boston.
EIN: 046089241

1214
Humane Society of the Commonwealth of Massachusetts
79 Milk St., No. 912
Boston 02109-3903

Established in 1785 in MA.
Foundation type: Independent
Financial data (yr. ended 03/31/91): Assets, $2,463,503 (M); expenditures, $162,030; qualifying distributions, $149,252, including $120,000 for 6 grants (high: $39,000; low: $4,000).
Fields of interest: Medical research, health services, drug abuse, medical sciences.
Limitations: Giving limited to MA. No grants to individuals directly.
Application information:

Initial approach: Letter
Deadline(s): None
Write: Charles F. Adams, Secy.
Officers and Trustees:* John E. Lawrence,* Pres.;
Charles F. Adams,* Secy.; Richard M. Cutler,*
Treas.; Francis H. Burr, Ferdinand
Colloredo-Mansfeld, Charles Devens, George P.
Gardner, Jr., Frederick S. Moseley III, Lawrence T.
Perera, Curtis Prout, M.D., William Saltonstall, W.
Nicholas Thorndike.
EIN: 042104291

1215
Hurdle Hill Foundation
c/o Woodstock Service Corp.
18 Tremont St.
Boston 02108

Established in 1960 in MA.
Donor(s): Edith M. Adams, Members of the
Phippen family.
Foundation type: Independent
Financial data (yr. ended 12/31/91): Assets,
$303,843 (M); gifts received, $185,702;
expenditures, $209,604; qualifying distributions,
$204,418, including $203,200 for 68 grants
(high: $17,500; low: $250).
Fields of interest: Conservation, environment,
hospitals, higher education, secondary education,
cultural programs.
Limitations: Giving primarily in MA. No grants to
individuals.
Application information: Contributes only to
pre-selected organizations. Applications not
accepted.
Trustees: Nelson J. Darling, Jr., Peter D. Phippen,
Richard D. Phippen, Susanne LaCroix Phippen,
William LaCroix Phippen.
EIN: 046012782

1216
The Hyams Foundation ▼
One Boston Place, 32nd Fl.
Boston 02108   (617) 720-2238
FAX: (617) 720-2434

Godfrey Hyams Trust and Sarah A. Hyams Fund
established in 1921 and 1929 in MA respectively.
Donor(s): Godfrey M. Hyams.‡
Foundation type: Independent
Financial data (yr. ended 12/31/90): Assets,
$64,638,315 (M); expenditures, $3,868,663;
qualifying distributions, $3,254,375, including
$3,254,375 for 224 grants (high: $85,000; low:
$1,194; average: $15,000-$25,000).
Purpose and activities: Giving for the benefit of
low income residents through support primarily
of neighborhood-based programs; support also for
other social service, youth service, community
organizing, advocacy, and community
development purposes, and for expenses capital
funds for summer youth programs. Priority
program areas initiated since 1984 include
housing, refugee services, adolescent pregnancy,
racial, ethnic and cultural diversity, and
neighborhood safety.
Fields of interest: Youth, community
development, social services, housing, family
planning, family services, homeless, immigration,
drug abuse, alcoholism, adult education.

Types of support: Operating budgets, continuing
support, matching funds, special projects, general
purposes, program-related investments, technical
assistance.
Limitations: Giving primarily in Boston,
Cambridge, Chelsea, Lynn, and Somerville, MA.
No support for municipal, state, or federal
agencies; institutions of higher learning for
standard educational programs; religious
organizations for sectarian religious purposes; or
national or regional health organizations; support
for medical research is being phased out. No
grants to individuals, or for endowment funds,
hospital capital campaigns, fellowships,
publications, conferences, or films or videos.
Publications: Annual report, grants list,
application guidelines.
Application information: Application form not
required.
Initial approach: Proposal, no more than 10
pages
Copies of proposal: 1
Deadline(s): None
Board meeting date(s): 10 times a year between
Sept. and June
Final notification: 1 to 6 months
Write: Elizabeth B. Smith, Exec. Dir.
Officers and Trustees:* John H. Clymer,* Chair.;
Elizabeth B. Smith, Exec. Dir.; James Jennings,
Theresa J. Morse, Deborah Prothrow-Stith, Lewis
H. Spence, Timothy L. Vaill, Roslyn M. Watson,
Boston Safe Deposit & Trust Co.
Number of staff: 3 full-time professional; 1
part-time professional; 2 full-time support; 1
part-time support.
Recent health grants:
1216-1 AIDS Action Committee of
Massachusetts, Boston, MA, $25,000. For
operating expenses. 1990.
1216-2 Bridge, The, Boston, MA, $10,000. For
AIDS program. 1990.
1216-3 Codman Square Health Center,
Dorchester, MA, $10,000. For Boston
Neighborhood Ventures' and for Boston Youth
Network Project. 1990.
1216-4 Coping With the Overall Pregnancy
Experience, Boston, MA, $10,000. For Boston
City Hospital Collaborative Project. 1990.
1216-5 Dimock Community Health Center,
Roxbury, MA, $25,000. For construction of
Child Care and Youth Services Building. 1990.
1216-6 Dorchester Mattapan Community Mental
Health Center, Dorchester, MA, $15,000. For
Multi-Cultural Team project. 1990.
1216-7 Elizabeth Stone House, Jamaica Plain,
MA, $10,000. For operating expenses. 1990.
1216-8 Fenway Community Health Center,
Boston, MA, $15,000. For construction of new
health center building. 1990.
1216-9 Harvard Street Neighborhood Health
Center, Dorchester, MA, $15,000. For
operating expenses of Adolescent and Child
Life Center. 1990.
1216-10 Harvard University, Harvard College,
Cambridge, MA, $40,000. For operating
expenses of Boston AIDS Consortium. 1990.
1216-11 Health Care for All, Boston, MA,
$15,000. For operating expenses. 1990.
1216-12 Judge Baker Guidance Center, Boston,
MA, $20,000. For salary of director of Camile
Cosby Ambulatory Care Center. 1990.
1216-13 Laboure Center, Boston, MA, $11,000.
For operating expenses. 1990.

1216-14 March of Dimes Birth Defects
Foundation, Boston, MA, $10,000. For salary
of project director for program to improve
pregnancy and birth outcomes for substance
abusing pregnant women. 1990.
1216-15 Medical Foundation, Boston, MA,
$37,000. For Medical Research Fellowships.
1990.
1216-16 Medical Foundation, Boston, MA,
$15,000. For Community Health Program,
Project Mattapan. 1990.
1216-17 Mental Health Association of
Somerville, Somerville, MA, $15,000. For
Welcome Project at Mystic Housing Project.
1990.
1216-18 Planned Parenthood League of
Massachusetts, Cambridge, MA, $30,000. For
operating expenses. 1990.
1216-19 Roxbury Comprehensive Community
Health Center, Roxbury, MA, $20,000. For
Adolescent Life Options Program. 1990.
1216-20 Somerville Hospital, Somerville, MA,
$30,000. For School-Based Health Center,
Teen Connection. 1990.
1216-21 Trustees of Health and Hospitals of the
City of Boston, Boston, MA, $15,000. For
salary of administrative assistant for WEATOC
Program. 1990.
1216-22 Trustees of Health and Hospitals of the
City of Boston, Boston, MA, $13,500. For job
training project of Lead Free Kids Program.
1990.

1217
The Iacocca Foundation
572 Washington St., Suite 17
Wellesley 02181   (617) 235-5632

Established in 1964 in MI; became active in 1985.
Donor(s): Lido A. Iacocca.
Foundation type: Independent
Financial data (yr. ended 12/31/90): Assets,
$10,393,782 (M); gifts received, $149,728;
expenditures, $1,097,767; qualifying
distributions, $1,022,232, including $754,245 for
9 grants (high: $200,000; low: $1,000; average:
$50-$100,000).
Purpose and activities: Support limited to
fellowships and endowed research positions in
diabetes research; also awards scholarships for
higher education for children of Chrysler
employees through the Citizen's Scholarship
Foundation of America.
Fields of interest: Medical research.
Types of support: Capital campaigns, endowment
funds, fellowships, professorships, research,
employee-related scholarships.
Limitations: No grants for building funds or
operating budgets.
Publications: 990-PF, informational brochure.
Application information: Application form not
required.
Initial approach: Letter
Deadline(s): None
Board meeting date(s): Quarterly
Write: Kathryn L. Hentz, Pres.
Officers and Trustees:* Kathryn L. Hentz,* Pres.;
Lido A. Iacocca,* V.P.; Joseph A. Califano, Jr.,
Secy.-Treas.; Leo-Arthur Kelmenson, William R.
Winn.
Number of staff: 2 full-time professional.
EIN: 386071154

1218
Island Foundation, Inc.
589 Mill St.
Marion 02738-1418   (508) 748-2809

Incorporated in 1979 in MA as Ram Island, Inc.; current entity formed in 1986 by merger with Green Island, Inc.
Donor(s): W. Van Alan Clark, Jr.‡
Foundation type: Independent
Financial data (yr. ended 12/31/90): Assets, $20,228,386 (M); expenditures, $1,167,879; qualifying distributions, $1,030,493, including $833,612 for 83 grants (high: $37,500; low: $1,500; average: $3,000-$20,000), $70,000 for 2 program-related investments and $3,000 for 1 in-kind gift.
Purpose and activities: Giving primarily for 1) alternative and appropriate treatment systems of wastewater; 2) building capacity of individuals and neighborhoods in the city of New Bedford, MA; and 3) expanding Montessori educational practices in public schools.
Fields of interest: Community development, education, environment, youth, women, education—early childhood, social services, family planning, conservation, public policy, human rights.
Types of support: General purposes, operating budgets, special projects, research, program-related investments.
Limitations: Giving primarily in the northeastern U.S., with program interest in New Bedford, MA. No support for religious organizations. No grants to individuals.
Publications: Annual report (including application guidelines).
Application information: Full proposals by invitation only.
  Initial approach: Telephone or letter
  Copies of proposal: 1
  Deadline(s): Rolling
  Board meeting date(s): Annually and as needed
  Write: Jenny D. Russell, Exec. Dir.
Officers and Board Member:* Lucy H. Nesbeda,* Pres.; Jenny D. Russell, Exec. Dir.
Number of staff: 1 full-time professional; 1 part-time support.
EIN: 042670567
Recent health grants:
1218-1 Adolescent Consultation Services, Cambridge, MA, $10,000. For diagnostic and therapeutic services to court involved youth and their families. 1990.
1218-2 AIDS Action Committee of Massachusetts, Boston, MA, $10,000. For general operating support for education, advocacy and client services to combat AIDS epidemic. 1990.
1218-3 Alliance for Better Nursing Home Care, Providence, RI, $10,000. For Building Bridges program which organizes visits and activities between nursing home residents and children. 1990.
1218-4 Anchorage, Beverly, MA, $10,000. For substance and sexual abuse counselor at this residential treatment center for adolescent youth. 1990.
1218-5 Bridge Over Troubled Waters, Boston, MA, $10,000. Toward expansion of residential facilities for runaways and street youth. 1990.
1218-6 Coping With the Overall Pregnancy Experience, Boston, MA, $25,000. For Child

Abuse Prevention Program which provides educational and counseling services for pregnant and parenting women. 1990.
1218-7 Crittenton Hastings House of Florence Crittenton League, Brighton, MA, $15,000. For life skills and job readiness initiative for pregnant and parenting teens. 1990.
1218-8 Highlander Research and Education Center, New Market, TN, $15,000. For Environmental Health Program which offers workshops to citizens directly affected by toxic pollution. 1990.
1218-9 Narconon, Malden, MA, $10,000. For educational drug prevention program presented in elementary schools in New Bedford, MA. 1990.
1218-10 National Toxics Campaign Fund, Boston, MA, $20,000. For Boston Harbor Toxics Project which researches toxic waste and promotes education of pollution sources and prevention around Boston Harbor. 1990.
1218-11 New Bedford Womens Center, New Bedford, MA, $10,000. For Health Project and Rape Crisis Center. 1990.
1218-12 Positive Action Against Chemical Addiction, New Bedford, MA, $10,550. For technical assistance for strategic planning, fundraising and board involvement. 1990.
1218-13 Suncoast Therapeutic Equitation Program, Sarasota, FL, $12,500. For general support for program that offers horseback riding as therapy for disabled individuals. 1990.

1219
Marion Gardner Jackson Charitable Trust
c/o Bank of Boston
P.O. Box 1861
Boston 02105   (617) 434-5669

Established in 1968.
Foundation type: Independent
Financial data (yr. ended 12/31/90): Assets, $6,579,621 (M); expenditures, $465,483; qualifying distributions, $404,473, including $381,500 for 31 grants (high: $25,000; low: $1,500).
Fields of interest: Youth, health services, hospitals, arts, cultural programs, social services.
Types of support: Building funds.
Limitations: Giving primarily in Adams County, IL. No grants to individuals.
Application information:
  Initial approach: Proposal
  Deadline(s): Sept. 1
  Write: Sharon M. Driscoll, Trust Officer, Bank of Boston
Trustee: Bank of Boston.
EIN: 046010559

1220
John Hancock Mutual Life Insurance Company Giving Program
John Hancock Place
P.O. Box 111
Boston 02117   (617) 572-6607

Financial data (yr. ended 12/31/90): Total giving, $3,000,000, including $2,115,000 for grants and $885,000 for employee matching gifts.
Purpose and activities: Supports United Way, civic and community affairs, education, health,

culture, AIDS programs, the disadvantaged, housing, and minorities.
Fields of interest: Community funds, civic affairs, community development, education, higher education, cultural programs, youth, hospitals, dance, AIDS, disadvantaged, housing, insurance education, minorities.
Types of support: Capital campaigns, endowment funds, general purposes, matching funds, research, special projects, employee matching gifts.
Limitations: Giving primarily in Boston, MA, except for employee matching gifts and support for the United Way; no support for organizations headquartered outside of Boston. No support for fraternal, political, or religious organizations. No grants to individuals.
Application information: Include goals and description of organization, population served and their socioeconomic position, board list, and 501(c)(3) status proof.
  Initial approach: Brief letter or proposal
  Deadline(s): None
  Final notification: One month
  Write: James H. Young, Gen. Dir. and Asst. Secy.
Number of staff: 1

1221
The Howard Johnson Foundation
P.O. Box 235
541 Main St.
South Weymouth 02190   (617) 337-2201
Application address: c/o Howard B. Johnson, 720 Fifth Ave., Suite 1304, New York, NY 10019

Trust established in 1961 in MA.
Donor(s): Howard D. Johnson.‡
Foundation type: Independent
Financial data (yr. ended 12/31/91): Assets, $3,235,932 (M); expenditures, $227,689; qualifying distributions, $209,226, including $168,000 for grants.
Purpose and activities: Giving primarily for higher and secondary education and health and hospitals; support also for museums, churches, religious welfare agencies, the environment, and animal welfare.
Fields of interest: Higher education, secondary education, education, health, hospitals, museums, religion, religious welfare, environment, animal welfare.
Types of support: General purposes.
Limitations: Giving primarily in MA, CT, and NY. No grants to individuals.
Application information: Application form not required.
  Initial approach: Letter
  Copies of proposal: 1
  Deadline(s): Submit letter early in calendar year
  Board meeting date(s): Varies
  Final notification: Indefinite
  Write: Eugene J. Durgin, Secy.
Officer: Eugene J. Durgin, Secy.
Trustees: Marissa J. Brock, Dorothy J. Henry, Howard B. Johnson, Howard Bates Johnson, Patricia Bates Johnson, Joshua J. Weeks, William H. Weeks.
Number of staff: 1 part-time support.
EIN: 046060965

1222
Edward Bangs Kelley and Elza Kelley Foundation, Inc.
243 South St.
P.O. Drawer M
Hyannis 02601   (508) 775-3117

Incorporated in 1954 in MA.
Donor(s): Edward Bangs Kelley,‡ Elza deHorvath Kelley.‡
Foundation type: Independent
Financial data (yr. ended 12/31/90): Assets, $3,294,015 (M); gifts received, $404,545; expenditures, $132,312; qualifying distributions, $115,553, including $53,480 for 16 grants (high: $7,500; low: $1,000) and $38,150 for 58 grants to individuals (high: $2,000; low: $150; average: $250-$4,000).
Purpose and activities: To promote health and welfare of inhabitants of Barnstable County, MA; grants for higher education, including scholarships, and particularly for medical and paramedical education; support also for health and hospitals, hospices, prevention of drug and alcohol abuse, child development and youth agencies, the elderly, libraries, the environment, marine sciences, and cultural programs, including museums, fine arts, theater, and the performing arts.
Fields of interest: Health, higher education, hospitals, drug abuse, youth, aged, libraries, environment, arts, performing arts.
Types of support: Operating budgets, seed money, emergency funds, building funds, equipment, matching funds, scholarship funds, special projects, research, student aid, capital campaigns, publications.
Limitations: Giving limited to Barnstable County, MA. No grants to individuals (except for scholarships), or for annual campaigns, deficit financing, land acquisition, endowment funds, exchange programs, fellowships, publications, or conferences; no loans.
Publications: Annual report (including application guidelines).
Application information: Application form required.
Initial approach: Letter, followed by proposal
Copies of proposal: 6
Deadline(s): Apr. 30 for scholarships; no deadline for grants; grants considered Apr., July, and Oct. if greater than $2,500
Board meeting date(s): Jan., Apr., July, and Oct.
Final notification: 3 weeks
Write: Henry L. Murphy, Jr., Admin. Mgr.
Officers and Directors:* Frank L. Nickerson,* Pres.; Milton L. Penn,* V.P. and Treas.; Thomas S. Olsen, Clerk; Henry L. Murphy, Jr., Admin. Mgr.; John F. Aylmer, Jocelyn Bowman, Palmer Davenport, Frank W. Garran, Jr., M.D., Townsend Hornor, John M. Kayajan, Kenneth S. MacAffer, Jr., Mary Louise Montgomery, Joshua A. Nickerson, Jr., Barbara H. Sheaffer.
Number of staff: 1 part-time professional.
EIN: 046039660

1223
Charles A. King Trust
c/o Fleet Bank of Massachusetts, N.A.
28 State St.
Boston 02107   (617) 573-6415

Trust established in 1938 in MA.
Donor(s): Charles A. King.‡
Foundation type: Independent
Financial data (yr. ended 12/31/91): Assets, $11,415,297 (M); expenditures, $675,202; qualifying distributions, $640,296, including $573,283 for 47 grants (high: $15,500; low: $500).
Purpose and activities: To encourage and support medical and surgical research projects carried on by charitable or educational corporations. Grants are awarded soley for postdoctoral research fellowships.
Fields of interest: Medical research.
Types of support: Research, fellowships.
Limitations: Giving limited to MA. No grants to individuals.
Publications: Application guidelines.
Application information: Fellowships are paid directly to sponsoring institutions. Application form required.
Initial approach: Telephone
Copies of proposal: 17
Deadline(s): Oct. 15 for projects to start on or after Feb. 1 of following year
Board meeting date(s): Dec.
Final notification: 2 months
Write: John M. Dolan, V.P., Fleet Bank of Massachusetts, N.A.
Trustees: Edward N. Dane, Richard H. Lovell, Fleet Bank of Massachusetts, N.A.
Number of staff: 4 full-time professional; 1 full-time support.
EIN: 046012742

1224
Lechmere Corporate Giving Program
275 Wildwood Street
Woburn 01801   (617) 935-8320

Financial data (yr. ended 01/31/90): Total giving, $200,000 for grants.
Purpose and activities: Each year Lechmere sets aside two percent of federal taxable income to fund nonprofit organizations in the communities and neighboring communities of Lechmere stores. Programs from cities will be considered if the organization provides outreach to those communities Lechmere is in. Lechmere has identified young people ages seven to nineteen, as the focus of the contribution program. The social action budget concentrates on prevention and intervention programs that reach youngsters before they become substance abusers. Grants are made to organizations or programs the primary mission of which is substance-abuse-prevention.
Fields of interest: Social services, arts, youth, drug abuse.
Types of support: General purposes, special projects, operating budgets.
Limitations: Giving limited to Cambridge, Dedham, Danver, Springfield, Framingham, Woburn, Weymouth, Worcester, Seekonk, MA; Manchester, Nashua, Salem, NH; Warwick, RI; Albany, Poughkeepsie, Greece, Henrietta, NY; Newington, CT. No support for health, including research, hospitals, mental health, counseling (except in prevention programs for youth) and therapeutic programs, training and education, including grants to colleges, scholarship programs and programs within colleges, churches or religious organizations, political organizations.

No grants to individuals, or for capital campaigns, endowment funds, fundraisers, including tournaments, raffles, roadraces, dinners, advertising space, tickets, and sponsorships.
Publications: Corporate giving report.
Application information: External Relations Department handles giving. Application form not required.
Initial approach: Telephone inquiry and proposal
Copies of proposal: 1
Deadline(s): None
Write: Elaine L. Ricci, Dir., External Rels.
Administrators: Elaine L. Ricci, Dir., External Rels.; Jerri Murray, External Rels. Admin.
Number of staff: 2 full-time professional; 1 full-time support.

1225
June Rockwell Levy Foundation, Inc.
99 High St., 30th Fl.
Boston 02110   (617) 357-8220

Incorporated in 1947 in CT.
Donor(s): Austin T. Levy.‡
Foundation type: Independent
Financial data (yr. ended 12/31/90): Assets, $14,793,362 (M); expenditures, $711,905; qualifying distributions, $649,562, including $580,700 for 90 grants (high: $50,000; low: $1,000; average: $2,000-$5,000).
Purpose and activities: Grants largely for hospitals, medical research, and higher and secondary education; support also for youth agencies, cultural programs, and the handicapped.
Fields of interest: Hospitals, medical research, higher education, secondary education, youth, cultural programs, handicapped.
Types of support: Scholarship funds, building funds, continuing support, seed money, capital campaigns, equipment, research, general purposes.
Limitations: Giving primarily in RI. No support for religious purposes. No grants to individuals.
Application information: Application form not required.
Initial approach: Letter
Copies of proposal: 1
Deadline(s): None
Board meeting date(s): Starting in Feb., lst Tuesday of every other month
Write: James W. Noonan, Secy.
Officers and Trustees:* Edward H. Osgood,* Chair. and Pres.; James W. Noonan,* Secy.; Jonathan B. Loring, Treas.; James K. Edwards, George T. Helm, Raymond N. Menard, Winifred H. Thompson, James M. White.
Number of staff: None.
EIN: 046074284

1226
Linnell Foundation
75 Second Ave.
Needham 02194

Established in 1977 in MA.
Foundation type: Independent
Financial data (yr. ended 12/31/91): Assets, $6,094,549 (M); expenditures, $318,790; qualifying distributions, $279,900, including

$279,900 for 14 grants (high: $220,000; low: $100).
Fields of interest: Crime and law enforcement, public policy, drug abuse.
Officer: Arthur G. Carlson, Jr., Exec. Dir.
Trustees: Russell N. Cox, Robert J. Richards, Robert C. Silver.
EIN: 042625173

1227
Fred & Sarah Lipsky Charitable Foundation
Six Pleasant St., Rm. 510
Malden 02148

Established in 1960 in MA.
Donor(s): Fred Lipsky.‡
Foundation type: Independent
Financial data (yr. ended 01/31/92): Assets, $2,248,803 (M); expenditures, $191,385; qualifying distributions, $175,407, including $139,200 for 75 grants (high: $20,000; low: $100).
Purpose and activities: Emphasis on Jewish welfare funds and temple support; support also for secondary and other education, including a high school-administered college scholarship program, hospitals, and youth agencies.
Fields of interest: Jewish giving, Jewish welfare, secondary education, hospitals, youth.
Types of support: Scholarship funds, general purposes.
Limitations: Giving primarily in MA. No grants to individuals.
Application information: Contributes only to pre-selected organizations. Applications not accepted.
Advisory Board: Benjamin L. Cline, Barbara L. Feinberg, Burton Gerson, Binna L. Golden, Evelyn E. Kosofsky.
Trustee: Malden Trust Co.
EIN: 046072512

1228
The Little Family Foundation
33 Broad St., 10th Fl.
Boston 02109   (617) 742-2790

Trust established in 1946 in RI.
Donor(s): Royal Little.‡
Foundation type: Independent
Financial data (yr. ended 12/31/90): Assets, $12,274,329 (M); expenditures, $935,367; qualifying distributions, $857,757, including $857,757 for 78 grants (high: $135,000; low: $1,000; average: $5,000).
Purpose and activities: Support for scholarship funds at designated business schools; Rhode Island Junior Achievement for programs in secondary schools; and various charities in New England, including youth agencies, cultural programs, and hospitals.
Fields of interest: Business education, secondary education, youth, cultural programs, hospitals.
Types of support: Operating budgets, continuing support, annual campaigns, emergency funds, building funds, equipment, matching funds, scholarship funds.
Limitations: Giving primarily in New England, including MA and RI, and the Pacific Northwest, including WA and OR. No grants to individuals,

or for seed money, deficit financing, or land acquisition; no loans.
Publications: Application guidelines.
Application information: For scholarships, application is by letter to designated business school; deadline Sept. 1. Application form not required.
   Initial approach: Letter
   Copies of proposal: 1
   Deadline(s): None
   Board meeting date(s): Quarterly
   Final notification: After board meetings
   Write: Arthur D. Little, Trustee
Trustees: Augusta Willoughby Little Bishop, E. Janice Leeming, Arthur D. Little, Cameron R. Little, The Rhode Island Hospital Trust National Bank.
Number of staff: None.
EIN: 056016740

1229
Lotus Development Corporation Philanthropy Program
55 Cambridge Parkway
Cambridge 02142   (617) 693-1667

Financial data (yr. ended 12/31/90): Total giving, $7,242,000, including $1,068,000 for grants (high: $25,000; low: $500; average: $5,000-$10,000), $174,000 for 465 employee matching gifts and $6,000,000 for 20,000 in-kind gifts.
Purpose and activities: "The Lotus Philanthropy Program combines a strong focus on the company's headquarters communities with programs of both national and international scope. Project grants are made through the Cambridge-based Lotus Philanthropy Committee to groups working in Boston, Cambridge, Sommerville and contiguous communities. The Committee funds community-based, innovative projects that provide individuals with the skills to control their own future, that provide both individuals and communities with the resources to effect ongoing change, and that remove barriers to an equitable distribution of wealth, power and opportunity. To these ends, the Committee focuses on programs which specifically address issues of racism or which promote access to information and computer technology for all. International grants are made by similar employee committees functioning within Lotus locations throughout Western Europe and concentrating on all programs and efforts in those local communities. Matching gifts of employees' individual contributions are made throughout the U.S., while donations of Lotus software are made to voluntary organizations operating throughout the world."
Fields of interest: Computer sciences, race relations, intercultural relations, international affairs, AIDS, community development, education—minorities, employment, civil rights, leadership development, minorities, public policy, United Kingdom, France, Italy, Spain, Germany, Australia, Europe, Canada.
Types of support: In-kind gifts, employee matching gifts, operating budgets, seed money, donated products, employee volunteer services.
Limitations: Giving primarily in Boston, Cambridge, and Somerville, MA for domestic programs; also support in PR, Ireland, UK, France,

Germany, Sweden, Italy, Spain, Australia. No support for organizations that "advocate, support or practice discrimination based on race, religion, national origin, language, sex, sexual preference, age or physical handicap". No grants to individuals.
Publications: Corporate report, corporate giving report (including application guidelines), informational brochure.
Application information: Company has a staff that only handles contributions. Application form required.
   Initial approach: Write for application form
   Copies of proposal: 1
   Deadline(s): Jan. 1, May 1, and Sept. 1
   Board meeting date(s): Apr. 30, Aug. 31, and Dec. 31
   Final notification: May 15, Sept. 15, and Jan. 15
   Write: Michael P. Durney, Dir., Corp. Giving
Number of staff: 3 full-time professional; 1 part-time professional; 1 part-time support.

1230
Stephen C. Luce Charitable Foundation
c/o Shawmut Bank N.A.
P.O. Box 15032
Worcester 01615-0032

Established in 1982 in MA.
Donor(s): Stephen C. Luce Annuity Trust.
Foundation type: Independent
Financial data (yr. ended 02/28/91): Assets, $3,592,497 (M); gifts received, $750; expenditures, $177,580; qualifying distributions, $157,102, including $143,880 for 12 grants (high: $38,439; low: $2,285).
Purpose and activities: Giving for a library, churches, a hospital, and Masonic charities.
Fields of interest: Libraries, religion—Christian, hospitals.
Limitations: Giving primarily in MA. No grants to individuals.
Application information: Contributes only to pre-selected organizations. Applications not accepted.
Trustee Bank: Shawmut Bank, N.A.
EIN: 237105691

1231
The M/A-Com Foundation, Inc.
(Formerly Microwave Associates Communities Foundation)
401 Edgewater Place, Suite 560
Wakefield 01880

Established in 1967.
Donor(s): M/A-COM, Inc.
Foundation type: Company-sponsored
Financial data (yr. ended 09/30/91): Assets, $65,457 (M); gifts received, $100,000; expenditures, $323,900; qualifying distributions, $323,785, including $181,225 for 85 grants (high: $20,150; low: $20) and $142,560 for grants to individuals.
Purpose and activities: Giving primarily for higher education, including scholarships for employees' children, and the United Way; support also for youth, culture, health, and hospitals.
Fields of interest: Higher education, community funds, youth, cultural programs, health, hospitals.
Types of support: Scholarship funds, student aid.

Limitations: Giving primarily in MA.
Application information:
Initial approach: Letter
Deadline(s): Apr. 1 for scholarships; no set deadline for grants
Write: Victoria B. Dillon, Trustee
Trustees: Kermit Birchfield, Victoria B. Dillion, Robert Galudel.
EIN: 046169568

1232
Nancy Lurie Marks Charitable Foundation
c/o Goulston & Storrs
400 Atlantic Ave.
Boston 02110-3333

Established in 1976 in MA.
Donor(s): Nancy Lurie Marks, Marian Smith.
Foundation type: Independent
Financial data (yr. ended 10/31/91): Assets, $3,025,974 (M); gifts received, $1,132,063; expenditures, $637,719; qualifying distributions, $611,614, including $563,800 for 47 grants (high: $330,000; low: $100).
Fields of interest: Higher education, social sciences, medical research, Jewish welfare, museums, arts.
Limitations: Giving primarily in Boston, MA. No grants to individuals; no loans or program-related investments.
Application information: Contributes only to pre-selected organizations. Applications not accepted.
Write: Jay E. Orlin, Trustee
Trustees: Cathy J. Lurie, Jeffrey R. Lurie, Harry L. Marks, Jay E. Orlin.
EIN: 042607232

1233
Massachusetts Mutual Life Insurance Company Contribution Plan
1295 State St.
Springfield 01111   (413) 788-8411

Financial data (yr. ended 12/31/90): Total giving, $1,343,000 for grants.
Purpose and activities: Support for health, the underprivileged, social services, employment, education, housing, community and civic affairs, arts and culture, and the United Way. Surplus furniture may be donated to Springfield organizations; employee volunteers can apply to recieve up to $500 for the nonprofit with which they work; in addition, employees are involved with helping students in two school programs.
Fields of interest: Health, social services, education, community development, civic affairs, arts, cultural programs, community funds, housing, employment.
Limitations: Giving limited to areas of home office in MA; some contributions to national and state agencies if contribution will benefit the home office area. No support for fraternal, labor, religious, and veterans organizations, trade and industry associations, and organizations with the sole purpose of providing entertainment. No grants to individuals; or for independent fund raising activities of United Way agencies, other than capital campaigns.
Publications: Application guidelines.

Application information: Application form required.
Initial approach: In writing
Deadline(s): None
Board meeting date(s): Contributions review committee meets once a month
Write: Annette Holmes, Community Relations Analyst

1234
Mildred H. McEvoy Foundation
370 Main St., Suite 1200
Worcester 01608   (508) 798-8621

Trust established in 1963 in MA.
Donor(s): Mildred H. McEvoy.‡
Foundation type: Independent
Financial data (yr. ended 12/31/91): Assets, $24,269,865 (M); expenditures, $1,158,635; qualifying distributions, $1,170,680, including $1,110,680 for 44 grants (average: $225-$190,000) and $60,000 for 1 loan.
Fields of interest: Higher education, museums, historic preservation, science and technology, medical research, hospitals.
Limitations: Giving primarily in Worcester, MA, and the Boothbay Harbor, ME, area. No grants to individuals, or for endowment funds.
Application information: Application form not required.
Initial approach: Letter
Copies of proposal: 1
Deadline(s): Submit proposal preferably in Apr.; deadline June
Board meeting date(s): During the summer and in Dec.
Final notification: Dec. 31
Write: Sumner B. Tilton, Jr., Trustee
Trustees: George H. McEvoy, Paul R. Rossley, Sumner B. Tilton, Jr.
Number of staff: 1 part-time professional.
EIN: 046069958

1235
The John Merck Fund ▼
11 Beacon St., Suite 600
Boston 02108   (617) 723-2932

Established in 1970 in NY as a trust.
Donor(s): Serena S. Merck.‡
Foundation type: Independent
Financial data (yr. ended 12/31/90): Assets, $93,758,748 (M); expenditures, $4,778,700; qualifying distributions, $4,190,918, including $3,747,567 for 98 grants (high: $225,000; low: $1,000; average: $25,000-$50,000).
Purpose and activities: Grants are made in the following areas: to medical teaching hospitals for research on developmental disabilities in children; to preserve environmental quality in rural New England and globally; to promote nonproliferation of weapons of mass destruction and conventional arms; to support population control policy and planning initiatives; and to advance international human rights.
Fields of interest: Medical research, child development, environment, conservation, ecology, energy, arms control, family planning, human rights.
Types of support: Research, publications, special projects, operating budgets, fellowships,

conferences and seminars, program-related investments.
Limitations: No grants to individuals.
Publications: Grants list, informational brochure.
Application information: Grants usually made at the initiation of the fund. Applications not accepted.
Board meeting date(s): Monthly
Write: Francis W. Hatch, Chair.
Officers and Trustees:* Francis W. Hatch,* Chair.; Richard A. Kimball, Jr.,* Secy.; Huyler C. Held,* Treas.; Judith M. Buechner, Serena M. Hatch, Arnold Hiatt, Robert M. Pennoyer.
Number of staff: 1 full-time professional; 1 part-time support.
EIN: 237082558
Recent health grants:
1235-1 Alan Guttmacher Institute, NYC, NY, $25,000. To disseminate booklet on RU 486. 1990.
1235-2 Catholics for a Free Choice, DC, $30,000. For Latin American program. 1990.
1235-3 Center for Population Options, DC, $25,000. For International Clearinghouse on Adolescent Fertility. 1990.
1235-4 Columbia University, Center for Population and Family Health, NYC, NY, $50,000. For general support of Development Law and Policy Program. 1990.
1235-5 Columbia University, College of Physicians and Surgeons, NYC, NY, $138,647. For research and treatment program in field of developmental disabilities. 1990.
1235-6 Duke University Medical Center, Durham, NC, $60,000. For John Merck Scholar. 1990.
1235-7 Equipo Argentino de Antropologia Forense, Buenos Aires, Argentina, $25,000. For general purpose grant. 1990.
1235-8 Feminist Majority Foundation, Arlington, VA, $25,000. To campaign for RU 486 and Contraceptive Research Project. 1990.
1235-9 Harvard University, School of Public Health, Boston, MA, $100,000. For AIDS and Reproductive Health Network. 1990.
1235-10 Johns Hopkins Medical Institutions, Baltimore, MD, $115,000. For research and treatment program in field of developmental disabilities. 1990.
1235-11 Merck Forest Foundation, Rupert, VT, $30,000. For general purpose grant. 1990.
1235-12 Planned Parenthood Federation of America, NYC, NY, $75,000. For Public Impact Litigation Project. 1990.
1235-13 Planned Parenthood Federation of America, NYC, NY, $50,000. For conference series on new contraceptive technologies. 1990.
1235-14 Population Crisis Committee, DC, $30,000. To promote availability of RU 486. 1990.
1235-15 Reproductive Health Technologies Project, DC, $39,800. To promote availability of RU 486. Grant administered by Tides Foundation. 1990.
1235-16 Stanford University Medical Center, Stanford, CA, $150,000. For research and treatment programs in field of developmental disabilities and autistic children. 1990.
1235-17 University of California, San Francisco, CA, $17,500. For research and treatment programs in field of developmental disabilities and autistic children. 1990.

1235-18 Women Judges Fund for Justice, DC, $20,000. For Bioethics Education Project. 1990.

1235-19 Yale University, Child Study Center, New Haven, CT, $225,000. For research and treatment programs in field of developmental disabilities. 1990.

1236
The E. F. Merkert Foundation
c/o Merkert Enterprises
500 Turnpike St.
Canton 02021   (617) 828-4800

Established in 1960.
Donor(s): Merkert Enterprises, Inc., Eugene F. Merkert.
Foundation type: Independent
Financial data (yr. ended 12/31/90): Assets, $1,122,775 (M); gifts received, $175,000; expenditures, $324,394; qualifying distributions, $323,869, including $323,869 for 49 grants (high: $50,000; low: $200).
Fields of interest: Education, higher education, medical research, hospitals, social services.
Types of support: Endowment funds, research.
Limitations: Giving primarily in MA.
Application information:
   Initial approach: Letter
   Deadline(s): None
   Write: Eugene F. Merkert, Trustee
Trustee: Eugene F. Merkert.
EIN: 046111832

1237
Middlecott Foundation
50 Congress St., Suite 800
Boston 02109

Established in 1967 in MA.
Donor(s): Members of the Saltonstall family.
Foundation type: Independent
Financial data (yr. ended 12/31/90): Assets, $944,645 (M); gifts received, $323,239; expenditures, $331,104; qualifying distributions, $319,045, including $319,045 for 277 grants (high: $25,000; low: $25; average: $100-$1,000).
Fields of interest: Education, social services, health associations, hospitals, cultural programs, child welfare, youth.
Limitations: No grants to individuals.
Application information: Contributes only to pre-selected organizations. Applications not accepted.
   Write: William L. Saltonstall, Trustee
Trustees: Robert A. Lawrence, George Lewis, William L. Saltonstall.
Number of staff: 1 part-time support.
EIN: 046155699

1238
The Millipore Foundation
80 Ashby Rd.
Bedford 01730-2271   (617) 275-9200

Established in 1985 in MA.
Donor(s): Millipore Corp.
Foundation type: Company-sponsored
Financial data (yr. ended 09/30/91): Assets, $953,818 (M); gifts received, $852,000;

expenditures, $894,154; qualifying distributions, $889,559, including $747,180 for 121 grants (high: $50,000; low: $500) and $139,904 for 517 employee matching gifts.
Purpose and activities: Giving primarily through grants and employee matching gifts to organizations involved in health, education, and social services.
Fields of interest: Education, health, hospitals, social services.
Types of support: Employee volunteer services, general purposes, employee matching gifts.
Limitations: No support for religious programs or political organizations.
Publications: Annual report, informational brochure (including application guidelines), application guidelines.
Application information: Application form not required.
   Initial approach: Full proposal
   Copies of proposal: 1
   Deadline(s): None
   Board meeting date(s): Quarterly
   Write: Charleen L. Johnson, Exec. Dir.
Officers and Trustees:* Geoffrey Nunes,* Chair.; Charleen L. Johnson, Exec. Dir.; John A. Gilmartin, Wayne J. Kennedy.
Number of staff: None.
EIN: 222583952

1239
Monarch Capital Corporate Giving Program
One Monarch Place
Springfield 01144   (413) 781-3000

Financial data (yr. ended 12/31/90): Total giving, $160,000 for grants.
Purpose and activities: Supports education; health, including AIDS programs; arts and culture; and civic affairs; employee matching gifts for higher education.
Fields of interest: AIDS, health, arts, civic affairs, education, cultural programs.
Types of support: Capital campaigns, operating budgets, employee matching gifts.
Limitations: Giving primarily in the Springfield, MA, area.
Publications: Informational brochure (including application guidelines), corporate report.
Application information: Application form required.
   Deadline(s): Quarterly
   Board meeting date(s): Quarterly
   Write: Gordon N. Oakes, Jr., Chair. of the Board

1240
NEBS Corporate Giving Program
New England Business Services
500 Main Street
Groton 01471   (508) 448-6111

Financial data (yr. ended 12/31/90): Total giving, $350,000, including $210,000 for grants and $140,000 for employee matching gifts.
Purpose and activities: Support for education, civic affairs, social services, health services, arts and culture, and community funds.
Fields of interest: Education, civic affairs, social services, health, arts.

Limitations: Giving primarily in areas of company facilities: Flagstaff, AZ, Groton, MA, Maryville, MO, Peterborough, NH, and Madison, WI. No support for churches. No grants to individuals.
Application information: Application form not required.
   Initial approach: Proposal
   Write: Paul Robinson, Legal Officer

1241
New England Biolabs Foundation
32 Tozer Rd.
Beverly 01915   (508) 927-2404

Established in 1982 in MA.
Donor(s): Donald G. Comb.
Foundation type: Independent
Financial data (yr. ended 11/30/91): Assets, $3,200,000 (M); gifts received, $50,000; expenditures, $200,000; qualifying distributions, $185,000, including $160,000 for 35 grants (high: $17,000; low: $100; average: $5,000-$7,000), $5,000 for 2 grants to individuals (high: $4,000; low: $1,000) and $20,000 for 1 foundation-administered program.
Purpose and activities: Giving primarily for environmental, educational, health, and social projects in New England and abroad, including Africa, Asia, the Caribbean, Central America, and the Philippines; some support for scientific research.
Fields of interest: Africa, Asia, Latin America, international development, science and technology, conservation, health, cultural programs, education, elementary education, human rights.
Types of support: Research, grants to individuals, matching funds, seed money, special projects.
Limitations: Giving primarily in New England, especially MA, and in less-developed countries, focusing on Tanzania, Cameroon, Papua New Guinea, and Central America. No support for religious activities, services for the elderly or the handicapped, or art projects outside the immediate community. No grants for capital endowment or building funds, operating costs, fellowships, projects normally funded by major agencies, movies or videos, scholarships, or conferences.
Publications: Informational brochure (including application guidelines), grants list.
Application information: Application form not required.
   Initial approach: Letter
   Deadline(s): Mar. 1, Sept. 1, and Dec. 1
   Board meeting date(s): Jan., Apr., and Oct.
   Final notification: 4 to 6 weeks after meeting
   Write: Martine Kellett, Exec. Dir.
Officer: Martine Kellett, Exec. Dir.
Trustees: Donald G. Comb, Douglas I. Foy, Henry P. Paulus.
Number of staff: 1 full-time professional; 1 part-time support.
EIN: 042776213

1242
New England Electric System Giving Program
25 Research Dr.
Westborough 01582   (508) 366-9011

Purpose and activities: Supports education, the arts, community affairs, general health care, the environment, economics, and youth.
Fields of interest: Education, arts, community funds, health, higher education, environment, hospitals, youth, economics.
Types of support: Matching funds, building funds, general purposes.
Limitations: Giving primarily in headquarters city and major operating locations.
Application information:
  Initial approach: Letter
  Write: Don F. Goodwin, Corp. Contribs. Coord.
Number of staff: None.

1243
The New England Foundation
c/o Stephen Clark
Ten Post Office Sq. South, Suite 1330
Boston 02109

Established in 1986 in MA.
Donor(s): Thomas E. Bass.
Foundation type: Independent
Financial data (yr. ended 12/31/90): Assets, $6,476,186 (M); gifts received, $1,805; expenditures, $434,150; qualifying distributions, $343,476, including $329,250 for 44 grants (high: $98,000; low: $500).
Fields of interest: Higher education, secondary education, hospitals, cultural programs.
Limitations: Giving limited to New England. No grants to individuals.
Application information: Contributes only to pre-selected organizations. Applications not accepted.
Trustees: Stephen R. Clark, Joseph McNay.
EIN: 222757391

1244
New England Telephone & Telegraph Company Giving Program
185 Franklin St., Room 1602
Boston 02107   (617) 743-4846

Financial data (yr. ended 12/31/90): Total giving, $4,650,000 for grants.
Purpose and activities: Supports health, human services, education, community services, the homeless, hunger programs, and drug abuse programs, and the arts and humanities. Employee matching gift program for education and the arts; recent emphasis has been on hunger, homelessness, and job training.
Fields of interest: Health, social services, education, community development, arts, humanities, community funds, drug abuse, adult education, cultural programs, homeless, hunger, performing arts, youth.
Types of support: Capital campaigns, employee matching gifts, special projects, employee volunteer services.
Limitations: Giving primarily in the northeast. No support for religious organizations when sectarian in purpose, political causes or organizations, elementary or secondary schools, national health organizations, or hospital building funds. No grants to individuals, or for general operating expenses, endowments, special occasion or good will advertising.
Publications: Application guidelines.

Application information: Include description and budget of organization and project, time frame for project, board and contributors list, financial statement, and 501(c)(3) status proof.
  Initial approach: Letter or phone
  Deadline(s): None
  Final notification: Two weeks
  Write: Stephan M. Norton, Contribs. Mgr.

1245
Deborah Munroe Noonan Memorial Fund u/w Frank Noonan
c/o Fleet Bank, N.A.
28 State St.
Boston 02107   (617) 573-6415

Trust established in 1947 in MA.
Donor(s): Frank M. Noonan.‡
Foundation type: Independent
Financial data (yr. ended 09/30/90): Assets, $4,124,325 (M); gifts received, $22,631; expenditures, $282,499; qualifying distributions, $261,373, including $228,450 for 5 grants (high: $66,959; low: $29,302; average: $25,000-$40,000).
Purpose and activities: Grants soley for medical services to handicapped children provided at local hospitals.
Fields of interest: Hospitals, handicapped.
Types of support: Special projects.
Limitations: Giving limited to the greater Boston, MA, area. No grants to individuals, or for scholarships or fellowships; no loans.
Publications: Application guidelines.
Application information: Call for deadline information. Application form required.
  Initial approach: Telephone
  Copies of proposal: 12
  Board meeting date(s): Distribution committee meets as required
  Final notification: Following annual meeting
  Write: John M. Dolan, V.P., Fleet Bank, N.A.
Trustee: Fleet Bank, N.A.
Number of staff: 4 full-time professional; 1 full-time support.
EIN: 046025957

1246
Old Colony Charitable Foundation
c/o Bank of Boston
P.O. Box 1890
Boston 02105   (617) 434-3768

Established in 1955 in MA by declaration of trust.
Foundation type: Community
Financial data (yr. ended 12/31/91): Assets, $4,509,996 (M); gifts received, $704,096; expenditures, $256,477; qualifying distributions, $177,865, including $177,865 for 31 grants (high: $40,522; low: $630).
Purpose and activities: Consideration given to core programming and capital support in the areas of human services, urban programs, youth and family services, and health care programs.
Fields of interest: Social services, urban affairs, youth, family services, education, health, general charitable giving.
Types of support: Operating budgets, continuing support, seed money, equipment, capital campaigns, general purposes.

Limitations: Giving limited to the greater Boston, MA, area. No support for national organizations or film production. No grants to individuals, or for conferences, travel, endowment funds, matching gifts, scholarships, research not under aegis of recognized charitable organizations, publications, or projects requiring multi-year commitment; no loans.
Publications: Annual report, application guidelines.
Application information: Application form required.
  Initial approach: Proposal
  Copies of proposal: 1
  Deadline(s): Jan. 15, May 15, and Sept. 15
  Board meeting date(s): Mar., July, and Nov.
  Final notification: 1 week
  Write: Sharon M. Driscoll, Exec. Account Mgr.
Trustee: Bank of Boston.
Number of staff: None.
EIN: 046010342

1247
Bessie Pappas Charitable Foundation, Inc.
P.O. Box 318
Belmont 02178   (617) 862-2851

Established in 1984 in MA as successor to the Pappas Family Foundation.
Donor(s): Thomas Anthony Pappas.
Foundation type: Independent
Financial data (yr. ended 12/31/90): Assets, $3,514,292 (M); expenditures, $224,298; qualifying distributions, $186,470, including $160,300 for 31 grants (high: $10,000; low: $500).
Purpose and activities: Support primarily for the arts, health, and family and social services; support also for education and religious welfare organizations.
Fields of interest: Arts, health, family services, social services, education, religious welfare.
Limitations: Giving primarily in MA. No grants to individuals.
Publications: Application guidelines.
Application information:
  Deadline(s): Sept. 30
  Final notification: Dec. 31
  Write: Betsy Pappas, V.P.
Officers and Directors: Charles A. Pappas,* Pres. and Treas.; Helen K. Pappas,* Exec. V.P.; Betsy Z. Pappas,* V.P. and Clerk; Sophia Pappas, Donald Young.
Number of staff: 2 full-time professional.
EIN: 222540702

1248
Thomas Anthony Pappas Charitable Foundation, Inc.
P.O. Box 463
Belmont 02178-0463   (617) 862-2802

Incorporated in 1975 in MA.
Donor(s): Thomas Anthony Pappas.‡
Foundation type: Independent
Financial data (yr. ended 12/31/90): Assets, $18,089,636 (M); expenditures, $1,009,638; qualifying distributions, $846,021, including $722,500 for 64 grants (high: $100,000; low: $1,000; average: $1,000-$100,000).

Purpose and activities: Emphasis on higher education, hospitals, cultural programs, Greek Orthodox church support, religious associations, and youth and social service agencies.
Fields of interest: Education, education—minorities, higher education, hospitals, cultural programs, religion, youth, social services, crime and law enforcement, drug abuse.
Types of support: Annual campaigns, building funds, endowment funds, research, professorships, scholarship funds, fellowships, continuing support, building funds.
Limitations: Giving primarily in MA. No grants to individuals.
Publications: Program policy statement, application guidelines.
Application information: Application form not required.
  Initial approach: Letter or proposal
  Deadline(s): Submit proposal preferably in Mar. or Sept.; deadline Sept. 30
  Board meeting date(s): Mar., June, Sept., Dec., and as required
  Final notification: Dec. 31
Officers and Directors:* Charles A. Pappas,* Pres. and Treas.; Helen K. Pappas,* Exec. V.P.; Betsy Z. Pappas,* V.P. and Clerk; Sophia Pappas, Donald Young.
Number of staff: 3 full-time professional.
EIN: 510153284

1249
Amelia Peabody Charitable Fund ▼
201 Devonshire St.
Boston 02110-1401   (617) 451-6178

Established in 1974.
Donor(s): Amelia Peabody,‡ Eaton Foundation.
Foundation type: Independent
Financial data (yr. ended 12/31/90): Assets, $87,197,283 (M); expenditures, $5,009,375; qualifying distributions, $4,682,301, including $4,476,460 for 128 grants (high: $1,500,000; low: $1,000; average: $5,000-$25,000).
Purpose and activities: Grants primarily for higher education; the environment; hospitals, medical research, and health and family services; and culture, including museums and historic preservation.
Fields of interest: Higher education, education—building funds, environment, conservation, medical research, hospitals, hospitals—building funds, health services, health, drug abuse, family services, disadvantaged, handicapped, homeless, cultural programs, museums, fine arts, historic preservation, general charitable giving.
Types of support: Building funds, endowment funds, capital campaigns, renovation projects, equipment, research.
Limitations: Giving primarily in New England. No support for tax-supported organizations or religious groups. No grants to individuals.
Publications: Application guidelines.
Application information: Application form not required.
  Initial approach: Letter or proposal
  Copies of proposal: 1
  Deadline(s): None
  Board meeting date(s): Quarterly

  Final notification: 8 weeks after each quarter closing
  Write: Jo Anne Borek, Exec. Dir.
Trustees: Richard A. Leahy, Harry F. Rice, Patricia E. Rice.
Number of staff: 1 part-time professional.
EIN: 237364949
Recent health grants:
1249-1 Beth Israel Hospital, Boston, MA, $50,000. 1990.
1249-2 Bridge Over Troubled Waters, Boston, MA, $10,000. 1990.
1249-3 Childrens Hospital, Boston, MA, $100,000. 1990.
1249-4 Dimock Community Health Center, Roxbury, MA, $50,000. 1990.
1249-5 Joslin Diabetes Center, Boston, MA, $1,500,000. 1990.
1249-6 Lahey Clinic Foundation, Burlington, MA, $86,000. 1990.
1249-7 Malden Hospital, Malden, MA, $50,000. 1990.
1249-8 Mental Health Association, North Suffolk, Chelsea, MA, $20,000. 1990.
1249-9 Mount Desert Island Hospital, Bar Harbor, ME, $50,000. 1990.
1249-10 Rogerson House, Boston, MA, $25,000. 1990.
1249-11 Saint Josephs Hospital, Lowell, MA, $10,000. 1990.
1249-12 Salem Hospital, Salem, MA, $10,000. 1990.
1249-13 Tri-City Community Mental Health Center, Malden, MA, $20,000. 1990.
1249-14 Visiting Nurse Association, Norwell, MA, $21,795. 1990.

1250
The Peabody Foundation, Inc.
c/o Sherburne, Powers & Needham
One Beacon St.
Boston 02108

Established in 1894 in MA.
Donor(s): Charles B. Jaixen,‡ Adla V. Jaixen.‡
Foundation type: Independent
Financial data (yr. ended 09/30/91): Assets, $10,942,068 (M); gifts received, $91,319; expenditures, $540,432; qualifying distributions, $496,429, including $473,927 for 14 grants (high: $100,000; low: $1,000).
Purpose and activities: Grants limited to providing care, treatment, rehabilitation, education, and assistance of children, to encourage and support medical research in the causes of crippling disease, particularly in children.
Fields of interest: Child welfare, handicapped, medical research.
Types of support: Research.
Limitations: Giving limited to MA, with emphasis on the Boston area. No grants to individuals.
Application information: Application form not required.
  Deadline(s): None
  Write: William V. Tripp III
Officers and Trustees:* William V. Tripp III,* Pres.; Norman C. Nicholson, Jr.,* V.P. and Treas.; Mrs. Francis B. Haydock,* Clerk; Harry C. Barr, Dorothy A. Brown, Mrs. Edwin F. Cave, Mrs. John L. Damon, John H. Hewitt, Sally D. Hurlbut, Andrew G. Jessiman, M.D., Mrs. Stephen D.

Paine, Sylvia L. Stevens, Mrs. W. Nicholas Thorndike.
EIN: 042104767

1251
Amelia Peabody Foundation ▼
c/o Hale and Dorr
60 State St.
Boston 02109   (617) 742-9100
Application address: 30 Western Ave., Gloucester, MA 01930; Tel.: (508) 283-0643

Trust established in 1942 in MA; absorbed a share of the assets of The Eaton Foundation, MA, in 1985.
Donor(s): Amelia Peabody.‡
Foundation type: Independent
Financial data (yr. ended 12/31/90): Assets, $90,383,525 (M); expenditures, $3,971,018; qualifying distributions, $3,444,055, including $3,257,030 for 71 grants (high: $333,000; low: $4,000; average: $10,000-$100,000).
Purpose and activities: To assist local charitable and educational organizations, with emphasis on education, hospitals, youth agencies, cultural programs, and conservation.
Fields of interest: Education, educational research, education—building funds, child development, child welfare, youth, medical education, hospitals, hospitals—building funds, cultural programs, conservation, general charitable giving.
Types of support: Building funds, matching funds, capital campaigns, operating budgets.
Limitations: Giving limited to MA. No grants to individuals, or for endowment funds, scholarships, or fellowships; no loans.
Publications: Annual report.
Application information: Application form not required.
  Initial approach: Letter
  Copies of proposal: 5
  Deadline(s): None
  Board meeting date(s): Quarterly
  Final notification: As required
  Write: James D. St. Clair or Bayard D. Waring, Co-Managing Trustees
Trustees: G. Dana Bill, James D. St. Clair, Margaret N. St. Clair, Bayard D. Waring, Lloyd B. Waring.
Number of staff: 3
EIN: 046036558

1252
Perini Memorial Foundation, Inc.
73 Mount Wayte Ave.
Framingham 01701   (508) 875-6171
Scholarship application address: Selection Comm., P.O. Box 31, Framingham, MA 01701

Incorporated in 1953 in MA.
Donor(s): Perini Corp.
Foundation type: Company-sponsored
Financial data (yr. ended 12/31/91): Assets, $2,288,505 (M); gifts received, $75,000; expenditures, $163,860; qualifying distributions, $153,435, including $121,933 for 44 grants (high: $25,000; low: $100) and $29,500 for 12 grants to individuals (high: $3,000; low: $1,500).
Purpose and activities: Emphasis on higher education, Roman Catholic church support and

religious associations, and hospitals and social services; also awards scholarships to children of employees of Perini Corp. and its subsidiaries.
Fields of interest: Higher education, Catholic giving, hospitals, cancer, social services.
Types of support: Employee-related scholarships, general purposes.
Limitations: Giving primarily in MA. No grants to individuals (except employee-related scholarships), or for research, scholarships, fellowships, or matching gifts; no loans.
Application information: Application form required for scholarships.
  Initial approach: Letter
  Copies of proposal: 1
  Write: Bart W. Perini, Treas.
Officers: David B. Perini, Pres.; Charles B. Perini, V.P.; Bart W. Perini, Treas.
EIN: 046118587

1253
Joseph Perini Memorial Foundation
73 Mt. Wayte Ave.
Framingham 01701   (508) 875-6171
Application address: P.O. Box 31, Framingham, MA 01701

Incorporated in 1953 in MA.
Donor(s): Joseph R. Perini.‡
Foundation type: Independent
Financial data (yr. ended 12/31/90): Assets, $3,760,625 (M); gifts received, $100,000; expenditures, $473,027; qualifying distributions, $457,805, including $420,340 for 73 grants (high: $35,000; low: $150; average: $1,000-$4,000) and $32,000 for 9 grants to individuals (high: $4,000; low: $2,000).
Purpose and activities: Giving for education, including scholarships to children of Perini Corp. employees, social services, including family and youth agencies, church support and religious associations; support also for hospices and hospitals.
Fields of interest: Education, family services, religion, youth, hospices, hospitals, cancer, health services.
Types of support: Employee-related scholarships, capital campaigns, endowment funds, matching funds.
Limitations: Giving primarily in MA. No grants to individuals (except for employee-related scholarships), or for research, scholarships, fellowships, or operating budgets; no loans.
Application information: Scholarships available only to sons and daughters of employees of Perini Corp. or its subsidiaries. Application form not required.
  Initial approach: Letter
  Copies of proposal: 1
  Deadline(s): Nov.
  Board meeting date(s): Dec.
  Write: Joseph R. Perini, Secy.
Officers: Thomas B. Perini, Pres.; Harold Ottobrini, V.P.; Joseph R. Perini, Secy.
Number of staff: None.
EIN: 046139986

1254
Perpetual Trust for Charitable Giving
c/o Fleet Bank of Massachusetts, N.A.
28 State St.
Boston 02109

Foundation type: Independent
Financial data (yr. ended 12/31/91): Assets, $10,748,711 (M); expenditures, $973,008; qualifying distributions, $908,465, including $830,340 for 63 grants (high: $60,000; low: $1,000).
Fields of interest: Hospitals, higher education.
Types of support: Capital campaigns, operating budgets.
Limitations: Giving primarily in MA. No grants to individuals.
Application information: Contributes only to pre-selected organizations. Applications not accepted.
Trustee: Fleet Bank of Massachusetts, N.A.
EIN: 046026301

1255
Joseph Persky Foundation
c/o Singer & Lusardi
370 Main St.
Worcester 01608   (413) 436-7704

Incorporated in 1944 in MA.
Donor(s): David Persky, Hardwick Knitted Fabrics, Inc.
Foundation type: Independent
Financial data (yr. ended 12/31/90): Assets, $2,026,844 (M); gifts received, $75,000; expenditures, $150,088; qualifying distributions, $148,478, including $144,250 for 28 grants (high: $55,000; low: $250).
Purpose and activities: Grants largely for Jewish welfare funds; support also for higher education, hospitals and health agencies, and biological research.
Fields of interest: Jewish welfare, higher education, hospitals, health services, biological sciences.
Limitations: Giving primarily in MA, with some emphasis on Worcester. No grants to individuals.
Application information: Contributes only to pre-selected organizations. Applications not accepted.
Officers: David A. Persky, Pres. and Treas.; Marlene Persky, Secy.
Directors: Marguerite Persky, Warren Persky, Suzanne Persky Tompkins.
EIN: 046057747

1256
Harold Whitworth Pierce Charitable Trust
c/o Nichols and Pratt
50 Congress St.
Boston 02109   (617) 523-6800

Trust established in 1960 in MA.
Donor(s): Harold Whitworth Pierce.‡
Foundation type: Independent
Financial data (yr. ended 12/31/91): Assets, $13,210,564 (M); expenditures, $717,490; qualifying distributions, $649,094, including $635,125 for 36 grants (high: $154,295; low: $3,000).

Fields of interest: Medical research, higher education, secondary education, youth, museums, cultural programs, family planning, environment.
Limitations: Giving primarily in MA. No grants to individuals.
Publications: Program policy statement, application guidelines.
Application information: Application form not required.
  Initial approach: Letter or telephone
  Copies of proposal: 1
  Deadline(s): May 1 and Nov. 1
  Board meeting date(s): May and Nov.
  Write: Elizabeth D. Nichols, Grant Administrator
Trustees: James R. Nichols, Harold I. Pratt.
Number of staff: None.
EIN: 046019896

1257
Poitras Charitable Foundation, Inc.
198 Highland St.
Holliston 01746   (508) 429-6281

Established in 1986 in MA.
Donor(s): James Poitras, Patricia Poitras.
Foundation type: Independent
Financial data (yr. ended 12/31/90): Assets, $304,365 (M); gifts received, $118; expenditures, $248,387; qualifying distributions, $246,615, including $245,000 for 18 grants (high: $100,000; low: $1,000).
Fields of interest: Hospitals, medical research, mental health, social services, conservation.
Types of support: Annual campaigns, continuing support, capital campaigns, emergency funds, building funds, research.
Limitations: Giving primarily in MA. No grants to individuals.
Application information: Application form not required.
  Initial approach: Letter
  Copies of proposal: 1
  Deadline(s): None
  Final notification: End of year
  Write: Patricia T. Poitras, Pres., or James Poitras, Treas.
Officers and Directors:* Patricia T. Poitras,* Pres.; James Poitras,* Treas.
Number of staff: None.
EIN: 222725927

1258
Polaroid Foundation, Inc. ▼
750 Main St., 2M
Cambridge 02139   (617) 577-4035

Incorporated in 1971 in MA.
Donor(s): Polaroid Corp.
Foundation type: Company-sponsored
Financial data (yr. ended 12/31/91): Assets, $0 (M); gifts received, $2,264,568; expenditures, $2,251,847; qualifying distributions, $2,251,847, including $1,808,618 for grants (high: $380,000; low: $50; average: $2,000-$10,000) and $443,035 for 3,249 employee matching gifts.
Purpose and activities: Support for community funds and social service agencies, including programs for the urban poor, and higher education, including matching gifts; grants also to

cultural programs, youth agencies, and health services.
Fields of interest: Community funds, urban affairs, community development, social services, family services, homeless, housing, minorities, women, education, education—early childhood, elementary education, secondary education, higher education, education—minorities, cultural programs, arts, museums, youth, health, health services, handicapped, hospices, AIDS.
Types of support: Matching funds, employee matching gifts, employee-related scholarships, seed money, emergency funds, fellowships, general purposes, annual campaigns, capital campaigns, continuing support, equipment, loans, operating budgets, publications, renovation projects, special projects, employee matching gifts, annual campaigns, scholarship funds.
Limitations: Giving primarily in MA, particularly greater Boston, Cambridge, and New Bedford. No grants to individuals (except for employee-related scholarships), or for endowment funds.
Publications: Biennial report, application guidelines, program policy statement.
Application information: Application form required.
> *Initial approach:* Proposal
> *Copies of proposal:* 1
> *Deadline(s):* None
> *Board meeting date(s):* Monthly
> *Final notification:* 3 to 4 months after board meeting
> *Write:* Jill Healy, Sr. Administrator
Officers: Robert Delahunt, Pres.; Marcia Schiff, Secy. and Exec. Dir.; Ralph Norwood, Treas.
Trustees: I. MacAllister Booth, Sheldon A. Buckler, Richard F. deLima, Milton S. Dietz, Owen J. Gaffney, Peter O. Kliem, Joseph Oldfield, William J. O'Neill, Jr.
Number of staff: 1 full-time professional; 2 part-time professional; 2 full-time support.
EIN: 237152261

1259
William Townsend Porter Foundation, Inc.
(Formerly Harvard Apparatus Foundation, Inc.)
c/o Palmer & Dodge
One Beacon St.
Boston 02108

Established in 1938.
Foundation type: Independent
Financial data (yr. ended 03/31/91): Assets, $2,057,482 (M); expenditures, $92,127; qualifying distributions, $92,127, including $92,127 for grants (average: $5,000-$40,000).
Purpose and activities: Grants to promote the teaching of physiology.
Fields of interest: Higher education, medical education, medical sciences.
Types of support: Continuing support, seed money, special projects.
Limitations: No grants to individuals.
Application information: Contributes only to pre-selected organizations. Applications not accepted.
> *Board meeting date(s):* Nov.
Officers and Trustees:* A. Clifford Barger,* Pres.; Nancy S. Milburn,* Treas.; Casimir de Rham, Jr.,* Clerk; Reinier Beewwkes III, John C.S. Fray, H. Maurice Goodman, Benjamin Kaminer, John A. Perkins.

EIN: 042104293

1260
Olive Higgins Prouty Foundation, Inc.
c/o State Street Bank & Trust Co.
P.O. Box 351, M-11
Boston 02101   (617) 654-3297

Incorporated in 1952 in MA.
Donor(s): Olive Higgins Prouty.‡
Foundation type: Independent
Financial data (yr. ended 12/31/91): Assets, $2,222,038 (M); expenditures, $143,572; qualifying distributions, $131,953, including $115,000 for 42 grants (high: $22,000; low: $1,000).
Fields of interest: Hospitals, youth, arts, music, higher education, secondary education.
Limitations: Giving primarily in the greater Worcester, MA, area. No grants to individuals.
Publications: Application guidelines.
Application information: Application form required.
> *Initial approach:* Telephone
> *Copies of proposal:* 1
> *Deadline(s):* Sept. 30
> *Board meeting date(s):* Oct. 31
> *Final notification:* Dec. 31
> *Write:* George Robbins, Sr., V.P., State Street Bank & Trust Co.
Officers and Trustees:* Richard Prouty,* Pres.; Lewis I. Prouty, Treas.; William Mason Smith III, Thomas P. Jalkut, One International Place.
EIN: 046046475

1261
Sidney & Esther Rabb Charitable Foundation
c/o Boston Safe Deposit & Trust Co.
One Boston Place
Boston 02108
Application address: c/o The Avcar Group, Ltd., 225 Franklin St., Suite 2700, Boston, MA 02110

Established in 1952 in MA.
Donor(s): Sidney R. Rabb.‡
Foundation type: Independent
Financial data (yr. ended 12/31/91): Assets, $3,779,503 (M); expenditures, $276,501; qualifying distributions, $252,766, including $249,697 for 21 grants (high: $68,253; low: $100).
Fields of interest: Higher education, Jewish welfare, cultural programs, hospitals.
Limitations: Giving primarily in Boston, MA.
Application information: Application form not required.
> *Initial approach:* Letter
> *Deadline(s):* None
> *Write:* Carol R. Goldberg, Trustee
Trustees: Helene R. Cahners-Kaplan, Carol R. Goldberg.
EIN: 046039595

1262
Raytheon Company Corporate Giving Program
141 Spring St.
Lexington 02173   (617) 862-6600

Financial data (yr. ended 12/31/90): Total giving, $5,750,000, including $5,350,000 for 1,000 grants (high: $100,000; low: $100; average: $5,000) and $400,000 for 4,000 employee matching gifts.
Purpose and activities: "Raytheon funds organizations dedicated to improving service in four areas: quality of education; quality of care quality of opportunity; and quality of life. Assuring quality services, building on proven success, meeting community needs, helping to build the management capactiy of nonprofit organizations, and supporting innovative problem-solving - these are the ways that the company seeks to be involved in its local communities. Raytheon Company believes it has a responsiblility to be an active member of its communites - by providing resources and expertise." Grant size varies, depending on the scope of the project and Raytheon Company's relationship to it. Multiple year grants will be considered for capital purposes. The range of one-year grants is $500 to $20,000; typical size is $5,000. Multi-year commitments paid over 3-5 years range from $10,000 to $250,000 Requests for product donations of kitchen and laundry appliances and marine electronics will be considered in lieu of, or as a supplement to, cash grants.
Fields of interest: Aged, arts, education, education—building funds, education—minorities, engineering, environment, handicapped, mathematics, science and technology, social services, cultural programs, disadvantaged, ecology, hospices, hospitals, intercultural relations, minorities, museums, performing arts, women, youth.
Types of support: Building funds, capital campaigns, employee matching gifts, operating budgets, special projects, equipment, renovation projects, technical assistance, in-kind gifts, donated equipment, donated products.
Limitations: Giving limited to local organizations in plant communities and to regional organizations benefiting plant communities. No support for religious, political, athletic, fraternal, or veterans' organiaztions, disease-specific organizations, independent elementary and secondary schools, organizations with primarily international activities, productions for public broadcasting, or private foundations. No grants to individuals, or for basic research projects, operating support for United Way affiliates, or organizations whose applications have been denied within the past 12 months.
Publications: Corporate giving report, application guidelines.
Application information: Raytheon has a staff that only handles contributions. Application form not required.
> *Initial approach:* Write to the Manager of Human Resources at the local Raytheon facility or send to headquarters; telephone inquiries discouraged and formal interviews not always possible; follow-up contact will be made by Raytheon as needed
> *Deadline(s):* Mar. 31, June 30, and Sept. 30
> *Final notification:* Generally within 3 months; volume of requests may delay notification
> *Write:* Janet Taylor, Mgr., Corp. Contribs.
Number of staff: 1 full-time professional; 1 full-time support.

1263
Sumner M. Redstone Charitable Foundation
c/o Pannell Kerr Forster
100 Summer St.
Boston 02110-2104
Application address: 200 Elm St., Dedham, MA
02026; Tel.: (617) 461-1600

Established in 1986 in MA.
Foundation type: Independent
Financial data (yr. ended 12/31/90): Assets,
$54,891 (M); expenditures, $248,369; qualifying
distributions, $248,325, including $248,325 for
31 grants (high: $30,500; low: $250).
Purpose and activities: Giving primarily for
Jewish organizations, including welfare funds;
support also for hospitals and medical centers.
Fields of interest: Jewish giving, Jewish welfare,
hospitals, health associations.
Limitations: Giving primarily in MA.
Application information:
    Deadline(s): None
    Write: Sumner M. Redstone, Trustee
Trustee: Sumner M. Redstone.
EIN: 222761621

1264
George C. & Evelyn R. Reisman Charitable Trust
c/o Lourie & Cutler
60 State St.
Boston 02109

Established in 1981 in MA.
Donor(s): George C. Reisman, Apparel Retail
Corp.
Foundation type: Independent
Financial data (yr. ended 12/31/90): Assets,
$9,410,936 (M); expenditures, $524,817;
qualifying distributions, $439,545, including
$439,545 for 41 grants (high: $350,000; low:
$50).
Purpose and activities: Giving primarily to a
Jewish welfare fund; also supports other Jewish
organizations and hospitals.
Fields of interest: Jewish welfare, Jewish giving,
hospitals.
Limitations: Giving limited to Boston, MA. No
grants to individuals.
Application information:
    Initial approach: Letter
    Deadline(s): None
    Write: David Andelman, Trustee
Trustees: David Andelman, Evelyn R. Reisman,
George C. Reisman, Howard Reisman, Robert
Reisman, David Rothstein.
EIN: 042743096

1265
The Mabel Louise Riley Foundation ▼
(also known as The Riley Foundation)
Grants Management Assocs.
230 Congress St., 3rd Fl.
Boston 02110   (617) 426-7172

Established in 1971 in MA as the Mabel Louise
Riley Charitable Trust.
Donor(s): Mabel Louise Riley.‡
Foundation type: Independent

Financial data (yr. ended 05/31/91): Assets,
$34,741,237 (M); expenditures, $2,130,464;
qualifying distributions, $1,901,468, including
$1,767,500 for 60 grants (high: $80,000; low:
$1,000; average: $30,000-$100,000).
Purpose and activities: Interest in new
approaches to important problems, with an
emphasis on improved social services and race
relations; special interest in programs for children
and youth; support for educational programs,
community and neighborhood development,
employment, housing programs, cultural activities
and energy conservation.
Fields of interest: Education, community
development, housing, social services, youth,
race relations, child welfare, employment, family
services, cultural programs, minorities.
Types of support: Seed money, building funds,
equipment, land acquisition, special projects,
renovation projects, technical assistance, capital
campaigns.
Limitations: Giving limited to the greater Boston,
MA, area, with strong emphasis on the city; and
to Cape Cod and Newton, MA. No grants to
individuals, or for operating budgets, continuing
support, annual campaigns, emergency funds,
deficit financing, research, publications,
conferences, professorships, internships,
exchange programs, fellowships, or matching
gifts; no loans.
Publications: Annual report, application
guidelines.
Application information: Application form not
required.
    Initial approach: Proposal or telephone
    Copies of proposal: 1
    Deadline(s): Feb. 15 and Aug. 15
    Board meeting date(s): Apr.-May and Oct.-Nov.
    Final notification: 1 month after board meetings
    Write: Newell Flather, Administrator, Naomi
    Tuchmann, Administrator, or Philip Hall,
    Foundation Asst.
Administrators: Newell Flather, Naomi Tuchmann.
Trustees: Andrew C. Bailey, Douglas Danner,
Robert W. Holmes, Jr., Boston Safe Deposit &
Trust Co.
Number of staff: 2 part-time professional; 1
part-time support.
EIN: 046278857
Recent health grants:
1265-1 Barry L. Price Rehabilitation Center, West
    Newton, MA, $10,000. For renovations. 1991.
1265-2 Dimock Community Health Center,
    Roxbury, MA, $50,000. For capital campaign.
    1991.
1265-3 Fenway Community Health Center,
    Boston, MA, $50,000. For construction of
    health care facility. 1991.
1265-4 Positive Lifestyles, Mattapan, MA,
    $35,000. For construction of housing for
    homeless substance abusers. 1991.
1265-5 Thom Clinic, Boston, MA, $40,000. For
    mental health service program. 1991.

1266
The Rogers Family Foundation
P.O. Box 100
Lawrence 01842   (508) 685-1000

Trust established in 1957 in MA.
Donor(s): Irving E. Rogers, Eagle-Tribune
Publishing Co., Martha B. Rogers.

Foundation type: Independent
Financial data (yr. ended 12/31/90): Assets,
$8,864,212 (M); gifts received, $401,982;
expenditures, $385,975; qualifying distributions,
$348,379, including $348,379 for 58 grants
(high: $30,000; low: $300).
Fields of interest: Hospitals, higher education,
secondary education, community development,
community funds, religion—Christian.
Limitations: Giving limited to the greater
Lawrence, MA, area, including Methuen,
Andover, and Haverhill, MA, and southeastern
NH. No grants to individuals, or for endowment
funds, research, scholarships, fellowships, or
matching gifts; no loans.
Application information: Funds largely
committed.
    Initial approach: Proposal
    Deadline(s): None
    Final notification: Within 2 or 3 months
    Write: Irving E. Rogers, Jr., Trustee
Trustees: Irving E. Rogers, Jr., Martha B. Rogers,
Richard M. Wyman.
EIN: 046063152

1267
Rowland Foundation, Inc. ▼
P.O. Box 13
Cambridge 02238

Incorporated in 1960 in DE.
Donor(s): Edwin H. Land, Helen M. Land.
Foundation type: Independent
Financial data (yr. ended 11/30/90): Assets,
$36,484,938 (M); expenditures, $2,141,144;
qualifying distributions, $1,959,536, including
$1,959,536 for 44 grants (high: $350,000;
average: $10,000-$50,000).
Purpose and activities: Grants primarily for
education including colleges and universities,
social services, health, medical research,
conservation, and cultural programs, including
museums and historical associations.
Fields of interest: Education, social services,
health, medical research, conservation, cultural
programs, museums, history.
Types of support: Professorships, general
purposes, research.
Limitations: Giving primarily in the
Boston-Cambridge, MA, area. No grants to
individuals, or for capital or endowment funds, or
matching gifts; no loans.
Publications: Annual report.
Application information: Application form not
required.
    Initial approach: Letter
    Copies of proposal: 1
    Deadline(s): None
    Board meeting date(s): As required
    Final notification: Varies
    Write: Philip DuBois, V.P.
Officers and Trustees:* Edwin H. Land,* Pres.;
Philip DuBois,* V.P.; Helen M. Land,* V.P.; Julius
Silver, Secy.; Jennifer Land DuBois.
Number of staff: None.
EIN: 046046756

1268
Lawrence J. and Anne Rubenstein Charitable Foundation
c/o Beacon Hill Capitol Corp.
One Boston Place, 31st Fl.
Boston 02108   (617) 973-0550

Trust established in 1963 in MA.
Donor(s): Lawrence J. Rubenstein,‡ Anne C. Rubenstein.
Foundation type: Independent
Financial data (yr. ended 05/31/91): Assets, $11,116,414 (M); gifts received, $1,997,004; expenditures, $513,126; qualifying distributions, $413,215, including $409,785 for 19 grants (high: $100,000; low: $1,000).
Purpose and activities: Giving for hospitals, early childhood, higher and medical education, science and technology, medical research, including cancer research, but with emphasis on medical care and research relating to children's illnesses; support also for programs for the homeless and the performing arts.
Fields of interest: Hospitals, medical research, cancer, science and technology, education—early childhood, higher education, child welfare, homeless, arts, general charitable giving.
Types of support: Annual campaigns, building funds, capital campaigns, emergency funds, endowment funds, equipment, general purposes, professorships, special projects.
Limitations: Giving primarily in MA.
Application information: Application form not required.
  Initial approach: Letter
  Copies of proposal: 1
  Deadline(s): Prior to May 1 of year grant requested
  Board meeting date(s): Quarterly
  Write: Richard I. Kaner, Trustee
Trustees: Richard I. Kaner, Frank Kopelman, Anne C. Rubenstein.
Number of staff: 1 part-time professional.
EIN: 046087371

1269
Josephine G. Russell Trust
70 East St.
Methuen 01844   (508) 687-0151
A copy of the application must also be sent to each of the following addresses: Archer L. Bolton, Jr., Trustee, P.O. Box 806, Rockport, ME 04856; Marsha E. Rich, Esq., Trustee, 59 Lucerne Dr., Andover, MA 01810

Trust established in 1934.
Donor(s): Josephine G. Russell.‡
Foundation type: Independent
Financial data (yr. ended 12/31/91): Assets, $5,621,192 (M); expenditures, $323,144; qualifying distributions, $284,200, including $284,200 for 35 grants (high: $66,700; low: $1,000; average: $5,000-$10,000).
Purpose and activities: Giving for hospitals, schools, and a community fund.
Fields of interest: Hospitals, education, community funds.
Types of support: General purposes, annual campaigns, emergency funds, building funds, equipment, publications, scholarship funds, special projects.

Limitations: Giving limited to the greater Lawrence, MA, area. No grants to individuals, or for matching gifts; no loans.
Publications: 990-PF, application guidelines.
Application information: Application form not required.
  Initial approach: Letter or proposal
  Copies of proposal: 3
  Deadline(s): Jan. 31
  Board meeting date(s): Quarterly
  Write: Clifford E. Elias, Esq., Trustee
Trustees: Archer L. Bolton, Jr., Clifford E. Elias, Marsha E. Rich.
Number of staff: 1 part-time professional; 1 part-time support.
EIN: 042136910

1270
Sailors' Snug Harbor of Boston
c/o Adams, Harkness and Hill
One Liberty Sq.
Boston 02109   (617) 423-6688

Established in 1852 in MA.
Foundation type: Independent
Financial data (yr. ended 04/30/90): Assets, $3,815,796 (M); expenditures, $279,096; qualifying distributions, $252,820, including $226,105 for 24 grants (high: $50,000; low: $2,500).
Purpose and activities: Giving for the health and welfare of the aged, sailors, and others; grants to institutions for the relief and support of aged sailors.
Fields of interest: Health, welfare, aged, seamen, welfare—indigent individuals, family services.
Limitations: Giving primarily in the Boston, MA, area. No grants to individuals.
Application information: Application form not required.
  Initial approach: Proposal
  Deadline(s): In time for approval at board meetings
  Board meeting date(s): Nov. 15, Feb. 15, and Apr. 15
  Write: Stephen Little, Pres.
Officers and Trustees:* Stephen Little,* Pres.; Charles E. Rogerson II,* Secy.-Treas.; Richard E. Byrd, Charles K. Cobb, Jr., G. Lincoln Dow, Jr., Joseph E. Eaton, Charles R. Eddy, Robert W. Loring, Francis B. Lothrop, Jr., Everett Morse, Jr., John A. Perkins, Thomas Rogerson, G. West Saltonstall, William L. Saltonstall, Henry Wheeler, Benjamin Williams, Thomas B. Williams, Jr.
EIN: 042104430

1271
Richard Saltonstall Charitable Foundation
c/o S & Co., Inc.
50 Congress St., Rm. 800
Boston 02109   (617) 227-8660

Established in 1964 in MA.
Foundation type: Independent
Financial data (yr. ended 12/31/90): Assets, $9,987,002 (M); expenditures, $505,474; qualifying distributions, $455,608, including $455,608 for 27 grants (high: $50,000; low: $2,000).

Fields of interest: Hospitals, medical research, youth, performing arts, museums, community funds.
Limitations: Giving primarily in MA.
Application information: Application form not required.
  Initial approach: Letter
  Deadline(s): None
  Write: Dudley H. Willis or Robert A. Lawrence, Trustees
Trustees: Robert A. Lawrence, Dudley H. Willis.
EIN: 046078934

1272
Sawyer Charitable Foundation
142 Berkeley St.
Boston 02116   (617) 267-2414

Trust established in 1957 in MA.
Donor(s): Frank Sawyer, William Sawyer, The Brattle Co. Corp., St. Botolph Holding Co., First Franklin Parking Corp., and others, First Federal Packing Corp.
Foundation type: Independent
Financial data (yr. ended 12/31/91): Assets, $5,156,492 (M); gifts received, $5,200; expenditures, $311,728; qualifying distributions, $272,794, including $232,950 for 76 grants (high: $25,250; low: $100).
Fields of interest: Jewish welfare, Catholic welfare, community funds, health services, hospitals, handicapped.
Limitations: Giving primarily in the greater New England area. No grants to individuals, or for operating budgets or building funds.
Application information:
  Initial approach: Proposal
  Deadline(s): Oct. 15
  Write: Carol S. Parks, Exec. Dir.
Officers: Carol S. Parks, Exec. Dir.; Frank Sawyer, Mgr.; Mildred F. Sawyer, Mgr.
EIN: 046088774

1273
William E. Schrafft and Bertha E. Schrafft Charitable Trust
One Financial Center, 26th Fl.
Boston 02111   (617) 457-7327

Trust established in 1946 in MA.
Donor(s): William E. Schrafft,‡ Bertha E. Schrafft.‡
Foundation type: Independent
Financial data (yr. ended 12/31/91): Assets, $16,176,192 (M); expenditures, $906,183; qualifying distributions, $798,000, including $798,000 for 92 grants (high: $80,000; low: $1,000; average: $1,000-$75,000).
Purpose and activities: Grants primarily for educational programs in the Boston metropolitan area, for minorities and higher and secondary education; support also for community funds, cultural programs, youth agencies, and hospitals.
Fields of interest: Higher education, secondary education, education—minorities, community funds, youth, cultural programs, hospitals.
Types of support: General purposes, operating budgets, continuing support, annual campaigns, endowment funds, scholarship funds.
Limitations: Giving limited to MA, with emphasis on the Boston metropolitan area. No grants to

individuals, or for matching gifts, seed money, emergency funds, or deficit financing; no loans.
Publications: Annual report, application guidelines.
Application information: Application form not required.
Initial approach: Proposal
Copies of proposal: 4
Deadline(s): None
Board meeting date(s): About 6 times a year
Final notification: 2 months
Write: Karen Faulkner, Exec. Dir.
Officer: Karen Faulkner, Exec. Dir.
Trustees: Lavania B. Chase, Arthur Parker, John M. Wood, Jr.
Number of staff: None.
EIN: 046065605
Recent health grants:
1273-1 Childrens Hospital, Boston, MA, $20,000. 1990.
1273-2 Dana-Farber Cancer Institute, Boston, MA, $35,000. 1990.
1273-3 Massachusetts Eye and Ear Infirmary, Boston, MA, $10,000. 1990.
1273-4 National Society to Prevent Blindness, Boston, MA, $15,000. 1990.
1273-5 New England Home for Little Wanderers, Brookline, MA, $10,000. 1990.
1273-6 Thom Clinic, Boston, MA, $10,000. 1990.
1273-7 Winchester Hospital Foundation, Winchester, MA, $10,000. 1990.

1274
Abraham Shapiro Charity Fund
65 Sprague St.
Readville 02137   (617) 361-1200

Trust established in 1945 in MA.
Donor(s): Abraham Shapiro, and various companies.
Foundation type: Independent
Financial data (yr. ended 12/31/90): Assets, $5,253,137 (M); expenditures, $365,119; qualifying distributions, $326,000, including $326,000 for 9 grants (high: $130,000; low: $500).
Fields of interest: Jewish welfare, higher education, hospitals.
Limitations: Giving primarily in MA. No grants to individuals, or for scholarships, fellowships, or matching gifts; no loans.
Application information: Contributes only to pre-selected organizations. Applications not accepted.
Board meeting date(s): Quarterly
Write: George Shapiro, Trustee
Trustees: Arthur S. Goldberg, George Shapiro, Philip Shir.
EIN: 046043588

1275
Carl and Ruth Shapiro Foundation
Two Commonwealth Ave.
Boston 02116-3134

Established around 1966 in MA as Carl Shapiro Foundation.
Donor(s): Carl Shapiro, Ruth Shapiro.
Foundation type: Independent

Financial data (yr. ended 12/31/90): Assets, $3,882,231 (M); gifts received, $175,000; expenditures, $500,187; qualifying distributions, $486,660, including $486,660 for grants.
Purpose and activities: Grants primarily for Jewish welfare funds, higher education, hospitals, art organizations, and museums. Scholarships also given for medical research concerning the mind and for religious study.
Fields of interest: Jewish welfare, higher education, hospitals, arts, museums.
Application information: Contributes only to pre-selected organizations. Applications not accepted.
Officers: Carl Shapiro, Pres.; Ruth Shapiro, Secy.
EIN: 046135027

1276
Shawmut National Corporation Direct Contributions Program
c/o Community Relations, Shawmut Bank
One Federal St., 35th Fl.
Boston 02211   (617) 292-3748
Address in CT: Maxine Dean, Community Rels., Connecticut Natl. Bank, 777 Main St., Hartford, CT 06115; Tel.: (203) 728-2274

Financial data (yr. ended 12/31/90): Total giving, $4,000,000 for 700 grants.
Purpose and activities: Shawmut National Corporation manages its corporate contributions through a direct giving program administered by its primary affiliates, Shawmut Bank and Connecticut National Bank. Support for the United Way, community services, education, health, cultural organizations, and economic development are major elements of the program.
Fields of interest: Community development, arts, community funds, cultural programs, health, homeless, education, literacy, social services, urban development.
Types of support: Employee matching gifts, operating budgets, capital campaigns.
Limitations: Giving primarily in MA, CT, and RI. No support for medical research, national health organizations, political, religious, or fraternal organizations or grantmaking organizations. No grants to individuals; or for conferences, benefits, special events.
Publications: Application guidelines.
Application information: Company has a staff that only handles contributions. Application form not required.
Initial approach: Telephone or letter to community relations department at nearest SNC bank branch or regional office; recommendations for grants are made on the local level to the main office in Boston offices and Hartford
Copies of proposal: 1
Deadline(s): Varies by state
Board meeting date(s): Varies by state
Final notification: Varies by state
Write: Dinah L. Waldsmith, Asst. V.P.
Administrators: Maxine Dean, Asst. V.P. and Admin., Charitable Contribs.; Dinah Waldsmith, Asst. V.P. and Admin., Charitable Contribs.
Number of staff: 2 full-time professional; 1 full-time support.

1277
Sheraton Foundation, Inc.
c/o The Sheraton Corp.
60 State St.
Boston 02109   (617) 367-5454

Incorporated in 1950 in MA.
Donor(s): ITT Sheraton Corp.
Foundation type: Company-sponsored
Financial data (yr. ended 12/31/90): Assets, $3,704,288 (M); expenditures, $253,785; qualifying distributions, $171,194, including $171,194 for 21 grants (high: $50,000; low: $100).
Purpose and activities: Support primarily for community funds; some grants to educational institutions, including scholarship funds, health agencies, youth agencies, and hospitals.
Fields of interest: Community funds, education, health services, youth, hospitals.
Types of support: General purposes, continuing support, annual campaigns, scholarship funds.
Limitations: Giving primarily in the greater Boston, MA, area. No grants to individuals, or for endowment or capital funds, research, or matching gifts; no loans.
Application information: Applicants for scholarship funds must be enrolled in hotel administration and/or restaurant management.
Initial approach: Proposal
Copies of proposal: 1
Board meeting date(s): Apr., July, Sept., and Dec.
Final notification: 6 months
Write: Brenda J. Furlong, Treas.
Officers and Directors:* John Kapioltas,* Pres.; Brenda J. Furlong,* Treas.; William D. Buxton.
Number of staff: 2
EIN: 046039510

1278
George and Beatrice Sherman Family Charitable Trust
c/o Goulston & Storrs
400 Atlantic Ave.
Boston 02110

Trust established in 1969.
Donor(s): George Sherman.‡
Foundation type: Independent
Financial data (yr. ended 06/30/91): Assets, $3,654,990 (M); expenditures, $542,297; qualifying distributions, $430,658, including $400,130 for 116 grants (high: $50,000; low: $50).
Purpose and activities: Emphasis on higher education; support also for Jewish welfare funds, temple support, and hospitals.
Fields of interest: Higher education, Jewish welfare, Jewish giving, hospitals.
Limitations: Giving primarily in MA. No grants to individuals.
Application information: Contributes only to pre-selected organizations. Applications not accepted.
Trustees: Jacob Lewiton, Alan W. Rottenberg, Norton L. Sherman, Marvin Sparrow.
EIN: 046223350

1279
Richard and Susan Smith Foundation
27 Boylston St., Box 1000
Chestnut Hill 02167   (617) 232-8200
To contact only when further clarification of the guidelines is needed: c/o Grants Management Assocs., 230 Congress St., Boston, MA 02110; Tel.: (617) 426-7172

Trust established in 1970 in MA.
Donor(s): Marian Smith,‡ Richard A. Smith.
Foundation type: Independent
Financial data (yr. ended 04/30/91): Assets, $3,668,805 (M); gifts received, $820,000; expenditures, $1,018,067; qualifying distributions, $1,001,067, including $959,024 for 55 grants (high: $320,000; low: $100).
Purpose and activities: Grants for health, education, children and youth programs; the arts are a secondary field of interest. Particularly interested in organizations providing opportunities for economically disadvantaged populations, especially children and youth, and cancer research.
Fields of interest: Health, cancer, medical research, hospitals—building funds, education, higher education, social services, youth, child welfare, disadvantaged, arts, museums.
Types of support: General purposes, building funds, capital campaigns, special projects, annual campaigns, fellowships, research, seed money.
Limitations: Giving primarily in the greater Boston, MA, area. No support for sectarian religious activities or political causes. No grants to individuals, or for deficit financing, endowment funds, operating budgets, efforts supported by the general public, or efforts in which the foundation may become the sole source of funding.
Publications: 990-PF, application guidelines.
Application information: Application form not required.
   Initial approach: Letter
   Copies of proposal: 2
   Deadline(s): None
   Board meeting date(s): Fall and spring
   Write: Kay M. Kilpatrick, Contribs.
      Administrator
Trustees: Amy S. Berylson, John G. Berylson, Brian J. Knez, Debra S. Knez, Dana W. Smith, Robert A. Smith, Susan F. Smith.
Number of staff: None.
EIN: 237090011

1280
State Street Foundation ▼
c/o State Street Bank & Trust Co.
P.O. Box 351
Boston 02101   (617) 654-3381
Application address: Public Affairs Division, State Street Boston Corp., 225 Franklin St., Boston, MA 02101

Trust established in 1963 in MA.
Donor(s): State Street Bank & Trust Co.
Foundation type: Company-sponsored
Financial data (yr. ended 12/31/90): Assets, $4,588,854 (M); gifts received, $2,236,943; expenditures, $1,893,311; qualifying distributions, $1,880,425, including $1,814,283 for 123 grants (high: $120,000; low: $1,368; average: $3,000-$20,000) and $57,905 for 440 employee matching gifts.

Purpose and activities: Grants to organizations helping to improve the quality of life for residents of the greater Boston area, with emphasis on community funds, neighborhood development, health and human services, public and secondary education, job training, and cultural programs.
Fields of interest: Cultural programs, social services, community development, health, education, secondary education, vocational education, community funds.
Types of support: Annual campaigns, building funds, capital campaigns, continuing support, emergency funds, employee matching gifts, endowment funds, equipment, general purposes, land acquisition, matching funds, operating budgets, program-related investments, renovation projects, special projects, technical assistance.
Limitations: Giving primarily in the greater Boston, MA, area. No grants to individuals, or for scholarships.
Publications: including application guidelines, 990-PF.
Application information: Application form not required.
   Initial approach: Proposal
   Copies of proposal: 1
   Deadline(s): None
   Board meeting date(s): Quarterly
   Final notification: 2 weeks after meeting
   Write: Madison Thompson, Asst. V.P., State
      Street Bank & Trust Co.
Trustee: State Street Bank & Trust Co.
Number of staff: 2 full-time professional; 2 full-time support.
EIN: 046401847
Recent health grants:
1280-1 Dimock Community Health Center, Roxbury, MA, $25,000. For capital campaign. 1990.
1280-2 Harvard Street Neighborhood Health Center, Dorchester, MA, $10,000. For additional physician time for Adolescent and Child Life Center. 1990.
1280-3 Lahey Clinic Foundation, Burlington, MA, $10,000. For 21st Century Fund Campaign. 1990.
1280-4 Massachusetts General Hospital, Boston, MA, $30,000. For capital campaign towards emergency room facilities. 1990.
1280-5 Mattapan Community Health Center, Mattapan, MA, $15,000. For general operating support. 1990.
1280-6 Quincy City Hospital, Quincy, MA, $10,000. For capital support for first major modernization project. 1990.
1280-7 Women, Inc., Dorchester, MA, $10,000. Toward educational and job placement programs. 1990.

1281
Stearns Charitable Trust
66 Commonwealth Ave.
Concord 01742

Trust established in 1947 in MA.
Donor(s): Russell B. Stearns.‡
Foundation type: Independent
Financial data (yr. ended 12/31/91): Assets, $4,182,120 (M); expenditures, $168,997; qualifying distributions, $148,825, including $142,500 for 46 grants (high: $10,000; low: $500).

Purpose and activities: Emphasis on cultural programs, including a science museum; support also for libraries, community funds, the environment, an aquarium corporation, and social services.
Fields of interest: Cultural programs, museums, libraries, health, alcoholism, community funds, environment, social services.
Types of support: Annual campaigns, general purposes, special projects, program-related investments.
Limitations: Giving primarily in MA. No grants to individuals.
Application information: Contributes only to pre-selected organizations. Applications not accepted.
   Board meeting date(s): As required
   Write: Russell S. Beede, Trustee
Trustees: Russell S. Beede, Virginia Stearns Gassel, Anne B. Jencks.
Number of staff: None.
EIN: 046036697

1282
Artemas W. Stearns Trust
70 East St.
Methuen 01844-4597   (508) 687-0151
A copy of the application must also be sent to each of the following addresses: Vincent P. Morton, Jr., Trustee, 14 Sunset Rock Rd., Andover, MA 01810; Marsha E. Rich, Esq., 59 Lucerne Dr., Andover, MA 01810

Trust established in 1896 in MA.
Donor(s): Artemas W. Stearns.‡
Foundation type: Independent
Financial data (yr. ended 12/31/91): Assets, $3,422,730 (M); expenditures, $213,658; qualifying distributions, $186,500, including $186,500 for 30 grants (high: $30,000; low: $500; average: $5,000).
Purpose and activities: Support for organizations which service and benefit the deserving poor and indigent aged people, including hospitals, community projects, and secondary schools.
Fields of interest: Welfare, aged, hospitals, community development, secondary education.
Types of support: Annual campaigns, building funds, emergency funds, equipment, general purposes, publications, scholarship funds, special projects.
Limitations: Giving limited to the greater Lawrence, MA, area. No grants to individuals, or for endowment funds or matching gifts; no loans.
Publications: 990-PF, application guidelines.
Application information: Contact foundation for addresses to which additional copies of request should be sent. Application form not required.
   Initial approach: Letter or proposal
   Copies of proposal: 3
   Deadline(s): Jan. 31
   Board meeting date(s): Quarterly
   Write: Clifford E. Elias, Esq., Trustee
Trustees: Clifford E. Elias, Vincent P. Morton, Jr., Marsha E. Rich.
Number of staff: 1 full-time professional; 1 part-time support.
EIN: 042137061

1283
The Abbot and Dorothy H. Stevens Foundation
P.O. Box 111
North Andover 01845   (508) 688-7211

Trust established in 1953 in MA.
Donor(s): Abbot Stevens.‡
Foundation type: Independent
Financial data (yr. ended 12/31/90): Assets, $12,374,528 (M); expenditures, $789,999; qualifying distributions, $1,274,005, including $676,280 for 81 grants (high: $50,000; low: $100; average: $2,000-$5,000) and $546,200 for loans.
Fields of interest: Health, education, youth, welfare, conservation, arts, historic preservation, humanities, museums.
Types of support: Building funds, capital campaigns, continuing support, endowment funds, equipment, matching funds, operating budgets, renovation projects, seed money, technical assistance.
Limitations: Giving limited to MA, with emphasis on the greater Lawrence area. No support for national organizations, or for state or federal agencies. No grants to individuals, or for annual campaigns, deficit financing, exchange programs, internships, professorships, scholarships, or fellowships; no loans.
Publications: Program policy statement, application guidelines.
Application information: Application form not required.
   Initial approach: Proposal
   Copies of proposal: 1
   Board meeting date(s): Monthly except July and Aug.
   Write: Elizabeth A. Beland, Administrator
Trustees: Phebe S. Miner, Christopher W. Rogers, Samuel S. Rogers.
Number of staff: 1 full-time professional.
EIN: 046107991

1284
The Nathaniel and Elizabeth P. Stevens Foundation
P.O. Box 111
North Andover 01845   (508) 688-7211

Trust established in 1943 in MA.
Donor(s): Nathaniel Stevens.‡
Foundation type: Independent
Financial data (yr. ended 12/31/90): Assets, $9,616,626 (M); expenditures, $662,915; qualifying distributions, $1,037,414, including $537,926 for 89 grants (high: $50,000; low: $100; average: $2,000-$10,000) and $453,800 for loans.
Fields of interest: Conservation, health, hospitals, social services, housing, minorities, arts, historic preservation, museums, education.
Types of support: General purposes, seed money, emergency funds, building funds, equipment, land acquisition, endowment funds, special projects, matching funds, capital campaigns, conferences and seminars, consulting services, continuing support, operating budgets, renovation projects, technical assistance.
Limitations: Giving limited to MA, with emphasis on the greater Lawrence area. No support for national organizations, or for state or federal

agencies. No grants to individuals, or for deficit financing, exchange programs, internships, lectureships, research, professorships, scholarships, fellowships, or annual campaigns; no loans.
Publications: Application guidelines, program policy statement.
Application information: Application form not required.
   Initial approach: Proposal
   Copies of proposal: 1
   Deadline(s): None
   Board meeting date(s): Monthly except July and Aug.
   Final notification: 2 months
   Write: Elizabeth A. Beland, Administrator
Trustees: Joshua L. Miner IV, Phebe S. Miner, Samuel S. Rogers.
Number of staff: 1 shared staff
EIN: 042236996

1285
The Stoddard Charitable Trust ▼
370 Main St., 12th Fl.
Worcester 01608   (508) 798-8621

Trust established in 1939 in MA.
Donor(s): Harry G. Stoddard.‡
Foundation type: Independent
Financial data (yr. ended 12/31/90): Assets, $39,164,894 (M); gifts received, $2,037,201; expenditures, $3,544,029; qualifying distributions, $3,229,269, including $3,205,500 for 83 grants (high: $400,000; low: $1,000; average: $5,000-$30,000).
Purpose and activities: Emphasis on education, cultural programs, historical associations, youth agencies, and a community fund; support also for social service agencies, the environment, and health associations.
Fields of interest: Education, cultural programs, youth, historic preservation, history, community funds, social services, environment, health associations.
Types of support: Annual campaigns, seed money, emergency funds, building funds, equipment, land acquisition, research, scholarship funds, fellowships, professorships, internships, matching funds, general purposes, continuing support, renovation projects.
Limitations: Giving primarily in Worcester, MA. No grants to individuals.
Application information: Application form not required.
   Initial approach: Proposal
   Copies of proposal: 5
   Deadline(s): Submit proposal between Jan. and Nov.; no set deadlines
   Board meeting date(s): As required
   Final notification: 3 months
   Write: Warner S. Fletcher, Chair.
Officers and Trustees: Warner S. Fletcher,* Chair.; Helen E. Stoddard,* Vice-Chair.; Valerie S. Loring,* Secy.; Judith S. King, Treas.; Allen W. Fletcher, Marion S. Fletcher.
Number of staff: None.
EIN: 046023791
Recent health grants:
1285-1 Great Brook Valley Health Center, Worcester, MA, $50,000. 1990.
1285-2 Health Awareness Services of Central Massachusetts, Worcester, MA, $10,000. 1990.

1285-3 Spectrum House, Westboro, MA, $30,000. 1990.
1285-4 Tufts University, School of Veterinary Medicine, Grafton, MA, $15,000. 1990.

1286
The Stone Charitable Foundation, Inc.
P.O. Box 728
Wareham 02571   (508) 759-3503

Incorporated in 1948 in MA.
Donor(s): Dewey D. Stone,‡ Stephen A. Stone, Anne A. Stone,‡ Thelma Finn, Jack Finn, Harry K. Stone.‡
Foundation type: Independent
Financial data (yr. ended 11/30/91): Assets, $6,408,031 (M); gifts received, $450,000; expenditures, $393,696; qualifying distributions, $356,614, including $352,650 for 48 grants (high: $65,000; low: $50).
Purpose and activities: Giving largely for Jewish organizations and welfare funds; grants also for hospitals, higher education, cultural programs, and the promotion of peace.
Fields of interest: Jewish welfare, Jewish giving, hospitals, health, higher education, cultural programs, peace.
Types of support: General purposes, research, endowment funds, scholarship funds, building funds, annual campaigns, equipment, capital campaigns.
Limitations: Giving primarily in MA. No grants to individuals.
Application information: Application form not required.
   Deadline(s): None
   Board meeting date(s): As required
   Write: Stephen A. Stone, Pres.
Officers: Stephen A. Stone, Pres.; Theodore H. Teplow, Secy.; Alford Rudnick, Treas.
Number of staff: None.
EIN: 046114683

1287
Anne and David Stoneman Charitable Foundation, Inc.
c/o Grants Mgmt. Assocs.
230 Congress St.
Boston 02110   (617) 426-7172

Incorporated in 1957 in MA.
Donor(s): Anne Stoneman.
Foundation type: Independent
Financial data (yr. ended 07/31/91): Assets, $1,952,781 (M); gifts received, $166,218; expenditures, $293,207; qualifying distributions, $256,130, including $244,550 for 62 grants (high: $17,000; low: $250).
Purpose and activities: "To strengthen the ability of economically deprived people to provide for themselves and their families, to help people achieve independence and self-sufficiency, and to improve the services and programs of nonprofit organizations." Giving primarily for Jewish welfare funds, hospitals, and the performing arts; some support also for education.
Fields of interest: Jewish welfare, hospitals, performing arts, education, education—minorities.
Types of support: Annual campaigns, seed money, capital campaigns, special projects, equipment.

Limitations: Giving primarily in Boston and Cape Cod, MA, Palm Beach County, FL, NC, KY, and the State of Israel. No grants to individuals.
Publications: Informational brochure (including application guidelines).
Application information: Application form required.
> *Initial approach:* Letter
> *Copies of proposal:* 2
> *Deadline(s):* Dec. 15
> *Board meeting date(s):* Winter and summer
> *Final notification:* July
> *Write:* Jean S. Whitney, Administrator
Officers and Directors:* Miriam H. Stoneman,* Pres.; Ala H. Reid, Treas.; Elizabeth Deknatel, Maria Deknatel, Jean R. Fitzpatrick, Alan Rottenberg, Robert Smith, Eric Stein, Jane Stein.
Number of staff: 2 part-time professional.
EIN: 046047379

1288
Stratford Foundation ▼
53 State St., 15th Fl.
Boston 02109   (617) 248-7426

Established in 1983 in MA.
Donor(s): Kenneth H. Olsen.
Foundation type: Independent
Financial data (yr. ended 12/31/91): Assets, $90,957,967 (M); gifts received, $124,200; expenditures, $6,237,543; qualifying distributions, $6,237,543, including $6,040,708 for 68 grants (high: $895,125; low: $2,355; average: $20,000-$100,000).
Purpose and activities: Grants primarily to institutions closely associated with the donor and the donor's family. However, non-donor associated grants are also actively considered.
Limitations: No grants to individuals.
Publications: Application guidelines, 990-PF.
Application information: Application form required.
> *Initial approach:* Letter
> *Copies of proposal:* 2
> *Deadline(s):* None
> *Board meeting date(s):* Periodically
> *Write:* Peter A. Wilson, Exec. Dir.
Trustees: Ava Lisa Memmen, Eeva-Liisa Aulikki Olsen, Kenneth H. Olsen, Richard J. Testa.
Custodial Bank: Investors Bank & Trust Co.
Number of staff: None.
EIN: 222524023
Recent health grants:
1288-1 American Cancer Society, NYC, NY, $36,400. 1990.
1288-2 Childrens Medical Center Research Foundation, Dayton, OH, $21,769. 1990.
1288-3 Christian Medical and Dental Society, Richardson, TX, $21,769. 1990.
1288-4 Emerson Hospital, Concord, MA, $21,769. 1990.
1288-5 Joslin Diabetes Center, Boston, MA, $72,562. 1990.
1288-6 Lancaster Cleft Palate Clinic, Lancaster, PA, $50,878. 1990.

1289
Thomas Thompson Trust
31 Milk St., Suite 201
Boston 02109-5104   (617) 338-2798

Trust established in 1869 in MA.
Donor(s): Thomas Thompson.‡
Foundation type: Independent
Financial data (yr. ended 05/31/91): Assets, $9,127,745 (M); expenditures, $417,997; qualifying distributions, $345,340, including $345,340 for 17 grants (high: $100,000; low: $1,400; average: $2,000-$20,000).
Purpose and activities: To assist poor seamstresses, needlewomen, and shop girls in temporary need. Funds may be distributed "to those charitable organizations...deemed to be directed toward the promotion of health, education, or the general social or civic betterment."
Fields of interest: Health, education, social services, welfare.
Types of support: Annual campaigns, emergency funds, building funds, equipment, land acquisition, matching funds, special projects, renovation projects.
Limitations: Giving limited to Windham County, VT, particularly in the town of Brattleboro, and to Dutchess County, NY, particularly in the town of Rhinebeck. No grants to individuals, or for operating budgets, continuing support, seed money, deficit financing, endowment funds, scholarships, or fellowships; no loans.
Publications: Application guidelines.
Application information: Grants awarded only to organizations that have been in operation for 3 consecutive years. Application form not required.
> *Initial approach:* Telephone
> *Copies of proposal:* 1
> *Deadline(s):* None
> *Board meeting date(s):* Monthly except Aug., and as required
> *Final notification:* 6 weeks
> *Write:* Daniel W. Fawcett or William B. Tyler, Trustees
Trustees: Daniel W. Fawcett, William B. Tyler.
Number of staff: 1 part-time professional.
EIN: 030179429

1290
The Tupancy-Harris Foundation of 1986
c/o Fiduciary Trust Co.
Box 1647
Boston 02105-1647
Application address: 175 Federal St., Boston, MA 02110; Tel.: (617) 482-5270

Established in 1986 in MA.
Donor(s): Oswald A. Tupancy.‡
Foundation type: Independent
Financial data (yr. ended 12/31/91): Assets, $11,771,417 (M); gifts received, $910,740; expenditures, $504,030; qualifying distributions, $440,042, including $439,996 for 22 grants (high: $193,087; low: $1,000).
Purpose and activities: Support for the activities of the Nantucket Conservation Foundation and the Nantucket Historical Association; grants also for welfare programs, medical research for hospitals, public television, and the University of Michigan.
Fields of interest: Conservation, historic preservation, social services, youth, medical research, hospitals, media and communications, higher education.
Limitations: Giving primarily in Nantucket, MA.

Application information: Application form not required.
> *Initial approach:* Letter
> *Copies of proposal:* 1
> *Deadline(s):* None
> *Write:* Robert N. Karelitz, V.P., Fiduciary Trust Co.
Trustee: Fiduciary Trust Co.
Number of staff: None.
EIN: 046547989

1291
Edwin S. Webster Foundation
c/o Grants Management Assocs., Inc.
230 Congress St., 3rd Fl.
Boston 02110   (617) 426-7172

Trust established in 1948 in MA.
Donor(s): Edwin S. Webster.‡
Foundation type: Independent
Financial data (yr. ended 12/31/91): Assets, $23,316,677 (M); expenditures, $1,003,500; qualifying distributions, $984,000, including $984,000 for 60 grants (high: $60,000; low: $2,000).
Fields of interest: Education, social services, minorities, cultural programs, youth, hospitals, medical research.
Types of support: Operating budgets, building funds, endowment funds, special projects, research, capital campaigns.
Limitations: Giving primarily in New England, with an emphasis on the Boston, MA, area. No grants to individuals, or for emergency funds, deficit financing, publications, or conferences; no loans.
Publications: Grants list, application guidelines.
Application information: Application form not required.
> *Initial approach:* Proposal
> *Copies of proposal:* 1
> *Deadline(s):* Submit proposal preferably in Mar. or Sept.; no set deadline
> *Board meeting date(s):* June and Dec.
> *Final notification:* 15 days after meetings on grant proposals
> *Write:* Administrator
Officer and Trustees:* Richard Harte, Jr.,* Secy.; Henry U. Harris, Jr., Henry U. Harris III, Edwin W. Hiam.
Number of staff: 2 shared staff
EIN: 046000647

1292
Fred W. Wells Trust Fund
c/o Fleet Bank of Massachusetts
P.O. Box 9003-MASPM18TRU
Springfield 01101   (413) 785-8524
Additional tel.: (413) 785-8570

Donor(s): Fred W. Wells.‡
Foundation type: Independent
Financial data (yr. ended 06/30/91): Assets, $2,946,189 (M); expenditures, $179,191; qualifying distributions, $152,906, including $13,343 for 5 grants (high: $6,193; low: $150) and $120,051 for 321 grants to individuals (high: $4,500; low: $50).
Purpose and activities: Grants for medical and other health care programs, and agricultural

accomplishment prizes; support also for scholarships.
Fields of interest: Hospitals, health services, agriculture.
Types of support: Scholarship funds.
Limitations: Giving limited to Franklin County, MA; scholarships limited to residents of Greenfield, Deerfield, Shelburne, Ashfield, Montague, Buckland, Charlemont, Heath, Leyden, Gill, Northfield, Conway, Bernardston, Hawley, Rowe, and Monroe, MA.
Publications: Application guidelines.
Application information: Application form required for education grants.
  Initial approach: Letter
  Copies of proposal: 1
  Deadline(s): Apr. 15 for education grants
  Board meeting date(s): May
  Final notification: May 31
  Write: Thea E. Katsounakis or Edna Walters
Officer and Trustees:* Theodore Penick,* Chair.; Gail Bissell, Douglas A. Chandler, Jean Cummings, Nancy Dole, Laurel Ann Glocheski, Ralph W. Haskins, Thomas Heywood, Donald J. LaPierre, Peter C. Mackin, Robert Merriam, Marsha Pratt, Louis Scott, Donald Smiaroski, Todd Sumner.
EIN: 046412350

1293
Arthur Ashley Williams Foundation
345 Union Ave.
P.O. Box 665
Framingham 01701   (508) 872-4334

Incorporated in 1951 in MA.
Donor(s): Arthur A. Williams.‡
Foundation type: Independent
Financial data (yr. ended 12/31/91): Assets, $3,126,914 (M); expenditures, $197,333; qualifying distributions, $70,170, including $70,170 for 14 grants (high: $8,000; low: $1,000; average: $5,000-$10,000).
Purpose and activities: Giving primarily in the areas of the arts, AIDS research, religion, and higher education. Financial aid for higher education to students in need.
Fields of interest: Arts, AIDS, religion, religion—Christian, higher education, education, social services, welfare, youth, cancer, animal welfare.
Types of support: Student aid, scholarship funds.
Publications: Application guidelines.
Application information: Application form required.
  Initial approach: Letter
  Copies of proposal: 1
  Deadline(s): Submit proposal preferably in Dec.; deadline 1 week prior to board meetings
  Board meeting date(s): Jan., Apr., July, and Oct.
  Write: Clement T. Lambert, Treas.
Officers and Trustees:* Frederick F. Cole,* Chair.; Elbert F. Tuttle,* Secy.; Clement T. Lambert,* Treas.; Martha Goodnow Anderson, Melissa Laverack, Nancy Rose, Harold Williams.
Number of staff: None.
EIN: 046044714

1294
Louis E. Wolfson Foundation
c/o Mintz, Levin, et al.
One Financial Ctr.
Boston 02111   (617) 638-4100
Application address: Boston Univ. School of Medicine, 80 East Concord St., Rm. 103, Boston, MA 02118

Trust established in 1951 in MA.
Donor(s): Louis E. Wolfson, M.D.‡
Foundation type: Independent
Financial data (yr. ended 06/30/91): Assets, $17,562,777 (M); expenditures, $1,052,794; qualifying distributions, $943,345, including $900,000 for 3 grants of $300,000 each.
Purpose and activities: Two-thirds of income is restricted to the support of student aid endowments at medical schools of Boston University, Harvard University, and Tufts University; remaining grants generally restricted to supporting medical education of M.D. degree candidates at medical schools.
Fields of interest: Medical education.
Limitations: No grants to individuals.
Publications: Application guidelines.
Application information: Application form not required.
  Initial approach: Letter
  Deadline(s): None
  Board meeting date(s): Varies; grants paid in late summer and in late Dec. or early Jan.
  Final notification: Within 3 months
  Write: John I. Sandson, Trustee
Trustees: Henry H. Banks, Allie Cohen, James Cohen, Albert F. Cullen, Jr., Daniel D. Federman, John Penn, John I. Sandson.
EIN: 046053295

1295
Greater Worcester Community
Foundation, Inc.
44 Front St., Suite 530
Worcester 01608-1782   (508) 755-0980

Incorporated in 1975 in MA.
Foundation type: Community
Financial data (yr. ended 12/31/91): Assets, $28,147,638 (M); gifts received, $1,739,558; expenditures, $2,062,331; qualifying distributions, $1,590,123, including $1,463,923 for 238 grants (high: $100,000; low: $54; average: $1,000-$4,000) and $126,200 for 135 grants to individuals (average: $1,000-$1,500).
Purpose and activities: "To help meet the health, educational, social welfare, cultural and civic needs of the people of Greater Worcester, including, but not limited to, assisting charitable and educational institutions; for the needy, sick, aged or helpless; for the care of children; for the betterment of living and working conditions; for recreation for all classes, and for such other public and/or charitable uses and purposes as will best make for mental, moral and physical improvement, or contribute to the public welfare."
Fields of interest: Health, education, civic affairs, cultural programs, social services, employment, homeless, housing, AIDS.
Types of support: Seed money, equipment, matching funds, scholarship funds, employee-related scholarships, special projects, technical assistance, student aid, general

purposes, operating budgets, program-related investments, renovation projects.
Limitations: Giving limited to the greater Worcester, MA, area.
Publications: Annual report, program policy statement, application guidelines, newsletter.
Application information: Submit 8 copies of Foundation summary sheet plus 2 copies of proposal. Scholarships are for residents of Worcester County, MA or for children of employees of Rotman's Furniture. Application form required.
  Initial approach: Telephone or letter
  Copies of proposal: 2
  Deadline(s): Educational grants, Apr. 1; women and children, June 1; discretionary awards, Dec. 1; and scholarships, Mar. 15
  Board meeting date(s): Mar., June, Sept., Nov., and as required
  Final notification: 3 1/2 months
  Write: Ms. Ann T. Lisi, Exec. Dir.
Officers and Directors:* John M. Nelson,* Pres.; David K. Woodbury,* V.P.; Stephen B. Loring,* Treas.; J. Robert Seder, Clerk; Joseph Hagan,* Chair., Distrib. Comm.; Vincent F. O'Rourke, Jr.,* Member, Distrib. Comm.; Richard B. Collins, Martha A. Cowan, William P. Densmore, Zoila Torres Feldman, Sarah B. Garfield, David R. Grenon, James H. Harrington, Michael D. Leavitt, John O. Mirick, Carol L. Seager, Edward D. Simsarian, Sumner B. Tilton, Jr., Margaret W. Traina.
Distribution Committee: Michael D. Brockelman, James F. Delahunty, Mary F. Fletcher, Corinne C. Turner, Shirley A. Wright.
Trustee Banks: Fleet Bank of Massachusetts, N.A., Mechanics Bank, Shawmut Bank, N.A.
Number of staff: 3 full-time professional; 1 part-time professional; 3 part-time support.
EIN: 042572276
Recent health grants:
1295-1 Great Brook Valley Health Center, Worcester, MA, $37,500. Toward campaign to construct new community health center. 1990.
1295-2 Health Awareness Services of Central Massachusetts, Worcester, MA, $10,000. For Access program, comprehensive counseling service for pregnant and parenting teens. 1990.
1295-3 Pernet Family Health Services, Worcester, MA, $16,000. To develop employment choices program for women. 1990.
1295-4 Rape Crisis Project of Worcester, Worcester, MA, $10,000. For challenge grant for crisis intervention and counseling. 1990.
1295-5 Visiting Nurses Association of Central Massachussetts, Worcester, MA, $10,350. For pilot program to develop home health support for women with young children. 1990.

1296
E. Stanley & Alice M. Wright Foundation
c/o Fleet Bank, N.A.
370 Main St.
Worcester 01608-1760

Established in 1986 in MA.
Foundation type: Independent
Financial data (yr. ended 12/31/90): Assets, $2,615,605 (M); expenditures, $194,627; qualifying distributions, $167,500, including $167,500 for 20 grants (high: $37,500; low: $1,000).

Fields of interest: Hospitals, museums, Protestant giving, community development.
Types of support: General purposes, capital campaigns.
Limitations: Giving primarily in MA. No grants to individuals.
Application information: Contributes only to pre-selected organizations. Applications not accepted.
Trustees: David M. Wright, Fleet Bank, N.A.
EIN: 222566627

1297
Wyman-Gordon Foundation
105 Madison St., Box 789
Worcester 01613-0789   (508) 756-7111

Established in 1966 in DE.
Donor(s): Wyman-Gordon Co.
Foundation type: Company-sponsored
Financial data (yr. ended 12/31/90): Assets, $4,771,215 (M); expenditures, $373,527; qualifying distributions, $331,600, including $320,634 for 39 grants (high: $145,250; low: $250) and $8,260 for employee matching gifts.
Fields of interest: Community funds, cultural programs, higher education, hospitals, youth.
Types of support: General purposes, operating budgets, continuing support, annual campaigns, seed money, emergency funds, deficit financing, building funds, equipment, land acquisition, employee matching gifts, scholarship funds, employee-related scholarships, fellowships.
Limitations: Giving primarily in MA, with emphasis on the Worcester area, and in plant communities in Danville, IL, Jackson, MI, and South Gate, CA. No grants to individuals, or for endowment funds, special projects, research, publications, or conferences; no loans.
Application information: Application form not required.
  Initial approach: Letter or proposal
  Copies of proposal: 1
  Deadline(s): None
  Board meeting date(s): Feb., Apr., June, Aug., Oct., and Dec.
  Write: Richard L. Stevens, Secy.-Treas.
Officers and Directors:* Joseph R. Carter,* Pres.; James E. Coyne,* V.P.; William S. Hurley,* V.P.; James S. Walsh,* V.P.; Richard L. Stevens,* Secy.-Treas.
Number of staff: 1 part-time professional; 1 part-time support.
EIN: 046142600

1298
Yawkey Foundation II
990 Washington St.
Dedham 02026-6716   (617) 329-7470

Established in 1983 in MA.
Donor(s): Jean R. Yawkey.‡
Foundation type: Independent
Financial data (yr. ended 06/30/91): Assets, $9,224,703 (M); gifts received, $1,839,665; expenditures, $412,678; qualifying distributions, $372,179, including $352,000 for 14 grants (high: $150,000; low: $2,000).
Fields of interest: Recreation, hospitals, higher education, youth.
Limitations: Giving primarily in MA, with emphasis on the greater metropolitan Boston area.
Application information: Primarily supports organizations favored by donor and donor's husband during his lifetime.
  Initial approach: Letter
  Deadline(s): None
  Write: John L. Harrington, Exec. Dir.
Officer and Trustees:* John L. Harrington,* Exec. Dir.; William P. Baldwin, Edward F. Kenney.
EIN: 042768239

MICHIGAN

1299
Allen Foundation, Inc.
P.O. Box 1606
Midland 48641-1606   (517) 832-5678

Established in 1975 in MI.
Foundation type: Independent
Financial data (yr. ended 12/31/91): Assets,
$7,839,507 (L); expenditures, $381,638;
qualifying distributions, $361,252, including
$361,252 for 16 grants (high: $100,000; low:
$1,400).
Purpose and activities: Giving primarily to
organizations for use in the human nutrition field,
including hospitals and universities.
Fields of interest: Nutrition, hospitals, higher
education.
Publications: Annual report.
Application information: Application form
required.
 Initial approach: Letter
 Copies of proposal: 9
 Board meeting date(s): Twice annually
 Write: Dale Baum, Secy.
Officers and Trustees:* Roberta R. Allen,* Chair.;
William J. Allen,* Pres.; William Lauderbach,*
V.P.-Finance; Dale Baum,* Secy.; W. Brock
Neely,* Treas.; Gail E. Allen, Marilyn Haeussler,
Mark Ostahowski, M.D.
Number of staff: 1 part-time support.
EIN: 510152562

1300
The Anderson Fund
(Formerly The Bundy Foundation)
333 West Fort St., Suite 2050
Detroit 48226

Incorporated in 1952 in MI.
Foundation type: Independent
Financial data (yr. ended 12/31/91): Assets,
$7,203,215 (M); expenditures, $785,602;
qualifying distributions, $785,000, including
$785,000 for 23 grants (high: $200,000; low:
$1,000).
Fields of interest: Education, cultural programs,
hospitals.
Types of support: Operating budgets.
Limitations: Giving primarily in MI. No support
for organizations currently receiving funds from
other organizations which the foundation
supports. No grants to individuals.
Application information: Contributes only to
pre-selected organizations. Applications not
accepted.
 Board meeting date(s): As required
Officers and Directors:* Wendell W. Anderson,
Jr.,* Pres.; John W. Anderson II,* V.P.; Mariam C.
Noland,* Secy.-Treas.; Joseph A. Hudson, W.
Warren Shelden.
Number of staff: 2 full-time professional.
EIN: 386053694

1301
Ann Arbor Area Community Foundation
(Formerly Ann Arbor Area Foundation)
121 West Washington, Suite 400
Ann Arbor 48104   (313) 663-0401

Incorporated in 1963 in MI.
Foundation type: Community
Financial data (yr. ended 12/31/91): Assets,
$6,164,534 (M); gifts received, $732,966;
expenditures, $291,933; qualifying distributions,
$153,399, including $153,399 for grants
(average: $500-$7,500).
Purpose and activities: Support for innovative
programs and projects encompassing charity,
civic affairs, culture, health and human services,
ecology, historic preservation, and education.
Fields of interest: Child welfare, youth, aged,
health, social services, higher education, ecology.
Types of support: Seed money, emergency funds,
building funds, equipment, matching funds,
scholarship funds, research, special projects,
publications, conferences and seminars.
Limitations: Giving limited to the Ann Arbor, MI,
area. No support for religious or sectarian
purposes. No grants to individuals (except for
limited scholarship funds), or for operating
budgets, continuing support, annual campaigns,
deficit financing, fundraising purposes, land
acquisition, endowment funds, consulting
services, technical assistance, fellowships; no
loans or program-related investments.
Publications: Annual report (including application
guidelines), program policy statement, application
guidelines.
Application information: Application form
required.
 Initial approach: Telephone
 Copies of proposal: 4
 Deadline(s): Feb. 7, May 20, and Oct. 7 for
  grants; Sept. 18 for youth projects
 Board meeting date(s): Jan., Mar., May, July,
  Sept., and Nov.
 Final notification: 60 days
 Write: Terry N. Foster, Pres.
Officers and Trustees:* Charles E. Leahy,* Chair.;
Terry N. Foster, Pres.; Charles Borgsdorf,* Secy.;
Pamela Horiszny,* Treas.; Don Chisholm, Albert
Coudron, Rosalie Edwards, Douglas Freeth, James
Frenza, Ruth Hatcher, William Herman, Henry
Landau, Gundar Myran, George Nichols, Willis
Patterson, Dennis Pearsall, Michael Radock,
Rudolph Reichert, Charles Reinhart, Norma
Sarns, David Wierman.
Distribution Committee: Barbara Balbach,
Charles Borgsdorf, Isaac Campbell, Constance
Cress, Jack Dobson, John Eman, Cynthia Grzelak,
Howdy Holmes, Grif McDonald, Ruth Whitaker.
Number of staff: 2 part-time professional; 1
full-time support.
EIN: 386087967

1302
ANR Foundation, Inc. ▼
One Woodward Ave.
Detroit 48226   (313) 965-1200

Incorporated in 1985 in MI.
Donor(s): American Natural Resources Co., and
its subsidiaries.
Foundation type: Company-sponsored

Financial data (yr. ended 12/31/91): Assets,
$1,002,040 (M); gifts received, $745,000;
expenditures, $1,075,785; qualifying
distributions, $1,074,974, including $1,073,944
for grants (high: $77,220; low: $65).
Purpose and activities: Support for health and
welfare, culture, education, and community
responsibility.
Fields of interest: Health, health services, welfare,
social services, community funds, cultural
programs, education, higher education,
community development, civic affairs.
Types of support: Employee matching gifts,
operating budgets, general purposes, scholarship
funds.
Limitations: Giving primarily in Detroit, MI. No
support for organizations supported by the United
Way, or for exclusively denominational or
sectarian purposes. No grants to individuals, or
for fundraising events, conventions, or goodwill
advertising.
Application information:
 Initial approach: Letter
 Deadline(s): None
 Write: James F. Cordes, Pres.
Officers and Directors:* James R. Paul,* Chair.;
James F. Cordes,* Pres.; Austin M. O'Toole, Secy.;
David A. Arledge, Treas.; Lawrence P. Doss.
EIN: 382602116

1303
Battle Creek Community Foundation
(Formerly Greater Battle Creek Foundation)
One Riverwalk Ctr.
34 West Jackson St.
Battle Creek 49017-3505   (616) 962-2181
FAX: (616) 962-2182

Established in 1974 in MI.
Foundation type: Community
Financial data (yr. ended 04/30/91): Assets,
$16,956,762 (M); gifts received, $4,460,770;
expenditures, $2,496,408; qualifying
distributions, $1,834,915, including $1,797,765
for 120 grants (high: $25,000; low: $100;
average: $14,980), $35,150 for 21 grants to
individuals (high: $2,000; low: $500) and $2,000
for in-kind gifts.
Purpose and activities: Support for charitable,
scientific, literary, and educational programs of all
kinds that will foster improvement of the physical
environment and living, working, and social
conditions.
Fields of interest: Community development,
public affairs, health, hospitals, education,
literacy, child development, youth, minorities,
cultural programs, arts.
Types of support: Seed money, emergency funds,
building funds, equipment, land acquisition,
scholarship funds, special projects, publications,
conferences and seminars, matching funds.
Limitations: Giving limited to the greater Battle
Creek, MI, area. No grants for operating budgets,
deficit financing, endowments, or research; no
loans.
Publications: Annual report, grants list, newsletter,
application guidelines, 990-PF, financial
statement, informational brochure.
Application information: Application form
required.
 Initial approach: Letter or telephone
 Copies of proposal: 15

Deadline(s): Quarterly
Board meeting date(s): Bimonthly
Write: Peter J. Christ, Pres. and C.E.O.
Officers and Trustees:* William E. LaMothe,*
Chair.; Barbara K. Hill,* Vice-Chair.; Peter J.
Christ, Pres. and C.E.O.; Sadie Penn,* Secy.;
Richard M. Tsoumas,* Treas.; Elizabeth H. Binda,
Chris T. Christ, Donald F. Estes, Dale G. Griffin,
Louis Martin, Susan E. Ordway, Charles L. Siefert,
M.D., Elizabeth J. Settles, Theodore E. Sovern,
William P. Winslow.
Number of staff: 2 full-time professional; 2
full-time support; 1 part-time support.
EIN: 382045459

1304
Bauervic-Paisley Foundation
2855 Coolidge Hwy., Suite 100
Troy 48084
Application address: P.O. Box 445, Milford, MI
48042

Established in 1984 in MI.
Foundation type: Independent
Financial data (yr. ended 12/31/91): Assets,
$2,760,572 (M); expenditures, $177,637;
qualifying distributions, $126,790, including
$98,490 for 16 grants (high: $25,000; low: $500).
Fields of interest: Higher education, secondary
education, religious schools, hospitals, health
associations.
Types of support: Renovation projects, operating
budgets, matching funds.
Limitations: No grants to individuals.
Application information: Application form
required.
Deadline(s): Oct. 1
Write: The Board of Directors
Officers and Directors:* Beverly Paisley,* Pres.
and Secy.; Peter W. Paisley,* Treas.; Rose
Bauervic-Wright.
EIN: 382494390

1305
Berrien Community Foundation, Inc.
515 Ship St., Suite A4
St. Joseph 49085-0092   (616) 983-3304
Application address: P.O. Box 92, St. Joseph, MI
49085

Incorporated in 1952 in MI.
Foundation type: Community
Financial data (yr. ended 12/31/91): Assets,
$3,675,834 (M); gifts received, $269,220;
expenditures, $166,334; qualifying distributions,
$110,435, including $110,435 for 32 grants (high:
$12,897; low: $175).
Purpose and activities: Primary areas of interest
include social services, youth, and general
charitable giving.
Fields of interest: Health, community
development, arts, humanities, education, social
services, youth, general charitable giving.
Types of support: Seed money, matching funds,
research, conferences and seminars, endowment
funds, special projects.
Limitations: Giving limited to Berrien County, MI.
No support for sectarian religious purposes. No
grants to individuals, or for consulting services,
technical assistance, operating funds, deficit

financing, or annual fund drives; no loans or
program-related investments.
Publications: Annual report, application
guidelines, program policy statement, 990-PF,
financial statement, newsletter.
Application information: Application guidelines
available on request. 20 copies of application
required for youth-oriented projects. Application
form required.
Initial approach: Telephone
Deadline(s): Sept. 15 for winter meeting; Mar. 1
for spring meeting
Board meeting date(s): Quarterly
Final notification: 6 weeks to 2 months
Write: Margaret Poole, Exec. Dir.
Officers and Trustees:* Richard Whiteman,*
Pres.; Larry Bubb,* V.P.; Mark A. Miller,* Secy.;
James P. DeLapa,* Treas.; Margaret Poole,* Exec.
Dir.; Greg Forbes, Jim Giffin, Malcolm S. Ross,
Marily Schanze, Stephen Sizer, John Steimle.
Number of staff: 1 full-time professional; 2
part-time support.
EIN: 386057160

1306
A. G. Bishop Charitable Trust
c/o NBD Bank, N.A.
One East First St.
Flint 48502   (313) 760-8451

Trust established in 1944 in MI.
Donor(s): Arthur Giles Bishop.‡
Foundation type: Independent
Financial data (yr. ended 12/31/90): Assets,
$5,684,865 (M); expenditures, $316,956;
qualifying distributions, $283,053, including
$277,172 for 58 grants (high: $33,333; low:
$500).
Fields of interest: Higher education, youth, social
services, hospitals, health services, community
funds, cultural programs.
Types of support: Operating budgets, continuing
support, annual campaigns, seed money,
emergency funds, deficit financing, building
funds, equipment, land acquisition, research.
Limitations: Giving limited to the Flint-Genesee
County, MI, community. No grants to individuals,
or for endowment funds, scholarships,
fellowships, or matching gifts; no loans.
Publications: Application guidelines.
Application information: Application form not
required.
Initial approach: Letter
Copies of proposal: 3
Deadline(s): None
Board meeting date(s): 3 to 4 times per year
Final notification: 1 month
Write: Pamela W. Taeckens, Trust Officer, NBD
Bank, N.A.
Trustees: Robert J. Bellairs, Jr., Elizabeth B.
Wentworth, NBD Bank, N.A.
Number of staff: 1 part-time professional.
EIN: 386040693

1307
Arnold and Gertrude Boutell Memorial
Fund
c/o Second National Bank of Saginaw
101 North Washington Ave.
Saginaw 48607   (517) 776-7582

Trust established in 1961 in MI.
Donor(s): Arnold Boutell,‡ Gertrude Boutell.‡
Foundation type: Independent
Financial data (yr. ended 03/31/91): Assets,
$7,562,379 (M); expenditures, $626,876;
qualifying distributions, $556,656, including
$522,092 for 18 grants (high: $125,000; low:
$500; average: $5,000-$20,000).
Purpose and activities: Support largely for a
community fund, education, cultural programs,
community development, and hospitals.
Fields of interest: Education, cultural programs,
hospitals, community development.
Limitations: Giving limited to Saginaw County,
MI. No grants to individuals, or for endowment
funds.
Application information: Application form
required.
Initial approach: Letter
Copies of proposal: 1
Deadline(s): None
Board meeting date(s): Bimonthly
Write: Denice McGlaughlin, Trust Admin.
    Officer, Second National Bank of Saginaw
Trustee: Second National Bank of Saginaw.
EIN: 386040492

1308
Chrysler Corporate Giving Program
12000 Chrysler Dr.
Highland Park 48288-1919   (313) 956-5194
Mailing Address: P.O. Box 1919, Detroit, MI
48288

Financial data (yr. ended 12/31/90): Total giving,
$9,500,000, including $5,500,000 for grants and
$4,000,000 for in-kind gifts.
Purpose and activities: Support for education,
especially secondary education, leadership
development, including Junior Achievement,
employment training, economic development,
minority affairs, and community funds. Chrysler
also has an ASSETS DONATION PROGRAM in
which the corporation donates vehicles and auto
parts to high schools and vocational schools for
the training of auto mechanics and technicians.
Fields of interest: Education, arts, community
funds, youth, minorities, higher education,
secondary education, education, leadership
development, employment, economics, business
education, crime and law enforcement, drug
abuse, engineering, family services, AIDS,
elementary education, homeless, hunger,
alcoholism, education—minorities, aged, health,
literacy, vocational education, military personnel,
volunteerism, law and justice.
Types of support: Equipment, donated products,
donated equipment, employee matching gifts,
operating budgets, employee volunteer services,
in-kind gifts, special projects, continuing support,
employee-related scholarships, fellowships,
emergency funds, scholarship funds, matching
funds.
Limitations: Giving primarily in headquarters city
and major operating areas. No grants to
individuals, or for endowments, or research; no
vehicle donations.
Publications: Corporate report, corporate giving
report, application guidelines.
Application information:
Initial approach: Letter to headquarters
Copies of proposal: 1

Deadline(s): None
Board meeting date(s): As soon as possible
Final notification: 3 months
Write: Ms. Lynn A. Feldhouse, Admin.
Administrators: Kim-Lan Trinh, Admin.; Lynn A. Feldhouse, Mgr.
Number of staff: 2 full-time professional; 1 full-time support.

1309
Chrysler Corporation Fund ▼
12000 Chrysler Dr.
Highland Park 48288-1919   (313) 956-5194

Incorporated in 1953 in MI.
Donor(s): Chrysler Corp.
Foundation type: Company-sponsored
Financial data (yr. ended 12/31/91): Assets, $17,000,000 (M); expenditures, $10,459,062; qualifying distributions, $14,875,529, including $9,552,529 for 1,098 grants (high: $400,000; low: $250; average: $1,000-$50,000), $823,000 for 3,100 employee matching gifts and $4,500,000 for in-kind gifts.
Purpose and activities: Support for community funds, health and human services, education, civic affairs, and cultural programs.
Fields of interest: Community funds, education, civic affairs, cultural programs, social services, health.
Types of support: Continuing support, annual campaigns, emergency funds, special projects, employee matching gifts, building funds, employee-related scholarships, scholarship funds, operating budgets.
Limitations: Giving primarily in areas where the company has a substantial number of employees. No support for primary or secondary schools, religious organizations for religious purposes, veterans' or labor organizations, fraternal associations, athletic groups, social clubs, political organizations or campaigns, or national health organizations, except through the United Way. No grants to individuals (except for scholarships to children of company employees), or for endowment funds, conferences, seminars, fellowships, deficit financing, equipment and materials, or research; no grants for operating expenses of organizations supported through the United Way; no loans.
Publications: Corporate giving report, program policy statement, application guidelines, annual report.
Application information: Application form not required.
Initial approach: Letter
Copies of proposal: 1
Deadline(s): None
Board meeting date(s): As required, usually quarterly; educational grants approved at fall meeting
Final notification: 4 months
Write: Ms. Lynn A. Feldhouse, Mgr., or Ms. Kim-Lan Trinh, Administrator
Officers and Trustees:* Thomas G. Denomme,* Pres.; S.W. Bergeron,* V.P. and Treas.; Lynn A. Feldhouse, Secy. and Mgr.; Richard E. Acosta, Francois J. Castaing, F.J. Farmer, M.M. Glusac, William J. O'Brien III, E. Thomas Pappert, Leroy C. Richie.
Number of staff: 2 full-time professional; 1 full-time support.

EIN: 386087371
Recent health grants:
1309-1 American Cancer Society, NYC, NY, $10,000. 1990.
1309-2 Baylor University Medical Center, Dallas, TX, $100,000. For ABC Hospital Fund. 1990.
1309-3 Boston University, Health Policy Institute, Boston, MA, $10,000. 1990.
1309-4 Childrens Hospital of Michigan, Pediatric Trauma Center, Detroit, MI, $50,000. 1990.
1309-5 Detroit Institute of Ophthalmology, Grosse Pointe Park, MI, $10,000. 1990.
1309-6 Easter Seal Society of Del-Mar, Wilmington, DE, $10,000. 1990.
1309-7 Greater Detroit Area Health Council, Detroit, MI, $25,500. 1990.
1309-8 Hospital for Special Surgery, NYC, NY, $10,000. 1990.
1309-9 Judson Center, Royal Oak, MI, $10,000. 1990.
1309-10 Kresge Eye Institute at Wayne State University, Detroit, MI, $10,000. 1990.
1309-11 Leukemia Society of America, Michigan Chapter, Harper Woods, MI, $10,000. 1990.
1309-12 Media-Advertising Partnership for a Drug-Free America, NYC, NY, $15,000. 1990.
1309-13 National Leadership Coalition for Health Care Reform, DC, $25,000. 1990.
1309-14 Palmer Drug Abuse Program, Milford, MI, $10,000. 1990.
1309-15 Rose Hill Center, Bloomfield Hills, MI, $50,000. 1990.
1309-16 W N E T Channel 13, NYC, NY, $100,000. For Borderline Medicine. 1990.

1310
Consumers Power Corporate Giving Program
212 West Michigan Ave.
Jackson 49201   (517) 788-0550

Financial data (yr. ended 12/31/90): Total giving, $600,000, including $584,000 for grants (high: $50,000; low: $50) and $16,000 for employee matching gifts.
Purpose and activities: Support for education, health care, social welfare, community issues, civic affairs, arts and culture, and Michigan growth and enhancement.
Fields of interest: Arts, education, civic affairs, community funds, education—building funds, education—minorities, general charitable giving, health, public affairs, cultural programs, health services, mental health, minorities, museums, music, community development, performing arts, theater, urban development, volunteerism, welfare, wildlife, women, youth.
Types of support: Capital campaigns, general purposes, seed money, equipment, building funds, annual campaigns, conferences and seminars, employee matching gifts, endowment funds, matching funds, publications, renovation projects, special projects, in-kind gifts.
Limitations: Giving primarily in headquarters location and service area. No support for fraternal organizations or churches. No grants to individuals.
Application information: Application form required.
Initial approach: Letter; proposal
Copies of proposal: 1
Deadline(s): Best time to apply is in first quarter

Board meeting date(s): As needed
Final notification: 8-10 weeks
Write: Dennis H. Marvin, Dir., Communs., Planning, and Programs
Staff: Marti Carpenter, Secy. to Admin.
Number of staff: 1 part-time professional.

1311
Consumers Power Foundation
212 West Michigan Ave.
Jackson 49201   (517) 788-0318

Established in 1990 in MI.
Donor(s): Consumers Power Co.
Foundation type: Company-sponsored
Financial data (yr. ended 12/31/90): Assets, $1,866,335 (M); expenditures, $1,032,363; qualifying distributions, $1,028,663, including $884,154 for 228 grants (high: $30,000; low: $55) and $131,575 for 167 employee matching gifts.
Purpose and activities: Support for organizations that 1) provide solutions to problems faced by individuals and families who need help to address their own needs; 2) protect the natural environment; 3) improve availability and quality of education; 4) back the improvement of public health care systems; 5) participate in community and civic activities; and 6) increase an awareness of the values of artistic and cultural achievements and encourage their growth. The foundation also matches the gifts of company employees and retirees to higher education, Michigan public broadcasting stations, and Michigan community foundations.
Fields of interest: Family services, environment, education, health, civic affairs, community development, arts, cultural programs.
Types of support: Capital campaigns, operating budgets, building funds, employee matching gifts, renovation projects.
Limitations: Giving primarily in MI. No support for religious organizations for religious purposes, labor or veterans' organizations, fraternal or social clubs, or organizations already supported by the United Way. No grants to individuals, or for endowments; no purchase of tickets for support of fundraising events or advertising for such events.
Application information:
Initial approach: Letter not exceeding 2 pages
Deadline(s): None
Write: Dennis H. Marvin, Secy.-Treas.
Officers and Directors:* William T. McCormick, Jr.,* Chair.; John W. Clark, Pres.; Dennis H. Marvin, Secy.-Treas.; Frederick W. Buckman, Victor J. Fryling, S. Kinnie Smith.
EIN: 382935534

1312
Dorothy U. Dalton Foundation, Inc. ▼
c/o Old Kent Bank of Kalamazoo
P.O. Box 4019
Kalamazoo 49003-4019   (616) 383-6940

Incorporated in 1978 in MI as successor to Dorothy U. Dalton Foundation Trust.
Donor(s): Dorothy U. Dalton.‡
Foundation type: Independent
Financial data (yr. ended 12/31/91): Assets, $26,310,115 (M); expenditures, $1,333,583; qualifying distributions, $1,260,493, including

$1,198,133 for 80 grants (high: $100,000; low: $500).

Purpose and activities: Emphasis on higher education, mental health, social service and youth agencies, and cultural programs.

Fields of interest: Higher education, youth, mental health, social services, community development, drug abuse, homeless, housing, cultural programs, performing arts, theater.

Types of support: Operating budgets, continuing support, seed money, emergency funds, deficit financing, building funds, equipment, land acquisition, matching funds, research, special projects, general purposes, capital campaigns, renovation projects.

Limitations: Giving primarily in Kalamazoo County, MI. No support for religious organizations. No grants to individuals, or for annual campaigns, scholarships, fellowships, publications, or conferences; no loans.

Publications: 990-PF.

Application information: Application form not required.

Initial approach: Proposal
Copies of proposal: 5
Deadline(s): Submit proposal preferably in Apr. and Oct.
Board meeting date(s): May and Nov.
Final notification: 30 days after board meetings
Write: Ronald N. Kilgore, Secy.-Treas.

Officers and Trustees:* Suzanne D. Parish,* Pres.; Howard Kalleward,* V.P.; Ronald N. Kilgore, Secy.-Treas.; Thompson Bennett, Arthur F. Homer.

Number of staff: None.
EIN: 382240062

1313
The Mignon Sherwood DeLano Foundation
c/o First of America Bank-Michigan, N.A.
108 East Michigan Ave.
Kalamazoo 49007-3931

Incorporated in 1985 in MI.
Donor(s): Mignon Sherwood Delano.‡
Foundation type: Independent
Financial data (yr. ended 12/31/91): Assets, $3,204,172 (M); expenditures, $142,403; qualifying distributions, $138,206, including $126,599 for 22 grants (high: $15,000; low: $500).

Fields of interest: Community development, civic affairs, social services, youth, child development, health, general charitable giving.

Limitations: Giving primarily in Allegan, MI. No grants to individuals.

Application information: Application form required.

Write: David Tichnor, Pres.

Board of Advisors: David Ticknor, Pres.; Ellen Altamore, Rebecca Burnett, G. Phillip Dietrich, Bernard Riker.

Trustee: First of America Bank.
EIN: 382557743

1314
DeRoy Testamentary Foundation
3274 Penobscot Bldg.
Detroit 48226   (313) 961-3814

Established in 1979 in MI.

Donor(s): Helen L. DeRoy.‡
Foundation type: Independent
Financial data (yr. ended 12/31/91): Assets, $20,223,095 (M); expenditures, $965,098; qualifying distributions, $871,675, including $804,228 for 73 grants (high: $100,000; low: $500).

Fields of interest: Higher education, arts, cultural programs, Jewish welfare, hospitals, social services, youth.

Types of support: Special projects.

Limitations: Giving primarily in MI. No grants to individuals.

Application information:

Deadline(s): None
Write: Leonard H. Weiner, Pres., or Arthur Rodecker, V.P.

Officers and Trustees:* Leonard H. Weiner,* Pres.; Arthur Rodecker,* V.P.; Bernice Michel,* Secy.

EIN: 382208833

1315
The Charles DeVlieg Foundation
(Formerly The Charles B. and Charles R. DeVlieg Foundation)
P.O. Box 33010
Bloomfield Hills 48303   (313) 961-0200

Incorporated in 1961 in MI.
Donor(s): Charles B. DeVlieg,‡ Charles R. DeVlieg, DeVlieg Machine Co., Kathryn S. DeVlieg.
Foundation type: Independent
Financial data (yr. ended 12/31/91): Assets, $3,707,938 (M); gifts received, $40,250; expenditures, $257,744; qualifying distributions, $200,972, including $191,288 for 32 grants (high: $25,000; low: $500) and $2,000 for 2 grants to individuals.

Purpose and activities: Support largely for higher and other education, including grants to a university for fellowships and a scholarship program for local high school graduates; grants for community funds, hospitals, youth agencies, family planning and services, the arts, environmental organizations, public policy, and science and technology.

Fields of interest: Educational associations, higher education, community funds, hospitals, youth, family services, arts, environment, public policy, science and technology.

Types of support: Fellowships, general purposes, scholarship funds, employee-related scholarships.

Limitations: Giving primarily in southeastern MI. No grants to individuals (except for employee-related scholarships), or for endowment funds, research programs, or matching gifts; no loans.

Application information: Application form required.

Initial approach: Proposal
Copies of proposal: 2
Deadline(s): None
Board meeting date(s): Semiannually
Write: Herbert A. Beyer, Exec. Dir.

Officers and Trustees:* Herbert A. Beyer,* Pres. and Exec. Dir.; Curt DeRoo, Treas.; Janet DeVlieg, Julia DeVlieg, Kathryn S. DeVlieg, Richard A. Jerue, Gerald Stetler.

Number of staff: 1 part-time professional.
EIN: 386075696

1316
The Richard and Helen DeVos Foundation
▼
190 Munive N.W., Suite 500
Grand Rapids 49503   (616) 454-4114

Incorporated in 1969 in MI.
Donor(s): Richard M. DeVos, Helen J. DeVos.
Foundation type: Independent
Financial data (yr. ended 12/31/90): Assets, $40,369,697 (M); gifts received, $500,000; expenditures, $4,272,209; qualifying distributions, $4,232,604, including $4,232,604 for 126 grants (high: $1,025,500; low: $50; average: $1,000-$25,000).

Purpose and activities: Giving largely for religious programs and associations, church support, music, and the performing arts, higher education, and social welfare.

Fields of interest: Denominational giving, music, performing arts, higher education, social services.

Types of support: General purposes.

Application information:

Initial approach: Letter
Deadline(s): None
Write: Jerry Tuherger, Administrator, or Jayne Wierenga, Exec. Asst.

Officers: Richard M. DeVos, Pres.; Helen J. DeVos, V.P.; Jerry Tuberger, Secy.-Treas.
EIN: 237066873

Recent health grants:

1316-1 Butterworth Hospital, Grand Rapids, MI, $1,025,500. 1990.

1316-2 Project HOPE, Millwood, VA, $10,000. 1990.

1316-3 Resthaven Care Center, Holland, MI, $25,000. 1990.

1317
Dow Corning Corporate Contributions Program
Midland 48686-0994   (517) 496-6290

Financial data (yr. ended 12/31/90): Total giving, $2,848,100, including $2,507,300 for grants (high: $62,500; low: $1,000; average: $5,000-$30,000) and $340,800 for 812 employee matching gifts.

Purpose and activities: "Dow Corning's vision recognizes that enduring success requires sensitivity to the public interest...not only through products and services that improve the quality of life, but also through our responsiveness to priority social issues. We recognize that there are many social issues worthy of our attention and many organizations addressing these issues. We cannot attempt to support them all, so we have invested our time and effort to focus on issues we consider to be of vital concern to Dow Corning employees, neighbors and to society." Commitments are maintained to Matching Gifts Programs in Education and the Arts, EEO Scholarships and Contributions, United Way and a number of scholarships for children of employees. Other support is divided into the following categories: K-12 Educational Reform, Higher Education, New Community Development in communities where Dow Corning has facilities, Local Arts and Culture and the Environment.

Fields of interest: Performing arts, education, arts, community funds, community development,

science and technology, engineering, chemistry, cultural programs, civic affairs, education—minorities, fine arts, hospitals, literacy, youth, Europe, Canada, Asia, Latin America.
Types of support: Capital campaigns, employee matching gifts, matching funds, seed money, general purposes, employee-related scholarships, special projects.
Limitations: Giving primarily in Midland, Bay and Saginaw Counties, MI; Carollton and Elizabethtown, KY; Greensboro, NC; and Springfield, OR; Huguenot, NY; Arlington, TN; where facilities are in Europe, Canada, Mexico, South America, Japan, and Pacific Rim. No support for political, veterans' or religious organizations, or athletic activities at the college/university level. Generally, no contributions of company products, materials, or equipment; no grants to individuals or for fundraising events.
Publications: Application guidelines.
Application information: Requests for less than $2,000 are usually handled by plant locations, as are overseas requests. Application form required.
  Initial approach: Letter
  Copies of proposal: 1
  Deadline(s): None
  Board meeting date(s): Within six months decisions are made
  Final notification: Within one month
  Write: Anne M. DeBoer, Mgr., Corp. Contribs.
Number of staff: 1 full-time professional; 1 part-time support.

1318
Earl-Beth Foundation
Nine Mack Ctr.
23223 Nine Mack Dr.
St. Clair Shores 48080   (313) 776-8030
FAX: (313) 776-8070

Incorporated in 1944 in MI.
Donor(s): Earl Holley,‡ Mrs. Earl Holley,‡ Holley Carburetor Co.
Foundation type: Independent
Financial data (yr. ended 12/31/91): Assets, $9,830,628 (M); expenditures, $527,820; qualifying distributions, $426,897, including $313,401 for 93 grants.
Purpose and activities: "To encourage and support creative programs primarily in the areas of education, health, human social services, and environmental concerns. Focus is to encourage innovative programs to benefit and improve the lives of children and disadvantaged adults with programs that will be beneficial to them and to communities in Detroit."
Fields of interest: Education, higher education, secondary education, youth, child welfare, cultural programs, music, health, hospitals.
Types of support: Seed money, special projects.
Limitations: Giving limited to the Detroit, MI, metropolitan area. No grants to individuals, or for endowment funds or capital programs.
Publications: Application guidelines.
Application information: Application form not required.
  Initial approach: Letter requesting guidelines
  Copies of proposal: 1
  Deadline(s): Mar. 1 and Sept. 1
  Board meeting date(s): Apr. and Oct.

Final notification: 4 weeks after meeting
  Write: Lisa Holley, Pres.
Officers and Trustees:* Lisa C. Holley,* Pres.; Danforth E. Holley,* Exec. V.P.; Theodore H. Oldham, Secy.; Mark Holley,* Treas.; Janie Holley Fleckenstein, Helen M. Fowler, Scott Holley, Deborah Holley Palms.
Number of staff: 1 full-time professional; 1 part-time support.
EIN: 386055542

1319
C. K. Eddy Family Memorial Fund
c/o Second National Bank of Saginaw
101 North Washington Ave.
Saginaw 48607   (517) 776-7583
Additional tel.: (517) 776-7368

Trust established in 1925 in MI.
Donor(s): Arthur D. Eddy.‡
Foundation type: Independent
Financial data (yr. ended 06/30/91): Assets, $9,943,292 (M); expenditures, $655,575; qualifying distributions, $591,366, including $240,017 for 17 grants (high: $69,195; low: $95) and $288,500 for 123 loans to individuals.
Purpose and activities: Giving for hospitals, a community fund, musical and cultural activities, and aid to Saginaw public schools.
Fields of interest: Hospitals, music, cultural programs, education.
Types of support: Student loans, special projects, equipment.
Limitations: Giving limited to Saginaw County, MI.
Publications: Application guidelines.
Application information: Application form required.
  Deadline(s): For student loans, May 1; for grants under $5,000, the Monday before the weekly Thursday meeting; for grants over $5,000, 2 weeks prior to the bimonthly meeting on the 3rd Wednesday of the month
  Write: Helen James (grants) or Marsha Sieggreen (student loans)
Trustee: Second National Bank of Saginaw.
EIN: 386040506

1320
Drusilla Farwell Foundation
c/o Manufacturers National Bank of Detroit
100 Renaissance Ctr., 7th Fl.
Detroit 48243
Application address: 1708 Ford Bldg., Detroit, MI 48236; Tel.: (313) 961-3091

Established in 1937 in MI.
Foundation type: Independent
Financial data (yr. ended 08/31/91): Assets, $2,280,082 (M); expenditures, $88,184; qualifying distributions, $80,027, including $75,075 for 127 grants (high: $4,250; low: $100).
Fields of interest: Protestant giving, religion—Christian, libraries, education, health, medical research.
Limitations: Giving primarily in MI.
Application information: Application form not required.
  Deadline(s): None
  Write: Hugo Krave, Pres.

Officers: Hugo Krave, Pres.; Randolph Fields, V.P.; Helmuth Krave, Secy.
EIN: 386082430

1321
Federal-Mogul Corporate Giving Program
P.O. Box 1966
Detroit 48235   (313) 354-9934

Purpose and activities: Supports arts and culture, higher and vocational education; also supports general health care, civic affairs, youth, welfare, and the United Way.
Fields of interest: Arts, cultural programs, higher education, vocational education, education, health, civic affairs, community funds, youth, welfare.
Limitations: Giving primarily in headquarters city and major operating locations. No support for political parties and elementary and secondary education.
Publications: Application guidelines.
Application information:
  Initial approach: Letter
  Deadline(s): None
  Write: Lonnie Ross, Contribs. Comm.
Staff: Christine Cusmano, Secy., Contribs. Comm.

1322
First of America Bank Corporate Giving Program
108 East Michigan Ave.
Kalamazoo 49007   (616) 376-9000

Purpose and activities: First of America, a multi-bank holding corporation, and its subsidiaries operate local contributions programs. 99 percent of support stems from the subsidiaries and one percent from the parent. Interests include health, family services and the United Way.
Fields of interest: Family services, health, community funds.
Limitations: Giving primarily in headquarters city and where there are affiliates and branches in MI, IN, and IL.
Application information:
  Initial approach: Letter to nearest bank
  Deadline(s): None
  Write: Richard D. Klein, Vice-Chair.

1323
Community Foundation of Greater Flint
Northbank Ctr., Suite 410
432 North Saginaw St.
Flint 48502-2013   (313) 767-8270

Established in MI in 1978.
Foundation type: Community
Financial data (yr. ended 12/31/91): Assets, $25,600,000 (M); gifts received, $3,327,738; expenditures, $3,337,904; qualifying distributions, $2,850,485, including $2,850,485 for 218 grants (high: $635,000; low: $75).
Purpose and activities: "To respond to current or emerging needs in the Genesee County, MI, area in conservation and environment, culture and the arts, education, health and human services, and leadership development."

Fields of interest: Conservation, environment, cultural programs, arts, education, health, AIDS, social services, leadership development.
Types of support: Annual campaigns, continuing support, general purposes, special projects, endowment funds, matching funds.
Limitations: Giving limited to Genesee County, MI. No grants to individuals.
Publications: Annual report, informational brochure (including application guidelines), newsletter.
Application information: Application form required.
  Initial approach: Telephone or personal contact
  Deadline(s): Varies
  Board meeting date(s): 1st Friday of even numbered months
  Write: Dorothy M. Reynolds, Pres.
Officers and Trustees:* Danny R. Gaydou,* Chair.; Olivia P. Maynard,* Vice-Chair.; Dorothy M. Reynolds, Pres.; David K. Swenson, Exec. V.P.; Laura B. Froats, C.F.O.; Arthur L. Tuuri, M.D.
Number of staff: 4 full-time professional; 2 full-time support; 1 part-time support.
EIN: 382190667
Recent health grants:
1323-1 Alzheimers Disease and Related Disorders Association, Ann Arbor, MI, $19,725. 1990.
1323-2 Flint Odyssey House, Flint, MI, $10,000. 1990.
1323-3 Genesee County Health Department, Flint, MI, $98,535. 1990.
1323-4 Genesee County Health Department, Flint, MI, $24,686. 1990.
1323-5 Hamilton Family Health Center, Flint, MI, $15,000. 1990.
1323-6 Hurley Medical Center, Flint, MI, $11,900. 1990.
1323-7 Medical Society Foundation, Flint, MI, $80,254. 1990.
1323-8 Planned Parenthood of Flint, Flint, MI, $18,589. 1990.
1323-9 Rotary Dyslexia Center, Flint, MI, $15,000. 1990.

1324
Benson and Edith Ford Fund
100 Renaissance Ctr., 34th Fl.
Detroit 48243   (313) 259-7777

Incorporated in 1943 in MI as the Hotchkiss Fund.
Donor(s): Benson Ford.‡
Foundation type: Independent
Financial data (yr. ended 12/31/91): Assets, $14,400,975 (M); gifts received, $941,578; expenditures, $632,553; qualifying distributions, $609,669, including $602,500 for 58 grants (high: $100,000; low: $1,000).
Fields of interest: Education, community funds, hospitals, arts, Catholic giving, child welfare, youth.
Limitations: Giving primarily in MI. No grants to individuals.
Application information: Awards generally limited to charities already favorably known to substantial contributors of the foundation.
  Initial approach: Letter
  Deadline(s): None
  Write: Pierre V. Heftler, Secy.

Officers and Trustees:* Lynn F. Alandt,* Pres.; Benson Ford, Jr.,* V.P.; Pierre V. Heftler,* Secy.; Richard M. Cundiff, Treas.
EIN: 386066333

1325
Walter and Josephine Ford Fund
100 Renaissance Ctr., 34th Fl.
Detroit 48243   (313) 259-7777

Incorporated in 1951 in MI.
Donor(s): Josephine F. Ford, Walter B. Ford II.
Foundation type: Independent
Financial data (yr. ended 12/31/91): Assets, $7,113,112 (M); gifts received, $418,195; expenditures, $624,677; qualifying distributions, $602,325, including $587,675 for 103 grants (high: $200,350; low: $50).
Fields of interest: Higher education, education, community funds, arts, museums, Protestant giving, medical research, hospitals, youth, social services.
Limitations: Giving primarily in MI. No grants to individuals.
Application information: Awards generally limited to charities already favorably known to substantial contributors of the foundation.
  Initial approach: Letter
  Deadline(s): None
  Write: Pierre V. Heftler, Secy.
Officers and Trustees:* Josephine F. Ford,* Pres.; Pierre V. Heftler,* Secy.; Richard M. Cundiff, Treas.
EIN: 386066334

1326
William and Martha Ford Fund
100 Renaissance Ctr., 34th Fl.
Detroit 48243   (313) 259-7777

Incorporated in 1953 in MI.
Donor(s): William Clay Ford, Martha Firestone Ford.
Foundation type: Independent
Financial data (yr. ended 12/31/91): Assets, $3,185,867 (M); gifts received, $145,492; expenditures, $852,533; qualifying distributions, $822,695, including $818,984 for 61 grants (high: $225,500; low: $100).
Purpose and activities: Giving primarily for higher and other education, hospitals and medical research and a freedom institute; support also for community funds, church support, the arts, and youth and social service agencies.
Fields of interest: Higher education, education, hospitals, medical research, freedom, community funds, religion, arts, youth, social services.
Limitations: Giving primarily in MI. No grants to individuals.
Application information: Awards generally limited to organizations known to the donors.
  Initial approach: Letter
  Deadline(s): None
  Write: Pierre V. Heftler, Secy.
Officers and Trustees:* William Clay Ford,* Pres.; Pierre V. Heftler,* Secy.; Richard M. Cundiff, Treas.; Martha F. Ford.
EIN: 386066335

1327
The Henry Ford II Fund
100 Renaissance Ctr., 34th Fl.
Detroit 48243   (313) 259-7777

Incorporated in 1953 in MI.
Donor(s): Henry Ford II.‡
Foundation type: Independent
Financial data (yr. ended 12/31/91): Assets, $13,326,814 (M); gifts received, $775,078; expenditures, $1,032,221; qualifying distributions, $1,007,555, including $1,001,500 for 23 grants (high: $200,000; low: $2,500; average: $500-$25,000).
Fields of interest: Higher education, education, hospitals, arts, community funds, social services.
Limitations: Giving primarily in MI, with some emphasis on Detroit. No grants to individuals.
Application information: Awards are generally limited to charitable organizations already favorably known to the foundation's contributors.
  Initial approach: Letter
  Deadline(s): None
  Board meeting date(s): As needed
  Write: Pierre V. Heftler, Secy.
Officers and Trustees:* Edsel B. Ford II,* Pres.; Pierre V. Heftler,* Secy.; Richard M. Cundiff,* Treas.
Number of staff: None.
EIN: 386066332

1328
Ford Motor Company Corporate Giving Program
The American Rd.
Dearborn 48121   (313) 845-8711

Financial data (yr. ended 12/31/90): Total giving, $7,899,025, including $7,633,506 for grants (high: $500,000; low: $100; average: $100-$5,000) and $265,519 for 12 in-kind gifts.
Purpose and activities: Makes contributions of land, buildings, equipment, and in-house services; gives to colleges and universities for specific research projects; also maintains memberships in Chambers of Commerce and other area organizations.
Fields of interest: Education, higher education, arts, community funds, youth, minorities, medical research, fine arts.
Types of support: Building funds, general purposes, employee matching gifts, technical assistance, donated equipment, donated products, use of facilities.
Limitations: No support for building funds, capital funds, or endowments. No grants to individuals.
Publications: Application guidelines.
Application information: Include project description and budget, list of major donors, financial report, and 501(c)(3) status.
  Initial approach: Letter
  Deadline(s): None
  Board meeting date(s): Monthly
  Write: Leo J. Brennan, Jr., Secy., Contribs. Comm.

1329
Ford Motor Company Fund ▼
The American Rd.
Dearborn 48121   (313) 845-8711

Incorporated in 1949 in MI.
Donor(s): Ford Motor Co.
Foundation type: Company-sponsored
Financial data (yr. ended 12/31/91): Assets, $40,853,762 (L); gifts received, $35,427; expenditures, $22,793,773; qualifying distributions, $22,265,131, including $20,028,448 for 1,456 grants (high: $1,300,000; low: $100; average: $1,000-$25,000) and $2,236,683 for 11,011 employee matching gifts.
Purpose and activities: Support for education, including matching gifts for colleges and universities and basic research grants; community funds and urban affairs; hospitals; and civic and cultural programs.
Fields of interest: Education, higher education, community funds, urban affairs, hospitals, AIDS, cultural programs, civic affairs.
Types of support: Matching funds, research, annual campaigns, equipment, general purposes, publications, conferences and seminars, employee matching gifts, continuing support, employee-related scholarships.
Limitations: Giving primarily in areas of company operations nationwide, with special emphasis on Detroit, MI. No grants to individuals, or for building funds, scholarships, or fellowships.
Publications: Annual report, application guidelines, informational brochure.
Application information: Application form not required.
  Initial approach: Letter
  Copies of proposal: 1
  Deadline(s): None
  Board meeting date(s): Apr. and Oct.
  Final notification: 6 months
  Write: Leo J. Brennan, Jr., Exec. Dir.
Officer and Trustees:* Harold A. Poling,* Pres.; Frank J. Darin, V.P.; David N. McCammon,* Treas.; Philip E. Benton, Allan D. Gilmour, Jack Martin, Peter J. Pestillo, David Scott, Stanley A. Seneker.
Number of staff: 3 full-time professional; 3 full-time support; 2 part-time support.
EIN: 381459376
Recent health grants:
1329-1 Beaumont Hospital Foundation, Royal Oak, MI, $200,000. For capital support. 1991.
1329-2 Caring Athletes Team for Childrens and Henry Ford Hospitals, Detroit, MI, $30,000. 1991.
1329-3 Child Guidance Center, Cleveland, OH, $10,000. 1991.
1329-4 Childrens Center of Wayne County, Detroit, MI, $50,000. 1991.
1329-5 Childrens Hospital of Michigan, Oak Park, MI, $15,000. For Festival of Trees. 1991.
1329-6 Childrens National Medical Center, DC, $25,000. 1991.
1329-7 Detroit Institute for Children, Detroit, MI, $40,000. 1991.
1329-8 Detroit Institute of Ophthalmology, Grosse Pointe Park, MI, $10,000. For Eyes on the Classics. 1991.
1329-9 Drug Abuse Resistance Education (DARE), Michigan Advisory Board, East Lansing, MI, $34,000. 1991.
1329-10 Eye Research Institute of Retina Foundation, Boston, MA, $50,000. 1991.
1329-11 Family Place, Ronald McDonald House, Chicago, IL, $15,000. For capital support. 1991.

1329-12 Harvard University, Cambridge, MA, $50,000. For health risk analysis. 1991.
1329-13 Lauri Strauss Leukemia Foundation, NYC, NY, $10,000. 1991.
1329-14 Media-Advertising Partnership for a Drug-Free America, NYC, NY, $100,000. 1991.
1329-15 Mercy Memorial Hospital Foundation, Monroe, MI, $25,000. 1991.
1329-16 National Fund for Medical Education, NYC, NY, $10,000. 1991.
1329-17 National Kidney Foundation, NYC, NY, $53,475. For Science Scholars Program. 1991.
1329-18 Occupational Physicians Scholarship Fund, NYC, NY, $100,000. 1991.
1329-19 Renaissance Health Care, Detroit, MI, $10,000. 1991.
1329-20 Saint Joseph Mercy Hospital, Ann Arbor, MI, $50,000. For capital support. 1991.
1329-21 University of Michigan Hospitals, Ann Arbor, MI, $100,000. For capital support. 1991.

1330
Four County Foundation
155 Rawles St.
Box 118
Romeo 48065-0118   (313) 752-4484

Established in 1987 in MI.
Foundation type: Community
Financial data (yr. ended 03/31/91): Assets, $2,719,369 (M); gifts received, $35,968; expenditures, $222,852; qualifying distributions, $179,897, including $179,897 for grants (high: $23,500; low: $650).
Fields of interest: Education, health, aged, youth.
Types of support: Continuing support, matching funds, seed money, special projects.
Limitations: Giving limited to southeast Lapeer, northwest Macomb, northeast Oakland, and southwest St. Clair counties, MI. No grants to individuals, or for operating expenses.
Publications: Annual report, financial statement, application guidelines, informational brochure, newsletter.
Application information: Application form required.
  Initial approach: Letter of inquiry
  Copies of proposal: 5
  Deadline(s): May, Aug., Nov., and Feb.
  Board meeting date(s): 4th Thursday monthly
  Write: Peggy Hamilton, Exec. Dir.
Officers: James T. Ligon, Pres.; Kathleen Eubank, Secy.; John S. Bishop, Treas.; Peggy Hamilton, Exec. Dir.
Number of staff: 1 full-time professional; 1 part-time support.
EIN: 382736601

1331
The Fremont Area Foundation
108 South Stewart
Fremont 49412   (616) 924-5350

Incorporated in 1951 in MI.
Foundation type: Community
Financial data (yr. ended 12/31/91): Assets, $80,123,950 (M); gifts received, $800,927; expenditures, $1,832,347; qualifying distributions, $1,479,084, including $1,368,114 for 139 grants (high: $364,621; low: $12; average: $12-$364,621) and $110,970 for 156

grants to individuals (high: $1,000; low: $250; average: $250-$1,000).
Purpose and activities: "The foundation has established six broad funding categories: 1) Newaygo County Community Services: to sustain operations of this autonomous agency established for the delivery of general social welfare services and educational programs; 2) Civic Responsibilities: to strengthen the municipal activities of villages, cities, governmental units, and other related organizations; 3) Education: to augment and promote the special projects of schools, libraries, and other organizations for instruction and training, and for scholarships to promote higher education and learning in specialized programs; 4) Fine Arts and Culture: to support activities that promote appreciation of and participation in artistic expression such as music, theater, dance, sculpture, and painting; 5) Human Services: to foster the delivery of services and the operation of programs to help meet basic human needs and to support the provision of rehabilitative services; and 6) Health and Hospitals: made to health care providers and other related organizations for activities designed to promote optimal well-being and to provide health-related education."
Fields of interest: Community development, civic affairs, education, libraries, fine arts, cultural programs, social services, aged, rehabilitation, health, hospitals.
Types of support: Operating budgets, seed money, emergency funds, student aid, matching funds, consulting services, equipment, general purposes, renovation projects, special projects, scholarship funds.
Limitations: Giving primarily in Newaygo County, MI. No grants to individuals (except for scholarships from specified funds of the foundation), or for endowments, contingencies, reserves, or deficit financing; no loans.
Publications: Annual report, application guidelines, informational brochure.
Application information: Application form not required.
  Initial approach: Letter or telephone to arrange interview
  Copies of proposal: 10
  Deadline(s): Feb. 15 and Sept. 15 except for emergencies
  Board meeting date(s): Usually in Feb., Apr., July, and Nov.
  Final notification: 3 months
  Write: Bertram W. Vermeulen, Exec. Dir.
Officers and Trustees:* Maynard DeKryger,* Pres.; Dean H. Morehouse,* V.P.; Bertram W. Vermeulen, Secy. and Exec. Dir.; Lana A. Ford,* Treas.; Stephen R. Clark, Andrew M. Cummings, Wendie Gerber, Richard L. Hogancamp, James H. McCormick, Cleland V. Methner, William A. Rottman, Eric W. Rudert, Ross G. Scott, Philip T. Smith, Norma A. Schuiteman, Rev. Richard K. Williams.
Number of staff: 4 full-time professional; 1 full-time support; 1 part-time support.
EIN: 381443367
Recent health grants:
1331-1 American Cancer Society, Newaygo County Chapter, Fremont, MI, $10,696. 1990.
1331-2 Duke University Medical Center, Durham, NC, $10,000. 1990.
1331-3 Gerber Memorial Hospital, Fremont, MI, $10,695. For equipment. 1990.

1331-4 Ronald McDonald House, Grand Rapids, MI, $15,000. For operational support. 1990.

1331-5 University of Michigan Hospitals, Ann Arbor, MI, $24,642. 1990.

1332
Frey Foundation
48 Fountain St., N.W.
Grand Rapids 49503-3023   (616) 451-0303

Established in 1974 in MI.
Donor(s): Edward J. Frey, Sr.,‡ Frances T. Frey.
Foundation type: Independent
Financial data (yr. ended 12/31/91): Assets, $58,838,032 (M); gifts received, $78,108; expenditures, $2,755,111; qualifying distributions, $2,109,435, including $2,109,435 for 89 grants (high: $250,000; low: $980).
Fields of interest: Child welfare, child development, family services, education—early childhood, environment.
Types of support: Seed money, special projects.
Limitations: Giving primarily in Emmet, Charlevoix, and Kent counties, MI. No grants to individuals, or for endowment funds, debt retirement, general operating expenses, or scholarships.
Publications: Biennial report, program policy statement, informational brochure, application guidelines.
Application information: Application form required.
  Initial approach: Letter or telephone
  Copies of proposal: 1
  Deadline(s): Contact foundation for deadline dates
  Board meeting date(s): Mar., June, Sept., and Dec.
  Write: James M. Richmond, Pres.
Officers and Directors:* Mary Frey Rottschafer,* Chair.; Edward J. Frey, Jr.,* Vice-Chair.; James M. Richmond,* Pres.; David G. Frey, Secy.; John M. Frey,* Treas.
Number of staff: 2 full-time professional; 1 part-time professional; 1 full-time support.
EIN: 237094777
Recent health grants:

1332-1 Alano Club, Grand Rapids, MI, $20,000. To improve and expand facility providing substance abuse recovery and recreational programs for adults, teens and family members. 1991.

1332-2 Blodgett Memorial Hospital, Grand Rapids, MI, $15,000. To purchase equipment to record emergency phone calls to Blodgett Regional Poison Center, providing poison control services to 65 Michigan counties. 1991.

1332-3 Catholic Secondary Schools, Grand Rapids, MI, $25,000. To train faculty to improve educational outcomes for children with learning disabilities and other special needs. 1991.

1332-4 Charlevoix Area Hospital, Charlevoix, MI, $75,000. To improve and expand ambulatory health care services. 1991.

1332-5 Cherry Street Services, Grand Rapids, MI, $24,697. To improve facilities for health care services to low-income elderly and indigent clients. 1991.

1332-6 Grand Rapids Child Guidance Clinic, Grand Rapids, MI, $12,000. To help establish comprehensive early childhood education and home-based family support program for disadvantaged urban families. 1991.

1332-7 Northern Michigan Hospital Foundation, Petoskey, MI, $70,000. To establish overnight accommodations and hospitality services for patients' families and guests. 1991.

1332-8 Planned Parenthood Association of Northern Michigan, Petoskey, MI, $10,000. To provide equipment and materials to launch fund development campaign for new offices. 1991.

1332-9 Planned Parenthood Centers of West Michigan, Grand Rapids, MI, $20,000. To relocate and expand family planning, preventive and primary health care clinic serving low-income women. 1991.

1332-10 Planned Parenthood Centers of West Michigan, Grand Rapids, MI, $12,500. To purchase and renovate combined central office, family planning and health care facility. 1991.

1332-11 Project Rehab, Grand Rapids, MI, $10,000. To establish residential, full day and outpatient substance abuse treatment program for troubled adolescents and their families. 1991.

1332-12 Saint Johns Home for Emotionally Disturbed Children, Grand Rapids, MI, $100,000. To build new residential treatment campus for emotionally disturbed adolescents. 1991.

1333
The Fruehauf Foundation
100 Maple Park Blvd., Suite 106
St. Clair Shores 48081-2254   (313) 774-5130

Incorporated in 1968 in MI.
Donor(s): Barbara F. Bristol, Angela Fruehauf, Harvey C. Fruehauf, Jr.
Foundation type: Independent
Financial data (yr. ended 12/31/91): Assets, $3,029,876 (M); expenditures, $151,677; qualifying distributions, $146,682 for 114 grants (high: $20,000; low: $50).
Fields of interest: Education, higher education, community development, religion—Christian, hospitals, health associations, social services.
Types of support: General purposes.
Limitations: Giving primarily in MI. No grants to individuals.
Application information:
  Initial approach: Letter
  Deadline(s): None; applications reviewed monthly
  Board meeting date(s): As required
  Write: Mrs. Elizabeth J. Woods, Asst. Secy.
Officers and Trustees:* Harvey C. Fruehauf, Jr.,* Pres. and Treas.; Barbara F. Bristol,* V.P.; Frederick R. Keydel,* Secy.; Robert W. Bowman, Robert B. Joslyn.
EIN: 237015744

1334
General Motors Cancer Research Foundation, Inc.
14-262 EB General Motors Bldg.
3044 West Grand Blvd.
Detroit 48202   (313) 556-4260

Established about 1978 in MI.
Donor(s): General Motors Corp.
Foundation type: Company-sponsored
Financial data (yr. ended 12/31/90): Assets, $810,819 (M); gifts received, $2,003,629; expenditures, $1,987,820; qualifying distributions, $1,985,234, including $180,000 for grants and $300,000 for 4 grants to individuals (high: $100,000; low: $50,000).
Purpose and activities: Awards to individuals for "contributions to the prevention, detection, or treatment of cancer in order to stimulate further research in this field." Candidates for prizes must be nominated by invited proposers.
Fields of interest: Cancer.
Types of support: Grants to individuals.
Limitations: Giving on a domestic and international basis. No grants for scholarships or fellowships; no loans.
Publications: Application guidelines.
Application information:
  Deadline(s): Oct. for prize nominations
  Board meeting date(s): Apr. or May
  Final notification: June
  Write: J.J. Nowicki, Mgr.
Officers and Trustees:* R.C. Stempel,* Chair.; J.G. Fortner,* Pres.; W.G. Quiley, Secy.; R.T. O'Connell,* Treas.; W.O. Baker, J.E. Rhoads, L.S. Rockefeller, B.C. Schmidt, R.B. Smith.
Number of staff: 1
EIN: 382219731

1335
General Motors Corporate Giving Program
3044 West General Motors Blvd.
Detroit 48202-3091   (313) 556-4260

Financial data (yr. ended 12/31/90): Total giving, $65,000,000 for grants.
Purpose and activities: "General Motors believes that corporate philanthropy is an integral part of corporate social responsibility. A sound philanthropic program is in the best interests of the Corporation, its stockholders, its employees, and the communities in which it operates." While GM seeks to contribute to worthy local activities in the cities and states in which GM facilities are located, it also works to benefit the nation as a whole. GM supports culture and arts, and public policy and economic education organizations that are located in GM communities or have a positive impact upon GM business. Figures represent combined foundation and corporate giving.
Fields of interest: Arts, community funds, cultural programs, education, health, higher education, public policy, education—minorities, secondary education, elementary education, science and technology, mathematics, engineering.
Types of support: Building funds, equipment, general purposes, operating budgets, renovation projects, special projects, employee volunteer services.
Limitations: Giving primarily in headquarters city and operating locations nationwide. No support for special interest groups or projects, or for elementary and secondary schools, medical and nursing schools, medical or other research not related to marketing or business, religious organizations when denominational or sectarian in purpose, or industrial affiliate programs. No

grants to individuals, or for conferences, workshops, or seminars, endowment funds, journal or "goodwill" advertisements. General Motors does not contribute its products for on-highway use.

Publications: Corporate giving report.

Application information:

Initial approach: Universities: contact GM Exec. Liaison. If no GM executive is assigned, contact the public affairs officer at the nearest GM facility; local organizations, contact nearest plant; national organizations, contact Detroit address

Deadline(s): None

Write: David Czarnecki, Mgr., Corp. Contribs. and Asst. Treas., GM Fdn.

1336
General Motors Foundation, Inc. ▼
13-145 General Motors Bldg.
3044 West Grand Blvd.
Detroit 48202-3091   (313) 556-4260

Incorporated in 1976 in MI.

Donor(s): General Motors Corp.

Foundation type: Company-sponsored

Financial data (yr. ended 12/31/90): Assets, $149,835,939 (M); expenditures, $24,091,145; qualifying distributions, $34,995,604, including $23,091,357 for grants (high: $2,000,000; low: $200; average: $10,000-$100,000) and $785,906 for employee matching gifts.

Purpose and activities: Grants largely for higher education, community funds, social services, hospitals, health, cancer research, cultural programs, and urban and civic affairs.

Fields of interest: Higher education, community funds, hospitals, cancer, health, urban affairs, civic affairs, cultural programs, social services.

Types of support: Operating budgets, continuing support, annual campaigns, seed money, emergency funds, building funds, equipment, land acquisition, research, publications, special projects, capital campaigns, renovation projects, technical assistance.

Limitations: Giving primarily in plant cities where company has significant operations. No support for special interest groups. No grants to individuals, or for deficit financing, endowment funds, or matching gifts; no loans.

Publications: Informational brochure.

Application information: Application form not required.

Initial approach: Letter

Copies of proposal: 1

Deadline(s): None

Board meeting date(s): Contributions committee meets annually

Final notification: 2 months

Write: D.R. Czarnecki

Officers and Trustees:* R.T. O'Connell,* Chair.; J.E. Mischi, Pres.; W.W. Creek, Secy.; L.J. Krain, Treas.; W.E. Hoglund, L.E. Reuss, F. Alan Smith, J.F. Smith, Jr., Robert C. Stempel.

Number of staff: 1 full-time professional; 1 full-time support.

EIN: 382132136

Recent health grants:

1336-1 Childrens Hospital of Michigan, Detroit, MI, $66,667. For capital grant. 1990.

1336-2 Detroit Institute of Ophthalmology, Grosse Pointe Park, MI, $10,000. For fundraising event sponsorship. 1990.

1336-3 Framingham Union Hospital, Framingham, MA, $20,000. For capital campaign. 1990.

1336-4 General Motors Cancer Research Foundation, NYC, NY, $2,000,000. 1990.

1336-5 Insight, Flint, MI, $100,000. For capital campaign. 1990.

1336-6 Media-Advertising Partnership for a Drug-Free America, NYC, NY, $10,000. For operating support. 1990.

1336-7 Menninger Foundation, Topeka, KS, $10,000. For unrestricted operating support. 1990.

1336-8 Michigan Community Blood Center, Saginaw, MI, $16,666. For capital campaign. 1990.

1336-9 National Head Injury Foundation, Southborough, MA, $10,000. For operating support. 1990.

1337
The Gerber Companies Foundation ▼
445 State St.
Fremont 49413   (616) 928-2759

Incorporated in 1952 in MI.

Donor(s): Gerber Products Co.

Foundation type: Company-sponsored

Financial data (yr. ended 05/31/91): Assets, $40,245,781 (M); gifts received, $282,625; expenditures, $1,732,374; qualifying distributions, $1,732,374, including $1,388,783 for 343 grants (high: $200,000; low: $36; average: $500-$5,000) and $230,800 for 294 grants to individuals (high: $1,200; low: $400; average: $400-$1,200).

Purpose and activities: Support for public and private higher education, including scholarships for children of company employees, scholarship grants in industry related fields of the company, and matching grants; health and human services, including the United Way; and selected projects in communities where Gerber Companies are located.

Fields of interest: Education, higher education, medical education, education—minorities, health, hospitals, nursing, hospices, health services, nutrition, medical research, child development, community funds, agriculture, government, economics.

Types of support: Continuing support, annual campaigns, matching funds, scholarship funds, employee-related scholarships, conferences and seminars, employee matching gifts, endowment funds, equipment, in-kind gifts.

Limitations: Giving limited to cities where company has major operations in AR, CA, IN, MI, NY, NC, SC, TN, and WI. No grants for seed money, emergency funds, deficit financing, land acquisition, renovations, demonstration projects, or publications; no loans.

Publications: Program policy statement.

Application information: Application form not required.

Initial approach: Telephone or letter

Copies of proposal: 1

Deadline(s): Submit proposal preferably in Dec. or Jan., Feb., or Mar.

Board meeting date(s): Jan., Apr., July, and Oct.

Write: Grace J. Deur, Secy., or Yvonne A. Lee, Pres.

Officers and Trustees:* Yvonne A. Lee,* Pres.; George A. Purvis,* V.P.; Grace J. Deur,* Secy. and Administrator; Richard E. Dunning,* Treas.; K. Larry Beemer, Stephen R. Clark, Jay B. Hartfield, Barbara J. Ivens, Robert L. Johnston, L. James Lovejoy, Fred K. Schomer, James T. Smith.

Number of staff: None.

EIN: 386068090

1338
The Rollin M. Gerstacker Foundation ▼
P.O. Box 1945
Midland 48640-1945   (517) 631-6097

Incorporated in 1957 in MI.

Donor(s): Eda U. Gerstacker,‡ Carl A. Gerstacker.

Foundation type: Independent

Financial data (yr. ended 12/31/90): Assets, $66,903,238 (M); expenditures, $1,978,481; qualifying distributions, $1,869,634, including $1,869,634 for 98 grants (high: $300,000; low: $1,000; average: $5,000-$25,000).

Purpose and activities: To assist community projects, with emphasis on the aged and youth; grants also for higher education (including seminaries), health care, medical research, hospitals, and churches.

Fields of interest: Aged, youth, higher education, theological education, social services, civic affairs, health, hospitals, religion—Christian.

Types of support: Annual campaigns, seed money, emergency funds, building funds, equipment, endowment funds, research, matching funds, general purposes, continuing support, land acquisition, capital campaigns.

Limitations: Giving primarily in MI and OH. No grants to individuals, or for scholarships or fellowships; no loans.

Publications: Annual report.

Application information: Application form not required.

Initial approach: Letter

Copies of proposal: 1

Deadline(s): May 15 and Nov. 15

Board meeting date(s): June and Dec.

Final notification: 1 month

Write: E.N. Brandt, V.P.

Officers and Trustees:* Gail E. Allen,* Pres.; E.N. Brandt,* V.P. and Secy.; Carl A. Gerstacker,* V.P. and Treas.; Gilbert A. Currie, Esther S. Gerstacker, Lisa J. Gerstacker, Julius Grosberg, Paul F. Oreffice, Alan W. Ott, Jean U. Popoff, William D. Schuette.

Number of staff: None.

EIN: 386060276

Recent health grants:

1338-1 American Council on Science and Health, Summit, NJ, $35,000. 1990.

1338-2 Association for Childrens Mental Health, East Lansing, MI, $15,000. 1990.

1338-3 Boulder County Dental Aid, Boulder, CO, $10,000. 1990.

1338-4 Drug Abuse Resistance Education (DARE), Midland, MI, $10,000. 1990.

1338-5 Michigan Eye Bank and Transplant Center, Ann Arbor, MI, $10,000. 1990.

1338-6 National Parkinson Foundation, Miami, FL, $10,000. 1990.

1338-7 Saginaw Valley Blood Program, Saginaw, MI, $12,500. 1990.

1338-8 Visiting Nurse Association of Midland, Midland, MI, $15,000. 1990.

1339
Irving S. Gilmore Foundation ▼
136 East Michigan Ave., Suite 615
Kalamazoo 49007   (616) 342-6411

Established in 1972 in MI.
Donor(s): Irving S. Gilmore.‡
Foundation type: Independent
Financial data (yr. ended 12/31/90): Assets, $115,380,414 (M); expenditures, $6,916,311; qualifying distributions, $6,191,306, including $5,804,463 for 112 grants (high: $1,250,000; low: $184; average: $5,000-$200,000).
Purpose and activities: Major support allocated for cultural and performing arts and human services; giving also for health and well-being, education and youth, and community development.
Fields of interest: Arts, performing arts, social services, health services, education, youth, community development.
Types of support: Capital campaigns, equipment, special projects, operating budgets, scholarship funds, building funds, matching funds, seed money, endowment funds, land acquisition, renovation projects, emergency funds, student aid.
Limitations: Giving primarily in the greater Kalamazoo, MI, area. No grants to individuals.
Publications: Annual report (including application guidelines), application guidelines.
Application information: Application form not required.
   Initial approach: Proposal
   Copies of proposal: 4
   Deadline(s): Feb. 1, Apr. 2, June 3, Aug. 1, Oct. 1, and Dec. 2
   Board meeting date(s): Jan., Mar., May, July, Sept., and Nov.
   Write: Frederick W. Freund, Exec. Dir.
Officers and Trustees:* Richard M. Hughey,* Pres.; Floyd L. Parks,* V.P. and Treas.; Harold H. Holland,* V.P.; Russell L. Gabier,* Secy. and Exec. Dir.
Number of staff: 1 full-time professional; 1 full-time support; 1 part-time support.
EIN: 237236057
Recent health grants:
1339-1 Bronson Health Foundation, Kalamazoo, MI, $200,000. For facilities. 1990.
1339-2 Kalamazoo Alcohol and Drug Abuse Council, Kalamazoo, MI, $125,000. For facilities. 1990.
1339-3 Planned Parenthood of Kalamazoo, Kalamazoo, MI, $34,566. For operations. 1990.
1339-4 Wellness Networks, Flint, MI, $22,000. For operations. 1990.

1340
The Grand Rapids Foundation ▼
209-C Waters Bldg.
161 Ottawa, N.W.
Grand Rapids 49503-2703   (616) 454-1751

Established in 1922 in MI by resolution and declaration of trust.
Foundation type: Community

Financial data (yr. ended 06/30/91): Assets, $48,949,704 (M); gifts received, $2,080,714; expenditures, $4,014,117; qualifying distributions, $3,352,231, including $3,171,460 for 100 grants (high: $250,000; low: $250; average: $10,000-$50,000), $110,771 for 155 grants to individuals (high: $5,000; low: $250; average: $250-$2,500) and $70,000 for loans.
Purpose and activities: To provide support for projects or causes designed to benefit the people and the quality of life in the Grand Rapids community and its environs, through grants for social welfare, youth agencies, cultural programs, health, recreation, neighborhood development, the environment, and education, including scholarships for Kent County residents to attend selected colleges.
Fields of interest: Arts, disadvantaged, AIDS, community development, education, youth, environment, health.
Types of support: Seed money, emergency funds, building funds, equipment, land acquisition, matching funds, scholarship funds, capital campaigns, consulting services, loans, renovation projects, special projects, technical assistance, student aid, employee-related scholarships.
Limitations: Giving limited to Grand Rapids, MI, and surrounding communities. No support for religious organizations, hospitals, K-12 schools, or nursing homes/retirement facilities. No grants to individuals (except for scholarships), or for continued operating support, annual campaigns, travel expenses, scholarly research, deficit financing, endowment funds, computers, or vehicles; no student loans.
Publications: Annual report, informational brochure, newsletter, application guidelines.
Application information: The student loan program has been discontinued; new loans will not be made. Application form required.
   Initial approach: Letter or telephone
   Copies of proposal: 11
   Deadline(s): Submit scholarship applications between Jan. 1 and Apr. 15; deadline for all other applications is 10 weeks preceding board meeting
   Board meeting date(s): Bimonthly beginning in Aug.
   Final notification: June 15 for scholarships; 1 month for other requests
   Write: Marcia Rapp, Prog. Officer
Officer: Diana R. Sieger, Exec. Dir.
Trustees: C. Christopher Worfel, Chair.; David G. Frey, Vice-Chair.; Ann M. Cooper, Dirk C. Hoffius, Robert L. Hooker, David B. LaClaire, Shirley K. Perkins, David J. Wagner, Casey Wondergem.
Trustee Banks: Michigan National Bank, NBD Grand Rapids, N.A., Old Kent Bank & Trust Co.
Number of staff: 2 full-time professional; 2 part-time professional; 1 full-time support.
EIN: 382877959
Recent health grants:
1340-1 AIDS Resource Center, Grand Rapids, MI, $83,000. To hire Executive Director. 1990.
1340-2 Alzheimers Disease and Related Disorders Association, Grand Rapids, MI, $15,000. To develop Family Support Project. 1991.
1340-3 Easter Seal Society, Grand Rapids, MI, $25,000. For child care for children with disabilities. 1990.

1340-4 Grand Rapids Child Guidance Clinic, Grand Rapids, MI, $38,000. For Project FOCUS start-up. 1991.
1340-5 Grand Rapids Child Guidance Clinic, Grand Rapids, MI, $30,000. For building renovation for Project FOCUS. 1991.
1340-6 Kent County Emergency Medical Services, Grand Rapids, MI, $55,000. To purchase automated defibrillators. 1991.
1340-7 Kent County Health Department, Grand Rapids, MI, $20,000. For plan to reduce infant mortality. 1991.
1340-8 M. J. Clark Memorial Home, Grand Rapids, MI, $25,500. To develop Alzheimer's program model. 1991.
1340-9 Parkinsons Education Program of West Michigan, Grand Rapids, MI, $20,000. To develop Resource Center. 1991.
1340-10 Planned Parenthood Centers of West Michigan, Grand Rapids, MI, $16,074. For new program to treat low-income women. 1990.
1340-11 Planned Parenthood Centers of West Michigan, Grand Rapids, MI, $14,000. From AIDS Foundation Trust Fund. 1991.
1340-12 Project Rehab, Grand Rapids, MI, $40,000. For Dakotah Family Treatment Center. 1990.
1340-13 Saint Johns Home for Emotionally Disturbed Children, Grand Rapids, MI, $125,000. For new facility. 1990.
1340-14 Vision Enrichment Services, Grand Rapids, MI, $13,100. For scanner to convert print to speech. 1990.
1340-15 Visiting Nurse Services of Grand Rapids, Grand Rapids, MI, $50,000. To increase home health care. 1990.

1341
Granger Foundation
P.O. Box 22187
Lansing 48909-2187   (517) 393-1670

Established in 1978.
Donor(s): Granger Assocs., Granger Construction Co., and members of the Granger family.
Foundation type: Independent
Financial data (yr. ended 06/30/92): Assets, $5,566,061 (M); gifts received, $657,869; expenditures, $309,592; qualifying distributions, $309,592, including $309,592 for 54 grants (high: $30,000; low: $250; average: $5,000-$10,000).
Fields of interest: Protestant giving, Protestant welfare, Catholic giving, social services, family services, disadvantaged, drug abuse, child welfare, handicapped, aged, community funds, general charitable giving.
Types of support: Annual campaigns, capital campaigns.
Limitations: Giving primarily in MI. No grants to individuals.
Publications: Annual report, 990-PF, program policy statement, application guidelines.
Application information: Application form required.
   Initial approach: Letter
   Copies of proposal: 4
   Deadline(s): None
   Board meeting date(s): Semiannually
   Write: Alton L. Granger, Trustee

Trustees: Alton L. Granger, Donna M. Granger, Janice M. Granger, Jerry P. Granger, Lynne C. Granger, Ronald K. Granger.
Number of staff: None.
EIN: 382251879

1342
Great Lakes Bancorp Corporate Giving Program
401 East Liberty
P.O. Box 8600
Ann Arbor 48107   (313) 769-8300

Financial data (yr. ended 12/31/90): Total giving, $120,000 for grants.
Purpose and activities: Supports health, welfare, the arts and culture, civic affairs, education, and community programs, and United Way. Giving only in headquarters city and branch office locations in MI and OH.
Fields of interest: Community funds, health, welfare, arts, civic affairs, education.
Types of support: Capital campaigns, special projects, operating budgets.
Limitations: Giving limited to headquarters city and branch office locations in MI and OH.
Publications: Application guidelines.
Application information:
    Initial approach: Letter; Send requests to headquarters
    Copies of proposal: 1
    Deadline(s): None
    Final notification: 8 weeks
    Write: James S. Patterson, Mgr., Corp. Communs.

1343
Herrick Foundation ▼
150 West Jefferson, Suite 2500
Detroit 48226   (313) 496-7656

Incorporated in 1949 in MI.
Donor(s): Ray W. Herrick,‡ Hazel M. Herrick.‡
Foundation type: Independent
Financial data (yr. ended 09/30/90): Assets, $126,916,179 (M); gifts received, $30,000; expenditures, $10,496,255; qualifying distributions, $10,241,483, including $10,187,933 for 192 grants (high: $1,300,000; low: $1,000; average: $5,000-$100,000).
Purpose and activities: Emphasis on higher and secondary education, including scholarship and capital funds, Protestant church support, cultural programs, youth agencies, hospitals, and health and welfare agencies.
Fields of interest: Higher education, secondary education, Protestant giving, hospitals, health services, youth, social services, cultural programs.
Types of support: Building funds, equipment, land acquisition, research, scholarship funds, special projects, general purposes.
Limitations: Giving primarily in MI. No grants to individuals.
Application information: Application form not required.
    Initial approach: Letter
    Deadline(s): None
    Board meeting date(s): Every 2 to 3 months
    Write: Delores de Galleford
Officers and Trustees:* Kenneth G. Herrick,* Chair., Pres., and Treas.; John W. Gelder,* V.P. and

Secy.; Richard B. Gushee,* V.P.; Todd W. Herrick,* V.P.; Catherine R. Cobb.
Number of staff: None.
EIN: 386041517
Recent health grants:
1343-1 Alzheimers Disease and Related Disorders Association, Chicago, IL, $25,000. For general, charitable, scientific and educational purposes. 1990.
1343-2 Beaumont Foundation, William Beaumont Hospital, Birmingham, MI, $15,000. For research in Department of Obstetrics and Gynecology. 1990.
1343-3 Beaumont Foundation, William Beaumont Hospital, Birmingham, MI, $15,000. For research in Department of Physical Medicine and Rehabilitation. 1990.
1343-4 Bixby Hospital Community Health Care Endowment Fund, Adrian, MI, $100,000. To relocate Critical Care Unit at Bixby Medical Center. 1990.
1343-5 Childrens Inn at the National Institutes of Health, Friends of, DC, $10,000. For general purposes. 1990.
1343-6 Dawn, Ypsilanti, MI, $25,000. For general, charitable and educational purposes. 1990.
1343-7 Gillette Childrens Hospital Foundation, Saint Paul, MN, $20,000. For general purposes and toward microvax computer system for Motion Analysis Laboratory. 1990.
1343-8 Greenwich Hospital Association, Greenwich, CT, $10,000. For general, charitable, educational and scientific purposes. 1990.
1343-9 Henry Ford Hospital, Detroit, MI, $355,000. Toward high-speed radiographic equipment for use in imaging joint motions to study instantaneous joint functions. 1990.
1343-10 Herrick Memorial Hospital, Tecumseh, MI, $1,300,000. For new office building. 1990.
1343-11 Hudson, City of, Hudson, MI, $235,000. For operating costs for Thorn Hospital. 1990.
1343-12 Hudson, City of, Hudson, MI, $165,000. For new roof and new furnace for Thorn Hospital. 1990.
1343-13 Judson Center, Royal Oak, MI, $25,000. Toward construction of Residential Support Center. 1990.
1343-14 Lake Cumberland Mental Health Mental Retardation Board, Vocational Evaluation Center, Somerset, KY, $45,000. For construction of Center. 1990.
1343-15 Lake Cumberland Mental Health Mental Retardation Board, Vocational Evaluation Center, Somerset, KY, $30,000. For instruments, equipment and software comprising vocational evaluation system. 1990.
1343-16 Lenawee, County of, Lenawee County Health Department, Adrian, MI, $15,000. To conduct health needs survey of County to enable Department to apply for federal program addressing health needs of significantly large uninsured or underinsured population. 1990.
1343-17 Michigan, State of, Lansing, MI, $10,000. For drug abuse resistance education program. 1990.
1343-18 Morenci Area Hospital, Morenci, MI, $300,000. For specific projects. 1990.

1343-19 Muscular Dystrophy Association, NYC, NY, $25,000. For general, charitable and educational purposes. 1990.
1343-20 National Institute for Burn Medicine, Ann Arbor, MI, $10,000. For general, charitable, educational and scientific purposes. 1990.
1343-21 National Kidney Foundation of Michigan, Ann Arbor, MI, $25,000. For Building Fund. 1990.
1343-22 National Sudden Infant Death Syndrome Foundation, Columbia, MD, $15,000. For general, charitable and educational purposes. 1990.
1343-23 Oaklawn Hospital, Marshall, MI, $25,000. For general purposes including purchase of medical equipment. 1990.
1343-24 Saint Jude Childrens Research Hospital, Memphis, TN, $100,000. To endow Herrick Foundation Chair in Biochemistry. 1990.
1343-25 University of Michigan, Ann Arbor, MI, $200,000. For preventive medicine project. 1990.
1343-26 University of Michigan, Ann Arbor, MI, $25,000. For Kidney and Pancreatic Transplant Program, including Liver Transplantation. 1990.
1343-27 University of Michigan, Ann Arbor, MI, $10,000. For Community Dental Center. 1990.

1344
Myrtle E. & William G. Hess Charitable Trust
c/o NBD Bank, N.A.
P.O. Box 330222
Detroit 48232-6222   (313) 225-3124

Established in 1984 in MI.
Donor(s): Myrtle E. Hess.‡
Foundation type: Independent
Financial data (yr. ended 09/30/91): Assets, $7,137,782 (M); expenditures, $504,671; qualifying distributions, $441,300, including $404,200 for 21 grants (high: $100,000; low: $1,200; average: $1,200-$85,000).
Purpose and activities: Giving to local area Catholic institutions and agencies, including Catholic hospitals and schools, or to those institutions which received grants during the donor's lifetime or designated for support in donor's will.
Fields of interest: Catholic giving, Catholic welfare, religious schools, hospitals.
Types of support: General purposes, special projects.
Limitations: Giving limited to Oakland County, MI, unless otherwise stipulated in donor's will.
Publications: 990-PF.
Application information: Application form not required.
    Initial approach: Proposal
    Copies of proposal: 2
    Deadline(s): Dec.
    Board meeting date(s): Jan.
    Write: Therese M. Thorn, 2nd V.P., NBD Bank, N.A.
Trustees: Thomas W. Payne, Therese M. Thorn.
Number of staff: None.
EIN: 382617770

1345
James and Lynelle Holden Fund
802 East Big Beaver
Troy 48083-1404

Incorporated in 1941 in MI.
Donor(s): James S. Holden,‡ Lynelle A. Holden.‡
Foundation type: Independent
Financial data (yr. ended 10/31/91): Assets, $8,529,757 (M); expenditures, $634,626; qualifying distributions, $580,978, including $559,750 for 34 grants (high: $100,000; low: $1,500; average: $2,500-$35,000).
Purpose and activities: Support for medical research, including medical schools and hospitals; aid to youth agencies, minority and underprivileged children, higher education, and care of the aged; grants also for cultural programs.
Fields of interest: Medical research, medical education, hospitals, youth, child welfare, minorities, higher education, aged, cultural programs.
Types of support: Annual campaigns, general purposes, building funds, equipment, research, scholarship funds, fellowships, matching funds, continuing support, operating budgets.
Limitations: Giving primarily in MI, with emphasis on Detroit. No grants to individuals, or for endowment funds; no loans.
Application information: Application form not required.
> *Initial approach:* Letter or proposal
> *Copies of proposal:* 1
> *Deadline(s):* None
> *Board meeting date(s):* Jan., Apr., July, and Oct.
> *Final notification:* Several weeks
> *Write:* Herbert J. Wilson, Pres.
Officers and Trustees:* Herbert J. Wilson,* Pres. and Secy.; Louis F. Dahling,* V.P.; Arthur Kaufmann,* Treas.
Number of staff: 1 full-time professional; 1 part-time professional.
EIN: 386052154

1346
Hudson-Webber Foundation ▼
333 West Fort St., Suite 1310
Detroit 48226   (313) 963-7777

Incorporated in 1943 in MI; on Jan. 1, 1984 absorbed the Richard H. and Eloise Jenks Webber Charitable Fund, Inc., and the Eloise and Richard Webber Foundation.
Donor(s): Eloise Webber,‡ Richard Webber,‡ The J.L. Hudson Co., The Richard H. and Eloise Jenks Webber Charitable Fund, Eloise and Richard Webber Foundation, and members of the Webber family.
Foundation type: Independent
Financial data (yr. ended 12/31/90): Assets, $79,133,643 (M); expenditures, $4,355,972; qualifying distributions, $4,016,501, including $3,504,400 for 73 grants (high: $313,000; low: $250; average: $20,000-$50,000), $47,396 for 48 grants to individuals (high: $2,980; low: $19; average: $400-$1,700), $41,556 for 1 foundation-administered program and $300,000 for loans.
Purpose and activities: Concentrates efforts and resources in support of projects within five program missions, which impact upon the vitality and quality of life of the metropolitan Detroit

community: 1)growth and development of the Detroit Medical Center; 2)economic development of southeastern MI, with emphasis on the creation of additional employment opportunities; 3)physical revitalization of downtown Detroit; 4)enhancement of major art and cultural resources in Detroit; and 5)reduction of crime in Detroit. The foundation also provides charitable assistance to J.L. Hudson Company employees or ex-employees needing help to overcome personal crises and misfortunes.
Fields of interest: Community development, civic affairs, community funds, hospitals, hospitals—building funds, employment, housing, welfare—indigent individuals, delinquency, arts, cultural programs, museums, theater, crime and law enforcement, general charitable giving.
Types of support: Operating budgets, continuing support, annual campaigns, seed money, building funds, matching funds, special projects, grants to individuals, equipment, consulting services, renovation projects, employee matching gifts, general purposes, program-related investments.
Limitations: Giving primarily in the Detroit, MI, metropolitan area. No support for educational institutions or neighborhood organizations, except for projects that fall within current program missions. No grants to individuals (except for J.L. Hudson Company employees and ex-employees), or for emergency funds, deficit financing, endowment funds, scholarships, fellowships, publications, conferences, fundraising social events, or exhibits; no loans.
Publications: Biennial report (including application guidelines).
Application information: Application form not required.
> *Initial approach:* Proposal
> *Copies of proposal:* 1
> *Deadline(s):* Apr. 15, Aug. 15 (for July and Dec. meetings), and Dec. 15 (for meeting in Apr. of following year)
> *Board meeting date(s):* July, Dec., and Apr.
> *Final notification:* 1 week after board decision
> *Write:* Gilbert Hudson, Pres.
Officers and Trustees:* Joseph L. Hudson, Jr.,* Chair.; Gilbert Hudson,* Pres. and C.E.O.; Hudson Holland, Jr.,* Secy.; Frank M. Hennessey,* Treas.; Lawrence P. Doss, Alfred R. Glancy III, Joseph L. Hudson IV, Philip J. Meathe, Theodore H. Mecke, Jr., Mrs. Alan E. Schwartz, William P. Vititoe.
Number of staff: 1 full-time professional; 1 full-time support; 1 part-time support.
EIN: 386052131
Recent health grants:
1346-1 Childrens Center of Wayne County, Detroit, MI, $150,000. For building renovations. 1991.
1346-2 Childrens Hospital of Michigan, Detroit, MI, $70,000. For Children's Helping Kids educational outreach program. 1991.
1346-3 Detroit Economic Growth Association, Detroit, MI, $25,000. For development studies for Grace Hospital facility. 1991.
1346-4 Greater Detroit Area Health Council, Detroit, MI, $49,000. For capital spending study for area hospitals. 1991.
1346-5 Michigan Cancer Foundation, Detroit, MI, $70,000. For strategic planning. 1991.
1346-6 Planned Parenthood League of Detroit, Detroit, MI, $12,000. For education programs for youth. 1991.

1346-7 Wayne State University, Detroit, MI, $100,000. For Elliman Medical Research Building Instrumentation. 1991.

1347
The Jackson Community Foundation
(Formerly The Jackson Foundation)
230 West Michigan Ave.
Jackson 49201-2230   (517) 787-1321

Incorporated in 1948 in MI.
Foundation type: Community
Financial data (yr. ended 12/31/91): Assets, $6,558,134 (M); gifts received, $1,536,039; expenditures, $245,000; qualifying distributions, $141,993, including $141,993 for 44 grants (high: $30,000; low: $100; average: $500-$18,000).
Purpose and activities: Support for community improvement and other programs for the benefit of the residents of Jackson County.
Fields of interest: Community development, family services, youth, drug abuse, education, health, cultural programs, arts, literacy, performing arts, humanities, historic preservation, environment.
Types of support: Seed money, building funds, equipment, land acquisition, matching funds, consulting services, technical assistance, loans, special projects, research, capital campaigns.
Limitations: Giving limited to Jackson County, MI. No support for religious purposes. No grants to individuals, or for endowment funds, scholarships, fellowships, publications, or conferences.
Publications: Annual report (including application guidelines), newsletter, application guidelines.
Application information: Application form not required.
> *Initial approach:* Letter or telephone
> *Copies of proposal:* 20
> *Deadline(s):* Submit proposal preferably in Jan., Apr., July, or Oct.; deadlines Feb. 1, May 1, Aug. 1, and Nov. 1
> *Board meeting date(s):* Mar., June, Sept., and Dec.
> *Final notification:* 6 weeks
> *Write:* Herbert E. Spieler, Pres.
Officers and Trustees:* Mark Rosenfeld,* Chair.; Charles H. Aymond,* Vice-Chair.; Herber E. Spieler,* Pres.; Jerry B. Booth,* Secy.-Treas.; Robert W. Ballantine, Georgia R. Fojtasek, Donna Hardy, Patricia B. Harris, Anthony P. Hurst, Gary L. Krupa, Raynard C. Lincoln, Jr., Clara D. Noble, William Sigmund, Geraldine M. Walker, Edward Woods, Susan Wrzesinski.
Number of staff: 2 full-time professional; 1 part-time professional; 1 full-time support; 1 part-time support.
EIN: 386070739
Recent health grants:
1347-1 Region Two Action Agency, Center for Healthy Beginners, Jackson, MI, $25,000. For establishment of prenatal clinic. 1991.

1348
K Mart Corporate Giving Program
Public Affairs
3100 West Big Beaver Rd.
Troy 48084   (313) 643-1000

Financial data (yr. ended 01/31/91): Total giving, $3,700,000, including $3,610,000 for 360 grants (high: $1,000,000; low: $25; average: $5,000-$10,000) and $90,000 for 950 employee matching gifts.

Purpose and activities: Supports higher education and educational associations, arts, business education, public affairs, health, welfare, minority programs, national disease associations, community funding and United Way. Types of support include volunteer programs with retired company employees, in-kind donations, and employee gift matching for education and the arts.

Fields of interest: Higher education, education, community funds, health, health associations, welfare, minorities, arts, business education, fine arts, public affairs.

Types of support: Employee matching gifts, general purposes, employee-related scholarships, in-kind gifts.

Limitations: Giving primarily in headquarters state and operating locations, including CA, CO, DE, FL, GA, IL, IN, IA, KY, NJ, NY, OH, PA, and PR. No support for religious organizations for religious purposes, charities supported by united funds, or secondary education. No grants to individuals, or for endowments or research.

Publications: Corporate report, application guidelines, corporate giving report.

Application information: Application form not required.

> *Initial approach:* Letter; Send requests to headquarters
> *Copies of proposal:* 1
> *Deadline(s):* 90 days prior to need
> *Board meeting date(s):* Committee meets quarterly
> *Write:* A. Robert Stevenson, V.P., Public and Govt. Affairs

Administrator: Linda M. Holser, Supvr., Corp. Contribs.

Number of staff: 1 full-time professional; 1 full-time support.

1349
Kalamazoo Foundation

151 South Rose St., Suite 332
Kalamazoo 49007   (616) 381-4416
FAX: (616) 381-3146

Established in 1925; incorporated in 1930 in MI.
Foundation type: Community
Financial data (yr. ended 12/31/91): Assets, $107,355,981 (M); gifts received, $7,295,235; expenditures, $7,511,281; qualifying distributions, $6,474,680, including $6,474,680 for grants.

Purpose and activities: Primary areas of giving include economic development, education, health, and housing. Grants largely for capital purposes.

Fields of interest: Economics, education, housing, health.

Types of support: Seed money, building funds, general purposes, emergency funds, matching funds, equipment, scholarship funds, capital campaigns, program-related investments, technical assistance, employee matching gifts, renovation projects, special projects.

Limitations: Giving limited to Kalamazoo County, MI. No grants to individuals, or for endowment funds.

Publications: Annual report (including application guidelines), informational brochure (including application guidelines), newsletter, application guidelines.

Application information: Application form required.

> *Initial approach:* Telephone
> *Copies of proposal:* 9
> *Deadline(s):* Mar. 1, July 1, and Nov. 1
> *Board meeting date(s):* May, Sept., and Jan.
> *Final notification:* 2 months
> *Write:* Nanette M. Williams, Fiscal and Admin. Officer

Officers, Trustees and Distribution Committee:*
Martha G. Parfet,* Pres.; Elizabeth S. Upjohn,* V.P.; John E. Hopkins, Secy.-Treas. and Exec. Dir.; Joseph J. Dunnigan, David L. Hatfield, William J. Lawrence, Jr.

Trustee Banks: Comerica Bank-Kalamazoo, First of America Bank-Michigan, N.A., Old Kent Bank of Kalamazoo.

Number of staff: 6 full-time professional; 3 full-time support.

EIN: 386048002

1350
Kellogg Corporate Giving Program

One Kellogg Square
Battle Creek 49016-3599   (616) 961-2235

Purpose and activities: Support for areas where the company has a plant, subsidiary, or other important operation. Emphasis on 1)Education—in addition to colleges and universities receiving support through the company's matching gift program, consideration may be given to such organizations as the United Negro College Fund, independent state college foundations, and other similar organizations; 2)Research—nutrition and/or certain programs conducted by universities related to research within the company's realm of interests; 3)Minority-oriented organizations—organizations designed to improve economic opportunities for members of minority groups; 4)Hospital building funds—funds for capital improvements to institutions (normally no funds contributed to support maintenance or operating funds); 5)Civic and Cultural—programs which are devoted to improving the quality of life and which have wide community and employee acceptance; 6)Health—organizations such as the American Dental Association for research related to the company's realm of interests. Occasional support is given to organizations such as Y Centers, Salvation Army, Boy Scouts, Girl Scouts, or similar programs which are popular in the community and do not receive funds from United Way in areas where the company has a significant operation; support also for disasters or emergencies and gifts of real or personal property.

Fields of interest: Higher education, arts, cultural programs, health, hospitals, community funds, community development, civic affairs, youth, minorities.

Types of support: Equipment, employee matching gifts, in-kind gifts.

Limitations: Giving primarily in headquarters city and major operating locations in CA, MI, NE, PA, and TN; national programs also considered. No support for sectarian organizations. No grants to

individuals, or for building or capital funds, operating budgets, or for United Way recipients.

Publications: Application guidelines.

Application information: Interviews or on-site visits are arranged for large requests. Plant locations have their own budgets and decide on smaller local grants; larger and national requests are handled by headquarters.

> *Initial approach:* Letter and proposal; local requests can be addressed to plants
> *Deadline(s):* Aug. 31
> *Board meeting date(s):* Committee meets in Apr. and Oct.
> *Final notification:* Within 4 months
> *Write:* Debra Price, Exec. Services Coord.

1351
W. K. Kellogg Foundation ▼

One Michigan Ave. East
Battle Creek 49017-4058   (616) 968-1611
FAX: (616) 968-0413

Incorporated in 1930 in MI.
Donor(s): W.K. Kellogg,‡ W.K. Kellogg Foundation Trust.
Foundation type: Independent
Financial data (yr. ended 08/31/91): Assets, $5,396,889,094 (M); expenditures, $196,077,706; qualifying distributions, $153,942,541, including $144,252,139 for 1,205 grants (high: $2,800,000; low: $300; average: $75,000-$250,000), $2,564,911 for 139 grants to individuals and $7,125,491 for foundation-administered programs.

Purpose and activities: "To receive and administer funds for educational and charitable purposes." Aid limited to programs concerned with application of existing knowledge rather than research. Supports pilot projects which, if successful, can be continued by initiating organization and emulated by other communities or organizations with similar problems. Current funding priorities include projects designed to improve human well-being through: youth, higher education, leadership, community-based, problem-focused health services, food systems, rural life, philanthropy, and volunteerism, and groundwater resources. In MI only, projects are supported for economic development. The following areas, which will receive limited funding, may become major interests in the future: families and neighborhoods and human resources for the management of information systems.

Fields of interest: Youth, higher education, leadership development, health services, agriculture, rural development, community development, volunteerism, aged, minorities, Southern Africa, Latin America, Caribbean, conservation.

Types of support: Seed money, fellowships.

Limitations: Giving primarily in the U.S., Latin America, the Caribbean, and southern Africa; support also for international fellowship programs in other countries. No support for religious purposes. No grants to individuals (except through fellowship programs), or for building or endowment funds, research, development campaigns, films, equipment, publications, conferences, or radio and television programs unless they are an integral part of a project already being funded; no grants for operating budgets, annual campaigns, emergency funds, deficit financing, land acquisition, or renovation projects; no loans.

Publications: Annual report (including application guidelines), informational brochure (including application guidelines), newsletter, occasional report.

Application information: Proposals must conform to specified program priorities. Application form not required.

Initial approach: Letter
Copies of proposal: 1
Deadline(s): None
Board meeting date(s): Monthly
Write: Nancy A. Sims, Exec. Asst.-Programming

Officers and Trustees:* Russell G. Mawby,* Chair. and C.E.O.; Norman A. Brown,* Pres. and C.O.O.; Laura A. Davis, V.P., Corp. Affairs and Corp. Secy.; William W. Fritz, V.P., Finance and Treas.; Karen R. Hollenbeck, V.P., Admin.; Helen K. Grace, V.P., Program; Dan E. Moore, V.P., Program; Valora Washington, V.P., Program; Katherine L. Saigeon, Asst. V.P., Finance; Shirley D. Bowser, Chris T. Christ, William E. La Mothe, Dorothy A. Johnson, Wenda Weeks Moore, Robert L. Raun, Howard F. Sims, Jonathan T. Walton.

Number of staff: 71 full-time professional; 1 part-time professional; 155 full-time support; 2 part-time support.

EIN: 381359264

Recent health grants:

1351-1 American Council for Drug Education, NYC, NY, $168,888. To reduce use of drugs among residents of Pittsfield, MA, by working with Berkshire Community College to implement communitywide drug demand reduction program. 1991.

1351-2 American Nurses Foundation, DC, $1,365,378. To improve health care by developing public leadership skills of nurses and consumers to enable them to better inform state and local policymakers. 1991.

1351-3 Ancianos, Taos, NM, $774,721. To increase elderly Hispanic rural residents' access to health care by preparing indigenous community members as health care providers and through mobile health services outreach. 1991.

1351-4 Au Sable Trails Institute of Environmental Studies, Mancelona, MI, $32,100. To improve and protect groundwater quality and human health through heightened public awareness of groundwater resource and protection strategies. Grant brings total of Foundation assistance for project to $66,250. 1991.

1351-5 Auburn University, Montgomery, AL, $1,262,555. To improve rural residents' health and quality of life through health services for elderly, tutoring/enrichment programs for children and human resource development. 1991.

1351-6 Auburn University, Montgomery, AL, $33,860. To establish integrated model to improve well-being of elderly in rural Alabama through holistic health assessment, health risk appraisal and human resource development. Grant brings total of Foundation assistance for project to $1,407,798. 1991.

1351-7 Austral University of Chile, Casilla, Chile, $110,000. To provide study/fellowship opportunities in areas addressing needs of community-based health. 1991.

1351-8 Baltimore Medical System, Baltimore, MD, $67,928. To improve southeast Baltimore adolescents' health and well-being through program of health services, recreation, counseling, leadership development and vocational options. Grant brings total of Foundation assistance for project to $840,377. 1991.

1351-9 Battle Creek Health System, Battle Creek, MI, $35,000. To improve health care for homeless and uninsured by developing nursing clinic. Grant made because of Foundation's response to special programming opportunities. It is unlikely Foundation would make such a grant otherwise. 1991.

1351-10 Brandeis University, Waltham, MA, $671,649. To strengthen Kellogg Foundation-assisted community-based health projects by planning, implementing, and evaluating networking meetings and providing technical assistance. 1991.

1351-11 Brandeis University, Waltham, MA, $201,250. To prepare leaders to better develop and manage county government health care programs. Grant brings total of Foundation assistance for project to $1,568,708. 1991.

1351-12 Brandeis University, Waltham, MA, $13,387. To strengthen Kellogg Foundation-assisted community-based health care projects through support of networking meeting. 1991.

1351-13 California State Department of Education, Sacramento, CA, $122,000. To develop ten state-of-the-art middle grade schools through collaborating statewide venture involving schools, health and social service agencies and colleges and universities. Grant brings total of Foundation assistance for project to $622,000. 1991.

1351-14 California State University, Long Beach, CA, $242,700. To disseminate internationally lessons learned from Kellogg Foundation-assisted distance learning and nursing education projects. 1991.

1351-15 California State University, Long Beach, CA, $76,000. To disseminate internationally lessons learned from Kellogg Foundation-assisted distance learning and nursing education projects. Grant brings total of Foundation assistance for project to $318,700. 1991.

1351-16 California State University, Long Beach, CA, $11,500. To disseminate internationally lessons learned from Foundation-assisted distance learning and nursing education projects. Grant brings total of Foundation assistance for project to $330,200. 1991.

1351-17 Caribbean Community School of the Virgin Islands Annual Conference of African Methodist Episcopal Church, Saint Croix, VI, $40,000. To improve health of K-12 students and their families by integrating interdisciplinary health education component across curriculum. Grant made because of Foundation's response to special programming opportunities. It is unlikely Foundation would make such a grant otherwise. 1991.

1351-18 Carnegie-Mellon University, Pittsburgh, PA, $11,785. To improve health of elderly patients by developing program of computer-generated individualized care information for patients, their families and health care providers. Grant brings total of

Foundation assistance for project to $381,306. 1991.

1351-19 Catholic University of Ecuador, Quito, Ecuador, $22,000. To provide study/fellowship opportunities in areas addressing needs of community-based health. 1991.

1351-20 Cayetano Heredia Peruvian University, Peru, $13,000. To provide study/fellowship opportunities in areas addressing needs of community-based health. 1991.

1351-21 Center for Public Resources, NYC, NY, $179,725. To reduce health care costs related to unnecessary legal conflict and litigation through alternative dispute resolutions. 1991.

1351-22 Center for Research in Ambulatory Health Care Administration, Denver, CO, $294,000. To develop support services to assist elderly to remain in home settings in community. 1991.

1351-23 Center of Information and Education for the Prevention of Drug Abuse, Lima, Peru, $11,500. To increase development opportunities for disadvantaged youth by enabling youth groups to establish neighborhood libraries and children's play activities. Grant made because of Foundation's response to special programming opportunities. It is unlikely Foundation would make such a grant otherwise. 1991.

1351-24 Central American Institute of Public Administration, San Jose, Costa Rica, $622,450. To improve delivery of health care for Central Americans through educational program for administrators of local health care services and health care systems. 1991.

1351-25 Central University of Venezuela, Caracas, Venezuela, $22,000. To provide study/fellowship opportunities in areas addressing needs of community-based health. 1991.

1351-26 Cheff Center for the Handicapped, Augusta, MI, $10,710. To develop educational videotapes for use in training instructors/operators of therapeutic horseback riding programs for the handicapped. Grant brings total of Foundation assistance for project to $22,710. 1991.

1351-27 Chippewa County Health Department, Sault Sainte Marie, MI, $336,670. To improve and protect groundwater quality and human health through heightened public awareness of groundwater resources and protection strategies. Grant made as part of Foundation's emergent programming. Very limited number of such grants will be made. 1991.

1351-28 Clinical Hospital of Porto Alegre, Porto Alegre, Brazil, $614,200. To improve delivery of health services to public through educational program for administrators of local health care facilities and systems. 1991.

1351-29 Codman Square Health Center, Dorchester, MA, $1,125,428. To improve health services for socioeconomically disadvantaged families in two South Boston communities. 1991.

1351-30 Columbia University, NYC, NY, $59,063. To improve inner-city residents' access to primary health care by enabling academic medical center to provide outreach program utilizing students in health professions. Grant brings total of Foundation assistance for project to $992,132. 1991.

1351-31 Community Action Agency, Region II, Jackson, MI, $22,396. To improve maternal and child health by establishing center for prenatal and child health care and developing educational outreach program to reduce teen pregnancies. 1991.

1351-32 Council of Michigan Foundations, Grand Haven, MI, $200,000. For Michigan AIDS Fund to provide support for state organizations' AIDS-related projects. Grant made because of Foundation's response to special programming opportunities. It is unlikely Foundation would make such a grant otherwise. 1991.

1351-33 East Carolina University, Greenville, NC, $32,000. To improve health of rural adolescents and their access to health care by implementing comprehensive, communitywide health services program. Grant brings total of Foundation assistance for project to $1,002,602. 1991.

1351-34 East Tennessee State University, Johnson City, TN, $6,000,000. To improve health of Americans by redirecting health professions education toward community-based primary health care practice. 1991.

1351-35 Eastern Center of Community Studies and Training, Tarapoto, Peru, $89,815. To improve health services for poor by implementing community-managed health care program and training community health agents. 1991.

1351-36 Education Development Center, Newton, MA, $1,215,488. To disseminate Foundation-assisted project to improve professional health teams' decisionmaking capacity regarding cessation of treatment for terminally ill patients. 1991.

1351-37 Eisenhower Medical Research and Education Center, Rancho Mirage, CA, $20,033. To address needs of underserved through video tapes linking health professions education with community-based, problem-focused health services. Grant brings total of Foundation assistance for project to $127,963. 1991.

1351-38 Eisenhower Medical Research and Education Center, Annenberg Center, Rancho Mirage, CA, $50,000. To increase public health professionals' involvement with community-based health services through support of invitational conference. 1991.

1351-39 Emanti Esive, Manzini, Swaziland, $228,477. To improve health status of rural community residents by developing health education and food production program. 1991.

1351-40 F.I.R.S.T. (For Individuals Recovering Sound Thinking), Dorchester, MA, $100,000. To help reduce spread of gang violence and other negative behaviors among at-risk black youth by providing leadership and peer counseling training. 1991.

1351-41 Family Place, DC, $144,650. To promote normal child health and development among low-income urban families through provision of health, social, parenting and educational services. 1991.

1351-42 Federal University of Minas Gerais, Belo Horizonte, Brazil, $105,000. To provide study/fellowship opportunities in areas addressing needs of community-based health. 1991.

1351-43 Federal University of Minas Gerais, Belo Horizonte, Brazil, $84,000. To improve maternal and infant health in South Africa by enabling group of nurses to observe education and birth attendant programs in Brazil. 1991.

1351-44 Federal University of Minas Gerais, Belo Horizonte, Brazil, $75,000. To provide study/fellowship opportunities in areas addressing needs of community-based health. 1991.

1351-45 Federal University of Parana, Curitiba, Brazil, $35,000. To provide study/fellowship opportunities in areas addressing needs of community-based health. 1991.

1351-46 Federal University of Parana, Curitiba, Brazil, $20,000. To provide study/fellowship opportunities in areas addressing needs of community-based health. 1991.

1351-47 Federal University of Rio de Janeiro, Rio de Janeiro, Brazil, $75,000. To provide study/fellowship opportunities in areas addressing needs of community-based health. 1991.

1351-48 Federal University of Rio de Janeiro, Rio de Janeiro, Brazil, $42,000. To provide study/fellowship opportunities in areas addressing needs of community-based health. 1991.

1351-49 Federal University of Rio de Janeiro, Rio de Janeiro, Brazil, $40,000. To provide study/fellowship opportunities in areas addressing needs of community-based health. 1991.

1351-50 George Washington University, DC, $723,441. To improve public's community-based health services by providing national and state health care policymakers with information from Foundation-assisted model projects. 1991.

1351-51 Georgetown University, DC, $426,383. To disseminate findings of health maintenance/disease prevention study of dietary components for individuals with chronic diseases. 1991.

1351-52 Greater Detroit Area Health Council, Detroit, MI, $10,400. To assist persons with AIDS in southeastern Michigan by establishing collaborative case management program and preparing specially-trained social workers. Grant made because of Foundation's response to special programming opportunities. It is unlikely Foundation would make such a grant otherwise. 1991.

1351-53 Greater Southeast Community Center for the Aging, Hillcrest Heights, MD, $1,121,443. To improve health of inner-city elderly by providing them with comprehensive services and utilizing their parenting and child care skills to help at-risk families. 1991.

1351-54 Group Health Cooperative of Puget Sound, Seattle, WA, $74,569. To improve health status of seniors through health promotion program in nonprofit health maintenance organization. Grant brings total of Foundation assistance for project to $1,093,868. 1991.

1351-55 Guanajuato, State of, Tamazuca, Mexico, $38,604. To provide group fellowship to enable professionals from various institutions to explore health professions education and primary care programs in Chile and Brazil. 1991.

1351-56 Haitian Community Health Information and Referral Center, Brooklyn, NY, $44,850. To improve health care for immigrant Haitian adolescents and their families by establishing culturally sensitive health care services. 1991.

1351-57 Hastings Center, Briarcliff Manor, NY, $316,926. To disseminate Foundation-assisted project to improve professional health teams' decisionmaking capacity regarding cessation of treatment for terminally ill patients. 1991.

1351-58 Henry Ford Hospital, Detroit, MI, $541,619. To improve health of middle-school youth through collaborative network of community and health care services. Grant made because of Foundation's responsibility as corporate entity of Michigan. It is unlikely Foundation would make such a grant in any other state. 1991.

1351-59 Hospital Research and Educational Trust, Chicago, IL, $89,450. To improve access, quality and efficiency of health services in rural areas by implementing community-oriented primary care models at rural sites. Grant brings total of Foundation assistance for project to $1,179,300. 1991.

1351-60 Ilimo Community Project, Phoenix, South Africa, $439,610. To improve health of black South Africans by constructing housing and latrines, purifying water and teaching individuals to care for themselves and their families. 1991.

1351-61 Indian Health Board of Minneapolis, Minneapolis, MN, $118,500. To increase educational opportunities for Indian youth and their families through community support systems, mentoring and educational programs. 1991.

1351-62 Indiana University, Bloomington, IN, $82,700. To improve health of indigent and minority citizens through information and referral center and health education workshops. Grant made because of Foundation's response to special programming opportunities. It is unlikely Foundation would make such a grant otherwise. 1991.

1351-63 Indiana University, Indianapolis, IN, $70,091. To develop governmental and public health leaders in six Indiana cities to help provide community-oriented primary health care for area residents. Grant brings total of Foundation assistance for this project to $534,291. 1991.

1351-64 Institute for the Development of Organization and Administration, Santiago, Chile, $286,900. To improve health of Latin Americans by strengthening and expanding network of Kellogg Foundation-assisted projects. 1991.

1351-65 Institute of Health of the State of Mexico, Toluca, Mexico, $39,000. To provide study/fellowship opportunities in areas addressing needs of community-based health. 1991.

1351-66 Institute of Nutrition of Central America and Panama, Guatemala City, Guatemala, $77,000. For study/fellowship opportunities in areas related to food systems. 1991.

1351-67 Institute of Nutrition of Central America and Panama, Guatemala City, Guatemala, $75,000. For study/fellowship opportunities in areas related to food systems. 1991.

1351-68 Institute of Nutrition of Central America and Panama, Guatemala City, Guatemala,

$75,000. To provide study/fellowship opportunities in areas addressing needs of community-based health. 1991.

1351-69 Institute of Public Administration, Dublin, Ireland, $40,000. To establish permanent secretariat for European Healthcare Management Association. Grant brings total of Foundation assistance for project to $429,720. 1991.

1351-70 Intergenerational Health Center, San Jose, CA, $848,813. To provide holistic health services to underserved populations by establishing health centers in Lutheran churches in 10 California communities. 1991.

1351-71 International Council of Nurses, Geneva, Switzerland, $21,004. To enable select nursing professionals in southern Africa to participate in review and revision of regulations that affect nursing education and practice. 1991.

1351-72 International Council of Nurses, Geneva, Switzerland, $19,456. To improve health care by sharing lessons learned from nursing regulation project. 1991.

1351-73 Israelita Center for Help to the Youth, Sao Paulo, Brazil, $31,500. To provide group fellowship to enable team to visit centers for learning disabilities in U.S.. 1991.

1351-74 Lake Superior State University, Sault Sainte Marie, MI, $971,225. To provide health education/primary care to mid-life adults, including outreach services to rural/isolated residents, and prepare community leaders and students to extend project outreach. 1991.

1351-75 Latin American Youth Center, DC, $671,676. To improve health of Hispanic youth through Teen Health Program, providing access to health care, health education, health career internships and leadership development. 1991.

1351-76 Lesotho Ministry of Health, Maseru, Lesotho, $82,656. To improve health of southern Africans by reorienting health professions education toward primary health care through education programs. 1991.

1351-77 Lesotho Nurses Association, Roura, Lesotho, $25,000. For study/fellowship opportunities in areas related to community-based health care. 1991.

1351-78 Lesotho Nurses Association, Roura, Lesotho, $25,000. For study/fellowship opportunities in areas related to community-based health care. 1991.

1351-79 Lincoln Community Health Center, Durham, NC, $60,000. To improve health of disadvantaged, inner-city youth by developing model health promotion program for adolescents and to disseminate results. Grant brings total of Foundation assistance for project to $1,049,471. 1991.

1351-80 Lions Foundation of District L.4, Sao Paulo, Brazil, $357,000. To prevent blindness in children by establishing model program of primary eye care in existing community health centers in 16 municipalities. Grant made because of Foundation's response to special programming opportunities. It is unlikely Foundation would make such a grant otherwise. 1991.

1351-81 Marquette General Hospital, Marquette, MI, $75,547. To improve early childhood education by establishing parent training program. 1991.

1351-82 Marshfield Clinic, Marshfield, WI, $20,000. To improve agricultural safety and health programs targeting children by enabling specialists nationwide to participate in conference. Grant made because of Foundation's response to special programming opportunities. It is unlikely Foundation would make such a grant otherwise. 1991.

1351-83 Medical College of Georgia, Augusta, GA, $1,736,762. To improve rural residents' access to comprehensive health and social services through mobile outreach clinic and individual referrals and monitoring. 1991.

1351-84 Medical College of Georgia, Augusta, GA, $197,912. To reduce infant mortality and improve maternal and infant health in rural east central Georgia through model community outreach and individual case management project. Grant brings total of Foundation assistance for project to $1,032,390. 1991.

1351-85 Medical University of Southern Africa, Medunsa, South Africa, $115,780. To improve black African leadership by providing scholarships to undergraduates, and/or fellowships to postgraduates, in areas needing further development. 1991.

1351-86 Medical University of Southern Africa, Medunsa, South Africa, $14,000. For study/fellowship opportunities in areas relating to leadership. 1991.

1351-87 Michigan State University, East Lansing, MI, $6,000,000. To improve health of Americans by redirecting health professions education toward community-based primary health care practice. 1991.

1351-88 Michigan State University, East Lansing, MI, $596,743. To improve and protect groundwater quality and human health through technical and networking assistance to locally based organizations in Michigan and Great Lakes Basin. 1991.

1351-89 Michigan State University, East Lansing, MI, $228,000. To encourage students, faculty and staff, and alumni to adapt healthy lifestyles by integrating health promotion into curricula and learning environment. Grant brings total of Foundation assistance for project to $2,224,370. 1991.

1351-90 Michigan Technological University, Houghton, MI, $595,401. To establish regional groundwater education center to improve and protect groundwater quality and human health through action-oriented groundwater protection programs. Grant made as part of Foundation's emergent programming. A very limited number of such grants will be made. 1991.

1351-91 Milwaukee Indian Health Board, Milwaukee, WI, $17,400. To improve maternal/infant health among urban Native Americans by identifying high-risk pregnant women and infants and providing network of health and education services. Grant brings total of Foundation assistance for project to $200,147. 1991.

1351-92 Ministry of Health, Cordoba, Argentina, $137,360. To expand primary health services in Cordoba and develop training program to improve quality of community nursing care. 1991.

1351-93 Ministry of Health, Maseru, Lesotho, $95,000. For study/fellowship opportunities in areas related to community-based health care. 1991.

1351-94 Ministry of Health, Maseru, Lesotho, $75,000. For study/fellowship opportunities in areas related to community-based health care. 1991.

1351-95 Ministry of Health, Maseru, Lesotho, $62,000. For study/fellowship opportunities in areas related to community-based health care. 1991.

1351-96 Ministry of Health, Maseru, Lesotho, $40,000. For study/fellowship opportunities in areas related to community-based health care. 1991.

1351-97 Ministry of Health, Mbabane, Swaziland, $25,000. For study/fellowship opportunities in areas related to community-based health care. 1991.

1351-98 Ministry of Health, Institute of Health, Mbabane, Swaziland, $94,000. For study/fellowship opportunities in areas related to community-based health care. 1991.

1351-99 Ministry of Health and the Environment, Kingstown, Saint Vincent & the Grenadines, $80,000. To provide study/fellowship opportunities in areas addressing needs of community-based health. 1991.

1351-100 Ministry of Health of Botswana, Gaborone, Botswana, $120,000. For study/fellowship opportunities in areas related to community-based health care. 1991.

1351-101 Ministry of Health of the State of Veracruz, Jalapa, Mexico, $712,605. To improve health of rural residents of southern Veracruz through support of integrated model of primary health care services and health personnel training. 1991.

1351-102 Ministry of Health of Trinidad & Tobago, San Fernando, Trinidad & Tobago, $80,000. To provide study/fellowship opportunities in areas addressing needs of community-based health. 1991.

1351-103 Ministry of Health of Trinidad & Tobago, San Fernando, Trinidad & Tobago, $30,000. To provide study/fellowship opportunities in areas addressing needs of community-based health. 1991.

1351-104 Ministry of Health of Zimbabwe, Harare, Zimbabwe, $1,310,450. To improve health care for southern Africans by strengthening nursing education and developing community outreach services. 1991.

1351-105 Ministry of Health of Zimbabwe, Harare, Zimbabwe, $125,000. For study/fellowship opportunities in areas relating to leadership. 1991.

1351-106 Ministry of Health of Zimbabwe, Harare, Zimbabwe, $120,000. For study/fellowship opportunities in areas related to community-based health care. 1991.

1351-107 Ministry of Health of Zimbabwe, Harare, Zimbabwe, $100,000. For study/fellowship opportunities in areas addressing needs of youth. 1991.

1351-108 Ministry of Health of Zimbabwe, Harare, Zimbabwe, $100,000. For study/fellowship opportunities in areas related to community-based health care. 1991.

1351-109 Ministry of Health of Zimbabwe, Harare, Zimbabwe, $60,000. For study/fellowship opportunities in areas related to community-based health care. 1991.

1351-110 Ministry of Health of Zimbabwe, Harare, Zimbabwe, $52,000. For study/fellowship opportunities in areas related to community-based health care. 1991.

1351-111 Ministry of Health of Zimbabwe, Harare, Zimbabwe, $47,000. For study/fellowship opportunities in areas related to community-based health care. 1991.

1351-112 Ministry of Health of Zimbabwe, Harare, Zimbabwe, $25,000. For study/fellowship opportunities in areas related to community-based health care. 1991.

1351-113 Ministry of Health of Zimbabwe, Harare, Zimbabwe, $25,000. For study/fellowship opportunities in areas related to community-based health care. 1991.

1351-114 Ministry of Health of Zimbabwe, Harare, Zimbabwe, $25,000. For study/fellowship opportunities in areas related to community-based health care. 1991.

1351-115 Morehouse School of Medicine, Atlanta, GA, $6,000,000. To improve health of Americans by redirecting health professions education toward community-based primary health care practice. 1991.

1351-116 Morris Heights Health Center, Bronx, NY, $456,412. To improve maternal and child health in low-income, urban community by integrating alternative childbearing services into community health clinic. 1991.

1351-117 Natal University Development Foundation, Durban, South Africa, $33,320. To improve maternal and child health in peri-urban and rural communities through training of nurse midwives. Grant brings total of Foundation assistance for project to $83,320. 1991.

1351-118 National Association of Rural Youth of Panama, Panama City, Panama, $155,232. To improve lives of rural families and youth through integrated project focused on nutrition, farm production and health. 1991.

1351-119 National Black Womens Health Project, Atlanta, GA, $1,579,992. To improve well-being of black adolescent women and their families through coordinated health and social services, education and career training. 1991.

1351-120 National Black Womens Health Project, Atlanta, GA, $38,365. To improve inner-city high school girl's health through self-help groups, using health professionals as educators and role models and summer health career internships. 1991.

1351-121 National Board of Literacy and Educational Extension, Mexico City, Mexico, $442,569. To improve lives of rural children and their families through support of program of elementary education, community development and health promotion. 1991.

1351-122 National Institute of Public Health, Mexico City, Mexico, $135,000. To provide study/fellowship opportunities in areas addressing needs of community-based health. 1991.

1351-123 National Institute of Public Health, Mexico City, Mexico, $105,691. To enable group of Latin American Health Administration Development Network members to observe patient care assessment for quality assurance systems in U.S.. 1991.

1351-124 National Institute of Public Health, Mexico City, Mexico, $25,000. To provide

study/fellowship opportunities in areas addressing needs of community-based health. 1991.

1351-125 National Retinitis Pigmentosa Foundation, Baltimore, MD, $50,349. To increase volunteer training and awareness of scientific discoveries and their impact on degenerative eye diseases through national meeting. Grant made because of Foundation's response to special programming opportunities. It is unlikely Foundation would make such a grant otherwise. 1991.

1351-126 National Rural Health Association, Kansas City, MO, $50,000. To improve access to health care for migrant farm workers by providing fellowships in migrant health to mid-level health care professionals. Grant made because of Foundation's response to special programming opportunities. It is unlikely Foundation would make such a grant otherwise. 1991.

1351-127 National School of Nursing, Lima, Peru, $78,000. To provide study/fellowship opportunities in areas addressing needs of community-based health. 1991.

1351-128 National Trust for the Development of African-American Men, DC, $97,250. To help black Americans develop positive life skills through culturally-focused training program of leadership, economic development, crime prevention and health information. Grant made because of Foundation's response to special programming opportunities. It is unlikely Foundation would make such a grant otherwise. 1991.

1351-129 National University of Colombia, Bogota, Colombia, $60,000. To provide study/fellowship opportunities in areas addressing needs of community-based health. 1991.

1351-130 National University of Colombia, Bogota, Colombia, $58,000. To provide study/fellowship opportunities in areas addressing needs of community-based health. 1991.

1351-131 National University of Lesotho, Lesotho, $85,000. For study/fellowship opportunities in areas related to community-based health care. 1991.

1351-132 National University of Loja, Ecuador, $35,000. To provide study/fellowship opportunities in areas addressing needs of community-based health. 1991.

1351-133 National University of Rosario, Rosario, Argentina, $488,925. To improve health care for Latin Americans by establishing off-campus bachelor's degree program in nursing. Grant administered by Faculty of Medical Sciences Cooperative Association. 1991.

1351-134 National University of Rosario, Rosario, Argentina, $25,000. To provide study/fellowship opportunities in areas addressing needs of community-based health. 1991.

1351-135 National University of San Agustin, Arequipa, Peru, $42,000. To provide study/fellowship opportunities in areas addressing needs of community-based health. 1991.

1351-136 North Avenue Womens Center, Battle Creek, MI, $1,027,400. To improve health of infants and children through on-site and

outreach prenatal care services, and to insure fiscal stability. 1991.

1351-137 North Central Technical Institute, Wausau, WI, $53,345. To help elderly maintain their independence by developing community-wide health promotion programs geared to their special needs. Grant brings total of Foundation assistance for project to $985,363. 1991.

1351-138 Northwest Aging Association, Spencer, IA, $71,110. To improve health of elderly by establishing nurse-led support services through structure of local churches. 1991.

1351-139 Northwest Michigan Resource Conservation and Development Council, Traverse City, MI, $64,998. To improve and protect groundwater quality and human health by developing computer system to improve land use decisionmaking. Grant made as part of Foundation's emergent programming. A very limited number of such grants will be made. 1991.

1351-140 Oregon State University, Corvallis, OR, $445,473. To increase number of minorities in health professions through enrichment program for elementary students in rural Hispanic and Native American communities. 1991.

1351-141 Oswaldo Cruz Foundation, Rio de Janeiro, Brazil, $85,000. To provide study/fellowship opportunities in areas addressing needs of community-based health. 1991.

1351-142 Pace University, NYC, NY, $183,866. To improve health of students, as well as staff and family, through university-wide, nurse-coordinated health promotion program and to disseminate results. 1991.

1351-143 Pacific Presbyterian Medical Center, San Francisco, CA, $11,940. To disseminate results of studies involving clinicians in hospital-based program that helps control health care costs while improving quality of care. 1991.

1351-144 Pan American Health Organization, DC, $211,220. To disseminate appropriate technology for perinatal care in primary health care settings throughout Latin America and Caribbean. 1991.

1351-145 Pan American Health Organization, DC, $165,000. To help selected Latin American countries develop public health policies by disseminating model health delivery systems. 1991.

1351-146 Pan American Health Organization, DC, $138,200. To strengthen and consolidate Latin American and Caribbean health-related information system to ensure availability of data for decision-making. Grant brings total of Foundation assistance for this project to $1,478,000. 1991.

1351-147 Paulista Society for the Development of Medicine, Sao Paulo, Brazil, $283,205. To enable Foundation-funded Brazilian projects to share information by continued support to national secretariat. 1991.

1351-148 Phoenix Memorial Hospital, Phoenix, AZ, $232,285. To improve health of infants born to poor women through program of outreach case management and educational support services, utilizing community volunteers. 1991.

1351-149 Potrero Hill Neighborhood House, San Francisco, CA, $100,000. To help prevent substance abuse and violence and improve academic skills among at-risk, black middle school students through program of youth activities and support services. 1991.

1351-150 Pullman Health Systems, Pullman, MI, $228,793. To provide educational programs on groundwater contamination to migrant farm workers, public and health care providers. 1991.

1351-151 Refengkgotso Community Project, Johannesburg, South Africa, $344,243. To improve health of black South Africans by constructing housing and latrines, purifying water and teaching individuals to care for themselves and their families. 1991.

1351-152 Research and Advanced Studies, Mexico City, Mexico, $470,721. To improve health conditions in Lerma, Mexico, communities by implementing primary care program. 1991.

1351-153 S.A.M.I.C. Pediatric Hospital, Buenos Aires, Argentina, $85,000. To provide study/fellowship opportunities in areas addressing needs of community-based health. 1991.

1351-154 Salvador Zubiran National Institute of Nutrition, Mexico City, Mexico, $749,321. To improve nutrition and health of Indians in Oaxaca, Mexico, by preparing local community residents to serve as health promoters. 1991.

1351-155 Salzburg Seminar in American Studies, Cambridge, MA, $50,000. To increase awareness of critical health care issues through international conference. 1991.

1351-156 Secretary of Health of the State of Tabasco, Villahermosa, Mexico, $40,000. To provide study/fellowship opportunities in areas addressing needs of community-based health. 1991.

1351-157 Secretary of Health of the State of Tabasco, Villahermosa, Mexico, $15,000. To provide study/fellowship opportunities in areas addressing needs of community-based health. 1991.

1351-158 South African Medical Research Council, Congella, South Africa, $12,940. To enable group of Fellows in Kellogg International Leadership Program to study role of water-related projects in empowering southern African communities. 1991.

1351-159 Southeastern University of the Health Sciences, North Miami Beach, FL, $50,000. To increase number of minority health care professionals in underserved communities by exposing minority youth to health care professions. Grant made because of Foundation's response to special programming opportunities. It is unlikely Foundation would make such a grant otherwise. 1991.

1351-160 Stephenson Community Schools, Stephenson, MI, $34,588. To improve coordination of health, educational and human services for high-risk families by establishing family health resource centers. Grant brings total Foundation assistance for this project to $134,239. 1991.

1351-161 Students Health and Welfare Centres Organisation (SHAWCO), Kensington, South Africa, $198,147. To improve health of housing settlement residents by developing comprehensive primary health care system. 1991.

1351-162 Substance Abuse Council of Greater Battle Creek, Battle Creek, MI, $10,000. To develop drug-free family entertainment program for New Year's Eve. Grant made because of Foundation's responsibility as corporate member of greater Battle Creek area. Foundation would not make such a grant in any other community. 1991.

1351-163 Swaziland Ministry of Health, Mbabane, Swaziland, $81,550. To involve nurses in strengthening primary health care and nurse licensure examination/registration procedures through series of workshops. 1991.

1351-164 Tchula Family Health Center, Tchula, MS, $34,000. To improve health care delivery for rural residents through enhanced medical and transportation services. Grant made because of Foundation's response to special programming opportunities. It is unlikely Foundation would make such a grant otherwise. 1991.

1351-165 Texas Tech University Health Sciences Center, Lubbock, TX, $314,524. To improve health of high-risk mothers and their infants by providing interactive video health education information in English and Spanish. 1991.

1351-166 Texas Womans University, Denton, TX, $587,666. To increase high-risk pregnant Hispanic women's access to prenatal/perinatal care through support of program utilizing volunteer neighborhood mothers. 1991.

1351-167 Trauma Foundation, San Francisco, CA, $35,750. To strengthen effectiveness of community-based violence prevention program for youth through evaluation component. Grant made because of Foundation's response to special programming opportunities. It is unlikely Foundation would make such a grant otherwise. 1991.

1351-168 Trustees of Health and Hospitals of the City of Boston, Boston, MA, $6,000,000. To improve health of Americans by redirecting health professions education toward community-based primary health care practice. 1991.

1351-169 Trustees of Health and Hospitals of the City of Boston, Boston, MA, $50,000. To improve health and human service delivery through conferences to initiate and support restructuring process. Grant made because of Foundation's response to special programming opportunities. It is unlikely Foundation would make such a grant otherwise. 1991.

1351-170 Umoja Care, Chicago, IL, $24,857. To improve health care for frail elderly by training community women as health care providers. 1991.

1351-171 United States-China Educational Institute, San Francisco, CA, $55,840. To strengthen community-based health and youth/education programs in China and U.S. by establishing Binational Fellowship Exchange Program. 1991.

1351-172 United States-China Educational Institute, San Francisco, CA, $50,000. To strengthen primary health care in China and U.S. by disseminating health professions education techniques and providing exchange opportunities. Grant made because of Foundation's response to special programming opportunities. It is unlikely Foundation would make such a grant otherwise. 1991.

1351-173 University of Buenos Aires, Buenos Aires, Argentina, $60,000. To provide study/fellowship opportunities in areas addressing needs of community-based health. 1991.

1351-174 University of California, Los Angeles, CA, $472,096. To improve quality of life for elderly adults and reduce costly services by providing community-based health care assessment and in-home preventive services. Grant brings total of Foundation assistance for project to $1,122,589. 1991.

1351-175 University of California, San Francisco, CA, $178,712. To disseminate results of project to increase access of health care services to uninsured and underinsured people through improved information systems. 1991.

1351-176 University of California, San Francisco, CA, $89,000. To improve health of elderly in long-term care facilities through preparation of geriatric nurse practitioners. 1991.

1351-177 University of Cape Town, Rondebosch, South Africa, $38,800. To improve maternal and infant health through distance learning program for midwives and physicians. 1991.

1351-178 University of Chile, Santiago, Chile, $704,473. To improve health of urban adolescents by establishing comprehensive health program and training health personnel. 1991.

1351-179 University of Chile, Santiago, Chile, $44,000. To improve health care for persons in five rural communities by establishing family-focused model for health professions education in medicine, nursing and nutrition. Grant brings total Foundation assistance for project to $277,146. 1991.

1351-180 University of Costa Rica, San Jose, Costa Rica, $25,000. To enable select faculty to visit model primary health care/teaching centers, including Foundation-assisted projects. 1991.

1351-181 University of El Valle, Cali, Colombia, $1,038,720. To improve health care for Latin Americans by establishing certificate level and continuing education programs and strengthening existing master's degree program for nurses. 1991.

1351-182 University of Florida, Gainesville, FL, $45,987. To strengthen southern African nurses' primary health care skills through leadership development and independent study program. 1991.

1351-183 University of Hawaii, Honolulu, HI, $6,000,000. To improve health of Americans by redirecting health professions education toward community-based primary health care practice. 1991.

1351-184 University of Illinois, Chicago, IL, $2,388,519. To evaluate Foundation-assisted comprehensive services projects through in-depth analysis of cross-project data. 1991.

1351-185 University of Illinois, Chicago, IL, $1,119,770. To improve community-based health care services by establishing leadership training program for staff of Foundation-assisted projects, community residents and health professionals. 1991.

1351-186 University of Illinois, Chicago, IL, $58,183. To strengthen preparation of nursing faculty and administration for southern African countries through faculty exchange with University of Botswana. Grant brings total of Foundation assistance for project to $201,454. 1991.

1351-187 University of Iowa, Iowa City, IA, $89,769. To disseminate results of project to educate agriculturalists and health professionals to deal effectively with farm-related occupational/environmental health problems. 1991.

1351-188 University of Massachusetts, Worcester, MA, $620,651. To help local health and human service agencies strengthen their delivery of services by providing training and technical assistance aimed at establishing community coalitions. 1991.

1351-189 University of Michigan, Ann Arbor, MI, $39,974. To enhance health professions education by placing student interns in grassroots community health agencies. 1991.

1351-190 University of Michigan, Ann Arbor, MI, $20,000. To inform Michigan policymakers of issues related to rising health care costs and medically uninsured through student-run seminar. 1991.

1351-191 University of Michigan, Ann Arbor, MI, $17,000. To strengthen role of nurses in community-based health care services in China and U.S. by establishing exchange program. 1991.

1351-192 University of Michigan, Ann Arbor, MI, $10,000. To provide research and technical support to produce study and presentation guide for conference on history of health sciences in Michigan. Grant made as part of Foundation's emergent programming. Very limited number of such grants will be made. 1991.

1351-193 University of Missouri, Columbia, MO, $1,788,040. To develop support services to assist elderly to remain in home settings in community and to disseminate results. 1991.

1351-194 University of Missouri, Columbia, MO, $18,266. To demonstrate and evaluate nurse-physician team training in family practice. 1991.

1351-195 University of Natal, Durban, South Africa, $386,454. To improve health care for South Africans through seminar series to help develop projects to prepare health professionals for community-based health services. 1991.

1351-196 University of Natal, Durban, South Africa, $95,000. For study/fellowship opportunities in areas related to community-based health care. 1991.

1351-197 University of Natal, Durban, South Africa, $50,000. To improve health of southern Africans by supporting southern African advisors' efforts to reorient health professions education toward primary health care. 1991.

1351-198 University of New Mexico, Albuquerque, NM, $307,556. To improve health of people of New Mexico by educating future teachers, nurses and physicians to provide health promotion services and disseminate results. 1991.

1351-199 University of Nuevo Leon, Monterrey, Mexico, $224,144. To improve health of Latin Americans and increase involvement of nurses in primary health care through nursing conference. 1991.

1351-200 University of Puerto Rico, San Juan, PR, $31,720. To prepare nurses for leadership roles in primary health care in Latin America. Grant brings total of Foundation assistance for project to $129,917. 1991.

1351-201 University of San Carlos, Guatemala City, Guatemala, $78,000. To provide study/fellowship opportunities in areas addressing needs of community-based health. 1991.

1351-202 University of Sao Paulo, Sao Paulo, Brazil, $353,960. To improve Brazilians' access to oral health data in Portuguese by establishing network of health information centers. 1991.

1351-203 University of Sao Paulo, Sao Paulo, Brazil, $110,000. To provide study/fellowship opportunities in areas addressing needs of community-based health. 1991.

1351-204 University of Sao Paulo, Sao Paulo, Brazil, $28,000. To provide study/fellowship opportunities in areas addressing needs of community-based health. 1991.

1351-205 University of Sao Paulo, Sao Paulo, Brazil, $18,500. To provide study/fellowship opportunities in areas addressing needs of community-based health. 1991.

1351-206 University of Texas, El Paso, TX, $6,000,000. To improve health of Americans by redirecting health professions education toward community-based primary health care practice. 1991.

1351-207 University of Texas, El Paso, TX, $940,172. To increase number of Hispanics in health professions and provide health education through educational/mentoring program for youth and their families. 1991.

1351-208 University of the Witwatersrand, Johannesburg, South Africa, $55,000. For study/fellowship opportunities in areas related to community-based health care. 1991.

1351-209 University of West Indies Hospital, Kingston, Jamaica, $250,000. To improve access to health-related data in Caribbean by establishing network of regional health information centers. 1991.

1351-210 University of Wisconsin, Madison, WI, $372,029. To improve health care in communities by training clinicians in administrative and leadership skills through nonresidential master's degree program. Grant brings total of Foundation assistance for this project to $1,135,282. 1991.

1351-211 University of Zimbabwe, Harare, Zimbabwe, $146,032. To improve community health by analyzing and educating traditional healers and public on proper use of medicinal plant extracts. 1991.

1351-212 University of Zimbabwe, Harare, Zimbabwe, $100,770. To increase access to health care in rural areas by providing community-based clinical experiences for pharmacy students. 1991.

1351-213 University of Zimbabwe, Harare, Zimbabwe, $90,000. For study/fellowship opportunities in areas related to community-based health care. 1991.

1351-214 University of Zimbabwe, Harare, Zimbabwe, $60,000. For study/fellowship opportunities in areas related to community-based health care. 1991.

1351-215 University of Zimbabwe, Harare, Zimbabwe, $25,000. For study/fellowship

opportunities in areas related to community-based health care. 1991.

1351-216 Urban League of Greater Tampa, Tampa, FL, $51,570. To improve health of urban black adolescent males by providing comprehensive health and social services and culturally relevant health education. Grant brings total of Foundation assistance for project to $1,040,140. 1991.

1351-217 Urban League, Metropolitan Tulsa, Tulsa, OK, $688,350. To improve health of inner-city infants and children by integrating community health, social and educational resources. 1991.

1351-218 Visiting Nurse Association of Evanston, Evanston, IL, $848,602. To improve well-being of ethnically-diverse frail adolescents and elderly by providing in-home volunteer and nurse-managed respite care. 1991.

1351-219 Visiting Nurse Services of Southern Michigan, Battle Creek, MI, $64,800. To help implement strategic plan and provide health care for homeless through local Nursing Clinic. Grant made because of Foundation's responsibility as corporate member of Greater Battle Creek Area. Foundation would not make such a grant in any other community. Grant brings total of Foundation assistance for project to $136,197. 1991.

1351-220 Wayne County Health Department, Detroit, MI, $1,108,640. To improve maternal/infant health in minority communities by developing outreach program in six Tulsa sites. 1991.

1351-221 West Virginia University System, Charleston, WV, $6,000,000. To improve health of Americans by redirecting health professions education toward community-based primary health care practice. 1991.

1351-222 Western Michigan University, Kalamazoo, MI, $40,000. To establish regional groundwater education center to improve and protect groundwater quality and human health through action-oriented groundwater protection programs. Grant made as part of Foundation's emergent programming. A very limited number of such grants will be made. Grant brings total of Foundation assistance for project to $610,975. 1991.

1351-223 Women Action Group, Zimbabwe, $318,525. To improve health of rural women through outreach program of health screenings and information and by promoting formation of village self-help groups. 1991.

1351-224 World Health Organization, Geneva, Switzerland, $96,100. To improve health care in southern Africa by enabling nurses to participate in leadership development workshop. 1991.

1351-225 World Vision, Monrovia, CA, $1,309,415. To mobilize volunteers from church congregations to provide assistance to clients of local Head Start and Women, Infants, and Children programs and start new volunteerism efforts. 1991.

1352
Elizabeth E. Kennedy Fund
110 Miller Ave., No. 300
Ann Arbor 48104-1339   (313) 761-3780

Incorporated in 1954 in MI.
Donor(s): Elizabeth E. Kennedy.
Foundation type: Independent
Financial data (yr. ended 12/31/90): Assets, $2,878,957 (M); expenditures, $166,544; qualifying distributions, $158,401, including $149,885 for 21 grants (high: $25,000; low: $780; average: $1,000-$10,000).
Purpose and activities: Emphasis on higher and other education, the arts, archaeology, conservation and the environment, health, family planning, medical research, and mental health; preference is to provide seed money.
Fields of interest: Education, higher education, education—minorities, arts, archaeology, conservation, environment, health, family planning, medical research, mental health.
Types of support: Seed money, operating budgets, renovation projects, capital campaigns, equipment, research.
Limitations: Giving limited to MI, with emphasis on less populated areas of the state. No grants to individuals.
Publications: Annual report (including application guidelines), 990-PF.
Application information: Application form not required.
> *Initial approach:* Letter
> *Copies of proposal:* 4
> *Deadline(s):* None
> *Board meeting date(s):* Mar. and Sept.
> *Write:* John S. Dobson, Secy.
Officers and Trustees: Elizabeth E. Kennedy,* Pres.; John S. Dobson,* Secy.; Ann K. Irish, Susan Kennedy Johnston, Joan K. Slocum, William W. Slocum.
Number of staff: None.
EIN: 386063463

1353
The Kresge Foundation ▼
3215 West Big Beaver Rd.
P.O. Box 3151
Troy 48007-3151   (313) 643-9630
FAX: (313) 643-0588

Incorporated in 1924 in MI.
Donor(s): Sebastian S. Kresge.‡
Foundation type: Independent
Financial data (yr. ended 12/31/90): Assets, $1,214,208,974 (M); expenditures, $55,166,247; qualifying distributions, $59,921,976, including $48,792,000 for 160 grants (high: $1,500,000; low: $40,000; average: $100,000-$500,000).
Purpose and activities: Challenge grants only for building construction or renovation projects, major capital equipment or an integrated system at a cost of at least $75,000 and purchase of real estate; grants generally to tax-exempt institutions involved in higher education (awarding baccalaureate and/or graduate degrees), health and long-term care, social services, science and environment, arts and humanities, and public affairs. Full accreditation is required for higher education and hospital applicants. The foundation does not grant initial funds or total project costs; grants are for a portion of the costs remaining at the time of grant approval. Special Program: The Kresge Foundation will accept applications for a challenge grant program to upgrade and endow scientific equipment and laboratories in colleges and universities, teaching

hospitals, medical schools, and research institutions. For details, request a pamphlet entitled "The Kresge Foundation Science Initiative."
Fields of interest: Higher education, health services, environment, arts, humanities, social services, science and technology, public affairs, AIDS.
Types of support: Building funds, equipment, land acquisition, matching funds, renovation projects.
Limitations: No support for elementary or secondary schools. No grants to individuals, operating or special project budgets, furnishings, conferences, seminars, church building projects, endowment funds, student aid, scholarships, fellowships, research, debt retirement, completed projects, or general purposes; no loans.
Publications: Annual report, informational brochure (including application guidelines).
Application information: Application form required.
> *Initial approach:* Letter or telephone
> *Copies of proposal:* 1
> *Deadline(s):* None
> *Board meeting date(s):* Monthly
> *Final notification:* Generally within 5 months; grants announced Feb. through June and Sept. through Dec. for approvals, throughout the year for rejections
> *Write:* Alfred H. Taylor, Jr., Chair.
Officers and Trustees: Alfred H. Taylor, Jr.,* Chair.; John E. Marshall III,* Pres. and Secy.; Miguel L. Satut, V.P.; Edward M. Hunia, Treas.; Jill K. Conway, Bruce A. Kresge, M.D., George D. Langdon, Jr., Edward H. Lerchen, David K. Page, Margaret T. Smith.
Number of staff: 9 full-time professional; 11 full-time support.
EIN: 381359217
Recent health grants:
1353-1 Abbott-Northwestern Hospital, Minneapolis, MN, $500,000. Toward Phase I renovation, expansion and equipping of radiation oncology unit of Virginia Piper Cancer Institute. 1991.
1353-2 Angela Hospice Home Care, Livonia, MI, $350,000. Toward construction of inpatient hospice facility. 1991.
1353-3 Area Substance Abuse Council, Cedar Rapids, IA, $150,000. Toward renovation and expansion of facility. 1991.
1353-4 Ashley, Havre de Grace, MD, $300,000. Toward construction of Bantle Hall. 1991.
1353-5 Baptist Medical Center, Jacksonville, FL, $850,000. Toward construction and renovation of facilities for new children's hospital. 1991.
1353-6 Bona Vista Comprehensive Rehabilitation Services, Kokomo, IN, $75,000. Toward renovation and expansion of Howard County facility, and construction of Miami County facility. 1991.
1353-7 Child Guidance Center, Cleveland, OH, $150,000. Toward renovation and expansion of main center facility. 1991.
1353-8 Childrens Hospital Medical Center of Akron, Akron, OH, $500,000. Toward construction and renovation of facilities. 1991.
1353-9 Childrens Hospital of Wisconsin, Milwaukee, WI, $500,000. Toward renovation and expansion of surgical facilities. 1991.

1353-10 Childrens Medical Foundation, Dallas, TX, $500,000. Toward renovation and expansion of facilities. 1991.
1353-11 Childrens Oncology Services of Alabama, Birmingham, AL, $100,000. Toward renovation and expansion of Ronald McDonald House of Alabama. 1991.
1353-12 Childs Hospital, Albany, NY, $250,000. Toward renovation and expansion of facilities. 1991.
1353-13 Crusaders Central Clinic Association, Rockford, IL, $90,000. Toward renovation of space within Crusaders Central Clinic for use as immediate care clinic. 1991.
1353-14 Dallas Child Guidance Clinic, Dallas, TX, $150,000. Toward construction of replacement facility. 1991.
1353-15 Epworth Childrens Home, Saint Louis, MO, $100,000. Toward construction of secure cottage. 1991.
1353-16 Hospital for Sick Children, DC, $250,000. Toward renovation and expansion of facilities. 1991.
1353-17 Infant Welfare Society of Chicago, Chicago, IL, $150,000. Toward renovation of facility. 1991.
1353-18 Judson Retirement Community, Cleveland Heights, OH, $150,000. Toward renovation of nursing care unit and construction of health care center. 1991.
1353-19 Kalamazoo Child Guidance Clinic, Kalamazoo, MI, $100,000. For renovation and expansion of clinic headquarters facilities. 1991.
1353-20 Mary Imogene Bassett Hospital and Clinics, Cooperstown, NY, $500,000. Toward construction of ambulatory care center. 1991.
1353-21 Mayo Foundation for Medical Education and Research, Rochester, MN, $500,000. Toward purchase of nuclear magnetic resonance equipment for biomedical imaging research program. 1991.
1353-22 Mount Sinai Hospital and Medical Center, NYC, NY, $500,000. For renovation and expansion of hospital facilities. 1991.
1353-23 Mount Sinai Hospital Medical Center of Chicago, Chicago, IL, $200,000. Toward construction of Cancer Treatment Center. 1991.
1353-24 New York Association for the Learning Disabled, Capital District Chapter, Schenectady, NY, $250,000. Toward construction of facility for Wildwood School. 1991.
1353-25 New York Eye and Ear Infirmary, NYC, NY, $250,000. Toward renovation of space and purchase of equipment for two Ambulatory Centers. 1991.
1353-26 Ottawa Civic Hospital, Ottawa, Canada, $200,000. Toward construction and renovation of hospital facilities. 1991.
1353-27 Pennsylvania State University, Hershey, PA, $600,000. Toward construction of biomedical research facility at Milton S. Hershey Medical Center. 1991.
1353-28 Rehabilitation Center, Evansville, IN, $300,000. Toward renovation and expansion of facilities. 1991.
1353-29 Rose Hill Center, Bloomfield Hills, MI, $500,000. Toward construction of facilities in Holly, MI. 1991.
1353-30 Saint Elizabeth Hospital, Elizabeth, NJ, $250,000. Toward construction of Patient Care Tower and renovation of facilities. 1991.

1353-31 Saint Lukes Hospital, Kansas City, MO, $500,000. Toward expansion of Mid America Heart Institute. 1991.

1353-32 University of Minnesota, Minneapolis, MN, $500,000. For Science Initiative grant toward purchase of Nuclear Magnetic Resonance Spectrometer for Biomedical Engineering Center. 1991.

1353-33 Wake Forest University, Bowman Gray School of Medicine, Winston-Salem, NC, $1,000,000. Toward construction and renovation of facilities. 1991.

1353-34 Wayne State University, School of Medicine, Detroit, MI, $350,000. Toward purchase of scientific equipment. 1991.

1353-35 Wheeling Hospital, Wheeling, WV, $400,000. Toward construction of Wellness Center. 1991.

1353-36 Wyandotte House, Kansas City, KS, $80,000. Toward expansion of Kaw Valley Children's Center and construction of emergency services building. 1991.

1354
The Greater Lansing Foundation
c/o First of America Bank-Central
P.O. Box 21007
Lansing 48909   (517) 334-5437

Established as community foundation in 1947 in MI; status changed in 1980 to independent foundation.
Foundation type: Independent
Financial data (yr. ended 12/31/91): Assets, $10,121,981 (M); expenditures, $530,751; qualifying distributions, $481,338, including $481,338 for 108 grants (high: $20,250; low: $94).
Purpose and activities: Support for charitable, public, or educational institutions, including support for health and the handicapped. Grants mainly for capital expenditures.
Fields of interest: Education, handicapped, health, arts, general charitable giving.
Types of support: Building funds, equipment, matching funds, seed money, special projects, publications, annual campaigns, conferences and seminars, consulting services, emergency funds, renovation projects, research, scholarship funds.
Limitations: Giving limited to Ingam, Clinton, and Eaton counties, MI. No grants to individuals, or for operating budgets, endowment funds, continuing support, deficit financing, land acquisition, or technical assistance; no loans.
Publications: 990-PF.
Application information: Application form required.
Initial approach: Telephone
Copies of proposal: 6
Deadline(s): Submit application form preferably in May; deadline June 30
Board meeting date(s): Aug.
Write: Dorothy L. Sullivan, Secy.
Officers: Ralph W. Bonner, Chair.; Robert K. Kinning, Vice-Chair.; Dorothy L. Sullivan, Secy.
Distribution Committee: Dick Ferris, Suzanne B. Mills, Jane White.
Trustee Bank: First of America Bank-Central.
Number of staff: None.
EIN: 386057513

1355
Edward C. Levy Foundation
8800 Dix Ave.
Detroit 48209

Established in 1973 in MI.
Donor(s): Edward C. Levy Co., Charitable Lead Trust.
Foundation type: Independent
Financial data (yr. ended 09/30/91): Assets, $1,091,227 (M); gifts received, $153,896; expenditures, $966,887; qualifying distributions, $947,728, including $941,240 for 87 grants (high: $375,000; low: $15).
Purpose and activities: Primary giving for child welfare; grants also for health associations, including those for cancer, and Jewish organizations, including welfare funds.
Fields of interest: Child welfare, health associations, cancer, Jewish giving, Jewish welfare.
Limitations: No grants to individuals.
Application information: Contributes only to pre-selected organizations. Applications not accepted.
Trustees: Edward C. Levy, Jr., Joshua J. Stone.
EIN: 386091368

1356
Lincoln Health Care Foundation
70 Hall Place
Grosse Pointe Farms 48236   (313) 882-0597

Foundation type: Independent
Financial data (yr. ended 12/31/91): Assets, $2,433,568 (M); expenditures, $116,625; qualifying distributions, $95,000, including $95,000 for 8 grants (high: $20,000; low: $5,000).
Fields of interest: Hospitals, higher education, medical education, health.
Types of support: Scholarship funds, research.
Limitations: Giving primarily in MI. No grants to individuals.
Application information: Contributes only to pre-selected organizations. Applications not accepted.
Officers: M.B. Landers, M.D., Pres. and Treas.; Stephen Landers, V.P.; Maxine Barr, Secy.
Trustees: Donald Barr, M.D. Landers III, M.D., Virginia V. Landers.
EIN: 381359220

1357
The Loutit Foundation
P.O. Box 491
Grand Haven 49417

Incorporated in 1957 in MI.
Donor(s): William R. Loutit.‡
Foundation type: Independent
Financial data (yr. ended 12/31/91): Assets, $2,021,500 (M); gifts received, $80,992; expenditures, $262,375; qualifying distributions, $243,264, including $236,300 for 40 grants (high: $65,000; low: $100).
Purpose and activities: Support for health, higher education, including buildings and equipment, youth agencies, aid to the handicapped, cultural programs, and community development.
Fields of interest: Youth, handicapped, cultural programs, higher education, community development, health.

Types of support: Capital campaigns, annual campaigns, seed money, emergency funds, building funds, equipment, land acquisition, matching funds, special projects.
Limitations: Giving limited to MI, with emphasis on the western area of the state. No grants to individuals, or for research; no loans.
Publications: Biennial report.
Application information: Application form not required.
Initial approach: Letter or proposal
Copies of proposal: 6
Deadline(s): 1 week prior to board meeting
Board meeting date(s): Feb., May, Aug., and Nov.
Final notification: 2 weeks after meeting
Write: Paul A. Johnson, Pres.
Officers and Trustees:* Paul A. Johnson,* Pres.; Jon W. Eshleman,* V.P.; C. Christopher Worfel,* Secy.-Treas.; Thomas M. Boven, Kennard Creason.
Number of staff: None.
EIN: 386053445

1358
McGregor Fund ▼
333 West Fort St., Suite 1380
Detroit 48226   (313) 963-3495

Incorporated in 1925 in MI.
Donor(s): Tracy W. McGregor,‡ Mrs. Tracy W. McGregor.‡
Foundation type: Independent
Financial data (yr. ended 06/30/91): Assets, $87,763,076 (M); expenditures, $3,534,931; qualifying distributions, $3,131,354, including $2,814,000 for 81 grants (high: $150,000; low: $500; average: $15,000-$50,000).
Purpose and activities: A general purpose foundation supporting education, welfare, including health and youth agencies, humanities, and sciences, with emphasis on the homeless and hungry and higher education; grants also to private colleges and universities in MI, OH, and IN.
Fields of interest: Education, higher education, social services, youth, homeless, hunger, health, cultural programs.
Types of support: Operating budgets, annual campaigns, building funds, equipment, special projects, capital campaigns, continuing support, general purposes, renovation projects.
Limitations: Giving primarily in Detroit, MI; grants to private colleges and universities limited to IN, MI, and OH. No grants to individuals, or for deficit financing, land acquisition, endowment funds, scholarships, fellowships, research, travel, workshops, publications, or conferences; no loans.
Publications: Annual report (including application guidelines).
Application information: Application form not required.
Initial approach: Letter
Copies of proposal: 1
Deadline(s): None
Board meeting date(s): Feb., Apr., June, Sept., and Nov.
Final notification: 60 days
Write: W. Calvin Patterson III, Exec. Dir.
Officers and Trustees:* Elliot H. Phillips,* Pres.; W. Warren Shelden, V.P.; Peter P. Thurber,* Secy.; Robert M. Surdam,* Treas.; W. Calvin Patterson

III, Exec. Dir.; Carlton M. Higbie, Jr., Eugene A. Miller, Bruce W. Steinhauer, M.D., Peter W. Stroh.
Number of staff: 1 part-time professional; 2 full-time support.
EIN: 380808800
Recent health grants:
1358-1 Alzheimers Disease and Related Disorders Association, Detroit Area Chapter, Detroit, MI, $20,000. For in-home respite program. 1991.
1358-2 Catholic Social Services of Wayne County, Detroit, MI, $25,000. For Voices program for services to victims of incest and sexual abuse. 1991.
1358-3 Childrens Home of Detroit, Grosse Pointe Woods, MI, $50,000. For residential program for emotionally troubled children. 1991.
1358-4 Cottage Hospital of Grosse Point, Grosse Point Farms, MI, $250,000. For obstetrics unit and for improvements at Pierson Clinic. 1991.
1358-5 Detroit Institute for Children, Detroit, MI, $40,000. To fund Institute for Physicians and Therapists. 1991.
1358-6 Mariners Inn, Detroit, MI, $150,000. For expansion and renovation of main facility. 1991.
1358-7 Michigan Cancer Foundation, Detroit, MI, $10,000. For summer student research. 1991.
1358-8 Rose Hill Center, Bloomfield Hills, MI, $150,000. For capital campaign. 1991.
1358-9 Southwest Detroit Community Mental Health Services, Detroit, MI, $25,000. For renovation of Fisher Center. 1991.
1358-10 World Medical Relief, Detroit, MI, $15,000. For prescription drugs for elderly in southeast Michigan. 1991.

1359
Michigan National Corporate Contributions Program
P.O. Box 9065
Farmington Hills 48333   (313) 473-3000

Purpose and activities: Major support for the aged; giving also for child welfare, drug abuse, the handicapped, health services, Jewish giving, the homeless, cancer and heart disease organizations, general and private higher education, fine arts institutes and the United Way.
Fields of interest: Community funds, arts, education, higher education, child welfare, drug abuse, community development, handicapped, heart disease, leadership development, health, homeless, Jewish giving, fine arts, cancer, aged, educational associations, health associations, child development, hospitals—building funds.
Types of support: General purposes, employee volunteer services.
Publications: Corporate report.
Application information: Public Relations handles giving.
  Write: Robert J. Mylod, Chair., Pres., and C.E.O.

1360
Frances Goll Mills Fund
c/o Second National Bank of Saginaw
101 North Washington Ave.
Saginaw 48607   (517) 776-7582

Established in 1982 in MI.
Donor(s): Frances Goll Mills.‡
Foundation type: Independent
Financial data (yr. ended 09/30/91): Assets, $3,363,196 (M); expenditures, $258,950; qualifying distributions, $237,979, including $218,450 for 15 grants (high: $100,000; low: $450).
Purpose and activities: Giving primarily for hospitals, social services, civic organizations, historic preservation, and a church.
Fields of interest: Hospitals, social services, civic affairs, historic preservation, religion.
Types of support: Operating budgets, continuing support, seed money, emergency funds, building funds, equipment, land acquisition, matching funds, consulting services.
Limitations: Giving primarily in Saginaw County, MI. No grants to individuals, or for annual campaigns, deficit financing, endowments, special programs, scholarships, fellowships, professorships, or internships; no loans.
Publications: Application guidelines.
Application information: Application form required.
  Initial approach: Letter or proposal
  Copies of proposal: 1
  Deadline(s): None
  Board meeting date(s): Bimonthly, beginning in Feb.
  Final notification: 1 week after meeting
  Write: Denice McGlaughlin, Trust Administration Officer, Second National Bank of Saginaw
Trustee: Second National Bank of Saginaw.
Number of staff: None.
EIN: 382434002

1361
Monroe Auto Equipment Company Giving Program
One International Dr.
Monroe 48161   (313) 243-8000

Financial data (yr. ended 12/31/90): Total giving, $85,000, including $82,000 for grants and $3,000 for employee matching gifts.
Purpose and activities: Support for education and the prevention of drug abuse.
Fields of interest: Drug abuse, education.
Limitations: Giving primarily in areas of company operations. No grants to individuals.
Application information:
  Initial approach: Letter
  Deadline(s): Quarterly
  Write: Kay Osgood, Secy., Monroe Auto Equipment Trust

1362
Morley Brothers Foundation
One Tuscola St.
P.O. Box 2485
Saginaw 48605-2485   (517) 792-1427
Additional tel.: (517) 753-3438

Incorporated in 1948 in MI.
Donor(s): Ralph Chase Morley, Sr.,‡ Mrs. Ralph Chase Morley, Sr.‡
Foundation type: Independent
Financial data (yr. ended 12/31/91): Assets, $4,051,467 (M); gifts received, $100,000;

expenditures, $311,277; qualifying distributions, $289,468, including $289,468 for 51 grants (high: $40,000; low: $130; average: $130-$40,000).
Purpose and activities: Giving primarily for arts and culture, including museums and fine arts; secondary and higher education; organizations providing assistance to minority students; youth; welfare; health and hospitals; and community development.
Fields of interest: Cultural programs, fine arts, secondary education, higher education, education—minorities, youth, welfare, health, hospitals, community development.
Types of support: Operating budgets, continuing support, annual campaigns, seed money, emergency funds, building funds, equipment, special projects, research, matching funds, capital campaigns.
Limitations: Giving primarily in the greater Saginaw, MI, area. No grants to individuals, or for endowment funds, deficit financing, land acquisition, renovation projects, publications, or conferences; no loans.
Application information: Application form not required.
  Initial approach: Letter
  Copies of proposal: 1
  Deadline(s): None
  Board meeting date(s): Feb., Apr., Aug., and Nov.
  Final notification: 3 months
  Write: Edward B. Morley, Jr., Pres.
Officers and Trustees:* Edward B. Morley, Jr.,* Pres.,* Lucy M. Thomson,* V.P.; Lois K. Guttowsky, Secy.; Peter B. Morley,* Treas.; Michael M. Brand, Burrows Morley, Jr., Jay D. Morley, Katharyn Morley, Robert S. Morley.
Number of staff: 2 part-time professional.
EIN: 386055569

1363
Charles Stewart Mott Foundation ▼
1200 Mott Foundation Bldg.
Flint 48502-1851   (313) 238-5651

Incorporated in 1926 in MI.
Donor(s): Charles Stewart Mott,‡ and family.
Foundation type: Independent
Financial data (yr. ended 12/31/90): Assets, $929,505,650 (M); expenditures, $38,980,597; qualifying distributions, $33,565,932, including $33,565,932 for 541 grants (high: $1,266,909; low: $2,000; average: $10,000-$100,000).
Purpose and activities: Supports community improvement through grants for expressing individuality; expanding personal horizons; citizenship; volunteer action; counteracting root causes of alienation; community identity and stability; community renewal; environmental management; fostering institutional openness; better delivery of services; and training in and improving practices of leadership. Pioneer in community education concept.
Fields of interest: Higher education, secondary education, education—early childhood, education—minorities, adult education, vocational education, citizenship, community development, leadership development, volunteerism, rural development, family services, delinquency, disadvantaged, youth, AIDS, environment, conservation, Southern Africa.

Types of support: Conferences and seminars, continuing support, loans, matching funds, operating budgets, program-related investments, publications, seed money, special projects, technical assistance, general purposes.
Limitations: No support for religious organizations or for religious purposes. No grants to individuals, or generally for building or endowment funds, research, scholarships, or fellowships.
Publications: Annual report (including application guidelines), newsletter, financial statement, informational brochure (including application guidelines), program policy statement, occasional report.
Application information: Application form not required.
  Initial approach: Proposal
  Copies of proposal: 1
  Deadline(s): None
  Board meeting date(s): Mar., June, Sept., and Dec.
  Final notification: 60 to 90 days
  Write: Judy Samelson, V.P., Communications
Officers and Trustees:* William S. White,* Chair., Pres. and C.E.O.; William H. Piper,* Vice-Chair.; Richard K. Rappleye, V.P. and Secy.-Treas.; Willard J. Hertz, V.P. and Senior Advisor; Judy Y. Samelson, V.P., Communications; Robert E. Swaney, Jr., V.P., Investments; Maureen H. Smyth, V.P., Programs; Marjorie P. Allen, Alonzo A. Crim, Katherine Fanning, Rushworth M. Kidder, C.S. Harding Mott II, Maryanne Mott, Willa B. Player, John W. Porter, Harold P. Rodes.
Number of staff: 28 full-time professional; 3 part-time professional; 16 full-time support.
EIN: 381211227
Recent health grants:
1363-1 Alaska Center for the Environment, Anchorage, AK, $33,500. For technical and scientific assistance to Alaskan citizen groups working to protect their communities from existing and future environmental health threats with focus on Kenai Peninsula, home to much of Alaska's petrochemical industry and site of widespread groundwater contamination. 1991.
1363-2 Alaska Health Project, Anchorage, AK, $50,000. For Small Business Waste Reduction Project. 1991.
1363-3 Alaska Native Health Board, Anchorage, AK, $52,340. For Community Hazardous Material Management Program. 1991.
1363-4 American Association for Marriage and Family Therapy Research and Education Foundation, DC, $34,264. For policy seminar on parent involvement in elementary school reform. 1991.
1363-5 Boy Scouts of America, Birmingham Area Council, Birmingham, AL, $45,096. For Tomorrow's Leaders program working with coed youth ages 14 to 20 who reside in 13 housing projects on events and activities that may include drug prevention, community service, employment development, tutoring and youth leadership. 1991.
1363-6 Brigham and Womens Hospital, Boston, MA, $100,000. For Patients-Clients Project, research and demonstration program to improve access to social benefits programs for poor medical patients. 1991.
1363-7 Center for Rural Affairs, Walthill, NE, $32,288. For Agricultural Chemical Reduction

Initiative to decrease use of agricultural chemicals by fostering development and adoption of farming practices that use fewer pesticides and commercial fertilizers. 1991.
1363-8 Child Trends, DC, $70,117. For study of state data on teenage pregnancies, abortion and births to determine impact of state family planning policies on adolescent pregnancy and childbearing. 1991.
1363-9 Colorado State University Foundation, Fort Collins, CO, $20,000. For Rocky Mountain Student Environmental Health Project for establishment of new toxics community assistance program. 1991.
1363-10 Community Service Society of New York, NYC, NY, $335,000. For replication of Cooperative Home Care Associates by developing curriculum establishing training institute and seeding at least four business starts in four diverse low-income communities over next seven years. 1991.
1363-11 Environmental Health Coalition, San Diego, CA, $30,000. For Toxics Information and Community Assistance Program which aims to remedy identified toxic problems and to empower citizens with appropriate and effective information. 1991.
1363-12 JSI Research and Training Institute, Boston, MA, $50,000. For Community Environmental Health Technical Resource Center to respond to toxics-related environmental health concerns. 1991.
1363-13 MAP International, Brunswick, GA, $25,000. For equipment and initial funding for Saint Xenia Hospital in the Soviet Union, which will specialize in gerontology. 1991.
1363-14 National Academy of Sciences, DC, $50,000. For conference and completion of study of high-risk youth giving particular attention to root causes of negative adolescent behavior and interrelationship among poor school performance, substance abuse, teen pregnancy and criminal or other antisocial behavior. 1991.
1363-15 National Child Labor Committee, NYC, NY, $25,000. Toward revitalized National Farmworker Health and Education Coalition as advocacy resource for migrant children and youth. 1991.
1363-16 National Commission to Prevent Infant Mortality, DC, $40,000. For plan to strengthen social agenda for minority children. 1991.
1363-17 National Safe Workplace Institute, Chicago, IL, $100,000. To establish Mexico-U.S. Occupational and Environmental Health Committee. 1991.
1363-18 National Toxics Campaign Fund, Boston, MA, $30,000. For growth and operation of new laboratory for providing low-cost, reliable testing for community groups and others with suspected danger from toxic contamination. 1991.
1363-19 Population Crisis Committee, DC, $80,000. For Population/Environment Program to strengthen ties between environmental and population movements. 1991.
1363-20 Research Foundation of the City University of New York, Hunter College School of Health, NYC, NY, $20,000. For Community Environmental Health Resource Center. 1991.
1363-21 Servicios Cientificos y Tecnicos, Hato Rey, PR, $35,000. For Puerto Rican

Community Environmental Health Program. 1991.
1363-22 Southwest District Health Department, Caldwell, ID, $35,000. Toward LINK: For Pregnant and Parenting Teens Project, designed to provide comprehensive services for pregnant and parenting teens in three rural counties of Idaho. 1991.
1363-23 Unison Institute, DC, $45,000. For training and technical assistance on computerized environmental data. 1991.
1363-24 University of Texas Medical Branch Hospitals, Galveston, TX, $30,000. For toxics technical assistance and community outreach. 1991.
1363-25 Western Carolina University, Cullowhee, NC, $25,000. To provide technical assistance for development of three rural intergenerational model programs, which will include health education, tutoring, counseling, work and volunteer opportunities for at-risk adolescents. 1991.

1364
Ruth Mott Fund ▼
1726 Genesee Towers
Flint 48502   (313) 232-3180

Incorporated in 1979 in MI.
Donor(s): Ruth R. Mott.
Foundation type: Independent
Financial data (yr. ended 11/30/91): Assets, $2,530,823 (M); gifts received, $2,216,838; expenditures, $2,143,147; qualifying distributions, $2,097,843, including $1,769,789 for 166 grants (high: $40,000; low: $1,000; average: $15,000-$25,000) and $575 for 13 employee matching gifts.
Purpose and activities: Support for programs with 501(c)(3) exempt status that focus on topics of emerging significance, exemplify originality, and offer the potential for application on a broader scale within four areas: 1) arts and special interests, especially art projects that seek to preserve cultural diversity and value cultural democracy, and for arts and beautification in Flint and Genesee County, MI; 2) environmental programs focusing on global deforestation, and alternative (sustainable) agriculture; environment guidelines currently under review, programmatic interests to be announced February 1993; 3) health promotion, with emphasis on preventive programs for low-income sectors of the population that emphasize one or more of the following: improved nutrition, stress control, exercise and fitness, smoking cessation, and reduced alcohol and drug use; the fund realizes that access to health care is a significant problem for low-income Americans and will, from time to time, consider applications that address equity and access concerns about health care for low-income people (proposals encouraged from new or small organizations with budgets of less than $500,000 per year); and 4) national and international security programs that foster public review and discussion of factors that contribute to the security of a nation. Currently the fund is especially interested in receiving applications that address the following: a) deepening of examination by the public of national and international security issues in terms of their implications for global security; b) strengthening

the process of accountability to the public of national security agencies; c) monitoring the impact of the Department of Energy and the Department of Defense on the environment and human health; and d) examining the level and quality of expenditures for national security.
Fields of interest: Arts, cultural programs, museums, music, theater, environment, conservation, ecology, agriculture, health, nutrition, family planning, disadvantaged, hunger, minorities, Native Americans, welfare—indigent individuals, public policy, peace, arms control, foreign policy.
Types of support: Operating budgets, continuing support, seed money, matching funds, special projects, general purposes, publications, conferences and seminars.
Limitations: Giving for domestic and international programs. No grants to individuals, or for capital or endowment funds, annual campaigns, emergency funds, major equipment, renovations, films and videos of low-priority, deficit financing, scholarships, or fellowships; no loans.
Publications: Application guidelines, multi-year report (including application guidelines), program policy statement.
Application information: Application form not required.
   Initial approach: Proposal (up to 12 pages)
   Copies of proposal: 2
   Deadline(s): Nov. 7, Mar. 15, and July 1
   Board meeting date(s): Feb., June, and Oct.
   Final notification: 3 to 4 weeks after board meeting
   Write: Deborah E. Tuck, Exec. Dir.
Officers and Trustees:* Leslie Dunbar,* Chair.; Joseph R. Robinson,* Vice-Chair. and Treas.; Maryanne Mott,* Pres.; Susan Kleinpell,* Secy.; Brooks Bollman III, Dudley Cocke, Jean E. Fairfax, Donna H. Metcalf, Ruth R. Mott, Melissa Patterson, Rafe Pomerance, Virginia M. Sullivan, Herman E. Warsh.
Number of staff: 2 full-time professional; 1 part-time professional; 1 full-time support; 1 part-time support.
EIN: 382284264

1365
Muskegon County Community Foundation, Inc.
Community Foundation Bldg.
425 West Western Ave.
Muskegon 49440   (616) 722-4538

Incorporated in 1961 in MI.
Donor(s): Harold Frauenthal,‡ Charles Goodnow.‡
Foundation type: Community
Financial data (yr. ended 12/31/90): Assets, $18,101,410 (M); gifts received, $853,571; expenditures, $1,623,493; qualifying distributions, $1,043,975, including $891,363 for 75 grants (high: $115,000; low: $50; average: $50-$115,000) and $152,612 for 310 grants to individuals (high: $2,500; low: $250; average: $250-$1,000).
Purpose and activities: To assist worthwhile projects, with emphasis on health and human services, the arts and culture, education, and community development and urban affairs. Priority support for pilot projects, seed money, and challenge gifts.

Fields of interest: Health, social services, arts, cultural programs, education, community development, urban development, general charitable giving.
Types of support: Seed money, special projects, matching funds, equipment, scholarship funds, loans, research, publications, conferences and seminars, endowment funds, student aid, consulting services, continuing support, emergency funds, exchange programs, internships, operating budgets, professorships, renovation projects.
Limitations: Giving limited to Muskegon County, MI. No grants to individuals (except for scholarships), or for deficit financing.
Publications: Annual report (including application guidelines), program policy statement, newsletter, financial statement, grants list, informational brochure (including application guidelines), application guidelines.
Application information: Application form required.
   Initial approach: Telephone
   Copies of proposal: 16
   Deadline(s): None
   Board meeting date(s): Feb., Apr., June, Aug., Oct., and Dec.
   Final notification: 2 to 3 weeks
   Write: Patricia B. Johnson, Pres.
Officers and Trustees:* John L. Hilt,* Chair.; Fred C. Culver, Jr.,* Vice-Chair.; Patricia B. Johnson,* Pres. and Secy.-Treas.; Josephine F. Anacker, Marilyn V. Andersen, Barbara Andrie, Douglas Bard, George W. Bartlett, Janie Brooks, Robert W. Christie, Bettye Clark-Cannon, Eugene Fisher, Robert Garrison, John Halmond, Robert Hilleary, Robert D. Hovey, Robert Jewell, Richard K. Kaufman, Robert Kersman, John H. Martin, Gary W. Ostrom, Daniel Thill, Robert D. Tuttle, Richard N. Witham.
Trustee Banks: Comerica Bank, First of America Bank, FMB Lumberman's Bank, Old Kent Bank of Grand Haven.
Number of staff: 3 full-time professional; 2 full-time support.
EIN: 386114135
Recent health grants:
1365-1 Mercy Hospital, Muskegon, MI, $10,000. For critical care unit capital campaign. 1990.
1365-2 Mercy Hospital, Muskegon, MI, $10,000. For critical care unit campaign. 1990.

1366
Northeast Michigan Community Foundation
c/o Alpena Shopping Arcade
150-B North State Ave.
Alpena 49707   (517) 354-2221
Additional address: P.O. Box 282, Alpena, MI 49707

Incorporated in 1974 in MI.
Foundation type: Community
Financial data (yr. ended 12/31/91): Assets, $2,212,222 (M); gifts received, $475,104; expenditures, $176,449; qualifying distributions, $125,521, including $125,321 for 46 grants (high: $35,000; low: $200) and $200 for 1 grant to an individual.
Fields of interest: Civic affairs, health, social services, arts, youth, education, libraries.

Types of support: Conferences and seminars, continuing support, equipment, land acquisition, matching funds, program-related investments, publications, renovation projects, scholarship funds, seed money.
Limitations: Giving limited to Alpena County, MI, and neighboring counties. No grants to individuals, or for operating needs or budget deficits.
Publications: Annual report, application guidelines, informational brochure, newsletter, program policy statement.
Application information: Application form required.
   Initial approach: Letter or telephone
   Copies of proposal: 1
   Deadline(s): Feb. 1, May 1, Aug. 1, and Nov. 1
   Board meeting date(s): Quarterly
   Final notification: Within days of board meeting
   Write: Elizabeth L. Connolly, Exec. Dir.
Officers and Trustees:* Robert Granum,* Pres.; Betty Krueger,* V.P.; Marianne Liddell,* Secy.; Gerald Jasinski,* Treas.; Richard Boyce, Avis Hinks, George LaFleche, Jack Leopard, M.D., David Nadolsky, Chantal Nevoret, Lucas Pfeiffenberger, Carolynne Wegmeyer, Charles Wiesen.
Number of staff: 2 part-time professional.
EIN: 237384822

1367
Louis & Helen Padnos Foundation
River Ave. at Bayside Dr.
Holland 49423

Established in 1959.
Donor(s): Louis Padnos Iron & Metal Co.
Foundation type: Independent
Financial data (yr. ended 05/31/91): Assets, $2,906,533 (M); gifts received, $138,030; expenditures, $140,509; qualifying distributions, $129,875, including $129,875 for grants (high: $40,000).
Purpose and activities: Support primarily for Jewish organizations and a recycling program; minor support also for health, education, and social services.
Fields of interest: Jewish giving, environment, health, education, social services.
Limitations: Giving primarily in MI. No grants to individuals.
Application information: Contributes only to pre-selected organizations. Applications not accepted.
Trustees: Seymour K. Padnos, Stuart B. Padnos.
EIN: 386053081

1368
William M. and Mary E. Pagel Trust
c/o NBD Bank, N.A.
611 Woodward Ave.
Detroit 48226   (313) 225-3124
Application address: c/o NBD Bank, N.A., P.O. Box 330222, Detroit, MI 48232-6222

Established in 1964 in MI.
Donor(s): Mary E. Pagel,‡ William M. Pagel.‡
Foundation type: Independent
Financial data (yr. ended 12/31/90): Assets, $6,218,041 (M); expenditures, $709,091; qualifying distributions, $677,200, including

$677,200 for 49 grants (high: $45,000; low: $1,000; average: $1,000-$45,000).
Purpose and activities: Emphasis on health and hospitals, the aged, child welfare, rehabilitation and aid to the handicapped, and Protestant church support; support also for a social service agency.
Fields of interest: Health, hospitals, aged, child welfare, rehabilitation, handicapped, Protestant giving, social services.
Types of support: Annual campaigns, continuing support, general purposes.
Limitations: Giving primarily in MI, with emphasis on the Detroit metropolitan tri-county area. No grants to individuals.
Application information: Application form not required.
  Initial approach: Letter
  Copies of proposal: 1
  Deadline(s): Oct. 30
  Board meeting date(s): Nov.
  Final notification: Nov. 15
  Write: Therese M. Thorn, 2nd V.P., NBD Bank, N.A.
Trustee: NBD Bank, N.A.
Number of staff: None.
EIN: 386046204

1369
Elsa U. Pardee Foundation ▼
P.O. Box 1866
Midland 48641-1866   (517) 832-3691

Incorporated in 1944 in MI.
Donor(s): Elsa U. Pardee.‡
Foundation type: Independent
Financial data (yr. ended 12/31/91): Assets, $62,145,099 (M); expenditures, $3,062,553; qualifying distributions, $2,940,471, including $2,940,471 for 59 grants (high: $200,000; low: $2,000; average: $25,000-$80,000).
Purpose and activities: To promote the cure and control of cancer; grants to hospitals, universities, and institutes for cancer research and control.
Fields of interest: Medical research, cancer.
Types of support: Research.
Limitations: No grants to individuals, or for capital, building, or endowment funds, equipment (except when used in a specific project), scholarships, fellowships, general purposes, matching gifts, or fundraising campaigns; no loans.
Publications: Annual report (including application guidelines).
Application information: Application form required.
  Initial approach: Letter
  Copies of proposal: 8
  Deadline(s): None
  Board meeting date(s): 3 times a year
  Final notification: 4 to 6 months
  Write: James A. Kendall, Secy.
Officers and Trustees: Gail E. Allen,* Pres.; Carl A. Gerstacker,* V.P. and Treas.; James A. Kendall,* Secy.; W. James Allen, Lisa J. Gerstacker, Richard J. Kociba, Michael S. Leahy, M.D., Patrick J. Oriel, Alan W. Ott, Norman C. Rumple, William D. Schuette.
Number of staff: 1 part-time support.
EIN: 386065799
Recent health grants:

1369-1 Colorado State University, Fort Collins, CO, $37,350. For research project, Enhancement of DNA Double Strand Cleavage. 1991.
1369-2 Duke University Medical Center, Durham, NC, $148,318. For research project, Expression and Regulation of Tissue Inhibitor of Metalloproteinases in Breast Carcinoma. 1991.
1369-3 Georgia Institute of Technology, Atlanta, GA, $21,060. For research project, Synthetic Studies of Antitumor Agent. 1991.
1369-4 Health Research, Roswell Park Division, Buffalo, NY, $120,303. For research project, Search for Metastasis Genes in Ovarian Carcinoma. 1991.
1369-5 Hipple Cancer Research Center, Dayton, OH, $32,000. For research project, Development of Orally-Active Stimulants of Human Hematopoiesis. 1991.
1369-6 Indiana University, Indianapolis, IN, $60,000. For research project, Isolation, Characterization and Sequencing of T-Cell ALL c-DNA. 1991.
1369-7 Mayo Foundation, Rochester, MN, $78,000. For research project, Ultrasonic Activation of Hematoporphyrin Derivative: Pilot Study. 1991.
1369-8 McLean Hospital, Belmont, MA, $25,130. For research project, Protein Kinase C Isoenzymes in Neuroblastoma Cell Differentiation. 1991.
1369-9 Medical College of Virginia, Massey Cancer Center, Richmond, VA, $30,834. For research project, Making Informed Choice about Adjuvant Chemotherapy for Node Negative Breast Cancer. 1991.
1369-10 Mercy Hospital of Pittsburgh, Pittsburgh, PA, $22,200. For research project, Control of Colorectal Metastases in Nude Mice. 1991.
1369-11 Michigan Cancer Foundation, Detroit, MI, $95,668. For research project, Development of an Immortal Line of Normal, Human Breast Epithelial Cells. 1991.
1369-12 New England Medical Center Hospitals, Boston, MA, $57,270. For research project, Cytotoxic Efficacy of Melanocyte Stimulating Hormone-Diphtheria Toxin Fusion Protein in Human Malignant Melanoma. 1991.
1369-13 New York University Medical Center, NYC, NY, $54,600. For research project, Role of Nuclear Receptors for Retinoic Acid in Human Carcinomas. 1991.
1369-14 Pennsylvania State University, Hershey, PA, $70,300. For research project, Isolation of Second-site Suppressor Mutations in Transformation-defective Alleles of Oncogene v-src. 1991.
1369-15 Rutgers, The State University of New Jersey, Piscataway, NJ, $46,248. For research project, Pyridoacridines: Synthesis, Antineoplastic Activity, and Structure-Activity Studies. 1991.
1369-16 Scripps Clinic, Research Institute of, La Jolla, CA, $38,000. For research project, Role of Phagocyte - Derived Oxygen Radicals in Pathogenesis of Hepatocellular Carcinoma with Chronic Hepatitis B Virus Infection. 1991.
1369-17 University of Arizona, Tucson, AZ, $54,186. For research project, Biological Effects of Taxol on Tumor Cell Invasion. 1991.

1369-18 University of Arizona, Tucson, AZ, $35,000. For research project, Syntheses of Carbohydrate Derivatives Relevant to Cancer Chemotherapy. 1991.
1369-19 University of California, Santa Barbara, CA, $86,180. For research project, New Diradicals as Anticancer Agents. 1991.
1369-20 University of Florida, Gainesville, FL, $62,158. For research project, Immune-deficient Mice as Model for the Study of Normal and Leukemic Human Hematopoiesis. 1991.
1369-21 University of Illinois, Chicago, IL, $30,300. For research project, Chemical and Bio-assay studies of Traditional Drug (CMS-87) used for Treatment of Cancer. 1991.
1369-22 University of Iowa Hospitals and Clinics, Iowa City, IA, $56,850. For research project, Effect of Hyperthermia on Dunning Prostate Tumor Model. 1991.
1369-23 University of Mississippi, University, MS, $60,000. For research project, Drug-Mediated Inhibition of Topoisomerase II. 1991.
1369-24 University of Missouri, Columbia, MO, $51,680. For research project, Developing DNA Binding Agents: A Unique Bis-Intercalator. 1991.
1369-25 University of North Carolina, Chapel Hill, NC, $11,750. For research project, Boronic Acid Derivatives of Thymidine and its Analogs as Potential Antitumor/Antiviral Agents. 1991.
1369-26 University of Pittsburgh, Pittsburgh, PA, $40,000. For research project, Measurement of Interstitial Fluid Pressure in Human Tumors. 1991.
1369-27 University of Tennessee, Memphis, TN, $11,200. For research project, Combination of Hyperthermia and Chemotherapy: Effect on Bladder Cancer Cell Lines. 1991.
1369-28 University of Wisconsin, Madison, WI, $100,000. For research project, Stepwise Transformation of Human Bronchial Epithelium. 1991.
1369-29 University of Wisconsin, Milwaukee, WI, $50,000. For research project, Immunological Basis of Highly Successful Murine Tumor Therapy. 1991.
1369-30 Wayne State University, Detroit, MI, $60,000. For research project, Expansion of Tumor Infiltrating Lymphocytes from Human Renal Cell Carcinoma in Hollow-Fiber Bioreactor. 1991.

1370
The Meyer and Anna Prentis Family Foundation, Inc.
P.O. Box 7037
Huntington Woods 48070   (313) 398-8415
Application address: 1700 Guardian Building, Detroit, MI 48226

Incorporated in 1955 in MI.
Donor(s): Members of the Prentis family.
Foundation type: Independent
Financial data (yr. ended 12/31/91): Assets, $4,321,869 (M); expenditures, $215,555; qualifying distributions, $215,555, including $195,805 for 46 grants (high: $60,000; low: $25).
Purpose and activities: Giving primarily for medical research, education, the disadvantaged,

and cultural programs; support also for Jewish giving, including Jewish welfare funds.
Fields of interest: Medical research, cancer, education, disadvantaged, cultural programs, arts, performing arts, Jewish giving, Jewish welfare.
Limitations: Giving primarily in MI. No grants to individuals, or for endowment funds, scholarships, fellowships, or matching gifts; no loans.
Application information:
   Initial approach: Letter
   Copies of proposal: 1
   Board meeting date(s): July and Dec.
   Write: Ralph Kliber
Officers and Trustees:* Barbara P. Frenkel,* Pres.; Denise L. Brown,* V.P.; Ronald E.P. Frenkel, M.D.,* V.P.; Dale P. Frenkel,* Secy.; Marvin A. Frenkel,* Treas.; Tom P. Frenkel, Cindy P. Kanter, Nelson P. Lande.
EIN: 386090332

1371
Ransom Fidelity Company
702 Michigan National Tower
Lansing 48933   (517) 482-1538

Incorporated in 1915 in MI.
Donor(s): Ransom E. Olds.‡
Foundation type: Independent
Financial data (yr. ended 12/31/91): Assets, $4,025,347 (M); expenditures, $199,559; qualifying distributions, $135,111, including $126,852 for 31 grants (high: $14,400; low: $30).
Fields of interest: Higher education, hospitals, religion—Christian, cultural programs, conservation.
Limitations: Giving primarily in MI. No grants to individuals.
Application information: Application form required.
   Deadline(s): None
   Write: R.E. Olds Anderson, Pres.
Officers and Directors:* R.E. Olds Anderson,* Pres.; Doris Boog, Secy.-Treas.; Katrina B. Anderson, Deborah Stephens, Diane Tarpoff.
EIN: 381485403

1372
Milton M. Ratner Foundation
c/o NBD Bank, N.A., Trust Div.
611 Woodward Ave.
Detroit 48226   (313) 424-9373
Application address: 17515 West Nine Mile, Suite 875, Southfield, MI 48075; Tel.: (313) 424-9373

Incorporated in 1968 in MI.
Donor(s): Milton M. Ratner.‡
Foundation type: Independent
Financial data (yr. ended 08/31/91): Assets, $6,341,733 (M); expenditures, $300,065; qualifying distributions, $265,498, including $245,300 for 42 grants (high: $40,000; low: $300; average: $200-$50,000).
Fields of interest: Medical research, hospitals, higher education.
Types of support: Building funds, equipment, publications, research, scholarship funds, special projects, general purposes.
Limitations: Giving primarily in MI and GA. No grants to individuals.

Publications: 990-PF.
Application information: Application form not required.
   Initial approach: Letter
   Copies of proposal: 1
   Deadline(s): Oct. 1
   Board meeting date(s): Oct.
   Write: Charles R. McDonald, V.P. and Secy.
Officers and Trustees:* Mary Jo Ratner Corley,* Pres.; Charles R. McDonald,* V.P. and Secy.; J. Beverly Langford,* Treas.
Agent: NBD Bank, N.A.
EIN: 386160330

1373
Edward F. Redies Foundation, Inc.
c/o R & B Machine Tool Co.
118 East Michigan Ave.
Saline 48176-1553   (313) 429-9421

Incorporated in 1981 in MI.
Donor(s): R & B Machine Tool Co.
Foundation type: Company-sponsored
Financial data (yr. ended 12/31/91): Assets, $2,406,610 (M); gifts received, $200,000; expenditures, $90,852; qualifying distributions, $86,500, including $86,500 for 12 grants (high: $50,000; low: $1,000; average: $1,000-$50,000).
Purpose and activities: Giving for civic affairs, higher education, public schools, social services, and a hospital.
Fields of interest: Civic affairs, social services, hospitals, higher education, education.
Types of support: Scholarship funds, capital campaigns, equipment.
Limitations: Giving primarily in MI, with emphasis on Saline and Washtenaw County. No grants to individuals.
Application information: Application form required.
   Initial approach: Letter
   Deadline(s): Mar. 30
   Write: Geoffrey L. Crosbie, Controller
Trustees: James D. Buhr, Wilbur K. Pierpont, Robert D. Redies, Milton E. Stemen.
Number of staff: None.
EIN: 382391326

1374
May Mitchell Royal Foundation
c/o Comerica Bank-Midland
201 McDonald St.
Midland 48640
Application address: 2266 Kings Lake Blvd., Naples, FL 33962; Tel.: (813) 774-0420

Established in 1981 in MI.
Donor(s): May Mitchell Royal Trust.
Foundation type: Independent
Financial data (yr. ended 09/30/91): Assets, $2,065,351 (M); expenditures, $138,427; qualifying distributions, $120,942, including $114,790 for 15 grants (high: $26,153; low: $1,300).
Purpose and activities: Giving for hospitals and eye research and treatment; support also for health associations, including those for the heart and cancer, the handicapped, drug abuse programs, hospices, and nursing training.

Fields of interest: Hospitals, ophthalmology, health associations, cancer, heart disease, handicapped, drug abuse, hospices, nursing.
Types of support: Equipment, scholarship funds, research.
Limitations: Giving primarily in MI, FL, and HI.
Application information: Application form required.
   Initial approach: Letter
   Deadline(s): May 31
   Write: Richard O. Hartley, Chair., Grant Comm.
Grant Committee: Richard O. Hartley, Chair.; Tyrone W. Gillespie, Ruth C. Lishman.
Trustee: Comerica Bank-Midland.
EIN: 382387140

1375
Sage Foundation ▼
34705 West 12 Mile, Suite 355
Farmington Hills 48331

Incorporated in 1954 in MI.
Donor(s): Charles F. Sage,‡ Effa L. Sage.‡
Foundation type: Independent
Financial data (yr. ended 12/31/90): Assets, $28,980,185 (M); expenditures, $2,456,363; qualifying distributions, $2,273,488, including $1,954,889 for 96 grants (high: $450,000; low: $1,000; average: $10,000-$25,000).
Purpose and activities: Emphasis on higher and secondary education and hospitals; grants also for aid to the handicapped, Roman Catholic religious and charitable organizations, youth and child welfare agencies, church support, and cultural programs.
Fields of interest: Higher education, secondary education, hospitals, handicapped, Catholic giving, Catholic welfare, youth, child welfare, social services, cultural programs.
Types of support: General purposes, scholarship funds, renovation projects, building funds, operating budgets, research, special projects.
Limitations: Giving primarily in MI.
Publications: Financial statement.
Application information: Application form not required.
   Initial approach: Letter
   Deadline(s): None
   Board meeting date(s): Approximately every 2 weeks
   Final notification: 6 to 8 weeks
Officers and Trustees:* Melissa Sage Booth,* Chair., Pres. and Treas.; John J. Ayaub,* V.P. and Secy.; John H. Booth, Genevieve R. Sage, James E. Van Doren.
Number of staff: None.
EIN: 386041518

1376
Saginaw Community Foundation
118 East Genesee
Saginaw 48607-1227   (517) 755-0545

Incorporated in 1984 in MI.
Foundation type: Community
Financial data (yr. ended 12/31/91): Assets, $3,303,840 (M); gifts received, $1,147,995; expenditures, $359,409; qualifying distributions, $228,191, including $222,191 for 63 grants (high: $76,000; low: $24) and $6,000 for 10 grants to individuals (high: $1,000; low: $500).

Purpose and activities: Support for projects not currently being served by existing community resources and projects providing leverage for generating other funds and community resources.
Fields of interest: Arts, community development, education, health, recreation, welfare, general charitable giving.
Types of support: Building funds, emergency funds, equipment, matching funds, publications, renovation projects, scholarship funds, technical assistance, seed money, special projects.
Limitations: Giving limited to Saginaw County, MI. No support for churches or sectarian religious programs. No grants to individuals (except for designated scholarship funds), or for operating budgets or basic municipal or educational services; generally no multi-year grants.
Publications: Annual report (including application guidelines), application guidelines, program policy statement, newsletter, occasional report.
Application information: Application form required.

Initial approach: Letter (1 page)
Copies of proposal: 10
Deadline(s): Feb. 1, May 1, Aug. 1, and Nov. 1
Board meeting date(s): Monthly
Final notification: 1 month after deadline
Write: Lucy R. Allen, Pres. and C.E.O.
Officers and Trustees:* William F. Nelson, Jr.,* Chair.; Curtis E. White,* Vice-Chair.; Lucy R. Allen,* Pres. and C.E.O.; Culli Damuth,* Secy.; Lloyd Fairbanks,* Treas.; Robert G. App, M.D., Thomas W. Barwin, Patricia F. Bierlein, Hugo E. Braun, Jr., Craig A. Chancellor, Joseph P. Day, David M. Hall, C.G. King, Jr., Joseph E. LaClair, Terry R. Niederstadt, Terry Pruitt, Ronald G. Schneider, Patricia A. Shaheen, Paul T. Virciglio.
Number of staff: 1 full-time professional; 1 part-time professional; 1 full-time support.
EIN: 382474297

1377
Sehn Foundation
23874 Kean Ave.
Dearborn 48124

Established in 1968 in MI.
Donor(s): Francis J. Sehn, James T. Sehn.
Foundation type: Independent
Financial data (yr. ended 12/31/90): Assets, $2,991,697 (M); gifts received, $19,274; expenditures, $381,009; qualifying distributions, $300,395, including $300,106 for 30 grants (high: $250,000; low: $60).
Fields of interest: Catholic giving, health, social services, education.
Types of support: General purposes.
Limitations: Giving primarily in Detroit, MI. No grants to individuals.
Application information: Contributes only to pre-selected organizations. Applications not accepted.
Officer: Francis J. Sehn, Pres.
EIN: 386160784

1378
Seidman Family Foundation
(Formerly The Thomas Erler Seidman Foundation)
99 Monroe Ave., N.W., Suite 800
Grand Rapids 49503   (616) 453-7719

Trust established in 1950 in MI.
Donor(s): Frank E. Seidman,‡ Esther L. Seidman.‡
Foundation type: Independent
Financial data (yr. ended 12/31/91): Assets, $2,805,470 (M); expenditures, $136,068; qualifying distributions, $129,996, including $122,000 for 34 grants (high: $50,000; low: $500).
Purpose and activities: Emphasis on cultural programs and higher education; support also for social service agencies and medical research.
Fields of interest: Cultural programs, higher education, social services, medical research.
Types of support: General purposes, building funds, endowment funds, annual campaigns, equipment.
Limitations: Giving on a national basis, with some emphasis on MI. No grants to Individuals.
Application information: Application form not required.

Deadline(s): None
Write: Augusta Eppinga, Trustee
Trustees: Augusta Eppinga, B. Thomas Seidman, L. William Seidman, Sarah B. Seidman.
EIN: 136098204

1379
The Shiffman Foundation
c/o Charles Nida
2290 First National Bldg.
Detroit 48226

Incorporated in 1948 in MI.
Donor(s): Abraham Shiffman.
Foundation type: Independent
Financial data (yr. ended 09/30/91): Assets, $2,035,719 (M); expenditures, $153,744; qualifying distributions, $149,531, including $134,786 for 51 grants (high: $25,100; low: $100).
Purpose and activities: Emphasis on Jewish welfare funds; giving also for peace issues and community development; some support for higher education in the U.S. and Israel, hospitals, community funds, and temple support.
Fields of interest: Jewish welfare, peace, community development, higher education, Israel, hospitals, community funds, Jewish giving.
Limitations: Giving primarily in Detroit, MI. No grants to individuals.
Application information: Contributes only to pre-selected organizations. Applications not accepted.
Officers and Trustees:* Norman James Levey,* Pres.; Robert I. Kohn, Jr.,* V.P.; Richard H. Levey,* V.P.; Janet S. Kohn,* Secy.; Bruce Gershenson,* Treas.; Beatrice Alexander, Edward Allardice, Lisa Kaichen, Lester Morris, Victor Shiffman.
Number of staff: 1 part-time professional.
EIN: 381396850

1380
The Skillman Foundation ▼
333 West Fort St., Suite 1350
Detroit 48226   (313) 961-8850

Incorporated in 1960 in MI.
Donor(s): Rose P. Skillman.‡
Foundation type: Independent
Financial data (yr. ended 12/31/91): Assets, $364,323,178 (M); gifts received, $2,243,549; expenditures, $19,507,002; qualifying distributions, $17,481,980, including $16,474,379 for 130 grants (high: $2,503,263; low: $500; average: $20,000-$100,000).
Purpose and activities: The purpose of the foundation is to improve the well-being of residents of Southeastern Michigan and, in particular, the Detroit metropolitan area. Developing children and youth to their maximum potential is the foundation's primary goal. A central concern is meeting the needs of the disadvantaged. The foundation functions both as a resource for the nonprofit community and as a catalyst for positive change.
Fields of interest: Child development, child welfare, education, health, law and justice, education—minorities, vocational education, youth, aged, welfare—indigent individuals, social services, disadvantaged, homeless, family services, delinquency, crime and law enforcement, hunger, handicapped, drug abuse, arts, performing arts, cultural programs, fine arts, recreation.
Types of support: Seed money, general purposes, employee matching gifts, special projects, scholarship funds, operating budgets.
Limitations: Giving primarily in southeastern MI, with emphasis on metropolitan Detroit, including Wayne, Macomb, and Oakland counties. No support for long-term projects not being aided by other sources, sectarian religious activities, political lobbying or legislative activities, or new organizations which do not have an operational and financial history. No grants to individuals, or for endowment funds, annual campaigns, basic research or deficit financing; no loans.
Publications: Annual report, informational brochure (including application guidelines), newsletter.
Application information: Application form not required.

Initial approach: Proposal
Copies of proposal: 1
Deadline(s): Apr. 1 for arts and culture organizations; for other grants no set deadline
Board meeting date(s): Feb., Apr., June, Sept., and Nov.
Final notification: 2 weeks after board meeting
Write: Program Office
Officers and Trustees:* William E. Hoglund,* Chair.; Leonard W. Smith,* Pres. and Secy.; Jean E. Gregory, V.P. and Treas.; Kari Schlachtenhaufen, V.P., Prog.; James A. Aliber, Lillian Bauder, William M. Brodhead, Bernadine N. Denning, Walter Douglas, Alan Schwartz, Jane R. Thomas.
Number of staff: 7 full-time professional; 4 full-time support; 1 part-time support.
EIN: 381675780
Recent health grants:
1380-1 Boys and Girls Club of Royal Oak, Royal Oak, MI, $20,000. For Fathers and Sons Together substance abuse prevention program. 1991.
1380-2 Boys and Girls Clubs of Pontiac, Pontiac, MI, $10,000. For Smart Moves program. 1991.
1380-3 Boysville of Michigan, Clinton, MI, $20,000. For substance abuse prevention program. 1991.
1380-4 Childrens Center of Wayne County, Detroit, MI, $70,000. To establish new program development unit. 1991.

1380-5 Common Ground, Royal Oak, MI, $15,000. For substance abuse prevention program. 1991.

1380-6 Community Services of Oakland, Madison Heights, MI, $18,500. For substance abuse prevention program. 1991.

1380-7 Detroit, City of, Health Department, Detroit, MI, $1,500,000. For Parenting Education and Advocacy Program. 1991.

1380-8 Development Centers, Detroit, MI, $180,000. For Project New Chance, teen parent education and training program. 1991.

1380-9 Girl Scouts of the U.S.A., Michigan Metro Council, Detroit, MI, $20,000. For substance abuse prevention program. 1991.

1380-10 Growth Works, Plymouth, MI, $42,000. To begin substance abuse early intervention program. 1991.

1380-11 Hadassah, Womens Zionist Organization of America, San Francisco Chapter, San Francisco, CA, $20,000. For oncology unit in memory of Milton Pilhashy. 1991.

1380-12 Hebrew Home for the Aged Disabled, San Francisco, CA, $50,000. For adult day care program. 1991.

1380-13 Macomb Intermediate School District, Mount Clemens, MI, $22,000. For Student Leadership Services of Michigan's substance abuse prevention project for middle school students. 1991.

1380-14 Macomb Intermediate School District, Student Leadership Services of Michigan, Mount Clemens, MI, $22,000. For substance abuse prevention project for middle school students. 1991.

1380-15 Michigan Communities in Action for Drug-Free Youth, Birmingham, MI, $15,000. For general operating support. 1991.

1380-16 Michigan Health Care Education and Research Foundation, Detroit, MI, $250,000. For Caring Program for Children, health insurance program for uninsured Michigan children. 1991.

1380-17 Michigan, State of, Department of Public Health, Lansing, MI, $573,000. For Project Uptown, participation program for parents of special needs children. 1991.

1380-18 Oakwood United Hospitals, Taylor Teen Health Center, Taylor, MI, $20,000. For substance abuse prevention peer education program. 1991.

1380-19 Palmer Drug Abuse Program, Milford, MI, $20,000. For general operating support. 1991.

1380-20 Planned Parenthood League of Detroit, Detroit, MI, $32,000. To continue HI-LITES Teen Theatre troupe. 1991.

1380-21 Saint Vincent and Sarah Fisher Home for Children, Farmington Hills, MI, $500,000. For emergency shelter and infant mortality prevention program. 1991.

1380-22 Salvation Army of Southfield, Southfield, MI, $56,000. For Youth Education Institute substance abuse prevention program. 1991.

1380-23 United Community Services of Metropolitan Detroit, PREVCO, Detroit, MI, $18,000. For substance abuse prevention project. 1991.

1380-24 Waterford School District, Waterford, MI, $270,000. For comprehensive substance abuse prevention and research programs. 1991.

1380-25 Wayne County Department of Health and Community Services, Youth Services Division, Detroit, MI, $410,000. To maintain youth assistance programs. 1991.

1380-26 Wayne State University, Merrill-Palmer Institute of Human and Family Life, Detroit, MI, $323,000. For Graduate Certificate Program in Infant Mental Health. 1991.

1380-27 World Medical Relief, Detroit, MI, $25,000. For general operating support. 1991.

1380-28 Young Adults Health Center, Ypsilanti, MI, $20,000. To continue Teen Theatre substance abuse prevention program. 1991.

1381

Community Foundation for Southeastern Michigan ▼

333 West Fort St., Suite 2010
Detroit 48226   (313) 961-6675

Established in 1984 in MI.
Foundation type: Community
Financial data (yr. ended 12/31/91): Assets, $35,588,364 (M); gifts received, $11,929,492; expenditures, $2,902,989; qualifying distributions, $2,443,282, including $2,269,889 for grants (average: $10,000), $66,100 for 51 grants to individuals (high: $3,500; low: $25; average: $25-$3,500) and $107,293 for 5 foundation-administered programs.
Purpose and activities: Supports projects in areas of civic affairs, social services, culture, health, and education.
Fields of interest: Civic affairs, social services, cultural programs, health, education.
Types of support: Seed money, special projects, scholarship funds, endowment funds.
Limitations: Giving limited to southeastern MI. No support for sectarian religious programs. No grants to individuals for unrestricted funds, or for capital projects, endowments, annual campaigns, or operating budgets (except in initial years of new ventures).
Publications: Annual report (including application guidelines), application guidelines.
Application information: Application form not required.
Initial approach: Proposal
Copies of proposal: 1
Deadline(s): None
Board meeting date(s): Quarterly
Final notification: Following board meetings
Write: C. David Campbell, V.P., Prog.
Officers and Trustees:* Joseph L. Hudson, Jr.,* Chair.; Wendell W. Anderson, Jr.,* Vice-Chair.; Max M. Fisher,* Vice-Chair.; Frank D. Stella,* Vice-Chair.; Mrs. R. Alexander Wrigley,* Secy.; Richard H. Austin,* Treas.; David K. Page, Chair., Prog. and Dist. Committee; Thomas V. Angott, Hon. Dennis W. Archer, Don H. Barden, Michael J. Brenner, Keith E. Crain, Lynn W. Day, Walter E. Douglas, C. Rupert Edwards, William Clay Ford, Jr., Ralph J. Gerson, Alfred R. Glancy III, David Handleman, Sr., David B. Hermelin, Hon. Damon J. Keith, Mrs. Charles Kessler, Thomas I. Klein, John E. Lobbia, Richard A. Manoogian, Florine Mark, David N. McCammon, Alonzo L. McDonald, Kenneth E. Millard, Edward J. Miller, Daniel T. Murphy, William J. O'Brien, William F. Pickard, Heinz Prechter, Douglas J. Rasmussen, Dean E. Richardson, Jack A. Robinson, Alan E. Schwartz, Edgar A. Scribner, W. Warren Shelden,

Neal Shine, F. Alan Smith, Roger B. Smith, A. Alfred Taubman, Hon. Anna Diggs Taylor, Peter P. Thurber, Mrs. Richard C. Van Dusen, Jonathan T. Walton, Joan B. Warren, Stanley J. Winkelman.
Number of staff: 5 full-time professional; 3 full-time support.
EIN: 382530980
Recent health grants:

1381-1 Beaumont Foundation, Southfield, MI, $22,500. 1990.

1381-2 Childrens Center of Wayne County, Detroit, MI, $46,000. For community outreach substance abuse prevention project. 1990.

1381-3 Childrens Home of Detroit, Grosse Pointe Woods, MI, $19,170. To purchase and install insulation in eight of agency's facilities. 1990.

1381-4 Childrens Hospital of Michigan, Detroit, MI, $30,900. 1990.

1381-5 Community Action on Substance Abuse, Ann Arbor, MI, $50,000. For Youth and Parents Together in Prevention program. 1990.

1381-6 Crittenton Hospital, Rochester, MI, $25,000. 1990.

1381-7 Deaf Hearing and Speech Center, Detroit, MI, $26,464. To meet specific needs of low-income, hearing-impaired individuals. 1990.

1381-8 Detroit Institute for Children, Detroit, MI, $10,000. For further development of AudioScan for use by multiple-handicapped persons. 1990.

1381-9 Easter Seal Society of Wayne County, Inkster, MI, $11,900. To purchase and install drop ceiling, ceiling insulation and heating and cooling units. 1990.

1381-10 Henry Ford Health Care Corporation, Troy, MI, $22,500. 1990.

1381-11 Henry Ford Hospital, Troy, MI, $10,000. 1990.

1381-12 Metropolitan Center for High Technology, Detroit, MI, $20,000. To refine test for drug exposure in infants. 1990.

1381-13 Michigan Cancer Foundation, Detroit, MI, $12,500. 1990.

1381-14 Michigan Cancer Foundation, Detroit, MI, $11,800. To conduct technical energy analysis of facility. 1990.

1381-15 Northeast Guidance Center, Detroit, MI, $15,000. To purchase and install energy conservation measures. 1990.

1381-16 Planned Parenthood League of Detroit, Detroit, MI, $11,750. 1990.

1381-17 Project Prevention, Detroit, MI, $28,210. Toward program activities. 1990.

1381-18 Sacred Heart Rehabilitation Center, Detroit, MI, $34,000. To purchase and install modular boiler system. 1990.

1381-19 Saint Joseph Mercy Hospital, Pontiac, MI, $11,783. To establish Parent Partners Program. 1990.

1381-20 Southeast Michigan Council of Governments (SEMCOG), Detroit, MI, $40,000. To help small businesses and governmental units create drug-free work environments. 1990.

1381-21 Troy Families for Safe Homes, Troy, MI, $52,500. To start Talking with Your Kids About Alcohol program. 1990.

1381-22 Victory Evangelical Lutheran Church, Detroit, MI, $20,000. For Youth Empowerment Service of Northwest Neighborhood Action Group. 1990.

1382
Jack D. and Fredda S. Sparks Foundation, Inc.
2704 Highland Court
St. Joseph 49085

Established in 1986 in MI.
Donor(s): Fredda S. Sparks, Jack D. Sparks.
Foundation type: Independent
Financial data (yr. ended 12/31/91): Assets, $753,677 (M); expenditures, $216,720; qualifying distributions, $214,695, including $210,350 for grants.
Fields of interest: Higher education, family planning, cultural programs, general charitable giving.
Types of support: General purposes.
Limitations: Giving primarily in MI. No grants to individuals.
Application information: Application form not required.
  Deadline(s): None
  Write: Jack D. Sparks, Pres.
Officers: Jack D. Sparks, Pres.; Jack D. Sparks, Jr., V.P.; Katherine S. Telgarshy, V.P.; Fredda S. Sparks, Secy.-Treas.
EIN: 382702293

1383
SPX Corporation Foundation
(Formerly Sealed Power Foundation)
700 Terrace Point Dr.
P.O. Box 3301
Muskegon 49443-3301   (616) 724-5000

Established in 1982 in MI.
Donor(s): SPX Corp.
Foundation type: Company-sponsored
Financial data (yr. ended 12/31/91): Assets, $657 (M); gifts received, $212,254; expenditures, $236,345; qualifying distributions, $235,058, including $192,859 for 37 grants (high: $37,000; low: $100) and $42,199 for 213 employee matching gifts.
Fields of interest: Cultural programs, education, higher education, health, welfare, civic affairs.
Types of support: Employee matching gifts, general purposes.
Limitations: Giving primarily in plant communities.
Publications: Informational brochure.
Application information:
  Write: James M. Sheridan, Pres.
Officers and Trustees:* James M. Sheridan,* Pres.; John D. Tyson,* Secy.; Dale A. Johnson, Donald H. Johnson, Stephen A. Lison, R. Budd Werner.
Number of staff: 1 part-time support.
EIN: 386058308

1384
Steelcase Foundation ▼
P.O. Box 1967
Grand Rapids 49507   (616) 246-4695

Trust established in 1951 in MI.
Donor(s): Steelcase, Inc.
Foundation type: Company-sponsored
Financial data (yr. ended 11/30/90): Assets, $44,418,180 (M); gifts received, $5,000,000; expenditures, $4,177,470; qualifying distributions, $3,967,855, including $3,967,855

for 127 grants (high: $300,000; low: $1,924; average: $2,000-$25,000).
Purpose and activities: Support for human services, including a community fund, health, education, arts, and the environment; particular concerns include helping the disadvantaged, disabled, young, and elderly to improve the quality of their lives.
Fields of interest: Social services, health, handicapped, AIDS, youth, aged, disadvantaged, community development, environment, education, secondary education, higher education, arts, cultural programs.
Types of support: Building funds, general purposes, capital campaigns, special projects, employee-related scholarships.
Limitations: Giving limited to areas of company operations, including Grand Rapids, MI; Orange County, CA; Asheville, NC; Athens, AL; and Toronto, Canada. No support for churches, or programs with substantial religious overtones of a sectarian nature. No grants to individuals, or for endowment funds.
Publications: Annual report (including application guidelines), application guidelines.
Application information: Application form required.
  Initial approach: Letter
  Copies of proposal: 1
  Deadline(s): None
  Board meeting date(s): Quarterly and as required
  Final notification: At least 90 days
  Write: Kate Pew Wolters, Exec. Dir.
Trustees: Robert C. Pew, Chair.; David D. Hunting, Sr., David D. Hunting, Jr., Roger L. Martin, Frank H. Merlotti, Jerry K. Meyers, Peter M. Wege, Old Kent Bank & Trust Co.
Staff: Kate Pew Wolters, Exec. Dir.
Number of staff: 1 full-time professional; 1 part-time support.
EIN: 386050470
Recent health grants:
1384-1 AIDS Foundation of Kent County, Grand Rapids, MI, $10,000. For programs. 1990.
1384-2 Childrens Oncology and Family Services of Western Michigan, Grand Rapids, MI, $65,000. For construction of Western Michigan Ronald McDonald House. 1990.
1384-3 Down Syndrome Association of West Michigan, Grand Rapids, MI, $12,700. To purchase computer for communication network and resource center. 1990.
1384-4 Easter Seal Society, Grand Rapids, MI, $27,000. To renovate site for day care program for children with and without disabilities. 1990.
1384-5 Grand Rapids Child Guidance Clinic, Grand Rapids, MI, $85,000. For Project Focus, early childhood development program for needy families. 1990.
1384-6 Hearing and Speech Center, Grand Rapids, MI, $32,950. For Deaf Services Center support. 1990.
1384-7 Inter-City Alcoholic Retreat, I-Care, Grand Rapids, MI, $10,000. For start-up funding for residential housing for alcoholic women. 1990.
1384-8 Jellema House, Grand Rapids, MI, $15,000. For substance abuse treatment. 1990.
1384-9 M. J. Clark Memorial Home, Grand Rapids, MI, $25,500. For start-up funding for Daybreak program for people with Alzheimer's disease. 1990.

1384-10 Planned Parenthood Centers of West Michigan, Grand Rapids, MI, $20,000. For low-income medical care and prevention. 1990.
1384-11 Rockford Ambulance, Lowell Ambulance Service, Grand Rapids, MI, $15,000. For capital support for new Lowell facility. 1990.
1384-12 Saint Johns Home for Emotionally Disturbed Children, Grand Rapids, MI, $200,000. For capital campaign support. 1990.
1384-13 United Cerebral Palsy Association of Orange County, Santa Ana, CA, $10,000. For capital expenditures in infant development center. 1990.
1384-14 Visiting Nurse Services of Western Michigan, Grand Rapids, MI, $50,000. For organizational refinancing. 1990.
1384-15 West Shore Health Services, Grand Rapids, MI, $74,500. To complete renovation of Transitions building. 1990.

1385
Sarah A. Stewart Foundation
19511 Mack Ave.
Grosse Pointe 48236   (313) 886-0450

Established in 1980 in CA.
Foundation type: Independent
Financial data (yr. ended 09/30/91): Assets, $4,587,449 (M); expenditures, $331,283; qualifying distributions, $322,443, including $301,000 for 13 grants (high: $85,000; low: $4,000; average: $5,000-$119,000).
Fields of interest: Education, social services, health services, medical research.
Limitations: Giving primarily in CA. No grants to individuals.
Application information: Contributes only to pre-selected organizations. Applications not accepted.
  Write: Richard K. Simonds
Officers: Daniel M. Gibbs, M.D., Pres.; Nancy Richard, V.P.; Mary P. Daniel, Secy.
Number of staff: 1 part-time professional.
EIN: 953705192

1386
A. Alfred Taubman Foundation ▼
P.O. Box 200
200 East Long Lake Rd.
Bloomfield Hills 48303-0200   (313) 258-6800

Established in 1979 in MI.
Donor(s): A. Alfred Taubman.
Foundation type: Independent
Financial data (yr. ended 07/31/91): Assets, $5,722 (M); gifts received, $1,215,969; expenditures, $1,216,912; qualifying distributions, $1,215,887, including $1,215,770 for 76 grants (high: $100,000; low: $20; average: $500-$10,000).
Purpose and activities: Giving for education, Jewish welfare funds, medical research, and human services.
Fields of interest: Education, Jewish welfare, medical research.
Types of support: Operating budgets.
Limitations: Giving primarily in MI, with emphasis on Detroit.

Application information: Application form not required.

> *Deadline(s):* None
> *Board meeting date(s):* As necessary
> *Final notification:* 3 weeks
> *Write:* Guy L. Schmidt

Officers and Trustees:* A. Alfred Taubman,* Chair. and Treas.; Max M. Fisher,* Pres.; Jeffrey H. Miro,* Secy.; Gayle T. Kalisman, Dean E. Richardson, Robert S. Taubman, William S. Taubman.
Number of staff: None.
EIN: 382219625

1387
The Thomas Foundation
32000 Northwestern Hwy., Suite 150
Farmington Hills 48334-1565   (313) 855-3955

Established in 1984 in MI.
Foundation type: Independent
Financial data (yr. ended 03/31/91): Assets, $3,785,071 (M); expenditures, $49,325; qualifying distributions, $33,518, including $31,750 for 11 grants (high: $10,000; low: $500).
Fields of interest: Health associations, hospitals, child welfare, Jewish welfare.
Limitations: Giving primarily in MI.
Application information:
> *Initial approach:* Letter
> *Deadline(s):* None
> *Final notification:* Within 60 days
> *Write:* Jay Brody, Trustee

Trustees: Jay Brody, Chester Uncapher.
EIN: 382510591

1388
The Tiscornia Foundation, Inc.
1010 Main St., Suite A
St. Joseph 49085   (616) 926-0812

Incorporated in 1942 in MI.
Donor(s): Auto Specialties Manufacturing Co., Lambert Brake Corp., James W. Tiscornia,‡ Waldo V. Tiscornia.‡
Foundation type: Independent
Financial data (yr. ended 11/30/90): Assets, $3,746,286 (M); expenditures, $264,169; qualifying distributions, $245,186, including $140,325 for 21 grants (high: $50,000; low: $150) and $33,250 for 8 grants to individuals (high: $9,250; low: $830).
Fields of interest: Community funds, higher education, health, youth, social services, family planning, arts.
Types of support: Continuing support, annual campaigns, seed money, emergency funds, building funds, equipment, scholarship funds.
Limitations: Giving primarily in southwestern MI. No grants to individuals (except committee-selected scholarship recipients), or for research or matching gifts; no loans.
Publications: Annual report (including application guidelines), 990-PF.
Application information: Scholarships only for Northern Berrien County high school students. Application form not required.
> *Initial approach:* Letter or proposal
> *Copies of proposal:* 1
> *Deadline(s):* Apr. 1 for scholarships; Oct. 31 for general grants

Board meeting date(s): Jan.
Final notification: Feb. for grants; May for scholarships
Write: Laurianne T. Davis, Secy.

Officers and Trustees:* Lester Tiscornia,* Pres.; Bernice Tiscornia,* V.P.; Laurianne T. Davis,* Secy.; Henry H. Tippett,* Treas.; Edward Tiscornia, James Tiscornia, Theodore Troff.
Number of staff: 1 part-time professional; 1 part-time support.
EIN: 381777343

1389
The Harry A. and Margaret D. Towsley Foundation ▼
Plymouth Orchard Bldg., Suite 200
3055 Plymouth Rd.
Ann Arbor 48105   (313) 662-6777

Incorporated in 1959 in MI.
Donor(s): Margaret D. Towsley.
Foundation type: Independent
Financial data (yr. ended 12/31/91): Assets, $36,349,824 (M); expenditures, $2,238,594; qualifying distributions, $2,191,477, including $2,155,349 for 39 grants (high: $250,000; low: $1,500; average: $5,000-$50,000).
Purpose and activities: Support for medical and pre-school education, social services, and continuing education and research in the health sciences.
Fields of interest: Education, medical education, education—early childhood, social services, medical research.
Types of support: Continuing support, annual campaigns, building funds, endowment funds, matching funds, special projects.
Limitations: Giving limited to MI, with emphasis on Ann Arbor and Washtenaw County. No grants to individuals, or for travel, scholarships, fellowships, conferences, books, publications, films, tapes, audio-visual, or other communication media; no loans.
Publications: Annual report, application guidelines.
Application information: Application form not required.
> *Initial approach:* Letter and proposal
> *Copies of proposal:* 2
> *Deadline(s):* Submit proposal between Jan. and Mar.; deadline Mar. 31
> *Board meeting date(s):* Apr., July, Sept., and Dec.
> *Final notification:* 60 to 90 days
> *Write:* Margaret Ann Riecker, Pres.

Officers and Trustees:* Harry A. Towsley, M.D.,* Chair.; Margaret Ann Riecker,* Pres.; Margaret D. Towsley,* 1st V.P.; Judith D. Alexander,* 2nd V.P; John E. Riecker, Secy.; C. Wendell Dunbar,* Treas.; Robert L. Bring, Jennifer Poteat-Flores, Lynn T. White, Susan T. Wyland.
Number of staff: None.
EIN: 386091798
Recent health grants:
1389-1 Asthma and Allergy Foundation of America, Michigan Chapter, Ann Arbor, MI, $20,000. For camperships and asthma training programs. 1990.
1389-2 Catherine McAuley Health Center, Ann Arbor, MI, $50,000. For cancer care pavilion outpatient oncology treatment facility. 1990.

1389-3 Community Dental Clinic, School of Dentistry, Ann Arbor, MI, $10,000. Grant shared with City of Ann Arbor and University of Michigan, School of Dentistry. 1990.
1389-4 Corner Health Center, Ypsilanti, MI, $10,000. For program support. 1990.
1389-5 Council of Michigan Foundations, Grand Haven, MI, $25,000. For Michigan AIDS Fund. 1990.
1389-6 Dawn Farm, Ypsilanti, MI, $34,000. For Recovery Place for substance abusers. 1990.
1389-7 Glacier Hills Nursing Center, Ann Arbor, MI, $100,000. For geriatric teaching/nursing home and adult respite day care. 1990.
1389-8 Kalamazoo College, Kalamazoo, MI, $50,000. For scholarship fund for health science students. 1990.
1389-9 Planned Parenthood of Mid-Michigan, Ann Arbor, MI, $37,473. For peer education program. 1990.
1389-10 Starr Commonwealth for Boys, Albion Campus, Albion, MI, $100,000. For health, physical education and recreation center. 1990.
1389-11 Student-Parent Center for Infants, Ann Arbor, MI, $10,000. For services for infants and toddlers. 1990.
1389-12 United Methodist Retirement Homes, Chelsea, MI, $20,000. For nursing center. 1990.
1389-13 University of Michigan, Department of Pediatrics, Ann Arbor, MI, $50,000. For David G. Dickenson Collegiate Professorship. 1990.
1389-14 University of Michigan, School of Dentistry, Ann Arbor, MI, $14,450. For Black Dentistry in the 21st Century Program. 1990.

1390
The Emmet and Frances Tracy Fund ▼
400 Renaissance Ctr., 35th Fl.
Detroit 48243

Incorporated in 1951 in MI.
Donor(s): Alma Piston Co., G.P.D., Inc., Snow Manufacturing Co.
Foundation type: Independent
Financial data (yr. ended 11/30/91): Assets, $1,710,212 (M); gifts received, $1,050,000; expenditures, $1,069,486; qualifying distributions, $1,067,660, including $1,065,337 for 135 grants (high: $150,000; low: $100; average: $1,000-$30,000).
Purpose and activities: Support for an academy and Roman Catholic organizations, including welfare groups; grants also for other social services and educational institutions, hospitals, and health agencies.
Fields of interest: Secondary education, Catholic giving, Catholic welfare, social services, education, hospitals, health.
Types of support: General purposes.
Limitations: Giving primarily in MI, with emphasis on Detroit. No grants to individuals.
Application information: Contributes only to pre-selected organizations. Applications not accepted.
> *Board meeting date(s):* As required
> *Write:* Emmet E. Tracy, Pres.

Officers: Emmet E. Tracy, Pres.; Frances A. Tracy, V.P.; Paul R. Trigg, Jr., Secy.; Emmet E. Tracy, Jr., Treas.
Number of staff: None.

EIN: 386057796

1391
Triford Foundation
20446 Harper Ave.
Harper Woods 48225

Established in 1968 in MI.
Foundation type: Independent
Financial data (yr. ended 12/31/91): Assets, $3,173,826 (M); expenditures, $136,370; qualifying distributions, $117,000, including $117,000 for 71 grants (high: $6,800; low: $100).
Fields of interest: Hospitals, health, Protestant giving, religion, secondary education, education.
Types of support: Annual campaigns, general purposes.
Limitations: No grants to individuals, or for building funds.
Application information: Funds currently committed; contributes only to pre-selected organizations. Applications not accepted.
Officers and Trustees:* Frederick S. Ford, Jr.,* Pres. and Secy.; Horace C. Ford,* V.P. and Treas.; Frederick B. Ford,* V.P. and Mgr.; Esther C. Ford, James W. Ford.
Number of staff: 1 part-time professional; 1 part-time support.
EIN: 237003478

1392
The Upjohn Company Foundation
7000 Portage Rd.
Kalamazoo 49001   (616) 323-7017

Established in 1988 in MI.
Donor(s): The Upjohn Co.
Foundation type: Company-sponsored
Financial data (yr. ended 12/31/91): Assets, $23,316,516 (M); expenditures, $1,131,969; qualifying distributions, $1,129,882, including $1,122,500 for 21 grants (high: $422,500; low: $500).
Fields of interest: Education, medical education, community funds, higher education, cultural programs, youth.
Types of support: Endowment funds, building funds, capital campaigns.
Limitations: Giving primarily in Kalamazoo, MI, and environs.
Application information:
  Initial approach: Letter and proposal
  Board meeting date(s): Monthly
  Write: Vickie G. Heerlyn, Exec. Dir. and Secy.
Officers and Directors:* Donald R. Parfet, Pres.; William U. Parfet, V.P. and Treas.; Vickie G. Heerlyn,* Exec. Dir. and Secy.; Roy D. Hudson, Mark Novitch, Robert C. Salisbury, Ley S. Smith.
EIN: 382784862

1393
The Upjohn Corporate Giving Program
7000 Portage Rd.
Kalamazoo 49001   (616) 323-4000

Financial data (yr. ended 12/31/90): Total giving, $19,101,204, including $6,075,000 for grants and $13,026,204 for in-kind gifts.
Purpose and activities: "The Upjohn Company believes that corporate contributions are an investment in the future of the company. The financial health of a corporation is dependent not only on the economic but also on the social environment in which it operates. We believe that business has a philanthropic obligation, especially in areas likely to be more effectively addressed by the private sector. The Upjohn Company makes contributions of money and merchandise to fulfill its acknowledged responsibility for assisting local, regional, national and international organizations engaged in nonprofit activities designed to improve the economic and social well-being of mankind. Contributions are made in fields of education, health, social, welfare, culture, and the arts, civic activities and public policy." Main giving areas are in local communities, with special consideration granted to agencies in which Upjohn employees play an active volunteer role. Consideration is also given to programs with the aim of improving the economic and social status of women. In 1990 the Upjohn Company Foundation gave $715,250.
Fields of interest: Health, welfare, community funds, arts, museums, higher education, health associations, education, medical research, minorities, performing arts, aged, medical sciences.
Types of support: Seed money, capital campaigns, matching funds, general purposes, scholarship funds, in-kind gifts.
Limitations: Giving primarily in areas of company operations in the U.S.; also support abroad; grants made for local, regional, national, and international agencies. No support for purely social, labor, fraternal, veterans (except when they provide services to nonmembers on a nondiscriminatory basis) or religious organizations (except when they provide humanitarian services on a nonsectarian basis), school-related sports and band events. No grants to individuals, or multi-year grants (except for capital grants), travel, tickets to dinners, publications, or good-will advertising (rare exceptions may be made where the company has larger operations and the donee is of special interest), or endowments.
Publications: Application guidelines.
Application information: The corporate contributions committee is composed of 3 corporate officers. In making its decision, the Committee asks: Is the purpose of the organization worthy? Is it set up to implement its program effectively? Does it have adequate budgetary controls? Can it provide a recent audit? What percentage of the funds collected are spent on fund-raising? What are other companies, foundations or individuals now contributing? Will it be a one-time contribution? Will it require a continuing commitment? For how long? What amount is being requested.
  Initial approach: Letter and copy of proposal
  Deadline(s): None
  Board meeting date(s): Monthly; budget for following year is drafted in Aug.
  Write: Vickie G. Heerlyn, Mgr., Corp. Contribs.

1394
Vlasic Foundation
710 North Woodward
Bloomfield Hills 48304

Established in 1958 in MI.
Donor(s): Robert J. Vlasic, Joseph Vlasic.‡
Foundation type: Independent
Financial data (yr. ended 05/31/91): Assets, $3,697,568 (M); gifts received, $25,000; expenditures, $348,704; qualifying distributions, $346,604, including $346,604 for 42 grants (high: $221,375; low: $100).
Purpose and activities: Grants primarily for education and health agencies; some support for social services, Roman Catholic welfare organizations, and cultural programs.
Fields of interest: Education, health, social services, Catholic welfare, cultural programs.
Types of support: General purposes.
Limitations: Giving primarily in MI. No grants to individuals.
Application information: Contributes only to pre-selected organizations. Applications not accepted.
  Write: Robert Vlasic, Pres.
Officers and Trustees:* Robert J. Vlasic,* Pres.; Richard R. Vlasic,* V.P.; William J. Vlasic,* V.P.; James J. Vlasic,* Secy.; Michael A. Vlasic,* Treas.
Number of staff: None.
EIN: 386077329

1395
Volkswagen of America Corporate Giving Program
888 West Big Beaver Rd.
Troy 48007   (313) 362-6120

Financial data (yr. ended 12/31/91): Total giving, $133,232 for 31 grants (high: $5,000; low: $100; average: $100-$1,000).
Purpose and activities: Supports general and economic education and private colleges. Also supports fine, literary, and performing arts, community arts, museums, and cultural and fine arts institutes. Community funding includes federated campaigns, minority programs, health, and United Way. Emphasizes special projects. Arts support through capital campaigns and special projects.
Fields of interest: Education, higher education, arts, museums, community funds, fine arts, minorities, cultural programs, performing arts, health.
Types of support: Capital campaigns, special projects.
Limitations: Giving primarily in headquarters city and operating locations. No support for chapters of national organizations or political activities. No grants to individuals, endowments or research.
Publications: Corporate report.
Application information: Public Relations handles giving.
  Initial approach: Letter describing project
  Deadline(s): None
  Board meeting date(s): Committee meets as needed; applications reviewed quarterly
  Write: Jennifer Hurshell, Dir., Pub. Rels.

1396
Wege Foundation

P.O. Box 6388
Grand Rapids 49516-6388   (616) 957-0480

Established about 1967 in MI.
Donor(s): Peter M. Wege.
Foundation type: Independent
Financial data (yr. ended 12/31/91): Assets,
$6,703,784 (M); gifts received, $147,040;
expenditures, $371,890; qualifying distributions,
$354,210, including $350,549 for 30 grants
(high: $200,000; low: $350).
Fields of interest: Hospitals, youth, social
services, cultural programs, education,
community development, environment.
Types of support: Equipment, special projects.
Limitations: Giving primarily in Greater Kent
County, MI, with emphasis on the Grand Rapids
area. No grants to individuals, or for operating
budgets.
Application information:
  Initial approach: Proposal
  Deadline(s): None
  Write: Peter M. Wege, Pres.
Officers: Peter M. Wege, Pres.; Peter M. Wege II,
V.P.; Charles Lundstrom, Secy.
EIN: 386124363

1397
Henry E. and Consuelo S. Wenger Foundation, Inc.

P.O. Box 43098
Detroit 48243

Incorporated in 1959 in MI.
Donor(s): Consuelo S. Wenger.
Foundation type: Independent
Financial data (yr. ended 12/31/90): Assets,
$7,508,823 (M); expenditures, $612,179;
qualifying distributions, $600,800, including
$600,800 for 88 grants (high: $100,000; low:
$250).
Fields of interest: Secondary education, higher
education, hospitals, health associations, cultural
programs, Protestant giving, environment,
conservation.
Limitations: Giving primarily in FL, IL, MI, and
NY. No grants to individuals.
Application information: Contributes only to
pre-selected organizations. Applications not
accepted.
Officers and Directors:* Henry Penn Wenger,*
Pres.; Diane Wenger,* V.P.; Miles Jaffe,* Secy.;
William E. Slaughter, Jr.,* Treas.
EIN: 386077419

1398
Samuel L. Westerman Foundation

1700 North Woodward, Suite A
Bloomfield Hills 48013   (313) 642-5770
Application address: 14532 Indian Trails Dr.,
Grand Haven, MI 49417; Tel.: (616) 847-1986

Established in 1971 in MI.
Foundation type: Independent
Financial data (yr. ended 01/31/90): Assets,
$6,583,963 (M); expenditures, $351,926;
qualifying distributions, $305,012, including
$305,012 for 80 grants (high: $20,000; low:
$500).

Fields of interest: Education, higher education,
religion, cultural programs, arts, health, youth,
child welfare, animal welfare, social services.
Limitations: Giving primarily in MI. No grants to
individuals.
Application information: Application form not
required.
  Initial approach: Letter
  Copies of proposal: 1
  Deadline(s): None
  Board meeting date(s): Quarterly
  Write: Mrs. Martha M. Muir, V.P.
Officers: James H. LoPrete, Pres.; Martha M.
Muir, V.P., Office of Grants; Keith H. Muir, Treas.
EIN: 237108795

1399
Whirlpool Foundation ▼

400 Riverview Dr., Suite 410
Benton Harbor 49022   (616) 923-5112

Incorporated in 1951 in MI.
Donor(s): Whirlpool Corp.
Foundation type: Company-sponsored
Financial data (yr. ended 12/31/91): Assets,
$14,852,269 (L); gifts received, $3,300,000;
expenditures, $3,860,240; qualifying
distributions, $3,734,578, including $3,248,593
for grants (average: $200-$25,000), $309,000 for
grants to individuals (average: $1,500-$3,000)
and $176,985 for employee matching gifts.
Purpose and activities: Giving primarily to
community funds, youth and social welfare
agencies, cultural programs, health services, and
higher education, including scholarships for
children of corporation employees and employee
matching gifts.
Fields of interest: Community funds, youth,
cultural programs, welfare, arts, higher education,
education, community development, health,
health services.
Types of support: Matching funds, operating
budgets, annual campaigns, emergency funds,
building funds, equipment, research,
employee-related scholarships, continuing
support, employee matching gifts, endowment
funds.
Limitations: Giving limited to communities where
major company units are located: Clyde, Findlay,
Greenville, and Marion, OH; Evansville, IN; Fort
Smith, AR; Lavergne, TN; Oxford, MS; and
Columbia, SC. No grants to individuals (except
employee-related scholarships), or for
endowment funds; no loans.
Application information: Application form not
required.
  Initial approach: Letter or telephone
  Copies of proposal: 1
  Deadline(s): Oct. 1
  Board meeting date(s): As required
  Final notification: 30 to 60 days
  Write: Sharron Krieger, Program Administrator
Officers and Trustees:* Stephen E. Upton,* Pres.;
Sharron Krieger, Secy. and Exec. Dir.; Bradley J.
Bell,* Treas.; Bruce K. Berger, William D. Marohn,
Jay Van Den Berg.
Number of staff: 1 full-time professional; 1
part-time support.
EIN: 386077342
Recent health grants:
1399-1 Birthright of Saint Joseph, Saint Joseph,
MI, $10,000. 1990.

1399-2 Hancock County Alcoholism Council,
Findlay, OH, $15,000. 1990.

1400
The Whiting Foundation

901 Citizens Bank Bldg.
328 South Saginaw St.
Flint 48502   (313) 767-3600

Incorporated in 1940 in MI.
Donor(s): Members of the Johnson family.
Foundation type: Independent
Financial data (yr. ended 06/30/91): Assets,
$12,273,921 (M); expenditures, $607,971;
qualifying distributions, $586,102, including
$545,412 for 39 grants (high: $100,000; low:
$100).
Purpose and activities: Giving to further secular
and religious education and research of all kinds;
to aid and improve the physical, financial,
mental, and moral condition of the poor, the sick,
the young, the aged, and the disabled among all
classes. Support nationally for cancer research.
Fields of interest: Religious schools, aged, youth,
handicapped, cancer.
Types of support: General purposes, special
projects.
Limitations: Giving limited to the greater Flint,
MI, area.
Application information:
  Initial approach: Concise proposal
  Copies of proposal: 1
  Deadline(s): Apr. 30
  Write: Donald E. Johnson, Jr., Pres.
Officers and Trustees:* Donald E. Johnson, Jr.,*
Pres.; John T. Lindholm,* Secy.-Treas.; Marsha A.
Kump, Exec. Dir.; Mary Alice J. Heaton, Linda
W.J. Utley.
EIN: 386056693

1401
Harvey Randall Wickes Foundation

Plaza North, Suite 472
4800 Fashion Sq. Blvd.
Saginaw 48604   (517) 799-1850

Incorporated in 1945 in MI.
Donor(s): Harvey Randall Wickes,‡ members of
the Wickes family and others.
Foundation type: Independent
Financial data (yr. ended 12/31/90): Assets,
$24,355,937 (M); expenditures, $1,218,119;
qualifying distributions, $1,122,517, including
$1,090,249 for 34 grants (high: $300,000; low:
$50; average: $5,000-$60,000).
Purpose and activities: Giving primarily for civic
affairs groups, especially parks and recreation
agencies and sports programs; support also for a
library, youth and social services, a community
fund, hospitals, and cultural programs.
Fields of interest: Civic affairs, recreation,
libraries, youth, social services, community funds,
hospitals, cultural programs.
Types of support: Building funds, equipment,
renovation projects, operating budgets.
Limitations: Giving limited to the Saginaw, MI,
area. No grants to individuals.
Application information: Application form not
required.
  Initial approach: Letter followed by proposal;
    no set deadline

Copies of proposal: 1
Deadline(s): Submit proposal preferably 1 month prior to meeting
Write: James V. Finkbeiner, Pres.
Officers and Trustees: Melvin J. Zahnow, Chair.; James V. Finkbeiner, Pres.; H.E. Braun, Jr., V.P. and Secy.; Lloyd J. Yeo, Treas.; Frank N. Andersen, Robert G. App, Craig Horn, Frank M. Johnson, William W. Kessel, William F. Nelson, Jr., David F. Wallace.
Number of staff: 1 full-time professional; 1 part-time support.
EIN: 386061470
Recent health grants:
1401-1 Saginaw Cooperative Hospital, Saginaw, MI, $125,000. For renovations. 1990.
1401-2 Saint Marys Medical Center, Saginaw, MI, $33,333. Toward purchase of radiotherapy linear accelerator. 1990.

1402
Wickson-Link Memorial Foundation
P.O. Box 3275
3023 Davenport St.
Saginaw 48605   (517) 793-9830

Donor(s): James Wickson,‡ Meta Wickson.‡
Foundation type: Independent
Financial data (yr. ended 12/31/91): Assets, $3,870,252 (M); expenditures, $197,124; qualifying distributions, $160,045, including $160,045 for 41 grants (high: $16,000; low: $500).
Purpose and activities: Support for community funds, social services and programs for the disadvantaged, youth and child welfare, cultural organizations, health, and education, including business and higher education, programs for minorities and early childhood education, and libraries.
Fields of interest: Community funds, social services, disadvantaged, child welfare, cultural programs, health, higher education, libraries, education—minorities, education—early childhood.
Types of support: Annual campaigns, operating budgets, equipment.
Limitations: Giving primarily in Saginaw County, MI.
Application information: Application form not required.
Initial approach: Letter
Copies of proposal: 3
Deadline(s): None
Board meeting date(s): Quarterly
Write: Lloyd J. Yeo, Pres.
Officers: Lloyd J. Yeo, Pres. and Treas.; B.J. Humphreys, V.P. and Secy.
Director: C. Ward Lauderbach.
Number of staff: 1 part-time professional.
EIN: 386083931

1403
Matilda R. Wilson Fund ▼
100 Renaissance Ctr., Suite 3377
Detroit 48243   (313) 259-7777

Incorporated in 1944 in MI.
Donor(s): Matilda R. Wilson,‡ Alfred G. Wilson.‡
Foundation type: Independent

Financial data (yr. ended 12/31/90): Assets, $32,598,493 (M); expenditures, $1,667,204; qualifying distributions, $1,431,408, including $1,345,662 for 32 grants (high: $415,291; low: $2,500; average: $10,000-$25,000).
Fields of interest: Higher education, arts, cultural programs, social services, youth, hospitals.
Types of support: Operating budgets, general purposes, building funds, equipment, endowment funds, research, special projects, scholarship funds, matching funds.
Limitations: Giving primarily in southeast MI. No grants to individuals; no loans.
Application information: Application form not required.
Initial approach: Proposal or letter
Copies of proposal: 1
Deadline(s): None
Board meeting date(s): Jan., Apr., July, and Oct.
Write: Frederick C. Nash, Pres.
Officers and Trustees:* Frederick C. Nash,* Pres.; Pierre V. Heftler,* V.P.; Robert M. Surdam,* Treas.
EIN: 386087665

1404
Lula C. Wilson Trust
c/o NBD Bank, N.A.
1116 West Long Lake Rd.
Bloomfield Hills 48013   (313) 645-7306

Trust established in 1963 in MI.
Donor(s): Lula C. Wilson.‡
Foundation type: Independent
Financial data (yr. ended 12/31/91): Assets, $2,015,617 (M); expenditures, $139,269; qualifying distributions, $110,530, including $110,530 for 22 grants (high: $10,000; low: $1,000; average: $1,000-$10,000).
Purpose and activities: Giving primarily for community development; support also for family and social services, youth and child welfare, women, the handicapped, hospices, performing arts groups and other cultural programs, and higher and secondary education.
Fields of interest: Community development, social services, family planning, disadvantaged, child development, youth, women, cultural programs, secondary education, higher education.
Types of support: Operating budgets, continuing support, annual campaigns, seed money, emergency funds, building funds, equipment, renovation projects, matching funds, capital campaigns, program-related investments.
Limitations: Giving restricted to Pontiac and Oakland County, MI. No grants to individuals, or for endowment funds, research, deficit financing, land acquisition, special projects, publications, conferences, scholarships, fellowships, or matching gifts.
Application information: Application form not required.
Initial approach: Letter
Copies of proposal: 1
Deadline(s): None
Board meeting date(s): As required
Final notification: 1 month
Write: Wilbur L. Avril, V.P., NBD Bank, N.A.
Trustee: NBD Bank, N.A.
Number of staff: None.
EIN: 386058895

1405
World Heritage Foundation
One Heritage Place, Suite 400
Southgate 48195   (313) 246-0563

Established in 1985 in MI.
Donor(s): Heinz C. Prechter, Heinz C. Prechter Charitable Lead Trust.
Foundation type: Independent
Financial data (yr. ended 12/31/90): Assets, $8,112,543 (M); gifts received, $100,000; expenditures, $283,223; qualifying distributions, $240,600, including $240,600 for 32 grants (high: $40,000; low: $100).
Fields of interest: Hospitals, community development, higher education, arts.
Types of support: Operating budgets, special projects.
Limitations: Giving primarily in MI. No grants to individuals.
Application information: Contributes only to pre-selected organizations. Applications not accepted.
Officers and Directors:* Heinz C. Prechter,* Chair.; Waltraud Prechter,* Pres.; Evangeline Redmer,* Secy.-Treas.; Gerald E. Szpotek,* Secy.-Treas.; Bruce C. Greening, Mgr.
EIN: 382640416

1406
Mary and George Herbert Zimmerman Foundation
220 Bagley, Suite 408
Detroit 48226

Established in 1937 in MI.
Donor(s): Members of the Zimmerman family.
Foundation type: Independent
Financial data (yr. ended 12/31/91): Assets, $2,482,569 (M); expenditures, $84,777; qualifying distributions, $68,100, including $68,100 for 26 grants (high: $12,500; low: $750).
Fields of interest: Religion—Christian, hospitals, health services, education.
Limitations: Giving primarily in MI. No grants to individuals.
Application information: Contributes only to pre-selected organizations. Applications not accepted.
Officers and Directors:* Elaine Z. Peck,* Pres.; Sheila P. Peck,* V.P.; Doris S. Bato,* Secy.; Rankin P. Peck, Treas.
EIN: 381685880

1407
Paul and Helen Zuckerman Family Foundation
(Formerly Paul Zuckerman Foundation)
280 Daines, Suite 100-B
Birmingham 48009

Established in 1953 in MI.
Donor(s): Paul Zuckerman,‡ Helen Zuckerman.
Foundation type: Independent
Financial data (yr. ended 12/31/90): Assets, $521,136 (M); expenditures, $113,014; qualifying distributions, $110,974, including $109,000 for 3 grants (high: $100,000; low: $4,000).
Purpose and activities: Giving primarily to a cancer research foundation.

Fields of interest: Cancer, medical education, general charitable giving.
Types of support: Research, general purposes.
Limitations: Giving primarily in Detroit, MI. No grants to individuals.
Application information: Contributes only to pre-selected organizations. Applications not accepted.
Officers: Helen Zuckerman, Pres.; Ira J. Jaffe, Secy.-Treas.
Trustees: Allan Cutler, Linda Klein, Thomas I. Klein, Arthur Weiss, Norbert Zuckerman.
EIN: 386064454

MINNESOTA

1408
Marshall H. and Nellie Alworth Memorial Fund

506 Alworth Bldg.
Duluth 55802   (218) 722-9366

Incorporated in 1949 in MN.
Donor(s): Marshall W. Alworth.‡
Foundation type: Independent
Financial data (yr. ended 12/31/90): Assets, $5,807,140 (M); gifts received, $699,527; expenditures, $958,834; qualifying distributions, $872,702, including $804,037 for 459 grants to individuals (high: $2,866; low: $666; average: $1,700-$2,500).
Purpose and activities: Awards scholarships for higher education to high school graduates who intend to specialize in the sciences, including chemistry, physics, mathematics, geology, biological sciences, engineering, nursing, and medicine.
Fields of interest: Science and technology, chemistry, physics, mathematics, physical sciences, biological sciences, engineering, medical sciences, medical education, nursing, pharmacy.
Types of support: Student aid.
Limitations: Giving limited to graduates for high schools in 15 northeastern MN counties. No grants for building or endowment funds or matching gifts; no loans.
Publications: Program policy statement, application guidelines.
Application information: Application form available from high schools in northern MN. Application form required.
   Initial approach: Letter
   Copies of proposal: 1
   Deadline(s): Submit proposal preferably in Dec. through Feb.; deadline Mar. 1
   Board meeting date(s): May
   Final notification: June
   Write: Richard H. Carlson, Exec. Dir.
Officers and Directors:* James Claypool, Pres.; John M. Donovan,* Secy.; Donald B. Crassweller,* Treas.; Richard H. Carlson, Exec. Dir.; Carol Fryberger, William E. Jacott, M.D., Mary Jo Jess, Peter J. Johnson.
Number of staff: 1 full-time professional; 1 full-time support.
EIN: 410797340

1409
American Express Minnesota Foundation ▼

c/o IDS Financial Services
IDS Tower Ten, Tax Dept. Unit 156
Minneapolis 55440   (612) 372-2643
Application address: IDS Tower Ten, Minneapolis, MN 55440

Established in 1987 in MN.
Donor(s): IDS Financial Corp.
Foundation type: Company-sponsored
Financial data (yr. ended 12/31/90): Assets, $37,430 (M); gifts received, $2,072,330; expenditures, $2,120,973; qualifying distributions, $2,120,755, including $2,120,720 for grants (average: $5,000-$60,000).
Purpose and activities: Main emphasis on cultural diversity and national heritage programs, higher education, employment and training, and child welfare. The foundation looks for programs that provide high-quality services, serve children and families, offer direct services to the public, find innovative solutions to community problems, involve IDS employees, and fit within the company's primary focus areas. Priority will be given to specific projects (as opposed to general operating support), to projects supported by public/private partnerships, to efforts that involve IDS beyond grant support (e.g., business/school/parent coalitions), and to distinctive projects where company involvement can make a noticeable difference. The IDS Matching Program matches IDS employees' individual gifts to various nonprofit organizations.
Fields of interest: Education, education—early childhood, education—minorities, higher education, welfare, family services, child welfare, youth, women, minorities, aged, employment, AIDS, community development, economics, volunteerism, cultural programs, fine arts, historic preservation, performing arts.
Types of support: Employee matching gifts, operating budgets, special projects.
Limitations: Giving primarily in MN. No support for religious, political, fraternal, or sports organizations, medical research or hospitals. No grants to individuals, or for books, magazines, endowments, capital campaigns, benefits, or charitable dinners.
Publications: Corporate giving report, 990-PF.
Application information: Application form not required.
   Initial approach: Proposal
   Deadline(s): July 1
   Board meeting date(s): Quarterly
   Final notification: Within six to eight weeks
   Write: Sue Gethin, Mgr., Public Affairs, IDS, or Marie Tobin, Community Relations Specialist
Officers and Directors:* Carol A. Kerner,* Pres.; Lynn I. Nelson, V.P.; Colleen C. Harvey, Secy.; Morris Goodwin, Jr.,* Treas.; Carl W. Gans, James D. Gaviglio, Harvey Golub, Samuel E. Kasuske, James A. Mitchell, Marty R. Shugarts, Stephen W. Swenson, John R. Thomas, Charlaine Tolkien.
Number of staff: 3 full-time professional; 1 part-time professional.
EIN: 411607944

1410
Andersen Foundation ▼

c/o Andersen Corp.
100 Fourth Ave. North
Bayport 55003   (612) 439-5150

Incorporated in 1959 in MN.
Donor(s): Fred C. Andersen.‡
Foundation type: Independent
Financial data (yr. ended 12/31/90): Assets, $209,995,194 (M); expenditures, $11,548,670; qualifying distributions, $11,062,810, including $11,052,982 for 117 grants (high: $1,150,000; low: $500; average: $10,000-$175,000).
Purpose and activities: Grants largely for higher education; support also for cultural programs, medical research, hospitals, and civic affairs.
Fields of interest: Higher education, cultural programs, medical research, hospitals, health services, civic affairs.
Limitations: No support for state or federally funded colleges or universities. No grants to individuals.
Application information:
   Deadline(s): None
   Board meeting date(s): 3 or 4 times a year, as required
   Final notification: Varies
   Write: Lisa Carlstrom, Asst. Secy.
Officers and Directors:* Katherine B. Andersen,* Pres.; Earl C. Swanson,* V.P. and Secy.; Keith R. Clements,* Treas.; W.R. Foster.
Number of staff: 1 part-time professional.
EIN: 416020920
Recent health grants:
1410-1 Childrens Hospital, Saint Paul, MN, $75,000. 1990.
1410-2 Gillette Childrens Hospital, Saint Paul, MN, $205,000. 1990.
1410-3 Hazelden Foundation, Center City, MN, $75,000. 1990.
1410-4 Institute for Orthopedic Research, Salt Lake City, UT, $25,000. 1990.
1410-5 Lakeview Memorial Hospital, Stillwater, MN, $125,000. 1990.
1410-6 Mayo Foundation, Rochester, MN, $250,000. 1990.
1410-7 Metropolitan-Mount Sinai Medical Center, Minneapolis, MN, $10,000. 1990.
1410-8 Ramsey Foundation, Saint Paul, MN, $50,000. 1990.
1410-9 River Falls Area Hospital and Kinnic Long-Term Unit, River Falls, WI, $100,000. 1990.
1410-10 University of Minnesota, Cancer Research Center, Minneapolis, MN, $750,000. 1990.

1411
Hugh J. Andersen Foundation ▼

287 Central Ave.
Bayport 55003   (612) 439-1557

Established in 1962.
Donor(s): Hugh J. Andersen,‡ Jane K. Andersen,‡ Katherine B. Andersen.
Foundation type: Independent
Financial data (yr. ended 02/28/92): Assets, $28,533,653 (M); expenditures, $1,320,423; qualifying distributions, $1,165,048, including $1,165,048 for 100 grants (high: $100,000; low: $500; average: $5,000-$25,000).
Purpose and activities: Emphasis on child and youth programs, community issues, and health and medical issues, including AIDS research.
Fields of interest: Disadvantaged, family services, youth, homeless, health services, AIDS.
Types of support: Operating budgets, special projects, general purposes, annual campaigns.
Limitations: Giving primarily in Washington County in MN and Pierce, Polk, and St. Croix counties in WI. No support for lobbying activities. No grants to individuals, or for fundraising dinners and events, travel, scholarships, or fellowships; no loans.

Publications: Annual report (including application guidelines).
Application information: Application form required.
 Initial approach: Letter or proposal
 Copies of proposal: 1
 Deadline(s): Apr. 1, July 1, Oct. 1, and Dec. 1
 Board meeting date(s): May, Aug., Nov., and Jan.
 Final notification: Approximately 3 months
 Write: Peggie Scott, Grants Consultant
Officers and Trustees:* Carol F. Andersen,* Pres.; Sarah J. Andersen,* V.P. and Secy.; Christine E. Andersen,* Treas.
Number of staff: 1 part-time professional.
EIN: 416020914
Recent health grants:
1411-1 AIDS Resource Foundation for Children, Newark, NJ, $24,570. 1991.
1411-2 American Cancer Society, Minnesota Division, Minneapolis, MN, $40,000. 1991.
1411-3 Childrens Hospital, Saint Paul, MN, $75,000. 1991.
1411-4 CommonHealth Clinic, Stillwater, MN, $20,000. 1991.
1411-5 Hazelden Foundation, Minneapolis, MN, $25,000. 1991.
1411-6 Health Start, Saint Paul, MN, $10,000. 1991.
1411-7 Hudson Memorial Hospital, Hudson, WI, $50,000. 1991.
1411-8 Hyacinth Foundation, Highland Park, NJ, $12,000. 1991.
1411-9 Lakeview Memorial Hospital Foundation, Stillwater, MN, $15,000. 1991.
1411-10 Learning Disabilities Association, Minneapolis, MN, $77,000. 1991.
1411-11 Learning Disabilities of Minnesota, Minneapolis, MN, $44,977. 1991.
1411-12 Minnesota AIDS Project, Minneapolis, MN, $10,000. 1991.
1411-13 Seva Foundation, Chelsea, MI, $10,000. 1991.

1412
Arthur H. Anderson Charitable Trust
c/o Norwest Bank Minnesota, N.A.
733 Marquette Ave.
Minneapolis 55479-0063

Foundation type: Independent
Financial data (yr. ended 06/30/91): Assets, $2,687,413 (M); expenditures, $156,855; qualifying distributions, $131,885, including $127,760 for 7 grants (high: $51,104; low: $12,776).
Fields of interest: Higher education, Protestant welfare, Protestant giving, social services, youth, hospitals.
Limitations: Giving primarily in MN. No grants to individuals.
Application information: Contributes only to pre-selected organizations. Applications not accepted.
Trustee: Norwest Bank Minnesota, N.A.
EIN: 416218548

1413
Baker Foundation
4900 IDS Ctr.
Minneapolis 55402   (612) 332-7479

Trust established in 1947; incorporated in 1954 in MN.
Donor(s): Morris T. Baker.‡
Foundation type: Independent
Financial data (yr. ended 12/31/91): Assets, $4,046,811 (M); expenditures, $280,017; qualifying distributions, $262,550, including $256,550 for 60 grants (high: $35,000; low: $100).
Fields of interest: Medical research, hospitals, higher education, conservation, youth, music.
Types of support: Annual campaigns, building funds, capital campaigns, general purposes, operating budgets.
Limitations: Giving primarily in MN. No grants to individuals.
Application information: Application form not required.
 Initial approach: Letter
 Copies of proposal: 1
 Deadline(s): None
 Board meeting date(s): As required
 Write: William M. Baker, Pres., or James W. Peter, Secy.
Officers and Directors:* William M. Baker,* Pres.; Roger L. Baker,* V.P.; David C. Sherman,* V.P.; James W. Peter,* Secy.-Treas.; Doris G. Baker, Morris T. Baker III, Nancy W. Baker, Mary Baker-Philbin, Tobias R. Philbin, Charles C. Pineo III, Linda Baker Pineo, Sandra B. Sherman.
Number of staff: 1 part-time professional; 1 part-time support.
EIN: 416022591

1414
Peggy Bauervic Foundation
(Formerly Bauervic-Carroll Foundation)
92 Mississippi River Blvd. North
St. Paul 55104-5613   (612) 293-0326
Application address: 26 East Exchange St., Suite 312, St. Paul, MN 55101

Established in 1984 in MI.
Foundation type: Independent
Financial data (yr. ended 12/31/91): Assets, $3,359,447 (M); expenditures, $120,254; qualifying distributions, $56,323, including $13,400 for 7 grants (high: $5,000; low: $100).
Fields of interest: Education, social services, medical research, medical sciences, arts.
Limitations: No grants to individuals.
Application information: Application form required.
 Initial approach: Letter requesting application
 Copies of proposal: 1
 Deadline(s): Oct. 1
 Write: Peggy Maitland, Pres.
Officers and Directors:* Peggy L. Maitland,* Pres. and Secy.; Jane Carroll,* V.P.; Stuart Maitland,* Treas.; Rose Bauervic-Wright, Jeffrey Carroll, Lynne M. Carroll.
Number of staff: 1 full-time professional.
EIN: 382494383

1415
James F. Bell Foundation
601 Lakeshore Pkwy., Suite 350
Minnetonka 55343   (612) 540-2295

Trust established in 1955 in MN.
Donor(s): James Ford Bell.‡

Foundation type: Independent
Financial data (yr. ended 12/31/90): Assets, $11,387,627 (M); expenditures, $655,558; qualifying distributions, $550,766, including $539,585 for 66 grants (high: $50,000; low: $500).
Purpose and activities: Emphasis on universities and cultural programs; support also for wildlife preservation and conservation, and youth agencies.
Fields of interest: Cultural programs, youth, conservation, wildlife, AIDS.
Types of support: Endowment funds, general purposes, scholarship funds, capital campaigns.
Limitations: Giving primarily in MN.
Application information:
 Initial approach: Proposal
 Deadline(s): None
 Write: Robert O. Mathson, Exec. Secy.
Officer: Robert O. Mathson, Exec. Secy.
Trustees: Ford W. Bell, Samuel H. Bell, Jr., David B. Hartwell.
EIN: 416023099

1416
Bemis Company Foundation
222 South Ninth St., No. 2300
Minneapolis 55402-4099   (612) 340-6198

Trust established in 1959 in MO.
Donor(s): Bemis Co., Inc.
Foundation type: Company-sponsored
Financial data (yr. ended 12/31/90): Assets, $1,714,423 (M); expenditures, $896,844; qualifying distributions, $887,707, including $804,318 for 215 grants (high: $92,655; low: $10; average: $500-$5,000) and $83,389 for 206 employee matching gifts.
Purpose and activities: Grants largely for scholarship programs for children of employees, state associations of independent colleges, an educational institution, an employee matching gift program, community funds, hospitals, and cultural and civic affairs programs.
Fields of interest: Higher education, education, community funds, cultural programs, civic affairs, hospitals, health, social services.
Types of support: Annual campaigns, building funds, employee-related scholarships, employee matching gifts, continuing support.
Limitations: Giving limited to areas of company operations. No support for religious or political purposes. No grants to individuals, or for endowment funds, research, educational capital programs, or trips or tours; no loans.
Publications: Corporate giving report, application guidelines.
Application information: Application form not required.
 Initial approach: Proposal
 Copies of proposal: 1
 Deadline(s): None
 Board meeting date(s): Mar., June, Aug., and Dec.
 Write: L.E. Schwanke, Trustee
Trustees: L.F. Bazany, B.R. Field, L.E. Schwanke.
Number of staff: 2 part-time professional.
EIN: 416038616

1417
F. R. Bigelow Foundation ▼
1120 Norwest Ctr.
St. Paul 55101   (612) 224-5463

Trust established in 1934; incorporated in 1946 in MN.
Donor(s): Frederick Russell Bigelow,‡ Eileen Bigelow.
Foundation type: Independent
Financial data (yr. ended 12/31/90): Assets, $68,973,345 (M); expenditures, $3,237,441; qualifying distributions, $2,809,945, including $2,809,945 for 117 grants (high: $375,000; low: $750; average: $10,000-$100,000).
Purpose and activities: Support for higher and secondary education, social services, including a community fund, arts and humanities, and health.
Fields of interest: Higher education, secondary education, social services, community funds, cultural programs, health, arts, humanities.
Types of support: Seed money, emergency funds, equipment, land acquisition, building funds, scholarship funds, matching funds, special projects, continuing support, renovation projects.
Limitations: Giving limited to the greater St. Paul, MN, metropolitan area. No grants to individuals, or for endowment funds; giving rarely for operating budgets; no loans.
Publications: Annual report (including application guidelines), application guidelines, informational brochure.
Application information: Application form required.
  Initial approach: Telephone, letter, or proposal
  Copies of proposal: 1
  Deadline(s): 3 months prior to board meetings
  Board meeting date(s): 3 times a year
  Final notification: 3 to 4 months
  Write: Paul A. Verret, Secy.-Treas.
Officer: Paul A. Verret, Secy.-Treas.
Trustees: Carl B. Drake, Jr., Chair.; Robert L. Bullard, Iris C. Cornelius, John N. Jackson, Constance B. Kunin, Malcolm W. McDonald, Mary Bigelow McMillian, Kathleen Culman Ridder, John A. Theobald.
Number of staff: None.
EIN: 510232651
Recent health grants:
1417-1 Center for Victims of Torture, Minneapolis, MN, $10,000. Toward renovation of new facility. 1990.
1417-2 Childrens Biomedical Research, Saint Paul, MN, $50,000. Toward adoptive T-cell immunotherapy research. 1990.
1417-3 Childrens Defense Fund, Saint Paul, MN, $25,000. Toward project to increase access to medical assistance for children and pregnant women in Minnesota. 1990.
1417-4 Chrysalis Center for Women, Minneapolis, MN, $10,000. Toward initiation of Family Recovery Program in Saint Paul, MN. 1990.
1417-5 Face to Face Health and Counseling Service, Saint Paul, MN, $18,000. Toward Pregnancy Prevention and Health Promotion Project for high-risk youth. 1990.
1417-6 Hazelden Foundation, Center City, MN, $25,000. For Pioneer House Capital Campaign. 1990.
1417-7 Model Cities Health Center, Saint Paul, MN, $20,000. Toward payment of outstanding accounts payable. 1990.

1417-8 Model Cities Health Center, Saint Paul, MN, $20,000. For Patient Subsidy Fund for low-income uninsured and underinsured patients. 1990.
1417-9 Planned Parenthood of Minnesota, Saint Paul, MN, $20,000. Toward clinic relocation to East Side. 1990.
1417-10 Ramsey Foundation, Saint Paul, MN, $20,000. Toward presentation of long-range funding strategy and to begin program for emergency medical dispatchers. 1990.
1417-11 Wayside House, Minneapolis, MN, $30,000. For Relocation Capital Campaign. 1990.
1417-12 Youth Emergency Service and Nighttime Emergency Outreach Network (YES/NEON), Minneapolis, MN, $10,000. Toward merger with Contact Twin Cities. 1990.

1418
The Blandin Foundation ▼
(Formerly Charles K. Blandin Foundation)
100 Pokegama Ave. North
Grand Rapids 55744   (218) 326-0523

Incorporated in 1941 in MN.
Donor(s): Charles K. Blandin.‡
Foundation type: Independent
Financial data (yr. ended 12/31/91): Assets, $220,000,000 (M); expenditures, $8,410,975; qualifying distributions, $8,410,975, including $5,392,173 for 174 grants (high: $855,000; low: $900), $284,367 for 541 grants to individuals (high: $2,000; low: $166; average: $500-$1,000), $1,093,972 for 22 foundation-administered programs and $600,000 for 2 program-related investments.
Purpose and activities: Giving in five priority areas for rural MN: 1)leadership development; 2)economic development; 3)arts and humanities; 4)the environment; and 5)educational opportunities, including scholarships for undergraduates and vocational study for recent graduates under the age of 22 who attended an Itasca County, Hill City, or Remer, MN, high school.
Fields of interest: Leadership development, economics, youth, rural development, Native Americans, community development, family services, arts, humanities, environment, education, higher education.
Types of support: Seed money, matching funds, scholarship funds, program-related investments, special projects, technical assistance, student aid.
Limitations: Giving limited to MN, with emphasis on rural areas; scholarships limited to graduates of an Itasca County, Hill City, or Remer high school. No support for religious activities or camping programs. No grants to individuals (other than for scholarships), or for operating budgets, continuing support, annual campaigns, deficit financing, government services, capital funds (outside home community), endowments, publications, travel, medical research, conferences, or seminars (outside of those sponsored by the foundation and related to its grantmaking).
Publications: Annual report, grants list, informational brochure (including application guidelines).
Application information: Scholarship applicants should call or write to the foundation for

deadlines and other information. Application form not required.
  Initial approach: Letter or visit
  Copies of proposal: 1
  Deadline(s): Jan. 2, May. 1, Sept. 1, and Nov. 1
  Board meeting date(s): During the first 2 weeks of Jan., Apr., and Aug.
  Final notification: 2 weeks after board meeting
  Write: Paul M. Olson, Pres.
Officers and Trustees:* Bruce Stender,* Chair.; Mary Jo Jess,* Vice-Chair.; Paul M. Olson, Pres.; Kathryn Jensen, V.P.; Vernae Hasbargen,* Secy.; Steve Shaler,* Treas.; Kathleen R. Annette, Robert L. Bullard, Robert L. Comstock, Jr., Henry Doerr, Peter A. Heegaard, James Hoolihan, James R. Oppenheimer, Brian Vergin.
Number of staff: 6 full-time professional; 1 part-time professional; 5 full-time support; 3 part-time support.
EIN: 416038619
Recent health grants:
1418-1 Block Nurse Program, Saint Paul, MN, $159,000. To help disseminate Block Nurse Program to rural communities in Minnesota. 1991.
1418-2 Community Memorial Hospital, Deer River, MN, $12,000. For purchase and installation of security system for Deer River Nursing Home. 1991.
1418-3 First Call for Help of Itasca County, Grand Rapids, MN, $25,000. For development of Access to Service Project. 1991.
1418-4 Franciscan Sisters Health Care, Little Falls, MN, $25,000. For North Star Hospital Consortium to develop educational program for six rural northwest Minnesota hospitals. 1991.
1418-5 Hope House, Grand Rapids, MN, $74,000. For transitional grant to enable Hope House to become fully licensed Halfway House. 1991.

1419
Blue Cross & Blue Shield of Minnesota Foundation, Inc.
3535 Blue Cross Rd.
St. Paul 55164   (612) 456-8401
Additional address: P.O. Box 64560, St. Paul, MN 55164

Established in 1986 in MN.
Donor(s): Blue Cross & Blue Shield of Minnesota.
Foundation type: Company-sponsored
Financial data (yr. ended 12/31/90): Assets, $5,540,173 (M); gifts received, $2,685,197; expenditures, $281,811; qualifying distributions, $278,163, including $278,163 for 10 grants (high: $195,632; low: $1,200).
Purpose and activities: To advance public health and the art and science of hospital, medical and health care. To support and enhance programs and activities that will have a beneficial impact on the lives of people living and working within the area served by Blue Cross and Blue Shield of Minnesota; support also for the United Way.
Fields of interest: Health, hospitals, community funds.
Limitations: Giving primarily in MN.
Application information:
  Initial approach: Proposal
  Deadline(s): None
  Write: Carol Laurent, Secy.

Officers and Directors:* Frank Johnson, M.D.,*
Chair.; Andrew P. Czajkowski,* Vice-Chair. and
Pres.; Carol Laurent,* Secy.; Stanley Ness,* Treas.;
William A. Jenison, Deborah Montgomery,
Richard M. Wageman, Francis Windsor.
EIN: 363525653

1420
Otto Bremer Foundation ▼
Suite 2000, 445 Minnesota St.
St. Paul 55101-2107   (612) 227-8036

Trust established in 1944 in MN.
Donor(s): Otto Bremer.‡
Foundation type: Independent
Financial data (yr. ended 12/31/90): Assets,
$95,805,165 (M); expenditures, $5,620,939;
qualifying distributions, $5,968,846, including
$5,244,443 for 536 grants (high: $150,000; low:
$130; average: $1,000-$25,000) and $307,000
for loans.
Purpose and activities: Emphasis on rural poverty
and combating racism. Support also for
postsecondary education, human services, health,
religion, and community affairs.
Fields of interest: Rural development, race
relations, education, welfare, social services,
disadvantaged, delinquency, hunger, homeless,
women, welfare—indigent individuals, Native
Americans, health services, immigration, public
affairs, civil rights, human rights, crime and law
enforcement, community funds, conservation.
Types of support: Seed money, emergency funds,
building funds, equipment, special projects,
matching funds, conferences and seminars,
technical assistance, program-related investments,
internships, continuing support, loans, operating
budgets.
Limitations: Giving limited to MN, ND, and WI
where there are Bremer Bank affiliates, and to
organizations addressing poverty in the city of St.
Paul. No support for national health
organizations. No grants to individuals, or for
endowment funds, medical research, or
professorships.
Publications: Annual report (including application
guidelines).
Application information: Application form not
required.
  Initial approach: Letter or telephone
  Copies of proposal: 1
  Deadline(s): Submit proposal at least 3 months
    before funding decision is desired
  Board meeting date(s): Monthly
  Final notification: 3 months
  Write: John Kostishack, Exec. Dir.
Officer and Trustees:* John Kostishack,* Exec.
Dir.; Charlotte S. Johnson, William H. Lipschultz,
Robert J. Reardon.
Number of staff: 3 full-time professional.
EIN: 416019050
Recent health grants:
1420-1 Center for Victims of Torture,
  Minneapolis, MN, $25,000. To develop
  volunteer program to assist refugees and exiles
  served by Center. 1991.
1420-2 CENTRE, Inc., Fargo, ND, $15,000. To
  remodel building used for chemical
  dependency day treatment program. 1991.
1420-3 Chrysalis Center for Women,
  Minneapolis, MN, $15,000. For operating
  support for Chrysalis East which provides

chemical dependency treatment and other
services to low-income women. 1991.
1420-4 Garrison Memorial Hospital, Garrison,
  ND, $12,000. For improvements to emergency
  room. 1991.
1420-5 Genesis 90s, Ashland, WI, $20,000. For
  operations of consumer controlled mental
  health center. 1991.
1420-6 Good Samaritan Hospital Association,
  Rugby, ND, $25,000. For construction of
  intensive care area. 1991.
1420-7 Help Enable Alcoholics Receive
  Treatment (HEART), Saint Paul, MN, $25,000.
  For chemical dependency treatment for
  individuals who lack coverage under health
  insurance or public assistance. 1991.
1420-8 Hispanos en Minnesota, Saint Paul, MN,
  $25,000. To expand chemical dependency
  counseling and prevention services to residents
  of Dakota County. 1991.
1420-9 Independent School District No. 196,
  Eagan, MN, $22,500. For parent support
  component of school-based mental health
  program. 1991.
1420-10 Indianhead Residential Care Facility
  and Sunshadows, Shell Lake, WI, $12,000. For
  additional staff and to purchase equipment for
  chemical dependency treatment program.
  1991.
1420-11 Lutheran Social Services of Wisconsin
  and Upper Michigan, Washburn, WI,
  $20,000. For development of adolescent
  chemical dependency treatment program.
  1991.
1420-12 Minnesota AIDS Project, Minneapolis,
  MN, $21,000. For Southwest AIDS Project,
  which provides referral and support services
  for people with AIDS in Marshall, MN. 1991.
1420-13 Minnesota AIDS Project, Central
  Minnesota AIDS Project, Saint Cloud, MN,
  $15,750. For operations of project. 1991.
1420-14 Minnesota Indian Primary Residential
  Treatment Center, Sawyer, MN, $20,000. For
  construction of new building for chemical
  dependency treatment center for Native
  American people. 1991.
1420-15 Minot State University, Minot, ND,
  $20,000. To purchase equipment for
  Communication Disorders Clinic which
  provides diagnosis and treatment services to
  residents of southwestern North Dakota. 1991.
1420-16 North Dakota Alliance for the Mentally
  Ill, Minot, ND, $20,000. For operations of
  organization that serves families dealing with
  mental illness. 1991.
1420-17 North Dakota State School of Science,
  Wahpeton, ND, $15,000. For Practical Nurse
  Satellite program which trains nurses to serve
  rural areas. 1991.
1420-18 Northwest Youth and Family Services,
  New Brighton, MN, $10,000. To increase
  health and nutrition educational service to
  youth at-risk. 1991.
1420-19 Richardton Health Center, Richardton,
  ND, $13,500. For purchase of equipment and
  to provide needed repairs for rural health
  clinic. 1991.
1420-20 University of Minnesota, Community
  University Health Care Center, Minneapolis,
  MN, $11,000. To continue mental health
  services to Laotian clients. 1991.

1421
The Bush Foundation ▼
E-900 First National Bank Bldg.
332 Minnesota St.
St. Paul 55101   (612) 227-0891

Incorporated in 1953 in MN.
Donor(s): Archibald Bush,‡ Mrs. Archibald Bush.‡
Foundation type: Independent
Financial data (yr. ended 11/30/91): Assets,
$428,332,547 (M); expenditures, $25,075,720;
qualifying distributions, $21,575,109, including
$17,706,224 for 242 grants (high: $1,000,000;
low: $2,325; average: $25,000-$50,000) and
$1,791,884 for grants to individuals.
Purpose and activities: Support largely for
education, arts and humanities, delivery of health
care, leadership development, minority
opportunity, and women and girls. Also operates
the Bush Leadership Fellows Program in MN,
ND, SD, and western WI, the Bush Fellowships
for Artists in MN, ND, and SD, and the Bush
Medical Fellows program in rural areas of MN,
ND, and SD.
Fields of interest: Higher education, education,
arts, humanities, media and communications,
health services, social services, leadership
development, minorities, women.
Types of support: Fellowships, matching funds,
endowment funds, special projects, seed money,
continuing support, capital campaigns,
renovation projects.
Limitations: Giving primarily in MN, ND, and
SD. No support for private foundations. No grants
to individuals (except for fellowships), or for
research in biomedical and health sciences;
generally no grants for continuing operating
support, for building construction of hospitals or
medical facilities, church sanctuaries, individual
daycare centers, municipal buildings, and
buildings in public colleges and universities; no
covering of operating deficits, or to retire
mortgages or other debts; no loans.
Publications: Annual report, application
guidelines, program policy statement, financial
statement.
Application information: Application form not
required.
  Initial approach: Letter or telephone
  Copies of proposal: 2
  Deadline(s): 3 1/2 months before board
    meetings
  Board meeting date(s): Feb., Apr.
    (odd-numbered years only), June, and Oct.
  Final notification: 10 days after board meetings
  Write: Humphrey Doermann, Pres.
Officers and Directors:* Thomas E. Holloran,*
Chair.; Frank B. Wilderson, Jr.,* 1st Vice-Chair.;
Anita M. Pampusch,* 2nd Vice-Chair.; Humphrey
Doermann, Pres.; Sharon Sayles Belton,* Secy.;
Richard D. McFarland,* Treas.; Merlin E. Dewing,
Phyllis B. France, Ellen Z. Green, Beatrix A.
Hamburg, John A. McHugh, Diana E. Murphy,
Kennon V. Rothchild, W. Richard West, Jr., C.
Angus Wurtele, Ann Wynia.
Number of staff: 7 full-time professional; 4
full-time support; 2 part-time support.
EIN: 416017815
Recent health grants:
1421-1 A Chance to Grow, Minneapolis, MN,
  $53,080. To evaluate Chance to Learn project.
  1991.

1421-2 Accessible Space, Saint Paul, MN, $50,000. For North Dakota Health Care Project. 1991.

1421-3 Apple Tree Dental, Minneapolis, MN, $25,000. For dental services for the aged. 1991.

1421-4 Block Nurse Program, Saint Paul, MN, $158,901. For program support. 1991.

1421-5 Community Clinic Consortium, Saint Paul, MN, $53,144. Toward Quality Assurance Program. 1991.

1421-6 Diabetes House, Saint Paul, MN, $30,000. For program start-up expenses. 1991.

1421-7 Family Networks, Minneapolis, MN, $25,000. For renovation project at Thorson Elementary School. 1991.

1421-8 Family Service of Greater Saint Paul, Saint Paul, MN, $55,984. To expand services to families suffering grief and loss. 1991.

1421-9 Fond du Lac Reservation Business Committee, Cloquet, MN, $35,000. For building renovation for mental health/human services programs. 1991.

1421-10 Mille Lacs Reservation Business Committee, Mille Lacs Band of Chippewa Indians, Onamia, MN, $60,000. For chemical abuse aftercare program. 1991.

1421-11 Minneapolis Crisis Nursery, Minneapolis, MN, $10,000. For program expansion. 1991.

1421-12 Minneapolis, City of, Minneapolis, MN, $69,990. For program to improve pregnancy outcomes for low-income women. 1991.

1421-13 Minnesota Indian Primary Residential Treatment Center, Mash-Ka-Wisen Treatment Center, Sawyer, MN, $10,000. For building expansion. 1991.

1421-14 Minnesota Institute on Black Chemical Abuse, Minneapolis, MN, $10,000. For building renovation. 1991.

1421-15 Outcomes, Saint Paul, MN, $60,000. For start-up support for program for autistic children and adults. 1991.

1421-16 Rapid City Foundation, Rapid City, SD, $11,790. To develop health and human services plan for Rapid City. 1991.

1421-17 Sarah Family Programs, Saint Paul, MN, $35,000. For capital project for transitional living program for women. 1991.

1421-18 Sexual Violence Center of Hennepin County, Minneapolis, MN, $75,000. Toward purchase of building. 1991.

1421-19 South Dakota Human Services Center, Yankton, SD, $30,130. For mental health program for Native Americans. 1991.

1421-20 Threshold, Sioux Falls, SD, $100,000. To help construct residential youth treatment facility. 1991.

1421-21 United Hospitals Foundation, Saint Paul, MN, $50,000. For renovation of community health center. 1991.

1421-22 University of Minnesota, Minneapolis, MN, $271,225. For day treatment program for Southeast Asian refugees. 1991.

1421-23 University of Minnesota, Minneapolis, MN, $216,580. For study of health care costs in Minnesota. 1991.

1421-24 University of North Dakota, Grand Forks, ND, $164,667. To establish joint pediatric preventive health residency program with University of North Carolina and Indian Health Service. 1991.

1421-25 Valley Rural Health Cooperative, Grand Forks, ND, $98,390. For continuing education program for rural health providers. 1991.

1421-26 Wellspring Therapeutic Communities, Minneapolis, MN, $10,000. For equipment and furnishings. 1991.

1421-27 White Earth Tribal Council, White Earth, MN, $31,987. Toward building renovation for chemical dependency program. 1991.

1422
Patrick and Aimee Butler Family Foundation

First National Bank Bldg.
332 Minnesota St., E-1420
St. Paul 55101-1369   (612) 222-2565

Incorporated in 1951 in MN.
Donor(s): Patrick Butler,‡ Aimee Mott Butler.
Foundation type: Independent
Financial data (yr. ended 12/31/91): Assets, $9,621,534 (M); gifts received, $350,000; expenditures, $913,146; qualifying distributions, $851,591, including $851,591 for 76 grants (high: $200,000; low: $500).
Purpose and activities: Primary areas of interest include chemical dependency, visual arts, museum, disadvantaged, women, family and children, housing, and the environment.
Fields of interest: Drug abuse, museums, disadvantaged, women, family services, housing, environment, humanities.
Types of support: Continuing support, annual campaigns, building funds, special projects, endowment funds, capital campaigns.
Limitations: Giving primarily in the St. Paul and Minneapolis, MN, area. No support for criminal justice, secondary and elementary education, health or hospitals, medical research, performing arts, film, employment or vocational programs, or economic education. No grants to individuals; no loans.
Publications: Informational brochure (including application guidelines).
Application information: Application form required.
  Initial approach: Letter or telephone requesting guidelines or letter of intent form
  Copies of proposal: 1
  Deadline(s): Apr. 30 for letter of intent form, Aug. for full proposal
  Board meeting date(s): June and Oct.
  Final notification: Nov. or Dec.
  Write: Sandra K. Butler, Prog. Officer
Officers and Trustees:* Peter M. Butler,* Pres.; Patrick Butler, Jr.,* V.P.; Terence N. Doyle, Secy.; John K. Butler,* Treas.; Sandra K. Butler, Prog. Officer; Cecelia M. Butler, Ellen M. Butler, Patricia Butler, Suzanne A. LeFevour, Hall James Peterson, Kate Butler Peterson.
Number of staff: 1 part-time professional; 1 part-time support.
EIN: 416009902

1423
Cargill Corporate Contributions Committee

P.O. Box 9300
Minneapolis 55440   (612) 475-6213

Financial data (yr. ended 05/31/90): Total giving, $2,605,000, including $2,368,000 for grants (high: $52,335; low: $250) and $237,000 for 16 grants to individuals (high: $4,000; low: $200).
Purpose and activities: Support for a broad spectrum of programs that help achieve a better informed, healthier, more productive and prosperous citizenry, in the areas of education, social services, culture, civic affairs, and health; special emphasis is placed on educational and social service programs that help individuals in becoming more self-reliant and on organizations that involve company volunteers. The Cargill Cares project involves employees in raising cash and in-kind donations for local community nonprofits and in giving their time and efforts. The Cargill Incorporated Volunteers in Community Service (CIVICS) and the SPICE retiree group also coordinate charitable activities. Giving figures represent cash grants by head quarters and divisions and do not include nonmonetary support. Current Giving reflects combined foundation and headquarters giving.
Fields of interest: Agriculture, business, child development, child welfare, citizenship, civic affairs, cultural programs, disadvantaged, economics, education, education—early childhood, education—minorities, employment, general charitable giving, handicapped, health, higher education, hunger, international affairs, international relief, public affairs, public policy, social services, volunteerism, youth, business education, environment, nutrition.
Types of support: In-kind gifts, annual campaigns, capital campaigns, continuing support, equipment, operating budgets, professorships, program-related investments, scholarship funds, employee-related scholarships, special projects, building funds, fellowships, internships, donated equipment, donated products, use of facilities, loaned talent, employee volunteer services.
Limitations: Giving primarily in the Twin Cities, greater MN area, and other areas in the U.S. where company has facilities.
Publications: Corporate giving report, application guidelines.
Application information: Corporate Contributions office handles giving for the Twin Cities. Application form not required.
  Initial approach: Write letter with supporting document; write to nearest company facility for local program
  Copies of proposal: 1
  Deadline(s): Grant requests reviewed year-round
  Board meeting date(s): Every 6-8 weeks
  Final notification: Immediately following contributions committee meetings for the Twin Cities; contact local facility for more information
  Write: James S. Hield, Secy., Contribs. Comm.
Administrator: James S. Hield, Secy.
Number of staff: 1 part-time professional; 1 full-time support.

1424
The Cargill Foundation ▼

P.O. Box 9300
Minneapolis 55440   (612) 475-6122

Incorporated in 1952 in MN.
Donor(s): Cargill Charitable Trust, Cargill, Inc.

Foundation type: Company-sponsored
Financial data (yr. ended 12/31/91): Assets, $41,088,000 (M); gifts received, $2,000,000; expenditures, $3,379,365; qualifying distributions, $3,168,211, including $3,167,822 for 145 grants (high: $400,000; low: $2,000; average: $2,500-$5,000).
Purpose and activities: Emphasis on education and social service programs; limited support for health, cultural programs, and civic affairs.
Fields of interest: Education, social services, cultural programs, civic affairs, health.
Types of support: Operating budgets, continuing support, general purposes, special projects, capital campaigns.
Limitations: Giving primarily in the seven-county Minneapolis-St. Paul, MN, metropolitan area. No support for religious organizations for religious purposes. No grants to individuals, or for endowment funds, matching gifts, research, demonstration projects, publications, films or videos, travel, conferences, or fellowships; no loans.
Publications: Informational brochure (including application guidelines).
Application information: Application form required.
  Initial approach: Telephone
  Copies of proposal: 1
  Deadline(s): Feb. 1 for educational grants; Apr. 1 for health grants; June 1 for social programs; Oct. 1 for cultural and civic programs
  Board meeting date(s): Apr., June, Sept., and Dec.
  Final notification: 2 weeks to 1 month after board meetings
  Write: Audrey Tulberg, Prog. and Admin. Dir.
Officers: Walter B. Saunders, Pres.; James R. Cargill, V.P.; Peter Dorsey, V.P.; Cargill MacMillan, Jr., V.P.; John E. Pearson, V.P.
Number of staff: 1 full-time professional; 1 full-time support; 1 part-time support.
EIN: 416020221
Recent health grants:
1424-1 Childrens Biomedical Research, Saint Paul, MN, $15,000. For general support. 1990.
1424-2 Help Enable Alcoholics Receive Treatment (HEART), Saint Paul, MN, $12,000. For general support. 1990.
1424-3 Indian Health Board of Minneapolis, Minneapolis, MN, $10,000. For general support. 1990.
1424-4 Metropolitan Achievement Center, Minneapolis, MN, $25,401. For general support. 1990.
1424-5 Minnesota Medical Foundation, Minneapolis, MN, $75,000. For general support. 1990.
1424-6 Planned Parenthood of Minnesota, Saint Paul, MN, $16,000. For general support. 1990.
1424-7 Washburn Child Guidance Center, Minneapolis, MN, $10,000. For general support. 1990.

1425
Caring and Sharing Foundation, Inc.
c/o LeRoy Kopp
6600 France Ave. South, Suite 235
Edina 55435

Established in 1986 in MN.

Donor(s): Leroy Kopp.
Foundation type: Independent
Financial data (yr. ended 12/31/90): Assets, $2,249,380 (M); gifts received, $150,000; expenditures, $112,245; qualifying distributions, $112,245, including $111,125 for 77 grants (high: $10,000; low: $25).
Fields of interest: Protestant giving, Catholic giving, health, social services, child welfare, youth.
Limitations: Giving primarily in MN.
Application information:
  Initial approach: Letter
  Deadline(s): None
Directors: Barbara Kopp, LeRoy Kopp.
EIN: 363485918

1426
Carolyn Foundation ▼
4800 First Bank Place
Minneapolis 55402   (612) 339-7101

Trust established in 1964 in MN.
Donor(s): Carolyn McKnight Christian.‡
Foundation type: Independent
Financial data (yr. ended 12/31/90): Assets, $22,427,850 (M); expenditures, $1,241,843; qualifying distributions, $1,065,598, including $1,065,598 for 45 grants (high: $100,000; low: $3,000; average: $4,000-$20,000).
Purpose and activities: Priorities include education, culture, health and welfare, including child welfare, the environment, women, and the disadvantaged.
Fields of interest: Education, cultural programs, health services, environment, youth, child welfare, social services, disadvantaged, women.
Types of support: General purposes.
Limitations: Giving primarily in the metropolitan areas of New Haven, CT, and Minneapolis-St. Paul, MN. No support for political or veterans' groups, fraternal societies, or religious organizations for religious purposes. No grants to individuals, or for endowment funds, annual fund drives, deficit funding, costs of litigation, or continuing support; no loans.
Publications: Annual report (including application guidelines).
Application information: Application form not required.
  Initial approach: Letter
  Copies of proposal: 7
  Deadline(s): Submit proposal Jan. and Feb. for minor grants (under $10,000) and between Jan. and June for major grants ($10,000 and larger); board awards major grants at Dec. meeting; deadlines Mar. 1 for minor grants; July 1 for major grants
  Board meeting date(s): June and Dec.
  Final notification: June and Dec.
  Write: Carol J. Fetzer, Exec. Dir.
Officers and Trustees:* Lucy C. Mitchell,* Chair.; Guido Calabresi,* Vice-Chair.; Carol J. Fetzer,* Secy. and Exec. Dir.; Edwin L. Crosby,* Treas.; Beatrice C. Booth, Benton J. Case, Jr., Eugenie T. Copp, Franklin M. Crosby III, G. Christian Crosby, Sumner McK. Crosby, Jr., Thomas M. Crosby, Jr., Carolyn C. Graham.
Number of staff: None.
EIN: 416044416
Recent health grants:

1426-1 American Cultural Traditions For Teen Suicide Prevention, Grand Prairie, TX, $10,000. 1990.
1426-2 Indian Health Board of Minneapolis, Minneapolis, MN, $17,500. 1990.
1426-3 Leeway, Hamden, CT, $35,000. 1990.
1426-4 Shirley Frank Foundation, New Haven, CT, $35,000. 1990.
1426-5 Zero Population Growth, DC, $15,000. 1990.

1427
Central Minnesota Community Foundation
619 St. Germain Mall, Suite 214
P.O. Box 1284
St. Cloud 56302-1284   (612) 253-4380

Established in 1985 in MN.
Foundation type: Community
Financial data (yr. ended 06/30/91): Assets, $8,821,294 (M); gifts received, $1,259,609; expenditures, $846,139; qualifying distributions, $705,340, including $705,340 for 58 grants (average: $250-$5,000).
Purpose and activities: "To make a continuing relevant contribution to the present and future vitality of Central Minnesota, building the independence and interdependence of people in the development of self-capacity and fullness of life."
Fields of interest: Education, arts, environment, health, social services.
Types of support: Scholarship funds, seed money, technical assistance, conferences and seminars.
Limitations: Giving primarily in Benton, Stearns, and Sherburne counties, MN. No support for religious, political, or fraternal organizations. No grants to individuals, or for medical research.
Publications: Annual report, informational brochure, application guidelines.
Application information: Application form required.
  Initial approach: Telephone or letter requesting guidelines
  Copies of proposal: 7
  Deadline(s): Mar. 1 and Sept. 1 for undesignated funds
  Board meeting date(s): 3rd Monday in May and Nov.
  Write: Leland Newman, Exec. Dir.
Officers and Directors:* Fr. Hilary Thimmesh,* Pres.; Andy Hilger,* V.P.; Caroline Boureson,* Secy.; John Weitzel,* Treas.; Leland E. Newman, Exec. Dir.; and 20 additional directors.
Number of staff: 2 full-time professional.
EIN: 363412544

1428
Chadwick Foundation
4122 IDS Ctr.
Minneapolis 55402

Established in 1967 in MN.
Donor(s): Members of the Dayton family.
Foundation type: Independent
Financial data (yr. ended 12/31/90): Assets, $5,319,881 (M); gifts received, $750,000; expenditures, $1,019,822; qualifying distributions, $1,008,562, including $1,008,250 for 59 grants (high: $260,000; low: $250).

Purpose and activities: Emphasis on secondary and higher education, community services, cultural programs, conservation, hospitals and medical research, the arts, and Protestant church support.
Fields of interest: Higher education, secondary education, arts, hospitals, medical research, Protestant giving, cultural programs, conservation, community development, social services.
Types of support: Research, general purposes.
Limitations: Giving primarily in MN. No grants to individuals.
Application information: Contributes only to pre-selected organizations. Applications not accepted.
Officers and Directors:* Lucy J. Dayton,* Pres. and Treas.; Robert J. Dayton,* V.P. and Secy.; Edward N. Dayton,* V.P.; John W. Dayton,* V.P.; Ronald N. Gross.
Number of staff: None.
EIN: 416080619

1429
Charlson Research Foundation
P.O. Box 369
Excelsior 55331   (612) 474-3216

Established in 1977 in MN.
Donor(s): Lynn L. Charlson.
Foundation type: Independent
Financial data (yr. ended 10/31/90): Assets, $10,870,752 (M); expenditures, $800,124; qualifying distributions, $791,609, including $525,934 for 8 grants (high: $108,934; low: $30,000).
Fields of interest: Energy, science and technology, medical research, medical education.
Types of support: Research.
Limitations: No grants to individuals.
Publications: 990-PF.
Application information: Contributes only to pre-selected organizations. Applications not accepted.
    Board meeting date(s): Varies as necessary
    Write: Craig McCoy, Prog. Coord.
Officers: Lynn L. Charlson, Pres.; Beverly C. Charlson, V.P.; Kim H. McCoy, Secy.; Leslie H. Stiles, Treas.
Directors: Karen McElrath, Mary L. Rippy.
Number of staff: 1 full-time professional; 2 part-time support.
EIN: 411313302

1430
Cowles Media Company Giving Program
329 Portland Ave.
Minneapolis 55415-1112   (612) 673-7051

Financial data (yr. ended 12/31/90): Total giving, $1,700,000, including $1,600,000 for grants and $100,000 for employee matching gifts.
Purpose and activities: Support for the arts, early childhood education, family services, literacy, media and communications, human services, and youth; employee matching gifts for art and education.
Fields of interest: Arts, education—early childhood, family planning, family services, literacy, media and communications, youth.

Types of support: Annual campaigns, capital campaigns, continuing support, employee matching gifts, endowment funds.
Limitations: Giving primarily in Minneapolis, MN. No support for religious, international or political programs, or organizations pricipally involved in medicine, health, research, substance abuse or rehabilitation. No grants to individuals, or for publications, conferences, travel, or fundraising events.
Application information: Application form not required.
    Initial approach: Letter and proposal
    Copies of proposal: 1
    Deadline(s): None
    Board meeting date(s): Calendar quarters
    Write: Jan Vitch, Contribs. Coord.

1431
Cowles Media Foundation ▼
329 Portland Ave.
Minneapolis 55415   (612) 375-7051

Incorporated in 1945 in MN.
Donor(s): Cowles Media Co.
Foundation type: Company-sponsored
Financial data (yr. ended 03/31/90): Assets, $7,949,545 (M); gifts received, $650,000; expenditures, $1,521,103; qualifying distributions, $1,427,240, including $1,427,240 for 124 grants (high: $250,000; low: $500; average: $1,000-$10,000).
Purpose and activities: Support of educational, scientific, and charitable organizations, including higher education, civic agencies, and journalism; support also for social service and youth organizations.
Fields of interest: Education, higher education, journalism, civic affairs, science and technology, social services, youth.
Limitations: Giving limited to the Minneapolis, MN, area. No grants to individuals, or for operating budgets or special projects.
Publications: 990-PF, program policy statement, application guidelines.
Application information:
    Initial approach: Letter or telephone
    Copies of proposal: 1
    Deadline(s): None
    Write: Janet L. Schwichtenberg
Officers and Directors:* David Kruidenier,* Chair.; Roger P. Parkinson,* Pres.; James A. Alcott,* V.P.; David C. Cox,* V.P.; Norton L. Armour, Secy.; John Cole, Treas.; Bette Fenton, Hazel Reinhardt.
EIN: 416031373
Recent health grants:
1431-1 Planned Parenthood of Minnesota, Saint Paul, MN, $100,000. For endowment campaign. 1991.
1431-2 Planned Parenthood of Minnesota, Saint Paul, MN, $10,000. For general operating support. 1991.

1432
Dain Bosworth Foundation
(Formerly Dain Bosworth/IFG Foundation)
Dain Bosworth Plaza
P.O. Box 1160
Minneapolis 55440-1160   (612) 371-2765

Incorporated in 1961 in MN.
Donor(s): Dain, Kalman and Quail, Inc., Inter-Regional Financial Group, Inc.
Foundation type: Company-sponsored
Financial data (yr. ended 12/31/90): Assets, $69,876 (M); gifts received, $286,805; expenditures, $363,641; qualifying distributions, $363,641, including $350,095 for grants.
Purpose and activities: The foundation's primary focus will be on grants benefiting youth development, with priority given to education programs. Other general areas supported by the foundation include health and social services, civic and community development, and the arts.
Fields of interest: Business, community funds, civic affairs, community development, health, health services, education, social services, family services, child welfare, child development, cultural programs, theater.
Types of support: Employee matching gifts, general purposes, continuing support, annual campaigns, seed money, building funds, operating budgets.
Limitations: Giving primarily in areas of company operations in MN. No support for religious groups. No grants to individuals, or for capital or endowment funds, research, scholarships, fellowships, travel, tours, conferences, fundraising events, or multi-year pledges; no loans.
Publications: Annual report (including application guidelines).
Application information: Only MN applications accepted by the foundation; other applications should be sent to the nearest branch office. Application form not required.
    Initial approach: Letter
    Copies of proposal: 1
    Deadline(s): Jan. 31 and July 31
    Board meeting date(s): Feb., Mar., Aug., and Sept.
    Final notification: 2 to 3 weeks following Mar. and Sept. meetings
    Write: Sherry Koster, Exec. Dir.
Officers and Directors:* Doug Coleman,* Chair.; Sherry Koster,* Exec. Dir.; Linda Fjeld, B.J. French, Judy Gaviser, Dawn Hyde, Gaylord May, Richard McFarland, Don Melton, Dennis Murray, John O'Malley, John Peyton, Kim Simensen, Claudia Zweber.
Number of staff: 11 part-time professional; 1 part-time support.
EIN: 416030639

1433
Dayton Hudson Foundation ▼
777 Nicollet Mall
Minneapolis 55402-2055   (612) 370-6555

Incorporated in 1918 in MN.
Donor(s): Dayton Hudson Corp., and operating divisions.
Foundation type: Company-sponsored
Financial data (yr. ended 01/31/92): Assets, $20,400,000 (M); gifts received, $10,941,000; expenditures, $11,305,033; qualifying distributions, $11,514,490, including $11,151,490 for 411 grants (high: $828,500; low: $1,000; average: $5,000-$100,000).
Purpose and activities: "The foundation manages the Minneapolis/St. Paul-based giving for the Dayton Hudson Corp. and its Twin Cities-based operating companies, a small national grants

program and major funding initiatives with all three operating companies (Target, Mervyn's and the Department Store Division of Dayton Hudson Corp.). Giving is concentrated on programs that are committed to achieving results and demonstrating leadership. The foundation's priorities are to social action programs that result in the economic and social progress of individuals, and that develop strategies that respond effectively to community, social, and economic concerns, and to arts programs that result in artistic excellence, community leadership in the arts, and increased access to, and use of, the arts as a means of community expression."

Fields of interest: Cultural programs, urban affairs, community development, arts, social services, disadvantaged.

Types of support: Operating budgets, continuing support, annual campaigns, matching funds, consulting services, technical assistance, special projects, publications, general purposes.

Limitations: Giving primarily in areas of company operations including MN, especially the Twin Cities metropolitan area, MI, CA, FL, IL, and TX; grants rarely for national organizations or programs. No support for religious organizations for religious purposes; grants rarely made to health organizations, educational institutions, or tax-supported activities. No grants to individuals, or for seed money, emergency funds, land acquisition, scholarships, fellowships, research, or conferences; grants rarely for endowment funds; no loans.

Publications: Corporate giving report, informational brochure (including application guidelines), program policy statement, application guidelines, annual report, grants list.

Application information: Organizations located outside of MN should apply to a Dayton Hudson operating company. The Grant Application Guide explains how and where to apply. Application form not required.

> *Initial approach:* Letter with proposal
> *Copies of proposal:* 1
> *Deadline(s):* None
> *Board meeting date(s):* Mar., June, and Dec.
> *Final notification:* Usually within 60 days, although decisions are generally not made between Jan. 31 and Apr. 15
> *Write:* Cynthia Mayeda, Chair.

Officers and Trustees:* Cynthia Mayeda,* Chair.; William E. Harder, Secy.; Karol D. Emmerich, Kenneth A. Macke, Walter T. Rossi, Robert J. Ulrich, Stephen E. Watson.

Number of staff: 6 full-time professional; 2 full-time support.

EIN: 416017088

Recent health grants:

1433-1 Arts Over AIDS Task Force, Minneapolis, MN, $31,000. For production and distribution of Arts Over AIDS video. 1991.

1433-2 Arts Over AIDS Task Force, Minneapolis, MN, $15,000. For general support for arts community's response to HIV/AIDS. 1991.

1433-3 CONTACT YES/NEON, Minneapolis, MN, $15,000. For costs associated with merger of YES/NEON and CONTACT Twin Cities. 1991.

1433-4 Face to Face Health and Counseling Service, Saint Paul, MN, $10,000. For Discovery employment preparation program for young women. 1991.

1433-5 Indian Health Board of Minneapolis, Minneapolis, MN, $40,000. For continuing support of Soaring Eagles youth leadership program. 1991.

1433-6 JV Films, Minneapolis, MN, $10,000. For completion of Caregivers documentary about person with AIDS and his care partners. 1991.

1433-7 Learning Disabilities Association, Minneapolis, MN, $30,000. For general support for adult literacy tutoring, employment and support services. 1991.

1433-8 Minneapolis Police Department, Minneapolis, MN, $10,000. For Project DARE (Drug Abuse Resistance Education). 1991.

1433-9 Planned Parenthood of Minnesota, Saint Paul, MN, $18,000. For community education on pregnancy prevention provided at non-clinical locations. 1991.

1433-10 Wayside House, Minneapolis, MN, $10,000. For employment development programming. 1991.

1434
Ecolab Corporate Contributions Program
c/o Ecolab Inc.
Ecolab Center
St. Paul 55102   (612) 293-2233

Financial data (yr. ended 12/31/91): Total giving, $779,601, including $739,196 for grants (high: $163,750; average: $500-$5,000) and $40,405 for employee matching gifts.

Purpose and activities: "We want to make a difference. In tough economic times, we believe it is especially important to invest in our communities because they are our future. By helping them become healthy and vital, we ensure our well-being." The company's operating and capital grants serve the categories of education, community development, health and human services, and arts and culture. However, Ecolab channels its resources primarily to agencies and programs that give disadvantaged groups and individuals the tools they need to become self-sufficient. The corporate contributions program addresses company concerns through charitable contribution, creative programming and employee volunteerism. Figures represent combined giving for the corporation and Ecolab Foundation.

Fields of interest: Health, social services, arts, cultural programs, community development, education, aged, homeless, women, child development, minorities.

Types of support: Capital campaigns, operating budgets, employee volunteer services, endowment funds, employee matching gifts, capital campaigns.

Limitations: Giving primarily in St.Paul-Minneapolis area in MN; support also in Garland, TX, Joliet, Il, Woodbridge, NJ, Beloit, WI, and Columbus, OH. No support for sectarian or denominational, religious organizations unless funds are to be used in direct interest of the whole community, political or lobbying organizations, or industry, trade or professional association memberships. No grants to individuals, or for fundraisers, loans, investments, luncheons, ticket purchases, or advertisements.

Application information:

> *Deadline(s):* July 1
> *Write:* Louise K. Thoreson, Program Consultant

1435
Ecolab Foundation
Ecolab Ctr., 10th Fl.
St. Paul 55102   (612) 293-2259
Application address: c/o CSFA-Midwest, P.O. Box 297, St. Peter, MN 56082

Established in 1982 in MN.

Foundation type: Company-sponsored

Financial data (yr. ended 12/31/90): Assets, $1,831,691 (M); gifts received, $191,679; expenditures, $815,523; qualifying distributions, $899,769, including $684,661 for 377 grants (high: $112,000; low: $25), $95,621 for grants to individuals and $61,600 for loans to individuals.

Purpose and activities: Gives one-year scholarships to dependents of active or retired Ecolab, Inc., employees for tuition and academic fees at accredited colleges or universities, and also at technical and community colleges; support also for higher education, human service organizations, the arts, and the environment.

Fields of interest: Education, arts, health, community development, environment.

Types of support: Employee-related scholarships, technical assistance, operating budgets, employee matching gifts.

Limitations: Giving primarily in Garland, TX; Beloit, WI; St. Paul, MN; Woodbridge, NJ; and Joliet, IL.

Publications: Corporate giving report (including application guidelines).

Application information: Application form not required.

> *Initial approach:* Letter of inquiry requesting application guidelines
> *Copies of proposal:* 1
> *Deadline(s):* July 1
> *Board meeting date(s):* Quarterly
> *Final notification:* Mar.
> *Write:* L.J. West, Dir., Community & Public Relations

Officers and Directors:* William R. Rosengren,* Sr. V.P., General Counsel, and Secy.; Arthur E. Henningsen,* V.P. and Controller; John G. Forsythe,* V.P., Tax and Public Affairs; Diana D. Lewis,* V.P., Human Relations; William A. Mathison,* V.P.

Number of staff: None.

EIN: 411372157

1436
Edwin H. Eddy Family Foundation
(Formerly Eddy Foundation)
c/o Norwest Bank, N.A.
Capital Management and Trust Dept.
Duluth 55802   (218) 723-2773

Established in 1982 in MN.

Donor(s): Edwin H. Eddy, Jr.‡

Foundation type: Independent

Financial data (yr. ended 06/30/91): Assets, $2,560,518 (M); expenditures, $161,593; qualifying distributions, $150,897, including $96,000 for 4 grants (high: $50,000; low: $5,000; average: $20,000) and $39,950 for 32 grants to individuals (high: $2,000; low: $1,000; average: $1,200).

Purpose and activities: Grants for research into and treatment of individuals with speech or hearing disorders. Also awards scholarships for students studying in the field of communication

disorders: first priority for Duluth, MN, area residents at the University of Minnesota, Duluth; second priority for area residents at other institutions; and third priority for non-residents at the University of Minnesota, Duluth.
Fields of interest: Handicapped, medical research, speech pathology.
Types of support: Student aid, conferences and seminars, continuing support, grants to individuals, internships, lectureships, matching funds, professorships, research, scholarship funds, technical assistance.
Limitations: Giving limited to the Duluth, MN, area. No grants for capital improvements or salaries.
Publications: Informational brochure (including application guidelines), program policy statement, application guidelines.
Application information: Application form required for scholarships.
Initial approach: Proposal
Copies of proposal: 8
Deadline(s): Mar. 31 for scholarships
Board meeting date(s): June 1 for scholarships
Trustees: Rodney J. Edwards, Eben S. Spencer, Norwest Bank, N.A.
EIN: 416242226

1437
Edwards Memorial Trust
c/o First Trust, N.A.
P.O. Box 64704
St. Paul 55164-0704   (612) 291-5115

Trust established in 1961 in MN.
Donor(s): Ray Edwards.‡
Foundation type: Independent
Financial data (yr. ended 12/31/91): Assets, $13,414,765 (M); expenditures, $709,472; qualifying distributions, $657,548, including $648,700 for 89 grants (high: $50,000; low: $500).
Purpose and activities: Emphasis on public hospitals, including the maintaining of free beds; some support for social services and health agencies, including those benefiting the handicapped.
Fields of interest: Hospitals, social services, health services, handicapped, mental health.
Types of support: General purposes.
Limitations: Giving primarily in the Minneapolis-St. Paul, MN, area. No grants to individuals.
Application information: Application form not required.
Initial approach: Letter
Deadline(s): None
Board meeting date(s): May and Nov.
Write: Leonard J. Ilges, V.P., First Trust, N.A.
Trustee: First Trust, N.A.
EIN: 416011292

1438
The Fingerhut Family Foundation
5354 Parkdale Dr., No. 310
Minneapolis 55416   (612) 545-3000

Incorporated in 1960 in MN.
Donor(s): Manny Fingerhut, Rose Fingerhut.
Foundation type: Independent

Financial data (yr. ended 12/31/90): Assets, $59,857 (M); expenditures, $651,996; qualifying distributions, $651,996, including $617,665 for 71 grants (high: $450,000; low: $100; average: $500-$10,000).
Fields of interest: Jewish giving, social services, medical research.
Types of support: Operating budgets, annual campaigns, continuing support, emergency funds, general purposes, research, special projects.
Limitations: Giving primarily in MN, especially the Twin Cities. No grants for building funds.
Application information: Application form not required.
Initial approach: Letter and brief proposal
Copies of proposal: 2
Deadline(s): None
Board meeting date(s): As necessary
Final notification: 4 weeks
Write: Ronald Fingerhut, Pres.
Officers and Directors:* Ronald Fingerhut,* Pres.; Stanley Nemer,* V.P. and Secy.-Treas.; Rose Fingerhut,* V.P.; Beverly Deikel, Manny Fingerhut.
Number of staff: 1 part-time professional; 1 part-time support.
EIN: 416030930

1439
Miles and Shirley Fiterman Charitable Foundation
5217 Wayzata Blvd., Suite 212
Minneapolis 55416

Established in 1986.
Donor(s): Miles Q. Fiterman, Shirley L. Fiterman.
Foundation type: Independent
Financial data (yr. ended 12/31/90): Assets, $1,972,314 (M); gifts received, $45,000; expenditures, $228,697; qualifying distributions, $223,414, including $223,348 for 39 grants (high: $125,000; low: $25).
Purpose and activities: Primary giving for Jewish welfare; support also for medical research and culture.
Fields of interest: Jewish giving, health associations, medical research, cultural programs.
Limitations: No grants to individuals.
Application information: Contributes only to pre-selected organizations. Applications not accepted.
Trustees: Miles Q. Fiterman, Shirley L. Fiterman, Steven C. Fiterman.
EIN: 411582224

1440
H. B. Fuller Community Affairs Program
2400 Energy Park Dr.
St. Paul 55108   (612) 647-3617

Financial data (yr. ended 12/31/90): Total giving, $299,710 for grants.
Purpose and activities: Support for social services/human relations, education, health and welfare, community development, environmental issues, and arts and humanities. The Company emphasizes youth development programs in the areas of education and crisis prevention both through grants and employee volunteerism in the U.S. and in plant locations abroad.
Fields of interest: Social services, education, welfare, health, community funds, environment,

arts, cultural programs, youth, Japan, Latin America, Canada, Mexico, Europe, Australia, child welfare, youth.
Types of support: Employee volunteer services.
Limitations: Giving primarily in operating locations in U.S., Argentina, Brazil, Chile, Costa Rica, Australia, Dominican Republic, El Salvador, Ecuador, Guatemala, Honduras, Mexico, Panama, Peru, Puerto Rico, Austria, Belgium, France, Germany, Netherlands, Spain, Sweden, United Kingdom, Canada, and Japan. No support for religious, political, fraternal or veterans' organizations, except those which benefit the entire community, or to lobbying groups, national or local disease associations. No grants to individuals, or for capital or endowment drives, fund-raising campaigns, courtesy advertising, travel, or basic or applied research.
Publications: Corporate giving report (including application guidelines).
Application information:
Initial approach: Letter or proposal
Board meeting date(s): Community Affairs Councils meet monthly
Final notification: Within 6 weeks
Write: Karen Muller, Exec. Dir.
Council Chairpersons: Shirley Draft, Lewis Flanagan, Beverly Krebs, Diane Strickland, Naida Kissner, Community Affairs Asst.

1441
General Mills Foundation ▼
P.O. Box 1113
Minneapolis 55440   (612) 540-7891
FAX: (612) 540-4925

Incorporated in 1954 in MN.
Donor(s): General Mills, Inc.
Foundation type: Company-sponsored
Financial data (yr. ended 05/31/91): Assets, $41,893,547 (L); gifts received, $13,864,000; expenditures, $10,994,062; qualifying distributions, $26,384,793, including $10,342,877 for 563 grants (high: $817,887; low: $1,000; average: $5,000-$15,000), $562,046 for 1,429 employee matching gifts and $15,479,870 for in-kind gifts.
Purpose and activities: Grants for higher and secondary education, social services, community funds, health, and civic and cultural activities.
Fields of interest: Cultural programs, arts, education, secondary education, higher education, health, social services, community funds.
Types of support: Operating budgets, employee matching gifts, scholarship funds, employee-related scholarships, special projects.
Limitations: Giving primarily in areas of major parent company operations, with emphasis on the Minneapolis, MN, area. No support for religious purposes, recreation, or national or local campaigns to eliminate or control specific diseases. No grants to individuals, or, generally, for endowment, research, publications, films, conferences, seminars, advertising, athletic events, testimonial dinners, workshops, symposia, travel, fundraising events, or deficit financing; no loans.
Publications: Corporate giving report (including application guidelines), informational brochure, application guidelines, annual report, occasional report.

Application information: Preliminary telephone calls or personal visits discouraged. Application form not required.

Initial approach: Proposal with brief cover letter
Copies of proposal: 1
Deadline(s): None
Board meeting date(s): 4 times a year and as required
Final notification: 4 weeks
Write: Reatha Clark King, Pres. and Exec. Dir.
Officers and Trustees:* H. Brewster Atwater, Jr.,* Chair.; Reatha Clark King,* Pres. and Exec. Dir.; David A. Nasby, V.P.; Clifford L. Whitehill,* Secy.; David B. Van Benschoten, Treas.; F. Caleb Blodgett, J.R. Lee, T.P. Nelson, A.R. Schulze, Mark H. Willes.
Number of staff: 2 full-time professional; 3 full-time support.
EIN: 416018495
Recent health grants:

1441-1 A Chance to Grow, Minneapolis, MN, $50,000. To develop techniques for educating developmentally delayed children. 1991.

1441-2 Amigos de las Americas, Houston, TX, $10,000. For leadership and development opportunities for student volunteers in Latin America. 1991.

1441-3 Birth, Education, Training, Acceptance (BETA), Orlando, FL, $20,000. For program for high-risk pregnant women, mothers and children. 1991.

1441-4 Center for Drug-Free Living, Orlando, FL, $15,000. For chemical dependency treatment and prevention agency. 1991.

1441-5 Community Clinic Consortium, Saint Paul, MN, $15,000. For health care for uninsured clients. 1991.

1441-6 Community Communications, Orlando, FL, $25,000. For production of anti-drug television program. 1991.

1441-7 Delnor Health Care Foundation, Saint Charles, IL, $20,000. For capital for hospital. 1991.

1441-8 Family Service of Greater Saint Paul, Saint Paul, MN, $10,000. For Minnesota Center for Grief and Loss. 1991.

1441-9 Indian Health Board of Minneapolis, Minneapolis, MN, $10,500. For Soaring Eagles Youth Leadership Project. 1991.

1441-10 Media-Advertising Partnership for a Drug-Free America, NYC, NY, $50,000. For campaign to reduce demand for illegal drugs. 1991.

1441-11 Minneapolis Childrens Foundation, Minneapolis, MN, $250,000. For capital for hospital expansion project. 1991.

1441-12 Minnesota AIDS Project, Minneapolis, MN, $10,000. For preventive education and client services. 1991.

1441-13 National Foundation for Depressive Illness, NYC, NY, $25,000. For education on diagnosis and treatment of depressive illness. 1991.

1441-14 National Marrow Donor Program, Saint Paul, MN, $15,000. For operating support to facilitate registry of marrow donors. 1991.

1441-15 Neighborhood Involvement Program, Minneapolis, MN, $12,500. For health care and social services to low-income individuals. 1991.

1441-16 Planned Parenthood of Minnesota, Saint Paul, MN, $18,000. For education and

family planning services for low-income clients. 1991.

1441-17 South Chicago Health Care Foundation, Chicago, IL, $10,000. For capital for hospital remodeling. 1991.

1441-18 Southside Community Clinic, Minneapolis, MN, $75,000. For prenatal care and services. 1991.

1441-19 Susan G. Komen Foundation, Dallas, TX, $50,000. To underwrite Breast Cancer Summit in Washington, D.C.. 1991.

1441-20 University of Minnesota Foundation, Institute for Disabilities Studies, Minneapolis, MN, $100,000. For study on effects of cocaine use by pregnant women. 1991.

1441-21 University of Texas M.D. Anderson Cancer Center, Houston, TX, $15,000. For conference to address cancer crisis in minority communities. 1991.

1441-22 Washburn Child Guidance Center, Minneapolis, MN, $50,000. For capital for remodeling. 1991.

1441-23 We Can Ride, Minnetonka, MN, $10,000. For therapeutic horseback riding lessons for individuals with disabilities. 1991.

1442
Grand Metropolitan Food Sector Corporate Giving Program

Mail Station 37X5
200 South Sixth St.
Minneapolis 55402-1464   (612) 330-4966

Financial data (yr. ended 12/31/90): Total giving, $16,000,000, including $10,000,000 for grants and $6,000,000 for in-kind gifts.
Purpose and activities: "GrandMet believes that it has a responsibility to provide support to charitable and community projects that help people in need to help themselves. Employees are encouraged to volunteer to serve in the communities in which they live and work. We place particular emphasis on initiatives that support the regeneration of inner cities and the strengthening of links between education and industry." The goal of "Children and Youth in Need: A Chance for Every Child," the GrandMet/Pillsbury program, is to prepare children and youth in need to participate in a skilled, culturally diverse workforce and become contributing members of society. The target population: children and youth in need are those young people, from birth through adolescence, who are unlikely to become self-sufficient without special assistance. The method of achieving goal: GrandMet/Pillsbury's focused giving targets three critical, interrelated components in the development of competent, productive and responsible people: 1. Necessary social, intellectual and psychological values and behaviors needed to take advantage of educational and employment opportunities and to succeed. 2. Adequate nutrition for health development and to take advantage of educational opportunities. 3. Sufficient adult support and guidance from family and other caring adults. The focus is on prevention programs for children in need, ages 0-18 in communities where GrandMet/Pillsbury has operations. Preference is shown to programs that deal with issues in an innovative way, maximizing all available resources, i.e. financial,

volunteers, and other in-kind contributions. GrandMet/Pillsbury also supports a limited number of broader efforts which undergird, supplement, and support the children's program by reducing or eliminating the underlying causes of child poverty and contributing toward the full development of children in need in the areas of health and welfare, education, arts and culture, and civic and community affairs. Most grants will be for direct services. While other GrandMet companies have different priorities (e.g. animal health and welfare in ALPO; youth education in Burger King; education in Heublein; vision correction benefits for hardship cases in Pearle; support for disadvantaged children in Pillsbury), all GrandMet companies and their employees actively support the United Way and there is an overall emphasis on disadvantaged children and youth, particulary among the food sector companies.
Fields of interest: Civic affairs, arts, cultural programs, dance, economics, education, medical research, minorities, higher education, theater, community funds, urban development, youth.
Types of support: Capital campaigns, endowment funds, special projects, employee matching gifts, equipment.
Limitations: Giving limited to areas of plant operations, particularly where there is a large business presence. No support for religious denominations or sects, academic, medical, or scientific research. No grants to individuals, or for debt financing, multi-year requests, sponsorships, fundraising events or advertising; generally no support for endowment or capital campaigns; no scholarships for higher education, except for the company-related programs. Pillsbury product donations are only made through the Second Harvest Food Bank; no promotional items.
Application information: Application form required.

Deadline(s): 1992 deadlines for GrandMet/Pillsbury: Arts/General Community - Nov. 15, 1991; Education/Training/Employment - Jan. 31, 1992; Health/Welfare - May 15, 1992; Fiscal year-end/miscellaneous - Aug. 14, 1992
Board meeting date(s): Contributions Committee meets Dec. 11, 1991 for Arts/General Community; Education/Training/Employment - Mar. 5, 1992; Health/Welfare - June 18, 1992;
Write: Kristin Larson, Dir., Community Affairs
Charitable Contributions Committee: Kristin Larson, Dir., Community Rels.; James R. Behnke, Sr. V.P., Growth and Technology; Ian A. Martin, Chair. and C.E.O.; Laura Marquardt, Secy.

1443
Grand Metropolitan Food Sector Foundation ▼

(Formerly The Pillsbury Foundation)
Mail Station 37X5
200 South Sixth St.
Minneapolis 55402-1464   (612) 330-5434

Incorporated in 1957 in MN.
Donor(s): Pillsbury, Inc.
Foundation type: Company-sponsored
Financial data (yr. ended 05/31/90): Assets, $9,089,339 (M); gifts received, $3,699,969; expenditures, $4,814,142; qualifying

distributions, $4,672,410, including $4,621,921 for 564 grants (high: $450,000; low: $23; average: $50-$50,000) and $50,489 for employee matching gifts.

Purpose and activities: The foundation focuses on prevention programs for disadvantaged children and youth, including support for exceptional programs in the communities of company operations and a limited number of national grants. In addition to focused giving, the foundation also supports a limited number of broader efforts in headquarters and plant communities that reduce or eliminate underlying causes of child poverty and contribute toward the full development of disadvantaged children and youth. Support also for health and welfare, mainly through the United Way, job scholarships through the Citizen's Scholarship Foundation of America and matching gifts, culture and art, and civic affairs and community development. Support for scholarship funds only at pre-selected institutions.

Fields of interest: Youth, leadership development, child development, child welfare, delinquency, disadvantaged, health, family services, community development, hunger, employment, higher education, secondary education, elementary education, education—early childhood, education—minorities, AIDS, cultural programs, performing arts, museums.

Types of support: Annual campaigns, scholarship funds, employee-related scholarships, matching funds, employee matching gifts, seed money, technical assistance, operating budgets, special projects.

Limitations: Giving primarily in areas where the company has plants and subsidiaries in the U.S. No support for religious denominations or sects or for health organizations. No grants to individuals, or for capital or endowment campaigns, fundraising, or travel; no loans; no product donations except through the Second Harvest Food Bank Network.

Publications: Corporate giving report (including application guidelines), informational brochure (including application guidelines).

Application information: Application form not required.
  Initial approach: Letter
  Copies of proposal: 1
  Deadline(s): None
  Board meeting date(s): Bimonthly
  Final notification: 1 to 4 months
  Write: Kristin Larson, Exec. Dir.

Officers and Directors:* Ian A. Martin,* Pres.; J. Howard Chandler,* V.P.; N. Jean Fountain, V.P.; Daniel F. Crowley, Secy.-Treas.; Kristin Larson, Exec. Dir.; Raymond R. Krause, John A. Powers.

Number of staff: 2 full-time professional; 2 full-time support.
EIN: 416021373

1444
The Greystone Foundation
400 Baker Bldg.
706 Second Ave. South
Minneapolis 55402   (612) 332-2454

Established in 1948 in MN.
Donor(s): Members of the Paul A. Brooks family.
Foundation type: Independent

Financial data (yr. ended 12/31/90): Assets, $1,037,453 (M); gifts received, $166,050; expenditures, $371,775; qualifying distributions, $352,485, including $352,485 for 119 grants (high: $100,000; low: $60; average: $1,000-$10,000).

Purpose and activities: Giving for health and medical research, community funds and a community foundation, private secondary education, animal care and preservation, and arts and cultural programs.

Fields of interest: Health services, medical research, community funds, secondary education, animal welfare, arts, cultural programs.

Types of support: Operating budgets, continuing support, annual campaigns, seed money, emergency funds, deficit financing, building funds, equipment, land acquisition, special projects, research, publications, conferences and seminars.

Limitations: Giving primarily in MN. No grants to individuals, or for endowment funds, matching gifts, scholarships, or fellowships; no loans.

Application information: Application form not required.
  Initial approach: Proposal
  Deadline(s): None
  Board meeting date(s): As required
  Write: John M. Hollern, Trustee
Trustees: John M. Hollern, Michael P. Hollern.
Number of staff: None.
EIN: 416027765

1445
Groves Foundation
10000 Hwy. 55 West
P.O. Box 1267
Minneapolis 55440   (612) 546-6943

Incorporated in 1952 in MN.
Donor(s): S.J. Groves & Sons Co., Frank M. Groves.‡
Foundation type: Company-sponsored
Financial data (yr. ended 09/30/90): Assets, $11,651,703 (M); expenditures, $433,193; qualifying distributions, $413,193, including $340,464 for 25 grants (high: $100,000; low: $25) and $12,500 for 6 grants to individuals (high: $2,500; low: $1,250).

Purpose and activities: Giving for the arts, medical research, and social services; support for education includes employee-related scholarships for dependents of S.J. Groves & Sons Co. and its subsidiaries.

Fields of interest: Education, arts, social services, medical research.

Types of support: Employee-related scholarships, annual campaigns.

Limitations: Giving primarily in the Minneapolis, MN, area. No grants to individuals (except for employee-related scholarships), or for capital or endowment funds or matching gifts; no loans.

Application information: Application form not required.
  Initial approach: Letter
  Copies of proposal: 1
  Deadline(s): None
  Board meeting date(s): Nov. and as required
  Write: Elfriede M. Lobeck, Exec. Dir.
Officers: Frank N. Groves, Pres. and Treas.; C.T. Groves, V.P.; Saundra A. Martell, Secy.; Elfriede M. Lobeck, Exec. Dir.

Number of staff: 1
EIN: 416038512

1446
Honeywell Corporate Giving Program
Honeywell Plaza
Minneapolis 55408   (612) 870-6821

Financial data (yr. ended 12/31/90): Total giving, $1,000,000 for grants.

Purpose and activities: Supports a wide variety of local organizations through a giving program that is one fourth of company's total contributions. Gives to elementary, secondary, business, and engineering education, public and private colleges, and performing and general arts, and a wide variety of programs and causes: hospices, the handicapped, the disabled, the aged, early childhood development, minorities, women, refugees, economic and job development, United Way, and civic affairs programs. Non-monetary support is given through an employee volunteer program, and in-kind gifts and services. The foundation allocates funds to the divisions for their communities, and the divisions supplement foundation allocations from operating budgets. Foundation allocations are not included in the figures.

Fields of interest: Arts, youth, cultural programs, welfare, community funds, health, education, higher education, civic affairs, education—early childhood, elementary education, community development, engineering, employment, leadership development, literacy, business, dance, disadvantaged, health, health services, higher education, hospices, museums, women, volunteerism, performing arts, science and technology, secondary education, youth, child development.

Types of support: Employee matching gifts, matching funds, scholarship funds, building funds, matching funds, operating budgets, scholarship funds, seed money, in-kind gifts, employee volunteer services, donated equipment.

Limitations: Giving primarily in headquarters city and operating locations. No support for religious organizations. No grants to individuals, or for dinners, or fundraising benefits.

Application information: Approach nearest facility; no formal process for applications. Application form not required.
  Initial approach: Proposal
  Copies of proposal: 1
  Deadline(s): None
  Write: Laurisa Sellers, Dir., Honeywell Fdn.

1447
The Emma B. Howe Memorial Foundation
▼
A200 Foshay Tower
821 Marquette Ave.
Minneapolis 55402   (612) 339-7343

Incorporated in 1985 in MN; supporting organization of The Minneapolis Foundation.
Donor(s): Emma B. Howe.‡
Foundation type: Independent
Financial data (yr. ended 03/31/91): Assets, $36,936,452 (M); expenditures, $1,822,075; qualifying distributions, $1,444,680, including

$1,444,680 for 82 grants (high: $43,500; low: $1,000; average: $5,000-$25,000).

Purpose and activities: Giving to organizations which serve the poor and disadvantaged, children, the handicapped, and victims of discrimination by 1)addressing the underlying causes of problems in the community rather than those which deal with only the symptoms of those problems; 2)focusing on the reduction of poverty by fostering individual and family self-sufficiency; 3)working to combat racism, sexism, and other forms of discrimination; 4)focusing on education of children and adults; 5)providing medical research or health services dealing with the prevention, diagnosis, and treatment of chronic diseases of children, in particular, heart and circulatory diseases and cancer; and 6)conducting research or policy analysis on the conditions that underlie poverty, in order to foster innovative approaches designed to improve the quality of life for disadvantaged groups.

Fields of interest: Disadvantaged, social services, employment, family services, race relations, minorities, education—minorities, Native Americans, women, education, education—early childhood, child welfare, youth, medical research, health services, handicapped, heart disease, cancer, AIDS, public policy.

Types of support: Seed money, special projects.

Limitations: Giving limited to MN. No support for religious organizations for religious purposes, or political, veterans', or fraternal organizations. No grants to individuals, or for capital or federated fund drives, annual contributions to general operating budgets, endowments, scholarships, conferences, deficit financing, memberships in civic or trade associations, courtesy advertising, tickets, or national fundraising efforts.

Publications: Annual report (including application guidelines).

Application information:

Initial approach: Letter of inquiry deadlines: Dec. 1 and June 1; if project is of interest, proposal will be requested

Copies of proposal: 10

Deadline(s): Jan. 15 and July 15 for proposals requested following letter of inquiry

Board meeting date(s): Mar. and Sept.

Write: Patricia A. Cummings, Mgr. - Support Orgs.

Officers and Trustees:* Richard O. Hanson,* Pres.; Hoover Grimsby,* V.P.; Marion G. Etzwiler, Secy.-Treas.; John Brown, Halsey Halls, Michele Keith, Kate A. Speltz, Flo Wiger.

Number of staff: 4 shared staff

Recent health grants:

1447-1 Childrens Defense Fund, Saint Paul, MN, $25,300. For project to remove bureaucratic barriers from medical assistance that keep low-income Minnesotans from receiving coverage. 1991.

1447-2 Clearwater County Memorial Hospital, Bagley, MN, $16,000. For Children's Center project, effort to start-up child care center in hospital, to serve families in Clearwater County. Grant made through Northwest Minnesota Initiative Fund. 1991.

1447-3 Continuum Center, Minneapolis, MN, $32,000. For start-up of Recovery of Self project, joint effort of Harrison School and Continuum Center to reduce drug use and related criminal activity by helping students develop internal behavioral controls. 1992.

1447-4 Courage Center, Golden Valley, MN, $40,000. For rehabilitation services for disabled residents of Northeastern Minnesota. 1992.

1447-5 Family Networks, Minneapolis, MN, $25,000. For new therapeutic preschool program serving children who are at-risk for abuse and neglect. 1991.

1447-6 Indian Health Board of Minneapolis, Minneapolis, MN, $20,000. For second year support for Home Instruction Program for Pre-school Youngsters. 1991.

1447-7 Learning Disabilities Association, Minneapolis, MN, $25,000. For The Next Step, demonstration program to assist learning disabled adults to advance into career-oriented jobs. 1991.

1447-8 Mille Lacs Band of Chippewa Indians, Onamia, MN, $20,000. For start-up support for culturally specific drug and alcohol aftercare program. 1991.

1447-9 Minnesota Citizens Organizations Acting Together (COACT), Saint Paul, MN, $25,000. For Health Care Campaign to mobilize campaign members in support of accessible and affordable health care. Grant made through North Area Training and Resource Institute. 1991.

1447-10 Minnesota Head Injury Association, Minneapolis, MN, $30,000. For development of Community Support Networks throughout Minnesota to assist head-injured persons and their families. 1991.

1447-11 Sexual Assault Services, Brainerd, MN, $10,900. For professional community education coordinator position. 1991.

1447-12 University of Minnesota, Institute for Disabilities Studies, Minneapolis, MN, $40,000. For pilot study of effects of prenatal cocaine exposure on learning in African-American infants. 1991.

1447-13 University of Minnesota, Minnesota Medical Foundation, Minneapolis, MN, $40,000. For research on B cell lymphoproliferative disorder. 1992.

1447-14 University of Minnesota, Minnesota Medical Foundation, Minneapolis, MN, $27,481. For Improved Hmong Health Care/Family Planning Project at Community University Health Care Center. 1992.

1447-15 University of Minnesota, Minnesota Medical Foundation, Minneapolis, MN, $19,000. For second year support for research study, The Natural History of Diabetic Nephropathy in Young Insulin-Dependent Diabetic Patients. 1991.

1447-16 University of Minnesota, School of Public Health, Minneapolis, MN, $29,500. For study analyzing whether 1987 Minnesota Parental Leave Law discriminates against working poor, single mothers and families with serious health problems. 1991.

1448
The Hubbard Foundation
3415 University Ave.
St. Paul 55114

Incorporated in 1958 in MN.

Donor(s): Stanley E. Hubbard, KSTP, Inc., Hubbard Broadcasting, Inc.

Foundation type: Company-sponsored

Financial data (yr. ended 11/30/90): Assets, $6,460,983 (M); expenditures, $353,932; qualifying distributions, $346,202, including $346,184 for 134 grants (high: $50,000; low: $50).

Fields of interest: Youth, hospitals, health associations, community funds, higher education, secondary education, cultural programs.

Types of support: Operating budgets, building funds.

Limitations: Giving primarily in MN. No grants to individuals.

Application information: Contributes only to pre-selected organizations. Applications not accepted.

Officers: Stanley E. Hubbard, Pres.; Stanley S. Hubbard, V.P. and Treas.; Karen H. Hubbard, V.P.; Gerald D. Deeney, Secy.

Trustees: Phillip A. Dufrene, Constance L. Eckert.

EIN: 416022291

1449
Helen Lang Charitable Trust
c/o First Trust, N.A.
P.O. Box 64704
St. Paul 55164-0704   (612) 291-5130

Established in 1980.

Donor(s): Helen Lang.‡

Foundation type: Independent

Financial data (yr. ended 08/31/90): Assets, $1,409,943 (M); expenditures, $410,040; qualifying distributions, $397,290, including $395,144 for 6 grants (high: $250,000; low: $10,000).

Fields of interest: Education, conservation, hospitals.

Types of support: Research, general purposes.

Limitations: Giving primarily in MN.

Application information:

Initial approach: Written form only

Deadline(s): None

Write: Rod Thein

Trustees: Andrew Scott, First Trust, N.A.

EIN: 416231202

1450
The MAHADH Foundation
287 Central Ave.
Bayport 55003   (612) 439-1557

Established in 1962.

Donor(s): Mary Andersen Hulings, Fred C. Andersen,‡ Katherine B. Andersen.

Foundation type: Independent

Financial data (yr. ended 02/28/92): Assets, $14,400,547 (M); gifts received, $1,215,000; expenditures, $1,975,337; qualifying distributions, $1,984,557, including $1,930,077 for 147 grants (high: $165,000; low: $500; average: $1,000-$20,000).

Fields of interest: Social services, disadvantaged, homeless, health, handicapped, youth, music.

Types of support: General purposes, operating budgets, capital campaigns, special projects, endowment funds, annual campaigns.

Limitations: Giving primarily in MN, with emphasis on the Bayport area and St. Paul, and in

western WI. No grants to individuals, or for scholarships or fellowships,; no loans.
Publications: Annual report (including application guidelines).
Application information: Application form required.

> *Initial approach:* Letter or proposal
> *Copies of proposal:* 1
> *Deadline(s):* Submit proposal preferably in Mar., June, Sept., or Nov.; no set deadline
> *Board meeting date(s):* Generally May, Aug., Nov., and Jan.
> *Final notification:* 3 months
> *Write:* Peggie Scott, Grants Consultant

Officers and Directors:* Mary Andersen Hulings,* Pres.; Albert D. Hulings,* V.P.; Arthur W. Kaemmer,* V.P.; Martha H. Kaemmer,* V.P.; Mary H. Rice,* V.P.; Kathleen R. Conley,* Secy.; William J. Begin,* Treas.
Number of staff: 1 part-time professional.
EIN: 416020911

1451
Marbrook Foundation
400 Baker Bldg.
Minneapolis 55402   (612) 332-2454

Established in 1948 in MN.
Donor(s): Edward Brooks,‡ Markell C. Brooks.‡
Foundation type: Independent
Financial data (yr. ended 12/31/91): Assets, $7,390,266 (M); expenditures, $332,933; qualifying distributions, $275,000, including $275,000 for 68 grants (high: $25,000; low: $500).
Purpose and activities: Support for elementary, business and medical education, physical and mental health, social services, including employment programs, community funds, visual and performing arts, including fine arts and theater, historical preservation, and programs on conservation and the environment.
Fields of interest: Education, elementary education, business education, social services, employment, community funds, arts, performing arts, conservation, health.
Types of support: Operating budgets, continuing support, annual campaigns, seed money, emergency funds, building funds, endowment funds, matching funds, professorships, research, conferences and seminars, special projects, capital campaigns, equipment, renovation projects, land acquisition.
Limitations: Giving limited to the Minneapolis-St. Paul, MN, area. No support for religious purposes. No grants to individuals, or for deficit financing, equipment, scholarships, fellowships, demonstration projects, or publications.
Publications: Annual report (including application guidelines), grants list.
Application information: Application form not required.

> *Initial approach:* Proposal
> *Copies of proposal:* 1
> *Deadline(s):* Submit proposal preferably in Mar. or Sept.; deadlines May 15 and Oct. 15
> *Board meeting date(s):* May and Nov.
> *Final notification:* 4 weeks after meeting
> *Write:* Conley Brooks, Jr., Exec. Dir.

Officer and Trustees:* Conley Brooks, Jr.,* Exec. Dir.; John E. Andrus III, Conley Brooks, Markell Brooks, William R. Humphrey, Jr.

Number of staff: None.
EIN: 416019899
Recent health grants:
1451-1 Abbott-Northwestern Hospital, Piper Cancer Institute, Minneapolis, MN, $10,000. 1991.
1451-2 Minneapolis Childrens Medical Center, Minneapolis, MN, $15,000. 1991.

1452
Mardag Foundation
1120 Norwest Ctr.
St. Paul 55101   (612) 224-5463

Established in 1969 in MN.
Donor(s): Agnes E. Ober.‡
Foundation type: Independent
Financial data (yr. ended 12/31/90): Assets, $25,151,845 (M); expenditures, $1,354,052; qualifying distributions, $1,251,882, including $1,133,118 for 68 grants (high: $80,000; low: $2,200; average: $2,200-$80,000).
Fields of interest: Fine arts, conservation, aged, youth, social services, cultural programs, education, arts, AIDS.
Types of support: Special projects, building funds, research, seed money, deficit financing, matching funds, equipment, emergency funds, general purposes, renovation projects.
Limitations: Giving limited to MN. No support for sectarian religious programs. No grants to individuals, or for annual campaigns, endowment funds, scholarships, fellowships, or generally for continuing support.
Publications: Annual report, 990-PF, program policy statement, application guidelines.
Application information: Application form not required.

> *Initial approach:* Letter or proposal
> *Copies of proposal:* 1
> *Deadline(s):* None
> *Board meeting date(s):* Quarterly and as required
> *Final notification:* 90 days
> *Write:* Paul A. Verret, Secy.

Officers and Directors:* Thomas G. Mairs,* Principal Officer; Richard B. Ober, Financial Officer; Paul A. Verret, Secy.; James E. Davidson, Constance M. Levi, Katherine V. Lilly, Gayle M. Ober, Timothy M. Ober.
Number of staff: None.
EIN: 237022429
Recent health grants:
1452-1 Clearwater County Memorial Hospital, Bagley, MN, $20,000. Toward operating expenses for Children's Center. 1990.
1452-2 Hazelden Foundation, Center City, MN, $10,000. For capital campaign for Pioneer House. 1990.
1452-3 Minnesota Alliance for Health Care Consumers, Minneapolis, MN, $10,000. Toward initiation of part-time development director position. 1990.
1452-4 Washburn Child Guidance Center, Minneapolis, MN, $10,000. Toward remodeling of facility. 1990.
1452-5 Wayside House, Minneapolis, MN, $20,000. For relocation and capital campaign. 1990.

1453
The McKnight Endowment Fund for Neuroscience ▼
600 TCF Tower, 121 South Eighth St.
Minneapolis 55402   (612) 333-4220

Established in 1987 in MN.
Donor(s): The McKnight Foundation.
Foundation type: Independent
Financial data (yr. ended 12/31/90): Assets, $1,598 (M); gifts received, $1,725,000; expenditures, $1,748,438; qualifying distributions, $1,570,000, including $1,570,000 for 39 grants to individuals (high: $50,000; low: $35,000).
Purpose and activities: Awards grants for neuroscience research, especially as it pertains to memory and to a clearer understanding of diseases affecting memory and its biological substrates.
Fields of interest: Medical research.
Types of support: Grants to individuals, research.
Limitations: Giving limited to U.S. citizens or permanent residents.
Publications: Application guidelines.
Application information: Applications for Development and Research Project Awards solicited by invitation only following nominating process. Application form required.

> *Initial approach:* Letter or telephone call for application forms and guidelines
> *Deadline(s):* Jan. 1 for Scholars Awards
> *Board meeting date(s):* Mar.
> *Final notification:* Apr. 1 for Scholars Awards
> *Write:* Marilyn J. Pidany, Administrator

Officers and Directors:* Samuel H. Barondes, M.D.,* Pres.; Ann M. Graybiel, Ph.D.,* V.P.; Michael O'Keefe,* Secy.-Treas.; Cynthia Boynton, Corey S. Goodman, Eric Kandel, M.D., Charles F. Stevens, M.D.
EIN: 411563321

1454
The McKnight Foundation ▼
600 TCF Tower
121 South Eighth St.
Minneapolis 55402   (612) 333-4220

Incorporated in 1953 in MN.
Donor(s): William L. McKnight,‡ Maude L. McKnight,‡ Virginia M. Binger, James H. Binger.
Foundation type: Independent
Financial data (yr. ended 12/31/90): Assets, $906,355,455 (M); expenditures, $39,808,384; qualifying distributions, $39,937,042, including $38,216,160 for 313 grants (high: $2,000,000; low: $1,500; average: $1,500-$2,000,000) and $50,000 for 10 grants to individuals.
Purpose and activities: Emphasis on grantmaking in the areas of human and social services; has multi-year comprehensive program in the arts, housing, and aid to families in poverty; has multi-year program for support of projects in non-metropolitan areas of MN; supports nationwide scientific research programs in areas of (1) neuroscience, particularly for research in memory and diseases affecting memory, and (2) basic plant biology (applications for these programs are solicited periodically through announcements in scientific journals and directly to institutions carrying out research programs).

Fields of interest: Social services, housing, family services, disadvantaged, homeless, rural development, child development, child welfare, women, youth, AIDS, arts, Africa, community funds, environment, energy, international development.

Types of support: Operating budgets, building funds, seed money, equipment, matching funds, capital campaigns, general purposes, renovation projects, special projects, technical assistance.

Limitations: Giving limited to organizations in MN, especially the seven-county Twin Cities, MN, area, except for special programs initiated by the board of directors. No support for religious organizations for religious purposes or biomedical research. No grants to individuals (except for the Human Service Awards), or for basic research in academic disciplines (except for stated programs in plant biology research), endowment funds, scholarships, fellowships, national fundraising campaigns, ticket sales, or conferences; no loans.

Publications: Annual report (including application guidelines), grants list, occasional report, application guidelines.

Application information: Human Service Awards are restricted to MN residents; nominations must be received by Oct. 1. Application form not required.

>   *Initial approach:* Letter
>   *Copies of proposal:* 3
>   *Deadline(s):* Mar. 1, June 1, Sept. 1, and Dec. 1
>   *Board meeting date(s):* June, Sept., Dec., and Mar.
>   *Final notification:* 2 1/2 months
>   *Write:* Michael O'Keefe, Exec. V.P.

Officers and Directors:* Cynthia Boynton,* Pres.; Michael O'Keefe, Exec. V.P.; Marilyn Pidany, V.P., Administration and Secy.; Carol Berde, V.P., Prog.; James M. Binger,* Treas.; James H. Binger, Patricia S. Binger, Virginia M. Binger, Noa Boynton.

Number of staff: 9 full-time professional; 8 full-time support.

EIN: 410754835

Recent health grants:

1454-1 Aid to Southeast Asia, Minneapolis, MN, $40,000. For start-up support for organization soliciting and transporting donated medical equipment and supplies to hospitals in Vietnam. 1991.

1454-2 Case Western Reserve University, Cleveland, OH, $170,000. For development of pilot project to strengthen health services for children in Laos. 1991.

1454-3 Center for Victims of Torture, Minneapolis, MN, $259,034. For bridge funding to expand services and establish reimbursement procedures for organization which supports and treats victims of torture by foreign governments. 1991.

1454-4 Family Resource and Experience Exchange, Minneapolis, MN, $15,000. For operating support for multi-purpose organization providing counseling, group support, information and referral and crisis intervention to low-income individuals and families in Northeast Minneapolis. 1991.

1454-5 Hope House of Saint Croix Valley, Bayport, MN, $50,000. For capital support for residential facility for people in later stages of AIDS. 1991.

1454-6 Jewish Family and Childrens Service of Minneapolis, Minneapolis, MN, $75,000. For operating support for Children's Mental Health

Demonstration Program, providing case management, community education programs and individual therapy to children and families with multiple problems attending Aquila Elementary school in Saint Louis Park. 1991.

1454-7 League of Women Voters of Minnesota Education Fund, Saint Paul, MN, $30,000. For public education project to train community leaders to monitor mental health programs in their counties. 1991.

1454-8 Minnesota AIDS Project, Minneapolis, MN, $175,000. For general support. 1991.

1454-9 Minnesota American Indian AIDS Task Force, Minneapolis, MN, $45,000. For outreach and education services to American Indians at risk for AIDS. 1991.

1454-10 Minnesota Hispanic AIDS Partnership, Saint Paul, MN, $60,798. For education and prevention services for Hispanic people at risk for AIDS and HIV. 1991.

1454-11 Sexual Violence Center of Hennepin County, Minneapolis, MN, $125,000. For capital support for building to house expanded counseling, advocacy and abuse prevention services for victims of sexual assault, their families and community. 1991.

1454-12 Twin Cities Society for Children and Adults with Autism, Saint Paul, MN, $45,000. For agency serving children and adults with autism during transition from volunteer to professional staff. 1991.

1455
Meadowood Foundation
4122 IDS Center
Minneapolis 55402

Established in 1968.
Foundation type: Independent
Financial data (yr. ended 12/31/90): Assets, $6,192,095 (M); expenditures, $363,226; qualifying distributions, $320,061, including $320,000 for 12 grants (high: $100,000; low: $3,000).
Fields of interest: Social services, conservation, higher education, hospitals, arts.
Types of support: General purposes, building funds.
Limitations: Giving primarily in Minneapolis, MN. No grants to individuals.
Application information: Contributes only to pre-selected organizations. Applications not accepted.
Officers and Directors:* Douglas J. Dayton,* Pres. and Treas.; Shirley D. Dayton,* V.P.; Ronald N. Gross,* Secy.; Bruce C. Dayton, David D. Dayton, Steven J. Melander-Dayton.
EIN: 410943749

1456
The Medtronic Foundation ▼
7000 Central Ave., N.E.
Minneapolis 55432   (612) 574-3024

Established in 1979 in MN.
Donor(s): Medtronic, Inc.
Foundation type: Company-sponsored
Financial data (yr. ended 04/30/90): Assets, $1,301,144 (M); gifts received, $1,000,000; expenditures, $1,185,016; qualifying distributions, $1,112,323, including $1,014,658

for 61 grants (high: $474,675; low: $1,000; average: $1,000-$20,000) and $94,141 for employee matching gifts.

Purpose and activities: Emphasis on physical health promotion and education, science education (especially at the pre-college level), the elderly, social service agencies, and community funds. Priority given to programs for people of color, the economically disadvantaged, or projects that use older adults as resources.

Fields of interest: Health, health associations, biological sciences, aged, education, education—minorities, elementary education, higher education, secondary education, cultural programs, arts, disadvantaged, social services, minorities, race relations, volunteerism, community funds.

Types of support: Operating budgets, continuing support, annual campaigns, seed money, matching funds, scholarship funds, special projects, employee matching gifts.

Limitations: Giving primarily in areas of company operations, including Phoenix and Tempe, AZ; Minneapolis, Brooklyn Center, Coon Rapids, Fridley, and Milaca, MN; Irvine, Anaheim, and San Diego, CA; Haverhill, and Danvers, MA; and Humacao and Vellalba, PR, or to national organizations having an effect on these areas. Generally no support for United Way member agencies, primarily social organizations, religious, political, or fraternal activities, primary health care, or health research. No grants to individuals, or for deficit financing, research, travel, fundraising events, advertising, conferences, operating support for smaller arts groups, or multiple-year commitments; grants seldom for capital or endowment funds.

Publications: Annual report (including application guidelines), grants list.

Application information: Requests from the Twin Cities to be sent to MN address; requests from other Medtronic communities to be sent to local manager who will forward them to headquarters with an assessment of the request. Application form not required.

>   *Initial approach:* Proposal with letter
>   *Copies of proposal:* 1
>   *Deadline(s):* Submit proposal between Aug. and Mar.; no set deadline; most decisions made in Oct., Dec., and Apr.
>   *Board meeting date(s):* June, Aug., Oct., Dec., and Apr.
>   *Final notification:* At least 60 days
>   *Write:* Jan Schwarz, Mgr.

Officers and Directors:* Bill Erickson,* Chair.; Janet Fiola,* Vice-Chair.; Ronald Lund,* Secy.; Mike Boris,* Treas.; Bill Hogan, Ron J. Meyer, Dennis Sellke, Mike Stevens, Steve Tranter.

Number of staff: 1 part-time professional; 1 part-time support.

EIN: 411306950

Recent health grants:

1456-1 Childrens Heart Fund, Minneapolis, MN, $20,000. For heart surgery in U.S. for third world children. 1990.

1456-2 Health Futures Institute, Minneapolis, MN, $25,500. For public and private alliance to study and promote policies/practices improving health. 1990.

1457
The Minneapolis Foundation ▼
A200 Foshay Tower
821 Marquette Ave. South
Minneapolis 55402   (612) 339-7343
*Application address for the Minnesota
Nonprofits Assistance Fund:* Susan Kenny
Stevens, Admin., Colonial Office Park Bldg.,
2700 University Ave. West, Suite 70, St. Paul,
MN 55114; Tel.: (612) 647-0013; FAX: (612)
672-3846

Incorporated in 1915 in MN.
Foundation type: Community
Financial data (yr. ended 03/31/91): Assets,
$135,224,840 (M); gifts received, $6,016,206;
expenditures, $11,696,157; qualifying
distributions, $10,610,957, including $9,123,657
for 1,514 grants (high: $4,213,438; low: $50;
average: $7,500-$35,000) and $1,487,300 for 59
loans.
Purpose and activities: "To attract and mobilize
community and philanthropic assets to promote
equal access to resources needed for every
individual, family and community in MN to reach
full potential. The foundation carries forward this
mission in the following ways: as Grantmaker,
providing direct financial resources to programs
that target immediate or emerging community
issues; as a Catalyst, mobilizing community
leaders and constituencies; as a Community
Resource, providing services to donors, nonprofit
organizations, and the community at large; as a
Resource Developer, building a permanent
unrestricted endowment; and as a Steward,
receiving and distributing community resources."
Fields of interest: Community development, civic
affairs, arts, social services, family services,
disadvantaged, race relations, Native Americans,
women, child development, child welfare, youth,
education, health services, AIDS.
Types of support: Seed money, emergency funds,
equipment, technical assistance, loans, special
projects, continuing support, general purposes,
operating budgets.
Limitations: Giving primarily in MN, with
emphasis on the Minneapolis-St. Paul,
seven-county metropolitan area. No support for
national campaigns, religious organizations for
religious purposes, veterans' or fraternal
organizations, or organizations within umbrella
organizations. No grants to individuals, or for
annual campaigns, deficit financing, building or
endowment funds, land acquisition, matching
gifts, scholarships, fellowships, research,
publications, conferences, courtesy advertising,
benefit tickets, telephone solicitations, or
memberships.
Publications: Annual report, newsletter, 990-PF,
application guidelines, informational brochure
(including application guidelines).
Application information: Undesignated funds
considered in May and Nov.; requests to the
McKnight-Neighborhood Self-Help Initiatives
Program and Emma B. Howe Memorial Fdn.
reviewed in Mar. and Sept.; Minnesota Women's
Fund considered in July and Jan.; B.C. Gamble
and P.W. Skogmo Fdn., June and Dec.
Application form required.
   Initial approach: Applicant should request
      guidelines for the appropriate fund
   Copies of proposal: 17

Deadline(s): Undesignated grants, Mar. 1 and
   Sept. 1; MNSHIP grants, Jan. 10 and July 10;
   Emma B. Howe Memorial Fdn. grants, letters
   of inquiry due June 1 and Dec. 1;
   Minnesota Women's Fund, May 15 and Nov.
   15; B.C. Gamble and P.W. Skogmo Fdn.,
   Apr. 1 and Oct. 1
Board meeting date(s): Quarterly; distribution
   committee meets 8 times a year
Write: Marion G. Etzwiler, Pres.
Officers and Trustees:* Richard W. Schoenke,*
Chair.; Clinton A. Schroeder,* Vice-Chair.; Sandra
Vargas, Vice-Chair.; Marion G. Etzwiler, Pres.;
Stuart J. Applebaum, V.P., Development; Curtis W.
Johnson, Secy.; Conley Brooks, Jr.,* Treas.; and 22
additional trustees.
Trustee Banks: First Bank Minneapolis, Norwest
Bank Minneapolis, N.A.
Number of staff: 13 full-time professional; 7
full-time support.
EIN: 416029402
Recent health grants:
1457-1 Abbott-Northwestern Hospital,
   Minneapolis, MN, $93,800. 1991.
1457-2 American Indian Services, Minneapolis,
   MN, $16,000. For expansion of outreach
   activities of residential alcohol treatment
   program. 1991.
1457-3 Cedar Riverside Peoples Center,
   Minneapolis, MN, $10,000. For staff physician
   at medical clinic, to increase primary health
   services for residents and families of West
   Bank community. 1991.
1457-4 Center for Victims of Torture,
   Minneapolis, MN, $17,500. For clinic
   manager to increase effectiveness of efforts to
   assist refugees who have been victims of
   torture. 1991.
1457-5 Eye Research Institute of Retina
   Foundation, Boston, MA, $160,000. 1991.
1457-6 Fremont Community Health Services,
   Minneapolis, MN, $10,000. For program to
   improve internal management of clinics
   through training of supervisory staff. 1991.
1457-7 Minneapolis Childrens Medical Center,
   Minneapolis, MN, $105,000. 1991.
1457-8 Minneapolis Childrens Medical Center,
   Minneapolis, MN, $25,000. For Homeless
   Youth Health Care Project, joint effort with
   Lutheran Social Services Street Outreach
   program. 1991.
1457-9 Minneapolis Heart Institute Foundation,
   Minneapolis, MN, $51,902. 1991.
1457-10 Minneapolis Youth Diversion Program,
   Minneapolis, MN, $20,000. For Teaching Early
   Acceptable Methods of Socialization
   (T.E.A.M.S.) program, to be offered in public
   schools to address problems with sexually
   aggressive children. 1992.
1457-11 Minnesota Hispanic AIDS Partnership,
   Saint Paul, MN, $10,600. For education,
   training and technical assistance. Grant made
   through Spanish Speaking Affairs Council.
   1991.
1457-12 Northside Residents Redevelopment
   Council, Minneapolis, MN, $25,000. For
   publication of neighborhood newsletter,
   mortgage foreclosure prevention, preservation
   of low-income housing, small business
   assistance and support of African American
   Men Against Narcotics (AAMAN). 1991.
1457-13 Planned Parenthood of Minnesota,
   Saint Paul, MN, $59,125. 1991.

1457-14 University of Minnesota, Minnesota
   Medical Foundation, Minneapolis, MN,
   $20,200. 1991.
1457-15 Vail Place, Minneapolis, MN, $10,000.
   For staff training. 1991.

1458
Minnesota Mining and Manufacturing Company Contributions Program
(also known as 3M Contributions Program)
c/o Community Affairs
Bldg. 521-11-01, 3M Ctr.
St. Paul 55144-1000   (612) 736-3781

Financial data (yr. ended 12/31/89): Total giving,
$17,590,559, including $3,445,951 for grants
(high: $90,000; low: $50; average: $50-$50,000)
and $14,144,608 for in-kind gifts.
Purpose and activities: Emphasis on projects
which meet one or more of the following
guidelines: projects which address specific needs
of the community and suggest solutions; offer
opportunities for enriched life, and provide
communities with the skills to accomplish
positive social goals; and seek self-support or
broad-based community support as their ultimate
goal. Support for educational institutions and
organizations, civic and community
organizations, the arts, media, culture, social
services, health care, federated campaigns, and
special projects/international activities. 3M
requests that organizations seeking grants be in
existence for at least one year. Also gives through
in-kind gifts, employee volunteerism, and
matching gifts for educational institutions and
public radio and television. Programs reflect
combined foundation and direct-giving and
in-kind support.
Fields of interest: Aged, biochemistry, biological
sciences, business, business education, chemistry,
child welfare, civic affairs, crime and law
enforcement, delinquency, dentistry, drug abuse,
ecology, economics, education—minorities,
family services, handicapped, health associations,
higher education, international relief, law and
justice, legal services, mental health, minorities,
music, physical sciences, vocational education,
volunteerism, youth.
Types of support: Employee matching gifts,
fellowships, matching funds, operating budgets,
research, scholarship funds, donated equipment,
donated products, use of facilities, public
relations services, employee volunteer services,
in-kind gifts, loaned talent, program-related
investments, general purposes.
Limitations: Giving limited to communities where
3M manufacturing, sales, and service activities
exist in AL, AZ, AR, CA, CT, DC, GA, IL, IA, KY,
MA, MI, MN, MS, NE, NJ, NC, ND, OH, OK, OR,
PA, SC, SD, TN, TX, UT, VA, WA, WV, WI. No
support for political, fraternal, social, veterans, or
military organizations, religious organizations for
religious purposes, cause-related marketing
programs, media promotion or sponsorship,
elementary or secondary schools, both public and
private (though special programs relating to
science, mathematics, economics, business, or
vocational education may receive consideration),
or subsidization of books, magazines,
newspapers, or articles in professional journals
(though publications related to 3M-supported
projects may be given consideration). No grants

to individuals, or for capital or endowment funds, emergency operating support, conferences, seminars, workshops, symposia, publication of conference-related proceedings, athletic events or associations, fund-raising and testimonial events/dinners, travel, advertising (though public service announcements may be considered), or for purchase of equipment not of 3M manufacture; 3M will not normally fund a program or project beyond 3 years.
Publications: Corporate giving report (including application guidelines).
Application information: 3M has a staff that only handles contributions. Application form required.
   Initial approach: Letter of inquiry including brief organizational history, project description, amount requested, timetable, and listing of directors and officers and their affiliations
   Deadline(s): Grant applications must be received at least 8 weeks prior to the month in which the request is to be reviewed
   Board meeting date(s): Mar., Aug., and Dec.
   Final notification: The requesting organization will receive notification of the results
   Write: Eugene W. Steele, Mgr., 3M Contrib. Prog. and Secy., 3M Foundation
Corporate Contribution Committee: Donald W. Larson, Pres. and Dir., Commun. Affairs; Arlo D. Levi, V.P. and V.P., Fdn.; Eugene W. Steele, Secy. and Mgr., 3M Educ. Contribs.; Dwight W. Peterson, Treas. and Treas., Fdn.; J. Marc Adam, Group V.P., Consumer and Advertising Markets; Ronald O. Baukol, Group V.P., Medical Products; Elva E. Christiansen, Mgr., Corp. Progs.; Livio D. DeSimone, Exec. V.P, Info. and Imaging Tech. Sector; Donald H. Frenette, Exec. Dir., Public Rels.; Harry A. Hammerly, Exec. V.P., Industrial & Electronic Sector; Allen F. Jacobson, Chair. and C.E.O.; Ronald A. Mitsch, Sr. V.P., Research and Development; Manuel J. Monteiro, Exec. V.P., International Opers.; L. James Schoenwetter, V.P. and Cont.; John J. Ursu, Gen. Coun.; Christopher J. Wheeler, V.P., Human Resources.
Number of staff: 7 full-time professional; 6 full-time support.

1459
Minnesota Mining and Manufacturing Foundation, Inc. ▼
(also known as 3M Foundation, Inc.)
3M Center Bldg. 591-30-02
St. Paul 55144-1000   (612) 736-3781

Incorporated in 1953 in MN.
Donor(s): Minnesota Mining & Manufacturing Co.
Foundation type: Company-sponsored
Financial data (yr. ended 12/31/91): Assets, $17,171,288 (M); gifts received, $506,680; expenditures, $13,911,037; qualifying distributions, $13,890,603, including $12,756,950 for 604 grants (high: $1,515,000; low: $50; average: $500-$25,000) and $601,653 for 660 employee matching gifts.
Purpose and activities: Primary areas of interest include community funds, higher and vocational education, educational programs for minorities, the performing arts, drug abuse programs, and the elderly. Support also for human services, including programs for alcohol abuse, the disabled and disadvantaged, women and youth,

rehabilitation, civic involvement, and preventive health care.
Fields of interest: Community funds, education, education—minorities, vocational education, higher education, business education, arts, performing arts, social services, rehabilitation, alcoholism, drug abuse, handicapped, women, aged, youth, hunger, homeless, Native Americans, health, medical research, environment.
Types of support: Operating budgets, annual campaigns, matching funds, employee matching gifts, scholarship funds, internships, fellowships, special projects, in-kind gifts, employee-related scholarships, emergency funds, research.
Limitations: Giving primarily in the 127 locations where the company has facilities in AL, CA, GA, IL, IN, IA, KY, MA, MI, MN, MS, MO, NE, NJ, NC, ND, OH, OK, OR, PA, SC, SD, TX, UT, VA, WA, WV, and WI. No support for projects of specific religious denominations or sects, athletic events, or conduit agencies. No grants to individuals, or for capital or endowment funds, loans or investments, propaganda and lobbying efforts, fundraising events and associated advertising, travel, publications unrelated to foundation-funded projects, seed money, deficit financing, or conferences.
Publications: Corporate giving report (including application guidelines), informational brochure (including application guidelines).
Application information: Application form required.
   Initial approach: Letter or personal visit by appointment
   Copies of proposal: 1
   Deadline(s): At least 8 weeks prior to month in which board meets
   Board meeting date(s): Mar., Aug., and Dec.
   Final notification: 3 months
   Write: Richard E. Hanson, V.P.
Officers and Directors: Arlo D. Levi,* Pres.; Richard E. Hanson,* V.P.; Eugene W. Steele,* Secy.; Dwight W. Peterson,* Treas.; J. Marc Adam, M. George Allen, Elva E. Christiansen, Livio D. DeSimone, Larry Eaton, Donald H. Frenette, M. Kay Grenz, Harry A. Hammerly, William J. McLellan, Ronald A. Mitsch, L. James Schoenwetter, John J. Ursu.
Number of staff: None.
EIN: 416038262
Recent health grants:
1459-1 Childrens Hospital, Saint Paul, MN, $35,000. 1991.
1459-2 Health Start, Saint Paul, MN, $11,000. 1991.
1459-3 Help Enable Alcoholics Receive Treatment (HEART), Saint Paul, MN, $10,000. 1991.
1459-4 Melpomene Institute for Womens Health Research, Minneapolis, MN, $10,000. 1991.
1459-5 Minnesota Medical Foundation, Minneapolis, MN, $200,000. 1991.
1459-6 Minnesota Medical Foundation, Minneapolis, MN, $32,000. 1991.
1459-7 Saint Anthony Park Block Nurse Program, Saint Paul, MN, $20,000. 1991.
1459-8 Surgical Infection Society, NYC, NY, $10,000. 1991.

1460
Wildey H. Mitchell Family Foundation
c/o Bruce Potter, Norwest Trust Dept.
230 West Superior St.
Duluth 55802

Established in 1979.
Donor(s): Wildey H. Mitchell,‡ Margaret Mitchell.‡
Foundation type: Independent
Financial data (yr. ended 12/31/90): Assets, $4,989,276 (M); gifts received, $4,627,375; expenditures, $67,451; qualifying distributions, $59,800, including $59,800 for 21 grants (high: $20,000; low: $500).
Purpose and activities: Support primarily for a community foundation; giving also for social services, including an emergency food program, hospitals, and higher education.
Fields of interest: Community development, social services, higher education, hospitals.
Limitations: Giving primarily in Duluth, MN. No grants to individuals.
Application information: Contributes only to pre-selected organizations. Applications not accepted.
Directors: Michael S. Altman, Bruce W. Potter, Robert J. Zallar.
EIN: 416222997

1461
Northern States Power Corporate Contributions
414 Nicollet Mall
Minneapolis 55401   (612) 330-6026
Additional tel.: (612) 330-7701

Financial data (yr. ended 12/31/90): Total giving, $3,512,745, including $3,182,745 for grants, $80,000 for employee matching gifts and $250,000 for in-kind gifts.
Purpose and activities: Support for community services, including the United Way, education, and health and civic affairs. Emphasis is on helping the needy and disadvantaged by targeting poverty, hunger, housing, child abuse, education, and career options. Projects supported include those dealing with crisis situations and those seeking long-term solutions. The following factors are considered when a proposal is evaluated: 1) How does the proposed program meet the Company's primary objective to provide the disadvantaged with access to opportunity? 2) How does the amount of the funding request relate to the total need? 3) Does the organization have a track record of success, stability, and sound management of human and financial resources? 4) Is there a need for the program or service? 5) Does the service target the cause of a problem or its effect? 6) Do other organizations in the same geographical area offer similar services? 7) Is there community support and involvement for the program? 8) Does the organization evaluate and measure the success of its programs?.
Fields of interest: Civic affairs, social services, community funds, education, health.
Types of support: Building funds, general purposes, capital campaigns, employee matching gifts, continuing support, emergency funds, operating budgets, special projects, scholarship funds, employee volunteer services, loaned talent.

Limitations: Giving limited to applicants within service area of Northern States Power; no support for national groups. No support for fraternal, religious or athletic organizations, elementary or secondary schools unless a specific need for disadvantaged students' is addressed, nursing homes, or hospitals. No grants to individuals, or for endowments, multiple year pledges, printing, research programs, conferences, advertising, fundraising, or travel.

Publications: Program policy statement, corporate giving report, application guidelines.

Application information: Completion of the application form is not required. The contributions staff reviews proposals on an ongoing basis before submitting them to the Corp. Contribs. Comm. which meets bimonthly. The Exec. Comm. makes the final decision for larger grants.

Initial approach: Letter
Copies of proposal: 1
Deadline(s): None
Final notification: 4 months
Write: Linda J. Granoien, Consultant, Corp. Contribs. or Bruce A. Palmer, Mgr., Corp. Contribs.

Number of staff: 2 full-time professional; 1 full-time support.

1462
Northwest Area Foundation ▼
E-1201 First National Bank Bldg.
332 Minnesota St.
St. Paul 55101-1373   (612) 224-9635
FAX: (612) 225-3881

Incorporated in 1934 in MN as Lexington Foundation; name changed to Louis W. and Maud Hill Family Foundation in 1950; present name adopted 1975.

Donor(s): Louis W. Hill, Sr.,‡ Maud Hill.‡

Foundation type: Independent

Financial data (yr. ended 02/28/92): Assets, $261,407,174 (M); expenditures, $13,482,731; qualifying distributions, $13,314,210, including $12,038,415 for grants (high: $930,000; low: $7,600; average: $25,000-$255,000).

Purpose and activities: Program directions include 1) regional economic development; 2) basic human needs; 3) natural resource conservation and management; and 4) the arts.

Fields of interest: Community development, urban development, rural development, public policy, health, social services, health services, disadvantaged, housing, Native Americans, ecology, environment, conservation, agriculture, arts, performing arts.

Types of support: Special projects, research, consulting services, technical assistance, program-related investments, seed money.

Limitations: Giving limited to ID, IA, MN, MT, ND, OR, SD, and WA. No support for religious programs or propaganda. No grants to individuals, scholarships, fellowships, endowments, annual fund drives, films, travel, physical plants, equipment, publications, operating budgets, capital campaigns, conferences, or expansion.

Publications: Annual report, newsletter, application guidelines.

Application information: Application form required.

Initial approach: Letter
Copies of proposal: 1
Deadline(s): None
Board meeting date(s): Bimonthly
Final notification: 3 to 4 months
Write: Terry Tinson Saario, Pres.

Officers and Directors:* Roger R. Conant,* Chair.; Marcia J. Bystrom,* Vice-Chair.; Terry Tinson Saario, Pres. and Secy.; Sandra Hokanson, V.P., Admin.; Karl N. Stauber, V.P., Prog.; Worth Bruntjen,* Treas.; Nina M. Archabal, W.E. Bye Barsness, Steven L. Belton, W. John Driscoll, David F. Hickok, M.D., Richard S. Levitt, James R. Scott.

Trustees: Irving Clark, W. John Driscoll, Sheila ffolliot, Louis W. Hill, Jr., Maud Hill Schroll.

Number of staff: 8 full-time professional; 6 full-time support; 1 part-time support.

EIN: 410719221

Recent health grants:

1462-1 Illusion Theater and School, Minneapolis, MN, $34,000. For symposium and subsequent educational outreach activities on Race, Prejudice and Health Care: The Lessons of the Tuskegee Syphilis Study. 1992.

1462-2 McLaughlin Research Institute for Biomedical Sciences, Great Falls, MT, $100,000. To establish development office. 1992.

1462-3 National Rural Health Association, Kansas City, MO, $193,495. To evaluate impact of Foundation grants designed to demonstrate ability of community decisionmaking projects to address survival of rural health care systems. 1992.

1462-4 Southwest District Health Department, Caldwell, ID, $90,000. For continued support for rural adolescent pregnancy prevention and parenting program. 1992.

1462-5 Washington Citizen Action Education and Research Fund, Seattle, WA, $26,000. To bring together business, labor and other constituency groups from across Washington state to discuss health care costs, access problems and possible solutions. 1992.

1463
Numero-Steinfeldt Foundation
c/o Apple & Apple
5353 Wayzata Blvd., Suite 600
Minneapolis 55416   (612) 545-0431

Established in 1951.

Donor(s): J.A. Numero.‡

Foundation type: Independent

Financial data (yr. ended 12/31/91): Assets, $219,414 (M); expenditures, $243,102; qualifying distributions, $237,400, including $237,400 for grants.

Purpose and activities: Giving primarily to Jewish organizations, including federated funds and temple support; some grants also for health and community organizations.

Fields of interest: Jewish giving, Jewish welfare, health, community development.

Limitations: Giving primarily in MN. No grants to individuals.

Application information:

Initial approach: Letter
Deadline(s): None
Write: B.M. Numero, Pres.

Officers: B.M. Numero, Pres.; O.J. Steinfeldt, V.P. and Treas.; S.J. Steinfeldt, Secy.

EIN: 416025897

1464
NWNL Companies Corporate Giving Program
(also known as Northwestern National Life Insurance Corporate Giving Program)
20 Washington Ave. South
Minneapolis 55440   (612) 342-5622

Financial data (yr. ended 12/31/90): Total giving, $5,595,739, including $1,171,423 for 636 grants (high: $216,000; low: $150), $19,000 for 9 grants to individuals (high: $2,400; low: $600), $138,251 for 373 employee matching gifts, $4,200,000 for 6 loans and $67,065 for 22 in-kind gifts.

Purpose and activities: "We believe it is the obligation of business to share its success and to use its human and financial resources to help society create a healthier, more fulfilling environment. This philosphy is woven into the fabric of our corporation and is one of the Guiding Values or principles under which we operate. It is our belief that companies sensitive in the social realm will be the companies that out-perform other firms in economic growth and financial return. Stated differently, we adhere to the view that financial returns and social goals are not mutually exclusive." The priorities are Urban and Civic Affairs, United Way, Health, Education, and Culture. In 1990 the company began an evaluation of its policies, resulting in a new emphasis on Health and Wellness, Aging, and Work and Family issues, on which more specific guidelines will become available. In addition to giving by headquarters, separate charitable contributions programs are administered by Northwestern National Life Insurance Company, Northern Life Insurance Company, North Atlantic Life Insurance Company and Merastar within their own communities. The in-kind costs represent the cost of supplies and materials and do not include the cost of loaned employees.

Fields of interest: Arts, cultural programs, museums, theater, performing arts, music, health, welfare, hunger, education, higher education, AIDS, child welfare, aged, child development, insurance education, volunteerism, women, youth.

Types of support: Employee-related scholarships, equipment, employee matching gifts, general purposes, capital campaigns, employee volunteer services, special projects, donated products, donated equipment, use of facilities.

Limitations: Giving primarily in immediate communities. NWNL makes grants in its headquarters community with additional support to organizations having metropolitan service orientation within the seven county area which includes the Twin Cities of Minneapolis and St. Paul. Grants may also be made outside of the Twin Cities where the company employs a substantial number of people. Northern Life Insurance grants are made within the greater Seattle, WA, area and North Atlantic Life Insurance makes grants in and around Jericho, NY. Merastar operates a limited program in Chattanooga, TN. Preference is first to local organizations, then national organizations with local affiliates, and lastly purely national organizations. No support for religious or political purposes, fraternal organizations,, social clubs, labor organizations. No grants to individuals, or for advertising, conferences, workshops, or other meetings, unless the meeting directly addresses a special emphasis or focus area of NWNL giving, travel, benefits, performances, testimonial dinners or other event-type fund raising activities.

Publications: Corporate giving report, corporate report, application guidelines.

Application information:

Initial approach: Proposal to nearest facility contributions manager; cover letters of no more than 3 pages should be included. Requests must be within focus areas

Deadline(s): Mar. 31, June 30, Sept. 30, and Dec. 1

Final notification: Within 10 weeks

Write: Alicia E. Ringstad, Exec. Dir.

Corporate Contributions Committee: John E. Pearson, Chair. and C.E.O.; John G. Turner, Pres. and C.O.O.; Steve W. Wishart, Sr. V.P., Investments and Pensions; James R. Miller, V.P., Corp. Devel.; Michael J. Dubes, Sr. V.P., Individual Insurance; R. Michael Conley, Sr. V.P., Group Div.; Susan J. Markovich, Pres., GIVE.

Number of staff: 2 full-time professional; 1 part-time support.

1465

Alice M. O'Brien Foundation

324 Forest

Mahtomedi 55115   (612) 426-2143

Incorporated in 1951 in MN.

Donor(s): Alice M. O'Brien.‡

Foundation type: Independent

Financial data (yr. ended 12/31/90): Assets, $2,794,193 (M); expenditures, $176,305; qualifying distributions, $144,854, including $144,854 for 23 grants (high: $25,000; low: $150).

Purpose and activities: Emphasis on secondary and higher education, including medical education and research; some support for social services and cultural programs.

Fields of interest: Secondary education, higher education, medical education, medical research, social services, cultural programs.

Types of support: Operating budgets, annual campaigns, seed money, building funds, equipment, research, endowment funds, continuing support.

Limitations: Giving primarily in MN. No grants to individuals, or for endowment funds, scholarships, fellowships, or matching gifts; no loans.

Application information: Application form not required.

Initial approach: Proposal

Copies of proposal: 1

Deadline(s): May 1 and Nov. 15

Board meeting date(s): June and Dec.

Final notification: 6 months

Write: Mrs. Julia O'Brien Wilcox, Dir.

Officer and Directors:* Thomond R. O'Brien,* Pres.; Eleanor M. O'Brien, Terrance G. O'Brien, Julia O'Brien Wilcox.

Number of staff: None.

EIN: 416018991

1466

I. A. O'Shaughnessy Foundation, Inc. ▼

c/o First Trust, N.A.

P.O. Box 64704

St. Paul 55164   (612) 222-2323

Incorporated in 1941 in MN.

Donor(s): I.A. O'Shaughnessy,‡ John F. O'Shaughnessy,‡ Globe Oil and Refining Companies, Lario Oil and Gas Co.

Foundation type: Independent

Financial data (yr. ended 12/31/90): Assets, $44,874,056 (M); expenditures, $2,495,668; qualifying distributions, $2,495,668, including $2,495,668 for 64 grants (high: $375,000; low: $1,000; average: $5,000-$50,000).

Purpose and activities: Giving for cultural programs, secondary and higher education, social services, medical research, and Roman Catholic religious organizations.

Fields of interest: Higher education, secondary education, social services, Catholic giving, performing arts, music, cultural programs, medical research.

Types of support: Annual campaigns, building funds, equipment, endowment funds, research, general purposes, continuing support.

Limitations: Giving limited to the U.S., with emphasis on MN, IL, KS, and TX. No support for religious missions or individual parishes. No grants to individuals; no loans.

Publications: Application guidelines.

Application information: Grants usually initiated by the directors. Application form not required.

Initial approach: Letter

Copies of proposal: 1

Deadline(s): None

Board meeting date(s): June and Nov.

Final notification: 6 months

Write: John Bultena

Officers and Directors:* Lawrence O'Shaughnessy,* Pres.; J. Garrett Lyman,* V.P.; Donald E. O'Shaughnessy,* V.P.; Eileen O'Shaughnessy,* V.P.; John F. O'Shaughnessy,* V.P.

EIN: 416011524

1467

Ordean Foundation

501 Ordean Bldg.

424 West Superior St.

Duluth 55802   (218) 726-4785

Incorporated in 1933 in MN.

Donor(s): Albert L. Ordean,‡ Louise Ordean.‡

Foundation type: Independent

Financial data (yr. ended 12/31/91): Assets, $23,949,387 (M); expenditures, $1,169,935; qualifying distributions, $1,186,464, including $909,464 for 40 grants (high: $145,800; low: $413) and $277,000 for 5 loans.

Purpose and activities: To administer and furnish relief and charity for the local poor, including the aged, minorities, and homeless; to make grants to local organizations performing services or providing facilities in certain areas of health and youth activities, including rehabilitation, drug and alcohol and juvenile deliquency programs, AIDS research, and mental illness institutions.

Fields of interest: Community development, aged, minorities, housing, social services, health, youth, rehabilitation, AIDS, disadvantaged.

Types of support: Building funds, scholarship funds, loans, operating budgets, matching funds, program-related investments, equipment, continuing support, renovation projects, special projects.

Limitations: Giving limited to Duluth and contiguous cities and townships in St. Louis County, MN. No support for national fundraising campaigns, direct religious purposes, or to supplant government funding. No grants to individuals, or for endowment funds, travel, conferences or workshops, benefits, research, including biomedical research, or deficit financing.

Publications: Annual report (including application guidelines), grants list.

Application information: Application form not required.

Initial approach: Telephone, letter, or proposal

Copies of proposal: 12

Deadline(s): 15th of each month

Board meeting date(s): Monthly

Final notification: Within 10 days of board meeting

Write: Antoinette Poupore-Haats, Exec. Dir.

Officers and Directors:* Arthur C. Josephs,* Pres.; Charles M. Bell,* V.P.; Antoinette Poupore-Haats,* Secy.-Treas. and Exec. Dir.; Roger M. Bowman, Howard P. Clarke, Robert M. Fischer, David G. Gartzke, Rita D. Hutchens, Marjorie T. Whitney, Donald G. Wirtanen.

Number of staff: 2 full-time professional; 2 part-time support.

EIN: 410711611

Recent health grants:

1467-1 Boys and Girls Club of Duluth, Duluth, MN, $10,000. For Smart Moves drug, alcohol and pregnancy prevention program. 1990.

1467-2 College of Saint Scholastica, Duluth, MN, $78,000. For scholarships for 38 low-income registered nursing and five low-income physical therapy students. 1990.

1467-3 Duluth Community Health Center, Duluth, MN, $52,000. For health care services for low-income people. 1990.

1467-4 Duluth Technical Institute, Duluth, MN, $10,200. For scholarships for 11 low-income Licensed Practical Nursing students. 1990.

1467-5 Lutheran Social Service of Minnesota, Duluth, MN, $170,000. For Ordean/Sharing Fund to provide medical, dental and emergency assistance to low-income people. 1990.

1467-6 Saint Lukes Hospital, Duluth, MN, $25,000. For market specialized Alzheimer services. Grant shared with Benedictine Health Center and Miller-Dwan Medical Center. 1990.

1467-7 United Cerebral Palsy of Northeastern Minnesota, Duluth, MN, $19,000. For apartment complex for people with physical disabilities. 1990.

1468

Otter Tail Power Company Corporate Giving Program

215 South Cascade St.

Fergus Falls 56537   (218) 739-8200

Financial data (yr. ended 12/31/90): Total giving, $400,000, including $320,000 for grants, $40,000 for employee matching gifts and $40,000 for in-kind gifts.

Purpose and activities: Giving for arts and culture, the elderly, child welfare, community development, the disadvantaged, the environment, the handicapped, mental health, volunteerism, recreation, minorities, health, including cancer, welfare, education, including secondary and business, and civic activities. Also gives through in-kind donations.
Fields of interest: Arts, cultural programs, health, welfare, education, civic affairs, aged, business education, cancer, child development, child welfare, community development, crime and law enforcement, disadvantaged, education—building funds, environment, fine arts, general charitable giving, handicapped, heart disease, historic preservation, hospices, hospitals—building funds, leadership development, libraries, mental health, minorities, museums, music, performing arts, recreation, secondary education, volunteerism.
Types of support: In-kind gifts, annual campaigns, building funds, conferences and seminars, continuing support, employee matching gifts, endowment funds, equipment, matching funds, renovation projects.
Limitations: Giving primarily in home and division offices in MN, ND, and SD.
Application information: Include contributors list. Application form not required.
Initial approach: Letter
Final notification: 1-4 weeks
Write: John MacFarlane, Pres. and C.E.O.

1469
Pax Christi Foundation
c/o Hutterer & Krenn
7900 Xerxes Ave., South, Suite 928
Minneapolis 55431

Established in 1987 in MN.
Donor(s): Joseph C. Pahl, Jeanne M. Pahl.
Foundation type: Independent
Financial data (yr. ended 06/30/91): Assets, $7,844,447 (M); gifts received, $2,161,650; expenditures, $211,716; qualifying distributions, $200,118, including $190,000 for 11 grants (high: $25,000; low: $10,000).
Purpose and activities: Giving primarily to organizations providing food, clothing, and shelter to needy people, including people with AIDS and children and families.
Fields of interest: Welfare, housing, AIDS, youth.
Limitations: Giving primarily in Minneapolis and St. Paul, MN. No grants to individuals.
Application information: Contributes only to pre-selected organizations. Applications not accepted.
Officers: Joseph C. Pahl, Pres.; Jeanne M. Pahl, Secy.-Treas.; Vincent K. Hutterer, C.F.O.
EIN: 363550495

1470
Pentair, Inc. Corporate Giving Program
1700 West Highway 36
St. Paul 55113   (612) 636-7920

Financial data (yr. ended 12/31/90): Total giving, $450,000, including $409,000 for grants and $41,000 for employee matching gifts.
Purpose and activities: Support for arts and culture, health and welfare, education, civic affairs and music.

Fields of interest: Arts, cultural programs, health, welfare, education, civic affairs, music, general charitable giving.
Types of support: Annual campaigns, capital campaigns, continuing support, employee matching gifts, endowment funds, fellowships.
Application information: Application form not required.
Initial approach: Letter of inquiry
Copies of proposal: 1
Board meeting date(s): Quarterly
Final notification: 12 weeks
Write: Helen Hallstadt, Corp. Office Leasing Coord.
Administrators: H.A. Hollstadt, Corp. Office. Leasing Coord.; D. Eugene Nugent, Chair.

1471
The Jay and Rose Phillips Family Foundation ▼
(Formerly The Phillips Foundation)
2345 N.E. Kennedy St.
Minneapolis 55413   (612) 331-6230

Incorporated in 1944 in MN.
Donor(s): Jay Phillips,‡ and members of the Phillips family.
Foundation type: Independent
Financial data (yr. ended 12/31/90): Assets, $65,905,527 (M); gifts received, $229,966; expenditures, $3,571,017; qualifying distributions, $3,307,808, including $3,152,410 for 228 grants (high: $1,050,973; low: $25; average: $1,000-$10,000).
Purpose and activities: Giving primarily for hospitals and medical research, Jewish religious organizations and welfare funds, higher education, social services, and cultural programs.
Fields of interest: Higher education, medical research, hospitals, cultural programs, community funds, Jewish welfare, Jewish giving, social services.
Types of support: Building funds, equipment, research, professorships, matching funds, lectureships, general purposes, operating budgets.
Limitations: Giving primarily in MN and the Midwest. No support for religious organizations for sectarian purposes. No grants to individuals, or for endowment funds.
Publications: Application guidelines.
Application information: Application form not required.
Initial approach: Letter
Copies of proposal: 1
Deadline(s): None
Board meeting date(s): As required
Final notification: 30 days
Write: Thomas P. Cook, Exec. Dir.
Officers and Trustees:* Morton B. Phillips,* Chair.; Rose Phillips,* Chair.; Thomas P. Cook,* Secy. and Exec. Dir.; Paula Bernstein, William Bernstein, Jack I. Levin, Pauline Phillips.
Number of staff: 3 full-time professional; 2 full-time support.
EIN: 416019578

1472
Gerald Rauenhorst Family Foundation
3434 Norwest Ctr.
Minneapolis 55402

Incorporated in 1965 in MN.
Donor(s): Gerald A. Rauenhorst, Henrietta Rauenhorst, Rauenhorst Corp.
Foundation type: Independent
Financial data (yr. ended 12/31/90): Assets, $13,457,377 (M); gifts received, $176,906; expenditures, $761,999; qualifying distributions, $690,000, including $690,000 for 25 grants (high: $200,000; low: $1,000).
Fields of interest: Higher education, Catholic giving, drug abuse, music.
Limitations: Giving primarily in MN. No grants to individuals.
Application information: Contributes only to pre-selected organizations. Applications not accepted.
Officers and Director:* Gerald A. Rauenhorst, Pres.; Henrietta Rauenhorst, Exec. V.P.; John H. Agee,* V.P. and Mgr.
EIN: 410080773

1473
Red Wing Shoe Company Foundation
314 Main St.
Red Wing 55066   (612) 388-8211

Incorporated in 1955 in MN.
Donor(s): Red Wing Shoe Co., Inc.
Foundation type: Company-sponsored
Financial data (yr. ended 12/31/90): Assets, $411,921 (M); gifts received, $300,000; expenditures, $297,407; qualifying distributions, $297,010, including $297,010 for 32 grants (high: $135,000; low: $200).
Purpose and activities: Emphasis on youth agencies; support also for environmental education, higher and secondary education, civic affairs, and health agencies.
Fields of interest: Youth, environment, higher education, secondary education, civic affairs, health.
Types of support: Annual campaigns, building funds, capital campaigns, exchange programs, general purposes, lectureships, matching funds, renovation projects, research, scholarship funds, seed money, special projects, continuing support.
Limitations: Giving primarily in the Red Wing, MN, area. No grants to individuals.
Publications: Annual report.
Application information:
Initial approach: Letter
Deadline(s): None
Write: Joseph P. Goggin, Secy.-Treas.
Officers: W.J. Sweasy, V.P.; Joseph P. Goggin, Secy.-Treas.
Number of staff: None.
EIN: 416020177

1474
Margaret Rivers Fund
P.O. Box C
Stillwater 55082

Incorporated in 1948 in MN.
Donor(s): Robert E. Slaughter.‡
Foundation type: Independent

Financial data (yr. ended 12/31/90): Assets, $15,999,997 (M); expenditures, $680,391; qualifying distributions, $644,915, including $612,400 for 162 grants (high: $80,000; low: $250).
Purpose and activities: Grants primarily for hospitals, church support, youth agencies, aid to the handicapped, and care of the aged; grants also for cultural programs and conservation.
Fields of interest: Religion—Christian, hospitals, youth, handicapped, aged, cultural programs, arts, conservation.
Types of support: General purposes.
Limitations: Giving primarily in MN. No grants to individuals.
Application information: Application form not required.
Initial approach: Letter
Deadline(s): None
Board meeting date(s): Monthly
Write: David F. Pohl, Pres.
Officers and Trustees:* David F. Pohl,* Pres.; Robert G. Briggs,* V.P.; Helen Moelter, Secy.; Lawrence Severson, Treas.
EIN: 416017102

1475
The Saint Paul Foundation, Inc. ▼
1120 Norwest Ctr.
St. Paul 55101-1797   (612) 224-5463

Established in 1940 in MN by adoption of a plan; incorporated in 1964.
Foundation type: Community
Financial data (yr. ended 12/31/91): Assets, $183,314,845 (M); gifts received, $14,975,374; expenditures, $14,210,064; qualifying distributions, $9,813,843, including $9,569,863 for grants (average: $100-$100,000) and $243,980 for grants to individuals.
Purpose and activities: Support for educational, charitable, cultural, or benevolent purposes of a public nature; interest in adult literacy, family sexual abuse, independent schools, neighborhood development, South East Asian refugees, cultural diversity, and access to healthcare.
Fields of interest: Education, health, health services, cultural programs, humanities, welfare.
Types of support: Seed money, emergency funds, building funds, equipment, research, matching funds, special projects, scholarship funds, renovation projects, capital campaigns, technical assistance, conferences and seminars, consulting services, deficit financing.
Limitations: Giving limited to Ramsey, Washington, and Dakota counties and the St. Paul, MN, metropolitan area. No support for sectarian religious programs, except from designated funds. No grants for annual operating budgets, land acquisition, endowment funds (except through designated funds) or generally, for continuing support; no student loans.
Publications: Annual report, application guidelines, newsletter.
Application information: Very few grants are made to individuals directly, but many are made to 501(c)(3) or educational organizations on behalf of individuals from funds designated for specific purposes. No general scholarships available. Applications not accepted. Application form required.

Initial approach: Letter of inquiry
Copies of proposal: 1
Deadline(s): 4 months before next board meeting
Board meeting date(s): Quarterly
Final notification: Within 1 month
Write: Paul A. Verret, Pres.
Officers and Directors:* Frederick T. Weyerhaeuser,* Chair.; Virginia D. Brooks,* Vice-Chair.; Paul A. Verret, Pres. and Secy.; Jean E. Hart, V.P.; Willis M. Forman,* Treas.; Tobin G. Barrozo, Nobert J. Conzemius, David M. Craig, M.D., Patrick J. Donovan, Curman L. Gaines, Marice L. Halper, Ann Huntrods, Joseph R. Kingman III, Thomas W. McKeown, Joseph T. O'Neill, Barbara B. Roy.
Corporate Trustees: American National Bank & Trust Co., First Trust, N.A., Norwest Bank Minnesota, N.A.
Number of staff: 12 full-time professional; 2 part-time professional; 10 full-time support; 3 part-time support.
EIN: 416031510
Recent health grants:
1475-1 Abbott-Northwestern Hospital, Minneapolis, MN, $10,000. For formation of Virginia Piper Cancer Institute. 1990.
1475-2 Accessible Space, Saint Paul, MN, $15,000. For expansion of services to brain-injured persons in East Metro area. 1990.
1475-3 Aid to Southeast Asia, Minneapolis, MN, $15,000. For operating budget, with preference for personnel costs. 1990.
1475-4 Block Nurse Program, Saint Paul, MN, $10,000. For operating expenses. 1990.
1475-5 Center for Victims of Torture, Minneapolis, MN, $35,000. For rehabilitation assessments for former re-education camp detainees. 1990.
1475-6 Childrens Defense Fund, Saint Paul, MN, $25,000. For project to increase access of pregnant women and children to medical assistance. 1990.
1475-7 Childrens Hospital, Saint Paul, MN, $10,000. For purchase of computer network. 1990.
1475-8 CommonHealth Clinic, Stillwater, MN, $10,000. For creation of revolving fund for Home Care Program. 1990.
1475-9 Contact Twin Cities, Minneapolis, MN, $12,750. For new staff position as part of three-year development program. 1990.
1475-10 Face to Face Health and Counseling Service, Saint Paul, MN, $15,000. For comprehensive program evaluation of Detached Youth Worker Program. 1990.
1475-11 Hazelden Foundation, Center City, MN, $20,000. For general support. 1990.
1475-12 Hazelden Foundation, Center City, MN, $10,000. For general support. 1990.
1475-13 Health One Corporation, Minneapolis, MN, $35,000. For Mount Sinai Capital Campaign. 1990.
1475-14 Health One Corporation, Minneapolis, MN, $35,000. For Mount Sinai Capital Campaign. 1990.
1475-15 Help Enable Alcoholics Receive Treatment (HEART), Saint Paul, MN, $20,000. For general support. 1990.
1475-16 Hudson Memorial Hospital, Hudson, WI, $10,000. For general support. 1990.
1475-17 Jamestown, Stillwater, MN, $25,000. For general support. 1990.

1475-18 Johns Hopkins University, Department of Neurology, Baltimore, MD, $25,000. 1990.
1475-19 Lakeview Memorial Hospital Foundation, Stillwater, MN, $10,000. For general support. 1990.
1475-20 Menninger Foundation, Topeka, KS, $100,000. For Charlee Program, for development of Over 18 Program in California. 1990.
1475-21 Minnesota Medical Foundation, Minneapolis, MN, $20,000. For bone marrow transplant research. 1990.
1475-22 Model Cities Health Center, Saint Paul, MN, $20,000. For Patient Subsidy Fund for low-income uninsured and underinsured patients. 1990.
1475-23 Model Cities Health Center, Saint Paul, MN, $13,060. For consultant expenses for developing joint strategic plan among East Metro community health clinics. 1990.
1475-24 National Foundation for Cancer Research, Bethesda, MD, $17,000. For general support. 1990.
1475-25 Planned Parenthood of Minnesota, Saint Paul, MN, $20,000. To help finance relocation expenses. 1990.
1475-26 Ramsey Foundation, Saint Paul, MN, $10,800. For implementation of fundraising strategy and training course for emergency medical dispatchers. 1990.
1475-27 SPRC, Saint Paul, MN, $25,000. For Families Together Program. 1990.
1475-28 United Hospitals Foundation, Saint Paul, MN, $60,000. For Cancer Management Center Fund. 1990.
1475-29 United Way of the Saint Croix Area, Stillwater, MN, $15,000. For health and social services needs assessment. 1990.
1475-30 Vail Place, Hopkins, MN, $15,000. For general support. 1990.

1476
St. Croix Foundation
c/o First Trust, N.A.
P.O. Box 64367
St. Paul 55164   (612) 291-5132

Established in 1950 in MN.
Donor(s): Ianthe B. Hardenbergh, I. Hardenbergh Charitable Annuity Trust, Gabrielle Hardenbergh.
Foundation type: Independent
Financial data (yr. ended 12/31/90): Assets, $3,356,186 (M); gifts received, $170,000; expenditures, $376,025; qualifying distributions, $353,281, including $344,760 for 68 grants (high: $25,000; low: $500).
Purpose and activities: Giving for health organizations and hospitals, cultural programs, social service and youth agencies, and education; support also for churches.
Fields of interest: Health, hospitals, cultural programs, social services, youth, education, denominational giving.
Types of support: General purposes, operating budgets.
Limitations: Giving limited to the Stillwater and St. Paul, MN, areas.
Application information: Application form not required.
Initial approach: Proposal
Copies of proposal: 1
Deadline(s): Nov. 15

Board meeting date(s): Dec.
Final notification: 3 to 4 weeks
Write: Jeffrey T. Peterson
Officers and Directors:* Robert S. Davis,* Pres.;
Quentin O. Heimerman,* V.P.; Gabrielle
Hardenbergh,* Secy.; Edgerton Bronson,* Treas.;
Raymond A. Reister.
Number of staff: None.
EIN: 416011826

1477
The St. Paul Companies, Inc. Corporate Contributions Program
385 Washington St.
St. Paul 55102-7359   (612) 221-7359

Financial data (yr. ended 12/31/91): Total giving,
$8,323,072, including $7,962,649 for 224 grants
(high: $500,000; low: $400) and $360,423 for
2,297 employee matching gifts.
Purpose and activities: "To accomplish its
business mission, The St. Paul is dependent on a
healthy and vital social, economic and political
environment. Therefore, it has a responsibility to
all its stakeholders to actively participate in
creating that environment. One way it does this is
through its community affairs efforts: volunteers,
corporate leadership, social purpose investments
and charitable grants." Support for Native
Americans, minority education, health, fine arts,
housing, the disadvantaged, race relations, urban
and economic development, cultural growth,
non-profit management, and programs which aid
families.
Fields of interest: Family services, economics,
community development, cultural programs,
social services, leadership development, Native
Americans, education, arts, health,
education—minorities, fine arts, gays and
lesbians, housing, disadvantaged, minorities,
secondary education, museums, theater, music,
ophthalmology, urban development, race
relations.
Types of support: Annual campaigns, continuing
support, employee matching gifts, matching
funds, employee-related scholarships, technical
assistance, capital campaigns, endowment funds.
Limitations: Giving primarily in the Twin Cities
region of MN; service centers and subsidiaries
give in their locations in AR, GA, IL, MO, NJ, and
NY. No support for religious organizations for
sectarian purposes, veterans' organizations, or
political or lobbying groups, or advertising.
Publications: Application guidelines, corporate
giving report.
Application information: In reviewing grant
requests from nonprofit organizations, the
company looks for: a clear program description,
quality delivery of a needed service, the
organization's willingness to cooperate with
others in the community, broad-based community
support, effective evaluation method, sound fiscal
policies, full financial disclosure, reasonable
administrative overhead, qualified staff, programs
in which those being served are actively involved
in decision-making and volunteer activities, and
programs which could have broader application
to the community, region, or county. Application
form required.
Initial approach: Obtain grant application
materials from Community Affairs Dept.
Copies of proposal: 1

Deadline(s): Completed application must be
submitted at least 2 months prior to meeting
dates
Board meeting date(s): Apr. 15, June 14, Sept.
16, Dec. 16; Oct. 30 (leadership program)
Final notification: 3 weeks after meetings
Write: Mary Pickard, Community Affairs Officer
Number of staff: 3 full-time professional; 1
full-time support; 1 part-time support.

1478
Sundet Foundation
7556 Washington Ave. South
Eden Prairie 55344
Scholarship application address: c/o Steve
Erbstoesser, 9231 Penn Ave. South,
Minneapolis, MN 55431

Established in 1980.
Donor(s): Century Manufacturing Co., Fountain
Industries Co., Goodall Manufacturing Co.
Foundation type: Independent
Financial data (yr. ended 12/31/90): Assets,
$3,360,155 (M); gifts received, $489,377;
expenditures, $193,340; qualifying distributions,
$186,591, including $181,691 for 86 grants
(high: $31,000; low: $100) and $4,900 for grants
to individuals.
Purpose and activities: Giving primarily for
community and social services, including
community funds and youth development; higher
and secondary education, including scholarships
to children of Century Manufacturing Co.
employees; Protestant churches and
organizations; and medical research.
Fields of interest: Community development,
social services, community funds, youth, higher
education, secondary education, education,
Protestant giving, medical research.
Types of support: General purposes,
employee-related scholarships.
Limitations: Giving primarily in MN.
Application information: Completion of
application form required for scholarships.
Deadline(s): Feb. 28
Officers and Directors:* Leland N. Sundet,* Pres.;
Louise C. Sundet,* V.P.; Scott A. Sundet,*
Secy.-Treas.
EIN: 411378654

1479
James R. Thorpe Foundation
8085 Wayzata Blvd.
Minneapolis 55426   (612) 545-1111

Incorporated in 1974 in MN.
Donor(s): James R. Thorpe.‡
Foundation type: Independent
Financial data (yr. ended 11/30/91): Assets,
$7,552,800 (M); expenditures, $397,645;
qualifying distributions, $368,070, including
$368,070 for 101 grants (high: $20,000; low:
$1,000; average: $3,000-$5,000).
Purpose and activities: Primary areas of interest
include the disadvantaged, youth, the elderly,
education, medical research, and cultural
programs. Giving for social service agencies and
higher and secondary education; support also for
community health care and AIDS research.
Fields of interest: Disadvantaged, social services,
youth, aged, handicapped, education, health

services, medical research, AIDS, arts, cultural
programs, performing arts.
Types of support: Operating budgets, equipment,
scholarship funds, capital campaigns, general
purposes, internships, research, special projects.
Limitations: Giving primarily in Minneapolis,
MN. No grants to individuals, or for continuing
support, emergency or endowment funds, deficit
financing, land acquisition, matching gifts,
publications, seminars, benefits, or conferences;
no loans.
Publications: Biennial report.
Application information: Application form not
required.
Initial approach: Telephone or letter of inquiry
Copies of proposal: 1
Deadline(s): Mar. 1 and Sept. 1
Board meeting date(s): May and Nov.
Final notification: 1 week
Write: Edith D. Thorpe, Pres., or Jane M.
Stamstad, Exec. Dir.
Officers and Directors:* Edith D. Thorpe,* Pres.;
Leonard M. Addington,* V.P.; Mary C. Boos,* V.P.;
Elizabeth A. Kelly,* V.P.; Samuel A. Cote,* Secy.;
Samuel S. Thorpe III,* Treas.
Number of staff: 1 part-time professional.
EIN: 416175293

1480
Tonka Corporate Giving Program
Interchange North Bldg.
300 South Hwy. 169, Suite 500
St. Louis Park 55426   (612) 525-3500

Purpose and activities: Primary giving is for
children in need, including toys for tots and
children's hospitals.
Fields of interest: Child welfare, child
development, hospitals.
Types of support: Annual campaigns, capital
campaigns.
Application information: Program has been
temporarily suspended.
Write: B.J. French, Dir., Corp. Communs.

1481
Archie D. and Bertha H. Walker Foundation
1121 Hennepin Ave.
Minneapolis 55403   (612) 332-3556

Incorporated in 1953 in MN.
Donor(s): Archie D. Walker,‡ Bertha H. Walker.‡
Foundation type: Independent
Financial data (yr. ended 12/31/91): Assets,
$5,858,217 (M); expenditures, $311,636;
qualifying distributions, $220,500, including
$220,500 for 48 grants (high: $21,000; low:
$1,000).
Purpose and activities: Support for programs
dealing with chemical dependency (chiefly
alcoholism); grants also for organizations that
combat white racism in the white community.
Fields of interest: Alcoholism, race relations, arts.
Types of support: Special projects, building funds,
research, annual campaigns, operating budgets,
conferences and seminars.
Limitations: Giving primarily in the seven-county
Minneapolis-St. Paul, MN, metropolitan area. No
support for private foundations. No grants to
individuals, or for endowment funds.

Publications: Annual report (including application guidelines).
Application information: Application form required.
Initial approach: Proposal
Copies of proposal: 1
Deadline(s): Submit proposal by Dec. 1
Board meeting date(s): Annually in Mar. and as required
Final notification: June
Write: Mary Powell or Joan Schoepke, Administrators
Officers and Trustees:* David H. Griffith,* Pres.; Louise Walker McCannel,* V.P.; Berta Walker,* V.P.; Walter W. Walker,* V.P.; Teri M. Lamb,* Secy.; Harriet W. Fitts,* Treas.; Louise W. Greene, Katherine W. Griffith, Dana D. McCannel, Laurie H. McCannel, Abigail M. Walker, Amy C. Walker, Archie D. Walker, Jr., Archie D. Walker III, Elaine B. Walker, Patricia Walker, Lita W. West.
Number of staff: 2 part-time professional.
EIN: 416022758

1482
Wallin Foundation
c/o Winston Wallin
7022 Tupa Circle
Edina 55435

Established in 1986 in MN.
Donor(s): Maxine H. Wallin, Winston R. Wallin.
Foundation type: Independent
Financial data (yr. ended 12/31/90): Assets, $2,244,902 (M); gifts received, $838,742; expenditures, $101,615; qualifying distributions, $83,484, including $80,150 for 54 grants (high: $13,500; low: $30).
Fields of interest: Community funds, family planning, higher education, child welfare, arts, general charitable giving.
Limitations: Giving primarily in MN. No grants to individuals.
Application information: Contributes only to pre-selected organizations. Applications not accepted.
Trustees: Maxine H. Wallin, Winston R. Wallin.
EIN: 416283068

1483
Lee and Rose Warner Foundation
444 Pine St.
St. Paul 55101 (612) 228-4444

Incorporated in 1959 in MN.
Donor(s): Rose Warner.‡
Foundation type: Independent
Financial data (yr. ended 12/31/90): Assets, $6,725,703 (M); expenditures, $307,219; qualifying distributions, $282,372, including $281,845 for grants.
Fields of interest: Higher education, religion, health, social services.
Limitations: Giving primarily in MN. No grants to individuals, or for endowment funds, research programs, scholarships, or fellowships; no loans.
Application information: Application form not required.
Initial approach: Letter
Copies of proposal: 1
Deadline(s): None
Board meeting date(s): Sept. and Dec.

Write: Malcolm W. McDonald
Trustees: Donald G. McNeely, Kevin McNeely, Kevin Richey, S.W. Richey.
Number of staff: None.
EIN: 416011523

1484
The Wasie Foundation
909 Foshay Tower
Minneapolis 55402 (612) 332-3883

Incorporated in 1966 in MN as Stan Don Mar Foundation.
Donor(s): Donald A. Wasie,‡ Stanley L. Wasie,‡ Marie F. Wasie.
Foundation type: Independent
Financial data (yr. ended 12/31/90): Assets, $12,987,430 (M); expenditures, $347,719; qualifying distributions, $347,719, including $139,520 for 26 grants (high: $37,000; low: $25; average: $25-$37,000).
Purpose and activities: Giving primarily for higher education, including scholarship funds at selected institutions for qualified students of Polish ancestry; support also for health organizations, mental health, the handicapped, and issues involving children and the family.
Fields of interest: Education, higher education, health, youth, child welfare, child development, mental health, handicapped.
Types of support: Operating budgets, continuing support, special projects, general purposes.
Limitations: Giving limited to the metropolitan area of Minneapolis and St. Paul. No grants to individuals; no loans.
Publications: Application guidelines, grants list, program policy statement.
Application information: Scholarship information available from the foundation or a participating institution. Application form required.
Initial approach: Telephone
Copies of proposal: 1
Deadline(s): Varies
Board meeting date(s): As required
Final notification: 60 days after board meetings
Write: Gregg D. Sjoquist, Exec. Dir.
Officers and Directors:* Marie F. Wasie,* Pres. and Treas.; J.J. Choromanski,* V.P. and Secy.; Gregg D. Sjoquist,* Exec. Dir.; Thelma G. Haynes, Andrew J. Leemhuis, M.D., David A. Odahowski, Ina N. Reed, Roy K. Sorensen.
Number of staff: 2 full-time professional; 1 full-time support; 1 part-time support.
EIN: 410911636

1485
Wedum Foundation
6860 Flying Cloud Dr.
Eden Prairie 55344 (612) 944-5547

Established in 1959 in MN.
Donor(s): Maynard C. Wedum,‡ John A. Wedum.
Foundation type: Independent
Financial data (yr. ended 12/31/90): Assets, $6,068,982 (M); gifts received, $95,000; expenditures, $648,882; qualifying distributions, $414,269, including $379,465 for 11 grants (high: $281,815; low: $150) and $12,280 for 38 grants to individuals (high: $1,200; low: $100).
Fields of interest: Social services, aged, education, business education, computer

sciences, health associations, alcoholism, community development, wildlife, rural development.
Types of support: Student aid, conferences and seminars, land acquisition, matching funds, program-related investments, seed money.
Limitations: Giving primarily in the Alexandria, MN, area.
Publications: 990-PF.
Application information: Student aid support beyond existing programs available through local "Dollars for Scholars" units. Application form required.
Copies of proposal: 1
Deadline(s): None
Board meeting date(s): Fall
Final notification: Late fall
Write: Mayo Johnson, Pres.
Officers: Mayo Johnson, Pres. and Treas.; Gary Slette, V.P.; John A. Wedum, V.P.; Mary Beth Wedum, Secy.
Number of staff: 1 part-time professional; 1 part-time support.
EIN: 416025661

1486
Weyerhaeuser Family Foundation, Inc.
(Formerly Weyerhaeuser Foundation)
2100 First National Bank Bldg.
St. Paul 55101 (612) 228-0935

Incorporated in 1950 in MN.
Donor(s): Members of the Weyerhaeuser family.
Foundation type: Independent
Financial data (yr. ended 12/31/91): Assets, $9,143,600 (M); gifts received, $229,744; expenditures, $503,510; qualifying distributions, $392,100, including $392,100 for 16 grants (high: $25,000; low: $10,000; average: $10,000-$20,000).
Purpose and activities: Grants restricted to support of national and international programs and services; emphasis on education for members of minority races, conservation, the environment, population control, self-help programs, and the promotion of world cooperation and understanding.
Fields of interest: Education—minorities, conservation, family planning, international affairs, environment.
Types of support: Seed money, special projects.
Limitations: No support for elementary or secondary education. No grants to individuals, or for building or endowment funds, annual campaigns, operating budgets, equipment, scholarships, fellowships, travel or matching gifts; no loans.
Publications: Annual report (including application guidelines).
Application information: Application form required.
Initial approach: Letter
Copies of proposal: 1
Deadline(s): Submit proposal from Jan. through Apr.; deadline May 1
Board meeting date(s): Program committee meets annually in early summer to review proposals; board meets usually in Nov.
Write: Nancy N. Weyerhaeuser, Pres.
Officers and Trustees:* Nancy N. Weyerhaeuser,* Pres.; George F. Jewett, Jr.,* V.P.; Elizabeth S. Driscoll,* Secy.; Walter S. Rosenberry III,* Treas.;

Lynn Weyerhaeuser Day, Julie W. Heidmann, W. Howard Meadowcraft, Bette D. Moorman, Robert J. Phares, Gregory W. Piasecki, Laura R. Rasmussen, Peter C. Titcomb, Charles A. Weyerhaeuser, Ginnie Weyerhaeuser, Nancy N. Weyerhaeuser, William T. Weyerhaeuser.
Number of staff: 1 part-time professional.
EIN: 416012062

1487
Whitney Foundation
1900 Foshay Tower
821 Marquette Ave.
Minneapolis 55402

Established in 1959 in MN.
Donor(s): Wheelock Whitney, and members of the Whitney family.
Foundation type: Independent
Financial data (yr. ended 12/31/91): Assets, $1,385,078 (M); gifts received, $23,847; expenditures, $273,869; qualifying distributions, $273,869, including $266,321 for 311 grants (high: $10,000; low: $15; average: $200-$1,000).

Fields of interest: Social services, child welfare, alcoholism, AIDS, drug abuse, education.
Types of support: Annual campaigns, continuing support.
Limitations: Giving limited to MN, with emphasis on Hennepin and Ramsey counties. No grants to individuals, or for publications, video productions, or trips.
Application information: The foundation does not consider unsolicited requests from outside MN. Application form not required.
  Initial approach: Letter
  Copies of proposal: 1
  Deadline(s): 2 weeks before designation meeting
  Board meeting date(s): Mar., May, Sept., and Nov.
  Write: Gladys Green
Officers: Wheelock Whitney, Pres.; Joseph H. Whitney, Secy.
Director: Benson K. Whitney.
Number of staff: 2 part-time support.
EIN: 416022514

1488
Wood-Rill Foundation
4122 IDS Ctr.
Minneapolis 55402

Established in 1967 in MN.
Donor(s): Bruce B. Dayton, Lucy B. Dayton.
Foundation type: Independent
Financial data (yr. ended 12/31/90): Assets, $515,747 (M); gifts received, $884,000; expenditures, $771,951; qualifying distributions, $771,436, including $771,400 for 21 grants (high: $395,000; low: $100).
Fields of interest: Arts, performing arts, fine arts, civic affairs, higher education, medical sciences.
Types of support: General purposes.
Limitations: No grants to individuals.
Application information: Contributes only to pre-selected oranizations. Applications not accepted.
Officers and Directors:* Bruce B. Dayton,* Pres.; Ann D. Buxton,* V.P.; Brandt N. Dayton,* V.P.; Lucy B. Dayton,* V.P.; Mark B. Dayton,* V.P.; Ronald N. Gross, Secy.-Treas.; Ruth Ann Stricker.
EIN: 416080487

MISSISSIPPI

1489
Deposit Guaranty Foundation
One Deposit Guaranty Plaza
P.O. Box 730
Jackson 39205

Incorporated in 1962 in MS.
Donor(s): Deposit Guaranty National Bank.
Foundation type: Company-sponsored
Financial data (yr. ended 01/31/91): Assets,
$91,676 (M); gifts received, $564,500;
expenditures, $486,061; qualifying distributions,
$486,053, including $483,924 for 60 grants
(high: $134,746; low: $200).
Purpose and activities: Emphasis on higher
education and a community fund; support also
for youth and social service agencies, hospitals,
and the arts.
Fields of interest: Higher education, youth,
hospitals, arts, social services.
Types of support: Annual campaigns, capital
campaigns, employee matching gifts, operating
budgets, program-related investments,
employee-related scholarships, scholarship funds.
Limitations: Giving limited to MS. No grants to
individuals.
Application information:
  Initial approach: Letter
  Copies of proposal: 1
  Board meeting date(s): Annually
  Write: William M. Jones, Sr. V.P., Deposit
    Guaranty National Bank
Officers and Directors:* E.B. Robinson, Jr.,* Pres.;
Howard L. McMillan, Jr.,* V.P.; Robert G. Barnett,
Secy.; Arlen L. McDonald, Treas.; William Jones,
James S. Lenoir, Lowell F. Stephens.
EIN: 646026793

1490
Feild Co-Operative Association, Inc.
P.O. Box 5054
Jackson 39296-5054   (601) 939-9295

Incorporated in 1919 in TN.
Donor(s): Sons of the late Dr. and Mrs. Monfort
Jones.
Foundation type: Independent
Financial data (yr. ended 12/31/90): Assets,
$8,350,552 (M); expenditures, $1,533,219;
qualifying distributions, $1,212,587, including
$1,089,996 for grants.
Purpose and activities: Awards interest-bearing
student loans to MS residents who are juniors or
seniors in college, graduate and professional
students, or students in special fields; some grants
to local hospitals and social service agencies.
Fields of interest: Hospitals, social services,
education.
Types of support: Student loans.
Limitations: Giving limited to MS residents. No
grants for building or endowment funds,
operating budgets, or special projects.
Publications: Informational brochure, application
guidelines.

Application information: Application form and
personal interview required for student loans.
  Initial approach: Letter
  Copies of proposal: 1
  Deadline(s): Submit proposal any time of the
    year
  Board meeting date(s): Semiannually
  Final notification: 4 to 6 weeks after applying
  Write: Mrs. Ann Stephenson
Officers and Directors:* Bernard B. Jones II,*
Chair.; Hobson C. McGehee, Jr.,* Pres.; B. Bryan
Jones III,* 1st V.P.; William M. Link,* 2nd V.P.;
Hobson C. McGehee III, Kenneth Wills.
Number of staff: 3
EIN: 640155700

1491
The Robert M. Hearin Foundation
P.O. Box 3348
Jackson 39207-3348   (601) 961-6879

Established in 1965.
Donor(s): Robert M. Hearin, Sr., Bay Street Corp.,
Yazoo Investment Corp.
Foundation type: Independent
Financial data (yr. ended 11/30/90): Assets,
$2,847,494 (M); gifts received, $450,000;
expenditures, $536,135; qualifying distributions,
$524,656, including $521,000 for 13 grants
(high: $100,000; low: $1,000).
Fields of interest: Higher education, hospitals.
Limitations: Giving primarily in MS.
Application information: Application form not
required.
  Deadline(s): None
  Write: Daisy Blackwell, Trustee
Trustees: Daisy S. Blackwell, Robert M. Hearin,
Jr., Matthew L. Holleman III, E.E. Laird, Jr., Annie
Laurie McRee.
EIN: 646027443

1492
Phillips Foundation
P.O. Box 471
Columbus 39703
Application address: 116 Fifth St. North,
Columbus, MS 39701; Tel.: (601) 327-8401

Established in 1941.
Donor(s): Phillips Foundation Trust.
Foundation type: Operating
Financial data (yr. ended 12/31/90): Assets,
$2,327,905 (M); gifts received, $1,474,185;
expenditures, $109,363; qualifying distributions,
$96,283, including $90,883 for grants to
individuals.
Purpose and activities: Giving "for the benefit of
the indigent sick, in payment of expenses for
medical, surgical, and hospital attention and
services other than doctors' bills or surgical fees."
Fields of interest: Welfare—indigent individuals,
health.
Types of support: Grants to individuals.
Limitations: Giving limited to Lowndes County,
MS.
Application information: Application form
required.
  Deadline(s): None
  Write: Atwell Andrews

Officers and Trustees:* George Hazard,* Pres.;
Hunter Gholson,* Secy.; T.E. Lott, Jr.,* Treas.
EIN: 646020136

1493
Vicksburg Hospital Medical Foundation
P.O. Box 1578
Vicksburg 39180-1578   (601) 636-5514

Established in 1956 in MS.
Foundation type: Independent
Financial data (yr. ended 12/31/91): Assets,
$9,094,376 (M); expenditures, $483,793;
qualifying distributions, $389,740, including
$373,000 for 6 grants (high: $143,000; low:
$25,000; average: $20,000-$75,000).
Fields of interest: Medical education, nursing,
medical research.
Types of support: Scholarship funds, endowment
funds.
Limitations: Giving primarily in MS and GA. No
grants to individuals.
Application information:
  Initial approach: Letter
  Deadline(s): None
  Board meeting date(s): Quarterly
  Write: Dr. W.K. Purks, Pres.
Officers: W.K. Purks, M.D., Pres.; I.C. Knox, Jr.,
V.P.; P.K. Watson, Secy.-Treas.
Trustees: H.D. Andrews, H.N. Gage, Jr.
EIN: 646025312

1494
W. E. Walker Foundation
1675 Lakeland Dr.
Riverhill Tower, Suite 400
Jackson 39216   (601) 362-9895

Established in 1972 in MS.
Donor(s): W.E. Walker, Jr., W.E. Walker Stores, Inc.
Foundation type: Independent
Financial data (yr. ended 12/31/90): Assets,
$7,733,305 (M); expenditures, $1,102,265;
qualifying distributions, $1,041,730, including
$1,005,170 for 58 grants (high: $330,000; low:
$100; average: $1,000-$15,000).
Purpose and activities: Giving for independent
schools, Protestant churches, higher education,
and youth agencies; grants also for cultural
programs, health and welfare agencies, and
medical research.
Fields of interest: Elementary education,
secondary education, higher education,
theological education, Protestant giving, youth,
cultural programs, welfare, health services,
medical research.
Types of support: General purposes, capital
campaigns, building funds, annual campaigns.
Limitations: Giving primarily in MS.
Application information: Application form
required for scholarships.
  Deadline(s): None
  Board meeting date(s): As needed
  Write: John Stone Jenkins
Trustees: Leigh B. Allen III, John S. Jenkins, Gloria
M. Walker, W.E. Walker, Jr., W.E. Walker III.
Number of staff: 1 part-time professional.
EIN: 237279902

MISSOURI

1495
Anheuser-Busch Charitable Trust ▼
c/o Anheuser-Busch Companies, Inc.
One Busch Place
St. Louis 63118   (314) 577-7368

Trust established in 1951 in MO.
Donor(s): Alice Busch,‡ Anheuser-Busch, Inc., August A. Busch & Co. of Massachusetts, Inc.
Foundation type: Company-sponsored
Financial data (yr. ended 09/30/90): Assets, $1,205,570 (M); expenditures, $1,688,391; qualifying distributions, $1,660,693, including $1,660,000 for 9 grants (high: $875,000; low: $8,333; average: $10,000-$250,000).
Purpose and activities: Support for higher education, cultural programs, programs for minorities and youth, health organizations and hospitals, and environmental protection groups.
Fields of interest: Higher education, hospitals, health, cultural programs, youth, minorities, environment.
Types of support: Building funds, equipment, professorships, capital campaigns, renovation projects.
Limitations: Giving primarily in areas of company operations, with emphasis on the St. Louis, MO, area. No support for political, religious, social, fraternal, or athletic organizations. No grants to individuals, or for hospital operating budgets; no loans.
Publications: Application guidelines.
Application information: Application form required.
  Initial approach: Proposal
  Copies of proposal: 1
  Deadline(s): None
  Board meeting date(s): As required
  Final notification: 6 to 8 weeks
  Write: Cynthia M. Garrone, Contribs. Admin.
Board of Control: JoBeth G. Brown, August A. Busch III, Jerry E. Ritter.
Trustee: Boatmen's Trust Co.
Number of staff: None.
EIN: 436023453
Recent health grants:
1495-1 University of Missouri, Veterinary School, Saint Louis, MO, $250,000. 1990.

1496
Anheuser-Busch Corporate Contributions Program
One Busch Place
St. Louis 63118-1852   (314) 577-2425

Purpose and activities: During 1991, Anheuser-Busch Companies and its charitable foundations contributed approximately $25 million to nonprofit organizations. The company as well as the foundation, supports education, health care, minorities, youth, cultural enrichment, and environmental protection. In addition, through the Anheuser-Busch Employee Volunteer Grant Program the company recognizes its employees who actively volunteer

their services to nonprofit organizations by making grants to these organizations. The company also offers an employee Matching Gift Program for educational institutions.
Fields of interest: Science and technology, alcoholism, education—minorities, education, health, minorities, youth, cultural programs, environment.
Limitations: Giving limited almost entirely to headquarters city and cities in which company has manufacturing facilities. No support for political, religious, social, fraternal, athletic, and non tax-exempt organizations. No grants to individuals, or for hospital operating budgets.
Publications: Application guidelines.
Application information: Application form required.
  Initial approach: Letter and proposal
  Deadline(s): None
  Board meeting date(s): Every 8 weeks
  Final notification: 8 weeks
  Write: Nancy Calcaterra, Contribs. Admin.

1497
Anheuser-Busch Foundation ▼
c/o Anheuser-Busch Companies, Inc.
One Busch Place
St. Louis 63118   (314) 577-7368

Established in 1975 in MO.
Donor(s): Anheuser-Busch, Inc.
Foundation type: Company-sponsored
Financial data (yr. ended 12/31/90): Assets, $65,316,788 (M); gifts received, $93,128; expenditures, $7,068,068; qualifying distributions, $6,866,214, including $6,849,899 for grants (high: $875,000; low: $25; average: $1,000-$25,000).
Purpose and activities: Giving primarily for United Way agencies and for higher education; support also for youth, community development, the arts, and health agencies.
Fields of interest: Community funds, higher education, youth, community development, arts, health associations.
Types of support: Building funds, capital campaigns, continuing support, employee matching gifts, matching funds.
Limitations: Giving primarily in areas of company operations. No support for political organizations, organizations whose activities are primarily religious in nature, social or fraternal groups, or athletic organizations. No grants to individuals, or for hospital operating budgets.
Publications: Application guidelines.
Application information: Application form required.
  Initial approach: Letter
  Copies of proposal: 1
  Deadline(s): None
  Board meeting date(s): Approximately every 2 months
  Final notification: Following board meetings
  Write: Cynthia M. Garrone, Contribs. Admin.
Trustees: JoBeth G. Brown, August A. Busch III, Jerry E. Ritter.
Trustee Bank: Boatmen's National Bank of St. Louis.
EIN: 510168084
Recent health grants:
1497-1 American Council on Alcoholism, Baltimore, MD, $60,000. 1990.

1497-2 American Council on Alcoholism, Baltimore, MD, $30,000. 1990.
1497-3 American Council on Science and Health, NYC, NY, $25,000. 1990.
1497-4 Central Medical Center, Saint Louis, MO, $10,000. 1990.
1497-5 Epworth Childrens Home, Saint Louis, MO, $25,000. 1990.
1497-6 Health Education Foundation, DC, $70,000. 1990.
1497-7 Jewish Hospital of Saint Louis, Saint Louis, MO, $25,000. For Older Adult Service and Information System. 1990.
1497-8 Jewish Hospital of Saint Louis, Walter Chalmers Reisinger Tribute Fund for Cancer Research, Saint Louis, MO, $25,000. 1990.
1497-9 Lake of the Ozarks General Hospital, Osage Beach, MO, $10,000. 1990.
1497-10 MaryGrove, Saint Louis, MO, $10,000. 1990.
1497-11 McKee Medical Center, Fort Collins, CO, $25,000. 1990.
1497-12 Queen of Peace Center, Saint Louis, MO, $12,000. 1990.
1497-13 Saint Josephs Medical Center of Stockton, Stockton, CA, $20,000. 1990.
1497-14 Saint Lukes Hospital, Roger Maris Cancer Center, Fargo, ND, $10,000. 1990.

1498
Geraldine & R. A. Barrows Foundation
c/o United Missouri Bank of Kansas City, N.A.
P.O. Box 226
Kansas City 64141
Application address: c/o United Missouri Bank of Kansas City, N.A., Trust Dept., P.O. Box 419226, Kansas City, MO 64141-6226; Tel.: (816) 556-7711

Established in 1979 in MO.
Donor(s): G.M. Barrows.‡
Foundation type: Independent
Financial data (yr. ended 02/28/91): Assets, $6,166,090 (M); gifts received, $73,266; expenditures, $309,473; qualifying distributions, $297,981, including $287,500 for 40 grants (high: $30,000; low: $500).
Purpose and activities: Giving primarily for underprivileged or handicapped children and cancer research; support also for health associations, a Methodist church, and higher education.
Fields of interest: Youth, child welfare, handicapped, cancer, health associations, Protestant giving, higher education.
Types of support: General purposes.
Limitations: Giving primarily in Kansas City, MO.
Application information:
  Initial approach: Letter
  Deadline(s): None
  Write: Stephen J. Campbell
Trustee: United Missouri Bank of Kansas City, N.A.
EIN: 431184875

1499
R. A. Bloch Cancer Foundation, Inc.
(Formerly Cancer Connection, Inc.)
4410 Main St.
Kansas City 64111-1888

Donor(s): R.A. Bloch, Annette M. Bloch.

Foundation type: Independent
Financial data (yr. ended 12/31/90): Assets, $5,494,622 (M); gifts received, $2,531,300; expenditures, $210,589; qualifying distributions, $0.
Fields of interest: Cancer.
Officer and Directors:* R.A. Bloch,* Pres.; Annette M. Bloch,* V.P.; Terry Ward,* Secy.; Linda Goldberg,* Treas.; L.E. Bloch, Jr., Roger Cohen, Dino Dinovitz, Nancy Jacob, Herbert Kohn.
EIN: 431213050

1500
The Henry W. and Marion H. Bloch Foundation
4410 Main St.
Kansas City 64111   (816) 753-6900

Established in 1983 in MO.
Donor(s): Henry W. Bloch, Marion H. Bloch.
Foundation type: Independent
Financial data (yr. ended 12/31/92): Assets, $9,065,850 (M); expenditures, $453,586; qualifying distributions, $380,140, including $380,140 for grants (average: $100-$5,000).
Purpose and activities: Emphasis on the arts, including museums, theater, ballet, and music, and hospitals; some support also for temples, civic affairs and community funds, and business education.
Fields of interest: Arts, cultural programs, museums, theater, dance, music, fine arts, hospitals, Jewish giving, civic affairs, community funds, education, literacy, business education.
Types of support: Building funds, capital campaigns, special projects.
Limitations: Giving limited to the 50-mile area around Kansas City, MO, including KS. No grants to individuals.
Application information: Contributes only to pre-selected organizations. Applications not accepted.
  Board meeting date(s): Dec.
  Write: Robert L. Bloch, V.P.
Officers and Directors:* Henry W. Bloch,* Pres. and C.E.O.; Robert L. Bloch,* V.P. and Secy.-Treas.; Marion H. Bloch,* V.P.; Thomas M. Bloch, Mary Jo Brown, Edward A. Smith, Elizabeth Bloch Uhlmann.
Number of staff: 2 part-time professional.
EIN: 431329803

1501
H & R Block Corporate Giving Program
4410 Main St.
Kansas City 64111   (816) 753-6900

Financial data (yr. ended 12/31/90): Total giving, $785,471, including $747,181 for 309 grants (high: $133,200; low: $50; average: $50-$20,000) and $38,290 for 113 employee matching gifts.
Purpose and activities: "Contributions made through the corporation are only to those organizations which cannot receive funds from the H & R Block Foundation, namely 501(c)(4) organizations or other private foundations. These contributions are limited and do not represent a significant sum.". Main support for arts, health, civic affairs, education, and youth.

Fields of interest: Arts, community development, AIDS, cultural programs, health, education—early childhood, homeless, Jewish giving, civic affairs, dance, employment, higher education, housing, aged, education, minorities, religious schools, secondary education, theater, vocational education, music, race relations, social services, urban development, youth.
Types of support: Annual campaigns, employee matching gifts, equipment, operating budgets, seed money, building funds, special projects, capital campaigns, continuing support, employee-related scholarships, program-related investments, emergency funds, general purposes, land acquisition, matching funds.
Limitations: Giving primarily in greater Kansas City area. No grants for organizations able to apply for funds through the H & R Block Foundation.
Publications: Corporate report, program policy statement, application guidelines, informational brochure (including application guidelines).
Application information: Application form not required.
  Initial approach: Letter; Send to headquarters
  Copies of proposal: 1
  Deadline(s): 45 days prior to quarterly board meetings- Mar., June, Sept., and Dec.
  Board meeting date(s): Quarterly
  Final notification: 2 weeks after board meeting
  Write: Barbara Allmon, Pres., H & R Block Fdn.
Number of staff: 2 full-time professional; 1 part-time professional; 2 full-time support.

1502
The H & R Block Foundation
4410 Main St.
Kansas City 64111   (816) 753-6900

Incorporated in 1974 in MO.
Donor(s): H & R Block, Inc.
Foundation type: Company-sponsored
Financial data (yr. ended 12/31/90): Assets, $17,707,624 (M); gifts received, $3,008,000; expenditures, $924,037; qualifying distributions, $829,725, including $684,076 for 140 grants (high: $133,200; low: $100), $63,105 for 32 grants to individuals (high: $2,000; low: $1,321) and $38,290 for 94 employee matching gifts.
Purpose and activities: Giving primarily for education, arts and culture, United Way, youth, neighborhood development, health, including AIDS programs and mental health, and civic endeavors; scholarships for children of company employees only.
Fields of interest: Higher education, secondary education, arts, cultural programs, community development, urban development, youth, social services, health services, AIDS.
Types of support: General purposes, building funds, equipment, land acquisition, matching funds, employee matching gifts, program-related investments, employee-related scholarships, operating budgets, continuing support, annual campaigns, seed money, emergency funds, capital campaigns, special projects.
Limitations: Giving limited to the 50-mile area around Kansas City, MO, including KS. No support for religious purposes, single-disease agencies, or historic preservation projects. No grants to individuals (except for scholarships to children of company employees), or for

endowment funds, travel, telethons, research, demonstration projects, publications, or conferences; no loans.
Publications: Informational brochure (including application guidelines), annual report.
Application information: Application form not required.
  Initial approach: 1- to 2-page letter
  Copies of proposal: 1
  Deadline(s): 45 days prior to meetings
  Board meeting date(s): Mar., June, Sept., and Dec.
  Final notification: 2 weeks after board meeting
  Write: Barbara Allmon, Pres.
Officers and Directors:* Henry W. Bloch,* Chair. and Treas.; Edward A. Smith,* Vice-Chair.; Barbara Allmon, Pres.; Robert L. Bloch, Secy.; Charles E. Curran, Morton I. Sosland.
Number of staff: 4 full-time professional; 2 full-time support.
EIN: 237378232

1503
Brown Group, Inc. Charitable Trust
8400 Maryland Ave.
Clayton 63105   (314) 854-4120

Trust established in 1951 in MO.
Donor(s): Brown Group, Inc.
Foundation type: Company-sponsored
Financial data (yr. ended 09/30/90): Assets, $4,747,867 (M); expenditures, $1,182,304; qualifying distributions, $1,159,323, including $1,156,767 for 411 grants (high: $125,000; low: $50; average: $100-$20,000).
Fields of interest: Community funds, hospitals, higher education, arts, youth, cultural programs.
Types of support: General purposes, operating budgets, continuing support, annual campaigns, emergency funds, building funds, equipment, land acquisition, employee matching gifts, scholarship funds, renovation projects.
Limitations: Giving limited to areas of company's major operations, with emphasis on St. Louis, MO. No grants to individuals, or for endowment funds, special projects, research, publications, or conferences; no loans.
Application information: Application form not required.
  Initial approach: Proposal
  Copies of proposal: 1
  Deadline(s): None
  Board meeting date(s): As needed
  Final notification: 1 to 3 months
  Write: Harry E. Rich, C.F.O., Brown Group, Inc.
Control Committee and Trustees:* Eugene F. Jordan, Secy.; B.A. Bridgewater, Jr.,* Member; W.L. Hadley Griffin,* Member; Harry E. Rich,* Member; Andrew M. Rosen, Member.
Trustee Bank: Boatmen's Trust Co.
Number of staff: 2 shared staff
EIN: 237443082

1504
The Commerce Bancshares Foundation
(Formerly The Commerce Foundation)
P.O. Box 13686
Kansas City 64199

Incorporated in 1952 in MO.

Donor(s): Commerce Bank of Kansas City, N.A., Commerce Bank of St. Louis, N.A., Commerce Bank of Springfield, and other affiliates.
Foundation type: Company-sponsored
Financial data (yr. ended 12/31/90): Assets, $4,709,368 (M); gifts received, $371,067; expenditures, $652,885; qualifying distributions, $644,520, including $644,520 for 245 grants (high: $30,750; low: $100).
Purpose and activities: Support for the fine and performing arts, including music; education, especially business and higher education and economics; youth and child development; community funds; and health and hospitals.
Fields of interest: Arts, fine arts, performing arts, education, higher education, child development, youth, community funds, health, hospitals.
Types of support: Continuing support, annual campaigns, seed money, building funds, endowment funds, special projects, professorships, general purposes, capital campaigns.
Limitations: Giving primarily in MO. No grants to individuals, or for operating budgets or matching gifts; no loans.
Application information:
 Initial approach: Letter
 Copies of proposal: 1
 Deadline(s): None
 Board meeting date(s): As required
 Write: Warren W. Weaver, Pres.
Officers and Directors:* Warren W. Weaver,* Pres.; Charles E. Templer, V.P. and Treas.; T. Alan Peschka,* Secy.; David W. Kemper, James M. Kemper, Jr.
Number of staff: None.
EIN: 446012453

1505
Community Foundation, Inc.
(Formerly Community Foundation of Greene County, Inc.)
901 St. Louis St., Suite 303
Springfield 65806   (417) 864-6199

Incorporated as a community foundation in 1973 in MO.
Foundation type: Community
Financial data (yr. ended 06/30/91): Assets, $3,128,836 (M); gifts received, $717,857; expenditures, $154,696; qualifying distributions, $127,219, including $127,219 for grants.
Purpose and activities: "To serve as a vehicle for the establishment of charitable funds in the community. A scholarship is offered to high school graduates of Greene County schools. Grants are made to nonprofit organizations."
Fields of interest: Higher education, secondary education, performing arts, museums, health, recreation, community development, youth, social services, family services, child welfare, alcoholism, leadership development, aged, homeless.
Types of support: Conferences and seminars, emergency funds, matching funds, renovation projects, scholarship funds, seed money.
Limitations: Giving primarily in southwest MO. No grants for capital campaigns or operating expenses.
Publications: Annual report, newsletter, application guidelines, informational brochure.

Application information: Application form required.
 Initial approach: Letter (1 page)
 Copies of proposal: 10
 Deadline(s): No set deadline, but grant recommendations are made in Nov. and May
 Board meeting date(s): 4th Tuesday of most months
 Final notification: Late May and late Nov.
 Write: Jan Horton, Exec. Dir.
Officers: John Courtney, Pres.; Pat Walker, V.P.; Art Haseltine, Secy.; Ken Carter, Treas.
Number of staff: 1 full-time professional; 1 part-time support.
EIN: 237290968

1506
The Contico International, Inc. Charitable Trust
1101 North Warson Rd.
St. Louis 63132   (314) 997-5900

Established in 1988 in MO.
Donor(s): Contico International, Inc.
Foundation type: Company-sponsored
Financial data (yr. ended 12/31/90): Assets, $2,468 (M); gifts received, $271,558; expenditures, $271,953; qualifying distributions, $271,833, including $271,833 for 23 grants (high: $100,000; low: $250).
Purpose and activities: Support primarily for medical research, hospitals, and Jewish welfare.
Fields of interest: Medical research, Jewish welfare.
Limitations: Giving primarily in St. Louis, MO. No grants to individuals.
Application information:
 Initial approach: Proposal
 Deadline(s): None
 Write: Lester Miller, Trustee
Trustee: Lester Miller.
EIN: 436353680

1507
Louetta M. Cowden Foundation
c/o Boatmen's First National Bank of Kansas City
14 West Tenth St.
Kansas City 64105   (816) 691-7481
Mailing address: P.O. Box 419038, Kansas City, MO 64183

Trust established in 1964 in MO.
Donor(s): Louetta M. Cowden.‡
Foundation type: Independent
Financial data (yr. ended 12/31/90): Assets, $6,043,636 (M); expenditures, $383,555; qualifying distributions, $342,469, including $335,000 for 7 grants (high: $100,000; low: $10,000; average: $10,000-$50,000).
Purpose and activities: Support for children's welfare and hospitals, with emphasis on capital fund grants.
Fields of interest: Child welfare, hospitals, museums, welfare.
Types of support: Building funds, equipment, land acquisition, seed money, emergency funds, capital campaigns, special projects.
Limitations: Giving limited to the metropolitan Kansas City, MO, area. No grants to individuals, or for endowment funds, scholarships, fellowships, or matching gifts; no loans.

Publications: 990-PF, application guidelines.
Application information: Application form not required.
 Initial approach: Telephone or letter (no more than 3 pages)
 Copies of proposal: 1
 Deadline(s): None
 Board meeting date(s): Mar., June, Sept., and Dec.
 Final notification: 2 months
 Write: David P. Ross, Sr. V.P., Boatmen's First National Bank of Kansas City
Trustees: Menefee D. Blackwell, Arthur H. Bowen, Jr., Boatmen's First National Bank of Kansas City.
Number of staff: 1 full-time professional.
EIN: 436052617

1508
CPI Corporate Giving Program
1706 Washington Ave.
St. Louis 63103   (314) 231-1575

Financial data (yr. ended 02/02/91): Total giving, $1,172,102, including $518,430 for 93 grants (high: $30,000; low: $100), $116,019 for 115 employee matching gifts and $537,653 for 102 in-kind gifts.
Purpose and activities: Support for education, including literacy, vocational, secondary and higher education, educational building funds, and minority education; culture and the arts, including museums, theater, and libraries; Jewish welfare; social services, including programs involving senior citizens, the handicapped, the disadvantaged, child welfare, and hunger; health, and hospitals.
Fields of interest: Arts, business education, child welfare, community funds, cultural programs, disadvantaged, education—building funds, education—minorities, handicapped, higher education, hospitals, hunger, Jewish welfare, libraries, mental health, museums, music, performing arts, race relations, social services, theater, welfare, youth, education, child development, general charitable giving, secondary education, minorities, Jewish giving, literacy, vocational education, education, child development, general charitable giving, secondary education, minorities, Jewish giving, literacy, vocational education.
Types of support: Employee-related scholarships, employee matching gifts, donated equipment, donated products, loaned talent, annual campaigns, operating budgets, in-kind gifts, capital campaigns, continuing support, general purposes, matching funds.
Limitations: Giving primarily in the metropolitan St. Louis, MO, area.
Publications: Corporate report, application guidelines, program policy statement.
Application information: Application form not required.
 Initial approach: Letter; send requests to headquarters
 Copies of proposal: 1
 Deadline(s): None
 Board meeting date(s): As needed
 Write: Fran Scheper, V.P., Human Resources
Number of staff: 1 part-time professional; 1 part-time support.

1509
The E. L. Craig Foundation, Inc.
P.O. Box 1404
Joplin 64802　　　　　　　　(417) 624-6644

Incorporated in 1960 in MO.
Donor(s): Tamko Asphalt Products, Inc., Royal Brand Roofing, Inc.
Foundation type: Independent
Financial data (yr. ended 07/31/90): Assets, $4,689,747 (M); gifts received, $100,000; expenditures, $318,617; qualifying distributions, $306,300, including $306,300 for 31 grants (high: $100,000; low: $100).
Purpose and activities: Interests include higher education, economics, freedom-liberty programs, youth agencies, hospitals, and cancer research.
Fields of interest: Higher education, economics, freedom, youth, hospitals, cancer.
Limitations: Giving primarily in Joplin, MO, and Washington, DC. No grants to individuals.
Application information: Contributes only to pre-selected organizations. Applications not accepted.
　Write: J.P. Humphreys, Pres.
Officers: J.P. Humphreys, Pres.; David Craig Humphreys, V.P.; Ethelmae Craig Humphreys, Secy.-Treas.
EIN: 446015127

1510
The Danforth Foundation ▼
231 South Bemiston Ave., Suite 1080
St. Louis 63105-1996　　　　　(314) 862-6200

Incorporated in 1927 in MO.
Donor(s): William H. Danforth,‡ Mrs. William H. Danforth.‡
Foundation type: Independent
Financial data (yr. ended 05/31/91): Assets, $254,897,016 (M); expenditures, $7,196,613; qualifying distributions, $7,140,789, including $5,121,266 for 105 grants (high: $625,000; low: $1,000; average: $30,000-$105,000), $89,600 for 63 employee matching gifts and $1,229,586 for 6 foundation-administered programs.
Purpose and activities: Dedicated to enhancing the humane dimensions of life through activities which emphasize the theme of improving the quality of teaching and learning. Serves pre-collegiate education through grantmaking and program activities, particularly those in support of administrators and legislators who are formulating public policy on elementary and secondary public education.
Fields of interest: Education, elementary education, secondary education, education—minorities, public policy.
Types of support: Consulting services, technical assistance, special projects.
Limitations: No support for colleges and universities (except for projects in elementary and secondary education). No grants to individuals, or for building or endowment funds, or operating budgets; no loans.
Publications: Annual report, informational brochure (including application guidelines), financial statement, grants list.
Application information: Grant proposals for higher education not accepted; fellowship applications available only through participating universities. Application form not required.

Initial approach: Letter
Copies of proposal: 1
Deadline(s): None
Board meeting date(s): May and Nov., and as required
Final notification: 4 weeks
Write: Dr. Bruce J. Anderson, Pres.
Officers and Trustees:* William H. Danforth,* Chair.; James R. Compton,* Vice-Chair. and Secy.; Bruce J. Anderson,* Pres.; Melvin C. Bahle, Treas.; Kathryn Nelson, Prog. Dir.; Peter Wilson, Prog. Dir.; Gary Wright, Prog. Dir.; John H. Biggs, Virginia S. Brown, Donald C. Danforth, Jr., Charles Guggenheim, George E. Pake, P. Roy Vagelos.
Number of staff: 4 full-time professional; 3 full-time support; 1 part-time support.
EIN: 430653297
Recent health grants:
1510-1 Florida Department of Health and Rehabilitative Services, Miami, FL, $75,000. For school and community coalition for child development project in South Miami Beach schools. 1992.
1510-2 Missouri, State of, Department of Mental Health, Jefferson City, MO, $58,500. For Caring Communities Project. 1992.
1510-3 Saint Louis County Department of Community Health and Medical Care, Clayton, MO, $26,976. For teenage health consultant program. 1992.
1510-4 Saint Louis County Department of Community Health and Medical Care, Clayton, MO, $24,000. For teenage health consultant program. 1991.

1511
Marion Merrell Dow Foundation
c/o Marion Merrell Dow, Inc.
9300 Ward Pkwy.
Kansas City 64114-3321　　　　(816) 966-4000

Established in 1988.
Donor(s): Merrell Dow Pharmaceuticals, Inc.
Foundation type: Company-sponsored
Financial data (yr. ended 06/30/91): Assets, $11,300,098 (M); gifts received, $180,500; expenditures, $462,095; qualifying distributions, $420,016, including $392,500 for grants.
Fields of interest: Medical research, medical education.
Limitations: Giving primarily in Kansas City, MO. No grants to individuals.
Application information:
Initial approach: Letter (1 or 2 pages)
Deadline(s): None
Write: Community Affairs Dept.
Officers and Trustees:* Robert B. Rogers,* Pres. and Treas.; John Deadwyler, V.P.; William K. Hoskins,* V.P.; Ken Lohr, V.P.; Charles D. Dalton, Secy.
EIN: 431503440

1512
Harry Edison Foundation ▼
501 North Broadway
St. Louis 63102-2196　　　　　(314) 331-6540

Incorporated in 1949 in IL.
Donor(s): Harry Edison.‡
Foundation type: Independent

Financial data (yr. ended 12/31/90): Assets, $29,604,573 (M); expenditures, $1,711,462; qualifying distributions, $1,531,171, including $1,529,650 for grants (average: $1,000-$50,000).
Purpose and activities: Support primarily for higher education, Jewish welfare funds, children's services, social services, cultural programs, hospitals, and medical research.
Fields of interest: Higher education, medical education, hospitals, medical research, Jewish welfare, social services, family planning, youth, cultural programs.
Types of support: Professorships, building funds, annual campaigns.
Limitations: Giving primarily in St. Louis, MO. No grants to individuals.
Application information: Contributes only to pre-selected organizations. Applications not accepted.
Board meeting date(s): As required
Write: Eric P. Newman, Pres.
Officers and Directors:* Eric P. Newman,* Pres.; Bernard Edison,* V.P. and Secy.; Henry Kohn.
Number of staff: None.
EIN: 436027017

1513
Irving and Beatrice C. Edison Foundation, Inc.
501 North Broadway
St. Louis 63102-2102

Established in 1961.
Donor(s): Irving Edison, Bernard Edison.
Foundation type: Independent
Financial data (yr. ended 07/31/91): Assets, $2,106,414 (M); expenditures, $69,321; qualifying distributions, $56,361, including $52,648 for 29 grants (high: $14,500; low: $25).
Purpose and activities: Giving primarily to higher and other education and hospitals; support also for Jewish organizations and a community fund.
Fields of interest: Higher education, education, hospitals, Jewish giving, community funds.
Limitations: Giving primarily in St. Louis, MO. No grants to individuals.
Application information: Contributes only to pre-selected organizations. Applications not accepted.
Officers and Directors:* Bernard Edison,* Pres.; Marilyn Edison,* V.P.; Peter A. Edison,* Secy.
EIN: 436027018

1514
Emerson Charitable Trust ▼
c/o Emerson Electric Co.
8000 West Florissant, P.O. Box 4100
St. Louis 63136　　　　　　　(314) 553-2000

Established in 1944 in MO as Emerson Electric Manufacturing Company Charitable Trust; present name adopted in 1981.
Donor(s): Emerson Electric Co.
Foundation type: Company-sponsored
Financial data (yr. ended 09/30/90): Assets, $15,832,764 (M); gifts received, $3,947,212; expenditures, $8,324,419; qualifying distributions, $7,998,886, including $7,836,220 for 1,744 grants (high: $750,000; low: $25; average: $100-$10,000) and $155,375 for 111 grants to individuals.

Purpose and activities: Grants for community funds, higher education, cultural programs, hospitals and health agencies, public policy organizations, and youth agencies.
Fields of interest: Education, higher education, community funds, cultural programs, hospitals, health services, public policy, youth.
Types of support: Employee matching gifts, employee-related scholarships.
Limitations: Giving primarily in areas of company operations.
Application information: Application form required.
  Initial approach: Letter
  Deadline(s): None
  Board meeting date(s): Distribution committee meets 3 times a year
  Write: R.W. Staley, Chair.
Officer: R.W. Staley, Chair. and Exec. V.P.
Trustee: Boatmen's Trust Co.
Number of staff: None.
EIN: 526200123

1515
Emerson Electric Corporate Contributions Program
c/o Emerson Electric Co.
8000 West Florissant, P.O. Box 4100
St. Louis 63136   (314) 553-2000

Purpose and activities: Supports education, through higher education and business and engineering education; health through hospitals, and research; social services, through the United Way, youth and family programs; arts and humanities, through the performing arts and historic preservation; and public affairs. The corporate contributions and the foundation support the same programs. At times very small grants may come through the divisions themselves, but generally giving is handled by headquarters.
Fields of interest: Education, higher education, business education, engineering, health, hospitals, medical research, social services, community funds, youth, family services, arts, humanities, performing arts, historic preservation.
Limitations: Giving primarily in St. Louis, MO, and operating areas.
Application information: Divisions recommend grants to headquarters. Whether a grant will be from the foundation or a direct contribution is decided after the grant is awarded. Application form required.
  Initial approach: Approach nearest operation
  Deadline(s): None
  Write: Jo Ann Harmon, V.P., Corp. Admin.

1516
Enright Foundation, Inc.
7508 Main
Kansas City 64114

Established in 1965.
Donor(s): Joseph J. Enright.
Foundation type: Independent
Financial data (yr. ended 03/31/91): Assets, $3,223,355 (M); gifts received, $861; expenditures, $187,333; qualifying distributions, $159,052, including $148,455 for 38 grants (high: $30,000; low: $100).

Fields of interest: Hospitals, Catholic giving, child welfare, social services.
Types of support: General purposes.
Limitations: Giving primarily in MO. No grants to individuals, or for scholarships or awards.
Application information: Contributes only to pre-selected organizations. Applications not accepted.
Officers and Directors:* Anna M. Cassidy,* Pres.; L.J. Cassidy,* V.P.; Thomas E. King,* Secy.; Kathleen Cassidy,* Treas.
EIN: 436067639

1517
Farmland Industries Corporate Contributions Program
3315 North Oak Traffic Way
P.O. Box 7305
Kansas City 64116   (816) 459-6352

Financial data (yr. ended 08/31/90): Total giving, $250,000, including $240,000 for grants and $10,000 for in-kind gifts.
Purpose and activities: Support for education, social services, United Way, arts and culture, youth programs and agencies, health agencies, and agricultural programs.
Fields of interest: Youth, agriculture, social services, education, arts, cultural programs, health.
Types of support: Annual campaigns, capital campaigns, continuing support.
Limitations: Giving primarily in headquarters city and major operating areas in MO.
Application information:
  Initial approach: Letter of inquiry
  Write: Fran Quinn, Mgr., Member Relations
Number of staff: 1 full-time professional.

1518
Milton W. Feld Charitable Trust
2345 Grand Ave., Suite 2800
Kansas City 64108   (816) 292-2124

Established in 1980 in MO.
Donor(s): Milton W. Feld.‡
Foundation type: Independent
Financial data (yr. ended 08/31/90): Assets, $1,194,923 (M); expenditures, $391,591; qualifying distributions, $371,035, including $327,845 for 38 grants (high: $50,000; low: $1,000; average: $1,000-$50,000).
Purpose and activities: Emphasis on hospitals, medicine, and AIDS research; higher education and educational programs for minorities; Jewish welfare organizations; cultural programs, including music; and social service agencies, including family services, drug abuse programs, and child welfare agencies.
Fields of interest: Medical sciences, AIDS, higher education, Jewish welfare, cultural programs, music, social services, family services, drug abuse, child welfare.
Types of support: Special projects, capital campaigns, continuing support, matching funds, operating budgets, scholarship funds, building funds.
Limitations: Giving primarily in Kansas City and St. Louis, MO. No support for private foundations. No grants to individuals, or for travel, conferences, or telethons.
Publications: Application guidelines.

Application information: Application form not required.
  Initial approach: Proposal
  Deadline(s): None
  Board meeting date(s): As necessary
  Write: Abraham E. Margolin, Trustee
Trustees: Selma S. Feld, Abraham E. Margolin, Irving H. Selber.
Number of staff: None.
EIN: 431155236

1519
The Francis Families Foundation ▼
800 West 47th St., Suite 604
Kansas City 64112   (816) 531-0077
Application address: Donald F. Tierney, M.D., Dir. of Fellowship Program, Dept. of Medicine, UCLA, Los Angeles, CA 90024-1690; Tel.: (213) 825-5316

Established in 1989 in MO from the merger of the Parker B. Francis Foundation (established in 1951 in MO) and the Parker B. Francis III Foundation (established in 1962 in MO).
Donor(s): Parker B. Francis,‡ Mary B. Francis,‡ Parker B. Francis III.‡
Foundation type: Independent
Financial data (yr. ended 12/31/91): Assets, $62,491,683 (M); expenditures, $3,378,640; qualifying distributions, $2,991,315, including $2,728,776 for 96 grants (high: $100,000; low: $275; average: $10,000-$12,000).
Purpose and activities: Giving primarily to fund medical fellowships in pulmonary medicine and anesthesiology, and to support educational institutions within the greater Kansas City, MO, metropolitan area.
Fields of interest: Medical research, education, higher education, performing arts, arts.
Types of support: Fellowships, capital campaigns, special projects.
Limitations: Giving limited to the U.S. and Canada for fellowships, and to the greater Kansas City, MO, metropolitan area for educational and cultural institutions.
Publications: Annual report, informational brochure.
Application information: Application form required for fellowship program.
  Initial approach: Letter
  Deadline(s): Sept. 15 for fellowships; Oct. 1 for grants
  Board meeting date(s): May and Dec.
  Final notification: Dec.
  Write: Linda K. French, Asst. Secy.-Treas.
Officers and Directors:* John B. Francis,* Pres.; Mary Harris Francis,* V.P.; Mary Shaw Branton,* Secy.-Treas.; Charles Curran, J. Scott Francis, Robert J. Reintjes, James P. Sunderland, Robert West.
Number of staff: 2 part-time support.
EIN: 431492132

1520
James H. Fullbright & Monroe L. Swyers Foundation
c/o Boatmen's Trust Co.
100 North Broadway, P.O. Box 14737
St. Louis 63178   (314) 466-3420

Established in 1981 in MO.

Foundation type: Independent
Financial data (yr. ended 09/30/90): Assets, $2,491,253 (M); expenditures, $199,287; qualifying distributions, $169,612, including $167,000 for 87 grants to individuals (high: $4,000; low: $1,000).
Purpose and activities: Awards scholarships to high school graduates residing in MO for higher education; special consideration for southwest MO students planning to pursue a medical education.
Fields of interest: Medical education.
Types of support: Student aid.
Limitations: Giving limited to MO.
Application information: Application form required.
   Deadline(s): Apr. 1
   Write: William R. Russell, Sr. Trust Officer, Boatmen's Trust Co.
Trustees: Clifford P. McKinney, Jr., Boatmen's Trust Co.
EIN: 436252766

1521
Clifford Willard Gaylord Foundation
c/o Boatmen's National Bank of St. Louis
100 North Broadway, P.O. Box 14737
St. Louis 63178   (314) 466-3454

Established in 1948 in MO.
Donor(s): Clifford W. Gaylord.‡
Foundation type: Independent
Financial data (yr. ended 12/31/90): Assets, $6,508,236 (M); expenditures, $582,085; qualifying distributions, $547,247, including $531,600 for 62 grants (high: $90,000; low: $1,000).
Purpose and activities: Giving primarily for higher education; support also for hospitals, social service and youth agencies, child welfare, health agencies, and cultural programs.
Fields of interest: Higher education, hospitals, health services, youth, child welfare, social services, cultural programs.
Limitations: Giving primarily in St. Louis, MO. No grants to individuals.
Application information: Application form not required.
   Deadline(s): None
   Write: George H. Halpin, Jr.
Trustees: Frances M. Barnes III, Clair S. Cullinbine, Robert G.H. Hoester, Barbara P. Lawton, Ethan A.H. Shepley, Jr.
Agent: Boatmen's National Bank of St. Louis.
EIN: 436027517

1522
The Goppert Foundation
9201 Ward Pkwy., Suite 310
Kansas City 64114   (816) 333-0110

Incorporated in 1958 in MO.
Donor(s): Clarence H. Goppert.
Foundation type: Independent
Financial data (yr. ended 10/31/91): Assets, $4,045,333 (M); expenditures, $169,914; qualifying distributions, $163,330, including $160,000 for 4 grants (high: $75,000; low: $15,000; average: $15,000-$75,000).

Fields of interest: Education, education—minorities, higher education, youth, hospitals, disadvantaged.
Types of support: Equipment, matching funds, building funds, general purposes, annual campaigns, continuing support, capital campaigns, endowment funds, renovation projects, special projects, emergency funds.
Limitations: Giving primarily in western MO and eastern KS. No grants to individuals.
Application information: Application form not required.
   Deadline(s): None
   Write: Thomas A. Goppert, Secy.-Treas.
Officers and Directors:* Clarence H. Goppert,* Chair. and Pres.; Richard D. Goppert,* Vice-Chair.; M. Charles Kellogg, V.P.; Thomas A. Goppert,* Secy.-Treas.; Howard E. Bunton, Carolyn Kellogg, Leon G. Kusnetzky.
Number of staff: None.
EIN: 446013933

1523
Allen P. & Josephine B. Green Foundation
P.O. Box 523
Mexico 65265   (314) 581-5568

Trust established in 1941 in MO.
Donor(s): Allen P. Green,‡ Josephine B. Green.‡
Foundation type: Independent
Financial data (yr. ended 12/31/90): Assets, $6,558,586 (M); expenditures, $491,367; qualifying distributions, $420,000, including $420,000 for 51 grants (high: $25,000; low: $1,000).
Purpose and activities: Giving for human services, with emphasis on child development and the family, women, and the elderly; health services, including rehabilitation programs for drug and alcohol abuse, cancer care, and nursing; arts and humanities, especially fine and performing arts groups and historic preservation; education, including early childhood, elementary and secondary, adult and vocational, theological and medical and other higher educational institutions, and libraries; community development and civic affairs; and environmental conservation and animal welfare.
Fields of interest: Social services, youth, aged, women, health, arts, elementary education, higher education, libraries, ecology.
Types of support: Seed money, emergency funds, building funds, equipment, endowment funds, scholarship funds, special projects, conferences and seminars, matching funds, capital campaigns, renovation projects.
Limitations: Giving primarily in the Mexico, MO, area; no giving outside the continental U.S. No grants to individuals, or for operating budgets; no loans.
Publications: Annual report.
Application information: Application form not required.
   Initial approach: Letter
   Copies of proposal: 1
   Deadline(s): Apr. 1 or Oct. 1
   Board meeting date(s): May and Nov.
   Final notification: 1 month
   Write: Walter G. Staley, Secy.-Treas.
Officers and Directors:* James F. McHenry,* Pres.; Robert R. Collins,* V.P.; Walter G. Staley,* Secy.-Treas.; A.D. Bond III, Christopher S. Bond,

Susan Green Foote, Martha S. Marks, Homer E. Sayad, Walter G. Staley, Jr., George C. Willson III, Robert A. Wood.
Number of staff: 1 part-time support.
EIN: 436030135
Recent health grants:
1523-1 Cedar Creek Therapeutic Riding Center, Columbia, MO, $10,000. For cover for riding arena. 1990.
1523-2 Grace Hill Neighborhood Health Center, Saint Louis, MO, $10,000. For videotape series on prenatal care education. 1990.
1523-3 Independence Center, Saint Louis, MO, $10,000. For housing program and employment services. 1990.

1524
Group Health Foundation of Greater St. Louis
3556 Caroline St.
St. Louis 63104   (314) 577-8105

Established in 1986 in MO.
Foundation type: Independent
Financial data (yr. ended 10/31/91): Assets, $4,000,000 (M); expenditures, $287,342; qualifying distributions, $190,580, including $190,580 for 11 grants (high: $35,000; low: $1,000; average: $1,000-$35,000).
Purpose and activities: Support primarily for health agencies and health services, emphasizing prevention and health promotion; interest in projects that have the potential to reduce health care costs.
Fields of interest: Health, health services.
Types of support: Conferences and seminars, lectureships, program-related investments, research, scholarship funds, seed money, special projects.
Limitations: Giving primarily in St. Louis, MO. No grants to individuals.
Publications: Annual report, application guidelines.
Application information: Application form not required.
   Initial approach: Letter
   Copies of proposal: 2
   Deadline(s): Feb., May, Aug., and Nov.
   Board meeting date(s): Feb., May, Aug., and Nov.
   Final notification: Following board meeting
   Write: Robert M. Swanson, Ph.D., Secy.
Officers and Directors:* Edward Edgerley,* Pres.; Marvin Mueller,* V.P.; Robert M. Swanson,* Secy.; Taylor Scott,* Treas.; Ralph L. Biddy, M.D., Richard Ellerbrocke, Martin Greenberg, Russ Guethle, Richard Stensrud, Kenneth Worley.
Number of staff: None.
EIN: 431141117

1525
Hall Family Foundations ▼
Charitable & Crown Investment - 323
P.O. Box 419580
Kansas City 64141-6580   (816) 274-8516

Hallmark Educational Foundation incorporated in 1943 in MO; Hallmark Education Foundation of KS incorporated in 1954 in KS; combined funds formerly known as Hallmark Educational Foundations.

Donor(s): Hallmark Cards, Inc., Joyce C. Hall,‡ E.A. Hall,‡ R.B. Hall.‡
Foundation type: Independent
Financial data (yr. ended 12/31/90): Assets, $407,362,996 (M); gifts received, $75,558,711; expenditures, $11,196,437; qualifying distributions, $10,624,680, including $8,132,513 for 70 grants (high: $2,000,000; low: $6,288; average: $20,000-$100,000), $273,082 for 147 grants to individuals (high: $29,050; low: $500; average: $1,500-$3,000) and $1,656,288 for program-related investments.
Purpose and activities: Giving within four main areas of interest: 1)the performing and visual arts; 2)youth, especially education, and programs that promote social well-being, health and character building of young people; 3)economic development, including programs for the homeless; and 4)the elderly.
Fields of interest: Arts, cultural programs, performing arts, education, education—early childhood, elementary education, secondary education, higher education, education—minorities, youth, child development, social services, aged, minorities, community development, homeless, housing, urban development, environment.
Types of support: Seed money, emergency funds, building funds, equipment, special projects, general purposes, renovation projects, program-related investments, capital campaigns.
Limitations: Giving limited to MO and KS, in the Kansas City area. No support for international or religious organizations or for political purposes. No grants to individuals (except for emergency aid to Hallmark Cards employees, and scholarships for their children and close relatives only), or for endowment funds, travel, operating deficits, conferences, scholarly research, or fundraising campaigns such as telethons.
Publications: Annual report, informational brochure (including application guidelines).
Application information: Scholarships are for the children and close relatives of Hallmark Cards employees only. Only eligible applicants should apply. Application form not required.
Initial approach: Letter
Copies of proposal: 1
Deadline(s): 6 weeks before board meetings
Board meeting date(s): Mar., June, Sept., and Dec.
Final notification: 4 to 6 weeks
Write: Wendy Burcham, Peggy Collins, John Laney, or Margaret Pence, Prog. Officers
Officers: William A. Hall, Pres.; John A. MacDonald, V.P. and Treas.; Eleanor Angelbeck, Secy.
Directors: Donald J. Hall, Chair.; Paul H. Henson, Irvine O. Hockaday, Jr.; David H. Hughes, Robert A. Kipp, John P. Mascotte, Margaret H. Pence, Morton I. Sosland.
Number of staff: 2 full-time professional; 2 part-time professional; 1 full-time support.
EIN: 446006291
Recent health grants:
1525-1 Adolescent Resources Corporation (ARC), Kansas City, MO, $25,000. For Health Track program. 1990.
1525-2 Childrens Mercy Hospital, Kansas City, MO, $421,000. For Molecular Genetic Technology program. 1990.

1525-3 Clinicare Family Health Services, Kansas City, KS, $26,050. For Wyandotte County Hospice program for the aging. 1990.
1525-4 Comprehensive Mental Health Services, Independence, MO, $10,000. For Families First project. 1990.
1525-5 Crittenton Center, Kansas City, MO, $62,500. For central city family clinic. 1990.
1525-6 N.E.W.S. House for Battered Women, Kansas City, MO, $50,000. For Domestic Violence Network Hotline. 1990.
1525-7 Swope Parkway Comprehensive and Mental Health Center, Kansas City, MO, $35,000. For feasibility study. 1990.
1525-8 Swope Parkway Comprehensive and Mental Health Center, Kansas City, MO, $12,500. For Health Ministry program for the aging. 1990.
1525-9 United Cerebral Palsy Association, Kansas City, MO, $50,000. For capital support. 1990.

1526
Hallmark Cards Corporate Contributions Program
P.O. Box 580
Kansas City 64141-6580   (816) 274-8515
Application address for products: Charitable Contribs. Mgr. Product, Kansas City, MO 64141-6580

Financial data (yr. ended 12/31/90): Total giving, $13,603,000, including $1,600,000 for grants, $3,000 for employee matching gifts, $1,600,000 for loans and $10,400,000 for in-kind gifts.
Purpose and activities: Hallmark's Corporate Contribution Program serves as a general purpose fund in support of a broad range of programs in areas such as social welfare, arts and humanities, health care, and civic affairs; main interests are the arts, family services, and education; in the majority of cases, Hallmark Cards participates with others in funding programs of community concern. Hallmark Cards also makes charitable donations of its products to qualifying agencies and loans or program related investments through its "Social Investments Program."
Fields of interest: AIDS, business education, child development, citizenship, cultural programs, education—early childhood, education—building funds, education—minorities, educational associations, employment, family services, general charitable giving, homeless, hospices, housing, immigration, journalism, leadership development, literacy, public affairs, rehabilitation, theater, urban development, volunteerism, humanities, disadvantaged, museums, youth, welfare.
Types of support: In-kind gifts, annual campaigns, building funds, capital campaigns, continuing support, employee matching gifts, internships, program-related investments, technical assistance, equipment, general purposes, matching funds, operating budgets, seed money, special projects, employee volunteer services, renovation projects, donated products.
Limitations: Giving limited to headquarters city and major operating locations in CT, GA, IL, KS, MO, NC, and TX. No support for religious, fraternal, international or veterans' organizations, atheletic, labor, or social clubs. No grants to individuals, or for United Way recipients,

endowment funds, for past operating deficits, travel, conferences, scholarly research, charitable advertisements, mass-media campaigns, and non tax-exempt organizations.
Publications: Application guidelines.
Application information: If the request falls within an area of company interest and meets the guidelines, applicants may be asked to submit a project description including the program goals and objectives, background information on the agency or organization, budget, information on the staff administering the program, list of current board members, information on the criteria for evaluating the program's effectiveness, financial plan, 501(C)(3). Requests are initially reviewed by the Plant Contribution Committee in non-Kansas City locations or the corporate contribution staff at headquaters. Application form not required.
Initial approach: Letter describing the need, purpose, and general activities of the requesting organizations; send to nearest company facility
Copies of proposal: 1
Deadline(s): None
Board meeting date(s): Periodic
Final notification: 4 to 6 weeks
Write: Jeanne M. Bates, Community Development Mgr.
Contributions Committee: Jeanne M. Bates, Community Development Mgr.; Walt Richards, Mgr., Charitable Contribs. (products).
Number of staff: 6 full-time professional; 2 full-time support.

1527
Hallmark Corporate Foundation ▼
P.O. Box 419580, Dept. 323
Kansas City 64141-6580   (816) 274-8515

Established in 1983 in MO.
Donor(s): Hallmark Cards, Inc.
Foundation type: Company-sponsored
Financial data (yr. ended 12/31/91): Assets, $27,631,987 (M); expenditures, $1,880,581; qualifying distributions, $7,895,452, including $6,595,452 for 900 grants (high: $540,000; low: $35; average: $200-$10,000) and $1,300,000 for 1 program-related investment.
Purpose and activities: Support for a wide range of programs, including AIDS, employment, journalism, literacy, urban affairs, youth (including the problem of delinquency), higher and pre-college education, arts, social welfare, and civic affairs.
Fields of interest: AIDS, handicapped, rehabilitation, drug abuse, employment, journalism, urban development, volunteerism, public policy, immigration, child development, family services, leadership development, child welfare, youth, education, education—early childhood, secondary education, higher education, business education, education—minorities, elementary education, literacy, business, economics, welfare, housing, hunger, aged, civic affairs, community development, cultural programs, historic preservation, museums, arts.
Types of support: Annual campaigns, building funds, continuing support, employee matching gifts, equipment, internships, matching funds, program-related investments, seed money, technical assistance, special projects, capital

campaigns, renovation projects, general purposes, operating budgets.
Limitations: Giving limited to Kansas City, MO, and cities where Hallmark facilities are located.
Publications: Application guidelines, 990-PF.
Application information: Application form not required.
  Initial approach: Written proposal
  Copies of proposal: 1
  Deadline(s): None
  Board meeting date(s): Periodic
  Final notification: Within 6 weeks
  Write: Jeanne Bates, V.P.
Officers and Directors:* Donald J. Hall,* Chair.; William A. Hall, Pres.; Jeanne M. Bates, V.P.; John A. MacDonald, Treas.; Hank Frigon, Irvine O. Hockaday, Jr., Robert A. Kipp, Robert L. Stark.
Number of staff: 4 full-time professional; 1 full-time support.
EIN: 431303258

1528
Florence P. Hamilton Foundation
One West Armour, Suite 300
Kansas City 64111-9989

Established about 1969 in CA.
Donor(s): Florence P. Hamilton, William H. Peterson Trust.
Foundation type: Independent
Financial data (yr. ended 12/31/90): Assets, $2,452,100 (M); expenditures, $198,127; qualifying distributions, $122,000, including $122,000 for 23 grants (high: $50,000; low: $500).
Fields of interest: Cultural programs, hospitals, social services, libraries.
Limitations: Giving primarily in CA, MO, and OK. No grants to individuals.
Application information:
  Initial approach: Letter
  Deadline(s): None
  Write: Charles H. Price II, Trustee
Trustees: Robert Hamilton, Carol Swanson Price, Charles H. Price II, Gerock H. Swanson, W. Clark Swanson, Jr.
EIN: 956235131

1529
May H. Ilgenfritz Testamentary Trust
108 West Pacific
Sedalia 65301   (816) 826-3310

Trust established in 1941 in MO.
Foundation type: Independent
Financial data (yr. ended 12/31/90): Assets, $2,948,069 (M); expenditures, $179,960; qualifying distributions, $171,710, including $25,000 for 1 grant and $143,125 for 120 grants to individuals (high: $4,200; low: $300).
Purpose and activities: Emphasis on scholarships to individuals and a rehabilitation center for handicapped children.
Fields of interest: Child welfare, handicapped, rehabilitation.
Types of support: Student aid, operating budgets.
Limitations: Giving primarily in MO; scholarships restricted to residents of Sedalia.
Application information: Application form required for scholarships.
  Deadline(s): None

Write: John Pelham, Trustee
Trustees: John Pelham, Third National Bank.
EIN: 440663403

1530
Interco, Inc. Charitable Trust ▼
P.O. Box 387
St. Louis 63166   (314) 863-1100
Application address: Interco, Inc., 101 South Hanley Rd., Clayton, MO 63105

Trust established in 1944 in MO.
Donor(s): Interco, Inc., and subsidiaries.
Foundation type: Company-sponsored
Financial data (yr. ended 12/31/90): Assets, $27,178,171 (M); expenditures, $1,154,275; qualifying distributions, $1,019,262, including $1,008,818 for 262 grants (high: $100,000; low: $25; average: $500-$30,000).
Purpose and activities: Emphasis on a community fund, higher education, and cultural programs; support also for hospitals, and social service and youth agencies.
Fields of interest: Community funds, higher education, cultural programs, hospitals, social services, youth.
Limitations: Giving primarily in St. Louis, MO. No grants to individuals.
Application information:
  Initial approach: Letter
  Deadline(s): None
  Write: Robert T. Hensley, Jr., Trustee
Trustees: Robert T. Hensley, Jr., Mercantile Bank of St. Louis, N.A.
Number of staff: None.
EIN: 436020530

1531
Jefferson Smurfit Corporation Charitable Trust
c/o Boatmen's Trust Co.
510 Locust St., P.O. Box 14737
St. Louis 63178
Application address: c/o Jefferson Smurfit Corp., P.O. Box 66820, St. Louis, MO 63166

Established in 1951.
Donor(s): Container Corp. of America, Jefferson Smurfit Corp.
Foundation type: Company-sponsored
Financial data (yr. ended 12/31/90): Assets, $1,369,130 (M); expenditures, $677,554; qualifying distributions, $668,604, including $667,850 for 24 grants (high: $500,000; low: $1,000).
Purpose and activities: Giving primarily for higher education; some support also for the arts, hospitals and health associations, and a zoological park.
Fields of interest: Higher education, arts, health associations, hospitals, animal welfare, recreation.
Limitations: Giving primarily in MO.
Application information:
  Initial approach: Proposal and organization profile
  Deadline(s): None
  Write: Lyle L. Meyer, Member, Admin. Comm.
Administrative Committee: James B. Mally, Jack McCarthy, Lyle L. Meyer, James E. Terrell, Bill M. Thompson.
Trustee: Boatmen's Trust Co.

EIN: 436023508

1532
Mary Ranken Jordan and Ettie A. Jordan Charitable Foundation
c/o Mercantile Bank, N.A.
P.O. Box 387
St. Louis 63166   (314) 231-7626

Trust established in 1957 in MO.
Donor(s): Mary Ranken Jordan.‡
Foundation type: Independent
Financial data (yr. ended 12/31/90): Assets, $16,114,293 (M); expenditures, $1,078,692; qualifying distributions, $1,014,493, including $1,001,120 for 87 grants (high: $100,000; low: $1,000).
Purpose and activities: Giving limited to charitable and eleemosynary institutions with emphasis on higher education and cultural programs; grants also for social services, secondary education, and hospitals and health services.
Fields of interest: Higher education, hospitals, cultural programs, social services, secondary education, health services.
Types of support: Building funds, operating budgets, special projects, continuing support.
Limitations: Giving limited to MO, with emphasis on St. Louis. No grants to individuals, or for endowment funds.
Publications: Application guidelines.
Application information: Application form not required.
  Initial approach: Letter
  Copies of proposal: 3
  Deadline(s): None
  Board meeting date(s): Jan.
  Final notification: After Jan. 15
  Write: H. Jill Fivecoat, V.P., Mercantile Bank, N.A.
Trustee: Mercantile Bank, N.A.
Number of staff: None.
EIN: 436020554
Recent health grants:
  1532-1 Grace Hill Neighborhood Health Center, Saint Louis, MO, $10,000. 1990.
  1532-2 Jewish Hospital of Saint Louis, Saint Louis, MO, $10,000. 1990.
  1532-3 Memorial Home, Saint Louis, MO, $20,000. 1990.
  1532-4 Ranken Jordan Home for Convalescent Crippled Children, Saint Louis, MO, $50,000. 1990.

1533
The Greater Kansas City Community Foundation and Its Affiliated Trusts
1055 Broadway, Suite 130
Kansas City 64105   (816) 842-0944
FAX: (816) 842-8079

Established in 1978 in MO.
Foundation type: Community
Financial data (yr. ended 01/31/91): Assets, $77,366,275 (M); expenditures, $8,447,986; qualifying distributions, $7,734,137, including $7,734,137 for grants.
Purpose and activities: Giving primarily to improve the quality of life in the metropolitan area in the fields of arts and culture, health,

welfare, community action, and education; giving also for matching and challenge grants.
Fields of interest: Cultural programs, arts, AIDS, health, social services, community development, civic affairs, education.
Types of support: Seed money, matching funds, general purposes, lectureships, program-related investments, renovation projects, scholarship funds, special projects.
Limitations: Giving primarily in the five-county greater Kansas City, MO, area. No grants to individuals (except through designated scholarship funds), or for deficit financing, endowments, capital or annual campaigns, or operating expenses.
Publications: Annual report, application guidelines, newsletter, informational brochure.
Application information: Application form not required.
> *Initial approach:* Proposal or letter
> *Copies of proposal:* 1
> *Deadline(s):* None
> *Board meeting date(s):* Mar., June, Sept., and Dec.
> *Final notification:* Within 2 weeks of board meeting
> *Write:* Janice C. Kreamer, Pres.
Officers and Directors:* Adele C. Hall,* Chair.; A. Drue Jennings,* Vice-Chair.; Janice C. Kreamer,* Pres.; George S. Bittner, V.P., Finance; Dalene D. Bradford, V.P., Program; Marion C. Kreamer,* Secy.; Richard C. Green,* Treas.; and 22 additional directors.
Number of staff: 8 full-time professional; 4 full-time support.
EIN: 431152398
Recent health grants:
1533-1 Crittenton Center, Kansas City, MO, $150,000. For school counselor training program. 1992.
1533-2 Domestic Violence Network, Kansas City, MO, $45,000. For family violence crisis hotline. 1992.
1533-3 Mental Health Association in Wyandotte County, Kansas City, MO, $20,000. For Kansas YouthNet start-up staffing. 1992.
1533-4 Midwest Christian Counseling Center, Kansas City, MO, $30,000. For Street Psych church outreach. 1992.
1533-5 Project Neighbors Helping Others Obtain Dignity (Neighbor-HOOD) Fund, Kansas City, MO, $500,000. For drug abuse prevention programming. 1992.
1533-6 Project Neighbors Helping Others Obtain Dignity (Neighbor-HOOD) Fund, Kansas City, MO, $16,000. For administrative support. 1992.
1533-7 Swope Ridge Geriatric Center, Kansas City, MO, $49,440. For certified nursing assistant training program. 1992.
1533-8 Tri-County Community Mental Health Services, North Kansas City, MO, $42,200. For families first crisis intervention. 1992.
1533-9 United Community Services of Johnson County, Overland Park, KS, $45,000. For Johnson County Health Partnership. 1992.
1533-10 Wyandotte House, Kansas City, KS, $115,000. For residential treatment programs. 1992.

1534
Ewing Marion Kauffman Foundation
4900 Oak
Kansas City 64112　　　　　(816) 932-1000

Established in 1966 in MO.
Donor(s): Ewing M. Kauffman.
Foundation type: Operating
Financial data (yr. ended 06/30/91): Assets, $8,770,151 (M); gifts received, $9,602,318; expenditures, $4,572,679; qualifying distributions, $4,547,739, including $1,327,047 for 47 grants (high: $250,000; low: $500) and $3,184,511 for 4 foundation-administered programs.
Purpose and activities: To "research and identify the unfulfilled needs of society and develop, implement and/or fund breakthrough solutions that have a lasting impact and offer people a choice and hope for the future. Objectives include: 1) educating and enhancing the ability of people at risk, particularly the young, to become self-sufficient and productive; and 2) increasing the understanding and appreciation of our free enterprise system and help to ensure that our spirit of entrepreneurism propagates to future generations."
Fields of interest: Health services, drug abuse, alcoholism, child development, education—early childhood, family services, disadvantaged.
Limitations: Giving primarily in KS and MO. No loans or program-related investments.
Publications: Annual report (including application guidelines), informational brochure (including application guidelines).
Application information: Funds primarily disbursed through foundation-administered programs; few grants awarded. Application form not required.
> *Initial approach:* Brief concept paper; no proposals
> *Copies of proposal:* 1
> *Deadline(s):* None
> *Board meeting date(s):* Sept. and Mar.
> *Write:* Robert L. Barrett, Dir. of Communications
Officers and Directors:* Ewing M. Kauffman,* Chair.; Robert Rogers,* Pres.; David Lady, Secy.-Treas.; Michael Herman, Charles L. Hughes, James E. McGraw, Louis W. Smith.
Number of staff: 54 full-time professional; 27 full-time support; 5 part-time support.
EIN: 436064859

1535
Enid and Crosby Kemper Foundation
c/o United Missouri Bank of Kansas City, N.A.
Tenth St. and Grand Ave., P.O. Box 226
Kansas City 64141　　　　　(816) 556-7722

Established in 1972 in MO.
Donor(s): Enid J. Kemper, R. Crosby Kemper, Sr.‡
Foundation type: Independent
Financial data (yr. ended 12/31/90): Assets, $30,193,518 (M); expenditures, $313,686; qualifying distributions, $190,035, including $123,539 for 9 grants (high: $36,000; low: $5,000).
Purpose and activities: Emphasis on secondary education and cultural programs, including museums and the performing arts; some support also for health and higher education.

Fields of interest: Higher education, secondary education, cultural programs, museums, performing arts, health.
Types of support: General purposes.
Limitations: Giving primarily in KS and MO. No support for medical institutions. No grants for capital funds.
Application information: Contributes only to pre-selected organizations. Applications not accepted.
> *Board meeting date(s):* Quarterly and as needed
Trustees: Malcolm M. Aslin, Mary S. Kemper, R. Crosby Kemper, Jr., United Missouri Bank of Kansas City, N.A.
EIN: 237279896

1536
William T. Kemper Foundation
c/o Commerce Bank of Kansas City, N.A.
Box 419248
Kansas City 64141-6248
Application address: c/o Commerce Bank of Kansas City, N.A., P.O. Box 13095, Kansas City, MO 64199-3095; Tel.: (816) 234-2985

Established in 1989 in MO.
Donor(s): William T. Kemper,‡ William T. Kemper Revocable Trust.
Foundation type: Independent
Financial data (yr. ended 10/31/90): Assets, $111,511,244 (M); gifts received, $112,035,121; expenditures, $2,295,242; qualifying distributions, $1,983,765, including $1,954,018 for 77 grants (high: $250,000; low: $500).
Purpose and activities: Support for education, including higher education and art education, health and human services, civic and economic development, and the arts, including fine and performing arts; some support for religious organizations.
Fields of interest: Education, health, social services, civic affairs, community development, arts, music, performing arts, fine arts, religion—Christian.
Limitations: Giving primarily in Kansas City, MO. No support for political purposes, veterans' or fraternal organizations, private foundations, fundraising activities, or for projects which provide direct funding to entities outside the U.S. No grants for indivduals; no loans.
Application information:
> *Initial approach:* Proposal
> *Deadline(s):* None
> *Write:* Exec. Dir.
Trustee: Commerce Bank of Kansas City, N.A.
EIN: 436345116

1537
The David Woods Kemper Memorial Foundation
1800 Commerce Bank Bldg.
P.O. Box 13686
Kansas City 64199　　　　　(816) 234-2346

Incorporated in 1946 in MO.
Donor(s): James M. Kemper, James M. Kemper, Jr.
Foundation type: Independent
Financial data (yr. ended 12/31/90): Assets, $5,021,436 (M); expenditures, $226,045; qualifying distributions, $210,069, including

$210,069 for 135 grants (high: $12,500; low: $50).
Fields of interest: Education, higher education, secondary education, arts, cultural programs, family planning, youth, community development, Protestant giving, public policy.
Limitations: Giving primarily in Kansas City, MO. No grants to individuals.
Application information: Contributes only to pre-selected organizations. Applications not accepted.
Write: James M. Kemper, Jr., Pres.
Officers: James M. Kemper, Jr., Pres.; David W. Kemper, V.P.; Laura Kemper Fields, Secy.-Treas.
Number of staff: None.
EIN: 446012535

1538
Laclede Gas Charitable Trust
720 Olive St., Rm. 1525
St. Louis 63101   (314) 342-0859

Trust established in 1966 in MO.
Donor(s): Laclede Gas Co.
Foundation type: Company-sponsored
Financial data (yr. ended 09/30/90): Assets, $5,716,798 (M); expenditures, $503,004; qualifying distributions, $497,253, including $459,800 for 109 grants (high: $220,725; low: $50) and $37,438 for 71 employee matching gifts.
Purpose and activities: Primary areas of interest include the arts, family services, community funds, higher education, and general charitable giving.
Fields of interest: Youth, family services, health, cultural programs, arts, public policy, civic affairs, community funds, higher education, secondary education, general charitable giving.
Types of support: Annual campaigns, general purposes, matching funds, employee-related scholarships, employee matching gifts, operating budgets, building funds, equipment, emergency funds, conferences and seminars, special projects.
Limitations: Giving primarily in areas of company operations. No support for religious or sectarian organizations or veterans' groups. No grants to individuals.
Publications: Informational brochure.
Application information: Application form required.
Initial approach: Letter
Copies of proposal: 1
Deadline(s): Apr. 15
Board meeting date(s): Mar., June, Sept., and Dec.
Write: Ruth Dreckshage, Trustee
Trustees: Ruth Dreckshage, Robert C. Jaudes, Lee M. Liberman.
Number of staff: None.
EIN: 436068197

1539
The Leader Foundation
7711 Carondelet Ave., 10th Fl.
St. Louis 63105   (314) 725-7300

Established in 1944.
Foundation type: Independent
Financial data (yr. ended 01/31/91): Assets, $2,714,118 (M); expenditures, $192,522; qualifying distributions, $171,864, including

$43,000 for 2 grants (high: $33,000; low: $10,000) and $112,025 for 38 grants to individuals (high: $6,371; low: $100).
Purpose and activities: Giving primarily to individuals for pensions and health organizations and family services.
Fields of interest: Welfare—indigent individuals, health, aged, family services.
Types of support: Grants to individuals, continuing support, special projects.
Limitations: Giving primarily in St. Louis, MO.
Application information: Application form not required.
Initial approach: Letter
Copies of proposal: 1
Deadline(s): None
Board meeting date(s): May and Nov.
Write: Edwin G. Shifrin, V.P.
Officers: Donald E. Ray, Pres.; J.A. Baer II, V.P.; Edwin G. Shifrin, V.P.; Steven M. Rafsky, Secy.-Treas.
Directors: Philip Marlo, Patricia Reaves.
Number of staff: None.
EIN: 436036864

1540
David B. Lichtenstein Foundation
P.O. Box 19740
St. Louis 63144

Established in 1947 in MO.
Donor(s): David Lichtenstein.‡
Foundation type: Independent
Financial data (yr. ended 12/31/90): Assets, $8,131,769 (M); expenditures, $395,826; qualifying distributions, $395,826, including $327,235 for 32 grants (high: $115,000; low: $25).
Fields of interest: Protestant giving, dentistry, hospitals, health associations, higher education, social services.
Limitations: Giving limited to MO.
Application information: Application form not required.
Deadline(s): None
Write: Daniel B. Lichtenstein, Mgr.
Officer and Trustees:* Daniel B. Lichtenstein,* Mgr.; Ken Cohen, Sheldon Cohen, Allene N. Lichtenstein, David B. Lichtenstein, Jr., Barney Reiss, Craig K. Reiss, Mary Lichtenstein Straub.
EIN: 436033786

1541
R. A. Long Foundation
600 Plaza West Bldg.
4600 Madison Ave.
Kansas City 64112   (816) 561-4600

Incorporated in 1958 in MO.
Donor(s): Loula Long Combs,‡ Sally Long Ellis,‡ R.A. Long Ellis.
Foundation type: Independent
Financial data (yr. ended 11/30/90): Assets, $3,514,134 (M); expenditures, $216,308; qualifying distributions, $183,866, including $155,250 for 52 grants (high: $7,500; low: $500).
Purpose and activities: Giving largely for services for youth, including child welfare, recreation, rehabilitation, and education.
Fields of interest: Youth, child welfare, recreation, rehabilitation, education.

Types of support: Capital campaigns, consulting services, operating budgets, renovation projects.
Limitations: Giving primarily in KS and MO. No grants to individuals, or for endowment funds, research programs, scholarships, or fellowships; no loans.
Publications: Application guidelines.
Application information: Application form not required.
Initial approach: Letter
Copies of proposal: 1
Deadline(s): Apr. 30 and Oct. 30
Board meeting date(s): May and Nov.
Write: James H. Bernard, Treas.
Officers and Directors:* R.A. Long Ellis,* Pres.; Hayne Ellis III,* V.P.; James H. Bernard, Jr.,* Secy.; James H. Bernard,* Treas.; Long Ellis, Linna Place, Janet Rickel, Ann J. Thompson.
Number of staff: None.
EIN: 446014081

1542
Carrie J. Loose Trust
c/o The Greater Kansas City Community Foundation
1055 Broadway St., No. 130
Kansas City 64105-1595   (816) 842-0944

Trust established in 1927 in MO.
Donor(s): Harry Wilson Loose,‡ Carrie J. Loose.‡
Foundation type: Independent
Financial data (yr. ended 12/31/90): Assets, $8,674,652 (M); expenditures, $529,425; qualifying distributions, $487,047, including $435,137 for 13 grants (high: $100,000; low: $10,000).
Purpose and activities: Grants to established local educational, health, and welfare institutions; support for research into the community's social and cultural needs and for experimental and demonstration projects. A member trust of the Kansas City Association of Trusts and Foundations.
Fields of interest: Education, health, welfare, cultural programs.
Types of support: Special projects.
Limitations: Giving limited to Kansas City, MO. No grants to individuals, or for building funds, matching gifts, endowment funds, deficit financing, annual or capital campaigns, general support, scholarships, or fellowships; no loans.
Publications: Application guidelines.
Application information: Application form not required.
Initial approach: Letter or proposal
Copies of proposal: 1
Deadline(s): 4 to 6 months prior to board meetings
Board meeting date(s): Mar., June, Sept., and Dec.
Final notification: Within 2 weeks of the board meetings
Write: Janice C. Kreamer, Pres., The Greater Kansas City Community Foundation
Officers and Directors:* James P. Sunderland,* Chair.; Edward A. Smith,* Vice-Chair.; Janice C. Kreamer, Pres.; George S. Bittner, V.P., Finance; Dalene D. Bradford, V.P., Prog.; Marion E. Kreamer,* Secy.; Charles A. Duboc,* Treas.; and 20 additional directors.
Trustee: Boatmen's First National Bank of Kansas City.
Number of staff: 12 shared staff

EIN: 446009246

1543
Harry Wilson Loose Trust
c/o The Greater Kansas City Community
Foundation
1055 Broadway St., No. 130
Kansas City 64105-1595   (816) 842-0944

Trust established in 1927 in MO.
Donor(s): Harry Wilson Loose.‡
Foundation type: Independent
Financial data (yr. ended 12/31/90): Assets,
$3,431,718 (M); expenditures, $234,706;
qualifying distributions, $217,808, including
$205,850 for 10 grants (high: $50,000; low:
$7,850).
Purpose and activities: Emphasis on civic and
community development in Kansas City,
including grants for health, social services, and
the arts and cultural programs. A member trust of
the Kansas City Association of Trusts and
Foundations.
Fields of interest: Community development, civic
affairs, arts, cultural programs, health, social
services.
Types of support: Research, special projects.
Limitations: Giving limited to Kansas City, MO.
No grants to individuals, or for endowment funds,
general support, building funds, matching gifts,
scholarships, or fellowships; no loans.
Publications: Annual report, application
guidelines.
Application information: Application form not
required.
   Initial approach: Letter or proposal
   Copies of proposal: 1
   Deadline(s): 4 months prior to full board
      meetings
   Board meeting date(s): Mar., June, Sept., and
      Dec.
   Final notification: Within 2 weeks of the full
      board meeting
   Write: Janice C. Kreamer, Pres., The Greater
      Kansas City Community Foundation
Officers: James P. Sunderland, Chair.; Edward A.
Smith, Vice-Chair.; Janice C. Kreamer, Pres.;
George S. Bittner, V.P.; Dalene D. Bradford, V.P.;
Marion E. Kreamer, Secy.; Charles A. Duboc,
Treas.
Trustees: Donald H. Chisolm, Robert T.H.
Davidson, Boatmen's First National Bank of
Kansas City.
Number of staff: None.
EIN: 446009245

1544
John Allan Love Charitable Foundation
c/o Edgar G. Boedecker
130 South Bemiston, 4th Fl.
St. Louis 63105   (314) 727-5822

Established in 1966 in MO.
Donor(s): John Allan Love Trusts.
Foundation type: Independent
Financial data (yr. ended 12/31/90): Assets,
$2,807,679 (M); expenditures, $180,907;
qualifying distributions, $155,290, including
$154,300 for 33 grants (high: $20,000; low:
$100).

Purpose and activities: Grants for medical
research concerning the handicapped, cultural
programs, education, community funds, and the
promotion of good citizenship.
Fields of interest: Medical research, handicapped,
cultural programs, education, community funds,
citizenship.
Limitations: Giving primarily in MO.
Officers: Rumsey Ewing, Pres.; W. Anderson
Payne, V.P.; James G. Forsyth, Treas.
Directors: John McKinney, John J. Owen, Jackson
C. Parriott.
EIN: 436066121

1545
Lowenstein Brothers Foundation
400 East Red Bridge Rd., Suite 206
Kansas City 64131   (816) 941-7939

Trust established in 1956 in MO.
Foundation type: Independent
Financial data (yr. ended 10/31/90): Assets,
$3,501,166 (M); expenditures, $201,793;
qualifying distributions, $197,588, including
$197,588 for 40 grants (high: $70,000; low: $25).
Purpose and activities: Support for education,
health, youth, and social services, with emphasis
on Jewish agencies.
Fields of interest: Jewish giving, Jewish welfare,
education, health, youth, social services.
Limitations: Giving primarily in MO.
Application information:
   Initial approach: Letter
   Deadline(s): None
   Write: William B. Lowenstein, Trustee
Trustees: Marjorie Sue Kaplan, Glenn L.
Lowenstein, Lon J. Lowenstein, William B.
Lowenstein.
EIN: 436055404

1546
Edward Mallinckrodt, Jr. Foundation
One North Jefferson
St. Louis 63105   (314) 289-3000

Incorporated in 1953 in MO.
Donor(s): Edward Mallinckrodt, Jr.‡
Foundation type: Independent
Financial data (yr. ended 09/30/91): Assets,
$19,765,195 (M); expenditures, $978,245;
qualifying distributions, $822,786, including
$811,110 for grants (high: $99,500; low: $8,000).
Purpose and activities: Grants largely for
biomedical education and research, including
grants to individual researchers under the Scholar
Program.
Fields of interest: Medical education, medical
research.
Types of support: Research, grants to individuals.
Publications: Annual report, 990-PF.
Application information:
   Deadline(s): None
   Write: Oliver M. Langenberg, Pres.
Officers and Directors:* Oliver M. Langenberg,*
Pres. and Treas.; Tom Cori,* V.P.; Charles C. Allen,
Jr.,* Secy.; Juan Traveras.
Number of staff: None.
EIN: 436030295

1547
**The May Department Stores Company
Foundation, Inc.**
(Formerly The May Stores Foundation, Inc.)
Sixth and Olive Sts.
St. Louis 63101   (314) 342-6403

Incorporated in 1945 in NY.
Donor(s): May Department Stores Co.
Foundation type: Company-sponsored
Financial data (yr. ended 12/31/90): Assets,
$20,047,487 (M); gifts received, $7,519,269;
expenditures, $10,208,963; qualifying
distributions, $10,117,431, including
$10,117,431 for grants (high: $625,000; low:
$10; average: $100-$25,000).
Purpose and activities: Grants to charitable and
educational institutions throughout the country,
with emphasis on community funds in areas of
company operations; support also for cultural
programs, hospitals and health care, and civic
affairs.
Fields of interest: Education, higher education,
community funds, cultural programs, hospitals,
health, AIDS, social services, civic affairs.
Limitations: Giving primarily in areas of company
operations.
Application information: Contributes only to
pre-selected organizations. Applications not
accepted.
   Write: Jan R. Kniffen, V.P., Secy., and Treas.
Officers and Directors:* Jerome T. Loeb,* Pres.;
Jan R. Kniffen,* V.P. and Secy.-Treas.; David C.
Farrell,* V.P.; Thomas A. Hayes,* V.P.; Robert F.
Cerulli.
Number of staff: None.
EIN: 436028949

1548
**McDonnell Douglas Corporation Giving
Program**
c/o McDonnell Douglas Community Rels.
P.O. Box 516 - Mail Code 1001510
St. Louis 63166   (314) 232-8464

Financial data (yr. ended 12/31/90): Total giving,
$1,178,083, including $178,083 for grants and
$1,000,000 for in-kind gifts.
Purpose and activities: "McDonnell Douglas has
a proud tradition of helping people in need and
providing them with the means to help
themselves. McDonnell Douglas supports a
variety of programs that help individuals realize
their full potential and become productive
members of society; programs designed to
eliminate the causes of societal problems, in
addition to treating the symptoms. In this way, we
move ever closer to our ultimate goal of making
the communities where McDonnell Douglas is
located better places in which to live and work.
Achieving that objective is no small task and
despite steady progress, there is still much work to
be done." Most giving is through the Foundation
and Employee Community Funds. Organized
geographically to serve specific communities in
which MDC employees live and work, the six
Employees' Community Funds are supported by
employee payroll deductions. Employee
Solicitations occur once a year and are
administered by McDonnell Douglas so that 100
percent of the donations are used for community
causes. While emloyee grants tend to be highly

localized by nature, common threads run through the six funds disbursements. In addition to supporting programs for the hungry and homeless, education and youth at risk, the Employees' Community Funds also focus their support on programs for the disabled, and arts, cultural, and health issues. To ensure that contributions are returned to the communities in which employees live each fund is governed by a board of directors consisting exclusively of employees. Their decisions are guided by the results of periodic surveys in which employees indicate the general categories of service they feel are most deserving of support. In 1990 the Employees Community Funds gave more than $11.1 million. Through the Community Help and Involvement Program (CHIP), employees volunteer for nonprofits. Winners of the McDonnell Douglas Volunteer of the Year Award receive $1,000 to be granted to their chosen nonprofit.

Fields of interest: Social services, youth, community development, handicapped, cultural programs, civic affairs, health, science and technology, performing arts, environment, engineering, citizenship.

Types of support: Capital campaigns, general purposes, research, scholarship funds, seed money, donated equipment, use of facilities, loaned talent, employee volunteer services.

Limitations: Giving primarily in operating areas in AZ, CA, FL, MO, OK, and TX.

Application information: Application form not required.

   Initial approach: Letter to nearest facility
   Write: Walter E. Diggs, Jr., Pres., McDonnell Douglas Foundation

1549
James S. McDonnell Foundation ▼
1034 South Brentwood Blvd., Suite 1610
St. Louis 63117   (314) 721-1532

Incorporated in 1950 in MO.
Donor(s): James S. McDonnell,‡ James S. McDonnell III, John F. McDonnell.
Foundation type: Independent
Financial data (yr. ended 12/31/90): Assets, $75,114,584 (M); expenditures, $12,666,499; qualifying distributions, $12,666,499, including $12,284,471 for 85 grants (high: $2,000,000; low: $1,000; average: $50,000-$200,000).
Purpose and activities: Giving for research in biomedical and cognitive neuroscience, research and application of cognitive psychology to education and research on issues related to global understanding; support also for cultural and educational activities in the St. Louis metropolitan area. Foundation-initiated programs include: Cognitive Studies for Educational Practice, Molecular Medicine in Cancer Research, and the McDonnell-Pew Program in Neuroscience.
Fields of interest: Medical research, international studies, educational research, science and technology, cancer.
Types of support: Special projects, research, conferences and seminars.
Limitations: No grants to individuals, or generally for endowment funds, capital campaigns, building funds, renovations, scholarships, or general purposes.

Publications: Annual report (including application guidelines).
Application information: Contact foundation for program information. Application form not required.
   Initial approach: Letter
   Copies of proposal: 1
   Deadline(s): None
   Board meeting date(s): As needed
   Final notification: Varies
   Write: John T. Bruer, Pres.
Officers and Directors:* John T. Bruer, Pres.; James S. McDonnell III,* V.P. and Secy.; John F. McDonnell,* Treas.; Michael Witunski.
Number of staff: 2 full-time professional; 1 full-time support.
EIN: 436030988
Recent health grants:

1549-1 Albert Einstein College of Medicine of Yeshiva University, Department of Cell Biology, Bronx, NY, $137,500. For McDonnell Scholar in Molecular Medicine in Cancer Research. 1991.

1549-2 California Institute of Technology, Division of Biology, Pasadena, CA, $57,916. For research grant as part of McDonnell-Pew Program in Cognitive Neuroscience. 1991.

1549-3 Cambridge University, Physiological Laboratory, Cambridge, England, $59,999. For research grant as part of McDonnell-Pew Program in Cognitive Neuroscience. 1991.

1549-4 Childrens Hospital, Boston, MA, $137,500. For McDonnell Scholar in Molecular Medicine in Cancer Research. 1991.

1549-5 Childrens Hospital, Boston, MA, $137,500. For research of McDonnell Fellow in Molecular Medicine in Cancer Research. 1991.

1549-6 Columbia University, Comprehensive Cancer Center, NYC, NY, $137,500. For work of McDonnell Fellow in Molecular Medicine in Cancer Research. 1991.

1549-7 Columbia University, Department of Biochemistry, NYC, NY, $137,500. For McDonnell Scholar in Molecular Medicine in Cancer Research. 1991.

1549-8 Dartmouth College, Medical School, Department of Psychiatry, Hanover, NH, $240,000. For McDonnell-Pew Program in Cognitive Neuroscience. 1991.

1549-9 Dartmouth Medical School, Department of Psychiatry, Hanover, NH, $177,889. For fifth McDonnell Summer Institute in Cognitive Neuroscience. 1991.

1549-10 Duke University Medical Center, Division of Hematology-Oncology, Durham, NC, $137,500. For research of McDonnell Fellow in Molecular Medicine in Cancer Research. 1991.

1549-11 Foundation for Advanced Education in the Sciences, Laboratory of Neuropsychiatry, National Institutes of Health, Bethesda, MD, $85,313. For training grant in McDonnell-Pew Program in Cognitive Neuroscience. 1991.

1549-12 Fred Hutchinson Cancer Research Center, Department of Genetics, Seattle, WA, $137,500. For work of McDonnell Fellow in Molecular Medicine in Cancer Research. 1991.

1549-13 Fred Hutchinson Cancer Research Center, Pediatric Oncology, Seattle, WA, $137,500. For research of McDonnell Fellow in Molecular Medicine in Cancer Research. 1991.

1549-14 Harvard University, Department of Psychiatry, Cambridge, MA, $107,353. For training grant for McDonnell-Pew Program in Cognitive Neuroscience. 1991.

1549-15 Johns Hopkins University, School of Medicine, Oncology Center, Baltimore, MD, $137,500. For work of McDonnell Fellow in Molecular Medicine in Cancer Research. 1991.

1549-16 Massachusetts General Hospital, Boston, MA, $137,500. For work of McDonnell Fellow in Molecular Medicine in Cancer Research. 1991.

1549-17 Massachusetts General Hospital, Cancer Center, Boston, MA, $137,500. For research of McDonnell Fellow in Molecular Medicine in Cancer Research. 1991.

1549-18 Massachusetts General Hospital, Neurolinguistics Laboratory, Boston, MA, $295,405. For development and operation of Laboratory. 1991.

1549-19 Massachusetts Institute of Technology, Department of Brain and Cognitive Science, Cambridge, MA, $37,500. For matching funds for research of Presidential Young Investigator. 1991.

1549-20 Massachusetts Institute of Technology, Department of Brain and Cognitive Science, Cambridge, MA, $27,500. For postdoctoral research in Cognitive Studies for Educational Practice Program. 1991.

1549-21 Medical Research Council, Cyclotron Unit, London, England, $59,678. For research grant as part of McDonnell-Pew Program in Cognitive Neuroscience. 1991.

1549-22 Montreal Neurological Institute and Hospital, Montreal, Canada, $240,000. For McDonnell-Pew Program in Cognitive Neuroscience. 1991.

1549-23 Princeton University, Princeton, NJ, $675,000. For renewed support for Phase II of Human Information Processing Group. 1991.

1549-24 Princeton University, Princeton, NJ, $293,938. For administrative costs of McDonnell-Pew Program in Cognitive Neuroscience. 1991.

1549-25 Program for Appropriate Technology in Health, Seattle, WA, $1,042,811. For renewed support for International Task Force on Hepatitis B Immunization. 1991.

1549-26 Program for Appropriate Technology in Health, Seattle, WA, $50,000. To develop initial operational plan for Consultative Group of Children's Vaccine Initiative. 1991.

1549-27 Program for Appropriate Technology in Health, Seattle, WA, $42,000. For initial work of Epstein-Barr Virus Vaccine Task Force. 1991.

1549-28 Rush-Presbyterian-Saint Lukes Medical Center, Department of Psychology and Social Sciences, Rush Medical College, Chicago, IL, $56,804. For research grant for McDonnell-Pew Program in Cognitive Neuroscience. 1991.

1549-29 Rutgers, The State University of New Jersey, Center for Molecular and Behavioral Neuroscience, Newark, NJ, $60,000. For research grant for McDonnell-Pew Program in Cognitive Neuroscience. 1991.

1549-30 Stanford University, School of Medicine, Department of Neurobiology, Stanford, CA, $117,826. For training grant for McDonnell-Pew Program for Cognitive Neuroscience. 1991.

1549-31 Stanford University, School of Medicine, Division of Oncology, Stanford, CA, $137,500. For research of McDonnell Fellow in Molecular Medicine for Cancer Research. 1991.

1549-32 University of California, Department of Anthropology, Santa Barbara, CA, $37,500. For matching funds for Presidential Young Investigator for research on learning and development that attempts to incorporate evolutionary theory into cognitive neuroscience. 1991.

1549-33 University of California, Department of Biology, La Jolla, CA, $400,000. For McDonnell-Pew Program in Cognitive Neuroscience. 1991.

1549-34 University of Medicine and Dentistry of New Jersey Foundation, Center for Neuroscience, Piscataway, NJ, $15,000. For inter-institutional course and conference on cognitive neuroscience of memory. 1991.

1549-35 University of Oxford, Laboratory of Physiology, Oxford, England, $400,000. For McDonnell-Pew Program in Cognitive Neuroscience. 1991.

1549-36 University of Texas, Southwestern Medical School, Department of Pathology, Dallas, TX, $137,500. For work of McDonnell Fellow in Molecular Medicine in Cancer Research. 1991.

1549-37 Washington University, Department of Philosophy, Saint Louis, MO, $90,000. For planning grant for Philosophy, Neuroscience and Psychology Program. 1991.

1549-38 Washington University, School of Medicine, Division of Hematology/Oncology, Saint Louis, MO, $234,153. For fellowship support and administrative costs as part of Molecular Medicine in Cancer Research Program. 1991.

1549-39 Yale University, School of Medicine, Department of Pathology, New Haven, CT, $137,500. For McDonnell Scholar in Molecular Medicine in Cancer Research. 1991.

1549-40 Yale University, School of Medicine, Section of Neurobiology, New Haven, CT, $116,516. For training grant for McDonnell-Pew Program in Cognitive Neuroscience. 1991.

1550
Mercantile Trust Company Charitable Trust

c/o Mercantile Bank, N.A.
P.O. Box 387
St. Louis 63166   (314) 425-2672

Trust established in 1952 in MO.
Donor(s): Mercantile Trust Co.
Foundation type: Company-sponsored
Financial data (yr. ended 02/28/91): Assets, $2,967,216 (M); expenditures, $824,580; qualifying distributions, $822,572, including $798,648 for 82 grants (high: $70,000; low: $30; average: $1,000-$7,000) and $23,909 for 133 employee matching gifts.
Purpose and activities: Emphasis on higher education, hospitals, and cultural programs; support also for youth agencies and community development.

Fields of interest: Higher education, hospitals, cultural programs, youth, community development.
Limitations: Giving primarily in MO.
Publications: Program policy statement.
Application information: Application form not required.
   Initial approach: Letter
   Copies of proposal: 1
   Deadline(s): None
   Write: Ms. H. Jill Fivecoat, V.P., Mercantile Bank, N.A.
Trustee: Mercantile Bank, N.A.
Number of staff: None.
EIN: 436020630

1551
Spencer T. and Ann W. Olin Foundation ▼

Pierre Laclede Bldg.
7701 Forsyth Blvd.
St. Louis 63105   (314) 727-6202

Incorporated in 1957 in DE.
Donor(s): Spencer T. Olin, Ann W. Olin.‡
Foundation type: Independent
Financial data (yr. ended 12/31/91): Assets, $41,635,989 (M); gifts received, $836,950; expenditures, $4,882,353; qualifying distributions, $4,480,575, including $4,480,575 for 30 grants (high: $1,500,000; low: $750; average: $1,000-$100,000).
Purpose and activities: Giving primarily for higher education, medical education, research, health services, and environmental conservation; support also for community service agencies.
Fields of interest: Higher education, medical education, health services, medical research, environment.
Types of support: Annual campaigns, research, general purposes.
Limitations: No support for national health or welfare organizations, religious groups, or generally for secondary education, or projects which are substantially financed by public tax funds. No grants to individuals, or for building or endowment funds, deficit financing, operating budgets, conferences, travel, exhibits, scholarships, fellowships, or matching gifts; no loans.
Publications: Annual report (including application guidelines).
Application information: Applications not accepted.
   Board meeting date(s): Usually in Apr.
   Write: Warren M. Shapleigh, Pres.
Officers and Trustees:* Warren M. Shapleigh,* Pres.; J. Lester Willemetz, Treas. and Exec. Dir.; Eunice Olin Higgins, William W. Higgins, Rolla J. Mottaz, John C. Pritzlaff, Jr., Mary Olin Pritzlaff, Barbara Olin Taylor, F. Morgan Taylor, Jr.
Number of staff: 2 part-time professional; 1 part-time support.
EIN: 376044148
Recent health grants:
1551-1 Harrington Arthritis Research Center, Phoenix, AZ, $50,000. 1990.
1551-2 Washington University, Saint Louis, MO, $1,500,000. For Spencer T. and Ann W. Olin Medical Scientist Fellowship Program. 1990.

1552
Oppenstein Brothers Foundation

911 Main St., Suite 100
P.O. Box 13095
Kansas City 64199-3095   (816) 234-8671

Trust established in 1975 in MO.
Donor(s): Michael Oppenstein.‡
Foundation type: Independent
Financial data (yr. ended 03/31/92): Assets, $19,076,056 (M); expenditures, $908,397; qualifying distributions, $886,592, including $886,592 for 89 grants (high: $80,000; low: $1,000).
Purpose and activities: Grants primarily for social services and early childhood, elementary, secondary, adult, vocational and higher education, emphasizing the prevention of illness and abuse, and programs which enhance the ability of individuals to remain or become self-sufficient; some support for community and leadership development, family planning and services, social services and welfare agencies, Jewish welfare organizations, programs for youth, minorities, the handicapped, disadvantaged, mentally ill, homeless and elderly, and arts education.
Fields of interest: Social services, elementary education, secondary education, higher education, youth, homeless, aged, arts, health, AIDS.
Types of support: Operating budgets, general purposes, seed money, emergency funds, special projects, matching funds, renovation projects, consulting services, lectureships, conferences and seminars.
Limitations: Giving limited to the Kansas City, MO, metropolitan area. No support for medical research. No grants to individuals, or for annual campaigns, building funds or expansion, scholarships, fellowships, medical equipment, or generally for endowment funds; limited operating funds for United Way or Jewish Federation supported agencies; no loans.
Publications: Multi-year report, informational brochure (including application guidelines).
Application information: Application form not required.
   Initial approach: Telephone or letter
   Copies of proposal: 2
   Deadline(s): Submit proposal with complete information approximately 2 weeks prior to board meetings; no set deadline
   Board meeting date(s): Usually bimonthly
   Final notification: 2 to 4 months
   Write: Candace L. Fowler, Prog. Officer
Officer: Candace L. Fowler, Prog. Officer.
Disbursement Committee: John Morgan, Chair.; Mary Bloch, Laura Fields, Roger Hurwitz, Estelle Sosland.
Trustee: Commerce Bank of Kansas City, N.A.
Number of staff: None.
EIN: 436203035
Recent health grants:
1552-1 Menorah Medical Center, Kansas City, MO, $25,000. For obstetric care for indigent women and to subsidize medical services for Jewish Russian immigrants. 1991.
1552-2 Midwest Christian Counseling Center, Kansas City, MO, $10,000. For Adolescent Substance Abuse Treatment Program. 1991.
1552-3 National Council on Alcoholism and Drug Abuse, Kansas City, MO, $12,500. To

help establish and operate asssessment center. 1991.

1552-4 Renaissance West, Kansas City, MO, $50,000. For Women's Intensive Outpatient Treatment Program. 1991.

1552-5 United Way, Heart of America, Kansas City, MO, $10,000. For development of Heart of America Community AIDS Partnership, collaborative AIDS programs in metropolitan area. 1991.

1553
Paul Patton Charitable Trust
c/o Boatmen's First National Bank of Kansas City
P.O. Box 419038
Kansas City 64183
Application address: c/o Boatmen's First National Bank, Trust Div., 14 West Tenth St., Kansas City, MO 64105; Tel.: (816) 691-7481

Established in 1989 in MO.
Foundation type: Independent
Financial data (yr. ended 12/31/90): Assets, $2,589,361 (M); expenditures, $127,953; qualifying distributions, $103,271, including $100,000 for 1 grant.
Purpose and activities: Giving limited to pediatric research and related causes.
Fields of interest: Medical education, medical research.
Types of support: Research.
Limitations: Giving primarily in the greater Kansas City area.
Application information:
  Initial approach: Letter of no more than 3 pages
  Deadline(s): Varies
  Write: David P. Ross, Sr. V.P., Boatmen's First National Bank of Kansas City
Trustees: William L. Evans, Jr., C. Ted McCarter, Boatmen's First National Bank of Kansas City.
EIN: 446009254

1554
Pet Incorporated Community Support Foundation
400 South Fourth St.
St. Louis 63102   (314) 621-5400

Established in 1959.
Donor(s): Pet, Inc.
Foundation type: Company-sponsored
Financial data (yr. ended 12/31/90): Assets, $218,058 (M); gifts received, $476,435; expenditures, $557,824; qualifying distributions, $557,579, including $557,500 for 60 grants (high: $175,000; low: $500).
Purpose and activities: Giving primarily for education, youth, cultural programs, health and welfare, and a community fund.
Fields of interest: Education, youth, cultural programs, health, welfare, community funds.
Types of support: General purposes, operating budgets, equipment, scholarship funds, capital campaigns.
Limitations: Giving primarily in MO, with emphasis on St. Louis.
Application information:
  Initial approach: Letter and proposal
  Deadline(s): None
  Write: Richard A. Mittelbusher, Pres.

Officers and Trustees:* Richard L. Mittelbusher,* Pres.; Anthony C. Knizel,* V.P. and Treas.; Myron W. Sheets, V.P.; James A. Wescott, V.P.; Phyllis P. Vogt, Secy.; Miles L. Marsh.
EIN: 436046149

1555
James T. Pettus, Jr. Foundation
c/o Guaranty Trust Co. of Missouri
7701 Forsyth, Suite 1200
Clayton 63105   (314) 725-9055
Additional mailing address: P.O. Box 16260, Clayton, MO 63105

Established in 1960 in MO.
Foundation type: Independent
Financial data (yr. ended 12/31/91): Assets, $2,500,000 (M); gifts received, $75,000; expenditures, $145,311; qualifying distributions, $131,900, including $131,900 for 41 grants (high: $12,900; low: $500; average: $2,000-$6,000).
Fields of interest: Social services, youth, child development, education, health associations, hospices, handicapped, community funds, general charitable giving.
Types of support: Annual campaigns, continuing support, general purposes.
Limitations: Giving primarily in HI.
Application information: Rarely funds new applicants; all new applications limited to HI.
  Initial approach: Letter
  Deadline(s): None
  Final notification: Within 60 days
  Write: James A. Finch III, Trustee
Trustees: James A. Finch III, Betty Pettus, James T. Pettus, Jr., Guaranty Trust Co. of Missouri.
Number of staff: None.
EIN: 436029569

1556
Pitzman Fund
c/o Boatmen's Trust Co.
100 North Broadway, P.O. Box 14737
St. Louis 63178   (314) 436-9042

Established in 1944.
Donor(s): Frederick Pitzman.‡
Foundation type: Independent
Financial data (yr. ended 09/30/90): Assets, $2,045,505 (M); expenditures, $66,517; qualifying distributions, $55,703, including $54,500 for 27 grants (high: $10,000; low: $500; average: $500-$1,500).
Fields of interest: Education, youth, social services, drug abuse, family planning, cultural programs, Protestant giving.
Types of support: Annual campaigns, continuing support, general purposes.
Limitations: Giving primarily in St. Louis, MO.
Application information: Application form not required.
  Copies of proposal: 1
  Deadline(s): None
  Write: Roy T. Blair
Trustees: Carol Elsaesser, Boatmen's Trust Co.
Number of staff: None.
EIN: 436023901

1557
Ralston Purina Trust Fund ▼
Checkerboard Sq.
St. Louis 63164   (314) 982-3230

Trust established in 1951 in MO.
Donor(s): Ralston Purina Co.
Foundation type: Company-sponsored
Financial data (yr. ended 08/31/90): Assets, $15,696,740 (M); gifts received, $1,500,000; expenditures, $2,322,914; qualifying distributions, $2,287,114, including $2,285,200 for 74 grants (high: $500,000; low: $1,000; average: $2,000-$20,000).
Purpose and activities: Grants principally to community funds; support also for higher education, health, education and human service agencies. Foundation support represents about one-half of the company's charitable giving, which includes funds for an employee matching gift program and employee-related scholarships.
Fields of interest: Community funds, higher education, social services, health, education.
Types of support: General purposes, building funds, capital campaigns, emergency funds, endowment funds.
Limitations: Giving limited to areas of company facilities, especially St. Louis, MO. No support for religious or politically partisan purposes. No grants to individuals, or for investment funds, advertisements, research which is not action-oriented, underwriting of deficits, or post-event funding; no loans.
Publications: Application guidelines.
Application information:
  Initial approach: Proposal
  Copies of proposal: 1
  Deadline(s): None
  Board meeting date(s): Quarterly
  Final notification: 6 to 8 weeks
  Write: Fred H. Perabo, Dir., Community Affairs
Board of Control: C.S. Sommer, Chair.; Fred H. Perabo.
Trustee: Boatmen's Trust Co.
Number of staff: 1 part-time professional; 1 part-time support.
EIN: 431209652

1558
The J. B. Reynolds Foundation
3520 Broadway
P.O. Box 139
Kansas City 64111   (816) 753-7000

Incorporated in 1961 in MO.
Donor(s): Walter Edwin Bixby, Sr., Pearl G. Reynolds.‡
Foundation type: Independent
Financial data (yr. ended 12/31/90): Assets, $10,304,646 (M); expenditures, $503,368; qualifying distributions, $493,544, including $493,544 for 96 grants (high: $30,000; low: $20; average: $1,000-$20,000).
Fields of interest: Medical research, youth, social services, arts, civic affairs.
Types of support: Annual campaigns, seed money, emergency funds, building funds, equipment, land acquisition, research, publications, conferences and seminars, continuing support.
Limitations: Giving primarily in a 150-mile radius of Kansas City, MO. No grants to individuals.

Application information: Contributes only to pre-selected organizations. Applications not accepted.

Board meeting date(s): Apr. and Dec.
Write: Walter E. Bixby, V.P.
Officers: Joseph Reynolds Bixby, Pres.; Walter E. Bixby, V.P. and Treas.; Richard L. Finn, Secy.
Board Members: Kathryn Bixby-Haddad, Ann Bixby-Oxler.
EIN: 446014359

1559
Joseph H. and Florence A. Roblee Foundation
c/o Boatmen's Trust Co.
510 Locust St., P.O. Box 14737
St. Louis 63178

Trust established in 1970 in MO.
Donor(s): Louise Roblee McCarthy,‡ Florence Roblee Trust.
Foundation type: Independent
Financial data (yr. ended 12/31/90): Assets, $10,783,827 (M); expenditures, $571,787; qualifying distributions, $509,185, including $478,325 for 50 grants (high: $10,000; low: $1,000; average: $500-$15,000).
Purpose and activities: Emphasis on ecumenical projects, educational projects generally outside the academic area (such as intercultural global understanding, citizen education, and leadership development), health (primarily mental health), and pressing social problems.
Fields of interest: Educational research, leadership development, mental health, religion, intercultural relations, citizenship, health, social sciences, AIDS, social services, religion—Christian, peace, Protestant giving.
Types of support: Seed money, building funds, equipment, endowment funds, scholarship funds, exchange programs, capital campaigns, emergency funds, special projects.
Limitations: Giving primarily in MO, CA, FL, NC, NY, and TX. No grants to individuals, or for research programs; no loans.
Application information: Application form not required.

Initial approach: Proposal
Copies of proposal: 4
Deadline(s): Feb. 28 and Aug. 31
Board meeting date(s): June and Oct.
Final notification: July 1 and Dec. 1
Write: Roy T. Blair, Trust Officer, Boatmen's Trust Co.
Officer and Trustees:* Carol M. Duhme,* Pres.; Marjorie M. Robins, Boatmen's Trust Co.
Board Members: Warren Duhme, Barbara R. Foorman, Roblee McCarthy, Jr., Nancy Richardson, Carol R. von Arx, Ann Welker.
Number of staff: 1 part-time professional.
EIN: 436109579

1560
Sachs Fund
400 Chesterfield Ctr., Suite 600
Chesterfield 63017   (314) 537-1000
Application address: P.O. Box 350, Chesterfield, MO 63006

Trust established in 1957 in MO.
Donor(s): Samuel C. Sachs, Sachs Electric Corp.

Foundation type: Independent
Financial data (yr. ended 04/30/91): Assets, $2,727,000 (M); expenditures, $187,800; qualifying distributions, $147,915, including $147,915 for 21 grants (high: $51,000; low: $150).
Fields of interest: Jewish welfare, hospitals, community funds, higher education, cultural programs.
Limitations: Giving primarily in MO. No grants to individuals.
Application information: Contributes only to pre-selected organizations. Applications not accepted.
Write: Louis S. Sachs, Trustee
Trustees: Louis S. Sachs, Mary L. Sachs, Jerome W. Sandweiss.
EIN: 436032385

1561
Schnuck Markets, Inc.
11420 Lackland Rd.
P.O. Box 46928
St. Louis 63146   (314) 994-9900

Purpose and activities: Supports general education, early childhood through higher education, and the development of youth; also gives for hunger programs and hospitals.
Fields of interest: Education, higher education, education—early childhood, elementary education, hunger, hospitals, youth.
Types of support: Annual campaigns, employee volunteer services, donated products, cause-related marketing.
Limitations: Giving primarily in St. Louis, MO, and other markets in which company operates.
Application information: Corporate secretary's office handles giving.
Write: Terry E. Schnuck, Secy. and Chief Legal Counsel

1562
Arch W. Shaw Foundation
Thomasville Route, Box 60B
Birch Tree 65438   (417) 764-3701

Trust established in 1949 in IL.
Foundation type: Independent
Financial data (yr. ended 12/31/90): Assets, $9,262,888 (M); expenditures, $415,376; qualifying distributions, $411,190, including $411,000 for 61 grants (high: $25,000; low: $1,000).
Fields of interest: Higher education, business education, education—building funds, libraries, hospitals, hospices, medical research, hospitals—building funds, cultural programs, museums.
Types of support: Building funds, equipment, annual campaigns, scholarship funds, matching funds, continuing support, endowment funds.
Limitations: Giving primarily in IL and MO. No support for private foundations. No grants to individuals.
Application information:
Initial approach: Letter
Deadline(s): None
Write: William W. Shaw, Trustee
Trustees: Arch W. Shaw II, Bruce P. Shaw, Roger D. Shaw, Jr., William W. Shaw.

EIN: 366055262

1563
Shelter Insurance Foundation
1817 West Broadway
Columbia 65218   (314) 874-4290

Established in 1981 in MO.
Foundation type: Company-sponsored
Financial data (yr. ended 06/30/91): Assets, $1,575,225 (M); gifts received, $193,490; expenditures, $257,181; qualifying distributions, $255,502, including $22,773 for 7 grants (high: $13,000; low: $273) and $232,729 for grants to individuals.
Purpose and activities: Support primarily for higher education, including scholarships to individuals, cancer research, and general charitable giving.
Fields of interest: Higher education, cancer, general charitable giving.
Types of support: Research, student aid, scholarship funds.
Limitations: Giving limited to AR, CO, IL, IN, IA, KS, KY, LA, MS, MO, NE, OK, and TN.
Application information:
Initial approach: Letter
Deadline(s): None
Write: Raymond E. Jones, Secy.
Officers and Directors:* Gustav J. Lehr,* Pres.; Robert W. Maupin,* V.P.; Raymond E. Jones,* Secy.; J. Donald Duello,* Treas.; Robert T. Cox, Howard B. Lang, John W. Lennox, Jean J. Madden, B.R. Minnick, James A. Offutt, Jack L. Pettit, Mark E. Zimmer.
EIN: 431224155

1564
Shoenberg Foundation, Inc.
200 North Broadway, Suite 1475
St. Louis 63102   (314) 421-2247

Incorporated in 1955 in MO.
Donor(s): Sydney M. Shoenberg.‡
Foundation type: Independent
Financial data (yr. ended 12/31/91): Assets, $5,178,870 (M); expenditures, $488,245; qualifying distributions, $478,900, including $478,900 for 32 grants (high: $130,000; low: $100).
Fields of interest: Arts, cultural programs, history, community funds, medical research, hospitals, speech pathology, Jewish giving.
Types of support: Annual campaigns, capital campaigns, continuing support.
Limitations: Giving primarily in MO. No grants to individuals.
Application information: Contributes only to pre-selected organizations. Applications not accepted.
Write: William W. Ross, Secy.-Treas.
Officers and Directors:* Sydney M. Shoenberg, Jr.,* Chair.; Robert H. Shoenberg,* Pres.; E.L. Langenberg,* V.P.; William W. Ross,* Secy.-Treas.
Number of staff: None.
EIN: 436028764

1565
Roy W. Slusher Charitable Foundation
c/o Mercantile Bank of Springfield, Trust Dept.
P.O. Box 10327
Springfield 65805-0327   (417) 868-4545

Established in 1988 in MO.
Foundation type: Independent
Financial data (yr. ended 02/28/91): Assets,
$6,102,350 (M); expenditures, $285,936;
qualifying distributions, $424,491, including
$137,022 for 11 grants (high: $20,000; low:
$1,000) and $200,000 for set-asides.
Purpose and activities: Funding to meet the needs
of disadvantaged youth and their families and to
increase the quality of life for the elderly through
the following broad areas: educational
scholarships, broad national health issues, youth
camps and programs, senior citizens programs,
and public radio and television.
Fields of interest: Hospitals, heart disease, cancer,
child welfare, youth, aged.
Types of support: Building funds, scholarship
funds, operating budgets, general purposes, seed
money.
Limitations: Giving primarily in MO. No grants to
individuals, or for routine operating needs, annual
fundraising, or endowments.
Application information: Application form not
required.
  Deadline(s): None
  Board meeting date(s): Mar. and Sept.
  Write: Charles A. Fuller, Jr., Mgr.
Officer: Charles A. Fuller, Jr., Mgr.
Trustee: Mercantile Bank of Springfield.
EIN: 436339151

1566
Ralph L. Smith Foundation
c/o Boatmen's First National Bank of Kansas City
14 West Tenth St.
Kansas City 64105   (816) 691-2800
Mailing address: P.O. Box 38, Kansas City, MO
64183

Trust established in 1952 in MO.
Donor(s): Harriet T. Smith,‡ Ralph L. Smith.‡
Foundation type: Independent
Financial data (yr. ended 12/31/90): Assets,
$8,307,858 (M); expenditures, $311,523;
qualifying distributions, $272,012, including
$259,998 for 77 grants (high: $15,000; low:
$262; average: $5,000-$30,000).
Fields of interest: Education, youth, conservation,
medical research, women.
Limitations: Giving primarily in the Kansas City,
MO, metropolitan area. No grants to individuals.
Publications: 990-PF.
Application information: Applications for grants
will not be acknowledged.
  Initial approach: Telephone followed by 3-page
    letter
  Copies of proposal: 1
  Deadline(s): None
  Board meeting date(s): Quarterly
  Final notification: 2 months
  Write: David P. Ross, Sr. V.P., Boatmen's First
    National Bank of Kansas City
Managers: Harriet Denison, Anne S. Douthat,
Ralph L. Smith, Jr.
Trustee: Boatmen's First National Bank of Kansas
City.

EIN: 446008508

1567
The Sosland Foundation ▼
4800 Main St., Suite 100
Kansas City 64112   (816) 756-1000
FAX: (816) 756-0494

Incorporated in 1955 in MO.
Donor(s): Members of the Sosland family.
Foundation type: Independent
Financial data (yr. ended 11/30/91): Assets,
$22,612,424 (M); expenditures, $1,438,589;
qualifying distributions, $1,291,102, including
$1,291,102 for 229 grants (high: $400,000; low:
$500; average: $1,000-$10,000).
Purpose and activities: Giving to Jewish and
social welfare funds, higher and secondary
education, the arts, and health organizations.
Fields of interest: Jewish giving, Jewish welfare,
higher education, secondary education, arts,
social services, health.
Types of support: Emergency funds, endowment
funds, special projects.
Limitations: Giving primarily in the metropolitan
Kansas City, MO, and KS areas. No grants to
individuals, or for publications, or conferences;
no loans.
Application information: Application form not
required.
  Initial approach: Letter
  Copies of proposal: 1
  Deadline(s): None
  Board meeting date(s): Mar., June, Sept., and
    Dec.
  Final notification: 3 months
  Write: Debbie Sosland-Edelman, Ph.D
Officers and Directors:* Morton I. Sosland,*
Pres.; H.J. Sosland, V.P.; Neil N. Sosland,*
Secy.-Treas.
Number of staff: 2 part-time professional.
EIN: 446007129

1568
Sidney W. and Sylvia N. Souers Charitable Trust
c/o Boatmen's Trust Co.
100 North Broadway, P.O. Box 14737
St. Louis 63178   (314) 436-9263

Trust established in 1955 in MO.
Donor(s): Sylvia N. Souers.
Foundation type: Independent
Financial data (yr. ended 12/31/90): Assets,
$12,595,340 (M); expenditures, $596,702;
qualifying distributions, $550,633, including
$547,000 for 25 grants (high: $100,000; low:
$1,000).
Fields of interest: Higher education, hospitals.
Limitations: Giving primarily in St. Louis, MO,
and Washington, DC. No grants to individuals.
Application information:
  Initial approach: Letter
  Deadline(s): None
Trustee: Boatmen's Trust Co.
EIN: 436079817

1569
Southwestern Bell Foundation
One Bell Center, Suite 223
St. Louis 63101   (314) 235-7040

Established in 1984 in MO.
Donor(s): Southwestern Bell Corp.
Foundation type: Company-sponsored
Financial data (yr. ended 12/31/89): Assets,
$42,012,377 (M); gifts received, $16,000,000;
expenditures, $15,654,813; qualifying
distributions, $15,580,000, including
$14,818,431 for 2,704 grants (high: $720,000;
low: $100) and $749,825 for 5,650 employee
matching gifts.
Purpose and activities: Giving largely for
education; support also for health, welfare, the
arts, and civic affairs.
Fields of interest: Education, health, welfare, arts,
cultural programs, civic affairs, community funds.
Types of support: Conferences and seminars,
employee matching gifts, lectureships, matching
funds, research, seed money, special projects,
technical assistance.
Limitations: Giving primarily in KS, MO, DC, TX,
AR, OK, and NY. No support for religious
organizations, fraternal, veterans', or labor groups.
No grants to individuals, or for operating funds for
hospitals, capital funds, operating funds for
United Way-supported organizations, special
advertising, or ticket/dinner purchases.
Publications: Annual report (including application
guidelines), informational brochure (including
application guidelines).
Application information: Unsuccessful applicants
may not reapply in same calendar year.
Application form not required.
  Initial approach: Letter
  Copies of proposal: 1
  Deadline(s): None
  Final notification: Four to six weeks
  Write: Charles DeRiemer, V.P. and Exec. Dir.
Officers and Directors:* Larry Alexander, Pres.;
Roger Wohlert, V.P. and Treas.; Charles
DeRiemer,* V.P. and Exec. Dir.; Gerald
Blatherwick, James Ellis, Robert G. Pope.
Number of staff: 4 full-time professional; 1
full-time support.
EIN: 431353948
Recent health grants:
1569-1 Baylor Medical Center at Ennis, Ennis,
  TX, $10,000. 1990.
1569-2 Childrens Foundation of Saint Louis,
  Saint Louis, MO, $35,000. 1990.
1569-3 Childrens Miracle Network Telethon of
  Greater Saint Louis, Saint Ann, MO, $10,000.
  1990.
1569-4 Circus Arts Foundation of Missouri, Saint
  Louis, MO, $20,000. 1990.
1569-5 Edgewood Childrens Center, Webster
  Groves, MO, $26,000. 1990.
1569-6 Harris Methodist Foundation, Fort Worth,
  TX, $10,500. 1990.
1569-7 Jewish Hospital of Saint Louis, Saint
  Louis, MO, $25,000. 1990.
1569-8 Lake of the Ozarks General Hospital,
  Osage Beach, MO, $10,000. 1990.
1569-9 Leukemia Society of America, Saint
  Louis, MO, $60,000. 1990.
1569-10 Mercy Health Center, Oklahoma City,
  OK, $20,000. 1990.
1569-11 Neighborhood Health Center, Saint
  Louis, MO, $22,000. 1990.

1569-12 Provident Counseling, Saint Louis, MO, $10,000. 1990.

1569-13 Quality of Life Foundation of Austin, Austin, TX, $23,000. 1990.

1569-14 Saint Louis Childrens Hospital, Saint Louis, MO, $35,000. 1990.

1569-15 Scottish Rite Childhood Language Disorder Clinic, Saint Louis, MO, $10,000. 1990.

1569-16 South Community Hospital, Oklahoma City, OK, $10,000. 1990.

1569-17 Texas Tech Medical Foundation, Lubbock, TX, $37,750. 1990.

1569-18 University Medical Center, Dallas, TX, $50,000. 1990.

1569-19 Wyandotte House, Kansas City, KS, $10,000. 1990.

1570
Victor E. Speas Foundation ▼
c/o Boatmen's First National Bank of Kansas City
14 West Tenth St.
Kansas City 64105   (816) 691-7481

Trust established in 1947 in MO.
Donor(s): Effie E. Speas,‡ Victor E. Speas,‡ Speas Co.
Foundation type: Independent
Financial data (yr. ended 12/31/90): Assets, $21,097,613 (M); expenditures, $1,475,770; qualifying distributions, $1,311,761, including $1,277,125 for 74 grants (high: $100,000; low: $45; average: $5,000-$50,000).
Purpose and activities: Giving restricted to improving the quality of health care in the Kansas City, MO, area. Support mainly for medically-related higher education, including loans for medical students at the University of Missouri at Kansas City, preventive health care, and medical research; grants also for agencies serving the health care needs of the elderly, youth, and the handicapped.
Fields of interest: Hospitals, rehabilitation, medical education, medical research, youth, child welfare, aged, health services, handicapped, AIDS, alcoholism, cancer, drug abuse, heart disease, hospices, mental health, safety, volunteerism, women, dentistry.
Types of support: Seed money, emergency funds, equipment, research, special projects, renovation projects, capital campaigns, matching funds, operating budgets, student loans.
Limitations: Giving limited to Jackson, Clay, Platte, and Cass counties, MO. No grants for endowment funds or scholarships (except to medical students at the University of Missouri at Kansas City); no loans.
Publications: 990-PF, program policy statement, application guidelines.
Application information: Application form not required.
  Initial approach: Telephone or letter (no longer than 3 pages)
  Copies of proposal: 1
  Deadline(s): None
  Board meeting date(s): Bimonthly
  Final notification: 2 months
  Write: David P. Ross, Sr. V.P., Boatmen's First National Bank of Kansas City ·
Trustee: Boatmen's First National Bank of Kansas City.
Number of staff: 1 full-time professional.

EIN: 446008340

1571
John W. and Effie E. Speas Memorial Trust
c/o Boatmen's First National Bank of Kansas City
14 West Tenth St.
Kansas City 64183   (816) 691-7481
Application address: Boatmen's First National Bank of Kansas City, P.O. Box 419038, Kansas City, MO 64183

Trust established in 1947 in MO.
Donor(s): Effie E. Speas,‡ Victor E. Speas,‡ Speas Co.
Foundation type: Independent
Financial data (yr. ended 12/31/90): Assets, $21,107,140 (M); expenditures, $1,446,146; qualifying distributions, $1,288,371, including $1,254,160 for 26 grants (high: $250,000; low: $3,000; average: $5,000-$100,000).
Purpose and activities: Giving primarily for hospitals and health services, including support for the aged and mentally disabled, higher education in the health professions, and medical research.
Fields of interest: Health services, hospitals, medical education, aged, mental health, medical research.
Types of support: Special projects, equipment, research, general purposes, operating budgets, seed money.
Limitations: Giving limited to the greater Kansas City metropolitan area.
Publications: 990-PF.
Application information: Application form not required.
  Initial approach: Letter of 3 pages or less
  Copies of proposal: 1
  Deadline(s): None
  Board meeting date(s): Biweekly
  Final notification: 2 months
  Write: David P. Ross, Sr. V.P., Boatmen's First National Bank of Kansas City
Trustee: Boatmen's First National Bank of Kansas City.
Number of staff: 1 full-time professional.
EIN: 446008249

1572
Stupp Brothers Bridge & Iron Company Foundation
P.O. Box 6600
St. Louis 63125   (314) 638-5000

Trust established about 1952 in MO.
Donor(s): Stupp Bros. Bridge & Iron Co.
Foundation type: Company-sponsored
Financial data (yr. ended 10/31/90): Assets, $6,319,439 (M); expenditures, $335,319; qualifying distributions, $323,120, including $323,120 for 160 grants (high: $46,000; low: $50).
Purpose and activities: Giving to hospitals, community funds, and higher education and educational associations; support also for cultural, health, and welfare programs.
Fields of interest: Hospitals, community funds, higher education, educational associations, cultural programs, health services, welfare.
Limitations: Giving primarily in MO. No grants to individuals.

Application information: Contributes only to pre-selected organizations. Applications not accepted.
Trustees: Erwin P. Stupp, Jr., John P. Stupp, Robert P. Stupp.
EIN: 237412437

1573
Norman J. Stupp Foundation
c/o Commerce Bank of St. Louis, N.A., Investment Management & Trust Services
P.O. Box 11356
Clayton 63105   (314) 746-7220

Established in 1952 in MO.
Donor(s): Norman J. Stupp.‡
Foundation type: Independent
Financial data (yr. ended 06/30/90): Assets, $11,000,000 (M); expenditures, $600,000; qualifying distributions, $500,000, including $500,000 for grants.
Fields of interest: Youth, social services, hospitals, medical research, education, public affairs, science and technology.
Types of support: Capital campaigns, endowment funds, operating budgets, research, scholarship funds, special projects.
Limitations: Giving primarily in St. Louis, MO.
Publications: 990-PF.
Application information: Non-MO applications usually not reviewed. Application form not required.
  Initial approach: Letter or proposal
  Deadline(s): Oct. 30 and Apr. 30
  Board meeting date(s): Apr. and Dec.
  Write: John W. North, V.P. and Trust Officer, Commerce Bank of St. Louis, N.A.
Trustee: Commerce Bank of St. Louis, N.A.
EIN: 436027433

1574
Lester T. Sunderland Foundation
8080 Ward Pkwy., Suite 155
Kansas City 64114   (913) 451-8900

Incorporated in 1945 in MO.
Donor(s): Lester T. Sunderland.‡
Foundation type: Independent
Financial data (yr. ended 12/31/91): Assets, $15,212,000 (M); expenditures, $690,184; qualifying distributions, $673,841, including $669,071 for grants.
Purpose and activities: Emphasis on building funds for higher education; support also for youth agencies, hospitals, and community funds.
Fields of interest: Education—building funds, youth, hospitals, community funds.
Types of support: Operating budgets, continuing support, annual campaigns, seed money, emergency funds, building funds, equipment, land acquisition, endowment funds.
Limitations: Giving primarily in MO, KS, NE, and AR. No grants to individuals; no loans.
Publications: 990-PF.
Application information: Application form not required.
  Initial approach: Letter
  Copies of proposal: 1
  Board meeting date(s): As required
  Write: James P. Sunderland, V.P.

Officers and Trustees:* Paul Sunderland,* Pres.; James P. Sunderland,* V.P. and Secy.; Robert Sunderland,* V.P. and Treas.; Charles Sunderland, Whitney P. Sunderland.
Number of staff: None.
EIN: 446011082

1575
Tension Envelope Foundation
819 East 19th St., 5th Fl.
Kansas City 64108 (816) 471-3800

Incorporated in 1954 in MO.
Donor(s): Tension Envelope Corp.
Foundation type: Company-sponsored
Financial data (yr. ended 11/30/90): Assets, $2,470,764 (M); expenditures, $336,803; qualifying distributions, $300,356, including $296,562 for 152 grants (high: $30,094; low: $200).
Purpose and activities: Emphasis on Jewish welfare funds; support also for community funds, higher education, health, civic affairs, culture and the arts, and youth.
Fields of interest: Jewish welfare, community funds, higher education, health, civic affairs, cultural programs, arts, youth.
Limitations: Giving primarily in areas of company operations. No grants to individuals.
Application information: Application form not required.
   Initial approach: Letter
   Deadline(s): None
   Write: Eliot S. Berkley, Secy.
Officers and Directors:* Richard L. Berkley,* Pres.; Walter L. Hiersteiner, V.P.; Eliot S. Berkley,* Secy.; E. Bertram Berkley,* Treas.; William Berkley, Abraham E. Margolin.
EIN: 446012554

1576
Union Electric Company Corporate
   Giving Program
1901 Chouteau St.
P.O. Box 149
St. Louis 63166 (314) 621-3222

Financial data (yr. ended 12/31/90): Total giving, $621,691, including $487,650 for grants (average: $5,000-$25,000) and $134,041 for 159 in-kind gifts.
Purpose and activities: The company supports the following general areas: civic, cultural and arts organizations, educational institutions and programs, medical facilities, social services, urban affairs, and youth activities. Considered are programs for the elderly, business, child welfare, community development, conservation, the disadvantaged, the handicapped, health, the homeless, hunger, minorities, museums, public policy, rural development, science and technology, urban affairs, volunteerism, women, welfare, and economics. Types of support include employee matching gifts for education. The company also makes in-kind donations of its salvage/surplus and materials. The corporate contributions program is specifically designated to provide small gifts of less than $2,500.
Fields of interest: Civic affairs, cultural programs, education, higher education, hospitals, social services, urban development, youth, aged, arts,

business, business education, child welfare, conservation, crime and law enforcement, performing arts, delinquency, disadvantaged, education—early childhood, education—building funds, educational research, elementary education, employment, energy, engineering, environment, family services, handicapped, health, homeless, hunger, leadership development, minorities, secondary education, literacy, science and technology, volunteerism, housing.
Types of support: Capital campaigns, operating budgets, building funds, employee matching gifts, annual campaigns, continuing support, emergency funds, endowment funds, equipment, general purposes, matching funds, renovation projects, research, special projects, technical assistance, scholarship funds, in-kind gifts, donated equipment, employee volunteer services.
Limitations: Giving primarily in the St. Louis, MO, area and operating locations. No support for political organizations or candidates, or social, religious, fraternal, veterans', or similar organizations.
Publications: Informational brochure (including application guidelines).
Application information: Company has a staff that only handles contributions. Application form not required.
   Initial approach: Proposal on organization letterhead; Send to headquarters
   Copies of proposal: 1
   Deadline(s): None
   Board meeting date(s): Applications reviewed as received
   Write: Patricia Barrett, V.P., Corp. Communs.
Administrators: M. Patricia Barrett, V.P., Corp. Communs.; Eugene M. McMahon, Supvr., Community Rels.
Number of staff: 1 full-time professional; 2 part-time professional; 1 full-time support.

1577
The Earl E. Walker and Myrtle E. Walker
   Foundation
12071 Carberry Place
St. Louis 63131-3123

Established in 1987 in MO.
Donor(s): CARR Lane Manufacturing.
Foundation type: Independent
Financial data (yr. ended 12/31/90): Assets, $1,057,399 (M); gifts received, $400,000; expenditures, $210,406; qualifying distributions, $209,500, including $206,000 for 5 grants (high: $100,000; low: $1,000) and $3,500 for 2 grants to individuals (high: $2,000; low: $1,500).
Fields of interest: Civic affairs, museums, health, education.
Types of support: Student aid.
Limitations: Giving primarily in MI and MO.
Application information: Contributes only to pre-selected organizations. Applications not accepted.
Trustees: Earl E. Walker, Myrtle E. Walker.
EIN: 431466121

1578
Louis L. and Adelaide C. Ward Foundation
1000 Walnut St.
Kansas City 64106

Established in 1966 in MO.
Donor(s): Louis L. Ward, Adelaide C. Ward.
Foundation type: Independent
Financial data (yr. ended 12/31/90): Assets, $4,780,665 (M); expenditures, $390,641; qualifying distributions, $382,010, including $382,010 for 32 grants (high: $250,000; low: $25; average: $5,000).
Purpose and activities: Support primarily for health and culture; some support for education.
Fields of interest: Health, cultural programs, education.
Types of support: Annual campaigns, capital campaigns, general purposes, scholarship funds, endowment funds.
Limitations: Giving primarily in KS and MO.
Application information: Application form not required.
   Initial approach: Letter
   Copies of proposal: 1
   Deadline(s): Dec. 31
   Write: Louis L. Ward, Pres.
Officers: Louis L. Ward, Pres.; Adelaide C. Ward, V.P. and Treas.; Scott H. Ward, Secy.
EIN: 436064548

1579
Webb Foundation
232 Kingshighway, Suite 205
St. Louis 63108 (314) 367-0232

Established in 1969 in MO.
Donor(s): Francis M. Webb,‡ Pearl M. Webb.‡
Foundation type: Independent
Financial data (yr. ended 12/31/91): Assets, $6,856,838 (M); expenditures, $516,906; qualifying distributions, $511,871, including $509,200 for 73 grants (high: $20,000; low: $1,000; average: $3,000-$15,000).
Purpose and activities: Support primarily for the welfare and education of children, particularly the indigent and handicapped; support also for social service agencies, especially those contributing to the improvement of society or for the care and support of disadvantaged people, higher and secondary education, and health and hospitals.
Fields of interest: Child welfare, social services, hospitals, health, higher education, secondary education, disadvantaged.
Types of support: Operating budgets, continuing support, annual campaigns, seed money, building funds, equipment, scholarship funds, fellowships, research.
Limitations: Giving limited to the Midwest. No grants to individuals, or for emergency funds, deficit financing, land acquisition, endowment funds, matching gifts, special projects, publications, or conferences; no loans.
Publications: Informational brochure (including application guidelines).
Application information: Application form not required.
   Initial approach: Letter, proposal, or telephone
   Copies of proposal: 2
   Deadline(s): Submit proposal preferably in Apr. or Sept.; deadlines end of May and Oct.

Board meeting date(s): June and Nov.
Final notification: After board meetings
Write: Richard E. Fister, Secy.
Officer, Advisory Committee and Trustees:*
Richard E. Fister,* Secy.; Virginia M. Fister,
Bernice Hock, Donald D. McDonald, Evelyn M.
McDonald.
Number of staff: None.
EIN: 237028768

1580
**Lyndon C. Whitaker Charitable
  Foundation**
120 South Central St., Suite 1122
St. Louis 63105   (314) 726-5734

Trust established in 1975 in MO.
Donor(s): Mae M. Whitaker.‡
Foundation type: Independent
Financial data (yr. ended 04/30/91): Assets,
$21,047,306 (M); expenditures, $1,107,462;
qualifying distributions, $896,653, including

$840,242 for 51 grants (high: $125,000; low:
$400).
Fields of interest: Medical education, medical
research, performing arts, fine arts, historic
preservation, higher education.
Types of support: Endowment funds, general
purposes, research.
Limitations: Giving primarily in St. Louis, MO.
No grants to individuals.
Application information:
  Initial approach: Proposal
  Deadline(s): None
  Write: Urban C. Bergbauer, Jr., Trustee
Trustee: Urban C. Bergbauer, Jr.
EIN: 510173109

1581
The John M. Wolff Foundation
c/o Commerce Bank of St. Louis, N.A.,
Investment Mgmt. & Trust Srvcs.
8000 Forsyth, P.O. Box 11356
Clayton 63105   (314) 746-7220

Trust established in 1956 in MO.
Donor(s): John M. Wolff.‡
Foundation type: Independent
Financial data (yr. ended 12/31/89): Assets,
$2,351,263 (M); expenditures, $283,631;
qualifying distributions, $271,332, including
$268,000 for 23 grants (high: $143,500; low:
$1,000).
Fields of interest: Hospitals, higher education,
education, performing arts, social services.
Types of support: Capital campaigns, general
purposes, operating budgets, research.
Limitations: Giving primarily in St. Louis, MO,
and some AZ organizations.
Publications: 990-PF.
Application information: Application form not
required.
  Initial approach: Letter
  Deadline(s): Oct. 1
  Board meeting date(s): Sept.
  Write: John M. Wolff III, Trustee
Trustees: John M. Wolff III, Commerce Bank of St.
Louis, N.A.
EIN: 436026247

MONTANA

1582
Charles M. Bair Memorial Trust
c/o First Trust Co. of Montana
P.O. Box 30678
Billings 59115   (406) 657-8122

Established in 1978.
Donor(s): Marguerite B. Lamb.‡
Foundation type: Independent
Financial data (yr. ended 01/31/91): Assets,
$18,867,441 (M); expenditures, $1,009,094;
qualifying distributions, $983,775, including
$825,000 for 5 grants (high: $400,000; low:
$10,000) and $136,602 for 35 grants to
individuals (high: $9,895; low: $309).
Purpose and activities: Giving primarily for
hospitals and Protestant churches; scholarships
limited to graduates or seniors of Harlowton and
White Sulphur Springs high schools, and to
graduates or seniors of high schools in Meagher
and Wheatland counties in MT.
Fields of interest: Hospitals, Protestant giving.
Types of support: Student aid, general purposes.
Limitations: Giving primarily in MT.
Application information: Application form
required.
   Deadline(s): Set yearly, but normally falls in Apr.
Trustees: Alberta M. Bair, First Trust Co. of
Montana.
EIN: 810370774

1583
MPCo/Entech Foundation, Inc.
c/o The M-P-Co.
40 East Broadway
Butte 59701   (406) 723-5421

Established in 1985 in MT.
Donor(s): MT Power Co., Entech, Inc.
Foundation type: Company-sponsored
Financial data (yr. ended 12/31/91): Assets,
$186,648 (M); gifts received, $417,489;
expenditures, $434,865; qualifying distributions,
$433,825, including $409,898 for 108 grants
(high: $30,000; low: $25; average: $25-$30,000)
and $22,460 for 25 employee matching gifts.
Purpose and activities: Support for colleges and
universities through grants and an employee
matching gift program; giving also for health
associations and hospitals.
Fields of interest: Higher education, education,
health associations, hospitals.
Types of support: Building funds, scholarship
funds, employee matching gifts, employee-related
scholarships, capital campaigns, continuing
support, equipment, general purposes.
Limitations: Giving primarily in MT and TX. No
support for United Way umbrella organizations
(except for capital funds) or fraternal, veterans', or
similar organizations. No grants to individuals, or
for operating funds (except for organizations such
as the United Way).
Publications: Annual report (including application
guidelines).
Application information: Application form
required.
   Initial approach: Letter or telephone
   Copies of proposal: 1
   Deadline(s): None
   Board meeting date(s): Quarterly
   Final notification: Following board meetings
   Write: Pamela Merrell, Secy.
Directors: D.T. Berube, John J. Burke, Alan Cain,
R.P. Gannon, Shag Miller, J.J. Murphy, A.K. Neill,
W.P. Schmechel.
Number of staff: 1 part-time support.
EIN: 810432484

1584
Sample Foundation, Inc.
14 North 24th St.
P.O. Box 279
Billings 59103   (406) 256-5667

Incorporated in 1956 in FL.
Donor(s): Helen S. Sample.
Foundation type: Independent
Financial data (yr. ended 10/31/90): Assets,
$3,209,633 (M); gifts received, $190,842;
expenditures, $221,615; qualifying distributions,
$204,240, including $204,240 for 41 grants
(high: $50,000; low: $500).
Purpose and activities: Grants for services for the
disadvantaged, social services, hospitals, and
community funds. Grant support primarily for
capital outlays or to assist in initiating a particular
project.
Fields of interest: Disadvantaged, hospitals,
community funds, social services.
Types of support: Capital campaigns, special
projects.
Limitations: Giving primarily in MT and Collier
County, FL. No support for religious organizations
or any group with political affiliations. No grants
to individuals.
Publications: Application guidelines.
Application information:
   Initial approach: Letter
   Board meeting date(s): Oct. 1
   Write: Miriam T. Sample, V.P.
Officers: Joseph S. Sample, Pres.; Michael S.
Sample, V.P.; Miriam T. Sample, V.P.; T.A. Cox,
Secy.-Treas.
Number of staff: None.
EIN: 596138602

NEBRASKA

1585
Thomas D. Buckley Trust
P.O. Box 647
Chappell 69129   (308) 874-2212

Established about 1980 in NE.
Donor(s): Thomas D. Buckley.‡
Foundation type: Independent
Financial data (yr. ended 05/31/90): Assets,
$8,199,856 (M); expenditures, $412,308;
qualifying distributions, $386,876, including
$356,946 for 71 grants (high: $28,000; low:
$250; average: $500-$10,000).
Fields of interest: Community development,
education, elementary education,
religion—Christian, health services, hospitals,
civic affairs, computer sciences, general
charitable giving.
Types of support: General purposes.
Limitations: Giving primarily in NE, particularly
Chappell, and CO. No grants to individuals.
Application information: Application form
required.
　Initial approach: Letter requesting application
　　form
　Copies of proposal: 1
　Deadline(s): None
　Board meeting date(s): 2nd Wednesday of each
　　month
　Write: Dwight E. Smith or Connie Loos
Trustees: Bill M. Hughes, D.F. Kripal, Walter W.
Peterson.
Number of staff: 1 part-time professional; 1
part-time support.
EIN: 476121041

1586
The Buffett Foundation ▼
222 Kiewit Plaza
Omaha 68131   (402) 345-9168

Incorporated in 1964 in NE.
Donor(s): Warren E. Buffett, Berkshire Hathaway,
Inc.
Foundation type: Independent
Financial data (yr. ended 06/30/91): Assets,
$17,918,276 (M); gifts received, $2,785,380;
expenditures, $2,455,147; qualifying
distributions, $2,376,574, including $2,115,960
for 80 grants (high: $219,473; low: $160;
average: $1,000-$100,000) and $150,000 for 15
grants to individuals of $10,000 each.
Purpose and activities: Grants primarily for family
planning programs.
Fields of interest: Family planning.
Types of support: General purposes.
Application information: Applications not
accepted.
　Write: Allen Greenberg
Officers and Directors:* Susan T. Buffett,* Pres.;
Warren E. Buffett,* V.P. and Treas.; Gladys Kaiser,
Secy.; Susan Greenberg, Carol Loomis, Thomas S.
Murphy.
Number of staff: 1 full-time professional; 1
part-time professional.

EIN: 476032365

1587
ConAgra Foundation, Inc.
c/o ConAgra, Inc.
One Central Park Plaza
Omaha 68102   (402) 595-4158

Donor(s): ConAgra, Inc.
Foundation type: Company-sponsored
Financial data (yr. ended 05/27/90): Assets,
$1,525,844 (M); gifts received, $1,546,407;
expenditures, $1,568,557; qualifying
distributions, $1,567,000, including $1,566,958
for 222 grants (high: $150,175; low: $100).
Purpose and activities: Emphasis on education,
community and civic betterment, health and
human services, arts and culture.
Fields of interest: Cultural programs, arts,
education, health, community development.
Types of support: Scholarship funds,
employee-related scholarships.
Limitations: Giving primarily in Omaha, NE. No
grants to individuals (except for scholarship
programs).
Application information: Grants are generally
pre-selected.
　Initial approach: Proposal
　Deadline(s): None
　Write: Patricia Schweiger, Secy.
Officers and Directors:* Lynn L. Phares,* Pres.;
Gerald B. Vernon,* V.P.; Patricia Schweiger,*
Secy.; James P. O'Donnell, Treas.; Philip B.
Fletcher, Charles M. Harper, L.B. Thomas.
EIN: 362899320

1588
Hazel R. Keene Trust
c/o Fremont National Bank & Trust Co., Trust
Dept.
P.O. Box 169
Fremont 68025   (402) 721-1050

Established in 1986 in NE.
Donor(s): Hazel Keene.
Foundation type: Independent
Financial data (yr. ended 06/30/90): Assets,
$2,249,905 (M); expenditures, $230,553;
qualifying distributions, $130,000, including
$130,000 for 16 grants (high: $65,000; low:
$500).
Purpose and activities: Primary areas of interest
include community development, the elderly,
child welfare, and early childhood education.
Giving for social services, adult and other
education, health, agriculture and animal welfare,
the arts, and historic preservation.
Fields of interest: Social services, aged, child
welfare, youth, crime and law enforcement,
education—early childhood, education,
community development, arts, nutrition, health.
Types of support: Building funds, capital
campaigns, general purposes, lectureships,
matching funds, scholarship funds, publications,
seed money, renovation projects, endowment
funds.
Limitations: Giving limited to Fremont and
Dodge County, NE. No grants to individuals.
Publications: Annual report, financial statement.

Application information: Grants must directly
serve residents of Fremont and Dodge County,
NE. Application form required.
　Initial approach: Letter
　Copies of proposal: 2
　Deadline(s): May 1
　Board meeting date(s): May 30
　Final notification: June 30
　Write: Joe Twidwell
Trustees: John Kerrigan, Stan Lundstrom, Jerry
Myers, Fremont National Bank & Trust Co.
Number of staff: None.
EIN: 476144486

1589
Peter Kiewit Foundation ▼
900 Woodmen Tower
17th and Farnam St.
Omaha 68102   (402) 344-7890

Established in 1975 in NE.
Donor(s): Peter Kiewit.‡
Foundation type: Independent
Financial data (yr. ended 06/30/90): Assets,
$219,831,687 (M); gifts received, $550;
expenditures, $11,179,751; qualifying
distributions, $10,228,157, including $9,178,275
for 90 grants (high: $1,236,004; low: $2,250;
average: $10,000-$100,000) and $403,521 for
126 grants to individuals (high: $4,000; low:
$500; average: $1,000-$4,000).
Purpose and activities: Giving primarily for
cultural programs, including the arts, civic affairs,
community development, higher and other
education, health and social service agencies,
and youth programs. Contributions almost always
made as challenge or matching grants.
Fields of interest: Civic affairs, community
development, rural development, education,
higher education, health services, social services,
youth, cultural programs, arts.
Types of support: Matching funds, student aid,
capital campaigns, equipment, general purposes,
land acquisition, program-related investments,
renovation projects, seed money, special projects.
Limitations: Giving limited to NE and western IA;
Sheridan, WY; and Rancho Mirage, CA; college
scholarships available to high school students in
the Omaha, NE—Council Bluffs, IA, area only.
No support for elementary or secondary schools,
churches, or religious groups. No grants to
individuals (except for scholarships), or for
endowment funds or annual campaigns.
Publications: Annual report, informational
brochure (including application guidelines),
application guidelines.
Application information: Application form
required.
　Initial approach: Letter or telephone
　Copies of proposal: 3
　Deadline(s): June 30, Sept. 30, Dec. 31, and
　　Mar. 31 for organizations; Mar. 1 for
　　scholarships
　Board meeting date(s): Sept., Dec., Mar., and
　　June
　Final notification: Within 30 days of board
　　meeting
　Write: Lyn Wallin Ziegenbein, Exec. Dir.
Officer: Lyn Wallin Ziegenbein, Exec. Dir. and
Secy.
Trustees: Robert B. Daugherty, Chair.; Ray L.
Daniel, Jr., Vice-Chair.; Richard L. Coyne,

Marjorie B. Kiewit, Peter Kiewit, Jr., FirsTier Bank Omaha.
Number of staff: 3 full-time professional; 2 full-time support.
EIN: 476098282
Recent health grants:
1589-1 Eisenhower Medical Center, Rancho Mirage, CA, $500,000. To develop new Emergency Department facility. 1990.
1589-2 Nebraska AIDS Project (NAP), Omaha, NE, $10,000. For operating support. 1990.
1589-3 Planned Parenthood of Omaha-Council Bluffs, Omaha, NE, $34,213. For start-up costs for new West Omaha facility. 1990.
1589-4 Planned Parenthood of Omaha-Council Bluffs, Omaha, NE, $20,000. To supplement cost of pregnancy testing services for clients. 1990.
1589-5 Sniffles, Lincoln, NE, $15,000. Toward start-up costs and basic renovation of facility. 1990.
1589-6 Wellness Council of Sheridan County, Sheridan, WY, $33,332. To establish and operate public wellness program and organization. 1990.
1589-7 Wellness Councils of America, Omaha, NE, $175,000. To establish national headquarters office. 1990.

1590
Lincoln Foundation, Inc.
215 Centennial Mall South, Rm. 200
Lincoln 68508   (402) 474-2345

Incorporated in 1955 in NE.
Foundation type: Community
Financial data (yr. ended 12/31/90): Assets, $17,679,823 (M); gifts received, $25,090; expenditures, $1,206,282; qualifying distributions, $880,513, including $880,513 for 144 grants (high: $285,690).
Purpose and activities: To promote the mental, moral, intellectual, and physical improvement, assistance, and relief of the inhabitants of Lincoln and Lancaster County in particular, and elsewhere in the U.S. where funds are available; giving mainly in the areas of civic and community affairs, cultural programs, health and welfare, and higher education.
Fields of interest: Community development, welfare, cultural programs, higher education, health, civic affairs.
Types of support: Scholarship funds, seed money, emergency funds, research, matching funds, special projects.
Limitations: Giving primarily in Lincoln and Lancaster County, NE. No grants to individuals, or for building or endowment funds or operating budgets.
Publications: Annual report, program policy statement, application guidelines, newsletter.
Application information: Application form required.
  Initial approach: Telephone
  Copies of proposal: 12
  Deadline(s): 8 weeks prior to board meetings
  Board meeting date(s): Jan., Apr., July, and Oct.
  Write: Kim Schuurmans, Prog. and Funds Officer

Officers and Directors:* Thomas C. Woods III,* Chair.; Virginia Johnson,* Vice-Chair.; Philip Heckman, Pres.; Cynthia Milligan,* Secy.; Tom Hayes,* Treas.; and 20 additional directors.
Number of staff: 3 full-time professional; 1 part-time professional; 2 full-time support; 1 part-time support.
EIN: 470458128

1591
Armstrong McDonald Foundation
600 The Atrium
1200 N St.
Lincoln 68508
Application address: 7340 East Shoeman Ln., Scottsdale, AZ 85251; Tel.: (602) 949-0974

Established in 1987 in NE.
Foundation type: Independent
Financial data (yr. ended 12/31/90): Assets, $10,585,729 (M); expenditures, $541,179; qualifying distributions, $465,782, including $451,000 for 21 grants (high: $100,000; low: $5,000).
Fields of interest: Higher education, health, youth, social services, handicapped, animal welfare.
Limitations: Giving primarily in southwestern U.S. No grants to individuals.
Application information:
  Initial approach: Proposal
  Deadline(s): Apr. 15 and Sept. 15
  Write: Future H. McDonald, Pres.
Officers: Future H. McDonald, Pres.; James M. McDonald, V.P. and Secy.; Laurie Bourchard, V.P. and Treas.
EIN: 363458711

1592
Omaha Community Foundation
Two Central Park Plaza
222 South 15th St.
Omaha 68102   (402) 342-3458

Established in 1982 in NE.
Donor(s): Harold W. Andersen.
Foundation type: Community
Financial data (yr. ended 12/31/91): Assets, $8,808,837 (M); gifts received, $1,975,343; expenditures, $1,092,281; qualifying distributions, $894,069, including $894,069 for 133 grants (high: $250,000; low: $100).
Fields of interest: Civic affairs, cultural programs, health, education, social services, women.
Types of support: Building funds, conferences and seminars, continuing support, emergency funds, matching funds, publications, renovation projects, seed money, equipment, special projects, technical assistance, scholarship funds.
Limitations: Giving limited to the metropolitan Omaha, NE, area. No grants to individuals, or for endowments, deficit financing, annual drives, dinners, or tickets.
Publications: Annual report (including application guidelines), 990-PF, program policy statement, application guidelines, grants list, newsletter, informational brochure.
Application information: Application form required.

Copies of proposal: 7
Deadline(s): Apr. 1 and Oct. 1
Board meeting date(s): June and Dec.
Final notification: June and Dec.
Write: W. Earl Taylor, Exec. Dir.
Officers and Directors:* Eugene A. Conley,* Pres.; Mimi S. Waldbaum,* V.P.; Mary S. Bernstein,* Secy.; George J. Kubat,* Treas.; W. Earl Taylor, Exec. Dir.; and 17 additional directors.
Number of staff: 1 full-time professional; 1 part-time professional; 1 full-time support.
EIN: 470645958

1593
Quivey-Bay State Foundation
1515 East 20th St.
Scottsbluff 69361   (308) 635-7701

Established in 1948 in NE.
Donor(s): M.B. Quivey, Mrs. M.B. Quivey.
Foundation type: Independent
Financial data (yr. ended 01/31/90): Assets, $2,359,916 (M); expenditures, $161,883; qualifying distributions, $147,932, including $147,932 for 55 grants (high: $15,000; low: $100).
Purpose and activities: Emphasis on higher education, Protestant church support, and youth and child welfare agencies; support also for historic preservation, health, and social services.
Fields of interest: Higher education, Protestant giving, youth, child welfare, historic preservation, health, social services.
Limitations: Giving primarily in western NE. No grants to individuals, or for endowment funds.
Application information: Application form not required.
  Initial approach: Letter
  Copies of proposal: 1
  Deadline(s): None
  Board meeting date(s): Oct. and Nov.
  Write: Ted Cannon, Secy.-Treas.
Officer: Ted Cannon, Secy.-Treas.
EIN: 476024159

1594
Robert Herman Storz Foundation
c/o Robert H. Storz
Kiewit Plaza Bldg., 8th Fl.
Omaha 68131

Established in 1957.
Donor(s): Robert Herman Storz.
Foundation type: Independent
Financial data (yr. ended 12/31/90): Assets, $6,653,618 (M); expenditures, $447,624; qualifying distributions, $305,510, including $305,510 for 41 grants (high: $114,700; low: $10).
Fields of interest: Religion—Christian, cultural programs, theater, hospitals, higher education, recreation.
Limitations: Giving primarily in NE. No grants to individuals.
Application information: Contributes only to pre-selected organizations. Applications not accepted.
Trustees: Susan Storz Butler, Robert Herman Storz.
EIN: 476025980

NEVADA

1595
Bing Fund Corporation ▼
302 East Carson Ave., Suite 617
Las Vegas 89101   (702) 386-6183
Application address: 9700 West Pico Blvd., Los
Angeles, CA 90035; Tel.: (213) 277-3222

Incorporated in 1977 in NV as partial successor
to Bing Fund, Inc., incorporated in NY.
Donor(s): Leo S. Bing,‡ Anna Bing Arnold, Peter
S. Bing.
Foundation type: Independent
Financial data (yr. ended 05/31/90): Assets,
$41,387,938 (M); gifts received, $325,000;
expenditures, $1,887,398; qualifying
distributions, $1,827,826, including $1,825,000
for 17 grants (high: $1,186,000; low: $500;
average: $5,000-$250,000).
Purpose and activities: Giving primarily for
higher education, museums, the arts, secondary
education, hospitals, and population control.
Fields of interest: Higher education, secondary
education, museums, arts, hospitals, family
planning.
Application information: Application form not
required.
   Deadline(s): None
   Write: Peter S. Bing, Pres.
Officers: Peter S. Bing, Pres.; Robert D. Burch,
Secy.
EIN: 942476169

1596
Conrad N. Hilton Foundation ▼
100 West Liberty St., Suite 840
Reno 89501   (702) 323-4221

Established in 1944; incorporated in 1950 in CA;
incorporated in 1989 in NV.
Donor(s): Conrad N. Hilton.‡
Foundation type: Independent
Financial data (yr. ended 02/28/91): Assets,
$428,692,519 (M); gifts received, $3,135,150;
expenditures, $15,475,412; qualifying
distributions, $15,475,412, including
$14,058,895 for 126 grants (high: $3,896,203;
low: $300; average: $5,000-$100,000) and
$24,830 for 1 in-kind gift.
Purpose and activities: The greater part of the
foundation's giving is devoted to several major
long-term projects, including the areas of drug
abuse prevention, hotel administration education,
and Catholic welfare; funding for smaller scale
miscellaneous grants very limited. Special areas
of interest are: 1)Works of Catholic Sisters funded
through Conrad N. Hilton Fund for Sisters;
2)Substance abuse education funded through the
Best Foundation for Drug Free Tomorrow;
3)Multihandicapped blind funded through
Perkins School for the Blind; and 4)Water
development in Ghana, Africa, funded through
World Vision.
Fields of interest: Drug abuse, hotel
administration, education, Catholic welfare,
health.

Types of support: Building funds, endowment
funds, equipment, operating budgets,
publications, scholarship funds, seed money,
technical assistance, continuing support.
Limitations: No support for religious
organizations for the benefit of their own
membership, medical research, the arts, the
elderly, political lobbying or legislative activities,
or local branches of national charities. No grants
to individuals, or for general fundraising events,
exhibits, travel, or surveys; no loans.
Publications: Annual report, application
guidelines, informational brochure.
Application information: The foundation accepts
applications primarily from its specified
beneficiaries. Application form not required.
   Initial approach: Letter
   Copies of proposal: 1
   Deadline(s): None
   Board meeting date(s): Quarterly
   Final notification: Within 30 days
   Write: Donald H. Hubbs, Pres.
Officers and Directors:* Donald H. Hubbs,*
Pres.; Steven M. Hilton,* V.P.; Patrick Modugno,
V.P.; Jean Van Sickle, Secy.; Deborah Kerr, Treas.;
Robert Buckley, M.D., William H. Edwards, James
R. Galbraith, Robert A. Groves, Barron Hilton,
Barry Hilton, Eric M. Hilton.
Number of staff: 8 full-time professional; 3
full-time support.
EIN: 943100217
Recent health grants:
1596-1 Barbara Sinatra Childrens Center at
   Eisenhower, Rancho Mirage, CA, $20,000.
   1991.
1596-2 Best Foundation for a Drug Free
   Tomorrow, Reno, NV, $340,000. 1991.
1596-3 Catholic Charities of the Archdiocese of
   Los Angeles, Angels Flight, Los Angeles, CA,
   $20,500. 1991.
1596-4 Childrens Hospital, Boston, MA,
   $15,000. 1991.
1596-5 Childrens Memorial Foundation,
   Chicago, IL, $50,000. 1991.
1596-6 Helen Keller International, NYC, NY,
   $165,000. 1991.
1596-7 Hospitaller Foundation of California, Los
   Angeles, CA, $20,000. 1991.
1596-8 House Ear Institute, Los Angeles, CA,
   $50,000. 1991.
1596-9 International Federation of Multiple
   Sclerosis Societies, NYC, NY, $25,000. 1991.
1596-10 Mayo Foundation, Rochester, MN,
   $500,000. 1991.
1596-11 National Health Foundation, Los
   Angeles, CA, $200,000. 1991.
1596-12 National Multiple Sclerosis Society,
   Southern California Chapter, Glendale, CA,
   $101,717. 1991.
1596-13 Project Orbis, NYC, NY, $25,000. 1991.
1596-14 Robert Steel Foundation for Pediatric
   Cancer Research, NYC, NY, $50,000. 1991.
1596-15 Saint Annes Maternity Home, Los
   Angeles, CA, $100,000. 1991.
1596-16 Salk Institute for Biological Studies, La
   Jolla, CA, $100,000. 1991.

1597
Nell J. Redfield Foundation
P.O. Box 61
1755 East Plumb Ln., Suite 212
Reno 89504   (702) 323-1373

Established in 1982 in NV.
Donor(s): Nell J. Redfield.‡
Foundation type: Independent
Financial data (yr. ended 12/31/91): Assets,
$6,256,861 (M); expenditures, $348,720;
qualifying distributions, $260,716, including
$260,716 for 34 grants (high: $50,000; low:
$1,000).
Purpose and activities: Support primarily for the
advancement of health care, medical research,
and the care of handicapped children; support
also for the aged, education, and religion.
Fields of interest: Health associations, health,
medical research, handicapped, aged, education,
religion.
Types of support: Building funds, equipment,
scholarship funds, endowment funds.
Limitations: Giving primarily in Reno, NV.
Application information: Application form
required.
   Initial approach: Letter
   Deadline(s): Jan. 15 through June 1
   Write: Gerald C. Smith, Dir.
Directors: Iris G. Brewerton, Betty Alyce Jones,
Helen Jeane Jones, Gerald C. Smith, Kenneth G.
Walker.
Trustee: Farmers & Merchants Trust Co.
EIN: 237399910

1598
Stearns-Blodgett Trust
c/o First Interstate Bank of Nevada
P.O. Box 30100
Reno 89520   (702) 784-3316

Established in 1979 in NV.
Donor(s): Edith Miller Blodgett.‡
Foundation type: Operating
Financial data (yr. ended 01/31/91): Assets,
$729,836 (M); expenditures, $222,124;
qualifying distributions, $212,683, including
$202,914 for 50 grants to individuals (high:
$20,055; low: $64).
Purpose and activities: To aid and assist indigent
persons in need of ophthalmologic care.
Fields of interest: Ophthalmology.
Types of support: Grants to individuals.
Limitations: Giving limited to NV and northern
CA.
Publications: Application guidelines.
Application information: Occasional grants to
institutions initiated by the administrators.
Application form required.
Administrative Committee: John Webster Brown,
Leo J. Humphries, Clarence Jones.
Trustee: First Interstate Bank of Nevada, N.A.
EIN: 886033781

1599
E. L. Wiegand Foundation ▼
Wiegand Ctr.
165 West Liberty St.
Reno 89501   (702) 333-0310

Established in 1982 in NV.
Donor(s): Ann K. Wiegand,‡ Edwin L. Wiegand.‡
Foundation type: Independent
Financial data (yr. ended 10/31/90): Assets,
$76,152,114 (M); gifts received, $22,142;
expenditures, $4,561,266; qualifying
distributions, $4,354,746, including $4,073,824

for 119 grants (high: $367,000; low: $150; average: $4,000-$100,000).

Purpose and activities: Grants primarily for education, health and medical research; also for public affairs, civic and community affairs, and arts and cultural affairs; emphasis on Roman Catholic institutions.

Fields of interest: Education, elementary education, secondary education, higher education, legal education, medical education, business education, health, medical research, hospitals, cancer, heart disease, chemistry, biology, biochemistry, biological sciences, ophthalmology, aged, civic affairs, community development, public affairs, arts, fine arts, museums, music, performing arts, theater, Catholic giving.

Types of support: Equipment, special projects.

Limitations: Giving primarily in NV and adjoining western states, including CA, AZ, OR, ID, and UT; Public Affairs grants giving primarily in CA, Washington, DC, and New York, NY. No support for organizations receiving significant support from public tax funds; organizations with beneficiaries of their own choosing; or federal, state, or local government agencies or institutions. No grants to individuals, or for endowment funds, fundraising campaigns, emergency funding, film or media presentations, or operating funds; no loans.

Publications: Informational brochure (including application guidelines).

Application information: Application form required.

Initial approach: Letter
Copies of proposal: 1
Deadline(s): None
Board meeting date(s): Feb., June, and Oct.
Write: Joanne C. Hildahl, V.P., Grants Prog.

Officers and Trustees:* Raymond C. Avansino, Jr.,* Chair. and Pres.; Michael J. Melarkey, V.P. and Secy.; Kristen A. Avansino, V.P., California Grants; Joann C. Hildahl, V.P., Grants Program; Norbert F. Stanny,* V.P.; James T. Carrico, Treas.; Harvey C. Fruehauf, Jr.

Number of staff: None.

EIN: 942839372

Recent health grants:

1599-1 American Cancer Society, Nevada Division, Las Vegas, NV, $19,000. For computer equipment. 1990.

1599-2 Good Shepherd Grace Center, San Francisco, CA, $10,000. For van. 1990.

1599-3 Holy Cross Hospital, Nogales, AZ, $73,000. For emergency department equipment. 1990.

1599-4 Holy Cross Jordan Valley Hospital, West Jordan, UT, $80,000. For operating room equipment. 1990.

1599-5 House Ear Institute, Los Angeles, CA, $80,000. For computer equipment. 1990.

1599-6 Houston Ear Research Foundation, Houston, TX, $16,000. For cochlear implant processors. 1990.

1599-7 Marian Medical Center, Santa Maria, CA, $31,000. For cardiac equipment. 1990.

1599-8 Mercy Medical Center, Redding, CA, $66,000. For cardiac telemetry monitoring system. 1990.

1599-9 Peace Harbor Hospital, Florence, OR, $36,000. For 20-passenger bus for cancer treatment program. 1990.

1599-10 Providence Hospital, Oakland, CA, $100,000. For Yag laser. 1990.

1599-11 Saint Benedicts Family Medical Center, Jerome, ID, $74,000. For cardiac monitoring equipment. 1990.

1599-12 Saint Benedicts Hospital, Ogden, UT, $96,000. For cardiac equipment. 1990.

1599-13 Saint Francis Hospital, Miami, FL, $100,000. For cardiac equipment. 1990.

1599-14 Saint Joseph Hospital, Tucson, AZ, $84,000. For ophthamology equipment. 1990.

1599-15 Saint Lukes Hospital, San Francisco, CA, $71,400. For computer sonography unit. 1990.

1599-16 Saint Marys Hospital and Medical Center, San Francisco, CA, $85,000. For cardiac equipment. 1990.

1599-17 Saint Vincent Medical Center, Los Angeles, CA, $19,000. For pediatric neonatal equipment. 1990.

1599-18 Saint Vincents/Santa Barbara, Santa Barbara, CA, $18,000. For therapy pool and dressing room. 1990.

1599-19 Sisters of Notre Dame, Saratoga, CA, $40,000. For infirmary equipment. 1990.

1599-20 West Texas Rehabilitation Center, Abilene, TX, $30,000. For rehabilitation equipment. 1990.

NEW HAMPSHIRE

1600
Norwin S. and Elizabeth N. Bean Foundation
c/o New Hampshire Charitable Foundation
One South St., P.O. Box 1335
Concord 03302-1335   (603) 225-6641

Trust established in 1957 in NH; later became an affiliated trust of the New Hampshire Charitable Fund.
Donor(s): Norwin S. Bean,‡ Elizabeth N. Bean.‡
Foundation type: Independent
Financial data (yr. ended 12/31/91): Assets, $7,505,999 (M); expenditures, $454,559; qualifying distributions, $386,559, including $386,559 for 41 grants (high: $26,000; low: $1,250; average: $2,500-$10,000).
Purpose and activities: Giving primarily for social and human services including low-income housing programs, and youth; support also for education, including secondary education, health associations, and the arts.
Fields of interest: Social services, housing, youth, education, secondary education, health, health associations, arts.
Types of support: General purposes, seed money, emergency funds, building funds, equipment, land acquisition, special projects, conferences and seminars, matching funds, loans, program-related investments, consulting services, scholarship funds.
Limitations: Giving limited to Amherst and Manchester, NH. No grants to individuals, or for scholarships, fellowships, operating budgets, deficit financing, or endowment funds.
Publications: Annual report, informational brochure (including application guidelines).
Application information: Application form not required.
Initial approach: Letter or telephone
Copies of proposal: 1
Deadline(s): Feb. 1, May 1, Aug. 1, and Nov. 1
Board meeting date(s): Mar., June, Sept., and Dec.
Write: Deborah Cowan, Prog. Dir.
Officer and Trustees:* John H. Hoben,* Chair.; Christy H. Belvin, Thomas Donovan, John R. McLane, Jr., James A. Shanahan, Jr.
Number of staff: 5 shared staff
EIN: 026013381

1601
Chatham, Inc. ▼
(Formerly Henley League, Ltd.)
Liberty Ln.
Hampton 03842   (603) 926-5911

Established in 1986.
Donor(s): The Henley Group, Inc.
Foundation type: Company-sponsored
Financial data (yr. ended 05/31/91): Assets, $7,681,072 (M); gifts received, $14,070; expenditures, $2,062,740; qualifying distributions, $1,924,392, including $1,633,372 for 284 grants (high: $150,000; low: $50;

average: $1,000-$10,000) and $249,750 for employee matching gifts.
Purpose and activities: Support primarily for arts and culture, youth development and health-related organizations.
Fields of interest: Arts, cultural programs, youth, health.
Types of support: Employee matching gifts, general purposes.
Application information:
Initial approach: Letter
Deadline(s): None
Write: William Coffey
Officers and Directors:* Spenser Stokes,* Pres.; Robert J. Barone,* V.P.; William E. Coffey, V.P.; Paul M. Montrone,* V.P.; Paul M. Meister,* V.P. and Treas.; Allison Pellegrino,* Secy.; Michael D. Dingman.
EIN: 330240692
Recent health grants:
1601-1 Big Apple Circus, NYC, NY, $10,000. For fundraiser. 1991.
1601-2 Childrens Hospital, Boston, MA, $10,000. For pledge payment. 1991.
1601-3 Dana-Farber Cancer Institute, Boston, MA, $20,000. For pledge payment. 1991.
1601-4 Juvenile Diabetes Foundation International, NYC, NY, $10,000. For fundraiser. 1991.
1601-5 Kenneth Norris, Jr. Cancer Hospital, Los Angeles, CA, $25,000. For William French-Smith Memorial Fund. 1991.
1601-6 Massachusetts Eye and Ear Infirmary, Boston, MA, $15,000. For general operating support. 1991.
1601-7 Massachusetts General Hospital, Boston, MA, $50,000. For pledge payment. 1991.
1601-8 Robert J. Mathews Foundation, Sacramento, CA, $10,000. For cancer research and general operating support. 1991.
1601-9 Robert Lurie Endowment Fund, Chicago, IL, $25,000. For Northwestern University Cancer Center. 1991.
1601-10 Salk Institute for Biological Studies, La Jolla, CA, $15,000. For general operating support. 1991.
1601-11 Sharp HealthCare, San Diego, CA, $50,000. For pledge payment. 1991.

1602
Cogswell Benevolent Trust
875 Elm St.
Manchester 03101   (603) 622-4013

Trust established in 1929 in NH.
Donor(s): Leander A. Cogswell.‡
Foundation type: Independent
Financial data (yr. ended 12/31/91): Assets, $11,925,812 (M); expenditures, $509,362; qualifying distributions, $478,013, including $421,215 for 62 grants (high: $100,000; low: $500; average: $1,000-$15,000).
Fields of interest: Higher education, youth, community funds, hospitals, religion, performing arts, health associations.
Limitations: Giving primarily in NH. No grants to individuals, or for endowment funds, operating budgets, or deficit financing.
Application information: The foundation no longer gives scholarships or loans to individuals; scholarship funds have been donated to the New Hampshire Charitable Fund-Student Aid Program,

One South St., Concord, NH 03301. Application form not required.
Initial approach: Letter
Copies of proposal: 1
Deadline(s): None
Board meeting date(s): Usually monthly and as required
Final notification: 30 days
Write: David P. Goodwin, Trustee
Trustees: David P. Goodwin, Mark Northridge, Theodore Wadleigh.
Number of staff: 1 part-time support.
EIN: 020235690

1603
Alexander Eastman Foundation
c/o New Hampshire Charitable Foundation
One South St., P.O. Box 1335
Concord 03302-1335   (603) 225-6641

Established in 1983 in NH.
Foundation type: Independent
Financial data (yr. ended 09/30/91): Assets, $5,027,798 (M); expenditures, $212,052; qualifying distributions, $187,197, including $152,187 for 18 grants (high: $45,000; low: $900; average: $5,000-$10,000).
Purpose and activities: Awards grants to improve the quality and availability of health care and to promote good health and well-being for residents of the greater Derry, NH, area; giving also includes scholarship assistance for area residents working in the health care field.
Fields of interest: Health, health services.
Types of support: Employee-related scholarships, conferences and seminars, consulting services, operating budgets, technical assistance, special projects.
Limitations: Giving primarily in Derry, Londonderry, Windham, Chester, Hampstead, and Sandown, NH. No grants to individuals.
Publications: Informational brochure (including application guidelines).
Application information: Application form not required.
Initial approach: Proposal
Copies of proposal: 1
Deadline(s): Feb. 1, May 1, Aug. 1, and Nov. 1
Board meeting date(s): Mar., June, Sept., and Dec.
Write: Deborah Cowan, Prog. Dir.
Trustees: Giacomo Agati, Thomas Buchanan, Craig Bulkley, Sharon Butterfield, Rose Colby, Janet Conroy, Margaret DeRedon, Oscar Greene, Patricia Plouff, James Reinhart, Elaine Rendo, Dolores Warhall.
Number of staff: None.
EIN: 020222124

1604
Foundation for Seacoast Health
P.O. Box 4606
Portsmouth 03801   (603) 433-4001
FAX: (603) 433-4091

Incorporated in 1984 in NH as the Portsmouth Hospital Foundation; name changed in 1986 to Foundation for Seacoast Health.
Foundation type: Independent
Financial data (yr. ended 12/31/91): Assets, $20,833,562 (M); gifts received, $81,125;

expenditures, $917,200; qualifying distributions, $663,622, including $576,122 for 49 grants (high: $205,000; low: $500) and $87,500 for 26 grants to individuals.
Purpose and activities: To support, develop, and promote health care in six areas: infants/children; adolescents; the elderly; through the discretionary fund for research and development, and health education and information, including drug abuse, AIDS, family planning and services; through scholarships for local students pursuing health-related fields of study. Giving also for volunteerism, hospices, and nursing.
Fields of interest: Health, youth, aged, medical education, nursing, child welfare, health services, AIDS, family planning, family services.
Types of support: Student aid, matching funds, seed money, special projects, technical assistance.
Limitations: Giving limited to Portsmouth, Rye, New Castle, Greenland, Newington, and North Hampton, NH; and Kittery, Eliot, and York, ME. No grants to individuals (except through the foundation scholarship program), or for operating expenses, deficit financing, or travels.
Publications: Annual report (including application guidelines), newsletter, application guidelines, occasional report.
Application information: Application form not required.
  Initial approach: Letter, not more than 2 pages
  Copies of proposal: 2
  Deadline(s): Feb. 15 for scholarships; last day of month for discretionary fund; Mar. 1 for infant/child/adolescent health; June 1 for general health; Sept. 1 for elderly health; and twice each month for medical financial assistance
  Board meeting date(s): 1st Tuesday of Mar., May, Aug., and Nov.; annual meeting, 3rd Tuesday in Apr.
  Final notification: Apr. for scholarships; 1 month for discretionary funds; May for infant/child/adolescent health; Aug. for general health; Nov. for elderly health; every two weeks for medical financial assistance
  Write: Susan Bunting, Exec. Dir.
Officers and Trustees:* Rodney G. Brock,* Pres.; Robert A. Allard,* V.P.; John H. Rodgers,* Treas.; Ferris G. Bavicchi, Eileen D. Foley, Thomas M. Keane, Susan Meister, Terry L. Morton, C. Peter Rasmussen, G. Warren Wilder.
Number of staff: 1 full-time professional; 1 full-time support.
EIN: 020386319
Recent health grants:
1604-1 Portsmouth Housing Authority, Portsmouth, NH, $65,000. For Respite Care Program for persons with Alzheimer's Disease. 1990.
1604-2 Portsmouth School Department, Portsmouth, NH, $141,700. For Clipper Health Center salaries, computer program and start-up costs. 1990.
1604-3 Portsmouth School Department, Portsmouth, NH, $10,000. For challenge grant to assist fundraising for construction of Clipper Health Center. 1990.
1604-4 Seacoast Mental Health Center, Portsmouth, NH, $100,000. For New Heights for Teens Program. 1990.
1604-5 Visiting Nurse Association, Portsmouth Regional, Portsmouth, NH, $60,000. For Elder Day Care Program. 1990.

1605
The Fuller Foundation, Inc.
Box 461
Rye Beach 03871   (603) 964-6998

Incorporated in 1936 in MA.
Donor(s): Alvan T. Fuller, Sr.‡
Foundation type: Independent
Financial data (yr. ended 12/31/90): Assets, $8,239,012 (M); expenditures, $514,321; qualifying distributions, $317,650, including $295,650 for 95 grants (high: $25,000; low: $100; average: $1,000-$5,000).
Fields of interest: Medical research, education, drug abuse.
Types of support: Operating budgets, continuing support, annual campaigns, matching funds, special projects, research.
Limitations: Giving primarily in Boston, MA, and the immediate seacoast area of NH. No grants to individuals, or for seed money, publications, or conferences; no loans.
Publications: Application guidelines.
Application information: Application form not required.
  Initial approach: Proposal
  Copies of proposal: 1
  Deadline(s): Mar. 15, Aug. 15, and Dec. 15
  Board meeting date(s): Feb., May, and Oct.
  Final notification: 1 to 6 months
  Write: John T. Bottomley, Exec. Dir.
Officers and Trustees:* Peter Fuller,* Pres.; Stephen D. Bottomley, Treas.; John T. Bottomley,* Exec. Dir.; Miranda Fuller Bocko, Lydia Fuller Bottomley, Ann Fuller Donovan, Peter D. Fuller, Jr., James D. Henderson, Hope Halsey Swasey, Samuel S. Talbot, Melinda F. Van den Heuvel.
Number of staff: 1 full-time professional; 1 full-time support.
EIN: 042241130

1606
Oleonda Jameson Trust
c/o Orr & Reno
One Eagle Sq., P.O. Box 709
Concord 03302-0709   (603) 224-2381

Established in 1977 in NH.
Foundation type: Independent
Financial data (yr. ended 12/31/91): Assets, $3,913,867 (M); expenditures, $158,090; qualifying distributions, $151,385, including $144,049 for 27 grants (high: $22,500; low: $414).
Fields of interest: Higher education, community funds, social services, hospitals, cultural programs.
Types of support: Scholarship funds, general purposes.
Limitations: Giving limited to NH, with emphasis on Concord. No grants for capital improvements, construction, or endowment funds.
Application information:
  Initial approach: Proposal
  Deadline(s): None
  Write: Malcolm McLane, Trustee
Trustees: Malcolm McLane, Dudley W. Orr, Robert H. Reno.
EIN: 026048930

1607
The New Hampshire Charitable Foundation ▼
One South St.
P.O. Box 1335
Concord 03302-1335   (603) 225-6641

Incorporated in 1962 in NH.
Foundation type: Community
Financial data (yr. ended 12/31/91): Assets, $67,595,763 (M); gifts received, $9,091,280; expenditures, $5,593,819; qualifying distributions, $4,551,326, including $2,986,737 for 813 grants (high: $50,000; low: $100; average: $1,000-$5,000), $1,161,924 for grants to individuals (average: $500-$1,000), $118,000 for loans to organizations and $284,665 for loans to individuals.
Purpose and activities: Giving for charitable and educational purposes including the arts, humanities, the environment and conservation, health, and social and community services; grants primarily to inaugurate new programs and strengthen existing charitable organizations, with emphasis on programs rather than capital needs; support also for college scholarships.
Fields of interest: Education, arts, humanities, environment, conservation, health, social services.
Types of support: Seed money, loans, student aid, fellowships, scholarship funds, student loans, general purposes, special projects, consulting services, technical assistance.
Limitations: Giving limited to NH. No support for sectarian or religious purposes. No grants to individuals (except for student aid); generally no grants for building funds, endowments, operating support, deficit financing, capital campaigns for acquisition of land or renovations to facilities, purchase of major equipment, academic research, or out-of-state travel.
Publications: Annual report, program policy statement, informational brochure (including application guidelines).
Application information: Application form not required.
  Initial approach: Telephone or letter
  Copies of proposal: 1
  Deadline(s): Feb. 1, May 1, Aug. 1, and Nov. 1; Apr. 24 for student aid applicants for upcoming school year
  Board meeting date(s): Mar., June, Sept., and Dec.
  Final notification: 4 to 6 weeks
  Write: Deborah Cowan, Assoc. Dir.
Officers and Directors:* Walter Peterson,* Chair.; Lewis Feldstein,* Pres.; Linda McGoldrick,* Secy.; Martin L. Gross,* Treas.; Maurice L. Arel, Kennett R. Kendall, Jr., J. Bonnie Newman, Kendra Stearns O'Donnell, John F. Weeks, Jr., Anne C. Zachos.
Number of staff: 8 full-time professional; 4 full-time support; 2 part-time support.
EIN: 026005625
Recent health grants:
1607-1 Alliance for the Mentally Ill of New Hampshire, Peterborough, NH, $20,000. For second year operating support and for management consultancy and resource guides. 1990.
1607-2 Child Health Services, Manchester, NH, $10,000. For consulting support to study current model of health care delivery. 1990.
1607-3 Crotched Mountain Community Care, Manchester, NH, $16,000. For interim

operating support for North Country Alzheimer's project. 1990.

1607-4 Governors Blue Ribbon Commission on Health, Concord, NH, $15,000. For staffing for nine months. 1990.

1607-5 New Hampshire Family Planning Council, Concord, NH, $15,500. For continued support for consultancy to assess family planning delivery system. 1990.

1607-6 Newport Hospital, Newport, NH, $35,000. For interim general support. 1990.

1607-7 Professional Fitness Associates, Meredith, NH, $10,000. For cardiovascular risk reduction program at Laconia and Gilford High Schools. 1990.

1608
The Penates Foundation
Liberty Ln.
Hampton 03842   (603) 926-5911

Established in 1984 in NH.
Donor(s): Paul M. Montrone, Henley Manufacturing Charitable Foundation, Inc.
Foundation type: Independent
Financial data (yr. ended 12/31/91): Assets, $3,910,659 (M); gifts received, $571,000; expenditures, $267,605; qualifying distributions, $223,500, including $223,500 for 31 grants (high: $50,000; low: $250).
Fields of interest: Higher education, secondary education, social services, medical research, music.
Limitations: Giving primarily in the Northeast.
Application information:
  Initial approach: Letter
  Deadline(s): None
  Write: Paul M. Montrone, Dir.
Officers and Directors:* Sandra G. Montrone, Pres.; Robert J. Barone,* V.P.; Karen L. Bond, Secy.; Michael J. Farrell,* Treas.; Michele M.

Montrone, Exec. Dir.; Theodore Kurz, Paul M. Montrone.
EIN: 222536075

1609
Lou and Lutza Smith Charitable Foundation
c/o New Hampshire Charitable Foundation
One South St., P.O. Box 1335
Concord 03302-1335   (603) 225-6641

Established in 1971 in NH.
Donor(s): Lutza Smith,‡ Louis Smith Marital Trust.
Foundation type: Independent
Financial data (yr. ended 12/31/90): Assets, $3,300,752 (M); expenditures, $577,014; qualifying distributions, $549,277, including $504,330 for 32 grants (high: $50,000; low: $500; average: $5,000-$10,000).
Purpose and activities: Giving for education, health, social services, and child welfare, as well as programs related to the conduct and operation of horse racing.
Fields of interest: Education, health, social services, child welfare, recreation.
Types of support: Building funds, capital campaigns, special projects.
Limitations: Giving primarily in NH, and to organizations providing services to NH residents. No support for religious organizations, except for programs of general social service. No grants to individuals, or for operating expenses for extended periods.
Publications: Informational brochure (including application guidelines).
Application information: Application form not required.
  Initial approach: Letter or telephone
  Copies of proposal: 1
  Deadline(s): Feb. 1, May 1, Aug. 1, Nov. 1

Board meeting date(s): Mar., June, Sept., and Dec.
  Write: Deborah Cowan, Prog. Dir.
Trustees: Charles A. DeGrandpre, Louise K. Newman, Kathleen M., Robinson.
Number of staff: 3 shared staff
EIN: 237162940

1610
The Trust Family Foundation
52 Stiles Rd.
Salem 03079   (603) 898-6670

Established in 1986 in NH.
Donor(s): Diane Trust, Martin Trust.
Foundation type: Independent
Financial data (yr. ended 12/31/91): Assets, $14,361,000 (M); gifts received, $3,500,000; expenditures, $407,000; qualifying distributions, $331,993, including $298,000 for grants (high: $120,000; low: $2,000).
Fields of interest: Education, Jewish giving, medical sciences, arts.
Types of support: Special projects.
Limitations: Giving primarily in New England. No grants for capital campaigns or operating budgets.
Publications: 990-PF, financial statement, informational brochure.
Application information: Application form not required.
  Initial approach: Summary letter
  Copies of proposal: 1
  Board meeting date(s): Varies
  Write: Ronald L. Roberts, Administrator
Officer: Ronald L. Roberts, Administrator.
Trustees: David Trust, Diane Trust, Laura Trust, Martin Trust.
Number of staff: 2 part-time professional.
EIN: 026070843

NEW JERSEY

1611
Allied-Signal Foundation ▼
(Formerly Allied Corporation Foundation)
101 Columbia Rd.
P.O. Box 2245
Morristown 07962-1057   (201) 455-5876

Incorporated in 1963 in NY; in 1982 absorbed
Bunker Ramo Foundation; in 1984 absorbed
Bendix Foundation; merged and incorporated in
1982 in NJ as Allied Corporation Foundation; in
1987 name changed to Allied-Signal Foundation.
Donor(s): Allied-Signal, Inc.
Foundation type: Company-sponsored
Financial data (yr. ended 12/31/90): Assets,
$282,940 (M); gifts received, $9,420,980;
expenditures, $9,430,113; qualifying
distributions, $9,400,896, including $8,049,220
for 724 grants (high: $445,000; low: $1,000;
average: $2,000-$15,000) and $1,351,601 for
employee matching gifts.
Purpose and activities: Support primarily for
higher education, including fellowship and
scholarship programs, and community funds;
grants also for health, aging, human services,
youth agencies, urban affairs, and cultural
programs.
Fields of interest: Higher education, community
funds, health, social services, aged, youth, urban
affairs, cultural programs.
Types of support: Operating budgets, continuing
support, annual campaigns, seed money, building
funds, equipment, employee matching gifts,
fellowships, scholarship funds, renovation
projects.
Limitations: Giving primarily in areas of company
operations. No support for church-related
programs. No grants to individuals, or for
endowment funds; no loans.
Application information: Application form not
required.
   Initial approach: Letter
   Copies of proposal: 1
   Deadline(s): Oct. 1
   Board meeting date(s): Feb.
   Final notification: Only if approved
   Write: Alan S. Painter, V.P. and Exec. Dir.
Officers and Directors:* Edward L. Hennessy, Jr.,
Chair.; David G. Powell,* Pres.; Alan S. Painter,
V.P. and Exec. Dir.; Brian D. Forrow,* V.P.;
Heather M. Mullett, Secy.; G. Peter D'Aloia,
Treas.; John W. Barter, Alan Belzer, John L. Day,
Roy H. Ekrom, Mary L. Good, Fred M. Poses,
James E. Sierk, James J. Verrant.
Number of staff: None.
EIN: 222416651
Recent health grants:
1611-1 Alliance for Aging Research, DC,
$10,000. 1990.
1611-2 American Diabetes Association,
Bridgewater, NJ, $100,000. 1990.
1611-3 American Federation for Aging Research,
NYC, NY, $115,000. For Creative Investigator
grants and for administrative grant. 1990.
1611-4 Boston University, Boston, MA, $10,000.
For Health Policy Institute. 1990.

1611-5 Daniel Freeman Memorial Hospital,
Inglewood, CA, $10,000. 1990.
1611-6 Deafness Research Foundation, NYC, NY,
$100,000. 1990.
1611-7 Gerontological Society of America, DC,
$10,000. 1990.
1611-8 Institute for Evaluating Health Risks, San
Francisco, CA, $10,000. For developing sound
risk assessment techniques for proper
environmental regulation. 1990.
1611-9 Johns Hopkins University, Center on
Aging, Baltimore, MD, $61,000. For
administrative grant. 1990.
1611-10 Johns Hopkins University, School of
Hygiene and Public Health, Baltimore, MD,
$25,000. 1990.
1611-11 Little Company of Mary Hospital,
Torrance, CA, $10,000. 1990.
1611-12 Loyola University Medical Center,
Maywood, IL, $10,000. For Heart Transplant
Unit. 1990.
1611-13 Memorial Sloan-Kettering Cancer
Center, NYC, NY, $20,000. 1990.
1611-14 Mercy-Memorial Medical Center, Saint
Joseph, MI, $10,000. For capital campaign for
cancer care. 1990.
1611-15 Morristown Memorial Health
Foundation, Morristown, NJ, $200,000. For
Era of Excellence Campaign. 1990.
1611-16 National Council on the Aging, DC,
$10,000. 1990.
1611-17 National Osteoporosis Foundation, DC,
$100,000. 1990.
1611-18 National Parkinson Foundation, Miami,
FL, $100,000. 1990.
1611-19 National Stroke Association,
Englewood, NJ, $100,000. 1990.
1611-20 Occupational Physicians Scholarship
Fund, Arlington Heights, IL, $20,000. For
physicians training in occupational medicine.
1990.
1611-21 Torrance Memorial Hospital, Torrance,
CA, $20,000. For capital grant. 1990.
1611-22 University of Medicine and Dentistry of
New Jersey Foundation, Newark, NJ,
$200,000. For capital campaign. 1990.
1611-23 Vistas for the Blind, Los Angeles, CA,
$10,000. For continuing annual support for
10K Run. 1990.

1612
American Cyanamid Company
Contributions Program
One Cyanamid Plaza
Wayne 07470   (201) 831-2714

Financial data (yr. ended 12/31/87): Total giving,
$3,647,000, including $3,515,000 for grants
(low: $25; average: $1,000-$5,000) and
$132,000 for employee matching gifts.
Purpose and activities: "Since contributions to
philanthropic or other qualified organizations
represent a distribution of assets being managed
for stockholders, the only theory upon which they
can be justified is that such contributions will
benefit Cyanamid directly or indirectly. Cyanamid
will establish an annual fund to be used to
support organizations which work to satisfy the
needs and interests of Cyanamid employees and
the communities in which they work and live.
Cyanamid will support United Ways; hospitals;
educational institutions; and health, social and

cultural programs which contribute to the welfare
of Cyanamid employees, their families and the
general public. Cyanamid will also selectively
support national and international organizations
when such support could enhance the economic
or social environment in which it operates.
Cyanamid considers its first contribution
obligation as being to those communities in
which it maintains operations; only under
unusual circumstances will it consider donations
in other communities." Criteria for support are:
(A) services to Cyanamid or its employees; (B)
services that enhance the economic or social
environment at Cyanamid locations; (C) support
for the free enterprise system; (D) an improved
technology base to which Cyanamid can have
access. Corporate contributions (national,
international, state, regional) should fall into four
categories: 1. contributions which serve to
support the free enterprise system; 2.
contributions; to educational/research institutions
which are accumulating technology in areas of
interest to Cyanamid; 3. contributions to
educational institutions which provide a source of
candidates for employment; 4. contributions to
institutions or organizations which provide a
service to Cyanamid employees.
Fields of interest: Education, science and
technology, health, welfare, civic affairs, arts,
humanities, biochemistry, business education.
Types of support: Building funds, capital
campaigns, conferences and seminars, employee
matching gifts, fellowships, general purposes,
operating budgets, research, scholarship funds,
special projects.
Limitations: Giving primarily in headquarters city
and major operating areas. No support for
sectarian, religious, political, veterans', special
interest groups, or for organizations participating
in the United Way. No grants to individuals, or
labor organizations.
Publications: Program policy statement.
Application information: Application form not
required.
   Initial approach: Letter
   Deadline(s): No deadlines but large requests
      preferred in Aug. or Sept.
   Final notification: 4-6 weeks for full review and
      decision
   Write: Dolores Stortz, Contribs. Mgr.
Number of staff: 1 full-time professional; 1
part-time support.

1613
American Re-Insurance Corporate Giving
Program
555 College Rd. East
Princeton 08543

Purpose and activities: Supports cultural
programs, education, community funds, health
and welfare.
Fields of interest: Cultural programs, education,
community funds, health, welfare.
Limitations: Giving primarily in headquarters city
and operating locations; primary focus - central
NJ.
Application information:
   Initial approach: Letter of inquiry or proposal to
      headquarters
   Copies of proposal: 1
   Deadline(s): Best time to apply is June to Aug.

Board meeting date(s): Oct.-Nov. for next fiscal year
Final notification: All requests will be answered
Write: Diane Vatalero, Chair., Charitable Contribs. Comm.

1614
Armco Foundation

300 Interpace Pkwy.
Parsippany 07054-0324   (201) 316-5274

Incorporated in 1951 in OH.
Donor(s): Armco Inc.
Foundation type: Company-sponsored
Financial data (yr. ended 12/31/91): Assets, $9,795,485 (M); expenditures, $546,184; qualifying distributions, $528,547, including $479,526 for 157 grants (high: $35,000; low: $200; average: $100-$5,000) and $38,996 for 201 employee matching gifts.
Purpose and activities: Grants for health and hospitals, welfare, and higher education, including a scholarship program for the children of active company employees administered by the College Scholarship Service; support also for public affairs and a matching gift program for higher educational and cultural institutions.
Fields of interest: Welfare, hospitals, health services, arts, environment, higher education.
Types of support: Continuing support, seed money, matching funds, employee-related scholarships, employee matching gifts, special projects, capital campaigns, general purposes, employee volunteer services.
Limitations: Giving primarily in areas of company operations. No support for religious organizations. No grants to individuals (except for employee-related scholarships), or for deficit financing, land acquisition, endowment funds, fellowships, demonstration projects, or publications; no loans.
Application information: Application form not required.
Initial approach: Letter
Copies of proposal: 1
Deadline(s): None
Board meeting date(s): Mar. and Dec.
Final notification: 4 to 6 weeks
Write: Ms. Loyce A. Martin, Fdn. Admin.
Officers and Trustees:* Brage Golding, Chair.; Robert L. Purdum,* Pres.; John M. Bilich, Exec. V.P.; Robert W. Kent, V.P. and Secy.; James L. Bertsch, Treas.; Frederick B. Dent, Harry Holiday, Jr., John H. Ladish.
Number of staff: 1 full-time professional; 1 part-time support.
EIN: 316026565

1615
The Corella & Bertram Bonner Foundation, Inc. ▼

22 Chambers St., Box 712
Princeton 08542   (609) 924-6663

Established in 1981 in NJ; reactivated in 1989.
Foundation type: Independent
Financial data (yr. ended 06/30/91): Assets, $43,325,799 (M); gifts received, $38,322,453; expenditures, $1,794,858; qualifying distributions, $1,769,625, including $1,376,394

for 353 grants (high: $125,000; low: $500; average: $1,000-$25,000).
Purpose and activities: Support primarily for higher and other education, including educational programs for minorities; religious organizations, including those operating missionary programs, and welfare programs; social services and hunger programs; and hospitals, the handicapped, medical research, and ophthalmology.
Fields of interest: Higher education, education, education—minorities, religion, religion—missionary programs, social services, hunger, hospitals, handicapped, medical research.
Types of support: Matching funds, scholarship funds, continuing support.
Limitations: Giving limited to domestic programs in the U.S. No grants to individuals, or for capital improvements, endowments, operating budgets, building funds, or renovations.
Publications: Informational brochure.
Application information: Application form required.
Initial approach: Telephone
Copies of proposal: 1
Deadline(s): Aug. 15
Write: Wayne Meisel, Exec. Dir.
Officers and Trustees:* Bertram F. Bonner,* Pres.; Corella A. Bonner,* V.P.
Number of staff: 3 full-time professional; 2 full-time support.
EIN: 222316452
Recent health grants:
1615-1 Foundation for Glaucoma Research, San Francisco, CA, $10,000. 1991.
1615-2 Foundation of the American Academy of Ophthalmology, San Francisco, CA, $10,000. 1991.
1615-3 Lahey Clinic Medical Center, Burlington, MA, $125,000. 1991.
1615-4 Mayo Foundation, Rochester, MN, $50,000. For Glaucoma Research. 1991.
1615-5 Mayo Foundation, Rochester, MN, $50,000. 1991.
1615-6 Retinitis Pigmentosa Foundation Fighting Blindness, NYC, NY, $10,000. 1991.

1616
The Mary Owen Borden Memorial Foundation

160 Hodge Rd.
Princeton 08540   (609) 924-3637

Incorporated in 1934 in NJ.
Donor(s): Bertram H. Borden,‡ Victory Memorial Park Foundation.
Foundation type: Independent
Financial data (yr. ended 12/31/90): Assets, $8,255,478 (M); expenditures, $534,527; qualifying distributions, $463,525, including $439,925 for 52 grants (high: $40,000; low: $200; average: $7,586).
Purpose and activities: Grants for programs focusing on special needs of youth which include: family planning counseling to teenagers; assistance to unwed, teenage mothers; day care centers for young, disadvantaged parents; assistance to families where instability prevails; assistance to institutions or programs aiding delinquent youth; and innovative or alternative forms of criminal justice for youthful offenders. Support also for human services, conservation

and the environment, nuclear disarmament, and substance abuse. Emphasis on grants for new and innovative projects and preference for support to organizations that are new, or established organizations undertaking new projects.
Fields of interest: Youth, family planning, education—early childhood, child welfare, social services, conservation, health, women, community development.
Types of support: Seed money, matching funds, special projects, general purposes, operating budgets, capital campaigns.
Limitations: Giving limited to Monmouth and Mercer counties, NJ. No grants to individuals, or for scholarships or fellowships; no loans.
Publications: Annual report (including application guidelines), application guidelines.
Application information: Application form required.
Initial approach: Write for form if request meets foundation guidelines
Copies of proposal: 1
Deadline(s): Jan. 1, Apr. 1, and Sept. 1
Board meeting date(s): Jan., May, and Oct.
Final notification: 2 weeks
Write: John C. Borden, Jr., Exec. Dir.
Officers and Trustees:* Mrs. Q.A. Shaw McKean, Jr.,* Pres.; Mrs. Marvin Broder,* V.P.; Mary L. Miles, Secy.; Joseph Lord,* Treas.; John C. Borden, Jr.,* Exec. Dir.; Thomas A. Borden, Gordon Litwin, Jerri Morrison, Dorothy Ransom.
Number of staff: 1 part-time professional; 1 part-time support.
EIN: 136137137
Recent health grants:
1616-1 Bayshore Youth and Family Services, Matawan, NJ, $10,000. For individual and family counseling program for youth who have been identified at high risk of becoming drug and substance abusers. 1990.
1616-2 Childrens Psychiatric Center, Eatontown, NJ, $15,000. To cover salary costs for life skills training staff who work with mentally disadvantaged adolescents. 1990.
1616-3 Epiphany House, Long Branch, NJ, $10,000. For operating expenses of residential and treatment home for recovering women alcoholics and their children. 1990.
1616-4 McOss Foundation, Red Bank, NJ, $10,000. For maternal and child health care and services for low income families in Long Branch, Asbury Park and Red Bank. 1990.
1616-5 Riverview Medical Center, Red Bank, NJ, $40,000. For capital campaign for new equipment and new computerized health care system. 1990.

1617
Brady Foundation

P.O. Box 351
Gladstone 07934   (908) 234-1900

Incorporated in 1953 in NJ.
Donor(s): Helen M. Cutting,‡ Nicholas Brady.
Foundation type: Independent
Financial data (yr. ended 12/31/90): Assets, $6,293,029 (M); expenditures, $255,399; qualifying distributions, $221,042, including $146,000 for 33 grants (high: $30,000; low: $500; average: $5,000).
Fields of interest: Hospitals, youth, museums, religion.

Limitations: Giving primarily in NJ.
Application information: Application form not required.
  Initial approach: Letter
  Deadline(s): None
  Board meeting date(s): Quarterly
  Write: Joseph A. Gaunt, Secy.
Officers and Trustees:* James C. Brady, Jr.,* Pres. and Treas.; Joseph A. Gaunt, Secy.; N.F. Brady, Anderson Fowler.
Number of staff: None.
EIN: 136167209

1618
Brawer Philanthropic Foundation
250 Belmont Ave.
Haledon 07508   (201) 942-5200

Established in 1962 in NJ.
Donor(s): Brawer Brothers, Inc.
Foundation type: Independent
Financial data (yr. ended 12/31/91): Assets, $38,044 (M); gifts received, $239,000; expenditures, $239,816; qualifying distributions, $239,816, including $239,758 for 32 grants (high: $125,000; low: $25).
Fields of interest: Jewish giving, Jewish welfare, hospitals, general charitable giving.
Types of support: Annual campaigns, building funds, continuing support.
Publications: 990-PF.
Application information: Application form not required.
  Deadline(s): None
  Write: Irving Brawer, Trustee
Trustees: Irving Brawer, Isaac Brawer, Louis Brawer, Sidney Brawer.
EIN: 226057242

1619
Robert E. Brennan Foundation, Inc.
c/o Mortenson, Fleming, et al.
340 North Ave.
Cranford 07016-2435

Incorporated in 1984 in NJ.
Donor(s): Robert E. Brennan.
Foundation type: Independent
Financial data (yr. ended 12/31/91): Assets, $24,354,786 (M); gifts received, $15,347,500; expenditures, $967,394; qualifying distributions, $889,305, including $884,330 for 39 grants (high: $200,000; low: $100; average: $5,000-$10,000).
Purpose and activities: Giving for parochial and other education, Christian churches, social services, health associations, and medical care for children.
Fields of interest: Education, religious schools, higher education, religion—Christian, social services, recreation, health, health associations.
Types of support: Capital campaigns, general purposes, scholarship funds, building funds.
Limitations: Giving primarily in NJ. No grants to individuals.
Application information: Contributes only to pre-selected organizations. Applications not accepted.
Officers and Trustees:* Robert E. Brennan,* Pres.; Patricia A. Brennan,* V.P.; Nora Aquilon, Secy.; Ronald J. Riccio,* Treas.

EIN: 222550509

1620
Brunetti Foundation
1655 U.S. Hwy. 9
Old Bridge 08857   (908) 679-1600

Established in 1974.
Donor(s): Aldercrest Development Corp., John J. Brunetti.
Foundation type: Independent
Financial data (yr. ended 12/31/90): Assets, $2,301,494 (M); gifts received, $275,000; expenditures, $95,112; qualifying distributions, $93,037, including $92,250 for 72 grants (high: $20,000; low: $100).
Purpose and activities: Support primarily for a military academy, higher education, medical research, and hospitals; minor support for Catholic churches.
Fields of interest: Education, higher education, medical research, hospitals, Catholic giving.
Types of support: Research, endowment funds, scholarship funds.
Limitations: Giving primarily in NJ, NY, and FL. No grants to individuals.
Application information: Application form not required.
  Deadline(s): None
  Write: John J. Brunetti, Pres.
Officers and Directors:* John J. Brunetti,* Pres.; John J. Brunetti, Jr., V.P. and Secy.; Anna G. Brunetti.
EIN: 237346205

1621
The Bunbury Company, Inc.
169 Nassau St.
Princeton 08542   (609) 683-1414

Incorporated in 1952 in NY.
Donor(s): Dean Mathey.‡
Foundation type: Independent
Financial data (yr. ended 12/31/90): Assets, $13,989,958 (M); expenditures, $807,209; qualifying distributions, $671,913, including $542,512 for 134 grants (high: $50,000; low: $50; average: $50-$10,000).
Purpose and activities: Grants primarily for higher and secondary education, including programs for minorities, the disadvantaged, the handicapped, youth agencies, health, family services and family planning, the fine arts and cultural organizations, the environment and ecology, and organizations benefiting women.
Fields of interest: Higher education, secondary education, disadvantaged, youth, women, family planning, health services, arts, environment, ecology.
Types of support: General purposes.
Limitations: Giving primarily in NJ. No grants to individuals, or for building funds or fellowships; no loans.
Publications: Annual report (including application guidelines).
Application information:
  Initial approach: Proposal
  Copies of proposal: 1
  Deadline(s): 1 month before board meetings
  Board meeting date(s): Feb., May, July, and Oct.

Final notification: 1 to 2 weeks after board meeting
  Write: Samuel W. Lambert, III, Pres., or Barbara L. Ruppert, Asst. Secy.
Officers and Directors:* Samuel W. Lambert III,* Pres.; Edward J. Toohey,* V.P.; Charles C. Townsend, Jr.,* Secy.; James R. Cogan,* Treas.; Charles B. Atwater, Stephan A. Morse, Robert M. Olmsted, William B. Wright, Edward R. Zuccaro.
Number of staff: 9 part-time professional; 1 full-time support; 1 part-time support.
EIN: 136066172

1622
Campbell Soup Foundation ▼
(Formerly Campbell Soup Fund)
Campbell Place
Camden 08103   (609) 342-6431

Incorporated in 1953 in NJ.
Donor(s): Campbell Soup Co.
Foundation type: Company-sponsored
Financial data (yr. ended 06/30/91): Assets, $13,134,458 (M); gifts received, $1,500,000; expenditures, $1,577,104; qualifying distributions, $1,491,150, including $1,491,150 for 86 grants (high: $175,000; low: $500; average: $5,000-$25,000).
Purpose and activities: Capital grants to private institutions of higher education and hospitals and other health care facilities; support also for cultural programs, social service and youth agencies, community funds, and public interest groups. Major interest in nutrition and health.
Fields of interest: Higher education, education—building funds, education—minorities, youth, social services, cultural programs, public policy, hospitals, health services.
Types of support: Building funds, renovation projects, capital campaigns.
Limitations: Giving primarily in areas of company operations, with emphasis on the Camden, NJ, and Philadelphia, PA, areas. No grants to individuals, or for operating budgets, continuing support, annual campaigns, seed money, emergency funds, deficit financing, land acquisition, endowment funds, matching gifts, equipment, or scholarships or fellowships; no loans.
Publications: Annual report, corporate giving report.
Application information: Application form not required.
  Initial approach: Letter
  Copies of proposal: 1
  Deadline(s): None
  Board meeting date(s): As required
  Final notification: 4 to 8 weeks
  Write: Jeremiah F. O'Brien, Vice-Chair.
Officers and Trustees:* J.M. Coleman,* Chair.; J.J. Baldwin, Vice-Chair.; J.F. O'Brien,* Vice-Chair.; J.J. Furey, Secy.; B.E. Edgerton,* Treas.; L.J. Greaney, Controller; R.F. Bernstock, J.R. Kirk, C.V. McCarthy.
Number of staff: 2 full-time professional; 2 part-time professional; 2 part-time support.
EIN: 216019196
Recent health grants:
1622-1 American Heart Association, Dallas, TX, $10,000. 1991.

1622-2 Columbia University, College of Physicians and Surgeons, NYC, NY, $50,000. For study, Heritable Markers of Salt Sensitivity in Human Subjects: A Pilot Project. 1991.

1622-3 Cooper Hospital-University Medical Center, Camden, NJ, $25,000. Toward purchase of Stable Xenon CT Scanner, used to measure cerebral blood flow. 1991.

1622-4 Kent and Queen Annes Hospital, Chestertown, MD, $10,000. 1991.

1622-5 Monell Chemical Senses Center, Philadelphia, PA, $12,500. 1991.

1622-6 National Kidney Foundation, NYC, NY, $14,000. For pilot project aimed at managing hypertension through dietary control. 1991.

1622-7 Navajo Community College, Tsaile, AZ, $34,000. For program to reduce obesity and prevent diabetes among Navajo school children. 1991.

1622-8 Oregon Health Sciences University, Portland, OR, $60,000. For study, Platelet Intracellular Calcium as A Predictor of Salt Sensitivity in Humans. 1991.

1622-9 Our Lady of Lourdes Medical Center, Camden, NJ, $35,000. For modernization of facility. 1991.

1622-10 Peninsula General Hospital, Salisbury, MD, $12,500. 1991.

1622-11 Public Voice for Food and Health Policy, DC, $15,000. For conference, Children and Nutrition: Building Our Nation's Health. 1991.

1622-12 University of Medicine and Dentistry of New Jersey, Camden, NJ, $25,000. Toward financial support for talented minority students seeking careers in health professions. 1991.

1622-13 West Jersey Health System, Camden, NJ, $60,000. For general support of four nurseries in System's obstetrics program. 1991.

1623
Emil Capita Charitable Trust
7020 Kennedy Blvd.
North Bergen 07047   (201) 869-7112

Established in 1984 in NJ.
Donor(s): Emil R. Capita.
Foundation type: Independent
Financial data (yr. ended 09/30/90): Assets, $2,226,780 (M); gifts received, $500; expenditures, $85,304; qualifying distributions, $80,000, including $80,000 for 1 grant.
Purpose and activities: "Grant recipients must be scientists affiliated with Columbia University engaged in hearing research."
Fields of interest: Science and technology, medical research.
Types of support: Research.
Application information:
    Write: Denise Meroni, Secy.
Officers: Anthony Del Spina, Pres.; Robert Capita, V.P.; Denise Meroni, Secy.; Roy A. Cohen, Treas.
Trustees: John Mach, Jules G. Walther, M.D.
EIN: 222669043

1624
CPC International Corporate Giving Program
International Plaza
P.O. Box 8000
Englewood Cliffs 07632-9976   (201) 894-2571

Financial data (yr. ended 12/31/91): Total giving, $14,000,000.
Purpose and activities: Support for a wide range of programs falling under these categories: education, health, welfare, community service, and culture; willing to consider programs for minorities, women, the handicapped, child welfare, the disadvantaged, law and justice, literacy, mental health, museums, race relations, drug abuse, and volunteerism. Regionally and nationally, company tends to focus on larger, well-established organizations; local giving sometimes goes to smaller, more innovative programs; support includes in-kind giving of surplus food products. 40 percent of giving is made to higher education.
Fields of interest: Civic affairs, cultural programs, disadvantaged, economics, fine arts, general charitable giving, health, international affairs, medical research, minorities, music, media and communications, rural development, theater, urban development, vocational education, welfare, youth, child welfare, community development, education, education—minorities, educational associations, environment, health associations, health services, hospitals, hunger, law and justice, literacy, mental health, museums, race relations, social services, volunteerism, drug abuse.
Types of support: Operating budgets, capital campaigns, employee matching gifts, general purposes, special projects, donated products.
Limitations: Giving primarily in headquarters city and major operating locations. No support for fraternal, political or religious organizations. No grants to individuals or for fundraising projects.
Publications: Program policy statement.
Application information: Application form not required.
    Initial approach: Letter to nearest facility
    Copies of proposal: 1
    Final notification: Month following meeting
    Write: Patrica Baile, Mgr., Personnel Services

1625
Crane Fund for Widows and Children
140 Sylvan Ave., Suite 1
Englewood Cliffs 07632-2509

Established in 1914 in IL.
Foundation type: Independent
Financial data (yr. ended 12/31/90): Assets, $10,705,969 (M); expenditures, $646,841; qualifying distributions, $609,480, including $508,983 for 240 grants (high: $24,000; low: $100) and $14,076 for 2 grants to individuals (high: $11,760; low: $2,316).
Purpose and activities: Support for community funds, hospitals, and higher education; limited support also to organizations in Canada and to needy and indigent persons in IL.
Fields of interest: Community funds, hospitals, higher education, Canada, welfare—indigent individuals.
Types of support: Grants to individuals.
Limitations: Giving primarily in the U.S. and Canada; grants for needy persons limited to IL.
Application information:
    Initial approach: Letter
    Deadline(s): None
    Write: Administrator

Trustees: J.P. Cronin, P.R. Hundt, R.B. Phillips, M.L. Raithel.
EIN: 366116543

1626
J. Fletcher Creamer Foundation
101 East Broadway
Hackensack 07601   (201) 488-9800

Established in 1980 in NJ.
Donor(s): J. Fletcher Creamer & Sons, Inc.
Foundation type: Independent
Financial data (yr. ended 03/31/92): Assets, $1,310,338 (M); gifts received, $100,700; expenditures, $1,316,736; qualifying distributions, $1,312,405, including $1,312,405 for 111 grants (high: $1,123,600; low: $50).
Fields of interest: Hospitals, health associations, Catholic giving, youth.
Limitations: Giving primarily in NJ. No grants to individuals.
Application information: Application form not required.
    Deadline(s): None
    Write: Robert Rogut, Trustee
Trustees: J. Fletcher Creamer, J. Fletcher Creamer, Jr., Robert Rogut.
EIN: 222335557

1627
Crum and Forster Foundation, Inc.
211 Mt. Airy Rd.
Basking Ridge 07920   (908) 204-3579

Incorporated in 1953 in CA as the Industrial Indemnity Foundation; the foundation is registered in CA and NJ.
Donor(s): Crum & Forster Corp., and affiliated companies.
Foundation type: Company-sponsored
Financial data (yr. ended 12/31/90): Assets, $14,911 (M); gifts received, $1,004,500; expenditures, $968,463; qualifying distributions, $968,408, including $880,340 for 586 grants (high: $69,285; low: $50; average: $500-$3,000) and $88,068 for 552 employee matching gifts.
Fields of interest: Health services, hospitals, youth, higher education, secondary education, cultural programs, arts, civic affairs, safety.
Types of support: Operating budgets, annual campaigns, seed money, emergency funds, equipment, building funds, scholarship funds, exchange programs, continuing support, capital campaigns, employee matching gifts, general purposes, in-kind gifts.
Limitations: No support for religious organizations or activities. No grants to individuals; no loans.
Application information: Application form not required.
    Initial approach: Letter or proposal
    Copies of proposal: 1
    Deadline(s): Submit proposal preferably from Sept. through Nov.; deadline Nov. 30
    Board meeting date(s): Mar. and as required
    Write: John A. Douglas, V.P.
Officers and Directors:* Joseph W. Brown, Jr.,* Chair., Pres., and C.E.O.; Robert A. Zito, V.P.; Doddridge H. Biaett, Secy.; R. Scott Donovan, Treas.; Anthony R. Biele, George J. Rachmiel.
Number of staff: 1 full-time professional.

EIN: 946065476

1628
The Diabetes Research & Education Foundation, Inc.
P.O. Box 6168
Bridgewater 08807-9998   (908) 658-9322

Established in 1984 in NJ.
Donor(s): Hoechst-Roussel Pharmaceuticals, Inc.
Foundation type: Independent
Financial data (yr. ended 12/31/90): Assets, $43,216 (M); gifts received, $1,000,000; expenditures, $1,196,501; qualifying distributions, $1,197,614, including $1,108,456 for 65 grants to individuals (high: $20,000; low: $2,359).
Purpose and activities: Awards grants to individuals for diabetes research and education initiatives that would seldom be considered for funding by traditional research foundations; the foundation underwrites projects in basic and clinical research and education.
Fields of interest: Medical research, health.
Types of support: Grants to individuals, research.
Publications: Annual report, informational brochure (including application guidelines).
Application information: Application form required.
  Initial approach: Proposal
  Copies of proposal: 7
  Deadline(s): Mar. 30 and Sept. 30
  Board meeting date(s): May and Nov.
  Final notification: Approximately 2 weeks after board meetings
  Write: Herbert C. Rosenkilde, M.D., Exec. Dir.
Officer: Leo P. Krall, M.D., Chair. and Pres.
Directors: Herbert C. Rosenkilde, M.D., Exec. Dir.; R. Keith Campbell, Donnell D. Etzwiler, M.D., Rachmiel Levine, M.D., Rita Nemchik.
Number of staff: 1
EIN: 222561975

1629
Fairleigh S. Dickinson, Jr., Foundation, Inc.
c/o Toner, DiBenedetto & Chiarella
Three ADP Blvd.
Roseland 07068

Incorporated in 1981 in NY.
Foundation type: Independent
Financial data (yr. ended 09/30/90): Assets, $147,015 (M); gifts received, $307,299; expenditures, $298,495; qualifying distributions, $294,429, including $252,250 for 39 grants (high: $42,500; low: $100).
Fields of interest: Higher education, secondary education, hospitals, health associations.
Limitations: Giving primarily in NJ.
Application information: Application form not required.
  Copies of proposal: 3
  Deadline(s): None
  Board meeting date(s): Apr. and Dec.
  Write: Roger L. Toner, Esq.
Officers: Jack King, Chair.; Harold Daitch, Vice-Chair.; Roger Toner, Secy.-Treas.
Number of staff: 1 part-time support.
EIN: 133118384

1630
Geraldine R. Dodge Foundation, Inc. ▼
163 Madison Ave., 6th Fl.
P.O. Box 1239
Morristown 07962-1239   (201) 540-8442

Incorporated in 1974 in NJ.
Donor(s): Geraldine R. Dodge.‡
Foundation type: Independent
Financial data (yr. ended 12/31/90): Assets, $137,953,811 (M); expenditures, $11,751,069; qualifying distributions, $10,093,211, including $8,757,594 for 306 grants (high: $209,651; low: $500; average: $15,000-$25,000), $125,000 for 25 grants to individuals, $5,890 for 52 employee matching gifts and $374,048 for 3 foundation-administered programs.
Purpose and activities: Grant-making emphasis in NJ on secondary education, performing and visual arts and other cultural activities, projects in population, environment, energy, and other critical areas, and programs in the public interest, including development of volunteerism, communications, and public issues. Interest in independent secondary schools in New England and Middle Atlantic states and in projects on the national level that are likely to lead to significant advances in secondary education. Projects that have implications beyond the school itself are of special interest. Support also for projects in welfare of animals on a national and local level which explore the human/animal bond, promote humane education, and address issues of cruelty, pet overpopulation, the protection of wildlife, farm animal abuse, and animal exploitation in laboratories.
Fields of interest: Education, secondary education, educational research, education—minorities, elementary education, arts, cultural programs, performing arts, theater, museums, environment, energy, public policy, volunteerism, media and communications, animal welfare, women, family planning, child development, youth.
Types of support: Seed money, conferences and seminars, matching funds, special projects, publications, continuing support, research, operating budgets, fellowships.
Limitations: Giving primarily in NJ, with support for the arts and local humane groups limited to NJ, and support for other local projects limited to the Morristown-Madison area; some giving in the other Middle Atlantic states and New England, and to national organizations. No support for religion, higher education, health, or conduit organizations. No grants for capital projects, equipment purchases, endowment funds, deficit financing, or scholarships.
Publications: Annual report (including application guidelines), application guidelines.
Application information: Application form not required.
  Initial approach: Letter or proposal
  Copies of proposal: 1
  Deadline(s): Submit proposal preferably in Mar., June, Sept., or Dec.; deadlines Dec. 15 for welfare of animals and local projects; Mar. 15 for secondary education; June 15 for the arts; and Sept. 15 for public issues
  Board meeting date(s): Mar., June, Sept., and Dec.
  Final notification: End of months in which board meets
  Write: Scott McVay, Exec. Dir.
Officers and Trustees:* Robert H.B. Baldwin,* Chair.; Robert LeBuhn,* Pres.; Scott McVay, Exec. Dir.; Barbara Knowles Debs, Christopher J. Elliman, Henry U. Harder, John Lloyd Huck, Nancy D. Lindsay, Walter J. Neppl, Paul J. O'Donnell.
Number of staff: 6 full-time professional; 2 part-time professional; 5 full-time support; 1 part-time support.
EIN: 237406010
Recent health grants:
1630-1 Auburn University, College of Veterinary Medicine, Auburn University, AL, $110,000. For third-year support of three-year program developing interactive video-computer simulations as alternatives to live animal experimentation in research and teaching. Grant shared with Tuskegee University School of Veterinary Medicine. 1990.
1630-2 Convince, East Lansing, MI, $75,000. For first-year operating costs of this veterinary school consortium which is coordinating development of interactive videodisc lessons as alternatives to sacrifice of animals in research and teaching. 1990.
1630-3 Cornell University, Ithaca, NY, $20,000. Toward symposium, Animal Pain and Its Control. Grant shared with New York State College of Veterinary Medicine. 1990.
1630-4 Cornell University, Baker Institute for Animal Health, Ithaca, NY, $31,500. For renewed support of two-year program of summer fellowships for eight veterinary students chosen from schools in U.S. and Canada. 1990.
1630-5 Cornell University, Baker Institute for Animal Health, Ithaca, NY, $15,000. For contribution in memory of William Rockefeller. 1990.
1630-6 Family Planning Association of New Jersey, Trenton, NJ, $19,000. For renewed support of Regulatory Affairs Program that works with state on regulations that have direct impact on quality, accessibility and cost effectiveness of New Jersey's reproductive health care services. 1990.
1630-7 Georgetown University, Kennedy Institute of Ethics, DC, $25,000. For seed support toward multi-year program entitled Bioethical Issues in Animal Experimentation: A New Academic Initiative. 1990.
1630-8 Memorial Sloan-Kettering Cancer Center, NYC, NY, $10,000. For contribution in memory of William D. Rockefeller. 1990.
1630-9 Mrs. Wilsons, Morristown, NJ, $20,000. For development of Community Education Program to help women cope with problems of recovery from drug and alcohol abuse. 1990.
1630-10 National Family Planning and Reproductive Health Association, DC, $30,000. For communication and education programs for more than 4,000 family planning clinics nationwide. 1990.
1630-11 Physicians Committee for Responsible Medicine, DC, $25,000. For second-year funding for project to develop alternatives to animal testing. 1990.
1630-12 Planned Parenthood Association of the Mercer Area, Trenton, NJ, $35,000. For public information program culminating in working manual that Planned Parenthood chapters

everywhere may use to counteract attacks on agency's mission of providing access to reproductive health services, including right to abortion. 1990.

1630-13 Planned Parenthood Federation of America, NYC, NY, $150,000. For public education programs in cooperation with 171 affiliates nationwide. 1990.

1630-14 Planned Parenthood of Essex County, Newark, NJ, $23,500. For continued support. 1990.

1630-15 Planned Parenthood of Essex County, Newark, NJ, $15,000. For family planning and health education programs in Essex County schools and its Haitian community. 1990.

1630-16 Planned Parenthood of Greater Camden, Camden, NJ, $45,000. For middle school peer counseling program that will introduce sexual responsibility at an early age and assist efforts to reduce adolescent pregnancy rates. 1990.

1630-17 Planned Parenthood of Greater Northern New Jersey, Morristown, NJ, $30,000. To help schools and child care centers develop policies and programs regarding early childhood sexuality education. 1990.

1630-18 Population Crisis Committee, DC, $50,000. To work with environment groups to reestablish U.S. government as leader in global population efforts, to advance access to family planning worldwide and to weave population policies and funding increases into government negotiations on environmental problems. 1990.

1630-19 Purdue University, School of Veterinary Medicine, West Lafayette, IN, $50,000. For renewed support of development of interactive videodisc and computer graphic alternatives to use of animals in teaching laboratories. 1990.

1630-20 Trenton, City of, Trenton, NJ, $30,000. For Trenton Office of Policy Studies, independently funded research and evaluation office that will provide informed, unbiased guidance to Trenton's new administration in finance, housing, health and education. 1990.

1630-21 Tufts University, School of Veterinary Medicine, Grafton, MA, $40,000. For establishment of computerized Wildlife Health Network for veterinarians, wildlife rehabilitators, educators and general public to include array of biomedical information and data on status of many wildlife species and survival problems they face. 1990.

1630-22 University of Illinois, College of Veterinary Medicine, Urbana, IL, $45,000. For interactive videodisc programs which develop psychomotor techniques and skills without using live animals to demonstrate standard surgical methods. 1990.

1630-23 University of Medicine and Dentistry of New Jersey, Newark, NJ, $32,000. For Domestic Violence Prevention Project which provides continuing education courses on domestic violence and elder maltreatment and which works closely with other organizations in New Jersey focusing on these issues. 1990.

1630-24 Zero Population Growth, DC, $40,000. For program of educating teachers and students from kindergarten through high school on environmental impact of population growth. 1990.

1631
Charles Edison Fund
101 South Harrison St.
East Orange 07018   (201) 675-9000

Incorporated in 1948 in DE.
Donor(s): Charles Edison,‡ and others.
Foundation type: Independent
Financial data (yr. ended 12/31/90): Assets, $23,577,348 (M); gifts received, $1,781; expenditures, $914,456; qualifying distributions, $917,742, including $432,092 for 31 grants (high: $82,280; low: $100) and $131,304 for 2 foundation-administered programs.
Purpose and activities: Grants largely for historic preservation, with emphasis on the homes of Thomas Alva Edison, and for education, medical research, and hospitals. Support also for foundation-sponsored exhibits at over 80 museums throughout the U.S., for science education teaching kits in over 50,000 classrooms, and for cassette re-recording of antique phonograph records for schools and museums.
Fields of interest: Historic preservation, education, medical research, hospitals, science and technology, cultural programs, museums.
Types of support: Operating budgets, continuing support, seed money, special projects, research, equipment.
Limitations: No grants to individuals, or for building or endowment funds, scholarships, fellowships, or matching gifts; no loans.
Publications: Informational brochure (including application guidelines).
Application information: Application form not required.
  Initial approach: Letter or proposal
  Copies of proposal: 1
  Deadline(s): 30 days prior to board meetings
  Board meeting date(s): Mar., June, Sept., and Dec.
  Write: Paul J. Christiansen, Pres.
Officers and Trustees:* Paul J. Christiansen,* Pres.; John P. Keegan,* V.P.; David O. Schantz,* Secy.-Treas.; Edward L. Allman, William M. Henderson, James E. Howe, Nancy M. Milligan, Robert E. Murray, John N. Schullinger, M.D., J. Thomas Smoot, Jr.
Number of staff: 2 full-time professional; 1 part-time professional; 1 full-time support; 2 part-time support.
EIN: 221514861

1632
Elizabethtown Gas Company Corporate Giving Program
One Elizabethtown Plaza
Union 07083   (201) 289-5000

Financial data (yr. ended 12/31/90): Total giving, $90,000, including $75,000 for grants and $15,000 for employee matching gifts.
Purpose and activities: Educational giving includes gifts to colleges and universities, vocational training, and technical/engineering education in service areas. Civic donations include support of local economic development. Social service contributions go to local United Way agencies, local rescue squads, local youth organizations, and community funds. The company also supports local hospitals and various local cultural concerns.
Fields of interest: Education, vocational education, engineering, social services, youth, community funds, cultural programs, hospitals, general charitable giving.
Limitations: Giving limited to service areas of Union, Middlesex, Warren, Suffix, and Hunterdon counties, NJ.
Application information:
  Initial approach: Letter or telephone
  Deadline(s): By end of Aug. for consideration
  Write: Carol Sliker, Asst. Corp. Secy.
Number of staff: None.

1633
The Charles Engelhard Foundation ▼
P.O. Box 427
Far Hills 07931   (201) 766-7224

Incorporated in 1940 in NJ.
Donor(s): Charles Engelhard,‡ Engelhard Hanovia, Inc., and others.
Foundation type: Independent
Financial data (yr. ended 12/31/90): Assets, $77,013,873 (M); expenditures, $5,569,595; qualifying distributions, $5,038,800, including $4,986,236 for 253 grants (high: $461,250; low: $500; average: $1,000-$100,000).
Purpose and activities: Emphasis on higher and secondary education, and cultural, medical, religious, wildlife, and conservation organizations.
Fields of interest: Religion, higher education, secondary education, cultural programs, medical sciences, wildlife, conservation.
Types of support: General purposes, special projects, continuing support, operating budgets.
Limitations: No grants to individuals, or for building funds.
Publications: Application guidelines.
Application information: Giving only to organizations known to the trustees. Applications not accepted.
  Board meeting date(s): Quarterly
  Write: Joan D. Ricci, Secy.
Officers and Trustees:* Jane B. Engelhard,* Pres.; Joan D. Ricci, Secy.; Edward G. Beimfohr,* Treas.; Charlene B. Engelhard, Sophie Engelhard, Mike Mansfield, Susan O'Connor, Sally E. Pingree, Anne E. Reed.
Number of staff: 1 full-time professional.
EIN: 226063032
Recent health grants:
1633-1 Beth Israel Hospital Association, Boston, MA, $50,000. 1990.
1633-2 Boca Grande Health Clinic, Boca Grande, FL, $25,000. 1990.
1633-3 Boston Womens Health Book Collective, Somerville, MA, $10,000. 1990.
1633-4 Delta Society, Renton, WA, $100,000. 1990.
1633-5 Georgetown University Medical Center, DC, $50,000. 1990.
1633-6 Institute for Homeopathy, Sugar Land, TX, $10,000. 1990.
1633-7 Massachusetts General Hospital, Boston, MA, $71,500. 1990.
1633-8 Mayo Foundation, Rochester, MN, $25,000. 1990.
1633-9 McLean Hospital, Belmont, MA, $40,000. 1990.

1633-10 Medical Education for South African Blacks, DC, $10,000. 1990.

1633-11 Missoula Community Hospital, Missoula, MT, $30,000. 1990.

1633-12 Nantucket Cottage Hospital, Nantucket, MA, $35,000. 1990.

1633-13 National Council on Alcoholism, NYC, NY, $10,000. 1990.

1633-14 New York Hospital-Cornell Medical Center, NYC, NY, $30,000. 1990.

1633-15 Newton-Wellesley Hospital, Newton, MA, $25,000. 1990.

1633-16 Planned Parenthood of New York City, NYC, NY, $15,000. 1990.

1633-17 Saint Lukes-Roosevelt Hospital Center, NYC, NY, $50,000. 1990.

1634
Englehard Corporate Giving Program
101 Wood Ave.
Iselin 08830-0770   (201) 205-6000

Purpose and activities: Maintains strong interest in technical programs, chemical engineering, and education, with most funds going for scholarships or general support. Health and welfare funding provided for diverse organizations, including United Way; giving also for cultural programs. Emphasis on projects that benefit customers, employees, or operating communities.
Fields of interest: Cultural programs, education—minorities, general charitable giving, higher education, education, welfare, community funds, health.
Types of support: Employee matching gifts, equipment, fellowships, matching funds, scholarship funds.
Limitations: Giving primarily in headquarters city and major operating locations. No support for political, religious, or veterans' organizations (except for programs which benefit the community at large). No grants to individuals.
Application information: Proposal including description of organization and project, amount requested, budget, 501(c)(3), budget and list of directors. Application form not required.
  Initial approach: Letter and proposal
  Copies of proposal: 1
  Deadline(s): Oct. 1 for funding the following year
  Board meeting date(s): As needed
  Final notification: Response within 3 months
  Write: William Dugle, V.P., Human Resources
Number of staff: 1 full-time professional; 1 full-time support.

1635
Fanwood Foundation
c/o King, King & Goldsack
450 Somerset St., P.O. Box 1106
North Plainfield 07061-1106   (201) 756-7804

Trust established in 1940 in NJ.
Donor(s): Dorothy W. Stevens.
Foundation type: Independent
Financial data (yr. ended 12/31/91): Assets, $11,537,453 (M); expenditures, $1,165,870; qualifying distributions, $1,081,921, including $1,071,800 for 166 grants (high: $370,000; low: $300).

Purpose and activities: Support primarily for secondary, business, and other education, including educational programs for minorities; support also for museums, the performing arts, and other cultural programs, hospitals and medical research, Christian organizations, wildlife and environmental conservation, economics and public policy, community development, and programs benefiting women, youth, Native Americans, and the disabled.
Fields of interest: Education, secondary education, cultural programs, religion—Christian, environment, health, public policy, women, youth, community development.
Types of support: Annual campaigns, endowment funds, operating budgets.
Limitations: No grants to individuals.
Application information:
  Initial approach: Letter
  Deadline(s): None
  Write: Victor R. King, Trustee
Trustees: Victor R. King, Robert T. Stevens, Jr., Whitney Stevens.
Number of staff: None.
EIN: 136051922

1636
The Frelinghuysen Foundation
P.O. Box 726
Far Hills 07931   (201) 439-3499

Incorporated in 1950 in NJ.
Donor(s): Members of the Frelinghuysen family.
Foundation type: Independent
Financial data (yr. ended 12/31/91): Assets, $2,194,270 (M); expenditures, $291,024; qualifying distributions, $261,893, including $259,050 for 45 grants (high: $50,000; low: $500).
Fields of interest: Higher education, secondary education, cultural programs, hospitals.
Types of support: General purposes, fellowships, internships, capital campaigns, equipment.
Limitations: Giving primarily in NJ and NY.
Application information:
  Initial approach: Letter
  Deadline(s): None
  Write: H.O.H. Frelinghuysen, Pres.
Officers: H.O.H. Frelinghuysen, Pres.; George L.K. Frelinghuysen, V.P. and Treas.; Peter Frelinghuysen, Secy.
EIN: 221723755

1637
The Fund for New Jersey
Kilmer Sq.
65 Church St., Suite 200
New Brunswick 08901   (908) 220-8656

Incorporated in 1969 in NJ as successor to The Florence Murray Wallace Fund established in 1958.
Donor(s): Charles F. Wallace,‡ and members of his family.
Foundation type: Independent
Financial data (yr. ended 12/31/91): Assets, $33,575,746 (M); expenditures, $1,337,112; qualifying distributions, $1,072,251, including $894,834 for 51 grants (high: $55,000; low: $759; average: $20,000) and $15,249 for foundation-administered programs.

Purpose and activities: Emphasis on projects which provide the basis for public action on state or local problems by way of research, litigation, citizen action, or supervision of government.
Fields of interest: Government, civic affairs, environment, urban affairs, minorities, public policy, education, AIDS.
Types of support: Seed money, research, special projects, publications, conferences and seminars, matching funds, general purposes, continuing support.
Limitations: Giving primarily in NJ or to regional programs that benefit NJ. No support for recreation, day care centers, drug treatment programs, health care delivery, or curricular changes in educational institutions. No grants to individuals, or for capital projects, equipment, endowment funds, scholarships, or fellowships.
Publications: Annual report (including application guidelines).
Application information: Application form not required.
  Initial approach: Letter
  Copies of proposal: 1
  Deadline(s): None
  Board meeting date(s): Mar., June, Sept., and Dec.
  Final notification: 2 weeks after board meeting
  Write: Mark M. Murphy, Exec. Dir.
Officers and Trustees:* Joseph C. Cornwall,* Chair. and Treas.; Richard J. Sullivan,* Pres.; Mark M. Murphy, Secy. and Exec. Dir.; William O. Baker, Candace McGee Ashmun, John W. Cornwall, Dickinson R. Debevoise, John J. Gibbons, Gustav Heningburg, Leonard Lieberman, Mary S. Strong, Jane W. Thorne.
Number of staff: 1 full-time professional; 1 part-time professional; 1 full-time support.
EIN: 221895028
Recent health grants:
1637-1 Citizens Committee on Biomedical Ethics, Oakes Outreach Center, Summit, NJ, $25,000. For civic education project involving public in analysis of availability, costs and quality of health care in U.S.. 1991.
1637-2 Hyacinth Foundation, New Brunswick, NJ, $10,000. For development of four pro se clinics, each devoted to an issue of particular importance to persons with AIDS. 1991.

1638
The Garfield Foundation
306 Carter Rd.
Princeton 08540

Foundation type: Independent
Financial data (yr. ended 11/30/90): Assets, $955,870 (M); gifts received, $136,000; expenditures, $316,218; qualifying distributions, $292,321, including $270,000 for 2 grants (high: $200,000; low: $70,000).
Purpose and activities: Support primarily for urban, regional and environmental research; support also for medical research and research on energy and arms control.
Fields of interest: Urban affairs, environment, medical research, energy, arms control.
Limitations: Giving primarily in Princeton, NJ. No grants to individuals.
Application information: Contributes only to pre-selected organizations. Applications not accepted.

Officers and Trustees:* George Garfield,* Pres.;
Elizabeth Garfield, Secy.; Brian Garfield.
EIN: 222285358

1639
General Public Utilities Corporate Giving
Program
100 Interpace Pkwy.
Parsippany 07054   (201) 263-6500

Purpose and activities: Supports civic programs,
economic and community development,
environmental issues, minority programs, energy
issues, scholarships, the United Way, health,
hospitals, education, and arts and culture and
social services.
Fields of interest: Civic affairs, economics,
environment, minorities, community funds, urban
development, energy, general charitable giving,
social services, health, hospitals, education, arts,
cultural programs, social services.
Types of support: Emergency funds, general
purposes, operating budgets, scholarship funds,
special projects.
Limitations: Giving primarily in headquarters city
and major operating locations.
Publications: Newsletter, informational brochure.
Application information: Application form not
required.
  Initial approach: Query letter describing
    project; complete proposal with budget
  Copies of proposal: 1
  Deadline(s): None
  Final notification: 6 weeks
  Write: Susan Schepman, V.P., Communs.
Number of staff: 1

1640
The Grand Marnier Foundation
One Whitman Court
Teaneck 07666   (201) 342-4663

Established in 1985 in NY.
Donor(s): The Carillon Importers, Ltd.
Foundation type: Company-sponsored
Financial data (yr. ended 12/31/90): Assets,
$11,275,720 (M); gifts received, $1,784,532;
expenditures, $1,125,870; qualifying
distributions, $1,015,013, including $834,756 for
43 grants (high: $153,000; low: $500).
Purpose and activities: Support primarily for arts
and cultural programs; some support also for
social services and health.
Fields of interest: Arts, performing arts, cultural
programs, social services, health.
Application information:
  Initial approach: Letter
  Deadline(s): None
  Write: Jerry Ciraulo, Treas.
Officers and Directors:* Michel Roux,* Pres.; Joel
Buchman,* Secy.; Jerry Ciraulo,* Treas.; Maxime
Coury, Francois de Gasperis, Jaques
Marnier-Lapostolle.
EIN: 133258414

1641
E. J. Grassmann Trust ▼
P.O. Box 4470
Warren 07059   (908) 753-2440

Trust established in 1979 in NJ.
Donor(s): Edward J. Grassmann.‡
Foundation type: Independent
Financial data (yr. ended 12/31/90): Assets,
$28,318,882 (M); expenditures, $2,501,812;
qualifying distributions, $2,386,386, including
$2,245,026 for 160 grants (high: $165,000; low:
$1,000; average: $5,000-$30,000).
Purpose and activities: Grants for higher and
secondary education, hospitals and health
organizations, historical associations,
environmental conservation, and social welfare
organizations, particularly those helping children.
Preference given to organizations with low
administration costs, and which show efforts to
achieve a broad funding base.
Fields of interest: Education, higher education,
secondary education, education—building funds,
health, hospitals—building funds, historic
preservation, environment, conservation, social
services, child welfare, youth.
Types of support: Endowment funds, scholarship
funds, building funds, equipment, land
acquisition, capital campaigns.
Limitations: Giving primarily in NJ, particularly
Union County, and in GA, primarily middle GA.
No grants to individuals, or for operating
expenses.
Publications: Application guidelines.
Application information: Application form not
required.
  Initial approach: Letter
  Copies of proposal: 1
  Deadline(s): Apr. 20 and Oct. 15
  Board meeting date(s): May or June and Nov.
  Final notification: After May or June meeting by
    July 31; after Nov. meeting by Dec. 31
  Write: William V. Engel, Exec. Dir.
Officer and Trustees:* William V. Engel,* Exec.
Dir.; Charles Danzig, Edward G. Engel, John B.
Harris, Jr., Haydn H. Murray.
Number of staff: 1 part-time professional; 2
part-time support.
EIN: 226326539

1642
Gulton Foundation, Inc.
c/o A. P. Bersohn & Co.
17 Arcadian Ave., Suite 108
Paramus 07652-1203

Incorporated in 1961 in NY.
Donor(s): Leslie K. Gulton,‡ Marian G. Malcolm,
Edith Gulton.
Foundation type: Independent
Financial data (yr. ended 10/31/91): Assets,
$8,796,134 (M); expenditures, $400,226;
qualifying distributions, $375,330, including
$375,330 for grants (high: $106,000).
Purpose and activities: Grants for higher
education and mental health services; support
also for scientific and medical research; some
giving in Israel.
Fields of interest: Higher education, mental
health, science and technology, medical research,
Israel.
Limitations: Giving primarily on the East Coast.
No grants to individuals.
Application information: Contributes only to
pre-selected organizations. Applications not
accepted.
  Write: Edith Gulton, Pres.

Officers: Edith Gulton, Pres.; Marian G. Malcolm,
V.P. and Treas.; Daniel Malcolm, Secy.
EIN: 136105207

1643
Harris Brothers Foundation
158 Sutton Rd.
Lebanon 08833   (908) 832-2761

Established in 1956 in DE.
Donor(s): Members of the Harris family.
Foundation type: Independent
Financial data (yr. ended 12/31/91): Assets,
$2,065,313 (M); expenditures, $120,084;
qualifying distributions, $105,050, including
$105,050 for 32 grants (high: $10,000; low:
$850).
Purpose and activities: Giving primarily for
Methodist and Presbyterian church support and
hospitals; support also for education.
Fields of interest: Protestant giving, hospitals,
education.
Limitations: Giving primarily in NJ. No grants to
individuals.
Application information:
  Deadline(s): None
  Write: Barbara L. Harris, Secy.-Treas.
Officers: Barbara L. Harris, Pres.; George W. Harris,
V.P.; O.H. Hewit III, V.P.; Frederick Scheidig, V.P.;
Barbara L. Harris, Secy.-Treas.
EIN: 136167230

1644
O. W. Havens Foundation
P.O. Box 106
Lakewood 08701

Established in 1978 in NJ.
Foundation type: Independent
Financial data (yr. ended 12/31/91): Assets,
$3,574,942 (M); expenditures, $163,573;
qualifying distributions, $155,000, including
$153,000 for 36 grants (high: $15,000; low:
$1,000).
Purpose and activities: Emphasis on social
services, including programs providing indigent
care; support also for education and health,
including a hospital and medical research.
Fields of interest: Social services, education,
health, hospitals, medical research.
Limitations: Giving primarily in Lakewood, NJ.
No grants to individuals.
Application information: Contributes only to
pre-selected organizations. Applications not
accepted.
Officers: Mabel E. Curtis, Pres.; Hermann
Winkelmann, V.P.; James Grandinetti, Secy.-Treas.
Trustees: Edward Rothstein, Robert Rothstein.
EIN: 222175726

1645
Hoechst Celanese Corporate Giving
Program
Route 202-206 North
P.O. Box 2500
Somerville 08876-1258   (201) 231-2880

Financial data (yr. ended 12/31/90): Total giving,
$3,000,000 for grants.

Purpose and activities: "Contributions are made to organizations that strengthen the communities in which Hoechst Celanese employees live and work, improve the environment in which Hoechst Celanese does business, or enhance the Corporation's opportunities to prosper and grow. Contributions should encourage Hoechst Celanese employees to be active citizens and to become involved in their communities. The contributions program is designed to support our own employees' charitable giving and volunteer activities. The link between employees and community organizations is an important criterion for giving. Contributions should enhance the public awareness and goodwill of Hoechst Celanese."
Fields of interest: Education—building funds, educational research, hospitals—building funds, biological sciences, cultural programs, chemistry, education, science and technology.
Types of support: Capital campaigns, employee matching gifts, equipment, operating budgets, building funds, professorships, fellowships, research, matching funds.
Limitations: Giving primarily in areas where plants are located. No support for religious or fraternal organizations. No grants to individuals.
Application information: Application form not required.
   Initial approach: Letter to headquarters
   Copies of proposal: 1
   Board meeting date(s): Quarterly
   Final notification: 4-6 weeks
   Write: Lewis Alpaugh, V.P., Fdn. and Dir., Corp. Rels.
Number of staff: 1 full-time professional; 1 part-time professional; 1 full-time support; 1 part-time support.

1646
Hoechst Celanese Foundation, Inc.
Rte. 202-206 North
P.O. Box 2500
Somerville 08876-1258　　　　(908) 231-2880

Established in 1984 in NJ.
Donor(s): Hoechst Celanese Corp.
Foundation type: Company-sponsored
Financial data (yr. ended 12/31/91): Assets, $10,000,000 (M); expenditures, $2,500,000; qualifying distributions, $2,500,000, including $2,500,000 for grants.
Purpose and activities: Giving for education, particularly the sciences; health and hospitals; and welfare and youth organizations. Support also for civic and public affairs, museums and other cultural programs, and the environment. Grants are based on an organization's influence on the community and the level of Hoechst employee involvement.
Fields of interest: Education, higher education, medical education, science and technology, medical sciences, hospitals, youth, social services, minorities, community development, cultural programs, arts, environment.
Types of support: Capital campaigns, operating budgets, research, special projects, continuing support, employee matching gifts, employee-related scholarships.
Limitations: Giving primarily in headquarters city and national operating locations; national organizations also considered. No support for

religious or fraternal organizations. No grants to individuals, or for operating expenses of United Way recipients; no commitments for more than five years; special projects of hospitals have low priority.
Application information: Application form not required.
   Initial approach: Letter
   Copies of proposal: 1
   Deadline(s): None
   Board meeting date(s): Feb., May, Aug., and Nov.
   Write: Lewis Alpaugh, V.P.
Officers: Karl Engels, Chair.; Lewis F. Alpaugh, V.P. and Exec. Dir.; E. Collins, Secy.; T. Denzer, Treas.
Number of staff: 1 full-time professional; 1 part-time professional.
EIN: 222577170

1647
Hoffmann-La Roche Corporate Giving Program
340 Kingsland Street, Dept. of Community Affairs
Nutley 07110　　　　(201) 235-3797

Purpose and activities: Support for 1) health programs (but not medical delivery) which address identified community needs; 2) educational programs which encourage math and science literacy; preference will be given, but not limited to teacher enrichment programs at the secondary level. Remedial education is not a priority, but programs targeted to non-traditional student populations are; 3) community social service programs which identify needs, propose solutions and involve community participants; and 4) art programs on a very limited basis. Contributions to local chapters of voluntary health and educational organizations with national affiliations will be based on the voluntary involvement of Roche employees in chapter activities. Requests for support must be submitted by the Roche employee. National headquarters of voluntary health organizations will be funded on an exception basis only. Preference will always be given to local chapters. In the case of seed money contributions for a new activity or organization, there should be reasonable chances that operating funds will be forthcoming from other sources because of the stimulus provided by the Roche contribution. Contributions are made on a one-time, non-renewable basis. Exceptions are at the discretion of the company.
Fields of interest: Health, animal welfare, mathematics, science and technology, volunteerism, youth, minorities, medical research.
Types of support: Operating budgets, seed money, employee matching gifts, general purposes, matching funds, special projects, technical assistance.
Limitations: Giving primarily in headquarters city and major operating locations in NY, CA, PA, and NC, with emphasis on NJ. No support for political, veterans', or labor organizations, or sectarian groups, except for programs which serve the general public. No grants to individuals, or for goodwill advertising, purchase, construction, expansion, or modification of facilities; purchase of equipment or other capital expenditures;

endowment funds, scholarships, matching gifts, special projects, publications, or conferences.
Publications: Informational brochure (including application guidelines).
Application information: Applications for research groups are very restricted. Company will request proposal if interested. Application form required.
   Initial approach: Ask for application form: telephone requests not honored
   Copies of proposal: 1
   Board meeting date(s): Contributions committee meets quarterly: Feb. 15, May 15, Aug. 15, and Nov. 15
   Final notification: Within 6 weeks of the closing quarterly date
   Write: Vivian L. Beetle, Dir. Community Affairs Dept.
Number of staff: 2 full-time professional; 2 full-time support; 1 part-time support.

1648
The Hoffmann-La Roche Foundation
P.O. Box 278
Nutley 07110　　　　(201) 235-2055

Trust established in 1945 in NJ.
Donor(s): Hoffmann-La Roche Inc.
Foundation type: Company-sponsored
Financial data (yr. ended 12/31/91): Assets, $28 (M); gifts received, $702,916; expenditures, $702,916; qualifying distributions, $702,916, including $702,916 for 34 grants (high: $102,500; low: $5,000; average: $2,500-$102,500).
Purpose and activities: Giving for medical and scientific research at leading universities and teaching hospitals and for general support of education programs in health, science and math; support also for teachers in communities where company has sites or employee populations.
Fields of interest: Medical research, higher education, science and technology, mathematics, education, biological sciences, AIDS.
Types of support: Research, fellowships.
Limitations: Giving primarily in the northeastern states, with emphasis on NY and NJ. No grants to individuals, or for general support, operating budgets, capital or endowment funds, matching gifts, special projects, publications, or conferences; no loans.
Application information: Application form not required.
   Initial approach: Letter
   Copies of proposal: 1
   Board meeting date(s): As required
   Final notification: 4 to 6 weeks
   Write: Vivian Beetle, Dir.
Officer: H.F. Boardman, Secy.
Trustees: I. Lerner, Martin F. Stadler.
Number of staff: None.
EIN: 226063790

1649
The Hoyt Foundation
Half Acre Rd.
Cranbury 08512　　　　(609) 655-6000

Incorporated in 1957 in DE.
Foundation type: Operating

Financial data (yr. ended 06/30/91): Assets, $3,065,579 (M); expenditures, $153,097; qualifying distributions, $144,098, including $137,100 for 15 grants (high: $36,700; low: $1,000).
Purpose and activities: Giving primarily for hospitals and medical research; support also for education and cultural programs.
Fields of interest: Hospitals, medical research, education, cultural programs.
Limitations: Giving primarily in NJ and NY. No grants to individuals.
Application information:
Initial approach: Letter
Deadline(s): None
Write: Charles O. Hoyt, Pres.
Officers: Charles O. Hoyt, Pres.; Frank M. Berger, M.D., V.P.; Suzanne H. Garcia, Secy.; Henry H. Hoyt, Jr., Treas.
EIN: 136110857

1650
The Huber Foundation ▼
P.O. Box 277
Rumson 07760   (201) 872-2322

Incorporated in 1949 in NJ.
Donor(s): Members of the Huber and Mertens families.
Foundation type: Independent
Financial data (yr. ended 12/31/90): Assets, $24,410,055 (M); expenditures, $1,413,007; qualifying distributions, $1,267,793, including $1,231,400 for 43 grants (high: $130,000; low: $1,500; average: $5,000-$50,000).
Purpose and activities: Grants primarily to organizations working in the areas of family planning, reproductive freedom, and population education.
Fields of interest: Family planning.
Types of support: Annual campaigns, operating budgets, seed money, special projects, publications.
Limitations: No support for foreign organizations or international projects. No grants to individuals, or for scholarships, fellowships, research, or building or endowment funds; no loans.
Publications: Annual report (including application guidelines).
Application information: Application form not required.
Initial approach: Letter
Copies of proposal: 1
Deadline(s): None
Board meeting date(s): 4 times a year; dates not fixed
Final notification: 3 months
Write: Lorraine Barnhart, Exec. Dir.
Officers and Trustees:* Hans A. Huber,* Pres.; David G. Huber,* V.P.; Michael W. Huber,* Secy.; Julia Ann Nagy, Treas.; Gertrude H. Mertens, Christopher W. Seely, Catherine Weiss.
Number of staff: 1 part-time professional.
EIN: 210737062

1651
The Hyde and Watson Foundation ▼
437 Southern Blvd.
Chatham 07928   (201) 966-6024

The Lillia Babbitt Hyde Foundation incorporated in 1924 in NY; The John Jay and Eliza Jane Watson Foundation incorporated in 1949; consolidation of two foundations into Hyde and Watson Foundation in 1983.
Donor(s): Lillia Babbitt Hyde,‡ Eliza Jane Watson.‡
Foundation type: Independent
Financial data (yr. ended 12/31/91): Assets, $58,828,088 (M); expenditures, $3,181,038; qualifying distributions, $2,884,433, including $2,478,520 for 225 grants (high: $50,000; low: $1,000; average: $5,000-$20,000).
Purpose and activities: "Support primarily for capital projects of lasting value which tend to increase quality, capacity or efficiency of a grantee's programs or services, such as purchase or relocation of facilities, facility improvements, capital equipment, instructive materials development, and certain medical research areas. Broad fields include health, education, religion, social services, arts, and humanities. A substantial proportion of grant funds each year will be allocated to projects for which the foundation's support makes a major contribution."
Fields of interest: Health, hospitals, medical research, drug abuse, mental health, education, education—early childhood, elementary education, secondary education, medical education, social services, welfare, disadvantaged, youth, child welfare, homeless.
Types of support: Building funds, equipment, land acquisition, matching funds, research, emergency funds, renovation projects, capital campaigns, special projects, technical assistance.
Limitations: Giving primarily in the New York, NY, metropolitan area and Essex, Union and Morris counties in NJ. No grants to individuals, or generally for operating budgets, continuing support, annual campaigns, general endowments, deficit financing, scholarships, or fellowships.
Publications: Annual report (including application guidelines), program policy statement, application guidelines.
Application information: Application format required if proposal is considered by grants committee. Application form required.
Initial approach: Letter
Copies of proposal: 1
Deadline(s): Submit preliminary letter of appeal by Feb. 15 for spring meeting and by Sept. 15 for fall meeting
Board meeting date(s): Apr./May and Nov./Dec.
Final notification: After grant or board meeting
Write: Robert W. Parsons, Jr., Pres.
Officers and Trustees:* John W. Holman, Jr.,* Chair. and Treas.; Robert W. Parsons, Jr.,* Pres.; Roger B. Parsons,* V.P. and Secy.; Hunter W. Corbin,* V.P.; H. Corbin Day, William V. Engel, David G. Ferguson, G. Morrison Hubbard, Jr., Richard W. KixMiller, John G. MacKechnie.
Number of staff: 7 full-time professional.
EIN: 222425725
Recent health grants:
1651-1 Adelphi University, Garden City, NY, $15,000. For cancer research project. 1990.
1651-2 Americas Keswick, Whiting, NJ, $15,000. For alteration and modernization of facilities to enhance and expand addiction recovery programs. 1990.
1651-3 Brooklyn Hospital/Caledonian Hospital, Brooklyn, NY, $20,000. For purchase of

surgical equipment to expand laparoscopy cholecystectomy program. 1990.
1651-4 Cerebral Palsy League of Union County, Union, NJ, $10,000. For construction of additional facilities to accomodate increased demand for services. 1990.
1651-5 Elizabeth General Medical Center Foundation, Elizabeth, NJ, $10,000. For construction of new parking garage. 1990.
1651-6 Hospital for Special Surgery Fund, NYC, NY, $20,000. For essential expansion and relocation of CAD/CAM system laboratory to enhance effectiveness of programs. 1990.
1651-7 International Center for the Disabled (ICD), NYC, NY, $75,000. For essential alterations, improvements and equipment for facilities. 1990.
1651-8 Muhlenberg Hospital Foundation, Plainfield, NJ, $25,000. For purchase of medical equipment for new Thomas S.P. Fitch Pavillion. 1990.
1651-9 New York Eye and Ear Infirmary, NYC, NY, $10,000. For facilities alterations and modernization to increase capacity and effectiveness of programs. 1990.
1651-10 New York Foundling Hospital, Center for Parent and Child Development, NYC, NY, $20,000. For purchase of equipment for new skilled nursing facilities for handicapped children. 1990.
1651-11 Riverview Hospital Foundation, Red Bank, NJ, $25,000. For purchase of equipment for hospital's new patient care information system. 1990.
1651-12 Saint Elizabeth Hospital, Elizabeth, NJ, $15,000. For major construction project to expand and modernize facilities. 1990.
1651-13 Saint Lukes-Roosevelt Hospital Center, NYC, NY, $20,000. For purchase of ultrasonic scanner equipment to improve effectiveness of programs. 1990.
1651-14 Saint Vincents Hospital and Medical Center of New York, NYC, NY, $15,000. For alterations of and equipment for facilities to provide Family Resource Room to enhance hospital's Parent Education programs. 1990.
1651-15 Stifel Paralysis Research Foundation, Short Hills, NJ, $10,000. For research toward cure and/or improved treatment for spinal cord injuries. 1990.
1651-16 Trudeau Institute, Saranac Lake, NY, $13,000. For purchase of laboratory equipment to enhance efficiency of cancer/AIDS research programs. 1990.
1651-17 Tulane Education Fund, Department of Medicine, Section of Allergy and Immunology, New Orleans, LA, $20,000. For asthma and allergy research. 1990.
1651-18 Welkind Rehabilitation Hospital, Chester, NJ, $15,000. For establishment of fund raising program. 1990.
1651-19 Youth Development Clinic of Newark, Newark, NJ, $10,000. For establishment of essential revolving working capital fund. 1990.

1652
Innovating Worthy Projects Foundation
426 Shore Rd., Suite E
Somers Point 08244   (609) 926-1111

Foundation type: Independent

Financial data (yr. ended 08/31/91): Assets, $5,283,962 (M); expenditures, $386,608; qualifying distributions, $297,773, including $200,104 for 31 grants (high: $45,000; low: $11).
Purpose and activities: Support primarily for the education, service or care of handicapped children, and programs to help the aged.
Fields of interest: Handicapped, aged, child welfare, education—early childhood, heart disease, mental health, recreation, disadvantaged, drug abuse.
Types of support: Seed money, special projects.
Application information: Application form required.
  Initial approach: Telephone
  Copies of proposal: 6
  Deadline(s): None
  Board meeting date(s): June, Sept., and Nov.
  Final notification: 90 days
  Write: Dr. Irving W. Packer, Chair.
Officers and Trustees:* Irving W. Packer,* Chair.; John McAfee,* Pres.; Stephen Weiss,* Secy.; Richard Culbertson, Treas.; David Crabtree, Edward E. Packer, Estelle Packer.
Number of staff: 2 full-time professional; 1 full-time support.
EIN: 226083636

1653
Abdol H. Islami, M.D. Foundation, Inc.
(Formerly Comprehensive Medical Review Course, Inc.)
c/o Collins, Toner & Rusen
123 Columbia Tpke.
Florham Park 07932
Application address: P.O. Box 796, Livingston, NJ 07039

Established in 1989 as a private foundation.
Foundation type: Independent
Financial data (yr. ended 12/31/91): Assets, $2,832,365 (M); gifts received, $7,207; expenditures, $173,888; qualifying distributions, $137,000, including $137,000 for 1 grant.
Fields of interest: Medical education, medical sciences.
Types of support: Scholarship funds, building funds.
Limitations: Giving primarily in NJ.
Application information: Application form required.
  Deadline(s): Mar. 15
  Write: Joan Islami, Pres.
Officer and Trustees:* Joan Islami,* Pres.; Robert A. Donahue, M.D., Susann Islami Donahue, John J. Henschel, Kim Islami, Yasmin Islami, David Schneider, M.D.
EIN: 222111419

1654
The Jaqua Foundation
One Garret Mountain Plaza
West Paterson 07424   (201) 278-9790

Established in 1977.
Donor(s): George R. Jaqua.‡
Foundation type: Independent
Financial data (yr. ended 12/31/91): Assets, $8,138,568 (M); gifts received, $5,500; expenditures, $388,169; qualifying distributions,

$328,547, including $314,166 for 26 grants (high: $50,000; low: $1,000).
Fields of interest: Higher education, hospitals, health services.
Limitations: No support for private foundations. No grants to individuals.
Application information:
  Initial approach: Letter
  Deadline(s): None
  Write: Eli Hoffman, Chair.
Officers: Eli Hoffman, Chair.; John Minnema, V.P.; W. Fletcher Hock, Jr., Secy.
EIN: 222086399

1655
The Jockey Hollow Foundation, Inc.
P.O. Box 462
Bernardsville 07924

Incorporated in 1960 in NJ.
Donor(s): Carl Shirley, Mrs. Carl Shirley.
Foundation type: Independent
Financial data (yr. ended 03/31/91): Assets, $10,560,294 (M); gifts received, $206,000; expenditures, $631,329; qualifying distributions, $581,897, including $571,540 for 69 grants (high: $75,000; low: $25).
Fields of interest: Conservation, hospitals, cultural programs.
Types of support: Scholarship funds.
Limitations: Giving primarily in NJ and MA. No grants to individuals.
Application information:
  Initial approach: Proposal
  Deadline(s): None
  Write: Betsy S. Michel, Pres.
Officers and Trustees:* Betsy S. Michel,* Pres. and Secy.; Joanne S. Forkner,* V.P.; Carl Shirley,* V.P.; Clifford L. Michel,* Treas.; Virginia L. Hartmann, Betsy B. Shirley.
EIN: 221724138

1656
Johnson & Johnson Corporate Giving Program
One Johnson & Johnson Plaza
New Brunswick 08933   (201) 524-3255

Financial data (yr. ended 12/31/90): Total giving, $32,300,000, including $16,400,000 for grants and $15,900,000 for in-kind gifts.
Purpose and activities: Supports projects or organizations which advance the science of medicine. Also supports higher educaton, civic affairs and public interest organizations, social welfare, including community funds and an employee matching gifts program for higher education, hospitals, health associations, drug and alcohol treatment centers and culture. Other support for arts and culture is limited and mainly in NJ, with some support for programs that are national in scope.
Fields of interest: Medical research, education, arts, cultural programs, civic affairs, social services, community funds, dance, museums, music, economics, minorities, science and technology, health, hospitals, drug abuse, youth.
Types of support: Operating budgets, continuing support, annual campaigns, emergency funds, matching funds, fellowships, research, technical assistance, operating budgets, employee matching

gifts, special projects, general purposes, scholarship funds, equipment, donated products.
Limitations: Giving primarily in areas where company has a major presence. No support for sectarian and religious organizations that do not serve the general public, political groups, groups receiving federated drive support, most preschool, elementary or secondary educational institutions. No grants to individuals, or for trips or tours, endowments of any kind, advertising for benefit purposes, deficit financing, capital funds, demonstration projects, conferences, sport sponsorships, publications, or loans.
Publications: Application guidelines.
Application information: Application form not required.
  Initial approach: Telephone or letter; if interested company will request full proposal
  Copies of proposal: 1
  Deadline(s): Aug. and Sept. for medical research grants
  Board meeting date(s): Trustees meet in Mar., June, Sept. and Dec.
  Final notification: Response within three months
  Write: Curtis G. Weeden, V.P., Corp. Contribs.
Number of staff: 1 full-time professional; 3 full-time support.

1657
Johnson & Johnson Family of Companies Contribution Fund ▼
One Johnson & Johnson Plaza
New Brunswick 08933   (908) 524-3255

Incorporated in 1953 in NJ.
Donor(s): Johnson and Johnson, and subsidiary companies.
Foundation type: Company-sponsored
Financial data (yr. ended 12/31/91): Assets, $2,043,000 (M); gifts received, $11,544,800; expenditures, $12,916,000; qualifying distributions, $12,782,000, including $10,148,000 for 850 grants (high: $300,000; low: $200; average: $1,000-$25,000) and $2,634,000 for 5,500 employee matching gifts.
Purpose and activities: Grants primarily directed toward health and health care programs. Foundation supports several specific programs including Johnson & Johnson Focused Giving Program, Johnson & Johnson Community Health Care Program, Head Start-Johnson & Johnson Management Education Program, Johnson & Johnson Wharton Nurse Fellows Program. Support also for education, family, and employment.
Fields of interest: Health services, medical sciences, science and technology, hospitals, medical research, nursing, health, nutrition, physical sciences, health associations, pharmacy, higher education, education, education—early childhood, medical education, educational research, education—minorities, secondary education, cultural programs, arts, media and communications, civic affairs, community funds, public policy, community development, urban development, urban affairs, social services, aged, child development, child welfare, youth, minorities, disadvantaged, welfare, family services, handicapped, employment, environment, conservation.
Types of support: Operating budgets, continuing support, annual campaigns, emergency funds,

matching funds, fellowships, research, technical assistance, special projects, employee matching gifts, general purposes, scholarship funds, cause-related marketing, building funds, seed money, renovation projects, conferences and seminars.

Limitations: Giving primarily in areas where company has facilities. National, state, regional gifts limited mainly to established programs; limited opportunity for unsolicited support. No grants to individuals, or for deficit financing, capital or endowment funds, or publications; no loans.

Publications: Application guidelines, program policy statement, corporate giving report, informational brochure.

Application information: Application form not required.

   Initial approach: Letter
   Copies of proposal: 1
   Deadline(s): None
   Board meeting date(s): Mar., June, Sept., and Dec.
   Final notification: 2 months
   Write: Curtis G. Weeden, V.P.

Officers and Trustees:* Roger S. Fine,* Pres.; F.A. Bolden,* V.P. and Secy.; Curtis G. Weeden,* V.P.; Andrew J. Markey,* Treas.

Number of staff: None.

EIN: 226062811

Recent health grants:

1657-1 Alliance for Aging Research, DC, $25,000. 1990.

1657-2 American Federation for Clinical Research, Boston, MA, $10,000. 1990.

1657-3 American Foundation for Pharmaceutical Education, North Plainfield, NJ, $20,000. 1990.

1657-4 American Health Foundation, NYC, NY, $59,500. 1990.

1657-5 Barrio Comprehensive Family Health Care Center, San Antonio, TX, $20,000. 1990.

1657-6 Brannon-McCulloch Primary Health Care, Memphis, TN, $25,000. 1990.

1657-7 Childrens Inn at the National Institutes of Health, Friends of, DC, $17,000. 1990.

1657-8 Christ Hospital and Medical Center, Oak Lawn, IL, $10,000. 1990.

1657-9 Community Hospital Group, Edison, NJ, $20,000. 1990.

1657-10 Cornell University Medical College, NYC, NY, $25,000. For minority education. 1990.

1657-11 Duke University, Health Promotion and Awareness Program, Durham, NC, $91,987. 1990.

1657-12 Educational Broadcasting Corporation, NYC, NY, $300,000. For Health Care Public Information program. 1990.

1657-13 George Washington University, National Health Policy Forum, DC, $10,000. 1990.

1657-14 Harvard University, Medical School, Boston, MA, $10,000. 1990.

1657-15 Harvard University, School of Public Health, Department of Health Policy and Management, Boston, MA, $50,000. 1990.

1657-16 Hospital Authority of Hall County and the City of Gainesville, Gainesville, GA, $10,000. 1990.

1657-17 Hunterdon Medical Center, Flemington, NJ, $15,000. 1990.

1657-18 Hunterdon Medical Center Foundation, Flemington, NJ, $30,000. 1990.

1657-19 Infant Welfare Society of Chicago, Chicago, IL, $20,000. 1990.

1657-20 Medical Center at Princeton Foundation, Princeton, NJ, $20,000. 1990.

1657-21 Medical Education for South African Blacks, DC, $25,000. 1990.

1657-22 Morristown Memorial Hospital, Morristown, NJ, $10,000. 1990.

1657-23 Muhlenberg Hospital Foundation, Plainfield, NJ, $10,000. 1990.

1657-24 Muhlenberg Regional Medical Center, Plainfield, NJ, $20,000. 1990.

1657-25 National Association of Community Health Centers, DC, $22,500. 1990.

1657-26 National Marfan Research Fund, Port Washington, NY, $10,000. 1990.

1657-27 New Brunswick Affiliated Hospitals, New Brunswick, NJ, $400,000. For grant administered by Saint Peter's Medical Center. 1990.

1657-28 New Brunswick Cultural Center, New Brunswick, NJ, $150,000. For Health Care Public Information program. 1990.

1657-29 Occupational Physicians Scholarship Fund, Arlington Heights, IL, $10,000. 1990.

1657-30 Overlook Hospital Foundation, Summit, NJ, $25,000. 1990.

1657-31 Pennsylvania State University, Department of Health Planning, University Park, PA, $50,000. For Eastern Europe Program. 1990.

1657-32 People-to-People Health Foundation, Project Hope Health Sciences Education Center, Millwood, VA, $46,000. For fellowships. 1990.

1657-33 Pharmaceutical Manufacturers Association Foundation, DC, $115,000. 1990.

1657-34 Preventive Medicine Research Institute, San Francisco, CA, $10,000. 1990.

1657-35 Raritan Bay Health Services Corporation, Perth Amboy, NJ, $20,000. 1990.

1657-36 Rutgers, The State University of New Jersey, Center of Alcohol Studies, New Brunswick, NJ, $31,625. 1990.

1657-37 Saint Barnabas Burn Foundation, West Orange, NJ, $10,000. 1990.

1657-38 San Antonio Community Hospital, Upland, CA, $11,700. 1990.

1657-39 Somerset Medical Center, Somerville, NJ, $40,000. 1990.

1657-40 South Cove Community Health Center, Boston, MA, $20,000. 1990.

1657-41 University of Medicine and Dentistry of New Jersey, Newark, NJ, $50,000. 1990.

1657-42 University of Minnesota, Graduate School of Health Service Administration, Minneapolis, MN, $20,000. For endowment of chair. 1990.

1657-43 University of Pennsylvania, Wharton School, Philadelphia, PA, $394,567. For Wharton Nurse Fellows Program. 1990.

1657-44 University of Puerto Rico, School of Dentistry, San Juan, PR, $40,000. 1990.

1657-45 W G B H Educational Foundation, Boston, MA, $1,083,000. For Health Care Public Information program. 1990.

1658

The Robert Wood Johnson Foundation ▼
P.O. Box 2316
Princeton 08543-2316   (609) 452-8701

Incorporated in 1936 in NJ; became a national philanthropy in 1972.

Donor(s): Robert Wood Johnson.‡

Foundation type: Independent

Financial data (yr. ended 12/31/90): Assets, $2,918,748,906 (M); expenditures, $84,264,407; qualifying distributions, $130,288,851, including $66,179,831 for grants (high: $3,465,263; average: $55,125-$200,000), $45,712,137 for set-asides and $3,105,575 for loans.

Purpose and activities: To improve the health and health care of Americans. To help the nation and its health care system identify and pursue new opportunities to address persistent health problems and to participate and respond to significant emerging problems. Three basic goals are pursued: 1)To assure that Americans of all ages have access to basic health care. 2)To improve the way services are organized and provided to people with chronic health conditions. 3)To promote health and prevent disease by reducing harm caused by substance abuse. Also seeks opportunities to help the nation address, effectively and fairly, the overarching problem of escalating health care expenditures.

Fields of interest: Health services, health, hospitals, nursing, mental health, dentistry, AIDS, aged, alcoholism, drug abuse, handicapped, homeless, minorities, child development, youth, medical education, education—minorities.

Types of support: Seed money, research, special projects, fellowships, program-related investments, matching funds.

Limitations: Giving limited to the U.S. No support for international activities, programs or institutions concerned solely with a specific disease, or basic biomedical research. No grants to individuals, or for ongoing general operating expenses, endowment funds, capital costs, including construction, renovation, or equipment, or research on unapproved drug therapies or devices.

Publications: Annual report (including application guidelines), informational brochure, application guidelines, occasional report, newsletter.

Application information: Application form not required.

   Initial approach: Letter
   Copies of proposal: 1
   Deadline(s): None
   Board meeting date(s): Quarterly
   Final notification: 6 to 12 months
   Write: Edward H. Robbins, Proposal Mgr.

Officers and Trustees:* Sydney F. Wentz,* Chair. and C.E.O.; Steven A. Schroeder, M.D.,* Pres.; Richard C. Reynolds, M.D., Exec. V.P.; J. Warren Wood III, V.P., General Counsel and Secy.; Andrew R. Greene, V.P. and Treas.; Thomas P. Gore, V.P. for Communications; Alan B. Cohen, V.P.; Ruby P. Hearn, V.P.; G. Russell Henshaw, Jr., Controller; Edward C. Andrews, Jr., M.D., James Burke, David R. Clare, Lawrence G. Foster, John J. Heldrich, Leonard F. Hill, Frank J. Hoenemeyer, John J. Horan, Hon. Thomas H. Kean, Jack W. Owen, Norman Rosenberg, M.D., Richard B. Sellars, John H. Steele, Rheba de Tornyay.

Number of staff: 43 full-time professional; 79 full-time support; 5 part-time support.

EIN: 226029397

Recent health grants:

1658-1 Abbott-Northwestern Hospital, Minneapolis, MN, $457,014. For Strengthening Hospital Nursing: A Program to Improve Patient Care. 1990.

1658-2 Ability Center of Greater Toledo, Sylvania, OH, $99,948. For Improving Service Systems for People with Disabilities. 1990.

1658-3 Ability Resources, Tulsa, OK, $100,000. For Improving Service Systems for People with Disabilities. 1990.

1658-4 Adaptive Living Programs for Handicapped Americans (ALPHA ONE), South Portland, ME, $98,649. For Improving Service Systems for People with Disabilities. 1990.

1658-5 Alabama State Health Department, Montgomery, AL, $461,207. For Healthy Futures Program, to coordinate and improve maternal, perinatal and infant care services. 1990.

1658-6 Alameda, County of, Oakland, CA, $200,000. For Fighting Back: Community Initiatives to Reduce Demand for Drugs and Alcohol. 1990.

1658-7 Alpha Center for Health Planning, DC, $278,596. For technical assistance and direction for Program on Changes in Health Care Financing and Organization. 1990.

1658-8 Alpha Center for Health Planning, DC, $199,444. For technical assistance and direction for Health Care for the Uninsured. 1990.

1658-9 Alum Rock Communication Center, San Jose, CA, $199,895. For Fighting Back: Community Initiatives to Reduce Demand for Drugs and Alcohol. 1990.

1658-10 Alzheimers Disease and Related Disorders Association, Atlanta, GA, $85,508. For Dementia Care and Respite Services Program. 1990.

1658-11 Alzheimers Disease and Related Disorders Association, Lexington, KY, $83,590. For Dementia Care and Respite Services Program. 1990.

1658-12 Alzheimers Disease and Related Disorders Association, Syracuse, NY, $84,134. For Dementia Care and Respite Services Program. 1990.

1658-13 American Academy of Pediatrics, Elk Grove Village, IL, $47,018. For international conference to compare child health care systems. 1990.

1658-14 American Baptist Homes of the West, Oakland, CA, $26,500. For feasibility study of supportive housing benefit in long-term care insurance. 1990.

1658-15 American Medical Student Association Foundation, Reston, VA, $24,840. For conference on recruiting physicians for underserved communities. 1990.

1658-16 Ann Arbor Center for Independent Living, Ann Arbor, MI, $100,000. For Improving Service Systems for People with Disabilities. 1990.

1658-17 Apache Drop-In Center, Lawton, OK, $91,485. For community-wide alcohol and substance abuse prevention and aftercare program. 1990.

1658-18 Arizona State University, College of Law, Tempe, AZ, $55,125. For Faculty Fellowships in Health Care Finance. 1990.

1658-19 Arkansas Childrens Hospital, Little Rock, AR, $204,699. For development of school health insurance plan in Arkansas. 1990.

1658-20 Arkansas Department of Health, Little Rock, AR, $568,552. For Healthy Futures Program, to coordinate and improve maternal, perinatal and infant care services. 1990.

1658-21 Asian Health Services, Oakland, CA, $100,000. For program to strengthen primary care health centers. 1990.

1658-22 Association of American Medical Colleges, DC, $42,887. For publication of information on minorities in medical education. 1990.

1658-23 Association of American Medical Colleges, DC, $26,195. For conference on historically black medical schools. 1990.

1658-24 Atlanta Jewish Community Center, Atlanta, GA, $98,683. For Dementia Care and Respite Services Program. 1990.

1658-25 Atlantis Community, Denver, CO, $92,887. For Improving Service Systems for People with Disabilities. 1990.

1658-26 Baltimore, City of, Office of the Mayor, Baltimore, MD, $300,000. For Homeless Families Program, initiative to help homeless families obtain needed health and supportive services. 1990.

1658-27 Bay Area Advocates for Nursing Home Reform, San Francisco, CA, $39,500. For residential health care information and referral service. 1990.

1658-28 Baylor College of Medicine, Houston, TX, $152,411. For Minority Medical Faculty Development Program. 1990.

1658-29 Baystate Medical Education and Research Foundation, Springfield, MA, $52,621. For technical assistance for research and development to improve long-term and ambulatory care quality. 1990.

1658-30 Beth Israel Hospital Association, Boston, MA, $610,793. For Strengthening Hospital Nursing: A Program to Improve Patient Care. 1990.

1658-31 Beth Israel Hospital Association, Boston, MA, $312,382. For Program on Care of Critically Ill Hospitalized Adults. 1990.

1658-32 Beth Israel Hospital Association, Boston, MA, $163,006. For Minority Medical Faculty Development Program. 1990.

1658-33 Boys and Girls Clubs of Newark, Newark, NJ, $199,996. For Fighting Back: Community Initiatives to Reduce Demand for Drugs and Alcohol. 1990.

1658-34 Brandeis University, Florence Heller Graduate School for Advanced Studies in Social Welfare, Waltham, MA, $140,438. For evaluation of Mental Health Services Program for Youth - Phase II. 1990.

1658-35 Brandeis University, Florence Heller Graduate School for Advanced Studies in Social Welfare, Waltham, MA, $81,000. For study of health service needs among developmentally disabled adults. 1990.

1658-36 Brigham and Womens Hospital, Boston, MA, $163,006. For Minority Medical Faculty Development Program. 1990.

1658-37 Brigham and Womens Hospital, Boston, MA, $45,000. For leadership development award for primary physicians in underserved areas. 1990.

1658-38 Brown University, Program in Medicine, Providence, RI, $150,000. For Preparing Physicians for the Future: A Program in Medical Education. 1990.

1658-39 California Health Decisions, Orange, CA, $87,559. For project to encourage use of Durable Power of Attorney for Health Care. 1990.

1658-40 California, State of, Health and Welfare Agency, Department of Mental Health, Sacramento, CA, $1,488,378. For Mental Health Services Program for Youth. 1990.

1658-41 Case Western Reserve University, School of Medicine, Cleveland, OH, $294,294. For Program on Care of Critically Ill Hospitalized Adults. 1990.

1658-42 Case Western Reserve University, School of Medicine, Cleveland, OH, $149,998. For Preparing Physicians for the Future: A Program in Medical Education. 1990.

1658-43 Catholic Charities of the Archdiocese of San Francisco, San Francisco, CA, $278,992. For Homeless Families Program, initiative to help homeless families obtain needed health and supportive services. 1990.

1658-44 Cedar Crest, Janesville, WI, $158,136. For Dementia Care and Respite Services Program. 1990.

1658-45 Center for Independence of the Disabled in New York, NYC, NY, $100,000. For Improving Service Systems for People with Disabilities. 1990.

1658-46 Center for Living and Working, Worcester, MA, $98,835. For Improving Service Systems for People with Disabilities. 1990.

1658-47 Cerebral Palsy Association of Middlesex County, Edison, NJ, $100,000. For expansion and renovation of treatment and educational facilities. 1990.

1658-48 Childrens Defense Fund, DC, $302,284. For improving child health and developmental services for low-income families. 1990.

1658-49 Childrens Hospital, Boston, MA, $74,960. For pilot project for technology dependent children. 1990.

1658-50 Childrens Hospital Medical Center of Northern California, Oakland, CA, $149,697. For program to improve health services for children in foster care. 1990.

1658-51 Childrens National Medical Center, DC, $398,033. For technical assistance and direction for School-Based Adolescent Health Care Program. 1990.

1658-52 Christian Community Health Fellowship, Philadelphia, PA, $20,000. For health careers development program in high-need communities. 1990.

1658-53 Colorado Coalition for the Homeless, Denver, CO, $299,982. For Homeless Families Program, initiative to help homeless families obtain needed health and supportive services. 1990.

1658-54 Columbia University, College of Physicians and Surgeons, NYC, NY, $149,192. For Preparing Physicians for the Future: A Program in Medical Education. 1990.

1658-55 Columbia University, Harlem Hospital Center, NYC, NY, $299,762. For hospital-led injury prevention for children and adolescents in Harlem. 1990.

1658-56 Committee for Economic Development, NYC, NY, $16,000. For analysis of effects of future health benefits for elderly. 1990.

1658-57 Community Family, Everett, MA, $71,958. For Dementia Care and Respite Services Program. 1990.

1658-58 Community Hospital of Indiana, Indianapolis, IN, $223,165. To improve quality of hospital care. 1990.

1658-59 Comprehensive AIDS Program, West Palm Beach, FL, $359,982. For AIDS Health Services Program. 1990.

1658-60 Confederated Tribes and Bands of the Yakima Indian Nation Reservation, Toppenish, WA, $247,837. For fetal alcohol syndrome prevention program. 1990.

1658-61 Copley Hospital, Montpelier, VT, $490,137. For Strengthening Hospital Nursing: A Program to Improve Patient Care. 1990.

1658-62 Cornell University, Ithaca, NY, $14,886. For Faculty Fellowships in Health Care Finance. 1990.

1658-63 Cornell University Medical College, NYC, NY, $133,479. For Minority Medical Faculty Development Program. 1990.

1658-64 Council of Community Services, Nashville, TN, $299,672. For Homeless Families Program, initiative to help homeless families obtain needed health and supportive services. 1990.

1658-65 District of Columbia General Hospital, DC, $573,285. For Strengthening Hospital Nursing: A Program to Improve Patient Care. 1990.

1658-66 Duke University Medical Center, School of Medicine, Durham, NC, $266,366. For Program on Care of Critically Ill Hospitalized Adults. 1990.

1658-67 Economic and Social Research Institute, Reston, VA, $968,141. For demonstration of alternative model for providing subacute care. 1990.

1658-68 Economic and Social Research Institute, Reston, VA, $94,155. For economic impact of restructuring employer-based health insurance system. 1990.

1658-69 Elijahs Promise, New Brunswick, NJ, $222,454. For expansion and coordination of health and human services to indigent in New Brunswick. 1990.

1658-70 Emory University, School of Medicine, Atlanta, GA, $54,243. For Faculty Fellowships in Health Care Finance. 1990.

1658-71 Enki Institute, Reseda, CA, $150,000. For youth health promotion program. 1990.

1658-72 Environmental Defense Fund, NYC, NY, $48,085. For analysis of environmental factor impact on health care. 1990.

1658-73 Fairfax, County of, District Health Department, Fairfax, VA, $59,244. For Dementia Care and Respite Services Program. 1990.

1658-74 Food and Nutrition Services, Aptos, CA, $103,761. For Dementia Care and Respite Services Program. 1990.

1658-75 Fort Berthold College Center, New Town, ND, $160,852. For alcoholism prevention combining traditional and conventional approaches. 1990.

1658-76 Foundation for Advanced Education in the Sciences, Bethesda, MD, $172,788. For Minority Medical Faculty Development Program. 1990.

1658-77 Foundation for Advanced Education in the Sciences, Bethesda, MD, $152,500. For

Minority Medical Faculty Development Program. 1990.

1658-78 Fremont Counseling Service, Lander, WY, $150,000. For substance abuse prevention project on Arapahoe and Shoshone reservations. 1990.

1658-79 General Hospital Corporation, Massachusetts General Hospital, Boston, MA, $260,969. For technical assistance and direction for Homeless Families Program, initiative to help homeless families obtain needed health and supportive services. 1990.

1658-80 George Washington University, DC, $498,168. For technical assistance and direction for Program on Care of Critically Ill Hospitalized Adults. 1990.

1658-81 George Washington University, DC, $140,512. For program to provide substance abuse policy information to states. 1990.

1658-82 George Washington University, DC, $93,219. For analysis of state policies affecting transition to work by disabled. 1990.

1658-83 Georgetown University, School of Medicine, DC, $350,015. For evaluation of Supportive Services in Senior Housing Program - Phase II. 1990.

1658-84 Georgetown University, School of Medicine, DC, $54,765. For Health Policy Fellowship Program. 1990.

1658-85 Grantmakers in Health, NYC, NY, $150,000. For educational program for staff and trustees in health philanthropy. 1990.

1658-86 Grow, Champaign, IL, $312,689. For statewide mutual self-help programs for chronically mentally ill. 1990.

1658-87 Hahnemann University, Philadelphia, PA, $69,471. For medical foster care by hospital staff for drug-addicted infants. 1990.

1658-88 Hale Hoola Hou, Kalihi-Palama Walk-In Clinic, Honolulu, HI, $94,408. For program to strengthen primary care health centers. 1990.

1658-89 Harvard University, Medical School, Boston, MA, $383,063. For technical assistance and direction for Program on Chronic Mental Illness. 1990.

1658-90 Harvard University, Medical School, Boston, MA, $308,614. For technical assistance and direction for Minority Medical Faculty Development Program. 1990.

1658-91 Harvard University, Medical School, Boston, MA, $178,315. For evaluation of effect of statewide perinatal program for uninsured. 1990.

1658-92 Harvard University, Medical School, Boston, MA, $151,900. For Minority Medical Faculty Development Program. 1990.

1658-93 Harvard University, Medical School, Boston, MA, $83,476. For technical assistance and direction for School-Based Adolescent Health Care Program. 1990.

1658-94 Harvard University, Medical School, Boston, MA, $55,575. For Health Policy Fellowship Program. 1990.

1658-95 Harvard University, Medical School, Boston, MA, $19,931. For U.S./UK conference on comparative mental health systems. 1990.

1658-96 Harvard University, School of Public Health, Boston, MA, $362,039. For evaluation of corporate managed care initiatives. 1990.

1658-97 Harvard University, School of Public Health, Boston, MA, $301,159. For evaluation

of team approach to providing home care for the aging in NYC housing projects. 1990.

1658-98 Harvard University, School of Public Health, Boston, MA, $150,119. For research on medical injury and on compensation and deterrence alternatives. 1990.

1658-99 Hawaii Island Adult Care, Hilo, HI, $33,945. For Dementia Care and Respite Services Program. 1990.

1658-100 Health Research, Albany, NY, $600,000. For regional demonstration of single-payer authority for health insurance. 1990.

1658-101 Health Research, Albany, NY, $359,835. For career advancement educational system for regional nurse manpower. 1990.

1658-102 Health Resources and Services Administration, Rockville, MD, $10,000. For second Primary Care Conference. 1990.

1658-103 Houston, City of, Houston, TX, $300,000. For Homeless Families Program, initiative to help homeless families obtain needed health and supportive services. 1990.

1658-104 Immanuel-Saint Josephs Hospital, Mankato, MN, $470,831. For Strengthening Hospital Nursing: A Program to Improve Patient Care. 1990.

1658-105 Indiana, State of, State Budget Agency, Indianapolis, IN, $99,980. For Program to Promote Long-Term Care Insurance for the Elderly. 1990.

1658-106 Institute for Rehabilitation and Research, Houston, TX, $272,554. For technical assistance and direction for Improving Service Systems for People with Disabilities. 1990.

1658-107 InterHealth Education and Research Foundation, Saint Paul, MN, $207,966. To improve quality of hospital care. 1990.

1658-108 International Center for Integrative Studies, The Door, NYC, NY, $51,520. For consolidated funding and reporting strategy for adolescent health services. 1990.

1658-109 Interwest Quality of Care, Salt Lake City, UT, $205,173. To improve quality of hospital care. 1990.

1658-110 Iowa Lakes Community College, Estherville, IA, $296,561. For regional Bachelor of Science in Nursing training program for rural nurses. 1990.

1658-111 Jamestown Band of Clallem Indians of Washington, Sequim, WA, $91,440. For Tribal Elders Health Protection Program. 1990.

1658-112 Jeff Davis Medical Care Center, Hazlehurst, GA, $37,585. For Rural Primary Care Health Care Project. 1990.

1658-113 Jersey City Health Care Corporation, Jersey City, NJ, $649,699. For Program to Improve Maternal and Infant Health in New Jersey. 1990.

1658-114 John F. Kennedy Medical Center Foundation, Edison, NJ, $265,202. For improving basic life skills of children with learning disabilities. 1990.

1658-115 Johns Hopkins University, School of Hygiene and Public Health, Baltimore, MD, $307,985. For technical assistance and direction for Faculty Fellowships in Health Care Finance Program. 1990.

1658-116 Johns Hopkins University, School of Hygiene and Public Health, Baltimore, MD, $284,457. For technical assistance for

Improving Quality of Hospital Care Program. 1990.

1658-117 Johns Hopkins University, School of Medicine, Baltimore, MD, $152,500. For Minority Medical Faculty Development Program. 1990.

1658-118 Johns Hopkins University, School of Medicine, Baltimore, MD, $152,479. For Minority Medical Faculty Development Program. 1990.

1658-119 Johns Hopkins University, School of Medicine, Baltimore, MD, $149,971. For Preparing Physicians for the Future: A Program in Medical Education. 1990.

1658-120 Kaiser Foundation Hospitals, Oakland, CA, $886,164. For evaluation of inpatient geriatric assessment program. 1990.

1658-121 Kentucky, Commonwealth of, Cabinet for Human Resources, Department of Mental Health and Mental Retardation Services, Frankfort, KY, $1,491,266. For Mental Health Services Program for Youth. 1990.

1658-122 Kokua Kalihi Valley Comprehensive Family Services, Honolulu, HI, $100,000. For Program to Strengthen Primary Care Health Centers. 1990.

1658-123 La Familia Medical Center, Santa Fe, NM, $99,999. For Program to Strengthen Primary Care Health Centers. 1990.

1658-124 Lexington/Richland Alcohol and Drug Abuse Council, Columbia, SC, $199,896. For Fighting Back: Community Initiatives to Reduce Demand for Drugs and Alcohol. 1990.

1658-125 Life Enrichment Center of Cleveland County, Shelby, NC, $50,197. For Dementia Care and Respite Services Program. 1990.

1658-126 Little Rock, City of, Little Rock, AR, $200,000. For Fighting Back: Community Initiatives to Reduce Demand for Drugs and Alcohol. 1990.

1658-127 Long-Term Care Data Institute, Waltham, MA, $174,922. For projecting long-term care use and cost. 1990.

1658-128 Madison Area Adult Day Centers, Madison, WI, $91,575. For Dementia Care and Respite Services Program. 1990.

1658-129 Mariposa Community Health Center, Nogales, AZ, $99,350. For Program to Strengthen Primary Care Health Centers. 1990.

1658-130 Marshall Heights Community Development Organization, DC, $99,983. For Fighting Back: Community Initiatives to Reduce Demand for Drugs and Alcohol. 1990.

1658-131 Marshfield Medical Research Foundation, Marshfield Clinic, Marshfield, WI, $246,822. For Program on Care of Critically Ill Hospitalized Adults. 1990.

1658-132 Maryland Hospital Education and Research Foundation, Lutherville, MD, $223,864. To improve quality of hospital care. 1990.

1658-133 Maryland, State of, Department of Health and Mental Hygiene, Baltimore, MD, $58,849. For evaluation of increased Medicaid fees on obstetrical care access in Maryland. 1990.

1658-134 Massachusetts General Hospital, Boston, MA, $200,400. To implement plans for architecturally-appropriate dementia care center. 1990.

1658-135 Massachusetts Health Research Institute, Boston, MA, $263,857. For Program

to Promote Long-Term Care Insurance for Elderly. 1990.

1658-136 Massachusetts Housing Finance Authority, Boston, MA, $196,000. For Supportive Services Program in Senior Housing. 1990.

1658-137 Mecklenburg County Area Mental Health/Mental Retardation Authority, Charlotte, NC, $197,386. For Fighting Back: Community Initiatives to Reduce Demand for Drugs and Alcohol. 1990.

1658-138 Medical and Health Research Association of New York City, NYC, NY, $109,458. For analysis and use of NHIS data on trends in health status and service use. 1990.

1658-139 Medical and Health Research Association of New York City, NYC, NY, $19,441. For establishment of mayoral advisory council on child health in NYC. 1990.

1658-140 Medical University of South Carolina, Charleston, SC, $14,911. For Faculty Fellowships in Health Care Finance. 1990.

1658-141 Medlantic Research Foundation, DC, $59,035. For feasibility of regional personal care attendants programs for disabled. 1990.

1658-142 Mental Health Center of Dane County, Madison, WI, $101,965. For technical assistance and direction for Mental Health Services Development Program. 1990.

1658-143 Mercy Hospital and Medical Center, Chicago, IL, $628,059. For Strengthening Hospital Nursing: A Program to Improve Patient Care. 1990.

1658-144 Methodist Hospitals, Gary, IN, $512,633. For accelerated nursing education program for minority high school students. 1990.

1658-145 Metro Atlanta Task Force for the Homeless, Atlanta, GA, $300,000. For Homeless Families Program, initiative to help homeless families obtain needed health and supportive services. 1990.

1658-146 Michigan State University, College of Osteopathic Medicine, East Lansing, MI, $57,870. For Health Policy Fellowship Program. 1990.

1658-147 Middlesex County Recreational Council, Edison, NJ, $65,000. For summer camp for children with health problems. 1990.

1658-148 Milwaukee, County of, Milwaukee, WI, $200,000. For Fighting Back: Community Initiatives to Reduce Demand for Drugs and Alcohol. 1990.

1658-149 Minneapolis American Indian Center, Minneapolis, MN, $96,328. For substance abuse prevention for American Indian high school students. 1990.

1658-150 Mississippi State Department of Health, Jackson, MS, $477,230. For Healthy Futures Program, to coordinate and improve maternal, perinatal and infant care services. 1990.

1658-151 Montana Hospital Research and Education Foundation, Helena, MT, $232,828. For Hospital-Based Rural Health Care Program. 1990.

1658-152 Montana Independent Living Project, Helena, MT, $92,818. For Improving Service Systems for People with Disabilities. 1990.

1658-153 Montefiore Medical Center, Bronx, NY, $426,022. For hospital-sponsored lead

poisoning prevention and treatment program. 1990.

1658-154 Morehouse School of Medicine, Atlanta, GA, $49,904. For developing new clinical training options. 1990.

1658-155 Morris County Organization for Hispanic Affairs, Dover, NJ, $10,000. For establishment of clinic for indigent Hispanic people. 1990.

1658-156 Morristown Memorial Hospital, Morristown, NJ, $743,836. For Program to Improve Maternal and Infant Health in New Jersey. 1990.

1658-157 Multnomah, County of, Portland, OR, $300,000. For Homeless Families Program, initiative to help homeless families obtain needed health and supportive services. 1990.

1658-158 National Academy of Sciences, Institute of Medicine, DC, $300,000. For technical assistance and direction for Health Policy Fellowships Program. 1990.

1658-159 National Academy of Sciences, Institute of Medicine, DC, $59,600. For Gustav O. Lienhard Award. 1990.

1658-160 National Academy of Sciences, Institute of Medicine, DC, $50,000. For distinguished scholar program. 1990.

1658-161 National Academy of Sciences, Institute of Medicine, DC, $34,700. For Robert Wood Johnson Health Policy Fellows: Workshop on Priority Issues. 1990.

1658-162 National Association of Community Health Centers, DC, $251,027. For technical assistance and direction for Program to Strengthen Primary Care Health Centers. 1990.

1658-163 National Council of State Boards of Nursing, Chicago, IL, $116,772. For study of feasibility of establishing national nurse database. 1990.

1658-164 National Leadership Coalition on AIDS, DC, $28,250. For corporate leadership conference on AIDS. 1990.

1658-165 National Network of Runaway and Youth Services, DC, $47,935. For training professionals in HIV prevention among high-risk youth. 1990.

1658-166 National Public Health and Hospital Institute, DC, $456,171. For program to monitor effects of AIDS on hospitals. 1990.

1658-167 National Public Health and Hospital Institute, DC, $48,768. For study of emergency room and trauma center services. 1990.

1658-168 Navajo Tribe of Arizona, Window Rock, AZ, $165,573. For child sexual abuse prevention and treatment. 1990.

1658-169 Nevada Health Facilities Education and Research Foundation, Reno, NV, $189,567. For hospital-based rural health care program for the aging. 1990.

1658-170 New Brunswick Affiliated Hospitals, New Brunswick, NJ, $3,465,263. For university-based cancer institute for Central New Jersey. 1990.

1658-171 New Brunswick Tomorrow, New Brunswick, NJ, $250,000. For program to address human service needs of New Brunswick community. 1990.

1658-172 New England Community Health Center Association, Boston, MA, $74,965. To develop model physician recruitment program for community health centers. 1990.

1658-173 New Haven, City of, New Haven, CT, $200,000. For Fighting Back: Community

Initiatives to Reduce Demand for Drugs and Alcohol. 1990.

1658-174 New York Academy of Medicine, NYC, NY, $21,238. For symposium for premed advisors on medical school admission procedures. 1990.

1658-175 New York University, NYC, NY, $160,881. For technical assistance and direction for Hospital-Based Rural Health Care Program. 1990.

1658-176 North Carolina, State of, Department of Human Resources, Raleigh, NC, $1,468,611. For Mental Health Services Program for Youth. 1990.

1658-177 Northwest New Mexico Council of Governments, Gallup, NM, $200,000. For Fighting Back: Community Initiatives to Reduce Demand for Drugs and Alcohol. 1990.

1658-178 Nursing Recruitment Coalition, Pittsburgh, PA, $480,013. For program to reduce attrition of minority and nontraditional students in nursing. 1990.

1658-179 Oak Cliff Clinics, Dallas, TX, $63,746. For establishment of family health center in South Dallas. 1990.

1658-180 Ocean County Board of Health, Toms River, NJ, $608,053. For Program to Improve Maternal and Infant Health in New Jersey. 1990.

1658-181 Ohio, State of, Department of Mental Health, Columbus, OH, $1,500,000. For Mental Health Services Program for Youth. 1990.

1658-182 Ohlone College, Fremont, CA, $406,520. To reduce attrition among minority, new immigrant and mature nursing students. 1990.

1658-183 Oklahoma State Department of Health, Oklahoma City, OK, $591,062. For Healthy Futures Program, to coordinate and improve maternal, perinatal and infant care services. 1990.

1658-184 On Lok Senior Health Services, San Francisco, CA, $416,929. For technical assistance for replication of On Lok model. 1990.

1658-185 Oneida Tribe of Indians of Wisconsin, Oneida, WI, $74,798. For health promotion, fitness and disease prevention for school-age children. 1990.

1658-186 Oregon Health Sciences University, School of Medicine, Portland, OR, $149,381. For Preparing Physicians for the Future: A Program in Medical Education. 1990.

1658-187 Oregon, State of, Department of Human Resources, Mental Health Division, Salem, OR, $1,369,192. For Mental Health Services Program for Youth. 1990.

1658-188 Ounce of Prevention Fund, Chicago, IL, $66,062. For school-based adolescent health clinic in Southside Chicago. 1990.

1658-189 Parents Against Drugs, Albuquerque, NM, $74,977. For planning alternative school for chemically-dependent students in recovery. 1990.

1658-190 Parker Jewish Geriatric Institute, New Hyde Park, NY, $47,252. For Dementia Care and Respite Services Program. 1990.

1658-191 Pennsylvania State University, University Park, PA, $55,125. For Faculty Fellowships in Health Care Finance. 1990.

1658-192 Pennsylvania State University, Milton S. Hershey Medical Center, Hershey, PA,

$410,025. For Strengthening Hospital Nursing: A Program to Improve Patient Care. 1990.

1658-193 Pennsylvania, Commonwealth of, Department of Public Welfare, Harrisburg, PA, $1,480,706. For Mental Health Services Program for Youth. 1990.

1658-194 People-to-People Health Foundation, Chevy Chase, MD, $45,743. For analysis of data on non-elderly people with physical disabilities. 1990.

1658-195 Planned Parenthood of Essex County, Newark, NJ, $632,666. For Program to Improve Maternal and Infant Health in New Jersey. 1990.

1658-196 Planned Parenthood of New York City, NYC, NY, $300,000. For program for adolescent and young adult women at risk of HIV infection. 1990.

1658-197 Policy Center, Denver, CO, $48,125. For further study of transitional care in nursing homes and swing-bed hospitals. 1990.

1658-198 Providence Medical Center, Portland, OR, $527,205. For Strengthening Hospital Nursing: A Program to Improve Patient Care. 1990.

1658-199 Prudential Insurance Company of America, Roseland, NJ, $377,121. For technical assistance and direction for Mental Health Services Program for Youth. 1990.

1658-200 Public Health Trust of Dade County, Miami, FL, $400,000. For school-based adolescent health care program at Miami Northwestern High School. 1990.

1658-201 Public Hospital Institute, San Mateo, CA, $314,536. To improve quality of hospital care. 1990.

1658-202 Puerto Rico, Commonwealth of, Department of Health, San Juan, PR, $574,790. For Healthy Futures Program, to coordinate and improve maternal, perinatal and infant care services. 1990.

1658-203 Regional Medical Center at Lubec, Lubec, ME, $200,000. To establish school health clinic in rural Maine. 1990.

1658-204 Research and Education Institute, Harbor UCLA Medical Center, Torrance, CA, $441,505. For Strengthening Hospital Nursing: A Program to Improve Patient Care. 1990.

1658-205 Resources for Independent Living, Sacramento, CA, $100,000. For Improving Service Systems for People with Disabilities. 1990.

1658-206 Richmond Unified School District, Richmond, CA, $49,992. For development of new model of managed health care. 1990.

1658-207 Robert Wood Johnson University Hospital, New Brunswick, NJ, $150,000. For advanced residency training program to prepare clergy as hospital chaplains. 1990.

1658-208 Rural Alaska Community Action Foundation, Anchorage, AK, $260,069. For child-parent substance abuse prevention and parenting program. 1990.

1658-209 Rural America Initiatives, Rapid City, SD, $129,600. For culturally-relevant maternal child health services. 1990.

1658-210 Saint Elizabeth Adult Day Care Center, Saint Louis, MO, $36,109. For Dementia Care and Respite Services Program. 1990.

1658-211 Saint Josephs Hospital and Medical Center, Paterson, NJ, $629,120. For Program to Improve Maternal and Infant Health in New Jersey. 1990.

1658-212 Saint Louis University, School of Public Health, Saint Louis, MO, $50,125. For Faculty Fellowships in Health Care Finance. 1990.

1658-213 Saint Lukes Hospital, Fargo, ND, $497,500. For Strengthening Hospital Nursing: A Program to Improve Patient Care. 1990.

1658-214 Saint Vincent Hospital and Health Center, Billings, MT, $507,410. For Strengthening Hospital Nursing: A Program to Improve Patient Care. 1990.

1658-215 Santa Barbara Council on Alcoholism and Drug Abuse, Santa Barbara, CA, $200,000. For Fighting Back: Community Initiatives to Reduce Demand for Drugs and Alcohol. 1990.

1658-216 Sauk Prairie Memorial Hospital Association, Prairie Du Sac, WI, $135,565. For Hospital-Based Rural Health Care Program. 1990.

1658-217 Seattle-King County Department of Public Health, Seattle, WA, $300,000. For Homeless Families Program, initiative to help homeless families obtain needed health and supportive services. 1990.

1658-218 Seneca Nation of Indians, New York Education Department, Salamanca, NY, $160,347. For substance abuse prevention for high-risk youth and families. 1990.

1658-219 Senior Services, Winston-Salem, NC, $100,940. For Dementia Care and Respite Services Program. 1990.

1658-220 Seton Hall University, South Orange, NJ, $14,879. For Faculty Fellowships in Health Care Finance. 1990.

1658-221 Shands Teaching Hospital and Clinics, Gainesville, FL, $261,379. For technical assistance and direction for Strengthening Hospital Nursing: A Program to Improve Patient Care. 1990.

1658-222 Sinai Samaritan Medical Center, Milwaukee, WI, $58,141. For Dementia Care and Respite Services Program. 1990.

1658-223 Southeastern Minnesota Center for Independent Living, Rochester, MN, $100,000. For Improving Service Systems for People with Disabilities. 1990.

1658-224 Southern New Jersey Perinatal Cooperative, Camden, NJ, $530,342. For Program to Improve Maternal and Infant Health in New Jersey. 1990.

1658-225 Stanford University, School of Medicine, Stanford, CA, $207,925. For two Clinical Scholars. 1990.

1658-226 Stanford University, School of Medicine, Stanford, CA, $152,456. For Minority Medical Faculty Development Program. 1990.

1658-227 Stavros Center for Independent Living, Amherst, MA, $100,000. For Improving Service Systems for People with Disabilities. 1990.

1658-228 Summit County Prevention Center, Park City, UT, $144,000. For program to reduce abuse of alcohol and other drugs. 1990.

1658-229 SUMMIT Independent Living Center, Missoula, MT, $99,925. For Improving Service Systems for People with Disabilities. 1990.

1658-230 Sunshine Terrace Foundation, Logan, UT, $189,653. For Dementia Care and Respite Services Program. 1990.

1658-231 Telespond Senior Services, Scranton, PA, $75,996. For Dementia Care and Respite Services Program. 1990.

1658-232 Texas Womans University, College of Nursing, Denton, TX, $398,067. For curriculum and support services to enable Licensed Vocational Nurses to advance to Bachelor of Science in Nursing degree. 1990.

1658-233 Trustees of Health and Hospitals of the City of Boston, Boston, MA, $557,547. For Strengthening Hospital Nursing: A Program to Improve Patient Care. 1990.

1658-234 United Hospital Fund of New York, NYC, NY, $286,756. For assessment of barriers to care leading to unnecessary hospitalization. 1990.

1658-235 United Hospital Fund of New York, NYC, NY, $14,417. For conference and proceedings on experience of AHSP grantees. 1990.

1658-236 United Seniors Health Cooperative, DC, $169,094. For development of benefits screening software for service agencies. 1990.

1658-237 United Way of Central Massachusetts, Worcester, MA, $200,000. For Fighting Back: Community Initiatives to Reduce Demand for Drugs and Alcohol. 1990.

1658-238 United Way of San Antonio and Bexar County, San Antonio, TX, $197,253. For Fighting Back: Community Initiatives to Reduce Demand for Drugs and Alcohol. 1990.

1658-239 University Hospitals of Cleveland, Cleveland, OH, $538,223. For Strengthening Hospital Nursing: A Program to Improve Patient Care. 1990.

1658-240 University of California, Graduate School of Management, Irvine, CA, $142,623. For research on rise in employer health care costs. 1990.

1658-241 University of California, Institute for Health and Aging, San Francisco, CA, $141,683. For evaluation of Improving Service Systems for People with Disabilities. 1990.

1658-242 University of California, School of Business Administration, Berkeley, CA, $54,900. For Health Policy Fellowship Program. 1990.

1658-243 University of California, School of Medicine, Los Angeles, CA, $316,246. For Program on Care of Critically Ill Hospitalized Adults. 1990.

1658-244 University of California, School of Medicine, Los Angeles, CA, $213,480. For two Clinical Scholars. 1990.

1658-245 University of California, School of Medicine, San Francisco, CA, $192,112. For two Clinical Scholars. 1990.

1658-246 University of California, School of Medicine, San Francisco, CA, $49,994. For study of women physicians at their career peak. 1990.

1658-247 University of California, School of Nursing, Los Angeles, CA, $14,746. For Faculty Fellowships in Health Care Finance. 1990.

1658-248 University of California, School of Nursing, San Francisco, CA, $152,400. For Clinical Nurse Scholars. 1990.

1658-249 University of California, School of Public Health, Los Angeles, CA, $128,137. For analysis of health status and service use by uninsured in California. 1990.

1658-250 University of Chicago, Pritzker School of Medicine, Chicago, IL, $149,728. For Preparing Physicians for the Future: A Program in Medical Education. 1990.

1658-251 University of Colorado Health Sciences Center, Denver, CO, $162,920. For Minority Medical Faculty Development Program. 1990.

1658-252 University of Colorado Health Sciences Center, Denver, CO, $157,373. For Minority Medical Faculty Development Program. 1990.

1658-253 University of Colorado Health Sciences Center, Denver, CO, $33,727. For supplement to evaluation of Teaching Nursing Home Program. 1990.

1658-254 University of Florida, College of Medicine, Gainesville, FL, $223,869. For technical assistance and direction for Healthy Futures Program, to coordinate and improve maternal, perinatal and infant care services. 1990.

1658-255 University of Florida, College of Medicine, Gainesville, FL, $55,800. For Health Policy Fellowship Program. 1990.

1658-256 University of Florida Foundation, Gainesville, FL, $468,677. For development of health policy center. 1990.

1658-257 University of Hawaii, John A. Burns School of Medicine, Honolulu, HI, $147,735. For Preparing Physicians for the Future: A Program in Medical Education. 1990.

1658-258 University of Illinois, College of Nursing, Chicago, IL, $380,773. For recruitment and retention of minority nursing students. 1990.

1658-259 University of Iowa, Iowa City, IA, $272,359. To improve quality of hospital care. 1990.

1658-260 University of Kentucky Research Foundation, Lexington, KY, $149,982. For Preparing Physicians for the Future: A Program in Medical Education. 1990.

1658-261 University of Maryland, Baltimore, MD, $275,231. For technical assistance and direction for AIDS Prevention and Service Program. 1990.

1658-262 University of Maryland, Baltimore, MD, $29,428. For implementation of health component for high-risk youth project. 1990.

1658-263 University of Maryland, Center on Aging, College Park, MD, $261,647. For technical assistance and direction for Program to Promote Long-Term Care Insurance for Elderly. 1990.

1658-264 University of Maryland, Center on Aging, College Park, MD, $38,757. For technical assistance and direction for Service Credit Banking Program. 1990.

1658-265 University of Medicine and Dentistry of New Jersey, Robert Wood Johnson Medical School, Piscataway, NJ, $485,286. For Program to Improve Maternal and Infant Health in New Jersey. 1990.

1658-266 University of Medicine and Dentistry of New Jersey, Robert Wood Johnson Medical School, Piscataway, NJ, $49,168. For statewide registry of patients with acute myocardial infarction. 1990.

1658-267 University of Medicine and Dentistry of New Jersey, School of Medicine, Newark, NJ, $250,000. For statewide study of feasibility and need for regional pediatric centers. 1990.

1658-268 University of Michigan, Medical School, Ann Arbor, MI, $77,077. For technical assistance for Preparing Physicians for the Future: A Program in Medical Education. 1990.

1658-269 University of Michigan, Medical School, Ann Arbor, MI, $51,279. For Health Policy Fellowship Program. 1990.

1658-270 University of Nebraska, College of Medicine, Omaha, NE, $149,947. For Preparing Physicians for the Future: A Program in Medical Education. 1990.

1658-271 University of New Mexico, School of Medicine, Albuquerque, NM, $148,509. For Preparing Physicians for the Future: A Program in Medical Education. 1990.

1658-272 University of North Carolina, Health Services Research Center, Chapel Hill, NC, $66,287. For Dental Services Research Scholars Communications Network. 1990.

1658-273 University of North Carolina, School of Medicine, Chapel Hill, NC, $371,436. For four Clinical Scholars. 1990.

1658-274 University of Oklahoma, College of Public Health, Oklahoma City, OK, $277,846. For technical assistance and direction for Improving Health of Native Americans. 1990.

1658-275 University of Oklahoma Health Sciences Center, School of Allied Health Sciences, Oklahoma City, OK, $221,234. For technical assistance and direction for Minority Medical Education Program. 1990.

1658-276 University of Pennsylvania, School of Medicine, Philadelphia, PA, $456,112. For four Clinical Scholars. 1990.

1658-277 University of Pennsylvania, School of Medicine, Philadelphia, PA, $391,190. For study of costs of care of critically ill adults. 1990.

1658-278 University of Pennsylvania, School of Nursing, Philadelphia, PA, $156,000. For stipends for Clinical Nurse Scholars Program. 1990.

1658-279 University of Puerto Rico, School of Public Health, San Juan, PR, $14,950. For Faculty Fellowships in Health Care Finance. 1990.

1658-280 University of Rochester, School of Medicine and Dentistry, Rochester, NY, $148,350. For Preparing Physicians for the Future: A Program in Medical Education. 1990.

1658-281 University of Rochester, School of Nursing, Rochester, NY, $151,200. For stipends for Clinical Nurse Scholars Program. 1990.

1658-282 University of South Carolina, College of Nursing, Columbia, SC, $54,243. For Faculty Fellowships in Health Care Finance. 1990.

1658-283 University of Utah, University Hospital, Salt Lake City, UT, $495,172. For Strengthening Hospital Nursing: A Program to Improve Patient Care. 1990.

1658-284 University of Virginia Law School Foundation, Charlottesville, VA, $100,525. For technical assistance to Medical Malpractice Program. 1990.

1658-285 University of Washington, School of Medicine, Seattle, WA, $442,221. For four Clinical Scholars. 1990.

1658-286 University of Washington, School of Medicine, Seattle, WA, $152,500. For Minority Medical Faculty Development Program. 1990.

1658-287 University of Washington, School of Medicine, Seattle, WA, $152,500. For Minority Medical Faculty Development Program. 1990.

1658-288 University of Washington, School of Nursing, Seattle, WA, $159,371. For technical assistance and direction for Clinical Nurse Scholars Program. 1990.

1658-289 University of Washington, School of Public Health and Community Medicine, Seattle, WA, $53,361. For Faculty Fellowships in Health Care Finance. 1990.

1658-290 University of Wisconsin, School of Medicine, Madison, WI, $72,267. For cost analysis of community treatment of people with chronic mental illness. 1990.

1658-291 Urban Institute, DC, $458,288. For analysis of options for restructuring U.S. health care financing system. 1990.

1658-292 Urban Institute, DC, $25,996. For special journal issue on medical malpractice reform. 1990.

1658-293 Vallejo, City of, Vallejo, CA, $198,661. For Fighting Back: Community Initiatives to Reduce Demand for Drugs and Alcohol. 1990.

1658-294 Vanderbilt University, Nashville, TN, $570,164. For evaluation of Homeless Families Program, initiative to help homeless families obtain needed health and supportive services. 1990.

1658-295 Vanderbilt University, School of Medicine, Nashville, TN, $380,349. For technical assistance and direction for Fighting Back: Community Initiatives to Reduce Demand for Drugs and Alcohol. 1990.

1658-296 Vanderbilt University, School of Medicine, Nashville, TN, $151,960. For Minority Medical Faculty Development Program. 1990.

1658-297 Vanderbilt University, Vanderbilt University Hospital, Nashville, TN, $410,960. For Strengthening Hospital Nursing: A Program to Improve Patient Care. 1990.

1658-298 Vermont Program for Quality in Health Care, Montpelier, VT, $291,436. To improve quality of hospital care. 1990.

1658-299 Vermont, State of, Department of Mental Health, Waterbury, VT, $1,460,041. For Mental Health Services Program for Youth. 1990.

1658-300 W G B H Educational Foundation, Boston, MA, $2,840,482. For PBS health quarterly series. 1990.

1658-301 Wake Forest University, Bowman Gray School of Medicine, Winston-Salem, NC, $270,982. For technical assistance and direction for Dementia Care and Respite Services Program. 1990.

1658-302 Wake Forest University, Bowman Gray School of Medicine, Winston-Salem, NC, $49,980. For follow-up of students who participated in Medicine as a Career Program. 1990.

1658-303 Washington University, School of Medicine, Saint Louis, MO, $152,498. For Minority Medical Faculty Development Program. 1990.

1658-304 West Virginia Department of Health and Human Resources, Charleston, WV, $440,656. For Healthy Futures Program, to coordinate and improve maternal, perinatal and infant care services. 1990.

1658-305 Western Consortium for Public Health, Berkeley, CA, $394,461. To evaluate effects of New Jersey hospital rate regulation on services for uninsured. 1990.

1658-306 Wisconsin, State of, Department of Health and Social Services, Madison, WI, $1,500,000. For Mental Health Services Program for Youth. 1990.

1658-307 Wisconsin, State of, Department of Health and Social Services, Madison, WI, $63,634. For Program to Promote Long-Term Care Insurance for Elderly. 1990.

1658-308 Womens City Club of New York, NYC, NY, $26,911. For survey of AIDS education for adolescents in New York City. 1990.

1658-309 Wright State University, Dayton, OH, $14,867. For Faculty Fellowships in Health Care Finance. 1990.

1658-310 Wrights Mesa Medical Services, Norwood, CO, $100,000. For Program to Strengthen Primary Care Health Centers. 1990.

1658-311 Yale University, School of Medicine, New Haven, CT, $185,335. For two Clinical Scholars. 1990.

1658-312 Yale University, School of Medicine, New Haven, CT, $156,102. For Minority Medical Faculty Development Program. 1990.

1658-313 Yale University, School of Medicine, New Haven, CT, $149,999. For Preparing Physicians for the Future: A Program in Medical Education. 1990.

1658-314 Yale University, School of Medicine, New Haven, CT, $25,687. For documentation of patients outcome research teams' origins and expectations. 1990.

1659
Quentin J. Kennedy Foundation
22 Old Smith Rd.
Tenafly 07670

Established in 1986 in NJ.
Donor(s): Quentin J. Kennedy.
Foundation type: Independent
Financial data (yr. ended 12/31/91): Assets, $5,654,880 (M); gifts received, $25,000; expenditures, $234,673; qualifying distributions, $229,750, including $229,750 for 23 grants (high: $68,750; low: $250).
Purpose and activities: Support primarily for Catholic organizations, including welfare agencies; support also for health and child welfare.
Fields of interest: Catholic giving, Catholic welfare, health, child welfare.
Limitations: Giving primarily in NY and NJ. No grants to individuals.
Application information: Contributes only to pre-selected organizations. Applications not accepted.
  Write: Quentin J. Kennedy, Pres.
Officers: Quentin J. Kennedy, Pres. and Treas.; Mary Elizabeth Kennedy, V.P.; Quentin J. Kennedy, Jr., Secy.
EIN: 222653050

1660
The James Kerney Foundation
P.O. Box 627
Princeton 08542   (609) 921-6336

Incorporated in 1934 in NJ.
Donor(s): Members of the Kerney family.
Foundation type: Independent
Financial data (yr. ended 12/31/91): Assets, $2,828,578 (M); expenditures, $124,317; qualifying distributions, $114,840, including $113,840 for 13 grants (high: $20,000; low: $4,000).
Fields of interest: Hospitals, youth, higher education, Catholic giving, family services, museums, fine arts.
Types of support: Scholarship funds, building funds, renovation projects, equipment.
Limitations: Giving limited to Trenton, NJ, and its surrounding area. No grants to individuals, or for operating budgets.
Publications: Annual report (including application guidelines).
Application information: Application form not required.
  Initial approach: Letter
  Copies of proposal: 1
  Deadline(s): Apr. and Oct.
  Board meeting date(s): May and Nov.
  Final notification: May and Nov.
  Write: J. Kerney Kuser II
Officers: Joseph P. Comley III, Pres.; Sheila McNeil Priory, V.P.; J. Regan Kerney, Secy.-Treas.
Trustees: Richard Bilotti, Albert B. Kahn, Jr., T. Lincoln Kerney II, Edward L. Meara III.
EIN: 226055884

1661
F. M. Kirby Foundation, Inc. ▼
17 DeHart St.
P.O. Box 151
Morristown 07963-0151   (201) 538-4800
Additional tel.: (212) 732-2265; IRS filing state: DE

Incorporated in 1931 in DE.
Donor(s): F.M. Kirby,‡ Allan P. Kirby, Sr.,‡ F.M. Kirby.
Foundation type: Independent
Financial data (yr. ended 12/31/91): Assets, $213,208,525 (M); expenditures, $8,360,173; qualifying distributions, $7,463,730, including $7,372,010 for 400 grants (high: $600,000; low: $500; average: $15,000-$25,000).
Purpose and activities: Support for higher and secondary education, health and hospitals, community funds, historic preservation, church support and church-related organizations, social services, conservation, public policy organizations, and population control. Grants almost entirely limited to organizations associated with personal interests of present or former foundation directors.
Fields of interest: Education, health, medical sciences, community funds, historic preservation, religion, family planning, youth, recreation, conservation, cultural programs, public policy, AIDS.
Types of support: Operating budgets, special projects, general purposes, equipment, renovation projects, research, seed money, annual campaigns, continuing support.
Limitations: Giving primarily in NY, NJ, PA, and VA. No grants to individuals, or for fundraising benefits; no loans or pledges.
Publications: Informational brochure.

Application information: Application form not required.
 Initial approach: Proposal with cover letter; no telephone solicitations accepted
 Copies of proposal: 1
 Deadline(s): Proposals received throughout the year; requests received after Oct. 31 are held over to the following year
 Board meeting date(s): Quarterly
 Final notification: Monthly for positive responses only
 Write: F.M. Kirby, Pres.
Officers and Directors:* F.M. Kirby,* Pres.; Walter D. Kirby,* V.P.; Thomas J. Bianchini,* Secy.-Treas.; Paul B. Mott, Jr., Exec. Dir.; Alice Kirby Horton, Fred M. Kirby III, S. Dillard Kirby, Jefferson W. Kirby.
Number of staff: 2 part-time professional; 2 part-time support.
EIN: 516017929
Recent health grants:
1661-1 Action on Smoking and Health, DC, $20,000. 1990.
1661-2 AIDS Resource Foundation for Children, Newark, NJ, $20,000. 1990.
1661-3 Alzheimers Disease and Related Disorders Association, Chicago, IL, $21,000. 1990.
1661-4 Alzheimers Disease and Related Disorders Association, Richmond, VA, $16,000. 1990.
1661-5 American Cancer Society, Atlanta, GA, $85,000. 1990.
1661-6 American Cancer Society, Morristown, NJ, $35,000. 1990.
1661-7 American Foundation for AIDS Research, NYC, NY, $10,000. 1990.
1661-8 American Heart Association, Bridgewater, NJ, $36,000. 1990.
1661-9 American Kidney Fund, Rockville, MD, $37,000. 1990.
1661-10 American Leprosy Missions, Elmwood Park, NJ, $10,000. 1990.
1661-11 American Parkinson Disease Association, Staten Island, NY, $15,000. 1990.
1661-12 Arthritis Foundation, Atlanta, GA, $30,000. 1990.
1661-13 Arthritis Foundation, Iselin, NJ, $10,000. 1990.
1661-14 Association for Voluntary Surgical Contraception, NYC, NY, $50,000. 1990.
1661-15 Big Apple Circus, NYC, NY, $10,000. For Clown Care Unit. 1990.
1661-16 Cancer Research Institute, NYC, NY, $60,000. 1990.
1661-17 Emory University, School of Medicine, Atlanta, GA, $350,000. For Culbertson Fund. 1990.
1661-18 Epilepsy Foundation of America, Landover, MD, $11,000. 1990.
1661-19 Happiness is Camping, Bronx, NY, $10,000. 1990.
1661-20 International Center for the Disabled (ICD), NYC, NY, $15,000. 1990.
1661-21 John Randolph Hospital, Hopewell, VA, $12,000. For desk top publishing unit. 1990.
1661-22 Leary Educational Foundation, Winchester, VA, $10,000. For Education and Crafts Pavilion. 1990.
1661-23 Leukemia Society of America, Maplewood, NJ, $12,500. 1990.

1661-24 Little Falls Hospital, Little Falls, NY, $12,000. For upgrade of Surgery and Imaging Departments. 1990.
1661-25 Manhattan Eye, Ear and Throat Hospital, NYC, NY, $10,000. For final payment to establish F.M. Kirby Retina Fellowship. 1990.
1661-26 Market Street Mission, Morristown, NJ, $32,500. 1990.
1661-27 Memorial Sloan-Kettering Cancer Center, NYC, NY, $12,000. 1990.
1661-28 Morris Council on Alcohol and Drug Abuse, Denville, NJ, $10,000. 1990.
1661-29 Morristown Memorial Health Foundation, Morristown, NJ, $56,000. 1990.
1661-30 Morristown Memorial Health Foundation, Morristown, NJ, $20,000. For Center for Cardiovascular Disease. 1990.
1661-31 Morristown Memorial Health Foundation, Morristown, NJ, $15,000. For HIV counseling and testing. 1990.
1661-32 Morristown Memorial Health Foundation, Morristown, NJ, $10,000. For Family Endowment. 1990.
1661-33 National AIDS Prevention Institute, Culpeper, VA, $15,000. 1990.
1661-34 National Council on Alcoholism, NYC, NY, $25,000. 1990.
1661-35 National Kidney Foundation, NYC, NY, $10,000. 1990.
1661-36 National Leukemia Association, Garden City, NY, $50,000. 1990.
1661-37 National Multiple Sclerosis Society, Montclair, NJ, $10,000. 1990.
1661-38 Overlook Hospital, Summit, NJ, $37,500. 1990.
1661-39 Planned Parenthood Federation of America, NYC, NY, $46,000. 1990.
1661-40 Planned Parenthood of Greater Northern New Jersey, Morristown, NJ, $23,000. 1990.
1661-41 Planned Parenthood of Northeastern Pennsylvania, Wilkes-Barre, PA, $12,500. 1990.
1661-42 Population Crisis Committee, DC, $29,000. 1990.
1661-43 Presbyterian Hospital in the City of New York, NYC, NY, $10,000. For Milstein Hospital. 1990.
1661-44 Research to Prevent Blindness, NYC, NY, $13,500. 1990.
1661-45 Skin Cancer Foundation, NYC, NY, $25,000. 1990.
1661-46 Strang Cancer Prevention Center, Strang Clinic, NYC, NY, $25,000. For Cancer Prevention Fund. 1990.
1661-47 Virginia Commonwealth University, Department of Psychiatry, Richmond, VA, $55,000. 1990.
1661-48 Virginia Polytechnic Institute and State University, Virginia-Maryland Regional College of Veterinary Medicine, Blacksburg, VA, $35,000. 1990.
1661-49 Visiting Health Service of Morris County, Dover, NJ, $15,000. 1990.
1661-50 Visiting Nurse Association of Morris County, Morristown, NJ, $12,000. 1990.
1661-51 Wilkes-Barre General Hospital, Wilkes-Barre, PA, $12,000. 1990.
1661-52 World Rehabilitation Fund, NYC, NY, $10,000. 1990.

1662
The Lynne & Charles Klatskin Foundation, Inc.
400 Hollister Rd.
Teterboro 07608-1183

Established in 1975.
Donor(s): Charles Klatskin.
Foundation type: Independent
Financial data (yr. ended 06/30/91): Assets, $172,333 (M); gifts received, $200,000; expenditures, $204,710; qualifying distributions, $204,035, including $204,035 for 42 grants (high: $100,000; low: $100).
Fields of interest: Jewish welfare, Jewish giving, hospitals, medical research, higher education.
Types of support: Endowment funds, research, general purposes.
Limitations: Giving primarily in NJ. No grants to individuals.
Application information: Contributes only to pre-selected organizations. Applications not accepted.
Officers and Trustees:* Charles Klatskin,* Pres.; Lynne Klatskin,* Secy.
EIN: 222083758

1663
Ernest Christian Klipstein Foundation
Village Rd.
New Vernon 07967   (201) 538-4445

Established in 1954 in NJ.
Donor(s): Kenneth H. Klipstein.‡
Foundation type: Independent
Financial data (yr. ended 12/31/91): Assets, $2,988,380 (M); gifts received, $351,000; expenditures, $127,144; qualifying distributions, $115,188, including $83,875 for 82 grants (high: $10,000; low: $50).
Fields of interest: Higher education, secondary education, cultural programs, conservation, media and communications, health.
Limitations: Giving primarily in NJ. No grants to individuals.
Application information: Application form not required.
 Deadline(s): None
 Write: David J. Klipstein, Pres.
Officers: David J. Klipstein, Pres.; Kenneth H. Klipstein II, V.P.; Marion C. White, Secy.; Constance M. Tebinka, Treas.
EIN: 226028529

1664
The Harold and Adeline Kramer Family Foundation, Inc.
85 Central Ave.
Clifton 07011-2309

Established in 1985.
Donor(s): Adeline Kramer, Harold Kramer.
Foundation type: Independent
Financial data (yr. ended 05/31/91): Assets, $1,328,699 (M); gifts received, $100,000; expenditures, $219,775; qualifying distributions, $220,524, including $215,500 for 28 grants (high: $20,000; low: $500).
Purpose and activities: Giving primarily for Jewish organizations, including temple support

and a seminary; support also for higher education and medical research and hospitals.

Fields of interest: Jewish giving, Jewish welfare, theological education, higher education, medical research, hospitals.

Types of support: General purposes, capital campaigns, endowment funds, building funds.

Limitations: Giving primarily in NY, NJ, and FL. No grants to individuals.

Application information: Contributes only to pre-selected organizations. Applications not accepted.

Officers and Trustees:* Harold Kramer,* Pres. and Mgr.; Frederick Kramer,* V.P.; George Kramer,* V.P.; Adeline Kramer,* Secy.; Arthur Kramer,* Treas.

EIN: 222615764

1665
The Stefano La Sala Foundation, Inc.
One Bridge Plaza North, Suite 105
Fort Lee 07024   (201) 947-9580

Incorporated in 1956 in NY.

Donor(s): Members of the La Sala family, La Sala Contracting Co., Inc., and others.

Foundation type: Independent

Financial data (yr. ended 11/30/91): Assets, $2,308,719 (M); expenditures, $156,975; qualifying distributions, $147,750, including $147,750 for 78 grants (high: $28,685; low: $10).

Purpose and activities: Emphasis on higher and secondary education and hospitals; grants also for Roman Catholic church support and social service agencies.

Fields of interest: Higher education, secondary education, hospitals, Catholic giving, religion, social services.

Limitations: Giving primarily in the New York, NY, area. No support for private foundations. No grants to individuals.

Publications: Annual report.

Application information: Contributes only to pre-selected organizations. Applications not accepted.

Write: A. Stephen La Sala, Dir.

Directors: A. Stephen La Sala, Andrew J. La Sala, Anthony La Sala, Frank La Sala.

Number of staff: 1 part-time professional; 1 part-time support.

EIN: 136110920

1666
The Lazarus Charitable Trust
c/o Toys 'R' Us
461 From Rd.
Paramus 07652

Established in 1986 in NJ.

Donor(s): Charles Lazarus.

Foundation type: Independent

Financial data (yr. ended 05/31/91): Assets, $2,712,829 (M); expenditures, $142,113; qualifying distributions, $134,159, including $133,874 for 38 grants (high: $25,000; low: $50).

Fields of interest: Health associations, cancer, hospitals, medical research, education, social services.

Limitations: Giving primarily in New York, NY and Washington, DC.

Application information:
Initial approach: Letter

Deadline(s): None
Write: Charles Lazarus, Trustee
Trustee: Charles Lazarus.
EIN: 133360876

1667
The Leavens Foundation
Llewellyn Park
West Orange 07052-4942

Established in 1959.

Donor(s): William B. Leavens, Jr.‡

Foundation type: Independent

Financial data (yr. ended 12/31/90): Assets, $3,026,065 (M); expenditures, $189,346; qualifying distributions, $150,625, including $150,625 for 43 grants (high: $15,000; low: $200; average: $100-$600).

Purpose and activities: Giving for the arts, a community fund, hospitals, health associations, and higher education.

Fields of interest: Arts, community funds, hospitals, higher education, environment.

Types of support: Continuing support, capital campaigns, special projects, general purposes.

Limitations: Giving primarily in NJ. No grants to individuals.

Application information: Contributes only to pre-selected organizations. Applications not accepted.

Write: Nancy L. Wright, Trustee

Trustees: Margaret R. Leavens, William B. Leavens III, Nancy L. Wright.

EIN: 226063089

1668
Thomas J. Lipton Foundation, Inc.
c/o Thomas J. Lipton, Inc.
800 Sylvan Ave.
Englewood Cliffs 07632

Incorporated in 1952 in DE.

Donor(s): Thomas J. Lipton, Inc., Calvin Klein Cosmetics.

Foundation type: Company-sponsored

Financial data (yr. ended 12/31/90): Assets, $112,188 (M); gifts received, $937,954; expenditures, $947,742; qualifying distributions, $939,443, including $939,298 for 561 grants (high: $52,500; low: $10).

Purpose and activities: Emphasis on research in nutrition, community funds, higher education, including scholarship aid, hospitals, cultural programs, social services, and youth agencies.

Fields of interest: Nutrition, community funds, higher education, youth, hospitals, cultural programs, social services.

Types of support: Research, scholarship funds, employee matching gifts.

Limitations: Giving primarily in areas of company operations, with some emphasis on NJ and NY.

Application information: Application form required.

Deadline(s): None
Write: Helen Siegle, Grant Administrator

Officers and Trustees:* Blaine R. Hess,* Pres.; D.W. St. Clair,* V.P. and Secy.; D.E. Grein,* V.P. and Treas.; W.J. Sellitti,* V.P. and Controller; W.K. Godfrey,* V.P.

EIN: 226063094

1669
The Magowan Family Foundation, Inc.
c/o Merrill Lynch & Co., Inc.
100 Union Ave.
Cresskill 07626
Application address: c/o Mary Ann Chapin, Asst. Treas., 2100 Washington St., San Francisco, CA 94109; Tel.: (415) 563-5581

Incorporated in 1954 in NY.

Donor(s): Charles E. Merrill, Sr.,‡ Robert A. Magowan, Sr.,‡ Doris M. Magowan, Merrill L. Magowan, Robert A. Magowan, Jr.

Foundation type: Independent

Financial data (yr. ended 10/31/91): Assets, $5,395,006 (M); gifts received, $57,417; expenditures, $468,188; qualifying distributions, $434,241, including $427,880 for 134 grants (high: $62,000; low: $500).

Fields of interest: Higher education, secondary education, religion—Christian, hospitals, cultural programs.

Limitations: Giving primarily in NY, CA, and FL. No grants to individuals.

Application information:
Initial approach: Letter
Deadline(s): None

Officers: Peter A. Magowan, Pres.; Doris M. Magowan, V.P.; Mark E. Magowan, V.P.; Merrill L. Magowan, V.P.; Stephen C. Magowan, V.P.; Bernat Rosner, Secy.; Thomas J. Lombardi, Treas.

EIN: 136085999

1670
Maneely Fund, Inc.
900 Haddon Ave., Suite 432
Collingswood 08108   (609) 854-5400

Incorporated in 1952 in PA.

Donor(s): Edward F. Maneely.‡

Foundation type: Independent

Financial data (yr. ended 12/31/91): Assets, $3,159,285 (M); expenditures, $181,069; qualifying distributions, $139,580, including $117,435 for 78 grants (high: $25,000; low: $100).

Fields of interest: Health, community funds, higher education, secondary education, social services, cultural programs, religion—Christian.

Types of support: Operating budgets, research, scholarship funds, annual campaigns.

Limitations: Giving primarily in NY, NJ, and PA. No grants to individuals.

Application information: Application form not required.

Initial approach: Letter
Deadline(s): None
Write: James E. O'Donnell, Pres.

Officers: James E. O'Donnell, Pres. and Treas.; Elizabeth J. Boylan, V.P.; Marie E. Dooner, Secy.

EIN: 231569917

1671
The Martin Family Fund, Inc.
c/o Robert Martin
P.O. Box 56
Saddle River 07458

Established in 1988.

Donor(s): Sylvia Martin.‡

Foundation type: Independent

Financial data (yr. ended 12/31/90): Assets, $3,572,079 (M); expenditures, $137,413; qualifying distributions, $112,817, including $102,950 for 42 grants (high: $20,000; low: $100).
Fields of interest: Higher education, medical research, health associations, hospitals, performing arts.
Limitations: Giving primarily in NJ and NY. No grants to individuals.
Application information: Contributes only to pre-selected organizations. Applications not accepted.
Officers: Robert Allan Martin, Pres.; Gertrude Ann Martin, Secy.
EIN: 222781283

1672
The Curtis W. McGraw Foundation
c/o Drinker, Biddle & Reath
P.O. Box 627
Princeton 08542   (609) 497-7011

Established in 1964 in NJ.
Donor(s): Elizabeth McGraw Webster.
Foundation type: Independent
Financial data (yr. ended 12/31/91): Assets, $13,187,767 (M); expenditures, $665,795; qualifying distributions, $647,111, including $643,889 for 76 grants (high: $50,000; low: $1,000; average: $8,955).
Purpose and activities: Support primarily for hospitals, mental health, AIDS research, elementary and other educational institutions, the arts, social services, and churches. Grants usually made to charities which are of interest to the officers.
Fields of interest: Hospitals, mental health, AIDS, education, elementary education, arts, performing arts, social services, drug abuse, religion, ecology.
Types of support: Annual campaigns, continuing support, operating budgets.
Limitations: Giving limited to the Princeton, NJ, Vail, CO, and Sun Valley, ID, areas. No grants to individuals, or for endowment funds, research, scholarships, fellowships, or matching gifts; no loans.
Publications: 990-PF.
Application information: Application form not required.
　Initial approach: Letter
　Copies of proposal: 1
　Deadline(s): Oct. 15
　Board meeting date(s): Nov. or Dec., and as required
　Final notification: By Dec. 31
　Write: Samuel W. Lambert III, Secy.-Treas.
Officers and Trustees:* Elizabeth McGraw Webster,* Pres.; Curtis M. Webster,* Exec. V.P.; Lisette S. Edmond,* V.P.; Marian S. Maricich,* V.P.; Dorothy H. Peyton,* V.P.; Samuel W. Lambert III,* Secy.-Treas.
Number of staff: None.
EIN: 221761678

1673
The MCJ Foundation ▼
330 South St., CN-1975
Morristown 07962-1975   (201) 540-0968

Application address: 375 Park Ave., Suite 301, New York, NY 10152; Tel: (212) 735-1125

Established in 1983 in NJ.
Donor(s): Raymond G. Chambers.
Foundation type: Independent
Financial data (yr. ended 11/30/90): Assets, $45,941,828 (M); expenditures, $7,752,195; qualifying distributions, $7,612,850, including $7,574,518 for 272 grants (high: $1,000,000; low: $200).
Purpose and activities: Giving primarily for education, human services, community funds, arts and philanthropy.
Fields of interest: Community funds, education, hospitals, health associations, child welfare, youth.
Types of support: Operating budgets, renovation projects.
Limitations: Giving primarily in NJ and NY. No grants to individuals.
Application information: Application form not required.
　Deadline(s): None
　Write: Christine Chambers, Exec. Dir.
Officers and Directors:* Raymond G. Chambers,* Pres.; Gary L. Moore,* V.P.; Donald R. Smith, Secy.; Christine Chambers, Co-Exec. Dir.; Martin S. Barber, Jennifer Chambers, Michael Chambers, Patricia Chambers, Frank H. Pearl, Frank E. Walsh, Jr.
EIN: 222497895
Recent health grants:
1673-1 American Holistic Health Association, Anaheim, CA, $10,000. For general operating support. 1990.
1673-2 American Paralysis Association, Springfield, NJ, $10,000. For general operating support. 1990.
1673-3 Morristown Memorial Hospital Foundation, Morristown, NJ, $10,000. For outreach worker at Morris Shelter. 1990.
1673-4 New Jersey Citizens Against Crime, Trenton, NJ, $25,000. For Drug Free School Zone Awareness Program. 1990.
1673-5 Princeton Child Development Institute, Princeton, NJ, $10,000. For Spring Sensations Benefit. 1990.
1673-6 University of Miami, Marc Buoniconti Fund, Miami, FL, $100,000. For general operating support. 1990.
1673-7 University of Miami, Marc Buoniconti Fund, Miami, FL, $85,000. For general operating support. 1990.

1674
Mercedes-Benz of North America
One Mercedes Dr.
Montvale 07645   (201) 573-0600

Purpose and activities: Main support for culture, community funds, civic affairs, and education.
Fields of interest: Community development, business education, education, environment, family services, fine arts, heart disease, higher education, historic preservation, homeless, hospitals, hospitals—building funds, humanities, hunger, libraries, literacy, medical research, minorities, museums, music, Native Americans, peace, public affairs, drug abuse, history, community funds, cultural programs, health, Jewish giving, alcoholism, cancer, civic affairs,

dance, education—minorities, child development, disadvantaged, youth.
Types of support: Annual campaigns, building funds, emergency funds, employee matching gifts, matching funds, publications, research, scholarship funds, in-kind gifts, donated equipment, employee volunteer services, use of facilities, general purposes.
Limitations: Giving primarily in major markets and areas near company facilities. No grants for religious organizations (excluding religious education or welfare).
Publications: Corporate report, program policy statement.
Application information: Application form not required.
　Initial approach: Letter; no requests by fax; send requests to nearest company facility
　Copies of proposal: 1
　Write: Maryalice Ritzmann, Press Info. Mgr.
Number of staff: 1 part-time professional; 1 part-time support.

1675
Merck & Company Corporate Giving Program
P.O. Box 2000
Rahway 07065-0900   (201) 855-2042

Financial data (yr. ended 12/31/90): Total giving, $28,800,000, including $9,000,000 for grants and $19,800,000 for in-kind gifts.
Purpose and activities: "The business of Merck is improving the quality of life throughout the world." Main emphasis is on the development of innovative products for the health and well-being of society. Support for medicine and science, with emphasis on creating opportunities for minorities; health and social services; and civic and cultural activities. In addition to cash grants, Merck also donates products to meet the needs of the ill and the indigent, and for victims of natural disasters. Together the foundation and corporation gave 794 grants totaling $18.4 million in 1990 (excluding nonmonetary gifts).
Fields of interest: Education, medical research, science and technology, engineering, health, social services, civic affairs, cultural programs, minorities, AIDS, higher education, secondary education, Australia, Canada, Latin America, United Kingdom, France, Germany, Europe, Italy, Japan, Mexico, Asia, Portugal, Spain, Scotland.
Types of support: Donated products, special projects, fellowships, program-related investments, research.
Limitations: Giving primarily in headquarters city and major operating locations in U.S. and abroad; plants exist in Australia, Canada, Costa Rica, England, France, Germany, Holland, Ireland, Italy, Japan, Mexico, Pakistan, Portugal, Scotland, S. Wales, Spain. No support for political, labor, fraternal, or veterans' groups. No grants to individuals, or for endowments, publications, or media productions.
Publications: Corporate giving report, application guidelines, informational brochure (including application guidelines).
Application information: Company has a staff that only handles contributions.
　Initial approach: Proposal no longer than 2 pages
　Copies of proposal: 1

Deadline(s): None
Board meeting date(s): As required
Final notification: Three months required for full review and decision
Write: Charles R. Hogan, Jr., Exec. V.P.
Contributions Staff: Charles R. Hogen, Jr., Sr. Dir.; John R. Taylor, Mgr., Fin. and Admin.; Shuang Ruy Huang, Mgr., Corp. Contribs.; Lois F. Schwartz, Coord.
Number of staff: 4 full-time professional; 4 full-time support.

1676
The Merck Company Foundation ▼
P.O. Box 100
One Merck Dr.
Whitehouse Station 08889-0100(908) 423-2042

Incorporated in 1957 in NJ.
Donor(s): Merck & Co., Inc.
Foundation type: Company-sponsored
Financial data (yr. ended 12/31/90): Assets, $31,338,140 (M); gifts received, $6,000,000; expenditures, $9,431,888; qualifying distributions, $9,393,253, including $8,049,245 for 320 grants (high: $279,700; low: $90; average: $10,000-$50,000), $343,297 for 12 grants to individuals and $989,844 for 1,206 employee matching gifts.
Purpose and activities: Support of education, primarily medical, and including the Merck Sharp & Dohme International Fellowships in Clinical Pharmacology; community programs, hospitals, medical, biological, and physical sciences, health agencies, public and civic organizations, and colleges in localities where the company has major operations; and an employee matching gift program for colleges, secondary schools, hospitals, public broadcasting and public libraries.
Fields of interest: Education, higher education, medical education, pharmacy, hospitals, medical sciences, physical sciences, health, biology, science and technology, chemistry, biochemistry, biological sciences, heart disease, ophthalmology, aged, public policy, engineering, environment, handicapped.
Types of support: Seed money, special projects, equipment, employee matching gifts, fellowships, publications.
Limitations: Giving primarily in areas of company operations, including NJ, PA, GA, VA, and CA. No support for labor, political, or sectarian groups. No grants to individuals (except for fellowships in clinical pharmacology), or for operating budgets, continuing support, annual campaigns, emergency or endowment funds, deficit financing, land acquisition, research, travel, conferences, publications, or media productions; no loans.
Publications: Corporate giving report.
Application information: Grants usually made at the initiative of the foundation. Application form not required.
Initial approach: Letter
Copies of proposal: 1
Deadline(s): Aug. 31 for fellowships in clinical pharmacology; no set deadline for other grants
Board meeting date(s): Semiannually and as required
Final notification: 2 months
Write: Charles R. Hogen, Jr., Exec. V.P.

Officers and Trustees:* P. Roy Vagelos, M.D.,* Chair.; Albert D. Angel,* Pres.; Charles R. Hogen, Jr., Exec. V.P.; Shuang Ruy Huang, V.P.; Clarence A. Abramson, Secy.; Larry W. Saufley, Treas.; H. Brewster Atwater, Jr., William G. Bowen, Frank T. Cary, Carolyne K. Davis, Lloyd C. Elam, Charles E. Exley, Jr., Jacques Genest, Marian S. Heiskell, John J. Horan, John E. Lyons, Albert W. Merck, Ruben F. Mettler, Paul G. Rogers, Richard S. Ross, Dennis Weatherstone.
Number of staff: 4 full-time professional; 4 full-time support.
EIN: 226028476
Recent health grants:
1676-1 American Association of Colleges of Pharmacy, Alexandria, VA, $17,000. 1990.
1676-2 American College of Cardiology, Bethesda, MD, $175,000. 1990.
1676-3 American Federation for Aging Research, NYC, NY, $147,500. 1990.
1676-4 American Federation for Aging Research, NYC, NY, $100,000. 1990.
1676-5 American Foundation for Pharmaceutical Education, Fair Lawn, NJ, $27,500. 1990.
1676-6 American Foundation for Pharmaceutical Education, Fair Lawn, NJ, $10,000. 1990.
1676-7 American Heart Association, Dallas, TX, $110,400. 1990.
1676-8 American Society of Hospital Pharmacists Research and Education Foundation, Bethesda, MD, $30,000. 1990.
1676-9 Association of Academic Health Centers, DC, $10,000. 1990.
1676-10 Association of University Professors of Ophthalmology, Dallas, TX, $35,000. 1990.
1676-11 Association of University Professors of Ophthalmology, Dallas, TX, $35,000. 1990.
1676-12 Campbell University, School of Pharmacy, Buies Creek, NC, $20,000. 1990.
1676-13 Cleveland Clinic Foundation, Cleveland, OH, $25,000. 1990.
1676-14 Cleveland Clinic Foundation, Cleveland, OH, $25,000. 1990.
1676-15 Colorado State University, College of Veterinary Medicine, Fort Collins, CO, $42,000. 1990.
1676-16 Cornell University, New York State College of Veterinary Medicine, Ithaca, NY, $43,000. 1990.
1676-17 Dartmouth-Hitchcock Medical Center, Hanover, NH, $50,000. 1990.
1676-18 Duke University Medical Center, Durham, NC, $50,000. 1990.
1676-19 Florida A & M University, College of Pharmacy and Pharmaceutical Sciences, Tallahassee, FL, $16,000. 1990.
1676-20 Harvard University, Medical School, Boston, MA, $100,000. 1990.
1676-21 Harvard University, School of Public Health, Boston, MA, $20,000. 1990.
1676-22 Hunterdon Medical Center, Flemington, NJ, $20,000. 1990.
1676-23 Institute for Evaluating Health Risks, San Francisco, CA, $25,000. 1990.
1676-24 International Stroke Foundation, Scottsdale, AZ, $18,000. 1990.
1676-25 Iowa State University of Science and Technology, College of Veterinary Medicine, Ames, IA, $45,000. 1990.
1676-26 Johns Hopkins Hospital, Baltimore, MD, $60,000. 1990.
1676-27 Johns Hopkins University, School of Medicine, Baltimore, MD, $100,000. 1990.

1676-28 Massachusetts General Hospital, Boston, MA, $250,000. 1990.
1676-29 Massachusetts Health Data Consortium, Waltham, MA, $12,000. 1990.
1676-30 Mayo Foundation, Rochester, MN, $60,000. 1990.
1676-31 Mayo Foundation, Rochester, MN, $36,500. 1990.
1676-32 Mayo Foundation, Rochester, MN, $36,500. 1990.
1676-33 Media-Advertising Partnership for a Drug-Free America, NYC, NY, $25,000. 1990.
1676-34 Medical University of South Carolina, Charleston, SC, $25,000. 1990.
1676-35 Medical University of South Carolina, Charleston, SC, $25,000. 1990.
1676-36 Meharry Medical College, Nashville, TN, $16,000. 1990.
1676-37 Mercer University, School of Medicine, Macon, GA, $15,000. 1990.
1676-38 Muhlenberg Regional Medical Center, Plainfield, NJ, $10,000. 1990.
1676-39 Muhlenberg Regional Medical Center, Plainfield, NJ, $10,000. 1990.
1676-40 National Academy of Sciences, Institute of Medicine, DC, $25,000. 1990.
1676-41 National Fund for Medical Education, Boston, MA, $30,000. 1990.
1676-42 National Womens Health Resource Center, DC, $15,000. 1990.
1676-43 New York University Medical Center, NYC, NY, $37,500. 1990.
1676-44 Ohio State University, College of Pharmacy, Columbus, OH, $22,500. 1990.
1676-45 Ohio State University, College of Veterinary Medicine, Columbus, OH, $44,000. 1990.
1676-46 Oregon Health Sciences University, Portland, OR, $16,000. 1990.
1676-47 Pharmaceutical Manufacturers Association Foundation, DC, $165,000. 1990.
1676-48 Purdue University, School of Pharmacy, West Lafayette, IN, $50,000. 1990.
1676-49 Rahway First Aid Emergency Squad, Rahway, NJ, $10,000. 1990.
1676-50 Rockefeller University, NYC, NY, $200,000. 1990.
1676-51 Saint Barnabas Medical Center, Livingston, NJ, $10,000. 1990.
1676-52 Saint Louis College of Pharmacy, Saint Louis, MO, $10,000. 1990.
1676-53 Stanley J. Sarnoff Fellowships for Cardiovascular Science, Bethesda, MD, $30,000. 1990.
1676-54 Student Osteopathic Medical Association, Philadelphia, PA, $15,000. 1990.
1676-55 Texas A & M University, College of Veterinary Medicine, College Station, TX, $30,300. 1990.
1676-56 Tuskegee University, School of Veterinary Medicine, Tuskegee, AL, $16,000. 1990.
1676-57 University of California, School of Veterinary Medicine, Davis, CA, $46,000. 1990.
1676-58 University of Colorado, School of Pharmacy, Boulder, CO, $10,000. 1990.
1676-59 University of Florida, College of Pharmacy, Gainesville, FL, $20,000. 1990.
1676-60 University of Illinois, College of Veterinary Medicine, Urbana, IL, $26,200. 1990.

1676-61 University of Illinois, College of Veterinary Medicine, Urbana, IL, $19,920. 1990.

1676-62 University of Medicine and Dentistry of New Jersey-University Hospital, Newark, NJ, $25,000. 1990.

1676-63 University of Medicine and Dentistry of New Jersey, Eye Institute of New Jersey, Newark, NJ, $10,000. 1990.

1676-64 University of Michigan, College of Pharmacy, Ann Arbor, MI, $50,000. 1990.

1676-65 University of Michigan, Medical School, Ann Arbor, MI, $15,000. 1990.

1676-66 University of North Carolina, School of Pharmacy, Chapel Hill, NC, $24,000. 1990.

1676-67 University of Pennsylvania, Leonard Davis Institute of Health Economics, Philadelphia, PA, $150,000. 1990.

1676-68 University of Pennsylvania, Leonard Davis Institute of Health Economics, Philadelphia, PA, $30,000. 1990.

1676-69 University of Pennsylvania, School of Veterinary Medicine, Kennett Square, PA, $29,370. 1990.

1676-70 University of Pittsburgh, School of Pharmacy, Pittsburgh, PA, $30,000. 1990.

1676-71 University of Southern California, College of Pharmacy, Los Angeles, CA, $20,000. 1990.

1676-72 University of Texas, College of Pharmacy, Austin, TX, $25,000. 1990.

1676-73 University of Texas Southwestern Medical Center, Dallas, TX, $100,000. 1990.

1676-74 University of Toledo, College of Pharmacy, Toledo, OH, $32,000. 1990.

1676-75 University of Washington, School of Pharmacy, Seattle, WA, $25,000. 1990.

1676-76 Virginia Commonwealth University, Medical College of Virginia, Richmond, VA, $20,000. 1990.

1676-77 Washington University, School of Medicine, Saint Louis, MO, $25,000. 1990.

1676-78 Wayne State University, College of Pharmacy, Detroit, MI, $14,500. 1990.

1676-79 West Virginia University, School of Pharmacy, Morgantown, WV, $12,000. 1990.

1677
Merck Family Fund

c/o Schumann, Hanlon, O'Connor & McCrossin
30 Montgomery St.
Jersey City 07302
Application address: P.O. Box 999, Charleston, SC 29402-0999; Tel.: (803) 722-3400

Incorporated in 1954 in NJ.
Donor(s): Members of the Merck family.
Foundation type: Independent
Financial data (yr. ended 12/31/91): Assets, $32,314,670 (M); expenditures, $1,036,413; qualifying distributions, $945,679, including $930,000 for 29 grants (high: $148,500; low: $5,000).
Purpose and activities: Grants largely for conservation, arts and culture, social services, and health associations, including hospitals; support also for education.
Fields of interest: Conservation, arts, cultural programs, social services, health associations, hospitals, medical research, handicapped, mental health, higher education, secondary education.
Types of support: Seed money, special projects.

Limitations: No grants to individuals; no loans.
Publications: Annual report, application guidelines.
Application information: Application form not required.
> *Initial approach:* Letter
> *Deadline(s):* Sept. 1
> *Board meeting date(s):* May and Oct.
> *Final notification:* Nov. 30
> *Write:* Antony M. Merck, Pres.
Officers and Trustees:* Antony M. Merck,* Pres.; Patience M. Chamberlin,* V.P.; Francis W. Hatch III,* Secy.; Wilhelm M. Merck, Treas.; Sharman B. Altshuler, Albert W. Merck, Jr., Josephine A. Merck, Anne Merck-Abeles.
Number of staff: 1 part-time support.
EIN: 226063382

1678
Aaron and Rachel Meyer Memorial Foundation, Inc.

c/o Mortenson & Assocs.
340 North Ave.
Cranford 07016   (908) 272-7000

Incorporated in 1964 in NJ.
Donor(s): Bertram Meyer.‡
Foundation type: Independent
Financial data (yr. ended 03/31/91): Assets, $5,306,067 (M); expenditures, $383,495; qualifying distributions, $337,664, including $301,350 for 25 grants (high: $20,000; low: $500).
Purpose and activities: Grants largely for hospitals and health organizations, and youth agencies; also some support for education, welfare, and Jewish organizations.
Fields of interest: Hospitals, health, youth, education, welfare, Jewish giving.
Limitations: Giving primarily in Passaic County, NJ. No grants to individuals.
Publications: 990-PF.
Application information: Application form not required.
> *Deadline(s):* None
> *Board meeting date(s):* 7 or 8 times a year
> *Write:* Robert S. Mortenson, Dir.
Directors: Al Levine, Philip B. Lowy, Robert S. Mortenson, Ruth Samuels.
Number of staff: None.
EIN: 226063514

1679
Midlantic Corporate Giving Program

Metro Park Plaza
P.O. Box 600
Edison 08818   (908) 321-8000

Financial data (yr. ended 12/31/90): Total giving, $900,000 for grants.
Purpose and activities: Charitable giving is one way Midlantic lives up to its community responsibilities. Support for housing, education, health, and hospitals; also giving for benefits and other fundraisers.
Fields of interest: Housing, education, hospitals.
Types of support: Employee volunteer services, loaned talent.
Limitations: Giving limited to NJ.
Application information: Application form not required.

Initial approach: Letter
Write: Marshal Wolf, Exec. V.P., Opers.

1680
Mutual Benefit Life Insurance Company Giving Program

520 Broad St. 1 Rm. AO5N
Newark 07101   (201) 481-8441

Financial data (yr. ended 12/31/90): Total giving, $1,836,000 for grants.
Purpose and activities: Supports education, housing, recreation, and employment, AIDS programs, child development and youth, volunteerism, hospitals, health, and arts and culture, including museums, libraries, and public broadcasting. Organizations with employee involvement receive special consideration. Also supports programs concerning minorities, community development, environment and urban revitalization; support includes in-kind donations.
Fields of interest: Education, housing, child development, arts, minorities, employment, museums, libraries, community development, urban development, youth, volunteerism, hospitals, AIDS.
Types of support: General purposes, employee matching gifts, building funds, capital campaigns, special projects, operating budgets, technical assistance.
Limitations: Giving primarily in Newark, NJ (eastern home office) and Kansas City, MO (western home office). No support for religious organizations for sectarian purposes or political organizations. No grants to individuals.
Application information:
> *Initial approach:* Brief letter and proposal
> *Deadline(s):* Submit by July 31 for consideration in the next year's budget
> *Board meeting date(s):* Quarterly
> *Final notification:* 12 weeks
> *Write:* Samuel M. Convissor, V.P., Govt. and Public Affairs
Administrators: Betty Lee Haggerty, Marilyn M. Jones.

1681
Nabisco Brands Corporate Giving Program

Seven Campus Dr.
Parsippany 07054   (201) 682-7098

Purpose and activities: Supports civic programs, cultural institutes, economic development, federated campaigns, fine arts institutes, general education, international groups, medical research, minority programs, music, scholarships, urban problems and women's issues; also gives products mainly to the Second Harvest Food Bank. The company does some promotional advertising for nonprofits and has employee volunteer programs.
Fields of interest: Civic affairs, cultural programs, economics, fine arts, education, international affairs, medical research, minorities, music, urban development, women.
Types of support: Employee volunteer services, donated products.
Limitations: Giving primarily in areas where the parent company maintains operating facilities; company will consider some national programs for funding.

Application information: Application form not required.

Initial approach: Brief letter or proposal
Deadline(s): Applications accepted throughout the year
Board meeting date(s): As needed
Write: Henry A. Sandbach, V.P., Public Rels.

1682
Nabisco Foundation ▼

(also known as The National Biscuit Company Foundation Trust)
Nabisco Brands Plaza
Parsippany 07054   (201) 682-7098

Incorporated in 1953 in NJ.
Donor(s): Nabisco Brands, Inc.
Foundation type: Company-sponsored
Financial data (yr. ended 12/31/90): Assets, $11,499,585 (M); expenditures, $2,905,330; qualifying distributions, $2,806,424, including $2,090,880 for 78 grants (high: $1,000,000; low: $1,000; average: $1,000-$10,000) and $715,544 for employee matching gifts.
Purpose and activities: Giving largely for higher education and united funds; support also for education, the aged, handicapped, the homeless, hospitals, youth agencies, and cultural programs, including the performing arts.
Fields of interest: Higher education, community funds, hospitals, cultural programs, performing arts, youth, aged, education, elementary education, literacy, handicapped, health, homeless, hunger.
Types of support: Building funds, scholarship funds, employee matching gifts, capital campaigns, emergency funds, employee-related scholarships.
Limitations: No grants to individuals.
Application information: Application form not required.

Copies of proposal: 1
Deadline(s): None
Board meeting date(s): As needed
Final notification: Varies
Write: Henry A. Sandbach, V.P., Public Relations
Administrative Committee: John F. Manfredi, Sr. V.P., Corp. Affairs; Henry A. Sandbach, V.P., Public Relations; Robert K. DeVries.
Trustee: Bankers Trust Co.
EIN: 136042595

1683
National Starch and Chemical Foundation, Inc. ▼

Ten Finderne Ave.
Bridgewater 08807   (908) 685-5201
Scholarship application address: Charles Jacot, National Merit Scholarship Corp., One American Plaza, Evanston, IL 60621; Tel.: (312) 866-5118

Incorporated in 1968 in NY.
Donor(s): National Starch & Chemical Corp.
Foundation type: Company-sponsored
Financial data (yr. ended 12/31/90): Assets, $861,188 (M); gifts received, $1,670,000; expenditures, $1,733,158; qualifying distributions, $1,634,834, including $1,608,961 for 355 grants (high: $50,000; low: $26; average:

$200-$5,000) and $25,873 for 103 employee matching gifts.
Purpose and activities: Giving for higher education, hospitals, community funds, and youth agencies; employee-related scholarships disbursed through National Merit Scholarship Corp.
Fields of interest: Higher education, hospitals, community funds, youth.
Types of support: Employee-related scholarships, employee matching gifts.
Limitations: Giving primarily in areas of company operations.
Application information:
Deadline(s): Dec. 31 for scholarships
Write: Mary Gagliardi
Officers and Directors:* J.B Doherty,* Chair.; R.B. Hennessey,* Pres.; H.J. Baumgarten, Secy.; D.L.E. Jones,* Treas.; James A. Kennedy, W.H. Powell, W.F. Schlauch.
EIN: 237010264

1684
Community Foundation of New Jersey

P.O. Box 317
Knox Hill Rd.
Morristown 07963-0317   (201) 267-5533

Incorporated in 1979 in NJ.
Foundation type: Community
Financial data (yr. ended 06/30/91): Assets, $8,594,748 (M); gifts received, $1,800,249; expenditures, $1,046,224; qualifying distributions, $744,974, including $744,974 for 180 grants (high: $85,000; low: $25).
Purpose and activities: Support "for innovative programs which can exert a multiplier effect or which through research may contribute to the solution or easing of important community problems."
Fields of interest: Education, health, AIDS, social services, arts, community development, leadership development, conservation, urban affairs, family services.
Types of support: Seed money, matching funds, technical assistance, special projects, program-related investments.
Limitations: Giving limited to NJ. No support for sectarian religious programs. No grants for capital or endowment funds, operating budgets, continuing support, annual campaigns, emergency funds, or deficit financing.
Publications: Annual report, application guidelines, newsletter, informational brochure.
Application information: Application form required.
Initial approach: Telephone
Copies of proposal: 1
Board meeting date(s): 4 times per year
Write: Sheila C. Williamson, Exec. Dir.
Officers and Trustees:* Christine Todd Whitman,* Pres.; Richard W. Roper,* V.P; Brenda W. Davis,* Secy.; John P. Quinn,* Treas.; Sheila C. Williamson, Exec. Dir.; Theodore L. Boyer, John B. Brescher, Hon. Brenden Byrne, Raymond G. Chambers, Timothy E. Felge, William S. Ford, Jr., Joseph S. Frelinghuysen, Jr., Aristides Georgantas, Hazel Gluck, Craig P. Heard, John L. Kidde, Gwendolyn I. Long, Warren Lummis, Jr., John D. Mack, Robert C. Neff, Robert B. O'Brien, John A. Piraneo, E. Burke Ross, Jr., Lawrence J. Schoenberg, Adrian Shelby.

Number of staff: 2 full-time professional; 1 part-time professional; 2 part-time support.
EIN: 222281783
Recent health grants:
1684-1 AIDS Coalition of Southern New Jersey, Camden, NJ, $15,600. To provide five support groups in three counties for HIV infected people. 1991.
1684-2 AIDS Resource Foundation for Children, Newark, NJ, $10,500. For residential camp for HIV positive children, their families and caregivers, and ARF staff and volunteers. 1991.
1684-3 American Red Cross, Cape May, NJ, $10,000. To hire coordinator to assist with community AIDS education outreach in target areas and establish network of AIDS providers. 1991.
1684-4 American Red Cross, Essex Chapter, East Orange, NJ, $20,000. To establish AIDS and HIV Education Posts within welfare hotels in Essex and Passaic Counties. 1991.
1684-5 Caribbean Haitian Council, East Orange, NJ, $10,000. For monthly one-half hour AIDS educational programs in Creole on three radio stations hosted by Haitian-American health professionals. 1991.
1684-6 Casa Prac, Vineland, NJ, $10,000. To recruit and train fifteen Hispanic teen peer leaders to disseminate AIDS education information. 1991.
1684-7 Choices, Newark, NJ, $17,000. For expansion of HIV/AIDS preventive education and counseling to women and their families recovering from drug and alcohol addiction. 1991.
1684-8 Comite de Apoyo a los Trabajadores Agricolas (CATA), Glassboro, NJ, $20,000. To provide AIDS educational programs, testing and counseling in migrant camps during farm season, in community during off season and in migrant health clinics. 1991.
1684-9 Family Planning Services of Cumberland, Gloucester and Salem Counties, Bridgeton, NJ, $11,300. To identify high-risk teens in 15 social service and juvenile agencies and provide these teens with AIDS education sessions. 1991.
1684-10 Family Service Bureau of Newark, Newark, NJ, $15,000. To establish two support groups, one for children orphaned by AIDS or with ill parent, the other for their care givers. 1991.
1684-11 Hyacinth Foundation, New Brunswick, NJ, $10,000. For position of Director of Volunteers and Training begun in first Partnership grant cycle. 1991.
1684-12 Jersey City Medical Center, AIDS Health Services, Jersey City, NJ, $10,000. For assessment coordinator to identify high-risk patients who will educate patients and refer them for counseling, testing and treatment. 1991.
1684-13 Joint Connection, Newark, NJ, $13,000. For HIV/AIDS information activities on buses taking inmates' families and friends for visits at state prisons. 1991.
1684-14 New Jersey Association on Correction, Trenton, NJ, $17,600. To fund three-agency outreach programs to educate women at high risk of HIV and refer them to coordinating agencies and also host two support groups in Perth Amboy and New Brunswick. 1991.

1684-15 New Jersey Women and AIDS Network, New Brunswick, NJ, $12,500. For coordinator for newly incorporated group devoted to problems of women and AIDS throughout State and to publish educational and advocacy newsletter. 1991.

1684-16 South Jersey AIDS Alliance, Atlantic City, NJ, $15,000. For case manager in Atlantic County to assist HIV infected individuals through support groups, referrals and education. 1991.

1684-17 Special Audiences, Newark, NJ, $15,000. For production and trouping of orginal AIDS education play written and performed by teens from Newark school system. 1991.

1684-18 United Family and Childrens Society, Plainfield, NJ, $20,000. To initiate weekly support groups for people living with AIDS and their caregivers. 1991.

1684-19 Westside AIDS Project, Redbank, NJ, $15,000. For expansion of HIV/AIDS prevention, education and outreach program in Long Branch. 1991.

1684-20 Women Aware, New Brunswick, NJ, $13,300. To produce AIDS training manual and provide technical assistance and intensive education to domestic violence centers in state. 1991.

1685
New Jersey Resources Foundation, Inc.
P.O. Box 1468
Wall 07719
Application address: P.O. Box 1464, Wall, NJ 07719; Tel.: (201) 938-1114

Established in 1987 in NJ.
Donor(s): New Jersey Resources Corp., and its affiliated companies.
Foundation type: Company-sponsored
Financial data (yr. ended 09/30/91): Assets, $119,834 (M); gifts received, $279,190; expenditures, $227,591; qualifying distributions, $227,591, including $227,591 for grants.
Purpose and activities: Support mainly for civic affairs, health, and human services; grants were given for fundraising, dinners, sponsorship of events, and advertisements.
Fields of interest: Civic affairs, social services, health, hospitals, education.
Limitations: Giving limited to NJ.
Application information:
Initial approach: Letter
Deadline(s): None
Write: Tom Kononowitz, V.P.
Officers and Trustees:* Oliver G. Richard III,* Pres.; Thomas J. Kononowitz, V.P.; Oleta J. Harden, Secy.; Lawrence M. Downes, Treas.; James M. Bollerman, Philip H. Reardon.
EIN: 222835065

1686
George A. Ohl, Jr. Trust
c/o First Fidelity Bank, N.A., NJ; Philanthropic Services Group
765 Broad St.
Newark 07102   (201) 430-4533

Trust established in 1947 in NJ.
Donor(s): George A. Ohl, Jr.‡

Foundation type: Independent
Financial data (yr. ended 12/31/91): Assets, $4,041,233 (M); expenditures, $218,804; qualifying distributions, $179,756, including $179,756 for 25 grants (high: $15,000; low: $1,000; average: $1,000-$20,000).
Purpose and activities: Giving primarily for hospitals, hospital building funds, medical research, and health organizations to improve and expand health care services; start-up or program support for unique projects that complement the educational system at the secondary school level and promote youth development with emphasis on inner-city youth and recreational activities; human service activities that provide care for the elderly, the economically disadvantaged and the homeless.
Fields of interest: Hospitals, health, medical research, secondary education, youth, recreation, social services, aged, disadvantaged, homeless.
Types of support: Seed money, equipment, research, capital campaigns, renovation projects, special projects.
Limitations: Giving limited to NJ. No grants to individuals, or for endowment funds or general operating support; no loans.
Publications: Application guidelines.
Application information: Application form not required.
Initial approach: Proposal
Copies of proposal: 1
Deadline(s): Feb. 1 and Aug. 1
Board meeting date(s): Mar. and Sept.
Final notification: 1 month after board meets
Write: James S. Hohn, Asst. V.P., First Fidelity Bank, N.A., NJ
Trustee: First Fidelity Bank, N.A., NJ.
EIN: 226024900

1687
Henry and Carolyn Sue Orenstein Foundation, Inc.
1140 Bloomfield Ave.
West Caldwell 07006-7126   (201) 882-9488

Established in 1986 in NJ.
Donor(s): Henry Orenstein, Carolyn Sue Orenstein.
Foundation type: Independent
Financial data (yr. ended 12/31/90): Assets, $24,759 (M); gifts received, $138,107; expenditures, $680,079; qualifying distributions, $679,690, including $679,681 for 11 grants (high: $618,881; low: $200).
Purpose and activities: Grants primarily for Jewish organizations, including support for elderly survivors of the Holocaust and educational activities; giving also for medical research.
Fields of interest: Jewish giving, educational associations, medical research.
Limitations: Giving primarily in New York, NY. No grants to individuals.
Application information: Contributes only to pre-selected organizations. Applications not accepted.
Write: Henry Orenstein, Trustee
Trustees: Carolyn Sue Orenstein, Frederick Orenstein, Henry Orenstein.
EIN: 222806030

1688
The Maurice Pate Institute for Human Survival
100 Watchtower Rd.
Denville 07834
Application address: 30 Putnam Rd., West Redding, CT 06896

Established in 1984 in NY.
Foundation type: Independent
Financial data (yr. ended 06/30/91): Assets, $3,297,760 (M); gifts received, $1,100; expenditures, $147,688; qualifying distributions, $146,057, including $26,712 for 3 grants (high: $18,257; low: $1,000).
Purpose and activities: Giving for "promoting peace and the survival of the nation."
Fields of interest: Peace, public policy, health.
Types of support: Conferences and seminars, publications.
Application information: Application form not required.
Deadline(s): None
Write: Joan Dydo, Pres.
Officers: Joan Dydo, Pres.; Dale S. Dydo, V.P.
Directors: Ruth S. Cohen, Robert F. Drinan, Joan Bel Geddes, Alvin Ruml, V. Tarzie Vittachi.
EIN: 112687491

1689
Petrie Foundation
70 Enterprise Ave.
Secaucus 07094-2567

Established in 1945 in NJ.
Donor(s): Milton Petrie.
Foundation type: Independent
Financial data (yr. ended 12/31/90): Assets, $76,292 (M); gifts received, $196,000; expenditures, $276,666; qualifying distributions, $275,825, including $275,775 for 88 grants (high: $20,000; low: $50).
Purpose and activities: Giving primarily for cultural programs, including museums, the performing arts, a historic preservation group, and intercultural institutions; support also for hospitals and health services, including physical rehabilitation.
Fields of interest: Cultural programs, museums, performing arts, historic preservation, intercultural relations, hospitals, health services, rehabilitation.
Limitations: Giving primarily in New York, NY.
Application information: Application form not required.
Deadline(s): None
Write: Milton Petrie, Dir.
Officers and Directors:* Joseph Flom,* V.P.; Bernard Petrie,* V.P.; Peter Left, Secy.-Treas.; H. Kirschenbaum Gerstein, Milton Petrie, D. Fink Stern.
EIN: 136108716

1690
Lucile and Maurice Pollak Fund
P.O. Box 398
West Long Branch 07764

Established in 1961 in NJ.
Donor(s): Maurice Pollak,‡ Lucile R. Pollak.‡
Foundation type: Independent

Financial data (yr. ended 12/31/91): Assets, $2,561,627 (M); gifts received, $395,881; expenditures, $116,399; qualifying distributions, $95,321, including $94,500 for 70 grants (high: $10,000; low: $300).

Purpose and activities: Giving in areas of special social concern, including higher education, Jewish organizations, health, and youth.

Fields of interest: Higher education, Jewish giving, health, youth.

Types of support: Building funds, seed money, special projects, equipment.

Limitations: Giving primarily in metropolitan New York and Westchester County, NY, and Monmouth County, NJ. No grants to individuals; no loans.

Application information: Giving primarily to pre-selected organizations in NY and NJ.

Initial approach: Letter with brief description of program
Deadline(s): None
Write: Henry Pollak II, Pres.

Officers and Directors:* Henry Pollak II,* Pres.; Lois P. Broder,* V.P.; Jean deB. Pollak,* Secy.; Marvin K. Broder,* Treas.; Thomas Pollak, William Pollak, Peter Stern, Peggy Wallach.

Number of staff: 1 part-time professional; 1 part-time support.

EIN: 226051671

1691
The Prudential Foundation ▼

Prudential Plaza
751 Broad St.
Newark 07102-3777   (201) 802-7354

Incorporated in 1977 in NJ.

Donor(s): Prudential Insurance Co. of America, Prudential Property & Casualty Co.

Foundation type: Company-sponsored

Financial data (yr. ended 12/31/91): Assets, $124,174,000 (M); expenditures, $15,918,000; qualifying distributions, $15,718,412, including $13,693,117 for 718 grants (high: $333,000; low: $1,000; average: $10,000-$75,000) and $2,025,295 for employee matching gifts.

Purpose and activities: Program interests include education, business and civic affairs, urban and community affairs, health and human services, including AIDS programs, arts and culture, and focus on children; support also for United Way drives in areas of company operations and matching gifts to education programs.

Fields of interest: Education, education—minorities, cultural programs, arts, civic affairs, urban affairs, minorities, community development, social services, public affairs, AIDS, health, health services, child development, homeless, urban development, youth, community funds.

Types of support: Operating budgets, continuing support, annual campaigns, seed money, emergency funds, equipment, matching funds, employee matching gifts, consulting services, technical assistance, employee-related scholarships, special projects, conferences and seminars, general purposes.

Limitations: Giving primarily in areas of company operations, especially Newark, NJ, and in CA, FL, MN, and PA. No support for labor, religious or athletic groups, or general operating funds for single-disease health organizations. No grants to individuals, or for endowment funds; no loans.

Publications: Annual report (including application guidelines).

Application information: Application form required.

Initial approach: Letter with brief description of program to determine eligibility and appropriate application form to complete
Copies of proposal: 1
Deadline(s): None
Board meeting date(s): Apr., Aug., and Dec.
Final notification: 4 to 6 weeks
Write: Deborah J. Gingher, V.P. and Secy.

Officers and Trustees:* William H. Tremayne,* Chair.; Elizabeth W. Scovill,* Vice-Chair.; Peter B. Goldberg, Pres.; Deborah J. Gingher, V.P. and Secy.; Paul G. O'Leary, V.P.; Joanne Brown Lee, Treas.; Eugene M. O'Hara, Comptroller; Lisle C. Carter, Jr., Carolyne K. Davis, James R. Gillen, Jon F., Hanson, Donald E. Procknow, Robert C. Winters, Edward D. Zinbarg.

Number of staff: 8 full-time professional; 7 full-time support.

EIN: 222175290

Recent health grants:

1691-1 Advertising Council, Partnership for a Drug Free America, NYC, NY, $50,000. For anti-drug education campaign. 1990.

1691-2 AIDS Resource Foundation for Children, Newark, NJ, $55,000. For staff development and medical care and housing for children with AIDS. 1990.

1691-3 AIDS Treatment Registry, NYC, NY, $10,000. For publications on clinical drug trials available in tri-state area. 1990.

1691-4 American Cancer Society, Jacksonville, FL, $10,000. For education and direct services in northeast Florida. 1990.

1691-5 American Foundation for AIDS Research, NYC, NY, $60,000. For AIDS-prevention education grants program and communications network. 1990.

1691-6 Association for Children of New Jersey, Invest in Children Coalition, Newark, NJ, $60,000. For funding for agencies delivering Women, Infants and Children (WIC) program in NJ, which ensures that low-income pregnant women, infants and children have access to prenatal and medical care, nutrition counseling and supplemental food programs. 1990.

1691-7 Boys and Girls Clubs of Newark, Broadway Unit, Newark, NJ, $25,000. For Smart Moves health education project. 1990.

1691-8 California Health Decisions, Orange, CA, $40,000. For staff expansion. 1990.

1691-9 Cathedral Healthcare System, Newark, NJ, $100,000. For AIDS services for women and children. Grant shared with Saint Michael's Medical Center. 1990.

1691-10 Center for Nonprofit Corporations, Princeton, NJ, $30,000. For self-insurance fund for employees of New Jersey nonprofits. 1990.

1691-11 Child Welfare League of America, DC, $10,000. For training program for pediatric AIDS caregivers. 1990.

1691-12 Community Health Law Project, East Orange, NJ, $15,000. For advocacy project on equal access for disabled. 1990.

1691-13 Design Industries Foundation for AIDS (DIFFA), Heart Strings: The National Tour,

NYC, NY, $65,000. For general support and fund-raising tour for community-based AIDS service delivery organizations. 1990.

1691-14 Design Industries Foundation for AIDS (DIFFA), Heart Strings: The National Tour, NYC, NY, $28,000. For theatrical tour to raise funds for local AIDS service organizations. 1990.

1691-15 Hastings Center, Briarcliff Manor, NY, $20,000. For research and public policy information on biomedical ethics issues. 1990.

1691-16 Hyacinth Foundation, Highland Park, NJ, $36,000. For volunteer management and communication programs for AIDS caregivers. 1990.

1691-17 Industrywide Network for Social, Urban and Rural Efforts (INSURE), DC, $125,000. For insurance industry fund for AIDS programs. 1990.

1691-18 International Youth Organization, Newark, NJ, $10,000. For advocacy for people with AIDS in Newark, NJ. Grant shared with Newark Community Project for People with AIDS. 1990.

1691-19 Joint Connection, Newark, NJ, $10,000. For AIDS-prevention education and service referral project. 1990.

1691-20 Life and Health Insurance Medical Research Fund, DC, $10,000. For AIDS research. 1990.

1691-21 Memorial Sloan-Kettering Cancer Center, NYC, NY, $52,500. For cancer treatment and rehabilitation. 1990.

1691-22 National AIDS Network, DC, $50,000. For general support. 1990.

1691-23 National Association of People with AIDS (NAPWA), DC, $115,000. For local self-help coalitions of people with AIDS. 1990.

1691-24 National Center for Health Education, NYC, NY, $50,000. For national Hispanic health conference. 1990.

1691-25 National Commission to Prevent Infant Mortality, DC, $75,000. For national Health-Education Consortium. Grant shared with Institute for Educational Leadership. 1990.

1691-26 National Commission to Prevent Infant Mortality, DC, $75,000. For national Health-Education Consortium. Grant shared with Institute for Educational Leadership. 1990.

1691-27 National Committee for Quality Assurance, DC, $20,000. For development of HMO quality standards and accreditation. 1990.

1691-28 National Fund for Medical Education, Boston, MA, $30,000. For needs assessment of AIDS education programs to primary care practitioners. 1990.

1691-29 National Health Policy Forum, DC, $10,000. For policy studies on Medicare and Medicaid. 1990.

1691-30 Newark Beth Israel Medical Center, Newark, NJ, $40,000. For modernization of cardiac and neonatal units. 1990.

1691-31 Planned Parenthood of Essex County, Newark, NJ, $10,000. For basic health services for poor women in Newark. 1990.

1691-32 Protestant Community Centers, Newark, NJ, $10,000. For health and social services. 1990.

1691-33 Rutgers, The State University of New Jersey, Center of Alcohol Studies, New Brunswick, NJ, $44,700. For scholarships and technical assistance to alcohol abuse professionals. 1990.

1691-34 Special Audiences, Newark, NJ, $20,000. For AIDS-prevention education through Teen-To-Teen theater troupe. 1990.

1691-35 Stop AIDS Project, San Francisco, CA, $15,000. For national AIDS education resource center. 1990.

1691-36 University of Medicine and Dentistry of New Jersey, Newark, NJ, $70,000. For mobile pediatric health-care program. 1990.

1691-37 Womens Action Alliance, NYC, NY, $50,000. For general support and for women's centers and AIDS project. 1990.

1691-38 Youth Development Clinic of Newark, Newark, NJ, $48,000. For general support and Zero to Three therapeutic parenting program for teen mothers and infants. 1990.

1692
Public Service Enterprise Group, Inc. Contributions Program

80 Park Plaza
Newark 07001   (201) 430-7000

Financial data (yr. ended 12/31/90): Total giving, $2,552,000, including $2,360,000 for 515 grants (high: $326,000; low: $100; average: $500-$7,500) and $192,000 for 1,500 employee matching gifts.

Purpose and activities: "In addition to being responsive to customers, it is also essential today to be a good corporate citizen. This means working in partnership with state, county and local authorities and many other public and private organizations in ways that are beneficial to the interests of the state and its citizens, and consistent with company interests." Emphasis is on fostering economic development within NJ particularly in the service territory, collaborating with the state, local governments, the development community and others to retain business already there, attract new companies, rebuild the state's cities, promote affordable housing, and with transportation officials to encourage development of an adequate transportation infrastructure. Involvement can also include direct assistance in the form of company personnel serving as directors on the boards of civic organizations. In addition to ecomomic development, the company concentrates on children's issues, including education, drug awareness and child care; with an emphasis on public education. Efforts in the commmunity also include working with the educational establishment to help improve the skill levels of the current and future work forces. Environmental issues are also of interest.

Fields of interest: Education, higher education, youth, minorities, hospitals, community funds, civic affairs, environment, health, homeless, education—minorities, housing, disadvantaged, educational associations, literacy, performing arts, volunteerism, business education, child welfare, community development, drug abuse, education—building funds, hospitals—building funds, leadership development, cultural programs, education—early childhood, elementary education.

Types of support: Research, scholarship funds, donated equipment, donated products, use of facilities, loaned talent, employee volunteer

services, in-kind gifts, seed money, matching funds, capital campaigns.

Limitations: Giving primarily in in headquarters and company locations. No support for United Way recipients for capital needs only. No grants to individuals.

Publications: Corporate report.

Application information: Company has a staff that only handles contributions.

Initial approach: Letter or telephone call
Deadline(s): None
Write: Maria B. Pinho, Mgr., Corp. Contribs.

Administrators: Frederick R. De Santi, Robert S. Smith, Frederick W. Schneider, John H. Maddocks, Robert W. Lockwood, E. James Ferland.

Number of staff: 3 full-time professional; 2 part-time support.

1693
The Charles L. Read Foundation

374 Millburn Ave.
P.O. Box 599
Millburn 07041

Trust established in 1954 in NJ.
Donor(s): Charles L. Read.
Foundation type: Independent
Financial data (yr. ended 12/31/91): Assets, $2,984,734 (M); expenditures, $195,189; qualifying distributions, $183,364, including $149,150 for 89 grants (high: $18,750; low: $500).

Fields of interest: Education, hospitals, religious welfare.

Limitations: Giving primarily in NJ and NY. No grants to individuals.

Publications: Financial statement.

Application information: Contributes only to pre-selected organizations. Applications not accepted.

Officers: Fred Herrigel III, Pres.; Richard Eisenberg, V.P.; Rodger K. Herrigel, Secy.; Saul Eisenberg, Treas.

Number of staff: None.
EIN: 226053510

1694
The Reeves Foundation, Inc.

115 Summit Ave.
Summit 07901-2899   (201) 273-2312

Established in 1988 as successor foundation to The Reeves Brothers Foundation, Inc.
Donor(s): Margie Hall.
Foundation type: Independent
Financial data (yr. ended 06/30/91): Assets, $19,273,421 (M); gifts received, $32,158; expenditures, $1,068,831; qualifying distributions, $986,966, including $883,093 for 23 grants (high: $250,000; low: $500).

Fields of interest: Higher education, hospitals, medical research, youth.

Limitations: Giving on the East Coast, especially NJ and NY, and in the South, especially in SC and NC. No grants to individuals.

Application information: Application form not required.

Deadline(s): None
Write: Margie Hall

Officers: J.E. Reeves, Jr., Pres. and Treas.; Jeneil Reeves, V.P. and Secy.; Joseph Moore, V.P.
EIN: 581792933

1695
Fannie E. Rippel Foundation ▼

The Concourse at Beaver Brook
P.O. Box 569
Annandale 08801-0569   (908) 735-0990

Incorporated in 1953 in NJ.
Donor(s): Julius S. Rippel.‡
Foundation type: Independent
Financial data (yr. ended 04/30/92): Assets, $60,325,530 (M); expenditures, $4,791,812; qualifying distributions, $4,791,812, including $4,345,352 for 26 grants (high: $500,000; low: $29,423; average: $100,000-$200,000).

Purpose and activities: The foundation's activities are legally restricted to aid to hospitals, for treatment of and/or research concerning cancer or heart disease and for institutions maintained for the relief and care of aged women.

Fields of interest: Hospitals, medical research, heart disease, cancer.

Types of support: Equipment, research, renovation projects, special projects.

Limitations: Giving primarily in the Eastern Seaboard states, particularly NJ and New York, NY. No grants to individuals, or for general purposes, operating budgets, continuing support, annual campaigns, deficit financing, scholarships, fellowships, endowment or building funds, or matching gifts; no loans.

Publications: Annual report, application guidelines.

Application information: Application form not required.

Initial approach: Letter
Copies of proposal: 1
Deadline(s): None
Board meeting date(s): Approximately 6 times a year
Final notification: Varies
Write: Edward W. Probert, V.P. and Secy.

Officers and Trustees:* Eric R. Rippel,* Pres.; Edward W. Probert, V.P. and Secy.; Janet E. Luther, Treas.; Bruce N. Bensley, S. Jervis Brinton, Jr., G. Frederick Hockenjos, John L. Kidde.

Number of staff: 4 full-time professional; 1 full-time support.

EIN: 221559427

Recent health grants:

1695-1 Arizona State University, Cancer Research Institute, Tempe, AZ, $137,000. For operating costs of collecting and recollecting various marine animal specimens which may contain anticancer agents. 1992.

1695-2 Arizona State University, Cancer Research Institute, Tempe, AZ, $130,000. Toward operating costs of collecting and recollecting various marine animal specimens which may contain anticancer agents. 1992.

1695-3 Childrens Hospital, Boston, MA, $125,000. Toward first two years' research efforts to develop radiopharmaceutical imaging agent to improve diagnosis and management of brain tumors. 1992.

1695-4 Clara Maass Medical Center, Department of Surgery, Belleville, NJ, $114,250. Toward purchase of Candela LaserTripter. 1992.

1695-5 Cooper Hospital-University Medical Center, Medical Center Coronary Care Unit, Camden, NJ, $150,000. Toward cost of Full-Disclosure Arrhythmia System. 1992.

1695-6 Coriell Institute for Medical Research, Camden, NJ, $188,460. Toward cost of laboratory equipment for cellular and molecular investigations into cancer disease. 1992.

1695-7 Duke University Medical Center, Durham, NC, $225,000. Toward first year's equipment and personnel expense to establish Macromolecular Crystallography and Modeling Center. 1992.

1695-8 Intersearch Institute, Annandale, NJ, $500,000. Toward cost of operations, drug development and research program expenses. 1992.

1695-9 Jackson Laboratory, Bar Harbor, ME, $226,000. Toward cost of equipping four new breeding rooms. 1992.

1695-10 John F. Kennedy Medical Center, Edison, NJ, $150,000. Toward purchase of High Dose Remote Afterloader System in Brachytherapy for radiation oncology patients. 1992.

1695-11 Kennedy Memorial Hospitals-University Medical Center, Gerontology Center, Cherry Hill, NJ, $155,400. Toward establishing Medication Awareness Program (MAP). 1992.

1695-12 Riverview Medical Center, Red Bank, NJ, $125,000. Toward cost of establishing eight bed Step-Down Unit and upgrading of Center's Outpatient Department. 1992.

1695-13 Trudeau Institute, Saranac Lake, NY, $150,000. Toward purchase of fluorescence activated cell sorter (FACStar Plus) to study cells of immune system. 1992.

1695-14 Tufts University, School of Medicine, Medford, MA, $147,000. Toward purchase of instrumentation to be used in basic and clinical research being carried out at Protein Sequencing Core Facility in Department of Physiology. 1992.

1695-15 United Hospitals Medical Center, Newark, NJ, $125,000. Toward Echo Doppler and other related equipment needed to develop cardiac non-invasive laboratory. 1992.

1695-16 University of California, Medical Center, San Francisco, CA, $100,000. Toward continued studies concerning coronary artery disease and relative utility of different noninvasive cardiac imaging methods being carried out at Nuclear Medicine Section. 1992.

1696
Stanley & Elsie Roth Foundation, Inc.
64 Weiss Rd.
Upper Saddle River 07758
Application address: c/o Paul, Weiss, Rifkind, Wharton & Garrison, 1285 6th Ave., New York, NY 10154

Incorporated in 1974 in NJ.
Donor(s): Stanley Roth, Sr.‡
Foundation type: Independent
Financial data (yr. ended 12/31/91): Assets, $1,134,248 (M); expenditures, $273,013; qualifying distributions, $259,581, including $259,000 for 29 grants (high: $100,000; low: $240).

Fields of interest: Higher education, business education, Jewish giving, hospitals.
Limitations: No grants to individuals.
Publications: 990-PF.
Application information: Application form not required.
Initial approach: Letter
Deadline(s): Sept. 30
Final notification: Dec. 31
Write: Richard S. Borisoff, Esq., V.P.
Officers and Directors:* Stanley Roth, Jr.,* Pres.; Richard S. Borisoff,* V.P.; Robert Roth,* V.P.; Joseph S. Iseman,* Secy.-Treas.
Number of staff: None.
EIN: 237400784

1697
David and Eleanore Rukin Philanthropic Foundation
17 Franklin Tpke.
Mahwah 07430   (201) 529-3666

Established in 1951 in NJ.
Donor(s): David Rukin, Eleanore Rukin, Barnett Rukin, Susan Eisen.
Foundation type: Independent
Financial data (yr. ended 12/31/90): Assets, $2,039,442 (M); expenditures, $265,068; qualifying distributions, $245,713, including $245,713 for 71 grants (high: $95,000; low: $10).
Purpose and activities: Giving primarily for Jewish welfare and education; some support also for other education, health and hospitals, and culture.
Fields of interest: Jewish welfare, Jewish giving, religious schools, education, health, hospitals, cultural programs.
Application information: Application form not required.
Deadline(s): None
Write: Julius Eisen, Dir.
Directors: Julius Eisen, Susan Eisen, Barnett Rukin, Eleanore Rukin.
EIN: 221715380

1698
Rutgers Community Health Foundation, Inc.
P.O. Box 10766
New Brunswick 08906-0766   (908) 572-5428

Established in 1986 in NJ from proceeds of sale of the Rutgers Community Health Plan, Inc.
Foundation type: Independent
Financial data (yr. ended 06/30/91): Assets, $4,895,506 (M); expenditures, $343,446; qualifying distributions, $343,196, including $289,884 for 34 grants (high: $10,000; low: $1,900).
Purpose and activities: Support for nonprofit organizations whose primary purpose is either 1) innovative delivery of needed health care services, or 2) innovative thinking and original investigation which hold promise of leading to the improvement of health care; support also for projects and programs that are on the cutting edge of health care, especially ones that are unable or unlikely to receive sufficient funding from alternative sources and for which the foundation's support will make a critical difference.

Fields of interest: Health, health services.
Types of support: Seed money.
Limitations: Giving limited to NJ, with emphasis on Central NJ. No grants to individuals.
Publications: Annual report, application guidelines.
Application information: Application form required.
Initial approach: Letter or telephone
Copies of proposal: 4
Deadline(s): Jan. 31
Board meeting date(s): Quarterly
Final notification: June 30
Write: Ann P. Parelius, Ph.D., Exec. Dir.
Officers and Trustees:* Nadine B. Shanler,* Pres.; Gary M. Gorran,* V.P. and Treas.; Robert H. Bierman, M.D.,* Secy.; Ann P. Parelius,* Exec. Dir.; Roger W. Birnbaum, Samuel H. Davis, Ivette Del Rio, David Harris, Robert G. Hughes, Ph.D., Judith M. Stern.
Number of staff: 1 part-time professional.
EIN: 222847302

1699
The Sandy Hill Foundation ▼
c/o Wesray Corp.
330 South St., CN 1975
Morristown 07960   (201) 540-9020

Incorporated in 1985 in NJ.
Donor(s): Frank E. Walsh, Jr.
Foundation type: Independent
Financial data (yr. ended 07/31/90): Assets, $11,591,114 (M); gifts received, $1,828,750; expenditures, $1,376,050; qualifying distributions, $1,175,789, including $1,170,955 for 76 grants (high: $210,000; low: $500; average: $1,000-$50,000).
Fields of interest: Education, higher education, social services.
Limitations: Giving primarily in NY, NJ, and PA.
Application information: Application form not required.
Deadline(s): None
Write: Rose Sciacca
Officers and Directors:* Frank E. Walsh, Jr.,* Pres.; Mary D. Walsh,* Secy.; Jeffrey R. Walsh, Mgr.
EIN: 222668774
Recent health grants:
1699-1 AIDS Resource Foundation for Children, Newark, NJ, $10,000. For general operating support. 1990.
1699-2 Morristown Memorial Hospital, A New Era of Excellence, Morristown, NJ, $20,000. For general operating support. 1990.
1699-3 Overlook Hospital Foundation, Summit, NJ, $10,000. For general operating expenses. 1990.
1699-4 Stop Cancer, Los Angeles, CA, $10,000. For general operating support. 1990.
1699-5 University of Miami, Buoniconti Fund, Coral Gables, FL, $10,000. For general fund. 1990.
1699-6 University of Miami, Buoniconti Fund, Coral Gables, FL, $10,000. For general fund. 1990.

1700
The Milton Schamach Foundation, Inc.
810 Belmont Ave.
North Haledon 07508   (201) 423-9494

Incorporated in 1969 in NJ.
Donor(s): Milton Schamach.‡
Foundation type: Independent
Financial data (yr. ended 08/31/91): Assets, $2,604,197 (M); expenditures, $204,760; qualifying distributions, $172,670, including $172,670 for 30 grants (high: $25,000; low: $1,000).
Fields of interest: Hospitals, health services, medical research.
Types of support: Equipment, research.
Limitations: Giving primarily in NJ. No grants to individuals.
Application information: Application form not required.
> *Initial approach:* Letter
> *Deadline(s):* May 31
> *Board meeting date(s):* 3 or 4 times a year as required
> *Final notification:* 3 to 4 months
> *Write:* Jack Goodman, Secy.-Treas.
Officers and Trustees:* Gene Schamach,* Pres.; Jack Goodman,* Secy.-Treas.; Andrew E.R. Frommelt, Jr., Alvin Goodman, Jay Rubenstein, Howard Schamach, Rhoda Schamach, Robert Schamach.
Number of staff: 2
EIN: 237051147

1701
Schering-Plough Corporate Giving Program
Corporate Contributions
Schering Plough Corp.
Madison 07940-1000   (201) 822-7408

Financial data (yr. ended 12/31/90): Total giving, $1,000,000 for grants.
Purpose and activities: "Schering-Plough has long recognized that our success as a business enterprise depends upon the vitality of the society in which we do business. Doing well financially as a business and doing good in a social sense are not separate concerns. One is dependent upon the other and both are important to the health of the Company and the well-being of the community. The Company believes that community responsibility is part of every manager's job. The way we conduct our day-to-day business, and the civic leadership of our management, set the pace for our involvement in local activities." Giving figures represent corporate and divisional cash gifts, including employee support to the United Way.
Fields of interest: Civic affairs, education, medical research, cultural programs, fine arts, general charitable giving, minorities, music, rural development, science and technology, theater, welfare, women, youth, health, hospitals, Latin America, Europe, United Kingdom, France, Australia, international affairs, international relief.
Types of support: In-kind gifts, employee-related scholarships, employee volunteer services.
Limitations: Giving primarily in areas where corporate sponsor has major facilities in CA, FL, IL, NE, NJ, PR, TN, and TX; also abroad in Argentina, Australia, Austria, Canada, Columbia,

Ecuador, France, Ireland, the United Kingdom, Venezuela. No grants to individuals.
Publications: Corporate giving report.
Application information: Application form required.
> *Initial approach:* Letter to nearest facility manager
> *Deadline(s):* None
> *Write:* Joan Henderson, Mgr.

1702
Schering-Plough Foundation, Inc. ▼
One Giralda Farms
P.O. Box 1000
Madison 07940-1000   (201) 822-7412

Incorporated in 1955 in DE.
Donor(s): Schering Corp., The Plough Foundation, Schering-Plough Corp.
Foundation type: Company-sponsored
Financial data (yr. ended 12/31/90): Assets, $15,973,670 (M); expenditures, $2,798,026; qualifying distributions, $2,726,257, including $2,358,499 for 116 grants (high: $100,000; low: $1,000; average: $10,000-$25,000) and $367,758 for 1,039 employee matching gifts.
Purpose and activities: Primary objective is support of institutional activities devoted to improving the quality and delivery of health care, through medical and allied education. Selective support to higher education, hospitals, health care programs, and cultural organizations in those communities where the corporation has major facilities. Grants made both directly and through national granting groups. Matching gift plan includes accredited higher and secondary educational institutions, and hospitals.
Fields of interest: Hospitals, hospitals—building funds, biochemistry, science and technology, health services, medical education, education, higher education, education—building funds, education—minorities, educational associations, cultural programs, museums, performing arts, Caribbean, safety, environment.
Types of support: Employee matching gifts, annual campaigns, seed money, building funds, equipment, internships, fellowships, general purposes, professorships, continuing support, operating budgets, scholarship funds, capital campaigns, endowment funds, renovation projects, employee-related scholarships, special projects.
Limitations: Giving primarily in areas where corporate sponsor has major facilities, especially NJ and TN. No grants to individuals, or for deficit financing, publications, or conferences; no loans.
Publications: Corporate giving report (including application guidelines).
Application information: Application form not required.
> *Initial approach:* Letter
> *Copies of proposal:* 1
> *Deadline(s):* Feb. 1 and Sept. 1
> *Board meeting date(s):* Spring and Fall
> *Final notification:* 6 months
> *Write:* Rita Sacco, Asst. Secy.
Officers and Trustees:* Allan S. Kushen,* Pres.; Joseph S. Roth, Secy.; Jack Wyszomierski, Treas.; David E. Collins, Donald R. Conklin, Hugh A. D'Andrade, Harold R. Hiser, Jr., Richard J. Kogan, Robert P. Luciano.

Number of staff: 1 full-time professional; 1 part-time professional; 1 part-time support.
EIN: 221711047
Recent health grants:
1702-1 American Foundation for Pharmaceutical Education, North Plainfield, NJ, $10,000. 1990.
1702-2 American Paralysis Association, Springfield, NJ, $12,500. 1990.
1702-3 Cleveland Clinic Foundation, Cleveland, OH, $25,000. 1990.
1702-4 Elizabeth General Medical Center Foundation, Elizabeth, NJ, $10,000. 1990.
1702-5 Epilepsy Foundation of New Jersey, Trenton, NJ, $15,000. 1990.
1702-6 Foundation for Biomedical Research, DC, $25,000. 1990.
1702-7 Harvard University, Medical School, Boston, MA, $25,000. 1990.
1702-8 Massachusetts General Hospital, Boston, MA, $10,000. 1990.
1702-9 Morris 2000, Morristown, NJ, $10,000. To track long-term senior citizen health care needs. 1990.
1702-10 Morristown Memorial Hospital, Morristown, NJ, $50,000. 1990.
1702-11 National Fund for Medical Education, Boston, MA, $20,000. 1990.
1702-12 Occupational Physicians Scholarship Fund, NYC, NY, $10,000. 1990.
1702-13 Overlook Hospital Foundation, Summit, NJ, $50,000. 1990.
1702-14 Partnership for a Drug Free America, NYC, NY, $50,000. 1990.
1702-15 People-to-People Health Foundation, Project HOPE, Millwood, VA, $50,000. 1990.
1702-16 Pharmaceutical Manufacturers Association Foundation, DC, $60,000. 1990.
1702-17 Rutgers, The State University of New Jersey, College of Pharmacy, Piscataway, NJ, $100,000. 1990.
1702-18 Saint Barnabas Development Foundation, Livingston, NJ, $100,000. 1990.
1702-19 Saint Elizabeth Hospital, Elizabeth, NJ, $40,000. 1990.
1702-20 Tufts University, Center for the Study of Drug Development, Boston, MA, $15,000. 1990.
1702-21 University of Florida, College of Pharmacy, Gainesville, FL, $15,000. 1990.
1702-22 University of Kansas, School of Pharmacy, Lawrence, KS, $15,000. 1990.
1702-23 University of Medicine and Dentistry of New Jersey Foundation, Newark, NJ, $100,000. 1990.
1702-24 University of Michigan, College of Pharmacy, Ann Arbor, MI, $95,000. 1990.
1702-25 University of Minnesota, College of Pharmacy, Minneapolis, MN, $10,000. 1990.
1702-26 University of Tennessee, College of Pharmacy, Memphis, TN, $25,000. 1990.
1702-27 University of Texas, College of Pharmacy, Austin, TX, $15,000. 1990.
1702-28 University of Wisconsin, School of Pharmacy, Madison, WI, $15,000. 1990.
1702-29 Urban Foundation U.S.A., NYC, NY, $10,000. For Tembisa Hospital Clinic. 1990.
1702-30 Yale University, School of Medicine, New Haven, CT, $25,000. 1990.

1703
The Schimmel Foundation, Inc.
c/o J.H. Cohn
75 Eisenhower Pkwy.
Roseland 07068

Established in 1990 in FL as a successor to the Schimmel Foundation.
Donor(s): Nobert Schimmel Grantor Trust.
Foundation type: Independent
Financial data (yr. ended 12/31/91): Assets, $4,845,640 (M); expenditures, $234,814; qualifying distributions, $135,824, including $101,600 for 5 grants (high: $40,000; low: $5,000).
Fields of interest: Museums, hospitals, religion.
Limitations: Giving primarily in Israel and the U.S. No grants to individuals.
Application information: Contributes only to pre-selected organizations. Applications not accepted.
Officers and Trustees:* Stephen B. Schimmel,* Pres.; Alan K. Bloom,* Secy.; Daniel Brooks.
EIN: 650170821

1704
The Schultz Foundation
1037 Route 46 East, Suite 207
Clifton 07013   (201) 614-8880

Incorporated in 1966 in DE; merged in 1987 with The William Lightfoot Schultz Foundation, which was incorporated in 1952.
Donor(s): Mabel L. Schultz,‡ and other members of the Schultz family.
Foundation type: Independent
Financial data (yr. ended 06/30/91): Assets, $18,594,720 (M); gifts received, $7,703; expenditures, $788,187; qualifying distributions, $748,159, including $673,564 for 41 grants (high: $100,000; low: $200; average: $100–$151,164).
Fields of interest: Medical research, drug abuse, hospices.
Types of support: General purposes, operating budgets, continuing support, seed money, building funds, matching funds, scholarship funds, internships, fellowships, research, special projects.
Limitations: Giving primarily in north central NJ. No grants to individuals, or for endowment funds, deficit financing, equipment, or land acquisition; no loans.
Application information: Application form not required.
   Initial approach: Telephone or letter
   Copies of proposal: 1
   Deadline(s): None
   Board meeting date(s): Board meets upon call
   Final notification: within 6 months
   Write: William L.S. Rigg, Exec. Dir.
Officers and Trustees:* George L. Schultz,* Pres. and Treas.; William L.S. Rigg,* V.P.; Margaret F. Schultz,* Secy.; John K. Bangs, John Barker, Margaret Schultz Bilotti, Marilyn Schultz Blackwell, Katharine Schultz Fieldhouse, Douglas C. Rigg, Elizabeth Schultz Rigg, Geoffrey B. Rigg, Elizabeth Schultz Vanderlinde.
Number of staff: 1 part-time professional; 1 part-time support.
EIN: 226103387

1705
The Schumann Fund for New Jersey, Inc.
33 Park St.
Montclair 07042   (201) 509-9883

Established in 1988 in NJ.
Donor(s): Florence and John Schumann Foundation.
Foundation type: Independent
Financial data (yr. ended 12/31/91): Assets, $21,099,234 (M); expenditures, $1,419,067; qualifying distributions, $1,193,111, including $1,193,111 for 66 grants.
Purpose and activities: Support primarily for 1) Early Childhood Development; 2) Environmental Protection; 3) Public Policy; and 4) local activities directed at solving community problems within Essex County, with emphasis on social services, children, and education.
Fields of interest: Education—early childhood, environment, conservation, public policy, social services, child welfare, education.
Types of support: Seed money, operating budgets, special projects.
Limitations: Giving limited to NJ. No grants to individuals, or for capital campaigns, annual giving, or endowments.
Publications: Annual report.
Application information: Application form not required.
   Initial approach: Proposal
   Copies of proposal: 1
   Deadline(s): 6 weeks prior to board meeting: Jan. 15, Apr. 15, Aug. 15, and Oct. 15
   Board meeting date(s): Feb., June, Sept., and Dec.
   Final notification: 4 to 8 weeks
   Write: Julie A. Keenan, Exec. Dir.
Officers and Trustees:* George R. Harris,* Chair.; Leonard S. Coleman, Vice-Chair.; Aubin Z. Ames, Treas.; Julie A. Keenan, Exec. Dir.; Christopher J. Daggett, Barbara H. Malcolm, Alan Rosenthal, Donald M. Wilson.
Number of staff: 1 full-time professional; 1 full-time support.
EIN: 521556076
Recent health grants:
1705-1 University of Medicine and Dentistry of New Jersey Foundation, Newark, NJ, $60,000. For project, Early Childhood Development Training for Day Care Teachers in Newark, which trains teachers in 17 Newark child care centers to identify developmentally appropriate behavior in toddlers. 1990.
1705-2 Youth Development Clinic of Newark, Newark, NJ, $45,000. To help establish Zero-to-Three, therapeutic mental health program for mothers and their newborn infants. 1990.
1705-3 Youth Development Clinic of Newark, Newark, NJ, $15,000. For Toddler Therapeutic Nursery. 1990.

1706
The Arnold A. Schwartz Foundation
c/o Kunzman, Coley, Yospin & Bernstein
15 Mountain Blvd.
Warren 07060   (908) 757-7927

Incorporated in 1953 in NJ.
Donor(s): Arnold A. Schwartz.‡
Foundation type: Independent

Financial data (yr. ended 11/30/91): Assets, $3,977,606 (M); expenditures, $212,714; qualifying distributions, $178,971, including $172,300 for 54 grants (high: $17,100; low: $1,000).
Fields of interest: Elementary education, secondary education, community development, youth, hospitals, child welfare.
Limitations: Giving primarily in northern NJ. No support for religious purposes. No grants to individuals, or for endowment funds; no loans.
Application information: Application form not required.
   Initial approach: Letter
   Copies of proposal: 2
   Deadline(s): Sept. 30
   Board meeting date(s): Feb., June, Sept., and Nov.
   Write: Edwin D. Kunzman, Pres.
Officers: Edwin D. Kunzman, Pres.; Louis Harding, V.P.; Steven Kunzman, Secy.-Treas.
Trustees: Victor DiLeo, David Lackland, Robert Shapiro, Kenneth Turnbull.
EIN: 226034152

1707
The Harold B. and Dorothy A. Snyder Foundation
P.O. Box 671
Moorestown 08057-0671   (609) 273-9745

Established in 1971 in NJ as a trust; incorporated in 1981 in NJ.
Donor(s): Harold B. Snyder, Sr.‡
Foundation type: Independent
Financial data (yr. ended 09/30/90): Assets, $6,779,258 (M); gifts received, $6,805; expenditures, $408,059; qualifying distributions, $283,519, including $179,607 for grants (high: $50,000; low: $200; average: $200-$50,000) and $30,630 for 11 grants to individuals (high: $5,564; low: $1,250).
Purpose and activities: Support for programs in Union County, NJ, and scholarships for NJ residents entering the Presbyterian or other Protestant ministries, nursing, and the building construction industry; for NJ nuns and priests who wish to further their secular education; and for NJ rabbinical students studying at the Jewish Theological Seminary of America.
Fields of interest: Nursing, heart disease, AIDS, health services, education, child welfare, women, housing, Protestant welfare, religion—Christian.
Types of support: Continuing support, equipment, general purposes, operating budgets, matching funds, renovation projects, seed money, special projects, loans, program-related investments, student aid, student loans.
Limitations: Giving primarily in the Union County, NJ, area. No grants to individuals directly; generally no capital campaigns.
Application information: Scholarships paid through institutions only. Application form not required.
   Initial approach: Letter or telephone
   Copies of proposal: 5
   Deadline(s): None
   Board meeting date(s): Bimonthly or quarterly
   Final notification: Aug.
   Write: Audrey Snyder, Exec. Dir

Officer and Trustees:* Audrey Snyder,* Exec. Dir.; Ethelyn Allison, Arline Snyder Cortese, Lillian Palumbo, Phyllis Johnson Snyder.
Number of staff: 1 full-time professional; 1 part-time support.
EIN: 222316043

1708
Subaru of America Foundation
Subaru Plaza
P.O. Box 6000
Cherry Hill 08034-6000   (609) 488-5099

Established in 1984 in NJ.
Donor(s): Subaru of America, Inc.
Foundation type: Company-sponsored
Financial data (yr. ended 12/31/91): Assets, $853,805 (M); expenditures, $244,923; qualifying distributions, $244,923, including $205,646 for 95 grants (high: $15,000; low: $500; average: $2,000-$3,000) and $39,277 for 295 employee matching gifts.
Purpose and activities: Giving primarily for social services targeted to children, especially the disadvantaged; primary areas of interest include literacy, cultural outreach, youth and drug abuse.
Fields of interest: Literacy, social services, disadvantaged, leadership development, youth, child welfare, family services, drug abuse, health services, cultural programs.
Types of support: Operating budgets, continuing support, annual campaigns, employee matching gifts, special projects, general purposes, matching funds, technical assistance, renovation projects.
Limitations: Giving limited to areas of company operations, primarily in the Cherry Hill/Moorestown, NJ, area, and immediate regional office communities in Addison, IL; Portland, OR; Aurora, CO; and Austell, GA. No support for religious, fraternal, or veterans' groups. No grants to individuals, or for land acquisition, endowment funds, scholarships, fellowships, research, publications, conferences and seminars, or vehicle donations; no loans.
Publications: Informational brochure (including application guidelines).
Application information: Application form not required.
  Initial approach: Letter, telephone, or proposal
  Copies of proposal: 1
  Deadline(s): Mar. 1, July 1, and Oct. 1
  Board meeting date(s): Mid- to end of Apr., Aug., and Nov.
  Final notification: Up to 5 months, depending on cycle
  Write: Denise L. Schwartz, Mgr.
Officers and Directors:* Takeshi Higurashi,* Chair.; George T. Muller,* Exec. V.P.; Joseph T. Scharff,* V.P. and Treas.
Staff: Denise L. Schwartz, Mgr.
Number of staff: 1 full-time professional; 1 full-time support.
EIN: 222531774

1709
Walter and Louise Sutcliffe Foundation
c/o First Fidelity Bank, N.A., NJ; Philanthropic Services Group
765 Broad St.
Newark 07102   (201) 430-2100

Established in 1990 in NJ as successor to the Walter and Louise Sutcliffe Foundation.
Donor(s): Louise Sutcliffe.‡
Foundation type: Independent
Financial data (yr. ended 12/31/91): Assets, $3,554,768 (M); expenditures, $98,119; qualifying distributions, $58,183, including $20,000 for 1 grant.
Purpose and activities: The foundation provides grants to institutions for nursing education and cancer research.
Fields of interest: Cancer, medical education, medical research, nursing.
Types of support: Scholarship funds, special projects, research, student aid.
Limitations: Giving primarily in NJ; no grants outside the U.S. No grants to individuals, or for endowments or general operating support; no loans.
Publications: Application guidelines.
Application information:
  Initial approach: Proposal
  Copies of proposal: 1
  Deadline(s): Nov. 1
  Board meeting date(s): Dec.
  Final notification: 1 month after board meeting
  Write: Christopher A. Ohmacht, Sr. Trust Officer, First Fidelity Bank, N.A., NJ
Trustee: First Fidelity Bank, N.A., NJ.
EIN: 521720225

1710
The Henry and Marilyn Taub Foundation
▼
c/o Wiss & Co.
354 Eisenhower Pkwy.
Livingston 07039

Established in 1967 in DE.
Donor(s): Henry Taub.
Foundation type: Independent
Financial data (yr. ended 12/31/90): Assets, $14,888,070 (M); gifts received, $794,262; expenditures, $2,049,960; qualifying distributions, $1,992,430, including $1,992,430 for 92 grants (high: $1,397,880; low: $25; average: $100-$5,000).
Purpose and activities: Grants largely for Jewish welfare funds; some support for higher and other education, social service and youth agencies, and hospitals.
Fields of interest: Jewish giving, Jewish welfare, higher education, education, social services, youth, hospitals.
Limitations: Giving primarily in NJ.
Application information: Contributes only to pre-selected organizations. Applications not accepted.
Officers and Directors:* Henry Taub,* Pres.; Fred S. Lafer, Secy.; Marilyn Taub,* Treas.
EIN: 226100525

1711
Terner Foundation, Inc.
P.O. Box 340
Oakhurst 07755

Established in 1953.
Donor(s): Emmanuel M. Terner, Mathilda Terner.
Foundation type: Independent

Financial data (yr. ended 07/31/91): Assets, $4,841,047 (M); gifts received, $300,000; expenditures, $716,384; qualifying distributions, $676,335, including $676,335 for 91 grants (high: $300,000; low: $100).
Fields of interest: Health services, hospitals, higher education, secondary education, Jewish giving, Jewish welfare.
Limitations: Giving primarily in NY and FL. No grants to individuals.
Application information: Contributes only to pre-selected organizations. Applications not accepted.
  Write: E.M. Terner, Chair.
Officers: Emmanuel M. Terner, Chair.; Mathilda Terner, Pres. and Treas.; Nancy Behrman, V.P.; Elaine Cooper, V.P.; Carol Lederman, V.P.; Winifred A. Packard, Secy.
EIN: 221605265

1712
The Thomas & Betts Charitable Trust
1001 Frontier Rd.
Bridgewater 08807-2941   (908) 685-1600

Trust established in 1948 in NJ.
Donor(s): Thomas & Betts Corp.
Foundation type: Company-sponsored
Financial data (yr. ended 12/31/91): Assets, $23,529 (M); gifts received, $250,000; expenditures, $429,449; qualifying distributions, $428,177, including $406,202 for 164 grants (high: $42,000; low: $227) and $21,975 for employee matching gifts.
Purpose and activities: Grants primarily for health and human services, including hospitals, youth clubs, and community funds; support also for museums and performing arts groups and higher and other education.
Fields of interest: Health, hospitals, social services, youth, community funds, museums, performing arts, education, higher education.
Types of support: Employee matching gifts, capital campaigns, annual campaigns, scholarship funds.
Limitations: Giving primarily in the area of company operations in Raritan, NJ. No grants to individuals, or for endowment funds, research, scholarships, or fellowships; no loans.
Publications: Annual report, application guidelines, informational brochure.
Application information:
  Initial approach: Letter
  Copies of proposal: 1
  Deadline(s): None
  Board meeting date(s): Oct. and Dec. and as required
  Write: Janice H. Way, Trustee
Trustees: Robert V. Berry, John F. Walsh, Janice H. Way.
EIN: 226032533

1713
Turrell Fund ▼
111 Northfield Ave.
West Orange 07052   (201) 325-5108

Incorporated in 1935 in NJ.
Donor(s): Herbert Turrell,‡ Margaret Turrell.‡
Foundation type: Independent

Financial data (yr. ended 12/31/90): Assets, $82,480,824 (M); expenditures, $4,970,369; qualifying distributions, $4,733,913, including $4,385,953 for 221 grants (high: $88,000; low: $500; average: $5,000-$50,000) and $347,960 for foundation-administered programs.

Purpose and activities: Grants to organizations dedicated to service to or care of children and youth under 18 years of age, with emphasis on the needy, the socially maladjusted, and the disadvantaged.

Fields of interest: Youth, child welfare, disadvantaged, delinquency, education, education—minorities, education—early childhood.

Types of support: Operating budgets, seed money, emergency funds, building funds, equipment, land acquisition, matching funds, scholarship funds, renovation projects, general purposes, special projects.

Limitations: Giving limited to NJ, particularly the northern urban areas centered in Essex County, and to VT. No support for advocacy work, most hospital work, or health delivery services; generally no support for cultural activities. No grants to individuals, or for endowment funds, publications, conferences, or research; no loans.

Publications: Annual report (including application guidelines).

Application information: Application form not required.

Initial approach: Letter
Copies of proposal: 1
Deadline(s): Submit proposal preferably in Jan. or Feb. or between June and Sept.; deadlines Feb. 1 and Sept. 1 for first-time applicants; Mar. 1 and Oct. 1 for others
Board meeting date(s): May and Nov. and/or Dec.
Final notification: 3 months after deadlines
Write: E. Belvin Williams, Exec. Dir.

Officers and Trustees:* Frank J. Hoenemeyer,* Chair.; Robert H. Grasmere,* Pres.; E. Belvin Williams,* Secy. and Exec. Dir.; Anne Marie A. Mills, Treas.; Paul J. Christiansen, Ann G. Dinse, Carl Fjellman, Richard R. Hough, Frank A. Hutson, Jr., S. Whitney Landon, Larry Prendergast, Vivian Shapiro.

Number of staff: 2 full-time professional; 1 part-time professional; 3 full-time support.

EIN: 221551936

Recent health grants:

1713-1 Ad House, Newark, NJ, $18,000. For prevention program. 1990.

1713-2 American Diabetes Association, Vermont Affiliate, Burlington, VT, $18,000. For camping program. 1990.

1713-3 Choices, Newark, NJ, $15,000. For children's services. 1990.

1713-4 Collier Services, Wickatunk, NJ, $30,000. For counseling and social services. 1990.

1713-5 Eden Institute, Princeton, NJ, $25,000. For summer program. 1990.

1713-6 Health Services of Hudson County, Jersey City, NJ, $11,400. For youth services. 1990.

1713-7 Integrity, Newark, NJ, $30,000. For adolescent rehabilitation and education. 1990.

1713-8 Main Street Counseling Center, West Orange, NJ, $15,000. For youth services. 1990.

1713-9 Mental Health Association of Essex County, East Orange, NJ, $18,000. For children's services. 1990.

1713-10 Middlesex Council on Alcoholism and Drug Abuse, East Brunswick, NJ, $15,000. For Hispanic outreach program. 1990.

1713-11 National Council on Alcoholism, Montclair, NJ, $20,000. For program support. 1990.

1713-12 Planned Parenthood Association of the Mercer Area, Trenton, NJ, $12,000. For teen advocacy program. 1990.

1713-13 Planned Parenthood of Essex County, Newark, NJ, $30,000. For youth education program. 1990.

1713-14 Planned Parenthood of Greater Northern New Jersey, Morristown, NJ, $16,000. For youth education program. 1990.

1713-15 United Cerebral Palsy of North Jersey, East Orange, NJ, $17,500. For pre-school program. 1990.

1713-16 United Cerebral Palsy of Vermont, Montpelier, VT, $18,000. For youth program. 1990.

1713-17 University of Medicine and Dentistry of New Jersey, Newark, NJ, $62,500. For inner-city gifted children program. 1990.

1713-18 Vermont Association for Mental Health, Montpelier, VT, $11,500. For camp program. 1990.

1714
Union Camp Charitable Trust
c/o Union Camp Corp.
1600 Valley Rd.
Wayne 07470   (201) 628-2248

Trust established in 1951 in NY.
Donor(s): Union Camp Corp.
Foundation type: Company-sponsored
Financial data (yr. ended 12/31/89): Assets, $1,803,585 (M); gifts received, $2,000,000; expenditures, $2,327,900; qualifying distributions, $2,304,284, including $2,302,461 for grants (high: $168,853; average: $200-$5,000).
Purpose and activities: Grants largely for community funds, higher and other education, including employee-related scholarships and matching gifts, hospitals and health services, social services, youth and women, civic affairs and public interest, civil rights and law and justice, Jewish giving and Protestant welfare, and cultural programs.
Fields of interest: Community funds, higher education, elementary education, hospitals, handicapped, drug abuse, social services, aged, women, youth, child welfare, community development, civil rights, international affairs, public policy, Protestant welfare, Jewish giving, cultural programs, media and communications, ecology.
Types of support: Employee matching gifts, employee-related scholarships, operating budgets, continuing support, annual campaigns, building funds, equipment, special projects, research, capital campaigns, consulting services, emergency funds, endowment funds, fellowships, matching funds, renovation projects, scholarship funds, seed money.
Limitations: Giving primarily in areas of company operations and to national organizations (generally east of the Mason-Dixon line). No grants to individuals (except employee-related scholarships); no loans.

Application information: Application form not required.
Initial approach: Proposal
Copies of proposal: 1
Deadline(s): Submit proposal preferably from Jan. through Aug.
Board meeting date(s): Nov.
Final notification: By Jan. 1
Write: Sydney N. Phin, Dir., Human Resources
Trustees: A. Calder, H.D. Camp, T.T. Dunn, Morgan Guaranty Trust Co. of New York.
Number of staff: 2 part-time professional.
EIN: 136034666
Recent health grants:

1714-1 Memorial Sloan-Kettering Cancer Center, NYC, NY, $10,000. 1990.

1714-2 University of Alabama in Birmingham Medical Center, Birmingham, AL, $10,000. 1990.

1714-3 University of Medicine and Dentistry of New Jersey, Newark, NJ, $10,000. 1990.

1715
Union Foundation
31C Mountain Blvd.
P.O. Box 4470
Warren 07059   (908) 753-2440

Incorporated in 1951 in NJ.
Donor(s): Edward J. Grassmann.‡
Foundation type: Independent
Financial data (yr. ended 11/30/90): Assets, $9,490,230 (M); expenditures, $727,899; qualifying distributions, $717,791, including $674,650 for 91 grants (high: $45,000; low: $300; average: $3,000-$10,000).
Purpose and activities: Grants to "local hospitals and health organziations, organizations engaged in ecological endeavors, educational institutions, especially privately supported ones, organizations that help the needy, particularly children and religious organizations. Preference given to organizations with low administration expenses, that show efforts to encourage individuals to help themselves, and which make efforts to achieve a broad base of funding."
Fields of interest: Hospitals, health services, environment, conservation, education, higher education, secondary education, youth, social services.
Types of support: Endowment funds, building funds, equipment, capital campaigns, land acquisition.
Limitations: Giving primarily in Union County, NJ. No grants to individuals, or for operating budgets.
Publications: Application guidelines.
Application information: Application form not required.
Initial approach: Proposal; less than 4 pages
Copies of proposal: 1
Deadline(s): Oct. 15
Board meeting date(s): Nov.
Final notification: Dec. 15
Write: William V. Engel, Esq., Pres.
Officers and Directors:* William V. Engel,* Pres.; Edward G. Engel,* V.P.; Suzanne B. Engel,* Secy.; Thomas H. Campbell,* Treas.
Trustees: Cynthia Q. Fuller, Haydn H. Murray, William O. Wuester, M.D.
Number of staff: 1 part-time professional; 2 part-time support.

EIN: 226046454

1716
Lucy and Eleanor S. Upton Charitable Foundation
c/o Thomas L. Morrissey
100 Mulberry St.
Newark 07102

Established in 1965.
Donor(s): Eleanor S. Upton.‡
Foundation type: Independent
Financial data (yr. ended 12/31/90): Assets,
$4,793,095 (M); expenditures, $288,059;
qualifying distributions, $228,000, including
$228,000 for 11 grants (high: $96,560; low:
$4,000).
Purpose and activities: Support primarily for a
university's fellowship program; giving also to
hospitals and cultural programs.
Fields of interest: Higher education, hospitals,
cultural programs.
Types of support: General purposes, research,
fellowships.
Limitations: Giving primarily in NJ. No grants to
individuals.
Application information: Contributes only to
pre-selected organizations. Applications not
accepted.
Trustees: William B. Cater, Thomas L. Morrissey,
Samuel C. Williams, Jr.
EIN: 226074947

1717
The Edward W. and Stella C. Van Houten Memorial Fund
c/o First Fidelity Bank, N.A., NJ; Philanthropic
Services Group
765 Broad St.
Newark 07102   (201) 430-4533

Established in 1979 in NJ.
Donor(s): Stella C. Van Houten.‡
Foundation type: Independent
Financial data (yr. ended 11/30/91): Assets,
$13,869,241 (M); expenditures, $957,238;
qualifying distributions, $851,030, including
$849,353 for 33 grants (high: $150,000; low:
$5,000; average: $5,000-$150,000).
Purpose and activities: Interests include: 1)
Human Service activities in Bergen and Passaic
Counties in NJ. Specific areas of interest include
orphaned children, the disabled, and the elderly;
2) Hospitals and health organizations in Bergen
and Passaic Counties in NJ to improve or expand
health-care services; 3) Higher education -
primarily medical and nursing training; and 4)
Education and care of children.
Fields of interest: Social services, child welfare,
aged, hospitals, hospitals—building funds, health,
higher education, medical education, nursing,
education—early childhood.
Types of support: Capital campaigns, equipment,
scholarship funds, special projects, seed money,
building funds, renovation projects.
Limitations: Giving primarily in Bergen and
Passaic counties, NJ. No grants to individuals, or
for general operating support or endowments; no
loans.
Publications: Application guidelines.

Application information: Application form not
required.
  Initial approach: Proposal
  Copies of proposal: 1
  Deadline(s): Feb. 1, May 1, Aug. 1, and Nov. 1
  Board meeting date(s): Mar., June, Sept., and
    Dec.
  Final notification: 1 month after board meets
  Write: James S. Hohn, Asst. V.P., First Fidelity
    Bank, N.A., NJ
Trustee: First Fidelity Bank, N.A., NJ.
EIN: 226311438

1718
Van Pelt Foundation
P.O. Box 823
Westwood 07675

Established in 1977 in NJ.
Donor(s): Edwin Van Pelt.
Foundation type: Independent
Financial data (yr. ended 09/30/91): Assets,
$4,691,816 (M); expenditures, $346,222;
qualifying distributions, $346,322, including
$330,900 for 72 grants (high: $51,000; low:
$200).
Purpose and activities: Support for smaller
organizations who have been hurt by cutbacks in
federal monies and/or individual contributions.
Fields of interest: Hospitals, hospitals—building
funds, child welfare, family services, homeless,
performing arts.
Types of support: Building funds, capital
campaigns, continuing support, employee
matching gifts, equipment, general purposes, seed
money.
Limitations: Giving primarily in NJ, NY, and FL.
No grants to individuals.
Application information: Application form not
required.
  Initial approach: Proposal
  Copies of proposal: 5
  Deadline(s): Before board meetings
  Board meeting date(s): May 1 and Nov. 1
Officers and Trustees:* Lawrence D. Bass,* Pres.;
Henry Gerke,* V.P.; Robert DuBois,* Secy.; Henry
Bass,* Treas.; Meredith Van Pelt.
Number of staff: 1 part-time support.
EIN: 222188141

1719
Victoria Foundation, Inc. ▼
40 South Fullerton Ave.
Montclair 07042   (201) 783-4450

Incorporated in 1924 in NJ.
Donor(s): Hendon Chubb.‡
Foundation type: Independent
Financial data (yr. ended 12/31/91): Assets,
$149,000,000 (M); expenditures, $6,785,306;
qualifying distributions, $6,785,306, including
$6,436,670 for 143 grants (high: $160,000; low:
$10,000; average: $20,000-$50,000).
Purpose and activities: Grants primarily for urban
activities and education programs, including early
childhood and elementary education; support
aslo for urban problems, leadership development,
youth agencies; and certain statewide
environmental projects.
Fields of interest: Community development,
urban development, urban affairs, education,

elementary education, educational research,
education—early childhood,
education—minorities, language and literature,
leadership development, youth, family planning,
social services, welfare, delinquency,
disadvantaged, minorities, housing, rehabilitation,
alcoholism, drug abuse, AIDS, environment.
Types of support: Operating budgets, continuing
support, emergency funds, building funds,
matching funds, special projects, research,
consulting services, technical assistance, general
purposes, land acquisition.
Limitations: Giving limited to Greater Newark,
NJ; environmental grants limited to NJ. No
support for organizations dealing with specific
diseases or afflictions, geriatric needs, or day care.
No grants to individuals, or for publications or
conferences; no loans.
Publications: Annual report (including application
guidelines), application guidelines.
Application information: Request application
guidelines. Application form required.
  Initial approach: Proposal or 2-page letter of
    introduction
  Copies of proposal: 1
  Deadline(s): Submit proposal prior to Feb. 1 or
    Sept. 1
  Board meeting date(s): May and Dec.
  Final notification: Within 3 weeks after board
    meeting if accepted
  Write: Catherine M. McFarland, Exec. Officer
Officers and Trustees:* Percy Chubb III,* Pres.;
Margaret H. Parker,* V.P.; Catherine M.
McFarland, Secy.; Kevin Shanley,* Treas.; Charles
Chapin III, Corinne A. Chubb, Sally Chubb, Mary
Coggeshall, Robert Curvin, Haliburton Fales II,
Gordon A. Millspaugh, Jr., William Turnbull,
Christine Todd Whitman.
Number of staff: 3 full-time professional; 2
full-time support.
EIN: 221554541
Recent health grants:
1719-1 Ad House, Newark, NJ, $20,000. To hire
  two part-time counselors for its prevention
  program, to purchase equipment and to offer
  stipend to participants. 1990.
1719-2 Choices, Newark, NJ, $40,000. For rising
  operational costs as well as for improved
  program supervision for substance-addicted
  mothers and their children. 1990.
1719-3 Easter Seal Society of New Jersey, Camp
  Merry Heart, Milltown, NJ, $20,000. For
  capital funds toward roof repairs on Victoria
  Hall, building originally donated to special
  camp for handicapped children. 1990.
1719-4 National Council on Alcoholism, North
  Jersey Area, Montclair, NJ, $16,000. To secure
  and extend present programs to
  disadvantaged. 1990.
1719-5 Newark Renaissance House, Newark, NJ,
  $20,000. Toward addition to existing modular
  unit. 1990.
1719-6 Planned Parenthood of Essex County,
  Newark, NJ, $42,000. For operating support
  and wages for high school students, well
  trained in health education, to discuss teen
  problems with their peers. 1990.
1719-7 Tom Skinner Associates Learning Center,
  Newark, NJ, $35,000. To provide Newark
  youth and adults with daytime, after-school
  and Saturday program of basic life skills
  training, and for parenting skills, your

body/your health and science awareness projects. 1990.

1719-8 Turning Point, Newark, NJ, $25,000. For operating funds for agency's Newark outpatient program. 1990.

1719-9 University of Medicine and Dentistry of New Jersey, Newark, NJ, $15,000. For Sexuality Today program, which provides full scholarships for 30 Newark educators, administrators and counselors and contributes toward printing of course handbook. 1990.

1719-10 University of Medicine and Dentistry of New Jersey, Young Fathers Program, Newark, NJ, $30,000. For project coordinator position and employment of needed administrative assistant. 1990.

1719-11 Youth Development Clinic of Newark, Newark, NJ, $55,000. To outreach satellite in Newark's Hispanic North Ward to deal with and treat family problems through counseling. 1990.

1720
Visceglia-Summit Associates Foundation

Raritan Plaza I
Raritan Ctr.
Edison 08818   (201) 225-2900

Incorporated in 1953 in NJ.
Donor(s): Vincent Visceglia, Diego R. Visceglia, John B. Visceglia.
Foundation type: Independent
Financial data (yr. ended 12/31/91): Assets, $1,548,982 (M); expenditures, $244,408; qualifying distributions, $209,328, including $203,328 for 133 grants (high: $26,500; low: $25) and $6,000 for 3 grants to individuals (high: $5,000; low: $500).
Purpose and activities: Support for hospitals, higher education, church support, and religious associations; some support also for community funds, music, opera, ballet, and other performing arts, and youth agencies.
Fields of interest: Hospitals, higher education, religion, religion—Christian, community funds, music, dance, performing arts, youth.
Limitations: Giving primarily in Essex and Middlesex counties, NJ.
Publications: Financial statement.
Application information: Contributes only to pre-selected organizations. Applications not accepted.
Officers: Diego R. Visceglia, Pres. and Treas.; John B. Visceglia, Secy.
EIN: 226041608

1721
Vollmer Foundation, Inc.

217 Gravel Hill Rd.
Kinnelon 07405   (201) 492-2309
Additional address: P.O. Box 704, Butler, NJ 07405

Incorporated in 1965 in NY.
Donor(s): Alberto F. Vollmer.‡
Foundation type: Independent
Financial data (yr. ended 12/31/91): Assets, $17,801,411 (M); expenditures, $1,706,436; qualifying distributions, $865,162, including $836,416 for 9 grants (high: $230,757; low: $8,224; average: $2,000-$30,000).

Purpose and activities: Emphasis on health and higher and other education; support also for the Catholic church in Venezuela.
Fields of interest: Health, higher education, education, religion—Christian, Catholic giving, Venezuela.
Types of support: Research, general purposes, continuing support.
Limitations: Giving limited to Venezuela. No grants to individuals, or for building funds or matching gifts; no loans.
Publications: Application guidelines.
Application information: Grants restricted to organizations established in Venezuela. Application form not required.
    Initial approach: Letter
    Copies of proposal: 2
    Deadline(s): None
    Board meeting date(s): As required
    Final notification: 2 to 3 months
    Write: Albert L. Ennist, Asst. Secy.
Officers and Directors:* Gustavo J. Vollmer,* Pres.; Ana Luisa Estrada,* V.P. and Treas.; Carolina V. de Eseverri,* Secy.; Ana M. de Estrada, Gustavo A. Vollmer.
Number of staff: 1 full-time professional; 2 part-time support.
EIN: 132620718

1722
Alberto Vollmer Foundation, Inc.

c/o Edward M. Phillips
35 West 43rd St.
Bayonne 07002

Established in 1988 in NJ.
Donor(s): Vollmer Foundation, Inc.
Foundation type: Independent
Financial data (yr. ended 12/31/91): Assets, $15,395,454 (M); expenditures, $761,208; qualifying distributions, $743,104, including $724,213 for 16 grants (high: $312,701; low: $1,880).
Fields of interest: Medical sciences, Catholic giving, higher education.
Types of support: General purposes.
Limitations: Giving primarily in Caracas, Venezuela. No grants to individuals.
Application information: Contributes only to pre-selected organizations. Applications not accepted.
Officers: Alberto J. Vollmer, Pres.; Christine de Vollmer, V.P.
EIN: 222872241

1723
The Warner-Lambert Charitable
Foundation ▼

201 Tabor Rd.
Morris Plains 07950   (201) 540-3652

Incorporated in 1969 in DE.
Donor(s): Warner-Lambert Co.
Foundation type: Company-sponsored
Financial data (yr. ended 12/31/90): Assets, $2,287,628 (M); gifts received, $5,500,250; expenditures, $4,907,100; qualifying distributions, $4,907,100, including $4,906,850 for 217 grants (high: $300,000; low: $1,500; average: $1,500-$50,000).

Purpose and activities: Emphasis on higher education, medical research and education, pharmacology, and community funds; some support for hospitals, civil rights, and social welfare and youth agencies.
Fields of interest: Community funds, higher education, medical research, medical education, pharmacy, civil rights, hospitals, youth, social services.
Types of support: Annual campaigns, building funds, continuing support, emergency funds, equipment, matching funds, operating budgets, professorships, seed money, research.
Limitations: Giving primarily in communities where company plants are located. No grants to individuals, or for endowment funds, demonstration projects, research (other than medical research), or conferences; no loans.
Application information: Application form not required.
    Initial approach: Letter
    Copies of proposal: 1
    Deadline(s): Submit proposal preferably between July and Sept.; deadline Sept.
    Board meeting date(s): Quarterly
    Write: Richard Keelty, Chair.
Officers and Directors:* Richard Keelty,* Chair.; Robert J. Dircks,* Pres.; David Alton, 1st V.P.; Raymond M. Fino,* 2nd V.P.; Donald E. O'Neill,* 3rd V.P.; Ronald E. Zier,* 4th V.P.; Stanley D. Grubman, Secy.; Paul Gerhart.
Number of staff: 1 full-time professional; 1 part-time professional; 1 part-time support.
EIN: 237038078
Recent health grants:

1723-1 American Academy of Neurology, Minneapolis, MN, $15,000. For fellowships. 1990.

1723-2 American College of Angiology, Roslyn, NY, $25,000. 1990.

1723-3 American Heart Association, North Brunswick, NJ, $250,000. 1990.

1723-4 American Paralysis Association, Short Hills, NJ, $10,000. 1990.

1723-5 Childrens Specialized Hospital, Mountainside, NJ, $25,000. 1990.

1723-6 Columbia University, Clinical Research Center, NYC, NY, $20,000. 1990.

1723-7 Dover General Hospital and Medical Center, Dover, NJ, $10,000. 1990.

1723-8 Epilepsy Foundation of New Jersey, Trenton, NJ, $40,000. For research fellowship. 1990.

1723-9 Florida A & M University, College of Pharmacy, Tallahassee, FL, $20,000. 1990.

1723-10 Hackensack Medical Center, Institute of Child Development, Hackensack, NJ, $18,000. 1990.

1723-11 Harvard University, Medical School, Cambridge, MA, $250,000. 1990.

1723-12 Hemophilia Association of New Jersey, Jersey City, NJ, $12,000. 1990.

1723-13 Institute of Medicine, DC, $20,000. 1990.

1723-14 Memorial Sloan-Kettering Cancer Center, NYC, NY, $15,000. 1990.

1723-15 Morristown Memorial Health Foundation, Morristown, NJ, $225,000. 1990.

1723-16 Mount Sinai Hospital and Medical Center, NYC, NY, $10,000. 1990.

1723-17 National Alliance for Research on Schizophrenia and Depression (NARSAD), Great Neck, NY, $10,000. 1990.

1723-18 National Council on Patient Information and Education, DC, $10,000. 1990.

1723-19 National Stroke Association, Englewood, NJ, $10,000. 1990.

1723-20 New York Hospital-Cornell Medical Center, NYC, NY, $50,000. 1990.

1723-21 Overlook Hospital, Summit, NJ, $25,000. 1990.

1723-22 Overlook Hospital, Summit, NJ, $10,050. 1990.

1723-23 Parenteral Drug Association Foundation for Pharmaceutical Sciences, Garden City, NY, $10,000. 1990.

1723-24 Pharmaceutical Manufacturers Association Foundation, DC, $150,000. 1990.

1723-25 Pharmaceutical Manufacturers Association Foundation, Alliance for Aging Research, DC, $25,000. 1990.

1723-26 Private Medical Care Foundation, Shawnee, OK, $10,000. 1990.

1723-27 Project HOPE, Chevy Chase, MD, $25,000. 1990.

1723-28 Self Memorial Hospital, Greenwood, SC, $10,000. 1990.

1723-29 Somerset Medical Center, Somerville, NJ, $25,000. 1990.

1723-30 United Cerebral Palsy Research and Education Foundation, NYC, NY, $50,000. For annual telethon. 1990.

1723-31 University of Maryland Foundation, School of Pharmacy, Baltimore, MD, $50,000. 1990.

1723-32 University of Medicine and Dentistry of New Jersey Foundation, Newark, NJ, $200,000. 1990.

1723-33 University of Michigan, Ann Arbor, MI, $23,000. For Biomedical Research Lecture Series. 1990.

1723-34 University of Michigan, College of Pharmacy, Ann Arbor, MI, $67,500. 1990.

1723-35 University of Michigan Foundation, School of Pharmacy, Ann Arbor, MI, $10,350. 1990.

1723-36 University of Minnesota, College of Pharmacy, Minneapolis, MN, $10,000. 1990.

1723-37 University of Nebraska, Pharmacy Department, Omaha, NE, $100,000. 1990.

1723-38 University of Southern California, School of Pharmacy, Los Angeles, CA, $10,000. 1990.

1723-39 University of Texas, College of Pharmacy, Austin, TX, $25,000. 1990.

1723-40 Xavier University, School of Pharmacy, Cincinnati, OH, $30,000. 1990.

1724
The Willits Foundation
730 Central Ave.
Murray Hill 07974   (201) 277-8259

Incorporated in 1963 in NJ.
Donor(s): Harris L. Willits,‡ John H. Evans, Members of the Willits family.
Foundation type: Independent
Financial data (yr. ended 11/30/91): Assets, $7,616,169 (M); gifts received, $147,534; expenditures, $318,897; qualifying distributions, $278,207, including $278,207 for 116 grants (high: $15,000; low: $100).
Purpose and activities: Emphasis on grants to higher educational institutions for scholarships; support also for hospitals, social service agencies, and Protestant church support and religious activities.
Fields of interest: Higher education, education, hospitals, social services, Protestant giving.
Types of support: Scholarship funds, general purposes.
Limitations: Giving primarily in NJ. No grants to individuals.
Application information:
  Initial approach: Proposal
  Copies of proposal: 1
  Deadline(s): None
  Board meeting date(s): Nov. and as required

Write: Mrs. Emily D. Lawrence, Secy.-Treas.
Officers and Trustees:* John H. Evans,* Pres.; Barbara W. Evans,* V.P.; Emily D. Lawrence,* Secy.-Treas.; Laura Evans, Caroline Jones, Geoffrey Jones, Lawrence E. Lindars, George T. Maloney, Robert H. McCaffrey, Itto A. Willits, John F. Willits.
EIN: 226063106

1725
The Winslow Foundation
(Formerly Windie Foundation)
c/o Drinker Biddle & Reath
P.O. Box 627
Princeton 08542-3712   (609) 921-6336

Established in 1987 in NJ.
Donor(s): Julia D. Winslow.‡
Foundation type: Operating
Financial data (yr. ended 12/31/90): Assets, $10,966,574 (M); gifts received, $9,249,043; expenditures, $122,308; qualifying distributions, $106,000, including $105,000 for 2 grants (high: $100,000; low: $5,000).
Purpose and activities: Giving "to resident homes for the purpose of assisting women alcoholics"; support also for ecology and the environment.
Fields of interest: Alcoholism, women, environment, ecology.
Types of support: Continuing support.
Limitations: Giving primarily in NJ. No grants to individuals.
Application information: Application form not required.
  Initial approach: Letter
  Deadline(s): None
  Write: Samuel W. Lambert III, Trustee
Trustees: Theresa Heinz, Samuel W. Lambert III, Wren Winslow Wirth.
Number of staff: None.
EIN: 222778703

NEW MEXICO

1726
Albuquerque Community Foundation
P.O. Box 36960
Albuquerque 87176-6960   (505) 883-6240

Established in 1981 in NM.
Foundation type: Community
Financial data (yr. ended 06/30/92): Assets, $5,310,031 (M); gifts received, $728,313; expenditures, $897,811; qualifying distributions, $732,384, including $704,649 for 70 grants (low: $500; average: $1,000-$3,000) and $27,735 for 4 in-kind gifts.
Purpose and activities: Support for cultural programs, including music, historic preservation, and the fine and performing arts; education; health services; conservation; and social services, including child welfare, leadership development, and programs for the homeless.
Fields of interest: Cultural programs, fine arts, performing arts, education, health, conservation, social services, child welfare, leadership development, homeless.
Types of support: Exchange programs, fellowships, publications, research, scholarship funds, seed money, special projects, technical assistance, consulting services, emergency funds, loans.
Limitations: Giving primarily in the greater Albuquerque, NM, area. No support for religious, political, or grantmaking organizations. No grants to individuals, or for purchase of equipment, debt requirement, or interest or tax payments.
Publications: Annual report (including application guidelines), newsletter, occasional report, informational brochure (including application guidelines).
Application information: Call for guidelines. Application form not required.
   Initial approach: Proposal
   Copies of proposal: 5
   Deadline(s): May 1
   Board meeting date(s): Quarterly
   Final notification: Annually in Sept.
   Write: Laura Hueter Bass, Exec. Dir.
Officers and Trustees:* Lee S. Blaugrund,* Pres.; James Collins,* V.P.; Randall Talbot,* Secy.; Karl Gustafson,* Treas.; Laura Hueter Bass, Exec. Dir.; Robert J. Stamm, and 8 additional trustees.
Number of staff: 1 full-time professional; 1 full-time support.
EIN: 850295444

1727
Dale J. Bellamah Foundation
P.O. Box 36600, Station D
Albuquerque 87176   (505) 293-1098

Established around 1972 in NM.

Donor(s): Dale J. Bellamah.‡
Foundation type: Independent
Financial data (yr. ended 12/31/91): Assets, $24,351,215 (M); expenditures, $1,405,849; qualifying distributions, $1,115,755, including $956,546 for 14 grants (high: $104,296; low: $1,000).
Purpose and activities: Giving for higher education including a military academy, hospitals and a diabetes association, social services and youth agencies, an organization providing care for the mentally retarded, and athletics.
Fields of interest: Higher education, military personnel, health, hospitals, health associations, youth, social services, handicapped, recreation.
Types of support: Scholarship funds, equipment, general purposes, capital campaigns, special projects, research.
Limitations: No grants to individuals.
Application information: Application form not required.
   Initial approach: Letter
   Deadline(s): None
   Board meeting date(s): As necessary
   Write: A.F. Potenziani, Chair. and Pres.
Officers and Directors:* A.F. Potenziani,* Chair. and Pres.; Frank A. Potenziani,* V.P.; William Potenziani,* Secy.-Treas.; Kathleen Guggimio, Martha M. Potenziani.
Number of staff: None.
EIN: 237177691

1728
Carlsbad Foundation, Inc.
116 South Canyon St.
Carlsbad 88220   (505) 887-1131

Incorporated in 1977 in NM.
Foundation type: Community
Financial data (yr. ended 06/30/91): Assets, $4,992,901 (M); gifts received, $553,040; expenditures, $488,157; qualifying distributions, $327,626, including $327,626 for grants.
Purpose and activities: Student loans to paramedical students and grants to local scholars; support also for civic groups and charitable organizations.
Fields of interest: Education, medical education, health, mental health, hospitals, hunger, community development, general charitable giving.
Types of support: Student loans, operating budgets, seed money, emergency funds, building funds, equipment, matching funds, renovation projects, student aid, continuing support, consulting services, technical assistance, scholarship funds, program-related investments, special projects, publications, conferences and seminars.
Limitations: Giving limited to South Eddy County, NM. No grants for annual campaigns.
Publications: Annual report (including application guidelines), newsletter.
Application information: Application form not required.
   Initial approach: Letter

Copies of proposal: 1
Deadline(s): 1 week in advance of board meetings
Board meeting date(s): Monthly
Write: John Mills, Exec. Dir.
Officers and Directors:* Nancy Beard,* Pres.; Linda Aycock,* V.P.; W.R. Williamson, Jr.,* Secy.; Harvey Hicks,* Treas.; John Mills, Exec. Dir.; Jay Forbes, Sherry Griffin, Bruce Pardue, Jere K. Reid, Barbara Webber.
Number of staff: 1 full-time professional; 3 part-time support.
EIN: 850206472

1729
J. F. Maddox Foundation ▼
P.O. Box 5410
Hobbs 88241   (505) 393-6338

Established in 1963 in NM.
Donor(s): J.F. Maddox,‡ Mabel S. Maddox.‡
Foundation type: Independent
Financial data (yr. ended 06/30/91): Assets, $75,384,121 (M); gifts received, $9,760; expenditures, $5,202,665; qualifying distributions, $4,407,112, including $4,145,406 for 84 grants (high: $2,500,000; low: $250; average: $1,000-$150,000) and $78,350 for 74 loans to individuals.
Purpose and activities: Giving for community projects where self-help is evident, activities benefiting the elderly, youth education and development programs, the arts, and higher education, including student loans.
Fields of interest: Education, higher education, cultural programs, arts, aged, youth, social services, drug abuse.
Types of support: Student loans, building funds, equipment, general purposes, matching funds, seed money, special projects, renovation projects.
Limitations: Giving primarily in NM and western TX; student loans limited to Lea County, NM, residents. No support for private foundations. No grants for operating budgets or endowment funds.
Publications: Application guidelines.
Application information: Application form required for student loans.
   Initial approach: Letter
   Copies of proposal: 1
   Deadline(s): None
   Board meeting date(s): As needed
   Final notification: Varies
   Write: Robert D. Socolofsky, Exec. Dir.
Officers and Directors:* Don Maddox,* Pres.; James M. Maddox,* V.P. and Treas.; Robert D. Socolofsky, Secy. and Exec. Dir.; Harry H. Lynch.
Number of staff: 1 full-time professional; 2 part-time professional; 2 full-time support.
EIN: 756023767
Recent health grants:
1729-1 Guidance Center of Lea County, Hobbs, NM, $189,850. For building. 1991.
1729-2 Palmer Drug Abuse Program, Hobbs, NM, $55,100. For operations, equipment and building. 1991.

NEW YORK

1730
Benjamin and Elizabeth Abrams Foundation, Inc.
645 Madison Ave.
New York 10022

Incorporated in 1943 in NY.
Donor(s): Benjamin Abrams,‡ Elizabeth Abrams Kramer.
Foundation type: Independent
Financial data (yr. ended 12/31/91): Assets, $2,230,740 (M); expenditures, $120,928; qualifying distributions, $103,729, including $65,660 for 43 grants (high: $11,000; low: $50).
Fields of interest: Higher education, hospitals, Jewish welfare, cultural programs.
Limitations: Giving primarily in NY and in Palm Beach County, FL. No grants to individuals.
Application information: Contributes only to pre-selected organizations. Applications not accepted.
Officers and Directors:* Elizabeth Abrams Kramer,* Pres. and Treas.; Marjorie A. Hyman,* V.P.; Geraldine A. Kory,* Secy.; Cynthia Bernstein.
EIN: 136092960

1731
Louis and Anne Abrons Foundation, Inc. ▼
c/o First Manhattan Co.
437 Madison Ave.
New York 10017   (212) 756-3376

Incorporated in 1950 in NY.
Donor(s): Anne S. Abrons,‡ Louis Abrons.‡
Foundation type: Independent
Financial data (yr. ended 12/31/91): Assets, $35,000,000 (M); expenditures, $3,177,214; qualifying distributions, $3,132,820, including $3,132,820 for 164 grants (high: $350,000; low: $500; average: $5,000-$50,000).
Purpose and activities: Giving primarily to social welfare agencies, Jewish charities, major New York City institutions, civic improvement programs, education, and environmental and cultural projects.
Fields of interest: Social services, disadvantaged, homeless, hunger, family services, youth, child welfare, family planning, minorities, aged, employment, hospitals, Jewish giving, Jewish welfare, Israel, civic affairs, community development, legal services, education, elementary education, higher education, libraries, environment, arts, cultural programs, museums, performing arts, theater.
Types of support: Operating budgets, continuing support, annual campaigns, seed money, general purposes, special projects, scholarship funds, research, technical assistance, building funds, consulting services.
Limitations: Giving primarily in the New York, NY, metropolitan area. No grants to individuals.
Application information: Contributes primarily to pre-selected organizations. Application form not required.
Copies of proposal: 1

Deadline(s): None
Board meeting date(s): Feb., June, and Oct.
Final notification: No notification to unsolicited applications
Write: Richard Abrons, Pres.
Officers and Directors:* Richard Abrons,* Pres.; Herbert L. Abrons,* V.P.; Rita Aranow,* V.P.; Edward Aranow, Secy.-Treas.; Alix Abrons, Anne Abrons, Henry Abrons, John Abrons, Leslie Abrons, Peter Abrons, Judith Aranow, Vicki Klein.
Number of staff: None.
EIN: 136061329
Recent health grants:
1731-1 Big Apple Circus, NYC, NY, $12,900. 1990.
1731-2 Blythedale Childrens Hospital, Valhalla, NY, $20,000. 1990.
1731-3 Center for Preventive Psychiatry, White Plains, NY, $15,000. 1990.
1731-4 Hardee Memorial Hospital, Wauchula, FL, $10,000. 1990.
1731-5 Memorial Sloan-Kettering Cancer Center, NYC, NY, $50,000. 1990.
1731-6 Mount Sinai Hospital and Medical Center, NYC, NY, $10,000. 1990.
1731-7 Planned Parenthood of New York City, NYC, NY, $117,000. 1990.
1731-8 Visiting Nurse Service of New York, NYC, NY, $25,000. 1990.
1731-9 White Plains Hospital Medical Center, White Plains, NY, $25,000. 1990.

1732
The Achelis Foundation
c/o Morris & McVeigh
767 Third Ave.
New York 10017   (212) 418-0588

Incorporated in 1940 in NY.
Donor(s): Elizabeth Achelis.‡
Foundation type: Independent
Financial data (yr. ended 12/31/91): Assets, $23,639,808 (M); gifts received, $14,650; expenditures, $981,277; qualifying distributions, $800,000, including $800,000 for 40 grants (high: $100,000; low: $10,000; average: $10,000-$30,000).
Purpose and activities: Giving for social services, including child welfare and youth, the elderly, the handicapped, and issues of hunger and the homeless; health, including hospitals, medical research, drug abuse, and rehabilitation programs; literacy projects and other educational agencies; and arts and culture.
Fields of interest: Social services, child welfare, aged, handicapped, health, hospitals, drug abuse, education, secondary education, literacy, arts.
Types of support: Building funds, general purposes, operating budgets, matching funds, equipment, land acquisition, annual campaigns, capital campaigns, endowment funds, renovation projects, research, fellowships.
Limitations: Giving primarily in the NY area. No grants to individuals, or for experimental projects, films, travel, publications, or conferences; no loans.
Publications: Biennial report (including application guidelines), financial statement.
Application information: Application form not required.
Initial approach: Letter and proposal
Copies of proposal: 1

Deadline(s): None
Board meeting date(s): Usually in May, July, and Dec.
Write: Mary Caslin Ross, Secy. and Exec. Dir.
Officers: Guy G. Rutherfurd, Pres.; Peter Frelinghuysen, V.P. and Treas.; Mary Caslin Ross, Secy. and Exec. Dir.
Trustees: Harry W. Albright, Jr., Mary B. Braga, Anthony Drexel Duke, John N. Irwin III, Leslie Lenkowsky, Marguerite Sykes Nichols, Russel Pennoyer, Mary S. Phipps.
Number of staff: None.
EIN: 136022018
Recent health grants:
1732-1 Cancer Care, NYC, NY, $15,000. Toward Field Work Training Program for graduate students in social work. 1991.
1732-2 International Center for the Disabled (ICD), NYC, NY, $30,000. For 75th Anniversary Campaign and to meet J.M. Foundation challenge award. 1991.
1732-3 Phoenix House Foundation, NYC, NY, $100,000. For purchase of new, young-adult- and adolescent-treatment facility, specifically Belle Terre property in South Kortright, NY. 1991.
1732-4 Saint Francis Friends of the Poor, NYC, NY, $15,000. For doctor from Saint Vincent's Hospital to serve this fragile population. 1991.
1732-5 Saint Vincents Hospital and Medical Center of New York, NYC, NY, $20,000. For community-outreach endowment fund. 1991.
1732-6 Trudeau Institute, Saranac Lake, NY, $20,000. For Young Investigator Fund. 1991.
1732-7 Veritas Therapeutic Community Foundation, NYC, NY, $15,000. For Family Therapy Program. 1991.

1733
The Julius Ada Foundation, Inc.
280 Park Ave., Suite 2750
New York 10017   (212) 972-1818

Established in 1987 in NY.
Foundation type: Independent
Financial data (yr. ended 10/31/91): Assets, $4,307,552 (M); gifts received, $32,244; expenditures, $382,807; qualifying distributions, $316,015, including $315,550 for 6 grants (high: $120,000; low: $2,500).
Purpose and activities: Giving primarily to a university for AIDS research and a medical foundation for genetic research; some support for a Jewish geriatric center.
Fields of interest: Higher education, AIDS, medical research, Jewish giving, aged.
Types of support: Research, general purposes.
Limitations: No grants to individuals.
Application information:
Initial approach: Proposal
Deadline(s): None
Write: Lewis Stein
Officers: Carl Seaman, Pres.; Linda Seaman, V.P.; Robert Krissoff, Secy.
EIN: 112897412

1734
Louis and Bessie Adler Foundation, Inc.
654 Madison Ave.
New York 10021

Incorporated in 1946 in NY.
Donor(s): Louis Adler,‡ Louis Adler Realty Co., Inc.
Foundation type: Independent
Financial data (yr. ended 12/31/90): Assets, $4,098,853 (M); expenditures, $214,774; qualifying distributions, $199,514, including $197,500 for 18 grants (high: $30,000; low: $500).
Purpose and activities: Support primarily for art museums; giving also for higher and secondary education, hospitals, and youth agencies.
Fields of interest: Museums, higher education, secondary education, hospitals, youth.
Limitations: Giving primarily in NY. No grants to individuals.
Application information: Applications not accepted.
  Deadline(s): None
  Write: Robert Liberman, Pres.
Officers: Jeffrey P. Klein, Chair.; Robert Liberman, Pres. and Treas.; Donald S. Klein, V.P. and Secy.; Louise Grunwald, V.P.
EIN: 131880122

1735
The Aeroflex Foundation
c/o Berman and Hecht
Ten East 40th St., Rm. 710
New York 10016   (212) 696-4235

Established in 1964 in NY.
Donor(s): The Aeroflex Corp.
Foundation type: Company-sponsored
Financial data (yr. ended 09/30/91): Assets, $3,904,483 (M); expenditures, $247,418; qualifying distributions, $187,535, including $160,800 for 12 grants (high: $29,800; low: $1,000).
Fields of interest: Performing arts, education, hospitals, general charitable giving.
Limitations: No grants to individuals.
Application information: Contributes only to pre-selected organizations. Applications not accepted.
Trustees: Kay Knight Clarke, Derrick M. Hussey, William A. Perlmuth.
EIN: 136168635

1736
Agway Foundation
333 Butternut Dr.
P.O. Box 4933
Syracuse 13221   (315) 449-6506

Established in 1967 in NY.
Donor(s): Agway, Inc.
Foundation type: Company-sponsored
Financial data (yr. ended 06/30/91): Assets, $2,289,304 (M); expenditures, $248,010; qualifying distributions, $240,757, including $240,757 for 125 grants (high: $51,287; low: $50).
Purpose and activities: Emphasis on areas of interest to its farmer-members, including

statewide and regional agricultural organizations, health, and rural youth organizations.
Fields of interest: Agriculture, rural development, youth, health.
Types of support: Continuing support, annual campaigns, seed money, emergency funds, building funds, equipment, endowment funds, lectureships, conferences and seminars.
Limitations: Giving primarily in the northeastern states of CT, DE, ME, MD, MA, NH, NJ, NY, OH, PA, RI, and VT. No support for educational or religious organizations. No grants to individuals, or for operating budgets.
Publications: Application guidelines.
Application information: Application form not required.
  Initial approach: Letter and proposal
  Copies of proposal: 1
  Deadline(s): None
  Board meeting date(s): Every 6 to 8 weeks
  Write: Arthur J. Fogerty, Chair.
Officers and Trustees:* Arthur J. Fogerty,* Chair.; Peter J. O'Neill,* Secy.-Treas.; Arnon C. Greif.
Number of staff: 1 part-time professional; 1 part-time support.
EIN: 166089932

1737
AKC Fund, Inc.
165 East 72nd St., Suite 1B
New York 10021   (212) 737-1011

Incorporated in 1955 in NY.
Donor(s): Members of the Childs and Lawrence families.
Foundation type: Independent
Financial data (yr. ended 12/31/91): Assets, $3,714,201 (M); gifts received, $100; expenditures, $209,922; qualifying distributions, $188,084, including $168,500 for 54 grants (high: $22,500; low: $500; average: $500-$25,000).
Purpose and activities: Grants largely for secondary and higher education; support also for conservation, health services, family planning, and the arts.
Fields of interest: Secondary education, higher education, conservation, wildlife, health services, family planning, arts.
Types of support: Annual campaigns, capital campaigns, continuing support, general purposes.
Limitations: No grants to individuals.
Application information: Currently supporting trustee-sponsored projects only. Applications not accepted.
  Write: Ann Brownell Sloane, Admin.
Officers and Directors:* Barbara Childs Lawrence,* Pres.; Hope S. Childs, Secy.; John W. Childs, Treas.; Edward Calder Childs, Anne Childs Collins, J. Vinton Lawrence, Jane L. Mali, Jenny Childs Preston, Susannah C.L. Wood.
Number of staff: None.
EIN: 136091321

1738
The Akzo America Foundation
666 Fifth Ave., 37th Fl.
New York 10103   (212) 541-3740
FAX: (212) 541-3745

Trust established in 1952 in NC.

Donor(s): Akzo America.
Foundation type: Company-sponsored
Financial data (yr. ended 12/31/90): Assets, $84,301 (M); gifts received, $50,000; expenditures, $291,027; qualifying distributions, $290,868, including $224,708 for 37 grants (high: $25,000; low: $95) and $65,961 for employee matching gifts.
Purpose and activities: Giving primarily for scholarships, fellowships, and matching contributions of employees to accredited colleges, universities, and preparatory schools; support also for community funds, health organizations, and youth agencies.
Fields of interest: Higher education, secondary education, community funds, health, youth.
Types of support: Employee matching gifts, scholarship funds, fellowships, building funds.
Limitations: No grants to individuals.
Application information: Beginning in 1991, the foundation's activites are limited to disbursements through employee matching gifts. Guidelines for general grants are not available. Applications not accepted.
  Board meeting date(s): Dec.
  Write: Judy Kuhlmann, Mgr.
Trustees: Richard M. Clarke, Peter S. Gold.
Number of staff: 1 part-time professional; 1 part-time support.
EIN: 566061194

1739
Albany International Corporate Contributions Program
P.O. Box 1907
Albany 12201   (518) 445-2200

Financial data (yr. ended 12/31/90): Total giving, $215,000, including $175,000 for grants (high: $10,000; low: $1,000; average: $1,000-$5,000) and $40,000 for employee matching gifts.
Purpose and activities: Giving for general and economic education, public and private colleges, civic programs, scientific research and hospitals including building funds.
Fields of interest: Education, higher education, economics, civic affairs, hospitals, science and technology, hospitals—building funds.
Types of support: Annual campaigns, building funds, capital campaigns, employee matching gifts, employee-related scholarships.
Limitations: Giving primarily in headquarters and company locations.
Publications: Corporate report.
Application information: Applications not accepted.
  Write: Charles Buchanan, V.P. and Secy.
Number of staff: None.

1740
Albany's Hospital for Incurables
P.O. Box 3628, Executive Park
Albany 12203-0628   (518) 459-7711

Established in 1974 in NY.
Foundation type: Operating
Financial data (yr. ended 12/31/90): Assets, $2,550,000 (M); expenditures, $289,000; qualifying distributions, $274,000, including $274,000 for 16 grants (high: $45,000; low: $3,000; average: $17,000).

Purpose and activities: Grants to facilitate the development of better health care; support for hospitals and hospital building funds, health services and associations, nursing homes, hospices, community health centers, nutrition and hunger, rehabilitation and AIDS programs, and family and regional health planning groups.
Fields of interest: Health, health services, health associations, hospitals, aged, hospices, rehabilitation, nutrition, family services, AIDS.
Types of support: General purposes, building funds, equipment, matching funds, renovation projects, seed money, continuing support, special projects, capital campaigns.
Limitations: Giving limited to Albany, Schenectady, Rensselaer, and Saratoga counties, NY. No grants to individuals, or for deficit financing, endowment funds, scholarships, or fellowships.
Publications: Program policy statement, application guidelines, multi-year report.
Application information: Application form required.
  Initial approach: Telephone, letter, or proposal
  Copies of proposal: 1
  Deadline(s): 30 days before board meetings
  Board meeting date(s): Jan., Apr., June, and Sept.
  Final notification: 5 days after board meets
  Write: Arnold Cogswell, Pres.
Officers and Trustees:* Arnold Cogswell,* Pres. and Treas.; Albert Hessberg II,* Secy.; William Barnet II, Mrs. Lewis Muhlfelder, Mrs. Freeman T. Putney, Jr., Robert H. Randles, M.D., Richard F. Sonneborn, Mrs. Dorann Zimicki.
Number of staff: None.
EIN: 141364443

1741
Joseph Alexander Foundation
400 Madison Ave., Suite 906
New York 10017   (212) 355-3688

Established in 1960 in NY.
Donor(s): Joseph Alexander.‡
Foundation type: Independent
Financial data (yr. ended 10/31/91): Assets, $14,303,382 (M); expenditures, $815,713; qualifying distributions, $728,752, including $640,250 for 69 grants (high: $50,000; low: $500).
Purpose and activities: Giving primarily for education, including libraries, law and medical schools, and other higher education; health, especially the medical sciences and research, AIDS programs, the elderly and hospices, cancer care, scientific organizations, and hospitals; museums and other arts groups; and Israel, and Jewish welfare and religious organizations.
Fields of interest: Higher education, libraries, medical sciences, AIDS, health, cancer, aged, arts, Israel, Jewish giving.
Types of support: General purposes, operating budgets, building funds, equipment, research, conferences and seminars, annual campaigns, capital campaigns, endowment funds, lectureships, renovation projects, scholarship funds, special projects, exchange programs.
Limitations: Giving primarily in Israel and the continental U.S., with emphasis on New York, NY. No grants to individuals.
Publications: Financial statement.

Application information: Application form not required.
  Initial approach: Proposal
  Copies of proposal: 1
  Deadline(s): Submit proposal preferably in Feb. through Aug.
  Board meeting date(s): Jan., Apr., July, and Oct.
  Write: Alfred Mackler, V.P.
Officers and Directors:* Arthur S. Alfert,* Pres.; Alfred Mackler,* V.P.; Robert M. Weintraub,* Secy.; Helen Mackler,* Treas.; Harvey A. Mackler.
EIN: 510175951

1742
Frances Allen Foundation
c/o Allen & Co.
711 Fifth Ave.
New York 10022

Trust established in 1959 in NY.
Donor(s): Members of the Allen family, Allen & Co., Inc.
Foundation type: Independent
Financial data (yr. ended 12/31/90): Assets, $2,733,480 (M); expenditures, $137,503; qualifying distributions, $121,944, including $117,500 for 27 grants (high: $25,000; low: $1,000).
Fields of interest: Youth, higher education, social services, hospitals, health, medical research.
Limitations: Giving primarily in NY. No grants to individuals.
Application information:
  Initial approach: Proposal
  Copies of proposal: 1
  Deadline(s): None
  Board meeting date(s): Monthly
  Write: Charles Allen, Jr., Trustee
Trustees: Charles Allen, Jr., Herbert Allen, Herbert Anthony Allen.
EIN: 136104670

1743
Rita Allen Foundation, Inc.
550 Park Ave.
New York 10021

Incorporated in 1953 in NY.
Donor(s): Rita Allen Cassel.‡
Foundation type: Independent
Financial data (yr. ended 12/31/90): Assets, $11,318,499 (M); expenditures, $717,983; qualifying distributions, $593,651, including $580,319 for 61 grants (high: $90,996; low: $100).
Purpose and activities: Primarily medical grants, with emphasis on research in the fields of cancer, multiple sclerosis, cerebral palsy, and euphorics and analgesics related to the terminally ill; some support for recognized welfare and religious organizations.
Fields of interest: Medical research, cancer, welfare, religion.
Limitations: No grants to individuals (except university research scientists), or for building funds, or operating budgets.
Application information:
  Copies of proposal: 1
  Deadline(s): Jan. 15
  Board meeting date(s): Annually and as required
  Write: Milton E. Cassel, Pres.

Officers and Directors:* Milton E. Cassel,* Pres. and Treas.; Moore Gates, Jr.,* Secy.; Harry M. Hitch.
Number of staff: None.
EIN: 136116429

1744
The Allyn Foundation, Inc.
P.O. Box 22
Skaneateles 13152
Grant application address: RD No. 1, Cayuga, NY 13034; Tel.: (315) 252-7618

Incorporated in 1956 in NY.
Donor(s): William N. Allyn,‡ Welch Allyn, Inc.
Foundation type: Independent
Financial data (yr. ended 12/31/90): Assets, $4,138,513 (M); gifts received, $100,000; expenditures, $267,921; qualifying distributions, $255,393, including $250,795 for 51 grants (high: $50,000; low: $150).
Purpose and activities: Emphasis on higher and other education, including medical education; support also for general charitable purposes, including youth and social service agencies, hospitals, and community development.
Fields of interest: Higher education, medical education, youth, child welfare, social services, hospitals, medical research, community development, general charitable giving.
Types of support: Building funds, equipment, fellowships, renovation projects, research, scholarship funds.
Limitations: Giving primarily in Skaneateles and the Onondaga and Cayuga counties, NY, area. No support for religious programs. No grants to individuals, or for endowment funds; no loans.
Publications: Application guidelines.
Application information: Application form not required.
  Initial approach: Letter
  Copies of proposal: 1
  Deadline(s): None
  Board meeting date(s): 4 times per year
  Write: Mrs. Marie Infanger, Exec. Dir.
Officers and Directors:* William G. Allyn,* Pres.; Lew F. Allyn,* V.P.; William F. Allyn,* V.P.; Marie Infanger,* Secy.-Treas. and Exec. Dir.; Dawn N. Allyn, Eric Allyn, Janet J. Allyn, Sonya Allyn, Tasha Falcone, Margaret M. O'Connell, Ruth C. Penchoen, Elsa A. Soderberg, Peter Soderberg, Robert C. Soderberg, Wilbur L. Townsend.
Number of staff: 1 part-time professional.
EIN: 156017723

1745
Alpern Family Foundation, Inc.
c/o Weitzman & Rubin, P.C.
400 Jericho Tpke., Suite 205
Jericho 11753

Established in 1952.
Donor(s): Bernard E. Alpern.‡
Foundation type: Independent
Financial data (yr. ended 12/31/90): Assets, $54,099 (M); gifts received, $525,000; expenditures, $528,693; qualifying distributions, $528,147, including $525,000 for 3 grants (high: $325,000; low: $100,000).
Purpose and activities: Support for medical research, including cancer and cerebral palsy.

Fields of interest: Medical research, cancer.
Types of support: Research.
Limitations: Giving primarily in NY and MA. No grants to individuals.
Application information: Contributes only to pre-selected organizations. Applications not accepted.
Officers and Directors:* Lloyd J. Alpern,* Pres.; Steven I. Rubin,* Secy.; Edward M. Alpern, Laura F. Pinzur.
EIN: 136100302

1746
Altman Foundation ▼
220 East 42nd St., Suite 411
New York 10017   (212) 682-0970

Incorporated in 1913 in NY.
Donor(s): Benjamin Altman,‡ Col. Michael Friedsam.‡
Foundation type: Independent
Financial data (yr. ended 12/31/90): Assets, $116,270,688 (M); expenditures, $5,878,791; qualifying distributions, $5,225,663, including $4,695,625 for 146 grants (high: $250,000; low: $2,500; average: $10,000-$100,000).
Purpose and activities: Support for non-public and independent schools and in particular, programs benefiting talented disadvantaged youth; private voluntary hospitals and health centers to extend medical services to the underserved; artistic and cultural institutions for outreach projects; and social welfare programs providing long-term solutions for the needs of the disadvantaged.
Fields of interest: Education, hospitals, health, AIDS, arts, cultural programs, welfare, disadvantaged.
Types of support: Special projects.
Limitations: Giving limited to NY, with emphasis on the boroughs of New York City. No grants to individuals, or for building funds.
Publications: Application guidelines.
Application information: Application form not required.
   Initial approach: Letter
   Copies of proposal: 1
   Deadline(s): None
   Board meeting date(s): 6 times a year
   Write: John S. Burke, Pres.
Officers and Trustees:* John S. Burke,* Pres.; Thomas C. Burke,* V.P and Treas.; Marion C. Baer, Secy.; Karen Rosa, Exec. Dir.; Bernard Finkelstein, Jane B. O'Connell, Maurice A. Selinger, Jr., Julia V. Shea, John W. Townsend IV, Victor D. Ziminsky, Jr.
Number of staff: 3 full-time professional; 4 full-time support.
EIN: 131623879
Recent health grants:
1746-1 Albert Einstein College of Medicine of Yeshiva University, Bronx, NY, $100,000. To expand and enhance services and outreach to disadvantaged children with developmental delay or disability. 1990.
1746-2 Benedictine Health Foundation, Kingston, NY, $50,000. For one-time-only grant toward endowment for Benedictine Hospital Prenatal Clinic. 1990.
1746-3 Big Apple Circus, NYC, NY, $25,000. For Clown Care Unit. 1990.

1746-4 Calvary Hospital, Calvary Fund, Bronx, NY, $50,000. For endowment. 1990.
1746-5 Catholic Home Bureau, NYC, NY, $100,000. For Maternity Birthcare program. 1990.
1746-6 Childrens Aid Society, NYC, NY, $25,000. For continued support of Mobile Medical/Dental Van. 1990.
1746-7 Fountain House, NYC, NY, $40,000. To continue support for New York City Clubhouse Network Program. 1990.
1746-8 Freedom Institute, NYC, NY, $10,000. For general support. 1990.
1746-9 Hospital Chaplaincy, NYC, NY, $15,000. To expand clinical education program. 1990.
1746-10 Lenox Hill Hospital, NYC, NY, $10,000. To support activities of Tropical Disease Center within New York State. 1990.
1746-11 Little Sisters of the Assumption Family Health Service, NYC, NY, $25,000. For Early Childhood Specialization. 1990.
1746-12 Manhattan Bowery Corporation, NYC, NY, $30,000. For continued support for Mobile Medical Outreach Clinic. 1990.
1746-13 Mental Health Association of New York and Bronx Counties, NYC, NY, $25,000. To continue support for project to design program models for community residences serving mentally ill children and adolescents. 1990.
1746-14 Mount Saint Ursula Speech Center, Bronx, NY, $35,000. To continue intensive rehabilitation program for young children suffering from speech, hearing and/or learning disabilities. 1990.
1746-15 Mount Sinai Hospital and Medical Center, NYC, NY, $75,000. For Early Child Health Project. 1990.
1746-16 New York Foundling Hospital, NYC, NY, $35,000. For transitional staffing to launch Sister Cecilia Schneider Community Housing Services project. 1990.
1746-17 New York Medical College, Valhalla, NY, $100,000. Toward capital campaign. 1990.
1746-18 Outreach Development Corporation, Outreach Project, Woodhaven, NY, $25,000. For development of Outpatient/Aftercare Program. 1990.
1746-19 Research Foundation of the City University of New York, NYC, NY, $53,000. For Evening/Weekend A.A.S. Degree in Nursing Program for part-time students at Borough of Manhattan Community College. 1990.
1746-20 Saint Dominics Home, Family Service Center, Bronx, NY, $30,000. For Grief and Bereavement Counseling Program for children in foster care. 1990.
1746-21 Saint Lukes-Roosevelt Hospital Center, NYC, NY, $100,000. To continue support for Palliative-Care Program and help build endowment for program. 1990.
1746-22 Saint Vincents Hospital and Medical Center of New York, NYC, NY, $10,000. For benefit of hospital. 1990.
1746-23 Saint Vincents Hospital and Medical Center of New York, NYC, NY, $10,000. For research and training programs in Department of Psychiatry. 1990.
1746-24 Steinway Mental Health Committee, Astoria, NY, $20,000. To continue support for Elder Care Project for homebound elderly in Queens. 1990.

1746-25 United Cerebral Palsy Research and Education Foundation, NYC, NY, $25,000. Toward research and professional education activities within New York State. 1990.
1746-26 Valentine Lane Family Practice Center, Yonkers, NY, $30,000. To develop services for HIV-infected patients and their families. 1990.
1746-27 Visiting Nurse Service of New York, NYC, NY, $100,000. To launch First Steps, comprehensive case management program working with substance abusing mothers and their infants in Harlem. 1990.
1746-28 Womens Action Alliance, NYC, NY, $25,000. To replicate Women's Alcohol and Drug Education Project for low-income women in New York City. 1990.

1747
The Altschul Foundation
342 Madison Ave., Suite 1002
New York 10017

Incorporated in 1941 in NY.
Donor(s): Louis Altschul,‡ Jeanette Cohen Altschul.‡
Foundation type: Independent
Financial data (yr. ended 06/30/91): Assets, $8,640,031 (M); expenditures, $282,450; qualifying distributions, $294,142, including $282,450 for 57 grants (high: $56,000; low: $500).
Purpose and activities: Emphasis on health associations, medical research, and Jewish organizations, including welfare funds; support also for youth and social services.
Fields of interest: Health associations, medical research, Jewish giving, Jewish welfare, youth, social services.
Limitations: Giving primarily in New York, NY, and FL. No grants to individuals.
Application information: Contributes only to pre-selected organizations. Applications not accepted.
   Board meeting date(s): June and Sept.
   Write: Leonard Rodney
Officers and Trustees:* Phyllis Rothstein,* Pres.; Louis Rothstein,* V.P.; Vivian C. Reichman,* Secy.-Treas.; Valerie Aspinwall, William Rothstein, Susan Rothstein-Schwimmer.
Number of staff: None.
EIN: 136400009

1748
Amax Foundation, Inc.
200 Park Ave.
New York 10166   (212) 856-4250

Incorporated in 1955 in NY.
Donor(s): Amax, Inc.
Foundation type: Company-sponsored
Financial data (yr. ended 12/31/90): Assets, $6,755,919 (M); gifts received, $2,000,000; expenditures, $1,158,751; qualifying distributions, $1,158,751, including $1,080,100 for 405 grants (high: $100,000; low: $250; average: $500-$2,000) and $44,480 for 204 employee matching gifts.
Purpose and activities: Grants for higher education, largely in the fields related to mining, metallurgy, geology, geophysics, and geochemistry; employee matching gift program

and Amax Earth Sciences Scholarships for children of employees only; health and welfare, especially United Way campaigns; cultural programs; and civic and public affairs.
Fields of interest: Higher education, physical sciences, engineering, science and technology, cultural programs, civic affairs, public policy, international affairs, community funds, social services, health, welfare.
Types of support: Building funds, continuing support, employee matching gifts, fellowships, general purposes, professorships, research, scholarship funds, employee-related scholarships, matching funds.
Limitations: Giving primarily in areas of company operations. No support for fraternal, religious, or sectarian organizations, primary or secondary education, creative arts groups, sports or athletic events, nursing homes, organizations supported by the United Way (unless permission has been granted by the United Way), or governmental or quasi-governmental agencies. No grants to individuals (except company-employee scholarships), or for memorial funds, goodwill advertisements in yearbooks or souvenir programs, charity dinners or special performance events, or endowment funds; no loans.
Publications: Application guidelines, program policy statement, informational brochure.
Application information: Employee-related scholarship program is not administered directly by the foundation; recipients are chosen by an outside organization. Application form not required.
> *Initial approach:* Letter
> *Copies of proposal:* 1
> *Deadline(s):* Submit proposal by Mar. 15 for civic and charitable projects and from July 1 to Sept. 1 for educational projects
> *Board meeting date(s):* May, Oct., and as required
> *Final notification:* 60 days
> *Write:* Sonja B. Michaud, Pres.
Officers and Directors:* Sonja B. Michaud,* Pres.; Helen M. Feeney,* V.P.; Raymond J. Cooke, Secy.; Charles E. Toder,* Controller.
Number of staff: 1 full-time professional; 1 full-time support.
EIN: 136111368

1749
AmBase Foundation, Inc.
(Formerly The Home Group Foundation)
59 Maiden Ln.
New York 10038   (212) 530-6208

Incorporated in 1963 in MO.
Foundation type: Company-sponsored
Financial data (yr. ended 12/31/90): Assets, $3,904,509 (M); gifts received, $30,500; expenditures, $394,998; qualifying distributions, $385,801, including $385,123 for 22 grants (high: $150,000; low: $500).
Fields of interest: Higher education, hospitals, youth, civic affairs, cultural programs, health associations.
Application information: The foundation has discontinued its employee-related scholarship program. Applications not accepted.
Officers and Directors:* George T. Scharffenberger,* Chair.; Robert L. Woodrum,* V.P.; Christine Werner, Secy.; Eben W. Pyne.

Number of staff: 1 part-time professional; 1 part-time support.
EIN: 133246657

1750
American Express Foundation ▼
c/o American Express Co.
American Express Tower, World Financial Ctr.
New York 10285-4710   (212) 640-5661

Incorporated in 1954 in NY.
Donor(s): American Express Co., and its subsidiaries.
Foundation type: Company-sponsored
Financial data (yr. ended 12/31/90): Assets, $1,075,128 (M); gifts received, $13,524,225; expenditures, $14,266,991; qualifying distributions, $14,260,692, including $12,604,684 for 811 grants (high: $890,000; low: $200; average: $1,000-$50,000), $423,485 for grants to individuals and $1,231,951 for employee matching gifts.
Purpose and activities: The foundation's philanthropic activities focus on three strategic themes: community service, education and employment, cultural programs, and historic preservation.
Fields of interest: Arts, museums, theater, cultural programs, historic preservation, education, secondary education, education—early childhood, elementary education, education—minorities, AIDS, drug abuse, child development, employment, child welfare, handicapped, minorities, civic affairs.
Types of support: Special projects, employee-related scholarships, employee matching gifts, seed money, annual campaigns, emergency funds, general purposes.
Limitations: Giving primarily in AZ, CA, CO, FL, GA, IL, MN, NC, NE, NY, TX, UT, MA, PA, and Washington, DC. International Committees include Asia/Pacific, Canada, Europe, Latin America, and Japan. No support for religious or fraternal organizations, sporting events or athletic programs, umbrella organizations with active grantmaking programs, or professional, trade, or marketing associations. No grants to individuals (except for employee-related scholarships), or for endowments, capital campaigns, advertising in journals or yearbooks, publication of books, magazines or articles in professional journals, or medical research; support for endorsements and capital campaigns on rare occasions only.
Publications: Grants list, informational brochure (including application guidelines).
Application information: Application form not required.
> *Initial approach:* Letter or proposal
> *Copies of proposal:* 1
> *Deadline(s):* None
> *Board meeting date(s):* Biannually
> *Final notification:* 3 to 4 months
> *Write:* Mary Beth Salerno, Pres. (Domestic Contact), or Cornelia W. Higginson, V.P. and Secy. (International Contact)
Senior Staff: Mary Beth Salerno, Pres. and V.P., Domestic Prog.; Cornelia Higginson, V.P., Intl. Prog. and Secy.; David A. Ruth, V.P., Philanthropic Prog. and Cult. Affairs; Susan Bloom, V.P., Cult. Affairs.
Trustees: Harvey Golub, Aldo Papone, James D. Robinson III, Joan E. Spero.

Number of staff: 10 full-time professional; 8 full-time support; 2 part-time support.
EIN: 136123529
Recent health grants:
1750-1 American Council for Drug Education, NYC, NY, $10,000. For drug education programs. 1990.
1750-2 American Foundation for AIDS Research, NYC, NY, $10,000. For AIDS prevention education. 1990.
1750-3 American Psychiatric Association, NYC, NY, $10,000. For volunteer services to the homeless. 1990.
1750-4 Black Leadership Commission on AIDS, NYC, NY, $10,000. For community education programs. 1990.
1750-5 Epilepsy Foundation of America, Landover, MD, $20,000. For Coelho Fund. 1990.
1750-6 Gay Mens Health Crisis (GMHC), NYC, NY, $20,000. For AIDS Crisis Fellowship Program. 1990.
1750-7 Hispanic AIDS Forum, NYC, NY, $15,000. For volunteer coordination. 1990.
1750-8 Hospital for Special Surgery, Sports Medicine Center, NYC, NY, $25,000. 1990.
1750-9 House Ear Institute, Los Angeles, CA, $10,000. For capital campaign for Los Angeles Medical Center. 1990.
1750-10 House Ear Institute, Los Angeles, CA, $10,000. For capital campaign for Los Angeles Medical Center. 1990.
1750-11 Learning Through an Expanded Arts Program (LEAP), NYC, NY, $10,000. For drug prevention program. 1990.
1750-12 Memorial Sloan-Kettering Cancer Center, NYC, NY, $50,000. For clinical research program. 1990.
1750-13 National Minority AIDS Council, DC, $20,000. For Project HEAL. 1990.
1750-14 New York Infirmary-Beekman Downtown Hospital, NYC, NY, $15,000. For general support. 1990.
1750-15 Occupational Physicians Scholarship Fund, Arlington Heights, IL, $12,500. For scholarship fund. 1990.
1750-16 Queens County Youth Development Corporation, Woodhaven, NY, $12,500. For outpatient/aftercare program. 1990.
1750-17 Variety Club Childrens Charities, London, England, $25,000. For Chailey Heritage School. 1990.
1750-18 Village Nursing Home, NYC, NY, $15,000. For AIDS pediatric care program. 1990.

1751
American Express Philanthropic Program
American Express Tower, World Financial Center
200 Vesey St.
New York 10285-4710   (212) 640-2000

Financial data (yr. ended 12/31/90): Total giving, $7,646,785 for grants.
Purpose and activities: "The American Express Philanthropic Program focuses on three themes: education and employment, cultural programs, and community service. Education and employment focuses on programs that prepare young people and others for employment, programs which promote educational reform from early childhood through secondary level and

address work/family issues such as increasing quality child care for working parents, and programs that increase geographic literacy. In the area of cultural programs we foster cultural diversity and cross-cultural communication. Our focus is on programs that provide arts education to young people, preserve historic, natural and cultural assets, and programs that increase the accessibility of the arts and help organizations develop new audiences. In addition to our comprehensive support to United Way, in the area of community service our focus is on local programs in communities with large numbers of American Express employees which address critical issues such as children at risk, drug abuse prevention, AIDS education, and homelessness; promote volunteerism; and strengthen the ability of the nonprofit sector to deliver services. In each of our philanthropic theme areas we encourage projects that advance the full participation of minorities, women, and the disabled in our society." Figures represent giving by all the direct giving programs, excluding foundations. Current Giving entries represent direct giving by all the subsidiaries, and also by the foundations: American Express Foundation and American Express Minnesota Foundation.
Fields of interest: Education, employment, cultural programs, community development, historic preservation, minorities, elementary education, education—minorities, secondary education, Asia, Japan, Europe, Canada, Latin America, AIDS, Africa, Caribbean, Australia, international relief.
Types of support: Employee matching gifts, seed money, special projects, general purposes.
Limitations: Giving primarily in operating locations and to national and international organizations: in U.S. geographic committees focus on AZ, CA, CO, DC, DE, FL, GA, IL, MA, MN, NC, NE, NY, PA, RI, TX, UT; international committees focus on Australia/South Pacific/South Asia, Canada, East Asia/Japan, Europe/Middle East/Africa, and Latin America/Carribbean. No support for organizations that discriminate on the basis of race, sex, or, religion, religious, fraternal or sports organizations, political causes, or hospitals, health, and disease-specific organizations with rare exceptions. No grants to individuals, or for fundraising events, goodwill advertising, travel, books, magazines, or articles, endowments or capital campaigns, with rare exceptions.
Publications: Grants list, application guidelines.
Application information: Funding decisions are made by Philanthropic Program trustees and staff. Local and regional committees in the U.S. and internationally originate proposals, participate in project development, and make recommendations. Application form not required.
  Initial approach: Letter of inquiry or proposal can be addressed to headquarters or local branch; Telephone for geography competition: (800) 395-GLOBE
  Deadline(s): Feb. 28th for geography competition
  Board meeting date(s): On an ongoing basis
  Final notification: 3 to 4 months
  Write: Cornelia W. Higginson, V.P., Philanthropic Prog. (International); Mary Beth Salerno, V.P., Philanthropic Prog. (Domestic); Sven Groennings, V.P., Education Programs

Administrators: Cornelia Higginson, V.P., Philanthropic Prog., International; Fran Kittredge, Sr. V.P., Shearson Lehman Hutton; Mary Beth Salerno, V.P., American Express Fdn., Domestic; Sven Groennings, V.P., Education Progs.
Number of staff: 7 full-time professional; 1 part-time professional; 7 full-time support.

1752
American Skin Association, Inc.
(Formerly The Skin Disease Society, Inc.)
150 East 58th St., 32nd Fl.
New York 10155   (212) 753-8260

Established in 1987 in NY.
Foundation type: Independent
Financial data (yr. ended 12/31/91): Assets, $804,722 (M); gifts received, $177,180; expenditures, $499,709; qualifying distributions, $368,093, including $351,093 for 6 grants (high: $333,334; low: $1,000) and $17,000 for 4 grants to individuals (high: $10,000; low: $1,000).
Fields of interest: Dermatology, medical research.
Types of support: Research, fellowships, professorships, annual campaigns.
Publications: Annual report, informational brochure.
Application information: Applications not accepted.
  Board meeting date(s): 4 times a year
  Write: Patricia Barrett, J.D., Exec. Dir.
Officers and Directors:* Peter Bentley,* Chair.; George W. Hambrick, Jr., M.D.,* Pres.; Edward O. Cole, V.P.; D. Martin Carter, M.D.,* Secy.; Donald G. Calder,* Treas.; Peggy A. Brooks-Bertram, Ph.D., Robert H. Burns, Mimi W. Coleman, S. Hazard Gillespie, John B. Lowry, Doris Merrill Magowan, Arthur J. Mahon, Oscar Robertson, Cecily B. Selby, Ph.D., Ruth S. Stanton, John S. Strauss, M.D., David D. Thompson, M.D., William H. Told, Jr., Anna Glen Vietor, Diane Wolf.
Number of staff: 2 full-time professional; 1 part-time support.
EIN: 133401320

1753
American Stock Exchange Corporate Giving Program
86 Trinity Place
New York 10006   (212) 306-1205

Financial data (yr. ended 12/31/90): Total giving, $500,000 for grants.
Purpose and activities: Supports arts, culture, theater, dance, health, all levels of education, children's and youth services, women's issues, minority programs, international groups, rural concerns, and urban problems. Community funding includes economic aid and job development, community organizing, and civic affairs; employee gift matching for education. Provides use of company facilities and donations of company's primary goods or services.
Fields of interest: Education, arts, performing arts, cultural programs, youth, minorities, women, rural development, urban development, civic affairs, economics, health.
Types of support: General purposes, special projects, technical assistance, in-kind gifts, use of facilities.

Limitations: Giving primarily in headquarters city. No grants to individuals.
Publications: Application guidelines.
Application information: Application form not required.
  Initial approach: Proposal
  Copies of proposal: 1
  Board meeting date(s): End of each quarter
  Final notification: Varies
  Write: Yvonne Harris Jones, Asst. V.P.
Number of staff: 1 full-time professional; 1 full-time support.

1754
Douglas G. Anderson - Leigh R. Evans Foundation
3575 Oakwood Ave.
Horseheads 14845   (607) 734-2281

Incorporated in 1960 in NY.
Donor(s): Hardinge Brothers, Inc.
Foundation type: Independent
Financial data (yr. ended 10/31/91): Assets, $1,457,161 (M); gifts received, $125,000; expenditures, $252,413; qualifying distributions, $249,126, including $242,595 for 31 grants (high: $55,000; low: $600).
Purpose and activities: Giving for higher education, hospitals, a community fund, and the performing arts.
Fields of interest: Higher education, hospitals, community funds, performing arts.
Types of support: General purposes, building funds, equipment, renovation projects.
Limitations: Giving primarily in Elmira, NY. No grants to individuals.
Application information:
  Initial approach: Proposal
  Copies of proposal: 1
  Board meeting date(s): Semiannually and as required
  Write: Robert G. Prochnow, Pres.
Officers and Trustees:* Robert G. Prochnow,* Pres.; Bertha A. Greenlee,* V.P.; Bela C. Tifft,* Secy.; Malcolm L. Gibson, Treas.; Robert E. Agan, James L. Flynn, E. Martin Gibson, Douglas A. Greenlee, Joseph C. Littleton, Boyd McDowell, Whitney Powers.
EIN: 166024690

1755
The Aquidneck Foundation
c/o Goldman Sachs & Co., Tax Dept.
85 Broad St.
New York 10004-2408

Established in 1981 in NY.
Donor(s): Stephen B. Kay.
Foundation type: Independent
Financial data (yr. ended 02/28/91): Assets, $1,852,215 (M); gifts received, $123,523; expenditures, $223,355; qualifying distributions, $206,394, including $206,305 for 57 grants (high: $50,000; low: $50).
Purpose and activities: Giving primarily for Jewish organizations and education, including universities; support also for cancer research.
Fields of interest: Jewish giving, Jewish welfare, education, higher education, cancer.
Limitations: Giving primarily in New York, NY, and Boston, MA. No grants to individuals.

Application information: Contributes only to pre-selected organizations. Applications not accepted.
Trustee: Stephen B. Kay.
EIN: 133102904

1756
Adrian & Jessie Archbold Charitable Trust
150 East 58th St., 32nd Fl.
New York 10155-0002   (212) 371-1152

Trust established in 1976 in NY.
Donor(s): Mrs. Adrian Archbold.‡
Foundation type: Independent
Financial data (yr. ended 11/30/90): Assets, $17,065,394 (M); expenditures, $944,290; qualifying distributions, $796,181, including $770,500 for 63 grants (high: $250,000; low: $500; average: $5,000-$10,000).
Purpose and activities: Grants primarily for the medical sciences, especially biology; support also for hospitals and health-related organizations, child welfare and youth programs, and social service agencies.
Fields of interest: Medical sciences, biological sciences, hospitals, health, dermatology, child welfare, youth, social services, education, cultural programs.
Types of support: General purposes, continuing support, conferences and seminars.
Limitations: No grants to individuals, or for endowment funds, scholarships, fellowships, or building funds; no loans.
Publications: Program policy statement.
Application information: Unsolicited proposals not encouraged. Application form not required.
   Initial approach: Letter
   Copies of proposal: 1
   Deadline(s): None
   Board meeting date(s): As required
   Final notification: 3 to 6 months
   Write: Arthur J. Mahon, Trustee
Trustees: Arthur J. Mahon, Chemical Bank.
Number of staff: 2 part-time professional.
EIN: 510179829

1757
Arkell Hall Foundation, Inc.
66 Montgomery St.
Canajoharie 13317   (518) 673-5417

Incorporated in 1948 in NY.
Donor(s): Mrs. F.E. Barbour,‡ and others.
Foundation type: Independent
Financial data (yr. ended 11/30/91): Assets, $32,445,307 (M); expenditures, $1,746,198; qualifying distributions, $1,370,149, including $760,621 for grants (average: $5,000-$10,000).
Purpose and activities: Maintains a residence and home for needy elderly women who are residents of Montgomery County; also general local giving, with emphasis on higher education, including scholarship funds, hospitals, and health and social services, including youth agencies.
Fields of interest: Education, higher education, medical education, health, health services, hospitals, social services, family services, youth, handicapped.
Types of support: Scholarship funds, building funds, equipment.

Limitations: Giving limited to the Canajoharie, NY, area. No grants to individuals, or for multi-year commitments, travel, conferences or other personal expenses; no loans.
Publications: Application guidelines.
Application information: Application form not required.
   Initial approach: Proposal
   Copies of proposal: 1
   Deadline(s): Sept. 15
   Board meeting date(s): Feb., May, Aug., and Oct.
   Final notification: Dec. 1
   Write: Joseph A. Santangelo, Administrator
Officers and Trustees:* Edward W. Shineman, Jr.,* Pres.; William B. MacKenzie,* V.P.; Ferdinand C. Kaiser,* Secy.; Robert H. Wille,* Treas.; Joseph A. Santangelo,* Administrator; James R. Dern, Joyce G. Dresser, Frances L. Howard, William T. Martin.
Number of staff: 1 full-time professional; 1 part-time professional; 1 full-time support; 1 part-time support.
EIN: 141343077

1758
J. Aron Charitable Foundation, Inc. ▼
126 East 56th St., Suite 2300
New York 10022   (212) 832-3405

Incorporated in 1934 in NY.
Donor(s): Members of the Aron family.
Foundation type: Independent
Financial data (yr. ended 12/31/91): Assets, $28,197,356 (M); expenditures, $2,958,637; qualifying distributions, $2,722,969, including $2,585,767 for 221 grants (high: $309,375; low: $100; average: $500-$25,000).
Purpose and activities: Giving primarily for hospitals and health associations, cultural programs, social service and youth agencies, Jewish welfare funds, and education, including medical schools.
Fields of interest: Hospitals, health associations, medical research, cultural programs, museums, historic preservation, social services, youth, Jewish welfare, education, medical education, general charitable giving.
Types of support: Annual campaigns, building funds, capital campaigns, general purposes, research, special projects.
Limitations: Giving primarily in New York, NY, and New Orleans, LA. No grants to individuals.
Application information: Application form not required.
   Initial approach: Proposal
   Copies of proposal: 1
   Deadline(s): None
   Board meeting date(s): Apr., July, Sept., and Dec.
   Write: Peter A. Aron, Exec. Dir.
Officers and Directors:* Jack R. Aron,* Pres.; Peter A. Aron,* V.P. and Exec. Dir.; Robert Aron,* V.P.; Hans G. Jepson,* Secy.-Treas.; Jacqueline A. Morrison, Ronald J. Stein.
Number of staff: 2 full-time professional; 1 full-time support; 1 part-time support.
EIN: 136068230

1759
ASARCO Foundation
180 Maiden Ln.
New York 10038   (212) 510-1813

Incorporated in 1956 in NY.
Donor(s): ASARCO Inc.
Foundation type: Company-sponsored
Financial data (yr. ended 12/31/90): Assets, $1,173,365 (M); expenditures, $418,343; qualifying distributions, $416,065, including $337,958 for 34 grants (high: $100,000; low: $50) and $76,587 for 154 employee matching gifts.
Purpose and activities: A limited program, including support for community funds, law and justice, including legal defense funds and societies, scholarship programs of colleges and universities with emphasis on mineral technology and engineering, hospitals, and cultural activities. The foundation also operates an employee matching gift program that matches gifts towards education, primarily higher education.
Fields of interest: Community funds, higher education, engineering, hospitals, cultural programs.
Types of support: Scholarship funds, fellowships, general purposes, continuing support, employee matching gifts.
Limitations: Giving limited to areas of company operations. No grants to individuals, or for endowment funds, research, or operating budgets; no loans.
Publications: Program policy statement, application guidelines.
Application information: Application form not required.
   Initial approach: Letter
   Deadline(s): None
   Board meeting date(s): As required
   Final notification: 2 to 3 months
   Write: D.M. Noyes, V.P.
Officers and Directors:* Robert J. Muth, Pres.; J.R. Corbett,* V.P.; Francis R. McAllister,* V.P.; D.M. Noyes, V.P.; K.A. Dockry, Secy.; R.J. O'Keefe, Controller; George W. Anderson, R.J. Bothwell, A.B. Kinsolving, Richard J. Osborne, T.C. Osborne.
Number of staff: 1 part-time support.
EIN: 136089860

1760
The ASDA Foundation
c/o First Spring Corp.
425 Park Ave., 28th Fl.
New York 10022   (212) 688-4010

Established in 1983.
Foundation type: Independent
Financial data (yr. ended 09/30/91): Assets, $8,919,949 (M); expenditures, $1,019,389; qualifying distributions, $783,418, including $783,418 for grants (high: $400,000).
Fields of interest: Higher education, medical research, AIDS.
Types of support: General purposes, research.
Application information: Application form not required.
   Deadline(s): None
   Write: Dr. Guido Goldman, Chair.
Officers and Directors:* Guido Goldman,* Chair.; B. Lance Sauerteig,* Pres.; Edward Neuburg, V.P. for Operations and Secy.; Lynne

Rodriquez, V.P. for Finance and Treas.; Jeanne Conley, Alain de Gunzburg, Charles de Gunzburg, Jean de Gunzburg, Ken Musen.
EIN: 521319624

1761
AT&T Company Corporate Giving Program
1301 Sixth Avenue
New York 10019   (212) 841-4747
University Equipment Prog.: Room 2F-111, P.O. Box 3044, 1100 E. Warrenville Rd., Naperville, IL 60566-7044

Financial data (yr. ended 12/31/91): Total giving, $27,200,000, including $5,100,000 for 1,477 grants and $22,100,000 for in-kind gifts.
Purpose and activities: "For more than one hendred years, AT&T has been steadfastly committed to public service and social responsibility. From the beginning, we've recognized that our business interests are entwined with the well-being of our society. As a result, AT&T has developed an ethic of not just doing well, but doing good. At the heart of our corporate citizenship is a set of beleiefs. We believe in innovation - in taking risks and trying new approaches. We believe in diversity - that we are richer when we embrace our differences, and learn from them. We believe in equality - that everyone should have an equal opportunity to achieve success and independence. We believe in human development - that investing in the talents and potential of people is the key to a better society. We believe in involvement - that people working together can make a difference." In addition to giving cash and equipment, the company also supports non-profit organizations through employee volunteerism.
Fields of interest: Higher education, education, health, hospitals, social services, community funds, arts, cultural programs.
Types of support: Use of facilities, employee volunteer services.
Limitations: Giving primarily in areas of company operations except for national organizations.
Publications: Informational brochure, biennial report.
Application information: National organizations, or universities, or organizations in New York City should write to NY office; local organizations should write for list of regional Contributions Coordinators. Application form not required.
  Initial approach: Letter of inquiry no more than 3 pages; Send requests to nearest company facility
  Copies of proposal: 1
  Deadline(s): None
  Write: Deb DeFago, AT&T Contribs. Coord.
Number of staff: 1 full-time professional; 8 part-time professional; 1 full-time support; 2 part-time support.

1762
AT&T Foundation ▼
1301 Ave. of the Americas, Rm. 3100
New York 10019   (212) 841-4747

Address for application guidelines and biennial report: P.O. Box 45284, Dept. FC, Jacksonville, FL 32232-5284
FAX: (212) 841-4683

Established in 1984 in NY.
Donor(s): American Telephone & Telegraph Co., Western Electric Fund.
Foundation type: Company-sponsored
Financial data (yr. ended 12/31/90): Assets, $98,900,000 (M); expenditures, $30,333,952; qualifying distributions, $30,333,952, including $26,139,946 for 847 grants (high: $1,000,000; low: $1,000; average: $5,000-$25,000) and $4,194,006 for 30,877.
Purpose and activities: Principal source of philanthropy for AT&T and its subsidiaries; scope is national, emphasizing support of private higher education, and institutions and projects in the areas of health care, social action, and the arts.
Fields of interest: Education, education—minorities, educational research, higher education, education—early childhood, secondary education, engineering, mathematics, science and technology, physical sciences, computer sciences, arts, performing arts, museums, dance, theater, music, AIDS, family services, minorities, youth, child welfare, child development, women, public policy, international affairs.
Types of support: Matching funds, employee matching gifts, special projects, research, annual campaigns, endowment funds, operating budgets, technical assistance, capital campaigns, scholarship funds.
Limitations: Giving on a national basis, including in CA, CO, Washington, DC, FL, GA, IL, MA, NJ, NY, OH, PA, and TX. No support for religious organizations for sectarian purposes, local chapters of national organizations, social sciences or health sciences programs, medical or nursing schools, or junior and community colleges, industrial affiliate programs or technical trade associations, medical research projects, disease-related health associations, operating expenses or capital campaigns of local health or human service agencies other than hospitals, or sports, teams, or athletic competitions. No grants to individuals, or for emergency funds, deficit financing, land acquisition, fellowships, publications, or conferences; does not purchase advertisements and sponsorships or donate equipment.
Publications: Biennial report, informational brochure (including application guidelines).
Application information: Detailed program limitations and addresses of regional Contributions Managers provided in guidelines. Application form not required.
  Initial approach: Letter (3 pages or less)
  Copies of proposal: 1
  Deadline(s): Jan., Apr., June, and Sept.
  Board meeting date(s): Mar., June, Sept., and Dec.
  Final notification: 90 days
  Write: Laura Abbott, Secy.
Officers and Trustees:* Marilyn Laurie,* Chair.; Reynold Levy,* Pres.; Anne Alexander, V.P., Education Programs; Gary Doran, V.P., Int'l. and Public Policy Programs; Timothy J. McClimon, V.P., Arts and Culture Program; Liza Parker, V.P., Policy and Administration; Gina Warren, V.P., Health and Social Action Programs; Sam A.

Gronner, Secy.; Sarah Jepsen, Exec. Dir.; Curtis R. Artis, Harold Burlingame, W. Frank Cobbin, Jr., Curtis J. Crawford, John C. Guerra, Jr., John A. Hinds, Judith A. Maynes, Thomas H. Norris, C. Kumar Patel, Robert J. Ranalli, Yvonne M. Shepard, Frederic S. Topor, Thomas C. Wajnert, Doreen S. Yochum, M. Kent Takeda.
Number of staff: 12 full-time professional; 2 part-time professional; 4 full-time support; 3 part-time support.
EIN: 133166495
Recent health grants:
1762-1 AIDS Foundation of Saint Louis, Saint Louis, MO, $10,000. 1990.
1762-2 AIDS Services Foundation for Orange County, Santa Ana, CA, $10,000. 1990.
1762-3 Beth Israel Medical Center, NYC, NY, $25,000. 1990.
1762-4 Childrens Hospital, Boston, MA, $50,000. 1990.
1762-5 Dartmouth-Hitchcock Medical Center, Hanover, NH, $25,000. 1990.
1762-6 Davies Medical Center, Institute for HIV Research and Treatment, San Francisco, CA, $10,000. 1990.
1762-7 Epworth Childrens Home, Saint Louis, MO, $10,000. 1990.
1762-8 Gay Mens Health Crisis (GMHC), NYC, NY, $25,000. 1990.
1762-9 Glide Memorial United Methodist Church, San Francisco, CA, $10,000. For health program. 1990.
1762-10 Greater Southeast Community Hospital Foundation, DC, $43,000. For family initiative. 1990.
1762-11 Hartford Action Plan on Infant Health, Hartford, CT, $10,000. 1990.
1762-12 Health South, Atlanta, GA, $10,000. For family initiative. 1990.
1762-13 International Center for the Disabled (ICD), NYC, NY, $12,500. 1990.
1762-14 International Childkind Foundation, Norcross, GA, $10,000. For health program. 1990.
1762-15 Irving Hospital Foundation, Irving, TX, $12,500. 1990.
1762-16 John F. Kennedy Medical Center, Edison, NJ, $15,000. 1990.
1762-17 La Rabida Childrens Hospital and Research Center, Chicago, IL, $15,000. For program for people with disabilities. 1990.
1762-18 Martin House, Community for Justice Foundation, Trenton, NJ, $10,000. For health program. 1990.
1762-19 Meharry Medical College, Nashville, TN, $50,000. 1990.
1762-20 Memorial Sloan-Kettering Cancer Center, NYC, NY, $25,000. 1990.
1762-21 Mercy Catholic Medical Center, Darby, PA, $10,000. 1990.
1762-22 Mount Sinai Hospital Medical Center of Chicago, Chicago, IL, $25,000. 1990.
1762-23 National Association of People with AIDS (NAPWA), DC, $10,000. 1990.
1762-24 National Medical Fellowships, NYC, NY, $62,500. 1990.
1762-25 National Minority AIDS Council, DC, $15,000. 1990.
1762-26 Northwest AIDS Foundation, Seattle, WA, $10,000. 1990.
1762-27 Overlook Hospital, Summit, NJ, $10,000. 1990.

1762-28 Pediatric AIDS Foundation, San Diego, CA, $15,000. 1990.

1762-29 Phoenix Memorial Hospital Foundation, Phoenix, AZ, $10,000. 1990.

1762-30 Riverview Medical Center, Red Bank, NJ, $12,500. 1990.

1762-31 San Francisco AIDS Foundation, San Francisco, CA, $20,000. 1990.

1762-32 Scottish Rite Childrens Medical Center, Atlanta, GA, $10,000. 1990.

1762-33 Southeastern Michigan Health Association, Southfield, MI, $45,000. For family initiative. 1990.

1763
The Atlantic Foundation of New York
c/o Price Waterhouse
153 East 53rd St., Rm. 3877
New York 10022

Established in 1989 in NY.
Donor(s): Atlan Management Corp., Interpacific Holdings, Inc.
Foundation type: Independent
Financial data (yr. ended 01/31/91): Assets, $14,479,904 (M); expenditures, $863,467; qualifying distributions, $969,146, including $767,000 for 27 grants (high: $100,000; low: $2,500) and $180,000 for set-asides.
Fields of interest: International affairs, intercultural relations, education, literacy, legal services, law and justice, public policy, volunteerism, health.
Limitations: Giving primarily to national and international organizations in New York, NY, and Washington, DC. No grants to individuals.
Application information: Contributes only to pre-selected organizations. Applications not accepted.
Officers and Directors:* Harvey P. Dale,* Pres.; Raymond L. Handlan,* Secy.-Treas.; Barbara C. Holley, Karen Merrill, Patricia T. Smalley.
EIN: 133562971

1764
Avon Products Foundation, Inc.
Nine West 57th St.
New York 10019   (212) 546-6731

Incorporated in 1955 in NY.
Donor(s): Avon Products, Inc.
Foundation type: Company-sponsored
Financial data (yr. ended 12/31/90): Assets, $50,770 (M); gifts received, $650,000; expenditures, $670,072; qualifying distributions, $670,072, including $396,500 for 22 grants (high: $107,500; low: $1,000; average: $2,000-$15,000), $150,717 for 61 grants to individuals (high: $6,000; low: $416) and $109,965 for 607 employee matching gifts.
Purpose and activities: Support for social services, including institutions and agencies whose main focus is on individuals, particularly youth, women, minorities and the disadvantaged; support also for hospitals, education (including employee-related scholarships and matching gifts), community funds, cultural organizations, urban programs, and civic projects.
Fields of interest: Social services, youth, women, minorities, disadvantaged, hospitals, education,

education—minorities, community funds, cultural programs, urban affairs, civic affairs.
Types of support: General purposes, operating budgets, employee-related scholarships, technical assistance, special projects, employee matching gifts, capital campaigns, scholarship funds, continuing support.
Limitations: Giving limited to areas immediately surrounding company operations in New York, Rye, and Suffern, NY; Newark, DE; Atlanta, GA; Springdale, OH; Pasadena, CA; and Morton Grove, IL. No support for individual member agencies of United Way and United Fund, or national health and welfare organizations. No grants to individuals (except for scholarships for children of company employees), or for capital or endowment funds; no loans.
Publications: Annual report, application guidelines, informational brochure (including application guidelines).
Application information: Application form required for scholarships only. Application form not required.
  Initial approach: Letter
  Copies of proposal: 1
  Deadline(s): Sept. 15
  Board meeting date(s): 3 times yearly
  Final notification: Oct. 15
  Write: Glenn S. Clarke, Pres.
Officers and Directors:* Glenn S. Clarke,* Pres.; Donna Blackwell,* V.P.; Phyllis B. Davis,* V.P.; James E. Preston,* V.P.; John F. Cox,* Secy.
Number of staff: 1 full-time professional; 1 full-time support.
EIN: 136128447

1765
The Bachmann Foundation, Inc.
230 Park Ave., Rm. 2525
New York 10169

Incorporated in 1949 in NY.
Donor(s): Louis Bachmann, Thomas W. Strauss.
Foundation type: Independent
Financial data (yr. ended 12/31/90): Assets, $4,476,892 (M); gifts received, $182,600; expenditures, $615,522; qualifying distributions, $596,499, including $590,216 for 134 grants (high: $77,400; low: $50).
Fields of interest: Secondary education, higher education, hospitals, child development, child welfare, Jewish welfare.
Limitations: Giving primarily in NY. No grants to individuals.
Application information: Contributes only to pre-selected organizations. Applications not accepted.
  Write: Louis Bachmann, Pres.
Officers: Louis Bachmann, Pres.; Barbara Bachmann Strauss, V.P.; Richard M. Danziger, Secy.; Thomas W. Strauss, Treas.
EIN: 136043497

1766
Rose M. Badgeley Residuary Charitable Trust
c/o Marine Midland Bank, N.A.
250 Park Ave.
New York 10177   (212) 503-2773

Trust established about 1977 in NY.

Donor(s): Rose Badgeley.‡
Foundation type: Independent
Financial data (yr. ended 01/31/91): Assets, $13,049,400 (M); gifts received, $84,908; expenditures, $957,081; qualifying distributions, $884,240, including $631,500 for 16 grants (high: $250,000; low: $5,000; average: $5,000-$25,000).
Purpose and activities: Emphasis on hospitals and health associations, particularly those concerned with medical research, including cancer and AIDS; support also for higher education, cultural programs, and social service and youth agencies.
Fields of interest: Hospitals, health associations, medical research, cancer, AIDS, alcoholism, higher education, cultural programs, social services, youth.
Types of support: Annual campaigns, building funds, equipment, general purposes, renovation projects, research, special projects, continuing support.
Limitations: Giving primarily in the five boroughs of New York, NY, and the greater metropolitan area. No grants to individuals.
Application information: Application form not required.
  Initial approach: Full written proposal
  Copies of proposal: 1
  Deadline(s): Submit proposal postmarked no earlier than Dec. 1 and no later than Mar. 15
  Board meeting date(s): Late Apr. or early May
  Final notification: Usually within a month after grant committee meeting if approved
  Write: Mr. Loren R. Sattinger, V.P., Marine Midland Bank, N.A.
Trustees: John J. Duffy, Marine Midland Bank, N.A.
Number of staff: None.
EIN: 136744781

1767
The Baird Foundation
P.O. Box 514
Williamsville 14221   (716) 633-5588

Trust established in 1947 in NY.
Donor(s): Flora M. Baird,‡ Frank B. Baird, Jr.,‡ Cameron Baird,‡ William C. Baird.‡
Foundation type: Independent
Financial data (yr. ended 12/31/90): Assets, $5,989,518 (M); expenditures, $428,501; qualifying distributions, $400,787, including $358,460 for 109 grants (high: $25,000; low: $250; average: $1,000-$2,000).
Purpose and activities: Primary areas of interest include the environment, hospitals, and medical research.
Fields of interest: Higher education, religion, arts, historic preservation, hospitals, medical research, social services, alcoholism, environment, community funds.
Types of support: Research, matching funds, general purposes, capital campaigns.
Limitations: Giving primarily in Erie County, NY. No grants to individuals; no loans.
Application information: Application form not required.
  Initial approach: Letter
  Copies of proposal: 1
  Deadline(s): None
  Board meeting date(s): About 4 times a year
  Final notification: 4 months

Write: Carl E. Gruber, Mgr.
Officer: Carl E. Gruber, Mgr.
Trustees: Arthur W. Cryer, Robert J.A. Irwin, William Baird Irwin.
Number of staff: 1 full-time professional; 1 part-time professional.
EIN: 166023080

1768
The Cameron Baird Foundation ▼
120 Delaware Ave.
Buffalo 14202
Application address: Box 564, Hamburg, NY 14075

Trust established in 1960 in NY.
Donor(s): Members of the family of Cameron Baird.
Foundation type: Independent
Financial data (yr. ended 12/31/91): Assets, $16,005,738 (M); expenditures, $980,084; qualifying distributions, $960,246, including $954,924 for 57 grants (high: $130,000; low: $274; average: $10,000-$50,000).
Purpose and activities: Emphasis on music and cultural programs, higher and secondary education, social services, population control, conservation, and civil rights.
Fields of interest: Cultural programs, music, higher education, secondary education, family planning, population studies, conservation, civil rights.
Limitations: Giving primarily in the Buffalo, NY, area. No support for religious organizations. No grants to individuals.
Application information: Generally contributes to pre-selected organizations. Application form not required.
　Initial approach: Letter
　Copies of proposal: 1
　Deadline(s): Submit proposal in the fall; most grants are made in Dec.
　Board meeting date(s): Annually
　Write: Brian D. Baird, Trustee
Trustees: Brian D. Baird, Bridget B. Baird, Bruce C. Baird, Jane D. Baird, Bronwyn Baird Clauson, Brenda Baird Senturia.
Number of staff: None.
EIN: 166029481

1769
The George F. Baker Trust ▼
767 Fifth Ave., Suite 2850
New York 10153　　　(212) 755-1890

Trust established in 1937 in NY.
Donor(s): George F. Baker.‡
Foundation type: Independent
Financial data (yr. ended 12/31/90): Assets, $19,159,304 (L); expenditures, $2,008,351; qualifying distributions, $1,537,400, including $1,537,400 for 58 grants (high: $250,000; low: $1,000; average: $5,000-$25,000).
Purpose and activities: Giving primarily for higher and secondary education, hospitals, social services, civic affairs, and religious and international affairs.
Fields of interest: Hospitals, conservation, secondary education, higher education, social services, civic affairs, religion, international affairs.

Types of support: Matching funds, general purposes.
Limitations: Giving primarily in the eastern U.S., with some emphasis on the New York, NY, area. No grants to individuals, or for scholarships; no loans.
Publications: Annual report.
Application information: Application form not required.
　Initial approach: Letter with brief outline of proposal
　Deadline(s): None
　Board meeting date(s): June and Nov.
　Final notification: Up to 6 months
　Write: Miss Rocio Suarez, Exec. Dir.
Officer: Rocio Suarez, Exec. Dir.
Trustees: Anthony K. Baker, George F. Baker III, Kane K. Baker, Citibank, N.A.
Number of staff: 1 full-time professional.
EIN: 136056818
Recent health grants:
1769-1 American Heart Association, Dallas, TX, $15,000. For general support of research programs to prevent stroke and cardiovascular disease. 1990.
1769-2 Community Hospital at Glen Cove, Glen Cove, NY, $25,000. For Emergency Department Expansion Program. 1990.
1769-3 Foundation for Depression and Manic Depression, NYC, NY, $10,000. For general support. 1990.
1769-4 Memorial Sloan-Kettering Cancer Center, NYC, NY, $25,000. For journal. 1990.
1769-5 New York Hospital-Cornell Medical Center, NYC, NY, $50,000. For research in field of hormones and their effects on brain function. 1990.
1769-6 New York Hospital-Cornell Medical Center, NYC, NY, $30,000. For general support to improve medical training and patient care. 1990.
1769-7 New York Hospital-Cornell Medical Center, NYC, NY, $25,000. For Chairman's Committee for Special Research of Department of Psychiatry. 1990.

1770
Banbury Fund, Inc.
c/o Tardino & Stewart
101 Park Ave., 35th Fl.
New York 10178

Incorporated in 1946 in NY.
Donor(s): Marie H. Robertson,‡ Charles S. Robertson.‡
Foundation type: Independent
Financial data (yr. ended 12/31/91): Assets, $27,672,417 (M); expenditures, $1,388,060; qualifying distributions, $1,292,833, including $1,234,879 for 81 grants (high: $120,000; low: $400; average: $3,000-$15,000).
Purpose and activities: Primary areas of interest include education, the environment, alcoholism, health, and medical research.
Fields of interest: Science and technology, marine sciences, education, higher education, secondary education, biochemistry, international studies, law and justice, welfare, disadvantaged, cancer, health, alcoholism, medical research, environment.
Types of support: Annual campaigns, building funds, capital campaigns, continuing support,

deficit financing, emergency funds, endowment funds, equipment, research, seed money.
Limitations: Giving primarily in NY. No grants to individuals.
Application information:
　Initial approach: Letter
　Copies of proposal: 3
　Deadline(s): None
　Board meeting date(s): July and Jan.
　Write: William S. Robertson, Pres.
Officers and Directors:* William S. Robertson,* Pres.; Walter C. Meier,* V.P.; John L. Robertson,* V.P.; Katherine R. Ernst,* Secy.; Anne R. Meier,* Treas.
Number of staff: 1 part-time professional.
EIN: 136062463

1771
The Bank of New York Corporate Contributions Program
48 Wall St., 10th Fl.
New York 10286　　　(212) 495-1730

Financial data (yr. ended 12/31/90): Total giving, $2,531,000, including $2,154,000 for grants (high: $80,000; low: $100; average: $1,000-$5,000) and $377,000 for 1,144 employee matching gifts.
Purpose and activities: Supports arts and culture, education, health, welfare and urban affairs. All types of support are considered on a case-by-case basis.
Fields of interest: Arts, cultural programs, education, health, welfare, urban affairs, museums, performing arts.
Types of support: Capital campaigns, continuing support, operating budgets, general purposes, employee matching gifts.
Limitations: Giving primarily in company operating areas in NY. No support for religious or political organizations. No grants to individuals.
Publications: Corporate report.
Application information: The office of the Secretary handles giving. Application form not required.
　Deadline(s): Applications are preferred in the fall
　Board meeting date(s): Jan.
　Final notification: Feb.
　Write: Katherine C. Hastings, Asst. V.P.
Number of staff: None.

1772
Bankers Trust Corporate Contributions Program
280 Park Ave.
New York 10017　　　(212) 454-3500

Financial data (yr. ended 12/31/90): Total giving, $1,900,000 for grants.
Purpose and activities: Supports social and public issues, education, community development, hospital building funds, urban development, volunteerism, and arts and culture. BT Foundation gave $4.1 million in 1990.
Fields of interest: Community development, cultural programs, hospitals—building funds, education—minorities, general charitable giving, performing arts, theater, urban development, volunteerism, social services, education, arts.

Types of support: Capital campaigns, employee matching gifts, general purposes, operating budgets, publications, renovation projects.
Limitations: Giving primarily in New York City. No grants to individuals, United Way recipients or to political, religious, fraternal, or veterans' organizations.
Publications: Informational brochure.
Application information: Application form not required.
  Initial approach: Letter
  Copies of proposal: 1
  Deadline(s): Applications accepted throughout the year
  Write: Nancy S. Ticktin, V.P. and Secy., Contribs. Comm. and Pres., Bankers Trust Fdn.
Number of staff: 1 full-time professional; 1 full-time support.

1773
C. R. Bard Foundation, Inc.
c/o U.S. Trust Co. of New York
114 West 47th St.
New York 10036
Application address: C.R. Bard, Inc., 730 Central Ave., Murray Hill, NJ 07974

Established in 1987 in NY.
Donor(s): C.R. Bard, Inc.
Foundation type: Company-sponsored
Financial data (yr. ended 12/31/91): Assets, $587,917 (M); gifts received, $1,000,000; expenditures, $808,655; qualifying distributions, $803,250, including $801,855 for 133 grants (high: $200,000; low: $1,000).
Purpose and activities: Support for higher education, community funds, health and medical research, and social services.
Fields of interest: Higher education, community funds, health, medical research, social services.
Types of support: General purposes, scholarship funds.
Limitations: Giving primarily in NY and NJ. No grants to individuals.
Application information:
  Initial approach: Proposal
  Deadline(s): None
  Write: Eugene Schultz, V.P.
Officers: George T. Malloney,* Pres.; George A. Davis, V.P. and Treas.; William H. Longfield,* V.P.; Eugene B. Schultz, V.P.; Richard A. Flink, Secy.
EIN: 222840708

1774
The Barker Welfare Foundation ▼
P.O. Box 2
Glen Head 11545   (516) 759-5592
Application address for Chicago agencies: c/o Philip D. Block III, One First National Plaza, Suite 2544, Chicago, IL 60603; Treasurer's Office: c/o Charles C. Hickox, 26 Broadway, New York, NY 10004

Incorporated in 1934 in IL.
Donor(s): Mrs. Charles V. Hickox.‡
Foundation type: Independent
Financial data (yr. ended 09/30/90): Assets, $30,205,104 (M); expenditures, $2,314,477; qualifying distributions, $1,902,306, including

$1,700,000 for 204 grants (high: $125,000; low: $1,000; average: $3,000-$9,000).
Purpose and activities: Grants to established organizations and charitable institutions, with emphasis on arts and culture, including museums and the fine and performing arts, child welfare and youth agencies, health services and rehabilitation, welfare, aid to the handicapped, family planning, libraries, the environment, and recreation.
Fields of interest: Cultural programs, fine arts, performing arts, museums, youth, child welfare, health, health services, rehabilitation, mental health, welfare, handicapped, family planning, libraries, environment, recreation.
Types of support: Operating budgets, continuing support, building funds, equipment, land acquisition, matching funds, special projects, renovation projects, annual campaigns.
Limitations: Giving primarily in Chicago, IL; Michigan City, IN; and New York, NY. No support for private elementary and secondary schools or for higher education. No grants to individuals, or for endowment funds, seed money, emergency funds, deficit financing, scholarships, fellowships, medical or scientific research, or conferences; no loans.
Publications: Program policy statement, application guidelines.
Application information: Proposals must be completed according to the foundation's guidelines in order to be considered for funding. Application form not required.
  Initial approach: Letter or telephone
  Copies of proposal: 1
  Deadline(s): Submit proposal preferably between Sept. and Dec.; deadline Feb. 1 for completed proposal
  Board meeting date(s): May
  Final notification: After annual meeting for positive response; from Sept. to May for negative response
  Write: Mrs. Walter L. Ross II, Pres. (NY and national agencies); Philip D. Block III (Chicago agencies)
Officers and Directors:* Sarane H. Ross,* Pres.; Katrina H. Becker,* V.P. and Secy.; Bettie P. Garrettson,* V.P.; Charles C. Hickox,* Treas.; Philip D. Block III, Diane Curtis, James R. Donnelley, John A. Garrettson, Julia S. Hansen, John B. Hickox, Linda J. Hickox, Alline Matheson, Alexander B. Ross.
Number of staff: 1 part-time professional; 1 full-time support.
EIN: 366018526

1775
Lawrence and Isabel Barnett Charitable Foundation
One Timber Trail
Rye 10580

Established in 1986 in CA.
Donor(s): Lawrence R. Barnett.
Foundation type: Independent
Financial data (yr. ended 09/30/91): Assets, $4,676,935 (M); gifts received, $6,670; expenditures, $320,136; qualifying distributions, $274,835, including $273,650 for 24 grants (high: $160,000; low: $50).
Fields of interest: Health associations, medical research, higher education.

Limitations: Giving primarily in NY. No grants to individuals.
Application information: Contributes only to pre-selected organizations. Applications not accepted.
Officers and Directors:* Lawrence R. Barnett,* Pres.; Isabel Barnett,* V.P. and C.F.O.; James Joseph Barnett.
EIN: 943031397

1776
The Theodore H. Barth Foundation, Inc.
1211 Ave. of the Americas
New York 10036   (212) 704-6000

Incorporated in 1953 in DE.
Donor(s): Theodore H. Barth.‡
Foundation type: Independent
Financial data (yr. ended 12/31/90): Assets, $17,588,872 (M); expenditures, $714,478; qualifying distributions, $631,840, including $555,750 for 68 grants (high: $75,000; low: $500; average: $1,000-$10,000) and $34,175 for 23 grants to individuals (high: $3,350; low: $500).
Purpose and activities: Grants for higher education, including scholarships, health and hospitals, religion, the arts and cultural organizations, social services, and child welfare; support also for civic affairs, aid to the handicapped, and conservation.
Fields of interest: Higher education, hospitals, health services, religion, arts, cultural programs, social services, child welfare, civic affairs, handicapped, conservation.
Limitations: Giving primarily in NY and MA. No grants to individuals.
Application information: The foundation's student aid program has been discontinued. Prior commitments will be paid; new applications will not be considered. Application form not required.
  Initial approach: Letter
  Deadline(s): None
  Write: Irving P. Berelson, Pres.
Officers and Directors:* Irving P. Berelson,* Pres. and Treas.; Thelma D. Berelson,* Secy.
EIN: 136103401

1777
Ruth Bartsch Memorial Trust
c/o The Chase Manhattan Bank, N.A., Tax Services Div.
1211 Ave. of the Americas, 36th Fl.
New York 10036   (212) 789-5334

Established in 1983 in NY.
Donor(s): Ruth Bartsch.‡
Foundation type: Independent
Financial data (yr. ended 11/30/91): Assets, $5,087,066 (M); expenditures, $244,455; qualifying distributions, $211,537, including $195,289 for 7 grants (high: $76,116; low: $5,000).
Fields of interest: Secondary education, hospitals, secondary education.
Limitations: No grants to individuals.
Application information:
  Initial approach: Letter
  Deadline(s): None
  Write: Joyce Schwartz
Trustees: Theodore Norman Richard, Sr., The Chase Manhattan Bank, N.A.

EIN: 133188775

1778
The Sandra Atlas Bass & Edythe & Sol G. Atlas Fund, Inc. ▼
185 Great Neck Rd.
Great Neck 11021   (516) 487-9030

Established in 1962 in NY.
Donor(s): Sol G. Atlas.
Foundation type: Independent
Financial data (yr. ended 12/31/90): Assets, $13,615,248 (M); gifts received, $1,166,578; expenditures, $1,499,168; qualifying distributions, $1,474,366, including $1,474,366 for 118 grants (high: $100,000; low: $200; average: $1,000-$15,000).
Purpose and activities: Giving primarily for social services, health, animal welfare, and Jewish welfare.
Fields of interest: Social services, animal welfare, Jewish welfare, health associations.
Limitations: Giving primarily in the New York, NY, metropolitan area, with emphasis on Long Island.
Application information: Application form not required.
Initial approach: Letter
Deadline(s): None
Write: Sandra A. Bass, Pres.
Officers: Sandra A. Bass, Pres.; Morton M. Bass, V.P.; Robert Zabelle, Secy.; Richard Cunningham, Treas.
EIN: 116036928
Recent health grants:
1778-1 American Kidney Fund, Rockville, MD, $15,000. 1990.
1778-2 Cancer Care, NYC, NY, $13,500. 1990.
1778-3 Childrens Oncology Society of New York, NYC, NY, $10,000. 1990.
1778-4 Cornell University, College of Veterinary Medicine, Ithaca, NY, $10,000. 1990.
1778-5 Hale House Center, NYC, NY, $17,500. 1990.
1778-6 Helen Keller International, NYC, NY, $28,000. 1990.
1778-7 Leukemia Society of America, NYC, NY, $12,000. 1990.
1778-8 Make-A-Wish Foundation of Metro New York, Port Washington, NY, $17,500. 1990.
1778-9 March of Dimes Birth Defects Foundation, NYC, NY, $13,000. 1990.
1778-10 Muscular Dystrophy Association, NYC, NY, $40,000. 1990.
1778-11 National Burn Victim Foundation, Orange, NJ, $15,000. 1990.
1778-12 National Federation of the Blind, Baltimore, MD, $11,500. 1990.
1778-13 National Jewish Center for Immunology and Respiratory Medicine, NYC, NY, $12,500. 1990.
1778-14 National Multiple Sclerosis Society, NYC, NY, $11,000. 1990.
1778-15 North Shore University Hospital, Manhasset, NY, $50,000. 1990.
1778-16 Ronald McDonald House of Long Island, New Hyde Park, NY, $10,000. 1990.
1778-17 Saint Francis Hospital Foundation, Roslyn, NY, $50,000. 1990.
1778-18 Saint Jude Childrens Research Hospital, NYC, NY, $21,000. 1990.
1778-19 United Cerebral Palsy, NYC, NY, $50,000. 1990.
1778-20 Variety, The Childrens Charity, NYC, NY, $25,000. 1990.

1779
Leo Cox Beach Philanthropic Foundation
c/o Thomas C. Beach, Jr.
P.O. Box 211
Middle Granville 12849

Established in 1989 in NY.
Donor(s): Thomas C. Beach, Jr.
Foundation type: Independent
Financial data (yr. ended 07/31/91): Assets, $2,053,732 (M); gifts received, $151,593; expenditures, $135,376; qualifying distributions, $108,500, including $108,500 for 7 grants (high: $44,000; low: $1,500).
Fields of interest: Hospitals, libraries, museums, arts.
Limitations: Giving primarily in Glen Falls, NY.
Application information: Contributes only to pre-selected organizations. Applications not accepted.
Directors: C. Randall Beach, Thomas C. Beach, Jr., Deborah Burnham, A. Desmond Fitzgerald, Dorothy Jackson, Pauline La Barge Palmer.
EIN: 141732259

1780
Beck Foundation
330 Madison Ave., 31st Fl.
New York 10017
Application address: P.O. Box 1566, Lexington, VA 24450

Established in 1954 in NY.
Donor(s): T. Edmund Beck.
Foundation type: Independent
Financial data (yr. ended 12/31/90): Assets, $3,060,381 (M); expenditures, $219,666; qualifying distributions, $202,808, including $198,493 for 46 grants (high: $75,600; low: $20).
Purpose and activities: Grants primarily for higher, secondary, and other education; child welfare agencies, alcohol abuse programs, and organizations benefiting minorities, the elderly, and the disabled; the arts, including historic preservation and museums; health and medical research; animal welfare; and religious giving.
Fields of interest: Higher education, secondary education, libraries, child welfare, alcoholism, aged, arts, health, medical research, animal welfare, religion.
Limitations: No grants to individuals.
Application information: Contributes only to pre-selected organizations. Applications not accepted.
Write: T. Edmund Beck, Pres.
Officer and Trustees:* T. Edmund Beck,* Pres.; John C. Beck, Madeline C. Beck, T.E. Beck, Jr., Susan Beck Wasch.
Number of staff: None.
EIN: 136082501

1781
The Bedford Fund, Inc.
c/o Marjorie E. Brody
Two Overhill Rd.
Scarsdale 10583   (914) 725-3591

Incorporated in 1919 in CT.
Donor(s): Edward T. Bedford.‡
Foundation type: Independent
Financial data (yr. ended 06/30/91): Assets, $5,743,145 (M); expenditures, $524,241; qualifying distributions, $499,624, including $491,000 for 19 grants (high: $100,000; low: $1,000).
Purpose and activities: Giving largely for hospitals, a youth agency, community funds, and the handicapped; support also for secondary education and conservation.
Fields of interest: Hospitals, community funds, secondary education, handicapped, conservation, social services.
Limitations: Giving limited to the local area surrounding Westport, CT. No grants to individuals.
Application information: Contributes only to pre-selected organizations. Applications not accepted.
Officers and Trustees:* Ruth T. Bedford,* Pres. and Mgr.; Marjorie E. Brody, Secy.; Mariana L. Clark, William B. Lloyd, Helen B. McCashin.
EIN: 066032006

1782
The Bedminster Fund, Inc.
1270 Ave. of the Americas, Rm. 2300
New York 10020   (212) 315-8300

Incorporated in 1948 in NY.
Foundation type: Independent
Financial data (yr. ended 06/30/91): Assets, $4,881,987 (M); gifts received, $18,999; expenditures, $645,907; qualifying distributions, $631,283, including $624,000 for 15 grants (high: $330,000; low: $2,000; average: $1,000-$100,000).
Purpose and activities: Emphasis on education, hospitals, the arts, and welfare agencies. Grants only to present beneficiary organizations and to special proposals developed by the directors; additional requests seldom considered.
Fields of interest: Education, hospitals, arts, welfare.
Types of support: General purposes.
Limitations: No grants to individuals; no loans.
Application information: Applications not accepted.
Board meeting date(s): Nov. and as required
Write: Robert F. Quick, Treas.
Officers and Directors:* Dorothy Dillon Eweson,* Pres.; Philip D. Allen,* V.P.; David H. Peipers,* V.P.; Joan Waldron, Secy.; Robert F. Quick, Treas.; Alexandra F. Allen, Christine Allen, Douglas E. Allen, Dorothy D. Caplow, Judith S. Leonard, Anne D. Zetterberg.
Number of staff: None.
EIN: 136083684

1783
The Beinecke Foundation, Inc. ▼
14-16 Elm Place
Rye 10580   (914) 967-2385

Incorporated in 1966 in NY as The Kerry Foundation, Inc.; absorbed Edwin J. Beinecke Trust, NY, in Apr., 1985; new name for combined foundations adopted in Dec., 1985.
Donor(s): Sylvia B. Robinson.
Foundation type: Independent
Financial data (yr. ended 12/31/90): Assets, $37,713,843 (M); expenditures, $2,404,330; qualifying distributions, $2,121,222, including $1,936,395 for 152 grants (high: $250,000; low: $100; average: $100-$30,000).
Fields of interest: Secondary education, higher education, medical education, conservation, Protestant giving.
Types of support: General purposes.
Limitations: Giving primarily in the NY-CT area. No grants to individuals; no loans.
Publications: Annual report.
Application information:
  Initial approach: 1 to 2 page letter
  Deadline(s): No deadline for unsolicited projects reflecting applicant's particular interest; contact foundation for deadline for projects reflecting applicant's interest which are developed in response to foundation's call for proposals
  Board meeting date(s): Spring and fall
  Final notification: 30 days
  Write: John R. Robinson, Pres.
Officers and Trustees:* John R. Robinson,* Pres. and Treas.; Sylvia B. Robinson, V.P.; Theodore H. Ashford, William O. Beers.
Number of staff: 2 full-time professional; 1 full-time support.
EIN: 136201175

1784
The Beir Foundation
110 East 59th St.
New York 10022   (212) 355-7733

Incorporated in 1944 in NY.
Donor(s): Members of the Beir family.
Foundation type: Independent
Financial data (yr. ended 12/31/90): Assets, $3,661,347 (M); expenditures, $310,382; qualifying distributions, $281,700, including $281,700 for 47 grants (high: $150,000; low: $30).
Purpose and activities: Support primarily for elementary, secondary, and higher education; support also for Jewish welfare funds, hospitals, and social service agencies.
Fields of interest: Elementary education, secondary education, higher education, Jewish welfare, hospitals, social services.
Limitations: Giving primarily in the New York, NY, area.
Application information: Applications not accepted.
  Write: Robert L. Beir, Pres.
Officers and Directors:* Robert L. Beir,* Pres.; Joan S. Beir,* V.P. and Secy.; James H. Mathias,* Treas.
EIN: 136084093

1785
The Belfer Foundation, Inc. ▼
One Dag Hammarskjold Plaza
New York 10017   (212) 644-2257

Incorporated in 1951 in NY.
Donor(s): members of the Belfer family, Belfer Corp.
Foundation type: Independent
Financial data (yr. ended 12/31/90): Assets, $28,566,798 (M); gifts received, $1,173,088; expenditures, $1,345,116; qualifying distributions, $1,018,370, including $1,016,705 for 176 grants (high: $155,000; low: $5; average: $100-$35,000).
Purpose and activities: Emphasis on health agencies, higher education, and Jewish welfare funds and religious organizations, also some giving for cultural organizations.
Fields of interest: Health, higher education, Jewish welfare, Jewish giving.
Limitations: Giving primarily in NY. No grants to individuals.
Application information: Applications not accepted.
  Write: Arthur B. Belfer, Pres.
Officers: Arthur B. Belfer, Pres.; Lawrence Ruben, V.P.; Robert A. Belfer, Secy.; Jack Saltz, Treas.
EIN: 136086711

1786
Frances & Benjamin Benenson Foundation, Inc.
708 Third Ave., 28th Fl.
New York 10017   (212) 867-0990

Established in 1983 in NY.
Donor(s): Charles B. Benenson.
Foundation type: Independent
Financial data (yr. ended 11/30/90): Assets, $15,085,039 (M); expenditures, $785,897; qualifying distributions, $683,977, including $683,227 for grants.
Fields of interest: Jewish giving, museums, arts, education, secondary education, health.
Limitations: No grants to individuals.
Application information: Contributes only to pre-selected organizations. Applications not accepted.
  Write: Anthony J. DiNome
Officers: Charles B. Benenson, Pres.; Emanuel Labin, V.P.
EIN: 133267113

1787
Louis Berkowitz Family Foundation, Inc.
51 Lexington Ave.
New York 10010   (212) 683-6342

Established in 1983 in NY.
Donor(s): Louis Berkowitz.‡
Foundation type: Independent
Financial data (yr. ended 12/31/91): Assets, $5,853,170 (M); expenditures, $109,999; qualifying distributions, $105,000, including $105,000 for 9 grants (high: $30,000; low: $1,000).
Purpose and activities: Giving primarily for hospitals and education; support also for Jewish organizations.
Fields of interest: Health, hospitals, cancer, education, Jewish giving.
Types of support: Equipment, research, special projects.
Limitations: Giving primarily in the New York, NY, metropolitan area.

Application information:
  Initial approach: Letter
  Deadline(s): None
  Write: John E. Tuchler, Pres.
Officers and Directors:* John E. Tuchler,* Pres.; Mollie Auerbach,* V.P.; Herbert Cohen,* V.P.; Blanche Heiling,* V.P.; Ruth Martin,* V.P.; Frederick Siegmund,* Secy.; Louis Katz,* Treas.
Number of staff: None.
EIN: 133190334

1788
Berlex Foundation, Inc.
530 Fifth Ave., 25th Fl.
New York 10036   (212) 719-5613
Application address: c/o The Center for Bio-Medical Communications, 80 West Madison Ave., Dumont, NJ 07628; Tel.: (201) 385-8080

Incorporated in 1986 in NY.
Donor(s): Berlex Laboratories, Inc.
Foundation type: Independent
Financial data (yr. ended 12/31/90): Assets, $219,408 (M); gifts received, $575,000; expenditures, $503,324; qualifying distributions, $475,377, including $249,163 for grants to individuals.
Purpose and activities: Awards research grants in the field of reproductive medicine to licensed physicians affiliated with a university or laboratory institution.
Fields of interest: Medical research.
Types of support: Grants to individuals, fellowships, publications, conferences and seminars, lectureships, matching funds.
Publications: Newsletter, informational brochure (including application guidelines), application guidelines.
Application information: Application form not required.
  Initial approach: Proposal
  Copies of proposal: 5
  Deadline(s): Oct. 15
  Board meeting date(s): Annually in Oct. or Nov.
  Final notification: Dec. 1
  Write: S. Lisanti
Officers: Robert S. Cohen, Pres.; Robert S. Chabora, Secy.; Howard W. Robin, Treas.
EIN: 133359746

1789
The Arnold Bernhard Foundation, Inc. ▼
711 Third Ave.
New York 10017   (212) 687-3965

Established in 1976.
Donor(s): Arnold Bernhard Charitable Annuity Trust I, Arnold Bernhard Charitable Annuity Trust II.
Foundation type: Independent
Financial data (yr. ended 12/31/90): Assets, $1,396,742 (M); gifts received, $1,200,000; expenditures, $1,943,261; qualifying distributions, $1,943,261, including $1,940,500 for 51 grants (high: $600,000; low: $500; average: $1,000-$25,000).
Purpose and activities: Giving primarily for education, with emphasis on private colleges and universities and a college preparatory school;

minor support also for hospitals, social services, and Christian organizations.
Fields of interest: Higher education, secondary education, hospitals, social services, religion—Christian.
Types of support: General purposes, capital campaigns, scholarship funds, annual campaigns, building funds, professorships.
Limitations: Giving on a national basis, with some emphasis on NY and CT. No grants to individuals.
Application information:
Initial approach: Letter
Deadline(s): None
Final notification: Nov. or Dec.
Write: Jean B. Buttner, Pres.
Officers and Directors:* Jean B. Buttner,* Pres.; Janet K. Bernhard,* V.P.; A. Van H. Bernhard.
EIN: 136100457
Recent health grants:
1789-1 Columbia University, College of Physicians and Surgeons, NYC, NY, $50,000. For biomedical research. 1990.
1789-2 Mount Sinai Hospital and Medical Center, NYC, NY, $55,000. For research in Parkinson's disease. 1990.
1789-3 Norwalk Hospital Foundation, Norwalk, CT, $50,000. For general funds. 1990.

1790
Sanford C. Bernstein & Company Foundation, Inc.
767 Fifth Ave.
New York 10153-0001

Established in 1968 in NY.
Donor(s): Zalman C. Bernstein, Sanford C. Bernstein & Co., Inc.
Foundation type: Company-sponsored
Financial data (yr. ended 12/31/91): Assets, $2,727,447 (M); gifts received, $304,000; expenditures, $359,558; qualifying distributions, $354,445, including $352,010 for 64 grants (high: $50,000; low: $100).
Fields of interest: Jewish giving, Jewish welfare, medical research, health associations, child welfare, social services, education.
Limitations: Giving primarily in New York, NY. No grants to individuals.
Application information: Contributes only to pre-selected organizations. Applications not accepted.
Trustees: Andrew Adelson, Zalman C. Bernstein, Kevin R. Brine, Charles C. Cahn, Peter Carmen, Joseph B. Greeley, Roger Hertog, Stuart K. Nelson, Lewis A. Sanders, Francis H. Trainer, Jr.
EIN: 136277976

1791
Margaret T. Biddle Foundation
c/o Cusack & Stiles
61 Broadway, Rm. 2912
New York 10006

Incorporated in 1952 in NY.
Donor(s): Margaret T. Biddle.‡
Foundation type: Independent
Financial data (yr. ended 12/31/91): Assets, $3,793,926 (M); expenditures, $188,616; qualifying distributions, $180,285, including

$180,000 for 9 grants (high: $50,000; low: $5,000).
Fields of interest: Hospitals, medical research, cancer, social services, child development, handicapped.
Types of support: General purposes.
Limitations: Giving on a national basis, with some emphasis on NY. No grants to individuals.
Application information: Contributes only to pre-selected organizations. Applications not accepted.
Officers and Directors:* Christian Hohenlohe,* Pres.; Richard A. Smith,* V.P. and Secy.; Catherine H. Jacobus,* V.P.; Peter Boyce Schulze,* V.P.
EIN: 131936016

1792
Lisa Bilotti Foundation, Inc.
c/o Kelley Drye & Warren
101 Park Ave.
New York 10178

Established in 1990 in NJ.
Donor(s): Lisa Bilotti.‡
Foundation type: Independent
Financial data (yr. ended 09/30/91): Assets, $299,233 (M); gifts received, $437,244; expenditures, $204,793; qualifying distributions, $204,000, including $204,000 for 2 grants (high: $200,000; low: $4,000).
Fields of interest: Hospitals, cancer.
Limitations: Giving primarily in New York, NY. No grants to individuals.
Application information: Contributes only to pre-selected organizations. Applications not accepted.
Officers and Directors:* Margaret S. Bilotti,* Pres. and Treas.; Carlo F. Bilotti,* V.P.; Talbot Miller,* Secy.
EIN: 133578733

1793
William Bingham 2nd Betterment Fund
c/o U.S. Trust Co. of New York
114 West 47th St.
New York 10036
Application address: 330 Madison Ave., Rm. 3500, New York, NY 10017

Foundation type: Independent
Financial data (yr. ended 12/31/91): Assets, $26,684,268 (M); expenditures, $1,418,341; qualifying distributions, $1,173,572, including $1,005,700 for 38 grants (high: $275,000; low: $1,500).
Purpose and activities: Giving primarily for the advancement of medicine; support also for higher education, a private academy, and a community foundation.
Fields of interest: Health services, medical research, education, higher education, secondary education, community development.
Types of support: Capital campaigns, scholarship funds, general purposes.
Limitations: Giving limited to ME. No grants to individuals.
Application information:
Initial approach: Letter
Deadline(s): None

Trustees: William M. Troop, Jr., William B. Windship, Carolyn S. Wollen, U.S. Trust Co. of New York.
EIN: 136072625

1794
Henry M. Blackmer Foundation, Inc.
c/o White & Case
1155 Ave. of the Americas
New York 10036

Incorporated in 1952 in DE.
Donor(s): Henry M. Blackmer.‡
Foundation type: Independent
Financial data (yr. ended 12/31/91): Assets, $2,557,104 (M); expenditures, $168,207; qualifying distributions, $147,345, including $121,000 for 29 grants (high: $20,000; low: $500).
Purpose and activities: Support for education, hospitals, cultural programs, and a zoological foundation; grants generally limited to a small list of institutional donees who have received grants from the foundation in the past.
Fields of interest: Education, higher education, secondary education, hospitals, cultural programs.
Limitations: No grants to individuals.
Application information: Contributes only to pre-selected organizations. Applications not accepted.
Officers and Trustees:* Morton Moskin,* Pres.; W. Perry Neff,* V.P.; David W. Swanson,* Secy.-Treas.; Margaret N. Blackmer.
EIN: 136097357

1795
Jacob Bleibtreu Foundation, Inc.
c/o Grant Thornton
Seven World Trade Ctr.
New York 10048

Incorporated in 1945 in NY.
Donor(s): Helen R. Bleibtreu,‡ Jacob Bleibtreu.‡
Foundation type: Independent
Financial data (yr. ended 09/30/91): Assets, $5,050,829 (M); expenditures, $934,462; qualifying distributions, $916,461, including $905,758 for 27 grants (high: $200,000; low: $500).
Fields of interest: Human rights, civil rights, public policy, hospitals, family planning, child welfare, Jewish welfare, social services.
Limitations: Giving primarily in New York, NY. No grants to individuals.
Application information: Contributes only to pre-selected organizations. Applications not accepted.
Officers and Directors:* Alexander Abraham,* Pres.; George H. Heyman, Jr.,* V.P.; Charles Looker.
EIN: 136065942

1796
Blinken Foundation, Inc.
c/o Donald Blinken
466 Lexington Ave.
New York 10017

Established in 1965 in NY.
Foundation type: Independent

Financial data (yr. ended 12/31/90): Assets, $2,234,913 (M); expenditures, $190,249; qualifying distributions, $189,222, including $187,650 for 36 grants (high: $26,000; low: $300; average: $500-$5,000).
Purpose and activities: Giving primarily for the performing arts and other cultural programs, education, and medical centers; support also for Jewish organizations.
Fields of interest: Arts, performing arts, cultural programs, hospitals, education, biological sciences, Jewish giving.
Types of support: Annual campaigns, fellowships, general purposes, internships, scholarship funds.
Limitations: Giving primarily in New York, NY. No grants to individuals.
Application information: Contributes only to pre-selected organizations. Applications not accepted.
Officers and Directors:* Donald M. Blinken,* Pres. and Treas.; Robert J. Blinken,* V.P. and Secy.; Alan J. Blinken,* V.P.
Number of staff: None.
EIN: 136190153

1797
Charles G. & Yvette Bluhdorn Charitable Trust

c/o Reminick, Aarons & Co.
685 Third Ave., 19th Fl.
New York 10017-4024   (212) 333-4300

Established in 1967 in NY.
Donor(s): Paul Bluhdorn.
Foundation type: Independent
Financial data (yr. ended 12/31/91): Assets, $6,949,505 (M); expenditures, $302,448; qualifying distributions, $262,678, including $206,300 for 60 grants (high: $25,000; low: $150).
Purpose and activities: Giving primarily for a school of design and other cultural programs, child welfare and social services, animal welfare and education, the environment, and hospitals and medical research, including AIDS research.
Fields of interest: Arts, social services, child welfare, historic preservation, education, environment, wildlife, hospitals, medical research, AIDS.
Types of support: General purposes, scholarship funds, special projects.
Limitations: Giving primarily in NY, with emphasis on the greater metropolitan New York area.
Application information: Application form not required.
  Initial approach: Letter
  Copies of proposal: 1
  Deadline(s): None
  Write: Dominique Bluhdorn, Trustee
Trustees: Dominique Bluhdorn, Paul Bluhdorn, Yvette Bluhdorn.
Number of staff: 1 full-time professional.
EIN: 136256769

1798
Edna F. Blum Foundation

4 Cradle Rock Rd.
Pound Ridge 10576-2208   (914) 764-0451

Established in 1989 in NY.

Donor(s): Edna F. Blum.‡
Foundation type: Independent
Financial data (yr. ended 07/31/91): Assets, $3,288,013 (M); gifts received, $866,768; expenditures, $178,717; qualifying distributions, $149,000, including $149,000 for 10 grants (high: $25,000; low: $6,000).
Purpose and activities: Support for a library, an adolescent pregnancy program, education, and social services, including projects concerned with the homeless and child welfare.
Fields of interest: Libraries, family planning, social services, homeless, child welfare, education, arts, AIDS.
Types of support: Equipment, special projects, operating budgets, research.
Limitations: Giving primarily in the metropolitan New York, NY, area. No grants to individuals.
Application information: Application form not required.
  Copies of proposal: 1
  Deadline(s): None
  Write: Jean L. Stern, Trustee
Trustees: Jean L. Stern, Robert A. Stern.
Number of staff: None.
EIN: 133563460

1799
The Elmer and Mamdouha Bobst Foundation, Inc. ▼

c/o The Elmer Holmes Bobst Library, New York Univ.
70 Washington Sq. South
New York 10012

Incorporated in 1968 in NY.
Donor(s): Elmer H. Bobst.‡
Foundation type: Independent
Financial data (yr. ended 12/31/90): Assets, $28,553,694 (M); expenditures, $1,466,495; qualifying distributions, $1,325,157, including $1,306,620 for 37 grants (high: $600,000; low: $100; average: $1,000-$60,000).
Purpose and activities: Emphasis on the promotion of health and medical research services, higher education, cultural programs, youth agencies, and national and international Islamic organizations.
Fields of interest: Health, medical research, higher education, cultural programs, youth, religion.
Publications: Annual report, informational brochure (including application guidelines).
Application information:
  Initial approach: Letter
  Deadline(s): None
  Write: Mamdouha S. Bobst, Pres.
Officers and Directors:* Mamdouha S. Bobst,* Pres. and Treas.; Arthur J. Mahon, Secy.; Farouk as-Sayid, Raja Kabbani, Mary Rockefeller, Milton C. Rose.
EIN: 132616114
Recent health grants:
1799-1 International Cancer Education Fund, NYC, NY, $600,000. 1990.
1799-2 Muslim Hospital of Tripoli, Tripoli, Lebanon, $60,000. 1990.
1799-3 New York University Medical Center, NYC, NY, $50,000. For fellowship fund. 1990.

1800
The Bodman Foundation ▼

c/o Morris & McVeigh
767 Third Ave., 22nd Fl.
New York 10017-2023   (212) 418-0500

Incorporated in 1945 in NJ.
Donor(s): George M. Bodman,‡ Louise C. Bodman.‡
Foundation type: Independent
Financial data (yr. ended 12/31/91): Assets, $40,194,323 (M); expenditures, $2,387,839; qualifying distributions, $2,100,000, including $2,100,000 for 67 grants (high: $200,000; low: $10,000; average: $20,000-$40,000).
Purpose and activities: Support largely for youth, the aged, and social service agencies, educational institutions, cultural programs, and health, including hospitals and rehabilitation programs.
Fields of interest: Social services, youth, child welfare, aged, handicapped, education, education—minorities, secondary education, cultural programs, health, hospitals, medical research, rehabilitation, drug abuse, AIDS, hunger.
Types of support: Building funds, equipment, annual campaigns, capital campaigns, general purposes, land acquisition, matching funds, operating budgets, research.
Limitations: Giving primarily in the New York, NY, area. Generally, no support for colleges or universities, performing arts groups, museums, or national health or mental health organizations. No grants to individuals, or for conferences, publications, travel, or film; no loans.
Publications: Biennial report (including application guidelines), program policy statement.
Application information: Application form not required.
  Initial approach: Letter and proposal
  Copies of proposal: 1
  Deadline(s): None
  Board meeting date(s): May, Sept., Dec., and as needed
  Final notification: Only when requested
  Write: Mary Caslin Ross, Secy. and Exec. Dir.
Officers and Trustees:* Guy G. Rutherfurd,* Pres. and Treas.; Marguerite Sykes Nichols,* V.P.; Mary Caslin Ross, Secy. and Exec. Dir.; Harry W. Albright, Jr., Mary B. Braga, Anthony Drexel Duke, Peter Frelinghuysen, John N. Irwin III, Leslie Lenkowsky, Russel Pennoyer, Mary S. Phipps.
Number of staff: 2 full-time professional.
EIN: 136022016
Recent health grants:
1800-1 Alzheimers Disease and Related Disorders Association, NYC, NY, $20,000. For Dementia Specialist Home Care Aides Training Program. 1991.
1800-2 Brooklyn Bureau of Community Service, Brooklyn, NY, $25,000. For Perinatal, Drug Treatment and Islands of Safety Programs. 1991.
1800-3 Cancer Care, NYC, NY, $31,668. Toward Field Work Training Program for graduate students in social work. 1991.
1800-4 Churchill Center for Learning Disabilities, NYC, NY, $30,000. For current capital campaign and to meet challenge grant. 1991.
1800-5 CPC Mental Health Services, Eatontown, NJ, $25,000. For current capital drive to construct school building. 1991.

1800-6 International Center for the Disabled (ICD), NYC, NY, $100,000. For medical area as part of 75th Anniversary Campaign. 1991.

1800-7 New York City School Volunteer Program, NYC, NY, $20,000. For Bridges to the Mainstream and Teens As School Volunteer Tutors Programs. 1991.

1800-8 New York Foundling Hospital, NYC, NY, $20,000. For equipment in skilled nursing facility for handicapped infants. 1991.

1800-9 Phoenix House Foundation, NYC, NY, $200,000. For challenge grant for purchase of Belle Terre property in South Kortright, NY for use as treatment facility for young adults and adolescents. 1991.

1800-10 Queens County Youth Development Corporation, Outreach Project, Woodhaven, NY, $25,000. For operating needs. 1991.

1800-11 Rockefeller University, NYC, NY, $40,000. For construction of laboratory for senior professor. 1991.

1800-12 Saint Francis Friends of the Poor, NYC, NY, $25,000. For doctor from Saint Vincent's Hospital to serve this fragile population over next two years. 1991.

1800-13 Saint Vincents Hospital and Medical Center of New York, NYC, NY, $40,000. For community outreach endowment fund. 1991.

1800-14 Veritas Therapeutic Community Foundation, NYC, NY, $25,000. For Family Therapy Program. 1991.

1800-15 World Rehabilitation Fund, NYC, NY, $20,000. For regional training center in prosthetics and orthotics in Latin America. 1991.

1800-16 Youth Counseling League, NYC, NY, $15,000. For on-site counseling program in public schools. 1991.

1801
Booth Ferris Foundation ▼

c/o Morgan Guaranty Trust Co. of NY
60 Wall St., 46th Fl.
New York 10260-0001   (212) 809-1630

Trusts established in 1957 and 1958 in NY; merged in 1964.
Donor(s): Chancie Ferris Booth,‡ Willis H. Booth.‡
Foundation type: Independent
Financial data (yr. ended 12/31/91): Assets, $151,924,900 (M); expenditures, $5,608,722; qualifying distributions, $4,716,223, including $4,231,000 for 76 grants (high: $150,000; low: $15,000; average: $25,000-$50,000).
Purpose and activities: Grants primarily for private education, especially theological education, smaller colleges, and independent secondary schools; limited support also for urban programs, social service agencies, and cultural activities.
Fields of interest: Theological education, education, educational associations, secondary education, higher education, urban affairs, social services, cultural programs, arts, child welfare.
Types of support: Continuing support, annual campaigns, seed money, emergency funds, building funds, equipment, renovation projects, endowment funds, matching funds, capital campaigns, general purposes.
Limitations: Giving limited to the New York, NY, metropolitan area for social service agencies and cultural organizations. No support for federated campaigns, community chests, or for work with specific diseases or disabilities. No grants to individuals, or for research; generally no grants to educational institutions for scholarships, fellowships, or unrestricted endowments; no loans.
Publications: Annual report (including application guidelines).
Application information: Application form not required.
Initial approach: Proposal
Copies of proposal: 1
Deadline(s): None
Board meeting date(s): Every 2 to 3 months, approximately 4 times per year
Final notification: 4 months
Write: Robert J. Murtagh, Trustee
Trustees: Robert J. Murtagh, Morgan Guaranty Trust Co. of New York.
Number of staff: 3 part-time professional.
EIN: 136170340
Recent health grants:
1801-1 Episcopal Health Services, Hempstead, NY, $100,000. For construction of Brooklyn health care facility. 1990.
1801-2 Legal Action Center of the City of New York, NYC, NY, $25,000. For AIDS Policy Project. 1990.
1801-3 Louise Wise Services, NYC, NY, $40,000. For implementation of Crisis Intervention Program. 1990.
1801-4 United Hospital Fund of New York, NYC, NY, $25,000. For New York City Health Care for the Homeless Program. 1990.

1802
Borden Corporate Contributions Program

277 Park Ave.
New York 10172   (212) 573-4000
Application address: 180 East Broad St., Columbus, OH 43215; Tel.: (614) 225-4340

Financial data (yr. ended 12/31/90): Total giving, $1,900,000, including $900,000 for grants and $1,000,000 for in-kind gifts.
Purpose and activities: Charitable contributions are an investment to improve people's lives in the communities in which Borden operates. Support for higher education, health, human services, civic affairs, United Way, community funds, youth agencies, and culture; also makes in-kind contributions of products, land, and equipment, as well as surplus foods for Second Harvest.
Fields of interest: Higher education, health, community funds, youth, cultural programs, hunger, civic affairs.
Types of support: In-kind gifts.
Limitations: Giving primarily in areas of company operations.
Application information: Corporate giving is administered by the Foundation. Requests for United Funds must be solicited through and recommended by the local plant manager.
Initial approach: Letter
Deadline(s): Mar. 1, July 1, and Oct. 1
Final notification: 3 to 6 months
Write: Judy Barker, Pres., Borden Foundation

1803
The Albert C. Bostwick Foundation

Hillside Ave. and Bacon Rd.
P.O. Box A
Old Westbury 11568   (516) 334-5566

Trust established in 1958 in NY.
Donor(s): Albert C. Bostwick.‡
Foundation type: Independent
Financial data (yr. ended 12/31/91): Assets, $2,700,735 (M); expenditures, $192,179; qualifying distributions, $174,700, including $174,700 for 46 grants (high: $25,000; low: $500).
Fields of interest: Medical research, hospitals, health, social services.
Types of support: Research.
Limitations: Giving primarily in NY. No grants to individuals.
Application information:
Initial approach: Letter
Deadline(s): None
Board meeting date(s): Annually
Write: Eleanor P. Bostwick, Trustee
Trustees: Albert C. Bostwick, Jr., Eleanor P. Bostwick, Andrew G.C. Sage III.
EIN: 116003740

1804
Botwinick-Wolfensohn Foundation, Inc. ▼

599 Lexington Ave.
New York 10022   (212) 909-8100

Established in 1952.
Donor(s): James D. Wolfensohn, Benjamin Botwinick, Edward Botwinick.
Foundation type: Independent
Financial data (yr. ended 12/31/90): Assets, $3,649,052 (M); gifts received, $1,614,614; expenditures, $1,893,045; qualifying distributions, $1,877,772, including $1,877,772 for 294 grants (high: $250,000; low: $10; average: $500-$5,000).
Purpose and activities: Emphasis on Israeli and Jewish interests, music education, minority education, medical research, social services, and the homeless.
Fields of interest: Israel, Jewish welfare, music, education, education—minorities, medical research, social services, homeless.
Types of support: Annual campaigns, building funds, capital campaigns, continuing support, general purposes, research, scholarship funds, seed money, special projects.
Limitations: Giving primarily in New York, NY. No grants to individuals.
Publications: 990-PF.
Application information: Discretionary funds are very limited; most contributions are longstanding commitments. Application form not required.
Initial approach: Letter or telephone
Copies of proposal: 1
Deadline(s): None
Board meeting date(s): Annually
Final notification: 3 to 6 months
Write: James D. Wolfensohn, Chair.
Officers: James D. Wolfensohn, Chair.; Benjamin Botwinick, Pres.; Edward Botwinick, V.P.; Elaine Wolfensohn, Secy.; Bessie Botwinick, Treas.; Jennifer Jacobson, Exec. Dir.
Number of staff: 1 full-time professional; 1 full-time support.

EIN: 136111833

1805
The Boxer Foundation
c/o George Rothkopf
366 North Broadway, Suite 310
Jericho 11753

Established in 1985.
Donor(s): Leonard Boxer.
Foundation type: Independent
Financial data (yr. ended 11/30/91): Assets,
$685,790 (M); gifts received, $790,813;
expenditures, $369,689; qualifying distributions,
$361,596, including $353,951 for 60 grants
(high: $250,000; low: $25).
Fields of interest: Health associations, higher
education, hospitals, medical education.
Types of support: General purposes.
Limitations: Giving primarily in the greater
metropolitan New York, NY, area, including Long
Island. No grants to individuals.
Application information: Contributes only to
pre-selected organizations. Applications not
accepted.
Officer: Leonard Boxer, Mgr.
EIN: 133345823

1806
Brain Trauma Foundation, Inc.
(Formerly The Sunny von Bulow Coma and
Head Trauma Research Foundation)
555 Madison Ave., Suite 2001
New York 10022-3303   (212) 753-5003
FAX: (212) 753-0149

Established in 1986 in NY.
Donor(s): Annie-Laurie Aitken Charitable Trust.
Foundation type: Independent
Financial data (yr. ended 12/31/90): Assets,
$659,409 (M); expenditures, $616,045; qualifying
distributions, $609,754, including $300,000 for
10 grants (high: $35,000; low: $8,750).
Purpose and activities: Support primarily for
medical research of coma and head trauma.
Fields of interest: Medical research.
Limitations: No grants to individuals.
Publications: Informational brochure (including
application guidelines), 990-PF, financial
statement.
Application information: Application form
required.
  Initial approach: 1- to 2-page letter of intent
  Copies of proposal: 8
  Deadline(s): July 31 and Jan. 31
  Board meeting date(s): Fall
  Final notification: One month after board
    meeting
  Write: Dominic Introcaso, Exec. Dir.
Officers and Directors:* Annie-Laurie Isham,*
Pres.; George Morris Gurley,* V.P.; Alexander von
Auersperg,* Secy.; Ralph Isham,* Treas.; Henry B.
Betts, M.D., Mrs. William McCormick Blair,
Yasmin Aga Khan Jeffries, Russel H. Paterson, Jr.,
M.D., Marilyn Price Spivack.
Number of staff: 1 full-time professional; 1
full-time support.
EIN: 133349779

1807
Branta Foundation, Inc.
c/o Perelson Johnson & Rones
560 Lexington Ave.
New York 10022

Established in 1955 in NY.
Donor(s): Harvey Picker.
Foundation type: Independent
Financial data (yr. ended 05/31/91): Assets,
$3,275,563 (M); gifts received, $606,838;
expenditures, $322,744; qualifying distributions,
$283,485, including $283,000 for 12 grants
(high: $60,000; low: $5,000).
Fields of interest: Higher education, health,
hospitals, cultural programs, international affairs.
Limitations: Giving primarily in NY. No grants to
individuals.
Application information: Contributes only to
pre-selected organizations. Applications not
accepted.
Officers and Directors:* Harvey Picker,* Pres.
and Treas.; Christine Beshar,* V.P. and Secy.
EIN: 136130955

1808
Bristol-Myers Squibb Company
Contributions Program
(Formerly Bristol-Myers Company Contributions
Program)
345 Park Ave., 43rd Fl.
New York 10154-0037   (212) 546-4000

Financial data (yr. ended 12/31/91): Total giving,
$19,000,000.
Purpose and activities: Charitable contributions
from the Bristol-Myers Squibb Foundation, the
company, and its subsidiaries and divisions
totaled more than $19 million during 1991.
Health-related, medical research and community
service organizations received 51 percent of
combined company and Foundation
contributions; educational institutions and
education-related programs received 31 percent;
and civic and cultural activities received 18
percent. The company supports medical research
with unrestricted grants to medical schools and
research institutions in North America, Europe,
and Asia. Annual Bristol-Myers Squibb Awards
are given to individuals selected by their medical
school or research institution. Individual
applications are not accepted. Bristol-Myers
Squibb also funds annual company symposia for
each category.
Fields of interest: Medical research, health,
nutrition, women, handicapped, minorities, AIDS,
heart disease, biological sciences, cancer, medical
research.
Types of support: Research, scholarship funds,
fellowships, conferences and seminars,
internships.
Limitations: Giving primarily in operating areas
nationally and internationally. No support for
political, fraternal, social or veterans'
organizations, religious or sectarian organizations,
unless project will benefit the community as a
whole. No grants to individuals, or for the United
Way and other federated campaign funding
recipients, endowments, courtesy advertising, non
tax-exempt organizations; no loans.
Application information:
  Initial approach: Letter outlining request

Write: Marilyn L. Gruber, Dir., Corp. Contribs.

1809
The Bristol-Myers Squibb Foundation, Inc.
▼
(Formerly The Bristol-Myers Fund, Inc.)
345 Park Ave., 43rd Fl.
New York 10154   (212) 546-4331

Trust established in 1953 in NY; successor fund
incorporated in 1982 in FL as Bristol-Myers Fund,
Inc.
Donor(s): Bristol-Myers Squibb Co., divisions and
subsidiaries.
Foundation type: Company-sponsored
Financial data (yr. ended 12/31/90): Assets,
$10,407,496 (M); gifts received, $3,000,000;
expenditures, $8,016,288; qualifying
distributions, $8,016,288, including $8,015,391
for 788 grants (high: $438,000; low: $25;
average: $5,000-$35,000).
Purpose and activities: Giving for medical
research, community funds, higher and other
education (including employee-related
scholarships administered by the National Merit
Scholarship Corp. and employee matching gifts),
and health care; support also for civic affairs and
community services, minority and women's
organizations, youth agencies, international
affairs, and arts and culture.
Fields of interest: Community development,
community funds, education, higher education,
education—minorities, secondary education,
civic affairs, minorities, women, youth, health
services, AIDS, medical research, cultural
programs, arts, international affairs.
Types of support: Annual campaigns, research,
employee-related scholarships, fellowships,
scholarship funds, general purposes, employee
matching gifts.
Limitations: Giving limited to areas of company
operations, and to national organizations. No
support for political, fraternal, social, or veterans'
organizations; religious or sectarian organizations
not engaged in a significant project benefiting the
entire community; specific public broadcast
programs or films; or organizations receiving
support through federated campaigns. No grants
to individuals, or for endowment funds; no loans.
Publications: Informational brochure.
Application information: Application form not
required.
  Initial approach: Proposal
  Copies of proposal: 1
  Deadline(s): Submit proposal preferably
    between Feb. and Sept.; deadline Oct. 1
  Board meeting date(s): Dec. and as needed
  Final notification: 2 to 3 months
  Write: Marilyn L. Gruber, V.P., or Nancy Arnst
    Taussig, Mgr.
Officers and Directors:* Patrick F. Crossman,*
Pres.; Marilyn L. Gruber, V.P.; J. Richard
Edmondson, Secy.; Jonathan B. Morris, Treas.;
Nancy Arnst Taussig, Mgr.; Michael E. Autera,
Richard L. Gelb.
Number of staff: 2 full-time professional; 1
part-time professional; 3 full-time support; 1
part-time support.
EIN: 133127947
Recent health grants:
1809-1 Albany College of Pharmacy, Albany, NY,
  $38,000. 1990.

1809-2 American Council for Drug Education, NYC, NY, $12,500. 1990.

1809-3 American Diabetes Association, NYC, NY, $10,000. 1990.

1809-4 American Foundation for AIDS Research, NYC, NY, $43,000. 1990.

1809-5 American Health Foundation, NYC, NY, $94,000. 1990.

1809-6 American Heart Association, Syracuse, NY, $40,000. 1990.

1809-7 American Society for Clinical Pharmacology and Therapeutics, Norristown, PA, $12,000. 1990.

1809-8 Childrens Hospital of Buffalo, Buffalo, NY, $21,100. 1990.

1809-9 Childrens Inn at the National Institutes of Health, Friends of, DC, $25,000. 1990.

1809-10 Columbia-Presbyterian Medical Center Fund, NYC, NY, $50,500. 1990.

1809-11 Floating Hospital, NYC, NY, $50,000. 1990.

1809-12 Foundation for Cancer Research and Education, Phoenix, AZ, $145,915. 1990.

1809-13 Fox Chase Cancer Center, Philadelphia, PA, $10,000. 1990.

1809-14 Garrison Volunteer Ambulance and First Aid Squad, Garrison, NY, $10,000. 1990.

1809-15 Grantmakers in Health, NYC, NY, $10,000. 1990.

1809-16 Harvard University, Medical School of Clinical Pharmacology, Cambridge, MA, $38,000. 1990.

1809-17 Harvard University, School of Public Health, Cambridge, MA, $12,100. 1990.

1809-18 Hispanic AIDS Forum, NYC, NY, $10,000. 1990.

1809-19 Hole in the Wall Gang Camp Fund, Westport, CT, $10,000. 1990.

1809-20 Hospital for Special Surgery Fund, NYC, NY, $31,000. 1990.

1809-21 International Pain Foundation, Seattle, WA, $15,000. 1990.

1809-22 International Society of Regulatory Toxicology and Pharmacolgy, DC, $20,000. 1990.

1809-23 Joslin Diabetes Center, Boston, MA, $20,000. 1990.

1809-24 Juvenile Diabetes Foundation International, NYC, NY, $25,000. 1990.

1809-25 Karolinska Institute, Stockholm, Sweden, $100,000. 1990.

1809-26 Manhattan Eye, Ear and Throat Hospital, NYC, NY, $10,000. 1990.

1809-27 Massachusetts General Hospital, Boston, MA, $100,000. 1990.

1809-28 Media-Advertising Partnership for a Drug-Free America, NYC, NY, $50,000. 1990.

1809-29 Memorial Sloan-Kettering Cancer Center, NYC, NY, $77,675. 1990.

1809-30 Morehouse School of Medicine, Atlanta, GA, $20,000. 1990.

1809-31 Mount Sinai Hospital and Medical Center, NYC, NY, $35,000. 1990.

1809-32 National Council on Patient Information and Education, DC, $25,000. 1990.

1809-33 National Foundation for Facial Reconstruction, NYC, NY, $18,000. 1990.

1809-34 National Medical Fellowships, NYC, NY, $10,000. 1990.

1809-35 New England Medical Center, Boston, MA, $25,000. 1990.

1809-36 New Milford Hospital, New Milford, CT, $10,250. 1990.

1809-37 New York Eye and Ear Infirmary, NYC, NY, $10,000. 1990.

1809-38 New York Health Careers Center, NYC, NY, $10,000. 1990.

1809-39 Occupational Physicians Scholarship Fund, NYC, NY, $15,000. 1990.

1809-40 Ossining Open Door Associates, Ossining, NY, $10,000. 1990.

1809-41 Pharmaceutical Manufacturers Association Foundation, DC, $200,000. 1990.

1809-42 Philadelphia College of Pharmacy and Science, Philadelphia, PA, $15,150. 1990.

1809-43 Saint Josephs Hospital Health Center, Syracuse, NY, $10,000. 1990.

1809-44 Salk Institute for Biological Studies, La Jolla, CA, $20,000. 1990.

1809-45 United Cerebral Palsy of New York City, NYC, NY, $13,000. 1990.

1809-46 Visiting Nurse Service of New York, NYC, NY, $10,000. 1990.

1810
The Carolyn & Kenneth D. Brody Foundation

(Formerly Kenneth D. Brody Foundation)
c/o Goldman Sachs & Co., Tax Dept.
85 Broad St.
New York 10004-2408

Established in 1980 in NY.
Donor(s): Kenneth D. Brody.
Foundation type: Independent
Financial data (yr. ended 09/30/91): Assets, $2,333,213 (M); gifts received, $700,000; expenditures, $484,656; qualifying distributions, $463,786, including $463,480 for 111 grants (high: $150,000; low: $60).
Fields of interest: Dance, cultural programs, higher education, health services, hospitals.
Limitations: Giving primarily in New York, NY. No grants to individuals, or for scholarships; no loans.
Application information: Contributes only to pre-selected organizations. Applications not accepted.
Trustees: Kenneth D. Brody, Donald R. Gant, H. Frederick Krimendahl II.
EIN: 133050750

1811
The Samuel Bronfman Foundation, Inc. ▼
375 Park Ave.
New York 10152-0192

Incorporated in 1951 in DE.
Donor(s): Joseph E. Seagram and Sons, Inc.
Foundation type: Company-sponsored
Financial data (yr. ended 12/31/90): Assets, $15,876,412 (M); gifts received, $1,025,500; expenditures, $6,263,300; qualifying distributions, $6,252,761, including $6,252,761 for 17 grants (high: $1,500,000; average: $50,000-$300,000).
Purpose and activities: To perpetuate the ideals of American democracy; finances research programs for the study of democratic business enterprise by means of fellowships and professorships in colleges and universities; grants also for Jewish welfare funds and medical education.

Fields of interest: Higher education, medical education, economics, Jewish giving, Jewish welfare, AIDS.
Types of support: General purposes, professorships, fellowships.
Limitations: No grants to individuals, or for building or endowment funds, or operating budgets.
Application information: Application form not required.
  Initial approach: Proposal
  Copies of proposal: 1
  Deadline(s): None
  Board meeting date(s): Jan., Apr., July, and Oct.
  Final notification: 6 to 8 weeks
  Write: William K. Friedman, V.P.
Officers and Trustees:* Edgar M. Bronfman,* Chair.; Samuel Bronfman II,* Pres.; William K. Friedman,* V.P.; Claire Cullen, Secy.; Richard Karl Goeltz,* Treas.; Charles R. Bronfman, Edgar Bronfman, Jr., David G. Sacks.
EIN: 136084708

1812
The Brookdale Foundation
126 East 56th St.
New York 10022-3668   (212) 308-7355

Incorporated in 1950 in NY.
Donor(s): Henry L. Schwartz,‡ and his brothers.
Foundation type: Independent
Financial data (yr. ended 06/30/91): Assets, $7,785,736 (M); gifts received, $726,366; expenditures, $1,288,735; qualifying distributions, $1,170,784, including $896,681 for 21 grants (high: $120,000; low: $3,000; average: $3,000-$50,000).
Purpose and activities: Support for gerontological and geriatric research and innovative service programs; giving also for higher education and youth.
Fields of interest: Aged, medical research, education, higher education, social services, youth, Jewish giving.
Types of support: Seed money, matching funds, conferences and seminars, special projects, research.
Limitations: No grants to individuals, or for operating budgets, continuing support, or annual campaigns; no loans.
Publications: Program policy statement, newsletter.
Application information: Application form not required.
  Initial approach: Letter of intent
  Copies of proposal: 1
  Deadline(s): None
  Board meeting date(s): Monthly
  Final notification: In writing
  Write: Stephen Schwartz, Pres.; or call Danylle Rudin, Asst. V.P. and Prog. Officer
Officers and Directors:* Stephen L. Schwartz,* Pres.; Mary Ann Van Clief, V.P. and Secy.; Jeanette Pereira, Treas.; Stanley Epstein, Arthur Norman Field, Lois Juliber, Rebecca Shaffer, John Winthrop, Roy Zuckerberg.
Number of staff: 2 full-time professional; 2 part-time support.
EIN: 136076863

1813
Gladys Brooks Foundation ▼
90 Broad St.
New York 10004   (212) 943-3217

Established in 1981 in NY.
Donor(s): Gladys Brooks Thayer.‡
Foundation type: Independent
Financial data (yr. ended 12/31/90): Assets,
$22,094,088 (M); expenditures, $1,292,837;
qualifying distributions, $1,233,185, including
$1,006,028 for 24 grants (high: $100,000; low:
$5,000; average: $5,000-$100,000).
Purpose and activities: Grants largely for libraries,
higher education, and hospitals and clinics.
Fields of interest: Libraries, higher education,
hospitals, health services.
Types of support: Endowment funds, building
funds, equipment, scholarship funds.
Limitations: Giving limited to the Northeast,
including NY, MA, CT, NH, VT, PA, ME, NJ, RI,
DE, and Washington, DC. No grants to
individuals, or for research.
Publications: Annual report (including application
guidelines), program policy statement.
Application information: Application form
required.
   Copies of proposal: 2
   Deadline(s): May 31
   Board meeting date(s): Bimonthly
   Final notification: Dec.
   Write: Ms. Jessica L. Rutledge, Admin. Asst.
Board of Governors and Trustees: James J. Daly,
Harman Hawkins, Robert E. Hill, U.S. Trust Co. of
New York.
Number of staff: 1 full-time professional.
EIN: 132955337
Recent health grants:
1813-1 CPC Mental Health Services, Eatontown,
   NJ, $100,000. 1991.
1813-2 Manhattan Institute for Cancer Research,
   NYC, NY, $50,000. 1991.
1813-3 New York Academy of Medicine, NYC,
   NY, $50,000. 1991.
1813-4 Winthrop-University Hospital, Mineola,
   NY, $100,000. 1991.

1814
The Milton V. Brown Foundation
2000 Plaza Ave.
P.O. Box 148
New Hyde Park 11040   (516) 328-1406

Established in 1986 in DE.
Donor(s): Milton V. Brown.‡
Foundation type: Independent
Financial data (yr. ended 12/31/91): Assets,
$2,037,610 (M); gifts received, $5,000;
expenditures, $130,723; qualifying distributions,
$130,173, including $129,213 for 25 grants
(high: $15,000; low: $553).
Fields of interest: Higher education, secondary
education, health, social services, youth.
Limitations: Giving primarily in NY.
Application information: Application form
required.
   Deadline(s): None
   Write: Ann M. Henken, Secy.
Officers and Directors:* Kalman I. Nulman,*
Pres.; Bruce Brown,* V.P.; Ann M. Henken,*
Secy.; Allan Brown,* Treas.
EIN: 112775808

1815
BT Foundation
280 Park Ave.
New York 10017   (212) 454-3086
Application address: P.O. Box 318, Church St.
Station, New York, NY 10012

Established in 1986 in NY.
Donor(s): BT Capital Corp.
Foundation type: Company-sponsored
Financial data (yr. ended 11/30/89): Assets,
$66,535 (M); gifts received, $2,600,000;
expenditures, $2,573,248; qualifying
distributions, $2,575,493, including $1,124,998
for 91 grants (high: $110,000; low: $250;
average: $5,000-$25,000) and $1,444,929 for
employee matching gifts (high: $45,660; low:
$50).
Purpose and activities: Support for arts and
culture, economic development, with emphasis
on community development and housing, social
and public services, and urban amenities.
Fields of interest: Theater, performing arts, arts,
cultural programs, urban development, urban
affairs, community development, housing, social
services.
Types of support: General purposes, operating
budgets, employee matching gifts, capital
campaigns, continuing support.
Limitations: Giving primarily in NY. No support
for religious purposes, veterans' and fraternal
organizations, or United Way agencies unless
they provide a fundraising waiver. No grants to
individuals, or for endowment campaigns.
Application information: Application form not
required.
   Initial approach: Proposal
   Deadline(s): None
   Write: Page Chapman, Pres.
Officers and Directors: Nancy S. Ticktin, Pres.;
Maureen S. Bateman, V.P.; James J. Baechle, Page
Chapman III.
Number of staff: 2 full-time professional; 3
full-time support.
EIN: 133321736
Recent health grants:
1815-1 American Council for Drug Education,
   NYC, NY, $10,000. For general operating
   support. 1990.
1815-2 American Council for Drug Education,
   NYC, NY, $10,000. 1990.
1815-3 Memorial Sloan-Kettering Cancer Center,
   NYC, NY, $30,000. For clinical research
   program. 1990.
1815-4 Memorial Sloan-Kettering Cancer Center,
   NYC, NY, $30,000. For clinical research
   program. 1990.
1815-5 Mid-Bronx Senior Citizens Council,
   Bronx, NY, $10,000. For drug counseling of
   at-risk youth. 1990.
1815-6 Puerto Rican Organization to Motivate,
   Enlighten, and Serve Addicts (PROMESA),
   Bronx, NY, $25,000. To provide range of social
   services to promote tenants' independent living
   skills. 1990.
1815-7 Saint Vincents Hospital and Medical
   Center of New York, NYC, NY, $10,000. For
   PRIDE Institute, Paramedic Mobile ICC,
   Department of Medicine's Education Fund and
   Berenson project on liver disease. 1990.

1816
Buffalo Forge Company Giving Program
490 Broadway
Buffalo 14204   (716) 847-5121

Purpose and activities: Supports civic programs,
the arts, education, research, culture, health,
United Way, and private colleges.
Fields of interest: Civic affairs, education, arts,
higher education, cultural programs, health,
community funds.
Types of support: Equipment, operating budgets,
capital campaigns, research.
Limitations: Giving primarily in Buffalo, NY.
Application information:
   Initial approach: Letter of inquiry describing
      project
   Copies of proposal: 1
   Deadline(s): Applications accepted throughout
      the year
   Board meeting date(s): Decisions made as
      needed
   Final notification: 4-6 weeks
   Write: Samuel A. Young, Pres. and C.E.O.
Number of staff: None.

1817
The Buffalo Foundation
1601 Main-Seneca Bldg.
237 Main St.
Buffalo 14203-2781   (716) 852-2857

Established in 1919 in NY by resolution and
declaration of trust.
Foundation type: Community
Financial data (yr. ended 12/31/90): Assets,
$34,152,782 (M); gifts received, $2,831,504;
expenditures, $2,792,060; qualifying
distributions, $2,301,513, including $2,301,513
for grants (high: $100,000; low: $82; average:
$3,000-$5,000).
Purpose and activities: To administer trust funds
for charitable, educational, and civic purposes.
Grants for educational institutions, scholarships,
family and child welfare, health services and
hospitals, the arts, and community development.
Fields of interest: Education, family services, child
welfare, health services, AIDS, hospitals, arts,
community development, general charitable
giving.
Types of support: Operating budgets, seed money,
emergency funds, building funds, equipment,
land acquisition, special projects, matching funds,
consulting services, technical assistance, research,
publications, conferences and seminars, general
purposes, renovation projects, student aid,
exchange programs, endowment funds,
internships, professorships.
Limitations: Giving limited to Erie County, NY;
scholarships awarded to local residents only. No
grants for annual campaigns or deficit financing;
no loans.
Publications: Annual report (including application
guidelines), application guidelines, informational
brochure, newsletter, program policy statement,
990-PF.
Application information: Application forms
required only for scholarships, and must be
requested between Mar. 1 and May 10.
Application form not required.
   Initial approach: Proposal
   Copies of proposal: 1

Deadline(s): Last business day of Mar., June, Sept., and Dec.; May 10 for scholarships
Board meeting date(s): 1st Wednesday of Feb., May, Aug., and Nov.
Final notification: 1st meeting after submission
Write: William L. Van Schoonhoven, Dir.
Officers: Mrs. Warren W. Lane, Chair.; Ronald J. Anthony, Vice-Chair.; William L. Van Schoonhoven, Dir. and Secy.
Governing Committee: James E. Denman, Mrs. Robert S. Grantham, Gordon R. Gross, Richard B. McCormick, John T. Smythe, Paul A. Willax.
Trustee Banks: Bank of Western New York, N.A., Fleet Bank, N.A., Manufacturers and Traders Trust Co., Marine Midland Bank Western Region, N.A.
Number of staff: 1 full-time professional; 2 full-time support; 1 part-time support.
EIN: 160743935
Recent health grants:
1817-1 Buffalo Hearing and Speech Center, Buffalo, NY, $10,000. Toward new center. 1990.
1817-2 Buffalo Hearing and Speech Center, Buffalo, NY, $10,000. Toward building of facility. 1990.
1817-3 Childrens Hospital of Buffalo, Womens and Childrens Health Research Foundation, Buffalo, NY, $20,000. For research. 1990.
1817-4 Medical Foundation of Buffalo, Buffalo, NY, $16,850. For cancer research. 1990.
1817-5 Medical Foundation of Buffalo, Buffalo, NY, $15,000. For equipment. 1990.
1817-6 Roswell Park Memorial Institute, Buffalo, NY, $37,500. For cancer research. 1990.
1817-7 Sisters Hospital Foundation, Buffalo, NY, $10,000. For equipment for Head and Neck Otolaryngology Center. 1990.

1818
Henrietta B. & Frederick H. Bugher Foundation

(also known as Bugher Foundation)
c/o Davis, Polk & Wardwell
One Chase Manhattan Plaza, 39th Fl.
New York 10022

Established in 1961 in DC.
Donor(s): Frederick McLean Bugher.‡
Foundation type: Independent
Financial data (yr. ended 08/31/91): Assets, $23,630,838 (M); expenditures, $520,115; qualifying distributions, $451,020, including $323,852 for 4 grants (high: $133,986; low: $25,000).
Purpose and activities: Giving limited to cardiovascular research.
Fields of interest: Medical research, heart disease.
Types of support: Research.
Limitations: No grants to individuals.
Application information:
Initial approach: Letter
Deadline(s): None
Write: D. Nelson Adams, Trustee
Trustees: D. Nelson Adams, Daniel N. Adams, Jr., Robert A. Robinson.
Agent: Crestar Bank, N.A.
Number of staff: None.
EIN: 526034266

1819
Alfred G. Burnham Donor Fund, Inc.

c/o Schlossberg Natale & Ahrenstein
41 East 42nd St.
New York 10017-5201

Incorporated in 1953 in NY.
Donor(s): Alfred G. Burnham,‡ Rae O. Burnham.
Foundation type: Independent
Financial data (yr. ended 10/31/91): Assets, $3,488,297 (M); expenditures, $217,370; qualifying distributions, $200,000, including $200,000 for 44 grants (high: $12,000; low: $500).
Fields of interest: Higher education, hospitals, medical research, family planning, Jewish giving, Jewish welfare, child welfare.
Types of support: Research, scholarship funds.
Limitations: No grants to individuals, or for building or endowment funds, or special projects.
Application information: Contributes only to pre-selected organizations. Applications not accepted.
Officers and Directors:* Patrick J. James,* Chair.; John M. Oppenheimer,* Secy.; Elizabeth B. Nevin, Alicia B. Winslow.
EIN: 136097278

1820
The Charitable Foundation of the Burns Family, Inc.

c/o Allen & Brown
295 Madison Ave., Suite 1228
New York 10017

Established in 1962 in NY.
Donor(s): Randal B. Borough.
Foundation type: Independent
Financial data (yr. ended 11/30/91): Assets, $2,365,713 (M); expenditures, $150,979; qualifying distributions, $115,726, including $83,500 for 41 grants (high: $6,250; low: $500).
Fields of interest: Secondary education, higher education, Catholic giving, hospitals, health associations, social services, arts.
Types of support: Building funds.
Limitations: Giving primarily in the New York, NY, metropolitan area, Charlotte, NC, Sheridan, WY, and FL. No grants to individuals.
Application information: Contributes only to pre-selected organizations. Applications not accepted.
Officers: Randal B. Borough, Pres.; William J. Burns, V.P.; William J. Ennis, Secy.; Jeremiah E. Brown, Treas.
Director: D. Bruce Burns.
EIN: 136114052

1821
Jacob Burns Foundation, Inc.

c/o Jacob Burns
60 East 42nd St.
New York 10165   (212) 867-0949

Incorporated in 1957 in NY.
Donor(s): Mary Elizabeth Hood,‡ Jacob Burns, Rosalie A. Goldberg.
Foundation type: Independent
Financial data (yr. ended 12/31/91): Assets, $12,728,657 (M); gifts received, $340,000; expenditures, $892,014; qualifying distributions,

$803,552, including $781,562 for 88 grants (high: $211,000; low: $50).
Purpose and activities: Giving primarily for Jewish organizations, including welfare funds and a yeshiva university, and cultural programs, especially an opera association and a public broadcasting network; minor support also for hospitals.
Fields of interest: Jewish giving, Jewish welfare, higher education, cultural programs, music, media and communications, hospitals.
Limitations: Giving primarily in NY. No grants to individuals.
Application information: Contributes only to pre-selected organizations. Applications not accepted.
Officers: Jacob Burns, Pres. and Treas.; Rosalie A. Goldberg, V.P. and Secy.
EIN: 136114245

1822
J. Homer Butler Foundation

P.O. Box 1841
Old Chelsea Station
New York 10011   (212) 242-7340
Additional tel.: (718) 209-2254

Incorporated in 1961 in NY.
Donor(s): Mabel A. Tod.‡
Foundation type: Independent
Financial data (yr. ended 12/31/90): Assets, $3,135,127 (M); expenditures, $191,951; qualifying distributions, $164,761, including $115,051 for 37 grants (high: $7,000; low: $1,000; average: $2,000-$5,000).
Purpose and activities: Grants to Roman Catholic missions and religious orders to help improve the quality of life for the sick in the missions, especially those afflicted with leprosy.
Fields of interest: Catholic giving, leprosy, religion—missionary programs.
Types of support: Continuing support, emergency funds, equipment, general purposes, scholarship funds, special projects.
Limitations: Giving to domestic organizations for programs in Central and South America, Africa, the Philippines, and India.
Publications: Informational brochure (including application guidelines).
Application information: Application form required.
Initial approach: Letter
Copies of proposal: 1
Deadline(s): June 30 and Dec. 31
Board meeting date(s): 1st Tuesday in Mar.
Write: Geraldine Fremer, Secy.-Treas.
Officers and Directors:* Rev. Joseph J. Walter, S.J.,* Pres.; Robert T. Ross,* V.P.; Geraldine Fremer,* Secy.-Treas.; Rev. Edwin J. Brooks, S.J., Daniel H. Coleman, M.D., Martha S. Collin, Rev. Timothy A. Curtin, S.J., Peter F. De Gaetano, Sr. Ann Edgar, Fausto Gonzalez, William F. Hibberd, Rev. James F. Keenan, Joan MacLean, F. Patrick Rogers, Rev. Henry J. Zenorini, S.J.
Number of staff: None.
EIN: 136126669

1823
The Louis Calder Foundation ▼

230 Park Ave., Rm. 1530
New York 10169   (212) 687-1680

Trust established in 1951 in NY.
Donor(s): Louis Calder.‡
Foundation type: Independent
Financial data (yr. ended 10/31/91): Assets, $112,637,738 (M); expenditures, $6,346,056; qualifying distributions, $5,725,372, including $5,278,750 for 159 grants (high: $200,000; low: $5,000; average: $15,000-$50,000).
Purpose and activities: To support mainly those programs deemed best calculated to promote health, education, and welfare of New York City residents through grants to established organizations. Current programs are designed to enhance the potential and increase self-sufficiency of children, youth, and their families.
Fields of interest: Education, higher education, disadvantaged, welfare, youth, social services, family services.
Types of support: Operating budgets, equipment, special projects, scholarship funds, general purposes.
Limitations: Giving primarily in New York, NY. No support for publicly-operated educational or medical institutions, private foundations, or governmental organizations; cultural grants only to well-known and established institutions. No grants to individuals; generally no grants for building or endowment funds, capital development, or continuing support.
Publications: Annual report (including application guidelines).
Application information: Application form not required.
  Initial approach: Letter (one to three pages)
  Copies of proposal: 1
  Deadline(s): Submit proposal between Nov. 1 and Mar. 31; deadline 5 months prior to end of organization's fiscal year or Mar. 31, whichever is earliest
  Board meeting date(s): As required
  Final notification: July 31
  Write: The Trustees
Trustees: Paul R. Brenner, Peter D. Calder, Manufacturers Hanover Trust Co.
Number of staff: 2 full-time support.
EIN: 136015562
Recent health grants:
1823-1 Big Apple Circus, NYC, NY, $10,000. For Clown Care Unit and expanded program activities for hospitalized children. 1991.
1823-2 Boys Club of New York, NYC, NY, $75,000. For Healthy Attitudes, new program to prevent alcohol, drug abuse and pregnancy among young people. 1991.
1823-3 Bronx-Lebanon Hospital Center, Bronx, NY, $50,000. For challenge grant for operation and expansion of neuro-developmental unit of Hospital's Pediatric AIDS Unit. 1991.
1823-4 Cancer Care, NYC, NY, $25,000. For adolescent outreach project. 1991.
1823-5 Citizens Committee for New York City, NYC, NY, $10,000. For 1991 Drug Prevention Awards program. 1991.
1823-6 Harlem Interfaith Counseling Service, NYC, NY, $15,000. For Family and Youth Support System. 1991.
1823-7 Little Sisters of the Assumption Family Health Service, NYC, NY, $25,000. For family life program. 1991.
1823-8 Manhattan Eye, Ear and Throat Hospital, NYC, NY, $25,000. For programs and activities

of Children's Learning Center and its programs for learning disabled children. 1991.
1823-9 Mount Sinai Hospital and Medical Center, NYC, NY, $100,000. For challenge grant to support Children's Heart Health Program and preventive education, screening and critical care services for children of East Harlem. 1991.
1823-10 New York Hospital-Cornell Medical Center, NYC, NY, $100,000. For first-year operating costs of primary health care clinic for women and children in western Queens. 1991.
1823-11 New York University Medical Center, NYC, NY, $110,000. For Pediatric AIDS Research Program. 1991.
1823-12 Office of Substance Abuse Ministry, Bronx, NY, $25,000. For Youth Dare to Care programs in Bronx. 1991.
1823-13 Rockefeller University, Laboratory of Biochemical Genetics and Metabolism, NYC, NY, $200,000. For heart disease research. 1991.
1823-14 Rogosin Institute, Comprehensive Lipid Control Center, NYC, NY, $100,000. For research and clinical programs. 1991.
1823-15 Saint Christophers-Jennie Clarkson Child Care Services, Dobbs Ferry, NY, $40,000. For Children's Health Services clinic. 1991.
1823-16 Seton Foundation for Learning, Staten Island, NY, $100,000. For challenge grant to establish operating fund endowment for educational programs for developmentally delaywed elementary school children. 1991.
1823-17 Visiting Nurse Service of New York, NYC, NY, $35,000. For operation of Maternal/Child Health and Pediatric Program. 1991.
1823-18 Youth Counseling League, NYC, NY, $25,000. For drop-out prevention program in New York City public schools. 1991.

1824
Leonard & Irma Canno Foundation, Inc.
870 Fifth Ave.
New York 10021-4953

Established in 1952.
Donor(s): Leonard E. Canno, Irma Canno, Equitable Bag Co., Inc.
Foundation type: Independent
Financial data (yr. ended 12/31/91): Assets, $831,095 (M); gifts received, $529,560; expenditures, $251,628; qualifying distributions, $251,628, including $247,057 for 28 grants (high: $100,000; low: $75).
Fields of interest: Jewish welfare, Jewish giving, hospitals, education.
Types of support: General purposes.
Limitations: Giving primarily in NY. No grants to individuals.
Application information: Contributes only to pre-selected organizations. Applications not accepted.
Officers and Directors:* Leonard E. Canno, Pres.; Irma Canno,* V.P.; Jonathan Canno.
EIN: 136161640

1825
Iris & B. Gerald Cantor Foundation
(Formerly The B. G. Cantor Art Foundation)
c/o Joel Rothstein
One World Trade Ctr., Suite 10500
New York 10048

Established in 1967 in NY.
Donor(s): B. Gerald Cantor, Iris Cantor, Cantor Fitzgerald Securities Corp., Market Data Corp.
Foundation type: Operating
Financial data (yr. ended 04/30/91): Assets, $21,686,786 (M); gifts received, $7,378,728; expenditures, $4,702,197; qualifying distributions, $5,378,454, including $4,447,222 for 43 grants (high: $1,050,000; low: $100; average: $1,000-$10,000) and $254,965 for foundation-administered programs.
Purpose and activities: A private operating foundation; support for exhibits and studies of the work of Rodin, higher education, a hospital, museums, and dance programs for young people.
Fields of interest: Fine arts, museums, dance, hospitals, youth, higher education.
Limitations: No grants to individuals.
Application information: Contributes only to pre-selected organizations. Applications not accepted.
Officers and Trustees:* Iris Cantor,* Pres.; B. Gerald Cantor,* V.P.; Harry Needleman, Secy.; Joel D. Rothstein,* Treas.; Peter Bing, Suzanne Fisher, Michelle Labozzetta, Michael Spero.
EIN: 136227347

1826
Capital Cities/ABC Foundation, Inc. ▼
77 West 66th St., Rm. 16-15
New York 10023   (212) 456-7498

Incorporated in 1974 in DE.
Donor(s): Capital Cities Communications, Inc.
Foundation type: Company-sponsored
Financial data (yr. ended 12/31/90): Assets, $2,025,808 (M); gifts received, $2,500,000; expenditures, $2,682,709; qualifying distributions, $2,671,973, including $2,671,973 for 245 grants (high: $114,000; low: $1,000; average: $1,000-$25,000).
Purpose and activities: Grants for higher education, hospitals, health agencies, and local minority development; some support for social service agencies, civic affairs, communications, cultural programs, and youth agencies.
Fields of interest: Education, higher education, hospitals, health services, education—minorities, minorities, social services, civic affairs, media and communications, cultural programs, youth.
Limitations: Giving primarily in areas where company properties are located. No grants to individuals, or for building funds.
Application information: Contributes only to pre-selected organizations. Applications not accepted.
  Board meeting date(s): Quarterly
  Write: Bernadette Longford Williams, Contribs. Admin.
Officers and Directors:* Thomas S. Murphy,* Pres.; Daniel B. Burke,* V.P. and Treas.; Ronald J. Doerfler,* V.P.; Andrew E. Jackson, V.P.; Michael P. Mallardi,* V.P.; Alfred R. Scheider, V.P.; David Westin,* V.P.; Philip R. Farmsworth, Secy.
EIN: 237443020

Recent health grants:

1826-1 Bedford-Stuyvesant Volunteer Ambulance Corps, Brooklyn, NY, $15,000. 1990.

1826-2 Childrens National Medical Center, DC, $15,000. 1990.

1826-3 Childrens National Medical Center, DC, $15,000. 1990.

1826-4 Houston Crackdown, Houston, TX, $15,000. 1990.

1826-5 Memorial Sloan-Kettering Cancer Center, NYC, NY, $25,000. 1990.

1826-6 New York Hospital-Cornell Medical Center, NYC, NY, $10,000. 1990.

1826-7 New York University Medical Center, NYC, NY, $100,000. 1990.

1826-8 Northern Lights Alternatives, NYC, NY, $10,000. 1990.

1826-9 Queen of Angels-Hollywood Presbyterian Medical Center, Los Angeles, CA, $10,789. 1990.

1826-10 United Cerebral Palsy, NYC, NY, $40,000. 1990.

1826-11 United Cerebral Palsy, NYC, NY, $40,000. 1990.

1826-12 Veterans Bedside Network, NYC, NY, $10,000. 1990.

1827
The Carmel Hill Fund
(Formerly Ruane Family Fund)
1370 Ave. of the Americas, 29th Fl.
New York 10019

Established in 1986 in NY.
Donor(s): William J. Ruane.
Foundation type: Independent
Financial data (yr. ended 12/31/91): Assets, $3,768,217 (M); gifts received, $2,603,317; expenditures, $894,994; qualifying distributions, $871,026, including $871,026 for 76 grants (high: $300,000; low: $100).
Fields of interest: Mental health, medical research, youth, social services, education, cultural programs.
Limitations: Giving primarily in NY. No grants to individuals.
Application information: Contributes only to pre-selected organizations. Applications not accepted.
Trustee: William J. Ruane.
EIN: 136881103

1828
Carnahan-Jackson Foundation
Fourth and Pine Bldg.
Jamestown 14701   (716) 483-1015
Additional address: P.O. Box 3326, Jamestown, NY 14702-3326

Trust established in 1972 in NY.
Donor(s): Katharine J. Carnahan.‡
Foundation type: Independent
Financial data (yr. ended 07/31/91): Assets, $9,782,113 (M); expenditures, $625,177; qualifying distributions, $581,283, including $531,116 for 42 grants (high: $120,000).
Purpose and activities: Primary areas of interest include higher and other education, libraries, hospitals, and youth; support also for and the handicapped, drug abuse programs, ecology,

housing, community development, dance and other performing arts groups, and church support; some support for certain prior interests of the donor.
Fields of interest: Higher education, education, hospitals, drug abuse, youth, community development, religion—Christian, handicapped, libraries, performing arts, dance, ecology, housing.
Types of support: Building funds, capital campaigns, continuing support, equipment, general purposes, lectureships, matching funds, scholarship funds, seed money, special projects.
Limitations: Giving primarily in western NY, particularly Chautauqua County. No grants to individuals.
Publications: Application guidelines, grants list.
Application information: Application form required.
Initial approach: Letter outlining needs and use of grant
Copies of proposal: 2
Deadline(s): Apr. 30 and Sept. 30
Board meeting date(s): June and Nov.
Final notification: July and Dec.
Write: David H. Carnahan, Exec. Secy.
Officers and Trustees:* David H. Carnahan,* Exec. Secy.; Samuel P. Price,* Secy.; Fleet Norstar Investment Services.
Advisory Committee: John D. Hamilton, Anne Kohl, Rebecca Robbins.
Number of staff: 1 part-time professional; 1 part-time support.
EIN: 166151608

1829
Carnegie Corporation of New York ▼
437 Madison Ave.
New York 10022   (212) 371-3200

Incorporated in 1911 in NY.
Donor(s): Andrew Carnegie.‡
Foundation type: Independent
Financial data (yr. ended 09/30/91): Assets, $981,014,472 (M); expenditures, $55,792,925; qualifying distributions, $51,996,272, including $42,540,276 for grants (high: $1,200,000; low: $975) and $4,008,049 for foundation-administered programs.
Purpose and activities: The advancement and diffusion of knowledge and understanding among the peoples of the U.S. and of certain countries that are or have been members of the British Overseas Commonwealth. The foundation's current program goals are as follows: 1) The education and healthy development of children and youth, including early childhood health and development, early adolescence educational achievement and health, science education, and education reform; 2) Strengthening human resources in developing countries; and 3) Cooperative security, which seeks to avoid catastrophic conflict among nations.
Fields of interest: Child development, youth, child welfare, minorities, race relations, education, education—early childhood, elementary education, literacy, education—minorities, educational associations, educational research, science and technology, health services, health associations, drug abuse, public policy, international affairs, international development, Southern Africa, Africa, Caribbean, peace, arms control, foreign policy.

Types of support: Continuing support, seed money, special projects, research, publications, conferences and seminars, exchange programs, general purposes.
Limitations: Giving primarily in the U.S. Some grants in Sub-Saharan Africa, South Africa, and the Caribbean. No support for facilities of educational or human service institutions. No grants for scholarships, fellowships, travel, basic operating expenses or endowments; no program-related investments.
Publications: Annual report, informational brochure, newsletter, grants list, occasional report.
Application information: Application form not required.
Initial approach: Telephone or letter
Deadline(s): None
Board meeting date(s): Oct., Jan., Apr., and June
Final notification: 6 months
Write: Dorothy W. Knapp, Secy.
Officers and Trustees:* Warren Christopher, Chair.; Sheila E. Widnall, Vice-Chair.; David A. Hamburg,* Pres.; Barbara D. Finberg, Exec. V.P. and Prog. Chair., Special Projects; Dorothy W. Knapp, Secy.; Cynthia E. Merritt, Assoc. Secy.; Jeanmarie C. Grisi, Treas.; Newton N. Minow, Counsel; Richard I. Beattie, James P. Comer, Eugene H. Cota-Robles, James Lowell Gibbs, Jr., Thomas H. Kean, Joshua Lederberg, Shirley M. Malcom, Ray Marshall, Mary Patterson McPherson, Henry Muller, Robert E. Rubin, Laurence A. Tisch, John C. Whitehead.
Number of staff: 60 full-time professional; 8 part-time professional; 22 full-time support; 2 part-time support.
EIN: 131628151
Recent health grants:

1829-1 African Medical and Research Foundation, Nairobi, Kenya, $25,000. Toward assessment of program on nonformal health education in eastern and southern Africa. 1991.

1829-2 Africare, DC, $193,000. Toward maternal health and child survival program in Imo State, Nigeria. 1991.

1829-3 American College of Obstetricians and Gynecologists, DC, $30,000. For collaborative program to improve maternal health in Nigeria. 1991.

1829-4 Case Western Reserve University, Cleveland, OH, $25,000. Toward Center for Adolescent Health. 1991.

1829-5 Center for Population Options, DC, $200,000. Toward projects concerned with electronic media and adolescent sexuality. 1991.

1829-6 Center on Addiction and Substance Abuse, NYC, NY, $25,000. For planning an institute on addiction and substance abuse. 1991.

1829-7 Childrens Defense Fund, DC, $700,000. Toward divisions of family support; health; and education, youth development and adolescent pregnancy prevention. 1991.

1829-8 Commonwealth Caribbean Medical Research Council, London, England, $250,000. Toward support. 1991.

1829-9 Defense for Children International-USA, NYC, NY, $23,000. For dissemination of The Effects of Maternal Mortality on Children in Africa. 1991.

1829-10 Family Care International, NYC, NY, $146,000. Toward technical assistance to safe motherhood initiatives in sub-Saharan Africa and advocacy in Caribbean. 1991.

1829-11 Fundacion Mexicana para la Salud, Mexico, $600,000. Toward research in maternal and child health and strengthening of health resources in Mexico. 1991.

1829-12 Fundacion Mexicana para la Salud, Mexico, $125,000. Toward planning and development unit. 1991.

1829-13 Fundacion Mexicana para la Salud, Mexico, $25,000. For planning and development unit to strengthen institutional philanthropy. 1991.

1829-14 Harvard University, Cambridge, MA, $25,000. Toward research and writing by Arnold S. Relman on health care policy. 1991.

1829-15 Harvard University, Cambridge, MA, $11,500. Toward collaborative training program with African institutions in health and behavioral research. 1991.

1829-16 Harvard University, Harvard School of Public Health, Cambridge, MA, $345,000. Toward Takemi Program in International Health. 1991.

1829-17 Institute of International Education, NYC, NY, $375,000. Toward International Health Policy Program. 1991.

1829-18 International Development Research Centre, Ottawa, Canada, $220,000. Toward Task Force on Health Research for Development. 1991.

1829-19 International Federation of Gynecology and Obstetrics, London, England, $25,000. Toward West African participation in precongress workshop at XIIIth World Congress on Obstetrics and Gynecology. 1991.

1829-20 International Womens Health Coalition, NYC, NY, $300,000. Toward program to improve reproductive health of women in Nigeria. 1991.

1829-21 International Womens Health Coalition, NYC, NY, $20,000. Toward reprinting and distributing of special issue of International Journal of Gynecology and Obstetrics on impact of unwanted pregnancy on health of women in developing countries. 1991.

1829-22 Johns Hopkins University, Baltimore, MD, $25,000. For estimating social and health impact of national economic changes on children and youth. 1991.

1829-23 Mental Health Law Project, DC, $250,000. Toward advocacy on behalf of preschool developmentally disabled children. 1991.

1829-24 Minority Health Professions Foundation, Silver Spring, MD, $15,000. Toward papers on prevention of youth violence in minority communities. 1991.

1829-25 National Center for Clinical Infant Programs, Arlington, VA, $100,000. Toward technical assistance conference for states on quality child-care programs for infants and toddlers. 1991.

1829-26 National Institute for Medical Research, Lagos, Nigeria, $25,000. Toward conference on health research priorities in Nigeria. 1991.

1829-27 National Progressive Primary Health Care Network, Parktown, South Africa, $200,000. Toward network of institutions and individuals concerned with primary health care in South Africa. 1991.

1829-28 New York Academy of Medicine, NYC, NY, $92,000. Toward project to strengthen

biomedical research and development in New York City. 1991.

1829-29 Nursing and Midwifery Council of Nigeria, Ikeja, Nigeria, $25,000. For planning continuing education courses for nurse-midwives. 1991.

1829-30 Paramedical School, Sierra Leone, $152,400. For research to reduce maternal mortality in Bo District of Sierra Leone. 1991.

1829-31 Sex Information and Education Council of the United States (SIECUS), NYC, NY, $25,000. Toward project to develop and disseminate national guidelines for sexuality education for children and adolescents. 1991.

1829-32 Stanford University, Stanford, CA, $25,000. Toward national long-range plan for research on sleep disorders by National Commission on Sleep Disorders Research. 1991.

1829-33 University of Benin, Teaching Hospital, Benin City, Nigeria, $165,000. For research on maternal mortality in rural Nigerian community. 1991.

1829-34 University of Bristol, Bristol, England, $23,500. Toward data analysis of study of pregnancy-induced hypertension in selected countries of Africa and Asia. 1991.

1829-35 University of California, San Francisco, CA, $25,000. Toward planning international health social science organization. 1991.

1829-36 University of Dar es Salaam, Dar es Salaam, Tanzania, $25,000. For interdisciplinary program in social science and medicine. 1991.

1829-37 University of Ghana, Medical School, Accra, Ghana, $150,000. Toward research on maternal mortality. 1991.

1829-38 University of Ibadan, Ibadan, Nigeria, $25,000. Toward symposium on molecular biology and human diseases. 1991.

1829-39 University of Michigan, Ann Arbor, MI, $25,000. Toward planning vesicovaginal fistulae intervention project in West Africa. 1991.

1829-40 University of Michigan, Ann Arbor, MI, $25,000. Toward planning vesicovaginal fistulae intervention project in West Africa. 1991.

1829-41 University of Nairobi, Nairobi, Kenya, $25,000. For interdisciplinary program in social science and medicine. 1991.

1829-42 University of Rochester, Rochester, NY, $330,000. Toward study of effectiveness of nurse home-visiting programs for low-income mothers and infants. 1991.

1829-43 University of Science and Technology, Kumasi, Ghana, $165,000. For research on maternal mortality in rural Ghana. 1991.

1829-44 University of Southern California, Los Angeles, CA, $99,000. Toward fellowships on U.S.-Mexico border health and environmental issues at Center for International Journalism. 1991.

1829-45 University of Zimbabwe, Harare, Zimbabwe, $80,000. Toward improvement of health information system of medical library. 1991.

1829-46 Womens International Public Health Network, Bethesda, MD, $19,200. For special newsletter issue about maternal health. 1991.

1829-47 World Health Organization, Geneva, Switzerland, $323,000. Toward monitoring and evaluation of functional literacy programs

for women in Zambia, Zimbabwe, Ghana and Nigeria. 1991.

1829-48 World Health Organization, Geneva, Switzerland, $250,000. For research and training on biobehavioral sciences and mental health. 1991.

1829-49 World Health Organization, Geneva, Switzerland, $250,000. Toward program to reduce health risks of childbearing in sub-Saharan Africa and Carribbean. 1991.

1830
Carrier Corporation Community Programs
Carrier Pkwy
P.O. Box 4808, ARC Bldg.
Syracuse 13221   (315) 433-4787

Purpose and activities: Supports education, health, hospitals, social services, volunteerism, culture and civic groups.

Fields of interest: Education, health, social services, cultural programs, civic affairs, hospitals, volunteerism.

Types of support: Matching funds, capital campaigns, general purposes, scholarship funds, employee matching gifts.

Limitations: Giving primarily in headquarters city and major operating locations.

Application information: Application form not required.

   Initial approach: Brief letter or proposal
   Copies of proposal: 1
   Deadline(s): None
   Board meeting date(s): Preliminary budget preparation-July through Sept. 15
   Final notification: Feb.
   Write: Patricia W. Gonzalez, Dir., Community Programs

Number of staff: 1 full-time professional; 1 full-time support.

1831
The Carter-Wallace Foundation
1345 Ave. of the Americas
New York 10105   (212) 339-5000

Established in 1986 in NY.

Donor(s): Carter-Wallace, Inc.

Foundation type: Company-sponsored

Financial data (yr. ended 03/31/91): Assets, $993,976 (M); expenditures, $1,048,586; qualifying distributions, $1,046,786, including $1,046,500 for 197 grants (high: $35,000; low: $65).

Fields of interest: Arts, health, welfare, higher education, hospitals.

Types of support: General purposes, capital campaigns, endowment funds, annual campaigns.

Limitations: Giving primarily in NY and NJ. No grants to individuals.

Application information: Contributes only to pre-selected organizations. Applications not accepted.

Officers: Henry H. Hoyt, Jr., Pres.; Charles O. Hoyt, Secy.; Daniel J. Black, Treas.; James L. Wagar, Mgr.

EIN: 133359226

1832
The Thomas & Agnes Carvel Foundation
430 East 57th St.
New York 10022
Application address: 222 Crestwood Ave., Crestwood, NY 10707; Tel.: (914) 793-7300

Established in 1976 in NY.
Donor(s): Thomas Carvel,‡ Agnes Carvel.
Foundation type: Independent
Financial data (yr. ended 11/30/90): Assets, $16,580,807 (M); expenditures, $574,629; qualifying distributions, $500,485, including $499,700 for 39 grants (high: $100,000; low: $200).
Purpose and activities: Support for general charitable purposes, including child welfare, youth programs, education, churches, and health associations and hospitals.
Fields of interest: Child welfare, youth, education, religion—Christian, health associations, hospitals.
Application information:
Initial approach: Letter
Deadline(s): Oct. 1
Write: Mildred Arcadipane, V.P.
Officers and Directors:* Agnes Carvel,* Chair.; Robert Davis,* Pres.; Mildred Arcadipane,* V.P. and Secy.; Ann McHugh,* V.P. and Treas.; Salvador Molella,* V.P.; Brendan Byrne, Anthony Cerrato, Thomas Reddy, Malcolm Wilson.
EIN: 132879673

1833
Mary Flagler Cary Charitable Trust ▼
350 Fifth Ave., Rm. 6622
New York 10118   (212) 563-6860

Trust established in 1968 in NY.
Donor(s): Mary Flagler Cary.‡
Foundation type: Independent
Financial data (yr. ended 06/30/91): Assets, $102,454,198 (M); expenditures, $8,165,116; qualifying distributions, $6,313,773, including $6,313,773 for 109 grants (high: $2,195,713; low: $2,500; average: $10,000-$50,000).
Purpose and activities: "The trust entertains grant proposals in three areas: for music in New York City (directed toward community music schools and professional performance institutions, with an emphasis on the commissioning, performance, and recording of contemporary music); for the conservation of natural resources on the Atlantic and Gulf coastlines (particularly the preservation of coastal barrier islands and associated wetlands, with grant funds directed toward land acquisition, legal defense, and citizen action); and for urban environmental programs in New York City (focused on support for community initiatives and to help develop local leadership to work on environmental problems within low-income neighborhoods of the city). The balance of the trust's grant budget is devoted primarily to support The Mary Flagler Cary Arboretum and its Institute of Ecosystem Studies in Millbrook, NY."
Fields of interest: Music, performing arts, conservation, environment, ecology, leadership development.
Types of support: Operating budgets, continuing support, land acquisition, matching funds, special projects, program-related investments, general purposes.

Limitations: Giving limited to New York, NY, for music and the urban environment, and the eastern coastal states for conservation. No support for private foundations, hospitals, religious organizations, primary or secondary schools, colleges and universities, libraries, or museums. No grants to individuals, or for scholarships, fellowships, capital funds, annual campaigns, seed money, emergency funds, deficit financing, or endowment funds; no loans to individuals.
Publications: Informational brochure (including application guidelines), grants list, financial statement.
Application information: Application form not required.
Initial approach: Letter with brief proposal
Copies of proposal: 1
Deadline(s): None
Board meeting date(s): Monthly
Final notification: 2 months
Write: Edward A. Ames, Trustee
Trustees: Edward A. Ames, William R. Grant, Phyllis J. Mills.
Number of staff: 2 full-time professional; 1 full-time support.
EIN: 136266964
Recent health grants:
1833-1 Rockefeller University, NYC, NY, $60,000. For post-doctoral fellowships at Field Research Center for Ecology and Ethology. 1992.
1833-2 Rockefeller University, NYC, NY, $60,000. For post-doctoral fellowships at Field Research Center for Ecology and Ethology. 1991.

1834
The Sara Chait Memorial Foundation, Inc.
860 Fifth Ave.
New York 10021   (212) 734-7894

Incorporated in 1959 in NY.
Donor(s): Abraham Chait,‡ Murray Backer,‡ Burton D. Chait, Marilyn Chait, and others.
Foundation type: Independent
Financial data (yr. ended 12/31/91): Assets, $2,462,890 (M); expenditures, $195,462; qualifying distributions, $195,462, including $193,400 for 13 grants (high: $50,000; low: $250).
Fields of interest: Medical research, heart disease, hospitals, health associations.
Limitations: Giving primarily in NY.
Application information:
Initial approach: Letter
Deadline(s): None
Write: Marilyn Chait, Secy.
Officers: Seymour Sobel, Pres.; Marilyn Chait, Secy.
EIN: 136121596

1835
Charina Foundation, Inc.
85 Broad St.
New York 10004

Incorporated in 1980 in NY.
Donor(s): Richard L. Menschel, The Menschel Foundation.
Foundation type: Independent

Financial data (yr. ended 08/31/91): Assets, $11,987,716 (M); expenditures, $635,556; qualifying distributions, $606,402, including $602,332 for 237 grants (high: $125,000; low: $100; average: $500-$5,000).
Purpose and activities: Emphasis on arts and culture, including museums; support also for health services, medical research, and hospitals; higher and other education; Jewish organizations, including welfare funds; recreation; and community development.
Fields of interest: Arts, cultural programs, health services, hospitals, rehabilitation, higher education, education, Jewish giving, recreation, legal services.
Types of support: Annual campaigns, building funds, capital campaigns, endowment funds, matching funds, seed money.
Limitations: Giving primarily in NY. No grants to individuals.
Application information: Foundation depends almost exclusively on self-initiated grants. Applications not accepted.
Write: Richard L. Menschel, Pres.
Officers and Directors:* Richard L. Menschel,* Pres. and Treas.; Ronay Menschel,* Secy.; Eugene P. Polk.
Number of staff: None.
EIN: 133050294

1836
Chase Lincoln First Bank, N.A. Corporate Contributions Program
One Lincoln First Sq.
Rochester 14643   (716) 258-5000

Financial data (yr. ended 12/31/90): Total giving, $587,000, including $447,500 for grants and $139,500 for employee matching gifts.
Purpose and activities: Support for arts and culture, health, human services, education, public policy, economic education, special interest in housing and the homeless. Funding also for general charitable giving which includes in-kind donations.
Fields of interest: Arts, health, education, public policy, housing, homeless, general charitable giving.
Types of support: Annual campaigns, building funds, capital campaigns, continuing support, employee matching gifts, endowment funds, general purposes, matching funds, scholarship funds, seed money, special projects, student aid, in-kind gifts.
Limitations: Giving primarily in areas of operations.
Publications: Application guidelines, financial statement.
Application information: Application form not required.
Write: Barbara J. Burns, Dir., Community Rels.
Number of staff: 1 full-time professional.

1837
Chase Manhattan Corporation Philanthropy Department
One Chase Manhattan Plaza, 9th fl.
New York 10081   (212) 676-7556

Applications from upstate NY: Public Affairs, Chase Lincoln First Bank, N.A., One Lincoln First Sq., Rochester NY 14643; Tel: (716) 258-5813

Financial data (yr. ended 12/31/91): Total giving, $7,696,036, including $6,743,682 for grants (high: $300,000), $879,492 for employee matching gifts and $72,862 for in-kind gifts.

Purpose and activities: "Through its philanthropic program, The Chase Manhattan Corporation aims to enhance the well-being of the communities it serves. Chase understands its responsibllities to its customers, employees, stockholders and the citizenry at large, and recognizes that the health and vitality of the larger community are crucial to the long-term success of the Corporation and its shareholders. In addition, Chase supports numerous not-for-porfit groups working in the fields of housing, economic development, health, human services and such urgent social concerns as homelessness and hunger." Specific objectives are: 1) To improve the quality of life in the communities Chase serves by: Fostering excellence in education, including precollege education and colleges and universities in the U.S. that are major Chase recruiting sources; Supporting local health, social welfare and community agencies; Helping to stablize neighborhoods through participation in housing rehabilitation, economic development and other community revitaization efforts; and Promoting the effective management of governmental and nonprofit organizations. 2) To support the development and promotion of public policies and economic education conducive to growth and community development. 3) To promote economic development and human well-being in the countries where Chase operates overseas, and to support organizations whose purpose is to foster international understanding. 4) To encourage charitable giving by the Corporation's employees through matching gift programs, 5) To encourage Chase employees to volunteer for nonprofit organizations.

Fields of interest: Cultural programs, arts, dance, music, museums, performing arts, theater, fine arts, education, higher education, secondary education, health, social services, homeless, hunger, housing, community development, community funds, economics, international relief.

Types of support: Scholarship funds, employee-related scholarships, employee matching gifts, capital campaigns, general purposes, operating budgets, special projects, continuing support, in-kind gifts, employee volunteer services, matching funds.

Limitations: Giving primarily in headquarters city and state and national operating locations in AZ, CA, CO, DE, FL, GA, IL, MD, MA, NY, OH, TX, UT. No support for religious, fraternal, veterans'or single disease organizations, or for medical research. No grants to individuals, or for member organizations of any United Way(s), to which the company already contributes.

Publications: Corporate giving report.

Application information: Contributions to U.S. organizations and contributions of an international nature are amde by The Chase Manhattan Corporations, with these exceptions: Contributions to organizations in upstate NY generally are made by Chase Lincoln First Bank, a subsidiary; contributions to organizations either

headquartered outside the continental U.S. or seeking funds for programs abroad generally are made by The Chase Manhattan Foundation. Application form required.
  Initial approach: Letter
  Write: David Ford, V.P. and Dir. of Philanthropy
Number of staff: 6 full-time professional; 2 full-time support.

1838
The Chase Manhattan Foundation
c/o The Chase Manhattan Bank, N.A.
Two Chase Manhattan Plaza, 29th Fl.
New York 10081   (212) 552-8205

Incorporated in 1969 in NY.
Donor(s): The Chase Manhattan Bank, N.A.
Foundation type: Company-sponsored
Financial data (yr. ended 12/31/91): Assets, $1,003,400 (M); gifts received, $507,150; expenditures, $2,524,586; qualifying distributions, $2,520,336, including $2,297,000 for grants (average: $5,000-$10,000) and $223,336 for grants to individuals.

Purpose and activities: Grants primarily for child welfare, health care, hunger and disaster relief, education, and for community, economic, and human resource development by organizations that operate largely outside the continental U.S. The foundation's employee-related scholarship program has been discontinued; final scholarships will be disbursed in 1995.

Fields of interest: International development, international relief, AIDS.

Types of support: Operating budgets, continuing support, annual campaigns, seed money, emergency funds, general purposes, employee-related scholarships, special projects.

Limitations: Giving primarily for projects outside the U.S. in countries where the company has an office. No support for religious, fraternal, or veterans' organizations, member organizations of the United Way, organizations serving people suffering from a single disease or medical condition, or medical research. No grants to individuals (except for scholarships to children of company employees), or for deficit financing, equipment, land acquisition, endowment funds, or matching gifts; no loans.

Publications: Annual report.

Application information: U.S. (except upstate NY) and foreign applicants: Philanthropic Activities Dept., Chase Manhattan Bank, N.A., 44 Wall St., 14th Fl., New York, NY 10005; Tel.: (212) 676-5081. Upstate NY applicants: Government Relations, Philanthropic Activities, Chase Lincoln First Bank, N.A., One Lincoln First Sq., Rochester, NY 14643; Tel.: (716) 258-5600. Application form required.
  Initial approach: Letter
  Copies of proposal: 1
  Deadline(s): Submit proposal preferably in Jan. or June; deadline Sept. 1
  Board meeting date(s): 3 times a year
  Final notification: 6 months
  Write: David S. Ford
Officers and Trustees:* Thomas G. LaBrecque,* Pres.; Donald L. Boudreau,* V.P.; Fraser P. Seitel,* V.P.; Francis X. Stankard,* V.P.; Elaine R. Bond, Richard J. Boyle, Robert R. Douglass, A. Wright Elliott, Michael P. Esposito, Jr., Thomas C. Lynch, James F. Murray, Arthur F. Ryan, John V.

Scicutella, L. Edward Shaw, Jr., Charles A. Smith, Deborah L. Talbot, Michael Urkowitz, J. Richard Zecher.
Number of staff: None.
EIN: 237049738
Recent health grants:
1838-1 Amigos de las Americas, Houston, TX, $12,000. 1991.
1838-2 Citizens Committee for New York City, NYC, NY, $15,000. For Drug Prevention Awards Program. 1991.
1838-3 New York Infirmary-Beekman Downtown Hospital, NYC, NY, $15,000. 1991.
1838-4 Saint Francis Friends of the Poor, NYC, NY, $20,000. For on-site medical services. 1991.
1838-5 Saint Vincents Hospital and Medical Center of New York, NYC, NY, $20,000. For Supportive Care Program. 1991.

1839
The Chazen Foundation
P.O. Box 801
Nyack 10960

Established in 1985 in NY.
Donor(s): Jerome A. Chazen.
Foundation type: Independent
Financial data (yr. ended 12/31/90): Assets, $9,101,506 (M); gifts received, $858,750; expenditures, $398,536; qualifying distributions, $378,082, including $332,122 for grants (high: $76,460) and $45,960 for 15 grants to individuals (high: $8,000; low: $900).
Purpose and activities: Giving primarily for Jewish welfare funds and other Jewish organizations; support also for social services, higher education, music, museums, and hospital building funds.
Fields of interest: Jewish giving, Jewish welfare, Israel, social services, higher education, business education, arts, music, museums, hospitals—building funds.
Types of support: Student aid.
Limitations: Giving primarily in the northeastern U.S.
Application information:
  Initial approach: Letter
  Deadline(s): None
Trustees: Jerome A. Chazen, Simona A. Chazen.
Number of staff: None.
EIN: 133229474

1840
Owen Cheatham Foundation
950 Third Ave.
New York 10022   (212) 753-4733

Incorporated in 1957 in NY as successor to Owen R. Cheatham Foundation, a trust established in 1934 in GA.
Donor(s): Owen Robertson Cheatham,‡ Celeste W. Cheatham.‡
Foundation type: Independent
Financial data (yr. ended 12/31/91): Assets, $6,814,279 (M); expenditures, $615,389; qualifying distributions, $477,946, including $350,000 for 77 grants (high: $29,000; low: $50).
Purpose and activities: Support primarily to assist programs that might not otherwise be achieved;

grants mainly for education, health, the arts, and welfare.
Fields of interest: Arts, welfare, education, medical research, health.
Officers and Directors:* Celeste C. Weisglass,* Pres.; Stephen S. Weisglass,* V.P. and Treas.; Ilse C. Meckauer, Secy.; MacDonald Budd.
EIN: 136097798

1841
Michael Chernow Trust f/b/o Charity Dated 3/13/75
c/o Schapiro, Wisan & Krassner
122 East 42nd St.
New York 10168-0057

Trust established in 1975.
Foundation type: Independent
Financial data (yr. ended 06/30/91): Assets, $3,739,262 (M); expenditures, $218,805; qualifying distributions, $163,120, including $145,500 for 12 grants (high: $50,000; low: $1,000).
Fields of interest: Jewish welfare, health, medical research, AIDS, higher education.
Limitations: Giving primarily in NY. No grants to individuals.
Application information: Application form not required.
Deadline(s): None
Trustees: Morris I. Chernofsky, Martin P. Krassner, Lynn A. Streim.
EIN: 136758226

1842
The China Medical Board of New York, Inc. ▼
750 Third Ave., 23rd Fl.
New York 10017   (212) 682-8000

Incorporated in 1928 in NY.
Donor(s): The Rockefeller Foundation.
Foundation type: Independent
Financial data (yr. ended 06/30/91): Assets, $122,428,192 (M); expenditures, $3,885,522; qualifying distributions, $3,583,109, including $2,589,948 for 31 grants (high: $561,000; low: $127; average: $10,000-$350,000).
Purpose and activities: "To extend financial aid to the Peking Union Medical College and/or like institutions in the Far East or the United States of America." The Board's activities are: 1) to assist institutions in improving the health levels and services in Asian societies, and 2) to assist institutions in improving the quality and increasing the numbers of appropriate health practitioners in these societies. Supports programs in medical research, staff development, cooperative planning, and library endowment only at designated national medical schools, nursing schools, and schools of public health in Hong Kong, Indonesia, Korea, Malaysia, the Philippines, Singapore, Taiwan, and the People's Republic of China.
Fields of interest: Nursing, health, medical education, medical research, libraries, Southeast Asia, Philippines, China.
Types of support: Conferences and seminars, research, fellowships, endowment funds, publications, scholarship funds, special projects, technical assistance.

Limitations: Giving limited to East and Southeast Asia, including the People's Republic of China, Hong Kong, Indonesia, Korea, Malaysia, the Philippines, Singapore, Taiwan, and Thailand. No support for governments, professional societies, or research institutes not directly under medical school control. No grants to individuals, or for capital funds, operating budgets for medical care, special projects, or the basic equipping of medical schools, nursing schools, or schools of public health that are the responsibility of various governments or universities; no loans.
Publications: Annual report.
Application information: Submit request through dean's office of Asian institution in which foundation has a program of support. Applications not accepted.
Deadline(s): None
Board meeting date(s): June and Dec.
Final notification: Immediately following board meetings
Write: William D. Sawyer, M.D., Pres.
Officers and Trustees:* J. Robert Buchanan, M.D., Chair.; William D. Sawyer, M.D.,* Pres.; Robert H.M. Ferguson, Secy.; Walter G. Ehlers,* Treas.; Mary Brown Bullock, Loring Catlin, Molly Joel Coye, M.D., Don Eugene Detmer, M.D., John R. Hogness, M.D., Tom G. Kessinger, Bayless A. Manning, Gloria H. Spivak.
Number of staff: 1 full-time professional; 4 full-time support.
EIN: 131659619
Recent health grants:
1842-1 Airlangga University, Faculty of Medicine, Surabaya, Indonesia, $500,000. For equal matching permanent endowment grant for Tropical Disease Center. 1991.
1842-2 Beijing Medical University, Beijing, China, $500,000. To develop and support fellowship programs for medical, nursing and public health faculty of health professions. Grant shared with Peking Union Medical College and Sun Yat-Sen University of Medical Sciences. 1991.
1842-3 China Medical University, Shenyang, China, $600,000. For matching grant to develop and support program in emergency medicine. 1991.
1842-4 China Medical University, Research Center for Medical Education, Shenyang, China, $570,000. For program on assessment of cognitive skill. 1992.
1842-5 Chulalongkorn University, Bangkok, Thailand, $600,000. For matching grant for program in Public Health Administration. 1991.
1842-6 Jiujiang Medical College, Jiujiang, China, $250,000. For development and operation of program for teaching and assessing competence of undergraduate medical students. 1991.
1842-7 Jiujiang Medical College, Jiujiang, China, $192,000. For equipment and acquisition for medical library. 1991.
1842-8 Peking Union Medical College, Beijing, China, $155,000. For renovation of roof of College Hospital. 1991.
1842-9 Peking Union Medical College, Medical College Hospital, Beijing, China, $156,000. For program of clinical epidemiology to establish organizations of quality assurance at both hospital and other levels, to establish and complete computer-microprocessor network

for information analysis and to determine issues of quality and appropriateness of patient care. 1991.
1842-10 Shanghai Medical University, Shanghai, China, $400,000. For Kidney Research Program. 1991.
1842-11 Shanghai Medical University, Shanghai, China, $350,000. For Hand Surgery and Microvascular Surgery Program, which consists of three projects, Microsurgery, Hand Surgery and Medical Rehabilitation. 1991.
1842-12 Shanghai Medical University, School of Public Health, Shanghai, China, $800,000. For Training Center for Health Management. 1991.
1842-13 Sun Yat-sen University of Medical Sciences, Guangzhou, China, $1,178,000. For joint, interdisciplinary program on Nasopharyngeal Cancer. Grant administered by Hunan Medical University. 1991.
1842-14 Sun Yat-sen University of Medical Sciences, Guangzhou, China, $455,000. For program in behavioral medicine. 1992.
1842-15 Sun Yat-sen University of Medical Sciences, Guangzhou, China, $300,000. To develop and support fellowship programs for medical, nursing and public health faculty of health professions. 1991.
1842-16 Sun Yat-sen University of Medical Sciences, Guangzhou, China, $250,000. To assist planning, production and distribution of audiovisual teaching materials. 1991.
1842-17 University of Health Sciences, Vientiane, Laos, $263,000. For staff and library development. 1992.
1842-18 West China University of Medical Sciences, Chengdu, China, $209,000. For development and operation of program for teaching and assessing competence of undergraduate medical students. 1991.
1842-19 Xian Medical University, Xian, China, $484,000. For interdisciplinary program on Environment-Related Bone and Tooth Disorders. 1991.
1842-20 Xian Medical University, Xian, China, $455,000. For three-year medical education program. 1992.
1842-21 Xian Medical University, Xian, China, $375,000. For program on cervical cancer, human papilloma virus and molecular epidemiology. 1992.
1842-22 Zhejiang Medical University, Hangzhou, China, $280,000. For development and operation of program for teaching and assessing competence of undergraduate medical students. 1991.

1843
The Chisholm Foundation
c/o U.S. Trust Co. of New York
114 West 47th St.
New York 10036-1532

Established in 1960 in MS.
Donor(s): A.F. Chisholm.‡
Foundation type: Independent
Financial data (yr. ended 12/31/90): Assets, $7,790,452 (M); expenditures, $376,223; qualifying distributions, $345,883, including $292,410 for 19 grants (high: $50,000; low: $1,000).

Purpose and activities: Giving for education and Episcopal organizations; support also for health, cultural programs, youth, and community funds.
Fields of interest: Education, Protestant giving, health, cultural programs, youth, community funds.
Types of support: General purposes.
Limitations: Giving primarily in MS and New York, NY. No grants to individuals.
Application information: Contributes only to pre-selected organizations. Applications not accepted.
Officers: Jean C. Lindsey, Pres.; Cynthia C. Saint-Amand, Secy.; Margaret A. Chisholm, Treas.
Director: Nathan E. Saint-Amand.
EIN: 646014272

1844
The CIT Group Foundation, Inc.
c/o The CIT Group Holding, Inc.
135 West 50th St.
New York 10020   (212) 408-6000

Incorporated in 1955 in NY.
Donor(s): CIT Financial Corp., and its subsidiaries.
Foundation type: Company-sponsored
Financial data (yr. ended 12/31/90): Assets, $109,304 (M); gifts received, $254,588; expenditures, $314,669; qualifying distributions, $313,545, including $296,285 for 139 grants (high: $20,000; low: $50) and $17,260 for employee matching gifts.
Fields of interest: Community funds, education, higher education, youth, health associations, cancer.
Types of support: Employee matching gifts, general purposes.
Limitations: Giving limited to areas of company operations. No grants to individuals.
Application information:
   Initial approach: Letter
   Deadline(s): None
   Write: Jay Simons, Asst. Secy.
Officers: Albert R. Gamper, Jr., Pres. and C.E.O.; Joseph A. Pollicino, Exec. V.P.; John J. Carroll, V.P. and Treas.; W. Baranoff, V.P.; H.A. Ittleson, V.P.; William M. O'Grady, V.P.; Thomas J. O'Rourke, V.P.
Number of staff: 1 part-time professional; 1 part-time support.
EIN: 136083856

1845
Citicorp/Citibank Corporate
Contributions Program
Citibank, N.A.
850 Third Ave., 13th Floor, Zone 10
New York 10043   (212) 559-8182

Financial data (yr. ended 12/31/91): Total giving, $23,400,955, including $18,265,839 for 748 grants (high: $1,000,000; low: $180) and $5,135,116 for employee matching gifts.
Purpose and activities: "Citibank's Contributions and Civic Responsibility programs focus heavily on education and other activities that promote stability and quality of life in our communities." Citibank makes grants to nonprofit organizations with the following characteristics: clearly delineated, measurable goals and innovative results-oriented programs falling within these

priority categories: education-research, community development, grants for children, arts education, culture, health and human services, and the global environment; strong leadership that significantly strengthens the communities in which Citibank operates and serves as a model for other nonprofit groups; sound administrative and financial status; and opportunities for Citibank volunteers to be involved with the program. Citibank also makes grants overseas for human services, education, and development.
Fields of interest: Cultural programs, education, health, community development, community funds, international affairs, AIDS, international relief.
Types of support: Continuing support, research, special projects, technical assistance, capital campaigns, general purposes, employee matching gifts, employee volunteer services.
Limitations: Giving primarily in New York City and operating locations nationwide. No support for religious, fraternal or veterans' organizations "unless they are engaged in a significant project benefiting the entire community"; political or national programs. No grants to individuals, or for fundraising dinners, telethons, marathons, races, benefits, events, or courtesy advertising.
Publications: Corporate giving report (including application guidelines), grants list.
Application information: Application form not required.
   Initial approach: "Contact the contributions committee representative in your area for the specific guidelines of that committee"
   Copies of proposal: 1
   Deadline(s): Generally review process is ongoing; certain areas have their own deadlines
   Final notification: Within 60 to 90 days
   Write: Paul M. Ostergard, V.P. and Dir., Corp. Contribs.
Number of staff: 3

1846
Liz Claiborne Foundation ▼
1441 Broadway
New York 10018   (212) 626-5424

Established in 1981 in NY.
Donor(s): Liz Claiborne, Inc., Elisabeth Claiborne Ortenberg, Arthur Ortenberg.
Foundation type: Company-sponsored
Financial data (yr. ended 12/31/91): Assets, $14,749,902 (M); gifts received, $2,436,229; expenditures, $1,516,970; qualifying distributions, $1,492,233, including $1,385,656 for 146 grants (high: $168,000; low: $300; average: $1,000-$10,000) and $106,577 for 435 employee matching gifts.
Purpose and activities: Grants primarily for human services, including child and family welfare, environmental programs, AIDS, and minority education; funding generally goes to programs serving the economically disadvantaged.
Fields of interest: Social services, disadvantaged, homeless, child welfare, environment, AIDS, education—minorities.
Types of support: Annual campaigns, employee matching gifts, operating budgets, employee volunteer services, special projects, matching funds.

Limitations: Giving limited to Hudson County, NJ, and New York, NY. No support for religious, fraternal, or veterans' organizations, media projects or fundraising events, sponsorships, or journal advertisements. No grants to individuals, or for capital campaigns, equipment, conferences or symposia, endowments, research, or technical assistance.
Publications: Application guidelines.
Application information: Product donations are strictly limited and are made only in support of significant volunteer involvement by company employees. Application form not required.
   Initial approach: Letter or proposal
   Copies of proposal: 1
   Deadline(s): 2 months in advance of desired review date
   Board meeting date(s): Approximately every 6 weeks
   Final notification: 2 months
   Write: Melanie Lyons, Dir.
Trustees: Jerome A. Chazen, Harvey L. Falk, Jay Margolis.
Number of staff: 2 full-time professional; 1 full-time support.
EIN: 133060673

1847
Frank E. Clark Charitable Trust
c/o Manufacturers Hanover Trust Co.
270 Park Ave.
New York 10017   (212) 270-9094

Trust established in 1936 in NY.
Donor(s): Frank E. Clark.‡
Foundation type: Independent
Financial data (yr. ended 12/31/90): Assets, $3,815,324 (M); expenditures, $434,909; qualifying distributions, $412,522, including $410,000 for 74 grants (high: $17,750; low: $2,000).
Purpose and activities: Income distributed to the parent body of major religious denominations for aid to needy churches; support also for health, welfare, and other charitable organizations.
Fields of interest: Religion—Christian, health, welfare, youth.
Limitations: Giving primarily in the New York, NY, metropolitan area.
Application information:
   Initial approach: Proposal
   Copies of proposal: 1
   Deadline(s): Oct. 31
   Board meeting date(s): Dec.
   Write: J.L. McKechnie, V.P., Manufacturers Hanover Trust Co.
Trustee: Manufacturers Hanover Trust Co.
EIN: 136049032

1848
Clark Family Charitable Trust
(Formerly Andrew L. Clark Family Charitable Trust)
c/o The Bank of New York, Tax Dept.
48 Wall St., 4th Fl.
New York 10286   (212) 495-1205

Established in 1989 in NJ.
Foundation type: Independent
Financial data (yr. ended 08/31/91): Assets, $3,509,077 (M); gifts received, $27,300;

expenditures, $117,027; qualifying distributions, $60,035, including $60,000 for 4 grants (high: $30,000; low: $10,000).

Fields of interest: Higher education, secondary education, cancer.

Limitations: Giving primarily in New York, NY, South Orange, NJ, and Cambridge, MA. No grants to individuals.

Application information: Application form not required.

Initial approach: Letter
Copies of proposal: 2
Deadline(s): May
Write: Carol Schneider Newitt

Trustees: Andrew L. Clark, The Bank of New York.
EIN: 136948420

1849
The Clark Foundation ▼
30 Wall St.
New York 10005   (212) 269-1833

Incorporated in 1931 in NY; merged with Scriven Foundation, Inc. in 1973.
Donor(s): Members of the Clark family.
Foundation type: Independent
Financial data (yr. ended 06/30/91): Assets, $251,418,869 (M); gifts received, $16,500; expenditures, $11,524,689; qualifying distributions, $11,393,813, including $5,988,367 for 122 grants (high: $473,722; low: $1,500; average: $5,000-$150,000), $2,014,545 for grants to individuals and $747,622 for 1 foundation-administered program.

Purpose and activities: Support for a hospital and museums in Cooperstown, NY; grants also for charitable and educational purposes, including undergraduate scholarships to students residing in the Cooperstown area. Support also for health, educational, youth, cultural, environmental, and community organizations and institutions.

Fields of interest: Museums, health services, health, AIDS, welfare, social services, welfare—indigent individuals, youth, employment, education, environment, general charitable giving.

Types of support: Operating budgets, continuing support, annual campaigns, seed money, emergency funds, building funds, equipment, special projects, student aid, general purposes, grants to individuals, capital campaigns.

Limitations: Giving primarily in upstate NY and New York City; scholarships restricted to students residing in the Cooperstown, NY, area. No grants to individuals (except as specified in restricted funds), or for deficit financing or matching gifts; no loans.

Publications: Program policy statement, application guidelines.

Application information: Application form not required.

Initial approach: Letter
Copies of proposal: 1
Deadline(s): None
Board meeting date(s): Oct. and May
Final notification: 2 to 6 months
Write: Edward W. Stack, Secy.

Officers and Directors:* Jane Forbes Clark II,* Pres.; Edward W. Stack,* V.P.; Joseph H. Cruickshank, Secy.; Kevin S. Moore, Treas.; Alfred C. Clark, William M. Evarts, Jr., Gates Helms Hawn, Archie F. MacAllaster, Mrs. Edward B.

McMenamin, Anne L. Peretz, John Hoyt Stookey, Clifton R. Wharton, Jr., A. Pennington Whitehead, Malcolm Wilson.

Number of staff: 4 full-time professional; 3 part-time professional; 43 full-time support; 20 part-time support.
EIN: 135616528

Recent health grants:

1849-1 Alzheimers Disease and Related Disorders Association, NYC, NY, $20,000. For home care aides training. 1992.

1849-2 Columbia University, School of Dental and Oral Surgery, NYC, NY, $35,000. For scholarship support. 1991.

1849-3 Harlem Interfaith Counseling Service, NYC, NY, $20,000. For general support. 1992.

1849-4 Hospital Chaplaincy, NYC, NY, $10,000. For general support. 1992.

1849-5 Hospital for Special Surgery, NYC, NY, $250,000. For capital campaign. 1991.

1849-6 International Center for the Disabled (ICD), NYC, NY, $25,000. For general support. 1991.

1849-7 Mary Imogene Bassett Hospital and Clinics, Cooperstown, NY, $100,000. For project outreach. 1991.

1849-8 Mary Imogene Bassett Hospital and Clinics, Cooperstown, NY, $12,000. For lifeline program. 1991.

1849-9 Memorial Sloan-Kettering Cancer Center, NYC, NY, $15,000. For patient non-medical expense fund. 1991.

1849-10 Memorial Sloan-Kettering Cancer Center, NYC, NY, $15,000. For patient non-medical expense fund. 1991.

1849-11 Memorial Sloan-Kettering Cancer Center, NYC, NY, $15,000. For patient non-medical expense fund. 1992.

1849-12 New England Deaconess Hospital, Boston, MA, $75,000. For AIDS research project. 1992.

1849-13 Phoenix House, NYC, NY, $25,000. For general support. 1992.

1849-14 Phoenix House Foundation, NYC, NY, $150,000. For expansion program and capital campaign. 1991.

1849-15 Planned Parenthood of New York City, NYC, NY, $15,000. For general support. 1991.

1849-16 Rogosin Institute, NYC, NY, $50,000. For general support. 1991.

1849-17 Russell Sage College, Troy, NY, $15,000. For scholarship assistance for undergraduate nursing students. 1991.

1849-18 Russell Sage College, Troy, NY, $10,000. For scholarship assistance for continuing nurse education. 1991.

1849-19 Saint Lukes-Roosevelt Hospital Center, NYC, NY, $150,000. For surgical research program. 1991.

1849-20 United Hospital Fund of New York, NYC, NY, $10,000. For general support. 1991.

1850
The Edna McConnell Clark Foundation ▼
250 Park Ave., Rm. 900
New York 10017   (212) 986-7050

Incorporated in 1950 in NY and 1969 in DE; the NY corporation merged into the DE corporation in 1974.
Donor(s): Edna McConnell Clark,‡ W. Van Alan Clark.‡

Foundation type: Independent
Financial data (yr. ended 09/30/90): Assets, $384,880,701 (M); expenditures, $25,373,765; qualifying distributions, $23,308,307, including $20,103,827 for 346 grants (high: $1,200,000; low: $5,000; average: $25,000-$250,000) and $258,072 for 4 foundation-administered programs.

Purpose and activities: Programs presently narrowly defined and directed toward five specific areas: 1) reducing unnecessary removal of children from troubled families by establishing family preservation services, supporting courts, agencies, and advocates in implementation of specific foster care and adoption reforms; 2) improving the educational opportunities of disadvantaged young people by designing intervention programs for the middle school years; 3) seeking a more rational, humane, and effective criminal justice system by establishing constitutional conditions in adult and juvenile correctional institutions, encouraging community-based sanctions for adults as alternatives to incarceration, and helping to dismantle large state training schools in favor of community-based programs for juveniles; 4) reducing the debilitating and deadly burden of illness in the poorest countries of the developing world through a targeted research program aimed at controlling the tropical diseases schistosomiasis, trachoma, and onchocerciasis; and 5) seeking to assist families in New York City to move out of emergency shelters and hotels into permanent housing by supporting projects to assess and plan for the needs of families before and immediately after they leave the shelters; supporting programs aimed at forming tenants associations and other mechanisms that give families a stake in their communities; and supporting efforts to create, improve, and expand public and social services in neighborhoods receiving large numbers of previously homeless families. The foundation also maintains a small program of Special Projects which primarily focuses on projects serving the poor and disadvantaged outside the established program areas that reflect their basic mission.

Fields of interest: Family services, child welfare, youth, secondary education, mathematics, crime and law enforcement, law and justice, medical research, schistosomiasis, ophthalmology, disadvantaged, homeless.

Types of support: Consulting services, continuing support, research, seed money, technical assistance, special projects.

Limitations: Giving internationally for Tropical Disease Research Program; nationally for the four other programs. No grants to individuals, or for capital funds, construction and equipment, endowments, scholarships, fellowships, annual appeals, deficit financing, or matching gifts; no loans to individuals.

Publications: Annual report, informational brochure (including application guidelines), grants list, occasional report.

Application information: Action-oriented projects preferred; research support primarily in Tropical Disease Program. Application form not required.

Initial approach: Letter
Copies of proposal: 1
Deadline(s): None
Board meeting date(s): Mar., May, June, Sept., and Dec.

Final notification: 1 month for declination; 2 to 3 months for positive action

Write: Patricia C. Stewart, V.P. and Secy.-Treas.

Officers and Trustees:* James McConnell Clark,* Chair.; Peter D. Bell,* Pres.; Patricia Carry Stewart, V.P. and Secy.-Treas.; Peter W. Forsythe, V.P.; Hays Clark, Drew S. Days III, Eleanor Thomas Elliott, John M. Emery, Lucy H. Nesbeda, Walter N. Rothschild, Jr., Edward C. Schmults, Sidney J. Weinberg, Jr., Ruth A. Wooden.

Number of staff: 16 full-time professional; 10 full-time support; 1 part-time support.

EIN: 237047034

Recent health grants:

1850-1 Adolescent Pregnancy Care and Prevention Program (TAPCAPP), Bronx, NY, $221,000. To continue Parent Education Project. 1991.

1850-2 Commonweal, Children and Philanthropy Project, Bolinas, CA, $20,000. To interview experts and then publish book examining attributes of diverse range of successful programs, as well as some that have fallen short of initial expectations. 1991.

1850-3 Commonwealth Agricultural Bureaux, International Institute of Parasitology, Saint Albans, England, $50,000. For research on onchocerciasis (river blindness). 1991.

1850-4 Foundation for Advanced Education in the Sciences, Oncho Task Force (OTF), Bethesda, MD, $295,000. For production and testing of selected antigens for screening in animal models, to facilitate testing of sera from individuals who are putatively immune to onchocerca infection, and to promote collaboration among researchers. 1991.

1850-5 Harvard University, Cambridge, MA, $35,000. For Dr. Joas Rugemalila of Tanzanian Institute of Medical Research in Mwanga and researchers from Harvard School of Public Health to conduct cost-effectiveness analysis of different schistosomiasis control strategies in order to design feasible and effective program for Tanzania. 1991.

1850-6 Harvard University, Harvard College, Cambridge, MA, $80,000. For committee to identify safe, effective, low-cost sources for tuberculosis drugs; explore alternative treatment strategies; and study causes of varying rates of case identification, diagnosis and treatment for men and women. Grant shared with World Health Organization. 1991.

1850-7 Harvard University, School of Public Health, Cambridge, MA, $26,000. For international team of public health researchers to examine capacity of several African countries to implement national schistosomiasis control program. 1991.

1850-8 Hesperian Foundation, Palo Alto, CA, $21,000. For publication of revised edition of Where There Is No Doctor, standard health reference book for people in developing world, providing information on prevention and treatment of many common illnesses. 1991.

1850-9 Institut Fur Tropenhygiene der Universitat Heidelberg, Heidelberg, Germany, $96,000. To assess immunological response of candidate antigens in jird model. 1991.

1850-10 Johns Hopkins University, Baltimore, MD, $140,000. For International Center for Preventative Ophthalmology Trachoma Vaccine Task Force to continue to provide

technical and administrative assistance and convene workshops on specific research areas. 1991.

1850-11 Juvenile Law Center, Philadelphia, PA, $55,000. To extend outreach beyond child welfare system by tapping potential support from mental health and juvenile justice systems. 1991.

1850-12 Marine Biological Laboratory, Woods Hole, MA, $70,000. For continued partial support for summer course, The Biology of Parasitism, curriculum which applies tools of molecular biology to study of parasitic diseases such as schistosomiasis and onchocerciasis. 1991.

1850-13 New England Biolabs, Beverly, MA, $100,000. To carry out standarized production of antigens. Antigens will then be tested in jird and mouse chamber models that constitute primary screening systems in onchocerciasis vaccine development. 1991.

1850-14 Pius XII School, Bronx, NY, $120,000. For family-centered services of Project Genesis, teaching math and language skills and offering both classroom-based and on-the-job training in computers, human services and health-related careers. 1991.

1850-15 Planned Parenthood of New York City, The Hub, NYC, NY, $50,000. To continue family support services which include human sexuality workshops, family counseling sessions designed to help improve communication skills between parents and their children, and pregnancy counseling sessions to assist women in making informed health decisions about pregnancy and family planning. 1991.

1850-16 Task Force for Child Survival, Atlanta, GA, $100,000. To work with Ghanaian Ministry of Health to plan and develop national control program for onchocerciasis and schistosomiasis, based on existing drug regimens and community education. 1991.

1850-17 Thomas Jefferson University, Philadelphia, PA, $190,000. To employ mouse chamber model as primary screening mechanism for testing oncho antigens. 1991.

1850-18 United Hospital Fund of New York, NYC, NY, $130,000. To work with public officials, social, health and housing providers to design strategy to improve and expand health care services in South Bronx. 1991.

1850-19 University of Connecticut, Farmington, CT, $140,000. To apply successful research experience with B. malayi antigen in attempt to identify antigen from O. volvulus. When identified, O. volvulus antigen will be tested on specially bred immunodeficient mice, called scid mice, which have been injected with O. volvulus. 1991.

1850-20 University of South Florida, Florida Mental Health Institute, Tampa, FL, $236,000. For continued support to assist eight states with which Children's Program is working. 1991.

1850-21 Vera Institute of Justice, NYC, NY, $100,000. To continue research and development of intermediate sanctions projects including treatment-oriented program for drug-dependent offenders, intensive supervision probation model and economic sanctions, or day-fine, programs. Institute will also use grant to support technical assistance and publication of educational materials. 1991.

1850-22 West Alabama Health Services, Eutaw, AL, $50,000. To expand 17th Judicial District sentencing advocacy project. 1991.

1850-23 World Health Organization, Geneva, Switzerland, $400,000. For Vanderbilt University's Schistosomiasis Vaccine Development Task Force to move to World Health Organization (WHO) in Geneva, Switzerland. 1991.

1851
Robert Sterling Clark Foundation, Inc. ▼
112 East 64th St.
New York 10021   (212) 308-0411
FAX: (212)755-2133

Incorporated in 1952 in NY.

Donor(s): Robert Sterling Clark.‡

Foundation type: Independent

Financial data (yr. ended 10/31/91): Assets, $69,364,539 (M); expenditures, $3,497,474; qualifying distributions, $2,621,977, including $2,621,977 for 101 grants (high: $100,000; low: $1,000; average: $10,000-$60,000).

Purpose and activities: The foundation supports projects that: 1) strengthen the management of cultural institutions in New York City and the greater metropolitan area; support arts advocacy; 2) ensure the effectiveness and accountability of public agencies in New York City and State; and 3) protect reproductive freedom and access to family planning services.

Fields of interest: Arts, cultural programs, fine arts, community development, urban development, government, public administration, public policy, education, environment, family services, family planning.

Limitations: Giving primarily in NY, with emphasis on New York City; giving nationally for reproductive freedom projects. No grants to individuals, or for operating budgets, annual campaigns, seed money, emergency funds, deficit financing, capital or endowment funds, matching gifts, scholarships, fellowships, conferences, or films.

Publications: Annual report, application guidelines.

Application information: Application form not required.

Initial approach: Proposal
Copies of proposal: 1
Deadline(s): None
Board meeting date(s): Jan., Apr., July, and Oct.
Final notification: 1 to 6 months
Write: Margaret C. Ayers, Exec. Dir.

Officers and Directors:* Winthrop R. Munyan,* Pres.; Miner D. Crary, Jr.,* Secy.; Richardson Pratt, Jr.,* Treas.; Margaret C. Ayers, Exec. Dir.; Raymond D. Horton, Charles G. Meyer, Jr., John N. Romans, Philip Svigals.

Number of staff: 3 full-time professional; 1 part-time professional; 1 full-time support.

EIN: 131957792

Recent health grants:

1851-1 Alan Guttmacher Institute, NYC, NY, $125,000. For research on state laws governing minors' rights to make independent decisions regarding health care and other life choices, how minors decide to have an abortion and involvement of parents and others in decision-making process. 1991.

1851-2 Catholics for a Free Choice, DC, $47,000. For research, production and dissemination of series of fact sheet/booklets on role of Catholic Church in shaping public policy on family planning services and availability of contraception. 1991.

1851-3 Center for Population Options, DC, $50,000. For research and publication of CPO's annual survey and report, Teenage Pregnancy and Too-early Childbearing: Public Costs, Personal Consequences. 1991.

1851-4 Citizens Budget Commission, NYC, NY, $24,000. For production of policy papers detailing proposals for reform of welfare and Medicaid financing, property taxation and union work rules in New York City. 1991.

1851-5 National Family Planning and Reproductive Health Association, DC, $50,000. For public education and advocacy efforts, services to membership and litigation to preserve ethical delivery of family planning services. 1991.

1851-6 National Organization for Women (NOW) Legal Defense and Education Fund, NYC, NY, $40,000. For work on clinic harassment lawsuits and provision of legal support and technical assistance on other reproductive rights issues to pro-choice groups around country. 1991.

1851-7 Planned Parenthood Federation of America, NYC, NY, $100,000. For public education and advocacy efforts aimed at defending and strengthening Title X federal family planning program, and for launching of new teen pregnancy prevention initiative, First Things First. 1991.

1851-8 Planned Parenthood of New York City, NYC, NY, $100,000. For public education and advocacy on behalf of school health, sex education and HIV-prevention programs in New York; and to preserve comprehensive family planning services for poor women and teenagers nationwide. 1991.

1851-9 Sex Information and Education Council of the United States (SIECUS), NYC, NY, $50,000. For public and professional education activities designed to promote and facilitate sexuality education for youngsters nationwide. 1991.

1851-10 State Communities Aid Association, Albany, NY, $30,000. For education and advocacy to promote government policies and funding that will support community-based psychiatric rehabilitation programs in NY State. 1991.

1852
Louis & Virginia Clemente Foundation, Inc.
c/o Townley & Updike
405 Lexington Ave.
New York 10174-0001

Established in 1975.
Foundation type: Independent
Financial data (yr. ended 12/31/91): Assets, $3,912,231 (M); expenditures, $293,628; qualifying distributions, $263,639, including $247,000 for 36 grants (high: $20,000; low: $2,000).
Fields of interest: Health, hospitals, higher education, social services, environment.

Limitations: Giving primarily in NY. No grants to individuals.
Application information: Contributes only to pre-selected organizations. Applications not accepted.
Officers and Directors:* Harry A. LeBien,* Pres.; Alfred J.W. LeBien, V.P.; Evelyn J. Lehman,* Secy.; Mary Ellen LeBein.
EIN: 510163549

1853
The Coleman Foundation
375 Park Ave., Suite 1901
New York 10152
FAX: (212) 980-5308

Trust established in 1962 in NY.
Donor(s): Janet M. Coleman, Martin S. Coleman.
Foundation type: Independent
Financial data (yr. ended 11/30/91): Assets, $2,334,590 (M); expenditures, $174,263; qualifying distributions, $139,646, including $131,110 for 50 grants (high: $50,000; low: $50).
Fields of interest: Jewish welfare, Jewish giving, hospitals, health, social services.
Limitations: Giving primarily in New York, NY. No grants to individuals, or for endowment funds.
Application information: Contributes only to pre-selected organizations. Applications not accepted.
Board meeting date(s): Semiannually
Trustees: Janet M. Coleman, Martin S. Coleman.
EIN: 136126040

1854
Sylvan C. Coleman Foundation
c/o The Bank of New York, Tax Dept.
One Wall St.
New York 10286
Application address: 2401 Merced St., San Leandro, CA 94577

Established about 1956.
Donor(s): Sylvan C. Coleman.
Foundation type: Independent
Financial data (yr. ended 11/30/91): Assets, $2,218,773 (M); expenditures, $112,244; qualifying distributions, $97,054, including $91,750 for 31 grants (high: $20,000; low: $150).
Fields of interest: Higher education, business education, cultural programs, health services, family planning, Jewish welfare, social services.
Application information:
Initial approach: Letter
Deadline(s): None
Write: Clarence B. Coleman, Trustee
Trustees: Clarence B. Coleman, Joan F. Coleman.
EIN: 136091160

1855
The Coles Foundation
40 East 84th St.
New York 10028   (212) 972-2500

Trust established in 1966 in NY.
Donor(s): Jerome S. Coles,‡ Geraldine H. Coles, Marilyn Haykin, Helene Stein.
Foundation type: Independent
Financial data (yr. ended 12/31/91): Assets, $43,807 (M); expenditures, $34,075; qualifying

distributions, $29,995, including $26,125 for 15 grants (high: $11,000; low: $25).
Fields of interest: Arts, Jewish welfare, Jewish giving, medical research, health associations, higher education.
Limitations: Giving primarily in New York, NY. No grants to individuals, or for matching gifts.
Application information: Applications for grants in excess of $5,000 generally not considered; major gifts awarded at the initiative of the trustees. Application form not required.
Initial approach: Letter and proposal
Copies of proposal: 1
Deadline(s): None
Board meeting date(s): Semiannually
Write: Howard L. Haykin, Trustee
Trustees: Geraldine H. Coles, Howard Haykin, Marilyn Haykin, Alvin H. Schulman, Helene Stein, Sidney Stein.
Number of staff: 1 part-time support.
EIN: 136213654

1856
Colgate-Palmolive Corporate Giving Program
300 Park Avenue
New York 10022   (212) 310-2000

Purpose and activities: Supports a variety of programs, including education, arts and culture, health care and hospitals, youth and minorities, civic and community programs, welfare and social services, and United Way.
Fields of interest: Education, arts, cultural programs, health, hospitals, civic affairs, community development, welfare, social services, community funds, youth, minorities.
Types of support: Annual campaigns, employee matching gifts, in-kind gifts, use of facilities.
Limitations: Giving primarily in headquarters city and operating locations; national programs also considered.
Publications: Application guidelines.
Application information: Company has a staff that only handles contributions. Application form not required.
Initial approach: Query letter; Send requests to headquarters or nearest company facility
Copies of proposal: 1
Deadline(s): Best time to apply is Aug.-Sept.
Final notification: Within 3 weeks; rejection sent if denied.
Write: Mary Lennor, Contribs. Admin.
Number of staff: 1 full-time professional.

1857
Joseph Collins Foundation
c/o Willkie Farr & Gallagher
153 East 53rd St.
New York 10022

Incorporated in 1951 in NY.
Donor(s): Joseph Collins, M.D.‡
Foundation type: Independent
Financial data (yr. ended 06/30/91): Assets, $12,769,378 (M); expenditures, $523,251; qualifying distributions, $458,677, including $434,450 for 179 grants to individuals (high: $4,000; low: $1,100; average: $2,000-$5,000).
Purpose and activities: The foundation makes annual grants only to students of inadequate

resources, in attendance at medical schools in states east of or contiguous to the Mississippi River, in sums not exceeding $5,000. Grants range from $1,000-$3,000 for tuition to needy second through fourth year, undergraduate medical students on the recommendation of medical school authorities.
Fields of interest: Medical education.
Types of support: Grants to individuals.
Limitations: No grants for pre-medical or postgraduate medical students.
Publications: Annual report, program policy statement, application guidelines.
Application information: Application form should be obtained from medical school. Application form required.
   Initial approach: Full proposal
   Copies of proposal: 1
   Deadline(s): Jan. 15 for application requests; Mar. 15 for filing
   Board meeting date(s): Nov. and as required
   Write: Mrs. Augusta L. Packer, Secy.-Treas.
Officers and Trustees:* Mark F. Hughes,* Pres.; W. Graham Knox, M.D.,* V.P.; Jack H. Nusbaum,* V.P.; Chester J. Straub, M.D.,* V.P.; Augusta L. Packer,* Secy.-Treas.
Number of staff: None.
EIN: 136404527

1858
Coltec Industries Charitable Foundation, Inc.

(Formerly Colt Industries Charitable Foundation, Inc.)
c/o Coltec Industries, Inc.
430 Park Ave.
New York 10022   (212) 940-0410

Incorporated in 1963 in DE.
Donor(s): Coltec Industries, Inc.
Foundation type: Company-sponsored
Financial data (yr. ended 06/30/91): Assets, $2,766 (M); gifts received, $305,000; expenditures, $308,785; qualifying distributions, $308,785, including $308,495 for 128 grants (high: $28,750; low: $350; average: $2,000-$3,000).
Purpose and activities: Giving for community funds, higher education, hospitals, cultural programs, and youth agencies; support also for civic affairs and public interest groups.
Fields of interest: Community funds, higher education, hospitals, cultural programs, youth, civic affairs, public policy.
Types of support: Building funds, operating budgets.
Limitations: Giving primarily in areas of company operations. No grants to individuals.
Application information: Application form not required.
   Initial approach: Letter
   Copies of proposal: 1
   Deadline(s): Submit proposal preferably in Sept. or Oct.
   Board meeting date(s): Quarterly
   Final notification: 3 months
   Write: Andrew C. Hilton, V.P.
Officers and Directors:* David I. Margolis,* Pres.; Anthony J. diBuono,* V.P. and Secy.; Salvatore J. Cozzolino,* V.P. and Treas.; Andrew C. Hilton,* V.P.
Number of staff: 2 part-time support.

EIN: 256057849

1859
The Common Giving Fund
666 Broadway, 5th Fl.
New York 10012-2317

Established in 1984 in NY.
Donor(s): Norman Lear, Frances Lear.
Foundation type: Independent
Financial data (yr. ended 04/30/90): Assets, $10,617,635 (M); expenditures, $1,168,224; qualifying distributions, $1,062,326, including $1,012,000 for 1 grant (average: $40,000-$200,000).
Purpose and activities: Giving primarily for public policy organizations; some support for hospitals and a university.
Fields of interest: Public policy, hospitals.
Types of support: General purposes, operating budgets.
Application information: Contributes only to donor-designated organizations. Applications not accepted.
   Initial approach: Proposal
   Deadline(s): None
Officers and Directors:* Margie Fine,* Pres.; Rosalie Sassano,* V.P.; June Makela,* Secy.-Treas.
Foundation Manager: Funding Exchange, Inc.
Number of staff: None.
EIN: 133269301

1860
The Commonwealth Fund ▼
One East 75th St.
New York 10021-2692   (212) 535-0400

Incorporated in 1918 in NY.
Donor(s): Mrs. Stephen V. Harkness,‡ Edward S. Harkness,‡ Mrs. Edward S. Harkness.‡
Foundation type: Independent
Financial data (yr. ended 06/30/90): Assets, $324,561,685 (M); expenditures, $16,663,318; qualifying distributions, $15,435,045, including $10,199,228 for 110 grants (high: $1,700,000; low: $1,000; average: $100,000), $248,200 for employee matching gifts and $438,000 for foundation-administered programs.
Purpose and activities: Supports new opportunities to improve Americans' health and well-being and to assist specific groups of Americans who have serious and neglected problems. The fund's five major programs strive to improve the efficacy and appropriateness of clinical care through patient's perceptions; help develop ways to enable all senior Americans to participate more fully in American life; help build a climate of respect and opportunity for skilled work training within the American education system, and to help non-college-bound youth shape a vision of themselves in careers as skilled workers; and foster a serious, sustained examination of the quality of urban life and ways to improve it. Grants also for related projects supporting these themes, including programs for minority medical students seeking careers in academic medicine and for nurses seeking to obtain advanced management training. Grants are provided to nonprofit institutions to generate service, educational, and research activities. Harkness Fellowships are awarded by selection

committees in each country to potential leaders from the United Kingdom, Australia, and New Zealand for study and research in the U.S.; applicants must be citizens of the United Kingdom, Australia, or New Zealand. Requirements and length of fellowship vary depending upon the country of origin.
Fields of interest: Health, health services, hospitals, medical education, nursing, aged, minorities, education—minorities, employment, public policy, youth.
Types of support: Research, special projects.
Limitations: No grants to individuals (except for Harkness Fellowships), or for building or endowment funds, general support, capital funds, construction or renovation of facilities, purchase of equipment, or assistance with operating budgets or deficits of established programs or institutions, scholarships, or matching gifts; no loans.
Publications: Annual report, application guidelines.
Application information: Application form not required.
   Initial approach: Letter or proposal
   Copies of proposal: 3
   Deadline(s): None
   Board meeting date(s): Apr., July, and Nov.
   Final notification: Immediately following board meeting
   Write: Adrienne A. Fisher, Grants Mgr.
Officers and Directors:* C. Sims Farr,* Chair.; Margaret E. Mahoney,* Pres.; Karen Davis, Exec. V.P.; John Craig, V.P. and Treas.; Robert L. Biblio, V.P.; Joseph Peri,* Secy.; Arthur Ashe, Lawrence S. Huntington, Helene Kaplan, Robert M. O'Neil, Roswell B. Perkins, Charles A. Sanders, M.D., Alfred R. Stern, Blenda J. Wilson.
Number of staff: 14 full-time professional; 1 part-time professional; 15 full-time support; 2 part-time support.
EIN: 131635260
Recent health grants:
1860-1 Alliance for Aging Research, DC, $340,000. For promoting better medical research and clinical care for older Americans. 1991.
1860-2 American College of Physicians, Philadelphia, PA, $200,000. To enhance physician's role in patient-centered care. 1991.
1860-3 American Foundation for AIDS Research, NYC, NY, $23,500. For educators with HIV Technical Assistance Project. 1991.
1860-4 American Geriatrics Society, New York Academy of Medicine, NYC, NY, $20,000. For Congress of Ethics in Clinical Medicine. 1991.
1860-5 Baylor College of Medicine, Houston, TX, $12,500. For Physician Assistant Oral History Project. 1991.
1860-6 Beth Israel Hospital, Boston, MA, $233,000. For Hospital Directors Task Force of Picker/Commonwealth Patient-Centered Care Program. 1991.
1860-7 Beth Israel Hospital, Division of General Medicine and Primary Care, Boston, MA, $500,000. For Picker/Commonwealth Patient-Centered Care Program: Phase V. 1991.
1860-8 Beth Israel Hospital, Division of General Medicine and Primary Care, Boston, MA, $280,000. For Patients' Perceptions of Hospital Care in Canada. 1991.
1860-9 Elliott White Springs Memorial Hospital, Lancaster, SC, $25,000. For Lancaster

Recovery Center Abuse Prevention Program for children of addicted and abusive parents. 1991.

1860-10 Freedom Institute, NYC, NY, $10,000. Toward support. 1991.

1860-11 Grantmakers in Health, NYC, NY, $20,500. Toward support. 1991.

1860-12 Harvard University, School of Public Health, Boston, MA, $15,000. For research on Canadian health care system and its relevance to U.S.. 1991.

1860-13 Harvard University, School of Public Health, Boston, MA, $10,000. For Mary W. Lasker Professorship and Research Program. 1991.

1860-14 Harvard University, School of Public Health, Department of Health and Social Behavior, Boston, MA, $141,172. For assessment of social marketing. 1991.

1860-15 Hastings Center, Briarcliff Manor, NY, $20,000. For conference on future of biomedical ethics. 1991.

1860-16 International Womens Health Coalition, NYC, NY, $25,000. For program on reproductive tract infections. 1991.

1860-17 Johns Hopkins University, School of Hygiene and Public Health, DC, $25,000. To develop Patient's Guide to World of Medicine. 1991.

1860-18 Johns Hopkins University, School of Hygiene and Public Health, Department of Health Policy and Management, Baltimore, MD, $333,000. For administration of Commonwealth Fund Commission on Elderly People Living Alone, 1990-91. 1991.

1860-19 Johns Hopkins University, School of Hygiene and Public Health, Department of Health Policy and Management, Baltimore, MD, $242,500. For Importance of Choice to Elderly People Receiving Home Care Services. 1991.

1860-20 Louis Harris and Associates, NYC, NY, $147,700. For Physicians' Perceptions of Medical Practice. 1991.

1860-21 Maine Health Information Center, Augusta, ME, $185,500. To examine Maine's Health Issues, Part Three. 1991.

1860-22 Manhattan Institute for Policy Research, NYC, NY, $496,500. To improve qualilty of life in New York City, Phase Two. 1991.

1860-23 Manhattan Institute for Policy Research, NYC, NY, $68,000. To improve qualilty of life in New York City. 1991.

1860-24 Massachusetts General Hospital, Boston, MA, $400,000. For more informed decision making for women with breast cancer. 1991.

1860-25 Massachusetts General Hospital, Women's Health Associates, Boston, MA, $15,000. To develop newsletter on women's health issues. 1991.

1860-26 Mount Sinai Hospital and Medical Center, NYC, NY, $500,000. To provide geriatric training throughout medical centers. 1991.

1860-27 National Public Health and Hospital Institute, DC, $91,000. To enable public hospitals to improve patient-centered care. 1991.

1860-28 New England Medical Center Hospitals, Boston, MA, $25,000. For examination of international health care technology transfer. 1991.

1860-29 New School for Social Research, Health Services Management and Policy Department, NYC, NY, $120,000. For study, Improving Graduate Education in Health Services Management: A New York City Focus. 1991.

1860-30 New York Academy of Medicine, NYC, NY, $300,000. To revitalize Academy. 1991.

1860-31 Rand Corporation, Health Sciences Program, Santa Monica, CA, $342,000. For study, More Appropriate Use of Cardiovascular Procedures in U.S. and Canada. 1991.

1860-32 Rand Corporation, Health Sciences Program, Santa Monica, CA, $325,000. For study, More Appropriate Use of Coronary Angioplasty in New York State. 1991.

1860-33 Rockefeller University, Rockefeller Archives Center, North Tarrytown, NY, $160,000. For part two of transfer and maintenance of Commonwealth Fund's Archives. 1991.

1860-34 Rush-Presbyterian-Saint Lukes Medical Center, Nursing Services Research and Support, Chicago, IL, $62,300. To improve patient-centered care through initiatives in nursing. 1991.

1860-35 United Hospital Fund of New York, NYC, NY, $250,000. For Responding to New York City's Hospital Crisis, Part Two. 1991.

1860-36 United Hospital Fund of New York, NYC, NY, $25,000. For study of AIDS epidemic in New York City by University of Minnesota Medical School, School of Public Health. 1991.

1860-37 University of California, Institute for Health Policy Studies, School of Medicine, San Francisco, CA, $50,000. To compare resource use in U.S. and Canada teaching hospitals. 1991.

1860-38 University of Connecticut, Roper Center for Public Opinion Research, Storrs, CT, $15,000. For expanding and publicizing collection of public opinion survey data on health and work issues. 1991.

1860-39 University of Pennsylvania, Philadelphia, PA, $60,483. To examine effects of teenage pregnancy. 1991.

1860-40 University of Virginia, Health Sciences Center, Charlottesville, VA, $10,000. For preparing Kerr White Collection on Health Services Research. 1991.

1860-41 Xavier University of Louisiana, New Orleans, LA, $25,000. To provide assistance to premedical students. 1991.

1861
Congel-Pyramid Trust
Four Clinton Sq., Suite 106
Syracuse 13202-1076   (315) 476-0532

Established in 1986 in NY.
Donor(s): Robert J. Congel, Pyramid Co., and subsidiaries.
Foundation type: Independent
Financial data (yr. ended 09/30/91): Assets, $1,171,312 (M); expenditures, $225,005; qualifying distributions, $221,039, including $215,500 for 9 grants (high: $100,000; low: $2,000).
Fields of interest: Welfare, higher education, hospitals, cultural programs.
Limitations: Giving primarily in Syracuse, NY. No grants to individuals.

Application information:
Initial approach: Letter
Deadline(s): None
Write: Robert V. Hunter, Trustee
Trustees: Timothy P. Ahern, Robert J. Congel, Suzanne M. Congel, Robert V. Hunter, Bruce A. Kenan, Leonard Leveen, George J. Schunck.
EIN: 166291475

1862
Leon & Toby Cooperman Foundation
c/o Goldman Sachs & Co., Tax Dept.
85 Broad St.
New York 10004-2408

Established in 1981.
Donor(s): Leon G. Cooperman.
Foundation type: Independent
Financial data (yr. ended 01/31/91): Assets, $2,573,655 (M); expenditures, $107,601; qualifying distributions, $76,001, including $75,925 for 86 grants (high: $25,000; low: $25).
Fields of interest: Jewish welfare, health, social services.
Types of support: General purposes.
Limitations: Giving primarily in New York, NY, and NJ. No grants to individuals.
Application information: Currently contributes only to pre-selected organizations. Applications not accepted.
Trustees: Leon G. Cooperman, Michael S. Cooperman, Toby F. Cooperman, Wayne M. Cooperman.
EIN: 133102941

1863
Peter C. Cornell Trust
c/o Fiduciary Services, Inc.
120 Delaware Ave., Suite 430
Buffalo 14202   (716) 854-1244

Established in 1949 in NY.
Donor(s): Peter C. Cornell, M.D.‡
Foundation type: Independent
Financial data (yr. ended 09/30/91): Assets, $4,335,457 (M); expenditures, $542,323; qualifying distributions, $514,500 for 57 grants (high: $90,000; low: $500; average: $3,000-$5,000).
Purpose and activities: Support for local eleemosynary, social, education, and health needs; some grants to national agencies in those fields.
Fields of interest: Social services, education, health, religion—Christian.
Types of support: Operating budgets, continuing support, annual campaigns, seed money, emergency funds, building funds, equipment, land acquisition, matching funds, capital campaigns.
Limitations: Giving primarily in Buffalo and Erie County, NY. No grants to individuals, or for program support, research, demonstration projects, publications, or conferences; no loans.
Publications: Application guidelines.
Application information: Application form not required.
Initial approach: Proposal
Copies of proposal: 4
Deadline(s): Oct. 1
Board meeting date(s): May and Nov.

Final notification: 6 months
Write: Joseph H. Morey, Jr., Trustee
Trustees: Wende A. Alford, S. Douglas Cornell, Joseph H. Morey, Jr.
Number of staff: None.
EIN: 951660344

1864
Corning Incorporated Foundation ▼
(Formerly Corning Glass Works Foundation)
MP-LB-02-1
Corning 14831   (607) 974-8746

Incorporated in 1952 in NY.
Donor(s): Corning Inc.
Foundation type: Company-sponsored
Financial data (yr. ended 12/31/91): Assets, $2,845,967 (M); gifts received, $2,544,248; expenditures, $2,550,258; qualifying distributions, $2,250,705, including $1,685,858 for 196 grants (high: $203,000; low: $100; average: $500-$2,500) and $564,847 for 4,246 employee matching gifts.
Purpose and activities: Support for educational, civic, cultural, health and human care institutions; scholarships and fellowships in selected educational fields at selected institutions.
Fields of interest: Education, higher education, secondary education, civic affairs, cultural programs, health, social services, community funds.
Types of support: Seed money, equipment, employee matching gifts, scholarship funds, fellowships, special projects.
Limitations: Giving primarily in communities where Corning Incorporated has operations. No support for elementary or secondary schools outside of school systems in plant communities, or for veterans' organizations, political parties, labor groups, or religious organizations. No grants to individuals; no loans.
Publications: Annual report (including application guidelines), application guidelines.
Application information: Application form not required.
Initial approach: Letter
Copies of proposal: 1
Deadline(s): None
Board meeting date(s): Mar., June, Sept., and Nov.
Final notification: 6 weeks
Write: Kristin A. Swain, Pres.
Officers and Trustees:* Susan B. King,* Chair.; Kristin A. Swain, Pres.; James L. Flynn, V.P.; A. John Peck, Jr., Secy.; Sandra Helton, Treas.; Roger G. Ackerman, Thomas S. Buechner, Van C. Campbell, David A. Duke, Richard Dulude, James R. Houghton, Richard E. Rahill, James E. Riesbeck, William C. Ughetta.
Number of staff: 2 full-time professional; 2 full-time support.
EIN: 166051394

1865
Jon & Joanne Corzine Foundation
c/o Goldman Sachs & Co., Tax Dept.
85 Broad St.
New York 10004

Established in 1981 in NJ.
Donor(s): Jon S. Corzine.

Foundation type: Independent
Financial data (yr. ended 01/31/91): Assets, $1,821,232 (M); gifts received, $629,632; expenditures, $300,104; qualifying distributions, $296,111, including $296,081 for 88 grants (high: $25,000; low: $20).
Fields of interest: Education, family services, religion—Christian, social services, health.
Types of support: Building funds, endowment funds, general purposes.
Limitations: Giving primarily in NY and NJ. No grants to individuals.
Application information: Contributes only to pre-selected organizations. Applications not accepted.
Trustees: Joanne Corzine, Jon S. Corzine, Robert A. Friedman.
EIN: 133103160

1866
The Cowles Charitable Trust
630 Fifth Ave., Suite 1612
New York 10111-0144   (212) 765-6262

Trust established in 1948 in NY.
Donor(s): Gardner Cowles.‡
Foundation type: Independent
Financial data (yr. ended 12/31/90): Assets, $13,644,630 (M); gifts received, $1,158,924; expenditures, $1,144,595; qualifying distributions, $1,063,341, including $923,400 for grants (high: $111,900).
Purpose and activities: Grants largely for arts and culture, including museums and the performing arts; education, including early childhood, higher, and secondary; hospitals and AIDS programs; social services, including family planning; and community funds.
Fields of interest: Arts, museums, education, education—early childhood, higher education, secondary education, health, AIDS, social services, family planning.
Types of support: Operating budgets, continuing support, annual campaigns, seed money, emergency funds, building funds, equipment, endowment funds, matching funds, capital campaigns, general purposes, renovation projects, special projects, professorships.
Limitations: Giving primarily in NY, FL, and the East Coast. No grants to individuals; no loans.
Publications: Annual report, application guidelines.
Application information: Application form not required.
Initial approach: Proposal or letter
Copies of proposal: 7
Deadline(s): Dec. 1, Mar. 1, June 1, and Sept. 1
Board meeting date(s): Jan., Apr., July, and Oct.
Final notification: Within 2 weeks of board meeting
Write: Martha Roby Stephens, Secy.
Officers and Trustees:* Gardner Cowles III,* Pres.; Martha Roby Stephens,* Secy.; Mary Croft, Treas.; Charles Cowles, Jan Cowles, Lois Cowles Harrison, Kate Cowles Nichols, Virginia Cowles Schroth.
Number of staff: 2 part-time professional.
EIN: 136090295
Recent health grants:
1866-1 Planned Parenthood Federation of America, NYC, NY, $39,000. 1990.

1866-2 Tampa Bay Research Institute, Saint Petersburg, FL, $35,000. 1990.

1867
The Crane Foundation
c/o Crane Co.
757 Third Ave.
New York 10017   (212) 415-7277

Established in 1951 in MO.
Donor(s): UMC Industries, Inc.
Foundation type: Company-sponsored
Financial data (yr. ended 12/31/90): Assets, $2,854,819 (M); expenditures, $127,315; qualifying distributions, $112,095, including $97,210 for 38 grants (high: $16,000; low: $500) and $14,885 for 55 employee matching gifts.
Purpose and activities: Emphasis on community funds, museums and the performing arts, families and youth, hospitals, and higher education, including research, business education, programs for minorities, and an employee matching gift program.
Fields of interest: Community funds, museums, performing arts, family services, child development, youth, employment, hospitals, drug abuse, higher education.
Types of support: General purposes, continuing support, annual campaigns, scholarship funds, employee matching gifts.
Limitations: Giving limited to areas of company operations. No grants to individuals, or for endowment funds, capital funds, or research; no loans.
Application information: Application form not required.
Initial approach: Letter
Deadline(s): None
Board meeting date(s): As required
Write: Gil A. Dickoff, Asst. Treas. and Mgr.
Officers and Directors:* Roberts S. Evans,* Chair. and Pres.; P.R. Hundt,* Exec. V.P. and Secy.; Jeremiah P. Cronin,* Exec. V.P. and Treas.; R. Phillips,* Exec. V.P.; G.A. Dickoff, Mgr.
EIN: 436051752

1868
Louise B. & Edgar M. Cullman Foundation
641 Lexington Ave., 29th Fl.
New York 10022-4599   (212) 838-0211
Application address: 387 Park Ave. South, New York, NY 10016; Tel.: (212) 561-8703

Established in 1956 in NY.
Donor(s): Edgar M. Cullman.
Foundation type: Independent
Financial data (yr. ended 12/31/90): Assets, $821,941 (M); gifts received, $114,275; expenditures, $806,010; qualifying distributions, $795,690, including $795,405 for 33 grants (high: $434,965; low: $100).
Fields of interest: Education, higher education, hospitals, cultural programs, wildlife, general charitable giving.
Application information: Application form required.
Copies of proposal: 1
Deadline(s): None
Board meeting date(s): Dec.
Write: Edgar M. Cullman, Chair.

Officers: Edgar M. Cullman, Chair.; Louise B. Cullman, V.P.
Number of staff: 1 part-time professional; 1 part-time support.
EIN: 136100041

1869
James H. Cummings Foundation, Inc.
1807 Elmwood Ave., Rm. 112
Buffalo 14207   (716) 874-0040

Incorporated in 1962 in NY.
Donor(s): James H. Cummings.‡
Foundation type: Independent
Financial data (yr. ended 05/31/91): Assets, $14,971,165 (M); expenditures, $777,038; qualifying distributions, $662,617, including $630,281 for 19 grants (high: $150,000; low: $190).
Purpose and activities: Exclusively for charitable purposes in advancing medical science, research, and education in the U.S. and Canada and for charitable work among underprivileged boys and girls and aged and infirm persons in designated areas. Priority is given to medical proposals.
Fields of interest: Medical sciences, medical research, medical education, hospitals, aged, youth, child welfare, Canada, disadvantaged.
Types of support: Building funds, seed money, equipment, land acquisition, matching funds, consulting services, research, renovation projects, annual campaigns, capital campaigns.
Limitations: Giving limited to the vicinity of the cities of Buffalo, NY; Hendersonville, NC; and Toronto, Ontario, Canada. No support for national health organizations. No grants to individuals, or for annual campaigns, program support, endowment funds, operating budgets, emergency funds, deficit financing, scholarships, fellowships, publications, conferences, or continuing support; no loans.
Publications: Annual report (including application guidelines).
Application information: Application form not required.
 Initial approach: Preliminary letter (not more than 2 pages) or telephone inquiry is encouraged
 Copies of proposal: 7
 Deadline(s): Feb. 15, May 15, Aug. 15, and Nov.15
 Board meeting date(s): Mar., June, Sept., and Dec.
 Final notification: 4 to 8 weeks
 Write: William J. McFarland, Exec. Dir.
Officers and Directors:* William G. Gisel,* Pres.; Kenneth M. Alford, M.D.,* V.P.; William J. McFarland, Secy. and Exec. Dir.; Robert J.A. Irwin,* Treas.; John Naughton, M.D., Robert S. Scheu, John N. Walsh, Jr.
Number of staff: 1 part-time professional; 1 part-time support.
EIN: 160864200
Recent health grants:
1869-1 Buffalo Hearing and Speech Center, Buffalo, NY, $25,000. 1991.
1869-2 Childrens Hospital of Buffalo, Buffalo, NY, $50,000. 1991.
1869-3 Hemophilia Center of Western New York, Buffalo, NY, $20,000. 1991.
1869-4 Medical Foundation of Buffalo, Buffalo, NY, $30,000. 1991.

1869-5 Memorial Mission Medical Center, Asheville, NC, $17,500. 1991.
1869-6 Millard Fillmore Hospital, Buffalo, NY, $250,000. 1991.
1869-7 Wellesley Hospital, Toronto, Canada, $35,320. 1991.

1870
The Nathan Cummings Foundation, Inc. ▼
885 Third Ave., Suite 3160
New York 10022   (212) 230-3377

Established in 1949 in NY.
Donor(s): Nathan Cummings.‡
Foundation type: Independent
Financial data (yr. ended 12/31/90): Assets, $188,833,527 (M); expenditures, $10,886,588; qualifying distributions, $7,843,863, including $7,843,863 for 196 grants (high: $1,075,000; low: $550; average: $5,000-$100,000).
Purpose and activities: The foundation is currently undergoing a review of grantmaking activities. Grants will focus on improving the environment on a global scale, supporting multi-cultural arts projects and making the arts more accessible to more people, improving the health-delivery system for the poor, and enhancing understanding between Jews and non-Jews.
Fields of interest: Environment, cultural programs, arts, health, health services, Jewish giving, Israel, Jewish welfare.
Types of support: Annual campaigns, building funds, capital campaigns, consulting services, general purposes, lectureships, special projects.
Publications: Grants list, application guidelines.
Application information: Application form required.
 Initial approach: Letter
 Deadline(s): None
 Board meeting date(s): 4 times a year
 Write: Charles R. Halpern, Pres.
Officers and Trustees:* Beatrice Cummings Mayer,* Chair.; Charles R. Halpern,* Pres.; Ruth Cummings Sorensen,* Vice-Chair.; Michael A. Cummings,* Secy.; Robert N. Mayer,* Treas.; Diane Cummings, Herbert K. Cummings, James K. Cummings.
Number of staff: 9 full-time professional; 5 full-time support.
EIN: 237093201
Recent health grants:
1870-1 Advocacy Institute, DC, $75,000. To train advocacy leaders in health and environment. 1990.
1870-2 Andrew Glover Youth Program, NYC, NY, $15,000. To provide health advocacy and prevention services to at-risk youth. 1990.
1870-3 Arizona State University, Cancer Research Institute, Phoenix, AZ, $10,000. For biomedical and chemical research into treatment and cure of cancer. 1990.
1870-4 Beth Israel Hospital, Boston, MA, $68,035. To determine extent to which people nationwide use and pay for alternative medical therapies. 1990.
1870-5 Bikur Cholim of New York, NYC, NY, $10,000. To publish teaching guide on visiting sick. 1990.
1870-6 Children of Alcoholics Foundation, NYC, NY, $35,800. To disseminate Images Within: Child's View of Parental Alcoholism. 1990.

1870-7 Childrens Defense Fund, DC, $50,000. For Southern Regional Maternal and Child Health Project. 1990.
1870-8 Commonweal, Bolinas, CA, $60,000. For Sustainable Futures Project. 1990.
1870-9 Communications Consortium, DC, $35,000. To develop information on attitudes of minority women about reproductive health issues. 1990.
1870-10 Environmental Health Coalition, San Diego, CA, $25,000. To improve local worker health and safety, water quality and environmental quality through Clean Bay Campaign and Ecological Safe Substitutes Program. 1990.
1870-11 Essential Information, DC, $35,000. For model Time Dollar Project, program that organizes individuals to exchange support services. 1990.
1870-12 Fetzer Institute, Kalamazoo, MI, $250,000. For Healing and the Mind, with Bill Moyers. 1990.
1870-13 First Nations Financial Project, Falmouth, VA, $50,000. For start-up funds for community controlled health clinic on Pine Ridge Reservation in South Dakota. 1990.
1870-14 Health Care for All, Boston, MA, $60,000. For public education about Massachusetts universal health care law. 1990.
1870-15 Institute for Social Justice, Little Rock, AR, $60,000. To organize low-income patients to work with hospital administrators to improve health care in Texas, Arkansas and New York. 1990.
1870-16 Institute for the Advancement of Health, San Francisco, CA, $24,200. For dialogue between Dalai Lama and American neuroscientists. 1990.
1870-17 Maternity Center Association, NYC, NY, $50,000. For Childbearing Center. 1990.
1870-18 Mental Health Law Project, DC, $35,000. To assure that eligible low-income mentally and physically disabled children receive benefits. 1990.
1870-19 Mind/Body Medical Institute, Boston, MA, $79,193. For school-based, relaxation-response curriculum for troubled and healthy children. 1990.
1870-20 Morse Geriatric Center, West Palm Beach, FL, $90,000. For Alan Cummings Memorial Unit. 1990.
1870-21 National Association of Community Health Centers, DC, $100,000. To recruit and retain doctors and health professionals. 1990.
1870-22 National Center for Health Education, NYC, NY, $20,000. For five-year strategic planning process. 1990.
1870-23 National Center for Policy Alternatives, DC, $150,000. For Collaborative Project on Health. 1990.
1870-24 New York Foundation for the Arts, NYC, NY, $37,000. For documentary film on Preventive Medicine Research Institute. 1990.
1870-25 Occupational Safety and Health Law Center, DC, $50,000. To produce occupational safety and health manual for workers. 1990.
1870-26 Preventive Medicine Research Institute, Sausalito, CA, $75,000. For clinical research into mind/body techniques for treating heart disease. 1990.
1870-27 Rape Foundation, Santa Monica, CA, $15,000. To assist victims of sexual assault, abuse and criminal violence. 1990.

1870-28 San Diego Youth and Community Services, San Diego, CA, $29,000. To provide direct services to runaway and street youth such as substance abuse counseling and drop-out prevention. 1990.

1870-29 Scottsdale Memorial Health Foundation, Scottsdale, AZ, $25,000. To establish Office of Community Health Education. 1990.

1870-30 Twentieth Century Fund, NYC, NY, $25,000. For Substance Abuse Strategy Initiative. 1990.

1870-31 University of Louisville, School of Medicine, Louisville, KY, $90,000. To develop medical school curricula on mind/body techniques and to encourage professional careers in clinical services and research related to mind/body medicine. 1990.

1870-32 Wellness Community-National, Santa Monica, CA, $75,000. To start new, local Wellness Communities for cancer patients across country. 1990.

1870-33 Wendy Paine OBrien Treatment Center, Scottsdale, AZ, $20,000. For capital contribution for family therapy room. 1990.

1871
The Frances L. & Edwin L. Cummings Memorial Fund ▼

501 Fifth Ave., Suite 1208
New York 10017-1602   (212) 286-1778

Established in 1982 in NY.
Donor(s): Edwin L. Cummings,‡ Frances L. Cummings.‡
Foundation type: Independent
Financial data (yr. ended 07/31/91): Assets, $28,110,147 (M); expenditures, $2,059,802; qualifying distributions, $1,846,748, including $1,620,000 for 58 grants (high: $150,000; low: $500; average: $1,000-$25,000).
Purpose and activities: Support for medical and disease research, specifically on the problems of aging, AIDS and cancer, rehabilitation and education of the physically and/or mentally handicapped, medical equipment for health care institutions demonstrating special needs, campaigns to build endowments through establishment of challenge grants, youth and child welfare concerns, especially child-abuse prevention, and higher education, particularly as it relates to student populations from disadvantaged backgrounds.
Fields of interest: Medical research, rehabilitation, mental health, handicapped, cancer, AIDS, youth, child welfare, disadvantaged, aged, delinquency, homeless, employment, family planning, higher education, literacy, education—early childhood, secondary education, vocational education, community development.
Types of support: Research, consulting services, endowment funds, professorships, scholarship funds, seed money, special projects, equipment, matching funds, publications.
Limitations: Giving primarily in the metropolitan New York, NY, area, including NJ and CT. No support for the cultural arts or private foundations, or for alcoholism or drug prevention, camping programs, day care programs, environmental programs, or public policy and/or lobbying groups. No grants to individuals (except for

scientific research projects which have been pre-screened by qualified scientific advisory committee), or for capital building campaigns, general operating expenses, general operating support, moving expenses, conferences, public opinion polls and surveys, or annual fundraising campaigns.
Publications: Biennial report (including application guidelines).
Application information: Application form not required.
  Initial approach: Letter, preferably 7 pages or less
  Copies of proposal: 8
  Deadline(s): Apr. 1 or Oct. 1
  Board meeting date(s): June and Dec.
  Final notification: 10 days after board meeting
  Write: Elizabeth Costas, Admin. Dir.
Trustees: J. Andrew Lark, The Bank of New York.
Board of Advisors: Lawrence J. Denson, Chair.; William Bricker, Fred J. Brotherton, Fairleigh Dickinson, Jr., Kathy Doyle, Anne Nordeman, Irving S. Wright.
Number of staff: 1 full-time professional; 1 full-time support.
EIN: 136814491

1872
Curtice-Burns/Pro-Fac Foundation

P.O. Box 681
Rochester 14603   (716) 383-1850

Trust established in 1966 in NY.
Donor(s): Curtice-Burns Foods, Inc.
Foundation type: Company-sponsored
Financial data (yr. ended 06/30/91): Assets, $401,034 (M); expenditures, $300,762; qualifying distributions, $300,762, including $296,730 for 191 grants (high: $21,000; low: $100; average: $1,000).
Purpose and activities: Emphasis on education, including higher education, building and scholarship funds, literacy and programs for minorities, and libraries; health agencies, hospital building funds, hospices, medical research, drug abuse and alcoholism, and rehabilitation; human services, including youth and child welfare, women and the elderly, minorities, the handicapped and the disadvantaged, and housing; community funds and development; and cultural programs including the fine and performing arts and historic preservation.
Fields of interest: Higher education, libraries, health, drug abuse, social services, youth, women, aged, community development, cultural programs.
Types of support: General purposes, operating budgets, annual campaigns, building funds, equipment, endowment funds, scholarship funds, fellowships, professorships, special projects, research, conferences and seminars, capital campaigns, continuing support, renovation projects.
Limitations: Giving primarily in areas of company operations. No support for religious organizations. No grants to individuals, or for seed money, emergency funds, deficit financing, land acquisition, matching gifts, or publications; no loans.
Application information: Application form not required.
  Initial approach: Proposal

  Copies of proposal: 1
  Deadline(s): None
  Board meeting date(s): Usually in Jan., Mar., May, Aug., Oct., and Dec.
  Final notification: 2 months
  Write: Marilyn T. Helmer, V.P.
Officer: Marilyn T. Helmer, V.P.
Trustees: Robert Call, Marilyn T. Hellmer, Edward Tobin.
Number of staff: 1 part-time support.
EIN: 166071142

1873
The Dammann Fund, Inc.

c/o John P. Engels & Associates
1740 Broadway, 25th Fl.
New York 10019   (212) 262-9154

Incorporated in 1946 in NY.
Donor(s): Members of the Dammann family.
Foundation type: Independent
Financial data (yr. ended 11/30/91): Assets, $7,944,526 (M); expenditures, $447,316; qualifying distributions, $344,059, including $292,225 for 132 grants (high: $76,775; low: $50).
Fields of interest: Hospitals, health services, welfare, religion, education.
Types of support: Continuing support, annual campaigns, seed money, building funds, endowment funds, general purposes, special projects.
Limitations: No grants to individuals, or for scholarships, fellowships, or matching gifts; no loans.
Application information:
  Initial approach: Letter
  Copies of proposal: 1
  Deadline(s): None
  Board meeting date(s): Mar., June, Sept., and Dec.
  Write: Penelope Johnston, Pres.
Officers and Directors:* Penelope D. Johnston,* Pres.; Pamela D. Adams,* Secy.-Treas.
Number of staff: 2 part-time support.
EIN: 136089896

1874
Eleanor Naylor Dana Charitable Trust ▼

375 Park Ave., 38th Fl.
New York 10152   (212) 754-2890

Established in 1979 in CT.
Donor(s): Eleanor Naylor Dana.‡
Foundation type: Independent
Financial data (yr. ended 05/31/91): Assets, $4,731,126 (M); gifts received, $4,197,092; expenditures, $5,291,642; qualifying distributions, $5,291,642, including $5,048,012 for 133 grants (high: $400,000; low: $1,204; average: $5,000-$100,000).
Purpose and activities: Grants are given mainly to foster and finance progress and the pursuit of excellence in two areas: 1)biomedical research, "to support clinical investigations by established scientists in qualified institutions in the U.S., to pursue innovative projects designed to improve medical practice or prevent disease," and 2)the performing arts, to assist the various performing arts fields in ways that could be of substantial

import to the grantees and the artists and the public which they serve.
Fields of interest: Medical research, performing arts, biological sciences.
Types of support: Research, special projects.
Limitations: Giving primarily in areas east of the Mississippi River. No grants to individuals, or for instrumentation other than that required for a specific project, large scale field studies of a therapeutic or epidemiological nature, or conferences (in biomedical research); or for deficit financing, exhibits, publications, or conclaves (in the arts).
Publications: Informational brochure.
Application information: Application form not required.
  Initial approach: Letter of intent under 1,000 words
  Copies of proposal: 6
  Deadline(s): None
  Board meeting date(s): Mar., June, Oct., and Dec.
  Final notification: After meetings
  Write: The Trustees
Officers and Trustees:* David J. Mahoney,* Chair.; A.J. Signorile,* Treas.; Robert A. Good, M.D., Carlos Moseley, Robert E. Wise, M.D.
Number of staff: 1 full-time professional.
EIN: 132992855
Recent health grants:
1874-1 All Childrens Hospital, Saint Petersburg, FL, $100,000. 1990.
1874-2 All Childrens Hospital, Saint Petersburg, FL, $100,000. 1990.
1874-3 All Childrens Hospital, Saint Petersburg, FL, $100,000. 1990.
1874-4 Beth Israel Hospital, Boston, MA, $100,000. 1990.
1874-5 Beth Israel Hospital, Boston, MA, $100,000. 1990.
1874-6 Beth Israel Hospital, Boston, MA, $88,563. 1990.
1874-7 Harvard University, Medical School, Boston, MA, $500,000. 1990.
1874-8 Jackson Laboratory, Bar Harbor, ME, $100,000. 1990.
1874-9 Jackson Laboratory, Bar Harbor, ME, $100,000. 1990.
1874-10 Kennebunkport Emergency Medical Service, Kennebunkport, ME, $10,000. 1990.
1874-11 Lahey Clinic Foundation, Burlington, MA, $350,000. 1990.
1874-12 Lahey Clinic Medical Center, Burlington, MA, $120,000. 1990.
1874-13 Lahey Clinic Medical Center, Burlington, MA, $100,000. 1990.
1874-14 Lahey Clinic Medical Center, Burlington, MA, $100,000. 1990.
1874-15 Lahey Clinic Medical Center, Burlington, MA, $100,000. 1990.
1874-16 Lahey Clinic Medical Center, Burlington, MA, $100,000. 1990.
1874-17 Lahey Clinic Medical Center, Burlington, MA, $90,000. 1990.
1874-18 Lahey Clinic Medical Center, Burlington, MA, $73,000. 1990.
1874-19 Lahey Clinic Medical Center, Burlington, MA, $50,000. 1990.
1874-20 Lahey Clinic Medical Center, Burlington, MA, $35,000. 1990.
1874-21 Lahey Clinic Medical Center, Burlington, MA, $25,000. 1990.

1874-22 Lahey Clinic Medical Center, Burlington, MA, $20,000. 1990.
1874-23 Lahey Clinic Medical Center, Burlington, MA, $11,000. 1990.
1874-24 Manic Depressive Illness Foundation, DC, $150,000. 1990.
1874-25 Manic Depressive Illness Foundation, DC, $20,000. 1990.
1874-26 Mayo Clinic, Rochester, MN, $10,500. 1990.
1874-27 Montefiore Medical Center, Bronx, NY, $10,000. 1990.
1874-28 National Osteoporosis Foundation, DC, $20,000. 1990.
1874-29 Neurosciences Research Foundation, NYC, NY, $25,000. 1990.
1874-30 New York University Medical Center, NYC, NY, $100,000. 1990.
1874-31 Northwestern University, Medical School, Chicago, IL, $50,000. 1990.
1874-32 Rockefeller University, NYC, NY, $50,000. 1990.
1874-33 Saint Elizabeths Hospital, Brighton, MA, $100,000. 1990.
1874-34 Saint Lukes-Roosevelt Hospital Center, NYC, NY, $100,000. 1990.
1874-35 Shriners Hospital for Crippled Children, Tampa, FL, $10,000. 1990.
1874-36 University of Iowa, College of Medicine, Iowa City, IA, $99,653. 1990.
1874-37 University of Miami, School of Medicine, Miami, FL, $89,651. 1990.
1874-38 University of Pennsylvania, David Mahoney Institute of Neurological Sciences, Philadelphia, PA, $500,000. 1990.
1874-39 University of Pennsylvania, School of Medicine, Philadelphia, PA, $95,579. 1990.
1874-40 University of South Florida, College of Medicine, Saint Petersburg, FL, $100,828. 1990.
1874-41 University of Virginia, Medical School, Charlottesville, VA, $100,000. 1990.

1875
The Charles A. Dana Foundation, Inc. ▼
745 Fifth Ave., Suite 700
New York 10151   (212) 223-4040

Incorporated in 1950 in CT.
Donor(s): Charles A. Dana,‡ Eleanor Naylor Dana.‡
Foundation type: Independent
Financial data (yr. ended 12/31/91): Assets, $211,020,905 (M); expenditures, $7,562,227; qualifying distributions, $5,558,446, including $3,583,785 for 44 grants (high: $331,266; low: $2,000; average: $50,000-$200,000), $641,130 for grants to individuals and $132,464 for foundation-administered programs.
Purpose and activities: Principal interests in education and health, particularly neuroscience, as well as the Charles A. Dana Awards for Pioneering Achievements in health and education. Support also for foundation-initiated cultural and civic projects in New York City.
Fields of interest: Education, health.
Types of support: Fellowships, general purposes.
Limitations: No support for professional organizations. No grants to individuals (except for the Charles A. Dana Awards), or for capital or endowment funds, operating budgets, continuing support, annual campaigns, building or

emergency funds, deficit financing, publications, conferences, demonstration projects, or colloquia; no loans.
Publications: Annual report (including application guidelines), newsletter.
Application information: Applications for the Charles A. Dana Awards by nomination only. Grants require matching support from the organizations involved. Application form not required.
  Initial approach: Letter (2 pages)
  Copies of proposal: 1
  Deadline(s): None
  Board meeting date(s): Apr., June, Oct., and Dec.
  Final notification: 2 to 3 months
  Write: Walter Donway, Prog. Officer (education), Stephen A. Foster, Exec. V.P. (health), Cynthia Read, Prog. Officer (Dana Awards), or Barbara Gill, Dir. Public Affairs
Officers and Directors:* David J. Mahoney,* Chair.; Stephen A. Foster, Exec. V.P.; Walter G. Corcoran,* V.P.; Clark M. Whittemore, Jr.,* Secy.-Treas.; Edward C. Andrews, Jr., Wallace L. Cook, Charles A. Dana, Jr., Donald B. Marron, Carlos Moseley, L. Guy Palmer II.
Number of staff: 9 full-time professional; 4 full-time support.
EIN: 066036761

1876
Day Family Foundation
c/o Goldman Sachs & Co., Tax Dept.
85 Broad St.
New York 10004

Established in 1979 in NY.
Donor(s): H. Corbin Day.
Foundation type: Independent
Financial data (yr. ended 07/31/91): Assets, $3,466,141 (M); gifts received, $244,500; expenditures, $449,212; qualifying distributions, $429,090, including $428,780 for 84 grants (high: $100,000; low: $50).
Fields of interest: Higher education, secondary education, youth, hospitals, health, museums.
Limitations: No grants to individuals.
Application information: Applications not accepted.
Trustees: Dorothy J. Day, H. Corbin Day, Stephen Friedman.
EIN: 133025969

1877
The Edmond de Rothschild Foundation
1585 Broadway, 20th Fl.
New York 10036   (212) 969-3250

Incorporated in 1963 in NY.
Donor(s): Edmond de Rothschild.
Foundation type: Independent
Financial data (yr. ended 02/28/91): Assets, $33,627,746 (M); gifts received, $1,550,000; expenditures, $2,284,327; qualifying distributions, $2,079,851, including $1,990,105 for 71 grants (high: $622,344; low: $57; average: $1,000-$50,000).
Purpose and activities: Grants largely for Jewish welfare funds, higher education, and organizations concerned with Israeli affairs in the

U.S. and abroad; support also for cultural programs, hospitals, and scientific research.
Fields of interest: Jewish giving, Jewish welfare, higher education, Israel, France, cultural programs, hospitals, science and technology, cancer, medical research.
Types of support: General purposes.
Limitations: Giving primarily in New York, NY, and in France; some giving in Israel. No grants to individuals.
Application information: Application form not required.
  Initial approach: Letter
  Copies of proposal: 1
  Deadline(s): None
  Board meeting date(s): As required
  Final notification: Varies
  Write: Paul H. Epstein, Secy.-Treas.
Officers and Directors:* Edmond de Rothschild,* Chair.; George M. Shapiro,* Pres.; Georges C. Karlweis,* V.P.; Paul H. Epstein,* Secy.-Treas.; Benjamin de Rothschild, Bernard Esambert, Stanley Komaroff.
Number of staff: None.
EIN: 136119422

1878
Dean Witter Financial Services Group Giving Program
2 World Trade Center, 17th Fl.
New York 10048   (212) 392-2914

Financial data (yr. ended 12/31/90): Total giving, $1,285,561.
Purpose and activities: Support for United Way, health and human services, education, arts and culture, and civic and community affairs.
Fields of interest: Health, social services, education, civic affairs, community funds.
Application information:
  Initial approach: Letter
  Write: Kenneth F. Mountcastle, Sr. V.P., Corp. Contribs.

1879
The Ira W. DeCamp Foundation ▼
c/o Mudge Rose Guthrie Alexander & Ferdon
630 Fifth Ave., Suite 1650
New York 10011   (212) 332-1613

Trust established in 1975 in NY.
Donor(s): Elizabeth DeCamp McInerny.‡
Foundation type: Independent
Financial data (yr. ended 10/31/91): Assets, $58,517,454 (M); expenditures, $3,998,754; qualifying distributions, $3,802,147, including $3,479,720 for 67 grants (high: $300,000; low: $10,000; average: $25,000-$100,000).
Purpose and activities: Grants for health care facilities and equipment and for medical research and education.
Fields of interest: Hospitals, medical education, medical research, health, AIDS.
Types of support: Building funds, equipment, seed money, research, special projects.
Limitations: No support for government-affiliated organizations. No grants to individuals, or for general support, land acquisition, publications, conferences, endowment funds, operating budgets, continuing support, annual campaigns, emergency funds, or deficit financing; no support

for research on live animals other than rats and mice; no loans.
Application information: Application form not required.
  Initial approach: Letter
  Copies of proposal: 3
  Deadline(s): None
  Board meeting date(s): Quarterly
  Final notification: 3 months
  Write: Arthur J. Mahon
Trustees: Herbert H. Faber, Manufacturers Hanover Trust Co.
Number of staff: None.
EIN: 510138577
Recent health grants:
1879-1 American Federation for Aging Research, NYC, NY, $25,000. For biomedical research on aging and related diseases. 1990.
1879-2 Boston College, Chestnut Hill, MA, $43,267. For research on ethics and mental health. 1990.
1879-3 Brooklyn College of the City University of New York, Brooklyn, NY, $10,000. For Bachelor of Arts and M.D. degree. 1990.
1879-4 Childrens Specialized Hospital, Mountainside, NJ, $50,000. Toward renovation of elementary school building for satellite outpatient center and construction of long-term care unit. 1990.
1879-5 Crotched Mountain Rehabilitation Center, Greenfield, NH, $50,000. For construction and endowment of aquatic and recreational swimming pool complex. 1990.
1879-6 Georgetown University Medical Center, Department of Psychiatry, DC, $25,000. For fellowship training in geriatrics. 1990.
1879-7 Hartwick College, Oneonta, NY, $25,000. For health care internships. 1990.
1879-8 Harvard University, Medical School, Boston, MA, $187,000. For Division of Medical Ethics. 1990.
1879-9 Hospital Chaplaincy, NYC, NY, $25,000. For matching grant for second major expansion of Clinical Pastoral Education Program. 1990.
1879-10 Hospital Chaplaincy, NYC, NY, $25,000. For matching grant for second major expansion of Clinical Pastoral Education Program. 1990.
1879-11 International Center for the Disabled (ICD), NYC, NY, $30,000. For Post-Trauma Clinic and Residency-In-Rehabilitation Program. 1990.
1879-12 Lighthouse, The, NYC, NY, $10,000. For Visual Impairment in Young Children Project. 1990.
1879-13 Little Flower Childrens Services, Brooklyn, NY, $25,000. For children with AIDS program. 1990.
1879-14 Manhattan Bowery Corporation, NYC, NY, $10,000. For Mobile Medical Outreach. 1990.
1879-15 Marquette University, Milwaukee, WI, $50,000. For challenge grant for construction and installation of biomedical engineering laboratories. 1990.
1879-16 Mather Memorial Hospital, Port Jefferson, NY, $50,000. For capital campaign for construction of Mather Emergency Pavillion. 1990.
1879-17 Memorial Sloan-Kettering Cancer Center, NYC, NY, $25,000. For challenge grant for clinical research facility and program. 1990.

1879-18 Mental Health Law Project, NYC, NY, $10,000. For supplemental income program demonstration project. 1990.
1879-19 Morristown Memorial Hospital, Morristown, NJ, $75,000. For challenge grant to Physician's Fund for Campaign for New Era of Excellence. 1990.
1879-20 National Alliance for Research on Schizophrenia and Depression (NARSAD), Great Neck, NY, $30,000. For Young Investigation Program. 1990.
1879-21 National Jewish Center for Immunology and Respiratory Medicine, Department of Pediatrics, NYC, NY, $25,000. For immunology research. 1990.
1879-22 National Judicial College, Reno, NV, $20,000. For Science and Bioethics Programs. 1990.
1879-23 National Retinitis Pigmentosa Foundation, Garden City, NY, $50,000. For research on inherited retinal degeneration, specifically DNA linkage studies. 1990.
1879-24 New York Foundling Hospital, NYC, NY, $50,000. Toward equipment for multi-handicapped children's skilled nursing facility. 1990.
1879-25 New York Hospital-Cornell Medical Center, NYC, NY, $125,000. For challenge grant for Joint Program in Molecular Neuroscience by Departments of Neurology and Psychiatry. 1990.
1879-26 New York Hospital-Cornell Medical Center, NYC, NY, $25,000. For educational program of pediatric cardiology. 1990.
1879-27 Princeton University, Princeton, NJ, $20,000. For start-up and program funds for professorship in ethics in life sciences. 1990.
1879-28 Rockefeller University, NYC, NY, $100,000. For laboratories conducting research in molecular and cell biology. 1990.
1879-29 Saint Barnabas Medical Center, Livingston, NJ, $100,000. For relocation and modernization of Elizabeth De Camp McInerny Burn Center. 1990.
1879-30 Saint Clares Hospital and Health Center, NYC, NY, $50,000. For challenge grant for renovation of hospital. 1990.
1879-31 Saint Vincents Hospital and Medical Center of New York, NYC, NY, $200,000. For James H. McInerny Endowment Fund for Health Care Outreach Programs for homeless in SRO hotels. 1990.
1879-32 Sigma Theta Tau, Indianapolis, IN, $25,000. For challenge grant to establish Center for Nursing Scholarship and International Nursing Library. 1990.
1879-33 University of Chicago, Chicago, IL, $33,720. For Junior Faculty Development Program of Center for Clinical Medical Ethics. 1990.
1879-34 Village Nursing Home, NYC, NY, $25,000. To establish skilled nursing facility for people with AIDS. 1990.
1879-35 Visiting Nurse Service of New York, NYC, NY, $25,000. For hospice program. 1990.
1879-36 W N E T Channel 13, NYC, NY, $25,000. For documentary on Health Care Across The Border. 1990.
1879-37 Yale University, New Haven, CT, $100,000. For construction of Center for Molecular Medicine and support of Medical Informatics Program. 1990.

1880
Dr. G. Clifford & Florence B. Decker Foundation
Galleria
Eight Hawley St.
Binghamton 13901 (607) 722-0211

Established in 1979 in NY.
Donor(s): G. Clifford Decker.‡
Foundation type: Independent
Financial data (yr. ended 12/31/91): Assets, $21,885,233 (M); gifts received, $1,544; expenditures, $920,076; qualifying distributions, $771,222, including $771,222 for 19 grants (high: $250,000; low: $2,648).
Fields of interest: Education, general charitable giving.
Types of support: Capital campaigns, seed money, special projects.
Limitations: Giving in the Broome County, NY, area. No support for religious organizations for religious purposes. No grants to individuals, or for endowments, operating expenses, continuing support, or for travel and trips.
Publications: Annual report, informational brochure (including application guidelines).
Application information: Submission of 1 copy of proposal required for funding requests under $5,000. Application form required.
Copies of proposal: 7
Deadline(s): Mar. 1, May 1, July 1, Sept. 1, and Nov. 1
Board meeting date(s): Apr., June, Aug., Oct., and Dec.
Write: Donna Bechdel, Exec. Dir.
Officers and Trustees: Ferris G. Akel,* Chair.; William S. Chittenden,* Vice-Chair.; Eugene E. Peckham,* Secy.; Douglas R. Johnson,* Treas.; Donna Bechdel, Exec. Dir.; Mary Lou Faust, Alice A. Wales.
Number of staff: 1 full-time professional; 1 part-time professional.
EIN: 161131704
Recent health grants:
1880-1 Broome Community College Foundation, Decker Health Science Center, Binghamton, NY, $45,000. For building project. 1991.
1880-2 Lourdes Hospital Foundation, Binghamton, NY, $25,000. For renovation and addition. 1991.
1880-3 State University of New York at Binghamton Foundation, Decker School of Nursing, Binghamton, NY, $200,000. For endowment to underwrite programs. 1991.
1880-4 United Health Services Foundation, Decker Center for Advanced Medical Treatment, Binghamton, NY, $250,000. For Pathway 2000 Capital Campaign. 1991.

1881
George Delacorte Fund
980 Fifth Ave., No. 11B
New York 10021-0126

Established about 1977 in NY.
Donor(s): George T. Delacorte, Jr.,‡ and others.
Foundation type: Independent
Financial data (yr. ended 12/31/90): Assets, $7,185,471 (M); gifts received, $102,338; expenditures, $294,684; qualifying distributions, $238,795, including $170,425 for 51 grants

(high: $25,000; low: $100) and $63,370 for foundation-administered programs.
Purpose and activities: Grants for cultural programs, youth, religious organizations, education, and health; program support annually to maintain and build public monuments in New York City.
Fields of interest: Cultural programs, youth, religion, education, health.
Limitations: Giving primarily in FL and the New York, NY, area. No grants to individuals.
Application information: Contributes only to pre-selected organizations. Applications not accepted.
Officers: Valerie Delacorte, V.P. and Treas.; Albert P. Delacorte, Secy.
EIN: 510202382

1882
Beatrice P. Delany Charitable Trust ▼
c/o The Chase Manhattan Bank, N.A.
1211 Ave. of the Americas, 35th Fl.
New York 10036

Trust established about 1977 in NY.
Donor(s): Beatrice P. Delany.‡
Foundation type: Independent
Financial data (yr. ended 10/31/89): Assets, $138,064,330 (M); expenditures, $11,189,009; qualifying distributions, $8,094,389, including $8,070,030 for 158 grants (high: $500,000; low: $30; average: $1,000-$20,000).
Purpose and activities: Giving largely for education, especially higher education, hospitals, health organizations, religion, and cultural programs.
Fields of interest: Education, higher education, hospitals, health, religion, cultural programs.
Types of support: General purposes.
Limitations: Giving primarily in the Chicago, IL, metropolitan area. No grants to individuals.
Application information:
Initial approach: Letter
Deadline(s): None
Write: John H.F. Enteman
Trust Committee: Thomas A. Reynolds, Jr., Mrs. Thomas A. Reynolds, Jr., Andrew Thomson, M.D.
Trustee: The Chase Manhattan Bank, N.A.
Number of staff: None.
EIN: 136748171
Recent health grants:
1882-1 Alexian Brothers Medical Center, Elk Grove Village, IL, $25,000. For general charitable purposes. 1991.
1882-2 Bishop Anderson House, Chicago, IL, $25,000. For general charitable purposes. 1991.
1882-3 Brain Research Foundation, Chicago, IL, $10,000. For general charitable purposes. 1991.
1882-4 Brain Research Foundation, Chicago, IL, $10,000. For general charitable purposes. 1991.
1882-5 Chicago Maternity Center, Chicago, IL, $10,000. For general charitable purposes. 1991.
1882-6 Childrens Memorial Hospital, Chicago, IL, $50,000. For general charitable purposes. 1991.
1882-7 Childrens Memorial Hospital, Chicago, IL, $25,000. For general charitable purposes. 1991.

1882-8 Childrens Memorial Hospital, Chicago, IL, $25,000. For general charitable purposes. 1991.
1882-9 Clearbrook Center Foundation, Rolling Meadows, IL, $10,000. For general charitable purposes. 1991.
1882-10 Dartmouth Medical School, Hanover, NH, $250,000. For general charitable purposes. 1991.
1882-11 Dartmouth Medical School, Hanover, NH, $250,000. For general charitable purposes. 1991.
1882-12 Dartmouth Medical School, Hanover, NH, $250,000. For general charitable purposes. 1991.
1882-13 Dartmouth Medical School, Hanover, NH, $250,000. For general charitable purposes. 1991.
1882-14 Esperanca, Phoenix, AZ, $15,000. For general charitable purposes. 1991.
1882-15 Hospital for Special Surgery Fund, NYC, NY, $10,000. For general charitable purposes. 1991.
1882-16 Indiana University, Medical School, Bloomington, IN, $25,000. For general charitable purposes. 1991.
1882-17 Indiana University, School of Medicine, Bloomington, IN, $15,000. For general charitable purposes. 1991.
1882-18 Jupiter Medical Center, Jupiter, FL, $10,000. For general charitable purposes. 1991.
1882-19 Jupiter Medical Center, Jupiter, FL, $10,000. For general charitable purposes. 1991.
1882-20 Northern Michigan Health Foundation, Petoskey, MI, $25,000. For general charitable purposes. 1991.
1882-21 Northern Michigan Hospital Foundation, Petoskey, MI, $10,000. For general charitable purposes. 1991.
1882-22 Old Peoples Home of Chicago, Chicago, IL, $50,000. For general charitable purposes. 1991.
1882-23 Old Peoples Home of Chicago, Chicago, IL, $50,000. For general charitable purposes. 1991.
1882-24 Old Peoples Home of Chicago, Chicago, IL, $50,000. For general charitable purposes. 1991.
1882-25 Rehabilitation Institute of Chicago, Chicago, IL, $15,000. For general charitable purposes. 1991.
1882-26 Rush-Presbyterian-Saint Lukes Medical Center, Chicago, IL, $250,000. For general charitable purposes. 1991.
1882-27 Rush-Presbyterian-Saint Lukes Medical Center, Chicago, IL, $250,000. For general charitable purposes. 1991.
1882-28 Rush-Presbyterian-Saint Lukes Medical Center, Chicago, IL, $250,000. For general charitable purposes. 1991.
1882-29 Rush-Presbyterian-Saint Lukes Medical Center, Chicago, IL, $250,000. For general charitable purposes. 1991.
1882-30 Rush-Presbyterian-Saint Lukes Medical Center, Department of Physiology, Chicago, IL, $50,000. For general charitable purposes. 1991.
1882-31 Rush-Presbyterian-Saint Lukes Medical Center, Student Scholarship Fund, Chicago, IL, $15,000. For general charitable purposes. 1991.

1882-32 Scottish Home, North Riverside, IL, $10,000. For general charitable purposes. 1991.

1883
Nelson B. Delavan Foundation
c/o Chase Lincoln First Bank, N.A.
P.O. Box 1412
Rochester 14603-1412
Application address: c/o Gary Shultz, Chase Lincoln First Bank, N.A., Five Seneca St., Geneva, NY 14456; Tel.: (315) 781-0280

Established in 1983 in NY.
Foundation type: Independent
Financial data (yr. ended 03/31/91): Assets, $4,267,084 (M); expenditures, $208,285; qualifying distributions, $191,739, including $189,950 for 54 grants (high: $10,000; low: $500).
Fields of interest: Cultural programs, performing arts, animal welfare, women, health, social services, international affairs.
Types of support: Operating budgets.
Limitations: Giving primarily in NY, with preference for the Seneca Falls region. No grants to individuals.
Application information:
Initial approach: Letter
Deadline(s): None
Trustee: Chase Lincoln First Bank, N.A.
EIN: 166260274

1884
Harry Dent Family Foundation, Inc.
P.O. Box 506
Lewiston 14092   (716) 754-8276

Incorporated in 1954 in NY.
Donor(s): Harry M. Dent.‡
Foundation type: Independent
Financial data (yr. ended 10/31/91): Assets, $4,671,911 (M); expenditures, $270,099; qualifying distributions, $221,984, including $199,168 for 1 grant.
Purpose and activities: Grants principally for medical research purposes, with emphasis on a neurological institute.
Fields of interest: Medical research, hospitals.
Limitations: Giving limited to western NY. No grants to individuals.
Application information: Funds presently committed. Applications not accepted.
Board meeting date(s): Semiannually
Write: Miss Jane E. Gailey, Secy.
Officers and Directors:* Harry M. Dent III,* Pres..; Graham Wood Smith,* V.P.; Jane E. Gailey,* Secy.; Susan L. Kimberly,* Treas.; Heidi D. Arthurs, Max Becker, Jr., Gloria G. Dent, Benjamin N. Hewitt, L. Nelson Hopkins, Jr., Helen Dent Lenahan.
Number of staff: 1
EIN: 160849923

1885
The Aaron Diamond Foundation, Inc. ▼
1270 Ave. of the Americas, Suite 2624
New York 10020   (212) 757-7680

Established in 1955 in NY.

Donor(s): Aaron Diamond.‡
Foundation type: Independent
Financial data (yr. ended 12/31/90): Assets, $87,189,594 (M); gifts received, $1,377,650; expenditures, $31,426,702; qualifying distributions, $29,401,941, including $28,147,783 for 518 grants (high: $1,000,000; low: $1,000; average: $10,000-$100,000).
Purpose and activities: Grants primarily for medical research, including AIDS research, minority education, cultural programs, and civil and human rights.
Fields of interest: Medical research, AIDS, nursing, education, minorities, education—minorities, education—early childhood, elementary education, secondary education, arts, cultural programs, performing arts, civil rights, human rights.
Types of support: Research, general purposes, continuing support, operating budgets, special projects.
Limitations: Giving limited to New York City. No support for theater projects. No grants to individuals, or for building funds, endowments, or other capital expenditures; no loans.
Publications: Annual report (including application guidelines), informational brochure (including application guidelines).
Application information: Application form not required.
Initial approach: Letter and proposal
Deadline(s): None
Board meeting date(s): Three times a year
Write: Vincent McGee, Exec. Dir.
Officers and Directors:* Irene Diamond,* Pres.; Robert L. Bernstein,* V.P.; Vincent McGee,* Secy. and Exec. Dir.; Peter Kimmelman,* Treas.; Noreen M. Clark, Adrian W. DeWind, Marian W. Edelman, Alfred Gellhorn, Vartan Gregorian, Howard H. Hiatt, Lewis Thomas.
Number of staff: 6 full-time professional; 6 full-time support; 1 part-time support.
EIN: 132678431
Recent health grants:
1885-1 Aaron Diamond AIDS Research Center for the City of New York, NYC, NY, $1,000,000. For general support for establishment and operation of AIDS research facility in New York City. 1990.
1885-2 Ackerman Institute for Family Therapy, NYC, NY, $75,000. For within-district cluster school strategy which trains teachers and educational staff to work with parents and students to advance student-school relationships and academic improvement. 1990.
1885-3 Adolescent Pregnancy Care and Prevention Program (TAPCAPP), Bronx, NY, $20,000. For general support. 1990.
1885-4 Albert Einstein College of Medicine of Yeshiva University, Bronx, NY, $100,000. For research on pediatric HIV infection. 1990.
1885-5 Albert Einstein College of Medicine of Yeshiva University, Department of Psychiatry, Bronx, NY, $189,730. For study, neurochemical mechanism of cocaine effects and action of potential antagonists. 1990.
1885-6 American Civil Liberties Union Foundation, NYC, NY, $25,000. For AIDS project. 1990.
1885-7 American Civil Liberties Union Foundation, National Prison Project, DC, $25,000. For AIDS in Prison Program. 1990.

1885-8 American Foundation for AIDS Research, NYC, NY, $25,000. For general support. 1990.
1885-9 American Foundation for AIDS Research, NYC, NY, $25,000. For scholars program, three-year scholarships to outstanding young investigators doing research on AIDS. 1990.
1885-10 Association for Drug Abuse Prevention and Treatment (ADAPT), NYC, NY, $25,000. For general support. 1990.
1885-11 Association for Research in Nervous and Mental Disease, NYC, NY, $10,000. For conference, Advances in Understanding the Addictive States. 1990.
1885-12 Association for the Help of Retarded Children, New York City Chapter, NYC, NY, $25,000. For preschool program for HIV-infected children. 1990.
1885-13 Bellevue Hospital Center, Emergency Medical Services, NYC, NY, $254,000. For hypo- and hyperthermia research project. 1990.
1885-14 Black Leadership Commission on AIDS, NYC, NY, $25,000. For advocacy and technical assistance. 1990.
1885-15 Brooklyn College of the City University of New York, Brooklyn, NY, $30,000. For health care internships in public health, medicine and research for students at SUNY Health Science Center. 1990.
1885-16 Capital District Center for Drug Abuse Research and Treatment, Albany, NY, $174,000. For creation of center for development and utilization of new drug treatments for addiction, with clinical trials in New York City. Grant administered by Albany Medical College. 1990.
1885-17 Childrens Health Fund, NYC, NY, $50,000. For general support. 1990.
1885-18 Citizens Commission on AIDS, NYC, NY, $25,000. For general support for efforts to increase public understanding of AIDS. 1990.
1885-19 City College of the City University of New York, NYC, NY, $300,000. For Gateway to Higher Education/Bridge to Medicine Program which helps minority students develop necessary skills for advanced study and careers in science, technology and medicine. 1990.
1885-20 City University of New York, Hunter-Bellevue School of Nursing, NYC, NY, $122,100. For Nursing Student Recruitment Project. 1990.
1885-21 City University of New York, Hunter-Bellevue School of Nursing, NYC, NY, $29,000. For special educational assistance program. 1990.
1885-22 City University of New York, Medical School, Sophie Davis School of Biomedical Education, NYC, NY, $100,000. For science education/medical research program for minority students from high school to graduate school to encourage them to choose careers in research sciences. 1990.
1885-23 City University of New York, Office of Academic Affairs: Division of Health and Education Programs, NYC, NY, $150,000. For Evening/Weekend Associate Degree Program in Nursing at Borough of Manhattan Community College. 1990.
1885-24 City University of New York, Office of Academic Affairs: Division of Health and Education Programs, NYC, NY, $25,000. For summer remediation program for minority

nursing students at New York City Technical College. 1990.

1885-25 Cold Spring Harbor Laboratory, Cold Spring Harbor, NY, $60,000. For study of three-dimensional structure of TAT protein of HIV virus using X-ray crystallography. 1990.

1885-26 Columbia University, College of Physicians and Surgeons, NYC, NY, $386,160. For research on basic biology of Alzheimer's disease. 1990.

1885-27 Columbia University, College of Physicians and Surgeons, NYC, NY, $218,000. For oncogene research. 1990.

1885-28 Columbia University, College of Physicians and Surgeons, NYC, NY, $90,000. For research into molecular mechanisms of latency in AIDS virus infection. 1990.

1885-29 Columbia University, College of Physicians and Surgeons, NYC, NY, $43,990. For visiting AIDS researcher from China. 1990.

1885-30 Columbia University, College of Physicians and Surgeons: Center for the Study of Society and Medicine, NYC, NY, $88,506. For Clinical Externship Program in Human Rights and Health Care which places fourth-year medical students with groups providing health care to refugees, rural migrants and isolated tribal and village residents in developing countries. 1990.

1885-31 Columbia University, School of Nursing, NYC, NY, $65,948. For clinical training program and minority recruitment effort. 1990.

1885-32 Cooperative Home Care Associates, Bronx, NY, $75,000. For Home Care Worker Education Project to train home care paraprofessionals to become licensed practical nurses. 1990.

1885-33 Cornell University Medical College, Department of Cell Biology and Anatomy, NYC, NY, $101,192. For study, heart embryogenesis and development. 1990.

1885-34 Cornell University Medical College, Department of Medicine, Division of Hematology-Oncology, NYC, NY, $85,000. For immunology research on macrophage deactivation factor. 1990.

1885-35 Correctional Association of New York, NYC, NY, $30,000. For AIDS in Prison Project. 1990.

1885-36 Dana-Farber Cancer Institute, Boston, MA, $75,000. For research into role of HIV glycoproteins in development of AIDS virus. 1990.

1885-37 Gay Mens Health Crisis (GMHC), NYC, NY, $25,000. For Music for Life benefit concert. 1990.

1885-38 Greater New York Hospital Association, NYC, NY, $143,100. For Project L.I.N.C. (Ladders in Nursing Careers) which will pay for educational expenses of 50 students, most of whom are from low-income minority backgrounds. 1990.

1885-39 Haitian Community Health Information and Referral Center, Brooklyn, NY, $25,000. For general support. 1990.

1885-40 Harlem Interfaith Counseling Service, NYC, NY, $50,000. For full-day pre-kindergarten learning laboratory which serves children from recently homeless families. 1990.

1885-41 Harvard University, School of Public Health, Boston, MA, $200,000. For

investigation into development of less virulent strain of AIDS virus, for use as potential natural vaccine. 1990.

1885-42 Health Action Resource Center, NYC, NY, $30,000. For West Harlem Community Health Planning Project. 1990.

1885-43 Helene Fuld School of Nursing, NYC, NY, $30,000. For nursing career advancement program. 1990.

1885-44 Hispanic AIDS Forum, NYC, NY, $25,000. For general support. 1990.

1885-45 Hospital Audiences, NYC, NY, $30,000. For AIDS prevention theater workshops to educate public school adolescents about AIDS prevention and drug addiction. 1990.

1885-46 Hospital League/Local 1199 Training and Upgrading Fund, NYC, NY, $20,000. For summer education program which trains parents who are working union members for higher-paying jobs in health care. 1990.

1885-47 Hunter College of the City University of New York, Division of Social Sciences, NYC, NY, $25,000. For expansion of Minority Access to Research Careers program which prepares undergraduate minority students for graduate school and research careers in alcohol, drug abuse and mental health. 1990.

1885-48 Hunter College of the City University of New York, School of Health Sciences, NYC, NY, $25,000. For Diego Lopez Center for action and research on AIDS and drugs. 1990.

1885-49 International Center for the Disabled (ICD), NYC, NY, $25,000. For vocational rehabilitation and educational work. 1990.

1885-50 International Womens Health Coalition, NYC, NY, $25,000. For general support. 1990.

1885-51 Irvington Institute for Medical Research, NYC, NY, $10,000. For symposium entitled Immunology in the 21st Century. 1990.

1885-52 John Jay College of Criminal Justice of the City University of New York, Office of Substance Abuse Prevention Programs, NYC, NY, $20,000. For Parent Leadership Project which provides education, resources and assistance to parents associations in eight school districts. 1990.

1885-53 Laban/Bartenieff Institute of Movement Studies, NYC, NY, $30,000. For summer workshops for New York City physical education teachers. 1990.

1885-54 Lambda Legal Defense and Education Fund, NYC, NY, $25,000. For AIDS project. 1990.

1885-55 Legal Action Center of the City of New York, NYC, NY, $20,000. For HIV Legal Services Initiative. 1990.

1885-56 Legal Aid Society, NYC, NY, $25,000. For Prisoner's Rights Project to protect rights of New York State prisoners infected with HIV virus, and to secure appropriate treatment and services. 1990.

1885-57 Little Sisters of the Assumption Family Health Service, NYC, NY, $20,000. For Family Life Program. 1990.

1885-58 Little Sisters of the Assumption Family Health Service, NYC, NY, $20,000. For Family Life Program. 1990.

1885-59 Long Island Jewish Medical Center, Division of Hematology-Oncology, New Hyde Park, NY, $174,048. For clinical trial of variety of chemicals on chronic lymphatic leukemia cells. 1990.

1885-60 MFY Legal Services, NYC, NY, $10,000. For AIDS Project which provides legal representation to poor people living with AIDS. 1990.

1885-61 Montefiore Medical Center, Bronx, NY, $290,067. For study of infants born to AIDS-infected mothers who are also intravenous drug users. 1990.

1885-62 Montefiore Medical Center, Bronx, NY, $81,180. For study, genetic basis for pathogenesis of colon cancer. 1990.

1885-63 Montefiore Medical Center, Bronx, NY, $48,650. For study, gene expression during cardiac hypertrophy. 1990.

1885-64 Montefiore Medical Center, Department of Epidemiology and Social Medicine, Bronx, NY, $235,000. For research program on infectious diseases and drug abuse at Rikers Island. 1990.

1885-65 Mount Sinai Hospital and Medical Center, NYC, NY, $117,990. For research on etiology of colon cancer. 1990.

1885-66 Mount Sinai Hospital and Medical Center, NYC, NY, $108,594. For infection-permissive immunization with influenza virus neuraminidase. 1990.

1885-67 Mount Sinai Hospital and Medical Center, NYC, NY, $90,000. For study, mechanisms for activating and inhibiting growth of oncogenes. 1990.

1885-68 Mount Sinai Hospital and Medical Center, NYC, NY, $65,000. For study, mucin-associated antigens in colon cancer. 1990.

1885-69 Mount Sinai Hospital and Medical Center, Department of Community Medicine, NYC, NY, $150,000. For research on AIDS reduction in East Harlem. 1990.

1885-70 Narcotic and Drug Research, Albany, NY, $23,819. For dissemination of information on activities of New York City cocaine-crack multidisciplinary research conferences. 1990.

1885-71 Narcotic and Drug Research, Albany, NY, $10,000. For International Working Group on AIDS and Drug Abuse. 1990.

1885-72 Natural Resources Defense Council, NYC, NY, $50,000. To identify sources of lead and other environmental toxins poisoning children of New York City. 1990.

1885-73 New York Academy of Medicine, NYC, NY, $75,000. For expansion of Being Healthy, junior high school program that includes lessons on substance abuse prevention, nutrition, adolescent growth and development, AIDS prevention and emotional health. 1990.

1885-74 New York Black Womens Health Project, Brooklyn, NY, $20,000. For general support. 1990.

1885-75 New York Hospital-Cornell Medical Center, Department of Medicine, Clinical Epidemiology Unit, NYC, NY, $30,000. For research and education program to increase voluntary HIV testing among women of child-bearing age. 1990.

1885-76 New York Hospital-Cornell Medical Center, Department of Medicine, Division of Infectious Diseases, NYC, NY, $100,000. For study, pathogenesis and interaction of human T cell leukemia virus type (HTLV-l) with AIDS virus. 1990.

1885-77 New York Hospital-Cornell Medical Center, Payne Whitney Psychiatric Clinic, NYC, NY, $130,000. For study, understanding relationship between drug use and violence. 1990.

1885-78 New York University, Division of Nursing, NYC, NY, $100,000. For recruitment program and Urban Health Care Project. 1990.

1885-79 New York University, Division of Nursing, NYC, NY, $18,500. For Urban Health Care Project to place teams of nursing and medical students in underserved communities during summer to provide health care to homeless, families on welfare and adolescent runaways. 1990.

1885-80 New York University Medical Center, NYC, NY, $160,000. For collaboration on new type of anti-HIV compound. 1990.

1885-81 New York University Medical Center, NYC, NY, $125,000. For study, pulmonary disorders and immune responses in HIV-infected individuals. 1990.

1885-82 New York University Medical Center, NYC, NY, $125,000. For New York Task Force on Immigrant Health to determine prevalence of various diseases among disparate immigrant groups and investigate cultural, linguistic and socioeconomic issues that erect barriers between physician and immigrant patient. 1990.

1885-83 New York University Medical Center, NYC, NY, $50,000. For transfer factor research. 1990.

1885-84 New York University Medical Center, Department of Cell Biology, NYC, NY, $55,000. For tumor rejection antigens. 1990.

1885-85 New York University Medical Center, Department of Medicine, NYC, NY, $117,207. For research into role of neutrophils in pathogenesis of coronary artery thrombosis. 1990.

1885-86 Osborne Association, NYC, NY, $10,000. For special project support for AIDS prevention among released inmates. 1990.

1885-87 Planned Parenthood of New York City, NYC, NY, $100,000. For AIDS prevention in Central Harlem and renewed general support. 1990.

1885-88 Public Health Research Institute of the City of New York, NYC, NY, $227,500. For study, molecular disruption of life cycle of HIV virus. 1990.

1885-89 Public Health Research Institute of the City of New York, NYC, NY, $121,540. For research on staphylococcus aureus. 1990.

1885-90 Public Health Research Institute of the City of New York, NYC, NY, $100,000. For development of more sensitive test for HIV infection using recombinant-RNA hybridization probes. 1990.

1885-91 Rockefeller University, NYC, NY, $200,000. For two studies on neuroendocrine function and endogenous opioid system in drug addicts. 1990.

1885-92 Rockefeller University, NYC, NY, $100,000. For research into immunobiology of AIDS. 1990.

1885-93 Saint Johns Episcopal Hospital-South Shore, Far Rockaway, NY, $25,000. For Teen Incentive Program, pregnancy prevention program which uses hospital staff as mentors for 9th and 10th graders. 1990.

1885-94 Saint Vincents Hospital and Medical Center of New York, NYC, NY, $50,000. For supplemental financial aid for nursing students. 1990.

1885-95 State University of New York, Health Science Center at Brooklyn, Brooklyn, NY, $25,000. For curriculum development for Physician's Assistant Training Program. 1990.

1886
Clarence and Anne Dillon Dunwalke Trust
1270 Ave. of the Americas, Rm. 2300
New York 10020   (212) 315-8343

Trust established in 1969 in NY.
Donor(s): Clarence Dillon.‡
Foundation type: Independent
Financial data (yr. ended 06/30/91): Assets, $17,711,065 (M); gifts received, $53,154; expenditures, $1,299,958; qualifying distributions, $1,139,700, including $1,126,000 for 52 grants (high: $250,000; low: $500).
Purpose and activities: Emphasis on hospitals, education, public affairs, the arts, and community funds. Grants primarily to present beneficiary organizations and for special proposals developed by the trustees.
Fields of interest: Education, hospitals, arts, medical research, public policy, community funds.
Types of support: Fellowships, endowment funds, equipment, research, annual campaigns, operating budgets, building funds, special projects, general purposes.
Limitations: Giving primarily in NJ and NY. No grants to individuals; no loans.
Application information: New requests seldom considered. Application form not required.
  Deadline(s): None
  Board meeting date(s): Nov. and as required
  Write: Crosby R. Smith, Trustee
Trustees: Philip D. Allen, Joan M. Bryan, Mark M. Collins, Jr., Phyllis Dillon Collins, C. Douglas Dillon, Dorothy Dillon Eweson, David H. Peipers, Crosby R. Smith.
Number of staff: 1 part-time professional.
EIN: 237043773
Recent health grants:
1886-1 American Federation for Aging Research, NYC, NY, $25,000. For general support. 1991.
1886-2 Morristown Memorial Hospital, Morristown, NJ, $150,000. For Photopheresis Program. 1991.

1887
Oliver S. and Jennie R. Donaldson Charitable Trust ▼
c/o U.S. Trust Co. of New York
114 West 47th St.
New York 10036-1530

Trust established in 1969 in NY.
Donor(s): Oliver S. Donaldson.‡
Foundation type: Independent
Financial data (yr. ended 12/31/90): Assets, $19,039,552 (M); expenditures, $1,640,738; qualifying distributions, $1,449,535, including $1,441,483 for 68 grants (high: $100,000; low: $3,000).
Purpose and activities: Interests include cancer research and treatment, child welfare and youth agencies, hospitals and health agencies, elementary, secondary, and higher education; support also for wildlife preservation, and the town of Pawling, NY; eleven named institutions are given first consideration.

Fields of interest: Medical research, cancer, hospitals, health services, child welfare, youth, elementary education, secondary education, higher education, wildlife.
Limitations: Giving primarily in the Northeast, with emphasis on MA. No grants to individuals.
Publications: Application guidelines.
Application information:
  Initial approach: Letter
  Deadline(s): None
  Board meeting date(s): Quarterly
  Write: Anne L. Smith-Ganey, Asst. V.P., U.S. Trust Co. of New York
Trustees: Wilson W. Curtis, William E. Murray, John F. Sisk, Pamela C. Smith.
EIN: 046229044

1888
Dorot Foundation
100 Park Ave.
New York 10017

Incorporated in 1958 in NY as Joy and Samuel Ungerleider Foundation.
Donor(s): Joy G. Ungerleider-Mayerson, D.S. and R.H. Gottesman Foundation.
Foundation type: Independent
Financial data (yr. ended 03/31/91): Assets, $23,633,935 (M); expenditures, $2,790,782; qualifying distributions, $2,505,472, including $2,421,462 for 72 grants (high: $1,000,000; low: $50; average: $2,000-$30,000) and $28,501 for 5 grants to individuals (high: $7,900; low: $3,660).
Purpose and activities: Grants primarily for higher education and educational organizations; support also for Jewish organizations.
Fields of interest: Higher education, medical education, educational associations, Israel, Jewish giving.
Limitations: Giving primarily in the U.S. and Israel.
Application information: Contributes only to pre-selected organizations. Applications not accepted.
Officers and Directors:* Joy G. Ungerleider-Mayerson,* Pres.; Philip Mayerson,* V.P.; Edgar Wachenheim III, V.P.; Peter C. Siegfried, Secy.; Benjamin Glowatz, Treas.
EIN: 136116927

1889
Paul P. Dosberg Foundation, Inc.
c/o M. Lewis, Esq.
1010 Times Square Bldg.
Rochester 14614

Established in 1956.
Donor(s): Paul P. Dosberg.‡
Foundation type: Independent
Financial data (yr. ended 12/31/90): Assets, $2,447,524 (M); gifts received, $25,000; expenditures, $565,956; qualifying distributions, $549,161, including $549,161 for 2 grants (high: $519,161; low: $30,000).
Fields of interest: Higher education, medical education, business education.
Types of support: Research, endowment funds.
Limitations: Giving primarily in NY and PA.
Application information:
  Initial approach: Letter
  Deadline(s): Sept. 1

Write: Myron S. Lewis, Secy.
Officer and Trustees:* Myron S. Lewis,* Secy.; Charlotte Kramer, Mark Kramer.
EIN: 166030605

1890
Dover Corporate Giving Program
280 Park Ave.
New York 10017   (212) 922-1640

Purpose and activities: Support for the New York City Urban Coalition, United Fund of Greater New York, and to selected national charities, many of which combat major diseases; employee matching gifts for education in technical fields. The giving program is decentralized with each Dover company making contributions in its community.
Fields of interest: Health, higher education.
Limitations: Giving primarily in headquarters city and major operating locations. No grants for testimonial dinners.
Application information:
Initial approach: Initial contact by letter or phone
Deadline(s): Parent company accepts applications throughout the year but Dover Elevator applications should be submitted by Aug. 1 for funding for the following year
Write: Cloyd Laporte Jr., Secy. and Legal Counsel
Administrators: Cloyd Laporte, Jr., Judy Harrison, Secy.

1891
The Dreitzer Foundation, Inc.
488 Madison Ave.
New York 10022   (212) 935-5500

Established in 1958 in NY.
Foundation type: Independent
Financial data (yr. ended 12/31/90): Assets, $6,116,906 (M); expenditures, $262,584; qualifying distributions, $239,369, including $190,500 for 27 grants (high: $30,000; low: $1,000).
Fields of interest: Jewish giving, youth, social services, health.
Limitations: Giving primarily in NY and FL.
Application information:
Write: Leonard Franklin, Pres.
Officers: Leonard Franklin, Pres.; David B. Goldfarb, Secy.-Treas.
Trustees: Shirley Dreitzer, Judith Wallach.
EIN: 136162509

1892
Dreyfus Charitable Foundation
(Formerly Dreyfus Medical Foundation)
Four West 58th St.
New York 10019

Established in 1961 in NY.
Donor(s): Jack J. Dreyfus, Jr., John Dreyfus, Joan D. Blout.
Foundation type: Operating
Financial data (yr. ended 12/31/90): Assets, $9,680,796 (M); expenditures, $3,778,049; qualifying distributions, $3,435,531, including

$500,000 for 1 grant and $2,873,913 for foundation-administered programs.
Purpose and activities: Grants limited to research of the drug Diphenylhydantoin (DPH), also known as Phenytoin (PHT).
Fields of interest: Medical research.
Types of support: Research.
Limitations: Giving primarily in NY. No grants to individuals.
Application information: Contributes only to pre-selected organizations. Applications not accepted.
Officers and Directors:* Jack Dreyfus,* Pres.; Helen C. Raudonat,* V.P.; Arnold D. Friedman,* Treas.; John Dreyfus.
EIN: 136086089

1893
Jean and Louis Dreyfus Foundation, Inc.
c/o Decker Hubbard and Welden
30 Rockefeller Plaza
New York 10112   (212) 581-7575

Incorporated about 1978 in NY.
Donor(s): Louis Dreyfus.‡
Foundation type: Independent
Financial data (yr. ended 12/31/90): Assets, $14,209,195 (M); expenditures, $834,869; qualifying distributions, $754,793, including $723,700 for 78 grants (high: $25,000; low: $1,700; average: $5,000-$10,000).
Purpose and activities: Grants primarily to established institutions of the arts and medical research; some support also for health and hospitals, and social services, including hospices, youth agencies, literacy, and programs for drug abuse.
Fields of interest: Arts, medical research, health, hospitals, social services, hospices, youth, literacy, drug abuse.
Limitations: Giving primarily in the New York, NY, area. No grants to individuals.
Application information: Application form not required.
Initial approach: Proposal
Copies of proposal: 2
Board meeting date(s): Spring and fall
Write: Thomas J. Hubbard, Secy.
Officers: Valli V. Dreyfus Firth, Pres.; Thomas J. Sweeney, V.P. and Treas.; Nicholas L.D. Firth, V.P.; Thomas J. Hubbard, Secy.
Number of staff: 1 part-time professional.
EIN: 132947180

1894
The Max and Victoria Dreyfus Foundation, Inc. ▼
575 Madison Ave.
New York 10022   (212) 605-0354

Incorporated in 1965 in NY.
Donor(s): Victoria Dreyfus,‡ Max Dreyfus.‡
Foundation type: Independent
Financial data (yr. ended 12/31/90): Assets, $41,325,517 (M); expenditures, $1,970,557; qualifying distributions, $1,483,070, including $1,483,070 for grants.
Purpose and activities: Support for hospitals, medical research, education, health and social services, with emphasis on youth and aid to the aged and handicapped, and cultural programs.

Fields of interest: Hospitals, medical research, health services, social services, youth, aged, handicapped, cultural programs, education.
Types of support: Research, special projects.
Limitations: No grants to individuals.
Application information:
Initial approach: Letter (not exceeding 5 pages)
Deadline(s): Mar. 31, July 31, and Nov. 30
Board meeting date(s): Usually in mid-Feb., June, and Oct.
Final notification: 2 weeks following board meetings
Write: Ms. Lucy Gioia, Admin. Asst.
Officers and Directors:* David J. Oppenheim,* Pres.; Nancy E. Oddo,* V.P.; Norman S. Portenoy,* V.P.; Mary P. Surrey, V.P.; Winifred Riggs Portenoy,* Secy.-Treas.
Number of staff: 1 full-time support; 1 part-time support.
EIN: 131687573

1895
The Caleb C. and Julia W. Dula Educational and Charitable Foundation
c/o Manufacturers Hanover Trust Co.
270 Park Ave., 21st Fl.
New York 10017   (212) 270-9066

Trust established in 1939 in NY.
Donor(s): Julia W. Dula.‡
Foundation type: Independent
Financial data (yr. ended 12/31/90): Assets, $22,052,548 (M); expenditures, $1,275,525; qualifying distributions, $1,141,862, including $957,000 for 70 grants (high: $200,000; low: $2,000).
Purpose and activities: Grants to charities which the Dulas supported during their lifetime, with emphasis on higher and secondary education, hospitals, libraries, social service agencies, child welfare, church support, cultural programs, and historic preservation.
Fields of interest: Higher education, secondary education, hospitals, libraries, social services, child welfare, religion, historic preservation, cultural programs, animal welfare.
Types of support: Operating budgets.
Limitations: No grants to individuals; no loans.
Application information: Application form not required.
Copies of proposal: 1
Deadline(s): None
Board meeting date(s): Usually spring and fall
Write: Ms. G. Price-Fitch, Trust Officer, Manufacturers Hanover Trust Co.
Trustees: Margaret C. Taylor, Julia P. Wightman, Orrin S. Wightman III, Manufacturers Hanover Trust Co.
EIN: 136045790

1896
The Dun & Bradstreet Corporation Foundation ▼
299 Park Ave.
New York 10171   (212) 593-6736

Incorporated in 1953 in DE.
Donor(s): The Dun & Bradstreet Group.
Foundation type: Company-sponsored
Financial data (yr. ended 12/31/90): Assets, $18,993,903 (M); expenditures, $3,050,780;

qualifying distributions, $3,027,859, including $962,980 for 347 grants (high: $186,100; low: $50; average: $200-$15,000) and $2,064,879 for employee matching gifts.

Purpose and activities: To assist charitable and educational institutions, with emphasis on cultural programs, community funds, higher education, health and welfare, and youth agencies.

Fields of interest: Community funds, higher education, health, youth, cultural programs, social services.

Types of support: Operating budgets, continuing support, annual campaigns, general purposes, employee-related scholarships, employee matching gifts.

Limitations: No grants to individuals (except for employee-related scholarships), or for building or endowment funds, or research; no loans.

Application information: Application form not required.

 Initial approach: Letter or proposal
 Copies of proposal: 1
 Deadline(s): Submit proposal preferably in
  Sept. or Oct.; no set deadline
 Board meeting date(s): Semiannually
 Final notification: 4 weeks
 Write: Juliann Gill, Admin.

Officers and Trustees:* Charles W. Moritz,* Pres.; David S. Fehr, V.P.; William O. Frohlich, V.P.; Virginia Simone, Secy.; Steven G. Klein, Treas.; Alan J. Klutch, Controller; Edwin A. Bescherer, Jr., Robert E. Weissman.

Number of staff: 2
EIN: 136148188

1897
Dyson Foundation ▼

230 Park Ave., Rm. 659
New York 10169   (518) 377-1576
Application address: 740 Union St., Schenectady, NY 12305; Tel.: (518) 377-1576

Trust established in 1949 in NY; incorporated in 1957 in DE.
Donor(s): Charles H. Dyson, Margaret M. Dyson,‡ The Dyson-Kissner-Moran Corp.
Foundation type: Independent
Financial data (yr. ended 12/31/90): Assets, $29,534 (M); gifts received, $4,788,520; expenditures, $4,819,294; qualifying distributions, $4,819,294, including $4,780,200 for 52 grants (high: $500,000; low: $500; average: $1,000-$50,000).
Purpose and activities: Grants that emphasize strategies and services that improve the lives and opportunities of poor and disadvantaged children; some support also for cultural programs, higher education and medical research; small targeted grants program in Dutchess County, NY.
Fields of interest: Arts, cultural programs, medical research, health services, medical education, education, disadvantaged, child welfare, youth.
Types of support: Building funds, endowment funds, research, special projects, scholarship funds, continuing support, fellowships.
Limitations: Giving primarily in the New York City metropolitan area and Dutchess County, NY. Other grant recipients are generally national in scope or impact. No grants to individuals.
Publications: Annual report (including application guidelines), 990-PF.

Application information: Unsolicited proposals are not accepted, but letter or telephone inquiries are welcomed. Application form not required.
 Copies of proposal: 1
 Deadline(s): None
 Board meeting date(s): Quarterly
 Write: Diana M. Gurieva, Exec. Dir.
Officers and Trustees:* Anne E. Dyson, M.D.,* Pres.; Ernest H. Lorch,* V.P.; John H. FitzSimons, Secy.; Robert R. Dyson,* Treas.; Charles H. Dyson, Joseph V. Mariner, Jr., John A. Moran.
Number of staff: 1 full-time professional; 1 part-time professional; 1 full-time support; 1 part-time support.
EIN: 136084888
Recent health grants:
1897-1 Big Apple Circus, NYC, NY, $50,000. For Clown Care Unit at Harlem Hospital. 1991.
1897-2 Childrens Defense Fund, DC, $50,000. For post-graduate fellowship program in Child Health Advocacy. 1991.
1897-3 Childrens Hospital, Division of General Pediatrics, Boston, MA, $258,135. For faculty development program to prepare young junior faculty members to address increasingly complex array of medical and social problems confronting children and their families (such as family disorganization, poverty, homelessness, and chronic disease, including HIV infection). 1991.
1897-4 Cornell University Medical College, Margaret M. Dyson Vision Research Institute, Departments of Ophthalmology and Pediatrics, NYC, NY, $1,500,000. For construction of and equipment for state-of-the-art research laboratory complex and toward operating support through endowment. 1991.
1897-5 Dana-Farber Cancer Institute, Department of Pediatrics, Boston, MA, $200,000. For continuing support for research in pediatric hematologic and oncologic diseases, with particular emphasis on bone marrow transplantation and engraftment. 1991.
1897-6 Hole in the Wall Gang Camp, Ashford, CT, $100,000. To establish and equip health care dispensary at recreational facility that provides year-round camping experiences for children who have cancer and other life-threatening blood disorders. 1991.
1897-7 Kildonan School, Amenia, NY, $19,500. For scholarship support for dyslexic students from Dutchess County at this specialized school. 1991.
1897-8 Northern Dutchess Hospital, Rhinebeck, NY, $10,000. Toward capital campaign. 1991.
1897-9 Planned Parenthood of Dutchess/Ulster, Poughkeepsie, NY, $25,000. For general support for pregnancy prevention programs. 1991.
1897-10 Yale University, Dwight Hall, New Haven, CT, $10,000. Toward development of book on experiences of children with cancer and other life-threatening blood disorders. 1991.

1898
Eastman Kodak Charitable Trust ▼

c/o Eastman Kodak Co.
343 State St.
Rochester 14650-0316   (716) 724-3127

Trust established in 1952 in NY.
Donor(s): Eastman Kodak Co.
Foundation type: Company-sponsored
Financial data (yr. ended 12/31/90): Assets, $21,542,883 (M); expenditures, $5,632,615; qualifying distributions, $5,611,023, including $5,611,023 for grants.
Purpose and activities: Support primarily for the United Way; pre-college, higher, and minority education; and environmental affairs.
Fields of interest: Community funds, education, education—minorities, higher education, environment.
Types of support: Continuing support, fellowships, scholarship funds, operating budgets.
Limitations: Giving primarily in high employment locations, including Rochester, NY; Kingsport, TN; Windsor, CO; Columbia, SC; and Longview, TX. Giving nationally only for higher education. No grants to individuals, or for matching gifts; no loans; low priority given to building or endowment funds.
Publications: Corporate giving report.
Application information: Contributes only to pre-selected organizations. Applications not accepted.
 Board meeting date(s): Monthly
 Write: Stanley C. Wright, Dir., Corp. Contribs.
Trustee: Chase Lincoln First Bank, N.A.
Number of staff: None.
EIN: 166015274
Recent health grants:
1898-1 Al Sigl Center for Rehabilitation Agencies, Rochester, NY, $75,000. 1990.
1898-2 Alzheimers Center for Upper East Tennessee, Kingsport, TN, $10,000. 1990.
1898-3 Compeer, Rochester, NY, $15,000. 1990.
1898-4 Highland Hospital Foundation, Rochester, NY, $40,000. 1990.
1898-5 Holston Valley Health Care Foundation, Kingsport, TN, $100,000. 1990.
1898-6 Holston Valley Health Care Foundation, Kingsport, TN, $100,000. 1990.
1898-7 Mountain Region Speech and Hearing Center, Kingsport, TN, $25,000. 1990.
1898-8 Occupational Physicians Scholarship Fund, NYC, NY, $12,500. 1990.
1898-9 Providence Hospital, Columbia, SC, $10,000. 1990.
1898-10 Richland Memorial Hospital, Columbia, SC, $15,000. 1990.
1898-11 University of Cincinnati Medical Center, Cincinnati, OH, $10,000. 1990.

1899
Eastman Kodak Company Giving Program

343 State St.
Rochester 14650-0316   (716) 724-9487

Financial data (yr. ended 12/31/91): Total giving, $17,800,000 for grants.
Purpose and activities: "Caring about communities - through the support of education, helath and human services, and community revitalization - is integral to our success and to our character. There are as many corporate philosophies of giving as there are corporate givers. When we describe our own, we say Kodak contributes time, energy and funding where we believe substantial gains can be made. We administer our corporate contributions in the same way we manage our business enterprises -

making investments with a dedication to achieving positive results. Most often, these investments are made in behalf of our employees, present and future, and the communities where they live and work." Focus is on education, health, human services, community revitalization, culture, and the arts. Products and services are donated when they better meet the need than cash. Figures include foundation giving.

Fields of interest: Secondary education, museums, public policy, science and technology, theater, music, performing arts, women, Native Americans, youth, arts, community development, educational research, engineering, humanities, community funds, cultural programs, environment, health, chemistry, computer sciences, education—minorities, higher education, conservation, health services, minorities, public affairs.

Types of support: Annual campaigns, continuing support, fellowships, operating budgets, research, employee-related scholarships, scholarship funds, seed money, employee volunteer services, donated products.

Limitations: Giving primarily in areas of company operations.

Publications: Corporate giving report.

Application information:
  Initial approach: Written request
  Copies of proposal: 1
  Deadline(s): None
  Board meeting date(s): Ongoing process
  Final notification: 2-4 weeks
  Write: Stanley C. Wright, Dir., Corp. Contribs.

Number of staff: 1 full-time professional; 1 full-time support.

1900
The Edouard Foundation, Inc. ▼
c/o Phillips Nizer et al.
31 West 52nd St., 19th Fl.
New York 10019   (212) 977-9700

Established in 1987 in NY.
Donor(s): Lyliane D. Finch.
Foundation type: Independent
Financial data (yr. ended 12/31/90): Assets, $1,500,181 (M); gifts received, $750,000; expenditures, $1,203,221; qualifying distributions, $1,193,946, including $1,192,000 for 31 grants (high: $200,000; low: $2,000; average: $10,000-$50,000).
Purpose and activities: Giving primarily for health, including hospitals, health associations and services, and AIDS research; support also for domestic and international human services, including youth, child welfare, social services, international relief, and human rights.
Fields of interest: Health, hospitals, health associations, health services, AIDS, youth, child welfare, social services, international relief, human rights, Native Americans.
Types of support: Research, general purposes.
Limitations: No grants to individuals.
Application information: Application form not required.
  Initial approach: Proposal
  Deadline(s): None
  Write: Gerald Meyer, Esq., Treas.
Officers and Directors:* Lyliane D. Finch,* Pres.; Edwin A. Margolius, Secy.; Gerald Meyer, Treas.; Arnold Finch, Beatrice Phillipe.

EIN: 133446831
Recent health grants:
1900-1 American Cancer Society, NYC, NY, $40,000. 1990.
1900-2 American Foundation for AIDS Research, NYC, NY, $40,000. 1990.
1900-3 Arthritis Foundation, NYC, NY, $30,000. 1990.
1900-4 International Child Health and Diarrheal Disease Foundation, Columbia, MD, $10,000. 1990.
1900-5 Juvenile Diabetes Foundation International, NYC, NY, $40,000. 1990.
1900-6 National Jewish Center for Immunology and Respiratory Medicine, NYC, NY, $15,000. 1990.
1900-7 National Kidney Foundation, NYC, NY, $30,000. 1990.
1900-8 Thomas A. Dooley Foundation, NYC, NY, $10,000. 1990.

1901
The Eisner Family Fund
c/o Executive Monetary Mgmt., Inc.
919 Third Ave.
New York 10022

Established in 1988 in NY.
Donor(s): Michael D. Eisner.
Foundation type: Independent
Financial data (yr. ended 12/31/91): Assets, $5,392,046 (M); expenditures, $454,748; qualifying distributions, $417,321, including $417,321 for 109 grants (high: $103,000; low: $85).
Purpose and activities: Support primarily for a Jewish home and hospital for the aged and higher education; giving also to hospitals, health organizations, medical research, museums and other cultural organizations, social services, and public media.
Fields of interest: Jewish welfare, aged, higher education, hospitals, health, medical research, cultural programs, museums, social services, media and communications.
Types of support: Continuing support.
Limitations: No grants to individuals.
Application information: Contributes only to pre-selected organizations. Applications not accepted.
Trustees: Margaret D. Eisner, Michael D. Eisner, Margot E. Freedman.
Number of staff: None.
EIN: 133486425

1902
W. H. Ellworth Trust for
Hawthorne-Cedar Knolls School, et al.
c/o U.S. Trust Co. of New York
114 West 47th St.
New York 10036

Foundation type: Independent
Financial data (yr. ended 01/31/91): Assets, $2,647,618 (M); expenditures, $139,793; qualifying distributions, $130,842, including $107,831 for 21 grants (high: $5,135; low: $5,134).
Fields of interest: Social services, education, health, religion—Christian.
Limitations: No grants to individuals.

Application information: Contributes only to pre-selected organizations. Applications not accepted.
Trustee: U.S. Trust Co. of New York.
EIN: 136073049

1903
Blanche T. Enders Charitable Trust
c/o Chemical Bank, Admin. Serv. Dept.
30 Rockefeller Plaza
New York 10112   (212) 621-2180

Foundation type: Independent
Financial data (yr. ended 12/31/91): Assets, $3,584,295 (M); expenditures, $136,609; qualifying distributions, $107,758, including $107,500 for 12 grants (high: $15,000; low: $2,500).
Purpose and activities: "Grants are restricted to organizations involved with children's education, care of the blind, crippled or aged, and the elimination of cruelty to animals."
Fields of interest: Child welfare, social services, Catholic giving, Catholic welfare, education, animal welfare, health, hospitals.
Limitations: Giving primarily in NY. No grants to individuals.
Application information: Application form not required.
  Initial approach: Letter
  Deadline(s): None
  Write: Patricia Kelly
Trustee: Chemical Bank.
EIN: 136164229

1904
The Equitable Foundation, Inc. ▼
787 Seventh Ave., 39th Fl.
New York 10019   (212) 554-3511

Established in 1986 in NY.
Donor(s): The Equitable.
Foundation type: Company-sponsored
Financial data (yr. ended 09/30/91): Assets, $920,626 (M); gifts received, $4,007,853; expenditures, $4,566,269; qualifying distributions, $4,566,269, including $1,325,000 for 115 grants (high: $75,000; low: $1,000; average: $5,000-$25,000), $65,000 for 35 grants to individuals (high: $4,000; low: $750) and $3,160,434 for employee matching gifts.
Purpose and activities: Giving primarily for minority education, arts and community services, AIDS, and equal opportunity programs.
Fields of interest: Higher education, education—minorities, arts, AIDS, minorities, secondary education, disadvantaged.
Types of support: Employee matching gifts, continuing support, general purposes, employee-related scholarships, special projects.
Limitations: No support for political, religious, or international purposes. No grants to individuals (other than employee-related scholarships).
Publications: Informational brochure.
Application information: Application form not required.
  Initial approach: Letter
  Copies of proposal: 1
  Deadline(s): None
  Board meeting date(s): Quarterly
  Write: Kathleen A. Carlson, Pres.

Officers and Directors:* Nancy H. Green,* Chair., Pres., and C.E.O.; Gordon G. Dinsmore, Sr. V.P.; Brian S. O'Neil, Sr. V.P.; Patricia A. Kelly, V.P.and Secy.; Katherine A. Mason, V.P. and Controller; William T. McCaffrey,* V.P.; Clifford M. Warren, V.P. and General Counsel; Kathleen A. Carlson, Exec. Dir.; Eleanor B. Sheldon.
Number of staff: 4 full-time professional; 2 full-time support.
EIN: 133340512
Recent health grants:
1904-1 American Foundation for AIDS Research, NYC, NY, $25,000. 1990.
1904-2 Design Industries Foundation for AIDS (DIFFA), NYC, NY, $10,000. 1990.
1904-3 Life and Health Insurance Medical Research Fund, DC, $65,000. 1990.
1904-4 National Medical Fellowships, NYC, NY, $10,000. 1990.

1905
Ernst & Young Foundation
c/o Ernst & Young
787 Seventh Ave.
New York 10019   (212) 773-3000

Established in 1990 in NY due to the merger of the Arthur Young Foundation and the Ernst & Whinney Foundation.
Foundation type: Company-sponsored
Financial data (yr. ended 06/30/90): Assets, $8,416,000 (M); gifts received, $1,044,000; expenditures, $3,556,000; qualifying distributions, $3,488,000, including $1,079,000 for grants, $258,000 for 13 grants to individuals (high: $37,200; low: $9,300) and $2,151,000 for 6,100 employee matching gifts.
Purpose and activities: Support for education, including business education, higher education, legal education, medical education and education for minorities; also support for accounting, mathematics, educational research, an employee matching gift program, fellowships, and lectureships. Special programs include the tax research grant program, accounting professorships, and doctoral dissertation grants.
Fields of interest: Accounting, business education, education—minorities, educational research, higher education, legal education, mathematics, medical education.
Types of support: Employee matching gifts, fellowships, grants to individuals, lectureships, professorships.
Publications: Informational brochure (including application guidelines).
Application information: Application form not required.
   Initial approach: Write to local office
   Board meeting date(s): Quarterly
   Write: Frank M. Preucil or Charles B. Eldridge
Officers: John J. Schornack, Pres.; Richard J. Dobkin, V.P.; Robert H. Donzelli, V.P.; Aaron Hipscher, V.P.; David B. Pearson, V.P.; Dennis R. Purdum, V.P.
Number of staff: 1 full-time professional; 1 part-time professional; 1 part-time support.
EIN: 136094489

1906
Essel Foundation, Inc.
2500 Westchester Ave., 4th Fl.
Purchase 10577

Established in 1966.
Donor(s): Stephen Lieber, Constance Lieber.
Foundation type: Independent
Financial data (yr. ended 11/30/91): Assets, $14,275,582 (M); gifts received, $2,664,088; expenditures, $1,519,161; qualifying distributions, $1,517,000, including $1,517,000 for 6 grants (high: $1,220,000; low: $2,000; average: $2,000-$1,220,000).
Fields of interest: Jewish giving, higher education, mental health, medical research, psychiatry.
Types of support: Research.
Limitations: No grants to individuals.
Application information: Contributes only to pre-selected organizations. Applications not accepted.
Officers: Constance Lieber, Pres.; Samuel Lieber, Secy.-Treas.
Number of staff: None.
EIN: 136191234

1907
The Ettinger Foundation, Inc.
665 Fifth Ave., No. 200
New York 10022-5305

Incorporated in 1949 in DE.
Donor(s): Members of the Ettinger family.
Foundation type: Independent
Financial data (yr. ended 12/31/90): Assets, $11,534,208 (M); gifts received, $71,554; expenditures, $788,606; qualifying distributions, $631,242, including $609,865 for grants.
Purpose and activities: Giving for higher and secondary education, including scholarships for the children of Prentice-Hall employees; grants also for community funds, health, and youth agencies.
Fields of interest: Higher education, secondary education, community funds, youth, health.
Types of support: Employee-related scholarships, scholarship funds.
Limitations: No grants to individuals (except for employee-related scholarships), or for general support, or building or endowment funds; no loans.
Publications: 990-PF.
Application information:
   Initial approach: Letter
   Copies of proposal: 1
   Deadline(s): None
   Board meeting date(s): Feb., May, Aug., and Nov.
   Write: Richard P. Ettinger, Trustee
Trustees: Lynn P. Babiuka, Richard P. Ettinger, Sharon Ettinger, Elaine P. Hapgood, Rocco Landesman, John P. Powers.
Number of staff: None.
EIN: 066038938

1908
Edward P. Evans Foundation
960 Fifth Ave.
New York 10021

Established in 1983 in VA.

Donor(s): Edward P. Evans.
Foundation type: Independent
Financial data (yr. ended 11/30/91): Assets, $3,125,801 (M); gifts received, $300,000; expenditures, $93,934; qualifying distributions, $60,460, including $58,750 for 9 grants (high: $30,000; low: $250).
Fields of interest: Secondary education, hospitals.
Types of support: General purposes.
Limitations: Giving primarily in VA and MA.
Application information: Application form not required.
   Deadline(s): None
   Write: Edward P. Evans, Trustee
Trustees: Edward P. Evans, Robert S. Evans, Dorsey R. Gardner, Charles J. Queenan, Jr.
EIN: 256232129

1909
The T. M. Evans Foundation, Inc. ▼
250 Park Ave.
New York 10177   (212) 557-5575

Incorporated in 1951 in DE.
Donor(s): Thomas Mellon Evans.
Foundation type: Independent
Financial data (yr. ended 12/31/90): Assets, $4,450,462 (M); expenditures, $1,104,418; qualifying distributions, $1,062,685, including $1,031,000 for 23 grants (high: $500,000; low: $500; average: $1,000).
Purpose and activities: Grants primarily for museums and historic preservation, higher education, hospitals, medical research, music, religion, youth guidance services, and literary activities.
Fields of interest: Museums, historic preservation, higher education, health associations, medical research, music, religion, youth, libraries, language and literature.
Types of support: Annual campaigns, building funds, capital campaigns, continuing support, emergency funds, equipment, general purposes, matching funds, operating budgets, renovation projects, research.
Limitations: Giving primarily in NY. No grants to individuals, or for scholarships or fellowships; no loans.
Application information: Application form not required.
   Initial approach: Proposal
   Copies of proposal: 1
   Deadline(s): None
   Board meeting date(s): Dec.
   Write: Luciano F. Cerrone, Secy.-Treas.
Officers and Trustees:* Thomas Mellon Evans,* Pres.; Luciano F. Cerrone,* Secy.-Treas.; Betty B. Evans, Edward P. Evans, Thomas M. Evans, Jr.
Number of staff: 1 part-time support.
EIN: 256012086
Recent health grants:
1909-1 Fountain House, NYC, NY, $100,000. 1990.
1909-2 New York University Medical Center, NYC, NY, $80,000. 1990.

1910
Fahey Family Foundation
c/o Goldman Sachs & Co., Tax Dept.
85 Broad St.
New York 10004

Established in 1987 in NY.
Donor(s): Peter M. Fahey.
Foundation type: Independent
Financial data (yr. ended 05/31/91): Assets, $279,598 (M); gifts received, $387,935; expenditures, $300,386; qualifying distributions, $295,648, including $295,400 for 53 grants (high: $150,000; low: $100).
Purpose and activities: Support primarily for a college; giving also for other education, medical research, hospitals, Catholic giving, and social services.
Fields of interest: Higher education, education, medical research, hospitals, social services, Catholic giving.
Types of support: General purposes.
Limitations: Giving primarily in NY. No grants to individuals.
Application information: Contributes to pre-selected organizations. Applications not accepted.
Trustees: Helen D. Fahey, Peter M. Fahey.
EIN: 133437921

1911
Michael David Falk Foundation, Inc.
P.O. Box 483, Canal St. Station, 10013
113 Spring St.
New York 10012

Established in 1968.
Donor(s): Isidore Falk.
Foundation type: Independent
Financial data (yr. ended 12/31/90): Assets, $3,885,886 (M); expenditures, $211,735; qualifying distributions, $200,400, including $200,150 for 4 grants (high: $180,000; low: $50).
Fields of interest: Jewish giving, Jewish welfare, higher education, medical education.
Limitations: Giving primarily in New York, NY. No grants to individuals.
Application information: Contributes only to pre-selected organizations. Applications not accepted.
Officers: Isidore Falk, Mgr.; Maurice Falk, Mgr.
EIN: 136265854

1912
Louis & Gertrude Feil Foundation, Inc.
370 Seventh Ave., Suite 618
New York 10001   (212) 563-6557

Established in 1977 in NY.
Donor(s): Louis Feil.
Foundation type: Independent
Financial data (yr. ended 06/30/91): Assets, $4,919,055 (M); expenditures, $279,108; qualifying distributions, $259,055, including $259,055 for 111 grants (high: $35,000; low: $50).
Fields of interest: Jewish giving, Jewish welfare, hospitals, medical education.
Limitations: Giving primarily in NY.
Application information:
  Deadline(s): None

Write: Louis Feil, Secy.-Treas.
Officers and Directors: Gertrude Feil,* Pres.; Jeffrey Feil,* V.P.; Louis Feil,* Secy.-Treas.
EIN: 132958414

1913
Fein Foundation
P.O. Box 99
Scarsdale 10583

Established in 1954 in NY.
Donor(s): Bernard Fein.
Foundation type: Independent
Financial data (yr. ended 12/31/90): Assets, $2,132,756 (M); expenditures, $107,663; qualifying distributions, $107,663, including $107,663 for 105 grants (high: $50,000; low: $10).
Fields of interest: Education, youth, health, media and communications.
Limitations: Giving primarily in the New York, NY, metropolitan area. No grants to individuals.
Application information: Contributes only to pre-selected organizations. Applications not accepted.
Trustees: Kathy Bierman, Adam Fein, Bernard Fein, David Fein.
Number of staff: None.
EIN: 136161610

1914
The Eugene and Estelle Ferkauf Foundation
67 Allenwood Rd.
Great Neck 11023-2213   (516) 773-3269

Established in 1967 in NY.
Donor(s): Eugene Ferkauf, Estelle Ferkauf.
Foundation type: Independent
Financial data (yr. ended 12/31/90): Assets, $3,928,753 (M); expenditures, $494,051; qualifying distributions, $452,593, including $339,750 for 48 grants (high: $35,000; low: $250; average: $10,350).
Fields of interest: Higher education, medical research, hospitals, fine arts, museums, music, theater.
Types of support: Research, building funds, continuing support.
Limitations: Giving limited to NY. No grants to individuals.
Publications: Application guidelines.
Application information: Application form not required.
  Initial approach: Letter of request
  Copies of proposal: 1
  Deadline(s): Submit proposal preferably in Jan., July, or Dec.
  Board meeting date(s): As required
  Write: The Trustees
Trustees: Lenore Bronstein, Robert Bronstein, Richard M. Dicke, Barbara Dor, Benny Dor, Estelle Ferkauf, Eugene Ferkauf, Amy Shapira, Israel Shapira.
Number of staff: 1 part-time professional.
EIN: 132621094

1915
The Donald M. Feuerstein Foundation
(Formerly The Feuerstein-Dryfoos Foundation, Inc.)
993 Fifth Ave.
New York 10028

Established in 1975 in NY.
Donor(s): Donald M. Feuerstein.
Foundation type: Independent
Financial data (yr. ended 06/30/91): Assets, $76,611 (M); gifts received, $75,000; expenditures, $256,487; qualifying distributions, $255,800, including $255,700 for 37 grants (high: $100,000; low: $100).
Fields of interest: Cultural programs, secondary education, higher education, health.
Limitations: Giving primarily in the New York, NY, metropolitan area. No grants to individuals.
Application information: Contributes only to pre-selected organizations. Applications not accepted.
Officers: Donald M. Feuerstein, Pres. and Treas.; Martin Lipton, V.P. and Secy.
EIN: 132838464

1916
Eugene V. Fife Family Foundation
c/o Goldman Sachs & Co., Tax Dept.
85 Broad St.
New York 10004-2408

Established in 1982.
Donor(s): Eugene V. Fife.
Foundation type: Independent
Financial data (yr. ended 01/31/91): Assets, $530,648 (M); gifts received, $282,945; expenditures, $393,866; qualifying distributions, $390,923, including $390,835 for 28 grants (high: $100,190; low: $500).
Fields of interest: Cultural programs, higher education, health associations, medical research.
Types of support: General purposes.
Limitations: Giving primarily in England and NY. No grants to individuals; no loans.
Application information: Contributes only to pre-selected organizations. Applications not accepted.
Trustees: Jonathan L. Cohen, Eugene V. Fife.
EIN: 133153715

1917
Elias and Bertha Fife Foundation, Inc.
Standard Motor Products, Inc.
37-18 Northern Blvd.
Long Island City 11101   (718) 392-0200

Incorporated in 1959 in NY.
Donor(s): Members of the Fife family, Standard Motor Products, Inc.
Foundation type: Independent
Financial data (yr. ended 04/30/91): Assets, $2,518,152 (M); gifts received, $120,000; expenditures, $202,751; qualifying distributions, $201,232, including $201,225 for 140 grants (high: $25,000; low: $100).
Fields of interest: Health services, hospitals, welfare, Jewish welfare, cultural programs.
Limitations: Giving primarily in NY.
Application information:
  Initial approach: Letter

Deadline(s): None
Write: Bernard Fife, Pres.
Officers and Directors:* Bernard Fife,* Pres.;
Nathaniel L. Sills,* Secy.-Treas.; Arlene Fife, Ruth
Sills.
EIN: 116035634

1918
Vain and Harry Fish Foundation, Inc.
c/o Vivian F. Gentleman, Esq.
66 East 79th St.
New York 10021   (212) 879-2520

Incorporated in 1972 in NY.
Donor(s): Vain B. Fish,‡ Harry Fish.‡
Foundation type: Independent
Financial data (yr. ended 12/31/91): Assets,
$3,736,581 (M); expenditures, $201,515;
qualifying distributions, $177,032, including
$140,000 for 49 grants (high: $25,000; low:
$500).
Purpose and activities: Grants for higher
education and hospitals; grants also for cultural
activities, youth agencies, the handicapped, and a
military academy.
Fields of interest: Higher education, hospitals,
cultural programs, youth, handicapped,
rehabilitation, secondary education.
Types of support: Endowment funds, seed money,
scholarship funds.
Limitations: No grants to individuals.
Application information:
Initial approach: Letter
Deadline(s): None
Write: Alexander W. Gentleman, Pres.
Officers: Alexander W. Gentleman, Pres.; Vivian
F. Gentleman, V.P.; Bernard Leegant, Treas.
EIN: 132723211

1919
John J. Flemm Foundation, Inc.
c/o Edward Owen Adler, Esq.
190 Willis Ave., Suite 240
Mineola 11501

Established in 1974.
Donor(s): John J. Flemm.‡
Foundation type: Independent
Financial data (yr. ended 01/31/91): Assets,
$2,612,139 (M); expenditures, $216,092;
qualifying distributions, $211,367, including
$178,310 for 157 grants (high: $8,100; low:
$100).
Fields of interest: Religion, education,
environment, ecology, animal welfare, health,
arts, law and justice, human rights.
Application information: Applications not
accepted.
Write: Edward Owen Adler, Esq., Counsel
Officers and Trustees:* Daniel Harris,* Pres.;
Judith Post,* Pres.; Robert Post,* Secy.; Michael
Harris,* Treas.; Avery Harris, Leona Post.
EIN: 237348789

1920
Forbes Foundation ▼
c/o Forbes Inc.
60 Fifth Ave.
New York 10011   (212) 620-2248

Established in 1979 in NJ.
Donor(s): Forbes, Inc.
Foundation type: Company-sponsored
Financial data (yr. ended 12/31/91): Assets,
$267,987 (M); expenditures, $1,687,493;
qualifying distributions, $1,686,630, including
$1,686,630 for 577 grants (high: $100,000; low:
$35; average: $100-$10,000).
Purpose and activities: Support for higher and
secondary education, hospitals, cultural programs
and museums, and welfare funds.
Fields of interest: Higher education, secondary
education, welfare, hospitals, cultural programs,
museums.
Types of support: General purposes, building
funds, endowment funds.
Limitations: No grants to individuals, or for
matching gifts; no loans.
Publications: 990-PF.
Application information: Contributes only to
pre-selected organizations. Applications not
accepted.
Board meeting date(s): As required
Write: Leonard H. Yablon, Secy.-Treas.
Officers: Malcolm S. Forbes, Jr., Pres.; Christopher
Forbes, V.P.; Leonard H. Yablon, Secy.-Treas.
Number of staff: None.
EIN: 237037319

1921
The Forchheimer Foundation
c/o Weitzner, Levine & Hamburg
230 Park Ave.
New York 10169   (212) 661-3140

Established about 1957 in NY.
Donor(s): Leo Forchheimer.‡
Foundation type: Independent
Financial data (yr. ended 12/31/90): Assets,
$13,510,640 (M); gifts received, $369,934;
expenditures, $1,416,341; qualifying
distributions, $1,339,500, including $1,339,500
for 19 grants (high: $500,000; low: $3,100;
average: $25,000-$75,000).
Purpose and activities: Giving primarily for
hospitals, health agencies, higher education,
including medical and technical education,
Jewish welfare funds, museums, and social
services.
Fields of interest: Hospitals, health, higher
education, medical education, Jewish welfare,
museums, social services, Israel.
Limitations: Giving primarily in Israel and New
York, NY.
Application information:
Deadline(s): None
Officers and Directors:* Ludwig Jesselson,* V.P.
and Treas.; Rudolph Forchheimer,* Secy.; Joseph
Levine.
EIN: 136075112

1922
The Ford Foundation ▼
320 East 43rd St.
New York 10017   (212) 573-5000

Incorporated in 1936 in MI.
Donor(s): Henry Ford,‡ Edsel Ford.‡
Foundation type: Independent
Financial data (yr. ended 09/30/91): Assets,
$6,253,006,737 (M); expenditures,

$288,213,002; qualifying distributions,
$301,499,409, including $236,490,143 for 1,568
grants (high: $5,200,000; low: $500; average:
$25,000-$1,500,000), $4,385,200 for 276 grants
to individuals (high: $73,000; low: $350; average:
$500-$20,000), $1,716,794 for 21
foundation-administered programs and
$13,286,407 for 10 program-related investments.
Purpose and activities: To advance the public
well-being by identifying and contributing to the
solution of problems of national and international
importance. Grants primarily to institutions for
experimental, demonstration, and development
efforts that are likely to produce significant
advances within the foundation's fields of interest:
Urban Poverty; Rural Poverty and Resources;
Rights and Social Justice; Governance and Public
Policy; Education and Culture; International
Affairs; and Reproductive Health and Population.
Fields of interest: Urban development,
community development, welfare, youth, rural
development, environment, agriculture,
employment, minorities, women, immigration,
legal services, government, public policy, higher
education, secondary education, arts,
international affairs, foreign policy, AIDS, aged.
Types of support: Conferences and seminars,
consulting services, exchange programs, general
purposes, matching funds, professorships,
program-related investments, publications,
research, seed money, special projects, technical
assistance, continuing support, endowment funds,
fellowships, grants to individuals.
Limitations: Giving on a worldwide basis,
including the U.S., Europe, Africa and the Middle
East, Asia, and Latin America and the Caribbean.
No support for programs for which substantial
support from government or other sources is
readily available, or for religious activities as
such. No grants for routine operating costs,
construction or maintenance of buildings, or
undergraduate scholarships; graduate fellowships
generally channeled through grants to universities
or other organizations; no grants for purely
personal or local needs.
Publications: Annual report, newsletter, program
policy statement (including application
guidelines), occasional report.
Application information: Foreign applicants
should contact foundation for addresses of its
overseas offices, through which they must apply.
Application form not required.
Initial approach: Letter, proposal, or telephone
Copies of proposal: 1
Deadline(s): None
Board meeting date(s): Dec., Mar., June, and
Sept.
Final notification: Initial indication as to
whether proposal falls within program
interests within 1 month
Write: Barron M. Tenny, Secy.
Officers and Trustees:* Edson W. Spencer,*
Chair.; Franklin A. Thomas,* Pres.; Barron M.
Tenny, V.P., General Counsel, and Secy.; Susan V.
Berresford, V.P.; John W. English, V.P.; Nancy
Feller, Assoc. Gen. Counsel and Dir., Legal
Services; John Koprowski, Treas.; Barry D.
Gaberman, Deputy V.P.; Diane Galloway-May,
Asst. Secy.; Yvonne Braithwaite Burke, Frances D.
Fergusson, Robert D. Haas, Sir Christopher Hogg,
Vernon E. Jordan, Jr., Donald F. McHenry, Paul F.
Miller, Jr., William G. Milliken, Luis G. Nogales,
Gen. Olusegun Obasanjo, Barbara Scott Preiskel,

Dorothy S. Ridings, Henry B. Schacht, M.S. Swaminathan, Thomas H. Wyman.
Number of staff: 227 full-time professional; 2 part-time professional; 331 full-time support; 8 part-time support.
EIN: 131684331
Recent health grants:

1922-1 Al-Azhar University, International Islamic Center for Population Studies and Research, Cairo, Egypt, $48,250. For family planning and reproductive health program. Grant administered by Government of Egypt. 1991.

1922-2 American Civil Liberties Union Foundation, NYC, NY, $1,000,000. For supplement to preserve access to reproductive health services, particularly for low-income women and teenagers, through Reproductive Freedom Project. 1991.

1922-3 American Civil Liberties Union Foundation, NYC, NY, $65,000. For supplement to publish book on legal and ethical dimensions of AIDS epidemic. 1991.

1922-4 American Society of Law and Medicine, Boston, MA, $86,000. For meeting in Washington, DC on regulatory, legal and ethical implications of use of antiprogestins in U.S. and for meeting in Toronto on other issues related to reproductive health. 1991.

1922-5 Asia Resource Center, DC, $111,600. For AIDS education and counseling for workers in Thai entertainment industries. 1991.

1922-6 Asian and Pacific Development Centre, Kuala Lumpur, Malaysia, $95,000. For family planning and reproductive health program. 1991.

1922-7 Bangladesh Association for the Prevention of Septic Abortion, Bangladesh, $49,438. For seminar on antiprogestins, drugs that induce early abortion. 1991.

1922-8 Bangladesh Womens Health Coalition, Bangladesh, $193,000. For supplement for evaluation of reproductive health training and service programs. 1991.

1922-9 Beijing Medical University, School of Public Health, Beijing, China, $24,000. To set up working group on reproductive health in Yunnan Province in southwest China to get better understanding of women's reproductive health needs in poorer parts of province and to devise programs to meet those needs. 1991.

1922-10 Birzeit University, Jordan, $150,000. For multidisciplinary community health research unit. 1991.

1922-11 Boston Womens Health Book Collective, Somerville, MA, $200,000. For family planning and reproductive health program. 1991.

1922-12 Brazilian Interdisciplinary AIDS Association, Rio de Janeiro, Brazil, $125,000. For national education, documentation and advocacy program on AIDS. 1991.

1922-13 Brigham and Womens Hospital, Boston, MA, $300,000. To study maternal-fetal policies related to AIDS, drug abuse and infant mortality programs and to develop integrated public policy agenda. 1991.

1922-14 Burkina Faso, Government of, Burkina Faso, $134,000. For research on maternal illness and death, and policies and programs that promote safe motherhood. 1991.

1922-15 C.B.C.I. Society for Medical Education, India, $82,000. To improve health care for children by training medical, paramedical,

nursing and health management personnel. 1991.

1922-16 Catholics for a Free Choice, DC, $300,000. For supplement for public policy and education programs on reproductive choice in U.S.. 1991.

1922-17 Catholics for a Free Choice, DC, $150,000. For family planning and reproductive health program in developing countries. 1991.

1922-18 Catholics for a Free Choice, DC, $50,000. For education on reproductive health and rights in Latin America. 1991.

1922-19 Center for Women Policy Studies, DC, $200,000. For supplement for research and policymaking projects of National Resource Center on Women and AIDS. 1991.

1922-20 Center for Womens Studies, Chile, $114,000. To include gender analysis in policymaking on health, housing and education. 1991.

1922-21 Child in Need Institute, India, $176,000. To develop job opportunities, women's reproductive health program and fundraising projects for voluntary health organization. 1991.

1922-22 College of Mexico, Mexico, $115,000. For research on social welfare and effects on health of inadequate housing in low-income settlements. 1991.

1922-23 Confederation of African Medical Associations and Societies, Nigeria, $42,000. For family planning and reproductive health program. 1991.

1922-24 Consumer Education and Research Centre, Ahmedabad, India, $150,000. To establish clearinghouse on policies related to industrial and environmental safety. 1991.

1922-25 Cornell University, Ithaca, NY, $50,000. To research affects of Vitamin A on children's growth in south India. 1991.

1922-26 Criminal Justice Policy Foundation, DC, $50,000. For book analyzing key issues of drug policy. 1991.

1922-27 Egypt, Government of, Ministry of Foreign Affairs, Egypt, $47,800. For supplement for educational television series on maternal and child health. 1991.

1922-28 Family Health International, Research Triangle Park, NC, $244,000. To determine extent of maternal morbidity in India, Bangladesh, Indonesia, and Egypt, and to identify responses to it. 1991.

1922-29 Family Health International, Research Triangle Park, NC, $105,237. For comparative study of safety, acceptability and efficacy of long-term contraceptive Norplant among Bangladeshi women. 1991.

1922-30 Family Planning Association of Kenya, Nairobi, Kenya, $49,978. For AIDS prevention program for adolescents and prostitutes. 1991.

1922-31 Foundation for Research in Health Systems, India, $134,000. For research and training program in community epidemiology, women's reproductive health and child survival. 1991.

1922-32 GELEDES Instituto de Mulher Negra, Sao Paulo, Brazil, $200,000. For research and public education on civil rights law and for legal services for victims of racial discrimination. 1991.

1922-33 George Washington University, DC, $435,387. For Intergovernmental AIDS Policy

Center, which gives state and local policy makers information and technical assistance on which to base responsible AIDS policies. 1991.

1922-34 Harvard University, Cambridge, MA, $250,000. For research on relation between household economics and reproductive health and child survival in India. 1991.

1922-35 Harvard University, Cambridge, MA, $50,000. For family planning and reproductive health program in China. 1991.

1922-36 Harvard University, Cambridge, MA, $45,000. For comparative study of maternal schooling and child survival in Nepal and Mexico. 1991.

1922-37 Industrial Cooperative Association (ICA), Somerville, MA, $45,000. To expand, with Community Services Society of New York, economic development project focused on home health care. 1991.

1922-38 Institute of Cultural Affairs, Chicago, IL, $14,500. To include consideration of women's reproductive health in conference on primary health care. 1991.

1922-39 Institute of Health Systems, India, $40,000. For child survival/fair start program. 1991.

1922-40 International Association for Maternal/Neonatal Health, Switzerland, $30,000. For child survival/fair start program in developing countries. 1991.

1922-41 International Centre for Diarrheal Disease Research, Bangladesh, $282,000. For supplement for rural maternity-care program. 1991.

1922-42 International Development Research Centre, Ottawa, Canada, $150,000. For supplement for regional information sharing network on AIDS in eastern and southern Africa. 1991.

1922-43 International Development Research Centre, Ottawa, Canada, $150,000. For family planning and reproductive health program in developing countries. 1991.

1922-44 International Federation of Gynecology and Obstetrics, London, England, $140,000. For family planning and reproductive health program in developing countries. 1991.

1922-45 International Nursing Services Association, India, $44,400. For AIDS education programs for school and college students. 1991.

1922-46 International Projects Assistance Services, Carrboro, NC, $50,000. For study of abortion services in Soviet Union, Romania and Hungary. 1991.

1922-47 Johns Hopkins University, Baltimore, MD, $27,500. For workshop on how health decisions are made in households in developing countries. 1991.

1922-48 KAHAYAG: Foundation for Development Support and Communications, Philippines, $32,000. For coalition of provincial NGO's (non-governmental organizations) that are working to involve local women in specifying reproductive health problems in their communities and in devising ways to overcome them. 1991.

1922-49 Kenya Medical Womens Association, Kenya, $31,856. To update laws affecting children so that they meet standards of U.N. Convention on Rights of the Child. 1991.

1922-50 Latin American Institute for Mental Health and Human Rights, Chile, $45,000. For supplement to research social and psychological effects of political repression. 1991.

1922-51 Matabeleland AIDS Council, Zimbabwe, $21,130. To direct study on HIV-infected patients and their families. 1991.

1922-52 Monroe, County of, Madisonville, TN, $100,000. For Monroe Maternity Center. 1991.

1922-53 Mrigendra Medical Trust, Nepal, $50,000. For supplement to develop health care plans for Tamang community. 1991.

1922-54 National Center for Clinical Infant Programs, Arlington, VA, $250,000. For supplement to complete Center's Better Care for the Babies Project, which involves technical assistance and public education on state programs aimed at improving quality of infant and toddler care. 1991.

1922-55 National Committee on United States-China Relations, NYC, NY, $32,000. For family planning and reproductive health program in China. 1991.

1922-56 National Council for International Health, DC, $95,000. To enable speakers from developing countries to participate in conference on women's health. 1991.

1922-57 National Council of Womens Societies of Nigeria, Nigeria, $250,000. For research, community awareness and health education activities of reproductive health program in Nigeria. 1991.

1922-58 National League for Nursing, NYC, NY, $200,000. To evaluate programs that train health care paraprofessionals to become nurses. 1991.

1922-59 National Medical Association, DC, $42,500. For public education and outreach for female African-American physicians on abortion and other reproductive health issues. 1991.

1922-60 National Research Institute for Family Planning, China, $30,000. For family planning and reproductive health program. 1991.

1922-61 New York University, NYC, NY, $2,000,000. To launch Substance Abuse Strategy Initiative, which will test series of drug abuse prevention and treatment programs for infants and pre-adolescents. 1991.

1922-62 Nigerian Association of Colleges of Medicine, Nigeria, $50,000. To integrate social sciences, reproductive health and primary health care into undergraduate medical training in Nigeria. 1991.

1922-63 Pacific Health and Development Resources, Kailua, HI, $44,000. For child survival/fair start program in developing countries. 1991.

1922-64 Panos Institute, DC, $194,000. For supplement to review AIDS Information and Development program and to produce two publications on AIDS in developing countries. 1991.

1922-65 Panos Institute, DC, $38,000. For dissemination of information on reproductive health in developing countries. 1991.

1922-66 Philippine Legislators Committee on Population and Development Foundation, Philippines, $60,000. For public information about reproductive health and population studies for legislators, government officials and media. 1991.

1922-67 Planned Parenthood Federation, International, London, England, $215,500. For research, education and exchange of information on issues of human sexuality in developing countries. 1991.

1922-68 Population and Community Development Association, Bangkok, Thailand, $85,000. For research on economic consequences of AIDS in Thailand, for AIDS-prevention educational services and for training program in AIDS prevention for community leaders from other Asian countries. 1991.

1922-69 Population and Community Development Association, Bangkok, Thailand, $49,000. For training program on AIDS prevention for Asian countries. 1991.

1922-70 Population Council, NYC, NY, $360,000. For supplement to develop reproductive health research network in Francophone West Africa. 1991.

1922-71 Population Council, NYC, NY, $359,614. For child survival/fair start program. 1991.

1922-72 Population Council, NYC, NY, $100,000. For employment generation program. 1991.

1922-73 Population Council, NYC, NY, $45,000. To study status of reproductive health in Eastern Europe. 1991.

1922-74 Population Crisis Committee, DC, $195,000. To expand international publication series. 1991.

1922-75 Population Services International India, India, $110,000. For marketing of condoms to help prevent AIDS. 1991.

1922-76 Program for Appropriate Technology in Health, Seattle, WA, $120,000. For supplement for publication of Outlook, quarterly journal on contraceptive developments, regulations and safety in developing countries. 1991.

1922-77 Resource Centre for Primary Health Care, Nepal, $50,000. For child survival/fair start program. 1991.

1922-78 San Diego, County of, San Diego, CA, $100,000. For Trauma Intervention Program. 1991.

1922-79 Sanchetna Community Health and Research Center, India, $120,000. For community-based research and outreach program providing health education for poor women and children. 1991.

1922-80 Sao Paulo Support Group for the Prevention of AIDS, Sao Paulo, Brazil, $70,980. For supplement for AIDS education, counseling and prevention activities. 1991.

1922-81 Society for Education, Action and Research in Community Health, Gadchiroli, India, $325,000. For community-based rural health services, training and research on maternal and childhood mortality. 1991.

1922-82 Society for Women and AIDS in Africa, Nigeria, $60,000. For public education on impact of AIDS on Nigeria. 1991.

1922-83 Society for Women and AIDS in Africa, Nigeria, $36,000. For public education on impact of AIDS on Nigerian women. 1991.

1922-84 Tribe Child Development Council, India, $70,000. For integrated health and development program for Jenu Kurubu tribe. 1991.

1922-85 Union of Palestinian Medical Relief Committees, Israel, $50,000. For family planning and reproductive health program. 1991.

1922-86 University of Benin, Togo, $250,000. For regional research and training network on population and reproductive health in Francophone, West Africa. 1991.

1922-87 University of California, San Francisco, CA, $127,000. For supplement to complete evaluation of California's Comprehensive Perinatal Service Program. 1991.

1922-88 University of Chile, Santiago, Chile, $30,000. For conference on social sciences and medicine in Latin America. 1991.

1922-89 University of Indonesia, Jakarta, Indonesia, $350,000. To establish capital fund. Grant made as part of Foundation's Reproductive Health and Population Program. 1991.

1922-90 University of Indonesia, Jakarta, Indonesia, $333,300. To strengthen university's program in medical anthropology. 1991.

1922-91 University of Limburg, Netherlands, $35,000. For meeting on restitution, compensation and rehabilitation for victims of human rights violations. 1991.

1922-92 University of London, London, England, $75,000. For supplement to coordinate collaborative research project in six developing countries on ways to measure maternal ill-health. 1991.

1922-93 University of Newcastle, Newcastle, Australia, $46,500. For development of international network for social scientists working on health issues. 1991.

1922-94 University of Nigeria, Nsukka, Nigeria, $50,000. To develop training program for non-literate women in eastern Nigeria on maternal health and income generation. 1991.

1922-95 Urmul Rural Health Research and Development Trust, India, $50,000. 1991.

1922-96 Voluntary Health Association of India, India, $160,000. For technical assistance to network of nongovernmental organizations sponsoring AIDS programs. 1991.

1922-97 Voluntary Health Association of India, India, $105,000. For supplement to analyze and distribute program materials of private voluntary health organizations. 1991.

1922-98 Voluntary Health Services Society, Bangladesh, $175,000. For supplement for publications, staff development and training for nongovernmental organizations concerned with children's health issues. 1991.

1922-99 W G B H Educational Foundation, Boston, MA, $300,000. For In the Shadow of Love, one-hour television drama about teenagers and AIDS. 1991.

1922-100 West Bengal Voluntary Health Association, India, $123,000. For education on proper use of prescription drugs and to expand self-financing and quality-control services of voluntary health organizations. 1991.

1922-101 West Bengal Voluntary Health Association, India, $123,000. For child survival/fair start program. 1991.

1922-102 WomanHealth Philippines, Quezon City, Philippines, $107,500. To enable specialists and women's health activists to attend conference on reproductive health and rights. 1991.

1922-103 Women Judges Fund for Justice, DC, $40,000. For family planning and reproductive health program. 1991.

1922-104 Womens Resource and Research Center, Philippines, $135,000. For program of participatory research on sexuality, reproductive health and women's rights. 1991.

1922-105 World Health Organization, Geneva, Switzerland, $45,000. For conference on reproductive health research in Eastern Europe. 1991.

1922-106 Zimbabwe International Book Fair Trust, Zimbabwe, $15,000. For AIDS prevention program for adolescents and prostitutes. 1991.

1923
Joseph C. and Esther Foster Foundation, Inc.
1088 Park Ave.
New York 10028

Established in 1961 in MA.
Donor(s): Esther J. Foster,‡ Joseph C. Foster.‡
Foundation type: Independent
Financial data (yr. ended 12/31/90): Assets, $2,061,377 (M); expenditures, $185,430; qualifying distributions, $136,800, including $136,800 for 29 grants (high: $50,000; low: $250; average: $250-$15,000).
Fields of interest: Higher education, educational research, Jewish welfare, fine arts, cultural programs, hospitals, medical research, race relations, minorities, freedom.
Types of support: Annual campaigns, matching funds, program-related investments.
Limitations: Giving primarily in NY and New England. No grants to individuals.
Application information: Telephone inquiries not considered. Application form not required.
Initial approach: Letter
Deadline(s): Prior to Dec. 31
Board meeting date(s): Dec. 31
Write: Jacqueline Foster, Pres.
Officers and Directors:* Jacqueline Foster,* Pres.; Daniel Foster Haft, Secy.; Lisa A. Bapter,* Treas.; Robin B. Abbott, Wendy L. Haft.
Number of staff: None.
EIN: 046114436

1924
Foundation for the Needs of Others, Inc.
c/o Patterson, Belknap, Webb & Tyler
30 Rockefeller Plaza, Suite 3500
New York 10112

Incorporated in 1953 in NY.
Donor(s): Helen W. Buckner, Walker G. Buckner, Thomas W. Buckner.
Foundation type: Independent
Financial data (yr. ended 12/31/91): Assets, $4,846,093 (M); expenditures, $335,034; qualifying distributions, $331,619, including $314,000 for 15 grants (high: $108,000; low: $5,000).
Purpose and activities: Giving priarily for a family planning organization and health associations; support also for music and other cultural programs.
Fields of interest: Family planning, health associations, music, cultural programs.

Limitations: Giving primarily in New York, NY. No grants to individuals.
Publications: 990-PF.
Application information: Contributes only to pre-selected organizations. Applications not accepted.
Officers and Trustees:* Elizabeth B. Buckner,* Pres. and Treas.; Thomas W. Buckner,* Secy.; Walker G. Buckner, Jr.
EIN: 136119874

1925
George and Elizabeth F. Frankel Foundation, Inc.
60 East 42nd St., Suite 1563
New York 10017

Incorporated in 1945 in NY.
Donor(s): George Frankel,‡ Elizabeth F. Frankel,‡ G. David Frankel, Charles Korn.
Foundation type: Independent
Financial data (yr. ended 03/31/91): Assets, $2,042,404 (M); gifts received, $152,034; expenditures, $487,323; qualifying distributions, $357,877, including $340,532 for 135 grants (high: $85,377; low: $50).
Fields of interest: Medical education, health associations, medical research, Jewish welfare.
Limitations: Giving primarily on the East Coast. No grants to individuals.
Application information: Contributes only to pre-selected organizations. Applications not accepted.
Officers and Trustees:* G. David Frankel,* Pres.; Doris F. Tulcin,* Secy.; Elizabeth F. Block, Geraldine F. Merksamer.
EIN: 136126076

1926
Samuel Freeman Charitable Trust ▼
c/o U.S. Trust Co. of New York
114 West 47th St.
New York 10036-1532   (212) 852-3683
Application address: c/o William E. Murray, Esq., 200 East 61st St., Suite 4G, New York, NY 10021

Established in 1981 in NY.
Donor(s): Samuel Freeman.‡
Foundation type: Independent
Financial data (yr. ended 12/31/91): Assets, $28,769,867 (M); gifts received, $570,312; expenditures, $1,738,422; qualifying distributions, $1,407,300, including $1,407,300 for 88 grants (high: $200,000; low: $300; average: $500-$25,000).
Purpose and activities: Giving primarily for health and education.
Fields of interest: Education, medical research, medical education, health associations, arts.
Types of support: Annual campaigns, continuing support, seed money, operating budgets, general purposes.
Limitations: Giving limited to the U.S., with emphasis on New York, NY.
Publications: Program policy statement.
Application information:
Initial approach: Proposal of not more than 2 pages
Deadline(s): None

Write: Anne L. Smith-Ganey, Asst. V.P., U.S. Trust Co. of New York
Trustees: William E. Murray, U.S. Trust Co. of New York.
EIN: 136803465

1927
Arnold D. Frese Foundation, Inc. ▼
30 Rockefeller Plaza, Suite 1938
New York 10112   (212) 757-6626

Established in 1966.
Donor(s): Arnold D. Frese.‡
Foundation type: Independent
Financial data (yr. ended 12/31/90): Assets, $12,169,952 (M); expenditures, $1,947,831; qualifying distributions, $1,315,000, including $1,215,000 for 40 grants (high: $365,000; average: $1,000-$35,000).
Purpose and activities: Support for hospitals, cultural programs, especially an opera company, and higher education.
Fields of interest: Hospitals, cultural programs, higher education.
Limitations: Giving primarily in New York, NY, and Greenwich, CT. No grants to individuals.
Application information:
Initial approach: Proposal
Deadline(s): None
Board meeting date(s): Quarterly
Final notification: 3 to 4 months
Write: James S. Smith, Pres.
Officers: Ines Frese, Chair.; James S. Smith, Pres. and Treas.; Hector G. Dowd, Secy.; E. Gayle Fisher, Exec. Dir.
Trustees: Henry D. Mercer, Jr., Emil Mosbacher, Jr.
Number of staff: 1 full-time professional.
EIN: 136212507

1928
Ludwig W. Frohlich Charitable Trust
c/o Chadbourne & Parke
30 Rockefeller Plaza
New York 10112

Trust established in 1969 in NY.
Donor(s): Ludwig W. Frohlich.‡
Foundation type: Independent
Financial data (yr. ended 12/31/90): Assets, $6,677,148 (M); expenditures, $744,819; qualifying distributions, $635,742, including $553,397 for 51 grants (high: $100,000; low: $250).
Fields of interest: Youth, medical research, hospitals, cultural programs, museums, social services.
Limitations: Giving primarily in New York, NY. No grants to individuals.
Application information: Contributes only to pre-selected organizations. Applications not accepted.
Trustees: Kathleen B. Buddenhagen, Ingrid Lilly Burns, Thomas R. Burns, Richard B. Leather.
EIN: 136288404

1929
Helene Fuld Health Trust ▼
c/o Townley & Updike
405 Lexington Ave.
New York 10174   (212) 973-6859

Trust established in 1951 in NJ; activated in 1969 as successor to Helene Fuld Health Foundation incorporated in 1935.

Donor(s): Leonhard Felix Fuld,‡ Florentine M. Fuld.‡

Foundation type: Independent

Financial data (yr. ended 09/30/90): Assets, $76,429,273 (M); expenditures, $6,192,905; qualifying distributions, $5,878,974, including $5,291,595 for 167 grants (high: $377,397; low: $5,000; average: $22,000).

Purpose and activities: Grants to state-accredited nursing schools affiliated with accredited hospitals to promote the health, education, and welfare of enrolled student nurses who are being taught to care for the sick and injured at bedside.

Fields of interest: Nursing, education.

Types of support: Equipment, publications, special projects.

Limitations: No grants to individuals, or for endowment funds, operating expenses, matching gifts, or general purposes; no loans.

Publications: Annual report (including application guidelines), application guidelines, grants list, financial statement.

Application information: Applications received by Oct. 31 deadline reviewed in spring of following year. Application form required.

Initial approach: Letter requesting application; no telephone or facsimile requests filled. Application updated every year and usually available in Aug.

Copies of proposal: 3

Deadline(s): Oct. 31

Board meeting date(s): Mar., June, Sept., and Dec.

Final notification: 8 months

Write: Robert C. Miller, Counsel, or Arlene J. Kennare, Grants Office Admin.

Trustee: Marine Midland Bank, N.A.

Number of staff: 1 full-time professional; 5 part-time professional.

EIN: 136309307

Recent health grants:

1929-1 Adelphi University, Garden City, NY, $20,000. For computer-assisted instruction equiment for nursing education. 1990.

1929-2 Albany State College, Albany, GA, $85,368. For computer-assisted instruction equiment for nursing education. 1990.

1929-3 American Friends of Assaf Harofeh School of Nursing, NYC, NY, $20,000. For audio-visual and computer-assisted instruction equipment, copier and library books for nursing education. 1990.

1929-4 Arizona State University, Tempe, AZ, $69,451. For interactive video equipment for nursing education. 1990.

1929-5 Armstrong State College, Savannah, GA, $10,000. For audio-visual equipment for nursing education. 1990.

1929-6 Augusta College, Augusta, GA, $20,000. For computer-assisted instruction and audio-visual equipment for nursing education. 1990.

1929-7 Aultman Hospital, Canton, OH, $17,159. For computer-assisted instruction equipment for nursing education. 1990.

1929-8 Barnes Hospital, Saint Louis, MO, $45,000. For computer-assisted instruction equipment for nursing education. 1990.

1929-9 Bay de Noc Community College, Escanaba, MI, $26,938. For interactive video

and computer-assisted instruction equipment for nursing education. 1990.

1929-10 Baystate Medical Center, Springfield, MA, $25,000. For computer-assisted instruction equipment for nursing education. 1990.

1929-11 Berkshire Community College, Pittsfield, MA, $12,407. For interactive video equipment for nursing education. 1990.

1929-12 Bishop Clarkson College of Nursing, Omaha, NE, $62,893. For interactive video equipment for nursing education. 1990.

1929-13 Blessing Hospital, Quincy, IL, $20,000. For computer-assisted instruction equipment for nursing education. 1990.

1929-14 Bluefield State College, Bluefield, WV, $10,000. For interactive video equipment for nursing education. 1990.

1929-15 Boise State University, Boise, ID, $45,213. For computer-assisted instruction, interactive video and audio visual equipment for nursing education. 1990.

1929-16 Bridgeport Hospital, Bridgeport, CT, $47,373. For nursing arts lab equipment, copier and classroom furnishings for nursing education. 1990.

1929-17 Burge School of Nursing, Springfield, MO, $15,834. For student lounge renovation. 1990.

1929-18 California State University, Chico, CA, $30,000. For nursing arts lab, computer-asssisted instruction and interactive video equipment for nursing education. 1990.

1929-19 California State University, Sacramento, CA, $25,000. For nursing arts lab and audio-visual equipment for nursing education. 1990.

1929-20 Cameron University, Lawton, OK, $10,000. For computer-assisted instruction equipment for nursing education. 1990.

1929-21 Cedar Crest College, Allentown, PA, $23,383. For nursing arts lab and audio-visual equipment for nursing education. 1990.

1929-22 Central School of Practical Nursing, Cleveland, OH, $19,290. For interactive video and audio-visual equipment. 1990.

1929-23 Chemeketa Community College, Salem, OR, $25,000. For interactive video equipment for nursing education. 1990.

1929-24 Chester County Hospital, West Chester, PA, $15,000. For interactive video equipment for nursing education. 1990.

1929-25 County College of Morris, Randolph, NJ, $10,000. For interactive video equipment for nursing education. 1990.

1929-26 East Stroudsburg University of Pennsylvania, East Stroudsburg, PA, $50,000. For computer-assisted instruction equipment for nursing education. 1990.

1929-27 Eastern Maine Technical College, Bangor, ME, $11,903. For computer-assisted instruction and audio-visual equipment for nursing education. 1990.

1929-28 Eastern Mennonite College, Harrisonburg, VA, $15,000. For interactive video equipment for nursing education. 1990.

1929-29 Edison State Community College, Piqua, OH, $15,000. For computer-assisted instruction, audio-visual and interactive video equipment for nursing education. 1990.

1929-30 Emory University, Atlanta, GA, $22,119. For audio-visual equipment for nursing education. 1990.

1929-31 Everett Community College, Everett, WA, $10,000. For interactive video equipment for nursing education. 1990.

1929-32 Fairfield University, Fairfield, CT, $30,000. For cardiac care unit simulation for nursing education. 1990.

1929-33 Gannon University, Erie, PA, $20,000. For interactive video and computer-assisted instruction equipment for nursing education. 1990.

1929-34 Geisinger Medical Center, Danville, PA, $45,000. For interactive video equipment, audio-visual software and library books for nursing education. 1990.

1929-35 Georgia College, Milledgeville, GA, $25,000. For interactive video equipment for nursing education. 1990.

1929-36 Helene Fuld School of Nursing, Camden, NJ, $187,500. For scholarships. 1990.

1929-37 Helene Fuld School of Nursing, NYC, NY, $187,500. For scholarships. Grant shared with North General Hospital for Joint Disease. 1990.

1929-38 Idaho State University, Pocatello, ID, $15,000. For audio-visual software for nursing education. 1990.

1929-39 Illinois Wesleyan University, Bloomington, IL, $15,403. For facsimile machine, copier and interactive video equipment for nursing education. 1990.

1929-40 Indiana State University, Terre Haute, IN, $12,752. For computer-assisted instruction equipment for nursing education. 1990.

1929-41 Indiana University of Pennsylvania, Indiana, PA, $50,000. For computer-assisted instruction equipment for nursing education. 1990.

1929-42 Indiana Vocational Technical College, Richmond, IN, $10,000. For computer-assisted instruction equipment for nursing education. 1990.

1929-43 Iowa Methodist School of Nursing, Des Moines, IA, $25,000. For interactive video and nursing arts lab equipment. 1990.

1929-44 Jameson Memorial Hospital, New Castle, PA, $15,000. For interactive video and nursing arts lab equipment for nursing education. 1990.

1929-45 Jefferson Community College, Watertown, NY, $15,000. For interactive video equipment for nursing education. 1990.

1929-46 Johns Hopkins University, Baltimore, MD, $30,000. For student lounge renovation and furnishings for nursing education. 1990.

1929-47 Kennebec Valley Technical College, Fairfield, ME, $10,000. For computer-assisted instruction equipment for nursing education. 1990.

1929-48 La Salle University, Philadelphia, PA, $17,552. For audio-visual equipment for nursing education. 1990.

1929-49 Lake Superior State University, Sault Sainte Marie, MI, $29,935. For interactive video equipment for nursing education. 1990.

1929-50 Lancaster General Hospital, Lancaster, PA, $41,432. For interactive video and audio-visual equipment for nursing education. 1990.

1929-51 Lansing Community College, Lansing, MI, $30,000. For audio-visual and computer-assisted instruction equipment for nursing education. 1990.

1929-52 Los Angeles County Medical Center, Los Angeles, CA, $40,000. For computer-assisted instruction equipment for nursing education. 1990.

1929-53 Louisiana College, Pineville, LA, $15,000. For computer-assisted instruction equipment for nursing education. 1990.

1929-54 Luzerne County Community College, Nanticoke, PA, $35,000. For interactive video equipment for nursing education. 1990.

1929-55 Lycoming College, Williamsport, PA, $31,725. For nursing arts lab equipment for nursing education. 1990.

1929-56 Mansfield General Hospital, Mansfield, OH, $15,000. For interactive video and computer-assisted instruction equipment for nursing education. 1990.

1929-57 Marion Technical College, Marion, OH, $15,000. For computer-assisted instruction equipment for nursing education. 1990.

1929-58 Massachusetts Bay Community College, Wellesley Hills, MA, $30,000. For computer-assisted instruction equipment for nursing education. 1990.

1929-59 Medical University of South Carolina, Charleston, SC, $20,000. For relief funds after Hurricane Hugo, used for student housing for nursing education. 1990.

1929-60 Memphis State University, Memphis, TN, $40,000. For interactive video equipment for nursing education. 1990.

1929-61 Mennonite College of Nursing, Bloomington, IL, $10,000. For computer-assisted instruction equipment. 1990.

1929-62 Meridian Community College, Meridian, MS, $15,000. For interactive video and computer-assisted instruction equipment for nursing education. 1990.

1929-63 Methodist Medical Center of Illinois, Peoria, IL, $13,347. For interactive video and computer-assisted instruction equipment for nursing education. 1990.

1929-64 Michigan State University, East Lansing, MI, $50,000. For interactive video equipment for nursing education. 1990.

1929-65 Millard Fillmore Hospital, Buffalo, NY, $25,000. For interactive video, computer-assisted instruction and audio-visual equipment for nursing education. 1990.

1929-66 Mississippi Gulf Coast Community College, Gulfport, MS, $64,294. For computer-assisted instruction, audio-visual and nursing arts lab equipment for nursing education. 1990.

1929-67 Missouri Baptist Medical Center, Saint Louis, MO, $25,644. For interactive video equipment for nursing education. 1990.

1929-68 Monroe Community College, Rochester, NY, $19,815. For interactive video equipment for nursing education. 1990.

1929-69 Monroe County Community College, Monroe, MI, $10,000. For nursing arts lab and computer-assisted instruction equipment for nursing education. 1990.

1929-70 Mount Carmel School of Nursing, Columbus, OH, $50,000. For nursing arts lab equipment for nursing education. 1990.

1929-71 Napa Valley College, Napa, CA, $30,000. For interactive video and computer-assisted instruction equipment for nursing education. 1990.

1929-72 National Student Nurses Association, NYC, NY, $17,000. For articles in Imprints and Dean's Notes for nursing education. 1990.

1929-73 Nazareth College, Kalamazoo, MI, $35,000. For interactive video equipment for nursing education. 1990.

1929-74 New Hampshire Technical Institute, Concord, NH, $29,280. For interactive video equipment for nursing education. 1990.

1929-75 New Mexico Junior College, Hobbs, NM, $20,000. For interactive video equipment for nursing education. 1990.

1929-76 North Iowa Area Community College, Mason City, IA, $15,000. For audio-visual and computer-assisted instruction software for nursing education. 1990.

1929-77 Northeast Louisiana University, Monroe, LA, $57,991. For interactive video equipment for nursing education. 1990.

1929-78 Northeast Missouri State University, Kirksville, MO, $25,000. For interactive video equipment for nursing education. 1990.

1929-79 Northeastern Hospital of Philadelphia, Philadelphia, PA, $36,249. For computer-assisted instruction, audio-visual and nursing arts lab equipment for nursing education. 1990.

1929-80 Northeastern Oklahoma A & M College, Miami, OK, $10,000. For computer-assisted instruction equipment for nursing education. 1990.

1929-81 Northern Kentucky University, Highland Heights, KY, $27,762. For interactive video equipment for nursing education. 1990.

1929-82 Northern Michigan University, Marquette, MI, $15,000. For interactive video equipment for nursing education. 1990.

1929-83 Northwestern Michigan College, Traverse City, MI, $32,145. For interactive video equipment for nursing education. 1990.

1929-84 Oakland University, Rochester, MI, $15,000. For nursing arts lab equipment for nursing education. 1990.

1929-85 Oklahoma State University, Oklahoma City, OK, $25,000. For interactive video equipment for nursing education. 1990.

1929-86 Oregon Health Sciences University, Portland, OR, $50,000. For long distance learning project for nursing education. 1990.

1929-87 Our Lady of the Lake Regional Medical Center, Baton Rouge, LA, $34,575. For audio-visual, computer-assisted instruction and nursing arts lab equipment for nursing education. 1990.

1929-88 Purdue University, West Lafayette, IN, $42,053. For interactive video and audio-visual equipment for nursing education. 1990.

1929-89 Riverside School of Professional Nursing, Newport News, VA, $25,000. For interactive video and computer-assisted instruction equipment for nursing education. 1990.

1929-90 Rochester General Hospital, Rochester, NY, $15,000. For computer-assisted instruction equipment for nursing education. 1990.

1929-91 Rock Valley College, Rockford, IL, $20,000. For interactive video and audio-visual equipment for nursing education. 1990.

1929-92 Roxborough Memorial Hospital, Philadelphia, PA, $39,695. For nursing arts lab, interactive video and classroom equipment and library books for nursing education. 1990.

1929-93 Royal Alexandria Hospitals, Edmonton, Canada, $50,000. For interactive video equipment for nursing education. 1990.

1929-94 Russell Sage College, Troy, NY, $15,000. For interactive video, computer-assisted instruction and nursing arts lab equipment for nursing education. 1990.

1929-95 Rutgers, The State University of New Jersey, Camden, NJ, $20,000. For interactive video equipment for nursing education. 1990.

1929-96 Sacred Heart Hospital, Norristown, PA, $16,160. For computer-assisted instruction equipment for nursing education. 1990.

1929-97 Saint Anselm College, Manchester, NH, $35,000. For computer-assisted instruction equipment for nursing education. 1990.

1929-98 Saint Johns Hospital, Springfield, IL, $15,000. For interactive video equipment for nursing education. 1990.

1929-99 Saint Joseph College, West Hartford, CT, $20,000. For interactive video equipment for nursing education. 1990.

1929-100 Saint Joseph Hospital, Nashua, NH, $35,000. For interactive video and long distance learning equipment for nursing education. 1990.

1929-101 Saint Marys Hospital, Waterbury, CT, $41,795. For copier, nursing arts lab and computer-assisted instruction equipment for nursing education. 1990.

1929-102 Saint Marys Hospital, Huntington, WV, $35,314. For computer-assisted instruction equipment for nursing education. 1990.

1929-103 Samaritan Hospital, Troy, NY, $20,000. For nursing arts lab and computer-assisted instruction equipment for nursing education. 1990.

1929-104 Samuel Merritt College of Nursing, Oakland, CA, $25,320. For computer-assisted instruction, audio-visual and interactive video equipment. 1990.

1929-105 San Francisco State University, San Francisco, CA, $20,000. For nursing arts lab, computer-assisted instruction and interactive video equipment for nursing education. 1990.

1929-106 Santa Barbara City College, Santa Barbara, CA, $30,000. For interactive video equipment for nursing education. 1990.

1929-107 Santa Rosa Junior College, Santa Rosa, CA, $20,000. For computer-assisted instruction and interactive video equipment for nursing education. 1990.

1929-108 Sarasota County Vocational Technical Center, Sarasota, FL, $15,055. For audio-visual, computer-assisted instruction and interactive video software for nursing education. 1990.

1929-109 Schoolcraft College, Livonia, MI, $20,000. For interactive video equipment for nursing education. 1990.

1929-110 Seattle University, Seattle, WA, $20,000. For computer-assisted instruction and audio-visual equipment for nursing education. 1990.

1929-111 Sewickley Valley Hospital, Sewickley, PA, $20,000. For computer-assisted instruction and interactive video equipment for nursing education. 1990.

1929-112 Sharon General Hospital, Sharon, PA, $44,311. For computer-assisted instruction, interactive video, audio-visual and nursing arts lab equipment for nursing education. 1990.

1929-113 Sinclair Community College, Dayton, OH, $10,000. For computer-assisted instruction and nursing arts lab equipment for nursing education. 1990.

1929-114 South Dakota State University, Brookings, SD, $10,000. For computer-assisted instruction equipment for nursing education. 1990.

1929-115 Southeastern Louisiana University, Hammond, LA, $47,319. For computer-assisted instruction and interactive video equipment for nursing education. 1990.

1929-116 Spokane Community College, Spokane, WA, $23,305. For audio-visual software for nursing education. 1990.

1929-117 State University of New York, Buffalo, NY, $20,000. For nursing arts lab equipment for nursing education. 1990.

1929-118 State University of New York, Stony Brook, NY, $51,720. For interactive video equipment for nursing education. 1990.

1929-119 State University of New York College of Technology, Utica, NY, $10,000. For audio-visual equipment for nursing education. 1990.

1929-120 Thomas Jefferson University, Philadelphia, PA, $20,000. For computer-assisted instruction and interactive video equipment for nursing education. 1990.

1929-121 Uniontown Hospital, Uniontown, PA, $10,000. For nursing arts lab equipment for nursing education. 1990.

1929-122 University of Alaska, Anchorage, AK, $45,000. For computer-assisted instruction equipment for nursing education. 1990.

1929-123 University of Arizona, Tucson, AZ, $40,000. For nursing arts lab and interactive video equipment for nursing education. 1990.

1929-124 University of British Columbia, Vancouver, Canada, $25,600. For interactive video equipment for nursing education. 1990.

1929-125 University of California, Los Angeles, CA, $18,628. For computer-assisted instruction equipment for nursing education. 1990.

1929-126 University of Cincinnati, Cincinnati, OH, $44,144. For computer-assisted instruction equipment for nursing education. 1990.

1929-127 University of Colorado, Denver, CO, $377,397. For evaluation and implementation of curriculum for National Model for Nursing Education. 1990.

1929-128 University of Delaware, Newark, DE, $10,000. For computer-assisted instruction equipment for nursing education. 1990.

1929-129 University of Illinois, Chicago, IL, $20,000. For audio-visual equipment for nursing education. 1990.

1929-130 University of Manitoba, Winnipeg, Canada, $40,000. For interactive video equipment for nursing education. 1990.

1929-131 University of Michigan, Ann Arbor, MI, $50,000. For long-distance learning equipment for nursing education. 1990.

1929-132 University of Minnesota, Minneapolis, MN, $10,000. For audio-visual and nursing arts lab equipment for nursing education. 1990.

1929-133 University of Nebraska, Omaha, NE, $35,984. For computer-assisted instruction equipment for nursing education. 1990.

1929-134 University of New Hampshire, Durham, NH, $32,199. For computer-assisted instruction, audio-visual and nursing arts lab equipment for nursing education. 1990.

1929-135 University of New Mexico, Albuquerque, NM, $20,000. For interactive video equipment for nursing education. 1990.

1929-136 University of Oklahoma, Oklahoma City, OK, $15,000. For interactive video equipment for nursing education. 1990.

1929-137 University of Pittsburgh, Pittsburgh, PA, $79,184. For interactive video equipment for nursing education. 1990.

1929-138 University of Puerto Rico, San Juan, PR, $25,000. For interactive video equipment for nursing education. 1990.

1929-139 University of Rhode Island, Kingston, RI, $15,000. For computer-assisted instruction and audio-visual equipment for nursing education. 1990.

1929-140 University of Scranton, Scranton, PA, $35,000. For interactive video equipment for nursing education. 1990.

1929-141 University of South Carolina, Spartanburg, SC, $25,000. For computer-assisted instruction, interactive video, audio-visual and nursing arts lab equipment for nursing education. 1990.

1929-142 University of Southwestern Louisiana, Lafayette, LA, $35,936. For computer-assisted instruction and nursing arts lab equipment for nursing education. 1990.

1929-143 University of Tennessee, Memphis, TN, $35,000. For computer-assisted instruction and audio-visual equipment for nursing education. 1990.

1929-144 University of the Virgin Islands, Kingshill, VI, $20,000. For interactive video and nursing arts lab equipment for nursing education. 1990.

1929-145 University of Vermont, Burlington, VT, $10,000. For interactive viddeo equipment for nursing education. 1990.

1929-146 University of Virginia, Charlottesville, VA, $51,300. For computer-assisted instruction and audio-visual equipment for nursing education. 1990.

1929-147 Villanova University, Villanova, PA, $15,000. For interactive video equipment for nursing education. 1990.

1929-148 Virginia Beach Vo-Tech, Virginia Beach, VA, $40,000. For audio-visual and computer-assisted instruction equipment and library books for nursing education. 1990.

1929-149 Walsh College, North Canton, OH, $20,550. For audio-visual, nursing arts lab, interactive video and computer-assisted instruction equipment for nursing education. 1990.

1929-150 Washington Hospital, Washington, PA, $25,000. For computer-assisted instruction equipment for nursing education. 1990.

1929-151 Watts School of Nursing, Durham, NC, $10,000. For computer-assisted instruction equipment for nursing education. 1990.

1929-152 Waukesha County Technical Institute, Pewaukee, WI, $15,000. For audio-visual equipment for nursing education. 1990.

1929-153 Wayne State University, Detroit, MI, $57,932. For interactive video equipment for nursing education. 1990.

1929-154 Westbrook College, Portland, ME, $19,108. For renovation of and furnishings for nursing arts lab and interactive equipment for nursing education. 1990.

1929-155 Western Kentucky University, Bowling Green, KY, $15,000. For interactive video equipment for nursing education. 1990.

1929-156 Wichita State University, Wichita, KS, $15,000. For interactive video equipment for nursing education. 1990.

1929-157 Yavapai College Foundation, Prescott, AZ, $10,000. For computer-assisted instruction equipment for nursing education. 1990.

1930
Fund for the City of New York, Inc.
121 Ave. of the Americas, 6th Fl.
New York 10013 (212) 925-6675

Incorporated in 1968 in NY.
Donor(s): The Ford Foundation.
Foundation type: Operating
Financial data (yr. ended 09/30/91): Assets, $9,484,566 (M); gifts received, $4,415,000; expenditures, $4,540,000; qualifying distributions, $6,785,000, including $430,000 for 56 grants (high: $25,000; low: $500; average: $5,000-$10,000), $30,000 for 6 grants to individuals of $5,000 each, $3,720,000 for foundation-administered programs and $2,605,000 for 221 loans.
Purpose and activities: The Fund for the City of New York was established by the Ford Foundation and given the mandate to be alert to the problems of the city and to opportunities to improve the performance of its government and the quality of life of its citizens. The fund seeks to improve the management of government agencies and nonprofit organizations and concentrates its programs in the areas of children and youth, housing, the urban environment and the AIDS epidemic. It operates a broad array of programs and acts as management and computer consultant, banker, grantmaker, neutral convener and broker, and incubator of new programs.
Fields of interest: Government, public policy, civic affairs, public administration, urban affairs, AIDS, housing, youth, race relations.
Types of support: Technical assistance, loans, exchange programs, consulting services, special projects, general purposes, seed money.
Limitations: Giving limited to New York City. No grants to individuals (except for public service awards), or for ongoing service programs, academic research, building or endowment funds, scholarships, fellowships, matching gifts, or studies that do not show promise of leading directly to policy or program improvement.
Publications: Multi-year report (including application guidelines), grants list, informational brochure, occasional report, application guidelines.
Application information: Application form not required.
  Initial approach: Proposal
  Copies of proposal: 1
  Deadline(s): None
  Board meeting date(s): Approximately 3 times a year in Jan., June, and Oct.
  Write: Nancy Rivera, Grants Prog. Asst.
Officers and Directors:* Frederick A.O. Schwarz, Jr.,* Chair.; Stephen Lefkowitz,* Vice-Chair.; Mary

McCormick,* Pres.; R. Palmer Baker,* Secy.; Paul Gibson,* Treas.; Roscoe Brown, Jr., Carolyn Chin, Simon P. Gourdine, Matina Horner, Nathan Quinones, Suzanne Schwerin, Esmeralda Simmons, Vaughn Williams.
Number of staff: 18 full-time professional; 1 part-time professional; 5 full-time support; 1 part-time support.
EIN: 132612524
Recent health grants:
1930-1 New York City AIDS Fund, NYC, NY, $20,000. Toward grant pool administered by New York City AIDS Fund which provides support for AIDS programs in New York City. Grant shared with New York Community Trust. 1991.

1931
The Catherine and Henry J. Gaisman Foundation
150 Ridge Rd.
P.O. Box 277
Hartsdale 10530-0277

Incorporated in 1934 in DE.
Donor(s): Henry J. Gaisman.‡
Foundation type: Independent
Financial data (yr. ended 12/31/91): Assets, $19,039,914 (M); expenditures, $363,078; qualifying distributions, $349,915, including $348,850 for 13 grants (high: $150,000; low: $200).
Purpose and activities: Giving for hospitals and medical research, including ophthalmologic and respiratory research, and Catholic church support.
Fields of interest: Hospitals, medical research, ophthalmology, Catholic giving.
Limitations: Giving primarily in NY. No grants to individuals.
Application information: Contributes only to pre-selected organizations. Applications not accepted.
Officer and Directors:* Catherine V. Gaisman,* Pres.; Robert Arias, Eric W. Waldman.
EIN: 136129464

1932
Galasso Foundation
P.O. Box 189
Cobleskill 12043-0189   (518) 234-2552

Established in 1963.
Donor(s): Susquehanna Motel Corp., August J. Galasso.
Foundation type: Independent
Financial data (yr. ended 12/31/91): Assets, $7,005,340 (M); expenditures, $192,951; qualifying distributions, $161,920, including $161,920 for 130 grants (high: $25,000; low: $25).
Fields of interest: Religion—Christian, religious schools, higher education, social services, health, child welfare.
Types of support: Student aid, general purposes.
Limitations: Giving primarily in central NY.
Application information:
  Initial approach: Letter
  Deadline(s): 6 months before funding is required
  Write: Martin A. Galasso, Trustee

Trustees: K.F. Burgin, Joseph R. Coppola, August J. Galasso, Martin A. Galasso, Paul M. Gonzalez, Michael J. Kelleher.
EIN: 166031447

1933
Gebbie Foundation, Inc. ▼
Hotel Jamestown Bldg., Rm. 308
P.O. Box 1277
Jamestown 14702-1277   (716) 487-1062

Incorporated in 1963 in NY.
Donor(s): Marion B. Gebbie,‡ Geraldine G. Bellinger.‡
Foundation type: Independent
Financial data (yr. ended 09/30/91): Assets, $62,075,054 (M); expenditures, $4,530,731; qualifying distributions, $4,446,085, including $4,309,085 for 91 grants (high: $500,000; low: $1,000; average: $1,000-$400,000) and $137,000 for loans.
Purpose and activities: Grants primarily for local organizations such as hospitals, libraries, youth agencies, cultural programs, social service agencies, and the United Way. Giving also to organizations that have shown an interest in medical and scientific research related to metabolic diseases of the bone and in detection of deafness in children and their education.
Fields of interest: Hospitals, libraries, youth, social services, cultural programs, theater, arts, community funds, education, education—early childhood, environment, community development, handicapped, medical sciences, medical research.
Types of support: Annual campaigns, seed money, building funds, equipment, matching funds, general purposes, loans, scholarship funds, continuing support, capital campaigns, renovation projects.
Limitations: Giving primarily in Chautauqua County and, secondarily, in neighboring areas of western NY; giving in other areas only when the project is consonant with program objectives that cannot be developed locally. No support for sectarian or religious organizations or for higher education, except to institutions that were recipients of lifetime contributions of the donor. No grants to individuals, or for endowment funds.
Publications: Occasional report, informational brochure.
Application information: Application form not required.
  Initial approach: Letter
  Copies of proposal: 10
  Deadline(s): Jan. 1, May 1, and Sept. 1
  Board meeting date(s): Mar., July, and Nov.
  Final notification: 1 to 4 months
  Write: John D. Hamilton, Pres.
Officers and Directors:* John D. Hamilton,* Pres.; Myron B. Franks,* V.P.; William I. Parker, Secy.; Gerald E. Hunt,* Treas.; Charles T. Hall, Kay Johnson, Lillian V. Ney, Geraldine Parker, Paul W. Sandberg.
Number of staff: 1 full-time professional; 1 part-time professional; 1 part-time support.
EIN: 166050287
Recent health grants:
1933-1 Buffalo Hearing and Speech Center, Buffalo, NY, $15,000. For instructional equipment for Interpreter training. 1991.

1933-2 Gateway Youth Center/Jamestown Ecumenical Ministries, Williamsville, NY, $10,000. To establish group therapy and hire certified alcoholism counselor. 1991.
1933-3 Lake Shore Hospital, Irving, NY, $11,500. For mammography equipment for radiology department. 1991.
1933-4 State University of New York, Fredonia, NY, $45,930. To purchase Auditory Evoked Potential equipment for Youngerman Center. 1991.

1934
The Geist Foundation
560 Lexington Ave., 17th Fl.
New York 10022   (212) 758-4999

Incorporated about 1959 in NJ.
Donor(s): Irving Geist.‡
Foundation type: Independent
Financial data (yr. ended 09/30/91): Assets, $2,569,472 (M); gifts received, $42,529; expenditures, $282,013; qualifying distributions, $269,691, including $265,787 for 61 grants (high: $45,000; low: $360; average: $275-$73,000).
Purpose and activities: Grants for Jewish welfare funds; support also for higher education and medical research, including cancer research.
Fields of interest: Jewish welfare, higher education, medical research, cancer.
Limitations: Giving primarily in NJ and NY. No grants to individuals.
Publications: 990-PF.
Application information: Application form not required.
  Initial approach: Letter
  Copies of proposal: 1
  Deadline(s): None
  Board meeting date(s): As required
  Write: Steven Rones, Trustee
Officers and Trustees:* Louis Rones,* Pres.; Steven Rones,* V.P.; Benjamin Alpert,* Secy.-Treas.
Number of staff: None.
EIN: 226059859

1935
Lawrence M. Gelb Foundation, Inc.
1585 Broadway
New York 10036   (212) 969-3285

Established in 1957 in NY.
Donor(s): Lawrence M. Gelb,‡ Richard L. Gelb, Bruce S. Gelb.
Foundation type: Independent
Financial data (yr. ended 12/31/90): Assets, $6,679,617 (M); gifts received, $250,000; expenditures, $697,273; qualifying distributions, $669,280, including $665,750 for 59 grants (high: $150,000; low: $500).
Purpose and activities: Support primarily for private secondary and higher education; some support also for cultural programs and hospitals.
Fields of interest: Secondary education, higher education, cultural programs, hospitals.
Limitations: No grants to individuals.
Application information: Application form not required.
  Initial approach: Letter
  Deadline(s): None
  Write: Robert M. Kaufman, Asst. Secy.

Officers and Directors:* Richard L. Gelb,* Chair.; Wilbur H. Friedman,* Secy.; Bruce S. Gelb, John T. Gelb, Lawrence N. Gelb, Robert M. Kaufman.
EIN: 136113586

1936
The Laurent and Alberta Gerschel Foundation, Inc.
1001 Fifth Ave.
New York 10028

Established in 1981.
Donor(s): Laurent Gerschel.
Foundation type: Independent
Financial data (yr. ended 12/31/90): Assets, $6,600,311 (M); expenditures, $291,032; qualifying distributions, $145,403, including $145,368 for 23 grants (high: $36,000; low: $110; average: $200-$5,000).
Purpose and activities: Support primarily for education, health, and the arts.
Fields of interest: Education, secondary education, higher education, Jewish giving, medical research.
Limitations: Giving primarily in NY.
Application information:
  Initial approach: Proposal
  Deadline(s): None
  Write: Laurent Gerschel, Pres.
Officers: Laurent Gerschel, Pres.; Alberta Gerschel, V.P.; Monica Hoffman, Secy.-Treas.
EIN: 133098507

1937
Patrick A. Gerschel Foundation
720 Fifth Ave., 10th Fl.
New York 10019-4107   (212) 490-4995

Established in 1986 in NY.
Foundation type: Independent
Financial data (yr. ended 12/31/90): Assets, $6,406,172 (M); expenditures, $612,471; qualifying distributions, $550,171, including $534,900 for 49 grants (high: $250,000; low: $100).
Purpose and activities: Support primarily for an Asian cultural institution; support also for the arts, medical research, community development, and higher and secondary education.
Fields of interest: Arts, museums, medical research, community development, higher education, secondary education, intercultural relations.
Types of support: Grants to individuals, research.
Limitations: Giving primarily in NY.
Application information:
  Write: Patrick A. Gerschel, Pres.
Officers: Patrick A. Gerschel, Chair. and Pres.; Charles H. Richter, Secy.-Treas.
EIN: 133317180

1938
Gibbs Brothers Foundation
c/o Morgan Guaranty Trust Co. of New York
Nine West 57th St.
New York 10019   (212) 826-7600
IRS filing state: DE

Trust established in 1957 in NY.
Donor(s): Gibbs & Cox, Inc.

Foundation type: Company-sponsored
Financial data (yr. ended 12/31/91): Assets, $341,221 (M); expenditures, $1,361,290; qualifying distributions, $1,346,018, including $1,345,000 for 27 grants (high: $350,000; low: $5,000).
Purpose and activities: Grants largely for continuing support of organizations including maritime museums and seamen's institutes, hospitals, colleges and universities, naval engineering societies, and legal organizations.
Fields of interest: Engineering, higher education, seamen, hospitals, museums, law and justice.
Types of support: Operating budgets, research.
Limitations: Giving primarily in New York, NY. No grants to individuals, or for annual campaigns, seed money, emergency funds, deficit financing, capital and endowment funds, matching gifts, scholarships, fellowships, program support, demonstration projects, publications, or conferences; no loans.
Application information: Application form not required.
  Initial approach: Letter with financial information
  Copies of proposal: 1
  Deadline(s): None
  Board meeting date(s): May
  Write: Richard Ehrlich, Trustee
Advisory Committee: M. Bernard Aidinoff, Richard M. Ehrlich, Walter Malstrom.
Trustee: Morgan Guaranty Trust Co. of New York.
Number of staff: None.
EIN: 136037653

1939
The Rosamond Gifford Charitable Corporation
731 James St., Rm. 404
Syracuse 13203   (315) 474-2489

Incorporated in 1954 in NY.
Donor(s): Rosamond Gifford.‡
Foundation type: Independent
Financial data (yr. ended 12/31/91): Assets, $17,959,512 (M); expenditures, $929,819; qualifying distributions, $863,659, including $780,167 for 30 grants (high: $89,900; low: $1,000; average: $4,000-$40,000).
Fields of interest: Social services, welfare, child welfare, aged, community funds, hospitals, health, medical research, higher education.
Types of support: Operating budgets, annual campaigns, seed money, emergency funds, building funds, equipment, research, renovation projects.
Limitations: Giving limited to organizations serving the residents of Syracuse and Onondaga County, NY. No grants to individuals, or for endowment funds, continuing support, deficit financing, land acquisition, special projects, matching gifts, scholarships, or fellowships; no loans.
Publications: Program policy statement, application guidelines, multi-year report.
Application information: Application form not required.
  Initial approach: Letter or telephone
  Copies of proposal: 2
  Deadline(s): None
  Board meeting date(s): Monthly
  Final notification: 2 months

Write: Dean A. Lesinski, Exec. Dir.
Officers and Trustees:* Robert F. Dewey,* Pres.; Roger L. MacDonald,* V.P. and Treas.; John H. Lynch,* Secy.; Dean A. Lesinski, Exec. Dir.; Donald M. Mills.
Number of staff: 2 full-time professional; 1 part-time support.
EIN: 150572881

1940
The Howard Gilman Foundation, Inc. ▼
111 West 50th St., 2nd Fl.
New York 10020   (212) 246-3300

Incorporated in 1981 in DE.
Donor(s): Gilman Investment Co., Gilman Paper Co.
Foundation type: Independent
Financial data (yr. ended 04/30/91): Assets, $22,659,676 (M); gifts received, $2,000,000; expenditures, $1,352,776; qualifying distributions, $1,276,809, including $1,132,588 for 107 grants (high: $200,000; low: $100; average: $100-$200,000).
Purpose and activities: Giving for AIDS programs and hospitals, medical and other higher education, the fine and performing arts and other cultural programs, religious organizations and support for Israel, social services, gays and lesbians, conservation, and wildlife preservation and animal welfare.
Fields of interest: AIDS, medical sciences, higher education, cultural programs, religion, Israel, social services, gays and lesbians, conservation, wildlife.
Limitations: Giving primarily in New York, NY.
Application information: Applications not accepted.
  Write: Howard Gilman, Pres.
Officer and Directors:* Howard Gilman,* Pres.; Bernard D. Bergreen, Sylvia P. Gilman.
Number of staff: 1 full-time professional; 1 part-time professional.
EIN: 133097486
Recent health grants:
1940-1 New York University Medical Center, NYC, NY, $185,000. For general support. 1990.
1940-2 Photographers and Friends United Against AIDS, NYC, NY, $10,000. For general support. 1990.

1941
Paul F. Glenn Foundation for Medical Research, Inc.
72 Virginia Dr.
Manhasset 11030
Application address: 1250 Coast Village Rd., Suite K, Santa Barbara, CA 93108; Tel.: (805) 565-3363

Established in 1965.
Foundation type: Independent
Financial data (yr. ended 09/30/91): Assets, $2,660,884 (M); gifts received, $204,750; expenditures, $220,505; qualifying distributions, $192,247, including $132,739 for 20 grants (high: $50,000; low: $125).
Purpose and activities: Grants to 1) encourage and accelerate research on the biology of aging; 2) assist those engaged in research on

mechanisms of the aging process, with the objective of delaying or preventing the onset of senility and prolonging the human life span; 3) increase the stature of the field of gerontology; 4) broaden scientific understanding of aging; and 5) advance the field of biogerontology through special award programs.
Fields of interest: Aged, medical research.
Types of support: Research, fellowships.
Limitations: No support for sociological, as opposed to biological, aging projects.
Application information: The foundation does not accept unsolicited grant applications or fellowship nominations.
Initial approach: Proposal
Copies of proposal: 3
Deadline(s): None
Write: Mark R. Collins, Exec. V.P.
Officers and Directors:* Paul F. Glenn,* Chair., Pres., and Treas.; Mark R. Collins, Exec. V.P.; Barbara Boyd,* V.P. and Secy.; Gary S. Kledzik, V.P.; Mary E. Ruth.
Number of staff: 3 part-time professional.
EIN: 136191732

1942
The Goldie-Anna Charitable Trust
c/o Greenfield, Eisenberg, Stein & Senior
99 Park Ave., 10th Fl.
New York 10016   (212) 818-9600

Established about 1977 in NY.
Foundation type: Independent
Financial data (yr. ended 12/31/90): Assets, $8,883,797 (M); expenditures, $438,094; qualifying distributions, $315,073, including $278,960 for 73 grants (high: $150,000; low: $150).
Purpose and activities: Emphasis on higher education, including some support in Israel, medical research, hospitals, Jewish giving, and cultural organizations.
Fields of interest: Higher education, Israel, medical research, hospitals, Jewish giving, cultural programs.
Limitations: Giving primarily in the New York, NY, metropolitan area.
Application information:
Initial approach: Proposal
Deadline(s): Nov. 30
Write: Kenneth L. Stein, Trustee
Trustees: Julius Greenfield, Kenneth L. Stein.
EIN: 132897474

1943
Faith Golding Foundation, Inc.
900 Third Ave., 35th Fl.
New York 10022

Established in 1984 in NY.
Donor(s): First Sterling Corp., Modern Properties, Inc., Faith Golding.
Foundation type: Independent
Financial data (yr. ended 11/30/91): Assets, $142,363 (M); gifts received, $265,000; expenditures, $263,743; qualifying distributions, $262,579, including $261,040 for 35 grants (high: $100,000; low: $20).
Fields of interest: Hospitals, museums.
Limitations: Giving primarily in New York, NY. No grants to individuals.

Application information: Contributes only to pre-selected organizations. Applications not accepted.
Trustees: Faith Golding, Bernard Greene, Ira W. Krauss.
EIN: 133260491

1944
The William P. Goldman and Brothers Foundation, Inc.
1270 Ave. of the Americas, Rm. 1801
New York 10020   (212) 489-9700

Incorporated in 1951 in NY.
Donor(s): William P. Goldman,‡ William P. Goldman & Bros., Inc.
Foundation type: Independent
Financial data (yr. ended 12/31/91): Assets, $2,721,126 (M); expenditures, $209,785; qualifying distributions, $205,710, including $205,710 for 74 grants (high: $25,000; low: $100).
Purpose and activities: Giving for Jewish welfare funds and temple support; support also for hospitals and medical research.
Fields of interest: Jewish welfare, Jewish giving, hospitals, medical research.
Limitations: Giving primarily in NY.
Application information: Application form not required.
Initial approach: Letter
Deadline(s): None
Write: Sidney Kraines, Pres.
Officers: Sidney Kraines, Pres. and Secy.; Byron Goldman, V.P.; Jeffrey L. Kraines, V.P.; Merrill Kraines, Treas.
EIN: 136163100

1945
Sol Goldman Charitable Trust
640 Fifth Ave.
New York 10019

Established in 1988 in NY; funded in fiscal 1990.
Donor(s): Sol Goldman.‡
Foundation type: Independent
Financial data (yr. ended 01/31/91): Assets, $27,665,190 (M); gifts received, $3,900,000; expenditures, $834,669; qualifying distributions, $771,138, including $769,308 for 4 grants (high: $240,000; low: $159,308).
Fields of interest: Hospitals, Jewish giving, Jewish welfare, higher education.
Limitations: Giving primarily in New York, NY. No grants to individuals.
Application information: Application form not required.
Initial approach: Proposal
Deadline(s): None
Write: Jane H. Goldman, Trustee
Trustees: Allan H. Goldman, Jane H. Goldman, Louisa Little.
EIN: 133577310

1946
Herman Goldman Foundation ▼
61 Broadway, 18th Fl.
New York 10006   (212) 797-9090

Incorporated in 1943 in NY.

Donor(s): Herman Goldman.‡
Foundation type: Independent
Financial data (yr. ended 02/28/91): Assets, $28,890,776 (M); gifts received, $6,780; expenditures, $2,296,314; qualifying distributions, $2,077,522, including $1,800,056 for 109 grants (high: $100,000; low: $500; average: $10,000-$50,000).
Purpose and activities: Emphasis on aiding economically and socially deprived persons through innovative grants in four main areas: Health - to achieve effective delivery of physical and mental health care services; Social Justice - to develop organizational, social, and legal approaches to aid deprived or handicapped people; Education - for new or improved counseling for effective pre-school, vocational and paraprofessional training; and the Arts - to increase opportunities for talented youth to receive training and for less affluent individuals to attend quality presentations; some aid for programs relating to nationwide problems.
Fields of interest: Health, mental health, handicapped, social services, disadvantaged, law and justice, education, education—early childhood, vocational education, performing arts.
Types of support: Continuing support.
Limitations: Giving primarily in the New York, NY, metropolitan area. No support for religious organizations. No grants to individuals.
Publications: Annual report (including application guidelines).
Application information: Application form not required.
Initial approach: Proposal
Copies of proposal: 1
Deadline(s): Middle of month preceding board meeting
Board meeting date(s): Monthly; grants considered every other month beginning in Apr.
Final notification: 1 to 2 months
Write: Richard K. Baron, Exec. Dir.
Officers and Directors:* Stanley M. Klein,* Pres.; David A. Brauner,* V.P.; Raymond S. Baron,* Secy.-Treas.; Richard K. Baron, Exec. Dir.; Jules M. Baron, Paul Bauman, Robert N. Davies, Emanuel Goldstein, Michael L. Goldstein, Seymour H. Kligler, Elias Rosenzweig, Gail Schneider, Norman H. Sparber.
Number of staff: 2 full-time professional.
EIN: 136066039
Recent health grants:
1946-1 AIDS Treatment Registry, NYC, NY, $10,000. Toward providing accurate, comprehensive and accessible information on AIDS and HIV-related clinical drug trials to persons in need of such information in New York metropolitan area. 1991.
1946-2 American Cancer Society, Florida Division, Miami, FL, $22,500. For renewed support. 1991.
1946-3 Cancer Care, NYC, NY, $10,000. For major Pain Initiative, three-year educational campaign designed to create greater awareness and improve patient care, oriented toward general public. 1991.
1946-4 Corporal Works Corporation, Hartford, CT, $25,000. For residential center for individuals living with AIDS. 1991.
1946-5 Cystic Fibrosis Foundation, NYC, NY, $15,000. For renewed funding. 1991.

1946-6 Fifty-Two Association, NYC, NY, $10,000. 1991.

1946-7 Fountain House, NYC, NY, $10,000. 1991.

1946-8 Franklin Hospital Medical Center, Valley Stream, NY, $15,000. Toward acquisition and maintenance of Picker 1200 SX 4th Generation CT scan for detection of abnormalities in early stages. 1991.

1946-9 Interplast, Palo Alto, CA, $10,000. 1991.

1946-10 Lenox Hill Hospital, Tropical Disease Center, NYC, NY, $25,000. 1991.

1946-11 Long Beach Memorial Hospital, Long Beach, NY, $50,000. Toward reconstruction of unit for patients suffering from head trauma, spinal injuries and debilitating injuries to extremities. 1991.

1946-12 Long Beach Memorial Hospital, Long Beach, NY, $50,000. Toward establishing new in-patient rehabilitation unit for disabled persons. 1991.

1946-13 Long Island Jewish Medical Center, New Hyde Park, NY, $50,000. Toward patient-oriented programs, including Alternate Level of Care Computer Tracking System, designed to track elderly patients waiting for discharge to match patients no longer in need of medical care with most effective and efficient discharge plan. 1991.

1946-14 March of Dimes Birth Defects Foundation, Greater New York Chapter, NYC, NY, $10,000. 1991.

1946-15 Miami Childrens Hospital, Miami, FL, $15,000. To complete key refinements to community-based support program, Ventilation-Assisted Children's Center Camp, and write how-to manual so that program can be replicated elsewhere. 1991.

1946-16 Mount Sinai Hospital and Medical Center, NYC, NY, $40,000. For development of differentiation therapy for breast cancer in animals to be translated into therapy for humans, in collaboration with Catholic Medical Center. 1991.

1946-17 National Council on Problem Gambling, NYC, NY, $10,000. 1991.

1946-18 North Shore University Hospital, Manhasset, NY, $50,000. For renewed support to develop mice and rats with genetic predisposition to rheumatoid arthritis, for research purposes. 1991.

1946-19 Queens Child Guidance Center, Jamaica, NY, $15,000. To organization that provides critical mental health intervention to troubled children and their families, without regard to ability to pay. 1991.

1946-20 Retinitis Pigmentosa Foundation Fighting Blindness, NYC, NY, $10,000. 1991.

1946-21 Rockefeller University, Laboratory of Human Behavior and Metabolism, NYC, NY, $50,000. Toward nutrition-related research into how body stores and processes fuel and how obesity may bring about certain kinds of heart disease. 1991.

1946-22 Saint Michaels Medical Center, Newark, NJ, $25,000. 1991.

1946-23 Trudeau Institute, Saranac Lake, NY, $15,000. 1991.

1946-24 Trudeau Institute, Saranac Lake, NY, $15,000. For research on opportunistic diseases which afflict AIDS patients and others—such as organ transplant

patients—whose immune systems have been damaged by disease or chemotherapy. 1991.

1946-25 United Cerebral Palsy, NYC, NY, $15,000. 1991.

1946-26 University of Florida Foundation, College of Veterinary Medicine, Gainesville, FL, $25,000. For new academic facility. 1991.

1946-27 West Bergen Mental Health Center, Ridgewood, NJ, $10,000. 1991.

1947
Goldome Foundation
c/o Goldome Tax Dept.
One Fountain Plaza
Buffalo 14203   (716) 847-5800

Established in 1969 in NY.
Donor(s): Goldome F.S.B.
Foundation type: Company-sponsored
Financial data (yr. ended 12/31/90): Assets, $2,314,782 (M); expenditures, $183,648; qualifying distributions, $183,648, including $169,185 for 10 grants (high: $75,000; low: $1,000) and $5,223 for 177 employee matching gifts.
Purpose and activities: Support for urban affairs, youth agencies, hospitals, educational organizations, social services, community development, culture, and the arts; also sponsors an employee matching gift program primarily for higher education.
Fields of interest: Urban affairs, social services, youth, hospitals, education, higher education, community development, cultural programs, arts.
Types of support: Operating budgets, continuing support, annual campaigns, building funds, employee matching gifts.
Limitations: Giving limited to NY, with emphasis on western NY (Buffalo, Syracuse, and Rochester); some support also in the New York City metropolitan area. No grants to individuals, or for seed money, emergency funds, deficit financing, equipment, land acquisition, renovations, endowment funds, scholarships, fellowships, special projects, research, publications, or conferences; no loans.
Application information: Contributes only to pre-selected organizations. Applications not accepted.
Officers: Sharon D. Randaccio, Pres.; Maureen A. Ronning, V.P.; William F. McLimmons, Secy.; Richard M. Hessinger, Treas.
Number of staff: None.
EIN: 237029266

1948
Horace W. Goldsmith Foundation ▼
c/o James C. Slaughter
437 Madison Ave., Suite 2009
New York 10022   (212) 308-9832

Incorporated in 1955 in NY.
Donor(s): Horace W. Goldsmith.‡
Foundation type: Independent
Financial data (yr. ended 12/31/90): Assets, $304,734,258 (M); expenditures, $13,918,658; qualifying distributions, $12,868,544, including $12,868,544 for 275 grants (high: $300,000; low: $8,333; average: $25,000-$100,000).
Purpose and activities: Support for cultural programs, including the performing arts and

museums; Jewish welfare funds and temple support; hospitals and a geriatric center; and education, especially higher education.
Fields of interest: Arts, fine arts, performing arts, museums, music, dance, Jewish giving, Jewish welfare, hospitals, rehabilitation, handicapped, AIDS, cancer, education, higher education, libraries, educational research, family planning, homeless, aged, conservation, international relief, law and justice, general charitable giving.
Types of support: Operating budgets, endowment funds, building funds, matching funds, general purposes, capital campaigns, scholarship funds, seed money.
Limitations: Giving primarily in New York, NY, MA, and AZ. No grants to individuals.
Application information: Foundation depends virtually exclusively on self-initiated grants. Applications not accepted.
   Board meeting date(s): 8 times a year
   Write: James C. Slaughter, C.E.O.
Officers and Directors:* Grace R. Goldsmith,* Chair. (Emeritus); James C. Slaughter, C.E.O.; Richard L. Menschel, Robert B. Menschel, William A. Slaughter.
Number of staff: None.
EIN: 136107758
Recent health grants:

1948-1 Alzheimers Disease and Related Disorders Association, NYC, NY, $25,000. 1990.

1948-2 American Federation for Aging Research, NYC, NY, $50,000. 1990.

1948-3 Beth Israel Medical Center, Surgical Endoscopy Fund, NYC, NY, $50,000. 1990.

1948-4 Boston AIDS Consortium, Boston, MA, $50,000. 1990.

1948-5 Burke Rehabilitation Center, White Plains, NY, $100,000. 1990.

1948-6 Chestnut Hill Hospital Healthcare, Philadelphia, PA, $50,000. 1990.

1948-7 Childrens Oncology Society of New York, NYC, NY, $150,000. 1990.

1948-8 College of Physicians of Philadelphia, Philadelphia, PA, $50,000. 1990.

1948-9 Columbia University, School of Nursing, NYC, NY, $25,000. 1990.

1948-10 Cystic Fibrosis Foundation, NYC, NY, $25,000. 1990.

1948-11 Dana-Farber Cancer Institute, Boston, MA, $500,000. 1990.

1948-12 Georgetown University, Vince Lombardi Medical Center, DC, $25,000. 1990.

1948-13 Guidance Center of New Rochelle, New Rochelle, NY, $25,000. 1990.

1948-14 Harlem Interfaith Counseling Service, NYC, NY, $25,000. 1990.

1948-15 Harvard University, Medical School, Boston, MA, $500,000. 1990.

1948-16 Hebrew Home for the Aged, Riverdale, NY, $25,000. 1990.

1948-17 Hospital Chaplaincy, NYC, NY, $25,000. 1990.

1948-18 Hospital for Special Surgery, NYC, NY, $1,500,000. 1990.

1948-19 Juvenile Diabetes Foundation, NYC, NY, $25,000. 1990.

1948-20 Lenox Hill Hospital, NYC, NY, $25,000. 1990.

1948-21 Leukemia Society of America, NYC, NY, $25,000. 1990.

1948-22 Lymphoma Cancer Society of America, Clifton, NJ, $100,000. 1990.

1948-23 Memorial Sloan-Kettering Cancer Center, Department of Surgery, NYC, NY, $50,000. 1990.

1948-24 Mercy Hospital, NYC, NY, $25,000. 1990.

1948-25 Mount Sinai Hospital and Medical Center, NYC, NY, $25,000. 1990.

1948-26 Nantucket Cottage Hospital, Nantucket, MA, $100,000. 1990.

1948-27 National Jewish Center for Immunology and Respiratory Medicine, NYC, NY, $25,000. 1990.

1948-28 Neurosciences Institute, NYC, NY, $25,000. 1990.

1948-29 New England Deaconess Hospital, Boston, MA, $500,000. 1990.

1948-30 New York Arthritis Foundation, NYC, NY, $50,000. 1990.

1948-31 New York Foundation for Nursing Homes, Jamaica, NY, $25,000. 1990.

1948-32 New York Hospital-Cornell Medical Center, NYC, NY, $400,000. 1990.

1948-33 New York School for Circus Arts, NYC, NY, $50,000. 1990.

1948-34 New York University, Center for Neurological Science, NYC, NY, $250,000. 1990.

1948-35 Planned Parenthood Association of Bucks County, Bristol, PA, $25,000. 1990.

1948-36 Planned Parenthood Association of Southeastern Pennsylvania, Philadelphia, PA, $75,000. 1990.

1948-37 Planned Parenthood of Central and Northern Arizona, Phoenix, AZ, $31,500. 1990.

1948-38 Planned Parenthood of Northwest New Jersey, Morristown, NJ, $100,000. 1990.

1948-39 Saint Francis Hospital, Roslyn, NY, $25,000. 1990.

1948-40 Saint Josephs Carondelet Child Center, Chicago, IL, $50,000. 1990.

1948-41 Saint Lukes-Roosevelt Hospital Center, NYC, NY, $25,000. 1990.

1948-42 Skin Cancer Foundation, NYC, NY, $25,000. 1990.

1948-43 Visiting Nurse Service of New York, NYC, NY, $25,000. 1990.

1949
The Leslie & Roslyn Goldstein Foundation
c/o Nathan Berkman & Co.
29 Broadway, Rm. 2800
New York 10006-3103

Established in 1980.
Donor(s): Leslie Goldstein, Roslyn Goldstein.
Foundation type: Independent
Financial data (yr. ended 11/30/91): Assets, $1,888,379 (M); expenditures, $106,703; qualifying distributions, $83,786, including $83,786 for grants (high: $35,200).
Purpose and activities: Primary areas of interest include education, the elderly, and Jewish organizations, including welfare funds and support for Israel.
Fields of interest: Jewish giving, Jewish welfare, Israel, aged, family services, medical sciences, cancer, education, general charitable giving.
Types of support: Annual campaigns, building funds, capital campaigns, program-related investments.

Application information: Application form not required.
Initial approach: Letter
Copies of proposal: 1
Deadline(s): None
Board meeting date(s): Varies
Trustees: Leslie Goldstein, Roslyn Goldstein.
EIN: 061035614

1950
N. S. Goldstein Foundation, Inc.
650 Park Ave.
New York 10021

Incorporated in 1956 in NY.
Donor(s): Nathan S. Goldstein,‡ Rosalie W. Goldstein.
Foundation type: Independent
Financial data (yr. ended 10/31/91): Assets, $2,202,473 (M); expenditures, $118,814; qualifying distributions, $102,660, including $102,660 for 35 grants (high: $25,000; low: $100).
Fields of interest: Jewish giving, Jewish welfare, hospitals.
Limitations: Giving primarily in NY. No grants to individuals.
Application information:
Initial approach: Letter
Deadline(s): None
Write: Rosalie W. Goldstein, Pres.
Officers and Directors:* Rosalie W. Goldstein,* Pres. and Treas.; Marjorie Doniger,* V.P. and Secy.; Burt J. Goldstein,* V.P.
Number of staff: None.
EIN: 136127750

1951
The Golub Foundation
501 Duanesburg Rd.
Schenectady 12306   (518) 356-9450
Scholarship application address: c/o Golub Corp., Scholarship Comm., P.O. Box 1074, Schenectady, NY 12301

Established in 1981 in NY.
Donor(s): Golub Corp., Jane Golub, Neil M. Golub.
Foundation type: Company-sponsored
Financial data (yr. ended 03/31/91): Assets, $510,851 (M); gifts received, $1,043,617; expenditures, $602,552; qualifying distributions, $602,346, including $535,391 for 418 grants (high: $83,333; low: $10) and $34,334 for 43 grants to individuals (high: $2,000; low: $200).
Purpose and activities: Support for the United Way, arts, health, and higher education; also awards scholarships to high school graduates in areas served by the company.
Fields of interest: Community funds, arts, health, higher education, education—minorities.
Types of support: Student aid.
Limitations: Giving limited to the Price Chopper Supermarket marketing area: the counties of Berkshire, Hampden, and Hampshire counties, MA; Lackawanna, Luzerne, Susquehanna, Wayne, and Wyoming, PA; Bennington, VT; and Albany, Broom, Clinton, Columbia, Delaware, Essex, Franklin, Fulton, Greene, Hamilton, Herkimer, Jefferson, Madison, Montgomery, Oneida, Onondaga, Oswego, Otsego, Rensselaer,

Saratoga, Schenectady, Schoharie, Warren, and Washington, NY.
Publications: Informational brochure.
Application information: Application form required for scholarships.
Deadline(s): Mar. 15 for full scholarship application packet
Write: Mary Lou Sennes, Admin.
Trustees: Margaret Davenport, Joanne Gage, Frank Lorch.
EIN: 222341421

1952
Mae Stone Goode Trust
c/o Marine Midland Bank, N.A.
P.O. Box 4203
Buffalo 14240

Foundation type: Independent
Financial data (yr. ended 09/30/91): Assets, $3,445,980 (M); expenditures, $217,423; qualifying distributions, $189,818, including $186,767 for 14 grants (high: $21,250; low: $10,490).
Fields of interest: Medical research, AIDS, cancer, hospitals.
Types of support: Grants to individuals, research.
Limitations: Giving primarily in Buffalo and Rochester, NY. No grants to individuals.
Application information: Contributes only to pre-selected individuals and organizations. Applications not accepted.
Trustees: William Yorks, Marine Midland Bank, N.A.
EIN: 237175053

1953
Joseph C. and Clare F. Goodman Memorial Foundation, Inc.
230 Park Ave., Rm. 2300
New York 10017

Incorporated in 1969 in NY.
Donor(s): Clare F. Goodman.‡
Foundation type: Independent
Financial data (yr. ended 09/30/91): Assets, $3,068,832 (M); expenditures, $159,807; qualifying distributions, $131,694, including $124,500 for 14 grants (high: $35,000; low: $1,500).
Fields of interest: Hospitals, health associations, youth.
Limitations: Giving primarily in New York, NY. No grants to individuals.
Application information: Contributes only to pre-selected organizations. Applications not accepted.
Officers: Joseph E. Seminara, Pres.; Joyce N. Eichenberg, V.P.; Sheldon Engelhardt, Treas.
EIN: 237039999

1954
David Goodstein Family Foundation, Inc.
c/o Milton Wolosoff CPA, P.C.
60 East 42nd St., Suite 823
New York 10165-0823   (212) 687-9515

Incorporated in 1944 in NY.
Donor(s): Members of the Goodstein family and family-related businesses.

Foundation type: Independent
Financial data (yr. ended 02/28/91): Assets, $5,476,705 (M); expenditures, $249,293; qualifying distributions, $230,184, including $220,000 for 57 grants (high: $42,000; low: $100).
Fields of interest: Jewish welfare, hospitals, higher education, medical education, cultural programs.
Types of support: General purposes, continuing support, annual campaigns, emergency funds, building funds, equipment, scholarship funds.
Limitations: Giving primarily in New York, NY and Chicago, IL. No support for private foundations. No grants to individuals, or for matching gifts; no loans.
Application information:
  Initial approach: Proposal
  Deadline(s): None
  Board meeting date(s): Quarterly
  Write: Robert Goodstein, Pres.
Officers: Robert Goodstein, Pres.; Marilyn Kushen, V.P.; Jeanne Goodwin, Secy.; Ivan Kushen, Treas.
EIN: 136094685

1955
Josephine Goodyear Foundation
1920 Liberty Bldg.
Buffalo 14202   (716) 856-2112

Incorporated in 1913 in NY.
Donor(s): Josephine L. Goodyear.
Foundation type: Independent
Financial data (yr. ended 12/31/90): Assets, $3,008,436 (M); gifts received, $50,000; expenditures, $200,713; qualifying distributions, $174,853, including $172,695 for 48 grants (high: $29,500; low: $152).
Purpose and activities: Giving to promote the health and welfare of indigent women and children, particularly to provide for their physical needs; emphasis on hospitals, child welfare, youth agencies, and community funds.
Fields of interest: Hospitals, child welfare, youth, community funds, women, disadvantaged.
Types of support: Seed money, emergency funds, building funds, equipment, land acquisition, matching funds, employee matching gifts, capital campaigns, research, special projects.
Limitations: Giving limited to the Buffalo, NY, area. No grants to individuals, or for continuing support, annual campaigns, deficit financing, endowment funds, scholarships, or fellowships; no loans.
Application information: Application form not required.
  Initial approach: Letter
  Copies of proposal: 7
  Deadline(s): Feb. 1, May 1, Sept. 1, and Dec. 1
  Board meeting date(s): May, Sept., and Dec.
  Final notification: 3 to 6 months
  Write: E.W. Dann Stevens, Secy.
Officers and Directors:* Clinton R. Wyckoff, Jr.,* Pres.; Edward F. Walsh, Jr.,* V.P.; E.W. Dann Stevens,* Secy.; Jean G. Bowen,* Treas.; Emma L.D. Churchill, Frank H. Goodyear, Robert M. Goodyear, Stanley A. Tirrell, Dorothy G. Wyckoff.
Number of staff: None.
EIN: 160755234

1956
Gordon/Rousmaniere/Roberts Fund ▼
10 Hanover Square
New York 10005

Established in 1985 in NY.
Donor(s): Albert H. Gordon.
Foundation type: Independent
Financial data (yr. ended 12/31/90): Assets, $14,225,441 (M); expenditures, $2,935,264; qualifying distributions, $2,805,400, including $2,751,500 for 85 grants (high: $250,000; low: $500; average: $5,000-$100,000).
Purpose and activities: Giving primarily for higher, secondary, and elementary education, including theological education; support also for a medical center and health associations, cultural programs and a historic preservation foundation, international relations, and environmental programs.
Fields of interest: Higher education, secondary education, elementary education, theological education, hospitals, health associations, cultural programs, historic preservation, international affairs, environment.
Limitations: Giving primarily in NY, MA, CA, and CT. No grants to individuals.
Application information:
  Initial approach: Proposal
  Deadline(s): None
  Write: William N. Loverd
Trustee: Mary G. Roberts.
EIN: 133257793
Recent health grants:
1956-1 Childrens Medical Center, Boston, MA, $50,000. 1990.
1956-2 Columbia Presbyterian Medical Center, NYC, NY, $100,000. 1990.
1956-3 Harvard University, School of Public Health, Boston, MA, $250,000. 1990.
1956-4 Institute for Aerobics Research, Dallas, TX, $50,000. 1990.
1956-5 Lawrence and Memorial Hospital, New London, CT, $50,000. 1990.
1956-6 Manhattan Eye, Ear and Throat Hospital, NYC, NY, $25,000. 1990.
1956-7 Memorial Sloan-Kettering Cancer Center, NYC, NY, $100,000. 1990.
1956-8 Stop Cancer, Los Angeles, CA, $62,500. 1990.
1956-9 Trudeau Institute, Saranac Lake, NY, $100,000. 1990.

1957
The Florence Gould Foundation ▼
c/o Cahill Gordon and Reindel
80 Pine St.
New York 10005   (212) 701-3400

Incorporated in 1957 in NY.
Donor(s): Florence J. Gould.‡
Foundation type: Independent
Financial data (yr. ended 12/31/90): Assets, $67,833,784 (M); gifts received, $10,799; expenditures, $4,170,990; qualifying distributions, $3,740,908, including $3,587,638 for 86 grants (high: $333,333; low: $1,100; average: $5,000-$100,000).
Purpose and activities: Established "to promote French-American amity and understanding" and for general charitable giving; support for

museums, higher education, and the arts in the U.S. and France, and for a hospital in Paris.
Fields of interest: France, museums, higher education, arts.
Limitations: Giving primarily in the U.S. and France. No grants to individuals.
Application information: Application form not required.
  Deadline(s): None
  Board meeting date(s): As necessary
  Final notification: Varies
  Write: John R. Young, Pres.
Officers and Directors:* John R. Young,* Pres.; William E. Hegarty,* V.P. and Secy.; Daniel Davison,* V.P. and Treas.; Daniel Wildenstein,* V.P.; Walter C. Cliff.
Number of staff: None.
EIN: 136176855
Recent health grants:
1957-1 American Hospital of Paris Foundation, NYC, NY, $333,333. 1990.
1957-2 Cornell University, Medical College, Ithaca, NY, $250,000. 1990.
1957-3 Mount Sinai Hospital and Medical Center, NYC, NY, $138,500. 1990.
1957-4 Pasteur Foundation, NYC, NY, $100,000. For GMHC. 1990.
1957-5 Rheumatology/Immunology and Allergy Research Fund, France, $98,500. 1990.

1958
Charles M. & Mary D. Grant Foundation
c/o Morgan Guaranty Trust Co. of New York
60 Wall St.
New York 10260   (212) 648-9664

Established in 1967 in NY.
Donor(s): Mary D. Grant.‡
Foundation type: Independent
Financial data (yr. ended 12/31/90): Assets, $5,516,625 (M); expenditures, $317,371; qualifying distributions, $275,752, including $270,000 for 13 grants (high: $50,000; low: $10,000).
Fields of interest: Higher education, hospitals, hospices, social services, youth.
Types of support: Operating budgets, continuing support, seed money, building funds, equipment, land acquisition, publications, special projects, general purposes.
Limitations: Giving primarily in the southern U.S. No grants to individuals, or for research, endowment funds, or matching gifts; generally no scholarships or fellowships; no loans.
Application information:
  Initial approach: Letter
  Copies of proposal: 1
  Deadline(s): None
  Board meeting date(s): May and Aug.
  Write: Hildy J. Simmons, V.P., Morgan Guaranty Trust Co. of New York
Trustee: Morgan Guaranty Trust Co. of New York.
Number of staff: 5
EIN: 136264329

1959
William T. Grant Foundation ▼
515 Madison Ave., 6th Fl.
New York 10022-5403   (212) 752-0071

Incorporated in 1936 in DE.

Donor(s): William T. Grant.‡
Foundation type: Independent
Financial data (yr. ended 12/31/90): Assets, $149,300,000 (M); expenditures, $7,800,000; qualifying distributions, $8,200,000, including $6,500,000 for 149 grants (high: $292,000; low: $329).

Purpose and activities: Supports research in any medical or social-behavioral scientific discipline on the development of school-age children, adolescents and youth. The foundation is especially interested in interdisciplinary research employing multiple methods to investigate several problems simultaneously. Support is available in four forms, all of which are investigator-initiated: 1) research grants; 2) evaluations of innovative community-based interventions aimed at reducing problem behaviors; 3) Faculty Scholars Program for junior investigators; and 4) a limited number of small one-time grants for child-related community service projects in the New York metropolitan area.

Fields of interest: Psychology, mental health, child development, youth, public policy, psychiatry, educational research, race relations, child welfare, delinquency, disadvantaged, education—minorities.

Types of support: Special projects, research.
Limitations: Giving limited to the metropolitan New York City area for community service grants. No grants to individuals, except for Faculty Scholars Program, or for annual fundraising campaigns, equipment and materials, land acquisition, building or renovation projects, operating budgets, endowments, or scholarships; no loans.

Publications: Annual report, informational brochure (including application guidelines), newsletter.

Application information: Application to Faculty Scholars Program by nomination only. All applicants will be notified as to required copies of proposals. Application form not required.

Initial approach: Letter
Copies of proposal: 6
Deadline(s): July 1 for Faculty Scholars Program nominations; no set deadline for grants
Board meeting date(s): Feb., June, Oct. and Dec.
Final notification: Immediately following board meeting; Mar. for Faculty Scholars Program
Write: Dr. Beatrix A. Hamburg, Pres.

Officers and Directors:* Robert P. Patterson, Jr.,* Chair.; Robert Johns Haggerty, M.D.,* Pres.; Lonnie R. Sherrod, V.P. for Prog.; Mary Goodley-Thomas, V.P. for Finance and Admin.; William H. Chisholm,* Treas.; Eileen Dorann, Controller; Ellis T. Gravette, Jr., Beatrix A. Hamburg, M.D., Martha L. Minow, Richard Price, Henry W. Riecken, Kenneth S. Rolland, Rivington R. Winant.

Number of staff: 5 full-time professional; 10 full-time support.
EIN: 131624021
Recent health grants:

1959-1 American Academy of Pediatrics, Elk Grove Village, IL, $10,000. For consensus conference on developmental issues related to children. 1991.

1959-2 Case Western Reserve University, Cleveland, OH, $175,000. For research on

AIDS education for African-American adolescents at risk. 1991.

1959-3 Childrens Hospital, Boston, MA, $10,000. For project on self-poisoning in high risk populations of adolescents. 1991.

1959-4 Community Health Project, NYC, NY, $10,000. For local programs that help children. 1991.

1959-5 Cornell University, Ithaca, NY, $57,500. For Consortium for Research Involving Stress Processes (CRISP) to review and critique methods used in stress research, focus on content area of research issues pertaining to family interactions in lifespan development and examine how families deal with chronic stress. 1991.

1959-6 Health Research, NYC, NY, $10,000. For local programs that help children. 1991.

1959-7 International Center for the Disabled (ICD), NYC, NY, $10,000. For local programs that help children. 1991.

1959-8 International Life Sciences Institute-Nutrition Foundation, DC, $10,000. For consultant to review work in psychometric instruments. 1991.

1959-9 Johns Hopkins University, Baltimore, MD, $10,000. For estimating impact of economic transition on health of children and youth in Eastern and Western Germany. 1991.

1959-10 Johns Hopkins University, School of Hygiene and Public Health, DC, $175,000. For research on timing and sequencing of marriage and motherhood implications for well-being of adolescent mothers. 1991.

1959-11 Montefiore Medical Center, NYC, NY, $94,147. For research on homeless, indigent children and their health, education and development. 1991.

1959-12 Montreal Childrens Hospital, Research Consortium on Chronic illness in Childhood, Montreal, Canada, $50,048. To continue to develop conceptual development of this field, enhance quality of empirical research in field and influence public policy and professional education in field. 1991.

1959-13 Mount Sinai Hospital and Medical Center, NYC, NY, $31,180. For workshop on child labor. 1991.

1959-14 National Association on Drug Abuse Problems, NYC, NY, $10,000. For local programs that help children. 1991.

1959-15 National Center for Clinical Infant Programs, Arlington, VA, $10,000. For report, Preventive Health Care for Young Children: A Ten Country Study with Analysis of Reference to U.S. Policy. 1991.

1959-16 National Health Policy Forum, DC, $154,216. For Children at Risk series, seminars on issues of child health and welfare, in which federal policymakers hear experts from variety of disciplines outline problems and options. 1991.

1959-17 National Jewish Center for Immunology and Respiratory Medicine, NYC, NY, $293,361. For assessment of psychological and physiological stressors in children at genetic risk for development of asthma. 1991.

1959-18 New York Academy of Medicine, NYC, NY, $10,000. For conference on pediatric poverty. 1991.

1959-19 Pennsylvania State University, University Park, PA, $10,000. For consortium

on depression in childhood and adolescence. 1991.

1959-20 San Diego State University, San Diego, CA, $175,000. For research on maltreated children and corresponding social maladjustment. 1991.

1959-21 Stanford University, Stanford, CA, $278,340. For research on verbal self-regulation in children at-risk for Attention Deficit Hyperactivity Disorder (ADHD). 1991.

1959-22 University of California, Los Angeles, CA, $338,172. For longitudinal study of adolescent women at-risk. 1991.

1959-23 University of California, Los Angeles, CA, $10,000. For consortium on developmental psychobiology of stress. 1991.

1959-24 University of California, Los Angeles, CA, $10,000. For consortium on adolescent bereavement. 1991.

1959-25 University of California, San Diego, CA, $10,000. For research on Comprehensive school health and educational reform. 1991.

1959-26 University of Colorado, Boulder, CO, $180,000. For research on contraceptive and health behavior over time in adolescents. 1991.

1959-27 University of Colorado, Boulder, CO, $53,699. For supplement to Pediatric Scientist Development Program, training for pediatricians in behavioral science research methods. 1991.

1959-28 University of Massachusetts Medical Center, Worcester, MA, $97,423. For research on community-based care for children with special needs and their families. 1991.

1959-29 University of Medicine and Dentistry of New Jersey, Newark, NJ, $67,504. For research project, Abused Child as Parent: Perceptions of Self and Others. 1991.

1959-30 University of Missouri, Saint Louis, MO, $10,000. For study, Levels and Dimensions of Evaluation of Stress Among School-age Children: America and Denmark. 1991.

1959-31 University of New Mexico, Albuquerque, NM, $59,470. For research on male fertility and parenting in New Mexico. 1991.

1959-32 University of North Carolina, Chapel Hill, NC, $175,000. For research on childhood peer rejection, aggression and academic adjustment and influence of family, neighborhood and cultural contexts on developmental pathways and mental health outcomes. 1991.

1959-33 University of North Carolina, Chapel Hill, NC, $16,100. For publication of monograph, Preventive Health Care for Young Children: Findings from Ten Country Study and Directions for U.S. Policy. 1991.

1959-34 University of Rochester, Rochester, NY, $498,355. For evaluation of maternal and child development outcomes in trial of pregnancy and infancy nurse-home visitation. 1991.

1959-35 University of Rochester, Rochester, NY, $322,500. For research on childhood maltreatment and developmental psychopathology. 1991.

1959-36 University of Washington, Seattle, WA, $10,000. For research on effects of traumatic parental death upon bereaved children and adolescents. 1991.

1959-37 Wake Forest University, Winston-Salem, NC, $175,000. For research on cognitive and psychiatric characteristics of adolescents at high risk for suicide attempts. 1991.

1959-38 Yale University, New Haven, CT, $200,082. For research on risk and protective factors in long-term life outcomes for adolescent mothers and their children. 1991.

1959-39 Yale University, New Haven, CT, $10,000. For social and health behavior survey for adolescents. 1991.

1959-40 Yale University, New Haven, CT, $10,000. For study of youth suicide in Israeli Defense Force. 1991.

1960
Graphic Controls Corporate Giving Program
P.O. Box 1271
Buffalo 14240   (716) 853-7500
Mailing Address: P.O. Box 1271, Buffalo, NY 14240

Financial data (yr. ended 12/31/90): Total giving, $116,385, including $104,355 for grants (high: $25,000; low: $100; average: $2,500-$5,000) and $12,030 for 141 employee matching gifts.
Purpose and activities: Main areas of interest are: the arts and humanities, business education, community development, and hospitals; also considers human services, including aid for the elderly, child welfare, drug abuse, the handicapped, education, including minority, and early childhood education, health, including AIDS, and medical research. Company also has employee volunteer programs.
Fields of interest: Aged, AIDS, alcoholism, arts, business, business education, child development, civic affairs, community development, community funds, conservation, drug abuse, employment, family services, government, handicapped, homeless, hospitals, humanities, international affairs, literacy, medical education, media and communications, mental health, minorities, rehabilitation, safety, science and technology, urban affairs, volunteerism, welfare, youth, women.
Types of support: Annual campaigns, building funds, capital campaigns, conferences and seminars, continuing support, emergency funds, employee matching gifts, internships, lectureships, matching funds, employee volunteer services, publications, renovation projects, research, employee-related scholarships, scholarship funds, seed money, special projects, technical assistance.
Limitations: Giving primarily in Buffalo, Clayton, and other parts of western NY; Cherry Hill, NJ; and Wilmerding, PA. No grants for operating funds.
Publications: Program policy statement, application guidelines.
Application information: Contributions are handled by Public Affairs. Application form not required.
  Initial approach: Request letter with financial information to headquarters
  Copies of proposal: 1
  Deadline(s): Nov. 1
  Board meeting date(s): Approx. Nov. 15
  Final notification: Dec. 30
  Write: May C. Randazzo, APR, Mgr., Public Affairs and Communs.

Administrators: Patricia Baubonis, Mgr., Legal Services; Rosanne Dee, Div. Human Resource Mgr.; James Menchette, Quality Control Technician; John Neuretuer, Sr. Inventory Planner.
Number of staff: 1 part-time professional; 1 part-time support.

1961
The Grateful Foundation, Inc.
280 Park Ave., West Bldg., Suite 2750
New York 10017   (212) 972-1818

Established in 1987 in DE.
Donor(s): Jordan Seaman.
Foundation type: Independent
Financial data (yr. ended 10/31/91): Assets, $2,632,663 (M); expenditures, $135,149; qualifying distributions, $102,015, including $101,550 for 4 grants (high: $50,000; low: $550).
Fields of interest: Medical research, AIDS.
Types of support: Research.
Limitations: Giving primarily in NY and CA. No grants to individuals.
Application information:
  Initial approach: Letter
  Deadline(s): None
  Write: Lewis Stein
Officers: Jordan Seaman, Pres.; Dana Seamon, V.P.; Robert Krissoff, Secy.
EIN: 112897411

1962
The Green Fund, Inc. ▼
501 Fifth Ave., Suite 1814
New York 10017   (212) 697-9531

Incorporated in 1947 in NY.
Donor(s): Evelyn Green Davis,‡ Louis A. Green.‡
Foundation type: Independent
Financial data (yr. ended 01/31/91): Assets, $23,152,121 (M); gifts received, $437,600; expenditures, $1,686,164; qualifying distributions, $1,525,290, including $1,414,645 for 207 grants (high: $275,036; low: $25; average: $250-$10,000).
Purpose and activities: Giving primarily for Jewish welfare funds, hospitals within the Jewish Federation network, services to the aged and mentally handicapped, higher and secondary education, the performing arts, social services, and youth agencies.
Fields of interest: Jewish giving, Jewish welfare, hospitals, performing arts, higher education, secondary education, youth, aged, social services, mental health.
Limitations: Giving primarily in the New York, NY, metropolitan area. No grants to individuals.
Application information: Grants initiated by the fund's members. Applications not accepted.
  Board meeting date(s): Varies
  Write: Cynthia Green Colin, Pres.
Officers and Directors:* Cynthia Green Colin,* Pres.; S. William Green,* Treas.; Patricia F. Green.
Number of staff: 1 part-time support.
EIN: 136160950

1963
The Alan C. Greenberg Foundation, Inc. ▼
c/o Bear Stearns & Co.
245 Park Ave.
New York 10167   (212) 272-2000

Established in 1964.
Donor(s): Alan C. Greenberg.
Foundation type: Independent
Financial data (yr. ended 12/31/90): Assets, $821,321 (M); gifts received, $2,175,935; expenditures, $1,657,427; qualifying distributions, $1,653,740, including $1,652,413 for 115 grants (high: $934,590; low: $50; average: $500-$20,000).
Purpose and activities: Emphasis on Jewish organizations, higher education, medical research, and cultural programs.
Fields of interest: Jewish giving, Israel, higher education, cultural programs, medical research.
Limitations: Giving primarily in NY and Israel.
Application information: Contributes only to pre-selected organizations. Applications not accepted.
  Board meeting date(s): As necessary
  Write: Alan C. Greenberg, Pres.
Officers and Directors: Alan C. Greenberg, Pres. and Treas.; Maynard Greenberg, V.P. and Secy.
Number of staff: None.
EIN: 136271740

1964
The David J. Greene Foundation, Inc.
c/o Ms. Barbara McBride
30 Wall St.
New York 10005   (212) 344-5180

Incorporated in 1966 in NY.
Donor(s): David J. Greene,‡ and members of the Greene family.
Foundation type: Independent
Financial data (yr. ended 12/31/91): Assets, $7,540,350 (M); gifts received, $6,250; expenditures, $408,323; qualifying distributions, $399,160, including $394,041 for 305 grants (high: $80,200; low: $25).
Fields of interest: Jewish welfare, hospitals, education, higher education, secondary education, social services, child welfare, youth, aged, environment.
Types of support: General purposes.
Limitations: Giving primarily in the New York, NY, metropolitan area. No grants to individuals.
Application information: Contributes only to pre-selected organizations. Applications not accepted.
  Board meeting date(s): Mar., June, Sept., and Dec.
Officers and Directors:* Alan I. Greene,* Pres.; Robert J. Ravitz,* V.P.; Barbara McBride,* Secy.; James R. Greene,* Treas.
Number of staff: None.
EIN: 136209280

1965
Robert Z. Greene Foundation ▼
c/o Parker Chapin Flattau & Klimpl
1211 Ave. of the Americas
New York 10036

Established in 1947 in NY.

Donor(s): Robert Z. Greene.‡
Foundation type: Independent
Financial data (yr. ended 12/31/91): Assets, $1,700,430 (M); expenditures, $258,419; qualifying distributions, $243,703, including $217,550 for 135 grants (high: $10,000; low: $39).
Fields of interest: Higher education, hospitals, health services, health associations, Jewish welfare.
Limitations: Giving primarily in FL and NY. No grants to individuals.
Application information: Contributes only to pre-selected organizations. Applications not accepted.
  Board meeting date(s): Monthly
  Write: Seymour Levine, Trustee
Trustees: Monroe Chapin, Seymour Levine.
Number of staff: None.
EIN: 136121751

1966
The Greenwall Foundation ▼
Two Park Ave., 24th Fl.
New York 10016   (212) 679-7266
FAX: (212) 679-7269

Incorporated in 1949 in NY.
Donor(s): Anna A. Greenwall,‡ Frank K. Greenwall.‡
Foundation type: Independent
Financial data (yr. ended 12/31/91): Assets, $58,095,986 (M); gifts received, $5,500; expenditures, $2,201,741; qualifying distributions, $2,201,741, including $1,698,829 for grants.
Purpose and activities: Giving primarily for medical research, especially in bone cancer, diabetes, and geriatrics; bioethics; education, especially for disadvantaged youth at the elementary and secondary school levels; and the arts and humanities; and to promote understanding of the concept of the free enterprise system.
Fields of interest: Medical research, education, arts, humanities.
Types of support: Program-related investments, special projects, research.
Limitations: Giving primarily in New York, NY, for arts and humanities; giving nationally for medical research, bioethics, and education. No grants to individuals, or for building or endowment funds, operating budgets, annual campaigns, deficit financing, publications, or conferences; no loans.
Publications: Annual report (including application guidelines).
Application information: Application form not required.
  Initial approach: Letter
  Copies of proposal: 1
  Deadline(s): Submit proposal preferably in Jan. or July; deadlines Feb. 1 and Aug. 1
  Board meeting date(s): May and Nov.
  Final notification: After next board meeting
  Write: William C. Stubing, Pres.
Officers and Directors:* George F. Cahill, Jr., M.D.,* Chair.; William C. Stubing,* Pres.; Richard L. Salzer,* V.P.; William S. Vaun, M.D.,* V.P.; Edith Levett, Corp. Secy.; C. Richard MacGrath,* Treas.; Chester Billings, Jr., George Bugliarello, Donald J. Donahue,* Beatrix A. Hamburg, M.D., Edward

M. Kresky, Andrew A. MacGrath, Francis F. MacGrath, Susan A. MacGrath, Carl B. Menges, Oscar M. Ruebhausen, Richard L. Salzer, Jr., M.D., Stephen Stamas.
Number of staff: 3 full-time professional; 1 full-time support.
EIN: 136082277
Recent health grants:
1966-1 Joslin Diabetes Center, Boston, MA, $192,000. For research, Transfection of Cells with Insulin Gene: A Combined Molecular and Cell Biology Approach. 1990.
1966-2 Joslin Diabetes Center, Boston, MA, $160,000. For research, Anti-Autoimmune Gene of Type I Diabetes: Potential Triggering of Autoimmunity by Somatic Mutations. 1990.
1966-3 Juvenile Diabetes Foundation International, Greater Bay Area Chapter, NYC, NY, $100,000. For research in diabetes. 1990.
1966-4 University of Texas Southwestern Medical Center, Dallas, TX, $100,000. For research, Evaluation of Novel Approaches for the Prevention of Diabetes. 1990.
1966-5 Virginia Mason Medical Center, Seattle, WA, $191,188. For research, Modulation of Immunologic Signals in IDDM. 1990.

1967
The Griffis Foundation, Inc.
c/o Pulsifer & Hutner, Inc.
14 Wall St.
New York 10005

Incorporated in 1943 in NY.
Donor(s): Stanton Griffis,‡ Nixon Griffis.
Foundation type: Independent
Financial data (yr. ended 12/31/90): Assets, $8,240,731 (M); expenditures, $505,301; qualifying distributions, $395,419, including $203,943 for 65 grants (high: $29,000; low: $20; average: $500-$2,000) and $20,073 for foundation-administered programs.
Purpose and activities: Emphasis on continuing projects in conservation, education, the humanities, health, and research in oceanographic fields; support also for religious purposes and social services.
Fields of interest: Conservation, education, humanities, health, marine sciences, biological sciences, religion, social services.
Types of support: Operating budgets, continuing support, seed money, deficit financing, professorships, fellowships, research, publications.
Limitations: Giving primarily in NY and CT. No grants to individuals, or for capital or endowment funds, annual campaigns, emergency funds, matching gifts, or conferences; no loans.
Publications: Program policy statement, application guidelines.
Application information: Application form not required.
  Initial approach: Letter
  Copies of proposal: 1
  Deadline(s): None
  Board meeting date(s): 10 times per year
  Final notification: 2 months
  Write: Nixon Griffis, Pres.
Officers and Directors:* Nixon Griffis,* Pres.; Hethea Nye,* V.P.; Hughes Griffis,* Secy.-Treas.; William G. Conway.
Number of staff: 1 part-time support.
EIN: 135678764

1968
Lila Gruber Research Foundation
19 Laurel Dr.
Great Neck 11021

Established in 1962.
Donor(s): Barry Gruber, Daryl Gruber, Murray P. Gruber.
Foundation type: Independent
Financial data (yr. ended 12/31/91): Assets, $2,010,901 (M); expenditures, $257,411; qualifying distributions, $243,806, including $243,806 for 58 grants (high: $100,000; low: $15).
Purpose and activities: Giving for Jewish religious and educational institutions and medical research; support also for social services, including a Jewish welfare fund.
Fields of interest: Jewish giving, religious schools, education, medical research, social services.
Types of support: Research, general purposes.
Limitations: Giving primarily in NY.
Application information: Application form not required.
  Initial approach: Letter
  Deadline(s): Nov. 15
  Write: Murray P. Gruber, Trustee
Trustee: Murray P. Gruber.
EIN: 116035223

1969
J. Gurwin Foundation, Inc.
P.O. Box 798
Great Neck 11022   (516) 466-3800

Incorporated in 1959 in NY.
Donor(s): Joseph Gurwin, Kings Point Industries, Inc.
Foundation type: Independent
Financial data (yr. ended 07/31/91): Assets, $11,579,249 (M); gifts received, $75,558; expenditures, $439,513; qualifying distributions, $423,932, including $422,590 for 60 grants (high: $246,000; low: $25).
Purpose and activities: Giving primarily for Jewish welfare funds; grants also for temple support and hospitals.
Fields of interest: Jewish welfare, Jewish giving, hospitals.
Limitations: Giving primarily in NY. No grants to individuals.
Application information: Contributes only to pre-selected organizations. Applications not accepted.
  Write: Joseph Gurwin, Pres.
Officers: Joseph Gurwin, Pres.; Rosalind Gurwin, Secy.-Treas.
Directors: Laura Gurwin Flug, Eric Gurwin.
EIN: 136059258

1970
Hagedorn Fund ▼
c/o Chemical Bank
270 Park Ave.
New York 10017   (212) 270-9107

Trust established in 1953 in NY.
Donor(s): William Hagedorn.‡
Foundation type: Independent
Financial data (yr. ended 12/31/91): Assets, $20,238,879 (M); expenditures, $1,946,899;

qualifying distributions, $1,561,628, including $1,289,000 for 116 grants (average: $5,000-$10,000).

Purpose and activities: Support for higher and secondary education, and church support; grants also for hospitals and health agencies, AIDS programs and medical research, the aged, youth agencies, social welfare, community funds, and cultural organizations.

Fields of interest: Higher education, secondary education, hospitals, health services, AIDS, medical research, aged, youth, child welfare, social services, welfare, disadvantaged, homeless, housing, community funds, cultural programs.

Types of support: Operating budgets, annual campaigns, building funds, capital campaigns, general purposes.

Limitations: Giving limited to the New York, NY, metropolitan area, including NJ and CT. No grants to individuals, or for continuing support, seed money, emergency funds, deficit financing, endowment funds, matching gifts, scholarships, fellowships, research, special projects, publications, or conferences; no loans.

Application information: Application form not required.

Initial approach: Proposal
Copies of proposal: 1
Deadline(s): Submit proposal preferably in Nov.; deadline Nov. 15
Board meeting date(s): Dec.
Final notification: 1 month
Write: Robert Rosenthal, V.P., Chemical Bank

Trustees: William J. Fischer, Jr., Charles B. Lauren, Chemical Bank.

Number of staff: 5 shared staff

EIN: 136048718

1971
Margaret Voorhies Haggin Trust in Memory of Her Late Husband, James Ben Ali Haggin

c/o The Bank of New York
One Wall St.
New York 10286

Trust established in 1938 in NY.

Donor(s): Margaret Voorhies Haggin.‡
Foundation type: Independent
Financial data (yr. ended 12/31/90): Assets, $16,115,944 (M); expenditures, $836,223; qualifying distributions, $733,922, including $719,299 for 14 grants (high: $363,785; low: $2,000).
Fields of interest: Higher education, hospitals.
Limitations: Giving limited to KY. No grants to individuals.
Application information: Contributes only to pre-selected organizations. Applications not accepted.
Trustee: The Bank of New York.
EIN: 136078494

1972
Irving A. Hansen Memorial Foundation

c/o Chemical Bank
30 Rockefeller Plaza
New York 10112-0002   (212) 621-2215

Established in 1983 in NY.

Donor(s): Irving A. Hansen.‡

Foundation type: Independent
Financial data (yr. ended 07/31/91): Assets, $2,394,930 (M); expenditures, $150,938; qualifying distributions, $100,250, including $100,000 for 10 grants (high: $15,000; low: $7,500).
Fields of interest: Medical research, cancer, medical education.
Limitations: No grants to individuals; no program-related investments.
Application information: Recipients chosen at the discretion of the trustees. Application form not required.

Initial approach: Letter
Deadline(s): None
Write: Ms. Diane McGuire

Trustees: Louis B. Frost, William B. Hibberd, Chemical Bank.
EIN: 133177338

1973
Gladys and Roland Harriman Foundation ▼

63 Wall St., 23rd Fl.
New York 10005   (212) 493-8182

Established in 1966 in NY.

Donor(s): Roland Harriman,‡ Gladys Harriman.‡
Foundation type: Independent
Financial data (yr. ended 12/31/90): Assets, $78,781,321 (M); gifts received, $3,053,167; expenditures, $5,135,553; qualifying distributions, $4,457,187, including $4,423,235 for 76 grants (high: $520,000; low: $1,000; average: $20,000-$50,000).
Purpose and activities: Giving primarily for education; support also for youth and social service agencies, and health agencies and hospitals.
Fields of interest: Education, youth, social services, health, hospitals.
Limitations: No grants to individuals.
Application information:

Initial approach: Letter
Copies of proposal: 1
Deadline(s): None
Board meeting date(s): Apr. and Oct.
Write: William F. Hibberd, Secy.

Officers and Directors:* Elbridge T. Gerry, Sr.,* Pres.; William Rich III, V.P.; William F. Hibberd, Secy.; William J. Corcoran, Treas.; Thomas F. Dixon, Terrence M. Farley, Elbridge T. Gerry, Jr., Edward H. Northrop.
Number of staff: 3
EIN: 510193915
Recent health grants:
1973-1 American Federation for Aging Research, NYC, NY, $62,000. 1990.
1973-2 Cornell University Medical College, NYC, NY, $50,000. 1990.
1973-3 Deafness Research Foundation, NYC, NY, $15,000. 1990.
1973-4 Good Samaritan Hospital, Suffern, NY, $25,000. 1990.
1973-5 Juvenile Diabetes Foundation, NYC, NY, $150,000. 1990.
1973-6 Long Island Council on Alcoholism, Mineola, NY, $10,000. 1990.
1973-7 New York Hospital-Cornell Medical Center, NYC, NY, $500,000. 1990.
1973-8 New York Infirmary-Beekman Downtown Hospital, NYC, NY, $10,000. 1990.

1973-9 Preventive Medicine Institute/Strang Clinic, NYC, NY, $200,000. 1990.
1973-10 Trudeau Institute, Saranac Lake, NY, $12,000. 1990.
1973-11 Visiting Nurse Service of New York, NYC, NY, $10,000. 1990.

1974
Mary W. Harriman Foundation

63 Wall St., 23rd Fl.
New York 10005   (212) 493-8182

Trust established in 1925 in NY; incorporated in 1973.

Donor(s): Mary W. Harriman.‡
Foundation type: Independent
Financial data (yr. ended 12/31/90): Assets, $17,927,846 (M); expenditures, $1,041,838; qualifying distributions, $914,873, including $867,500 for 91 grants (high: $60,000; low: $1,000; average: $1,000-$10,000).
Fields of interest: Higher education, secondary education, hospitals, health services, cultural programs, public policy, civic affairs, social services, youth.
Types of support: Annual campaigns, capital campaigns, general purposes, operating budgets.
Limitations: Giving primarily in the New York, NY, metropolitan area. No grants to individuals.
Publications: 990-PF.
Application information:

Initial approach: Proposal
Copies of proposal: 1
Deadline(s): Sept. 15
Board meeting date(s): Dec.
Final notification: 1 month
Write: William F. Hibberd, Secy.

Officers and Directors:* Kathleen L.H. Mortimer,* Pres.; William Rich III, V.P.; William F. Hibberd, Secy.; William J. Corcoran, Treas.; Mary A. Fisk, Elbridge T. Gerry, Sr., Pamela C. Harriman, Edward H. Northrop.
Number of staff: 2 full-time professional; 2 full-time support.
EIN: 237356000

1975
The John A. Hartford Foundation, Inc. ▼

55 East 59th St.
New York 10022   (212) 832-7788
FAX: (212) 593-4913

Established in 1929; incorporated in 1942 in NY.

Donor(s): John A. Hartford,‡ George L. Hartford.‡
Foundation type: Independent
Financial data (yr. ended 12/31/90): Assets, $247,916,866 (M); expenditures, $12,662,910; qualifying distributions, $9,643,942, including $9,305,199 for 82 grants (high: $271,348; low: $1,000; average: $50,000-$200,000), $292,745 for employee matching gifts and $45,998 for 2 foundation-administered programs.
Purpose and activities: The foundation provides support through 1)the Aging and Health Program, to address the unique health needs of the elderly, including long-term care, the use of medication in chronic health problems, increasing the nation's geriatric research and training capability, and improving hospital outcomes for frail elderly inpatients; and 2)the Health Care Cost and Quality Program concerned with balancing the

quality and cost of medical procedures, particularly by developing systems for assessing their appropriateness, quality, and value. The Health Care Financing Program and the John A. and George L. Hartford Fellowship Program were both terminated in 1985; the Hartford Geriatric Faculty Development Award Program was terminated in 1987.

Fields of interest: Health services, aged.

Types of support: Operating budgets, continuing support, program-related investments, special projects, research, publications, conferences and seminars, loans, employee matching gifts.

Limitations: No grants to individuals, or for annual or capital campaigns, seed money, research, emergency or endowment funds, or deficit financing.

Publications: Annual report, program policy statement, application guidelines.

Application information: No new grants to individuals will be awarded. Application form not required.

   Initial approach: Letter or proposal
   Copies of proposal: 1
   Deadline(s): No set deadline, but initial inquiry should be made at least 6 months before funding is required
   Board meeting date(s): Mar., May, Sept., and Dec.
   Final notification: 6 weeks
   Write: Richard S. Sharpe, Prog. Dir.

Officers and Trustees:* James D. Farley,* Chair.; Charles E. Murphy, Jr.,* Vice-Chair.; Norman H. Volk,* Vice-Chair.; Robert H. Mulreany,* Secy.; Stephen C. Eyre, Exec. Dir. and Treas.; Samuel R. Gische, Finance Dir. and Controller; Richard S. Sharpe, Prog. Dir.; Richard A. Cramer, Michael D. Dingman, Alexander M. Laughlin, Nuala Pell, Thomas A. Reynolds, Jr., Matthew E. Welsh, Kathryn D. Wriston.

Number of staff: 6 full-time professional; 6 full-time support.

EIN: 131667057

Recent health grants:

1975-1 American Federation for Aging Research, NYC, NY, $598,400. For fellowships for geriatric training to physicians in selected non-medical specialties. Stipends may be used for aging-related research and/or development of curricular materials for medical student and resident training. 1990.

1975-2 American Federation for Aging Research, NYC, NY, $535,700. For geriatric pharmacology scholarships for medical students. 1990.

1975-3 Cleveland Tomorrow, Cleveland, OH, $400,000. For Greater Cleveland Health Quality Choice program. 1990.

1975-4 Foundation for Health Care Quality, Seattle, WA, $331,000. For Health Care Effectiveness Information Utility - Obstetrics Quality and Access Demonstration Project. 1990.

1975-5 Health Care Purchasers Association of Puget Sound, Seattle, WA, $100,000. For Employer-Sponsored Managed Care System. 1990.

1975-6 Indiana University, Indianapolis, IN, $623,511. For study, Medication Use and Depressed Elderly Patients in Primary Care. 1990.

1975-7 Monroe, County of, Rochester, NY, $626,544. For pilot testing of Innovative

Financing and Delivery Systems for Long-Term Care for Elderly. 1990.

1975-8 National Academy of Sciences, Institute of Medicine, DC, $300,000. For design of Structured Approach to Medical Practice Guidelines. 1990.

1975-9 On Lok Senior Health Services, San Francisco, CA, $214,122. For implementation of Multi-Site Initiative for Risk-based Long-Term Care. 1990.

1975-10 San Diego Hospital Association, Sharp HealthCare, San Diego, CA, $624,752. To evaluate feasibility of developing comprehensive insurance products for elderly, including long-term care coverage. 1990.

1975-11 Society for Academic Emergency Medicine, University Association for Emergency Medicine, Lansing, MI, $90,309. To conduct surveys of physicians, patients and emergency medicine program directors in variety of hospitals to identify areas of greatest need in geriatric emergency medicine. 1990.

1975-12 University of California, San Francisco, CA, $207,252. To plan major project to enable health care consumers and purchasers to make better informed decisions in choosing among Bay Area providers for their surgery. 1990.

1975-13 University of Michigan, Ann Arbor, MI, $69,234. To plan second session of Academic Geriatrics Recruitment Program at which medical students discuss their research at 1991 American Geriatrics Society meeting. 1990.

1975-14 University of Pennsylvania, Leonard Davis Institute, Philadelphia, PA, $750,000. For continued support for development of system for rating hospital quality. 1990.

1976
Margaret Milliken Hatch Charitable Trust ▼

c/o The Bank of New York, Tax Dept.
One Wall St.
New York 10286

Trust established in 1970 in NY.
Donor(s): Margaret Milliken Hatch.‡
Foundation type: Independent
Financial data (yr. ended 10/31/90): Assets, $7,426,402 (M); gifts received, $95,799; expenditures, $2,565,299; qualifying distributions, $2,496,879, including $2,475,635 for 32 grants (high: $750,000; low: $2,000; average: $10,000-$50,000).
Purpose and activities: Emphasis on higher education, international welfare and understanding, and hospitals; support also for the aged, social service agencies, and Protestant churches. Grants almost entirely limited to institutions originally favored by creators of the trust.
Fields of interest: Higher education, international development, hospitals, aged, Protestant giving, social services.
Limitations: Giving primarily in NY and CT. No grants to individuals, or for building funds.
Application information:
   Initial approach: Letter
   Copies of proposal: 1
   Deadline(s): None
   Board meeting date(s): Apr. and Sept.
   Write: Donna Daniels, V.P., The Bank of New York

Trustees: Rakia I. Hatch, Richard L. Hatch, The Bank of New York, Irving Trust Co.
EIN: 136330533
Recent health grants:

1976-1 Cancer Research Institute, NYC, NY, $15,000. 1990.

1976-2 Columbia Presbyterian Medical Center, NYC, NY, $280,000. 1990.

1976-3 Columbia University, NYC, NY, $50,000. For cancer research. 1990.

1976-4 Columbia University, NYC, NY, $50,000. For Nursing School. 1990.

1976-5 Maine Medical Center, Portland, ME, $50,000. For Hatch Pavillion. 1990.

1976-6 Mount Sinai Hospital and Medical Center, NYC, NY, $503,635. 1990.

1976-7 Mount Sinai Hospital and Medical Center, NYC, NY, $300,000. For interdenominational chapel. 1990.

1976-8 Mount Sinai Hospital and Medical Center, NYC, NY, $250,000. For Hatch Lectureship in Geriatrics. 1990.

1976-9 Saint Vincents Hospital and Medical Center of New York, NYC, NY, $10,000. 1990.

1976-10 University of Virginia Medical Center, Charlottesville, VA, $10,000. 1990.

1977
Hausman Belding Foundation, Inc.

1430 Broadway
New York 10018   (212) 944-6040

Established in 1953.
Donor(s): Belding Heminway Co., Inc.
Foundation type: Company-sponsored
Financial data (yr. ended 12/31/90): Assets, $113 (M); gifts received, $251,000; expenditures, $380,637; qualifying distributions, $380,637, including $380,155 for 149 grants (high: $36,200; low: $25; average: $500-$1,000).
Purpose and activities: Grants primarily for Jewish welfare funds; support also for hospitals, health agencies, cancer research, education, and child development and welfare.
Fields of interest: Jewish welfare, hospitals, health services, cancer, education, child development, child welfare.
Limitations: Giving primarily in NY. No grants to individuals.
Application information: Contributes only to pre-selected organizations. Applications not accepted.
   Write: Cynthia Grushack
Officer: Jack Hausman, Administrator.
EIN: 136119189

1978
Charles Hayden Foundation ▼

One Bankers Trust Plaza
130 Liberty St.
New York 10006   (212) 938-0790

Incorporated in 1937 in NY.
Donor(s): Charles Hayden.‡
Foundation type: Independent
Financial data (yr. ended 09/30/91): Assets, $175,415,000 (M); expenditures, $7,970,000; qualifying distributions, $6,654,573, including $5,967,545 for grants.
Purpose and activities: To assist young people: emphasis on helping to provide physical facilities

and equipment for organizations primarily concerned with the mental, moral, and physical development of youth; some limited program support available for experimental projects with well-defined goals and the potential for replication by others.

Fields of interest: Youth, child development, child welfare, delinquency, education, elementary education, secondary education, higher education, education—building funds, social services, drug abuse, ecology, vocational education.

Types of support: Building funds, equipment, land acquisition, matching funds, renovation projects, special projects, seed money, technical assistance, capital campaigns.

Limitations: Giving limited to the New York, NY (including northern NJ), and Boston, MA, metropolitan areas. No support for fraternal groups, religious organizations for other than community youth-related projects, or hospitals, hospices, and projects essentially medical in nature. No grants to individuals, or for endowment funds, operating budgets, general support, continuing support, fellowships, annual campaigns, emergency funds, deficit financing, publications, or conferences; no loans.

Publications: Annual report (including application guidelines), application guidelines.

Application information: Application form not required.

Initial approach: Proposal
Copies of proposal: 1
Deadline(s): None
Board meeting date(s): Monthly
Final notification: 4 to 6 weeks
Write: William T. Wachenfeld, Pres.

Officers and Trustees:* William T. Wachenfeld,* Pres.; David B. Stone,* V.P.; Gilda G. Wray, V.P., Program; Howard F. Cerny,* Secy.-Treas.; John C. Esty, Jr., Malcolm MacKay, Kenneth D. Merrin.

Number of staff: 3 full-time professional; 7 part-time professional; 1 full-time support.

EIN: 135562237

Recent health grants:

1978-1 Ad House, Newark, NJ, $10,000. Toward renovation of basement area. 1991.

1978-2 Boys and Girls Clubs of Newark, Newark, NJ, $200,000. Toward implementation expenses for drug and alcohol reduction program. 1991.

1978-3 Center for Population and Family Health, NYC, NY, $25,000. To support construction costs relating to mental health work of clinic at IS 143. Grant shared with Columbia University and Presbyterian Hospital. 1991.

1978-4 Dynamite Youth Center Foundation, Fallsburg Residential Facility, Brooklyn, NY, $50,000. For matching grant toward construction of new Education Center for Fallsburg facility. 1991.

1978-5 Freedom Institute, NYC, NY, $40,000. Toward pilot school-based student and faculty assistance program. 1991.

1978-6 Integrity, Newark, NJ, $50,000. Toward purchase of kitchen equipment. 1991.

1978-7 International Center for the Disabled (ICD), NYC, NY, $45,000. Toward new rehabilitation and pre-vocational children's program. 1991.

1978-8 Learning Disabilities Foundation, Landmark School, Prides Crossing, MA,

$20,000. To renovate North Campus facility. 1991.

1978-9 New England Home for Little Wanderers, Brookline, MA, $175,000. To repair and increase dormitory space for boys at long term residential treatment center. 1991.

1978-10 Planned Parenthood of Nassau County, Mineola, NY, $75,000. Toward construction of new facility in Hempstead. 1991.

1978-11 Winston School, Short Hills, NJ, $25,000. To support relocation of school to new facilities. 1991.

1979
Joseph H. Hazen Foundation

110 East 59th St.
New York 10022

Incorporated in 1957 in NY.
Donor(s): Joseph H. Hazen.
Foundation type: Independent
Financial data (yr. ended 12/31/91): Assets, $3,592,457 (M); expenditures, $1,380,695; qualifying distributions, $1,380,695, including $1,375,260 for 31 grants (high: $1,000,000; low: $110).
Fields of interest: Jewish giving, higher education, museums, cultural programs, hospitals.
Limitations: Giving primarily in New York, NY. No grants to individuals.
Application information: Contributes only to pre-selected organizations. Applications not accepted.
Officers and Directors:* Joseph H. Hazen,* Pres.; Cynthia Hazen Polsky,* V.P.
EIN: 136161536

1980
The Hearst Foundation, Inc. ▼

888 Seventh Ave., 45th Fl.
New York 10106-0057   (212) 586-5404
Address for applicants from west of the Mississippi River: Thomas Eastham, V.P. and Western Dir., 90 New Montgomery St., Suite 1212, San Francisco, CA 94105; Tel.: (415) 543-0400

Incorporated in 1945 in NY.
Donor(s): William Randolph Hearst.‡
Foundation type: Independent
Financial data (yr. ended 12/31/91): Assets, $160,755,000 (M); expenditures, $6,514,000; qualifying distributions, $6,112,742, including $6,014,000 for 235 grants (high: $50,000; low: $10,000; average: $10,000-$50,000).
Purpose and activities: Giving for programs to aid poverty-level and minority groups, educational programs with emphasis on higher education and private secondary education, health-delivery systems, and cultural programs with records of public support. Organizations serving larger geographic areas generally favored over those of a narrow community nature.
Fields of interest: Education, health, social services, disadvantaged, cultural programs.
Types of support: Special projects, scholarship funds, endowment funds, general purposes, matching funds.
Limitations: Giving limited to the U.S. and its possessions. No support for political purposes. No grants to individuals or private foundations, or for

the purchase of tickets, tables, or advertising for fundraising events.
Publications: Application guidelines.
Application information: Only fully documented appeals will be considered. Application form not required.
Initial approach: Letter
Copies of proposal: 1
Deadline(s): None
Board meeting date(s): Mar., June, Sept., and Dec.
Final notification: 4 to 6 weeks
Write: Robert M. Frehse, Jr., V.P. and Exec. Dir. (east of the Mississippi River); Thomas Eastham, V.P. and Western Dir. (west of the Mississippi River)
Officers and Directors:* George R. Hearst, Jr.,* Pres.; Harvey L. Lipton,* V.P. and Secy.; Robert M. Frehse, Jr., V.P. and Exec. Dir.; Thomas Eastham, V.P. and Western Dir.; Frank A. Bennack, Jr.,* V.P.; Millicent H. Boudjakdji,* V.P.; John G. Conomikes,* V.P.; Richard E. Deems,* V.P.; John R. Hearst, Jr.,* V.P.; Randolph A. Hearst,* V.P.; William R. Hearst, Jr.,* V.P.; J. Kingsbury-Smith,* V.P.; Frank Massi,* V.P.; Gilbert C. Maurer,* V.P.; Raymond J. Petersen,* V.P.; Ralph J. Cuomo, Treas.
Number of staff: 10 full-time professional; 3 full-time support; 2 part-time support.
EIN: 136161746
Recent health grants:

1980-1 Alliance House, Salt Lake City, UT, $25,000. For general support for programs for mentally ill. 1991.

1980-2 Archdiocese of San Francisco, San Francisco, CA, $35,000. Toward Phoenix Project, drug rehabilitation and parenting skills program for pregnant women and girls. 1991.

1980-3 Baylor University Medical Center Foundation, Dallas, TX, $35,000. Toward pediatric center to provide care for children with chronic illnesses. 1991.

1980-4 Beaumont Foundation, William Beaumont Hospital, Birmingham, MI, $35,000. Toward programs in Department of Older Adult Services. 1991.

1980-5 Bellefaire Residential Treatment Center for Children, Shaker Heights, OH, $30,000. Toward meeting Kresge Foundation challenge grant to expand residential treatment services for emotionally disturbed adolescents. 1991.

1980-6 Boyer Childrens Clinic, Seattle, WA, $25,000. For early intervention services for children with neuromuscular disorders. 1991.

1980-7 Brain Research Foundation, Chicago, IL, $40,000. Toward endowment for Seed Research Grant Program at Brain Research Institute. 1991.

1980-8 Carney Hospital, Boston, MA, $35,000. For Community Oriented Primary Care Program initiated by Kellogg Foundation to expand community-based health care services in inner-city neighborhoods. 1991.

1980-9 Children of Alcoholics Foundation, NYC, NY, $20,000. For general support. 1991.

1980-10 Childrens Dental Foundation, Long Beach, CA, $25,000. Toward expansion of facilities to increase ability to serve larger numbers of uninsured children. 1991.

1980-11 Community Hospice Foundation of the Bay Area, Daly City, CA, $25,000. For programs for children with cancer or HIV infection and their families. 1991.

1980-12 Cornell University Medical College, NYC, NY, $35,000. For perinatal medical research in collaboration with United Cerebral Palsy Research and Educational Foundation. 1991.

1980-13 Craig Hospital Foundation, Englewood, CO, $25,000. For patient and family education programs. 1991.

1980-14 Deafness Research Foundation, NYC, NY, $35,000. Toward William Randolph Hearst Endowed Otologic Fellowship. 1991.

1980-15 Detroit Institute for Children, Detroit, MI, $30,000. For Educational Enrichment Fund to provide advanced training for clinical staff serving children with developmental disabilities. 1991.

1980-16 Eastchester Volunteer Ambulance Corps, Eastchester, NY, $15,000. For general support. 1991.

1980-17 Eastern Long Island Hospital, Greenport, NY, $35,000. Toward purchase of ultrasound equipment for Radiology Service. 1991.

1980-18 Family Institute of Philadelphia, Philadelphia, PA, $15,000. Toward Hispanic Family Mental Health Training Program for case workers. 1991.

1980-19 Family Services, Seattle, WA, $10,000. To expand programs for low-income stroke victims. 1991.

1980-20 Floating Hospital, NYC, NY, $30,000. Toward establishing revolving fund to alleviate cash flow problems and develop new programs. 1991.

1980-21 Friendship House Association of American Indians, San Francisco, CA, $10,000. Toward renovations to expand drug and alcohol rehabilitation programs for Native Americans. 1991.

1980-22 Grantmakers in Health, NYC, NY, $30,000. For general support. 1991.

1980-23 Greenwich Hospital Association, Greenwich, CT, $35,000. Toward purchase of Linear Accelerator for Outpatient Cancer Center. 1991.

1980-24 Hospice of Red River Valley, Fargo, ND, $25,000. For rural hospice training program. 1991.

1980-25 International Center for the Disabled (ICD), NYC, NY, $50,000. For Outpatient Stroke Rehabilitation Program. 1991.

1980-26 Leary Educational Foundation, Winchester, VA, $15,000. Toward construction of new academic building. 1991.

1980-27 Lupus Foundation of America, DC, $25,000. For general support. 1991.

1980-28 Mental Health Association of Houston and Harris County, Houston, TX, $25,000. Toward educational programs, with emphasis on programs to meet needs of culturally diverse communities. 1991.

1980-29 Mercy Hospital and Medical Center, Chicago, IL, $25,000. For health education programs at Alivio Medical Center. 1991.

1980-30 Neighborhood Health Clinics, Portland, OR, $10,000. For well-child clinic programs. 1991.

1980-31 Nellie Thomas Institute of Learning, Monterey, CA, $25,000. Toward community literacy programs in drug and alcohol rehabilitation centers for youth. 1991.

1980-32 New York Association for the Learning Disabled, Wildwood School, Schenectady, NY, $25,000. Toward construction of new facility. 1991.

1980-33 Northern Michigan Health Foundation, Petoskey, MI, $30,000. Toward establishing Hospitality House to serve families of patients at Northern Michigan Hospital. 1991.

1980-34 Norwalk Hospital Development Fund, Norwalk, CT, $35,000. Toward hospital-based and community-based outreach clinics. 1991.

1980-35 Outreach Project, Woodhaven, NY, $30,000. For general support of programs for youth with substance abuse problems. 1991.

1980-36 Palmer Drug Abuse Program, McAllen, TX, $10,000. For general support of counseling services for chemically-addicted adolescents and their families. 1991.

1980-37 Peninsula Counseling Center, Woodmere, NY, $30,000. For general support. 1991.

1980-38 Project Open Hand, San Francisco, CA, $15,000. To expand meal delivery programs to persons with AIDS throughout Bay Area. 1991.

1980-39 S.L.E. Foundation, NYC, NY, $15,000. For social service programs. 1991.

1980-40 Saginaw Valley State University, University Center, MI, $15,000. Toward training programs for occupational therapists. 1991.

1980-41 Saint Joseph Health Center Foundation, Kansas City, MO, $25,000. Toward endowment fund for community health care services. 1991.

1980-42 Saint Marys Foundation, Reno, NV, $50,000. For cardiac intensive care center. 1991.

1980-43 Saint Vincent de Paul Center, San Diego, CA, $25,000. For education and medical programs for homeless. 1991.

1980-44 Sansum Medical Research Foundation, Santa Barbara, CA, $25,000. For general support of research in cancer and diabetes. 1991.

1980-45 Slingerland Institute, Bellevue, WA, $25,000. For training programs for teachers working with dyslexic children. 1991.

1980-46 South Central Family Health Center, Los Angeles, CA, $20,000. For expansion of comprehensive health care and educational services. 1991.

1980-47 Southampton Hospital Association, Southampton, NY, $30,000. For equipment. 1991.

1980-48 Union Hospital Society of Mayville, Valley Rural Health Cooperative, Mayville, ND, $25,000. Toward programs to strengthen healthcare delivery at ten rural hospitals. 1991.

1981
William Randolph Hearst Foundation ▼
888 Seventh Ave., 45th Fl.
New York 10106-0057   (212) 586-5404
Address for applicants from west of the Mississippi River: Thomas Eastham, V.P. and Western Dir., 90 New Montgomery St., Suite 1212, San Francisco, CA 94105; Tel.: (415) 543-0400

Incorporated in 1948 in CA.
Donor(s): William Randolph Hearst.‡
Foundation type: Independent
Financial data (yr. ended 12/31/91): Assets, $352,277,537 (M); expenditures, $15,660,930; qualifying distributions, $14,317,040, including $12,565,800 for grants (high: $400,000; low: $10,000; average: $25,000-$50,000).
Purpose and activities: Programs to aid poverty-level and minority groups, educational programs with emphasis on private secondary and higher education, health delivery systems, and cultural programs with records of public support. Organizations serving larger geographic areas are generally favored over those of a narrow community nature. Support also through two independent scholarship programs: Journalism Awards Program and United States Senate Youth Program.
Fields of interest: Cultural programs, education, health, social services, disadvantaged.
Types of support: Endowment funds, scholarship funds, general purposes, special projects.
Limitations: Giving limited to the U.S. and its possessions. No support for political purposes. No grants to individuals, or for the purchase of tickets, tables, or advertising for fundraising events.
Publications: Application guidelines.
Application information: Only fully documented appeals will be considered. Application form not required.
  Initial approach: Letter or proposal
  Copies of proposal: 1
  Deadline(s): None
  Board meeting date(s): Mar., June, Sept., and Dec.
  Final notification: 4 to 6 weeks
  Write: Robert M. Frehse, Jr., V.P. and Exec. Dir. (east of the Mississippi River); Thomas Eastham, V.P. and Western Dir. (west of the Mississippi River)
Officers and Directors:* Randolph A. Hearst,* Pres.; Harvey L. Lipton,* V.P. and Secy.; Robert M. Frehse, Jr., V.P. and Exec. Dir.; Thomas Eastham, V.P. and Western Dir.; Frank A. Bennack, Jr.,* V.P.; Millicent H. Boudjakdji,* V.P.; John G. Conomikes,* V.P.; Richard E. Deems,* V.P.; George R. Hearst, Jr.,* V.P.; John R. Hearst, Jr.,* V.P.; William R. Hearst, Jr.,* V.P.; J. Kingsbury-Smith,* V.P.; Frank Massi,* V.P.; Gilbert C. Maurer,* V.P.; Raymond J. Petersen,* V.P.; Ralph J. Cuomo, Treas.
Number of staff: 14 full-time professional; 3 full-time support; 2 part-time support.
EIN: 136019226
Recent health grants:

1981-1 Adjustment Training Center, Aberdeen, SD, $10,000. Toward new facility to house programs for developmentally disabled clients. 1991.

1981-2 AMC Cancer Research Center, Denver, CO, $10,000. Toward cancer screening programs for low-income communities. 1991.

1981-3 American Foundation for AIDS Research, NYC, NY, $25,000. Toward Kresge Foundation challenge grant to establish new Community-Based Clinical Trial Groups. 1991.

1981-4 Arkansas Childrens Hospital, Little Rock, AR, $50,000. For state-wide ECMO (extracorporeal membrane oxygenation) program, treating life-threatening respiratory failure in infants. 1991.

1981-5 Association in Manhattan for Autistic Children, NYC, NY, $20,000. Toward salary of additional social worker. 1991.

1981-6 Brigham and Womens Hospital, Boston, MA, $35,000. Toward Obstetrical Impact

Team at Brookside Community Health Center. 1991.

1981-7 Cancer Care, Inc. and The National Cancer Foundation, NYC, NY, $35,000. For Pain Initiative Project, public education campaign for patients, family members and health care professionals in effort to design effective pain management programs. 1991.

1981-8 Childrens Museum of Utah, Salt Lake City, UT, $25,000. Toward educational programs emphasizing disability and health awareness. 1991.

1981-9 Childs Hospital, Albany, NY, $20,000. Toward modernization capital campaign. 1991.

1981-10 City University of New York, Medical School, NYC, NY, $35,000. Toward Gateway to Higher Education Program, preparing junior high and high school students for college and professional careers in medicine, research science and engineering. 1991.

1981-11 Columbia Presbyterian Medical Center, NYC, NY, $20,000. For conference for Varicella-Zoster Foundation on current research concerning virus and resulting diseases (shingles and chicken pox). 1991.

1981-12 Dartmouth College, Medical School, Hanover, NH, $75,000. To complete William Randolph Hearst Endowed Fund in Department of Maternal and Child Health of Dartmouth-Hitchcock Medical Center. 1991.

1981-13 Easter Seal Society for Crippled Children and Adults of San Mateo County, Burlingame, CA, $25,000. Toward computerizing vocational rehabilitation programs for disabled. 1991.

1981-14 Emory University, Carter Center, Decatur, GA, $150,000. For Health Risk Appraisal Program for health providers and health educators concerned with preventive healthcare. 1991.

1981-15 Episcopal Health Services, Hempstead, NY, $35,000. For capital campaign to build nursing home in Bedford-Stuyvesant, Brooklyn. 1991.

1981-16 Foundation for Depression and Manic Depression, NYC, NY, $10,000. For general support. 1991.

1981-17 Fred Hutchinson Cancer Research Center, Seattle, WA, $100,000. Toward construction of new campus to bring all scientific staff to one location. 1991.

1981-18 Haight Ashbury Free Medical Clinic, San Francisco, CA, $20,000. For general support of medical services for uninsured and homeless patients. 1991.

1981-19 Harmarville Rehabilitation Center, Pittsburgh, PA, $35,000. For Neuroscience Co-treatment Program for stroke patients. 1991.

1981-20 Howard University, College of Medicine, DC, $30,000. To complete William Randolph Hearst Endowed Scholarship Fund for Prospective Medical Students. 1991.

1981-21 Independence Center, Saint Louis, MO, $25,000. For general support of programs at psychiatric rehabilitation facility. 1991.

1981-22 Iowa Methodist Health Foundation, Des Moines, IA, $50,000. For programs at Family Ecology Center for at-risk infants and families. 1991.

1981-23 Jericho Project, NYC, NY, $25,000. For general support of programs for homeless adults with addictions. 1991.

1981-24 JESM Baromedical Research Institute, New Orleans, LA, $20,000. For research project concerning diagnosis and treatment of head injuries. 1991.

1981-25 Johns Hopkins University, Baltimore, MD, $35,000. Toward William Randolph Hearst Endowed Scholarship Fund in Accelerated Nursing Program. 1991.

1981-26 Los Angeles Free Clinic, Los Angeles, CA, $25,000. Toward endowment for new Homeless Services Clinic. 1991.

1981-27 Missouri River Home Health Agency, Jefferson City, MO, $25,000. Toward Medicare-certified hospice program. 1991.

1981-28 Montefiore Medical Center, Bronx, NY, $40,000. Toward expansion of services at Child Protection Center. 1991.

1981-29 National Association for Visually Handicapped, NYC, NY, $15,000. For general support. 1991.

1981-30 New England Community Health Center Association, Boston, MA, $25,000. Toward Physician Recruitment and Retention Program. 1991.

1981-31 New York Hospital-Cornell Medical Center, NYC, NY, $2,000,000. For leadership grant toward Hospital's Major Modernization Project. 1991.

1981-32 Pace University, NYC, NY, $35,000. To establish William Randolph Hearst Endowed Scholarship Fund for Minority Students in Science, Nursing and Education. 1991.

1981-33 Postgraduate Center for Mental Health, NYC, NY, $25,000. For Social and Vocational Rehabilitation Clinic for homeless mentally ill clients. 1991.

1981-34 Presbyterian-University Hospital, Pittsburgh, PA, $100,000. Toward research study on Aneurysm Detection Screening. 1991.

1981-35 Providence Medical Center, Seattle, WA, $25,000. Toward capital campaign to renovate nursing and education facilities. 1991.

1981-36 Psoriasis Research Institute, Palo Alto, CA, $10,000. Toward research on factors and causes of psoriasis as well as research leading to new treatment approaches. 1991.

1981-37 Sacred Heart Medical Center Foundation, Eugene, OR, $25,000. For prenatal services for low-income women. 1991.

1981-38 Saint Christophers-Jennie Clarkson Child Care Services, Dobbs Ferry, NY, $25,000. Toward Children's Health Service. 1991.

1981-39 Saint John-Bon Secours Continuing Care Center, Detroit, MI, $35,000. To complete funding toward Senior Community Med Tech Program. 1991.

1981-40 Saint Josephs Medical Center, Yonkers, NY, $35,000. Toward equipment needs for William Randolph Hearst Renal Center. 1991.

1981-41 Saint Lukes Episcopal Hospital, Texas Medical Center, Houston, TX, $35,000. Toward William Randolph Hearst Endowment Fund for Nursing Fellowships. 1991.

1981-42 Scott Newman Center, Los Angeles, CA, $35,000. Toward adapting Neighborhoods in Action, drug abuse prevention program, for use in minority communities. 1991.

1981-43 Sioux Valley Hospital Foundation, Sioux Falls, SD, $25,000. For Hospice Cottage Project. 1991.

1981-44 Teens Kick Off, San Francisco, CA, $20,000. Toward theater programs designed to help prevent drug abuse among teens. 1991.

1981-45 Texas Tech University Health Sciences Center, Lubbock, TX, $25,000. To complete William Randolph Hearst Endowed Scholarship Fund for Minority Students in Nursing and Allied Health programs. 1991.

1981-46 Thomas Jefferson University, College of Allied Health Sciences, Philadelphia, PA, $25,000. Toward William Randolph Hearst Endowed Scholarship Fund for Minority Students. 1991.

1981-47 Tulane University, School of Medicine, New Orleans, LA, $50,000. To complete William Randolph Hearst Scholarship Fund for Minority Students. 1991.

1981-48 United Cerebral Palsy, NYC, NY, $50,000. Toward general operating costs of Millicent Hearst Children's Center at Brooklyn Rehabilitation Campus. 1991.

1981-49 United Cerebral Palsy Associations, DC, $40,000. Toward establishment of Regional Technology Training Centers. 1991.

1981-50 University of California San Diego Medical Center, San Diego, CA, $35,000. For Hospice Volunteer Coordinator position. 1991.

1981-51 University of Maryland, Baltimore, MD, $25,000. For perinatal medical research in collaboration with United Cerebral Palsy Research and Educational Foundation. 1991.

1981-52 University of Miami, School of Nursing, Coral Gables, FL, $35,000. To complete William Randolph Hearst Endowed Scholarship Fund. 1991.

1981-53 West Virginia University, Department of Community Medicine, Morgantown, WV, $35,000. For W.K. Kellogg Foundation West Virginia Community Health Care Project. 1991.

1981-54 Wyandotte House, Kansas City, KS, $30,000. Toward Mabee Foundation challenge grant to expand residential treatment programs for emotionally distrubed youth. 1991.

1982

The Heckscher Foundation for Children ▼
17 East 47th St.
New York 10017   (212) 371-7775

Incorporated in 1921 in NY.
Donor(s): August Heckscher.‡
Foundation type: Independent
Financial data (yr. ended 12/31/91): Assets, $32,899,025 (M); expenditures, $1,867,779; qualifying distributions, $1,841,884, including $1,722,749 for 182 grants (high: $100,000; low: $52; average: $100-$25,000).

Purpose and activities: To promote the welfare of children; grants particularly for child welfare and family service agencies, education, recreation, music and the performing arts, health and hospitals, summer youth programs and camps, and aid to the handicapped.
Fields of interest: Child welfare, youth, social services, family services, homeless, education, libraries, recreation, arts, music, dance, museums, performing arts, theater, hospitals, health, drug abuse, AIDS, handicapped, environment.
Types of support: Seed money, building funds, equipment, land acquisition, renovation projects, special projects, scholarship funds.

Limitations: Giving primarily in the greater New York, NY, area. No grants to individuals, or for operating budgets, annual campaigns, deficit financing, fellowships, or endowment funds; no loans.
Publications: Application guidelines.
Application information: Application form not required.
  Initial approach: Letter or proposal
  Copies of proposal: 1
  Deadline(s): None
  Board meeting date(s): Monthly except July and Aug.
  Final notification: 1 month
  Write: Virginia Sloane, Pres.
Officers and Trustees: Louis Smadbeck,* Chair.; Virginia Sloane,* Pres.; Howard G. Sloane,* V.P. and Treas.; William D. Hart, Jr.,* Secy.; Richard N. Kerst, Carole S. Landman, John D. MacNeary, Gail Meyers, John M. O'Mara, Fred Obser, Howard Grant Sloane, Arthur J. Smadbeck, Mina Smadbeck, Paul Smadbeck.
Number of staff: 1 full-time professional; 1 part-time professional; 1 part-time support.
EIN: 131820170
Recent health grants:
1982-1 Ackerman Institute for Family Therapy, NYC, NY, $30,000. 1990.
1982-2 Ecumenical Narcotics Treatment for Effective Rehabilitation (ENTER), NYC, NY, $15,000. 1990.
1982-3 Floating Hospital, NYC, NY, $14,211. 1990.
1982-4 Happiness is Camping, Bronx, NY, $15,000. 1990.
1982-5 Memorial Sloan-Kettering Cancer Center, NYC, NY, $83,187. 1990.
1982-6 Memorial Sloan-Kettering Cancer Center, NYC, NY, $83,186. 1990.
1982-7 Mount Sinai Hospital and Medical Center, NYC, NY, $100,000. 1990.
1982-8 North Shore University Hospital, Manhasset, NY, $33,333. 1990.
1982-9 Ronald McDonald House of South Florida, Miami, FL, $50,000. 1990.
1982-10 United Cerebral Palsy, NYC, NY, $25,000. 1990.

1983
Justus Heijmans Foundation
641 Lexington Ave., 29th Fl.
New York 10022
Application address: 387 Park Ave., New York, NY 10016; Tel.: (212) 561-8700

Established in 1968.
Foundation type: Independent
Financial data (yr. ended 08/31/91): Assets, $395,587 (M); expenditures, $404,726; qualifying distributions, $404,537, including $324,310 for 5 grants (high: $324,310; low: $500).
Fields of interest: Secondary education, higher education, hospitals.
Limitations: Giving primarily in NY and CT.
Application information: Application form not required.
  Initial approach: Proposal
  Deadline(s): None
  Write: Edgar M. Cullman, Trustee
Trustees: Edgar M. Cullman, Edgar M. Cullman, Jr.
EIN: 136272082

1984
Heineman Foundation for Research, Educational, Charitable and Scientific Purposes, Inc.
c/o Brown Brothers Harriman Trust Co.
63 Wall St.
New York 10005

Incorporated in 1947 in DE.
Donor(s): Dannie N. Heineman.‡
Foundation type: Independent
Financial data (yr. ended 12/31/91): Assets, $9,341,063 (M); expenditures, $366,962; qualifying distributions, $342,542, including $340,000 for 12 grants (high: $100,000; low: $5,000).
Purpose and activities: Support for research programs in mathematical sciences and medicine; grants for higher education, specialized libraries (including the Heineman Library of Rare Books and Manuscripts given to the Pierpont Morgan Library, New York), music schools and two annual physics awards.
Fields of interest: Mathematics, science and technology, medical sciences, medical research, higher education, libraries, music, physics, energy, youth, race relations.
Types of support: Special projects.
Limitations: No grants to individuals.
Application information: Contributes only to pre-selected organizations. Applications not accepted.
  Board meeting date(s): Apr. and Nov.
Officers: David Rose, Pres.; Agnes Gautier, V.P.; Ann R. Podlipny, Secy.; Simon M.D. Rose, Treas.
Directors: Robert O. Fehr, Cecillie Froehlich, James H. Heineman, Marian Rose, Hans Tauber, M.D.
Number of staff: None.
EIN: 136082899

1985
The Harry B. Helmsley Foundation, Inc. ▼
60 East 42nd St.
New York 10165

Incorporated in 1954 in NY.
Donor(s): Harry B. Helmsley.
Foundation type: Independent
Financial data (yr. ended 05/31/91): Assets, $21,975,728 (M); expenditures, $6,897,498; qualifying distributions, $6,892,250, including $6,891,500 for 21 grants (high: $6,000,000; low: $100; average: $500-$10,000).
Purpose and activities: Grants largely for hospitals, higher education, medical research, and religious organizations.
Fields of interest: Hospitals, medical research, religion, higher education.
Application information: Contributes only to pre-selected organizations. Applications not accepted.
  Deadline(s): None
Officers and Directors: Harry B. Helmsley,* Pres.; Leona M. Helmsley,* V.P.; Frances Becker.
EIN: 136123336
Recent health grants:
1985-1 Alzheimers Disease Research, NYC, NY, $100,000. 1991.
1985-2 New York Hospital-Cornell Medical Center, NYC, NY, $10,000. 1991.

1985-3 Orentreich Foundation for the Advancement of Science, NYC, NY, $750,000. 1991.
1985-4 Society of New York Hospital, NYC, NY, $6,000,000. 1991.

1986
Hess Foundation, Inc. ▼
1185 Ave. of the Americas
New York 10036   (212) 997-8500

Incorporated in 1954 in DE.
Donor(s): Leon Hess.
Foundation type: Independent
Financial data (yr. ended 11/30/90): Assets, $110,864,489 (M); gifts received, $2,600,000; expenditures, $4,071,960; qualifying distributions, $4,036,303, including $4,028,788 for 92 grants (high: $1,000,000; low: $1,000; average: $5,000-$25,000).
Purpose and activities: Emphasis on higher education, a disaster relief fund, and hospitals; grants also for a football foundation, performing arts organizations, synagogues, and social welfare agencies.
Fields of interest: Higher education, hospitals, Jewish giving, performing arts, social services.
Limitations: No grants to individuals.
Application information: Contributes only to pre-selected organizations. Applications not accepted.
  Board meeting date(s): As required
  Final notification: Varies
  Write: Leon Hess, Pres.
Officers and Directors: Leon Hess, Pres.; Steven Gutman, V.P. and Secy.; Norma Hess, V.P. and Treas.; John B. Hess, V.P.
Number of staff: 1 full-time professional.
EIN: 221713046
Recent health grants:
1986-1 Alzheimers Association, Boca Raton, FL, $12,500. 1990.
1986-2 American Cancer Society, NYC, NY, $10,000. 1990.
1986-3 Lenox Hill Hospital, NYC, NY, $1,000,000. 1990.
1986-4 Marty Lyons Foundation, Hempstead, NY, $10,000. 1990.
1986-5 McLean Hospital, Belmont, MA, $35,000. 1990.
1986-6 Memorial Sloan-Kettering Cancer Center, NYC, NY, $11,000. 1990.
1986-7 Mount Sinai Childrens Center Foundation, NYC, NY, $10,000. 1990.
1986-8 Mount Sinai Hospital and Medical Center, NYC, NY, $157,135. 1990.
1986-9 Oslo Sanitetsforenings Reumatismesykehus, Oslo, Norway, $200,000. 1990.
1986-10 United Cerebral Palsy, NYC, NY, $33,333. 1990.

1987
Hettinger Foundation
c/o Oberfest
P.O. Box 318
Chappaqua 10514

Trust established in 1961 in NY.
Donor(s): Albert J. Hettinger, Jr.‡
Foundation type: Independent

Financial data (yr. ended 12/31/90): Assets, $10,518,240 (M); expenditures, $604,536; qualifying distributions, $555,800, including $555,800 for 21 grants (high: $235,000; low: $1,000).
Purpose and activities: Grants largely for secondary education at certain schools with which there is a long-standing relationship, including scholarship funds; support also for hospitals, cancer research, and welfare agencies.
Fields of interest: Secondary education, cancer, hospitals, welfare.
Types of support: General purposes, scholarship funds.
Limitations: Giving primarily in New York, NY, and CT. No grants to individuals.
Application information: Contributes only to pre-selected organizations. Applications not accepted.
Trustees: Betty Hettinger, John Hettinger, William R. Hettinger.
EIN: 136097726

1988
The DuBose and Dorothy Heyward Memorial Fund
c/o The Bank of New York
48 Wall St., 4-M
New York 10015   (212) 495-1177

Established in 1985 in NY.
Donor(s): Jenifer Heyward.‡
Foundation type: Independent
Financial data (yr. ended 12/31/90): Assets, $2,731,889 (M); expenditures, $2,056,000; qualifying distributions, $1,935,000, including $1,935,000 for 90 grants (high: $300,000; low: $1,000).
Purpose and activities: Grants to arts organizations and cancer research and treatment.
Fields of interest: Arts, dance, cancer.
Types of support: General purposes, research, grants to individuals.
Publications: Program policy statement.
Application information:
  Initial approach: Letter
  Copies of proposal: 2
  Deadline(s): None
  Write: Katherine W. Floyd
Trustees: Albert Cardinali, Thacher, Proffitt & Wood, The Bank of New York.
Number of staff: None.
EIN: 136840999

1989
The Hilson Fund, Inc.
c/o Wertheim Schroder Holdings, Inc.
787 Seventh Ave., 6th Fl.
New York 10019-6016   (212) 492-6910

Established in 1947 in NY.
Donor(s): John S. Hilson,‡ Mildred S. Hilson.
Foundation type: Independent
Financial data (yr. ended 11/30/91): Assets, $2,016,993 (M); expenditures, $72,203; qualifying distributions, $61,217, including $60,905 for 19 grants (high: $40,100; low: $50).
Fields of interest: Hospitals, medical research.
Limitations: Giving primarily in New York, NY.
Application information:
  Initial approach: Letter

  Deadline(s): None
Officers: Dwight R. Hilson, V.P.; William E. Hilson, V.P.; Richard J. Cunningham, Secy.; John Pyne, Treas.
EIN: 136028783

1990
Irma T. Hirschl Trust for Charitable Purposes ▼
c/o Manufacturers Hanover Trust Co.
600 Fifth Ave.
New York 10020   (212) 957-1654

Trust established in 1973 in NY.
Donor(s): Irma T. Hirschl.‡
Foundation type: Independent
Financial data (yr. ended 10/31/91): Assets, $35,043,665 (M); gifts received, $23,356; expenditures, $2,160,086; qualifying distributions, $1,990,513, including $1,820,000 for 24 grants (high: $110,000; low: $20,000; average: $20,000-$50,000).
Purpose and activities: Grants primarily to six medical schools for partial funding of selected medical research projects; annual medical scholarships to six designated medical schools; support also for 14 designated social service and health agencies.
Fields of interest: Medical education, medical research, social services, health services.
Types of support: Research, scholarship funds.
Limitations: Giving primarily in New York, NY. No support for private foundations. No grants to individuals.
Application information: All applications submitted by designated medical schools. Application form required.
  Deadline(s): Oct. 15
  Final notification: After Dec. 10
  Write: Uwe Linder, V.P., Manufacturers Hanover Trust Co.
Trustees: Robert Todd Lang, John M. Lewis, Manufacturers Hanover Trust Co.
EIN: 136356381

1991
A. W. Hoernle Foundation
630 Central Park Ave.
Yonkers 10704

Established in 1978 in NY.
Donor(s): Adolph W. Hoernle.
Foundation type: Independent
Financial data (yr. ended 05/31/89): Assets, $6,126,283 (M); expenditures, $288,254; qualifying distributions, $260,910, including $258,405 for 26 grants (high: $154,500; low: $80).
Fields of interest: Hospitals, health, cultural programs, education, social services.
Limitations: Giving limited to NY and FL. No grants to individuals.
Application information: Application form not required.
  Board meeting date(s): Annually
  Write: Fred W. Lessing, Secy.-Treas.
Officers: Adolph W. Hoernle, Pres.; Fred W. Lessing, Secy.-Treas.
Number of staff: None.
EIN: 132945331

1992
Josephine Lawrence Hopkins Foundation
61 Broadway, Suite 2912
New York 10006

Incorporated in 1968 in NY.
Donor(s): Josephine H. Graeber.‡
Foundation type: Independent
Financial data (yr. ended 12/31/91): Assets, $3,268,133 (M); expenditures, $306,079; qualifying distributions, $243,400, including $219,325 for 37 grants (high: $45,000; low: $500).
Fields of interest: Hospitals, Catholic giving, youth, performing arts, cultural programs, animal welfare, social services.
Limitations: Giving primarily in New York, NY. No grants to individuals; no loans.
Application information: Contributes only to pre-selected organizations. Applications not accepted.
  Board meeting date(s): Once a year, usually in Oct.
Officers and Directors:* Ivan Obolensky,* Pres. and Treas.; Vera L. Colage,* V.P.; Meredith N. Stiles, Jr.,* V.P.; Susan H. Whitmore,* V.P.; Lee Harrison Corbin, William P. Hurley.
EIN: 136277593

1993
Horncrest Foundation, Inc.
Six Sleator Dr.
Ossining 10562   (914) 941-5533

Established in 1960 in NY.
Foundation type: Independent
Financial data (yr. ended 09/30/91): Assets, $2,316,378 (M); gifts received, $27,000; expenditures, $140,728; qualifying distributions, $122,361, including $117,039 for 13 grants (high: $25,000; low: $500; average: $500-$25,000).
Purpose and activities: Scholarship programs primarily for minorities; support also for programs for the disadvantaged, cultural programs, medical education, and organizations that develop social change issues, including arms control, housing, and civil rights.
Fields of interest: Arts, education—minorities, medical education, housing, arms control.
Types of support: General purposes, matching funds, scholarship funds, seed money.
Limitations: Giving primarily in St. Louis, MO; Madison, WI; and the Twin Cities, MN. No grants to individuals.
Publications: Annual report, informational brochure (including application guidelines).
Application information: Application form not required.
  Initial approach: Letter requesting guidelines
  Copies of proposal: 1
  Deadline(s): June 1 and Dec. 1
  Write: Lawrence Blau, Pres.
Officers and Directors: Lawrence Blau,* Pres.; Olivia Blau,* V.P. and Secy.
EIN: 136021261

1994
The Howard and Bush Foundation, Inc. ▼
Two Belle Ave.
Troy 12180   (518) 273-6005

Incorporated in 1961 in CT.
Donor(s): Edith Mason Howard,‡ Julia Howard Bush.‡
Foundation type: Independent
Financial data (yr. ended 12/31/90): Assets, $7,753,075 (M); gifts received, $2,448; expenditures, $543,894; qualifying distributions, $502,913, including $460,716 for 28 grants (high: $62,500; low: $1,000; average: $5,000-$25,000).
Purpose and activities: Emphasis on social service and youth agencies, cultural programs, education, civic and urban affairs, and health agencies that benefit residents of Rensselaer County, NY.
Fields of interest: Social services, youth, child welfare, homeless, disadvantaged, cultural programs, arts, education, literacy, urban affairs, civic affairs, health services, AIDS.
Types of support: Special projects, equipment, matching funds.
Limitations: Giving primarily in Rensselaer County, NY. No support for government or largely tax-supported agencies, or to colleges, schools, or churches not connected with the founders. No grants to individuals, or for endowment funds, operating budgets, reserve or revolving funds, or deficit financing.
Publications: Annual report, application guidelines.
Application information: Contact staff well before submitting proposal; applications sent on request. Application form required.
  Initial approach: Letter or telephone, and 1- to 2-page concept paper
  Copies of proposal: 6
  Deadline(s): Jan. 15, May 15, and Sept. 10
  Board meeting date(s): Mar., July, and Nov.
  Final notification: Within 10 days after board meeting
  Write: Deborah Byers
Officers, Directors and Trustees:* Sara H. Catlin,* Pres.; Margaret Mochan,* V.P.; Donald Bowes,* Secy.; David Parmelee,* Treas.; David Haviland, Dean Leith, Jr., Fleet Bank, N.A.
Number of staff: 1 part-time professional.
EIN: 066059063

1995
Stewart W. & Willma C. Hoyt Foundation
300 Security Mutual Bldg.
105-107 Court St., Suite 400
Binghamton 13901   (607) 722-6706

Established in 1970 in NY.
Donor(s): Willma C. Hoyt.‡
Foundation type: Independent
Financial data (yr. ended 12/31/91): Assets, $13,455,690 (M); expenditures, $480,393; qualifying distributions, $344,898, including $330,507 for 34 grants (high: $100,000; low: $1,800; average: $1,500-$30,000) and $14,391 for 2 loans.
Purpose and activities: Primary areas of interest include the arts and humanities, health, and social and human services, with preference for capital campaigns, special projects, seed money, and operating expenses.
Fields of interest: Arts, cultural programs, humanities, education, higher education, health, AIDS, social services.

Types of support: General purposes, building funds, matching funds, seed money, special projects, operating budgets, continuing support, emergency funds, equipment, technical assistance, consulting services, scholarship funds, capital campaigns, loans.
Limitations: Giving limited to Broome County, NY. No support for religious purposes. No grants to individuals, or for annual campaigns, deficit financing, general endowments, research, or publications.
Publications: Annual report, application guidelines.
Application information: No grants considered at Jan., May, and Sept. meetings. Application form required.
  Initial approach: Telephone or letter
  Copies of proposal: 1
  Deadline(s): The 1st of months prior to board meetings
  Board meeting date(s): Bimonthly, beginning in Jan.; no grants awarded in Jan., May, and Sept.
  Final notification: 1 to 3 days following board meetings
  Write: Judith C. Peckham, Exec. Dir.
Officers and Directors:* John F. Russell,* Chair.; John M. Keeler,* Vice-Chair.; William Rincker,* Secy.-Treas.; Denise M. Balkas, Silvia Fenton, Fannie Linder, Albert Mamary, Jacqueline Visser.
Trustee: Chase Lincoln First Bank, N.A.
Number of staff: 1 full-time professional; 1 part-time support.
EIN: 237072539
Recent health grants:
1995-1 American Red Cross, Blood Services, Binghamton, NY, $15,000. For relocation, renovation of blood center. 1990.
1995-2 Broome Community College Foundation, Binghamton, NY, $200,000. Toward new health sciences building. 1990.

1996
The Charles Evans Hughes Memorial Foundation, Inc.
175 Water St., 10th Fl.
New York 10038-4924   (212) 858-6732

Incorporated in 1962 in NY.
Donor(s): Mrs. Chauncey L. Waddell,‡ Chauncey L. Waddell.‡
Foundation type: Independent
Financial data (yr. ended 07/31/91): Assets, $10,732,915 (M); gifts received, $55,014; expenditures, $564,515; qualifying distributions, $486,966, including $445,000 for 18 grants (high: $75,000; low: $5,000).
Purpose and activities: Giving primarily to organizations engaged in education, including legal education and the social sciences, legal aid, and organizations combatting prejudice based on race, color, or religious belief; support also for the arts, health, AIDS research, child welfare, and the environment.
Fields of interest: Education, legal education, civil rights, race relations, law and justice, arts, health, AIDS, environment.
Types of support: Continuing support, general purposes, research, scholarship funds, seed money, special projects.
Limitations: Giving primarily in NY. No grants to individuals.

Application information: Application form not required.
  Initial approach: Letter or telephone
  Copies of proposal: 6
  Deadline(s): June 1
  Board meeting date(s): Oct.
  Write: Mitchel J. Valicenti, Exec. V.P.
Officers and Directors:* Theodore H. Waddell, Pres.; Mitchel J. Valicenti,* Exec. V.P. and Treas.; Suzanne T. Reardon, Secy.; Marjory Hughes Johnson, William G. Kirkland, Betty J. Stebman.
Number of staff: None.
EIN: 136159445

1997
Hugoton Foundation
900 Park Ave.
New York 10021   (212) 734-5447

Established in 1981 in DE.
Donor(s): Wallace Gilroy.‡
Foundation type: Independent
Financial data (yr. ended 12/31/90): Assets, $26,920,568 (M); expenditures, $1,498,449; qualifying distributions, $1,484,930, including $1,346,000 for 43 grants (high: $300,000; low: $1,000; average: $5,000-$25,000).
Purpose and activities: Giving primarily for hospitals, medical research, and equipment needs; some support for higher and pre-college education and religious welfare.
Fields of interest: Medical research, hospitals, nursing, higher education, religious welfare.
Types of support: Equipment, special projects, research.
Limitations: Giving primarily in New York, NY, and Miami, FL. No grants to individuals.
Application information:
  Initial approach: Proposal
  Deadline(s): None
  Board meeting date(s): As necessary
  Final notification: 2 months
  Write: Joan K. Stout, Pres.
Officers and Directors:* Joan K. Stout,* Pres. and Treas.; Arthur Jansen,* V.P.; Joan M. Stout,* Secy.; Frank S. Fejes.
Number of staff: None.
EIN: 341351062

1998
Nila B. Hulbert Foundation
Six Ford Ave.
Oneonta 13820-1898   (607) 432-6720

Established about 1971.
Donor(s): Nila B. Hulbert.
Foundation type: Independent
Financial data (yr. ended 12/31/91): Assets, $3,336,907 (M); gifts received, $94,333; expenditures, $140,186; qualifying distributions, $137,174, including $101,600 for 17 grants (high: $25,000; low: $100).
Fields of interest: Hospitals, higher education, recreation, libraries, community development.
Limitations: Giving primarily in Oneonta, NY.
Application information:
  Initial approach: Letter
  Deadline(s): Sept. 30
  Write: Henry L. Hulbert, Trustee
Trustees: Henry L. Hulbert, J. Burton Hulbert, William H. Hulbert.

EIN: 237039996

1999
Hultquist Foundation, Inc.

c/o Price, Miller, Evans & Flowers
Fenton Bldg.
Jamestown 14701   (716) 664-7414

Established in 1965 in NY.
Foundation type: Independent
Financial data (yr. ended 06/30/91): Assets,
$11,132,736 (M); gifts received, $3,190,359;
expenditures, $422,635; qualifying distributions,
$407,048, including $390,087 for 11 grants (high:
$134,050; low: $1,000).
Fields of interest: Hospitals, social services,
youth, higher education.
Types of support: Building funds, capital
campaigns, annual campaigns.
Limitations: Giving primarily in Chautauqua
County, NY. No grants to individuals.
Application information:
Initial approach: Letter
Deadline(s): June 1 and Dec. 1
Write: Thomas I. Flowers, Pres.
Officers and Directors:* Thomas I. Flowers,*
Pres.; Charles H. Price,* V.P.; William L. Wright,*
V.P.; Robert F. Rohm, Jr.,* Secy.-Treas.
EIN: 160907729

2000
The Hunt Alternatives Fund ▼

1255 Fifth Ave.
New York 10029   (212) 722-7606
Denver application address: 500 East Eighth
Ave., Denver, CO 80203; Tel.: (303) 839-1933

Established in 1981 in NY.
Donor(s): Helen Hunt, Swanee Hunt.
Foundation type: Independent
Financial data (yr. ended 11/30/91): Assets,
$10,420,860 (M); gifts received, $2,122,000;
expenditures, $1,494,006; qualifying
distributions, $1,176,568, including $1,152,736
for grants (high: $150,000; low: $2,000; average:
$3,000-$30,000).
Purpose and activities: Support for human service
programs that strengthen the voices of individuals
and communities silenced because of social and
economic barriers, especially those concerned
with justice and dignity. The empowerment of
women is a primary focus area, including the
economic development of women and girls, the
elimination of violence in communities and
families, contributions to women's health and
reproductive rights, and challenges to the
oppression and discrimination against women,
particularly women of color. Denver grants
support leveraging institutional change as well as
neighborhood coalitions and the arts as a catalyst
and communicator of social change. In New
York, special emphasis is lent to programs serving
women and girls in East Harlem. Priority is given
to grassroots organizations that emphasize
prevention, leadership, development, and
advocacy for institutional change.
Fields of interest: Social services, disadvantaged,
child welfare, family services, women, youth,
minorities, AIDS, community development,
education, literacy, family planning, leadership

development, welfare—indigent individuals,
homeless, hunger, civil rights.
Types of support: Technical assistance, special
projects, operating budgets, seed money,
matching funds, general purposes.
Limitations: Giving limited to the Denver, CO,
Dallas, TX, and New York, NY, metropolitan
areas. No support for federal, state, or municipal
agencies, or cultural, educational, or religious
projects except those concerned with the
disabilities stated in the fund's purpose. No grants
to individuals, or for institutional or general
program needs.
Publications: Annual report (including application
guidelines), informational brochure (including
application guidelines).
Application information: Application form
required for Denver applicants only.
Initial approach: Proposal for New York and
Dallas; letter for Denver
Copies of proposal: 1
Deadline(s): Contact fund for dates
Board meeting date(s): Three times a year:
Spring, summer, and fall
Final notification: Following board meeting
Write: Kimberly Otis, Exec. Dir. for New York
and Dallas applicants, at the NY address;
Lauren Casteel for Denver applicants, at the
CO address
Officers and Directors:* Lauren Casteel,* Exec.
Dir. (Denver); Kimberly Otis, Exec. Dir. (New
York); Helen Hunt, Swanee Hunt, Vincent McGee.
Number of staff: 3 full-time professional; 2
part-time professional; 3 full-time support; 1
part-time support.
EIN: 751763787
Recent health grants:
2000-1 Colorado Alliance for the Mentally Ill,
Denver, CO, $10,000. For general support and
staff support. 1990.
2000-2 Commerce City Community Health
Services, Commerce City, CO, $15,000. For
school-based community clinic. 1990.
2000-3 Hunter College of the City University of
New York, Center for Community Action to
Prevent AIDS, NYC, NY, $15,000. To work
with women's organizations in East Harlem.
1990.
2000-4 New York Black Womens Health Project,
Brooklyn, NY, $20,000. For Wellness
Campaign. 1990.
2000-5 University of Colorado, Graduate School
of Public Affairs, Center for Health, Ethics and
Policy, Denver, CO, $10,000. For general
support. 1990.
2000-6 University of Colorado Health Sciences
Center, Denver School-Based Clinics, Denver,
CO, $10,000. For general support. 1990.

2001
Mary J. Hutchins Foundation, Inc.

110 William St.
New York 10038

Incorporated in 1935 in NY.
Donor(s): Mary J. Hutchins,‡ Caspar J. Voorhis,‡
Waldo H. Hutchins, Jr.‡
Foundation type: Independent
Financial data (yr. ended 12/31/90): Assets,
$21,700,287 (M); gifts received, $283,010;
expenditures, $1,177,538; qualifying
distributions, $1,058,083, including $977,200 for

54 grants (high: $60,000; low: $5,000) and
$49,440 for 13 grants to individuals (high:
$5,040; low: $2,640).
Purpose and activities: Support for health services
and hospitals, youth organizations, community
funds and development, and social services,
including religious welfare funds; also grants to
poor and needy individuals.
Fields of interest: Health services, hospitals,
youth, community funds, community
development, social services, religious welfare,
welfare—indigent individuals.
Types of support: Grants to individuals, general
purposes.
Limitations: Giving primarily in the New York,
NY, area. No support for educational purposes or
national health funds. No grants for for seed
money, scholarships, or annual campaigns.
Application information: Contributes only to
pre-selected organizations. Applications not
accepted.
Officers and Directors:* Waldo Hutchins III,*
Pres.; Richard J. Mirabella,* V.P. and Treas.; Robert
A. Fromel,* V.P.; Elizabeth Hatfield, Secy.;
Elizabeth E. Hutchins, John N. Huwer, Richard G.
Mulholland.
EIN: 136083578
Recent health grants:
2001-1 Brooklyn Hospital/Caledonian Hospital,
Brooklyn, NY, $30,000. 1990.
2001-2 Floating Hospital, NYC, NY, $15,000.
1990.
2001-3 Manhattan Eye, Ear and Throat Hospital,
NYC, NY, $25,000. 1990.
2001-4 Methodist Hospital of Brooklyn,
Brooklyn, NY, $25,000. 1990.
2001-5 Morristown Memorial Hospital,
Morristown, NJ, $60,000. 1990.
2001-6 New York Eye and Ear Infirmary, NYC,
NY, $15,000. 1990.
2001-7 New York Infirmary-Beekman
Downtown Hospital, NYC, NY, $40,000. 1990.
2001-8 North Shore University Hospital,
Manhasset, NY, $60,000. 1990.
2001-9 Overlook Hospital, Summit, NJ, $50,000.
1990.
2001-10 Planned Parenthood of Nassau County,
Mineola, NY, $25,000. 1990.
2001-11 Research Fund for Cystic Fibrosis,
Englewood, NJ, $20,000. 1990.
2001-12 Richmond Memorial Hospital and
Health Center, Staten Island, NY, $10,000.
1990.
2001-13 Saint Barnabas Hospital, Bronx, NY,
$20,000. 1990.
2001-14 Saint Lukes-Roosevelt Hospital Center,
NYC, NY, $30,000. For emergency room.
1990.
2001-15 Saint Vincents Hospital and Medical
Center of New York, NYC, NY, $40,000. 1990.
2001-16 Saint Vincents Medical Center of
Richmond, Staten Island, NY, $15,000. 1990.
2001-17 Staten Island Hospital, Staten Island,
NY, $10,000. 1990.
2001-18 United Hospital Fund of New York,
NYC, NY, $30,000. 1990.

2002
IBM Corporate Support Program

(Formerly IBM Corporate Contributions Program)
Old Orchard Rd.
Armonk 10504   (914) 765-7617

Financial data (yr. ended 12/31/90): Total giving, $152,300,000, including $102,000,000 for grants, $4,300,000 for grants to individuals and $46,000,000 for in-kind gifts.

Purpose and activities: For IBM, corporate contributions are a way of strenghtening its partnership with the communities in which IBM employees and customers live and work. "Our philanthrhopic activities are founded in the corporation's self-interest. We endeavor to be responsive to community efforts, within the limits of financial ability, in all locations where we operate. We only consider requests from publicly supported organizations exempt from Federal income tax under Section 501 (C)(3) of the Internal Revenue Code. Our equipment donations are limited primarily to agency programs engaged in job training for the economically disadvantaged and the physically disabled, and to selected institutions of higher learning for use in educational activities."

Fields of interest: Education, women, minorities, handicapped, computer sciences, business education, education—minorities, health, welfare, civic affairs, cultural programs, arts, science and technology, youth, social services, environment, elementary education, secondary education, engineering, public policy, language and literature, mathematics, United Kingdom, Canada, Mexico, Japan, Australia, Latin America, Germany.

Types of support: Donated products, donated equipment, employee volunteer services, in-kind gifts, loaned talent, fellowships, employee-related scholarships.

Limitations: Giving primarily in headquarters city and company operating locations; company also gives nationally and internationally where it has operations in Europe, Asia, Latin America, and Australia. No support for political, religious, fraternal, or animal welfare organizations, or athletic and competitive events. No grants to individuals, or for telethons, raffles, or auctions.

Publications: Application guidelines, corporate report.

Application information: Local or regional organizations should contact the local IBM plant or branch office; organizations national in scope should write to Armonk.

Initial approach: Query letter and complete proposal
Deadline(s): None
Board meeting date(s): As needed by senior officials and directors
Final notification: Varies, averages 2 to 3 months
Write: D.J. Kelly, Dir., Corp. Support Plans and Controls

Number of staff: 38 full-time professional.

2003
The Carl C. Icahn Foundation ▼

c/o Icahn & Co., Inc.
100 South Bedford Rd.
Mount Kisco 10549   (914) 242-4100

Established in 1980 in NY and DE.
Donor(s): Carl C. Icahn.
Foundation type: Independent
Financial data (yr. ended 11/30/90): Assets, $12,730,126 (M); expenditures, $1,184,760; qualifying distributions, $1,122,177, including

$1,066,134 for 99 grants (high: $150,000; low: $50; average: $1,000-$25,000).

Purpose and activities: Giving for cultural programs, hospitals, and for child welfare, including a child abuse prevention clinic.

Fields of interest: Hospitals, child welfare, youth, cultural programs.

Types of support: Building funds, annual campaigns, general purposes, matching funds.

Limitations: Giving primarily in New York, NY. No grants to individuals.

Application information:
Initial approach: Letter
Deadline(s): None
Board meeting date(s): As necessary
Write: Gail Golden, Secy.

Officers and Directors:* Carl C. Icahn,* Pres.; Gail Golden, Secy.; Liba Icahn,* Treas.; Robert Osborne, C.O.O.

Number of staff: 1
EIN: 133091588

Recent health grants:

2003-1 Alzheimers Disease and Related Disorders Association, NYC, NY, $25,000. For general purposes. 1990.

2003-2 Friends of Karen, Croton Falls, NY, $10,000. For programs. 1990.

2003-3 Northern Westchester Hospital Center, Mount Kisco, NY, $25,000. For Trustee's Year End Gift. 1990.

2003-4 Society of New York Hospital, NYC, NY, $75,000. For CCI program for prevention of child abuse. 1990.

2004
The IFF Foundation, Inc.

521 West 57th St.
New York 10019

Incorporated in 1963 in NY.
Donor(s): International Flavors & Fragrances, Inc.
Foundation type: Company-sponsored
Financial data (yr. ended 12/31/91): Assets, $315,539 (M); gifts received, $645,000; expenditures, $794,492; qualifying distributions, $793,517, including $766,108 for 84 grants (high: $250,000; low: $200) and $27,409 for 5 employee matching gifts.

Purpose and activities: Grants primarily for higher education, including medical education and matching gifts; support also for research in chemistry and international affairs, for hospitals and mental health services, civic affairs agencies, and cultural activities.

Fields of interest: Higher education, medical education, chemistry, international affairs, hospitals, cancer, medical research, mental health, civic affairs, cultural programs.

Types of support: Research, employee matching gifts.

Limitations: Giving primarily in New York, NY, and NJ. No grants to individuals.

Application information: Contributes only to pre-selected organizations. Applications not accepted.

Officers: Eugene P. Grisanti, Pres.; W. Dempsey, Secy.; T.H. Hoppel, Treas.
EIN: 136159094

2005
International Paper Company Foundation
▼

Two Manhattanville Rd.
Purchase 10577   (914) 397-1500

Incorporated in 1952 in NY.
Donor(s): International Paper Co.
Foundation type: Company-sponsored
Financial data (yr. ended 12/31/90): Assets, $33,346,152 (M); gifts received, $144,418; expenditures, $2,715,928; qualifying distributions, $2,447,003, including $2,260,682 for 1,291 grants (high: $100,000; average: $2,500-$5,000).

Purpose and activities: Grants primarily for model projects in company communities and selected programs with potential national impact, with focus on pre-college levels of education, programs for minorities and women in engineering, health and welfare, and community and cultural affairs. Operates own program EDCORE (Education and Community Resource Program) in selected International Paper communities for public schools by invitation only.

Fields of interest: Secondary education, elementary education, education—minorities, rural development, youth, community development, health.

Types of support: Seed money, special projects, annual campaigns, research, publications, matching funds, employee matching gifts, continuing support, fellowships, operating budgets, capital campaigns, program-related investments.

Limitations: Giving primarily in communities where there are company plants and mills, New York, NY and Memphis, TN. No support for athletic organizations or religious groups. No grants to individuals, or for endowment funds or capital expenses (except for health care facilities in company communities); no loans.

Publications: Occasional report, informational brochure (including application guidelines), grants list, application guidelines, annual report.

Application information: Address requests from organizations in company communities to the local company contact person; no applications accepted for EDCORE (Education and Community Resource Program) or for fellowships. Application form required.

Initial approach: Letter, telephone, or proposal with application to local facility
Copies of proposal: 1
Deadline(s): Prior to Oct. for consideration in following year's budget
Board meeting date(s): June
Final notification: Varies
Write: Arthur Wallace, Pres.

Officers: Arthur Wallace, Pres.; Sandra Wilson, V.P.; Tracy Doolittle, Secy.; Patricia Freda-Chan, Treas.

Directors: John A. Georges, James P. Melican, Jr., David W. Oskin.

Trustee: State Street Bank & Trust Co.

Number of staff: 2 full-time professional; 1 part-time support.

EIN: 136155080

Recent health grants:

2005-1 Mount Sinai Hospital and Medical Center, NYC, NY, $10,000. 1990.

2006
Iroquois Avenue Foundation
c/o White & Case
1155 Ave. of the Americas
New York 10036

Established in 1989 in DE.
Donor(s): Lydia B. Mann.
Foundation type: Independent
Financial data (yr. ended 12/31/90): Assets, $2,058,604 (M); expenditures, $58,927; qualifying distributions, $19,169, including $18,250 for 9 grants (high: $3,000; low: $1,000).
Purpose and activities: Giving primarily for medical research and hospitals; support also for youth groups and an arts association.
Fields of interest: Hospitals, medical research, youth, arts.
Types of support: General purposes.
Limitations: Giving primarily in Palm Beach, FL, and New York, NY. No grants to individuals.
Application information: Contributes only to pre-selected organizations. Applications not accepted.
Officers and Directors:* Lydia B. Mann,* Pres.; Peter A.B. Melhado,* V.P. and Secy.; Christian A. Melhado,* V.P. and Treas.; C. Sims Farr,* V.P.
EIN: 133562887

2007
A. C. Israel Foundation, Inc.
707 Westchester Ave.
White Plains 10604   (914) 681-4410

Incorporated in 1967 in DE as successor to the foundation of the same name incorporated in 1946 in NY.
Donor(s): Adrian C. Israel.
Foundation type: Independent
Financial data (yr. ended 12/31/90): Assets, $11,328,109 (M); gifts received, $915,513; expenditures, $382,534; qualifying distributions, $361,778, including $304,032 for 34 grants (high: $200,000; low: $100).
Fields of interest: Hospitals, higher education, secondary education.
Types of support: General purposes.
Limitations: Giving primarily in CT. No grants to individuals.
Application information:
 Initial approach: Letter
 Deadline(s): None
 Write: Barry W. Gray, V.P.
Officers and Directors:* Adrian C. Israel,* Pres.; Barry W. Gray,* V.P.; Thomas C. Israel,* V.P.; Jay M. Howard, Secy.
EIN: 516021414

2008
Ittleson Foundation, Inc.
645 Madison Ave., 16th Fl.
New York 10022   (212) 838-5010

Trust established in 1932 in NY.
Donor(s): Henry Ittleson,‡ Blanche F. Ittleson,‡ Henry Ittleson, Jr.,‡ Lee F. Ittleson,‡ Nancy S. Ittleson.‡
Foundation type: Independent
Financial data (yr. ended 12/31/90): Assets, $16,542,741 (M); expenditures, $1,773,541; qualifying distributions, $1,446,157, including $1,164,832 for 99 grants (high: $200,000; low: $50).
Purpose and activities: For the promotion of the well-being of mankind throughout the world, including research, publication, and the establishment, maintenance, and aid of charitable activities and institutions. Current areas of particular interest are: mental health, including the consequences of AIDS on the mental health of people; the environment; the elderly and other underserved populations, such as the poor and minority communities; and crime and justice, including the prevention of crime and assisting youthful offenders to outgrow criminality.
Fields of interest: Welfare, mental health, AIDS, environment, aged, disadvantaged, minorities, crime and law enforcement, delinquency.
Types of support: Seed money, matching funds, special projects, research, publications, technical assistance.
Limitations: No support for the humanities or cultural projects, general education, social service agencies offering direct service to people in local communities, or projects or organizations that are international in scope or purpose. No grants to individuals, or for continuing support, scholarships, fellowships, internships, annual or capital campaigns, travel, emergency or endowment funds, or deficit financing; no loans.
Publications: Annual report (including application guidelines).
Application information: Application form not required.
 Initial approach: Letter
 Copies of proposal: 1
 Deadline(s): None
 Board meeting date(s): May and Dec.
 Final notification: 3 weeks to 3 months
 Write: David M. Nee, Exec. Dir.
Officers and Directors:* H. Anthony Ittleson,* Chair. and Pres.; Pamela Lee Syrmis,* V.P.; David M. Nee,* Secy. and Exec. Dir.; Bernard W. Schwartz,* Treas.; Marianne S. Ittleson, Lionel I. Pincus, Victor Syrmis, M.D.
Number of staff: 1 full-time professional; 1 part-time support.
EIN: 510172757

2009
The Benjamin Jacobson and Sons Foundation
61 Broadway
New York 10006

Established in 1968 in NY and DE.
Donor(s): Benjamin Jacobson & Sons.
Foundation type: Company-sponsored
Financial data (yr. ended 06/30/91): Assets, $204,049 (M); gifts received, $10,000; expenditures, $305,094; qualifying distributions, $301,470, including $301,470 for 345 grants (high: $25,000; low: $10).
Purpose and activities: Grants primarily for health services and medical research, religious support, with emphasis on Jewish giving, education, youth programs, and social services.
Fields of interest: Health services, medical research, religion, Jewish giving, Jewish welfare, education, youth, social services.
Limitations: Giving primarily in the New York, NY, metropolitan area. No grants to individuals.
Application information: Contributes only to pre-selected organizations. Applications not accepted.
Officers and Directors:* Robert J. Jacobson, Sr.,* Pres.; Benjamin J. Jacobson, Jr.,* V.P.; Robert J. Jacobson, Jr.,* Secy.; Arthur L. Jacobson,* Treas.
EIN: 132630862

2010
Jesselson Foundation ▼
1301 Ave. of the Americas, Suite 4101
New York 10019   (212) 459-9600

Incorporated in 1955 in NY.
Donor(s): Ludwig Jesselson.
Foundation type: Independent
Financial data (yr. ended 04/30/91): Assets, $23,478,745 (M); expenditures, $1,607,888; qualifying distributions, $1,566,995, including $1,566,210 for 322 grants (high: $241,950; low: $36; average: $100-$10,000).
Purpose and activities: Grants largely for higher and Jewish education, welfare funds, health agencies, and synagogues; some support for cultural programs.
Fields of interest: Higher education, Jewish welfare, Jewish giving, Israel, theological education, health, cultural programs.
Application information:
 Initial approach: Letter
 Deadline(s): None
 Write: Ludwig Jesselson, Pres.
Officers: Ludwig Jesselson, Pres. and Treas.; Erica Jesselson, V.P. and Secy.; Michael Jesselson, 2nd V.P.
EIN: 136075098

2011
The JM Foundation ▼
60 East 42nd St., Rm. 1651
New York 10165   (212) 687-7735

Incorporated in 1924 in NY.
Donor(s): Jeremiah Milbank,‡ Katharine S. Milbank.‡
Foundation type: Independent
Financial data (yr. ended 12/31/91): Assets, $23,589,935 (M); expenditures, $3,098,018; qualifying distributions, $2,276,300, including $2,146,190 for 85 grants (high: $250,000; low: $1,000; average: $15,000-$35,000); $70,110 for 46 employee matching gifts and $60,000 for 1 foundation-administered program.
Purpose and activities: Giving primarily for rehabilitation of people with disabilities; prevention and wellness; education, prevention, and early intervention in alcohol and other drug abuse, and health-related public policy research. The foundation also has a strong interest in educational activities which strengthen America's pluralistic system of free markets, entrepreneurship, voluntarism, and private enterprise. It also supports organizations that enhance the quality of family life, and provide today's youth with meaningful life experiences, productive employment opportunities, healthy lifestyles, and positive character development.
Fields of interest: Handicapped, rehabilitation, education, youth, economics, alcoholism, drug abuse, volunteerism, public policy, health, disadvantaged.

Types of support: Research, special projects, publications, internships, matching funds, technical assistance, seed money.
Limitations: No support for the arts or international activities. No grants to individuals, or for operating expenses, annual fundraising campaigns, capital campaigns, or endowment funds; no loans.
Publications: Annual report (including application guidelines), application guidelines, occasional report.
Application information: Application form not required.
  Initial approach: Summary letter accompanied by proposal
  Copies of proposal: 1
  Deadline(s): Submit proposal preferably in Feb., July, or Oct.; deadline 45 days prior to meetings
  Board meeting date(s): Jan., May, and Oct.
  Final notification: Preliminary response within 20 working days
  Write: Chris K. Olander, Exec. Dir.
Officers and Directors:* Jeremiah Milbank, Jr.,* Pres.; Mrs. H. Lawrence Bogert,* V.P.; Daniel G. Tenney, Jr.,* Secy.; William Lee Hanley, Jr.,* Treas.; Chris K. Olander, Exec. Dir.; Jack Brauntuch, Special Counselor; Jeremiah M. Bogert, Lynn R. Bruhn, Mary E. Caslin, Jeremiah Milbank III, Peter C. Morse, Michael Sanger.
Number of staff: 2 full-time professional; 3 full-time support; 1 part-time support.
EIN: 136068340
Recent health grants:
2011-1 Allied Services Corporation, Scranton, PA, $15,000. To investigate effects of neuromuscular rehabilitation on patients with spinal cord injuries. 1991.
2011-2 American Enterprise Institute for Public Policy Research, DC, $35,000. Toward Health Policy Research Program. 1991.
2011-3 American Legislative Exchange Council, DC, $25,000. For programs to reform America's health care system and empower urban poor. 1991.
2011-4 American Occupational Therapy Foundation, Rockville, MD, $15,000. Toward research in occupational therapy. 1991.
2011-5 American Society of Addiction Medicine, DC, $50,000. For subspecialty program in primary care, medical student program follow-up, and toward Ruth Fox Memorial Fund. 1991.
2011-6 Boston University, Boston University/Chelsea Public Schools Partnership, Boston, MA, $25,000. Toward comprehensive health programs in Chelsea Public Schools. 1991.
2011-7 Cooper Union for the Advancement of Science and Art, NYC, NY, $25,000. Toward comprehensive, interdisciplinary program in biomedical engineering. 1991.
2011-8 Corporation Against Drug Abuse, DC, $20,000. For Small Business Project and School/Youth Prevention Program. 1991.
2011-9 Heritage Foundation, DC, $75,000. For Health Care Reform Project. 1991.
2011-10 International Center for Integrative Studies, The Door - A Center of Alternatives, NYC, NY, $15,000. Toward health programs and other activities for physically challenged teenagers. 1991.

2011-11 International Center for the Disabled (ICD), NYC, NY, $75,000. For sixth annual J.M. Foundation National Search for Excellence Awards in rehabilitation in collaboration with Dole Foundation. 1991.
2011-12 Jupiter Medical Center, Jupiter, FL, $50,000. For continuing medical education program for attending physicians. 1991.
2011-13 Mackinac Center, Midland, MI, $10,000. For Michigan: An Agenda for 90's, focusing on health care and growth of government. 1991.
2011-14 March of Dimes Birth Defects Foundation, NYC, NY, $25,000. To initiate OB/GYN and pediatric residency training program in identification and treatment of women with chemical dependency. 1991.
2011-15 National Foundation for Facial Reconstruction, NYC, NY, $25,000. For research on microsurgery and wound healing at the Margaret Milbank Bogert Laboratory. 1991.
2011-16 New York University Medical Center, Division of Alcoholism and Drug Abuse, NYC, NY, $20,000. Toward evaluation of Rational Recovery, new self-help movement for chemically dependent people. 1991.
2011-17 Outreach Project, Woodhaven, NY, $10,000. For Bridge to Careers and Substance Abuse Ministry Programs. 1991.
2011-18 Partners for Disabled Youth, Boston, MA, $10,000. For Youth in Preparation for Independence program. 1991.
2011-19 Planned Parenthood of New York City, NYC, NY, $25,000. Toward public education programs. 1991.
2011-20 Reason Foundation, Santa Monica, CA, $15,000. For New Paradigms in Health-Care Policy including special issue of Reason magazine. 1991.
2011-21 Stanford University, School of Medicine/Health Promotion Resource Center, Stanford, CA, $25,000. Toward Taking a Stand, Standing Together, national television documentary profiling leaders and community coalitions which prevent alcohol and drug problems. 1991.
2011-22 Straight, Saint Petersburg, FL, $15,000. For Education and Prevention Outreach Program in elementary, secondary and high schools. 1991.
2011-23 Washington Legal Foundation, DC, $20,000. To market and disseminate In Whose Interest, major WLF study on public interest law in nation's law schools. 1991.

2012
Joelson Foundation
c/o Reid & Priest
40 West 57th St.
New York 10019

Established in 1966.
Donor(s): Julius Joelson.‡
Foundation type: Independent
Financial data (yr. ended 03/31/91): Assets, $2,892,121 (M); gifts received, $157,500; expenditures, $238,027; qualifying distributions, $211,132, including $205,542 for 137 grants (high: $20,000; low: $50).
Fields of interest: Jewish giving, hospitals, child welfare, hunger, arts, general charitable giving.

Limitations: Giving primarily in New York, NY. No grants to individuals.
Application information: Contributes only to pre-selected organizations. Applications not accepted.
Officers: Stella Joelson, Pres.; Barbara J. Fife, V.P.; Joseph C. Mitchell, Treas.
EIN: 136220799

2013
Johnson & Higgins Corporate Responsibility
125 Broad St.
New York 10004   (212) 574-7028

Financial data (yr. ended 12/31/90): Total giving, $3,200,000 for grants.
Purpose and activities: Support for culture and arts, health and human services, education, and civic affairs.
Fields of interest: Civic affairs, cultural programs, higher education, health, social services.
Types of support: Scholarship funds.
Limitations: Giving limited to areas of company operations. No support for political, lobbying, religious, or fraternal organizations. No grants to individuals.
Application information: Guidelines are set by headquarters; decisions on grants are made at the local level.
  Initial approach: Letter or proposal; write to nearest company office
  Deadline(s): Sept.-Nov.
  Write: Frederick H. Kingsbury III, V.P.

2014
The Keith Wold Johnson Charitable Trust
c/o The Johnson Co., Inc.
630 Fifth Ave., Suite 918
New York 10111

Established in 1986 in NY.
Donor(s): Betty Wold Johnson.
Foundation type: Independent
Financial data (yr. ended 12/31/90): Assets, $2,565,602 (M); expenditures, $120,915; qualifying distributions, $112,580, including $111,500 for 5 grants (high: $50,000; low: $3,000).
Purpose and activities: Support for higher education, youth organizations, juvenile diabetes research, and a zoological society.
Fields of interest: Higher education, youth, medical research, health associations, AIDS, minorities, animal welfare.
Limitations: No grants to individuals.
Application information: Application form not required.
  Deadline(s): None
  Write: Robert W. Johnson IV, Trustee
Trustees: Christopher W. Johnson, Elizabeth Ross Johnson, Robert W. Johnson IV.
EIN: 112845826

2015
Daisy Marquis Jones Foundation ▼
620 Granite Bldg.
130 East Main St.
Rochester 14604-1620   (716) 263-3331

Established in 1968 in NY.
Donor(s): Daisy Marquis Jones.‡
Foundation type: Independent
Financial data (yr. ended 12/31/91): Assets,
$22,126,947 (M); gifts received, $1,000;
expenditures, $726,509; qualifying distributions,
$592,268, including $514,491 for 84 grants
(high: $37,500; low: $150; average:
$5,000-$10,000).
Purpose and activities: Grants primarily to
improve the quality of health care for local
residents; support also for services for senior
citizens, women and youth, with special
emphasis on the disadvantaged; support also
toward improving the administration of justice.
Special attention to preventive programs.
Fields of interest: Health, hospitals, aged,
women, youth, disadvantaged, child welfare, law
and justice, community development, public
affairs, education, education—early childhood,
civic affairs, legal services.
Types of support: Operating budgets, seed money,
emergency funds, building funds, equipment,
land acquisition, matching funds, technical
assistance, special projects, publications,
renovation projects, conferences and seminars,
capital campaigns.
Limitations: Giving limited to Monroe and Yates
counties, NY. No support for the arts or for
religious purposes. No grants to individuals, or for
endowment funds, research, continuing support,
scholarships, fellowships, annual campaigns, or
deficit financing; no loans.
Publications: Annual report (including application
guidelines), application guidelines, grants list,
program policy statement.
Application information: Application form
required.
  Initial approach: Letter
  Copies of proposal: 1
  Deadline(s): None
  Board meeting date(s): Monthly (except
    summer)
  Final notification: 2 to 3 months
  Write: Pearl W. Rubin, Pres.
Officers and Trustees: Leo M. Lyons,* Chair.;
Helen G. Whitney,* Vice-Chair.; Pearl W. Rubin,*
Pres.; Sydney R. Rubin,* Gen. Counsel; Marine
Midland Bank, N.A.
Number of staff: 2 full-time professional; 1
part-time support.
EIN: 237000227
Recent health grants:
2015-1 Kids Adjusting Through Support,
  Rochester, NY, $30,000. For support group
  programs for children and families in which a
  member has life threatening illness. 1991.
2015-2 Planned Parenthood of Rochester and
  Monroe County, Rochester, NY, $10,000. For
  emergency contribution to support mission to
  continue providing full range of family
  planning services. 1991.
2015-3 Rochester Primary Care Network,
  Rochester, NY, $25,000. To help develop
  collaborative automated clinical information
  system. 1991.

2016
Joy Family Foundation
107-111 Goundry St.
North Tonawanda 14120   (716) 692-6665

Established in 1989 in NY.
Donor(s): Paul W. Joy, H. Joan Joy.
Foundation type: Independent
Financial data (yr. ended 12/31/91): Assets,
$2,996,502 (M); gifts received, $2,870,957;
expenditures, $147,890; qualifying distributions,
$140,828, including $140,828 for 24 grants
(high: $20,000; low: $250; average:
$1,000-$15,000).
Fields of interest: Child welfare, youth, drug
abuse, alcoholism, women, AIDS, housing,
welfare—indigent individuals.
Types of support: Building funds, operating
budgets, grants to individuals, special projects,
consulting services.
Limitations: Giving primarily in the city of Buffalo
and Genesse, Erie, and Niagara counties, NY.
Application information: Application form
required.
  Initial approach: Letter requesting application
    form
  Copies of proposal: 1
  Deadline(s): None
  Write: Mrs. Marsha J. Sullivan, Exec. Dir.
Trustees: H. Joan Joy, Paul W. Joy, Stephen T. Joy,
John D. Reinhold, Paula Joy Reinhold, Marsha Joy
Sullivan, Michael F. Sullivan.
Number of staff: 1 part-time support.
EIN: 166335211

2017
The John M. and Mary A. Joyce
Foundation
37 Seminary Rd.
Bedford 10506   (914) 234-0720

Incorporated in 1956 in IL.
Donor(s): John M. Joyce,‡ Mary McCann Joyce,‡
Seven-Up Bottling Co.
Foundation type: Independent
Financial data (yr. ended 07/31/91): Assets,
$5,196,189 (M); expenditures, $324,633;
qualifying distributions, $593,633, including
$304,000 for 23 grants (high: $60,000; low:
$1,000).
Fields of interest: Catholic giving, secondary
education, higher education, social services,
hospitals.
Types of support: Matching funds, continuing
support, emergency funds, building funds,
scholarship funds.
Limitations: Giving primarily in NY. No grants to
individuals.
Application information: Contributes only to
pre-selected organizations. Applications not
accepted.
  Board meeting date(s): Mar., June, Sept., and
    Dec.
  Write: Timothy J. Joyce, Secy.
Officers and Trustees: Catherine P. Joyce,* Pres.;
Timothy J. Joyce,* V.P. and Treas.; George J.
Gillespie,* Secy.
Number of staff: None.
EIN: 366054112

2018
Julia R. and Estelle L. Foundation, Inc. ▼
817 Washington St.
Buffalo 14203   (716) 857-3325

Incorporated in 1941 in NY.

Donor(s): Peter C. Cornell Trust, R. John Oishei.‡
Foundation type: Independent
Financial data (yr. ended 12/31/90): Assets,
$21,185,179 (M); gifts received, $1,045,238;
expenditures, $2,126,919; qualifying
distributions, $2,105,333, including $2,094,419
for 137 grants (high: $105,000; low: $250;
average: $4,500-$25,000).
Purpose and activities: Emphasis on hospitals and
medical research, higher and secondary
education, and social services, including
programs for the aged and youth; some support
for health agencies and cultural programs.
Fields of interest: Hospitals, medical research,
health services, higher education, secondary
education, social services, aged, youth,
handicapped, child welfare, cultural programs.
Types of support: General purposes, research,
building funds.
Limitations: Giving primarily in Buffalo, NY.
Generally, no grants to individuals.
Application information: Application form not
required.
  Deadline(s): None
  Write: Richard L. Wolf, V.P.
Officers and Directors: Rupert Warren,* Pres.;
Richard L. Wolf,* V.P. and Secy.-Treas.; Carl E.
Larson,* V.P.
Members: Patricia O. Colby, Julian R. Oishei.
Number of staff: None.
EIN: 160874319

2019
Jurodin Fund, Inc.
630 Fifth Ave., Rm. 1418
New York 10111

Incorporated in 1960 in DE.
Donor(s): Julius Silver.
Foundation type: Independent
Financial data (yr. ended 12/31/91): Assets,
$14,586,054 (M); expenditures, $765,475;
qualifying distributions, $724,144, including
$711,286 for grants (high: $102,000).
Fields of interest: Jewish welfare, Jewish giving,
higher education, hospitals.
Limitations: Giving primarily in NY.
Application information: Application form not
required.
  Deadline(s): None
  Write: Julius Silver, Pres.
Officers and Trustees: Julius Silver,* Pres. and
Treas.; Roslyn S. Silver,* V.P.; Enid Winslow, V.P.;
David C. Oxman, Secy.; Carl Kaysen.
EIN: 136169166

2020
Max Kade Foundation, Inc. ▼
100 Church St., Rm. 1604
New York 10007   (212) 964-7980

Incorporated in 1944 in NY.
Donor(s): Max Kade.‡
Foundation type: Independent
Financial data (yr. ended 12/31/90): Assets,
$48,465,489 (M); expenditures, $1,986,427;
qualifying distributions, $1,857,101, including
$1,568,023 for 106 grants (high: $75,000; low:
$800; average: $1,000-$30,000).
Purpose and activities: Grants primarily to higher
educational institutions, with present emphasis on

postdoctoral research exchange programs between the U.S. and Europe in medicine or in the natural and physical sciences. Foreign scholars and scientists are selected by the sponsoring universities upon nomination by the respective Academy of Sciences. Grants also for visiting faculty exchange programs, the training of language teachers, and the development of language centers at qualified colleges and universities.

Fields of interest: Higher education, Europe, medical sciences, biological sciences, chemistry, engineering, physical sciences, language and literature.

Types of support: Exchange programs.

Limitations: Giving primarily in the U.S. and Europe. No grants to individuals, or for operating budgets, capital funds, development campaigns, or endowment funds; no loans.

Application information:
Initial approach: Letter or proposal
Deadline(s): None
Board meeting date(s): As required
Write: Erich H. Markel, Pres.

Officers and Directors:* Erich H. Markel,* Pres.; Reimer Koch-Weser,* V.P.; Berteline Dale-Baier, Secy.; Hans G. Hachmann,* Treas.; Fritz Kade, Jr., M.D.

Number of staff: 4 full-time professional.

EIN: 135658082

Recent health grants:

2020-1 Dartmouth College, Medical School, Department of Physiology, Hanover, NH, $13,875. For research and training in field of renal physiology, focusing on studies of electrophysical properties of renal intercalated cells. 1990.

2020-2 Duke University, Department of Medicine, Durham, NC, $11,800. For research and training in field of biochemistry/medicine, focusing on studies of cardiovascular adenosine receptors. 1990.

2020-3 Fred Hutchinson Cancer Research Center, Department of Clinical Research, Seattle, WA, $25,950. For research and training in field of bone marrow transplantation, focusing on studies of modification of transfusions products to prevent sensitization to marrow transplants. 1990.

2020-4 Fred Hutchinson Cancer Research Center, Department of Clinical Research, Seattle, WA, $11,800. For research and training in field of bone marrow transplantation, focusing on studies of antibody induced aplasia. 1990.

2020-5 Massachusetts General Hospital, Department of Developmental Chronobiology, Boston, MA, $31,600. For research and training in field of neurobiology, focusing on studies of cellular and molecular mechanisms of hormone action in hypothalamic suprachiasmatic nucleus. 1990.

2020-6 Massachusetts General Hospital, Department of Neurology, Boston, MA, $11,800. For research and training in field of molecular neurogenetics, focusing on studies of genetic regulation and variation in monomine oxidase B. 1990.

2020-7 Mayo Foundation, Department of Orthopedics, Rochester, MN, $14,300. For research and training in field of biomechanics/orthopedic surgery, focusing on

studies of soft tissue attachment to porous-coated segmental bone defect replacement prosthesis. 1990.

2020-8 Mayo Foundation, Department of Pharmacology, Rochester, MN, $32,700. For research and training in field of pharmacology, focusing on studies of regulation of potassium channels in MDCK cells by epinephrine. 1990.

2020-9 Medical College of Hampton Roads, Department of Plastic Surgery, Norfolk, VA, $32,700. For research and training in field of reconstructive microsurgery, focusing on studies of degree of fibrosis on peripheral nerve model following epineurotomy and perineurotomy procedures. 1990.

2020-10 Rockefeller University, Department of Cellular Physiology and Immunology, NYC, NY, $15,950. For research and training in field of cellular physiology and immunology, focusing on studies of molecular approaches to epidermal Langerhans' cell function. 1990.

2020-11 Stanford University, Department of Medicine, Stanford, CA, $14,300. For research and training in field of nephrology, focusing on studies of glomerular function and structure in experimental nephrosis. 1990.

2020-12 University of Alabama, Department of Medicine, Birmingham, AL, $11,800. For research and training in field of pathogenesis of rheumatoid arthritis, focusing on studies of immunoelectromicroscopy of oncogene products and transforming growth factors in synovial cells. 1990.

2020-13 University of California, Department of Cellular and Molecular Medicine, San Diego, CA, $25,950. For research and training in field of cellular and molecular biology of vacular endothelium, focusing on studies of identifying and localizing by immunocytochemistry and other surface glycoproteins. 1990.

2020-14 University of California, Department of Medicine, San Diego, CA, $32,850. For research and training in field of immunology, focusing on studies of autoimmunity and heat shock proteins 60 family of proteins. 1990.

2020-15 University of California, Department of Medicine, San Diego, CA, $14,300. For research and training in field of immunology and arthritis, focusing on studies of molecular basis of rheumatoid arthritis. 1990.

2020-16 University of California, Department of Medicine, San Diego, CA, $12,225. For research and training in field of pulmonary thromboembolism, focusing on studies of characterization of thrombolytic system in patients with thromboembolism. 1990.

2020-17 University of California, Department of Medicine, Division of Rheumatology/Clinical Immunology, San Francisco, CA, $25,950. For research and training in field of immunology, focusing on studies of molecular mechanisms in NK-Cell recognition of target cells. 1990.

2020-18 University of California, Department of Radiological Sciences, Los Angeles, CA, $14,300. For research and training in field of cardiovascular nuclear medicine, focusing on studies of positron emission tomography of heart. 1990.

2020-19 University of Nebraska Medical Center, Department of Internal Medicine, Omaha, NE, $13,875. For research and training in field of pulmonary cell biology, focusing on studies of

vitronectin levels present in lower respiratory tract in health and disease. 1990.

2020-20 University of Pittsburgh, Department of Pathology, Pittsburgh, PA, $14,300. For research and training in field of cancer immunology, focusing on studies of in vitro and in vivo antitumor effects of human adherent lymphokine-activated killer cells. 1990.

2020-21 University of Texas Southwestern Medical Center, Department of Internal Medicine, Dallas, TX, $31,400. For research and training in field of medicine and diabetes, focusing on studies of secretion of amylin by pancreatic islets. 1990.

2020-22 University of Vermont, Department of Pharmacology, Burlington, VT, $13,875. For research and training in field of pharmacology of anesthetics, focusing on studies of action of anesthetic drugs on brain blood vessels. 1990.

2020-23 University of Washington, Department of Anesthesiology, Seattle, WA, $34,175. For research and training in field of medicine, focusing on studies of pain enhancement of opioid analgesia. 1990.

2020-24 University of Washington, Department of Orthopaedics, Seattle, WA, $26,550. For research and training in field of orthopaedics, focusing on studies of biomechanics of hindfoot-contact and pressure measurement in subtalar joint. 1990.

2020-25 University of Washington, Department of Pharmacology, Seattle, WA, $14,300. For research and training in field of molecular pharmacology, focusing on studies of role of post-translational modifications of dihydropyridine-sensitive calcium channels. 1990.

2020-26 University of Wisconsin, Department of Veterinary Science, Madison, WI, $31,600. For research and training in field of mammalian embryology (animal), focusing on studies of biochemical and molecular analyses of embryo metabolism and development. 1990.

2020-27 Yale University, Department of Pharmacology, New Haven, CT, $25,900. For research and training in field of immunopharmacology, focusing on studies of determination of structural properties and localization of cyclosporin receptor, cyclophilin. 1990.

2021
Peter S. Kalikow Foundation, Inc.
101 Park Ave.
New York 10178-0002

Established in 1983 in NY.
Donor(s): Peter S. Kalikow.
Foundation type: Independent
Financial data (yr. ended 06/30/91): Assets, $295,278 (M); gifts received, $174,973; expenditures, $355,349; qualifying distributions, $355,349, including $354,940 for 59 grants (high: $40,000; low: $100; average: $1,000-$10,000).

Purpose and activities: Support primarily for Jewish organizations, hospitals and medical research, cultural programs, child welfare, and higher and other education.

Fields of interest: Jewish giving, Jewish welfare, hospitals, child welfare, higher education, education, health associations.
Types of support: Building funds.
Limitations: Giving primarily in NY.
Application information: Application form not required.
Initial approach: Letter
Deadline(s): None
Officers: Peter S. Kalikow, Pres.; Mary Kalikow, Exec. V.P.; Gerald Shrager, V.P.; Regina Mastrangelo, Secy.; Daniel F. Cremins, Treas.
EIN: 133182633

2022
Rita J. and Stanley H. Kaplan Foundation, Inc.
866 United Nations Plaza, Suite 547
New York 10017   (212) 688-1047

Incorporated in 1984 in NY.
Donor(s): Stanley H. Kaplan, Rita J. Kaplan.
Foundation type: Independent
Financial data (yr. ended 12/31/90): Assets, $12,761,909 (M); gifts received, $200,000; expenditures, $910,603; qualifying distributions, $778,570, including $752,618 for 180 grants (high: $100,000; low: $20).
Purpose and activities: Support for cultural programs, including music, arts, theater, performing arts, and museums; libraries; medical research and education, including mental illness, AIDS and cancer research, and hospital building funds; social and family services, including programs for the homeless, for children, and for women; Jewish giving; and organizations promoting human rights.
Fields of interest: Cultural programs, arts, medical research, cancer, AIDS, social services, family services, women, Jewish giving, human rights.
Types of support: Annual campaigns, capital campaigns, building funds, continuing support, general purposes, research, seed money.
Limitations: Giving primarily in NY. No grants to individuals.
Application information: Contributes only to pre-selected organizations. Applications not accepted.
Officers and Directors:* Stanley H. Kaplan,* Pres.; Rita J. Kaplan,* Secy.; Tara-Shelomith K. Freeman, Exec. Dir.; Nancy Kaplan Belsky, Paul Alan Kaplan, Susan Beth Kaplan.
Number of staff: 1 part-time professional; 1 part-time support.
EIN: 133221298

2023
The J. M. Kaplan Fund, Inc. ▼
30 Rockefeller Plaza, Suite 4250
New York 10112   (212) 767-0630
FAX: (212)767-0639

Incorporated in 1948 in NY as Faigel Leah Foundation, Inc.; The J.M. Kaplan Fund, Inc., a DE corporation, merged with it in 1975 and was renamed The J.M. Kaplan Fund, Inc.
Donor(s): Members of the J.M. Kaplan family.
Foundation type: Independent
Financial data (yr. ended 11/30/90): Assets, $85,564,577 (M); expenditures, $8,965,496; qualifying distributions, $11,702,451, including

$7,247,000 for 232 grants (high: $500,000; low: $1,000; average: $5,000-$50,000) and $4,023,025 for loans.
Purpose and activities: Giving in five areas: 1) conservation of the natural environment; 2) historic preservation; 3) improvement of land use; 4) civil liberties; 5) and the arts in New York City.
Fields of interest: Environment, agriculture, historic preservation, architecture, rural development, urban affairs, civic affairs, civil rights, human rights, homeless, arts, music, museums, libraries.
Types of support: Continuing support, seed money, special projects, publications, technical assistance, general purposes, land acquisition, program-related investments.
Limitations: Giving primarily in NY, with emphasis on New York City. No support for medicine, science, theater, or dance. No grants to individuals, or for films or video, building or endowment funds, operating budgets, annual campaigns, deficit financing, equipment and materials, renovation projects, scholarships, fellowships, conferences, research, prizes, study, or travel.
Publications: Annual report (including application guidelines).
Application information: Application form required.
Initial approach: Telephone or letter
Copies of proposal: 1
Deadline(s): Submit proposal only from Mar. 1 to Oct. 15; Music proposals in Sept. only
Board meeting date(s): As required
Final notification: 2 months
Write: Joan K. Davidson, Pres.
Officers and Trustees:* Joan K. Davidson,* Pres.; Elizabeth K. Fonseca,* V.P.; Mary E. Kaplan,* V.P.; Richard D. Kaplan,* V.P.; John Matthew Davidson,* Secy.; Henry Ng, Treas. and Chief Admin. Officer; Suzanne Davis, Exec. Dir.; Anthony C. Wood, Prog. Officer; Maurice Austin, Betsy Davidson, Bradford Davidson, Peter Davidson, Bruno Fonseca, Caio Fonseca, Isabel Fonseca, Quina Fonseca, Maurice C. Kaplan.
Number of staff: 3 full-time professional; 5 full-time support.
EIN: 136090286
Recent health grants:
2023-1 AIDS Treatment Registry, NYC, NY, $10,000. For general support. 1990.
2023-2 Gay Mens Health Crisis (GMHC), NYC, NY, $30,000. For general support. 1990.
2023-3 Planned Parenthood of New York City, NYC, NY, $100,000. For general support. 1990.

2024
Howard & Holly Katz Foundation
c/o Goldman Sachs & Co., Tax Dept.
85 Broad St.
New York 10004-2408

Established in 1983 in NY.
Donor(s): Howard C. Katz.
Foundation type: Independent
Financial data (yr. ended 08/31/91): Assets, $619,327 (M); gifts received, $250,000; expenditures, $241,154; qualifying distributions, $236,526, including $236,171 for 51 grants (high: $50,000; low: $25).

Fields of interest: Jewish welfare, hospitals, cultural programs, education, higher education.
Limitations: Giving primarily in New York, NY. No grants to individuals, or for scholarships; no loans.
Application information: Contributes only to pre-selected organizations. Applications not accepted.
Trustees: Holly M. Katz, Howard C. Katz, Ronald S. Tauber.
EIN: 133199938

2025
Henry Kaufmann Foundation
1585 Broadway
New York 10036   (212) 969-3229

Incorporated in 1928 in NY.
Donor(s): Henry Kaufmann.‡
Foundation type: Independent
Financial data (yr. ended 12/31/90): Assets, $6,253,030 (M); expenditures, $754,789; qualifying distributions, $730,018, including $673,706 for 17 grants (high: $150,000; low: $1,000; average: $15,000-$100,000).
Purpose and activities: Capital grants principally for geriatric care facilities, arts and educational institutions, Jewish giving and welfare funds, and camping and community centers.
Fields of interest: Recreation, aged, health, arts, education, Jewish giving, Jewish welfare.
Types of support: Building funds, equipment, general purposes, capital campaigns, land acquisition, professorships, renovation projects.
Limitations: Giving primarily in the New York, NY, and Pittsburgh, PA, metropolitan areas. No grants to individuals, or for endowment funds, operating budgets, scholarships, fellowships, or matching gifts; no loans.
Publications: 990-PF, annual report.
Application information: Application form not required.
Initial approach: Written proposal
Copies of proposal: 2
Deadline(s): Submit written proposal preferably 1 or 2 months before board meeting dates; no set deadline
Board meeting date(s): May and Nov.
Final notification: After board meetings (positive replies only)
Write: Jeffrey A. Horwitz, Asst. Secy.
Officers and Directors:* Philip J. Hirsch,* Pres.; Leonard N. Block,* V.P.; Daniel D. Mielnicki, Secy.; William T. Golden,* Treas.; Jerome Goldsmith, Exec. Dir.; Charles Looker, Walter Mendelsohn, Frederick P. Rose, John M. Wolf, Sr.
Number of staff: None.
EIN: 136034179

2026
Marion Esser Kaufmann Foundation
c/o Weber & Cardillo
2525 Palmer Ave.
New Rochelle 10801   (914) 636-8400

Established in 1986 in NY.
Donor(s): Marion Esser Kaufmann.‡
Foundation type: Independent
Financial data (yr. ended 12/31/91): Assets, $6,149,470 (M); expenditures, $385,047; qualifying distributions, $306,000, including

$306,000 for 8 grants (high: $100,000; low: $10,000).
Purpose and activities: Giving for higher education and research in the fields of Sudden Infant Death Syndrome, and Alzheimer's disease.
Fields of interest: Higher education, medical research, hospitals, aged, child development.
Types of support: Research, scholarship funds.
Limitations: No grants to individuals.
Application information:
  Deadline(s): None
  Final notification: Within 3 months
  Write: Allen Weber
Trustees: Frederick L. Bissinger, Richard Esser.
EIN: 133339941

2027
The Kekst Family Foundation
784 Park Ave.
New York 10021

Established in 1986 in NY.
Donor(s): Gershon Kekst.
Foundation type: Independent
Financial data (yr. ended 12/31/91): Assets, $2,024,307 (M); gifts received, $800,035; expenditures, $547,056; qualifying distributions, $545,877, including $545,500 for 8 grants (high: $400,000; low: $3,000).
Purpose and activities: Giving primarily to foster, support, and strengthen the study of Jewish religion, music, art, philosophy, values, traditions, and history, including grants to organizations to enable gifted teachers and students to continue their teaching activities. Support also for medical and scientific research and educational programs intended to combat medical and genetic diseases and afflictions which primarily affect Jewish infants and children.
Fields of interest: Jewish giving, Jewish welfare, theological education, medical research, religious schools, education.
Types of support: Research, scholarship funds.
Limitations: Giving primarily in NY. No grants to individuals.
Application information:
  Initial approach: Proposal
  Deadline(s): None
  Final notification: 3 months
  Write: Gershon Kekst, Pres.
Officers: Gershon Kekst, Pres.; Carol Kekst, Secy.-Treas.
EIN: 133382250

2028
J. C. Kellogg Foundation
c/o Spear, Leeds & Kellogg
115 Broadway
New York 10006   (212) 587-6129

Established in 1954 in NY.
Donor(s): Morris W. Kellogg, James C. Kellogg IV, Elizabeth I. Kellogg.
Foundation type: Independent
Financial data (yr. ended 08/31/91): Assets, $2,723,875 (M); gifts received, $220,775; expenditures, $206,084; qualifying distributions, $167,849, including $167,600 for 46 grants (high: $37,500; low: $100).
Fields of interest: Youth, secondary education, elementary education, hospitals.

Limitations: No grants to individuals.
Application information: Contributes only to pre-selected organizations. Applications not accepted.
  Write: William G. Peskoff
Officers and Trustees:* Elizabeth I. Kellogg,* Pres.; James C. Kellogg IV,* Secy.; Nancy K. Gifford, Morris W. Kellogg, Richard I. Kellogg.
Number of staff: None.
EIN: 136092448

2029
Ethel Kennedy Foundation
Box 82
Cold Spring Harbor 11724

Established in 1986 in DE and NY.
Foundation type: Independent
Financial data (yr. ended 12/31/91): Assets, $5,411,360 (M); expenditures, $193,220; qualifying distributions, $190,875, including $190,000 for 53 grants (high: $31,000; low: $500).
Fields of interest: Higher education, secondary education, social services, family services, child welfare, handicapped, health associations, hospitals.
Limitations: Giving primarily in NY. No grants to individuals.
Application information:
  Initial approach: Letter
  Deadline(s): None
  Write: Ethel K. Marran, Pres.
Officers: Ethel K. Marran, Pres. and Treas.; Elizabeth Marran, V.P.; Laura Marran, Secy.
EIN: 112768682

2030
The Kidder Peabody Foundation ▼
c/o Kidder, Peabody & Co., Inc.
Ten Hanover Sq., 19th Fl.
New York 10005   (212) 510-4720

Incorporated in 1959 in NY.
Donor(s): Kidder, Peabody and Co., Inc.
Foundation type: Company-sponsored
Financial data (yr. ended 12/31/90): Assets, $1,487,345 (M); expenditures, $1,622,529; qualifying distributions, $1,606,200, including $1,606,200 for 1,660 grants (high: $192,360; low: $100; average: $250-$5,000).
Purpose and activities: Emphasis on higher and secondary education; support also for arts, culture, and hospitals.
Fields of interest: Higher education, secondary education, arts, hospitals.
Limitations: Giving primarily in NY and areas where company maintains offices. No support for religious organizations. No grants to individuals; no loans.
Application information: Application form not required.
  Initial approach: Letter
  Deadline(s): None
  Board meeting date(s): Annually
  Write: Helen B. Platt, Pres.
Officers and Directors:* Silas S. Cathcart,* Chair.; Helen B. Platt,* Pres.; John Liftin,* Secy.; Joseph Martorella,* Treas.
Number of staff: None.
EIN: 136085918

2031
Walter H. D. Killough Trust
c/o Marine Midland Bank, N.A.
250 Park Ave., 4th Fl.
New York 10177   (212) 503-2768

Trust established in 1929 in NY.
Donor(s): Walter H.D. Killough.‡
Foundation type: Independent
Financial data (yr. ended 07/31/91): Assets, $2,631,893 (M); expenditures, $198,423; qualifying distributions, $166,808, including $121,063 for 18 grants (high: $34,199; low: $1,000).
Purpose and activities: Specific grants to designated educational and humane organizations; discretionary grants restricted primarily to hospitals and homes for the aged; scholarships limited to graduates of Erasmus High School, Brooklyn, New York.
Fields of interest: Hospitals, aged.
Types of support: Equipment, general purposes, operating budgets, research, special projects, building funds, renovation projects, emergency funds.
Limitations: Giving primarily in NJ and NY. No grants to individuals.
Application information: Application form not required.
  Initial approach: Proposal
  Copies of proposal: 1
  Deadline(s): Oct. 15
  Board meeting date(s): Nov. 30
  Final notification: Jan. 15
  Write: Deborah S. Metrick, Trust Officer, Marine Midland Bank, N.A.
Trustees: Norman S. Fink, Rt. Rev. Robert C. Witcher, Marine Midland Bank, N.A.
Number of staff: None.
EIN: 136063894

2032
Helen & Milton Kimmelman Foundation ▼
445 Park Ave., Suite 2100
New York 10022

Established in 1982 in NY.
Donor(s): Milton Kimmelman.‡
Foundation type: Independent
Financial data (yr. ended 11/30/90): Assets, $12,275,718 (M); gifts received, $2,417,080; expenditures, $4,783,632; qualifying distributions, $4,671,537, including $4,671,537 for 99 grants (high: $2,500,000; low: $25; average: $5,000-$50,000).
Purpose and activities: Giving primarily for Jewish welfare funds and other Jewish organizations, and the visual and performing arts, including museums; support also for medical research and education, and the environment.
Fields of interest: Jewish giving, Jewish welfare, arts, museums, performing arts, medical research, medical education, education, environment.
Types of support: Matching funds, general purposes, program-related investments, building funds.
Limitations: Giving primarily in New York, NY. No grants to individuals.
Application information: Contributes only to pre-selected organizations. Applications not accepted.
Trustee: Helen Kimmel.

EIN: 133110688
Recent health grants:
2032-1 Eye Research Institute of Central New York, Syracuse, NY, $25,000. 1990.
2032-2 Hebrew Home for the Aged, Riverdale, NY, $50,000. 1990.

2033
The Kirby Family Foundation

c/o W. Michael Reickert, The Ayco Corp.
One Wall St.
Albany 12205

Established in 1985 in PA.
Donor(s): Robert E. Kirby.
Foundation type: Independent
Financial data (yr. ended 12/31/91): Assets, $382,190 (M); gifts received, $194,035; expenditures, $97,054; qualifying distributions, $94,000, including $94,000 for 4 grants (high: $34,000; low: $10,000).
Fields of interest: Higher education, business education, hospices.
Limitations: No grants to individuals.
Application information: Contributes only to pre-selected organizations. Applications not accepted.
Officers and Directors:* Robert E. Kirby,* Pres.; Linda Mewshaw,* Secy.-Treas.
EIN: 251513507

2034
The David and Sadie Klau Foundation

c/o Rochlin, Lipsky, Goodkin, Stoler & Co., P.C.
125 West 45th St., 7th Fl.
New York 10036-4003   (212) 840-6444
Application address: 993 Fifth Ave., New York, NY 10028

Incorporated in 1942 in NY.
Donor(s): David W. Klau.‡
Foundation type: Independent
Financial data (yr. ended 12/31/91): Assets, $25,828,470 (M); expenditures, $1,620,379; qualifying distributions, $1,444,207, including $1,438,094 for 214 grants (high: $200,000; low: $5).
Purpose and activities: Emphasis on health and hospitals, AIDS programs, psychiatry and mental health issues, higher, early childhood, adult, minority, and other education, libraries, Jewish welfare funds and temple support, child development and welfare, family planning, the handicapped, human services, culture, including music and museums, religion, and civil rights groups.
Fields of interest: Health, AIDS, higher education, education—early childhood, libraries, Jewish giving, child welfare, disadvantaged, museums, religion.
Types of support: General purposes, annual campaigns, building funds, capital campaigns.
Limitations: Giving primarily in New York, NY.
Application information:
    Initial approach: Written request
    Deadline(s): None
    Board meeting date(s): As required
    Write: Sadie K. Klau, Pres.
Officers and Directors:* Sadie K. Klau,* Pres.; Paula K. Oppenheim,* V.P. and Secy.-Treas.;

Lucille K. Carothers, James D. Klau, Felice K. Shea.
Number of staff: None.
EIN: 136161378

2035
David L. Klein, Jr. Memorial Foundation, Inc.

c/o Miriam Klein
700 Park Ave.
New York 10021

Incorporated in 1959 in NY.
Donor(s): David L. Klein,‡ Miriam Klein, Endo Laboratories, Inc.
Foundation type: Independent
Financial data (yr. ended 02/28/91): Assets, $2,913,497 (M); expenditures, $131,156; qualifying distributions, $113,536, including $95,915 for 123 grants (high: $25,000; low: $50).
Purpose and activities: Emphasis on hospitals, medical research, and Jewish welfare funds; support also for temple support, higher education, and cultural activities.
Fields of interest: Hospitals, medical research, Jewish welfare, Jewish giving, higher education, cultural programs.
Limitations: Giving primarily in NY. No grants to individuals.
Application information: Contributes only to pre-selected organizations. Applications not accepted.
Officer and Trustees:* Miriam Klein,* Pres.; Saretta Barnet, Marjorie Traub.
EIN: 136085432

2036
The Esther A. and Joseph Klingenstein Fund, Inc. ▼

787 Seventh Ave., 6th Fl.
New York 10019-6016   (212) 492-6181

Incorporated in 1945 in NY.
Donor(s): Esther A. Klingenstein,‡ Joseph Klingenstein.‡
Foundation type: Independent
Financial data (yr. ended 09/30/91): Assets, $70,658,033 (M); gifts received, $65,613; expenditures, $4,114,670; qualifying distributions, $3,757,446, including $2,558,675 for 69 grants (high: $440,176; low: $3,000; average: $20,000-$50,000) and $900,002 for 27 grants to individuals.
Purpose and activities: Primary interests in neuroscientific research bearing on epilepsy and independent secondary education. Some support also for health, animal research, church and state separation, public and social policy, communications and journalism, population and family planning, environment, and minority affairs.
Fields of interest: Medical research, secondary education, education, health, public policy, journalism, media and communications, family planning, population studies, environment, minorities.
Types of support: Research, special projects, publications, conferences and seminars, fellowships, operating budgets, seed money, general purposes, continuing support.

Limitations: No grants to individuals (except in fund's own programs in neuroscience and independent secondary education), or for building or endowment funds.
Publications: Informational brochure.
Application information: Application forms are required for The Klingenstein Fellowship Awards, and are available from department heads or from the foundation. Application form not required.
    Initial approach: Letter or proposal
    Copies of proposal: 1
    Deadline(s): None
    Board meeting date(s): Generally 5 or 6 times a year
    Write: John Klingenstein, Pres.
Officers and Directors:* John Klingenstein,* Pres. and Treas.; Frederick A. Klingenstein,* V.P. and Secy.; Claire List, V.P.; Patricia D. Klingenstein, Sharon L. Klingenstein.
Number of staff: 2 full-time professional; 1 part-time professional; 1 full-time support.
EIN: 136028788

2037
Jay E. Klock and Lucia De L. Klock Kingston Foundation

(Formerly Klock Company Trust)
c/o Key Trust Co.
54 State St.
Albany 12207
Application address: 267 Wall St., Kingston, NY 12401

Established in 1966 in NY.
Foundation type: Independent
Financial data (yr. ended 12/31/91): Assets, $4,224,521 (M); expenditures, $315,463; qualifying distributions, $291,464, including $291,213 for 52 grants (high: $12,000; low: $500).
Fields of interest: Hospitals, health services, youth, child welfare, social services, community funds.
Limitations: Giving limited to Kingston and Ulster counties, NY. No grants to individuals.
Application information:
    Initial approach: Letter
    Deadline(s): Mar. 31, June 30, Sept. 30, and Dec. 31
Trustee: Key Trust Co.
EIN: 146038479

2038
Louis & Rose Klosk Fund

c/o Chemical Bank, Admin. Svcs. Dept.
30 Rockefeller Plaza, 60th Fl.
New York 10112   (212) 621-2148

Trust established in 1970 in NY.
Donor(s): Louis Klosk.‡
Foundation type: Independent
Financial data (yr. ended 12/31/91): Assets, $4,236,525 (M); expenditures, $217,057; qualifying distributions, $155,948, including $153,100 for 44 grants (high: $12,500; low: $500).
Fields of interest: Medical education, higher education, health associations, Jewish welfare, Jewish giving, aged, arts.
Limitations: Giving primarily in New York, NY. No grants to individuals.

Application information: Application form not required.

Deadline(s): None

Write: Barbara Strohmeier, V.P., Chemical Bank

Trustees: Barry C. Cooper, Nathan Cooper, Chemical Bank.

EIN: 136328994

2039
Knox Family Foundation
P.O. Box 387
Johnstown 12095

Incorporated in 1961 in NY.

Donor(s): Eleanor E. Knox,‡ Knox Gelatine, Inc.

Foundation type: Independent

Financial data (yr. ended 12/31/90): Assets, $5,054,300 (M); expenditures, $272,246; qualifying distributions, $231,500, including $231,500 for 175 grants (high: $19,500; low: $100).

Fields of interest: Higher education, secondary education, hospitals, Protestant giving, welfare, social services.

Limitations: No grants to individuals.

Application information: Contributes only to pre-selected organizations. Applications not accepted.

Officers and Directors:* Eleanor G. Nalle,* Pres. and Treas.; John K. Graham,* V.P. and Secy.; Paul Armstrong,* V.P.; Rose Ann Armstrong,* V.P.; Roseann K. Beaudoin,* V.P.; Rosemary Birchard,* V.P.; Charles K. Brumley,* V.P.; Richard W. Hallock,* V.P.

EIN: 146017797

2040
The Seymour H. Knox Foundation, Inc.
3750 Marine Midland Ctr.
Buffalo 14203   (716) 854-6811

Incorporated in 1945 in NY.

Donor(s): Seymour H. Knox,‡ Marjorie K.C. Klopp,‡ Dorothy K.G. Rogers.‡

Foundation type: Independent

Financial data (yr. ended 12/31/91): Assets, $20,430,713 (M); expenditures, $1,205,505; qualifying distributions, $1,087,328, including $988,650 for 98 grants (high: $205,600; low: $100).

Purpose and activities: Giving primarily for the fine and performing arts and higher and secondary education; support also for hospitals and health associations, civic and social service organizations, and community funds.

Fields of interest: Arts, performing arts, higher education, secondary education, hospitals, health associations, civic affairs, social services, community funds.

Types of support: General purposes.

Limitations: Giving primarily in the Buffalo, NY, area. No grants to individuals.

Application information:

Initial approach: Letter

Deadline(s): None

Write: Seymour H. Knox, Pres.

Officers: Seymour H. Knox III, Chair.; Hazard K. Campbell, V.P. and Secy.; Northrup R. Knox, V.P. and Treas.

Directors: Benjamin K. Campbell, Northrup R. Knox, Jr., Seymour H. Knox IV, Randolph A. Marks, Henry Z. Urban.

EIN: 160839066

2041
The Kohlberg Foundation, Inc. ▼
116 Radio Circle
Mount Kisco 10549

Established in 1989 in NY.

Donor(s): The Kohlberg Foundation.

Foundation type: Independent

Financial data (yr. ended 12/31/90): Assets, $26,562,765 (M); gifts received, $44,044; expenditures, $1,497,240; qualifying distributions, $1,306,484, including $1,305,734 for 95 grants (high: $568,759; low: $50; average: $500-$5,000).

Purpose and activities: Support for higher education, social services, and cultural organizations.

Fields of interest: Higher education, education, Jewish giving, museums, child welfare, health associations, hospitals, medical research.

Limitations: Giving primarily in NY. No grants to individuals.

Application information: Contributes only to pre-selected organizations. Applications not accepted.

Trustees: Karen K. Davis, Andrew Kohlberg, James Kohlberg, Jerome Kohlberg, Jr., Nancy S. Kohlberg, Pamela K. Vinal.

EIN: 133496263

Recent health grants:

2041-1 American Diabetes Association, NYC, NY, $50,000. 1990.

2041-2 Northern Westchester Hospital Center, Mount Kisco, NY, $10,000. 1990.

2042
Kopf Foundation, Inc.
c/o Kelley, Drye & Warren
101 Park Ave.
New York 10178

Incorporated in 1967 in NY.

Foundation type: Independent

Financial data (yr. ended 12/31/91): Assets, $4,487,883 (M); expenditures, $211,222; qualifying distributions, $155,035, including $154,500 for 9 grants (high: $100,000; low: $1,500).

Fields of interest: Higher education, health associations, hospitals.

Limitations: Giving primarily in NY. No grants to individuals.

Application information: Contributes only to pre-selected organizations. Applications not accepted.

Officers: Patricia Ann Colagiuri, Pres.; Nancy Sue Mueller, V.P.; Michael S. Insel, Secy.; Brenda Christy Helies, Treas.

EIN: 136228036

2043
Elizabeth Christy Kopf Foundation
c/o Kelley Drye & Warren
101 Park Ave.
New York 10178

Established in 1982 in NY.

Donor(s): R.C. Kopf.

Foundation type: Independent

Financial data (yr. ended 12/31/91): Assets, $3,027,831 (M); expenditures, $225,061; qualifying distributions, $163,425, including $162,300 for 10 grants (high: $100,000; low: $100).

Fields of interest: Higher education, hospitals, Protestant giving.

Limitations: Giving primarily in NY and MA. No grants to individuals.

Application information: Contributes only to pre-selected organizations. Applications not accepted.

Officers: Patricia Ann Colagiuri, Pres.; Nancy Sue Mueller, V.P.; Michael S. Insel, Secy.; Brenda Christy Helies, Treas.

EIN: 133127936

2044
Kramer Foundation
One Penn Plaza, Suite 1830
New York 10119-0001

Established about 1951 in NY.

Donor(s): Saul Kramer.

Foundation type: Independent

Financial data (yr. ended 12/31/90): Assets, $2,688,006 (M); expenditures, $181,368; qualifying distributions, $175,368, including $166,519 for 129 grants (high: $20,000; low: $10).

Fields of interest: Jewish welfare, Jewish giving, social services, higher education, medical education, health services.

Limitations: Giving primarily in NY.

Application information:

Initial approach: Letter

Deadline(s): None

Write: Saul Kramer, Mgr.

Officers: Saul Kramer, Mgr.; Bernard Wald, Mgr.

EIN: 221713053

2045
C. L. C. Kramer Foundation
c/o Zabelle, Shechter & Marks
P.O. Box 431
Millerton 12546

Established in 1966.

Donor(s): Catherine Kramer.‡

Foundation type: Independent

Financial data (yr. ended 09/30/91): Assets, $5,761,764 (M); expenditures, $459,010; qualifying distributions, $434,818, including $430,500 for 22 grants (high: $80,000; low: $1,000).

Purpose and activities: Giving primarily for hospitals, associations for the blind, and Jewish organizations; support also for the performing arts.

Fields of interest: Hospitals, health associations, handicapped, performing arts, Jewish giving.

Types of support: General purposes.

Limitations: Giving primarily in New York, NY. No grants to individuals.
Application information: Contributes only to pre-selected organizations. Applications not accepted.
  Write: Robert Zabelle, Pres., or David Marks, Treas.
Officers: Robert Zabelle, Pres.; Charles Looker, Secy.; David J. Marks, Treas.
EIN: 136226513

2046
Henry R. Kravis Foundation, Inc. ▼
c/o Kohlberg Kravis Roberts & Co.
Nine West 57th St.
New York 10019-2601

Established in 1985 in NY.
Donor(s): Henry R. Kravis.
Foundation type: Independent
Financial data (yr. ended 11/30/90): Assets, $3,040,376 (M); gifts received, $1,197,441; expenditures, $8,316,523; qualifying distributions, $8,296,312, including $8,295,390 for 80 grants (high: $2,130,000; low: $100; average: $10,000-$100,000).
Purpose and activities: Support primarily for arts and culture, including a museum, and for Jewish welfare.
Fields of interest: Jewish welfare, museums, arts.
Types of support: General purposes.
Limitations: No grants to individuals.
Application information: Contributes only to pre-selected organizations. Applications not accepted.
Officers and Directors:* Henry R. Kravis,* Chair. and Pres.; Thomas Hudson, Secy.; Richard I. Beattie, Jerome Kohlberg, Jr.
Number of staff: None.
EIN: 133341521
Recent health grants:
2046-1 Juvenile Diabetes Foundation, NYC, NY, $25,000. For general support. 1991.
2046-2 Mount Sinai Hospital and Medical Center, NYC, NY, $1,860,000. For general support. 1991.

2047
Roger Kresge Foundation, Inc.
320 North McKinley Ave.
Endicott 13760   (607) 748-4040

Established in 1970.
Donor(s): Roger L. Kresge.‡
Foundation type: Independent
Financial data (yr. ended 12/31/90): Assets, $2,986,293 (M); gifts received, $2,094,336; expenditures, $100,587; qualifying distributions, $90,954, including $77,084 for 9 grants (high: $20,000; low: $2,500; average: $1-$20,000).
Purpose and activities: "For the physical, mental, and educational development of children and young adults."
Fields of interest: Child development, child welfare, youth, education, education—early childhood, elementary education, education—minorities, vocational education, drug abuse.
Types of support: Scholarship funds, matching funds, capital campaigns, operating budgets, renovation projects, special projects.

Limitations: Giving limited to Broome County, NY. No grants to individuals.
Publications: 990-PF, informational brochure (including application guidelines), application guidelines.
Application information: Application form required.
  Initial approach: Letter
  Copies of proposal: 1
  Deadline(s): Oct. 15
  Board meeting date(s): Nov. 15
  Write: Carol Kresge, Pres.
Officers and Directors:* Carol Kresge,* Pres. and Exec. Dir.; Darwin R. Wales,* Secy.; James Lee, Robert Lindridge, John Spence.
Number of staff: 1 full-time professional.
EIN: 237081254

2048
The Mathilde and Arthur B. Krim Foundation, Inc.
33 East 69th St.
New York 10021

Donor(s): Arthur B. Krim.
Foundation type: Independent
Financial data (yr. ended 12/31/91): Assets, $67,931 (M); gifts received, $92,250; expenditures, $125,360; qualifying distributions, $124,275, including $124,275 for 121 grants (high: $52,500; low: $17).
Purpose and activities: Emphasis on higher education, medical research, including AIDS research, health agencies, cultural programs, public policy, social services, civil rights, Jewish organizations, and an institute of sociology.
Fields of interest: Higher education, medical research, AIDS, health, cultural programs, public policy, arms control, social services, civil rights, minorities, Africa, Jewish giving.
Types of support: Continuing support, research.
Limitations: Giving primarily in NY. No grants to individuals.
Publications: 990-PF.
Application information: Applications not accepted.
  Write: Arthur B. Krim, Chair.
Director: Arthur B. Krim, Chair.
Number of staff: None.
EIN: 136219851

2049
L and L Foundation
570 Park Ave., Suite 1A
New York 10021   (212) 758-7764

Incorporated in 1963 in NY.
Donor(s): Lawrence E. Brinn.‡
Foundation type: Independent
Financial data (yr. ended 12/31/91): Assets, $6,152,693 (M); expenditures, $312,349; qualifying distributions, $295,976, including $290,100 for 42 grants (high: $125,000; low: $100).
Fields of interest: Hospitals, higher education, cultural programs, performing arts, fine arts, youth, child welfare.
Limitations: Giving primarily in NY. No grants to individuals.
Application information: Application form not required.

  Initial approach: Letter
  Deadline(s): None
  Write: Mildred C. Brinn, Pres.
Officers and Directors:* Mildred Cunningham Brinn,* Pres. and Treas.; Peter F. De Gaetano,* Secy.
EIN: 136155758

2050
Asmund S. Laerdal Foundation, Inc.
One Labriola Court
Armonk 10504

Established in 1977 in NY.
Donor(s): Laerdal Medical Corp.
Foundation type: Independent
Financial data (yr. ended 12/31/90): Assets, $4,260,888 (M); gifts received, $100,000; expenditures, $247,215; qualifying distributions, $198,209, including $197,259 for 5 grants (high: $95,000; low: $2,000).
Purpose and activities: Giving primarily for medicine, emergency medical services, and medical research.
Fields of interest: Medical research, health services.
Types of support: Research.
Limitations: No grants to individuals.
Application information: Contributes only to pre-selected organizations. Applications not accepted.
Officer: Hans H. Dahll, Pres.
EIN: 132885659

2051
Eugene M. Lang Foundation ▼
155 East 38th St.
New York 10016   (212) 687-4741

Established in 1968 in NY.
Donor(s): Eugene M. Lang.
Foundation type: Independent
Financial data (yr. ended 12/31/90): Assets, $24,767,652 (M); expenditures, $2,634,672; qualifying distributions, $2,527,639, including $2,503,001 for 75 grants (high: $1,142,694; low: $50; average: $100-$20,000).
Purpose and activities: Support for higher and other education, cultural programs, and health and hospitals, including medical research.
Fields of interest: Cultural programs, education, education—early childhood, education—minorities, higher education, hospitals, health, medical research.
Types of support: Operating budgets, continuing support, annual campaigns, seed money, emergency funds, scholarship funds, professorships, internships, fellowships, special projects, conferences and seminars, land acquisition.
Limitations: Giving primarily in NY and neighboring area, including PA. No grants to individuals, or for building funds, equipment and materials, capital or endowment funds, deficit financing, publications, or matching gifts; no loans.
Application information: Application form not required.
  Initial approach: Letter
  Deadline(s): None
  Board meeting date(s): Apr. and Nov.

Write: Chris Hermanek
Trustees: David A. Lang, Eugene M. Lang, Stephen Lang, Theresa Lang, Jane Lang.
Number of staff: 1 part-time professional; 1 full-time support.
EIN: 136153412
Recent health grants:
2051-1 Booth Memorial Medical Center, Flushing, NY, $25,300. 1990.
2051-2 Rockefeller University, NYC, NY, $100,000. 1990.

2052
The Jacob and Valeria Langeloth Foundation ▼
One East 42nd St.
New York 10017   (212) 687-3760

Incorporated in 1915 in NY as the Valeria Home; renamed in 1975.
Donor(s): Jacob Langeloth.‡
Foundation type: Independent
Financial data (yr. ended 11/30/91): Assets, $36,405,320 (M); expenditures, $2,195,828; qualifying distributions, $1,832,814, including $1,705,000 for 32 grants (high: $100,000; low: $10,000; average: $25,000-$100,000).
Purpose and activities: Grants to nonprofit hospitals and health-care facilities, primarily to defray costs incurred by in-patients who are "people of education," or are involved in the arts, who normally would not ask for or be justified in accepting charity, but who nevertheless have difficulty in meeting their obligations.
Fields of interest: Hospitals, health services, hospices.
Types of support: Continuing support.
Limitations: Giving limited to NY, with emphasis on New York City and Westchester County. No grants to individuals.
Application information: Applications for grants are not invited except from previous recipients. Application form not required.
  Initial approach: Letter
  Copies of proposal: 1
  Deadline(s): Sept. 1
  Board meeting date(s): Feb. and Sept.
  Final notification: Varies
  Write: William R. Cross, Jr., Pres.
Officers and Directors:* John L. Loeb,* Chair.; William R. Cross, Jr.,* Pres. and Exec. Dir.; George Labalme, Jr.,* V.P.; Julian B. Beaty, Jr.,* Secy.; Henry A. Loeb,* Treas.; Mrs. Claude Boillot, Adam Hochschild, John L. Loeb, Jr., Peter K. Loeb, Richard G. Poole.
Number of staff: 1 part-time professional; 2 full-time support.
EIN: 131773646
Recent health grants:
2052-1 Adirondack Tri-County Nursing Home, North Creek, NY, $80,000. For patient care. 1990.
2052-2 Brooklyn Hospital, Brooklyn, NY, $30,000. For patient care. 1990.
2052-3 Burke Rehabilitation Center, White Plains, NY, $80,000. For patient care. 1990.
2052-4 District Nursing Association of Northern Westchester, Mount Kisco, NY, $15,000. For patient care. 1990.
2052-5 Family Service of Westchester, White Plains, NY, $50,000. For patient care. 1990.

2052-6 Glens Falls Hospital, Glens Falls, NY, $30,000. For patient care. 1990.
2052-7 Hospital for Joint Diseases, Orthopedic Institute, NYC, NY, $60,000. For patient care. 1990.
2052-8 International Center for the Disabled (ICD), NYC, NY, $100,000. For patient care. 1990.
2052-9 Jamaica Hospital Nursing Home, Jamaica, NY, $25,000. For patient care. 1990.
2052-10 Jewish Home and Hospital for the Aged, NYC, NY, $50,000. For patient care. 1990.
2052-11 Lenox Hill Hospital, NYC, NY, $100,000. For patient care. 1990.
2052-12 Memorial Sloan-Kettering Cancer Center, NYC, NY, $60,000. For patient care. 1990.
2052-13 Montefiore Medical Center, Hospital of Albert Einstein College of Medicine, Bronx, NY, $60,000. For patient care. 1990.
2052-14 Mount Sinai Hospital and Medical Center, NYC, NY, $100,000. For patient care. 1990.
2052-15 National Foundation for Facial Reconstruction, NYC, NY, $10,000. For patient care. 1990.
2052-16 New York University Medical Center, NYC, NY, $20,000. For patient care. 1990.
2052-17 Northern Westchester Hospital Center, Mount Kisco, NY, $50,000. For patient care. 1990.
2052-18 Peekskill Community Hospital, Peekskill, NY, $65,000. For patient care. 1990.
2052-19 Phelps Memorial Hospital, North Tarrytown, NY, $10,000. For patient care. 1990.
2052-20 Presbyterian Hospital in the City of New York, NYC, NY, $100,000. For patient care. 1990.
2052-21 Rockefeller University Hospital, NYC, NY, $100,000. For patient care. 1990.
2052-22 Rusk Institute of Rehabilitation Medicine, NYC, NY, $20,000. For patient care. 1990.
2052-23 Saint Agnes Hospital, White Plains, NY, $25,000. For patient care. 1990.
2052-24 Saint Lukes-Roosevelt Hospital Center, NYC, NY, $15,000. For patient care. 1990.
2052-25 Society of the New York Hospital, NYC, NY, $100,000. For patient care. 1990.
2052-26 Southampton Hospital, Southampton, NY, $50,000. For patient care. 1990.
2052-27 United Hospital, Port Chester, NY, $25,000. For patient care. 1990.
2052-28 Westchester Community Opportunity Program, Archway, White Plains, NY, $15,000. For patient care. 1990.
2052-29 White Plains Hospital Medical Center, White Plains, NY, $50,000. For patient care. 1990.

2053
Larsen Fund, Inc.
c/o Marcelle Coudrai
Time & Life Bldg., Rm. 4335, Rockefeller Ctr.
New York 10020
Application address: Grants Admin., 2960 Post Rd., Suite 100, Southport, CT 06490; Tel.: (203) 255-5318

Incorporated in 1941 in NY.

Donor(s): Roy E. Larsen.‡
Foundation type: Independent
Financial data (yr. ended 12/31/90): Assets, $7,092,524 (M); expenditures, $504,469; qualifying distributions, $437,790, including $384,884 for 53 grants (high: $35,000; low: $1,000).
Purpose and activities: Support for education, including medical and secondary schools, educational research, computer sciences, and social sciences; human services, including youth, family services, and family planning; hospitals and population studies; law and justice and urban affairs; intercultural relations; conservation, ecology, and wildlife preservation; and the arts, including museums, theater, and the media.
Fields of interest: Higher education, secondary education, youth, family services, hospitals, libraries, law and justice, intercultural relations, conservation, arts.
Types of support: General purposes, fellowships, professorships, research, annual campaigns, building funds, capital campaigns, conferences and seminars, consulting services, endowment funds, internships, land acquisition, lectureships, scholarship funds, seed money, special projects.
Limitations: Giving primarily in the New York, NY, area, the Minneapolis, MN, area, and CT. No grants to individuals.
Publications: Annual report (including application guidelines).
Application information: Application form not required.
  Initial approach: Letter
  Copies of proposal: 1
  Deadline(s): Submit proposal at least 60 days prior to meeting dates
  Board meeting date(s): Beginning of June and Dec.
  Write: Mrs. Patricia S. Palmer
Officers and Directors:* Robert R. Larsen,* Pres. and Treas.; Christopher Larsen,* V.P.; Ann Larsen Simonson,* V.P.; Jonathan Z. Larsen,* Secy.; Marcelle Coudrai.
Number of staff: 2 full-time support.
EIN: 136104430
Recent health grants:
2053-1 American Foundation for AIDS Research, NYC, NY, $10,000. 1990.
2053-2 Planned Parenthood of Minnesota, Saint Paul, MN, $11,000. 1990.

2054
Lasdon Foundation, Inc.
Ten Rockefeller Plaza, Suite 1111
New York 10020-1903   (212) 977-8420

Incorporated in 1946 in DE.
Donor(s): W.S. Lasdon,‡ Stanley S. Lasdon,‡ J.S. Lasdon,‡ M.S. Lasdon.‡
Foundation type: Independent
Financial data (yr. ended 11/30/91): Assets, $2,952,423 (M); expenditures, $250,813; qualifying distributions, $232,807, including $168,990 for 50 grants (high: $30,000; low: $40).
Purpose and activities: To further research in the medical sciences through grants to universities and medical institutions; support also for the performing arts, general civic projects, and Jewish organizations.

Fields of interest: Medical sciences, higher education, performing arts, civic affairs, Jewish giving.
Types of support: Research, matching funds, continuing support, annual campaigns.
Limitations: No grants to individuals, or for building or endowment funds, operating budgets, or program support.
Application information: Application form not required.
   Initial approach: Letter
   Copies of proposal: 1
   Deadline(s): Submit proposal preferably in Mar. or Sept.; no set deadline
   Board meeting date(s): Annually
   Final notification: Application for grants not necessarily acknowledged
Officers and Directors:* Gene S. Lasdon,* V.P.; Jeffrey S. Lasdon,* V.P.; Mildred D. Lasdon,* V.P.; Mildred L. Benson, Secy.
Number of staff: 1 full-time support.
EIN: 131739997

2055
William and Mildred Lasdon Foundation, Inc.
c/o N.L. Laitman
650 Park Ave., Apt. 6F
New York 10021

Established in 1947 in DE.
Donor(s): Jacob S. Lasdon, William S. Lasdon, Mildred D. Lasdan, Nanetta L. Leitman.
Foundation type: Independent
Financial data (yr. ended 12/31/91): Assets, $9,353,642 (M); expenditures, $193,493; qualifying distributions, $176,793, including $152,585 for 112 grants (high: $8,500; low: $100).
Fields of interest: Hospitals, arts, museums.
Limitations: Giving primarily in New York, NY. No grants to individuals.
Application information: Contributes only to pre-selected organizations. Applications not accepted.
Officers: Mildred D. Lasdon, Pres.; Bonnie Eletz, V.P.; Cathy Sorkin, V.P.; Nanette L. Laitman, Secy.-Treas.
EIN: 237380362

2056
Albert and Mary Lasker Foundation, Inc.
865 First Ave., Apt. 15E
New York 10017   (212) 421-9010

Incorporated in 1942 in NY.
Donor(s): Albert D. Lasker,‡ Mary W. Lasker.
Foundation type: Operating
Financial data (yr. ended 12/31/90): Assets, $2,621,966 (M); gifts received, $1,135,413; expenditures, $471,745; qualifying distributions, $322,821, including $18,035 for 8 grants (high: $10,000; low: $100) and $304,786 for foundation-administered programs.
Purpose and activities: Primarily concerned with medical research; annual Lasker awards given to honor and encourage outstanding medical research; support also for a beautification program, and health programs.
Fields of interest: Medical research, health, biological sciences, medical sciences.

Types of support: Continuing support.
Publications: 990-PF.
Application information: Applications not accepted.
   Write: Mary W. Lasker, Pres.
Officers and Directors:* Mary W. Lasker,* Pres.; Jordan Gutterman,* Exec. V.P.; Catherine G. Blair, V.P.; William McC. Blair, V.P.; James W. Fordyce,* Secy.-Treas.; Christopher Brody, Anne B. Fordyce, James E. Hughes, Jr.
EIN: 131680062

2057
B. J. Lasker Foundation, Inc.
1585 Broadway
New York 10036

Established in 1957 in NY.
Donor(s): Bernard J. Lasker.‡
Foundation type: Independent
Financial data (yr. ended 11/30/91): Assets, $1,509,103 (M); expenditures, $384,438; qualifying distributions, $380,719, including $379,350 for 29 grants (high: $11,000; low: $100).
Fields of interest: Hospitals, medical research, community funds, Jewish welfare, animal welfare.
Limitations: No grants to individuals.
Application information: Contributes only to pre-selected organizations. Applications not accepted.
Officer and Directors:* James J. Fuld,* V.P.; George G. Gallantz.
EIN: 136051635

2058
The Lauder Foundation, Inc.
767 Fifth Ave.
New York 10153   (212) 572-4426

Incorporated in 1962 in NY.
Donor(s): Estee Lauder, Joseph H. Lauder,‡ Leonard A. Lauder, Ronald S. Lauder.
Foundation type: Independent
Financial data (yr. ended 11/30/91): Assets, $7,401,470 (M); gifts received, $524,206; expenditures, $673,901; qualifying distributions, $668,616, including $668,616 for 90 grants (high: $25,000; low: $100; average: $1,000-$5,000).
Purpose and activities: Emphasis on museums and cultural programs, education, medical research, Jewish organizations, social service agencies, and conservation; some support for public affairs organizations and hospitals.
Fields of interest: Museums, cultural programs, arts, education, education—building funds, medical research, cancer, Jewish giving, social services, conservation, public policy, hospitals.
Limitations: Giving primarily in the New York, NY, metropolitan area. No grants to individuals.
Application information: Application form not required.
   Initial approach: Proposal
   Copies of proposal: 1
   Deadline(s): None
   Board meeting date(s): As needed
   Final notification: 4 to 8 weeks
   Write: Barbara E. Dobres
Officers and Directors:* Estee Lauder,* Pres.; Leonard A. Lauder,* Secy.-Treas.

Number of staff: None.
EIN: 136153743

2059
Lawrence Foundation
c/o Lawrence Aviation Industries, Inc.
Sheep Pasture Rd.
Port Jefferson Station 11776   (516) 473-1800

Established in 1943 in MA and NY.
Donor(s): Lawrence Aviation Industries, Inc.
Foundation type: Independent
Financial data (yr. ended 12/31/90): Assets, $2,480,489 (M); expenditures, $104,003; qualifying distributions, $101,829, including $85,854 for 59 grants (high: $10,000; low: $100).
Fields of interest: Higher education, hospitals, health associations, social services, cultural programs, Jewish giving.
Limitations: Giving primarily in NY, with emphasis on Long Island.
Application information: Application form not required.
   Deadline(s): None
   Write: Gerald Cohen, Trustee
Trustee: Gerald Cohen.
EIN: 116035412

2060
The Lazar Foundation
c/o Helen Lazar
680 Madison Ave.
New York 10021

Incorporated in 1957 in DE.
Donor(s): Jack Lazar,‡ Helen B. Lazar.
Foundation type: Independent
Financial data (yr. ended 12/31/91): Assets, $6,813,604 (M); gifts received, $720,000; expenditures, $699,663; qualifying distributions, $674,500, including $669,550 for 81 grants (high: $75,000; low: $100).
Fields of interest: Jewish welfare, higher education, environment, hospitals, social services.
Types of support: Special projects.
Limitations: Giving primarily in NY. No grants to individuals.
Publications: 990-PF.
Application information: Contributes only to pre-selected organizations. Applications not accepted.
Officers and Trustees:* Helen B. Lazar,* Pres.; William B. Lazar,* V.P. and Secy.; Jeanne L. Morency,* Treas.
Number of staff: 1 part-time professional.
EIN: 136088182

2061
James T. Lee Foundation, Inc.
P.O. Box 1856
New York 10185

Incorporated in 1958 in NY.
Donor(s): James T. Lee.‡
Foundation type: Independent
Financial data (yr. ended 11/30/91): Assets, $4,685,833 (M); expenditures, $306,415; qualifying distributions, $277,791, including $275,000 for 22 grants (high: $25,000; low: $5,000).

Fields of interest: Higher education, medical education, hospitals, religion, child welfare.
Types of support: Continuing support, annual campaigns, emergency funds, deficit financing, scholarship funds, special projects, research.
Limitations: Giving primarily in NY. No grants to individuals, or for operating budgets, seed money, capital or endowment funds, publications, or conferences; no loans.
Application information: Contributes only to pre-selected organizations. Applications not accepted.
   Board meeting date(s): Feb., May, Aug., and Nov.
   Write: Raymond T. O'Keefe, Pres.
Officers and Directors:* Raymond T. O'Keefe,* Pres.; Robert Rivel, V.P. and Treas.; John J. Duffy,* Secy.; Thomas Appleby, Verne S. Atwater, James Bloor, Robert Graber, Delcour Potter, Wesley Rivel.
Number of staff: None.
EIN: 131878496

2062
Samuel J. & Ethel Lefrak Foundation, Inc.
97-77 Queens Blvd.
Rego Park 11374   (718) 495-9021

Established in 1963.
Donor(s): Samuel J. Lefrak, L.S.S. Leasing Corp.
Foundation type: Independent
Financial data (yr. ended 12/31/90): Assets, $181,567 (M); gifts received, $43,247; expenditures, $205,476; qualifying distributions, $205,069, including $205,069 for 92 grants (high: $26,200; low: $10).
Purpose and activities: Giving primarily for education, hospitals and health agencies, and cultural institutions; some support for Jewish giving and general charitable giving.
Fields of interest: Education, health, cultural programs, Jewish giving, general charitable giving.
Limitations: Giving primarily in New York, NY. No grants to individuals.
Application information:
   Initial approach: Letter
   Deadline(s): None
   Write: Maxwell Goldpin, Admin. Asst.
Officer: Samuel J. Lefrak, Pres.
EIN: 116043788

2063
The Morris P. Leibovitz Foundation
19 East 70th St.
New York 10021

Established in 1988 in NY.
Donor(s): Morris P. Leibovitz.
Foundation type: Independent
Financial data (yr. ended 12/31/90): Assets, $2,143,199 (M); gifts received, $500,000; expenditures, $68,214; qualifying distributions, $66,100, including $66,100 for 8 grants (high: $23,000; low: $1,000).
Fields of interest: Jewish giving, higher education, aged, drug abuse.
Limitations: Giving primarily in NY. No grants to individuals.
Application information: Contributes only to pre-selected organizations. Applications not accepted.

Trustee: Morris P. Leibovitz.
EIN: 133442686

2064
The Dorothea L. Leonhardt Foundation, Inc.
One Chase Manhattan Plaza, 47th Fl.
New York 10005   (212) 530-5016
Application address: c/o Joanne L. Cassullo, Pres., 755 Park Ave., Apt. 3C, New York, NY 10021

Incorporated in 1988 in NY.
Donor(s): Frederick H. Leonhardt.‡
Foundation type: Independent
Financial data (yr. ended 07/31/91): Assets, $8,105,277 (M); expenditures, $538,164; qualifying distributions, $463,035, including $395,358 for 47 grants (high: $65,000; low: $200).
Fields of interest: Higher education, medical research, arts, cultural programs, music, performing arts, theater.
Types of support: General purposes, research, continuing support, endowment funds, professorships.
Limitations: Giving primarily in NY. No grants to individuals.
Application information: Generally contributes only to pre-selected organizations.
   Write: Guilford W. Gaylord, Secy.
Officers and Directors:* Joanne L. Cassullo,* Pres.; Alexander D. Forger,* V.P.; Guilford W. Gaylord,* Secy.-Treas.; Richard A. Stark.
Number of staff: 1 full-time professional.
EIN: 133420520

2065
Elisabeth & John Levin Fund
c/o Richard A. Eisner & Co.
575 Madison Ave.
New York 10022

Established in 1964.
Donor(s): Elisabeth L. Levin.
Foundation type: Independent
Financial data (yr. ended 11/30/90): Assets, $220,409 (M); gifts received, $494,348; expenditures, $345,512; qualifying distributions, $341,338, including $340,800 for grants (high: $50,000).
Fields of interest: Higher education, hospitals, Jewish giving, Jewish welfare.
Limitations: Giving primarily in New York, NY. No grants to individuals.
Application information: Contributes only to pre-selected organizations. Applications not accepted.
Officers: Elisabeth L. Levin, Pres.; Henry A. Loeb, V.P.; John A. Levin, Secy.-Treas.
EIN: 136168345

2066
Leviton Foundation, Inc. - New York
59-25 Little Neck Pkwy.
Little Neck 11362

Incorporated in 1952 in NY.
Donor(s): Leviton Manufacturing Co., American Insulated Wire Corp.

Foundation type: Company-sponsored
Financial data (yr. ended 12/31/91): Assets, $469,807 (M); expenditures, $407,080; qualifying distributions, $407,080, including $406,550 for 30 grants (high: $175,000; low: $100).
Purpose and activities: Emphasis on Jewish welfare funds; some support for education, community funds, and hospitals.
Fields of interest: Jewish welfare, higher education, community funds, hospitals.
Limitations: Giving primarily in NY and RI. No grants to individuals.
Application information: Contributes only to pre-selected organizations. Applications not accepted.
Officers and Directors:* Harold Leviton,* Pres.; Jack Amsterdam,* Secy.-Treas.; Shirley Leviton,* Treas.; Donald Mendier.
EIN: 116006368

2067
The Betty & Norman F. Levy Foundation, Inc.
c/o Norman F. Levy
30 Rockefeller Plaza, 59th Fl.
New York 10112

Established in 1965 in NY.
Donor(s): Norman F. Levy.
Foundation type: Independent
Financial data (yr. ended 09/30/92): Assets, $5,415,202 (M); expenditures, $323,045; qualifying distributions, $301,635, including $300,375 for 21 grants (high: $100,500; low: $250).
Purpose and activities: "Giving to any charity within the manager's focus, including both Jewish and non-Jewish organizations."
Fields of interest: Jewish welfare, Jewish giving, health, higher education.
Limitations: Giving primarily in New York, NY. No grants to individuals.
Application information: Contributes only to pre-selected organizations. Applications not accepted.
Officers and Directors:* Norman F. Levy,* Pres.; Francis N. Levy,* V.P.; Albert L. Maltz,* Secy.
EIN: 132553674

2068
Reginald F. Lewis Foundation
Nine West 57th St., 48th Fl.
New York 10019

Established in 1987 in NY.
Donor(s): Reginald F. Lewis,‡ TLC Group.
Foundation type: Independent
Financial data (yr. ended 06/30/91): Assets, $824,715 (M); expenditures, $959,866; qualifying distributions, $959,335, including $932,500 for 84 grants (high: $25,000; low: $1,000).
Fields of interest: Higher education, medical education, hospitals, minorities, race relations, performing arts, social services, youth.
Limitations: Giving primarily in New York, NY. No grants to individuals.
Application information: Contributes only to pre-selected organizations. Applications not accepted.

Directors: Beverly A. Cooper, Loida N. Lewis.
EIN: 133429965

2069
David L. Lieb Foundation, Inc.
274 Madison Ave., Suite 402
New York 10016-0601   (212) 683-7110

Donor(s): David L. Lieb.
Foundation type: Independent
Financial data (yr. ended 09/30/91): Assets,
$1,261,860 (M); expenditures, $244,233;
qualifying distributions, $239,703, including
$238,109 for 25 grants (high: $162,746; low:
$20).
Purpose and activities: Giving primarily for a
Jewish welfare fund and other Jewish
organizations; support also for higher education
and hospitals.
Fields of interest: Jewish welfare, Jewish giving,
higher education, hospitals.
Limitations: Giving primarily in NY. No grants to
individuals.
Application information: Contributes only to
pre-selected organizations. Applications not
accepted.
Officers: David L. Lieb, Pres.; Charles H. Lieb,
Secy.
EIN: 136077728

2070
Lighting Research Institute, Inc.
345 East 47th St.
New York 10017

Established in 1983.
Donor(s): National Electric Manufacturers Assn.,
General Electric Co.
Foundation type: Operating
Financial data (yr. ended 12/31/90): Assets,
$229,424 (M); gifts received, $335,386;
expenditures, $426,201; qualifying distributions,
$417,872, including $251,807 for grants (high:
$52,000).
Purpose and activities: A private operating
foundation; grants to organizations for video
development and lighting engineering, medical
and other higher education, and medical research.
Fields of interest: Film, higher education, medical
education, medical research.
Types of support: Research.
Limitations: No grants to individuals.
Application information: Contributes only to
pre-selected organizations. Applications not
accepted.
Officers and Director:* Pieter Von Herrman,
Pres.; Richard Vincent,* Secy.
EIN: 133147071

2071
Fay J. Lindner Foundation
1161 Meadowbrook Rd.
North Merrick 11566

Established in 1966.
Donor(s): Fay J. Lindner.
Foundation type: Independent
Financial data (yr. ended 08/31/91): Assets,
$16,787,979 (M); gifts received, $2,109,025;
expenditures, $665,807; qualifying distributions,

$665,216, including $655,270 for 50 grants
(high: $150,000; low: $1,000).
Purpose and activities: Giving primarily for
hospitals and health agencies; grants also to a
university, social services, the elderly, and Jewish
organizations, including a welfare fund.
Fields of interest: Hospitals, health, social
services, Jewish giving, aged.
Types of support: Program-related investments,
building funds, fellowships, seed money, special
projects.
Limitations: Giving primarily in Long Island, NY.
No grants to individuals.
Application information: Contributes only to
pre-selected organizations. Applications not
accepted.
Write: Robert M. Goldberg, Pres.
Officer: Robert M. Goldberg, Pres.
EIN: 116043320

2072
George Link, Jr. Foundation, Inc. ▼
c/o Emmet, Marvin and Martin
48 Wall St.
New York 10005   (212) 422-2974

Incorporated in 1980 in NY.
Donor(s): George Link, Jr.‡
Foundation type: Independent
Financial data (yr. ended 12/31/90): Assets,
$22,411,349 (M); expenditures, $1,670,842;
qualifying distributions, $1,492,245, including
$1,465,600 for 108 grants (high: $111,000; low:
$1,000; average: $5,000-$10,000).
Purpose and activities: Giving primarily for
hospitals and medical research, higher and
secondary education, welfare, culture and fine
arts, and Christian religious giving.
Fields of interest: Hospitals, medical research,
higher education, secondary education, welfare,
religion—Christian, cultural programs, fine arts.
Types of support: Building funds, scholarship
funds, fellowships, endowment funds.
Limitations: Giving primarily in NY, MA, and NJ.
No grants to individuals, or for general support,
operating budgets, continuing support, annual
campaigns, seed money, emergency funds, deficit
financing, equipment, land acquisition,
renovation projects, or matching gifts; no loans.
Application information: Application form not
required.
Initial approach: Proposal
Copies of proposal: 5
Deadline(s): None
Board meeting date(s): Monthly except July and
Aug.
Final notification: 6 weeks
Write: Michael J. Catanzaro, V.P.
Officers and Directors: Eleanor Irene Link, Chair.;
Robert Emmet Link, Vice-Chair.; Bernard F. Joyce,
V.P. and Secy.; Michael J. Catanzaro, V.P. and
Treas.; Coleman Clougherty, V.P.
Number of staff: None.
EIN: 133041396

2073
Lippman Rose Schnurmacher Fund, Inc.
1114 First Ave.
New York 10021   (212) 838-7766

Incorporated in 1945 in NY.

Donor(s): Rose Schnurmacher.‡
Foundation type: Independent
Financial data (yr. ended 12/31/91): Assets,
$1,244,510 (M); gifts received, $54,000;
expenditures, $325,289; qualifying distributions,
$324,390, including $324,390 for 56 grants
(high: $100,000; low: $100).
Fields of interest: Jewish welfare, Jewish giving,
hospitals, health.
Limitations: Giving primarily in NY.
Application information:
Write: Adolph Schnurmacher, Mgr.
Officers: Adolph Schnurmacher, Mgr.; Irwin
Schnurmacher, Mgr.
EIN: 136126002

2074
Frances and John L. Loeb Foundation
c/o Loeb Partners Corp.
61 Broadway
New York 10006

Incorporated in 1937 in NY.
Donor(s): John L. Loeb, Frances L. Loeb.
Foundation type: Independent
Financial data (yr. ended 10/31/90): Assets,
$4,383,474 (M); gifts received, $240,082;
expenditures, $832,995; qualifying distributions,
$827,800, including $814,850 for 162 grants
(high: $306,000; low: $100; average:
$100-$10,000).
Purpose and activities: Giving for higher
education and a private secondary school,
hospitals and health services, and cultural
programs, including museums and the performing
arts; some support also for social services and
international affairs and foreign relations.
Fields of interest: Higher education, secondary
education, hospitals, health services, cultural
programs, museums, performing arts, social
services, international affairs, foreign policy.
Limitations: Giving primarily in New York, NY.
No grants to individuals.
Application information: Contributes only to
pre-selected organizations. Applications not
accepted.
Officers and Directors:* Frances L. Loeb,* Pres.
and Treas.; John L. Loeb,* V.P. and Secy.; Deborah
L. Brice, Ann L. Bronfman, Judith L. Chiara,
Arthur L. Loeb, John L. Loeb, Jr.
Number of staff: None.
EIN: 136085598

2075
Loewenberg Foundation, Inc.
450 Park Ave.
New York 10022   (212) 753-4100

Established in 1959 in NY.
Donor(s): Ralph E. Loewenberg, Kurt
Loewenberg.‡
Foundation type: Independent
Financial data (yr. ended 10/31/91): Assets,
$2,235,978 (M); expenditures, $153,846;
qualifying distributions, $111,750, including
$111,750 for 13 grants (high: $80,000; low: $250).
Purpose and activities: Support primarily for
Jewish welfare; giving also for the arts, higher and
secondary education, and medical research.

Fields of interest: Jewish welfare, arts, higher education, secondary education, medical research.
Types of support: Research.
Limitations: Giving primarily in New York, NY. No grants to individuals.
Application information:
Initial approach: Proposal
Deadline(s): None
Write: Ralph E. Loewenberg, Pres.
Officers and Directors:* Ralph E. Loewenberg,* Pres. and Treas.; Jeffrey N. Grabel,* Secy.; Frederick Lubeker.
EIN: 136075586

2076
Loews Foundation ▼
One Park Ave., 15th Fl.
New York 10016   (212) 545-2643

Trust established in 1957 in NY.
Donor(s): Loews Corp., and subsidiaries.
Foundation type: Company-sponsored
Financial data (yr. ended 12/31/90): Assets, $7,739 (M); gifts received, $1,585,000; expenditures, $1,687,125; qualifying distributions, $1,687,125, including $1,673,965 for 75 grants (high: $725,000; low: $200; average: $1,000-$25,000) and $13,075 for employee matching gifts.
Purpose and activities: Grants primarily for Jewish welfare funds, higher education, including employee matching gifts and employee-related scholarships through the National Merit Scholarship Corporation., and cultural organizations.
Fields of interest: Higher education, cultural programs, Jewish welfare.
Types of support: Employee matching gifts, employee-related scholarships.
Limitations: No grants to individuals.
Application information: Applications for employee-related scholarship program available from the foundation, otherwise no application form required.
Initial approach: Letter, telephone or proposal
Deadline(s): None
Board meeting date(s): As required
Write: Daria Mychajluk
Trustees: J. Kenny, Roy Posner, Laurence A. Tisch, Preston R. Tisch.
EIN: 136082817
Recent health grants:
2076-1 Gay Mens Health Crisis (GMHC), NYC, NY, $25,000. For AIDS Walk. 1990.
2076-2 Gay Mens Health Crisis (GMHC), NYC, NY, $25,000. For Music For Life. 1990.
2076-3 New York University Medical Center, NYC, NY, $25,000. For Ovarian Cancer Research. 1990.
2076-4 Will Rogers Memorial Fund, White Plains, NY, $10,000. 1990.

2077
Richard Lounsbery Foundation, Inc. ▼
159A East 61st St.
New York 10021   (212) 319-7033

Incorporated in 1959 in NY.
Donor(s): Richard Lounsbery Foundation Trust, Inc.

Foundation type: Independent
Financial data (yr. ended 12/31/90): Assets, $14,945,833 (M); gifts received, $1,075,579; expenditures, $2,323,644; qualifying distributions, $2,085,538, including $1,757,298 for 131 grants (high: $60,000; low: $35; average: $1,000-$25,000).
Purpose and activities: Support primarily for biomedical research, the improvement of the teaching and learning of science and mathematics at the secondary and elementary levels, and human rights.
Fields of interest: Medical research, biology, secondary education, science and technology, elementary education, mathematics, human rights.
Types of support: Seed money, matching funds, fellowships, research.
Limitations: No grants to individuals, or for capital or building funds, conferences or seminars, or endowment funds; no loans.
Application information: Funds mainly committed to projects developed by the directors; other projects sometimes considered, but applications not encouraged. Application form not required.
Initial approach: Letter
Copies of proposal: 1
Deadline(s): 6 weeks prior to board meetings
Board meeting date(s): Last Wednesday of Jan., Apr., July, and Oct.
Final notification: 2 weeks
Write: Alan F. McHenry, Pres.
Officers and Directors:* Alan F. McHenry,* Pres. and Treas.; Benjamin J. Borden,* V.P. and Secy.; William J. McGill, M.D., Frederick Seitz, M.D., Lewis Thomas, M.D.
Number of staff: 1 full-time professional; 1 full-time support.
EIN: 136081860
Recent health grants:
2077-1 Columbia University, NYC, NY, $35,000. For research on anti-hypertensive effects of cocaine. 1990.
2077-2 Columbia University, NYC, NY, $25,000. For project, Cardiovascular Effects of Cocaine. 1990.
2077-3 Cornell University Medical Center, Hypertension and Cardiovascular Center, NYC, NY, $32,000. 1990.
2077-4 Cornell University Medical College, NYC, NY, $50,000. For Genesis 2000 DNA Sequencer. 1990.
2077-5 Institut de la Vie, Paris, France, $30,000. For AIDS research. 1990.
2077-6 Manhattan Eye, Ear and Throat Hospital, NYC, NY, $50,000. For CHI/Cochlear Implant. 1990.
2077-7 Masonic Medical Research Laboratory, NYC, NY, $15,000. For research on antihypertension effects of IL-2. 1990.
2077-8 Monell Chemical Senses Center, Philadelphia, PA, $60,000. For project, Body Odor and Cancer. 1990.
2077-9 Rockefeller University, NYC, NY, $25,000. For Bar Project. 1990.
2077-10 Saint Josephs Hospital, Flushing, NY, $50,000. For Project Excel. 1990.
2077-11 Whittier Institute for Diabetes and Endocrinology, La Jolla, CA, $25,000. For research on pituitary peptides. 1990.

2078
Leon Lowenstein Foundation, Inc. ▼
126 East 56th St., 28th Fl.
New York 10022   (212) 319-0670
FAX: (212) 688-0134

Incorporated in 1941 in NY.
Donor(s): Leon Lowenstein.‡
Foundation type: Independent
Financial data (yr. ended 12/31/91): Assets, $74,859,596 (M); expenditures, $3,697,033; qualifying distributions, $2,993,545, including $2,398,550 for 100 grants (high: $500,000; low: $100; average: $1,000-$25,000).
Purpose and activities: Support primarily for New York City public education and medical research, with emphasis on child and adolescent psychiatry and Parkinson's Disease.
Fields of interest: Medical research, education, secondary education, elementary education, youth.
Types of support: General purposes, research, seed money, special projects.
Limitations: Giving primarily in the New York, NY, metropolitan area.
Application information: Application form not required.
Initial approach: Letter
Copies of proposal: 1
Deadline(s): None
Board meeting date(s): As necessary
Final notification: 3 months
Write: John F. Van Gorder, Exec. Dir.
Officers and Directors:* Robert Bendheim,* Pres.; John M. Bendheim,* V.P.; Bernard R. Rapoport,* Secy.-Treas.; John F. Van Gorder, Exec. Dir.
Number of staff: 2 full-time professional.
EIN: 136015951
Recent health grants:
2078-1 Arthritis Foundation, New York Chapter, NYC, NY, $10,000. 1990.
2078-2 Columbia University, College of Physicians and Surgeons, NYC, NY, $70,000. 1990.
2078-3 Greenwich Hospital Association, Greenwich, CT, $200,000. 1990.
2078-4 Harvard University, Cambridge, MA, $115,000. For medical research. 1990.
2078-5 International Center for the Disabled (ICD), NYC, NY, $25,000. 1990.
2078-6 Long Island Jewish Medical Center, New Hyde Park, NY, $100,000. 1990.
2078-7 Mount Sinai Hospital and Medical Center, NYC, NY, $250,000. For capital support. 1990.
2078-8 White Plains Hospital Medical Center, White Plains, NY, $75,000. 1990.

2079
Theodore Luce Charitable Trust
c/o Chemical Bank, Admin. Services Dept.
30 Rockefeller Plaza
New York 10112   (212) 621-2148

Foundation type: Independent
Financial data (yr. ended 07/31/91): Assets, $7,652,627 (M); expenditures, $415,067; qualifying distributions, $358,250, including $358,000 for grants (average: $6,000).

Fields of interest: Hospitals, health associations, animal welfare, social services, youth, child welfare.
Limitations: Giving primarily in New York, NY. No grants to individuals, or for conferences or research papers.
Application information: Application form not required.
  Deadline(s): None
  Write: Mrs. M. Peterson
Trustee: Chemical Bank.
EIN: 136029703

2080
James A. Macdonald Foundation
One North Broadway
White Plains 10601   (914) 428-9305

Incorporated in 1966 in NY.
Donor(s): Flora Macdonald Bonney.‡
Foundation type: Independent
Financial data (yr. ended 12/31/91): Assets, $5,941,716 (M); expenditures, $399,592; qualifying distributions, $374,780, including $353,780 for 265 grants (high: $20,000; low: $150; average: $300-$800) and $21,000 for 2 loans.
Fields of interest: Protestant giving, secondary education, community funds, hospitals, youth, historic preservation.
Types of support: Operating budgets, continuing support, annual campaigns, seed money, emergency funds, building funds, equipment, land acquisition, endowment funds, scholarship funds, special projects, research, fellowships, renovation projects.
Limitations: Giving primarily in NY. No grants to individuals, or for matching gifts; no loans.
Application information: Application form not required.
  Initial approach: Letter
  Copies of proposal: 1
  Deadline(s): None
  Board meeting date(s): Irregularly, but at least quarterly
  Write: Walter J. Handelman, Secy.
Officers and Directors:* Alice H. Model,* Pres.; Walter J. Handelman,* V.P. and Secy.; Alan L. Model,* Treas.
Number of staff: None.
EIN: 136199690

2081
Marquis George MacDonald Foundation, Inc.
c/o UBS Asset Management (NY), Inc.
1211 Ave. of the Americas, 38th Fl.
New York 10036-8796   (212) 789-7034

Incorporated in 1951 in NY.
Donor(s): Marquis George MacDonald.‡
Foundation type: Independent
Financial data (yr. ended 12/31/91): Assets, $5,738,130 (M); expenditures, $274,406; qualifying distributions, $230,142, including $205,200 for 128 grants (high: $10,000; low: $500).
Purpose and activities: Giving for the arts, environment, higher and secondary education, church support, religious associations, hospitals, health, cancer and AIDS research, welfare funds,

and organizations providing benefit to the community and serving the public interest.
Fields of interest: Arts, environment, higher education, secondary education, religion, hospitals, health, AIDS, welfare, community development.
Types of support: Special projects.
Limitations: No grants to individuals, or for matching gifts; no loans.
Application information: Contributes only to pre-selected organizations; unsolicited proposals not considered. Applications not accepted.
  Board meeting date(s): May 7, Aug. 6, and Dec. 10
  Write: Jeannine Merrien, Admin.
Officers and Directors:* Catherine MacDonald,* Pres.; Kevin McDonald,* V.P. and Secy.; John L. McDonald, Jr.,* V.P. and Treas.; Helen McDonald, Joseph MacDonald.
Number of staff: 1 part-time professional.
EIN: 131957181

2082
The Paul MacKall & Evanina Evans Bell MacKall Trust
c/o Morgan Guaranty Trust Co. of New York
Nine West 57th St.
New York 10019   (212) 826-7628

Established in 1982 in NY.
Foundation type: Independent
Financial data (yr. ended 08/31/91): Assets, $9,945,940 (M); expenditures, $986,015; qualifying distributions, $911,980, including $911,980 for 1 grant.
Purpose and activities: Giving limited to medical facilities for ophthalmological research.
Fields of interest: Ophthalmology.
Limitations: No grants to individuals.
Application information:
  Initial approach: Letter
  Deadline(s): None
  Write: James J. Watson, V.P., Morgan Guaranty Trust Co. of New York
Trustees: Stuart Fine, Morgan Guaranty Trust Co. of New York.
EIN: 136794686

2083
Josiah Macy, Jr. Foundation ▼
44 East 64th St.
New York 10021   (212) 486-2424

Incorporated in 1930 in NY.
Donor(s): Kate Macy Ladd.‡
Foundation type: Independent
Financial data (yr. ended 06/30/91): Assets, $102,537,885 (M); expenditures, $5,254,341; qualifying distributions, $4,727,845, including $3,554,976 for 41 grants (high: $756,078; low: $1,000; average: $10,000-$300,000), $87,175 for 63 employee matching gifts and $248,179 for 1 foundation-administered program.
Purpose and activities: Major interest in medicine and health. Major grant programs are Minorities in Medicine, Medical Education, with emphasis on improving its effectiveness, and training of physicians and other health care professionals; support also for Macy Conferences, usually on issues relevant to current program areas.

Fields of interest: Medical sciences, education—minorities, health, medical education, biological sciences, nursing.
Types of support: Special projects.
Limitations: No grants to individuals, or for travel, capital or endowment funds, operating budgets, annual fund appeals, seed money, emergency funds, deficit financing, research, publications, conferences not run by the foundation, scholarships, or fellowships; no loans.
Publications: Annual report.
Application information: The Pathobiology Program has been discontinued. Receipt of proposal acknowledged; no interviews. Application form not required.
  Initial approach: Letter
  Copies of proposal: 1
  Deadline(s): None
  Board meeting date(s): Jan., May, and Sept.
  Final notification: Within 1 month
  Write: Thomas H. Meikle, Jr., M.D., Pres.
Officers and Directors:* Clarence F. Michalis,* Chair.; Thomas H. Meikle, Jr., M.D.,* Pres.; Rina Forlini, Secy.-Treas.; Lawrence K. Altman, M.D., Louis S. Auchincloss, Alexander G. Bearn, M.D., E. Virgil Conway, Charles B. Finch, S. Parker Gilbert, Patricia Albjerg Graham, Ph.D., Bernard W. Harleston, Ph.D., Arthur H. Hayes, Jr., M.D., Lawrence S. Huntington, John Jay Iselin, Ph.D., David L. Luke III, Mary Patterson McPherson, Ph.D., Walter N. Rothschild, Jr.
Number of staff: 2 full-time professional; 4 full-time support.
EIN: 135596895
Recent health grants:
2083-1 American Medical Student Association Foundation, Reston, VA, $10,900. Toward national conference, Financing Medical Education. 1991.
2083-2 Association of Academic Health Centers, DC, $15,000. Toward meeting, Human Resources for Health: Challenging the Future. 1991.
2083-3 City College of the City University of New York, CUNY Medical School, Sophie Davis School of Biomedical Education, NYC, NY, $20,000. For development of enhanced program to recruit and retain minority students. 1991.
2083-4 Columbia University, NYC, NY, $20,000. For planning of four-year curriculum in medical ethics at Harvard Medical School and Columbia University College of Physicians and Surgeons. 1991.
2083-5 Columbia University, College of Physicians and Surgeons, NYC, NY, $100,000. For conference, Taking Charge of Graduate Medical Education: To Meet Nation's Needs in the 21st Century. 1991.
2083-6 Cornell University, Ithaca, NY, $15,000. For development and dissemination of educational materials to be used in ethics courses with video tapes of play, Miss Ever's Boys. 1991.
2083-7 Johns Hopkins University, School of Medicine, Baltimore, MD, $100,000. For conference, The Obstetrician and Gynecologist in the 21st Century—Meeting Society's Needs. 1991.
2083-8 Mount Sinai School of Medicine, NYC, NY, $750,000. For project to develop Standardized Patient Program, whereby medical students are taught and tested for

clinical skills essential in the patient-doctor encounter. 1991.

2083-9 National Academy of Sciences, DC, $24,600. Toward workshop on minority careers in academic medicine and science. 1991.

2083-10 National Womens Health Resource Center, DC, $15,000. For publication of final report of symposium, Forging Women's Health Research Agenda. 1991.

2083-11 New Haven Public Schools, New Haven, CT, $159,027. For Precollegiate Enrichment Program (PREP) at James J. Hillhouse High School. 1991.

2083-12 New York State Council on Graduate Medical Education, Troy, NY, $20,000. For evaluation of impact of 405 Regulations on graduate medical education and quality of patient care in New York State. 1991.

2083-13 Southern Illinois University, School of Medicine, Carbondale, IL, $10,000. For review of six years of experience with clinical practice examination (CPX). 1991.

2083-14 University of California, School of Nursing, San Francisco, CA, $14,000. For conference on AIDS/HIV infection for nurse educators. 1991.

2084
The Mailman Foundation, Inc.
150 East 58th St., 14th Fl.
New York 10155   (212) 421-3131
FAX: (212) 421-3163

Incorporated in 1943 in DE.
Donor(s): Joseph L. Mailman,‡ Abraham L. Mailman.‡
Foundation type: Independent
Financial data (yr. ended 12/31/90): Assets, $4,672,209 (M); gifts received, $410,000; expenditures, $543,110; qualifying distributions, $501,412, including $500,902 for 55 grants (high: $250,000; low: $68).
Fields of interest: Jewish giving, Jewish welfare, hospitals, higher education, arts.
Limitations: No grants to individuals.
Application information: Contributes only to pre-selected organizations. Applications not accepted.
Write: Joseph V. Hastings, Secy.-Treas.
Officers and Trustees:* Phyllis Mailman,* Pres.; Joshua L. Mailman,* V.P.; Joan M. Wolfe,* V.P.; Judson A. Wolfe,* V.P.; Joseph V. Hastings, Secy.-Treas.
EIN: 136161556

2085
F. T. and Anna C. Manley Memorial Fund
c/o The Bank of New York, Tax Dept.
One Wall St., 28th Fl.
New York 10286
Application address: c/o Key Trust Co., Trust Dept., Olean, NY 14760; Tel.: (716) 372-0415

Established in 1987 in NY.
Foundation type: Independent
Financial data (yr. ended 12/31/91): Assets, $2,537,097 (M); expenditures, $124,309; qualifying distributions, $106,588, including $102,500 for 18 grants (high: $7,500; low: $2,500).

Fields of interest: Hospitals, higher education, social services, child welfare, Protestant giving, libraries.
Limitations: Giving primarily in NY.
Application information: Application form not required.
Initial approach: Letter
Deadline(s): None
Trustee: The Bank of New York.
EIN: 136905221

2086
The James Hilton Manning and Emma Austin Manning Foundation
45 Fifth Ave.
New York 10003

Incorporated in 1958 in NY.
Donor(s): Beatrice Austin Manning,‡ Alfred M. Hoelzer.‡
Foundation type: Independent
Financial data (yr. ended 07/31/91): Assets, $4,419,272 (M); gifts received, $2,000; expenditures, $327,000; qualifying distributions, $270,162, including $254,500 for 9 grants (high: $100,000; low: $5,000).
Purpose and activities: Support only for "medical research in human physiology and the diseases thereof."
Fields of interest: Medical research.
Types of support: Research.
Limitations: No grants to individuals, or for student aid, general support, capital or endowment funds, scholarships, fellowships, or matching gifts; no loans.
Publications: Annual report.
Application information: Contributes only to pre-selected organizations. Applications not accepted.
Board meeting date(s): Semiannually
Officers and Directors:* Leonard T. Scully,* Pres.; Jean T.J. Scully,* Secy.; Ann Kissel Grun,* Treas.; Frank Veith.
Number of staff: 1 part-time professional.
EIN: 136123540

2087
Manufacturers Hanover Foundation ▼
270 Park Ave.
New York 10017   (212) 286-7124

Trust established in 1956 in NY.
Donor(s): Manufacturers Hanover Trust Co.
Foundation type: Company-sponsored
Financial data (yr. ended 12/31/90): Assets, $16,683,962 (M); expenditures, $1,226,867; qualifying distributions, $1,180,466, including $750,500 for grants and $429,966 for employee matching gifts.
Purpose and activities: Interests include a community fund, civic affairs, higher and secondary education, educational research, hospitals, cultural programs, youth agencies, public policy and community development organizations, and health agencies.
Fields of interest: Civic affairs, education, educational research, hospitals, health services, cultural programs, youth, public policy, community development.

Types of support: Employee matching gifts, annual campaigns, building funds, general purposes, continuing support.
Limitations: Giving primarily in areas in which the company operates, primarily the New York, NY, metropolitan area. No support for private foundations. No grants to individuals, or for scholarships, fellowships, or special projects; no loans.
Publications: Annual report.
Application information: Application form not required.
Initial approach: Letter
Copies of proposal: 1
Deadline(s): Submit proposal preferably between Sept. and Dec.; deadline Mar. 31
Board meeting date(s): May
Final notification: June 1
Write: Matthew Trachtenberg, Agent
Advisory Committee: John F. McGillicuddy, Chair.
Trustee: Manufacturers Hanover Trust Co.
EIN: 136143284

2088
Robert Mapplethorpe Foundation, Inc. ▼
120 Wooster St., 4th Fl.
New York 10012   (212) 941-4760
FAX: (212) 941-4764

Established in 1988 in NY.
Donor(s): Robert Mapplethorpe.‡
Foundation type: Independent
Financial data (yr. ended 05/31/92): Assets, $3,105,342 (M); expenditures, $1,214,178; qualifying distributions, $1,064,953, including $755,800 for 18 grants (high: $320,000; low: $100; average: $2,500-$20,000).
Purpose and activities: Support for medical research to advance the cure and treatment of AIDS and HIV infection, and for photography as an art form through assisting museums, universities, and other institutions, and by publishing quality books and materials.
Fields of interest: AIDS, medical research, arts.
Types of support: Publications, special projects, equipment, research.
Limitations: No support for social services. No grants to individuals.
Publications: Application guidelines, annual report, grants list.
Application information: Application form not required.
Initial approach: Letter
Deadline(s): None
Board meeting date(s): Approximately every 6 weeks
Final notification: Approximately 1 week after board
Write: Mame Kennedy, Exec. Dir.
Officers and Directors:* Michael Ward Stout,* Pres.; Lynn Davis,* V.P.; Dimitri Levas,* V.P.; Burton Lipsky,* Secy.-Treas.; Mame Kennedy, Exec. Dir.
Number of staff: 2 full-time professional; 1 part-time professional.
EIN: 133480472

2089
Mark IV Industries Foundation, Inc.
c/o Mark IV Industries
P.O. Box 810
Buffalo 14226-0810   (716) 689-4972

Established in 1976 in NY.
Donor(s): Mark IV Industries, Inc.
Foundation type: Company-sponsored
Financial data (yr. ended 04/30/91): Assets, $2,143,316 (M); expenditures, $199,772; qualifying distributions, $199,772, including $188,625 for 46 grants (high: $20,000; low: $25; average: $1,000-$1,500) and $3,841 for 41 employee matching gifts.
Purpose and activities: Giving for higher education, youth and child welfare, the performing arts and other cultural programs, community development, and Jewish organizations.
Fields of interest: Child development, child welfare, community development, general charitable giving, museums, performing arts, youth, cultural programs, education, hospitals, Jewish giving, higher education.
Types of support: Continuing support, employee matching gifts.
Limitations: Giving primarily in Buffalo, NY.
Publications: Annual report.
Application information: Application form not required.
  Initial approach: Letter
  Copies of proposal: 1
  Deadline(s): None
  Board meeting date(s): Apr.
  Write: Carol Ann Richthammer
Officers: Sal H. Alfiero, Chair.; Clement R. Arrison, Pres.; Gerald S. Lippes, Secy.
Number of staff: 1
EIN: 161082605

2090
Marks Family Foundation
c/o Carl Marks & Co.
135 East 57th St.
New York 10022

Established in 1986.
Donor(s): Edwin S. Marks, Nancy A. Marks.
Foundation type: Independent
Financial data (yr. ended 06/30/91): Assets, $379,279 (M); gifts received, $102,000; expenditures, $385,585; qualifying distributions, $383,040, including $381,690 for 35 grants (high: $100,000).
Fields of interest: Museums, arts, performing arts, social services, child welfare, hospitals.
Limitations: Giving primarily in NY. No grants to individuals.
Application information: Contributes only to pre-selected organizations. Applications not accepted.
Officers: Edwin S. Marks, Pres. and Treas.; Nancy A. Marks, V.P. and Secy.
EIN: 133385770

2091
The William Marx Foundation
215 Lexington Ave., No. 202
New York 10016-6023

Donor(s): Helen Schulman Marx.
Foundation type: Independent
Financial data (yr. ended 10/31/91): Assets, $2,230 (M); gifts received, $805,000; expenditures, $859,347; qualifying distributions, $859,347, including $858,000 for 9 grants (high: $260,000; low: $3,000).
Purpose and activities: Giving primarily to services for the developmentally disabled, hospice care, and medical sciences; support also for Jewish welfare organizations.
Fields of interest: Handicapped, hospices, medical sciences, Jewish welfare.
Limitations: No grants to individuals.
Application information: Contributes only to pre-selected organizations. Applications not accepted.
Officers: Helen Schulman Marx, Pres.; Cynthia Marks, V.P.; Harry Marx, Secy.-Treas.
EIN: 116020448

2092
The Charles A. Mastronardi Charitable Foundation
c/o Morgan Guaranty Trust Co. of New York
Nine West 57th St.
New York 10019   (212) 826-7603

Established in 1964 in NY.
Donor(s): Charles A. Mastronardi.‡
Foundation type: Independent
Financial data (yr. ended 12/31/90): Assets, $8,959,692 (M); expenditures, $486,322; qualifying distributions, $425,475, including $391,600 for 99 grants (high: $60,000; low: $100).
Purpose and activities: Giving largely for higher education, specific disease health associations, hospitals, Roman Catholic welfare and church support, and child welfare and development, including programs for special needs children.
Fields of interest: Higher education, health associations, hospitals, Catholic giving, Catholic welfare, child welfare, child development, handicapped.
Limitations: Giving primarily in NY and FL. No grants to individuals.
Application information:
  Initial approach: Letter or proposal
  Deadline(s): None
  Write: Edward F. Bennett, V.P.
Officers: Carrie Mastronardi, Pres.; Olga DeFelippo, Exec. V.P.; Edward F. Bennett, V.P.; Margaret Mastronardi, V.P.; Nicholas D. Mastronardi, V.P.; Mary Turino, V.P.
EIN: 136167916

2093
G. Harold & Leila Y. Mathers Charitable Foundation ▼
103 South Bedford Rd., Suite 101
Mount Kisco 10549-3440   (914) 242-0465

Established in 1975 in NY.
Donor(s): G. Harold Mathers,‡ Leila Y. Mathers.‡
Foundation type: Independent

Financial data (yr. ended 12/31/91): Assets, $120,526,763 (M); expenditures, $10,273,864; qualifying distributions, $9,692,864, including $9,692,134 for 70 grants (high: $600,000; low: $2,500; average: $2,500-$600,000).
Purpose and activities: Giving primarily for basic medical research.
Fields of interest: Medical research.
Types of support: Research, general purposes.
Limitations: No grants to individuals.
Application information: Application form not required.
  Initial approach: Letter, with 1 copy of research proposal
  Copies of proposal: 1
  Deadline(s): None
  Board meeting date(s): 2 or 3 times a year
  Final notification: Varies
  Write: James H. Handelman, Exec. Dir.
Officers and Directors:* Donald E. Handelman,* Pres.; William R. Handelman,* V.P.; John Hay,* V.P.; Don Fizer,* Secy.; Joseph W. Handelman,* Treas.; John R. Young.
Number of staff: 1 full-time professional; 1 full-time support.
EIN: 237441901
Recent health grants:
2093-1 American Red Cross, Rockville, MD, $191,408. For medical research. 1990.
2093-2 American Red Cross, Rockville, MD, $127,695. For medical research. 1990.
2093-3 American Red Cross, Rockville, MD, $93,694. For medical research. 1990.
2093-4 Beth Israel Hospital, Boston, MA, $47,692. For medical research. 1990.
2093-5 Brown University, Providence, RI, $45,521. For medical research. 1990.
2093-6 Burke Rehabilitation Center, White Plains, NY, $250,012. For medical research. 1990.
2093-7 Case Western Reserve University, School of Medicine, Cleveland, OH, $178,400. For medical research. 1990.
2093-8 Childrens Hospital of Philadelphia, Philadelphia, PA, $240,000. For medical research. 1990.
2093-9 Columbia University, College of Physicians and Surgeons, NYC, NY, $75,000. For medical research. 1990.
2093-10 Dana-Farber Cancer Institute, Boston, MA, $332,829. For medical research. 1990.
2093-11 Doctors Services Foundation, Houston, TX, $35,000. For general support. 1990.
2093-12 Downstate Medical Center, Brooklyn, NY, $54,029. For medical research. 1990.
2093-13 Georgetown University Medical Center, DC, $265,817. For medical research. 1990.
2093-14 Harvard University, Boston, MA, $593,000. For medical research. 1990.
2093-15 Hospital for Joint Diseases, NYC, NY, $63,293. For medical research. 1990.
2093-16 La Jolla Cancer Research Foundation, La Jolla, CA, $143,000. For medical research. 1990.
2093-17 Massachusetts General Hospital, Boston, MA, $97,064. For medical research. 1990.
2093-18 Memorial Sloan-Kettering Cancer Center, NYC, NY, $137,500. For medical research. 1990.
2093-19 Montefiore Medical Center, Bronx, NY, $112,104. For medical research. 1990.

2093-20 Montefiore Medical Center, Bronx, NY, $54,295. For medical research. 1990.

2093-21 Montefiore Medical Center, Bronx, NY, $50,000. For medical research. 1990.

2093-22 National Cancer Institute, Bethesda, MD, $254,000. For medical research. 1990.

2093-23 National Cancer Institute, Bethesda, MD, $173,540. For medical research. 1990.

2093-24 National Cancer Institute, Bethesda, MD, $66,485. For medical research. 1990.

2093-25 National Heart, Lung, and Blood Institute, Bethesda, MD, $10,000. For medical research. 1990.

2093-26 National Institute of Health, National Heart, Lung and Blood Institute, Bethesda, MD, $10,000. For medical research. 1990.

2093-27 New York Hospital-Cornell Medical Center, NYC, NY, $50,000. For medical research. 1990.

2093-28 New York Hospital-Cornell Medical Center, NYC, NY, $49,590. For medical research. 1990.

2093-29 New York Hospital-Cornell Medical Center, White Plains, NY, $24,967. For clinical study. 1990.

2093-30 New York Medical College, Valhalla, NY, $150,000. For medical research. 1990.

2093-31 New York Medical College, Valhalla, NY, $60,995. For medical research. 1990.

2093-32 New York Medical College, Valhalla, NY, $57,059. For medical research. 1990.

2093-33 New York State Department of Health, Stony Brook, NY, $56,347. For medical research. 1990.

2093-34 Northwestern University, Evanston, IL, $49,677. For medical research. 1990.

2093-35 Saint Francis Hospital, Santa Barbara, CA, $375,000. For purchase of cardiac catheterization laboratory equipment. 1990.

2093-36 Salk Institute for Biological Studies, La Jolla, CA, $666,667. For new construction. 1990.

2093-37 Salk Institute for Biological Studies, La Jolla, CA, $340,500. For medical research. 1990.

2093-38 Salk Institute for Biological Studies, La Jolla, CA, $10,000. For medical research. 1990.

2093-39 Santa Barbara Council on Alcoholism and Drug Abuse, Santa Barbara, CA, $25,000. For general support. 1990.

2093-40 Scripps Clinic and Research Foundation, La Jolla, CA, $467,825. For medical research. 1990.

2093-41 Stanford University Medical Center, Stanford, CA, $500,000. For medical research. 1990.

2093-42 Tulane University Medical Center, New Orleans, LA, $98,000. For medical research. 1990.

2093-43 University of California, San Francisco, CA, $54,603. For medical research. 1990.

2093-44 University of Chicago Medical Center, Chicago, IL, $127,367. For medical research. 1990.

2093-45 University of Colorado, Health Science Center, Denver, CO, $25,000. For medical research. 1990.

2093-46 University of Iowa, College of Medicine, Iowa City, IA, $137,467. For medical research. 1990.

2093-47 University of Nevada, School of Medicine, Reno, NV, $100,215. For medical research. 1990.

2093-48 University of North Carolina, Chapel Hill, NC, $55,009. For medical research. 1990.

2093-49 University of Rochester Medical Center, Rochester, NY, $37,148. For medical research. 1990.

2093-50 University of Tennessee, College of Veterinary Medicine, Knoxville, TN, $39,700. For medical research. 1990.

2093-51 University of Texas, Health Science Center, Houston, TX, $154,361. For medical research. 1990.

2093-52 University of Texas, Health Science Center, San Antonio, TX, $262,326. For medical research. 1990.

2093-53 Worcester Foundation for Experimental Biology, Shrewsbury, MA, $265,000. For medical research. 1990.

2093-54 Yale University, New Haven, CT, $517,131. For medical research. 1990.

2093-55 Yale University, School of Medicine, New Haven, CT, $239,067. For medical research. 1990.

2094
Helen Mayer Charitable Trust
c/o Fleet Bank, N.A.
One East Ave.
Rochester 14638   (716) 546-9105

Established in 1959 in NY.
Donor(s): Helen Shumway Mayer.
Foundation type: Independent
Financial data (yr. ended 11/30/91): Assets, $706,845 (M); gifts received, $142,500; expenditures, $274,549; qualifying distributions, $270,800, including $270,500 for 30 grants (high: $50,000; low: $500).
Fields of interest: Environment, conservation, historic preservation, cancer, hospitals, religion—Christian.
Limitations: Giving primarily in the New England states. No grants to individuals.
Application information: Application form not required.
  Deadline(s): None
  Write: Jack Murphy, Trust Officer, Fleet Bank, N.A.
Trustees: Helen Shumway Mayer, Fleet Bank, N.A.
EIN: 166022958

2095
The Louis B. Mayer Foundation
165 East 72nd St., Suite 1B
New York 10021   (212) 737-1011

Trust established in 1947 in CA.
Donor(s): Louis B. Mayer.‡
Foundation type: Independent
Financial data (yr. ended 12/31/91): Assets, $8,736,956 (M); expenditures, $1,134,700; qualifying distributions, $1,054,213, including $1,030,000 for 3 grants (high: $1,000,000; low: $5,000; average: $5,000-$1,000,000).
Purpose and activities: Support for basic innovation, research, and development in areas of film preservation and medical research.
Fields of interest: Film, medical research.

Types of support: Building funds, continuing support, endowment funds, equipment, research, seed money, special projects.
Limitations: No grants to individuals; no loans.
Publications: 990-PF.
Application information: Contributes only to pre-selected organizations. Applications not accepted.
  Board meeting date(s): Quarterly
  Write: Ann Brownell Sloane, Administrator
Officers and Trustees:* L. Jeffrey Selznick,* Pres.; Robert A. Gottlieb,* Secy.; Carol Farkas,* Treas.
Number of staff: 4 shared staff
EIN: 952232340

2096
The Mayrock Foundation, Inc.
c/o C. Wise
1300 Old Country Rd.
Westbury 11590

Donor(s): M. Fortunoff of Westbury Corp., Harry Mayrock, Birdie Samson.
Foundation type: Operating
Financial data (yr. ended 05/31/91): Assets, $208,635 (M); gifts received, $1,200; expenditures, $235,060; qualifying distributions, $235,060, including $233,169 for 54 grants (high: $50,000; low: $50).
Purpose and activities: Support primarily for Jewish giving and Jewish welfare programs, hospitals, a single disease association, and an international affairs institute; some support also for education and other charitable giving.
Fields of interest: Jewish giving, Jewish welfare, hospitals, health associations, international affairs, education, general charitable giving.
Types of support: Endowment funds.
Limitations: Giving primarily in NY and NJ.
Application information:
  Initial approach: Request on letterhead
  Deadline(s): None
  Write: Isidore Mayrock, V.P.
Officers: Alan Fortunoff, V.P.; Isidore Mayrock, V.P.; Rachel Sands, Secy.; Elliot Mayrock, Treas.
EIN: 112646558

2097
James J. McCann Charitable Trust and McCann Foundation, Inc. ▼
(also known as McCann Foundation)
35 Market St.
Poughkeepsie 12601   (914) 452-3085

McCann Foundation, Inc. established in NY in 1967; trust established in 1969 in NY; foundations function as single unit and financial data is combined.
Donor(s): James J. McCann.‡
Foundation type: Independent
Financial data (yr. ended 12/31/90): Assets, $25,355,747 (M); expenditures, $2,113,684; qualifying distributions, $1,921,604, including $1,787,728 for 41 grants (high: $668,485; low: $50; average: $100-$1,000,000).
Purpose and activities: Giving primarily for secondary and higher education (including scholarship funds), recreation, civic projects, social services, cultural programs, church support and religious associations, and hospitals.

Fields of interest: Higher education, secondary education, recreation, civic affairs, social services, religion—Christian, cultural programs, hospitals.
Types of support: Continuing support, annual campaigns, seed money, building funds, equipment, land acquisition, scholarship funds, fellowships, publications, conferences and seminars.
Limitations: Giving limited to Poughkeepsie and Dutchess County, NY. No grants to individuals, or for operating budgets, emergency or endowment funds, deficit financing, or matching gifts; generally no loans.
Publications: Annual report.
Application information: Application form not required.
  Initial approach: Letter or proposal
  Copies of proposal: 1
  Deadline(s): Submit proposal preferably in Feb. or Aug.; no deadline
  Board meeting date(s): Jan. and July
  Final notification: 60 days
  Write: John J. Gartland, Jr., Pres.
Officers and Trustees:* John J. Gartland, Jr.,* Pres.; William L. Gardner, Jr.,* V.P.; Richard V. Corbally, Secy.
Number of staff: 1 part-time professional; 1 part-time support.
EIN: 146050628

2098
The McCarthy Charities, Inc.
P.O. Box 576
Troy 12181

Incorporated in 1917 in NY.
Donor(s): Robert H. McCarthy, Lucy A. McCarthy.‡
Foundation type: Independent
Financial data (yr. ended 12/31/90): Assets, $3,468,307 (M); gifts received, $1,000; expenditures, $241,840; qualifying distributions, $233,434, including $229,809 for 82 grants (high: $25,000; low: $10).
Purpose and activities: Giving for Roman Catholic church support and church-related education and welfare agencies; support also for community funds, social service agencies, and hospitals.
Fields of interest: Catholic giving, Catholic welfare, community funds, social services, hospitals.
Limitations: Giving primarily in the Albany Capital District, NY, area. No grants to individuals.
Application information:
  Initial approach: Letter
  Write: Peter F. McCarthy, Pres.
Officers: Peter F. McCarthy, Pres. and Treas.; James A. McCarthy, V.P.; Marion P. McCarthy, Secy.
EIN: 146019064

2099
Mary A. and John M. McCarthy Foundation
69 First St.
Garden City 11530   (516) 742-7895

Established in 1985.
Donor(s): Mary A. McCarthy, John M. McCarthy.
Foundation type: Independent

Financial data (yr. ended 11/30/91): Assets, $2,200,000 (M); gifts received, $100,000; expenditures, $100,000; qualifying distributions, $100,000, including $100,000 for 12 grants (high: $25,000; low: $1,000).
Fields of interest: Education, education—minorities, health, hospitals, animal welfare, arts, theater, Catholic giving.
Types of support: Scholarship funds, capital campaigns.
Limitations: No grants to individuals.
Publications: 990-PF.
Application information: Contributes only to pre-selected organizations. Applications not accepted.
  Board meeting date(s): End of each quarter
  Write: John M. McCarthy, Trustee
Trustees: John M. McCarthy, Mary A. McCarthy, Neil M. McCarthy, Stephen J. McCarthy.
Number of staff: None.
EIN: 136863980

2100
Neil A. McConnell Foundation, Inc.
113 East 55th St.
New York 10022-3502   (212) 980-9090

Incorporated in 1960 in NY.
Donor(s): Neil A. McConnell.
Foundation type: Independent
Financial data (yr. ended 03/31/91): Assets, $2,645,556 (L); expenditures, $554,884; qualifying distributions, $527,042, including $499,500 for 26 grants (high: $90,000; low: $1,650; average: $5,000-$35,000).
Purpose and activities: Giving for special educational projects identified or developed by the foundation; interests include the arts, medical sciences, child development, and the aged.
Fields of interest: Education, Africa, aged, arts, cancer, child development, child welfare, educational research, medical sciences, museums, music, psychology, recreation, theater, hospitals.
Types of support: Special projects, annual campaigns, conferences and seminars, general purposes, research.
Limitations: Giving limited to the northeastern U.S. and the New York, NY, metropolitan area. No grants to individuals; no loans or program-related investments.
Application information: Application form not required.
  Initial approach: Letter
  Copies of proposal: 1
  Deadline(s): None
  Board meeting date(s): Annually and as required
  Write: James G. Niven, V.P.
Officers and Trustees:* Neil A. McConnell,* Pres.; James G. Niven,* V.P. and Treas.; B. Scott McConnell,* V.P.; Douglas F. Williamson, Jr., Secy.; Concetta Matranga, Exec. Dir.
Number of staff: 1 full-time professional.
EIN: 136114121

2101
J. M. McDonald Foundation, Inc.
2057 East River Rd.
Cortland 13045-9752   (607) 756-9283

Incorporated in 1952 in NE.

Donor(s): James M. McDonald, Sr.‡
Foundation type: Independent
Financial data (yr. ended 12/31/90): Assets, $10,316,683 (M); expenditures, $662,802; qualifying distributions, $580,648, including $570,000 for 28 grants (high: $60,000; low: $9,000; average: $10,000-$30,000).
Purpose and activities: Grants for the aged, orphans, and children who are sick, infirm, blind, or crippled; support for youth and child care in an effort to combat juvenile delinquency and to aid underprivileged, mentally or physically handicapped children; other interests include health and hospitals and education, especially higher education.
Fields of interest: Aged, child welfare, social services, youth, crime and law enforcement, handicapped, hospitals, health services, education, higher education.
Types of support: Annual campaigns, building funds, equipment, general purposes, continuing support, renovation projects.
Limitations: Giving limited to the U.S. No grants to individuals, or for seminars, workshops, endowment funds, scholarships, fellowships, travel, exhibits, or conferences; no loans.
Publications: Application guidelines.
Application information: Application form not required.
  Initial approach: Letter, proposal, or telephone
  Copies of proposal: 1
  Deadline(s): Apr. 15 and Sept. 15
  Board meeting date(s): May and Oct.
  Final notification: May 30 or Oct. 30 for positive responses
  Write: Reed L. McJunkin, Secy.
Officers and Trustees:* Eleanor F. McJunkin,* Pres.; Donald R. McJunkin,* V.P.; Reed L. McJunkin,* Secy.; Donald C. Berry, Jr.,* Treas.
Number of staff: 1 part-time support.
EIN: 471431059

2102
Dextra Baldwin McGonagle Foundation, Inc.
445 Park Ave.
New York 10022   (212) 758-8970
Additional address: 40 Crossing at Blind Brook, Purchase, NY 10577-2210

Incorporated in 1967 in NY.
Donor(s): Mrs. Dextra Baldwin McGonagle.‡
Foundation type: Independent
Financial data (yr. ended 12/31/91): Assets, $7,988,756 (M); expenditures, $533,873; qualifying distributions, $475,892, including $460,075 for 83 grants (high: $120,000; low: $25; average: $25-$120,000).
Purpose and activities: Primary areas of interest include hospitals, the medical sciences, and medical research, including cancer research; grants also for higher and medical education, social service agencies, religious organizations, and cultural programs.
Fields of interest: Hospitals, health services, medical sciences, cancer, biological sciences, medical research, medical education, higher education, social services, religion, cultural programs.
Types of support: Annual campaigns, seed money, building funds, equipment, research, endowment funds.

Limitations: Giving primarily in NY and CA. No grants to individuals, or for matching gifts.
Application information: Applications not accepted.
 Board meeting date(s): As required
 Write: David B. Spanier, Pres.
Officers and Directors:* Maury L. Spanier,* Chair.; David B. Spanier,* Pres.; Helen G. Spanier,* V.P. and Secy.-Treas.
Number of staff: 3 part-time support.
EIN: 136219236

2103
The Donald C. McGraw Foundation, Inc.
46 Summit Ave.
Bronxville 10708 (914) 779-1691

Incorporated in 1963 in NY.
Donor(s): Donald C. McGraw.‡
Foundation type: Independent
Financial data (yr. ended 01/31/91): Assets, $5,459,661 (M); gifts received, $160,729; expenditures, $335,789; qualifying distributions, $321,535, including $311,500 for 29 grants (high: $50,000; low: $1,000).
Fields of interest: Hospitals, medical research, higher education, secondary education, religion—Christian.
Limitations: Giving primarily in NY, NJ, and MA. No grants to individuals.
Application information: Available funds for new applicants are very limited.
 Initial approach: Letter
 Deadline(s): None
 Write: John L. Cady, V.P.
Officers: Donald C. McGraw, Jr., Pres.; John L. Cady, V.P.; John L. McGraw, Secy.-Treas.
EIN: 136165603

2104
The McGraw-Hill Foundation, Inc. ▼
1221 Ave. of the Americas, Rm. 2917
New York 10020 (212) 512-6113

Incorporated in 1979 in NY.
Donor(s): McGraw-Hill, Inc.
Foundation type: Company-sponsored
Financial data (yr. ended 12/31/91): Assets, $24,095 (M); gifts received, $2,200,000; expenditures, $2,190,506; qualifying distributions, $2,190,076, including $1,207,239 for 157 grants (high: $170,000; low: $100; average: $1,000-$5,000) and $982,752 for 3,295 employee matching gifts.
Purpose and activities: Program emphasis is on education; significant support also given in the areas of health and welfare, arts and cultural organizations, and civic activities.
Fields of interest: Health, disadvantaged, civic affairs, arts, cultural programs, libraries, literacy, adult education, education.
Types of support: General purposes, operating budgets, continuing support, annual campaigns, research, scholarship funds, employee-related scholarships, matching funds, employee matching gifts, employee volunteer services.
Limitations: Giving limited to areas of company operations, or to national organizations. No support for religious or political organizations or United Way member agencies. No grants to individuals, or for capital, building, or

endowment funds, conferences, travel, courtesy advertising, films, or publications; no loans.
Publications: Annual report.
Application information: Application form not required.
 Initial approach: Proposal
 Copies of proposal: 1
 Deadline(s): None
 Board meeting date(s): Quarterly
 Final notification: 4 to 6 weeks
 Write: Susan A. Wallman, V.P.
Officers and Directors:* Barbara A. Munder,* Pres.; Susan A. Wallman, V.P. and Secy.; Frank D. Penglase, V.P. and Treas.; Susan S. Buchanan, V.P.; Frank J. Kaufman, V.P.; Robert N. Landes, V.P.; Donald S. Rubin, V.P.; Thomas J. Sullivan, V.P.
Number of staff: 2 full-time professional; 2 full-time support.
EIN: 132955464

2105
Mellam Family Foundation
c/o U.S. Trust Co. of New York
114 West 47th St.
New York 10036

Established in 1987 in NY.
Donor(s): Laura M. Mellam.
Foundation type: Independent
Financial data (yr. ended 12/31/91): Assets, $4,807,300 (M); gifts received, $20,000; expenditures, $327,744; qualifying distributions, $316,259, including $299,100 for 21 grants (high: $50,000; low: $5,000).
Fields of interest: Hospitals, health associations, social services, general charitable giving.
Limitations: Giving primarily in New York, NY. No grants to individuals.
Application information: Contributes only to pre-selected organizations. Applications not accepted.
Trustee: U.S. Trust Co. of New York.
EIN: 136894208

2106
The Andrew W. Mellon Foundation ▼
140 East 62nd St.
New York 10021 (212) 838-8400

Trust established in 1940 in DE as Avalon Foundation; incorporated in 1954 in NY; merged with Old Dominion Foundation and renamed the Andrew W. Mellon Foundation in 1969.
Donor(s): Ailsa Mellon Bruce,‡ Paul Mellon.
Foundation type: Independent
Financial data (yr. ended 12/31/90): Assets, $1,831,235,504 (M); expenditures, $94,608,320; qualifying distributions, $78,786,420, including $74,467,370 for 369 grants (high: $5,000,000; low: $2,900; average: $50,000-$100,000).
Purpose and activities: Grants on selective basis in higher education, cultural affairs, including the humanities, museums, performing arts, population, and in certain environmental and public affairs areas. Graduate fellowship program in the humanities administered by the Woodrow Wilson National Fellowship Foundation, which makes all awards.
Fields of interest: Higher education, cultural programs, humanities, museums, performing arts,

population studies, environment, conservation, public policy, public affairs.
Types of support: Continuing support, endowment funds, research, internships, fellowships, matching funds, special projects.
Limitations: No support for primarily local organizations. No grants to individuals (including scholarships and fellowships); no loans.
Publications: Annual report (including application guidelines).
Application information: Application form not required.
 Initial approach: Descriptive letter or proposal
 Copies of proposal: 1
 Deadline(s): None
 Board meeting date(s): Mar., June, Oct., and Dec.
 Final notification: After board meetings
 Write: Richard Ekman, Secy.
Officers and Trustees:* John C. Whitehead,* Chair.; William G. Bowen,* Pres.; T. Dennis Sullivan, Financial V.P.; Richard Ekman, Secy.; Kenneth J. Herr, Treas.; Charles E. Exley, Jr., Hanna Holborn Gray, Timothy Mellon, Frank H.T. Rhodes, Charles A. Ryskamp, John R. Stevenson.
Number of staff: 13 full-time professional; 20 full-time support.
EIN: 131879954
Recent health grants:
2106-1 Alan Guttmacher Institute, NYC, NY, $100,000. For population research and analysis. 1991.
2106-2 Better World Society, DC, $140,000. Toward disseminating information on development of new contraceptives. 1991.
2106-3 Center for Population Options, DC, $200,000. For research and other activities concerned with prevention of adolescent pregnancy. 1991.
2106-4 International Womens Health Coalition, NYC, NY, $500,000. Toward providing training, technical assistance and other forms of support to reproductive health projects in developing countries. 1991.
2106-5 Population Council, NYC, NY, $750,000. For social science fellowship program and for fellowships for population specialists from Eastern Europe and Soviet Union. 1991.
2106-6 Population Council, NYC, NY, $600,000. For junior investigators in reproductive biology. 1991.
2106-7 Population Council, NYC, NY, $330,000. For use by its MEA awards program toward Middle Eastern population studies program. 1991.
2106-8 Population Council, Research Division, NYC, NY, $900,000. For social science research. 1991.
2106-9 Population Resource Center, DC, $95,000. For technical assistance to African Development Bank. 1991.
2106-10 University of Connecticut, Storrs, CT, $300,000. For postdoctoral fellowships in contraceptive-development research. 1991.
2106-11 University of Virginia, Charlottesville, VA, $300,000. For postdoctoral fellowships in contraceptive-development research. 1991.

2107
L. Thomas Melly Foundation
c/o Goldman Sachs & Co., Tax Dept.
85 Broad St.
New York 10004-2408

Established in 1969 in NY.
Donor(s): L. Thomas Melly.
Foundation type: Independent
Financial data (yr. ended 05/31/91): Assets,
$2,629,025 (M); gifts received, $96,015;
expenditures, $90,987; qualifying distributions,
$84,862, including $84,550 for 36 grants (high:
$30,000; low: $50).
Fields of interest: Higher education, youth, social
services, health, health associations.
Limitations: Giving primarily in CT, NY. No grants
to individuals.
Application information: Applications not
accepted.
Trustees: Alice P. Melly, L. Thomas Melly, Laura
A. Melly, Thomas L. Melly.
EIN: 237059703

2108
Memorial Fund, Inc.
Ten Downing Dr. South
White Plains 10607-2011

Established in 1937.
Donor(s): Beth Rosenthal, Doris Rosenthal,
Edward Rosenthal, Peter Rosenthal, Kenneth
Sarnoff, Jelp Assocs.
Foundation type: Independent
Financial data (yr. ended 12/31/90): Assets,
$2,577,210 (M); gifts received, $777;
expenditures, $159,109; qualifying distributions,
$114,802, including $114,752 for 121 grants
(high: $27,800; low: $10).
Fields of interest: Hospitals, Jewish giving, family
services, health associations, education, general
charitable giving.
Limitations: Giving primarily in NY. No grants to
individuals.
Application information: Contributes only to
pre-selected organizations. Applications not
accepted.
Write: Doris Rosenthal, Pres.
Officers: Doris Rosenthal, Pres.; Peter Rosenthal,
V.P. and Secy.; Carol Maslow, V.P. and Treas.
EIN: 136185716

2109
The Memton Fund, Inc.
527 Madison Ave., 15th Fl.
New York 10022   (212) 644-4915

Incorporated in 1936 in NY.
Donor(s): Albert G. Milbank,‡ Charles M.
Cauldwell.‡
Foundation type: Independent
Financial data (yr. ended 12/31/91): Assets,
$6,796,163 (M); expenditures, $347,721;
qualifying distributions, $317,059, including
$297,250 for 115 grants (high: $13,500; low:
$250; average: $1,000-$5,000).
Fields of interest: Education, environment, health,
social services, cultural programs.
Types of support: General purposes, annual
campaigns, endowment funds, capital campaigns,
special projects.

Limitations: No grants to individuals.
Application information: Contributes only to
pre-selected organizations. Applications not
accepted.
Board meeting date(s): Spring and fall
Write: Lillian Daniels, Secy.-Treas.
Officers and Directors:* Daphne M. White,*
Pres.; Elenita M. Drumwright,* V.P.; Lillian I.
Daniels,* Secy.-Treas.; Marjorie M. Farrar, Olivia
Farrar-Wellman, Ellen White Levy, David M.
Milbank, Samuel L. Milbank, Samuel S. Polk,
Barrie M. White.
Number of staff: 1 part-time professional.
EIN: 136096608

2110
The Mendik Foundation
c/o Mendik Realty Co., Inc.
330 Madison Ave.
New York 10017

Established in 1988 in DE.
Donor(s): Bernard H. Mendik.
Foundation type: Company-sponsored
Financial data (yr. ended 11/30/90): Assets,
$1,367,637 (M); gifts received, $460,000;
expenditures, $574,779; qualifying distributions,
$562,000, including $562,000 for 7 grants (high:
$200,000; low: $12,000).
Fields of interest: Legal education, education,
hospitals, Jewish giving.
Limitations: Giving primarily in New York, NY.
No grants to individuals.
Application information: Contributes only to
pre-selected organizations. Applications not
accepted.
Officers and Director:* Bernard H. Mendik,*
Pres.; Susan Mendik, V.P. and Secy.; David R.
Greenbaum, Treas.
EIN: 133499450

2111
The Robert and Joyce Menschel
Foundation
c/o Goldman Sachs & Co.
85 Broad St.
New York 10004   (212) 902-6913

Established in 1958 in NY.
Donor(s): Robert B. Menschel.
Foundation type: Independent
Financial data (yr. ended 10/31/91): Assets,
$6,342,161 (M); expenditures, $151,180;
qualifying distributions, $151,180, including
$150,900 for 140 grants (high: $15,000; low:
$100).
Fields of interest: Social services, arts, higher
education, hospitals.
Application information: All grants initiated by
the foundation. Applications not accepted.
Officers: Robert B. Menschel, Pres. and Treas.;
Joyce F. Menschel, V.P. and Secy.
Directors: Henry Christensen III, David F.
Menschel.
Number of staff: None.
EIN: 136098443

2112
The Sue and Eugene Mercy, Jr. Foundation
c/o Goldman Sachs & Co., Tax Dept.
85 Broad St.
New York 10004

Established in 1967 in NY.
Donor(s): Eugene Mercy, Jr.
Foundation type: Independent
Financial data (yr. ended 12/31/90): Assets,
$3,222,733 (M); expenditures, $578,621;
qualifying distributions, $504,321, including
$504,041 for 150 grants (high: $135,000; low:
$50).
Purpose and activities: Emphasis on Jewish
giving, including welfare funds, secondary
education, and hospitals; support also for higher
education and culture, particularly music.
Fields of interest: Jewish giving, Jewish welfare,
secondary education, hospitals, higher education,
cultural programs, music.
Limitations: Giving primarily in New York, NY.
No grants to individuals.
Application information: Contributes only to
pre-selected organizations. Applications not
accepted.
Officers and Directors:* Eugene Mercy, Jr.,* Pres.
and Treas.; Sue Mercy,* V.P.; Robert E. Mnuchin,*
Secy.
EIN: 136217050

2113
Merrill Lynch & Company Foundation, Inc. ▼
South Tower, 6th Fl.
World Financial Ctr.
New York 10080-0614   (212) 236-4319

Incorporated in 1950 in DE.
Donor(s): Merrill Lynch, Pierce, Fenner & Smith,
Inc.
Foundation type: Company-sponsored
Financial data (yr. ended 12/31/90): Assets,
$21,245,629 (M); gifts received, $2,001,147;
expenditures, $3,236,917; qualifying
distributions, $3,149,749, including $3,101,000
for grants (high: $440,000; low: $500).
Purpose and activities: Emphasis on education,
especially higher education; support also for the
arts, cultural programs, health, civic affairs, and
community services.
Fields of interest: Education, higher education,
arts, cultural programs, health, AIDS, civic affairs,
social services.
Types of support: General purposes, operating
budgets, special projects, research, capital
campaigns, continuing support, endowment
funds, publications, renovation projects,
scholarship funds.
Limitations: No support for religious purposes or
social, fraternal, or athletic organizations. No
grants to individuals, or for deficit financing,
matching gifts, or conferences; no loans.
Publications: Corporate giving report, 990-PF,
application guidelines.
Application information: Application form not
required.
Initial approach: Letter
Copies of proposal: 1
Deadline(s): None
Board meeting date(s): Mar., June, Sept., and
Dec.

Final notification: 3 months
Write: Westina L. Matthews, Secy.
Officers and Trustees:* John A. Fitzgerald,* Pres.;
Paul W. Critchlow, V.P.; William A. Schreyer,*
V.P.; Daniel P. Tully,* V.P.; Westina L. Matthews,
Secy.; Thomas J. Lombardi, Treas.
Number of staff: 3 full-time professional; 1
part-time professional; 3 full-time support; 2
part-time support.
EIN: 136139556
Recent health grants:
2113-1 Brookings Institution, DC, $25,000. For
long-term care financing study. 1990.
2113-2 Daytop Village Foundation, NYC, NY,
$125,000. For general operating purposes.
1990.
2113-3 Martin House, Community for Justice
Foundation, Trenton, NJ, $25,000. For health
care delivery program. 1990.
2113-4 Media-Advertising Partnership for a
Drug-Free America, NYC, NY, $25,000. For
general operating purposes. 1990.

2114
Merrill Lynch & Company, Inc. Corporate Contributions Program
World Financial Center
World Headquarters
New York 10080-6106   (212) 236-4319

Financial data (yr. ended 12/31/90): Total giving,
$8,507,768, including $7,020,534 for 2,424
grants (high: $100,000; low: $1,000) and
$1,487,234 for 5,911 employee matching gifts.
Purpose and activities: Merrill Lynch and
subsidiaries support health, culture and the arts,
civic and community affairs, and community
development. In addition to direct cash grants,
the company underwrites cultural events, and
awards grants on behalf of employee volunteers
through the Employee Community Involvement
Program. Priority for giving for headquarters is in
higher education. Local offices are the primary
sources of support for community-based
organizations.
Fields of interest: Higher education, health,
cultural programs, arts, civic affairs, community
development, elementary education, community
funds.
Types of support: Employee matching gifts,
scholarship funds, capital campaigns, donated
equipment, general purposes.
Limitations: Giving primarily in the main
headquarters area of New York City and the
greater NY area and in other cities where the
company has offices. No support for fraternal,
social, athletic, political, or religious
organizations. No grants to individuals, or for
operating support of government agencies, or to
reduce an operating deficit or liquidate a debt.
Publications: Corporate giving report (including
application guidelines).
Application information: Company has a staff
that only handles contributions. Application form
not required.
  Initial approach: Letter (3 page maximum)
  Copies of proposal: 1
  Deadline(s): No deadlines; decisions are made
  continuously
  Final notification: Within 60 days
  Write: Westina L. Matthews, Philanthropic
  Programs

Administrators: John A. Fitzgerald, Pres., Merill
Lynch and Co. Fdn., Inc.; Westina L. Matthews,
Mgr., Philanthropic Progs. and Secy. of the Fdn.
Number of staff: 3 full-time professional; 1
part-time professional; 3 full-time support.

2115
Joyce Mertz-Gilmore Foundation ▼
218 East 18th St.
New York 10003   (212) 475-1137

Incorporated in 1959 in NY.
Donor(s): Joyce Mertz Gilmore.‡
Foundation type: Independent
Financial data (yr. ended 12/31/91): Assets,
$60,435,707 (M); gifts received, $4,990,000;
expenditures, $7,983,536; qualifying
distributions, $8,849,618, including $7,208,600
for 473 grants (high: $375,000; low: $500;
average: $5,000-$25,000).
Purpose and activities: Current concerns include
human rights, the environment, world security
issues, and New York City cultural, social, and
civic concerns.
Fields of interest: Arts, energy, human rights.
Types of support: Operating budgets, general
purposes, special projects, technical assistance,
donated equipment, continuing support, seed
money.
Limitations: Giving nationally, with the exception
of the New York City Program. No grants to
individuals, or for capital or endowment funds,
conferences, film or television production,
scholarships, fellowships, or matching gifts.
Publications: Biennial report (including
application guidelines), informational brochure,
grants list.
Application information: Submit proposal upon
request of foundation only. Application form
required.
  Initial approach: Letter
  Copies of proposal: 1
  Deadline(s): Jan. 31 and July 31
  Board meeting date(s): Apr. and Nov. for grant
  decisions
  Final notification: Within 2 weeks of meeting
  Write: Robert Crane, V.P., Prog., or Penny
  Fujiko Willgerodt, Prog. Assoc.
Officers and Directors:* Larry E. Condon,* Pres.;
Elizabeth Burke Gilmore,* Secy.; Charles
Bloomstein,* Treas.; Harlan Cleveland, Hal
Harvey, C. Virgil Martin, Richard J. Mertz, Patricia
Ramsay, Franklin W. Wallin.
Number of staff: 6 full-time professional; 1
part-time professional; 6 full-time support.
EIN: 132872722
Recent health grants:
2115-1 AIDSFilms, NYC, NY, $10,000. For
general support. 1990.
2115-2 Alpha School, Brooklyn, NY, $10,000.
For HIV Program Outreach project to conduct
one-to-one outreach with HIV-infected
adolescents who lack basic information about
available services. 1990.
2115-3 American Civil Liberties Union
Foundation, NYC, NY, $15,000. For AIDS and
Civil Liberties Project to improve access to
new medical treatments, combat
discrimination and ensure access to frank,
effective AIDS education and information.
1990.

2115-4 Citizens Commission on AIDS, NYC, NY,
$10,000. For general support. 1990.
2115-5 Faith Hope and Charity Community
Services, Brooklyn, NY, $15,000. For Day Care
HIV/AIDS Awareness Program to provide
prevention methodology training to five
teachers, who will then counsel and educate
children and their families about disease. 1990.
2115-6 Gay Mens Health Crisis (GMHC), NYC,
NY, $25,500. For Office of Public Policy to
combat discrimination against people (homo-
and heterosexual) with AIDS and AIDS-Related
Complex (ARC), especially with regard to such
issues as insurance coverage and mandatory
AIDS testing. 1990.
2115-7 Haitian Centers Council, NYC, NY,
$10,000. For Haitian Coalition on AIDS for
feasibility and planning process for HIV/AIDS
primary care center. 1990.
2115-8 Latino Commission on AIDS, NYC, NY,
$50,000. For general support. 1990.
2115-9 Medical Education for South African
Blacks, DC, $25,000. For general support.
1990.
2115-10 Medicare Beneficiaries Defense Fund,
NYC, NY, $10,000. For general support. 1990.
2115-11 MFY Legal Services, NYC, NY, $10,000.
For AIDS Legal Project to defend women and
people of color against discrimination in
public housing treatment and benefits. 1990.
2115-12 Neuroscience Education and Research
Foundation, La Jolla, CA, $75,000. 1990.
2115-13 New Brighton Community Local
Development Corporation, Staten Island, NY,
$15,000. For HIV/AIDS Prevention Program to
reach at-risk youth and other residents with
AIDS education and referral information. 1990.
2115-14 New York AIDS Coalition, NYC, NY,
$10,000. For general support. 1990.
2115-15 New York AIDS Coalition, NYC, NY,
$10,000. For Community-Based Technical
Assistance project to foster greater
participation of community organizations in
AIDS policy debate. 1990.
2115-16 Phoenix House Development Fund,
NYC, NY, $35,000. 1990.
2115-17 Planned Parenthood Association of
Southwest Florida, Sarasota, FL, $60,000.
1990.
2115-18 Saint Lukes-Roosevelt Hospital Center,
NYC, NY, $25,000. 1990.
2115-19 Women and AIDS Resource Network,
NYC, NY, $10,000. For general support. 1990.

2116
Stanley W. Metcalf Foundation, Inc.
120 Genesee St., Rm. 503
Auburn 13021   (315) 253-9321

Established in 1962.
Donor(s): Stanley W. Metcalf.‡
Foundation type: Independent
Financial data (yr. ended 12/31/91): Assets,
$5,747,993 (M); expenditures, $386,983;
qualifying distributions, $371,408, including
$335,505 for 83 grants (high: $30,000; low:
$200; average: $500-$50,000).
Purpose and activities: Emphasis on youth
organizations and church support; grants also for
hospitals, welfare, and education.
Fields of interest: Youth, Protestant giving,
hospitals, welfare, education.

Types of support: Annual campaigns, building funds, capital campaigns, continuing support, emergency funds, endowment funds, general purposes, matching funds, operating budgets, scholarship funds.
Limitations: Giving primarily in Cayuga County, NY.
Application information: Application form not required.
  Deadline(s): None
  Write: J. Douglas Pedley, Pres.
Officer and Directors:* J. Douglas Pedley,* Pres.; Herbert T. Anderson, James P. Costello, Marjorie S. Pedley, Madeline M. Schneider, Ronald D. West.
Number of staff: 1 shared staff
EIN: 156017859

2117
Metropolitan Life Foundation ▼
One Madison Ave.
New York 10010-3690   (212) 578-6272

Incorporated in 1976 in NY.
Donor(s): Metropolitan Life Insurance Co.
Foundation type: Company-sponsored
Financial data (yr. ended 12/31/90): Assets, $100,270,265 (M); expenditures, $8,721,301; qualifying distributions, $17,183,562, including $7,317,271 for 506 grants (high: $800,000; low: $1,000; average: $1,000-$25,000), $120,000 for 1 grant to an individual, $633,930 for 700 employee matching gifts, $489,646 for foundation-administered programs and $7,988,785 for loans.
Purpose and activities: To make donations for higher education, health, including substance abuse programs, civic purposes, social services, and United Way chapters; grants also for cultural programs, including public broadcasting, music, dance, and theater, and urban development, including housing and public policy; also makes program-related investments.
Fields of interest: Education, higher education, medical education, insurance education, health, drug abuse, alcoholism, AIDS, handicapped, social services, family services, child welfare, minorities, women, cultural programs, arts, urban development, community development, public policy, libraries.
Types of support: Operating budgets, continuing support, employee matching gifts, research, program-related investments, general purposes, publications, special projects, scholarship funds, employee-related scholarships, seed money.
Limitations: No support for private foundations, religious, fraternal, athletic, political, social, or veterans' organizations; organizations already receiving support through United Way campaigns; local chapters of national organizations; disease-specific organizations; labor groups; organizations with international programs; organizations primarily engaged in patient care or direct treatment, drug treatment centers and community health clinics; hospital capital fund campaigns; or elementary or secondary schools. No grants to individuals (except for 1 medical research award), or for endowment funds, courtesy advertising, or festival participation.
Publications: Corporate giving report, application guidelines, program policy statement, informational brochure (including application guidelines).
Application information: Application form required for special programs where requests for proposals are issued.
  Initial approach: Letter
  Deadline(s): Varies for competitive awards programs; none for grants
  Board meeting date(s): About 6 times a year
  Final notification: 4 to 6 weeks
  Write: Sibyl C. Jacobson, Pres. and C.E.O.
Officers and Directors:* John J. Creedon,* Chair.; Sibyl C. Jacobson,* Pres. and C.E.O.; William J. Howard, Counsel and Secy.; Arthur G. Typermass,* Treas.; Kenneth W. Malcolm, Controller; Robert J. Crimmins, William T. Friedwald, M.D., John D. Moynahan, Jr., Vincent P. Reusing.
Number of staff: None.
EIN: 132878224
Recent health grants:
2117-1 Ackerman Institute for Family Therapy, NYC, NY, $20,000. 1990.
2117-2 American Association of Community and Junior Colleges, DC, $100,000. For health research and illness prevention. 1990.
2117-3 American Association of Community and Junior Colleges, DC, $15,000. For Community College Substance Abuse Training Initiative. 1990.
2117-4 American Association of School Administrators, Arlington, VA, $21,140. For Health and Safety Education Program. 1990.
2117-5 American Council for Drug Education, NYC, NY, $25,000. For health education. 1990.
2117-6 Association of Science Technology Centers, DC, $50,000. For Vision Exhibit. 1990.
2117-7 Barton County Community College, Great Bend, KS, $10,000. For Community College Substance Abuse Training Initiative. 1990.
2117-8 Brevard Community College, Cocoa, FL, $10,000. For Community College Substance Abuse Training Initiative. 1990.
2117-9 Central Community College, Grand Island, NE, $10,000. For Community College Substance Abuse Training Initiative. 1990.
2117-10 Cold Spring Harbor Laboratory, Banbury Center, Cold Spring Harbor, NY, $10,000. For health research and illness prevention. 1990.
2117-11 College of DuPage, Glen Ellyn, IL, $10,000. For Community College Substance Abuse Training Initiative. 1990.
2117-12 Greenfield Community College, Greenfield, MA, $10,000. For Community College Substance Abuse Training Initiative. 1990.
2117-13 Institute for Aerobics Research, Dallas, TX, $12,000. 1990.
2117-14 Life and Health Insurance Medical Research Fund, DC, $50,000. For health research and illness prevention. 1990.
2117-15 Long Beach City College, Long Beach, CA, $10,000. For Community College Substance Abuse Training Initiative. 1990.
2117-16 Luzerne County Community College, Nanticoke, PA, $10,000. For Community College Substance Abuse Training Initiative. 1990.
2117-17 March of Dimes Birth Defects Foundation, Healthy Mothers, Healthy Babies, White Plains, NY, $70,000. For Minority Health Promotion Project. 1990.
2117-18 Miami-Dade Community College, Miami, FL, $10,000. For Community College Substance Abuse Training Initiative. 1990.
2117-19 National Association for Children of Alcoholics, South Laguna, CA, $53,000. 1990.
2117-20 National Center for Health Education, NYC, NY, $45,000. 1990.
2117-21 National Fund for Medical Education, NYC, NY, $25,000. 1990.
2117-22 National Medical Fellowships, NYC, NY, $20,000. 1990.
2117-23 New York Blood Center, NYC, NY, $25,000. For health research and illness prevention. 1990.
2117-24 New York Botanical Garden, Bronx, NY, $50,000. For health research and illness prevention. 1990.
2117-25 Northern Essex Community College, Haverhill, MA, $10,000. For Community College Substance Abuse Training Initiative. 1990.
2117-26 Occupational Physicians Scholarship Fund, NYC, NY, $25,000. 1990.
2117-27 Partnership for a Drug Free America, NYC, NY, $35,000. 1990.
2117-28 Presentation College, Aberdeen, SD, $10,000. For Community College Substance Abuse Training Initiative. 1990.
2117-29 San Juan College, Farmington, NM, $10,000. For Community College Substance Abuse Training Initiative. 1990.
2117-30 South Suburban College, South Holland, IL, $10,000. For Community College Substance Abuse Training Initiative. 1990.
2117-31 Southeastern Community College, Whiteville, NC, $10,000. For Community College Substance Abuse Training Initiative. 1990.
2117-32 Triton College, River Grove, IL, $10,000. For Community College Substance Abuse Training Initiative. 1990.
2117-33 University of California, La Jolla, CA, $200,000. For award for medical research. 1990.
2117-34 University of Heidelberg, Heidelberg, Germany, $200,000. For award for medical research. 1990.
2117-35 W Q E D Metropolitan Pittsburgh Public Broadcasting, Pittsburgh, PA, $75,000. For Health and Safety Education Program. 1990.
2117-36 YMCA of Greater New York, NYC, NY, $100,000. For health education. 1990.

2118
The Meyer Foundation
c/o Lazard Freres & Co.
One Rockefeller Plaza
New York 10020

Established in 1985 in NY.
Foundation type: Independent
Financial data (yr. ended 12/31/91): Assets, $8,774,694 (M); expenditures, $411,875; qualifying distributions, $404,718, including $400,750 for 6 grants (high: $200,000; low: $750).
Fields of interest: Higher education, medical research, arts, social services.
Types of support: General purposes, research.
Limitations: No grants to individuals.

Application information: Applications not accepted.
Write: George J. Ames, Secy.-Treas.
Officers and Directors:* Phillipe Meyer,* Pres.; Vincent Meyer,* V.P.; George J. Ames,* Secy.-Treas.
Number of staff: None.
EIN: 133317912

2119
The Dunlevy Milbank Foundation, Inc.
c/o Sullivan & Cromwell
125 Broad St.
New York 10004   (212) 558-3724

Incorporated in 1941 in NY.
Donor(s): Dunlevy Milbank.‡
Foundation type: Independent
Financial data (yr. ended 12/31/91): Assets, $1,393,844 (M); expenditures, $325,216; qualifying distributions, $312,542, including $296,750 for 16 grants (high: $135,000; low: $250; average: $250-$100,000).
Purpose and activities: Emphasis on hospitals, a zoological society, a medical center, and local community organizations.
Fields of interest: Hospitals, medical research, cancer, community development, general charitable giving.
Types of support: Building funds, general purposes, capital campaigns, endowment funds, special projects.
Limitations: Giving primarily in New York, NY, and FL. No grants to individuals.
Application information: Application form not required.
Initial approach: Letter
Copies of proposal: 1
Deadline(s): Oct.
Board meeting date(s): Nov. or Dec. and as required
Final notification: 1 to 2 months
Write: Donald R. Osborn, Secy.-Treas.
Officers and Directors:* Barbara Foshay Duke,* V.P.; Donald R. Osborn,* Secy.-Treas.
Number of staff: None.
EIN: 136096738

2120
Milbank Memorial Fund
One East 75th St.
New York 10021   (212) 570-4800

Incorporated in 1905 in NY.
Donor(s): Elizabeth Milbank Anderson.‡
Foundation type: Operating
Financial data (yr. ended 12/31/91): Assets, $46,692,998 (M); expenditures, $2,358,224; qualifying distributions, $1,945,407, including $370,085 for 55 grants (high: $50,000; low: $500) and $803,102 for 4 foundation-administered programs.
Purpose and activities: A private operating foundation that supports its program activities through a variety of means, including grants, commissions and the work of members of the staff. The program of the fund emphasizes the implications of social and clinical research for health and related policy. Program activities are organized around the Milbank Health Policy Reviews, through which the fund seeks to inform policy making by precisely defining selected

issues, by clarifying the social, political, and professional context of important policy questions, and by evaluating the critical choices raised by these questions. The fund also publishes the Milbank Quarterly, a peer-reviewed international journal in the field of health policy that was established in 1923.
Fields of interest: Health, health services, social services, public affairs.
Types of support: Research.
Limitations: No grants to individuals, or for annual campaigns, building or endowment funds, deficit financing, operating budgets, general purposes, matching gifts, or scholarships; no loans.
Publications: Annual report, informational brochure (including application guidelines).
Application information: Application form not required.
Initial approach: Letter describing proposal research project
Copies of proposal: 1
Board meeting date(s): May, Oct., and Feb.
Write: Daniel M. Fox, Ph.D., Pres.
Officers and Directors:* Samuel L. Milbank,* Chair.; Francis H. Musselman,* Vice-Chair.; Daniel M. Fox,* Pres.; Sara C. Romano, Secy.-Treas.; Kathleen S. Andersen, Prog. Officer; Robert H. Ebert, Peter M. Gottsegen, Thomas E. Harvey, Jeremiah Milbank, Jr., Carl J. Schramm, Jr., Rosemary A. Stevens, John D. Stoeckle, Alan T. Wenzell.
Number of staff: 4 full-time professional; 2 part-time professional; 4 full-time support.
EIN: 135562282

2121
Millbrook Tribute Garden, Inc. ▼
c/o George T. Whalen, Inc.
P.O. Box AC
Millbrook 12545   (914) 677-3434

Incorporated in 1943 in NY.
Foundation type: Independent
Financial data (yr. ended 09/30/91): Assets, $15,857,516 (M); expenditures, $1,188,340; qualifying distributions, $1,157,365, including $1,063,668 for 38 grants (high: $200,000; low: $1,000; average: $1,000-$30,000).
Purpose and activities: Emphasis on secondary education, church support, child welfare, hospitals, and civic projects; operates and maintains a playground and memorial park in honor of war veterans.
Fields of interest: Secondary education, religion—Christian, child welfare, hospitals, civic affairs.
Types of support: General purposes, capital campaigns, equipment.
Limitations: Giving limited to Millbrook, NY. No grants to individuals.
Application information:
Initial approach: Proposal
Deadline(s): None
Write: George T. Whalen, Jr., Trustee
Officers: Oakleigh B. Thorne, Pres.; Daryl Parshall, V.P.
Trustees: Felicitas S. Thorne, Vincent N. Turletes, George T. Whalen, Jr., Robert W. Whalen.
EIN: 141340079

2122
Kathryn & Gilbert Miller Fund, Inc.
c/o Proskauer, Rose, Goetz & Mendelsohn
1585 Broadway
New York 10036   (212) 969-3000

Incorporated in 1952 in NY.
Donor(s): Kathryn B. Miller.‡
Foundation type: Independent
Financial data (yr. ended 03/31/91): Assets, $1,719,308 (M); expenditures, $441,148; qualifying distributions, $434,060, including $427,167 for 29 grants (high: $118,667; low: $500; average: $5,000-$25,000).
Fields of interest: Cultural programs, performing arts, hospitals, medical research, higher education, secondary education.
Limitations: Giving primarily in New York, NY. No grants to individuals.
Application information: Application form not required.
Deadline(s): None
Write: Charles Looker, Pres.
Officers and Directors:* Charles Looker,* Pres.; Philip J. Hirsch,* V.P. and Treas.; Jerold Zieselman,* Secy.
EIN: 136121254

2123
Milstein Family Foundation, Inc. ▼
1271 Ave. of the Americas, Suite 4200
New York 10020   (212) 708-0800

Established in 1975 in NY.
Donor(s): Builtland Partners, Seymour Milstein, Paul Milstein, Gloria M. Flanzer.
Foundation type: Independent
Financial data (yr. ended 09/30/90): Assets, $4,417,804 (M); gifts received, $7,400,000; expenditures, $6,089,498; qualifying distributions, $6,088,798, including $6,022,518 for 63 grants (high: $5,105,000; low: $250; average: $1,000-$10,000).
Purpose and activities: For at least the next five years, the foundation will give primarily for medicine, including medical research.
Fields of interest: Medical research.
Types of support: Research.
Limitations: Giving primarily in NY.
Application information:
Initial approach: Letter
Write: Seymour Milstein, Chair.
Officers and Directors:* Seymour Milstein,* Chair.; Paul Milstein, Pres.; David V. Habif, V.P.; Philip L. Milstein, Secy.-Treas.; Gloria M. Flanzer, Constance M. Lederman, Roslyn M. Meyer, Edward L. Milstein, Howard P. Milstein, Irma P. Milstein, Vivian Milstein, Barbara M. Zalaznick.
EIN: 510190133

2124
Mohawk-Hudson Community Foundation, Inc.
P.O. Box 3198
Albany 12203-0198   (518) 273-8596
Application address: 270 River St., Suite 2R, Troy, NY 12189

Incorporated in 1968 in NY.
Foundation type: Community

Financial data (yr. ended 12/31/90): Assets, $2,030,313 (M); gifts received, $437,504; expenditures, $1,023,212; qualifying distributions, $799,760, including $799,760 for 654 grants (high: $14,000; low: $25; average: $500-$2,500).

Purpose and activities: Some funds restricted by donor designation; for others, emphasis on giving to otherwise unfinanced projects in the public interest.

Fields of interest: Arts, dance, museums, performing arts, education, literacy, adult education, education—early childhood, child welfare, child development, volunteerism, community development, civic affairs, drug abuse, aged, mental health, rehabilitation, hunger, homeless, AIDS, hospitals, Jewish giving, energy, conservation, wildlife.

Types of support: Special projects, equipment, scholarship funds, seed money.

Limitations: Giving primarily in Albany, Renssalaer and Saratoga counties, NY. No support for sectarian religious purposes. No grants to individuals, or for endowment or building funds, operating budgets, deficit financing, consulting services, continuing support, emergency funds, land acquisition, annual campaigns, or fellowships; no loans.

Publications: Annual report, application guidelines, newsletter, informational brochure.

Application information: Application form required.

>   *Initial approach:* Proposal
>   *Copies of proposal:* 12
>   *Deadline(s):* Apr. 1 and Oct. 1
>   *Board meeting date(s):* Apr. and Oct.
>   *Write:* Judith Lyons, Exec. Dir.

Officers and Directors:* Charles C. Freihofer III,* Pres.; Weston F. Cowles, 1st V.P.; Susan S. Clarke,* 2nd V.P.; Ellen K. Lang,* Secy.; Edward R. McEwan, Treas.; Judith Lyons,* Exec. Dir.; and 21 additional directors.

Number of staff: 2 full-time professional; 2 part-time support.

EIN: 141505623

Recent health grants:

2124-1 James A. Eddy Memorial Geriatric Long Term Home Health Care Program, Troy, NY, $10,000. 1990.

2124-2 Samaritan Hospital Foundation, Troy, NY, $11,097. 1990.

2125

The Ambrose Monell Foundation ▼

c/o Fulton, Duncombe & Rowe
30 Rockefeller Plaza, Rm. 3217
New York 10112   (212) 586-0700

Incorporated in 1952 in NY.

Donor(s): Maude Monell Vetlesen.‡

Foundation type: Independent

Financial data (yr. ended 12/31/90): Assets, $142,045,591 (M); expenditures, $6,689,726; qualifying distributions, $6,457,115, including $6,339,985 for 86 grants (high: $500,000; low: $1,000; average: $5,000-$100,000).

Purpose and activities: For the "improvement of the physical, mental, and moral condition of humanity throughout the world." Giving largely for hospitals and health services, scientific research, museums, performing arts, and other cultural activities, and higher and secondary education; support also for social services, research in political science, mental health, and aid to the handicapped.

Fields of interest: Hospitals, health, health services, AIDS, alcoholism, mental health, handicapped, medical research, physical sciences, education, higher education, secondary education, social services, aged, animal welfare, political science, public policy, mental health, handicapped, physical sciences.

Types of support: General purposes, research, building funds, endowment funds.

Limitations: No grants to individuals.

Application information: Application form not required.

>   *Initial approach:* Proposal
>   *Copies of proposal:* 1
>   *Deadline(s):* None
>   *Board meeting date(s):* Dec.
>   *Write:* Harmon Duncombe, Pres.

Officers and Directors:* Harmon Duncombe,* Pres. and Treas.; George Rowe, Jr.,* V.P. and Secy.; Eugene P. Grisanti, Henry G. Walter, Jr.

Number of staff: None.

EIN: 131982683

Recent health grants:

2125-1 Alzheimers Disease and Related Disorders Association, Chicago, IL, $150,000. 1990.

2125-2 American Federation for Aging Research, NYC, NY, $100,000. 1990.

2125-3 American Foundation for AIDS Research, NYC, NY, $150,000. 1990.

2125-4 Cancer Research Institute, NYC, NY, $150,000. 1990.

2125-5 Columbia University, NYC, NY, $25,000. For cancer research. 1990.

2125-6 Deafness Research Foundation, NYC, NY, $25,000. 1990.

2125-7 Fountain House, NYC, NY, $300,000. 1990.

2125-8 Good Samaritan Hospital, West Palm Beach, FL, $10,000. 1990.

2125-9 Harvard University, School of Public Health, Cambridge, MA, $500,000. 1990.

2125-10 Harvard University, School of Public Health, Department of Tropical Medicine, Cambridge, MA, $100,000. 1990.

2125-11 Hospital Audiences, NYC, NY, $10,000. 1990.

2125-12 Howard University, College of Medicine, DC, $50,000. 1990.

2125-13 International Center for the Disabled (ICD), Rehabilitation and Research Center, NYC, NY, $20,000. 1990.

2125-14 Johns Hopkins University, Project on Alcoholism, Baltimore, MD, $62,000. 1990.

2125-15 Lenox Hill Hospital, NYC, NY, $50,000. 1990.

2125-16 Massachusetts General Hospital, Cancer Center, Boston, MA, $101,985. 1990.

2125-17 Memorial Sloan-Kettering Cancer Center, NYC, NY, $100,000. 1990.

2125-18 Menninger Foundation, Topeka, KS, $150,000. 1990.

2125-19 Monell Chemical Senses Center, Philadelphia, PA, $500,000. 1990.

2125-20 National Council on Alcoholism, NYC, NY, $15,000. 1990.

2125-21 National Jewish Center for Immunology and Respiratory Medicine, Denver, CO, $100,000. 1990.

2125-22 National Multiple Sclerosis Society, NYC, NY, $75,000. 1990.

2125-23 National Retinitis Pigmentosa Foundation, Garden City, NY, $100,000. 1990.

2125-24 New York Arthritis Foundation, NYC, NY, $50,000. 1990.

2125-25 Orton Dyslexia Society, NYC, NY, $25,000. 1990.

2125-26 Population Crisis Committee, DC, $50,000. 1990.

2125-27 Psoriasis Research Institute, Palo Alto, CA, $125,000. 1990.

2125-28 Southampton Hospital, Southampton, NY, $10,000. 1990.

2126

Monterey Fund, Inc.

c/o Bear, Stearns & Co.
866 U.N. Plaza, 6th Fl.
New York 10017

Incorporated in 1967 in NY.

Donor(s): Bear Stearns & Co., employees of Bear, Stearns & Co.

Foundation type: Independent

Financial data (yr. ended 04/30/90): Assets, $5,205,568 (M); gifts received, $7,795,950; expenditures, $7,506,511; qualifying distributions, $7,506,511, including $7,505,655 for grants (high: $350,000; low: $10; average: $100-$1,000).

Purpose and activities: Grants primarily for Jewish welfare funds and other Jewish organizations; support also for hospitals, health services, community funds, higher and other education, social services, and youth and child welfare.

Fields of interest: Jewish giving, Jewish welfare, hospitals, health services, community funds, education, higher education, social services, youth, child welfare.

Limitations: No grants to individuals.

Application information:

>   *Deadline(s):* None
>   *Board meeting date(s):* As required
>   *Final notification:* Varies
>   *Write:* William J. Montgoris, Treas.

Officers: Kenneth Edlow, Pres.; Alvin Einbender, V.P.; William J. Montgoris, Treas.

EIN: 136255661

2127

Edward S. Moore Foundation, Inc. ▼

c/o Walter, Conston, Alexander and Green
90 Park Ave.
New York 10016   (212) 210-9400
Application address: 55 Old Field Point Rd., Greenwich, CT 06830; Tel.: (203) 629-4591

Established in 1957 in NY.

Donor(s): Edward S. Moore, Jr.,‡ Evelyn N. Moore,‡ Carolyn N. Moore, and others.

Foundation type: Independent

Financial data (yr. ended 12/31/91): Assets, $30,939,656 (M); expenditures, $1,600,529; qualifying distributions, $1,498,803, including $1,388,270 for 89 grants (high: $150,000; low: $1,000; average: $1,000-$30,000).

Purpose and activities: Support for youth agencies, hospitals, education, and cultural programs, including museums, and churches.

Fields of interest: Hospitals, youth, education, cultural programs, museums, religion—Christian.
Types of support: Operating budgets, continuing support, annual campaigns, seed money, emergency funds, building funds, equipment, land acquisition, endowment funds, matching funds, internships, scholarship funds, special projects, research.
Limitations: Giving primarily in NY and CT. No grants to individuals, or for deficit financing, publications, or conferences; no loans.
Publications: Annual report, 990-PF.
Application information: Application form not required.
> *Initial approach:* Letter
> *Copies of proposal:* 1
> *Deadline(s):* None
> *Board meeting date(s):* Jan., Apr., July, and Oct.
> *Final notification:* 3 to 6 months
> *Write:* John W. Cross III, Pres.

Officers and Directors:* John W. Cross III,* Pres.; Marion Moore Gilbert,* V.P.; Donald Vail,* Secy.; Alexander Jackson,* Treas.; Louisa Gilbert, Lois Cross Willis.
Number of staff: 1 full-time professional.
EIN: 136127365

2128
J. P. Morgan and Company Corporate Giving Program

60 Wall St.
New York 10260   (212) 648-9673

Financial data (yr. ended 12/31/90): Total giving, $2,530,965 for grants.
Purpose and activities: "Our overall philanthropic objective is to improve the quality of life in the communities in which we live and work. We focus our efforts on increasing the capacity of people and organizations to help themselves, and stress long-term solutions to problems rather than short-term remedies." Emphasis is on helping to find solutions to social problems and needs through support of competent agencies in fields of health, social services, culture, education, the environment, and international affairs. Special attention is given to job training, youth programs, international relief, housing, economic development, and advocacy and citizen involvement programs in New York City. Employee gifts to educational programs, cultural institutions, hospitals and health care agencies, human services and local development organizations, environmental and international organizations are matched. The Company is often able to supplement the effect of financial contributions in other ways. Sometimes it provides management and training and equipment. Through the Volunteer Center hundreds of employees are placed in off-hours volunteer assignments and on the boards of nonprofit organizations.
Fields of interest: Arts, education, health, international affairs, urban affairs.
Types of support: Annual campaigns, donated equipment, employee matching gifts, equipment, operating budgets, seed money, technical assistance, building funds, renovation projects, special projects, capital campaigns, general purposes, matching funds, employee volunteer services, loaned talent.

Limitations: Giving primarily in New York, NY, except for selected institutions of higher education and international affairs. No support for religious organizations unless their programs are secular in nature, for work with specific diseases and disabilities, programs dealing with chemical dependency, or for scholarly research. No grants to individuals, or for scholarships and fellowships.
Publications: Corporate giving report (including application guidelines), application guidelines.
Application information: Charitable activities are administered by Community Relations and Public Affairs. Application form required.
> *Initial approach:* Request application from bank
> *Deadline(s):* Grants are made on a calendar-year basis; for proposal to be considered in the same year in which it is submitted, it must be received by Sept. 15
> *Board meeting date(s):* Monthly
> *Final notification:* 3 months; proposals will not be considered until all requested information has been received; Morgan will discontinue consideration of any proposal that remains incomplete 2 months after acknowledgement of its receipt
> *Write:* Roberta A. Ruocco, V.P., Community Relations and Public Affairs Dept.

Community Relations and Public Affairs Dept.: Karen A. Erdos, Lorraine A. Fowler, Laura D. Roosevelt, Roberta A. Ruocco, Hildy J. Simmons, Barbara H. Spruell.

2129
Morgan Guaranty Trust Company of New York Charitable Trust ▼

60 Wall St., 46th Fl.
New York 10260   (212) 648-9673

Trust established in 1961 in NY.
Donor(s): Morgan Guaranty Trust Co. of New York.
Foundation type: Company-sponsored
Financial data (yr. ended 12/31/90): Assets, $2,341,203 (M); gifts received, $5,000,000; expenditures, $7,576,225; qualifying distributions, $7,576,225, including $5,659,500 for 392 grants (high: $650,000; low: $500; average: $2,000-$25,000) and $1,916,445 for employee matching gifts.
Purpose and activities: Emphasis is on helping to find solutions to social problems and needs through support of competent agencies in fields of health, social services, culture, education, the environment, and international affairs. Special attention to job training, youth programs, international relief, housing, economic development, and advocacy and citizen involvement programs in New York City. Matches employee gifts to educational programs, cultural institutions, hospitals and health care agencies, human services and local development organizations, environmental and international organizations.
Fields of interest: Health, hospitals, AIDS, social services, housing, aged, child welfare, minorities, cultural programs, arts, performing arts, education, higher education, elementary education, community development, libraries, international relief, international affairs, environment, wildlife.
Types of support: Employee matching gifts, operating budgets, annual campaigns, seed

money, building funds, equipment, special projects, matching funds, technical assistance, general purposes, capital campaigns, endowment funds, renovation projects.
Limitations: Giving limited to New York, NY, except for selected institutions of higher education, and international affairs. No support for organizations working with chemical dependency, specific disabilities or diseases (except AIDS), or churches, for non-secular purposes. No grants to individuals, or scholarly research for scholarships, fellowships, or conferences; no loans.
Publications: Corporate giving report, application guidelines, program policy statement.
Application information: Application form required.
> *Initial approach:* Letter
> *Copies of proposal:* 1
> *Deadline(s):* Sept. 15
> *Board meeting date(s):* Monthly
> *Final notification:* 3 months
> *Write:* Roberta Ruocco, V.P., Morgan Guaranty Trust Co. of New York

Advisory Committee: Roberto G. Mendoza, Jr., John F. Ruffle, Kurt F. Viermetz, Douglas Warner, Dennis Weatherstone.
Trustee: Morgan Guaranty Trust Co. of New York.
Number of staff: 4 full-time professional; 4 full-time support.
EIN: 136037931
Recent health grants:
2129-1 Albert Einstein College of Medicine of Yeshiva University, Bronx, NY, $15,000. For programs promoting health and accessible high-quality health care services. 1990.
2129-2 Bedford Stuyvesant Volunteer Ambulance Corps, Brooklyn, NY, $10,000. For programs promoting health and accessible high-quality health care services. 1990.
2129-3 Center for Immigrants Rights, NYC, NY, $10,000. For programs promoting health and accessible high-quality health care services. 1990.
2129-4 Citizens Commission on AIDS, NYC, NY, $10,000. 1990.
2129-5 Columbia-Presbyterian Medical Center Fund, NYC, NY, $20,000. For programs promoting health and accessible high-quality health care services. 1990.
2129-6 Episcopal Health Services, Hempstead, NY, $25,000. For programs for the aging. 1990.
2129-7 Friends and Relatives of Institutionalized Aged, NYC, NY, $15,000. 1990.
2129-8 Highbridge Community Life Center, Bronx, NY, $20,000. For programs addressing AIDS. 1990.
2129-9 Hispanic AIDS Forum, NYC, NY, $10,000. 1990.
2129-10 Legal Action Center of the City of New York, NYC, NY, $15,000. For programs addressing AIDS. 1990.
2129-11 Little Sisters of the Assumption Family Health Service, NYC, NY, $25,000. For programs promoting health and accessible high-quality health care services. 1990.
2129-12 March of Dimes Birth Defects Foundation, Campaign for Healthier Babies, NYC, NY, $15,000. For programs promoting health and accessible high-quality health care services. 1990.
2129-13 Montefiore Medical Center, Women's Center, Bronx, NY, $15,000. For programs

promoting health and accessible high-quality health care services. 1990.

2129-14 Mount Sinai Hospital and Medical Center, NYC, NY, $30,000. For Volunteer Program for the aging. 1990.

2129-15 New York Academy of Medicine, NYC, NY, $20,000. For programs promoting health and accessible high-quality health care services. 1990.

2129-16 New York Blood Center, NYC, NY, $25,000. For operating support. 1990.

2129-17 New York Business Group on Health, NYC, NY, $15,000. For programs promoting health and accessible high-quality health care services. 1990.

2129-18 New York Infirmary-Beekman Downtown Hospital, NYC, NY, $25,000. For operating support. 1990.

2129-19 Pastoral and Educational Services, Brooklyn, NY, $10,000. 1990.

2129-20 Planetree Health Resource Center, San Francisco, CA, $15,000. For programs promoting health and accessible high-quality health care services. 1990.

2129-21 Planned Parenthood of New York City, NYC, NY, $30,000. For operating support. 1990.

2129-22 Rand Corporation, Santa Monica, CA, $20,000. For programs promoting health and accessible high-quality health care services. 1990.

2129-23 Retired Senior Volunteer Program (RSVP), Friends of, NYC, NY, $10,000. For programs addressing AIDS. 1990.

2129-24 Rockefeller University, NYC, NY, $32,500. For capital support. 1990.

2129-25 Saint Lukes-Roosevelt Hospital Center, NYC, NY, $80,000. For medical care leadership. 1990.

2129-26 TAPCAPP, Bronx, NY, $15,000. For programs promoting health and accessible high-quality health care services. 1990.

2129-27 United Hospital Fund of New York, NYC, NY, $15,000. For programs promoting health and accessible high-quality health care services. 1990.

2129-28 United Way of Tri-State, NYC, NY, $650,000. For programs promoting health and accessible high-quality health care services. 1990.

2130
Morgan Stanley Foundation ▼
1251 Ave. of the Americas, 31st Fl.
New York 10020   (212) 703-6610

Trust established in 1961 in NY.
Donor(s): Morgan Stanley & Co., Inc.
Foundation type: Company-sponsored
Financial data (yr. ended 12/31/91): Assets, $10,000,000 (M); expenditures, $1,680,000; qualifying distributions, $1,680,000, including $1,415,000 for 300 grants (high: $25,000; low: $1,000; average: $3,500-$10,000) and $265,000 for employee matching gifts.
Purpose and activities: Giving primarily for programs in social welfare, including programs for housing and employment; grants also for hospitals.
Fields of interest: Welfare, child welfare, youth, housing, employment, community development, education—minorities, hospitals.

Types of support: Operating budgets, continuing support, employee matching gifts, general purposes.
Limitations: Giving primarily in the New York, NY, metropolitan area. No support for United Way member agencies. No grants to individuals, or for emergency, endowment or building funds, deficit financing, equipment, land acquisition, scholarships, fellowships, special projects, research, publications, or conferences; no loans.
Publications: Program policy statement.
Application information: Application form not required.
Initial approach: Letter
Copies of proposal: 1
Deadline(s): None
Board meeting date(s): Quarterly and as required
Final notification: 6 months to 1 year
Write: Patricia Schaefer
Trustees: Anson Beard, Jr., Kenneth DeRegt, Robert Feduniak, John Wilson.
Number of staff: 2 full-time professional.
EIN: 136155650

2131
Morgan Stanley Group Corporate Giving Program
1251 Ave. of the Americas, 31st Fl.
New York 10020   (212) 703-6610

Purpose and activities: Support for business, minority and higher education, child welfare and youth, the homeless, housing the disadvantaged, hunger, employment, AIDS programs, and the aged. The direct giving program contributed approximately as much as the foundation in 1990.
Fields of interest: Arts, business education, child welfare, community development, disadvantaged, education, education—minorities, employment, homeless, hospitals, housing, hunger, social services, youth, AIDS, aged, minorities.
Types of support: Employee volunteer services.
Limitations: Giving primarily in New York City, NY. No support for United Way member agencies.
Application information:
Initial approach: Letter to headquarters
Copies of proposal: 1
Final notification: 3-6 months
Write: Patricia Schaefer, Fdn. Officer

2132
Morris Morgenstern Foundation
100 Merrick Rd., Rm. 506E
Rockville Centre 11570   (516) 536-3030

Trust established in 1949 in NY.
Donor(s): Morris Morgenstern.‡
Foundation type: Independent
Financial data (yr. ended 12/31/91): Assets, $11,285,913 (M); gifts received, $59,575; expenditures, $1,281,268; qualifying distributions, $1,267,115, including $1,222,253 for 151 grants (high: $225,000; low: $18; average: $50-$10,000).
Purpose and activities: Support for Jewish organizations, including welfare funds, synagogues and other religious institutions, hospitals, and yeshivas.
Fields of interest: Jewish welfare, Jewish giving, hospitals, religious schools, higher education.

Types of support: General purposes.
Limitations: Giving primarily in the New York, NY, metropolitan area. No grants to individuals.
Application information:
Initial approach: Letter
Deadline(s): None
Final notification: Within 1 month after board meeting
Write: Hannah Klein, Exec. Dir.
Trustee: Frank N. Morgenstern.
EIN: 131635719

2133
Norman M. Morris Foundation, Inc.
Six Corporate Park Dr.
White Plains 10604   (914) 694-1380

Incorporated in 1947 in NY.
Donor(s): Norman M. Morris.
Foundation type: Independent
Financial data (yr. ended 12/31/91): Assets, $6,781,353 (M); expenditures, $307,637; qualifying distributions, $289,555, including $289,555 for 199 grants (high: $152,500; low: $20).
Fields of interest: Jewish giving, Jewish welfare, higher education, hospitals, medical research.
Limitations: Giving primarily in NY.
Application information: Application form not required.
Initial approach: Letter
Deadline(s): None
Write: Norman M. Morris, Pres.
Officers and Trustees:* Norman M. Morris,* Pres.; Marvin Lubin,* V.P.; Robert E. Morris,* Secy.-Treas.; Arline J. Lubin, Kenneth A. Lubin, Leland M. Morris.
EIN: 136119134

2134
The William T. Morris Foundation, Inc. ▼
230 Park Ave., Suite 622
New York 10169   (212) 986-8036
Scholarship application address: Roberta Ripa, Wyoming Area High School, Exeter, PA 18643

Trust established in 1937; incorporated in 1941 in DE.
Donor(s): William T. Morris.‡
Foundation type: Independent
Financial data (yr. ended 06/30/91): Assets, $40,335,230 (M); expenditures, $2,634,371; qualifying distributions, $2,363,726, including $2,079,000 for 69 grants (high: $250,000; low: $5,000; average: $5,000-$20,000) and $16,000 for 1 grant to an individual.
Purpose and activities: Giving primarily to charitable, scientific, and/or educational institutions.
Fields of interest: Higher education, cultural programs, hospitals, health services, youth.
Limitations: Giving primarily in the northeastern states, especially NY and CT; scholarships limited to residents of West Pittston, PA.
Application information: Applications for student aid must be made through local high school.
Initial approach: Letter and proposal
Copies of proposal: 1
Deadline(s): July 31 for scholarships; None for grants
Board meeting date(s): As required

Final notification: 6 to 8 weeks
Write: Edward A. Antonelli, Pres.
Officers and Directors:* Edward A. Antonelli,*
Pres.; W.F. Wheeler, Jr.,* V.P.; Bruce A. August,*
Secy.; A.C. Laske, Jr.,* Treas.; Arthur C. Laske.
Number of staff: 3 full-time professional.
EIN: 131600908
Recent health grants:
2134-1 Arthritis Foundation, NYC, NY, $15,000.
1991.
2134-2 Bridgeport Hospital Foundation,
Bridgeport, CT, $75,000. 1991.
2134-3 Cabrini Medical Center, NYC, NY,
$50,000. 1991.
2134-4 Deafness Research Foundation, NYC,
NY, $15,000. 1991.
2134-5 Eye Bank for Sight Restoration, NYC, NY,
$20,000. 1991.
2134-6 Hospital for Special Surgery, NYC, NY,
$25,000. 1991.
2134-7 Joslin Diabetes Center, Boston, MA,
$20,000. 1991.
2134-8 Memorial Sloan-Kettering Cancer Center,
NYC, NY, $30,000. For Morris Fellows. 1991.
2134-9 Memorial Sloan-Kettering Cancer Center,
NYC, NY, $10,000. For benefit. 1991.
2134-10 National Foundation for Facial
Reconstruction, NYC, NY, $25,000. 1991.
2134-11 New York Hospital-Cornell Medical
Center, NYC, NY, $50,000. For James B. Brady
Foundation. 1991.
2134-12 New York Infirmary-Beekman
Downtown Hospital, NYC, NY, $25,000. 1991.
2134-13 New York Lung Association, NYC, NY,
$10,000. 1991.
2134-14 North Broward Hospital District, Fort
Lauderdale, FL, $15,000. 1991.
2134-15 Saint Vincents Medical Center
Foundation, Bridgeport, CT, $75,000. 1991.
2134-16 United Hospital Fund of New York,
NYC, NY, $10,000. 1991.

2135
Henry and Lucy Moses Fund, Inc. ▼
c/o Moses and Singer
1301 Ave. of the Americas
New York 10019   (212) 554-7800

Incorporated in 1942 in NY.
Donor(s): Henry L. Moses,‡ Lucy G. Moses.‡
Foundation type: Independent
Financial data (yr. ended 12/31/90): Assets,
$7,142,335 (M); gifts received, $2,000,000;
expenditures, $3,726,701; qualifying
distributions, $3,687,187, including $3,682,922
for 179 grants (high: $500,000; low: $50;
average: $1,000-$10,000).
Purpose and activities: Support for hospitals,
including building funds, and rehabilitation and
medical schools; Jewish and other welfare funds;
higher and legal education and educational
programs for minorities; social service agencies,
including those for youth, child welfare,
minorities, the aged, and the handicapped; the
arts and cultural programs, including dance;
environmental concerns, including Central Park
in New York City; and AIDS programs.
Fields of interest: Hospitals, medical education,
rehabilitation, Jewish welfare, higher education,
education—minorities, legal education, social
services, youth, minorities, aged, handicapped,

child welfare, Israel, cultural programs, arts,
performing arts, music, environment, AIDS.
Types of support: Building funds, endowment
funds, research, scholarship funds, fellowships,
general purposes, matching funds, professorships,
continuing support, annual campaigns, capital
campaigns, operating budgets.
Limitations: Giving primarily in the metropolitan
New York, NY, area. No grants to individuals; no
loans.
Application information: Support generally
limited to previous grant recipients. Applications
not accepted.
   Board meeting date(s): Usually in Feb., May,
   Aug., and Oct.
Write: Irving Sitnick, Secy.
Officers and Directors:* Felix A. Fischman,*
Pres.; Alfred W. Bressler,* V.P.; Joseph Fishman,
V.P.; Irving Sitnick, Secy.; Henry Schneider,* Treas.
Number of staff: None.
EIN: 136092967
Recent health grants:
2135-1 Columbia University, NYC, NY,
$500,000. For Neurology. 1990.
2135-2 Columbia University, NYC, NY,
$250,000. For Parkinson's Disease. 1990.
2135-3 Floating Hospital, NYC, NY, $15,000.
1990.
2135-4 Massachusetts Institute of Technology,
Whitehead Institute for Biomedical Research,
Cambridge, MA, $500,000. 1990.
2135-5 Mount Sinai Hospital and Medical
Center, NYC, NY, $500,000. 1990.
2135-6 Mount Sinai Hospital and Medical
Center, NYC, NY, $10,000. 1990.
2135-7 Parker Jewish Geriatric Institute, New
Hyde Park, NY, $10,000. 1990.
2135-8 Planned Parenthood of New York City,
NYC, NY, $10,000. 1990.

2136
Stewart R. Mott Charitable Trust
(Formerly Stewart R. Mott Charitable
Trust/Spectemur Agendo)
14 East 96th St., No. 2
New York 10128   (212) 289-0006

Trust established in 1968 in NY; reorganized in
1989 in NY.
Donor(s): Stewart R. Mott, Ruth R. Mott.
Foundation type: Independent
Financial data (yr. ended 12/31/91): Assets,
$6,588,413 (M); expenditures, $353,683;
qualifying distributions, $260,748, including
$153,675 for 89 grants (high: $50,000; low:
$100; average: $500-$2,000).
Fields of interest: Arms control, public policy,
foreign policy, government, civil rights,
population studies, family planning.
Types of support: General purposes.
Limitations: No support for local or state
organizations. No grants to individuals, or for
media or direct services.
Application information: Application form not
required.
   Initial approach: Proposal
   Copies of proposal: 1
   Deadline(s): None
   Write: Steve Cheifetz, Admin. Dir.
Trustees: Stewart R. Mott, Kappy J. Wells.
Number of staff: 4 part-time professional; 2
part-time support.

EIN: 237002554

2137
Mary S. Mulligan Charitable Trust
c/o Fleet Bank, N.A.
One East Ave.
Rochester 14638   (716) 546-9105

Established in 1967 in NY.
Donor(s): Mary S. Mulligan.‡
Foundation type: Independent
Financial data (yr. ended 05/31/91): Assets,
$2,567,169 (M); gifts received, $85,635;
expenditures, $139,381; qualifying distributions,
$124,517, including $123,000 for 20 grants
(high: $20,000; low: $1,000).
Fields of interest: Museums, hospitals, youth.
Types of support: Building funds, continuing
support, endowment funds, research, scholarship
funds.
Limitations: Giving primarily in Rochester, NY.
No grants to individuals.
Application information:
   Initial approach: Letter
   Deadline(s): None
   Write: Jack Murphy
Trustee: Fleet Bank, N.A.
EIN: 166076169

2138
**Charles & Constance Murcott Charitable
Trust**
Ten Matinecock Farms Rd.
Glen Cove 11542

Established in 1986 in NY.
Foundation type: Independent
Financial data (yr. ended 08/31/91): Assets,
$1,609,925 (M); expenditures, $227,257;
qualifying distributions, $220,485, including
$220,485 for 32 grants (high: $120,350; low:
$50).
Purpose and activities: Giving primarily for health
associations and hospitals and secondary and
higher education; some support for conservatories.
Fields of interest: Hospitals, health associations,
health services, secondary education, higher
education, conservation.
Limitations: Giving primarily in the greater
metropolitan New York, NY, area, including Long
Island. No grants to individuals.
Application information: Contributes only to
pre-selected organizations. Applications not
accepted.
Trustees: Charles Murcott, Constance Murcott.
EIN: 112826619

2139
**The Murray Foundation for Eye Research,
Inc.**
(Formerly John P. Murray, Jr. Foundation, Inc.)
c/o Pegg & Pegg
370 Lexington Ave., Rm. 1007
New York 10017-6503   (212) 532-4287

Donor(s): John P. Murray.
Foundation type: Independent
Financial data (yr. ended 12/31/90): Assets,
$5,604,727 (M); gifts received, $55,250;
expenditures, $244,877; qualifying distributions,

$163,640, including $160,450 for 2 grants (high: $140,450; low: $20,000).
Purpose and activities: Giving for eye research and programs for the blind.
Fields of interest: Medical research, handicapped.
Types of support: Research, general purposes.
Application information: Application form not required.
 Deadline(s): None
 Write: Robert R. Pegg
Officers and Directors:* John P. Murray,* Pres.; James M. Murray,* V.P. and Secy.; Elizabeth Husfa,* V.P. and Treas.; Ellen Kelsey,* V.P.; John P. Murray III,* V.P.
EIN: 133421590

2140
Mutual Of New York Foundation
(Formerly MONY Financial Services Foundation)
1740 Broadway, MD 9-5
New York 10019   (212) 708-2136

Established in 1987 in NY; direct corporate giving since the early 1940's.
Donor(s): The Mutual Life Insurance Co. of New York.
Foundation type: Company-sponsored
Financial data (yr. ended 12/31/91): Assets, $0 (M); expenditures, $879,361; qualifying distributions, $866,684, including $607,232 for grants (high: $10,000; low: $500; average: $1,000-$10,000) and $259,452 for employee matching gifts.
Purpose and activities: The foundation seeks to apply available resources in specific, well-defined areas of the philanthropic community. The foundation's resources are targeted towards innovative, need-responsible projects and programs within priority areas of funding. Each site has strategic funding priorities which seek to address the specific needs of the communities in which they are located. The funding focuses are as follows: 1) New York City: Funding for AIDS Care and Training Services (FACTS) Program; 2) Teaneck, NJ: Meeting the Essential Needs of Families with Children; 3) Purchase, NY: Funding for Senior Citizens Program; and 4) Syracuse, NY: The Essential Needs of Children & Teens at Risk. These focuses are geographically limited to those areas.
Fields of interest: Family services, child welfare, child development, youth, aged, homeless, volunteerism, AIDS, hospices.
Types of support: Employee matching gifts, special projects, employee-related scholarships, matching funds, in-kind gifts, loaned talent.
Limitations: Giving only in communities where MONY maintains offices, including Teaneck, NJ; Purchase, Syracuse, and New York, NY. No support for private foundations, fully participating members of the United Way, or religious, fraternal, athletic, social, or veterans' organizations. No grants to individuals, or for capital fund drives, endowments, or deficit financing.
Publications: Application guidelines.
Application information: Application form not required.
 Initial approach: Letter of inquiry for guideline brochures
 Copies of proposal: 1

Deadline(s): Varies for grants; Feb. 3 for V.I.P. Award
Board meeting date(s): Sept. 15
Final notification: Varies
 Write: Lynn Stekas, Pres.
Officers: Lynn Stekas, Pres.; Gerald J. Carroll, Secy.; Richard Daddario, C.F.O.
Directors: James B. Farley, Chair.; Thomas J. Conklin, Samuel Foti, Michael Roth, Thomas Schlossberg.
Number of staff: None.
EIN: 133398852

2141
The Napier Foundation
c/o Chemical Bank
30 Rockefeller Plaza, 60th Fl.
New York 10112   (212) 621-2148
Application address: Michael Consolini, Napier Co., Napier Park, Meriden, CT 06450

Donor(s): Napier Co.
Foundation type: Company-sponsored
Financial data (yr. ended 07/31/91): Assets, $2,624,211 (M); gifts received, $25,551; expenditures, $155,470; qualifying distributions, $127,767, including $127,625 for 73 grants (high: $12,500; low: $100).
Fields of interest: Higher education, secondary education, youth, social services, hospitals, cultural programs.
Limitations: Giving primarily in the Meriden, CT, area. No loans or program-related investments.
Application information: Application form not required.
 Deadline(s): None
 Write: Barbara Strohmeier, V.P., Chemical Bank
Trustees: John E. Benison, Eugene E. Bertolli, Michael G. Consolini, Eleanor S. Cooney, Ronald J. Meoni, Robert M. Meyers, Howard C. Schaefer, John A. Shulga, Carter H. White, Chemical Bank.
EIN: 136029883

2142
National Fuel Gas Corporate Giving Program
10 Lafayette Sq.
Buffalo 14203   (607) 857-6928

Purpose and activities: Supports fine arts institutes and general education, including private colleges and employee-related scholarships. Support also for community development, crime and law enforcement, hospital building funds, theater, and women's programs; includes in-kind donations.
Fields of interest: Fine arts, education, higher education, community development, crime and law enforcement, hospitals—building funds, theater, women, general charitable giving.
Types of support: Annual campaigns, building funds, capital campaigns, conferences and seminars, employee-related scholarships, scholarship funds, student aid, in-kind gifts.
Limitations: Giving primarily in headquarters city and major operating locations in 22 counties in western NY state and northwestern PA.
Publications: Newsletter.
Application information:
 Write: Bernard J. Kennedy, Pres. and C.E.O.
Administrator: Roger Wilkecks, Assist. V.P., Risk Mgt.

Number of staff: 2 part-time professional; 2 part-time support.

2143
Hugo and Doris Neu Foundation, Inc.
c/o Hugo Neu & Sons
1185 Ave. of the Americas, Suite 310
New York 10036

Incorporated in 1955 in NY.
Donor(s): Hugo Neu, Union Minerals & Alloys Corp., Hugo Neu & Sons, Inc.
Foundation type: Independent
Financial data (yr. ended 12/31/90): Assets, $6,825,312 (M); gifts received, $1,000,000; expenditures, $387,248; qualifying distributions, $365,185, including $363,900 for 74 grants (high: $80,000; low: $50).
Purpose and activities: Emphasis on Jewish welfare funds; support also for hospitals and higher and secondary education.
Fields of interest: Jewish giving, Jewish welfare, hospitals, higher education, secondary education, educational associations.
Types of support: General purposes.
Limitations: Giving primarily in NY. No grants to individuals.
Application information: Contributes only to pre-selected organizations. Applications not accepted.
Officers and Directors:* Doris Neu,* Pres. and Treas.; John L. Neu,* V.P. and Secy.; Richard W. Neu,* V.P.; Herman Caro, Donald Schapiro.
EIN: 136107504

2144
New Street Foundation, Inc. ▼
(Formerly The Drexel Burnham Lambert Foundation, Inc.)
450 Lexington Ave., 14th Fl.
New York 10017   (212) 450-7926

Established in 1986 in NY.
Donor(s): Drexel Burnham Lambert, Inc.
Foundation type: Independent
Financial data (yr. ended 12/31/91): Assets, $19,000,000 (M); expenditures, $1,240,000; qualifying distributions, $1,088,129, including $1,088,129 for 34 grants (high: $85,000; low: $5,000; average: $20-$30,000).
Fields of interest: Education, education—early childhood, elementary education, education—minorities, health, aged, youth, child welfare.
Types of support: Consulting services, technical assistance, general purposes, operating budgets.
Limitations: Giving primarily in New York, NY metropolitan area. No grants to individuals.
Publications: Informational brochure (including application guidelines).
Application information:
 Board meeting date(s): Monthly except July and Aug.
 Write: Alexa M. Silberkleit, Consultant
Number of staff: 1 part-time professional.
EIN: 133377947
Recent health grants:
2144-1 Alzheimers Disease and Related Disorders Association, NYC, NY, $100,000. 1990.

2144-2 American Federation for Aging Research, NYC, NY, $50,000. 1990.

2144-3 American Foundation for AIDS Research, NYC, NY, $250,000. 1990.

2144-4 American Paralysis Association, Springfield, NJ, $25,000. 1990.

2144-5 Retinitis Pigmentosa Foundation, International, Baltimore, MD, $60,000. 1990.

2144-6 United Cerebral Palsy, NYC, NY, $15,000. 1990.

2145
The New World Foundation ▼
100 East 85th St.
New York 10028   (212) 249-1023

Incorporated in 1954 in IL.
Donor(s): Anita McCormick Blaine.‡
Foundation type: Independent
Financial data (yr. ended 09/30/91): Assets, $29,221,559 (M); gifts received, $4,800; expenditures, $3,846,148; qualifying distributions, $1,898,827, including $1,458,000 for 118 grants (high: $125,000; low: $250; average: $1,000-$25,000).
Purpose and activities: Program places emphasis on 1) equal rights and opportunity, with emphasis on minorities' rights; 2) public education, especially the roles of parents and the community working together; 3) public health, particularly helping the disadvantaged, raising occupational health and safety standards, and reducing environmental hazards to health; 4) community initiative for rural and urban communities; and 5) avoidance of war, especially nuclear war, and seeking peace; some support also for youth advocacy and child welfare agencies.
Fields of interest: Civil rights, race relations, minorities, education, health services, social services, child welfare, AIDS, community development, public policy, peace, arms control.
Types of support: Special projects, conferences and seminars, program-related investments, technical assistance, seed money, loans.
Limitations: No support for community fund drives, schools, hospitals, or cultural, arts, or media programs, organizations which discriminate against women or members of ethnic minority groups, or that do not have an affirmative action policy and practice. No grants to individuals, or for general operating budgets, deficit financing, continuing support, capital, building, or endowment funds, research that is not action- or policy-oriented with regard to current issues and is not of limited scope or duration, scholarships, fellowships, or matching gifts; emergency loans to current grantees only.
Publications: Biennial report (including application guidelines).
Application information: Application form not required.
  Initial approach: Letter
  Copies of proposal: 1
  Deadline(s): None
  Board meeting date(s): 3 times a year
  Final notification: 3 months
  Write: Colin Greer, Pres.
Officers and Directors:* David B. Harrison,* Chair.; Colin Greer, Pres. and Exec. Dir.; Adrian W. DeWind, Charles Heymaestre, Phyllis Ross Schloss.

Number of staff: 3 full-time professional; 3 full-time support.
EIN: 131919791

2146
The New York Community Trust ▼
Two Park Ave., 24th Fl.
New York 10016-9385   (212) 686-0010
FAX: (212) 532-8528

Established in 1923 in NY by resolution and declaration of trust.
Foundation type: Community
Financial data (yr. ended 12/31/91): Assets, $1,030,740,628 (M); gifts received, $21,133,964; expenditures, $72,350,208; qualifying distributions, $68,139,252, including $68,009,479 for grants (high: $4,586,634; low: $100; average: $5,000-$35,000) and $129,773 for employee matching gifts.
Purpose and activities: An administrator of many individual charitable funds. Priority given to applications for special support for projects having particular significance for the New York City area. Loan guarantee program improves access to commercial lending. Program areas of major interest are 1) Children, youth and families - includes issues of hunger and homelessness, substance abuse, and youth development; 2) Community development and the environment - includes civic affairs, conservation, economic development, housing, neighborhood revitalization, and technical assistance; 3) Education, arts and the humanities - includes arts and culture, education, and human justice; and 4) Health and people with special needs - includes health services systems, and policies, biomedical research, AIDS, visual handicaps, children with disabilities, and mental health and retardation.
Fields of interest: Social services, family services, child welfare, homeless, employment, women, aged, drug abuse, community development, urban development, energy, environment, education, arts, human rights, immigration, legal services, health, AIDS.
Types of support: Seed money, consulting services, technical assistance, special projects, research, publications, conferences and seminars, loans, scholarship funds, employee matching gifts, fellowships.
Limitations: Giving limited to the New York, NY, metropolitan area. No support for religious purposes, or for transportation, or manpower development by non-advised grant program. No grants to individuals, or for deficit financing, emergency funds, building campaigns, endowment funds, or general operating support.
Publications: Informational brochure (including application guidelines), annual report, application guidelines (including application guidelines), newsletter, occasional report, financial statement.
Application information: Application form required.
  Initial approach: Proposal with cover letter
  Copies of proposal: 1
  Deadline(s): None
  Board meeting date(s): Feb., Apr., June, July, Oct., and Dec.
  Final notification: 15 weeks
  Write: Lorie A. Slutsky, Dir.
Officers and Distribution Committee:* Barbara Scott Preiskel,* Chair.; Lorie A. Slutsky,* Pres. and

Dir.; Karen Metcalf, V.P., Finance and Admin.; Joyce M. Bove, V.P., Program and Projects; Sidney S. Whelan, Jr., V.P., Donor Relations; Kieran J. Lawlor, Controller; William Parsons, Consulting member; Bernard J. Pisani, M.D., Consulting member; Arthur G. Altschul, Aida Alvarez, Bruce L. Ballard, M.D., William M. Evarts, Jr., Charlotte M. Fischman, Barry H. Garfinkel, Judah Gribetz, Robert M. Kaufman, Mrs. Laurance S. Rockefeller, Carroll L. Wainwright, Jr.
Trustees: The Bank of New York, Bankers Trust Co., Barclays Bank of New York, N.A., Bessemer Trust Co., N.A., Brown Brothers Harriman Trust Co., The Chase Manhattan Bank, N.A., Chemical Bank, Citibank, N.A., Fiduciary Trust Co. International, IBJ Schroder Bank & Trust Co., Manufacturers Hanover Trust Co., Marine Midland Bank, N.A., Morgan Guaranty Trust Co. of New York, Republic National Bank of New York, Rockefeller Trust Co., J. & W. Seligman Trust Co., U.S. Trust Co. of New York.
Number of staff: 21 full-time professional; 5 part-time professional; 18 full-time support; 3 part-time support.
EIN: 133062214
Recent health grants:
2146-1 Academy for Educational Development, NYC, NY, $10,000. For inventory of school health programs in New York City public schools. 1991.

2146-2 Access Development Fund Corporation, NYC, NY, $26,000. To create low-cost housing for homeless mentally ill persons, specifically for salaries of housing developer/client advocate. 1991.

2146-3 Ackerman Institute for Family Therapy, NYC, NY, $25,000. To continue support for Family-School Collaboration Model. 1991.

2146-4 Advocates for Children of New York, NYC, NY, $30,000. To ensure implementation of comprehensive AIDS education support and outreach programs for children in New York City public schools. 1991.

2146-5 AIDS and Adolescents Network of New York City, NYC, NY, $50,000. To coordinate and link human service organizations and health care providers that serve youth at risk of HIV infection. 1991.

2146-6 AIDS Task Force, Lower Manhattan, NYC, NY, $60,000. To develop linkages between community-based agencies and hospitals serving people with AIDS in lower Manhattan. 1991.

2146-7 American Indian Community House, NYC, NY, $60,000. To develop culturally appropriate HIV prevention and education intervention for Native American community in New York City. 1991.

2146-8 Arthritis Foundation, New York Chapter, NYC, NY, $45,000. To provide direct assistance for needy people suffering from arthritis. 1991.

2146-9 Bedford Stuyvesant Restoration Corporation, Brooklyn, NY, $40,000. To establish youth drug prevention program in Bedford Stuyvesant. 1991.

2146-10 Betances Health Unit, NYC, NY, $60,000. For physician House Call Program for elderly residents and homebound persons with AIDS on Lower East Side. 1991.

2146-11 Beth Israel Medical Center, NYC, NY, $50,000. To test new model of medical and nursing care for hospitalized patients. 1991.

2146-12 Beth Israel Medical Center, NYC, NY, $50,000. For model substance abuse treatment program for women with children living in family shelters. 1991.

2146-13 Black Leadership Commission on AIDS, NYC, NY, $65,000. To strengthen commission's ability to provide technical assistance to community-based organizations. 1991.

2146-14 Bronx Community College of the City University of New York, Bronx, NY, $40,000. For Health Force: Women Against AIDS, to train women affected by AIDS to become care givers and advocates. 1991.

2146-15 Bronx-Lebanon Hospital Center, Bronx, NY, $50,000. To begin model health care program for women with AIDS. 1991.

2146-16 Brooklyn Legal Services Corporation, Brooklyn, NY, $39,500. To expand legal service program for poor young women and children with AIDS. 1991.

2146-17 Cancer Care, NYC, NY, $532,000. To expand financial support program for indigent cancer patients. 1991.

2146-18 Caribbean Womens Health Association, NYC, NY, $25,000. To enhance capabilities of organization serving Caribbean-American community in New York City. 1991.

2146-19 Center for Health Policy Studies, Albany, NY, $10,000. To identify strategies to link substance abuse and health care providers. 1991.

2146-20 Citizens Committee for New York City, NYC, NY, $50,000. To stimulate and develop grassroots volunteer-initiated HIV prevention/education care program for low-income neighborhoods. 1991.

2146-21 Coalition of Voluntary Mental Health, Mental Retardation, and Alcoholism Agencies, NYC, NY, $80,000. To develop linkages between community-based AIDS organizations and traditional providers of mental health services. 1991.

2146-22 Columbia University, School of Public Health, NYC, NY, $25,800. To study results of managed health care demonstration program. 1991.

2146-23 Committee to Aid Ethiopian Refugees, NYC, NY, $25,000. To initiate AIDS Education and Referral program for Ethiopian and other African refugees. 1991.

2146-24 Community Health Project, NYC, NY, $60,000. For mobile health program targeted to street youth in Manhattan at risk of HIV infection. 1991.

2146-25 Community Resource Exchange, NYC, NY, $65,000. To provide technical assistance in organizational development to community-based AIDS service organizations. 1991.

2146-26 Community Resource Exchange, NYC, NY, $30,000. To improve management of community-based drug programs. 1991.

2146-27 Concerned Citizens of Queens, Queens, NY, $65,000. For AIDS education program for Central and South American communities in Queens. 1991.

2146-28 Correctional Association of New York, NYC, NY, $40,000. To make clinical trials of HIV therapies/treatments available to prisoners and parolees with HIV/AIDS. 1991.

2146-29 East Harlem Interfaith, NYC, NY, $60,000. To link church groups and AIDS service providers in upper Manhattan. 1991.

2146-30 East Williamsburg Valley Industrial Development Company, Brooklyn, NY, $25,000. To launch workplace safety program for manufacturing companies in Williamsburg, Brooklyn. 1991.

2146-31 Family Health Project, NYC, NY, $25,000. To initiate education and care program for Asian and Pacific Islanders at risk of HIV infection. 1991.

2146-32 Federation of Protestant Welfare Agencies, NYC, NY, $35,000. For technical assistance to agencies serving children affected by AIDS. 1991.

2146-33 Floating Hospital, NYC, NY, $35,000. For citywide measles immunization campaign. 1991.

2146-34 Gay Men of African Descent, NYC, NY, $25,000. To expand HIV education and care program serving gay African-American men. 1991.

2146-35 Gay Mens Health Crisis (GMHC), NYC, NY, $50,000. For AIDS education and relapse prevention program targeted to gay men. 1991.

2146-36 Goddard-Riverside Community Center, NYC, NY, $50,000. To train staff of single room occupancy hotels in HIV prevention and case management procedures. 1991.

2146-37 Happiness is Camping, Bronx, NY, $40,000. To initiate Families Living With Cancer Program. 1991.

2146-38 Harlem Interfaith Counseling Service, NYC, NY, $40,000. To expand supportive services to relocated families in Harlem community. 1991.

2146-39 Health Systems Agency of New York City, NYC, NY, $40,000. To study supportive housing for elderly. 1991.

2146-40 Heiser Program for Research in Leprosy, NYC, NY, $13,393. 1991.

2146-41 Hetrick-Martin Institute, NYC, NY, $50,000. To provide education, counseling and health services to gay and lesbian youth at risk of HIV infection. 1991.

2146-42 Hetrick-Martin Institute, NYC, NY, $25,000. To initiate program of AIDS prevention and life planning for lesbian and gay street youth between ages 21-25. 1991.

2146-43 Hospital Audiences, NYC, NY, $10,000. For transportation costs of job program for disabled young people surveying arts organizations. 1991.

2146-44 Housing Works, NYC, NY, $75,000. To locate and secure housing for homeless, HIV-infected persons with AIDS. 1991.

2146-45 Hunter College of the City University of New York, Brookdale Center on Aging, NYC, NY, $10,000. For citywide aging and AIDS task force. 1991.

2146-46 Institute for the Puerto Rican/Hispanic Elderly, NYC, NY, $25,000. To initiate AIDS education and support program for elderly Latinos. 1991.

2146-47 Johns Hopkins University, School of Public Health, Baltimore, MD, $20,000. 1991.

2146-48 Korean Community Services of Metropolitan New York, Flushing, NY, $25,000. To initiate program to educate Koreans about risks of HIV infection. 1991.

2146-49 Latino Commission on AIDS, NYC, NY, $50,000. To develop coordinated response to AIDS from within New York City's Latino Community. 1991.

2146-50 Learning Through an Expanded Arts Program (LEAP), NYC, NY, $25,000. To expand drug prevention program in elementary and junior high schools. 1991.

2146-51 Legal Action Center of the City of New York, NYC, NY, $25,000. To provide legal assistance to AIDS service organizations. 1991.

2146-52 Lesbian and Gay Community Services Center, NYC, NY, $50,000. For comprehensive AIDS bereavement program for gay community. 1991.

2146-53 Malkin and Ross, Albany, NY, $10,000. To advocate for increased funding of local AIDS services. 1991.

2146-54 Manhattan Eye, Ear and Throat Hospital, NYC, NY, $40,000. To increase outreach activities for children's eye and learning centers. 1991.

2146-55 Medicare Beneficiaries Defense Fund, NYC, NY, $27,000. To expand program to help elderly people receive medicare benefits. 1991.

2146-56 MFY Legal Services, NYC, NY, $75,000. To expand legal services program for poor women with AIDS. 1991.

2146-57 MFY Legal Services, NYC, NY, $60,000. To provide legal services and advocacy to poor HIV-infected women and children. 1991.

2146-58 Montefiore Medical Center, NYC, NY, $30,000. To establish hospital-based prevention and treatment center for victims of child abuse and neglect. 1991.

2146-59 Mount Saint Ursula Speech Center, Bronx, NY, $25,000. To expand dropout prevention program for children with speech and learning disabilities. 1991.

2146-60 Mount Sinai Hospital and Medical Center, NYC, NY, $55,000. For model health and social services project for children and families in East Harlem. 1991.

2146-61 Mount Sinai Hospital and Medical Center, NYC, NY, $35,000. For intergenerational demonstration that provides housing for elderly people and day care for children. 1991.

2146-62 NARCO Freedom, Bronx, NY, $50,000. To include preventive services in treatment program for crack-addicted women with children. 1991.

2146-63 New England Medical Center Hospitals, Boston, MA, $51,500. 1991.

2146-64 New Hope Guild Centers, Brooklyn, NY, $50,000. For developing and coordinating health and social service support programs for persons with HIV infection in East New York. 1991.

2146-65 New York Academy of Medicine, NYC, NY, $72,000. For research fellowships in ophthalmology. 1991.

2146-66 New York Academy of Medicine, NYC, NY, $38,000. For commission to study status of biomedical research in New York City. 1991.

2146-67 New York Academy of Medicine, NYC, NY, $32,000. To evaluate model health education program for junior high schools. 1991.

2146-68 New York Academy of Medicine, NYC, NY, $10,000. For development of AIDS policy positions. 1991.

2146-69 New York AIDS Coalition, NYC, NY, $50,000. For comprehensive, community-based advocacy efforts that increase funding and knowledge about AIDS. 1991.

2146-70 New York Association for Ambulatory Care, NYC, NY, $10,000. To strengthen skills of managers of primary health care services. 1991.

2146-71 New York Business Group on Health, NYC, NY, $20,000. To help small businesses develop support programs for their employees who care for elderly relatives. 1991.

2146-72 New York Society for the Prevention of Cruelty to Children, NYC, NY, $10,000. To prepare child and health care workers to address treatment issues faced by drug exposed infants/families. 1991.

2146-73 New York State Task Force on Life and the Law, NYC, NY, $10,000. For public education campaign on health care proxy law. 1991.

2146-74 Northside Center for Child Development, NYC, NY, $40,000. To expand mental health and supportive services to formerly homeless, emotionally disturbed children. 1991.

2146-75 Norwegian Radium Hospital, Oslo, Norway, $20,000. 1991.

2146-76 Nursing Home Community Coalition of New York State, NYC, NY, $30,000. To study New York State nursing home quality assurance and surveillance system. 1991.

2146-77 Nursing Home Community Coalition of New York State, NYC, NY, $10,000. To train AIDS advocates on issues of quality long-term care. 1991.

2146-78 Partnership for a Drug Free America, NYC, NY, $65,000. To develop local anti-drug media campaign for children and youth. 1991.

2146-79 People for the American Way, NYC, NY, $50,000. To educate public on effects of Supreme Court decision regarding women's health care and privacy rights. 1991.

2146-80 Pregones Touring Puerto Rican Theater Collection, NYC, NY, $60,000. For interactive AIDS education and prevention theater workshop targeted to Latino community. 1991.

2146-81 Project Return Foundation, NYC, NY, $58,000. For AIDS education/service program targeted to chronically mentally ill, substance abusing women. 1991.

2146-82 Public Policy and Education Fund, Albany, NY, $35,000. To examine feasibility of universal health insurance in New York State. 1991.

2146-83 Queens Child Guidance Center, Jamaica, NY, $40,000. To help families achieve successful adoptions of troubled foster children. 1991.

2146-84 Saint Lukes-Roosevelt Hospital Center, NYC, NY, $35,000. To provide medical and rehabilitation services to injured, needy classical ballet dancers. 1991.

2146-85 Senior Action in a Gay Environment (SAGE), NYC, NY, $40,000. To provide education, prevention and social services for older gay persons with AIDS or at risk of HIV infection. 1991.

2146-86 Southeast Queens Clergy for Community Empowerment, Jamaica, NY, $35,000. To plan and develop community church-sponsored supportive housing program for persons with AIDS. 1991.

2146-87 United Hospital Fund of New York, NYC, NY, $75,000. For primary care development fund. 1991.

2146-88 United Hospital Fund of New York, NYC, NY, $40,000. To study home care in New York City. 1991.

2146-89 United Hospital Fund of New York, NYC, NY, $10,000. To recruit volunteers to work in hospitals and nursing homes. 1991.

2146-90 University Hospital Leiden, Leiden, Netherlands, $24,500. 1991.

2146-91 Upper Room AIDS Ministry, NYC, NY, $50,000. To expand day care program for persons with AIDS in upper Manhattan. 1991.

2146-92 Upward Fund, NYC, NY, $25,000. For model AIDS Education and Prevention Program for Youth. 1991.

2146-93 Vision Services for the Blind and Visually Impaired, NYC, NY, $42,200. To train paraprofessionals to work with elderly people with visual disabilities. 1991.

2146-94 Visiting Nurse Association of Brooklyn, Brooklyn, NY, $34,500. To establish ethics committee in certified home health care agency. 1991.

2146-95 Visiting Nurse Service of New York, NYC, NY, $50,000. For model psychiatric program for homebound persons with AIDS. 1991.

2146-96 Volunteers of America in Greater New York, NYC, NY, $25,000. For Neighborhood Drug Prevention Program in Bushwick section of Brooklyn. 1991.

2146-97 W G B H Educational Foundation, Boston, MA, $10,000. For television drama with local follow-up about teenagers and AIDS. 1991.

2146-98 West Side Federation for Senior Housing, NYC, NY, $75,000. To develop supportive residence for homeless persons with AIDS. 1991.

2146-99 Women and Foundations/Corporate Philanthropy, NYC, NY, $10,000. For national conference for grantmakers to focus attention on women's health issues. 1991.

2146-100 Womens City Club of New York, NYC, NY, $21,000. For coalition that supports responsible AIDS education. 1991.

2146-101 Womens City Club of New York, NYC, NY, $10,000. To support and monitor development and implementation of comprehensive HIV/AIDS education programs in public schools. 1991.

2147
New York Foundation ▼
350 Fifth Ave., No. 2901
New York 10118   (212) 594-8009

Incorporated in 1909 in NY.
Donor(s): Louis A. Heinsheimer,‡ Alfred M. Heinsheimer,‡ Lionel J. Salomon.‡
Foundation type: Independent
Financial data (yr. ended 12/31/91): Assets, $54,358,000 (M); expenditures, $3,826,208; qualifying distributions, $3,031,553, including $2,686,553 for 82 grants (high: $50,000; low: $10,000; average: $20,000-$35,000) and $345,000 for 2 loans.
Purpose and activities: Support for projects designed to improve the quality of life for disadvantaged, handicapped, and minority populations, with extra emphasis on youth and the elderly, especially projects with a strong community base. Some support for advocacy and coalition work and health services, including AIDS programs.
Fields of interest: Community development, aged, disadvantaged, minorities, youth, handicapped, health, health services, AIDS, welfare—indigent individuals, employment, hunger, homeless, child welfare, women, public policy, housing, immigration, education, leadership development, environment.
Types of support: Operating budgets, continuing support, seed money, matching funds, technical assistance, general purposes, special projects.
Limitations: Giving limited to local programs in the New York, NY, metropolitan area. No support for the arts, medical research, or films. No grants to individuals, or for annual campaigns, renovations, emergency funds, deficit financing, building or endowment funds, equipment, scholarships, fellowships, land acquisition, research, conferences, publications, or demonstration projects.
Publications: Annual report (including application guidelines).
Application information: Application form not required.
  Initial approach: Letter
  Copies of proposal: 1
  Deadline(s): Nov. 1, Mar. 1, and July 1
  Board meeting date(s): Feb., June, and Oct.
  Final notification: 3 to 6 months
  Write: Madeline Lee, Exec. Dir.
Officers and Trustees:* William M. Kelly,* Chair.; Joan Leiman,* Vice-Chair.; M.D. Taracido,* Secy.; Malcolm Smith,* Treas.; R. Harcourt Dodds, Angelo Falcon, Margaret Fung, Marilyn Gittell, Stephen D. Heyman, Michael M. Kellen, Mack Lipkin, Jr., Archibald R. Murray, Stephanie K. Newman, Robert Pollack, Alice Radosh, Helen Rehr, Rebecca S. Straus, Edward Wachenheim III.
Number of staff: 4 full-time professional; 4 full-time support.
EIN: 135626345
Recent health grants:

2147-1 Bedford-Stuyvesant Volunteer Ambulance Corps, Brooklyn, NY, $25,000. To enhance and expand Youth Corps Training Program of all-volunteer, minority-run ambulance corps. 1990.

2147-2 Body Positive of New York, NYC, NY, $30,000. For staff support for self-help, advocacy and peer counseling organization of HIV-sero-positive individuals, their families and friends. 1990.

2147-3 Bronx Committee for the Communitys Health, Bronx, NY, $30,000. To extend neighborhood assessment and advocacy work in AIDS and child health issues. 1990.

2147-4 Citizens Committee for New York City, NYC, NY, $30,000. For salary of Training and Technical Assistance Coordinator for Committee's Anti-Crime Center, city-wide anti-drug effort that brings together grassroots activists, law enforcement personnel, and prevention and treatment specialists. 1990.

2147-5 Highbridge Community Life Center, Bronx, NY, $30,600. For two staff positions to recruit and train community residents to work at new AIDS residence in South Bronx. 1990.

2147-6 Medicare Beneficiaries Defense Fund, NYC, NY, $35,000. For organization providing direct legal assistance and advocacy, as well as information and referral services to Medicare beneficiaries. 1990.

2147-7 New York AIDS Coalition, NYC, NY, $35,000. For general support. 1990.

2147-8 People With AIDS Coalition, NYC, NY, $25,000. Toward Speakers Bureau and Hotline programs. 1990.

2147-9 Steinway Mental Health Committee, Astoria, NY, $30,000. For services to frail and homebound elderly in three Queens housing projects. 1990.

2147-10 Women and AIDS Resource Network, Brooklyn, NY, $30,000. For renewed general support. 1990.

2147-11 Womens Health Education Project, NYC, NY, $27,500. For salary of Coordinator for Project (formerly Women's Health Network), self-help health care project aimed at women in public shelter system. 1990.

2147-12 Youth Communications, NYC, NY, $35,696. For New Youth Connections, newspaper published and written by young people, to publish two special supplements, one on responsible sexuality and one on violence and conflict resolution. 1990.

2148
New York Life Foundation ▼

51 Madison Ave.
New York 10010   (212) 576-7341

Established in 1979 in NY.
Donor(s): New York Life Insurance Co.
Foundation type: Company-sponsored
Financial data (yr. ended 12/31/90): Assets, $35,736,870 (M); expenditures, $2,503,062; qualifying distributions, $2,446,340, including $2,444,050 for 632 grants (high: $400,000; low: $50; average: $500-$10,000).
Purpose and activities: Grants to national and local organizations. Priority areas are AIDS and literacy; support also for higher education, including insurance education, in both direct grants and employee matching gifts; community funds; community development and urban affairs; hospitals; cultural programs; and youth and social service agencies.
Fields of interest: AIDS, literacy, higher education, medical education, insurance education, community funds, community development, urban affairs, hospitals, cultural programs, social services.
Types of support: Scholarship funds, general purposes, operating budgets, building funds, special projects, employee matching gifts.
Limitations: No support for public educational institutions; fraternal, social, professional, veterans', or athletic organizations; religious or sectarian organizations or activities whose services are limited to members of any one religious group; grantmaking foundations; pre-school, primary, or secondary educational institutions; or United Way-member organizations already receiving foundation support. No grants to individuals, or for seminars, conferences, trips, memorials, endowments, capital campaigns, research-related programs, or matching gifts; no loans.
Publications: Application guidelines.
Application information: Application form not required.

Initial approach: Letter
Copies of proposal: 1
Deadline(s): None
Board meeting date(s): No formal schedule
Final notification: Varies
Write: Carol J. Reuter, Pres.
Officers and Directors:* Harry G. Hohn,* Chair.; Carol J. Reuter, Pres.; Walter C. Weissinger, Jr., Secy.; Anne Pollack, Treas.; George A.W. Bundschuh.
Number of staff: 3 full-time professional; 1 full-time support.
EIN: 132989476

2149
New York Telephone Company Giving Program

1095 Ave. of the Americas, Room 4120
New York 10036   (212) 395-2295

Purpose and activities: New York Telephone evaluates each applicant organization on its merits. Specifically, the company reviews the quality of the program, its service to the public, the size and type of constituency it serves, the organization's management, and its accountability, finances and fundraising practices. Because the company considers it important that an applicant receive widespread support from the community in which it functions, the applicant organization's community impact and interest are also assessed. To assure that its contributions are used where they have the greatest value, New York Telephone gives only where a genuine need for funding is demonstrated, and only to programs that do not duplicate the work of public agencies. The contributions program covers three general areas: health and welfare, education, and culture and civic affairs. The grants are disbursed in the following categories: General Operating Expense-for day-to-day expenses of the organization; Capital Grants-for construction, remodeling or restoration of physical facilities; Leadership Grants-for noteworthy projects of certain non-profit organizations; Special Grants-for a specific project by an organization are in some cases sponsored 100 percent by the company.
Fields of interest: Health, welfare, higher education, education, civic affairs, cultural programs.
Types of support: Capital campaigns, employee matching gifts, operating budgets, special projects, equipment, conferences and seminars, matching funds, research, seed money.
Limitations: Giving primarily in NY. No support for discriminatory organizations, political groups, national health organizations, elementary or secondary education, or religious groups for denominational purposes, or organizations that are not 501(C)(3) certified. No grants to individuals, or for goodwill or special occasion advertising, or operating expenses of United Way recipients.
Application information:
Initial approach: Letter, phone or full application
Deadline(s): Applications accepted throughout the year
Board meeting date(s): Charitable Contributions Committee meets as needed

Final notification: Minimum of 12 weeks to process applications
Write: Beth Pendergast, Staff Dir., Contribs.

2150
The New-Land Foundation, Inc. ▼

1345 Ave. of the Americas, 45th Fl.
New York 10105   (212) 841-6000

Incorporated in 1941 in NY.
Donor(s): Muriel M. Buttinger.‡
Foundation type: Independent
Financial data (yr. ended 12/31/91): Assets, $19,000,000 (M); expenditures, $1,600,000; qualifying distributions, $1,400,000, including $1,400,000 for 130 grants (high: $50,000; low: $1,000; average: $5,000-$15,000).
Purpose and activities: Grants for civil rights, mental health, population control, environmental preservation, arms control and disarmament, arts for children, leadership development and minority education.
Fields of interest: Civil rights, human rights, mental health, population studies, environment, energy, arms control, peace, public policy, education—minorities, leadership development.
Types of support: General purposes, annual campaigns, seed money, research, continuing support, internships, matching funds, operating budgets, special projects.
Limitations: No grants to individuals; no loans.
Publications: Application guidelines.
Application information: Application form required.
Initial approach: Letter requesting guidelines
Copies of proposal: 1
Deadline(s): Feb. 1 and Aug. 1
Board meeting date(s): Spring and fall
Final notification: For positive responses only
Write: Robert Wolf, Esq., Pres.
Officers and Directors:* Robert Wolf,* Pres.; Constance Harvey,* V.P.; Hal Harvey,* V.P.; Renee G. Schwartz,* Secy.-Treas.; Joan Harvey, Joseph Harvey, Anna Frank Loeb, Albert Solnit.
Number of staff: None.
EIN: 136086562
Recent health grants:
2150-1 All Childrens Hospital, Saint Petersburg, FL, $30,000. For University of South Florida Doctor Day. 1990.
2150-2 Howard University, School of Medicine, DC, $15,000. 1990.
2150-3 Mental Health Law Project, NYC, NY, $10,000. 1990.
2150-4 Planned Parenthood of New York City, NYC, NY, $25,000. 1990.
2150-5 Western New England Institute for Psychoanalysis, New Haven, CT, $10,000. 1990.

2151
Samuel I. Newhouse Foundation, Inc. ▼

c/o Paul Scherer & Co.
330 Madison Ave.
New York 10017

Incorporated in 1945 in NY.
Donor(s): Samuel I. Newhouse,‡ Mitzi E. Newhouse.‡
Foundation type: Independent

Financial data (yr. ended 10/31/90): Assets, $60,794,674 (M); expenditures, $6,126,937; qualifying distributions, $6,075,605, including $6,075,605 for 422 grants (high: $321,500; low: $100; average: $1,000-$10,000).
Purpose and activities: Establishment of Newhouse Communications Center at Syracuse University for education and research in mass communications; giving for community funds, hospitals, Jewish welfare funds, higher and secondary education, music and the arts, and youth agencies; support also for journalism associations.
Fields of interest: Community funds, hospitals, Jewish welfare, higher education, secondary education, music, arts, youth, media and communications, journalism.
Limitations: No grants to individuals.
Application information: Contributes only to pre-selected organizations. Applications not accepted.
Officers and Directors:* Samuel I. Newhouse, Jr.,* Pres. and Treas.; Donald E. Newhouse,* V.P. and Secy.; Richard E. Diamond.
Number of staff: None.
EIN: 116006296
Recent health grants:
2151-1 American Cancer Society, NYC, NY, $10,450. 1990.
2151-2 Bronson Health Foundation, Kalamazoo, MI, $10,000. 1990.
2151-3 Childrens Oncology and Family Services of Western Michigan, Grand Rapids, MI, $25,000. 1990.
2151-4 Columbia University, NYC, NY, $10,000. For urological research fund. 1990.
2151-5 Cornell University Medical College, NYC, NY, $20,000. For Richard T. Silver Endowment Fund. 1990.
2151-6 Crouse Irving Memorial Foundation, Syracuse, NY, $100,000. 1990.
2151-7 Hebrew Home for the Aged, Riverdale, NY, $10,000. 1990.
2151-8 Memorial Sloan-Kettering Cancer Center, NYC, NY, $100,000. 1990.
2151-9 Mercy Respite Care Corporation, Grand Rapids, MI, $10,000. 1990.
2151-10 Rosenfeld Heart Foundation, NYC, NY, $50,500. 1990.
2151-11 United Jewish Appeal, NYC, NY, $200,000. For capital campaign for Mount Sinai Medical Center. 1990.

2152
Jerome A. and Estelle R. Newman Assistance Fund, Inc.
925 Westchester Ave., Suite 308
White Plains 10604-3507   (914) 993-0777

Incorporated in 1954 in NY.
Donor(s): Howard A. Newman, Jerome A. Newman.‡
Foundation type: Independent
Financial data (yr. ended 06/30/91): Assets, $7,923,391 (M); expenditures, $589,488; qualifying distributions, $554,500, including $554,500 for 21 grants (high: $150,000; low: $500; average: $250-$15,000).
Purpose and activities: Giving primarily to Jewish education and welfare organizations, including a guild for the blind; support also for higher and other education and hospitals.

Fields of interest: Jewish welfare, handicapped, higher education, education, hospitals.
Limitations: Giving primarily in NY. No loans or grants to individuals.
Application information:
    Initial approach: Letter
    Deadline(s): None
    Board meeting date(s): Sept.
    Final notification: Varies
    Write: Howard A. Newman, Chair.
Officers and Directors:* Howard A. Newman,* Chair.; William C. Newman,* Pres.; Patricia Nanon,* V.P.; Elizabeth L. Newman,* V.P.; Robert H. Haines,* Secy.; Michael Greenberg, Treas.; Andrew H. Levy, Victoria Woolner Samuels, William C. Scott.
Number of staff: None.
EIN: 136096241

2153
Nichols Foundation, Inc.
630 Fifth Ave., Rm. 1964
New York 10111   (212) 581-1160

Incorporated in 1923 in NY.
Donor(s): Members of the Nichols family.
Foundation type: Independent
Financial data (yr. ended 01/31/91): Assets, $8,574,029 (M); gifts received, $20,000; expenditures, $738,500; qualifying distributions, $607,127, including $556,105 for 63 grants (high: $40,000; low: $75).
Fields of interest: Higher education, secondary education, chemistry, biological sciences, medical sciences, cancer, hospitals, child welfare, youth, social services, environment, conservation.
Types of support: Research, matching funds, continuing support, annual campaigns, building funds, equipment, endowment funds, scholarship funds, fellowships.
Limitations: Giving primarily in the New York, NY, metropolitan area. No grants to individuals; no loans.
Application information: Application form not required.
    Initial approach: Letter
    Copies of proposal: 1
    Deadline(s): Submit proposal preferably in Apr. or Oct.; deadlines Apr. 30 and Oct. 31
    Board meeting date(s): June and Jan.
    Final notification: 4 months to 1 year
    Write: Peter C. Coxhead, Pres.
Officers and Directors:* Peter C. Coxhead,* Pres.; David H. Nichols,* V.P.; C. Walter Nichols III,* Treas.; Ralph N. Coxhead, Kathleen C. Moseley, Joan N. Rizzo.
Number of staff: 1 full-time professional.
EIN: 136400615

2154
Edward John Noble Foundation, Inc. ▼
32 East 57th St.
New York 10022   (212) 759-4212
Business office address: P.O. Box 162, Washington Depot, CT 06794

Trust established in 1940 in CT; incorporated in 1982.
Donor(s): Edward John Noble.‡
Foundation type: Independent

Financial data (yr. ended 12/31/90): Assets, $94,943,112 (M); expenditures, $8,283,131; qualifying distributions, $8,283,131, including $7,708,570 for 71 grants (high: $600,000; low: $250; average: $5,000-$50,000).
Purpose and activities: Grants to major cultural organizations in New York City, especially for their educational programs. Selected projects concerned with conservation and ecology primarily related to activities on an island off the coast of GA. Supports private college and university environmental studies programs in the Northeast and programs to improve educational opportunity for gifted and talented disadvantaged children in New York City. Programs in health education efforts related to family planning and the problems of overpopulation.
Fields of interest: Arts, music, conservation, environment, ecology, family planning, education.
Types of support: Continuing support, matching funds, general purposes, endowment funds, special projects.
Limitations: Giving primarily in the New York, NY, metropolitan area for arts organizations and their educational programs; St. Catherine's Island, GA, and the eastern states for conservation projects and population control; and the Northeast for private colleges and universities. No grants to individuals, or for publications, building funds, equipment, television, films, or performances; no loans.
Publications: Biennial report (including application guidelines).
Application information: Application form not required.
    Initial approach: Letter or proposal
    Copies of proposal: 1
    Deadline(s): None
    Board meeting date(s): Dec.
    Final notification: 3 months
    Write: June Noble Larkin, Chair.
Officers and Directors:* June Noble Larkin,* Chair. and Pres.; Shirley M. Crowell,* Secy.; E.J. Noble Smith,* Treas. and Exec. Dir.; Nancy K. Breslin, Mimi Coleman, Robert G. Goelet, Marion E. Hawley, Frank Y. Larkin, Howard Phipps, Jr., Frank P. Piskor, David Smith, Carroll L. Wainwright, Jr.
Number of staff: 3 full-time professional; 2 full-time support.
EIN: 061055586
Recent health grants:
2154-1 Canton-Potsdam Hospital, Potsdam, NY, $10,000. For general support of Edward John Noble Guild which raises funds for hospital. 1991.
2154-2 Center for Population Options, DC, $15,000. For continuation of Partnership Program. 1991.
2154-3 Greenwich Hospital Association, Greenwich, CT, $25,000. For Noble Lecture Fund and education for health care providers. 1991.
2154-4 International Center for Integrative Studies, The Door - A Center of Alternatives, NYC, NY, $40,000. For Sexual Health and Awareness Program. 1991.
2154-5 Inwood House, NYC, NY, $20,000. For general support of community outreach program. 1991.
2154-6 National Family Planning and Reproductive Health Association, DC, $20,000. For general support. 1991.

2154-7 North Country Childrens Clinic, Watertown, NY, $10,000. For start-up funds to establish development office. 1991.

2154-8 Phillips Academy, Andover, MA, $10,000. For MS2 (Math and Sciences for Minority Students) Program. 1991.

2154-9 Planned Parenthood League of Connecticut, New Haven, CT, $15,000. For general support. 1991.

2154-10 Planned Parenthood of New York City, NYC, NY, $75,000. For Hub Center located in South Bronx. 1991.

2154-11 Population Council, NYC, NY, $50,000. For contraceptive research. 1991.

2154-12 Research Foundation of the State University of New York, Albany, NY, $50,000. For expanded rural practice-based training for medical students. 1991.

2154-13 Vocational Foundation, NYC, NY, $20,000. Toward salary of full-time health educator. 1991.

2154-14 Washington Ambulance Association, Washington, CT, $10,000. For general support. 1991.

2154-15 Worcester Foundation for Experimental Biology, Shrewsbury, MA, $84,000. Toward contraceptive research for males. 1991.

2154-16 Zero Population Growth, DC, $20,000. For Population Education Program. 1991.

2155
Norcross Wildlife Foundation, Inc.
P.O. Box 0414, Planetarium Station
New York 10024-0414   (212) 362-4831
FAX: (212) 362-4783

Established in 1964 in NY.
Donor(s): Arthur D. Norcross,‡ June Norcross Webster.‡
Foundation type: Independent
Financial data (yr. ended 12/31/90): Assets, $33,455,686 (M); expenditures, $4,250,932; qualifying distributions, $1,661,911, including $882,085 for 79 grants (high: $65,000; low: $50) and $633,726 for foundation-administered programs.
Purpose and activities: Support for social services, conservation, environmental and wildlife organizations, community development, civic affairs, and historical preservation; support also for health organizations, rehabilitation programs, assistance for the handicapped, drug abuse programs, education, including early childhood and elementary education, aid for minority students, youth, child welfare and development, Native Americans, and media and communications.
Fields of interest: Social services, conservation, environment, ecology, wildlife, civic affairs, health, education, elementary education, youth, media and communications.
Types of support: Building funds, publications, seed money, capital campaigns, land acquisition, renovation projects, special projects, equipment.
Limitations: Giving primarily in the Northeast, but not restricted.
Publications: Application guidelines.
Application information: Express mail applications not encouraged. Application form not required.
   Initial approach: Letter requesting guidelines
   Copies of proposal: 11

   Deadline(s): Aug. 15
   Board meeting date(s): Varies
   Final notification: Oct. 30
   Write: Richard S. Reagan, Pres.
Officers and Directors:* Richard S. Reagan,* Pres. and Treas.; Ethel Stella,* Exec. V.P.; Fred C. Anderson,* Secy.; Warren Balgooyen, Jos. A. Catalano, Arthur Douglass, Edward Gallagher, Arthur D. Norcross, Jr., Anthony Schoendorf.
Number of staff: 2 full-time professional.
EIN: 132041622

2156
North American Reassurance Corporate Giving Program
237 Park Ave.
New York 10017   (212) 907-8000

Purpose and activities: Supports civic programs, cultural institutes, education, medical research, minority programs, urban affairs, and welfare programs.
Fields of interest: Civic affairs, cultural programs, education, medical research, minorities, urban affairs, welfare.
Application information: Giving has been allocated for 1991.
   Initial approach: Letter
   Write: Michel Sales, Pres. and C.E.O.

2157
Northern Chautauqua Community Foundation, Inc.
212 Lake Shore Dr. West
Dunkirk 14048   (716) 366-4892

Incorporated in 1986 in NY.
Foundation type: Community
Financial data (yr. ended 12/31/91): Assets, $2,346,366 (M); gifts received, $151,553; expenditures, $130,718; qualifying distributions, $91,325, including $91,325 for grants (average: $500-$5,000).
Purpose and activities: Primary areas of interest include education, libraries, family services, community funds, cultural programs, and other general charitable activities.
Fields of interest: Community development, community funds, environment, arts, cultural programs, hospitals, family services, aged, higher education, education, libraries, general charitable giving.
Types of support: Matching funds, scholarship funds, general purposes, special projects.
Limitations: Giving limited to northern Chautauqua County, NY. No support for religious organizations. No grants to individuals (except for designated scholarship funds), or for capital campaigns, general operating budgets, publication of books, conferences, or annual fundraising campaigns.
Publications: Annual report (including application guidelines), application guidelines.
Application information: Application form required.
   Initial approach: Letter or telephone
   Copies of proposal: 4
   Deadline(s): 30 days prior to grants committee meetings
   Board meeting date(s): Quarterly
   Final notification: 10 days following meetings

   Write: David J. Doino, Exec. Dir.
Officers and Directors:* Rocco R. Doino,* Pres.; Thomas Reed,* V.P.; Ann Manly,* Secy.; Andrew W. Dorn, Jr.,* Treas.; David J. Doino, Exec. Dir.; James F. Carpenter, Maxine Cole, Richard S. Johnson, John D. Koch, Donald A. MacPhee, Douglas A. Newman, Horace Pantano, Perry F. Reininga, Joseph J. Ricotta, George B. Weaver, Jr., Thomas K. Webb, Jr., William Wells, H.K. Williams III.
Number of staff: 1 part-time professional; 1 part-time support.
EIN: 161271663

2158
Northern New York Community Foundation, Inc.
(Formerly Watertown Foundation, Inc.)
120 Washington St.
Watertown 13601   (315) 782-7110

Incorporated in 1929 in NY.
Foundation type: Community
Financial data (yr. ended 12/31/91): Assets, $3,613,563 (M); gifts received, $149,483; expenditures, $886,604; qualifying distributions, $716,835, including $464,411 for 48 grants (high: $76,985; low: $334) and $252,424 for 283 grants to individuals (high: $2,700; low: $500).
Purpose and activities: To promote charitable, educational, cultural, recreational, and health programs through grants to community organizations and agencies and a student scholarship program.
Fields of interest: Community funds, education, cultural programs, recreation, health.
Types of support: Annual campaigns, seed money, building funds, equipment, land acquisition, matching funds, student aid, special projects, research, publications, conferences and seminars, renovation projects, capital campaigns.
Limitations: Giving limited to Jefferson and Lewis counties, NY. No grants for endowment funds or deficit financing.
Publications: Annual report, newsletter.
Application information: Application form not required.
   Initial approach: Letter
   Copies of proposal: 1
   Deadline(s): Feb. 1, May 1, Aug. 1, and Nov. 1
   Board meeting date(s): Mar., June, Sept., and Dec.
   Final notification: 1 to 2 months
   Write: Alex C. Velto, Exec. Dir.
Officers and Directors:* Everett G. Foster,* Pres.; Anderson Wise,* V.P.; Floyd J. Chandler,* Secy.-Treas.; Alex C. Velto, Exec. Dir.; Norman R. Ahlheim, John Doldo, Jr., Barbara D. Hanrahan, Lee T. Hirschey, Robert G. Horr, Jr., Jane N. Lormore, James L. O'Donnell, Richard E. Smith, P. Owen Willaman, Grace A. Wright.
Number of staff: 1 full-time professional; 1 part-time professional; 2 full-time support.
EIN: 156020989
Recent health grants:

2158-1 House of the Good Samaritan, Watertown, NY, $25,000. Toward Cancer Treatment Center. 1990.

2158-2 North Country Childrens Clinic, Watertown, NY, $16,000. For new development office. 1990.

2158-3 Visiting Nurse Association, Watertown, NY, $48,178. For scholarships in nursing and related health fields. 1990.

2159
Norwood Foundation, Inc.
c/o Bessemer Trust Co.
630 Fifth Ave.
New York 10111
Mailing address: P.O. Box 238, East Norwich, NY 11732; Tel.: (516) 626-0288

Incorporated in 1952 in NY.
Donor(s): Thomas M. Bancroft,‡ Edith W. Bancroft.‡
Foundation type: Independent
Financial data (yr. ended 12/31/91): Assets, $2,240,011 (M); expenditures, $116,379; qualifying distributions, $94,500, including $94,500 for 20 grants (high: $25,000; low: $1,000; average: $1,000-$25,000).
Fields of interest: Education, secondary education, hospitals, health associations, drug abuse, museums, Protestant giving.
Types of support: Operating budgets, continuing support, annual campaigns, seed money, building funds, equipment, endowment funds, scholarship funds, deficit financing, capital campaigns.
Limitations: Giving primarily in NY. No grants to individuals, or for emergency funds, exchange programs, land acquisition, matching gifts, fellowships, professorships, internships, special projects, research, publications, or conferences; no loans.
Application information: Limited available funding. Application form not required.
  Initial approach: Letter
  Deadline(s): None
Officer: Thomas M. Bancroft, Jr., Pres. and Treas.
Number of staff: None.
EIN: 136111530

2160
Jessie Smith Noyes Foundation, Inc. ▼
16 East 34th St.
New York 10016   (212) 684-6577

Incorporated in 1947 in NY.
Donor(s): Charles F. Noyes.‡
Foundation type: Independent
Financial data (yr. ended 12/31/91): Assets, $63,991,097 (M); expenditures, $3,956,988; qualifying distributions, $3,316,289, including $3,316,289 for 150 grants (high: $55,000; low: $1,000; average: $10,000-$30,000).
Purpose and activities: Basic goal is to prevent irreversible damage to the natural systems upon which all life depends through grants in the following areas: 1) tropical ecology, with special interest in preventing the destruction of tropical ecosystems, in particular, tropical forests in the Amazonian region of Latin America; 2) sustainable agriculture promoting long-term sustainability in the U.S., particularly the South, and in Latin America; 3) water and toxics, especially the protection of groundwater in the U.S.; and 4) reproductive rights in the U.S. and Latin America. Grants, which are to institutions only, emphasize the strengthening of individuals and institutions committed to sustaining natural systems and a sustainable society.

Fields of interest: Environment, family planning, agriculture, ecology, Latin America, conservation, women.
Types of support: Continuing support, special projects, seed money.
Limitations: Giving primarily in southeast, southcentral and southwestern U.S.; Amazonian region of Latin America. No grants to individuals, or for endowment funds, capital construction funds, land acquisition, or general fundraising drives; generally no support for conferences, research, or media; no loans.
Publications: Annual report (including application guidelines), program policy statement, application guidelines.
Application information: Applications not accepted for discretionary or founder-designated funds. Application form required.
  Initial approach: 1- or 2-page letter of inquiry, including budget estimate, timetable, and other potential sources of support; if project is of interest, full proposal will be requested
  Copies of proposal: 1
  Deadline(s): Letters of inquiry will be received at any time during the year; proposals will usually be due 1 month after being requested
  Board meeting date(s): Jan., May, and Oct.
  Final notification: Within 6 weeks of receipt of letters; within 2 weeks of board meetings for final proposals
  Write: Stephen Viederman, Pres.
Officers and Directors:* Nicholas Jacangelo,* Chair.; Dorothy E. Muma,* Vice-Chair.; Timothy Raphael,* Vice-Chair.; Stephen Viederman,* Pres.; Nicholas Jacangelo,* Secy.-Treas.; Dorothy Anderson, Catherine Bedell, John Carroll, Donna Chavis, Edith N. Muma, David Orr, Emily Smith, Edward Tasch, Greg Watson.
Number of staff: 2 full-time professional; 2 part-time professional; 2 full-time support; 1 part-time support.
EIN: 135600408
Recent health grants:
2160-1 Council on the Concerns of Women Physicians, DC, $20,000. To increase knowledge among reproductive health care providers on reproductive health issues from Afro-American perspective and to formulate medical strategies to address public health crisis. 1991.
2160-2 Grupo CURUMIN, Boa Vista, Brazil, $10,100. To improve women's reproductive health care in Brazil through development of communications systems. 1991.
2160-3 International Projects Assistance Services, Carrboro, NC, $18,257. To improve reproductive health care for women by making manual vacuum aspiration services available at hospitals in Mexico. 1991.
2160-4 Madre, NYC, NY, $50,000. To ensure that access to full range of reproductive services, including abortion, is part of any package of national health care. 1991.
2160-5 National Black Womens Health Project, Atlanta, GA, $45,000. To increase awareness of African-Americans about reproductive rights issues and to mobilizing them for action. 1991.
2160-6 National Council of Negro Women, DC, $50,000. To build informed constituency to advocate for reproductive rights of African-American women. 1991.
2160-7 National Organization for Women (NOW) Legal Defense and Education Fund,

NYC, NY, $40,000. To protect reproductive freedom against nationwide assaults by Operation Rescue and other state and local adversaries. 1991.
2160-8 National Womens Law Center, DC, $45,000. To provide public policy analysis at federal and state level, assistance to national and local womens groups and public education on reproductive rights issues. 1991.

2161
A. Lindsay and Olive B. O'Connor Foundation
P.O. Box D
Hobart 13788   (607) 538-9248

Trust established in 1965 in NY.
Donor(s): Olive B. O'Connor.‡
Foundation type: Independent
Financial data (yr. ended 12/31/91): Assets, $40,859,615 (M); expenditures, $1,563,405; qualifying distributions, $1,385,890, including $1,208,938 for 120 grants (high: $400,000; low: $102; average: $1,000-$20,000).
Purpose and activities: Emphasis on "quality of life," including hospitals, libraries, community centers, higher education, nursing and other vocational education, child development and youth agencies, religious organizations, museums, and historic restoration; support also for civic affairs and town, village, and environmental conservation and improvement.
Fields of interest: Hospitals, libraries, higher education, child development, denominational giving, historic preservation, community development, civic affairs, environment, conservation.
Types of support: General purposes, continuing support, annual campaigns, seed money, emergency funds, building funds, equipment, land acquisition, endowment funds, special projects, research, publications, conferences and seminars, scholarship funds, matching funds, loans, technical assistance, program-related investments, renovation projects.
Limitations: Giving primarily in Delaware County, NY, and contiguous rural counties in upstate NY. No grants to individuals, or for operating budgets or deficit financing.
Publications: Program policy statement.
Application information: Limited funding available until 1992. Application form required.
  Initial approach: Letter
  Copies of proposal: 1
  Deadline(s): Apr. 1 and Sept. 1
  Board meeting date(s): May or June and Sept. or Oct.; committee meets monthly to consider grants under $10,000
  Final notification: 1 week to 10 days after semiannual meeting
  Write: Donald F. Bishop II, Exec. Dir.
Officer: Donald F. Bishop II, Exec. Dir.
Advisory Committee: Robert L. Bishop II, Vice-Chair.; Robert L. Bishop, Exec. Secy.; Donald F. Bishop, Charlotte Bishop Hill, William J. Murphy, Eugene E. Peckham.
Trustee: Chase Lincoln First Bank, N.A.
Number of staff: 2 full-time professional.
EIN: 166063485

2162
Jonathan & Shirley O'Herron Foundation
c/o Lazard Freres & Co.
One Rockefeller Plaza
New York 10020-1902

Established in 1984 in NY.
Donor(s): Jonathan O'Herron, Shirley O'Herron.
Foundation type: Independent
Financial data (yr. ended 06/30/91): Assets,
$228,767 (M); gifts received, $193,166;
expenditures, $250,722; qualifying distributions,
$247,885, including $245,800 for 53 grants
(high: $48,000; low: $500).
Purpose and activities: Giving primarily for
Catholic churches, secondary and higher
education; support also for hospitals and social
services.
Fields of interest: Catholic giving, secondary
education, higher education, social services,
hospitals.
Limitations: Giving primarily in MA, CT, VT, and
NY. No grants to individuals.
Application information: Application form not
required.
  Initial approach: Letter
  Deadline(s): None
  Write: Jonathan O'Herron, Pres.
Officers: Jonathan O'Herron, Pres.; Shirley
O'Herron, V.P.; Thomas F.X. Mullarkey,
Secy.-Treas.
EIN: 133244207

2163
The O'Sullivan Children Foundation, Inc.
c/o Kevin P. O'Sullivan
355 Post Ave.
Westbury 11590

Established in 1981.
Donor(s): Kevin P. O'Sullivan, Carole O'Sullivan.
Foundation type: Independent
Financial data (yr. ended 09/30/91): Assets,
$5,881,840 (M); gifts received, $201,400;
expenditures, $751,925; qualifying distributions,
$740,519, including $516,681 for 83 grants
(high: $125,000; low: $25).
Purpose and activities: Giving primarily for
Catholic organizations, including churches and a
school; support also for hospitals and health
associations.
Fields of interest: Catholic giving, religious
schools, health services, hospitals, medical
research, handicapped, child welfare, community
funds, general charitable giving.
Types of support: Capital campaigns, endowment
funds.
Limitations: Giving primarily in the greater
metropolitan New York, NY, area, with some
emphasis on Long Island. No grants to individuals.
Application information: Contributes only to
pre-selected organizations. Applications not
accepted.
Officers and Directors:* Kevin P. O'Sullivan,*
Pres.; Carole O'Sullivan,* V.P. and Treas.; Neil M.
Delman,* Secy.
Number of staff: 1 full-time professional.
EIN: 133126389

2164
Theresa and Edward O'Toole Foundation
c/o The Bank of New York, Trust Dept.
48 Wall St., 4th Fl.
New York 10286   (212) 495-1183
Application address: 99 Kinderkamack Rd.,
Suite 208, Westwood, NJ 07675

Established in 1971.
Donor(s): Theresa O'Toole.‡
Foundation type: Independent
Financial data (yr. ended 06/30/91): Assets,
$20,399,632 (M); expenditures, $1,139,108;
qualifying distributions, $1,034,789, including
$970,400 for 208 grants (high: $100,000; low:
$500).
Fields of interest: Catholic giving, Catholic
welfare, education, higher education, hospitals.
Types of support: Continuing support, annual
campaigns, emergency funds, building funds,
special projects, research, matching funds,
general purposes.
Limitations: Giving primarily in NY, NJ, and FL.
No grants to individuals, or for endowment funds,
scholarships, or fellowships; no loans.
Application information: Application form not
required.
  Initial approach: Letter
  Copies of proposal: 2
  Deadline(s): None
  Board meeting date(s): Apr. and Oct.
  Final notification: 1 month after board meeting
  Write: Chris Degheri or Katherine Floyd,
    Trustees
Trustees: Chris Degheri, The Bank of New York.
Number of staff: None.
EIN: 136350175

2165
Sylvan and Ann Oestreicher Foundation, Inc.
645 Madison Ave.
New York 10022   (212) 759-8500

Incorporated in 1948 in NY.
Donor(s): Sylvan Oestreicher.‡
Foundation type: Independent
Financial data (yr. ended 04/30/91): Assets,
$3,915,525 (M); expenditures, $182,329;
qualifying distributions, $170,318, including
$163,245 for 185 grants (high: $10,000; low:
$75).
Purpose and activities: Grants primarily for
religious welfare funds, hospitals, and higher
education; support also for the handicapped,
youth agencies, religious associations, and
cultural programs.
Fields of interest: Religious welfare, hospitals,
higher education, handicapped, youth, religion,
cultural programs.
Limitations: Giving primarily in NY.
Application information: Application form not
required.
  Deadline(s): None
  Write: Robert F. Welch, Secy.
Officers: Ann Oestreicher, Pres.; Merwin Lewis,
V.P.; Robert F. Welch, Secy.
EIN: 136085974

2166
Open Society Fund, Inc. ▼
888 Seventh Ave., 33rd Fl.
New York 10106   (212) 262-6300

Established about 1981 in NY.
Donor(s): George Soros, Tivadar Charitable Lead
Trust.
Foundation type: Independent
Financial data (yr. ended 12/31/90): Assets,
$6,652,676 (M); gifts received, $6,009,835;
expenditures, $4,148,673; qualifying
distributions, $4,048,030, including $3,702,320
for 40 grants (high: $1,068,025; low: $1,000;
average: $5,000-$25,000) and $63,985 for 18
grants to individuals.
Purpose and activities: Grants for higher
education, including scholarships for
disadvantaged or minority students and
fellowships for scholarly research or analysis;
international studies and affairs; human rights;
and the medical sciences. Applicants must be
affiliated with an institution.
Fields of interest: Higher education,
education—minorities, disadvantaged,
international studies, international affairs, human
rights, medical sciences.
Types of support: Fellowships, scholarship funds,
student aid, research, grants to individuals.
Limitations: No loans for individuals.
Application information: Applicants will be
solicited through contacts with educational
institutions.
  Write: Susan Weber Soros, V.P., Treas., and Dir.
Officers and Directors:* George Soros,* Pres.;
Gary Gladstein, V.P. and Secy.; Susan Weber
Soros,* Exec. V.P. and Treas.; Aryeh Neier, William
D. Zabel.*
EIN: 133095822
Recent health grants:
2166-1 Community Family Planning Council,
  NYC, NY, $30,000. 1990.

2167
Orange and Rockland Utilities Corporate Giving Program
One Blue Hill Plaza
Pearl River 10965   (914) 577-2470
Additional tel.: (914) 577-2719

Financial data (yr. ended 12/31/90): Total giving,
$354,000, including $250,000 for grants and
$104,000 for employee matching gifts.
Purpose and activities: Main emphasis on United
Way, including matching employee contributions,
hospitals, and education; giving also for fine arts,
conservation, crime and law enforcement, mental
health, and religious schools.
Fields of interest: Higher education, education,
crime and law enforcement, handicapped,
hospitals, environment, civic affairs,
education—minorities, fine arts, conservation,
education, general charitable giving, mental
health, religious schools.
Types of support: Annual campaigns, donated
equipment, employee matching gifts, equipment,
technical assistance, employee volunteer services,
in-kind gifts, special projects, use of facilities,
donated products, employee-related scholarships,
general purposes, public relations services,
scholarship funds.

Limitations: Giving limited to service territory in Rockland, Orange, and Sullivan counties, NY; Bergen County, NJ; and Pike County, PA.
Publications: Corporate report.
Application information: Office of V.P., Corporate Policy and External Affairs handles contributions.
 Initial approach: Send requests to headquarters
 Write: Diana Hess-Porath, Mgr., Public Affairs
Administrators: Diana Hess-Porath, Mgr., Public Affairs; Linda Winikow, V.P.
Number of staff: 1 full-time support.

2168
The Orentreich Family Foundation
909 Fifth Ave.
New York 10021

Established in 1986 in NY.
Donor(s): Orentreich Medical Group, David Orentreich, Norman Orentreich.
Foundation type: Independent
Financial data (yr. ended 09/30/91): Assets, $5,457,887 (M); gifts received, $10,000; expenditures, $257,486; qualifying distributions, $245,108, including $242,289 for grants (high: $140,765).
Fields of interest: Hospitals, health associations, medical research, Jewish giving.
Limitations: Giving primarily in New York, NY. No grants to individuals.
Application information: Contributes only to pre-selected organzations. Applications not accepted.
Officers and Trustees:* N. Orentreich,* Pres.; D. Orentreich,* Treas.
EIN: 136879797

2169
Edward B. Osborn Charitable Trust
c/o U.S. Trust Co. of New York
114 West 47th St.
New York 10036-1532   (212) 852-1000

Trust established in 1961 in NY.
Donor(s): Edward B. Osborn.
Foundation type: Independent
Financial data (yr. ended 10/31/91): Assets, $4,135,933 (M); expenditures, $250,220; qualifying distributions, $235,212, including $220,525 for 45 grants (high: $22,475; low: $400).
Fields of interest: Hospitals, medical research, cultural programs, higher education.
Limitations: Giving primarily in NY and FL.
Application information: Application form not required.
 Deadline(s): None
Trustee: U.S. Trust Co. of New York.
EIN: 136071296

2170
OSG Foundation
1114 Ave. of the Americas, 12th Fl.
New York 10036

Donor(s): Overseas Shipholding Group, Inc., Glander International, Inc.
Foundation type: Company-sponsored
Financial data (yr. ended 12/31/91): Assets, $313,506 (M); gifts received, $1,042,270;

expenditures, $933,326; qualifying distributions, $933,451, including $932,971 for 164 grants (high: $125,000; low: $20).
Fields of interest: Jewish welfare, Jewish giving, hospitals, health associations, education, arts.
Limitations: Giving primarily in NY. No grants to individuals.
Application information: Contributes only to pre-selected organizations. Applications not accepted.
Officers and Directors:* Raphael Recanati,* Pres.; Michael A. Recanati,* V.P. and Secy.-Treas.; Morton P. Hyman,* V.P.; Ran Hettena.
EIN: 133099337

2171
The Overbrook Foundation ▼
521 Fifth Ave., Rm. 1501
New York 10175   (212) 661-8710

Incorporated in 1948 in NY.
Donor(s): Frank Altschul,‡ Helen G. Altschul,‡ Arthur G. Altschul, Margaret A. Lang.
Foundation type: Independent
Financial data (yr. ended 12/31/90): Assets, $60,639,560 (M); expenditures, $3,404,665; qualifying distributions, $2,916,967, including $2,839,466 for 182 grants (high: $222,900; low: $250; average: $1,000-$10,000).
Purpose and activities: Giving primarily for conservation and environment; grants also for arts and cultural programs, child welfare, civil rights, community funds, elementary, secondary, and higher education, hospitals, international affairs, medical research, museums, and social services.
Fields of interest: Arts, cultural programs, museums, child welfare, civil rights, community funds, conservation, environment, elementary education, secondary education, higher education, hospitals, medical research, international affairs, social services.
Types of support: General purposes.
Limitations: Giving primarily in NY and CT. No grants to individuals.
Application information: Application form not required.
 Initial approach: Letter
 Deadline(s): None
 Board meeting date(s): Usually in Apr. and Nov.
 Final notification: Within 3 months
 Write: M. Sheila McGoldrick
Officers and Directors:* Arthur G. Altschul,* Pres. and Treas.; Edith A. Graham,* V.P.; Margaret A. Lang,* V.P.; Diana L. Altschul,* Secy.; Stephen F. Altschul, Robert C. Graham, Jr., Frances L. Labaree.
Number of staff: None.
EIN: 136088860
Recent health grants:
 2171-1 AIDS Resource Center, NYC, NY, $25,000. 1990.
 2171-2 Boston City Hospital, Boston, MA, $10,000. 1990.
 2171-3 Burke Rehabilitation Center, White Plains, NY, $75,166. 1990.
 2171-4 Conservation International Foundation, DC, $50,000. 1990.
 2171-5 Gay Mens Health Crisis (GMHC), NYC, NY, $25,000. 1990.
 2171-6 Hole in the Wall Gang Camp Fund, Westport, CT, $10,000. 1990.

 2171-7 Marthas Vineyard Hospital Foundation, Oak Bluffs, MA, $10,000. 1990.
 2171-8 Planned Parenthood of New York City, NYC, NY, $100,000. 1990.
 2171-9 Planned Parenthood of New York City, NYC, NY, $50,000. 1990.
 2171-10 Stamford Hospital, Stamford, CT, $45,000. 1990.
 2171-11 United States Cancer Research Council, Bethesda, MD, $10,000. 1990.
 2171-12 Village Nursing Home, NYC, NY, $10,000. 1990.
 2171-13 Visiting Nurse Service of New York, NYC, NY, $15,000. 1990.

2172
PaineWebber Foundation
1285 Ave. of the Americas
New York 10019   (212) 713-4545

Established in 1983 in NY.
Donor(s): PaineWebber, Inc.
Foundation type: Company-sponsored
Financial data (yr. ended 12/31/90): Assets, $5,456,677 (M); expenditures, $283,449; qualifying distributions, $283,449, including $207,000 for 40 grants (high: $50,000; low: $1,000).
Fields of interest: Hospitals, libraries, hunger, welfare, religious welfare.
Limitations: Giving primarily in NY. No grants to individuals.
Application information:
 Initial approach: Letter
 Deadline(s): Dec. 1
 Write: Monika Dillon, Trustee
Trustees: Monika Dillon, Paul Guenther, Donald B. Marron.
EIN: 046032804

2173
William S. Paley Foundation, Inc.
One East 53rd St.. Rm. 1400
New York 10022   (212) 888-2520

Incorporated in 1936 in NY.
Donor(s): William S. Paley.‡
Foundation type: Independent
Financial data (yr. ended 12/31/90): Assets, $66,444,188 (M); gifts received, $47,615,299; expenditures, $4,147,290; qualifying distributions, $3,628,921, including $3,620,150 for 23 grants (high: $2,000,000; low: $150).
Purpose and activities: Emphasis on a museum of broadcasting, education, cultural programs, and health services and hospitals.
Fields of interest: Education, cultural programs, libraries, museums, health services, hospitals.
Types of support: General purposes, annual campaigns, continuing support.
Limitations: Giving primarily in New York, NY. No grants to individuals.
Application information: Application form not required.
 Initial approach: Proposal
 Copies of proposal: 1
 Deadline(s): None
 Board meeting date(s): 3rd Wednesday in Oct.
 Write: Patrick S. Gallagher, Exec. Dir.
Officers and Directors:* Henry A. Kissinger,* Chair.; Sidney W. Harl,* V.P. and Treas.; John S.

Minary,* V.P.; Daniel L. Mosley,* Secy.; Patrick S. Gallagher,* Exec. Dir.; George J. Gillespie III, Arthur L. Liman, Kate C. Paley, William C. Paley.
Number of staff: None.
EIN: 136085929

2174
The Palisades Educational Foundation, Inc.
(Formerly The Pren-Hall Foundation, Inc.)
c/o Gibney, Anthony & Flaherty
665 Fifth Ave., 2nd Fl.
New York 10022   (201) 461-0170
Application address: 2050 Center Ave., Suite 200, Fort Lee, NJ 07024

Incorporated in 1949 in DE.
Donor(s): Prentice-Hall, Inc.
Foundation type: Independent
Financial data (yr. ended 12/31/90): Assets, $4,640,154 (M); expenditures, $444,006; qualifying distributions, $440,017, including $391,000 for 27 grants (high: $80,000; low: $2,000).
Purpose and activities: Support for higher and secondary education, health and hospitals, community funds, church support and church-related organizations, social services, and conservation.
Fields of interest: Education, higher education, secondary education, health, hospitals, medical research, community funds, religion, social services, conservation.
Types of support: Continuing support, operating budgets, scholarship funds, special projects, general purposes, professorships, research, seed money, annual campaigns.
Limitations: Giving primarily in NY, NJ, and CT. No grants to individuals, or for fellowships or pledges; no loans.
Application information: Grants limited almost entirely to organizations associated with interests of present or former directors.
  Initial approach: Letter
  Deadline(s): None
  Board meeting date(s): Nov. or Dec.
  Write: Ralph F. Anthony, Pres.
Officers and Trustees:* Ralph F. Anthony,* Pres.; Donald A. Schaefer,* V.P.; Frederick W. Anthony,* Secy.; Gerald J. Dunworth, Jr.,* Treas.; Colin Gunn.
Number of staff: None.
EIN: 516015053

2175
Moses L. Parshelsky Foundation
26 Court St., Rm. 904
Brooklyn 11242   (718) 875-8883

Trust established in 1949 in NY.
Donor(s): Moses L. Parshelsky.‡
Foundation type: Independent
Financial data (yr. ended 12/31/91): Assets, $5,581,088 (M); expenditures, $383,556; qualifying distributions, $308,919, including $278,350 for 60 grants (high: $40,000; low: $100; average: $100-$40,000).
Purpose and activities: Emphasis on the aged, the handicapped, and hospitals; support also for higher and secondary education, temple support and religious activities, youth agencies, mental health, and Jewish welfare funds.

Fields of interest: Hospitals, higher education, secondary education, Jewish giving, aged, handicapped, youth, mental health, Jewish welfare.
Limitations: Giving primarily in Brooklyn and Queens, NY. No grants to individuals, or for building or endowment funds, or operating budgets.
Application information: Application form not required.
  Initial approach: Letter
  Copies of proposal: 1
  Deadline(s): May 31
  Board meeting date(s): Monthly
  Write: Tony B. Berk, Trustee
Trustees: Tony B. Berk, Josephine B. Krinsky, Robert D. Krinsky.
Number of staff: 1 part-time professional.
EIN: 111848260

2176
Patrina Foundation
P.O. Box 777
Manhasset 11030

Established in 1990 in NY.
Donor(s): Lorinda P. de Roulet.
Foundation type: Independent
Financial data (yr. ended 12/31/91): Assets, $5,761,516 (M); expenditures, $54,129; qualifying distributions, $14,663.
Purpose and activities: Giving with emphasis on secondary and higher education, particularly women's, cultural programs, and special interests of the donor.
Fields of interest: Arts, education—early childhood, family planning, women, general charitable giving.
Types of support: Scholarship funds, special projects.
Limitations: Giving primarily in the Northeast. No grants to individuals.
Application information: Application form not required.
  Initial approach: Proposal
  Copies of proposal: 6
  Deadline(s): Mar. 1 and Oct. 1
  Board meeting date(s): Apr. and Nov.
  Write: Mary Jo McLoughlin, Exec. Dir.
Officers and Directors:* Lorinda P. de Roulet, Pres.; Sandra de Roulet,* V.P. and Secy.; Daniel C. de Roulet,* Treas.; Elizabeth Rainoff.
Number of staff: 1 part-time professional.
EIN: 113035018

2177
The Peierls Foundation, Inc.
c/o Bankers Trust Co.
P.O. Box 1297, Church St. Station
New York 10008
Application address: 73 South Holman Way, Golden, CO 80401

Incorporated in 1956 in NY.
Donor(s): Edgar S. Peierls,‡ Ethel F. Peierls.
Foundation type: Independent
Financial data (yr. ended 10/31/90): Assets, $3,687,206 (M); gifts received, $6,700; expenditures, $252,570; qualifying distributions, $232,500, including $232,500 for 31 grants (high: $33,000; low: $2,400).

Fields of interest: Youth, social services, handicapped, minorities, higher education, medical research, family planning.
Limitations: No grants to individuals.
Application information: Application form not required.
  Deadline(s): None
  Final notification: Positive responses only
  Write: E.J. Peierls, Pres.
Officers: E.J. Peierls, Pres.; Brian Eliot Peierls, V.P. and Treas.; Ethel F. Peierls, Secy.
EIN: 136082503

2178
Albert Penick Fund
c/o Chase Manhattan Bank, N.A.
1211 Ave. of the Americas
New York 10036

Trust established in 1951 in NY.
Donor(s): A.D. Penick,‡ Mrs. Albert D. Penick.
Foundation type: Independent
Financial data (yr. ended 12/31/91): Assets, $2,088,111 (M); expenditures, $153,986; qualifying distributions, $137,810, including $126,500 for 30 grants (high: $50,000; low: $1,000).
Fields of interest: Higher education, secondary education, nursing, health associations, hospitals, cultural programs, animal welfare, conservation.
Limitations: Giving primarily in NY, CT, and MA.
Application information: Application form not required.
  Initial approach: Letter
  Deadline(s): None
Trustees: Nancy P. Corcoran, K. Philip Dresdner, V. Susan Penick.
EIN: 136161137

2179
PepsiCo Foundation, Inc. ▼
700 Anderson Hill Rd.
Purchase 10577   (914) 253-3153

Incorporated in 1962 in NY.
Donor(s): PepsiCo, Inc.
Foundation type: Company-sponsored
Financial data (yr. ended 12/31/90): Assets, $24,866,813 (M); gifts received, $18,000,000; expenditures, $7,469,848; qualifying distributions, $7,452,748, including $6,397,803 for 288 grants (high: $730,313; low: $35; average: $10,000-$50,000) and $1,054,926 for employee matching gifts.
Purpose and activities: Support for education, preventive medicine, the arts and other nonprofit organizations where employees are involved as volunteers.
Fields of interest: Education, higher education, education—minorities, business education, health services, economics, youth, community funds, civic affairs, cultural programs, performing arts, arts, international affairs, medical sciences.
Types of support: Employee matching gifts.
Limitations: Giving primarily in communities where operating divisions are located including Irvine, CA; Wichita, KS; Louisville, KY; Somers, NY; and Plano, TX. No grants to individuals.
Publications: Informational brochure (including application guidelines).
Application information:

Initial approach: Proposal
Deadline(s): None
Board meeting date(s): At least annually
Final notification: Within 3 months
Write: Jacqueline R. Millan, V.P., Contribs.
Officers and Directors: Donald M. Kendall,*
Chair.; Joseph F. McCann,* Pres.; Jacqueline R.
Millan, V.P., Contribs.; Douglas M. Cram, Secy.;
Claudia Morf, Treas.; D. Wayne Calloway, Robert
G. Dettmer, Roger A. Enrico, Ronald E. Harrison,
Michael H. Jordan, Steven S. Reinemund.
Number of staff: 2 full-time professional; 2
full-time support.
EIN: 136163174
Recent health grants:
2179-1 American Council on Science and
    Health, NYC, NY, $20,000. 1990.
2179-2 Duke University Medical Center,
    Durham, NC, $250,000. 1990.
2179-3 Presbyterian Hospital in the City of New
    York, NYC, NY, $10,000. 1990.
2179-4 United Hospitals Medical Center,
    Newark, NJ, $10,000. 1990.

2180
The George W. Perkins Memorial Foundation
c/o Mrs. George W. Perkins
One East 66th St.
New York 10021   (212) 879-2370
Additional tel.: (212) 879-8196

Incorporated in 1961 in NY.
Donor(s): Mrs. George W. Perkins.
Foundation type: Independent
Financial data (yr. ended 12/31/91): Assets,
$13,337,606 (M); expenditures, $586,382;
qualifying distributions, $515,785, including
$515,500 for 54 grants (high: $50,000; low:
$1,000).
Fields of interest: Higher education, secondary
education, hospitals, conservation.
Limitations: No grants to individuals.
Application information: Contributes only to
pre-selected organizations. Applications not
accepted.
    Board meeting date(s): Oct.
    Write: Helen Kartis, Secy.
Officers: Anne P. Cabot, Pres.; George W. Perkins,
Jr., V.P.; Linn M. Perkins, V.P.; Penelope P. Wilson,
V.P.; Helen Kartis, Secy.
Trustee: Arthur V. Savage.
Number of staff: 1 full-time professional.
EIN: 136085859

2181
The Pfizer Foundation, Inc.
235 East 42nd St.
New York 10017   (212) 573-3351

Incorporated in 1953 in NY.
Donor(s): Pfizer Inc.
Foundation type: Company-sponsored
Financial data (yr. ended 12/31/91): Assets,
$7,535,427 (M); gifts received, $1,500,000;
expenditures, $1,292,021; qualifying
distributions, $1,290,250, including $1,290,250
for 155 grants (high: $100,000; low: $1,000;
average: $1,000-$5,000).
Purpose and activities: Support in the following
areas: 1) Education, especially higher education,

with consideration given to educational
associations; 2) Health care, including research
and rehabilitation programs for the handicapped,
substance abuse, and hospices; 3) Civic and
community services, including programs for the
elderly, youth, women, and conservation; 4)
Culture, including the fine and performing arts,
libraries, and public broadcasting; and 5)
International affairs.
Fields of interest: Higher education, health, civic
affairs, community development, women, aged,
youth, cultural programs, libraries, international
affairs.
Types of support: Operating budgets, continuing
support, annual campaigns, seed money,
emergency funds, building funds, equipment,
matching funds, professorships, internships,
scholarship funds, fellowships, special projects,
research, publications, conferences and seminars,
capital campaigns, endowment funds, exchange
programs, technical assistance.
Limitations: Giving primarily in areas of company
operations, with emphasis on local New York City
or national organizations. No support for religious
organizations for religious purposes, veterans',
fraternal or labor organizations, non tax-exempt
foundations, or anti-business organizations. No
grants to individuals, or for deficit financing,
employee matching gifts, goodwill advertising, or
land acquisition; no loans.
Publications: Corporate giving report (including
application guidelines).
Application information: Application form not
required.
    Initial approach: Proposal
    Copies of proposal: 1
    Deadline(s): None
    Board meeting date(s): As required
    Final notification: 3 months
    Write: Wyndham Anderson, Exec. V.P.
Officers and Directors: Robert A. Wilson,* Pres.;
Wyndham Anderson,* Exec. V.P.; James R.
Gardner, V.P.; Terence J. Gallagher,* Secy.; Kevin
S. Keating,* Treas.
Number of staff: None.
EIN: 136083839
Recent health grants:
2181-1 Institute of Medicine, DC, $30,000. 1990.
2181-2 International Center for the Disabled
    (ICD), NYC, NY, $10,000. 1990.
2181-3 Partnership for a Drug Free America,
    NYC, NY, $25,000. 1990.
2181-4 Pharmaceutical Manufacturers
    Association Foundation, DC, $90,000. 1990.
2181-5 Rockefeller University, NYC, NY,
    $10,000. 1990.

2182
Pfizer Inc. Corporate Giving Program
Pfizer, Inc.
235 East 42nd St.
New York 10017   (212) 573-7578

Financial data (yr. ended 12/31/90): Total giving,
$8,775,000, including $7,475,000 for grants and
$1,300,000 for employee matching gifts.
Purpose and activities: The broad objectives of
Pfizer's corporate giving program are: to improve
educational, health, cultural, social, and other
community services, in areas of company
facilities; to make grants to educational and
research institutions, academic departments, and

programs which involve significant mutual,
intellectual, or scientific interests; and to support
selected national organizations and institutions
whose programs address social problems of
interest to Pfizer. Support for nonprofit
organizations whose programs are of interest to
the company as a whole or to the company's
particular divisions, such as pharmaceuticals,
chemicals, agriculture, materials science,
consumer and hospital products. Programs in
which Pfizer employees are active volunteers
receive special consideration; Pfizer encourages
individual employee support of health care and
social service organizations through the United
Way. Part of the contributions program focuses on
encouraging studies, analyses, and discussions of
policy issues; Pfizer seeks to recognize academic
and other institutions engaged in research,
writing, and publishing on policy issues.
Additional support for organizations engaged in
international activities, focusing on projects that
enrich the development process worldwide and
that directly relate to international public policy
concerns; also support for organizations and
institutions overseas through Pfizer International.
The company often responds to emergencies and
natural disasters with donations of medicine
and/or equipment; this assistance is generally
coordinated through established international
relief agencies.
Fields of interest: Adult education, aged, arts,
biochemistry, business education, cancer,
business, child welfare, community development,
crime and law enforcement, cultural programs,
civic affairs, child development, conservation,
delinquency, disadvantaged, drug abuse,
education—building funds, educational research,
handicapped, heart disease, hospitals,
international relief, libraries, minorities, political
science, public affairs, rehabilitation,
welfare—indigent individuals, ecology,
education—early childhood, education,
environment, general charitable giving, homeless,
international affairs, international studies, literacy,
medical education, foreign policy.
Limitations: Giving primarily in areas of company
operations; support also for national
organizations. No support for religious
organizations, fraternal, labor, or veterans'
organizations, political parties or candidates,
partisan political organizations, anti-business
organizations, or organizations related to the
business interests of Pfizer Inc. No grants to
individuals, or for goodwill advertising; no loans.
Publications: Corporate giving report (including
application guidelines), grants list.
Application information: Organizations serving
regional interests in Pfizer communities are
handled by local facility management;
organizations whose programs complement
Pfizer's business areas are handled by
headquarters staff under the auspices of the
division whose interests relate to the program;
contributions to organizations with a
broad-based, corporate-wide focus are handled
by the Corporate Contributions Committee,
which is comprised of Pfizer employees who
meet regularly to review proposals; international
contributions are handled by management in that
country. Application form not required.
    Initial approach: Proposal
    Copies of proposal: 1
    Deadline(s): None

Board meeting date(s): Monthly
Final notification: 3 months
Write: Ann M. Hardwick, Mgr., Corp. Support
Programs

2183
The Carl and Lily Pforzheimer Foundation, Inc. ▼
650 Madison Ave., 23rd Fl.
New York 10022   (212) 223-6500

Incorporated in 1942 in NY.
Donor(s): Members of the Pforzheimer family.
Foundation type: Independent
Financial data (yr. ended 12/31/90): Assets,
$33,591,915 (M); expenditures, $1,912,204;
qualifying distributions, $1,806,960, including
$1,552,259 for 29 grants (high: $292,132; low:
$2,000; average: $10,000-$50,000).
Purpose and activities: Maintains publishing and
research activities in connection with the Carl H.
Pforzheimer Library collection at the New York
Public Library in the general field of American
and English literature; giving primarily for higher
and secondary education; support also for
cultural programs, public administration, a
national municipal organization, and health care.
Fields of interest: Education, higher education,
secondary education, libraries, literacy, language
and literature, arts, performing arts, theater, public
administration, government, citizenship, civic
affairs, health, hospitals, nursing.
Types of support: Seed money, professorships,
internships, scholarship funds, endowment funds,
fellowships, matching funds, program-related
investments, publications, special projects,
student aid.
Limitations: No grants to individuals, or for
building funds; no loans.
Application information:
  Initial approach: Letter or proposal
  Copies of proposal: 1
  Deadline(s): None
  Board meeting date(s): Apr., June, Oct., and
  Dec.
  Final notification: Immediately following board
  meeting, generally
  Write: Carl H. Pforzheimer, Jr., Pres.
Officers and Directors:* Carl H. Pforzheimer, Jr.,*
Pres.; Carl H. Pforzheimer III,* V.P. and Treas.;
Martin F. Richman, Secy.; Anthony Ferranti,*
Controller; Nancy P. Aronson, Richard W. Couper,
George L.K. Frelinghuysen,* Carol K. Pforzheimer.
Number of staff: 3 full-time professional; 2
full-time support.
EIN: 135624374
Recent health grants:
2183-1 Mount Sinai Hospital and Medical
  Center, NYC, NY, $292,132. 1990.
2183-2 Visiting Nurse Service of New York, NYC,
  NY, $105,000. 1990.

2184
Philip Morris Companies Corporate Contributions Program
120 Park Ave.
New York 10017   (212) 880-3489

Financial data (yr. ended 12/31/90): Total giving,
$46,300,000 for grants.

Purpose and activities: Philip Morris Companies
corporate headquarters and the subsidiaries
(except for Kraft General Foods, which has its
own foundation) follow the same guidelines for
giving. Philip Morris commits itself to assisting
organizations that enrich the quality of life in
areas of company operations, stimulating the
growth of new knowledge, creating a social
atmosphere conducive to equal opportunities for
all, and strengthening public confidence in the
business sector. Support is for higher education,
health and welfare, culture and humanities, and
conservation and the environment; also for the
United Way, employee matching gifts, and
scholarships for employees' dependents. Special
support for people of color. Giving figures are for
headquarters and subsidiaries, including Kraft
General Foods Foundation.
Fields of interest: Higher education, health,
cultural programs, welfare, humanities,
environment, AIDS, minorities, Native Americans.
Types of support: Employee matching gifts,
general purposes, operating budgets, special
projects, continuing support, emergency funds,
endowment funds, matching funds,
professorships, scholarship funds, research,
employee-related scholarships.
Limitations: No support for religious or fraternal
organizations, United Way recipients, public
television or radio, elementary and secondary
schools, or youth organizations. No grants to
individuals, or for capital or building fund drives.
Publications: Informational brochure.
Application information:
  Initial approach: Local requests to the nearest
  operating company for local managers to
  assess and recommend to headquarters
  office as seen fit. Other requests to
  headquarters
  Write: Anne T. Dowling, Dir., Corp. Contribs.

2185
Charlotte Palmer Phillips Foundation, Inc.
c/o Walter, Conston, Alexander & Green
90 Park Ave.
New York 10016   (212) 210-9400

Incorporated in 1958 in NY.
Donor(s): Charlotte Palmer Phillips.‡
Foundation type: Independent
Financial data (yr. ended 12/31/91): Assets,
$2,539,629 (M); expenditures, $110,080;
qualifying distributions, $84,958, including
$64,000 for 34 grants (high: $10,800; low: $100).
Fields of interest: Higher education, secondary
education, religion, hospitals, medical research.
Types of support: Operating budgets, continuing
support, building funds, equipment, endowment
funds, scholarship funds.
Limitations: Giving primarily in NY. No loans.
Application information: Contributes only to
pre-selected organizations. Applications not
accepted.
  Board meeting date(s): May
  Write: Robert L. Strong, Pres.
Officers and Trustees:* Robert L. Strong,* Pres.
and Treas.; James R. Cogan,* V.P. and Secy.; Rev.
George T. Cook, Paul M. Frank, Stevens L. Frost,
Louise H. Kerr, Charles E. Rogers, Mary S. Strong.
Number of staff: 1 part-time professional.
EIN: 136100994

2186
Phillips-Van Heusen Foundation, Inc.
1290 Ave. of the Americas
New York 10104   (212) 541-5200

Incorporated in NY in 1969.
Donor(s): Phillips-Van Heusen Corp.
Foundation type: Company-sponsored
Financial data (yr. ended 12/31/90): Assets,
$1,739,231 (M); gifts received, $23,000;
expenditures, $370,468; qualifying distributions,
$365,176, including $364,850 for 101 grants
(high: $100,000; low: $100).
Purpose and activities: Emphasis on Jewish
organizations, including those in Israel,
community funds, health and hospitals, and
higher education; support also for child welfare,
youth and social service agencies, and
international affairs; the corporation runs a
clothing bank and donates clothes and shoes to
the homeless.
Fields of interest: Jewish giving, Israel,
community funds, health, hospitals, higher
education, international affairs, social services,
child welfare.
Types of support: Operating budgets, continuing
support, annual campaigns, emergency funds,
special projects, research.
Limitations: No grants to individuals.
Application information: The foundation no
longer accepts unsolicited grant requests.
  Board meeting date(s): Sept.
  Write: Lawrence S. Phillips, Chair.
Officers: Lawrence S. Phillips, Chair.; Bruce J.
Klatsky, Pres.; Irwin W. Winter, V.P. and Treas.;
Pamela N. Hootkin, Secy.
Number of staff: None.
EIN: 237104639

2187
The Pines Bridge Foundation
c/o Swig Weiler & Arnow
1114 Ave. of the Americas, Suite 3400
New York 10036

Established in 1986 in NY.
Donor(s): Alan G. Weiler, The Weiler-Arnow
Investment Co.
Foundation type: Independent
Financial data (yr. ended 12/31/91): Assets,
$2,237,474 (M); gifts received, $500,000;
expenditures, $326,312; qualifying distributions,
$324,292, including $323,972 for 37 grants
(high: $50,000; low: $1,000).
Fields of interest: Higher education, hospitals,
health, cultural programs, performing arts, theater.
Limitations: Giving primarily in New York, NY.
No grants to individuals.
Application information: Contributes only to
pre-selected organizations. Applications not
accepted.
Trustees: Alan G. Weiler, Elaine Weiler.
EIN: 136872045

2188
Pinewood Foundation
100 Park Ave.
New York 10017

Incorporated in 1956 in NY as Celeste and
Armand Bartos Foundation.

Donor(s): Celeste G. Bartos, D.S. and R.H. Gottesman Foundation.
Foundation type: Independent
Financial data (yr. ended 09/30/91): Assets, $11,607,000 (M); expenditures, $1,377,797; qualifying distributions, $1,281,905, including $1,253,508 for 64 grants (high: $195,000; low: $100).
Fields of interest: Higher education, cultural programs, arts, child welfare, health, hospitals, community development, recreation.
Limitations: Giving on a national basis, with some emphasis on the greater metropolitan New York, NY, area. No grants to individuals.
Application information: Contributes only to pre-selected organizations. Applications not accepted.
Officers and Directors: Celeste G. Bartos,* Pres.; Armand P. Bartos,* V.P.; Edgar Wachenheim III, V.P.; Peter C. Siegfried, Secy.; Benjamin Glowatz, Treas.; Adam Bartos.
EIN: 136101581

2189
Henry B. Plant Memorial Fund, Inc.
c/o U.S. Trust Co. of New York
114 West 47th St.
New York 10036-1532

Incorporated in 1947 in NY.
Donor(s): Amy P. Statter.
Foundation type: Independent
Financial data (yr. ended 12/31/90): Assets, $5,591,913 (M); expenditures, $331,655; qualifying distributions, $280,935, including $277,000 for 85 grants (high: $50,000; low: $500).
Fields of interest: Hospitals, health services, family planning, cultural programs, environment.
Limitations: Giving primarily in NY. No grants to individuals.
Application information:
  Initial approach: Letter
  Deadline(s): None
  Write: Edward Sullivan
Officers: Mrs. J. Phillip Lee, Pres.; Phyllis S. Oxman, V.P.
Advisor: U.S. Trust Co. of New York.
EIN: 136077327

2190
Pluta Family Foundation, Inc.
3385 Brighton Henriette Town Line Rd.
Rochester 14623

Incorporated in 1966 in NY.
Donor(s): James Pluta, Helen Pluta, Peter Pluta, Mrs. Peter Pluta, General Circuits, Inc., Pluta Manufacturing Corp.
Foundation type: Independent
Financial data (yr. ended 12/31/90): Assets, $4,308,523 (M); expenditures, $138,989; qualifying distributions, $126,612, including $116,667 for 2 grants (high: $100,000; low: $16,667) and $980 for 2 grants to individuals (high: $600; low: $380).
Purpose and activities: Support for hospitals and higher education, including scholarship funds and student aid for General Circuits employees and their families.
Fields of interest: Hospitals, higher education.

Types of support: Scholarship funds, employee-related scholarships.
Limitations: Giving limited to Monroe County, NY.
Application information:
  Initial approach: Letter
  Board meeting date(s): Semiannually
Officer and Directors: Peter Pluta,* Pres.; Andrew Pluta, John Pluta.
EIN: 510176213

2191
The Pomerantz Foundation
1400 Broadway, 16th Fl.
New York 10018   (212) 221-4000

Established in 1961.
Donor(s): John J. Pomerantz.
Foundation type: Independent
Financial data (yr. ended 04/30/91): Assets, $1,007,759 (M); gifts received, $1,461,563; expenditures, $1,667,409; qualifying distributions, $1,667,409, including $1,667,309 for 15 grants (high: $257,978; low: $24,448).
Fields of interest: Higher education, Jewish giving, medical research, youth.
Application information:
  Initial approach: Letter
  Deadline(s): None
  Write: John J. Pomerantz, Treas.
Officer: John J. Pomerantz, Treas.
EIN: 136161231

2192
The Pope Foundation
211 West 56th St., Suite 5-E
New York 10019   (212) 765-4156

Incorporated in 1947 in NY.
Donor(s): Generoso Pope.‡
Foundation type: Independent
Financial data (yr. ended 12/31/91): Assets, $27,589,715 (M); expenditures, $1,510,720; qualifying distributions, $1,251,974, including $1,083,227 for 58 grants (high: $195,000; low: $500; average: $1,000-$50,000).
Purpose and activities: Emphasis on Roman Catholic church support, religious associations and welfare funds, higher and secondary education, and hospitals. Commencing in 1992, applications are invited for a music award providing a fellowship to an American musical composer or singer in mid-career with a demonstrated record of accomplishment.
Fields of interest: Catholic giving, Catholic welfare, social services, higher education, secondary education, hospitals, music.
Types of support: Fellowships, general purposes.
Limitations: Giving primarily in the New York, NY, metropolitan area, including Westchester County. No grants to individuals.
Application information: Application form required for the foundation's Awards for the Arts program.
  Initial approach: Letter
  Deadline(s): Dec. 31 for Awards for the Arts program; no set deadlines for other grants
  Write: Anthony Pope, V.P., for grants, and Catherine E. Pope, Pres. and Prog. Dir., for Awards for the Arts program

Officers and Directors: Catherine Pope,* Pres.; Anthony Pope,* V.P. and Secy.; Fortune Pope,* V.P. and Treas.
EIN: 136096193

2193
The Lois B. Pope Foundation, Inc.
c/o Townley & Updike
405 Lexington Ave.
New York 10174

Established in 1989 in NY.
Donor(s): Lois B. Pope.
Foundation type: Independent
Financial data (yr. ended 11/13/91): Assets, $2,372,606 (M); gifts received, $2,005,235; expenditures, $675,403; qualifying distributions, $651,021, including $439,902 for 20 grants (high: $283,573; low: $300).
Fields of interest: Higher education, hospitals.
Limitations: Giving primarily in FL and PA. No grants to individuals.
Application information: Contributes only to pre-selected organizations. Applications not accepted.
Officers and Directors: Lois B. Pope,* Pres.; Anastasia M. Berrodin,* V.P.; Robert C. Miller, Secy.; Frank Berrodin,* Treas.
EIN: 133542769

2194
Port Royal Foundation, Inc.
419 Park Ave. South, Suite 1302
New York 10016   (212) 481-8770

Incorporated in 1983 in NY.
Foundation type: Independent
Financial data (yr. ended 10/31/90): Assets, $526,589 (M); expenditures, $274,098; qualifying distributions, $261,601, including $259,500 for 32 grants (high: $61,000; low: $500).
Purpose and activities: Support primarily for higher education, historical preservation, and cultural programs; minor support for medical research.
Fields of interest: Higher education, historic preservation, cultural programs, medical research.
Types of support: General purposes.
Limitations: Giving primarily in NY and HI. No grants to individuals.
Application information:
  Initial approach: Letter
  Deadline(s): None
  Write: Ta Cox, V.P.
Officers: Sally Sample Aall, Pres.; Ta Cox, V.P. and Secy.; Maureen Anderson, Treas.
EIN: 133162050

2195
Mrs. Cheever Porter Foundation
c/o Adams & Becker
Seven High St.
Huntington 11743
Application address: c/o Kelley, Drye & Warren, 101 Park Ave., New York, NY 10178

Established in 1962 in NY.
Foundation type: Independent

Financial data (yr. ended 06/30/91): Assets, $2,952,801 (M); expenditures, $239,060; qualifying distributions, $209,900, including $209,900 for 42 grants (high: $14,000; low: $100).
Fields of interest: Higher education, cultural programs, performing arts, hospitals, animal welfare.
Limitations: Giving primarily on the East Coast.
Application information:
Initial approach: Letter
Deadline(s): None
Write: Alton E. Peters, Dir.
Directors: Alton E. Peters, Edgar Scott, Jr., Clifford E. Starkins.
EIN: 136093181

2196
The Potts Memorial Foundation
P.O. Box 1015
Hudson 12534   (518) 828-3366

Incorporated in 1922 in NY.
Foundation type: Independent
Financial data (yr. ended 12/31/90): Assets, $2,757,089 (M); expenditures, $198,061; qualifying distributions, $179,395, including $174,328 for 9 grants (high: $61,100; low: $5,000).
Purpose and activities: A private foundation established to provide for the care, treatment, and rehabilitation of persons afflicted with tuberculosis; support for tuberculosis eradication, including fellowship programs for physicians.
Fields of interest: Medical education, health services, rehabilitation, medical research.
Types of support: Seed money, building funds, equipment, research, special projects, publications, conferences and seminars, internships, scholarship funds, fellowships.
Limitations: No grants to individuals, or for endowment funds or matching gifts; no loans.
Application information:
Initial approach: Proposal
Copies of proposal: 8
Deadline(s): One month prior to board meeting
Board meeting date(s): May and Oct.
Write: Charles E. Inman, Esq., Secy.
Officers and Trustees:* Carl G. Whitbeck, M.D.,* Pres.; James M. Blake, M.D.,* V.P.; Charles E. Inman,* Secy.; J. Warren Van Deusen,* Treas.; Stanley Bardwell, M.D., Gerald D. Dorman, M.D., Frank C. Maxon, Jr., M.D.
EIN: 141347714

2197
The Louis and Harold Price Foundation, Inc. ▼
654 Madison Ave., Suite 2005
New York 10021   (212) 753-0240
Additional tel.: (212) 752-9335

Incorporated in 1951 in NY.
Donor(s): Louis Price,‡ Harold Price.
Foundation type: Independent
Financial data (yr. ended 12/31/91): Assets, $67,730,730 (M); expenditures, $2,091,728; qualifying distributions, $1,450,661, including $1,450,661 for 147 grants (high: $961,300; low: $50; average: $100-$5,000).

Purpose and activities: Support for a business institute, Jewish welfare funds, hospitals, community funds, and higher education, including scholarship funds; grants also for youth agencies, camps for children, temple support, medical research, the arts, and services for the handicapped, including the blind.
Fields of interest: Jewish giving, Jewish welfare, Israel, hospitals, health associations, medical sciences, mental health, rehabilitation, community funds, homeless, minorities, family services, education, literacy, libraries, higher education, medical education, youth, recreation, arts.
Types of support: Endowment funds, operating budgets, scholarship funds, special projects, continuing support, research, annual campaigns.
Limitations: Giving primarily in the metropolitan New York, NY, area and Los Angeles, CA. No grants to individuals, or for building funds.
Application information: Application form not required.
Initial approach: Letter
Copies of proposal: 1
Deadline(s): None
Board meeting date(s): Feb., May, and as required
Final notification: 1 to 3 months
Write: Harold Price, Pres., or Rosemary L. Guidone, V.P. and Exec. Dir.
Officers and Trustees:* Harold Price,* Pres.; Pauline Price,* V.P. and Secy.; Rosemary L. Guidone,* V.P. and Exec. Dir.; David Gerstein,* Secy.; Gloria W. Appel, George Asch, Linda Vitti.
Number of staff: 1 full-time professional.
EIN: 136121358

2198
William E. and Maude S. Pritschard Charitable Trust
c/o The Chase Manhattan Bank, N.A.
1211 Ave. of the Americas
New York 10036   (212) 789-5325

Established in 1983 in NY.
Foundation type: Independent
Financial data (yr. ended 12/31/91): Assets, $12,994,957 (M); gifts received, $3,032; expenditures, $230,917; qualifying distributions, $130,631, including $106,500 for 14 grants (high: $62,500; low: $1,000).
Fields of interest: Social services, religion, education, hospitals, general charitable giving.
Types of support: General purposes.
Application information: Applications not accepted.
Write: Michael H. Spiegel
Trustees: Edward J. Cunnigle, Herbert C. Wellington, The Chase Manhattan Bank, N.A.
EIN: 136824965

2199
The Prospect Hill Foundation, Inc. ▼
420 Lexington Ave., Suite 3020
New York 10170   (212) 370-1144

Incorporated in 1960 in NY; absorbed The Frederick W. Beinecke Fund in 1983.
Donor(s): William S. Beinecke.
Foundation type: Independent

Financial data (yr. ended 06/30/91): Assets, $40,296,231 (M); gifts received, $208,638; expenditures, $2,325,239; qualifying distributions, $1,933,401, including $1,641,014 for 90 grants (high: $300,000; low: $2,500; average: $5,000-$25,000) and $115,300 for 130 employee matching gifts.
Purpose and activities: The Prospect Hill Foundation has a broad range of philanthropic interests. Prospective applicants are requested to obtain guidelines prior to submitting an inquiry.
Fields of interest: Arms control, family planning, environment, conservation, social services.
Types of support: Matching funds, operating budgets, general purposes, seed money, special projects.
Limitations: Giving primarily in the northeastern U.S., including NY and RI. No support for religious activities. No grants to individuals, or for research.
Publications: Grants list, informational brochure (including application guidelines).
Application information: Application form not required.
Initial approach: Letter
Copies of proposal: 2
Deadline(s): None
Board meeting date(s): 4 or 5 times annually
Final notification: 4 weeks
Write: Constance Eiseman, Exec. Dir.
Officers and Directors:* William S. Beinecke,* Pres.; Elizabeth G. Beinecke,* V.P.; John B. Beinecke,* V.P.; Constance Eiseman, Secy. and Exec. Dir.; Michael A. Yesko, Treas.; Frederick W. Beinecke, Frances Beinecke Elston, Sarah Beinecke Richardson.
Number of staff: 1 full-time professional; 1 full-time support.
EIN: 136075567
Recent health grants:
2199-1 Alan Guttmacher Institute, NYC, NY, $15,000. Toward study, Preventing Pregnancy, Protecting Health: A New Look at Birth Control Choices in the United States. 1991.
2199-2 American Civil Liberties Union Foundation, Reproductive Freedom Project, NYC, NY, $17,500. For litigation on behalf of reproductive choice. 1991.
2199-3 Catholics for a Free Choice, DC, $10,000. To promote reproductive choice in Latin America. 1991.
2199-4 Center for Population Options, DC, $25,000. For adolescent pregnancy prevention activities in Latin America. 1991.
2199-5 Center for Population Options, DC, $10,715. To enable Asociacion Guatemalteca de Educacion Sexual in Guatemala to expand Mayan girls scholarship program. 1991.
2199-6 Easter Seal Society of Rhode Island, Meeting Street School, East Providence, RI, $10,000. For capital campaign. 1991.
2199-7 International Projects Assistance Services, Carrboro, NC, $15,000. To train medical professionals in Nicaragua to use manual vacuum aspiration equipment and provide contraceptive counseling. 1991.
2199-8 International Womens Health Coalition, NYC, NY, $30,000. For reproductive health activities in Latin America. 1991.
2199-9 Planned Parenthood of New York City, NYC, NY, $40,000. Toward pregnancy prevention and public education activities. 1991.

2199-10 Population Council, NYC, NY, $13,000. To print in Spanish and disseminate in Latin America, Meeting Male Reproductive Health Needs in Latin America. 1991.

2199-11 Population Crisis Committee, DC, $15,000. Toward preparation costs of U.S. Population Assistance: Issues for the 1990s, evaluation of United States Agency for International Development's population program. 1991.

2199-12 Saint Lukes-Roosevelt Hospital Center, NYC, NY, $20,000. Toward purchase of flow cytometer. 1991.

2199-13 Stamford Hospital, Stamford, CT, $10,000. To purchase special beds for acutely ill patients. 1991.

2200
Prudential-Bache Foundation
100 Gold St.
New York 10292   (212) 214-7507

Incorporated in 1965 in NY.
Donor(s): Bache Halsey Stuart Shields, Inc.
Foundation type: Company-sponsored
Financial data (yr. ended 01/31/91): Assets, $31,786 (M); gifts received, $440,000; expenditures, $446,266; qualifying distributions, $446,266, including $446,190 for 95 grants (high: $100,000; low: $100).
Fields of interest: Higher education, health, social services, youth, cultural programs.
Types of support: Scholarship funds, general purposes.
Limitations: Giving primarily in New York, NY.
Application information: Application form not required.
  Deadline(s): None
  Write: Bruno G. Bissetta, Treas.
Officers: H. Virgil Sherrill, Pres.; James J. Rizzo, V.P. and Secy.; Bruno G. Bissetta, Treas.
EIN: 136193023

2201
Quantum Chemical Corporation
Contributions Committee
99 Park Avenue
New York 10016-1502   (212) 551-0438

Financial data (yr. ended 12/31/90): Total giving, $985,027 for 154 grants (high: $30,000; low: $170).
Purpose and activities: Supports education, the arts and sciences, cultural programs, health care and hospitals, youth, welfare, United Way, and religious welfare. Quantum also supports emergency medical services organizations that are based in community areas of operations.
Fields of interest: Community funds, education, arts, science and technology, cultural programs, health, hospitals, civic affairs, welfare, higher education, education—early childhood, education—building funds, education—minorities, educational associations, elementary education, health associations, hospices, hospitals—building funds, museums, music, youth, religious welfare.
Types of support: General purposes, employee matching gifts, annual campaigns, building funds, capital campaigns, conferences and seminars, continuing support, endowment funds,

equipment, fellowships, grants to individuals, research, scholarship funds, employee-related scholarships, special projects, scholarship funds, student loans.
Limitations: Giving primarily in operating areas.
Publications: Informational brochure.
Application information: Contributions are handled by the Corporate Communications department. Applications not accepted.
  Copies of proposal: 1
  Write: Kirsten Fowles, Dir., Corp. Communs.
Administrators: Kirsten Fowles, Dir., Corp. Communs.; Carlotta Wilsen, Comm. Rels. Admin.; Anne Rudder, Secy.
Number of staff: 3 full-time professional; 2 full-time support.

2202
Charles S. Raizen Foundation, Inc.
31 Meadow Rd.
Scarsdale 10583

Established in 1945 in NY.
Donor(s): Charles S. Raizen,‡ Patricia T. Raizen.‡
Foundation type: Independent
Financial data (yr. ended 12/31/90): Assets, $2,124,478 (M); expenditures, $149,555; qualifying distributions, $136,550, including $136,550 for 93 grants (high: $45,000; low: $50).
Fields of interest: Jewish giving, Jewish welfare, medical research, social services.
Limitations: No grants to individuals.
Application information: Contributes only to pre-selected organizations. Applications not accepted.
  Board meeting date(s): Annually
Officers: Roy Raizen, Pres.; Edna Mae Fadem, V.P.; Nancy Raizen, Secy.; Leroy Fadem, Treas.
EIN: 136122579

2203
Ramapo Trust ▼
126 East 56th St.
New York 10022   (212) 308-7355

Trust established in 1973 in NY.
Donor(s): Henry L. Schwartz,‡ Montebello Trust.
Foundation type: Independent
Financial data (yr. ended 06/30/91): Assets, $43,996,274 (M); expenditures, $3,113,047; qualifying distributions, $2,822,106, including $2,286,732 for 58 grants (high: $350,000; low: $600; average: $7,500-$55,000).
Purpose and activities: Giving for gerontological and geriatric research and innovative services; support also for health, higher and other education, and youth and child welfare.
Fields of interest: Aged, medical research, health, higher education, education—early childhood, elementary education, youth, child welfare.
Types of support: Seed money, matching funds, special projects, research, conferences and seminars, emergency funds.
Limitations: No grants to individuals, or for capital or building campaigns, operating budgets, continuing support, annual campaigns, or deficit financing; no loans.
Publications: Newsletter, application guidelines.
Application information: Application form not required.
  Initial approach: Letter of intent

  Deadline(s): None
  Board meeting date(s): Monthly
  Write: Danylle Rudin by telephone, or Stephen L. Schwartz, Trustee, by mail
Trustees: Arthur Norman Field, Karen Schwartz Hart, Harold Resnik, Andrew M. Schreier, William Schreier, Rebecca Schwartz, Stephen L. Schwartz, Mary Ann Van Clief.
Number of staff: 1 full-time professional; 1 part-time professional; 2 part-time support.
EIN: 136594279
Recent health grants:

2203-1 Duke University Medical Center, Durham, NC, $60,000. 1991.

2203-2 Harvard University, Medical School, Boston, MA, $120,000. 1991.

2203-3 Medicare Beneficiaries Defense Fund, NYC, NY, $49,058. 1991.

2203-4 Memorial Sloan-Kettering Cancer Center, NYC, NY, $93,821. 1991.

2203-5 Mental Health Association of New York and Bronx Counties, NYC, NY, $10,000. 1991.

2203-6 Mount Sinai Hospital and Medical Center, NYC, NY, $178,369. 1991.

2203-7 Rockefeller University, NYC, NY, $86,058. 1991.

2203-8 Saint Lukes-Roosevelt Hospital Center, NYC, NY, $114,940. 1991.

2203-9 University of Arizona, Health Sciences Center, Tucson, AZ, $67,935. 1991.

2203-10 University of Illinois, Department of Medicine, Chicago, IL, $55,000. 1991.

2203-11 Vision Services for the Blind and Visually Impaired, NYC, NY, $71,012. 1991.

2203-12 Wake Forest University, Bowman Gray School of Medicine, Winston-Salem, NC, $56,286. 1991.

2204
The Paul Rapoport Foundation, Inc.
220 East 60th St., Suite 14K
New York 10022   (212) 888-6578

Established in 1987 in NY.
Donor(s): Paul Rapoport.‡
Foundation type: Independent
Financial data (yr. ended 06/30/91): Assets, $8,316,943 (M); gifts received, $75; expenditures, $404,433; qualifying distributions, $356,998, including $339,840 for 41 grants (high: $25,000; low: $115).
Purpose and activities: Support for organizations which provide care, support, and services, primarily within the gay community, to individuals with the HIV infection or AIDS; giving also to organizations that aid the lesbian and gay community by promoting and supporting the community's development, social and legal rights, identity, and general well-being.
Fields of interest: AIDS, gays and lesbians.
Types of support: Seed money, operating budgets, continuing support, matching funds, publications, general purposes, special projects, conferences and seminars.
Limitations: Giving primarily in the New York, NY, metropolitan area. No support for medical research, cultural or artistic activities, or other foundations. No grants to individuals, or for endowment funds or building campaigns.
Publications: Grants list, application guidelines.
Application information: Application form not required.

Initial approach: Letter or telephone
Copies of proposal: 9
Deadline(s): Mar. 1, June 1, Sept. 1, and Dec. 1 (or previous Friday if the 1st falls on a weekend)
Board meeting date(s): June, Sept., Dec., and Mar.
Final notification: One to two weeks after board meeting
Write: Jane D. Schwartz, Exec. Dir.
Officers and Directors:* Joseph E. Mattes,* Pres.; Joel B. Ifcher,* V.P.; James M. Rosenberg,* Treas.; Jane D. Schwartz, Exec. Dir.; Michael Fischer, Diana Leo, Daniel Rapoport, Jerry Rumain, Rosalie J. Wolf.
Number of staff: 1 shared staff
EIN: 136892333

2205
Rauch Foundation, Inc.
400 Post Ave.
Westbury 11590   (516) 997-2756

Incorporated in 1960 in NY.
Donor(s): Philip J. Rauch, Louis J. Rauch.
Foundation type: Independent
Financial data (yr. ended 11/30/90): Assets, $13,434,795 (M); gifts received, $400,216; expenditures, $986,680; qualifying distributions, $905,637, including $880,480 for 73 grants (high: $500,000; low: $8).
Purpose and activities: Support for innovative programs in the area of early childhood and day-care. Funds for local ongoing support of educational, cultural, health, and social service organizations currently fully committed.
Fields of interest: Child development, higher education, cultural programs, health, social services, Protestant giving.
Types of support: Seed money, special projects, research, publications, conferences and seminars, matching funds.
Limitations: Giving primarily in the eastern states between Boston, MA, and Washington, DC. No support for religious purposes. No grants to individuals, or for deficit financing, building funds, land acquisition, scholarships, or fellowships; no loans.
Application information: Contributes only to pre-selected organizations. Applications not accepted.
Board meeting date(s): Jan., July, and Oct.
Officers: Louis J. Rauch, Pres.; Philip J. Rauch, V.P. and Secy.-Treas.; Nancy R. Douzinas, V.P.; Gerald I. Lustig, V.P.; Philip J. Rauch, V.P.
Number of staff: 1 part-time support.
EIN: 112001717

2206
Reader's Digest Association Giving Program
Roaring Brook Rd.
Pleasantville 10570   (914) 241-5370

Purpose and activities: "Reader's Digest strives to be a responsible corporate citizen in the communities where we work and most of our employees live. Our involvement includes contributing financially to charitable organizations and, from time to time, providing inkind gifts. This local particiption helps bring life

to our corporate theme, 'We make a difference in 100 million lives worldwide.'" Whether an organization's objectives are complementary to the company's objectives is a major factor in determining funding. The company also considers whether employees are involved, if they recommend support, and if the organization provides services that employees use. It is important that the organization document its successful efforts. Readers's Digest has established budget limitations for each contribution area. Generally, no organization which receives funding through the Reader's Digest Foundation, the DeWitt Wallace-Reader's Digest Fund or the Lila Wallace-Reader's Digest Fund may also receive a corporate contribution.
Fields of interest: Arts, civic affairs, community funds, cultural programs, education, education—minorities, health, social services, public policy, youth.
Types of support: Continuing support, program-related investments, general purposes.
Limitations: Giving primarily in communities where employees live. No support for sports events, with the exception of the Ken Venturi Guiding Eyes Classic, religious organizations or endeavors, veterans, political, or fraternal organizations. No grants for advertisements, public television, film, or media projects, capital or building campaigns. No loaned executives; however a Volunteer Support Program is sponsored by the foundation.
Publications: Informational brochure.
Application information: Application form not required.
Initial approach: Letter of inquiry
Deadline(s): None
Write: J. Edward Hall, V.P. for Contribs.; Carole M. Howard, in Public Rels. for Sponsorships/Special Events
Number of staff: 2 part-time professional; 2 part-time support.

2207
Recanati Foundation
511 Fifth Ave.
New York 10017   (212) 578-1845

Incorporated in 1956 in NY.
Donor(s): Israel Discount Bank Ltd., Jewish Communal Fund.
Foundation type: Independent
Financial data (yr. ended 06/30/91): Assets, $4,705,940 (M); gifts received, $2,437,742; expenditures, $690,365; qualifying distributions, $667,639, including $667,300 for 85 grants (high: $100,000; low: $50).
Purpose and activities: Giving primarily to a medical school and Jewish organizations, including welfare funds.
Fields of interest: Medical education, Jewish giving, Jewish welfare, Israel.
Limitations: Giving primarily in NY. No grants to individuals, or for building funds.
Application information: Contributes only to pre-selected organizations. Applications not accepted.
Write: Marvin Alexander
Directors: Eliahu Cohen, Ran Hettena, Morton P. Hyman, Diane Recanati, Michael A. Recanati, Raphael Recanati, Gertrud Stark.
EIN: 136113080

2208
Philip D. Reed Foundation, Inc. ▼
570 Lexington Ave., Rm. 923
New York 10022

Incorporated in 1955 in NY.
Donor(s): Philip D. Reed.‡
Foundation type: Independent
Financial data (yr. ended 06/30/91): Assets, $7,852,853 (M); gifts received, $64,313; expenditures, $1,517,251; qualifying distributions, $1,440,527, including $1,405,500 for 29 grants (high: $400,000; low: $1,000; average: $10,000-$50,000).
Purpose and activities: Grants mainly for higher education, international studies, public policy organizations, with emphasis on major exchange and study programs, energy and the environment, natural resources conservation, minority education advancement, and family planning.
Fields of interest: Higher education, international studies, international affairs, public policy, energy, environment, conservation, family planning.
Limitations: No grants to individuals.
Application information:
Deadline(s): None
Write: Patricia Anderson, Secy.
Officers and Trustees:* Philip D. Reed, Jr.,* Chair. and Pres.; Harold A. Segall,* V.P. and Treas.; Patricia Anderson,* Secy.; Kathryn R. Smith.
EIN: 136098916

2209
Anne & Harry J. Reicher Foundation
1173-A Second Ave.
Box 363
New York 10021

Established in 1961 in PA.
Donor(s): Harry D. Reicher, Sydell Markelson.‡
Foundation type: Independent
Financial data (yr. ended 12/31/91): Assets, $5,249,827 (M); gifts received, $1,764,509; expenditures, $1,088,447; qualifying distributions, $1,040,000, including $1,040,000 for 40 grants (high: $600,000; low: $500).
Purpose and activities: Giving primarily to hospitals and health organizations, particularly a hospital for joint diseases, to Jewish welfare funds, and a housing organization.
Fields of interest: Hospitals, health, Jewish welfare, housing.
Limitations: Giving primarily in the greater New York, NY, metropolitan area. No grants to individuals.
Application information: Contributes only to pre-selected organizations. Applications not accepted.
Officers: Harold Lamberg, Pres.; Leonard Zalkin, V.P. and Treas.; Rabbi Balfour Brickner, Secy.
EIN: 136115086

2210
Jacob L. Reiss Foundation
c/o The Bank of New York, Tax Dept.
One Wall St.
New York 10286

Trust established in 1953 in NY.
Donor(s): Jacob L. Reiss.‡
Foundation type: Independent

Financial data (yr. ended 12/31/91): Assets, $3,741,440 (M); expenditures, $153,953; qualifying distributions, $150,009, including $150,000 for 27 grants (high: $30,000; low: $1,000).
Fields of interest: Hospitals, Catholic giving, religious schools, welfare, handicapped.
Limitations: Giving primarily in NY, NJ, and WI. No grants to individuals.
Application information: Contributes only to pre-selected organizations. Applications not accepted.
Directors: Mary Beth Tietje Murray, Robert R. Reiss, Theodore J. Reiss.
Trustee: The Bank of New York.
EIN: 136064123

2211
Republic New York Corporate Giving Program
452 Fifth Ave.
New York 10018   (212) 515-6597

Purpose and activities: Main areas of interest are arts, education, Jewish welfare, health and human services and urban development. Support also for performing arts, cultural institutes, economic development, business and minority education, and private colleges. Provides employee matching gifts for higher education, advertising and public relations, general operation expenses, and donations of in-kind goods and services.
Fields of interest: Performing arts, arts, higher education, education, cultural programs, minorities, business education, child welfare, community development, drug abuse, family services, handicapped, adult education, AIDS, homeless, hunger, international affairs, education—minorities, aged, disadvantaged, Jewish welfare, urban development.
Types of support: Operating budgets, capital campaigns, special projects, in-kind gifts.
Limitations: Giving primarily in the metropolitan New York, NY, area. No support for political organizations.
Application information: Letter describing program.
  Initial approach: Letter
  Deadline(s): None
  Final notification: 2-3 weeks required for full review and decision
  Write: J. Phillip Burgess, V.P.

2212
Revlon Foundation, Inc. ▼
c/o MacAndrews & Forbes Group, Inc.
36 East 63rd St.
New York 10021

Incorporated in 1955 in NY.
Donor(s): Revlon, Inc., and its subsidiaries.
Foundation type: Company-sponsored
Financial data (yr. ended 12/31/90): Assets, $1,686,295 (M); gifts received, $3,214,000; expenditures, $1,730,414; qualifying distributions, $1,709,962, including $1,669,250 for 28 grants (high: $800,000; low: $500; average: $10,000-$100,000) and $40,712 for 126 employee matching gifts (high: $2,975).
Purpose and activities: Emphasis on women's interest groups, minorities, and health care which

are national in scope or where company has subsidiaries, and cultural organizations which focus on main areas of interest listed above; support also for higher education, including an employee matching gift program, Jewish giving and welfare funds, conservation, and community funds.
Fields of interest: Women, minorities, health, cultural programs, higher education, Jewish welfare, Jewish giving, conservation, community funds, AIDS.
Types of support: Employee matching gifts.
Limitations: No grants to individuals; employee matching gifts awarded to educational institutions only.
Application information: Contributes only to pre-selected organizations. Applications not accepted.
Officers and Directors:* Richard E. Halperin,* Pres.; Nancy T. Gardiner, Exec. V.P.; William J. Fox, Sr. V.P.; Wade H. Nichols III, V.P. and Secy.; William H. Frank, V.P. and Treas.; James T. Conroy, V.P.; Howard Gittis, Ronald O. Perelman.
EIN: 136126130
Recent health grants:
2212-1 Childrens Health Fund, NYC, NY, $30,000. For grant shared with New York Hospital-Cornell Medical Center. 1990.
2212-2 John F. Kennedy Medical Center, Edison, NJ, $50,000. 1990.
2212-3 New England Deaconess Hospital, Boston, MA, $10,000. 1990.
2212-4 University of California, School of Medicine, Los Angeles, CA, $800,000. 1990.

2213
Charles H. Revson Foundation, Inc. ▼
444 Madison Ave., 30th Fl.
New York 10022   (212) 935-3340

Incorporated in 1956 in NY.
Donor(s): Charles H. Revson.‡
Foundation type: Independent
Financial data (yr. ended 12/31/90): Assets, $82,721,152 (M); expenditures, $7,286,371; qualifying distributions, $5,216,791, including $5,216,791 for 54 grants (high: $1,000,000; low: $1,000; average: $5,000-$150,000).
Purpose and activities: Grants for urban affairs and public policy, with a special emphasis on New York City problems as well as national policy issues; education, including higher education; biomedical research policy; and Jewish philanthropy and education. Particular emphasis within these program areas on the future of New York City, accountability of government, the changing role of women (especially leadership development for public life), minority groups, and the role of modern communications in education and other aspects of society.
Fields of interest: Urban affairs, public policy, government, community development, civil rights, education, higher education, biological sciences, medical research, AIDS, Jewish giving, Jewish welfare, women, minorities, media and communications.
Types of support: Research, fellowships, internships, special projects.
Limitations: Giving primarily in New York, NY. No support for local health appeals. No grants to

individuals, or for building or endowment funds, general support, or matching gifts; no loans.
Publications: Biennial report, application guidelines.
Application information: Application form not required.
  Initial approach: Letter or full proposal
  Copies of proposal: 1
  Deadline(s): None
  Board meeting date(s): Apr., June, Oct., and Dec.
  Final notification: 6 months
  Write: Eli N. Evans, Pres.
Officers and Directors:* Adrian W. DeWind,* Chair.; Eli N. Evans,* Pres.; Lisa E. Goldberg,* V.P.; Charles H. Revson, Jr., Secy.-Treas.; Helaine Barnett, Alice Chandler, Beatrix A. Hamburg, M.D., Matina S. Horner, Joshua Lederberg, Arthur Levitt, Jr., Matthew Nimetz, John C. Revson, Robert S. Rifkind.
Number of staff: 3 full-time professional; 1 part-time professional; 4 full-time support; 1 part-time support.
EIN: 136126105
Recent health grants:
2213-1 State Communities Aid Association, Albany, NY, $20,000. For Fair Financial Plan and SCAA's work in area of economic security including welfare reform, tax policy, nutrition assistance and health policy including broadening health coverage options for poor. 1990.

2214
Rhodebeck Charitable Trust ▼
c/o Turk, Marsh, Kelly & Hoare
575 Lexington Ave.
New York 10022-6102

Established in 1987 in AZ.
Donor(s): Mildred T. Rhodebeck.‡
Foundation type: Independent
Financial data (yr. ended 04/30/91): Assets, $16,956,422 (M); expenditures, $1,824,847; qualifying distributions, $1,679,732, including $1,679,732 for 21 grants (high: $1,050,000; low: $5,000; average: $5,000-$25,000).
Purpose and activities: "To alleviate the plight of disadvantaged people including homeless, hungry, elderly, children, and sick by making grants to publicly supported tax-exempt organizations concerned with one or more of these objectives."
Fields of interest: Disadvantaged, welfare, legal services, community funds, family services, homeless, hunger, aged, child welfare, youth, mental health, drug abuse.
Types of support: General purposes, special projects.
Limitations: Giving limited to AZ and New York, NY. No grants to individuals.
Application information: Unsolicited applications are discouraged.
  Write: Huyler C. Held, Trustee
Trustee: Huyler C. Held.
Number of staff: 1 part-time support.
EIN: 133413293
Recent health grants:
2214-1 Fountain House, NYC, NY, $1,050,000. For general operating support. 1991.
2214-2 Mental Health Law Project, NYC, NY, $25,000. For Access Development Fund. 1991.

2214-3 Phoenix House Foundation, NYC, NY, $25,000. For general operations. 1991.

2215
Rich Foundation, Inc.
1150 Niagara St.
P.O. Box 245
Buffalo 14240　　　　　　　(716) 878-8000

Established in 1961.
Donor(s): Rich Products Corp.
Foundation type: Company-sponsored
Financial data (yr. ended 12/31/90): Assets, $815,559 (M); gifts received, $220,000; expenditures, $314,051; qualifying distributions, $303,441, including $300,842 for 124 grants (high: $100,000; low: $50).
Fields of interest: Community funds, arts, hospitals, religion—Christian, education, higher education, youth.
Limitations: Giving primarily in Buffalo and western NY.
Application information:
Initial approach: Letter
Deadline(s): None
Write: David A. Rich, Exec. Dir.
Officer: David A. Rich, Exec. Dir.
EIN: 166026199

2216
Smith Richardson Foundation, Inc. ▼
477 Madison Ave., 17th Fl.
New York 10022　　　　　　(212) 688-3392
Application address for Early Intervention, Education and Indigenous Self-Help projects: c/o Peter L. Richardson, V.P., 266 Post Rd. East, Westport, CT 06880

Incorporated in 1935 in NC.
Donor(s): H.S. Richardson, Sr.,‡ Grace Jones Richardson.‡
Foundation type: Independent
Financial data (yr. ended 12/31/90): Assets, $265,650,040 (M); expenditures, $11,428,150; qualifying distributions, $10,289,873, including $7,861,150 for 223 grants (high: $600,000; average: $10,000-$100,000).
Purpose and activities: The main thrusts of grants-in-aid program are a public affairs program, aimed at supporting and promoting a vigorous economy and free society, mainly through support of public policy research projects and educational programs focusing on business and the economy; early intervention/education projects for at-risk children; and indigenous self-help/mutual aid projects which would include community oriented efforts that focus on child development and family support issues in economically disadvantaged areas.
Fields of interest: Public policy, government, economics, freedom, foreign policy, social sciences, political science, international studies, international affairs, educational associations, education—early childhood, family services, child development.
Types of support: Research, publications, seed money, matching funds, special projects, internships.
Limitations: No support for programs in the arts, historic restoration, or regional or community programs concerning employment, recreation, or

regional or community health and welfare. No grants to individuals, or for deficit financing, building or endowment funds, scholarships, fellowships, operating budgets, or research in the physical sciences; no loans.
Publications: Annual report (including application guidelines).
Application information: Most projects funded are initiated by the foundation. Application form not required.
Initial approach: Proposal
Copies of proposal: 1
Deadline(s): None
Board meeting date(s): Usually in Mar., June, Sept., and Dec.
Final notification: 30 to 60 days
Write: Mrs. Devon Gaffney Cross, Dir. of Foreign Policy Studies, or Mr. John O'Bryan, Prog. Officer, Domestic Policy Studies
Officers and Trustees:* H. Smith Richardson, Jr.,* Chair.; R. Randolph Richardson,* Vice-Chair. and Pres.; Peter L. Richardson,* V.P.; R. Larry Coble,* Treas.; Robert H. DeMichele, Robert H. Mulreany, Heather Richardson, Stuart S. Richardson.
Governors: William E. Odon, L. Richardson Preyer, Lundsford Richardson, Jr., Roderick R. Richardson, Henry S. Rowen, E. William Stetson III, James Q. Wilson.
Number of staff: 5 full-time professional; 2 full-time support.
EIN: 560611550
Recent health grants:
2216-1 American Psychiatric Association, NYC, NY, $40,000. 1990.
2216-2 Mid-Fairfield Child Guidance Center, Norwalk, CT, $15,000. 1990.
2216-3 National Center for Clinical Infant Programs, Arlington, VA, $150,042. 1990.
2216-4 New York Hospital-Cornell Medical Center, Society of the, NYC, NY, $43,274. 1990.
2216-5 Overlook Hospital Foundation, Summit, NJ, $17,000. 1990.
2216-6 Wakeman Memorial Association, Southport, CT, $15,000. 1990.
2216-7 Women and Infants Hospital of Rhode Island, Providence, RI, $163,275. 1990.

2217
The Frederick W. Richmond Foundation, Inc.
P.O. Box 33
Wantagh 11793　　　　　　(516) 579-3373

Incorporated in 1962 in NY.
Donor(s): Frederick W. Richmond.
Foundation type: Independent
Financial data (yr. ended 06/30/91): Assets, $3,328,769 (M); expenditures, $402,145; qualifying distributions, $349,771, including $318,151 for 91 grants (high: $72,600; low: $100; average: $2,000).
Fields of interest: Education, arts, cultural programs, museums, AIDS.
Types of support: Special projects, seed money, fellowships.
Limitations: No grants to individuals.
Publications: 990-PF, program policy statement.
Application information: Application form not required.
Initial approach: Letter
Copies of proposal: 1

Deadline(s): None
Board meeting date(s): Biannually
Final notification: 3 months
Write: Pauline Nunen, Exec. Dir.
Officers and Directors:* Timothy E. Wyman,* Pres.; William J. Butler,* Secy.; Pauline Nunen, Exec. Dir.; Barbara Bode, Helen Fioratti, Steven N. Kaufmann, Frederick W. Richmond.
Number of staff: 1 full-time professional; 1 part-time professional; 1 part-time support.
EIN: 136124582

2218
The Ring Foundation, Inc.
20 West 47th St.
New York 10036-3303

Established in 1979 in NY.
Donor(s): Frank Ring, Leo Ring, Michael Ring, Freeda Ring.
Foundation type: Independent
Financial data (yr. ended 05/31/91): Assets, $2,758,651 (M); gifts received, $248,620; expenditures, $112,380; qualifying distributions, $107,203, including $107,203 for grants (high: $53,444).
Purpose and activities: Support primarily for Jewish giving; support also for medical organizations and higher and secondary education.
Fields of interest: Jewish giving, higher education, secondary education, medical sciences.
Types of support: Building funds.
Limitations: Giving primarily in NY. No grants to individuals.
Application information: Contributes only to pre-selected organizations. Applications not accepted.
Officers: Frank Ring, Pres.; Freeda Ring, V.P.; Michael Ring, Secy.
EIN: 133015418

2219
The Ritter Foundation, Inc.
1776 Broadway, Suite 1700
New York 10019　　　　　　(212) 757-4646

Incorporated in 1947 in NY.
Donor(s): Gladys Ritter Livingston, Irene Ritter,‡ Lena Ritter,‡ Louis Ritter,‡ Sidney Ritter.‡
Foundation type: Independent
Financial data (yr. ended 11/30/91): Assets, $5,413,738 (M); expenditures, $437,333; qualifying distributions, $380,293, including $339,948 for 124 grants (high: $45,400; low: $50).
Purpose and activities: Grants for higher education, including medical education; giving also to Israel, mental health, and local Jewish welfare funds.
Fields of interest: Higher education, medical education, Jewish welfare, Israel, mental health.
Types of support: Building funds, capital campaigns, endowment funds, general purposes, emergency funds, research, scholarship funds.
Limitations: No grants to individuals.
Publications: Annual report.
Application information: Funds committed through 1995. Applications not accepted.
Board meeting date(s): May and Nov.
Write: Toby G. Ritter, V.P.

Officers and Trustees: Gladys Ritter Livingston,* Pres.; Toby G. Ritter,* V.P. and Secy.; David Ritter,* V.P.; Alan I. Ritter,* Treas.; Frances R. Weisman.
Number of staff: 1 part-time support.
EIN: 136082276

2220
May Ellen and Gerald Ritter Foundation
9411 Shore Rd.
Brooklyn 11209

Foundation established in 1980 in NY.
Donor(s): Gerald Ritter,‡ May Ellen Ritter.‡
Foundation type: Independent
Financial data (yr. ended 12/31/90): Assets, $7,172,713 (M); expenditures, $358,954; qualifying distributions, $300,056, including $255,473 for 33 grants (high: $111,000; low: $100).
Purpose and activities: Giving primarily for health agencies and Roman Catholic welfare funds.
Fields of interest: Health services, hospitals, Catholic welfare.
Limitations: Giving primarily in NY. No grants to individuals.
Application information: Application form not required.
  Initial approach: Letter and proposal
  Deadline(s): None
  Board meeting date(s): Quarterly
  Write: Emma A. Daniels, Pres.
Officers: Emma A. Daniels, Pres.; John Parker, V.P.; Helen Rohan, Secy.; Sophie Distanovich, Treas.
Number of staff: None.
EIN: 136114269

2221
Rochester Area Foundation
335 Main St. East, Suite 402
Rochester 14604   (716) 325-4353

Incorporated in 1972 in NY.
Foundation type: Community
Financial data (yr. ended 02/28/92): Assets, $30,176,286 (M); gifts received, $4,483,027; expenditures, $2,885,238; qualifying distributions, $2,431,924, including $2,211,800 for 709 grants (high: $69,000; low: $100) and $98,485 for 205 grants to individuals (high: $2,000; low: $180).
Purpose and activities: Giving for broad purposes related to community betterment, including education, the environment, cultural programs, health services, community development, and social services, including family and legal services, minorities, women, and youth; scholarship recipients chosen by institutions. Primary interests in 1993 will be in early childhood education; community development, including leadership programs for young people; and strengthening families and children through expansion of housing counseling and resource management counseling to low income families.
Fields of interest: Education—early childhood, cultural programs, health services, AIDS, community development, social services, family services, women, youth, housing.
Types of support: Seed money, equipment, fellowships, renovation projects, technical assistance, consulting services, scholarship funds, publications, student aid, special projects, building funds, conferences and seminars.
Limitations: Giving limited to Monroe, Livingston, Ontario, Orleans, Genesee, and Wayne counties, NY. No support for partisan political organizations or religious projects. No grants to individuals (except from restricted funds), or for operating budgets, continuing support, annual campaigns, deficit financing, land acquisition, endowment or emergency funds, matching or challenge grants, or research.
Publications: Annual report, program policy statement, application guidelines, financial statement, newsletter, informational brochure.
Application information: Scholarship recipients chosen by institutions. Application form required.
  Initial approach: Letter
  Copies of proposal: 3
  Board meeting date(s): Jan., Mar., May, July, Sept., and Nov.
  Write: Linda S. Weinstein, Pres.
Officers and Directors: Ruth H. Scott,* Chair.; Joseph C. Briggs,* Vice-Chair.; Jon L. Schumacher,* Vice-Chair.; Mary-Francis Winters,* Vice-Chair.; Linda S. Weinstein, Pres.; Dorothy Luebke,* Secy.; Richard Gray,* Treas.; and 26 additional directors.
Number of staff: 4 full-time professional; 1 part-time professional; 4 full-time support; 1 part-time support.
EIN: 237250641

2222
Rochester Gas and Electric Corporate Giving Program
89 East Avenue
Rochester 14649   (716) 546-2700

Financial data (yr. ended 12/31/90): Total giving, $517,302 for 46 grants (high: $295,000; low: $100).
Purpose and activities: Support for health and welfare (75 percent), education (19 percent), civic affairs (3 percent), and the arts and culture (3 percent).
Fields of interest: Arts, civic affairs, cultural programs, education, health, welfare.
Types of support: Annual campaigns, building funds, capital campaigns, continuing support.
Limitations: Giving primarily in the franchise area: nine counties centering around Rochester, NY.
Application information: Applications not accepted.
  Write: David C. Heiligman, V.P. and Secy.-Treas.

2223
Rockefeller Brothers Fund ▼
1290 Ave. of the Americas
New York 10104   (212) 373-4200

Incorporated in 1940 in NY.
Donor(s): John D. Rockefeller, Jr.,‡ Martha Baird Rockefeller,‡ Abby Rockefeller Mauze,‡ David Rockefeller, John D. Rockefeller, 3rd,‡ Laurance S. Rockefeller, Nelson A. Rockefeller,‡ Winthrop Rockefeller.‡
Foundation type: Independent
Financial data (yr. ended 12/31/91): Assets, $317,926,715 (M); expenditures, $16,349,843; qualifying distributions, $15,439,321, including $10,887,465 for 209 grants (high: $285,000; low: $1,000; average: $25,000-$300,000) and $22,865 for employee matching gifts.
Purpose and activities: "Support of efforts in the U.S. and abroad that contribute ideas, develop leaders, and encourage institutions in the transition to global interdependence and that counter world trends of resource depletion, militarization, protectionism, and isolation which now threaten to move humankind everywhere further away from cooperation, trade and economic growth, arms restraint, and conservation." There are five major giving categories: 1) One World, with two major components: sustainable resource use and world security, including issues related to arms control, international relations, development, trade, and finance; 2) New York City; 3) Nonprofit Sector; 4) Education; and 5) Special Concerns: South Africa.
Fields of interest: International development, international affairs, arms control, conservation, environment, intercultural relations, agriculture, economics, urban development, AIDS, Southern Africa, education, education—minorities.
Types of support: General purposes, seed money, special projects, conferences and seminars, internships, exchange programs, matching funds, consulting services, continuing support, research, technical assistance.
Limitations: Giving on a domestic and international basis. No support for churches, hospitals, or community centers. No grants to individuals (including research, graduate study, or the writing of books or dissertations, with two exceptions: the RBF Fellowships and the Program for Asian Projects), no grants for land acquisitions or building funds; no loans.
Publications: Annual report (including application guidelines).
Application information: Application form not required.
  Initial approach: Letter no more than two or three pages
  Copies of proposal: 1
  Deadline(s): None
  Board meeting date(s): Feb., June, and Nov.
  Final notification: 3 months
  Write: Benjamin R. Shute, Jr., Secy.-Treas.
Officers and Trustees: Abby M. O'Neill,* Chair.; Steven C. Rockefeller,* Vice-Chair.; Colin G. Campbell,* Pres.; Russell A. Phillips, Jr., Exec. V.P.; Benjamin R. Shute, Jr., Secy.-Treas.; Leora E. Landmesser, Comptroller; Catharine O. Broderick, Jonathan F. Fanton, Neva R. Goodwin, T. George Harris, William H. Luers, Jessica T. Mathews, Richard D. Parsons, David Rockefeller, Jr., Richard G. Rockefeller, Rodman C. Rockefeller, S. Frederick Starr.
Number of staff: 5 full-time professional; 2 part-time professional; 16 full-time support; 1 part-time support.
EIN: 131760106
Recent health grants:
2223-1 Beth Israel Medical Center, NYC, NY, $40,000. For continued support for Helping Hands Program, which trains stabilized Methadone Maintenance Treatment Program patients to serve as buddies to homebound methadone patients with AIDS. 1991.
2223-2 Black Leadership Commission on AIDS, NYC, NY, $100,000. For general support. 1991.

2223-3 Correctional Association of New York, NYC, NY, $50,000. Toward AIDS in Prison Project's work with AIDS-infected inmates being discharged from New York State and City correctional institutions. Project works to provide inmates at time of their release with AIDS education and with assistance in gaining access to health care, housing, support groups, substance abuse treatment and personal counseling. 1991.

2223-4 Latino Commission on AIDS, NYC, NY, $100,000. Toward initial program operations. 1991.

2224
The Rockefeller Foundation ▼
1133 Ave. of the Americas
New York 10036   (212) 869-8500

Incorporated in 1913 in NY.
Donor(s): John D. Rockefeller, Sr.‡
Foundation type: Independent
Financial data (yr. ended 12/31/91): Assets, $2,171,548,237 (M); gifts received, $1,607,640; expenditures, $107,391,985; qualifying distributions, $111,914,246, including $68,409,950 for 915 grants (high: $1,750,000; low: $357), $7,614,916 for 424 grants to individuals (high: $92,800; low: $180), $36,743 for 207 employee matching gifts, $10,845,160 for 76 foundation-administered programs and $4,357,000 for program-related investments.
Purpose and activities: The foundation offers grants and fellowships in three principal areas: international science-based development, the arts and humanities, and equal opportunities. Within science-based development, the focus is on the developing world and emphases are on the global environment; on the agricultural, health and population sciences; and on a very limited number of special African initiatives. The foundation also has smaller grant programs in international security and U.S. school reform. In addition, the foundation maintains the Bellagio Study and Conference Center in northern Italy for conferences of international scope and for residencies for artists and scholars.
Types of support: Fellowships, research, publications, conferences and seminars, special projects, grants to individuals, program-related investments, employee matching gifts, seed money, technical assistance.
Limitations: No support for the establishment of local hospitals, churches, schools, libraries, or welfare agencies or their building or operating funds; financing altruistic movements involving private profit; or attempts to influence legislation. No grants for personal aid to individuals, or for capital or endowment funds, general support, or scholarships; no loans, except program-related investments.
Publications: Annual report, program policy statement, application guidelines.
Application information: Application forms required for certain programs and fellowships; orgainzations may be asked to supply information on their own affirmative action efforts, including data on the gender and minority composition of the leadership of the institution.
Initial approach: Letter or proposal
Copies of proposal: 1

Deadline(s): None unless specified in special notices for certain programs and fellowships
Board meeting date(s): Usually in Mar., June, Sept., and Dec.
Write: Lynda Mullen, Secy.
Officers and Trustees:* John R. Evans,* Chair.; Peter C. Goldmark, Jr.,* Pres.; Kenneth Prewitt, Sr. V.P.; Frank Karel, V.P. for Communications; Hugh B. Price, V.P.; Lynda Mullen, Secy.; David A. White, Treas.; Sally Ferris, Dir. for Administration; Alan Alda, Harold Brown, Henry G. Cisneros, Johnnetta Cole, Peggy Dulany, Frances FitzGerald, Daniel P. Garcia, Ronald E. Goldsberry, W. David Hopper, Karen N. Horn, Alice Stone Ilchman, Richard H. Jenrette, Tom Johnson, Arthur Levitt, Jr., Robert C. Maynard, Alvaro Umana, Harry Woolf.
Number of staff: 738 full-time professional; 1 part-time professional; 65 full-time support; 3 part-time support.
EIN: 131659629
Recent health grants:

2224-1 Addis Ababa University, Addis Ababa, Ethiopia, $50,000. For core support of its Clinical Epidemiology Unit. 1991.

2224-2 Africa Press Trust, Lusaka, Zambia, $17,800. For meeting and publication costs in connection with formation of network of African journalists interested in population issues. 1991.

2224-3 African Medical and Research Foundation, Nairobi, Kenya, $34,200. To enable member of its staff to receive advanced training at School of Hygiene and Public Health, Johns Hopkins University. 1991.

2224-4 Aga Khan Foundation U.S.A., DC, $100,000. Toward continuation of Primary Health Care Management Advancement Programme. 1991.

2224-5 Al-Azhar University, Cairo, Egypt, $25,000. Toward conference on bioethics in human reproduction research in Muslim world, held at International Islamic Center for Population Studies and Research. 1991.

2224-6 Alexandria University, Faculty of Medicine, Alexandria, Egypt, $34,000. For research on male fertility. 1991.

2224-7 American Society of Tropical Medicine and Hygiene, Cleveland, OH, $13,000. For activities of Program Planning Committee for XIII International Congress for Tropical Medicine and Malaria. 1991.

2224-8 Asociacion Dominicana Pro-Bienestar de la Familia, Santo Domingo, Dominican Republic, $100,000. To enable Profamilia to conduct survey on sexual experience and contraceptive practice among young people in Dominican Republic. 1991.

2224-9 Asociacion Dominicana Pro-Bienestar de la Familia, Santo Domingo, Dominican Republic, $65,390. To participate in international study to develop single contraceptive implant using nomegestrol acetate. 1991.

2224-10 Australian National University, Canberra, Australia, $120,000. For continued support for international journal, Health Transition Review. 1991.

2224-11 Australian National University, Canberra, Australia, $120,000. For continued support for international journal, Health Transition Review. 1991.

2224-12 Australian National University, Canberra, Australia, $59,920. To study women's status and differences in fertility among Pygmies, rural villagers and townsfolk in southern Cameroon. Grant shared with Institute for Human Sciences, Cameroon. 1991.

2224-13 Bangladesh Institute of Development Studies, Dhaka, Bangladesh, $58,200. For study of causes and consequences of change in family structure and women's status in Bangladesh. Grant shared with Population Council. 1991.

2224-14 Beijing University, Beijing, China, $20,700. For study of differences in fertility patterns between Han and Mongolian herdsmen in Inner Mongolia Autonomous Region of China. 1991.

2224-15 Cambridge University, Cambridge, England, $50,000. For research and training project, collaborative with Molteno Laboratories of Parasitology, Institut Pasteur, Lille, France and Kenya Medical Research Institute to develop vaccine against schistosomiasis. 1991.

2224-16 Carvajal Foundation, Cali, Colombia, $43,750. Toward external evaluation of Health and Population Program. 1991.

2224-17 Carvajal Foundation, Cali, Colombia, $43,750. Toward external evaluation of its Health and Population Program. 1991.

2224-18 Carvajal Foundation, Cali, Colombia, $35,000. For environmental recycling program. 1991.

2224-19 Case Western Reserve University, Cleveland, OH, $190,000. For continued funding of program to help Uganda develop capacity for training increased numbers of nurse-midwives and upgrading their skills and status as way of bringing about sustained reduction in maternal mortality and morbidity. 1991.

2224-20 Case Western Reserve University, Cleveland, OH, $140,000. For continued funding of program to help Uganda develop capacity for training increased numbers of nurse-midwives and upgrading their skills and status as way of bringing about sustained reduction in maternal mortality and morbidity. 1991.

2224-21 Catholic University of Chile, Santiago, Chile, $300,000. For research and training program organized by Reproductive and Developmental Biology Unit and Laboratory of Endocrinology. 1991.

2224-22 Catholic University of Chile, Santiago, Chile, $67,510. For comparative study of fertilization in animals, to be conducted in its Faculty of Biological Sciences. 1991.

2224-23 Catholic University of Chile, Santiago, Chile, $20,000. For study, to be conducted at Faculty of Biological Sciences, on interaction between sperm and human oviduct. 1991.

2224-24 Catholic University of Chile, Department of Endocrinology, Santiago, Chile, $16,120. To train colleague from Shanghai Institute of Planned Parenthood Research. 1991.

2224-25 Catholic University of Chile, Faculty of Biological Sciences, Santiago, Chile, $27,820. For study of ciliary movement in fallopian tube. 1991.

2224-26 Center for Genetic Engineering and Biotechnology Investigations, Cuernavaca,

Mexico, $134,115. For research and training project, collaborative with Stanford University School of Medicine's Division of Geographic Medicine, on acute infectious diarrheas of childhood. 1991.

2224-27 Center for Population Options, DC, $50,000. Toward conference on adolescent health in Africa, held in collaboration with Centre for the Study of Adolescence, Nairobi. 1991.

2224-28 Center on Addiction and Substance Abuse, NYC, NY, $50,000. Toward development of Center. 1991.

2224-29 Centro de Estudios de Poblacion, Buenos Aires, Argentina, $59,730. To study how gender images affect adolescent reproductive behavior in Argentina. 1991.

2224-30 Centro de Investigacion y de Estudios Avanzados del IPN, Mexico City, Mexico, $99,344. For research project, collaborative with University of California at San Francisco, on protozoan intestinal diseases. 1991.

2224-31 Centro de Pesquisa e Assistencia em Reproducao Humana, Salvador, Brazil, $63,200. For study of hormone levels in women using single contraceptive implant containing nomegestrol acetate. 1991.

2224-32 Centro de Pesquisas e Controle das Doencas Materno-Infantis de Campinas, Campinas, Brazil, $29,600. For study of precocious cortical granule release, zona pellucida modifications and sperm-zona pellucida interactions during maturation of human oocyte. 1991.

2224-33 Cheikh Anta Diop University, Dakar, Senegal, $12,500. Toward Sixth International Conference on AIDS in Africa. 1991.

2224-34 Cheikh Anta Diop University, Dakar, Senegal, $12,500. Toward Sixth International Conference on AIDS in Africa. 1991.

2224-35 Chiang Mai University, Chiang Mai, Thailand, $83,705. For AIDS research project entitled Thai Military Male Health Study. 1991.

2224-36 Chiang Mai University, Chiang Mai, Thailand, $83,705. For AIDS research project entitled Thai Military Male Health Study. 1991.

2224-37 Chinese Academy of Sciences, Beijing, China, $10,200. To enable Shanghai Institute of Materia Medica to participate in international study to develop single contraceptive implant using nomegestrol acetate. 1991.

2224-38 Christian Medical College and Hospital, Vellore, India, $79,750. For research and training project, collaborative with Geographic Medicine and Infectious Diseases Division of New England Medical Center, Boston, on clinical, epidemiologic, pathogenic and etiological aspects of diarrheal diseases in India. 1991.

2224-39 Chulalongkorn University, Bangkok, Thailand, $25,000. For core support of its Clinical Epidemiology Unit. 1991.

2224-40 Chulalongkorn University, Institute of Population Studies, Bangkok, Thailand, $40,975. For pilot project on Thailand as part of multi-site intervention study of commercial sex workers and HIV transmission. 1991.

2224-41 Chulalongkorn University, Institute of Population Studies, Bangkok, Thailand, $40,975. For pilot project in Thailand as part of multi-site intervention study of commercial sex workers and HIV transmission. 1991.

2224-42 Columbia University, Center for Population and Family Health, NYC, NY, $200,000. To provide selected African institutions with technical assistance that strengthens their ability both to carry out and to improve family planning and health programs. 1991.

2224-43 Commonwealth Regional Health Secretariat for East, Central, and Southern Africa, Arusha, Tanzania, $400,000. To encourage greater integration of reproductive health and population issues in development policies of African countries. 1991.

2224-44 Commonwealth Regional Health Secretariat for East, Central, and Southern Africa, Arusha, Tanzania, $400,000. To encourage greater integration of reproductive health and population issues in development policies of African countries. 1991.

2224-45 Commonwealth Regional Health Secretariat for East, Central, and Southern Africa, Arusha, Tanzania, $85,640. For study of patterns of contraceptive use and health of women in Kenya, Mauritius, Swaziland, Uganda and Zambia. 1991.

2224-46 Council for Responsible Genetics, NYC, NY, $25,000. Toward program to educate international biomedical research community, public and policymakers about growing threat of biological weapons. 1991.

2224-47 Educational Commission for Foreign Medical Graduates, Philadelphia, PA, $35,000. For International Medical Scholars Program. 1991.

2224-48 Emory University, Carter Center, Atlanta, GA, $50,000. For planning program aimed at reducing tobacco use in developing countries. 1991.

2224-49 Escola Paulista de Medicina, Sao Paulo, Brazil, $51,670. For research on how hormones and other factors regulate Sertoli cell. 1991.

2224-50 Escola Paulista de Medicina, Sao Paulo, Brazil, $25,000. For core support of its Clinical Epidemiology Unit. 1991.

2224-51 Escola Paulista de Medicina, Sao Paulo, Brazil, $10,000. For research project entitled Repetitive Strain Injuries in Keyboard Operators: A Cross-Sectional Study. 1991.

2224-52 Family Care International, NYC, NY, $10,000. For collaborative effort with African Medical and Research Foundation to improve maternal health services in Kenya by working through private sector. 1991.

2224-53 Family Care International, NYC, NY, $10,000. For collaborative effort with African Medical and Research Foundation to improve maternal health services in Kenya by working through private sector. 1991.

2224-54 Federal University of Bahia, Brazil, $300,000. For research and training program in fertility regulation and reproductive health based at its maternity hospital. 1991.

2224-55 Foundation for International Scientific Cooperation, Ann Arbor, MI, $65,000. For continued funding of program to improve disease surveillance systems of Vietnam and Laos. 1991.

2224-56 Gadjah Mada University, Yogyakarta, Indonesia, $25,000. For core support of its Clinical Epidemiology Unit. 1991.

2224-57 Harvard University, Cambridge, MA, $100,000. Toward workshop, Good Health in Africa. 1991.

2224-58 Harvard University, Cambridge, MA, $99,300. For project entitled Strengthening and Replicating New Programs in International Health. 1991.

2224-59 Harvard University, Cambridge, MA, $62,000. To study how preference for sons and differential treatment of children by sex affects fertility in Morocco and Tunisia. 1991.

2224-60 Harvard University, Cambridge, MA, $15,300. For diarrheal diseases study relevant to Cameroon. 1991.

2224-61 Hospital General de Mexico, Mexico City, Mexico, $25,000. For core support of its Clinical Epidemiology Unit. 1991.

2224-62 Institut du Sahel, Bamako, Mali, $100,000. For use by Centre d'Etudes et de Recherche sur la Population pour le Developpement (CERPOD) for development of demographic surveillance system. 1991.

2224-63 Institut du Sahel, Bamako, Mali, $100,000. For use by Centre d'Etudes et de Recherche sur la Population pour le Developpement (CERPOD) for development of demographic surveillance system. 1991.

2224-64 Institut Pasteur de Lille, Lille, France, $50,000. For research and training project, collaborative with University of Colombo, Sri Lanka and University of Edinburgh, on epidemiology of malaria transmission. 1991.

2224-65 Institut Pasteur de Lille, Lille, France, $36,000. For research and training project, collaborative with Molteno Laboratories of Parasitology, University of Cambridge, England, and Kenya Medical Research Institute, to develop vaccine against schistosomiasis. 1991.

2224-66 Instituto de Biologia y Medicina Experimental, Buenos Aires, Argentina, $36,220. For study of regulation of testicular steroidogenesis by endocrine and paracrine factors. 1991.

2224-67 Instituto de Biologia y Medicina Experimental, Buenos Aires, Argentina, $35,000. For study of factors from human follicular fluid which affects follicular maturation and capacitation of sperm. 1991.

2224-68 Instituto Nacional de la Nutricion, Mexico City, Mexico, $35,500. For study of physiological effects of follicle-stimulating hormone on function of pituitary-gonadal axis. 1991.

2224-69 Instituto Nacional de la Nutricion, Mexico City, Mexico, $10,000. To enable scientists from developing countries to attend meeting of Latin American Association of Research in Human Reproduction, in Caracas, Venezuela. 1991.

2224-70 International Clinical Epidemiology Network (INCLEN), Philadelphia, PA, $648,300. For Executive Office. 1991.

2224-71 International Clinical Epidemiology Network (INCLEN), Philadelphia, PA, $50,000. For start-up of Phase II activities in Latin America and Asia. 1991.

2224-72 International Epidemiological Association, Los Angeles, CA, $15,000. Toward Southeast Asia regional meeting in Indonesia. 1991.

2224-73 International Food Policy Research Institute, DC, $70,300. To study role of women's status in determining marital fertility and nutritional and health status in rural Kenya. 1991.

2224-74 International Health and Biomedicine Limited, DC, $19,300. Toward organizing photographic exhibition on World Health Organization/UNICEF campaign for child immunization. 1991.

2224-75 International Health and Biomedicine Limited, United Kingdom, $25,000. For media project focusing on relationships between rapid population growth, status and health of women and the environment. 1991.

2224-76 International Potato Center, Lima, Peru, $181,510. For research project on health effects of pesticide use in Ecuadorian potato production. 1991.

2224-77 International Society for Infectious Diseases, Boston, MA, $24,410. For upcoming Congress in Nairobi, Kenya. 1991.

2224-78 International Union for the Scientific Study of Population, Liege, Belgium, $40,000. For seminar on course of fertility transition in sub-Saharan Africa, held in Harare, Zimbabwe. 1991.

2224-79 International Union for the Scientific Study of Population, Liege, Belgium, $10,000. Toward conference, held in Veracruz, Mexico, on peopling of the Americas. 1991.

2224-80 International Womens Health Coalition, NYC, NY, $25,000. Toward program to stimulate international health policy interest in problem of reproductive tract infections among women in third world. 1991.

2224-81 International Womens Health Coalition, NYC, NY, $25,000. Toward program to stimulate international health policy interest in problem of reproductive tract infections among women in third world. 1991.

2224-82 Johns Hopkins University, Baltimore, MD, $159,800. For research and training in community-based approaches to control of Aedes aegypti, urban mosquito vector of dengue fever. 1991.

2224-83 Johns Hopkins University, Baltimore, MD, $25,000. For in-country workshops in Mexico, Indonesia and Nigeria at which participants will develop methodologies for studies aimed at establishing national-level priorities with regard to disease control. 1991.

2224-84 Johns Hopkins University, Baltimore, MD, $23,000. Toward investigation of Chinese paralytic syndrome, new clinical entity that originally was described as Guillain-Barre syndrome. 1991.

2224-85 Johns Hopkins University, School of Medicine, Baltimore, MD, $74,440. For research on luteal angiogenic factor. 1991.

2224-86 Khon Kaen University, Khon Kaen, Thailand, $30,700. For study of efficacy of new drug, AC-17, in treatment of dengue hemorrhagic fever. 1991.

2224-87 Khon Kaen University, Khon Kaen, Thailand, $25,000. For core support of its Clinical Epidemiology Unit. 1991.

2224-88 Mahidol University, Bangkok, Thailand, $25,000. For core support of its Clinical Epidemiology Unit. 1991.

2224-89 Mahidol University, Bangkok, Thailand, $15,000. Toward developing-country scientists participating in Second Asia-Pacific Congress of Medical Virology, held in Bangkok. 1991.

2224-90 Mahidol University, Center for Vaccine Development, Bangkok, Thailand, $450,000. For dengue vaccine development project. 1991.

2224-91 Makerere University, Kampala, Uganda, $52,330. To strengthen population research and training program. 1991.

2224-92 Makerere University, Kampala, Uganda, $12,500. For research study on acyclovir for treatment of chronic genital and perianal ulceration due to herpes simplex virus infection in patients with HIV infection. 1991.

2224-93 Makerere University, Kampala, Uganda, $12,500. For research study on acyclovir for treatment of chronic genital and perianal ulceration due to herpes simplex virus infection in patients with HIV infection. 1991.

2224-94 Marine Biological Laboratory, Woods Hole, MA, $35,000. For research on anti-toxin produced in ovary of marine mollusk which may be useful in treatment of septic shock and cholera. 1991.

2224-95 Marine Biological Laboratory, Woods Hole, MA, $35,000. For research on anti-toxin produced in ovary of marine mollusk which may be useful in treatment of septic shock and cholera. 1991.

2224-96 McMaster University, Hamilton, Canada, $638,000. To continue support of Clinical Epidemiology Resource and Training Center. 1991.

2224-97 Medical Research Council, Banjul, Gambia, $36,000. For research and training project, collaborative with Department of Immunology, Wenner-Gren Institute, University of Stockholm and Department of Community Medicine, Chulalongkorn University, Bangkok, to develop vaccine against malaria. 1991.

2224-98 Ministry of Health of Mexico, Mexico, $284,630. For community-based Aedes aegypti control program in Mexico. 1991.

2224-99 Ministry of Health of Mexico, Mexico, $59,344. For pilot project in Mexico launching multi-country trial of interventions aimed at reducing role of commercial sex workers in transmission of HIV and other sexually transmitted diseases. 1991.

2224-100 Ministry of Health of Mexico, Mexico, $59,344. For pilot project in Mexico launching multi-country trial of interventions aimed at reducing role of commercial sex workers in transmission of HIV and other sexually transmitted diseases. 1991.

2224-101 Ministry of Public Health, Yaounde, Cameroon, $26,000. For site visits and information gathering by members of Cameroon's newly established Advisory Board in Epidemiology, preparatory to initiating formal operations. 1991.

2224-102 Ministry of Public Health, Bangkok, Thailand, $350,000. For continued support of grant-making activities and further development of National Epidemiology Board of Thailand. 1991.

2224-103 Ministry of Public Health, Bangkok, Thailand, $350,000. For continued support of grantmaking activities and further development of National Epidemiology Board of Thailand. 1991.

2224-104 Moi University, Geography Department, Eldoret, Kenya, $37,000. For continuing study of indigenous medical

systems for maternal and child health in Kenya. 1991.

2224-105 National Academy of Sciences, Institute of Medicine, DC, $50,000. Toward project, Microbial Threats to Health. 1991.

2224-106 National Archives Trust Fund, DC, $15,000. Toward Margaret Sanger Papers Project. 1991.

2224-107 National Archives Trust Fund, DC, $15,000. Toward Margaret Sanger Papers Project. 1991.

2224-108 National Bureau of Economic Research, Cambridge, MA, $27,140. For study of effects of restrictive abortion laws on adolescent childbearing in Tennessee. 1991.

2224-109 National Epidemiology Board of Cameroon, Yaounde, Cameroon, $300,000. Toward grantmaking activities and further development. 1991.

2224-110 National Epidemiology Board of Cameroon, Yaounde, Cameroon, $50,000. Toward grantmaking activities and further development. 1991.

2224-111 National Institute for Medical Research, Lagos, Nigeria, $10,000. Toward international conference on health research priorities for Nigeria. 1991.

2224-112 National Research Institute of Health, Addis Ababa, Ethiopia, $23,925. For pilot project in Ethiopia as part of multi-site intervention study of commercial sex workers and HIV transmission. 1991.

2224-113 National Research Institute of Health, Addis Ababa, Ethiopia, $23,925. For pilot project in Ethiopia as part of multi-site intervention study of commercial sex workers and HIV transmission. 1991.

2224-114 NCI Research, Evanston, IL, $100,000. Toward study entitled Increasing Employment Opportunities in Allied Health Care Occupations for Inner-City Residents. 1991.

2224-115 New England Medical Center Hospitals, Boston, MA, $79,750. For research and training project, collaborative with Christian Medical College Hospital, Vellore, India, on clinical, epidemiologic, pathogenic and etiological aspects of diarrheal diseases in India. 1991.

2224-116 New York University, NYC, NY, $200,000. To support analysis of implementation of project aimed at ameliorating problem of substance abuse in key target groups of inner-city residents. 1991.

2224-117 New York University, NYC, NY, $29,435. For use by medical center for research study on immunological tissue responses to malaria infections. 1991.

2224-118 Nigerian Institute of Social and Economic Research, Nigeria, $122,265. For baseline research in Nigeria on social and cultural factors that contribute to inequitable health outcomes. 1991.

2224-119 Nigerian Institute of Social and Economic Research, Nigeria, $122,265. To support baseline research in Nigeria on social and cultural factors that contribute to inequitable health outcomes. 1991.

2224-120 North-Eastern Hill University, Shillong, India, $26,000. For research on elective killing of gonadal cells by hormonotoxins. 1991.

2224-121 Ohio State University, Columbus, OH, $50,000. For continuation of INCLEN

Pharmacoepidemiology Seed Grants Program. 1991.

2224-122 Organizacao Internacional de Pesquisa em Saude Reprodutiva, Salvador, Brazil, $1,000,000. For program of South-to-South cooperation to develop new contraceptive methods and improve reproductive health. 1991.

2224-123 Partnership for a Drug Free America, NYC, NY, $100,000. For Inner-City Initiative. 1991.

2224-124 Pontificia Universidad Javeriana, Bogota, Colombia, $25,000. For core support of Clinical Epidemiology Unit. 1991.

2224-125 Population and Community Development Association, Bangkok, Thailand, $50,000. For second phase of initiative to prevent spread of AIDS in Thailand. 1991.

2224-126 Population and Community Development Association, Bangkok, Thailand, $50,000. For second phase of initiative to prevent spread of AIDS in Thailand. 1991.

2224-127 Population Council, NYC, NY, $400,000. To enable Council to participate in postmarketing surveillance of Norplant contraceptive implants in developing countries. 1991.

2224-128 Population Council, NYC, NY, $65,000. To compile and publish report identifying major findings from international research on family planning programs. 1991.

2224-129 Population Council, NYC, NY, $25,000. For in vitro study of sexual transmission of HIV across intact epithelia. 1991.

2224-130 Population Council, NYC, NY, $25,000. For in vitro study of sexual transmission of HIV across intact epithelia. 1991.

2224-131 Princeton University, Office of Population Research, Princeton, NJ, $25,000. For study of contraceptive efficacy of diaphragm, sponge and cervical cap. 1991.

2224-132 Princeton University, Office of Population Research, Princeton, NJ, $20,000. For research on fertility transition in Africa. 1991.

2224-133 Program for Appropriate Technology in Health, Seattle, WA, $50,000. Toward international conference on control of hepatitis B in developing countries, held in Cameroon. 1991.

2224-134 Program for Appropriate Technology in Health, Seattle, WA, $42,000. For initial work of Epstein-Barr Virus Vaccine Task Force. 1991.

2224-135 Program for Appropriate Technology in Health, Seattle, WA, $29,150. For planning study in Zimbabwe for technology transfer of HIV dipstick. 1991.

2224-136 Program for Appropriate Technology in Health, Seattle, WA, $29,150. For planning study in Zimbabwe for technology transfer of HIV dipstick. 1991.

2224-137 Program for Appropriate Technology in Health, Seattle, WA, $12,254. Toward meeting on prospects for developing vaccine against Epstein Barr virus, held in New York City. 1991.

2224-138 Programa Latinoamericano de Capacitacion e Investigacion en Reproduccion Humana, Mexico City, Mexico, $14,560. To participate in international multicenter clinical trial using anti-hCG vaccine in patients with lung cancer. 1991.

2224-139 Rand Corporation, Santa Monica, CA, $98,000. Toward pilot study entitled Reducing Inner City Drug Markets and Violence. 1991.

2224-140 Rockefeller University, NYC, NY, $489,225. To cover operating costs associated with preservation and continuing use for future generations of Foundation records deposited at Rockefeller Archive Center. 1991.

2224-141 Rockefeller University, Laboratory of Plant Molecular Biology, NYC, NY, $600,000. For research on molecular genetics of rice. 1991.

2224-142 Rockefeller University, Rockefeller Archive Center, NYC, NY, $30,000. Toward conference entitled Philanthropy in the African-American Experience. 1991.

2224-143 Salk Institute for Biological Studies, La Jolla, CA, $382,800. For research on molecular mechanisms for induction of rice defense responses to microbial disease. 1991.

2224-144 Scripps Clinic, Research Institute of, La Jolla, CA, $304,500. For research on molecular biology of rice tungro virus and rice yellow mottle virus, and genetic engineering of rice for virus resistance. 1991.

2224-145 Scripps Clinic, Research Institute of, La Jolla, CA, $237,800. For research on genetic engineering of cassava for virus resistance. 1991.

2224-146 Shanghai Medical University, Shanghai, China, $25,000. For core support of Clinical Epidemiology Unit. 1991.

2224-147 Social Science Research Council, NYC, NY, $11,805. For project designed to improve our understanding of relationships between population growth and quality of the environment. 1991.

2224-148 Sriwijaya University, Palembang, Indonesia, $35,350. For study of family structure, female autonomy and fertility in rural South Sumatra, Indonesia. 1991.

2224-149 Stanford University, Stanford, CA, $72,000. For research and training project on enteric infections of childhood, collaborative between its Division of Geographic Medicine and Center for Genetic Engineering and Biotechnology Investigations, Cuernavaca, Mexico. 1991.

2224-150 State Family Planning Commission, Beijing, China, $100,000. To enable Commission to demonstrate advantages of enhanced rural family planning system that integrates improved methods of contraception with better training of local family planning personnel. 1991.

2224-151 Suez Canal University, Ismailia, Egypt, $25,000. For core support of Clinical Epidemiology Unit. 1991.

2224-152 Taiwan Provincial Institute of Family Planning, Taiwan, $57,110. To study how declines in fertility have affected status of women in Taiwan. Grant shared with Georgetown University. 1991.

2224-153 Task Force for Child Survival, Atlanta, GA, $98,900. Toward third-year of Vaccine Development Project. 1991.

2224-154 Texas Tech University Health Sciences Center, Lubbock, TX, $15,000. For study on nutritional management of growth retardation in developing-country children recovering from Shigella dysentery. 1991.

2224-155 Thailand Development Research Institute Foundation, Bangkok, Thailand, $249,300. For study of environmental and health effects of pesticide use on rice fields in selected Thai villages. 1991.

2224-156 Tropical Diseases Research Center, Ndola, Zambia, $37,680. Toward project, Schooling and Maternal Behavior in Zambian Township. 1991.

2224-157 United Nations Population Fund, NYC, NY, $200,000. For studies of contraceptive requirements and logistics management needs in selected developing countries. 1991.

2224-158 Universidad de la Frontera, Temuco, Chile, $25,000. For core support of Clinical Epidemiology Unit. 1991.

2224-159 Universidad de los Andes, Bogota, Colombia, $12,250. For study comparing fertility transition in Colombia and Venezuela, countries with markedly different patterns of development. 1991.

2224-160 Universidad Nacional Autonoma de Mexico, Department of Developmental Biology, Mexico City, Mexico, $35,200. For study of gossypol's effects on interactions between spermatogenic and Sertoli cells. 1991.

2224-161 Universidad Nacional de Tucuman, Medical School, San Miguel de Tucuman, Argentina, $25,000. For study on how cholesterol and other sperm membrane lipids affect acrosome reaction. 1991.

2224-162 Universidade Federal do Rio de Janeiro, Rio de Janeiro, Brazil, $25,000. For core support of Clinical Epidemiology Unit. 1991.

2224-163 University of Arizona, Tucson, AZ, $24,000. For technical field assistance with social science research activities at INCLEN sites in the Philippines, Indonesia, Thailand and India. 1991.

2224-164 University of Benin, Benin City, Nigeria, $48,630. For comparative study of rural community structure and contraceptive use in selected Nigerian communities. 1991.

2224-165 University of Botswana, Gaborone, Botswana, $33,700. To study consequences of population growth for economic development in Botswana. 1991.

2224-166 University of Buenos Aires, Faculty of Pharmacy and Biochemistry, Buenos Aires, Argentina, $35,000. For study on oxidative damage to sperm and its relevance to human fertility. 1991.

2224-167 University of Buenos Aires, School of Medicine, Buenos Aires, Argentina, $35,050. For study of reproductive abnormalities in progeny of diabetic rats. 1991.

2224-168 University of California, San Francisco, CA, $1,239,601. To complete support for Pew Charitable Trusts/Rockefeller Foundation program on Health of the Public, five-year program aimed at mobilizing North American academic institutions to lead in implementing equitable, cost-effective health care and health promotion practices. 1991.

2224-169 University of California, San Francisco, CA, $29,500. For continued support for child survival program in selected African countries. 1991.

2224-170 University of Chile, Santiago, Chile, $274,950. For research and training program in reproductive biology and endocrinology. 1991.

2224-171 University of Chile, Santiago, Chile, $35,000. For study of endocrinology of human corpus luteum. 1991.

2224-172 University of Chile, Faculty of Medicine, Santiago, Chile, $14,100. To participate in international multicenter clinical trial using anti-hCG vaccine in patients with lung cancer. 1991.

2224-173 University of Dar es Salaam, Dar es Salaam, Tanzania, $22,610. For study of how social and environmental factors affect child mortality rates among refugees from Burundi living in Tanzania. 1991.

2224-174 University of Dhaka, Dhaka, Bangladesh, $69,980. For phase two of study of family planning program effort and performance in Bangladesh. 1991.

2224-175 University of Health Sciences, Madras, India, $50,000. For core support for Madras Medical College's Clinical Epidemiology Unit. 1991.

2224-176 University of Ilorin, Department of Epidemiology and Community Health, Nigeria, $16,938. For further analysis of data collected on determinants of fertility in Ilorin. 1991.

2224-177 University of Kinshasa, Zaire, $14,180. For study of interrelationships between employment, education and fertility in urban Zaire. 1991.

2224-178 University of Lagos, Lagos, Nigeria, $25,000. For study of effects of chloroquine, antimalarial drug, on spermatogenesis and fertility in rats. 1991.

2224-179 University of Lagos, Department of Obstetrics and Gynaecology, Lagos, Nigeria, $21,870. To participate in international study to develop single contraceptive implant containing nomegestrol acetate. 1991.

2224-180 University of Michigan, Population Studies Center, Ann Arbor, MI, $60,000. To study relationship between women's education, labor force participation and fertility decline in Brazil. Grant shared with Instituto de Planejamento Economico e Social/Instituto de Pesquisas, Rio de Janeiro, Brazil. 1991.

2224-181 University of Nairobi, Nairobi, Kenya, $90,000. For study conducted at Population Studies and Research Institute on fertility decline in rural Kenya. 1991.

2224-182 University of Nairobi, Department of Psychology, Nairobi, Kenya, $12,750. For evaluation of group counseling as therapeutic intervention for people who are HIV-positive. 1991.

2224-183 University of Nairobi, Department of Psychology, Nairobi, Kenya, $12,750. For evaluation of group counseling as therapeutic intervention for people who are HIV-positive. 1991.

2224-184 University of Nairobi, Population Studies and Research Institute, Nairobi, Kenya, $49,910. To study impact of migration on women's status in Kenya. 1991.

2224-185 University of North Carolina, Chapel Hill, NC, $65,900. To study how high fertility and women's status affect education of Philippine children. Grant shared with University of the Philippines, Manila. 1991.

2224-186 University of North Carolina, Chapel Hill, NC, $40,000. For continued support of internal evaluation of INCLEN program. 1991.

2224-187 University of Oxford, Oxford, England, $104,800. For collaborative research and training project with University of Papua, New Guinea, to study clinical, pathophysiological and genetic aspects of Plasmodium falciparum malaria in Melanesia and Polynesia. 1991.

2224-188 University of Pennsylvania, Philadelphia, PA, $160,000. To help Malawi develop capacity for training increased numbers of nurse-midwives and upgrading their skills and status as way of bringing about sustained reduction in maternal mortality and morbidity. 1991.

2224-189 University of Pennsylvania, Philadelphia, PA, $160,000. To help Malawi develop capacity for training increased numbers of nurse-midwives and upgrading their skills and status as way of bringing about sustained reduction in maternal mortality and morbidity. 1991.

2224-190 University of Pennsylvania, Philadelphia, PA, $140,000. For International Clinical Epidemiology Network (INCLEN) Executive Office. 1991.

2224-191 University of Pennsylvania, Philadelphia, PA, $47,560. To study demand for children among married women in rural area of Tanzania. Grant shared with University of Dar es Salaam, Tanzania. 1991.

2224-192 University of Pennsylvania, Philadelphia, PA, $20,000. To enable developing-country scientists to attend conference on scientific and ethical issues surrounding gametes, fertilization and fallopian tube. 1991.

2224-193 University of Pennsylvania, Population Studies Center, Philadelphia, PA, $51,750. To provide technical assistance to Chinese State Family Planning Commission as latter undertakes field experiment in family planning in rural China. 1991.

2224-194 University of Surrey, Guildford, England, $84,400. For research project entitled Development of Live-Attenuated Japanese Encephalitis Vaccine Adapted to Growth in Primary Chick Embryo Fibroblast Cell Culture. 1991.

2224-195 University of Texas Medical Branch Hospitals, Galveston, TX, $35,000. For continued support of research project on pathogenesis of Dengue Hemorrhagic Fever (DHF) infection. 1991.

2224-196 University of the Philippines, Manila, Philippines, $25,000. For core support of its Clinical Epidemiology Unit. 1991.

2224-197 University of Uppsala, Uppsala, Sweden, $42,000. For research and training project, collaborative between Department of Genetics and Instituto de Investigaciones Bioquimicas and Universidad Nacional de Salta, Buenos Aires, Argentina, on development of vaccine against Trypanosoma cruzi. 1991.

2224-198 University of Virginia, Charlottesville, VA, $26,000. For research and training project, collaborative between Division of Geographic Medicine and Federal University of Ceara Health Center, Fortaleza, Brazil, to reduce morbidity and mortality of enteric diseases in northern Brazil. 1991.

2224-199 University of Washington, Seattle, WA, $31,845. For study, collaborative with University of Nairobi, Kenya, to assess nutritional status of children born to HIV-1 seropositive and seronegative mothers in Nairobi. 1991.

2224-200 University of Washington, Seattle, WA, $31,845. For study, collaborative with University of Nairobi, Kenya, to assess nutritional status of children born to HIV-1 seropositive and seronegative mothers in Nairobi. 1991.

2224-201 University of Western Australia, Nedlands, Australia, $20,000. For publication and dissemination of Southeast Asia and Western Pacific region health systems newsletter entitled Virus Information Exchange. 1991.

2224-202 University of Wisconsin, Madison, WI, $86,050. To study determinants of infant and child mortality in Yaounde, Cameroon. Grant shared with Institut de Formation et de Recherche Demographiques, Yaounde, Cameroon. 1991.

2224-203 University of Yaounde, Yaounde, Cameroon, $40,500. For international conference on health technology procurement, assessment and repair in developing countries. 1991.

2224-204 University of Yaounde, Yaounde, Cameroon, $25,000. For core support of its Clinical Epidemiology Unit. 1991.

2224-205 Walter Reed Army Institute of Research, DC, $38,200. For use by U.S. and Thai components of Armed Forces Research Institute of Medical Science (AFRIMS) in establishing collaborative program of research on virology in Thailand. 1991.

2224-206 West China University of Medical Sciences, Chengdu, China, $25,000. For core support of its Clinical Epidemiology Unit. 1991.

2224-207 World Bank, DC, $50,000. For regional consultation on family planning program-effectiveness in tropical Africa. 1991.

2224-208 World Health Organization, Geneva, Switzerland, $700,000. To monitor health, safety and acceptability issues of Norplant contraceptive method. 1991.

2224-209 World Health Organization, Geneva, Switzerland, $350,000. To continue support for Special Programme on Vaccine Development. 1991.

2224-210 World Health Organization, Geneva, Switzerland, $300,000. To continue program to reduce high rate of maternal mortality in developing countries. 1991.

2224-211 World Health Organization, Geneva, Switzerland, $300,000. For continued support for Expanded Programme on Immunization and Trans-Diseases Vaccinology Programme. 1991.

2224-212 World Health Organization, Geneva, Switzerland, $300,000. To continue program to reduce high rate of maternal mortality in developing countries. 1991.

2224-213 World Health Organization, Geneva, Switzerland, $250,000. Toward Secretariat of Children's Vaccine Initiative. 1991.

2224-214 World Health Organization, Geneva, Switzerland, $200,000. To continue support for Expanded Programme on Immunization and Trans-Diseases Vaccinology Programme. 1991.

2224-215 World Health Organization, Geneva, Switzerland, $60,000. Toward meeting on organization of community-oriented outpatient services and referral systems in developing-country cities. 1991.

2224-216 World Health Organization, Geneva, Switzerland, $60,000. For renewed support for international health systems newsletter, Bridge. 1991.

2224-217 Zhejiang Academy of Medical Sciences, Hangzhou, China, $28,650. For study of gossypol antifertility-sensitive enzymes as warning indicators for monitoring occurrence of gossypol-induced sterility. 1991.

2225
Richard & Dorothy Rodgers Foundation
1633 Broadway, Suite 3801
New York 10019

Established in 1952 in NY.
Donor(s): Richard Rodgers,‡ Dorothy F. Rodgers.‡
Foundation type: Independent
Financial data (yr. ended 12/31/90): Assets, $2,480,190 (M); gifts received, $508,205; expenditures, $392,418; qualifying distributions, $378,449, including $375,125 for 114 grants (high: $75,000; low: $110; average: $1,000-$10,000).
Purpose and activities: Support for hospitals, culture, including museums, Jewish organizations, and general charitable giving.
Fields of interest: Hospitals, cultural programs, museums, Jewish giving, general charitable giving.
Limitations: Giving primarily in New York, NY. No grants to individuals.
Application information: Contributes only to pre-selected organizations. Applications not accepted.
Officers: Lawrence B. Buttenwieser, Secy.
EIN: 136062852

2226
Billy Rose Foundation, Inc. ▼
One Dag Hammarskjold Plaza, 47th Fl.
New York 10163   (212) 349-4141

Incorporated in 1958 in NY.
Donor(s): Billy Rose.‡
Foundation type: Independent
Financial data (yr. ended 12/31/91): Assets, $9,112,402 (M); expenditures, $1,433,613; qualifying distributions, $1,358,030, including $1,334,500 for 89 grants (high: $325,000; low: $2,000; average: $5,000-$25,000).
Purpose and activities: Support for museums, particularly a museum in Israel, the performing and fine arts, higher education, and medical research.
Fields of interest: Museums, fine arts, performing arts, higher education, medical research.
Types of support: Research, special projects.
Limitations: Giving primarily in New York, NY. No grants to individuals.
Application information: Application form not required.
  Initial approach: Letter
  Deadline(s): None
  Board meeting date(s): Usually in June

Final notification: Varies
  Write: Terri C. Mangino, Exec. Dir.
Officers and Directors:* Arthur Cantor,* Chair.; Charles Wohlstetter, Pres.; James R. Cherry,* V.P. and Treas.; Edward T. Walsh, Jr., Secy.; Terri C. Mangino, Exec. Dir.
Number of staff: 1 full-time professional.
EIN: 136165466

2227
Susan and Elihu Rose Foundation, Inc.
c/o Rose Assocs.
380 Madison Ave., 4th Fl.
New York 10017

Established in 1988 in DE.
Donor(s): Elihu Rose, Samuel and David Rose Charitable Foundation
Foundation type: Independent
Financial data (yr. ended 12/31/90): Assets, $24,259,638 (M); gifts received, $25,303,768; expenditures, $1,297,690; qualifying distributions, $1,245,450, including $1,215,450 for 130 grants (high: $250,000; low: $75).
Fields of interest: Higher education, arts, performing arts, historic preservation, health associations, cancer, Jewish giving, Jewish welfare.
Limitations: Giving primarily in New York, NY. No grants to individuals.
Application information: Contributes only to pre-selected organizations. Applications not accepted.
Officer and Directors:* Elihu Rose,* Pres. and Secy.; Susan Rose.
EIN: 133484181

2228
Sunny and Abe Rosenberg Foundation, Inc.
c/o Robert S. Gassman
350 Fifth Ave.
New York 10118
Application address: c/o Star Industries, Inc., 345 Underhill Blvd., Syosset, NY 11791; Tel.: (718) 895-8950

Incorporated in 1966 in NY.
Donor(s): Abraham Rosenberg.
Foundation type: Independent
Financial data (yr. ended 12/31/90): Assets, $9,327,385 (M); expenditures, $384,155; qualifying distributions, $307,570, including $307,285 for 95 grants (high: $50,000; low: $50).
Fields of interest: Jewish welfare, higher education, hospitals, health associations.
Limitations: Giving primarily in NY.
Application information:
  Initial approach: Letter
  Deadline(s): None
  Write: Mrs. Sonia Rosenberg, V.P.
Officers: Abraham Rosenberg, Pres. and Treas.; Sonia Rosenberg, V.P. and Secy.
EIN: 136210591

2229
The Rosenstiel Foundation
c/o Roseman & Colin
575 Madison Ave.
New York 10022   (212) 940-8839

Incorporated in 1950 in OH.
Donor(s): Lewis S. Rosenstiel.‡
Foundation type: Independent
Financial data (yr. ended 12/31/91): Assets, $14,918,478 (M); expenditures, $754,782; qualifying distributions, $614,625, including $614,625 for 83 grants (high: $145,000; low: $500).
Purpose and activities: Grants largely for Polish cultural programs, the performing arts, health organizations, hospitals, and higher education.
Fields of interest: Poland, performing arts, health, higher education, rehabilitation.
Types of support: Seed money, general purposes.
Limitations: Giving primarily in NY and FL. No grants to individuals.
Application information: Contributes only to pre-selected organizations. Applications not accepted.
  Write: Rosanne Panzer, Asst. Secy.
Officers and Directors:* Blanka A. Rosenstiel,* Pres.; Elizabeth R. Kabler,* V.P.; Maurice C. Greenbaum,* Secy.
Number of staff: None.
EIN: 066034536

2230
The William Rosenwald Family Fund, Inc.
122 East 42nd St., 24th Fl.
New York 10168   (212) 697-2420

Incorporated in 1938 in CT.
Donor(s): William Rosenwald, and family.
Foundation type: Independent
Financial data (yr. ended 12/31/91): Assets, $15,032,216 (M); expenditures, $1,406,875; qualifying distributions, $1,159,802, including $1,128,150 for 44 grants (high: $814,100; low: $100).
Purpose and activities: Emphasis on Jewish welfare funds; some support for medical education and hospitals.
Fields of interest: Jewish welfare, medical education, hospitals.
Types of support: General purposes.
Limitations: Giving primarily in NY. No grants to individuals.
Application information: Contributes only to pre-selected organizations. Applications not accepted.
  Write: David P. Steinmann, Secy.
Officers and Directors:* William Rosenwald,* Pres. and Treas.; Nina Rosenwald,* V.P.; Alice R. Sigelman,* V.P.; Elizabeth R. Varet,* V.P.; David P. Steinmann, Secy.
EIN: 131635289

2231
Ross Family Charitable Foundation
c/o Oded Aboodi
75 Rockefeller Plaza, Suite 900
New York 10019

Established in 1989 in NY.
Donor(s): Steven J. Ross.
Foundation type: Independent
Financial data (yr. ended 11/30/91): Assets, $7,911,295 (M); gifts received, $45,000; expenditures, $524,680; qualifying distributions, $366,510, including $366,210 for 63 grants (high: $70,000; low: $100).

Fields of interest: Hospitals, health associations, social services, education, cultural programs, public policy, Jewish giving, community development.
Limitations: Giving primarily in the greater metropolitan New York, NY, area, including Long Island. No grants to individuals.
Application information: Contributes only to pre-selected organizations. Applications not accepted.
Trustees: Oded Aboodi, Steven J. Ross.
EIN: 133552082

2232
The Dorothea Haus Ross Foundation
1036 Monroe Ave.
Rochester 14620   (716) 473-6006

Established in 1979 in NY.
Donor(s): Dorothea Haus Ross.
Foundation type: Independent
Financial data (yr. ended 05/31/91): Assets, $2,595,766 (M); gifts received, $250,000; expenditures, $156,850; qualifying distributions, $84,019, including $84,019 for 26 grants (high: $6,000; low: $499; average: $2,723).
Purpose and activities: To advance the moral, mental, and physical well-being of children of all races and creeds in all parts of the world; to aid and assist in providing for the basic needs of food, shelter, and education of such children by whatever means and methods necessary or advisable; to prevent by medical research or otherwise the mental and physical handicaps of children.
Fields of interest: Child welfare, medical research, handicapped, hunger, youth, rehabilitation, child development, disadvantaged.
Types of support: Seed money, equipment, matching funds, special projects, research, publications, emergency funds, endowment funds, technical assistance, renovation projects.
Limitations: No grants to individuals, or for operating budgets, continuing support, annual campaigns, deficit financing, land acquisition, conferences, scholarships, or fellowships; no emergency funds outside Monroe County, NY; no loans.
Publications: Application guidelines.
Application information: 1 copy only of appendix material. Application form not required.
  Initial approach: Telephone, letter, or proposal
  Copies of proposal: 4
  Deadline(s): None
  Board meeting date(s): Quarterly
  Final notification: 2 months
  Write: Wayne S. Cook, Exec. Dir.
Trustees: Catherine Chamberlain, Philetus M. Chamberlain, Marine Midland Bank, N.A.
Officer: Wayne S. Cook, Ph.D., Exec. Dir.
Number of staff: 1 part-time professional.
EIN: 161080458

2233
Robert E. & Judith O. Rubin Foundation
c/o Goldman Sachs & Co., Tax Dept.
85 Broad St., 30th Fl.
New York 10004

Established in 1980 in NY.
Donor(s): Robert E. Rubin.

Foundation type: Independent
Financial data (yr. ended 08/31/91): Assets, $3,163,256 (M); gifts received, $1,000,000; expenditures, $534,965; qualifying distributions, $508,365, including $508,085 for 44 grants (high: $100,000; low: $100).
Fields of interest: Hospitals, education, Jewish welfare, cultural programs, theater.
Limitations: Giving primarily in New York, NY. No grants to individuals.
Application information: Applications not accepted.
Trustees: Judith O. Rubin, Robert E. Rubin, Roy J. Zuckerberg.
EIN: 133050749

2234
Helena Rubinstein Foundation, Inc. ▼
405 Lexington Ave.
New York 10174   (212) 986-0806

Incorporated in 1953 in NY.
Donor(s): Helena Rubinstein Gourielli.‡
Foundation type: Independent
Financial data (yr. ended 05/31/91): Assets, $33,589,039 (M); expenditures, $5,385,777; qualifying distributions, $5,047,266, including $4,588,457 for 248 grants (high: $300,000; average: $5,000-$25,000).
Purpose and activities: Focus on projects that benefit women and children. Funding primarily for higher and other education, community and social services, health care and medical research, and the arts.
Fields of interest: Women, child welfare, youth, education, education—minorities, higher education, legal education, social services, minorities, disadvantaged, drug abuse, homeless, health services, medical research, AIDS, Israel, arts, cultural programs, performing arts.
Types of support: Operating budgets, seed money, internships, scholarship funds, fellowships, research, continuing support, general purposes.
Limitations: Giving primarily in New York, NY. No grants to individuals, or for emergency funds or film or video projects; no loans.
Publications: Annual report (including application guidelines), application guidelines.
Application information: Application form not required.
  Initial approach: Letter
  Copies of proposal: 1
  Deadline(s): None
  Board meeting date(s): Nov. and May
  Final notification: 1 to 3 months
  Write: Diane Moss, Exec. Dir.
Officers and Directors:* Oscar Kolin,* Pres.; Diane Moss,* V.P. and Exec. Dir.; Robert S. Friedman,* Secy.-Treas.; Gertrude G. Michelson, Martin E. Segal, Louis E. Slesin, Suzanne Slesin.
Number of staff: 4 full-time professional; 1 full-time support; 1 part-time support.
EIN: 136102666
Recent health grants:
2234-1 Beth Israel Medical Center, NYC, NY, $25,000. For scholarships at Phillips Beth Israel School of Nursing. 1992.
2234-2 Childrens Blood Foundation, NYC, NY, $60,000. For Immunology Laboratory and general support. 1992.
2234-3 Childrens Health Fund, NYC, NY, $20,000. For New York Children's Health

Project, medical outreach for homeless and indigent children. 1992.
2234-4 Dartmouth Medical School, Hanover, NH, $15,000. For scholarships for women medical students. 1991.
2234-5 Door - A Center of Alternatives, NYC, NY, $15,000. For general support of sexual health and awareness program. 1992.
2234-6 Harvard University, School of Public Health, Boston, MA, $75,000. For stipends for Minority Fellowship Programs. 1991.
2234-7 Home Care Associates Training Institute, Bronx, NY, $10,000. For general support. 1992.
2234-8 March of Dimes Birth Defects Foundation, Greater New York Chapter, NYC, NY, $25,000. For Campaign for Healthier Babies. 1991.
2234-9 National Foundation for Facial Reconstruction, NYC, NY, $15,000. For Family Support Fund which assists needy patients to pay for incidental expenses associated with treatment. 1991.
2234-10 National Jewish Center for Immunology and Respiratory Medicine, NYC, NY, $10,000. For AIDS research. 1991.
2234-11 New York Alliance for the Public Schools, NYC, NY, $10,000. For Careers in Contemporary Health Care, program that encourages high school students to enter field of nursing. 1991.
2234-12 Phoenix House Foundation, NYC, NY, $45,000. For general support. 1992.
2234-13 Planned Parenthood Federation of America, NYC, NY, $25,000. For litigation program. 1992.
2234-14 Planned Parenthood of New York City, NYC, NY, $25,000. For the Hub: A Center for Change for South Bronx teens. 1992.
2234-15 Saint Francis Friends of the Poor, NYC, NY, $15,000. For psychiatric care for residents. 1991.
2234-16 South Dakota State University, College of Nursing, Brookings, SD, $10,000. For tuition assistance for nurses from Rosebud and Pine Ridge Reservations in RN Upward Mobility Program in Martin, South Dakota. 1991.
2234-17 University of Washington, Seattle, WA, $25,000. For cancer research. 1991.

2235
The Louis and Rachel Rudin Foundation, Inc. ▼
345 Park Ave.
New York 10154   (212) 644-8473

Incorporated in 1968 in NY.
Foundation type: Independent
Financial data (yr. ended 07/31/91): Assets, $20,695,824 (M); expenditures, $1,398,620; qualifying distributions, $1,378,858, including $1,277,500 for 31 grants (high: $95,000; low: $5,000; average: $15,000-$60,000).
Purpose and activities: Grants to medical and nursing schools only for educational training programs.
Fields of interest: Medical education, nursing.
Types of support: Scholarship funds.
Limitations: Giving primarily in New York, NY. No grants to individuals, or for building funds.
Application information:
  Initial approach: Letter

Write: Susan H. Rapaport, Admin.
Officers and Directors:* Jack Rudin,* Pres.; Lewis Steinman,* V.P.; Lewis Rudin,* Secy.; Natalie Lewin,* Treas.; Beth Rudin DeWoody, Donald Heimlich, Stephen Lewin.
EIN: 237039549
Recent health grants:
2235-1 Adelphi University, School of Nursing, Garden City, NY, $10,000. For scholarships. 1991.
2235-2 Alfred University, College of Nursing, Alfred, NY, $10,000. For scholarships. 1991.
2235-3 Bellevue Hospital Center, Hunter-Bellevue School of Nursing, NYC, NY, $50,000. For scholarships. 1991.
2235-4 Bronx Community College of the City University of New York, Department of Nursing, Bronx, NY, $62,000. For scholarships. 1991.
2235-5 Columbia University, College of Physicians and Surgeons, NYC, NY, $94,000. For medical scholarships. 1991.
2235-6 Columbia University, College of Physicians and Surgeons, NYC, NY, $32,000. For School of Nursing RN/MS Program scholarships. 1991.
2235-7 Columbia University, College of Physicians and Surgeons, NYC, NY, $19,000. For School of Nursing scholarships. 1991.
2235-8 Columbia University, College of Physicians and Surgeons, NYC, NY, $10,000. For Nephrology Fellowship. 1991.
2235-9 Columbia University, School of Nursing, NYC, NY, $50,000. For joint program with Memorial Sloan-Kettering Cancer Center in Graduate Oncology for scholarships to nurses in NYC hospitals. 1991.
2235-10 Cornell University, Medical College, Ithaca, NY, $55,000. For medical scholarships. 1991.
2235-11 Cornell University, Medical College, Ithaca, NY, $41,000. For Endocrinology Fellowship. 1991.
2235-12 Cornell University, Medical College, Ithaca, NY, $32,000. For fellowships for M.D.s and Ph.D.s. Grant shared with Memorial Sloan-Kettering Cancer Center. 1991.
2235-13 Mount Sinai School of Medicine, NYC, NY, $50,000. For nursing scholarships. 1991.
2235-14 Mount Sinai School of Medicine, NYC, NY, $44,700. For medical scholarships. 1991.
2235-15 Mount Sinai School of Medicine, NYC, NY, $29,800. For M.D./Ph.D. program. 1991.
2235-16 Mount Sinai School of Medicine, NYC, NY, $20,000. For City College of New York Bio-Medical Program. 1991.
2235-17 Mount Sinai School of Medicine, NYC, NY, $20,000. For Pre-Med Research Program with City University of New York. 1991.
2235-18 Mount Sinai School of Medicine, NYC, NY, $15,000. For Cancer Radiation Treatment Teaching Program. 1991.
2235-19 New York Medical College, Valhalla, NY, $42,000. For joint program with Saint Vincents Hospital in Pediatric Residency Scholarships. 1991.
2235-20 New York University, Nursing Division of the School of Education, NYC, NY, $67,000. For scholarships. 1991.
2235-21 New York University, School of Medicine, NYC, NY, $88,000. For medical scholarships. 1991.

2235-22 New York University, School of Medicine, NYC, NY, $20,000. For City College of New York Bio-Medical Program. 1991.
2235-23 North General Hospital, Helen Fuld School of Nursing, NYC, NY, $57,000. For scholarships. 1991.
2235-24 North General Hospital, Helen Fuld School of Nursing, NYC, NY, $38,000. For Tutorial Program. 1991.
2235-25 Phillips Beth Israel School of Nursing, NYC, NY, $60,000. For scholarships. 1991.
2235-26 Rutgers, The State University of New Jersey, College of Nursing, Newark, NJ, $40,000. For nursing scholarships. 1991.
2235-27 Saint Lukes-Roosevelt Hospital Center, NYC, NY, $20,000. For joint program with Columbia University in Drug Rehabilitation Training in Emergency Room. 1991.
2235-28 Saint Vincents Hospital and Medical Center of New York, School of Nursing, NYC, NY, $86,000. For scholarships. 1991.
2235-29 Saint Vincents Hospital and Medical Center of New York, School of Nursing, NYC, NY, $15,000. For special education program in nursing care of patients with chronic diseases. 1991.
2235-30 Yeshiva University, Albert Einstein College of Medicine, NYC, NY, $95,000. For medical scholarships. 1991.

2236
Samuel and May Rudin Foundation, Inc. ▼
345 Park Ave.
New York 10154   (212) 644-8473

Incorporated in 1976 in NY.
Donor(s): Samuel Rudin.‡
Foundation type: Independent
Financial data (yr. ended 06/30/91): Assets, $2,743,797 (M); gifts received, $6,239,055; expenditures, $7,284,817; qualifying distributions, $7,223,692, including $6,977,797 for 219 grants (high: $1,300,000; low: $50; average: $10,000-$50,000).
Purpose and activities: Support primarily for higher education, social service and religious welfare agencies, hospitals and health associations, and museums, performing arts groups, and other cultural programs.
Fields of interest: Higher education, social services, religious welfare, hospitals, health associations, museums, performing arts, cultural programs.
Limitations: Giving primarily in New York, NY.
Application information:
  Initial approach: Letter
  Deadline(s): None
  Write: Susan H. Rapaport, Admin.
Officers and Directors:* Jack Rudin,* Pres.; Lewis Rudin,* Exec V.P. and Secy.-Treas.; Beth Rudin DeWoody,* V.P.; Eric C. Rudin,* V.P.; Madeleine Rudin Johnson, Katherine L. Rudin, William Rudin.
EIN: 132906946
Recent health grants:
2236-1 American Narcolepsy Association, NYC, NY, $20,000. For general support. 1991.
2236-2 Cedars-Sinai Medical Center, Los Angeles, CA, $20,000. For hospice for leukemia patients. 1991.

2236-3 Cedars-Sinai Medical Center, Department of Transfusion Medicine, Los Angeles, CA, $20,000. For research. 1991.
2236-4 Children of Alcoholics Foundation, NYC, NY, $10,000. For Helpline. 1991.
2236-5 Cleveland Clinic, Cleveland, OH, $300,000. For general support. 1991.
2236-6 Columbia University, NYC, NY, $162,000. For Incarnation Children's Center for Homeless. Grant shared with Harlem Hospital. 1991.
2236-7 Columbia University, NYC, NY, $65,000. For pediatric injury prevention arts program. Grant shared with Harlem Hospital. 1991.
2236-8 Columbia University, College of Physicians and Surgeons, NYC, NY, $150,000. For May Rudin Fellowship at Center for the Study of Society and Medicine. 1991.
2236-9 Columbia University, College of Physicians and Surgeons, NYC, NY, $30,000. For interdepartmental graduate program. 1991.
2236-10 Columbia University, College of Physicians and Surgeons, NYC, NY, $15,000. For Samuel Rudin Distinguished Visiting Professorship Endowment. 1991.
2236-11 Columbia University, College of Physicians and Surgeons, NYC, NY, $10,000. For Amyotrophic Lateral Sclerosis (ALS) research. 1991.
2236-12 Columbia University, School of Nursing, NYC, NY, $20,000. For May Rudin Clinical Research Program. 1991.
2236-13 Damon Runyon-Walter Winchell Cancer Fund, NYC, NY, $25,000. For fellowship. 1991.
2236-14 Damon Runyon-Walter Winchell Cancer Fund, NYC, NY, $20,000. For general support for research. 1991.
2236-15 Daytop Village Foundation, NYC, NY, $10,000. For general support for drug rehabilitation. 1991.
2236-16 Gay Mens Health Crisis (GMHC), NYC, NY, $116,000. For family services. 1991.
2236-17 Happiness is Camping, Bronx, NY, $10,000. To improve facility. 1991.
2236-18 Juvenile Diabetes Foundation, NYC, NY, $10,000. For Casey Johnson Research Fund. 1991.
2236-19 Lenox Hill Hospital, NYC, NY, $125,000. For Interventional Cardiology Project. 1991.
2236-20 Memorial Sloan-Kettering Cancer Center, NYC, NY, $143,332. For Roberta C. Rudin Leukemia Research Fund. 1991.
2236-21 Memorial Sloan-Kettering Cancer Center, NYC, NY, $50,000. For Model Psychology Support Service Program. 1991.
2236-22 Memorial Sloan-Kettering Cancer Center, NYC, NY, $20,000. For AIDS research. 1991.
2236-23 Memorial Sloan-Kettering Cancer Center, NYC, NY, $10,000. For Graduate Oncology Nursing. Grant shared with Columbia University College of Physicians and Surgeons. 1991.
2236-24 Memorial Sloan-Kettering Cancer Center, NYC, NY, $10,000. For I Have A Dream. 1991.
2236-25 Mount Sinai Hospital and Medical Center, NYC, NY, $50,000. For North General AIDS Fellowship. 1991.

2236-26 Mount Sinai Hospital and Medical Center, NYC, NY, $35,000. For Adolescent AIDS Health Center in Harlem. 1991.

2236-27 Mount Sinai Hospital and Medical Center, NYC, NY, $27,000. For medical scholarships. 1991.

2236-28 Mount Sinai Hospital and Medical Center, NYC, NY, $10,000. For Pediatric Prevention Initiative. 1991.

2236-29 Mount Sinai Hospital and Medical Center, Department of Radiotherapy, NYC, NY, $10,000. For scholarships. 1991.

2236-30 National Association for Visually Handicapped, NYC, NY, $15,000. For information and referral service. 1991.

2236-31 New York Blood Center, NYC, NY, $25,000. For minority donor campaign. 1991.

2236-32 New York School for Circus Arts, NYC, NY, $13,008. For Big Apple Circus. 1991.

2236-33 North General Hospital, NYC, NY, $20,000. For management development program. 1991.

2236-34 North General Hospital, Helene Fuld School of Nursing, NYC, NY, $30,000. For nursing scholarships. 1991.

2236-35 Nurses House, NYC, NY, $10,000. For support for nurses. 1991.

2236-36 Phoenix House Development Fund, NYC, NY, $50,000. For AIDS and drug education. 1991.

2236-37 Planned Parenthood of New York City, NYC, NY, $30,000. For general support. 1991.

2236-38 Planned Parenthood of New York City, NYC, NY, $10,000. For general support. 1991.

2236-39 Planned Parenthood of New York City, NYC, NY, $10,000. For Project Beat Street. 1991.

2236-40 Research to Prevent Blindness, NYC, NY, $10,000. For general support. 1991.

2236-41 Ronald McDonald House, NYC, NY, $25,000. For stipends for underprivileged families. Grant shared with Children's Oncology Society of New York. 1991.

2236-42 Saint Vincents Hospital and Medical Center of New York, NYC, NY, $150,000. For supportive care program for people with AIDS. 1991.

2236-43 Southampton Hospital Association, Southampton, NY, $10,000. For surgical equipment. 1991.

2236-44 Veritas Therapeutic Community, NYC, NY, $10,000. For forgotten youngsters program. 1991.

2236-45 Visiting Nurse Service of New York, NYC, NY, $10,000. For hospice. 1991.

2236-46 Wellness Community-National, Santa Monica, CA, $10,000. For general support. 1991.

2236-47 Yeshiva University, Albert Einstein College of Medicine, NYC, NY, $150,000. For scholarship for Ph.D research. 1991.

2236-48 Youth Counseling League, NYC, NY, $15,000. For counseling at New York City Public Schools. 1991.

2237
Mary A. H. Rumsey Foundation
63 Wall St., 23rd Fl.
New York 10005-3062

Established in 1984 in NY.
Donor(s): Mary A.H. Rumsey.‡

Foundation type: Independent
Financial data (yr. ended 09/30/90): Assets, $5,168,356 (M); gifts received, $2,484,200; expenditures, $494,109; qualifying distributions, $422,459, including $389,000 for 66 grants (high: $75,000; low: $500).
Fields of interest: Cultural programs, health, hospitals, conservation, animal welfare, higher education.
Limitations: Giving on a national basis, with some emphasis on the greater metropolitan New York, NY, area. No grants to individuals.
Application information: Application form not required.
  Initial approach: Letter
  Deadline(s): None
  Write: William F. Hibberd, Secy.
Officers and Directors:* Charles C. Rumsey,* Pres.; William Rich III,* V.P.; William F. Hibberd, Secy.; William J. Corcoran, Treas.; Mary M. Rumsey, Douglas F. Williamson, Jr.
EIN: 133244314

2238
The Peter M. Sacerdote Foundation
c/o Goldman Sachs & Co., Tax Dept.
85 Broad St.
New York 10004

Established in 1981.
Foundation type: Independent
Financial data (yr. ended 02/28/91): Assets, $1,405,710 (M); expenditures, $234,643; qualifying distributions, $226,580, including $226,300 for 45 grants (high: $62,500; low: $100).
Fields of interest: Business education, higher education, secondary education, theater, hospitals, community funds.
Limitations: Giving primarily in New York, NY. No grants to individuals.
Application information: Contributes only to pre-selected organizations. Applications not accepted.
Trustee: Peter M. Sacerdote.
EIN: 133102940

2239
Raymond and Beverly Sackler Foundation, Inc.
15 East 62nd St.
New York 10021-7204

Established in 1967 in NY.
Donor(s): Raymond R. Sackler, R.S. Sackler, J.D. Sackler.
Foundation type: Operating
Financial data (yr. ended 12/31/90): Assets, $10,765,445 (M); gifts received, $900,000; expenditures, $636,539; qualifying distributions, $594,226, including $42,708 for 3 grants (high: $20,000; low: $2,708; average: $2,708-$20,000) and $551,518 for 4 foundation-administered programs.
Fields of interest: Medical research, biological sciences, physical sciences, medical education, hospitals, mathematics, museums.
Application information: Applications not accepted.
Officers: Raymond R. Sackler, Pres.; J.D. Sackler, V.P.; R.S. Sackler, V.P.; B. Sackler, Secy.-Treas.

Number of staff: 7 full-time professional; 4 part-time professional.
EIN: 237022467

2240
Saks Fifth Avenue Corporate Giving Program
611 Fifth Avenue
New York 10022   (212) 940-4240

Purpose and activities: Supports humanities and culture, civic affairs, literacy, arts, and health and social services, including AIDS and drug abuse programs.
Fields of interest: Arts, museums, civic affairs, health, hospitals, humanities, social services, drug abuse, AIDS, literacy.
Limitations: Giving limited to areas where Saks operates. No support for political or religious causes.
Application information: Each store has its own contributions budget and concentrates on its own community. The Saks in NY city prefers not to receive applications. In NY Special Events/Publicity handles contributions.
  Initial approach: Brief letter to director of Corporate Contributions Committee or local manager of nearest branch store
  Deadline(s): None
  Write: Helen O'Hagan, Dir., Corp. Contribs. Comm.

2241
The William R. and Virginia F. Salomon Family Foundation, Inc.
1301 Ave. of the Americas, 41st Fl.
New York 10019

Incorporated in 1954 in NY.
Donor(s): William R. Salomon.
Foundation type: Independent
Financial data (yr. ended 12/31/91): Assets, $1,915,336 (M); expenditures, $445,317; qualifying distributions, $429,995, including $424,670 for 97 grants (high: $100,000; low: $10).
Fields of interest: Higher education, hospitals, social services, cultural programs, civic affairs, Jewish welfare.
Types of support: Annual campaigns, building funds, general purposes, research.
Limitations: Giving primarily in New York, NY. No grants to individuals.
Application information: Contributes only to pre-selected organizations. Applications not accepted.
  Board meeting date(s): Annually
  Write: William R. Salomon, Pres.
Officers and Directors:* William R. Salomon,* Pres. and Treas.; Virginia F. Salomon,* V.P.; Susan S. Havens, Peter F. Salomon.
Number of staff: None.
EIN: 136088823

2242
The Salomon Foundation Inc. ▼
Seven World Trade Center
New York 10048   (212) 783-7434

Established in 1985 in NY.

Donor(s): Salomon, Inc.
Foundation type: Company-sponsored
Financial data (yr. ended 12/31/90): Assets, $3,855,011 (M); gifts received, $701,258; expenditures, $2,611,170; qualifying distributions, $2,611,170, including $1,164,208 for 217 grants (high: $107,500; low: $1,000; average: $1,000-$10,000) and $1,318,789 for employee matching gifts.
Purpose and activities: Support for higher, elementary, and secondary education; arts and culture; community activities; libraries; and medical research and health. The foundation also sponsors an employee matching gift program for education. During 1990, the foundation expanded its program to include the Salomon Robeson Scholarship Fund, which awards a limited number of scholarships to graduating seniors who were chosen by a prestigious independent selection service to receive four-year scholarships.
Fields of interest: Education, elementary education, secondary education, education—minorities, business education, arts, cultural programs, community development, health, women, youth, disadvantaged.
Types of support: Employee matching gifts, scholarship funds.
Limitations: Giving primarily in the New York, NY, area and other geographic locations where branch offices are situated, notably Los Angeles and San Francisco, CA; Dallas, TX; Chicago, IL; Atlanta, GA; and Boston, MA. No grants to individuals.
Application information: Application form not required.
Initial approach: 3 page letter
Copies of proposal: 1
Deadline(s): None
Write: Jane Heffner, V.P. and Secy.
Officers and Directors:* Jane E. Heffner, V.P. and Secy.; Donald M. Feuerstein, Treas.; Warren E. Buffett, Andrew J. Hall, Gedale B. Horowitz, James L. Massey, William F. May.
Number of staff: 1 full-time professional; 1 full-time support.
EIN: 133388259

2243
Salomon, Inc. Corporate Contributions Program
Seven World Trade Center
New York 10048   (212) 783-7000

Purpose and activities: Support for higher and secondary education, libraries, literacy, business and minority education, the arts, medical research, drug abuse programs, employment, hospitals and health associations, women, minorities, and youth. Combined foundation and corporate giving totaled $4.6 million in 1990. Approximately half stemmed from the foundation and the other part from the corporation.
Fields of interest: Drug abuse, business education, secondary education, elementary education, disadvantaged, museums, hospitals, arts, environment, hunger, civic affairs, dance, education—minorities, employment, education, libraries, minorities, literacy, performing arts, social services, women, youth.
Types of support: Annual campaigns, employee matching gifts, operating budgets, special

projects, continuing support, student aid, general purposes, scholarship funds.
Limitations: Giving primarily in New York, NY, Atlanta, GA, Boston, MA, Chicago, IL, Dallas, TX, and Los Angeles and San Francisco, CA.
Application information: Application form not required.
Initial approach: Letter and back-up information to headquarters
Copies of proposal: 1
Deadline(s): None
Board meeting date(s): All year round
Write: Warren Buffett, Chair., Pres., and C.E.O.
Administrator: Jane Heffner, V.P., Corp. Contribs.
Number of staff: 1 full-time professional; 1 full-time support; 1 part-time support.

2244
The Gary Saltz Foundation, Inc.
600 Madison Ave., 20th Fl.
New York 10022   (212) 980-0910

Incorporated in 1985 in NY.
Donor(s): Jack Saltz, Anita Saltz.
Foundation type: Independent
Financial data (yr. ended 04/30/90): Assets, $4,459,187 (M); gifts received, $1,000,000; expenditures, $26,641; qualifying distributions, $0.
Purpose and activities: Grants primarily for medical research with emphasis on juvenile diabetes and cancer in children.
Fields of interest: Cancer, medical research.
Types of support: Research.
Limitations: No grants to individuals.
Application information: Contributes only to pre-selected organizations. Applications not accepted.
Write: Anita Saltz, Pres.
Officers: Anita Saltz, Pres.; Ronald Saltz, V.P.; Susan Saltz, Secy.; Leonard Saltz, Treas.
EIN: 133267114

2245
The Fan Fox and Leslie R. Samuels Foundation, Inc. ▼
630 Fifth Ave., Suite 2255
New York 10111-0002   (212) 315-2940
FAX: (212) 765-3319

Incorporated in 1959 in UT; reincorporated in 1981 in NY.
Donor(s): Leslie R. Samuels,‡ Fan Fox Samuels.‡
Foundation type: Independent
Financial data (yr. ended 07/31/90): Assets, $101,510,082 (M); gifts received, $1,150,000; expenditures, $4,732,138; qualifying distributions, $4,131,483, including $3,785,622 for 99 grants (high: $300,000; low: $280; average: $5,000-$200,000).
Purpose and activities: Grants largely for the performing arts and other cultural programs; hospitals and health care, especially programs for the young and elderly, including AIDS and cancer research; and arts-in-education.
Fields of interest: Performing arts, museums, cultural programs, dance, music, theater, health, drug abuse, hospices, hospitals, hospitals—building funds, aged, youth, AIDS, cancer, education, libraries.

Types of support: Continuing support, seed money, building funds, equipment, research, matching funds, special projects.
Limitations: Giving primarily in New York, NY. No grants to individuals, or for scholarships or fellowships; no loans.
Publications: Biennial report (including application guidelines).
Application information: Application form not required.
Initial approach: Letter
Copies of proposal: 1
Deadline(s): None
Board meeting date(s): Oct., Jan., Apr., July, and as necessary
Final notification: 2 months
Write: Adam Bernstein, Prog. Officer
Officers and Directors:* Morton J. Bernstein,* Chair.; Marvin A. Kaufman,* Pres.; Joseph C. Mitchell,* V.P. and Treas.; Carlos D. Moseley,* V.P.; Muriel Nasser,* Secy.
Number of staff: 3 full-time professional; 2 full-time support.
EIN: 133124818
Recent health grants:
2245-1 American Foundation for AIDS Research, NYC, NY, $50,000. Toward services to New York City based community clinical trial centers and toward creation of capital development program. 1991.
2245-2 Beth Israel Medical Center, NYC, NY, $200,000. Toward construction, renovation and furnishing of Samuels Planetree Model Hospital Unit. 1991.
2245-3 Childrens House of Long Island, New Hyde Park, NY, $10,000. Toward Hearts for the House program for Ronald McDonald House on campus of Long Island Jewish Hospital Medical Center. 1991.
2245-4 Happiness is Camping, Bronx, NY, $20,000. Toward general support for facility in Blairstown, NJ for children with cancer. 1991.
2245-5 Harlem Interfaith Counseling Service, NYC, NY, $25,000. Toward Pre-Kindergarten Learning Laboratory. 1991.
2245-6 Hospital Audiences, NYC, NY, $10,000. Toward OMNIBUS program to transport people with physical limitations to cultural and sports events. 1991.
2245-7 Hospital for Joint Diseases, NYC, NY, $20,000. Toward Geriatric Hip Fracture Program. 1991.
2245-8 Jewish Board of Family and Childrens Services, NYC, NY, $50,000. Toward Learning Center in Brooklyn for diagnosis and treatment of learning disabilities in children. 1991.
2245-9 Long Island Jewish Medical Center, New Hyde Park, NY, $98,875. Toward Geriatric Assessment Team program to study care of geriatric patients to improve their treatment and reduce their stay in hospital. 1991.
2245-10 Long Island Jewish Medical Center, New Hyde Park, NY, $50,000. Toward Psychosocial Program in Oncology for patients and out-patients. 1991.
2245-11 Long Island Jewish Medical Center, Schneider Children's Hospital, New Hyde Park, NY, $106,100. Toward establishment of Genetics Laboratory to facilitate improved and increased testing of high-risk pregnant women. 1991.
2245-12 Long Island Jewish Medical Center, Schneider Children's Hospital, New Hyde

Park, NY, $81,000. Toward Regional Neonatal Satellite program. 1991.

2245-13 Long Island Jewish Medical Center, Schneider Children's Hospital, New Hyde Park, NY, $37,500. Toward Pediatric Asthma Center. 1991.

2245-14 Medical and Health Research Association of New York City, NYC, NY, $30,000. Toward Infant Mortality Initiative of New York City Department of Health. 1991.

2245-15 Mount Sinai Hospital and Medical Center, NYC, NY, $75,000. Toward Geriatrics Fellowship Program for Subspecialties. 1991.

2245-16 Mount Sinai Hospital and Medical Center, NYC, NY, $50,000. Toward spasticity and fertility programs for individuals paralyzed by spinal cord injury. 1991.

2245-17 National Center for Learning Disabilities, NYC, NY, $20,000. Toward making videos and publications on training of probation officers in dealing with learning-disabled, at-risk youth in juvenile and family court systems. 1991.

2245-18 New York University Medical Center, NYC, NY, $10,000. Toward Cardiovascular and Hemodynamics Research project. 1991.

2245-19 Pride of Judea Mental Health Center, Douglaston, NY, $16,000. Toward producing play Halfway There by Periwinkle National Theater for Young Audiences on alcohol and substance abuse. 1991.

2245-20 Saint Lukes-Roosevelt Hospital Center, NYC, NY, $200,000. Toward construction of Samuels Immunodeficiency Center for treatment of people with AIDS in new building and clinic in Winston Building at Roosevelt Hospital. 1991.

2246
Sandoz Foundation of America
608 Fifth Ave.
New York 10020   (201) 386-0880

Incorporated in 1965 in DE.
Donor(s): Sandoz Corp.
Foundation type: Company-sponsored
Financial data (yr. ended 12/31/91): Assets, $5,820,161 (M); expenditures, $234,556; qualifying distributions, $191,968, including $188,900 for 13 grants (high: $35,000; low: $650).
Purpose and activities: Grants primarily to educational and charitable institutions engaged in medical and scientific research.
Fields of interest: Medical research, medical education, science and technology.
Limitations: No grants to individuals, or for building or endowment funds or operating budgets.
Publications: Application guidelines.
Application information:
   Initial approach: Letter
   Copies of proposal: 1
   Deadline(s): None
   Board meeting date(s): As required
   Write: Craig D. Burrell, M.D., V.P.
Officers: Daniel C. Wagniere, Pres.; Kenneth L. Brewton, Jr., V.P.; Craig D. Burrell, M.D., V.P.; Herbert J. Brennan, Secy.
Trustees: Marc Moret, M.D., Ulrich H. Oppikofer, M.D.
EIN: 136193034

2247
Joseph E. & Norma G. Saul Foundation, Inc.
c/o Saul Partners
630 Fifth Ave., Suite 2518
New York 10111

Established in 1984 in NY.
Donor(s): Joseph E. Saul.
Foundation type: Independent
Financial data (yr. ended 09/30/91): Assets, $2,046,213 (M); gifts received, $19,925; expenditures, $1,507,723; qualifying distributions, $1,502,503, including $1,502,218 for 24 grants (high: $675,000; low: $35; average: $35-$675,000).
Fields of interest: Jewish welfare, Jewish giving, higher education, cultural programs, hospitals.
Limitations: Giving primarily in New York, NY, and PA. No grants to individuals.
Publications: 990-PF.
Application information: Contributes only to pre-selected organizations. Applications not accepted.
Officers and Trustees:* Joseph E. Saul,* Pres. and Treas.; Andrew M. Saul,* V.P.; Norma G. Saul,* Secy.; Lynn T. Fischer, Sidney J. Silberman.
EIN: 133254180

2248
Michael & Helen Schaffer Foundation, Inc.
295 Madison Ave.
New York 10017

Established in 1961 in NY.
Donor(s): Michael I. Schaffer, Helen Schaffer.
Foundation type: Independent
Financial data (yr. ended 07/31/91): Assets, $7,855,808 (M); gifts received, $2,000,000; expenditures, $695,501; qualifying distributions, $625,506, including $619,326 for 67 grants (high: $51,000; low: $75).
Fields of interest: Health, education.
Limitations: Giving primarily in NY, with some emphasis on New York City. No grants to individuals.
Application information: Contributes only to pre-selected organizations. Applications not accepted.
Officers: Michael I. Schaffer, Pres.; Helen Schaffer, V.P.; Wendy Appel, Secy.; Peter Schaffer, Treas.
EIN: 136159235

2249
The Scherman Foundation, Inc. ▼
315 West 57th St., Suite 204
New York 10019   (212) 489-7143

Incorporated in 1941 in NY.
Donor(s): Members of the Scherman family.
Foundation type: Independent
Financial data (yr. ended 12/31/91): Assets, $73,772,134 (M); expenditures, $4,350,505; qualifying distributions, $4,090,378, including $3,779,685 for 132 grants (high: $200,000; low: $5,000; average: $5,000-$25,000) and $40,000 for program-related investments.
Purpose and activities: Grants largely for conservation, disarmament and peace, family planning, human rights and liberties, the arts, and social welfare. In the last two areas, priority is given to organizations in New York City. In the social welfare field, grants are made to organizations concerned with social justice, housing, public affairs, and community self-help.
Fields of interest: Conservation, environment, arms control, peace, human rights, civil rights, family planning, performing arts, cultural programs, arts, music, theater, social services, family services, homeless, hunger, housing, community development, libraries, legal services.
Types of support: Operating budgets, continuing support, seed money, emergency funds, matching funds, program-related investments, special projects, general purposes, technical assistance.
Limitations: Giving primarily in New York, NY, for arts and social welfare. No support for colleges, universities, or other higher educational institutions. No grants to individuals, or for building or endowment funds, scholarships, or fellowships.
Publications: Annual report (including application guidelines), application guidelines.
Application information: Application form not required.
   Initial approach: Letter
   Copies of proposal: 1
   Deadline(s): None
   Board meeting date(s): Quarterly
   Final notification: 3 months
   Write: David F. Freeman, Exec. Dir.
Officers and Directors:* Axel G. Rosin,* Pres.; Katharine S. Rosin,* Secy.; David F. Freeman, Treas. and Exec. Dir.; Helen Edey, M.D., Susanna Sahatdjian, Anthony M. Schulte, Sandra Silverman, Karen R. Sollins, Marcia Thompson.
Number of staff: 1 full-time professional; 1 part-time professional; 1 full-time support.
EIN: 136098464
Recent health grants:
2249-1 Big Apple Circus, NYC, NY, $10,000. For general support. 1990.
2249-2 Catholics for a Free Choice, DC, $50,000. For general support. 1990.
2249-3 Columbia University, Center for Population and Family Health, NYC, NY, $60,000. For general support. 1990.
2249-4 Emmaus House, NYC, NY, $15,000. For housing program for homeless people with AIDS. 1990.
2249-5 Friends and Relatives of Institutionalized Aged, NYC, NY, $25,000. For general support. 1990.
2249-6 Johns Hopkins Hospital, Baltimore, MD, $10,000. For research on alcoholism. 1990.
2249-7 Mental Health Law Project, DC, $20,000. For ACCESS Development Fund. 1990.
2249-8 Physicians for Social Responsibility, DC, $15,000. For general support. 1990.
2249-9 Planned Parenthood Federation of America, NYC, NY, $25,000. For Family Planning International Assistance program. 1990.
2249-10 Population Institute, DC, $20,000. For general support. 1990.
2249-11 Village Nursing Home, NYC, NY, $20,000. For budget for Rivington House. 1990.
2249-12 World Neighbors, Oklahoma City, OK, $20,000. For Reproductive Health Care Program. 1990.

2250
S. H. and Helen R. Scheuer Family Foundation, Inc. ▼
104 East 40th St.
New York 10016-1801   (212) 573-8350

Incorporated in 1943 in NY.
Donor(s): Members of the Scheuer family.
Foundation type: Independent
Financial data (yr. ended 11/30/90): Assets, $27,799,665 (M); gifts received, $6,322,816; expenditures, $14,013,890; qualifying distributions, $14,109,177, including $13,081,495 for 292 grants (high: $3,340,430; low: $100; average: $5,000-$50,000).
Purpose and activities: Emphasis on local Jewish welfare funds, higher education, and cultural programs.
Fields of interest: Jewish giving, Jewish welfare, higher education, cultural programs.
Limitations: Giving primarily in New York, NY.
Application information: The foundation only makes contributions to pre-selected organizations. However, the foundation does review unsolicited applications for funds.
 Board meeting date(s): As necessary
 Write: Wilbur Daniels, Exec. Dir.
Officers: Amy Scheuer Cohen, Pres.; Richard J. Scheuer, V.P.; Harvey Brecher, Secy.; Harold Cohen, Treas.
Number of staff: 1 full-time professional.
EIN: 136062661
Recent health grants:
2250-1 American Friends of Jerusalem Mental Health Center, NYC, NY, $125,000. 1990.
2250-2 Beth Abraham Foundation, Bronx, NY, $151,648. 1990.
2250-3 Beth Abraham Hospital, Bronx, NY, $125,000. 1990.
2250-4 Bikur Cholim of New York, NYC, NY, $10,000. 1990.
2250-5 Center for Preventive Psychiatry, White Plains, NY, $10,000. 1990.
2250-6 Metropolitan Jewish Geriatric Center, Brooklyn, NY, $40,254. 1990.
2250-7 National Gaucher Foundation, DC, $25,000. 1990.

2251
Sarah I. Schieffelin Residuary Trust
c/o The Bank of New York
48 Wall St.
New York 10286

Established in 1976.
Donor(s): Sarah I. Schieffelin.‡
Foundation type: Independent
Financial data (yr. ended 03/31/91): Assets, $7,008,486 (M); expenditures, $365,450; qualifying distributions, $320,576, including $296,949 for 29 grants (high: $30,000; low: $1,000).
Fields of interest: Conservation, wildlife, cultural programs, health, social services, Protestant giving.
Types of support: Continuing support.
Limitations: Giving primarily in New York, NY. No grants to individuals.
Application information:
 Initial approach: Proposal
 Copies of proposal: 1
 Deadline(s): Mar. 31
 Board meeting date(s): May 31

 Final notification: June 30
 Write: Grace Allen
Trustees: Thomas B. Fenlon, The Bank of New York.
EIN: 136724459

2252
The Dorothy Schiff Foundation
(Formerly The Pisces Foundation)
c/o Chemical Bank
30 Rockefeller Plaza
New York 10112   (212) 621-2146

Incorporated in 1951 in NY.
Donor(s): Dorothy Schiff,‡ New York Post Corp.
Foundation type: Independent
Financial data (yr. ended 12/31/90): Assets, $8,249,841 (M); expenditures, $487,561; qualifying distributions, $442,450, including $401,500 for 40 grants (high: $25,000; low: $1,000).
Fields of interest: Media and communications, education, hospitals, delinquency, AIDS, environment, family planning.
Limitations: Giving primarily in NY. No grants to individuals, or for endowment or capital funds or matching gifts; no loans.
Application information:
 Initial approach: Letter
 Deadline(s): None
 Board meeting date(s): Monthly except Aug.
 Write: Adele Hall Sweet, Pres.
Officers: Adele Hall Sweet, Pres.; Sarah-Ann Kramarsky, Secy.; Mortimer W. Hall, Treas.
Trustee: Chemical Bank.
Number of staff: None.
EIN: 136018311

2253
Priscilla & Richard J. Schmeelk Foundation, Inc.
c/o Noble, Speer, & Fulvio
60 East 42nd St.
New York 10165

Established in 1983 in NY.
Donor(s): Richard J. Schmeelk.
Foundation type: Independent
Financial data (yr. ended 12/31/90): Assets, $980,955 (M); gifts received, $144,850; expenditures, $225,820; qualifying distributions, $225,820, including $223,570 for 71 grants (high: $50,000; low: $20).
Fields of interest: Social services, hospitals, youth, Jewish giving, public affairs.
Limitations: Giving primarily in New York, NY. No grants to individuals.
Application information: Contributes only to pre-selected organizations. Applications not accepted.
Officers and Directors:* Richard J. Schmeelk,* Pres. and Treas.; Priscilla M. Schmeelk,* V.P. and Secy.; George DeSipio.
EIN: 133126387

2254
Charles & Mildred Schnurmacher Foundation, Inc.
1114 First Ave.
New York 10021

Established in 1977 in NY.
Donor(s): Charles M. Schnurmacher.‡
Foundation type: Independent
Financial data (yr. ended 11/30/91): Assets, $21,394,282 (M); expenditures, $1,140,061; qualifying distributions, $1,089,294, including $1,058,000 for 45 grants (high: $276,000; low: $500).
Fields of interest: Medical research, hospitals, Jewish giving, higher education.
Limitations: Giving primarily in NY. No grants to individuals.
Application information:
 Initial approach: Letter
 Deadline(s): None
Officers: Adolph Schnurmacher, Pres.; Fred Plotkin, Secy.; Ira J. Weinstein, Treas.
EIN: 132937218

2255
David Schwartz Foundation, Inc. ▼
c/o Siegel, Sacks & Co.
630 Third Ave.
New York 10017   (212) 682-6640

Incorporated in 1945 in NY.
Donor(s): Jonathan Logan, Inc., David Schwartz, and others.
Foundation type: Independent
Financial data (yr. ended 05/31/91): Assets, $14,139,407 (M); expenditures, $1,675,869; qualifying distributions, $1,486,363, including $1,486,363 for 81 grants (high: $417,625; low: $50; average: $500-$25,000).
Purpose and activities: Emphasis on higher education, cultural programs, and social welfare; support also for hospitals, health agencies, and Jewish organizations.
Fields of interest: Higher education, cultural programs, welfare, hospitals, health services, Jewish giving.
Types of support: General purposes.
Limitations: Giving primarily in NY, with emphasis on New York City. No grants to individuals.
Application information: Funds currently committed; contributes only to pre-selected organizations. Applications not accepted.
 Board meeting date(s): At least once a year, usually in May or June
Officers and Directors:* Richard J. Schwartz,* Pres.; Sheila Schwartz,* V.P. and Treas.; Stephen D. Gardner,* Secy.; Irene Schwartz.
Number of staff: None.
EIN: 226075974

2256
Arnold and Marie Schwartz Fund for Education and Health Research
465 Park Ave.
New York 10022

Incorporated in 1971 in DE.
Donor(s): Arnold Schwartz Charitable Trust.
Foundation type: Independent

Financial data (yr. ended 03/31/91): Assets, $4,897,272 (M); expenditures, $616,395; qualifying distributions, $552,665, including $502,344 for 78 grants (high: $156,000; low: $25; average: $500-$10,000).
Fields of interest: Higher education, medical research, hospitals, music, religion, historic preservation.
Types of support: General purposes, building funds, scholarship funds.
Limitations: Giving primarily in the New York, NY, metropolitan area.
Application information:
Deadline(s): None
Officers and Directors:* Marie D. Schwartz, Pres.; Ruth Kerstein,* Secy.; Sylvia Kassel, Nellie Jane MacDonald.
EIN: 237115019

2257
The Schwarzman Charitable Foundation
c/o Barry Strauss Assocs., Ltd.
245 Fifth Ave., Suite 1102
New York 10016-8775

Established in 1986 in NY.
Donor(s): Stephen A. Schwarzman.
Foundation type: Independent
Financial data (yr. ended 11/30/91): Assets, $32,768 (M); gifts received, $481,166; expenditures, $496,609; qualifying distributions, $496,534, including $494,674 for 54 grants (high: $100,000; low: $20).
Fields of interest: Jewish giving, cultural programs, performing arts, film, higher education, secondary education, hospitals.
Limitations: Giving primarily in New York, NY; some giving also in Boston, MA. No grants to individuals.
Application information: Contributes only to pre-selected organizations. Applications not accepted.
Write: Stephen A. Schwarzman, Trustee
Trustees: Joseph Schwarzman, Stephen A. Schwarzman.
EIN: 133460672

2258
Edith M. Schweckendieck Trusts
c/o Citibank, N.A.
One Court Sq., 22nd Fl.
Long Island City 11120
Application address: PBG Trusts, 153 East 53rd St., New York, NY 10043; Tel.: (212) 715-0100

Trust established in 1922 in NY; second trust established in 1936 in NY.
Donor(s): Edith M. Schweckendieck.‡
Foundation type: Independent
Financial data (yr. ended 12/31/90): Assets, $2,314,159 (M); expenditures, $145,882; qualifying distributions, $123,085, including $122,800 for grants.
Purpose and activities: Grants to charitable institutions to provide assistance for care and maintenance of the aged and feeble; care, maintenance, and education of crippled children; and prevention and relief of cancer.
Fields of interest: Aged, child welfare, handicapped, cancer.

Types of support: General purposes, building funds, endowment funds.
Limitations: Giving limited to NY. No grants to individuals.
Application information:
Initial approach: Letter
Deadline(s): Submit proposal preferably in July; deadline Aug. 31
Board meeting date(s): Oct.
Write: Joseph P. Valentine, V.P., Citibank, N.A.
Trustee: Citibank, N.A.
EIN: 136055135

2259
Julius Seaman Family Foundation, Inc.
1010 Northern Blvd.
Great Neck 11021   (516) 466-2002

Established in 1987 in NY.
Foundation type: Independent
Financial data (yr. ended 10/31/91): Assets, $3,153,101 (M); expenditures, $141,604; qualifying distributions, $140,810, including $140,525 for 8 grants (high: $105,000; low: $100).
Fields of interest: Jewish giving, Jewish welfare, hospitals, health associations.
Limitations: Giving primarily in NY. No grants to individuals.
Application information:
Initial approach: Letter
Deadline(s): None
Write: Lewis Stein
Officers: Morton Seaman, Pres.; Jill Plancher, V.P.; Jeffrey Seaman, V.P.; Lois Seaman, V.P.
EIN: 112951057

2260
Beatrice & Samuel A. Seaver Foundation
c/o Eisner & Lubin
250 Park Ave.
New York 10177

Established in 1986 in NY.
Donor(s): Beatrice Seaver.
Foundation type: Independent
Financial data (yr. ended 11/30/91): Assets, $345,966 (M); gifts received, $479,107; expenditures, $448,664; qualifying distributions, $448,103, including $448,103 for 7 grants (high: $309,528; low: $8,575).
Fields of interest: Hospitals, museums, performing arts.
Limitations: Giving primarily in New York, NY. No grants to individuals.
Application information: Contributes only to pre-selected organizations. Applications not accepted.
Trustees: John Cohen, Hirschell E. Levine, Beatrice Seaver.
EIN: 133251432

2261
Sequa Foundation of Delaware
(Formerly Sun Chemical Foundation)
200 Park Ave.
New York 10166

Established in 1967.
Donor(s): Sun Chemical Corp., Sequa Corp.

Foundation type: Company-sponsored
Financial data (yr. ended 12/31/90): Assets, $367,905 (M); gifts received, $765,527; expenditures, $627,575; qualifying distributions, $627,525 for 44 grants (high: $250,000; low: $50).
Purpose and activities: Giving primarily to Jewish welfare funds and higher education; support also for hospitals and the arts.
Fields of interest: Higher education, Jewish welfare, hospitals, arts.
Types of support: Capital campaigns, continuing support, general purposes.
Limitations: Giving primarily in NY. No grants to individuals.
Publications: 990-PF.
Application information: Application form not required.
Initial approach: Proposal
Deadline(s): None
Write: Monroe Adlman, Asst. Secy.
Officers and Trustees:* Norman E. Alexander,* Pres.; Gerald S. Gutterman,* V.P.; S.Z. Krinsly,* Secy.; K.A. Drucker, Treas.
Number of staff: 1 part-time support.
EIN: 237000821

2262
The Sexauer Foundation
531 Central Park Ave.
Scarsdale 10583

Incorporated in 1961 in DE.
Donor(s): John A. Sexauer.‡
Foundation type: Independent
Financial data (yr. ended 08/31/91): Assets, $2,277,177 (M); expenditures, $139,286; qualifying distributions, $106,145, including $97,250 for 66 grants (high: $10,000; low: $250).
Purpose and activities: Emphasis on hospitals; support also for health associations and higher education.
Fields of interest: Hospitals, health associations, higher education.
Limitations: No grants to individuals.
Application information: Contributes only to pre-selected organizations. Applications not accepted.
Officers: James M. Sexauer, Pres. and Treas.; Nancy S. Walsh, V.P. and Secy.
Trustee: Thomas J. Abbamont.
EIN: 136156256

2263
The Evelyn Sharp Foundation
1370 Ave. of the Americas
New York 10019   (212) 603-1333

Incorporated in 1952 in NY.
Donor(s): Evelyn Sharp, and others.
Foundation type: Independent
Financial data (yr. ended 06/30/91): Assets, $5,745,936 (M); expenditures, $266,061; qualifying distributions, $246,195, including $244,910 for 37 grants (high: $50,000; low: $200).
Fields of interest: Museums, performing arts, education, family planning, hospitals, medical research.
Limitations: Giving primarily in New York, NY.
Application information:

Initial approach: Letter
Deadline(s): None
Write: Mrs. Evelyn Sharp, Pres.
Officers and Trustees:* Mary Cronson,* Pres.;
Paul Cronson,* V.P.; Albert Francke III,* V.P.;
Jeremiah Milbank, Jr.,* V.P.; Peter J. Sharp,* V.P.
EIN: 136119532

2264
Eric P. Sheinberg Foundation
c/o Goldman Sachs & Co., Tax Dept.
85 Broad St., 30th Fl.
New York 10004

Donor(s): Eric P. Sheinberg.
Foundation type: Independent
Financial data (yr. ended 06/30/91): Assets,
$3,144,301 (M); gifts received, $300,000;
expenditures, $170,468; qualifying distributions,
$157,950, including $157,700 for 67 grants
(high: $35,000; low: $50).
Fields of interest: Health associations, hospitals,
civic affairs, arts, cultural programs, higher
education, social services, youth, Jewish giving.
Types of support: General purposes.
Limitations: Giving primarily in New York, NY.
No grants to individuals.
Application information: Contributes only to
pre-selected organizations. Applications not
accepted.
Trustees: Eric P. Sheinberg, Michael Steinhardt.
EIN: 137004291

2265
Ralph C. Sheldon Foundation, Inc. ▼
P.O. Box 417
Jamestown 14702-0417   (716) 664-9890
Application address: 710 Hotel Jamestown
Bldg., Jamestown, NY 14701

Incorporated in 1948 in NY.
Donor(s): Julia S. Livengood,‡ Isabell M.
Sheldon.‡
Foundation type: Independent
Financial data (yr. ended 05/31/91): Assets,
$5,422,908 (M); gifts received, $1,095,923;
expenditures, $1,527,805; qualifying
distributions, $1,510,047, including $1,483,540
for 28 grants (high: $250,000; low: $3,000;
average: $10,000-$50,000).
Purpose and activities: Support for youth
development organizations, community
improvement, cultural organizations, hospital,
and social service organizations.
Fields of interest: Youth, community
development, community funds, cultural
programs, fine arts, performing arts, theater,
hospitals, social services, environment, libraries.
Types of support: General purposes, building
funds, equipment, annual campaigns, capital
campaigns, emergency funds, renovation projects.
Limitations: Giving primarily in southern
Chautauqua County, NY. No support for religious
organizations. No grants to individuals.
Application information: Application form
required.
   Copies of proposal: 1
   Deadline(s): None
   Board meeting date(s): Varies, approximately 5
   times a year

Final notification: Immediately after
determination
Write: Paul B. Sullivan, Exec. Dir.
Officers and Directors:* J. Elizabeth Sheldon,*
Pres.; Walter L. Miller,* V.P.; Robert G. Wright,
V.P.; Paul B. Sullivan, Secy. and Exec. Dir.; Miles
L. Lasser,* Treas.; Barclay O. Wellman.
Number of staff: 1 part-time professional; 1
part-time support.
EIN: 166030502
Recent health grants:
2265-1 Womens Christian Association Hospital,
Jamestown, NY, $250,000. For Jones Hill.
1991.

2266
David and Lyn Silfen Foundation
c/o Goldman Sachs & Co., Tax Dept.
85 Broad St., 30th Fl.
New York 10004-2106

Established in 1981 in NY.
Donor(s): David M. Silfen.
Foundation type: Independent
Financial data (yr. ended 03/31/91): Assets,
$1,609,952 (M); gifts received, $700,000;
expenditures, $546,656; qualifying distributions,
$547,132, including $546,656 for 101 grants
(high: $200,000; low: $100).
Purpose and activities: Support primarily for
higher education; giving also for secondary
education, medical research, Jewish welfare
funds, and recreation programs.
Fields of interest: Higher education, secondary
education, medical research, Jewish welfare,
recreation, general charitable giving.
Limitations: Giving primarily in New York, NY,
CT, and PA. No grants to individuals.
Application information: Presently contributes
only to pre-selected organizations. Applications
not accepted.
Trustees: Robert M. Freeman, Patricia Gordon,
Ellen S. Margolin, David M. Silfen, Lyn Silfen.
EIN: 133103011

2267
Louis & Martha Silver Foundation, Inc.
c/o Gassman Rebhun & Co., P.C.
350 Fifth Ave.
New York 10118
Application address: 345 Underhill Blvd.,
Syosset, NY 11791; Tel.: (718) 895-8950

Established in 1964 in NY.
Donor(s): Louis Silver, Martha Silver.
Foundation type: Independent
Financial data (yr. ended 12/31/90): Assets,
$2,850,037 (M); expenditures, $75,124;
qualifying distributions, $45,418, including
$45,418 for 107 grants (high: $5,000; low: $18).
Purpose and activities: Emphasis on Jewish
giving, including temple support, welfare funds,
hospitals, and yeshivas and seminaries.
Fields of interest: Jewish giving, Jewish welfare,
hospitals, religious schools.
Limitations: Giving primarily in the greater
metropolitan New York, NY, area.
Application information: Application form not
required.
   Initial approach: Letter
   Deadline(s): None

Write: Louis Silver, Pres.
Officers: Louis Silver, Pres.; Martha Silver,
Secy.-Treas.
EIN: 136165326

2268
Louis P. Singer Fund, Inc.
c/o Christy & Viener
620 Fifth Ave.
New York 10020

Established in 1961.
Donor(s): Berkshire Hathaway, Inc.
Foundation type: Independent
Financial data (yr. ended 08/31/91): Assets,
$2,001,319 (M); gifts received, $9,696;
expenditures, $211,649; qualifying distributions,
$200,840, including $195,445 for 97 grants
(high: $25,000; low: $20).
Purpose and activities: Support primarily for
Jewish welfare, including support for Israel; giving
also for public television and radio and other
cultural programs, hospitals, health associations,
medical research, and education.
Fields of interest: Jewish welfare, media and
communications, cultural programs, hospitals,
medical research, health associations, education.
Limitations: Giving primarily in the greater
metropolitan New York, NY, area, including
Nassau county. No grants to individuals.
Application information: Contributes only to
pre-selected organizations. Applications not
accepted.
Officers: Paula Singer, Pres.; Midge Korczak, V.P.;
John D. Viener, Secy.-Treas.
EIN: 136077788

2269
The Alexandrine and Alexander L.
Sinsheimer Fund
c/o Manufacturers Hanover Trust Co.
270 Park Ave.
New York 10017   (212) 270-9111

Trust established in 1959 in NY.
Donor(s): Alexander L. Sinsheimer,‡ Alexandrine
Sinsheimer.‡
Foundation type: Independent
Financial data (yr. ended 04/30/91): Assets,
$8,576,625 (M); expenditures, $397,978;
qualifying distributions, $357,620, including
$354,319 for 10 grants (high: $64,773; low:
$20,000).
Purpose and activities: Grants to medical schools
to support scientific research relating to
prevention and cure of human diseases.
Fields of interest: Medical research.
Types of support: Research.
Limitations: Giving limited to the New York, NY,
metropolitan area.
Application information: Application form
required.
   Deadline(s): Feb. 15
   Write: T.E. Roepe, V.P., Manufacturers Hanover
   Trust Co.
Trustee: Manufacturers Hanover Trust Co.
EIN: 136047421

2270
The Slaner Foundation, Inc.
645 Fifth Ave.
New York 10022

Established in 1960 in NY.
Donor(s): Alfred P. Slaner, Felix Zandman.
Foundation type: Independent
Financial data (yr. ended 11/30/91): Assets,
$2,808,009 (M); expenditures, $132,648;
qualifying distributions, $125,535, including
$123,500 for 15 grants (high: $50,000; low:
$100).
Fields of interest: Jewish welfare, public policy,
peace, health associations, family planning.
Types of support: Endowment funds, general
purposes.
Limitations: Giving primarily in New York, NY.
No grants to individuals.
Application information: Contributes only to
pre-selected organizations. Applications not
accepted.
  Write: Alfred P. Slaner, Pres.
Officers and Directors:* Alfred P. Slaner,* Pres.
and Treas.; Luella Slaner,* V.P. and Secy.; Millie
Bluth Allinson, Eugenia Ames, Milton N. Scofield.
EIN: 136143119

2271
The Charles Slaughter Foundation
c/o Milgrim Thomajan & Lee
53 Wall St.
New York 10005-2815   (212) 858-5342

Established in 1980 in NY.
Foundation type: Independent
Financial data (yr. ended 10/31/90): Assets,
$2,405,757 (M); expenditures, $180,191;
qualifying distributions, $120,400, including
$110,000 for 2 grants (high: $80,000; low:
$30,000).
Fields of interest: Hospitals, medical research.
Types of support: Research.
Limitations: Giving primarily in New York, NY.
No grants to individuals.
Publications: Financial statement.
Application information: Contributes only to
pre-selected organizations. Applications not
accepted.
  Write: Myles A. Cane, Pres.
Officers: Myles A. Cane, Pres.; William E.
Friedman, Secy.-Treas.
Director: Kenneth T. Donaldson.
Number of staff: 1 part-time professional; 1
part-time support.
EIN: 133055995

2272
Joseph & Sylvia Slifka Foundation
477 Madison Ave., Rm. 704
New York 10022   (212) 753-5766

Established in 1944 in NY.
Donor(s): Joseph Slifka, Sylvia Slifka.
Foundation type: Independent
Financial data (yr. ended 10/31/91): Assets,
$3,661,002 (M); gifts received, $806,915;
expenditures, $323,970; qualifying distributions,
$312,945, including $312,660 for 104 grants
(high: $60,000; low: $50).

Fields of interest: Jewish welfare, hospitals,
cultural programs, arts, higher education.
Limitations: Giving primarily in the New York,
NY, metropolitan area. No grants to individuals.
Application information:
  Initial approach: Letter
  Deadline(s): None
  Write: Joseph Slifka, Pres.
Officers: Joseph Slifka, Pres.; Sylvia Slifka, V.P.;
Barbara Slifka, Secy.; Alan B. Slifka, Treas.
EIN: 136106433

2273
Alfred P. Sloan Foundation ▼
630 Fifth Ave., Suite 2550
New York 10111-0242   (212) 649-1649

Incorporated in 1934 in DE.
Donor(s): Alfred P. Sloan, Jr.,‡ Irene Jackson
Sloan,‡ New Castle Corp.
Foundation type: Independent
Financial data (yr. ended 12/31/91): Assets,
$727,641,989 (M); expenditures, $31,370,421;
qualifying distributions, $30,078,294, including
$24,803,395 for grants (average:
$10,000-$3,000,000) and $3,823,000 for 130
grants to individuals (high: $30,000).
Purpose and activities: Foundation is interested in
science and technology; education in science,
technology, and management; economic growth
and industrial competitiveness; and selected
national issues.
Fields of interest: Science and technology,
education—minorities, higher education,
economics, mathematics, physical sciences,
women, immigration.
Types of support: Seed money, research,
fellowships, conferences and seminars, special
projects.
Limitations: No support for the creative or
performing arts, humanities, medical research,
religion, or primary or secondary education. No
grants to individuals directly, or for endowment or
building funds, or equipment not related directly
to foundation-supported projects; no loans.
Publications: Informational brochure (including
application guidelines), annual report, newsletter.
Application information: Nomination forms
available for fellowship candidates; direct
applications not accepted. Application form not
required.
  Initial approach: Letter
  Copies of proposal: 1
  Deadline(s): Sept. 15 for fellowship program;
    no deadline for others
  Board meeting date(s): Throughout the year
    (grants of $30,000 or less); 5 times a year
    (grants over $30,000)
  Final notification: Early in year for research
    fellowships; within 3 months for others
  Write: Ralph E. Gomory, Pres.
Officers and Trustees:* Howard W. Johnson,
Chair.; Ralph E. Gomory,* Pres.; Stewart F.
Campbell, Financial V.P. and Secy.; Arthur L.
Singer, Jr., V.P.; Lucy Wilson Benson, Stephen L.
Brown, Lloyd C. Elam, S. Parker Gilbert, Howard
H. Kehrl, Donald N. Langengerg, Cathleen Synge
Morawetz, Frank Press, Lewis T. Preston, Harold
T. Shapiro, Roger B. Smith.
Number of staff: 19
EIN: 131623877
Recent health grants:

2273-1 Harvard University, Cambridge, MA,
$300,000. For final grant for Journalism
Fellowship for Advanced Study in Public
Health. 1991.
2273-2 Massachusetts Institute of Technology,
Cambridge, MA, $2,527,640. For new
program for the study of the pharmaceutical
industry. 1991.
2273-3 Rockefeller University, NYC, NY,
$25,000. For writings on history of science.
1991.
2273-4 Whitehead Institute for Biomedical
Research, Cambridge, MA, $25,000. For
public seminar series on social, ethical and
environmental consequences of molecular
biology revolution. 1991.

2274
George D. Smith Fund, Inc. ▼
c/o Lawrence W. Milas, V.P.
805 Third Ave., 20th Fl.
New York 10022

Incorporated in 1956 in DE.
Donor(s): George D. Smith, Sr.‡
Foundation type: Independent
Financial data (yr. ended 12/31/90): Assets,
$27,845,181 (M); expenditures, $1,386,470;
qualifying distributions, $1,355,900, including
$1,355,900 for 8 grants (high: $577,800; low:
$100; average: $25,000-$75,000).
Purpose and activities: Primarily supports basic
research in molecular and cellular physiology and
in cardiovascular diagnostic methods at two
university medical centers; support also for higher
education and public television.
Fields of interest: Medical sciences, media and
communications, higher education.
Types of support: Research.
Limitations: Giving primarily in CA and UT.
Application information: Unsolicited applications
are not considered. Applications not accepted.
Officers and Trustees:* George D. Smith, Jr.,*
Pres. and Secy.-Treas.; Lawrence W. Milas, V.P.;
Camilla M. Smith,* V.P.
EIN: 136138728

2275
Gerardus Smith-John G. Green Trust
Schenectady Trust Co.
P.O. Box 380
Schenectady 12301

Established in 1987 in NY.
Foundation type: Independent
Financial data (yr. ended 12/31/91): Assets,
$4,202,297 (M); expenditures, $225,686;
qualifying distributions, $215,746, including
$208,825 for 9 grants (high: $25,059; low:
$8,553).
Fields of interest: Protestant giving, women,
higher education, hospitals.
Limitations: Giving primarily in NY. No grants to
individuals.
Application information: Contributes only to
pre-selected organizations. Applications not
accepted.
Trustee: Trustco Bank.
EIN: 222507158

2276

The Christopher D. Smithers Foundation, Inc.

P.O. Box 67, Oyster Bay Rd.
Mill Neck 11765   (516) 676-0067

Incorporated in 1952 in NY.
Donor(s): Christopher D. Smithers,‡ Mabel B. Smithers,‡ R. Brinkley Smithers.
Foundation type: Independent
Financial data (yr. ended 12/31/91): Assets, $6,735,620 (M); gifts received, $137,741; expenditures, $724,002; qualifying distributions, $692,736, including $624,198 for 42 grants (high: $250,000; low: $50; average: $50-$250,000).
Purpose and activities: Supports organizations performing prevention, educational service, treatment, and research in the field of alcoholism; initiates its own projects in this field primarily by writing and publishing specialized booklets for industry, educational organizations, and the general public.
Fields of interest: Alcoholism.
Types of support: Operating budgets, special projects, research, conferences and seminars.
Limitations: No grants to individuals, or for building or endowment funds, or matching gifts; no loans.
Publications: Annual report.
Application information: Application form not required.
 Initial approach: Proposal
 Copies of proposal: 2
 Deadline(s): Submit proposal between Sept. and Dec.; no set deadline
 Board meeting date(s): May
 Write: Adele C. Smithers, Pres.
Officers and Directors:* R. Brinkley Smithers,* Chair.; Adele C. Smithers,* Pres.; M. Elizabeth Brothers,* V.P.; Henry S. Ziegler,* Secy.; Charles F. Smithers, Jr.,* Treas.; Shirley B. Klusener, Christopher B. Smithers.
Number of staff: 1 part-time professional.
EIN: 131861928

2277

John Ben Snow Memorial Trust

P.O. Box 378
Pulaski 13142   (315) 298-6401

Trust established in 1974 in NY.
Donor(s): John Ben Snow.‡
Foundation type: Independent
Financial data (yr. ended 12/31/91): Assets, $19,854,043 (M); expenditures, $1,385,136; qualifying distributions, $1,032,858, including $917,100 for 43 grants (high: $75,000; low: $3,485; average: $15,000-$25,000).
Purpose and activities: Support primarily for higher education, especially for research, scholarship funds, business education, and minority students; the humanities and cultural institutions, especially libraries, the performing arts, theater, and historical preservation; medical and health organizations; environmental groups; media and communications; community development; and recreation. Support also for the handicapped, Native Americans, and science and technology.
Fields of interest: Higher education, education—minorities, libraries, cultural programs, health, medical research, environment, community development, Native Americans, recreation.
Types of support: Seed money, equipment, research, publications, scholarship funds, fellowships, matching funds, renovation projects, internships.
Limitations: Giving primarily in the metropolitan New York and central, NY, areas, and NV. No support for government agencies or unspecified projects. No grants to individuals, or for operating budgets or endowment funds; no loans.
Publications: Annual report (including application guidelines).
Application information: Application form required.
 Initial approach: Letter
 Copies of proposal: 1
 Deadline(s): Submit proposal preferably from July through Mar.; deadline Mar. 15
 Board meeting date(s): June
 Final notification: 3 months
 Write: Vernon F. Snow, Trustee
Trustees: Allen R. Malcolm, Rollan D. Melton, Vernon F. Snow, The Bank of New York.
Number of staff: 2 part-time support.
EIN: 136633814

2278

The SO Charitable Trust

c/o Oded Aboodi
75 Rockefeller Plaza, Suite 1501
New York 10019

Established in 1980 in NJ.
Donor(s): Summer Assocs., Oded Aboodi.
Foundation type: Independent
Financial data (yr. ended 11/30/91): Assets, $2,064,007 (M); gifts received, $1,446,078; expenditures, $287,968; qualifying distributions, $278,351, including $278,301 for 64 grants (high: $25,000; low: $50).
Fields of interest: Jewish giving, Jewish welfare, religious schools, animal welfare, medical research, hospitals, higher education, general charitable giving.
Limitations: Giving primarily in NY. No grants to individuals.
Application information: Contributes only to pre-selected organizations. Applications not accepted.
Trustees: Oded Aboodi, Solomon M. Weiss.
EIN: 133050892

2279

Solow Foundation

Nine West 57th St.
New York 10019-2601   (212) 935-7529

Established in 1978 in DE.
Donor(s): Sheldon H. Solow.
Foundation type: Independent
Financial data (yr. ended 10/31/90): Assets, $7,576,339 (M); expenditures, $49,035; qualifying distributions, $24,732, including $24,001 for grants.
Fields of interest: Education, higher education, libraries, cultural programs, Jewish giving, cancer, youth.
Types of support: General purposes.

Application information: Application form not required.
 Deadline(s): None
 Write: Sheldon H. Solow, Pres.
Officers: Sheldon H. Solow, Pres. and Treas.; Rosalie S. Wolff, V.P.; Leonard Lazarus, Secy.
EIN: 132950685

2280

Sony Corporation of America Foundation, Inc.

Nine West 57th St.
New York 10019   (212) 418-9404

Established in 1972 in NY.
Donor(s): Sony Corp. of America.
Foundation type: Company-sponsored
Financial data (yr. ended 12/31/90): Assets, $745,400 (M); gifts received, $285,856; expenditures, $1,078,602; qualifying distributions, $1,074,979, including $1,074,979 for 463 grants (high: $50,000; low: $25).
Purpose and activities: Grants largely for hospitals, higher education, including scholarships for children of company employees, community funds, the performing arts, and Japanese and other cultural programs.
Fields of interest: Hospitals, higher education, community funds, performing arts, cultural programs, intercultural relations.
Types of support: General purposes, operating budgets, continuing support, annual campaigns, seed money, emergency funds, deficit financing, building funds, equipment, land acquisition, endowment funds, employee matching gifts, internships, employee-related scholarships.
Limitations: No grants to individuals (except for scholarships for children of company employees), or for special projects, research, publications, or conferences; no loans.
Application information: Application form not required.
 Initial approach: Letter
 Copies of proposal: 1
 Deadline(s): None
 Board meeting date(s): Quarterly
 Final notification: 1 week
 Write: Kenneth L. Nees, Pres.
Officers and Directors:* Masaaki Morita,* Chair.; Kenneth L. Nees,* Pres. and Secy.; Robert D. Dillon, Jr.,* V.P.; Norio Ohga,* V.P.; Harvey L. Schein,* V.P.; John Stern,* V.P.; Kenji Tamiya,* V.P.; Neil Vander Dussen,* V.P.; Akio Morita.
Number of staff: None.
EIN: 237181637

2281

The Soros Foundation-Hungary, Inc. ▼

888 Seventh Ave., Suite 1901
New York 10106   (212) 757-2323
FAX: (212) 974-0367

Established in 1983 in NY.
Donor(s): George Soros, George Soros Charitable Lead Trust, Tivadar Charitable Lead Trust.
Foundation type: Independent
Financial data (yr. ended 12/31/90): Assets, $3,345,080 (M); gifts received, $3,322,149; expenditures, $5,936,311; qualifying distributions, $5,918,123, including $5,224,942 for 142 grants (high: $750,000; low: $15;

average: $2,000-$20,000) and $166,843 for 119 grants to individuals (high: $7,000; low: $65).

Purpose and activities: Supports Hungarian organizations and projects, including the fields of language, culture, and education; also awards grants and scholarships to individuals for higher education and medical research.

Fields of interest: Europe, language and literature, cultural programs, journalism, education, community development, civic affairs, journalism.

Types of support: Exchange programs, grants to individuals, student aid, research, fellowships, internships, conferences and seminars, special projects.

Limitations: Giving primarily in Hungary.

Publications: Annual report.

Application information:
  Copies of proposal: 1
  Deadline(s): None
  Board meeting date(s): Usually within 1 month
  Write: Elizabeth Lorant, Exec. Dir., James McLain, Prog. Officer, or Eva Zorandy, Prog. Officer

Officers and Directors:* George Soros,* Pres.; Philip Kaiser,* V.P.; William D. Zabel,* V.P.; Elizabeth Lorant, Exec. Dir.; Wassily Leontief.

Number of staff: 4 full-time professional; 2 full-time support.

EIN: 133210361

Recent health grants:

2281-1 Brothers Brother Foundation, Pittsburgh, PA, $19,357. To distribute medicines and medical supplies to Hungary. 1990.

2281-2 Hastings Center, Briarcliff Manor, NY, $30,000. For biomedical ethics project. 1990.

2281-3 National Medical Institute and Library, Budapest, Hungary, $12,953. For in-kind donation. 1990.

2281-4 Pecs University Medical School, Pecs, Hungary, $39,025. For medical project. 1990.

2281-5 Semmelweis Medical University, Budapest, Hungary, $28,859. For medical project. 1990.

2281-6 SOTE-Pharmacy, Budapest, Hungary, $30,378. For in-kind donation. 1990.

2282
Jerry and Emily Spiegel Family Foundation, Inc.

(Formerly Jerry Spiegel Foundation, Inc.)
Two East 88th St.
New York 10128

Established in 1958 in NY.
Donor(s): Jerry Spiegel, Emily Spiegel.
Foundation type: Independent
Financial data (yr. ended 03/31/91): Assets, $5,151,322 (M); gifts received, $1,035,000; expenditures, $288,597; qualifying distributions, $284,597, including $280,359 for 91 grants (high: $88,500; low: $24).
Purpose and activities: Giving primarily for Jewish welfare organizations and temples; support also for health associations, hospitals, and higher education.
Fields of interest: Jewish welfare, Jewish giving, hospitals, health associations, higher education.
Limitations: Giving primarily in NY. No grants to individuals.
Application information: Contributes only to pre-selected organizations. Applications not accepted.

Officers: Jerry Spiegel, Pres.; Emily Spiegel, V.P.; Lise Spiegel, Secy.-Treas.; Arthur D. Sanders, Treas.
EIN: 116006020

2283
The Spiritus Gladius Foundation

(Formerly D.C. Foundation, Inc.)
c/o Meyer Handelman Co.
P.O. Box 817
Purchase 10577-0817   (914) 939-4060

Established in 1959 in NY.
Donor(s): Nedenia H. Hartley.
Foundation type: Independent
Financial data (yr. ended 08/31/92): Assets, $2,698,789 (M); expenditures, $160,839; qualifying distributions, $147,535, including $147,250 for 34 grants (high: $35,000; low: $250; average: $250-$35,000).
Fields of interest: Higher education, arts, medical research, child welfare, youth.
Limitations: Giving primarily in NY, CT, and MA. No grants to individuals.
Application information: Contributes only to pre-selected organizations. Applications not accepted.
  Write: Donald E. Handelman, V.P. and Secy.-Treas.
Officers: Nedenia H. Hartley, Pres.; Donald E. Handelman, V.P. and Secy.-Treas.
Trustees: Nedenia R. Craig, Joseph W. Handelman, William R. Handelman, Heather M. Robertson, Stanley H. Rumbough.
Number of staff: None.
EIN: 136113272

2284
The Bernard & Anne Spitzer Foundation, Inc.

800 Fifth Ave.
New York 10021-7299

Donor(s): Bernard Spitzer.
Foundation type: Independent
Financial data (yr. ended 12/31/91): Assets, $3,122,323 (M); gifts received, $30,000; expenditures, $186,996; qualifying distributions, $183,035, including $182,750 for grants (high: $100,000).
Purpose and activities: Support primarily for juvenile diabetes research, family planning, and education; giving also for cultural programs.
Fields of interest: Medical research, family planning, education, cultural programs.
Types of support: General purposes.
Limitations: Giving primarily in NY. No grants to individuals.
Application information: Contributes only to pre-selected organizations. Applications not accepted.
Officers: Bernard Spitzer, Pres.; Anne Spitzer, V.P.
EIN: 133098005

2285
The Seth Sprague Educational and Charitable Foundation ▼

c/o U.S. Trust Co. of New York
114 West 47th St.
New York 10036-1532   (212) 852-3683

Trust established in 1939 in NY.
Donor(s): Seth Sprague.‡
Foundation type: Independent
Financial data (yr. ended 12/31/90): Assets, $36,831,033 (M); expenditures, $2,229,552; qualifying distributions, $1,965,599, including $1,556,500 for 376 grants (high: $46,000; low: $500; average: $1,000-$5,000).
Purpose and activities: Emphasis on health and human services, education, culture and the arts, and civic affairs and community development.
Fields of interest: Health services, hospitals, social services, youth, child welfare, cultural programs, performing arts, museums, education, higher education, secondary education.
Types of support: Operating budgets, seed money, general purposes, matching funds, special projects.
Limitations: Giving primarily in NY and MA. No grants to individuals, or for building funds; no loans.
Publications: Application guidelines.
Application information: Application form not required.
  Initial approach: Proposal or letter
  Copies of proposal: 1
  Deadline(s): Apr. 15 and Oct. 1
  Board meeting date(s): Mar., June, Sept., and Nov. (grants awarded at June and Nov. meetings)
  Final notification: No notice unless grant is made
  Write: Maureen Augusciak, Sr. V.P., or Anne L. Smith-Ganey, Asst. V.P., U.S. Trust Co. of New York
Trustees: Walter G. Dunnington, Jr., Arline Ripley Greenleaf, Jacqueline D. Simpkins, U.S. Trust Co. of New York.
Number of staff: None.
EIN: 136071886

Recent health grants:

2285-1 Alcoholism Council of Greater New York, NYC, NY, $10,000. 1990.

2285-2 Society of the New York Hospital, NYC, NY, $20,000. 1990.

2285-3 Society of the New York Hospital, NYC, NY, $20,000. 1990.

2285-4 Spectrum House, Westboro, MA, $20,000. 1990.

2286
The Spunk Fund, Inc.

675 Third Ave., Suite 1510
New York 10017   (212) 972-8330

Incorporated in 1981 in NY.
Donor(s): Marianne Gerschel.
Foundation type: Independent
Financial data (yr. ended 06/30/91): Assets, $10,381,086 (M); gifts received, $520,000; expenditures, $1,935,238; qualifying distributions, $1,481,447, including $1,415,940 for 27 grants (high: $64,800; low: $1,000; average: $1,000-$65,000).
Purpose and activities: Support initiatives that contribute to the enrichment and well-being of children and adolescents, including medical research, education, cultural programs, and programs for the prevention and treatment of child abuse and neglect. Total giving figures for odd-numbered fiscal years represent two granting

cycles; total giving for even-numbered fiscal years will equal zero.

Fields of interest: Youth, child development, child welfare, medical research, AIDS, cultural programs, education, education—early childhood, elementary education, education—minorities, family services.

Types of support: General purposes, research.

Limitations: Giving primarily in NY, with support for international grants growing. No grants to individuals, or for capital programs.

Publications: Informational brochure (including application guidelines).

Application information: Proposals must be requested by the fund to receive consideration. Application form not required.

Initial approach: Letter of inquiry
Copies of proposal: 1
Deadline(s): Letters of inquiry accepted year round; requested proposals due Apr. 1
Board meeting date(s): June
Final notification: July 1
Write: Ms. Marianne Gerschel, Pres.

Officer: Marianne Gerschel, Pres. and Treas.

Number of staff: 2 full-time professional; 1 full-time support; 2 part-time support.

EIN: 133116094

2287
St. Giles Foundation
(Formerly The House of St. Giles the Cripple)
One Hanson Place
Brooklyn 11243   (718) 638-1996

Foundation type: Independent
Financial data (yr. ended 03/31/92): Assets, $16,816,101 (M); gifts received, $3,565; expenditures, $708,627; qualifying distributions, $613,377, including $532,000 for 8 grants (high: $125,000; low: $25,000).

Purpose and activities: Grants for hospitals and organizations to help the handicapped; special interest in childrens' orthopedics.

Fields of interest: Hospitals, handicapped, youth.

Types of support: Equipment, research, general purposes.

Application information:
Initial approach: Proposal
Deadline(s): None
Write: Richard Crocker

Officers: Richard T. Arkwright, Pres.; John H. Livingston, V.P.; John J. Bennett, Jr., Secy.; Samuel H. Owens, Treas.

Trustees: William B. Falconer, Jr., Robert B. Mackay.

EIN: 111630806

2288
The Starr Foundation ▼
70 Pine St.
New York 10270   (212) 770-6882

Incorporated in 1955 in NY.
Donor(s): Cornelius V. Starr.‡
Foundation type: Independent
Financial data (yr. ended 12/31/90): Assets, $616,002,007 (M); gifts received, $4,001,500; expenditures, $31,675,530; qualifying distributions, $31,675,530, including $29,242,416 for 342 grants (high: $500,000; low: $1,000; average: $1,000-$25,000) and

$1,561,629 for 448 grants to individuals (high: $9,000; low: $100).

Purpose and activities: Grants largely for education with emphasis on higher education, including scholarships under specific programs; support also for culture, health, welfare, and social sciences.

Fields of interest: Education, higher education, hospitals, health, social services, cultural programs, social sciences, AIDS.

Types of support: Continuing support, building funds, endowment funds, professorships, student aid, scholarship funds, fellowships, research, general purposes.

Limitations: No grants to individuals (except through foundation's scholarship programs), or for matching gifts; no loans.

Publications: 990-PF.

Application information: Application form not required.

Initial approach: Letter
Copies of proposal: 1
Deadline(s): None
Board meeting date(s): Feb. and Sept.
Final notification: Varies
Write: Mr. Ta Chun Hsu, Pres.

Officers and Directors:* Maurice R. Greenberg,* Chair.; Ta Chun Hsu,* Pres.; Marion I. Breen,* V.P.; Gladys Thomas, V.P.; Ida E. Galler, Secy.; Frank R. Tengi, Treas.; Houghton Freeman, Edwin A.G. Manton, John J. Roberts, Ernest E. Stempel.

Number of staff: 2 full-time professional; 3 full-time support.

EIN: 136151545

Recent health grants:

2288-1 Ackerman Institute for Family Therapy, NYC, NY, $50,000. For Family-School Collaboration Project. 1991.

2288-2 Ackerman Institute for Family Therapy, NYC, NY, $50,000. For counseling and education. 1991.

2288-3 Alzheimers Disease and Related Disorders Association, New York City Chapter, NYC, NY, $15,000. For programs. 1991.

2288-4 American Council on Science and Health, NYC, NY, $30,000. For renewed general support. 1991.

2288-5 American Medico-Legal Foundation, Philadelphia, PA, $75,000. For review of ten hospitals. 1991.

2288-6 Amyotrophic Lateral Sclerosis (ALS) Association, Laguna Hills, CA, $50,000. For matching support of research and service programs. 1991.

2288-7 Beekman Downtown Hospital, NYC, NY, $1,500,000. For programs for Chinese patients. 1991.

2288-8 Cancer Support and Education Center, Menlo Park, CA, $50,000. For Hugh M. Blake Scholarship Fund. 1991.

2288-9 Childrens Blood Foundation, NYC, NY, $500,000. For capital improvements program. 1991.

2288-10 Childrens Oncology Society of New York, NYC, NY, $200,000. For challenge grant to help complete funding of library of Ronald McDonald House. 1991.

2288-11 Cobble Hill Nursing Home, Brooklyn, NY, $300,000. For expansion of Andrew J. Stein Alzheimer's Resource Center. 1991.

2288-12 Cooper Union for the Advancement of Science and Art, Albert Nerken School of

Engineering, NYC, NY, $300,000. Toward biomedical engineering program. 1991.

2288-13 Danbury Hospital Development Fund, Danbury, CT, $80,000. For general support. 1991.

2288-14 Dartmouth-Hitchcock Medical Center, Hanover, NH, $1,000,000. For capital campaign to establish C.V. Starr Magnetic Resonance Imaging Center. 1991.

2288-15 Deborah Hospital Foundation, Electrophysiology Department, Browns Mills, NJ, $50,000. Toward purchase of Telemetry Monitoring System. 1991.

2288-16 Devereux Foundation, Devon, PA, $300,000. For Direct-Care Curriculum. 1991.

2288-17 Greater New York Hospital Foundation, NYC, NY, $280,000. For Project Ladders in Nursing Careers. 1991.

2288-18 Harlem Interfaith Counseling Service, NYC, NY, $15,000. For renewed support of Family and Youth Support Systems. 1991.

2288-19 Heart Research Foundation, NYC, NY, $10,000. For continued support of cardiovascular research. 1991.

2288-20 Hebrew Home for the Aged, Riverdale, NY, $500,000. For expansion and renovation project for new Link Building between two pavilions. 1991.

2288-21 International Center for the Disabled (ICD), NYC, NY, $150,000. For 75th anniversary campaign. 1991.

2288-22 International Center for the Disabled (ICD), NYC, NY, $25,000. For Annual Gala Dinner. 1991.

2288-23 Medical College of Wisconsin, International Bone Marrow Transplant Registry, Milwaukee, WI, $225,000. For research program. 1991.

2288-24 Meharry Medical College, Nashville, TN, $250,000. For endowed scholarship support. 1991.

2288-25 National Center for Learning Disabilities, NYC, NY, $25,000. For renewed support of programs for learning disabled children. 1991.

2288-26 National Marrow Donor Program, Minneapolis, MN, $150,000. For general support. 1991.

2288-27 Neighborhood Coalition for Shelter, NYC, NY, $15,000. For renewed support for substance abuse specialist. 1991.

2288-28 New York Hospital-Cornell Medical Center, NYC, NY, $5,000,000. For additional grant in support of major modernization campaign. 1991.

2288-29 Orentreich Foundation for the Advancement of Science, NYC, NY, $25,000. For renewed support of activities in basic biomedical research. 1991.

2288-30 Phoenix House Foundation, NYC, NY, $45,000. For continued support and to meet challenge grant. 1991.

2288-31 Project Orbis, NYC, NY, $25,000. For renewed support. 1991.

2288-32 Rogosin Institute, Comprehensive Lipid Control Center, NYC, NY, $500,000. For Lipid program. 1991.

2288-33 University of Rochester, Paul N. Yu Cardiovascular Institute, Rochester, NY, $500,000. For proposed Institute to be established at University of Rochester Medical Center. 1991.

2288-34 University of Southern California, Kenneth Norris, Jr. Comprehensive Cancer Unit, Los Angeles, CA, $40,000. For intensive care unit. 1991.

2288-35 Village Nursing Home, NYC, NY, $60,000. For seed money for Phase II of AIDS Home Care Program. 1991.

2288-36 Yale University, New Haven, CT, $200,000. To augment C.V. Starr Scholarship Fund, one half of grant for benefit of Medical School students only. 1991.

2288-37 Youth Counseling League, NYC, NY, $50,000. For program support. 1991.

2289
Amy Plant Statter Foundation
598 Madison Ave., 9th Fl.
New York 10022

Established in 1958 in NY.
Donor(s): Amy Plant Statter Clark.
Foundation type: Independent
Financial data (yr. ended 12/31/90): Assets, $2,711,414 (M); expenditures, $188,658; qualifying distributions, $168,500, including $168,500 for 43 grants (high: $8,000; low: $500).
Fields of interest: Hospitals, health services, social services, youth, handicapped.
Limitations: Giving on a national basis, with some emphasis on the greater metropolitan New York, NY, area and Seattle, WA. No grants to individuals.
Application information: Contributes only to pre-selected organizations. Applications not accepted.
　Write: John H. Reilly, Jr., Trustee
Trustees: Amy Plant Statter Clark, John H. Reilly, Jr.
EIN: 136152801

2290
Philip H. & Lois R. Steckler Foundation, Inc.
c/o Philip H. Steckler, Jr.
522 Fifth Ave.
New York 10036

Established in 1969 in NY.
Donor(s): Philip H. Steckler, Jr.
Foundation type: Independent
Financial data (yr. ended 07/31/91): Assets, $1,459,983 (M); expenditures, $518,469; qualifying distributions, $491,365, including $491,115 for 176 grants (high: $200,000; low: $7).
Purpose and activities: Giving primarily for hospitals and health services, especially cancer related organizations and higher and secondary education; some support for churches, youth services, and cultural activities.
Fields of interest: Hospitals, health services, cancer, higher education, secondary education, education, religion—Christian, youth, cultural programs.
Limitations: Giving primarily in NY. No grants to individuals.
Application information: Contributes only to pre-selected organizations. Applications not accepted.
Officers: Lois R. Steckler, Pres.; Philip H. Steckler III, V.P.; Allan Steckler, Secy.; Donald H. Steckler, Treas.

EIN: 132621420

2291
The Steele-Reese Foundation
c/o Messrs. Davidson, Dawson & Clark
330 Madison Ave.
New York 10017　　　　　　(212) 557-7700
Application addresses: John R. Bryden, 760 Malabu Dr., Lexington, KY 40502; Christine Brady, P.O. Box 7263, Boise, ID 83707

Trust established in 1955 in NY.
Donor(s): Eleanor Steele Reese,‡ Emmet P. Reese.‡
Foundation type: Independent
Financial data (yr. ended 08/31/91): Assets, $29,965,358 (M); expenditures, $1,506,980; qualifying distributions, $1,277,857, including $1,104,821 for 43 grants (high: $81,250; low: $2,000).
Purpose and activities: Principally to aid organized charities in southern Appalachia and ID and adjacent states. Support for education, including scholarships, health and hospices, welfare, including programs for drug abuse and youth, conservation, and the humanities, with a strong preference for rural projects; student aid paid through institutions.
Fields of interest: Conservation, higher education, education, health, welfare, child welfare, humanities, rural development, drug abuse, hospices, youth.
Types of support: General purposes, operating budgets, equipment, endowment funds, matching funds, professorships, scholarship funds.
Limitations: Giving primarily in southern Appalachia, particularly KY, and in the northwest, with emphasis on ID; scholarship program limited to students from Lemhi and Custer counties, ID. No grants to individuals, or for continuing support, annual campaigns, seed money, emergency or building funds, deficit financing, research, or land acquisition; no loans; grants to individuals confined to scholarships and paid through institutions.
Publications: Annual report (including application guidelines).
Application information: High school seniors in Lemhi and Custer counties, ID, should apply for scholarships through their schools. Application form not required.
　Initial approach: Letter
　Copies of proposal: 3
　Deadline(s): None; payments are generally made in Feb. and Aug.
　Board meeting date(s): Monthly
　Final notification: 3 to 6 months
　Write: William T. Buice, III, Trustee (in NY for general matters), Dr. John R. Bryden (for southern Appalachian applicants), and Mrs. Christine Brady (for northwestern applicants)
Trustees: William T. Buice III, Robert T.H. Davidson, Morgan Guaranty Trust Co. of New York.
Number of staff: 3 part-time support.
EIN: 136034763

2292
Joseph F. Stein Foundation, Inc.
28 Aspen Rd.
Scarsdale 10583　　　　　　(914) 725-1770

Incorporated in 1954 in NY.
Donor(s): Joseph F. Stein,‡ Allen A. Stein,‡ and others.
Foundation type: Independent
Financial data (yr. ended 12/31/91): Assets, $9,959,828 (M); gifts received, $399,997; expenditures, $638,103; qualifying distributions, $628,405, including $624,019 for 175 grants (high: $268,000; low: $25).
Purpose and activities: Grants largely for local Jewish welfare and social activities; some support for higher and secondary education, including religious education, and medical research.
Fields of interest: Jewish welfare, Jewish giving, higher education, secondary education, medical research.
Types of support: General purposes, equipment, research.
Limitations: Giving primarily in NY and FL. No grants to individuals (including scholarships), or for matching gifts; no loans.
Application information:
　Initial approach: Letter
　Copies of proposal: 1
　Board meeting date(s): Monthly
　Write: Melvin M. Stein, Pres.
Officers and Directors:* Melvin M. Stein,* Pres.; Roger H. Stein,* V.P. and Treas.; Elaine S. Stein,* V.P.; Stuart M. Stein,* Secy.
Number of staff: None.
EIN: 136097095

2293
The Harold & Mimi Steinberg Charitable Trust
527 West 34th St.
New York 10001

Established in 1986 in NY.
Donor(s): Harold Steinberg.‡
Foundation type: Independent
Financial data (yr. ended 12/31/90): Assets, $6,342,306 (M); gifts received, $149,000; expenditures, $342,634; qualifying distributions, $333,364, including $310,000 for 5 grants (high: $150,000; low: $10,000).
Fields of interest: Libraries, Jewish welfare, hospitals, higher education.
Limitations: Giving primarily in New York, NY. No grants to individuals.
Application information: Contributes only to pre-selected organizations. Applications not accepted.
Trustees: Charles Benenson, Seth Weingarten, William D. Zabel.
EIN: 133383348

2294
Sterling Drug Corporate Giving Program
90 Park Avenue
New York 10016　　　　　　(212) 907-3087

Financial data (yr. ended 12/31/90): Total giving, $2,052,000, including $1,005,000 for 165 grants (high: $50,000; low: $250; average: $1,000-$5,000), $347,000 for 756 employee matching gifts and $700,000 for in-kind gifts.
Purpose and activities: Support for human welfare, drug abuse and health education programs, pharmaceutical programs and other business and industry interests, education,

including medical education, medical sciences, and health and welfare. Other forms of support include product donations, services, and employee volunteerism.

Fields of interest: Education, health, welfare, cultural programs, hospitals, higher education, child welfare, disadvantaged, drug abuse, medical education, medical sciences, museums, performing arts, pharmacy, AIDS, family services, homeless, handicapped, education—minorities, urban development, health services.

Types of support: In-kind gifts, matching funds, employee matching gifts, scholarship funds, fellowships, general purposes, special projects, professorships, operating budgets, lectureships, donated products, employee volunteer services.

Limitations: Giving primarily in New York City and to selected national organizations. No support for veterans' groups, or social or fraternal organizations, or sectarian or denominational groups. No grants to individuals, or for goodwill advertising, or United-Way affiliated agencies.

Application information: Company has a staff that only handles contributions. Application form not required.

> *Initial approach:* Letter and proposal; send requests to nearest facility
> *Copies of proposal:* 1
> *Deadline(s):* None
> *Board meeting date(s):* Approximately quarterly
> *Final notification:* Varies-usually 1 to 3 months after receipt of proposal
> *Write:* Heather Hollowell, Dir., Community and Industry Relations

Number of staff: 2 full-time professional; 1 full-time support.

2295
Gustav and Irene Stern Foundation, Inc.
(Formerly Gustav Stern Foundation, Inc.)
c/o Braver, Stern Securities Corp.
641 Lexington Ave.
New York 10022

Donor(s): Ray Stern.
Foundation type: Independent
Financial data (yr. ended 03/31/91): Assets, $9,218,382 (M); expenditures, $510,181; qualifying distributions, $486,700, including $440,858 for 145 grants (high: $75,000; low: $25).
Fields of interest: Jewish giving, Jewish welfare, hospitals.
Limitations: Giving primarily in New York, NY.
Application information:
> *Initial approach:* Letter
> *Deadline(s):* None

Officers: Irene Stern, Pres.; Steven Stern, V.P.; Joyce Herland, Secy.; Roy Stern, Treas.
Director: Ralph Suskind.
EIN: 136121155

2296
Stony Wold-Herbert Fund, Inc.
136 East 57th St., Rm. 1705
New York 10022   (212) 753-6565

Incorporated in 1974 in NY.
Foundation type: Independent
Financial data (yr. ended 12/31/90): Assets, $4,344,865 (M); gifts received, $2,550;

expenditures, $308,699; qualifying distributions, $265,045, including $159,440 for 13 grants (high: $25,000; low: $3,000) and $49,970 for 36 grants to individuals (high: $2,370; low: $150).

Purpose and activities: Support for four programs: research grants to doctors within the greater New York area involved in studying respiratory diseases; pulmonary fellowships to doctors in the greater New York area training in the respiratory field; grants for community service projects in the pulmonary field; and supplementary scholarships for college or vocational school students, 16 years or older, living in the greater New York area only, with respiratory illnesses.

Fields of interest: Hospitals, medical research, medical education, disadvantaged, general charitable giving.

Types of support: Continuing support, deficit financing, fellowships, special projects, research, conferences and seminars, student aid.

Limitations: Giving primarily in NY. No grants for capital or endowment funds, operating budgets, annual campaigns, seed money, emergency funds, or matching gifts; no loans.

Publications: Annual report, application guidelines, newsletter, informational brochure.

Application information: Application form required.

> *Initial approach:* Letter or telephone
> *Copies of proposal:* 8
> *Deadline(s):* Oct. 15 for research and fellowship grants; Mar. 1 for community service proposals
> *Board meeting date(s):* Nov., Mar., and May
> *Final notification:* 2 to 3 weeks
> *Write:* Cheryl S. Friedman, Exec. Dir.

Officers: Mrs. Charles S. Whitman, Jr., Pres.; Mrs. George C. Moore, V.P.; Anne Logan Davis, M.D., Secy.; Adams H. Nickerson, Treas.; Cheryl S. Friedman, Exec. Dir.

Board Members: Mrs. Douglas F. Allen, H. Kent Atkins, Robert Beekman, M.D., A.L. Loomis Bell, Jr., M.D., William C. Breed III, Mrs. Ronald Carr, Sheila C. Davidson, Francis G. Geer, M.D., Mrs. James L. German III, Milena Lewis, M.D., Lawrence L. Scharer, M.D., Mrs. William Schuette, Jr., Nicholas A. Shephens, Henry M. Thomas III, M.D.

Number of staff: 2 part-time professional.
EIN: 132784124

2297
Robert L. Stott Foundation, Inc.
c/o Wagner, Stott & Co.
20 Broad St.
New York 10005

Incorporated in 1957 in NY.
Donor(s): Robert L. Stott.‡
Foundation type: Independent
Financial data (yr. ended 12/31/91): Assets, $2,784,435 (M); expenditures, $136,974; qualifying distributions, $134,850, including $132,500 for 33 grants (high: $25,000; low: $500).
Fields of interest: Religion—Christian, secondary education, hospitals.
Limitations: Giving primarily in NY and FL. No grants to individuals.
Application information: Contributes only to pre-selected organizations. Applications not accepted.

Officers and Directors:* Robert L. Stott, Jr.,* Pres.; Donald B. Stott,* Secy.-Treas.
EIN: 136061943

2298
Martha Washington Straus & Harry H. Straus Foundation, Inc.
Sky Meadow Farm
Lincoln Ave.
Port Chester 10573

Incorporated in 1949 in NC.
Donor(s): Harry H. Straus, Sr.,‡ Louise Straus King.
Foundation type: Independent
Financial data (yr. ended 12/31/90): Assets, $3,990,461 (M); gifts received, $32,174; expenditures, $230,958; qualifying distributions, $219,100, including $219,100 for 115 grants (high: $20,000; low: $100).
Purpose and activities: Giving primarily for health, including medical research and education, hospitals, and health associations; some support also for Jewish organizations, the handicapped, and social services.
Fields of interest: Medical research, medical education, hospitals, health services, health associations, Jewish giving, handicapped, social services.
Limitations: Giving primarily in New York, NY, and the metropolitan Washington, DC, area. No grants to individuals.
Application information: Contributes only to pre-selected organizations. Applications not accepted.

> *Board meeting date(s):* As required
> *Write:* Roger J. King, Secy.-Treas.

Officers: Louise Straus King, Pres.; Betty B. Straus, V.P.; Roger J. King, Secy.-Treas. and Mgr.
EIN: 560645526

2299
The Stuart Foundation, Inc.
126 East 56th St., 6th Fl.
New York 10022   (212) 753-0800

Incorporated in 1951 in NY.
Donor(s): Members of the Stuart family.
Foundation type: Independent
Financial data (yr. ended 12/31/91): Assets, $2,950,000 (M); expenditures, $164,800; qualifying distributions, $128,000, including $125,400 for 74 grants (high: $37,500; low: $30; average: $30-$37,500).
Purpose and activities: Giving primarily for education, including educational research and associations, building funds, organizations providing assistance to minority students, early childhood, elementary, secondary, higher and medical education; support also for the arts, including museums, theaters, and the fine and performing arts, libraries, cancer research and hospitals, and family services, including child welfare and development.
Fields of interest: Educational associations, education—minorities, secondary education, higher education, arts, performing arts, libraries, hospitals, family services, child welfare.
Types of support: Annual campaigns, scholarship funds, building funds, fellowships, capital campaigns, endowment funds, special projects, equipment, research, general purposes.

Limitations: Giving primarily in NY and New England. No grants to individuals.
Application information: Contributes only to pre-selected organizations. Applications not accepted.
Board meeting date(s): Annually
Officers and Directors:* Alan L. Stuart,* Pres.; Ronda H. Lubin, Corp. Secy.; Carolyn A. Stuart, James M. Stuart, Jr.
Number of staff: 1 full-time professional; 1 part-time professional.
EIN: 136066191

2300
The Sulzberger Foundation, Inc.
229 West 43rd St.
New York 10036   (212) 556-1750

Incorporated in 1956 in NY.
Donor(s): Arthur Hays Sulzberger,‡ Iphigene Ochs Sulzberger.‡
Foundation type: Independent
Financial data (yr. ended 12/31/91): Assets, $21,955,902 (M); expenditures, $1,101,861; qualifying distributions, $1,043,062, including $1,001,148 for 206 grants (high: $77,150; low: $100).
Fields of interest: Education, cultural programs, hospitals, community funds, welfare, conservation.
Types of support: Annual campaigns, building funds, capital campaigns, conferences and seminars, consulting services, continuing support, emergency funds, endowment funds, equipment, exchange programs, fellowships, general purposes, internships, lectureships, operating budgets, professorships, program-related investments, renovation projects, scholarship funds, seed money, special projects, technical assistance.
Limitations: Giving primarily in NY and Chattanooga, TN. No grants to individuals, or for matching gifts; no loans.
Application information:
Initial approach: Telephone
Deadline(s): None
Board meeting date(s): Jan. and as required
Write: Marian S. Heiskell, Pres.
Officers and Directors:* Marian S. Heiskell,* Pres.; Arthur Ochs Sulzberger,* V.P. and Secy.-Treas.; Ruth S. Holmberg,* V.P.; Judith P. Sulzberger,* V.P.
Number of staff: 3 part-time support.
EIN: 136083166

2301
Solon E. Summerfield Foundation, Inc. ▼
270 Madison Ave., Room 1201
New York 10016   (212) 685-5529

Incorporated in 1939 in NY.
Donor(s): Solon E. Summerfield.‡
Foundation type: Independent
Financial data (yr. ended 12/31/90): Assets, $34,364,057 (M); expenditures, $1,803,433; qualifying distributions, $1,647,501, including $1,415,183 for 122 grants (high: $554,139; low: $250; average: $500-$10,000).
Purpose and activities: Three-fourths of funds paid to designated recipients; remaining one-fourth distributed largely for higher

education; some support for social services and hospitals and health.
Fields of interest: Higher education, social services, hospitals, health, child welfare.
Types of support: Endowment funds, scholarship funds.
Application information: Contributes only to pre-selected organizations. Applications not accepted.
Write: Joseph A. Tiano, Secy.-Treas.
Officers and Trustees:* William W. Prager,* Pres.; Clarence R. Treeger,* V.P.; Joseph A. Tiano,* Secy.-Treas.
Number of staff: None.
EIN: 131797260
Recent health grants:
2301-1 Visiting Nurse Service of New York, NYC, NY, $55,414. 1990.

2302
Surdna Foundation, Inc. ▼
1155 Ave. of the Americas, 16th Fl.
New York 10036   (212) 730-0030
FAX: (212) 391-4384

Incorporated in 1917 in NY.
Donor(s): John E. Andrus.‡
Foundation type: Independent
Financial data (yr. ended 06/30/91): Assets, $329,991,327 (M); gifts received, $1,571,993; expenditures, $14,851,158; qualifying distributions, $9,277,742, including $8,127,942 for 59 grants (high: $1,081,750; low: $9,000).
Purpose and activities: "The foundation's guidelines focus on two areas: 1) the Environment, specifically transportation and energy, urban and suburban issues, and biological and cultural diversity; and 2) Community Revitalization, which takes a comprehensive and holistic approach to restoring communities in America. The foundation is particularly interested in fostering catalytic, entreprenurial programs that offer solutions to difficult systemic problems."
Fields of interest: Community development, conservation, ecology, energy, environment, housing, urban development.
Types of support: Seed money, special projects, technical assistance, continuing support, general purposes.
Limitations: No grants to individuals, or for annual campaigns, building funds, endowments, or land acquisition.
Publications: Annual report (including application guidelines).
Application information: Application form not required.
Initial approach: Letter and preliminary outline
Copies of proposal: 1
Deadline(s): None
Board meeting date(s): Sept., Nov., Feb., and May
Final notification: 90 days
Write: Edward Skloot, Exec. Dir.
Officers and Directors:* Peter B. Benedict,* Chair.; Samuel S. Thorpe III, Pres.; John J. Lynagh,* V.P. and Secy.; Lawrence S.C. Griffith, V.P.; Frederick F. Moon III,* Treas.; John E. Andrus III, Julia Moon Aubry, Christopher F. Davenport, Sandra T. Kaupe, Elizabeth Andrus Kelly, Edith D. Thorpe.
Number of staff: 5 full-time professional; 2 full-time support; 1 part-time support.

EIN: 136108163
Recent health grants:
2302-1 AIDS Resource Center, NYC, NY, $64,212. 1990.
2302-2 Community Health Project, NYC, NY, $35,000. 1990.
2302-3 Living With AIDS Fund, NYC, NY, $10,000. 1990.
2302-4 Northern Lights Alternatives, NYC, NY, $50,000. 1990.

2303
The Sussman Family Foundation
1370 Ave. of the Americas, Rm. 3100
New York 10019   (212) 262-6162

Established in 1989 in DE.
Donor(s): S. Donald Sussman.
Foundation type: Independent
Financial data (yr. ended 09/30/91): Assets, $1,326,700 (M); gifts received, $1,487,086; expenditures, $787,906; qualifying distributions, $782,253, including $779,463 for 71 grants (high: $200,000; low: $45).
Fields of interest: Museums, youth, Jewish giving, AIDS.
Limitations: Giving primarily in NY.
Application information: Application form not required.
Deadline(s): None
Write: Leon M. Metzger
Officers: S. Donald Sussman, Chair.; Laurie T. Sussman, Pres.; Beatrice L. Sussman, V.P.; Felice R. Sussman, V.P.; Arlene Ferrara, Secy.-Treas.
EIN: 133558788

2304
The Swanson Foundation
122 East 42nd St.
New York 10168   (212) 687-8360

Incorporated in 1952 in NY.
Donor(s): Glen E. Swanson.‡
Foundation type: Independent
Financial data (yr. ended 12/31/91): Assets, $4,184,869 (M); expenditures, $157,301; qualifying distributions, $130,000, including $130,000 for 3 grants (high: $100,000; low: $5,000).
Fields of interest: Medical research, hospitals, youth.
Limitations: Giving primarily in New York, NY. No grants to individuals.
Application information:
Initial approach: Letter
Deadline(s): None
Write: Arthur Richenthal, Dir.
Director: Arthur Richenthal.
EIN: 136108509

2305
Stephen C. Swid and Nan G. Swid Foundation
c/o SCS Communications
1290 Ave. of the Americas
New York 10104

Established in 1985 in NY.
Donor(s): Stephen C. Swid, Charles Koppleman, Martin Bandier.

Foundation type: Independent
Financial data (yr. ended 09/30/91): Assets, $1,597,580 (M); expenditures, $295,623; qualifying distributions, $292,321, including $291,723 for 45 grants (high: $50,000; low: $100).
Purpose and activities: Giving primarily for an international studies institute; support also for Jewish organizations, including institutes of higher education, a museum and other cultural programs, a hospital, and health associations.
Fields of interest: International studies, Jewish giving, higher education, museums, cultural programs, hospitals, health associations.
Limitations: Giving primarily in New York, NY. No grants to individuals.
Application information: Contributes only to pre-selected organizations. Applications not accepted.
Officers: Stephen C. Swid, Pres.; Nan G. Swid, Secy.
EIN: 133369493

2306
J. T. Tai & Company Foundation, Inc.
18 East 67th St.
New York 10021

Incorporated in 1983 in DE.
Donor(s): Jun Tsei Tai, J.T. Tai & Co.
Foundation type: Independent
Financial data (yr. ended 12/31/90): Assets, $11,964,070 (M); gifts received, $4,286; expenditures, $569,876; qualifying distributions, $541,748, including $541,748 for 52 grants (high: $180,900; low: $290).
Fields of interest: Higher education, medical education, health associations.
Types of support: Student aid, general purposes.
Application information: Application form not required.
Initial approach: Letter
Deadline(s): None
Write: Jun Tsei Tai, Pres.
Officers and Directors:* Jun Tsei Tai,* Pres. and Managing Dir.; F. Richard Hsu, Secy.; Ping Y. Tai.
EIN: 133157279

2307
Fred and Harriett Taylor Foundation
c/o Chase Lincoln First Bank, N.A.
P.O. Box 1412
Rochester 14603-1412

Trust established in 1976 in NY.
Donor(s): Fred C. Taylor.‡
Foundation type: Independent
Financial data (yr. ended 12/31/90): Assets, $6,299,820 (M); expenditures, $495,906; qualifying distributions, $462,467, including $459,600 for 38 grants (high: $100,000; low: $1,000).
Fields of interest: Education, hospitals, health associations, youth, Protestant giving, community development.
Limitations: Giving limited to the Hammondsport, NY, area. No grants to individuals.
Application information: Contributes only to pre-selected organizations. Applications not accepted.

Trustee: Chase Lincoln First Bank, N.A.
EIN: 166205365

2308
The Teagle Foundation, Inc. ▼
30 Rockefeller Plaza, Rm. 2835
New York 10112   (212) 247-1946

Incorporated in 1944 in CT.
Donor(s): Walter C. Teagle,‡ Rowena Lee Teagle,‡ Walter C. Teagle, Jr.‡
Foundation type: Independent
Financial data (yr. ended 05/31/91): Assets, $93,855,526 (M); expenditures, $5,430,946; qualifying distributions, $3,981,073, including $3,859,192 for 220 grants (high: $103,700; low: $3,400; average: $25,000-$75,000), $40,559 for 10 grants to individuals and $81,322 for 365 employee matching gifts.
Purpose and activities: General and project grants in support of higher education. Scholarships for children of employees of Exxon Corp. and its affiliates (program administered by College Scholarship Service, Princeton, NJ). Limited support for New York City community organizations with youth activities. Direct assistance grants to needy employees, annuitants, and widows of deceased employees of Exxon Corp.
Fields of interest: Theological education, nursing, youth, higher education.
Types of support: Employee-related scholarships, continuing support, matching funds, special projects, employee matching gifts, general purposes, seed money.
Limitations: Giving limited to the U.S. and (for Exxon Scholarship Program only) Canada. No grants to community organizations outside New York City. No grants to U.S. organizations for foreign programmatic activities. No grants to individuals not connected with Exxon Corp.; no loans.
Publications: Annual report (including application guidelines).
Application information: Application form not required.
Initial approach: Letter
Copies of proposal: 1
Deadline(s): Applications for Exxon Scholarship Program due Nov. 1 at College Scholarship Service; no deadline for other grants
Board meeting date(s): Feb., May, and Nov.
Final notification: Promptly after decision
Write: Richard W. Kimball, Pres.
Officers and Directors:* Donald M. Cox,* Chair.; Richard W. Kimball,* Pres. and C.E.O.; Margaret B. Sullivan, Secy.; James C. Anderson, Treas.; George Bugliarello, Elliot R. Cattarulla, John S. Chalsty, Peter O. Crisp, Robert G. Engel, Richard L. Morrill, Walter C. Teagle III.
Number of staff: 2 full-time professional; 1 part-time professional; 2 full-time support.
EIN: 131773645
Recent health grants:
2308-1 Hampton University, Hampton, VA, $90,000. To help licensed practical nurses (LPNs) and licensed vocational nurses (LVNs) attain Bachelor of Science in Nursing degrees through other than traditional four-year format. 1991.
2308-2 Hospital Chaplaincy, NYC, NY, $25,000. For strategic planning study. 1991.

2308-3 Hospital Chaplaincy, NYC, NY, $25,000. For training of clinical pastoral education supervisors. 1991.
2308-4 Incarnate Word College, San Antonio, TX, $25,000. For start-up of Bachelor of Science in Nursing and Masters of Science in Nursing program in Laredo, Texas, which will eventually provide faculty for local nursing schools. 1991.
2308-5 Johns Hopkins University, Baltimore, MD, $50,000. For accelerated Bachelor of Science in Nursing program for students who already have baccalaureate degree in other disciplines. 1991.
2308-6 Kearney State College, Kearney, NE, $90,000. To help licensed practical nurses (LPNs) and licensed vocational nurses (LVNs) attain Bachelor of Science in Nursing degrees through other than traditional four-year format. 1991.
2308-7 Medical University of South Carolina, Charleston, SC, $90,000. To help licensed practical nurses (LPNs) and licensed vocational nurses (LVNs) attain Bachelor of Science in Nursing degrees through other than traditional four-year format. 1991.
2308-8 North Carolina A & T State University, Greensboro, NC, $91,000. For technical assistance and direction of Teagle LPN-to-BSN Initiative. 1991.
2308-9 Otterbein College, Westerville, OH, $90,000. To help licensed practical nurses (LPNs) and licensed vocational nurses (LVNs) attain Bachelor of Science in Nursing degrees through other than traditional four-year format. 1991.
2308-10 Salem State College, Salem, MA, $90,000. To help licensed practical nurses (LPNs) and licensed vocational nurses (LVNs) attain Bachelor of Science in Nursing degrees through other than traditional four-year format. 1991.
2308-11 San Jose State University, San Jose, CA, $90,000. To help licensed practical nurses (LPNs) and licensed vocational nurses (LVNs) attain Bachelor of Science in Nursing degrees through other than traditional four-year format. 1991.
2308-12 United Negro College Fund, NYC, NY, $25,000. For premedical summer institute at Fisk University. 1991.
2308-13 University of Pennsylvania, School of Nursing, Philadelphia, PA, $25,000. For Leadership Venture Fund. 1991.

2309
Texaco Foundation ▼
(Formerly Texaco Philanthropic Foundation Inc.)
2000 Westchester Ave.
White Plains 10650   (914) 253-4150

Incorporated in 1979 in DE.
Donor(s): Texaco, Inc.
Foundation type: Company-sponsored
Financial data (yr. ended 12/31/91): Assets, $35,543,605 (M); expenditures, $11,222,493; qualifying distributions, $11,120,746, including $9,702,324 for 617 grants (high: $500,000; low: $500; average: $5,000-$15,000) and $1,378,945 for 2,816 employee matching gifts.
Purpose and activities: To enhance the quality of life by providing support for cultural programs,

higher education, social welfare, public and civic organizations, hospitals and health agencies, and environmental protection.

Fields of interest: Arts, education, environment, science and technology, social services, youth, health services, health, hospitals, public policy, civic affairs.

Types of support: Employee matching gifts, fellowships, research, employee-related scholarships, special projects, scholarship funds.

Limitations: Giving primarily in areas of company operations to local organizations; support also for national organizations that serve a large segment of the population. No support for religious organizations, private foundations, fraternal, social, or veterans' organizations, social functions, commemorative journals, or meetings, or political activities. No grants to individuals (except for employee-related scholarships), or for general operating support, capital funds (except for selected private nonprofit hospitals), or endowments; no loans.

Publications: Annual report (including application guidelines).

Application information: Application form not required.

Initial approach: Proposal
Copies of proposal: 1
Deadline(s): None
Board meeting date(s): Mar. and Sept.
Final notification: 2 months
Write: Maria Mike-Mayer, Secy.

Officers and Directors:* J. Brademas, Chair.; Carl B. Davidson,* Pres.; Maria Mike-Mayer, Secy.; Robert W. Ulrich, Treas.; George Eaton, Comptroller.

Number of staff: 5
EIN: 133007516

Recent health grants:

2309-1 American Academy of Clinical Toxicology, Pittsburgh, PA, $15,000. 1990.

2309-2 American Society of the Most Venerable Order of the Hospital of Saint John of Jerusalem, NYC, NY, $30,000. 1990.

2309-3 Childrens Hospital, New Orleans, LA, $12,000. 1990.

2309-4 Goleta Valley Community Hospital, Santa Barbara, CA, $25,000. 1990.

2309-5 Institute for Evaluating Health Risks, San Francisco, CA, $25,000. 1990.

2309-6 Juvenile Diabetes Foundation, NYC, NY, $25,000. 1990.

2309-7 League Against Cancer, Miami, FL, $10,000. 1990.

2309-8 Media-Advertising Partnership for a Drug-Free America, NYC, NY, $25,000. 1990.

2309-9 Memorial Sloan-Kettering Cancer Center, NYC, NY, $145,000. 1990.

2309-10 National Jewish Center for Immunology and Respiratory Medicine, Denver, CO, $70,000. 1990.

2309-11 National Multiple Sclerosis Society, Wichita, KS, $15,000. 1990.

2309-12 National Multiple Sclerosis Society, Tulsa, OK, $18,000. 1990.

2309-13 New York Association for the Blind, Westchester Lighthouse, White Plains, NY, $15,000. 1990.

2309-14 New York Blood Center, NYC, NY, $10,000. 1990.

2309-15 New York Hospital Burn Center, NYC, NY, $10,000. 1990.

2309-16 Pan American Association of Eye Banks, Houston, TX, $10,000. 1990.

2309-17 Saint Agnes Hospital, White Plains, NY, $10,000. 1990.

2309-18 Saint Francis Regional Medical Center, Wichita, KS, $30,000. 1990.

2309-19 Samaritan Institute, Denver, CO, $10,000. 1990.

2309-20 University of Hawaii, School of Public Health, Honolulu, HI, $15,000. 1990.

2309-21 University of Miami, Miami, FL, $10,000. For Miami Project to Cure Paralysis. Grant shared with Jackson Memorial Medical Center. 1990.

2309-22 University of Virginia, Department of Plastic and Maxillofacial Surgery, Charlottesville, VA, $10,000. 1990.

2309-23 Vassar Brothers Hospital, Poughkeepsie, NY, $14,000. 1990.

2310
Thanksgiving Foundation

c/o Fiduciary Trust Co. of New York
Two World Trade Ctr.
New York 10048

Established in 1985 in NJ.
Donor(s): Thomas M. Peters, Marion Post Peters.
Foundation type: Independent
Financial data (yr. ended 07/31/91): Assets, $5,854,454 (M); expenditures, $286,812; qualifying distributions, $261,901, including $245,500 for 56 grants (high: $25,000; low: $1,000).
Purpose and activities: Giving primarily for elementary and secondary education and human services, including child welfare; some support also for museums and the fine arts, hospitals, and environmental conservation, including reforestation and wildlife preservation.
Fields of interest: Elementary education, secondary education, social services, child welfare, museums, fine arts, hospitals, environment, wildlife.
Limitations: Giving primarily in New York, NY, and NJ. No grants to individuals.
Application information: Contributes only to pre-selected organizations. Applications not accepted.
Trustees: Thomas Henry Stine, Mark C. Winmill, Fiduciary Trust Co. of New York.
EIN: 136861874

2311
Thompson Medical Foundation

919 Third Ave.
New York 10022

Established in 1974.
Donor(s): Thompson Medical Co., Inc.
Foundation type: Independent
Financial data (yr. ended 12/31/90): Assets, $168,205 (M); gifts received, $2,650,000; expenditures, $2,584,055; qualifying distributions, $2,552,391, including $2,552,391 for 127 grants (high: $381,250; low: $100).
Purpose and activities: Giving primarily for Israel; support also for Jewish organizations, including welfare funds, and medical research.
Fields of interest: Israel, Jewish giving, Jewish welfare, medical research.

Types of support: General purposes.
Limitations: Giving in the U.S. and Israel. No grants to individuals.
Application information: Contributes only to pre-selected organizations. Applications not accepted.
Directors: S. Daniel Abraham, Moses Ratowsky, Edward L. Steinberg.
EIN: 237414925

2312
The Thorne Foundation

435 East 52nd St.
New York 10022   (212) 758-2425

Incorporated in 1930 in NY.
Donor(s): Landon K. Thorne,‡ Julia L. Thorne.‡
Foundation type: Independent
Financial data (yr. ended 12/31/91): Assets, $2,206,527 (M); expenditures, $487,214; qualifying distributions, $463,954, including $463,954 for 53 grants (high: $100,000; low: $100).
Purpose and activities: Emphasis on higher and secondary education, museums, cultural programs, youth development organizations, a library, and a zoological society; support also for hospitals.
Fields of interest: Higher education, secondary education, museums, cultural programs, youth, recreation, libraries, hospitals.
Limitations: Giving primarily in NY.
Application information:
Initial approach: Proposal
Deadline(s): None
Write: Miriam A. Thorne, Pres.
Officers: Miriam A. Thorne, Pres.; David H. Thorne,* V.P.; John B. Jessup, Secy.
EIN: 136109955

2313
The Oakleigh L. Thorne Foundation

1633 Broadway, 30th Fl.
New York 10019   (212) 246-5070

Incorporated in 1959 in NY.
Donor(s): Commerce Clearing House, Inc.
Foundation type: Company-sponsored
Financial data (yr. ended 12/31/91): Assets, $158,345 (M); gifts received, $300,000; expenditures, $294,765; qualifying distributions, $294,500, including $294,500 for 90 grants (high: $100,000; low: $500).
Fields of interest: Community funds, hospitals, health services, higher education, secondary education, youth, conservation, cultural programs.
Types of support: General purposes, operating budgets, continuing support, annual campaigns, seed money, emergency funds, deficit financing, building funds, equipment, land acquisition, endowment funds, special projects, research, publications, capital campaigns, renovation projects.
Limitations: Giving primarily in NY. No grants to individuals, or for scholarships, fellowships, or matching gifts; no loans.
Application information: Application form not required.
Initial approach: Letter
Copies of proposal: 1
Deadline(s): None

Board meeting date(s): Quarterly
Final notification: 6 months
Write: Oakleigh B. Thorne, Pres.
Officers and Directors: Oakleigh B. Thorne,*
Chair., Pres., and Treas.; Oakleigh Thorne,* V.P.
and Secy.; Theresa A. Milone,* V.P.
Number of staff: None.
EIN: 510243758

2314
Tiger Foundation
101 Park Ave.
New York 10178   (212) 984-2565

Established in 1989 in NY.
Donor(s): Julian H. Robertson, Jr.
Foundation type: Independent
Financial data (yr. ended 06/30/91): Assets,
$3,586,907 (M); gifts received, $2,569,651;
expenditures, $1,840,151; qualifying
distributions, $1,836,188, including $1,828,500
for 14 grants (high: $400,000; low: $10,000).
Purpose and activities: Giving primarily for
cancer research; support also for education and
child welfare and youth programs, including job
training.
Fields of interest: Cancer, education, youth,
employment.
Limitations: Giving primarily in New York, NY.
No grants to individuals.
Application information: Contributes only to
pre-selected organizations. Applications not
accepted.
   Write: Tref Wolcott, Exec. Dir.
Trustees: Michael D. Bills, Patrick D. Duff, John
A. Griffin, D. Christine King, Edward J. McAree,
Steven C. Olson, Julian H. Robertson, Jr., Timothy
R. Schlit, Arnold H. Snider, and 8 additional
trustees.
EIN: 133555671
Recent health grants:
2314-1 Preventive Medicine Institute/Strang
   Clinic, NYC, NY, $400,000. 1991.
2314-2 Strang Cancer Prevention Center, NYC,
   NY, $400,000. 1991.

2315
Time Warner, Inc. Foundation
(Formerly Warner Communications Foundation,
Inc.)
c/o Time Warner, Inc.
75 Rockefeller Plaza, 14th Fl.
New York 10019   (212) 484-8022

Established in 1959 in NY.
Donor(s): Warner Communications, Inc.
Foundation type: Company-sponsored
Financial data (yr. ended 09/30/90): Assets,
$481,841 (M); expenditures, $360,000;
qualifying distributions, $360,000, including
$360,000 for 4 grants (high: $250,000; low:
$10,000).
Fields of interest: Hospitals, cultural programs,
dance, higher education.
Limitations: Giving primarily in NY and CA.
Application information: Applications not
accepted.
   Write: Mary E. McCarthy, Dir. of Corp. Contribs.
Officers and Directors: Deane F. Johnson,*
Chair.; Warren A. Christie, V.P.; Eli T. Bruno, Secy.;
David R. Haas,* Treas.

Administrator: Mary E. McCarthy, Dir. of Corp.
Contribs.
EIN: 136085361

2316
Tisch Foundation, Inc. ▼
667 Madison Ave.
New York 10021-8087   (212) 545-2000

Incorporated in 1957 in FL.
Donor(s): Hotel Americana, Tisch Hotels, Inc.,
members of the Tisch family, and closely held
corporations.
Foundation type: Independent
Financial data (yr. ended 12/31/90): Assets,
$79,108,351 (M); expenditures, $7,497,210;
qualifying distributions, $7,327,233, including
$7,322,033 for 114 grants (high: $2,000,000;
low: $100; average: $1,000-$25,000).
Purpose and activities: Emphasis on higher
education, including institutions in Israel, and
research-related programs; support also for Jewish
organizations and welfare funds, museums, and
secondary education.
Fields of interest: Higher education, museums,
Israel, Jewish welfare, Jewish giving, secondary
education.
Types of support: Continuing support, building
funds, equipment, research.
Limitations: No grants to individuals, or for
endowment funds, scholarships, fellowships, or
matching gifts; no loans.
Application information: Contributes only to
pre-selected organizations. Applications not
accepted.
   Board meeting date(s): Mar., June, Sept., Dec.,
   and as required
   Write: Laurence A. Tisch, Sr. V.P.
Officers and Directors: Preston R. Tisch, Pres.;
Laurence A. Tisch, Sr. V.P.; E. Jack Beatus,*
Secy.-Treas.; Joan M. Tisch, Wilma S. Tisch.
Number of staff: None.
EIN: 591002844
Recent health grants:
2316-1 AIDS Project Los Angeles, Los Angeles,
   CA, $10,000. 1990.
2316-2 Big Apple Circus, NYC, NY, $15,000.
   1990.
2316-3 Childrens Hearing Institute, NYC, NY,
   $10,000. 1990.
2316-4 Gay Mens Health Crisis (GMHC), NYC,
   NY, $50,000. 1990.
2316-5 Montefiore Medical Center, NYC, NY,
   $20,000. For unrestricted support. 1990.
2316-6 Mount Sinai Hospital and Medical
   Center, NYC, NY, $500,000. 1990.
2316-7 New York University Medical Center,
   Tisch Hospital, NYC, NY, $2,000,000. For
   unrestricted support. 1990.
2316-8 Pediatric AIDS Foundation, Santa
   Monica, CA, $40,000. 1990.
2316-9 United Hospital, Port Chester, NY,
   $20,000. For campaign. 1990.
2316-10 White Plains Hospital Medical Center,
   White Plains, NY, $13,625. 1990.

2317
Rose & John Tishman Fund, Inc.
666 Fifth Ave.
New York 10103-0001

Established in 1957 in NY.
Donor(s): Rose F. Tishman.
Foundation type: Independent
Financial data (yr. ended 12/31/91): Assets,
$925,302 (M); gifts received, $165,000;
expenditures, $247,955; qualifying distributions,
$242,888, including $240,410 for 44 grants
(high: $150,000; low: $25).
Fields of interest: Higher education, science and
technology, social services, health, Jewish giving.
Limitations: Giving primarily in NY.
Application information:
   Initial approach: Letter
   Deadline(s): None
   Write: John L. Tishman, Pres.
Officers: John Tishman, Pres.; Daniel R. Tishman,
V.P. and Treas.; Katherine Blacklock, V.P.; Rose F.
Tishman, V.P.; Kathleen E. Kotown, Secy.
EIN: 136151766

2318
Tortuga Foundation
c/o Siegel, Sacks & Co.
630 Third Ave., 22nd Fl.
New York 10017

Established in 1979 in NY.
Donor(s): William C. Breed III, J.L. Tweedy.
Foundation type: Independent
Financial data (yr. ended 09/30/91): Assets,
$5,425,475 (M); gifts received, $600,000;
expenditures, $598,286; qualifying distributions,
$563,000, including $550,000 for 23 grants
(high: $50,000; low: $5,000).
Purpose and activities: Support primarily for land
preservation, the environment, and women's and
family planning groups; support also for health
organizations and education.
Fields of interest: Environment, conservation,
women, family planning, health associations,
education, general charitable giving.
Limitations: No grants to individuals.
Application information: Contributes only to
pre-selected organizations. Applications not
accepted.
Officers and Trustees: George H.P. Dwight,*
Pres.; Hugh J. Freund,* V.P. and Secy.-Treas.;
Patricia P. Livingston,* V.P.; Robert C. Livingston,
Millie L. Siceloff.
Number of staff: 2 shared staff
EIN: 510245279

2319
Ray W. and Ildah Totman Medical
Research Fund
c/o National Bank & Trust Co. of Norwich
52 South Broad St.
Norwich 13815-1699

Established in 1988 in NY.
Donor(s): Ray W. Totman.‡
Foundation type: Independent
Financial data (yr. ended 03/31/91): Assets,
$3,098,553 (M); expenditures, $292,324;
qualifying distributions, $237,500, including
$237,500 for 1 grant.

Fields of interest: Medical research.
Types of support: Research.
Limitations: Giving primarily in VT. No grants to individuals.
Application information: Contributes only to pre-selected organizations. Applications not accepted.
Trustees: Marguerite Boyer, William J. Herron, Donald E. Stone.
EIN: 161328003

2320
Robert Mize & Isa White Trimble Family Foundation
c/o Gerard L. Finneran
50 East 77th St., Apt 12D
New York 10021

Established in 1978 in NY.
Donor(s): Mary Ray Finneran.‡
Foundation type: Independent
Financial data (yr. ended 06/30/91): Assets, $2,473,591 (M); expenditures, $104,900; qualifying distributions, $102,005, including $96,000 for 15 grants (high: $10,000; low: $1,000).
Purpose and activities: Giving primarily for hospitals; support also for social services, including child welfare programs, and Catholic religious and welfare organizations.
Fields of interest: Hospitals, Catholic giving, religious welfare, child welfare, social services.
Limitations: Giving primarily in NY. No grants to individuals, or for scholarships or fellowships; no loans.
Application information: Contributes only to pre-selected organizations. Applications not accepted.
Officers and Directors:* Gerard L. Finneran,* Pres.; Daniel J. Ashley,* V.P.; Rita H. Rowan,* Secy.; Gerard B. Finneran,* Treas.
EIN: 132972532

2321
Ruth Turner Fund, Inc.
c/o Kridel & Neuwirth
360 Lexington Ave.
New York 10017-6502

Established in 1973.
Donor(s): Ruth Turner.‡
Foundation type: Independent
Financial data (yr. ended 12/31/90): Assets, $4,172,099 (M); expenditures, $220,744; qualifying distributions, $185,505, including $172,000 for 13 grants (high: $25,000; low: $3,000).
Purpose and activities: Support for medical research, including AIDS research, and programs for the visually impaired; grants also for youth and social services, and primary and secondary education.
Fields of interest: Medical research, AIDS, handicapped, youth, social services, homeless, education—early childhood, secondary education.
Types of support: Research, scholarship funds.
Limitations: Giving primarily in New York, NY. No grants to individuals.
Officers: William J. Kridel, Pres.; Daniel L. Hartman, V.P.; Gloria S. Neuwirth, Secy.

Number of staff: None.
EIN: 237240889

2322
'21' International Holding Inc. Foundation
▼
(Formerly KIHI Foundation)
153 East 53rd St., Suite 5900
New York 10022   (212) 230-0400

Established around 1983 in NY as GFI/Knoll Foundation; name changed to KIHI Foundation in 1988; present name adopted in 1990.
Donor(s): '21' International Holding, Inc.
Foundation type: Company-sponsored
Financial data (yr. ended 12/31/90): Assets, $78,381 (M); gifts received, $1,150,000; expenditures, $1,087,150; qualifying distributions, $1,087,150, including $1,065,355 for grants and $21,795 for 60 employee matching gifts.
Purpose and activities: Primary areas of interest include museums and other arts groups, Jewish welfare funds, and medical research.
Fields of interest: Cultural programs, Jewish welfare, Jewish giving, higher education, secondary education, political science, Israel, arts, child development, disadvantaged, education, museums, medical research, human rights, religious welfare.
Types of support: General purposes, annual campaigns, capital campaigns, matching funds.
Limitations: Giving primarily in New York, NY. No grants to individuals.
Application information: Contributes only to pre-selected organizations. Applications not accepted.
    Board meeting date(s): As required
    Write: Judy Hershon, V.P.
Director: Marshall S. Cogan.
Number of staff: None.
EIN: 222518739

2323
Unilever United States Foundation
(Formerly Lever Brothers Company Foundation)
390 Park Ave.
New York 10022   (212) 906-4685

Incorporated in 1952 in NY.
Donor(s): Lever Brothers Co., Van den Bergh Foods Co., Unilever United States, Inc.
Foundation type: Company-sponsored
Financial data (yr. ended 12/31/90): Assets, $623,068 (M); expenditures, $1,018,000; qualifying distributions, $1,018,000, including $925,000 for 175 grants (high: $50,000; low: $500) and $93,000 for 629 employee matching gifts.
Fields of interest: Civil rights, health, community development, education, elementary education, housing, environment.
Types of support: Operating budgets, employee-related scholarships, employee matching gifts, donated products, in-kind gifts.
Limitations: Giving primarily in areas of company operations in NY, CA, GA, IN, MD, MO, and NJ. No support for religious, political, or international organizations. No grants to individuals (except for employee-related scholarships), or for building funds or endowment funds; no loans.

Publications: Application guidelines.
Application information: Application form not required.
    Initial approach: Letter or proposal
    Copies of proposal: 1
    Deadline(s): None
    Board meeting date(s): May, Oct., and Dec.
    Final notification: 1 month after meeting
    Write: Rachel R. Greenstein, Community Affairs Mgr., Unilever United States, Inc.
Officers and Directors:* Ned W. Bandler,* Pres.; John T. Gould, Jr., V.P.; John Lamantia, Paul Mayer, T.C. Mullins, W.M. Volpi.
Number of staff: 2 part-time professional; 1 part-time support.
EIN: 136122117

2324
Bella & Israel Unterberg Foundation, Inc.
c/o Leipziger & Breskin
230 Park Ave.
New York 10169

Incorporated in 1948 in NY.
Donor(s): Members of the Unterberg family.
Foundation type: Independent
Financial data (yr. ended 12/31/91): Assets, $1,070,274 (M); gifts received, $197,685; expenditures, $465,746; qualifying distributions, $437,285, including $437,285 for 102 grants (high: $50,000; low: $40).
Fields of interest: Social services, Jewish welfare, higher education, hospitals.
Limitations: Giving primarily in NY, with emphasis on the greater metropolitan New York area. No grants to individuals.
Application information: Contributes only to pre-selected organizations. Applications not accepted.
Officers: Edgar J. Nathan III, Pres.; Selma S. Unterberg, 1st V.P.; Carol R. Meyer, 2nd V.P.; Thomas I. Unterberg, 3rd V.P.; James H. Powell, 4th V.P.; Frank E. Joseph, Jr., 5th V.P.; Lilian V. Desecktor, Secy.
EIN: 136099080

2325
Ushkow Foundation, Inc.
c/o Sedco Industries, Inc.
98 Cutter Mill Rd., Suite 475N
Great Neck 11021

Incorporated in 1956 in NY.
Donor(s): Joseph Ushkow.
Foundation type: Independent
Financial data (yr. ended 10/31/90): Assets, $2,784,497 (M); expenditures, $16,205; qualifying distributions, $8,125, including $7,985 for 16 grants (high: $2,500; low: $25).
Fields of interest: Hospitals, higher education, Jewish welfare.
Limitations: Giving primarily in NY, with some emphasis on Nassau County. No grants to individuals.
Application information: Contributes only to pre-selected organizations. Applications not accepted.
Officers: Barbara Deane, Pres.; Maurice A. Deane, Secy.-Treas.
EIN: 116006274

2326
van Ameringen Foundation, Inc. ▼
509 Madison Ave.
New York 10022   (212) 758-6221

Incorporated in 1950 in NY.
Donor(s): Arnold Louis van Ameringen.‡
Foundation type: Independent
Financial data (yr. ended 12/31/91): Assets, $42,100,266 (M); expenditures, $1,925,067; qualifying distributions, $1,682,487, including $1,682,487 for 48 grants (high: $80,000; low: $2,500; average: $20,000-$50,000).
Purpose and activities: Grants chiefly to promote mental health and social welfare through preventive measures, treatment, and rehabilitation; support also for child development, medical education, and health, including the fields of psychology and psychiatry.
Fields of interest: Mental health, child development, health services, medical education, psychology, psychiatry.
Types of support: Operating budgets, seed money, matching funds, special projects, research, publications, endowment funds.
Limitations: Giving primarily in the urban Northeast from Boston, MA, to Washington, DC, including NY and PA. No support for international activities and institutions in other countries, or for mental retardation, the physically handicapped, drug abuse, or alcoholism. No grants to individuals, or for annual campaigns, deficit financing, emergency funds, capital campaigns, scholarships, or fellowships; no loans.
Publications: Annual report.
Application information: Application form not required.
Initial approach: Proposal
Copies of proposal: 1
Deadline(s): 2 months before board meetings
Board meeting date(s): Mar., June, and Nov.
Final notification: Within 60 days
Write: Henry van Ameringen, Pres.
Officers and Directors:* Henry P. van Ameringen,* Pres. and Treas.; Lily vA. Auchincloss,* V.P.; Harmon Duncombe,* Secy.; Mrs. Arnold Louis van Ameringen,* Honorary Chair.; Eleanor K. Sypher, Exec. Dir.; Patricia Kind, Henry G. Walter, Jr.
Number of staff: 1 full-time professional; 1 full-time support.
EIN: 136125699
Recent health grants:
2326-1 Alliance for the Mentally Ill of Pennsylvania, Harrisburg, PA, $60,000. For state-wide effort to train families to educate public on stigma of mental illness. 1991.
2326-2 American Orthopsychiatric Association, NYC, NY, $10,000. For production and distribution of journal, Readings. 1991.
2326-3 Columbia University, Columbia University Community Services, NYC, NY, $107,378. For social and mental health services to seven formerly homeless families at The Rio. 1991.
2326-4 Emory University, Carter Center, Atlanta, GA, $28,000. For annual Rosalyn Carter Symposium on Mental Health Policy. 1991.
2326-5 Federation of Parents and Friends of Lesbians and Gays, DC, $50,000. For network of volunteer organizers and educators, serving families and caregivers of people with HIV/AIDS. 1991.

2326-6 Fountain House, van Ameringen Center for Education and Research, NYC, NY, $240,000. For continued support for research, training and rehabilitation programs. 1991.
2326-7 Gay Mens Health Crisis (GMHC), NYC, NY, $90,000. For group therapy and psychological interventions to help staff at GMHC deal with stress and anxiety. 1991.
2326-8 Green Chimneys Childrens Services, Brewster, NY, $20,000. For how-to manual on animal-assisted therapy for emotionally disturbed children. 1991.
2326-9 Green Door, DC, $50,000. For kitchen renovation and vocational equipment for cafe in clubhouse program. 1991.
2326-10 Institute of Living, Hartford, CT, $150,000. For bilingual, family outreach clinical case manager to deliver outpatient mental health services to Hartford's disadvantaged children and adolescents before, during and after treatment. 1991.
2326-11 National Center for Clinical Infant Programs, Arlington, VA, $150,000. For Fellowship Program to promote leadership and innovation in field of infant health, mental health and development. 1991.
2326-12 Resources for Human Development, Norristown, PA, $144,600. For salary of Director of Compeer, which matches mentally-ill client to volunteer friend as adjunct to therapy. 1991.
2326-13 Vermont Liberation Organization, White Light Communications, Burlington, VT, $35,000. For salary support for this TV production business (managed by recovering mentally ill) to educate public about issues and concerns of ex-patients. 1991.
2326-14 Way Station, Frederick, MD, $50,000. For start-up operational funding for Training and Education Center of community-based organization's rehabilitation and outreach to deinstitutionalized mentally-ill. 1991.
2326-15 West Side Federation for Senior Housing, Valley Lodge, NYC, NY, $30,000. For case management services to mentally-disabled residents. 1991.

2327
H. van Ameringen Foundation
509 Madison Ave.
New York 10022

Established in 1950.
Donor(s): Henry P. van Ameringen.
Foundation type: Independent
Financial data (yr. ended 12/31/90): Assets, $949,154 (M); gifts received, $700,000; expenditures, $336,031; qualifying distributions, $335,683, including $335,365 for 57 grants (high: $50,000; low: $100).
Fields of interest: Mental health, AIDS, homeless, general charitable giving.
Limitations: Giving primarily in NY. No grants to individuals.
Application information: Unsolicited applications not accepted.
Trustee: Henry P. van Ameringen.
EIN: 136215329

2328
The Vanneck-Bailey Foundation
100 Park Ave.
New York 10017

Established in 1971 in NY through the consolidation of The Vanneck Foundation, incorporated in 1949 in NY, and The Frank and Marie Bailey Foundation.
Donor(s): John Vanneck,‡ Barbara Bailey Vanneck.
Foundation type: Independent
Financial data (yr. ended 12/31/91): Assets, $5,989,724 (M); expenditures, $275,581; qualifying distributions, $270,162, including $269,860 for 101 grants (high: $42,000; low: $50).
Fields of interest: Higher education, hospitals, community development, Protestant giving, conservation.
Types of support: Continuing support, research.
Limitations: Giving primarily in the East Coast. No grants to individuals.
Application information: Contributes only to pre-selected organizations. Applications not accepted.
Write: John B. Vanneck, V.P.
Officers: Barbara Bailey Vanneck, Pres.; John B. Vanneck, V.P.; Jeanne M. Wiedeman, Secy.; William P. Vanneck, Treas.
EIN: 237165285

2329
Miles Hodsdon Vernon Fund, Inc.
49 Beekman Ave.
North Tarrytown 10591   (914) 631-4226

Incorporated in 1953 in NY.
Donor(s): Miles Hodsdon Vernon,‡ Martha Hodsdon Kinney,‡ Louise Hodsdon.‡
Foundation type: Independent
Financial data (yr. ended 12/31/90): Assets, $4,809,305 (M); expenditures, $257,537; qualifying distributions, $229,600, including $221,450 for 51 grants (high: $30,000; low: $250).
Purpose and activities: Grants for medical research, especially on encephalitis and other brain disorders; support also for youth agencies, aid for the aged, and education.
Fields of interest: Medical research, handicapped, youth, aged, higher education, secondary education.
Types of support: Scholarship funds, research.
Limitations: Giving primarily in NY. No grants to individuals.
Application information:
Initial approach: Proposal
Deadline(s): None
Write: Robert C. Thomson, Jr., Pres.
Officers and Directors:* Robert C. Thomson, Jr.,* Pres. and Treas.; Dennis M. Fitzgerald,* V.P. and Secy.; Eleanor C. Thomson, Gertrude Whalen.
EIN: 136076836

2330
The Vidda Foundation
c/o Carter, Carter & Rupp
Ten East 40th St., Suite 2103
New York 10016   (212) 696-4052

Established in 1979 in NY.
Donor(s): Ursula Corning.
Foundation type: Independent
Financial data (yr. ended 05/31/92): Assets, $1,689,844 (M); gifts received, $1,000,000; expenditures, $1,222,679; qualifying distributions, $1,097,001, including $1,097,001 for 37 grants (high: $500,000; low: $500; average: $500-$500,000).
Purpose and activities: Giving primarily to higher education and educational projects, cultural programs, including fine arts and museums, an educational film-making company, church music funds, animal welfare, the environment and conservation, hospitals, and social services, including child welfare and the elderly.
Fields of interest: Higher education, cultural programs, fine arts, museums, music, Catholic giving, Protestant giving, animal welfare, conservation, hospitals, social services, child welfare, aged.
Types of support: General purposes, building funds, special projects, endowment funds, research, operating budgets.
Limitations: Giving primarily in NY. No grants to individuals.
Application information: Application form not required.
  Initial approach: Letter or proposal
  Copies of proposal: 1
  Deadline(s): None
  Board meeting date(s): Nov. and May
  Final notification: Approximately 2 months
  Write: Gerald E. Rupp, Mgr.
Officer and Trustees:* Gerald E. Rupp,* Mgr.; Ann Fraser Brewer, Ursula Corning, Thomas T. Fraser, Christophe Velay.
Number of staff: 2 part-time professional; 2 part-time support.
EIN: 132981105

2331
The Laura B. Vogler Foundation, Inc.
P.O. Box 94
Bayside 11361   (718) 423-3000

Incorporated in 1959 in NY.
Donor(s): Laura B. Vogler,‡ John J. Vogler.‡
Foundation type: Independent
Financial data (yr. ended 10/31/91): Assets, $3,851,985 (M); expenditures, $233,998; qualifying distributions, $204,424, including $163,683 for 62 grants (high: $5,000; low: $1,000; average: $1,000-$5,000).
Purpose and activities: "Awards one-time non-renewable grants for new programs in the areas of health, youth, child welfare, the elderly, the disadvantaged, and other related services."
Fields of interest: Health, youth, child welfare, aged, disadvantaged.
Types of support: Seed money, emergency funds, special projects, research, scholarship funds.
Limitations: Giving limited to New York City and Long Island. No grants to individuals, or for building or endowment funds, annual fundraising campaigns, or matching gifts; no loans.
Publications: Annual report (including application guidelines).
Application information: Application form required.
  Initial approach: Letter
  Copies of proposal: 1

Deadline(s): Jan. 1, Apr. 1, July 1, and Oct. 1
Board meeting date(s): Jan., Apr., July, and Oct.
Final notification: 2 to 3 months
Write: D. Donald D'Amato, Pres.
Officers and Trustees:* D. Donald D'Amato,* Pres. and C.E.O.; Lawrence L. D'Amato,* Secy.-Treas.; Max L. Kupferberg, I. Jerry Lasurdo, Stanley C. Pearson, Robert T. Waldbauer, Karen M. Yost.
Number of staff: 2 part-time professional; 1 part-time support.
EIN: 116022241

2332
Mary Jane & William J. Voute Foundation, Inc.
31 Masterton Rd.
Bronxville 10708

Established in 1977 in NY.
Donor(s): Mary Jane Voute, William J. Voute.‡
Foundation type: Independent
Financial data (yr. ended 06/30/91): Assets, $2,114 (M); gifts received, $422,000; expenditures, $425,405; qualifying distributions, $420,531, including $420,353 for 44 grants (high: $200,000; low: $25).
Purpose and activities: Grants primarily for Catholic church support and higher education; giving also for health and hospitals and social services.
Fields of interest: Catholic giving, higher education, health, hospitals, social services.
Types of support: Scholarship funds.
Limitations: Giving primarily in the New York, NY, metropolitan area, including Westchester County. No grants to individuals.
Application information: Contributes only to pre-selected organizations. Applications not accepted.
Officers: Mary Jane Voute, V.P. and Secy.
Directors: Stanley L. Cohen, Salvatore Traini, Michael Walsh.
EIN: 510249510

2333
George P. Wakefield Residuary Trust
c/o The Bank of New York, Tax Dept.
One Wall St., 28th Fl.
New York 10286
Application address: 437 Madison Ave., New York, NY 10022

Foundation type: Independent
Financial data (yr. ended 06/30/91): Assets, $2,216,277 (M); expenditures, $118,.75; qualifying distributions, $117,270, including $116,770 for 22 grants (high: $9,350; low: $2,420).
Purpose and activities: Support primarily for Jewish welfare agencies; giving also to child welfare organizations, hospitals and medical research.
Fields of interest: Jewish welfare, child welfare, hospitals, medical research.
Limitations: Giving primarily in New York, NY.
Application information:
  Initial approach: Letter
  Deadline(s): None
  Write: Samuel Weinberg, Trustee

Trustees: Samuel Weinberg, The Bank of New York.
EIN: 136079388

2334
Wallace Genetic Foundation, Inc. ▼
c/o Stanley Rosenberg
660 White Plains Rd.
Tarrytown 10591
Grant application address: Polly Lawrence, Research Secy., 4801 Massachusetts Ave., Suite 400, Washington, DC 20016; Tel.: (202) 966-2932

Incorporated in 1959 in NY.
Donor(s): Henry A. Wallace.‡
Foundation type: Independent
Financial data (yr. ended 12/31/90): Assets, $50,884,858 (M); gifts received, $310,000; expenditures, $2,545,344; qualifying distributions, $2,437,271, including $2,360,794 for 65 grants (high: $550,000; low: $3,000; average: $5,000-$75,000).
Purpose and activities: Support for agricultural research and preservation of farmland, higher education, nutritional research, conservation, and environmental activities.
Fields of interest: Agriculture, conservation, environment, higher education, nutrition.
Types of support: Research.
Limitations: No grants to individuals, or for scholarships or overhead expenses; no loans.
Application information: Application form required.
  Initial approach: Letter and proposal
  Copies of proposal: 1
  Deadline(s): None
  Board meeting date(s): As required
  Final notification: Sept. 1
Directors: Jean W. Douglas, Henry B. Wallace, Robert B. Wallace.
Number of staff: 3
EIN: 136162575
Recent health grants:
2334-1 Dermatology Foundation of Miami, Miami, FL, $125,000. 1990.
2334-2 Harlan E. Moore Heart Research Foundation, Champaign, IL, $90,000. 1990.
2334-3 Physicians for Social Responsibility, DC, $15,000. 1990.
2334-4 Population Crisis Committee, DC, $550,000. 1990.
2334-5 United States Cancer Research Council, Bethesda, MD, $50,000. 1990.

2335
Miriam G. and Ira D. Wallach Foundation ▼
100 Park Ave.
New York 10017   (212) 532-7306

Incorporated in 1956 in NY.
Foundation type: Independent
Financial data (yr. ended 10/31/91): Assets, $16,373,340 (M); gifts received, $100,085; expenditures, $1,286,519; qualifying distributions, $1,087,356, including $1,082,188 for 91 grants (high: $150,000; low: $50; average: $1,000-$10,000).
Purpose and activities: Support primarily for higher education, and international relations,

including peace; support also for social services, Jewish organizations, and cultural programs.
Fields of interest: Higher education, international affairs, peace, social services, Jewish giving, Jewish welfare, cultural programs, AIDS.
Limitations: Giving primarily in NY.
Application information: Contributes only to pre-selected organizations. Applications not accepted.
Officers and Directors:* Ira D. Wallach,* Pres.; Edgar Wachenheim III,* V.P.; James G. Wallach,* V.P.; Kenneth L. Wallach,* V.P.; Miriam G. Wallach,* V.P.; Peter C. Siegfried, Secy.; Benjamin Glowatz, Treas.; Sue W. Wachenheim, Kate B. Wallach, Mary K. Wallach, Susan S. Wallach.
EIN: 136101702

2336
Riley J. and Lillian N. Warren and Beatrice W. Blanding Foundation
Six Ford Ave.
Oneonta 13820   (607) 432-6720

Trust established in 1972 in NY.
Donor(s): Beatrice W. Blanding.
Foundation type: Independent
Financial data (yr. ended 12/31/91): Assets, $5,612,847 (M); expenditures, $240,202; qualifying distributions, $230,034, including $189,000 for 24 grants (high: $75,000; low: $500).
Purpose and activities: Emphasis on higher and secondary education; support also for hospitals, churches, and organizations benefiting youth.
Fields of interest: Higher education, secondary education, religious schools, religion—Christian, hospitals, youth.
Limitations: Giving primarily in the Oneonta, NY, area.
Application information:
 Initial approach: Letter
 Deadline(s): Nov. 1
 Write: Henry L. Hulbert. Esq., Mgr.
Officer and Trustees:* Henry L. Hulbert,* Mgr.; Beatrice W. Blanding, Robert A. Harlem.
EIN: 237203341

2337
Washington Square Fund
P.O. Box 7938, F.D.R. Station
New York 10150

Foundation type: Independent
Financial data (yr. ended 09/30/90): Assets, $2,364,072 (M); gifts received, $1,500; expenditures, $150,545; qualifying distributions, $124,691, including $119,200 for 8 grants (high: $34,700; low: $5,000).
Purpose and activities: Grants for child welfare, youth agencies, and families, including welfare and social programs, education about health, teenage pregnancy prevention, guidance of troubled teenagers, and family planning and counseling; preference is for pilot and special projects, usually of 2 to 3 years duration.
Fields of interest: Child welfare, youth, family services, education, family planning, social services.
Types of support: Seed money, special projects.

Limitations: Giving limited to New York, NY. No grants to individuals, or for operating funds or ongoing programs.
Application information:
 Initial approach: Letter or proposal
 Deadline(s): None
 Write: L. Kirk Payne, Pres.
Officers: L. Kirk Payne, Pres.; Theresa R. Schaff, V.P.; Louise Chinn, Secy.; Susan J. Baisley, Treas.
Directors: James D. Johnson, Mrs. James D. Johnson, Margo Lynden, William Taggart, Theresa Thompson, Jeff Wallis.
EIN: 131624213

2338
Monique Weill-Caulier Trust
c/o Weil, Gotshal & Manges
767 Fifth Ave.
New York 10153

Established in 1981 in NY.
Foundation type: Independent
Financial data (yr. ended 10/31/91): Assets, $2,093,785 (M); gifts received, $10,833; expenditures, $124,696; qualifying distributions, $92,604, including $80,000 for 3 grants (high: $26,667; low: $26,666).
Fields of interest: Medical education, higher education.
Limitations: Giving primarily in NY. No grants to individuals.
Application information: Contributes only to pre-selected organizations. Applications not accepted.
Trustees: Robert Todd Lang, John M. Lewis.
EIN: 133020092

2339
The John L. Weinberg Foundation
c/o Goldman Sachs & Co.
85 Broad St., 22nd Fl.
New York 10004

Trust established in 1959 in NY.
Donor(s): John L. Weinberg.
Foundation type: Independent
Financial data (yr. ended 04/30/91): Assets, $19,221,421 (M); gifts received, $2,680,000; expenditures, $648,048; qualifying distributions, $611,940, including $610,887 for 126 grants (high: $200,000; low: $15).
Fields of interest: Hospitals, medical research, secondary education, higher education, Jewish welfare.
Types of support: Annual campaigns, operating budgets, professorships, program-related investments, renovation projects, research.
Limitations: Giving primarily in New York, NY, and Greenwich, CT. No grants to individuals.
Application information: Application form not required.
 Initial approach: Letter
 Copies of proposal: 1
 Board meeting date(s): N
 Write: John L. Weinberg, Trustee
Trustees: Arthur G. Altschul, Jean H. Weinberg, John L. Weinberg, John S. Weinberg, Sue Ann Weinberg.
Number of staff: 2 part-time support.
EIN: 136028813

2340
Sidney J. Weinberg, Jr. Foundation
c/o Goldman Sachs & Co., Tax Dept.
85 Broad St.
New York 10004

Established in 1979 in NY.
Donor(s): Sidney J. Weinberg, Jr.
Foundation type: Independent
Financial data (yr. ended 05/31/91): Assets, $14,732,497 (M); gifts received, $2,000,082; expenditures, $1,158,642; qualifying distributions, $1,119,130, including $1,118,400 for 68 grants (high: $250,000; low: $100).
Fields of interest: Higher education, hospitals.
Types of support: General purposes.
Limitations: Giving primarily in the eastern U.S., especially New York, NY. No grants to individuals.
Application information: Contributes only to pre-selected organizations. Applications not accepted.
Trustees: Elizabeth W. Smith, Peter A. Weinberg, Sidney J. Weinberg, Jr., Sydney H. Weinberg.
Number of staff: None.
EIN: 132998603

2341
The Alex J. Weinstein Foundation, Inc.
c/o Herbert Feinberg
60 Cutter Mill Rd., No. 504
Great Neck 11021

Established in 1953.
Foundation type: Independent
Financial data (yr. ended 11/30/90): Assets, $2,409,626 (M); expenditures, $115,589; qualifying distributions, $105,384, including $101,250 for 19 grants (high: $35,000; low: $50).
Fields of interest: Hospitals, higher education, Jewish giving, museums, performing arts.
Limitations: Giving primarily in NY and CT. No grants to individuals.
Application information: Contributes only to pre-selected organizations. Applications not accepted.
Directors and Trustees: Herbert D. Feinberg, Barrie J. Solesko.
EIN: 136160964

2342
J. Weinstein Foundation, Inc.
Rockridge Farm, Route 52
Carmel 10512

Incorporated in 1948 in NY.
Donor(s): Joe Weinstein,‡ J.W. Mays, Inc.
Foundation type: Independent
Financial data (yr. ended 12/31/90): Assets, $3,739,001 (M); gifts received, $30,000; expenditures, $121,715; qualifying distributions, $121,715, including $120,566 for 37 grants (high: $61,551; low: $25).
Purpose and activities: Support for higher education in the U.S. and Israel, temple support, hospitals, and Jewish welfare funds.
Fields of interest: Higher education, Israel, Jewish giving, hospitals, Jewish welfare.
Types of support: Continuing support, endowment funds, general purposes.
Limitations: Giving primarily in NY.

Application information: Contributes only to pre-selected organizations. Applications not accepted.
Officers and Directors:* Max L. Shulman,* Pres.; Lloyd J. Shulman,* V.P.; Sylvia W. Shulman,* V.P.; Salvatore Cappuzzo,* Secy.-Treas.
EIN: 116003595

2343
Wellington Foundation, Inc.
14 Wall St., Suite 1702
New York 10005

Incorporated in 1955 in NY.
Donor(s): Herbert G. Wellington,‡ Herbert G. Wellington, Jr., Elizabeth D. Wellington.‡
Foundation type: Independent
Financial data (yr. ended 12/31/90): Assets, $1,415,599 (M); expenditures, $280,500; qualifying distributions, $276,975, including $276,000 for grants.
Fields of interest: Medical research, education, cultural programs.
Limitations: Giving primarily in the greater New York, NY, metropolitan area. No grants to individuals.
Application information: Contributes only to pre-selected organizations. Applications not accepted.
Officers: Herbert G. Wellington, Jr., Pres. and Treas.; Patricia B. Wellington, V.P.; Thomas D. Wellington, Secy.
EIN: 136110175

2344
The Margaret L. Wendt Foundation ▼
40 Fountain Plaza, Suite 277
Buffalo 14202-2220   (716) 855-2146

Trust established in 1956 in NY.
Donor(s): Margaret L. Wendt.‡
Foundation type: Independent
Financial data (yr. ended 01/31/91): Assets, $47,737,307 (M); expenditures, $3,115,774; qualifying distributions, $4,839,274, including $2,548,351 for 107 grants (high: $300,000; low: $400; average: $5,000-$15,000) and $2,290,923 for program-related investments.
Purpose and activities: Emphasis on education, the arts, and social services; support also for churches and religious organizations, health associations, public interest organizations, and youth agencies.
Fields of interest: Arts, health associations, religion, social services, higher education, education, youth, child welfare, public affairs, political science, hospitals, AIDS, aged, handicapped, medical sciences, mental health, community development, conservation, law and justice, minorities.
Limitations: Giving primarily in Buffalo and western NY. No grants to individuals, or for scholarships.
Publications: Application guidelines.
Application information: Application form not required.
  Initial approach: Letter or application form
  Copies of proposal: 4
  Deadline(s): 1 month prior to board meeting
  Board meeting date(s): Quarterly; no fixed dates
  Final notification: Usually 4 to 6 months

Write: Robert J. Kresse, Secy.
Officers and Trustees:* Ralph W. Loew,* Chair.; Robert J. Kresse,* Secy.; Thomas D. Lunt.
Number of staff: 1 part-time support.
EIN: 166030037
Recent health grants:
2344-1 Alcoholism Services Foundation, Buffalo, NY, $150,000. For construction of adolescent treatment facility. 1991.
2344-2 Arthritis Foundation of Western New York, Buffalo, NY, $15,000. For three local research projects. 1991.
2344-3 Brooks Memorial Hospital, Dunkirk, NY, $10,000. For cardiac rehabilitation program. 1991.
2344-4 Buffalo Columbus Hospital, Buffalo, NY, $75,000. For new construction and rehabilitation. 1991.
2344-5 Buffalo Council on Alcohol Abuse, Buffalo, NY, $11,000. For prevention program for deaf residents of Western New York. 1991.
2344-6 DYouville College, Buffalo, NY, $42,012. For physical and occupational therapy equipment. 1991.
2344-7 Episcopal Church Home of Western New York, Buffalo, NY, $250,000. For equity contribution required by New York State for construction. 1991.
2344-8 Erie Alliance for the Mentally Ill, Snyder, NY, $15,000. For repairs to building. 1991.
2344-9 Life Transition Center, Buffalo, NY, $10,000. For operational expenses of Ravlin Clinic. 1991.
2344-10 Millard Fillmore Health, Education and Research Foundation, Buffalo, NY, $300,000. For neurological intensive care unit. 1991.
2344-11 Mount Saint Marys Hospital, Lewiston, NY, $50,000. For expansion and renovation project. 1991.
2344-12 Nazarene Nursing Home, Buffalo, NY, $13,500. For purchase of 100 kilowatt emergency generator. 1991.
2344-13 Planned Parenthood of Buffalo and Erie County, Buffalo, NY, $19,784. For family program specialist for teen drop-in center. 1991.
2344-14 Roswell Park Memorial Institute, Buffalo, NY, $69,895. For diffractometer head and for chromatography system. 1991.
2344-15 Saint Francis Home, Williamsville, NY, $20,000. For computer network for five skilled nursing facilities. 1991.
2344-16 Samaritan Pastoral Counseling Center, Buffalo, NY, $10,000. For general operating purposes. 1991.
2344-17 Transitional Services, Buffalo, NY, $25,000. For down payment for purchase of larger house. 1991.
2344-18 United Cerebral Palsy Association of Western New York, Buffalo, NY, $30,000. For voice recognition system for severely disabled. 1991.
2344-19 Western New York AIDS Program, Buffalo, NY, $32,980. For regional case management coordinator. 1991.
2344-20 Wyoming Foundation, Perry, NY, $15,000. For expansion of skilled nursing facility. 1991.

2345
Nina W. Werblow Charitable Trust
c/o Ehrenkranz, Ehrenkranz and Schultz
375 Park Ave.
New York 10152   (212) 751-5959

Trust established in 1977 in NY.
Donor(s): Nina W. Werblow.‡
Foundation type: Independent
Financial data (yr. ended 02/28/91): Assets, $5,404,338 (M); expenditures, $301,561; qualifying distributions, $247,496, including $215,000 for 52 grants (high: $25,000; low: $1,000).
Fields of interest: Jewish welfare, arts, hospitals, higher education, social services.
Limitations: Giving limited to New York, NY.
Application information:
  Initial approach: Letter
  Deadline(s): Sept. 30
  Write: Roger A. Goldman, Esq., Trustee
Trustees: Lillian Ahrens Carver, Joel S. Ehrenkranz, Roger A. Goldman.
EIN: 136742999

2346
Westvaco Foundation Trust ▼
c/o Westvaco Corp.
299 Park Ave.
New York 10171   (212) 688-5000

Trust established in 1951 in NY.
Donor(s): Westvaco Corp.
Foundation type: Company-sponsored
Financial data (yr. ended 09/30/90): Assets, $3,486,861 (M); gifts received, $1,276,103; expenditures, $1,296,728; qualifying distributions, $1,296,350, including $1,117,086 for 180 grants (high: $72,232; low: $125; average: $1,000-$10,000) and $179,234 for 807 employee matching gifts.
Purpose and activities: Support primarily for community funds, education (including colleges and universities), hospitals, and a cancer center; also matches employee gifts to educational institutions.
Fields of interest: Community funds, education, higher education, hospitals.
Types of support: Employee matching gifts, general purposes.
Limitations: Giving primarily in areas of plant operations. No grants to individuals, or in-kind gifts.
Publications: Multi-year report.
Application information: Contributions initiated primarily by plant managers; unsolicited requests usually not granted.
  Initial approach: Letter
  Deadline(s): None
  Write: Roger A. Holmes
Trustees: William S. Bearer, George E. Cruser, The Bank of New York.
Number of staff: 1 part-time professional; 1 part-time support.
EIN: 136021319
Recent health grants:
2346-1 Columbia Presbyterian Medical Center, NYC, NY, $50,000. 1990.
2346-2 Garrett Memorial Hospital, Oakland, MD, $10,000. 1990.
2346-3 Medical University of South Carolina, Charleston, SC, $50,000. 1990.

2346-4 W P S D-TV, Paducah, KY, $12,500. For Lions Club Crippled Children Telethon. 1990.

2347
The Whitehead Foundation ▼
65 East 55th St.
New York 10022   (212) 755-3131

Established in 1982 in NY.
Donor(s): John C. Whitehead Foundation.
Foundation type: Independent
Financial data (yr. ended 06/30/91): Assets, $17,616,405 (M); gifts received, $1,000,000; expenditures, $2,529,606; qualifying distributions, $2,447,158, including $2,446,072 for 187 grants (high: $400,000; low: $50; average: $1,000-$25,000).
Purpose and activities: General categories of interest: international affairs, economic and public policy, the arts, and higher education.
Fields of interest: International affairs, Europe, public policy, public affairs, civic affairs, arts, higher education.
Types of support: Annual campaigns, capital campaigns.
Limitations: Giving primarily in NY.
Application information: Unsolicited proposals are rarely approved.
  Board meeting date(s): Quarterly
  Write: Denise Emmett
Trustees: Arthur G. Altschul, Anne Whitehead Crawford, John L. Weinberg, John Gregory Whitehead, John C. Whitehead, Nancy Dickerson Whitehead.
EIN: 133119344
Recent health grants:
2347-1 Daytop Village Foundation, NYC, NY, $75,000. 1991.
2347-2 Rockefeller University, NYC, NY, $50,000. 1991.
2347-3 Rockefeller University, NYC, NY, $10,000. 1991.
2347-4 Scleroderma Federation, NYC, NY, $25,000. 1991.

2348
The Helen Hay Whitney Foundation ▼
450 East 63rd St.
New York 10021-7999   (212) 751-8228

Trust established in 1947; incorporated in 1951 in NY.
Donor(s): Mrs. Charles S. Payson.‡
Foundation type: Independent
Financial data (yr. ended 06/30/91): Assets, $28,832,360 (M); gifts received, $50,000; expenditures, $1,660,615; qualifying distributions, $1,487,952, including $1,257,586 for 68 grants to individuals.
Purpose and activities: To support beginning postdoctoral training in basic biomedical research through research fellowships for residents of the U.S., Canada, or Mexico who are under 35 years of age. Fellowships are awarded to individuals but funds are administered largely by research institutions. American citizenship is not required, but applications are not accepted from individuals or organizations outside North America.
Fields of interest: Medical research.
Types of support: Fellowships.

Limitations: Giving limited to North America. No grants to individuals over 35 years of age.
Publications: Annual report, informational brochure (including application guidelines).
Application information: Application form required.
  Initial approach: Letter or telephone
  Copies of proposal: 7
  Deadline(s): Submit proposal in Aug.; deadline Aug. 15
  Board meeting date(s): Jan. and June
  Final notification: 5 months
  Write: Barbara M. Hugonnet, Admin. Dir.
Officers and Trustees:* Mrs. Henry B. Middleton, Pres.; Maclyn McCarty, M.D.,* V.P. and Chair., Scientific Advisory Comm.; Thomas A. Melfe,* Secy.; Sandra de Roulet, M.D.,* Treas.; Alexander G. Bearn, M.D., Charles L. Christian, M.D., Lisa A. Steiner, M.D., W. Perry Welch.
Number of staff: 1 full-time professional; 6 part-time professional; 1 part-time support.
EIN: 131677403

2349
John Wiley & Sons Corporate
Contributions Program
605 Third Ave.
New York 10158   (212) 850-6000

Financial data (yr. ended 04/30/90): Total giving, $279,372, including $96,000 for grants (high: $10,000; low: $500), $173,372 for employee matching gifts and $10,000 for in-kind gifts.
Purpose and activities: Emphasis on culture, education, libraries, and literacy.
Fields of interest: AIDS, arts, fine arts, education, education—minorities, international affairs, literacy, performing arts, museums, music, theater, community development, international relief, biological sciences, cultural programs, elementary education, environment, chemistry, higher education, educational associations, human rights, international law, libraries, secondary education, literacy, physics.
Types of support: Annual campaigns, capital campaigns, employee matching gifts, fellowships, lectureships, publications, scholarship funds, conferences and seminars, in-kind gifts, donated products, emergency funds, endowment funds.
Limitations: Giving primarily in New York City, NY.
Publications: Corporate report.
Application information: Giving handled by office of Vice-Chairman.
  Initial approach: Letter to headquarters
  Write: Deborah E. Wiley, Vice-Chair.
Number of staff: 2 part-time support.

2350
Marie C. and Joseph C. Wilson Foundation
160 Allens Creek Rd.
Rochester 14618   (716) 461-4699

Trust established in 1963 in NY.
Donor(s): Katherine M. Wilson,‡ Joseph C. Wilson.‡
Foundation type: Independent
Financial data (yr. ended 12/31/91): Assets, $11,058,461 (M); expenditures, $1,404,873; qualifying distributions, $1,319,527, including

$1,240,959 for 47 grants (high: $896,707; low: $100; average: $1,000-$25,000).
Purpose and activities: Giving primarily for social services, health and medical research, education, housing, and youth agencies; some support for the arts.
Fields of interest: Social services, homeless, housing, youth, education, health, medical research, arts.
Types of support: Operating budgets, continuing support, annual campaigns, seed money, emergency funds, endowment funds, matching funds, internships, scholarship funds, fellowships, special projects, research, conferences and seminars.
Limitations: Giving primarily in Rochester, NY. No support for political organizations. No grants to individuals.
Publications: Annual report (including application guidelines).
Application information: Application form not required.
  Initial approach: 1-page letter; submit full proposal only at request of foundation
  Copies of proposal: 2
  Deadline(s): None
  Board meeting date(s): May and Oct.; grants considered in Oct. only
  Final notification: 3 months
  Write: Ruth H. Fleischmann, Exec. Dir.
Officers and Board of Managers:* Katherine W. Roby, Chair.; Ruth H. Fleischmann,* Exec. Dir.; Joan W. Dalbey, R. Thomas Dalbey, Jr., Katherine Dalbey Ensign, Deirdre Wilson Garton, Breckenridge Kling, Judith W. Martin, Janet C. Wilson, Joseph R. Wilson.
Trustee: Chase Lincoln First Bank, N.A.
Number of staff: 1 part-time professional; 1 part-time support.
EIN: 166042022
Recent health grants:
2350-1 Highland Hospital Foundation, Rochester, NY, $35,100. To establish Diabetes Health Source, comprehensive diabetes education program. 1990.
2350-2 Rochester Friendly Home, Rochester, NY, $16,666. To create specialized unit for care and treatment of Alzheimer's patients. 1990.

2351
Winkler Foundation
2514 East Seventh St., No. 4B
Brooklyn 11235-6257   (718) 934-2760

Foundation type: Operating
Financial data (yr. ended 03/31/91): Assets, $470,718 (M); gifts received, $18,000; expenditures, $214,239; qualifying distributions, $214,239, including $207,750 for 7 grants (high: $101,000; low: $250).
Fields of interest: Israel, hospitals.
Types of support: Scholarship funds, general purposes.
Limitations: Giving primarily in Israel.
Application information:
  Deadline(s): None
  Write: Irving Loeb, Trustee
Trustees: Irving Loeb, Neal Myerberg, Ephraim F. Rubin.
EIN: 112729601

2352
The Norman and Rosita Winston Foundation, Inc. ▼
1740 Broadway, 2nd Fl
New York 10019   (212) 698-4380

Incorporated in 1954 in NY.
Donor(s): Norman K. Winston,‡ The N.K. Winston Foundation, Inc.
Foundation type: Independent
Financial data (yr. ended 12/31/90): Assets, $48,111,020 (M); expenditures, $3,047,251; qualifying distributions, $2,449,300, including $2,449,300 for 98 grants (high: $100,000; low: $1,000; average: $5,000-$100,000).
Purpose and activities: Emphasis on higher education, including medical and theological education, hospitals, and cultural programs.
Fields of interest: Higher education, medical education, theological education, secondary education, hospitals, cultural programs.
Types of support: General purposes.
Limitations: Giving primarily in NY. No grants to individuals.
Application information: Application form not required.
   Initial approach: Proposal
   Copies of proposal: 1
   Deadline(s): None
   Board meeting date(s): 2 to 4 times a year
   Final notification: By the end of Dec.
   Write: Julian S. Perlman, Pres.
Officers and Directors:* Julian S. Perlman,* Pres.; Arthur Levitt, Jr.,* V.P. and Treas.; Simon H. Rifkind.
Number of staff: None.
EIN: 136161672

2353
Harry Winston Research Foundation, Inc.
718 Fifth Ave.
New York 10019   (212) 245-2000

Incorporated in 1964 in NY.
Donor(s): Harry Winston,‡ Ronald Winston.
Foundation type: Independent
Financial data (yr. ended 12/31/90): Assets, $9,572,089 (M); expenditures, $972,814; qualifying distributions, $889,098, including $872,815 for 23 grants (high: $425,000; low: $50).
Purpose and activities: Giving for programs of scientific research in the field of genetics and related medical research, including support for hospitals and higher education; giving also to a museum of natural history.
Fields of interest: Hospitals, medical research, higher education, medical sciences, museums.
Types of support: Research.
Limitations: Giving primarily in NY, with emphasis on the greater metropolitan New York area. No grants to individuals.
Application information: Contributes only to pre-selected organizations. Applications not accepted.
Officers: Ronald Winston, Pres.; Robert Holtzman, V.P.; Richard Copaken, Secy.
EIN: 136168266

2354
Robert Winthrop Charitable Trust
c/o Wood, Struthers & Winthrop
P.O. Box 18
New York 10005

Donor(s): Robert Winthrop.
Foundation type: Independent
Financial data (yr. ended 11/30/90): Assets, $2,086,001 (M); gifts received, $306,605; expenditures, $247,494; qualifying distributions, $220,570, including $220,570 for 86 grants (high: $25,000; low: $25).
Purpose and activities: Support primarily for wildlife preservation; support also for higher education, historic preservation, medical research, and museums.
Fields of interest: Wildlife, higher education, historic preservation, medical research, museums.
Limitations: No grants to individuals.
Application information: Contributes only to pre-selected organizations. Applications not accepted.
Trustees: Cornelia Bonnie, Robert Winthrop.
EIN: 237441147

2355
Robert I. Wishnick Foundation
(Formerly The Witco Foundation)
520 Madison Ave.
New York 10022
Application address: 375 Park Ave., New York, NY 10152; Tel.: (212) 371-1844

Incorporated in 1951 in IL.
Donor(s): Witco Chemical Corp.
Foundation type: Company-sponsored
Financial data (yr. ended 12/31/90): Assets, $8,919,754 (M); expenditures, $581,773; qualifying distributions, $559,065, including $559,065 for 139 grants (high: $125,000; low: $100).
Purpose and activities: Grants largely for hospitals, higher education, community funds, and Jewish welfare funds; employee-related scholarships awarded through National Merit Scholarship Corp.
Fields of interest: Higher education, hospitals, community funds, Jewish welfare, social services.
Types of support: Annual campaigns, endowment funds, research, conferences and seminars, scholarship funds, fellowships, employee-related scholarships, general purposes.
Limitations: Giving in areas of company operations. No grants to individuals (except for employee-related scholarships), or for matching gifts; no loans.
Application information: Requests from outside New York City must be forwarded through local offices of the corporation. Application form not required.
   Initial approach: Proposal
   Copies of proposal: 1
   Deadline(s): None
   Board meeting date(s): Monthly
   Final notification: 6 to 8 weeks
   Write: William Wishnick, Pres.
Officers and Directors:* William Wishnick,* Pres.; William R. Toller,* V.P.; Joseph Russo,* Secy.; Robert L. Bachner, Simeon Brinberg.
EIN: 136068668

2356
Esther & Morton Wohlgemuth Foundation, Inc.
1501 Broadway, Rm. 1503
New York 10036

Incorporated in 1956 in NY.
Donor(s): Morton Wohlgemuth,‡ Esther Wohlgemuth, Alexander Wohlgemuth, Robert Wohlgemuth.
Foundation type: Independent
Financial data (yr. ended 12/31/91): Assets, $2,501,010 (M); expenditures, $104,623; qualifying distributions, $99,307, including $90,500 for 65 grants (high: $15,000; low: $100).
Fields of interest: Higher education, health, hospitals, social services, youth, Jewish welfare.
Limitations: Giving primarily in NY. No grants to individuals.
Application information: Contributes only to pre-selected organizations. Applications not accepted.
Officers: Samuel Zinman, Pres. and Treas.; Alexander Wohlgemuth, V.P.; Robert Wohlgemuth, V.P.; Irwin M. Thrope, Secy.
EIN: 136086849

2357
Woodland Foundation, Inc.
c/o Bankers Trust Co.
280 Park Ave.
New York 10017

Incorporated in 1950 in DE.
Donor(s): William Durant Campbell.
Foundation type: Independent
Financial data (yr. ended 12/31/91): Assets, $4,333,176 (M); expenditures, $221,181; qualifying distributions, $170,000, including $170,000 for 39 grants (high: $25,000; low: $250).
Purpose and activities: Giving for higher and secondary education; grants also for youth agencies, Protestant church support, and hospitals.
Fields of interest: Higher education, secondary education, youth, Protestant giving, hospitals.
Types of support: Annual campaigns, building funds, capital campaigns, endowment funds.
Limitations: No grants to individuals.
Application information: Applications not accepted.
   Write: Harvey G. Burney, Treas.
Officers and Trustees:* Margot C. Bogert,* Pres.; Jeremiah M. Bogert,* V.P.; Winthrop Rutherford, Jr.,* Secy.; Harvey G. Burney,* Treas.; William Durant Campbell, George W. Knight, Frank J. Nulty.
Number of staff: None.
EIN: 136018244

2358
Woodstock Foundation, Inc.
30 Rockefeller Plaza, Rm. 5600
New York 10112
Application address: 18 Elm St., Woodstock, VT 05091; Tel.: (802) 457-3000

Established in 1968 in VT.
Donor(s): Laurance S. Rockefeller.
Foundation type: Operating

Financial data (yr. ended 12/31/90): Assets, $5,010,629 (M); gifts received, $4,206,030; expenditures, $1,172,117; qualifying distributions, $1,305,782, including $168,555 for 33 grants (high: $51,000; low: $200) and $890,333 for foundation-administered programs.
Purpose and activities: "The principle activity of the foundation is to operate and maintain a public building (farm museum) in the town of Woodstock, VT for the benefit of the general public."
Fields of interest: Health, welfare, education, community development, conservation.
Limitations: Giving limited to regional organizations and towns surrounding the Woodstock, VT, area.
Application information: Application form not required.
   Initial approach: Letter
   Deadline(s): Prior to Labor Day
   Board meeting date(s): Annually
   Write: Thomas M. Debevoise, Pres.
Officers and Trustees:* Laurance S. Rockefeller,* Chair.; C. Wesley Frye, Jr.,* Vice-Chair.; Mary F. Rockefeller,* Vice-Chair.; Thomas M. Debevoise,* Pres.; Janice E. Barron, Secy.; Joseph D. Flores, Treas.; and 7 additional trustees.
EIN: 030221142

2359
Ann Eden Woodward Foundation
c/o J.A. Lapatin, Esq.
989 Ave. of the Americas
New York 10018

Established in 1963 in NY.
Donor(s): Ann Eden Woodward.‡
Foundation type: Independent
Financial data (yr. ended 05/31/91): Assets, $379,200 (M); gifts received, $190,000; expenditures, $207,501; qualifying distributions, $203,659, including $200,050 for 25 grants (high: $25,000; low: $800).
Purpose and activities: Giving for the performing arts and museums, hospitals, environmental and wildlife preservation, and a public library.
Fields of interest: Museums, performing arts, hospitals, conservation, wildlife, libraries.
Limitations: Giving primarily in New York, NY. No grants to individuals.
Application information: Grants awarded at discretion of managers. Applications not accepted.
Officers: J.A. Lapatin, Mgr.; J.A. Woods, Mgr.
EIN: 136126021

2360
Youths' Friends Association, Inc.
c/o Seidman & Seidman
15 Columbus Circle
New York 10023-7711
Application address: P.O. Box 5387, Hilton Head, SC 29938; Tel.: (803) 671-5060

Incorporated in 1950 in NY.
Donor(s): Johan J. Smit,‡ Mrs. Johan J. Smit.‡
Foundation type: Independent
Financial data (yr. ended 12/31/91): Assets, $6,661,527 (M); expenditures, $352,085; qualifying distributions, $291,620, including $263,500 for 95 grants (high: $20,000; low: $1,000).

Purpose and activities: Grants largely for international relief, and higher and secondary education, through scholarship support earmarked for NJ high school students; support also for social services, youth, health, and cultural programs.
Fields of interest: International relief, higher education, secondary education, social services, youth, health, cultural programs.
Types of support: Scholarship funds, general purposes.
Limitations: No grants to individuals.
Application information: Application form not required.
   Initial approach: Letter
   Copies of proposal: 1
   Deadline(s): None
   Board meeting date(s): Semiannually
   Write: Walter J. Graver, Secy.-Treas.
Officers and Directors:* Peta Smit,* Pres.; Sheila Smit,* V.P.; Walter J. Graver,* Secy.-Treas.; Erna Graver, Helen Kirchen, Robert Kirchen, Marion Meinert, Stephen C. Smit.
EIN: 136097828

2361
Charles Zarkin Memorial Foundation, Inc.
c/o Wachtell, Lipton, Rosen & Katz
299 Park Ave.
New York 10171

Incorporated in 1969 in NY.
Donor(s): Fay Zarkin.‡
Foundation type: Independent
Financial data (yr. ended 12/31/91): Assets, $3,877,256 (M); expenditures, $248,611; qualifying distributions, $245,535, including $240,250 for 9 grants (high: $50,000; low: $250).
Fields of interest: Jewish giving, Jewish welfare, hospitals, animal welfare, secondary education.
Limitations: Giving primarily in New York, NY. No grants to individuals.
Application information: Contributes only to pre-selected organizations. Applications not accepted.
   Board meeting date(s): Dec.
Officers and Trustees:* Martin Lipton,* Pres. and Treas.; Leonard M. Rosen,* V.P.; Susan Lipton, Constance Monte.
Number of staff: None.
EIN: 237149277

2362
Zenkel Foundation
15 West 53rd St.
New York 10019-5410   (212) 333-5730

Established in 1987 in NY.
Foundation type: Independent
Financial data (yr. ended 12/31/90): Assets, $3,820,567 (M); expenditures, $240,115; qualifying distributions, $208,252, including $202,353 for 90 grants (high: $40,000; low: $18).
Purpose and activities: Giving primarily for Jewish welfare, the arts, and museums; support also for health associations, AIDS and other medical research, race relations and human rights, the environment, and higher education.
Fields of interest: Jewish welfare, arts, museums, health associations, AIDS, medical research,

environment, race relations, human rights, higher education.
Types of support: Annual campaigns, building funds, general purposes, scholarship funds.
Limitations: No grants to individuals.
Application information: Contributes only to pre-selected organizations. Applications not accepted.
   Write: Lois Zenkel, Pres.
Officers and Directors:* Lois S. Zenkel,* Pres.; Daniel R. Zenkel,* Secy.; Bruce L. Zenkel,* Treas.; Gary B. Zenkel, Lisa R. Zenkel.
Number of staff: None.
EIN: 133380631

2363
Ziff Communications Corporate Giving Program
One Park Avenue
New York 10016   (212) 503-3500

Purpose and activities: Support for children's programs, funding for AIDS research, funds for victims of natural disasters and famine, relief aid in Africa.
Fields of interest: Africa, AIDS, alcoholism, child welfare, drug abuse, environment, handicapped, homeless, volunteerism.
Types of support: Annual campaigns, emergency funds, employee matching gifts.
Limitations: No grants to individuals.
Application information: Application form not required.
   Initial approach: Written requests only
   Copies of proposal: 1
   Deadline(s): Oct. 31
   Write: Dorothy Boston, Dir., Community Rels.

2364
Marie and John Zimmermann Fund, Inc.
c/o U.S. Trust Co. of New York
114 West 47th St.
New York 10036-1532   (212) 852-1000

Incorporated in 1942 in NY.
Donor(s): Marie Zimmermann.‡
Foundation type: Independent
Financial data (yr. ended 12/31/91): Assets, $6,171,277 (M); expenditures, $246,993; qualifying distributions, $190,000, including $190,000 for 3 grants (high: $110,700; low: $31,300).
Fields of interest: Higher education, medical education.
Limitations: No grants to individuals.
Application information: Contributes only to pre-selected organizations. Applications not accepted.
   Board meeting date(s): June
   Write: Anne L. Smith-Ganey, Asst. V.P., U.S. Trust Co. of New York
Officers and Directors:* John C. Zimmermann III,* Pres.; Robert Perret, Jr.,* Secy.; Henry W. Grady, Jr.,* Treas.; J. Robert Buchanan, M.D., Anne C. Heller, A. Parks McCombs, Thomas H. Meikle, Jr., Anne L. Smith-Ganey.
Number of staff: None.
EIN: 136158767

2365
Sergei S. Zlinkoff Fund for Medical Research and Education, Inc.
c/o Carter, Ledyard & Milburn
Two Wall St.
New York 10005

Incorporated in 1956 in NY.
Donor(s): Sergei S. Zlinkoff.‡
Foundation type: Independent
Financial data (yr. ended 10/31/91): Assets, $2,510,845 (M); expenditures, $257,593; qualifying distributions, $255,483, including $235,000 for 10 grants (high: $40,000; low: $5,000).
Purpose and activities: Grants primarily for medical and other higher education and medical research; some support for family planning services and research.
Fields of interest: Medical education, medical research, higher education, family planning.
Types of support: General purposes.

Limitations: Giving on a national basis, with some emphasis on New York, NY. No grants to individuals.
Application information: Contributes only to pre-selected organizations. Applications not accepted.
Officers and Directors:* Milton W. Hamolsky, M.D.,* Pres.; Ralph E. Hansmann,* V.P. and Treas.; John O. Lipkin, M.D.,* V.P.; Mack Lipkin, Jr., M.D.,* V.P.; Iris Berliner Alster, Secy.; Jerome J. Cohen,* Secy.; Robert Goldstein, M.D., Sandra Z. Hamolsky.
EIN: 136094651

2366
Roy J. Zuckerberg Foundation
c/o Goldman Sachs & Co., Tax Dept.
85 Broad St., 30th Fl.
New York 10004-2408

Established in 1980 in NY.
Donor(s): Roy J. Zuckerberg.

Foundation type: Independent
Financial data (yr. ended 09/30/91): Assets, $1,973,727 (M); gifts received, $600,000; expenditures, $692,570; qualifying distributions, $685,125, including $684,845 for 137 grants (high: $100,000; low: $50).
Fields of interest: Jewish welfare, health associations, hospitals.
Limitations: Giving primarily in the greater metropolitan New York, NY, area. No grants to individuals.
Application information: Contributes only to pre-selected organizations. Applications not accepted.
Trustees: James C. Kautz, Barbara Zuckerberg, Dina R. Zuckerberg, Lloyd P. Zuckerberg, Roy J. Zuckerberg.
EIN: 133052489

NORTH CAROLINA

2367
American Schlafhorst Foundation, Inc.
c/o American Schlafhorst Co.
P.O. Box 240275
Charlotte 28224　　　　　　　(704) 554-0800

Established in 1987 in NC.
Donor(s): American Schlafhorst Co.
Foundation type: Company-sponsored
Financial data (yr. ended 12/31/91): Assets,
$2,500,000 (M); expenditures, $120,000;
qualifying distributions, $115,000, including
$115,000 for 5 grants (high: $30,000; low:
$15,000).
Fields of interest: Child welfare, hospitals, aged,
arts.
Limitations: Giving limited to NC, with emphasis
on Charlotte and Mecklenburg County. No grants
to individuals.
Application information: Applications not
accepted.
　Write: Helmut Deussen, Pres.
Officers and Directors: Helmut Deussen,* Pres.;
Joel H. Myers, Secy.; Melk M. Lehner, Frank
Paetzold, Charles B. Park III, Tracy E. Tindal.
Number of staff: None.
EIN: 561590110

2368
Mary Reynolds Babcock Foundation, Inc.
▼
102 Reynolda Village
Winston-Salem 27106-5123　　(919) 748-9222
FAX: (919) 777-0095

Incorporated in 1953 in NC.
Donor(s): Mary Reynolds Babcock,‡ Charles H.
Babcock.‡
Foundation type: Independent
Financial data (yr. ended 08/31/90): Assets,
$61,204,714 (M); expenditures, $5,131,419;
qualifying distributions, $4,824,740, including
$4,382,695 for 158 grants (high: $1,000,000;
low: $800; average: $5,000-$35,000).
Purpose and activities: Supports active
participation by citizens in the protection of the
environment, the development of public policy,
the well-being of children and adolescents,
education, grassroots organizing, opportunity for
women, rural issues, and the arts.
Fields of interest: Environment, citizenship,
public policy, government, law and justice, social
services, family planning, youth, child
development, education—early childhood,
education, literacy, rural development, legal
services, race relations, human rights, women,
arts, media and communications, general
charitable giving.
Types of support: Operating budgets, seed
money, emergency funds, special projects,
program-related investments, matching funds,
general purposes.
Limitations: Giving primarily in NC and the
southeastern U.S., and to national organizations.
No support for medical or health programs,

research, film or video production, international
activities, local or community programs (except
where the program is a model for the region or
nation), or for tax-supported educational
institutions outside NC. No grants to individuals,
or for endowment funds, building funds,
renovation projects, scholarships, or fellowships;
no student loans.
Publications: Annual report (including application
guidelines), program policy statement, application
guidelines.
Application information: Application form
required.
　Initial approach: Proposal
　Copies of proposal: 1
　Deadline(s): Mar. 1 and Sept. 1
　Board meeting date(s): May and Nov.
　Final notification: 1st week of months following
　　board meetings
　Write: Sandra Mikush, Acting Exec. Dir.
Officers and Directors: William L. Rogers,*
Pres.; Barbara B. Millhouse,* V.P.; Kenneth F.
Mountcastle, Jr.,* Secy.; L. Richardson Preyer,*
Treas.; William L. Bondurant, Exec. Dir.; Betsy M.
Babcock, Bruce M. Babcock, David Dodson,
Reynolds Lassiter, Katharine B. Mountcastle,
Katharine R. Mountcastle, Kenneth Mountcastle
III, Laura Mountcastle, Mary Mountcastle,
Zachary T. Smith, Isabel C. Stewart, Paul N.
Ylvisaker.
Number of staff: 3 full-time professional; 2
full-time support.
EIN: 560690140
Recent health grants:
2368-1 Childhood Cancer Research Institute,
　Arlington, MA, $10,000. To enhance public
　awareness of health risks from radiation
　exposure with speaking tours, public relations
　and educational activities. 1990.
2368-2 Freedom From Hunger Foundation,
　Davis, CA, $10,000. For Partners for Improved
　Nutrition and Health (PINAH), program which
　encourages local residents to initiate
　improvements in their diet, health and
　community well-being. 1990.
2368-3 Interreligious Foundation for Community
　Organizations, NYC, NY, $10,000. For literacy
　programs for children and to assist coal miners
　seeking enforcement of health and safety
　regulations to limit mining accidents. 1990.
2368-4 Kentucky Youth Advocates, Building
　Arks: A Public Campaign to Support Early
　Childhood Programs, Louisville, KY, $55,000.
　For plans to publicize need for perinatal care,
　parenting education, preschool programs,
　health care and adequate nutrition to diminish
　risk of failure in school. 1990.
2368-5 Mental Health Law Project, DC,
　$30,000. For foster care reform in Alabama.
　1990.
2368-6 North Carolina, State of, Department of
　Public Instruction, Raleigh, NC, $40,000. For
　early childhood education program which
　incorporates parent education, health services
　and prenatal care. 1990.

2369
The Belk Foundation
2801 West Tyvola Rd.
Charlotte 28217-4500　　　　(704) 357-1000

Trust established in 1928 in NC.

Donor(s): The Belk Mercantile Corps., Matthews
Belk, Belk Enterprises.
Foundation type: Company-sponsored
Financial data (yr. ended 05/31/91): Assets,
$25,272,308 (M); gifts received, $940,333;
expenditures, $1,140,082; qualifying
distributions, $1,026,113, including $1,024,500
for 45 grants (high: $250,000; low: $900).
Purpose and activities: Grants largely for higher
education; support also for youth agencies,
hospitals, and cultural programs.
Fields of interest: Higher education, youth,
cultural programs, hospitals.
Types of support: Building funds, annual
campaigns, operating budgets.
Limitations: Giving primarily in NC and SC. No
grants to individuals.
Application information:
　Initial approach: Letter
　Deadline(s): None
　Write: John W. Lassiter, Trustee
Trustees: John W. Lassiter, First Union National
Bank.
Advisors: Thomas M. Belk, Chair.; Claudia Belk,
and 6 additional advisors.
EIN: 566046450

2370
Blue Bell Foundation
c/o Wachovia Bank & Trust Co., N.A.
P.O. Box 3099
Winston-Salem 27150-1022　　(919) 373-3580
Application address: P.O. Box 21488,
Greensboro, NC 27420; Tel.: (919) 373-3412

Trust established in 1944 in NC.
Donor(s): Blue Bell, Inc.
Foundation type: Company-sponsored
Financial data (yr. ended 12/31/90): Assets,
$3,898,711 (M); expenditures, $367,571;
qualifying distributions, $344,926, including
$328,195 for 148 grants (high: $50,000; low:
$50) and $15,626 for 47 employee matching gifts.
Purpose and activities: Grants for higher and
secondary education, including matching gifts,
community funds, hospitals, and cultural
programs.
Fields of interest: Higher education, secondary
education, community funds, cultural programs,
hospitals.
Types of support: Employee matching gifts.
Limitations: Giving primarily in areas where
corporation has plants.
Application information:
　Initial approach: Letter
　Deadline(s): None
　Write: Charles Conkin, V.P., Human Resources
Advisory Committee: D.P. Laws, H.V. Moore, T.L.
Weatherford.
Trustee: Wachovia Bank & Trust Co., N.A.
EIN: 566041057

2371
Brenner Foundation, Inc.
c/o Ion Inc.
3415 Glenn Ave.
Winston-Salem 27105

Incorporated in 1960 in NC.

Donor(s): Abe Brenner, Morris Brenner, Sanco Corp., Brenner Companies, Inc., United Metal Recyclers.
Foundation type: Independent
Financial data (yr. ended 04/30/91): Assets, $2,302,833 (M); gifts received, $550,000; expenditures, $685,828; qualifying distributions, $681,267, including $681,267 for 47 grants (high: $572,000; low: $100).
Fields of interest: Hospitals, Jewish giving, Jewish welfare, general charitable giving.
Limitations: Giving primarily in NC.
Officers: Abe Brenner, Pres.; Herb Brenner, V.P.; Gertrude Brenner, Secy.-Treas.
Director: C. Max Storey.
EIN: 566058174

2372
Broyhill Family Foundation, Inc. ▼
P.O. Box 500, Golfview Park
Lenoir 28645   (704) 758-6120

Incorporated in 1945 in NC.
Donor(s): Broyhill Furniture Industries, Inc., James E. Broyhill, and family.
Foundation type: Independent
Financial data (yr. ended 12/31/90): Assets, $30,077,907 (M); expenditures, $1,683,890; qualifying distributions, $1,287,695, including $1,287,695 for 193 grants (high: $131,000; low: $60; average: $200-$5,000).
Purpose and activities: Support for scholarship loans through the College Foundation, Inc.; support also for health, child development and welfare, civic and community services, and the free enterprise system.
Fields of interest: Health, child development, child welfare, social services, community funds, civic affairs, public policy, higher education.
Types of support: Scholarship funds, special projects.
Limitations: Giving primarily in NC. No grants to individuals.
Application information:
  Initial approach: Letter
  Deadline(s): June 15 and Dec. 15
  Board meeting date(s): Quarterly
  Final notification: Within calendar year
  Write: Paul H. Broyhill, Pres., or Mrs. Lee E. Pritchard, Asst. Secy.-Treas.
Officers and Directors:* Paul H. Broyhill,* Pres.; E.D. Beach,* Secy.-Treas.; Clarence E. Beach, Faye A. Broyhill, M. Hunt Broyhill, Mrs. Lee E. Pritchard.
Number of staff: 2 full-time professional.
EIN: 566054119

2373
Kathleen Price and Joseph M. Bryan Family Foundation ▼
One North Pointe, Suite 170
3101 North Elm St.
Greensboro 27408   (919) 288-5455

Incorporated in 1955 in NC.
Donor(s): Kathleen Price Bryan,‡ Joseph M. Bryan, Sr., Kathleen Bryan Edwards, Nancy Bryan Faircloth, Joseph M. Bryan, Jr.
Foundation type: Independent
Financial data (yr. ended 12/31/90): Assets, $33,981,574 (M); expenditures, $1,913,930;

qualifying distributions, $1,683,843, including $1,519,945 for 92 grants (high: $200,000; low: $1,500; average: $5,000-$100,000).
Purpose and activities: Grants principally in the fields of higher, secondary, and early childhood education; community and performing arts; health and human services, including AIDS programs; public interest; and youth.
Fields of interest: Social services, arts, health, disadvantaged, education—early childhood, aged.
Types of support: Continuing support, seed money, equipment, operating budgets, scholarship funds, technical assistance, special projects, endowment funds, program-related investments, building funds, renovation projects, internships.
Limitations: Giving primarily in NC, with emphasis on Greensboro and Guilford County. No support for private foundations, conferences, or for film or video production. No grants to individuals, or generally for annual fund drives or research; no loans.
Publications: Application guidelines, annual report.
Application information: Telephone or personal interviews with Exec. Dir. are encouraged prior to deadlines; site visits are made when possible. Proposals should be no more than two pages. Application form required.
  Initial approach: Telephone or write for application form and for annual report
  Copies of proposal: 1
  Deadline(s): Mar. 1 and Sept. 1
  Board meeting date(s): May and Nov.
  Final notification: 2 weeks after board meetings
  Write: Robert K. Hampton, Exec. Dir.
Officers and Trustees:* Kathleen Bryan Edwards,* Pres.; Joseph M. Bryan, Jr.,* V.P. and Treas.; Robert K. Hampton, Secy. and Exec. Dir.; William C. Friday, Jane C. Kendall, S. Davis Phillips, Kathleen Clay Taylor.
Number of staff: 1 full-time professional; 1 full-time support.
EIN: 566046952
Recent health grants:
2373-1 AIDS Community Residence Association, Durham, NC, $25,000. For challenge grant for operating support of residential-care facility serving homeless people with AIDS from across North Carolina. 1990.
2373-2 Alexander Childrens Center, Charlotte, NC, $10,000. Toward capital improvements at residential care facility for emotionally disturbed children. 1990.
2373-3 Exchange Club Center for the Prevention of Child Abuse, Statesville, NC, $10,000. For expansion of counseling and other support services to abused children and their abusers. 1990.
2373-4 Family Service of High Point, High Point, NC, $25,000. For challenge grant toward new facility for organization providing counseling, education, and other support services to victims of domestic violence and sexual assault and their abusers. 1990.
2373-5 Florence Crittenton Services, Charlotte, NC, $25,000. For challenge grant for programs assisting single, pregnant young women in North and South Carolina. 1990.
2373-6 Human Service Alliance, Winston-Salem, NC, $25,000. For challenge grant toward start-up and construction of completely volunteer-operated residential care facility for

terminally ill with one-third of residential space to be reserved for people with AIDS. 1990.
2373-7 Links Adolescent Services, Greensboro, NC, $25,000. For challenge grant toward start-up of residential treatment center for adolescents with drug or alcohol dependencies. 1990.
2373-8 Maryfield Nursing Home, High Point, NC, $100,000. For challenge grant toward expansion of this skilled and intermediate care nursing home. 1990.
2373-9 Sisters of Mercy of North Carolina, Belmont, NC, $75,000. Toward start-up and operating support for House of Mercy, convent-based residential care facility for homeless and other needy people with AIDS. 1990.
2373-10 Southeastern Family Violence Center, Lumberton, NC, $10,000. For challenge grant for counseling, education and support services for children who are victims of domestic violence or sexual assault. 1990.
2373-11 Triad Health Project, Greensboro, NC, $25,000. For challenge grant to expand AIDS support services and public education about AIDS prevention. 1990.
2373-12 United Cerebral Palsy Triad Adult Center, Greensboro, NC, $10,000. Toward expansion of job training and employment opportunities for disabled adults. 1990.
2373-13 Uwharrie Homes, Albemarle, NC, $10,000. Toward purchase and renovation of residential facility used for short-term treatment of emotionally disturbed and troubled youth from Cabarrus, Stanly and Union Counties. 1990.

2374
Burlington Industries Corporate Giving Program
3330 West Friendly Ave.
Greensboro 27410   (919) 379-2000

Financial data (yr. ended 09/30/90): Total giving, $1,520,000 for grants.
Purpose and activities: Support for community and urban programs, culture, education, united campaigns, health care, public broadcasting, hospitals and clinics, arts and United Way. Types of support include loaned staff, gifts of used or surplus equipment or furniture and the donation of products manufactured by the company.
Fields of interest: Urban development, cultural programs, arts, education, health, minorities, media and communications, community funds, women.
Types of support: In-kind gifts, consulting services, equipment, donated equipment, loaned talent, donated products.
Limitations: Giving primarily in headquarters city, major U.S. operating areas and operating locations in foreign countries. No grants to individuals, or for general operating budgets or endowments.
Publications: Informational brochure (including application guidelines).
Application information: Application form not required.
  Initial approach: Letter of inquiry or by telephone
  Copies of proposal: 1

Board meeting date(s): Decisions made in Mar., June, Sept., and Dec. by Donations Committee
Write: Park R. Davidson, Treas.

2375
Burlington Industries Foundation
P.O. Box 21207
3330 West Friendly Ave.
Greensboro 27420   (919) 379-2515

Trust established in 1943 in NC.
Donor(s): Burlington Industries, Inc., and subsidiary companies.
Foundation type: Company-sponsored
Financial data (yr. ended 09/30/91): Assets, $6,785,845 (M); expenditures, $856,250; qualifying distributions, $825,414, including $601,299 for 145 grants (high: $50,000; low: $100; average: $500-$5,000), $18,700 for 28 grants to individuals (high: $1,000; low: $300; average: $250-$1,000) and $194,993 for 311 employee matching gifts.
Purpose and activities: To support educational, charitable, cultural, and similar causes. Grants to colleges and universities generally in the geographical area of plants, where the company recruits annually for employees. Grants to various community and civic causes based upon recommendation of the company's local management; includes support for youth agencies, hospitals, and some health associations. Grants to individuals are only to help employees cope with hardship caused by disasters.
Fields of interest: Higher education, community funds, civic affairs, youth, cultural programs, health, hospitals.
Types of support: Matching funds, annual campaigns, building funds, professorships, scholarship funds, fellowships, employee matching gifts.
Limitations: Giving primarily in areas of company operations in NC, SC, and VA. Generally no grants for sectarian or denominational religious organizations, national organizations, private secondary schools, or historic preservation projects. No grants to individuals (except for company employees and their families in distress), or for conferences, seminars, workshops, outdoor dramas, films, documentaries, endowment funds, or medical research operating expenses; no loans.
Publications: Program policy statement, application guidelines.
Application information: Application form not required.
  Initial approach: Letter
  Copies of proposal: 1
  Deadline(s): None
  Board meeting date(s): Annually
  Final notification: Within 30 days
  Write: Park R. Davidson, Exec. Dir.
Officer and Trustees:* Park R. Davidson,* Exec. Dir.; J.C. Cowan, Jr., Donald R. Hughes, J. Kenneth Lesley, Charles A. McLendon, Jr.
Number of staff: None.
EIN: 566043142

2376
Burroughs Wellcome Contributions Program
Burroughs Wellcome Co.
3030 Cornwallis Rd.
Research Triangle Park 27709   (919) 248-4177

Financial data (yr. ended 08/31/90): Total giving, $5,907,122, including $3,722,344 for 1,000 grants (high: $250,000; low: $10; average: $10-$250,000), $153,423 for 1,408 employee matching gifts and $2,031,355 for 82 in-kind gifts.
Purpose and activities: Support for medical education and biomedical research, AIDS information and research, medical education, arts and cultural programs, elementary, secondary, and higher education, civic organizations, health and human service organizations through employee matching gifts to United Way, and scholarships to children of company employees through the National Merit Scholarship Corporation; other forms of support include employee matching gifts to schools, foundations, hospitals, and public radio and television stations, in-kind donations of employee talent, surplus materials, and products; international health care projects receive product donations. Education, health and sciences, including research and professional organizations related to health matters, are major areas of support.
Fields of interest: AIDS, medical research, medical education, nursing, pharmacy, welfare—indigent individuals, education, higher education, international relief, arts.
Types of support: In-kind gifts, annual campaigns, building funds, conferences and seminars, employee matching gifts, fellowships, lectureships, matching funds, publications, special projects, seed money, professorships, capital campaigns, donated products, cause-related marketing.
Limitations: Giving primarily in Research Triangle Park and Greenville, NC, for health and human services, and civic and cultural programs; some support for national organizations. No support for political or religious groups. No grants to individuals.
Publications: Corporate giving report (including application guidelines).
Application information: Letters requesting contributions for NC charities should be addressed to Arline Erwin; requests for charities outside NC should be addressed to Joan Guilkey; biomedical research requests may be referred to The Burroughs Wellcome Fund; Contributions and Business Donations Dept. handles philanthropy as well as other payments to non-profits. Application form not required.
  Initial approach: Letter, including IRS exemption number
  Copies of proposal: 1
  Deadline(s): None
  Board meeting date(s): As needed
  Final notification: 8-12 weeks
  Write: Joan Guilkey, Contribs./Business Donations Mgr.
Contribs. and Business Donations Comm.: Josiah Whitehead, Chair. and V.P., Corp. Affairs; Peter Reckert, V.P., Mktg. and Sls.; Joan Guilkey, Contribs. and Bus. Donations Mgr.
Number of staff: 1 full-time professional; 4 full-time support.

2377
The Burroughs Wellcome Fund ▼
3030 Cornwallis Rd.
Research Triangle Park 27709   (919) 248-4136

Incorporated in 1955 in NY.
Donor(s): Burroughs Wellcome Co.
Foundation type: Company-sponsored
Financial data (yr. ended 08/31/91): Assets, $25,692,054 (M); gifts received, $5,000,000; expenditures, $5,549,300; qualifying distributions, $5,699,089, including $5,064,471 for 202 grants (high: $385,000; low: $500; average: $1,000-$50,000).
Purpose and activities: Primarily to give financial aid for the advancement of research in the basic medical sciences within the U.S.: (1) an annual Experimental Therapeutics Scholar Award of $350,000, paid over five years; (2) an annual competitive Toxicology Scholar Award of $350,000, paid over five years; (3) an annual competitive Molecular Parasitology Scholar Award of $350,000, paid over five years; (4) Wellcome Visiting Professorships in the Basic Medical Sciences administered by the Federation of American Societies for Experimental Biology; (5) Wellcome Visiting Professorships in Microbiological Sciences administered by the American Society of Microbiology; (6) Wellcome Research Travel Grants to Britain/Ireland; (7) competitive awards for postdoctoral research fellowships administered by national medical, pharmacy, and life sciences organizations; (8) an annual competitive Scholar Award of $350,000 for Immunopharmacology of Allergic Diseases; (9) New Investigator Awards in virology of $90,000; anesthesiology of $70,000; molecular parasitology and clinical oncology of $60,000; occasional, modest grants made on a short-term basis to institutions for specially talented investigators and innovative research projects in the basic medical sciences.
Fields of interest: Medical education, medical research, biological sciences, medical sciences, educational research, pharmacy.
Types of support: Scholarship funds, special projects, research, professorships, fellowships, lectureships.
Limitations: Giving limited to the U.S. No grants to individuals, or for building or endowment funds, equipment, operating budgets, continuing support, annual campaigns, deficit financing, publications, conferences, matching gifts; no loans.
Publications: Annual report, application guidelines, newsletter, informational brochure (including application guidelines).
Application information: Application form required only for Wellcome Research Travel Grants Program.
  Initial approach: Letter
  Copies of proposal: 2
  Deadline(s): varies
  Board meeting date(s): Bimonthly, beginning in Feb.
  Final notification: 6 weeks
  Write: Martha G. Peck, Exec. Dir.
Officers and Directors:* Howard J. Schaeffer,* Pres.; Martha G. Peck, Secy. and Exec. Dir.; Stephen D. Corman,* Treas.; Anne W. Alderson, Controller; David W. Barry, M.D., George H. Hitchings, Trevor M. Jones, Thomas Krenitsky, Philip R. Tracy.

Number of staff: 3 full-time professional; 2 full-time support.
EIN: 237225395
Recent health grants:

2377-1 American Association of Obstetricians and Gynecologists Foundation, Rochester, NY, $70,000. For Research Fellowships in Perinatal Transmission of HIV-1 and continued support for 1989 and 1990 Fellows. 1991.

2377-2 American Association of Obstetricians and Gynecologists Foundation, Houston, TX, $70,000. For post-doctoral research fellowship in obstetrics and gynecology. 1991.

2377-3 American Federation for Clinical Research Foundation, Thorofare, NJ, $40,000. For Young Investigator Award for Clinical Research and support for 1991 recipient. 1991.

2377-4 American Foundation for Pharmaceutical Education, Fair Lawn, NJ, $50,350. For eighteen new investigator awards to support research by junior faculty at U.S. pharmacy schools. 1991.

2377-5 American Foundation for Pharmaceutical Education, Fair Lawn, NJ, $20,000. For Burroughs Pharmacology/Toxicology Graduate Fellow and Wellcome Pharmaceutics/Biopharmaceutics Graduate Fellow. 1991.

2377-6 American Foundation for Pharmaceutical Education, North Plainfield, NJ, $10,000. For industry-oriented fellowship program. 1991.

2377-7 American Social Health Association, Durham, NC, $53,750. For post-doctoral research fellowship in sexually transmitted diseases. 1991.

2377-8 American Society of Clinical Oncology, Chicago, IL, $30,000. For Young Investigator Award to study immunization of colon cancer patients with mucin antigens. 1991.

2377-9 American Society of Clinical Oncology, Chicago, IL, $30,000. For Young Investigator Award in Clinical Oncologic Research. 1991.

2377-10 American Society of Hospital Pharmacists, Bethesda, MD, $54,000. For Research Fellowship in Effect of Gender and Menstrual Cycle-Ciprofloxacin's Ability to Alter Genetic Polymorphic and Nonpolymorphic Pathway of Drug Metabolism, and continued support of 1990 Fellow. 1991.

2377-11 Dana-Farber Cancer Institute, Boston, MA, $12,000. For supplemental stipend for third-year fellow, for research on granulocyte-macrophage colony stimulating factor. 1991.

2377-12 Dartmouth College, Hanover, NH, $29,884. For bridging grant to study role of urokinase in modifying tumor cell growth. 1991.

2377-13 Deafness Research Foundation, NYC, NY, $27,000. For Research Fellowship in Cochlear Blood Flow and Noise Exposure Effects on the Autonomic Nervous System, and support for 1991 Fellow. 1991.

2377-14 Dermatology Foundation, Evanston, IL, $27,000. For Research Fellowship in Interaction Between Ultraviolet Radiation and Papilloma Viruses in Transgenic Mice, and continued support for 1990 Fellow. 1991.

2377-15 Dermatology Foundation, Evanston, IL, $27,000. For dermatology research fellowship in honor of Dr. Marion B. Sulzberger. 1991.

2377-16 Epilepsy Foundation of America, Landover, MD, $60,000. For clinical epilepsy post-doctoral research fellowship. 1991.

2377-17 Foundation for Anesthesia Education and Research, Park Ridge, IL, $140,000. For Young Investigator Awards in Anesthesiology to study hormone sensitive lipase: gene candidate in malignant hyperthermia susceptibility, and to study mechanism of general anesthetics depression of central excitatory synapses. 1991.

2377-18 Foundation for Anesthesia Education and Research, Baltimore, MD, $140,000. For Anesthesiology Young Investigator Award. 1991.

2377-19 Infectious Diseases Society of America, New Haven, CT, $90,000. For Young Investigator Award in Virology to study co-expression of E4 and L1 open reading frames in human papilloma virus infections and continued support for 1988-90 New Investigators. 1991.

2377-20 Infectious Diseases Society of America, New Haven, CT, $90,000. For new investigator award in infectious diseases. 1991.

2377-21 Infectious Diseases Society of America, New Haven, CT, $63,600. For Research Fellowships in capacity of Mycobacterium leprae to Invade Nerves and continued support for 1989 Fellow. 1991.

2377-22 Jackson Laboratory, Bar Harbor, ME, $25,000. For 1990 Summer Research Program to introduce undergraduate and graduate students to biomedical research. 1991.

2377-23 Johns Hopkins University, School of Medicine, DC, $60,000. For Pharmacoepidemiology Scholar Award. 1991.

2377-24 Marine Biological Laboratory, Woods Hole, MA, $30,000. For 1990 Biology of Parasitism Summer Program to teach students how to apply molecular biology, immunology and biochemistry to study of parasites. 1991.

2377-25 Michigan State University, East Lansing, MI, $300,000. For Toxicology Scholar Award. 1991.

2377-26 Mount Desert Island Biological Laboratory, Salisbury Cove, ME, $25,000. For education in biomedical sciences for faculty and students at liberal arts colleges. 1991.

2377-27 National Foundation for Infectious Diseases, DC, $39,600. For fifteen young investigator matching grants to support pilot research in infectious diseases by junior faculty at U.S. medical schools. 1991.

2377-28 National Kidney Foundation, NYC, NY, $60,000. For Research Fellowship in Role of Polymorphonuclear Neutrophils in Ischemia Reperfusion Injury. 1991.

2377-29 National Medical Fellowships, NYC, NY, $12,000. For need-based scholarship program for minority medical students. 1991.

2377-30 National Society to Prevent Blindness, NYC, NY, $54,000. For Research Fellowship in Cost Effectiveness of Screening and Treatment of Glaucoma, and continued support for 1989 and 1990 Fellows. 1991.

2377-31 Oregon Health Sciences University, Vollum Institute for Biomedical Research, Portland, OR, $150,000. For Hitchings Award for Innovative Methods in Drug Design and Discovery on behalf of Dr. Susan Amara. 1991.

2377-32 Tufts University, School of Medicine, Medford, MA, $300,000. For Experimental Therapeutics Scholar Award. 1991.

2377-33 University of Alabama, Birmingham, AL, $300,000. For Molecular Parasitology Scholar Award. 1991.

2377-34 University of California, Davis, CA, $300,000. For Experimental Therapeutics Scholar Award. 1991.

2377-35 University of Colorado Health Sciences Center, Denver, CO, $300,000. For Immunopharmacology of Allergic Diseases Scholar Award. 1991.

2377-36 University of Michigan, Department of Medicinal Chemistry and Pharmacognosy, Ann Arbor, MI, $150,000. For Hitchings Award for Innovative Methods in Drug Design and Discovery on behalf of Dr. Michael Marletta. 1991.

2377-37 University of North Carolina, School of Medicine, Chapel Hill, NC, $500,000. To establish Graduate Scholar Award Program to support one Ph.D. and one M.D. student per year to advance their training. 1992.

2377-38 Washington University, School of Medicine, Saint Louis, MO, $30,000. For seed grant to study in vitro fertilization. 1991.

2377-39 Yale University, New Haven, CT, $12,000. For supplemental stipend to study identification and characterization of unique phenothiazine targets in multidrug resistant cells. 1991.

2377-40 Yale University, School of Medicine, New Haven, CT, $300,000. For Innovative Methods in Drug Design Scholar Award. 1991.

2377-41 Yale University, School of Medicine, New Haven, CT, $60,000. For New Investigator Award in Molecular Parasitology to study strategies used by parasites to survive inside host cells. 1991.

2378
The Cannon Foundation, Inc. ▼
P.O. Box 548
Concord 28026-0548   (704) 786-8216

Incorporated in 1943 in NC.
Donor(s): Charles A. Cannon,‡ Cannon Mills Co.
Foundation type: Independent
Financial data (yr. ended 09/30/91): Assets, $105,825,402 (M); expenditures, $5,049,667; qualifying distributions, $4,557,717, including $4,394,266 for 102 grants (high: $800,000; low: $500; average: $500-$800,000).
Purpose and activities: Support for hospitals, higher and secondary education, and cultural programs; grants also for Protestant church support, and social service and youth agencies.
Fields of interest: Hospitals, higher education, secondary education, cultural programs, Protestant giving, social services, youth.
Types of support: Annual campaigns, building funds, equipment, matching funds, renovation projects.
Limitations: Giving primarily in NC, especially in the Cabarrus County area. No grants to individuals, or for operating budgets, seed money, emergency funds, deficit financing, land acquisition, endowment funds, demonstration projects, research, publications, conferences, seminars, scholarships, or fellowships; no loans.
Publications: Application guidelines.

Application information: Application form required.

Initial approach: Letter
Copies of proposal: 1
Deadline(s): Submit proposal in Jan., Apr., July, and Oct.; deadline Jan. 15, Apr. 15, July 15, and Oct. 15
Board meeting date(s): Mar., June, Sept., and Dec.
Final notification: Within 2 weeks of board action
Write: Dan L. Gray, Exec. Dir.

Officers and Directors:* Mariam C. Hayes,* Pres.; W.S. Fisher,* V.P.; T.C. Haywood,* Secy.-Treas.; Dan L. Gray,* Exec. Dir.; G.A. Batte, Jr., W.C. Cannon, Jr., R.C. Hayes, Elizabeth L. Quick, T.L. Ross.

Number of staff: 1 full-time professional; 2 full-time support.

EIN: 566042532

Recent health grants:

2378-1 Alexander Childrens Center, Charlotte, NC, $25,000. For asbestos removal and renovation. 1990.

2378-2 Alice Aycock Poe Center for Health Education, Raleigh, NC, $50,000. To construct and equip Poe Center for Health Education. 1990.

2378-3 Alzheimers Disease and Related Disorders Association of Western North Carolina, Asheville, NC, $10,000. For Care-giver Support Center and Thrift Shop Network. 1990.

2378-4 Alzheimers Disease and Related Disorders Association of Greater Charlotte, Southern Piedmont Chapter, Charlotte, NC, $20,000. For operating funds. 1990.

2378-5 Blowing Rock Hospital, Blowing Rock, NC, $25,000. For renovation to hospital building to meet Life/Safety Code. 1990.

2378-6 Cabarrus County Schools, Concord, NC, $51,400. For Health Education Program. 1990.

2378-7 Cabarrus Memorial Hospital, Concord, NC, $1,150,000. For new patient care services. 1990.

2378-8 Cabarrus Memorial Hospital, Concord, NC, $430,000. For Duke-Cabarrus Professional Education Program. 1990.

2378-9 Charles A. Cannon, Jr. Memorial Hospital, Banner Elk, NC, $25,000. To purchase replacement equipment. 1990.

2378-10 Easter Seal Society of North Carolina, Raleigh, NC, $10,000. For Comprehensive Respite Care Program serving Irdell County. 1990.

2378-11 Florence Crittenton Services, Charlotte, NC, $10,000. To assist in covering short fall in State Maternity Home Fund. 1990.

2379
Carolina Power & Light Company Corporate Giving Program

411 Fayetteville St.
P.O. Box 1551
Raleigh 27602   (919) 546-6309

Financial data (yr. ended 12/31/90): Total giving, $2,091,810 for grants (average: $1,000-$10,000).

Purpose and activities: Supports the social sciences, education, civic and public affairs, arts and humanities, and health.

Fields of interest: Social services, education, civic affairs, arts, humanities, health.

Types of support: Employee matching gifts, capital campaigns, building funds, special projects, research, loaned talent, use of facilities, donated equipment.

Limitations: Giving primarily in headquarters city and major operating locations in NC and SC. No support for religious organizations. No grants to individuals.

Publications: Application guidelines, corporate report.

Application information: Community Relations Dept. handles giving. Application form required.

Initial approach: Letter or proposal; Send requests to nearest company facility
Copies of proposal: 1
Deadline(s): Applications accepted throughout the year
Board meeting date(s): Monthly
Final notification: 14 weeks
Write: Barbara K. Allen, Mgr., Community Rels.

2380
The Donald & Elizabeth Cooke Foundation

P.O. Box 540
Southern Pines 28388
Application address: 235 East Penn. Ave., Southern Pines, NC 28387; Tel.: (919) 692-7811

Established in 1980 in NC.

Donor(s): Elizabeth G. Cooke.‡

Foundation type: Independent

Financial data (yr. ended 12/31/90): Assets, $3,866,525 (M); expenditures, $271,310; qualifying distributions, $221,114, including $221,114 for 34 grants (high: $50,000; low: $1,000).

Fields of interest: Education, higher education, health, general charitable giving.

Limitations: Giving primarily in NC.

Application information: Application form not required.

Deadline(s): Dec. 15
Write: W. Harry Fullenwider, Pres., or Sandy Patterson, V.P.

Officers and Directors:* W. Harry Fullenwilder,* Pres.; Sandy Patterson,* V.P.

EIN: 581408721

2381
Harry L. Dalton Foundation, Inc.

736 Wachovia Ctr.
Charlotte 28285   (704) 332-5380

Established about 1979 in NC.

Foundation type: Independent

Financial data (yr. ended 07/31/91): Assets, $2,687,927 (M); expenditures, $114,398; qualifying distributions, $109,840, including $109,840 for 30 grants (high: $26,000; low: $25).

Purpose and activities: Giving primarily for education, including higher education and libraries; support also for cultural programs, youth, family planning, drug abuse programs, mental health, and historic preservation.

Fields of interest: Education, higher education, libraries, cultural programs, family planning, fine arts, historic preservation, mental health, museums, drug abuse, youth.

Application information: Application form not required.

Deadline(s): None
Write: Mary K. Dalton, Pres.

Officers and Directors:* Mary K. Dalton,* Pres. and Treas.; Elizabeth D. Brand,* Secy.

Number of staff: 1 part-time support.

EIN: 566061267

2382
The Josephus Daniels Charitable Foundation

215 South McDowell St.
Raleigh 27601-1331   (919) 829-4694

Established in 1964 in NC.

Donor(s): The News and Observer Publishing Co.

Foundation type: Company-sponsored

Financial data (yr. ended 12/31/90): Assets, $2,987,927 (M); gifts received, $298,500; expenditures, $608,084; qualifying distributions, $585,010, including $578,551 for 87 grants (high: $56,250; low: $10).

Purpose and activities: Grants primarily for higher education, other educational associations, and community development; support also for the fine and performing arts, other cultural programs, and social services.

Fields of interest: Higher education, educational associations, community development, community funds, arts, media and communications, journalism, language and literature, disadvantaged, handicapped, homeless, AIDS, child development, women, wildlife.

Types of support: Annual campaigns, building funds, capital campaigns, continuing support, emergency funds, endowment funds, equipment, publications, renovation projects, scholarship funds, seed money, special projects, in-kind gifts, land acquisition.

Limitations: Giving primarily in NC. No support for religious organizations. No grants to individuals, or for conferences or seminars.

Publications: Informational brochure (including application guidelines).

Application information: Application form not required.

Initial approach: Letter
Deadline(s): None
Board meeting date(s): Quarterly
Write: Witt Clarke, Secy.-Treas.

Officers: Frank A. Daniels, Jr., Pres.; Melvin L. Finch, V.P.; Witt Clarke, Secy.-Treas.

EIN: 566065260

2383
Lucy Daniels Foundation, Inc.

3019 Essex Circle
Raleigh 27608   (919) 881-0182

Established in 1989 in NC.

Donor(s): Lucy D. Inman.

Foundation type: Independent

Financial data (yr. ended 09/30/91): Assets, $7,104,387 (M); gifts received, $600,019; expenditures, $250,320; qualifying distributions, $331,341, including $199,583 for 1 foundation-administered program.

Purpose and activities: Giving for psychoanalytic treatment with an emphasis on creativity, research, and community education.

Fields of interest: Psychology, psychiatry, arts.
Types of support: Conferences and seminars, grants to individuals, research.
Limitations: Giving primarily in the Raleigh, Durham, Chapel Hill, NC, area.
Publications: Informational brochure.
Application information: Application procedures are being developed.
  Deadline(s): None
  Write: Lucy D. Inman, Chair.
Officer and Directors:* Lucy D. Inman, Ph.D.,* Chair.; Melvin G. Shimm,* V.P.; Lucy Noble Inman, Patrick B. Inman, Ingrid B. Pisetsky, M.D., and 4 additional directors.
Number of staff: 2 part-time professional; 1 part-time support.
EIN: 581854794

2384
Deichman-Lerner Foundation
118 South Main St.
Salisbury 28144

Foundation type: Independent
Financial data (yr. ended 02/02/91): Assets, $64,633 (M); gifts received, $276,000; expenditures, $219,742; qualifying distributions, $219,742, including $219,700 for 11 grants (high: $88,200; low: $200).
Purpose and activities: Giving primarily for an organization providing relief in India; support also for medical and higher education.
Fields of interest: International relief, medical education, higher education.
Limitations: No grants to individuals.
Application information: Contributes only to pre-selected organizations. Applications not accepted.
Officers and Directors:* H.H. Deichmann,* Chair.; Bernice L. Lerner, Pres.; James Y. Preston,* Secy.; Morton S. Lerner, Treas.; Debra L. Foster, H. Byron Ives III.
EIN: 581615694

2385
The Dickson Foundation, Inc.
2000 Two First Union Ctr.
Charlotte 28282   (704) 372-5404

Incorporated in 1944 in NC.
Donor(s): American and Efird Mills, Inc.
Foundation type: Independent
Financial data (yr. ended 12/31/90): Assets, $20,638,191 (M); expenditures, $1,106,204; qualifying distributions, $1,137,034, including $1,106,070 for 268 grants (high: $50,000; low: $100).
Fields of interest: Community funds, youth, secondary education, higher education, educational associations, hospitals, social services.
Types of support: Scholarship funds, general purposes.
Limitations: Giving primarily in NC. No grants to individuals, or for building or endowment funds.
Application information:
  Initial approach: Letter
  Deadline(s): None
  Board meeting date(s): Annually and as required
Officers and Directors:* R. Stuart Dickson,* Chair.; Alan T. Dickson,* Pres.; Rush S. Dickson

III,* V.P.; Thomas W. Dickson,* V.P.; Colleen S. Colbert, Secy.-Treas.
EIN: 566022339

2386
The Duke Endowment ▼
200 South Tryon St., Suite 1100
Charlotte 28202-3200   (704) 376-0291
Rural Church Division: 3329 Chapel Hill Blvd., P.O. Box 51307, Durham, NC 27707-1307; Tel.: (919)489-3359

Trust established in 1924 in NJ.
Donor(s): James Buchanan Duke.‡
Foundation type: Independent
Financial data (yr. ended 12/31/91): Assets, $1,211,947,564 (M); expenditures, $55,291,565; qualifying distributions, $51,499,166, including $48,292,555 for 969 grants.
Purpose and activities: "To make provision in some measure for the needs of mankind along physical, mental, and spiritual lines." Grants to nonprofit hospitals and child care institutions in NC and SC; rural United Methodist churches and retired ministers in NC and their dependents; and Duke, Furman, and Johnson C. Smith universities, and Davidson College.
Fields of interest: Hospitals, child welfare, Protestant giving, education.
Types of support: Operating budgets, seed money, emergency funds, matching funds, professorships, internships, scholarship funds, fellowships, endowment funds, research, special projects, publications, conferences and seminars, consulting services, technical assistance, continuing support, annual campaigns, building funds, capital campaigns, equipment, general purposes, renovation projects, grants to individuals.
Limitations: Giving limited to NC and SC. No grants to individuals (except for retired ministers and their dependents), or for deficit financing; no loans.
Publications: Annual report (including application guidelines), newsletter, informational brochure (including application guidelines).
Application information: Application form not required.
  Initial approach: Letter
  Deadline(s): None
  Board meeting date(s): Monthly
  Final notification: Immediately after trustees' meeting
  Write: Jere W. Witherspoon, Exec. Dir.
Officers and Trustees:* Mary D.B.T. Semans,* Chair.; Hugh M. Chapman,* Vice-Chair.; Louis C. Stephens, Jr.,* Vice-Chair.; Myrna C. Fourcher, Secy.; Janice C. Walker, Treas.; Jere W. Witherspoon, Exec. Dir.; William G. Anlyan, M.D., Archie K. Davis, Doris Duke, Mary D.T. Jones, Thomas Stephen Kenan III, Juanita M. Kreps, Thomas Anderson Langford, Charles F. Myers, Jr., Richard W. Riley, Russell M. Robinson II, James C. Self, Charles B. Wade, Jr.
Number of staff: 17 full-time professional; 16 full-time support.
EIN: 560529965
Recent health grants:
2386-1 Abbeville County Memorial Hospital, Abbeville, SC, $150,000. To establish midwifery-assisted obstetrical program. 1991.

2386-2 Alamance Health Services, Burlington, NC, $30,000. For chaplaincy program. 1991.
2386-3 Alamance Memorial Hospital, Burlington, NC, $18,062. For operating support toward charity care. 1991.
2386-4 Albemarle Hospital, Elizabeth City, NC, $175,000. For addition to expand patient services, radiology, training, education and cafeteria. 1991.
2386-5 Albemarle Hospital, Elizabeth City, NC, $14,610. For operating support toward charity care. 1991.
2386-6 Alexander Childrens Center, Charlotte, NC, $31,770. For general support. 1991.
2386-7 Allen Bennett Memorial Hospital, Greer, SC, $13,155. For operating support toward charity care. 1991.
2386-8 Anderson Memorial Hospital, Anderson, SC, $34,930. For operating support toward charity care. 1991.
2386-9 Angel Community Hospital, Franklin, NC, $175,000. For renovation program to construct new operating room, intensive care unit, and labor and delivery. 1991.
2386-10 Annie Penn Memorial Hospital, Reidsville, NC, $200,000. For construction program. 1991.
2386-11 Annie Penn Memorial Hospital, Reidsville, NC, $15,000. To establish development office. 1991.
2386-12 Annie Penn Memorial Hospital, Reidsville, NC, $14,494. For operating support toward charity care. 1991.
2386-13 Anson County Hospital, Wadesboro, NC, $14,586. For operating support toward charity care. 1991.
2386-14 Baker Hospital, North Charleston, SC, $150,000. For newly-completed addition. 1991.
2386-15 Baptist Medical Center at Columbia, Columbia, SC, $34,284. For operating support toward charity care. 1991.
2386-16 Baptist Retirement Homes of North Carolina, Winston-Salem, NC, $115,000. To construct 100-bed nursing care addition to North Carolina Baptist Home in Asheville, NC. 1991.
2386-17 Barnwell County Hospital, Barnwell, SC, $120,000. For renovation program to relocate and expand emergency department and to replace some furniture in patients' rooms. 1991.
2386-18 Beaufort County Hospital Association, Washington, NC, $125,000. To purchase CT scanner and other medical equipment and for renovations to Beaufort County Hospital. 1991.
2386-19 Beaufort County Memorial Hospital, Beaufort, SC, $200,000. For construction of new patient tower and renovation of 72 beds for long-term care. 1991.
2386-20 Beaufort County Memorial Hospital, Beaufort, SC, $10,000. For continued support of development program. 1991.
2386-21 Bon Secours Saint Francis Xavier Hospital, Charleston, SC, $17,967. For operating support toward charity care. 1991.
2386-22 Bruce Hospital System, Florence, SC, $10,700. For operating support toward charity care. 1991.
2386-23 C. J. Harris Community Hospital, Sylva, NC, $11,686. For operating support for charity care. 1991.

2386-24 Cabarrus Memorial Hospital, Concord, NC, $17,814. For operating support toward charity care. 1991.

2386-25 Cannon Memorial Hospital, Pickens, SC, $15,000. To establish fund development program. 1991.

2386-26 Cape Fear Memorial Hospital, Wilmington, NC, $125,000. For construction program to expand radiology, laboratory and ambulatory surgery areas. 1991.

2386-27 Cape Fear Valley Medical Center, Fayetteville, NC, $48,942. For operating support toward charity care. 1991.

2386-28 Carolina Medicorp, Winston-Salem, NC, $200,000. To assist in operation of health technology education center. 1991.

2386-29 Carolina Medicorp, Winston-Salem, NC, $175,000. To construct women's center and to renovate and expand laboratory, radiology, intensive care and rehabilitation center at Forsyth Memorial Hospital. 1991.

2386-30 Carolina Medicorp, Winston-Salem, NC, $13,000. To establish Welcome Baby, child-abuse prevention program providing support and early intervention to first-time mothers. 1991.

2386-31 Carolinas Health Care Conference, Charlotte, NC, $60,000. For program on Health Care's Economic Climate: A Growing Sentiment for Reform. 1991.

2386-32 Carolinas Hospital System, Florence, SC, $250,000. Toward construction of 20-bed women's center that will provide obstetrical, gynecological and newborn care. 1991.

2386-33 Carolinas Medical Center, Charlotte, NC, $57,523. For operating support toward charity care. 1991.

2386-34 Carteret County General Hospital Corporation, Morehead City, NC, $175,000. To construct new operating suite and to purchase new computer system. 1991.

2386-35 Catawba Memorial Hospital, Hickory, NC, $150,000. To establish nursing unit for adolescent psychiatry and to renovate hospital facility. 1991.

2386-36 Catawba Memorial Hospital, Hickory, NC, $14,519. For operating support toward charity care. 1991.

2386-37 Charles A. Cannon, Jr. Memorial Hospital, Banner Elk, NC, $77,500. To establish geriatric assessment program. 1991.

2386-38 Charles A. Cannon, Jr. Memorial Hospital, Banner Elk, NC, $15,000. To establish fund development program. 1991.

2386-39 Charleston Memorial Hospital, Charleston, SC, $225,000. For renovation program to include obstetrical services addition and construction of ambulatory care facility. 1991.

2386-40 Charleston Memorial Hospital, Charleston, SC, $18,753. For operating support toward charity care. 1991.

2386-41 Charlotte-Mecklenburg Hospital Authority, Charlotte, NC, $175,000. To construct 11-story addition to replace 288 patient beds and to construct clinical research building at Carolinas Medical Center. 1991.

2386-42 Chester County Hospital, Chester, SC, $12,763. For operating support toward charity care. 1991.

2386-43 Chowan Hospital, Edenton, NC, $10,247. For operating support toward charity care. 1991.

2386-44 Cleveland Memorial Hospital, Shelby, NC, $175,000. To construct new patient care tower, new 120-bed skilled nursing facility and to renovate existing hospital. 1991.

2386-45 Cleveland Memorial Hospital, Shelby, NC, $19,489. For operating support toward charity care. 1991.

2386-46 Columbus County Hospital, Whiteville, NC, $35,000. To develop computer laboratory network for Columbus County Hospital, Bladen County Hospital and Pender Memorial Hospital. 1991.

2386-47 Columbus County Hospital, Whiteville, NC, $13,281. For operating support toward charity care. 1991.

2386-48 Community General Hospital, Thomasville, NC, $150,000. To renovate birthing suite and to purchase major medical equipment. 1991.

2386-49 Conway Hospital, Conway, SC, $10,000. To establish development program. 1991.

2386-50 Craven Regional Medical Center, New Bern, NC, $175,000. For 26-bed nursing unit, 110-bed nursing home, management information system, oncology unit, cardiac catheterization room and centralized outpatient service. 1991.

2386-51 Craven Regional Medical Center, New Bern, NC, $23,314. For operating support toward charity care. 1991.

2386-52 Cumberland County Hospital System, Fayetteville, NC, $175,000. For expansion program to include new patient services tower. 1991.

2386-53 Duke University, Fuqua School of Business, Durham, NC, $50,000. For Health Administration program. 1991.

2386-54 Duke University Medical Center, Durham, NC, $250,000. For transition expenses in moving Master's Degree in Health Administration program to Fuqua School of Business. 1991.

2386-55 Duke University Medical Center, Durham, NC, $200,000. To assist in consolidation of family medicine activities on Duke campus. 1991.

2386-56 Duke University Medical Center, Durham, NC, $100,000. For Medical School curriculum development. 1991.

2386-57 Duke University Medical Center, Durham, NC, $100,000. For master plan for newly-acquired seven and one-half acre tract of land. 1991.

2386-58 Duke University Medical Center, Durham, NC, $52,745. For operating support toward charity care. 1991.

2386-59 Duke University Medical Center, Durham, NC, $25,000. For Chancellor's Forum, which will host private-sector conferences. 1991.

2386-60 Duke University Medical Center, Durham, NC, $25,000. For Neighborhood Advisors project, program that provides information and referral services to elderly. 1991.

2386-61 Duke University Medical Center, Durham, NC, $10,000. To publish proceedings of Twenty-Seventh Annual National Forum on Hospital and Health Affairs. 1991.

2386-62 Duke University Medical Center, Center for Youth, Durham, NC, $12,500. For multidisciplinary effort to find remedies for problems of American youth. 1991.

2386-63 Duke University Medical Center, Office of Science and Technology, Durham, NC, $152,500. To transfer into clinical practice its medical discoveries, to maximize commercial opportunities for Duke research, and to coordinate activities with Duke Management Corporation, University Council and Office of Technology Transfer. 1991.

2386-64 Durham Regional Hospital, Durham, NC, $34,000. To establish child development education project at Lincoln Community Health Center. 1991.

2386-65 Durham Regional Hospital Corporation, Durham, NC, $16,868. For operating support toward charity care. 1991.

2386-66 Edgefield County Hospital, Edgefield, SC, $30,000. To purchase equipment. 1991.

2386-67 Elliott White Springs Memorial Hospital, Lancaster, SC, $11,455. For operating support toward charity care. 1991.

2386-68 Florence General Hospital, Florence, SC, $90,000. To purchase CT scanner and other major medical equipment, and for renovations to hospital. 1991.

2386-69 Florence General Hospital, Florence, SC, $11,459. For operating support toward charity care. 1991.

2386-70 Forsyth Memorial Hospital, Winston-Salem, NC, $40,362. For operating support toward charity care. 1991.

2386-71 Gaston Health Care Support, Gastonia, NC, $175,000. To construct 96-bed nursing home and to renovate Gaston Memorial Hospital. 1991.

2386-72 Gaston Memorial Hospital, Gastonia, NC, $34,111. For operating support toward charity care. 1991.

2386-73 Georgetown Memorial Hospital, Georgetown, SC, $100,000. To purchase hospital information system and radiology equipment. 1991.

2386-74 Georgetown Memorial Hospital, Georgetown, SC, $14,445. For operating support toward charity care. 1991.

2386-75 Georgetown Memorial Hospital, Georgetown, SC, $10,000. To establish development program. 1991.

2386-76 Greenville Memorial Hospital, Greenville, SC, $62,671. For operating support toward charity care. 1991.

2386-77 Halifax Memorial Hospital, Roanoke Rapids, NC, $20,886. For operating support toward charity care. 1991.

2386-78 Haywood County Hospital, Clyde, NC, $30,000. To establish fund development program. 1991.

2386-79 High Point Regional Hospital, High Point, NC, $21,192. For operating support toward charity care. 1991.

2386-80 Holy Angels, Belmont, NC, $75,000. To construct three Intermediate Care Facilities for children and adults with severe profound mental retardation and/or physical disabilities. 1991.

2386-81 Hugh Chatham Memorial Hospital, Elkin, NC, $175,000. To expand and upgrade outpatient and intensive/coronary care services and to construct medical office building. 1991.

2386-82 Huntersville Oaks Nursing Home, Huntersville, NC, $24,489. For operating support toward charity care. 1991.

2386-83 Iredell Memorial Hospital, Statesville, NC, $17,570. For operating support toward charity care. 1991.

2386-84 Johnston Memorial Hospital, Smithfield, NC, $11,882. For operating support toward charity care. 1991.

2386-85 Kershaw County Memorial Hospital, Camden, SC, $50,000. To purchase home health care agency, which includes staff of 17 providers. 1991.

2386-86 Kershaw County Memorial Hospital, Camden, SC, $15,031. For operating support toward charity care. 1991.

2386-87 Kershaw County Memorial Hospital, Camden, SC, $15,000. To establish fund development program to assist hospital foundation. 1991.

2386-88 Kings Mountain Hospital, Kings Mountain, NC, $75,000. To renovate facilities to add psychiatric services and to purchase major medical equipment. 1991.

2386-89 Laurens County Health Care System, Laurens, SC, $175,000. For construction and equipment of new 90-bed replacement hospital. 1991.

2386-90 Laurens County Hospital, Clinton, SC, $11,961. For operating support toward charity care. 1991.

2386-91 Lenoir Memorial Hospital, Kinston, NC, $34,422. For operating support toward charity care. 1991.

2386-92 Lexington County Health Services District, West Columbia, SC, $175,000. To expand Lexington Medical Center and to build replacement 132-bed nursing home. 1991.

2386-93 Lexington County Health Services District, West Columbia, SC, $60,000. To establish health promotion programs in rural hospitals, in conjunction with South Carolina Hospital Association. 1991.

2386-94 Lexington Medical Center, West Columbia, SC, $23,851. For operating support toward charity care. 1991.

2386-95 Lexington Memorial Hospital, Lexington, NC, $140,000. Toward construction cost in first phase of long-range facilities expansion project. 1991.

2386-96 Loris Community Hospital, Loris, SC, $12,304. For operating support toward charity care. 1991.

2386-97 Lower Florence County Hospital, Lake City, SC, $90,000. For renovation program. 1991.

2386-98 Lutheran Retirement Ministries of Alamance County, Burlington, NC, $30,000. To renovate Twin Lakes Center Nursing Home and to build new community building. 1991.

2386-99 Margaret R. Pardee Memorial Hospital, Hendersonville, NC, $175,000. To construct new radiation therapy center and renovation program to provide maternal/child health unit and medical/surgical unit. 1991.

2386-100 Margaret R. Pardee Memorial Hospital, Hendersonville, NC, $14,141. For operating support toward charity care. 1991.

2386-101 Mary Black Health Systems, Spartanburg, SC, $29,000. To develop community educational program on living wills. 1991.

2386-102 McLeod Regional Medical Center of the Pee Dee, Florence, SC, $175,000. To construct new patient tower devoted to high-risk obstetrics and neonatal services. 1991.

2386-103 McLeod Regional Medical Center of the Pee Dee, Florence, SC, $125,000. Toward employment of perinatologist for regional perinatal program. 1991.

2386-104 McLeod Regional Medical Center of the Pee Dee, Florence, SC, $36,768. For operating support toward charity care. 1991.

2386-105 McLeod Regional Medical Center of the Pee Dee, Florence, SC, $35,000. To establish health careers programs for high school students. 1991.

2386-106 Memorial Mission Medical Center, Asheville, NC, $22,055. For operating support toward charity care. 1991.

2386-107 Mental Health Center, Charlotte, NC, $11,803. For operating support toward charity care. 1991.

2386-108 Mercy Hospital, Charlotte, NC, $15,496. For operating support toward charity care. 1991.

2386-109 Montgomery Memorial Hospital, Troy, NC, $185,000. To convert acute-care beds to long-term care beds and to expand outpatient facilities. 1991.

2386-110 Moore Regional Hospital, Pinehurst, NC, $175,000. For new surgical/intensive care facility addition. 1991.

2386-111 Moore Regional Hospital, Pinehurst, NC, $24,266. For operating support toward charity care. 1991.

2386-112 Morehead Memorial Hospital, Eden, NC, $175,000. For new two-story addition. 1991.

2386-113 Morehead Memorial Hospital, Eden, NC, $12,284. For operating support toward charity care. 1991.

2386-114 Moses H. Cone Memorial Hospital, Greensboro, NC, $175,000. To create women's hospital and to construct 150-bed nursing home. 1991.

2386-115 Moses H. Cone Memorial Hospital, Greensboro, NC, $40,075. For operating support toward charity care. 1991.

2386-116 Moses H. Cone Memorial Hospital, Greensboro, NC, $30,000. To provide social worker for Greensboro Urban Ministry Free Clinic, which provides free medical and dental care to medically indigent of Guilford County. 1991.

2386-117 Murphy Medical Center, Murphy, NC, $15,603. For operating support toward charity care. 1991.

2386-118 MUSC Medical Center of South Carolina, Charleston, SC, $45,892. For operating support toward charity care. 1991.

2386-119 Nash General Hospital, Rocky Mount, NC, $31,403. For operating support toward charity care. 1991.

2386-120 New Hanover Regional Medical Center, Wilmington, NC, $37,411. For operating support toward charity care. 1991.

2386-121 North Carolina Baptist Hospital, Winston-Salem, NC, $25,628. For operating support toward charity care. 1991.

2386-122 North Carolina Hospital Foundation, Raleigh, NC, $200,000. Toward construction of new office building. 1991.

2386-123 North Carolina Hospital Foundation, Raleigh, NC, $25,000. To establish quality indicators project for North Carolina. 1991.

2386-124 North Carolina Hospital Foundation, Raleigh, NC, $20,000. To develop public education program concerning death with dignity. 1991.

2386-125 Oconee Memorial Hospital, Seneca, SC, $22,296. For operating support toward charity care. 1991.

2386-126 Pender Memorial Hospital, Burgaw, NC, $80,000. For major medical equipment, including fluoroscopic x-ray unit, ultrasound, chemistry analyzer and computer and to renovate operating room and x-ray area. 1991.

2386-127 Pitt County Memorial Hospital, Greenville, NC, $225,000. For major expansion and renovation program to add 143 additional beds and 51 replacement beds. 1991.

2386-128 Pitt County Memorial Hospital, Greenville, NC, $36,720. For operating support toward charity care. 1991.

2386-129 Presbyterian Health Services Corporation, Charlotte, NC, $59,000. For Parish Nurse Program. 1991.

2386-130 Presbyterian Hospital, Charlotte, NC, $31,859. For operating support toward charity care. 1991.

2386-131 Providence Hospital, Columbia, SC, $14,181. For operating support toward charity care. 1991.

2386-132 Pungo District Hospital Corporation, Belhaven, NC, $60,000. Toward purchase of CT scanner and establishment of ventilation-dependent patient services. 1991.

2386-133 Randolph Hospital, Asheboro, NC, $175,000. To construct major addition to hospital. 1991.

2386-134 Regional Medical Center of Orangeburg and Calhoun Counties, Orangeburg, SC, $26,448. For operating support toward charity care. 1991.

2386-135 Rex Hospital, Raleigh, NC, $22,368. For operating support toward charity care. 1991.

2386-136 Richland Memorial Hospital, Columbia, SC, $200,000. To construct and equip Cancer Treatment and Research Center, new operating rooms, catheterization laboratory, outpatient areas, delivery suite and parking garage. 1991.

2386-137 Richland Memorial Hospital, Columbia, SC, $57,919. For operating support toward charity care. 1991.

2386-138 Richmond Memorial Hospital, Rockingham, NC, $11,316. For operating support toward charity care. 1991.

2386-139 Roanoke-Chowan Alliance, Ahoskie, NC, $175,000. To construct and equip 16-bed obstetrical/gynecological unit, 40-bed medical/surgical/pediatric unit and ambulatory care center. 1991.

2386-140 Roanoke-Chowan Hospital, Ahoskie, NC, $11,629. For operating support toward charity care. 1991.

2386-141 Roper Hospital, Charleston, SC, $28,342. For operating support toward charity care. 1991.

2386-142 Saint Francis Hospital, Greenville, SC, $200,000. Toward construction of new 50-bed Women's Hospital. 1991.

2386-143 Saint Francis Hospital, Greenville, SC, $17,774. For operating support toward charity care. 1991.

2386-144 Saint Joseph of the Pines Hospital, Southern Pines, NC, $150,000. To build new facility containing 60 long-term care beds and 20 beds for aged. 1991.

2386-145 Saint Josephs Health Services, Asheville, NC, $60,000. To establish decentralized pharmacy system. 1991.

2386-146 Saint Josephs Hospital, Asheville, NC, $22,439. For operating support toward charity care. 1991.

2386-147 Saint Lukes Hospital, Columbus, NC, $30,000. To establish fund development program. 1991.

2386-148 Sampson County Memorial Hospital, Clinton, NC, $100,000. To operate three rural health clinics in Sampson County. 1991.

2386-149 Sampson County Memorial Hospital, Clinton, NC, $11,309. For operating support toward charity care. 1991.

2386-150 Scotland Health Group, Laurinburg, NC, $15,000. To establish hospice program. 1991.

2386-151 Scotland Memorial Hospital, Laurinburg, NC, $15,314. For operating support toward charity care. 1991.

2386-152 Scotland Memorial Hospital, Laurinburg, NC, $15,000. For development office. 1991.

2386-153 Sea Level Hospital, Sea Level, NC, $175,000. To construct facility housing 40 long-term care beds. 1991.

2386-154 Self Memorial Hospital, Greenwood, SC, $100,000. For comprehensive maternal and infant care service system for medically indigent in six-county area. 1991.

2386-155 Self Memorial Hospital, Greenwood, SC, $28,218. For operating support toward charity care. 1991.

2386-156 Shriners Hospital for Crippled Children, Greenville, SC, $13,716. For operating support toward charity care. 1991.

2386-157 Sloop Memorial Hospital, Crossnore, NC, $30,000. To implement development program. 1991.

2386-158 South Carolina Hospital Research and Education Foundation, West Columbia, SC, $50,000. To develop series of educational programs focusing on job redesign, work restructuring and registered nurse retention in South Carolina hospitals. 1991.

2386-159 Southeastern General Hospital, Lumberton, NC, $36,663. For operating support toward charity care. 1991.

2386-160 Spartanburg Regional Medical Center, Spartanburg, SC, $53,796. For operating support toward charity care. 1991.

2386-161 Stanly Health Services, Albemarle, NC, $15,000. To establish development program. 1991.

2386-162 Transylvania Community Hospital, Brevard, NC, $15,000. To establish hospice program. 1991.

2386-163 Tuomey Hospital, Sumter, SC, $175,000. To construct new radiation therapy center. 1991.

2386-164 Tuomey Hospital, Sumter, SC, $25,113. For operating support toward charity care. 1991.

2386-165 Tuomey Hospital, Sumter, SC, $15,000. For hospice program. 1991.

2386-166 Union Memorial Hospital, Monroe, NC, $15,071. For operating support toward charity care. 1991.

2386-167 University of North Carolina Hospitals, Chapel Hill, NC, $36,135. For operating support toward charity care. 1991.

2386-168 University of North Carolina Hospitals, Chapel Hill, NC, $30,000. To expand pediatric pastoral care services. 1991.

2386-169 Wake County Hospital System, Raleigh, NC, $225,000. To construct 80-bed hospital in Cary, NC. 1991.

2386-170 Wake County Hospital System, Raleigh, NC, $200,000. To construct new educational and indigent care clinic building. 1991.

2386-171 Wake County Medical Center, Raleigh, NC, $35,472. For operating support toward charity care. 1991.

2386-172 Wallace Thomson Hospital, Union, SC, $80,000. To purchase equipment for newly-recruited physicians in urology and orthopedics. 1991.

2386-173 Wallace Thomson Hospital, Union, SC, $15,678. For operating support toward charity care. 1991.

2386-174 Wayne County Memorial Hospital, Goldsboro, NC, $25,943. For operating support toward charity care. 1991.

2386-175 Wesley Long Community Hospital, Greensboro, NC, $15,014. For operating support toward charity care. 1991.

2386-176 Western North Carolina Rural Hospital Alliance, Boone, NC, $50,000. For mobile screening and primary care program for residents of Alliance four-county area. 1991.

2386-177 Wilson Memorial Hospital, Wilson, NC, $23,766. For operating support toward charity care. 1991.

2387
Duke Power Company Foundation ▼
422 South Church St.
Charlotte 28242   (704) 373-3224
Scholarship application address: Scholastic Excellence Awards Program, P.O. Box 33189, Charlotte, NC 28242

Established in 1984 in NC.
Donor(s): Duke Power Co.
Foundation type: Company-sponsored
Financial data (yr. ended 12/31/90): Assets, $5,591,380 (M); gifts received, $6,236,620; expenditures, $5,724,498; qualifying distributions, $5,722,948, including $5,657,393 for 1,731 grants (high: $100,000; low: $10; average: $500-$10,000) and $65,555 for 166 grants to individuals.
Purpose and activities: Supports those organizations, institutions, and programs that are able to demonstrate a broad base of support among the business and civic community. Support is directed to: health and human services, education, civic programs, the homeless, environment, engineering, and culture and art. Awards competitive scholarships to students whose parents live in company areas and to employees' or retirees' children.
Fields of interest: Health, education, civic affairs, cultural programs, arts, historic preservation, social services, homeless, hospices, safety, community funds, engineering, environment, general charitable giving.

Types of support: Employee-related scholarships, student aid, capital campaigns, employee matching gifts, general purposes, matching funds.
Limitations: Giving primarily in the company's headquarters and service areas in NC and SC. No support for single sectarian or denominational religious, veterans', or fraternal organizations; organizations where the foundation would be the only donor; hospitals supported by the Duke Endowment; or to organizations primarily supported by tax dollars (education excepted). No grants to individuals (except for scholarships).
Application information: Application form required for scholarships only; students must be nominated by school official.
Initial approach: Proposal
Copies of proposal: 1
Deadline(s): Scholarships: Oct. 15; all others anytime
Write: Robert C. Allen, V.P.
Officers and Trustees:* William S. Lee,* Chair.; William H. Grigg,* Pres.; Robert C. Allen, V.P. and Exec. Dir.; John P. O'Keefe, Secy.; David L. Hauser, Treas.; Steve C. Griffith, Jr., Warren H. Owen.
EIN: 581586283
Recent health grants:
2387-1 Alexander Childrens Center, Charlotte, NC, $10,000. 1990.
2387-2 Amethyst Foundation, Charlotte, NC, $50,000. 1990.
2387-3 Partnership for a Drug Free America, NYC, NY, $10,000. 1990.

2388
Durham Corporation Giving Program
2610 Wycliff Road
Raleigh 27607   (919) 881-2219
Mailing address: P.O. Box 27807, Raleigh, NC 27611

Financial data (yr. ended 12/31/90): Total giving, $124,752, including $119,912 for grants and $4,840 for 30 employee matching gifts.
Purpose and activities: Support for United Way, private higher education, health and welfare, community development, and arts and culture. Types of support include loaned staff and use of company printing facilities.
Fields of interest: Community funds, higher education, health, welfare, arts, community development, business education.
Types of support: Employee matching gifts, capital campaigns, building funds, in-kind gifts.
Limitations: No grants to individuals, or for endowments.
Application information:
Initial approach: Letter; Send requests to headquarters
Final notification: 4 weeks
Write: Floyd E. Skipper, V.P. and Secy.

2389
Horatio B. Ebert Charitable Foundation
c/o Mark B. Edwards
128 South Tryon St., Suite 1600
Charlotte 28202

Established in 1985.
Donor(s): Lyda G. Ebert,‡ Robert O. Ebert.
Foundation type: Independent

Financial data (yr. ended 12/31/90): Assets, $9,216,200 (M); expenditures, $373,304; qualifying distributions, $360,867, including $360,867 for grants.
Fields of interest: Hospitals, higher education, religion—Christian, child welfare.
Types of support: Building funds.
Limitations: Giving primarily in NC, OH, KY, and FL.
Application information: Contributes only to pre-selected organizations. Applications not accepted.
   Write: Robert O. Ebert, Trustee
Trustees: Adrienne Ebert, Robert O. Ebert, Viola R. Ebert, Cathy Harkless.
Number of staff: 1 part-time support.
EIN: 592602801

2390
Thomas Austin Finch Foundation
c/o Wachovia Bank & Trust Co., N.A.
P.O. Box 3099
Winston-Salem 27150-1022

Trust established in 1944 in NC.
Donor(s): Ernestine L. Finch Mobley,‡ Thomas Austin Finch, Jr.‡
Foundation type: Independent
Financial data (yr. ended 12/31/90): Assets, $6,160,863 (M); expenditures, $393,128; qualifying distributions, $342,616, including $340,861 for 22 grants (high: $58,500; low: $400).
Fields of interest: Secondary education, religious schools, Protestant giving, community funds, civic affairs, libraries, hospitals.
Types of support: Operating budgets, continuing support, annual campaigns, building funds, equipment, scholarship funds, special projects.
Limitations: Giving limited to Thomasville, NC. No grants to individuals, or for emergency funds, deficit financing, endowment funds, or fellowships; no loans.
Publications: Informational brochure (including application guidelines).
Application information: Application form required.
   Initial approach: Letter
   Copies of proposal: 1
   Deadline(s): None
   Board meeting date(s): Mar. and Nov.
   Final notification: 2 weeks
   Write: J. Lee Knight, Administrator
Foundation Committee: David Finch, Chair.; Kermit Cloninger, John L. Finch, Sumner Finch, Meredith Slane Person.
Trustee: Wachovia Bank & Trust Co., N.A.
Number of staff: None.
EIN: 566037907

2391
First Gaston Foundation, Inc.
(Formerly Myers-Ti-Caro Foundation, Inc.)
P.O. Box 2696
Gastonia 28053   (704) 865-6111

Incorporated in 1950 in NC.
Donor(s): Textiles, Inc., Threads, Inc.
Foundation type: Independent
Financial data (yr. ended 09/30/90): Assets, $6,750,372 (M); expenditures, $488,718;

qualifying distributions, $395,500, including $303,352 for 37 grants (average: $1,000-$20,000) and $92,148 for 40 grants to individuals (high: $4,500; low: $100).
Purpose and activities: Grants for higher and secondary education, including scholarships to students in Gaston County; support also for social services and youth, religious welfare, health and hospitals, and arts and culture.
Fields of interest: Higher education, secondary education, social services, youth, religious welfare, health, hospitals, arts, cultural programs.
Types of support: Student aid, scholarship funds, building funds, capital campaigns.
Limitations: Giving limited to communities in NC, with emphasis on Gaston County.
Application information: Application form required for scholarships.
   Copies of proposal: 1
   Deadline(s): None
   Board meeting date(s): May and Dec.
   Write: Albert G. Myers III, Chair., or Nina Greene, Secy.
Officers and Trustees:* Albert G. Myers III,* Chair.; B. Frank Matthews II,* Vice-Chair.; J. Mack Holland, Jr.,* Secy.; Robert P. Caldwell, Jr.,* Treas.; A. Leonel Brunnemer, Tom D. Effird, J.C. Fry, Albert G. Myers, Jr.
Number of staff: 1 full-time support.
EIN: 560770083

2392
The First Union Foundation ▼
Two First Union
Charlotte 28288-0143   (704) 374-6649
Contrib. Coord. at the following First Union Natl. Banks: SC, Finance Div. T-2, Box 1329, Greenville, SC 29602; GA, P.O. Box 740074, Atlanta, GA 30374; FL, 0561, P.O. Box 2080, Jacksonville, FL 32231; NC, 0143, Charlotte, NC 28288

Established in 1987 in NC.
Donor(s): First Union Corp.
Foundation type: Company-sponsored
Financial data (yr. ended 12/31/91): Assets, $385,908 (M); gifts received, $3,635,781; expenditures, $4,256,257; qualifying distributions, $4,229,141, including $4,010,934 for 1,426 grants (high: $300,000; low: $25; average: $100-$20,000) and $218,207 for 1,018 employee matching gifts.
Purpose and activities: Support for higher education and special programs for public elementary and secondary schools; arts funds or councils; community improvement; family and social services, minorities, and the handicapped. Special consideration for children and youth and the disadvantaged to help them become productive and self-sufficient. Types of support include capital grants, made only when there is a community-wide fundraising campaign that includes the entire business community. A grant is made for one year only and does not imply that a grant will be made the following year unless a multi-year pledge is made.
Fields of interest: Community development, social services, health, education, cultural programs, arts, hospitals—building funds, housing.
Types of support: Building funds, capital campaigns, endowment funds, operating budgets, renovation projects, special projects, employee

matching gifts, scholarship funds, seed money, general purposes.
Limitations: Giving limited to FL, GA, NC, and SC. No support for religious, veterans', or fraternal organizations, retirement homes, pre-college level private schools except through employee matching gifts, or organizations supported through the United Way, except for approved capital campaigns.
Publications: Informational brochure (including application guidelines).
Application information: Application form not required.
   Initial approach: Proposal to the nearest First Union Bank
   Copies of proposal: 1
   Deadline(s): Sept. 1 for consideration in next year's budget
   Board meeting date(s): Mar., June, Sept., and Dec.
   Write: Ann D. Thomas, Dir., Corp. Contribs.
Directors: Ann D. Thomas, Dir., Corp. Contribs.; Robert Atwood, Marion A. Cowell, Jr., Edward E. Crutchfield, Jr., John R. Georgius, B.J. Walker.
Trustee: First Union National Bank of North Carolina.
EIN: 566288589

2393
Foundation For The Carolinas ▼
301 South Brevard St.
Charlotte 28202   (704) 376-9541

Incorporated in 1958 in NC.
Foundation type: Community
Financial data (yr. ended 12/31/91): Assets, $61,483,187 (M); gifts received, $6,810,501; expenditures, $6,253,462; qualifying distributions, $5,221,572, including $5,221,572 for grants (high: $10,000; low: $100; average: $1,000-$5,000).
Purpose and activities: Support primarily for education, human services, religion, the arts, and health.
Fields of interest: Education, social services, religion, arts, health.
Types of support: Seed money, matching funds, scholarship funds.
Limitations: Giving primarily to organizations serving the citizens of NC and SC, with emphasis on the Central Piedmont region. No grants to individuals, or for deficit financing, capital campaigns, operating budgets, publications, conferences, videos, travel, or endowment funds.
Publications: Annual report (including application guidelines), newsletter.
Application information: Application form required.
   Initial approach: Letter
   Copies of proposal: 1
   Deadline(s): Feb. 1, June 1, and Oct. 1
   Board meeting date(s): Quarterly, with annual meeting in Mar.; distribution committee meets monthly
   Final notification: 2 months
   Write: Marilyn M. Bradburg, V.P.
Officers and Directors:* Robin L. Hinson,* Chair.; William H. Grigg,* 1st Vice-Chair.; Edwin L. Jones, Jr.,* Vice-Chair.; William L. Spencer, Pres.; Marilyn Bradbury,* V.P.; James Thompson,* Secy.; Crandall Close Bowles,* Treas.; John M. Belk, Larry J. Dagenhart, Charles T. Davidson,

James S. Howell, F. Kenneth Iverson, C. Don Steger, and 32 additional directors.
Number of staff: 6 full-time professional; 2 part-time professional; 5 full-time support; 1 part-time support.
EIN: 566047886
Recent health grants:
2393-1 Alexander Childrens Center, Charlotte, NC, $42,360. 1990.
2393-2 Central House, Charlotte, NC, $18,000. 1990.
2393-3 Charlotte-Mecklenburg Hospital Authority Foundation, Charlotte, NC, $10,500. 1990.
2393-4 Community Health Services, Charlotte, NC, $48,593. 1990.
2393-5 Heineman Medical Research Center of Charlotte, Charlotte, NC, $47,000. 1990.
2393-6 Planned Parenthood of Greater Charlotte, Charlotte, NC, $16,787. 1990.
2393-7 Presbyterian Hospital Foundation, Charlotte, NC, $38,200. 1990.
2393-8 Richmond Memorial Hospital, Rockingham, NC, $50,000. 1990.
2393-9 Richmond, County of, Rockingham, NC, $45,000. For health program. 1990.

2394
Gilmer-Smith Foundation
P.O. Box 251
Mount Airy 27030

Foundation type: Independent
Financial data (yr. ended 11/30/91): Assets, $2,941,327 (M); expenditures, $250,976; qualifying distributions, $188,176, including $64,050 for 16 grants (high: $19,730; low: $120) and $105,454 for 2 foundation-administered programs.
Purpose and activities: Giving primarily for a park and a historical preservation society; support also for health.
Fields of interest: Community development, historic preservation, health, medical education.
Limitations: Giving primarily in Mount Airy, NC. No grants to individuals.
Application information: Contributes only to pre-selected organizations. Applications not accepted.
Officers: Edward N. Swanson, Pres.; P.M. Sharpe, Secy.
Trustees: David Beal, George T. Fawcett, Jr., Rachel B. Smith.
EIN: 581463411

2395
Glaxo Corporate Giving Program
Five Moore Dr.
Research Triangle Park 27709   (919) 248-2588

Purpose and activities: Glaxo believes "in being a conscientious corporate citizen as well as a contributing and active member of the communities within which we work." While the foundation emphasizes projects having a statewide effect, the corporate giving program concentrates on three counties in NC: Durham, Wake, and Orange. Support for health, welfare, education, culture and the arts, and civic and community services. Programs reflect foundation and corporate giving.

Fields of interest: Arts, civic affairs, community development, community funds, cultural programs, education, educational associations, elementary education, health, higher education, secondary education.
Types of support: Program-related investments, seed money, special projects, donated products.
Limitations: Giving primarily in Durham, Wake, and Orange Counties, NC.
Application information: Include funds, in hand or pledged, and from whom; line-item budget for the project, and list of board members.
Application form not required.
  Initial approach: Proposal
  Copies of proposal: 1
  Board meeting date(s): Monthly
  Write: Kathryn H. Wallace, Contribs. Admin.
Number of staff: 1 full-time professional; 1 full-time support.

2396
The Glaxo Foundation
Five Moore Dr.
Research Triangle Park 27709   (919) 248-2140

Established in 1986 in NC.
Donor(s): Glaxo, Inc.
Foundation type: Company-sponsored
Financial data (yr. ended 06/30/91): Assets, $19,787,552 (M); gifts received, $3,150,000; expenditures, $717,719; qualifying distributions, $702,369, including $696,269 for 7 grants (high: $300,000; low: $17,894).
Purpose and activities: Primary areas of interest include math, science, and health education.
Fields of interest: Education, education—early childhood, elementary education, secondary education, education—minorities, science and technology, mathematics, child development, community development, civic affairs, disadvantaged, health.
Types of support: Operating budgets, seed money.
Limitations: No support for religious or fraternal organizations, or international programs. No grants to individuals, or for capital campaigns or building funds.
Publications: Informational brochure (including application guidelines).
Application information: Application form required.
  Initial approach: Proposal
  Copies of proposal: 2
  Deadline(s): Apr. 1 and Oct. 1
  Board meeting date(s): June and Dec.
  Final notification: June 30 and Dec. 31
  Write: Elliott M. Sogol, Fdn. Admin.
Officers and Directors:* Charles Sanders,* C.E.O.; Ernest Mario,* Deputy Chair.; Thomas R. Haber,* Sr. V.P. and C.F.O.; Thomas W. D'Alonzo,* Group V.P.; Robert A. Ingram,* Group V.P.; Michael Bongiovani, Joseph Ruvane.
Number of staff: None.
EIN: 581698610

2397
Carrie C. & Lena V. Glenn Foundation
c/o Branch Banking & Trust Co.
223 West Nash St.
Wilson 27893

Established in 1971 in NC.

Foundation type: Independent
Financial data (yr. ended 09/30/91): Assets, $5,007,300 (M); expenditures, $269,377; qualifying distributions, $218,510, including $200,000 for 24 grants (high: $18,500; low: $1,000).
Fields of interest: Libraries, education, medical education, health, drug abuse, community development, religious welfare.
Types of support: General purposes.
Limitations: Giving primarily in Gaston County, NC.
Application information: Application form not required.
  Deadline(s): None
Directors: Sarah Abernathy, Hugh F. Bryant, W.W. Dickson, Craig Fielding, Judith M. Miller, Elizabeth T. Stewart, James G. Stuart.
Trustee: Branch Banking & Trust Co.
EIN: 237140170

2398
The Foundation of Greater Greensboro, Inc.
First Citizens Bank, Suite 307
P.O. Box 207
Greensboro 27402   (919) 379-9100

Established in 1983.
Foundation type: Community
Financial data (yr. ended 06/30/91): Assets, $9,619,401 (M); gifts received, $2,000,000; expenditures, $960,000; qualifying distributions, $952,646, including $952,646 for grants.
Fields of interest: Cultural programs, arts, civic affairs, community development, education, health, social services.
Types of support: Emergency funds, equipment, general purposes, seed money, special projects.
Limitations: Giving limited to the Greater Greensboro, NC, area.
Publications: Annual report, application guidelines, program policy statement, newsletter.
Application information: Application form required.
  Initial approach: Proposal (3 pages or less)
  Copies of proposal: 1
  Deadline(s): 30 days prior to monthly meeting
  Board meeting date(s): Monthly
  Final notification: Within 60 days
  Write: Wentworth L. Durgin, Exec. Dir.
Officers and Directors:* Philip Gelzer,* Pres.; Joseph F. Bond,* Treas.; and 27 additional directors.
Number of staff: 3 full-time professional; 1 full-time support; 1 part-time support.
EIN: 561380249

2399
The John W. and Anna H. Hanes Foundation
c/o Wachovia Bank of North Carolina
P.O. Box 3099, MC 31022
Winston-Salem 27150   (919) 770-5274

Trust established in 1947 in NC.
Foundation type: Independent
Financial data (yr. ended 12/31/91): Assets, $16,169,348 (M); expenditures, $763,644; qualifying distributions, $676,773, including

$672,001 for 41 grants (high: $166,667; low: $1,000; average: $1,000-$25,000).

Fields of interest: Cultural programs, arts, historic preservation, conservation, environment, child welfare, social services, health.

Types of support: Annual campaigns, seed money, emergency funds, building funds, equipment, land acquisition, endowment funds, matching funds, special projects, publications, capital campaigns.

Limitations: Giving limited to NC, particularly Forsyth County. No grants to individuals, or for operating expenses.

Publications: Program policy statement, application guidelines.

Application information: Application form required.

  Initial approach: Telephone or letter
  Copies of proposal: 1
  Deadline(s): 15th day of month preceding board meeting
  Board meeting date(s): Jan., Apr., July, and Oct.
  Final notification: 10 days
  Write: Joyce T. Adger, Sr. V.P., Wachovia Bank of North Carolina

Trustees: Frank Borden Hanes, Sr., Frank Borden Hanes, Jr., Gordon Hanes, R. Philip Hanes, Jr., Wachovia Bank of North Carolina, N.A.

Number of staff: None.

EIN: 566037589

2400
James G. Hanes Memorial Fund/Foundation

c/o NationsBank
One NCNB Plaza TO9-1
Charlotte 28255   (704) 386-8477

Trusts established in 1957 and 1972 in NC.

Foundation type: Independent

Financial data (yr. ended 10/31/90): Assets, $1,503,257 (M); gifts received, $180,307; expenditures, $526,297; qualifying distributions, $1,033,830, including $497,200 for 21 grants (high: $116,700; low: $1,000; average: $1,000-$25,000).

Fields of interest: Health, cultural programs, conservation, community development, arts.

Types of support: Annual campaigns, seed money, emergency funds, building funds, equipment, land acquisition, matching funds, special projects, research, publications, endowment funds.

Limitations: Giving primarily in NC and the Southeast. No grants to individuals, or for general operational or maintenance purposes.

Publications: Informational brochure (including application guidelines).

Application information: Application form required.

  Initial approach: Proposal
  Copies of proposal: 1
  Deadline(s): Mar. 15, June 15, Sept. 15, and Dec. 15
  Board meeting date(s): Jan., Apr., July, and Oct.
  Final notification: 10 days
  Write: Mgr., Foundations/Endowments

Distribution Committee: Eldridge C. Hanes, Chair.; Edward K. Crawford, James G. Hanes III, Douglas R. Lewis, Drewry Hanes Nostitz, Frank F. Willingham.

Trustee: Nationsbank.

Number of staff: None.

EIN: 566036987

2401
James J. and Angelia M. Harris Foundation

c/o Wachovia Bank and Trust Co., N.A.
P.O. Box 3099
Winston-Salem 27150   (704) 364-6046
Application address: P.O Box 220427, Charlotte, NC 28222

Established as a trust in 1984 in NC.

Donor(s): James J. Harris.‡

Foundation type: Independent

Financial data (yr. ended 11/30/91): Assets, $13,240,752 (M); gifts received, $321,146; expenditures, $818,824; qualifying distributions, $735,189, including $732,299 for 51 grants (high: $50,000; low: $500).

Purpose and activities: Primary areas of interest include higher and other education, health services and hospitals, social services, and youth.

Fields of interest: Education, higher education, adult education, education—early childhood, youth, social services, Protestant giving, health services, hospitals, arts.

Types of support: Scholarship funds, matching funds, capital campaigns, special projects.

Limitations: Giving limited to Clarke County, GA, and Mechlenburg County, NC (except where otherwise provided in trust agreement). No grants to individuals.

Publications: Application guidelines, informational brochure.

Application information: Application form not required.

  Initial approach: Letter (no more than 3 pages)
  Copies of proposal: 1
  Deadline(s): None
  Board meeting date(s): May and Nov.
  Write: Lillian Seaman

Officer and Managers:* William S. Lee III,* Chair.; Sara Harris Bissell, Cameron M. Harris, John W. Harris, James E.S. Hynes.

Number of staff: None.

EIN: 561465696

2402
Alex Hemby Foundation

4419 Sharon Rd.
Charlotte 28211

Established in 1950 in NC.

Donor(s): Hemby Investment Co.

Foundation type: Independent

Financial data (yr. ended 12/31/90): Assets, $7,884,972 (M); expenditures, $435,692; qualifying distributions, $390,325, including $390,325 for 36 grants (high: $125,000; low: $250).

Purpose and activities: Giving primarily for health associations and hospitals, especially a medical center's trauma unit; support also for higher education and Presbyterian churches and cultural programs.

Fields of interest: Health associations, hospitals, higher education, Protestant giving.

Limitations: Giving primarily in NC.

Application information:

  Initial approach: Letter
  Deadline(s): None

  Write: T.E. Hemby, Jr., Trustee

Trustees: T.E. Hemby, Jr., Beverly H. Leahy, Beverly H. Sheaff.

EIN: 566046767

2403
Lance Foundation

c/o NationsBank
One NationsBank Plaza, T09-1
Charlotte 28255
Application address: c/o Lance, Inc., P.O. Box 32368, Charlotte, NC 28232

Trust established in 1956 in NC.

Donor(s): Lance, Inc., and members of the Van Every family.

Foundation type: Company-sponsored

Financial data (yr. ended 06/30/91): Assets, $4,842,481 (M); gifts received, $54,782; expenditures, $547,906; qualifying distributions, $525,025, including $516,322 for grants (average: $2,000-$5,000).

Purpose and activities: Emphasis on higher education, medical research, and community services, particularly in an area where donor is engaged in business.

Fields of interest: Higher education, medical research, social services.

Types of support: General purposes, operating budgets.

Limitations: Giving primarily in NC, SC, and southeastern states. No grants to individuals, or for scholarships or fellowships; no loans.

Application information: Application form not required.

  Initial approach: Proposal or letter
  Copies of proposal: 1
  Deadline(s): None
  Board meeting date(s): As required
  Final notification: 2 to 3 months
  Write: Zean Jamison, Dir.

Directors: J.W. Disher, Thom B. Horack, Zean Jamison, J.S. Moore, Albert F. Sloan, Paul A. Stroup.

Trustee: NationsBank.

Number of staff: 1

EIN: 566039487

2404
Nickel Producers Environmental Research Association, Inc.

100 Capitola Dr., Suite 104
Durham 27713   (919) 544-8500

Foundation type: Independent

Financial data (yr. ended 12/31/90): Assets, $807,306 (M); gifts received, $1,108,766; expenditures, $1,363,931; qualifying distributions, $1,362,941, including $938,959 for grants.

Purpose and activities: Grants "for research investigations, studies, and surveys relating to occupational health and safety aspects of the nickel producing industries and related environmental matters."

Fields of interest: Environment, science and technology, health, safety.

Types of support: Research.

Limitations: Giving primarily in Europe, Canada, and the U.S.

Application information:

Initial approach: Proposal
Write: Donna J. Sivulka, Secy.
Officer: Donna J. Sivulka, Secy.
EIN: 133070077

2405
North Carolina Community Foundation
2626 Glenwood Ave., Suite 170
Raleigh 27608   (919) 781-2797
FAX: (919) 781-1618; Western Regional Office
address: 502-A Valley River Ave., P.O. Box
1094, Murphy, NC 28906; Tel.: (704) 837-4483

Established in 1985 in NC.
Foundation type: Community
Financial data (yr. ended 03/31/92): Assets,
$3,400,000 (M); gifts received, $1,350,000;
expenditures, $640,000; qualifying distributions,
$113,415, including $77,415 for 31 grants (high:
$40,000; low: $100; average: $100-$40,000) and
$36,000 for 4 in-kind gifts.
Fields of interest: Education, higher education,
health services, drug abuse, historic preservation,
environment, homeless, aged, youth,
religion—Christian.
Limitations: Giving limited to NC.
Publications: Annual report, informational
brochure.
Application information:
Board meeting date(s): June and Dec.
Write: Elizabeth C. Fentress, Exec. Dir.
Officers and Directors:* Lewis R. Holding,* Pres.;
Charles W. Gaddy,* V.P.; Victor E. Bell, Jr.,* 2nd
V.P.; William J. Cathecart,* Secy.; John A.
Williams, Jr.,* Treas.; Waverly F. Akins, John A.
Allison IV, R. Marks Arnold, and 20 additional
directors.
Number of staff: 5

2406
O'Herron Foundation, Inc.
6525 Morrison Blvd., Suite 500
Charlotte 28211

Established in 1962 in NC.
Foundation type: Independent
Financial data (yr. ended 12/31/90): Assets,
$3,428,969 (M); gifts received, $87,600;
expenditures, $186,950; qualifying distributions,
$170,800, including $170,800 for 22 grants
(high: $50,000; low: $200).
Fields of interest: Higher education, elementary
education, heart disease, social services,
religion—Christian.
Limitations: Giving limited to Mecklenburg and
Wake counties, NC, and Horry County, SC, and
Palm Beach County, FL. No grants to individuals.
Application information:
Initial approach: Proposal
Deadline(s): None
Write: Edward M. O'Herron, Pres.
Officers: Edward M. O'Herron, Jr., Pres. and
Treas.; Margaret B. O'Herron, V.P.; B. Irvin Boyle,
Secy.
EIN: 566061256

2407
James J. and Mamie R. Perkins Memorial Fund
c/o NationsBank, Trust Group
P.O. Box 1807
Greenville 27835-1807   (919) 758-4116
Application address: P.O. Box 7166, Greenville,
NC 27835

Established in 1989 in NC.
Foundation type: Independent
Financial data (yr. ended 09/30/91): Assets,
$8,211,158 (M); expenditures, $487,438;
qualifying distributions, $428,264, including
$406,197 for 34 grants (high: $44,528; low:
$1,000).
Fields of interest: Community development, civic
affairs, health, social services, youth, higher
education, secondary education, cultural
programs.
Limitations: Giving limited to Pitt County, NC. No
grants to individuals.
Application information: Application form
required.
Deadline(s): None
Write: James G. Sullivan, Dir.
Officers and Directors:* Louis W. Gaylord, Jr.,*
Chair.; Lawrence P. Houston, Jr., Secy.; James G.
Sullivan.
EIN: 566325764

2408
Polk County Community Foundation, Inc.
One Depot St.
Tryon 28782   (704) 859-5314

Incorporated in 1975 in NC.
Foundation type: Community
Financial data (yr. ended 12/31/90): Assets,
$2,897,047 (M); gifts received, $294,943;
expenditures, $138,774; qualifying distributions,
$114,037, including $114,037 for grants.
Fields of interest: Health, hospices, education,
medical education, community development,
general charitable giving.
Types of support: Scholarship funds, matching
funds, seed money.
Limitations: Giving limited to the Polk County,
NC, area.
Publications: Annual report, application
guidelines, newsletter, financial statement,
informational brochure (including application
guidelines).
Application information: Application form
required.
Copies of proposal: 5
Deadline(s): 3 weeks prior to end of each
quarter
Board meeting date(s): 2nd Thursday in Apr.,
June, Oct., and Dec.
Final notification: Immediately following board
meetings
Write: Paul E. Culberson, Exec. Dir.
Officers and Directors:* Joseph Claud,* Chair.;
Thomas Connell,* Vice-Chair.; Howard
McIntyre,* Pres.; Margaret Forbes,* Secy.; Mrs.
Joseph W. Stayman, Jr., Treas.; Paul E. Culberson,
Exec. Dir.; Mrs. Henry W. Welch, Admin. Dir.;
and 12 additional directors.
Number of staff: None.
EIN: 510168751

2409
Provident Benevolent Foundation
(Formerly Providence Charitable Foundation)
4500 Cameron Valley Pkwy., Suite 450
Charlotte 28211

Established in 1989 in NC.
Donor(s): Jesse J. Thompson.
Foundation type: Independent
Financial data (yr. ended 06/30/91): Assets,
$3,232,098 (M); gifts received, $2,962,000;
expenditures, $199,709; qualifying distributions,
$182,780, including $170,000 for 2 grants (high:
$100,000; low: $70,000).
Fields of interest: Higher education, hospitals,
social services.
Types of support: Operating budgets.
Limitations: Giving limited to NC, TN, KY, and
VA. No grants for endowments or deficit
financing.
Application information:
Initial approach: Letter not exceeding 2 pages
Deadline(s): Mar. 31, June 30, Sept. 30, and
Dec. 31
Write: Jesse J. Thompson, Pres.
Officers and Directors:* Jesse J. Thompson,*
Pres.; Sylvia M. Thompson,* V.P.; Robert S.
Marquis, Secy.; Jessie T. Derham, JoAnne T.
Manofsky, Mary Virginia Thompson.
EIN: 581881092

2410
Kate B. Reynolds Charitable Trust ▼
2422 Reynolda Rd.
Winston-Salem 27106-4606   (919) 723-1456

Established in 1947 in NC.
Donor(s): Kate B. Reynolds.‡
Foundation type: Independent
Financial data (yr. ended 08/31/91): Assets,
$289,949,928 (M); expenditures, $14,566,555;
qualifying distributions, $13,922,449, including
$13,536,677 for 141 grants (high: $336,694; low:
$2,800; average: $20,000-$200,000).
Purpose and activities: Seventy-five percent of net
income to be distributed for the health care of
those in need statewide: to increase the
availability of health services to underserved
groups, to address the problems of health services
in rural areas, to reduce the rate of the infant
mortality/morbidity, and to promote good health
and prevent illness. Twenty-five plercent for the
benefit of poor and needy residents of
Winston-Salem and Forsyth County: to support
organizations which provide for basic neeeds
(food, clothing, shelter), to support organizations
which provide services that improve the quality of
life for needy residents, and to fund efforts that
promote self-sufficiency.
Fields of interest: Health, health services, health
associations, AIDS, cancer, heart disease, rural
development, social services, welfare—indigent
individuals, alcoholism, drug abuse, family
services, family planning, nutrition, child welfare,
aged, homeless, hunger, housing.
Types of support: Operating budgets, continuing
support, annual campaigns, seed money,
matching funds, building funds, capital
campaigns, equipment, general purposes,
renovation projects, special projects.
Limitations: Giving limited to NC; social welfare
grants limited to Winston-Salem and Forsyth

County; health care giving, statewide. No grants to individuals, or for endowment funds or medical research; grants on a highly selective basis for construction of facilities or purchase of equipment.

Publications: Annual report (including application guidelines), informational brochure, application guidelines.

Application information: Applicant should contact the Exec. Dir., Deputy Exec. Dir., or Assoc. Dir. prior to submitting a written application. Application form required.

   Initial approach: Telephone to inquire about guidelines and to receive application
   Copies of proposal: 1
   Deadline(s): Jan. 1, May. 1, and Aug. 1 for Poor and Needy Division; Mar. 15 and Sept 15 for Health Care Division, or the 1st business day thereafter if the deadline falls on a weekend or holiday
   Board meeting date(s): Advisory committee for Poor and Needy Division meets in Feb., June, and Sept.; for Health Care grants in May and Nov.
   Final notification: Within 2 weeks after Advisory Board meeting
   Write: E. Ray Cope, Exec Dir., or W. Vance Frye, Dir., Health Care Division

Trustee: Wachovia Bank & Trust Co., N.A.
Number of staff: 3 full-time professional; 2 full-time support.
EIN: 566036515
Recent health grants:

2410-1 Alamance Coalition Against Drug Abuse, Burlington, NC, $160,000. For start-up expenses of full-time program to reduce alcohol and drug abuse in Alamance County. 1991.

2410-2 Alcohol/Drug Council of North Carolina, Durham, NC, $270,553. For development of local coalitions to address alcohol/drug abuse. 1991.

2410-3 Alzheimers Disease and Related Disorders Association, Triad North Carolina Chapter, Winston-Salem, NC, $37,840. To develop long-term funding plan for state's four ADRDA chapters. 1991.

2410-4 American Cancer Society, Forsyth County Unit, Winston-Salem, NC, $19,500. To assist with patients' medicines, supplies and transportation needs as well as staff expansion. 1991.

2410-5 Amos Cottage Rehabilitation Hospital, Winston-Salem, NC, $75,000. For medical treatment fees for financially needy Forsyth County residents. 1991.

2410-6 Autism Services, Raleigh, NC, $25,405. For staff expansion. 1991.

2410-7 Bethany House, Southern Pines, NC, $20,000. To renovate facility for female substance abusers. 1991.

2410-8 Blue Ridge Community Health Services, Hendersonville, NC, $484,100. For start-up expenses of program to improve obstetrical care in four-county region. 1991.

2410-9 Caldwell Community College and Technical Institute, Lenoir, NC, $140,875. To expand associate degree nursing program. 1991.

2410-10 Cancer Services, Winston-Salem, NC, $29,000. For direct client assistance funds and prescription medicine purchase. 1991.

2410-11 Charles A. Cannon, Jr. Memorial Hospital, Banner Elk, NC, $157,500. To initiate geriatric assessment and intervention program. 1991.

2410-12 Charlotte-Mecklenburg Schools, Charlotte, NC, $24,000. For operating expenses of project UPLIFT, program of prevention and early intervention directed at pregnant women in low-income housing developments. 1991.

2410-13 Child Guidance Center, Winston-Salem, NC, $25,000. For operating expenses related to clinic's termination of operations and transfer of programs to other community providers. 1991.

2410-14 Christian Love Ministries, Murphy, NC, $17,162. To renovate and purchase equipment for facility serving alcohol/drug abusers. 1991.

2410-15 Christian Rehabilitation Center, Charlotte, NC, $164,890. For start-up expenses of residential facility for female substance abusers. 1991.

2410-16 Chrysalis Counseling Center, New Bern, NC, $52,500. To expand mental health counseling service. 1991.

2410-17 Cleveland-Rutherford Kidney Association, Shelby, NC, $49,994. For facility renovation. 1991.

2410-18 Contact: Winston-Salem, Winston-Salem, NC, $15,000. For operating expenses, publication expenses and renovation costs. 1991.

2410-19 Crisis Control Ministry, Winston-Salem, NC, $151,509. For operating expenses of free pharmacy. 1991.

2410-20 Davie, County of, Mocksville, NC, $59,800. To develop additional information for determining appropriate system of health care for county. 1991.

2410-21 District Memorial Hospital of Southwestern North Carolina, Andrews, NC, $70,000. To expand and equip ambulatory care facility. 1991.

2410-22 Duplin General Hospital, Kenansville, NC, $250,000. To expand facilities used by home care operations. 1991.

2410-23 Durham County Advocates for the Mentally Ill, Durham, NC, $50,000. Toward purchase of larger facility to house day treatment program. 1991.

2410-24 Durham Regional Hospital Corporation, Durham, NC, $180,000. For start-up expenses of program of Durham Academy of Medicine, Dentistry and Pharmacy to reduce preventable disease among black population. 1991.

2410-25 East Carolina University, School of Medicine, Greenville, NC, $197,410. To develop regional child abuse evaluation program by Department of Pediatrics. 1991.

2410-26 East Carolina University, School of Nursing, Greenville, NC, $520,160. To establish mid-wifery training program. 1991.

2410-27 Forsyth County Health Department, Winston-Salem, NC, $20,000. To initiate AIDS prevention education program for Hispanics. 1991.

2410-28 Forsyth Technical College, Winston-Salem, NC, $200,000. For operating expenses of health technology center. 1991.

2410-29 Forsyth, County of, Winston-Salem, NC, $40,386. To develop definitive information about long-term care needs of county's elderly population. 1991.

2410-30 Friendship House, Winston-Salem, NC, $22,000. Toward operating expenses. 1991.

2410-31 Goshen Medical Center, Faison, NC, $17,286. To purchase vehicle for transporting low-income patients. 1991.

2410-32 Greensboro Urban Ministry, Greensboro, NC, $75,000. Toward construction and operating expenses of infirmary for homeless individuals. 1991.

2410-33 Hertford-Gates District Health Department, Winton, NC, $43,145. For operating expenses of adolescent pregnancy prevention program. 1991.

2410-34 Holy Angels, Belmont, NC, $100,000. Toward construction and operating expenses of three Intermediate Care Facilities for mentally retarded. 1991.

2410-35 Hope Haven, Charlotte, NC, $200,000. Toward construction of residential facility for male substance abusers. 1991.

2410-36 Hospital Hospitality House of Wilmington, Wilmington, NC, $25,000. For program for cancer outpatients. 1991.

2410-37 Hot Springs Health Program, Hot Springs, NC, $73,000. To renovate and expand ambulatory medical facility at Mars Hill. 1991.

2410-38 Human Service Alliance, Winston-Salem, NC, $100,000. Toward construction of facility for terminally ill. 1991.

2410-39 Hyde, County of, Swan Quarter, NC, $74,750. To transport low-income patients to regional health care providers. 1991.

2410-40 Isothermal Community College, Spindale, NC, $199,560. To establish associate degree programs in nursing at Cleveland Community College, Isothermal Community College and McDowell Technical Community College. 1991.

2410-41 Lutheran Family Services, Raleigh, NC, $70,000. To expand community group home program for mentally disabled individuals. 1991.

2410-42 Mecklenburg Adolescent Health Center, Charlotte, NC, $290,706. For start-up operating expenses. 1991.

2410-43 Mental Health Association, Winston-Salem, NC, $32,978. For start-up expenses of case management program for severely emotionally and behaviorally handicapped children. 1991.

2410-44 Mental Health Association in North Carolina, Raleigh, NC, $274,188. To expand community-based housing program. 1991.

2410-45 Metrolina Association for the Blind, Charlotte, NC, $69,945. To expand staff of low-vision clinic. 1991.

2410-46 Migrant Benevolent Association, Newton Grove, NC, $74,000. For purchase and operating expenses of two vehicles to transport migrant families to health care providers. 1991.

2410-47 MMAEs Inn Corporation, Charlotte, NC, $50,000. To furnish, equip and operate additional hospital hospitality house. 1991.

2410-48 Mountain Home Nursing Service, Hayesville, NC, $40,000. Toward construction of office and storage facility. 1991.

2410-49 National Society to Prevent Blindness, North Carolina Affiliate, Raleigh, NC, $95,526. For start-up expenses of program to provide vision screening for children enrolled in day care and kindergarten. 1991.

2410-50 Natural Science Center of Greensboro, Greensboro, NC, $99,900. For equipment purchase and start-up operating expenses of wellness center and nutrition education program. 1991.

2410-51 North Carolina Academy of Family Physicians Foundation, Raleigh, NC, $150,000. For operating expenses of North Carolina Student Rural Health Coalition. 1991.

2410-52 North Carolina Accreditation Commission for In-Home Aide Services, Raleigh, NC, $162,042. For staff expansion. 1991.

2410-53 North Carolina Baptist Hospital, Winston-Salem, NC, $269,807. To expand organ procurement program. 1991.

2410-54 North Carolina Department of Environment, Health and Natural Resources, Raleigh, NC, $98,167. For operating expenses of task force to develop health promotion/disease prevention agenda for North Carolina. 1991.

2410-55 North Carolina Department of Environment, Health and Natural Resources, Division of Adult Health, Raleigh, NC, $173,369. To develop information to assist in reducing mortality/morbidity from cervical cancer. 1991.

2410-56 North Carolina Department of Environment, Health and Natural Resources, Division of Maternal and Child Health, Raleigh, NC, $2,862,706. To establish lay health advisors for Baby Love program. 1991.

2410-57 North Carolina Department of Environment, Health and Natural Resources, Division of Maternal and Child Health, Raleigh, NC, $148,464. To provide specialized nutrition services for developmentally disabled children through Rocky Mount Developmental Evaluation Center. 1991.

2410-58 North Carolina Foundation for Alternative Health Programs, Raleigh, NC, $46,000. To develop appropriate lay health advisor model to be used in conjunction with state's Baby Love program. 1991.

2410-59 North Carolina High School Athletic Association, Chapel Hill, NC, $75,000. For start-up expenses of substance abuse prevention program. 1991.

2410-60 North Carolina Hospital Foundation, Raleigh, NC, $20,450. For project to determine feasibility of rural hospitals providing inpatient-psychiatric care. 1991.

2410-61 North Carolina Institute of Medicine, Durham, NC, $423,877. To address health access in state for uninsured and underinsured individuals. 1991.

2410-62 North Carolina Medical Society Foundation, Raleigh, NC, $740,838. To determine whether back-up staff from family residency programs will reduce burn-out of physicians practicing in isolated areas. 1991.

2410-63 Northampton County Schools, Jackson, NC, $82,546. To continue school-based adolescent health program. 1991.

2410-64 Our Community Hospital, Scotland Neck, NC, $138,500. For facility modification. 1991.

2410-65 Pungo District Hospital Corporation, Belhaven, NC, $100,000. To purchase computerized tomography scanner. 1991.

2410-66 Relatives, The, Charlotte, NC, $120,000. For start-up expenses of telephone hotline for teenagers. 1991.

2410-67 REMMSCO, Reidsville, NC, $40,000. To expand half-way facility for recovering alcoholic men. 1991.

2410-68 Reynolds Health Center, Winston-Salem, NC, $149,280. To add physician extender to Obstetrics Clinic. 1991.

2410-69 Reynolds Health Center, Winston-Salem, NC, $143,194. To establish computer-supported patient information and management system. 1991.

2410-70 Robersonville Community Hospital, Robersonville, NC, $43,776. To establish primary outpatient care system for community and Oak City. 1991.

2410-71 Robeson Health Care Corporation, Pembroke, NC, $184,744. For start-up expenses of geriatric preventive health care program. 1991.

2410-72 Saint Marks Center, Charlotte, NC, $50,000. Toward construction expenses of two Intermediate Care Facilities for Mentally Retarded Adults. 1991.

2410-73 Senior Services, Winston-Salem, NC, $110,085. To provide Meals-on-Wheels and HomeCare services for clients unable to pay fees. 1991.

2410-74 Serenity House, Concord, NC, $25,000. To expand facility serving male substance abusers. 1991.

2410-75 Services for Older Adults of Rowan County, Salisbury, NC, $45,000. For operating expenses of two adult day care/health centers. 1991.

2410-76 University of North Carolina, School of Medicine, Chapel Hill, NC, $328,469. For Department of Community Pediatrics to establish computer network with local support groups of families with developmentally disabled children. 1991.

2410-77 University of North Carolina, School of Medicine, Chapel Hill, NC, $224,546. For Area Health Education Center to establish education and recruitment program for rural and minority students into health careers. 1991.

2410-78 University of North Carolina, School of Medicine, Chapel Hill, NC, $40,360. For Departments of Psychiatry, Obstetrics/Gynecology and Community Pediatrics to conduct project for identifying and referring sexually abused adolescents in public health family planning clinics. 1991.

2410-79 University of North Carolina, School of Medicine, Chapel Hill, NC, $23,000. For Department of Pathology to establish digitized image/audio communications system with Area Health Education Center at Charlotte Memorial Hospital. 1991.

2410-80 Western North Carolina AIDS Project, Asheville, NC, $21,400. For expenses of support services coordinator. 1991.

2410-81 Wilkes Regional Medical Center, North Wilkesboro, NC, $354,357. For start-up expenses of comprehensive program to reduce infant mortality in Wilkes County. 1991.

2410-82 Winston-Salem State University, Winston-Salem, NC, $695,950. To establish baccalaureate program in physical therapy. 1991.

2411

Z. Smith Reynolds Foundation, Inc. ▼
101 Reynolda Village
Winston-Salem 27106-5199   (919) 725-7541
FAX: (919) 725-6069

Incorporated in 1936 in NC.
Donor(s): Nancy S. Reynolds,‡ Mary Reynolds Babcock,‡ Richard J. Reynolds, Jr.,‡ William N. Reynolds.‡
Foundation type: Independent
Financial data (yr. ended 12/31/91): Assets, $245,536,253 (M); gifts received, $11,028,863; expenditures, $11,954,660; qualifying distributions, $11,954,660, including $10,972,443 for 303 grants (high: $1,000,000; low: $1,000; average: $15,000-$35,000) and $87,000 for 9 grants to individuals (high: $12,000; low: $5,000).
Purpose and activities: Giving primarily for primary and secondary education, community and economic development, social services, child welfare and development, citizenship and leadership development, public policy and affairs, conservation of the environment, improvement of the criminal justice system, and minority and women's issues.
Fields of interest: Education, education—early childhood, elementary education, secondary education, education—minorities, literacy, vocational education, community development, citizenship, rural development, social services, disadvantaged, welfare, welfare—indigent individuals, child development, delinquency, youth, child welfare, housing, leadership development, public policy, law and justice, crime and law enforcement, public affairs, civil rights, human rights, environment, conservation, minorities, race relations, Native Americans, women.
Types of support: Operating budgets, continuing support, seed money, matching funds, special projects, conferences and seminars, general purposes, technical assistance.
Limitations: Giving limited to NC. No grants to individuals (except for Nancy Susan Reynolds Awards for community leadership and sabbatical program), or for research; no loans or program-related investments.
Publications: Annual report (including application guidelines), occasional report.
Application information: Application form required.
    Initial approach: Letter or telephone
    Copies of proposal: 1
    Deadline(s): For grants, Feb. 1 and Aug. 1; for Sabbatical Program, Dec. 1; for Nancy Susan Reynolds Awards, June 1
    Board meeting date(s): 3rd Friday in May and Nov.
    Final notification: 4 months after deadline
    Write: Thomas W. Lambeth, Exec. Dir.
Officers and Trustees:* Mary Mountcastle, Pres.; Zachary T. Smith,* V.P.; Thomas W. Lambeth, Secy. and Exec. Dir.; Joseph G. Gordon,* Treas.; Smith W. Bagley,* Josephine D. Clement, Daniel G. Clodfelter, Hubert Humphrey, Katharine B. Mountcastle, Stephen L. Neal, Jane S. Patterson, Sherwood H. Smith, Jr., Lloyd P. Tate, Jr.
Number of staff: 3 full-time professional; 1 part-time professional; 4 full-time support; 1 part-time support.
EIN: 586038145

Recent health grants:

2411-1 Alice Aycock Poe Center for Health Education, Raleigh, NC, $30,000. To provide information and inducement for children to choose healthy lifestyles and learn how to take care of their bodies. 1990.

2411-2 Blue Ridge Community Health Services, Hendersonville, NC, $15,000. For development of AIDS education programs for prison population, blue-collar workers and teens. 1990.

2411-3 Child Guidance Center, Winston-Salem, NC, $20,000. For Parent Skills Training Program to assist families of children with severe emotional problems through group discussions, problem-solving, providing emotional support to involved parents. 1990.

2411-4 Cleveland Psychosocial Services, Shelby, NC, $20,000. For expansion of Adventure House, rehabilitation day program for persons with severe and persistent mental illness. 1990.

2411-5 Creative Health Ministry, Pembroke, NC, $20,000. To improve well-being of Native Americans in Robeson County by providing counseling, educational and advocacy services, holding classes on parenting skills and child development; and production of Directory of Services for Indians in Robeson County. 1990.

2411-6 Durham County Advocates for the Mentally Ill, Durham, NC, $15,000. For housing development project to assist mentally ill people gain and retain decent, affordable housing. 1990.

2411-7 Forsyth County Health Department, Winston-Salem, NC, $15,000. For ManTalk, targeted male adolescent pregnancy prevention program. 1990.

2411-8 Guilford College, Community Justice Resource Center, Greensboro, NC, $20,000. For FIRST Project, effort to create residential facility in Forsyth County to address root causes within individuals of both drug abuse and criminal behavior. 1990.

2411-9 Helpline of Carteret County, Moorehead City, NC, $15,000. For staff and office support for 24-hour crisis line/information and referral service for victims of rape and domestic violence. 1990.

2411-10 Hope Harbor Home, Supply, NC, $10,000. For substance abuse counselor/transition counselor for clients of shelter for abused women and children. 1990.

2411-11 Lincoln Community Health Center, Durham, NC, $50,000. For Reaching Adolescent Program (RAP), outreach program to inner city middle schools that targets at-risk minority youth. 1990.

2411-12 NAACP Special Contribution Fund, Greensboro, NC, $50,000. For conference entitled Black Males in Jeopardy and to establish local community coalitions to combat problems through after-school peer tutorials, health education, mentor programs, African-American history and cultural education. 1990.

2411-13 National Toxics Campaign Fund, Boston, MA, $20,000. For toxics campaign in North Carolina, help in developing and advancing statewide policies for waste reduction and toxics use reduction and to involve North Carolina residents in national issue campaigns around incineration, military toxics and safe foods. 1990.

2411-14 North Carolina Outward Bound School, Morganton, NC, $25,000. For development of Survivors of Violence recovery program for women who have endured sexual assault, incest and domestic violence. 1990.

2411-15 North Carolina Student Rural Health Coalition, Durham, NC, $20,000. For African-American Occupational Safety and Health Project. 1990.

2411-16 Planned Parenthood of Greater Raleigh, Raleigh, NC, $25,000. To establish self-sustaining health care in Wilmington. 1990.

2411-17 Save the Children Federation, Asheville, NC, $60,000. For Mothers Too!, project to address needs of pregnant and lactating women. 1990.

2412
The Florence Rogers Charitable Trust
P.O. Box 36006
Fayetteville 28303   (919) 484-2033

Trust established in 1961 in NC.
Donor(s): Florence L. Rogers.‡
Foundation type: Independent
Financial data (yr. ended 03/31/91): Assets, $4,020,154 (M); expenditures, $241,151; qualifying distributions, $192,174, including $141,300 for 64 grants (high: $15,000; low: $250; average: $2,975).
Purpose and activities: Support for music and the arts, education, recreation, hunger programs, child welfare, nursing and hospices, wildlife, and the general quality of life in the area. Preference is given to seed money for new ideas.
Fields of interest: Music, arts, theater, education, recreation, hunger, child welfare, nursing, hospices, wildlife.
Types of support: Conferences and seminars, emergency funds, matching funds, operating budgets, publications, renovation projects, research, seed money, special projects.
Limitations: Giving primarily in Fayetteville, Cumberland County, and southeastern NC. No grants to individuals, or for building or endowment funds, scholarships, or fellowships; no loans.
Publications: Informational brochure (including application guidelines).
Application information: Application form not required.
   Initial approach: Letter or telephone
   Copies of proposal: 1
   Deadline(s): Feb. 28, Apr. 30, July 31, Oct. 31, and Dec. 31
   Board meeting date(s): Monthly
   Final notification: By the end of the following month
   Write: Nolan P. Clark, Trustee
Trustees: Nolan P. Clark, John C. Tally.
Number of staff: 1 full-time professional; 1 part-time professional; 2 part-time support.
EIN: 566074515

2413
Salisbury Community Foundation, Inc.
P.O. Box 2189
Salisbury 28145-2189   (704) 633-7800

Incorporated in 1944 in NC.
Foundation type: Community
Financial data (yr. ended 12/31/91): Assets, $15,997,346 (M); gifts received, $5,195,480; expenditures, $9,293,596; qualifying distributions, $9,288,573, including $9,288,573 for 425 grants (high: $1,000,000; low: $100; average: $3,518).
Purpose and activities: Grants primarily for capital projects in Rowan County; some seed-money grants for special projects. Primary areas of interest include education and hospital building funds, the environment, public administration, and religion.
Fields of interest: Education, education—building funds, environment, arts, public administration, hospitals—building funds, hospices, religion, social services.
Types of support: Building funds, special projects, seed money.
Limitations: Giving primarily in NC. No grants to individuals, or for endowment funds or operating budgets.
Publications: Annual report, financial statement.
Application information: Application form required.
   Initial approach: Proposal
   Copies of proposal: 1
   Deadline(s): 3 weeks before board meetings
   Board meeting date(s): Feb., May, Aug., and Nov.
   Write: Fred Rodenbeck, Treas.
Officers and Trustees:* James G. Whitton,* Pres.; W.A. Sherrill,* Secy.; Fred Rodenbeck, Treas.; Irvin Oestreicher, Patsy Rendelman, Fred J. Stanback, Jr., W.C. Stanback.
EIN: 560772117

2414
The General William A. Smith Trust, Item XXII
c/o United Carolina Bank, Trust Dept.
212 South Tryon St.
Charlotte 28200   (704) 372-9938

Trust established in 1940 in NC.
Donor(s): Gen. William A. Smith.
Foundation type: Independent
Financial data (yr. ended 12/31/91): Assets, $3,931,033 (M); expenditures, $264,858; qualifying distributions, $237,754, including $235,254 for 17 grants (high: $55,500; low: $100).
Fields of interest: Education, higher education, Protestant giving, hospitals, medical research.
Types of support: Annual campaigns, building funds, capital campaigns, continuing support, emergency funds, endowment funds, equipment, general purposes, professorships, renovation projects, scholarship funds, special projects.
Limitations: Giving primarily in Anson County, NC. No grants to individuals.
Application information: Application form not required.
   Deadline(s): Dec. 31
Administrative Trustees: Bennett M. Edwards, Jr., Joe Gaddy, James A. Hardison, Jr.
Trustee Bank: United Carolina Bank.
EIN: 566042630

2415
Adele M. Thomas Trust
2214 Carol Woods
Chapel Hill 27514   (919) 942-8198

Established in 1961 in IN.
Donor(s): Claude A. Thomas,‡ Adele M. Thomas.
Foundation type: Independent
Financial data (yr. ended 12/31/90): Assets,
$1,703,053 (M); expenditures, $212,272;
qualifying distributions, $212,272, including
$206,836 for 38 grants (high: $136,000; low:
$25; average: $25-$11,140).
Purpose and activities: Giving for social services,
including child welfare and family planning and
services; support also for cultural programs,
Christian religious organizations, and citizenship.
Fields of interest: Social services, family planning,
family services, child welfare, cultural programs,
religion—Christian, citizenship.
Types of support: Annual campaigns, continuing
support, general purposes.
Limitations: Giving primarily in Orange County,
NC, Marion County, IN, and Washington, DC.
Application information: Application form not
required.
  Deadline(s): None
  Board meeting date(s): On call
  Write: Adele M. Thomas, Trustee
Trustees: Adele M. Thomas, John V. Thomas.
Number of staff: None.
EIN: 356042836

2416
Thomasville Furniture Industries Foundation
c/o Wachovia Bank & Trust Co., N.A.
P.O. Box 3099
Winston-Salem 27150   (919) 770-6222
Application address: c/o Carlyle A. Nance, Jr.,
V.P., Personnel, Thomasville Furniture Industries
Inc., Thomasville, NC 27360

Trust established in 1960 in NC.
Donor(s): Thomasville Furniture Industries, Inc.
Foundation type: Company-sponsored
Financial data (yr. ended 12/31/90): Assets,
$3,248,376 (M); expenditures, $298,888;
qualifying distributions, $271,369, including
$269,312 for 106 grants (high: $25,000; low:
$10; average: $1,500-$2,000).
Purpose and activities: Grants largely for higher
and secondary education, including scholarships
for children of employees of Thomasville
Furniture Industries, and for hospitals, mainly in
areas of company operations.
Fields of interest: Higher education, secondary
education, hospitals.
Types of support: Employee-related scholarships,
annual campaigns.
Limitations: Giving primarily in NC.
Application information:
  Initial approach: Letter
  Deadline(s): None
  Write: Susan Wiles
Administrative Committee: Frederick B. Starr,
Chair.; Carlyle A. Nance, Jr., Secy.; Frank B. Burr,
Charles G. O'Brien.
Trustee: Wachovia Bank & Trust Co., N.A.
EIN: 566047870

2417
Greater Triangle Community Foundation
100 Park Offices, Suite 209
P.O. Box 12834
Research Triangle Park 27709   (919) 549-9840

Incorporated in 1983 in NC.
Foundation type: Community
Financial data (yr. ended 06/30/91): Assets,
$7,706,710 (M); gifts received, $1,442,172;
expenditures, $836,054; qualifying distributions,
$605,432, including $519,136 for grants (high:
$25,000; low: $100), $67,496 for grants to
individuals (high: $5,000; low: $100), $17,000
for loans and $1,800 for in-kind gifts.
Fields of interest: Education, arts, conservation,
health, social services.
Types of support: Scholarship funds, seed money,
special projects.
Limitations: Giving limited to Durham, Orange,
and Wake counties, NC. No grants for annual
campaigns, continuing support, or operating
budgets.
Publications: Annual report, newsletter,
application guidelines.
Application information: Application form
required.
  Copies of proposal: 4
  Deadline(s): Feb. 1 and Aug. 1
  Board meeting date(s): Apr. and Dec.
  Final notification: June 1 and Dec. 1
  Write: Linda Ironside, Assoc. Dir.
Officers and Directors:* Frank A. Daniels, Jr.,*
Pres.; Arthur W. Clark,* V.P.; Jane "Coolie"
Monroe,* Secy.; Carl G. Ward,* Treas.; Richard
McEnally,* Finance Chair.; Mary L. Hill,* Distrib.
Chair.; and 23 additional directors.
Number of staff: 2 full-time professional; 1
part-time professional; 1 full-time support.
EIN: 561380796
Recent health grants:
2417-1 Threshold, Durham, NC, $17,000. 1991.

2418
United Dominion Industries Limited Corporate Giving Program
(Formerly AMCA International Corporate Giving
Program)
301 S. College St.
2300 One First Union Ctr.
Charlotte 28202   (704) 347-6875

Purpose and activities: Giving for science and
education including, higher, elementary, and
continuing education.
Fields of interest: Education, higher education,
science and technology, adult education,
elementary education, hospitals.
Types of support: General purposes.
Limitations: Giving primarily in headquarters city
area.
Publications: Corporate report.
Application information: Applications not
accepted.
  Write: Robert L. Shaffer, Chair., Donations
  Comm.
Number of staff: None.

2419
Philip L. Van Every Foundation ▼
c/o NationsBank
One NCNB Plaza, T09-1
Charlotte 28255
Application address: c/o Lance, Inc., P.O. Box
32368, Charlotte, NC 28232; Tel.: (704)
554-1421

Established in 1961 in NC.
Donor(s): Philip Van Every.
Foundation type: Independent
Financial data (yr. ended 12/31/90): Assets,
$22,022,740 (M); expenditures, $1,540,548;
qualifying distributions, $1,466,039, including
$1,445,150 for 102 grants (high: $250,000; low:
$750; average: $5,000-$10,000).
Purpose and activities: Giving for social services,
health and medical research, and education,
especially higher education.
Fields of interest: Social services, health,
education, higher education, medical research.
Limitations: Giving primarily in NC and SC.
Application information: Application form not
required.
  Initial approach: Letter or proposal
  Deadline(s): None
  Final notification: Immediately after board
  meeting
  Write: Zeann Jamison, Pres.
Officer and Administrators: Zean Jamison, Exec.
Dir.; J.W. Disher, T.B. Horack, J.S. Moore, Albert
F. Sloan, Paul A. Stroup.
Trustee: NationsBank.
Number of staff: 1
EIN: 566039337

2420
Volvo GM Heavy Truck Corporate Giving Program
P.O. Box 26115
Greensboro 27402-6115   (919) 279-2000

Purpose and activities: Support for community
development, ecology, education, health, and arts
and culture.
Fields of interest: Civic affairs, community
development, community funds, ecology,
education, education—building funds, fine arts,
general charitable giving, health,
hospitals—building funds, libraries, literacy,
mental health, museums, performing arts, theater.
Types of support: Annual campaigns, building
funds, emergency funds, general purposes.
Limitations: Giving primarily in NC, OH, UT, and
VA. No support for religious or governmental
agencies. No grants to individuals.
Application information: Application form not
required.Applications not accepted.
  Initial approach: Letter
  Write: Maureen F. Hartigan, Dir., Communs.
Administrators: Thage Berggren, Pres.; Rudolph
Spik, Mgr., Public Rels.
Number of staff: 1 part-time support.

2421
The Wachovia Foundation Inc. ▼
c/o Wachovia Bank & Trust Co., N.A.
P.O. Box 3099
Winston-Salem 27150-0001

Incorporated in 1982 in NC.
Donor(s): Wachovia Bank & Trust Co., N.A.
Foundation type: Company-sponsored
Financial data (yr. ended 12/31/90): Assets, $0
(M); gifts received, $2,530,000; expenditures,
$1,221,014; qualifying distributions, $1,217,933,
including $1,217,909 for grants (average:
$2,000-$20,000).
Purpose and activities: Emphasis on higher
education and community projects, including
community funds.
Fields of interest: Higher education, education,
libraries, community funds, community
development, crime and law enforcement, social
services, child welfare, recreation, humanities,
historic preservation, media and
communications, performing arts, ecology,
handicapped, health, drug abuse, hospitals.
Types of support: Building funds, capital
campaigns, special projects, endowment funds,
research, operating budgets, annual campaigns,
renovation projects.
Limitations: Giving primarily in NC. No grants to
individuals.
Application information:
  Initial approach: Contact local bank office
  Deadline(s): None
  Board meeting date(s): Monthly
  Write: L.M. Baker, Jr., Pres. and C.E.O.,
    Wachovia Bank & Trust Co., N.A.
Officers: John G. Medlin, Jr., Pres.; L.M. Baker, Jr.,
V.P.; Thomas A. Bennett, V.P.; Kenneth W.
McAllister, Secy.; Graham P. Dozier, Treas.
Number of staff: None.
EIN: 581485946

2422
Weaver Foundation, Inc.
324 West Wendover, Suite 300
Greensboro 27408   (919) 275-9600
Application address: P.O. Box 26040,
Greensboro, NC 27420-6040

Incorporated in 1967 in NC.
Donor(s): W.H. Weaver,‡ E.H. Weaver.
Foundation type: Independent
Financial data (yr. ended 12/31/90): Assets,
$11,653,860 (M); gifts received, $368,724;
expenditures, $500,127; qualifying distributions,
$447,745, including $446,968 for 48 grants
(high: $217,000; low: $50).
Purpose and activities: Giving primarily for arts
and culture and higher education; support also
for social services, low-income housing,
Protestant ministries, and health.
Fields of interest: Arts, higher education,
education—early childhood, social services,
housing, homeless, Protestant giving, health.
Limitations: Giving primarily in NC. No grants to
individuals.
Application information: Application form not
required.
  Initial approach: Proposal
  Copies of proposal: 1
  Deadline(s): None
  Board meeting date(s): Varies

  Write: Robert G. Kelley, V.P.
Officers and Trustees:* H.M. Weaver,* Pres. and
Chair.; Robert G. Kelley,* V.P. and Secy.-Treas.;
Ashley W. Hodges, Edith H. Weaver, Michele D.
Weaver.
Number of staff: None.
EIN: 566093527

2423
The Community Foundation of Western North Carolina, Inc.
14 College St.
Asheville 28802   (704) 254-4960
Mailing address: P.O. Box 1888, Asheville, NC
28802

Incorporated in 1978 in NC as the Community
Foundation of Greater Asheville, Inc.
Foundation type: Community
Financial data (yr. ended 06/30/91): Assets,
$9,307,083 (M); gifts received, $4,518,591;
expenditures, $1,575,883; qualifying
distributions, $1,331,958, including $1,331,958
for grants (high: $105,000; low: $50; average:
$50-$105,000).
Fields of interest: Social services, youth, arts,
education, environment, health.
Types of support: Matching funds, seed money,
scholarship funds, technical assistance, special
projects.
Limitations: Giving limited to western NC. No
support for religious organizations or sectarian
purposes. No grants to individuals, or for capital
campaigns or endowment funds.
Publications: Annual report, newsletter,
application guidelines, informational brochure.
Application information: Application form
required.
  Initial approach: Telephone or letter
  Copies of proposal: 7
  Deadline(s): Nov. 30
  Board meeting date(s): Quarterly, last
    Wednesday in Jan., Apr., July, and Oct.
  Final notification: May 31
  Write: Pat Smith, Exec. Dir.
Officers and Directors:* Mimi Cecil,* Chair.;
Thomas C. Arnold,* Vice-Chair.; Susan Kosma,*
Secy.; Jerry L. Cole,* Treas.; Pat Smith, Exec. Dir.;
and 22 additional directors.
Number of staff: 1 full-time professional; 1
part-time professional; 1 full-time support.
EIN: 561223384

2424
The Winston-Salem Foundation ▼
310 West Fourth St., Suite 229
Winston-Salem 27101   (919) 725-2382

Established in 1919 in NC by declaration of trust.
Foundation type: Community
Financial data (yr. ended 12/31/90): Assets,
$56,919,696 (M); gifts received, $2,804,028;
expenditures, $6,148,188; qualifying
distributions, $6,051,994, including $5,489,994
for grants (high: $622,358; low: $25; average:
$1,000-$12,000), $175,000 for 128 grants to
individuals and $387,000 for 165 loans to
individuals.
Purpose and activities: Student aid primarily to
bona fide residents of Forsyth County, NC;
support also for nonprofit organizations of all

types, especially educational, social service and
health programs, the arts, and civic affairs.
Fields of interest: Education, social services,
youth, health, aged, community development,
drug abuse, arts, civic affairs.
Types of support: Seed money, emergency funds,
student aid, special projects, matching funds,
general purposes, student loans, fellowships,
research, continuing support.
Limitations: Giving primarily in the greater
Forsyth County, NC, area; some support for
northwest NC. No grants for annual campaigns,
land acquisition, publications, or conferences.
Publications: Annual report, application
guidelines, newsletter, grants list, informational
brochure (including application guidelines).
Application information: Application form
required for student aid or student loans and
includes $20 application fee.
  Initial approach: Telephone
  Copies of proposal: 1
  Deadline(s): Jan. 1, Apr. 1, July 1, and Oct. 1
  Board meeting date(s): Mar., June, Sept., and
    Dec.
  Final notification: 1 month
  Write: Henry M. Carter, Jr., Exec. Dir.
Officer: Henry M. Carter, Jr., Exec. Dir.
Foundation Committee: Barbara K. Phillips,
Chair.; Graham F. Bennett, Herbert Brenner,
Victor I. Flow, Jr., Robert C. Gulledge, Roberta W.
Irwin, Joseph F. Neely, C. Edward Pleasants, Jr., A.
Tab Williams III.
Trustees: Branch Banking & Trust Co., Central
Carolina Bank & Trust Co., First Citizens Bank &
Trust Co., First Union National Bank,
NationsBank, Southern National Bank, Wachovia
Bank & Trust Co., N.A.
Number of staff: 5 full-time professional; 1
part-time professional; 4 full-time support.
EIN: 566037615
Recent health grants:
2424-1 Addiction Recovery Care Association,
Winston-Salem, NC, $21,200. To continue
funding for second year position of
Development Director and for materials to
supplement the position. 1991.
2424-2 Boys Club of Winston-Salem, Salvation
Army, Winston-Salem, NC, $40,000. To
provide continuing support for Smart Moves
programming in outreach sites. 1991.
2424-3 Cancer Services, Winston-Salem, NC,
$41,300. To initiate new position of Volunteer
Coordinator and to add to emergency
assistance funds. 1991.
2424-4 Forsyth County Health Department,
Winston-Salem, NC, $34,400. To develop and
implement community-based health education
project targeting older adults in low-income
housing communities. 1991.
2424-5 Forsyth County Health Department,
Winston-Salem, NC, $13,000. To continue for
third year, start-up funding for drug prevention
outreach programming targeting high-risk
youth. 1991.
2424-6 Forsyth Initiative for Residential Self-Help
Treatment, Winston-Salem, NC, $50,000. To
help initiate alternative to incarceration for
hard core offenders and substance abusers.
1991.
2424-7 Forsyth Technical College,
Winston-Salem, NC, $30,000. To help fund
operations of new Health Technologies Center
by hiring faculty. 1991.

2424-8 Girls Club of Winston-Salem, Salvation Army, Winston-Salem, NC, $13,000. For expansion of Friendly PEERsuasion drug education and prevention program. 1991.

2424-9 Mental Health Association, Winston-Salem, NC, $33,000. To help initiate Childrens Advocacy Group to provide case management for emotionally and behaviorally handicapped children and their parents. 1991.

2424-10 Nature Science Center, Winston-Salem, NC, $17,025. To fund permanent exhibit of effects of drug use. 1991.

2424-11 STEP ONE, Winston Salem, NC, $66,000. For prevention and education training programs for churches and medical, human service professionals and educators. 1991.

2424-12 STEP ONE, Winston-Salem, NC, $36,100. To continue Parenting Training Program for second year. 1991.

2424-13 STEP ONE, Winston-Salem, NC, $25,000. To continue, for third year, start-up support for Parents for Drug Free Youth. Grant shared with Safe Initiative. 1991.

2424-14 YMCA of High Point, High Point, NC, $20,000. To provide drug prevention programming to high risk teens. 1991.

2425
Margaret C. Woodson Foundation, Inc.
P.O. Box 829
Salisbury 28145 (704) 633-5000

Incorporated in 1954 in NC.
Donor(s): Margaret C. Woodson.‡
Foundation type: Independent
Financial data (yr. ended 12/31/91): Assets, $364,881 (M); gifts received, $415,084; expenditures, $453,142; qualifying distributions, $437,942, including $421,000 for 31 grants (high: $70,000; low: $1,000).
Fields of interest: Higher education, cultural programs, child welfare, hospitals, social services.
Limitations: Giving primarily in Davie and Rowan counties, NC. No grants for research.
Application information: Application form not required.
 Deadline(s): None
 Write: James L. Woodson, Pres.
Officers and Directors:* James L. Woodson,* Pres.; Esther C. Shay,* V.P.; Roy C. Hoffner, Secy.; Charles Cunningham,* Treas.; Paul I. Bernhardt, Beulah Hillard, Mary Holt W. Woodson, Paul B. Woodson, Jr.
Trustee: U.S. Trust Co. of New York.
EIN: 566064938

NORTH DAKOTA

2426
Fargo-Moorhead Area Foundation
609-1/2 First Ave. North, No. 205
Fargo 58102   (701) 234-0756

Established in 1960 in ND.
Foundation type: Community
Financial data (yr. ended 12/31/91): Assets,
$6,729,162 (L); gifts received, $947,584;
expenditures, $571,887; qualifying distributions,
$352,706 for 142 grants
(high: $20,520; low: $10; average:
$500-$10,000).
Fields of interest: Arts, civic affairs, social
services, education, health, youth.
Types of support: Seed money, emergency funds,
equipment, scholarship funds, renovation
projects, capital campaigns, conferences and
seminars, consulting services, exchange
programs, general purposes, operating budgets,
publications, special projects, technical
assistance, continuing support, matching funds.
Limitations: Giving primarily in the counties of
Cass, ND, and Clay, MN. No grants to
individuals, or for deficit financing, land
acquisition, or medical research; no loans.
Publications: Program policy statement,
application guidelines, informational brochure,
annual report.
Application information: Application form
required.
   Initial approach: Letter or telephone
   Copies of proposal: 10
   Deadline(s): Dec. 31
   Board meeting date(s): Quarterly
   Final notification: May 30
   Write: Susan M. Hunke, Exec. Dir.
Officer: Jim Swedback, Pres.
Distribution Committee and Directors: Esther
Allen, Elizabeth Bushell, Betsy Dalrymple, Mary
Davies, Robert Dawson, Annelee Donnelly,
Edward Ellenson, J. Phillip Johnson, William
Schlossman, Jr.
Trustee Banks: American Bank & Trust Co., First
Interstate Bank, First Trust Co. of North Dakota,
N.A., Norwest Capital Bank North Dakota, N.A.
Number of staff: 1 full-time professional; 1
part-time professional; 1 full-time support.
EIN: 456010377

2427
Tom & Frances Leach Foundation, Inc.
P.O. Box 1136
Bismarck 58502   (701) 255-0479

Established in 1955 in ND.
Donor(s): Thomas W. Leach,‡ Frances V. Leach.‡
Foundation type: Independent
Financial data (yr. ended 12/31/91): Assets,
$7,201,032 (M); expenditures, $445,007;
qualifying distributions, $270,463, including
$255,600 for 44 grants (high: $50,000; low:
$1,000; average: $1,000-$10,000).
Fields of interest: Higher education, education,
social services, youth, child development,
hospitals, health services, cultural programs,
performing arts, arts, general charitable giving.
Types of support: Scholarship funds, capital
campaigns, continuing support, endowment
funds, general purposes, operating budgets,
special projects.
Limitations: Giving primarily in ND, particularly
in Bismarck and Mandan, and in Tulsa, OK.
Publications: Annual report, informational
brochure, application guidelines.
Application information: Application form
required.
   Initial approach: Letter
   Copies of proposal: 1
   Deadline(s): Sept. 15
   Board meeting date(s): Nov.
   Final notification: Dec.
   Write: Clement C. Weber, Exec. Dir.
Officers and Directors:* Ernest R. Fleck,* Pres.;
James P. Wachter,* V.P.; Russell R. Mather,*
Secy.-Treas.; Clement C. Weber, Exec. Dir.; Frank
J. Bavendick, Robert P. Hendrickson, Gilbert N.
Olson, Paul D. Schliesman.
Number of staff: 1 full-time professional; 1
full-time support.
EIN: 456012703

2428
Myra Foundation
P.O. Box 1536
Grand Forks 58206-1536   (701) 775-9420

Incorporated in 1941 in ND.
Donor(s): John E. Myra.‡
Foundation type: Independent
Financial data (yr. ended 12/31/90): Assets,
$2,603,743 (M); expenditures, $265,676;
qualifying distributions, $207,716, including
$200,216 for 28 grants (high: $27,000; low:
$1,000).
Fields of interest: Higher education, secondary
education, social services, youth, aged, civic
affairs, health, cultural programs.
Types of support: Scholarship funds, renovation
projects, equipment.
Limitations: Giving limited to Grand Forks
County, ND. No grants to individuals, or for
endowment funds, research, or matching gifts; no
loans.
Publications: Informational brochure (including
application guidelines).

Application information: Application form
required.
   Initial approach: Letter
   Copies of proposal: 1
   Deadline(s): None
   Board meeting date(s): Quarterly
   Write: Edward C. Gillig, Pres.
Officers: Edward C. Gillig, Pres.; Hilda Johnson,
V.P.; Robert F. Hansen, Secy.-Treas.
EIN: 450215088

2429
Alex Stern Family Foundation
Bill Stern Bldg., Suite 205
609-1/2 First Ave., North
Fargo 58102   (701) 237-0170

Established in 1964 in ND.
Donor(s): William Stern,‡ Sam Stern,‡ Edward A.
Stern.‡
Foundation type: Independent
Financial data (yr. ended 12/31/91): Assets,
$8,026,003 (M); expenditures, $422,635;
qualifying distributions, $352,915, including
$352,915 for 55 grants (high: $50,000; low:
$200; average: $6,417).
Purpose and activities: Giving primarily for arts
and culture, including museums and the
performing arts; child welfare and youth
organizations; family and social services,
including legal services, alcohol abuse programs,
and welfare for the homeless, aged, and disabled;
community organizations; higher, business,
minority, and other education; and hospices and
cancer research.
Fields of interest: Arts, child welfare, family
services, aged, social services, handicapped,
alcoholism, community funds, education, higher
education, hospices, cancer.
Types of support: Special projects, continuing
support, annual campaigns, emergency funds,
building funds, equipment, research, conferences
and seminars, professorships, matching funds,
lectureships, operating budgets, publications,
scholarship funds.
Limitations: Giving limited to the Fargo, ND, and
Moorhead, MN, areas. No grants to individuals,
or for endowment funds; no loans.
Publications: Application guidelines.
Application information: Application form
required.
   Initial approach: Letter, telephone, or proposal
   Copies of proposal: 4
   Deadline(s): Submit application preferably
     between Apr. and Dec.; no set deadline
   Board meeting date(s): Varies
   Final notification: Within a few months
   Write: W.R. Amundson, Exec. Dir.
Officer and Trustees:* W.R. Amundson,* Exec.
Dir.; J.L. McCormick, E.G. Preston, S. Stroud.
Number of staff: 1 part-time professional.
EIN: 456013981

OHIO

2430
Akron Community Foundation
900 Society Bldg.
159 South Main St., Suite 900
Akron 44308-1318   (216) 376-8522
FAX: (216) 376-0202

Incorporated in 1955 in OH.
Foundation type: Community
Financial data (yr. ended 03/31/92): Assets, $21,756,522 (M); gifts received, $1,096,593; expenditures, $1,294,204; qualifying distributions, $867,367, including $867,367 for 190 grants (high: $164,900; low: $50; average: $50-$164,900).
Purpose and activities: To promote charitable, benevolent, educational, recreational, health, esthetic, cultural, and public welfare activities; to support a program of research leading to the improvement of the health, education, and general well-being of all citizens of the Akron area; to give toward the support of experimental and demonstration programs, through established or new agencies; to test the validity of research findings in various fields of community planning directed toward the efficient and adequate coordination of public and private services organized to meet human needs.
Fields of interest: Education, recreation, health, cultural programs, arts, welfare, youth, social services, community development.
Types of support: Matching funds, research, special projects, scholarship funds, seed money.
Limitations: Giving primarily in Akron, and Summit County, OH. No grants to individuals, or for endowment funds, capital campaigns, or fellowships; no loans.
Publications: Annual report, application guidelines, newsletter.
Application information: No more than 1 grant to an organization in a 12-month period. Application form not required.
  Initial approach: Letter or telephone; request application guidelines
  Copies of proposal: 20
  Deadline(s): Jan. 2, Apr. 1, July 1, and Oct. 1
  Board meeting date(s): Generally Feb., May, Aug., and Nov.
  Final notification: 6 weeks
  Write: D.J. Catrow, Asst. Treas.
Officers and Trustees:* Ann Amer Brennan,* Chair.; Donald R. Fair,* Vice-Chair.; Jody Bacon, Exec. V.P.; Allan Johnson, Secy.; Ernest J. Novack, Jr.,* Treas.; Ronald C. Allan, Edward S. Gaffney, J. Harvey Graves, Judith Isroff, Arthur E. Kemp, Tom Merryweather, Mary Myers, Janise B. Parry, Bruce F. Rothmann, M.D., Edwin Schrank, Sandra Smith, Robert Stefanko, Gale R. Urda, James R. Williams.
Trustee Banks: Bank One Akron, N.A., First National Bank of Ohio, National City Bank, Society National Bank.
Number of staff: 2 full-time professional; 3 part-time professional; 2 full-time support.
EIN: 237029875
Recent health grants:

2430-1 Boys Village, Smithville, OH, $10,000. For Treatment Foster Care Network in Akron-Canton area. 1991.
2430-2 Edwin Shaw Hospital Development Foundation, Akron, OH, $23,028. For equipment. 1991.
2430-3 Mental Health Association of Summit County, Summit County, Akron, OH, $10,000. To reactivate adolescent Suicide Prevention Program. 1991.
2430-4 Say Yes To Tennis, Akron, OH, $10,000. For substance abuse/tennis development program in Elizabeth Park Development. 1991.

2431
The Allyn Foundation
2211 South Dixie Ave., Suite 302
Dayton 45409   (513) 299-2295

Incorporated in 1955 in OH.
Donor(s): S.C. Allyn.‡
Foundation type: Independent
Financial data (yr. ended 12/31/91): Assets, $2,180,733 (M); expenditures, $129,391; qualifying distributions, $115,881, including $107,000 for 54 grants (high: $10,000; low: $500).
Fields of interest: Higher education, secondary education, education, hospitals, social services, handicapped, community funds, family planning, health services.
Types of support: Capital campaigns, continuing support, general purposes, scholarship funds.
Limitations: Giving primarily in southern OH, with the exception of certain schools and universities. No grants to individuals, or for endowment funds.
Publications: 990-PF, annual report (including application guidelines).
Application information: Contributes only to pre-selected organizations. Applications not accepted.
  Board meeting date(s): Nov.3 ; executive board meeting in June
  Write: Charles S. Allyn, Jr., Pres.
Officers and Trustees:* Charles S. Allyn, Jr.,* Pres.; Mary Louise Sunderland,* V.P.; Compton Allyn,* Secy.-Treas.; Elizabeth C. Allyn, Sarah Allyn Bahlman, Anne Reed Sunderland, Louise Allyn Sunderland, Mary Compton Sunderland.
Number of staff: None.
EIN: 316030791

2432
The American Financial Corporation Foundation ▼
One East Fourth St.
Cincinnati 45202   (513) 579-2400

Established in 1971 in OH.
Donor(s): American Financial Corp.
Foundation type: Company-sponsored
Financial data (yr. ended 12/31/90): Assets, $71,790 (M); gifts received, $1,400,000; expenditures, $1,478,262; qualifying distributions, $1,478,207, including $1,478,207 for 86 grants (high: $150,000; low: $75; average: $250-$25,000).
Purpose and activities: The foundation is primarily a conduit for corporate contributions to local charities. Giving primarily for organizations

promoting social change, economic study, and social welfare, including hospitals, and public interest organizations; grants also for education and the arts.
Fields of interest: Social services, welfare, economics, hospitals, public policy, higher education, arts.
Types of support: Building funds, endowment funds, operating budgets, special projects.
Limitations: Giving primarily in the Cincinnati, OH, area. No grants to individuals.
Application information:
  Initial approach: Letter
  Copies of proposal: 1
  Deadline(s): None
  Board meeting date(s): As required
  Final notification: 60 days
  Write: Sandra W. Heimann, V.P.
Officers and Directors:* Carl H. Lindner,* Pres.; Sandra W. Heimann, V.P.; Robert D. Lindner,* V.P.; James C. Kennedy, Secy.; Fred J. Runk, Treas.
Number of staff: None.
EIN: 237153009

2433
American Greetings Corporate Giving Program
10500 American Rd.
Cleveland 44144-2388   (216) 252-7300

Purpose and activities: Supports arts and culture, health and welfare, education, and civic affairs.
Fields of interest: Arts, cultural programs, health, welfare, education, civic affairs.
Types of support: Capital campaigns, matching funds, operating budgets.
Limitations: Giving primarily in corporate headquarters and major operating areas.
Publications: Corporate report.
Application information: Application form not required.
  Initial approach: Letter
  Deadline(s): None
  Final notification: 6 weeks. All requests will be answered
  Write: Harvey Levin, V.P.

2434
William P. Anderson Foundation
c/o The Central Trust Co.
Fifth and Main Sts.
Cincinnati 45202   (513) 651-8439

Incorporated in 1941 in OH.
Foundation type: Independent
Financial data (yr. ended 10/31/91): Assets, $4,649,775 (M); expenditures, $247,631; qualifying distributions, $225,036, including $220,820 for 49 grants (high: $16,000; low: $720).
Fields of interest: Hospitals, health services, community funds, education, child welfare, youth, delinquency, conservation, arts, fine arts.
Types of support: Annual campaigns, building funds, capital campaigns.
Limitations: Giving primarily in Cincinnati, OH. No grants to individuals.
Application information: The foundation no longer awards scholarships to individual students; existing commitments will be paid out. Application form not required.

Initial approach: Letter
Deadline(s): None
Board meeting date(s): Oct. and Nov.
Write: Paul D. Myers, Secy.
Officers and Trustees:* William P. Anderson V,* Pres.; Vachael Anderson Coombe,* V.P.; Harry W. Whittaker,* V.P.; Paul D. Myers,* Secy.; Grenville Anderson,* Treas.; William G. Anderson, Eva Jane Coombe, Michael A. Coombe, James A. Myers, Margot A. Pattison, Dorothy W. Reed, Katharine W. Taft.
Number of staff: None.
EIN: 316034059

2435
The Andrews Foundation
1127 Euclid Ave., Suite 210
Cleveland 44115   (216) 621-3215

Incorporated in 1951 in OH.
Donor(s): Mrs. Matthew Andrews.‡
Foundation type: Independent
Financial data (yr. ended 12/31/91): Assets, $6,456,099 (M); expenditures, $296,759; qualifying distributions, $280,414, including $249,838 for 36 grants (high: $25,000; low: $1,000; average: $1,000-$25,000).
Fields of interest: Higher education, secondary education, performing arts, alcoholism, handicapped.
Types of support: Annual campaigns, building funds, capital campaigns, endowment funds, general purposes.
Limitations: Giving limited to northeastern OH. No grants to individuals.
Application information: Application form not required.
Initial approach: Letter
Copies of proposal: 1
Deadline(s): None
Board meeting date(s): Usually in Nov.
Write: Richard S. Tomer, Pres.
Officers and Trustees:* Richard S. Tomer,* Pres.; Barbara J. Baxter,* V.P.; James H. Dempsey, Jr.,* Secy.; Laura S. Baxter, Treas.
Number of staff: None.
EIN: 346515110

2436
The Evenor Armington Fund
c/o The Huntington Trust Co., N.A.
P.O. Box 1558
Columbus 43260

Established in 1954 in OH.
Donor(s): Everett Armington, and members of the Armington family.
Foundation type: Independent
Financial data (yr. ended 06/30/91): Assets, $5,174,133 (M); expenditures, $332,220; qualifying distributions, $308,043, including $299,432 for 31 grants (high: $25,000; low: $2,000).
Purpose and activities: Grants primarily for special projects, usually short-term, in education, child welfare, medical research, health, the arts, the environment, and public policy organizations, including human rights, peace and justice, and the struggle against poverty.
Fields of interest: Education, child welfare, medical research, health services, arts,

environment, public policy, human rights, peace, social services.
Types of support: Consulting services, operating budgets, continuing support, annual campaigns, emergency funds, research, publications, special projects.
Limitations: No grants to individuals, or for deficit financing or general purposes.
Application information: Contributes only to pre-selected organizations. Applications not accepted.
Board meeting date(s): Summer
Trustee: The Huntington Trust Co., N.A.
Number of staff: None.
EIN: 346525508

2437
The Ashtabula Foundation, Inc.
c/o Society National Bank
4717 Main Ave.
Ashtabula 44004   (216) 992-6818

Incorporated in 1922 in OH.
Foundation type: Community
Financial data (yr. ended 12/31/91): Assets, $10,778,468 (M); gifts received, $5,589; expenditures, $494,106; qualifying distributions, $406,656, including $384,612 for 31 grants (high: $100,000; low: $126).
Purpose and activities: To administer charitable trusts; support for health, welfare, and cultural programs, with emphasis on a community fund and church support.
Fields of interest: Health, welfare, cultural programs, religion.
Types of support: Building funds, land acquisition, renovation projects, equipment, matching funds.
Limitations: Giving limited to the Ashtabula, OH, area.
Publications: Annual report, application guidelines.
Application information: Application guidelines for scholarship funds available. Application form required.
Initial approach: Proposal
Copies of proposal: 4
Deadline(s): Feb. 1, May 1, Aug. 1, and Nov. 1
Board meeting date(s): Jan., Mar., Apr., June, July, Sept., Oct., and Dec.
Write: Robert E. Martin, Jr., Secy.-Treas.
Officers and Trustees:* Wilbur Anderson,* Pres.; William C. Zweier,* V.P.; Robert E. Martin, Jr., Secy.-Treas.; Roy H. Bean, Jerry Brockway, Thad Hague, Douglas Hedberg, Eleanor A. Jammal, Glen W. Warner, Barbara P. Wiese.
Trustee Bank: Society National Bank.
Number of staff: None.
EIN: 346538130

2438
The Austin Memorial Foundation
Aurora Commons Office Bldg., Suite 230
Aurora 44202   (216) 562-5515

Incorporated in 1961 in OH.
Donor(s): Members of the Austin family.
Foundation type: Independent
Financial data (yr. ended 12/31/91): Assets, $5,418,679 (M); gifts received, $101,000; expenditures, $370,106; qualifying distributions,

$323,919, including $280,200 for 27 grants (high: $75,000; low: $300).
Fields of interest: Education, higher education, secondary education, hospitals, Protestant giving, social services, environment.
Limitations: No grants to individuals.
Application information: Contributes only to pre-selected organizations. Applications not accepted.
Board meeting date(s): Semiannually
Write: Donald G. Austin, Jr., Pres.
Officers and Trustees:* Donald G. Austin, Jr.,* Pres.; Donald G. Austin, Sr.,* V.P.; Winifred N. Austin,* V.P.; Margaret A. Grumhaus,* V.P.; Colette Mylott, Secy.; David A. Rodgers,* Treas.; James W. Austin, Richard C. Austin, Stewart G. Austin, Thomas G. Austin, Sarah R. Cole, Ann R. Loeffler.
Number of staff: 1 part-time professional.
EIN: 346528879

2439
Baird Brothers Company Foundation
c/o The Huntington Trust Co., N.A.
P.O. Box 1558
Columbus 43260
Application address: c/o The Huntington Trust Co., N.A., 41 South High St., Columbus, OH 43215; Tel.: (614) 463-3707

Foundation type: Independent
Financial data (yr. ended 06/30/91): Assets, $3,553,954 (M); expenditures, $216,874; qualifying distributions, $172,342, including $166,415 for 10 grants (high: $84,313; low: $982).
Fields of interest: Civic affairs, religion—Christian, hospitals.
Limitations: Giving limited to Nelsonville, OH. No grants to individuals.
Application information: Application form not required.
Deadline(s): None
Directors: David S. Fraedrich, Arlene B. Powell, Wilbert W. Warren.
Trustee: The Huntington Trust Co., N.A.
EIN: 316194844

2440
Battelle Distribution Program
(Formerly Battelle Memorial Program)
505 King Ave.
Columbus 43201   (614) 424-6424

Financial data (yr. ended 12/31/90): Total giving, $1,932,000, including $1,500,000 for grants and $432,000 for 45 in-kind gifts.
Purpose and activities: Supports civic affairs, culture, education, health and human services. "Our corporate financial support, as reflected through our distribution program, as well as our staff's involvement in public leadership roles and their countless hours of voluntary community service, all demonstrate Battelle's continuing role as a concerned and responsible corporate citizen." Battelle's distribution program funds charitable activities in the major categories of Arts and Culture, Health and Human Services, Education, and Civic and Community, emphasizing educational programs in these areas. In addition, when equipment and personal

property are upgraded at Battelle, items become available for distribution to eligible organizations. The major portion of the annual distribution budget is allocated to established organizations with reputations for meeting community needs, demonstrating cost-effectiveness, and implementing quality programs and services. A small portion is available for newly established organizations that are attempting to address new areas of concern identified by the community. Rather than being the sole source of funding, Battelle prefers to join with other corporations and foundations in providing a broad base of support for major community initiatives. Batelle's representation at fundraisers will be based primarily on the following criteria: a fundraiser is a major annual event; the fund-raiser is sponsored by an established organization; and a Battelle staff member serves on the organization's governing board.
Fields of interest: Civic affairs, cultural programs, education, health, humanities, arts, educational associations.
Types of support: Annual campaigns, capital campaigns, conferences and seminars, donated equipment.
Limitations: Giving primarily in Columbus, OH, and the Tri-Cities in WA and other communities where major facilities are located. No support for extracurricular school activities, fraternal, political, or religious organizations. Generally no general operating support for United Way member agencies; capital campaigns and special projects are considered on a case-by-case basis; no support for individuals, or for advertisements.
Publications: Informational brochure (including application guidelines).
Application information: Community Relations handles giving. Application form not required.
Initial approach: Letter requesting guidelines to nearest office
Copies of proposal: 1
Deadline(s): None
Board meeting date(s): Quarterly Distribution Committee meetings
Final notification: Within 2 weeks of each meeting
Write: Barbara A. Sills, Dir., Commun. Rels.
Number of staff: 1 full-time professional; 1 full-time support.

2441
Ward Beecher Foundation
c/o Mahoning National Bank of Youngstown, Trust Dept.
P.O. Box 479
Youngstown 44501   (216) 742-7000

Established in 1958 in OH.
Donor(s): Ward Beecher.‡
Foundation type: Independent
Financial data (yr. ended 12/31/91): Assets, $2,639,444 (M); expenditures, $132,850; qualifying distributions, $122,697, including $116,000 for 10 grants (high: $25,000; low: $2,500).
Purpose and activities: Support for capital building drives for hospitals, community funds, and youth agencies.
Fields of interest: Hospitals, community funds, youth.

Types of support: Building funds, annual campaigns, capital campaigns, equipment, renovation projects.
Limitations: Giving limited to the Youngstown, OH, area. No grants to individuals, or for scholarships, fellowships, matching gifts, endowment funds, or research; no loans.
Application information: Application form not required.
Initial approach: Letter or proposal
Copies of proposal: 1
Deadline(s): Submit proposal in the 1st quarter of the calendar year
Board meeting date(s): As required
Write: Patrick A. Sebastiano, Sr. V.P. and Sr. Trust Officer, Mahoning National Bank of Youngstown
Directors: Eleanor Beecher Flad, Erle L. Flad, Ward Beecher Flad, Gregory L. Ridler.
Trustee: Mahoning National Bank of Youngstown.
Number of staff: None.
EIN: 346516441

2442
Bicknell Fund
c/o Advisory Services, Inc.
1422 Euclid Ave., Rm. 1010
Cleveland 44115-2078   (216) 363-6482

Incorporated in 1949 in OH.
Donor(s): Kate H. Bicknell, Warren Bicknell, Jr.,‡ Warren Bicknell III, Kate B. Kirkham.
Foundation type: Independent
Financial data (yr. ended 12/31/91): Assets, $5,486,164 (M); gifts received, $20,219; expenditures, $261,774; qualifying distributions, $232,012, including $228,900 for 59 grants (high: $32,000; low: $1,000; average: $1,000-$5,000).
Fields of interest: Higher education, secondary education, health, social services, hunger, fine arts.
Types of support: Scholarship funds, continuing support, special projects.
Limitations: Giving primarily in northeast OH. No grants to individuals; no loans.
Publications: Application guidelines.
Application information: Multi-year grants not awarded. Application form not required.
Initial approach: Proposal
Copies of proposal: 1
Deadline(s): Submit proposal prior to May or Nov.
Board meeting date(s): June and Dec.
Write: Robert G. Acklin, Secy.-Treas.
Officers and Trustees:* Kate B. Kirkham,* Pres.; Warren Bicknell III,* V.P.; Robert G. Acklin, Secy.-Treas.; Wendy H. Bicknell, Donald J. Hofman, Henry L. Meyer III, Alexander S. Taylor II, Lyman H. Treadway III.
EIN: 346513799

2443
BP America Corporate Giving Program
200 Public Square 36-A
Cleveland 44114-2375   (216) 586-8621

Financial data (yr. ended 12/31/90): Total giving, $16,547,010, including $11,900,913 for grants, $1,110,604 for 6,028 employee matching gifts and $3,535,493 for loans.

Purpose and activities: Supports education, health and human services, civic and community affairs, urban development, and culture and the arts. Types of support include employee matching gifts for higher education, hospitals and culture, in-kind donations; and program-related investments for the social investments program.
Fields of interest: Urban development, education, higher education, health, civic affairs, social services, cultural programs, arts, community development, hospitals, environment, education—minorities.
Types of support: Capital campaigns, building funds, employee matching gifts, equipment, fellowships, general purposes, matching funds, operating budgets, research, scholarship funds, special projects.
Limitations: No support for religious, political, or fraternal organizations. No grants to individuals.
Publications: Corporate giving report (including application guidelines).
Application information: Company has a staff that only handles contributions. Application form not required.
Initial approach: Phone or letter
Copies of proposal: 1
Deadline(s): Applications accepted throughout the year
Write: Barry Doggett, Dir., Corp. Contribs.
Number of staff: 5 full-time professional; 1 part-time professional; 1 full-time support.

2444
The Bremer Foundation
709 Bank One Bldg.
Youngstown 44503

Incorporated in 1953 in OH.
Donor(s): Richard P. Bremer.‡
Foundation type: Independent
Financial data (yr. ended 12/31/91): Assets, $1,868,205 (M); expenditures, $281,894; qualifying distributions, $276,075, including $272,960 for 21 grants (high: $136,730; low: $600).
Purpose and activities: Giving primarily for higher and medical education; support also for social services.
Fields of interest: Higher education, medical education, social services.
Limitations: Giving primarily in OH. No grants to individuals.
Application information: Contributes only to pre-selected organizations. Applications not accepted.
Write: James E. Mitchell, Secy.
Officers and Trustees:* Jonas S. Bremer,* Pres.; George Woodman,* V.P.; James E. Mitchell,* Secy.; Morris S. Rosenblum, M.D.,* Treas.; Henry G. Cramblett, M.D., Joan L. McCoy, W. Brooks Reed.
EIN: 346514168

2445
Bridgestone/Firestone Trust Fund ▼
(Formerly The Firestone Trust Fund)
1200 Firestone Pkwy.
Akron 44317   (216) 379-6802

Trust established in 1952 in OH.
Donor(s): Bridgestone/Firestone, Inc.

Foundation type: Company-sponsored
Financial data (yr. ended 12/31/90): Assets, $9,718,286 (M); expenditures, $2,417,081; qualifying distributions, $2,326,763, including $2,276,563 for 776 grants (high: $251,004; low: $50; average: $1,000-$35,000).
Purpose and activities: Support for higher and other education, including employee matching gifts; community funds, health, and welfare; also supports civic and community affairs, and culture, including the fine and performing arts.
Fields of interest: Education, education—building funds, higher education, community funds, welfare, youth, hospitals, health, civic affairs, cultural programs, arts, fine arts, museums, music, performing arts, theater.
Types of support: Continuing support, annual campaigns, seed money, emergency funds, building funds, endowment funds, matching funds, employee matching gifts, research, special projects, capital campaigns, employee-related scholarships.
Limitations: Giving primarily in areas of company operations. No grants to individuals, or for operating budgets, deficit financing, equipment, land acquisition, fellowships, publications, or conferences; no loans.
Publications: Application guidelines.
Application information: Application form not required.
> *Initial approach:* Letter
> *Copies of proposal:* 1
> *Deadline(s):* Submit proposal preferably by July; no set deadline
> *Board meeting date(s):* As required
> *Final notification:* 3 to 4 weeks
> *Write:* Frances C. Houser, Secy.
Bridgestone/Firestone Trust Fund Committee: D.A. Thomas, Chair.; Frances C. Houser, Secy.
Trustee: Society National Bank.
Number of staff: 1 full-time support.
EIN: 346505181

2446
Britton Fund
c/o Advisory Services, Inc.
1010 Hanna Bldg., 1422 Euclid Ave.
Cleveland 44115-2078   (216) 363-6487

Incorporated in 1952 in OH.
Donor(s): Gertrude H. Britton, Charles S. Britton, Brigham Britton.‡
Foundation type: Independent
Financial data (yr. ended 12/31/91): Assets, $6,919,702 (M); gifts received, $70,000; expenditures, $375,798; qualifying distributions, $352,315, including $347,900 for 41 grants (high: $68,000; low: $2,000; average: $2,000-$5,000).
Fields of interest: Community funds, social services, educational research, secondary education, higher education, handicapped, health services, hospitals, youth, general charitable giving.
Types of support: General purposes, operating budgets, emergency funds, annual campaigns, continuing support, endowment funds, scholarship funds.
Limitations: Giving primarily in OH. No grants to individuals.
Publications: Annual report.

Application information: Funds substantially committed. Application form not required.
> *Initial approach:* Letter
> *Copies of proposal:* 1
> *Deadline(s):* Prior to board meetings
> *Board meeting date(s):* May and Nov.
> *Write:* Elizabeth C. Reed, Secy.
Officers and Trustees:* Charles S. Britton II,* Pres.; Gertrude H. Britton,* V.P.; Elizabeth C. Reed, Secy.; Donald C. Cook, Treas.; Lynda R. Britton.
Number of staff: None.
EIN: 346513616

2447
Eva L. and Joseph M. Bruening Foundation ▼
627 Hanna Bldg.
1422 Euclid Ave.
Cleveland 44115   (216) 621-2632

Established in 1988 in OH.
Donor(s): Joseph M. Bruening,‡ Eva L. Bruening.‡
Foundation type: Independent
Financial data (yr. ended 12/31/90): Assets, $33,689,835 (M); gifts received, $3,151,490; expenditures, $2,609,112; qualifying distributions, $2,290,933, including $2,205,815 for 83 grants (high: $200,000; low: $400; average: $15,000-$100,000).
Fields of interest: Education, higher education, child welfare, youth, aged, disadvantaged, social services, health, community development, recreation.
Types of support: Capital campaigns, building funds, equipment, renovation projects, seed money.
Limitations: Giving limited to the greater Cleveland, OH, area. No grants to individuals, or for endowment funds, general operating budgets, research, publications, or symposiums and seminars.
Publications: Informational brochure.
Application information: The foundation does not respond to mass mailings or annual campaign appeals. Application form not required.
> *Initial approach:* Proposal
> *Copies of proposal:* 1
> *Deadline(s):* Mar. 1, July 1, and Nov. 1
> *Board meeting date(s):* Apr., Aug, and Dec.
> *Final notification:* Within several weeks of board meeting
> *Write:* Janet E. Narten, Exec. Secy.
Distribution Committee: John R. Cunin, Chair.; Robert T. Blaine, E. Lorrie Robertson.
Trustee: Ameritrust Co., N.A.
Number of staff: 1 full-time professional; 1 part-time professional; 1 part-time support.
EIN: 341584378
Recent health grants:
2447-1 AIDS Housing Council of Greater Cleveland, Cleveland, OH, $20,000. For purchase, renovation and start-up operations of Kamana Place: assisted living facility for AIDS patients. 1990.
2447-2 Alcoholism Services of Cleveland, Cleveland, OH, $45,000. For family alcoholism intervention and rehabilitation program. 1990.
2447-3 Beech Brook, Pepper Pike, OH, $10,000. For renovation of playground. 1990.

2447-4 Bellefaire Residential Treatment Center for Children, Cleveland, OH, $60,000. For remodeling residence buildings. 1990.
2447-5 Cleveland Health Education Museum, Cleveland, OH, $15,000. To purchase teaching walls for Education Center. 1990.
2447-6 Federation for Community Planning, Cleveland, OH, $10,904. For reprinting It's Your Move: health information directory for adolescents. 1990.
2447-7 Free Medical Clinic of Greater Cleveland, Cleveland, OH, $17,500. For remodeling to provide additional counseling rooms. 1990.
2447-8 Parmadale, Cleveland, OH, $25,000. For family therapy for violent K-3 students project in Cleveland Public Schools. 1990.

2448
Kenneth Calhoun Charitable Trust
c/o Society National Bank
P.O. Box 9950
Canton 44711-0950
Application address: c/o Society National Bank, 157 South Main St., Akron, OH 44308; Tel.: (216) 379-1647

Established in 1982 in OH.
Donor(s): Kenneth Calhoun.‡
Foundation type: Independent
Financial data (yr. ended 07/31/91): Assets, $4,031,297 (M); expenditures, $279,295; qualifying distributions, $253,554, including $247,487 for 78 grants (high: $50,500; low: $500; average: $500-$5,000).
Fields of interest: Hospitals, cultural programs, education, youth, social services.
Limitations: Giving limited to the greater Akron, OH, area with an emphasis on Summit County. No grants to individuals.
Application information: Application form not required.
> *Initial approach:* Letter
> *Copies of proposal:* 1
> *Deadline(s):* Jan. 15, Apr. 15, July 15, and Oct. 15
> *Board meeting date(s):* At the end of Jan., Apr., July, and Oct.
> *Write:* Karen Krino, Sr. Trust Officer, Society National Bank
Trustee: Society National Bank.
EIN: 341370330

2449
The Robert Campeau Family Foundation (U.S.) ▼
(Formerly Federated Department Stores Foundation)
Seven West Seventh St.
Cincinnati 45202   (513) 579-7166
Administration office: 64 The Bridal Path, Don Mills, Ontario, Canada M3B 2B1

Originally incorporated in 1952 in OH as Federated Department Stores Foundation and later dissolved; reestablished in 1980 in OH; new name adopted in 1989.
Donor(s): Federated Department Stores, Inc.
Foundation type: Company-sponsored
Financial data (yr. ended 01/31/91): Assets, $11,410,660 (M); expenditures, $5,101,844;

qualifying distributions, $6,429,823, including $4,261,539 for 579 grants (high: $328,854; low: $1,000; average: $1,000-$50,000) and $741,396 for employee matching gifts.

Purpose and activities: Emphasis on higher education, and cultural, civic, and health and welfare programs; matching employee gifts to educational and cultural organizations and contributions of $1,000 or more to local organizations at the request of the divisions of the company.

Fields of interest: Education, higher education, social services, urban affairs, civic affairs, cultural programs, fine arts, performing arts.

Types of support: Employee matching gifts, general purposes, building funds, matching funds, special projects.

Limitations: Giving primarily in communities of company operations: Miami, FL; Atlanta, GA; Boston and Somerville, MA; Brooklyn and New York, NY; Cincinnati and Columbus, OH; Memphis, TN; Seattle, WA; and Paramus, NJ. No support for religious organizations for religious purposes or educational institutions for non-scholastic programs. No grants to individuals.

Publications: Annual report.

Application information: Local organizations should apply directly to local division of Federated Department Stores. Application form not required.

Initial approach: Proposal
Copies of proposal: 1
Deadline(s): None
Board meeting date(s): Approximately the 15th of each month
Final notification: 6 to 8 weeks
Write: Patricia Ikeda, Exec. Dir.

Officers and Trustees:* Ilse Campeau,* Chair. and Pres.; Robert Campeau,* Vice-Chair.; Ronald W. Tysoe,* Sr. V.P.; Roland Villemaire, V.P. and Treas.; J. Roy Weir,* Secy.; Patricia Ikeda, Exec. Dir.; Daniel Campeau, Cardinal G. Emmett Carter, Rita Epperson.

Number of staff: 1 part-time professional; 2 part-time support.

EIN: 310996760

Recent health grants:

2449-1 American Foundation for AIDS Research, NYC, NY, $10,000. For 90 Minutes for Life event at Carnegie Hall. 1991.

2449-2 Dana-Farber Cancer Institute, Boston, MA, $10,000. For capital development campaign. 1991.

2449-3 Providence Foundation, Seattle, WA, $25,000. For campaign to improve medical center. 1991.

2449-4 Saint Jude Childrens Research Hospital, Memphis, TN, $10,000. For capital fund drive for expansion efforts of hospital. 1991.

2449-5 Sheriffs Youth Foundation, Los Angeles, CA, $25,000. Toward expansion of Substance Abuse and Narcotics Education (SANE) Program. 1991.

2449-6 Trustees of Health and Hospitals of the City of Boston, Boston, MA, $40,000. For annual support. 1991.

2450

Case Western Reserve University Department of Surgery Foundation

(also known as CWRU Department of Surgery Foundation)
2074 Abington Rd.
Cleveland 44106-2602

Foundation type: Independent

Financial data (yr. ended 12/31/91): Assets, $1,592,155 (M); gifts received, $329,008; expenditures, $226,242; qualifying distributions, $215,000, including $215,000 for 1 grant.

Fields of interest: Medical research.

Limitations: Giving primarily in Cleveland, OH. No grants to individuals.

Application information: Contributes only to pre-selected organizations. Applications not accepted.

Officers and Trustees:* Jerry M. Shuck, M.D.,* Pres.; Michael W.L. Gauderer, M.D.,* V.P.; Mark Malangoni, M.D.,* V.P.; Edward Purnell, M.D.,* V.P.; Martin Resnick, M.D.,* V.P.; Alexander S. Geha, M.D.,* Secy.; Robert Ratcheson, M.D.,* Treas.; Alan Shons, M.D.

EIN: 341583598

2451

Centerior Energy Company Giving Program

(Formerly The Cleveland Electric Illuminating Company Giving Program)
P.O. Box 5000
Cleveland 44101   (216) 447-3100

Financial data (yr. ended 12/31/90): Total giving, $334,539 for grants.

Purpose and activities: Supports civic and community affairs, the arts, including museums and music, education, youth, and United Way.

Fields of interest: Civic affairs, arts, education, health, community funds, higher education, museums, music, youth.

Types of support: Annual campaigns, building funds, capital campaigns.

Limitations: Giving primarily in Northeastern OH, mostly in Cleveland. No grants to individuals, or for endowments or scholarships.

Application information: Application form not required.

Initial approach: Summary of proposal, one-two pages
Copies of proposal: 1
Deadline(s): None
Board meeting date(s): Committee meetings monthly
Final notification: All requests will be answered

Contributions Committee: Jacquita Hauserman, Chair.; Tanzie D. Adams, Secy.; Gary Greben.

2452

Centerior Energy Foundation ▼

(Formerly The Cleveland Electric Illuminating Foundation)
6200 Oaktree Blvd.
Independence 44131   (216) 622-9800
Application address: 55 Public Sq., Cleveland, OH 44113; Tel.: (216) 479-4907

Incorporated in 1961 in OH.

Donor(s): The Cleveland Electric Illuminating Co., Centerior Energy Corp.

Foundation type: Company-sponsored

Financial data (yr. ended 12/31/91): Assets, $17,990,971 (M); expenditures, $1,648,924; qualifying distributions, $1,640,216, including $1,637,362 for 304 grants (high: $439,000; low: $10; average: $25-$3,500).

Purpose and activities: Emphasis on qualifying nonprofit organizations in health, welfare, civic, cultural, or educational endeavors; support also for community funds; giving only within the Centerior Corporation's service area.

Fields of interest: Education, higher education, secondary education, hospitals, health, health associations, health services, cultural programs, museums, theater, welfare, civic affairs, community funds, law and justice, human rights.

Types of support: Annual campaigns, building funds, equipment, operating budgets, employee matching gifts, continuing support, in-kind gifts, matching funds, capital campaigns, renovation projects, special projects.

Limitations: Giving limited to northeastern and northwestern OH, with emphasis on Cleveland and Toledo. Generally, no grants to individuals, or for endowment funds, deficit financing, research, scholarships, or fellowships; no loans.

Publications: Informational brochure (including application guidelines), program policy statement.

Application information: Application form not required.

Initial approach: Cover letter with proposal
Copies of proposal: 1
Deadline(s): None
Board meeting date(s): Contributions Committee usually meets monthly
Final notification: 8 weeks
Write: Jacquita K. Hauserman, Chair., Contribs. Comm.

Officers and Trustees:* Robert J. Farling,* Chair.; Lyman C. Phillips,* Vice-Chair.; Jacquita K. Hauserman, Pres.; Terrence Linnert, V.P.; E. Lyle Pepin, Secy.; Gary M. Hawkinson, Treas.; Richard B. Anderson, Albert C. Bersticken, Leigh Carter, Thomas A. Commes, Wayne Embry, George H. Kaull, Richard A. Miller, Frank E. Mosier, Sister Mary Martha Reinhard, S.N.D., Robert Savage, Paul M. Smart, William J. Williams.

Number of staff: 2 part-time professional; 1 part-time support.

EIN: 346514181

2453

Charities Foundation

One Sea Gate, 22nd Fl.
Toledo 43666   (419) 247-1888

Trust established in 1937 in OH.

Donor(s): Owens-Illinois, Inc., William E. Levis,‡ Harold Boeschenstein,‡ and others.

Foundation type: Company-sponsored

Financial data (yr. ended 12/31/91): Assets, $4,483,070 (M); gifts received, $813,450; expenditures, $813,450; qualifying distributions, $789,046, including $623,265 for 70 grants (high: $300,000; low: $60; average: $750-$20,000) and $165,781 for 231 employee matching gifts.

Purpose and activities: Contributions from the foundation are initiated internally, with emphasis on higher and other education, community funds,

hospitals, cultural programs, including museums and performing arts, conservation, youth and social service agencies, and civic and public affairs organizations.
Fields of interest: Higher education, community funds, cultural programs, conservation, youth, public affairs, education, social services, civic affairs, hospitals, museums, performing arts.
Types of support: General purposes, employee matching gifts.
Limitations: Giving primarily in OH, with emphasis on Toledo. No grants to individuals, or for scholarships.
Publications: Annual report, 990-PF.
Application information: All funds presently committed. Applications not accepted.
  Write: Grayce A. Neimy, Secy.
Officer: David Van Hooser, Mgr.
Trustees: Jerome A. Bohland, Henry A. Page, Jr., Carter Smith.
Number of staff: 1 part-time support.
EIN: 346554560

2454
Alvah S. & Adele C. Chisholm Memorial Fund
c/o National City Bank
P.O. Box 5756
Cleveland 44101

Established in 1968 in OH.
Foundation type: Independent
Financial data (yr. ended 12/31/90): Assets, $0 (M); expenditures, $250,546; qualifying distributions, $235,889, including $234,386 for 22 grants (high: $200,386; low: $500).
Fields of interest: Music, higher education, hospitals.
Limitations: Giving primarily in Cleveland, OH.
Trustee: National City Bank.
EIN: 346599093

2455
Cincinnati Bell Foundation, Inc.
201 East Fourth St.
Cincinnati 45202   (513) 397-1228

Established in 1984 in OH.
Donor(s): Cincinnati Bell, Inc.
Foundation type: Company-sponsored
Financial data (yr. ended 12/31/91): Assets, $1,304,322 (M); gifts received, $1,000,000; expenditures, $883,421; qualifying distributions, $883,174, including $843,700 for 51 grants (high: $275,000; low: $100) and $38,259 for 124 employee matching gifts.
Purpose and activities: Support for the arts; education, including higher education; health and hospitals; welfare and youth; media and communications, and community funds. Priority to programs that are broadly supported by other organizations.
Fields of interest: Arts, education, higher education, health, hospitals, hospitals—building funds, welfare, youth, media and communications, community funds.
Types of support: Annual campaigns, capital campaigns, employee matching gifts, operating budgets, matching funds.
Limitations: Giving primarily in the greater Cincinnati, OH, area, and in northern KY, and

any other city in which company has a significant corporate presence.
Publications: Informational brochure (including application guidelines).
Application information: Application form not required.
  Initial approach: Letter
  Copies of proposal: 1
  Deadline(s): None
  Board meeting date(s): 3 or 4 times per year
  Write: James F. Eichmann, Exec. Dir.
Officers: Dwight H. Hibbard, Pres.; Janet S. Neidhard, Secy.-Treas.; James F. Eichmann, Exec. Dir.
Trustees: Scott Aiken, John T. LaMacchia, Dennis J. Sullivan, Jr.
Number of staff: None.
EIN: 311125542

2456
The Greater Cincinnati Foundation
Star Bank Center
425 Walnut St., Suite 1110
Cincinnati 45202-3915   (513) 241-2880

Established in 1963 in OH by bank resolution and declaration of trust.
Foundation type: Community
Financial data (yr. ended 12/31/90): Assets, $84,591,802 (M); gifts received, $5,659,197; expenditures, $6,345,413; qualifying distributions, $5,793,614, including $5,793,614 for grants.
Purpose and activities: Grants for a broad range of both new and existing activities in general categories of arts and culture and humanities, civic affairs, economic development, education, health, and social and human services, including youth agencies.
Fields of interest: Community development, volunteerism, education, social services, arts, youth, civic affairs, health.
Types of support: Seed money, capital campaigns, building funds, equipment, program-related investments, special projects, matching funds, loans, technical assistance, renovation projects.
Limitations: Giving limited to the greater Cincinnati, OH, area. No support for sectarian religious purposes. No grants to individuals, or for operating budgets, annual campaigns, deficit financing, scholarships, fellowships, internships, exchange programs, or scholarly research.
Publications: Annual report (including application guidelines), newsletter, application guidelines, informational brochure.
Application information: Application form required.
  Initial approach: Letter or telephone, followed by interview with foundation staff
  Copies of proposal: 22
  Deadline(s): 90 days prior to board meetings
  Board meeting date(s): Feb., May, Aug., and Nov.
  Final notification: Immediately following board meetings
  Write: Ruth A. Cronenberg, Prog. Officer
Officers: William A. Friedlander, Dir.; Herbert R. Brown, Assoc. Dir.; Charles W. Goering, Assoc. Dir.; Elizabeth D. Goldsmith, Assoc. Dir.; Thomas S. Heldman, Assoc. Dir.; Daniel LeBlond, Assoc. Dir.; Walter L. Lingle, Jr., Assoc. Dir.; Nelson

Schwab, Jr., Assoc. Dir.; Robert Westheimer, Assoc. Dir.
Governing Board: Kay Pettengill, Chair.; William D. Atteberry, Vice-Chair.; Cynthia Booth, V.P.; Louise A. Head, Charles S. Mechem, Jr., Sidney Peerless, M.D., John G. Smale, Robert G. Stachler, John L. Strubbe.
Trustee Banks: Ameritrust Co., N.A., BancOne Ohio Corp., The Central Trust Co. of Northern Ohio, N.A., Fifth Third Bank, Huntington National Bank, Kentucky National Bank, The Lebanon-Citizens National Bank, The Northside Bank & Trust Co., Peoples Liberty Bank of Northern Kentucky, Provident Bank, Society Bank, N.A., Star Bank, N.A., Cincinnati.
Number of staff: 2 full-time professional; 3 full-time support.
EIN: 310669700
Recent health grants:
2456-1 Alzheimers Disease Association of Cincinnati, Cincinnati, OH, $10,000. For Partners in Care training program. 1990.
2456-2 Babies Milk Fund Association and Maternity Society, Cincinnati, OH, $18,578. For renovation of new clinic facilities. 1990.
2456-3 Center for Comprehensive Alcoholic Treatment, Cincinnati, OH, $20,000. 1990.
2456-4 Samaritan Counseling Center of Greater Cincinnati, Cincinnati, OH, $10,000. 1990.
2456-5 Urban Appalachian Council, Cincinnati, OH, $10,000. 1990.

2457
The Cleveland Foundation ▼
1422 Euclid Ave., Suite 1400
Cleveland 44115-2001   (216) 861-3810
FAX: (216)861-1729

Established in 1914 in OH by bank resolution and declaration of trust.
Foundation type: Community
Financial data (yr. ended 12/31/90): Assets, $573,012,252 (M); gifts received, $9,432,555; expenditures, $33,924,323; qualifying distributions, $33,247,607, including $30,487,607 for 869 grants (high: $2,100,000; low: $45; average: $1,000-$595,000), $2,650,000 for 4 foundation-administered programs and $110,000 for loans.
Purpose and activities: The pioneer community foundation which has served as a model for most community foundations in the U.S.; grants are made to private tax-exempt and governmental agencies and programs serving the greater Cleveland area in the fields of civic and cultural affairs, education and economic development, and health and social services. Current priorities are in economic development, neighborhood development, downtown revitalization, lakefront enhancement, programs dealing with the young, the aged and special constituencies, health care for the medically indigent and for underserved populations, and the professional performing and visual arts. Grants mainly as seed money for innovative projects or to developing institutions or services addressing unmet needs in the community. Very limited support for capital purposes for highly selective construction or equipment projects which serve the program priorities listed above.
Fields of interest: Community development, civic affairs, urban development, arts, cultural

programs, performing arts, fine arts, elementary education, secondary education, higher education, economics, health, hospitals, AIDS, social services, aged, youth.

Types of support: Seed money, special projects, matching funds, consulting services, technical assistance, program-related investments, renovation projects.

Limitations: Giving limited to the greater Cleveland area, with primary emphasis on Cleveland, Cuyahoga, Lake, and Geauga counties, OH, unless specified by donor. No support for sectarian or religious activities, community services such as fire and police protection, and library and welfare services. No grants to individuals, or for endowment funds, operating costs, debt reduction, fundraising campaigns, publications, films and audiovisual materials (unless they are an integral part of a program already being supported), memberships, travel for bands, sports teams, classes and similar groups; capital support for planning, construction, renovation, or purchase of buildings, equipment and materials, land acquisition, or renovation of public space unless there is strong evidence that the program is of priority to the foundation.

Publications: Annual report (including application guidelines), newsletter, occasional report, application guidelines, informational brochure.

Application information: Application form not required.

> *Initial approach:* Letter
> *Copies of proposal:* 2
> *Deadline(s):* Mar. 31, June 30, Sept. 15, and Dec. 31
> *Board meeting date(s):* Distribution committee meets in Mar., June, Sept., and Dec.
> *Final notification:* 1 month
> *Write:* Steven A. Minter, Exec. Dir.

Officers: Steven A. Minter, Exec. Dir.; Roberta W. Allport, Secy.; Philip T. Tobin, Admin. Officer and Treas.

Distribution Committee: Alfred M. Rankin, Jr., Chair.; Annie Lewis Garda, Vice-Chair.; Rev. Elmo A. Bean, James M. Delaney, Russell R. Gifford, Henry J. Goodman, Jerry V. Jarrett, Adrienne L. Jones, Lindsay J. Morgenthaler, James V. Patton.

Trustees: Ameritrust Co., N.A., Bank One, Cleveland, N.A., First National Bank of Ohio, Huntington National Bank, National City Bank, Society National Bank.

Number of staff: 19 full-time professional; 2 part-time professional; 23 full-time support.

EIN: 340714588

Recent health grants:

2457-1 Alzheimers Disease and Related Disorders Association, Cleveland, OH, $29,108. For expanded programming in Lake and Geauga Counties. 1991.

2457-2 American School Health Association, Kent, OH, $106,977. For multidisciplinary school health program in Cleveland Public Schools. 1991.

2457-3 Beech Brook, Pepper Pike, OH, $20,000. For playground renovation contingent on raising balance needed. 1991.

2457-4 Bellefaire-Jewish Childrens Bureau, Shaker Heights, OH, $182,779. For start-up support for Intensive Treatment and Diagnostic Center. 1991.

2457-5 Bellefaire-Jewish Childrens Bureau, Shaker Heights, OH, $30,000. For Children's Change, The Art of Living Fund. 1991.

2457-6 Bellefaire-Jewish Childrens Bureau, Shaker Heights, OH, $10,000. For Reserve Fund - A Gift to the Bellefaire Fund. 1991.

2457-7 Benjamin Rose Institute, Cleveland, OH, $114,808. For study of nursing assistant and resident interactions in four local nursing homes. 1991.

2457-8 Case Western Reserve University, Frances Payne Bolton School of Nursing, Cleveland, OH, $135,585. For nursing Informatics Program. 1991.

2457-9 Central School of Practical Nursing, Cleveland, OH, $20,777. For salary support for home nursing program. 1991.

2457-10 Cleveland Health Education Museum, Cleveland, OH, $114,595. Toward increased costs associated with new executive director and new position of director of adult education. 1991.

2457-11 Cleveland State University, Cleveland, OH, $100,000. For professional health training in physical/occupational therapy and speech and hearing programs. 1991.

2457-12 Cleveland, City of, Cleveland, OH, $67,667. For development of lead abatement program for city, in association with Environmental Health Watch. 1991.

2457-13 Community United Headstart, Cleveland, OH, $15,358. For prenatal education and support program. 1991.

2457-14 Cuyahoga County Board of Commissioners, Department of Human Services, Cleveland, OH, $23,250. For Home Health Aide training program in geriatrics. 1991.

2457-15 Cuyahoga County District Board of Health, Cleveland, OH, $60,926. For assessment of health needs in East Cleveland. 1991.

2457-16 Epilepsy Foundation of Northeast Ohio, Cleveland, OH, $93,067. For Epilepsy Family Action Services Program. 1991.

2457-17 Epilepsy Foundation of Northeast Ohio, Cleveland, OH, $91,998. For teen transition program expansion in Cleveland Public Schools. 1991.

2457-18 Health Hill Hospital for Children, Cleveland, OH, $60,000. For The Family Center. 1991.

2457-19 Lake County Free Medical Clinic, Painesville, OH, $20,000. For prescription medication subsidy program. 1991.

2457-20 Malachi House, Cleveland, OH, $150,000. For bridge funding for community health programs. 1991.

2457-21 Menorah Park Jewish Home for Aged, Beachwood, OH, $116,557. For restraint reduction program in at least four area nursing homes. 1991.

2457-22 MetroHealth Foundation, Cleveland, OH, $126,000. For wellness program at MetroHealth Clement Center for Family Care. 1991.

2457-23 Neighborhood Health Care, Cleveland, OH, $57,330. For pilot physician retention program at Neighborhood Family Practice. 1991.

2457-24 Star of the Sea, Cleveland, OH, $92,550. For renovation of Stella Maris dependency treatment center. 1991.

2457-25 Task Force on Violent Crime Charitable Fund, Cleveland, OH, $38,843. For substance abuse public education, prevention and

corrections programs by Substance Abuse Initiative for Greater Cleveland. 1991.

2457-26 United Cerebral Palsy Association of Greater Cleveland, Cleveland, OH, $22,000. For organizational study. 1991.

2457-27 Witness/Victim Service Center, Family Violence Program, Cleveland, OH, $27,000. For clinical treatment services for perpetrators of family violence. 1991.

2458
The Cleveland-Cliffs Foundation
1100 Superior Ave.
Cleveland 44114-2589   (216) 694-5700

Established in 1960 in OH.

Donor(s): Cleveland-Cliffs, Inc., Tilden Mining Co., Empire Iron Mining Partnership, Hibbing Taconite Co.

Foundation type: Company-sponsored

Financial data (yr. ended 12/31/91): Assets, $800,169 (M); gifts received, $600,000; expenditures, $406,612; qualifying distributions, $405,694, including $320,030 for 127 grants (high: $39,878; low: $100) and $85,370 for 96 employee matching gifts.

Purpose and activities: Support for higher education, including an employee matching gift program, community funds, museums, hospitals, and social services, including youth agencies. Priority given to innovative educational projects.

Fields of interest: Hospitals, community funds, higher education, youth, social services, education, hospitals—building funds, museums.

Types of support: General purposes, building funds, research, professorships, scholarship funds, employee matching gifts, annual campaigns, capital campaigns.

Limitations: Giving primarily in areas of company operations, with emphasis on Cleveland, OH, MI, and MN. No grants to individuals; no loans.

Publications: Application guidelines.

Application information: Application form not required.

> *Initial approach:* Proposal
> *Copies of proposal:* 1
> *Deadline(s):* None
> *Board meeting date(s):* Jan. and July; disbursement committee meets monthly
> *Final notification:* 3 months
> *Write:* David L. Gardner, Secy.

Officers and Trustees:* M.T. Moore,* Chair. and C.E.O.; John L. Kelly,* V.P., Public Affairs; David L. Gardner, Secy.-Treas.; Robert S. Colman, E. Mandell de Windt, James D. Ireland III, E. Bradley Jones, Leslie Lazar Kanuk, Gilbert H. Lamphere, Stephen B. Oresman, David V. Ragone, Alan Schwartz, Samuel K. Scovil, Jeptha H. Wade, Alton W. Whitehouse, Jr.

Number of staff: None.

EIN: 346525124

2459
The George W. Codrington Charitable Foundation
c/o Ameritrust Co., N.A., Trust Tax
P.O. Box 5937
Cleveland 44101   (216) 566-5837

Application address: 1100 National City Bank Bldg., Cleveland, OH 44114

Trust established in 1955 in OH.
Donor(s): George W. Codrington.‡
Foundation type: Independent
Financial data (yr. ended 12/31/91): Assets, $10,607,747 (M); expenditures, $536,999; qualifying distributions, $470,400, including $470,400 for 75 grants (high: $57,000; low: $200; average: $200-$57,000).
Purpose and activities: Giving primarily for higher education and hospitals; support also for community funds, museums and other arts groups, and youth.
Fields of interest: Education, higher education, hospitals, AIDS, community funds, arts, museums, youth, child development.
Types of support: Annual campaigns, continuing support, capital campaigns, special projects, equipment, research.
Limitations: Giving limited to Cuyahoga County, OH, and the surrounding area. No grants to individuals, or for endowment funds; no loans.
Publications: Annual report (including application guidelines).
Application information: Application form not required.
  Initial approach: Full proposal
  Copies of proposal: 6
  Deadline(s): Submit proposal preferably the month before board meetings
  Board meeting date(s): Apr., June, Sept., and Dec.
  Final notification: Promptly after board meeting
  Write: Raymond T. Sawyer, Chair.
Officers and Supervisory Board:* Raymond T. Sawyer, Chair.; Douglas O. Cooper,* Secy.; John J. Dwyer, William E. McDonald, Curtis E. Moll, William Seelboch.
Trustee: Ameritrust Co., N.A.
Number of staff: None.
EIN: 346507457

2460
The Columbus Foundation ▼
1234 East Broad St.
Columbus 43205   (614) 251-4000

Established in 1943 in OH by resolution and declaration of trust.
Foundation type: Community
Financial data (yr. ended 12/31/90): Assets, $150,581,845 (M); gifts received, $21,481,262; expenditures, $14,394,249; qualifying distributions, $11,439,352, including $11,439,352 for 1,906 grants (high: $800,000; low: $50; average: $1,000-$50,000).
Purpose and activities: A public charitable foundation for receiving funds for distribution to charitable organizations mainly in the central OH region. Grants made to strengthen existing agencies or to initiate new programs in the following categories: arts and humanities, civic affairs, conservation and environmental protection, education, health, mental health and retardation, and social service agencies.
Fields of interest: Arts, humanities, civic affairs, conservation, environment, education, health, AIDS, mental health, social services.
Types of support: Seed money, matching funds, capital campaigns, land acquisition, publications,

renovation projects, special projects, technical assistance, continuing support.
Limitations: Giving limited to central OH from unrestricted funds. No support for religious purposes, or for projects normally the responsibility of a public agency. No grants to individuals, or generally for budget deficits, conferences, scholarly research, or endowment funds.
Publications: Annual report, application guidelines, newsletter, informational brochure.
Application information: Grant requests to the Columbus Youth Foundation must be submitted by the 1st Fridays in Feb. and Oct. for consideration at meetings held in Apr. and Dec.; requests to the Ingram-White Castle Foundation must be submitted by the 1st Fridays in Feb. and Sept. for consideration in Apr. and Nov. Application form required.
  Initial approach: Meeting with staff
  Copies of proposal: 4
  Deadline(s): For 1991: Health- Jan., Social Services- Feb., Arts and Conservation- Apr., Social Services- July, Civic Affairs- Sept., Education- Nov.
  Board meeting date(s): Jan., Feb., Apr., July, Sept., Nov.
  Final notification: Approximately three months after the given deadline
  Write: James I. Luck, Pres.
Officers: James I. Luck, Pres.; Raymond J Biddiscombe, V.P.; Barbara K. Brandt, V.P.; Tullia Brown Hamilton, V.P.
Governing Committee: John B. Gerlach, Chair.; Leslie H. Wexner, Vice-Chair.; J.W. Wolfe, Vice-Chair.; Don M. Casto III, Charlotte P. Kessler, Flora Delle A. Pfahl, Alex Shumate, Attorney.
Trustee Banks and Trustee Committee: Ameritrust Co., N.A., BancOhio National Bank, Bank One Ohio Trust Co., N.A., Huntington Trust Co., N.A., Society Bank, N.A.
Number of staff: 12 full-time professional; 11 full-time support.
EIN: 316044264
Recent health grants:
2460-1 Childrens Hospital, Columbus, OH, $65,000. To assist in providing indigent care to Franklin County families in clinic program. 1991.
2460-2 Childrens Hospital, Columbus, OH, $14,981. For operations. 1991.
2460-3 Columbus Area Council on Alcoholism, Columbus, OH, $150,000. For technical assistance to schools that want to establish Student Assistance Programs for drug and alcohol dependence. 1991.
2460-4 Columbus Speech and Hearing Center, Columbus, OH, $46,500. To establish pediatric hearing services program for children ages birth to three. 1991.
2460-5 Columbus, City of, Columbus Health Department, Columbus, OH, $70,000. For Children of Alcoholics Prevention Program. 1991.
2460-6 Columbus, City of, Columbus Health Department, Columbus, OH, $70,000. For Lifestyle Risk Reduction Prevention Program for children and youth. 1991.
2460-7 Columbus, City of, Columbus Health Department, Columbus, OH, $50,000. For case management coordinator for AIDS case management plan. 1991.

2460-8 Columbus, City of, Office of the Mayor, Columbus, OH, $40,000. For four inner-city neighborhood coalitions engaged in substance abuse prevention activities for one year. 1991.
2460-9 Ecco Family Health Center, Columbus, OH, $25,000. To provide comprehensive prenatal care, education and support for inner-city teens. 1991.
2460-10 Hannah Neil Center for Children, Columbus, OH, $52,500. For Willson Family and Child Guidance Clinic for mental health services to children. 1991.
2460-11 Health Coalition of Central Ohio, Columbus, OH, $40,000. For development and implementation of health planning process. 1991.
2460-12 Heinzerling Foundation, Columbus, OH, $100,000. For renovation and expansion of facility. 1991.
2460-13 House of Hope for Alcoholics, Columbus, OH, $75,000. For start-up funding for alcoholism counseling, education and treatment program for deaf and hearing impaired residents of Franklin County. 1991.
2460-14 Johns Hopkins University, School of Public Health and Hygiene, Baltimore, MD, $24,000. For scholarships to students in master's degree program who will provide medical care to residents of Uganda and Taiwan. 1991.
2460-15 North Side Child Development Center, Columbus, OH, $20,000. For Preschool Alcohol and Drug Abuse Prevention Program. 1991.
2460-16 Ohio Caring Foundation, Columbus, OH, $30,000. To match dollars raised from new sources in community to provide basic health care services at no cost to children of Franklin County working poor. 1991.
2460-17 Planned Parenthood of Central Ohio, Columbus, OH, $48,200. To provide education and support services to teenage mothers. 1991.
2460-18 Seneca County General Health District, Tiffin, OH, $12,000. For Homemaker/Aide Program for aging. 1991.

2461
Mary S. & David C. Corbin Foundation
1036 Society Bldg.
Akron 44308   (216) 762-6427

Established about 1970.
Donor(s): David C. Corbin.‡
Foundation type: Independent
Financial data (yr. ended 12/31/91): Assets, $11,244,862 (M); expenditures, $610,742; qualifying distributions, $511,585, including $511,585 for 36 grants (high: $125,000; low: $50).
Fields of interest: Hospitals, secondary education, social services.
Types of support: General purposes.
Limitations: Giving primarily in Akron, OH. No support for organizations which in turn make grants to others. No grants to individuals, or for annual fundraising campaigns, ongoing requests for general operating support, or operating deficits.
Application information: Application form not required.
  Deadline(s): Mar. 1 for consideration in Apr.; Sept. 1 for consideration in Oct.

Write: Valerie Clauss, Treas.
Officers: Joseph M. Holden, Pres. and Secy.;
James L. Hartenstein, V.P.; Valerie Clauss, Treas.
EIN: 237052280

2462
Coshocton Foundation
222 South Fourth St.
P.O. Box 6
Coshocton 43812   (614) 622-0010

Established in 1966 in OH.
Donor(s): Adolph Golden,‡ Edward E.
Montgomery.
Foundation type: Community
Financial data (yr. ended 09/30/91): Assets,
$3,449,203 (M); gifts received, $731,611;
expenditures, $259,470; qualifying distributions,
$200,652, including $200,652 for grants
(average: $3,000).
Purpose and activities: Support largely for the
improvement of a park and the downtown area;
giving also for a museum, health services, and
higher education.
Fields of interest: Civic affairs, education, higher
education, secondary education, health services,
hospitals, alcoholism.
Types of support: Capital campaigns, continuing
support, equipment, renovation projects, special
projects, student aid, matching funds, employee
matching gifts.
Limitations: Giving limited to Coshocton County,
OH.
Publications: Annual report.
Application information: Application form not
required.
  Initial approach: Letter
  Deadline(s): None
  Board meeting date(s): Quarterly
  Write: Orville Fuller, Treas.
Officers and Trustees:* Robert M. Thomas, Pres.;
Paul Bryant, V.P.; Randall H. Peddicord, Secy.;
Orville Fuller,* Treas.; Willard S. Breon, Samuel
C. Clow, Seward D. Schooler.
Distribution Committee: Fred E. Johnston, Chair.;
Mrs. Howard Gross, R. Leo Prindle, Bruce
Wallace, Harry Zink.
Number of staff: None.
EIN: 316064567

2463
James M. Cox, Jr. Foundation, Inc.
Fourth and Ludlow Sts.
Dayton 45402
Application address: c/o Cox Enterprises, Inc.,
P.O. Box 105720, Atlanta, GA 30348

Established in 1969 in GA.
Donor(s): James M. Cox, Jr.‡
Foundation type: Independent
Financial data (yr. ended 12/31/91): Assets,
$26,123,289 (M); expenditures, $1,337,851;
qualifying distributions, $1,211,333, including
$1,211,333 for 24 grants (high: $300,000; low:
$3,000).
Purpose and activities: Support for environmental
conservation, higher education, including schools
of journalism and media communications and
medical schools, and hospitals.

Fields of interest: Conservation, environment,
higher education, medical education, journalism,
hospitals.
Types of support: General purposes.
Limitations: Giving primarily in OH and GA.
Application information:
  Deadline(s): None
  Board meeting date(s): Annually
  Write: Carl R. Gross, Treas.
Officers and Trustees:* James Cox Kennedy,*
Pres.; Barbara Cox Anthony,* V.P.; James A.
Hatcher, Secy.; Carl R. Gross,* Treas.
EIN: 237256190

2464
J. Ford Crandall Memorial Foundation
311 Mahoning Bank Bldg.
Youngstown 44503   (216) 744-2125

Trust established in 1975 in OH.
Donor(s): J. Ford Crandall.‡
Foundation type: Independent
Financial data (yr. ended 12/31/91): Assets,
$4,311,000 (M); expenditures, $296,999;
qualifying distributions, $242,474, including
$230,379 for 15 grants (high: $60,000; low:
$2,150).
Fields of interest: Hospitals, social services, arts,
education, higher education, family services,
citizenship, community funds.
Types of support: Building funds, equipment,
endowment funds, scholarship funds.
Limitations: Giving limited to Mahoning County,
OH. No grants to individuals, or for operating
budgets or research; no loans.
Publications: 990-PF.
Application information: Application form not
required.
  Initial approach: Letter
  Copies of proposal: 3
  Deadline(s): None
  Board meeting date(s): Bimonthly
  Write: R.M. Hammond, Secy. and Counsel
Officers and Trustees:* Amy H. Gambrel,* Chair.;
William G. Marshall,* Vice-Chair.; Andrew
Bresko,* 2nd Vice-Chair.; R.M. Hammond,* Secy.
Number of staff: None.
EIN: 346513634

2465
Charles H. Dater Foundation, Inc.
508 Atlas Bank Bldg.
Cincinnati 45202   (513) 241-1234

Established in 1985 in OH.
Foundation type: Independent
Financial data (yr. ended 08/31/91): Assets,
$5,569,064 (M); gifts received, $175,750;
expenditures, $434,684; qualifying distributions,
$349,175, including $228,400 for 50 grants
(high: $20,000; low: $500).
Purpose and activities: Support primarily for
social and family services, with emphasis on
services for children and the disadvantaged;
support also for hospitals, education, including
libraries, and museums and other fine arts groups.
Fields of interest: Social services, child
development, child welfare, youth, family
services, hospitals, education, libraries, fine arts,
museums.

Types of support: Annual campaigns, building
funds, consulting services, continuing support,
equipment, general purposes, program-related
investments, scholarship funds, seed money,
special projects.
Limitations: Giving primarily in the greater
Cincinnati, OH, area.
Publications: 990-PF.
Application information: Application form
required.
  Initial approach: Letter requesting application
  form
  Copies of proposal: 4
  Deadline(s): None
  Board meeting date(s): Monthly
  Final notification: Within 2 months
  Write: Bruce A. Krone, Secy.
Officers and Trustees:* Paul W. Krone,* Pres.;
Bruce A. Krone,* Secy.; Stanley J. Frank, Jr., David
L. Olberding, John D. Silvati.
EIN: 311150951

2466
The Dayton Foundation
2100 Kettering Tower
Dayton 45423-1395   (513) 222-0410
FAX: (513) 222-0636

Established in 1921 in OH by resolution and
declaration of trust.
Foundation type: Community
Financial data (yr. ended 12/31/90): Assets,
$39,986,947 (M); gifts received, $7,901,819;
expenditures, $7,744,075; qualifying
distributions, $7,927,554, including $7,232,896
for grants (average: $1,000-$10,000) and $60,700
for 27 grants to individuals (high: $30,510; low:
$90; average: $300-$1,500).
Purpose and activities: To assist public charitable,
benevolent and educational purposes which
benefit local citizens and respond to a wide
variety of community needs, including cultural
programs, community development, health and
social services, and youth; "to help launch new
projects which represent a unique and
unduplicated opportunity for the community,"
and to generate matching funds.
Fields of interest: Community development, civic
affairs, health services, hospitals, cultural
programs, arts, humanities, conservation,
environment, education, youth, social services.
Types of support: Seed money, building funds,
equipment, matching funds, technical assistance,
special projects, capital campaigns, conferences
and seminars, consulting services, emergency
funds, endowment funds, renovation projects,
internships, land acquisition, publications,
research, scholarship funds.
Limitations: Giving limited to the greater Dayton,
OH, area. No support for religious organizations
for religious purposes. No grants to individuals
(except for awards to teachers and municipal
employees), or for operating budgets, exchange
programs, professorships, continuing support,
annual campaigns, or deficit financing; no loans
or program-related investments.
Publications: Annual report (including application
guidelines), newsletter, program policy statement,
application guidelines, informational brochure.
Application information: Application form not
required.
  Initial approach: Proposal, telephone, or letter

Copies of proposal: 1
Deadline(s): Mar., July, Sept., and Nov.
Board meeting date(s): 4 times per year
Final notification: 4 to 6 weeks
Write: Janet Henry, V.P., Prog.
Officers and Governing Board:* Jesse Philips,* Chair.; Thomas Danis,* Vice-Chair.; Darrell L. Murphy, Secy.; James A. Cash, Treas.; Charles Abramovitz, John W. Berry, Sr., Charles S. Brown, Richard F. Glennon, Lloyd E. Lewis, Jr., Burnell R. Roberts, Betsey Whitney.
Trustees and Bank Trustees: Avery Allen, Thomas G. Becker, Hudson Green, William A. Harrell, Donald H. Kasle, Dan Sadlier, Frederick W. Schantz, Bank One, Dayton, N.A., The Central Trust Co., N.A., Citizens Federal Savings and Loan Assn., Fifth Third Bank, The First National Bank, Dayton, Ohio, Huntington National Bank, Society Bank, N.A.
Number of staff: 8 full-time professional; 5 part-time professional; 3 full-time support; 2 part-time support.
EIN: 316027287
Recent health grants:
2466-1 Childrens Medical Center, Dayton, OH, $17,906. 1990.
2466-2 Memorial Sloan-Kettering Cancer Center, NYC, NY, $105,150. 1990.
2466-3 Miami Valley Health Foundation, Dayton, OH, $15,470. 1990.
2466-4 Miami Valley Regional Planning Commission, Dayton, OH, $10,000. Toward work program of Partnership, including major efforts in affordable housing, homelessness, young adult self-sufficiency and prevention of substance abuse. 1990.
2466-5 Planned Parenthood Association of Miami Valley, Dayton, OH, $22,868. 1990.

2467
The Dayton Power & Light Company Foundation
Courthouse Plaza, S.W.
P.O. Box 1247
Dayton 45402   (513) 259-7131

Established in 1984 in OH.
Donor(s): Dayton Power & Light Co.
Foundation type: Company-sponsored
Financial data (yr. ended 12/31/91): Assets, $17,619,151 (M); expenditures, $734,524; qualifying distributions, $610,828, including $610,828 for grants (average: $25-$250,000).
Fields of interest: Civic affairs, race relations, community development, energy, engineering, health, welfare, museums, cultural programs, arts, environment, education, literacy, general charitable giving.
Types of support: Capital campaigns, operating budgets, scholarship funds, general purposes, annual campaigns.
Limitations: Giving primarily in west central OH.
Application information:
Copies of proposal: 1
Deadline(s): None
Board meeting date(s): Quarterly
Write: Sharon M. Tolliver
Officers and Trustees:* Stephen F. Kozair,* Pres.; Judy W. Lansaw,* Secy.; Thomas M. Jenkins,* Treas.
Number of staff: 1 full-time professional.
EIN: 311138883

2468
George H. Deuble Foundation
c/o Ameritrust Co., N.A.
Box 5937
Cleveland 44101
Mailing address: c/o DCC Corp., P.O. Box 2288, North Canton, OH 44720; Tel.: (216) 494-0494

Trust established in 1947 in OH.
Donor(s): George H. Deuble.‡
Foundation type: Independent
Financial data (yr. ended 12/31/90): Assets, $15,486,875 (M); expenditures, $786,204; qualifying distributions, $714,966, including $699,860 for 110 grants (high: $63,667; low: $49).
Fields of interest: Youth, higher education, cultural programs, hospitals.
Types of support: Continuing support, annual campaigns, emergency funds, building funds, equipment, endowment funds, matching funds, scholarship funds, loans, conferences and seminars.
Limitations: Giving primarily in the Stark County, OH, area. No grants to individuals, or for operating budgets, seed money, deficit financing, general endowments, land acquisition, research, or publications.
Application information: Application form not required.
Initial approach: Letter
Copies of proposal: 1
Deadline(s): None
Board meeting date(s): Monthly
Final notification: 1 month
Write: Andrew H. Deuble, Trustee
Officer and Trustees:* Walter C. Deuble,* Pres.; Andrew H. Deuble, Stephen G. Deuble, Charles A. Morgan, Ameritrust Co., N.A.
Number of staff: None.
EIN: 346500426

2469
The East Ohio Gas Company Giving Program
1717 E. 9th St.
Cleveland 44114   (216) 432-3232
Application address: Corp. Relations Dept., P.O. Box 5759, Cleveland, OH 44101; Tel.: (216) 736-6505

Financial data (yr. ended 12/31/90): Total giving, $960,000, including $935,000 for 100 grants (high: $20,000; low: $100) and $25,000 for 8 in-kind gifts.
Purpose and activities: "As part of our mission of strengthening the economic climate and the well being of the communities we serve, the East Ohio Gas Company has established the following objectives: To enhance the livability of communities throughout our service area; To strengthen housing, commercial, and industrial markets to enhance the economic vitality of our service area; To develop educational programs to improve opportunities for young people; and To expand opportunities for young people with disadvantaged backgrounds." Priorities are Community and Economic Development; Education; Health Care; Human Services; and Culture and the Arts. Most support is through the East Ohio Gas Company Fund of the

Consolidated Natural Gas Company Foundation of the parent company. East Ohio Gas has also developed large non-foundation programs to respond to: 1) Weatherization - East Ohio Gas in conjunction with the Ohio Department of Development provides the Housewarming Program for 4,000 low income customers each year; and 2) Housing for low income families - East Ohio Gas is a major participant in the Cleveland Housing Partnership which provides equity funds for development of housing by community development corporations.
Fields of interest: Business education, community development, hospitals—building funds, intercultural relations, elementary education, environment, homeless, hunger, civic affairs, disadvantaged, education, energy, hospitals, leadership development, minorities, literacy, public policy, urban affairs, urban development.
Types of support: Annual campaigns, conferences and seminars, donated equipment, equipment, technical assistance, building funds, in-kind gifts, capital campaigns, donated products.
Limitations: Giving limited to areas where the company has a customer base or a major facility in OH.
Publications: Program policy statement, application guidelines.
Application information: Application form required.
Initial approach: Letter; send to headquarters
Copies of proposal: 1
Deadline(s): Accepted throughout the year
Board meeting date(s): 6 times a year
Write: John Wilbur, Mgr., Corp. Relations
Number of staff: 2 full-time professional; 1 full-time support.

2470
The Eaton Charitable Fund ▼
Eaton Corp.
Eaton Ctr.
Cleveland 44114-2584   (216) 523-4822

Trust established in 1953 in OH.
Donor(s): Eaton Corp.
Foundation type: Company-sponsored
Financial data (yr. ended 12/31/90): Assets, $7,594,956 (M); expenditures, $3,386,655; qualifying distributions, $3,360,026, including $3,354,815 for 1,490 grants (high: $243,551; low: $50; average: $1,000-$10,000).
Purpose and activities: High priority to local organizations which serve the needs of company's employees and offer them opportunity to provide leadership, voluntary service, and personal financial support, including vigorous support for the United Way concept. General operating support and capital grants to health, human services, medical research, civic and cultural organizations, and independent college funds. Support for educational institutions preferably for engineering, scientific, technological, and business-related projects; capital campaigns limited to educational institutions with programs of direct interest to Eaton. Capital grants to health care facilities limited to geographic areas where there is a shortage of beds, facilities which serve needs of employees, and have reduced their ratio of beds to general public and shortened average stay, and

projects that will increase productivity and lower cost of health care.

Fields of interest: Community funds, higher education, education—building funds, health services, hospitals—building funds, youth, cultural programs, civic affairs.

Types of support: Operating budgets, building funds, employee matching gifts, annual campaigns, special projects, in-kind gifts.

Limitations: Giving primarily in areas of company operations. No support for religious denominations, fraternal organizations, and organizations which could be members of a United Fund or federated community fund but who choose not to participate. No grants to individuals, or for endowment funds, or fundraising events outside of specific company interests; no loans.

Publications: Corporate giving report, annual report, application guidelines.

Application information: Contribution requests should be made through a local Eaton manager wherever possible. Application form not required.

   Initial approach: Letter or proposal
   Copies of proposal: 1
   Deadline(s): None
   Board meeting date(s): Quarterly
   Final notification: 60 to 90 days
   Write: Frederick B. Unger, Dir. of Community Affairs

Officer: Frederick B. Unger, Dir. of Community Affairs.

Corporate Contributions Committee: Marshall Wright, Chair.; William E. Butler, John D. Evans, Floyd M. Wilkerson.

Trustee: Society National Bank.

Number of staff: 2 part-time professional; 1 part-time support.

EIN: 346501856

Recent health grants:

2470-1 Mayo Foundation, Rochester, MN, $10,000. 1990.

2471
Elisha-Bolton Foundation
c/o Advisory Services
1422 Euclid Ave., 1010 Hanna Bldg.
Cleveland 44115-2078   (216) 363-6485

Established in 1986 in OH.
Donor(s): Betsy Bolton Schafer.
Foundation type: Independent
Financial data (yr. ended 12/31/91): Assets, $3,501,400 (M); expenditures, $202,460; qualifying distributions, $170,000, including $170,000 for 33 grants (high: $25,000; low: $500).
Purpose and activities: Emphasis on health, higher education, and Christian religious organizations.
Fields of interest: Religion—Christian, religious schools, health, nursing, higher education, international relief, ecology, community funds, music.
Types of support: Scholarship funds, continuing support, special projects, student aid.
Limitations: No grants to individuals.
Publications: Financial statement.
Application information: Application form not required.
   Initial approach: Proposal
   Deadline(s): None

Board meeting date(s): Sept., Oct., Nov., and Dec.
   Write: Paulette Kitko, Secy.-Treas.
Officers and Trustees:* Betsy Bolton Schafer,* Pres.; Gilbert P. Schafer III,* V.P.; Julian B. Schafer,* V.P.; Paulette Kitko, Secy.-Treas.
Number of staff: None.
EIN: 341500135

2472
The Thomas J. Emery Memorial
c/o Frost and Jacobs
2500 Central Trust Ctr.
Cincinnati 45202   (513) 621-3124

Incorporated in 1925 in OH.
Donor(s): Mary Muhlenberg Emery.‡
Foundation type: Independent
Financial data (yr. ended 12/31/90): Assets, $17,664,060 (M); expenditures, $932,141; qualifying distributions, $801,473, including $759,506 for 49 grants (high: $55,000; low: $1,000).
Fields of interest: Higher education, secondary education, cultural programs, youth, hospitals, social services.
Limitations: Giving primarily in Cincinnati, OH.
Application information: Application form not required.
   Initial approach: Letter
   Deadline(s): None
   Board meeting date(s): 4 times a year
   Final notification: 30 days to 3 months
   Write: Henry W. Hobson, Jr., Pres.
Officers and Trustees:* Henry W. Hobson, Jr.,* Pres.; Walter L. Lingle, Jr.,* V.P.; Frank T. Hamilton,* Secy.; Lee A. Carter,* Treas.; John T. Lawrence, Jr.
Number of staff: 2 part-time support.
EIN: 310536711

2473
Walter and Marian English Foundation
2744 Bexley Park Rd.
Columbus 43209-2232   (614) 239-1183

Established about 1978 in Ohio.
Donor(s): Walter English.
Foundation type: Independent
Financial data (yr. ended 12/31/91): Assets, $2,179,299 (M); expenditures, $98,655; qualifying distributions, $96,505, including $89,040 for 23 grants (high: $25,000; low: $35).
Fields of interest: Civic affairs, cultural programs, education, health, social services.
Limitations: Giving limited to Franklin County, OH. No grants to individuals.
Application information: Not accepting any new requests currently.
   Write: Ellen E. Wiseman, Trustee
Trustees: Walter English, Ellen E. Wiseman.
EIN: 310921799

2474
Bob Evans Farms Corporate Giving Program
3776 S. High St.
Columbus 43207   (614) 491-2225

Purpose and activities: Supports youth, education, including higher and business education, hospitals, agriculture, and conservation.
Fields of interest: Agriculture, business education, conservation, education, hospitals, youth, higher education.
Types of support: Annual campaigns, continuing support, endowment funds, general purposes, capital campaigns.
Limitations: Giving primarily in marketing areas in FL, GA, IL, IN, KY, MD, MI, MO, OH, PA, TN, TX, and WV.
Publications: Corporate report.
Application information: Corporate Communications department handles giving. Application form not required.
   Copies of proposal: 1
   Deadline(s): Mar. 1
   Board meeting date(s): Apr.
   Final notification: May
   Write: Mary L. Cusick, V.P., Corp. Communs.
Number of staff: 1 part-time professional; 1 part-time support.

2475
The Thomas J. Evans Foundation
36 North Second St.
P.O. Box 919
Newark 43055-0764   (614) 345-3431

Established in 1965 in OH.
Donor(s): Thomas J. Evans.‡
Foundation type: Independent
Financial data (yr. ended 10/31/91): Assets, $14,293,898 (M); expenditures, $287,979; qualifying distributions, $376,880, including $227,267 for 9 grants (high: $92,767; low: $1,000) and $128,627 for 4 program-related investments.
Purpose and activities: Grants in the areas of public health, education, recreation, social services, church support, and protection of the environment; also land and buildings held for use by charitable organizations.
Fields of interest: Health, education, recreation, religion—Christian, social services, environment.
Types of support: Seed money, building funds, general purposes, scholarship funds, operating budgets.
Limitations: Giving primarily in Licking County, OH. No grants to individuals.
Application information: Application form not required.
   Initial approach: Letter
   Deadline(s): None
   Board meeting date(s): Quarterly
   Write: J. Gilbert Reese, Pres.
Officers and Trustees:* John W. Alford,* Chair.; J. Gilbert Reese,* Pres.; Sarah R. Wallace,* Secy.
EIN: 316055767

2476
Fairfield County Foundation
P.O. Box 2450
Lancaster 43130   (614) 653-8251

Established in 1989 in OH.
Foundation type: Community
Financial data (yr. ended 12/31/91): Assets, $2,857,213 (M); gifts received, $2,562,476;

expenditures, $115,471; qualifying distributions, $115,471, including $112,771 for 17 grants (high: $10,000; low: $150) and $2,700 for 2 loans to individuals.

Fields of interest: Aged, disadvantaged, recreation, drug abuse, hospitals, health, health associations, general charitable giving.

Types of support: Donated equipment, use of facilities, scholarship funds, continuing support, matching funds, seed money.

Limitations: Giving limited to Fairfield County, OH. No grants to individuals.

Publications: Annual report, application guidelines, informational brochure.

Application information: Contact foundation for application form. Application form required.

   Copies of proposal: 3
   Deadline(s): Dec., Mar., June, and Sept.
   Board meeting date(s): 3rd Thursday in Jan., Apr., July, and Oct.
   Write: Nancy J. Frick, Exec. Dir.

Officers: Donald C. Wendel, Chair.; Nancy J. Frick, Exec. Dir.

Number of staff: 1 part-time support.

EIN: 341623983

2477
Ferro Corporate Giving Program

1000 Lakeside Ave.
Cleveland 44114-1183   (216) 641-8580

Purpose and activities: Supports community and civic affairs, environmental issues, education, minority programs, United Way, welfare programs, health, and arts and culture.

Fields of interest: Civic affairs, environment, education, higher education, minorities, community funds, welfare, arts, cultural programs, health.

Limitations: Giving primarily in headquarters city and major operating locations. No support for fraternal and religious organizations. No grants to individuals.

Application information:
   Initial approach: Proposal
   Write: James M. Hill, Risk Mgr.

2478
Ferro Foundation

1000 Lakeside Ave.
Cleveland 44114-1183   (216) 641-8580

Incorporated in 1959 in OH.

Donor(s): Ferro Corp.

Foundation type: Company-sponsored

Financial data (yr. ended 04/30/92): Assets, $30,420 (M); gifts received, $275,000; expenditures, $250,200; qualifying distributions, $250,297, including $250,200 for grants.

Purpose and activities: Emphasis on a community fund, higher education, cultural programs, and hospitals.

Fields of interest: Higher education, cultural programs, arts, hospitals.

Types of support: Operating budgets, building funds, annual campaigns, capital campaigns.

Limitations: Giving primarily in OH.

Application information: Application form not required.

   Write: James M. Hill, Secy.-Treas.

Officers and Trustees:* A.C. Bersticker,* Pres.; H.R. Ortino,* V.P.; J.M. Hill, Secy.-Treas.

EIN: 346554832

2479
The Fifth Third Foundation

c/o Fifth Third Bank
Dept. 00864, Fifth Third Ctr.
Cincinnati 45263   (513) 579-6034

Trust established in 1948 in OH.

Donor(s): Fifth Third Bank.

Foundation type: Company-sponsored

Financial data (yr. ended 09/30/91): Assets, $11,615,892 (M); gifts received, $1,665,800; expenditures, $1,241,930; qualifying distributions, $1,187,198, including $1,131,419 for 227 grants (high: $56,950; low: $100) and $20,773 for 116 employee matching gifts.

Purpose and activities: Emphasis on higher education, hospitals, health agencies, youth, social services, cultural programs, and community development.

Fields of interest: Higher education, education—minorities, literacy, health services, hospitals, youth, social services, community development, cultural programs, arts, performing arts.

Types of support: Continuing support, annual campaigns, seed money, building funds, equipment, special projects, publications, capital campaigns, renovation projects, scholarship funds, employee matching gifts.

Limitations: Giving primarily in the Cincinnati, OH, area, and other operating areas of the corporation. No grants to individuals, or for endowment funds or fellowships; no loans.

Publications: Application guidelines, informational brochure, program policy statement.

Application information: Application form not required.

   Initial approach: Proposal
   Copies of proposal: 1
   Deadline(s): None
   Board meeting date(s): Monthly
   Write: Carolyn F. McCoy, Foundation Officer

Trustee: Fifth Third Bank.

Number of staff: 1 full-time professional; 1 full-time support.

EIN: 316024135

2480
Harvey Firestone, Jr. Foundation

c/o Bank One Akron, N.A.
50 South Main St.
Akron 44308

Established in 1983 in OH.

Foundation type: Independent

Financial data (yr. ended 12/31/90): Assets, $10,474,707 (M); expenditures, $446,059; qualifying distributions, $348,850, including $344,500 for 41 grants (high: $65,000; low: $500).

Purpose and activities: Emphasis on hospitals and education; support also for cultural programs, social services, and denominational giving.

Fields of interest: Hospitals, education, cultural programs, social services, denominational giving.

Types of support: General purposes.

Limitations: Giving primarily in the eastern U.S. No grants to individuals.

Application information: Contributes only to pre-selected organizations. Applications not accepted.

   Write: C.J. Goldthorpe

Trustees: Anne F. Ball, Martha F. Ford.

EIN: 341388254

2481
Firman Fund

c/o H & I Advisors
1030 Hanna Bldg., 1422 Euclid Ave.
Cleveland 44115-2078   (216) 363-1035

Incorporated in 1951 in OH.

Donor(s): Pamela H. Firman.

Foundation type: Independent

Financial data (yr. ended 12/31/90): Assets, $7,477,219 (M); expenditures, $351,646; qualifying distributions, $325,696, including $320,200 for 106 grants (high: $30,000; low: $50; average: $100-$50,000).

Fields of interest: Hospitals, medical education, higher education, secondary education, youth, community funds, cultural programs.

Types of support: Annual campaigns, general purposes, building funds.

Limitations: Giving primarily in OH. No grants to individuals, or for research; no loans.

Application information:
   Initial approach: Proposal or letter
   Copies of proposal: 1
   Deadline(s): 6 weeks prior to meetings
   Board meeting date(s): Apr. and Nov.
   Write: Pamela H. Firman, Pres., or Neil A. Brown, Secy.

Officers: Pamela H. Firman, Pres.; Neil A. Brown, Secy.; M.G. Mikolaj, Treas.

Trustees: Royal Firman III, Cynthia F. Webster.

EIN: 346513655

2482
Forest City Enterprises Charitable Foundation, Inc.

10800 Brookpark Rd.
Cleveland 44130

Trust established in 1976 in OH.

Donor(s): Forest City Enterprises, Inc.

Foundation type: Company-sponsored

Financial data (yr. ended 01/31/91): Assets, $28,016 (M); gifts received, $715,000; expenditures, $746,059; qualifying distributions, $746,059, including $745,975 for 281 grants (high: $210,500; low: $20).

Purpose and activities: Support for Jewish welfare funds, a community fund, and several other fields, including crime and law enforcement, leadership development, drug abuse programs, the homeless, and hunger. Additional support for education, including adult and elementary education, and cultural programs.

Fields of interest: Homeless, hunger, leadership development, elementary education, drug abuse, crime and law enforcement, Jewish welfare, education, cultural programs, community development.

Types of support: Annual campaigns, employee-related scholarships.

Limitations: Giving primarily in OH. No grants to individuals.
Application information:
Copies of proposal: 1
Deadline(s): None
Write: Nathan Shafran
Officers and Trustees:* Max Ratner,* Pres.; Sam Miller,* V.P.; Helen F. Morgan, Secy.; Albert Ratner, Charles Ratner, J. Struchen.
Number of staff: 3
EIN: 341218895

2483
The Harry K. & Emma R. Fox Charitable Foundation
c/o National City Bank
P.O. Box 5756
Cleveland 44101   (216) 621-8400
Application address: 900 Bond Court Bldg., Cleveland, OH 44114

Trust established in 1959 in OH.
Donor(s): Emma R. Fox.‡
Foundation type: Independent
Financial data (yr. ended 12/31/91): Assets, $5,688,879 (M); expenditures, $355,262; qualifying distributions, $308,574, including $301,100 for 70 grants (high: $20,000; low: $500; average: $1,000-$10,000).
Fields of interest: Hospitals, education, cultural programs, youth, social services.
Types of support: General purposes, special projects, equipment.
Limitations: Giving primarily in northeastern OH, with emphasis on the greater Cleveland area. No grants to individuals; no loans.
Publications: Application guidelines.
Application information: Application form not required.
Initial approach: Full proposal
Copies of proposal: 4
Deadline(s): May 15 and Nov. 15
Board meeting date(s): June and Dec.
Final notification: 6 months
Write: Harold E. Friedman, Secy.
Officer: Harold E. Friedman, Secy.
Trustees: Marjorie S. Schweid, Chair.; George Rosenfeld, Vice-Chair.; National City Bank.
Number of staff: 1 part-time professional.
EIN: 346511198

2484
France Stone Foundation
1000 National Bank Bldg.
Toledo 43604   (419) 241-2201

Established in 1952 in OH.
Donor(s): George A. France,‡ The France Stone Co., and subsidiaries.
Foundation type: Independent
Financial data (yr. ended 12/31/90): Assets, $8,016,530 (M); expenditures, $345,518; qualifying distributions, $291,750, including $285,750 for 24 grants (high: $122,000; low: $1,000).
Fields of interest: Youth, higher education, medical education.
Types of support: Continuing support, annual campaigns, research, scholarship funds.

Limitations: Giving primarily in northwest OH. No grants to individuals, or for operating budgets or special projects.
Application information: Application form not required.
Initial approach: Proposal
Copies of proposal: 1
Deadline(s): Oct. 1
Board meeting date(s): June
Final notification: 6 months
Write: Joseph S. Heyman, Pres.
Officers and Trustees:* Joseph S. Heyman,* Pres.; Ollie J. Risner,* V.P.; Andrew E. Anderson,* Secy.-Treas.
Number of staff: 1 part-time support.
EIN: 346523033

2485
Laura B. Frick Trust
c/o Wayne County National Bank
P.O. Box 550
Wooster 44691   (216) 264-1222

Foundation type: Independent
Financial data (yr. ended 12/31/91): Assets, $2,117,188 (M); expenditures, $125,337; qualifying distributions, $119,899, including $114,220 for 37 grants (high: $25,000; low: $250).
Purpose and activities: Giving primarily to a library, a hospital, and elementary and secondary education; some support also for social services and health.
Fields of interest: Libraries, hospitals, elementary education, secondary education, social services, health.
Types of support: General purposes.
Limitations: Giving primarily in the Wooster, OH, area.
Application information: Application form not required.
Initial approach: Letter
Deadline(s): None
Write: Stephen Kitchen, Sr. Trust Officer, Wayne County National Bank
Trustee: Wayne County National Bank.
EIN: 346513247

2486
The Sidney Frohman Foundation
c/o Muehlauser & Moore
P.O. Box 790
Sandusky 44871

Trust established in 1952 in OH.
Donor(s): Sidney Frohman,‡ Blanche P. Frohman.‡
Foundation type: Independent
Financial data (yr. ended 12/31/91): Assets, $8,478,784 (M); expenditures, $400,437; qualifying distributions, $348,703, including $336,712 for 44 grants (high: $25,000; low: $750).
Purpose and activities: To promote the well-being of humanity through assistance to the sick, aged, and needy, guidance of youth, aid to higher and secondary education, support of public health and recreation, and the furtherance of research.
Fields of interest: Welfare, aged, youth, higher education, secondary education, hospitals, recreation.

Types of support: Equipment, capital campaigns, general purposes, operating budgets.
Limitations: Giving primarily in OH, with emphasis on Erie County. No grants to individuals.
Application information: Contributes only to pre-selected organizations. Applications not accepted.
Trustees: Daniel C. Frohman, George T. Henderson, D.G. Koch.
EIN: 346517809

2487
Paul & Maxine Frohring Foundation, Inc.
3200 National City Ctr.
Cleveland 44114

Established in 1958 in OH.
Donor(s): Paul R. Frohring, Maxine A. Frohring.
Foundation type: Independent
Financial data (yr. ended 12/31/90): Assets, $3,477,238 (M); expenditures, $195,839; qualifying distributions, $186,209, including $184,000 for 22 grants (high: $100,000; low: $500).
Purpose and activities: Support primarily for higher and secondary education; support also for health and social service agencies.
Fields of interest: Higher education, secondary education, health, social services.
Types of support: General purposes, building funds.
Limitations: Giving primarily in OH. No grants to individuals; no loans or program-related investments.
Application information: Application form not required.
Deadline(s): None
Write: William W. Falsgraf, Secy.
Officers and Trustees:* Paul R. Frohring,* Pres.; Maxine A. Frohring,* V.P. and Treas.; William W. Falsgraf,* Secy.; Elmer Jagow, Paula Frohring Kuslan.
EIN: 346513729

2488
The William O. and Gertrude Lewis Frohring Foundation, Inc.
3200 National City Ctr.
Cleveland 44114   (216) 621-0200

Trust established in 1958 in OH; incorporated in 1963.
Donor(s): William O. Frohring,‡ Gertrude L. Frohring.‡
Foundation type: Independent
Financial data (yr. ended 12/31/90): Assets, $4,160,642 (M); expenditures, $255,806; qualifying distributions, $216,518, including $210,950 for 52 grants (high: $50,000; low: $500).
Fields of interest: Health, education, arts.
Types of support: Operating budgets, continuing support, annual campaigns, seed money, emergency funds, building funds, equipment, land acquisition.
Limitations: Giving primarily in Geauga, Lake, and Cuyahoga counties, OH. No grants to individuals, or for deficit financing, endowment funds, matching gifts, scholarships, or fellowships; no loans.

Application information: Application form not required.
> *Initial approach:* Letter
> *Copies of proposal:* 1
> *Deadline(s):* Submit proposal preferably in Mar. and Aug.; deadline 1 week before board meetings
> *Board meeting date(s):* May and Oct.
> *Final notification:* 3 weeks after board meetings
> *Write:* William W. Falsgraf, Asst. Secy.

Officers and Trustees:* Glenn H. Frohring,* Chair.; Elaine A. Szilagyi,* Secy.; Lloyd W. Frohring,* Treas.; William W. Falsgraf.
Number of staff: None.
EIN: 346516526

2489
The Lewis P. Gallagher Family Foundation
c/o Society National Bank, Trust Dept.
800 Superior Ave.
Cleveland 44114
Application address: 2817 Second Ave. North, Suite 207, Billings, MT 59101

Established in 1980.
Donor(s): Lewis P. Gallagher Family Charitable Income Trust.
Foundation type: Independent
Financial data (yr. ended 12/31/90): Assets, $5,297,342 (M); gifts received, $893,689; expenditures, $908,876; qualifying distributions, $869,807, including $751,047 for 23 grants (high: $200,000; low: $2,500) and $100,000 for loans.
Fields of interest: Higher education, secondary education, hospitals, youth, welfare.
Types of support: Scholarship funds, operating budgets, general purposes, equipment, endowment funds, capital campaigns.
Limitations: Giving primarily in OH and MT. No grants to individuals.
Application information:
> *Initial approach:* Letter
> *Deadline(s):* Sept. 1
> *Write:* Gilbert V. Kelling, Jr., Secy.

Officers: Howard H. Fraser, Pres.; Gilbert V. Kelling, Jr., Secy.; Monford D. Custer III, M.D., Treas.
EIN: 341325313

2490
The GAR Foundation ▼
50 South Main St.
P.O. Box 1500
Akron 44309   (216) 376-5300

Trust established in 1967 in OH.
Donor(s): Ruth C. Roush,‡ Galen Roush.‡
Foundation type: Independent
Financial data (yr. ended 12/31/90): Assets, $126,032,252 (M); expenditures, $5,808,257; qualifying distributions, $5,637,108, including $5,310,086 for 146 grants (high: $1,000,000; low: $900; average: $10,000-$50,000).
Purpose and activities: Grants to higher and secondary educational institutions for programs promoting the private enterprise economic system, and for the arts, hospitals, and civic and social service agencies, including youth activities.

Fields of interest: Education, higher education, secondary education, economics, arts, civic affairs, hospitals, social services, youth.
Types of support: Equipment, general purposes, endowment funds, matching funds, research, scholarship funds, seed money.
Limitations: Giving primarily in northeastern OH, with emphasis on Akron. No support for medical research or private non-operating foundations. No grants to individuals, or for fundraising campaigns or general operating expenses of the donee not directly related to its exempt purpose.
Publications: Application guidelines.
Application information: Application form required.
> *Initial approach:* Proposal
> *Copies of proposal:* 1
> *Deadline(s):* 1st of month prior to board meeting date
> *Board meeting date(s):* Feb., May, Aug., and Nov.
> *Final notification:* Jan. 1, Apr. 1, July 1 and Oct. 1
> *Write:* Hugh Colopy, Member of Distrib. Comm.

Distribution Committee: Joseph Clapp, Hugh Colopy, John L. Tormey, S.R. Werner, Charles F. Zodrow.
Trustee: National City Bank, Akron.
Number of staff: 1 full-time professional; 4 part-time professional.
EIN: 346577710
Recent health grants:
2490-1 Boys Village, Smithville, OH, $10,000. For Caring Family Fund. 1990.
2490-2 Childrens Hospital Foundation, Akron, OH, $300,000. For modernization program which will benefit all hospital patients regardless of their ability to pay. 1990.
2490-3 Cuyahoga Falls General Hospital, Cuyahoga Falls, OH, $25,000. For Easy Street program. 1990.
2490-4 Health Education Center of Akron, Akron, OH, $20,000. For endowment fund. 1990.
2490-5 International Health Services Foundation, Chardon, OH, $25,000. For endowment fund for Rehabilitation Center. 1990.
2490-6 Occupational Health Centers of America Educational Foundation, Worthington, OH, $10,000. To establish nursing scholarship program. 1990.
2490-7 Pegasus Farm, Hartville, OH, $25,000. Toward completion of office, restroom, classroom and viewing area facilities in their new indoor riding arena; for main driveway from road into new facilities in order to benefit both mentally and physically handicapped people. 1990.
2490-8 Saint Elizabeth Hospital Medical Center, Youngstown, OH, $15,000. Toward retiring Phase II expenses of Centralized Outpatient Oncology Program. 1990.
2490-9 Samaritan Hospital, Ashland, OH, $10,000. For equipment. 1990.
2490-10 United Way, Barberton Area, Barberton, OH, $25,000. To target critical areas of human service need with specific emphasis on assisting the poor through work of Hospital Care Committee, Barberton-Summit County Free Clinic and other agencies serving needs of the poor. 1990.

2490-11 Visiting Nurse Service, Akron, OH, $25,000. For endowment fund. 1990.
2490-12 Wooster Community Hospital, Wooster, OH, $10,000. Toward construction of antepartum exam room in new obstetrics unit of hospital. 1990.

2491
GenCorp Corporate Giving Program
175 Ghent Rd.
Fairlawn 44333-3300   (216) 869-4292

Financial data (yr. ended 12/31/90): Total giving, $431,729, including $422,729 for grants and $9,000 for in-kind gifts.
Purpose and activities: Support for education, including elementary and higher education, literacy, community service, arts and culture, and civic affairs.
Fields of interest: Civic affairs, arts, health, social services, literacy, elementary education, higher education.
Types of support: Annual campaigns, employee matching gifts, general purposes, donated products.
Limitations: Giving primarily in areas where GenCorp has facilities.
Application information: Company has a staff that only handles contributions. Application form not required.
> *Initial approach:* Letter to nearest facility
> *Copies of proposal:* 1
> *Deadline(s):* None
> *Board meeting date(s):* Frequently
> *Final notification:* 4-6 weeks
> *Write:* Karen Ingraham, Dir.

Staff: Karen Ingraham, Exec. Dir., GenCorp Found.
Number of staff: 1 full-time professional; 1 part-time support.

2492
The Goodyear Tire & Rubber Company Giving Program
1144 East Market St.
Akron 44316-0001   (216) 796-2121

Purpose and activities: Supports health and human services, education, civic, and cultural programs; also matches employee gifts for education only.
Fields of interest: Health, education, civic affairs, cultural programs.
Types of support: Employee matching gifts.
Limitations: Giving primarily in headquarters city and all operating locations. No support for religion. No grants to individuals, or for endorsements.
Application information: Application form not required.
> *Initial approach:* Letter
> *Deadline(s):* None
> *Board meeting date(s):* As needed
> *Write:* Patricia A. Kemph, Asst. Secy.

2493
Robert Gould Foundation, Inc.
P.O. Box 44338
Cincinnati 45244
Application address: c/o James J. Ryan, Esq., Taft
Stettinius & Hollister, Star Bank Ctr., Cincinnati,
OH 45202; Tel.: (513) 381-2838

Established about 1973.
Donor(s): Robert Gould.‡
Foundation type: Independent
Financial data (yr. ended 07/31/91): Assets,
$523,702 (M); gifts received, $363,500;
expenditures, $274,976; qualifying distributions,
$273,940, including $252,850 for 18 grants
(high: $200,050; low: $25).
Purpose and activities: Giving primarily to a heart
institute; some support also for cancer research,
cultural programs, and general charitable
activities.
Fields of interest: Heart disease, cancer, cultural
programs, general charitable giving.
Limitations: Giving primarily in Cincinnati, OH.
No grants to individuals.
Application information:
   Initial approach: Letter
   Deadline(s): None
Trustees: Alvin Gould, Helen Gould, James J.
Ryan.
EIN: 316064275

2494
Gould Inc. Foundation
35129 Curtis Blvd.
Eastlake 44094   (216) 953-5000

Incorporated in 1951 in OH.
Donor(s): Gould, Inc.
Foundation type: Company-sponsored
Financial data (yr. ended 12/31/91): Assets,
$2,897,843 (M); expenditures, $192,518;
qualifying distributions, $189,291, including
$189,291 for 112 grants (high: $20,053; low:
$20; average: $2,000-$5,000).
Purpose and activities: To strengthen the
socio-economic environment in areas of
corporate operations and of selected educational
and scientific institutions; grants largely for
scholarships for children of employees, hospitals,
cultural activities, and youth agencies; support
also for national organizations recognized as
beneficial to the broader national community.
Fields of interest: Hospitals, cultural programs,
youth, civic affairs, education, science and
technology, social services.
Types of support: Employee-related scholarships,
annual campaigns, research, employee matching
gifts.
Limitations: Giving primarily in areas of corporate
operations: Chandler, AZ; Pocatello, ID; Glen
Burnie, MD; Newburyport, MA; and Cleveland,
Eastlake, and McConnelsville, OH. No support
for groups that discriminate against minorities;
disease-related organizations, other than special
projects undertaken within Gould Inc.; or
religious and fraternal groups which do not
benefit entire commmunities. No grants to
individuals (except employee-related
scholarships); no loans.
Publications: Application guidelines.

Application information: Write to principal
manager of local Gould facility. Application form
not required.
   Initial approach: Letter or proposal
   Copies of proposal: 1
   Deadline(s): Jan. 31 for scholarships; Mar. 31
   for general requests
   Board meeting date(s): Apr. and as required
   Write: Joseph Huss, V.P., Human Resources,
   Gould Inc.
Officers and Directors: C.D. Ferguson,* Pres.;
M.C. Veysey,* V.P. and Secy.; J.W. Gaskin,* V.P.;
L.J. Huss,* V.P.
Number of staff: None.
EIN: 346525555

2495
The Grimes Foundation
200 South Main St.
Urbana 43078
Application address: 166 Tanglewood Dr.,
Urbana, OH 43078; Tel.: (513) 653-4865

Incorporated about 1951 in OH.
Donor(s): Warren G. Grimes.
Foundation type: Independent
Financial data (yr. ended 12/31/90): Assets,
$2,416,641 (M); expenditures, $205,159;
qualifying distributions, $182,002, including
$175,150 for 29 grants (high: $27,000; low:
$700).
Fields of interest: Higher education, secondary
education, elementary education, civic affairs,
hospitals.
Types of support: General purposes, scholarship
funds, building funds.
Limitations: Giving primarily in OH and FL. No
grants to individuals, or for endowment funds,
research, or matching gifts; no loans.
Application information: Application form not
required.
   Initial approach: Letter or telephone
   Copies of proposal: 1
   Deadline(s): None
   Write: Lewis B. Moore
Trustees: Clarence J. Brown, Jr., James S. Mihori,
Lewis B. Moore, Robert S. Oelman.
Number of staff: None.
EIN: 346528288

2496
Walter L. and Nell R. Gross Charitable Trust
105 East Fourth St., Rm. 710
Cincinnati 45202   (513) 721-5086

Established in 1955 in OH.
Donor(s): Members of the Gross family.
Foundation type: Independent
Financial data (yr. ended 12/31/91): Assets,
$4,233,558 (M); expenditures, $218,824;
qualifying distributions, $200,150, including
$199,950 for 56 grants (high: $40,000; low:
$100).
Fields of interest: Protestant giving, youth,
cultural programs, hospitals, health, higher
education, secondary education.
Limitations: Giving primarily in OH. No grants to
individuals.
Application information: Application form not
required.

   Initial approach: Letter
   Write: Walter L. Gross, Jr. or Thomas R. Gross,
   Trustees
Advisory Board: Thomas R. Gross, Walter L.
Gross, Jr., Patricia G. Linnemann.
Number of staff: None.
EIN: 316033247

2497
The George Gund Foundation ▼
1845 Guildhall Bldg.
45 Prospect Ave. West
Cleveland 44115   (216) 241-3114
FAX: (216) 241-6560

Incorporated in 1952 in OH.
Donor(s): George Gund.‡
Foundation type: Independent
Financial data (yr. ended 12/31/90): Assets,
$310,698,007 (M); expenditures, $13,171,843;
qualifying distributions, $11,996,651, including
$11,996,651 for 353 grants (high: $520,000; low:
$600; average: $10,000-$25,000).
Purpose and activities: Priority to education
projects, with emphasis on new concepts and
methods of teaching and learning, and on
increasing educational opportunities for the
disadvantaged; programs advancing economic
revitalization and job creation; projects
promoting neighborhood development; projects
for improving human services, employment
opportunities, housing for minority and
low-income groups, and meeting the special
needs of women; support also for ecology, civic
affairs, and the arts.
Fields of interest: Educational research, higher
education, elementary education, secondary
education, employment, community
development, social services, housing, minorities,
women, youth, AIDS, disadvantaged, ecology,
civic affairs, arts.
Types of support: Operating budgets, continuing
support, seed money, emergency funds, land
acquisition, matching funds, internships,
scholarship funds, special projects, publications,
conferences and seminars, program-related
investments, exchange programs, research.
Limitations: Giving primarily in northeastern OH.
Generally no grants to individuals, or for building
or endowment funds, equipment, or renovation
projects.
Publications: Annual report (including application
guidelines), application guidelines.
Application information: Application form not
required.
   Initial approach: Proposal
   Copies of proposal: 1
   Deadline(s): Jan. 15, Mar. 30, June 30, and
   Sept. 30
   Board meeting date(s): Mar., June, Oct., and
   Dec.
   Final notification: 8 weeks
   Write: David Bergholz, Exec. Dir.
Officers and Trustees: Frederick K. Cox,* Pres.
and Treas.; Geoffrey Gund,* V.P.; Ann L. Gund,
Secy.; David Bergholz, Exec. Dir.; Kathleen L.
Barber, George Gund III, Llura A. Gund.
Number of staff: 3 full-time professional; 3
full-time support.
EIN: 346519769
Recent health grants:

2497-1 AIDS Action Foundation, DC, $35,000. To study public financing options for health care for people with AIDS. 1991.

2497-2 American Foundation for AIDS Research, NYC, NY, $35,000. For Washington-based public policy office. 1991.

2497-3 Baylor College of Medicine, Houston, TX, $102,015. For mouse models for retinal degenerations. 1991.

2497-4 Baylor College of Medicine, Houston, TX, $55,000. For mapping and isolation of genes for recessively inherited retinal dystrophies. 1991.

2497-5 Catholics for a Free Choice, DC, $41,708. For operating support. 1991.

2497-6 Center for Policy Alternatives, DC, $40,000. For state-based legislative network for reproductive health. 1991.

2497-7 Center for Women Policy Studies, DC, $20,000. For national collaboration for AIDS Policy for Women. 1991.

2497-8 Child Guidance Center, Cleveland, OH, $33,340. For second-year support for ALERTeam. 1991.

2497-9 Cleveland Department of Public Health and Welfare, Cleveland, OH, $60,000. For lead hazard abatement project. 1991.

2497-10 Cleveland Rape Crisis Center, Cleveland, OH, $41,708. For strategic planning and second-year support for Pre-School Child Assault Prevention program. 1991.

2497-11 Communications Consortium, DC, $25,000. For Reproductive Health Media Strategies Project. 1991.

2497-12 Environmental Health Watch, Cleveland, OH, $25,000. For operating support. 1991.

2497-13 Environmental Health Watch, Cleveland, OH, $25,000. For lead poisoning project and organizational development. 1991.

2497-14 Father Flanagans Boys Home, Boys Town, NE, $66,080. For gene localization of Usher syndrome. 1991.

2497-15 Harvard University, Medical School, Boston, MA, $122,440. For candidate gene approach to hereditary retinal degenerations. 1991.

2497-16 Harvard University, Medical School, Boston, MA, $29,400. For investigation of genetic basis of autosomal dominant Retinitis Pigmentosa. 1991.

2497-17 Johns Hopkins University, Baltimore, MD, $79,550. For molecular genetics of human retinal dystrophies. 1991.

2497-18 MetroHealth Medical Center, Cleveland, OH, $205,000. For comprehensive family services at King-Kennedy estates. 1991.

2497-19 National Association of People with AIDS (NAPWA), DC, $25,000. To train local coalitions of policy advocates. 1991.

2497-20 National Black Womens Health Project, Atlanta, GA, $25,000. For national policy office staff. 1991.

2497-21 National Community AIDS Partnership, DC, $20,000. For local public policy activities. 1991.

2497-22 National Family Planning and Reproductive Health Association, DC, $15,000. For operating support. 1991.

2497-23 National Institute of Health, Bethesda, MD, $28,900. For molecular genetic study of Usher syndrome. 1991.

2497-24 National Medical Association, DC, $15,000. For videotape for African-American physicians on reproductive rights. 1991.

2497-25 National Minority AIDS Council, DC, $22,500. To increase minority involvement in AIDS policy issues. 1991.

2497-26 National Retinitis Pigmentosa Foundation, Baltimore, MD, $431,071. For retinitis pigmentosa research. 1991.

2497-27 Neighborhood Health Care, Cleveland, OH, $35,000. For Hispanic outreach worker. 1991.

2497-28 Planned Parenthood of Greater Cleveland, Cleveland, OH, $40,000. For public affairs programming. 1991.

2497-29 Preterm-Cleveland, Cleveland, OH, $130,000. For revolving loan fund for indigent women. 1991.

2497-30 Public Citizen Foundation, DC, $35,000. For litigation related to AIDS drug AZT. 1991.

2497-31 Rainbow Babies and Childrens Hospital, Cleveland, OH, $125,000. For second year of perinatal cocaine abuse project. 1991.

2497-32 University of California, Los Angeles, CA, $132,810. For molecular genetics studies in Retinitis Pigmentosa. 1991.

2497-33 University of Chicago, Chicago, IL, $133,221. For molecular genetics of inherited retinal defects. 1991.

2497-34 University of Iowa, Iowa City, IA, $74,275. For molecular genetic study of Usher syndrome. 1991.

2497-35 University of Iowa, Iowa City, IA, $35,035. For molecular genetic study of Usher Syndrome. 1991.

2497-36 University of Iowa Hospitals and Clinics, Iowa City, IA, $50,000. For clinical features and molecular biology of mutation-associated dominant and recessive Retinitis Pigmentosa. 1991.

2497-37 University of Michigan, Ann Arbor, MI, $90,956. For alternate reverse genetics strategy to isolate genetic loci for x-linked Retinitis Pigmentosa. 1991.

2497-38 University of Texas, Houston, TX, $86,321. For DNA linkage studies of degenerative retinal diseases. 1991.

2497-39 University of Texas, Houston, TX, $70,000. For molecular characterization of retinal degeneration slow gene product. 1991.

2498

H.C.S. Foundation ▼

1801 East 9th St., Suite 1035
Cleveland 44114-3103   (216) 781-3502

Trust established in 1959 in OH.
Donor(s): Harold C. Schott.‡
Foundation type: Independent
Financial data (yr. ended 12/31/91): Assets, $47,763,397 (M); gifts received, $4,937,278; expenditures, $2,089,790; qualifying distributions, $1,782,986, including $1,445,436 for 14 grants (high: $500,000; low: $5,000; average: $5,000-$500,000).
Purpose and activities: Grants primarily for a hospital, health organizations, and education.
Fields of interest: Health, education, handicapped.

Types of support: Operating budgets, scholarship funds, endowment funds, building funds.
Limitations: Giving limited to OH. No grants to individuals.
Application information: Application form not required.
  Initial approach: Letter
  Copies of proposal: 1
  Deadline(s): None
  Write: Trustees
Trustees: Francie S. Hiltz, L. Thomas Hiltz, Betty Jane Mulcahy, William Dunne Saal, Milton D. Schott, Jr.
Number of staff: 1 full-time professional.
EIN: 346514235

2499

The Hamilton Community Foundation, Inc.

319 North Third St.
Hamilton 45011   (513) 863-1389

Incorporated in 1951 in OH.
Foundation type: Community
Financial data (yr. ended 12/31/91): Assets, $17,461,730 (M); gifts received, $2,577,684; expenditures, $1,686,144; qualifying distributions, $1,616,566, including $1,590,768 for 250 grants (high: $180,000; low: $20) and $25,798 for foundation-administered programs.
Purpose and activities: Grants for local institutions, with emphasis on youth and child welfare agencies and scholarships. Grants also for health agencies including alcohol and drug rehabilitation programs, and cultural programs.
Fields of interest: Youth, child welfare, elementary education, community development, health, drug abuse, alcoholism, cultural programs, arts.
Types of support: Seed money, emergency funds, scholarship funds, conferences and seminars, special projects.
Limitations: Giving limited to Butler County, OH. No grants to individuals, or for operating budgets, continuing support, annual campaigns, deficit financing, capital or endowment funds, matching gifts, research, demonstration projects, or publications; no loans.
Publications: Annual report, application guidelines, newsletter.
Application information: Application form not required.
  Initial approach: Proposal
  Copies of proposal: 12
  Deadline(s): Submit proposal 30 days prior to 1st Monday of months in which board meets
  Board meeting date(s): Feb., Apr., June, Oct., and Dec.
  Final notification: Immediately
  Write: Cynthia V. Parrish, Exec. Dir.
Officers: John A. Whalen, Pres.; Cynthia V. Parrish, Exec. Dir.
Trustees: David Belew, Don W. Fitton, Jr., Richard J. Fitton, William Hartford, William Keck, Joseph L. Marcum, Richard Niehaus, Lee H. Parrish, Charles Roesch, Mary Ann Willis.
Trustee Banks: First National Bank of Southwestern Ohio, Society Bank, N.A., Star Bank, N.A., Butler County.
Number of staff: 2 part-time professional; 1 full-time support.
EIN: 316038277

2500
Hartzell-Norris Charitable Trust
c/o Fifth Third Bank of Western Ohio
326 North Main St., Trust Dept.
Piqua 45356

Trust established in 1943 in OH.
Donor(s): Hartzell Industries, Inc.
Foundation type: Company-sponsored
Financial data (yr. ended 10/31/91): Assets,
$4,289,927 (M); expenditures, $287,318;
qualifying distributions, $249,613, including
$248,473 for 756 grants (high: $25,000; low:
$10).
Purpose and activities: Giving for youth agencies,
social services, including the Salvation Army,
health and hospitals, community funds, Protestant
church support and religious associations, and
higher education.
Fields of interest: Youth, social services, health,
hospitals, community funds, Protestant giving,
higher education.
Limitations: Giving primarily in OH.
Distribution Committee: G.W. Hartzell, Chair.;
Roy H. DePriest, Miriam H. Hartzell.
Trustee: Fifth Third Bank of Western Ohio, N.A.
EIN: 316024521

2501
Haskell Fund
1010 Hanna Bldg.
Cleveland 44115   (216) 363-6481

Incorporated in 1955 in OH.
Donor(s): Melville H. Haskell,‡ Coburn Haskell,
Melville H. Haskell, Jr., Mark Haskell.
Foundation type: Independent
Financial data (yr. ended 12/31/91): Assets,
$2,671,133 (M); expenditures, $143,742;
qualifying distributions, $125,428, including
$123,700 for 57 grants (high: $16,000; low:
$500; average: $1,000-$5,000).
Purpose and activities: Giving locally for
community services; support nationally for:
education, including medical and other higher,
secondary and elementary institutions, building
funds, research, and adult education programs;
hospitals, health agencies, and medical research;
family planning, the elderly, and hunger
programs; theater; and the environment.
Fields of interest: Environment, community
development, community funds, social services,
higher education, secondary education, aged,
family planning, cultural programs, health
services.
Types of support: Annual campaigns, building
funds, continuing support, endowment funds,
general purposes, operating budgets, scholarship
funds, special projects.
Limitations: Giving primarily in the Cleveland,
OH, area for community service grants; other
grants awarded nationally. No grants to
individuals.
Publications: Annual report.
Application information: Application form not
required.
   Initial approach: Proposal
   Copies of proposal: 1
   Deadline(s): May 31
   Board meeting date(s): Within the 1st 2 weeks
    of June
   Write: Donald C. Cook, Treas.

Officers and Trustees:* Coburn Haskell,* Pres.;
Schuyler A. Haskell,* V.P.; Elizabeth C. Reed,
Secy.; Donald C. Cook, Treas.; Melville H.
Haskell, Jr., Mary H. Haywood.
Number of staff: None.
EIN: 346513797

2502
Heed Ophthalmic Foundation
c/o F.A. Gutman, M.D., Cleveland Clinic
Foundation
9500 Euclid Ave.
Cleveland 44195-5024

Trust established in 1946 in IL.
Donor(s): Thomas D. Heed,‡ Mrs. Thomas D.
Heed,‡ Society of Heed Fellows.
Foundation type: Independent
Financial data (yr. ended 07/31/91): Assets,
$3,952,937 (M); gifts received, $9,600;
expenditures, $295,061; qualifying distributions,
$229,007, including $200,800 for 42 grants to
individuals (average: $4,800).
Purpose and activities: Fellowships to U.S.
citizens who are graduates of medical schools
accredited by the American Medical Association,
and who show exceptional ability to further their
education in the field of diseases of the eye and
eye surgery or to do research in ophthalmology.
Fields of interest: Ophthalmology.
Types of support: Fellowships.
Limitations: Giving limited to U.S. citizens.
Publications: Application guidelines.
Application information: Application form
required.
   Initial approach: Letter
   Copies of proposal: 1
   Deadline(s): Dec. 31
   Board meeting date(s): Aug. and Nov.
   Write: Mary Jevnikar
Trustee: First National Bank of Chicago.
Number of staff: 1 full-time support.
EIN: 366012426

2503
Robert E. Hillier Family Charitable Trust
1365 Sharon-Copley Rd.
P.O. Box 70
Sharon Center 44274   (216) 239-2711

Established in 1974 in OH.
Donor(s): Pleadis Hillier,‡ Colon C. Hillier,‡ Ruth
E. Hillier.‡
Foundation type: Independent
Financial data (yr. ended 11/30/91): Assets,
$7,171,633 (M); gifts received, $1,343,320;
expenditures, $622,932; qualifying distributions,
$523,768, including $475,344 for 27 grants
(high: $79,463; low: $100; average:
$500-$10,000).
Fields of interest: Health, youth, social services,
aged, education, religion.
Types of support: General purposes, scholarship
funds, annual campaigns, special projects.
Limitations: Giving primarily in Medina and
Summit counties, OH.
Application information: Application form not
required.
   Initial approach: Letter
   Write: Robert C. Bolon, Exec. Dir.

Officer and Trustees:* Robert C. Bolon,* Exec.
Dir.; Henry S. Belden, Henry L. Metzger, John C.
Swartz.
Number of staff: None.
EIN: 237425779

2504
Honda of America Foundation
Honda Pkwy.
Marysville 43040   (513) 644-7899

Established in 1981 in OH.
Donor(s): Honda of America Manufacturing, Inc.
Foundation type: Company-sponsored
Financial data (yr. ended 12/31/90): Assets,
$3,146,477 (M); gifts received, $1,000,000;
expenditures, $192,687; qualifying distributions,
$188,205, including $187,721 for 15 grants
(high: $27,750; low: $50; average:
$978-$36,000).
Purpose and activities: Support for educational
institutions, cultural exchange, including an
educators to Japan program, and medical
research at a children's hospital.
Fields of interest: Education, Japan, medical
research, cultural programs.
Types of support: Scholarship funds.
Limitations: Giving primarily in areas where
Honda of America facilities are located and
associates reside in OH.
Application information: Application form not
required.
   Initial approach: Letter with proposal
   Copies of proposal: 1
   Write: Lourene Hoy or Sondra Fleming,
    Administrator
Officers and Trustees:* Hiroyuki Yoshino,* Pres.;
Toshi Amino,* Exec. V.P.; Susan Insley,* Exec. Dir.;
Tetsuo Chino.
Number of staff: None.
EIN: 311006130

2505
The Hoover Foundation ▼
101 East Maple St.
North Canton 44720   (216) 499-9200

Trust established in 1945 in OH.
Donor(s): Members of the Hoover family.
Foundation type: Independent
Financial data (yr. ended 12/31/91): Assets,
$35,638,304 (M); expenditures, $1,839,430;
qualifying distributions, $1,686,305, including
$1,595,267 for 75 grants (high: $213,935; low:
$75; average: $5,000-$50,000) and $12,851 for
19 employee matching gifts.
Purpose and activities: Grants for youth agencies,
hospital building funds, community funds, and
higher, secondary, and elementary education.
Fields of interest: Youth, hospitals—building
funds, community funds, higher education,
secondary education, education—early
childhood, elementary education, hunger.
Types of support: Building funds, operating
budgets, annual campaigns, scholarship funds,
general purposes.
Limitations: Giving primarily in Stark County,
OH. No grants to individuals, or for endowment
funds.
Application information: Application form not
required.

Initial approach: Letter
Deadline(s): None
Board meeting date(s): As required
Final notification: 1 week to 1 month
Write: L.R. Hoover, Chair.
Trust Committee: Lawrence R. Hoover,* Chair.; Ronald K. Bennington, Thomas H. Hoover, M.D., Joyce U. Niffenegger, Timothy D. Schlitz.
Trustee: Society National Bank.
Number of staff: None.
EIN: 346510994

2506
The Herbert W. Hoover Foundation
c/o Society National Bank
126 Central Plaza North
Canton 44702
Application address: United Bank Plaza, Suite 40, Canton, OH 44702; Tel.: (216) 453-5555

Established in 1947.
Donor(s): The Hoover Foundation.
Foundation type: Independent
Financial data (yr. ended 12/31/91): Assets, $12,865,054 (M); expenditures, $740,757; qualifying distributions, $669,001, including $590,637 for 29 grants (high: $85,000; low: $1,000).
Fields of interest: Environment, historic preservation, higher education, religious schools, health services, heart disease, social services.
Types of support: Building funds, equipment, general purposes.
Limitations: Giving primarily in OH. No grants to individuals, or for continuing support.
Application information:
Initial approach: Letter
Deadline(s): None
Write: Herbert W. Hoover, Jr., Chair.
Officer and Trustees:* Herbert W. Hoover, Jr.,* Chair.; Ruth H. Basner, Walter W. Johnson, Jr., Robert S. O'Brien, Blair C. Woodside, Jr., Society National Bank.
EIN: 346905388

2507
The Huffy Foundation, Inc.
P.O. Box 1204
Dayton 45401   (513) 866-6251

Incorporated in OH in 1959 as Huffman Foundation; name changed in 1978.
Donor(s): Huffy Corp.
Foundation type: Company-sponsored
Financial data (yr. ended 06/30/92): Assets, $665,075 (M); gifts received, $500,000; expenditures, $327,106; qualifying distributions, $324,009, including $308,815 for 111 grants (high: $35,000; low: $50; average: $1,000) and $15,194 for 42 employee matching gifts.
Purpose and activities: Support for museums, theaters, the fine arts, and other cultural programs; human services, including youth and child welfare, women, and recreation; health and hospitals; programs for drug abusers and alcoholics; community funds and civic affairs; and higher education.
Fields of interest: Arts, youth, women, recreation, health, drug abuse, community funds, civic affairs, higher education.

Types of support: Operating budgets, continuing support, annual campaigns, seed money, emergency funds, matching funds, scholarship funds, special projects, employee matching gifts, building funds, capital campaigns, consulting services, general purposes.
Limitations: Giving primarily in areas of company operations in OH, CO, CA, PA, and WI. No grants to individuals, or for deficit financing, endowment funds, research, or fellowships; no loans.
Publications: Informational brochure (including application guidelines).
Application information: Application form not required.
Initial approach: Letter or proposal
Copies of proposal: 1
Deadline(s): None
Board meeting date(s): Apr., Aug., and Dec.
Final notification: Approximately 2 weeks after board meetings
Write: Robert R. Wieland, Secy.
Officers and Trustees:* F.C. Smith,* Chair.; Harry A. Shaw III,* Pres.; Robert R. Wieland, Secy.; Richard L. Molen, S.J. Northrop.
Number of staff: None.
EIN: 316023716

2508
George M. and Pamela S. Humphrey Fund
c/o Advisory Services, Inc.
1010 Hanna Bldg., 1422 Euclid Ave.
Cleveland 44115-2078   (216) 363-6483

Incorporated in 1951 in OH.
Donor(s): George M. Humphrey,‡ Pamela S. Humphrey.‡
Foundation type: Independent
Financial data (yr. ended 12/31/91): Assets, $8,758,014 (M); expenditures, $421,994; qualifying distributions, $390,440, including $383,900 for 58 grants (high: $50,000; low: $500).
Purpose and activities: Support for hospitals, higher and secondary education, and community funds; support also for cultural programs and health agencies.
Fields of interest: Hospitals, higher education, secondary education, community funds, cultural programs, health services.
Types of support: Operating budgets, continuing support, annual campaigns, emergency funds, building funds, equipment, endowment funds, matching funds, professorships, internships, research, technical assistance.
Limitations: Giving primarily in OH, with emphasis on Cleveland. No grants to individuals; no loans.
Publications: Annual report.
Application information: Application form not required.
Initial approach: Letter or proposal
Copies of proposal: 1
Deadline(s): Prior to board meetings
Board meeting date(s): Apr., Nov., and Dec.
Final notification: 1 month
Write: Jackie A. Horning, Secy.-Treas.
Officers and Trustees:* Carol H. Butler,* Pres.; John G. Butler,* V.P.; Jackie A. Horning, Secy.-Treas.; Pamela B. Rutter.
EIN: 346513798

2509
Iddings Foundation
Kettering Tower, Suite 1620
Dayton 45423   (513) 224-1773

Trust established in 1973 in OH.
Donor(s): Roscoe C. Iddings,‡ Andrew S. Iddings.‡
Foundation type: Independent
Financial data (yr. ended 12/31/90): Assets, $8,199,586 (M); expenditures, $550,010; qualifying distributions, $611,426, including $464,038 for 82 grants (high: $20,000; low: $300; average: $5-$10,000).
Purpose and activities: Grants for pre-college and higher education, health care, mental health, care of the aged and handicapped, youth agencies, cultural programs, the environment, community welfare, and population control.
Fields of interest: Secondary education, higher education, health, mental health, aged, handicapped, youth, cultural programs, environment, community funds, family planning.
Types of support: Operating budgets, continuing support, annual campaigns, seed money, emergency funds, building funds, equipment, land acquisition, scholarship funds, special projects, publications, consulting services, capital campaigns, conferences and seminars, general purposes, matching funds, renovation projects.
Limitations: Giving limited to OH, with emphasis on the Dayton metropolitan area. No grants to individuals, or for endowment funds or deficit financing; no loans.
Publications: Informational brochure (including application guidelines), multi-year report.
Application information: Application form not required.
Initial approach: Letter or telephone
Copies of proposal: 8
Deadline(s): Mar. 1, June 1, Sept. 1, or Nov. 1
Board meeting date(s): Apr., July, Oct., and Dec.
Final notification: 1 week following meeting of distribution committee
Write: Maribeth A. Eiken, Admin. Secy.
Trustee: Bank One, Dayton, N.A.
Number of staff: 1 part-time professional.
EIN: 316135058

2510
The Louise H. and David S. Ingalls Foundation, Inc.
301 Tower East
20600 Chagrin Blvd.
Shaker Heights 44122   (216) 921-6000

Incorporated in 1953 in OH.
Donor(s): Louise H. Ingalls,‡ Edith Ingalls Vignos, Louise Ingalls Brown, David S. Ingalls,‡ David S. Ingalls, Jr., Jane I. Davison, Anne I. Lawrence.
Foundation type: Independent
Financial data (yr. ended 12/31/91): Assets, $17,583,000 (M); expenditures, $705,000; qualifying distributions, $670,000, including $670,000 for 23 grants (high: $150,000; low: $2,666).
Purpose and activities: Support mainly to organizations known to the trustees for "the improvement of the physical, educational, mental, and moral condition of humanity throughout the world"; grants largely for elementary, secondary, higher and medical education, school building funds, educational

research; support also for community funds and civic affairs, humanities programs, arts and culture, including museums, fine arts, dance, theater, performing arts and music, historical preservation, archaeology and anthropology, the environment and conservation, health programs, hospitals and hospital building funds, medical research, rehabilitation programs, the disadvantaged, and child development.
Fields of interest: Elementary education, secondary education, higher education, education, cultural programs, museums, health, medical research, disadvantaged, child development.
Types of support: Special projects, building funds, capital campaigns, research, endowment funds, equipment.
Limitations: Giving primarily in Cleveland, OH. No grants to individuals.
Application information: Application form not required.
  Initial approach: Proposal
  Copies of proposal: 5
  Deadline(s): None
  Board meeting date(s): As required
  Write: David S. Ingalls, Jr., Pres.
Officers and Trustees:* David S. Ingalls, Jr.,* Pres. and Treas.; Louise Ingalls Brown,* V.P.; Edith Ingalls Vignos,* V.P.; James H. Dempsey, Jr., Secy.; Jane I. Davidson, Anne I. Lawrence.
Number of staff: 2 part-time support.
EIN: 346516550

2511
The Ireland Foundation
c/o H & I Advisors
1030 Hanna Bldg., 1422 Euclid Ave.
Cleveland 44115-2004   (216) 363-1033

Incorporated in 1951 in OH.
Donor(s): Margaret Allen Ireland,‡ R. Livingston Ireland,‡ Kate Ireland, and members of the Ireland family.
Foundation type: Independent
Financial data (yr. ended 12/31/90): Assets, $8,199,188 (M); expenditures, $463,823; qualifying distributions, $394,292, including $388,350 for grants (high: $104,750; low: $100; average: $1,000-$5,000).
Purpose and activities: Grants largely for educational and charitable programs, with emphasis on nursing, higher and secondary education, and hospitals; grants also for music.
Fields of interest: Nursing, higher education, secondary education, education, hospitals, music.
Types of support: General purposes.
Limitations: Giving primarily in Cleveland, OH. No grants to individuals.
Application information: Funds committed to the same charities each year; foundation rarely considers new appeals.
  Initial approach: Letter and brief proposal
  Board meeting date(s): 1st Tuesday of Nov.
  Write: Louise Ireland Humphrey, Pres.
Officers and Trustees:* Louise Ireland Humphrey,* Pres. and Treas.; Kate Ireland,* V.P.; M.G. Mikolaj, Secy.; R.L. Ireland III.
EIN: 346525817

2512
Isaac & Esther Jarson - Stanley & Mickey Kaplan Foundation
(Formerly Isaac N. and Esther M. Jarson Charitable Trust)
105 East Fourth St., Suite 710
Cincinnati 45202   (513) 721-5086

Trust established in 1955 in OH.
Foundation type: Independent
Financial data (yr. ended 12/31/90): Assets, $3,324,067 (M); expenditures, $146,778; qualifying distributions, $130,857, including $130,757 for 84 grants (high: $30,250; low: $12).
Fields of interest: Civic affairs, community development, education, cultural programs, Jewish giving, health.
Limitations: Giving primarily in the greater Cincinnati, OH, area. No grants to individuals.
Application information:
  Initial approach: Letter
  Deadline(s): None
  Write: Stanley M. Kaplan or Myran J. Kaplan, Trustees
Trustees: Myran J. Kaplan, Stanley M. Kaplan.
Number of staff: None.
EIN: 316033453

2513
The Jochum-Moll Foundation
c/o David J. Hessler
6100 Rockside Woods Blvd., No. 345
Cleveland 44131

Incorporated in 1961 in OH.
Donor(s): MTD Products, Inc., and its subsidiaries.
Foundation type: Company-sponsored
Financial data (yr. ended 07/31/91): Assets, $14,370,626 (M); gifts received, $187,265; expenditures, $650,300; qualifying distributions, $579,834, including $579,834 for 46 grants (high: $83,334; low: $1,000).
Purpose and activities: Emphasis on higher and secondary education and hospitals; grants also for a community fund, welfare, and church support.
Fields of interest: Higher education, secondary education, hospitals, welfare, religion—Christian.
Limitations: Giving primarily in OH. No grants to individuals.
Application information: Contributes only to pre-selected organizations. Applications not accepted.
Officers and Trustees:* Theo Moll,* Pres.; Emil Jochum,* V.P.; David J. Hessler,* Secy.; Curtis E. Moll,* Treas.; Emma Gerhard, Darrell Moll.
EIN: 346538304

2514
The Robert E., Harry A., and M. Sylvia Kangesser Foundation
1801 East Ninth St., No. 1220
Cleveland 44114   (216) 621-5752

Incorporated in 1947 in OH.
Donor(s): Robert E. Kangesser,‡ Harry A. Kangesser,‡ M. Sylvia Kangesser.‡
Foundation type: Independent
Financial data (yr. ended 12/31/91): Assets, $3,164,906 (M); expenditures, $293,053; qualifying distributions, $252,010, including

$236,025 for 19 grants (high: $165,000; low: $200).
Purpose and activities: Support largely for Jewish educational organizations; support also for non-denominational health and medical services and civic affairs.
Fields of interest: Jewish welfare, Jewish giving, religious schools, theological education, health services, Israel, medical sciences, ophthalmology, hospitals—building funds, civic affairs.
Types of support: General purposes, building funds, annual campaigns, continuing support, operating budgets, capital campaigns.
Limitations: Giving primarily in the greater Cleveland, OH, area. No grants to individuals.
Application information: Application form not required.
  Initial approach: Proposal
  Deadline(s): Aug. 31
  Board meeting date(s): Usually in Sept. or Oct.
  Write: David G. Kangesser, Pres.
Officers and Trustees:* David G. Kangesser,* Pres.; Helen Kangesser,* V.P.; Hedy Kangesser,* Treas.
EIN: 346529478

2515
The Kettering Family Foundation
1440 Kettering Tower
Dayton 45423   (513) 228-1021

Incorporated in 1955 in IL; reincorporated in 1966 in OH.
Donor(s): E.W. Kettering,‡ Virginia W. Kettering, J.K. Lombard, S.K. Williamson, P.D. Williamson, M.D., Richard D. Lombard,‡ B. Weiffenbach,‡ Charles F. Kettering III.
Foundation type: Independent
Financial data (yr. ended 12/31/90): Assets, $7,431,928 (M); gifts received, $16,000; expenditures, $388,746; qualifying distributions, $310,900, including $310,900 for 25 grants (high: $50,000; low: $400; average: $5,000-$25,000).
Fields of interest: Education, higher education, arts, cultural programs, fine arts, conservation, environment, medical research, handicapped.
Types of support: Operating budgets, annual campaigns, seed money, deficit financing, building funds, equipment, land acquisition, endowment funds, special projects, research, publications, capital campaigns, continuing support, general purposes, matching funds.
Limitations: No support for foreign purposes, or religious organizations, public elementary or secondary schools; Ohio-based organizations, or for purposes within Ohio. No grants to individuals, or for scholarships or fellowships; no loans.
Publications: Annual report.
Application information: Application form not required.
  Initial approach: 1- to 3-page letter stating purpose and amount requested
  Copies of proposal: 1
  Deadline(s): Mar. 1 and Sept. 1
  Board meeting date(s): Mid-May and mid-Nov.
  Final notification: 1 month after board meetings
  Write: Jack L. Fischer, Secy.
Officers and Trustees:* Charles F. Kettering III,* Pres.; Susan K. Beck,* V.P.; Debra L. Williamson,* V.P.; Jack L. Fischer, Secy.; Jonathan G. Verity,

Treas.; Matthew B. Beck, Kyle W. Cox, Mark A. Cox, Douglas J. Cushnie, Karen W. Cushnie, Linda K. Danneberg, William H. Danneberg, Jean S. Kettering, Lisa S. Kettering, Virginia W. Kettering, Richard J. Lombard, Douglas E. Williamson, Leslie G. Williamson, P.D. Williamson, M.D., Susan K. Williamson.
Number of staff: None.
EIN: 310727384

2516
The Kettering Fund ▼
1440 Kettering Tower
Dayton 45423   (513) 228-1021

Established in 1958 in OH.
Donor(s): Charles F. Kettering.‡
Foundation type: Independent
Financial data (yr. ended 06/30/91): Assets, $83,870,762 (M); expenditures, $2,282,248; qualifying distributions, $2,263,728, including $2,214,500 for 38 grants (high: $1,000,000; low: $500; average: $5,000-$10,000).
Purpose and activities: Grants for scientific, medical, social, and educational studies and research; support also for community development and cultural programs, including the performing arts.
Fields of interest: Higher education, education, hospitals, health services, social services, community development, cultural programs, performing arts.
Limitations: Giving primarily in OH. No support for religious purposes or public elementary or secondary schools. No grants to individuals, or for fellowships or scholarships; no loans.
Application information: Application form not required.
   Initial approach: Brief outline of proposal in letter form
   Copies of proposal: 1
   Deadline(s): Apr. 1 and Sept. 1
   Board meeting date(s): Usually in mid-May and mid-Nov.
   Final notification: 10 days to 2 weeks after meeting date
   Write: Jack L. Fischer
Distribution Committee and Trustees:* Susan K. Beck, Member; Virginia W. Kettering,* Member; Jane K. Lombard, Member; Susan K. Williamson, Member; Bank One, Dayton, N.A.
Number of staff: None.
EIN: 316027115
Recent health grants:
2516-1 Mary Scott Nursing Center, Dayton, OH, $15,000. For general support. 1991.
2516-2 National Society to Prevent Blindness, Ohio Affiliate, Columbus, OH, $14,000. For general support. 1991.
2516-3 Planned Parenthood Association of Miami Valley, Dayton, OH, $30,000. For continued support. 1991.

2517
William H. Kilcawley Fund
c/o The Dollar Savings & Trust Co.
P.O. Box 450
Youngstown 44501-0450   (216) 744-9000

Established in 1946.
Foundation type: Independent

Financial data (yr. ended 12/31/91): Assets, $2,108,739 (M); expenditures, $308,875; qualifying distributions, $292,273, including $292,000 for 47 grants (high: $50,000; low: $500; average: $500-$25,000).
Purpose and activities: Giving primarily for higher and other education, Christian churches, community funds, performing and other arts, including museums, and health and social services, including youth and child development, programs for the aged and the homeless, and alcohol abuse programs.
Fields of interest: Education, higher education, religion—Christian, community funds, community development, arts, youth, aged, health services, health.
Types of support: Annual campaigns, building funds, capital campaigns, equipment, general purposes.
Limitations: Giving primarily in Youngstown, OH. No grants to individuals.
Application information: Application form not required.
   Initial approach: Letter or proposal
   Copies of proposal: 1
   Deadline(s): None
   Write: Herbert H. Pridham
Appointing Committee: Anne K. Christman.
Trustee: The Dollar Savings & Trust Co.
Number of staff: None.
EIN: 346515643

2518
Louise Kramer Foundation
c/o Society Bank, Trust Dept.
34 North Main St.
Dayton 45402   (513) 226-6076

Established in 1965 in OH.
Donor(s): Louise Kramer.‡
Foundation type: Independent
Financial data (yr. ended 12/31/91): Assets, $4,027,803 (M); expenditures, $214,891; qualifying distributions, $190,470, including $190,250 for 28 grants (high: $35,500; low: $1,000).
Fields of interest: Higher education, education, youth, child welfare, health services, hospices, hospitals, handicapped, arts, community funds, religion—Christian.
Types of support: Building funds, capital campaigns, operating budgets.
Limitations: Giving primarily in Dayton, OH.
Application information: Application form not required.
   Initial approach: Letter
   Copies of proposal: 1
   Deadline(s): Mar. 31
   Board meeting date(s): Varies
   Final notification: Varies
   Write: P.G. Gillespie, V.P. and Trust Officer, Society Bank, Trust Dept.
Officers and Trustees:* Joseph F. Connelly,* Pres.; Hugh Wall III,* Secy.; P.G. Gillespie, Treas.; W.T. Lincoln.
Number of staff: None.
EIN: 316055729

2519
The Kroger Company Foundation ▼
1014 Vine St.
Cincinnati 45201   (513) 762-4443

Established in 1987 in OH.
Donor(s): The Kroger Co.
Foundation type: Company-sponsored
Financial data (yr. ended 12/31/91): Assets, $7,693,000 (M); expenditures, $4,513,000; qualifying distributions, $4,420,000, including $4,420,000 for 1,313 grants (high: $334,450; low: $250; average: $1,000-$20,000).
Purpose and activities: To improve the quality of life in communities of company operations through support for united campaigns in communities which provide assistance and services to Kroger employees and customers, human services and substance abuse programs, cultural programs, educational institutions, and civic groups.
Fields of interest: Social services, drug abuse, cultural programs, education, civic affairs.
Types of support: Operating budgets, capital campaigns, seed money, general purposes, annual campaigns.
Limitations: Giving primarily in areas of company operations; certain national and regional groups will also be supported, but only to the extent to which they provide services to areas of company operations. No grants to individuals, or for endowment campaigns (but exceptions will be considered on a case-by-case basis where an endowment is an important part of a broader campaign that meets the foundation's objectives).
Publications: Application guidelines.
Application information: Application form not required.
   Initial approach: Proposal
   Copies of proposal: 1
   Deadline(s): None
   Final notification: Within 6 to 8 weeks
   Write: Paul Bernish, V.P.
Officers and Trustees:* Jack W. Partridge, Pres.; Paul Bernish,* V.P. and Secy.; Mary K. Hager,* Treas.; William Boehm, Donald F. Dufek, Paul Heldman, Patrick Kenney, Thomas E. Murphy, Lawrence M. Turner.
Number of staff: 1 part-time professional.
EIN: 311192929

2520
The Kuntz Foundation
2100 Kettering Tower
Dayton 45423   (513) 461-3870

Incorporated in 1946 in OH.
Donor(s): The Peter Kuntz Sr. family, The Peter Kuntz Co., and affiliated companies.
Foundation type: Independent
Financial data (yr. ended 12/31/91): Assets, $3,163,622 (M); expenditures, $232,051; qualifying distributions, $231,424, including $211,055 for 104 grants (high: $25,000; low: $80).
Fields of interest: Higher education, hospitals, Catholic giving, youth.
Limitations: Giving primarily in OH. No grants to individuals.
Application information:
   Initial approach: Letter
   Deadline(s): None

Write: Peter H. Kuntz, Pres.
Officers and Trustees:* Peter H. Kuntz,* Pres.;
Martin Kuntz,* Secy.; Richard P. Kuntz,* Treas.;
Dorothy Hobstetter, Edward Kuntz.
EIN: 316016465

2521
Fred A. Lennon Foundation ▼
29500 Solon Rd.
Solon 44139   (216) 248-4600

Established in 1965 in OH.
Foundation type: Independent
Financial data (yr. ended 11/30/90): Assets,
$8,163,783 (M); gifts received, $2,097,868;
expenditures, $3,502,836; qualifying
distributions, $3,478,630, including $3,478,630
for 202 grants (high: $500,000; low: $100;
average: $1,000-$10,000).
Purpose and activities: Giving for higher
education and Roman Catholic church support;
grants also for public policy, hospitals, cultural
programs, social services, and community funds.
Fields of interest: Higher education, Catholic
giving, hospitals, community funds, cultural
programs, public policy, civic affairs, social
services.
Limitations: Giving primarily in OH.
Application information: Contributes only to
pre-selected organizations. Applications not
accepted.
Officers: Fred A. Lennon, Pres.; A.P. Lennon, V.P.;
F.J. Callahan, Secy.
EIN: 346572287
Recent health grants:
2521-1 Cleveland Clinic Foundation, Cleveland,
OH, $500,000. For Ophthalmology Research
Fund. 1990.
2521-2 Cleveland Clinic Foundation, Cleveland,
OH, $300,000. For Bone Marrow
Transplantation Fund. 1990.
2521-3 Holy Family Cancer Home, Cleveland,
OH, $11,000. 1990.
2521-4 Huron Road Hospital, Cleveland, OH,
$50,000. For Lennon Diabetes Teaching
Center. 1990.
2521-5 Marymount Hospital, Garfield Heights,
OH, $10,000. 1990.
2521-6 National Psoriasis Foundation, Portland,
OR, $10,000. 1990.
2521-7 Rainbow Babies and Childrens Hospital,
Cleveland, OH, $28,000. 1990.
2521-8 University Hospital of Cleveland,
Cleveland, OH, $100,000. For J. L. Ankeney
Professorship Fund. 1990.

2522
Licking County Foundation
P.O. Box 4212
Newark 43055   (614) 349-3863

Established in 1956 in OH.
Foundation type: Community
Financial data (yr. ended 10/31/91): Assets,
$4,496,698 (M); gifts received, $308,110;
expenditures, $249,711; qualifying distributions,
$151,038, including $132,055 for 19 grants
(high: $50,000; low: $125; average:
$125-$50,000) and $18,983 for 30 grants to
individuals (high: $900; low: $500; average:
$500-$900).

Fields of interest: Youth, health, education, social
services.
Types of support: Scholarship funds, seed money,
student aid.
Limitations: Giving limited to Licking County, OH.
Publications: Annual report, informational
brochure.
Application information: Application form
required.
  Copies of proposal: 4
  Deadline(s): Varies
  Write: Sharon Schreiber
Officer: Frank B. Murphy, Chair.
Number of staff: None.
EIN: 316018618

2523
The Lincoln Electric Foundation
22801 St. Clair Ave.
Cleveland 44117   (216) 481-8100

Trust established in 1952 in OH.
Donor(s): The Lincoln Electric Co.
Foundation type: Company-sponsored
Financial data (yr. ended 12/31/90): Assets,
$721,592 (M); expenditures, $659,946;
qualifying distributions, $657,355, including
$656,750 for 53 grants (high: $110,000; low:
$250; average: $500-$20,000).
Purpose and activities: Emphasis on higher
education and a community fund; grants also for
hospitals and medical services, social service
agencies, cultural programs, and civic institutions.
Fields of interest: Higher education, community
funds, hospitals, health services, cultural
programs, social services, civic affairs.
Limitations: Giving primarily in OH, with
emphasis on Cleveland. No loans or
program-related investments.
Application information: Application form not
required.
  Initial approach: Letter
  Deadline(s): Sept. 1
  Board meeting date(s): Nov.
  Write: Ellis F. Smolik, Secy.
Officer: Ellis F. Smolik, Secy.
Trustee: Society National Bank.
Number of staff: 1
EIN: 346518355

2524
The Community Foundation of Greater Lorain County
1865 North Ridge Rd. East, Suite A
Lorain 44055   (216) 277-0142
Additional tel.: (216) 323-4445

Incorporated in 1980 in OH.
Foundation type: Community
Financial data (yr. ended 12/31/91): Assets,
$19,555,992 (M); gifts received, $1,404,550;
expenditures, $999,231; qualifying distributions,
$651,691, including $516,553 for grants
(average: $1,500-$10,000), $39,500 for 41 grants
to individuals (high: $2,000; low: $100; average:
$100-$2,000) and $95,638 for
foundation-administered programs.
Fields of interest: Social services, education,
health, civic affairs, cultural programs.

Types of support: Student aid, special projects,
general purposes, matching funds, technical
assistance, scholarship funds, seed money.
Limitations: Giving limited to Lorain County, OH,
and its immediate vicinity. No grants to
individuals (except for scholarships), or for annual
campaigns, deficit financing, or capital
campaigns.
Publications: Annual report, informational
brochure (including application guidelines),
application guidelines, newsletter.
Application information: Application form not
required.
  Initial approach: Proposal, letter, or telephone
  Copies of proposal: 1
  Deadline(s): Apr. 15, Aug. 15, and Dec. 15
  Board meeting date(s): Feb., June, and Oct.
  Final notification: 1 to 2 weeks following board
  meeting
  Write: Carol G. Simonetti, Exec. Dir.
Officers and Trustees:* John S. Corogin,* Pres.;
Billy S. Rowland,* V.P.; Larry D. Jones,* Secy.;
Robert S. Cook,* Treas.; Laurie Hoke, James W.
McGlamery, Fannie Moore-Hopkins, Benjamin
Norton, Celestino Rivera, Robert C. Singleton,
Kenneth S. Stumphauzer, Elizabeth W. Thomas,
Rickie Weiss, J. Milton Yinger.
Number of staff: 2 full-time professional; 1
part-time professional; 2 full-time support.
EIN: 341322781

2525
The Lubrizol Foundation
29400 Lakeland Blvd.
Wickliffe 44092   (216) 943-4200
Application address: 29425 Chagrin Blvd., Suite
303, Pepper Pike, OH 44122; Tel.: (216)
591-1404

Incorporated in 1952 in OH.
Donor(s): The Lubrizol Corp.
Foundation type: Company-sponsored
Financial data (yr. ended 12/31/91): Assets,
$3,896,988 (M); expenditures, $1,142,805;
qualifying distributions, $1,139,254, including
$932,700 for grants and $206,554 for 800
employee matching gifts.
Purpose and activities: Emphasis on higher
education, social services, civic affairs and
cultural programs, youth agencies, and health; the
foundation also conducts an employee matching
gift program.
Fields of interest: Youth, social services, civic
affairs, family services, general charitable giving,
hospitals, health, education, higher education,
secondary education, literacy, science and
technology, agriculture, engineering,
biochemistry, cultural programs, arts, fine arts,
performing arts.
Types of support: Operating budgets, continuing
support, annual campaigns, building funds,
equipment, matching funds, scholarship funds,
fellowships, research, employee matching gifts,
capital campaigns, general purposes.
Limitations: Giving primarily in areas of major
company operations, particularly the greater
Cleveland, OH, and Houston, TX, areas. No
support for religious purposes. No grants to
individuals, or for seed money, deficit financing,
endowment funds, demonstration projects,
publications, or conferences; no loans.
Publications: Annual report, 990-PF.

Application information: Application form not required.
  Initial approach: Proposal
  Copies of proposal: 1
  Deadline(s): None
  Board meeting date(s): As required, usually 4 times a year
  Final notification: 2 weeks after meeting
  Write: Martha L. Berens, Secy. and Foundation Mgr.
Officers and Trustees:* L.E. Coleman,* Chair. and C.E.O.; Douglas W. Richardson,* Pres. and C.O.O.; Martha L. Berens, Secy. and Foundation Mgr.; Jeffrey P. Hollis, Treas.; W.T. Beargie, J. Cody Davis, David K. Ford, George R. Hill, K.H. Hopping, J.F. Klemens, W.M. LeSuer.
Number of staff: 2 full-time professional; 1 full-time support.
EIN: 346500595

2526
M/B Foundation
c/o W.W. Boeschenstein
Fiberglas Tower, SG/15
Toledo 43659

Established in 1986.
Donor(s): William W. Boeschenstein, Elizabeth M. Boeschenstein.
Foundation type: Independent
Financial data (yr. ended 12/31/90): Assets, $254,883 (M); gifts received, $119,538; expenditures, $206,472; qualifying distributions, $206,472, including $206,000 for 24 grants (high: $50,000; low: $500).
Purpose and activities: Giving for health, including a medical center and substance addiction services, historic preservation and other cultural programs, and pre-college private education.
Fields of interest: Health, hospitals, alcoholism, historic preservation, cultural programs, elementary education, secondary education.
Limitations: Giving primarily in Toledo, OH; some giving also on the East Coast. No grants to individuals.
Application information: Contributes only to pre-selected organizations. Applications not accepted.
Trustees: Josephine M. Boeschenstein, William W. Boeschenstein.
EIN: 311195114

2527
The John C. Markey Charitable Fund
P.O. Box 623
Bryan 43506

Established in 1966 in OH.
Donor(s): John C. Markey.‡
Foundation type: Independent
Financial data (yr. ended 06/30/91): Assets, $3,554,820 (M); expenditures, $234,426; qualifying distributions, $206,884, including $206,350 for 65 grants (high: $25,000; low: $100).
Fields of interest: Higher education, Protestant giving, libraries, hospitals, arts, cultural programs, education, social services.
Limitations: No grants to individuals.

Application information: Application form not required.
  Initial approach: Letter
  Deadline(s): None
  Write: John R. Markey, Pres.
Officers: John R. Markey, Pres. and Treas.; Catherine M. Anderson, V.P. and Treas.; Arthur S. Newcomer, Secy.; L.W. Lisle, Treas.
EIN: 346572724

2528
Elizabeth Ring Mather and William Gwinn Mather Fund
650 Citizens Bldg.
850 Euclid Ave.
Cleveland 44114   (216) 861-5341

Incorporated in 1954 in OH.
Donor(s): Elizabeth Ring Mather.‡
Foundation type: Independent
Financial data (yr. ended 12/31/91): Assets, $7,957,984 (M); gifts received, $573,938; expenditures, $913,224; qualifying distributions, $890,741, including $848,138 for 41 grants (high: $539,612; low: $300).
Purpose and activities: Giving generally for specific civic purposes, including the arts, hospitals and health agencies, higher and secondary education, conservation, and social welfare.
Fields of interest: Civic affairs, arts, hospitals, health services, higher education, secondary education, conservation, social services.
Types of support: Annual campaigns, building funds, equipment, general purposes, publications, endowment funds.
Limitations: Giving primarily in OH, with emphasis on the greater Cleveland area. No grants to individuals, or for scholarships, fellowships, or matching gifts; no loans.
Application information: Application form not required.
  Initial approach: Letter
  Copies of proposal: 1
  Deadline(s): None
  Board meeting date(s): June and Dec.
  Write: Jane J. Masters, Asst. Secy.-Treas.
Officers and Trustees:* James D. Ireland III,* Pres.; Lucy E. Ireland,* V.P.; Theodore R. Colborn,* Secy.; George R. Ireland,* Treas.; Cornelia I. Hallinan, Cornelia W. Ireland, R. Henry Norweb, Jr.
Number of staff: 1 part-time professional.
EIN: 346519863

2529
Manuel D. & Rhoda Mayerson Foundation
312 Walnut St., Suite 3600
Cincinnati 45202   (513) 621-2300

Established in 1986 in FL.
Donor(s): Manuel D. Mayerson, Rhoda Mayerson.
Foundation type: Independent
Financial data (yr. ended 10/31/91): Assets, $3,686,006 (M); gifts received, $971,372; expenditures, $1,039,890; qualifying distributions, $1,491,617, including $968,095 for 70 grants (high: $240,000; low: $90).
Purpose and activities: Primary areas of interest include social services, the disadvantaged, youth, the handicapped, and education. Giving for

health; the performing and fine arts, including museums, theater, and music groups; Jewish welfare funds and other organizations; vocational and other education; and family and social services, including programs for the aged, the disabled and disadvantaged, the homeless, hunger, rehabilitation, women, and youth.
Fields of interest: Health, arts, Jewish giving, education, social services, family services, aged, disadvantaged, women, youth, handicapped.
Types of support: Capital campaigns, emergency funds, matching funds, seed money, special projects, technical assistance.
Limitations: Giving primarily in Cincinnati, OH, and South Palm Beach County, FL.
Publications: Multi-year report, application guidelines, informational brochure (including application guidelines).
Application information: Application form not required.
  Initial approach: Telephone
  Copies of proposal: 1
  Deadline(s): None
  Board meeting date(s): Bimonthly
  Final notification: Following meeting
  Write: Peter M. Bloch, Exec. Dir.
Officer: Peter M. Bloch, Exec. Dir.
Number of staff: 1 full-time professional; 1 part-time support.
EIN: 311310431

2530
John A. McAlonan Trust
c/o National City Bank
One Cascade Plaza
Akron 44309-2130   (216) 375-8398

Trust established in 1958 in OH.
Donor(s): John A. McAlonan.‡
Foundation type: Independent
Financial data (yr. ended 12/31/91): Assets, $5,184,795 (M); expenditures, $248,660; qualifying distributions, $214,794, including $214,261 for 49 grants (high: $10,000; low: $100).
Fields of interest: Cultural programs, hospitals, youth, education, handicapped.
Limitations: Giving limited to the Akron, OH, area. No grants to individuals.
Application information:
  Initial approach: Letter or proposal
  Copies of proposal: 6
  Board meeting date(s): May and Nov.
  Write: Mary H. Hembree, Trust Officer, National City Bank
Trustee: National City Bank.
EIN: 346513095

2531
The Mead Corporate Giving Program
Courthouse Plaza N.E.
Dayton 45463   (513) 459-6323

Financial data (yr. ended 12/31/90): Total giving, $1,381,668 for grants.
Purpose and activities: Supports civic and community affairs, the environment, libraries, performing arts, dance, theater, wildlife, youth, federated campaigns, education, health, hospitals, science, United Way. "At the Mead Corporation, the activity of charitable giving is a partnership

between the people of Mead and the communities where we live and work. Through charitable giving, Mead strives to assist communities in identifying the most pressing local needs and the best choices for meeting those needs. In all cases, the fundamental belief that guides Mead's charitable contributions is simple: Individuals can make a difference in improving the quality of peoples lives, and through individuals, the Mead Corporation can make a difference in the communities we serve." Mead's charitable contributions directly support organizations through financial grants and through in-kind contributions of Mead paper, products, or services. In providing support, Mead places the emphasis of its giving on meeting local needs in the communities where it operates, rather than supporting national programs. Further, Mead emphasizes contributions that will assist individual communities in identifying the most urgent needs among their citizens and ranking which needs ought to be met first. Mead also encourages an active and efficient collaboration among organizations to meet community needs. Practically, this means an emphasis on support for umbrella agencies, which generally serve a broad spectrum of citizens. Mead also emphasizes support for organizations that encourage citizen involvement and volunteerism. Combined foundation and corporate giving totaled $4,615,000 in 1990.
Fields of interest: Aged, arts, dance, disadvantaged, drug abuse, education—minorities, elementary education, environment, family services, handicapped, health associations, health services, hospices, law and justice, leadership development, libraries, literacy, mathematics, museums, music, performing arts, public affairs, public policy, rehabilitation, secondary education, social services, theater, volunteerism, wildlife, youth.
Types of support: In-kind gifts.
Limitations: Giving primarily in areas of company operations; no support for national organizations. No grants to individuals.
Publications: Informational brochure.
Application information: Dayton area groups contact the main address; others should contact their local business unit manager. Application form not required.
Initial approach: Letter
Copies of proposal: 1
Deadline(s): None
Write: Ronald F. Budzik, Exec. Dir.
Number of staff: None.

2532
Medusa Corporate Giving Program
3008 Lee and Monticello Blvds.
Cleveland Heights 44118   (216) 371-4000
Mailing address: P.O. Box 5668, Cleveland, OH 44101

Financial data (yr. ended 12/31/90): Total giving, $71,429 for in-kind gifts.
Purpose and activities: Support for arts, child welfare, handicapped, health, and education.
Fields of interest: Arts, child welfare, handicapped, health, education.
Types of support: Annual campaigns, continuing support, emergency funds.

Limitations: Giving primarily in headquarters and company locations.
Application information: Human Resources office handles giving. Applications not accepted.
Write: Daniel E. Somes, Pres. and C.O.O.
Number of staff: 1 part-time professional; 1 part-time support.

2533
Merrell Dow Pharmaceuticals Corporate Giving Program
10123 Alliance Road
Cincinnati 45242   (513) 948-9111

Purpose and activities: Support for higher and other education, fine arts, community development, health and human services, civic affairs, and arts and culture.
Fields of interest: Community development, community funds, education, fine arts, higher education, health, civic affairs, arts, cultural programs.
Limitations: Giving primarily in greater Cincinnati, OH and greater Indianapolis, IN, areas. No support for organizations receiving support from the United Way.
Application information: Application form not required.
Initial approach: Direct request to K.A. Lohr
Copies of proposal: 1
Write: Kenneth A. Lohr, Dir., Comm. Affairs
Administrators: Kenneth A. Lohr, Dir., Community Affairs; Janet Grubb, Secy. to Dir.
Number of staff: 1 part-time professional; 1 part-time support.

2534
Lewis N. Miller Charitable Trust
c/o Elyria Savings & Trust National Bank
105 Court St.
Elyria 44035

Established in 1985 in OH.
Foundation type: Independent
Financial data (yr. ended 12/31/91): Assets, $3,014,246 (M); expenditures, $157,291; qualifying distributions, $149,708, including $142,124 for 9 grants (average: $15,792).
Fields of interest: Animal welfare, higher education, social services, health, libraries, religion—Christian, historic preservation.
Limitations: Giving primarily in OH. No grants to individuals.
Application information: Contributes only to pre-selected organizations. Applications not accepted.
Trustee: Elyria Savings & Trust National Bank.
EIN: 346834475

2535
George Lee Miller Memorial Trust
c/o Society National Bank
P.O. Box 9950
Canton 44711-0950   (216) 489-5422

Established about 1982 in OH.
Foundation type: Independent
Financial data (yr. ended 12/31/91): Assets, $2,838,096 (M); expenditures, $128,233; qualifying distributions, $106,627, including

$106,627 for 16 grants (high: $8,975; low: $4,043).
Purpose and activities: Grants for hospitals, youth agencies, and Protestant church support; grants also for a university and a historical society.
Fields of interest: Hospitals, youth, Protestant giving, higher education, history.
Limitations: Giving primarily in the Canton, OH, area.
Application information:
Initial approach: Letter
Deadline(s): None
Write: Stephen C. Donatini
Trustee: Society National Bank.
EIN: 346748261

2536
Monarch Machine Tool Company Foundation
615 North Oak St.
Sidney 45365

Trust established in 1952 in OH.
Donor(s): Monarch Machine Tool Co.
Foundation type: Company-sponsored
Financial data (yr. ended 12/31/90): Assets, $2,365,980 (M); gifts received, $82; expenditures, $159,819; qualifying distributions, $150,125, including $144,450 for 33 grants (high: $25,000; low: $100).
Fields of interest: Higher education, youth, community funds, hospitals, community development, aged, social services.
Types of support: Building funds, general purposes.
Limitations: Giving primarily in OH, with some emphasis on Sidney.
Application information: Application form not required.
Deadline(s): Dec.
Write: Robert M. Peters, Treas.
Officers: N.V. Gushing, Pres.; R.J. Siewert, Pres.; R.B. Riethman, Secy.-Treas.; Robert M. Peters, Treas.
Trustee: J.A. Dunlop.
EIN: 346556088

2537
The Harry C. Moores Foundation
3010 Hayden Rd.
Columbus 43235   (614) 764-8999

Trust established in 1961 in OH.
Donor(s): Harry C. Moores.‡
Foundation type: Independent
Financial data (yr. ended 09/30/91): Assets, $23,776,816 (M); expenditures, $1,158,826; qualifying distributions, $1,132,109, including $1,130,000 for 76 grants (high: $100,000; low: $2,000; average: $1,000-$20,000).
Purpose and activities: Grants largely for rehabilitation of the handicapped, Protestant church support, hospitals, higher education, cultural programs, and social service agencies concerned with the aged, child welfare, and the retarded.
Fields of interest: Handicapped, cultural programs, Protestant giving, hospitals, health, higher education, aged, child welfare, social services.

Types of support: Seed money, scholarship funds, general purposes, capital campaigns, annual campaigns.
Limitations: Giving primarily in the Columbus, OH, area. No support for private foundations. No grants to individuals, or for endowment funds, or matching gifts; no loans.
Application information: Application form not required.
  Initial approach: Proposal in letter form
  Copies of proposal: 1
  Deadline(s): Submit proposal between Oct. and July; deadline Aug. 1
  Board meeting date(s): Apr. or May and Aug. or Sept.
  Final notification: By Oct. 15 (if affirmative)
  Write: David L. Fenner, Secy.
Officers and Trustees:* Francis E. Caldwell,* Chair.; David L. Fenner, Secy.; William H. Leighner,* Treas.; Ronald D. Bardon, William C. Jones.
Number of staff: None.
EIN: 316035344

2538
Burton D. Morgan Foundation, Inc.
P.O. Box 1500
Akron 44309-1500   (216) 258-6512

Established in 1967 in OH.
Donor(s): Burton D. Morgan.
Foundation type: Independent
Financial data (yr. ended 12/31/91): Assets, $21,142,404 (M); gifts received, $500,000; expenditures, $722,043; qualifying distributions, $597,335, including $553,000 for 9 grants (high: $553,000; low: $600).
Fields of interest: Education, higher education, business education, educational research, education—building funds, health services, mental health, family planning, religion, cultural programs, arts, general charitable giving.
Types of support: General purposes, building funds, special projects, research, endowment funds, operating budgets.
Limitations: Giving primarily in Summit County, OH. No grants to individuals.
Publications: Application guidelines, 990-PF.
Application information: Application form not required.
  Initial approach: Letter
  Copies of proposal: 1
  Board meeting date(s): 3 times a year
  Write: John V. Frank, Pres. and Trustee
Officers and Trustees:* John V. Frank,* Pres.; Weldon W. Case,* V.P.; Richard A. Chenoweth,* Secy.-Treas.; J. Martin Erbaugh, Thomas G. Murdough.
Number of staff: 1 part-time professional.
EIN: 346598971

2539
The Mount Vernon Community Trust
c/o First-Knox National Bank
One South Main St., P.O. Box 871
Mount Vernon 43050   (614) 393-5500

Established in 1944 in OH by declaration of trust.
Foundation type: Community
Financial data (yr. ended 12/31/91): Assets, $9,832,386 (M); gifts received, $484,032;

expenditures, $678,797; qualifying distributions, $560,198, including $560,198 for grants (high: $32,500; low: $300; average: $300-$25,000).
Purpose and activities: "To assist public, educational, charitable or benevolent enterprises." Grants, in accordance with the donors' wishes, for student loan and scholarship funds, Protestant church support, community funds, youth agencies, nursing and the health profession, and museums.
Fields of interest: Protestant giving, community funds, education, youth, nursing, health, museums.
Types of support: Scholarship funds, building funds, capital campaigns, continuing support, equipment, matching funds, seed money.
Limitations: Giving primarily in Knox County, OH. No support for religious purposes. No grants for endowment funds or research; no loans.
Publications: Annual report, informational brochure.
Application information: Application form required.
  Initial approach: Letter
  Copies of proposal: 7
  Board meeting date(s): Monthly
  Write: William Stroud, Chair., Dist. Comm.
Officers and Distribution Committee:* William A. Stroud,* Chair.; Helen M. Zelkowitz,* Vice-Chair.; James J. Cullers, Secy.; Maureen Buchwald, Winslow Curry, Kenneth Stevenson.
Trustee: The First-Knox National Bank.
Number of staff: None.
EIN: 316024796

2540
The Murch Foundation
830 Hanna Bldg.
Cleveland 44115

Incorporated in 1956 in OH.
Donor(s): Maynard H. Murch.‡
Foundation type: Independent
Financial data (yr. ended 12/31/91): Assets, $11,202,828 (M); expenditures, $486,000; qualifying distributions, $471,200, including $471,000 for 72 grants (high: $45,000; low: $1,000; average: $1,000-$90,000).
Fields of interest: Museums, cultural programs, higher education, secondary education, hospitals, health, recreation.
Types of support: Annual campaigns, capital campaigns, endowment funds, general purposes, renovation projects, scholarship funds.
Limitations: Giving primarily in OH. No grants to individuals.
Application information: Contributes only to pre-selected organizations. Applications not accepted.
  Write: Maynard H. Murch IV, Pres.
Officers and Trustees:* Maynard H. Murch IV,* Pres. and Treas.; Creighton B. Murch,* V.P. and Secy.; Robert B. Murch,* V.P.
Number of staff: 1 part-time support.
EIN: 346520188

2541
The Murdough Foundation
(Formerly Thomas G. & Joy P. Murdough Foundation)
2200 Highland Rd.
P.O. Box 444
Twinsburg 44087

Established in 1984.
Donor(s): Thomas G. Murdough, Jr.
Foundation type: Independent
Financial data (yr. ended 12/31/91): Assets, $4,016,768 (M); gifts received, $303,188; expenditures, $191,052; qualifying distributions, $153,424, including $143,900 for 45 grants (high: $30,000; low: $100).
Purpose and activities: Giving primarily for higher education, youth agencies and child welfare, and hospitals; support also for an Episcopal church and cultural programs.
Fields of interest: Hospitals, child welfare, youth, Protestant giving, cultural programs.
Types of support: Building funds, annual campaigns, general purposes.
Limitations: Giving primarily in OH, with emphasis on the northeastern OH area. No grants to individuals.
Application information: Application form not required.
  Deadline(s): None
  Write: Thomas G. Murdough, Jr., Pres.
Officers and Trustees:* Thomas G. Murdough, Jr.,* Pres. and Treas.; Joy P. Murdough,* Secy.; William M. Oldham.
EIN: 341454379

2542
John P. Murphy Foundation ▼
Tower City Ctr., Suite 610 Terminal Tower
50 Public Square
Cleveland 44113-2203   (216) 623-4770
FAX: (216) 623-4773

Incorporated in 1960 in OH.
Donor(s): John P. Murphy.‡
Foundation type: Independent
Financial data (yr. ended 12/31/91): Assets, $40,260,408 (M); expenditures, $1,959,829; qualifying distributions, $1,781,906, including $1,693,675 for 98 grants (high: $100,000; low: $1,000; average: $5,000-$50,000).
Purpose and activities: Giving primarily for higher education, civic affairs, community development and health; support also for the arts, social services and youth.
Fields of interest: Higher education, arts, civic affairs, community development, social services, youth, public affairs, health, nursing.
Types of support: Operating budgets, building funds, equipment, general purposes, capital campaigns, continuing support, annual campaigns, exchange programs, matching funds, publications, renovation projects, research, special projects.
Limitations: Giving primarily in the greater Cleveland, OH, area. No grants to individuals, or for endowment funds; no loans.
Publications: Annual report, informational brochure.
Application information: Application form not required.
  Initial approach: Letter

Copies of proposal: 1
Deadline(s): 3 weeks before meeting
Board meeting date(s): Bimonthly
Final notification: Within 2 weeks of meeting
Write: Herbert E. Strawbridge, Pres. and
Secy.-Treas.
Officers and Trustees:* Herbert E. Strawbridge,*
Pres. and Secy.-Treas.; Claude M. Blair,* V.P.;
Robert R. Broadbent,* V.P.; Marie S. Strawbridge,*
V.P.; Robert G. Wright,* V.P.
Number of staff: 1 part-time support.
EIN: 346528308

2543
R. C. and Katharine M. Musson Charitable Foundation
Box 5140
Akron 44334-0140   (216) 864-5515

Established in 1984 in OH as R. C. and Katharine
M. Musson Charitable Trust; successor foundation
established in 1988.
Donor(s): R.C. Musson.‡
Foundation type: Independent
Financial data (yr. ended 06/30/91): Assets,
$3,857,008 (M); expenditures, $347,421;
qualifying distributions, $341,384, including
$320,257 for 44 grants (high: $85,000; low:
$500; average: $1,000-$10,000).
Fields of interest: Catholic giving, Protestant
giving, Jewish giving, community funds, social
services, housing, rehabilitation, arts.
Types of support: General purposes.
Limitations: Giving primarily in Summit County,
OH.
Application information: Application form not
required.
Initial approach: Proposal
Copies of proposal: 1
Deadline(s): None
Write: Robert B. Palmer, Trustee
Trustees: Irvin J. Musson, Jr., Robert B. Palmer,
Ben Segers.
Number of staff: 1 part-time support.
EIN: 341549070

2544
National City Corporate Giving Program
National City Ctr.
1900 East Ninth St.
Cleveland 44114   (216) 575-2000

Financial data (yr. ended 12/31/90): Total giving,
$4,800,000 for grants (high: $10,000; low:
$1,000; average: $1,000-$5,000).
Purpose and activities: "We believe the prosperity
of National City Corporation is directly tied to the
prosperity of the communities we serve.
Therefore, our member banks are strongly
committed to improving the quality of life,
physical development and overall economy of
their markets. We recognize that our community
involvement must go beyond providing quality
products and services. It extends to the financial
and personal support of community programs in
housing, economic development, human
services, education, and neighborhood
revitalization." The member banks of National
City Corporation manage contributions programs
in their communities. All the banks support in this
order: health and human services, education, arts

and culture, civic and community affairs, and
other programs not falling into the named
categories. In addition to giving cash grants, the
banks also make low interest rate loans to support
housing, business and job development, and
general neighborhood improvement and
revitalization and have extensive employee
volunteer programs. Employees participate in
school partnerships, fundraising events, donating
gifts at holiday time, and other events.
Fields of interest: Housing, hunger, museums,
performing arts, urban affairs, urban
development, women, youth, alcoholism, drug
abuse, dance, economics, education, arts, higher
education, health, handicapped, medical
research, minorities, music, media and
communications, theater, community funds.
Types of support: Employee volunteer services,
loaned talent, loans, program-related investments.
Limitations: Giving primarily in headquarters city
and operating locations in OH, KY, and Southern
IN for local organizations; some support for
national or regional organizations when their
programs support the National City's goals.
Publications: Informational brochure (including
application guidelines), program policy statement.
Application information: Application form not
required.
Initial approach: Letter to nearest branch
Copies of proposal: 1
Deadline(s): Before Nov. 10 is the best time to
apply
Board meeting date(s): Quarterly
Write: Allen C. Waddle, Sr. V.P., Public Affairs
Dept.

2545
Nationwide Insurance Foundation ▼
One Nationwide Plaza
Columbus 43216   (614) 249-4310

Incorporated in 1959 in OH.
Donor(s): Nationwide Mutual Insurance Co., and
affiliates.
Foundation type: Company-sponsored
Financial data (yr. ended 12/31/90): Assets,
$30,347,773 (M); gifts received, $5,836,400;
expenditures, $5,533,999; qualifying
distributions, $5,496,158, including $5,139,841
for 208 grants (high: $1,512,515; low: $52;
average: $1,000-$20,000) and $285,637 for
1,424 employee matching gifts.
Purpose and activities: Giving primarily for
human services agencies; support also for cultural
programs, community funds, and higher
education, including employee matching gifts.
Fields of interest: Social services, aged,
disadvantaged, family services, handicapped,
health, youth, arts, cultural programs, performing
arts, community funds, higher education,
insurance education, education—minorities,
educational associations.
Types of support: Operating budgets, continuing
support, annual campaigns, seed money,
emergency funds, special projects, scholarship
funds, employee matching gifts, capital
campaigns.
Limitations: Giving primarily in OH, particularly
Columbus, and other communities where the
company maintains offices. No support for public
elementary and secondary schools, or fraternal or

veterans' organizations. No grants to individuals,
or for building funds; no loans.
Publications: Informational brochure (including
application guidelines).
Application information: The foundation has a
specific format for requests for funding, which is
listed in the Guidelines for Grant Consideration
brochure. Application form not required.
Initial approach: Letter
Copies of proposal: 1
Deadline(s): Sept. 1
Board meeting date(s): Feb., May, Aug., and
Nov.
Final notification: Feb.
Write: Stephen A. Rish, V.P., Public Relations
Officers and Trustees:* John E. Fisher,* Chair.;
Thomas E. Kryshak,* Exec. V.P., Fin.; Peter F.
Frenzer, Exec. V.P., Investments; Gordon E.
McCutchan, Exec. V.P., General Counsel, and
Secy.; Douglas C. Robinette, V.P. and Treas.;
Stephen A. Rish, V.P., Public Relations; Charles L.
Fuellgraf, Jr., Henry S. Holloway, D. Richard
McFerson, W. Barton Montgomery, Dwight W.
Oberschlake, Arden L. Shisler.
Number of staff: 1 part-time professional; 1
full-time support.
EIN: 316022301
Recent health grants:
2545-1 Alliance for the Mentally Ill, Columbus,
OH, $21,400. 1990.
2545-2 Childrens Hospital Foundation,
Columbus, OH, $10,000. 1990.
2545-3 Childrens Hospital Research Foundation,
DC, $100,000. 1990.
2545-4 CompDrug, Columbus, OH, $10,000.
1990.
2545-5 Life and Health Insurance Medical
Research Fund, DC, $250,000. 1990.
2545-6 Lifecare Alliance, Columbus, OH,
$150,000. 1990.
2545-7 Planned Parenthood of Central Ohio,
Columbus, OH, $20,000. 1990.
2545-8 University of Alabama, Injury Prevention
Research Center, Birmingham, AL, $15,000.
1990.
2545-9 Vision Center of Central Ohio,
Columbus, OH, $16,760. 1990.

2546
The L. and L. Nippert Charitable Foundation
c/o The Central Trust Co. of Northern Ohio, N.A.
P.O. Box 1198
Cincinnati 45201   (513) 651-8428

Established in 1981.
Donor(s): Louis Nippert, Louise D. Nippert.
Foundation type: Independent
Financial data (yr. ended 12/31/91): Assets,
$4,370,806 (M); expenditures, $277,667;
qualifying distributions, $254,766, including
$249,800 for 28 grants (high: $100,000; low:
$300).
Fields of interest: Higher education, medical
education, fine arts, social services, community
funds.
Types of support: Annual campaigns, building
funds, capital campaigns, endowment funds,
equipment, land acquisition, operating budgets,
publications, renovation projects, scholarship
funds, seed money, special projects.

Limitations: Giving primarily in Cincinnati, OH. No grants to individuals.
Publications: Application guidelines.
Application information:
  Initial approach: Proposal
  Copies of proposal: 4
  Deadline(s): None
  Board meeting date(s): Apr., Aug., and Dec.
  Final notification: 1 month after meetings
  Write: Diane Collins, Trust Officer, The Central Trust Co. of Northern Ohio, N.A.
Trustees: Louis Nippert, Louise D. Nippert, The Central Trust Co. of Northern Ohio, N.A.
Number of staff: 1 shared staff
EIN: 316219757

2547

The Nord Family Foundation ▼
(Formerly Nordson Foundation)
347 Midway Blvd.
Elyria 44035   (216) 324-2822
Additional tel.: (216) 233-8401

Trust established in 1952 in OH; reorganized in 1988 under current name.
Donor(s): Walter G. Nord,‡ Mrs. Walter G. Nord,‡ Nordson Corp., Evan W. Nord.
Foundation type: Independent
Financial data (yr. ended 10/31/91): Assets, $64,030,343 (M); expenditures, $3,030,640; qualifying distributions, $3,030,640, including $2,591,501 for 180 grants (high: $150,000; low: $800; average: $5,000-$50,000), $3,245 for 34 employee matching gifts, $50,000 for 1 loan and $81,500 for 1 in-kind gift.
Purpose and activities: Emphasis on projects to assist the disadvantaged and minorities, including giving for early childhood, secondary, and higher education, social services, health, cultural affairs, and civic activities. New initiatives in 1990 were a project to establish a common agenda to address factors which inhibit social and economic progress within the county and a program to strengthen nonprofit organizations which address family issues.
Fields of interest: Minorities, disadvantaged, education, education—early childhood, secondary education, higher education, social services, urban development, civic affairs, health, arts, cultural programs.
Types of support: Operating budgets, continuing support, seed money, emergency funds, equipment, matching funds, consulting services, technical assistance, loans, special projects, publications, employee matching gifts, general purposes, program-related investments, donated land.
Limitations: Giving primarily in the Lorain and Cuyahoga county areas, OH. No grants to individuals, or for deficit financing, research, scholarships, fellowships, or conferences.
Publications: Annual report (including application guidelines), informational brochure (including application guidelines).
Application information: Application form not required.
  Initial approach: Proposal
  Copies of proposal: 1
  Deadline(s): Submit proposal at least 6 weeks before meetings
  Board meeting date(s): Feb., June, and Oct.
  Final notification: 1 to 3 months

Write: Henry C. Doll, Exec. Dir.
Officers and Trustees:* David Ignat, Pres.; Evan W. Nord,* V.P.; William D. Ginn,* Secy.; Virginia M. Barbato,* Treas.; Henry C. Doll, Exec. Dir.
Number of staff: 3 full-time professional; 1 part-time professional; 2 full-time support.
EIN: 341595929
Recent health grants:
2547-1 Art Studio, Cleveland, OH, $15,000. For production start-up costs for Wheelart Studio to support art therapy. 1991.
2547-2 Arthritis Foundation, Northeast Ohio Chapter, Wooster, OH, $18,000. For relocation expenses and rent assistance. 1991.
2547-3 Epilepsy Foundation of Northeast Ohio, Cleveland, OH, $18,000. For relocation expenses and rent assistance. 1991.
2547-4 Lorain County Blood Bank, Elyria, OH, $30,000. To purchase new blood bank software program. 1991.
2547-5 Lorain County Council on Alcoholism and Drug Abuse, Elyria, OH, $20,000. For Children's Program of Women's Renaissance Project. 1991.
2547-6 Our Lady of the Wayside Childrens Home, Avon, OH, $27,000. For creation of occupational therapist staff position. 1991.
2547-7 W. G. Nord Community Mental Health Center, Lorain, OH, $150,000. For capital campaign to build site for emergency stabilization program. 1991.
2547-8 W. G. Nord Community Mental Health Center, Lorain, OH, $26,200. For collaboration with center for children and youth services to provide mental health services for family violence project. 1991.

2548

The Nordson Corporation Foundation
28601 Clemens Rd.
Westlake 44145-1148   (216) 892-1580
Additional tel.: (216) 988-9411

Established in 1988 in OH.
Donor(s): Nordson Corp.
Foundation type: Company-sponsored
Financial data (yr. ended 10/31/91): Assets, $3,585,531 (M); expenditures, $1,052,520; qualifying distributions, $1,026,265, including $1,018,506 for 87 grants (high: $100,000; low: $350; average: $550-$25,000).
Purpose and activities: To provide a source of stable funding for community programs and projects in the areas of education, human welfare, civics, and art and culture. Educational support is generally limited to improving elementary and secondary public schools and certain programs for public and private higher education. The foundation is willing to consider a number of funding areas, including urban affairs, volunteerism, public policy, and literacy.
Fields of interest: Adult education, aged, alcoholism, business education, citizenship, civic affairs, community development, community funds, disadvantaged, education—building funds, education—early childhood, education—minorities, educational associations, educational research, elementary education, employment, environment, fine arts, handicapped, health, health services, higher education, homeless, humanities, hunger, international affairs, leadership development,

literacy, mathematics, mental health, minorities, performing arts, public affairs, public policy, race relations, secondary education, social services, urban affairs, volunteerism, youth.
Types of support: Annual campaigns, building funds, capital campaigns, continuing support, emergency funds, employee matching gifts, equipment, in-kind gifts, matching funds, operating budgets, seed money.
Limitations: Giving limited to the northern OH and Atlanta, GA, areas.
Publications: Corporate giving report
Application information: Application form not required.
  Initial approach: Letter or proposal
  Copies of proposal: 1
  Deadline(s): None
  Board meeting date(s): 4 times yearly, one each calendar quarter
  Write: James C. Doughman, Dir., Public Affairs
Trustees: Edward C. Campbell, John E. Jackson, William P. Madar, Thomas L. Moorhead.
Number of staff: None.
EIN: 341596194

2549

Charles G. O'Bleness Foundation No. 3
c/o Huntington National Bank, Trust Dept.
41 South High St.
Columbus 43216   (614) 463-3707

Established in 1963 in OH.
Donor(s): Charles O'Bleness,‡ Charles O'Bleness Foundation No. 1.
Foundation type: Independent
Financial data (yr. ended 06/30/91): Assets, $2,697,879 (M); expenditures, $193,323; qualifying distributions, $176,679, including $161,706 for 13 grants (high: $35,714; low: $1,000).
Fields of interest: Hospitals, social services, higher education, secondary education.
Types of support: General purposes.
Limitations: Giving limited to Athens County, OH.
Application information: Application form not required.
  Deadline(s): Oct. 15
Advisors: John M. Jones, Theodore Vogt.
Trustee: Huntington National Bank.
EIN: 316042978

2550

The F. J. O'Neill Charitable Corporation ▼
3550 Lander Rd.
Cleveland 44124

Established in 1979 in OH.
Donor(s): Francis J. O'Neill.‡
Foundation type: Independent
Financial data (yr. ended 12/31/90): Assets, $89,610,599 (M); expenditures, $6,145,363; qualifying distributions, $4,241,173, including $4,183,345 for 74 grants (high: $1,500,000; low: $500; average: $5,000-$25,000).
Purpose and activities: Giving for higher and secondary education, medical research, and Roman Catholic organizations.
Fields of interest: Secondary education, higher education, Catholic giving, medical research.
Types of support: General purposes.

Limitations: Giving primarily in greater Cleveland, OH. No grants for scholarships, fellowships, prizes, or similar benefits.
Application information: Applications not accepted.
Officers: Hugh O'Neill, Pres.; Nancy M. O'Neill, V.P.; Rev. E.P. Joyce, Secy.-Treas.
EIN: 341286022

2551
The William J. and Dorothy K. O'Neill Foundation, Inc.
30195 Chagrin Blvd., Suite 123
Cleveland 44124   (216) 831-9667

Established in 1987 in OH.
Donor(s): Dorothy K. O'Neill, Cleveland Research Institute.
Foundation type: Independent
Financial data (yr. ended 12/31/90): Assets, $1,824,827 (M); gifts received, $706,807; expenditures, $526,051; qualifying distributions, $526,051, including $514,200 for 54 grants (high: $100,000; low: $500).
Purpose and activities: Giving primarily for Catholic organizations and higher and other education; support also for health.
Fields of interest: Catholic giving, higher education, education, health.
Types of support: Endowment funds, general purposes, annual campaigns.
Limitations: Giving primarily in OH.
Application information: Application form not required.
 Initial approach: Letter
 Deadline(s): None
 Write: William J. O'Neill, Jr., Pres.
Officers and Trustees:* William J. O'Neill, Jr.,* Pres. and Treas.; Sheldon M. Sager,* Secy.; Dorothy K. O'Neill.
EIN: 341560893

2552
Ohio Bell Foundation ▼
45 Erieview Plaza, Rm. 870
Cleveland 44114   (216) 822-2423

Established in 1987 in OH.
Donor(s): Ohio Bell.
Foundation type: Company-sponsored
Financial data (yr. ended 12/31/90): Assets, $23,765,901 (M); gifts received, $2,750,000; expenditures, $2,626,037; qualifying distributions, $2,497,918, including $2,102,240 for 181 grants (high: $180,000; low: $350; average: $150-$180,000) and $391,242 for 1,751 employee matching gifts.
Purpose and activities: Support for civic affairs, community development, science and technology, art and culture, higher, secondary, and elementary education, and health; support also for programs for literacy and the aged.
Fields of interest: Community development, science and technology, arts, cultural programs, education, elementary education, secondary education, higher education, health services, literacy, museums.
Types of support: Continuing support, employee matching gifts, general purposes, special projects, capital campaigns.

Limitations: Giving limited to the Ohio Bell serving area, except for employee matching gifts for education. No support for religious organizations for religious purposes, lobbying, veterans' or military organizations, direct patient care, United Way member agencies, or sports or athletic events. No grants to individuals, or for special event advertising.
Application information: Application form not required.
 Initial approach: Proposal
 Copies of proposal: 1
 Deadline(s): None
 Board meeting date(s): Periodic
 Final notification: Varies
 Write: William W. Boag, Jr., Exec. Dir.
Officers and Trustees:* Thomas L. Elliott,* Pres.; Michael J. Karson,* Secy.; Robert E. Cogan,* Treas.; William W. Boag, Jr., Exec. Dir.; Theodore B. Garrison, William J. Schlageter.
Number of staff: None.
EIN: 341536258
Recent health grants:
2552-1 American Heart Association, Cleveland, OH, $30,000. Toward renovation of building. 1990.
2552-2 Cleveland Clinic Foundation, Cleveland, OH, $75,000. For deWindt Family Cancer Research Laboratories Health Sciences Center Capital Building Campaign. 1990.
2552-3 Saint Lukes Hospital Association, Cleveland, OH, $20,000. For Adolescent Chemical Dependency Program. 1990.

2553
The Ohio Valley Foundation
c/o Fifth Third Bank
Dept. 00864
Cincinnati 45263   (513) 579-6034

Incorporated in 1946 in OH.
Donor(s): John J. Rowe,‡ Wm. L. McGrath, John W. Warrington.
Foundation type: Independent
Financial data (yr. ended 09/30/91): Assets, $4,062,531 (M); expenditures, $205,114; qualifying distributions, $189,547, including $175,180 for 19 grants (high: $25,000; low: $3,000).
Fields of interest: Education, youth, cultural programs, museums, hospitals, health services, legal services.
Types of support: Building funds, capital campaigns, renovation projects.
Limitations: Giving primarily in the greater Cincinnati, OH, area. No support for religious organizations. No grants to individuals, or for endowment funds or operating budgets.
Publications: Annual report.
Application information: Application form required.
 Initial approach: Proposal
 Copies of proposal: 1
 Deadline(s): July 1
 Board meeting date(s): Aug.
 Final notification: Immediately after meeting
 Write: Carolyn F. McCoy, Fdn. Officer
Trustees: Clement Buenger, Philip C. Long, David Sharrock, N. Beverly Tucker, John W. Warrington.
Number of staff: 1 full-time professional; 1 full-time support.
EIN: 316008508

Recent health grants:
2553-1 Wellness Community Center, Cincinnati, OH, $10,000. For start-up costs of service providing adult cancer victims with emotional and psychological support. 1990.

2554
The Parker-Hannifin Foundation
17325 Euclid Ave.
Cleveland 44112   (216) 531-3000

Incorporated in 1953 in OH.
Donor(s): Parker-Hannifin Corp.
Foundation type: Company-sponsored
Financial data (yr. ended 06/30/91): Assets, $36,601 (M); gifts received, $1,341,470; expenditures, $1,315,617; qualifying distributions, $1,315,617, including $1,137,549 for 317 grants (high: $100,000; low: $50; average: $100-$1,000) and $174,804 for 579 employee matching gifts.
Fields of interest: Higher education, community funds, civic affairs, hospitals, youth, health services, arts.
Types of support: Employee matching gifts.
Limitations: No support for fraternal or labor organizations.
Application information: Application form not required.
 Copies of proposal: 1
 Board meeting date(s): Jan. and July
 Write: Joseph D. Whiteman, V.P.
Officers and Trustees:* Patrick S. Parker,* Chair.; Paul G. Schloemer,* Pres. and C.E.O.; Joseph D. Whiteman, V.P., Secy., and General Counsel.
Number of staff: None.
EIN: 346555686

2555
Penn Central Corporate Giving Program
One East Fourth St.
Cincinnati 45202   (513) 579-6600

Financial data (yr. ended 12/31/90): Total giving, $1,200,000 for grants.
Purpose and activities: Grants only for tax-exempt organizations; supports education, health, welfare, culture, arts, civic and social activities. The subsidiaries have contributions budgets and handle giving in their areas.
Fields of interest: Education, health, welfare, cultural programs, arts, civic affairs, social services, general charitable giving.
Types of support: Employee matching gifts, general purposes.
Limitations: Giving primarily in headquarters city and major operating areas. No support for religious or fraternal organizations unless engaged in projects that benefit whole community, hospitals, or patient care, or organizations that don't conduct their business in a way consistent with equal opportunity guidelines, or religious or ethnic organizations. No grants to individuals, or for indirect support, or fundraising luncheons or dinners.
Application information:
 Initial approach: Query letter describing project
 Deadline(s): None
 Final notification: 6-8 weeks
 Write: David H. Street, Sr. V.P., Fin.

2556
The Perkins Charitable Foundation
1030 Hanna Bldg.
1422 Euclid Ave.
Cleveland 44115   (216) 621-0465

Trust established in 1950 in OH.
Donor(s): Members of the Perkins family.
Foundation type: Independent
Financial data (yr. ended 12/31/91): Assets,
$11,967,102 (M); expenditures, $474,468;
qualifying distributions, $453,300, including
$450,200 for 46 grants (high: $74,000; low:
$200).
Fields of interest: Higher education, secondary
education, hospitals, community funds,
conservation.
Limitations: No grants to individuals.
Application information: Application form not
required.
　Deadline(s): None
　Write: Marilyn Best, Secy.-Treas.
Officer: Marilyn Best, Secy.-Treas.
Trustees: George Oliva III, Jacob B. Perkins, Leigh
H. Perkins, Sallie P. Sullivan.
EIN: 346549753

2557
Jesse Philips Foundation ▼
4801 Springfield St.
Dayton 45401
Scholarship application address: c/o Ruth
Richardson, Dayton Board of Education, Dayton
Public Schools, 348 West First St., Dayton, OH
45402

Incorporated in 1960 in OH.
Donor(s): Jesse Philips, Philips Industries, Inc.,
and subsidiaries.
Foundation type: Company-sponsored
Financial data (yr. ended 02/28/91): Assets,
$17,445,460 (M); gifts received, $60,292;
expenditures, $1,258,858; qualifying
distributions, $1,151,485, including $1,151,485
for 173 grants (high: $62,925; low: $10; average:
$1,000-$25,000).
Purpose and activities: Giving for Jewish welfare
funds, hospitals, higher education, cultural
programs, social services, and community
development. Scholarships or study loans limited
to high school students in Montgomery County,
OH, or to Jesse Phillips Scholars and paid through
institutions.
Fields of interest: Jewish welfare, hospitals, higher
education, cultural programs, social services,
community development.
Types of support: Scholarship funds, general
purposes.
Limitations: Giving primarily in Dayton, OH.
Application information: Application forms
required for scholarship program.
　Deadline(s): May I for scholarships, none for
　　others
　Board meeting date(s): As necessary
　Final notification: Within one month
　Write: Jesse Philips, Pres.
Officers and Trustees:* Jesse Philips,* Pres.;
David T. Jeanmougin, V.P.; Caryl Philips,* V.P.;
Milton Roisman,* V.P.; E.L. Ryan, Jr.,* Secy.;
Thomas C. Haas,* Treas.
EIN: 316023380

2558
Pizzuti Family Foundation
250 East Broad St., Suite 1900
Columbus 43215-3708

Established in 1985 in OH.
Donor(s): Ronald A. Pizzuti.
Foundation type: Independent
Financial data (yr. ended 06/30/91): Assets,
$2,190,393 (M); gifts received, $513,750;
expenditures, $93,564; qualifying distributions,
$91,000, including $91,000 for 8 grants (high:
$30,000; low: $3,000).
Purpose and activities: Supports educational
organizations, organizations established to
improve health and welfare of children, those that
foster and promote visual and performing arts,
and medical research facilities.
Fields of interest: Higher education, education,
social services, child welfare, performing arts,
medical research.
Limitations: Giving primarily in OH. No grants to
individuals.
Application information: Contributes only to
pre-selected organizations. Applications not
accepted.
Officers: Ronald A. Pizzuti, Pres.; Ann L. Pizzuti,
Treas.
Trustee: Fredric L. Smith.
EIN: 311144793

2559
The William B. Pollock II and Kathryn Challiss Pollock Foundation
c/o Bank One, Youngstown, N.A.
Six Federal Plaza West
Youngstown 44503

Trust established in 1952 in OH.
Donor(s): William B. Pollock II, Kathryn Challiss
Pollock.
Foundation type: Independent
Financial data (yr. ended 12/31/91): Assets,
$2,573,446 (M); expenditures, $108,055;
qualifying distributions, $90,326, including
$84,600 for 22 grants (high: $10,000; low: $100;
average: $50-$7,000).
Fields of interest: Hospitals, health services,
family planning, cultural programs, education,
youth, Protestant giving, community funds.
Types of support: Operating budgets, continuing
support, annual campaigns, seed money,
emergency funds, deficit financing, building
funds, equipment, land acquisition, endowment
funds, research, special projects, publications,
conferences and seminars.
Limitations: Giving limited to the Youngstown,
OH, area. No grants to individuals, or for
matching gifts, scholarships, or fellowships; no
loans.
Publications: 990-PF.
Trustees: Franklin S. Bennett, Jr., Bank One,
Youngstown, N.A.
Number of staff: None.
EIN: 346514079

2560
The Elisabeth Severance Prentiss Foundation ▼
c/o National City Bank
P.O. Box 5756
Cleveland 44101   (216) 575-2760

Trust established in 1944 in OH.
Donor(s): Elisabeth Severance Prentiss,‡ Luther L.
Miller, Kate W. Miller.
Foundation type: Independent
Financial data (yr. ended 12/31/90): Assets,
$48,643,265 (M); gifts received, $2,410,028;
expenditures, $2,410,028; qualifying
distributions, $2,211,327, including $2,211,327
for 26 grants (high: $990,327; low: $3,000;
average: $5,000-$100,000).
Purpose and activities: To promote medical and
surgical research and to assist in the acquisition,
advancement and dissemination of knowledge of
medicine and surgery, and of means of
maintaining health; to promote public health; to
aid hospitals and health institutions in Cuyahoga
County, OH, that are organized and operated
exclusively for public charitable purposes by
contributions for capital improvements or
equipment, purchase of rare and expensive drugs,
and expenses of operation or maintenance; to
improve methods of hospital management and
administration; to support programs to make
hospital and medical care available to all,
especially those of low income.
Fields of interest: Medical research, hospitals,
health services, health associations.
Types of support: Research, operating budgets,
continuing support, seed money, building funds,
equipment, endowment funds, special projects,
renovation projects.
Limitations: Giving primarily in the greater
Cleveland, OH, area. No support for national
fundraising organizations and foundations. No
grants to individuals, or for scholarships,
fellowships, or matching gifts; no loans.
Publications: Annual report (including application
guidelines).
Application information: Application form not
required.
　Initial approach: Proposal or letter
　Copies of proposal: 1
　Deadline(s): Submit proposal prior to May 15
　　and Nov. 15
　Board meeting date(s): June and Dec.
　Final notification: 1 week to 10 days following
　　board meetings
　Write: Frank Dinda
Officers and Managers:* Quentin Alexander,*
Pres.; Richard A. Beeman, Secy.; Harry J. Bolwell,
William J. DeLancey, J. Robert Killpack, William
A. Mattie.
Trustee: National City Bank.
Number of staff: None.
EIN: 346512433
Recent health grants:
2560-1 American Red Cross, Northern Ohio
　Region, Cleveland, OH, $10,000. For
　expansion of local unrelated marrow donor
　registry. 1990.
2560-2 Association for Retarded Citizens,
　Cleveland, OH, $25,000. For first payment on
　three-year grant to develop multi-disciplinary
　center for persons with Down's Syndrome and
　their families. In collaboration with Cuyahoga

County and Case Western Reserve University School of Medicine. 1990.

2560-3 Benjamin Rose Institute, Cleveland, OH, $10,000. For renovations to meet health needs of elderly residents. 1990.

2560-4 Berea Childrens Home and Family Services, Akron, OH, $10,000. For final payment on three-year grant to complete Diagnostic Assessment Service in Secure Treatment Center. 1990.

2560-5 Case Western Reserve University, Department of Medicine, Cleveland, OH, $200,000. For five-year grant to develop academic and clinical base of cardiology at University Hospitals. 1990.

2560-6 Case Western Reserve University, Frances Payne Bolton School of Nursing, Cleveland, OH, $100,000. For first payment on two-year grant to revitalize Learning Resources Laboratory. 1990.

2560-7 Case Western Reserve University, Frances Payne Bolton School of Nursing, Cleveland, OH, $50,000. For final payment on two-year grant to fund two Irish nursing students' enrollment in M.S. in Nursing Program. 1990.

2560-8 Case Western Reserve University, School of Medicine, Cleveland, OH, $25,000. For third payment on four-year grant to support research program in schizophrenia. Grant shared with University Hospitals of Cleveland. 1990.

2560-9 Central School of Practical Nursing, Cleveland, OH, $20,000. For training program for practical nurses. 1990.

2560-10 Cleveland Clinic Foundation, Cleveland, OH, $200,000. For payment on five-year grant for construction of dedicated cancer research facility within DeWindt Family Cancer Research Laboratories in new Health Sciences Center. 1990.

2560-11 Cleveland Eye Bank, Cleveland, OH, $10,000. For final payment on three-year grant to further develop public awareness of need for eye donations. 1990.

2560-12 Community AIDS Partnership Project, Cleveland, OH, $10,000. For first payment on three-year grant requested by United Way to support public health programs addressing problem of AIDS in Cleveland community. 1990.

2560-13 Free Medical Clinic of Greater Cleveland, Cleveland, OH, $23,000. For first payment on three-year grant to establish Adolescent Clinic to make health care more accessible to teenagers and provide atmosphere for preventive education. 1990.

2560-14 Health Hill Hospital for Children, Cleveland, OH, $10,000. For customized van to transport patients to acute care hospitals for follow-up care. 1990.

2560-15 Heather Hill, Chardon, OH, $20,000. For second payment on three-year grant to construct, furnish and equip Corinne Dolan Alzheimer's Center. 1990.

2560-16 Judson Retirement Community, Cleveland Heights, OH, $20,000. For first payment on five-year grant for construction of Health Care Center and renovation of present health care center into Alzheimer's Unit and Assisted Living Unit. 1990.

2560-17 Lutheran Medical Center Foundation, Cleveland, OH, $10,000. For Eye Clinic with equipment and facility modernization. 1990.

2560-18 Planned Parenthood of Greater Cleveland, Cleveland, OH, $15,000. For final payment on three-year grant to support 60th Anniversary Campaign for capital endowment and program expansion. 1990.

2560-19 Saint Lukes Hospital Association, Cleveland, OH, $990,327. 1990.

2560-20 University Hospitals of Cleveland, Cleveland, OH, $380,000. For payment on five-year grant for R. Livingston Ireland Cancer Center and Alzheimer's programs. 1990.

2560-21 Vocational Guidance and Rehabilitation Services, Cleveland, OH, $20,000. For first payment on six-year grant restricted to medical services to help disadvantaged Clevelanders gain health needed to live independent, productive lives. 1990.

2561
The Procter & Gamble Company Corporate Giving Program
P.O. Box 599
Cincinnati 45201   (513) 983-1100

Financial data (yr. ended 06/30/90): Total giving, $16,680,000, including $7,300,000 for grants, $3,947,000 for grants to individuals and $5,433,000 for in-kind gifts.
Purpose and activities: Support for education, including research and development and engineering fellowships and grants to colleges and universities; social service agencies and civic groups; donations to charitable organizations through promotion events; product, equipment, and land donations; support also for other programs benefiting society such as equal opportunity programs to support minority recruitment and development, secondary education programs, and a tuition refund program for additional employee education.
Fields of interest: Community development, business education, drug abuse, education, handicapped, health, health associations, hunger, minorities, secondary education, social services, civic affairs.
Types of support: Fellowships, in-kind gifts, research, donated products, loaned talent, annual campaigns, donated land, capital campaigns.
Limitations: Giving limited to headquarters and areas of company operations.
Publications: Grants list, informational brochure.
Application information: Contributions are handled by the Public Affairs Department.
Write: R.R. Fitzpatrick, Mgr., Contribs.
Number of staff: 5 full-time professional.

2562
The Procter & Gamble Fund ▼
P.O. Box 599
Cincinnati 45201   (513) 983-3913

Incorporated in 1952 in OH.
Donor(s): The Proctor & Gamble Co.
Foundation type: Company-sponsored
Financial data (yr. ended 06/30/91): Assets, $47,611,925 (M); expenditures, $16,456,326; qualifying distributions, $16,360,381, including $16,306,242 for 5,374 grants (high: $1,880,000; low: $50; average: $5,000-$100,000).
Purpose and activities: Grants nationally for private higher education and economic and public policy research organizations; support also for community funds, hospitals, youth agencies, urban affairs, and aid to the handicapped; generally limited to areas of domestic company operations.
Fields of interest: Higher education, economics, educational associations, public policy, social services, youth, handicapped, urban affairs, civic affairs.
Types of support: Annual campaigns, building funds, continuing support, emergency funds, equipment, land acquisition, matching funds, employee-related scholarships, employee matching gifts.
Limitations: Giving primarily in areas in the U.S. and where the company and its subsidiaries have large concentrations of employees; national giving for higher education and economic and public affairs. No grants to individuals.
Publications: Informational brochure.
Application information: Grant requests from colleges and universities are discouraged, as most grants are initiated by the trustees within specified programs. Application form not required.
Initial approach: Proposal
Copies of proposal: 1
Deadline(s): None
Board meeting date(s): Jan., Apr., July, and Oct.
Final notification: 1 month
Write: R.R. Fitzpatrick, V.P.
Officers and Trustees:* R.L. Wehling,* Pres.; R.R. Fitzpatrick,* V.P. and Secy.; R.A. Bachhuber, V.P.; S.J. Fitch,* V.P.; George M. Gibson, Treas.; E.L. Nelson.
Number of staff: 3 full-time professional; 1 full-time support.
EIN: 316019594
Recent health grants:
2562-1 American Council on Science and Health, NYC, NY, $12,500. 1991.
2562-2 American Foundation for Pharmaceutical Education, Fair Lawn, NJ, $15,000. 1991.
2562-3 American Red Cross, Blood Services, Wilkes-Barre, PA, $12,500. 1991.
2562-4 Chenango Memorial Hospital, Norwich, NY, $100,000. 1991.
2562-5 Community Counseling Center, Cape Girardeau, MO, $15,000. 1991.
2562-6 Community Memorial Hospital, Cheboygan, MI, $25,000. 1991.
2562-7 Institute for Mental Health Initiatives, DC, $10,000. 1991.
2562-8 Media-Advertising Partnership for a Drug-Free America, NYC, NY, $50,000. 1991.
2562-9 N.E.W. Community Clinic, Green Bay, WI, $10,000. 1991.
2562-10 National Medical Association, DC, $75,000. 1991.
2562-11 Occupational Physicians Scholarship Fund, NYC, NY, $25,000. 1991.
2562-12 Resident Home for the Mentally Retarded of Hamilton County, Cincinnati, OH, $12,000. 1991.
2562-13 Tunkhannock Community Ambulance Association, Tunkhannock, PA, $25,000. 1991.

2563
Progressive Corporate Contributions Program
6000 Parkland Blvd.
Mayfield Heights 44143   (216) 464-8000

Mailing address: P.O. Box 5070, Cleveland, OH 44101

Financial data (yr. ended 12/31/90): Total giving, $772,050, including $752,050 for 47 grants (high: $40,000; low: $244) and $20,000 for employee matching gifts.

Purpose and activities: "Our goal is to support philanthropic activities that: represent new directions and entrepreneurial risks, stimulate creative use of talent, knowledge, expertise and resources, challenge people to think outside the lines, would be difficult to fund through traditional sources, reach new audiences and constituencies, and address important or new community needs." Emphasis is on special projects as opposed to operating, benefit, capital, and endowment support. Criteria for evaluating proposals include: risk-taking, honesty, innovation, creativity, and performance-evaluation. Projects should be in line with the company's policy. Supports the arts and culture, civic affairs, education, environment, health, minority programs, and social sciences.

Fields of interest: Environment, minorities, social services, arts, civic affairs, cultural programs, education, health, welfare.

Types of support: Employee matching gifts, matching funds, employee-related scholarships, seed money, special projects.

Limitations: Giving primarily in the greater Cleveland, OH area; Colorado Springs, CO; and Sacramento, CA; some support also in Richmond, VA, Tampa, FL, and Austin, TX. No support for religious organizations for religious purposes. No grants to individuals.

Publications: Application guidelines, corporate giving report.

Application information: Application form not required.

Initial approach: Letter with complete proposal
Copies of proposal: 1
Deadline(s): None
Board meeting date(s): Monthly
Final notification: 8 weeks
Write: Barbara Pine, Contribs. Mgr.

Number of staff: 1 full-time professional; 1 part-time support.

2564
RB&W Corporate Giving Program
5970 Heisley Rd.
Mentor 44060   (216) 357-1200

Financial data (yr. ended 12/31/90): Total giving, $24,190, including $18,770 for 57 grants (high: $2,800; low: $25; average: $25-$2,800) and $5,420 for 3 grants to individuals (high: $2,500; low: $1,000; average: $1,000-$2,500).

Purpose and activities: Supports arts, community development, health, youth and hospital building funds.

Fields of interest: Arts, community development, hospitals—building funds, health, youth, higher education, performing arts.

Types of support: Annual campaigns, building funds, employee-related scholarships.

Publications: Corporate report, program policy statement.

Application information: Application form not required.

Initial approach: Letter; Send requests to headquarters
Board meeting date(s): Approximately bi-monthly
Write: John J. Lohrman, Chair., Pres. and C.E.O.
Administrator: Kent M. Holcomb, V.P., Human Resources and Corp. Secy.
Number of staff: 1 part-time professional; 1 part-time support.

2565
Reeves Foundation
232-4 West Third St.
P.O. Box 441
Dover 44622   (216) 364-4660

Trust established in 1966 in OH.
Donor(s): Margaret J. Reeves,‡ Helen F. Reeves,‡ Samuel J. Reeves.‡
Foundation type: Independent
Financial data (yr. ended 12/31/91): Assets, $15,833,464 (M); expenditures, $886,703; qualifying distributions, $769,720, including $731,493 for 14 grants (high: $400,000; low: $3,000).
Purpose and activities: Emphasis on historical societies and health agencies, including hospitals; grants also for youth agencies, education, and public administration. Priority given to capital improvement projects.
Fields of interest: Historic preservation, health, hospitals, youth, education, education—building funds, public administration.
Types of support: Continuing support, building funds, equipment, matching funds, special projects.
Limitations: Giving primarily in OH, with emphasis on the Dover area. No grants to individuals, or for annual campaigns, seed money, emergency funds, deficit financing, land acquisition, renovation projects, endowment funds, fellowships, special projects, publications, or conferences; no loans.
Application information: Application form not required.

Initial approach: Proposal
Copies of proposal: 2
Deadline(s): 10 days prior to those months when board meets
Board meeting date(s): Bimonthly starting in Feb.
Final notification: 1 month
Write: Don A. Ulrich, Exec. Dir.
Officers and Trustees: * Margaret H. Reeves,* Pres.; W.E. Zimmerman,* Exec. V.P.; Thomas R. Scheffer,* V.P.; W.E. Lieser,* Treas.; Don A. Ulrich, Exec. Dir.; Thomas J. Patton, Ronald L. Pissocra, Jeffry Wagner.
Number of staff: 1 part-time professional; 1 part-time support.
EIN: 346575477

2566
The Reinberger Foundation ▼
27600 Chagrin Blvd.
Cleveland 44122   (216) 292-2790

Established in 1968 in OH.
Donor(s): Clarence T. Reinberger,‡ Louise F. Reinberger.‡
Foundation type: Independent

Financial data (yr. ended 12/31/90): Assets, $47,119,128 (M); expenditures, $2,625,735; qualifying distributions, $2,215,968, including $2,063,500 for 54 grants (high: $200,000; low: $1,000; average: $20,000-$100,000).
Purpose and activities: Support for the arts, social welfare, Protestant churches, higher education, and medical research.
Fields of interest: Arts, cultural programs, Protestant giving, higher education, medical research, social services.
Types of support: Operating budgets, continuing support, annual campaigns, building funds, equipment, endowment funds, matching funds, scholarship funds, research, publications, special projects, deficit financing, capital campaigns, renovation projects, general purposes.
Limitations: Giving primarily in the Cleveland and Columbus, OH, areas. No grants to individuals, or for seed money, emergency funds, land acquisition, demonstration projects, or conferences; no loans.
Publications: 990-PF, grants list, informational brochure (including application guidelines).
Application information: Application form not required.

Initial approach: Proposal
Copies of proposal: 1
Deadline(s): None
Board meeting date(s): Mar., June, Sept., and Dec.
Final notification: 6 months
Write: Robert N. Reinberger, Co-Dir.
Officer: Richard H. Oman, Secy.
Directors: Robert N. Reinberger, William C. Reinberger.
Trustee: Ameritrust Co., N.A.
Number of staff: 2 full-time professional.
EIN: 346574879

2567
Reliance Electric Company Charitable, Scientific and Educational Trust
6065 Parkland Blvd.
Cleveland 44124   (216) 266-5826

Trust established in 1952 in OH.
Donor(s): Reliance Electric Co.
Foundation type: Company-sponsored
Financial data (yr. ended 12/31/91): Assets, $76,060 (M); gifts received, $800,000; expenditures, $884,259; qualifying distributions, $878,634, including $878,634 for 623 grants (high: $25,000; low: $20; average: $500-$5,000).
Purpose and activities: Emphasis on community funds, higher education, hospitals, cultural programs, and social services; also funds an employee matching gift program.
Fields of interest: Community funds, higher education, social services, hospitals, cultural programs.
Types of support: Employee matching gifts, capital campaigns, continuing support.
Limitations: Giving primarily in areas of major company facilities. No support for national health organizations. No grants to individuals, or for dinners or special events.
Publications: Program policy statement.
Application information: Application form not required.

Initial approach: Proposal
Copies of proposal: 1

Deadline(s): None
Board meeting date(s): Quarterly
Write: Edward R. Towns, Secy.
Officer: Edward R. Towns, Secy.
Trustee: Ameritrust Co., N.A.
Number of staff: None.
EIN: 346505329

2568
Renner Foundation
1422 Euclid Ave., K-No. 1146
Cleveland 44115-1951

Incorporated in 1947 in OH as Renner Clinic
Foundation.
Donor(s): R. Richard Renner, M.D.‡
Foundation type: Independent
Financial data (yr. ended 05/31/91): Assets,
$2,902,052 (M); gifts received, $100;
expenditures, $175,994; qualifying distributions,
$130,504, including $130,000 for 2 grants (high:
$120,000; low: $10,000).
Purpose and activities: Primary area of interest is
higher education.
Fields of interest: Higher education, medical
education, hospitals, medical sciences,
conservation, environment, wildlife.
Types of support: Scholarship funds, general
purposes, professorships.
Limitations: Giving primarily in WV and OH. No
grants to individuals.
Application information: Frequently contributes
to pre-selected organizations. Application form
required.
Copies of proposal: 3
Deadline(s): Feb. 1
Board meeting date(s): May
Write: John W. Renner, Pres.
Officers and Trustees:* John W. Renner,* Pres.;
Richard R. Renner,* Treas.; Brett Percy, David F.
Percy, Jennifer S. Percy, Ruth A. Percy, Daniel S.
Renner, J. Robert Renner, Karen L. Renner, Mary
A. Renner, Robert R. Renner, Steven Renner, Tami
Renner, Tara Renner, Jane R. See, Ann Stillwater.
Number of staff: None.
EIN: 340684303

2569
The Reynolds and Reynolds Company Foundation
P.O. Box 2608
Dayton 45401   (513) 449-4490

Established in 1986 in OH.
Donor(s): The Reynolds and Reynolds Co.
Foundation type: Company-sponsored
Financial data (yr. ended 09/30/90): Assets,
$45,177 (M); gifts received, $865,000;
expenditures, $834,040; qualifying distributions,
$833,915, including $831,165 for 64 grants
(high: $253,750; low: $100).
Purpose and activities: "The foundation focuses
attention on a program of giving to promote a
healthy environment for neighbors, employees
and their families, and the business community."
Support for health, education, arts, and
community activities; organizations not falling
precisely into these categories may also be
considered for grants. Programs will be judged on
their impact in the local community and how
they fit into the total contributions program.

Support is given to traditional, established
organizations and to organizations which propose
worthy, innovative programs. At times, when the
foundation sees a need for a specific program for
which it has not received an application, it may
solicit a grant that addresses the perceived need.
The United Way is also strongly supported.
Fields of interest: Cultural programs, arts, social
services, community funds, health, education,
higher education, community development.
Types of support: Annual campaigns, capital
campaigns, operating budgets, program-related
investments, special projects, endowment funds.
Limitations: Giving primarily in areas of company
operations, with emphasis on Dayton, OH. No
support for sectarian organizations with an
exclusively religious purpose, fraternal or
veterans' organizations, primary or secondary
schools (except for occasional special projects), or
tax-supported universities and colleges (except for
occasional special projects); organizations
receiving funds from the United Way generally
not considered. No grants to individuals, or for
courtesy advertising.
Publications: Application guidelines.
Application information: Outside of Dayton area,
write to local facility manager. Application form
not required.
Initial approach: Proposal
Copies of proposal: 1
Board meeting date(s): Every other month
beginning in Oct.
Final notification: 3 months
Write: Mary Green, Admin.
Officer and Trustee:* John R. Martin,* Chair.
EIN: 311168299

2570
The Charles E. and Mabel M. Ritchie Memorial Foundation
c/o First National Bank of Ohio
106 South Main St.
Akron 44308   (216) 384-7313

Trust established in 1954 in OH.
Donor(s): Mabel M. Ritchie.‡
Foundation type: Independent
Financial data (yr. ended 12/31/90): Assets,
$4,930,998 (M); expenditures, $253,783;
qualifying distributions, $233,386, including
$226,850 for 42 grants (high: $20,000; low:
$1,000).
Fields of interest: Community development, civic
affairs, hospitals, cultural programs, youth,
education, higher education.
Types of support: Capital campaigns, scholarship
funds, building funds.
Limitations: Giving limited to Summit County,
OH. No grants to individuals.
Application information: Application form not
required.
Initial approach: Proposal
Copies of proposal: 4
Deadline(s): Jan. 1, Apr. 1, July 1, and Oct. 1
Board meeting date(s): Distribution Committee
meets first week of Feb., May, Aug., and Nov.
Write: Ronald B. Tynan, V.P., First National
Bank of Ohio
Advisory Committee: Edward F. Carter, Kathryn
M. Hunter, John D. Ong.
Trustee: First National Bank of Ohio.
EIN: 346500802

2571
George W. & Mary F. Ritter Charitable Trust
c/o Society Bank & Trust
P.O. Box 10099
Toledo 43699-0099
Application address: c/o Society Bank & Trust,
Three Seagate, Toledo, OH 43699; Tel.: (419)
259-8217

Established in 1982 in OH.
Foundation type: Independent
Financial data (yr. ended 11/30/91): Assets,
$5,166,818 (M); expenditures, $285,676;
qualifying distributions, $265,200, including
$264,650 for 25 grants (high: $35,464; low: $12).
Purpose and activities: Giving primarily for
Protestant churches; support also for hospitals,
higher education, a library, a museum, and social
services. Student aid limited to male graduates of
Ottawa Hills High School and Vermillion High
School attending Baldwin-Wallace College.
Fields of interest: Protestant giving, hospitals,
higher education, libraries, museums, social
services.
Types of support: Operating budgets, student aid.
Limitations: Giving primarily in the Toledo, OH,
area.
Application information: Completion of
application form required for scholarships.
Deadline(s): None
Write: Michael D. Wilkins, Selection
Committee Member
Trustee: Society Bank & Trust.
Scholarship Selection Committee: Larry Firestien,
Edgar A. Gibson, James D. Harvey, Michael D.
Wilkins.
EIN: 346781636

2572
The Samuel Rosenthal Foundation
Halle Bldg., Suite 310
1228 Euclid Ave.
Cleveland 44115-1802   (216) 523-8125

Trust established in 1959 in OH.
Foundation type: Independent
Financial data (yr. ended 03/31/91): Assets,
$10,018,391 (M); expenditures, $957,378;
qualifying distributions, $919,334, including
$893,681 for 51 grants (high: $415,000; low:
$25).
Purpose and activities: Giving primarily for social
services programs, including vocational guidance
and rehabilitation, Jewish federated philanthropic
campaigns, United Way, Foodbank, Sight Center,
entertainment enrichment and special events of
childrens' hospitals, and Cleveland Works; health
programs, including research in multiple
sclerosis, cerebral palsy, and deafness; education
programs, including nursing scholarships and
support for local inner-city scholarship programs,
Jewish religious education, and institutions for
musical education; arts and humanities programs,
including local cultural institutions, museums,
orchestra, ballet, theater, and opera.
Fields of interest: Social services, welfare, Jewish
giving, aged, youth, health, hospitals, education,
secondary education, cultural programs.
Types of support: General purposes.
Limitations: Giving primarily in Cleveland, OH.
No grants to individuals.

Application information: Application form not required.
> *Initial approach:* Letter
> *Copies of proposal:* 1
> *Deadline(s):* None
> *Board meeting date(s):* 4 times a year
> *Final notification:* After meeting
> *Write:* Charlotte R. Kramer, Trustee

Trustees: Cynthia R. Boardman, Jane R. Horvitz, Charlotte R. Kramer, Mark R. Kramer, Leighton A. Rosenthal.
Number of staff: 1 part-time professional; 1 part-time support.
EIN: 346558832

2573
The Rubbermaid Foundation
1147 Akron Rd.
Wooster 44691-0800   (216) 264-6464

Established in 1986 in OH.
Donor(s): Rubbermaid, Inc.
Foundation type: Company-sponsored
Financial data (yr. ended 12/31/90): Assets, $5,180,263 (M); expenditures, $1,264,372; qualifying distributions, $1,260,854, including $1,252,689 for grants (high: $288,598).
Fields of interest: Arts, fine arts, education, secondary education, higher education, business education, health, economics.
Types of support: Annual campaigns.
Limitations: Giving primarily in OH, with emphasis on Wooster. No grants to individuals.
Application information: Application form not required.
> *Initial approach:* Letter
> *Copies of proposal:* 1
> *Deadline(s):* None
> *Write:* Richard Gates, Pres.

Officers and Trustees:* Richard D. Gates,* Pres.; Joseph G. Meehan,* V.P.; James A. Morgan,* Secy.; John W. Dean, Treas.; Wolfgang R. Schmitt, Thomas W. Ward, Walter W. Williams.
EIN: 341533729

2574
Josephine S. Russell Charitable Trust
c/o The Central Trust Co., N.A.
P.O. Box 1198
Cincinnati 45201   (513) 651-8377

Trust established in 1976 in OH.
Donor(s): Josephine Schell Russell.‡
Foundation type: Independent
Financial data (yr. ended 06/30/91): Assets, $6,186,158 (M); expenditures, $348,070; qualifying distributions, $312,430, including $307,639 for 62 grants (high: $15,000; low: $1,500; average: $5,000-$10,000).
Purpose and activities: Emphasis on education; support also for social service agencies, cultural programs, health, and scientific and literary purposes.
Fields of interest: Education, social services, cultural programs, health, science and technology, language and literature.
Types of support: Seed money, equipment, land acquisition, special projects, building funds, capital campaigns, renovation projects.
Limitations: Giving limited to the greater Cincinnati, OH, area. No grants to individuals, or

for endowment funds, operating budgets, continuing support, annual campaigns, deficit financing, scholarships, or conferences; no loans.
Publications: Informational brochure (including application guidelines).
Application information: Application form not required.
> *Initial approach:* Letter, telephone, or proposal
> *Copies of proposal:* 8
> *Deadline(s):* Dec. 1 and June 1
> *Board meeting date(s):* Jan. and July
> *Final notification:* 6 weeks after meetings
> *Write:* Mrs. Nancy C. Gurney, Foundation Administrator

Trustee: The Central Trust Co., N.A.
Number of staff: 1 part-time professional.
EIN: 316195446

2575
John J. and Mary R. Schiff Foundation
P.O. Box 145496
Cincinnati 45250-5496

Established in 1983 in OH.
Donor(s): John J. Schiff, Mary R. Schiff.
Foundation type: Independent
Financial data (yr. ended 06/30/90): Assets, $9,597,031 (M); expenditures, $343,719; qualifying distributions, $334,948, including $329,888 for 8 grants (high: $192,188; low: $2,000).
Purpose and activities: Support primarily for a museum; support also for other cultural programs, higher education, and hospitals.
Fields of interest: Museums, cultural programs, hospitals, higher education.
Limitations: Giving primarily in Cincinnati, OH.
Officer and Trustees:* John J. Schiff, Jr.,* Chair.; Susan S. Rheingold, Thomas R. Schiff.
EIN: 311077222

2576
Albert G. and Olive H. Schlink Foundation
401 Citizens National Bank Bldg.
Norwalk 44857

Established in 1966 in OH.
Foundation type: Independent
Financial data (yr. ended 12/31/91): Assets, $8,189,872 (M); expenditures, $417,131; qualifying distributions, $384,713, including $365,200 for 17 grants (high: $143,000; low: $2,500).
Purpose and activities: Grants to organizations providing aid to the indigent, aged, including health agencies and hospitals; support also for the blind.
Fields of interest: Disadvantaged, aged, health services, hospitals, handicapped, nursing, medical research, medical education.
Limitations: Giving primarily in OH. No grants to individuals.
Application information: Application form not required.
> *Initial approach:* Letter
> *Copies of proposal:* 1
> *Deadline(s):* None
> *Board meeting date(s):* Bimonthly
> *Final notification:* Dec.
> *Write:* Robert A. Wiedemann, Pres.

Officers and Trustees:* Robert A. Wiedemann,* Pres. and Secy.; Dorothy E. Wiedemann,* V.P.; John D. Allton,* Treas.; Lawrence P. Furlong, Curtis J. Koch.
Number of staff: None.
EIN: 346574722

2577
Charlotte R. Schmidlapp Fund
c/o Fifth Third Bank
Dept. 00864
Cincinnati 45263   (513) 579-6034

Trust established in 1907 in OH.
Donor(s): Jacob G. Schmidlapp.‡
Foundation type: Independent
Financial data (yr. ended 09/30/91): Assets, $18,981,878 (M); gifts received, $204,888; expenditures, $978,771; qualifying distributions, $909,475, including $819,581 for 27 grants (high: $250,000; low: $3,503) and $19,905 for 28 loans to individuals.
Purpose and activities: "To aid young girls in the preparation for womanhood, by bringing their minds and hearts under the influence of education, relieving their bodies from disease, suffering or constraint and assisting them to establish themselves in life." Student loan program recently discontinued, however, prior commitments are still being honored; the foundation will make direct grants, primarily to colleges, universities, and nursing schools.
Fields of interest: Women, education, higher education, nursing, health, leadership development.
Types of support: Seed money, special projects.
Limitations: Giving primarily in Cincinnati, OH. No grants for building or endowment funds, or operating budgets.
Publications: Application guidelines.
Application information:
> *Initial approach:* Letter
> *Copies of proposal:* 1
> *Deadline(s):* Feb. 1, May 1, Aug. 1, and Nov. 1
> *Board meeting date(s):* Mar, June, Sept., and Dec.
> *Final notification:* Immediately following board meetings
> *Write:* Carolyn F. McCoy, Fdn. Officer

Trustee: Fifth Third Bank.
Number of staff: 1 full-time professional; 1 full-time support.
EIN: 310532641
Recent health grants:
2577-1 Christ Hospital, Cincinnati, OH, $20,000. For student loans. 1990.
2577-2 Good Samaritan Hospital, Cincinnati, OH, $20,000. For student loans. 1990.

2578
Jacob G. Schmidlapp Trust No. 1 ▼
c/o Fifth Third Bank
Dept. 00864, Foundation Office
Cincinnati 45263   (513) 579-6034

Trust established in 1927 in OH.
Donor(s): Jacob G. Schmidlapp.‡
Foundation type: Independent
Financial data (yr. ended 09/30/91): Assets, $37,201,671 (M); expenditures, $1,884,633; qualifying distributions, $1,761,423, including

$1,611,242 for 76 grants (high: $100,000; low: $287; average: $10,000-$50,000).

Purpose and activities: Grants for the relief of sickness, suffering, and distress, and for care of young children or the helpless and afflicted; support also for education related to the care of young children, including child care training.

Fields of interest: Health, hospitals, welfare, social services, child welfare, child development, youth, aged, education—minorities, homeless, housing, hunger, education.

Types of support: Seed money, building funds, equipment, land acquisition, capital campaigns.

Limitations: Giving primarily in the greater Cincinnati, OH, area. No support for religious purposes. No grants to individuals, or for annual campaigns, emergency funds, deficit financing, general support, scholarships, fellowships, operating budgets, or continuing support; no loans.

Publications: Annual report (including application guidelines).

Application information: Application form not required.

   Initial approach: Letter, telephone, or proposal
   Copies of proposal: 1
   Deadline(s): Feb. 10, May 10, Aug. 10, and Nov. 10
   Board meeting date(s): Mar., June, Sept., and Dec.
   Final notification: Middle of months in which board meets
   Write: Carolyn McCoy

Trustee: Fifth Third Bank.

Number of staff: 1 full-time professional; 1 full-time support.

EIN: 316019680

2579
SCOA Foundation, Inc.
41 South High St., Suite 3310
Columbus 43215

Established in 1969 in OH.

Donor(s): SCOA Industries, Inc.

Foundation type: Company-sponsored

Financial data (yr. ended 12/31/91): Assets, $4,889,154 (M); expenditures, $716,710; qualifying distributions, $673,200, including $673,200 for 49 grants (high: $91,200; low: $300).

Purpose and activities: Giving primarily for Jewish welfare, child welfare, and community funds; support also for higher education, hospitals, and cultural activities.

Fields of interest: Jewish welfare, Jewish giving, child welfare, community funds, higher education, hospitals, cultural programs.

Limitations: Giving primarily in communities where Hills Department Stores are located; in 13 states in the Midwest. No grants to individuals.

Application information: Contributes only to pre-selected organizations. Applications not accepted.

   Write: William K. Friend, Secy.

Officers and Trustees:* Herbert H. Schiff,* Chair.; William K. Friend, Secy.; George R. Friese, Murray Gallant, Harvey M. Krueger, Thomas H. Lee, Larry Voelker.

EIN: 237002220

2580
The Sears Family Foundation
907 Park Bldg.
Cleveland 44114   (216) 241-6434

Trust established in 1949 in OH.

Donor(s): Anna L. Sears,‡ Lester M. Sears,‡ Ruth P. Sears,‡ Mary Ann Swetland.‡

Foundation type: Independent

Financial data (yr. ended 12/31/91): Assets, $2,458,847 (M); gifts received, $48,355; expenditures, $127,896; qualifying distributions, $118,583, including $118,583 for 48 grants (high: $25,000; low: $500).

Fields of interest: Education, health, welfare, environment, arts.

Types of support: General purposes, operating budgets, continuing support, annual campaigns, seed money, emergency funds, deficit financing, building funds, equipment, land acquisition, matching funds, research, capital campaigns.

Limitations: Giving limited to the Cleveland, OH, area. No grants to individuals, or for scholarships or fellowships; no loans.

Publications: 990-PF, application guidelines.

Application information: Application form not required.

   Initial approach: Letter
   Copies of proposal: 1
   Deadline(s): Submit proposal preferably before Dec.
   Board meeting date(s): As needed
   Final notification: 60 days
   Write: David W. Swetland, Trustee

Officer and Trustees:* Polly M. Swetland,* Secy.; Ruth Swetland Eppig, David Sears Swetland, David W. Swetland.

Number of staff: 2 part-time support.

EIN: 346522143

2581
The Della Selsor Trust
P.O. Box 1488
Springfield 45501   (513) 324-5541

Established in 1966 in OH.

Donor(s): Della Selsor.‡

Foundation type: Independent

Financial data (yr. ended 12/31/90): Assets, $2,529,660 (M); expenditures, $114,928; qualifying distributions, $110,709, including $110,100 for 60 grants (high: $15,000; low: $50).

Fields of interest: Youth, cultural programs, hospitals, education.

Types of support: Annual campaigns, building funds, capital campaigns.

Limitations: Giving limited to Clark and Madison counties, OH.

Application information:

   Initial approach: Letter or telephone call
   Deadline(s): None
   Write: Trustees

Trustees: Glenn W. Collier, Oscar T. Martin.

EIN: 510163338

2582
The Louise Taft Semple Foundation
1800 Star Bank Ctr.
Cincinnati 45202   (513) 381-2838

Application address: 1808 Cincinnati Commerce Ctr., 600 Vine St., Cincinnati, OH 45202

Incorporated in 1941 in OH.

Donor(s): Louise Taft Semple.‡

Foundation type: Independent

Financial data (yr. ended 12/31/91): Assets, $14,917,389 (M); expenditures, $609,321; qualifying distributions, $499,894, including $483,200 for 31 grants (high: $75,000; low: $1,500; average: $1,000-$75,000).

Fields of interest: Higher education, secondary education, fine arts, social services, health.

Types of support: Building funds, endowment funds, scholarship funds, matching funds.

Limitations: Giving primarily in the Cincinnati or Hamilton County, OH, area. No grants to individuals, or for general purposes or research; no loans.

Application information: Application form not required.

   Initial approach: Letter
   Deadline(s): None
   Board meeting date(s): 1st Monday in Apr., July, Oct., and Dec.
   Final notification: 3 months
   Write: Dudley S. Taft, Pres. and Trustee

Officers and Trustees:* Dudley S. Taft,* Pres.; James R. Bridgeland, Jr.,* Secy.; Norma F. Gentzler, Treas.; Mrs. John T. Lawrence, Jr., Walter L. Lingle, Jr., Nellie L. Taft, Robert A. Taft, Jr., Mrs. Robert A. Taft II.

Number of staff: None.

EIN: 310653526

2583
The Sherwick Fund
c/o The Cleveland Foundation
1422 Euclid Ave., Suite 1400
Cleveland 44115-2001   (216) 861-3810

Incorporated in 1953 in OH; a supporting organization of The Cleveland Foundation.

Donor(s): John Sherwin,‡ Frances Wick Sherwin.

Foundation type: Independent

Financial data (yr. ended 12/31/90): Assets, $11,847,432 (M); expenditures, $508,258; qualifying distributions, $412,106, including $412,106 for 40 grants (high: $80,006; low: $500; average: $500-$80,006).

Purpose and activities: A supporting fund of The Cleveland Foundation; emphasis on youth agencies, health, education, social services, cultural programs, and community funds.

Fields of interest: Youth, health, education, social services, cultural programs, community funds, AIDS.

Types of support: Seed money, technical assistance, capital campaigns, special projects.

Limitations: Giving limited to the greater Cleveland, OH, area and Lake County. No grants to individuals, or for endowment funds, general operating budgets, or deficit financing; no loans.

Publications: Application guidelines, program policy statement, biennial report.

Application information: Application form not required.

   Initial approach: Full proposal or letter of inquiry
   Copies of proposal: 2
   Deadline(s): Apr. 1 and Oct. 1

Board meeting date(s): Usually in June and Dec.
Final notification: 1 month after board meets
Write: Michael J. Hoffmann, Secy.-Treas.
Officers and Trustees:* John Sherwin, Jr.,* Pres.;
Homer C. Wadsworth,* V.P.; Michael J.
Hoffmann, Secy.-Treas.; James M. Delaney, Sally
K. Griswold, Richard W. Pogue.
Number of staff: None.
EIN: 346526395

2584
The Sisler McFawn Foundation
(Formerly Lois Sisler McFawn Trust No. 2)
3925 Embassy Pkwy.
Akron 44333-1799   (216) 374-2628

Trust established in 1956 in OH.
Donor(s): Lois Sisler McFawn.‡
Foundation type: Independent
Financial data (yr. ended 12/31/91): Assets,
$12,172,061 (M); expenditures, $899,849;
qualifying distributions, $796,390, including
$781,033 for 90 grants (high: $50,000; low:
$500).
Purpose and activities: Emphasis on education,
public health and programs for the sick, aged,
needy, disabled, and youth.
Fields of interest: Education, health, aged,
welfare, handicapped, youth.
Types of support: General purposes, building
funds, equipment, seed money, capital
campaigns, endowment funds, operating budgets,
renovation projects, special projects.
Limitations: Giving primarily in Summit County,
OH. No grants to individuals; no loans.
Application information: Application form not
required.
  Initial approach: Proposal
  Copies of proposal: 1
  Deadline(s): None
  Board meeting date(s): 3 times a year; call for
    schedule
  Write: Sarah S. Wright, Grants Mgr.
Distribution Committee: Michael J. Connor,
Howard L. Flood, Patricia A. Kemph, John D.
Ong, Justin T. Rogers, Jr.
Trustee: Society National Bank.
Number of staff: 1 part-time professional.
EIN: 346508111

2585
The Eleanor Armstrong Smith Charitable
Fund
1100 National City Bank Bldg.
Cleveland 44114   (216) 566-5500

Established in 1974 in OH.
Donor(s): Kelvin Smith.‡
Foundation type: Independent
Financial data (yr. ended 12/31/91): Assets,
$3,873,704 (M); expenditures, $112,764;
qualifying distributions, $92,372, including
$92,154 for 20 grants (high: $40,000; low: $79).
Purpose and activities: Support primarily for
nature and horticulture, health care,
non-sectarian education, and the performing and
visual arts.
Fields of interest: Environment, wildlife, health,
hospitals, arts, performing arts, education.
Types of support: General purposes.

Limitations: Giving primarily in the Cleveland,
OH, area. No grants to individuals; no loans.
Application information: Telephone inquiries
discouraged. Application form not required.
  Initial approach: Letter
  Copies of proposal: 1
  Deadline(s): None
  Write: Andrew L. Fabens, III
Trustee: Eleanor A. Smith.
Number of staff: None.
EIN: 237374137

2586
The Kelvin and Eleanor Smith Foundation
▼
1100 National City Bank Bldg.
Cleveland 44114   (216) 566-5500
Application address: 29425 Chagrin Blvd., Suite
303, Pepper Pike, OH 44122

Incorporated in 1955 in OH.
Donor(s): Kelvin Smith.‡
Foundation type: Independent
Financial data (yr. ended 10/31/91): Assets,
$57,458,687 (M); expenditures, $2,412,873;
qualifying distributions, $2,247,571, including
$2,129,278 for 34 grants (high: $1,000,000; low:
$1,200; average: $5,000-$25,000).
Purpose and activities: The foundation's principal
interests are in the fields of non-sectarian
education, the free enterprise system, the
performing and visual arts, health care, and other
activities of the type supported by the United Way
Services of Cleveland.
Fields of interest: Education, performing arts, arts,
health, community funds.
Types of support: Operating budgets, continuing
support, annual campaigns, seed money, building
funds, equipment.
Limitations: Giving primarily in the greater
Cleveland, OH, area. No grants to individuals, or
for endowment funds, scholarships, fellowships,
or matching gifts; no loans.
Publications: Application guidelines.
Application information: Application form not
required.
  Initial approach: Letter
  Copies of proposal: 2
  Deadline(s): None
  Board meeting date(s): Varies
  Final notification: 2 to 3 months
  Write: Douglas W. Richardson, Pres.
Officers and Trustees: John L. Dampeer,* Chair.
and Treas.; Douglas W. Richardson, Pres.; Lucia S.
Nash, V.P.; Cara S. Stirn, V.P.; Ellen Mavec, Secy.;
Michael D. Eppig, M.D., Lincoln Reavis.
Number of staff: None.
EIN: 346555349

2587
J. M. Smucker Company Giving Program
Strawberry Ln.
P.O. Box 280
Orrville 44667   (216) 682-0015

Financial data (yr. ended 04/30/90): Total giving,
$647,000, including $439,000 for grants
(average: $1,000), $9,000 for 45 employee
matching gifts and $199,000 for in-kind gifts.

Purpose and activities: Supports education, the
arts and culture, health, human services and civic
and public affairs.
Fields of interest: Education, cultural programs,
arts, health, civic affairs.
Types of support: General purposes, donated
products.
Limitations: Giving primarily in OH.
Application information: Contributions handled
by Human Resources Dept.
  Initial approach: Letter or proposal
  Deadline(s): Applications accepted throughout
    the year
  Write: Tim Miller, Mgr., Emloyee Development

2588
Willard E. Smucker Foundation
2026 Wayne St., Route 2
Orrville 44667

Established in 1968 in OH.
Donor(s): J.M. Smucker Co., and members of the
Smucker family.
Foundation type: Company-sponsored
Financial data (yr. ended 12/31/91): Assets,
$7,626,020 (M); gifts received, $126,000;
expenditures, $205,477; qualifying distributions,
$204,408, including $203,608 for 32 grants
(high: $33,334; low: $500).
Fields of interest: Higher education, education,
hospitals, social services.
Types of support: General purposes.
Limitations: Giving primarily in OH. No grants to
individuals.
Application information: Contributes only to
pre-selected organizations. Applications not
accepted.
Officers and Trustees:* Paul H. Smucker,* Pres.
and Treas.; Marcella S. Clark,* Exec. V.P.; H. Ray
Clark,* V.P.; Lorraine E. Smucker,* V.P.; Steven J.
Ellcessor, Secy.; Richard K. Smucker, Timothy P.
Smucker.
EIN: 346610889

2589
Society Bank Corporate Giving Program
c/o Community Rels.
800 Superior Ave.
Cleveland 44114   (216) 622-9000

Financial data (yr. ended 12/31/90): Total giving,
$3,043,657, including $3,016,657 for 928 grants
(high: $510,000; low: $100; average:
$500-$10,000) and $27,000 for loans.
Purpose and activities: "Building excellence in
our schools, improving race relations, revitalizing
our neighborhoods, helping entrepreneurs
succeed are among the tough challenges we face
in our communities. As a corporate citizen who
cares, Society attacks these issues head-on,
always striving to find ways to make our
communities stronger." Society supports civic
programs, culture, health, social services, arts and
education through contributions and program
related investments. In 1988, program related
investments were made for low-income housing
and economic revitalization in depressed areas.
Fields of interest: Civic affairs, community funds,
arts, education, hospitals, higher education.
Types of support: Program-related investments,
annual campaigns, employee matching gifts,

operating budgets, seed money, building funds, employee volunteer services, loaned talent, capital campaigns, continuing support, matching funds.
Limitations: Giving primarily in OH.
Publications: Informational brochure (including application guidelines), corporate report.
Application information: Community Relations handles giving. Application form not required.
   Initial approach: Send requests to nearest company facility
   Copies of proposal: 1
   Deadline(s): None
   Board meeting date(s): Weekly
   Final notification: One month
   Write: Anne M. Grove
Number of staff: 2 part-time professional; 4 part-time support.

2590
Star Bank, N.A., Cincinnati Foundation
(Formerly The First National Bank of Cincinnati Foundation)
c/o Star Bank Corp.
P.O. Box 1038
Cincinnati 45201   (513) 632-4610

Trust established in 1967 in OH.
Foundation type: Company-sponsored
Financial data (yr. ended 12/31/90): Assets, $1,538,835 (M); gifts received, $950,000; expenditures, $582,352; qualifying distributions, $580,673, including $580,473 for 49 grants (high: $225,000; low: $490).
Fields of interest: Community funds, hospitals, cultural programs, arts, business, business education, higher education, child welfare, family services, citizenship.
Types of support: General purposes, building funds, equipment, land acquisition, operating budgets.
Limitations: Giving limited to the greater Cincinnati, OH, area. No grants to individuals, or for endowment funds, research, scholarships, fellowships, or matching gifts; no loans.
Application information: Application form not required.
   Initial approach: Letter
   Deadline(s): None
   Board meeting date(s): Monthly
   Write: Ms. Peggy A. Woods
Officers and Trustees:* Samuel M. Cassidy,* Pres.; Oliver W. Waddell,* V.P.; Raymond Beck,* Secy.; James R. Bridgeland, Jr., J.P. Hayden, Jr., Thomas J. Klinedinst, William N. Liggett, Charles S. Mechem, Jr., Thomas E. Petry, William Portman, William W. Wommack.
Number of staff: None.
EIN: 316079013

2591
The Stark County Foundation
United Bank Bldg., Suite 350
220 Market Ave. South
Canton 44702   (216) 454-3426
FAX: (216) 452-2009

Established in 1964 in OH by resolution and declaration of trust.
Foundation type: Community

Financial data (yr. ended 12/31/91): Assets, $46,946,887 (M); gifts received, $528,030; expenditures, $1,864,083; qualifying distributions, $1,384,649, including $1,197,220 for 140 grants (high: $210,000; low: $50; average: $2,500-$20,000); $68,979 for grants to individuals and $118,450 for loans to individuals.
Purpose and activities: To maintain the sound health and general welfare of the citizens through support for civic improvement programs, including the Newmarket Project for redevelopment of downtown Canton, hospitals, and educational institutions.
Fields of interest: Civic affairs, community development, hospitals, education, higher education, legal education, social services, youth, arts, fine arts.
Types of support: Seed money, emergency funds, building funds, equipment, land acquisition, matching funds, scholarship funds, special projects, research, conferences and seminars, consulting services, technical assistance, capital campaigns, general purposes, student loans, student aid, loans.
Limitations: Giving limited to Stark County, OH. No grants for endowment funds, operating budgets, continuing support, annual campaigns, publications, or deficit financing; no grants or loans to individuals (except to college students who are residents of Stark County).
Publications: Multi-year report, program policy statement, application guidelines, financial statement, grants list.
Application information: Application form not required.
   Initial approach: Letter or proposal
   Copies of proposal: 8
   Deadline(s): Mar. 1 for student aid; none for other grants
   Board meeting date(s): Monthly
   Final notification: 60 to 90 days
   Write: James A. Bower, Exec. Dir.
Officers: Patricia C. Quick, Financial Officer; James A. Bower, Exec. Dir.
Distribution Committee: William H. Belden, Jr., Donald L. Hart, Thomas H. Hoover, William L. Luntz, Randolph L. Snow.
Trustee Banks: Ameritrust Co. of Stark County, Bank One of Alliance, The Central Trust Co. of Northern Ohio, N.A., First National Bank in Massillon, Society National Bank, United National Bank.
Number of staff: 1 full-time professional; 1 part-time professional; 1 full-time support.
EIN: 340943665

2592
Justine Sterkel Trust
c/o Bank One, Mansfield, N.A.
28 Park Ave. West
Mansfield 44902

Trust established in 1966 in OH.
Donor(s): Justine Sterkel.‡
Foundation type: Independent
Financial data (yr. ended 12/31/91): Assets, $3,490,624 (M); expenditures, $162,584; qualifying distributions, $138,031, including $136,760 for 7 grants (high: $59,380; low: $1,000).
Fields of interest: Rehabilitation, family services, child welfare, social services.

Limitations: Giving primarily in the city of Mansfield and Richland County, OH.
Application information: Application form not required.
   Deadline(s): None
Trustees: H. Eugene Ryan, Bank One, Mansfield, N.A.
EIN: 346576810

2593
Robert A. Stranahan, Jr. Charitable Trust
c/o Society Bank & Trust
P.O. Box 10099
Toledo 43699-0099

Established in 1959.
Donor(s): Robert A. Stranahan, Jr., Nancy S. Jones, Lynn S. Butler.
Foundation type: Independent
Financial data (yr. ended 12/31/91): Assets, $5,411,228 (M); expenditures, $197,723; qualifying distributions, $185,005, including $182,500 for 9 grants (high: $30,000; low: $2,500).
Fields of interest: Child development, youth, religion—Christian, higher education, handicapped, cancer.
Types of support: General purposes, special projects.
Limitations: Giving primarily in Toledo, OH. No loans or program-related investments.
Application information: Contributes only to pre-selected organizations. Applications not accepted.
Advisors: Robert Brotje, Gerald W. Miller, Roberta M. Pawlak, Francis G. Pletz, Mescal S. Stranahan.
Trustee: Society Bank & Trust.
EIN: 346504818

2594
Tamarkin Foundation
20 Federal Plaza West
Youngstown 44503   (216) 743-1786

Established in 1968.
Donor(s): Tamarkin Co., Project Four, Inc., S & H Co., Giant Eagle Markets, Inc., and members of the Tamarkin family.
Foundation type: Company-sponsored
Financial data (yr. ended 12/31/90): Assets, $379,814 (M); gifts received, $200,000; expenditures, $268,667; qualifying distributions, $265,430, including $265,430 for 30 grants (high: $79,000; low: $180).
Fields of interest: Jewish giving, Jewish welfare, cultural programs, hospitals, education, social services.
Types of support: Operating budgets, special projects, building funds.
Limitations: Giving primarily in OH.
Application information: Application form not required.
   Deadline(s): None
   Write: Bertram Tamarkin, Pres., or Nathan H. Monus, Secy.
Officers and Trustees:* Bertram Tamarkin,* Pres.; Jerry P. Tamarkin,* V.P.; Nathan H. Monus,* Secy.; Jack B. Tamarkin,* Treas.; Arthur N.K. Friedman, Michael I. Monus.
EIN: 341023645

2595
Timken Foundation of Canton ▼
236 Third St., S.W.
Canton 44702   (216) 455-5281

Incorporated in 1934 in OH.
Donor(s): Members of the Timken family.
Foundation type: Independent
Financial data (yr. ended 09/30/91): Assets,
$125,651,551 (M); expenditures, $5,673,487;
qualifying distributions, $5,489,703, including
$5,430,321 for 46 grants (high: $625,000; low:
$5,724; average: $10,000-$300,000).
Purpose and activities: To promote broad civic
betterment by capital fund grants; grants largely
for colleges, schools, hospitals, cultural centers,
conservation and recreation, and other charitable
institutions.
Fields of interest: Community funds, community
development, leadership development,
education, higher education,
education—minorities, computer sciences,
secondary education, elementary education,
education—early childhood, libraries, hospitals,
hospitals—building funds, cultural programs,
conservation, recreation, child development,
Australia, Canada, Europe.
Types of support: Building funds, equipment,
capital campaigns, endowment funds, land
acquisition.
Limitations: Giving primarily in areas of Timken
Co. domestic operations in Canton, Columbus,
Ashland, Bucyrus, and Wooster, OH; Gaffney, SC;
Lincolnton, NC; Latrobe, PA; and Concord,
Keene, and Lebanon, NH. Giving also in
Australia, Brazil, Canada, France, Great Britain,
and South Africa. No grants to individuals, or for
operating budgets.
Application information: Proposal. Application
form not required.
    Deadline(s): None
    Board meeting date(s): As required
    Final notification: As soon as possible
    Write: Don D. Dickes, Secy.-Treas.
Officers and Trustees* Ward J. Timken,* Pres.;
W.R. Timken,* V.P.; W.R. Timken, Jr.,* V.P.; Don
D. Dickes,* Secy.-Treas.
Number of staff: 1 full-time professional; 1
part-time support.
EIN: 346520254
Recent health grants:
2595-1 Ashland Hospital Association, Ashland,
OH, $50,000. For capital campaign. 1990.
2595-2 Cleveland Clinic Foundation, Cleveland,
OH, $250,000. For capital campaign. 1990.
2595-3 Planned Parenthood of Stark County,
Canton, OH, $125,000. Toward acquisition of
new facility. 1990.
2595-4 Saint Thomas-Elgin General Hospital
Foundation, Canada, $43,363. For hospital
modernization. 1990.
2595-5 South African Red Cross Society, South
Africa, $19,631. To purchase ambulance.
1990.
2595-6 Wooster Community Hospital, Hospital
Auxilary, Wooster, OH, $50,000. For
expansion and renovation. 1990.

2596
The C. Carlisle and Margaret M. Tippit Charitable Trust
2000 Huntington Bldg.
Cleveland 44115

Established in 1989.
Foundation type: Independent
Financial data (yr. ended 08/31/91): Assets,
$2,605,201 (M); expenditures, $197,662;
qualifying distributions, $190,600, including
$184,600 for grants.
Fields of interest: Health, civic affairs, religion,
education.
Limitations: Giving primarily in Cleveland, OH.
No grants to individuals.
Application information: Contributes only to
pre-selected organizations. Applications not
accepted.
Trustees: James R. Bright, Carl J. Tippit.
EIN: 341627297

2597
Toledo Community Foundation, Inc.
608 Madison Ave., Suite 1540
Toledo 43604-1151   (419) 241-5049

Established in 1924 in OH by trust agreement;
reactivated in 1973.
Foundation type: Community
Financial data (yr. ended 12/31/91): Assets,
$20,766,369 (L); gifts received, $1,933,948;
expenditures, $3,495,738; qualifying
distributions, $3,151,815, including $3,151,815
for grants.
Purpose and activities: Support for projects which
promise to affect a broad segment of the citizens
of northwestern OH or which tend to help those
living in an area not being adequately served by
local community resources. Areas of interest
include social services and youth programs, arts
and culture, health associations, education,
conservation, religion, government and urban
affairs, and united funds.
Fields of interest: Arts, conservation,
environment, health, education, youth, social
services, public affairs, urban affairs.
Types of support: Seed money, matching funds,
special projects.
Limitations: Giving primarily in northwestern
OH, with emphasis on the greater Toledo area.
No grants to individuals, or for annual campaigns,
operating budgets, or endowment funds.
Publications: Annual report (including application
guidelines), informational brochure, application
guidelines.
Application information: Application form
required.
    Initial approach: Telephone
    Copies of proposal: 1
    Deadline(s): Mar. 1, June 1, Sept. 1, and Dec. 1
    Board meeting date(s): Jan., Apr., July, and Oct.
    Final notification: 2 months
    Write: Pam Howell-Beach, Dir.
Officers and Trustees:* Steven Timonere,* Pres.;
Ardath Danford,* V.P.; Thomas H. Anderson,*
Secy.; Lawrence T. Foster,* Treas.; Ronald C.
Boller, Elizabeth Brady, Robert V. Franklin, Jr., Joel
Levine, Duane Stranahan, Jr., Julie Taylor, Mary
Wolfe.
Number of staff: 2 full-time professional; 2
part-time professional; 2 part-time support.

EIN: 237284004

2598
Tranzonic Companies Corporate Giving Program
30195 Chagrin Blvd., Suite 224E
Pepper Pike 44124   (216) 831-5757

Purpose and activities: Support for the United
Way and health and social services.
Fields of interest: Health, social services,
community funds.
Types of support: In-kind gifts.
Limitations: Giving primarily in local areas of
operations.
Application information: Applications not
accepted.
    Write: Robert Reitman, Chair. and C.E.O.

2599
Tranzonic Foundation
c/o The Tranzonic Companies
30195 Chagrin Blvd., Suite 224E
Pepper Pike 44124   (216) 831-5757

Established in 1976 in OH.
Donor(s): The Tranzonic Companies.
Foundation type: Company-sponsored
Financial data (yr. ended 06/30/91): Assets,
$7,164 (M); gifts received, $369,500;
expenditures, $369,500; qualifying distributions,
$369,500, including $369,500 for 30 grants
(high: $50,000; low: $100).
Fields of interest: Jewish welfare, community
funds, health, community development.
Limitations: Giving primarily in northern OH. No
grants to individuals.
Application information: Application form
required.
    Initial approach: Letter
    Copies of proposal: 1
    Deadline(s): None
    Board meeting date(s): Quarterly
    Final notification: Late Feb. or early Mar.
    Write: Robert S. Reitman, V.P.
Officers: James H. Berick, Pres.; Robert S.
Reitman, V.P.; Sam Pearlman, Secy.-Treas.
Number of staff: None.
EIN: 341193613

2600
The Treu-Mart Fund
c/o The Cleveland Foundation
1422 Euclid Ave., Suite 1400
Cleveland 44115-2001   (216) 861-3810
Additional address: c/o R. Michael Cole, The
Jewish Community Federation of Cleveland,
1750 Euclid Ave., Cleveland, OH 44115; Tel.:
(216) 566-9200

Established in 1980 in OH; a supporting
organization of The Cleveland Foundation.
Donor(s): Elizabeth M. Treuhaft, William C.
Treuhaft.‡
Foundation type: Independent
Financial data (yr. ended 12/31/90): Assets,
$5,040,689 (M); expenditures, $153,676;
qualifying distributions, $122,500, including
$122,500 for 5 grants (high: $50,000; low:
$7,500; average: $7,500-$50,000).

Purpose and activities: Supporting organization of The Cleveland Foundation and The Jewish Community Federation of Cleveland; organization grants primarily for projects benefitting residents of the greater Cleveland area, especially those incorporating demonstration or research elements. Support largely for community development, cultural programs, health planning, and social service activities, including Jewish welfare agencies.
Fields of interest: Jewish giving, Jewish welfare, community development, cultural programs, health, social services, Jewish welfare, youth.
Types of support: Research, special projects.
Limitations: Giving primarily in Cleveland, OH. No grants to individuals, or for operating budgets or annual campaigns.
Publications: Biennial report (including application guidelines).
Application information: Application form not required.
  Initial approach: Proposal
  Copies of proposal: 2
  Deadline(s): Apr. 1 and Sept. 15
  Board meeting date(s): Usually in June and Oct.
  Final notification: Within 1 month of board meeting dates
  Write: Michael J. Hoffmann, Treas.
Officers and Trustees:* Arthur W. Treuhaft,* Pres.; Henry L. Zucker,* V.P.; R. Michael Cole, Secy.; Michael J. Hoffmann, Treas.; Mary Louise Hahn, Jerry V. Jarrett, Frances M. King, Albert B. Ratner, Milton A. Wolf.
Number of staff: None.
EIN: 341323364

2601
Trinova Corporate Giving Program
c/o Community Relations
3000 Strayer
Maumee 43537   (419) 867-2200
Application addresses: Organizations in northwest OH, write to the Maumee OH, address. Others write to the nearest subsidiary or plant

Purpose and activities: Trinova has a highly decentralized giving program. Contributions of $5,000 or more are paid through Trinova Foundation. Contributions less than $5,000 are paid through the direct giving program, with the exception of grants for Junior Achievement, the United Way, and higher education which are always made through the foundation, regardless of the amount. Areas of interest include the arts, business, higher education, educational research, health, and youth. Aerogroup and Vickers at times make donations of equipment to schools. Each division has its own giving guidelines and budget.
Fields of interest: Arts, business education, civic affairs, cultural programs, educational associations, educational research, health, higher education, hospitals, museums, music, youth.
Types of support: Annual campaigns, building funds, continuing support, employee matching gifts, general purposes.
Limitations: Giving limited to northwest OH for giving by headquarters; operating companies handle requests in their areas. No support for religious organizations. No grants to individuals; generally no support for fundraisers.

Application information: Requests should be addressed to the nearest plant or subsidiary. At Trinova headquarters, responsibility for Community Relations is rotated among the different departments of the company. Grantseekers should find out which department is currently in charge before writing. Application form not required.
  Initial approach: Letter; write to nearest operating company of Trinova, Vickers, or Aeroquip
  Copies of proposal: 1
  Deadline(s): None
  Board meeting date(s): Contribs. Comm. meets monthly
  Final notification: As soon as proposal is received
  Write: Richard G. Rump, Mgr., Fin. Communs.

2602
TRW Corporate Giving Program
1900 Richmond Rd.
Cleveland 44124   (216) 291-7164

Financial data (yr. ended 12/31/90): Total giving, $1,050,000 for grants.
Purpose and activities: Supports civic affairs, arts and culture, youth programs, education, united funds and hospitals. The foundation handles gifts of more than $5,000, those of $5,000 or less are handled directly by operating units. Support is also given through in-kind gifts.
Fields of interest: Civic affairs, community development, cultural programs, youth, education, hospitals, community funds.
Types of support: In-kind gifts, employee volunteer services.
Limitations: Giving limited to areas with significant company presence: Cleveland, OH; Los Angeles, San Bernardino, San Diego, San Luis Obispo, Sunnyville, CA; Boston, MA; Colorado Springs, CO; Detroit, MI; Eastern, TN; Fairfax, VA; Fairfield and Parsippany, NJ; Houston, TX; Huntsville, AL; Lafayette, IN; Ogden, IA, and Washington DC. No support for religious or fraternal organizations or, hospitals for regular operating support. No grants to individuals.
Application information: Application form not required.
  Initial approach: One to two page letter outlining project
  Write: Al Senger, Dir., Community Affairs

2603
TRW Foundation ▼
1900 Richmond Rd.
Cleveland 44124   (216) 291-7166

Incorporated in 1953 in OH as the Thompson Products Foundation; became the Thompson Ramo Wooldridge Foundation in 1958, and adopted its present name in 1965.
Donor(s): TRW, Inc.
Foundation type: Company-sponsored
Financial data (yr. ended 12/31/90): Assets, $19,333,044 (M); gifts received, $2,400,000; expenditures, $8,062,762; qualifying distributions, $7,997,780, including $6,191,602 for 375 grants (high: $382,500; low: $1,000; average: $5,000-$25,000), $60,000 for 6 grants

to individuals and $1,701,126 for employee matching gifts.
Purpose and activities: Grants largely for higher education, particularly for engineering, technical, science, and/or business administration programs, and community funds; limited support for hospitals, welfare agencies, youth agencies, and civic and cultural organizations.
Fields of interest: Education, education—early childhood, elementary education, education—minorities, secondary education, higher education, computer sciences, science and technology, engineering, business education, community funds, hospitals, welfare, disadvantaged, volunteerism, youth, civic affairs, cultural programs.
Types of support: Employee matching gifts, scholarship funds, professorships, fellowships, research, operating budgets, general purposes, matching funds, special projects, employee-related scholarships.
Limitations: Giving primarily in TRW plant communities, with some emphasis on Cleveland, OH. No support for religious purposes, fraternal or labor organizations, or private elementary or secondary schools. No grants to individuals (except for employee-related scholarships and TRW Presidential Young Investigators Awards), or for endowment funds.
Publications: Annual report, program policy statement, application guidelines, grants list.
Application information: Application form not required.
  Initial approach: Proposal
  Copies of proposal: 1
  Deadline(s): Submit proposals any time; deadline Sept. 1 for organizations already receiving support from the foundation
  Board meeting date(s): Dec.
  Final notification: 30 to 90 days
  Write: Alan F. Senger, V.P.
Officers and Trustees:* Howard V. Knicely,* Pres.; C.G. Miller, V.P. and Controller; Robert M. Hamje,* V.P.; William H. Oliver, V.P.; Alan F. Senger, V.P.; William A. Warren, V.P.; James M. Roosevelt, Secy.; Martin A. Coyle, Edsel D. Dunford, Joseph T. Gorman.
Number of staff: None.
EIN: 346556217
Recent health grants:
2603-1 Cerebral Palsy of Essex and West Hudson, Belleville, NJ, $16,430. 1990.
2603-2 Cleveland Clinic Foundation, Cleveland, OH, $50,000. 1990.
2603-3 Cleveland Hearing and Speech Center, Cleveland, OH, $10,000. 1990.
2603-4 Crippled Childrens Society, Long Beach, CA, $36,300. 1990.
2603-5 El Camino Hospital, Mountain View, CA, $20,000. 1990.
2603-6 Freeman Hospitals Foundation, Inglewood, CA, $25,000. 1990.
2603-7 Heather Hill, Chardon, OH, $10,000. 1990.
2603-8 Lorain County Community Hospital, Lorain, OH, $20,000. 1990.
2603-9 Neighboring: Support Services for Mental Health, Cleveland, OH, $11,118. 1990.
2603-10 Saint Lukes Hospital Association, Cleveland, OH, $25,000. 1990.
2603-11 South Bay Free Clinic, Manhattan Beach, CA, $10,000. 1990.

2604
The Van Wert County Foundation
101-1/2 East Main St.
Van Wert 45891   (419) 238-1743

Incorporated in 1925 in OH.
Donor(s): Charles F. Wassenberg,‡ Gaylord
Saltzgaber,‡ John D. Ault,‡ Kernan Wright,‡
Richard L. Klein,‡ Hazel Gleason,‡ Constance
Eirich.‡
Foundation type: Independent
Financial data (yr. ended 12/31/90): Assets,
$7,095,429 (M); expenditures, $392,787;
qualifying distributions, $298,238, including
$209,950 for 18 grants (high: $59,543; low: $40;
average: $500); $66,288 for 97 grants to
individuals (high: $1,500; low: $200; average:
$200-$1,500) and $22,000 for 1 loan to an
individual.
Purpose and activities: Emphasis on scholarships
in art, music, agriculture, and home economics;
support also for elementary, secondary and higher
education, youth agencies, an art center,
recreational facilities, and programs dealing with
alcoholism and drug abuse.
Fields of interest: Arts, music, agriculture,
elementary education, secondary education,
higher education, youth, recreation, drug abuse,
alcoholism.
Types of support: General purposes, equipment,
student aid.
Limitations: Giving limited to Van Wert County,
OH. No grants for endowment funds or matching
gifts; no loans.
Publications: 990-PF, application guidelines.
Application information: Application forms and
guidelines issued for scholarship program;
application form not required for organizations.
Initial approach: Letter or proposal
Copies of proposal: 1
Deadline(s): Submit proposal in May or Nov.;
deadlines May 15 and Nov. 15
Board meeting date(s): Semiannually
Final notification: 1 week
Write: Robert W. Games, Exec. Secy.
Officers and Trustees:* Larry L. Wendel,* Pres.;
D.L. Brumback, Jr.,* V.P.; C. Allan Runser,* Secy.;
William S. Derry, Bruce Kennedy, Kenneth Koch,
Gaylord E. Leslie, Watson Ley, Paul W. Purmort,
Jr., Charles F. Ross, Donald C. Sutton, Roger K.
Thompson, Sumner J. Walters, G. Dale Wilson,
Michael R. Zedaker.
Number of staff: 1 full-time professional; 1
full-time support.
EIN: 340907558

2605
Walter E. and Caroline H. Watson
Foundation
c/o The Dollar Savings & Trust Co.
P.O. Box 450
Youngstown 44501   (216) 744-9000

Trust established in 1964 in OH.
Donor(s): Walter E. Watson.‡
Foundation type: Independent
Financial data (yr. ended 12/31/91): Assets,
$5,283,419 (M); expenditures, $251,774;
qualifying distributions, $230,403, including
$230,152 for 38 grants (high: $45,030; low:
$500; average: $500-$5,000).

Purpose and activities: To support public
institutions of learning in OH and public and
charitable institutions in the Mahoning Valley,
OH, area; emphasis on health and hospitals,
child development and youth agencies,
community development, health and family
services, housing and other programs for the
disadvantaged, Jewish welfare funds, and arts and
cultural programs, including the fine and
performing arts.
Fields of interest: Hospitals, health, child
development, youth, education, community
development, family services, disadvantaged, arts,
Jewish welfare.
Types of support: Annual campaigns, equipment,
general purposes, renovation projects, special
projects, building funds, continuing support,
capital campaigns.
Limitations: Giving primarily in Youngstown, OH.
No grants to individuals, or for endowment funds
or operating budgets.
Application information: Application form not
required.
Initial approach: Letter and proposal
Copies of proposal: 3
Board meeting date(s): Semiannually
Write: Herbert H. Pridham
Trustee: The Dollar Savings & Trust Co.
Number of staff: None.
EIN: 346547726

2606
The Raymond John Wean Foundation ▼
P.O. Box 760
Warren 44482   (216) 394-5600

Trust established in 1949 in OH.
Donor(s): Raymond J. Wean.‡
Foundation type: Independent
Financial data (yr. ended 12/31/90): Assets,
$42,048,416 (M); expenditures, $2,574,234;
qualifying distributions, $2,363,731, including
$2,363,731 for 687 grants (high: $200,000; low:
$100; average: $200-$5,000).
Purpose and activities: Grants for higher and
secondary education, hospitals, health agencies,
youth agencies, Protestant church support,
cultural programs, and social services.
Fields of interest: Higher education, secondary
education, hospitals, health services, youth,
community funds, Protestant giving, cultural
programs, social services.
Types of support: Continuing support.
Limitations: Giving primarily in OH, Palm Beach,
FL, and PA, especially Pittsburgh.
Application information: Contributes only to
pre-selected organizations. Applications not
accepted.
Board meeting date(s): As required
Write: Raymond J. Wean, Jr., Chair.
Administrators: Raymond J. Wean, Jr., Chair.;
Raymond J. Wean III, Vice-Chair.; Clara G.
Petrosky, Secy.; Gordon B. Wean.
Trustee: Second National Bank of Warren.
Number of staff: None.
EIN: 346505038
Recent health grants:
2606-1 Planned Parenthood of Western
Pennsylvania, Pittsburgh, PA, $15,000. 1990.
2606-2 Saint Joseph Riverside Hospital, Warren,
OH, $10,000. For New Start Endowment
Fund. 1990.

2606-3 Trumbull Memorial Hospital, Warren,
OH, $45,000. For building fund. 1990.
2606-4 Trumbull Memorial Hospital, Warren,
OH, $25,000. For special grant. 1990.

2607
White Consolidated Industries
Foundation, Inc.
c/o White Consolidated Industries, Inc.
11770 Berea Rd.
Cleveland 44111   (216) 252-3700

Established in 1951 in OH.
Donor(s): White Consolidated Industries, Inc.,
The Tappan Co.
Foundation type: Company-sponsored
Financial data (yr. ended 12/31/90): Assets,
$817,360 (M); gifts received, $109,931;
expenditures, $324,213; qualifying distributions,
$320,786, including $309,431 for grants (high:
$45,000; low: $80) and $11,355 for 45 employee
matching gifts.
Fields of interest: Child welfare, disadvantaged,
hunger, law and justice, higher education,
education—minorities, community funds,
hospitals, drug abuse, cultural programs.
Types of support: General purposes, building
funds, equipment, research, continuing support,
operating budgets, employee matching gifts.
Limitations: Giving primarily in Cleveland and
Columbus, OH. No grants to individuals.
Application information: Application form
required.
Initial approach: Proposal
Copies of proposal: 1
Deadline(s): None
Board meeting date(s): As required
Write: Daniel R. Elliott, Jr., Chair.
Officers and Trustees:* Daniel R. Elliott, Jr.,*
Chair.; Wayne D. Schierbaum,* V.P. and Treas.;
Donald C. Blasius,* V.P.; W.G. Bleakley,* V.P.
EIN: 046032840

2608
The E. F. Wildermuth Foundation
c/o Robert W. Lee
4770 Indianola Ave., Suite 240
Columbus 43214   (614) 846-5838

Established in 1962.
Foundation type: Independent
Financial data (yr. ended 12/31/91): Assets,
$3,271,310 (M); expenditures, $240,767;
qualifying distributions, $190,974, including
$180,039 for 23 grants (high: $50,000; low:
$100).
Purpose and activities: Grants primarily for higher
education, particularly optometric schools and
research; support also for the arts and a church.
Fields of interest: Higher education,
ophthalmology, arts, religion—Christian.
Limitations: Giving primarily in OH and
contiguous states. No grants to individuals.
Application information: Application form not
required.
Initial approach: Letter
Deadline(s): Aug. 1
Write: Homer W. Lee, Treas.
Officers and Trustees:* H. Ward Ewalt,* Pres.;
Faurest Borton,* V.P.; Bettie A. Kalb,* V.P.;
Genevieve Connable,* Secy.; Homer W. Lee,*

Treas.; Karl Borton, J. Patrick Campbell, Robert W. Lee, David R. Patterson, David T. Patterson, Phillip N. Phillipson.
EIN: 316050202

2609
Wodecroft Foundation
1900 Chemed Ctr.
225 East Fifth St.
Cincinnati 45202-3172   (513) 977-8250

Established in 1958 in OH.
Donor(s): Roger Drackett.‡
Foundation type: Independent
Financial data (yr. ended 12/31/91): Assets, $11,193,351 (M); expenditures, $368,890; qualifying distributions, $359,433, including $356,100 for 50 grants (high: $50,000; low: $1,000).
Purpose and activities: Giving primarily for health and hospitals and the arts, including a philharmonic orchestra; support also for schools, conservation, and human services.
Fields of interest: Health, hospitals, cultural programs, education, conservation, social services, general charitable giving.
Types of support: Annual campaigns, building funds, capital campaigns, equipment.
Limitations: Giving primarily in Hamilton County, OH, and Collier County, FL. No grants to individuals.
Application information: Application form not required.
   Initial approach: Letter
   Deadline(s): None
   Board meeting date(s): As required
   Final notification: Prior to Dec. 31
   Write: H. Truxtun Emerson, Jr., Secy.
Officers and Trustees:* Richard W. Barrett,* Chair.; H. Truxton Emerson, Jr.,* Secy.; Jeanne H. Drackett.
EIN: 316047601

2610
Wolfe Associates, Inc. ▼
34 South Third St.
Columbus 43215   (614) 461-5220

Incorporated in 1973 in OH.
Donor(s): The Dispatch Printing Co., The Ohio Co., WBNS TV, Inc., RadiOhio, Inc., Video Indiana, Inc.
Foundation type: Company-sponsored
Financial data (yr. ended 06/30/91): Assets, $5,728,111 (M); gifts received, $811,700; expenditures, $2,249,769; qualifying distributions, $2,249,769, including $2,235,533 for 108 grants (high: $100,000; low: $100; average: $1,000-$10,000).
Purpose and activities: Giving for a community fund, higher and secondary education, hospitals and medical research, cultural activities, and youth and social service agencies.
Fields of interest: Higher education, secondary education, educational associations, medical research, hospitals, health, cultural programs, youth, social services, community development.
Types of support: Operating budgets, continuing support, annual campaigns, emergency funds, building funds, equipment, matching funds, professorships, scholarship funds.

Limitations: Giving primarily in central OH. No grants to individuals, or for research, demonstration projects, publications, or conferences.
Publications: Program policy statement, application guidelines.
Application information: Application form not required.
   Initial approach: Letter
   Deadline(s): None
   Board meeting date(s): Mar., June, Sept., and Dec.
   Final notification: After board meeting
   Write: A. Kenneth Pierce, Jr., V.P.
Officers: John W. Wolfe, Chair.; John F. Wolfe, Pres.; A. Kenneth Pierce, Jr., V.P. and Secy.-Treas.; Nancy Wolfe Lane, V.P.; William C. Wolfe, Jr., V.P.
Number of staff: None.
EIN: 237303111
Recent health grants:
2610-1 American Cancer Society, Columbus, OH, $15,000. 1991.
2610-2 Franciscan Health System of Central Ohio, Saint Anthony Medical Center, Columbus, OH, $10,000. 1991.
2610-3 Lifecare Alliance, Columbus, OH, $20,000. For capital campaign. 1991.

2611
Women's Project Foundation
c/o Society National Bank
P.O. Box 5937
Cleveland 44101-0937   (216) 737-5283

Established in 1986.
Foundation type: Independent
Financial data (yr. ended 11/30/91): Assets, $7,504,021 (M); expenditures, $407,557; qualifying distributions, $339,167, including $336,000 for 4 grants (high: $160,000; low: $11,000).
Purpose and activities: Support for projects for women's and children's issues, including women filmmakers and domestic violence.
Fields of interest: Women, child welfare, film, arts, family planning, education—minorities, minorities, adult education, alcoholism.
Types of support: Special projects, research.
Application information: Application form not required.
   Initial approach: Letter
   Copies of proposal: 1
   Deadline(s): Nov. 1
   Board meeting date(s): Late fall
   Final notification: Only notified if approved
   Write: Joyce K. Alexander
Trustees: Louise L. Gund, Maximilian Kempner, Society National Bank.
Number of staff: None.
EIN: 133417304

2612
The Wuliger Foundation, Inc. ▼
Halle Bldg. Suite 760
1228 Euclid Ave.
Cleveland 44115   (216) 522-0106

Incorporated in 1956 in OH.
Donor(s): Ernest M. Wuliger, Allan M. Unger, Ohio-Sealy Mattress Manufacturing Co.
Foundation type: Independent

Financial data (yr. ended 12/31/90): Assets, $5,221,345 (M); expenditures, $1,059,367; qualifying distributions, $1,007,689, including $997,892 for 96 grants (high: $450,000; low: $100; average: $1,000-$10,000).
Purpose and activities: Giving for Jewish welfare funds; support also for higher education, hospitals, and the arts.
Fields of interest: Jewish welfare, higher education, hospitals, arts.
Limitations: Giving primarily in OH. No grants to individuals.
Application information:
   Initial approach: Proposal
   Deadline(s): None
   Board meeting date(s): As necessary
   Final notification: Within 2 weeks if possible
   Write: Ernest M. Wuliger, Pres.
Officers: Ernest M. Wuliger, Pres.; E. Jeffrey Wuliger, V.P.; Timothy F. Wuliger, Secy.; Gregory Wuliger, Treas.
Number of staff: None.
EIN: 346527281
Recent health grants:
2612-1 Bowman Gray School of Medicine, Winston-Salem, NC, $50,000. 1990.
2612-2 Cleveland Clinic Foundation, Cleveland, OH, $10,000. 1990.
2612-3 Shepherd Center for Treatment of Spinal Injuries, Atlanta, GA, $50,000. 1990.

2613
The Leo Yassenoff Foundation ▼
16 East Broad St., Suite 403
Columbus 43215   (614) 221-4315

Incorporated in 1947 in DE.
Donor(s): Leo Yassenoff.‡
Foundation type: Independent
Financial data (yr. ended 12/31/90): Assets, $5,770,026 (M); expenditures, $818,744; qualifying distributions, $818,744, including $666,368 for 105 grants (high: $200,000; low: $200; average: $1,000-$20,000).
Purpose and activities: Support primarily for social services, including programs for minorities and the disadvantaged, education, health and hospitals, youth agencies, civic affairs, and arts and cultural programs.
Fields of interest: Social services, minorities, disadvantaged, education, health, hospitals, youth, civic affairs, arts, cultural programs.
Types of support: Seed money, emergency funds, equipment, matching funds, special projects, renovation projects, building funds.
Limitations: Giving limited to Franklin County, OH. No support for religious purposes, except to donor-designated recipients. No grants to individuals, or for operating support, annual campaigns, endowments, deficit financing, or debt reduction; no loans.
Publications: Application guidelines.
Application information: Application must follow foundation guidelines. Application form not required.
   Initial approach: Telephone or letter
   Copies of proposal: 1
   Deadline(s): Jan. 1, Apr. 1, July 1, and Oct. 1
   Board meeting date(s): Mar., June, Sept. and Dec.
   Final notification: 3 months
   Write: Cynthia Cecil Lazarus, Exec. Dir.

Officers and Trustees:* Melvin L. Schottenstein,*
Chair.; Frederick E. Dauterman, Jr.,* Vice-Chair.;
Cynthia A. Cecil Lazarus,* Exec. Dir. and
Secy.-Treas.
Number of staff: 1 full-time professional; 1
full-time support; 1 part-time support.
EIN: 310829426

2614
Hugo H. and Mabel B. Young Foundation
416 North Wood St.
Loudonville 44842   (419) 994-4501

Incorporated in 1963 in OH.
Foundation type: Independent
Financial data (yr. ended 04/30/91): Assets,
$4,055,165 (M); expenditures, $290,569;
qualifying distributions, $258,492, including
$253,952 for 9 grants (high: $106,069; low:
$2,500).
Fields of interest: Civic affairs, education, health.
Types of support: Building funds, equipment,
scholarship funds.
Limitations: Giving primarily in Ashland County,
OH. No grants to individuals, or for general
purposes or matching gifts; no loans.
Application information: Application form not
required.
   Initial approach: Letter
   Copies of proposal: 7
   Deadline(s): Submit proposal preferably in Mar.
   Board meeting date(s): 3rd Tuesday in June
   Write: R.D. Mayer, Secy.-Treas.
Officers and Trustees:* Phillip Ranney,* Chair.;
James Dudte,* Pres.; Avery Hand,* V.P.; R.D.
Mayer,* Secy.-Treas.; Robert Dubler, James
Lingenfelter.
Number of staff: None.
EIN: 346560664

2615
The Youngstown Foundation
c/o The Dollar Savings & Trust Co.
P.O. Box 450
Youngstown 44501   (216) 744-9000

Established in 1918 in OH by bank resolution.
Foundation type: Community
Financial data (yr. ended 12/31/90): Assets,
$37,898,367 (M); gifts received, $1,123,811;
expenditures, $2,565,880; qualifying
distributions, $2,320,432, including $2,320,432
for 57 grants (high: $330,000; low: $500;
average: $1,000-$10,000).
Purpose and activities: To support local charitable
and educational agencies for the betterment of
the community; grants for capital purposes, with
emphasis on aid to crippled children, community
funds, youth agencies, music and cultural
programs, and hospitals.
Fields of interest: Handicapped, child
development, community funds, youth, music,
cultural programs, hospitals, health services,
educational associations, Jewish welfare.
Types of support: Building funds, equipment,
annual campaigns, student loans, general
purposes, renovation projects, special projects,
conferences and seminars, continuing support,
research.
Limitations: Giving limited to Mahoning County,
OH, with emphasis on Youngstown. No grants to
individuals (except for limited student loans), or
for endowment funds, operating budgets, seed
money, emergency funds, deficit financing, land
acquisition, demonstration projects, publications,
scholarships, fellowships, or matching gifts.
Publications: Informational brochure, annual
report.
Application information: Application form not
required.

   Initial approach: Proposal
   Copies of proposal: 5
   Deadline(s): None
   Board meeting date(s): Jan., Mar., May, July,
      Sept., Nov., and Dec.
   Write: Herbert H. Pridham, Secy.
Officer: Herbert H. Pridham, Secy.
Distribution Committee: William R. Powell,
Chair.; Thomas R. Hollern, Vice-Chair.; Franklin
S. Bennett, Jr., Ann Hudak, Joseph S. Nohra.
Trustee: The Dollar Savings & Trust Co.
Number of staff: None.
EIN: 346515788
Recent health grants:
2615-1 Alcoholic Clinic of Youngstown,
   Youngstown, OH, $10,000. 1990.
2615-2 Childrens Rehabilitation Center, Warren,
   OH, $22,000. 1990.
2615-3 Easter Seal Society, Youngstown, OH,
   $330,000. 1990.
2615-4 Easter Seal Society, Youngstown, OH,
   $19,158. 1990.
2615-5 Fanconis Anemia Research Fund,
   Eugene, OR, $84,368. 1990.
2615-6 Saint Elizabeth Hospital Medical Center,
   Youngstown, OH, $111,221. 1990.
2615-7 Saint Elizabeth Hospital Medical Center,
   Youngstown, OH, $10,000. 1990.
2615-8 Visiting Nurses Association, Youngstown,
   OH, $98,129. 1990.
2615-9 Western Reserve Care System,
   Youngstown, OH, $47,671. 1990.
2615-10 Youngstown Area Association for
   Children and Adults with Learning Disabilities,
   Youngstown, OH, $25,000. 1990.
2615-11 Youngstown Hearing and Speech
   Center, Youngstown, OH, $226,000. 1990.
2615-12 Youngstown Osteopathic Hospital,
   Youngstown, OH, $10,000. 1990.

OKLAHOMA

2616
American Fidelity Corporation Founders Fund, Inc.
2000 Classen Ctr.
Oklahoma City 73106
Application address: P.O. Box 25523,
Oklahoma City, OK 73125; Tel.: (405) 523-5111

Established in 1984 in OK.
Donor(s): American Fidelity Assurance Co.
Foundation type: Company-sponsored
Financial data (yr. ended 06/30/91): Assets,
$2,906,290 (M); gifts received, $335,162;
expenditures, $263,175; qualifying distributions,
$261,304, including $259,762 for 108 grants
(high: $37,541; low: $25; average: $25-$37,499).
Purpose and activities: Support for various arts
councils, local cultural events and museums;
community funds and civic affairs groups such as
the Junior League, the Rotary, Chamber of
Commerce and YMCA; AIDS programs, health
associations and clinics; welfare programs; and
education, including higher education and
educational research.
Fields of interest: Arts, community funds, civic
affairs, cultural programs, education, higher
education, educational research, health, health
associations, AIDS, religion, environment.
Types of support: General purposes, research,
employee matching gifts, endowment funds,
operating budgets.
Limitations: Giving limited to OK. No grants to
individuals.
Application information: Application form
required.
   Initial approach: Letter
   Copies of proposal: 5
   Board meeting date(s): Varies
   Write: Dortha Dever, Secy.
Officers: William Durrett, Pres.; Dortha Deaver,
Secy.; John Rex, Treas.
Number of staff: None.
EIN: 731236059

2617
Grace & Franklin Bernsen Foundation ▼
1308 Fourth National Bank Bldg.
Tulsa 74119   (918) 584-4711

Established in 1985 in OK.
Donor(s): Grace Bernsen,‡ Franklin Bernsen.‡
Foundation type: Independent
Financial data (yr. ended 09/30/91): Assets,
$22,304,049 (M); expenditures, $1,067,650;
qualifying distributions, $812,600, including
$812,600 for 33 grants (high: $150,000; low:
$1,000; average: $5,000-$25,000).
Fields of interest: Arts, humanities, theater,
biological sciences, medical sciences, youth,
education, health, crime and law enforcement,
welfare.
Types of support: Building funds, continuing
support, matching funds.
Limitations: Giving primarily in the Tulsa, OK,
area.

Application information: Application form not
required.
   Copies of proposal: 1
   Deadline(s): None
   Board meeting date(s): Monthly
   Write: Howard M. Maher, Trustee
Trustees: Howard M. Maher, Donald F. Marlar,
Donald E. Pray, John D. Strong.
Number of staff: 2 full-time professional.
EIN: 237009414

2618
Boatmen's First National Bank of Oklahoma Foundation
(Formerly First Interstate Bank of Oklahoma
Foundation)
P.O. Box 25189
Oklahoma City 73125   (405) 272-5216

Established in 1987 in OK.
Donor(s): Boatmen's First National Bank of
Oklahoma.
Foundation type: Company-sponsored
Financial data (yr. ended 12/31/90): Assets,
$354,420 (M); gifts received, $107,288;
expenditures, $431,182; qualifying distributions,
$429,670, including $429,670 for 95 grants
(high: $70,000; low: $400).
Purpose and activities: Support for health and
welfare, education, civic afairs, and arts and
cultural programs. Major supporter of United
Way and Allied Arts.
Fields of interest: Health, welfare, education,
civic affairs, arts, cultural programs.
Types of support: Capital campaigns, equipment,
operating budgets.
Limitations: Giving limited to OK. No support for
sectarian organizations or other grantmaking
foundations. No grants to individuals, or for trips
or tours, advertising, or endowments.
Application information: Letter or telephone call
for guidelines and application form. Application
form required.
   Deadline(s): None
   Board meeting date(s): Monthly
   Write: Sheila Mayberry, Secy.
Officers and Directors:* Ken Schuerman,* Chair.
and Pres.; Sheila Mayberry, Secy.; Brett Dean,
Charles Finsel, Mariana Pearson, Trudy Perry.
EIN: 736237244

2619
The Mervin Bovaird Foundation ▼
800 Oneok Plaza
100 West Fifth St.
Tulsa 74103   (918) 583-1777

Established about 1956.
Donor(s): Mabel W. Bovaird.‡
Foundation type: Independent
Financial data (yr. ended 12/31/90): Assets,
$29,293,020 (M); expenditures, $1,520,273;
qualifying distributions, $1,376,701, including
$878,000 for 64 grants (high: $150,000; low:
$500; average: $500-$35,000) and $422,540 for
76 grants to individuals (high: $7,950; low:
$1,450; average: $5,000-$7,950).
Purpose and activities: Supports scholarship
funds at the University of Tulsa and Oklahoma
Baptist University; support also for community

development, social services, education, and
health.
Fields of interest: Community development,
social services, education, health.
Types of support: Scholarship funds, general
purposes.
Limitations: Giving primarily in Tulsa, OK.
Application information: Scholarship recipients
are chosen by the universities and subsequently
approved by the foundation; scholarship awards
are made directly to the universities.
   Deadline(s): Between May 1 and Aug. 1 for
      scholarships
   Board meeting date(s): Irregularly
   Final notification: Dec. 20
   Write: Fenelon Boesche, Pres.
Officers and Trustees:* Fenelon Boesche,* Pres.;
Tilford Eskridge,* V.P.; Thomas H. Trower,* V.P.;
Franklin D. Hettinger,* Secy.-Treas.
Number of staff: 2
EIN: 736102163

2620
C. Harold & Constance Brand Foundation
1708 Camden Way
Oklahoma City 73116

Established in 1985 in OK.
Donor(s): Constance M. Brand.
Foundation type: Independent
Financial data (yr. ended 12/31/91): Assets,
$551,932 (M); expenditures, $301,133;
qualifying distributions, $301,133, including
$277,000 for 6 grants (high: $250,000; low:
$1,000).
Purpose and activities: Giving primarily for
health, especially a health center; some support
also for child welfare and Christian organizations.
Fields of interest: Health, child welfare,
religion—Christian.
Limitations: Giving primarily in Oklahoma City,
OK. No grants to individuals.
Application information: Contributes only to
pre-selected organizations. Applications not
accepted.
Officers: Constance M. Brand, Pres. and Treas.;
Robert C. Fuegner, V.P.; Clara R. Stevens, Secy.
Directors: Gerald L. Gamble, John F. Wilkinson, Jr.
EIN: 726095799

2621
Broadhurst Foundation
401 South Boston, Suite 100
Tulsa 74103   (918) 584-0661

Trust established in 1951 in OK.
Donor(s): William Broadhurst.‡
Foundation type: Independent
Financial data (yr. ended 12/31/91): Assets,
$6,009,758 (M); expenditures, $393,548;
qualifying distributions, $703,405, including
$135,902 for 46 grants (high: $12,500; low: $50)
and $523,656 for 11 loans.
Purpose and activities: Support for scholarship
funds at institutions selected by the foundation,
for students training for the Christian ministry;
grants also to educational and religious
institutions, and to medical research institutions,
especially related to pediatric diseases; loans to
churches for building projects.

Fields of interest: Religion—Christian, theological education, medical research, education.
Types of support: Continuing support, seed money, building funds, equipment, scholarship funds, fellowships, loans, renovation projects.
Limitations: Giving primarily in the Midwest, particularly OK. No grants to individuals, or for scholarship funds, except at 31 schools the foundation currently supports.
Application information: Application form not required.
> *Initial approach:* Letter or proposal
> *Copies of proposal:* 1
> *Deadline(s):* None
> *Board meeting date(s):* Quarterly
> *Final notification:* 1 month
> *Write:* Ann Cassidy Baker, Chair.
Trustees: Ann Cassidy Baker, Chair.; John Cassidy, Jr., Clint V. Cox, Ernestine Broadhurst Howard, Wishard Lemons.
Number of staff: 1 full-time professional; 1 part-time professional; 1 part-time support.
EIN: 736061115

2622
Max and Tookah Campbell Foundation
P.O. Box 701051
Tulsa 74170

Trust established in 1964 in OK.
Donor(s): Max W. Campbell.‡
Foundation type: Independent
Financial data (yr. ended 12/31/90): Assets, $5,193,731 (M); expenditures, $426,529; qualifying distributions, $292,164, including $267,984 for 34 grants (high: $49,478; low: $300).
Purpose and activities: Emphasis on Protestant church support and higher education; grants also for hospitals and health agencies, museums and the arts, and youth agencies.
Fields of interest: Protestant giving, higher education, hospitals, health services, museums, arts, youth.
Limitations: Giving primarily in OK. No grants to individuals.
Application information: Contributes only to pre-selected organizations. Applications not accepted.
Trustees: Pauline Holderman, Joan Lepley Hunt, Robert G. Hunt, Bobbie Tomlins.
EIN: 736111626

2623
H. A. and Mary K. Chapman Charitable Trust ▼
One Warren Place, Suite 1816
6100 South Yale
Tulsa 74136   (918) 496-7882

Trust established in 1976 in OK.
Donor(s): H.A. Chapman.‡
Foundation type: Independent
Financial data (yr. ended 12/31/91): Assets, $47,224,596 (M); expenditures, $2,355,044; qualifying distributions, $2,079,041, including $1,982,000 for 41 grants (high: $465,000; low: $2,500; average: $10,000-$50,000).
Purpose and activities: Grants largely for education, particularly higher education, health, social services, and cultural programs.

Fields of interest: Higher education, education, social services, cultural programs, health.
Limitations: Giving primarily in Tulsa, OK.
Application information: Application form required.
> *Initial approach:* Letter or telephone
> *Copies of proposal:* 2
> *Deadline(s):* None
> *Board meeting date(s):* Quarterly and as needed
> *Write:* Ralph L. Abercrombie or Donne Pitman, Trustees
Trustees: Ralph L. Abercrombie, Donne W. Pitman.
Number of staff: None.
EIN: 736177739

2624
The Charles B. Goddard Foundation
1000 Energy Ctr., Suite 102
P.O. Box 1485
Ardmore 73402   (405) 226-6040

Trust established in 1958 in OK.
Donor(s): Charles B. Goddard.‡
Foundation type: Independent
Financial data (yr. ended 06/30/91): Assets, $5,385,767 (M); expenditures, $331,307; qualifying distributions, $304,860, including $304,860 for 42 grants (high: $50,000; low: $25).
Purpose and activities: Primary areas of interest include community funds and elementary education.
Fields of interest: Community funds, education, elementary education, secondary education, child development, child welfare, youth, health services, health associations, hospitals.
Types of support: Operating budgets, continuing support, annual campaigns, seed money, emergency funds, building funds, equipment, land acquisition, research.
Limitations: Giving limited to southern OK and northern TX, or to programs of nationwide impact. No grants to individuals, no loans.
Application information: The foundation's philanthropic activities have been greatly reduced.
> *Board meeting date(s):* Apr. and Oct.
> *Write:* William R. Goddard, Jr., Chair.
Officers and Trustees:* William R. Goddard, Jr.,* Chair.; William M. Johns,* Secy.-Treas.; Elizabeth E. Cashman, Ann G. Corrigan, William R. Goddard.
Number of staff: None.
EIN: 756005868

2625
Dexter G. Johnson Educational and Benevolent Trust
204 North Robinson, Suite 900
900 First City Place
Oklahoma City 73102   (405) 232-3340

Trust established in 1971 in OK.
Foundation type: Independent
Financial data (yr. ended 12/31/90): Assets, $5,194,107 (M); expenditures, $478,606; qualifying distributions, $410,638, including $330,487 for 74 grants to individuals (high: $200,000; low: $100) and $34,600 for loans to individuals.
Purpose and activities: Giving for student loans to physically handicapped students and students

who by misfortune or calamity cannot otherwise complete their education in OK high schools, Oklahoma A & M College, Oklahoma City University, the University of Oklahoma; grants or loans to handicapped individuals for audiological evaluations, corrective surgery, vocational training, speech therapy, and medical equipment.
Fields of interest: Handicapped, vocational education, speech pathology, health services, welfare—indigent individuals.
Types of support: Student aid, equipment, grants to individuals, student loans.
Limitations: Giving limited to OK.
Application information: Application form required.
> *Deadline(s):* None
> *Write:* Phil C. Daugherty, Esq., Trustee
Trustee: Phil C. Daugherty.
EIN: 237389204

2626
The Kerr Foundation, Inc.
6301 North Western, Suite 130
Oklahoma City 73118   (405) 842-1510

Incorporated in 1963 in OK, and reincorporated in 1985.
Donor(s): Grayce B. Kerr Flynn.‡
Foundation type: Independent
Financial data (yr. ended 12/31/90): Assets, $19,840,442 (M); gifts received, $5,868; expenditures, $1,678,825; qualifying distributions, $1,186,927, including $1,005,186 for 53 grants (high: $115,000; low: $300; average: $10,000-$50,000).
Purpose and activities: Giving primarily for education, the fine arts and other cultural activities, and health. Generally all grants are challenge grants.
Fields of interest: Education, cultural programs, arts, fine arts, museums, health, libraries, public administration, youth.
Types of support: Matching funds.
Limitations: Giving primarily in TX, AR, KS, CO, MO, NM, and OK. No grants to individuals, or generally for continuing support.
Publications: Application guidelines.
Application information: Application form required.
> *Initial approach:* Letter
> *Copies of proposal:* 4
> *Deadline(s):* None
> *Board meeting date(s):* Quarterly
> *Write:* Anne Holzberlein, Admin. Asst.
Officers and Trustees:* Robert S. Kerr, Jr.,* Chair. and Pres.; Lou C. Kerr,* V.P. and Secy.; Gerald R. Marshall,* Treas.; Royce Hammons, Sharon Kerr, Steven Kerr, Elmer B. Staats.
Number of staff: 2 part-time professional; 1 full-time support.
EIN: 731256122

2627
The J. E. and L. E. Mabee Foundation, Inc. ▼
3000 Mid-Continent Tower
401 South Boston
Tulsa 74103   (918) 584-4286

Incorporated in 1948 in DE.
Donor(s): J.E. Mabee,‡ L.E. Mabee.‡

Foundation type: Independent
Financial data (yr. ended 08/31/91): Assets, $544,657,220 (M); expenditures, $23,688,406; qualifying distributions, $22,050,280, including $21,808,560 for 80 grants (high: $1,000,000; low: $2,500; average: $100,000-$500,000).
Purpose and activities: To aid Christian religious organizations, charitable organizations, and institutions of higher learning; and to support hospitals and other agencies and institutions engaged in the discovery, treatment, and care of diseases.
Fields of interest: Religion—Christian, higher education, youth, education—building funds, hospitals.
Types of support: Building funds, capital campaigns, renovation projects.
Limitations: Giving limited to OK, TX, KS, AR, MO, and NM. No support for secondary or elementary education, or tax-supported institutions. No grants to individuals, or for research, endowment funds, scholarships, fellowships, or operating expenses; no loans.
Publications: Program policy statement, application guidelines.
Application information: Application form not required.
  Initial approach: Proposal
  Copies of proposal: 1
  Deadline(s): Mar. 1, June 1, Sept. 1, and Dec. 1
  Board meeting date(s): Jan., Apr., July, and Oct.
  Final notification: After board meetings
  Write: John H. Conway, Jr., Vice-Chair.
Officers and Trustees:* Guy R. Mabee,* Chair.; John H. Conway, Jr.,* Vice-Chair. and Secy.-Treas.; John W. Cox,* Vice-Chair.; Joe Mabee,* Vice-Chair.; Donald P. Moyers,* Vice-Chair.; James L. Houghton, H. Alan Nelson.
Number of staff: 1 full-time professional; 6 part-time professional; 7 full-time support.
EIN: 736090162
Recent health grants:

2627-1 Barrio Comprehensive Family Health Care Center, San Antonio, TX, $200,000. For treatment center building renovation. 1990.
2627-2 Bay Area Rehabilitation Center, Baytown, TX, $250,000. For new treatment center building. 1990.
2627-3 Cenikor Foundation, Fort Worth, TX, $60,000. For treatment center building renovation. 1990.
2627-4 Dean A. McGee Eye Institute, Oklahoma City, OK, $60,000. For medical equipment. 1990.
2627-5 Driscoll Foundation Childrens Hospital, Corpus Christi, TX, $75,000. For treatment center building renovation. 1990.
2627-6 Foundation for Sheltered Living, Topeka, KS, $100,000. For cottages and lodges. 1990.
2627-7 Hillcrest Medical Center, Tulsa, OK, $300,000. For medical equipment. 1990.
2627-8 Irving Community Hospital Foundation, Irving, TX, $500,000. For new building. 1990.
2627-9 Marbridge Foundation, Manchaca, TX, $375,000. For retirement/nursing center building. 1990.
2627-10 Mental Health Association in Tulsa, Tulsa, OK, $40,000. For cottages and lodges. 1990.
2627-11 Ozanam Home for Boys, Kansas City, MO, $80,000. For building. 1990.

2627-12 Problem Pregnancy Center of Midland, Midland, TX, $32,500. For administration building renovation. 1990.
2627-13 University Medical Center, Dallas, TX, $400,000. For medical equipment. 1990.

2628
McCasland Foundation ▼
McCasland Bldg.
P.O. Box 400
Duncan 73534   (405) 252-5580

Trust established in 1952 in OK.
Donor(s): Members of the McCasland family, Mack Oil Co., Jath Oil Co.
Foundation type: Independent
Financial data (yr. ended 12/31/91): Assets, $26,832,317 (M); gifts received, $3,023; expenditures, $1,290,084; qualifying distributions, $1,226,136, including $1,211,624 for 128 grants (high: $70,000; low: $150; average: $1,000-$50,000).
Fields of interest: Higher education, social services, cultural programs, hospitals.
Types of support: Scholarship funds, general purposes, building funds.
Limitations: Giving primarily in OK and the Southwest, including TX and KS.
Application information:
  Initial approach: Letter
  Deadline(s): None
  Board meeting date(s): Varies; usually quarterly
  Final notification: After board meetings
  Write: W.H. Phelps, Trustee
Trustees: Mary Frances Maurer, T.H. McCasland, Jr., W.H. Phelps.
Number of staff: None.
EIN: 736096032

2629
The McGee Foundation, Inc.
P.O. Box 18127
Oklahoma City 73154   (405) 842-6266

Incorporated in 1963 in OK.
Donor(s): Dean A. McGee.‡
Foundation type: Independent
Financial data (yr. ended 06/30/91): Assets, $5,873,640 (M); expenditures, $281,511; qualifying distributions, $229,000, including $229,000 for 9 grants (high: $75,000; low: $1,000).
Fields of interest: Higher education, physical sciences, arts, family planning.
Types of support: Renovation projects, building funds, general purposes.
Limitations: Giving primarily in OK and CA. No grants to individuals, or for endowment funds.
Application information: Application form not required.
  Deadline(s): None
  Write: Miss Elizabeth Zoernig, Secy.-Treas.
Officers and Directors:* Marcia McGee Bieber,* Pres.; Patricia McGee Maino,* V.P.; Elizabeth Zoernig,* Secy.-Treas.
EIN: 736099203

2630
The Merrick Foundation
P.O. Box 998
Ardmore 73402   (405) 226-7000

Trust established in 1947 in OK; incorporated in 1968.
Donor(s): Mrs. Frank W. Merrick,‡ and others.
Foundation type: Independent
Financial data (yr. ended 12/31/90): Assets, $6,049,404 (M); expenditures, $301,982; qualifying distributions, $237,489, including $197,700 for 32 grants (high: $18,000; low: $250; average: $1,000-$20,000).
Purpose and activities: Giving for higher education and hospitals; grants also for medical research, youth agencies, and a community fund.
Fields of interest: Higher education, hospitals, medical research, youth, community funds.
Types of support: Seed money, building funds, matching funds, annual campaigns.
Limitations: Giving primarily in OK, with emphasis on southern OK. No grants to individuals, or for endowment or operating funds.
Publications: Application guidelines, informational brochure.
Application information: Application form not required.
  Initial approach: Letter
  Copies of proposal: 1
  Deadline(s): Submit proposal in Sept.
  Board meeting date(s): Nov.
  Final notification: Nov.
  Write: Frank W. Merrick, V.P.
Officers and Trustees:* Elizabeth Merrick Coe,* Pres.; Frank W. Merrick, V.P.; Valda M. Buchanan,* Secy.; Michael A. Cawley, Charles R. Coe, Jr., Ross Coe, Ward I. Coe, Bill Goddard, Robert B. Merrick, Ward S. Merrick, Jr., Johnnie Rolen, Jack D. Wilkes.
Number of staff: 3 part-time professional.
EIN: 736111622

2631
The Samuel Roberts Noble Foundation, Inc. ▼
P.O. Box 2180
2510 State Hwy. 199 East
Ardmore 73402   (405) 223-5810

Trust established in 1945 in OK; incorporated in 1952.
Donor(s): Lloyd Noble.‡
Foundation type: Independent
Financial data (yr. ended 10/31/91): Assets, $387,739,488 (M); gifts received, $100; expenditures, $20,597,989; qualifying distributions, $19,755,380, including $6,805,257 for 147 grants (high: $598,320; low: $100; average: $5,000-$150,000), $68,000 for 47 grants to individuals (high: $2,000; low: $1,000; average: $1,000-$2,000), $37,078 for 28 employee matching gifts and $12,845,045 for 3 foundation-administered programs.
Purpose and activities: Supports its own three operating programs: 1) basic biomedical research pertaining to cancer and degenerative diseases; 2) plant research, with the objective of genetic engineering of plants; and 3) agricultural research, consultation, and demonstration, along with wildlife management, for the benefit of rural and urban people. Primarily, grants are for higher

education, for health research pertaining to cancer and degenerative diseases, and for health delivery systems. Matching gift program for Noble Company employees.
Fields of interest: Medical research, health services, cancer, agriculture, social services, higher education.
Types of support: Research, employee-related scholarships, seed money, building funds, equipment, endowment funds, matching funds, employee matching gifts.
Limitations: Giving primarily in the Southwest, with emphasis on OK. No grants to individuals (except through the scholarship program for children of employees of Noble organizations); no loans.
Publications: Annual report, application guidelines.
Application information: Application form required.
> *Initial approach:* Letter
> *Copies of proposal:* 1
> *Deadline(s):* 6 weeks prior to board meeting dates
> *Board meeting date(s):* Usually in Jan., Apr., July, and Oct.
> *Final notification:* 2 weeks after board meetings
> *Write:* Michael A. Cawley, Pres.
Officers and Trustees:* Michael A. Cawley,* Pres.; Larry Pulliam, V.P. and Treas.; M.K. Patterson, Jr., V.P.; Elizabeth A. Aldridge, Secy.; Ann Noble Brown, David R. Brown, Vivian N. Dubose, William R. Goddard, John R. March, Shelley Mullins, Edward E. Noble, Mary Jane Noble, Sam Noble, Susan Ruppert, John F. Snodgrass.
Number of staff: 71 full-time professional; 90 full-time support; 14 part-time support.
EIN: 730606209
Recent health grants:

2631-1 American Mental Health Fund, DC, $35,000. For national public education and awareness program. 1990.

2631-2 American Paralysis Association, Short Hills, NJ, $10,000. For research program in regeneration of damage to central nervous system. 1990.

2631-3 Baptist Medical Center of Oklahoma Foundation, Oklahoma City, OK, $200,000. For purchase of Cardiac Excimer Laser. 1990.

2631-4 Childrens Medical Foundation, Dallas, TX, $166,666. Toward construction, expansion and renovation project. 1990.

2631-5 Childrens Medical Foundation, Dallas, TX, $75,000. For lobby renovation project. 1990.

2631-6 Hillcrest Medical Center Foundation, Tulsa, OK, $150,000. For Intensive Care Clinical Information Project. 1990.

2631-7 Hospital Hospitality House Foundation, Oklahoma City, OK, $10,000. For endowment fund. 1990.

2631-8 Murray State College Foundation, Veterinary Technology and Department of Agriculture Programs, Tishomingo, OK, $80,000. Toward building addition, renovation and equipment purchases. 1990.

2631-9 Norman Alcohol Information Center, Norman, OK, $30,000. For general operating support. 1990.

2631-10 Oklahoma Association of the Deaf, Sulphur, OK, $20,000. For greenhouse

construction at Oklahoma School for the Deaf. 1990.

2631-11 Oklahoma Medical Research Foundation, Oklahoma City, OK, $30,000. For Oklahoma Department of Education Science Teacher Workshop. 1990.

2631-12 Piedmont Hospital, Atlanta, GA, $50,000. Toward endowment of Chair of Surgery with Emory University. 1990.

2631-13 Salk Institute for Biological Studies, La Jolla, CA, $621,336. For operating and equipment costs associated with joint Plant Cell Biology Project. 1990.

2631-14 Salk Institute for Biological Studies, La Jolla, CA, $97,547. For Plant Cell Biology Fellowships. 1990.

2631-15 Salk Institute for Biological Studies, La Jolla, CA, $67,500. For equipment purchase for Plant Cell Biology Project. 1990.

2631-16 Salk Institute for Biological Studies, La Jolla, CA, $11,948. For operating and equipment costs associated with joint Plant Cell Biology Project. 1990.

2631-17 Scott and White Memorial Hospital, Temple, TX, $175,000. For purchase of Spectranetics CVX-300 Laser Surgical system. 1990.

2631-18 Shepherd Center for Treatment of Spinal Injuries, Atlanta, GA, $50,000. For facilities expansion and equipment purchases. 1990.

2631-19 Southern Oklahoma Ambulance Service, Ardmore, OK, $65,000. For paramedic ambulance and related equipment. 1990.

2631-20 Southwestern Diabetic Foundation, Gainesville, TX, $10,000. For Camp Sweeney renovations and repairs. 1990.

2631-21 Stehlin Foundation for Cancer Research, Houston, TX, $50,000. For testing of cancer drug 9-amino camptothecin. 1990.

2631-22 University of Texas Health Science Center, Dallas, TX, $100,000. For Clinical Nutrition Scholars Program, program of research and teaching role of nutrition in treatment and prevention of disease. 1990.

2632
Occidental Oil and Gas Charitable Foundation
(Formerly Cities Service Foundation)
110 West Seventh St.
P.O. Box 300
Tulsa 74102   (918) 561-4745

Incorporated in 1954 in DE.
Donor(s): Occidental Oil and Gas Co.
Foundation type: Company-sponsored
Financial data (yr. ended 12/31/90): Assets, $9,194,423 (M); expenditures, $724,485; qualifying distributions, $675,508, including $525,917 for 183 grants (high: $90,000; low: $100; average: $5,000) and $149,569 for 215 employee matching gifts.
Purpose and activities: Giving primarily for higher education (including an employee matching gift program), cultural programs and the arts, health and welfare organizations, and community funds.
Fields of interest: Higher education, cultural programs, arts, health, health services, welfare, community funds.

Types of support: Annual campaigns, employee matching gifts, operating budgets, renovation projects, employee-related scholarships.
Limitations: Giving limited to areas of company operations: Tulsa and Oklahoma City, OK, and Houston and Midland, TX. No grants to individuals.
Application information: Application form not required.
> *Initial approach:* Letter
> *Copies of proposal:* 1
> *Deadline(s):* Sept. 1
> *Write:* Joanne G. Sellers, Contribs. Coord.
Officers and Trustees:* David A. Hentschel,* Pres.; R.W. Archibald, V.P.; D.A. Kelsey, V.P.; R.G. Peters,* Exec. Secy.; G.D. Luthey, Secy.; C.P. Marlowe,* Treas.; J.R. Niehaus, J.G. Sellers.
Number of staff: 2 part-time professional.
EIN: 136081799

2633
Oklahoma City Community Foundation, Inc.
115 Park Ave.
Oklahoma City 73103   (405) 235-5603
Additional address: P.O. Box 1146, Oklahoma City, OK 73101

Incorporated in 1968 in OK.
Foundation type: Community
Financial data (yr. ended 06/30/91): Assets, $66,230,090 (M); gifts received, $13,027,416; expenditures, $2,726,122; qualifying distributions, $2,449,383, including $2,449,383 for 357 grants (high: $603,438; low: $25; average: $3,000-$10,000).
Fields of interest: Education, cultural programs, health, social services.
Types of support: Scholarship funds, fellowships, matching funds, operating budgets, continuing support, annual campaigns, seed money, emergency funds, building funds, equipment, research, special projects.
Limitations: Giving primarily in greater Oklahoma City, OK. No grants to individuals, or for endowment funds or deficit financing; no loans.
Publications: Annual report, newsletter.
Application information:
> *Initial approach:* Telephone
> *Copies of proposal:* 6
> *Deadline(s):* July 31 and Jan. 31
> *Board meeting date(s):* Jan., Apr., July, and Oct.
> *Write:* Nancy B. Anthony, Exec. Dir.
Officers and Trustees:* George J. Records,* Pres.; J. Edward Barth,* V.P.; John L. Belt, Secy. and General Counsel; Eleanor J. Maurer, Treas.; Carla S. Pickrell, Comptroller; Nancy B. Anthony, Exec. Dir.; Ray T. Anthony, Nancy Payne Ellis, Dan Hogan III, John E. Kirkpatrick, Frank McPherson, James R. Tolbert III, Richard Van Horn.
Trustee Banks: Bank of Oklahoma, Boatman's First National Bank, Liberty National Bank, Trust Co. of Oklahoma.
Number of staff: 2 full-time professional; 1 full-time support; 1 part-time support.
EIN: 237024262
Recent health grants:

2633-1 American Red Cross, Oklahoma County Chapter, Oklahoma City, OK, $23,000. For establishment of centrally located surgical retrival site for division of Tissue Services. 1991.

2633-2 Baptist Medical Center of Oklahoma, Oklahoma City, OK, $11,804. 1991.

2633-3 Mercy Health Center, Oklahoma City, OK, $10,000. 1991.

2634
Oklahoma Gas and Electric Company Foundation, Inc.
101 North Robinson
P.O. Box 321
Oklahoma City 73101   (405) 272-3196

Incorporated in 1957 in OK.
Donor(s): Oklahoma Gas and Electric Co.
Foundation type: Company-sponsored
Financial data (yr. ended 12/31/91): Assets, $883,665 (M); gifts received, $400,000; expenditures, $633,283; qualifying distributions, $630,641, including $588,299 for 57 grants (high: $50,000; low: $200; average: $3,000-$10,000) and $42,342 for 163 employee matching gifts.
Fields of interest: Higher education, hospitals, youth, arts, community funds.
Types of support: Operating budgets, continuing support, annual campaigns, building funds, equipment, employee matching gifts, professorships, scholarship funds.
Limitations: Giving limited to OK, in areas of company operations. No grants to individuals; no loans.
Application information: Application form not required.
  Initial approach: Letter or proposal
  Copies of proposal: 1
  Deadline(s): None
  Board meeting date(s): As required
  Final notification: 1 month
  Write: James G. Harlow, Jr., Pres.
Officers and Directors:* James G. Harlow, Jr.,* Pres.; Patrick J. Ryan,* V.P.; Al M. Strecker,* V.P.; Irma B. Elliott,* Secy.-Treas.
Number of staff: None.
EIN: 736093572

2635
Oklahoma Gas and Electric Company Giving Program
P.O. Box 321
Oklahoma City 73101   (405) 272-3195

Financial data (yr. ended 12/31/90): Total giving, $334,029 for 64 grants (high: $112,000; low: $25; average: $1,000-$30,000).
Purpose and activities: Supports civic affairs, health associations, hospital building funds, education, the arts including fine arts and museums, and general charitable giving.
Fields of interest: Civic affairs, arts, fine arts, education, general charitable giving, health associations, hospitals—building funds, museums.
Types of support: Loaned talent.
Application information: Applications not accepted.
  Write: James G. Harlow, Jr., Chair., Pres., and C.E.O.

2636
Phillips Petroleum Foundation, Inc. ▼
16 C4 Phillips Bldg.
Bartlesville 74001   (918) 661-6248

Incorporated in 1973 in OK.
Donor(s): Phillips Petroleum Co.
Foundation type: Company-sponsored
Financial data (yr. ended 12/31/90): Assets, $857,065 (M); gifts received, $4,790,429; expenditures, $4,372,995; qualifying distributions, $4,358,556, including $3,372,919 for 552 grants (high: $100,000; low: $25; average: $1,000-$25,000) and $994,536 for employee matching gifts.
Purpose and activities: Support for education, civic and youth organizations, cultural programs, and social service and health agencies.
Fields of interest: Youth, civic affairs, cultural programs, education, health, social services.
Types of support: Employee matching gifts, operating budgets, annual campaigns, seed money, building funds, equipment, land acquisition, renovation projects, research, conferences and seminars, scholarship funds, fellowships, professorships, internships, exchange programs, matching funds, continuing support, general purposes, capital campaigns.
Limitations: Giving primarily in areas of company operations, particularly OK, TX, CO, and other states in the South and Southwest. Generally no grants to religious organizations or specialized health agencies. No grants to individuals, or for trips or fundraising dinners; no loans.
Publications: Application guidelines.
Application information: Application form not required.
  Initial approach: Proposal, letter, or telephone
  Copies of proposal: 1
  Deadline(s): None
  Board meeting date(s): Mar. and as required
  Final notification: 8 to 12 weeks
  Write: John C. West, Exec. Mgr.
Officers and Directors:* R.W. Peters, Jr.,* Pres.; R.W. Holsapple,* V.P. and Treas.; J. Bryan Whitworth,* V.P.; G.C. Meese, Secy.; J.M. Bork, Controller; J.W. O'Toole, General Tax Officer; John C. West, Exec. Mgr.; Dale J. Billam, Stanley R. Mueller.
Number of staff: 1 part-time professional; 1 part-time support.
EIN: 237326611
Recent health grants:

2636-1 Alcohol and Drug Center, Bartlesville, OK, $35,000. For unrestricted support. 1990.

2636-2 Bluestem Regional Medical Development Foundation, Bartlesville, OK, $100,000. For unrestricted support. 1990.

2636-3 Mental Health Association of Washington County, Bartlesville, OK, $10,000. For unrestricted support. 1990.

2636-4 Oklahoma State Department of Health, Oklahoma City, OK, $50,000. For unrestricted support. 1990.

2636-5 Saint Francis Hospital, Greenville, SC, $10,000. For unrestricted support. 1990.

2636-6 University of Oklahoma, College of Medicine, Tulsa, OK, $17,500. For unrestricted support. 1990.

2636-7 Washington County Family Planning, Bartlesville, OK, $10,000. For unrestricted support. 1990.

2636-8 Women and Children in Crisis, Bartlesville, OK, $10,000. For unrestricted support. 1990.

2637
Puterbaugh Foundation
215 East Choctaw, First National Ctr., Suite 117
P.O. Box 729
McAlester 74502   (918) 426-1591

Trust established in 1949 in OK.
Donor(s): Jay Garfield Puterbaugh,‡ Leela Oliver Puterbaugh.‡
Foundation type: Independent
Financial data (yr. ended 12/31/91): Assets, $7,111,997 (L); expenditures, $343,365; qualifying distributions, $271,068, including $229,403 for 29 grants (high: $50,000; low: $25) and $41,665 for 1 foundation-administered program.
Purpose and activities: Primary areas of interest include child welfare, community funds, health associations, and higher education.
Fields of interest: Medical research, health associations, higher education, education, youth, social services, child welfare, government, community funds.
Types of support: Annual campaigns, building funds, endowment funds, equipment, exchange programs, matching funds, professorships, scholarship funds, special projects.
Limitations: Giving primarily in OK. No grants to individuals.
Publications: Financial statement.
Application information: Budgets are set 1 year in advance of year of payment. Application form not required.
  Initial approach: Letter
  Deadline(s): Jan. 15 for payment in Dec.
  Board meeting date(s): As necessary
  Write: Don C. Phelps, Managing Trustee
Trustees: Don C. Phelps, Managing Trustee; Frank G. Edwards, Norris J. Welker.
Number of staff: 2 part-time support.
EIN: 736092193

2638
Robert Glenn Rapp Foundation
2301 N.W. 39th Expressway, Suite 300
Oklahoma City 73112   (405) 525-8331

Trust established about 1953 in OK.
Donor(s): Florence B. Clark.‡
Foundation type: Independent
Financial data (yr. ended 12/31/90): Assets, $6,742,819 (M); expenditures, $223,242; qualifying distributions, $40,605, including $21,500 for 10 grants (high: $5,000; low: $500; average: $500-$5,000).
Fields of interest: Education, higher education, secondary education, education—building funds, educational research, medical research, hospitals.
Types of support: Scholarship funds, building funds, seed money, capital campaigns, endowment funds.
Limitations: Giving primarily in OK, with emphasis on Oklahoma City. No grants to individuals.
Publications: Informational brochure (including application guidelines), application guidelines.

Application information: Application form required.

Initial approach: Letter
Copies of proposal: 6
Deadline(s): Sept. 1
Board meeting date(s): Annually, usually in the latter part of the year
Final notification: Dec. 31
Write: Trustees

Trustees: Jilene K. Boghetich, Merry L. Knowles, James H. Milligan, Lois Darlene Milligan, Margaret L. Milligan, Michael J. Milligan.
Number of staff: 1 part-time support.
EIN: 730616840

2639
Sarkeys Foundation ▼
116 South Peters, Suite 219
Norman 73069   (405) 364-3703

Established in 1962 in OK.
Donor(s): S.J. Sarkeys.‡
Foundation type: Independent
Financial data (yr. ended 11/30/90): Assets, $49,490,520 (M); expenditures, $2,449,400; qualifying distributions, $2,248,244, including $2,067,447 for 34 grants (high: $660,000; low: $3,000; average: $10,000-$125,000).
Purpose and activities: Emphasis on higher education; grants also for community services, health and welfare, and general charitable support. Preference given to project-oriented grants over general budgetary support.
Fields of interest: Higher education, education, education—building funds, educational research, education—early childhood, social services, welfare, homeless, health, AIDS, arts, cultural programs, museums, ecology, environment.
Types of support: Endowment funds, capital campaigns, professorships, research, scholarship funds, special projects.
Limitations: Giving primarily in OK and the Southwest. Generally, no support for local programs appropriately financed within the community, or direct mail solicitations. No grants to individuals.
Publications: Informational brochure (including application guidelines).
Application information: Application form not required.

Initial approach: Proposal or letter
Copies of proposal: 10
Deadline(s): Mar. 15 and Sept. 15
Board meeting date(s): Jan., Apr., July, and Oct.; grants considered at Apr. and Oct. meeting
Final notification: Shortly after Apr. and Oct. board meetings
Write: Cheri D. Cartwright, Dir. of Grants

Officers and Trustees:* Robert Rennie,* Pres.; Robert S. Rizley,* V.P.; Jane Janroe,* Secy.-Treas.; Richard J. Hefler, Mgr.; Cheri D. Cartwright, Dir. of Grants; Richard Bell, Joseph W. Morris, Paul F. Sharp, Lee Anne Wilson.
Number of staff: 2 full-time professional; 1 full-time support.
EIN: 730736496
Recent health grants:
2639-1 American Diabetes Association, Tulsa, OK, $30,000. To help install centralized computer system. 1990.
2639-2 Community Council of Central Oklahoma, Oklahoma City, OK, $25,000. For

post-natal care for underprivileged mothers. 1990.
2639-3 Help in Crisis, Tahlequah, OK, $10,000. For job training for battered women. 1990.
2639-4 Norman Alcohol Information Center, Norman, OK, $87,000. For start-up costs for Codependency Treatment Program. 1990.
2639-5 Norman Regional Hospital Foundation, Norman, OK, $115,600. To purchase equipment and expand cardiology services. 1990.
2639-6 Oklahoma Medical Research Foundation, Oklahoma City, OK, $75,000. For research laboratory. 1990.

2640
Scrivner Corporate Giving Program
5701 North Shartel
Box 26030
Oklahoma City 73126   (405) 841-5500

Financial data (yr. ended 12/31/90): Total giving, $75,000, including $60,000 for grants, $5,000 for 2 employee matching gifts and $10,000 for in-kind gifts.
Purpose and activities: Support for adult, business, secondary, and higher education, literacy, family and child welfare, community development, crime and law enforcement, health associations, homeless, medical research, social services, and youth programs; includes in-kind giving.
Fields of interest: Adult education, business education, child welfare, civic affairs, community development, crime and law enforcement, educational associations, engineering, family services, general charitable giving, health, health associations, higher education, homeless, hunger, literacy, medical research, secondary education, social services, youth.
Types of support: In-kind gifts, annual campaigns, building funds, capital campaigns, continuing support, employee matching gifts, endowment funds, equipment, program-related investments, scholarship funds.
Limitations: Giving primarily in communities where company does business, especially in central OK.
Application information: Application form not required.

Initial approach: Letter
Copies of proposal: 1
Write: Marybeth Sloan, Dir. of Corp. Communs.

Number of staff: 1

2641
Charles Morton Share Trust
c/o Liberty National Bank & Trust Co.
P.O. Box 25848, Trust Dept.
Oklahoma City 73125-0848   (405) 231-6815

Trust established in 1959 in OK.
Donor(s): Charles Morton Share.‡
Foundation type: Independent
Financial data (yr. ended 06/30/91): Assets, $8,788,245 (M); expenditures, $541,802; qualifying distributions, $377,831, including $344,000 for 19 grants (high: $70,000; low: $2,000; average: $15,000-$25,000).

Purpose and activities: Emphasis on higher education and hospitals; support also for community projects and a museum.
Fields of interest: Higher education, hospitals, community development, museums.
Types of support: Scholarship funds, general purposes.
Limitations: Giving primarily in OK. No grants to individuals, or for operating budgets, continuing support, annual campaigns, seed money, emergency, building, or endowment funds; deficit financing, equipment, land acquisition, renovations, matching gifts, special projects, research, publications, or conferences; no loans.
Application information: Application form not required.

Initial approach: Proposal
Copies of proposal: 5
Deadline(s): None
Board meeting date(s): Quarterly and as required
Final notification: 6 weeks

Trustees: J.R. Holder, C.E. Johnson, Gertrude Myers, B.H. Thornton, Liberty National Bank & Trust Co. of Oklahoma City.
Number of staff: None.
EIN: 736090984

2642
Herman P. and Sophia Taubman Foundation
c/o Mrs. Billie Coffee
P.O. Box 2300
Tulsa 74192   (918) 588-6423

Trust established in 1955 in OK.
Donor(s): Herman P. Taubman,‡ Sophia Taubman.‡
Foundation type: Independent
Financial data (yr. ended 12/31/90): Assets, $3,828,721 (M); expenditures, $560,204; qualifying distributions, $525,451, including $525,451 for 32 grants (high: $200,000; low: $250).
Purpose and activities: Primary fields of interest include medical sciences and research, mental health, and Jewish giving.
Fields of interest: Jewish welfare, Jewish giving, hospitals, medical research, medical sciences, mental health, psychiatry, education, adult education, education—building funds, education—minorities, community development.
Types of support: Research, building funds, general purposes, special projects.
Limitations: Giving primarily in OK, CA, and NY. No grants to individuals.
Application information: Application form not required.

Initial approach: Letter
Copies of proposal: 3
Deadline(s): None
Board meeting date(s): As required
Write: Louis B. Taubman, Trustee

Trustees: David Fist, Louis Taubman.
Number of staff: None.
EIN: 736092820

2643
C. W. Titus Foundation
1801 Philtower Bldg.
Tulsa 74103   (918) 582-8095

Established in 1968 in OK.
Foundation type: Independent
Financial data (yr. ended 12/31/90): Assets, $9,521,425 (M); expenditures, $421,022; qualifying distributions, $389,792, including $368,124 for 48 grants (high: $80,000; low: $1,000; average: $1,000-$10,000).
Purpose and activities: Giving primarily for hospitals and health services; support also for the arts and cultural programs, the handicapped, and social service agencies.
Fields of interest: Hospitals, health services, cultural programs, arts, handicapped, social services.
Types of support: Operating budgets.
Limitations: Giving primarily in OK and MO.
Application information: Application form not required.
  Deadline(s): None
Trustees: Rosemary T. Reynolds, Timothy T. Reynolds.
EIN: 237016981

2644
Warren Charite
P.O. Box 470372
Tulsa 74147-0372   (918) 492-8100

Established in 1968 in OK.
Donor(s): William K. Warren.
Foundation type: Independent
Financial data (yr. ended 11/30/90): Assets, $6,312,639 (M); gifts received, $200,000; expenditures, $373,628; qualifying distributions, $367,869, including $366,050 for 35 grants (high: $102,000; low: $250).
Purpose and activities: Grants for a cancer research center and a hospital; preference given to local Catholic health care facilities.
Fields of interest: Cancer, medical research, hospitals, Catholic giving, health services.
Types of support: General purposes.
Limitations: Giving primarily in OK. No grants to individuals.
Application information: Application form not required.
  Initial approach: Letter
  Deadline(s): None
  Write: W.R. Lissau, Secy.
Officers and Directors:* W.K. Warren, Jr.,* Pres.; W.R. Lissau,* V.P.; P.K. Griffith, Secy.; W.E. Weeks,* Treas.
EIN: 730776064

2645
The William K. Warren Foundation ▼
P.O. Box 470372
Tulsa 74147-0372   (918) 492-8100

Incorporated in 1945 in OK.
Donor(s): William K. Warren,‡ Mrs. William K. Warren.
Foundation type: Independent
Financial data (yr. ended 12/31/90): Assets, $297,295,926 (M); gifts received, $3,557,483; expenditures, $20,117,746; qualifying distributions, $18,481,447, including $18,359,249 for 67 grants (high: $10,000,000; low: $150; average: $5,000-$50,000).

Purpose and activities: Grants for local Catholic health care facilities, education, and social services; substantial support for a medical research program.
Fields of interest: Health services, Catholic welfare, education, social services, medical research.
Types of support: Building funds, endowment funds, operating budgets, special projects.
Limitations: Giving primarily in OK. No grants to individuals.
Application information: Application form not required.
  Initial approach: Letter
  Deadline(s): None
  Board meeting date(s): Semiannually
  Write: W.R. Lissau, Pres.
Officers and Directors:* Robert J. Stanton,* Chair.; Natalie O. Warren,* Vice-Chair.; W.K. Warren, Jr.,* Vice-Chair.; W.R. Lissau,* Pres.; John A. Naughton, V.P. and Treas.; Dorothy Warren King,* Secy.; John A. Gaberino, Jr., John J. King, Jr., Patricia Warren Swindle.
Number of staff: 10
EIN: 730609599
Recent health grants:
2645-1 American Heart Association, Tulsa, OK, $10,000. 1990.
2645-2 Arthritis Foundation, Tulsa, OK, $10,000. 1990.
2645-3 Laureate Mental Health Corporation, Tulsa, OK, $10,000,000. For research in field of psychiatry. 1990.
2645-4 William K. Warren Medical Research Center, Tulsa, OK, $7,000,000. For medical research. 1990.

2646
The Herman and Mary Wegener Foundation, Inc.
1711 First National Bldg.
Oklahoma City 73102   (405) 235-7200

Incorporated in 1954 in OK.
Donor(s): Herman H. Wegener.‡
Foundation type: Independent
Financial data (yr. ended 12/31/90): Assets, $2,879,770 (M); gifts received, $25,475; expenditures, $349,599; qualifying distributions, $286,588, including $278,200 for 31 grants (high: $15,000; low: $200).
Purpose and activities: Emphasis on hospitals and education; grants also for cultural programs, youth agencies, and social service agencies.
Fields of interest: Hospitals, education, secondary education, cultural programs, youth, social services.
Types of support: Building funds, operating budgets, special projects.
Limitations: Giving primarily in Oklahoma City, OK. No grants to individuals, or for endowment funds.
Application information:
  Initial approach: Letter
  Deadline(s): Nov. 1
  Board meeting date(s): Quarterly
  Write: The Trustees
Officers and Trustees:* Willis B. Sherin,* Pres.; Lee Holmes,* V.P.; May Fry, Secy.; Clenard

Wegener,* Treas.; Rosemary Fields, Kenneth Wegener, Raymond Lee Wegener, Willis B. Wegener.
EIN: 736095407

2647
The Williams Companies Corporate Giving Program
P.O. Box 2400
Tulsa 74102   (908) 588-2000

Financial data (yr. ended 12/31/90): Total giving, $751,077, including $620,936 for grants, $126,141 for employee matching gifts and $4,000 for in-kind gifts.
Purpose and activities: Support for education, health and human services, civic affairs, and culture; also printing services made available for nonprofit organizations.
Fields of interest: Education, health, civic affairs, cultural programs.
Types of support: In-kind gifts.
Limitations: Giving primarily in areas of company operations. No support for political campaigns, religious denominations, or fraternal organizations. No grants to individuals.
Application information: Application form not required.
  Initial approach: Letters
  Copies of proposal: 1
  Board meeting date(s): Monthly
  Write: Hannah D. Robson, Mgr., The Williams Companies Foundation

2648
The Anne and Henry Zarrow Foundation
Mid-Continent Tower
P.O. Box 1530
Tulsa 74101   (918) 587-3391

Established in 1986 in OK.
Donor(s): Henry H. Zarrow.
Foundation type: Independent
Financial data (yr. ended 12/31/90): Assets, $4,073,149 (M); expenditures, $367,152; qualifying distributions, $362,171, including $359,000 for 55 grants (high: $25,000; low: $500).
Fields of interest: Education, handicapped, health, medical research, mental health, disadvantaged, homeless, hunger, aged.
Types of support: Annual campaigns, emergency funds, operating budgets.
Limitations: Giving primarily in the Tulsa, OK, area. No grants to individuals.
Application information: Application form not required.
  Initial approach: Letter
  Copies of proposal: 1
  Deadline(s): None
  Board meeting date(s): Fall and spring
  Write: Judith Z. Kishner
Officers and Directors:* Henry H. Zarrow,* Pres.; Anne S. Zarrow,* V.P.; Robert H. Elliott,* Secy.; J.W. Kerby,* Treas.; Judith Z. Kishner, Stuart A. Zarrow.
EIN: 731286874

OREGON

2649
The Carpenter Foundation
711 East Main St., Suite 10
P.O. Box 816
Medford 97501   (503) 772-5851

Incorporated in 1957 in OR.
Donor(s): Helen Bundy Carpenter,‡ Alfred S.V. Carpenter,‡ Harlow Carpenter.
Foundation type: Independent
Financial data (yr. ended 06/30/91): Assets, $10,134,298 (M); expenditures, $584,527; qualifying distributions, $475,231, including $451,538 for 62 grants (high: $25,000; low: $500; average: $3,000-$6,000).
Fields of interest: Arts, community development, child development, child welfare, conservation, education, secondary education, higher education, social services, drug abuse.
Types of support: Operating budgets, seed money, equipment, matching funds, technical assistance, scholarship funds, research.
Limitations: Giving primarily in Jackson and Josephine counties, OR. No grants to individuals, or for deficit financing, endowment funds, or demonstration projects.
Publications: Annual report (including application guidelines).
Application information: Application form not required.
  Initial approach: Proposal
  Copies of proposal: 1
  Deadline(s): Submit proposal 4 weeks before board meeting
  Board meeting date(s): Usually in Mar., June, Sept., and Dec.
  Final notification: 1 to 2 weeks
  Write: Dunbar Carpenter, Treas., or Jane Carpenter, Pres., Treas.
Officers and Trustees:* Jane H. Carpenter,* Pres.; Emily C. Mostue,* V.P.; Karen C. Allan,* Secy.; Dunbar Carpenter,* Treas.
Associate Trustees: Barbara Bean, Sheila Kimball, Bill Moffat, Shirley Petton, David Sevlian.
Number of staff: 1 part-time support.
EIN: 930491360
Recent health grants:
2649-1 Womens Crisis Support Team, Grants Pass, OR, $12,000. For protection, advocacy and service to women, children and families subject to abuse. 1990.

2650
Chiles Foundation ▼
111 S.W. Fifth Ave., Suite 4050
Portland 97204-3643   (503) 222-2143

Incorporated in 1949 in OR.
Donor(s): Eva Chiles Meyer,‡ Earle A. Chiles,‡ Virginia H. Chiles.
Foundation type: Independent
Financial data (yr. ended 12/31/90): Assets, $20,007,267 (M); expenditures, $4,030,939; qualifying distributions, $3,766,109, including $3,386,550 for 70 grants (high: $523,800; low: $500; average: $1,000-$100,000).
Purpose and activities: Grants traditionally to institutions of higher education for business schools and medical research.
Fields of interest: Higher education, medical research, business education.
Types of support: Building funds, equipment.
Limitations: Giving primarily in OR, with emphasis on Portland, and the Pacific Northwest. No grants to individuals, or for deficit financing, mortgage retirement, projects involving litigation, or projects and conferences already completed; no loans.
Application information: Application form required.
  Initial approach: Telephone
  Deadline(s): Submit proposal by telephone between Jan. 1 and Feb. 15
  Board meeting date(s): As required
  Final notification: By Dec. 31
Officer and Trustees:* Earle M. Chiles,* Pres.; Virginia H. Chiles, Frank E. Nash.
Number of staff: 2 full-time professional; 2 part-time professional.
EIN: 936031125
Recent health grants:
2650-1 Cystic Fibrosis Foundation, Portland, OR, $49,200. For general operating support. 1990.
2650-2 Providence Medical Foundation, Portland, OR, $222,400. For general operating support and building construction. 1990.
2650-3 Saint Vincent Medical Foundation, Portland, OR, $220,000. For general operating support. 1990.

2651
The Collins Foundation ▼
1618 S.W. First Ave., Suite 305
Portland 97201   (503) 227-7171

Incorporated in 1947 in OR.
Donor(s): Members of the Collins family.
Foundation type: Independent
Financial data (yr. ended 12/31/90): Assets, $80,237,203 (M); expenditures, $4,378,921; qualifying distributions, $4,067,350, including $4,067,350 for 212 grants (high: $550,000; low: $500; average: $5,000-$25,000).
Purpose and activities: Emphasis on higher education, youth, hospices and health agencies, social welfare, and the arts and cultural programs.
Fields of interest: Higher education, youth, arts, cultural programs, health services, social services, homeless, hospices.
Types of support: Building funds, equipment, research, matching funds, program-related investments, special projects.
Limitations: Giving limited to OR, with emphasis on Portland. No support for legislative lobbying or delayed projects. No grants to individuals, or for deficit financing, endowment funds, general purposes, scholarships, fellowships, operating budgets, or annual campaigns.
Publications: Annual report (including application guidelines), informational brochure.
Application information: Application form not required.
  Initial approach: Letter
  Copies of proposal: 1
  Deadline(s): None

  Board meeting date(s): Approximately 6 times a year
  Final notification: 4 to 8 weeks
  Write: William C. Pine, Exec. V.P.
Officers and Trustees:* Maribeth W. Collins,* Pres.; William C. Pine, Exec. V.P.; Ralph Bolliger,* V.P.; Grace Collins Goudy,* V.P.; Thomas B. Stoel, Secy.; Timothy R. Bishop, Treas.
Number of staff: 1 part-time professional; 1 part-time support.
EIN: 936021893
Recent health grants:
2651-1 Alano Club of Portland, Portland, OR, $15,000. For rehabilitation of facility. 1990.
2651-2 Mental Health Association of Oregon, Salem, OR, $25,000. For Keepwell, Inc. workshops. 1990.
2651-3 Metropolitan Family Services, Portland, OR, $15,000. For medication management program. 1990.
2651-4 Neighborhood Health Clinics, Portland, OR, $10,000. For prenatal care project. 1990.
2651-5 Nurse Practitioner Community Health Clinic, Portland, OR, $10,000. For medically needy children's fund. 1990.
2651-6 Oregon Health Sciences University, Department of Ophthalmology, Portland, OR, $100,000. For Dr. Lester T. Jones Chair. 1990.
2651-7 Orton Dyslexia Society, Oregon Branch, Portland, OR, $10,000. For 1991 national conference in Portland. 1990.
2651-8 Providence Milwaukie Hospital Foundation, Milwaukie, OR, $15,000. For equipment for Providence Milwaukie Hospital. 1990.
2651-9 Saint Vincent Medical Foundation, Portland, OR, $50,000. For Outcomes Management for heart disease study. 1990.

2652
Collins Medical Trust
1618 S.W. First Ave., Suite 300
Portland 97201   (503) 227-1219

Established in 1956 in OR.
Donor(s): Truman W. Collins.‡
Foundation type: Independent
Financial data (yr. ended 09/30/91): Assets, $3,514,800 (M); expenditures, $136,225; qualifying distributions, $126,931, including $125,404 for 12 grants (high: $25,000; low: $2,160; average: $2,160-$25,000).
Purpose and activities: Grants limited to medical research and medical education.
Fields of interest: Education, higher education, medical research, medical sciences, medical education, nursing, health services, cancer, aged.
Types of support: Equipment, research, scholarship funds, fellowships, special projects, lectureships, endowment funds.
Limitations: Giving limited to OR.
Publications: Informational brochure (including application guidelines), application guidelines.
Application information: Application form not required.
  Initial approach: Letter or telephone
  Copies of proposal: 1
  Deadline(s): Jan. 1, May 1, and Sept. 1
  Board meeting date(s): 3rd Thursday in Jan., May, and Sept.
  Final notification: 7 days after meeting
  Write: Joseph A. Connolly, Administrator

Officers: Timothy R. Bishop, Treas.; Joseph A. Connolly, Administrator.
Trustees: Maribeth W. Collins, Truman W. Collins, Jr., Joseph F. Paquet, M.D., James R. Patterson, M.D.
Number of staff: None.
EIN: 936021895

2653
The Jackson Foundation
c/o U.S. Bank, Trust Dept.
P.O. Box 3168
Portland 97208   (503) 275-5718

Trust established in 1960 in OR; Philip Ludwell Jackson Charitable and Residual Trusts were merged into The Jackson Foundation in 1981.
Donor(s): Maria C. Jackson.‡
Foundation type: Independent
Financial data (yr. ended 06/30/91): Assets, $9,118,620 (M); expenditures, $629,428; qualifying distributions, $553,427, including $509,477 for 116 grants (high: $41,716; low: $500; average: $1,000-$25,000).
Purpose and activities: Support largely to aid needy persons through social service agencies; grants for higher and secondary education, cultural programs, hospitals, community and civic organizations, and youth agencies. "Priority is given to one-time special projects and development projects."
Fields of interest: Social services, housing, minorities, youth, aged, women, drug abuse, health, education, arts.
Types of support: Continuing support, program-related investments, endowment funds, capital campaigns, research, matching funds.
Limitations: Giving limited to OR. No support for churches or temples. No grants to individuals, or for endowment funds, matching gifts, scholarships, fellowships, or building or equipment funds for religious organizations; no loans to individuals.
Publications: Annual report.
Application information: Application form required.
  Initial approach: Request for application form
  Copies of proposal: 4
  Deadline(s): Aug. 25, Nov. 25, and Mar. 25
  Board meeting date(s): Sept., Dec., Apr., and as required
  Final notification: 3 or 4 weeks
  Write: Frank E. Staich, Asst. V.P., U.S. Bank
Directors: Milo E. Ormseth, Gordon M. Tretheway, U.S. Bank.
Number of staff: 3
EIN: 936020752

2654
The Jeld-Wen Foundation
(Formerly Jeld-Wen, Wenco Foundation)
P.O. Box 1329
Klamath Falls 97601

Established in 1969.
Donor(s): Jeld-Wen Fiber Products, Inc. of Iowa, Jeld-Wen Co. of Arizona, Wenco, Inc. of North Carolina, Wenco, Inc. of Ohio, and other Jeld-Wen, Wenco companies.
Foundation type: Company-sponsored

Financial data (yr. ended 12/31/91): Assets, $15,882,483 (M); expenditures, $646,349; qualifying distributions, $594,836, including $590,568 for 119 grants (high: $42,800; low: $300).
Purpose and activities: The foundation prioritizes requests on the basis of demonstrated impact toward making our communities better places to live. An assessment is also made as to how many company employees will use the services. Projects that improve the existing service or provide new ones, usually involving capital or seed money, and annual support for existing organizations through the United Way are major categories for giving.
Fields of interest: Community funds, higher education, health services, health, youth, arts, museums.
Types of support: General purposes, seed money, building funds, equipment, land acquisition, special projects, scholarship funds, matching funds.
Limitations: Giving primarily in areas of company operations; in AZ, FL, IA, KY, NC, OH, OR, SD, and WA projects should serve communities in which company plants exist; projects in adjacent communities may be accepted if sufficient numbers of employees reside in the area and would benefit. No support for activities that are specifically religious or that duplicate services provided by other government or private agencies. No grants to individuals; no loans.
Publications: Program policy statement, application guidelines.
Application information: Application form required.
  Initial approach: Proposal or letter; prefers not to receive telephone calls
  Copies of proposal: 1
  Deadline(s): None
  Board meeting date(s): Mar., June, Sept., and Dec.
  Final notification: 2 weeks after meetings
  Write: R.C. Wendt, Secy.
Officer and Trustees:* R.C. Wendt,* Secy.; W.B. Early, Nancy Wendt, R.L. Wendt, L.V. Wetter.
Number of staff: None.
EIN: 936054272

2655
The Samuel S. Johnson Foundation
(Formerly The S. S. Johnson Foundation)
P.O. Box 356
Redmond 97756   (503) 548-8104
FAX: (503) 548-2014

Incorporated in 1948 in CA.
Donor(s): Samuel S. Johnson,‡ Elizabeth Hill Johnson.
Foundation type: Independent
Financial data (yr. ended 05/31/92): Assets, $4,245,603 (M); expenditures, $193,942; qualifying distributions, $197,433, including $159,920 for 139 grants (high: $8,500; low: $100; average: $100-$1,000) and $30,790 for grants to individuals (average: $500-$1,000).
Purpose and activities: Giving for higher, medical, legal, vocational, secondary, and early childhood education, including research associations, language and literacy programs, social services, including community development funds, family services, drug abuse

prevention, and programs for the aged, women, youth and child welfare and development; civic affairs, including humanities programs, volunteerism, and leadership development; public policy; science and technology; health and hospitals, including nursing, cancer and other medical research, and the medical sciences; the environment, conservation, and ecology; animal welfare; the fine and performing arts and other cultural programs, including museums and historical preservation; and religious organizations. Support primarily for limited emergency operational funds and limited non-recurring emergency grants or loans to students through educational institutions, with a focus on health care fields.
Fields of interest: Higher education, medical education, secondary education, educational associations, social services, family services, drug abuse, aged, women, youth, community development, civic affairs, health, hospitals, medical sciences, conservation, cultural programs, arts, religion—Christian.
Types of support: Operating budgets, seed money, emergency funds, matching funds, scholarship funds, conferences and seminars, equipment, special projects, continuing support, lectureships, professorships, publications, research, in-kind gifts, renovation projects.
Limitations: Giving primarily in the Pacific Northwest, primarily OR, northern CA, and WA. No support for foreign organizations. No grants for annual campaigns, deficit financing, construction, sole underwriting of major proposals or projects, or endowments.
Publications: 990-PF, program policy statement, application guidelines, informational brochure (including application guidelines).
Application information: Application form required for scholarships and loans. Application form not required.
  Initial approach: Letter
  Copies of proposal: 1
  Deadline(s): June 1 for July meeting and Nov. 15 for Jan. meeting
  Board meeting date(s): July and Jan.
  Final notification: 2 to 3 weeks after board meeting
  Write: Elizabeth Hill Johnson, Pres.
Officers and Directors:* Elizabeth Hill Johnson,* Pres.; Elizabeth K. Johnson-Helm,* V.P. and Secy.; Mary A. Krenowicz, Exec. Secy.; Patricia Johnson Nelson,* C.F.O.; Robert W. Hill, Ralf H. Stinson.
Number of staff: 1 part-time professional.
EIN: 946062478

2656
Louisiana-Pacific Foundation
111 S.W. Fifth Ave.
Portland 97204   (503) 221-0800

Established in 1973 in OR.
Donor(s): Louisiana-Pacific Corp.
Foundation type: Company-sponsored
Financial data (yr. ended 12/31/91): Assets, $18,646 (M); gifts received, $1,161,000; expenditures, $1,148,109; qualifying distributions, $1,148,109, including $1,148,109 for 223 grants (high: $302,795; low: $100; average: $500-$5,000).
Purpose and activities: Giving for higher education, including employee-related

scholarships, and community funds; some support for health and social services, the medical sciences, youth agencies, and the arts, including the performing arts.
Fields of interest: Higher education, community funds, civic affairs, health services, handicapped, medical sciences, social services, youth, arts, performing arts.
Types of support: Annual campaigns, capital campaigns, continuing support, general purposes, employee-related scholarships, emergency funds.
Limitations: Giving primarily in areas of plant locations.
Application information: Application form required for scholarships.
Initial approach: Letter
Copies of proposal: 1
Board meeting date(s): Quarterly
Write: Pamela A. Selis, Trustee
Officers and Trustees:* Harry A. Merlo,* Chair. and Pres.; Pamela A. Selis,* V.P.; Anton C. Kirchhof, Secy.; John C. Hart, Treas.; Anita M. Davis, Gary R. Maffei.
Number of staff: None.
EIN: 237268660

2657
Meyer Memorial Trust ▼
(Formerly Fred Meyer Charitable Trust)
1515 S.W. Fifth Ave., Suite 500
Portland 97201   (503) 228-5512

Trust established by will in 1978; obtained IRS status in 1982 in OR.
Donor(s): Fred G. Meyer.‡
Foundation type: Independent
Financial data (yr. ended 03/31/91): Assets, $278,572,830 (M); expenditures, $16,957,007; qualifying distributions, $14,948,273, including $13,994,107 for 187 grants (high: $1,000,000; low: $1,000; average: $20,000-$200,000).
Purpose and activities: The trust provides two types of funding: 1) general purpose grants, primarily in OR for education, the arts and humanities, health, and social welfare; and 2) special program grants, primarily in AK, ID, MT, OR, and WA, for the Support for Children at Risk program. Under general purpose, the trust operates the Small Grants Program, which provides awards of $500 to $8,000 for small projects in OR. The Aging and Independence Program has been terminated.
Fields of interest: Arts, museums, humanities, performing arts, education, higher education, social services, family services, youth, aged, child welfare, child development, health, delinquency.
Types of support: Seed money, building funds, equipment, matching funds, technical assistance, program-related investments, special projects, research, general purposes, operating budgets, renovation projects.
Limitations: Giving primarily in OR, except for special programs which also include WA, ID, MT, and AK. No support for sectarian or religious organizations for religious purposes. No grants to individuals, or for operating budgets, endowment funds, annual campaigns, deficit financing, scholarships, fellowships, or indirect or overhead costs, except as specifically and essentially related to the grant project; occasional program-related loans only.

Publications: Annual report, informational brochure (including application guidelines), program policy statement.
Application information: Special guidelines for Children at Risk program and Small Grants Program. Application form required.
Initial approach: Proposal
Copies of proposal: 1
Deadline(s): Apr. 1 and Sept. 1 for Children at Risk program; Jan. 15, Apr. 15, July 15, and Oct. 15 for Small Grants Program; no set deadline for other grants
Board meeting date(s): Monthly
Final notification: 3 to 5 months for proposals that pass first screening; 1 to 2 months for those that do not
Write: Charles S. Rooks, Exec. Dir.
Officers: Charles S. Rooks, Secy. and Exec. Dir.; Wayne G. Pierson, Treas.
Trustees: Travis Cross, Pauline Lawrence, Warne Nunn, G. Gerald Pratt, Oran B. Robertson.
Number of staff: 5 full-time professional; 5 full-time support.
EIN: 930806316
Recent health grants:
2657-1 Bend-La Pine School District, Bend, OR, $55,000. For drug and alcohol intervention program for students in kindergarten through high school. 1992.
2657-2 Carondelet Psychiatric Care Center, Richland, WA, $179,000. For early intervention program which provides intensive home and school-based delinquency prevention activities for young children exhibiting high-risk characteristics. 1992.
2657-3 Community Health Center, Ashland, OR, $38,000. To enable clinic to obtain certification as primary care organization. 1992.
2657-4 Fanconis Anemia Research Fund, Eugene, OR, $197,000. To expand and improve support program for families whose children are affected by Fanconi's anemia, rare genetic disorder which causes bone marrow failure and cancers in children. 1992.
2657-5 Good Samaritan Hospital and Medical Center, Portland, OR, $118,500. For three videos on care for elderly heart patients and their families to improve quality of life in recovery. 1992.
2657-6 Mental Health Association of Oregon, Salem, OR, $180,000. For Oregon Family Support Network for families with children with serious emotional or behavioral disorders. 1992.
2657-7 Oregon Health Sciences University, Portland, OR, $536,000. For audio visual telecommunications equipment to broadcast educational programs to nursing students. 1992.
2657-8 Portland Adventist Medical Center, Portland, OR, $158,000. To establish and equip adult psychiatric day hospital program. 1992.
2657-9 Saint Charles Medical Center, Bend, OR, $83,600. To establish network that will link cardiac services at Saint Charles Hospital with eight rural hospitals in Central and Eastern Oregon. 1992.
2657-10 Tualatin Valley Mental Health Center, Portland, OR, $231,000. For start-up costs for Hispanic Training and Employment Program, partnership program with Centro Cultural,

which provides low-income Hispanics with language and employment skills. 1992.
2657-11 Umatilla County Mental Health, Pendleton, OR, $80,000. To establish countywide network of support services for families with children at-risk of social, behavorial, and emotional problems. 1992.

2658
Northwest Natural Gas Company Contributions Program
220 N.W. Second Ave.
Portland 97209   (503) 226-4211

Financial data (yr. ended 12/31/90): Total giving, $403,000, including $393,000 for 600 grants (high: $10,000; low: $25; average: $100-$5,000) and $10,000 for 31 in-kind gifts.
Purpose and activities: Supports education, including public and private colleges, civic affairs and community development, arts and culture, welfare, and health programs.
Fields of interest: Education, civic affairs, community development, community funds, cultural programs, health, welfare, arts.
Types of support: General purposes, annual campaigns, capital campaigns, employee-related scholarships, donated equipment.
Limitations: Giving primarily in company service area: Willamette Valley of OR, north and central coast, southwest WA. No support for programs already funded under the United Way umbrella.
Publications: Application guidelines.
Application information: Contributions are handled by the Corporate Secretary. Application form required.
Initial approach: Letter to chairman of Contributions Committee asking for application and guidelines
Copies of proposal: 1
Final notification: After committee's review-generally 4 to 6 weeks
Write: C.J. Rue, Chair., Contribs. Comm.
Administrator: C.J. Rue, Chair., Contribs. Comm.
Number of staff: 2 part-time professional.

2659
OCRI Foundation
P.O. Box 1705
Lake Oswego 97035-0575   (503) 635-8010
FAX: (503) 635-6544

Established in 1971 in OR.
Donor(s): Members of the Lamb family.
Foundation type: Independent
Financial data (yr. ended 12/31/91): Assets, $4,420,689 (M); expenditures, $307,880; qualifying distributions, $294,521, including $270,010 for 90 grants (high: $32,000; low: $75).
Purpose and activities: Primary areas of interest include ecology, housing, hunger, youth, and Christian religious organizations.
Fields of interest: Religion—Christian, Protestant giving, higher education, youth, environment, conservation, ecology, agriculture, hunger, homeless, housing, health, humanities, wildlife.
Types of support: Emergency funds, general purposes, matching funds, seed money, special projects.
Limitations: Giving limited to OR and the Northwest. No grants to individuals.

Publications: Program policy statement, application guidelines.
Application information: Application form not required.

Initial approach: Proposal
Copies of proposal: 1
Deadline(s): None
Board meeting date(s): Mar., July, Sept., and Dec.
Write: Judith Anderson, Administrator

Officers and Directors:* Anita Lamb Bailey,* Chair.; Maryann Lamb,* Vice-Chair.; Helen Lamb,* Secy.; F. Gilbert Lamb,* Treas.; Dorothy Lamb, Frank G. Lamb, Paula L. Lamb, Peter Lamb, Walter Minnick.
Number of staff: 1 part-time support.
EIN: 237120564

2660
The Oregon Community Foundation ▼
621 S.W. Morrison, Suite 725
Portland 97205   (503) 227-6846

Established in 1973 in OR.
Foundation type: Community
Financial data (yr. ended 06/30/91): Assets, $75,602,877 (M); gifts received, $10,101,287; expenditures, $9,931,217; qualifying distributions, $8,975,693, including $8,426,987 for 638 grants (high: $1,477,140; low: $100; average: $1,000-$10,000), $476,385 for 92 grants to individuals (high: $1,883; low: $200) and $72,321 for 1 foundation-administered program.
Purpose and activities: To "meet educational, cultural, medical, social and civic needs in all areas and at all levels of society throughout the state."
Fields of interest: Education, cultural programs, health, social services, youth, aged, disadvantaged, civic affairs, community development, leadership development.
Types of support: Operating budgets, seed money, building funds, equipment, land acquisition, technical assistance, scholarship funds, special projects, matching funds, renovation projects.
Limitations: Giving limited to OR. No support for religious organizations for religious purposes. No grants to individuals (except for scholarships), or for emergency funding, endowments, annual campaigns, deficit financing, research, publications, films, or conferences, unless so designated by a donor; no loans.
Publications: Annual report, newsletter, program policy statement, application guidelines.
Application information: Application form required.

Initial approach: 1-page letter
Copies of proposal: 12
Deadline(s): Submit application preferably in Mar. or Aug.; deadlines Apr. 1 and Sept. 1
Board meeting date(s): Jan., June, Sept., and Nov.
Final notification: 3 months
Write: Gregory A. Chaille, Pres.

Officers and Directors:* Robert W. Chandler,* Chair.; Richard F. Hensley,* Vice-Chair.; Sally McCracken,* Vice-Chair.; Gregory A. Chaille, Pres.; Alex M. Byler,* Secy.; Robert Murray,* Treas.; Clifford N. Carlsen, Jr., John D. Gray, Alice Koehler, Carolyn McMurchie, Walter C.

Reynolds, M.D., David Rhoten, Ethel Simon-McWilliams, Donna P. Woolley.
Investment Managers: The Bank of California, N.A., First Interstate Bank of Oregon, N.A., The Oregon Bank, Provident Investment Counsel, Scudder, Stevens, Clark, U.S. National Bank of Oregon.
Number of staff: 6 full-time professional; 1 part-time professional; 3 full-time support.
EIN: 237315673
Recent health grants:
2660-1 American Academy of Environmental Medicine, Denver, CO, $17,660. 1991.
2660-2 American Heart Association, Oregon Affiliate, Portland, OR, $54,887. 1991.
2660-3 Child Development and Rehabilitation Center, Portland, OR, $32,850. 1991.
2660-4 Deschutes County Mental Health Services, Bend, OR, $10,000. 1991.
2660-5 Devers Eye Clinic, Portland, OR, $26,294. 1991.
2660-6 Easter Seal Society for Crippled Children and Adults of Oregon, Portland, OR, $16,859. 1991.
2660-7 Emanuel Medical Center Foundation, Portland, OR, $35,000. 1991.
2660-8 Good Samaritan Hospital, Portland, OR, $20,934. 1991.
2660-9 Good Samaritan Hospital, Portland, OR, $10,000. 1991.
2660-10 Health Bridge Northwest, Portland, OR, $48,500. 1991.
2660-11 Healthy Start, Hillsboro, OR, $10,000. 1991.
2660-12 Kidney Association of Oregon, Portland, OR, $16,534. 1991.
2660-13 Medical Research Foundation of Oregon, Portland, OR, $50,500. 1991.
2660-14 Mental Health Services West, Portland, OR, $10,000. 1991.
2660-15 Oregon Health Sciences University Foundation, Portland, OR, $246,799. 1991.
2660-16 Oregon Stroke Clubs Association, Portland, OR, $10,000. 1991.
2660-17 Providence Milwaukie Hospital Foundation, Milwaukie, OR, $10,000. 1991.
2660-18 Rogue Valley Health Foundation, Medford, OR, $10,000. 1991.
2660-19 William Temple House, Portland, OR, $36,440. 1991.
2660-20 Yamhill County Mental Health, McMinnville, OR, $13,000. 1991.

2661
PacifiCorp Foundation ▼
700 N.E. Multnomah, Suite 700
Portland 97232-4107   (503) 464-6000
Application address: 500 N.E. Multnomah, Suite 1500, Portland, OR 97232; Tel.: (503) 731-6676

Established in 1988 in OR.
Donor(s): Pacific Power & Light Co., Utah Power & Light Co., NERCO, Inc., Pacific Telecom, Inc., PacifiCorp Financial Services, Pacific Development, Inc.
Foundation type: Company-sponsored
Financial data (yr. ended 12/31/90): Assets, $2,896,693 (M); gifts received, $3,914,360; expenditures, $2,387,463; qualifying distributions, $2,377,534, including $2,378,736 for 578 grants (high: $100,000; low: $100).

Purpose and activities: Support primarily for health and welfare, the United Way, and education, especially colleges and universities; giving also for civic and social affairs and culture and the arts.
Fields of interest: Health, welfare, community funds, civic affairs, community development, education, higher education, cultural programs, arts.
Limitations: Giving primarily in major operating areas in the West. No support for religious organizations for religious purposes or veterans' or fraternal organizations. No grants to individuals, or for endowments, or coverage of operating deficits.
Application information:

Initial approach: Letter or proposal
Deadline(s): None
Write: Ernest Bloch II, Exec. Dir.

Officers: Gerard K. Drummond, Chair.; Sally A. Nofziger, Secy.; Ernest Bloch II, Exec. Dir.
Directors: David F. Bolender, William J. Glasgow, Lawrence E. Heiner, Robert W. Moench.
Contributions Committee: Kandis Brewer, Paul G. Lorenzini, William W. Lyons, David Mead, William E. Peressini, Brian M. Wirkkala.
EIN: 943089826
Recent health grants:
2661-1 Alaska Health Fair, Anchorage, AK, $10,000. 1990.
2661-2 Center for Ethics in Health Care, Portland, OR, $25,000. 1990.
2661-3 Doembecher Childrens Hospital, Portland, OR, $13,500. 1990.
2661-4 Holy Cross Hospital Foundation of Utah, Salt Lake City, UT, $10,000. 1990.
2661-5 IHC Hospitals, Salt Lake City, UT, $12,500. 1990.
2661-6 Providence Medical Foundation, Portland, OR, $15,000. 1990.

2662
Rose E. Tucker Charitable Trust
900 S.W. Fifth Ave., 24th Fl.
Portland 97204   (503) 224-3380

Trust established in 1976 in OR.
Donor(s): Rose E. Tucker,‡ Max and Rose Tucker Foundation.
Foundation type: Independent
Financial data (yr. ended 06/30/91): Assets, $14,777,238 (M); expenditures, $924,800; qualifying distributions, $807,619, including $764,577 for 165 grants (high: $30,000; low: $500; average: $2,500-$10,000).
Fields of interest: Disadvantaged, handicapped, welfare, education, hospitals, health, arts, cultural programs, community development.
Types of support: Building funds, scholarship funds, general purposes, operating budgets, equipment, special projects, capital campaigns, land acquisition.
Limitations: Giving primarily in OR, with emphasis on the Portland metropolitan area. No support for religion or private foundations. No grants to individuals, or for fellowships, operating budgets, or debt reduction; no loans.
Publications: Application guidelines, annual report (including application guidelines), grants list.
Application information: Application form not required.

Initial approach: Proposal
Copies of proposal: 1
Deadline(s): None
Board meeting date(s): Approximately every 2 months
Final notification: Within 10 days of board meetings
Write: Thomas B. Stoel or Milo Ormseth, Trustees
Trustees: Milo E. Ormseth, Thomas B. Stoel, U.S. National Bank of Oregon.
Number of staff: 1 part-time support.
EIN: 936119091

2663
U.S. Bancorp Corporate Giving Program
P.O. Box 8837
Portland 97208   (503) 275-5776

Financial data (yr. ended 12/31/90): Total giving, $2,024,115 for grants (high: $95,000; low: $500).
Purpose and activities: Supports educational, health and welfare, and civic and cultural programs.
Fields of interest: Education, higher education, health, welfare, civic affairs, cultural programs, minorities, music, arts.
Types of support: Grants to individuals, seed money, building funds, special projects, donated equipment, employee volunteer services, matching funds, equipment, capital campaigns, continuing support, general purposes, employee matching gifts, scholarship funds, student loans.
Limitations: Giving primarily in headquarters and major operating areas in OR. No support for religious organizations and tax supported groups. No grants for conventions and conferences.
Publications: Corporate report, application guidelines.
Application information: The Social Responsibility Department handles giving. Application form not required.
Initial approach: Letter to nearest company facility
Copies of proposal: 1
Deadline(s): Monthly
Board meeting date(s): Monthly
Final notification: 4-8 weeks
Write: Linda Wright, Secy., Contribs. Comm.
Administrators: Linda Wright, V.P., Public Affairs; Molly Reed, V.P., Social Responsibility.
Number of staff: 2 full-time professional.

2664
Wheeler Foundation
1211 S.W. Fifth Ave., Suite 2906
Portland 97204-1911   (503) 228-0261

Established in 1965 in OR.
Donor(s): Coleman H. Wheeler,‡ Coleman H. Wheeler, Jr.‡
Foundation type: Independent
Financial data (yr. ended 12/31/91): Assets, $5,415,668 (M); gifts received, $20,000; expenditures, $272,424; qualifying distributions, $260,533, including $252,600 for 72 grants (high: $17,500; low: $1,000; average: $1,000).
Fields of interest: Higher education, secondary education, youth, medical research, health services, cultural programs.
Types of support: General purposes.
Limitations: Giving primarily in OR. No grants to individuals, or for endowment funds.
Application information: Application form not required.
Initial approach: Letter
Copies of proposal: 1
Deadline(s): None
Board meeting date(s): Mar., June, Sept., and Dec.
Write: Samuel C. Wheeler, Pres.
Officers and Directors:* Samuel C. Wheeler,* Pres.; Charles B. Wheeler,* V.P.; John C. Wheeler,* V.P.; Edward T. Wheeler,* Secy.; Thomas K. Wheeler,* Treas.
Number of staff: 1 part-time professional.
EIN: 930553801

PENNSYLVANIA

2665
Air Products and Chemicals, Inc.
Corporate Giving Program
c/o Corp. Philanthropy
7201 Hamilton Blvd.
Allentown 18195-1501   (215) 481-8079

Financial data (yr. ended 09/30/90): Total giving, $2,600,000, including $2,200,000 for grants and $400,000 for employee matching gifts.
Purpose and activities: Supports education, health, welfare, community investment, civic improvement, culture and the arts.
Fields of interest: Community development, drug abuse, education, health, welfare, civic affairs, cultural programs, arts.
Types of support: Capital campaigns, employee matching gifts, operating budgets, matching funds, special projects.
Limitations: Giving primarily in headquarters city and major operating areas.
Publications: Informational brochure.
Application information: Application form not required.
  Initial approach: Letter and proposal
  Copies of proposal: 1
  Deadline(s): None
  Board meeting date(s): Monthly
  Final notification: Within 3 months
  Write: Charlotte Walker, Contribs. Officer
Number of staff: 1 full-time professional.

2666
The Air Products Foundation ▼
7201 Hamilton Blvd.
Allentown 18195-1501   (215) 481-8079

Incorporated in 1979 in PA.
Donor(s): Air Products and Chemicals, Inc.
Foundation type: Company-sponsored
Financial data (yr. ended 09/30/90): Assets, $3,091,452 (M); gifts received, $1,000,000; expenditures, $1,337,354; qualifying distributions, $1,332,123, including $1,331,825 for 413 grants (high: $150,000; low: $100; average: $500-$5,000).
Purpose and activities: Support for the areas of higher and other education, including programs for minorities, health associations, drug abuse prevention, welfare, community investment, housing for low income families, and culture and the arts, including the fine arts.
Fields of interest: Cultural programs, arts, fine arts, education, higher education, educational associations, education—minorities, health, health associations, drug abuse, welfare, child welfare, housing, community development, community funds, public policy.
Types of support: Operating budgets, continuing support, annual campaigns, seed money, emergency funds, building funds, equipment, special projects, capital campaigns, renovation projects, general purposes.
Limitations: Giving primarily in areas where major company operations exist throughout the

U.S. No support for sectarian religious purposes, political or veterans' organizations, labor groups, national capital campaigns of health organizations, hospital capital campaigns or operating expenses, elementary or secondary schools, or organizations receiving support from the United Way. No grants to individuals; no loans.
Publications: Informational brochure (including application guidelines).
Application information: Application form not required.
  Initial approach: Proposal
  Copies of proposal: 1
  Deadline(s): None
  Board meeting date(s): Monthly
  Final notification: 3 months
  Write: Charlotte Walker, Contribs. Officer
Officers and Trustees:* D.T. Shire,* Chair.; C.P. Powell, Vice-Chair.; J.H. Agger, Secy.; D.H. Kelly, Treas.; P.L. Thibaut Brian, R.M. Davis, R.F. Dee, Walter F. Light, Harold A. Wagner.
Number of staff: None.
EIN: 232130928
Recent health grants:
2666-1 Easter Seal Society of Lehigh Valley, Bethlehem, PA, $30,000. For Money Walks capital fund. 1990.

2667
Alco Standard Foundation
P.O. Box 834
Valley Forge 19482-0834   (215) 296-8000

Established in 1974 in PA.
Donor(s): Alco Standard Corp.
Foundation type: Company-sponsored
Financial data (yr. ended 12/31/91): Assets, $3,788,371 (M); expenditures, $393,967; qualifying distributions, $376,355, including $252,693 for 219 grants (high: $23,538; low: $9) and $123,662 for 555 employee matching gifts.
Purpose and activities: Emphasis on community funds, education, including an employee matching gift program, hospitals, health, youth, and cultural programs.
Fields of interest: Community funds, education, health, youth, cultural programs, hospitals.
Types of support: Employee matching gifts, matching funds.
Limitations: Giving primarily in areas of company operations. No grants to individuals.
Application information: Contributes only to pre-selected organizations. Applications not accepted.
  Board meeting date(s): 2nd Tuesday in Feb.
Officers and Directors:* Ray B. Mundt,* Pres.; William F. Drake, Jr.,* V.P.; Hugh G. Moulton, Secy.; O. Gordon Brewer, Jr., Treas.
EIN: 237378726

2668
Alcoa Foundation ▼
1501 Alcoa Bldg.
Pittsburgh 15219-1850   (412) 553-2348

Trust established in 1952 in PA; incorporated in 1964.
Donor(s): Aluminum Co. of America.
Foundation type: Company-sponsored

Financial data (yr. ended 12/31/90): Assets, $234,637,554 (M); expenditures, $13,602,935; qualifying distributions, $12,569,665, including $10,276,465 for 1,424 grants (high: $300,000; low: $125; average: $5,000-$25,000), $448,000 for 224 grants to individuals, $1,330,200 for 2,912 employee matching gifts, $257,500 for 1 foundation-administered program and $257,500 for loans.
Purpose and activities: Grants chiefly for education, especially higher education, arts and cultural programs, health and welfare organizations, hospitals, civic and community development, and youth organizations.
Fields of interest: Education, higher education, educational associations, cultural programs, arts, health associations, hospitals, welfare, community development, civic affairs, youth.
Types of support: Annual campaigns, building funds, conferences and seminars, continuing support, emergency funds, employee matching gifts, equipment, fellowships, matching funds, operating budgets, research, scholarship funds, seed money, employee-related scholarships, capital campaigns, general purposes, renovation projects, special projects.
Limitations: Giving primarily in areas of company operations, including: Davenport, IA; Knoxville, TN; Massena, NY; Pittsburgh, PA; Evansville, IN; Cleveland, OH; and Rockdale, TX. No support for sectarian or religious organizations, political purposes, or elementary or secondary schools. No grants to individuals (except for employee-related scholarships), or for endowment funds, tickets, souvenir programs, advertising, golf outings, trips, tours, or student exchange programs.
Publications: Annual report, informational brochure (including application guidelines).
Application information: Application form not required.
  Initial approach: Proposal
  Copies of proposal: 1
  Deadline(s): None
  Board meeting date(s): Monthly
  Final notification: 1 to 4 months
  Write: F. Worth Hobbs, Pres.
Officers and Directors:* F. Worth Hobbs,* Pres.; Kathleen W. Buechel, V.P.; Kathleen R. Burgan, Secy.-Treas.; Ernest J. Edwards, Richard L. Fischer, Vincent R. Scorsone, Robert F. Slagle, Donald R. Whitlow.
Corporate Trustee: Mellon Bank, N.A.
Number of staff: 3 full-time professional; 1 part-time professional; 3 full-time support.
EIN: 251128857
Recent health grants:
2668-1 Alice Hyde Hospital Association Foundation, Malone, NJ, $15,000. 1990.
2668-2 Allegheny Valley Hospital, Natrona Heights, PA, $25,000. 1990.
2668-3 American British Cowdray Hospital Foundation, Dallas, TX, $30,000. 1990.
2668-4 Associacao de Pais e Amigos dos Excepcionais, Pocos de Caldas, Brazil, $15,000. 1990.
2668-5 Bellefaire Residential Treatment Center for Children, Shaker Heights, OH, $10,000. 1990.
2668-6 Childrens Hospital of Pittsburgh, Pittsburgh, PA, $40,000. 1990.
2668-7 Cleveland Clinic Foundation, Cleveland, OH, $10,000. 1990.

2668-8 Easter Seal Society for Crippled Children and Adults of Allegheny County, Pittsburgh, PA, $25,000. 1990.

2668-9 Gateway Rehabilitation Center, Aliquippa, PA, $60,000. 1990.

2668-10 Good Samaritan Hospital, Lebanon, PA, $13,633. 1990.

2668-11 Harmarville Foundation, Harmarville Rehabilitation Center, Pittsburgh, PA, $45,000. 1990.

2668-12 Health and Welfare Planning Association, Pittsburgh, PA, $10,000. 1990.

2668-13 Jupiter Medical Center, Jupiter, FL, $15,000. 1990.

2668-14 Magee-Womens Health Foundation, Pittsburgh, PA, $30,000. 1990.

2668-15 Memorial Sloan-Kettering Cancer Center, NYC, NY, $40,000. 1990.

2668-16 Mount Carmel Hospital Foundation, Colville, WA, $25,000. 1990.

2668-17 National Fund for Medical Education, Boston, MA, $10,000. 1990.

2668-18 Occupational Physicians Scholarship Fund, Arlington Heights, IL, $25,000. 1990.

2668-19 Parent and Child Guidance Center, Pittsburgh, PA, $25,000. 1990.

2668-20 Persad Center, Pittsburgh, PA, $10,000. 1990.

2668-21 Planned Parenthood of Western Pennsylvania, Pittsburgh, PA, $10,000. 1990.

2668-22 Population Crisis Committee, DC, $22,000. 1990.

2668-23 Rehabilitation Center, Evansville, IN, $10,000. 1990.

2668-24 Rehabilitation Center and Workshop, New Kensington, PA, $10,000. 1990.

2668-25 Rock Island County Council on Addictions, East Moline, IL, $10,000. 1990.

2668-26 Saint Francis Health Foundation, Pittsburgh, PA, $41,000. 1990.

2668-27 Scott and White Memorial Hospital, Temple, TX, $15,000. 1990.

2668-28 Thompson Cancer Survival Center, Knoxville, TN, $25,000. 1990.

2668-29 University of Pittsburgh, Pittsburgh Cancer Institute, Pittsburgh, PA, $50,000. 1990.

2668-30 Wagner Institute, Whittier, CA, $10,000. 1990.

2668-31 West Glamorgan Health Authority, Wales, $38,000. 1990.

2668-32 Western Pennsylvania Hospital, Pittsburgh, PA, $30,000. 1990.

2669
Allegheny Ludlum Corporate Giving Program
1000 Six PPG Pl.
Pittsburgh 15222-5479   (412) 394-2836

Financial data (yr. ended 12/31/90): Total giving, $401,857, including $355,282 for 152 grants (high: $76,000; low: $50; average: $50-$1,000) and $46,575 for 85 employee matching gifts.
Purpose and activities: Support for civic affairs, community development, cultural programs, social services, Jewish welfare, urban affairs, youth, women, and general charitable giving.
Fields of interest: Arts, civic affairs, community development, cultural programs, disadvantaged, fine arts, general charitable giving, health, health associations, Jewish giving, music, hospitals,

performing arts, rehabilitation, safety, social services, urban affairs, women, youth.
Types of support: Annual campaigns, continuing support, employee-related scholarships.
Limitations: Giving primarily in operating locations in CT, IN, NY, OK and PA. No grants to individuals.
Application information: Application form not required.
  Initial approach: By mail to headquarters
  Copies of proposal: 1
  Deadline(s): None
  Write: Jon D. Walton, Chair., Contribs. Comm.
Number of staff: None.

2670
Allegheny Ludlum Foundation
1000 Six PPG Place
Pittsburgh 15222-5479   (412) 394-2836

Established in 1981 in PA.
Donor(s): Allegheny Ludlum Corp.
Foundation type: Company-sponsored
Financial data (yr. ended 12/31/91): Assets, $3,050,280 (M); gifts received, $1,000,000; expenditures, $1,172,253; qualifying distributions, $1,161,364, including $1,161,364 for 132 grants (high: $346,792; low: $200; average: $1,000-$10,000).
Purpose and activities: Giving primarily for community funds, youth agencies, and hospitals and medical research; some support for higher and other education, cultural programs, including the fine and performing arts, and social services benefiting the aged, the disabled, minorities, and women.
Fields of interest: Community funds, community development, youth, child welfare, hospitals, medical research, handicapped, nursing, rehabilitation, higher education, secondary education, libraries, arts, fine arts, performing arts, museums, social services, aged, women, minorities.
Types of support: Annual campaigns, building funds, capital campaigns, continuing support, emergency funds, publications, employee-related scholarships, scholarship funds, special projects.
Limitations: Giving primarily in PA, IN, CT, NY, and OK. No support for private foundations. No grants to individuals.
Application information: Application form not required.
  Initial approach: Letter
  Copies of proposal: 1
  Deadline(s): None
  Write: Jon D. Walton, Chair. Contribs. Comm.
Trustees: J.L. Murdy, R.P. Simmons, Jon D. Walton, Pittsburgh National Bank.
Number of staff: None.
EIN: 256228755

2671
Harriett Ames Charitable Trust ▼
c/o St. Davids Ctr.
150 Radnor Chester Rd., A-200
St. Davids 19087   (215) 341-9270

Trust established in 1952 in NY.
Donor(s): Harriett Ames.‡
Foundation type: Independent

Financial data (yr. ended 12/31/91): Assets, $11,236,018 (M); expenditures, $940,440; qualifying distributions, $929,444, including $897,500 for 32 grants (high: $150,000; low: $2,500; average: $2,500-$20,000).
Purpose and activities: Grants to educational and charitable organizations, with emphasis on medical research, education, health associations, cultural organizations, and Jewish welfare.
Fields of interest: Medical research, health associations, education, Jewish welfare, cultural programs.
Types of support: General purposes.
Limitations: Giving primarily in the New York, NY, metropolitan area. No grants to individuals.
Application information: Applications not accepted.
  Board meeting date(s): Varies
  Write: Leanne M. Workman
Trustee: Walter H. Annenberg.
Number of staff: 11 shared staff
EIN: 236286757

2672
AMETEK Foundation, Inc.
Station Sq. Two
Paoli 19301   (215) 647-2121

Incorporated in 1960 in NY.
Donor(s): AMETEK, Inc.
Foundation type: Company-sponsored
Financial data (yr. ended 12/31/90): Assets, $3,798,288 (M); gifts received, $650,000; expenditures, $946,103; qualifying distributions, $926,680, including $926,680 for 120 grants (high: $100,000; low: $500; average: $1,000-$25,000).
Fields of interest: Community funds, hospitals, hospitals—building funds, medical research, cancer, higher education, education—building funds, education—minorities, elementary education, history, welfare, human rights, Jewish giving, arts.
Types of support: Annual campaigns, building funds, research, employee-related scholarships, scholarship funds, technical assistance, matching funds, general purposes, exchange programs, equipment, endowment funds.
Limitations: No grants to individuals, or for matching funds (except for the United Way); no loans.
Application information: Application form not required.
  Initial approach: Letter
  Copies of proposal: 1
  Deadline(s): Submit proposal preferably in Feb. or Sept.; deadlines Feb. 28 and Sept. 30
  Board meeting date(s): Apr. and Nov.
  Final notification: 2 weeks after board meets
  Write: Robert W. Yannarell, Asst. Secy.-Treas.
Officers and Directors:* John H. Lux,* Pres.; Walter Blankley, V.P.; Bernard E. Brandes,* Secy.-Treas.; Wallace E. Cowan, Helmut N. Friedlaender, Anthony A. Sirna III.
Number of staff: None.
EIN: 136095939

2673
AMP Foundation

c/o Dauphin Deposit Bank & Trust Co.
P.O. Box 2961
Harrisburg 17105-2961   (717) 564-0100
Application address: c/o AMP, Inc., Eisenhower
Blvd., Harrisburg, PA 17108

Established in 1977 in PA.
Donor(s): AMP, Inc.
Foundation type: Company-sponsored
Financial data (yr. ended 12/31/91): Assets,
$13,437,976 (M); expenditures, $804,723;
qualifying distributions, $778,006, including
$777,549 for 357 grants (high: $110,500; low:
$50; average: $5,000-$15,000).
Fields of interest: Hospitals, youth, higher
education, community funds, social services.
Limitations: Giving primarily in PA, with some
emphasis on the Harrisburg and Carlisle areas.
No grants to individuals.
Application information:
Initial approach: Proposal
Deadline(s): Submit proposal preferably in
Nov.; no set deadline
Board meeting date(s): Jan. and July
Final notification: 4 to 6 weeks after Jan.
meeting
Write: Merrill A. Yohe, Esq.
Trustee: Dauphin Deposit Bank & Trust Co.
Number of staff: 2 part-time professional; 1
part-time support.
EIN: 232022928

2674
Bessie F. Anathan Foundation

Oliver Bldg.
535 Smithfield St.
Pittsburgh 15222-2304   (412) 391-1270

Established in 1957 in PA.
Foundation type: Independent
Financial data (yr. ended 12/31/91): Assets,
$2,716,216 (M); expenditures, $80,004;
qualifying distributions, $76,973, including
$76,000 for 13 grants (high: $45,000; low: $500).
Purpose and activities: Giving primarily for a
hospital; support also for the arts and social
services.
Fields of interest: Hospitals, arts, social services.
Limitations: Giving primarily in PA. No grants to
individuals.
Application information: Application form not
required.
Deadline(s): None
Write: Alan G. Lehman, Trustee
Trustees: Alan G. Lehman, Jane A. Lehman, Joel
Spear, Jr., Carol S. Williams.
EIN: 256028686

2675
The Annenberg Foundation ▼

St. Davids Ctr.
150 Radnor-Chester Rd., Suite A-200
St. Davids 19087

Established in 1989 in PA.
Donor(s): Walter H. Annenberg.
Foundation type: Independent
Financial data (yr. ended 06/30/91): Assets,
$1,302,778,581 (M); gifts received, $495,256;

expenditures, $70,166,115; qualifying
distributions, $63,500,719, including
$54,551,660 for 171 grants (high: $9,020,000;
low: $250; average: $25,000-$250,000).
Purpose and activities: Supports efforts to
advance the public well-being through improved
communication, and encourages the
development of more effective ways to share
ideas and knowledge. Support primarily for early
childhood and K-12 education. Some support for
cultural programs and health.
Fields of interest: Education—early childhood,
elementary education, secondary education,
cultural programs.
Types of support: Seed money, special projects.
Limitations: No grants to individuals, or for basic
research, capital construction, or general
operating expenses.
Publications: Application guidelines.
Application information:
Initial approach: Letter
Copies of proposal: 1
Board meeting date(s): Apr. and Nov.
Final notification: Within 6 months
Write: Dr. Mary Ann Meyers, Pres.
Officers and Trustees:* Walter H. Annenberg,*
Chair.; Leonore A. Annenberg,* Vice-Chair.; Mary
Ann Meyers, Pres. and Secy.; William J. Heinrich,
Jr.,* V.P.; Donald Mullen, Treas.; Daniel Kelly,
Gen. Counsel; Wallis Annenberg, Charles
Weingarten, Gregory Weingarten, Lauren
Weingarten.
Number of staff: 3 full-time professional; 3
full-time support.
EIN: 236257083
Recent health grants:
2675-1 Bryn Mawr Hospital, Bryn Mawr, PA,
$50,100. 1991.
2675-2 Dermatology Foundation, Evanston, IL,
$50,000. 1991.
2675-3 Devereux Foundation, Devon, PA,
$166,667. 1991.
2675-4 Eisenhower Medical Research and
Education Center, Rancho Mirage, CA,
$400,000. 1991.
2675-5 Eisenhower Medical Research and
Education Center, Rancho Mirage, CA,
$125,000. 1991.
2675-6 Eisenhower Medical Research and
Education Center, Rancho Mirage, CA,
$125,000. 1991.
2675-7 Eisenhower Memorial Hospital at
Eisenhower Medical Center, Rancho Mirage,
CA, $500,000. 1991.
2675-8 Linus Pauling Institute of Science and
Medicine, Palo Alto, CA, $150,000. 1991.
2675-9 Meharry Medical College, Nashville, TN,
$50,000. 1991.
2675-10 Mount Sinai Hospital and Medical
Center, NYC, NY, $1,100,000. 1991.
2675-11 Stratford Friends School, Havertown,
PA, $12,000. 1991.
2675-12 Western Community Drug
Rehabilitation Foundation, Los Angeles, CA,
$10,000. 1991.

2676
The Annenberg Fund, Inc. ▼

St. Davids Ctr.
150 Radnor Chester Rd., Suite A-200
St. Davids 19087   (215) 341-9270

Incorporated in 1951 in DE.
Donor(s): Walter H. Annenberg.
Foundation type: Independent
Financial data (yr. ended 12/31/90): Assets,
$22,152,848 (M); expenditures, $2,575,717;
qualifying distributions, $2,547,651, including
$2,510,682 for 138 grants (high: $1,000,000;
low: $100; average: $100-$100,000).
Purpose and activities: Emphasis on higher
education, health and medical research,
including medical education, cultural programs,
and community services.
Fields of interest: Education, higher education,
medical education, medical research, medical
sciences, cultural programs, social services.
Types of support: Research, building funds,
general purposes.
Limitations: Giving primarily in PA, CA, and NY.
No grants to individuals.
Application information: Applications not
accepted.
Board meeting date(s): Varies
Write: Donald Mullen, Treas.
Officers and Directors:* Walter H. Annenberg,*
Chair.; Leonore A. Annenberg,* Vice-Chair.; Mary
Ann Meyers, Pres. and Secy.; William J. Henrich,
Jr.,* V.P.; Donald Mullen, Treas.; Wallis
Annenberg, Gregory Weingarten.
Number of staff: None.
EIN: 236286756
Recent health grants:
2676-1 Eisenhower Medical Research and
Education Center, Rancho Mirage, CA,
$400,000. 1990.
2676-2 Eisenhower Medical Research and
Education Center, Rancho Mirage, CA,
$250,000. 1990.

2677
The Arcadia Foundation ▼

105 East Logan St.
Norristown 19401   (215) 275-8460

Incorporated in 1964 in PA.
Donor(s): Edith C. Steinbright, Marilyn Lee
Steinbright.
Foundation type: Independent
Financial data (yr. ended 09/30/91): Assets,
$36,116,295 (M); gifts received, $3,222;
expenditures, $1,935,857; qualifying
distributions, $1,923,240, including $1,923,240
for 208 grants (high: $50,000; low: $350;
average: $500-$20,000).
Purpose and activities: Emphasis on hospitals and
hospital building funds, health agencies and
services, nursing, and hospices, early childhood,
adult and higher education, libraries, child
development and welfare agencies, youth
organizations, and social service and general
welfare agencies, including care of the
handicapped, aged, and hungry; support also for
family services, the environment and
conservation, wildlife and animal welfare,
religious organizations, historical preservation,
and music organizations.
Fields of interest: Hospitals, health, higher
education, libraries, child welfare, handicapped,
aged, family services, environment,
religion—Christian.
Types of support: Operating budgets, annual
campaigns, continuing support, emergency funds,
building funds, equipment, endowment funds,

research, special projects, scholarship funds, capital campaigns, general purposes, renovation projects.
Limitations: Giving limited to PA. Generally, no support for cultural programs. No grants to individuals, or for deficit financing, land acquisition, fellowships, demonstration projects, publications, or conferences; no loans.
Publications: Application guidelines.
Application information: Application form not required.
  Initial approach: Telephone, letter, or proposal (not exceeding 2 pages)
  Copies of proposal: 1
  Deadline(s): Submit proposal only between July 1 and Aug. 15; deadline Aug. 15
  Board meeting date(s): Sept. and Nov.
  Final notification: 3 months
  Write: Marilyn Lee Steinbright, Pres.
Officers and Directors:* Marilyn Lee Steinbright,* Pres.; Tanya Hashorva,* V.P.; David P. Sandler,* Secy.; Harvey S.S. Miller,* Treas.; Edward L. Jones, Jr., Kathleen Shellington, Edith C. Steinbright.
Number of staff: None.
EIN: 236399772
Recent health grants:
2677-1 Alzheimers Disease and Related Disorders Association, Philadelphia, PA, $10,000. 1991.
2677-2 American Heart Association, Philadelphia, PA, $10,000. 1991.
2677-3 Arthritis Foundation, Philadelphia, PA, $11,000. 1991.
2677-4 Bryn Mawr Rehabilitation Hospital, Malvern, PA, $10,000. 1991.
2677-5 Community Health Affiliates, Ardmore, PA, $10,000. 1991.
2677-6 Devereux Foundation, Devon, PA, $15,000. 1991.
2677-7 Grand View Hospital, Sellersville, PA, $10,000. 1991.
2677-8 Hayes Manor, Philadelphia, PA, $10,000. 1991.
2677-9 Lancaster AIDS Project, Lancaster, PA, $10,000. 1991.
2677-10 Lancaster Cleft Palate Clinic, Lancaster, PA, $10,000. 1991.
2677-11 Make-A-Wish Foundation of Philadelphia, Philadelphia, PA, $10,000. 1991.
2677-12 Montgomery Health Foundation, Norristown, PA, $12,000. 1991.
2677-13 North Penn Hospital, Lansdale, PA, $10,000. 1991.
2677-14 Paoli Memorial Hospital, Paoli, PA, $20,000. 1991.
2677-15 Scleroderma Association of Delaware Valley, Narbeth, PA, $10,000. 1991.
2677-16 United Cerebral Palsy of Lehigh Valley, Bethlehem, PA, $15,000. 1991.
2677-17 Visiting Nurse Association of Greater Philadelphia, Philadelphia, PA, $15,500. 1991.
2677-18 Warrington Community Ambulance Corps, Warrington, PA, $10,000. 1991.

2678
The Arronson Foundation
1101 Market St.
Philadelphia 19107   (215) 238-1700

Established in 1957 in DE.
Donor(s): Gertrude Arronson.‡
Foundation type: Independent

Financial data (yr. ended 10/31/91): Assets, $6,796,838 (M); expenditures, $633,887; qualifying distributions, $633,887, including $622,614 for 57 grants (high: $100,000; low: $100).
Purpose and activities: Emphasis on Jewish organizations and education, particularly higher education; support also for the performing arts and other cultural programs, hospitals and hospices, nursing and medical research, women's issues, and family planning.
Fields of interest: Jewish giving, Israel, education, higher education, cultural programs, hospitals, hospices, medical research, women, family planning.
Types of support: Annual campaigns, endowment funds, scholarship funds, seed money.
Limitations: Giving primarily in Philadelphia, PA.
Application information: Application form required.
  Initial approach: Letter
  Copies of proposal: 1
  Deadline(s): None
  Write: Harold E. Kohn, Pres.
Officers: Harold E. Kohn, Pres. and Treas.; Edith Kohn, V.P. and Secy.; Joseph C. Kohn, V.P.
Number of staff: None.
EIN: 236259604

2679
Asplundh Foundation
708 Blair Mill Rd.
Willow Grove 19090   (215) 784-4200

Incorporated in 1953 in PA.
Donor(s): Carl Hj. Asplundh,‡ Lester Asplundh.
Foundation type: Independent
Financial data (yr. ended 12/31/91): Assets, $5,368,728 (M); gifts received, $100,500; expenditures, $261,456; qualifying distributions, $256,583, including $256,583 for 75 grants (high: $120,000; low: $40).
Purpose and activities: Giving primarily for Protestant church support; some support also for health care, historic preservation societies, and other cultural programs.
Fields of interest: Protestant giving, health, historic preservation, cultural programs.
Limitations: Giving primarily in PA. No grants to individuals.
Application information:
  Initial approach: Letter
  Deadline(s): None
  Write: E. Boyd Asplundh
Officer and Directors:* Edward K. Asplundh,* Pres.; Barr E. Asplundh, Robert H. Asplundh.
EIN: 236297246

2680
Barra Foundation, Inc. ▼
8200 Flourtown Ave., Suite 12
Wyndmoor 19118   (215) 233-5115

Incorporated in 1963 in DE.
Donor(s): Robert L. McNeil, Jr.
Foundation type: Independent
Financial data (yr. ended 12/31/91): Assets, $28,415,504 (M); expenditures, $2,024,528; qualifying distributions, $1,848,122, including $1,741,397 for 244 grants (high: $250,000; low: $500; average: $1,000-$10,000).

Purpose and activities: Giving for the advancement and diffusion of knowledge and its effective application to human needs in certain fields, particularly in Eighteenth Century American art and material culture. Projects must be pilot studies or enterprises requiring foresight, not supported by other agencies or individuals; publication or studies required.
Fields of interest: Arts, education, health, social services.
Types of support: Matching funds, special projects.
Limitations: Giving primarily in the Philadelphia, PA, area. No grants to individuals, or for annual or capital campaigns, building or endowment funds, operating budgets, deficit drives, scholarships, fellowships, or ongoing programs; no loans.
Publications: Program policy statement.
Application information: Application form required.
  Initial approach: Letter
  Copies of proposal: 3
  Deadline(s): None
  Board meeting date(s): Dec. and as appropriate
  Final notification: 3 to 6 months
  Write: Robert L. McNeil, Jr., Pres.
Officers and Directors:* Robert L. McNeil, Jr.,* Pres. and Treas.; William T. Tredennick,* V.P.; Frank R. Donahue, Jr.,* Secy.; Herman R. Hutchinson, E. Marshall Nichols, Jr.
Number of staff: 1 part-time support.
EIN: 236277885

2681
Helen D. Groome Beatty Trust
c/o Mellon Bank (East), N.A.
P.O. Box 7236
Philadelphia 19101-7236   (215) 553-3208

Trust established in 1951 in PA.
Donor(s): Helen D. Groome Beatty.‡
Foundation type: Independent
Financial data (yr. ended 09/30/91): Assets, $6,322,770 (M); gifts received, $2,105; expenditures, $339,540; qualifying distributions, $334,247, including $315,250 for 119 grants (high: $20,000; low: $800).
Purpose and activities: To provide capital support for charitable and educational institutions, with emphasis on higher education, hospitals, and cultural programs.
Fields of interest: Higher education, hospitals, cultural programs.
Types of support: Building funds, renovation projects, capital campaigns.
Limitations: Giving primarily in the Philadelphia, PA, metropolitan area. No grants to individuals, or for endowment funds or operating budgets.
Publications: Application guidelines.
Application information:
  Initial approach: Proposal
  Copies of proposal: 1
  Deadline(s): Apr. 15
  Board meeting date(s): May 15 and Nov. 15
  Write: Patricia M. Kling, Trust Officer, Mellon Bank (East), N.A.
Trustee: Mellon Bank (East), N.A.
EIN: 236224798

2682
Bell Telephone Company of Pennsylvania Giving Program

One Pkwy., 9th FL-A
Philadelphia 19102   (215) 466-2257

Financial data (yr. ended 12/31/90): Total giving, $4,000,000, including $3,830,000 for grants and $170,000 for employee matching gifts.
Purpose and activities: Emphasis on education, particularly telecommunications programs in colleges and universities in Pennsylvania. Support also for business, engineering, science, and economic education. The company also runs a matching gifts program for education. Support for health and human services, primarily through United Way, with limited funding for youth organizations, hospitals, family services, and health organizations. Limited support also for the arts, primarily museums, libraries, and community arts.
Fields of interest: Education, higher education, health, welfare, civic affairs, cultural programs, arts, historic preservation, libraries, museums, business education, youth.
Types of support: General purposes, capital campaigns, special projects, employee matching gifts.
Limitations: Giving primarily in operating territory, Harrisburg, Philadelphia, and Pittsburgh, PA. No support for political, fraternal, religious, and veterans' organizations. No grants to individuals.
Application information: Application form not required.
  Initial approach: Letter and proposal on organization's letterhead, along with IRS form indicating nonprofit, 501(c)(3) status
  Copies of proposal: 1
  Deadline(s): None
  Board meeting date(s): Jan. of each year
  Final notification: 2 weeks
  Write: Charles D. Fulton, Corp. Contribs. Mgr.
Number of staff: 7

2683
Claude Worthington Benedum Foundation ▼

1400 Benedum-Trees Bldg.
Pittsburgh 15222   (412) 288-0360

Incorporated in 1944 in PA.
Donor(s): Michael Late Benedum,‡ Sarah N. Benedum.‡
Foundation type: Independent
Financial data (yr. ended 12/31/91): Assets, $195,020,105 (M); expenditures, $9,795,481; qualifying distributions, $8,817,070, including $7,978,262 for grants (average: $20,000-$50,000).
Purpose and activities: Grants are made primarily to WV organizations in the areas of education, health and human services, community and economic development, and the arts. Local initiatives and partnerships are encouraged. Grants in Pittsburgh are generally limited to university-based projects that address regional issues and support for the creation of the new cultural district, including the Benedum Center for the Performing Arts.
Fields of interest: Education, elementary education, secondary education, higher education, health, health services, social services, child welfare, community development, arts.
Types of support: Matching funds, consulting services, building funds, operating budgets, technical assistance, special projects, program-related investments, seed money, capital campaigns, conferences and seminars, research.
Limitations: Giving limited to WV and southwestern PA. No support for national health and welfare campaigns, medical research, or religious activities. No grants to individuals.
Publications: Application guidelines, multi-year report.
Application information: Application form not required.
  Initial approach: Letter or telephone
  Copies of proposal: 1
  Deadline(s): None
  Board meeting date(s): Mar., June, Sept., and Dec.
  Final notification: Up to 6 months
  Write: Paul R. Jenkins, Pres.
Officers and Trustees:* Paul G. Benedum, Jr.,* Chair.; Paul R. Jenkins,* Pres.; David L. Wagner, V.P. and Treas.; Elizabeth Pusateri, Secy.; G. Nicholas Beckwith, Henry A. Bergstrom, Robert E. Maxwell, L. Newton Thomas, Jr.
Number of staff: 5 full-time professional; 1 part-time professional; 3 full-time support.
EIN: 251086799
Recent health grants:
2683-1 Alderson-Broaddus College, Philippi, WV, $750,000. For development of Master's Degree program for physician assistants and purchase of related equipment, computers and library acquisitions. 1991.
2683-2 Boone Memorial Hospital, Madison, WV, $155,000. For establishment of Boone Memorial Wellness Initiative, community-based, health promotion/disease prevention program serving all ages. 1991.
2683-3 Boys and Girls Club of Huntington, Huntington, WV, $162,928. To initiate Smart Moves, youth leadership development and health promotion program in Charleston, Huntington, Martinsburg and Parkersburg. 1991.
2683-4 Clay County Health Department, Clay, WV, $10,000. For program costs of Parent Aide program for Clay and Braxton counties. 1991.
2683-5 Daymark, Charleston, WV, $60,000. For renovation of facilities to house Patchwork program, crisis intervention program for youth. 1991.
2683-6 Intercounty Health, Martinsburg, WV, $50,000. For renovation and equipment costs to Shenandoah Community Health Center to expand primary care, particularly maternal and child health services. 1991.
2683-7 Lincoln County Primary Care Center, Hamlin, WV, $50,000. For start-up funds to establish, in conjunction with Southern West Virginia Community College, associate degree in nursing program in Hamlin, WV. 1991.
2683-8 Lions Sight Conservation Foundation, Charleston, WV, $60,000. To purchase mobile clinic for statewide vision screening program. 1991.
2683-9 Minnie Hamilton Health Care Center, Grantsville, WV, $50,000. For renovations to facility to enable addition of physician and certified nurse midwife to address serious shortage of obstetrical providers. 1991.
2683-10 National Council of Jewish Women, Charleston, WV, $86,203. To initiate and carry out policy study on how AFDC program can more effectively be used to address health care and economic development issues in West Virginia. 1991.
2683-11 New River Health Association, Scarbro, WV, $109,553. For establishment of birthing center for low-income women. 1991.
2683-12 New River Health Association, Scarbro, WV, $38,450. To expand Maternal/Infant Health Outreach Worker Program, providing education and other support services in prenatal and early childhood care to low-income women and infants. 1991.
2683-13 Saint George Medical Clinic, Saint George, WV, $50,000. To construct expanded facility to house existing rural primary care center and to enable addition of certified nurse midwife services. 1991.
2683-14 West Virginia Commission for the Hearing Impaired, Charleston, WV, $50,000. For development of statewide interpreter training program. 1991.
2683-15 West Virginia Department of Health and Human Resources, Charleston, WV, $55,300. For Perinatal Task Force project coordinator salary. 1991.
2683-16 West Virginia Department of Health and Human Resources, Charleston, WV, $40,000. To study incidence of substance abuse among West Virginia mothers. 1991.
2683-17 West Virginia Department of Health and Human Resources, Charleston, WV, $33,000. To develop Pilot Transportation Program to provide Medicaid-eligible women and infants with transportation stipends to obtain health care, social and enhanced educational and medical services. 1991.
2683-18 West Virginia Department of Health and Human Resources, Charleston, WV, $30,000. To evaluate Adolescent Pregnancy Prevention Program. 1991.
2683-19 West Virginia Health Care Planning Commission, Charleston, WV, $160,000. For community educational aspect of Commission's goals by building awareness of health and health care delivery problems in West Virginia and encouraging community-based involvement in potential solutions. 1991.
2683-20 West Virginia Hospital Research and Education Foundation, Charleston, WV, $10,000. To develop concurrent program for children and adolescents in conjunction with statewide conference of hearing impaired, their families, and education and health providers. 1991.
2683-21 West Virginia University Foundation, Morgantown, WV, $44,250. For statewide rural health conference and development of videotape portraying successful, community-based rural health projects in West Virginia to be used for community education and as tool to recruit health professions manpower. 1991.
2683-22 Wheeling Hospital, Wheeling, WV, $100,000. For continued program development and evaluation of Well Prepared Progam, health promotion/disease prevention program for children and their families. 1991.

2683-23 Wirt County Health Services Association, Elizabeth, WV, $30,000. For renovation of rural primary care center to enable it to serve as clinical education site for medical education. 1991.

2684
Allen H. & Selma W. Berkman Charitable Trust
1500 Oliver Bldg.
Pittsburgh 15232 (412) 355-8640
Application address: 5000 Fifth Ave., Apt. 207, Pittsburgh, PA 15232

Established in 1972 in PA.
Donor(s): Allen H. Berkman, Selma W. Berkman.
Foundation type: Independent
Financial data (yr. ended 10/31/91): Assets, $1,843,270 (M); gifts received, $583,273; expenditures, $574,034; qualifying distributions, $573,404, including $573,334 for 18 grants (high: $250,000; low: $500; average: $1,500).
Purpose and activities: Giving primarily for higher and other educational institutions, and social services, including programs for the aged, child development, and the handicapped; support also for health and hospitals, the performing arts, historic preservation, and other cultural programs, and community and urban development.
Fields of interest: Higher education, education, social services, aged, family planning, handicapped, health associations, cultural programs, community development, urban development, intercultural relations, international relief.
Types of support: Special projects, annual campaigns, building funds, capital campaigns, continuing support, emergency funds, endowment funds, fellowships, general purposes, operating budgets, scholarship funds, technical assistance, research, program-related investments.
Limitations: Giving primarily in the Pittsburgh, PA, area. No grants to individuals.
Publications: Annual report, 990-PF.
Application information: Application form not required.
   Initial approach: Letter
   Copies of proposal: 1
   Deadline(s): Sept. 1
   Write: Allen H. Berkman, Trustee
Trustees: Barbara B. Ackerman, Allen H. Berkman, Richard L. Berkman, Selma W. Berkman, Susan B. Rahm.
Number of staff: None.
EIN: 256144060

2685
Archie W. and Grace Berry Foundation
1030 Continental Dr., Box 1551
King of Prussia 19406-0951

Established in 1988 in PA.
Donor(s): A.W. Berry, Sr.
Foundation type: Independent
Financial data (yr. ended 06/30/91): Assets, $3,044,693 (M); gifts received, $1,000,000; expenditures, $217,512; qualifying distributions, $213,761, including $213,000 for 14 grants (high: $50,000; low: $2,000).

Purpose and activities: Giving primarily to a hospital and a medical foundation; some support for an archdiocese and other Catholic organizations.
Fields of interest: Hospitals, medical research, Catholic giving.
Limitations: Giving primarily in PA. No grants to individuals.
Application information: Contributes only to pre-selected organizations. Applications not accepted.
Trustees: A.W. Berry, Sr., A.W. Berry, Jr., Robert B. Berry, Louis F. Riuituso.
EIN: 236951678

2686
Theodora B. Betz Foundation
1617 John F. Kennedy Blvd.
Philadelphia 19103 (215) 568-5450

Established in 1989 in PA.
Foundation type: Independent
Financial data (yr. ended 04/30/91): Assets, $10,523,636 (M); expenditures, $523,014; qualifying distributions, $454,769, including $417,000 for 4 grants (high: $150,000; low: $67,000).
Fields of interest: Hospitals, cancer.
Limitations: Giving primarily in Philadelphia, PA.
Application information: Application form not required.
   Deadline(s): None
   Write: Jane Bishop, Trustee
Trustees: Jane Bishop.
EIN: 236965187

2687
The Raymond and Elizabeth Bloch Foundation
830 Frick Bldg.
Pittsburgh 15219

Established in 1989 in PA.
Donor(s): Raymond Bloch.‡
Foundation type: Independent
Financial data (yr. ended 12/31/90): Assets, $4,099,310 (M); gifts received, $23; expenditures, $245,793; qualifying distributions, $200,000, including $200,000 for 9 grants (high: $80,000; low: $4,000).
Purpose and activities: Giving primarily to organizations concerned with issues of world peace through international law and arms control; some support also for medical research to relieve pain caused primarily by headaches.
Fields of interest: Arms control, peace, medical sciences, international law.
Limitations: Giving primarily in Pittsburgh, PA, and Washington, DC.
Application information: Application form not required.
   Deadline(s): None
   Write: Bernard L. Bloch, Pres. and C.E.O.
Officer: Bernard L. Bloch, Pres. and C.E.O.

2688
Boiron Research Foundation, Inc.
1208 Amosland Rd.
Norwood 19074-0000

Established in 1987 in MD.
Donor(s): Boiron, Inc.
Foundation type: Company-sponsored
Financial data (yr. ended 12/31/91): Assets, $511,798 (M); gifts received, $35,983; expenditures, $133,522; qualifying distributions, $212,092, including $5,000 for 1 grant, $83,500 for 2 grants to individuals (high: $60,000; low: $23,500) and $123,592 for foundation-administered programs.
Purpose and activities: Support limited to homeopathic medical research.
Fields of interest: Medical research.
Types of support: Grants to individuals.
Application information:
   Initial approach: Proposal
   Deadline(s): Sept. 30
   Write: Thierry Montfort, V.P.
Officers: Christian Brown, Pres.; Jean Boiron, V.P.; Thierry Montfort, V.P.
Trustee: Townsend W. Hoopes.
EIN: 521268329

2689
Caroline Alexander Buck Foundation
1600 Market St., Suite 3600
Philadelphia 19103 (215) 751-2080

Established in 1960.
Donor(s): Caroline A. Churchman.‡
Foundation type: Independent
Financial data (yr. ended 12/31/91): Assets, $3,267,480 (M); gifts received, $2,000,000; expenditures, $138,606; qualifying distributions, $122,980, including $113,000 for 49 grants (high: $25,000; low: $1,000).
Purpose and activities: Giving primarily for social services, including programs aiding minorities, the aged, women, children, and the disabled; support also for higher and other education, and hospitals and health associations, including research on cancer and heart disease.
Fields of interest: Social services, minorities, aged, women, child welfare, higher education, elementary education, hospitals, health, museums.
Types of support: In-kind gifts.
Limitations: Giving primarily in PA, with emphasis on the Philadelphia greater metropolitan area. No grants to individuals.
Application information: Application form required.
   Initial approach: Letter
   Deadline(s): May and Nov.
   Board meeting date(s): Spring and fall
   Write: Bruce A. Rosenfield, Dir.
Directors: Deborah P. Churchman, John Alexander Churchman, W. Morgan Churchman III, George Connell, Gordon Kerns, Bruce A. Rosenfield, J. Pennington Straus.
Number of staff: None.
EIN: 236257115

2690
Buncher Family Foundation
5600 Forward Ave.
Pittsburgh 15217 (412) 422-9900

Established in 1974 in PA.
Donor(s): The Buncher Co., Jack G. Buncher, Buncher Management Agency, Buncher Rail Car Service Co.
Foundation type: Independent
Financial data (yr. ended 11/30/91): Assets, $859,410 (M); gifts received, $1,418,092; expenditures, $841,175; qualifying distributions, $840,235, including $839,019 for 80 grants (high: $200,000; low: $20).
Fields of interest: Jewish giving, Jewish welfare, medical research, civic affairs.
Limitations: Giving primarily in PA, with emphasis on Pittsburgh. No grants to individuals.
Application information:
    Initial approach: Letter
    Deadline(s): None
    Write: Bernita B. Balter, Secy.-Treas.
Officers: Joanne K. Buncher, Pres.; Bernita B. Balter, Secy.-Treas.
EIN: 237366998

2691
William B. Butz Memorial Fund
(Formerly William A. & Alice Butz Memorial Fund)
R.D. 2, Box 120
Oley 19547   (215) 987-9416

Established in 1954 in PA.
Donor(s): William B. Butz.‡
Foundation type: Independent
Financial data (yr. ended 12/31/91): Assets, $3,407,377 (M); expenditures, $120,035; qualifying distributions, $109,270, including $87,000 for 7 grants (high: $30,000; low: $2,000).
Purpose and activities: Giving primarily for cultural programs, including the fine and performing arts; support for medical centers and conservation.
Fields of interest: Cultural programs, arts, hospitals, medical research, conservation.
Types of support: Research.
Limitations: No grants to individuals.
Publications: 990-PF.
Application information: Contributes only to pre-selected organizations. Applications not accepted.
    Write: Ilse Morning, Secy.
Trustees: William L. Massey III, Ingrid Morning, Ober Morning II.
Number of staff: None.
EIN: 236259515

2692
The Byers Foundation
290 Bristol Rd.
Chalfont 18914

Established in 1986 in PA.
Donor(s): Byers Choice Ltd.
Foundation type: Independent
Financial data (yr. ended 12/31/91): Assets, $1,368,455 (M); gifts received, $710,000; expenditures, $906,766; qualifying distributions, $906,766, including $900,556 for 34 grants (high: $225,000; low: $250).
Fields of interest: Historic preservation, arts, higher education, hospitals, social services, youth.
Types of support: Building funds, renovation projects, equipment.

Limitations: Giving primarily in PA.
Application information: Applications not accepted.
    Board meeting date(s): Biannually
    Write: Bob Byers, Secy.-Treas.
Officers and Directors:* Joyce F. Byers, Pres.; Robert L. Byers, Secy.-Treas.
Number of staff: None.
EIN: 232406657

2693
Alpin J. and Alpin W. Cameron Memorial Fund
c/o CoreStates Bank, N.A.
P.O. Box 7618/FCI-3-10-30
Philadelphia 19101-7618   (215) 786-7624

Trust established in 1957 in PA.
Donor(s): Alpin W. Cameron,‡ Alpin J. Cameron,‡ Emma D. Dwier.‡
Foundation type: Independent
Financial data (yr. ended 09/30/91): Assets, $2,919,969 (M); gifts received, $103,083; expenditures, $167,544; qualifying distributions, $153,507, including $143,250 for 47 grants (high: $7,500; low: $500).
Purpose and activities: Primary areas of interest include education and cultural programs.
Fields of interest: Cultural programs, education, higher education, hospitals, youth, social services, environment.
Limitations: Giving primarily in the Philadelphia, PA, area.
Application information: Application form not required.
    Initial approach: Letter
    Board meeting date(s): Monthly
    Write: Paul L. Keperling, Trust Administrator, CoreStates Bank, N.A.
Trustee: CoreStates Bank, N.A.
Number of staff: None.
EIN: 236213225

2694
Charles Talbot Campbell Foundation
c/o Integra Trust Co.
300 Fourth Ave.
Pittsburgh 15278-2121   (412) 644-8332

Trust established in 1975 in PA.
Donor(s): Charles Talbot Campbell.‡
Foundation type: Independent
Financial data (yr. ended 12/31/92): Assets, $3,785,000 (M); expenditures, $282,700; qualifying distributions, $275,000, including $275,000 for 15 grants (high: $50,000; low: $5,000; average: $10,000).
Purpose and activities: Emphasis on hospitals and ophthalmological research, agencies for the handicapped, and music.
Fields of interest: Hospitals, ophthalmology, handicapped, music.
Types of support: General purposes, research.
Limitations: Giving primarily in western PA. No support for community funds, including United Way. No grants to individuals; no loans.
Application information: Application form not required.
    Copies of proposal: 1
    Board meeting date(s): Varies
    Final notification: Affirmative replies only

Write: William M. Schmidt, V.P.
Trustee: Integra Trust Co., N.A.
Number of staff: None.
EIN: 251287221

2695
Julius H. Caplan Charity Foundation, Inc.
14th & Cumberland Sts.
P.O. Box 208
Lebanon 17042   (717) 272-4665

Incorporated in 1944 in NY.
Donor(s): Hyman S. Caplan,‡ Keystone Weaving Mills, Inc.
Foundation type: Independent
Financial data (yr. ended 12/31/90): Assets, $4,796,080 (M); expenditures, $170,227; qualifying distributions, $137,757, including $131,344 for 36 grants (high: $50,000; low: $25).
Fields of interest: Jewish welfare, higher education, hospitals.
Limitations: Giving primarily in PA. No grants to individuals.
Application information: Application form not required.
    Deadline(s): None
    Write: Eli Caplan, Dir.
Directors: Eli Caplan, Helen Caplan, Perry Caplan.
EIN: 136067379

2696
E. Rhodes & Leona B. Carpenter Foundation ▼
c/o Joseph A. O'Connor, Jr., Morgan, Lewis & Bockius
2000 One Logan Sq.
Philadelphia 19103   (215) 963-5212
Application address: P.O. Box 58880, Philadelphia, PA 19102-8880; Tel.: (215) 963-5212

Established in 1975 in VA.
Donor(s): E. Rhodes Carpenter,‡ Leona B. Carpenter.‡
Foundation type: Independent
Financial data (yr. ended 12/31/90): Assets, $88,192,198 (M); expenditures, $4,806,928; qualifying distributions, $3,887,639, including $3,733,804 for 78 grants (high: $500,000; low: $772; average: $5,000-$50,000).
Purpose and activities: Main areas of interest include the arts, including the performing arts and museums; education, including graduate theological education; and health.
Fields of interest: Arts, health, education, theological education, museums.
Limitations: Giving primarily in areas east of the Mississippi River. No support for local church congregations or parishes, private secondary education, or large public charities. No grants to individuals.
Application information:
    Initial approach: Letter
    Deadline(s): None
Officers: Ann B. Day, Pres.; Paul B. Day, Jr., V.P. and Secy.-Treas.
Director: M.H. Reinhart.
EIN: 510155772
Recent health grants:

2696-1 Catawba Memorial Hospital, Hickory, NC, $106,000. For purchase of pool for Rehabilitation Center. 1990.

2696-2 Cen-Tex Alcoholic Rehabilitation Center, Temple, TX, $12,450. To purchase pick-up truck. 1990.

2696-3 Cross-Over Ministry, Richmond, VA, $10,000. For modernization of medical building. 1990.

2696-4 Johns Hopkins University, School of Nursing, Baltimore, MD, $500,000. For endowed scholarship fund. 1990.

2696-5 Johns Hopkins University, School of Nursing, Baltimore, MD, $311,000. For building renovation for lecture hall, lounge and practice lab. 1990.

2696-6 Mary Baldwin College, Staunton, VA, $174,600. For health care and ministry program. 1990.

2696-7 Scott and White Memorial Hospital, Temple, TX, $70,000. For Cell Imaging Laboratory. 1990.

2696-8 Valdese General Hospital, Valdese, NC, $100,000. For modernization and renovation program. 1990.

2697
Carpenter Technology Corporation Foundation

101 West Bern St.
Reading 19601   (215) 371-2214

Incorporated in 1953 in NJ; re-incorporated in 1981 in DE as the Carpenter Technology Corporation Foundation.
Donor(s): Carpenter Technology Corp.
Foundation type: Company-sponsored
Financial data (yr. ended 09/30/91): Assets, $419,487 (M); expenditures, $375,414; qualifying distributions, $374,991, including $294,959 for 92 grants (high: $105,000; low: $100) and $80,032 for 273 employee matching gifts.
Purpose and activities: Support for community funds, health and welfare, culture and the arts, civic and public affairs, and higher education, including scholarship funds, an employee matching gift program, and employee-related scholarships through National Merit Scholarship Corp.
Fields of interest: Community funds, hospitals, health, welfare, social services, youth, cultural programs, arts, civic affairs, public affairs, higher education.
Types of support: Employee matching gifts, scholarship funds, building funds, general purposes, fellowships, research, special projects, employee-related scholarships.
Limitations: Giving primarily in areas of company operations, especially the Reading, PA, area. No grants to individuals.
Publications: Program policy statement, application guidelines.
Application information: Application form required for scholarships.
  Initial approach: Letter
  Deadline(s): Dec. of preceding academic year for scholarships
  Board meeting date(s): Semiannually
  Write: W.J. Pendleton, V.P.
Officers and Directors:* Paul R. Roedel,* Chair.; Robert W. Cardy, Pres.; William J. Pendleton, V.P.

and Secy.; John A. Schuler, Treas.; Howard O. Beaver, Jr., Thomas Beaver, Jr., William E.C. Dearden, C. McCollister Evarts, M.D., James A. Flick, Jr., Carl R. Garr, Arthur E. Humphrey, Joseph L. Jones, Edward W. Kay, Frederick C. Langenberg, Marlin M. Miller, Jr., S. James Spitz, Jr., Harry W. Walker II.
EIN: 232191214

2698
Louis N. Cassett Foundation

One Penn Ctr., Suite 335
1617 JFK Blvd.
Philadelphia 19103

Trust established in 1946 in PA.
Donor(s): Louis N. Cassett.‡
Foundation type: Independent
Financial data (yr. ended 12/31/91): Assets, $6,396,854 (M); expenditures, $442,374; qualifying distributions, $373,998, including $366,800 for 161 grants (high: $25,000; low: $200; average: $3,000).
Purpose and activities: Giving primarily for social service and youth agencies, higher education, community development, hospitals, medical research, and health agencies, including aid to the handicapped; some support also for cultural programs and Protestant churches.
Fields of interest: Social services, youth, higher education, community development, hospitals, medical research, health services, handicapped, cultural programs, arts, Protestant giving.
Types of support: Annual campaigns, building funds.
Limitations: Giving primarily in the northeastern U.S. No grants to individuals, or for endowment funds.
Application information: Application form not required.
  Initial approach: Proposal
  Copies of proposal: 1
  Deadline(s): None
  Board meeting date(s): As required
  Write: Malcolm B. Jacobson, Trustee
Trustees: Albert J. Elias, Carol Gerstley Hofheimer, Malcolm B. Jacobson.
Number of staff: None.
EIN: 236274038

2699
Julius and Ray Charlestein Foundation, Inc.

1710 Romano Dr.
Norristown 19401   (215) 277-3800

Established in 1963.
Donor(s): Premier Dental Products Co., Premier Medical Co.
Foundation type: Company-sponsored
Financial data (yr. ended 06/30/91): Assets, $3,318,018 (M); gifts received, $300,000; expenditures, $365,974; qualifying distributions, $317,989, including $317,955 for grants.
Purpose and activities: Giving primarily to Jewish associations, including welfare funds; support also for education and health organizations.
Fields of interest: Jewish welfare, health, education, Jewish giving.
Limitations: Giving primarily in the Philadelphia, PA, area. No grants to individuals.

Application information: Contributes only to pre-selected organizations. Applications not accepted.
  Write: Morton Charlestein, Pres.
Officers: Morton Charlestein, Pres.; Jerrold A. Frezel, V.P.; Gary Charlestein, Secy.-Treas.
Number of staff: None.
EIN: 232310090

2700
CIGNA Corporate Giving Program

One Liberty Place
1650 Market St.
Philadelphia 19192-1540   (215) 761-6055
Application address in CT: James N. Mason, Jr., Dir., Civic Affairs, CIGNA Corp., W-A, 900 Cottage Grove Ave., Bloomfield, CT 06002

Financial data (yr. ended 12/31/90): Total giving, $1,025,000, including $657,000 for grants and $368,000 for in-kind gifts.
Purpose and activities: CIGNA sometimes complements Foundation programs with direct contributions to community relations projects, including support for civic and cultural events, in-kind donations of materials and services, and memberships in civic organizations. CIGNA recognizes the efforts of employee volunteers who work in educational and social service organizations through the Grants-for-Givers program, Volunteer of the Month Award, and the Annual Community Service Award.
Fields of interest: Education, health, civic affairs, community development, cultural programs, arts, housing, economics.
Types of support: In-kind gifts, donated equipment.
Limitations: Giving primarily in the greater Philadelphia, PA, area, and the greater Hartford, CT, area. No support for sectarian religious activities, or research and treatment of specific diseases, political organizations or campaigns, lobbying groups, or organizations primarily funded by United Way. No grants to individuals, or for capital campaigns, endowment drives, improvements or expansions, or hospital campaigns.
Application information: Contributions are handled by the foundation staff and by various departments depending on the type of grant request. Application form not required.
  Initial approach: Letter; Send to headquarters
  Copies of proposal: 1
  Deadline(s): None
  Write: Arnold W. Wright, Jr., Exec. Dir., CIGNA Fdn.

2701
CIGNA Foundation ▼

One Liberty Place
1650 Market St.
Philadelphia 19192-1540   (215) 761-6055
Organizations in the greater Hartford area, write to: James N. Mason, Dir., Civic Affairs, CIGNA Foundation, W-A, Hartford, CT 06152-5001

Incorporated in 1962 in PA; merged with Connecticut General Contributions and Civic Affairs Department in 1982.
Donor(s): CIGNA Corp.
Foundation type: Company-sponsored

Financial data (yr. ended 12/31/91): Assets, $2,728,183 (M); gifts received, $8,195,096; expenditures, $8,292,811; qualifying distributions, $8,131,463, including $6,705,836 for grants (high: $725,000; low: $100; average: $2,000-$100,000) and $1,425,627 for 3,138 employee matching gifts.

Purpose and activities: Support for a broad range of programs in education, health and human services, civic affairs, and the arts, with priority placed on public secondary education, higher education for minority students, programs which favorably influence CIGNA's business environment, community economic development, and culture and the arts. Special emphasis on increasing literacy, career education, and minority higher education, programs which contribute to an improved understanding of societal issues significant to business and economic development in Philadelphia, PA, and Hartford, CT.

Fields of interest: Education, education—early childhood, elementary education, education—minorities, business education, literacy, higher education, arts, cultural programs, social services, youth, women, civic affairs, health.

Types of support: Employee matching gifts, general purposes, annual campaigns, emergency funds, fellowships, matching funds, operating budgets, scholarship funds, employee-related scholarships, special projects.

Limitations: Giving primarily in Hartford, CT, and Philadelphia, PA; and to selected national organizations. No support for religious organizations for religious purposes, political organizations or campaigns, or disease-specific research or treatment organizations. No grants to individuals, or endowment drives, capital campaigns, organizations receiving major support through the United Way or other CIGNA-supported federated funding agencies, or hospital capital improvements and expansions.

Publications: Corporate giving report (including application guidelines), annual report, grants list.

Application information: In the greater Hartford area, direct requests to Bloomfield, CT, office; other requests go to Philadelphia, PA, office. Application form not required.

Initial approach: Letter of 1 or 2 pages
Copies of proposal: 1
Deadline(s): None
Board meeting date(s): Biennially
Final notification: 6 weeks
Write: Arnold W. Wright, Jr., Exec. Dir.

Officers: Barry F. Wiksten, Pres.; Arnold W. Wright, Jr., Exec. Dir.

Directors: Thomas J. Wagner, Chair.; Caleb L. Fowler, Donald M. Levinson, G. Robert O'Brien, James G. Stewart, George R. Trumbull.

Number of staff: 5 full-time professional; 3 full-time support.

EIN: 236261726

Recent health grants:

2701-1 Academy of Natural Sciences of Philadelphia, Philadelphia, PA, $60,000. For capital campaign, Biological Research Fund, World Health Project and general operations. 1990.

2701-2 American Fund for Dental Health, Chicago, IL, $10,000. For advancements of dentistry and improvements in oral health. 1990.

2701-3 American Red Cross, Bloodmobile Program, Hartford, CT, $10,000. For promotion and overhead for blood drives, enabling employees of CIGNA companies to donate blood. 1990.

2701-4 Community Health Services, Hartford, CT, $15,000. For special projects and equipment acquisition at neighborhood health clinic in Hartford, which provides medical care for indigent. 1990.

2701-5 Hartford Action Plan on Infant Health, Hartford, CT, $45,000. To support project to reduce incidence of infant mortality and low birthweight in Hartford's low-income neighborhoods. 1990.

2701-6 Hartford Hospital, Hartford, CT, $100,000. For multi-year grant supporting AIDS project and capital improvements. 1990.

2701-7 High Risk Counseling Project, Hartford, CT, $45,000. To enable special guidance counselor to work with high-risk students at Hartford Public High School. 1990.

2701-8 National Fund for Medical Education, Hartford, CT, $15,000. For medical education and research programs. 1990.

2701-9 National Health Policy Forum, DC, $10,000. For program on managed health care administered through George Washington University. 1990.

2701-10 University of Connecticut, Hartford, CT, $12,000. For Health Children Initiative. 1990.

2701-11 University of Pennsylvania, School of Dental Medicine, Philadelphia, PA, $10,000. 1990.

2702
Claneil Foundation, Inc.
630 West Germantown Pike, Suite 400
Plymouth Meeting 19462-1059

Incorporated in 1968 in DE.
Donor(s): Henry S. McNeil,‡ Langhorne B. Smith.
Foundation type: Independent
Financial data (yr. ended 12/31/90): Assets, $6,259,805 (M); expenditures, $419,019; qualifying distributions, $350,873, including $350,150 for 66 grants (high: $75,000; low: $350; average: $350-$75,000).
Fields of interest: Higher education, secondary education, cultural programs, fine arts, health services, social services, family planning, conservation, historic preservation.
Limitations: Giving primarily in PA. No grants to individuals.
Application information: Application form not required.

Initial approach: Proposal
Copies of proposal: 1
Deadline(s): Sept. 30
Board meeting date(s): Oct.
Final notification: Nov.
Write: Dr. Henry A. Jordan, Exec. Dir.

Officers and Directors:* Lois F. McNeil,* Pres.; Barbara M. Jordan,* V.P.; Warrin C. Meyers,* V.P.; George M. Brodhead,* Secy.; Langhorne B. Smith,* Treas.; Henry A. Jordan,* Exec. Dir.
EIN: 236445450

2703
G.H. Clapp Dec'd Charitable and Educational Trust
(Formerly The Anne L. and George H. Clapp Charitable and Educational Trust)
c/o Mellon Bank, N.A.
One Mellon Bank Ctr.
Pittsburgh 15230
Application address: c/o Mellon Bank, N.A., Three Mellon Bank Ctr., Pittsburgh, PA 15260; Tel.: (412) 234-7210

Donor(s): George H. Clapp.‡
Foundation type: Independent
Financial data (yr. ended 09/30/91): Assets, $13,029,955 (M); expenditures, $557,296; qualifying distributions, $508,922, including $486,000 for 42 grants (high: $30,500; low: $1,000).
Fields of interest: Education, secondary education, hospitals, health associations, social services, child welfare, youth, cultural programs, community funds.
Limitations: Giving primarily in the Pittsburgh, PA, area.
Application information:

Initial approach: Letter; application form provided after initial contact
Deadline(s): None
Write: Norbert Pail, V.P., Mellon Bank, N.A.
Trustees: William E. Collins, William A. Galbraith, Jr., Mellon Bank, N.A.
EIN: 256018976

2704
Charles S. & Mary Coen Family Foundation
1100 West Chestnut St.
Washington 15301

Established in 1959 in PA.
Donor(s): C.S. Coen,‡ Mary Coen,‡ Charles R. Coen, C.S. Coen Land Co.
Foundation type: Independent
Financial data (yr. ended 02/29/92): Assets, $5,698,807 (M); gifts received, $36,000; expenditures, $272,338; qualifying distributions, $266,994, including $264,125 for 78 grants (high: $50,000; low: $25).
Fields of interest: Higher education, health associations, hospitals, social services, aged.
Limitations: Giving primarily in PA. No grants to individuals.
Application information: Contributes only to pre-selected organizations. Applications not accepted.
Trustees: Earl Coen, Mona Thompson.
EIN: 256033877

2705
Ethel D. Colket Foundation
c/o Provident National Bank
1632 Chestnut St.
Philadelphia 19103

Established in 1964 in PA.
Foundation type: Independent
Financial data (yr. ended 08/31/91): Assets, $2,209,922 (M); expenditures, $71,255; qualifying distributions, $58,084, including

$58,000 for 13 grants (high: $12,500; low: $1,000).
Fields of interest: Higher education, museums, hospitals, religion.
Types of support: General purposes, building funds.
Limitations: Giving primarily in the Delaware Valley, PA, area.
Application information:
Initial approach: Letter
Deadline(s): None
Trustees: Ruth Colket, Tristram Colket, Jr., Provident National Bank.
EIN: 236292917

2706
Colonial Penn Group Corporate Giving Program
Colonial Penn Plaza
11 Penn Center Plaza
Philadelphia 19181   (215) 988-8000

Financial data (yr. ended 12/31/90): Total giving, $400,000 for grants (high: $190,000; low: $250; average: $1,000-$1,500).
Purpose and activities: Support for 1) Health-emphasis on research programs designed to improve the health care of the elderly; also considers support for programs that work toward the reduction of health care costs through either preventive medicine or other types of programs; 2) Education-emphasis on higher education, with particular emphasis upon those institutions located in primary operating areas. Also focus attention and contributions upon gerontological programs within higher education. Additional support through employee matching gifts to education; 3) Welfare-support for organizations that aid underprivileged citizens in the community and that help to promote general social improvement; particular attention to those requests that do not duplicate, overlap or neutralize the efforts of the community-wide endeavors to which Colonial Penn has already contributed; in addition, support to new community organizations which do not qualify for participation in community-federated drives; 4) Human Rights-striving for the elimination of discrimination based on stereotypes; contributions in this area are made to organizations that address themselves to the inequities and discriminations against the elderly, blacks, women and others; 5) Civic-support for nonprofit organizations and causes that work together to help solve the more pressing needs of communities; 6) Cultural-in order to help provide a wholesome environment in which to live, work, and conduct business, corporate giving in this area is focused on community organizations and institutions, outside of the area of higher education as such, in the visual and performing arts, the humanities, and the physical and natural sciences. It is Colonial Penn's policy that exceptions to the guidelines as outlined above should not be made unless extreme exigencies accompany the requests.
Fields of interest: Health, welfare, education, human rights, cultural programs, civic affairs.
Types of support: Matching funds, general purposes.
Limitations: Giving primarily in major operating areas.

Application information: The administration of Colonial Penn Group's corporate giving program is the responsibility of the Corporate Contributions Committee, which consists of six persons, is appointed by the Chair., and is chaired by the Sr. V.P. of Corporate Affairs. Funds have been committed for 1991.
Initial approach: Proposal
Write: Maryann Haynes, V.P. and Chair., Contribs. Comm.
Administrators: Maryann Haynes, V.P. and Chair., Contribs. Comm.; Michelle Vitanza, Sr. Exec. Secy.

2707
Connelly Foundation ▼
One Tower Bridge, Suite 1450
West Conshohocken 19428   (215) 834-3222

Incorporated·in 1955 in PA.
Donor(s): John F. Connelly,‡ Josephine C. Connelly.
Foundation type: Independent
Financial data (yr. ended 12/31/90): Assets, $219,422,011 (M); expenditures, $10,162,142; qualifying distributions, $10,016,225, including $9,870,309 for 216 grants (high: $1,147,500; low: $100; average: $1,000-$10,000).
Purpose and activities: Giving to higher education; Christian religious institutions, including churches, schools and colleges, and welfare programs; hospitals; and social services.
Fields of interest: Higher education, elementary education, secondary education, religion—Christian, Catholic giving, Protestant giving, Catholic welfare, religious welfare, religious schools, education, hospitals, AIDS, social services, disadvantaged, handicapped, aged, youth, homeless, women, community development, cultural programs.
Types of support: Scholarship funds, capital campaigns, endowment funds, operating budgets, renovation projects, special projects, emergency funds.
Limitations: Giving primarily in the Philadelphia, PA, and Delaware Valley area. No grants to individuals, or for research; no loans.
Publications: 990-PF, application guidelines.
Application information: Application form not required.
Initial approach: Letter
Copies of proposal: 1
Deadline(s): Submit proposal preferably early in the year
Board meeting date(s): Jan., Mar., May, July, Sept., Nov., and Dec.
Final notification: 3 to 6 months after receiving proposal
Write: Victoria K. Flaville, V.P.
Officers and Trustees:* Josephine C. Connelly,* Chair.; Josephine C. Mandeville,* Pres. and C.E.O.; Victoria K. Flaville, V.P. and Secy.; Chester C. Hilinski,* V.P. and General Counsel; Emily L. Riley,* V.P.; Reda Amiry, Treas.; William Avery, Lewis W. Bluemle, Jr., Christine C. Connelly, Danielle Connelly, John F. Connelly, Jr., Thomas S. Connelly, Judith Delouvrier, Philippe Delouvrier, Owen A. Mandeville, Jr.
Number of staff: 5 full-time professional; 3 part-time support.
EIN: 236296825
Recent health grants:

2707-1 Eastern Mercy Health System, Philadelphia, PA, $10,000. 1990.
2707-2 Immaculate Mary Home, Philadelphia, PA, $28,750. For contribution made in form of stock. 1990.
2707-3 Mercy Catholic Medical Center, Darby, PA, $500,625. For contribution made in form of stock. 1990.
2707-4 National Foundation for Ileitis and Colitis, Philadelphia, PA, $10,000. 1990.
2707-5 Nazareth Hospital, Philadelphia, PA, $1,020,000. For contribution made in form of stock. 1990.
2707-6 Pennsylvania Hospital, Philadelphia, PA, $50,000. For neurological research. 1990.

2708
Consolidated Natural Gas Company Foundation ▼
c/o CNG Tower
625 Liberty Ave.
Pittsburgh 15222-3199   (412) 227-1185

Established about 1985 in PA.
Donor(s): Consolidated Natural Gas Co.
Foundation type: Company-sponsored
Financial data (yr. ended 12/31/90): Assets, $792,587 (M); expenditures, $3,521,221; qualifying distributions, $3,538,312, including $3,254,411 for 528 grants (high: $125,000; low: $250; average: $500-$100,000) and $231,994 for 1,017 employee matching gifts.
Purpose and activities: Support for health human services, community funds and development, education, and culture and the arts.
Fields of interest: Social services, community funds, community development, education, cultural programs, arts, health services.
Types of support: Employee matching gifts, operating budgets, matching funds, annual campaigns, building funds, capital campaigns, conferences and seminars, continuing support, equipment, general purposes, matching funds, operating budgets, renovation projects, special projects.
Limitations: Giving primarily in PA, OH, WV, NY, LA, VA, and areas where the company has business interests. No support for fraternal, political, or labor organizations, or organizations for strictly sectarian purposes. No grants to individuals, or for operating funds of United Way-supported organizations, fundraising activities, or courtesy advertising.
Publications: Informational brochure (including application guidelines).
Application information: Application form not required.
Initial approach: Letter
Copies of proposal: 1
Deadline(s): Sept. 1 for support renewal requests
Board meeting date(s): Varies
Write: Ray N. Ivey, V.P. and Exec. Dir.
Officers and Directors:* David E. Weatherwax,* Pres.; Ray N. Ivey,* V.P. and Exec. Dir.; S.M. Banda, Secy. and Mgr.; R.J. Bean, Jr., W.F. Fritsche, Jr., R.R. Gifford, D.P. Hunt, L.J. Timms, Jr., R.E. Wright.
Trustee: Mellon Bank, N.A.
Number of staff: 2 full-time professional; 1 full-time support.
EIN: 136077762

Recent health grants:

2708-1 Childrens Hospital, New Orleans, LA, $10,000. For operating support. 1990.

2708-2 Cleveland Clinic Foundation, Cleveland, OH, $16,500. For capital support. 1990.

2708-3 Cleveland Clinic Foundation, Cleveland, OH, $10,000. For operating support. 1990.

2708-4 Heather Hill, Corinne Dolan Alzheimer Center, Chardon, OH, $10,000. For operating support. 1990.

2708-5 Saint Lukes Hospital, Cleveland, OH, $10,000. For operating support. 1990.

2709
Consolidated Rail Contributions Program

(also known as Conrail)
6 Penn Center Plaza, Rm. 1820
Philadelphia 19103   (215) 977-4699

Financial data (yr. ended 12/31/90): Total giving, $1,161,000, including $234,000 for grants, $546,000 for employee matching gifts and $381,000 for in-kind gifts.

Purpose and activities: Support for civic and urban affairs, public policy, transportation, engineering, health, business and higher education, culture and the arts, community development, human services, economic revitalization, and minority programs.

Fields of interest: Business education, civic affairs, education, educational research, engineering, health, higher education, minorities, public policy, transportation, urban affairs, community development, cultural programs, arts.

Types of support: Annual campaigns, continuing support, employee matching gifts, general purposes, employee-related scholarships.

Limitations: Giving primarily in areas served by Conrail, which include IL, IN, MI, OH, PA, NY, MA, CT, NJ, WV, MD, DE, and Washington, DC. No support for religious or fraternal organizations, or political campaigns. No grants to individuals.

Application information: Application form not required.

> *Initial approach:* Letter to Contributions Committee Chairman
> *Copies of proposal:* 1
> *Deadline(s):* None
> *Board meeting date(s):* Monthly
> *Final notification:* Within two weeks of board meeting
> *Write:* Beth Maggio, Mrg. Contribs. Comm.

Administrators: Allen Schimmel, V.P., Admin. Services and Corp. Secy.; Beth Maggio, Mgr., Contribs. Comm.

Number of staff: 1 part-time professional; 1 part-time support.

2710
The Craig-Dalsimer Fund

Packard Bldg., 12th Fl.
Philadelphia 19102

Established in 1987 in PA.
Donor(s): Janet Craig Dalsimer.‡
Foundation type: Independent
Financial data (yr. ended 02/28/92): Assets, $2,572,475 (M); expenditures, $108,856; qualifying distributions, $96,607, including $87,154 for 1 grant.

Purpose and activities: Giving to a university for the study of adolescent medicine.

Fields of interest: Higher education, medical research.

Limitations: Giving primarily in Philadelphia, PA. No grants to individuals.

Application information: Application form not required.

> *Deadline(s):* None

Trustees: Anne Marie Chirco, Lida Freeman, David J. Kaufman.
EIN: 236875197

2711
E. R. Crawford Estate

Trust Fund "A", P.O. Box 487
McKeesport 15134   (412) 672-6670

Trust established in 1936 in PA.
Donor(s): E.R. Crawford.‡
Foundation type: Independent
Financial data (yr. ended 12/31/90): Assets, $5,674,802 (M); expenditures, $506,334; qualifying distributions, $490,239, including $437,050 for 99 grants (high: $50,000; low: $500) and $27,618 for 27 grants to individuals (high: $1,440; low: $288).

Purpose and activities: Giving for hospitals, higher education, Protestant church support, and community funds; scholarship aid to McKeesport Area High School and Duquesne High School seniors to attend the University of Pittsburgh or Pennsylvania State University, McKeesport Campus; grants to indigent individuals are limited to former employees of McKeesport Tin Plate Co. who meet income requirements.

Fields of interest: Hospitals, Protestant giving, community funds, higher education.

Types of support: Operating budgets, scholarship funds, grants to individuals.

Limitations: Giving primarily in PA, with emphasis on Allegheny County. No grants to individuals (except former employees of the McKeesport Tin Plate Co.).

Application information: Application form required for needy individuals.

> *Initial approach:* Proposal
> *Deadline(s):* None
> *Write:* Francis E. Neish, Jr., Trustee

Trustees: William O. Hunter, Francis E. Neish, Jr., George F. Young, Jr.
Number of staff: 4
EIN: 256031554

2712
The Crels Foundation

P.O. Box 275
New Holland 17557   (717) 354-7901

Trust established in 1953 in PA.
Donor(s): Edwin B. Nolt.‡
Foundation type: Independent
Financial data (yr. ended 12/31/91): Assets, $5,824,371 (M); expenditures, $226,404; qualifying distributions, $226,404, including $225,000 for 41 grants (high: $38,000; low: $1,000; average: $1,000-$38,000).

Purpose and activities: Support for hospitals, nursing homes, Mennonite-related religious associations, and parochial elementary education.

Fields of interest: Hospitals, aged, Protestant giving, denominational giving, education, elementary education, religious schools.

Types of support: General purposes, building funds, equipment, operating budgets.

Limitations: Giving primarily in the Lancaster County, PA, area. No grants to individuals, or for endowment funds, research programs, scholarships, fellowships, continuing support, annual campaigns, seed money, emergency funds, land acquisition, renovation projects, publications, conferences, matching gifts, or special projects; no loans.

Application information: Applications not encouraged. Application form not required.

> *Initial approach:* Letter
> *Copies of proposal:* 1
> *Deadline(s):* Sept. 15
> *Board meeting date(s):* Oct. and as required
> *Write:* George C. Delp, Chair.

Officers and Trustees:* George C. Delp,* Chair.; Clarence J. Nelson,* Secy.; Eugene N. Burkholder, Kenneth N. Burkholder, John H. Frey.
Number of staff: None.
EIN: 236243577

2713
Crown American Corporate Giving Program

Pasquerilla Plaza
Johnstown 15907   (814) 536-4441

Financial data (yr. ended 01/31/90): Total giving, $106,700 for 105 grants (high: $10,000; low: $10).

Purpose and activities: Supports higher, secondary, business, elementary, and adult education, arts, catholic giving, community development, fine arts, historic preservation, libraries, literacy, museums, recreation, and youth.

Fields of interest: Adult education, arts, business education, Catholic giving, community development, cultural programs, elementary education, fine arts, higher education, historic preservation, libraries, literacy, museums, music, performing arts, recreation, secondary education, youth, community funds, architecture, employment, crime and law enforcement, education—building funds, educational research, family services, hospitals—building funds, community funds, government, conservation, education, general charitable giving, Italy, public affairs, medical education, public policy, religion, theater.

Types of support: Capital campaigns, consulting services, general purposes, matching funds, scholarship funds, special projects, employee-related scholarships, donated equipment, building funds, donated land.

Limitations: Giving primarily in Johnstown, PA and other areas where Crown America Corp. has properties in PA, NY, NJ, KY, TN, WV, VA, NC, GA, MD, and IN.

Publications: Corporate report.

Application information: Executive Offices and Corporate Communications Department handle giving. Application form not required.

> *Initial approach:* Must be written request; Send requests to headquarters
> *Deadline(s):* None
> *Write:* Donna Gambol, V.P., Communs.

Number of staff: None.

2714
Cyclops Foundation
650 Washington Rd.
Pittsburgh 15228   (412) 571-6331

Trust established in 1953 in PA.
Donor(s): Cyclops Corp.
Foundation type: Company-sponsored
Financial data (yr. ended 12/31/90): Assets,
$288,903 (M); gifts received, $400,000;
expenditures, $319,766; qualifying distributions,
$319,766, including $292,684 for 57 grants
(high: $60,000; low: $500) and $26,695 for
employee matching gifts.
Fields of interest: Community funds, community
development, higher education, hospitals, health
services, cultural programs, arts, aged, child
welfare, environment.
Types of support: Annual campaigns, seed
money, building funds, equipment, land
acquisition, employee matching gifts, capital
campaigns, scholarship funds.
Limitations: Giving primarily in areas of company
operations in PA and OH. No grants to
individuals, or for endowment funds, research,
fellowships, challenge grants, special projects,
deficit financing, operating budgets, continuing
support, emergency funds, publications, or
conferences; no loans.
Application information: Application form not
required.
 Initial approach: Letter
 Copies of proposal: 1
 Deadline(s): None
 Final notification: 1 to 2 months
 Write: Ed Romanoff
Trustees: Joseph J. Nowak, James F. Will.
Number of staff: None.
EIN: 256067354

2715
William B. Dietrich Foundation
1811 Chestnut St., Suite 304
Philadelphia 19103   (215) 988-0050

Incorporated in 1936 in DE.
Donor(s): Daniel W. Dietrich Foundation, Inc.,
Henry D. Dietrich,‡ Dietrich American
Foundation.
Foundation type: Independent
Financial data (yr. ended 12/31/91): Assets,
$8,377,754 (M); gifts received, $375,350;
expenditures, $362,627; qualifying distributions,
$312,890, including $284,500 for 8 grants (high:
$150,000; low: $500; average: $15,000).
Fields of interest: Conservation, education, higher
education, secondary education, museums,
historic preservation, community funds, AIDS,
general charitable giving.
Types of support: Research, operating budgets,
special projects, building funds, capital
campaigns, matching funds.
Limitations: Giving primarily in PA. No grants to
individuals.
Application information: Application form not
required.
 Initial approach: Letter
 Copies of proposal: 1
 Board meeting date(s): Jan., Apr., July, and Oct.
 Write: William B. Dietrich, Pres.

Officers and Directors:* William B. Dietrich,*
Pres. and Treas.; Frank G. Cooper,* Secy.; Frederic
C. Barth.
Number of staff: 2 shared staff
EIN: 231515616

2716
Dolfinger-McMahon Foundation
c/o Duane, Morris & Heckscher
One Liberty Place
Philadelphia 19103-7396   (215) 979-1768

Trust established in 1957 in PA, and originally
comprised of four separate trusts: T/W of Henry
Dolfinger as modified by will of Mary McMahon;
1935 D/T of Henry Dolfinger as modified by will
of Caroline D. McMahon; Residuary T/W of
Caroline D. McMahon; Dolfinger-McMahon Trust
for Greater Philadelphia. In 1986 the 1935 D/T
of H. Dolfinger was merged with the residuary
T/W of C. McMahon.
Donor(s): Caroline D. McMahon,‡ Mary M.
McMahon.‡
Foundation type: Independent
Financial data (yr. ended 09/30/91): Assets,
$12,116,611 (M); expenditures, $665,201;
qualifying distributions, $506,722, including
$497,749 for 102 grants (high: $15,000; low:
$1,000).
Purpose and activities: Emphasis on
experimental, demonstration, or "seed money"
projects in race relations, aid to the handicapped,
higher and secondary education, social and
urban programs, church programs, and health
agencies. Since 1981, the foundation has given
increased consideration to true emergency
situations. Emergency funding will be rarely made
and, once made, will disqualify the agency from
receiving any additional funding for the
succeeding three years. Grants limited to $20,000
in any one year to a single project or program.
Fields of interest: Race relations, minorities,
handicapped, education, theological education,
literacy, higher education, secondary education,
social services, disadvantaged, welfare, urban
affairs, civic affairs, urban development,
community development, leadership
development, volunteerism, religion, religious
welfare, health, nutrition, AIDS.
Types of support: Operating budgets, seed
money, emergency funds, matching funds, special
projects, publications, conferences and seminars,
deficit financing, scholarship funds.
Limitations: Giving limited to the greater
Philadelphia, PA, area. No support for medical or
scientific research or for special interest advocacy
through legislative lobbying or solicitation of
government agencies. No grants to individuals, or
for endowment funds, physical facilities, ordinary
operating expenses, renovations or building
repairs, building funds, scholarships, or
fellowships.
Publications: Annual report (including application
guidelines), application guidelines.
Application information: See guidelines for
format required for requests. Application form not
required.
 Initial approach: Letter requesting guidelines,
  followed by proposal
 Copies of proposal: 2
 Deadline(s): Submit proposal preferably in Mar.
  or Sept.; must actually be received on or

before Apr. 1 or Oct. 1 (or the preceding
 Friday if the 1st falls on a weekend)
 Board meeting date(s): Spring, fall, and as
  required
 Final notification: 1 week to 10 days following
  semiannual meeting
 Write: Marlene Valcich, Exec. Secy.
Officer: Marlene Valcich, Exec. Secy.
Trustees: Martin A. Heckscher, Roland Morris.
Number of staff: None.
Recent health grants:
2716-1 Christ Church Hospital, Kearsley Home,
 Philadelphia, PA, $11,550. To fund land use
 survey for expansion of Kearsley/Christ Church
 Hospital's campus which currently offers 87
 rent-subsidized independent living apartments
 for older adults and 20 bed nursing home.
 1990.
2716-2 Eastern Mercy Health System,
 Philadelphia, PA, $11,000. For project entitled
 Salud y Misericordia which will send medical
 team from Philadelphia area to perform
 surgery and teaching at regional hospital in
 Piura, Peru. 1990.

2717
Drueding Foundation
c/o Mrs. James J. Stokes III
411 State Rd.
Gladwyne 19035

Established in 1986 in PA.
Foundation type: Independent
Financial data (yr. ended 06/30/91): Assets,
$4,580,194 (M); expenditures, $237,338;
qualifying distributions, $210,289, including
$205,000 for 1 grant.
Fields of interest: Health, homeless.
Limitations: Giving primarily in PA. No grants to
individuals.
Application information: Contributes only to
pre-selected organizations. Applications not
accepted.
Officers: Frank Drueding, Pres.; Bernard J.
Drueding, Jr., V.P.; Diana S. Gifford, Secy.; Patricia
Stokes, Treas.
EIN: 232418214

2718
John E. duPont Foundation
13 Paoli Court
Paoli 19301   (215) 296-9900

Established in 1988 in PA.
Donor(s): John E. duPont.
Foundation type: Independent
Financial data (yr. ended 12/31/90): Assets,
$223,217 (M); gifts received, $575,206;
expenditures, $472,756; qualifying distributions,
$470,000, including $470,000 for 6 grants (high:
$350,000; low: $10,000).
Purpose and activities: Giving primarily to
professional and amateur athletics and sports
organizations.
Fields of interest: Recreation, hospitals.
Limitations: Giving on a national basis, with
some emphasis on PA. No grants to individuals.
Application information:
 Initial approach: Proposal
 Deadline(s): None
 Write: Taras M. Wochok, Esq., Trustee

Trustees: John E. duPont, Taras M. Wochok.
EIN: 232499540

2719
Dynamet Foundation
195 Museum Rd.
Washington 15301   (412) 228-1000

Established in 1989 in PA.
Donor(s): Dynamet Inc.
Foundation type: Company-sponsored
Financial data (yr. ended 12/31/91): Assets,
$4,644,804 (M); gifts received, $2,000,000;
expenditures, $349,248; qualifying distributions,
$332,294, including $332,217 for 65 grants
(high: $250,000; low: $50).
Purpose and activities: Giving primarily for
higher education; support also for health
associations, medical research, and youth
programs.
Fields of interest: Higher education, health
associations, medical research, youth.
Types of support: Research, general purposes.
Limitations: Giving primarily in PA, with some
empahsis on Washington. No grants to
individuals.
Application information:
    Initial approach: Letter
    Deadline(s): None
    Write: Viola G. Taboni, Treas.
Officers and Trustees:* Peter C. Rossin,* Chair.;
Peter N. Stephans,* Pres.; J. Robert Van Kirk,*
Secy.; Viola G. Taboni,* Treas.; Ada E. Rossin,
Joan R. Stephans.
EIN: 256327217

2720
Eden Hall Foundation ▼
Pittsburgh Office and Research Park
5500 Corporate Dr., Suite 210
Pittsburgh 15237   (412) 364-6670

Established in 1984 in PA.
Donor(s): Eden Hall Farm.
Foundation type: Independent
Financial data (yr. ended 12/31/90): Assets,
$102,179,221 (M); expenditures, $5,022,219;
qualifying distributions, $4,967,125, including
$4,810,050 for 77 grants (high: $300,000; low:
$2,500; average: $25,000-$100,000).
Purpose and activities: Support for higher
education, the prevention and alleviation of
sickness and disease, the improvement of
conditions of the poor and needy, and the
advancement of good morals.
Fields of interest: Higher education, hospitals,
health services, social services, disadvantaged.
Types of support: Capital campaigns, scholarship
funds, endowment funds, research.
Limitations: Giving limited to western PA. No
support for private foundations. No grants to
individuals, or for operating budgets, deficit
financing, or general fundraising campaigns.
Publications: Application guidelines.
Application information: Application form not
required.
    Initial approach: Letter
    Board meeting date(s): Quarterly
    Write: Arthur H. Andersen, Secy.

Officers: Richard F. Herr, Chair.; George R. Shifler,
V.P. and Treas.; Arthur H. Andersen, Secy.; Ralph
D. McCracken, Gen. Mgr.
Number of staff: 2
EIN: 251384468
Recent health grants:
2720-1 Abraxas Foundation, Pittsburgh, PA,
$50,000. For rebuilding program. 1990.
2720-2 Allegheny Valley Hospital, Natrona
Heights, PA, $100,000. For facilities
improvement. 1990.
2720-3 American Cancer Society, Pittsburgh, PA,
$25,000. For assistance programs. 1990.
2720-4 Butler Memorial Hospital Foundation,
Butler, PA, $180,000. For renovation. 1990.
2720-5 Childrens Hospital of Pittsburgh,
Pittsburgh, PA, $100,000. For centennial
campaign for endowed chair. 1990.
2720-6 D.T. Watson Rehabilitation Hospital,
Sewickley, PA, $150,000. For expansion of
Center. 1990.
2720-7 Easter Seal Society for Crippled Children
and Adults of Allegheny County, Pittsburgh,
PA, $100,000. For renovation of dining area.
1990.
2720-8 Easter Seal Society of Butler County,
Butler, PA, $30,000. For elevator in new
facility. 1990.
2720-9 Gateway Rehabilitation Center,
Aliquippa, PA, $50,000. For new services and
to expand treatment capacity. 1990.
2720-10 Gibbs Rest Home, Pittsburgh, PA,
$12,400. For renovations. 1990.
2720-11 McGee-Womens Health Foundation,
Pittsburgh, PA, $100,000. To fund new
program. 1990.
2720-12 Medical Center of Beaver County,
Beaver, PA, $100,000. For construction. 1990.
2720-13 Mercy Hospital of Pittsburgh,
Pittsburgh, PA, $80,000. To purchase
computer/video tape. 1990.
2720-14 North Hills Passavant Hospital,
Pittsburgh, PA, $20,000. For equipment for
ophthalmic laser center. 1990.
2720-15 Ohio Valley General Hospital, McKees
Rocks, PA, $50,000. For educational
endowment fund. 1990.
2720-16 Rehabilitation Institute of Pittsburgh,
Pittsburgh, PA, $34,000. For building addition
program. 1990.
2720-17 Saint Clair Memorial Hospital
Foundation, Pittsburgh, PA, $50,000. For
geriatic services endowment fund. 1990.
2720-18 Spina Bifida Association of Western
Pennsylvania, Pittsburgh, PA, $20,000. For
construction and renovation project. 1990.
2720-19 Visiting Nurse Association of Allegheny
County, Pittsburgh, PA, $15,000. To purchase
computer and laser printer. 1990.
2720-20 Waynesburg College, Waynesburg, PA,
$50,000. For scholarships in nursing. 1990.
2720-21 Western Pennsylvania Hospital
Foundation, Pittsburgh, PA, $50,000. For
renovations. 1990.

2721
Elf Atochem North America Foundation ▼
(Formerly Atochem North America Foundation)
Pennwalt Bldg.
Three Benjamin Franklin Pkwy.
Philadelphia 19102   (215) 587-7000

Trust established in 1957 in PA.
Donor(s): Atochem North America.
Foundation type: Company-sponsored
Financial data (yr. ended 12/31/91): Assets,
$1,204,493 (M); gifts received, $780,000;
expenditures, $1,422,438; qualifying
distributions, $1,417,782, including $1,071,477
for grants (high: $82,290; low: $30; average:
$100-$1,000), $127,600 for grants to individuals
and $211,861 for employee matching gifts.
Purpose and activities: Grants primarily for
community funds; higher education, including
employee-related scholarships and matching gifts;
and cultural programs, including museums and
public broadcasting; support also for civic affairs,
and health and medicine.
Fields of interest: Community funds, education,
higher education, cultural programs, health,
media and communications, museums, hospitals,
civic affairs.
Types of support: Operating budgets, general
purposes, continuing support, annual campaigns,
seed money, emergency funds, deficit financing,
building funds, equipment, land acquisition,
matching funds, employee matching gifts,
employee-related scholarships, renovation
projects.
Limitations: Giving primarily in areas of company
operations, with some emphasis on the
Philadelphia, PA, area. No support for public
education; veterans', fraternal, or labor
organizations; or sectarian religious organizations.
No grants to individuals (except for
employee-related scholarships), or for
endowment funds, special projects, research,
publications, conferences, courtesy advertising, or
entertainment promotions; no loans.
Application information: Application form not
required.
    Initial approach: Proposal
    Copies of proposal: 1
    Deadline(s): None
    Board meeting date(s): Mar., June, Sept., and
    Dec.
    Final notification: 1 to 3 months
    Write: George L. Hagar, Exec. Secy.
Trustees: George Reath, Jr., Chair.; Anthony P.
Deluca, Seymour S. Preston III.
Number of staff: 1 part-time professional; 1
full-time support.
EIN: 236256818

2722
The Erie Community Foundation
502 G. Daniel Baldwin Bldg.
Erie 16501   (814) 454-0843

Established in 1935 in PA as Erie Endowment
Foundation; renamed in 1970.
Foundation type: Community
Financial data (yr. ended 12/31/91): Assets,
$25,352,486 (M); gifts received, $756,570;
expenditures, $1,365,574; qualifying
distributions, $1,113,979, including $1,113,979
for 237 grants (high: $100,000; low: $100;
average: $5,000-$10,000).
Fields of interest: Education, performing arts,
health services, social services, youth.
Types of support: Seed money, emergency funds,
building funds, equipment, matching funds,
annual campaigns, capital campaigns,
conferences and seminars.

Limitations: Giving limited to Erie County, PA. No grants to individuals (except for scholarships from restricted funds), or for deficit financing or land acquisition; no loans.
Publications: Annual report, newsletter.
Application information: Application form required.
  Initial approach: Letter or telephone
  Copies of proposal: 10
  Deadline(s): Submit proposal preferably in Feb., May, Aug., or Nov.; deadlines, 15th of the month prior to the board meetings
  Board meeting date(s): Mar., June, Sept., and Dec.
  Final notification: 4 to 6 weeks
  Write: Michael L. Batchelor, Exec. Dir.
Officers and Trustees:* Charles H. Bracken,* Chair.; Albert F. Duval,* Pres.; William F. Grant,* V.P.; Ray L. McGarvey,* Secy.-Treas.; David W. Doupe, M.D., John R. Falcone, Ann V. Greene, F. William Hirt, Edward P. Junker III.
Trustee Banks: First National Bank of Pennsylvania, Integra Financial Corp., Marine Bank, Mellon Bank, N.A.
Number of staff: 1 full-time professional; 1 full-time support.
EIN: 256032032
Recent health grants:
2722-1 Abraxas Foundation, Pittsburgh, PA, $20,000. For purchase and renovation of facility. 1990.
2722-2 AIDS Council of Erie, Erie, PA, $10,000. For Erie County HIV Outreach. 1990.
2722-3 Florence Crittenton Services, Erie, PA, $14,500. 1990.
2722-4 Gannondale School for Girls, Erie, PA, $13,300. For computers and training. 1990.
2722-5 Hamot Medical Center, Erie, PA, $10,100. 1990.
2722-6 Martin Luther King Center, Erie, PA, $10,000. For Bayfront NATO Dental Unit Project. 1990.
2722-7 Saint Marys Home of Erie, Erie, PA, $26,330. For Alzheimer Center. 1990.

2723
Maurice Falk Medical Fund
3315 Grant Bldg.
Pittsburgh 15219   (412) 261-2485

Incorporated in 1960 in PA.
Donor(s): Maurice and Laura Falk Foundation.
Foundation type: Independent
Financial data (yr. ended 08/31/91): Assets, $9,961,495 (M); expenditures, $481,501; qualifying distributions, $434,638, including $203,530 for 74 grants (high: $72,000; low: $200; average: $2,000), $56,183 for 1 foundation-administered program and $100,320 for 2 in-kind gifts.
Purpose and activities: Grants program is limited to programs in mental health, public policy, and minority affairs, including programs combatting racism.
Fields of interest: Mental health, psychiatry, public policy, civil rights, minorities, race relations.
Types of support: Continuing support, seed money, consulting services, technical assistance, special projects, publications, conferences and seminars.

Limitations: No grants to individuals, or for operating budgets, annual campaigns, deficit financing, capital funds, scholarships, fellowships, or matching gifts; no loans.
Publications: Occasional report.
Application information: Application form not required.
  Initial approach: Letter or telephone
  Copies of proposal: 1
  Deadline(s): None
  Board meeting date(s): Biannually
  Final notification: 2 to 3 weeks
  Write: Philip B. Hallen, Pres.
Officers and Trustees:* Sigo Falk,* Chair.; Philip B. Hallen, Pres.; Julian Ruslander,* Secy.-Treas.; Philip Baskin, Bertram S. Brown, M.D., Eric W. Springer.
Number of staff: 2 full-time professional; 1 full-time support.
EIN: 251099658
Recent health grants:
2723-1 University of Pittsburgh, Graduate School of Public Health, Pittsburgh, PA, $17,000. For Coordinator for Supportive Services and Minority Affairs. 1991.
2723-2 University of Pittsburgh, Graduate School of Public Health, Pittsburgh, PA, $10,000. For 1992 Public Health Careers Summer Opportunity Program. 1991.
2723-3 University of Pittsburgh, School of Medicine, Pittsburgh, PA, $10,000. For Black Scholarship Initiative Endowment Fund. 1991.

2724
Farber Foundation
1401 Walnut St.
Philadelphia 19102

Foundation type: Company-sponsored
Financial data (yr. ended 12/31/90): Assets, $2,658,162 (M); gifts received, $100,000; expenditures, $133,058; qualifying distributions, $132,958, including $132,840 for 37 grants (high: $40,000; low: $100; average: $50-$30,000).
Fields of interest: Jewish giving, higher education, health associations, hospitals, social services, performing arts.
Limitations: Giving primarily in Philadelphia, PA. No grants to individuals.
Application information: Contributes only to pre-selected organizations. Applications not accepted.
Officers: Jack Farber, Pres.; Stephen V. Dubin, V.P. and Secy.; James G. Baxter, V.P. and Treas.
EIN: 236254221

2725
Samuel S. Fels Fund ▼
1616 Walnut St., Suite 800
Philadelphia 19103   (215) 731-9455

Incorporated in 1935 in PA.
Donor(s): Samuel S. Fels.‡
Foundation type: Independent
Financial data (yr. ended 12/31/91): Assets, $35,802,636 (M); expenditures, $1,327,798; qualifying distributions, $963,288, including $963,288 for 160 grants (high: $250,000; low: $500; average: $3,000-$20,000).

Purpose and activities: Grants for continuing support of two major projects instituted by the fund itself: the Fels Research Institute, Temple University Medical School and the Fels Center of Government, University of Pennsylvania. Additional grants for short-term assistance to projects and organizations that help to demonstrate and evaluate ways to prevent, lessen, or resolve contemporary social problems, or that seek to provide permanent improvements in the provision of services for the improvement of daily life; to increase the stability of arts organizations and enrich the cultural life of the city of Philadelphia; limited aid to locally based university presses.
Fields of interest: Education, arts, community development, health services, AIDS.
Types of support: Seed money, emergency funds, matching funds, technical assistance, special projects, research, conferences and seminars, continuing support, general purposes, internships, publications.
Limitations: Giving limited to the city of Philadelphia, PA. No support for national organizations. No grants to individuals, or for endowment or building funds, travel, scholarships, or fellowships.
Publications: Annual report, application guidelines.
Application information: Applicant must request guidelines before submitting proposals. Application form required.
  Initial approach: Proposal
  Copies of proposal: 1
  Board meeting date(s): Monthly except Aug.
  Write: Helen Cunningham, Exec. Dir.
Officers and Member-Directors:* Iso Briselli,* Pres.; Helen Cunningham,* Secy. and Exec. Dir.; David C. Melnicoff,* Treas.; Brother Daniel Burke, F.S.C., Raymond K. Denworth, Jr., Sandra Featherman, Wilbur E. Hobbs, David H. Wice.
Number of staff: 1 full-time professional; 1 part-time support.
EIN: 231365325
Recent health grants:
2725-1 ActionAIDS, Philadelphia, PA, $15,000. For education and advocacy work on public policies related to AIDS. 1990.
2725-2 Center for Fair Employment, Philadelphia, PA, $10,000. For health insurance in workplace project. 1990.
2725-3 CHOICE: Concern for Health Options-Information, Care and Education, Philadelphia, PA, $19,000. To develop maternity care resource component of CHOICE Hotline. 1990.
2725-4 Elizabeth Blackwell Health Center for Women, Philadelphia, PA, $20,000. For general support. 1990.
2725-5 Episcopal Community Services of the Diocese of Pennsylvania, Philadelphia, PA, $20,000. For Courtwatch Program in collaboration with United Neighbors Against Drugs. 1990.
2725-6 Lutheran Social Mission Society of Philadelphia, Philadelphia, PA, $15,579. To train staff at hospitals and other agencies which encounter battered women. 1990.
2725-7 Philadelphia Parenting Associates, Philadelphia, PA, $14,000. To provide technical assistance to staff working with formerly cocaine addicted mothers and their children. 1990.

2725-8 Unemployment Information Center, Philadelphia, PA, $10,000. For Health Care Access Project. 1990.

2725-9 United Presbyterian Church of the U.S.A., Philadelphia, PA, $10,000. For Ecumenical Information AIDS Resource Center. 1990.

2726
Percival E. and Ethel Brown Foerderer Foundation

P.O. Box 7734
Philadelphia 19101-7734   (215) 828-8145

Trust established in 1962 in PA.
Donor(s): Ethel Brown Foerderer,‡ Percival E. Foerderer.‡
Foundation type: Independent
Financial data (yr. ended 12/31/91): Assets, $9,076,410 (M); expenditures, $429,024; qualifying distributions, $375,905, including $366,200 for 11 grants (high: $286,200; low: $1,000).
Purpose and activities: Funds largely committed to the Foerderer Fellowship Program for students in the College of Graduate Studies of Thomas Jefferson University; remainder currently focused on a research project concerning achondroplasia, the failure of normal development of cartilage resulting in dwarfism.
Fields of interest: Medical research, medical education.
Types of support: Fellowships, research.
Limitations: Giving primarily in the Philadelphia, PA, area. No grants to individuals.
Publications: Biennial report.
Application information: Fund presently committed; no new proposals are being considered at this time. Applications not accepted.
   Deadline(s): Sept. 1 (for previous commitments)
   Board meeting date(s): Apr., Sept., and Nov.
   Write: Judith Bardes, Administrator
Officers and Trustees:* Shirley Foerderer Murray,* Chair.; Ethel Foerderer Davis,* Vice-Chair.; N. Ramsay Pennypacker,* Secy.; Spencer D. Wright III,* Treas.; John M.K. Davis, Mignon Foerderer Davis, Shelley A. Hartz, James W. Stratton.
Number of staff: 1 shared staff
EIN: 236296084

2727
Foster Charitable Trust

P.O. Box 67
Pittsburgh 15230

Established in 1962 in PA.
Donor(s): Foster Industries, Inc.
Foundation type: Independent
Financial data (yr. ended 12/31/90): Assets, $2,180,446 (M); expenditures, $529,720; qualifying distributions, $508,850, including $508,850 for 59 grants (high: $210,000; low: $500).
Fields of interest: Jewish welfare, hospitals, higher education, arts.
Limitations: Giving primarily in PA. No grants to individuals, or for endowment funds or operating budgets.
Application information: Application form not required.
   Initial approach: Letter

Copies of proposal: 1
Deadline(s): None
Board meeting date(s): As required
Write: Bernard S. Mars, Trustee
Trustees: J.L. Foster, J.R. Foster, H.R. Gordon, B.S. Mars, M. Porter.
Number of staff: None.
EIN: 256064791

2728
The Foundation for Basic Cutaneous Research

210 West Rittenhouse Sq., Suite 3302
Philadelphia 19103

Donor(s): Ortho Pharmaceutical, Ajinomoto U.S.A., Inc., Clairol-Gelb Foundation, Hoechst Co., Johnson & Johnson Baby Products, Lever Brothers Co., The Upjohn Co.
Foundation type: Independent
Financial data (yr. ended 07/31/90): Assets, $474,577 (M); gifts received, $370,000; expenditures, $541,356; qualifying distributions, $541,356, including $313,735 for 17 grants (high: $75,000; low: $1,440) and $132,800 for 18 grants to individuals (high: $25,000; low: $500).
Fields of interest: Dermatology.
Types of support: Research.
Application information:
   Initial approach: Proposal
   Deadline(s): None
   Write: Dr. Lorraine H. Kligman, Pres.
Officer: Lorraine H. Kligman, M.D., Pres. and Secy.
EIN: 232439001

2729
The Fourjay Foundation

2300 Computer Ave., Bldg. G
Willow Grove 19090
Application address: Waterworks Unit A-8, 350 South River Rd., New Hope, PA 18938

Established in 1988 in PA.
Donor(s): Eugene W. Jackson.
Foundation type: Independent
Financial data (yr. ended 12/31/91): Assets, $6,038,308 (M); gifts received, $404,365; expenditures, $448,694; qualifying distributions, $396,525, including $389,980 for 2,743 grants (high: $31,008).
Fields of interest: Higher education, hospitals, health associations, nursing.
Types of support: Scholarship funds, matching funds, capital campaigns, research, general purposes.
Limitations: Giving primarily in PA and OK. No support for religious organizations. No grants to individuals.
Application information:
   Initial approach: Letter
   Deadline(s): None
   Write: Eugene W. Jackson, Trustee
Trustees: Eugene W. Jackson, Marie Louis Jackson.
EIN: 232537126

2730
Addison H. Gibson Foundation

c/o Integra Financial Corp.
Fourth Ave. and Wood St.
Pittsburgh 15222   (412) 261-1611

Trust established in 1936 in PA.
Donor(s): Addison H. Gibson.‡
Foundation type: Independent
Financial data (yr. ended 12/31/91): Assets, $19,429,197 (M); gifts received, $1,835; expenditures, $1,613,537; qualifying distributions, $1,388,581, including $626,000 for 29 grants (high: $27,000; low: $14,000), $146,921 for 42 grants to individuals (high: $15,726; low: $32) and $474,005 for 80 loans to individuals.
Purpose and activities: To provide (1) medical and hospital care for local needy persons and (2) loans to male students residing in western PA for college or university expenses after at least one year's self-maintenance; grants also to hospitals and rehabilitation institutions.
Fields of interest: Hospitals, welfare—indigent individuals, rehabilitation.
Types of support: Grants to individuals, student loans.
Limitations: Giving limited to western PA. No grants for building funds, endowments, operating budgets, or special projects.
Publications: Informational brochure (including application guidelines).
Application information: Application form required.
   Initial approach: For loans, letter or telephone to schedule personal interview; for medical assistance, letter or telephone from referring physician or agency prior to patient interview
   Deadline(s): None
   Board meeting date(s): About 10 times a year
   Final notification: Varies
   Write: Rebecca Wallace Sapiente, Dir.
Officer: Charlotte G. Kisseleff, Secy.
Trustees: Frank J. Gaffney, Earl F. Reed, Jr., Integra Financial Corp.
Number of staff: 1 full-time professional; 2 full-time support.
EIN: 250965379

2731
Glendorn Foundation

78 Main St.
Bradford 16701   (814) 368-7171

Trust established in 1953 in TX.
Donor(s): Forest Oil Corp., Ruth H. Dorn.‡
Foundation type: Company-sponsored
Financial data (yr. ended 12/31/91): Assets, $2,621,702 (M); gifts received, $27,100; expenditures, $140,924; qualifying distributions, $134,500, including $134,500 for 8 grants (high: $100,000; low: $1,000).
Fields of interest: Medical research, education.
Types of support: Research, capital campaigns.
Publications: Financial statement.
Application information: Funds currently committed. Applications not accepted.
   Write: William F. Higie, Mgr.
Officer and Trustees:* William F. Higie,* Mgr.; Clayton D. Chisum, David F. Dorn, Frederick M. Dorn, John C. Dorn, Wendy M. Hitt, Jay Bird Lawson, Leslie D. Young.

Number of staff: None.
EIN: 251024349

2732
William Goldman Foundation
1700 Walnut St., Suite 800
Philadelphia 19103   (215) 546-2779

Trust established in 1952 in PA.
Donor(s): William Goldman,‡ Helen L. Goldman.‡
Foundation type: Independent
Financial data (yr. ended 12/31/90): Assets, $2,802,056 (M); expenditures, $153,631; qualifying distributions, $110,601, including $30,250 for 33 grants (high: $8,500; low: $250; average: $250-$3,000) and $58,100 for 65 grants to individuals (high: $2,000; low: $500; average: $1,000).
Purpose and activities: Grants for graduate studies (including medical education and graduate school scholarships), hospitals, child welfare, community funds, and Jewish welfare funds.
Fields of interest: Higher education, medical education, education, hospitals, child welfare, community funds, Jewish welfare.
Types of support: Operating budgets, annual campaigns, research, scholarship funds, continuing support, special projects, student aid.
Limitations: Giving primarily in the metropolitan Philadelphia, PA, area. No grants for endowment funds or matching gifts; generally no loans.
Publications: Application guidelines.
Application information: Application form required for scholarships.
  Initial approach: Letter
  Copies of proposal: 1
  Deadline(s): Mar. 15 for scholarships; no deadline for other requests
  Board meeting date(s): Quarterly
  Write: William R. Goldman, Vice-Chair.
Officers and Trustees:* Alice S. Goldman,* Chair.; William R. Goldman,* Vice-Chair. and Secy.; Lowell H. Dubrow, Randolph Louis Goldman, Anne Goldman Kravitz, Barbara G. Susman, Ronald M. Wiener.
Number of staff: 1 part-time professional.
EIN: 236266261

2733
Grable Foundation
650 Smithfield St., Suite 240
Pittsburgh 15222   (412) 471-4550

Established in 1977 in PA.
Donor(s): Minnie K. Grable.‡
Foundation type: Independent
Financial data (yr. ended 12/31/91): Assets, $6,680,701 (M); gifts received, $2,309,341; expenditures, $335,357; qualifying distributions, $271,292, including $229,700 for 25 grants (high: $75,000; low: $1,000).
Fields of interest: Health, family planning, social services, youth, child development, family services, education.
Types of support: Annual campaigns, building funds, capital campaigns, continuing support, general purposes, operating budgets, program-related investments, special projects.

Limitations: Giving primarily in Pittsburgh, PA, Orlando, FL, and their vicinities.
Publications: 990-PF.
Application information: Application form not required.
  Initial approach: Proposal
  Copies of proposal: 1
  Deadline(s): None
  Board meeting date(s): Varies
  Write: Charles R. Burke, Chair.
Officers and Trustees:* Charles R. Burke,* Chair. and Secy.; Jan Nicholson,* Pres.; Charles R. Burke, Jr.,* V.P.; Steven E. Burke,* V.P.; William B. Nicholson,* Treas.; Patricia G. Burke, Barbara N. McFadyen, Marion G. Nicholson.
Number of staff: None.
EIN: 251309888

2734
Greensburg Foundation
P.O. Box 71
Greensburg 15601   (412) 834-8090

Established in 1947 in PA.
Foundation type: Community
Financial data (yr. ended 12/31/90): Assets, $2,000,000 (M); expenditures, $132,003; qualifying distributions, $129,950, including $129,950 for grants.
Purpose and activities: Primary areas of interest include community development, recreation, youth, and the performing arts.
Fields of interest: Education, elementary education, secondary education, higher education, medical education, libraries, community development, safety, family services, aged, youth, women, fine arts, museums, performing arts, health associations, recreation, general charitable giving.
Types of support: Scholarship funds, capital campaigns, general purposes, equipment, special projects.
Limitations: Giving limited to Greensburg, PA.
Publications: Informational brochure (including application guidelines).
Application information: Application form not required.
  Initial approach: Letter
  Copies of proposal: 1
  Deadline(s): Dec. 30 and June 30
  Board meeting date(s): Feb. and Aug.
  Write: Helen B. Kersten, Dir.
Officer and Directors:* Hugh Dempsey,* Chair.; Helen Kersten.
Number of staff: 1 part-time support.
EIN: 256052355

2735
The Grundy Foundation ▼
680 Radcliffe St.
P.O. Box 701
Bristol 19007   (215) 788-5460

Trust established in 1961 in PA.
Donor(s): Joseph R. Grundy.‡
Foundation type: Independent
Financial data (yr. ended 12/31/91): Assets, $42,761,003 (M); expenditures, $1,948,377; qualifying distributions, $1,691,582, including $824,547 for grants (high: $95,000; low: $500; average: $1,000-$30,000).

Purpose and activities: Grants for civic affairs and community planning; social service and youth agencies, including a community fund; cultural programs, higher education, and health. Giving restricted to activities in which the donor was interested during his lifetime.
Fields of interest: Higher education, hospitals, child welfare, youth, community development, community funds, civic affairs.
Types of support: Building funds, equipment, land acquisition, seed money, conferences and seminars, special projects, renovation projects, operating budgets.
Limitations: Giving limited to Bucks County, PA. No grants to individuals, or for endowment funds, research, scholarships, or fellowships; no loans.
Application information: Application form not required.
  Initial approach: Letter
  Copies of proposal: 1
  Deadline(s): None
  Board meeting date(s): Monthly except in Aug.
  Final notification: 1 week
  Write: Robert M. Kelly, Exec. Dir.
Officer and Trustees:* Robert M. Kelly,* Exec. Dir.; James M. Gassaway, Stanton C. Kelton, Jr., William P. Wood, Fidelity Bank, N.A.
Number of staff: 2 full-time professional.
EIN: 231609243

2736
Evelyn A. J. Hall Charitable Trust
150 Radnor Chester Rd., Suite A200
St. Davids 19087   (215) 341-9270

Trust established in 1952 in NY.
Donor(s): Evelyn A. Hall.
Foundation type: Independent
Financial data (yr. ended 12/31/91): Assets, $10,638,896 (M); expenditures, $1,313,638; qualifying distributions, $1,302,618, including $1,265,300 for 56 grants (high: $400,750; low: $100; average: $1,000-$25,000).
Purpose and activities: Primary areas of interest include cultural programs, hospitals, and medical research.
Fields of interest: Cultural programs, museums, hospitals, medical research, higher education, conservation, historic preservation, social services, youth, community development.
Types of support: General purposes.
Limitations: Giving primarily in New York, NY, and FL. No grants to individuals.
Application information: Applications not accepted.
  Board meeting date(s): Varies
  Write: Leanne M. Workman
Trustee: Walter H. Annenberg.
Number of staff: None.
EIN: 236286760

2737
The Hallowell Foundation
c/o The Philadelphia National Bank, Tax Dept.,
FC 1-24-7
P.O. Box 7618
Philadelphia 19101

Trust established in 1956 in PA.
Donor(s): Members of the Hallowell family.
Foundation type: Independent

Financial data (yr. ended 12/31/90): Assets, $4,529,316 (M); expenditures, $42,323; qualifying distributions, $5,445.
Fields of interest: Hospitals, higher education, secondary education.
Types of support: Building funds, operating budgets.
Limitations: Giving primarily in PA. No grants to individuals.
Application information: Contributes only to pre-selected organizations. Applications not accepted.
Trustees: Dorothy W. Hallowell, Howard T. Hallowell III, Merritt W. Hallowell, Anne H. Miller.
EIN: 236234545

2738
Hamilton Bank Foundation
(Formerly The National Central Foundation)
c/o Hamilton Bank
P.O. Box 3959
Lancaster 17604
Application address: c/o Hamilton Bank, 100 North Queen St., Lancaster, PA 17604

Incorporated in 1965 in PA.
Donor(s): Hamilton Bank.
Foundation type: Company-sponsored
Financial data (yr. ended 12/31/91): Assets, $97,737 (M); gifts received, $613,600; expenditures, $608,123; qualifying distributions, $607,962, including $607,943 for 438 grants (high: $57,575; low: $10).
Purpose and activities: Emphasis on community funds and higher education, including employee matching gifts; support also for hospitals, youth agencies, and arts organizations.
Fields of interest: Community funds, higher education, hospitals, youth, arts.
Types of support: Employee matching gifts, general purposes.
Limitations: Giving limited to seven counties of southcentral PA.
Application information:
  Deadline(s): None
  Write: Thomas Bamford, Corp. Communs. Officer
Trustee: Hamilton Bank.
EIN: 236444555

2739
The Greater Harrisburg Foundation
P.O. Box 678
Harrisburg 17108-0678   (717) 236-5040

Established in 1920 in PA; assets first acquired in 1940; grants first made in the mid-1940's.
Foundation type: Community
Financial data (yr. ended 12/31/91): Assets, $4,424,722 (L); gifts received, $753,617; expenditures, $374,486; qualifying distributions, $318,064, including $318,064 for 158 grants (high: $32,109; low: $10).
Purpose and activities: Giving for education, health, human services, community development, and the arts; priority assigned to funding new projects and awarding seed money to organizations which may not be eligible for support elsewhere.

Fields of interest: Education, health, social services, community development, arts.
Types of support: Seed money, special projects, publications, scholarship funds.
Limitations: Giving primarily in PA, with emphasis on Dauphin, Cumberland, Franklin, and Perry counties in central PA. No grants to individuals, or for operating or capital expenses.
Publications: Annual report (including application guidelines), informational brochure, application guidelines, newsletter.
Application information: Contact foundation for application forms. Application form required.
  Initial approach: Proposal or telephone
  Copies of proposal: 1
  Deadline(s): Apr. 15 for spring round; Sept. 1 for fall round
  Board meeting date(s): June and Nov. for grantmaking; Jan. and Mar. for policy review
  Final notification: 2 weeks following meeting date
  Write: Diane Sandquist, Pres.
Officers and Distribution Committee:* Lois Lehrman Grass,* Chair.; Gerald H. Hempt,* Vice-Chair.; William H. Alexander, Tita Eberly, Claude E. Nichols, M.D., Rod J. Pera, John M. Schrantz, John McD. Sharpe, Conrad M. Siegel, Elsie W. Swenson, Nathan H. Waters, Jr., Esq.
Staff: Diane Sandquist, Pres.; Cassandra W. Pepinsky, Prog. Officer; Linda K. Bugden, Fiscal Officer.
Trustee Banks: CCNB Bank, N.A., Citizens National Bank & Trust Co., Citizens National Bank of Greencastle, Commonwealth National Bank, Dauphin Deposit Bank & Trust Co., Farmers and Merchants Trust Co., Farmers Trust Co. of Carlisle, The First Bank and Trust Co. of Mechanicsburg, First National Bank and Trust Co. of Waynesboro, First National Bank of Greencastle, Fulton Bank, GHF, Inc., Hamilton Bank, Hershey Trust Co., The Juniata Valley Bank, Pennsylvania National Bank & Trust Co., Valley Bank and Trust Co.
Number of staff: 1 full-time professional; 2 part-time professional; 2 full-time support.
EIN: 236294219

2740
Harsco Corporation Fund
c/o Harsco Corp.
P.O. Box 8888
Camp Hill 17011-8888   (717) 763-7064

Trust established in 1956 in PA.
Donor(s): Harsco Corp.
Foundation type: Company-sponsored
Financial data (yr. ended 12/31/91): Assets, $8,657,210 (M); expenditures, $561,477; qualifying distributions, $552,152, including $552,152 for 222 grants (high: $97,930; low: $25).
Purpose and activities: Support for hospitals and health associations, higher education, human services, and a community fund; some giving also for the arts. Requests for contributions originate with local operating management and are approved or disapproved at the fund's central office. Employee-related scholarships administered through National Merit Scholarship Corp.
Fields of interest: Hospitals, health associations, higher education, welfare, community funds, arts.

Types of support: General purposes, operating budgets, continuing support, employee-related scholarships, employee matching gifts.
Limitations: Giving primarily in areas of company operations. No grants to individuals, or for special projects, building or endowment funds, or research programs; no loans.
Publications: Program policy statement.
Application information: Application form required for employee-related scholarships.
  Initial approach: Letter
  Deadline(s): Jan. 10 for scholarships; no set deadline for grants
  Board meeting date(s): Apr. and as required
  Write: Robert G. Yocum, Secy. (Grants), or David M. Sarkozy, Dir., Employee Relations (Scholarship Prog.)
Officers and Trustees:* Malcolm W. Gambill,* Pres.; D.C. Hathaway,* V.P.; R.G. Yocum, Secy.; George F. Rezich, Treas.; Robert F. Nation.
EIN: 236278376

2741
The Hassel Foundation
1760 Market St., 13th Fl.
Philadelphia 19103   (215) 561-6400

Trust established in 1961 in PA.
Donor(s): Morris Hassel,‡ Calvin Hassel.‡
Foundation type: Independent
Financial data (yr. ended 12/31/91): Assets, $5,120,640 (M); expenditures, $307,017; qualifying distributions, $296,748, including $273,000 for 19 grants (high: $60,000; low: $1,000) and $13,000 for 8 grants to individuals (high: $2,500; low: $1,000).
Purpose and activities: Support for hospitals, and higher and other education; two scholarships are awarded annually to graduating seniors of two specific high schools.
Fields of interest: Hospitals, education, higher education.
Types of support: General purposes, building funds, student aid.
Limitations: Giving primarily in PA. No grants to individuals (except for scholarships at specified high schools).
Application information: Scholarship applications are available from the high school principal's office; no application form for grants.
  Initial approach: Letter
  Deadline(s): None
  Board meeting date(s): June and as required
  Write: Michael H. Krekstein, Esq., Trustee
Trustees: Barbara Cohen, Sarle H. Cohen, Jay L. Goldberg, Marilyn Khoury, Theodore Kobrin, I.H. Krekstein, Michael H. Krekstein, Ephram Royfe, Morton M. Silton, Merle Wolfson.
EIN: 236251862

2742
Lita Annenberg Hazen Charitable Trust ▼
150 Radnor Chester Rd., Suite A200
St. Davids 19087   (215) 341-9270

Trust established in 1952 in NY.
Donor(s): Lita A. Hazen.
Foundation type: Independent
Financial data (yr. ended 12/31/91): Assets, $4,635,786 (M); expenditures, $651,812; qualifying distributions, $649,892, including

$623,775 for 39 grants (high: $95,800; low: $100; average: $1,000-$5,000).

Purpose and activities: Grants largely for medical research, hospitals, education, and cultural programs; some support for social services, especially Jewish welfare agencies.

Fields of interest: Medical research, hospitals, education, cultural programs, social services, Jewish welfare, conservation, community development.

Types of support: Annual campaigns, general purposes, scholarship funds.

Limitations: Giving primarily in New York, NY. No grants to individuals.

Application information: Contributes only to pre-selected organizations. Applications not accepted.

> *Board meeting date(s):* Varies
> *Write:* Leanne M. Workman

Trustee: Walter H. Annenberg.
Number of staff: 11 shared staff
EIN: 236286759

2743
H. J. Heinz Company Foundation ▼

P.O. Box 57
Pittsburgh 15230   (412) 456-5772

Trust established in 1951 in PA.
Donor(s): H.J. Heinz Co.
Foundation type: Company-sponsored
Financial data (yr. ended 12/31/90): Assets, $5,895,368 (M); gifts received, $5,178,776; expenditures, $7,363,286; qualifying distributions, $7,340,153, including $7,240,900 for grants (high: $200,000; low: $20; average: $1,000-$10,000).

Purpose and activities: Support mainly for community funds; grants also for higher education, including employee matching gifts, hospitals, youth and social service agencies, cultural programs, medical and nutritional research and prevention of cruelty to animals and children.

Fields of interest: Community funds, higher education, hospitals, social services, cultural programs, education, youth, child welfare, animal welfare, nutrition, medical research.

Types of support: Annual campaigns, building funds, continuing support, employee matching gifts, operating budgets, seed money, technical assistance, emergency funds, equipment, internships, scholarship funds, fellowships, special projects, research, publications, conferences and seminars, professorships, endowment funds, capital campaigns.

Limitations: Giving primarily in areas of company operations. No grants to individuals, or for deficit financing, or land acquisition; no loans.

Publications: Program policy statement, application guidelines.

Application information: Application form not required.

> *Initial approach:* Letter
> *Copies of proposal:* 1
> *Deadline(s):* None
> *Board meeting date(s):* As necessary
> *Final notification:* Varies
> *Write:* Loretta M. Oken, Admin.

Officers and Trustees:* Anthony J.F. O'Reilly,* Chair.; S.D. Wiley,* Vice-Chair.; Karyll A. Davis,* Secy.; R. Derek Finlay, Mellon Bank, N.A.

Number of staff: 1 full-time professional; 1 full-time support.
EIN: 256018924
Recent health grants:

2743-1 Allegheny Health Services, Pittsburgh, PA, $50,000. For capital support. 1990.

2743-2 American British Cowdray Hospital, Las Americas, Mexico, $10,000. For general support. 1990.

2743-3 American Cancer Society, New York City Division, NYC, NY, $10,000. For general support. 1990.

2743-4 Child Health Association of Sewickley, Sewickley, PA, $10,000. For general support. 1990.

2743-5 Childrens Hospital, Columbus, OH, $10,575. For general support. 1990.

2743-6 Childrens Hospital Medical Center of Akron, Akron, OH, $12,560. For general support. 1990.

2743-7 Childrens Hospital of Pittsburgh, Pittsburgh, PA, $50,000. For research. 1990.

2743-8 Childrens Hospital of Pittsburgh, Pittsburgh, PA, $19,295. For general support. 1990.

2743-9 D.T. Watson Rehabilitation Hospital, Sewickley, PA, $20,000. For general support. 1990.

2743-10 Eye and Ear Institute, Pittsburgh, PA, $35,000. For capital support. 1990.

2743-11 Gateway Rehabilitation Center, Aliquippa, PA, $25,000. For general support. 1990.

2743-12 Harmarville Foundation, Pittsburgh, PA, $100,000. For capital support. 1990.

2743-13 Hospital De La Concepcion, San German, PR, $10,000. For general support. 1990.

2743-14 International Life Sciences Institute Pennsylvania, Pittsburgh, PA, $100,000. For research. 1990.

2743-15 International Life Sciences Institute-Nutrition Foundation, DC, $66,105. For general support. 1990.

2743-16 International Life Sciences Institute-Nutrition Foundation, DC, $10,000. For research. 1990.

2743-17 Irish and American Paediatric Society, Cleveland, OH, $20,000. For scholarships and fellowships. 1990.

2743-18 Make-A-Wish Foundation of Western Pennsylvania, Pittsburgh, PA, $10,000. For general support. 1990.

2743-19 Media-Advertising Partnership for a Drug-Free America, NYC, NY, $50,000. For general support. 1990.

2743-20 Mercy Hospital Foundation, Pittsburgh, PA, $10,000. For capital support. 1990.

2743-21 National Foundation for Ileitis and Colitis, NYC, NY, $25,000. For capital support. 1990.

2743-22 Pittsburgh Recovery Center, Pittsburgh, PA, $12,000. For general support. 1990.

2743-23 Presbyterian-University Hospital, Pittsburgh, PA, $50,000. For capital support. 1990.

2743-24 Rainbow Babies and Childrens Hospital, Cleveland, OH, $11,975. For general support. 1990.

2743-25 Rehabilitation Institute of Pittsburgh, Pittsburgh, PA, $40,000. For capital support. 1990.

2743-26 Rush-Presbyterian-Saint Lukes Medical Center, Department of Preventative Medicine, Chicago, IL, $156,700. For general support. 1990.

2743-27 Singing River Hospital System, Pascagoula, MS, $20,000. For capital support. 1990.

2743-28 Spina Bifida Association of Western Pennsylvania, Pittsburgh, PA, $10,000. For general support. 1990.

2744
Howard Heinz Endowment ▼

30 CNG Tower
625 Liberty Ave.
Pittsburgh 15222-3115   (412) 391-5122

Trust established in 1941 in PA.
Donor(s): Howard Heinz,‡ Elizabeth Rust Heinz.‡
Foundation type: Independent
Financial data (yr. ended 12/31/90): Assets, $622,403,561 (M); expenditures, $24,219,066; qualifying distributions, $37,370,743, including $21,932,562 for 126 grants (high: $3,974,693; low: $2,000; average: $20,000-$500,000) and $15,438,181 for loans.

Purpose and activities: After gifts to certain agencies with which Mr. Heinz was associated during his life, the endowment supports music and the arts, education, health, nutrition, and urban affairs, usually with one-time, non-renewable grants for new programs, seed money, and capital projects.

Fields of interest: Arts, education, health, nutrition, community development, urban development, child welfare, child development.

Types of support: Seed money, building funds, equipment, research, matching funds, program-related investments, renovation projects, capital campaigns, special projects.

Limitations: Giving limited to PA, with emphasis on Pittsburgh and the Allegheny County area. No grants to individuals.

Publications: Annual report (including application guidelines), application guidelines.

Application information: Application form required.

> *Initial approach:* Letter or proposal
> *Copies of proposal:* 1
> *Deadline(s):* 90 days before meeting date
> *Board meeting date(s):* May and Nov.
> *Final notification:* Within several weeks of board meeting
> *Write:* Alfred W. Wishart, Jr., Exec. Dir.

Officers: J.E. Kime, Assoc. Dir., Chief Financial and Admin. Officer; Alfred W. Wishart, Jr., Exec. Dir.

Trustees: Drue Heinz, H. John Heinz IV, Teresa Heinz, Joseph W. Oliver, William H. Rea, William W. Scranton, Mellon Bank, N.A.

Number of staff: 23 shared staff
EIN: 251064784
Recent health grants:

2744-1 Allegheny Health Services, Pittsburgh, PA, $270,000. For Healthy Tomorrows Partnership For Children, pilot to develop Family Growth Center on North Side that will target teen parents and their children. 1991.

2744-2 Allentown Hospital, Allentown, PA, $600,000. To develop prenatal outreach program targeting Latino and homeless women in Allentown. Grant shared with Lehigh Valley Hospital Center. 1991.

2744-3 California Area Senior Center, California, PA, $252,805. For health study for elderly and support for new building construction. 1991.

2744-4 Childrens Hospital of Pittsburgh, Pittsburgh, PA, $500,000. To develop Family Drop-In Centers in three high-risk communities. 1991.

2744-5 Community Medical Center of Northwest Washington County, Burgettstown, PA, $50,000. For capital campaign for addition to existing building. 1991.

2744-6 East End Cooperative Ministry, Pittsburgh, PA, $75,000. For Sojourner House, residential treatment facility for low-income women recovering from drug and/or alcohol addiction. 1991.

2744-7 Family Health Council of Western Pennsylvania, Pittsburgh, PA, $600,000. To deliver comprehensive prenatal care to rural low-income women in Indiana County through use of Prenatal Mobile Unit. 1991.

2744-8 Magee-Womens Hospital, Pittsburgh, PA, $600,000. To develop prenatal outreach program targeting two high-risk communities in Pittsburgh: Terrace Village and Clairton. 1991.

2744-9 Marian Manor Nursing Home, Pittsburgh, PA, $100,000. For comprehensive senior services program. 1991.

2744-10 Presbyterian Association on Aging, Pittsburgh, PA, $165,000. For evaluation of Woodside Place Residential Alzheimer's Facility. 1991.

2744-11 Primary Care Health Services, Pittsburgh, PA, $600,000. To develop prenatal outreach program in Pittsburgh and Allegheny County public housing communities. 1991.

2744-12 Saint Francis Health Foundation, Pittsburgh, PA, $60,000. For Elderly Outreach Project (EOP). 1991.

2744-13 Thomas Jefferson University, Jefferson Medical College, Philadelphia, PA, $11,375. For meeting of Pennsylvania Nutrition Interurban Club. 1991.

2744-14 University of Pittsburgh, Office of Child Development, Pittsburgh, PA, $448,526. To evaluate and disseminate results of A Better Start, initiative to enhance prenatal care services for low-income women in Pennsylvania. 1991.

2744-15 University of Pittsburgh, Office of Child Development, Pittsburgh, PA, $151,474. For Project Coordinator position for A Better Start, initiative to enhance prenatal care services for low-income women in Pennsylvania. 1991.

2744-16 Western Pennsylvania Hospital, Pittsburgh, PA, $755,060. For Primary Care for Medically Underserved Populations Program. 1991.

2745
Vira I. Heinz Endowment ▼
30 CNG Tower
625 Liberty Ave.
Pittsburgh 15222-3115   (412) 391-5122

Established in 1986 in PA.
Donor(s): Vira I. Heinz.‡
Foundation type: Independent

Financial data (yr. ended 12/31/90): Assets, $298,736,446 (M); expenditures, $13,674,656; qualifying distributions, $13,151,619, including $12,563,286 for 120 grants (high: $4,500,000; low: $325; average: $10,000-$300,000).
Purpose and activities: Support for education, human services, arts and humanities, health, AIDS research, nutrition, religion and values, community affairs, and economic development.
Fields of interest: Education, social services, arts, humanities, health, AIDS, nutrition, religion, community development.
Types of support: Capital campaigns, general purposes, renovation projects, seed money, special projects, technical assistance, building funds.
Limitations: Giving limited to Pittsburgh and western PA, although in certain cases support may be considered on a national or international basis. No grants for general endowments.
Publications: Annual report, informational brochure, application guidelines.
Application information: Application form required.
  Initial approach: Letter or proposal
  Deadline(s): 90 days prior to board meeting
  Board meeting date(s): Apr. and Oct.
  Final notification: Within several weeks of board meeting
  Write: Alfred W. Wishart, Jr., Exec. Dir.
Officers: Alfred W. Wishart, Jr., Exec. Dir.; J.E. Kime, C.F.O.
Trustees: James M. Walton, Chair.; Teresa F. Heinz, William H. Rea, Helen P. Rush, John T. Ryan, Jr., S. Donald Wiley, Mellon Bank, N.A.
Number of staff: None.
EIN: 256235878
Recent health grants:
2745-1 National Council on the Aging, DC, $131,158. To develop, test, print, publish and disseminate training manuals for staff working in Adult Daycare Centers. 1991.

2745-2 Presbyterian Association on Aging, Pittsburgh, PA, $165,000. For evaluation of Woodside Place Residential Alzheimer Facility. 1991.

2745-3 Rehabilitation Institute of Pittsburgh, Pittsburgh, PA, $250,000. For capital funding drive, Miracles in Progress. 1991.

2745-4 University of Pittsburgh, Alzheimer's Disease Research Center, Pittsburgh, PA, $316,760. To initiate program of education, training and clinical consultation for Alzheimer's disease and other memory disorders in Hill District. 1991.

2745-5 University of Pittsburgh, School of Medicine, Pittsburgh, PA, $264,600. For research and primary care service delivery for under-represented minority medical school students. 1991.

2746
Drue Heinz Foundation ▼
(Formerly H. J. & Drue Heinz Foundation)
606 Oliver Bldg.
535 Smithfield St.
Pittsburgh 15222   (412) 281-5737

Established in 1954 in PA.
Foundation type: Independent
Financial data (yr. ended 12/31/90): Assets, $54,843,176 (M); gifts received, $38,613,277;

expenditures, $4,423,295; qualifying distributions, $4,303,389, including $4,303,389 for 79 grants (high: $1,610,000; low: $300; average: $1,000-$25,000).
Purpose and activities: Emphasis on higher education, medical research, conservation, recreation, fine arts, and prevention of cruelty to children and animals.
Fields of interest: Higher education, libraries, medical research, conservation, arts, cultural programs, museums, fine arts, recreation, architecture, child welfare, animal welfare.
Types of support: Special projects, general purposes.
Limitations: Giving primarily in PA, NY, and Washington, DC.
Application information: Contributes only to pre-selected organizations. Applications not accepted.
  Board meeting date(s): Nov.
  Write: Harry A. Thompson II, Mgr.
Trustees: James F. Dolan, Drue Heinz, William H. Rea, Mellon Bank, N.A.
Number of staff: 1 full-time professional; 1 part-time professional; 1 full-time support.
EIN: 256018930

2747
Hershey Foods Corporate Giving Program
14 East Chocolate Ave.
Hershey 17033   (717) 534-7574

Financial data (yr. ended 12/31/90): Total giving, $300,000 for grants (average: $1,000-$5,000).
Purpose and activities: "The Corporation recognizes that it has an inherent responsibility to be a good neighbor and responsible corporate citizen. It is corporate policy to make voluntary contributions in support of worthy educational, health, human service, civic and community, and arts and cultural organizations. Employees also are encouraged to take an active part in improving the quality of community life." Particular emphasis is placed on the needs of communities in which the Corporation employs a substantial number of people and on programs and institutions reasonably related to its business purposes and needs. Many factors are considered in determining the level of support for individual activities, including the total budget for the program or organization, its financial viability and importance to Hershey Foods and/or its employees. The Corporation's goal is to make aggregate contributions at a level approximating those of other responsible businesses, with particular emphasis on manufacturers in the food industry. Most contributions will be made in the form of money. However, donations of product, used equipment, services or facilities may be appropriate. Food bank donations, accounting for the largest portion of product donations, are generally directed to Second Harvest affiliates. On a rare occasion, it may be appropriate to support fundraising dinners both financially and by attendance when there are compelling reasons to be represented. In most instances, however, the Corporation declines to support such dinners. Golf tournaments, outside the immediate Hershey area, are rarely considered for support. The use of "goodwill" advertising for charitable causes (space in souvenir publications, yearbooks event programs and other special occasion

publications) is seldom considered an effective use of funds for advertising or public relations purposes. Such requests are declined except in special and limited circumstances where there is clear evidence of corporate benefit or appropriateness.

Fields of interest: Health, welfare, youth, education, community funds, arts, cultural programs, minorities, civic affairs, higher education, business education.

Types of support: Building funds, capital campaigns, employee matching gifts, general purposes, special projects, donated equipment, donated products.

Limitations: Giving primarily in local plant sites. No support for religious, sectarian, or veterans' organizations. No grants to individuals.

Publications: Corporate giving report (including application guidelines), application guidelines.

Application information: Company has a staff that only handles contributions. Application form not required.

> *Initial approach:* Letter to nearest plant; requests are then sent to headquarters to be reviewed by the corporate contributions committee
> *Deadline(s):* 60 days advance notice preferred
> *Board meeting date(s):* 10 times a year
> *Final notification:* Two months
> *Write:* Michael Berney, Corporate Contributions Mgr.

2748
The Hershey Foods Corporation Fund ▼
100 Crystal A Dr.
Hershey 17033   (717) 534-7574

Trust established in 1960 in PA.
Donor(s): Hershey Foods Corp.
Foundation type: Company-sponsored
Financial data (yr. ended 12/31/90): Assets, $3,118,158 (M); expenditures, $2,185,534; qualifying distributions, $2,182,245, including $1,798,461 for 218 grants (high: $125,000; low: $300; average: $500-$5,000) and $383,516 for 782 employee matching gifts.
Purpose and activities: Emphasis on education, including employee matching gifts, human services, civic affairs, and community funds; some support for cultural programs; emphasis on local plant-site communities.
Fields of interest: Higher education, civic affairs, community funds, community development, cultural programs, education.
Types of support: Employee matching gifts, operating budgets, continuing support, annual campaigns, seed money, emergency funds, building funds, equipment, endowment funds, fellowships, research, publications, conferences and seminars, capital campaigns, general purposes, scholarship funds.
Limitations: Giving primarily in PA, and local plant site communities. No grants to individuals, or for endowment funds that are not part of the higher education capital funds campaign; no loans.
Application information: Application form not required.
> *Initial approach:* Letter
> *Copies of proposal:* 1
> *Deadline(s):* At least 60 days prior to board meeting date

Board meeting date(s): Monthly, with some exceptions
Final notification: 1 to 2 months after receipt of letter
Write: M.L. Berney, Mgr., Corp. Contribs., Hershey Foods Corp.
Officer and Trustees:* Richard A. Zimmerman,* Chair.; J.P. Viviano, Kenneth L. Wolfe.
Number of staff: 1 full-time professional; 1 full-time support.
EIN: 236239132
Recent health grants:
2748-1 American Council on Science and Health, NYC, NY, $25,000. 1990.
2748-2 Central Pennsylvania Blood Bank, Hershey, PA, $15,000. 1990.
2748-3 International Life Sciences Institute-Nutrition Foundation, DC, $32,000. 1990.
2748-4 International Life Sciences Institute-Nutrition Foundation, DC, $14,000. 1990.
2748-5 International Life Sciences Institute-Nutrition Foundation, A and I Institute, DC, $18,000. 1990.
2748-6 International Life Sciences Institute-Nutrition Foundation, Risk Science Institute, DC, $18,000. 1990.
2748-7 Milton S. Hershey Medical Center, Hershey, PA, $20,000. 1990.
2748-8 Milton S. Hershey Medical Center, Hershey, PA, $20,000. 1990.
2748-9 Polyclinic Medical Center, Harrisburg, PA, $12,000. 1990.

2749
The Hillman Foundation, Inc. ▼
2000 Grant Bldg.
Pittsburgh 15219   (412) 338-3466

Incorporated in 1951 in DE.
Donor(s): John Hartwell Hillman, Jr.,‡ J.H. Hillman & Sons Co., Hillman Land Co., and family-owned corporations.
Foundation type: Independent
Financial data (yr. ended 12/31/91): Assets, $46,626,325 (M); expenditures, $3,228,194; qualifying distributions, $3,103,021, including $2,796,950 for 57 grants (high: $500,000; low: $2,500; average: $4,000-$200,000).
Purpose and activities: Program areas include cultural advancement and the arts, education, health and medicine, civic and community affairs, social services, and youth.
Fields of interest: Cultural programs, arts, education, higher education, health, community development, civic affairs, social services, youth.
Types of support: Continuing support, seed money, endowment funds, matching funds, professorships, special projects, building funds, equipment, land acquisition, capital campaigns, renovation projects.
Limitations: Giving primarily in Pittsburgh and southwestern PA. No grants to individuals, or for operating budgets, annual campaigns, deficit financing, travel, or conferences; no loans.
Publications: Annual report (including application guidelines).
Application information: Application form not required.
> *Initial approach:* Letter
> *Copies of proposal:* 1

Deadline(s): None
Board meeting date(s): Apr., June, Oct., and Dec., and at annual meeting in May
Write: Ronald W. Wertz, Pres.
Officers and Directors:* Henry L. Hillman,* Chair.; Ronald W. Wertz, Pres.; C.G. Grefenstette,* V.P.; H. Vaughan Blaxter III, Secy.; David H. Ross, Treas.; Elsie H. Hillman, Lawrence M. Wagner.
Number of staff: 2 full-time professional; 1 full-time support.
EIN: 256011462
Recent health grants:
2749-1 Association for Retarded Citizens of Allegheny County Foundation, Pittsburgh, PA, $35,000. Toward establishing Personal Care Residence Program designed to provide residential care for elderly people with retardation. 1991.
2749-2 Contact Pittsburgh, Pittsburgh, PA, $21,800. Toward start-up telecommunications and information management costs of new satellite phoneroom in donated space at Southwood Hospital in South Hills. 1991.
2749-3 D.T. Watson Rehabilitation Hospital, Sewickley, PA, $25,000. Toward renovation and expansion of Harry S. Tack Education Center. 1991.
2749-4 East End Cooperative Ministry, Pittsburgh, PA, $35,000. Toward establishment of Sojourner House, new residential center/halfway house for women recovering from drug and alcohol addiction and their children. 1991.

2750
The Henry L. Hillman Foundation
2000 Grant Bldg.
Pittsburgh 15219   (412) 338-3466

Established in 1964 in PA.
Donor(s): Henry L. Hillman.
Foundation type: Independent
Financial data (yr. ended 12/31/91): Assets, $15,631,642 (M); expenditures, $732,550; qualifying distributions, $704,995, including $694,250 for 51 grants (high: $235,000; low: $250; average: $1,000-$5,000).
Purpose and activities: Support primarily for the arts and cultural programs, and higher and secondary education; support also for youth, conservation, civic affairs, community development, church support, social services, and hospitals.
Fields of interest: Cultural programs, higher education, secondary education, youth, conservation, civic affairs, community development, religion—Christian, social services, hospitals.
Types of support: Operating budgets, continuing support, annual campaigns, seed money, emergency funds, building funds, equipment, matching funds, special projects, renovation projects, capital campaigns.
Limitations: Giving primarily in Pittsburgh and southwestern PA. No grants to individuals, or for deficit financing, land acquisition, endowment funds, research, publications, or conferences; no loans.
Publications: Financial statement.
Application information: Application form not required.

Initial approach: Letter
Copies of proposal: 1
Deadline(s): None
Board meeting date(s): Mar. and Dec.
Final notification: 3 to 4 months
Write: Ronald W. Wertz, Exec. Dir. and Secy.
Officers and Directors:* Henry L. Hillman,*
Pres.; Ronald W. Wertz,* Exec. Dir. and Secy.;
David H. Ross, Treas.; H. Vaughan Blaxter III.
Number of staff: 1 part-time professional; 2
part-time support.
EIN: 256065959

2751
The Holstrom Family Foundation
c/o Carleton A. Holstrom
20 East Court St., P.O. Box 1310
Doylestown 18901   (215) 340-1850

Established in 1984 in NY.
Donor(s): Carleton A. Holstrom.
Foundation type: Independent
Financial data (yr. ended 11/30/91): Assets,
$379,340 (M); gifts received, $99,400;
expenditures, $226,155; qualifying distributions,
$221,167, including $220,400 for 23 grants
(high: $100,000; low: $100).
Fields of interest: Cultural programs, arts,
performing arts, education, history, environment,
conservation, family planning, social services,
hospitals.
Types of support: Annual campaigns, capital
campaigns, endowment funds, research.
Limitations: Giving primarily in New York, NY,
and NJ. No grants to individuals.
Application information: Contributes only to
pre-selected organizations. Applications not
accepted.
Officers: Carleton A. Holstrom, Pres.; Christina L.
Holstrom, V.P.; Mary Beth Kineke, V.P.; Marcia O.
Holstrom, Secy.; Cynthia J. Cawthorne, Treas.
EIN: 222611162

2752
Janet A. Hooker Charitable Trust
150 Radnor Chester Rd., Suite A200
St. Davids 19087   (215) 341-9270

Trust established in 1952 in NY.
Donor(s): Janet A. Neff Hooker.
Foundation type: Independent
Financial data (yr. ended 12/31/91): Assets,
$8,395,873 (M); expenditures, $630,446;
qualifying distributions, $627,305, including
$592,000 for 36 grants (high: $60,000; low:
$1,000; average: $1,000-$25,000).
Purpose and activities: Primary areas of interest
include education, community development, and
cultural programs. Support for historic
preservation, conservation, medical research and
health services, and social service agencies;
giving also for animal welfare.
Fields of interest: Arts, cultural programs, historic
preservation, conservation, medical research,
health services, social services, animal welfare,
education, community development.
Types of support: Annual campaigns, general
purposes.
Limitations: Giving primarily in NY, FL, and
Washington, DC. No grants to individuals.

Application information: Applications not
accepted.
   Board meeting date(s): Varies
   Write: Leanne M. Workman
Trustee: Walter H. Annenberg.
Number of staff: None.
EIN: 236286762

2753
Elizabeth S. Hooper Foundation
223 West Lancaster Ave., Suite 200
Devon 19333

Established in 1967.
Donor(s): Interstate Marine Transport Co.,
Interstate Towing Co., Interstate Ocean Transport
Co., and members of the Hooper family.
Foundation type: Independent
Financial data (yr. ended 06/30/91): Assets,
$1,438,102 (M); gifts received, $325,000;
expenditures, $717,603; qualifying distributions,
$707,000, including $707,000 for 95 grants
(high: $400,000; low: $250).
Purpose and activities: Giving largely for higher
and secondary education; grants also for cultural
programs, public policy organizations, health,
and Protestant church support.
Fields of interest: Higher education, secondary
education, cultural programs, public policy,
health, Protestant giving.
Types of support: Building funds, special projects,
general purposes, emergency funds, research,
scholarship funds, operating budgets.
Application information: Foundation is not
considering any new grant requests. Applications
not accepted.
Officers and Directors:* Adrian S. Hooper,* Pres.;
Thomas Hooper,* V.P.; Bruce H. Hooper,* Secy.;
Ralph W. Hooper,* Treas.; John P. Lally.
EIN: 236434997

2754
John M. Hopwood Charitable Trust
c/o Pittsburgh National Bank, Charitable &
Institutional Trust Dept.
One Oliver Plaza, 27th Fl.
Pittsburgh 15265   (412) 762-3502

Trust established about 1948 in PA.
Donor(s): John M. Hopwood,‡ Mary S.
Hopwood,‡ William T. Hopwood.
Foundation type: Independent
Financial data (yr. ended 12/31/91): Assets,
$17,518,575 (M); expenditures, $719,337;
qualifying distributions, $679,286, including
$653,000 for 80 grants (high: $48,800; low:
$1,000).
Purpose and activities: Primary areas of interest
include conservation, education, and hospitals.
Fields of interest: Hospitals, education, higher
education, youth, cultural programs, social
services, energy, conservation, environment.
Types of support: Seed money, endowment funds,
special projects, matching funds.
Limitations: Giving primarily in PA and FL.
Application information:
   Initial approach: Letter
   Deadline(s): None
   Write: R. Bruce Bickel, V.P., Pittsburgh National
   Bank

Trustees: William T. Hopwood, Pittsburgh
National Bank.
EIN: 256022634

2755
Horsehead Community Development Fund, Inc.
P.O. Box 351
Palmerton 18071
Application address: 304 Princeton Ave.,
Palmerton, PA 18071; Tel.: (215) 826-4377

Established in 1989 in PA.
Donor(s): Horsehead Resources.
Foundation type: Independent
Financial data (yr. ended 12/31/91): Assets,
$21,996 (M); gifts received, $232,232;
expenditures, $294,660; qualifying distributions,
$294,660, including $293,647 for 45 grants
(high: $50,000; low: $500).
Purpose and activities: Giving primarily to a
hospital and a library association; support also for
community development and sports activities for
youth.
Fields of interest: Community development,
community funds, libraries, recreation, youth,
hospitals, environment, conservation, performing
arts.
Types of support: Capital campaigns, renovation
projects, special projects, emergency funds,
equipment.
Limitations: Giving primarily in Palmerton, PA,
and surrounding communities.
Publications: Annual report, 990-PF, grants list,
occasional report, program policy statement,
application guidelines.
Application information: Grants must be used in
same year awarded. Application form required.
   Initial approach: Letter or telephone
   Copies of proposal: 2
   Deadline(s): None
   Board meeting date(s): Quarterly
   Final notification: After board meeting
   Write: Charles H. Campton, Chair.
Officers and Directors:* Charles H. Campton,*
Chair.; Rev. Doris Bray,* Vice-Chair.; Peter Kern,*
Secy.; James A. Wimmer,* Treas.; William
Bechdolt, Harold A. Queen, William A. Smelas.
Number of staff: None.
EIN: 232588172

2756
The Hoyt Foundation
c/o First National Bank of Western Pennsylvania
P.O. Box 1488
New Castle 16103-1488
Application address: 101 East Washington St.,
New Castle, PA 16101; Tel.: (412) 652-5511

Incorporated in 1962 in PA.
Donor(s): May Emma Hoyt,‡ Alex Crawford Hoyt.
Foundation type: Independent
Financial data (yr. ended 10/31/91): Assets,
$9,683,159 (M); expenditures, $581,083;
qualifying distributions, $486,191, including
$385,000 for 34 grants (high: $75,000; low:
$100) and $101,191 for 158 grants to individuals
(high: $3,943; low: $150).
Purpose and activities: Emphasis on higher
education, including scholarships, and a hospital;
some support also for cultural programs.

Fields of interest: Higher education, hospitals, cultural programs.
Types of support: Student aid, annual campaigns, building funds, capital campaigns, continuing support, seed money.
Limitations: Giving limited to residents and organizations in Lawrence County, PA.
Application information: Application form required for scholarships.
Deadline(s): June 4
Board meeting date(s): Monthly
Write: Linda Pierog
Officer and Directors:* Thomas V. Mansell,* Pres.; Wayne Cole, Thomas J. O'Shane, Paul H. Reed, Jack Sant, Steve Warner.
Number of staff: 1 part-time support.
EIN: 256064468

2757
Milton G. Hulme Charitable Foundation
519 Frick Bldg.
Pittsburgh 15219   (412) 281-2007

Established in 1960 in PA.
Donor(s): Glover & MacGregor, Inc.
Foundation type: Independent
Financial data (yr. ended 12/31/91): Assets, $4,595,050 (M); expenditures, $210,328; qualifying distributions, $206,109, including $205,000 for 42 grants (high: $15,000; low: $1,000).
Fields of interest: Protestant giving, rehabilitation, health associations, social services.
Types of support: Operating budgets, capital campaigns.
Limitations: Giving primarily in Pittsburgh, PA. No grants to individuals.
Application information: Application form not required.
Initial approach: Letter, proposal, or telephone
Copies of proposal: 1
Deadline(s): June 30
Board meeting date(s): Dec.
Final notification: 2 weeks after application deadline
Write: Milton G. Hulme, Trustee
Trustees: Natalie H. Curry, Aura P. Hulme, Helen C. Hulme, Jocelyn H. MacConnell, Helen H. Shoup.
Number of staff: 2 part-time support.
EIN: 256062896

2758
The Roy A. Hunt Foundation
One Bigelow Sq., Suite 630
Pittsburgh 15219   (412) 281-8734

Established in 1966 in PA.
Donor(s): Roy A. Hunt.‡
Foundation type: Independent
Financial data (yr. ended 05/31/91): Assets, $28,638,854 (M); expenditures, $808,378; qualifying distributions, $688,440, including $616,065 for 83 grants (high: $100,000; low: $1,000; average: $7,500-$50,000).
Purpose and activities: Grants initiated by the trustees, primarily to support the Hunt Institute for Botanical Documentation at Carnegie-Mellon University; smaller grants for higher and secondary education, Protestant church support,

the arts and cultural programs, social services, the environment, health services, and hospitals.
Fields of interest: Higher education, secondary education, Protestant giving, cultural programs, arts, social services, environment, health associations, hospitals.
Types of support: Annual campaigns, building funds, endowment funds, general purposes.
Limitations: Giving primarily in the Pittsburgh, PA, and Boston, MA, areas. No grants to individuals.
Application information: Application form not required.
Initial approach: Letter
Copies of proposal: 1
Deadline(s): May 1 and Oct. 1 for solicited proposals only
Board meeting date(s): June and Nov.
Final notification: July and Dec.
Write: Torrence M. Hunt, Jr., Admin. Trustee
Trustees: Susan Hunt Hollingsworth, Andrew McQ. Hunt, Christopher M. Hunt, Daniel K. Hunt, Helen M. Hunt, John B. Hunt, Richard M. Hunt, Roy A. Hunt III, Torrence M. Hunt, Sr., Torrence M. Hunt, Jr., Marion M. Hunt-Badiner, Rachel Hunt Knowles.
Number of staff: 2 part-time professional.
EIN: 256105162

2759
Independence Foundation ▼
2500 Philadelphia National Bank Bldg.
Philadelphia 19107-3493   (215) 563-8105
FAX: (215) 563-8107

Established in 1932 as International Cancer Research Foundation; incorporated as Donner Foundation in 1945 in DE; divided in 1961 into Independence Foundation and a newly formed William H. Donner Foundation.
Donor(s): William H. Donner.‡
Foundation type: Independent
Financial data (yr. ended 12/31/91): Assets, $92,514,367 (M); expenditures, $4,055,233; qualifying distributions, $3,738,410, including $3,738,410 for 30 grants (high: $250,000; low: $1,000; average: $10,000-$30,000).
Purpose and activities: Support for educational and cultural organizations; support also for student aid in nursing education.
Fields of interest: Education, cultural programs, nursing.
Types of support: Endowment funds, professorships, general purposes, scholarship funds, fellowships.
Limitations: No grants to individuals, or for building and development funds, travel, research, publications, operating budgets, college scholarships, graduate fellowships, or matching gifts.
Publications: Annual report (including application guidelines).
Application information: Exhibit material, if sent, should be in single form. Receipt of proposals is acknowledged. Should the original prove to be within the scope of the foundation's interests, interviews with the board will be arranged prior to final determination. Application form not required.
Initial approach: Letter
Copies of proposal: 5
Deadline(s): 3 weeks before meetings

Board meeting date(s): Mar., June, Sept., and Dec.
Final notification: 3 to 6 weeks
Write: Frank H. Goodyear, Jr., Pres.
Officers and Directors:* Alexander F. Barbieri,* Chair. and Secy.; Frederick H. Donner, V.P.; Viola MacInnes,* Treas. and Acting C.E.O.; Theodore K. Warner, Jr.
Number of staff: 3 full-time professional.
EIN: 231352110
Recent health grants:
2759-1 Case Western Reserve University, School of Nursing, Cleveland, OH, $250,000. For teaching endowment. 1990.
2759-2 Case Western Reserve University, School of Nursing, Cleveland, OH, $100,000. For scholarship and loan funds. 1990.
2759-3 Emory University, School of Nursing, Atlanta, GA, $250,000. For teaching endowment. 1990.
2759-4 Emory University, School of Nursing, Atlanta, GA, $100,000. For scholarship and loan funds. 1990.
2759-5 Hampton University, School of Nursing, Hampton, VA, $50,000. For scholarship and loan funds. 1990.
2759-6 Johns Hopkins University, School of Nursing, Baltimore, MD, $250,000. For teaching endowment. 1990.
2759-7 Johns Hopkins University, School of Nursing, Baltimore, MD, $100,000. For scholarship and loan funds. 1990.
2759-8 New York University, Division of Nursing, NYC, NY, $250,000. For teaching endowment. 1990.
2759-9 New York University, Division of Nursing, NYC, NY, $100,000. For scholarship and loan funds. 1990.
2759-10 Planned Parenthood Association of Southeastern Pennsylvania, Philadelphia, PA, $35,000. For general support. 1990.
2759-11 Rush University, College of Nursing, Chicago, IL, $250,000. For teaching endowment. 1990.
2759-12 Rush University, College of Nursing, Chicago, IL, $100,000. For scholarship and loan funds. 1990.
2759-13 University of Pennsylvania, School of Nursing, Philadelphia, PA, $250,000. For teaching endowment. 1990.
2759-14 University of Pennsylvania, School of Nursing, Philadelphia, PA, $125,000. For scholarship and loan funds. 1990.
2759-15 University of Rochester, School of Nursing, Rochester, NY, $250,000. For teaching endowment. 1990.
2759-16 University of Rochester, School of Nursing, Rochester, NY, $100,000. For scholarship and loan funds. 1990.
2759-17 Vanderbilt University, School of Nursing, Nashville, TN, $250,000. For teaching endowment. 1990.
2759-18 Vanderbilt University, School of Nursing, Nashville, TN, $100,000. For scholarship and loan funds. 1990.
2759-19 Yale University, School of Nursing, New Haven, CT, $250,000. For teaching endowment. 1990.
2759-20 Yale University, School of Nursing, New Haven, CT, $100,000. For scholarship and loan funds. 1990.

2760
The J.D.B. Fund ▼
404 South Swedesford Rd.
P.O. Box 157
Gwynedd 19436   (215) 699-2233

Trust established in 1966 in PA.
Donor(s): John Drew Betz.
Foundation type: Independent
Financial data (yr. ended 12/31/90): Assets,
$7,406,067 (M); expenditures, $1,085,008;
qualifying distributions, $1,067,810, including
$1,067,810 for 44 grants (high: $595,560; low:
$300).
Fields of interest: Health associations, hospitals,
conservation, civic affairs, historic preservation.
Types of support: Building funds, equipment,
land acquisition, matching funds.
Limitations: Giving primarily in Philadelphia, PA,
and the surrounding area. No support for arts and
sciences or medical research. No grants to
individuals, or for endowment funds,
scholarships, fellowships, demonstration projects,
publications, or conferences; no loans for general
support of established universities, charities,
foundations, or hospitals.
Application information: Contributes only to
pre-selected organizations. Applications not
accepted.
   Board meeting date(s): Monthly
   Write: Paul J. Corr, Mgr.
Officer: Paul J. Corr, Mgr.
Trustee: Claire S. Betz.
Number of staff: 2
EIN: 236418867
Recent health grants:
2760-1 Indigent Fund of Home Oncology
   Therapies, Rockville, MD, $10,000. For
   memorial contribution. 1990.

2761
Henry Janssen Foundation, Inc.
2650 Westview Dr.
Wyomissing 19610

Incorporated in 1931 in DE.
Donor(s): Members of the Janssen family, Helen
Wetzel.
Foundation type: Independent
Financial data (yr. ended 12/31/91): Assets,
$12,753,388 (M); gifts received, $59,090;
expenditures, $658,297; qualifying distributions,
$580,453, including $576,500 for 48 grants
(high: $88,500; low: $1,000).
Fields of interest: Hospitals, health services,
cultural programs, higher education, community
funds.
Limitations: Giving primarily in PA, particularly
Reading and Berks County. No grants to
individuals.
Application information: Contributes only to
pre-selected organizations. Applications not
accepted.
Officers and Trustees: * Elsa L. Bowman,* Pres.;
Helene L. Master,* V.P.; John W. Bowman,* Secy.;
El Roy P. Master,* Treas.; David F. Rick, F. Eugene
Stapleton.
EIN: 231476340

2762
The Mary Hillman Jennings Foundation ▼
2325 Pittsburgh National Bldg.
Pittsburgh 15222   (412) 566-2510

Incorporated in 1968 in PA.
Donor(s): Mary Hillman Jennings.‡
Foundation type: Independent
Financial data (yr. ended 12/31/90): Assets,
$24,287,127 (M); expenditures, $1,572,717;
qualifying distributions, $1,404,766, including
$1,283,475 for 128 grants (high: $100,000; low:
$375; average: $1,000-$50,000).
Purpose and activities: Grants to schools, youth
agencies, and hospitals and health associations.
Fields of interest: Education, youth, hospitals,
health.
Types of support: Annual campaigns, building
funds, capital campaigns, endowment funds,
equipment, general purposes, renovation
projects, research, special projects.
Limitations: Giving primarily in the Pittsburgh,
PA, area. No grants to individuals.
Application information: Application form not
required.
   Initial approach: Letter
   Deadline(s): Submit proposal by May or Nov.
   Board meeting date(s): June and Dec.
   Final notification: 3 to 6 months
   Write: Paul Euwer, Jr., Exec. Dir.
Officers and Directors: * Evan D. Jennings II,*
Pres.; Andrew L. Weil,* Secy.; Irving A.
Wechsler,* Treas.; Paul Euwer, Jr.,* Exec. Dir.;
Christina Jennings.
Number of staff: 1 full-time professional; 1
part-time support.
EIN: 237002091
Recent health grants:
2762-1 Alzheimers Disease Alliance of Western
   Pennsylvania, Pittsburgh, PA, $25,000. 1990.
2762-2 Childrens Hospital of Pittsburgh,
   Pittsburgh, PA, $25,000. 1990.
2762-3 D.T. Watson Rehabilitation Hospital,
   Sewickley, PA, $25,000. 1990.
2762-4 Eye and Ear Institute, Pittsburgh, PA,
   $50,000. 1990.
2762-5 Harmarville Foundation, Pittsburgh, PA,
   $30,000. 1990.
2762-6 Magee-Womens Health Foundation,
   Pittsburgh, PA, $25,000. 1990.
2762-7 Marian Manor Nursing Home,
   Pittsburgh, PA, $10,000. 1990.
2762-8 Ocean Reef Medical Center, Key Largo,
   FL, $10,000. 1990.
2762-9 Oxford House, Great Falls, VA, $10,000.
   1990.
2762-10 Pittsburgh Cancer Institute, Pittsburgh,
   PA, $30,000. 1990.
2762-11 Pittsburgh Leadership Foundation,
   Pittsburgh, PA, $10,000. For Coalition for
   Addictive Diseases in Southwestern
   Pennsylvania. 1990.
2762-12 Saint Clair Memorial Hospital
   Foundation, Pittsburgh, PA, $16,000. 1990.
2762-13 Spina Bifida Association of Western
   Pennsylvania, Pittsburgh, PA, $25,000. 1990.
2762-14 West Penn Hospital Foundation,
   Pittsburgh, PA, $33,000. 1990.

2763
The Jewish Healthcare Foundation of Pittsburgh
Centre City Tower, Suite 2550
650 Smithfield St.
Pittsburgh 15222

Established in 1990 in PA.
Donor(s): Presbyterian University Health Systems,
Inc.
Foundation type: Independent
Financial data (yr. ended 12/31/91): Assets,
$82,978,208 (M); gifts received, $410;
expenditures, $2,517,230; qualifying
distributions, $2,085,749, including $1,623,457
for grants (high: $750,000; low: $500).
Purpose and activities: To support and foster the
provision of health care services, health care
education, and health care research, and to
respond to the health-related needs of the elderly,
underprivileged, indigent, and underserved
populations in western PA. The foundation will
assist in the treatment and care of those who are
elderly, sick, infirm, or in any way afflicted with
physical or mental disease, in both the Jewish and
general community. Current foundation priorities
include: 1) the health of children at risk; 2) special
needs of the elderly and chronically ill; and 3)
women's health.
Fields of interest: Health, aged, AIDS, health
services, family planning, hospitals, drug abuse,
nutrition, Jewish welfare, women.
Types of support: Matching funds, seed money,
emergency funds, special projects.
Limitations: Giving limited to western PA. No
grants to individuals, or for general operations,
endowment programs, capital needs, operating
deficits or retirement of debt, scholarships,
fellowships, research, or travel.
Publications: Annual report, application
guidelines, newsletter, program policy statement.
Application information: Application form not
required.
   Initial approach: Preliminary letter of intent not
      to exceed 6 pages
   Copies of proposal: 4
   Deadline(s): None
   Write: Karen Feinstein, Ph.D., Pres.
Officers and Trustees: * Alvin Rogal,* Chair.;
William K. Lieberman,* Vice-Chair.; Robert
Patton,* Vice-Chair.; Karen Wolk Feinstein,
Ph.D.,* Pres.; Rita Perlow,* Secy.; Robert A.
Paul,* Treas.; and 55 additional trustees.
Number of staff: 5 full-time professional; 1
part-time professional; 3 full-time support.
EIN: 251624347

2764
Edith C. Justus Trust
National Transit Bldg.
Oil City 16301   (814) 677-5085

Trust established in 1931 in PA.
Donor(s): Edith C. Justus.‡
Foundation type: Independent
Financial data (yr. ended 12/31/90): Assets,
$3,561,588 (M); gifts received, $201;
expenditures, $262,243; qualifying distributions,
$244,244, including $230,091 for 22 grants
(high: $38,780; low: $25; average:
$5,000-$20,000).

Purpose and activities: Giving largely for community development and civic affairs, including a library and public parks, and for social service and health agencies.
Fields of interest: Civic affairs, social services, health services, community development, aged, alcoholism, education, employment, family services, libraries.
Types of support: General purposes, operating budgets, building funds, equipment, land acquisition, continuing support, annual campaigns, seed money, emergency funds, deficit financing, matching funds, renovation projects.
Limitations: Giving primarily in Venango County, PA, with emphasis on Oil City. No grants to individuals, or for endowment funds, matching gifts, scholarships, fellowships, special projects, research, publications, or conferences; no loans.
Publications: Application guidelines, 990-PF, grants list.
Application information: Application form required.
  Initial approach: Letter
  Copies of proposal: 3
  Deadline(s): Submit proposal in Apr., Aug., or Nov.; no set deadline
  Board meeting date(s): May, Sept., and Dec.
  Final notification: 2 months
  Write: Stephen P. Kosak, Consultant
Trustee: Integra Financial Corp.
Number of staff: 1 full-time professional; 1 part-time support.
EIN: 256031057

2765
Samuel and Rebecca Kardon Foundation
c/o Landsburg Platt & Flax
117 South 17th St.
Philadelphia 19103   (215) 561-6633

Trust established in 1952 in PA.
Donor(s): Emanuel S. Kardon, American Bag & Paper Corp.
Foundation type: Independent
Financial data (yr. ended 12/31/91): Assets, $8,257,583 (M); expenditures, $261,572; qualifying distributions, $245,300, including $245,300 for 38 grants (high: $66,200; low: $100).
Purpose and activities: Emphasis on a music institute for the handicapped, higher and secondary education, and Jewish welfare funds; support also for hospitals and social service agencies.
Fields of interest: Education, music, handicapped, higher education, secondary education, Jewish welfare, hospitals, social services.
Limitations: Giving primarily in PA.
Application information:
  Initial approach: Letter
  Deadline(s): None
  Write: Emanuel S. Kardon, Pres.
Officer and Trustee:* Emanuel S. Kardon,* Pres.
EIN: 236278123

2766
Kennametal Foundation
P.O. Box 231
Latrobe 15650   (412) 539-5203

Trust established in 1955 in PA.
Foundation type: Company-sponsored
Financial data (yr. ended 06/30/91): Assets, $1,173,433 (M); gifts received, $800,000; expenditures, $317,150; qualifying distributions, $315,475, including $315,475 for 141 grants (high: $52,355; low: $25).
Purpose and activities: Emphasis on higher education, hospitals, museums, and social services, including community funds.
Fields of interest: Higher education, hospitals, community funds, social services, museums.
Types of support: Continuing support, building funds, equipment, endowment funds, program-related investments, matching funds.
Limitations: No grants to individuals, or for scholarships or fellowships; no loans.
Application information: Contributes only to pre-selected organizations. Applications not accepted.
  Board meeting date(s): Monthly
  Write: Alex G. McKenna, Trustee
Trustees: James R. Breisinger, Robert L. McGeehan, Alex G. McKenna, Quentin C. McKenna, Richard J. Orwig.
EIN: 256036009

2767
The Robert L. Kift-Thomas R. Mullen, Jr. Memorial Foundation, Inc.
P.O. Box 626
Allentown 18101

Established in 1949.
Foundation type: Independent
Financial data (yr. ended 12/31/91): Assets, $642,402 (M); expenditures, $44,614; qualifying distributions, $43,820, including $43,650 for 43 grants (high: $5,800; low: $50).
Fields of interest: Education, civic affairs, health, youth, community funds.
Limitations: Giving primarily in Allentown, PA, area. No grants to individuals.
Application information:
  Initial approach: Proposal
  Deadline(s): Feb. 1
  Write: J.C. Klein, V.P.
Officers and Trustees:* M.L. Mullen,* Pres.; T.H. Mohr,* V.P.; J.C. Klein,* Secy.; W.W. Toth,* Treas.; H.C. Weisel, Jr.
EIN: 236265407

2768
Josiah W. and Bessie H. Kline Foundation, Inc.
42 Kline Village
Harrisburg 17104   (717) 232-0266

Incorporated in 1952 in DE.
Donor(s): Josiah W. Kline,‡ Bessie H. Kline.‡
Foundation type: Independent
Financial data (yr. ended 12/31/91): Assets, $20,424,140 (M); expenditures, $1,059,053; qualifying distributions, $942,744, including $924,820 for 52 grants (high: $200,000; low: $500).
Purpose and activities: Support primarily for higher education, hospitals, and the handicapped; support also for scientific or medical research, educational associations and building funds, health associations, child welfare

organizations, historic preservation, and legal education and projects for the improvement of the law.
Fields of interest: Higher education, hospitals, science and technology, medical research, educational associations, education—building funds, health associations, child welfare, historic preservation, law and justice.
Types of support: General purposes, continuing support, annual campaigns, emergency funds, building funds, equipment, scholarship funds, matching funds, renovation projects, capital campaigns, land acquisition, lectureships, research.
Limitations: Giving primarily in south central PA. No grants to individuals, or for endowment funds, operating budgets, special projects, publications, conferences, or fellowships; no loans.
Publications: 990-PF.
Application information: Application form not required.
  Initial approach: Proposal
  Copies of proposal: 2
  Deadline(s): None
  Board meeting date(s): Semiannually
  Final notification: 6 months
  Write: Harry R. Bughman, Secy.
Officers and Directors:* Robert F. Nation,* Pres.; Richard E. Jordan,* V.P.; Harry R. Bughman,* Secy.; William J. King,* Treas.; William D. Boswell, Jeffrey J. Burdge, James A. Marley, Samuel D. Ross, David A. Smith, John C. Tuten.
Number of staff: 1 full-time professional.
EIN: 236245783

2769
John Crain Kunkel Foundation
1400 Market St., Suite 203
Camp Hill 17011   (717) 763-1784

Established in 1965 in PA.
Foundation type: Independent
Financial data (yr. ended 12/31/91): Assets, $9,257,381 (M); expenditures, $423,654; qualifying distributions, $332,955, including $298,500 for 20 grants (high: $50,000; low: $1,000).
Fields of interest: Higher education, secondary education, social services, health.
Types of support: General purposes.
Limitations: Giving primarily in PA.
Application information: Application form not required.
  Initial approach: Letter
  Deadline(s): None
  Write: Hasbrouck S. Wright, Exec. Trustee
Trustees: Hasbrouck S. Wright, Exec. Trustee; W. Minster Kunkel, K.R. Stark.
EIN: 237026914

2770
Edna G. Kynett Memorial Foundation, Inc.
P.O. Box 8228
Philadelphia 19101-8228   (215) 828-8145

Incorporated in 1954 in DE.
Donor(s): Harold H. Kynett.‡
Foundation type: Independent
Financial data (yr. ended 12/31/90): Assets, $2,354,475 (L); expenditures, $110,211;

qualifying distributions, $101,816, including $92,700 for 5 grants (high: $25,000; low: $2,700).
Purpose and activities: Grants to hospitals for medical education and research, to help educate primary care physicians in the field of cardiovascular disease.
Fields of interest: Hospitals, medical education, heart disease, medical research.
Types of support: Conferences and seminars, fellowships, special projects.
Limitations: Giving primarily in the Philadelphia, PA, area. No grants for endowment purposes.
Application information: Application form not required.
 Initial approach: Proposal
 Copies of proposal: 12
 Write: Judith L. Bardes, Mgr.
Officers and Trustees:* Joseph B. VanderVeer, M.D.,* Pres.; F.W. Elliott Farr,* V.P.; Barclay Hallowell,* Secy.; Michael W. Walsh,* Treas.; Judith Bardes, Mgr.; Elmer H. Funk, Jr., M.D., Davis W. Gregg, Norman B. Makous, M.D., James Shea, Edward J. Stemmler, M.D., Edward S. Weyl, D. Stratton Woodruff, Jr., M.D.
Number of staff: 1 part-time professional.
EIN: 236296592

2771
Laurel Foundation
Three Gateway Ctr., 6 North
Pittsburgh 15222   (412) 765-2400

Incorporated in 1951 in PA.
Donor(s): Cordelia S. May.
Foundation type: Independent
Financial data (yr. ended 12/31/91): Assets, $22,979,408 (M); expenditures, $1,246,101; qualifying distributions, $1,076,701, including $1,000,595 for 48 grants (high: $37,000; low: $610).
Purpose and activities: Grants largely to organizations operating in the fields of higher and secondary education, the environment and conservation, health, and medical research, welfare, family planning, cultural programs, including museums and the performing arts, and population planning, with concentration on projects originating in the Pittsburgh area; support also for immigration reform and media and communications.
Fields of interest: Higher education, secondary education, conservation, health, medical research, welfare, family planning, cultural programs, immigration, media and communications.
Types of support: General purposes, building funds, special projects, conferences and seminars, equipment, land acquisition, operating budgets, publications, lectureships.
Limitations: Giving primarily in western PA. No grants to individuals.
Publications: Annual report, application guidelines.
Application information: Application form not required.
 Initial approach: Letter
 Copies of proposal: 1
 Deadline(s): Submit proposal preferably between Jan. and Apr. or July and Oct.; deadlines are May 1 and Nov. 1
 Board meeting date(s): June and Dec.
 Final notification: June 20 and Dec. 20

Write: Gregory D. Curtis, Pres.
Officers and Trustees:* Cordelia S. May,* Chair.; Gregory D. Curtis, Pres. and Secy.; Roger F. Meyer, V.P. and Treas.; Mrs. John F. Kraft, Jr.,* V.P.; Curtis S. Scaife, Robert E. Willison.
Number of staff: 2 part-time professional; 2 part-time support.
EIN: 256008073

2772
Lehigh Valley Community Foundation
(Formerly Bethlehem Area Foundation)
961 Marcon Blvd., Suite 110
Allentown 18103-9521   (215) 266-4284

Established in 1967 in PA.
Foundation type: Community
Financial data (yr. ended 06/30/92): Assets, $3,022,534 (M); gifts received, $76,620; expenditures, $313,760; qualifying distributions, $223,507, including $223,507 for 51 grants (high: $24,250; low: $50; average: $1,000-$24,250).
Purpose and activities: Primary areas of interest include education and training, programs for the disadvantaged, social services, and welfare; support also for cultural programs.
Fields of interest: Health, nutrition, education, education—minorities, social services, disadvantaged, welfare, cultural programs, theater, historic preservation.
Types of support: Seed money, emergency funds, building funds, equipment, land acquisition, matching funds, special projects, capital campaigns, renovation projects, publications.
Limitations: Giving limited to the Bethlehem, PA, area. No support for sectarian religious purposes. No grants to individuals, or for operating budgets, continuing support, annual campaigns, deficit financing, endowments, scholarships, or research; no loans.
Publications: Annual report (including application guidelines), grants list, application guidelines, program policy statement.
Application information: Capital funding: must submit invoice copies when requesting release of funds. Program: brief progress report in June; program evaluation by Oct. Application form not required.
 Initial approach: Letter or telephone requesting application brochure
 Copies of proposal: 5
 Deadline(s): Submit proposal from June 1 to Aug. 1
 Board meeting date(s): Oct.
 Final notification: Oct.
 Write: Eleanor A. Boylston, Exec. Dir.
Officers and Board of Governors:* John R. Mendenhall,* Chair.; Martha Cusimano,* Vice-Chair.; Eleanor A. Boylston, Secy. and Exec. Dir.; Joseph Conroy, Joan Dealtrey, Paul Franz, Elmer Gates, Deborah Haight, Joseph F. Leeson, Jr., Helen Magee, William Matz, Chadwick Paol, Jose Perna, Terence Theman.
Trustee Banks: First Valley Bank, Lehigh Valley Bank, Meridian Bank.
Number of staff: 1 full-time professional; 1 full-time support.
EIN: 231686634

2773
Margaret and Irvin Lesher Foundation
National Transit Bldg.
Oil City 16301   (814) 677-5085

Trust established in 1963 in PA.
Donor(s): Margaret W. Lesher.‡
Foundation type: Independent
Financial data (yr. ended 12/31/91): Assets, $2,039,590 (M); expenditures, $119,460; qualifying distributions, $106,762, including $96,150 for 166 grants to individuals (high: $1,500; low: $2; average: $100-$2,000).
Purpose and activities: Giving limited to scholarships for graduates of Union Joint School District, Clarion County; support also for a rural medical center, and for research concerning the treatment of cancer and heart diseases.
Fields of interest: Medical research, cancer, heart disease.
Types of support: Student aid.
Limitations: Giving limited to Union School District of Clarion County, PA. No grants to individuals (except for scholarships), or for endowment funds; no loans.
Publications: 990-PF, application guidelines.
Application information: Application form required.
 Initial approach: Letter
 Copies of proposal: 2
 Deadline(s): Mar. 15 for initial applications; May 20 for renewals
 Board meeting date(s): May and Sept. and Dec. if needed
 Final notification: 2 months after board meeting
 Write: Stephen P. Kosak, Consultant
Trustee: Integra Financial Corp.
Number of staff: 1 full-time professional; 1 part-time support.
EIN: 256067843

2774
Polly Annenberg Levee Charitable Trust
St. Davids Ctr., Suite A-200
150 Radnor-Chester Rd.
St. Davids 19087

Trust established in 1952 in NY.
Donor(s): Polly Annenberg Levee.‡
Foundation type: Independent
Financial data (yr. ended 12/31/91): Assets, $10,395,130 (M); expenditures, $799,942; qualifying distributions, $788,202, including $755,000 for 25 grants (high: $135,000; low: $5,000; average: $5,000-$25,000).
Fields of interest: Hospitals, medical research.
Types of support: General purposes.
Limitations: Giving primarily in the Philadelphia, PA, and New York, NY, metropolitan areas and in FL. No grants to individuals.
Application information: Contributes only to pre-selected organizations. Applications not accepted.
 Board meeting date(s): Irregularly
 Write: Leanne M. Workman
Trustee: Walter H. Annenberg.
Number of staff: None.
EIN: 236286761

2775
Lindback Foundation
(also known as Christian R. and Mary F. Lindback Foundation)
c/o Fidelity Bank, N.A.
Broad & Walnut Sts.
Philadelphia 19109
Application address: One Liberty Place, Philadelphia, PA 19103-7396; Tel.: (215) 979-1978

Trust established in 1955, registered in NJ.
Donor(s): Mary F. Lindback,‡ Christian R. Lindback.‡
Foundation type: Independent
Financial data (yr. ended 12/31/91): Assets, $13,048,070 (M); expenditures, $111,691; qualifying distributions, $11.
Purpose and activities: Support primarily for higher education, including medical education, and hospitals and medical research; giving also for museums.
Fields of interest: Education, higher education, hospitals, medical education, medical research, museums.
Types of support: Fellowships, scholarship funds, capital campaigns, endowment funds.
Limitations: Giving primarily in PA and NJ. No grants to individuals, or for building or endowment funds.
Application information: Applications not accepted.
  Write: Maureen B. Evans, Sr. Trust Officer
Trustees: Martin A. Heckscher, Roland Morris, Fidelity Bank, N.A.
Number of staff: None.
EIN: 236290348

2776
Live Oak Foundation
c/o CoreStates Bank, N.A.
P.O. Box 7618, FC 1-1-24-7
Philadelphia 19101   (215) 973-2616

Established in 1966 in PA.
Donor(s): Charlotte C. Weber.
Foundation type: Independent
Financial data (yr. ended 08/31/91): Assets, $2,602,713 (M); expenditures, $25,391; qualifying distributions, $20,235, including $20,000 for 1 grant.
Purpose and activities: Support for hospitals and medical research projects; art museums and collections of paintings, sculptures, antiques, and other art objects; churches and other religious institutions; theater, opera, ballet, and other performing arts groups; and other educational activities, including animal welfare and wildlife preservation.
Fields of interest: Hospitals, medical research, fine arts, museums, theater, performing arts, religion, education, animal welfare, wildlife.
Application information: Application form not required.
  Initial approach: Letter
  Deadline(s): Feb. 28 for July awards
  Write: Nancy H. Garrison, V.P., CoreStates Bank, N.A.
Trustees: Charlotte C. Weber, John C. Weber, CoreStates Bank, N.A.
EIN: 236424637

2777
Lord Corporate Giving Program
2000 West Grandview Blvd.
P.O. Box 10038
Erie 16514   (814) 868-0924

Purpose and activities: Supports education, arts and culture, civic and community affairs, health and science, humanities and social services programs. Donations include company equipment and products.
Fields of interest: Education, higher education, cultural programs, civic affairs, community funds, health, science and technology, humanities.
Types of support: Seed money, equipment, special projects, building funds, endowment funds.
Limitations: Giving primarily in headquarters city and state and major operating locations.
Application information: Include project description and budget, an annual report and donor list; a contributions committee handles giving.
  Initial approach: Letter
  Write: Donald W. Saurer, Mgr., Public Rels.

2778
George H. and Margaret McClintic Love Foundation
Mellon Bank, N.A.
One Mellon Bank Ctr., Rm. 3845
Pittsburgh 15258-0001

Trust established in 1952 in PA.
Donor(s): George H. Love, Margaret McClintic Love, Howard M. Love.
Foundation type: Independent
Financial data (yr. ended 12/31/90): Assets, $4,289,413 (M); gifts received, $284,467; expenditures, $1,750,110; qualifying distributions, $1,684,375, including $1,667,175 for 58 grants (high: $450,000; low: $125).
Fields of interest: Higher education, secondary education, education, youth, child welfare, social services, women, hospitals.
Types of support: Annual campaigns, building funds, capital campaigns.
Limitations: Giving primarily in PA and on the East Coast.
Application information:
  Initial approach: Letter
  Deadline(s): None
Officers: George H. Love, Dir. of Distrib.; Lois R. O'Connor, Asst. Dir. of Distrib.
Trustee: Mellon Bank, N.A.
EIN: 256018655

2779
The Lukens Foundation
50 South First Ave.
Coatesville 19320   (215) 383-2159

Trust established in 1966 in PA.
Donor(s): Lukens Inc.
Foundation type: Company-sponsored
Financial data (yr. ended 12/31/90): Assets, $2,150,182 (L); gifts received, $847,000; expenditures, $808,056; qualifying distributions, $806,523, including $792,296 for 102 grants (high: $70,125; low: $330).

Purpose and activities: Emphasis on community funds; conservation; cultural programs, including museums and performing arts; health and welfare efforts; human service projects; and education, including an employee matching gift program supporting institutions of secondary and higher education.
Fields of interest: Community funds, conservation, cultural programs, museums, performing arts, health, health services, welfare, secondary education, higher education.
Types of support: Continuing support, annual campaigns, emergency funds, building funds, equipment, matching funds, employee matching gifts, employee-related scholarships.
Limitations: Giving primarily in areas of domestic company operations. No support for religious or fraternal organizations. No grants to individuals, or for endowment funds or research; no loans.
Publications: Informational brochure (including application guidelines).
Application information: Application form required.
  Initial approach: Letter
  Copies of proposal: 1
  Deadline(s): Submit proposal preferably in Oct.; deadline Dec. 1
  Board meeting date(s): Dec.
  Final notification: 4 months
  Write: W. Evelyn Walker, Administrator and Secy.
Officer: W. Evelyn Walker, Secy. and Administrator.
Trustees: R.W. Van Sant, Chair.; John R. Bartholdson, John Maier, Dennis Oats, Robert Schaal, William D. Sprague, John Van Roden.
EIN: 236424112

2780
Mack Trucks Corporate Giving Program
P.O. Box M
Allentown 18105-5000   (215) 439-3121

Purpose and activities: Main support for business and general education, community development, health and welfare; giving also for cultural and civic activities, the environment, and housing.
Fields of interest: Health, hospitals, welfare, education, business education, literacy, education—minorities, arts, humanities, cultural programs, environment, housing, safety, community development.
Types of support: Student aid, in-kind gifts, annual campaigns, donated equipment, technical assistance, loaned talent, use of facilities, donated products, employee volunteer services.
Limitations: Giving primarily in headquarters city and operating locations. No support for political, sectarian, veterans, fraternal, or labor organizations. No grants for programs, yearbooks, directory advertising, tables at benefits, past operating deficits, conferences, scholarly research, charitable advertisements, or mass media campaigns.
Application information: Contributions are handled by the Corporate Affairs Department.
  Initial approach: Letter to nearest company facility
  Deadline(s): End of third quarter
  Board meeting date(s): Beginning of year
  Write: Robin Crawford, Chair., Contribs. Comm.

Administrator: Robin Crawford, Chair., Cont. Comm., Govt. and Commun. Rels. Mgr.

2781
Massey Charitable Trust
P.O. Box 1178
Coraopolis 15108   (412) 262-5992

Established in 1968.
Donor(s): H.B. Massey,‡ Doris J. Massey, Massey Rental.
Foundation type: Independent
Financial data (yr. ended 12/31/91): Assets, $28,791,788 (M); expenditures, $1,580,316; qualifying distributions, $1,447,652, including $1,401,230 for 89 grants (high: $225,000; low: $910; average: $5,000-$50,000).
Purpose and activities: Giving primarily for higher education and the medical sciences, including medical research, hospitals, and health agencies and associations; support also for Protestant and Catholic church support, the arts, and social services.
Fields of interest: Higher education, medical research, hospitals, health, health associations, religion—Christian, arts, social services, family services, aged.
Limitations: Giving primarily in Pittsburgh, PA.
Application information: Application form not required.
    Copies of proposal: 1
    Deadline(s): None
    Board meeting date(s): May and Oct.
    Write: Walter J. Carroll, Exec. Dir. and Trustee
Officer and Trustees:* Walter J. Carroll,* Exec. Dir.; Daniel B. Carroll, Joe B. Massey.
Number of staff: 1 full-time professional; 1 full-time support.
EIN: 237007897

2782
James Frances McCandless Trust
c/o Pittsburgh National Bank, Trust Dept. 970
One Oliver Plaza
Pittsburgh 15265
Application address: c/o Pittsburgh National Bank, Trust Dept. 965, One Oliver Plaza, Pittsburgh, PA 15265

Foundation type: Independent
Financial data (yr. ended 12/31/91): Assets, $3,837,211 (M); expenditures, $146,382; qualifying distributions, $130,744, including $127,338 for 16 grants (high: $20,000; low: $2,500).
Fields of interest: Hospitals, child welfare, community funds, health associations, social services.
Types of support: General purposes.
Limitations: Giving primarily in Pittsburgh, PA.
Application information: Application form not required.
    Deadline(s): None
    Write: Henry C. Flood, V.P., Pittsburgh National Bank
Trustee: Pittsburgh National Bank.
EIN: 251347840

2783
Anne McCormick Trust
c/o Dauphin Deposit Bank & Trust Co.
P.O. Box 2961
Harrisburg 17105-2961   (717) 255-2045

Trust established in PA.
Donor(s): Anne McCormick.‡
Foundation type: Independent
Financial data (yr. ended 12/31/91): Assets, $4,709,886 (M); expenditures, $280,658; qualifying distributions, $229,756, including $229,297 for 30 grants (high: $50,000; low: $500).
Fields of interest: Hospitals, youth, higher education, cultural programs.
Limitations: Giving limited to Dauphin, Cumberland, Perry, York, and Franklin counties, PA. No grants to individuals.
Application information:
    Initial approach: Proposal
    Deadline(s): None
    Write: Larry A. Hartman, V.P. and Trust Officer, Dauphin Deposit Bank & Trust Co.
Trustee: Dauphin Deposit Bank & Trust Co.
EIN: 236471389

2784
McCune Foundation ▼
1104 Commonwealth Bldg.
316 Fourth Ave.
Pittsburgh 15222   (412) 644-8779

Established in 1979 in PA.
Donor(s): Charles L. McCune.‡
Foundation type: Independent
Financial data (yr. ended 09/30/91): Assets, $264,761,480 (M); expenditures, $14,456,001; qualifying distributions, $13,753,116, including $13,358,171 for 42 grants (high: $2,000,000; low: $40,000; average: $100,000-$500,000).
Purpose and activities: Giving primarily for independent higher education, health, and social services; support includes challenge grants. Preference is given to the organizations supported by the donor.
Fields of interest: Higher education, health services, social services.
Types of support: Equipment, endowment funds, building funds, capital campaigns, renovation projects, scholarship funds, seed money, special projects, professorships.
Limitations: Giving primarily in southwestern PA, with emphasis on the Pittsburgh area. No grants to individuals, or for general operating purposes; no loans.
Publications: Annual report (including application guidelines), grants list, financial statement.
Application information: Applicants are encouraged to wait 3 years after receiving a grant before reapplying. Application form not required.
    Initial approach: Letter of inquiry
    Copies of proposal: 1
    Deadline(s): Nov. 1 and Mar. 15
    Board meeting date(s): Jan. and June
    Final notification: 4 months
    Write: Henry S. Beukema, Exec. Dir.
Officer and Directors:* Martha J. Perry, Assoc. Exec. Dir.; Martha J. Muetzel, Secy.; Henry S. Beukema, Exec. Dir.

Distribution Committee: James M. Edwards, Richard D. Edwards, John R. McCune, John R. McCune, Jr., Robert F. Patton.
Trustee: Integra Financial Corp.
Number of staff: 2 full-time professional; 2 full-time support.
EIN: 256210269
Recent health grants:
2784-1 Allegheny Valley Hospital Foundation, Natrona Heights, PA, $300,000. Toward purchase of linear accelerator. 1990.
2784-2 Butler Memorial Hospital Foundation, Butler, PA, $200,000. Toward renovation of surgical suite. 1990.
2784-3 Childrens Hospital of Pittsburgh, Pittsburgh, PA, $1,200,000. Toward purchase and maintenance of research equipment. 1990.
2784-4 Easter Seal Society of Butler County, Butler, PA, $100,000. Toward construction of central program facility. 1990.
2784-5 Forbes Health Foundation, Pittsburgh, PA, $125,000. For endowment of Forbes Hospice. 1990.
2784-6 Gateway Rehabilitation Center, Pittsburgh, PA, $300,000. Toward renovation of facilities. 1990.
2784-7 Marian Manor Nursing Home, Pittsburgh, PA, $350,000. Toward expansion of facilities. 1990.
2784-8 McKeesport Hospital Foundation, McKeesport, PA, $75,000. Toward start-up of cancer care program. 1990.
2784-9 Mercy Hospital Foundation, Pittsburgh, PA, $250,000. Toward start-up of Parish Nurse Program. 1990.
2784-10 Saint Clair Memorial Hospital Foundation, Pittsburgh, PA, $500,000. For geriatric services endowment fund. 1990.
2784-11 Saint Francis Health Foundation, Pittsburgh, PA, $200,000. Toward start-up of Medical Center's Competency Clinic. 1990.
2784-12 Spina Bifida Association of Western Pennsylvania, Pittsburgh, PA, $300,000. Toward construction and renovation of residential camping facility. 1990.
2784-13 United Cerebral Palsy of Southwestern Pennsylvania, Pittsburgh, PA, $125,000. Toward purchase and renovation of headquarters building. 1990.
2784-14 West Penn Hospital Foundation, Pittsburgh, PA, $500,000. Toward renovation and construction of Cardiology Institute. 1990.

2785
McFeely-Rogers Foundation
1110 Ligonier St., Suite 300
P.O. Box 110
Latrobe 15650   (412) 537-5588

Incorporated in 1953 in PA.
Donor(s): James H. Rogers,‡ Nancy K. McFeely,‡ Nancy M. Rogers.‡
Foundation type: Independent
Financial data (yr. ended 12/31/91): Assets, $12,220,638 (M); expenditures, $724,283; qualifying distributions, $607,606, including $533,259 for 79 grants (high: $100,000; low: $300; average: $500-$1,000).
Purpose and activities: Support mainly to local educational and charitable institutions, including civic affairs, community development, recreation

programs, Protestant giving, hunger projects, cultural programs, and hospitals.
Fields of interest: Education, civic affairs, community development, recreation, Protestant giving, hunger, cultural programs, hospitals, hospitals—building funds, general charitable giving.
Types of support: Operating budgets, annual campaigns, seed money, emergency funds, deficit financing, building funds, equipment, matching funds, scholarship funds, general purposes, endowment funds, capital campaigns.
Limitations: Giving primarily in the Latrobe and Pittsburgh, PA, areas. No grants to individuals, or for land acquisition, special projects, research, publications, or conferences; no loans.
Publications: Program policy statement, application guidelines.
Application information: Application form not required.
  Initial approach: Letter or telephone
  Copies of proposal: 2
  Deadline(s): Apr. 15 and Nov. 1
  Board meeting date(s): End of May, and Nov.
  Final notification: 2 weeks after board meeting
  Write: James R. Okonak, Exec. Dir.
Officers and Trustees:* Fred M. Rogers,* Pres.; Nancy R. Crozier,* V.P.; James R. Okonak,* Secy. and Exec. Dir.; Grant F. Neely,* Treas.; William P. Barker, Douglas R. Nowicki, James B. Rogers.
Number of staff: 1 full-time professional; 2 part-time professional.
EIN: 251120947

2786
Katherine Mabis McKenna Foundation, Inc.
P.O. Box 186
Latrobe 15650   (412) 537-6900

Incorporated in 1969 in PA.
Donor(s): Katherine M. McKenna.‡
Foundation type: Independent
Financial data (yr. ended 12/31/90): Assets, $17,338,005 (M); gifts received, $63,895; expenditures, $934,061; qualifying distributions, $795,921, including $716,000 for 47 grants (high: $115,000; low: $200; average: $1,000-$10,000).
Fields of interest: Higher education, medical sciences, cultural programs, civic affairs, conservation.
Types of support: General purposes, operating budgets, annual campaigns, seed money, building funds, equipment, endowment funds, special projects, scholarship funds, capital campaigns, internships, land acquisition.
Limitations: Giving primarily in Westmoreland County, PA. No grants to individuals, or for matching gifts; no loans.
Publications: Program policy statement.
Application information: Application form not required.
  Initial approach: Letter
  Copies of proposal: 1
  Deadline(s): Submit proposal preferably in Jan. through July; deadline Oct. 1
  Board meeting date(s): Mar., June, Sept., and Dec.
  Final notification: 3 to 6 months
  Write: Linda M. Boxx, Secy.

Officers and Directors:* Alex G. McKenna,* Chair.; Wilma F. McKenna,* Vice-Chair.; Linda McKenna Boxx,* Secy.; T. William Boxx, Treas.; Zan McKenna Rich.
Trustee: Mellon Bank, N.A.
Number of staff: 1 part-time professional.
EIN: 237042752

2787
The McLean Contributionship
945 Haverford Rd.
Bryn Mawr 19010   (215) 527-6330

Trust established in 1951 in PA.
Donor(s): William L. McLean, Jr.,‡ Robert McLean, Bulletin Co.
Foundation type: Independent
Financial data (yr. ended 12/31/91): Assets, $23,514,546 (M); gifts received, $10,149; expenditures, $1,181,719; qualifying distributions, $1,050,582, including $1,020,000 for 72 grants (high: $50,000; low: $500; average: $10,000-$15,000).
Purpose and activities: Giving primarily for education, hospitals, youth agencies, and conservation. Trustees prefer special projects rather than continuing programs.
Fields of interest: Education, hospitals, conservation, youth.
Types of support: Special projects, building funds, capital campaigns, conferences and seminars, consulting services, endowment funds, equipment, land acquisition, publications, renovation projects, scholarship funds, seed money.
Limitations: Giving primarily in the greater Philadelphia, PA, metropolitan area.
Publications: Application guidelines.
Application information: Application form not required.
  Initial approach: Proposal
  Copies of proposal: 2
  Board meeting date(s): Quarterly
  Write: John H. Buhsmer, Pres.
Officers and Trustees:* William L. McLean III,* Chair.; John H. Buhsmer,* Pres.; Charles E. Catherwood, Treas.; Jean Bodine, R. Jean Brownlee, Joseph K. Gordon.
Number of staff: None.
EIN: 236396940

2788
The Benjamin and Mary Siddons Measey Foundation
225 North Olive St.
P.O. Box 258
Media 19063   (215) 566-5800

Trust established in 1958 in PA.
Donor(s): William Maul Measey.‡
Foundation type: Independent
Financial data (yr. ended 12/31/90): Assets, $13,277,278 (M); expenditures, $1,371,688; qualifying distributions, $1,255,826, including $1,255,826 for 16 grants (high: $500,000; low: $1,826).
Purpose and activities: Grants to medical schools in Philadelphia for scholarships and fellowships.
Fields of interest: Medical education, dentistry.
Types of support: Scholarship funds, fellowships.

Limitations: Giving limited to Philadelphia, PA. No grants to individuals.
Application information: Applications should be made to the dean of the particular medical school. Application form not required.
  Copies of proposal: 6
  Deadline(s): 1 month prior to meeting
  Board meeting date(s): 2nd Tuesday in Mar., June, Sept., and Dec.
  Final notification: 1 month following meeting
  Write: James C. Brennan, Mgr.
Officer: Matthew S. Donaldson, Jr., Secy.
Board of Managers: Jonathan E. Rhoads, M.D., Chair.; James C. Brennan, Brooke Roberts, M.D., Truman G. Schnabel, M.D., Willis J. Winn, Ph.D.
Number of staff: 1 part-time support.
EIN: 236298781

2789
Mellon Bank Corporate Giving Program
One Mellon Bank Center, Rm. 1830
Pittsburgh 15258   (412) 234-5000

Financial data (yr. ended 12/31/90): Total giving, $12,734,000 for grants.
Purpose and activities: "Through corporate contributions, employee involvement, and sponsorship of community activities and events, Mellon Bank Corporation seeks to be a constructive force which actively contributes to the quality of life in the communities in which we do business." Mellon supports the efforts of communities and nonprofit groups to help themselves. Preference is given to groups that demonstrate: 1) active board leadership; 2) comprehensive resource development plan; 3) clear definition of goals and how organization success is evaluated; and 4) collaboration with other nonprofits, particularly with respect to the management of the organization. A new funding initiative, Fund for Collaboration, requires nonprofits to collaborate in order to receive grants. Mellon's support is divided into three areas: grants, community activities, and inkind support. Giving figures represent combined foundation and corporation support, including grants, underwriting of community activities, donated items, employee support for the United Way, and employee support through walk-a-thons, etc., and employee volunteer time.
Fields of interest: Health, welfare, education, higher education, economics, community development, cultural programs, community funds, literacy, housing, elementary education, secondary education.
Types of support: Employee matching gifts, operating budgets, capital campaigns, general purposes, building funds, seed money, in-kind gifts, donated equipment, use of facilities, public relations services, employee volunteer services, loaned talent.
Limitations: Giving primarily in PA, MD, and DE where Mellon Bank Corporation operates offices; no support for national organizations or those which operate outside the U.S. No support for fraternal organizations, political parties, religious programs, individual United Way agencies which receive funds from the United Way, or specialized health campaigns. No grants to individuals (loans or assistance), or for scholarships, fellowships or travel grants, endowments, or multiple-year commitments.

Application information: Requests must be made in writing and directed to the bank in the organization's area. In 1991, Mellon is consolidating its PA banks. Although local management in each region will continue to make its own decisions regarding funding, the bank is particularly interested in receiving proposals from Pittsburgh that have statewide impact.

Initial approach: Proposal or letter
Board meeting date(s): Monthly
Final notification: 6 weeks
Write: Sylvia Clark, V.P.

2790
Mellon Bank Foundation

c/o Mellon Bank, N.A.
P.O. Box 185
Pittsburgh 15230   (412) 234-6380

Established in 1974 in PA.
Donor(s): Mellon Bank, N.A.
Foundation type: Company-sponsored
Financial data (yr. ended 12/31/91): Assets, $7,664,874 (M); gifts received, $922,250; expenditures, $931,055; qualifying distributions, $922,255, including $922,250 for 24 grants (high: $125,000; low: $4,000; average: $1,500-$10,000).
Purpose and activities: Giving primarily to serve the overall vitality of local communities, with emphasis on economic development, including business development, employment and retraining initiatives, health and welfare, higher education, and cultural programs.
Fields of interest: Community funds, community development, business, employment, health, welfare, hospitals, higher education, cultural programs, youth.
Types of support: Operating budgets, continuing support, annual campaigns, building funds, matching funds, technical assistance, special projects, capital campaigns, general purposes, seed money.
Limitations: Giving primarily in southwestern PA. No support for fraternal or religious organizations, specialized health campaigns or other highly specialized projects with little or no positive impact on local communities, or United Way agencies (unless authorized to solicit corporations). No grants to individuals, or for emergency funds, deficit financing, equipment, land acquisition, scholarships, fellowships, research, publications, or conferences; no loans.
Publications: Corporate giving report (including application guidelines), informational brochure.
Application information: Application form not required.
Initial approach: Proposal
Copies of proposal: 1
Deadline(s): None
Board meeting date(s): Monthly
Final notification: 2 months
Write: Richard S. Thomas, V.P., Mellon Bank
Officers and Trustees:* Sandra J. McLaughlin,* Chair. and Pres.; Sylvia Clark, V.P. and Secy.; Steven G. Elliott, Treas.; Joseph F. DiMario, Thomas F. Donovan, Richard A. Gaugh, Martin G. McGuinn, W. Keith Smith.
Number of staff: None.
EIN: 257423500

2791
Richard King Mellon Foundation ▼

One Mellon Bank Center
500 Grant St., 41st Fl.
Pittsburgh 15219-2502   (412) 392-2800
Mailing address: P.O. Box 2930, Pittsburgh, PA 15230-2930

Trust established in 1947 in PA; incorporated in 1971 in PA.
Donor(s): Richard K. Mellon.‡
Foundation type: Independent
Financial data (yr. ended 12/31/90): Assets, $836,121,061 (M); expenditures, $37,900,227; qualifying distributions, $37,914,528, including $31,885,307 for 135 grants (high: $1,000,000; low: $7,200) and $3,368,313 for program-related investments.
Purpose and activities: Local grant programs emphasize conservation, higher education, cultural and civic affairs, social services, medical research and health care; support also for conservation of natural areas and wildlife preservation elsewhere in the U.S.
Fields of interest: Conservation, wildlife, environment, civic affairs, education, higher education, cultural programs, social services, medical sciences, health.
Types of support: Seed money, building funds, equipment, land acquisition, research, matching funds, general purposes, continuing support, operating budgets, renovation projects.
Limitations: Giving primarily in Pittsburgh and western PA, except for nationwide conservation programs. No grants to individuals, or for fellowships or scholarships.
Publications: Annual report (including application guidelines), informational brochure.
Application information: Application form not required.
Initial approach: Proposal
Copies of proposal: 1
Deadline(s): Apr. 1 and Oct. 1; submit proposal between Jan. and Mar. or July and Sept.
Board meeting date(s): June and Dec.
Final notification: 1 to 6 months
Write: George H. Taber, V.P.
Officers and Trustees:* Richard P. Mellon,* Chair.; Seward Prosser Mellon,* Pres.; George H. Taber,* V.P. and Dir.; Robert B. Burr, Jr., Secy.; Andrew W. Mathieson,* Treas.; Arthur M. Scully, Jr., Mason Walsh, Jr.
Number of staff: 1 full-time professional; 8 part-time professional; 1 full-time support; 14 part-time support.
EIN: 251127705
Recent health grants:
2791-1 American Chronic Pain Association, Pittsburgh, PA, $25,000. For expansion support. 1990.
2791-2 Chemical People Institute, Pittsburgh, PA, $20,000. For community programs on prevention of alcohol and drug abuse. 1990.
2791-3 Childrens Hospital of Pittsburgh, Pittsburgh, PA, $1,500,000. To endow chair in pediatric hematology/oncology research. 1990.
2791-4 Gateway Rehabilitation Center, Aliquippa, PA, $300,000. Toward capital campaign. 1990.
2791-5 Make-A-Wish Foundation of Western Pennsylvania, Pittsburgh, PA, $10,000. For direct mail campaign. 1990.

2791-6 Marian Manor Nursing Home, Pittsburgh, PA, $100,000. Toward capital campaign. 1990.
2791-7 Parental Stress Center, Pittsburgh, PA, $150,000. For expanding and upgrading Bright Beginnings Warmline. 1990.
2791-8 Pittsburgh Recovery Center, Pittsburgh, PA, $20,000. For operating support of Penn Avenue location. 1990.
2791-9 Planned Parenthood of Western Pennsylvania, Pittsburgh, PA, $60,000. For family educational program. 1990.
2791-10 Presbyterian-University Hospital, Pittsburgh, PA, $45,000. For unrestricted support. 1990.
2791-11 Rehabilitation Institute of Pittsburgh, Pittsburgh, PA, $500,000. Toward capital campaign. 1990.
2791-12 Southwest Services, Pittsburgh, PA, $37,000. Toward implementing mental health outreach program for elderly in Southwest Allegheny County. 1990.
2791-13 Spina Bifida Association of Western Pennsylvania, Pittsburgh, PA, $300,000. Toward capital campaign for renovation and construction of camp. 1990.
2791-14 Support Center for Cancer, Pittsburgh, PA, $45,000. For operating support. 1990.
2791-15 Threshold, Greensburg, PA, $40,000. Toward down payment on home for mentally disadvantaged. 1990.
2791-16 Transplant Recipients International Organization, Pittsburgh, PA, $25,000. For operating support. 1990.
2791-17 University of Pittsburgh, Pittsburgh, PA, $77,000. For collaborative effort between Latrobe Area Hospital and Pittsburgh Cancer Institute for breast cancer screening program in rural areas. 1990.
2791-18 Urban League of Pittsburgh, Pittsburgh, PA, $50,000. To expand youth motivation and drug education and prevention program in two public housing projects. 1990.
2791-19 Visiting Nurse Association of Allegheny County, Pittsburgh, PA, $30,000. Toward expansion of stroke rehabilitation group program. 1990.

2792
Glenn and Ruth Mengle Foundation

c/o First Commonwealth Trust Co.
P.O. Box 1046
DuBois 15801

Trust established in 1956 in PA.
Donor(s): Glenn A. Mengle,‡ Ruth E. Mengle Blake.‡
Foundation type: Independent
Financial data (yr. ended 12/31/91): Assets, $9,976,228 (M); expenditures, $579,513; qualifying distributions, $579,513, including $438,381 for 38 grants (high: $69,050; low: $400).
Fields of interest: Youth, hospitals, civic affairs, higher education, community funds.
Types of support: Operating budgets, capital campaigns.
Limitations: Giving limited to the Brockway, Dubois, and Erie, PA, areas. No grants to individuals.

Application information: Contributes only to pre-selected organizations. Applications not accepted.

Write: D. Edward Chaplin, Exec. V.P. and Trust Officer, First Commonwealth Trust Co.

Trustees: DeVere L. Sheesley, First Commonwealth Trust Co.

EIN: 256067616

2793
Meridian Foundation
(Formerly American Bank & Trust Co. Foundation)
c/o Meridian Bancorp, Inc.
P.O. Box 7588
Philadelphia 19101-9732   (215) 854-3114

Established in 1956 in PA as the American Bank Foundation.

Donor(s): Meridian Bancorp, Inc.
Foundation type: Company-sponsored
Financial data (yr. ended 12/31/91): Assets, $94,558 (M); gifts received, $607,916; expenditures, $582,005; qualifying distributions, $581,944, including $581,692 for 112 grants (high: $41,616; low: $18).
Purpose and activities: Support for community funds, higher education, health and welfare, arts and culture, and civic affairs. Maximum grant for capital campaigns is 5 percent of goal; special emphasis on economic and community development.
Fields of interest: Community funds, higher education, health, welfare, arts, cultural programs, civic affairs, community development, economics.
Types of support: Annual campaigns, building funds, capital campaigns.
Limitations: Giving primarily in southeastern PA: Berks, Bucks, Chester, Dauphin, Delaware, Lancaster, Lebanon, Lehigh, Montgomery, Philadelphia, and Schuykill counties. No grants to individuals, or for endowment funds, scholarships, or fellowships; no loans.
Publications: Application guidelines.
Application information: Requests for multi-year support, capital campaigns, or grants over $5,000 handled by foundation directly. Smaller, single-year gifts are decided on by the local foundation committee for each subsidiary.
Initial approach: Proposal
Copies of proposal: 1
Deadline(s): 1 month prior to board meetings
Board meeting date(s): Feb., May, Aug., and Nov.
Write: Nora Mead Brownell, Dir., Corp. Communs. and Commun. Rels.
Trustee: Meridian Bancorp, Inc.
Number of staff: None.
EIN: 231976387

2794
The Merit Gasoline Foundation
551 West Lancaster Ave.
Haverford 19041   (215) 527-7900

Trust established in 1956 in PA.
Donor(s): Merit Oil Co., and affiliates.
Foundation type: Company-sponsored
Financial data (yr. ended 08/31/91): Assets, $404,030 (M); gifts received, $125,000; expenditures, $246,347; qualifying distributions, $245,510, including $228,130 for grants (average: $3,000-$7,000) and $16,960 for employee matching gifts.
Purpose and activities: Support for scholarship aid to children (including step-children) of employees of donor companies, civic affairs, higher education, social service programs, health agencies, and Jewish welfare.
Fields of interest: Health, social services, civic affairs, higher education, Jewish welfare.
Types of support: Operating budgets, continuing support, employee-related scholarships, employee matching gifts.
Limitations: Giving primarily in the urban areas of the New England and mid-Atlantic states where Merit Oil Co. has gas stations. No grants to individuals, or for building or endowment funds, research, or special projects; no loans.
Publications: Program policy statement, application guidelines.
Application information: Application form not required.
Initial approach: Proposal
Copies of proposal: 1
Deadline(s): Submit proposal preferably in Jan. and July; no set deadline
Board meeting date(s): Usually in Aug.
Write: Robert M. Harting, Exec. Dir.
Officer: Robert M. Harting, Exec. Dir.
Trustees: Lois B. Victor, Chair.; Ivan H. Gabel, Leonard Gilmar, Robert M. Harting, Joseph M. Jerome, Carl A. Levinson, Morton Sand.
Number of staff: None.
EIN: 236282846

2795
Miles Inc. Foundation
One Mellon Ctr.
500 Grant St.
Pittsburgh 15219-2502   (412) 394-6725

Established in 1985 in PA.
Donor(s): Miles Inc.
Foundation type: Company-sponsored
Financial data (yr. ended 12/31/90): Assets, $12,652,922 (M); gifts received, $2,163,395; expenditures, $914,667; qualifying distributions, $853,741, including $853,741 for 148 grants (high: $203,200; low: $100; average: $500-$10,000).
Purpose and activities: Primary areas of interest include education, including science programs, chemistry, and arts and cultural programs in the communities in which Miles Inc. operates.
Fields of interest: Community funds, community development, education, higher education, cultural programs, arts, civic affairs, chemistry, science and technology, medical sciences.
Types of support: In-kind gifts, operating budgets, special projects, lectureships, professorships, research.
Limitations: Giving primarily in PA for civic groups; nationwide to selected universities.
Application information: Request updated 1993 guidelines. Application form required.
Initial approach: Letter
Copies of proposal: 1
Deadline(s): Mid-June and mid-Dec.
Board meeting date(s): Spring and fall
Final notification: After board meeting
Write: Sande Deitch, Exec. Dir.

Officers: Gerd D. Mueller, Pres.; Fred Giel, Secy.; Jon R. Wyne, Treas.
Trustees: Sande K. Deitch, Elliot S. Schreiber, Helge H. Wehmeier.
Number of staff: 1 full-time professional; 1 full-time support.
EIN: 251508079

2796
The Millstein Charitable Foundation
North Fourth St. & Gaskill Ave.
Jeannette 15644

Established in 1964.
Foundation type: Independent
Financial data (yr. ended 09/30/91): Assets, $2,917,053 (M); gifts received, $2,500; expenditures, $147,460; qualifying distributions, $130,438, including $130,438 for 134 grants (high: $75,000; low: $10).
Purpose and activities: Grants primarily for Jewish welfare funds and temple support.
Fields of interest: Jewish giving, Jewish welfare, education, general charitable giving, Israel, medical research, homeless, hospices, hospitals, humanities.
Types of support: Annual campaigns, building funds, capital campaigns, emergency funds, research, special projects.
Limitations: Giving primarily in western PA.
Application information: Requests are reviewed as they are received. Application form not required.
Initial approach: Letter
Copies of proposal: 1
Board meeting date(s): Annually, usually in Sept.
Officer and Trustees:* David J. Millstein,* Exec. Secy.; Jack H. Millstein, Jr.
Number of staff: 1 part-time support.
EIN: 256064981

2797
Mudge Foundation
c/o Pittsburgh National Bank, Trust Dept. 970
One Oliver Plaza
Pittsburgh 15265   (412) 762-3866

Established in 1955 in PA.
Foundation type: Independent
Financial data (yr. ended 12/31/91): Assets, $2,462,711 (M); gifts received, $395; expenditures, $142,889; qualifying distributions, $131,658, including $127,590 for 13 grants (high: $30,000; low: $1,000).
Purpose and activities: Grants for natural resources and science projects, including medical research; support also for museums of natural history, a public policy organization, and higher education.
Fields of interest: Environment, science and technology, medical research, museums, public policy, higher education.
Types of support: General purposes, research.
Limitations: Giving primarily in TX, ME, and PA. No grants to individuals.
Application information: Application form not required.
Initial approach: Letter
Deadline(s): None
Write: Henry Flood, V.P., Pittsburgh National Bank

Trustee: Pittsburgh National Bank.
EIN: 256023150

2798
G. C. Murphy Company Foundation
211 Oberdick Dr.
McKeesport 15135   (412) 751-6649

Incorporated in 1952 in PA.
Foundation type: Independent
Financial data (yr. ended 12/31/91): Assets, $3,458,134 (M); gifts received, $100; expenditures, $167,814; qualifying distributions, $134,200, including $128,200 for 22 grants (high: $15,000; low: $1,000).
Purpose and activities: Emphasis on youth and social services, including women, child welfare, family services, and hunger; support also for health associations and services, hospital building funds, and programs for cancer care and the mentally ill, community funds and development, the arts, and higher education.
Fields of interest: Youth, social services, women, child welfare, health, hospitals—building funds, community funds, community development, arts, higher education.
Types of support: Annual campaigns, building funds, renovation projects, capital campaigns, continuing support, endowment funds.
Limitations: Giving primarily in southeastern Allegheny County, PA. No grants to individuals.
Application information: Application form not required.
   Initial approach: Proposal
   Copies of proposal: 1
   Deadline(s): None
   Board meeting date(s): Mar., July, and Nov.
   Write: Edwin W. Davis, Secy.
Officers and Directors:* T.F. Hudak,* Pres. and Treas.; R.T. Messner,* V.P.; Edwin W. Davis,* Secy.; M.M. Lewis, C.H. Lytle, S.W. Robinson.
Number of staff: 1 part-time professional.
EIN: 256028651

2799
Oberkotter Family Foundation ▼
1600 Market St., Suite 3600
Philadelphia 19103   (215) 751-2464

Established in 1985 in PA.
Donor(s): Paul Oberkotter, Louise Oberkotter,‡ Mildred L. Oberkotter.
Foundation type: Independent
Financial data (yr. ended 11/30/90): Assets, $9,403,284 (M); gifts received, $2,098,053; expenditures, $3,005,716; qualifying distributions, $2,915,336, including $2,817,815 for 27 grants (high: $331,000; low: $5,000; average: $5,000-$200,000).
Purpose and activities: Giving for the deaf and diabetes.
Fields of interest: Medical research, health, education.
Types of support: Matching funds, operating budgets, research.
Limitations: No grants to individuals.
Application information: Application form not required.
   Deadline(s): None
   Write: George H. Nofer, Esq., Dir.

Director and Trustees: George H. Nofer,* Dir.; Mildred Oberkotter, Paul Oberkotter, Bernard G. Segal.
EIN: 222694822
Recent health grants:
2799-1 Alzheimers Disease and Related Disorders Association, Greater Philadelphia Chapter, Philadelphia, PA, $50,000. For general support. 1990.
2799-2 American Diabetes Association, NYC, NY, $25,000. For general support. 1990.
2799-3 American Institute for Voice, Philadelphia, PA, $120,000. For general support. 1990.
2799-4 Auditory Verbal International, Easton, PA, $51,500. For general support. 1990.
2799-5 Beth Israel Medical Center, Department of Medicine-Diabetes, NYC, NY, $10,000. For general support. 1990.
2799-6 Childrens Hospital Medical Center of Northern California, Oakland, CA, $100,000. For general support. 1990.
2799-7 Deafness Research Foundation, NYC, NY, $75,615. For general support. 1990.
2799-8 Garfield G. Duncan Research Foundation, Philadelphia, PA, $50,000. For general support. 1990.
2799-9 Hospital for Special Surgery, Dana Center, NYC, NY, $100,000. For general support. 1990.
2799-10 John Tracy Clinic, Los Angeles, CA, $100,000. For program on video correspondence. 1990.
2799-11 Long Island Jewish Medical Center, Hearing and Speech Center, New Hyde Park, NY, $35,000. For building program. 1990.
2799-12 Mount Sinai Hospital and Medical Center, Department of Medicine, NYC, NY, $10,000. For general support. 1990.
2799-13 Rochester Institute of Technology, International Center for Hearing and Research, Rochester, NY, $250,000. For general support. 1990.
2799-14 University of California at Los Angeles Foundation, Medical School, Los Angeles, CA, $200,000. For diabetes research project. 1990.
2799-15 University of Pennsylvania, School of Medicine-George S. Cox Institute, Philadelphia, PA, $200,000. For general support. 1990.

2800
Gustav Oberlaender Foundation, Inc.
P.O. Box 896
Reading 19603

Incorporated in 1934 in DE.
Donor(s): Gustav Oberlaender.‡
Foundation type: Independent
Financial data (yr. ended 12/31/91): Assets, $2,292,999 (M); expenditures, $119,360; qualifying distributions, $102,642, including $101,830 for 42 grants (high: $10,000; low: $500).
Fields of interest: Cultural programs, hospitals, community funds, social services, higher education, youth.
Types of support: Annual campaigns, scholarship funds, building funds, continuing support, capital campaigns, renovation projects, special projects.
Limitations: Giving primarily in Berks County, PA. No grants to individuals.

Application information:
   Initial approach: Letter or proposal
   Deadline(s): None
   Write: Harold O. Leinbach, Pres.
Officers and Trustees:* Harold O. Leinbach,* Pres.; Richard O. Leinbach,* V.P.; John M. Ennis,* Secy.-Treas.; James R. Houck, Peter Leinbach, Douglas F. Smith, Greta L. Smith, Jean L. Ziemer, Meridian Trust Co.
EIN: 236282493

2801
Oxford Foundation, Inc. ▼
55 South Third St.
Oxford 19363

Incorporated in 1947 in DE.
Donor(s): John H. Ware III, Marian S. Ware.
Foundation type: Independent
Financial data (yr. ended 12/31/90): Assets, $23,481,566 (M); expenditures, $1,292,082; qualifying distributions, $1,276,800, including $1,276,800 for 120 grants (high: $250,000; low: $500; average: $500-$1,000).
Purpose and activities: Emphasis on human services and church support; support also for higher education, health and hospitals, and environmental conservation.
Fields of interest: Social services, youth, child welfare, Protestant giving, higher education, hospitals, health services, conservation.
Limitations: Giving primarily in PA. No grants to individuals, or for scholarships; no loans.
Application information:
   Initial approach: Letter
   Deadline(s): None
   Final notification: Only to applications approved by the trustees
   Write: Marian S. Ware, Chair. and Pres.
Officers and Trustees:* John H. Ware III,* Pres.; Marian S. Ware,* V.P.; Marilyn W. Lewis,* Secy.; John H. Ware IV,* Treas.; Carol W. Gates, Paul W. Ware.
EIN: 236278067
Recent health grants:
2801-1 Planned Parenthood of Chester County, West Chester, PA, $13,000. 1990.
2801-2 Planned Parenthood of Lancaster County, Lancaster, PA, $27,000. 1990.
2801-3 Southern Chester County Medical Center, West Grove, PA, $100,000. 1990.
2801-4 University of Pennsylvania, School of Nursing, Philadelphia, PA, $20,000. 1990.

2802
W. I. Patterson Charitable Fund
407 Oliver Bldg.
Pittsburgh 15222   (412) 281-5580

Trust established in 1955 in PA.
Donor(s): W.I. Patterson.‡
Foundation type: Independent
Financial data (yr. ended 07/31/91): Assets, $3,084,868 (M); expenditures, $155,274; qualifying distributions, $132,732, including $123,178 for 51 grants (high: $24,636; low: $500; average: $500-$7,000).
Purpose and activities: Support for higher and other education, a library, health associations and hospitals, and welfare funds.

Fields of interest: Higher education, education, libraries, health associations, hospitals, welfare.

Types of support: Operating budgets, continuing support, annual campaigns, seed money, emergency funds, deficit financing, building funds, equipment, land acquisition, research, publications, capital campaigns, general purposes.

Limitations: Giving primarily in Allegheny County, PA. No grants to individuals, or for endowment funds, special projects, scholarships, fellowships, or matching gifts; no loans.

Application information: Application form not required.

> *Initial approach:* Proposal
> *Copies of proposal:* 1
> *Deadline(s):* Submit proposal preferably in May or June; deadline June 30
> *Board meeting date(s):* At least 6 times a year, including Feb., May, July, Sept., and Nov.
> *Write:* Robert B. Shust, Trustee

Trustees: Martin L. Moore, Jr., Robert B. Shust, Lester K. Wolf.

Number of staff: None.

EIN: 256028639

2803

The William Penn Foundation ▼

1630 Locust St.
Philadelphia 19103-6305 (215) 732-5114

Incorporated in 1945 in DE.

Donor(s): Otto Haas,‡ Phoebe W. Haas,‡ Otto Haas & Phoebe W. Haas Charitable Trusts.

Foundation type: Independent

Financial data (yr. ended 12/31/91): Assets, $550,372,405 (M); gifts received, $11,570,245; expenditures, $34,946,793; qualifying distributions, $32,440,589, including $30,549,447 for 356 grants (high: $3,000,000; low: $2,000; average: $10,000-$100,000).

Purpose and activities: The foundation supports the following categories: (1)environment; (2)culture; (3)human development, including programs for children, adolescents, and the elderly; and (4)community fabric (institutions, services, and intergroup relations). Also sponsors a matching gift program for board members, former board members and employees of the foundation.

Fields of interest: Conservation, environment, arts, performing arts, cultural programs, social services, disadvantaged, child development, youth, family services, homeless, welfare, aged, employment, minorities, community development, urban development, housing, health, education, elementary education, higher education, secondary education.

Types of support: Seed money, equipment, matching funds, special projects, emergency funds, land acquisition, renovation projects, technical assistance, employee matching gifts, capital campaigns.

Limitations: Giving limited to the Philadelphia, PA, area, and Camden County, NJ; environmental giving in southeastern PA and southern NJ. No support for sectarian religious activities, recreational programs, or programs focusing on a particular disease or treatment for addiction. No grants to individuals, or for operating budgets, continuing support, annual campaigns, deficit financing, hospital building funds, endowment funds, scholarships, fellowships, research,

publications, travel, films, or conferences; no loans.

Publications: Annual report (including application guidelines), informational brochure (including application guidelines).

Application information: Application form not required.

> *Initial approach:* Proposal
> *Copies of proposal:* 1
> *Deadline(s):* None
> *Board meeting date(s):* Jan., Apr., July, Sept., and Dec.
> *Final notification:* 2 to 3 months
> *Write:* Bernard C. Watson, Ph.D., Pres. and C.E.O.

Officers and Directors:* John C. Haas,* Chair.; Thomas W. Haas,* Vice-Chair.; Bernard C. Watson,* Pres. and C.E.O.; Fran M. Coopersmith, V.P. for Finance and Treas.; Harry E. Cerino, V.P. for Progs.; Roland H. Johnson, Secy. and Sr. Prog. Officer; Ernesta Drinker Ballard, Mary C. Carroll, Gloria Twine Chisum, Richard G. Gilmore, Carole F. Haas, Chara C. Haas, David W. Haas, Frederick R. Haas, Janet F. Haas, William D. Haas, Philip C. Herr II, Stephanie W. Naidoff, Edmund B. Spaeth, Jr., Paul M. Washington.

Staff: C. Richard Cox, Sr., Prog. Officer; Helen Davis Pilcher, Prog. Officer; Fasaha M. Traylor, Prog. Officer; Cathy M. Weiss, Prog. Officer; Nancy K. Zimmerman, Prog. Officer.

Number of staff: 12 full-time professional; 3 part-time professional; 7 full-time support.

EIN: 231503488

Recent health grants:

2803-1 Diagnostic and Rehabilitation Center of Philadelphia, Philadelphia, PA, $100,000. For emergency capital repairs to Arch Street facility. 1991.

2803-2 Gwynedd-Mercy College, Gwynedd Valley, PA, $256,684. For enhancement of allied health careers programs. 1991.

2803-3 Juvenile Law Center, Philadelphia, PA, $300,000. To develop plan for full and coordinated implementation of three child-health laws in Philadelphia. Grant shared with Pennsylvania Children's Health Coalition. 1991.

2803-4 La Salle University, Philadelphia, PA, $44,747. For preparation of operational plan for its Neighborhood Nursing Center. 1991.

2803-5 Moss Rehabilitation Hospital, Philadelphia, PA, $134,225. To implement Stroke Transition After Inpatient Rehabilitation Project. 1991.

2803-6 Pathfinder Fund, Watertown, MA, $204,500. To address threat that overpopulation poses to global environment. 1991.

2803-7 Women Organized Against Rape, Philadelphia, PA, $50,000. For general support. 1991.

2804

Pennsylvania Power & Light Company Giving Program

Two North Ninth Street, Rte. 22&301, P.O. Box 3500
Allentown 18106 (215) 770-5151

Purpose and activities: "The company has a charitable contributions committee composed of our Chief Executive Officer, three

Executive/Senior Vice Presidents, one Division Vice President, and a Secretary. Due to the nature of our business, our contributions are directed to organizations within, or principally benefiting, our service area. Solicitations for funds directed to national, regional, or metropolitan areas outside our service territory area are, with few exceptions, declined." The company is organized into 6 divisions and specific funds are allocated for recipients in each division. Funds are also allocated to recipients of a systemwide nature. Supports education, the arts, civic and community affairs, health, human services, United Way, and youth.

Fields of interest: Education, higher education, arts, civic affairs, health, community funds, environment, youth, economics, hospitals.

Types of support: Equipment, building funds, scholarship funds, special projects, employee matching gifts, employee-related scholarships.

Limitations: Giving primarily in service area, approximately 1,000 square miles in central eastern PA.

Application information:

> *Initial approach:* Letter
> *Board meeting date(s):* At least twice annually, once to review policies, and in Sept. to approve budget for coming year
> *Write:* Robert K. Campbell, Pres. and C.E.O.

Administrator: Bert Daday, Spec. Asst. to Pres. for Community Affairs.

Number of staff: None.

2805

The Peterson Foundation

c/o John D. Iskrant
1600 Market St., Suite 3600
Philadelphia 19103
Application address: 175 East Clinton Ave., Tenafly, NJ 07670

Established in 1986 in PA.

Donor(s): Lee M. Peterson, J. Robert Peterson.

Foundation type: Independent

Financial data (yr. ended 11/30/90): Assets, $18,031 (M); gifts received, $250,038; expenditures, $331,050; qualifying distributions, $326,245, including $298,513 for 24 grants (high: $202,798; low: $275).

Fields of interest: Medical research, mental health, psychology.

Limitations: No grants to individuals.

Application information: Application form not required.

> *Deadline(s):* None
> *Write:* J. Robert Peterson, Trustee

Trustees: J. Robert Peterson, Lee M. Peterson.

EIN: 236766019

2806

The Pew Charitable Trusts ▼

One Commerce Sq.
2005 Market St., Suite 1700
Philadelphia 19103-7017 (215) 575-9050

Pew Memorial Trust, J.N. Pew, Jr. Charitable Trust, J. Howard Pew Freedom Trust, Mabel Pew Myrin Trust, Medical Trust, Knollbrook Trust, and Mary Anderson Trust, created in 1948, 1956, 1957, 1957, 1975, 1965, and 1957 respectively.

Donor(s): Mary Ethel Pew,‡ Mabel Pew Myrin,‡ J. Howard Pew,‡ Joseph N. Pew, Jr.‡

Foundation type: Independent

Financial data (yr. ended 12/31/91): Assets, $3,338,048,594 (M); expenditures, $117,272,068; qualifying distributions, $118,250,635, including $109,919,608 for grants (high: $2,250,000; low: $1,500; average: $50,000-$200,000) and $1,340,000 for program-related investments.

Purpose and activities: Giving primarily in arts and culture, education (including theology), health and human services, conservation and the environment, public and foreign policy, religion, and the newly formed interdisciplinary fund. In each of these areas the trusts stress the importance of developing capable and committed leadership.

Fields of interest: Conservation, environment, religion, religion—missionary programs, religion—Christian, theological education, international affairs, foreign policy, public policy, international relief, international affairs, public affairs, leadership development, citizenship, immigration, minorities, volunteerism, social services, child development, youth, family services, employment, disadvantaged, aged, handicapped, medical sciences, mental health, AIDS, health, drug abuse, media and communications, education, educational associations, higher education, secondary education, cultural programs, arts, performing arts.

Types of support: Seed money, matching funds, continuing support, renovation projects, research, operating budgets, special projects, general purposes, internships, technical assistance, exchange programs, program-related investments, fellowships, publications, conferences and seminars.

Limitations: No grants to individuals, or for endowment funds, deficit financing, scholarships, or fellowships (except those identified or initiated by the trusts).

Publications: Annual report, grants list, occasional report, informational brochure (including application guidelines), application guidelines.

Application information: Contact foundation for brochure on specific guidelines and limitations in each program area. Application form required.

Initial approach: Letter of inquiry (2 to 3 pages)
Copies of proposal: 1
Deadline(s): Culture: Music - Dec. 1, Museums/Visual Arts - Feb. 1, Theater - May 1, and Dance - Aug. 1
Board meeting date(s): Mar., June, Sept., and Dec.
Final notification: Approximately 3 weeks after board meetings
Write: Rebecca W. Rimel, Exec. Dir.

Officers and Board:* Thomas W. Langfitt, M.D.,* Pres.; Rebecca W. Rimel, Exec. Dir.; Susan W. Catherwood, Robert G. Dunlop, Robert E. McDonald, J. Howard Pew II, J.N. Pew III, Joseph N. Pew IV, M.D., R. Anderson Pew, William C. Richardson.

Trustee: The Glenmede Trust Co.

Number of staff: 66 full-time professional; 34 full-time support.

Recent health grants:

2806-1 Alzheimers Disease and Related Disorders Association, Greater Philadelphia Chapter, Philadelphia, PA, $100,000. To expand education and support services for families of Alzheimer's disease patients in low-income, minority neighborhoods in Philadelphia. 1991.

2806-2 American Association of Colleges of Pharmacy, Alexandria, VA, $150,000. For study of scope of practice in pharmacy. 1991.

2806-3 American Cancer Society, Bucks County Unit, Doylestown, PA, $12,000. For continued support of Final Care terminal nursing care program. 1991.

2806-4 American Cancer Society, Chester County Unit, Exton, PA, $36,000. For continued support of Patient Service and Rehabilitation Program for low-income cancer patients. 1991.

2806-5 American Cancer Society, Delaware County Unit, Media, PA, $94,000. For Terminal Nursing Care Program. 1991.

2806-6 American Cancer Society, Philadelphia Division, Philadelphia, PA, $90,000. For homemaker and home health aid services for elderly cancer patients in Philadelphia and Montgomery Counties. 1991.

2806-7 American College of Obstetricians and Gynecologists, DC, $120,000. For production and distribution of Baby on the Way: BASICS low-literacy edition of magazine for first-time mothers. 1991.

2806-8 American Medical Student Association, Reston, VA, $350,000. For International Partnership Program in Community-based Medical Education, exchange program between medical schools in U.S., Mexico, Central America and the Caribbean. 1991.

2806-9 Amigos de las Americas, Houston, TX, $120,000. To strengthen youth training and leadership programs in rural health and development in Mexico and Central America. 1991.

2806-10 Association for Independent Growth, Philadelphia Alliance of Mental Health/Mental Retardation Agencies, Philadelphia, PA, $50,000. For program to provide training and education services to staff of mental health/mental retardation agencies in Philadelphia. 1991.

2806-11 Baylor College of Medicine, Division of Allied Health Sciences, Houston, TX, $350,000. For Summer Medical and Research Training Program. 1991.

2806-12 Baylor College of Medicine, Division of Allied Health Sciences, Houston, TX, $200,000. For scholarship for work in regulation of human cell cycle. 1991.

2806-13 Boston University, Boston, MA, $60,000. For McDonnell-Pew research program in cognitive neuroscience. 1991.

2806-14 Brandeis University, Bigel Institute for Health Policy, The Heller School, Waltham, MA, $1,500,000. For curriculum development, teaching and fellowships for doctoral program, in collaboration with Boston University. 1991.

2806-15 Carnegie-Mellon University, School of Computer Science, Pittsburgh, PA, $82,251. For training program in cognitive neuroscience. 1991.

2806-16 Case Western Reserve University, Health Systems Management Center, Weatherhead School of Management, Cleveland, OH, $251,100. To provide research support for evaluation of Strengthening Hospital Nursing Program. 1991.

2806-17 Center for Health Education Research of Southeastern Pennsylvania, Philadelphia, PA, $240,000. For Caring Program for Children. 1991.

2806-18 Center in the Park, Philadelphia, PA, $90,000. For operations to continue in-home care, counseling and health promotion services for elderly. 1991.

2806-19 Center in the Park, Philadelphia, PA, $44,000. For general operations to continue and enhance in-home care, counseling and health promotion services. 1991.

2806-20 Cold Spring Harbor Laboratory, Cold Spring Harbor, NY, $200,000. For scholarship for study of enzyme function in cell cycle. 1991.

2806-21 Columbia University, Center for Population and Family Health, School of Public Health, NYC, NY, $410,000. To strengthen International Public Health Internship Program in Maternal and Child Health. 1991.

2806-22 Community Health Affiliates, Ardmore, PA, $125,000. For Independent Living Program, serving infirm elderly in subsidized housing. 1991.

2806-23 Contact Philadelphia, Philadelphia, PA, $12,000. To increase number of telephone reassurance calls to homebound elderly. 1991.

2806-24 Contact Philadelphia, Philadelphia, PA, $10,000. For telecommunications for deaf and Telephone Reassurance Program for homebound elderly and disabled individuals. 1991.

2806-25 Cornell University, Medical College, Ithaca, NY, $200,000. For scholarship for study of helix-loop-helix system in fruit flies. 1991.

2806-26 Corporate Alliance for Drug Education, Philadelphia, PA, $85,000. For drug prevention education program in Philadelphia public elementary schools. 1991.

2806-27 Dartmouth College, Medical School, Hanover, NH, $50,000. To improve laboratory sessions at Summer Institute for Cognitive Neuroscience in Department of Psychiatry. 1991.

2806-28 Delco Blind/Sight Center, Chester, PA, $65,000. For Homebound Rehabilitation Program for visually impaired and blind elderly. 1991.

2806-29 Duke University, Durham, NC, $512,000. For administrative costs and annual conference of scholarship program in biomedical sciences. 1991.

2806-30 Duke University, Durham, NC, $185,000. For enhanced leadership development program in veterinary education. 1991.

2806-31 Easter Seal Society for Crippled Children and Adults of Pennsylvania, Philadelphia, PA, $150,000. For summer camp program. 1991.

2806-32 Educational and Scientific Trust of the Pennsylvania Medical Society, Harrisburg, PA, $12,000. To produce educational video to inform elderly of their rights and resources under Medicare. 1991.

2806-33 Episcopal Community Services of the Diocese of Pennsylvania, Philadelphia, PA, $195,000. To provide in-home health and social services to low-income elderly in Philadelphia. 1991.

2806-34 Family and Community Service of Delaware County, Media, PA, $84,000. To provide geriatric and mental health counseling to frail, homebound elderly. 1991.

2806-35 Family Care International, NYC, NY, $200,000. For series of policy workshops in Mexico, Central America and Caribbean as part of Safe Motherhood Initiative, global effort to reduce maternal morbidity and mortality. 1991.

2806-36 Family Institute of Philadelphia, Philadelphia, PA, $45,000. For Hispanic Family Therapy Training Program. 1991.

2806-37 Foundation for Health Services Research, DC, $370,000. To develop and implement information system on ongoing health services research project. 1991.

2806-38 Foundation for State Legislatures, National Conference of State Legislatures, Denver, CO, $168,000. For project to inform and provide technical assistance to state legislators and their staffs to better design health policy to improve birth outcomes in at-risk households. 1991.

2806-39 Foundation for State Legislatures, National Conference of State Legislatures, Denver, CO, $64,500. To identify best-practice models of state workers' compensation systems and to assist in their replication. 1991.

2806-40 General Hospital Corporation, Boston, MA, $164,439. For training program in cognitive neuroscience. 1991.

2806-41 Harvard University, Harvard Medical School, Cambridge, MA, $35,000. For fellowships for outstanding young scientists from Latin America that enable them to work collaboratively with U.S. investigators and set up research laboratories in their home countries. 1991.

2806-42 Harvard University, Harvard Medical School, Cambridge, MA, $35,000. For fellowships for outstanding young scientists from Latin America that enable them to work collaboratively with U.S. investigators and set up research laboratories in their home countries. 1991.

2806-43 Harvard University, Harvard Program in Refugee Trauma, Harvard School of Public Health, Cambridge, MA, $220,000. To disseminate survey results on health and disability among Khmer refugees and to develop training program in mental health for Khmer refugees in Thailand. 1991.

2806-44 Harvard University, Office of Sponsored Research, Cambridge, MA, $59,969. For training program in cognitive neuroscience. 1991.

2806-45 Horizons Unlimited Geriatric Education Corporation, Media, PA, $30,000. To provide cognitive stimulation to frail and isolated elderly in Philadelphia nursing homes, senior centers and adult day care facilities. 1991.

2806-46 Horizons Unlimited Geriatric Education Corporation, Media, PA, $20,000. For Philadelphia County Cognitive Stimulation Program for isolated and frail elderly. 1991.

2806-47 Institute of International Education, NYC, NY, $95,000. For evaluation of Phase II of trust-initiated International Health Policy Program. 1991.

2806-48 International Catholic Child Bureau, NYC, NY, $40,000. For international seminar, The Psychological Well-being of Refugee Children: Research and Policy Issues. 1991.

2806-49 International Nutrition Foundation for Developing Countries, Cambridge, MA, $67,000. For training materials on nutrition and health policies in Costa Rica and compilation of policy-relevant community health research projects conducted in Mexico, Central America and the Caribbean. 1991.

2806-50 International Rescue Committee, NYC, NY, $50,000. For public health project for Ethiopian refugees in Eastern Sudan. 1991.

2806-51 Johns Hopkins University, Johns Hopkins Program for Medical Technology and Practice Assessment, School of Medicine, Baltimore, MD, $155,000. For survey of Medicaid-eligible women and their access to prenatal care services. 1991.

2806-52 Johns Hopkins University, School of Hygiene and Public Health, Baltimore, MD, $475,000. For second phase of renovation of Hampton House. 1991.

2806-53 Johns Hopkins University, School of Hygiene and Public Health, Baltimore, MD, $49,699. For faculty fellowship in nutrition. 1991.

2806-54 Lankenau Hospital, Philadelphia, PA, $1,000,000. For research and general operations. 1991.

2806-55 Lankenau Medical Research Center, Philadelphia, PA, $400,000. For construction of new Medical Research Center building. 1991.

2806-56 Marine Biological Laboratory, Woods Hole, MA, $27,100. For training in computational neuroscience. 1991.

2806-57 Memorial Sloan-Kettering Cancer Center, NYC, NY, $200,000. For scholarship for work in T-cell development in normal and transgenic mice. 1991.

2806-58 Mental Health Association, National, Alexandria, VA, $362,500. To strengthen community implementation of mental/emotional disability prevention strategies through increased state government support and expanded research and technical assistance. 1991.

2806-59 Michigan State University, East Lansing, MI, $132,000. For development of graduate summer food safety program. Grant made as part of Trust's National Veterinary Education Program. 1991.

2806-60 Montgomery County Association for the Blind, Norristown, PA, $60,000. For home-based rehabilitation, orientation and mobility instruction and for social worker. 1991.

2806-61 Montgomery County Emergency Services, Norristown, PA, $56,000. For Intensive Care Community Liaison Program, which provides array of mental health and general services to chronically mentally ill. 1991.

2806-62 Mount Sinai Hospital and Medical Center, School of Medicine, NYC, NY, $200,000. For scholarship for work on effects of nerve growth factor on gene expression. 1991.

2806-63 National Academy of Sciences, Institute of Medicine, DC, $50,000. For project to increase minority participation in health professions. 1991.

2806-64 National Coalition of Hispanic Health and Human Services Organizations, DC, $385,000. For research project, Growing Up Hispanic: Maternal and Child Health in Hispanic Communities. 1991.

2806-65 National Health Lawyers Association, DC, $25,000. For production and dissemination of The Patient Self-Determination Directory and Resource Guide. 1991.

2806-66 National Library of Medicine, Friends of, DC, $30,000. For pilot program, Health Sciences Education Project. 1991.

2806-67 National Public Health and Hospital Institute, DC, $235,000. For national survey of models developed by public hospitals and community organizations to respond to crisis of cocaine-involved infants. 1991.

2806-68 Neighborhood Services Center, Oxford, PA, $12,000. For Adopt a Friend, volunteer program providing friendly visits and in-home care to homebound elderly. 1991.

2806-69 Neighborhood Visiting Nurse Association of Chester County, West Chester, PA, $31,000. For Adult Health Supervision project, to prevent rehospitalization of elderly discharged from in-home skilled care. 1991.

2806-70 New England Medical Center, Boston, MA, $200,000. For scholarship for study of cytotoxic T-cell response to HIV-1. 1991.

2806-71 New York University, New York University Medical Center, NYC, NY, $200,000. For scholarship for work in cell biology and study of interferon-alpha signal transduction. 1991.

2806-72 New York University, Robert F. Wagner Graduate School of Public Service, NYC, NY, $1,000,000. For development of research and demonstration project on substance abuse prevention program among high-risk adolescents. 1991.

2806-73 North Carolina State University, College of Agriculture and Life Science, Raleigh, NC, $39,000. For faculty fellowship in nutrition. 1991.

2806-74 North Philadelphia Health System, Philadelphia, PA, $190,000. To support informal caregivers of elderly. 1991.

2806-75 Northeastern Hospital of Philadelphia, Philadelphia, PA, $75,000. For start-up of adult day care center. 1991.

2806-76 Northwestern University, Center for Health Services and Policy Research, Evanston, IL, $330,000. To evaluate two hospital-based outcomes management projects. 1991.

2806-77 Our Lady of Lourdes Medical Center, Camden, NJ, $75,000. For continued support of Helping Hands program. 1991.

2806-78 Pan American Health and Education Foundation, Mexican Foundation for Health, DC, $118,000. For project to improve nutrition teaching in Mexican medical schools and to develop collaborative network of nutrition researchers in Mexico. 1991.

2806-79 Pennington Biomedical Research Center, Baton Rouge, LA, $30,681. For faculty fellowship in nutrition. 1991.

2806-80 Pennsylvania Care Management Institute, Philadelphia, PA, $50,000. For training of care managers who provide services to frail, homebound elderly in Philadelphia and surrounding counties. 1991.

2806-81 Pennsylvania Hospital, Hall-Mercer Community Mental Health/Mental Retardation Center, Philadelphia, PA, $190,000. To provide health and mental health services to homebound, frail elderly. 1991.

2806-82 Pennsylvania State University, Institute for Policy Research and Evaluation, Graduate School of Public Policy and Administration, University Park, PA, $200,000. To organize and conduct seminar series on health and human services policy issues impacting families. 1991.

2806-83 Philadelphia AIDS Consortium, Philadelphia, PA, $300,000. For core administrative and planning expenses. 1991.

2806-84 Philadelphia Citizens for Children and Youth, Philadelphia, PA, $137,500. To continue and expand Child Health Watch project, community-based health education and outreach efffort. 1991.

2806-85 Philadelphia Geriatric Center, Philadelphia, PA, $121,000. For Counseling for Caregivers Program to strengthen efforts of family caregivers and relieve strain associated with caregiving. 1991.

2806-86 Philadelphia Geriatric Center, Philadelphia, PA, $75,000. For Counseling for Caregivers, program to strengthen efforts of caregivers for elderly who are themselves elderly. 1991.

2806-87 Philadelphia Health Management Corporation, Philadelphia, PA, $990,000. For Neighborhood Health Care Database Project. 1991.

2806-88 Philadelphia Mental Health Care Corporation, Philadelphia, PA, $95,000. To increase knowledge and awareness about mental disabilities and to enhance public acceptance of community-based housing and programs for people with mental disabilities. 1991.

2806-89 Planned Parenthood Association of Bucks County, Bristol, PA, $35,000. For human sexuality education programs. 1991.

2806-90 Planned Parenthood Federation of America, Family Planning International Assistance, NYC, NY, $2,700,000. For family planning services, training and institutional development in Mexico, Haiti and Nicaragua. 1991.

2806-91 Planned Parenthood of Greater Camden, Camden, NJ, $75,000. For educational programs. 1991.

2806-92 Population Crisis Committee, DC, $300,000. To educate U.S. public and inform policy makers about relationship between population growth and environmental degradation. 1991.

2806-93 Princeton University, Princeton, NJ, $200,000. For scholarship for study of cell fate control during generation of neuronal diversity. 1991.

2806-94 Saint Anthonys Health Care Foundation, Saint Petersburg, FL, $261,819. To administer program to enable nonprofit hospitals to undertake institution-wide changes that will strengthen their nursing services and improve quality of patient care. Funded in collaboration with Robert Wood Johnson Foundation. 1991.

2806-95 Salk Institute for Biological Studies, La Jolla, CA, $75,000. For fellowships for outstanding young scientists from Latin America that enable them to work collaboratively with U.S. investigators and set up research laboratories in their home countries. 1991.

2806-96 Saunders House, Wynnewood, PA, $50,000. To provide therapeutic activities for residents with memory impairment, Alzheimer's disease and other forms of senile dementia. 1991.

2806-97 Special Equestrians, Pineville, PA, $10,000. For operations for program that provides horseback riding therapy to broad range of disabled persons. 1991.

2806-98 Stanford University, Stanford, CA, $60,000. For research project in cognitive neuroscience. 1991.

2806-99 Texas A & M University, College Station, TX, $36,300. For faculty fellowship in nutrition. 1991.

2806-100 Tufts University, Medford, MA, $200,000. For scholarship for study of regulation of eukaryotic cell cycle. 1991.

2806-101 Tulane University, School of Medicine, New Orleans, LA, $300,000. For continuation and expansion of Medical Education and Enrichment Program for Minority and Disadvantaged Students. 1991.

2806-102 United Hospital Fund of New York, NYC, NY, $200,000. To develop and implement research and demonstration program to improve capacities of home-care agencies to respond more effectively to needs of their clients. 1991.

2806-103 University of Arizona, Tucson, AZ, $200,000. For scholarship for work in molecular analysis of acting proteins in yeast. 1991.

2806-104 University of Arizona, Tucson, AZ, $31,685. For faculty fellowship in nutrition. 1991.

2806-105 University of California, Irvine, CA, $200,000. For scholarship for study of molecular characterization of Borna disease virus. 1991.

2806-106 University of California, La Jolla, CA, $200,000. For scholarship for study of embryonic vertebrate visual system in vivo. 1991.

2806-107 University of California, Institute for Health Policy Studies, School of Medicine, San Francisco, CA, $1,250,000. For program for mid-career education in health policy including, but not limited to, post-doctoral research in collaboration with University of California at Los Angeles and Rand Corporation. 1991.

2806-108 University of California, Language Resource Program, Los Angeles, CA, $200,000. For scholarship for work in purification and characterization of Shaker K channel of fruit fly. 1991.

2806-109 University of California, School of Medicine, San Francisco, CA, $309,000. For program enhancements including interschool exchange, information dissemination, workshops and development of program casebook and video. Grant made as part of Trust's Health of the Public Program, to develop model educational programs, drawing on resources of schools of medicine, public health and social sciences, that will help orient medical and health professions to broader issues affecting health of the public.

Cosponsored with Rockefeller Foundation. 1991.

2806-110 University of Chicago, Chicago, IL, $700,000. For Pew Program in Medicine, Arts and the Social Sciences. 1991.

2806-111 University of Chicago, Chicago, IL, $200,000. For scholarship for study of structure and function of telomeres, ends of linear eukaryotic chromosomes. 1991.

2806-112 University of Chicago, Center for Clinical Medical Ethics, Chicago, IL, $500,000. To continue implementation of clinical medical ethics training network for senior clinical faculty. 1991.

2806-113 University of Florida, College of Medicine, Gainesville, FL, $200,000. For scholarship for work in pathogenesis of Prader-Willi syndrome and Angelman syndrome. 1991.

2806-114 University of Illinois, Urbana, IL, $28,894. For faculty fellowship in nutrition. 1991.

2806-115 University of Iowa, Iowa City, IA, $114,566. For research project in cognitive neuroscience. 1991.

2806-116 University of Maryland, School of Medicine, Baltimore, MD, $26,650. For faculty fellowship in nutrition. 1991.

2806-117 University of Medicine and Dentistry of New Jersey, Institute for the Study of Child Development, Robert Wood Johnson Medical School, Newark, NJ, $90,000. To conduct study on how incentives to recruit and retain people in health care are used and how they can improve health care delivery to low-income people. 1991.

2806-118 University of Michigan, Ann Arbor, MI, $200,000. For scholarship for study of cellular and molecular mechanisms that cause acute inflammation. 1991.

2806-119 University of Minnesota, Saint Paul, MN, $29,368. For faculty fellowship in nutrition. 1991.

2806-120 University of Minnesota, School of Mathematics, Minneapolis, MN, $200,000. For scholarship for work in developmental regulation and function of Drosphilia cytoplasmic dyneins. 1991.

2806-121 University of Pennsylvania, Leonard Davis Institute of Health Economics, Philadelphia, PA, $98,800. For evaluation of Pew National Dental Education Program. 1991.

2806-122 University of Pennsylvania, School of Medicine, Philadelphia, PA, $150,000. For summer internship program in community health for first-year medical students. 1991.

2806-123 University of Pennsylvania, Technical Assistance Education Center, Section of Public Psychiatry and Mental Health Services Research, Philadelphia, PA, $150,000. To improve mental health services for children and youth in Philadelphia and surrounding counties. 1991.

2806-124 University of Pittsburgh, Office of Research, Pittsburgh, PA, $59,702. For research project in cognitive neuroscience. 1991.

2806-125 University of Texas, Medical Branch, Austin, TX, $23,501. For faculty fellowship in nutrition. 1991.

2806-126 University of Washington, Seattle, WA, $200,000. For scholarship for study of physiological function of main inhibitory neurotransmitter. 1991.

2806-127 University of Washington, School of Public Health and Community Medicine, Seattle, WA, $230,000. For International Primary Health Care Fellowship Program. 1991.

2806-128 Urban Affairs Coalition of Greater Philadelphia, Philadelphia, PA, $138,400. To strengthen capacity of health and social service delivery organizations in Philadelphia and surrounding Pennsylvania counties. 1991.

2806-129 Visiting Nurse Association of Greater Philadelphia, Philadelphia, PA, $250,000. For general operations to provide for in-home health services to low-income and indigent elderly. 1991.

2806-130 Visiting Nurse Association of Greater Philadelphia, Philadelphia, PA, $110,000. For general operations to permit delivery of home-care services to low-income patients. 1991.

2806-131 Visiting Nurse Association-Community Services, Abington, PA, $50,000. For in-home personal care and home support services to low-income elderly and disabled individuals. 1991.

2806-132 VNA-Community Services, Abington, PA, $80,000. For in-home personal care and home support services to low-income elderly. 1991.

2806-133 Whitehead Institute for Biomedical Research, Cambridge, MA, $75,000. For fellowships for outstanding young scientists from Latin America that enable them to work collaboratively with U.S. investigators and set up research laboratories in their home countries. 1991.

2806-134 Wissahickon Hospice, Philadelphia, PA, $105,000. For Living Alone Program, to provide hospice services to terminally ill individuals without caregivers in residence. 1991.

2806-135 Wistar Institute of Anatomy and Biology, Philadelphia, PA, $300,000. For final phase of development of Biotechnology Center. 1991.

2806-136 Wistar Institute of Anatomy and Biology, Philadelphia, PA, $200,000. For scholarship for study of protein in human Wilm's tumors. 1991.

2806-137 Yale University, New Haven, CT, $200,000. For scholarship for study of genetic mutation in formation of undersized, inviable oocytes. 1991.

2806-138 Yeshiva University, Albert Einstein College of Medicine, NYC, NY, $2,700,000. For Infant Health and Development Program, longitudinal study on impact of early and regular health care on childhood development. 1991.

2807
Philadelphia Electric Company Giving Program
2301 Market St., 513-1
P.O. Box 8699
Philadelphia 19101   (215) 841-4000

Financial data (yr. ended 12/31/90): Total giving, $2,090,000, including $2,000,000 for grants and $90,000 for in-kind gifts.

Purpose and activities: Supports health and welfare, civic affairs, education, and arts and culture, minorities, the handicapped, and the elderly.

Fields of interest: Health, welfare, civic affairs, education, higher education, arts, cultural programs, handicapped, aged.

Types of support: Capital campaigns, general purposes, operating budgets, scholarship funds.

Limitations: Giving primarily in headquarters city and major operating locations. No grants to individuals.

Application information: Application form not required.

Initial approach: Letter
Board meeting date(s): Monthly
Final notification: 6-8 weeks
Write: William Taylor, Pres. and C.O.O.

2808
The Philadelphia Foundation ▼
1234 Market St., Suite 1900
Philadelphia 19107-3794   (215) 563-6417
FAX: (215) 563-6882

Established in 1918 in PA by bank resolution.
Donor(s): 140 different funds.
Foundation type: Community
Financial data (yr. ended 04/30/91): Assets, $70,600,000 (M); gifts received, $2,881,579; expenditures, $5,884,009; qualifying distributions, $4,926,257, including $4,926,257 for 483 grants (high: $128,031; low: $287; average: $5,000-$20,000).

Purpose and activities: For the purpose of promoting charitable, educational, and civic activities; most of the funds have specific purposes or named beneficiary institutions, with emphasis on health and welfare, including hospitals and community activities; grants also for education and cultural programs.

Fields of interest: Health, hospitals, AIDS, welfare, social services, community development, disadvantaged, handicapped, housing, minorities, civic affairs, civil rights, public policy, legal services, urban development, urban affairs, education, education—minorities, cultural programs, dance.

Types of support: Operating budgets, continuing support, seed money, emergency funds, matching funds, special projects, consulting services, technical assistance.

Limitations: Giving limited to Philadelphia and to Bucks, Chester, Delaware, and Montgomery counties in southeastern PA, except for designated funds. Generally, low priority given to national organizations, government agencies, large budget agencies, private schools, religious organizations, or umbrella-funding organizations. No grants to individuals, or for annual or capital campaigns, building funds, land acquisition, endowment funds, scholarships, fellowships, research, publications, tours or trips, conferences, or deficit financing; no loans.

Publications: Annual report, application guidelines, informational brochure, newsletter.

Application information: Application form required.

Initial approach: Proposal, including cover sheet and statistical form
Copies of proposal: 1

Deadline(s): Submit proposal preferably during May and June or Nov. and Dec.; proposals not accepted Aug.-Oct. and Feb.-Apr.; deadlines July 31 and Jan. 15
Board meeting date(s): Apr. and Nov.
Final notification: 3 to 4 months
Write: Carrolle Perry, Dir.

Managers: Ernesta Drinker Ballard, Chair.; James F. Bodine, David Brenner, William C. Bullitt, Rev. Joan Salmon Campbell, Carmen Febo-San Miguel, M.D., Barbara D. Hauptfuhrer, Dona Kahn, Garry Maddox, Christine Murphy, Don Jose Stovall, Leon C. Sunstein, Jr., Sheilah Vance-Lewis, Peter Vaughan, Flora Barth Wolf.

Trustees: Bryn Mawr Trust Co., Continental Bank, N.A., CoreStates Financial Corp., Fidelity Bank, N.A., First National Bank & Trust of Newtown, The Glenmede Trust Co., Mellon Bank, N.A., Meridian Trust Co., Provident National Bank.

Number of staff: 6 full-time professional; 4 full-time support.

EIN: 231581832

Recent health grants:

2808-1 American Cancer Society, Philadelphia Division, Philadelphia, PA, $10,000. 1991.

2808-2 Asociacion de Puertorriquenos en Marcha, Philadelphia, PA, $10,000. For health program. 1991.

2808-3 Brandywine School of Nursing, Philadelphia, PA, $12,000. 1991.

2808-4 Bryn Mawr Rehabilitation Hospital, Malvern, PA, $10,000. 1991.

2808-5 Childrens Hospital of Philadelphia, Philadelphia, PA, $56,331. 1991.

2808-6 Childrens Rehabilitation Hospital, Philadelphia, PA, $57,690. 1991.

2808-7 Clara Bell Duvall Education Fund, Philadelphia, PA, $14,000. 1991.

2808-8 Delaware County Legal Assistance Association, Philadelphia, PA, $35,000. For Pennsylvania Health Law Project. 1991.

2808-9 Family Institute of Philadelphia, Philadelphia, PA, $14,000. For Hispanic family therapy training. 1991.

2808-10 Fox Chase Cancer Center, Philadelphia, PA, $15,000. 1991.

2808-11 Friends Hospital, Philadelphia, PA, $13,273. 1991.

2808-12 Hahnemann University, School of Medicine, Philadelphia, PA, $44,653. 1991.

2808-13 Health Promotion Council of Southeast Pennsylvania, Philadelphia, PA, $17,784. 1991.

2808-14 HERS Foundation, Philadelphia, PA, $10,000. 1991.

2808-15 Home of the Merciful Saviour for Crippled Children, Philadelphia, PA, $13,645. 1991.

2808-16 Inglis House: The Philadelphia Home for Physically Disabled Persons, Philadelphia, PA, $13,239. 1991.

2808-17 Institute for Cancer Research, Philadelphia, PA, $21,852. 1991.

2808-18 Lankenau Hospital, Philadelphia, PA, $27,791. 1991.

2808-19 Livengrin Foundation, Eddington, PA, $20,216. 1991.

2808-20 Maternity Care Coalition of Greater Philadelphia, Philadelphia, PA, $20,000. 1991.

2808-21 Monmouth Medical Center, Long Branch, NJ, $15,500. 1991.

2808-22 Painted Bride Art Center, Philadelphia, PA, $10,000. For Our Living Legacy, An Arts Festival on AIDS. 1991.

2808-23 Pennsylvania College of Optometry, Philadelphia, PA, $15,000. 1991.

2808-24 Philadelphia Area Project on Occupational Safety and Health, Philadelphia, PA, $15,001. 1991.

2808-25 Philadelphia Black Womens Health Project, Philadelphia, PA, $15,508. 1991.

2808-26 Philadelphia College of Pharmacy and Science, Philadelphia, PA, $11,000. 1991.

2808-27 Philadelphia School District, Board of Education, Philadelphia, PA, $67,559. For health program. 1991.

2808-28 Planned Parenthood Association of Bucks County, Bristol, PA, $10,000. 1991.

2808-29 Planned Parenthood Association of Southeastern Pennsylvania, Philadelphia, PA, $25,001. 1991.

2808-30 Planned Parenthood of Chester County, West Chester, PA, $23,750. 1991.

2808-31 Presbyterian Medical Center of Philadelphia, Philadelphia, PA, $29,562. 1991.

2808-32 Presbyterian Medical Center of Philadelphia, Philadelphia, PA, $17,500. For Sickle Cell Anemia Program. 1991.

2808-33 Resources for Human Development, Philadelphia, PA, $13,000. For Greater Philadelphia Women's Medical Fund. 1991.

2808-34 Saint Christophers Hospital for Children, Philadelphia, PA, $59,344. 1991.

2808-35 Teaching Family Corporation, Erdenheim, PA, $12,000. For Marian Homes. 1991.

2808-36 Temple University, School of Medicine, Philadelphia, PA, $10,000. 1991.

2808-37 Women Organized Against Rape, Philadelphia, PA, $20,000. 1991.

2808-38 Women-In-Transition Project, Philadelphia, PA, $10,000. 1991.

2808-39 Woodrock, Sanatoga, PA, $35,000. For United Neighbors Against Drugs. 1991.

2809
The Pittsburgh Foundation ▼

30 CNG Tower
625 Liberty Ave.
Pittsburgh 15222-3115   (412) 391-5122

Established in 1945 in PA by bank resolution and declaration of trust.
Foundation type: Community
Financial data (yr. ended 12/31/91): Assets, $193,000,000 (M); gifts received, $17,000,000; expenditures, $7,400,000; qualifying distributions, $6,200,000, including $6,200,000 for 450 grants (high: $300,000; low: $100; average: $5,000-$70,000).
Purpose and activities: Organized for the permanent administration of funds placed in trust for public charitable and educational purposes; funds used for programs to support special projects of regularly established agencies, capital and equipment needs, research of a nontechnical nature, and demonstration projects. Grants primarily for human services, health, education, urban affairs, and the arts. Unless specified by the donor, grants are generally nonrecurring.
Fields of interest: Health, education, arts, social services, urban affairs, youth, AIDS.

Types of support: Special projects, seed money, building funds, equipment, research, renovation projects, technical assistance.
Limitations: Giving limited to Pittsburgh and Allegheny County, PA. No support for churches, private schools, or hospitals. No grants to individuals, or for annual campaigns, endowment funds, travel, operating budgets, scholarships, fellowships, or research of a highly technical or specialized nature; no loans to individuals.
Publications: Annual report, application guidelines, newsletter.
Application information: Application form required.
    Initial approach: Letter or proposal
    Copies of proposal: 1
    Deadline(s): Jan. 1, Apr. 1, July 1, and Oct. 1
    Board meeting date(s): Mar., June, Sept., and Dec.
    Final notification: 4 to 6 weeks
    Write: Alfred W. Wishart, Jr., Pres. and Exec. Dir.
Officers: Alfred W. Wishart, Jr., Exec. Dir.; J.E. Kime, Assoc. Dir. and Chief Financial and Admin. Officer.
Distribution Committee: William J. Copeland, Chair.; Frieda G. Shapira, Vice-Chair.; Dorothy R. Williams, Treas.; Byrd R. Brown, Jeanne C. Caliguiri, Douglas D. Danforth, George A. Davidson, Robert Dickey III, Arthur J. Edmunds, Benjamin R. Fisher, Jr., Phyllis Moorman Goode, Sherin H. Knowles, John L. Propst, Alvin Rogal, Samuel Y. Stroh.
Trustee Banks: Integra Financial Corp., Mellon Bank, N.A., Pittsburgh National Bank.
Number of staff: None.
EIN: 250965466
Recent health grants:

2809-1 American Cancer Society, Allegheny County Unit, Pittsburgh, PA, $11,243. For general support. 1991.

2809-2 Chestnut Ridge Counsel Services, Uniontown, PA, $12,000. For renovations to heating/cooling system of Health Center. 1991.

2809-3 Childrens Advocacy Center, Pittsburgh, PA, $30,000. To assist with programs and library, plus children's counselor, for sexually abused children. 1991.

2809-4 Childrens Hospital of Los Angeles, Los Angeles, CA, $66,000. For research of biologic therapy of neuroblastoma after bone marrow transplantation. 1991.

2809-5 Childrens Hospital of Pittsburgh, Pittsburgh, PA, $14,000. For research technician to be specimen coordinator. 1991.

2809-6 East End Cooperative Ministry, Pittsburgh, PA, $50,000. For renovations to Sojourner House, halfway house for women recovering from drug and alcohol addictions. 1991.

2809-7 Lemington Home for the Aged, Pittsburgh, PA, $102,444. To close transactions involved in refinancing its first mortgage. 1991.

2809-8 Mothers Against Drunk Driving (MADD), Fairless Hills, PA, $10,000. Toward drug and alcohol prevention program, called Alcohol, Drugs, Driving and You, designed for students in grades K-12. 1991.

2809-9 Nursing Recruitment Coalition, Pittsburgh, PA, $27,532. For nursing scholarships. 1991.

2809-10 Parents League for Emotional Adjustment, Pittsburgh, PA, $23,032. For training component of Friends-2-Gether, peer

support program for mentally ill children. 1991.

2809-11 Pittsburgh AIDS Task Force, Pittsburgh, PA, $75,000. For re-funding of outreach program for men at high risk of HIV infection. 1991.

2809-12 Planned Parenthood of Western Pennsylvania, Pittsburgh, PA, $65,175. To implement teen pregnancy prevention program in four high-risk communities. 1991.

2809-13 Presbyterian Association on Aging, Pittsburgh, PA, $70,000. For staff training and evaluation of Woodside Place Residential Alzheimer Facility. 1991.

2809-14 Regency Hall Nursing Home, Pittsburgh, PA, $15,000. For renovating facility and updating much-needed equipment. 1991.

2809-15 Rehabilitation Institute of Pittsburgh, Pittsburgh, PA, $50,000. For capital campaign. 1991.

2809-16 United Cerebral Palsy Association of Pittsburgh, Pittsburgh, PA, $24,530. Toward Support Circles project, two-year demonstration project which seeks to foster supportive relationships between persons with and without disabilities. 1991.

2809-17 United Cerebral Palsy of Southern Alleghenies, Johnstown, PA, $19,568. For purchase and installation of windows, boiler, door, stove and water heater at agency's facility. 1991.

2809-18 University of Pittsburgh, Health Policy Institute, Pittsburgh, PA, $23,052. 1991.

2809-19 University of Pittsburgh, School of Medicine, Pittsburgh, PA, $45,164. For direct interdisciplinary research in field of neuropsychobiology of mental disorders. 1991.

2809-20 Visiting Nurse Association of Allegheny County, Pittsburgh, PA, $20,000. For purchase of Actronics Interactive Learning System for CPR. 1991.

2810
Pittsburgh National Bank Foundation ▼

(Formerly Pittsburgh National Foundation)
c/o Pittsburgh National Bldg., 14th Fl.
Fifth Ave. and Wood St.
Pittsburgh 15222   (412) 762-3137

Established in 1970 in PA.
Donor(s): Pittsburgh National Bank.
Foundation type: Company-sponsored
Financial data (yr. ended 12/31/90): Assets, $5,386,895 (M); gifts received, $1,521,419; expenditures, $1,678,778; qualifying distributions, $1,673,768, including $1,624,425 for 244 grants (high: $500,000; low: $25; average: $1,000-$35,000) and $49,343 for 86 employee matching gifts.
Purpose and activities: Giving for community funds, education, hospitals and health, cultural programs, youth agencies, public policy, community development, and social services.
Fields of interest: Community funds, cultural programs, youth, social services, hospitals, health services, public policy, community development.
Types of support: Operating budgets, continuing support, annual campaigns, seed money, emergency funds, deficit financing, general purposes, building funds, equipment, land acquisition, matching funds, employee matching gifts.

Limitations: Giving limited to southwestern PA. No support for religious purposes. No grants to individuals, or for endowment funds; no loans.
Application information: Application form not required.
  Initial approach: Letter
  Copies of proposal: 1
  Deadline(s): None
  Board meeting date(s): Monthly
  Final notification: Approximately 6 weeks
  Write: Gere Edward Grimm, Secy.
Officer: D. Paul Beard, Secy.
Trustee: Pittsburgh National Bank.
Number of staff: 2 part-time professional; 2 part-time support.
EIN: 251202255
Recent health grants:
2810-1 Childrens Hospital of Pittsburgh, Pittsburgh, PA, $21,000. For general support. 1991.
2810-2 Gateway Rehabilitation Center, Aliquippa, PA, $15,000. For general support. 1991.
2810-3 Geisinger Foundation, Danville, PA, $20,000. For general support. 1991.
2810-4 Harmarville Rehabilitation Center, Pittsburgh, PA, $12,500. For general support. 1991.
2810-5 North Hills Passavant Hospital, Pittsburgh, PA, $12,000. For general support. 1991.
2810-6 Pittsburgh Cancer Institute, Pittsburgh, PA, $25,000. For general support. 1991.
2810-7 Rehabilitation Institute of Pittsburgh, Pittsburgh, PA, $21,250. For general support. 1991.
2810-8 Saint Margaret Memorial Hospital Foundation, Pittsburgh, PA, $10,000. For general support. 1991.

2811
The Polk Foundation, Inc.
2000 Grant Bldg.
Pittsburgh 15219   (412) 338-3466

Incorporated in 1957 in PA.
Donor(s): Patricia Hillman Miller.‡
Foundation type: Independent
Financial data (yr. ended 12/31/91): Assets, $3,731,737 (M); expenditures, $208,175; qualifying distributions, $169,212, including $163,000 for 3 grants (high: $100,000; low: $3,000).
Purpose and activities: Emphasis on a school for exceptional children, programs for mentally or physically handicapped youth, and medical research.
Fields of interest: Handicapped, youth, medical research.
Types of support: Seed money, building funds, equipment, capital campaigns, renovation projects.
Limitations: Giving limited to Pittsburgh and southwestern PA. No grants to individuals, or for operating budgets, continuing support, annual campaigns, emergency funds, deficit financing, land acquisition, endowment funds, matching gifts, scholarships, fellowships, research, special projects, publications, or conferences; no loans.
Publications: Financial statement.
Application information: Application form not required.

Initial approach: Letter
Copies of proposal: 1
Deadline(s): None
Board meeting date(s): May and Dec.
Final notification: 4 to 6 months
Write: Ronald W. Wertz, Secy.
Officers and Directors:* Henry L. Hillman,* Pres.; C.G. Grefenstette,* V.P.; Ronald W. Wertz,* Secy.; Lawrence M. Wagner, Treas.; Patricia M. Duggan.
Number of staff: 1 part-time professional; 2 part-time support.
EIN: 251113733

2812
PPG Industries Foundation ▼
One PPG Place
Pittsburgh 15272   (412) 434-2962

Incorporated in 1951 in PA.
Donor(s): PPG Industries, Inc.
Foundation type: Company-sponsored
Financial data (yr. ended 12/31/90): Assets, $7,182,633 (M); gifts received, $198,337; expenditures, $4,795,765; qualifying distributions, $4,647,725, including $3,881,139 for 961 grants (high: $420,000; low: $100; average: $5,000-$20,000) and $664,721 for 3,751 employee matching gifts.
Purpose and activities: Giving primarily for social services, including youth organizations, higher education, health and safety organizations, cultural programs, and civic and community affairs.
Fields of interest: Higher education, civic affairs, cultural programs, health services, safety, social services, youth, community development.
Types of support: Annual campaigns, capital campaigns, operating budgets, emergency funds, research, scholarship funds, employee-related scholarships, employee matching gifts, continuing support, special projects.
Limitations: Giving primarily in areas of company operations, with emphasis on the Pittsburgh, PA, region. No support for religious groups for religious purposes. No grants to individuals, or for endowment funds, advertising, benefits, grants (other than matching gifts) of less than $100, or operating support of United Way member agencies; no loans.
Publications: Annual report (including application guidelines).
Application information: Grant decisions made by the Screening Committee and the Board of Directors. Application form not required.
  Initial approach: Letter
  Copies of proposal: 1
  Deadline(s): Sept. 1
  Board meeting date(s): Usually in June and Dec.
  Final notification: Following board meetings
  Write: Roslyn Rosenblatt, Exec. Dir.
Officers and Directors:* Vincent A. Sarni,* Chair.; Raymond W. LeBoeuf,* V.P.; Joseph E. Rowe,* V.P.; Sue Sloan, Secy.; Roslyn Rosenblatt,* Exec. Dir.
Number of staff: 1 full-time professional; 1 full-time support; 1 part-time support.
EIN: 256037790
Recent health grants:
2812-1 Allegheny Health Education and Research Corporation, Pittsburgh, PA, $30,000. 1990.

2812-2 Allegheny Health Services, Pittsburgh, PA, $50,000. For special project. 1990.
2812-3 Childrens Hospital of Pittsburgh, Pittsburgh, PA, $25,000. 1990.
2812-4 Easter Seal Society for Crippled Children and Adults of Allegheny County, Pittsburgh, PA, $10,000. 1990.
2812-5 Gateway Rehabilitation Center, Pittsburgh, PA, $10,000. 1990.
2812-6 Harmarville Rehabilitation Center, Pittsburgh, PA, $10,000. 1990.
2812-7 Juvenile Diabetes Foundation International, Greater Pittsburgh Chapter, Pittsburgh, PA, $10,000. 1990.
2812-8 Magee-Womens Health Foundation, Pittsburgh, PA, $20,000. For Campaign for Women and Infants. 1990.
2812-9 Media-Advertising Partnership for a Drug-Free America, NYC, NY, $10,000. 1990.
2812-10 Memorial Sloan-Kettering Cancer Center, NYC, NY, $10,000. 1990.
2812-11 Parent and Child Guidance Center, Pittsburgh, PA, $12,500. 1990.
2812-12 Project Orbis, NYC, NY, $10,000. 1990.
2812-13 Wetzel County Hospital, New Martinsville, WV, $10,000. 1990.

2813
Provident Mutual Life Insurance Company Giving Program
1600 Market Street
P.O. Box 7378
Philadelphia 19101   (215) 636-5000

Financial data (yr. ended 12/31/90): Total giving, $575,000, including $535,000 for grants and $40,000 for employee matching gifts.
Purpose and activities: Supports arts and culture, health and welfare, education and civic affairs.
Fields of interest: Arts, cultural programs, health, welfare, education, civic affairs, education—minorities.
Types of support: Matching funds, employee matching gifts.
Limitations: Giving primarily in headquarters city. No support for fraternal and religious organizations. No grants to individuals.
Application information:
  Initial approach: Letter and proposal
  Deadline(s): Sept. and Oct.
  Final notification: 4-6 weeks
  Write: Keith Bratz, Dir., Communs.

2814
Provident National Bank Giving Program
Public Affairs Dept.
Broad and Chestnut Sts.
Philadelphia 19110   (215) 585-5445

Financial data (yr. ended 12/31/90): Total giving, $1,400,000, including $1,260,000 for grants and $140,000 for employee matching gifts.
Purpose and activities: Supports arts and culture, health and welfare, employment and community development, and education and civic affairs.
Fields of interest: Arts, cultural programs, health, welfare, education, civic affairs, community development, employment.
Types of support: Annual campaigns, building funds, capital campaigns, continuing support,

employee matching gifts, general purposes, operating budgets, special projects.
Limitations: Giving primarily in headquarters city and major operating locations in Philadelphia, Bucks, Montgomery, Delaware, and Chester counties, PA. No support for religious and for profit organizations. No grants to individuals.
Publications: Corporate giving report.
Application information: Application form not required.
    Initial approach: Letter and proposal
    Copies of proposal: 1
    Deadline(s): Sept.-Oct.
    Board meeting date(s): Jan. and May
    Final notification: Within 12 weeks
    Write: Brian Goerky, Dir., Corp. Affairs
Administrators: Brian Goerky, Dir., Corp. Affairs; Donna Raiford, Exec. Secy.
Number of staff: 1

2815
The Quaker Chemical Foundation
Elm and Lee Sts.
Conshohocken 19428   (215) 823-4313

Trust established in 1959 in PA.
Donor(s): Quaker Chemical Corp.
Foundation type: Company-sponsored
Financial data (yr. ended 06/30/91): Assets, $313,547 (M); gifts received, $378,000; expenditures, $394,362; qualifying distributions, $393,447, including $199,420 for 164 grants (high: $5,250; low: $50; average: $2,500), $93,711 for 28 grants to individuals (high: $8,000; low: $1,000; average: $1,000-$4,000) and $99,666 for 301 employee matching gifts.
Purpose and activities: Grants largely for higher education, including scholarships and employee matching gifts, local community funds, health, hospitals, social services, and cultural programs.
Fields of interest: Higher education, education, community funds, cultural programs, health, hospitals, social services.
Types of support: Scholarship funds, employee matching gifts, employee-related scholarships, matching funds.
Limitations: Giving primarily in areas of company operations, including CA, MI, and PA. No grants to individuals (except for employee-related scholarships), or for building or endowment funds; no loans.
Publications: Application guidelines.
Application information: Application form not required.
    Initial approach: Letter requesting guidelines
    Copies of proposal: 1
    Deadline(s): Apr. 30
    Board meeting date(s): Quarterly
    Final notification: July
    Write: Karen Miller
Trustees: Karl H. Spaeth, Chair.; Katherine N. Coughenour, Edwin J. Delattre, Alan G. Keyser, J. Everett Wick, Jane Williams.
Number of staff: None.
EIN: 236245803

2816
The RAF Foundation
8380 Old York Rd., Bldg. One, Suite 200
Elkins Park 19117

Established in 1984 in PA.
Donor(s): Robert A. Fox, Bar Plate Manufacturing, Ferche Millwork, Hardware Supply, Vinyl Building Products, Inc.
Foundation type: Independent
Financial data (yr. ended 11/30/91): Assets, $1,391,004 (M); gifts received, $250,000; expenditures, $261,229; qualifying distributions, $253,770, including $253,666 for 7 grants (high: $100,000; low: $5,000).
Fields of interest: Higher education, Jewish giving, Jewish welfare, biological sciences, medical research.
Limitations: Giving primarily in Philadelphia, PA. No grants to individuals.
Application information:
    Initial approach: Letter
    Deadline(s): None
    Write: Board of Trustees
Trustees: Esther G. Fox, Robert A. Fox.
EIN: 232331199

2817
Rite Aid Corporate Giving Program
431 Railroad Ave.
Shiremanstown 17011   (717) 761-2633
Application address: P.O. Box 3165, Harrisburg, PA 17105

Purpose and activities: Supports education, including higher education, health, arts and culture, civic affairs, and general charitable giving.
Fields of interest: Education, higher education, arts, cultural programs, civic affairs, general charitable giving, health.
Limitations: Giving primarily in the east coast including the middle and southern states: AL, CT, DE, DC, FL, GA, IN, KY, MD, MA, MI, NH, NJ, NY, NC, OH, PA, RI, SC, TN, VT, VA, and WV.
Application information: Application form required.
    Initial approach: Letter; Send to headquarters
    Write: Suzanne Mead, V.P., Corp. Communs.
Administrators: Suzanne Mead, V.P. Corp. Communs.; Jolene Zelinski, Donations Coord.

2818
The Rockwell Foundation
c/o Pittsburgh Bank, C & I Trust Dept.
One Oliver Plaza, 27th Fl.
Pittsburgh 15265   (412) 762-3390

Trust established in 1956 in PA.
Donor(s): Willard F. Rockwell,‡ and family.
Foundation type: Independent
Financial data (yr. ended 12/31/91): Assets, $11,013,348 (M); expenditures, $516,410; qualifying distributions, $496,000, including $496,000 for 107 grants (high: $75,000; low: $500).
Purpose and activities: Giving primarily for higher and secondary education; support also for the fine and performing arts, museums, music and dance organizations, child welfare and family services, conservation, hospitals and health agencies, including drug abuse programs, cancer

research, mental illness and hospices, biology, science and technology, historic preservation, and religion.
Fields of interest: Higher education, secondary education, arts, performing arts, child welfare, family services, hospitals, health, historic preservation, religion.
Types of support: Annual campaigns, building funds, capital campaigns, continuing support, endowment funds, equipment, general purposes, operating budgets, scholarship funds, seed money.
Limitations: Giving primarily in PA. No grants to individuals, or for fellowships; no loans.
Application information: Application form not required.
    Initial approach: Letter or telephone
    Copies of proposal: 1
    Board meeting date(s): As required
Officer and Trustees:* H. Campbell Stuckeman,* Secy.; George Peter Rockwell, Russell A. Rockwell, Willard F. Rockwell, Jr.
Number of staff: None.
EIN: 256035975

2819
Rockwell International Corporation Trust
▼
625 Liberty Ave.
Pittsburgh 15222-3123   (412) 565-4039

Trust established in 1959 in PA.
Donor(s): Rockwell International Corp.
Foundation type: Company-sponsored
Financial data (yr. ended 09/30/90): Assets, $15,243,036 (M); expenditures, $12,760,382; qualifying distributions, $12,642,800, including $12,627,198 for 3,560 grants (high: $500,000; low: $25; average: $1,000-$50,000).
Purpose and activities: Giving for higher education, primarily engineering education, and organizations which provide services in communities where donor has facilities; support also for cultural programs, health, and human services.
Fields of interest: Higher education, engineering.
Types of support: Operating budgets, building funds, employee matching gifts, scholarship funds, fellowships, professorships.
Limitations: Giving primarily in areas of corporate operations, except for selected national organizations and universities which are sources of recruits. No grants to individuals, or for hospital building campaigns or general endowments; no loans.
Publications: Informational brochure.
Application information: Application form not required.
    Initial approach: Proposal
    Copies of proposal: 1
    Deadline(s): None
    Board meeting date(s): Monthly
    Final notification: 60 to 90 days
    Write: Larry D. McMillen
Trust Committee: W.M. Barnes, Secy.; Donald R. Beall, R.L. Cattoy, Robert A. dePalma, Richard R. Mau.
Trustee: Pittsburgh National Bank.
Number of staff: 4
EIN: 251072431
Recent health grants:
2819-1 Allegheny Heart Institute, Pittsburgh, PA, $15,000. 1991.

2819-2 American Cancer Society, Costa Mesa, CA, $14,000. 1991.

2819-3 Blood Center of Southeastern Wisconsin, Milwaukee, WI, $10,000. 1991.

2819-4 Childrens Hospital of Wisconsin, Milwaukee, WI, $30,000. 1991.

2819-5 De Paul Hospital Foundation, Milwaukee, WI, $25,000. 1991.

2819-6 Juvenile Diabetes Foundation International, Los Angeles Chapter, Los Angeles, CA, $15,000. 1991.

2819-7 Media-Advertising Partnership for a Drug-Free America, NYC, NY, $10,000. 1991.

2819-8 Medical College of Wisconsin, Milwaukee, WI, $10,000. 1991.

2819-9 Richardson Health System, Richardson, TX, $20,000. 1991.

2819-10 Richland Hospital Foundation, Richland Center, WI, $10,000. 1991.

2819-11 Saint Joseph Hospital of Orange, Orange, CA, $16,300. 1991.

2819-12 Salk Institute for Biological Studies, La Jolla, CA, $25,000. 1991.

2819-13 Tanager Place Endowment Foundation, Children's Home of Cedar Rapids, Cedar Rapids, IA, $10,000. 1991.

2820
R. Rockwell Memorial Combined Trust
c/o Mellon Bank, N.A.
P.O. Box 185
Pittsburgh 15230
Application address: c/o Mellon Bank, N.A., One Mellon Bank Ctr., Rm 3845, Pittsburgh, PA 15258-0001, Tel.: (412) 234-4695

Donor(s): Lindsey J. Rockwell.‡
Foundation type: Independent
Financial data (yr. ended 12/31/90): Assets, $2,295,725 (M); gifts received, $866,035; expenditures, $377,250; qualifying distributions, $368,760, including $352,624 for 11 grants (high: $49,494; low: $2,045).
Fields of interest: Medical research, health associations, religion—Christian, religious welfare, social services.
Types of support: Operating budgets, general purposes.
Limitations: Giving primarily in PA.
Application information: Letter requesting guidelines.
Write: Helen M. Collins, Trust Officer, Mellon Bank, N.A.
Trustee: Mellon Bank, N.A.
EIN: 256220241

2821
Alexis Rosenberg Foundation
Seven Tohopeka Ln.
Philadelphia 19118   (215) 247-4829

Established in 1983 in PA.
Donor(s): Alexis Rosenberg.‡
Foundation type: Independent
Financial data (yr. ended 06/30/91): Assets, $2,349,977 (M); expenditures, $149,484; qualifying distributions, $124,902, including $124,902 for 48 grants (high: $10,000; low: $200).
Purpose and activities: Giving only to organizations to aid "Youth of America," including

grants for higher education, hospitals and rehabilitation, and cultural programs.
Fields of interest: Higher education, hospitals, rehabilitation, cultural programs, youth, rehabilitation.
Limitations: Giving primarily in the greater metropolitan Philadelphia, PA, area. No grants to individuals.
Application information: Application form required.
Initial approach: Proposal
Copies of proposal: 6
Deadline(s): 3 weeks prior to meeting
Board meeting date(s): Mar., June, Sept., and Dec.
Write: Paul B. Kurtz, Administrator
Trustees: William Epstein, William S. Greenfield, M.D., Charles Kahn, Jr.
Trustee Bank: Fidelity Bank, N.A.
Number of staff: 1 part-time professional.
EIN: 232222722

2822
Roth Foundation
Huntingdon Plaza, Suite 310
Huntingdon Valley 19006   (215) 947-3750

Established in 1953 in PA.
Donor(s): Edythe M. Roth, Abraham Roth.‡
Foundation type: Independent
Financial data (yr. ended 10/31/91): Assets, $917,585 (M); gifts received, $30,000; expenditures, $460,140; qualifying distributions, $459,446, including $250,000 for 1 grant and $208,123 for grants to individuals (high: $31,800; low: $26,323).
Purpose and activities: Scholarships for nursing education; some support also for medical research.
Fields of interest: Nursing, medical research.
Types of support: Student aid, research.
Limitations: Giving primarily in PA.
Application information: Applicants must have completed 1 year in a recognized school of nursing. Scholarship awards are made directly to nursing institution on recipient's behalf. Application form not required.
Initial approach: Letter
Deadline(s): None
Write: Edythe M. Roth, Trustee
Trustees: Henry Rosenberger, Edythe M. Roth, Roland P. Roth, Linda Schwartz.
EIN: 236271428

2823
Scaife Family Foundation ▼
Three Mellon Bank Ctr.
525 William Penn Place, Suite 3900
Pittsburgh 15219-1708   (412) 392-2900

Established in 1983 in PA.
Donor(s): Sarah Mellon Scaife.‡
Foundation type: Independent
Financial data (yr. ended 12/31/91): Assets, $115,620,000 (M); gifts received, $12,536,474; expenditures, $6,413,569; qualifying distributions, $6,181,683, including $5,970,950 for 79 grants (high: $1,000,000; low: $1,000; average: $25,000-$50,000).
Purpose and activities: Grants for programs that address issues relating to the family, education,

alcoholism, drug abuse, and community development.
Fields of interest: Family services, education, alcoholism, drug abuse, community development.
Types of support: General purposes, operating budgets, research, special projects.
Limitations: No grants to individuals; no loans.
Publications: 990-PF.
Application information: Application form not required.
Initial approach: Letter
Copies of proposal: 1
Deadline(s): Grant applications are normally considered in June and Dec.; no set deadline
Board meeting date(s): Quarterly
Final notification: Following board meetings
Write: Joanne B. Beyer, V.P.
Officers and Trustees:* David N. Scaife, Co-Chair.; Jennie K. Scaife, Co-Chair.; Sanford B. Ferguson, Pres.; Joanne B. Beyer, V.P. and Secy.-Treas.; Donald A. Collins, James M. Walton.
Number of staff: 1 part-time professional; 1 full-time support.
EIN: 251427015
Recent health grants:

2823-1 American Alliance for Rights and Responsibilities, DC, $151,000. For grassroots drug enforcement assistance. 1990.

2823-2 American Council for Drug Education, Rockville, MD, $136,000. For public education program. 1990.

2823-3 American Legislative Exchange Council, DC, $25,000. For Task Force on Substance Abuse. 1990.

2823-4 Contact Pittsburgh, Pittsburgh, PA, $36,000. For operating support. 1990.

2823-5 Gateway Rehabilitation Center, Aliquippa, PA, $200,000. For adolescent treatment program. 1990.

2823-6 Golden Key National Honor Society, Atlanta, GA, $50,000. For The Best of America Say No program. 1990.

2823-7 Make-A-Wish Foundation of Western Pennsylvania, Pittsburgh, PA, $15,000. For Funds for Wishes. 1990.

2823-8 National Kidney Foundation of Western Pennsylvania, Pittsburgh, PA, $108,000. For transportation for selected dialysis patients. 1990.

2823-9 Oxford House, DC, $40,000. For Pittsburgh Oxford Houses. 1990.

2823-10 Spina Bifida Association of Western Pennsylvania, Pittsburgh, PA, $75,000. For capital support. 1990.

2823-11 Straight, Murrysville, PA, $10,000. For Family Service Center. 1990.

2823-12 Whales Tale, Pittsburgh, PA, $75,000. For emergency shelter and counseling services. 1990.

2824
Sarah Scaife Foundation, Inc. ▼
Three Mellon Bank Ctr.
525 William Penn Place, Suite 3900
Pittsburgh 15219-1708   (412) 392-2900

Trust established in 1941; incorporated in 1959 in PA; present name adopted in 1974.
Donor(s): Sarah Mellon Scaife.‡
Foundation type: Independent
Financial data (yr. ended 12/31/91): Assets, $224,771,296 (M); expenditures, $13,354,109;

qualifying distributions, $12,410,966, including $11,206,000 for 119 grants (high: $1,000,000; low: $1,000; average: $25,000-$100,000).

Purpose and activities: Grants primarily directed toward public policy programs that address major international and domestic issues.

Fields of interest: Government, higher education, education, public policy, economics, international law, political science, crime and law enforcement, international affairs, international studies.

Types of support: Operating budgets, continuing support, seed money, matching funds, fellowships, research, special projects, publications, conferences and seminars, general purposes.

Limitations: No support for national organizations for general fundraising campaigns. No grants to individuals, or for deficit financing or scholarships; no loans.

Publications: Annual report (including application guidelines).

Application information: Application form not required.

> *Initial approach:* Letter or proposal
> *Copies of proposal:* 1
> *Deadline(s):* None
> *Board meeting date(s):* Feb., May, Sept., and Nov.
> *Final notification:* 2 to 4 weeks
> *Write:* Richard M. Larry, Pres.

Officers and Trustees:* Richard M. Scaife,* Chair.; Richard M. Larry,* Pres.; Donald C. Sipp, V.P., Investments and Treas.; Barbara L. Slaney, V.P.; R. Daniel McMichael, Secy.; William J. Bennett, Anthony J.A. Bryan, Edwin J. Feulner, Jr., Allan H. Meltzer, James M. Walton.

Number of staff: 6 shared staff

EIN: 251113452

Recent health grants:

2824-1 American Council on Science and Health, NYC, NY, $35,000. For general operating support. 1990.

2824-2 Betty Ford Center at Eisenhower Medical Center, Rancho Mirage, CA, $250,000. For program support. 1990.

2825
The Scholler Foundation

1100 One Penn Ctr. Plaza
Philadelphia 19103   (215) 568-7500

Trust established in 1939 in PA.

Donor(s): F.C. Scholler.‡

Foundation type: Independent

Financial data (yr. ended 12/31/91): Assets, $11,397,622 (M); expenditures, $610,199; qualifying distributions, $482,294, including $461,854 for 27 grants (high: $50,000; low: $3,460; average: $10,000-$25,000).

Purpose and activities: Giving for the alleviation of poverty and destitution, for the promotion of scientific research, including the branches of chemistry, and for other literary, educational, and public purposes; support largely for hospitals, with emphasis on grants for small community hospitals to purchase medical equipment.

Fields of interest: Hospitals.

Limitations: Giving limited to the Delaware Valley, PA. No grants to individuals, or for general support, endowment funds, scholarships, fellowships, or matching gifts; no loans.

Application information: Application form not required.

> *Initial approach:* Proposal
> *Copies of proposal:* 1
> *Deadline(s):* Feb. 1, May 1, Aug. 1, and Nov. 1
> *Board meeting date(s):* Feb., May, Aug., and Nov.
> *Write:* Frederick L. Fuges, Secy.

Officer and Trustees:* Frederick L. Fuges,* Secy.; Edwin C. Dreby III, E. Brooks Keffer, Jr., Charles S. Strickler.

Number of staff: None.

EIN: 236245158

2826
Scott Paper Company Foundation ▼

One Scott Plaza
Philadelphia 19113   (215) 522-6160

Trust established in 1954 in PA.

Donor(s): Scott Paper Co.

Foundation type: Company-sponsored

Financial data (yr. ended 12/31/91): Assets, $5,389 (M); gifts received, $3,150,862; expenditures, $3,182,567; qualifying distributions, $3,181,688, including $1,874,951 for 308 grants (high: $125,000; low: $55; average: $5,000-$10,000), $196,440 for 87 grants to individuals (high: $3,500; low: $1,000; average: $1,000-$3,500), $354,665 for 1,990 employee matching gifts and $755,632 for 2 foundation-administered programs.

Purpose and activities: Primary focus is on helping children in Scott communities reach their full potential through grants in education, including programs concerned with school reform and employee-related scholarships through Citizens' Scholarship Foundation of America, health and human services, and arts and culture.

Fields of interest: Child development, youth, volunteerism, education—early childhood, secondary education, literacy, disadvantaged, Europe.

Types of support: Seed money, employee-related scholarships, consulting services, continuing support, emergency funds, equipment, matching funds, special projects, technical assistance.

Limitations: Giving limited to areas of major company operations in Chester, PA; Dover, DE; Everett, WA; Fort Edward, NY; Hattiesburg, MS; Marinette and Oconto Falls, WI; Mobile, AL; Muskegon, MI; Rogers, AR; Skowhegan, Westbrook and Winslow, ME. No support for veterans', labor, or fraternal organizations, government agencies, religious organizations for religious purposes, national health funds, or entertainment groups. No grants to individuals, or for endowment funds, deficit financing, land acquisition, good-will advertising, research, or generally, for capital campaigns; no loans.

Publications: Annual report.

Application information: Scholarship program for children of Scott Paper Co. employees administered through Citizens' Scholarship Corp. of America. The employee matching gift program has been temporarily discontinued. Application form required.

> *Initial approach:* Letter requesting guidelines
> *Copies of proposal:* 1
> *Deadline(s):* None
> *Board meeting date(s):* June and Dec.

Final notification: 3 months
Write: Fran Rizzardi Urso, Mgr., Corp. Contrib.

Trustees: John J. Butler, Chair.; Thomas P. Czepial, Philip E. Lippincott, James A. Morrill, Paul N. Schregel.

Number of staff: 1 full-time professional; 1 full-time support.

EIN: 236231564

Recent health grants:

2826-1 Bingham Area Health Council, Bingham, ME, $10,000. 1990.

2826-2 Coalition for a Drug Free Mobile, Mobile, Al, $30,000. 1990.

2826-3 Community Alcohol and Drug Service, Everett, PA, $15,000. 1990.

2826-4 Corporate Alliance for Drug Education, Philadelphia, PA, $30,000. 1990.

2826-5 Maternity Care Coalition of Greater Philadelphia, Philadelphia, PA, $50,000. 1990.

2826-6 Mercy Hospital, Muskegon, MI, $30,430. 1990.

2826-7 Mid-Maine Medical Center, Waterville, ME, $20,000. 1990.

2826-8 Muskie Center, Waterville, ME, $20,000. 1990.

2826-9 Project Orbis, NYC, NY, $250,000. 1990.

2826-10 Shoulder, The, Mobile, AL, $10,000. 1990.

2826-11 Waterville Osteopathic Hospital, Waterville, ME, $30,000. 1990.

2827
The Scranton Area Foundation

204 Wyoming Ave.
Scranton 18503   (717) 347-6203

Established in 1954 in PA by resolution and declaration of trust.

Foundation type: Community

Financial data (yr. ended 12/31/90): Assets, $5,668,418 (M); gifts received, $192,789; expenditures, $535,877; qualifying distributions, $422,876, including $422,876 for grants (high: $55,000; low: $1,500).

Purpose and activities: Encourages and helps to build community endowment through grants for new projects and services to address unmet needs; provides a variety of donor services.

Fields of interest: Religion, community development, leadership development, human rights, libraries, higher education, conservation, youth, health, arts.

Types of support: Seed money, general purposes, research, special projects, publications, conferences and seminars, matching funds, consulting services, renovation projects, scholarship funds.

Limitations: Giving limited to the Scranton, PA, area. No grants to individuals, or for building or endowment funds, operating budgets, annual campaigns, continuing support, deficit financing, or emergency funds; no loans.

Publications: Informational brochure (including application guidelines), annual report, newsletter, grants list, application guidelines.

Application information: Application form required.

> *Initial approach:* Telephone
> *Copies of proposal:* 11
> *Deadline(s):* Submit proposal by 1st of month preceding board meeting
> *Board meeting date(s):* Jan., Apr., July, and Oct.

Final notification: Jan., Apr., July, and Oct.
Write: Jeanne A. Bovard, Exec. Dir.
Officers: Jeanne A. Bovard, Exec. Dir.; William J. Calpin, Jr., Secy.
Governors: Marion M. Isaacs, Chair.; Francis E. Crowley, Vice-Chair.; Venald W. Bovard, Eugene Cosgrove, Donald J. Fendrick, Mary Graham, Judith Graziano, Eugene J. Kane, William Lynett.
Trustee: Northeastern Bank.
Number of staff: 1 full-time professional; 1 full-time support.
EIN: 246022055

2828
Sharon Steel Foundation
Roemer Blvd. & Broadway
Farrell 16121   (412) 981-1375

Established in 1953 in PA.
Donor(s): Sharon Steel Corp.
Foundation type: Company-sponsored
Financial data (yr. ended 12/31/90): Assets, $2,928,727 (M); expenditures, $185,456; qualifying distributions, $177,075, including $177,075 for 29 grants (high: $100,000; low: $100).
Fields of interest: Higher education, museums, community funds, hospitals, medical research, civic affairs, youth, Jewish welfare.
Officers and Trustees: Victor Posner,* Chair.; Steven Posner, Mgr.; Jack Coppersmith.
EIN: 256063133

2829
Lawrence B. Sheppard Foundation, Inc.
c/o Hanover Shoe Farms, Inc.
P.O. Box 339
Hanover 17331   (717) 637-8931

Incorporated in 1946 in PA.
Donor(s): Lawrence B. Sheppard, Charlotte N. Sheppard.‡
Foundation type: Independent
Financial data (yr. ended 11/30/91): Assets, $2,628,518 (M); expenditures, $107,284; qualifying distributions, $88,000, including $88,000 for 27 grants (high: $12,500; low: $1,000).
Fields of interest: Religious schools, secondary education, health, Protestant giving, youth, community development, social services.
Types of support: General purposes, building funds, land acquisition, endowment funds.
Limitations: Giving primarily in the Hanover, PA, area. No grants to individuals.
Application information:
  Initial approach: Letter
  Deadline(s): Oct. 31
  Write: Paul E. Spears, Pres.
Officers: Paul E. Spears, Pres. and Treas.; Charlotte S. DeVan, V.P.; Russell C. Williams, Secy.
Directors: Lawrence S. DeVan, W. Todd DeVan, Patricia S. Winder.
EIN: 236251690

2830
Esther Simon Charitable Trust
150 Radnor Chester Rd., A200
Radnor 19087   (215) 341-9270

Trust established in 1952 in NY.
Donor(s): Esther Simon.‡
Foundation type: Independent
Financial data (yr. ended 12/31/91): Assets, $9,008,711 (M); expenditures, $941,980; qualifying distributions, $932,041, including $902,600 for 73 grants (high: $100,000; low: $1,000; average: $1,000-$25,000).
Purpose and activities: Primary areas of interest include education, cultural programs and the arts, hospitals, and Jewish welfare.
Fields of interest: Education, cultural programs, arts, social services, hospitals, conservation, historic preservation, Jewish welfare.
Types of support: Annual campaigns, general purposes.
Limitations: Giving primarily in New York, NY. No grants to individuals.
Application information: Applications not accepted.
  Deadline(s): Varies
  Write: L.M. Workman
Trustee: Walter H. Annenberg.
Number of staff: None.
EIN: 236286763

2831
W. W. Smith Charitable Trust ▼
101 Bryn Mawr Ave., Suite 200
Bryn Mawr 19010   (215) 525-9667

Trust established in 1977 in PA.
Donor(s): William Wikoff Smith.‡
Foundation type: Independent
Financial data (yr. ended 06/30/91): Assets, $98,959,466 (M); expenditures, $5,848,504; qualifying distributions, $5,547,808, including $5,325,295 for 123 grants (high: $277,000; low: $4,000; average: $5,000-$100,000).
Purpose and activities: Support for colleges' financial aid programs for qualified needy undergraduate students at accredited universities and colleges, hospital programs for the medical care of the poor and needy, basic scientific medical research programs dealing with cancer, AIDS, and heart disease, and programs of organizations providing shelter, food, and clothing for children and the aged.
Fields of interest: Education, higher education, health, health services, hospitals, medical sciences, medical research, cancer, AIDS, heart disease, social services, disadvantaged, welfare, homeless, hunger, minorities, women, child welfare, youth, aged.
Types of support: Scholarship funds, research, operating budgets, seed money, emergency funds, building funds, equipment, land acquisition, special projects, matching funds, general purposes, continuing support, renovation projects.
Limitations: Giving primarily in the Delaware Valley, including Philadelphia and its six neighboring counties; grants to colleges and hospitals (for indigent care) by invitation only. No grants to individuals, or for deficit financing, existing endowment funds, or retroactive funding for non-emergencies; no loans; no grants over three consecutive years; no funding of events such as dinners, golf tournaments, and program ads.
Publications: Biennial report (including application guidelines).

Application information: Free medical care and college financial aid programs by invitation only; applications for medical research grants must be submitted in quadruplicate; application forms required for medical research only.
  Initial approach: Proposal, or letter or telephone requesting guidelines
  Copies of proposal: 1
  Deadline(s): For free medical care, Feb. 1; no deadline for social service programs; for college scholarships, May 1; for cancer and AIDS research, June 15; and for heart research, Sept. 15
  Board meeting date(s): For medical care, Mar.; social services, Mar. and Sept.; scholarships, June; cancer and AIDS research, Sept.; heart research, Dec.
  Final notification: 1 month after trustees meet
  Write: Bruce M. Brown, Trust Admin.
Trustees: Mary L. Smith, CoreStates, N.A.
Number of staff: None.
EIN: 236648841
Recent health grants:
2831-1 Childrens Hospital of Philadelphia, Philadelphia, PA, $207,000. For research project, Endocardial Receptors in Congenital Cardiovascular Disease. 1991.
2831-2 Childrens Hospital of Philadelphia, Philadelphia, PA, $139,000. For indigent medical care. 1991.
2831-3 Coriell Institute for Medical Research, Camden, NJ, $129,000. For research project, Analysis of PDGF-Receptor-Related Protein in Tumor Cells. 1991.
2831-4 Coriell Institute for Medical Research, Camden, NJ, $60,000. For research project, Association of Cryptic Mycoplasma with AIDS. 1991.
2831-5 Crozer-Chester Medical Center, Chester, PA, $57,000. For indigent medical care. 1991.
2831-6 Fox Chase Cancer Center, Philadelphia, PA, $82,000. For research project, Effect of HIV I TAT on Deregulation of c-myc in AIDS-related B-cell Lymphoma. 1991.
2831-7 Graduate Hospital, Philadelphia, PA, $277,000. For research project, Altered Ion Channels and Atherosclerotic Vascular Dysfunction. 1991.
2831-8 Graduate Hospital, Philadelphia, PA, $118,300. For indigent medical care. 1991.
2831-9 Hahnemann University, Philadelphia, PA, $37,000. For hospital indigent medical care. 1991.
2831-10 Johns Hopkins University, Baltimore, MD, $144,000. For research project, Biologic Role of Hpr in Malignancy. 1991.
2831-11 Johns Hopkins University, Baltimore, MD, $58,000. For research project, Model to Test Chemoprophylaxis Against HIV Infection. 1991.
2831-12 Johns Hopkins University, Baltimore, MD, $50,000. For research project, Gene Expression in Marrow Granulocytes. 1991.
2831-13 Ken-Crest Centers for Exceptional Persons, Philadelphia, PA, $35,000. To help purchase and renovate model transitional home for technology-dependent boarder babies. 1991.
2831-14 Lankenau Medical Research Center, Philadelphia, PA, $215,000. For research project, Role of N-Cadherin and Associated Proteins in Heart. 1991.

2831-15 Mercy Catholic Medical Center, Darby, PA, $50,000. For indigent medical care. 1991.

2831-16 Pegasus Therapeutic Riding, Philadelphia, PA, $50,000. To construct indoor therapeutic facility. 1991.

2831-17 Philadelphia College of Pharmacy and Science, Philadelphia, PA, $62,000. For research project, Steroid Inducible RAS Genes and Second Messenger Interactions. 1991.

2831-18 Philadelphia College of Pharmacy and Science, Philadelphia, PA, $38,000. For scholars program. 1991.

2831-19 Philadelphia College of Pharmacy and Science, Philadelphia, PA, $10,000. For prize program. 1991.

2831-20 Presbyterian Home at Fifty-Eighth Street, Philadelphia, PA, $50,000. To construct, equip and furnish new central kitchen and dining room. 1991.

2831-21 Saint Ignatius Nursing Home, Philadelphia, PA, $50,000. For elevator repairs and kitchen equipment. 1991.

2831-22 Southern Chester County Community Health Services, West Grove, PA, $12,000. For operating support and purchase of emergency medical assistance in-home units for elderly. 1991.

2831-23 Temple University, Philadelphia, PA, $61,487. For hospital indigent medical care. 1991.

2831-24 Thomas Jefferson University, Philadelphia, PA, $182,000. For research project, Molecular Mechanisms Underlying Cardiovascular Homeostasis. 1991.

2831-25 Thomas Jefferson University, Philadelphia, PA, $162,000. For research project, Analysis of Camptothecin-DNA Topoisomerane I Interactions. 1991.

2831-26 Thomas Jefferson University, Philadelphia, PA, $108,000. For hospital indigent medical care. 1991.

2831-27 University of Pennsylvania, Philadelphia, PA, $106,000. For research project, Cardiomyoplasty for Acute Myocardial Infarction. 1991.

2831-28 Wistar Institute of Anatomy and Biology, Philadelphia, PA, $175,000. For research project, Biomedical Analysis of Wilms' Tumor Gene Product. 1991.

2831-29 Wistar Institute of Anatomy and Biology, Philadelphia, PA, $171,000. For research project, Role of Tumor-Derived TGF-Alpha in Carcinoma Growth. 1991.

2832
Hoxie Harrison Smith Foundation

(Formerly Smith Foundation)
210 Fairlamb Ave.
Havertown 19083   (215) 446-4651

Incorporated in 1920 in PA.
Donor(s): W. Hinckle Smith,‡ H. Harrison Smith.‡
Foundation type: Independent
Financial data (yr. ended 12/31/91): Assets, $6,680,109 (M); expenditures, $419,316; qualifying distributions, $389,995, including $365,975 for 45 grants (high: $25,000; low: $1,000).
Purpose and activities: To aid the sick, aged, and poor, as well as to aid in the education of needy boys and girls through local organizations

engaged in such work; grants for hospitals, child welfare, the aged, and the handicapped.
Fields of interest: Hospitals, child welfare, handicapped, aged, education.
Types of support: Building funds, operating budgets, special projects.
Limitations: Giving limited to southeastern PA. No grants to individuals, or for endowment funds.
Publications: Annual report.
Application information: Application form not required.
  Initial approach: Letter
  Copies of proposal: 1
  Deadline(s): Before Sept. 1
  Board meeting date(s): Semiannually
  Write: Joseph H. Barber, Secy.-Treas.
Officers and Directors:* Roger P. Hollingsworth,* Pres.; Robert L. Strayer,* V.P.; Joseph H. Barber,* Secy.-Treas.; Phillip C. Burnham, Howard W. Busch, William Buchanan Gold, Jr., William Powell, Francis R. Veale.
Trustee Bank: Philadelphia National Bank.
EIN: 236238148

2833
SmithKline Beecham Corporate Giving Program

P.O. Box 7929
Philadelphia 19101   (215) 751-4000

Financial data (yr. ended 12/31/90): Total giving, $7,176,925, including $3,706,925 for grants and $3,470,000 for in-kind gifts.
Purpose and activities: "As a leader in healthcare on a global scale, SmithKline Beecham aims to have its contributions enhance the company's role in healthcare, strenghten its business performance and invigorate the health and business environments in which the Company and its business sectors operate. We will ensure that SmithKline Beecham is correctly identified as a responsive, postive presence in all its communities. In employment and contracting, as well as in our giving, we are intent on combatting disadvantage due to ethnic heritage, sex, age and handicap. We are especially alert to such needs in host communities where social and economic condiditons are unusually difficult." The long-range priorities we have established are: 1) Medicine and Medical Research and Develpment; 2) Pharmacy; 3) Medical and Pharmacy Education; 4) Allied Health-Related/Scientific Fields; 5) Health and civic needs, especially in communities where SmithKline Beecham has a major presence, including agencies serving less-develped countries; 6) The health and welfare of disadvantaged minorities, handicapped persons and women; 7) Programs in which SmithKline Beecham employees are actively involved for the betterment of their communities. U.S. contributions are made through the Foundtion, the Company and other countries, contributions are made by the Company and its business sectors.
Fields of interest: Arts, health, social services, cultural programs, civic affairs.
Limitations: No grants to individuals.
Application information: In U.S. send requests to Foundation; in United Kingdom proposals to contributions coordinator.
  Initial approach: Letter

Board meeting date(s): Quarterly
Write: Jean Glenn, Dir., Public Affairs
Administrators: Jean Glenn, Dir., Public Affairs; Francis Fredrick, Sr. Prog. Assoc.

2834
SmithKline Beecham Foundation ▼

(Formerly SmithKline Beckman Foundation)
One Franklin Plaza
P.O. Box 7929
Philadelphia 19101   (215) 751-7024

Trust established in 1967 in DE.
Donor(s): SmithKline Beecham.
Foundation type: Company-sponsored
Financial data (yr. ended 12/31/90): Assets, $1,995,761 (M); gifts received, $1,985,000; expenditures, $5,711,286; qualifying distributions, $3,586,984, including $2,886,054 for 116 grants (high: $525,000; low: $500), $25,520 for 11 grants to individuals (high: $4,900; low: $518) and $675,410 for 1,058 employee matching gifts.
Purpose and activities: Foundation maintains an employee matching gift program for qualifying educational institutions and hospitals; support also for community funds, the arts, health and medicine, and public policy.
Fields of interest: Community funds, arts, fine arts, education, health, medical education, medical research, medical sciences, public policy, Southern Africa, civic affairs.
Types of support: Employee matching gifts, general purposes, operating budgets, research, special projects.
Limitations: No grants to individuals.
Publications: Annual report, 990-PF.
Application information: The scholarship program has been terminated.
  Initial approach: Proposal
  Board meeting date(s): May, and as required to review proposals
Officers and Directors:* Albert J. White,* Secy.; Henry J. King,* Treas.; Norman H. Blanchard, Ralph Christoffersen, J.P. Garnier, Harry Groome, Tod R. Hullin, Frederick W. Kyle, John B. Ziegler.
Number of staff: 1 full-time professional; 1 part-time professional; 3 full-time support.
EIN: 232120418

2835
Snee-Reinhardt Charitable Foundation

2101 One Mellon Bank Ctr.
500 Grant St.
Pittsburgh 15219   (412) 471-2944

Established in 1987 in PA.
Donor(s): Katherine E. Snee.
Foundation type: Independent
Financial data (yr. ended 12/31/91): Assets, $5,404,891 (M); gifts received, $662,143; expenditures, $287,112; qualifying distributions, $255,795, including $231,425 for 28 grants (high: $25,000; low: $1,000).
Fields of interest: Cancer, health, aged, youth, education, libraries, drug abuse, environment, community development, cultural programs.
Types of support: Seed money, renovation projects, special projects, equipment.
Limitations: Giving primarily in PA (especially the southwestern region), northeast WV, and northern

MD. No support for sectarian or religious organizations or organizations that promote abortion or euthanasia. No grants to individuals, or for capital improvement, endowment funds, or general operating expenses.
Publications: 990-PF, application guidelines, informational brochure (including application guidelines), grants list.
Application information: Application form not required.
- *Copies of proposal:* 1
- *Deadline(s):* Jan. 31, Apr. 30, July 31, and Oct. 31
- *Board meeting date(s):* 3rd Tuesday of Feb., May, Aug., and Nov.
- *Final notification:* 2 weeks after board meeting
- *Write:* Joan E. Boni, Admin. Asst.

Officer and Directors:* Paul A. Heasley,* Chair.; Virginia M. Davis, Karen L. Heasley, Timothy Heasley, James W. Ummer, Richard T. Vail.
Trustee: Mellon Bank, N.A.
Number of staff: 2 full-time support.
EIN: 256292908

2836
G. Whitney Snyder Charitable Fund
3720 One Oliver Plaza
Pittsburgh 15222   (412) 471-1331

Established in 1990 in PA as partial successor to The W. P. Snyder Charitable Fund.
Foundation type: Independent
Financial data (yr. ended 12/31/90): Assets, $4,720,522 (M); expenditures, $243,284; qualifying distributions, $228,452, including $219,500 for 20 grants (high: $50,000; low: $500).
Fields of interest: Higher education, secondary education, health, social services, youth, Protestant giving.
Types of support: Annual campaigns, operating budgets, general purposes.
Limitations: Giving primarily in PA.
Application information: Application form not required.
- *Deadline(s):* None
- *Write:* Charles E. Ellison, Secy.

Officer: Charles E. Ellison, Secy.
Trustee: J.K. Foster, G. Whitney Snyder, G. Whitney Snyder, Jr.
EIN: 251611761

2837
Sordoni Foundation, Inc.
45 Owen St.
Forty Fort 18704   (717) 283-1211

Incorporated in 1946 in PA.
Donor(s): Andrew J. Sordoni, Sr.,‡ Andrew J. Sordoni, Jr.,‡ Andrew J. Sordoni III, Mrs. Andrew J. Sordoni, Sr.,‡ Mrs. Andrew J. Sordoni, Jr.,‡ Mrs. Andrew J. Sordoni III, Helen Mary Sekera.
Foundation type: Independent
Financial data (yr. ended 07/31/91): Assets, $6,310,814 (M); gifts received, $47,000; expenditures, $1,112,611; qualifying distributions, $1,067,459, including $1,048,562 for 30 grants (high: $664,426; low: $100).
Purpose and activities: Giving for education; support also for cultural programs, health, social services, and civic affairs.

Fields of interest: Education, cultural programs, health, social services, civic affairs.
Types of support: Building funds, equipment, capital campaigns, continuing support, seed money, special projects, annual campaigns, endowment funds.
Limitations: Giving primarily in northeastern PA. No grants to individuals, or for scholarships.
Application information: The foundation has discontinued the scholarships to individuals program. No new grants will be awarded. Application form not required.
- *Initial approach:* Letter
- *Copies of proposal:* 1
- *Deadline(s):* None
- *Board meeting date(s):* As required
- *Write:* Benjamin Badman, Jr., Exec. V.P.

Officers and Directors:* Andrew J. Sordoni III,* Pres.; Benjamin Badman, Jr.,* Exec. V.P. and Secy.-Treas.; Richard Allan, Jule Ayers, Ruth Hitchner, Roy E. Morgan, Patrick Solano, Stephen Sordoni, Susan F. Sordoni, William B. Sordoni, William J. Umphred.
Number of staff: 1 full-time professional; 1 part-time support.
EIN: 246017505
Recent health grants:
2837-1   Geisinger Foundation, Danville, PA, $45,000. 1991.

2838
SPS Foundation
c/o SPS Technologies
P.O. Box 1000
Newtown 18940   (215) 860-3057

Trust established in 1953 in PA.
Donor(s): SPS Technologies, Inc.
Foundation type: Company-sponsored
Financial data (yr. ended 12/31/90): Assets, $564,492 (M); expenditures, $245,297; qualifying distributions, $244,997, including $243,016 for 167 grants (high: $63,000; low: $25; average: $100-$500).
Purpose and activities: Giving for community funds, higher education, health and hospitals, youth activities and child welfare, the arts and culture, law and justice, science, and welfare.
Fields of interest: Community funds, higher education, education, health, child welfare, family services, welfare, arts, fine arts, performing arts, law and justice, civic affairs.
Types of support: Operating budgets, continuing support, annual campaigns, emergency funds, building funds, equipment, employee matching gifts, special projects, research, capital campaigns, matching funds.
Limitations: Giving primarily in PA; Cleveland, OH; Santa Ana, CA; Muskegon, MI; Marengo, IL; and Mayaguez, PR. No grants to individuals, or for seed money, land acquisition, matching funds, scholarships, fellowships, demonstration projects, publications, or conferences and seminars; no loans.
Application information: Application form not required.
- *Initial approach:* Letter
- *Copies of proposal:* 1
- *Deadline(s):* None
- *Final notification:* 1 month
- *Write:* John P. McGrath, Trustee

Trustees: A.B. Belden, John P. McGrath, John R. Selby, Jr., Harry J. Wilkinson.
Number of staff: None.
EIN: 236294553

2839
The Donald B. and Dorothy L. Stabler Foundation
c/o Dauphin Deposit Bank & Trust Co.
213 Market St.
Harrisburg 17105

Established in 1966 in PA.
Donor(s): Stabler Companies, Inc., Donald B. Stabler, Dorothy L. Stabler.
Foundation type: Independent
Financial data (yr. ended 12/31/91): Assets, $6,795,507 (M); gifts received, $138,500; expenditures, $560,501; qualifying distributions, $533,037, including $532,525 for 71 grants (high: $100,000; low: $250; average: $1,400).
Fields of interest: Higher education, secondary education, hospitals, Catholic giving.
Types of support: Operating budgets, continuing support, annual campaigns, building funds, equipment, endowment funds, matching funds, scholarship funds, professorships.
Limitations: Giving primarily in PA, with some emphasis on Harrisburg. No grants to individuals, or for seed money, research programs, land acquisition, special projects, publications, conferences, deficit financing, or emergency funds; no loans.
Application information: Application form not required.
- *Initial approach:* Letter
- *Copies of proposal:* 1
- *Deadline(s):* 1 month prior to board meetings
- *Board meeting date(s):* Usually in May, Sept., and Oct.
- *Final notification:* 1 month after board meetings
- *Write:* William King, Chair.

Officers and Trustees:* William King,* Chair.; Frank A. Sinon,* Secy.; Richard E. Jordan, David Schaper, Richard Zimmerman.
Number of staff: None.
EIN: 236422944

2840
Stackpole-Hall Foundation
44 South St. Marys St.
St. Marys 15857   (814) 834-1845

Trust established in 1951 in PA.
Donor(s): Lyle G. Hall,‡ J. Hall Stackpole,‡ Harrison C. Stackpole.
Foundation type: Independent
Financial data (yr. ended 12/31/90): Assets, $17,852,116 (M); expenditures, $815,324; qualifying distributions, $713,785, including $606,357 for 63 grants (high: $69,741; low: $225).
Purpose and activities: Support for higher and secondary education, and literacy and vocational projects; social services, including youth and child welfare agencies; the arts and cultural programs; health services, including mental health and drug abuse issues; and community development, including civic affairs and leadership development, conservation concerns, rural development, and volunteerism.

Fields of interest: Higher education, secondary education, social services, youth, child welfare, arts, health services, mental health, community development, conservation.

Types of support: Building funds, annual campaigns, seed money, equipment, matching funds, capital campaigns, renovation projects, special projects.

Limitations: Giving primarily in Elk County, PA. No grants to individuals, or for scholarships or fellowships; generally, no grants for operating budgets or endowment funds; no loans.

Publications: Annual report (including application guidelines), newsletter, Informational brochure.

Application information: Application form not required.

Initial approach: Letter
Copies of proposal: 1
Deadline(s): 6 weeks prior to meeting dates
Board meeting date(s): Feb., May, Aug., and Dec.
Final notification: 8 to 12 weeks
Write: William C. Conrad, Exec. Secy.

Officer: William C. Conrad, Exec. Secy.

Trustees: Harrison C. Stackpole, Chair.; Douglas R. Dobson, Helen Hall Drew, Lyle G. Hall, Jr., J.M. Hamlin Johnson, Alexander Sheble-Hall, R. Dauer Stackpole.

Number of staff: 1 full-time professional; 2 part-time support.

EIN: 256006650

Recent health grants:

2840-1 Charleston Interfaith Crisis Ministry, Charleston, SC, $25,000. For construction of new Family Shelter designed to accommodate increasing number of homeless and hungry people in Charleston area. 1990.

2840-2 Geisinger Medical Center, Danville, PA, $12,000. For pastoral care residency program, designed to allow pastoral residents to devote more time to hospital activities, thereby obtaining specialized clinical training. 1990.

2840-3 Southside Community Hospital, Farmville, VA, $10,000. For completion of hospital's obstetric unit. 1990.

2840-4 University of Pittsburgh, Nursing Department, Bradford, PA, $16,667. To purchase equipment and other educational materials. 1990.

2841
Louis & Bessie Stein Foundation
1700 Walnut St., Suite 819
Philadelphia 19103

Established in 1953 in NJ.
Donor(s): Louis Stein, Walter Leventhal, Stanley Merves, Stein, Stein & Engel.
Foundation type: Independent
Financial data (yr. ended 12/31/91): Assets, $2,979,581 (M); gifts received, $443,596; expenditures, $304,334; qualifying distributions, $298,819, including $293,098 for 67 grants (high: $75,000; low: $14).
Fields of interest: Health, higher education, Jewish giving, Jewish welfare.
Limitations: Giving primarily in PA.
Application information:
Initial approach: Letter
Deadline(s): None
Write: Louis Stein, Trustee
Trustees: Marilyn Bellet, Louis Stein.

EIN: 236395253

2842
James Hale Steinman Foundation
P.O. Box 128
Lancaster 17603
Scholarship application address: Eight West King St., Lancaster, PA 17603

Trust established in 1952 in PA.
Donor(s): James Hale Steinman,‡ Louise Steinman von Hess,‡ Lancaster Newspapers, Inc., and others.
Foundation type: Independent
Financial data (yr. ended 12/31/91): Assets, $8,886,638 (M); gifts received, $440,000; expenditures, $497,878; qualifying distributions, $439,650, including $402,650 for 39 grants (high: $293,375; low: $250) and $37,000 for 24 grants to individuals (high: $2,000; low: $1,000).
Purpose and activities: Giving for the arts and historic preservation, higher and other education (including scholarships to newspaper carriers and children of employees of Steiman Enterprises), youth and social services, health, family planning, and a community fund.
Fields of interest: Arts, historic preservation, education, higher education, secondary education, youth, social services, health, family planning, community funds.
Types of support: Employee-related scholarships, annual campaigns, capital campaigns.
Limitations: Giving primarily in Lancaster, PA.
Application information: Application form available for employee-related scholarships.
Deadline(s): For scholarships, Feb. 28 of senior year of high school
Board meeting date(s): Dec.
Write: Dennis A. Getz, Secy.
Officers and Trustees:* Caroline S. Nunan,* Chair.; Beverly R. Steinman,* Vice-Chair.; Dennis A. Getz,* Secy.; Willis W. Shenk,* Treas.; John M. Buckwalter, Jack S. Gerhart, Caroline N. Hill, Hale S. Krasne.
Number of staff: None.
EIN: 236266377

2843
John Frederick Steinman Foundation
P.O. Box 128
Lancaster 17603
Additional address: Eight West King St., Lancaster, PA 17603

Trust established in 1952 in PA.
Donor(s): John Frederick Steinman,‡ Shirley W. Steinman,‡ Lancaster Newspapers, Inc., and others.
Foundation type: Independent
Financial data (yr. ended 12/31/91): Assets, $12,516,566 (M); gifts received, $160,000; expenditures, $597,588; qualifying distributions, $506,750, including $475,750 for 95 grants (high: $75,000; low: $100) and $30,000 for grants to individuals.
Purpose and activities: Giving for higher and secondary education, the arts, community funds, family planning and other social services, youth, health services and hospitals, and the handicapped; also funds a fellowship program

limited to graduate study in mental health or a related field.
Fields of interest: Higher education, secondary education, arts, community funds, social services, youth, hospitals, handicapped, mental health, psychiatry.
Types of support: Fellowships, annual campaigns, capital campaigns.
Limitations: Giving primarily in PA, with emphasis on the Lancaster area.
Application information: Application for fellowship program available upon request.
Deadline(s): Feb. 1 for fellowships
Board meeting date(s): Dec.
Write: Dennis A. Getz, Secy., or Jay H. Wenrich, Fellowship Prog. Secy. for fellowships
Officers and Trustees:* Pamela M. Thye,* Chair.; Dennis A. Getz,* Secy.; Willis W. Shenk, Treas.; John M. Buckwalter, Jack S. Gerhart, Henry Pildner, Jr.
Number of staff: None.
EIN: 236266378

2844
The Louis L. Stott Foundation
2000 One Logan Sq.
Philadelphia 19103   (215) 963-5281
Mailing address: 1400 Waverly Rd., Blair 225, Gladwyne, PA 19035

Trust established in 1968 in PA.
Donor(s): Martha Stott Diener.
Foundation type: Independent
Financial data (yr. ended 09/30/91): Assets, $2,411,531 (M); expenditures, $167,549; qualifying distributions, $144,259, including $128,500 for 38 grants (high: $20,000; low: $1,000; average: $1,000-$5,000).
Purpose and activities: Support for scientific and technological research, health services and medical research, and preservation of wildlife; giving also for elementary and secondary education, population and environmental control, law and justice, women, and family planning.
Fields of interest: Science and technology, medical research, wildlife, elementary education, secondary education, population studies, environment, law and justice, women, family planning.
Types of support: Operating budgets, continuing support, annual campaigns, seed money, emergency funds, building funds, equipment, land acquisition, special projects, research, publications, renovation projects.
Limitations: No grants to individuals, or for endowment funds, scholarships, fellowships, conferences, or matching gifts; no loans.
Publications: Application guidelines, program policy statement.
Application information: Application form not required.
Initial approach: Letter
Copies of proposal: 1
Deadline(s): Submit proposal preferably between Jan. and Aug.; no set deadline
Board meeting date(s): July and Aug.
Final notification: 2 to 3 months
Write: William P. Wood, Esq., Secy.
Officers and Trustees:* Martha Stott Diener,* Chair.; William P. Wood,* Secy.; Brady O. Bryson, Benjamin W. Stott, Edward Barrington Stott.

Number of staff: 1 part-time professional; 1 part-time support.
EIN: 237009027

2845
Strauss Foundation ▼
c/o Fidelity Bank, N.A.
Broad & Walnut Sts.
Philadelphia 19109   (215) 985-8031

Trust established in 1951 in PA.
Donor(s): Maurice L. Strauss.
Foundation type: Independent
Financial data (yr. ended 12/31/91): Assets, $40,389,984 (M); gifts received, $66,431; expenditures, $1,551,602; qualifying distributions, $1,447,074, including $1,438,371 for 432 grants (high: $100,000; low: $100; average: $1,000-$10,000).
Purpose and activities: Emphasis on Jewish welfare funds in the U.S. and Israel, child welfare and youth agencies, education, hospitals, and cultural programs.
Fields of interest: Jewish welfare, Israel, hospitals, cultural programs, child welfare, youth, higher education, education.
Limitations: Giving primarily in PA and for organizations in Israel. No grants to individuals.
Application information: Unsolicited applications are not encouraged.
  Initial approach: Letter
  Deadline(s): None
  Write: Judy Prenberg
Trustees: Henry A. Gladstone, Scott R. Isdaner, Sandra S. Krause, Benjamin Strauss, Robert Perry Strauss.
Corporate Trustee: Fidelity Bank, N.A.
EIN: 236219939

2846
Margaret Dorrance Strawbridge Foundation of Pennsylvania I, Inc.
c/o Robert L. Freedman, Dechert Price & Rhoads
3400 Center Sq. West, 1500 Market St.
Philadelphia 19102
Mailing address: P.O. Box 135, Mendenhall, PA 19357

Established in 1985 in PA.
Donor(s): Margaret Dorrance Strawbridge Foundation.
Foundation type: Independent
Financial data (yr. ended 12/31/90): Assets, $4,600,329 (M); gifts received, $113,460; expenditures, $225,601; qualifying distributions, $214,313, including $200,500 for 17 grants (high: $100,000; low: $1,000).
Fields of interest: Hospitals, medical research, cancer, cultural programs, education, animal welfare.
Limitations: No grants to individuals, or for endowment funds.
Application information: Applications not accepted.
  Write: George Strawbridge, Jr., Pres.
Officers: George Strawbridge, Jr., Pres. and Treas.; Nina S. Strawbridge, V.P. and Secy.
EIN: 232373081

2847
Margaret Dorrance Strawbridge Foundation of Pennsylvania II, Inc.
125 Strafford Ave.
Bldg. 3, Suite 108
Wayne 19087-3367   (215) 688-9261

Established in 1985 in PA.
Donor(s): Margaret Dorrance Strawbridge Foundation.
Foundation type: Independent
Financial data (yr. ended 12/31/90): Assets, $3,221,846 (M); gifts received, $109,887; expenditures, $230,735; qualifying distributions, $200,118, including $180,165 for 62 grants (high: $26,000; low: $300; average: $1,000-$5,000).
Purpose and activities: Emphasis on higher and secondary education, hospitals and medical research, and the environment. Nearly all grants are for operating expenses.
Fields of interest: Higher education, secondary education, hospitals, medical research, environment.
Types of support: Operating budgets, continuing support, research, annual campaigns.
Limitations: Giving primarily in the eastern U.S., especially PA and FL. No grants to individuals, or for capital or endowment funds, scholarships, or fellowships; no loans.
Application information: Application form not required.
  Initial approach: Letter
  Deadline(s): None
  Write: Diana Norris, Pres.
Officer and Director:* Diana S. Norris,* Pres.
Number of staff: None.
EIN: 232371943

2848
Superior-Pacific Fund
Seven Wynnewood Rd.
Wynnewood 19096
Scholarship application address: Superior Tube Co. Scholarship Comm., P.O. Box 616, Devault, PA 19432; Tel.: (215) 647-2701

Trust established in 1952 in PA.
Donor(s): Superior Tube Co., Pacific Tube Co., Cawsl Enterprises, Inc.
Foundation type: Company-sponsored
Financial data (yr. ended 12/31/91): Assets, $12,402,442 (M); expenditures, $551,551; qualifying distributions, $527,524, including $514,524 for 87 grants (high: $125,000; low: $25) and $13,000 for 14 grants to individuals (high: $1,500; low: $500).
Purpose and activities: Grants primarily for higher and secondary education, including scholarships for children of company employees, community funds, hospitals, health agencies, and the performing arts, including music.
Fields of interest: Higher education, secondary education, community funds, hospitals, health services, performing arts, music.
Types of support: Employee-related scholarships.
Limitations: Giving primarily in PA.
Application information: Application form required.
  Deadline(s): Jan. 2 for Personal Data Form A; Jan. 9 for High School Certification Form B

Officer and Directors:* Paul E. Kelly,* Pres.; Paul E. Kelly, Jr., William G. Warden III.
EIN: 236298237

2849
Charles L. Tabas Foundation
c/o Lawrence S. Chane, Blank, Rome, Comisky and McCauley
Four Penn Ctr. Plaza
Philadelphia 19103-1639   (215) 569-5721

Established in 1984 in PA.
Donor(s): Charles L. Tabas Memorial Lead Trust.
Foundation type: Independent
Financial data (yr. ended 03/31/92): Assets, $184,961 (M); expenditures, $52,675; qualifying distributions, $50,900, including $50,900 for 14 grants (high: $25,000; low: $100).
Fields of interest: Medical research, Jewish giving, museums.
Limitations: No grants to individuals.
Application information: Application form not required.
  Initial approach: Letter
  Deadline(s): None
  Write: Marriette S. Tabas, Pres.
Officers: Harriet S. Tabas, Pres.; Andrew R. Tabas, V.P.; Nancy C. Fleming, V.P.; Richard S. Tabas, Secy.; Gerald Levinson, Exec. Dir.
EIN: 222630429

2850
Harry C. Trexler Trust ▼
33 South Seventh St., Suite 205
Allentown 18101   (215) 434-9645
FAX: (215) 437-5721

Trust established in 1934 in PA.
Donor(s): Harry C. Trexler,‡ Mary M. Trexler.‡
Foundation type: Independent
Financial data (yr. ended 03/31/91): Assets, $64,319,581 (M); expenditures, $2,306,975; qualifying distributions, $1,962,742, including $1,755,347 for 65 grants (high: $599,889; low: $500; average: $10,000-$20,000).
Purpose and activities: The will provides that one-fourth of the income shall be added to the corpus, one-fourth paid to the City of Allentown for park purposes, and the remainder distributed to such charitable organizations and objects as shall be "of the most benefit to humanity," but limited to Allentown and Lehigh County, particularly for hospitals, churches, institutions for the care of the crippled and orphans, youth agencies, social services, cultural programs, and support of ministerial students at two named PA institutions.
Fields of interest: Hospitals, religion, handicapped, youth, civic affairs, social services, education, higher education, cultural programs, aged, health, recreation, disadvantaged.
Types of support: Building funds, matching funds, general purposes, operating budgets, continuing support, land acquisition, capital campaigns, renovation projects.
Limitations: Giving limited to Lehigh County, PA. No grants to individuals, or for endowment funds, research, scholarships, or fellowships; no loans.
Publications: Annual report, application guidelines.

Application information: Application form not required.

Initial approach: Letter
Copies of proposal: 3
Deadline(s): Jan. 31 for consideration at annual fund distribution
Board meeting date(s): Monthly; however, grant distribution takes place annually after Mar. 31
Final notification: June 1
Write: Thomas H. Christman, Secy. to the Trustees

Trustees: Dexter F. Baker, Chair.; Philip I. Berman, Carl J.W. Hessinger, Richard K. White, M.D., Kathryn Stephanoff.
Staff: Thomas H. Christman, Secy. to the Trustees.
Number of staff: 2 full-time professional.
EIN: 231162215
Recent health grants:

2850-1 Haven House, Philadelphia, PA, $12,500. Toward basement renovation. 1990.

2850-2 Visiting Nurse Association of Lehigh County, Allentown, PA, $35,000. Toward elderly and infant care programs. 1990.

2851
Union Pacific Corporate Giving Program
Martin Tower
Eighth and Eaton Aves.
Bethlehem 18018   (215) 861-3215

Financial data (yr. ended 12/31/90): Total giving, $3,295,000, including $2,639,000 for grants and $656,000 for employee matching gifts.
Purpose and activities: Union Pacific Foundation administers the wide-ranging philanthropic activities of Union Pacific Corporation and its operating companies - Union Pacific Railroad Company, Union Pacific Resources Company and Union Pacific Realty Company. Union Pacific Foundation grants are made primarily to private institutions of higher education, health, social welfare, and arts, located in communities served by the Union Pacific companies, which are principally in the West; the foundation has more implicit guidelines than the direct giving program which considers programs not filling the foundation's specifications. In addition to direct grants, the non-foundation giving program consists of scholarship aid to the children of employees and employee matching gifts programs.
Fields of interest: Arts, cultural programs, dance, education, energy, handicapped, health, health services, higher education, homeless, hospices, hospitals, hospitals—building funds, literacy, minorities, museums, performing arts, rehabilitation, theater, welfare, women, youth.
Types of support: Building funds, capital campaigns, employee matching gifts, equipment, matching funds, renovation projects, employee-related scholarships, special projects.
Limitations: Giving primarily in locations where Union Pacific maintains operations. No support for religious, political parties, and fraternal organizations. No grants to individuals.
Application information: Application form required.
Initial approach: Letter/proposal; company considers unsolicited requests for funding
Copies of proposal: 1
Deadline(s): August 15th
Board meeting date(s): End of Jan.

Final notification: Formal notification to accepted applicants
Write: Judy L. Swantak, Pres., Union Pacific Foundation

Administrators: Judy L. Swantak, Pres., Union Pacific Fdn.; Carol Mesko, Admin.

2852
Union Pacific Foundation ▼
Martin Tower
Eighth and Eaton Aves.
Bethlehem 18018   (215) 861-3225

Incorporated in 1955 in UT.
Donor(s): Union Pacific Corp.
Foundation type: Company-sponsored
Financial data (yr. ended 12/31/91): Assets, $1,672,000 (M); gifts received, $7,200,000; expenditures, $6,774,000; qualifying distributions, $6,984,000, including $6,769,000 for 750 grants (high: $227,500; low: $250; average: $1,000-$10,000) and $215,000 for program-related investments.
Purpose and activities: Grants primarily to non-tax-supported institutions of higher education, health (including hospitals and hospices), social services, and fine and performing arts groups and other cultural programs.
Fields of interest: Education, education—minorities, libraries, higher education, rehabilitation, hospitals, drug abuse, social services, minorities, disadvantaged, family services, handicapped, youth, performing arts, cultural programs, arts, museums, historic preservation, performing arts, theater.
Types of support: Continuing support, building funds, equipment, matching funds, scholarship funds, renovation projects, capital campaigns, special projects, program-related investments.
Limitations: Giving primarily in areas of company operations, particularly in the midwestern and western U.S. in AR, CA, CO, ID, IL, KS, LA, MO, NE, NV, OK, OR, TX, UT, WA, and WY. No support for tax-supported institutions or affiliates (other than United Ways); specialized national health and welfare organizations; religious or labor groups; social clubs, fraternal or veterans' organizations; support for United Way-affiliated organizations restricted to capital projects. No grants to individuals, or for sponsorship of dinners, benefits, seminars, or other special events.
Publications: Application guidelines.
Application information: The foundation does not sponsor an employee matching gift program. Application form required.
Initial approach: Letter
Copies of proposal: 1
Deadline(s): Aug. 15
Board meeting date(s): Late Jan. for consideration for the following year
Final notification: Feb. through May
Write: Mrs. Judy L. Swantak, Pres.
Officers and Trustees:* Drew Lewis,* Chair.; Judy L. Swantak, Pres. and Secy.; L. White Matthews III, V.P., Finance; J.B. Gremillion, Jr., V.P., Taxes; Gary M. Stuart, Treas.; C.E. Billingsley, Controller; C.W. von Bernuth, Gen. Counsel; W.L. Adams, R.P. Bauman, E.V. Conway, E.V. Eccles, E.T. Gerry, Jr., J.R. Hope, L.M. Jones, H.A. Kissinger, C.B. Malone, J.R. Meyer, T.A. Reynolds, Jr., J.D.

Robinson III, R.W. Roth, W.M. Shapleigh, R.D. Simmons.
Number of staff: 1 full-time professional; 4 full-time support.
EIN: 136406825
Recent health grants:

2852-1 All Saints Episcopal Hospital, Fort Worth, TX, $32,000. Toward construction of new hospital building. 1990.

2852-2 American Heart Association, Fort Worth, TX, $10,000. For unrestricted support. 1990.

2852-3 Bannock Regional Medical Center, Pocatello, ID, $15,000. For purchase of radiation treatment planning computer for Intermountain Cancer Center. 1990.

2852-4 Catholic Health Association of the United States, DC, $25,000. 1990.

2852-5 Child Study Center, Fort Worth, TX, $12,000. To upgrade computer equipment. 1990.

2852-6 Childrens Hospital, New Orleans, LA, $10,000. To support Autologous Bone Marrow Transplant Program for young leukemia patients. 1990.

2852-7 Cook-Fort Worth Childrens Medical Center, Fort Worth, TX, $40,000. Toward construction of pre-adolescent psychiatric unit. 1990.

2852-8 Cottonwood Alta View Health Care Foundation, Murray, UT, $60,000. To construct building and therapy pool for Back Institute/Work Hardening Program at Cottonwood Hospital. 1990.

2852-9 Crittenton Center, Kansas City, MO, $12,500. Toward building campaign. 1990.

2852-10 Emanuel Medical Center Foundation, Portland, OR, $10,000. To assist with relocation and expansion of Child Abuse Response and Evaluation Service. 1990.

2852-11 Fort Worth Challenge, Fort Worth, TX, $10,000. To support organization addressing problems of substance abuse. 1990.

2852-12 Great Plains Medical Center, North Platte, NE, $20,000. Toward renovations and improvements. 1990.

2852-13 Harris Methodist-Fort Worth, Emergency Medicine Department, Fort Worth, TX, $50,000. Toward expansion. 1990.

2852-14 Holy Cross Hospitals, Salt Lake City, UT, $30,000. To purchase equipment for occupational rehabilitation. 1990.

2852-15 Hospital Development Fund, Kansas City, MO, $15,000. Toward construction and equipping of Health and Rehabilitation Pavilion for Baptist Medical Center. 1990.

2852-16 Hospital of the Good Samaritan, Los Angeles, CA, $15,000. To purchase equipment for treatment of vascular disease. 1990.

2852-17 Intermountain Health Care, Salt Lake City, UT, $25,000. To construct new Primary Children's Medical Center adjacent to University of Utah Health Sciences Center. 1990.

2852-18 LDS Hospital-Deseret Foundation, Salt Lake City, UT, $10,000. To purchase equipment. 1990.

2852-19 Menninger Foundation, Topeka, KS, $12,500. For unrestricted support. 1990.

2852-20 Mental Health Association of Tarrant County, Fort Worth, TX, $20,000. Toward building expansion project to increase library and office space. 1990.

2852-21 Milford Valley Memorial Hospital, Milford, UT, $20,000. For unrestricted support. 1990.

2852-22 National Federation of State High School Associations, Kansas City, MO, $20,000. For TARGET Program that seeks to prevent drug and alcohol abuse among school-aged youth nationwide. 1990.

2852-23 Nebraska AIDS Project (NAP), Omaha, NE, $10,000. For salary for staff position for Case Manager. 1990.

2852-24 Pocatello Regional Medical Center, Pocatello, ID, $10,000. Toward construction of Cardiac Catheterization Laboratory. 1990.

2852-25 Quality Living, Omaha, NE, $25,000. Toward construction of long-term residential and active treatment facility for physically disabled. 1990.

2852-26 Saint Francis Medical Center, Grand Island, NE, $10,000. To develop cancer treatment center. 1990.

2852-27 Saint Joseph Hospital, Fort Worth, TX, $32,000. Toward completion of two surgical rooms in new operating room suite. 1990.

2853
USX Foundation, Inc. ▼
(Formerly United States Steel Foundation, Inc.)
600 Grant St., Rm. 2640
Pittsburgh 15219-4776   (412) 433-5237

Incorporated in 1953 in DE.
Donor(s): USX Corp., and certain subsidiaries.
Foundation type: Company-sponsored
Financial data (yr. ended 11/30/91): Assets, $12,292,184 (M); gifts received, $8,500,000; expenditures, $6,686,147; qualifying distributions, $6,441,971, including $5,009,675 for grants (high: $725,000; low: $100; average: $1,000-$25,000), $424,800 for 89 grants to individuals (high: $2,000; low: $500) and $1,007,496 for 853 employee matching gifts.
Purpose and activities: Support for higher education, primarily in the private sector, including college and university development grants, special purpose grants, project assistance, matching gifts, manpower development grants, and support to educational associations; scientific and research grants, including capital, operating, project, and research support; civic and cultural grants for capital and operating needs; medicine and health grants for research, capital, and operating purposes; and national and community social services support, including the United Way and other voluntary agencies.
Fields of interest: Higher education, science and technology, education, libraries, community development, cultural programs, performing arts, historic preservation, media and communications, health, mental health, rehabilitation, social services, legal services, minorities, community funds, volunteerism, human rights, environment, historic preservation, media and communications.
Types of support: Operating budgets, general purposes, continuing support, annual campaigns, seed money, emergency funds, building funds, equipment, special projects, research, employee matching gifts, capital campaigns, renovation projects, matching funds, employee-related scholarships, scholarship funds.

Limitations: Giving primarily in areas of company operations in the U.S. and Canada. No support for religious organizations for religious purposes. No grants to individuals, or for conferences, seminars, travel, scholarships, fellowships, publications, or films; no loans.
Publications: Annual report (including application guidelines), application guidelines.
Application information: Application form not required.
   Initial approach: 1- or 2-page proposal letter
   Copies of proposal: 1
   Deadline(s): Public, cultural, and scientific affairs, Jan. 15; aid to education, Apr. 15; medical, health, and national and community social services, July 15
   Board meeting date(s): Apr., July, and Oct.
   Final notification: Following board meetings
   Write: James L. Hamilton, III, Gen. Mgr.
Officers and Trustees:* Charles A. Corry,* Chair.; Robert H. Hernandez, C.F.O.; Peter B. Mulloney, Pres.; Rex D. Cooley,* V.P. and Comptroller; Gretchen R. Haggerty, V.P. and Treas.; Gary A. Glynn, V.P., Investments; Richard M. Hays, Secy.; James L. Hamilton III, Gen. Mgr.; Dominic B. King, General Counsel; John T. Mills, Tax Counsel; Ron S. Keisler, Dan D. Sandman, Thomas J. Usher, Louis A. Valli, Richard E. White.
Number of staff: 2 full-time professional; 2 full-time support.
EIN: 136093185
Recent health grants:

2853-1 Baylor University Medical Center Foundation, Dallas, TX, $12,000. For capital grant. 1990.

2853-2 Contact Pittsburgh, Pittsburgh, PA, $10,000. For capital grant. 1990.

2853-3 D.T. Watson Rehabilitation Hospital, Sewickley, PA, $20,000. For capital grant. 1990.

2853-4 Foundation for Abraxas, Pittsburgh, PA, $15,000. For capital grant. 1990.

2853-5 Gateway Rehabilitation Center, Aliquippa, PA, $20,000. For capital grant. 1990.

2853-6 Harmarville Rehabilitation Center, Pittsburgh, PA, $25,000. For capital grant. 1990.

2853-7 Harvard University, School of Public Health, Boston, MA, $50,000. For capital grant. 1990.

2853-8 National Medical Fellowships, NYC, NY, $10,000. For current operating needs. 1990.

2853-9 Parental Stress Center, Pittsburgh, PA, $10,000. For capital and operating needs. 1990.

2853-10 Southern Research Institute, Birmingham, AL, $75,000. For capital campaign. 1990.

2853-11 Spina Bifida Association of Western Pennsylvania, Pittsburgh, PA, $25,000. For capital grant. 1990.

2853-12 Visiting Nurse Association of Northwest Indiana, Hammond, IN, $25,000. For capital grant. 1990.

2854
Robert and Mary Weisbrod Foundation
c/o Integra Financial Corp.
Fourth Ave. and Wood St.
Pittsburgh 15222

Established in 1968 in PA.
Donor(s): Mary E. Weisbrod.‡
Foundation type: Independent
Financial data (yr. ended 12/31/91): Assets, $9,291,726 (M); gifts received, $146,569; expenditures, $514,981; qualifying distributions, $460,073, including $450,630 for 26 grants (high: $100,000; low: $1,000).
Fields of interest: Hospitals, medical research, social services, child welfare, music, historic preservation, general charitable giving.
Types of support: Capital campaigns, equipment.
Limitations: Giving primarily in the Pittsburgh, PA, area.
Application information: Application form not required.
   Initial approach: Proposal
   Copies of proposal: 1
   Deadline(s): None
   Board meeting date(s): As required
   Write: The Distribution Committee
Distribution Committee: John R. Echement, Donald L. McCaskey, Francis B. Nimick.
Trustee: Integra Financial Corp.
Number of staff: None.
EIN: 256105924

2855
Franklin H. & Ruth L. Wells Foundation
4718 Old Gettysburg Rd., Suite 405
Mechanicsburg 17055-4380   (717) 763-1157

Established in 1983 in PA.
Donor(s): Ruth L. Wells Annuity Trust, Frank Wells Marital Trust.
Foundation type: Independent
Financial data (yr. ended 05/31/91): Assets, $5,190,430 (M); gifts received, $195,267; expenditures, $537,666; qualifying distributions, $491,289, including $419,964 for 51 grants (high: $100,000; low: $500; average: $5,000-$20,000).
Purpose and activities: Support for social service agencies; health associations, hospices, and hospitals; cultural programs, including museums and historic preservation; and education, including elementary and secondary education, libraries, and literacy programs.
Fields of interest: Social services, health associations, hospices, hospitals, cultural programs, education, elementary education, secondary education, libraries, literacy.
Types of support: Building funds, capital campaigns, emergency funds, equipment, land acquisition, renovation projects, seed money, special projects.
Limitations: Giving primarily in Dauphin, Cumberland, and Perry counties, PA. No support for religious activities. No grants for operating expenses, endowments, or debts.
Application information: Application form not required.
   Initial approach: Letter
   Copies of proposal: 1
   Deadline(s): None
   Write: Miles J. Gibbons, Jr., Exec. Dir

Committee: Miles J. Gibbons, Jr., Exec. Dir.; Clifford S. Charles, Gladys R. Charles, Ellen R. Cramer.
Trustee: Dauphin Deposit Bank & Trust Co.
Number of staff: 2 part-time professional; 1 part-time support.
EIN: 222541749

2856
The H. O. West Foundation
(Formerly Herman O. West Foundation)
P.O. Box 808
Phoenixville 19460   (215) 935-4500

Established in 1972 in PA.
Donor(s): The West Co., and members of the West family.
Foundation type: Company-sponsored
Financial data (yr. ended 11/30/91): Assets, $213,918 (M); gifts received, $58,367; expenditures, $231,916; qualifying distributions, $231,916, including $179,252 for 28 grants, $39,982 for 26 grants to individuals and $9,675 for 51 employee matching gifts.
Purpose and activities: Giving primarily for hospitals, pharmacy and health care, and social services; support also for the arts, science and technology, and higher education, including an employee-related scholarship program and an employee matching gift program. Supports building funds for education and hospitals.
Fields of interest: Health, hospitals, pharmacy, social services, cultural programs, science and technology, education, higher education, community funds, community development.
Types of support: Employee matching gifts, building funds, research, employee-related scholarships, matching funds, annual campaigns, capital campaigns.
Limitations: Giving primarily in areas of company operations in FL, NJ, NE, NC, and PA.
Publications: Application guidelines.
Application information:
  Initial approach: Proposal
  Copies of proposal: 1
  Deadline(s): 2 weeks prior to meeting
  Board meeting date(s): Varies yearly
  Write: Mr. Geo Bennyhoff, Trustee
Trustees: James A. West, Chair.; Geo R. Bennyhoff, Franklin H. West, Victor E. Ziegler.
Number of staff: None.
EIN: 237173901

2857
The Whitaker Foundation ▼
4718 Old Gettysburg Rd., Suite 405
Mechanicsburg 17055-8411   (717) 763-1391

Trust established in 1975 in NY.
Donor(s): U.A. Whitaker,‡ Helen F. Whitaker.‡
Foundation type: Independent
Financial data (yr. ended 12/31/91): Assets, $365,152,660 (M); expenditures, $16,549,811; qualifying distributions, $15,972,604, including $15,277,715 for 278 grants (high: $1,650,000; low: $250; average: $40,000-$60,000).
Purpose and activities: Support for projects which integrate engineering with biomedical research; grants also to local human service agencies and educational institutions.

Fields of interest: Education, engineering, social services, medical research, biological sciences, physical sciences, mathematics, medical sciences.
Types of support: Seed money, research, special projects, fellowships.
Limitations: Giving primarily in the U.S. and Canada for Biomedical Engineering Research Program; and in the Harrisburg, PA, area for service and educational organizations; Regional Program limited to Cumberland, Dauphin, and Perry Counties, PA. No support for sectarian religious purposes. No grants to individuals, or for operating budgets of established programs, deficit financing, annual campaigns, emergency funds, publications, conferences, seminars, or endowment funds; no loans.
Publications: Program policy statement, informational brochure (including application guidelines).
Application information: Application procedures are outlined in program policy statements for medical research grants and Regional Program. Application form not required.
  Initial approach: Preliminary letter for Regional Program; preliminary application for medical research program
  Copies of proposal: 1
  Deadline(s): Apr. 30, Aug. 31, and Dec. 31 for regional program proposals, and Feb. 15, June 15, and Oct. 15 for Biomedical Engineering Research Program
  Board meeting date(s): Feb., June, and Oct. for governing committee
  Final notification: 5 months
  Write: Miles J. Gibbons, Jr., Pres.
Officer: Miles J. Gibbons, Jr., Pres.
Committee Members: Ruth W. Holmes, Chair.; Allen W. Cowley, M.D., Eckley B. Coxe IV, G. Burton Holmes, O.D., Richard J. Johns, M.D., Portia W. Shumaker.
Trustee: Chemical Bank.
Number of staff: 4 full-time professional; 2 full-time support.
EIN: 222096948
Recent health grants:
2857-1 Al-Anon Association of Harrisburg, Harrisburg, PA, $30,000. For expansion of Fellowship House. 1991.
2857-2 American Institute for Medical and Biological Engineering, Atlanta, GA, $20,000. For inaugural meeting. 1991.
2857-3 Arizona State University, Tempe, AZ, $180,000. For biomedical engineering research in modeling and experimental analysis of low-intensity electric field enhancement of nerve regeneration. 1991.
2857-4 Baylor College of Medicine, Houston, TX, $178,920. For biomedical engineering research in confocal laser scanning microscope with high temporal resolution for optical recording of neural activity. 1991.
2857-5 Beth Israel Hospital, Boston, MA, $180,000. For biomedical engineering research in magnetic resonance imaging of bone structure with metastatic defects in bone. 1991.
2857-6 Beth Israel Hospital, Boston, MA, $180,000. For biomedical engineering research in modulation of growth factor expression by mechanical forces in vascular endothelium. 1991.
2857-7 Biomedical Engineering Society, Culver City, CA, $19,000. For meeting. 1991.

2857-8 Biomedical Engineering Society, Culver City, CA, $15,000. For annual meeting. 1991.
2857-9 Boston University, Boston, MA, $178,866. For biomedical engineering research in mechanical properties of airway walls and their impact on impedance measurements. 1991.
2857-10 Brown University, Providence, RI, $148,413. For biomedical engineering research in theoretical and experimental analysis of multilayered microspheres to modulate release of bioactive materials. 1991.
2857-11 Capital Area Health Foundation, Harrisburg, PA, $10,000. For purchase of transesophageal echocardiography equipment. 1991.
2857-12 Case Western Reserve University, Cleveland, OH, $179,983. For biomedical engineering research in atomic force microscopy studies of interactions of plasma protein molecules with model surfaces and biomedical polymers. 1991.
2857-13 Columbia University, NYC, NY, $56,759. For biomedical engineering research in shape computations for bioengineering. 1991.
2857-14 Community General Osteopathic Hospital, Harrisburg, PA, $10,000. For construction of Bloom Diagnostic Center. 1991.
2857-15 Cornell University, Ithaca, NY, $179,840. For biomedical engineering research in manipulating peptide-mediated fusion to produce model viruses for targeted drug delivery. 1991.
2857-16 Easter Seal Society for the Handicapped of Tri-County, Harrisburg, PA, $11,130. For start-up costs for development center in Perry County. 1991.
2857-17 Eastern Virginia Medical School, Norfolk, VA, $177,000. For biomedical engineering research in noninvasive real-time determination of pulmonary mechanics in premature infants. 1991.
2857-18 Edgewater Psychiatric Center, Harrisburg, PA, $20,000. To purchase furniture and equipment for River View Center. 1991.
2857-19 Georgetown University Medical Center, DC, $179,938. For biomedical engineering research in image data compression for clinical digital radiography. 1991.
2857-20 Georgia Tech Foundation, Atlanta, GA, $179,999. For biomedical engineering research in role of hemodynamics and endothelial cell activation in atherosclerosis. 1991.
2857-21 Georgia Tech Foundation, Atlanta, GA, $179,810. For biomedical engineering research in development and characterization of flexible prototype for NMR studies of mammalian cells. 1991.
2857-22 Georgia Tech Foundation, Atlanta, GA, $178,450. For biomedical engineering research in near-infrared-raman sensor for laser cardiovascular surgery. 1991.
2857-23 Graduate Hospital, Philadelphia, PA, $180,000. For biomedical engineering research in development of rapid concentration clamp. 1991.
2857-24 Harvard University, Medical School, Boston, MA, $120,248. For biomedical engineering research in mechanical properties of intracellular biopolymer networks. Grant

shared with Brigham and Womens Hospital. 1991.

2857-25 Henry Ford Bone and Joint Specialty Center, Detroit, MI, $120,000. For biomedical engineering research in functional and morphological adaptation of skeleton during development of osteoporosis. 1991.

2857-26 Indiana University Foundation, Bloomington, IN, $88,015. For biomedical engineering research in characteristics of electro-mechanical stimulation of osteoblast. 1991.

2857-27 Institute of Electrical and Electronic Engineers (IEEE), Engineering in Medicine and Biology, Fargo, ND, $50,000. For student paper competition. 1991.

2857-28 John P. Robarts Research Institute, London, Canada, $174,613. For biomedical engineering research in 3-D architecture and micromechanical modeling of aortic valve leaflet. 1991.

2857-29 Johns Hopkins University, Baltimore, MD, $179,996. For biomedical engineering research in molecular basis of sodium channel inactivation. 1991.

2857-30 Johns Hopkins University, Baltimore, MD, $179,901. For biomedical engineering research in integrated algorithmic and neural network approach for detection of epilepticform activity in electroencephalogram. 1991.

2857-31 Johns Hopkins University, Baltimore, MD, $179,707. For biomedical engineering research in cardiac motion analysis using magnetic resonance tagging and optical flow. 1991.

2857-32 Johns Hopkins University, Baltimore, MD, $179,373. For biomedical engineering research in proton magnetic resonance spectroscopy of ischemic stroke. 1991.

2857-33 Johns Hopkins University, Baltimore, MD, $171,249. For biomedical engineering research in bioengineered pseudovirions: viruslike structures for vaccines and drug delivery. 1991.

2857-34 Massachusetts General Hospital, Boston, MA, $178,120. For biomedical engineering research in three-dimensional mapping of cardiac arrhythmias using flexible electrode array. 1991.

2857-35 Massachusetts General Hospital, Boston, MA, $60,000. For biomedical engineering research in new approach to preservation of biological materials by non-freezing methods. 1991.

2857-36 Mayo Foundation, Rochester, MN, $176,908. For biomedical engineering research in theoretical study of medical ultrasonic nondiffracting transducers. 1991.

2857-37 Minneapolis Medical Research Foundation, Minneapolis, MN, $179,667. For biomedical engineering research in mechanical pressures on human patella. 1991.

2857-38 Mount Sinai Hospital, Toronto, Canada, $117,874. For biomedical engineering research in development of computer model of fetal umbilical circulation. 1991.

2857-39 New York University, NYC, NY, $180,000. For biomedical engineering research in computer simulations and visualization of supercoiled DNA folding. 1991.

2857-40 Northwestern University, Evanston, IL, $179,937. For biomedical engineering research in linear electrostatic microactuator development: potential building blocks for artificial muscles. 1991.

2857-41 Northwestern University, Evanston, IL, $177,994. For biomedical engineering research in thin film dynamics of pulmonary airways. 1991.

2857-42 Ohio State University Research Foundation, Columbus, OH, $180,000. For biomedical engineering research in magnetic resonance imaging of abdominal and lower extremity arteries. 1991.

2857-43 Ohio State University Research Foundation, Columbus, OH, $180,000. For biomedical engineering research in analysis and quantification of laser-induced vascular injury using image processing and 3-D reconstruction techniques. 1991.

2857-44 Ohio State University Research Foundation, Columbus, OH, $118,523. For biomedical engineering research in biomechanical modeling of human tongue. 1991.

2857-45 Oregon Graduate Institute of Science and Technology, Beaverton, OR, $178,501. For biomedical engineering research in targeted drug delivery: photorelease from liposomes using diode laser-coupled fiber optic excitation. 1991.

2857-46 Oregon State University, Corvallis, OR, $167,777. For biomedical engineering research in quantifying molecular origins of protein surface activity. 1991.

2857-47 Pennsylvania State University, Milton S. Hershey Medical Center, Hershey, PA, $146,269. For biomedical engineering research in ultrasonic pharyngeal imaging system for study of obstructive sleep apnea. 1991.

2857-48 Polyclinic Medical Center, Harrisburg, PA, $10,000. For delivery table for childbirth center. 1991.

2857-49 Rehabilitation Institute of Chicago, Research Corporation, Chicago, IL, $179,958. For biomedical engineering research in surgery simulation: building computer graphics models to analyze and design musculoskeletal reconstructions. 1991.

2857-50 Research Foundation of the State University of New York, Buffalo, NY, $169,097. For biomedical engineering research in soft x-ray real-time microtomographic system for high resolution 3-D medical imaging. 1991.

2857-51 River Rescue of Harrisburg, Harrisburg, PA, $20,000. For new ambulance. 1991.

2857-52 Rutgers, The State University of New Jersey, New Brunswick, NJ, $179,880. For biomedical engineering research in neuronal growth cone motility at substrate boundaries. 1991.

2857-53 Southern Methodist University, Dallas, TX, $179,934. For biomedical engineering research in study of gait stability of normals and post-polio patients using nonlinear theory. 1991.

2857-54 University of California, Irvine, CA, $179,995. For biomedical engineering research in applications of optical laser trapping to the study of biological media and cellular interactions. 1991.

2857-55 University of California, Irvine, CA, $176,382. For biomedical engineering research in pulsed photothermal radiometry of port wine stains. 1991.

2857-56 University of California, La Jolla, CA, $179,298. For biomedical engineering research in ellipsometric measurement of retinal nerve fiber layer thickness. 1991.

2857-57 University of California, La Jolla, CA, $178,596. For biomedical engineering research in evaluation and modeling of subcutaneous tissue for glucose sensor implantation. 1991.

2857-58 University of California, San Francisco, CA, $179,068. For biomedical engineering research in metabolite imaging of humans using magnetic resonance spectroscopy. 1991.

2857-59 University of California, San Francisco, CA, $178,749. For biomedical engineering research in miniature ultrasound applicators for interstitial hyperthermia cancer therapy. 1991.

2857-60 University of California, San Francisco, CA, $174,912. For biomedical engineering research in ultrasound assessment of bone strength. 1991.

2857-61 University of Chicago, Chicago, IL, $180,000. For biomedical engineering research in study of molecular structure of ionic channels with atomic force microscope and scanning tunneling microscope. 1991.

2857-62 University of Chicago, Chicago, IL, $179,279. For biomedical engineering research in development of intelligent workstation for mammographic breast cancer detection. 1991.

2857-63 University of Chicago, Chicago, IL, $178,973. For biomedical engineering research in case-based approach to radiation treatment planning. 1991.

2857-64 University of Colorado, Boulder, CO, $46,319. For biomedical engineering research in noninvasive 3D imaging of human brain function using combined neuromagnetic and neuroelectric measurement and modeling. 1991.

2857-65 University of Connecticut, Storrs, CT, $180,000. For biomedical engineering research in combining high-speed video imaging and photometry of fluorescent probes with perforated patch recording to study pituitary cell physiology. 1991.

2857-66 University of Illinois, Urbana, IL, $180,000. For biomedical engineering research in optimal reconstruction technique for biochemical imaging using magnetic resonance. 1991.

2857-67 University of Iowa, Iowa City, IA, $179,996. For biomedical engineering research in modeling of dynamic coronary obstructions and their physiological impact. 1991.

2857-68 University of Maryland, Catonsville, MD, $114,325. For biomedical engineering research in determination of physical characteristics of collagen proteoglycan int in solutions at physiological concentrations. 1991.

2857-69 University of Michigan, Ann Arbor, MI, $179,954. For biomedical engineering research in cross-bridge kinetics in isolated cardiac myocytes utilizing laser based sarcomere length servo control system. 1991.

2857-70 University of Michigan, Ann Arbor, MI, $179,906. For biomedical engineering research in quantive and kinetic analysis of antigen presentation. 1991.

2857-71 University of Michigan, Ann Arbor, MI, $178,177. For biomedical engineering research in real-time adaptive control of hyperthermia treatments using ultrasound phased-array. 1991.

2857-72 University of Minnesota, Minneapolis, MN, $179,395. For biomedical engineering research in reduction of truncation artifacts and noise in NMR chemical shift imaging. 1991.

2857-73 University of Mississippi Medical Center, Jackson, MS, $176,387. For biomedical engineering research in linear systems analysis of lateral vestibular nuclei neuron responses. 1991.

2857-74 University of Missouri, Kansas City, MO, $169,580. For biomedical engineering research in high precision preparation of bone for uncemented prosthesis fixation. 1991.

2857-75 University of Montreal, Montreal, Canada, $119,200. For biomedical engineering research in role of structural and passive electrical properties on conduction of impulses in cardiac tissue. 1991.

2857-76 University of Nebraska, Lincoln, NE, $60,000. For biomedical engineering research in examination and characterization of interfacial phenomena at surface of prosthetic materials. 1991.

2857-77 University of New Brunswick, Fredericton, Canada, $96,686. For biomedical engineering research in development of elbow prosthesis. 1991.

2857-78 University of North Carolina, Chapel Hill, NC, $179,949. For biomedical engineering research in high-speed iterative reconstruction methods for quantitative SPECT imaging. 1991.

2857-79 University of North Carolina, Chapel Hill, NC, $179,647. For biomedical engineering research in development of automatic three dimensional microscopic imaging of fluorescent stained clinical specimens. 1991.

2857-80 University of North Carolina, Chapel Hill, NC, $179,402. For biomedical engineering research in development and application of high voltage pulsed field system for DNA sequencing. 1991.

2857-81 University of Pennsylvania, Philadelphia, PA, $180,000. For biomedical engineering research in wavelet analysis of ECG. 1991.

2857-82 University of Rochester, Rochester, NY, $180,000. For biomedical engineering research in two-compartment packed bed bioreactor with porous microsphere for long-term bone marrow culture. 1991.

2857-83 University of Southern California, Los Angeles, CA, $180,000. For biomedical engineering research in incorporation of anatomical MR data for improved functional imaging with PET. 1991.

2857-84 University of Tennessee-Calspan Center for Aerospace Research, Tullahoma, TN, $179,895. For biomedical engineering research in quantitative ultra-sensitive detection for biosciences applications. 1991.

2857-85 University of Texas, Austin, TX, $179,925. For biomedical engineering research in novel screening method for cervical neoplasia based on fluorescence spectroscopy. 1991.

2857-86 University of Texas Medical Branch Hospitals, Galveston, TX, $180,000. For biomedical engineering research in mathematical programming of radiotherapy plans. 1991.

2857-87 University of Texas System Cancer Center, Houston, TX, $179,990. For biomedical engineering research in assay of lymphocyte function and immunological disorders based on time-resolved morphological measurements. 1991.

2857-88 University of Toronto, Toronto, Canada, $170,860. For biomedical engineering research in ocular drug delivery systems for systemic and ocular therapy. 1991.

2857-89 University of Utah, Salt Lake City, UT, $180,000. For biomedical engineering research in cone beam reconstruction algorithms for single photon emission computed tomography. 1991.

2857-90 University of Utah, Salt Lake City, UT, $180,000. For biomedical engineering research in electrical current flow in human thorax: a computational, experimental and theorectical study. 1991.

2857-91 University of Utah, Salt Lake City, UT, $178,958. For biomedical engineering research in propagation model to study spatial distribution of repolarization in ventricular myocardium. 1991.

2857-92 University of Wisconsin, Madison, WI, $180,000. For biomedical engineering research in spectral editing techniques for 1H MR spectroscopy and chemical shift imaging of human brain in vivo. 1991.

2857-93 University of Wisconsin, Madison, WI, $176,288. For biomedical engineering research in reconstruction of femur: determination of optimal method of fixation following incremental resection of femur. 1991.

2857-94 University of Wisconsin, Madison, WI, $141,206. For biomedical engineering research in muscle force enhancement: kinematic and structural considerations. 1991.

2857-95 Virginia Commonwealth University, Richmond, VA, $177,340. For biomedical engineering research in angle independent flow map using color doppler flow imaging. 1991.

2857-96 Yale University, School of Medicine, New Haven, CT, $180,000. For biomedical engineering research in confocal imaging and mathematical modeling of calcium dynamics in hepatocyte. 1991.

2857-97 Yale University, School of Medicine, New Haven, CT, $179,904. For biomedical engineering research in improved measurement of diffusion and microcirculation in tissues by nuclear magnetic resonance (NMR). 1991.

2857-98 Yale University, School of Medicine, New Haven, CT, $164,995. For biomedical engineering research in new approaches to measurement of tissue perfusion in vivo by nuclear magnetic resonance. 1991.

2858
Widener Memorial Foundation in Aid of Handicapped Children

665 Thomas Rd.
P.O. Box 178
Lafayette Hill 19444-0178   (215) 836-7500

Incorporated in 1912 in PA.
Donor(s): Peter A.B. Widener,‡ Provident National Bank.
Foundation type: Independent
Financial data (yr. ended 12/31/91): Assets, $5,153,428 (M); gifts received, $553,516; expenditures, $725,310; qualifying distributions, $715,555, including $714,182 for 19 grants (high: $145,000; low: $4,000; average: $15,000-$100,000).
Purpose and activities: Support for research into the causes, treatment, and prevention of diseases and conditions which handicap children orthopedically; to aid and assist public and private charitable institutions and associations in the care, education, and rehabilitation of children so handicapped.
Fields of interest: Medical research, child welfare, handicapped.
Types of support: Seed money, building funds, equipment, special projects, research, renovation projects.
Limitations: Giving limited to Delaware Valley, PA, for projects relating to orthopedically handicapped children. No grants to individuals, or for endowment funds, scholarships, fellowships, or matching gifts; no loans.
Application information: Application form not required.
   Initial approach: Letter
   Copies of proposal: 1
   Deadline(s): Apr. 15 and Oct. 15
   Board meeting date(s): May and Nov.
   Final notification: Immediately after board meetings
   Write: F. Eugene Dixon, Jr., Pres.
Officers and Trustees:* F. Eugene Dixon, Jr.,* Pres.; Peter M. Mattoon,* V.P.; Edith Robb Dixon,* Secy.-Treas.; Bruce L. Castor, George Widener Dixon.
Number of staff: None.
EIN: 236267223

2859
Widgeon Foundation, Inc.

c/o George V. Strong, Jr.
1700 Two Mellon Bank Ctr.
Philadelphia 19102
Application address: P.O. Box 1084, Easton, MD 21601; Tel.: (301) 822-7707

Established in 1969 in PA.
Donor(s): Elizabeth H. Robinson.
Foundation type: Independent
Financial data (yr. ended 12/31/90): Assets, $2,008,790 (M); expenditures, $100,967; qualifying distributions, $99,918, including $91,465 for 36 grants (high: $15,000; low: $25).
Fields of interest: Higher education, religion—Christian, hospitals, social services.
Types of support: General purposes.
Limitations: Giving primarily in MD, VA, and PA. No grants to individuals.
Application information: Application form not required.

Initial approach: Proposal
Deadline(s): None
Write: Elizabeth H. Robinson, Pres.
Officers and Directors:* Elizabeth H. Robinson,* Pres. and Treas.; Richard Robinson,* V.P.; George V. Strong, Jr.,* Secy.
EIN: 136113927

2860
John C. Williams Charitable Trust
c/o Pittsburgh National Bank, Charitable & Institutional Trust Dept.
One Oliver Plaza, 27th Fl.
Pittsburgh 15265   (412) 762-3502

Trust established in 1936 in PA.
Donor(s): John C. Williams.‡
Foundation type: Independent
Financial data (yr. ended 12/31/91): Assets, $4,804,924 (M); gifts received, $5,142; expenditures, $177,193; qualifying distributions, $154,941, including $150,000 for 2 grants of $75,000 each.
Purpose and activities: Emphasis on higher education, hospitals, a community center, and youth agencies.
Fields of interest: Higher education, hospitals, youth.
Types of support: General purposes, renovation projects, capital campaigns, equipment.
Limitations: Giving limited to Steubenville, OH, and Weirton, WV. No grants to individuals, or for fellowships; no loans.
Publications: Application guidelines.
Application information: Application form required.
  Initial approach: Letter
  Copies of proposal: 3
  Deadline(s): Mar. and Oct.
  Board meeting date(s): Mar. and Oct.
  Write: Bruce Bickel, V.P., Pittsburgh National Bank
Trustee: Pittsburgh National Bank.
EIN: 256024153

2861
Williamsport-Lycoming Foundation
(Formerly Williamsport Foundation)
321 Pine St., Suite 207
Williamsport 17701   (717) 321-1500
FAX: (717) 321-6434

Established in 1916 in PA by bank resolution.
Foundation type: Community
Financial data (yr. ended 12/31/91): Assets, $19,905,282 (M); expenditures, $1,981,071; qualifying distributions, $1,537,294, including $1,537,294 for 48 grants (high: $500,000; low: $100; average: $1,000-$30,000).
Fields of interest: Education, higher education, recreation, youth, civic affairs, community development, cultural programs, arts, theater, historic preservation, conservation, hospitals, drug abuse.
Types of support: Building funds, emergency funds, equipment, general purposes, matching

funds, program-related investments, research, seed money, special projects, loans.
Limitations: Giving limited to organizations located in the greater Williamsport, PA, area. No grants to individuals, or for endowment funds or operating budgets.
Publications: Annual report, informational brochure.
Application information: Application form required.
  Initial approach: Letter
  Copies of proposal: 1
  Deadline(s): None
  Board meeting date(s): Monthly
  Final notification: 2 months
  Write: Mary Lou Kavelak, Admin. Secy.
Officers and Directors:* Robert L. Shangraw,* Pres.; Harold D. Hershberger, Jr.,* V.P. and Secy.; James W. Bower, Sr.,* V.P.; Theodore H. Reich,* Treas.; Dudley N. Anderson, Richard H. Confair, Timothy J. Crotty.
Trustees: Commonwealth Bank & Trust Co., Northern Central Bank, Williamsport National Bank.
Number of staff: 1 part-time support.
EIN: 246013117

2862
Thomas A. Wilson Foundation
c/o Integra Trust Co.
300 Fourth Ave.
Pittsburgh 15278   (412) 644-8359

Established in 1971 in PA.
Foundation type: Independent
Financial data (yr. ended 12/31/91): Assets, $4,964,202 (M); expenditures, $310,933; qualifying distributions, $280,122, including $270,000 for grants.
Fields of interest: Religion—Christian, hospitals.
Application information:
  Initial approach: Proposal
  Deadline(s): None
  Write: Barbara L. Beech, Asst. V.P., Integra Trust Co.
Trustee: Integra Trust Co., N.A.
Number of staff: None.
EIN: 237358862

2863
The Wood Foundation of Chambersburg, PA
273 Lincoln Way East
Chambersburg 17201   (717) 267-3174

Established in 1989 as successor foundation to the Wood Foundation of Chambersburg, PA.
Foundation type: Independent
Financial data (yr. ended 12/31/91): Assets, $6,751,961 (M); expenditures, $339,081; qualifying distributions, $320,922, including $271,742 for 60 grants (high: $50,000; low: $100).
Fields of interest: Social services, arts, hospitals, higher education, secondary education.
Limitations: Giving primarily in Chambersburg and Franklin counties, PA.

Application information: Proposal. Application form not required.
  Deadline(s): None
  Write: C.O. Wood III, Trustee
Trustees: Emilie W. Myers, C.O. Wood III, David S. Wood, Miriam M. Wood.
EIN: 251607838

2864
The Wyomissing Foundation, Inc.
1015 Penn Ave.
Wyomissing 19610   (215) 376-7496

Incorporated in 1929 in DE.
Donor(s): Ferdinand Thun,‡ and family.
Foundation type: Independent
Financial data (yr. ended 12/31/91): Assets, $17,151,097 (M); expenditures, $897,117; qualifying distributions, $582,866, including $554,525 for 49 grants (high: $440,000; low: $250; average: $1,000-$20,000).
Purpose and activities: Giving primarily for hospitals and health services, higher education and building funds for schools, civic affairs, youth and social service agencies, child welfare, and family planning and services; support also for the environment and conservation, and the arts, including performing arts and music.
Fields of interest: Health, higher education, education—building funds, civic affairs, youth, social services, child welfare, family services, conservation, arts.
Types of support: Operating budgets, continuing support, annual campaigns, seed money, emergency funds, building funds, equipment, matching funds, capital campaigns.
Limitations: Giving primarily in Berks County, PA, and contiguous counties; limited support also in the mid-Atlantic area. No grants to individuals, or for endowment funds, deficit financing, land acquisition, publications, conferences, scholarships, or fellowships; no loans.
Publications: Program policy statement, application guidelines, annual report, financial statement.
Application information: Application form not required.
  Initial approach: Proposal not exceeding 2 pages (excluding supporting materials)
  Copies of proposal: 1
  Deadline(s): Submit proposal preferably in Feb., May, Aug., or Oct.; deadline 25th of month preceding board meeting
  Board meeting date(s): Mar., June, Sept., and Nov.
  Final notification: 3 months
  Write: Lawrence A. Walsky, Secy.
Officers and Trustees:* Paul R. Roedel,* Pres.; David L. Thun,* V.P.; Lawrence A. Walsky, Secy.; Alfred Hemmerich,* Treas.; Thomas A. Beaver, Julia Buckman, Fred D. Hafer, Sidney D. Kline, Jr., Timothy K. Lake, Nicholas Muhlenberg.
Number of staff: 1 part-time professional; 1 part-time support.
EIN: 231980570

PUERTO RICO

2865
Puerto Rico Community Foundation
Royal Bank Ctr. Bldg., Suite 1417
Hato Rey 00917   (809) 751-3822
Additional tel.: (809) 751-3885

Incorporated in 1984 in PR; began operations in 1985.
Foundation type: Community
Financial data (yr. ended 12/31/90): Assets, $7,857,423 (M); gifts received, $2,361,874; expenditures, $1,922,539; qualifying distributions, $1,316,117, including $1,316,117 for 42 grants (high: $136,030; low: $2,500).
Purpose and activities: The foundation "seeks to contribute to the achievement of a healthier economy and enhance quality of life in Puerto Rico"; giving in areas such as economic development, educational associations, the elderly, community development, science and technological innovation, health, including AIDS programs, drug and alcohol abuse programs, arts and cultural activities, including dance and fine arts, criminal justice, agriculture, animal welfare, and civic affairs.
Fields of interest: Education, community development, science and technology, health, AIDS, arts, fine arts, agriculture, aged, disadvantaged.
Types of support: Conferences and seminars, continuing support, matching funds, operating budgets, professorships, publications, renovation projects, research, program-related investments, consulting services, technical assistance, emergency funds.
Limitations: Giving limited to Puerto Rico. No support for religious organizations or commonly accepted community services. No grants to individuals, or for annual campaigns, seed money, endowments, deficit financing, or scholarships; generally no grants for building funds.
Publications: Annual report, newsletter, informational brochure (including application guidelines), 990-PF, financial statement.
Application information: Application form required.
  Initial approach: Letter
  Deadline(s): None
  Board meeting date(s): June, Sept., Dec., and Mar.
  Final notification: Within 2 weeks after board meetings
  Write: Jose R. Crespo, Administrator
Officers: Manuel H. Dubon, Chair.; Ethel Rios de Betancourt, Pres.; Jose R. Crespo, Administrator; Nelson I. Colon, Prog. Dir.
Directors: Amalia Betanzos, and 18 additional directors.
Number of staff: 6 full-time professional; 4 full-time support.
EIN: 660413230

RHODE ISLAND

2866
Allendale Insurance Foundation
c/o The R.I. Hospital Trust National Bank
One Hospital Trust Plaza
Providence 02903   (401) 278-8700

Established in 1986 in RI.
Foundation type: Company-sponsored
Financial data (yr. ended 12/31/91): Assets, $4,574,150 (M); expenditures, $741,508; qualifying distributions, $716,274, including $716,274 for 744 grants (high: $163,509; low: $25).
Fields of interest: Community funds, education, higher education, health, social services, arts.
Application information:
  Initial approach: Proposal
  Deadline(s): None
Agent: The Rhode Island Hospital Trust National Bank.
EIN: 222773230

2867
Chace Fund, Inc.
731 Hospital Trust Bldg.
Providence 02903

Established in 1947 in RI.
Donor(s): Malcolm G. Chace III, Arnold B. Chace, Berkshire Hathaway, Inc., Kathleen Osborne.‡
Foundation type: Independent
Financial data (yr. ended 12/31/90): Assets, $713,275 (M); gifts received, $339,430; expenditures, $321,075; qualifying distributions, $315,114, including $311,264 for 104 grants (high: $50,000; low: $50).
Purpose and activities: Support primarily for community organizations; support also for education, social services, child welfare organizations, hospitals, and the arts.
Fields of interest: Community development, education, social services, child welfare, hospitals, arts.
Types of support: General purposes.
Limitations: Giving primarily in NY, RI, and MA. No grants to individuals.
Application information:
  Initial approach: Letter
  Deadline(s): None
  Write: Malcolm G. Chace, III, Pres.
Officers: Malcolm G. Chace III, Pres.; Arnold B. Chace, Jr., V.P.; Catherine McCarthy, Secy.-Treas.
EIN: 056008849

2868
The Champlin Foundations ▼
P.O. Box 637
Providence 02901-0637   (401) 421-3719

Trusts established in 1932, 1947, and 1975 in DE.
Donor(s): George S. Champlin,‡ Florence C. Hamilton,‡ Hope C. Neaves.‡
Foundation type: Independent

Financial data (yr. ended 12/31/91): Assets, $293,971,384 (M); gifts received, $750; expenditures, $15,965,040; qualifying distributions, $15,011,583, including $14,591,881 for 177 grants (high: $1,500,000; low: $1,000).
Purpose and activities: Giving primarily for conservation; higher, secondary, and other education, including libraries; health and hospitals; support also for cultural activities, including historic preservation; scientific activities; and social and family sevices, including programs for youth and the elderly.
Fields of interest: Conservation, environment, education, higher education, secondary education, libraries, health, hospitals, cultural programs, historic preservation, science and technology, social services, family planning, youth, aged, animal welfare.
Types of support: Building funds, equipment, land acquisition, renovation projects, scholarship funds, capital campaigns.
Limitations: Giving primarily in RI. No grants to individuals, or for general support, program or operating budgets, matching gifts, special projects, research, publications, conferences, or continuing support; no loans.
Publications: Program policy statement, application guidelines, annual report, grants list.
Application information: Application form not required.
  Initial approach: 1-page letter
  Copies of proposal: 1
  Deadline(s): Submit proposal preferably between Apr. 1 and Aug. 31; deadline Aug. 31
  Board meeting date(s): Nov.
  Final notification: After Nov. meeting
  Write: David A. King, Exec. Dir.
Distribution Committee: David A. King, Exec. Dir.; Francis C. Carter, John Gorham, Louis R. Hampton, Earl W. Harrington, Jr., Robert W. Kenyon, Norma B. LaFreniere, John W. Linnell.
Trustee: Bank of Delaware.
Number of staff: 1 full-time professional; 2 part-time professional; 1 full-time support.
EIN: 516010168
Recent health grants:
2868-1 Bethany Home of Rhode Island, Providence, RI, $25,000. For equipment and construction. 1990.
2868-2 Butler Hospital, Providence, RI, $50,000. For equipment and construction. 1990.
2868-3 Carolina Fire Association, Carolina, RI, $25,000. For rescue and ambulance vehicles. 1990.
2868-4 Cranston General Hospital, Cranston, RI, $25,000. For equipment and construction. 1990.
2868-5 Hattie Ide Chaffee Nursing Home, East Providence, RI, $25,000. For equipment and construction. 1990.
2868-6 Health Center of South County, Wakefield, RI, $50,000. For equipment and construction. 1990.
2868-7 Kent County Memorial Hospital, Warwick, RI, $100,000. For equipment and construction. 1990.
2868-8 Marathon House, Providence, RI, $100,000. 1990.
2868-9 Memorial Hospital, Pawtucket, RI, $200,000. For acquisition of assets of Notre Dame Hospital in Central Falls, and successful

transition of Notre Dame to facility for occupational health services, one-day surgery, physical therapy, x-ray and lab services and ambulatory and emergency treatment for walk-in patients. 1990.
2868-10 Miriam Hospital, Providence, RI, $200,000. For equipment and construction. 1990.
2868-11 Planned Parenthood of Rhode Island, Providence, RI, $150,000. For new facility. 1990.
2868-12 Providence Ambulatory Health Care Foundation, Providence, RI, $119,375. For new telephone system to connect six Health Centers. 1990.
2868-13 Rhode Island Blood Center, Providence, RI, $135,000. To establish DNA testing program in conjunction with technical modernization of HLA tissue typing lab. Grant shared with Vector Health Systems. 1990.
2868-14 Rhode Island Hospital, Providence, RI, $150,000. For equipment and construction. 1990.
2868-15 Roger Williams General Hospital, Providence, RI, $200,000. For equipment and construction. 1990.
2868-16 Saint Elizabeth Home, Providence, RI, $250,000. Toward acquisition of Metacom Manor, 129-bed health care facility. 1990.
2868-17 Saint Joseph Living Center, Providence, RI, $100,000. 1990.
2868-18 Salvation Army of Pawtucket, Adult Rehabilitation Center, Pawtucket, RI, $89,366. Toward recreational and study facilities. 1990.
2868-19 Sargent Rehabilitation Center for Disorders, Providence, RI, $24,600. For equipment and construction. 1990.
2868-20 Scituate Ambulance and Rescue Corps, North Scituate, RI, $25,000. For rescue and ambulance vehicles. 1990.
2868-21 Self-Help, Riverside, RI, $12,852. For equipment and construction. 1990.
2868-22 South County Hospital, Wakefield, RI, $100,000. For equipment and construction. 1990.
2868-23 Steere House-Home for the Aged, Providence, RI, $250,000. Toward construction of new facility on Rhode Island Hospital campus. 1990.
2868-24 Talbot Treatment Centers, Providence, RI, $32,500. 1990.
2868-25 Westerly Hospital, Westerly, RI, $100,000. For equipment and construction. 1990.
2868-26 Women and Infants Hospital of Rhode Island, Breast Care Center, Providence, RI, $150,000. For stereotactic imaging device. 1990.
2868-27 Wood River Health Services, Hope Valley, RI, $25,000. For equipment and construction. 1990.

2869
The Cranston Foundation
1381 Cranston St.
Cranston 02920   (401) 943-4800

Trust established in 1960 in RI.
Donor(s): Cranston Print Works Co.
Foundation type: Company-sponsored
Financial data (yr. ended 06/30/91): Assets, $785,175 (M); gifts received, $233,298;

expenditures, $330,592; qualifying distributions, $328,813, including $165,450 for 159 grants (high: $10,500; low: $100), $144,684 for 59 grants to individuals (high: $8,800; low: $109) and $18,679 for employee matching gifts.
Purpose and activities: Grants largely for higher education, including a scholarship program for children of Cranston Corporation employees. Support also for community funds, hospitals, and cultural programs.
Fields of interest: Higher education, community funds, hospitals, cultural programs.
Types of support: Employee-related scholarships, operating budgets, scholarship funds, employee matching gifts.
Limitations: Giving primarily in RI and MA.
Application information: Application form not required.
  Initial approach: Proposal
  Deadline(s): May 15
  Board meeting date(s): At least quarterly
  Write: The Trustees
Trustees: R. Mandeville, Frederic L. Rockefeller, Richard Schein, George W. Shuster, J. Wright.
EIN: 056015348

2870
Fleet/Norstar Charitable Trust ▼
(Formerly Fleet Charitable Trust)
c/o Fleet National Bank
111 Westminster St.
Providence 02903   (401) 278-6325

Trust established in 1955 in RI.
Donor(s): Fleet Bank, N.A.
Foundation type: Company-sponsored
Financial data (yr. ended 12/31/91): Assets, $36,373,738 (M); expenditures, $2,148,163; qualifying distributions, $2,065,263, including $1,964,498 for 416 grants (high: $200,000; average: $1,000-$20,000).
Purpose and activities: Giving primarily for capital purposes of major charities, including the United Way, health and hospitals, higher education, including an employee matching gift program, and the arts and museums. Support also for work/study scholarships paid to colleges on behalf of RI high school seniors from minority groups.
Fields of interest: Community funds, health services, hospitals, education, higher education, education—minorities, hunger, youth, arts.
Types of support: Annual campaigns, emergency funds, building funds, equipment, employee matching gifts, capital campaigns, matching funds, loaned talent, renovation projects, use of facilities, employee-related scholarships, research, scholarship funds.
Limitations: Giving limited to nonprofit organizations in CT, MA, ME, NH, NY, and RI. No grants for endowment or operating funds; no loans.
Publications: Application guidelines, program policy statement.
Application information: Scholarship candidates must be nominated by high school guidance counselor and submit a letter stating needs and provide financial information (RI only). Application form not required.
  Initial approach: Proposal
  Copies of proposal: 1
  Deadline(s): None

Board meeting date(s): Quarterly
Final notification: 2 months after board meeting
Write: Ms. Sheila Devin McDonald, Secy.
Trustee: Fleet Bank, N.A.
Number of staff: None.
EIN: 056007619

2871
Ira S. and Anna Galkin Charitable Trust
c/o Rosenstein Midwood & Co.
27 Dryden Ln.
Providence 02904   (401) 331-6851

Trust established in 1947 in RI.
Donor(s): Ira S. Galkin.
Foundation type: Independent
Financial data (yr. ended 12/31/91): Assets, $3,194,469 (M); expenditures, $180,238; qualifying distributions, $135,013, including $135,013 for 80 grants (high: $50,000; low: $25).
Fields of interest: Jewish welfare, Jewish giving, hospitals, higher education, social services.
Limitations: Giving primarily in RI.
Application information:
  Initial approach: Proposal
  Deadline(s): None
  Write: Arnold T. Galkin, Trustee
Trustees: Arnold T. Galkin, Herbert S. Galkin, Irwin S. Galkin.
EIN: 056006231

2872
Hasbro Children's Foundation ▼
200 Narragansett Park Dr.
Pawtucket 02862-0200   (401) 431-8697
Application address: 32 West 23rd St., New York, NY 10010; Tel.: (212) 645-2400

Established in 1985 in RI.
Donor(s): Hasbro, Inc.
Foundation type: Company-sponsored
Financial data (yr. ended 12/30/90): Assets, $4,857,075 (M); gifts received, $2,024,638; expenditures, $2,906,815; qualifying distributions, $2,903,940, including $2,682,954 for 87 grants (high: $225,000; low: $100; average: $5,000-$75,000).
Purpose and activities: Giving to improve the quality of life of children; emphasis on health, including pediatric AIDS, and special education, with focus on handicapped, abused, and neglected children, literacy, the impact of homelessness on children, minority education, and hunger. The foundation contributes to direct service programs on a national basis for children under the age of twelve.
Fields of interest: Child welfare, child development, health, hospitals, AIDS, handicapped, education—early childhood, education—minorities, homeless, hunger.
Types of support: Seed money, special projects.
Limitations: No grants to individuals, or for operating expenses or capital improvements.
Publications: Informational brochure (including application guidelines).
Application information: Application form not required.
  Initial approach: Letter and proposal
  Copies of proposal: 3
  Deadline(s): 2 months prior to meeting
  Board meeting date(s): Feb., June, and Oct.

Final notification: 1 week following meeting
  Write: Eve Weiss, Exec. Dir.
Officers and Trustees:* Ellen Block,* Chair.; Barry J. Alperin,* Secy.; Eve Weiss, Exec. Dir.; Carole Lewis Anderson, William Birenbaum, Roger Hart, Alan G. Hassenfeld, Samuel Katz, Jerome Lowenstein, Alvin Poussaint, B.J. Seabury, William Whaley.
Number of staff: 1 full-time professional; 1 full-time support.
EIN: 222570516

2873
Hasbro Industries Charitable Trust, Inc.
c/o Hasbro, Inc.
1027 Newport Ave.
Pawtucket 02861   (401) 727-5429

Established in 1984 in RI.
Donor(s): Hasbro, Inc.
Foundation type: Company-sponsored
Financial data (yr. ended 12/28/90): Assets, $3,312,367 (M); gifts received, $500,000; expenditures, $794,806; qualifying distributions, $785,104, including $785,104 for 96 grants (high: $145,000; low: $200; average: $500-$5,000).
Fields of interest: Education, education—early childhood, health, social services, family services, youth, child development, child welfare.
Types of support: Capital campaigns, program-related investments, donated products.
Limitations: Giving in RI, and areas of major company operations. No grants for scholarships, endowments, fundraising events, conferences, or other special event sponsorships.
Publications: Application guidelines.
Application information: Application form not required.
  Initial approach: Letter
  Copies of proposal: 1
  Deadline(s): July 1
  Board meeting date(s): Throughout spring and summer
  Write: Mary Louise Fazzano
Officers: Alan G. Hassenfeld, Pres.; Alfred J. Verrecchia, C.F.O.
Number of staff: 1 full-time professional; 1 full-time support.
EIN: 222538470

2874
Mary E. Hodges Fund
2115 Broad St.
Cranston 02905   (401) 467-2970

Foundation type: Independent
Financial data (yr. ended 10/31/91): Assets, $2,947,175 (M); expenditures, $230,180; qualifying distributions, $202,547, including $174,947 for grants (average: $1,000-$10,000) and $27,600 for grants to individuals.
Purpose and activities: Grants primarily for education, hospitals, and health and social services. Student aid for individuals who have a Masonic affiliation or who have been residents of RI for 5 years or more.
Fields of interest: Education, hospitals, health services, social services.
Types of support: Student aid.
Limitations: Giving limited to RI.

Application information:
Deadline(s): June 1
Write: Julio A. Paniccia, Secy.
Officers: Donald Hopkins, Pres.; Julio A. Paniccia, Secy.; Norman P. Jehan, Treas.
EIN: 056049444

2875
The Jaffe Foundation
300 Richmond St., Suite 204
Providence 02903-4222   (401) 421-2920

Established in 1962 in MA.
Donor(s): Meyer Jaffe,‡ Edwin A. Jaffe.
Foundation type: Independent
Financial data (yr. ended 06/30/91): Assets, $5,238,321 (M); expenditures, $568,342; qualifying distributions, $524,590, including $505,960 for 69 grants (high: $137,000; low: $100; average: $2,000).
Purpose and activities: "Dedicated to the support of disadvantaged peoples in the U.S. and other parts of the world, and commited to the survival of the Jewish people as a cultural unity." In persuing these goals the foundation focuses it's support mainly in the areas of health, education, and the arts.
Fields of interest: Higher education, Jewish giving, Jewish welfare, hospitals, health, performing arts, fine arts.
Limitations: Giving primarily in Fall River, MA, and Providence, RI. No grants to individuals.
Application information: Proposal.
Deadline(s): None
Board meeting date(s): Jan. and July
Write: Holly Seagrove, Exec. Secy.
Officers and Trustees:* Edwin A. Jaffe,* Chair.; Lola Jaffe,* Vice-Chair.; Donna Jaffe Fishbein, David S. Greer, Robert Jaffe.
EIN: 046049261

2876
Phyllis Kimball Johnstone and H. Earle Kimball Foundation
c/o The R.I. Hospital Trust National Bank
One Hospital Trust Plaza
Providence 02903   (401) 278-8700

Established in 1957 in DE.
Donor(s): Phyllis Kimball Johnstone.‡
Foundation type: Independent
Financial data (yr. ended 11/30/90): Assets, $2,988,274 (M); expenditures, $156,650; qualifying distributions, $130,752, including $127,950 for 22 grants (high: $25,000; low: $1,000).
Fields of interest: Hospitals, education, social services.
Limitations: Giving primarily in RI.
Application information:
Initial approach: Proposal
Deadline(s): None
Trustees: John R. Fales, Jr., Gordon A. Feiner, Avery Seaman, Jr., The Rhode Island Hospital Trust National Bank.
EIN: 056015723

2877
The Koffler Family Foundation
c/o The Koffler Corp.
170 Westminster St., Suite 1200
Providence 02903

Established in 1978 in RI.
Donor(s): The Koffler Corp.
Foundation type: Independent
Financial data (yr. ended 07/31/91): Assets, $5,168,316 (M); expenditures, $311,048; qualifying distributions, $296,361, including $296,361 for 94 grants (high: $181,050; low: $5).
Purpose and activities: Giving primarily to Jewish organizations, including welfare funds, congregations, and yeshivas; support also for higher education and hospitals.
Fields of interest: Jewish welfare, Jewish giving, religious schools, higher education, hospitals.
Limitations: Giving primarily in RI. No grants to individuals.
Application information: Contributes only to pre-selected organizations. Applications not accepted.
Trustees: Richard S. Bornstein, Leonard Granoff, Lillian Koffler, Sol Koffler.
EIN: 050376269

2878
Ida Ballou Littlefield Memorial Trust
1500 Fleet Ctr.
Providence 02903

Established in 1989 in RI.
Foundation type: Independent
Financial data (yr. ended 12/31/90): Assets, $5,869,619 (M); expenditures, $300,107; qualifying distributions, $249,328, including $220,265 for 18 grants (high: $40,000; low: $3,000).
Fields of interest: Medical research, higher education, museums.
Types of support: Renovation projects, capital campaigns.
Limitations: Giving primarily in RI. No grants to individuals.
Application information: Application form not required.
Deadline(s): None
Write: Joachim A. Weissfeld, Trustee
Trustees: William A. Viall, Joachim A. Weissfeld, Citizens Trust Co.
EIN: 223022799

2879
The Roy T. Morgan Foundation, Inc.
c/o Armstrong Gibbons
155 South Main St.
Providence 02903

Trust established in RI.
Donor(s): Roy T. Morgan.‡
Foundation type: Independent
Financial data (yr. ended 03/31/91): Assets, $3,577,774 (M); expenditures, $153,562; qualifying distributions, $109,200, including $103,200 for 6 grants (high: $50,000; low: $200).
Fields of interest: Secondary education, hospitals, community funds.
Limitations: Giving primarily in New England. No grants to individuals, or for endowment funds,

scholarships, fellowships, or matching gifts; no loans.
Application information: Contributes only to pre-selected organizations. Applications not accepted.
Board meeting date(s): Mar., June, Sept., and Dec.
Trustees: Russell S. Boles, Walter F. Gibbons, Vaughn G. Gooding.
EIN: 050413370

2880
Old Stone Bank Charitable Foundation
150 South Main St.
Providence 02903   (401) 278-2213

Established in 1969 in RI.
Donor(s): Old Stone Bank.
Foundation type: Company-sponsored
Financial data (yr. ended 12/31/91): Assets, $50,752 (M); gifts received, $100,000; expenditures, $355,663; qualifying distributions, $335,295, including $328,300 for 22 grants (high: $195,000; low: $550; average: $550-$195,000) and $6,995 for 64 employee matching gifts.
Fields of interest: Community funds, education, cultural programs, social services, health, civic affairs.
Types of support: Seed money, building funds, land acquisition, program-related investments, employee matching gifts, special projects, capital campaigns, matching funds, renovation projects.
Limitations: Giving limited to RI. No support for member agencies of United Way or other united appeals, or religious organizations. No grants to individuals, or for endowment funds, scholarships, fellowships, publications, conferences, or general operating support; no loans.
Publications: Annual report (including application guidelines), financial statement, grants list, program policy statement, informational brochure, application guidelines.
Application information: Out-of-state applications are not considered. Application form not required.
Initial approach: Letter or telephone
Copies of proposal: 1
Deadline(s): 1st day of month when board meets
Board meeting date(s): Bimonthly beginning in Jan.
Final notification: 4 to 6 weeks
Write: Kay H. Low, Coord.
Distribution Committee: Thomas P. Schutte, Chair.; Kay H. Low, Coord.; Thomas P. Dimeo, Winfield W. Major, James V. Rosati, Thomas F. Schutte, Richmond Viall, Jr.
Number of staff: 1 part-time professional.
EIN: 237029175

2881
Providence Journal Charitable Foundation
75 Fountain St.
Providence 02902   (401) 277-7286

Trust established in 1956 in RI.
Donor(s): Providence Journal Co.
Foundation type: Company-sponsored

Financial data (yr. ended 12/31/91): Assets, $2,778,898 (M); expenditures, $647,916; qualifying distributions, $619,849, including $619,849 for 74 grants (high: $191,000; low: $1,000).
Purpose and activities: Emphasis on higher education and a community fund; support also for youth agencies, cultural programs, and hospitals.
Fields of interest: Higher education, community funds, youth, cultural programs, hospitals.
Types of support: Capital campaigns, operating budgets.
Limitations: Giving primarily in RI. No grants to individuals.
Application information:
Initial approach: Letter or proposal
Copies of proposal: 1
Deadline(s): None
Board meeting date(s): Monthly
Write: Harry Dyson, Treas.
Officer and Trustees:* Harry Dyson,* Treas.; Stephen Hamblett, John C.A. Watkins.
EIN: 056015372

2882
The Rhode Island Foundation/The Rhode Island Community Foundation
70 Elm St.
Providence 02903   (401) 274-4564

Incorporated in 1916 in RI (includes The Rhode Island Community Foundation in 1984).
Foundation type: Community
Financial data (yr. ended 12/31/91): Assets, $175,971,555 (M); gifts received, $46,428,462; expenditures, $7,860,781; qualifying distributions, $6,667,397, including $6,667,397 for grants.
Purpose and activities: To promote educational and charitable activities which will tend to improve the living conditions and well-being of the inhabitants of RI; grants for capital and operating purposes principally to agencies working in the fields of education, health care, the arts and cultural affairs, youth, the aged, social services, urban affairs, historic preservation, and the environment. Some restricted grants for scholarships and medical research.
Fields of interest: Education, libraries, arts, social services, child welfare, family services, aged, health, AIDS, environment.
Types of support: Fellowships, operating budgets, seed money, emergency funds, building funds, equipment, land acquisition, matching funds, consulting services, technical assistance, special projects, scholarship funds, research, publications, conferences and seminars, renovation projects, capital campaigns, general purposes.
Limitations: Giving limited to RI. No support for sectarian purposes, or medical research (except as specified by donors). No grants to individuals (except designated funds), or for endowment funds, annual campaigns, or deficit financing; no loans.
Publications: Annual report (including application guidelines), program policy statement, application guidelines, newsletter, informational brochure.
Application information: Priority given to first 25 applications received prior to each board meeting. Application form not required.

Initial approach: Letter
Copies of proposal: 5
Deadline(s): None
Board meeting date(s): Jan., Mar., May, July, Sept., and Nov.
Final notification: 3 to 6 months
Write: Robert D. Rosendale, Treas.
Officers: Douglas M. Jansson, Secy. and Exec. Dir.; Robert D. Rosendale, Treas.
Distribution Committee and Board of Directors: Robert H.I. Goddard, Chair.; Melvin Alperin, Paul J. Choquette, B. Jae Clanton, Ann F. Conner, William H. Heisler, Edward Maggiacomo.
Trustees: Citizens Bank, Fleet National Bank, Old Stone Trust Co., The Rhode Island Hospital Trust National Bank, Van Liew Trust, The Washington Trust Co.
Number of staff: 6 full-time professional; 3 part-time professional; 4 full-time support; 1 part-time support.
EIN: 050208270
Recent health grants:
2882-1 Alliance for Better Nursing Home Care, Providence, RI, $10,000. Toward continuation of Residents' Council program. 1990.
2882-2 Alzheimers Disease and Related Disorders Association, Narragansett Chapter, Narragansett, RI, $30,000. For general support. 1990.
2882-3 American Cancer Society, Rhode Island Division, Providence, RI, $11,030. 1990.
2882-4 Family AIDS Center for Treatment and Support (FACTS), Providence, RI, $25,000. For residential program for children with AIDS. 1990.
2882-5 Health Center of South County, Wakefield, RI, $50,000. Toward capital campaign for new facility. 1990.
2882-6 Kent County Mental Health Center, Warwick, RI, $21,375. Toward community mental health/outreach program for West Warwick at-risk youth. 1990.
2882-7 Mental Health Services of Cranston, Johnston and Northwestern Rhode Island, Johnston, RI, $12,000. For Independent Living Program for frail elderly. 1990.
2882-8 Methodist Health and Welfare Services, East Providence, RI, $10,000. Toward replacement of commercial dishwasher. 1990.
2882-9 Miriam Hospital, Providence, RI, $100,000. For capital campaign. 1990.
2882-10 Northwest Community Nursing and Health Services, Harmony, RI, $14,350. 1990.
2882-11 Planned Parenthood of Rhode Island, Providence, RI, $25,000. For capital campaign to purchase and renovate new headquarters building. 1990.
2882-12 Progreso Latino, Central Falls, RI, $68,773. For prevention program for Spanish-speakers at risk of acquiring or transmitting HIV virus. Grant shared with Memorial Hospital and Brown University. 1990.
2882-13 Rhode Island Foundation of Dentistry for the Handicapped, Providence, RI, $12,500. For program of free dentistry for homebound and institutionalized. 1990.
2882-14 Rhode Island Health Center Association, Providence, RI, $10,125. For development of recruitment and retention plan for primary care personnel in state's community health centers. 1990.

2882-15 Rhode Island Hospital, Providence, RI, $56,358. 1990.
2882-16 Rhode Island Hospital, Child Development Center, Providence, RI, $17,000. Toward language development outreach program for Down Syndrome children. Grant shared with Down Syndrome Society. 1990.
2882-17 Rhode Island Lung Association, Providence, RI, $19,150. To purchase computer equipment and for staff training. 1990.
2882-18 Rhode Island Project AIDS, Providence, RI, $20,000. To develop and staff volunteer program. 1990.
2882-19 Rhode Island Rape Crisis Center, Providence, RI, $31,250. For operating support for development effort. 1990.
2882-20 ROAD Counseling Program, Woonsocket, RI, $14,200. To purchase computer equipment and services toward implementation of client database system. 1990.
2882-21 Robert J. Wilson House, Providence, RI, $10,000. Toward purchase of new van. 1990.
2882-22 Roger Williams General Hospital, Providence, RI, $17,700. 1990.
2882-23 Saint Francis Home, Woonsocket, RI, $15,000. Toward purchase and installation of nurses' call boxes. 1990.
2882-24 Saint Joseph Hospital, North Providence, RI, $14,000. For mental health services for Southeast Asian youth. 1990.
2882-25 Samaritans, Providence, RI, $10,000. Toward second year of Volunteer Recruitment Project. 1990.
2882-26 Self-Help, Riverside, RI, $20,000. To begin daycare for three-and four-year-old Head Start children in Warren. 1990.
2882-27 Socio-Economic Development Corporation (SEDC), Providence, RI, $23,700. For hiring consultants to help with re-organization of Corporation, which provides mental health and drug/alcohol abuse counseling on sliding fee scale for state's Southeast Asian community. 1990.
2882-28 Tri-Hab House, Woonsocket, RI, $13,750. Toward purchase of van for agency's residence for recovering alcoholics. 1990.
2882-29 Visiting Nurse Association, Providence, RI, $41,800. 1990.
2882-30 Warwick Community Action, Warwick, RI, $50,000. For Senior Wellness Program. 1990.
2882-31 Westerly Hospital, Westerly, RI, $30,000. For renovations to emergency room and out-patient facilities. 1990.

2883
Rhode Island Hospital Trust Corporate Giving Program
One Hospital Trust Plaza
Providence 02903   (401) 278-7683

Financial data (yr. ended 12/31/90): Total giving, $410,000 for grants.
Purpose and activities: Support for United Way, education, social services, employment, and training, higher education, health and human services, culture and the arts, civic and community affairs, social services, memberships, benefits, and program ads; also provides in-kind

donations of personnel time, products, and facilities.
Fields of interest: Community funds, education, employment, vocational education, higher education, health, social services, cultural programs, arts, civic affairs, community development, social services.
Types of support: In-kind gifts, employee volunteer services.
Limitations: Giving limited to RI. No support for churches, parishes, or political parties. No grants to individuals.
Application information:
  Initial approach: Letter
  Write: Susan Baxter, V.P. and Dir., Commun. and Govt. Affairs

2884
Fred M. Roddy Foundation, Inc.
c/o The R.I. Hospital Trust National Bank
One Hospital Trust Plaza
Providence 02903   (401) 278-8700

Trust established in 1969.
Donor(s): Fred M. Roddy.‡
Foundation type: Independent
Financial data (yr. ended 12/31/90): Assets, $8,555,176 (M); expenditures, $590,892; qualifying distributions, $498,483, including $489,542 for 33 grants (high: $50,000; low: $2,500; average: $5,000-$15,000).
Purpose and activities: Grants for higher education and medical research; support also for hospitals.

Fields of interest: Higher education, medical research, hospitals.
Limitations: Giving primarily in RI and MA.
Application information: Application form required.
  Initial approach: Letter
  Copies of proposal: 1
  Deadline(s): None
  Write: Shawn P. Buckless, Trustee
Trustees: Shawn P. Buckless, Lee Kintzel, John W. McIntyre.
Number of staff: None.
EIN: 056037528

2885
The Textron Charitable Trust ▼
P.O. Box 878
Providence 02901   (401) 457-2430
Scholarship application addresses: Jeffrey Little, National Merit Scholarship Corp., 1560 Sherman Ave., Suite 200, Evanston, IL 60201; Elaine Jacob, College Scholarship Service, P.O. Box CN6730, Princeton, NJ 08541

Trust established in 1953 in VT.
Donor(s): Textron, Inc.
Foundation type: Company-sponsored
Financial data (yr. ended 12/31/90): Assets, $12,715,514 (M); expenditures, $2,634,819; qualifying distributions, $2,590,891, including $1,864,393 for 376 grants (high: $123,750; low: $250; average: $500-$50,000) and $726,498 for 833 employee matching gifts.

Purpose and activities: Giving primarily for community funds, higher education, including scholarship programs, and hospitals and health agencies; support also for youth clubs, urban programs, minorities, and cultural programs.
Fields of interest: Community funds, higher education, hospitals, youth, urban affairs, minorities, health services, cultural programs.
Types of support: Building funds, equipment, matching funds, employee matching gifts, technical assistance, employee-related scholarships, capital campaigns, general purposes, special projects.
Limitations: Giving primarily in areas of company operations nationwide. No grants to individuals, or for endowment funds, land acquisition, deficit financing, or demonstration projects; no loans.
Publications: Application guidelines.
Application information: Application form not required.
  Initial approach: Proposal
  Copies of proposal: 1
  Deadline(s): None
  Board meeting date(s): Quarterly
  Final notification: 8 weeks
  Write: Elizabeth W. Monahan, Contribs. Coord.
Contributions Committee: Raymond W. Caine, Jr., Chair.
Trustee: The Rhode Island Hospital Trust National Bank.
Number of staff: 1 full-time professional.
EIN: 256115832

SOUTH CAROLINA

2886
Belk-Simpson Foundation
P.O. Box 528
Greenville 29602   (803) 235-3148

Trust established in 1944 in SC.
Donor(s): Belk-Simpson Co.
Foundation type: Company-sponsored
Financial data (yr. ended 12/31/90): Assets,
$4,475,627 (M); gifts received, $37,566;
expenditures, $223,249; qualifying distributions,
$216,125, including $212,125 for 85 grants
(high: $15,000; low: $25).
Fields of interest: Protestant giving, social
services, youth, hospitals, cultural programs.
Limitations: Giving primarily in SC. No grants to
individuals.
Application information:
  Initial approach: Letter
  Copies of proposal: 1
  Board meeting date(s): May 1 and Nov. 1
  Write: Willou Bichel, Trustee
Trustee: Willou R. Bichel.
Board of Advisors: Claire Efird, Lucy S. Kuhne,
Nell M. Rice, Kate M. Simpson.
EIN: 576020261

2887
W. W. Burgiss Charities, Inc.
c/o South Carolina National Bank
101 Greystone Blvd., Unit 9344
Columbia 29226
Application address: P.O. Box 969, Greenville,
SC 29602

Incorporated in 1952 in SC.
Donor(s): W.W. Burgiss.
Foundation type: Independent
Financial data (yr. ended 12/31/90): Assets,
$2,605,570 (M); expenditures, $194,181;
qualifying distributions, $54,145, including
$41,667 for 2 grants (high: $25,000; low:
$16,667).
Fields of interest: Youth, social services, health,
hospitals, education, higher education, science
and technology.
Limitations: Giving primarily in SC, with
emphasis on Greenville. No grants to individuals.
Application information: Application form not
required.
  Initial approach: Letter
  Deadline(s): None
Officers and Directors:* Arthur C. McCall,*
Chair.; P.J. Potter,* Vice-Chair.
Trustees: T.C. Cleveland, Jr., South Carolina
National Bank.
EIN: 576020262

2888
Central Carolina Community Foundation
P.O. Box 11222
Columbia 29211   (803) 254-5601

Incorporated in 1984 in SC.
Foundation type: Community

Financial data (yr. ended 06/30/91): Assets,
$5,630,232 (M); gifts received, $1,797,923;
expenditures, $367,609; qualifying distributions,
$235,478, including $235,478 for 52 grants
(high: $25,000; low: $25; average:
$3,000-$5,000).
Purpose and activities: Giving primarily for the
arts, early childhood education, drug abuse
programs, the homeless, health services, and
youth; support also for community development,
literacy programs, AIDS research, nutrition, and
the disadvantaged, including delinquency and
child welfare, child development and family
services, family planning, and recreation.
Fields of interest: Arts, education—early
childhood, homeless, drug abuse, health services,
youth.
Types of support: Equipment, seed money, special
projects, loans, program-related investments,
scholarship funds, conferences and seminars.
Limitations: Giving limited to Calhoun,
Clarendon, Fairfield, Kershaw, Lee, Lexington,
Newberry, Orangeburg, Richland, Saluda and
Sumter counties, SC. No grants to individuals
(except for designated awards or prizes), or for
endowments, debt reduction, fundraising
projects, medical research, publications, annual
appeals, or routine operating expenses.
Publications: Annual report, application
guidelines, newsletter, grants list.
Application information: Application form
required.
  Initial approach: Letter or telephone
  Copies of proposal: 9
  Deadline(s): Feb.
  Board meeting date(s): Quarterly
  Final notification: June
  Write: Mary Choate, Prog. Off.
Officers and Directors:* Arthur M. Bjontegard,
Jr.,* Pres.; Evan W. Nord,* V.P.; Jacqueline Miller,*
Secy.-Treas.; J. Mac Bennett, Exec. Dir.; J. Richard
Allison, Jr., Joe M. Anderson, Jr., Gayle O. Averyt,
Clinch H. Belser, Jr., J. Key Powell, and 26
additional directors.
Number of staff: 1 full-time professional; 2
part-time professional; 2 part-time support.
EIN: 570793960

2889
Close Foundation, Inc.
104 East Springs St.
Lancaster 29721   (803) 286-2196
Mailing address: P.O. Drawer 460, Lancaster,
SC 29721

Incorporated in 1968 in SC as Frances Ley Springs
Foundation, Inc.; renamed Close Foundation in
1985.
Donor(s): Members of the Springs and Close
families.
Foundation type: Independent
Financial data (yr. ended 12/31/91): Assets,
$9,019,308 (M); gifts received, $10,350;
expenditures, $750,435; qualifying distributions,
$619,540, including $619,540 for 39 grants
(high: $144,950; low: $1,000; average:
$1,000-$144,950).
Purpose and activities: Giving primarily for
higher education, including student loans and
health services; support also for recreation and
community services.

Fields of interest: Higher education, education,
recreation, health services, social services, arts.
Types of support: General purposes, annual
campaigns, seed money, building funds, land
acquisition, renovation projects, endowment
funds, conferences and seminars, professorships,
matching funds, student loans.
Limitations: Giving primarily in Lancaster County,
Chester Township of Chester County, and Fort
Mill Township, SC, and NC.
Publications: Annual report.
Application information: Application form
required for student loans.
  Initial approach: Proposal
  Copies of proposal: 1
  Board meeting date(s): Apr. and Dec.
  Final notification: 3 months
  Write: Charles A. Bundy, Pres.
Officers and Directors:* Anne Springs Close,*
Chair.; Charles A. Bundy,* Pres.; Crandall Close
Bowles,* V.P. and Treas.; James Bradley, Derick S.
Close, Elliott Springs Close, H.W. Close, Jr.,
Katherine Anne Close, Leroy Springs Close, Pat
Close, Frances Close Hart, R.C. Hubbard.
Number of staff: 2 shared staff
EIN: 237013986
Recent health grants:
2889-1 Amethyst Foundation, Charlotte, NC,
  $25,000. 1990.
2889-2 South Carolina Hospital Research and
  Education Foundation, West Columbia, SC,
  $13,000. 1990.

2890
Colonial Life and Accident Insurance Company Contributions Program
1200 Colonial Life Blvd. West
Columbia 29210   (803) 798-7000
Application address: P.O. Box 1365, Columbia,
SC 29202

Financial data (yr. ended 12/31/90): Total giving,
$468,791.
Purpose and activities: Support for a wide variety
of programs: business, higher education,
including minority, elementary, vocational, legal,
medical, and secondary education, literacy,
educational research, humanities, arts and
culture, housing, crime and law enforcement,
human rights, freedom, volunteerism, recreation,
hospitals and health associations, family services,
child welfare, hunger, the aged, urban
development, and conservation and ecology.
Fields of interest: Arts, business education, adult
education, aged, AIDS, alcoholism, animal
welfare, cancer, child welfare, citizenship, civic
affairs, crime and law enforcement, cultural
programs, conservation, drug abuse, ecology,
disadvantaged, education—building funds,
education—early childhood,
education—minorities, educational associations,
educational research, elementary education,
family planning, family services, fine arts,
freedom, handicapped, heart disease, health,
hospitals, historic preservation, humanities,
hunger, housing, human rights, insurance
education, libraries, mental health, nursing.
Types of support: Annual campaigns, conferences
and seminars, employee matching gifts, operating
budgets, building funds, employee volunteer
services, loaned talent, use of facilities, capital
campaigns, continuing support, fellowships,

internships, emergency funds, endowment funds, general purposes, land acquisition, scholarship funds.
Limitations: Giving limited to cities and counties in SC, with emphasis on headquarters area.
Application information: Contributions handled by office of Vice-Chair.
  Initial approach: Send requests to headquarters
  Write: Stephen G. Hall, Pres. and C.O.O.
Number of staff: 1 full-time professional; 1 full-time support.

2891
C. G. Fuller Foundation
c/o NationsBank
P.O. Box 2307
Columbia 29202-2307   (803) 758-2317

Established in 1972 in SC.
Donor(s): Cornell G. Fuller.‡
Foundation type: Independent
Financial data (yr. ended 12/31/90): Assets, $2,562,276 (M); expenditures, $177,968; qualifying distributions, $167,154, including $160,450 for grants.
Purpose and activities: Scholarships only for residents of SC attending colleges or universities in the state; some support also for children's welfare organizations, medical research, and religious organizations.
Fields of interest: Higher education, child welfare, medical research, religion.
Types of support: Annual campaigns, seed money, building funds, equipment, student aid.
Limitations: Giving limited to SC. No grants for endowment funds or matching gifts; no loans.
Publications: 990-PF.
Application information: Application form required.
  Initial approach: Letter
  Deadline(s): Feb. 15 for scholarships
  Board meeting date(s): Quarterly
  Final notification: 6 to 9 months
  Write: R. Westmoreland Clarkson
Trustees: Victor B. John, Clinton Lemon, NationsBank.
Number of staff: None.
EIN: 576050492

2892
The Fullerton Foundation, Inc. ▼
515 West Buford St.
Gaffney 29340   (803) 489-6678
Application address: P.O. Box 1146, Gaffney, SC 29342

Established in 1954 in NY.
Donor(s): Alma H. Fullerton.‡
Foundation type: Independent
Financial data (yr. ended 11/30/91): Assets, $29,139,353 (M); expenditures, $1,557,194; qualifying distributions, $1,347,819, including $1,301,097 for 26 grants (high: $150,000; low: $2,000; average: $20,000-$100,000).
Purpose and activities: Giving for hospitals, health care, and medical research; some support for higher education.
Fields of interest: Hospitals, health, higher education.
Types of support: Equipment, scholarship funds, special projects, matching funds, seed money.

Limitations: Giving primarily in NC and SC. No grants to individuals.
Application information:
  Initial approach: Letter
  Deadline(s): Apr. 1 and Aug. 1
  Board meeting date(s): Twice yearly
  Final notification: No set time
  Write: Walter E. Cavell, Exec. Dir.
Officers and Directors:* John M. Hamrick,* Chair.; Wylie L. Hamrick,* Vice-Chair. and Treas.; Volina Cline Valentine,* Secy.; Walter E. Cavell, Exec. Dir.; Catherine Hamrick Beattie, Charles F. Hamrick.
Number of staff: 1 part-time professional; 1 part-time support.
EIN: 570847444

2893
Gregg-Graniteville Foundation, Inc.
P.O. Box 418
Graniteville 29829   (803) 663-7552

Incorporated in 1949 in SC.
Foundation type: Independent
Financial data (yr. ended 12/31/91): Assets, $14,722,374 (M); expenditures, $818,129; qualifying distributions, $682,879, including $202,325 for 35 grants (high: $50,000; low: $375; average: $5,000), $86,416 for 45 grants to individuals (high: $2,500; low: $600) and $342,682 for 1 foundation-administered program.
Purpose and activities: Emphasis on education, recreation, religion, health, youth agencies, community funds, community development, and cultural programs; scholarships only for children of Graniteville Co. employees and residents of Graniteville, Vaucluse, and Warrenville, SC.
Fields of interest: Education, recreation, religion, health, youth, community funds, community development, cultural programs.
Types of support: Continuing support, emergency funds, building funds, endowment funds, matching funds, employee-related scholarships, research, special projects, capital campaigns, equipment, renovation projects.
Limitations: Giving primarily in Aiken County, SC, and Richmond County, GA. No grants to individuals (except for scholarships for children of company employees and residents of specified areas), or for operating budgets, deficit financing, land acquisition, publications, or conferences; no loans.
Publications: Annual report.
Application information: Application form required.
  Initial approach: Letter
  Copies of proposal: 1
  Deadline(s): None
  Board meeting date(s): Bimonthly or as required
  Final notification: 1 month
  Write: Joan F. Phibbs, Secy.
Officers and Directors:* Robert P. Timmerman,* Pres.; John W. Cunningham,* V.P.; Jerry R. Johnson,* V.P.; Joan F. Phibbs, Secy.-Treas.; Robert M. Bell, Carl W. Littlejohn, Jr., William C. Lott, Charles H. Marvin III, James A. Randall, J.Paul Reeves.
Number of staff: 1 full-time professional.
EIN: 570314400
Recent health grants:
2893-1 Greenwood Methodist Home, Greenwood, SC, $12,500. 1990.

2893-2 Hitchcock Rehabilitation Center, Aiken, SC, $20,000. 1990.
2893-3 Saint Joseph Foundation, Augusta, GA, $12,000. 1990.

2894
Inman-Riverdale Foundation
Inman Mills
Inman 29349   (803) 472-2121

Incorporated in 1946 in SC.
Donor(s): Inman Mills.
Foundation type: Company-sponsored
Financial data (yr. ended 11/30/91): Assets, $4,390,607 (M); gifts received, $50,000; expenditures, $502,246; qualifying distributions, $534,244, including $143,950 for 48 grants and $196,508 for grants to individuals.
Purpose and activities: Grants for higher education, including an employee-related scholarship fund, Protestant church support, youth agencies, community funds, recreation, and health activities.
Fields of interest: Higher education, Protestant giving, youth, community funds, recreation, health.
Types of support: Employee-related scholarships.
Limitations: Giving primarily in Inman and Enoree, SC.
Application information: Contributes only to pre-selected organizations. Applications not accepted.
  Write: W. Marshall Chapman, Chair.
Officers and Trustees:* W. Marshall Chapman,* Chair.; Robert H. Chapman, Jr.,* Vice-Chair.; Patricia H. Bird, Secy.; John F. Renfro, Jr.,* Treas.; Robert H. Chapman III, James C. Pace, Jr.
EIN: 576019736

2895
Everett N. McDonnell Foundation
c/o Wallace Evans, Managing Agent
16 Starboard Tack
Salem 29676

Incorporated in 1946 in IL.
Donor(s): Everett N. McDonnell.‡
Foundation type: Independent
Financial data (yr. ended 10/31/91): Assets, $3,173,886 (M); expenditures, $99,428; qualifying distributions, $88,330, including $83,320 for 62 grants (high: $30,000; low: $100).
Fields of interest: Hospitals, health associations, religion, cultural programs, general charitable giving.
Types of support: Endowment funds.
Limitations: Giving primarily in IL and GA.
Application information: Applications not accepted.
Officers and Directors:* Florence L. McDonnell,* Pres. and Treas.; Gwyneth O. Moran,* V.P.; John D. Marshall,* Secy.
EIN: 366109359

2896
Alfred Moore Foundation
c/o C.L. Page Enterprises, Inc.
P.O. Box 18426
Spartanburg 29318   (803) 583-3635

Incorporated in 1949 in SC.
Donor(s): Jackson Mills.
Foundation type: Company-sponsored
Financial data (yr. ended 12/31/90): Assets, $2,099,562 (M); expenditures, $134,797; qualifying distributions, $115,063, including $67,000 for 31 grants (high: $8,000; low: $200) and $48,063 for 21 grants to individuals (high: $7,500; low: $1,250).
Purpose and activities: Emphasis on higher education, including scholarships limited to high school students in the Spartanburg and Iva, SC, areas; support also for youth, health, and social services.
Fields of interest: Higher education, youth, social services, health.
Types of support: Student aid, general purposes.
Limitations: Giving limited to Anderson and Spartanburg counties, SC.
Application information:
   Initial approach: Letter
   Deadline(s): Scholarships, Mar. 29; loans, varies
   Write: Cary L. Page, Jr., Chair.
Officers and Directors:* Cary L. Page, Jr.,* Chair.; Bernelle Demo,* Vice-Chair.; John M. Hendrix.
EIN: 576018424

2897
Piedmont Health City Foundation, Inc.
P.O. Box 2585
Greenville 29602   (803) 242-5133

Established in 1985 in SC.
Foundation type: Independent
Financial data (yr. ended 12/31/90): Assets, $2,299,724 (M); expenditures, $187,705; qualifying distributions, $187,705, including $133,483 for 9 grants (high: $30,600; low: $4,000).
Purpose and activities: "To promote health education, provide effective and economical means of providing health care through health maintenance concepts, and to promote social, clinical, and medical research concerning health needs and the effectiveness of the care."
Fields of interest: Health, hospitals, cultural programs.
Limitations: Giving limited to the Piedmont and Greenville, SC, areas.
Application information: Application form required.
   Initial approach: Letter
   Copies of proposal: 7
   Deadline(s): Aug. 15
   Board meeting date(s): Mar., June, Sept., and Dec.
   Write: Schaefer Kendrick, Dean
Officers and Directors:* Leonard R. Byrne,* Chair.; Grady E. Wyatt, Jr.,* Vice-Chair.; N. David Evans,* Secy.; Robert E. Hamby, Jr.,* Treas.; and 10 additional directors.
Number of staff: 1
EIN: 570782523

2898
Sargent Foundation
P.O. Box 3706 Park Place
Greenville 29608   (803) 233-2769

Established in 1954.
Donor(s): Earle W. Sargent,‡ Eleanor G. Sargent.‡

Foundation type: Independent
Financial data (yr. ended 04/30/91): Assets, $2,073,590 (M); expenditures, $77,561; qualifying distributions, $59,263, including $59,263 for 14 grants (high: $12,500; low: $500).
Fields of interest: Community funds, hospitals, child welfare, literacy, performing arts.
Limitations: Giving primarily in SC. No grants to individuals.
Application information: Application form not required.
   Initial approach: Proposal
   Copies of proposal: 1
   Deadline(s): Apr. 1
   Board meeting date(s): Mid-Apr. and as required
   Final notification: Apr. 30
   Write: Ruth Nicholson, Pres.
Officers and Trustees:* Ruth Nicholson,* Pres. and Secy.; Robert A. Wilson,* V.P.; Margaret Lewis, Treas.; John R. McAdams,* Treas.
Number of staff: None.
EIN: 576019317

2899
The Self Foundation
P.O. Drawer 1017
Greenwood 29648   (803) 941-4063

Incorporated in 1942 in SC.
Donor(s): James C. Self.‡
Foundation type: Independent
Financial data (yr. ended 12/31/91): Assets, $29,323,216 (M); expenditures, $1,518,940; qualifying distributions, $1,313,636, including $1,219,180 for 32 grants (high: $250,000; low: $1,300; average: $20,000).
Purpose and activities: Primary interest in health and higher educational support also for civic and community service, activities for youth and the elderly, and cultural and historical activities; grants mainly for capital or special purposes.
Fields of interest: Health services, higher education, education, cultural programs, youth, aged.
Types of support: Seed money, emergency funds, building funds, equipment, matching funds, technical assistance, special projects, renovation projects.
Limitations: Giving limited to SC, with primary emphasis on Greenwood. No grants to individuals, or for endowment funds, land acquisition, operating budgets, continuing support, annual campaigns, deficit financing, publications, conferences, scholarships, fellowships, or research-related programs; no loans.
Publications: Annual report (including application guidelines).
Application information: Application form not required.
   Initial approach: Proposal
   Copies of proposal: 1
   Deadline(s): Submit proposal preferably in the 2 months prior to board meetings; deadlines, 1st day of month in which board meets
   Board meeting date(s): 3rd week in Mar., June, Sept., and Dec.
   Final notification: 10 days after board meeting
   Write: Frank J. Wideman, Jr., Exec. V.P.
Officers and Trustees:* James C. Self,* Pres.; Frank J. Wideman, Jr., Exec. V.P.; James C. Self, Jr.,* V.P.; W.M. Self,* Secy.; William B. Allin,

Treas.; Joe M. Anderson, Virginia S. Brennan, Carroll H. Brooks, Lynn W. Hodge, Sally E. Self, M.D., Paul E. Welder.
Number of staff: 1 full-time professional.
EIN: 570400594
Recent health grants:
2899-1 Greenwood Genetics Center, Greenwood, SC, $200,000. For architectural and engineering drawings and related documents to go with grant requests to establish Research Institute. 1991.
2899-2 S.O.S. Health Care, Myrtle Beach, SC, $10,000. Toward health care for poor and uninsured. 1991.
2899-3 South Carolina Organ Procurement Agency, Charleston, SC, $10,000. To help with creative and conceptive development phase of awareness program. 1991.

2900
The Simpson Foundation
P.O. Box 528
Greenville 29602   (803) 235-3148

Trust established in 1956 in SC.
Donor(s): W.H.B. Simpson,‡ Mrs. W.H.B. Simpson.
Foundation type: Independent
Financial data (yr. ended 12/31/90): Assets, $2,801,457 (M); expenditures, $114,617; qualifying distributions, $107,450, including $104,350 for 29 grants (high: $15,000; low: $500).
Fields of interest: Protestant giving, religion—missionary programs, health services, medical sciences.
Limitations: Giving primarily in SC. No support for educational purposes. No grants to individuals, or for scholarships; no loans.
Application information: Application form not required.
   Initial approach: Letter
   Deadline(s): Before board meetings
   Board meeting date(s): Nov. 1 and May 1
   Write: Mrs. Willou Bichel
Directors: Frances Dudley, Claire Efird, Wilma Johnson, Nell M. Rice.
Trustee: Willou R. Bichel.
EIN: 576017451

2901
John I. Smith Charities, Inc.
c/o NationsBank, Trust Dept.
P.O. Box 608
Greenville 29602   (803) 271-5934

Established in 1985 in SC.
Donor(s): John I. Smith.‡
Foundation type: Independent
Financial data (yr. ended 07/31/90): Assets, $16,511,799 (M); gifts received, $415,869; expenditures, $1,033,158; qualifying distributions, $956,398, including $942,992 for 25 grants (high: $250,000; low: $42).
Purpose and activities: Support for higher and other education, including medical and theological education, and literacy programs; museums and other fine and performing arts groups; religious associations; and community funds, child welfare, and programs for the handicapped.

Fields of interest: Education, higher education, medical education, literacy, religion, child welfare, handicapped, arts, community funds, general charitable giving.
Types of support: Capital campaigns, emergency funds, endowment funds, general purposes, scholarship funds.
Limitations: Giving primarily in SC.
Application information: Application form not required.
   Initial approach: Letter
   Board meeting date(s): Quarterly
   Write: Wilbur Y. Bridgers, Pres.
Officers: Wilbur Y. Bridgers, Pres. and Secy.; W. Thomas Smith, V.P. and Treas.
Director: Jefferson V. Smith III.
Agent: NationsBank.
Number of staff: None.
EIN: 570806327

2902
The Spartanburg County Foundation
320 East Main St.
Spartanburg 29302-1943   (803) 582-0138

Incorporated in 1943 in SC.
Foundation type: Community
Financial data (yr. ended 12/31/91): Assets, $18,520,454 (M); gifts received, $843,925; expenditures, $1,086,068; qualifying distributions, $828,556, including $828,556 for 152 grants (high: $50,000; low: $300; average: $5,000-$10,000).
Purpose and activities: To provide "for the mental, moral, intellectual and physical improvement, assistance and relief of the inhabitants of Spartanburg County." Support for local projects in education, arts, humanities, recreation, health, and welfare.
Fields of interest: Education, higher education, adult education, child welfare, recreation, welfare, health, humanities, arts, cultural programs.
Types of support: Continuing support, seed money, emergency funds, building funds, equipment, matching funds, conferences and seminars, consulting services, scholarship funds, renovation projects, lectureships.
Limitations: Giving limited to Spartanburg County, SC. No grants to individuals, or for operating budgets, annual campaigns, deficit financing, land acquisition, or endowment funds; no loans.
Publications: Annual report (including application guidelines), informational brochure.
Application information: Application form not required.
   Initial approach: Telephone
   Copies of proposal: 1
   Deadline(s): Submit proposal preferably in 1st 6 months of year, and at least 40 days before board meetings. Grants are considered in Mar., June, Sept., and Dec.
   Board meeting date(s): Monthly
   Final notification: 1 month following board meeting
   Write: James S. Barrett, Exec. Dir.
Officers and Trustees:* John E. Keith,* Chair.; Elaine Freeman,* Vice-Chair.; Joab M. Lesesne, Jr.,* Secy.; Kurt Zimmerli,* Treas.; James S. Barrett, Exec. Dir.; Richard H. Pennell, Robert V. Pinson, Ben Willard.

Number of staff: 1 full-time professional; 1 full-time support; 1 part-time support.
EIN: 570351398
Recent health grants:
2902-1 Carolina Pregnancy Center, Spartanburg, SC, $10,000. For challenge grant. 1990.
2902-2 Charles Lea Center for Rehabilitation and Special Education, Spartanburg, SC, $30,000. For matching grant for computer equipment. 1990.
2902-3 Mental Health Association of Spartanburg County, Spartanburg, SC, $18,000. For Caring Line program. 1990.

2903
Spring Industries Corporate Giving Program
Executive Office Bldg.
P.O. Box 70
Fort Mill 29715   (803) 547-2901

Financial data (yr. ended 12/31/90): Total giving, $1,006,653, including $946,464 for 454 grants (high: $10,000; low: $500; average: $500-$1,000) and $60,189 for 211 employee matching gifts.
Purpose and activities: Supports community and civic service programs, federated campaigns, culture and arts, health, hospitals, education and youth service. Provides company in-house services and donations of the company's primary goods or services; dominant focus on operating communities.
Fields of interest: Community development, civic affairs, cultural programs, arts, health, hospitals, education, youth.
Types of support: Donated products, in-kind gifts, use of facilities.
Limitations: Giving primarily in areas of company operations.
Application information: Corporate Communications office handles giving.
   Write: Robert L. Thompson Jr., V.P., Public Affairs

2904
Springs Foundation, Inc. ▼
104 East Springs St.
Lancaster 29721   (803) 286-2196
Mailing address: P.O. Drawer 460, Lancaster, SC 29721

Incorporated in 1942 in DE.
Donor(s): Elliott W. Springs,‡ Anne Springs Close, Frances Ley Springs.‡
Foundation type: Independent
Financial data (yr. ended 12/31/91): Assets, $20,326,869 (M); gifts received, $400; expenditures, $2,085,036; qualifying distributions, $1,885,065, including $1,625,699 for 40 grants (high: $1,130,050; low: $500; average: $5,000-$50,000) and $259,366 for 142 loans to individuals.
Purpose and activities: Support largely for hospitals, recreation, and education, including public schools and student loans; support also for community services, churches, and medical scholarships.
Fields of interest: Recreation, education, elementary education, medical education, hospitals, social services.

Types of support: Building funds, equipment, endowment funds, publications, professorships, matching funds, general purposes, special projects, student aid, student loans, operating budgets.
Limitations: Giving limited to Lancaster County and/or the townships of Fort Mill and Chester, SC. No grants to individuals (except through the Springs Medical Scholarship Program).
Publications: Annual report (including application guidelines).
Application information: Application form required for student loans. Application form not required.
   Initial approach: Telephone or brief letter
   Copies of proposal: 1
   Deadline(s): None
   Board meeting date(s): Apr. and Dec.
   Final notification: 3 months
   Write: Charles A. Bundy, Pres.
Officers and Directors:* Anne Springs Close,* Chair.; Charles A. Bundy,* Pres.; Crandall Close Bowles,* V.P. and Treas.; James Bradley, Derick S. Close, Elliott Springs Close, H.W. Close, Jr., Katherine Anne Close, Leroy Springs Close, Pat Close, Frances Close Hart, R.C. Hubbard.
Number of staff: 2 shared staff
EIN: 570426344
Recent health grants:
2904-1 Chester County Hospital, Chester, SC, $50,000. For physicians' office building. 1990.
2904-2 Chester County Hospital, Chester, SC, $25,000. For physicians' salary guarantees. 1990.
2904-3 Lancaster County Healthy Mothers/Healthy Babies Coalition, Lancaster, SC, $150,000. 1990.

2905
John T. Stevens Foundation
P.O. Box 158
Kershaw 29067

Established in 1948 in SC.
Donor(s): John T. Stevens.‡
Foundation type: Independent
Financial data (yr. ended 05/31/91): Assets, $3,953,259 (M); expenditures, $242,431; qualifying distributions, $214,398, including $199,398 for grants.
Fields of interest: Protestant giving, religion—Christian, medical education, secondary education, youth.
Limitations: Giving primarily in Kershaw and Lancaster County, SC.
Officers: Steve G. Williams, Sr., Pres.; Douglas H. Williams, V.P.
EIN: 576005554

2906
F. W. Symmes Foundation
c/o South Carolina National Bank
1401 Main St., Suite 501
Columbia 29226

Trust established in 1954 in SC.
Donor(s): F.W. Symmes.‡
Foundation type: Independent
Financial data (yr. ended 03/31/91): Assets, $9,058,582 (M); expenditures, $363,127; qualifying distributions, $313,250, including

$313,250 for 14 grants (high: $50,000; low: $2,250; average: $36,000).
Fields of interest: Religion, child welfare, hospitals, youth, music, fine arts, recreation, education, libraries.
Limitations: Giving primarily in the Greenville, SC, area. No grants to individuals.
Publications: Application guidelines, informational brochure.
Application information: Application form not required.
  Initial approach: Letter or telephone
  Copies of proposal: 10
  Deadline(s): 4 weeks before board meetings
  Board meeting date(s): Semiannually
  Final notification: 2 weeks following meeting
Trustees: William H. Orders, Wilson C. Wearn, F. McKinnon Wilkinson, South Carolina National Bank.
Number of staff: None.
EIN: 576017472

2907
Trident Community Foundation
456 King St.
Charleston 29403-6230   (803) 723-3635
Additional tel.: (803) 723-2124; FAX: (803) 577-3671

Incorporated in 1974 in SC.
Foundation type: Community
Financial data (yr. ended 06/30/92): Assets, $6,070,000 (M); gifts received, $1,337,897; expenditures, $1,469,901; qualifying distributions, $1,184,330, including $1,084,050 for 472 grants (high: $280,000; low: $100; average: $100-$280,000), $26,600 for 15 grants to individuals (average: $2,500), $63,680 for 7 foundation-administered programs and $10,000 for 1 loan.
Fields of interest: Arts, humanities, education, environment, social services, housing, health services, AIDS, child development.
Types of support: Emergency funds, program-related investments, publications, renovation projects, scholarship funds, seed money, special projects, technical assistance, student aid, operating budgets.

Limitations: Giving primarily in Berkeley, Charleston, and Dorchester counties, SC. No grants for annual campaigns, endowments, deficit financing, or generally for building funds.
Publications: Annual report (including application guidelines), newsletter.
Application information: Application form required.
  Initial approach: Submit letter of intent by July 15 for general grants cycle
  Copies of proposal: 5
  Board meeting date(s): 2nd Wednesday every month
  Final notification: Within 3 months of each proposal deadline
  Write: Ruth Heffron, Exec. Dir.
Officers and Directors:* J. Conrad Zimmerman, Jr.,* Pres.; Charlton deSaussure, Jr.,* V.P.; June Bradham,* Secy.; Thomas P. Anderson,* Treas.; Ruth H. Heffron,* Exec. Dir.; Richard Hendry, Prog. Dir.; Bernett Mazyck, Dir. of Neighborhood Grants.
Number of staff: 4 full-time professional; 1 full-time support; 1 part-time support.
EIN: 237390313

SOUTH DAKOTA

2908
Sioux Falls Area Foundation
141 North Main Ave., Suite 500
Sioux Falls 57102   (605) 336-7055

Established in 1976 in SD.
Foundation type: Community
Financial data (yr. ended 06/30/91): Assets,
$3,128,242 (M); gifts received, $254,946;
expenditures, $133,702; qualifying distributions,
$90,995, including $85,145 for 46 grants (high:
$20,000; low: $100; average: $500-$2,000) and
$5,850 for 15 grants to individuals (high: $2,500;
low: $200; average: $200-$2,500).
Fields of interest: Community development, arts,
environment, health, education, welfare.
Types of support: Scholarship funds, seed money,
technical assistance, general purposes, renovation
projects, special projects, equipment.
Limitations: Giving limited to the Sioux Falls, SD,
area. No support for sectarian religious purposes,
advocacy projects, or telephone solicitations. No
grants for national fundraising campaigns,
endowment funds, or travel for individuals or
groups.
Publications: Annual report, application
guidelines.
Application information: Application form
required.
  Initial approach: Letter or telephone
  Copies of proposal: 1
  Deadline(s): 2 months prior to quarter in which
    grant is sought
  Board meeting date(s): Quarterly to review
    proposals
  Write: Rosemary S. Draeger, Pres.
Officers: Larry Ritz, Chair.; Karl Wegner,
Vice-Chair.; Rosemary S. Draeger, Pres.; Ron
Staebell, Secy.; Richard Auld, Treas.
Number of staff: 1 part-time professional.
EIN: 466041694

2909
South Dakota Community Foundation
207 East Capitol
P.O. Box 296
Pierre 57501   (605) 224-1025

Incorporated in 1987 in SD.
Foundation type: Community
Financial data (yr. ended 12/31/91): Assets,
$11,499,209 (M); expenditures, $619,904;
qualifying distributions, $450,000, including
$450,000 for 71 grants (high: $37,712; low: $82;
average: $15-$17,000).
Fields of interest: Arts, citizenship,
education—minorities, Native Americans,
disadvantaged, community development,
community funds, health services, health.
Types of support: Matching funds, publications,
endowment funds.
Limitations: Giving limited to SD. No grants to
individuals.
Publications: Annual report (including application
guidelines), newsletter.
Application information: Application form
required.
  Copies of proposal: 7
  Deadline(s): Feb. 1 and Sept. 1
  Board meeting date(s): Apr. and Nov.
  Write: Bernard W. Christenson, Exec. Dir.
Officer: Bernard W. Christenson, Exec. Dir.
Number of staff: 1 full-time professional; 1
full-time support.
EIN: 460398115
Recent health grants:
2909-1 Black Hills Regional Eye Institute
    Foundation, Rapid City, SD, $15,000. Toward
    constructing research/education facility to treat
    diseases of eye. 1991.

TENNESSEE

2910
Dantzler Bond Ansley Foundation
c/o Third National Bank, Trust Dept.
P.O. Box 305110
Nashville 37230-5110   (615) 748-5207

Incorporated in 1980 in TN.
Donor(s): Mildred B. Ansley.‡
Foundation type: Independent
Financial data (yr. ended 04/30/91): Assets,
$6,452,231 (M); expenditures, $290,456;
qualifying distributions, $264,812, including
$246,500 for 51 grants (high: $50,000; low:
$500).
Fields of interest: Health, medical research,
alcoholism, higher education, secondary
education, cultural programs, social services.
Types of support: Annual campaigns, capital
campaigns.
Limitations: Giving primarily in central TN,
including Nashville.
Application information: Application form not
required.
  Copies of proposal: 3
  Deadline(s): May 31
  Write: Kim Williams, Trust Officer, Third
    National Bank
Trustees: Frank Drowota, Thomas F. Frist, Fred
Russell.
EIN: 592111990

2911
Belz Foundation
P.O. Box 171199
Memphis 38187-1199

Incorporated in 1952 in TN.
Donor(s): Philip Belz, Martin Belz, Ron Belz.
Foundation type: Independent
Financial data (yr. ended 12/31/90): Assets,
$4,962,703 (M); gifts received, $301,875;
expenditures, $782,969; qualifying distributions,
$775,368, including $774,992 for 455 grants
(high: $242,300; low: $5).
Purpose and activities: Emphasis on Jewish
welfare funds, temple support, Israel, education,
including higher education and yeshivas, cultural
organizations, and health and welfare
organizations.
Fields of interest: Jewish giving, Jewish welfare,
Israel, religious schools, higher education,
cultural programs, health, social services.
Limitations: Giving primarily in Memphis, TN.
No grants to individuals.
Application information: Contributes only to
pre-selected organizations. Applications not
accepted.
Officers: Jack A. Belz, Mgr.; Martin S. Belz, Mgr.;
Philip Belz, Mgr.; Ronald A. Belz, Mgr.; Jan B.
Groveman, Mgr.; Raymond Shainberg, Mgr.;
Jimmie D. Williams, Mgr.
EIN: 626046715

2912
Benwood Foundation, Inc. ▼
1600 American National Bank Bldg.
736 Market St.
Chattanooga 37402   (615) 267-4311

Incorporated in 1944 in DE, and 1945 in TN.
Donor(s): George Thomas Hunter.‡
Foundation type: Independent
Financial data (yr. ended 12/31/91): Assets,
$70,203,972 (M); expenditures, $6,911,588;
qualifying distributions, $6,611,979, including
$6,439,973 for 116 grants (high: $1,125,000;
low: $200; average: $1,000-$100,000) and
$45,000 for loans.
Purpose and activities: Support for higher and
secondary education, welfare, health agencies
and hospitals, cultural programs, including the
performing arts, beautification, and Christian
organizations.
Fields of interest: Education, higher education,
secondary education, arts, humanities, cultural
programs, performing arts, health, social services,
religion—Christian, environment.
Types of support: Research, seed money,
emergency funds, equipment, land acquisition,
conferences and seminars, professorships,
scholarship funds, matching funds, general
purposes, renovation projects.
Limitations: Giving primarily in the Chattanooga,
TN, area. No grants to individuals, or for building
or operating funds of churches; no loans.
Publications: Application guidelines, financial
statement.
Application information: Application form
required.
  Initial approach: Letter
  Copies of proposal: 6
  Deadline(s): 25th day of each month preceding
    board meetings
  Board meeting date(s): Jan., Mar., May, July,
    Sept., and Nov.
  Final notification: 3 days after board meeting,
    board reserves privilege of delaying decision
    for two months
  Write: Jean R. McDaniel, Exec. Dir.
Officers and Trustees:* Robert J. Sudderth, Jr.,*
Chair.; Walter R. Randolph, Jr.,* Pres.; Sebert
Brewer, Jr.,* V.P.; E.Y. Chapin III,* Secy.-Treas.;
Jean R. McDaniel, Exec. Dir.
Number of staff: 1 full-time professional; 1
full-time support.
EIN: 620476283
Recent health grants:
2912-1 Alton Park/Dodson Avenue Community
  Health Center, Chattanooga, TN, $100,000.
  1990.
2912-2 National Association for the
  Craniofacially Handicapped, Chattanooga,
  TN, $10,000. 1990.
2912-3 Project 714, Chattanooga, TN,
  $100,000. 1990.
2912-4 Scottish Rite Childrens Medical Center,
  Atlanta, GA, $10,000. 1990.
2912-5 Siskin Memorial Foundation,
  Chattanooga, TN, $300,000. 1990.
2912-6 Siskin Memorial Foundation,
  Chattanooga, TN, $25,000. 1990.
2912-7 University of Tennessee, Medical School,
  Memphis, TN, $15,000. 1990.
2912-8 Waldens Ridge Emergency Services,
  Signal Mountain, TN, $15,000. 1990.

2913
Thomas W. Briggs Foundation, Inc.
(Formerly T. W. Briggs Welcome Wagon
Foundation)
2670 Union Ave. Extension, Suite 1122
Memphis 38112-4402   (901) 323-0213

Established in 1957.
Donor(s): Thomas W. Briggs Residuary Trust.
Foundation type: Independent
Financial data (yr. ended 09/30/91): Assets,
$5,612,284 (M); gifts received, $301,320;
expenditures, $319,328; qualifying distributions,
$272,970, including $231,800 for 35 grants
(high: $38,000; low: $300).
Purpose and activities: Emphasis on youth and
education; support also for the arts, health, and
social services.
Fields of interest: Youth, education, arts, social
services, health.
Limitations: Giving primarily in AR, MS, and TN,
with emphasis on the Memphis, TN, area.
Application information:
  Initial approach: Proposal
  Deadline(s): None
Officers and Directors:* William T. Morris,*
Chair.; Harry J. Phillips, Sr.,* Pres.; Eleanor Prest,*
Secy.; S. Herbert Rhea,* Treas.; Margaret Hyde,
Hubert A. McBride, Spence Wilson.
EIN: 626039986

2914
The Brinkley Foundation
c/o National Bank of Commerce, Trust Div.
One Commerce Sq.
Memphis 38103   (901) 523-3270

Trust established in 1968 in TN.
Donor(s): Hugh M. Brinkley.‡
Foundation type: Independent
Financial data (yr. ended 12/31/91): Assets,
$2,220,455 (M); gifts received, $11,710;
expenditures, $129,643; qualifying distributions,
$120,008, including $120,000 for 16 grants
(high: $20,000; low: $2,000; average:
$5,000-$10,000).
Fields of interest: Hospitals, higher education,
arts, music.
Limitations: Giving primarily in the Memphis,
TN, area.
Application information: Application form not
required.
  Initial approach: Letter
  Deadline(s): None
  Write: Yvetie Marion, Trust Officer, National
    Bank of Commerce
Trustee: National Bank of Commerce.
EIN: 626079631

2915
L. P. Brown Foundation
119 Racine St.
P.O. Box 11514
Memphis 38111   (901) 323-0333

Established in 1956.
Donor(s): L.P. Brown III.
Foundation type: Independent
Financial data (yr. ended 05/31/91): Assets,
$2,302,034 (M); expenditures, $84,686;

qualifying distributions, $81,610, including $81,610 for 46 grants (high: $15,000; low: $25).
Purpose and activities: Giving for health associations, hospitals, higher education, and churches; support also for the arts and a community foundation.
Fields of interest: Health associations, hospitals, Protestant giving, higher education, arts, community development.
Limitations: Giving primarily in Memphis, TN.
Application information: Application form not required.
 Deadline(s): None
 Write: L.P. Brown III, Pres.
Officers: L.P. Brown III, Pres.; Bryan Morgan, V.P.; Stella A. Lowery, Secy.
Directors: Hubert A. McBride, Axson Brown Morgan.
EIN: 626036338

2916
The Community Foundation of Greater Chattanooga, Inc.
736 Market St., Suite 1701
Chattanooga 37402   (615) 265-0586

Incorporated in 1963 in TN.
Foundation type: Community
Financial data (yr. ended 12/31/91): Assets, $16,476,246 (M); gifts received, $1,181,657; expenditures, $1,299,600; qualifying distributions, $1,084,706, including $1,084,706 for 133 grants (high: $34,000; low: $100; average: $1,500-$10,000).
Purpose and activities: "To promote and enhance the well-being of the inhabitants of the greater Chattanooga area." Primary areas of interest include education and community development.
Fields of interest: Health, health services, education, higher education, education—minorities, elementary education, education—early childhood, community development, arts, environment.
Types of support: Student aid, seed money, building funds, conferences and seminars, matching funds, renovation projects, scholarship funds, capital campaigns, special projects, equipment, emergency funds.
Limitations: Giving limited to the greater Chattanooga, TN, area. No support for private schools or religious causes. No loans.
Publications: Annual report, program policy statement, application guidelines.
Application information: Application form required.
 Initial approach: Brief letter, visit, or application form
 Copies of proposal: 10
 Deadline(s): Jan. 25, Apr. 25, July 25, and Oct. 25
 Board meeting date(s): Quarterly; Grants Committee meets in Feb., May, Aug., and Nov.
 Final notification: 3 weeks after meeting
 Write: Peter T. Cooper, Exec. Dir.
Officers and Directors:* J. Guy Beatty,* Pres.; Alton Chapman, V.P.; Jane W. Harbaugh,* V.P.; Ruth Holmberg, V.P.; Robert J. Sudderth,* V.P.; Liston Bishop, Secy.; S.L. Probasco, Jr.,* Treas.; Jerry V. Adams, Frank A. Brock, P.K. Brock, Jr., Emmy Casey, Kay K. Chitty, Claudie Clark, Jr., Susan Davenport, R. Allan Edgar, John P. Guerry,

Zan Guerry, Spencer McCallie III, Sharon Mills, Yuji Noma, P. Robert Philip, David P. Phillips, Benjamin R. Probusco, Harold Ruck, Virginia Anne Sharber, Frances Smith, Yvonne Smith, Robert J. Sudderth, Jr., William P. Sudderth.
Number of staff: 2 full-time professional; 1 full-time support.
EIN: 626045999

2917
Christy-Houston Foundation, Inc.
122 North Spring St.
Murfreesboro 37129   (615) 898-1140

Established in 1987 in TN.
Donor(s): Lady Houston Brown Trust.
Foundation type: Independent
Financial data (yr. ended 04/30/91): Assets, $55,947,181 (M); gifts received, $536,630; expenditures, $1,270,119; qualifying distributions, $530,642, including $501,476 for 4 grants (high: $225,000; low: $876).
Fields of interest: Health, health associations, health services, hospices, hospitals, hospitals—building funds, nursing, nutrition, community development.
Types of support: Building funds, equipment, matching funds.
Limitations: Giving limited to Rutherford County, TN. No support for religious or veterans' organizations or historical societies. No grants to individuals.
Publications: Grants list, application guidelines.
Application information: Application form not required.
 Initial approach: Proposal, less than 5 pages
 Copies of proposal: 1
 Deadline(s): None
 Board meeting date(s): Mar., June, Sept., and Dec.
 Final notification: Apr. 1
 Write: James R. Arnhart, Exec. Dir.
Directors: James R. Arnhart, Exec. Dir.; Granville S.R. Bouldin, Henry King Butler, Ed Delbridge, Ed Elam, Clyde Fite, Larry N. Haynes, John S. Holmes, Jr., William H. Huddleston, Louis C. Jennings, Roger C. Maples, Hubert McCullough, Edward E. Miller, Jr., Matt B. Murfree III, Myers B. Parsons.
Number of staff: 1 part-time support.
EIN: 621280998

2918
The Robert H. and Monica M. Cole Foundation
c/o First American Trust Co., Trust Dept.
505 South Gay St.
Knoxville 37902

Established in 1976.
Foundation type: Independent
Financial data (yr. ended 09/30/90): Assets, $3,322,524 (M); gifts received, $1,008,401; expenditures, $185,306; qualifying distributions, $164,216, including $163,190 for 41 grants (high: $60,000; low: $500; average: $1,000-$5,000).
Purpose and activities: Grants for medical research on Parkinson's disease, cultural programs, and civic affairs.

Fields of interest: Medical research, cultural programs, civic affairs.
Types of support: Operating budgets, research.
Limitations: Giving limited to eastern TN, including Knoxville, and southeast KY.
Application information:
 Write: Mark A. Goodson, Trust Officer, First American Trust Co.
Trustees: Monica M. Cole, W.W. Davis, Sr., First American Trust Co.
EIN: 626137973

2919
Joe C. Davis Foundation
28 White Bridge Rd.
Nashville 37205
Application address: 908 Audubon Rd., Nashville, TN 37204; Tel.: (615) 297-1030

Established in 1976 in TN.
Donor(s): Joe C. Davis.‡
Foundation type: Independent
Financial data (yr. ended 09/30/90): Assets, $3,728,910 (M); gifts received, $209,996; expenditures, $312,092; qualifying distributions, $293,133, including $291,703 for 67 grants (high: $50,000; low: $200).
Fields of interest: Education—early childhood, elementary education, health, medical research, cancer, alcoholism, drug abuse, general charitable giving.
Types of support: Matching funds, research, seed money, special projects, student loans.
Limitations: Giving primarily in the Nashville, TN, area.
Application information: Send copy of application to Dr. and Mrs. William R. DeLoache, 72 Round Pond Rd., Greenville, SC 29607. Application form not required.
 Initial approach: Letter
 Copies of proposal: 2
 Deadline(s): Aug. 15
 Board meeting date(s): Sept. 10
 Final notification: Sept. 15
 Write: Mrs. Anne Fergerson
Trustees: Bond Davis DeLoache, William DeLoache, M.D., William R. DeLoache, Jr.
Number of staff: 1 part-time support.
EIN: 626125481

2920
H. W. Durham Foundation
5050 Poplar Ave., Suite 1522
Memphis 38157   (901) 683-3583

Incorporated in 1955 in TN.
Donor(s): H.W. Durham.‡
Foundation type: Independent
Financial data (yr. ended 09/30/91): Assets, $10,201,890 (M); gifts received, $73,616; expenditures, $763,886; qualifying distributions, $673,643, including $535,880 for 31 grants (high: $78,500; low: $200; average: $1,500-$64,101).
Purpose and activities: Giving primarily for the elderly and issues relating to the aging process.
Fields of interest: Aged, mental health, health, adult education, cultural programs, employment, disadvantaged, social services, leadership development, recreation, volunteerism.

Types of support: Program-related investments, scholarship funds, fellowships, publications, seed money, technical assistance, special projects, conferences and seminars, research.
Limitations: Giving primarily in Memphis, TN.
Publications: Application guidelines, informational brochure (including application guidelines).
Application information: Application form required.
  Initial approach: Letter
  Copies of proposal: 5
  Deadline(s): Jan. 1, Apr. 1, and Aug. 1
  Board meeting date(s): Feb., May, and Sept.
  Final notification: Immediately after board meeting
  Write: Jenks McCrory, Prog. Dir.
Officers: Thomas H. Durham, Jr., Pres.; Ralph Lawrence, V.P.; Jo Scott, Secy.; Jerry Allison, Treas.
Directors: Jenks McCrory, Hugh McHenry, Philip Morrison, Linda Nichols, A. Earl Priest.
Number of staff: 2 full-time professional; 2 part-time support.
EIN: 620583854

2921
First Tennessee Bank Corporate Giving Program
165 Madison Ave.
P.O. Box 84
Memphis 38101   (901) 523-4444

Financial data (yr. ended 12/31/90): Total giving, $470,000 for grants.
Purpose and activities: Support for arts and culture, health welfare, civic affairs, community development, economic development, and education.
Fields of interest: Arts, health, welfare, civic affairs, cultural programs, community development, economics, education.
Types of support: In-kind gifts, technical assistance, operating budgets, annual campaigns, seed money, special projects.
Limitations: Giving primarily in headquarters city and major operating locations. No support for charities sponsored by a single civic organization, agencies supported by the United Way, or united arts funds, religious, veteran, social, athletic, or fraternal organizations, or charities which redistribute funds to other charities, except for united fund-type organizations. No grants to individuals, or for deficit financing, endowments, or multi-year commitments of 4 years or more.
Publications: Application guidelines.
Application information: Application form not required.
  Initial approach: Letter of inquiry with description of project
  Copies of proposal: 1
  Deadline(s): Applications accepted throughout the year
  Final notification: 4 weeks
  Write: Susan Apple, Community Investment Rep.
Number of staff: 2 part-time professional.

2922
Genesco Corporate Giving Program
c/o Genesco Park, Suite 498
P.O. Box 731
Nashville 37202-0731   (615) 367-8281

Financial data (yr. ended 01/31/91): Total giving, $145,662 for 57 grants (high: $9,750; low: $80).
Purpose and activities: "In our society, a citizen has certain responsibilities as well as rights and privileges. The same is true for a corporation. GENESCO is committed to being a good corporate citizen. As one aspect of that commitment, the Company makes contributions of corporate funds and encourages participation in civic and charitable activities by its employees. All charitable contributions are to be made with the following goals in mind: 1. To meet the civic, social and community responsibilities of the Company and to set an example for employees and others. 2. To improve the overall quality of life in our various communities. 3. To promote the health and welfare of GENESCO employees and their families. 4. To promote an environment in which GENESCO, its employees, customers and suppliers continue to prosper." The C.E.O., subject to the approval of the Finance Committee, will establish an annual contributions budget, based on consideration given to the level of earnings of the Company, past history, and the size and scope of other company programs. Special consideration will be given to charities or organizations in which GENESCO employees are personally involved in a leadership position. Payments that are not strictly of a contributory nature, such as the cost of tickets to benefits, and program advertisements, shall be considered to be business expenses, not charitable grants, and will be the responsibility of the appropriate GENESCO company or corporate staff department. Nationwide employee grants to United Way totaled $214,038 in 1990.
Fields of interest: Cultural programs, arts, education, alcoholism, drug abuse, business education, education—minorities, employment, foreign policy, health, literacy, community funds.
Types of support: Annual campaigns, capital campaigns, internships, in-kind gifts.
Limitations: Giving primarily in Nashville, TN and Allentown, PA; as a general rule the company considers grants where there are over 50 employees. No support for political parties, campaigns or organizations; religious organizations. No grants to individuals, or for advertising or dinners.
Publications: Corporate giving report (including application guidelines), corporate report.
Application information: Corporate Relations department handles giving. The C.E.O. approves all grants in advance. Application form not required.
  Initial approach: Must be in writing; Send requests to headquarters
  Copies of proposal: 1
  Deadline(s): First of each month
  Board meeting date(s): First week of each month
  Final notification: Will send rejection notice
  Write: Teresa N. Miller, Dir., Pub. Rels.
Number of staff: None.

2923
Goldsmith Foundation, Inc.
1755 Lynnfield Rd., Suite 285
Memphis 38119

Incorporated in 1944 in TN.
Donor(s): Members of the Goldsmith family.
Foundation type: Independent
Financial data (yr. ended 12/31/90): Assets, $4,234,584 (M); gifts received, $1,985; expenditures, $291,389; qualifying distributions, $264,027, including $264,027 for 248 grants (high: $50,250; low: $25; average: $1,000-$10,000).
Fields of interest: Jewish welfare, Jewish giving, health, education, higher education, social services.
Limitations: Giving primarily in TN.
Officers and Trustees:* Robert T. Goldsmith,* Pres.; Fred Goldsmith, Jr., V.P.; Fred Goldsmith III,* V.P.; Larry J. Goldsmith, V.P.; Thomas B. Goldsmith, V.P.; Edwin M. Marks,* V.P.; Elias J. Goldsmith, Jr., Secy.-Treas.
EIN: 626039604

2924
Hamico, Inc.
1715 West 38th St.
Chattanooga 37409

Incorporated in 1956 in TN.
Donor(s): Chattem, Inc.
Foundation type: Independent
Financial data (yr. ended 12/31/90): Assets, $3,715,181 (M); expenditures, $94,708; qualifying distributions, $92,794, including $82,536 for 35 grants (high: $10,610; low: $300).
Fields of interest: Higher education, secondary education, elementary education, cultural programs, fine arts, health.
Types of support: Continuing support, endowment funds.
Limitations: Giving primarily in Chattanooga, TN. No grants to individuals.
Application information: Contributes only to pre-selected organizations. Applications not accepted.
Officers and Trustees:* Vernon L. Staggs,* Pres.; Herbert B. Barks,* V.P.; Durwood C. Harvey,* Secy.-Treas.; James M. Holbert, Bertram E. LeNoir, Jr., Howard E. Ottley.
Number of staff: None.
EIN: 626040782

2925
The HCA Foundation ▼
c/o Hospital Corp. of America
One Park Plaza, P.O. Box 550
Nashville 37202-0550   (615) 320-2165
FAX: (615) 320-2017

Established in 1982 in TN.
Donor(s): Hospital Corp. of America.
Foundation type: Company-sponsored
Financial data (yr. ended 12/31/90): Assets, $55,434,212 (L); expenditures, $2,816,348; qualifying distributions, $2,513,423, including $2,410,048 for 252 grants (high: $432,000; low: $100; average: $1,000-$20,000) and $103,375 for 523 employee matching gifts.

Purpose and activities: Giving primarily for health management and policy exploration; support also for education, especially higher education, the arts and cultural programs, social services, civic and community affairs, and the United Way.

Fields of interest: Health, health services, public policy, education, higher education, educational associations, arts, cultural programs, performing arts, fine arts, social services, civic affairs, community funds.

Types of support: Matching funds, general purposes, land acquisition, special projects, building funds, professorships, publications, conferences and seminars, renovation projects, capital campaigns, equipment, continuing support, employee matching gifts, operating budgets, research, employee-related scholarships.

Limitations: Giving primarily in Nashville, TN, and to HCA hospital communities in AR, AZ, CA, CO, DE, FL, GA, IL, KS, KY, LA, MO, NC, NH, NM, OK, SC, TN, TX, UT, VA, WI, and WV. No support for social, religious, fraternal, labor, athletic, or veterans' groups (except for specific programs of broad public benefit), schools below the college level, private foundations, or individual United Way agencies. No grants to individuals (except for employee-related scholarships), or for endowment funds, dinners, tables, or tickets to fundraising events, promotional materials including goodwill advertising, publications, trips, or tours.

Publications: Annual report (including application guidelines).

Application information: Information brochures available for HCA Teacher Awards Program, HCA Volunteer Service Awards, HCA Achievement Awards for Non-Profit Management, HCA Fund for Collaboration, and employee-related scholarship program. Application form not required.

Initial approach: Telephone or letter
Copies of proposal: 1
Deadline(s): None
Board meeting date(s): Jan., Apr., July, and Oct.
Final notification: Within 4 months
Write: Kenneth L. Roberts, Pres.

Officers and Directors:* Thomas F. Frist, Jr.,* Chair.; Kenneth L. Roberts, Pres.; Peter F. Bird, Secy. and Sr. Prog. Officer; William McInnes, Treas.; Robert C. Crosby, Frank F. Drowota III, Charles J. Kane, R. Clayton McWhorter, Roger E. Mick.

Number of staff: 4 full-time professional; 1 full-time support.

EIN: 621134070

Recent health grants:

2925-1 American College of Psychiatrists, Greenbelt, MD, $10,000. For annual meeting. 1990.

2925-2 American Liver Foundation, Cedar Grove, NJ, $20,000. For challenge grant to help establish San Diego chapter. 1990.

2925-3 American Nurses Foundation, Milwaukee, WI, $40,000. For national campaign supplying information to prospective nurses. 1990.

2925-4 Center for Health Education, Raleigh, NC, $18,679. For curriculum for nervous system/substance abuse classroom. 1990.

2925-5 Crisis Intervention Center, Nashville, TN, $25,000. For unrestricted support for top winner of HCA Award of Achievement competition. 1990.

2925-6 Cross-Over Ministry, Richmond, VA, $15,000. For medical services for homeless. 1990.

2925-7 Foundation for State Legislatures, Denver, CO, $46,700. For Tennessee Healthcare Exchange. 1990.

2925-8 Friends in General, Nashville, TN, $10,000. For prenatal care program at Metro General Hospital offering incentives to expectant mothers for each prenatal visit. 1990.

2925-9 Home For Awhile, Nashville, TN, $10,000. For capital campaign to build Ronald McDonald House. 1990.

2925-10 Hospital Hospitality House, Nashville, TN, $15,000. Toward renovation of guest facilities. 1990.

2925-11 Legal Services of Middle Tennessee, Nashville, TN, $13,700. For publication of updated consumer guide to Medicare supplemental insurance. 1990.

2925-12 Medical College of Virginia Foundation, Richmond, VA, $11,400. For Department of Health Administration in School of Allied Health Professions. 1990.

2925-13 New Mexico Junior College, Hobbs, NM, $22,770. For preceptorship program for associate degree candidates in nursing. 1990.

2925-14 Tennessee Hospital Education and Research Foundation, Nashville, TN, $21,510. For Tennessee Healthcare Exchange. 1990.

2925-15 Texas Back Institute Research Foundation, Plano, TX, $10,000. For general support. 1990.

2925-16 Vanderbilt University, Nashville, TN, $28,484. For research and symposiums on health policy issues. 1990.

2925-17 Westminster College, School of Nursing, Salt Lake City, UT, $50,000. For general support. 1990.

2925-18 Womans Hospital of Texas Research and Education Foundation, Houston, TX, $10,000. For breast health awareness project. 1990.

2925-19 Womens Health Research and Education Foundation, Nashville, TN, $15,000. For educational materials for patients and physicians. 1990.

2926
Hospital Corporation of America Corporate Giving Program
One Park Plaza
P.O. Box 550
Nashville 37202-0550   (615) 327-9551

Financial data (yr. ended 12/31/90): Total giving, $2,558,880 for grants.

Purpose and activities: HCA affiliates provide direct and in-kind contributions to charitable organizations in the areas of health research, civic and community affairs, and youth. In communities nationwide where HCA has operations, each affiliate has its own program of contributions or direct service based on its assessment of local needs. Scholarships for the children of HCA employees through the National Merit Scholarship Program.

Fields of interest: Civic affairs, education, youth, health.

Types of support: In-kind gifts, employee volunteer services.

Limitations: Giving limited to AZ, AR, CA, CO, DE, FL, GA, IL, KS, KY, LA, MO, NV, NH, NM, NC, OK, SC, TN, TX, UT, VA, WV and WI.

Application information:

Initial approach: Write to nearest HCA affiliate
Write: Ida Cooney, Exec. Dir.

2927
Orion L. & Emma B. Hurlbut Memorial Fund
c/o First Tennessee Bank
701 Market St.
Chattanooga 37401
Application address: Jo Ann Clifford, c/o Chattanooga Tumor Clinic, 975 East Third St., Chattanooga, TN 37403; Tel.: (615) 266-3029

Established in 1937 in TN.

Foundation type: Independent

Financial data (yr. ended 04/30/91): Assets, $11,980,338 (M); expenditures, $588,082; qualifying distributions, $509,200, including $291,316 for 1 grant and $148,141 for grants to individuals.

Purpose and activities: Giving primarily for a tumor clinic; support also for treatment of cancer patients.

Fields of interest: Cancer, welfare—indigent individuals.

Types of support: Grants to individuals.

Limitations: Giving primarily in TN.

Application information:

Deadline(s): None

Director: C. Windom Kimsey, M.D.

Administrators: Harry Stone, M.D., First Tennessee Bank, N.A.

EIN: 626034546

2928
William P. and Marie R. Lowenstein Foundation
100 North Main Bldg., Rm. 3020
Memphis 38103   (901) 525-5744

Incorporated about 1959 in TN.

Donor(s): Marie R. Lowenstein.‡

Foundation type: Independent

Financial data (yr. ended 12/31/90): Assets, $2,892,953 (M); expenditures, $227,880; qualifying distributions, $347,263, including $156,939 for 39 grants (high: $42,350; low: $100).

Fields of interest: Higher education, hospitals, health services, Jewish welfare, Israel.

Types of support: Operating budgets, seed money, equipment, scholarship funds, fellowships.

Limitations: Giving limited to TN and Israel. No grants to individuals, or for endowment funds or matching gifts; no loans.

Application information: Application form required.

Initial approach: Letter or proposal
Copies of proposal: 1
Deadline(s): None
Board meeting date(s): May and Dec.
Final notification: 10 months
Write: Alvin A. Gordon, Exec. Dir.

Officer and Directors:* Alvin A. Gordon,* Pres. and Exec. Dir.; Elaine K. Gordon, Marshall D. Gordon, Robert Gordon, Ed Marlowe, Ted M. Winestone.

Number of staff: 1 full-time professional; 1 full-time support.
EIN: 626037976

2929
Massengill-DeFriece Foundation, Inc.
Holston Plaza, Suite 208
516 Holston Ave.
Bristol 37620   (615) 764-3833

Incorporated in 1949 in TN.
Donor(s): Frank W. DeFriece,‡ Pauline M. DeFriece,‡ Frank W. DeFriece, Jr., Josephine D. Wilson.
Foundation type: Independent
Financial data (yr. ended 12/31/90): Assets, $3,911,294 (M); expenditures, $210,413; qualifying distributions, $178,066, including $172,850 for 18 grants (high: $75,750; low: $500; average: $12,000).
Purpose and activities: Support for a historical association, private higher education, museums, health, youth, and religion.
Fields of interest: Historic preservation, higher education, museums, health, youth, religion.
Types of support: Continuing support, annual campaigns, equipment, matching funds, capital campaigns, operating budgets, special projects.
Limitations: Giving primarily in the Bristol, TN, and Bristol, VA, areas. No grants to individuals; no loans.
Application information: Application form not required.
Initial approach: 1- to 2-page letter
Copies of proposal: 1
Deadline(s): None
Board meeting date(s): Usually quarterly
Final notification: 2 to 4 months
Write: Frank W. DeFriece, Jr., V.P.
Officers and Directors:* Albert S. Kelly, Jr.,* Pres.; Frank W. DeFriece, Jr.,* V.P.; Josephine D. Wilson,* V.P.; John C. Paty, Jr.,* Secy.-Treas.; Mark W. DeFriece, Paul E. DeFriece, C. Richard Hagerstrom, Jr.
Number of staff: 1 part-time support.
EIN: 626044873

2930
Jack C. Massey Foundation ▼
111 Westwood Pl., No. 203
Brentwood 37027-5021

Trust established in 1966 in TN.
Donor(s): Jack C. Massey.‡
Foundation type: Independent
Financial data (yr. ended 12/31/90): Assets, $3,438,856 (M); expenditures, $2,130,011; qualifying distributions, $2,038,532, including $2,030,200 for 54 grants (high: $1,000,000; low: $50; average: $1,000-$10,000).
Purpose and activities: Emphasis on higher and secondary education and medical research; grants also for cultural programs.
Fields of interest: Higher education, secondary education, medical research, cultural programs.
Types of support: Research.
Limitations: Giving primarily in TN. No grants to individuals.
Application information: Contributes only to pre-selected organizations. Applications not accepted.

Officers and Trustee:* Elizabeth Queener, Secy.; Clarence Edmonds,* Treas.
EIN: 626065672
Recent health grants:
2930-1 Holcomb Medical Research Institute, Nashville, TN, $10,000. 1990.
2930-2 Institute of Neurological Science, NYC, NY, $10,000. 1990.
2930-3 Planned Parenthood Association of Nashville, Nashville, TN, $40,000. 1990.

2931
Melrose Foundation, Inc.
P.O. Box 18184
Knoxville 37928-2184

Incorporated in 1945 in TN.
Foundation type: Independent
Financial data (yr. ended 12/31/90): Assets, $961,908 (M); expenditures, $276,771; qualifying distributions, $265,150, including $265,150 for 58 grants (high: $25,000; low: $200).
Fields of interest: Higher education, youth, social services, health associations, hospitals.
Limitations: Giving primarily in TN, with emphasis on Knoxville. No grants to individuals.
Application information: Contributes only to pre-selected organizations. Applications not accepted.
Officers and Directors:* J.E. Gettys,* Pres.; J.C. Kramer, V.P.; J.B. Woolsey, Secy.-Treas.; E.H. Rayson.
EIN: 626037984

2932
Plough Foundation ▼
6077 Primacy Pkwy., Suite 230
Memphis 38119   (901) 761-9180

Trust established in 1972 in TN.
Donor(s): Abe Plough.‡
Foundation type: Independent
Financial data (yr. ended 12/31/91): Assets, $89,264,428 (M); gifts received, $732,820; expenditures, $4,607,167; qualifying distributions, $3,798,239, including $3,798,239 for 67 grants (high: $500,000; low: $500; average: $5,000-$250,000).
Purpose and activities: Grants to community projects, including a community fund, early childhood and elementary education, substance abuse prevention-early intervention, social service agencies, civic affairs groups, and the arts.
Fields of interest: Education—early childhood, elementary education, social services, drug abuse, family services, youth.
Types of support: Operating budgets, continuing support, annual campaigns, seed money, emergency funds, deficit financing, equipment, matching funds, general purposes, building funds, capital campaigns, endowment funds, professorships.
Limitations: Giving primarily in Memphis and Shelby counties, TN. No grants to individuals, and generally no grants for annual operating funds; no loans.
Publications: Application guidelines, informational brochure.
Application information: Application form required.

Initial approach: Proposal
Copies of proposal: 1
Deadline(s): 15th of month prior to board meeting
Board meeting date(s): Feb., May, Aug., and Nov.
Final notification: Generally within two weeks
Write: Noris R. Haynes, Jr., Exec. Dir.
Officer and Trustees:* Noris R. Haynes, Jr.,* Exec. Dir.; Patricia R. Burnham, Eugene J. Callahan, Sharon R. Eisenberg, Diane R. Goldstein, Cecil C. Humphreys, Jocelyn P. Rudner, James Sprinfield, Steve Wishnia, National Bank of Commerce.
Number of staff: 1 full-time professional; 1 full-time support.
EIN: 237175983
Recent health grants:
2932-1 Auburn University, School of Pharmacy, Auburn University, AL, $22,500. 1990.
2932-2 Bnai Brith Home and Hospital for the Aged, Memphis, TN, $250,500. 1990.
2932-3 Childrens Oncology Group of Memphis, Memphis, TN, $50,000. 1990.
2932-4 Church Health Center of Memphis, Memphis, TN, $38,000. 1990.
2932-5 Drake University, School of Pharmacy, Des Moines, IA, $45,000. 1990.
2932-6 Saint Jude Childrens Research Hospital, Memphis, TN, $45,000. 1990.
2932-7 University of Cincinnati, School of Pharmacy, Cincinnati, OH, $45,000. 1990.
2932-8 University of Kansas, School of Pharmacy, Lawrence, KS, $22,500. 1990.
2932-9 University of Maryland, School of Pharmacy, Baltimore, MD, $67,500. 1990.
2932-10 University of Michigan, School of Pharmacy, Ann Arbor, MI, $45,000. 1990.
2932-11 University of Nebraska, School of Pharmacy, Omaha, NE, $45,000. 1990.
2932-12 University of South Carolina, School of Pharmacy, Columbia, SC, $45,000. 1990.
2932-13 University of Tennessee, Center for Health Sciences, Memphis, TN, $100,000. 1990.
2932-14 University of Tennessee, School of Pharmacy, Memphis, TN, $25,000. 1990.

2933
The Justin and Valere Potter Foundation
c/o NationsBank Personal Trust
One NationsBank Plaza M-7
Nashville 37239-1697   (615) 749-3586

Trust established in 1951 in TN.
Donor(s): Justin Potter,‡ Valere Blair Potter.‡
Foundation type: Independent
Financial data (yr. ended 12/31/91): Assets, $25,463,878 (M); expenditures, $1,089,093; qualifying distributions, $1,027,500, including $1,027,500 for 30 grants (high: $245,000; low: $5,000; average: $10,000-$75,000).
Purpose and activities: Giving primarily for higher education, including scholarship funds and medical education; support also for cultural programs, social services, and medical research.
Fields of interest: Higher education, medical education, cultural programs, social services, medical research.
Types of support: Scholarship funds, operating budgets, special projects, research.
Limitations: Giving primarily in Nashville, TN. No grants to individuals.

Application information:
Initial approach: Letter
Deadline(s): None
Board meeting date(s): As needed
Write: Lois Squires, Asst. V.P. and Trust Officer, NationsBank
Distribution Committee: Justin P. Wilson, Chair.; Albert L. Menefee, Jr.
Trustee: NationsBank.
Number of staff: None.
EIN: 626033081

2934
M. B. Seretean Foundation, Inc.
12424 Creek Hollow Ln.
Soddy-Daisy 37379

Established in 1964 in GA.
Donor(s): M.B. Seretean.
Foundation type: Independent
Financial data (yr. ended 06/30/90): Assets, $558,875 (M); expenditures, $553,326; qualifying distributions, $540,783, including $540,783 for 20 grants (high: $508,283; low: $250).
Fields of interest: Higher education, education, hospitals.
Limitations: Giving primarily in TN, FL, GA, and OK.
Officers: M.B. Seretean, Pres. and Treas.; Shirley Seretean, V.P.; Sue C. Moore, Secy.
EIN: 620725600

2935
Dorothy Snider Foundation
c/o First Tennessee Bank, N.A.
P.O. Box 84
Memphis 38101-0084
Application address: Clarke Tower, 5100 Poplar Ave., Suite 2929, Memphis, TN 38137

Foundation type: Independent
Financial data (yr. ended 01/31/91): Assets, $2,340,157 (M); expenditures, $196,870; qualifying distributions, $162,901, including $155,000 for 2 grants (high: $116,500; low: $38,500).
Purpose and activities: Giving primarily to the study of health care.
Fields of interest: Medical education.
Limitations: Giving limited to western TN and AR.
Application information:
Initial approach: Letter, including statement of need and major field of study
Deadline(s): None
Write: Jack Magids, Asst. Secy.
Trustee: First Tennessee Bank, N.A.
EIN: 526120444

2936
The William B. Stokely, Jr. Foundation
620 Campbell Station Rd.
Station West, Suite 27
Knoxville 37922   (615) 966-4878

Incorporated in 1951 in IN.
Donor(s): William B. Stokely, Jr.‡
Foundation type: Independent
Financial data (yr. ended 12/31/91): Assets, $9,120,682 (M); expenditures, $514,214;

qualifying distributions, $476,608, including $466,943 for 92 grants (high: $100,000; low: $10).
Fields of interest: Higher education, hospitals, health services, cultural programs, museums, youth.
Limitations: Giving primarily in eastern TN. No grants to individuals.
Application information: Application form not required.
Initial approach: Letter or proposal
Copies of proposal: 1
Deadline(s): Submit proposal preferably in the fall
Board meeting date(s): Feb., May, Aug., and Nov.
Write: William B. Stokely III, Pres.
Officers and Directors:* William B. Stokely III,* Pres.; Kay H. Stokely,* Exec. V.P.; Andrea A. White-Randall, V.P. and Secy.-Treas.; Stacy S. Byerly, William B. Stokely IV.
Number of staff: 1 full-time professional.
EIN: 356016402

2937
The Thompson Charitable Foundation ▼
P.O. Box 10516
Knoxville 37939   (615) 588-0491

Established in 1987 in TN.
Donor(s): B.R. Thompson, Sr.‡
Foundation type: Independent
Financial data (yr. ended 06/30/90): Assets, $17,503,147 (M); gifts received, $4,350,000; expenditures, $4,316,753; qualifying distributions, $4,268,614, including $4,230,000 for 7 grants (high: $3,380,000; low: $20,000; average: $50,000-$150,000).
Purpose and activities: Support primarily for a cancer center; grants also to a university, a symphony, and a youth center.
Fields of interest: Cancer, higher education, music, hospitals, housing.
Types of support: General purposes.
Limitations: Giving limited to Knox, Anderson, Scott and Blount counties, TN; Bell, Clay, Laurel and Leslie counties, KY; and Buchanan and Tazewell counties, VA. No grants for operating deficits or endowments.
Application information:
Initial approach: Letter (no more than 2 pages)
Deadline(s): Mar. 31, June 30, Sept. 30, and Dec. 31
Write: Velma Latham, Admin.
Officer and Directors:* Merle Wolfe,* Pres.; Carl Ensor, B. Ray Thompson, Jr., Jesse J. Thompson, Lindsay Young.
EIN: 581754763
Recent health grants:
2937-1 Thompson Cancer Survival Center, Knoxville, TN, $3,380,000. For general support and purchase of MRI equipment. 1990.

2938
The Toms Foundation
Valley Fidelity Bank Bldg., 9th Fl.
P.O. Box 2466
Knoxville 37901   (615) 544-3000

Trust established in 1954 in TN.
Donor(s): W.P. Toms.‡

Foundation type: Independent
Financial data (yr. ended 06/30/91): Assets, $3,286,496 (M); expenditures, $134,161; qualifying distributions, $117,919, including $16,050 for 14 grants (high: $5,000; low: $200; average: $650) and $100,140 for 1 foundation-administered program.
Purpose and activities: Emphasis on cancer research and higher education; foundation also operates a museum and gardens.
Fields of interest: Cancer, higher education, general charitable giving.
Types of support: Seed money, emergency funds, building funds, equipment, land acquisition, professorships, research.
Limitations: Giving primarily in eastern TN. No grants to individuals, or for endowment funds, operating budgets, continuing support, annual campaigns, publications, demonstration projects, conferences, deficit financing, matching gifts, scholarships, or fellowships; no loans.
Publications: Annual report.
Application information: Application form not required.
Initial approach: Letter of inquiry followed by proposal
Copies of proposal: 1
Deadline(s): Submit proposal preferably in June; deadline June 30
Board meeting date(s): Aug. and as required
Final notification: 1 month after annual meeting
Write: William C. Wilson, Pres., or Ronald L. Grimm, Secy.-Treas.
Officers and Trustees:* William C. Wilson,* Chair. and Pres.; Eleanor C. Krug,* V.P.; Ronald L. Grimm,* Secy.-Treas.; Mary Mayne Perry, Dorothy B. Wilson.
EIN: 626037668

2939
Tonya Memorial Foundation ▼
c/o American National Bank & Trust Co.
736 Market St.
Chattanooga 37402

Incorporated in 1949 in DE.
Donor(s): Burkett Miller.‡
Foundation type: Independent
Financial data (yr. ended 12/31/90): Assets, $11,190,972 (M); expenditures, $3,145,412; qualifying distributions, $3,046,033, including $2,942,591 for 14 grants (high: $1,000,000; low: $10,000; average: $15,000-$250,000).
Purpose and activities: Grants to new donees limited to capital projects of a nonsectarian nature; emphasis on downtown rehabilitation, parks, hospitals, and community educational projects; continuing support for a few existing projects approved during the founder's lifetime.
Fields of interest: Hospitals, recreation, urban development, education.
Types of support: Building funds, land acquisition, equipment.
Limitations: Giving primarily in Chattanooga, TN, for new grant recipients. No grants to individuals, or for scholarships, endowment funds, or operating budgets; no loans.
Application information: Application form not required.
Initial approach: Letter
Copies of proposal: 4
Deadline(s): None

Board meeting date(s): Jan., Apr., July, and Oct.
Final notification: 6 months
  Write: Maurice H. Martin, Pres., or H. James
    Hitching, Chair.
Officers and Trustees:* H. James Hitching,*
Chair.; Maurice H. Martin,* Pres. and Treas.;
James R. Hedges III,* V.P.; H. Whitney Durand,*
Secy.
Number of staff: 1 part-time professional.
EIN: 626042269

2940
Louise B. Wallace Foundation
c/o Equitable Trust Co.
P.O. Box 2727
Nashville 37219-0727   (615) 780-9318

Established in 1989 in TN.
Donor(s): George Newton Bullard Foundation.
Foundation type: Independent
Financial data (yr. ended 12/31/90): Assets,
$4,921,948 (M); gifts received, $335,512;
expenditures, $298,893; qualifying distributions,
$239,237, including $237,500 for 21 grants
(high: $60,000; low: $500).

Fields of interest: Social services, youth, hospitals,
arts.
Limitations: Giving primarily in Nashville, TN.
No grants to individuals.
Application information:
  Initial approach: Letter
  Deadline(s): None
  Board meeting date(s): Twice yearly
  Write: M. Kirk Scobey, Exec. V.P., Equitable
    Trust Co.
Trustees: Eleana Wallace Graves, Anne Wallace
Nesbitt, Elizabeth Bullard Wallace, J. Bransford
Wallace, Jr.
Number of staff: None.
EIN: 581797048

TEXAS

2941
Abell-Hanger Foundation ▼
303 West Wall, Rm. 615
Midland 79701   (915) 684-6655
Mailing address: P.O. Box 430, Midland, TX
79702

Incorporated in 1954 in TX.
Donor(s): George T. Abell,‡ Gladys H. Abell.‡
Foundation type: Independent
Financial data (yr. ended 06/30/91): Assets,
$97,679,515 (M); gifts received, $2,174,812;
expenditures, $6,824,329; qualifying
distributions, $6,415,755, including $5,909,404
for 120 grants (high: $1,000,000; low: $500;
average: $25,000-$50,000).
Purpose and activities: Support primarily for
higher education, youth activities, cultural
programs, health services, the handicapped, and
social welfare agencies.
Fields of interest: Higher education, business
education, cultural programs, arts, social services,
youth, family services, handicapped, aged,
disadvantaged, drug abuse, health services,
nursing, community development, civic affairs,
volunteerism.
Types of support: General purposes, operating
budgets, continuing support, annual campaigns,
seed money, building funds, endowment funds,
matching funds, scholarship funds, research,
equipment, capital campaigns, special projects.
Limitations: Giving limited to TX, preferably
within the Permian Basin. No grants to
individuals, or for individual scholarships or
fellowships; no loans.
Publications: 990-PF, annual report (including
application guidelines).
Application information: Application form
required.
   Initial approach: Telephone or letter
   Copies of proposal: 1
   Deadline(s): May 30, Feb. 28, Nov. 30, and
   Aug. 30
   Board meeting date(s): June 30, Mar. 30, Dec.
   30, and Sept. 30
   Final notification: 1 month
   Write: David L. Smith, Exec. Dir.
Officers and Trustees:* James I. Trott,* Pres.;
Robert L. Leibrock,* V.P.; Lester Van Pelt, Jr.,*
Secy.-Treas.; David L. Smith, Exec. Dir.; Duane H.
Abell, Jerome M. Fullinwider, John F. Younger.
Number of staff: 1 full-time professional; 2
part-time professional; 2 full-time support.
EIN: 756020781
Recent health grants:
2941-1 American Cancer Society, Midland Unit,
   Midland, TX, $10,000. For Round-Up '91.
   1991.
2941-2 American Heart Association, Midland
   County Division, Midland, TX, $10,000. For
   general operating support. 1991.
2941-3 Benign Essential Blepharospasm
   Research Fund, Beaumont, TX, $20,000. For
   training patients in outreach programs. 1991.

2941-4 Brewster Memorial Hospital, Alpine, TX,
   $100,000. For accounts payable reduction.
   1991.
2941-5 Cancer Patients Services, Laredo, TX,
   $11,000. For transportation expenses for
   patients. 1991.
2941-6 Casa de Amigos, Midland, TX, $15,000.
   For scholarships to Diabetic Youth Camp.
   1991.
2941-7 Midland Cerebral Palsy Center, Midland,
   TX, $60,000. To renovate Center and construct
   outdoor Hippotherapy Riding Facility. 1991.
2941-8 Midland Cerebral Palsy Center, Midland,
   TX, $30,000. For general operating support.
   1991.
2941-9 Midland Cerebral Palsy Center, Midland,
   TX, $10,000. For general operating support.
   1991.
2941-10 Midland Memorial Foundation,
   Midland, TX, $150,000. For expansion of
   School of Nursing Program. 1991.
2941-11 Midland Memorial Foundation,
   Midland, TX, $100,000. For nursing
   scholarships and stipends. 1991.
2941-12 Midland Rape Crisis Center, Midland,
   TX, $16,000. For general operating support.
   1991.
2941-13 Muscular Dystrophy Association,
   Midland, TX, $11,000. For annual summer
   camp. 1991.
2941-14 Palmer Drug Abuse Program, Midland,
   TX, $68,000. For general operating support.
   1991.
2941-15 Permian Basin Regional Council of
   Alcohol and Drug Abuse, Midland, TX,
   $20,000. For general operating support. 1991.
2941-16 Planned Parenthood of West Texas,
   Odessa, TX, $22,000. For start-up funding for
   prenatal services. 1991.
2941-17 Samaritan Counseling Center of West
   Texas, Midland, TX, $20,000. For general
   operating support. 1991.
2941-18 Scott and White Memorial Hospital,
   Temple, TX, $50,000. To establish Cardiac
   Imaging Center. 1991.
2941-19 Texas Society to Prevent Blindness,
   Houston, TX, $25,000. For general operating
   support, Vision Van maintenance and eye
   safety literature. 1991.
2941-20 Texas Tech University Health Sciences
   Center, Permian Basin School of Nursing,
   Lubbock, TX, $50,000. For operating support.
   1991.
2941-21 University of Texas System Cancer
   Center, Houston, TX, $50,000. For
   chemoprevention research at M.D. Anderson
   Cancer Center. 1991.
2941-22 West Texas Rehabilitation Center,
   Abilene, TX, $30,000. For capital
   improvement campaign. 1991.

2942
The Abercrombie Foundation
5005 Riverway, Suite 500
Houston 77056   (713) 627-2500

Established in 1988 in TX as partial successor to
The J.S. Abercrombie Foundation.
Donor(s): Josephine E. Abercrombie.
Foundation type: Independent
Financial data (yr. ended 12/31/90): Assets,
$6,761,595 (M); expenditures, $570,768;

qualifying distributions, $506,667, including
$506,667 for 10 grants (high: $150,000; low:
$5,000).
Purpose and activities: Support primarily for
higher and secondary education, including
medical education; giving also for child welfare.
Fields of interest: Medical education, higher
education, secondary education, child welfare.
Types of support: Building funds, operating
budgets, research.
Limitations: Giving primarily in Houston, TX.
Application information: Application form not
required.
   Initial approach: Proposal
   Copies of proposal: 1
   Deadline(s): May 15 and Nov. 15
   Write: Thomas M. Weaver, Mgr.
Officer: Thomas M. Weaver, V.P., Secy.-Treas.,
and Mgr.
Trustees: Josephine E. Abercrombie, Freda Bowen.
EIN: 760229183

2943
Community Foundation of Abilene
500 Chestnut, Suite 1509
P.O. Box 1001
Abilene 79604   (915) 676-3883

Incorporated in 1985 in TX.
Foundation type: Community
Financial data (yr. ended 06/30/91): Assets,
$7,475,198 (M); gifts received, $1,912,042;
expenditures, $1,331,370; qualifying
distributions, $1,197,110, including $1,143,316
for grants (average: $2,000-$8,000) and $53,794
for foundation-administered programs.
Fields of interest: Social services, health,
education, civic affairs, historic preservation.
Types of support: Annual campaigns, building
funds, conferences and seminars, consulting
services, equipment, matching funds, operating
budgets, publications, renovation projects,
scholarship funds, seed money, technical
assistance.
Limitations: Giving primarily in the Abilene, TX,
area. No grants to individuals, or for continuing
support, deficit financing, endowment funds; no
loans or program-related investments.
Publications: Annual report.
Application information: Application form
required.
   Initial approach: Letter
   Board meeting date(s): 1st Tuesday of every
   month
   Write: Nancy E. Dark Jones, Exec. Dir.
Officers and Trustees:* Peggy Beckham,* Chair.;
Jesse C. Fletcher,* Vice-Chair.; Jack D. Ramsey,*
Secy.; John L. Shelton, Jr.,* Treas.; Nancy E. Dark
Jones, Exec. Dir.; Joe Canon, and 12 additional
trustees.
Number of staff: 1 full-time professional; 1
full-time support; 1 part-time support.
EIN: 752045832

2944
Alcon Foundation
6201 South Freeway
Fort Worth 76134   (817) 551-8789

Established in 1962 in TX.
Donor(s): Alcon Laboratories, Inc.

Foundation type: Company-sponsored
Financial data (yr. ended 12/31/91): Assets, $12,484 (M); gifts received, $430,000; expenditures, $427,995; qualifying distributions, $427,917, including $427,917 for 206 grants.
Purpose and activities: Contributions mostly limited to education and research within areas of specialization of Alcon Laboratories, with emphasis on ophthalmology and vision care; grants also to community activities that benefit company employees.
Fields of interest: Health associations, ophthalmology, education, education—minorities, medical education, medical research, disadvantaged, arts, performing arts.
Types of support: Annual campaigns, lectureships, research, scholarship funds, conferences and seminars.
Limitations: No grants for building programs.
Application information: Application form not required.
Initial approach: Letter
Copies of proposal: 1
Deadline(s): None
Board meeting date(s): Feb., Apr., June, Aug., Oct., and Dec.
Write: John A. Walters, Co-Chair.
Trustees: Mary K. O'Neill, Co-Chair.; John A. Walters, Co-Chair.; C.H. Beasley, M.D., R. Halprin, J. Hiddemen, L. Liguori, R. Nelson, R.H. Sisson.
EIN: 756034736

2945
The Stanford & Joan Alexander Foundation
203 Timberwilde
Houston 77024

Established in 1986 in TX.
Donor(s): Stanford Alexander, Joan Alexander.
Foundation type: Independent
Financial data (yr. ended 12/31/90): Assets, $3,114,481 (M); gifts received, $718,638; expenditures, $88,354; qualifying distributions, $86,100, including $86,100 for 29 grants (high: $40,000; low: $100).
Fields of interest: Higher education, elementary education, medical education, health, medical research, mental health, community development, civil rights, religion, Jewish giving.
Types of support: Operating budgets, research, general purposes.
Limitations: Giving primarily in Houston, TX.
Application information: Contributes only to pre-selected organizations. Applications not accepted.
Officers and Directors:* Stanford Alexander,* Pres. and Treas.; Joan Alexander,* V.P. and Secy.; Andrew M. Alexander, Eric P. Alexander, Ilene S. Alexander, Melvin Dow.
EIN: 760204170

2946
Amarillo Area Foundation, Inc. ▼
700 First National Place I
801 South Fillmore
Amarillo 79101   (806) 376-4521

Established as a trust in 1957 in TX.

Foundation type: Community
Financial data (yr. ended 12/31/91): Assets, $21,891,837 (M); gifts received, $636,323; expenditures, $1,876,184; qualifying distributions, $1,506,410, including $1,462,061 for 56 grants (high: $400,000; low: $72; average: $2,500-$25,000) and $44,349 for grants to individuals.
Purpose and activities: Support for community development, including education, arts and cultural programs, and health organizations, especially a medical center.
Fields of interest: Community development, education, arts, cultural programs, health.
Types of support: Seed money, emergency funds, building funds, equipment, land acquisition, matching funds, consulting services, technical assistance, scholarship funds, special projects, research, student aid.
Limitations: Giving limited to the 26 most northern counties of the TX Panhandle. No grants to individuals (except for limited scholarships from designated funds), or for operating budgets, annual campaigns, deficit financing, endowment funds, publications, or conferences; no loans.
Publications: Annual report, application guidelines, newsletter.
Application information: Specific application format required. Application form required.
Initial approach: Letter or telephone
Copies of proposal: 1
Deadline(s): Quarterly - Jan. 15, Mar. 20, July 31, and Sept. 18
Board meeting date(s): Board meets bimonthly - Feb., Apr., June, Aug., Oct., and Dec. Executive Committee meets bimonthly - Mar., May, July, Sept., and Nov.
Write: Jim Allison, Pres. and Exec. Dir.
Officers and Directors:* Greg Mitchell,* Chair.; Jay O'Brien,* 1st Vice-Chair.; Lawrence Pickens,* 2nd Vice-Chair.; Danny Conklin,* Secy.; John Marmaduke,* Treas.; and 20 additional directors.
Number of staff: 3 full-time professional.
EIN: 750978220
Recent health grants:
2946-1 Don and Sybil Harrington Regional Medical Center, Amarillo, TX, $400,000. For general operating support. 1991.
2946-2 High Plains Epilepsy Association, Amarillo, TX, $17,248. For general operating support. 1991.

2947
Josephine Anderson Charitable Trust
P.O. Box 8
Amarillo 79105   (806) 376-7873

Donor(s): Josephine Anderson.‡
Foundation type: Independent
Financial data (yr. ended 02/28/91): Assets, $5,243,543 (M); expenditures, $370,237; qualifying distributions, $241,848, including $203,600 for 43 grants (high: $20,000; low: $50).
Fields of interest: Handicapped, health associations, hospitals, performing arts, cultural programs, religion—Christian, social services, child welfare, youth, education.
Types of support: Building funds.
Limitations: Giving primarily in Amarillo, TX. No grants to individuals.
Application information:
Initial approach: Letter

Deadline(s): None
Write: L.A. White, Managing Trustee, or Imadell Carter, Secy.
Officers and Trustees: L.A. White, Managing Trustee; Imadell Carter, Secy.
EIN: 751469596

2948
M. D. Anderson Foundation ▼
1301 Fannin St., 21st Fl.
P.O. Box 809
Houston 77001   (713) 658-2316

Trust established in 1936 in TX.
Donor(s): M.D. Anderson.‡
Foundation type: Independent
Financial data (yr. ended 12/31/90): Assets, $79,756,904 (M); gifts received, $3,848; expenditures, $3,688,840; qualifying distributions, $3,356,223, including $3,330,100 for 94 grants (high: $320,000; low: $1,000; average: $10,000-$50,000).
Purpose and activities: "The improvement of working conditions among workers generally...; the establishment, support and maintenance of hospitals, homes, and institutions for the care of the sick, the young, the aged, the incompetent and the helpless among the people; the improvement of living conditions among people generally." Support for a large local medical center and for educational and related projects.
Fields of interest: Health, education, youth, social services, aged, public policy, civic affairs.
Types of support: Building funds, equipment, matching funds, research, seed money.
Limitations: Giving limited to TX, primarily the Houston area. No grants to individuals, or for endowment funds or operating budgets.
Publications: Multi-year report, application guidelines.
Application information: Application form not required.
Initial approach: Letter
Copies of proposal: 5
Deadline(s): None
Board meeting date(s): Monthly
Final notification: 1 month
Write: John W. Lowrie, Secy.-Treas.
Officers and Trustees: A.G. McNeese, Jr., Pres.; Uriel E. Dutton, V.P.; Gibson Gayle, Jr., V.P.; Charles W. Hall, V.P.; John W. Lowrie, Secy.-Treas.
Number of staff: None.
EIN: 746035669
Recent health grants:
2948-1 Baylor College of Medicine, Houston, TX, $215,000. 1990.
2948-2 Cancer Counseling, Houston, TX, $10,000. 1990.
2948-3 Good Neighbor Healthcare Center, Houston, TX, $25,000. 1990.
2948-4 Hermann Eye Center, Houston, TX, $17,100. 1990.
2948-5 Holly Hall, Houston, TX, $25,000. 1990.
2948-6 Institute for Rehabilitation and Research, Houston, TX, $50,000. 1990.
2948-7 Institute of Religion, Houston, TX, $10,000. 1990.
2948-8 Living Bank International, Houston, TX, $15,000. 1990.
2948-9 Memorial Hospital Foundation of Houston, Houston, TX, $50,000. 1990.

2948-10 Palmer Drug Abuse Program, Houston, TX, $25,000. 1990.

2948-11 Retina Research Foundation, Houston, TX, $25,000. 1990.

2948-12 Saint Joseph Hospital Foundation, Houston, TX, $50,000. 1990.

2948-13 Saint Lukes Episcopal Hospital, Houston, TX, $30,000. 1990.

2948-14 San Jose Clinic, Houston, TX, $100,000. 1990.

2948-15 Texas Childrens Hospital, Houston, TX, $25,000. 1990.

2948-16 Texas Medical Center, Houston, TX, $320,000. 1990.

2948-17 University of Texas Health Science Center, Houston, TX, $200,000. 1990.

2948-18 University of Texas Health Science Center, Dental Branch, Houston, TX, $200,000. 1990.

2948-19 University of Texas Medical Branch Hospitals, Galveston, TX, $50,000. 1990.

2948-20 Visiting Nurse Association of Houston, Houston, TX, $50,000. 1990.

2949
Apache Corporation Giving Program
2000 Post Oak Blvd., Suite 100
Houston 77056-4400

Purpose and activities: Supports arts and culture, education, health, social services, community development, and civic and urban programs; includes in-kind giving.
Fields of interest: Education, arts, dance, theater, urban development, urban affairs, performing arts, community development, civic affairs, health, social services.
Types of support: In-kind gifts, special projects, employee matching gifts, operating budgets, special projects, employee volunteer services.
Limitations: Giving primarily in major operating locations in Denver, CO, Tulsa, OK, Houston, TX, and WY.
Publications: Application guidelines.
Application information:
  Initial approach: Send requests to headquarters
  Deadline(s): Jan., Apr., July, and Oct.
  Board meeting date(s): In ten weeks
  Write: Bruce Thomson, Mgr., Community Rels.
Number of staff: 2

2950
Associates Corporation of North America Corporate Giving Program
250 Carpenter Frwy.
Irving 75062   (214) 541-3000
Mailing Address: P.O. Box 660237, Dallas, TX 75266

Purpose and activities: Giving for education, health, arts and culture, civic affairs, and the United Way.
Fields of interest: Education, health, arts, cultural programs, civic affairs, general charitable giving.
Types of support: In-kind gifts, employee volunteer services.
Limitations: Giving limited to communities of operation.
Application information:
  Write: Neal Moore, Asst. V.P., Corp. Rels.

2951
Austin Community Foundation
P.O. Box 5159
Austin 78763   (512) 472-4483

Established in 1977 in TX.
Foundation type: Community
Financial data (yr. ended 12/31/89): Assets, $5,331,554 (M); gifts received, $353,084; expenditures, $727,644; qualifying distributions, $602,622, including $602,622 for 176 grants (high: $73,992).
Purpose and activities: Support for general charitable purposes, including education, community affairs and services, history, religious giving, medical research and rehabilitation, beautification, public health, child development, and recreation.
Fields of interest: Education, community development, history, religion, medical research, rehabilitation, recreation, child development.
Types of support: Seed money, capital campaigns, general purposes, annual campaigns, building funds, conferences and seminars, consulting services, continuing support, equipment, land acquisition, matching funds, professorships, publications, renovation projects, research, technical assistance.
Limitations: Giving limited to Travis County, TX, for discretionary grants. No grants to individuals, or for deficit financing, emergency funds, endowments, operating budgets, scholarships, or fellowships; no loans.
Publications: Newsletter, program policy statement, application guidelines.
Application information: Application form required.
  Initial approach: Letter
  Copies of proposal: 1
  Deadline(s): Dec. 1
  Board meeting date(s): Quarterly
  Write: Richard G. Slaughter, Exec. Dir.
Officers and Board of Governors: Sander Shapiro,* Pres.; Dorothy Rowland,* V.P.; Priscilla Pond Flawn,* Secy.; Robert E. Mettlen,* Treas.; Richard G. Slaughter, Exec. Dir.; Mrs. Sam A. Wilson, and 13 additional governors.
Number of staff: 2 full-time professional; 1 part-time support.
EIN: 741934031

2952
Anne T. & Robert M. Bass Foundation
201 Main St., Suite 2300
Fort Worth 76102-3199

Established in 1984 in TX.
Donor(s): Robert M. Bass.
Foundation type: Operating
Financial data (yr. ended 12/31/90): Assets, $9,225,998 (M); expenditures, $434,552; qualifying distributions, $415,000, including $415,000 for 8 grants (high: $150,000; low: $10,000).
Purpose and activities: Giving primarily for youth development organizations and a medical center; support also for social services, including those benefiting women, children and the homeless.
Fields of interest: Youth, hospitals, social services, women, child welfare, homeless.
Limitations: Giving primarily in Fort Worth, TX. No grants to individuals.

Application information: Contributes only to pre-selected organizations. Applications not accepted.
Officers and Directors:* Anne T. Bass,* Pres.; Robert M. Bass,* V.P.; Chester W. Carlock,* Secy.-Treas.
EIN: 752001892

2953
Harry Bass Foundation
8333 Douglas Ave., Suite 1400
Dallas 75225   (214) 696-0557

Established in 1983 in TX.
Donor(s): Harry W. Bass, Jr.
Foundation type: Independent
Financial data (yr. ended 12/31/90): Assets, $5,440,002 (M); expenditures, $264,529; qualifying distributions, $261,849, including $261,849 for 63 grants (high: $183,099; low: $100; average: $100-$10,000).
Purpose and activities: Support for numismatic organizations nationwide; support for education, museums, religious organizations, and health associations and hospitals in the Dallas, TX, area.
Fields of interest: Education, museums, libraries, civic affairs, religion, health associations, hospitals, general charitable giving.
Types of support: General purposes, annual campaigns, continuing support, equipment, scholarship funds.
Limitations: Giving primarily in the Dallas, TX, area. No grants to individuals.
Publications: 990-PF.
Application information: Contributes only to pre-selected organizations. Applications not accepted.
  Board meeting date(s): Dec.
  Write: Harry W. Bass, Jr., Trustee
Trustees: Doris L. Bass, Harry W. Bass, Jr., Carol Ann McLean.
Number of staff: None.
EIN: 751876307

2954
The Beal Foundation
c/o NCNB Texas-Midland, Trust Dept.
P.O. Box 270
Midland 79702-0270   (915) 685-2063
Additional address: c/o Carlton E. Beal, Chair., 104 South Pecos, Midland, TX 79701; Tel.: (915) 682-3753

Incorporated in 1962 in TX.
Donor(s): Carlton Beal, W.R. Davis.
Foundation type: Independent
Financial data (yr. ended 12/31/90): Assets, $2,827,072 (M); expenditures, $595,234; qualifying distributions, $377,000, including $377,000 for 36 grants (high: $70,000; low: $2,000).
Purpose and activities: Emphasis on education, social services, including programs for women and children, youth agencies, health associations and hospitals, and a community fund.
Fields of interest: Education, social services, women, child welfare, youth, health associations, hospitals, community funds.
Limitations: Giving primarily in the Midland, TX, area.

Application information: 1st-time applicants complete longer application form. Application form required.

Deadline(s): 1 month before meetings for 1st-time applicants; 2 weeks for repeat applicants
Board meeting date(s): Apr. 1 and Nov. 1
Write: Bill Hill, Trustee

Officers and Trustees:* Carlton Beal,* Chair.; Keleen Beal,* Vice-Chair.; Bill J. Hill,* Secy.-Treas.; Barry A. Beal, Carlton E. Beal, Jr., Spencer Beal, Mitchell A. Cappadonna, Robert J. Cowen, Karlene Beal Garber, Jane B. Ramsland, Pomeroy Smith, Tom Welch.
EIN: 756034480

2955
Theodore and Beulah Beasley Foundation, Inc.
3811 Turtle Creek Village, Suite 940
Dallas 75219-4419   (214) 522-8790

Incorporated in 1957 in TX.
Donor(s): Theodore P. Beasley.
Foundation type: Independent
Financial data (yr. ended 12/31/90): Assets, $7,340,888 (M); expenditures, $435,454; qualifying distributions, $280,347, including $280,347 for grants (high: $100,000; average: $1,000-$10,000).
Fields of interest: Higher education, youth, Protestant giving, hospitals.
Types of support: Capital campaigns, operating budgets, building funds, general purposes.
Limitations: Giving primarily in the Dallas, TX, area. No grants to individuals.
Application information: Contributes only to pre-selected organizations. Applications not accepted.
Board meeting date(s): As required
Write: Mary Beasley, Pres.
Officers: Mary E. Beasley, Pres.; Samuel Dashefsky, V.P. and Treas.; Linda Tinney, Secy.
Number of staff: None.
EIN: 756035806

2956
Bertha Foundation
P.O. Box 1110
Graham 76450   (817) 549-1400

Established in 1967 in TX.
Donor(s): E. Bruce Street, M. Boyd Street.
Foundation type: Independent
Financial data (yr. ended 12/31/91): Assets, $3,748,205 (M); gifts received, $861,600; expenditures, $217,657; qualifying distributions, $199,504, including $193,454 for 23 grants (high: $50,000; low: $23).
Fields of interest: Education, recreation, civic affairs, social services, libraries, hospitals.
Types of support: Operating budgets, scholarship funds, building funds.
Limitations: Giving primarily in TX, with emphasis on Graham. No grants to individuals.
Application information:
Initial approach: Letter
Deadline(s): None
Write: Douglas A. Stroud, V.P.

Officers and Directors:* Alice Ann Street,* Pres.; Douglas A. Stroud,* V.P.; J.R. Montgomery,* Secy.; E. Bruce Street, M. Boyd Street.
EIN: 756050023

2957
Sarah Campbell Blaffer Foundation
12 Greenway Plaza, Suite 716
Houston 77046   (713) 623-8690

Incorporated in 1964 in TX.
Donor(s): Sarah C. Blaffer.‡
Foundation type: Operating
Financial data (yr. ended 12/31/90): Assets, $59,988,157 (M); gifts received, $1,341,810; expenditures, $848,619; qualifying distributions, $782,079, including $240,000 for 39 grants (high: $24,000; low: $500) and $485,798 for 1 foundation-administered program.
Purpose and activities: A private operating foundation; grants for cultural programs, medical research, church support, and secondary and higher education; also operates a program of art exhibits.
Fields of interest: Arts, cultural programs, fine arts, medical research, religion—Christian, Protestant giving, secondary education, higher education.
Limitations: Giving primarily in TX. No grants to individuals, or for endowment funds, scholarships, or fellowships; no loans.
Application information: Application form not required.
Initial approach: Letter
Copies of proposal: 1
Deadline(s): Submit proposal from Jan. through Aug.; deadline Aug. 31
Board meeting date(s): Mar. and Oct.
Final notification: Dec.
Write: Edward Joseph Hudson, Jr., Secy.
Officers and Trustees:* Charles W. Hall,* Pres.; Jane Blaffer Owen,* V.P. and Treas.; Cecil Blaffer von Furstenberg,* V.P.; Edward Joseph Hudson, Jr.,* Secy.; Gilbert M. Denman, Jr.
Number of staff: 2 full-time professional.
EIN: 746065234

2958
Bosque Foundation ▼
(Formerly Bosque Charitable Foundation)
2911 Turtle Creek Blvd., Suite 900
Dallas 75219   (214) 559-0088

Established in 1983 in TX.
Donor(s): Julia T. Beecherl, Louis A. Beecherl, Jr.
Foundation type: Independent
Financial data (yr. ended 12/31/90): Assets, $5,173,739 (M); expenditures, $1,079,470; qualifying distributions, $1,065,873, including $1,065,873 for 17 grants (high: $500,000; low: $1,000; average: $5,000-$20,000).
Purpose and activities: Grants primarily for higher education and medical research.
Fields of interest: Higher education, medical research.
Types of support: Capital campaigns, building funds, research.
Limitations: Giving primarily in TX. No grants to individuals.
Application information:
Initial approach: 1-page letter

Copies of proposal: 1
Deadline(s): None
Board meeting date(s): As required
Final notification: Within 2 weeks
Write: Louis A. Beecherl, Jr., Trustee
Trustees: John T. Beecherl, Julia T. Beecherl, Louis A. Beecherl, Jr., Louis A. Beecherl III, William C. Beecherl, Julianna B. Davis, Mary B. Dillard.
Number of staff: None.
EIN: 756380232

2959
The Brown Foundation, Inc. ▼
2217 Welch Ave.
P.O. Box 130646
Houston 77219-0646   (713) 523-6867

Incorporated in 1951 in TX.
Donor(s): Herman Brown,‡ Margarett Root Brown,‡ George R. Brown,‡ Alice Pratt Brown.‡
Foundation type: Independent
Financial data (yr. ended 06/30/91): Assets, $496,877,087 (M); expenditures, $21,553,678; qualifying distributions, $20,082,363, including $19,820,628 for 181 grants (high: $2,850,000; low: $1,000; average: $10,000-$100,000) and $21,175 for employee matching gifts.
Purpose and activities: Support principally for the encouragement and assistance to education and the arts. The projects selected for funding most likely will have the potential of long-lasting significant impact in the community. The foundation's current emphasis is in the field of public education at the primary and secondary levels. It will focus on searching out and supporting non-traditional and innovative approaches designed to improve public education primarily within the state of Texas. Other areas of interest continue to be the visual and performing arts, and also include community service projects focused upon the needs of children and youth, especially in the Houston area.
Fields of interest: Arts, education.
Types of support: Operating budgets, continuing support, annual campaigns, building funds, endowment funds, matching funds, professorships, special projects, capital campaigns, renovation projects.
Limitations: Giving primarily in TX, with emphasis on Houston. No support for religious organizations or private foundations. No grants to individuals, or for advertising, testimonial dinners, deficit financing, or fundraising events; no loans.
Publications: Application guidelines, annual report (including application guidelines).
Application information: Will consider 1 grant proposal per 12 month period from an organization. No grant funds pledged beyond the current year. Application form not required.
Initial approach: Proposal
Copies of proposal: 1
Deadline(s): None
Board meeting date(s): Feb., May, Aug., and Nov.
Final notification: 3 months
Write: Katherine B. Dobelman, Exec. Dir.
Officers and Trustees:* Maconda Brown O'Connor,* Chair.; Isabel Brown Wilson,* Pres.; Louisa Stude Sarofim,* 1st V.P.; M.S. Stude,* V.P.; Nancy Brown Wellin,* V.P.; Edgar W. Monteith,* Secy.; Katherine B. Dobelman, Treas. and Exec.

Dir.; Travis A. Mathis, John H. O'Connor, James R. Paden, Christopher B. Sarofim.
Number of staff: 1 full-time professional; 5 full-time support; 2 part-time support.
EIN: 746036466
Recent health grants:
2959-1 Childrens Respiratory Summer Camp Foundation, Baytown, TX, $15,000. For Camp expenses. 1991.
2959-2 Cystic Fibrosis Foundation, Houston, TX, $15,000. Toward general operating fund. 1991.
2959-3 Good Samaritan Foundation, Houston, TX, $25,000. For matching grant toward scholarship program for student nurses. 1991.
2959-4 Group Psychotherapy Foundation, NYC, NY, $30,000. For research in group psychotherapy. 1991.
2959-5 Houston Academy of Medicine, Texas Medical Center Library, Houston, TX, $40,000. Toward purchase of books and periodicals. 1991.
2959-6 Mental Health Association of Houston and Harris County, Houston, TX, $83,798. Toward Houston Independent School District We Help Ourselves program. 1991.
2959-7 Methodist Hospital, Houston, TX, $25,000. Toward organ transplantation research program. 1991.
2959-8 Planned Parenthood Federation of America, NYC, NY, $10,000. Toward International Service program. 1991.
2959-9 Planned Parenthood of Houston and Southeast Texas, Houston, TX, $450,000. Toward capital campaign. 1991.
2959-10 Planned Parenthood of Houston and Southeast Texas, Houston, TX, $75,000. Toward general operating fund. 1991.
2959-11 San Jacinto Methodist Hospital, Baytown, TX, $50,000. For family practice program. 1991.
2959-12 Texas Medical Center, Houston, TX, $15,000. Toward water feature and park. 1991.
2959-13 University of Texas, M.D. Anderson Cancer Center, Houston, TX, $150,000. Toward lung cancer research. 1991.
2959-14 University of Texas Health Science Center, Houston, TX, $10,000. Toward scholarships for student nurses. 1991.

2960
William and Catherine Bryce Memorial Fund
c/o Team Bank, N.A.
P.O. Box 2050
Fort Worth 76113   (817) 884-4153

Trust established in 1944 in TX.
Foundation type: Independent
Financial data (yr. ended 09/30/91): Assets, $12,015,802 (M); expenditures, $683,922; qualifying distributions, $599,956, including $595,450 for 52 grants (high: $75,000; low: $350).
Fields of interest: Child welfare, child development, youth, higher education, secondary education, hospitals, cultural programs, social services, civic affairs.
Limitations: Giving limited to TX, particularly in the Fort Worth area. No grants to individuals.
Application information:
   Initial approach: Letter
   Copies of proposal: 1

Deadline(s): Sept.
Board meeting date(s): Nov.
Write: Jane Gallo, Trust Officer, Team Bank, N.A.
Trustee: Team Bank, N.A.
EIN: 756013845

2961
Burlington Northern Foundation ▼
3700 Continental Plaza
777 Main St.
Fort Worth 76102   (817) 878-2265

Incorporated in 1953 in MN; renamed in 1970.
Donor(s): Burlington Northern, Inc.
Foundation type: Company-sponsored
Financial data (yr. ended 12/31/91): Assets, $5,551,016 (M); gifts received, $595,954; expenditures, $4,147,721; qualifying distributions, $4,090,223, including $3,686,925 for 915 grants (high: $50,000; low: $50; average: $1,000-$25,000) and $355,298 for 176 employee matching gifts.
Purpose and activities: Grants primarily for higher education, cultural programs, community funds, social services, including the American Red Cross, civic and recreation programs, and hospitals.
Fields of interest: Higher education, cultural programs, civic affairs, community funds, social services, recreation, health, hospitals.
Types of support: Employee matching gifts, annual campaigns, building funds, equipment, general purposes.
Limitations: Giving primarily in areas of company operations, particularly Seattle, WA. No support for religious organizations for religious purposes, veterans' or fraternal organizations, national health organizations and programs, chambers of commerce, taxpayer associations, state railroad associations, or other bodies whose activities might benefit the company. No grants to individuals, or for operating budgets of hospitals, fundraising events, corporate memberships, endowment funds, scholarships, or fellowships; no loans.
Publications: Program policy statement, application guidelines.
Application information: Application form required.
   Initial approach: Letter requesting application form
   Copies of proposal: 1
   Deadline(s): None
   Board meeting date(s): Quarterly
   Final notification: 4 to 5 months
   Write: Pat Dickinson, Administrator
Officers and Directors:* John N. Etchart, Chair. and Pres.; Ronald H. Reimann, V.P.; Pat Dickinson, Secy.-Treas.
Trustees: First Trust, St. Paul.
Number of staff: 1 full-time professional.
EIN: 416022304
Recent health grants:
2961-1 Cook-Fort Worth Childrens Medical Center, Fort Worth, TX, $50,000. 1990.
2961-2 Oxford House, Great Falls, VA, $20,000. 1990.
2961-3 Quality Living, Omaha, NE, $25,000. 1990.
2961-4 Southern Wasco County Ambulance Service, Maupin, OR, $15,000. 1990.

2961-5 United Cerebral Palsy of Northeastern Minnesota, Duluth, MN, $10,000. 1990.

2962
The Effie and Wofford Cain Foundation ▼
4131 Spicewood Springs Rd.
Austin 78759   (512) 346-7490

Incorporated in 1952 in TX.
Donor(s): Effie Marie Cain, R. Wofford Cain.‡
Foundation type: Independent
Financial data (yr. ended 10/31/91): Assets, $51,582,664 (M); gifts received, $27,000; expenditures, $2,580,717; qualifying distributions, $2,180,410, including $1,985,336 for 82 grants (high: $500,000; low: $250; average: $2,000-$500,000).
Purpose and activities: Giving primarily for higher and secondary education, public service organizations, and cultural programs; grants also for religious organizations, aid to the handicapped, and medical services and research. The foundation has a major annual committment to the Cain Community Center in Athens, GA, and to Texas A&M University.
Fields of interest: Higher education, medical education, secondary education, education, community development, civic affairs, child development, arts, cultural programs, museums, fine arts, performing arts, religious schools, religious welfare, handicapped, disadvantaged, health, health services, hospitals, medical research.
Types of support: Building funds, endowment funds, seed money, operating budgets, research, scholarship funds, annual campaigns, continuing support, fellowships, internships, capital campaigns, professorships.
Limitations: Giving limited to TX. No grants to individuals.
Publications: Application guidelines.
Application information: Application form required.
   Initial approach: Telephone call or letter of inquiry
   Copies of proposal: 1
   Deadline(s): Aug. 31 for Oct. meeting; budget usually fully committed by July 1
   Board meeting date(s): Oct. (annual); 4 to 6 interim meetings (dates vary)
   Final notification: Varies
   Write: Harvey L. Walker, Exec. Dir.
Officers and Directors:* Effie Marie Cain,* Pres.; Franklin W. Denius,* Exec. V.P.; James B. Cain,* V.P.; R.J. Smith, Jr.,* V.P.; Harvey L. Walker, Secy., Treas. and Exec. Dir.; John C. Cain, Chamaine D. McGill.
Number of staff: 2 full-time professional; 1 full-time support; 1 part-time support.
EIN: 756030774
Recent health grants:
2962-1 Arthritis Foundation, North Texas Chapter, Dallas, TX, $15,000. For arthritis research. 1991.
2962-2 Austin Groups for the Elderly (AGE), Austin, TX, $10,000. For debt reduction for nursing home. 1991.
2962-3 Baylor College of Medicine, Houston, TX, $250,000. For research chair in cardiology. 1991.

2962-4 Baylor College of Medicine, Houston, TX, $50,000. For student exchange program. 1991.

2963
The Gordon and Mary Cain Foundation ▼
Eight Greenway Plaza, Suite 702
Houston 77046   (713) 960-9283

Established in 1988 in TX.
Donor(s): Gordon A. Cain, Mary H. Cain.
Foundation type: Independent
Financial data (yr. ended 12/31/90): Assets, $25,582,237 (M); gifts received, $25,000; expenditures, $1,375,538; qualifying distributions, $1,239,096, including $1,142,250 for 84 grants (high: $250,000; low: $250).
Purpose and activities: Giving primarily for higher and secondary educations, social services, health associations, arts, and denominational giving.
Fields of interest: Higher education, secondary education, family services, social services, child welfare, health associations, AIDS, arts, denominational giving.
Types of support: General purposes, annual campaigns, scholarship funds, building funds, continuing support, operating budgets, renovation projects, research.
Limitations: Giving primarily in Houston, TX. No grants to individuals.
Publications: Application guidelines.
Application information: Application form not required.
> *Initial approach:* Proposal
> *Copies of proposal:* 1
> *Deadline(s):* None
> *Board meeting date(s):* Spring and fall
> *Write:* James D. Weaver, Pres.

Officers: Gordon A. Cain, Chair.; James D. Weaver, Pres. and C.O.O.; Mary H. Cain, V.P.; Margaret W. Oehmig, V.P.; Sharyn A. Weaver, V.P.; William C. Oehmig, Secy.-Treas. and C.F.O.
Number of staff: 1 full-time professional; 1 part-time support.
EIN: 760251558
Recent health grants:
2963-1 American Cancer Society, Houston, TX, $10,000. For general operations. 1990.
2963-2 Good Samaritan Foundation, Houston, TX, $70,000. For general operations. 1990.
2963-3 Good Samaritan Foundation, Houston, TX, $30,000. 1990.
2963-4 Planned Parenthood Center of Houston, Houston, TX, $15,000. For general operations. 1990.
2963-5 Texas Childrens Hospital, Houston, TX, $250,000. For building fund. 1990.
2963-6 University of Texas, Medical School, Houston, TX, $10,000. For scholarship fund and student assistant program. 1990.

2964
Harry S. and Isabel C. Cameron Foundation
c/o NationsBank
P.O. Box 298502
Houston 77298-0502   (713) 787-4551

Established in 1966 in TX.
Donor(s): Isabel C. Cameron.‡

Foundation type: Independent
Financial data (yr. ended 06/30/91): Assets, $16,597,118 (M); expenditures, $1,018,699; qualifying distributions, $887,946, including $868,801 for 125 grants (high: $117,000; low: $200; average: $100-$10,000).
Fields of interest: Higher education, elementary education, secondary education, Catholic giving, health, social services, youth.
Types of support: Building funds, research, equipment, general purposes.
Limitations: Giving primarily in TX, especially Houston. No grants to individuals, or for operating support, endowment funds, or matching gifts; no loans.
Application information: Application form not required.
> *Initial approach:* Letter
> *Copies of proposal:* 6
> *Deadline(s):* Prior to board meetings
> *Board meeting date(s):* Apr., Aug., and Dec.
> *Final notification:* 2 weeks after board meetings, when action is favorable
> *Write:* Carl W. Schumacher, Jr. or Sally Braddy

Directors: Charlotte Cameron, David W. Cameron, Estelle Cameron Maloney, Frances Cameron Miller, Sylvia Cameron.
Trustee: NationsBank.
Number of staff: None.
EIN: 746073312

2965
Amon G. Carter Foundation ▼
1212 NCNB Ctr.
P.O. Box 1036
Fort Worth 76101   (817) 332-2783

Incorporated in 1945 in TX.
Donor(s): Amon G. Carter,‡ N.B. Carter,‡ Star-Telegram Employees Fund, Carter Foundation Production Co.
Foundation type: Independent
Financial data (yr. ended 12/31/90): Assets, $182,785,896 (M); expenditures, $9,709,948; qualifying distributions, $13,763,646, including $7,929,010 for 134 grants (high: $3,728,089; low: $250; average: $20,000-$100,000).
Purpose and activities: Grants primarily for the visual and performing arts, education, health care, social service and youth agencies, programs for the aged, and civic and community endeavors that enhance the quality of life. The foundation sponsors and largely supports an art museum.
Fields of interest: Arts, cultural programs, performing arts, museums, education, higher education, health services, hospitals, social services, youth, aged, civic affairs.
Types of support: Continuing support, annual campaigns, seed money, emergency funds, building funds, equipment, land acquisition, matching funds, professorships, research, renovation projects, capital campaigns, general purposes, special projects.
Limitations: Giving largely restricted to Fort Worth and Tarrant County, TX. No grants to individuals, or for ongoing operating budgets, deficit financing, publications, or conferences; no loans.
Publications: Program policy statement.
Application information: Grants outside local geographic area usually initiated by board. Application form not required.

> *Initial approach:* Letter
> *Copies of proposal:* 1
> *Deadline(s):* None
> *Board meeting date(s):* Apr., Sept., and Dec.
> *Final notification:* Within 10 days of board meeting
> *Write:* Bob J. Crow, Exec. Dir.

Officers and Directors:* Ruth Carter Stevenson,* Pres.; Robert W. Brown, M.D.,* V.P.; Paul W. Mason,* Secy.-Treas.; Bob J. Crow, Exec. Dir.; J. Lee Johnson IV, Mark L. Johnson.
Number of staff: 3 full-time professional; 3 full-time support.
EIN: 756000331
Recent health grants:
2965-1 American Heart Association, Fort Worth, TX, $50,000. For building fund. 1990.
2965-2 Because We Care, Fort Worth, TX, $50,000. For special program. 1990.
2965-3 Cenikor Foundation, Fort Worth, TX, $25,000. For special program. 1990.
2965-4 Child Study Center, Fort Worth, TX, $245,000. For building fund. 1990.
2965-5 Easter Seal Society for Crippled Children and Adults of Tarrant County, Fort Worth, TX, $35,400. For general support. 1990.
2965-6 Harlingen Community Emergency Care Foundation, Harlingen, TX, $20,000. For special program. 1990.
2965-7 John Peter Smith Hospital, Fort Worth, TX, $88,365. For special program. 1990.
2965-8 National Federation Target Program, Kansas City, MO, $109,856. For special program. 1990.
2965-9 Planned Parenthood of North Texas, Fort Worth, TX, $50,000. For special program. 1990.
2965-10 Texas Society to Prevent Blindness, Fort Worth, TX, $25,000. For building fund. 1990.
2965-11 Wellway Centers, Fort Worth, TX, $12,000. For special program. 1990.
2965-12 What About Remembering Me (WARM) Center, Fort Worth, TX, $45,000. For general support. 1990.

2966
The Chilton Foundation Trust
c/o NationsBank
P.O. Box 830241
Dallas 75283-0241   (214) 559-6413
Application address: c/o NationsBank, P.O. Box 831515, Dallas, TX 75283-1515

Trust established in 1945 in TX.
Donor(s): Arthur L. Chilton,‡ Leonore Chilton.‡
Foundation type: Independent
Financial data (yr. ended 12/31/90): Assets, $8,162,327 (M); expenditures, $849,328; qualifying distributions, $798,293, including $791,650 for 50 grants (high: $126,200; low: $500; average: $5,000-$25,000).
Fields of interest: Youth, hospitals, health, education, social services.
Limitations: Giving primarily in TX. No grants to individuals.
Application information: Application form not required.
> *Deadline(s):* None
> *Board meeting date(s):* As necessary
> *Final notification:* 2 months
> *Write:* Alice J. Gayle, Trust Officer, NationsBank

Trustee: NationsBank.

Number of staff: None.
EIN: 756006996

2967
The Cimarron Foundation
c/o Texas Commerce Bank
P.O. Drawer 140
El Paso 79980   (915) 546-6515

Established in 1987 in TX.
Donor(s): Woody L. Hunt.
Foundation type: Independent
Financial data (yr. ended 12/31/90): Assets,
$2,895,760 (M); gifts received, $2,000,000;
expenditures, $70,659; qualifying distributions,
$62,743, including $61,245 for 5 grants (high:
$25,000; low: $2,000).
Fields of interest: Medical research, education,
child welfare, child development, disadvantaged,
handicapped, social services.
Types of support: Research, general purposes,
building funds, capital campaigns, operating
budgets.
Limitations: Giving primarily in TX. No grants to
individuals.
Application information:
  Initial approach: Letter
  Deadline(s): None
  Write: Miss Terry Crenshaw, Trust Officer, Texas
    Commerce Bank
Officers and Trustees:* Woody L. Hunt,* Pres.;
Gayle G. Hunt,* V.P.; Jack L. Hunt, Texas
Commerce Bank.
EIN: 742489868

2968
The Clayton Fund, Inc.
c/o First City, Texas-Houston
P.O. Box 809
Houston 77001

Trust established in 1952 in TX.
Donor(s): William L. Clayton,‡ Susan V. Clayton.‡
Foundation type: Independent
Financial data (yr. ended 12/31/90): Assets,
$25,007,195 (M); expenditures, $1,194,426;
qualifying distributions, $1,049,915, including
$1,016,607 for 58 grants (high: $200,000; low:
$300; average: $5,000-$25,000).
Purpose and activities: Support largely for higher
education, including medical education and
scholarships; grants also for hospitals, medical
research, social services, population control, and
cultural programs.
Fields of interest: Higher education, medical
education, hospitals, medical research, nursing,
social services, family planning, cultural programs.
Types of support: Scholarship funds, continuing
support, operating budgets, program-related
investments, employee-related scholarships.
Limitations: Giving primarily in TX.
Application information: Request application
guidelines for scholarship program. Application
form not required.
  Copies of proposal: 1
  Write: Joe Patane, Trust Officer, First City,
    Texas-Houston
Officers and Trustees:* S.M. McAshan, Jr.,* Pres.;
Burdine Venghiattis,* V.P.; W.W. Vann,
Secy.-Treas. and Exec. Dir.; William C. Baker,
William L. Garwood, Jr.

Number of staff: 1 full-time professional; 1
full-time support.
EIN: 760285764

2969
Coastal Bend Community Foundation
860 First City Bank Tower - FCB 276
Corpus Christi 78477   (512) 882-9745

Established in 1980 in TX.
Foundation type: Community
Financial data (yr. ended 12/31/91): Assets,
$8,427,351 (M); gifts received, $834,240;
expenditures, $739,639; qualifying distributions,
$583,424, including $576,448 for 200 grants
(high: $25,000; low: $800; average:
$1,000-$5,000) and $6,976 for 29 grants to
individuals (high: $500; low: $125; average:
$200-$400).
Purpose and activities: Giving primarily for social
services, including alcohol and drug abuse
programs, youth and child welfare, the
disadvantaged, the homeless and hungry, and
welfare; hospitals; volunteerism; community
development; animal welfare; higher and other
education, including scholarship funds, literacy,
and libraries; arts and culture, including museums
and history.
Fields of interest: Drug abuse, alcoholism, youth,
higher education, libraries, cultural programs,
community development, disadvantaged, arts,
animal welfare.
Types of support: Seed money, scholarship funds,
equipment, general purposes, special projects,
fellowships.
Limitations: Giving limited to Aransas, Bee, Jim
Wells, Kleberg, Nueces, Refugio, and San Patricio
counties, TX.
Publications: Grants list, newsletter, informational
brochure (including application guidelines).
Application information: Application form not
required.
  Initial approach: Letter requesting guidelines
  Copies of proposal: 1
  Deadline(s): Sept. 15
  Board meeting date(s): Feb., May, Aug., and
    Nov.
  Final notification: Nov.
  Write: Dana Williams, Exec. V.P.
Officer and Director:* Dana Williams,* Exec. V.P.
Number of staff: 1 full-time professional; 1
full-time support.
EIN: 742190039

2970
Cockrell Foundation ▼
1600 Smith, Suite 4600
Houston 77002-7348   (713) 651-1271

Trust established in 1957 in TX; incorporated in
1966.
Donor(s): Mrs. Dula Cockrell,‡ Ernest Cockrell,
Jr.,‡ Virginia H. Cockrell.‡
Foundation type: Independent
Financial data (yr. ended 12/31/90): Assets,
$63,382,279 (M); expenditures, $3,092,106;
qualifying distributions, $2,812,885, including
$2,797,940 for 51 grants (high: $900,000; low:
$700; average: $1,000-$10,000).

Purpose and activities: Giving for higher
education; support also for cultural programs,
social services, youth, religion, and hospitals.
Fields of interest: Higher education, social
services, youth, child welfare, hospitals, cultural
programs, museums, religion—Christian.
Types of support: Annual campaigns, building
funds, capital campaigns, endowment funds,
fellowships, general purposes, matching funds,
operating budgets, professorships, research,
scholarship funds, special projects.
Limitations: Giving primarily in Houston, TX. No
grants to individuals.
Publications: Annual report, 990-PF.
Application information: Application form not
required.
  Initial approach: Proposal
  Copies of proposal: 1
  Deadline(s): None
  Board meeting date(s): Mar. and Oct.
  Final notification: 6 weeks
  Write: Mary McIntier, Exec. V.P.
Officers and Directors:* Alf Roark,* Pres.; Mary
McIntier, Exec. V.P.; Ernest H. Cockrell,* V.P.; W.F.
Wright, Jr., Secy.-Treas.; Janet S. Cockrell, Carol
Cockrell Curran, Richard B. Curran.
Number of staff: None.
EIN: 746076993
Recent health grants:
2970-1 Covenant House, Houston, TX, $30,000.
  For Medical Director's position. 1990.
2970-2 Holly Hall, Houston, TX, $10,000. For
  building fund. 1990.
2970-3 M. D. Anderson Cancer Center, Houston,
  TX, $100,000. For Scientific Achievement
  Fund. 1990.
2970-4 Saint Johns Hospital and Nursing Home,
  Jackson, WY, $10,000. For capital campaign.
  1990.
2970-5 Texas Childrens Hospital, Houston, TX,
  $250,000. For building for children. 1990.

2971
The James M. Collins Foundation
3131 Turtle Creek Blvd., Suite 810
Dallas 75219   (214) 522-0671

Established in 1964 in TX.
Donor(s): James M. Collins.‡
Foundation type: Independent
Financial data (yr. ended 12/31/90): Assets,
$5,704,272 (M); expenditures, $331,083;
qualifying distributions, $304,461, including
$300,875 for 132 grants (high: $150,000; low:
$50).
Purpose and activities: Emphasis on higher
education, including business and medical
education; church support and religious
associations; and hospitals and medical research.
Fields of interest: Higher education, business
education, medical education, religion, hospitals,
medical research.
Limitations: Giving primarily in TX. No grants to
individuals; no loans.
Application information: Applications not
accepted.
  Write: Dorothy Collins, Pres.
Officers and Trustees:* Dorothy Dann Collins,*
Pres.; Michael J. Collins,* V.P.; Kimberly K.
Karalija,* Secy.; Hubbard Hardy, Treas.
Number of staff: None.
EIN: 756040743

2972
Communities Foundation of Texas, Inc. ▼
4605 Live Oak St.
Dallas 75204 (214) 826-5231

Established in 1953 in TX; incorporated in 1960.
Foundation type: Community
Financial data (yr. ended 06/30/90): Assets, $205,225,229 (M); gifts received, $34,434,581; expenditures, $27,031,638; qualifying distributions, $24,627,460, including $24,627,460 for 1,162 grants (high: $4,144,175; low: $10; average: $500-$25,000).
Purpose and activities: Grants from unrestricted funds are generally for education, health and hospitals, social services, youth, and cultural programs.
Fields of interest: Education, health, hospitals, cultural programs, social services, youth.
Types of support: Seed money, emergency funds, building funds, equipment, land acquisition, matching funds, technical assistance, special projects, research, capital campaigns.
Limitations: Giving primarily in the Dallas, TX, area. No support for religious purposes from general fund, media projects, publications, or organizations which redistribute funds to other organizations. No grants to individuals, or for continuing support, deficit financing, endowment funds, scholarships, or fellowships.
Publications: Program policy statement, application guidelines, financial statement, newsletter, annual report, 990-PF.
Application information: Application form not required.
  Initial approach: Letter requesting guidelines
  Copies of proposal: 1
  Deadline(s): Feb. 1, July 1, and Oct. 1
  Board meeting date(s): Distribution committee for unrestricted funds meets in Mar., Aug., and Nov.
  Final notification: 1 week after distribution committee meeting
  Write: Kimberly Floyd, Grant Administrator
Officers and Trustees:* John Stephens,* Chair. and C.E.O.; Ruth Sharp Altshuler, Vice-Chair.; Edward M. Fjordbak,* Pres.; Margaret E. Shumake, Corp. Secy.; J. Michael Redfearn, Controller; Charlotte A. Nelson, Dir., Finance; Kimberly Floyd, Grant Admin.; Ebby Halliday Acers, Louis A. Beecherl, Jr., Durwood Chalker, Joe D. Denton, Jack B. Jackson, Thomas C. Unis.
Number of staff: 10 full-time professional; 1 part-time professional; 15 full-time support; 4 part-time support.
EIN: 750964565
Recent health grants:
2972-1 American Cancer Society, Dallas, TX, $22,775. 1991.
2972-2 American Cancer Society, Midland, TX, $15,000. 1991.
2972-3 American Diabetes Association, Dallas, TX, $10,000. 1991.
2972-4 Baylor College of Dentistry, Dallas, TX, $30,780. 1991.
2972-5 Baylor University Medical Center, Dallas, TX, $13,500. 1991.
2972-6 Benign Essential Blepharospasm Research Foundation, Beaumont, TX, $12,700. 1991.
2972-7 Children of Alcoholics Foundation, NYC, NY, $50,000. 1991.

2972-8 Childrens Cancer Fund of Dallas, Dallas, TX, $27,070. 1991.
2972-9 Childrens Medical Foundation, Dallas, TX, $19,867. 1991.
2972-10 Cook-Fort Worth Childrens Medical Center, Fort Worth, TX, $30,100. 1991.
2972-11 Cystic Fibrosis Foundation, Dallas, TX, $10,850. 1991.
2972-12 Dallas Area Parkinsonism Society, Dallas, TX, $16,594. 1991.
2972-13 Dallas Child Guidance Clinic, Dallas, TX, $34,541. 1991.
2972-14 Dallas Home for Jewish Aged, Dallas, TX, $63,000. 1991.
2972-15 Easter Seal Society for Children, Dallas, TX, $26,700. 1991.
2972-16 Fort Worth, City of, Public Health Department, Fort Worth, TX, $10,000. 1991.
2972-17 Herrin House, Dallas, TX, $30,200. 1991.
2972-18 Incest Recovery Association, Dallas, TX, $31,875. 1991.
2972-19 Kelsey-Seybold Foundation, Houston, TX, $15,000. 1991.
2972-20 Leaves, The, Richardson, TX, $10,000. 1991.
2972-21 Lions Sight and Tissue Foundation, Dallas, TX, $25,000. 1991.
2972-22 Maternity Cottage, Wichita Falls, TX, $10,000. 1991.
2972-23 Parkland Memorial Hospital Foundation, Dallas, TX, $10,000. 1991.
2972-24 Quality of Life Foundation of Austin, Austin, TX, $118,000. For capitol salute to the troops. 1991.
2972-25 Rockefeller University, NYC, NY, $260,000. 1991.
2972-26 Ross Centers, Lakewood, CO, $94,691. 1991.
2972-27 Saint Paul Medical Center, Dallas, TX, $16,666. 1991.
2972-28 Samuel Waxman Cancer Research Foundation, NYC, NY, $25,000. 1991.
2972-29 Shriners Hospital for Crippled Children, Chicago, IL, $25,000. 1991.
2972-30 Susan G. Komen Foundation, Dallas, TX, $17,550. 1991.
2972-31 Texas Society to Prevent Blindness, Houston, TX, $38,102. 1991.
2972-32 Third World Prosthetic Foundation, DC, $37,000. 1991.
2972-33 University of Texas Southwestern Medical Center, Dallas, TX, $343,750. 1991.
2972-34 University of Texas Southwestern Medical Center, Dallas, TX, $155,075. 1991.
2972-35 Wadley Institutes of Molecular Medicine, Dallas, TX, $155,200. 1991.
2972-36 Zale Lipshy University Hospital, Dallas, TX, $351,000. 1991.

2973
Community Hospital Foundation, Inc.
P.O. Box 24185
Houston 77229

Incorporated in 1986 in TX.
Foundation type: Independent
Financial data (yr. ended 05/31/91): Assets, $4,601,060 (M); expenditures, $328,671; qualifying distributions, $292,412, including $213,000 for 30 grants (high: $25,000; low: $500) and $52,000 for grants to individuals.

Purpose and activities: Giving primarily for higher education and Protestant churches; also provides scholarships to individuals for medical-related education.
Fields of interest: Higher education, Protestant giving, medical education.
Types of support: Student aid, capital campaigns, scholarship funds.
Limitations: Giving primarily in TX.
Application information:
  Initial approach: Proposal
  Deadline(s): None
  Write: Dr. Loren Rohr, Pres.
Officers: Loren Rohr, Pres.; J.H. Kritzler, V.P.; Edythe Tompson, Secy.-Treas.
Directors: G. Cobb, J. Ward.
EIN: 741470290

2974
Compaq Computer Foundation ▼
20555 SH 249
Houston 77070 (713) 370-0670

Established in 1988 in TX.
Donor(s): Compaq Computer Corp.
Foundation type: Company-sponsored
Financial data (yr. ended 12/31/90): Assets, $7,982,580 (M); gifts received, $7,090,097; expenditures, $2,825,081; qualifying distributions, $2,821,792, including $765,688 for 47 grants (high: $240,000; low: $500; average: $10,000-$25,000), $13,055 for 102 employee matching gifts and $2,043,049 for 1,448 in-kind gifts.
Purpose and activities: Supports health and human services, arts and culture, civic affairs, and welfare; also makes in-kind gifts and employee-matching gifts.
Fields of interest: Health, welfare, arts, cultural programs, civic affairs.
Types of support: In-kind gifts, employee matching gifts.
Limitations: Giving primarily in Houston, TX, but also giving in other areas of company operations.
Application information: Application form not required.
  Initial approach: Letter or telephone
  Copies of proposal: 1
  Deadline(s): None
  Write: Lou Ann Champ, Corp. Contribs. Administrator
Officers and Trustees:* James M. Eckhart,* Pres.; Dave Schempf,* V.P. and Treas.; Wilson D. Fargo, Secy.; Joseph R. Canion, James Harris.
EIN: 760264597
Recent health grants:
2974-1 Palmer Drug Abuse Program, Houston, TX, $54,555. For operating expenses. 1990.
2974-2 Stehlin Foundation for Cancer Research, Houston, TX, $150,000. For final payment. 1990.

2975
The Constantin Foundation ▼
3811 Turtle Creek Blvd., Suite 320-LB 39
Dallas 75219 (214) 522-9300

Trust established in 1947 in TX.
Donor(s): E. Constantin, Jr.,‡ Mrs. E. Constantin, Jr.‡
Foundation type: Independent

Financial data (yr. ended 12/31/90): Assets, $31,935,839 (M); expenditures, $1,760,539; qualifying distributions, $1,531,261, including $1,512,162 for 34 grants (high: $450,000; low: $5,000).

Purpose and activities: Emphasis on higher and other education; some support for cultural programs, social service and youth agencies, and hospitals and health, including alcohol and drug abuse programs.

Fields of interest: Higher education, secondary education, libraries, humanities, cultural programs, social services, youth, health, rehabilitation, media and communications.

Types of support: Building funds, matching funds, general purposes, land acquisition, equipment, capital campaigns, continuing support, renovation projects.

Limitations: Giving limited to the Dallas, TX, metropolitan area. No support for state schools, the theater, or churches. No grants to individuals, or for research; no loans.

Publications: Application guidelines.

Application information: Application form not required.

> *Initial approach:* Request guidelines
> *Copies of proposal:* 1
> *Deadline(s):* Sept. 30; grants reviewed at quarterly meetings; grant meeting in Dec.
> *Board meeting date(s):* Feb., May, Aug., Nov., and Dec.
> *Final notification:* Jan.
> *Write:* Betty S. Hillin, Exec. Dir.

Officer: Betty S. Hillin, Exec. Dir.

Trustees: Henry C. Beck, Jr., Gene H. Bishop, Walter L. Fleming, Jr., Paul A. Lockhart, Jr., Joel T. Williams, Jr.

Number of staff: 1 full-time professional; 1 full-time support.

EIN: 756011289

Recent health grants:

2975-1 Childrens Medical Center of Dallas, Dallas, TX, $50,000. 1990.

2975-2 Dallas Challenge, Dallas, TX, $40,000. 1990.

2975-3 Dallas Child Guidance Clinic, Dallas, TX, $50,000. 1990.

2975-4 Daytop Village Foundation, Dallas, TX, $50,000. 1990.

2975-5 Herrin House, Dallas, TX, $50,000. 1990.

2975-6 Nexus, Dallas, TX, $25,000. 1990.

2975-7 Saint Paul Medical Center, Dallas, TX, $40,000. 1990.

2975-8 University Medical Center, Dallas, TX, $30,000. 1990.

2976
The Denton A. Cooley Foundation

6624 Fannin, No. 2700
Houston 77030 (713) 799-2700

Incorporated in 1960 in TX.

Donor(s): Denton A. Cooley, M.D., Louise T. Cooley.

Foundation type: Independent

Financial data (yr. ended 11/30/91): Assets, $793,026 (M); gifts received, $155,000; expenditures, $281,701; qualifying distributions, $262,040, including $262,040 for 68 grants (high: $150,000; low: $40).

Fields of interest: Medical education, medical research, higher education, health services.

Types of support: Operating budgets, building funds, endowment funds, special projects, research.

Limitations: Giving primarily in the Houston, TX, area. No grants to individuals, or for scholarships, fellowships, publications, or conferences; no loans.

Publications: 990-PF.

Application information: Application form not required.

> *Initial approach:* Proposal
> *Copies of proposal:* 1
> *Deadline(s):* None
> *Board meeting date(s):* Quarterly
> *Final notification:* 4 to 6 months
> *Write:* Gerald Maley, Secy.-Treas.

Officers and Trustees:* Denton A. Cooley, M.D.,* Pres.; Louise T. Cooley,* V.P.; Gerald A. Maley,* Secy.-Treas.; Richard C. Hudson.

Number of staff: None.

EIN: 746053213

2977
Cooper Industries Foundation ▼

First City Tower, Suite 4000
P.O. Box 4446
Houston 77210 (713) 739-5607

Incorporated in 1964; absorbed Crouse-Hinds Foundation in 1982; absorbed McGraw-Edison Foundation in 1985.

Donor(s): Cooper Industries, Inc.

Foundation type: Company-sponsored

Financial data (yr. ended 12/31/90): Assets, $449,942 (M); gifts received, $3,300,000; expenditures, $3,990,712; qualifying distributions, $3,981,705, including $3,567,573 for 862 grants (high: $312,500; low: $15; average: $1,000-$5,000) and $413,094 for employee matching gifts.

Purpose and activities: Functions solely as a conduit through which Cooper Industries, Inc. and its operating units throughout the country make contributions to local charities, United Funds, education, civic and community affairs and limited health and welfare programs where company's operations are located; emergency funds are for local organizations only.

Fields of interest: Community funds, higher education, vocational education, youth, performing arts, arts, museums, health, conservation.

Types of support: Operating budgets, continuing support, annual campaigns, seed money, emergency funds, matching funds, employee matching gifts, employee-related scholarships, special projects, building funds, capital campaigns, general purposes.

Limitations: Giving primarily in Houston, TX, and other communities of company operations in AL, CA, CT, GA, IL, IN, ME, MI, MO, MS, NJ, NY, NC, OH, OK, PA, SC, TN, TX, and VA. No support for religious, fraternal, veterans', or lobbying organizations; national or state health and welfare organizations (except through the United Way and the company's matching gift program); or private elementary and secondary schools. No grants to individuals (except for scholarships to children of company employees), or for endowment funds, publications, conferences and seminars, or, generally, for hospital capital fund drives or their operating campaigns; no loans.

Publications: Application guidelines.

Application information: Requests that are local in nature will be referred to the nearest local operation for recommendation. Application form not required.

> *Initial approach:* Letter
> *Copies of proposal:* 1
> *Deadline(s):* Fall for funding the following year
> *Board meeting date(s):* Feb.; distribution committee meets semiannually
> *Final notification:* Within 90 days
> *Write:* Margie Joe, Secy.

Officers and Trustees:* Robert Cizik,* Chair.; Thomas W. Campbell,* Pres.; Alan E. Riedel,* Sr. V.P.; Margie Joe, Secy.; Dewain K. Cross,* Treas.

Number of staff: 2 part-time professional; 1 full-time support.

EIN: 316060698

Recent health grants:

2977-1 American Lung Association, Houston, TX, $12,000. For TB Elimination Project. 1990.

2977-2 Canonsburg General Hospital Foundation, Canonsburg, PA, $25,000. 1990.

2977-3 Odyssey House, Houston, TX, $10,000. 1990.

2977-4 Sturgis Hospital, Sturgis, MI, $12,000. 1990.

2977-5 Womens Christian Home, Houston, TX, $10,000. 1990.

2978
Ed Cox Foundation

2200 Ross Ave., Suite 3600
Dallas 75201

Established in 1985 in TX.

Donor(s): Elizabeth Cox,‡ Edwin L. Cox.

Foundation type: Independent

Financial data (yr. ended 12/31/90): Assets, $821,727 (M); gifts received, $442,000; expenditures, $232,748; qualifying distributions, $232,142, including $212,630 for 23 grants (high: $90,000; low: $100).

Fields of interest: Higher education, medical research, museums, general charitable giving.

Types of support: General purposes.

Limitations: Giving primarily in Dallas, TX. No grants to individuals.

Application information: Contributes only to pre-selected organizations. Applications not accepted.

Officer and Trustees:* J. Oliver McGonigle,* Mgr.; Berry R. Cox, Edwin L. Cox, Edwin L. Cox, Jr.

EIN: 752042913

2979
Joe and Jessie Crump Fund

c/o Team Bank, N.A.
P.O. Box 2050
Fort Worth 76113 (817) 884-4151

Trust established in 1965 in TX.

Foundation type: Independent

Financial data (yr. ended 09/30/91): Assets, $10,096,984 (M); expenditures, $1,308,153; qualifying distributions, $1,111,411, including $804,000 for 11 grants (high: $204,000; low: $5,000) and $290,441 for 4 loans.

Purpose and activities: Giving primarily for an Episcopal theological seminary; support also for cancer research, aid to handicapped children, and the Episcopal church.

Fields of interest: Theological education, cancer, medical research, handicapped.

Types of support: Research, scholarship funds, loans, lectureships.

Limitations: Giving limited to TX. No grants to individuals, or for building or endowment funds, matching gifts, or general purposes.

Application information: Application form not required.

> *Initial approach:* Letter
> *Copies of proposal:* 1
> *Deadline(s):* None
> *Board meeting date(s):* As required
> *Write:* Robert M. Lansford, Sr. V.P., Team Bank, N.A.

Trustees: Robert M. Lansford, Team Bank, N.A.

Number of staff: 1 shared staff

EIN: 756045044

2980
The Cullen Foundation ▼
601 Jefferson, 40th Fl.
Houston 77002   (713) 651-8600
Mailing address: P.O. Box 1600, Houston, TX 77251

Trust established in 1947 in TX.

Donor(s): Hugh Roy Cullen,‡ Lillie Cullen.‡

Foundation type: Independent

Financial data (yr. ended 12/31/90): Assets, $164,449,606 (M); expenditures, $13,360,194; qualifying distributions, $11,178,790, including $10,981,000 for 36 grants (high: $6,000,000; low: $5,000; average: $30,000-$110,000).

Purpose and activities: Giving for charitable, educational, medical, and other eleemosynary purposes; grants for hospitals, medical, including eye, research, and higher education; support also for music, the performing arts, social services, drug abuse prevention, community funds, and conservation.

Fields of interest: Health, hospitals, medical research, ophthalmology, higher education, music, performing arts, social services, drug abuse, community funds, conservation.

Types of support: Annual campaigns, deficit financing, building funds, equipment, land acquisition, general purposes, matching funds, professorships, research, renovation projects.

Limitations: Giving limited to TX, with emphasis on Houston. No grants to individuals; no loans.

Publications: 990-PF, application guidelines.

Application information: Application form not required.

> *Initial approach:* Proposal, letter, or telephone
> *Copies of proposal:* 1
> *Deadline(s):* None
> *Board meeting date(s):* Usually in Jan., Apr., July, Oct., and as required
> *Final notification:* Varies
> *Write:* Joseph C. Graf, Exec. Secy.

Officers and Trustees:* Wilhelmina Cullen Robertson,* Pres.; Roy Henry Cullen,* V.P.; Isaac Arnold, Jr.,* Secy.-Treas.; Joseph C. Graf, Exec. Secy.; Bert Campbell, Douglas B. Marshall, Jr.

Number of staff: 1 full-time professional; 1 full-time support.

EIN: 746048769

Recent health grants:

2980-1 Baylor College of Medicine, Houston, TX, $580,000. For second installment on grant toward endowment in molecular genetic research. 1990.

2980-2 Baylor College of Medicine, Houston, TX, $300,000. For Parkinson's Disease research. 1990.

2980-3 Baylor College of Medicine, Houston, TX, $200,000. For Parkinson's Disease research. 1990.

2980-4 Institute for Rehabilitation and Research Foundation, Houston, TX, $100,000. Toward patient tower. 1990.

2980-5 Methodist Hospital, Cardiovascular Patient Register, Houston, TX, $100,000. For development and implementation of computerized patient register. 1990.

2980-6 Stehlin Foundation for Cancer Research, Houston, TX, $244,000. For purchase of Preparative Flow Cytometer. 1990.

2980-7 Texas Childrens Hospital, Houston, TX, $600,000. Toward construction of facilities. 1990.

2980-8 Texas Heart Institute, Houston, TX, $200,000. Toward Campaign for the Texas Heart Institute. 1990.

2981
The Dallas Foundation
400 South Record St., Suite 600
Dallas 75202-4818   (214) 977-6676

Established in 1929 in TX.

Foundation type: Community

Financial data (yr. ended 12/31/90): Assets, $14,561,111 (M); gifts received, $489,350; expenditures, $1,346,670; qualifying distributions, $1,110,121, including $1,110,121 for 44 grants (high: $171,858; low: $3,500; average: $20,000-$100,000).

Purpose and activities: Giving to promote charitable, educational, cultural, civic, and health programs, including those for the disadvantaged, through grants to community organizations and agencies, principally for capital purposes.

Fields of interest: Education, cultural programs, civic affairs, health, disadvantaged.

Types of support: Building funds, capital campaigns, equipment, general purposes, special projects, matching funds, renovation projects.

Limitations: Giving limited to the City and County of Dallas, TX. No grants to individuals, or for endowment or emergency funds, operating budgets, annual campaigns, seed money, land acquisition, conferences and seminars, continuing support, publications, deficit financing, consulting services, technical assistance, research, scholarships, or fellowships; no loans.

Publications: Program policy statement, application guidelines, informational brochure, grants list.

Application information: Application form not required.

> *Initial approach:* 1-page proposal
> *Copies of proposal:* 1
> *Deadline(s):* Apr. 15 and Oct. 1
> *Board meeting date(s):* Usually in Feb., May, and Nov.
> *Final notification:* Following Nov. board meeting
> *Write:* Mary M. Jalonick, Exec. Dir.

Officer: Mary M. Jalonick, Exec. Dir.

Governors: George Schrader, Chair.; Robert W. Decherd, David G. Fox, Rev. Zan W. Holmes, Jr., Joseph R. Musolino, Joe Boyd Neuhoff, Caren H. Prothro, Margaret J. Rogers, John Field Scovell.

Trustee Bank: Bank One, Texas, N.A., NationsBank.

Number of staff: 1 full-time professional; 1 full-time support.

EIN: 756038529

2982
Davidson Family Charitable Foundation ▼
310 West Texas, Suite 709
Midland 79701   (915) 687-0995

Trust established in 1961 in TX.

Donor(s): C.J. Davidson.‡

Foundation type: Independent

Financial data (yr. ended 06/30/91): Assets, $19,999,869 (M); expenditures, $1,582,729; qualifying distributions, $1,393,383, including $1,338,731 for 77 grants (high: $100,000; low: $350).

Purpose and activities: Emphasis on higher and other education, welfare, medical research, hospitals, health services, community services, and youth.

Fields of interest: Higher education, education, welfare, medical research, hospitals, health services, youth.

Types of support: Building funds, equipment, scholarship funds, endowment funds, general purposes.

Limitations: Giving limited to TX. No grants to individuals.

Application information: Apply at school financial office for scholarships. Application form required.

> *Initial approach:* Letter
> *Copies of proposal:* 6
> *Deadline(s):* 45 days before semiannual meetings
> *Board meeting date(s):* June and Dec.
> *Final notification:* 2 weeks after meetings
> *Write:* Steve Davidson, Vice-Chair.

Officers and Trustees:* H.W. Davidson, Chair.; Steve Davidson,* Vice-Chair.; Barry A. McClenahan, Hilton T. Ray, James H. Stewart, Jr., John J. Wilson.

Trustee Bank: Team Bank, N.A.

Number of staff: 1 full-time professional.

EIN: 237440630

2983
Ken W. Davis Foundation
P.O. Box 3419
Fort Worth 76113   (817) 332-4081

Incorporated in 1954 in TX.

Donor(s): Members of the Ken W. Davis family.

Foundation type: Independent

Financial data (yr. ended 10/31/91): Assets, $3,355,317 (M); expenditures, $153,175; qualifying distributions, $128,592, including $125,400 for 31 grants (high: $30,000; low: $100).

Purpose and activities: Primary areas of interest are health and welfare, general education, culture and art, civic activities, and issue-oriented giving.

Fields of interest: Health, hospitals, handicapped, rehabilitation, animal welfare, homeless, community development, civic affairs, arts.
Types of support: Continuing support, general purposes, matching funds, program-related investments.
Limitations: Giving primarily in Fort Worth and Midland, TX, and Tulsa, OK. No support for religious organizations or drug or alcohol abuse programs. No loans or grants to individuals.
Publications: 990-PF.
Application information: Application form not required.
    Initial approach: Written proposal
    Copies of proposal: 1
    Deadline(s): None; however, fiscal year end is Oct. 31 for present year funding
    Board meeting date(s): Varies
    Final notification: Positive responses only
    Write: Kay Davis, V.P.
Officers and Directors:* Ken W. Davis, Jr.,* Pres.; Kay Davis,* V.P. and Secy.-Treas.; T.C. Davis,* V.P.
Number of staff: None.
EIN: 756012722

2984
The Raymond Dickson Foundation
P.O. Box 406
Hallettsville 77964   (512) 798-2531

Trust established in 1958 in TX.
Donor(s): Raymond Dickson,‡ Alton C. Allen.‡
Foundation type: Independent
Financial data (yr. ended 12/31/91): Assets, $2,778,599 (M); expenditures, $134,148; qualifying distributions, $118,500, including $118,500 for 31 grants (high: $50,000; low: $500).
Purpose and activities: Primary areas of interest include education, medical research, and medical facilities.
Fields of interest: Education, youth, child welfare, medical research, hospitals, arts, libraries.
Types of support: Operating budgets, building funds.
Limitations: Giving limited to TX. No grants to individuals, or for building funds.
Publications: Program policy statement, application guidelines.
Application information: Application form not required.
    Initial approach: Proposal
    Copies of proposal: 1
    Board meeting date(s): Nov. or Dec.
    Write: Robert K. Jewett, Chair.
Officer and Trustees:* Robert K. Jewett,* Chair.; Lewis Allen, Jr., Wilbur H. Baber, Jr., G. Cameron Duncan, Vaughan B. Meyer.
EIN: 746052983

2985
H. E. and Kate Dishman Charitable Foundation Trust
c/o First City, Texas-Beaumont, N.A.
P.O. Box 3391
Beaumont 77704   (409) 838-9398

Established in 1985 in TX.
Donor(s): The Dishman Foundation, H.E. Dishman,‡ Kate Dishman.
Foundation type: Independent

Financial data (yr. ended 12/31/90): Assets, $2,215,830 (M); expenditures, $88,595; qualifying distributions, $69,000, including $69,000 for 7 grants (high: $25,000; low: $3,000).
Fields of interest: Higher education, family services, minorities, disadvantaged, homeless, hospices, humanities.
Limitations: Giving primarily in Jefferson County, TX. No grants to individuals.
Publications: Application guidelines.
Application information: Application form required.
    Initial approach: Letter
    Copies of proposal: 1
    Deadline(s): May 31
    Final notification: Aug.
    Write: Pam Parish, V.P. and Trust Officer, First City, Texas-Beaumont, N.A.
Trustee: First City, Texas-Beaumont, N.A.
Number of staff: None.
EIN: 766024806

2986
Dodge Jones Foundation ▼
P.O. Box 176
Abilene 79604   (915) 673-6429

Incorporated in 1954 in TX.
Donor(s): Ruth Leggett Jones,‡ and others.
Foundation type: Independent
Financial data (yr. ended 12/31/91): Assets, $43,041,582 (M); expenditures, $3,079,907; qualifying distributions, $2,497,975, including $2,497,975 for 90 grants (high: $350,000; low: $250).
Purpose and activities: Support for education, the arts, health, community funds, and youth programs.
Fields of interest: Education, arts, health, community funds, youth.
Types of support: General purposes.
Limitations: Giving primarily in Abilene, TX. No grants to individuals.
Application information: Application form not required.
    Initial approach: Letter
    Copies of proposal: 1
    Deadline(s): None
    Board meeting date(s): Varies
    Final notification: Varies; rejections are immediate
    Write: Lawrence E. Gill, V.P., Grants Administration
Officers and Directors:* Julia Jones Matthews, Pres.; Joseph E. Canon,* V.P. and Exec. Dir.; Lawrence E. Gill, V.P., Grants Administration; Melvin W. Holt, V.P.; Eugene Allen, Secy.-Treas.; Joe B. Matthews, John A. Matthews, Jr., Kade L. Matthews, Julia Matthews Wilkinson.
Number of staff: 2 full-time professional; 1 part-time support.
EIN: 756006386

2987
The James R. Dougherty, Jr., Foundation
P.O. Box 640
Beeville 78104-0640   (512) 358-3560

Trust established in 1950 in TX.
Donor(s): James R. Dougherty,‡ Mrs. James R. Dougherty.‡

Foundation type: Independent
Financial data (yr. ended 11/30/91): Assets, $8,708,800 (M); expenditures, $789,944; qualifying distributions, $666,692, including $641,106 for 280 grants (high: $25,000; low: $200; average: $1,000-$5,000).
Purpose and activities: Support for Roman Catholic church-related institutions, including higher, secondary, and other education; cultural programs, including museums and the performing arts; health and hospitals; youth and social service agencies, particularly those benefiting the homeless, hunger, and women; and civil and human rights and international relief.
Fields of interest: Catholic giving, higher education, secondary education, arts, health, AIDS, child development, social services, women, international relief.
Types of support: Operating budgets, land acquisition, research, endowment funds, building funds, scholarship funds, equipment, annual campaigns, capital campaigns, conferences and seminars, general purposes, renovation projects.
Limitations: Giving primarily in TX. No grants to individuals; no loans.
Application information: Application form not required.
    Initial approach: Proposal
    Copies of proposal: 1
    Deadline(s): 10 days prior to board meeting
    Board meeting date(s): Semiannually
    Final notification: 6 months or less
    Write: Hugh Grove, Jr., Asst. Secy.
Officers and Trustees:* May Dougherty King,* Chair.; Mary Patricia Dougherty,* Secy.-Treas.; F. William Carr, Jr., Stephen T. Dougherty, Ben F. Vaughan III, Genevieve Vaughan.
Number of staff: 3
EIN: 746039858

2988
Dr. Pepper Corporate Giving Program
P.O. Box 655086
Dallas 75265-5086   (214) 360-7000

Purpose and activities: Dr. Pepper supports civic programs, environmental issues, arts and culture, hospitals, minority programs, science, United Way, urban problems, and especially education. The company has created the Grace Lyon Dr. Pepper Endowed Scholarship Fund for students majoring in business administration.
Fields of interest: Civic affairs, education, environment, arts, cultural programs, hospitals, minorities, political science, science and technology, community funds, urban development, business education.
Limitations: Giving primarily in headquarters city, headquarters state, entire U.S. and international locations.
Application information:
    Initial approach: Letter of inquiry
    Final notification: If rejected, will send notification
    Write: Ira M. Rosenstein, Exec. V.P. and C.F.O.

2989
Dresser Foundation, Inc. ▼
P.O. Box 718
Dallas 75221   (214) 740-6078

Harbison-Walker scholarship program application address: Scholarship Comm., One Gateway Ctr., Pittsburgh, PA 15222; Dresser Harbison Fdn. scholarship program application address: c/o Assoc. of Universities and Colleges of Canada, 151 Slater St., Ottawa, Canada KIP 5N1

Trust established in 1953 in TX.
Donor(s): Dresser Industries, Inc.
Foundation type: Company-sponsored
Financial data (yr. ended 10/31/90): Assets, $8,946,555 (M); expenditures, $1,579,104; qualifying distributions, $1,527,046, including $1,302,492 for 247 grants (high: $100,000; low: $300; average: $1,000-$5,000), $55,985 for 81 grants to individuals (high: $1,350; low: $300; average: $300-$900) and $165,823 for 207 employee matching gifts.
Purpose and activities: Emphasis on community funds and higher education, including employee-related scholarships through National Merit Scholarship Corp. and through two foundation programs; support also for hospitals, youth agencies, and cultural programs; provides minor welfare assistance to retired employees.
Fields of interest: Community funds, higher education, hospitals, health, youth, cultural programs.
Types of support: Employee matching gifts, general purposes, building funds, employee-related scholarships.
Limitations: Giving primarily in areas of company operations, particularly Pittsburgh, PA; Waukesha, WI; Marion, OH; and Houston and Dallas, TX. No grants to individuals (except for employee-related scholarships and old age assistance payments), or for endowment funds; no loans.
Publications: Application guidelines.
Application information: Completion of application forms required for all employee-related scholarship programs but not for other programs.
Initial approach: Proposal
Copies of proposal: 1
Deadline(s): None for general grants; Feb. 14 for Harbison-Walker employee scholarships, and June 1 for Dresser Canada, Inc. employee scholarships
Board meeting date(s): As required
Final notification: 3 months
Write: Richard E. Hauslein, Chair. of Contrib. Comm.
Officers and Directors:* John J. Murphy,* Chair.; J.J. Corboy,* Pres.; R.E. Hauslein,* V.P.; Bill D. St. John,* V.P.; M.S. Nickson, Secy.; Paul W. Willey, Treas.
Trustees: NCNB Bank of Dallas, Merrill Lynch Asset Management, Inc.
Number of staff: 1 full-time support.
EIN: 237309548
Recent health grants:
2989-1 Childrens Medical Center of Dallas, Dallas, TX, $10,000. 1990.
2989-2 Richardson Medical Center, Richardson, TX, $15,000. 1990.
2989-3 Waukesha Memorial Hospital, Waukesha, WI, $10,000. 1990.
2989-4 Zale Lipshy University Hospital, Dallas, TX, $25,000. 1990.

2990
Dresser Industries Corporate Giving Program
P.O. Box 718
Dallas 75221   (214) 740-6078

Financial data (yr. ended 10/31/90): Total giving, $43,791 for grants.
Purpose and activities: Supports civic and community programs, education, environmental issues, arts and culture, hospitals, minority organizations, the United Way, women's affairs, youth service, science, and projects/organizations concerned with urban problems.
Fields of interest: Social services, civic affairs, education, higher education, environment, arts, cultural programs, hospitals, minorities, community funds, women, youth, science and technology, urban development.
Types of support: Building funds, equipment.
Limitations: Giving primarily in areas of company operations.
Application information: Grants are handled on the divisional level.
Initial approach: Contact nearest division
Write: Richard E. Hauslein, Chair., Contribs. Comm.

2991
Dunagan Foundation, Inc.
P.O. Box 387
Monahans 79756

Established in 1976 in TX.
Donor(s): J. Conrad Dunagan, Kathlyn C. Dunagan, John C. Dunagan.
Foundation type: Independent
Financial data (yr. ended 12/31/90): Assets, $2,246,644 (M); gifts received, $51,500; expenditures, $210,450; qualifying distributions, $200,700, including $200,700 for 23 grants (high: $101,600; low: $250).
Fields of interest: Education, family planning, handicapped, history.
Types of support: Continuing support, professorships, scholarship funds, special projects.
Limitations: Giving primarily in TX; limited support in IL, CT, and MO. No grants to individuals.
Application information: Contributes only to pre-selected organizations. Applications not accepted.
Write: J. Conrad Dunagan, Pres.
Officers: J. Conrad Dunagan, Pres.; Kathlyn C. Dunagan, V.P.; John C. Dunagan, Secy.-Treas.
Number of staff: None.
EIN: 751561848

2992
The Lillian H. and C. W. Duncan Foundation
c/o Texas Commerce Bank, N.A.
P.O. Box 2558
Houston 77252-8037   (713) 236-4457

Established in 1964 in TX.
Donor(s): C.W. Duncan.‡
Foundation type: Independent
Financial data (yr. ended 09/30/91): Assets, $4,482,666 (M); expenditures, $382,965; qualifying distributions, $360,322, including

$346,436 for 51 grants (high: $21,000; low: $275).
Fields of interest: Hospitals, higher education, youth, child welfare, arts.
Limitations: Giving primarily in TX. No grants to individuals.
Application information:
Initial approach: Letter
Deadline(s): None
Board meeting date(s): Semiannually
Write: Inez Winston
Officers and Directors:* John H. Duncan,* Chair.; Charles W. Duncan, Jr.,* Pres.; Jeaneane Duncan, V.P.; Robert J. Faust, Secy.-Treas.; Anne S. Duncan, Brenda Duncan, C.W. Duncan III, John H. Duncan, Jr., Mary Anne Duncan.
EIN: 746064215

2993
John S. Dunn Research Foundation ▼
3355 West Alabama, Suite 720
Houston 77098-1718   (713) 626-0368

Established in 1985 in TX.
Donor(s): John S. Dunn, Sr.‡
Foundation type: Independent
Financial data (yr. ended 12/31/90): Assets, $75,224,155 (M); gifts received, $3,065; expenditures, $3,862,991; qualifying distributions, $3,494,850, including $3,268,508 for 16 grants (high: $1,000,000; low: $5,000; average: $5,000-$250,000).
Purpose and activities: Giving limited to health and medical-related organizations, especially hospitals; support also for cancer and other medical research.
Fields of interest: Hospitals, cancer, medical research, health.
Types of support: Endowment funds, matching funds.
Limitations: Giving limited to TX. No grants to individuals.
Publications: Informational brochure (including application guidelines).
Application information: Application form not required.
Initial approach: Letter
Copies of proposal: 1
Deadline(s): None
Board meeting date(s): Full board meets quarterly; Executive Committee meets on the third Wednesday of each month
Final notification: Written notice one week following meeting
Write: Robert D. Moreton, M.D., Exec. V.P. and Medical Advisor
Officers and Trustees:* Milby Dow Dunn,* Pres.; Robert D. Moreton, M.D.,* Exec. V.P. and Medical Advisor; Murry D. Kennedy,* V.P. and Secy.; John S. Dunn, Jr.,* V.P. and Treas.; Dagmar Dunn Pickens Gipe,* V.P.; Jerome L. Howard,* V.P.
Number of staff: 1 full-time professional; 2 full-time support.
EIN: 741933660
Recent health grants:
2993-1 Baylor College of Medicine, Houston, TX, $117,425. 1990.
2993-2 Houston Ear Research Foundation, Houston, TX, $75,000. For medical research. 1990.

2993-3 Methodist Hospital Foundation, Houston, TX, $1,300,000. For medical research. 1990.

2993-4 Saint Joseph Hospital Foundation, Houston, TX, $250,000. For medical research. 1990.

2993-5 San Jose Clinic, Houston, TX, $12,500. 1990.

2993-6 Texas Institute for Rehabilitation and Research, Houston, TX, $500,000. For medical research. 1990.

2993-7 University of Texas Health Science Center, Houston, TX, $13,834. 1990.

2993-8 University of Texas M.D. Anderson Cancer Center, Houston, TX, $424,749. For medical research. 1990.

2994
J. E. S. Edwards Foundation
4413 Cumberland Rd. North
Fort Worth 76116   (817) 737-6924

Established about 1975 in TX.
Donor(s): Jareen E. Schmidt.
Foundation type: Independent
Financial data (yr. ended 07/31/91): Assets, $2,064,895 (M); gifts received, $103,829; expenditures, $104,661; qualifying distributions, $85,000, including $85,000 for 21 grants (high: $20,000; low: $1,000).
Purpose and activities: Grants largely for social services, including programs for women, hunger, the disadvantaged, and child welfare; support also for health and youth agencies and Protestant giving, including churches, schools, and missionary programs.
Fields of interest: Social services, disadvantaged, women, child development, youth, hunger, health services, medical research, Protestant giving, religion—missionary programs.
Types of support: Operating budgets.
Limitations: Giving primarily in Fort Worth, TX. No grants to individuals.
Application information: Application form not required.
   Initial approach: Letter
   Copies of proposal: 1
   Deadline(s): None
   Board meeting date(s): June
   Write: Mrs. Jareen E. Schmidt, Pres.
Officers: Jareen E. Schmidt, Pres.; Stace Sewell, V.P.; Clifford Schmidt, Secy.; Sheryl E. Bowen, Treas.
Number of staff: 1
EIN: 510173260

2995
Kirk Edwards Foundation
Nine Valley Wood Court
Roanoke 76262

Established in 1966 in TX.
Donor(s): A.B. Kirk Edwards.‡
Foundation type: Independent
Financial data (yr. ended 10/31/91): Assets, $2,808,548 (M); expenditures, $221,308; qualifying distributions, $196,800, including $192,000 for 13 grants (high: $75,000; low: $1,000).
Fields of interest: Hospitals, health, cancer, religion—Christian, general charitable giving.
Types of support: Operating budgets.

Limitations: Giving primarily in TX. No grants to individuals.
Application information: Contributes only to pre-selected organizations. Applications not accepted.
Officers and Directors:* Lucian Parrish,* Pres.; Carolyn Sullivan,* V.P.; Elizabeth Young,* Secy.; Wayne Lafevre,* Treas.; Frank Gibson, Herbert B. Story.
EIN: 756054922

2996
El Paso Community Foundation
Texas Commerce Bank Bldg., Suite 1616
El Paso 79901   (915) 533-4020
FAX: (915) 532-0716

Incorporated in 1977 in TX.
Foundation type: Community
Financial data (yr. ended 12/31/90): Assets, $21,381,148 (M); gifts received, $2,521,209; expenditures, $5,018,825; qualifying distributions, $4,142,426, including $4,113,385 for 226 grants (high: $65,000; low: $50; average: $50-$25,000), $10,250 for 12 grants to individuals (high: $2,000; low: $250; average: $450-$2,000) and $18,791 for program-related investments.
Purpose and activities: Giving for education, social services, health, arts and humanities, the environment, community development, and the disabled.
Types of support: Matching funds, special projects, continuing support, technical assistance, program-related investments, seed money.
Limitations: Giving limited to the El Paso, TX, area. No grants to individuals (except for scholarships), or for deficit financing.
Publications: Annual report, application guidelines, 990-PF, newsletter, informational brochure.
Application information: Application form not required.
   Initial approach: Letter requesting guidelines
   Copies of proposal: 1
   Deadline(s): No set deadline; board considers requests quarterly
   Board meeting date(s): Feb., May, Sept., and Nov.
   Final notification: Following board consideration
   Write: Janice W. Windle, Pres.
Officers and Trustees:* Guillermo Ochoa,* Chair.; Mary Carmen Saucedo,* Vice-Chair.; Janice W. Windle, Pres.; Carl E. Ryan,* Secy.; Joe Kidd,* Treas.; Joe Alcantar, Jr., Luis Chavez, Jackson Curlin, Jr., Maybel Fayant, Richard H. Feuille, Bette Hervey, Betty M. MacGuire, Charles Mais, Mary Lou Moreno, James Phillips, Patricia Rogers, Alfredo Martinez Urdal.
Number of staff: 4 full-time professional; 3 full-time support; 1 part-time support.
EIN: 741839536
Recent health grants:

2996-1 Border Childrens Health Clinic, El Paso, TX, $40,000. For health care services to indigent children. 1990.

2996-2 El Paso Guidance Center, El Paso, TX, $20,000. For partial salary for psychologist. 1990.

2996-3 El Paso Rehabilitation Center, El Paso, TX, $65,000. For services for handicapped children. 1990.

2996-4 El Paso Rehabilitation Center, El Paso, TX, $19,000. For hearing services for low-income elderly. 1990.

2996-5 El Paso Rehabilitation Center, El Paso, TX, $10,000. For day care for handicapped children. 1990.

2996-6 Hospice of El Paso, El Paso, TX, $10,000. For services for children who are patients. 1990.

2996-7 Planned Parenthood Center of El Paso, El Paso, TX, $12,500. For capital grant. 1990.

2996-8 Shriners Hospital for Crippled Children, El Paso, TX, $10,000. For services for El Paso area children. 1990.

2996-9 Southwest AIDS Committee, El Paso, TX, $10,000. For Carnell House. 1990.

2996-10 Texas Tech University Medical Center, El Paso, TX, $20,000. For counseling for handicapped children. 1990.

2996-11 Texas Tech University Medical Center, El Paso, TX, $15,000. For counseling for handicapped children. 1990.

2996-12 Visiting Nurse Association of El Paso, El Paso, TX, $15,000. For care for indigent children. 1990.

2997
J. A. and Isabel M. Elkins Foundation
1166 First City Tower
1001 Fannin St.
Houston 77002

Trust established in 1956 in TX.
Foundation type: Independent
Financial data (yr. ended 08/31/91): Assets, $2,824,355 (M); gifts received, $11,459; expenditures, $164,578; qualifying distributions, $155,135, including $153,500 for 8 grants (high: $50,000; low: $5,000).
Purpose and activities: "Grants primarily for religious, charitable, scientific, or educational agencies, institutions, and corporations. General focus on churches and religious associations; child welfare, hospitals, and health agencies; scientific organizations sponsoring research; and schools and universities.
Fields of interest: Religion, child welfare, hospitals, health associations, medical research, science and technology, education, higher education.
Limitations: Giving primarily in TX, especially the greater Houston area. No grants to individuals, or for deficit financing; generally no grants for continuing operating support.
Application information: Contributes only to pre-selected organizations. Applications not accepted.
   Write: Ms. Velma Farris or Ms. Lauren Baird
Trustees: Joseph C. Dilg, J.A. Elkins, Jr., J.A. Elkins III.
EIN: 746047894

2998
Margaret & James A. Elkins, Jr. Foundation
1166 First City Tower
1001 Fannin St.
Houston 77002

Established in 1956 in TX.
Foundation type: Independent
Financial data (yr. ended 10/31/91): Assets, $4,380,036 (M); expenditures, $213,464; qualifying distributions, $183,063, including $183,000 for 6 grants (high: $95,000; low: $3,000).
Purpose and activities: "Grants primarily for charitable, religious, scientific, literary, or educational purposes, testing for public safety, or prevention of cruelty to children or animals. General focus on churches and religious associations; child welfare, hospitals and health agencies; scientific organizations sponsoring research; and schools and universities."
Fields of interest: Safety, religion, religion—Christian, child welfare, child development, animal welfare, hospitals, medical research, health associations, science and technology, biological sciences, medical education, education, higher education, secondary education, elementary education.
Types of support: Building funds, capital campaigns, endowment funds, special projects, emergency funds, equipment, research.
Limitations: Giving primarily in TX, especially the greater Houston area. No grants to individuals, or for deficit financing; generally no grants for continuing operating support.
Application information: Application form not required.
Initial approach: Letter
Copies of proposal: 1
Deadline(s): None
Write: Ms. Velma Farris or Ms. Lauren Baird
Trustees: J.A. Elkins, Jr., James A. Elkins III, R.A. Seale, Jr.
Number of staff: 1 shared staff
EIN: 746051746

2999
The Ellwood Foundation
P.O. Box 52482
Houston 77052 (713) 652-0613

Trust established in 1958 in TX.
Donor(s): D.C. Ellwood,‡ Irene L. Ellwood.‡
Foundation type: Independent
Financial data (yr. ended 09/30/91): Assets, $17,575,327 (M); expenditures, $790,311; qualifying distributions, $737,500, including $737,500 for 36 grants (high: $75,000; low: $5,000).
Fields of interest: Medical sciences, medical research, mental health, health services, hospitals, medical education, higher education, social services, youth.
Types of support: Renovation projects, operating budgets, scholarship funds, research.
Limitations: Giving primarily in the Houston, TX, area.
Application information: Application form not required.
Initial approach: Letter
Deadline(s): None
Write: H. Wayne Hightower, Pres.

Officers: H. Wayne Hightower, Pres.; Raybourne Thompson, Jr., V.P. and Secy.; Louis E. Scherck, V.P. and Treas.
EIN: 746039237

3000
Enron Foundation ▼
(Formerly The Enron Foundation - Omaha)
1400 Smith
P.O. Box 1188
Houston 77251-1188 (713) 853-5400

Established in 1979 in NE as InterNorth Foundation; in 1986 name changed to Enron Foundation - Omaha; in 1988 absorbed Enron Foundation - Houston (name changed from HNG Foundation) and name changed to Enron Foundation.
Donor(s): Enron Corp.
Foundation type: Company-sponsored
Financial data (yr. ended 12/31/90): Assets, $10,508,952 (M); expenditures, $3,847,747; qualifying distributions, $3,815,999, including $2,827,182 for 296 grants (high: $125,000; low: $100; average: $5,000-$10,000) and $843,081 for employee matching gifts.
Purpose and activities: Support primarily for higher education, arts and culture, community funds and civic organizations, and social service and youth agencies.
Fields of interest: Higher education, community funds, civic affairs, social services, youth, cultural programs, arts.
Types of support: Operating budgets, general purposes, continuing support, annual campaigns, seed money, emergency funds, building funds, matching funds, employee matching gifts, capital campaigns, equipment, renovation projects, research.
Limitations: Giving limited to areas of company operations, with preference given to the Midwest and the Houston, TX, area; giving also in Omaha, NE, and Winter Park, FL. No support for non-educational religious organizations. No grants to individuals, or for fellowships; generally no grants for endowment funds or advertising for benefit purposes; no loans.
Publications: Annual report, informational brochure (including application guidelines).
Application information: Application form not required.
Initial approach: Letter
Copies of proposal: 1
Deadline(s): 30 days before board meeting
Board meeting date(s): May, Aug., Nov., and Feb.
Final notification: Generally, within 30 days; grants for over $10,000 are considered at quarterly board meetings and may require a longer response period
Write: A. Hardie Davis, V.P. and General Mgr.
Officers and Directors: Kenneth L. Lay,* Chair. and Pres.; Peggy Menchaca,* V.P. and Secy.; William C. Moore,* V.P., Education and Community Relations; Robert J. Hermann, V.P., Tax; Elizabeth Labanowski,* V.P. and Gen. Counsel; A. Hardie Davis,* V.P. and Gen. Mgr.; Betty Studzinski, Treas.; Richard D. Kinder, Edmund P. Segner III, P. Leon Ullrich.
Number of staff: 2 full-time professional; 1 full-time support; 1 part-time support.
EIN: 470615943

Recent health grants:
3000-1 American Lung Association, San Jacinto Area, Houston, TX, $10,000. 1990.
3000-2 Baylor College of Medicine, Houston, TX, $25,000. 1990.
3000-3 Juvenile Diabetes Foundation, Houston Chapter, Houston, TX, $14,420. 1990.
3000-4 University of Texas M.D. Anderson Cancer Center, M.D. Anderson Cancer Center, Houston, TX, $70,000. 1990.

3001
Enserch Corporate Contributions Program
Enserch Center
300 South St. Paul St.
Dallas 75201 (214) 651-8700

Purpose and activities: Supports education, social welfare, public health, and the arts.
Fields of interest: Education, higher education, social services, welfare, health, arts.
Limitations: Giving limited to areas of operation. No grants for religious activities, individuals, or scholarships administered solely through institutions.
Application information:
Initial approach: Brief letter
Deadline(s): None
Write: Richard B. Williams, Sr. V.P., Administration

3002
Exxon Company, U.S.A. Corporate Contributions Program
P.O. Box 2180
Houston 77252 (713) 656-6379

Purpose and activities: Supports community and civic affairs, culture and the arts, minority education, environmental issues, equal rights, federated campaigns, general health care, science, urban problems, public policy, social services, volunteerism, wildlife, rehabilitation, leadership development, homeless, drug abuse, economics, welfare organizations, youth service, and women's programs. Support of education is through the Exxon Education Foundation. Also available are volunteer recruitment and employee volunteer programs.
Fields of interest: Community development, civic affairs, cultural programs, arts, education, higher education, environment, health, science and technology, urban development, welfare, youth, women, education—minorities, fine arts, homeless, leadership development, minorities, museums, Native Americans, performing arts, public policy, rehabilitation, social services, volunteerism, wildlife, drug abuse, economics, engineering, elementary education, secondary education.
Types of support: Employee matching gifts, equipment, capital campaigns, emergency funds, program-related investments, special projects, donated equipment, operating budgets, employee volunteer services, continuing support, fellowships, internships, general purposes, employee volunteer services.
Limitations: Giving primarily in locations where company has operations, employees, and retirees. No grants to individuals.
Publications: Corporate giving report.

Application information: Application form not required.

Initial approach: Letter of inquiry; Send requests to headquarters

Copies of proposal: 1

Deadline(s): Applications accepted throughout the year

Write: Michael C. Quinn, Coord., Public Affairs

3003
Exxon Corporate Giving Program
225 E. John W. Carpenter Fwy.
Irving 75062-2298   (214) 444-1000

Financial data (yr. ended 12/31/90): Total giving, $37,164,527 for 722 grants (high: $1,527,400; average: $5,000-$50,000).

Purpose and activities: Supports arts and culture, civic and community service. Figures represent giving by headquarters, divisions, and affiliates (excluding the foundation). Number of grants (722) is only for those of $5,000 and up. High grant is for the United Way. Exxon divides its giving into the following categories: Environment; Public Information and Policy Research; Education; United Appeals and Federated Drives; Health; Civic and Community Service Organizations; Minority and Women-Oriented Service Organizations; Arts, Museums, Historical Associations, Public Broadcasting Programming; and Contributions Outside the United States; emphasis on improving the socioeconomic status of women and minorities through Education and employment; and on research issues.

Fields of interest: Arts, cultural programs, civic affairs, community development, public policy, education, higher education, environment, minorities, health, welfare.

Types of support: Capital campaigns, employee matching gifts, equipment, general purposes, renovation projects, research, scholarship funds, special projects, employee-related scholarships.

Limitations: Giving primarily in areas of company operations. No grants to individuals.

Application information:

Initial approach: Initial contact by letter to the local Exxon facility or to headquarters

Deadline(s): None

Write: Leonard Fleischen, Mgr., Contribs.

3004
The R. W. Fair Foundation ▼
P.O. Box 689
Tyler 75710   (903) 592-3811

Trust established in 1936; incorporated in 1959 in TX.

Donor(s): R.W. Fair,‡ Mattie Allen Fair.‡

Foundation type: Independent

Financial data (yr. ended 12/31/90): Assets, $14,517,580 (M); expenditures, $1,838,693; qualifying distributions, $1,268,451, including $1,261,812 for 142 grants (high: $117,000; low: $100; average: $10,000-$50,000).

Purpose and activities: Grants largely for Protestant church support and church-related programs and secondary and higher education, including legal education; some support for hospitals, youth and social service agencies, libraries, and cultural activities.

Fields of interest: Protestant giving, education, secondary education, higher education, education—building funds, legal education, hospitals, cancer, heart disease, youth, social services, libraries, cultural programs.

Types of support: Seed money, building funds, equipment, general purposes, endowment funds, research, special projects, scholarship funds, matching funds.

Limitations: Giving primarily in the Southwest, with emphasis on TX. No grants to individuals, or for operating budgets.

Publications: Application guidelines.

Application information: Application form required.

Initial approach: Letter

Copies of proposal: 1

Deadline(s): Mar. 1, June 1, Sept. 1, and Dec. 1

Board meeting date(s): Mar., June, Sept., and Dec.

Final notification: 3 months

Write: Wilton H. Fair, Pres.

Officers and Directors:* Wilton H. Fair,* Pres.; James W. Fair,* Sr. V.P.; Sam Bright,* V.P.; Marvin N. Wilson,* Secy.-Treas.; Will A. Knight, B.B. Palmore, C.E. Peeples, Richard L. Ray.

Number of staff: 2 part-time professional.

EIN: 756015270

Recent health grants:

3004-1 Stewart Blood Bank Center, Tyler, TX, $25,000. 1990.

3004-2 University of Texas Health Science Center, Tyler, TX, $10,000. 1990.

3005
The William Stamps Farish Fund ▼
1100 Louisiana, Suite 1250
Houston 77002   (713) 757-7313

Incorporated in 1951 in TX.

Donor(s): Libbie Rice Farish.

Foundation type: Independent

Financial data (yr. ended 06/30/91): Assets, $90,766,926 (M); expenditures, $4,431,434; qualifying distributions, $4,236,738, including $4,180,000 for 112 grants (high: $200,000; low: $1,200; average: $10,000-$60,000).

Purpose and activities: Giving primarily for education, including colleges and universities, medical research, and social services.

Fields of interest: Education, medical research, social services.

Types of support: Research, general purposes.

Limitations: Giving primarily in TX. No grants to individuals, or for annual campaigns, deficit financing, operating budgets, exchange programs, consulting services, or endowment funds; no loans.

Publications: Application guidelines.

Application information: Application form not required.

Initial approach: Proposal

Copies of proposal: 1

Board meeting date(s): Annually

Write: W.S. Farish, Pres.

Officers and Trustees:* W.S. Farish,* Pres.; Martha Farish Gerry,* V.P.; Caroline Rotan, Secy.; Terry W. Ward, Treas.; Cornelia G. Corbett, Dan R. Japhet.

Number of staff: 1 full-time professional.

EIN: 746043019

Recent health grants:

3005-1 American Cancer Society, Texas Division, Area IV, Houston, TX, $10,000. For building campaign for new quarters and resource center. 1991.

3005-2 Baylor College of Medicine, Department of Hematology-Oncology, Houston, TX, $40,000. For bone marrow transplant program. 1991.

3005-3 Baylor College of Medicine, Department of Ophthalmology, Houston, TX, $100,000. To establish imaging analysis center and surgical lab. 1991.

3005-4 Baylor College of Medicine, Department of Pediatric Hematology-Oncology, Houston, TX, $40,000. For children's research. 1991.

3005-5 Blue Bird Circle Clinic for Pediatric Neurology, Houston, TX, $10,000. To provide medication for indigent patients. 1991.

3005-6 Cancer Counseling, Houston, TX, $15,000. For counseling for patient and family. 1991.

3005-7 Cold Spring Harbor Laboratory, Cold Spring Harbor, NY, $50,000. For medical seminars. 1991.

3005-8 Columbia Presbyterian Medical Center Fund, NYC, NY, $100,000. For hospital renovation and expansion. 1991.

3005-9 DePelchin Childrens Center, Houston, TX, $30,000. For psychiatric services for indigent children. 1991.

3005-10 Ephraim McDowell Cancer Research Foundation, Lexington, KY, $100,000. For magnetic resource imaging and spectroscopy facility at Markey Cancer Center. 1991.

3005-11 Episcopal Health Services, Hempstead, NY, $50,000. For cornerstone gift for Smithtown facility. 1991.

3005-12 Good Samaritan Foundation, Houston, TX, $10,000. For nursing scholarships. 1991.

3005-13 Healthways, Monticello, FL, $20,000. For health center. 1991.

3005-14 Hermann Eye Center, Hermann Eye Fund, Houston, TX, $50,000. For research on retina transplantation. 1991.

3005-15 Houston Ear Research Foundation, Houston, TX, $30,000. For research study of children with multi-channel cochlear implant. 1991.

3005-16 March of Dimes Birth Defects Foundation, Houston, TX, $10,000. For education program for males on pregnancy. 1991.

3005-17 Memorial Hospital Foundation of Houston, Houston, TX, $30,000. For new clinic for cancer treatment. 1991.

3005-18 Menninger Foundation, Topeka, KS, $10,000. For schizophrenic research. 1991.

3005-19 Morehouse School of Medicine, Atlanta, GA, $50,000. For scholarships. 1991.

3005-20 New York Botanical Garden, Bronx, NY, $10,000. For growing plants used in medical research. 1991.

3005-21 Palmer Drug Abuse Program, Houston, TX, $30,000. For drug abuse counselor for Memorial/Spring Branch Counseling Center and annual giving. 1991.

3005-22 Planned Parenthood Center of Houston, Houston, TX, $110,000. For new center. 1991.

3005-23 Retina Research Foundation, Houston, TX, $30,000. For retinal research. 1991.

3005-24 Saint Lukes Episcopal Hospital, Houston, TX, $12,000. For nursing scholarships. 1991.

3005-25 Saint Lukes-Roosevelt Hospital Center, NYC, NY, $40,000. For construction of cardiac care facilities. 1991.

3005-26 Stehlin Foundation for Cancer Research, Houston, TX, $50,000. For breast and colon research program. 1991.

3005-27 University of Texas Health Science Center, Houston, TX, $35,000. For colon cancer research. 1991.

3005-28 Visiting Nurse Service of New York, NYC, NY, $15,000. For home nursing care. 1991.

3006
The Fasken Foundation
500 West Texas Ave., Suite 1160
Midland 79701   (915) 683-5401

Incorporated in 1955 in TX.
Donor(s): Andrew A. Fasken,‡ Helen Fasken House,‡ Vickie Mallison,‡ Howard Marshall Johnson,‡ Ruth Shelton.‡
Foundation type: Independent
Financial data (yr. ended 12/31/90): Assets, $13,310,119 (M); gifts received, $500; expenditures, $1,209,077; qualifying distributions, $985,354, including $664,616 for 57 grants (high: $75,000; low: $500; average: $1,500-$25,000) and $286,085 for 128 grants to individuals (high: $3,000; low: $653).
Purpose and activities: Support for higher education, including scholarships to TX institutions for graduates of Midland County high schools and Midland Community College; support also for health and social services, including hospices and programs for alcoholism, drug abuse, mental health, and rehabilitation.
Fields of interest: Higher education, youth, child welfare, community funds, social services, health services, alcoholism, drug abuse, mental health, rehabilitation.
Types of support: Operating budgets, student aid.
Limitations: Giving limited to the Midland, TX, area. No grants to individuals (except scholarships limited to graduates of Midland high schools and junior college); no loans.
Publications: Application guidelines.
Application information: Application form required.
 Initial approach: Letter
 Copies of proposal: 1
 Deadline(s): Submit proposal in Dec. or July; no set deadline
 Board meeting date(s): Feb. and Sept.
 Final notification: 6 months
 Write: B.L. Jones, Exec. Dir.
Officers and Trustees:* Murray Fasken,* Pres.; Steven P. Fasken,* Secy.-Treas.; B.L. Jones,* Exec. Dir.; F. Andrew Fasken, William P. Franklin, Durward M. Goolsby.
Number of staff: 1 full-time professional; 1 part-time support.
EIN: 756023680

3007
The Favrot Fund
909 Wirt Rd., Suite 101
Houston 77024-3444   (713) 956-4009

Incorporated in 1952 in TX.

Donor(s): Laurence H. Favrot,‡ Johanna A. Favrot, George B. Strong.
Foundation type: Independent
Financial data (yr. ended 12/31/91): Assets, $13,000,000 (M); expenditures, $592,055; qualifying distributions, $486,000, including $486,000 for 35 grants (high: $50,000; low: $2,000; average: $2,000-$50,000).
Purpose and activities: Emphasis on community-based programs directed toward ecology, animal welfare, social services, family planning, and the arts, including the performing arts; grants also for education, health services, and youth agencies.
Fields of interest: Ecology, animal welfare, social services, family planning, arts, performing arts, education, health services, community development, youth.
Types of support: Operating budgets, building funds, equipment, general purposes.
Limitations: Giving primarily in TX, CA, NY, and Washington, DC. No grants to individuals.
Application information: Application form not required.
 Initial approach: Letter
 Copies of proposal: 1
 Deadline(s): None
 Board meeting date(s): Annually in Sept. or Oct.
 Write: Pam Garrett
Officers and Directors:* Johanna A. Favrot,* Pres. and Mgr.; Lenoir Moody Josey,* V.P.; Celestine Favrot Arndt, Laurence de Kanter Favrot, Leo Mortimer Favrot, Marcia Favrot, Romelia Favrot, Jeanette Favrot Peterson.
Number of staff: 1 part-time support.
EIN: 746045648

3008
The Feldman Foundation
7800 Stemmons Freeway
P.O. Box 1046
Dallas 75221   (214) 689-4337

Trust established in 1946 in TX.
Donor(s): Commercial Metals Co. subsidiaries.
Foundation type: Company-sponsored
Financial data (yr. ended 12/31/90): Assets, $13,393,863 (M); gifts received, $1,461,749; expenditures, $1,392,340; qualifying distributions, $1,327,176, including $1,140,950 for grants (average: $1,000-$100,000).
Purpose and activities: Giving primarily for Jewish welfare funds; some support for cultural programs, medical research, hospitals, higher education, and social service agencies.
Fields of interest: Jewish welfare, Jewish giving, cultural programs, medical research, hospitals, higher education, social services.
Types of support: Research, building funds, general purposes, scholarship funds, special projects, annual campaigns.
Limitations: Giving primarily in TX and NY.
Application information: Application form not required.
 Initial approach: Proposal
 Copies of proposal: 1
 Deadline(s): None
 Board meeting date(s): As needed
 Final notification: Upon receipt of proposal
 Write: Robert L. Feldman, Trustee
Trustees: Daniel E. Feldman, Moses Feldman, Robert L. Feldman.

Number of staff: 1 full-time support.
EIN: 756011578

3009
Leland Fikes Foundation, Inc. ▼
3050 Lincoln Plaza
500 North Akard
Dallas 75201-6696   (214) 754-0144

Incorporated in 1952 in DE.
Donor(s): Leland Fikes,‡ Catherine W. Fikes.
Foundation type: Independent
Financial data (yr. ended 12/31/90): Assets, $47,214,536 (M); expenditures, $8,294,925; qualifying distributions, $7,786,228, including $7,557,496 for 139 grants (high: $3,131,057; low: $100; average: $1,000-$10,000).
Purpose and activities: Giving primarily for medical research, health, youth, and social services, public interest groups, and education; grants also for population research and control, and cultural programs.
Fields of interest: Medical research, AIDS, mental health, child welfare, youth, social services, family planning, homeless, drug abuse, public policy, immigration, conservation, environment, education, elementary education, secondary education, higher education, medical education, cultural programs, performing arts.
Types of support: Annual campaigns, seed money, emergency funds, building funds, equipment, land acquisition, endowment funds, research, scholarship funds, matching funds, continuing support, capital campaigns, general purposes, operating budgets, professorships, special projects.
Limitations: Giving primarily in the Dallas, TX, area. No grants to individuals; no loans.
Publications: Application guidelines.
Application information: Submit proposal upon request. Application form not required.
 Initial approach: Letter
 Copies of proposal: 1
 Deadline(s): None
 Board meeting date(s): Bimonthly
 Final notification: By letter
 Write: Nancy Solana, Research and Grant Administration
Officers and Trustees:* Catherine W. Fikes,* Chair.; Lee Fikes,* Pres. and Treas.; Nancy J. Solana, Secy.; Amy L. Fikes.
Number of staff: 1 full-time professional; 3 part-time professional; 1 full-time support; 1 part-time support.
EIN: 756035984
Recent health grants:
3009-1 AIDS Arms Network, Dallas, TX, $20,000. For general support. 1990.
3009-2 Alan Guttmacher Institute, NYC, NY, $10,000. For analysis of family planning data. 1990.
3009-3 Association for Voluntary Surgical Contraception, NYC, NY, $10,000. To develop consumer education of new vasectomy technique. Grant shared with Association for Voluntary Sterilization. 1990.
3009-4 Catholics for a Free Choice, DC, $25,000. For general support. 1990.
3009-5 Center for Population Options, DC, $25,000. For general support. 1990.

3009-6 Center for Research on Population and Security, Chapel Hill, NC, $10,000. For family planning program in India. 1990.

3009-7 Childrens Defense Fund, DC, $10,000. For Texas Project which will study barriers to local maternal health programs. 1990.

3009-8 Childrens Medical Center of Dallas, Dallas, TX, $100,000. For expansion and renovation. 1990.

3009-9 Dallas Foundation for Health Education and Research, Dallas, TX, $250,000. For Sesame Street PEP Project. 1990.

3009-10 Foundation for Biomedical Research, DC, $10,000. For general support. 1990.

3009-11 Mental Health Association of Dallas County, Dallas, TX, $20,000. For general support. 1990.

3009-12 Planned Parenthood Federation of America, NYC, NY, $40,000. For general support. 1990.

3009-13 Planned Parenthood of Dallas and Northeast Texas, Dallas, TX, $46,264. For TACT program and Parent Teen Communication Project. Grant shared with Planned Parenthood of Greater Dallas. 1990.

3009-14 Population Crisis Committee, DC, $25,000. For general support. 1990.

3009-15 Population Institute, DC, $25,000. For general support. 1990.

3009-16 Population Services International, DC, $15,000. To market condoms in Haiti. 1990.

3009-17 Southwestern Medical Foundation, Dallas, TX, $16,667. For Bryan Williams Student Assistance Fund. 1990.

3009-18 Suicide and Crisis Center, Dallas, TX, $12,000. For general support. 1990.

3009-19 Texas Foundation for Health Science, Dallas, TX, $110,000. To buy medical coach as mobile clinic for homeless. 1990.

3009-20 Texas Society for Biomedical Research, Austin, TX, $10,000. For general support. 1990.

3009-21 University of Texas Southwestern Medical Center, Dallas, TX, $250,000. For research in molecular genetics. 1990.

3009-22 University of Texas Southwestern Medical Center, Dallas, TX, $130,000. To purchase fermentor for research in pathology. 1990.

3009-23 University of Texas Southwestern Medical Center, Dallas, TX, $116,666. For diabetes research. 1990.

3009-24 University of Texas Southwestern Medical Center, Dallas, TX, $100,000. For research in obstetrics and gynecology. 1990.

3009-25 University of Texas Southwestern Medical Center, Dallas, TX, $95,213. For research project in ophthalmology. 1990.

3009-26 University of Texas Southwestern Medical Center, Dallas, TX, $50,000. For two research projects in neurology. 1990.

3009-27 University of Texas Southwestern Medical Center, Dallas, TX, $33,333. To endow chair for Mineral Metabolism (Pak). 1990.

3009-28 YWCA of Metropolitan Dallas, Dallas, TX, $10,000. For Positive Enrichment for Teens Program. 1990.

3010
FINA Foundation
(Formerly American Petrofina Foundation)
8350 North Central Expressway
Dallas 75206   (214) 750-2400
Application address: P.O. Box 2159, Dallas, TX 75221

Incorporated in 1974 in TX.
Donor(s): American Petrofina, Inc.
Foundation type: Company-sponsored
Financial data (yr. ended 06/30/91): Assets, $5,073 (M); expenditures, $325,076; qualifying distributions, $314,917, including $314,917 for 59 grants (high: $31,980; low: $25).
Purpose and activities: Interests include health, especially hospitals and cancer and other medical research; community funds and civic affairs; the fine and performing arts, museums, and other cultural programs; higher and other education; family and social services; and the environment.
Fields of interest: Community funds, civic affairs, education, higher education, cultural programs, environment, family services, social services, medical research, hospitals.
Types of support: Continuing support, annual campaigns, seed money, emergency funds, building funds, equipment, research, scholarship funds, employee matching gifts, matching funds.
Limitations: Giving primarily in TX. No grants to individuals.
Publications: Annual report (including application guidelines).
Application information: Application form required for employee matching gifts.
   Initial approach: Proposal
   Copies of proposal: 1
   Deadline(s): None
   Board meeting date(s): Approximately once per calendar quarter
   Write: Brendan O'Connor, V.P.
Officers and Directors:* Ronald W. Haddock,* Pres.; Brendan O'Connor,* V.P. and Treas.; Kenneth W. Perry,* V.P.; Glenn E. Selvidge,* V.P.
EIN: 237391423

3011
First Interstate Foundation
(Formerly Allied Banks Foundation, Inc.)
815 Walker
P.O. Box 3326, MS No. 584
Houston 77253-3326   (713) 226-1850

Incorporated in 1979 in TX.
Donor(s): Allied Bank of Texas, First Interstate Bank of Texas.
Foundation type: Company-sponsored
Financial data (yr. ended 12/31/90): Assets, $754,825 (M); gifts received, $775,000; expenditures, $512,897; qualifying distributions, $512,897, including $512,781 for 109 grants (high: $100,000; low: $100).
Purpose and activities: Emphasis on cultural programs, including the performing arts, community funds, and social service agencies; support also for civic affairs, youth agencies, health, and education.
Fields of interest: Cultural programs, performing arts, community funds, social services, civic affairs, health, education, youth.
Types of support: Scholarship funds, general purposes.

Limitations: Giving primarily in TX.
Application information: Application form not required.
   Deadline(s): None
   Write: Bob Ward, V.P. and Treas.
Officers and Directors:* Linnet F. Deily,* Pres.; Bob D. Ward,* V.P. and Treas.; Michael B. Cahill,* V.P.; D. Kent Anderson.
EIN: 742066478

3012
Ray C. Fish Foundation
2001 Kirby Dr., Suite 1005
Houston 77019   (713) 522-0741

Incorporated in 1957 in TX.
Donor(s): Raymond Clinton Fish,‡ Mirtha G. Fish.‡
Foundation type: Independent
Financial data (yr. ended 06/30/91): Assets, $21,021,856 (M); gifts received, $74,857; expenditures, $1,314,989; qualifying distributions, $992,328, including $908,750 for 120 grants (high: $110,000; low: $500).
Fields of interest: Higher education, hospitals, medical research, youth, social services, cultural programs, performing arts.
Types of support: General purposes, operating budgets.
Limitations: Giving primarily in TX, with emphasis on Houston. No grants to individuals.
Application information: Contributes only to pre-selected organizations. Applications not accepted.
Officers: Barbara F. Daniel, Pres.; Robert J. Cruikshank, V.P.; James L. Daniel, Jr., V.P.; Paula Hooton, Secy.; Christopher J. Daniel, Treas.
Number of staff: 1
EIN: 746043047

3013
The Florence Foundation
c/o NationsBank, Trust Dept.
P.O. Box 830241
Dallas 75283-0241   (214) 508-1931
Additional tel.: (214) 508-1932

Established in 1956.
Donor(s): The Fred F. Florence Trust.
Foundation type: Independent
Financial data (yr. ended 11/30/90): Assets, $2,842,629 (M); expenditures, $109,996; qualifying distributions, $97,108, including $96,000 for 24 grants (high: $15,000; low: $1,000).
Fields of interest: Social services, higher education, cultural programs, religion, medical research.
Types of support: General purposes, matching funds, equipment, building funds, special projects.
Limitations: Giving primarily in TX. No grants for scholarships; no loans.
Application information: Application form not required.
   Initial approach: Letter
   Copies of proposal: 1
   Deadline(s): Feb. 1 and Aug. 1
   Board meeting date(s): Spring and fall
   Write: Dan M. White, Secy.

Members: Cecile Cook, Chair.; Dan M. White, Secy.; James Aston, David Florence, Paul Harris, John T. Stuart.
Trustee: NationsBank.
EIN: 756008029

3014
The Fondren Foundation ▼
7 TCT 37
P.O. Box 2558
Houston 77252-8037   (713) 236-4403

Trust established in 1948 in TX.
Donor(s): Mrs. W.W. Fondren, Sr.,‡ and others.
Foundation type: Independent
Financial data (yr. ended 10/31/90): Assets, $84,632,160 (M); expenditures, $3,413,128; qualifying distributions, $2,915,795, including $2,907,108 for 69 grants (high: $1,500,000; low: $2,000; average: $5,000-$50,000).
Purpose and activities: Emphasis on higher and secondary education, social service and youth agencies, cultural organizations, and health.
Fields of interest: Higher education, secondary education, social services, health services, cultural programs, youth.
Limitations: Giving primarily in TX, with emphasis on Houston, and in the Southwest. No grants to individuals, or for annual or operating fund drives.
Application information: Application form not required.
  Initial approach: Letter
  Copies of proposal: 1
  Deadline(s): None
  Board meeting date(s): Quarterly
  Write: Melanie A. Boone, Asst. Secy.
Officers and Trustees:* Sue Trammell Whitfield,* Chair.; Linda Knapp Underwood,* Vice-Chair.; Walter W. Fondren III,* Secy.-Treas.; Doris Fondren Allday, R. Edwin Allday, Melanie A. Boone, Ann Gordon Trammell, David M. Underwood, William F. Whitfield, Sr.
Number of staff: None.
EIN: 746042565
Recent health grants:
3014-1 Blue Bird Circle Clinic for Pediatric Neurology, Houston, TX, $25,000. For microscope. 1991.
3014-2 Can Care of Houston, Houston, TX, $15,000. For ministry to cancer patients and families. 1991.
3014-3 Center, Houston, TX, $60,000. For purchase of new facility. 1991.
3014-4 Epilepsy Association of Houston, Houston, TX, $11,000. For School Alert program. 1991.
3014-5 Good Neighbor Healthcare Center, Houston, TX, $10,000. For general operating support. 1991.
3014-6 Houston Child Guidance Center, Houston, TX, $50,000. For land expansion. 1991.
3014-7 Lions Eye Bank Foundation, Houston, TX, $25,000. For research and education campaign. 1991.
3014-8 Methodist Hospital Foundation, Houston, TX, $625,000. For pavillion renovation. 1991.
3014-9 Saint James House of Baytown, Baytown, TX, $25,000. 1991.

3014-10 Shoulder, The, Houston, TX, $10,200. For patient expenses. 1991.
3014-11 Texas Medical Center, Houston, TX, $1,000,000. For acquisition of properties. 1991.
3014-12 University of Texas M.D. Anderson Cancer Center, Houston, TX, $50,000. For Volunteer Service Endowment. 1991.

3015
Ershel Franklin Charitable Trust
P.O. Box 790
Post 79356   (806) 495-2051

Established in 1985 in TX.
Foundation type: Independent
Financial data (yr. ended 12/31/90): Assets, $2,016,853 (M); expenditures, $305,397; qualifying distributions, $305,397, including $305,397 for 72 grants (high: $50,312; low: $20).
Fields of interest: Medical education, hospitals, hospitals—building funds, nursing, cancer, civic affairs, higher education, religion.
Types of support: Scholarship funds, student loans, endowment funds, research, student aid.
Limitations: Giving primarily in TX. No grants to individuals.
Application information: Contributes only to pre-selected organizations. Applications not accepted.
  Board meeting date(s): As needed
  Write: Giles C. McCrary, Trustee
Trustee: Giles C. McCrary.
EIN: 756305761

3016
The Frees Foundation
5373 West Alabama, Suite 404
Houston 77056   (713) 623-0515

Established in 1983 in TX.
Donor(s): C. Norman Frees, Shirley B. Frees, Cumamex, S.A.
Foundation type: Independent
Financial data (yr. ended 12/31/91): Assets, $8,968,762 (M); gifts received, $1,205,000; expenditures, $536,798; qualifying distributions, $402,473, including $338,823 for 24 grants (high: $102,000; low: $1,000; average: $1,000-$125,000).
Purpose and activities: "Focus on community organizations in TX and the Republic of Mexico," including hospitals and health services; support also for organizations benefiting families, women, youth, the homeless and disadvantaged, and minorities and intercultural relations and international relief.
Fields of interest: Hospitals, Mexico, child welfare, child development, family services, general charitable giving, health, health associations, health services, Latin America, mental health, minorities, race relations, community development, disadvantaged, drug abuse, homeless, hospices, hunger, intercultural relations, international relief, nursing, nutrition, volunteerism, welfare—indigent individuals, women, youth.
Types of support: Building funds, continuing support, equipment, land acquisition, special projects.

Limitations: Giving primarily in TX and Mexico. No grants to individuals, or for endowment funds, deficit financing, or ongoing operating expenses.
Publications: Biennial report, occasional report, informational brochure (including application guidelines).
Application information: Application form not required.
  Initial approach: Proposal
  Copies of proposal: 1
  Deadline(s): None
  Board meeting date(s): Feb. 14
  Write: Nancy Frees Rosser, Dir.
Directors: C. Norman Frees, C. Norman Frees, Jr., Shirley B. Frees, Nancy Frees Rosser, Carol Frees Watkins.
Number of staff: 1 full-time professional; 1 full-time support.
EIN: 760053200

3017
Frost National Bank of San Antonio Corporate Giving Program
c/o Exec. Comm.
Frost National Bank, 100 West Houston St.
San Antonio 78205   (512) 220-4011

Purpose and activities: Bulk of giving for health and human services and education; general charitable support.
Fields of interest: Health, social services.
Types of support: Donated equipment, employee volunteer services.
Limitations: Giving limited to San Antonio, TX.
Application information:
  Write: Lon Carpenter, Sr. V.P.

3018
The Fuller Foundation, Inc.
500 Throckmorton St., Suite 2020
Fort Worth 76102   (817) 336-2020

Incorporated in 1951 in TX and in DE.
Donor(s): Andrew P. Fuller, William M. Fuller.
Foundation type: Independent
Financial data (yr. ended 12/31/90): Assets, $5,176,859 (M); gifts received, $42,740; expenditures, $479,391; qualifying distributions, $432,600, including $432,600 for 17 grants (high: $376,000; low: $250).
Purpose and activities: Giving primarily for a botanical garden conservatory; grants also for hospitals and the arts.
Fields of interest: Conservation, hospitals, arts.
Limitations: Giving primarily in TX.
Application information:
  Initial approach: Proposal
  Deadline(s): None
  Write: William M. Fuller, V.P.
Officers: Andrew P. Fuller, Pres.; William M. Fuller, V.P.; R.L. Bowen, Treas.
EIN: 756015942

3019
Garvey Texas Foundation, Inc.
P.O. Box 9600
Fort Worth 76147-0600

Incorporated in 1962 in TX.

Donor(s): James S. Garvey, Shirley F. Garvey, Garvey Foundation.
Foundation type: Independent
Financial data (yr. ended 12/31/90): Assets, $5,692,125 (M); gifts received, $33,000; expenditures, $325,310; qualifying distributions, $280,882, including $280,882 for 101 grants (high: $50,100; low: $13).
Fields of interest: Child welfare, youth, education, higher education, business education, cultural programs, community funds, hospitals, cancer, general charitable giving.
Types of support: Capital campaigns, program-related investments.
Limitations: Giving primarily in TX, OK, KS, NE, and CO. No grants to individuals.
Publications: 990-PF.
Application information: Application form required.
  Initial approach: Letter
  Copies of proposal: 1
  Deadline(s): None
  Write: Shirley F. Garvey, Pres.
Officers: Shirley F. Garvey, Pres.; James S. Garvey, V.P.; Debra J. Quillan, Treas.
Trustees: Richard F. Garvey, Carol G. Sweat.
EIN: 756031547

3020
The Cecil and Ida Green Foundation
(Formerly The Green Foundation)
3300 First City Ctr.
Dallas 75201   (214) 969-1700

Established in 1958 in TX.
Donor(s): Cecil H. Green, Ida M. Green.‡
Foundation type: Independent
Financial data (yr. ended 12/31/90): Assets, $5,863,431 (M); expenditures, $455,256; qualifying distributions, $437,149, including $428,200 for 30 grants (high: $50,000; low: $200).
Purpose and activities: Emphasis on hospitals and medical services, a museum, historical preservation, higher education, a secondary school, and a community fund.
Fields of interest: Hospitals, health services, cultural programs, museums, historic preservation, higher education, secondary education, community funds.
Types of support: Operating budgets, scholarship funds, building funds, capital campaigns, special projects, lectureships, professorships.
Limitations: Giving primarily in the Dallas, TX, area.
Application information: Application form not required.
  Deadline(s): None
  Write: William E. Collins, Trustee
Trustees: William E. Collins, Cecil H. Green, Bryan Smith.
EIN: 752263168

3021
Rosa May Griffin Foundation
P.O. Box 1775
Kilgore 75662   (214) 983-2051

Incorporated in 1960 in TX.
Donor(s): Rosa May Griffin.‡
Foundation type: Independent

Financial data (yr. ended 12/31/90): Assets, $3,858,614 (M); expenditures, $240,382; qualifying distributions, $173,702, including $173,702 for 17 grants (high: $25,000; low: $500; average: $1,200).
Purpose and activities: Giving for Presbyterian church support, higher education, and hospitals.
Fields of interest: Protestant giving, religion—Christian, higher education, hospitals.
Types of support: General purposes, operating budgets, continuing support, annual campaigns, emergency funds, building funds, equipment, matching funds.
Limitations: Giving limited to TX. No grants to individuals, or for endowment funds, scholarships, or fellowships; no loans.
Publications: Program policy statement.
Application information: Application form not required.
  Initial approach: Letter or proposal
  Copies of proposal: 1
  Deadline(s): Submit proposal in Oct.
  Board meeting date(s): Monthly
  Final notification: 1 month
  Write: Dan Phillips, Secy.-Treas.
Officers and Trustees:* O.N. Pederson,* Pres.; E.B. Mobley,* V.P.; Dan Phillips,* Secy.-Treas. and Mgr.
Number of staff: None.
EIN: 756011866

3022
Gulf Coast Medical Foundation
P.O. Box 30
Wharton 77488   (409) 532-0904

Established in 1983 in TX.
Foundation type: Independent
Financial data (yr. ended 05/31/91): Assets, $12,534,151 (M); gifts received, $300; expenditures, $714,941; qualifying distributions, $562,691, including $516,950 for 18 grants (high: $87,000; low: $100).
Fields of interest: Medical education, medical research, mental health.
Types of support: Capital campaigns, operating budgets, building funds, continuing support, matching funds, endowment funds, special projects.
Limitations: Giving primarily in Wharton, Matagorda, Jackson, Colorado, Fort Bend, and Brazoria counties, TX. No grants to individuals.
Publications: 990-PF.
Application information: Application form required.
  Initial approach: Letter
  Copies of proposal: 1
  Deadline(s): None
  Write: Dee McElroy, Exec. V.P.
Officers and Trustees:* Laurance H. Armour,* Pres.; Dee McElroy, Exec. V.P.; Kent Hill,* V.P.; Irving Moore, Secy.; Charles Davis, Treas.; R.B. Caraway, M.D., Charles F. Drees, Bert Huebner, and ten additional trustees.
Number of staff: None.
EIN: 741285242

3023
Gulf States Utilities Corporate Giving Program
350 Pine Street
Beaumont 77701   (409) 838-6631
Mailing Address: P.O. Box 2951, Beaumont TX 77704

Financial data (yr. ended 12/31/90): Total giving, $69,000.
Purpose and activities: Giving has been suspended for an indefinite period. Regular interests include higher, technical and engineering education, health and hospitals, social services, arts and humanities, public affairs, environmental issues, urban affairs, programs for children and youth.
Fields of interest: Arts, community development, community funds, economics, education, health.
Types of support: Use of facilities, public relations services, employee volunteer services, annual campaigns, employee matching gifts, operating budgets, loaned talent.
Limitations: Giving primarily in headquarters city, headquarters state, and major U.S. operating areas (only for economic development and energy awareness). No grants to individuals, primary or secondary schools, local organizations outside service areas, operating funds to hospitals.
Application information: Giving has been suspended; at present no date for resumption; Corporate Services Office handles giving. Applications not accepted.
  Write: Leslie D. Cobb, Corp. Secy.
Contributions Committee: E. Linn Draper, Jr., Chair., Pres., and C.E.O.; Edward M. Loggins, Sr. Exec. V.P.; L.D. Cobb, Secy.; C.J. Hebert, Sr. V.P.
Number of staff: 3 part-time support.

3024
Paul and Mary Haas Foundation
P.O. Box 2928
Corpus Christi 78403   (512) 887-6955

Trust established in 1954 in TX.
Donor(s): Paul R. Haas, Mary F. Haas.
Foundation type: Independent
Financial data (yr. ended 12/31/91): Assets, $1,125,576 (M); gifts received, $495,000; expenditures, $634,841; qualifying distributions, $575,676, including $331,050 for 101 grants (high: $22,765; low: $50; average: $5,000) and $244,625 for 50 grants to individuals (high: $750; low: $75; average: $750).
Purpose and activities: Primary areas of interest include social services, the disadvantaged and the homeless, higher and other education, and civic affairs. Grants also for youth agencies, housing, child development, alcohol abuse programs, early childhood, vocational, and adult education, the fine arts and other cultural programs, and community funds; scholarships only to undergraduates and vocational school students; limited medical support, including cancer and other medical research.
Fields of interest: Social services, disadvantaged, homeless, youth, rehabilitation, education, higher education, education—early childhood, arts, community funds, civic affairs.
Types of support: Special projects, student aid, annual campaigns, capital campaigns, emergency funds, equipment, general purposes, renovation

---

projects, seed money, operating budgets, scholarship funds, matching funds.
Limitations: Giving primarily in the Corpus Christi, TX, area. No grants to individuals (except for student aid); no support for graduate students.
Publications: Annual report (including application guidelines), application guidelines, 990-PF, grants list.
Application information: Application form provided for scholarship applicants. Application form not required.
Initial approach: Proposal
Copies of proposal: 1
Deadline(s): For scholarships preference is 3 months before the semester; none for other grants
Board meeting date(s): 1st quarter of the year
Final notification: Within a few weeks of receipt of proposal
Write: Nancy Wise Somers, Exec. Dir.
Trustees: Mary F. Haas, Paul R. Haas, Raymond P. Haas, Rene Haas, Rheta Haas Page.
Number of staff: 1 part-time professional; 1 part-time support.
EIN: 746031614
Recent health grants:
3024-1 HALO-Flight, Corpus Christi, TX, $10,000. For operational money for emergency helicopter ambulance covering 12 counties. 1990.
3024-2 University of Texas M.D. Anderson Cancer Center, Houston, TX, $147,500. For urology research and support of Scientific Achievement Fund. 1990.

3025
The Haggar Foundation ▼
6113 Lemmon Ave.
Dallas 75209 (214) 956-0241
Scholarship application address: Haggar Scholarship Program, The Univ. of North Texas, P.O. Box 13707, Denton, TX 76203-3707

Trust established in 1950 in TX.
Donor(s): Joseph M. Haggar, Sr., Rose M. Haggar, Haggar Co., and others.
Foundation type: Independent
Financial data (yr. ended 06/30/91): Assets, $17,205,599 (M); expenditures, $1,511,751; qualifying distributions, $1,303,947, including $1,303,947 for 216 grants (high: $250,000; low: $30; average: $500-$20,000).
Purpose and activities: Emphasis on higher and secondary education, including a scholarship program for children of company employees, and hospitals; contributions also for youth agencies and cultural programs.
Fields of interest: Higher education, secondary education, hospitals, youth, Catholic giving, cultural programs, theater, music, performing arts.
Types of support: Employee-related scholarships, building funds, general purposes, operating budgets, special projects.
Limitations: Giving limited to Dallas and south TX, in areas of company operations.
Publications: Application guidelines.
Application information: Application guidelines available for employee-related scholarship program. Application form required.
Copies of proposal: 1
Deadline(s): Submit scholarship application on or before Apr. 30; deadline Mar. 31

Board meeting date(s): Nov., Feb., May, and Aug.
Write: Rosemary Haggar Vaughan, Exec. Dir.
Trustees: Rosemary Haggar Vaughan, Exec. Dir.; Marty Vaughan Rumble, Assoc. Dir.; Marian Haggar Bryan, Edmond R. Haggar, Sr., Joseph M. Haggar, Jr., Robert C. Qualls, Patty Jo Haggar Turner.
Number of staff: 2
EIN: 756019237

3026
G. A. C. Halff Foundation
745 East Mulberry, Suite 400
San Antonio 78212 (512) 735-3300

Incorporated in 1951 in TX.
Donor(s): G.A.C. Halff.‡
Foundation type: Independent
Financial data (yr. ended 02/28/91): Assets, $5,727,696 (M); expenditures, $296,459; qualifying distributions, $256,000, including $256,000 for 37 grants (high: $25,000; low: $2,000).
Fields of interest: Social services, drug abuse, handicapped, youth, child welfare, family planning, community development, cancer.
Types of support: Continuing support.
Limitations: Giving primarily in San Antonio, TX. No grants to individuals.
Publications: Application guidelines.
Application information: Application form not required.
Initial approach: Letter
Copies of proposal: 1
Deadline(s): May 15
Board meeting date(s): End of June
Final notification: May 15
Write: Thomas F. Bibb, V.P.
Officers and Trustees:* Hugh Halff, Jr.,* Pres.; Thomas F. Bibb,* V.P. and Treas.; Catherine H. Edson,* Secy.; Roland R. Arnold, Thomas H. Edson, Marie M. Halff, Catherine H. Luhn, George M. Luhn.
EIN: 746042432

3027
The Ewing Halsell Foundation ▼
711 Navarro St.
San Antonio Bank and Trust Bldg., Suite 537
San Antonio 78205 (512) 223-2640

Trust established in 1957 in TX.
Donor(s): Ewing Halsell,‡ Mrs. Ewing Halsell,‡ Grace F. Rider.‡
Foundation type: Independent
Financial data (yr. ended 06/30/91): Assets, $44,308,515 (M); expenditures, $2,155,957; qualifying distributions, $1,836,882, including $1,680,472 for 81 grants (high: $186,000; low: $50; average: $1,500-$50,000).
Purpose and activities: Grants primarily for education, cultural programs, health organizations, and social service and youth agencies.
Fields of interest: Education, cultural programs, health associations, medical research, youth, social services.
Types of support: Operating budgets, annual campaigns, building funds, equipment, land

acquisition, research, publications, technical assistance, seed money.
Limitations: Giving limited to TX, with emphasis on southwestern TX, and particularly San Antonio. No grants to individuals, or for deficit financing, emergency funds, general endowments, matching gifts, scholarships, fellowships, demonstration projects, general purposes, or conferences; no loans.
Publications: Biennial report (including application guidelines), program policy statement.
Application information: Application form not required.
Initial approach: Letter or proposal
Copies of proposal: 1
Deadline(s): None
Board meeting date(s): Quarterly
Final notification: 3 months
Officers and Trustees: Gilbert M. Denman, Jr.,* Chair.; Helen Campbell,* Secy.-Treas.; Jean Deacy, Leroy G. Denman, Jr., Hugh A. Fitzsimmons, Jr.
Number of staff: 1 full-time professional; 2 part-time support.
EIN: 746063016
Recent health grants:
3027-1 Baptist Memorial Hospital System, San Antonio, TX, $25,000. For renovation of LVN nursing school. 1991.
3027-2 Community Council of South Central Texas, Seguin, TX, $30,000. For family planning network in eight rural southern Texas counties. 1991.
3027-3 Family Service Association of San Antonio, San Antonio, TX, $15,000. For health programs for homebound elderly. 1991.
3027-4 Good Samaritan Center of San Antonio, San Antonio, TX, $15,000. For multi-lingual videotapes of health lectures. 1991.
3027-5 Mission Road Development Center, San Antonio, TX, $15,000. To renovate group home for mentally retarded children. 1991.
3027-6 Planned Parenthood of San Antonio, San Antonio, TX, $30,000. For office management computer system. 1991.
3027-7 Saint Francis Nursing Home, San Antonio, TX, $50,000. For acquisition of patient furnishings. 1991.
3027-8 Texas Society to Prevent Blindness, San Antonio, TX, $25,000. For general support. 1991.

3028
George and Mary Josephine Hamman Foundation
910 Travis St., No. 1438
Houston 77002-5816 (713) 658-8345

Incorporated in 1954 in TX.
Donor(s): Mary Josephine Hamman,‡ George Hamman.
Foundation type: Independent
Financial data (yr. ended 04/30/91): Assets, $26,755,780 (M); expenditures, $1,633,522; qualifying distributions, $1,035,901, including $643,895 for 107 grants (high: $65,000; low: $500; average: $1,000-$10,000) and $266,250 for 102 grants to individuals (high: $10,000; low: $2,500; average: $2,500).
Purpose and activities: Giving for construction and operation of hospitals, medical treatment, and research organizations and programs; grants

to churches and affiliated religious organizations (nondenominational); individual scholarship program for local high school students; grants to building programs or special educational projects at colleges and universities, mostly local; contributions also to cultural programs, social services, and youth agencies.
Fields of interest: Hospitals, health services, medical research, religion, education, higher education, social services, cultural programs, youth, general charitable giving.
Types of support: Annual campaigns, building funds, equipment, research, scholarship funds, continuing support, matching funds, student aid.
Limitations: Giving limited to TX. No support for postgraduate education. No grants to individuals (except for scholarships).
Publications: Application guidelines.
Application information: Application form required for scholarships; none for other grants.
    Initial approach: Letter
    Copies of proposal: 1
    Deadline(s): Feb. 28 for scholarships, none for other grants
    Board meeting date(s): Monthly
    Final notification: 60 days
    Write: Stephen I. Gelsey, Admin.
Officers and Directors:* Charles D. Milby,* Pres.; Henry R. Hamman,* Secy.; Louise Milby Feagin.
Number of staff: 5 full-time professional.
EIN: 746061447

3029
The Curtis & Doris K. Hankamer Foundation
9039 Katy Freeway, Suite 430
Houston 77024-1623

Established in 1981 in TX.
Donor(s): Doris K. Hankamer, Earl Curtis Hankamer, Jr.
Foundation type: Independent
Financial data (yr. ended 12/31/90): Assets, $6,695,190 (M); expenditures, $473,001; qualifying distributions, $399,737, including $394,566 for 10 grants (high: $207,066; low: $2,500).
Purpose and activities: Giving primarily to a medical school for geriatrics fellowships and cancer research; some support also for ministry programs.
Fields of interest: Medical research, aged, cancer, religion—Christian.
Types of support: Fellowships, general purposes.
Limitations: Giving primarily in Houston, TX. No grants to individuals.
Application information: Contributes only to pre-selected organizations. Applications not accepted.
Trustees: S. Terry Bracken, Doris K. Hankamer, Scott Hunsaker.
EIN: 760022687

3030
The Don and Sybil Harrington Foundation ▼
700 First National Place I
801 South Fillmore
Amarillo 79101   (806) 373-8353

Trust established in 1951 in TX; incorporated in 1971.
Donor(s): Donald D. Harrington,‡ Mrs. Sybil B. Harrington.
Foundation type: Independent
Financial data (yr. ended 12/31/91): Assets, $70,892,460 (M); expenditures, $6,465,612; qualifying distributions, $6,465,612, including $4,937,459 for 54 grants (high: $1,745,370; low: $2,000; average: $10,000-$100,000).
Purpose and activities: Interests include hospitals and health agencies, medical research, the arts and cultural programs, higher and other education, including scholarship funds, youth agencies, social services, and civic affairs.
Fields of interest: Hospitals, health, health services, medical research, cancer, arts, cultural programs, media and communications, higher education, education, education—early childhood, elementary education, secondary education, youth, child development, social services, civic affairs.
Types of support: Scholarship funds, equipment, research, renovation projects, building funds.
Limitations: Giving limited to the 26 northernmost counties of the Texas Panhandle. No grants to individuals, or for operating budgets.
Publications: Application guidelines.
Application information: Application form not required.
    Initial approach: Letter requesting guidelines from Grants Coord.
    Copies of proposal: 1
    Deadline(s): At least 1 month prior to board meeting; Jan. 15, Mar. 20, July 31, and Sept. 16
    Board meeting date(s): Quarterly
    Final notification: 2 months
    Write: Jim Allison, Pres., or Evelyn Solonynka, Grants Coord.
Officers and Directors:* Gene Edwards,* Chair.; Don L. Patterson,* Vice-Chair.; Jim Allison, Pres. and Exec. Dir.; Patricia M. Smith, Secy.-Treas.
Number of staff: 1 full-time professional.
EIN: 751336604
Recent health grants:
3030-1 Amarillo Medical Center, Amarillo, TX, $94,232. 1990.
3030-2 Childrens Rehabilitation Center, Amarillo, TX, $188,463. 1990.
3030-3 Don and Sybil Harrington Cancer Center, Amarillo, TX, $1,884,634. 1990.
3030-4 Harrington Arthritis Research Center, Phoenix, AZ, $471,158. 1990.
3030-5 High Plains Baptist Hospital, Amarillo, TX, $25,000. Toward Easy Street Environment. 1990.
3030-6 Panhandle AIDS Support Organization, Amarillo, TX, $26,049. For salary and operating expenses. 1990.
3030-7 Panhandle Maternal/Child Health Foundation, Amarillo, TX, $48,000. To purchase pulmonary diagnostic machine. 1990.
3030-8 Texas Tech University Health Science Center, Amarillo, TX, $68,051. For study of molecular mechanism of killer cells in liver. 1990.

3031
Hawn Foundation, Inc.
300 North Ervay, Tower One, Suite 1540
Dallas 75201   (214) 220-2828

Incorporated in 1962 in TX.
Donor(s): Mildred Hawn.‡
Foundation type: Independent
Financial data (yr. ended 08/31/91): Assets, $22,279,648 (M); expenditures, $1,178,431; qualifying distributions, $922,171, including $862,250 for 43 grants (high: $350,000; low: $1,000; average: $3,500-$30,000).
Fields of interest: Medical research, health services, hospitals, higher education, social services, cultural programs.
Limitations: Giving primarily in TX, with emphasis on Dallas.
Application information: Application form not required.
    Initial approach: Letter
    Deadline(s): None
    Board meeting date(s): Aug. and as necessary
    Final notification: Between 30 and 90 days
    Write: Joe V. Hawn, Jr., Secy.-Treas.
Officers and Directors:* William Russell Hawn,* Pres.; Joe V. Hawn, Jr.,* Secy.-Treas.; W.A. Hawn, Jr., William Russell Hawn, Jr., R.S. Strauss, I.N. Taylor.
Number of staff: None.
EIN: 756036761

3032
Simon and Louise Henderson Foundation
P.O. Box 1365
Lufkin 75902   (409) 634-3448

Established in 1958 in TX.
Donor(s): Louise Henderson.‡
Foundation type: Independent
Financial data (yr. ended 12/31/90): Assets, $2,575,324 (M); expenditures, $146,830; qualifying distributions, $137,771, including $128,800 for 23 grants (high: $30,000; low: $50).
Fields of interest: Protestant giving, Protestant welfare, drug abuse, alcoholism, social services.
Types of support: General purposes, building funds.
Limitations: Giving primarily in East TX.
Application information: Application form not required.
    Deadline(s): None
    Board meeting date(s): Dec. and as required
    Write: Simon W. Henderson, Jr., Pres.
Officers: Simon W. Henderson, Jr., Pres.; Loucile J. Henderson, V.P.; Simon W. Henderson III, Secy.-Treas.
EIN: 756022769

3033
Albert & Ethel Herzstein Charitable Foundation ▼
6131 Westview
Houston 77055-5421   (713) 681-7868

Established in 1965 in TX.
Donor(s): Members of the Herzstein family.
Foundation type: Independent
Financial data (yr. ended 12/31/90): Assets, $26,977,149 (M); expenditures, $1,319,365; qualifying distributions, $1,283,071, including

$1,256,172 for 87 grants (high: $500,000; low: $10; average: $500-$25,000).
Purpose and activities: Giving primarily to a temple and medical research, including projects conducted at medical schools.
Fields of interest: Jewish giving, medical research, medical education.
Limitations: Giving primarily in TX.
Application information:
 Initial approach: Letter or proposal
 Deadline(s): None
 Write: Albert H. Herzstein, Mgr.
Officer and Trustee:* Albert H. Herzstein,* Mgr.
EIN: 746070484
Recent health grants:
3033-1 Baylor College of Medicine, Houston, TX, $120,000. 1990.
3033-2 Shoulder, The, Houston, TX, $20,000. 1990.

3034
Hillcrest Foundation ▼
c/o NationsBank, Trust Div.
P.O. Box 830241
Dallas 75283-0241   (214) 508-1965

Trust established in 1959 in TX.
Donor(s): Mrs. W.W. Caruth, Sr.‡
Foundation type: Independent
Financial data (yr. ended 05/31/91): Assets, $85,436,357 (M); expenditures, $3,679,406; qualifying distributions, $3,403,971, including $3,376,432 for 141 grants (high: $200,000; low: $1,000; average: $10,000-$50,000).
Purpose and activities: To relieve poverty, advance education, and promote health; support for higher and other education, health and hospitals, social services, including programs for youth and child welfare, drug abuse, rehabilitation and housing.
Fields of interest: Higher education, education, business education, secondary education, vocational education, adult education, education—building funds, health, hospitals, medical research, cancer, dentistry, social services, hunger, youth, child welfare, drug abuse, rehabilitation, handicapped, housing.
Types of support: Building funds, equipment, land acquisition, seed money, research, matching funds, continuing support, special projects, general purposes, renovation projects.
Limitations: Giving limited to TX, with emphasis on Dallas. No grants to individuals, or for endowment funds, scholarships, or fellowships; no loans.
Publications: Application guidelines, informational brochure (including application guidelines).
Application information: Application form required.
 Initial approach: Letter
 Copies of proposal: 1
 Deadline(s): End of Mar., Aug., and Nov.
 Board meeting date(s): As required, usually 3 times annually; May, Oct., and Jan.
 Write: Daniel Kelly, V.P., NationsBank
Trustees: D. Harold Byrd, Jr., Mabel P. Caruth, Donald Case, Harry A. Shuford, NationsBank.
Number of staff: 1 part-time professional.
EIN: 756007565
Recent health grants:

3034-1 American Heart Association, Texas Affiliate, Dallas Division, Dallas, TX, $25,000. To expand national research headquarters facility in Dallas. 1991.
3034-2 Baylor College of Dentistry, Dallas, TX, $200,000. For research and treatment of abnormal craniofacial problems. 1991.
3034-3 Dallas Challenge, Dallas, TX, $25,000. To provide alcohol and drug services to adolescents and family. 1991.
3034-4 Dallas Child Guidance Clinic, Dallas, TX, $50,000. Toward construction of new treatment center. 1991.
3034-5 Dallas County Community College District Foundation, Dallas, TX, $25,000. To purchase equipment for nursing programs. 1991.
3034-6 Daytop Village Foundation, Dallas, TX, $10,000. To provide affordable drug treatment to youths and families. 1991.
3034-7 Dental Health Programs, Dallas, TX, $50,000. For dental equipment for care of low-income families. 1991.
3034-8 Herrin House, Dallas, TX, $25,000. To renovate and expand home on Gaston Avenue and for rehabilitation programs for mentally ill adults. 1991.
3034-9 Incest Recovery Association, Dallas, TX, $20,000. To provide services and programs to victims of incest. 1991.
3034-10 Kent Waldrep National Paralysis Foundation, Dallas, TX, $50,000. For research and treatment of paralysis. 1991.
3034-11 Komen Alliance, Dallas, TX, $112,500. For Mammotest System to detect and treat breast cancer. 1991.
3034-12 Los Barrios Unidos Community Clinic, Dallas, TX, $25,000. To purchase and upgrade computer system. 1991.
3034-13 Mental Health Association of Dallas County, Dallas, TX, $15,000. For W.H.O. Program, primary prevention of child abuse. 1991.
3034-14 Methodist Hospitals of Dallas, Methodist Medical Center, Dallas, TX, $100,000. For Care Nursery for critically-ill babies. 1991.
3034-15 Save the Children Federation, Dallas, TX, $50,000. For child healthcare services in East Dallas. 1991.
3034-16 Texas Alcohol Narcotics Education, Dallas, TX, $20,000. To replace press equipment, distribute and support drug prevention materials. 1991.
3034-17 Texas Scottish Rite Hospital for Crippled Children, Dallas, TX, $25,000. To produce literacy program for high school students. 1991.
3034-18 Turtle Creek Manor, Dallas, TX, $25,000. To renovate and equip kitchen. 1991.
3034-19 University of North Texas, Center for Network Neuroscience, Denton, TX, $165,442. For neuroscience research project. 1991.
3034-20 University of Texas, Community Service Development Center, Arlington, TX, $25,000. For health care to low-income and homeless people. 1991.
3034-21 University of Texas Southwestern Medical Center, Dallas, TX, $50,000. For emphysema pulmonary disease research. 1991.

3035
Hobby Foundation
3050 Post Oak Blvd., Suite 1330
Houston 77056   (713) 993-2580

Incorporated in 1945 in TX.
Donor(s): W.P. Hobby,‡ Oveta Culp Hobby, The Houston Post Co.
Foundation type: Independent
Financial data (yr. ended 12/31/91): Assets, $30,091,838 (M); gifts received, $100,918; expenditures, $1,265,756; qualifying distributions, $1,123,025, including $1,107,348 for 150 grants (high: $300,500; low: $50).
Fields of interest: Higher education, secondary education, cultural programs, museums, hospitals, libraries.
Limitations: Giving primarily in TX.
Publications: Application guidelines.
Application information: Application form not required.
 Deadline(s): None
 Write: Mrs. Oveta Culp Hobby, Pres.
Officers and Trustees:* Oveta Culp Hobby,* Pres.; William P. Hobby, Jr.,* V.P.; Audrey Horn, Secy.; Peggy C. Buchanan, Treas.; Jessica Hobby Catto, Diana P. Hobby.
EIN: 746026606

3036
Hoblitzelle Foundation ▼
5956 Sherry Ln., Suite 901
Dallas 75225-6522   (214) 373-0462

Trust established in 1942 in TX; incorporated in 1953.
Donor(s): Karl St. John Hoblitzelle,‡ Esther T. Hoblitzelle.‡
Foundation type: Independent
Financial data (yr. ended 04/30/91): Assets, $73,918,751 (M); expenditures, $3,424,417; qualifying distributions, $3,424,417, including $3,023,625 for 78 grants (high: $241,000; low: $250; average: $5,000-$50,000).
Purpose and activities: Grants for higher, secondary, vocational, and medical education, hospitals and health services, youth agencies, cultural programs, social services, and community development.
Fields of interest: Education, higher education, secondary education, literacy, adult education, education—minorities, medical education, vocational education, hospitals, health services, rehabilitation, AIDS, alcoholism, youth, social services, child welfare, disadvantaged, aged, housing, community development, arts, cultural programs, historic preservation, fine arts.
Types of support: Seed money, building funds, equipment, land acquisition, matching funds, general purposes, renovation projects, capital campaigns, special projects.
Limitations: Giving limited to TX, primarily Dallas. No support for religious organizations for sectarian purposes. No grants to individuals; only occasional board-initiated support for operating budgets, debt reduction, research, scholarships, or endowments; no loans.
Publications: Annual report, program policy statement, application guidelines, newsletter.
Application information: Application form not required.
 Initial approach: Letter

Copies of proposal: 1
Deadline(s): Apr. 15, Aug. 15, and Dec. 15
Board meeting date(s): Latter part of May, Sept., and Jan.
Final notification: After next board meeting
Write: Paul W. Harris, Exec. V.P.
Officers and Directors:* James W. Aston,* C.E.O. and Chair.; James W. Keay,* Pres.; Paul W. Harris, Exec. V.P.; Mary Stacy, Secy.; John M. Stemmons,* Treas.; James D. Berry, Lillian M. Bradshaw, Dorothy R. Cullum, Gerald W. Fronterhouse, Robert Lynn Harris, Charles C. Sprague, M.D.
Number of staff: 1 full-time professional; 1 full-time support.
EIN: 756003984
Recent health grants:
3036-1 American Diabetes Association, Dallas, TX, $21,000. For two vehicles for Dallas area use. 1991.
3036-2 American Heart Association, Dallas, TX, $50,000. Toward additional building. 1991.
3036-3 Children and Youth Clinic, Robstown, TX, $40,000. Toward renovation and furnishing of new facility. 1991.
3036-4 Dallas Challenge, Dallas, TX, $50,000. For renovations to new facility. 1991.
3036-5 Dallas Challenge, South Dallas/Fair Park, Dallas, TX, $10,000. Toward facility renovations and furnishings. 1991.
3036-6 Dallas Child Guidance Clinic, Dallas, TX, $260,000. Toward new facility. 1991.
3036-7 Dallas County Community College District Foundation, Dallas, TX, $50,000. Toward nursing skills training equipment and materials. 1991.
3036-8 Herrin House, Dallas, TX, $30,000. Toward renovation of new East Dallas facility. 1991.
3036-9 March of Dimes Birth Defects Foundation, Dallas, TX, $21,535. Toward education program in work place. 1991.
3036-10 Southwestern Medical Foundation, Dallas, TX, $60,000. For national conference on broad moral, legal and health-related implications of medical malpractice. 1991.
3036-11 Southwestern Medical Foundation, Dental Health Programs/Parkland's Bluitt-Flowers Health Clinic, Dallas, TX, $50,000. For furnishings and equipment for dental health treatment and care facility. 1991.
3036-12 Turtle Creek Manor, Dallas, TX, $30,000. For computers for job training. 1991.

3037
Houston Endowment, Inc. ▼
P.O. Box 52338
Houston 77052   (713) 238-8100

Incorporated in 1937 in TX.
Donor(s): Jesse H. Jones,‡ Mrs. Jesse H. Jones.‡
Foundation type: Independent
Financial data (yr. ended 12/31/91): Assets, $773,000,000 (M); expenditures, $33,105,908; qualifying distributions, $33,163,663, including $31,768,080 for 287 grants (high: $2,000,000; low: $500; average: $1,000-$1,000,000).
Purpose and activities: For "the support of any charitable, educational or religious undertaking."
Types of support: Building funds, equipment, scholarship funds, special projects, fellowships, professorships, continuing support, annual campaigns, employee matching gifts, capital campaigns, endowment funds, general purposes, land acquisition, operating budgets, renovation projects.
Limitations: Giving primarily in TX; no grants outside the continental U.S. No grants to individuals; no loans.
Publications: Informational brochure (including application guidelines), annual report.
Application information: Application form not required.
Initial approach: Letter
Copies of proposal: 1
Deadline(s): None
Board meeting date(s): At least quarterly
Final notification: 2 to 4 months
Write: H. Joe Nelson III, Pres.
Officers and Directors* Jack S. Blanton,* Chair.; H.J. Nelson,* Pres.; Sheryl L. Johns, V.P. and Treas.; David L. Nelson, V.P. and Grant Dir.; Audrey Jones Beck, Milton Carroll, Jo Murphy, Philip G. Warner.
Number of staff: 10 full-time professional; 1 part-time professional; 7 full-time support.
EIN: 746013920
Recent health grants:
3037-1 American Cancer Society, Houston, TX, $10,000. For operating funds. 1990.
3037-2 Arthritis Institute of the National Hospital, Arlington, VA, $10,000. For operating funds. 1990.
3037-3 Baylor College of Medicine, Houston, TX, $10,000. For student instruction. 1990.
3037-4 Berea College, Berea, KY, $10,000. For Mary Gibbs Jones educational grant, scholarships in nursing. 1990.
3037-5 Blue Bird Circle Clinic for Pediatric Neurology, Houston, TX, $10,000. For Pediatric Neurological Clinic at Methodist Hospital, Houston. 1990.
3037-6 Childrens Heart Institute of South Texas, Corpus Christi, TX, $25,000. For operating funds. 1990.
3037-7 Cystic Fibrosis Foundation, Texas Gulf Coast Chapter, Houston, TX, $25,000. For operating funds. 1990.
3037-8 DeBakey Medical Foundation, Houston, TX, $1,000,000. Toward research on cardiovascular diseases. 1990.
3037-9 Fayette County Mental Health and Mental Retardation Agency, Schulenburg, TX, $100,000. For operating funds. 1990.
3037-10 Gulf Coast Regional Blood Center, Houston, TX, $6,000,000. Toward building expansion. 1990.
3037-11 Gulf Coast Regional Blood Center, Houston, TX, $100,000. For operating funds. 1990.
3037-12 Gulf Coast Regional Mental Health/Mental Retardation Center, Galveston, TX, $150,000. Toward purchase of equipment for facility in Pearland. 1990.
3037-13 Houston Baptist University, School of Nursing, Houston, TX, $150,000. 1990.
3037-14 Houston Child Guidance Center, Houston, TX, $25,000. For operating funds. 1990.
3037-15 Houston Council on Alcoholism and Drug Abuse, Houston, TX, $10,000. For operating funds. 1990.
3037-16 Institute of Religion, Houston, TX, $30,000. For scholarships in ministry and medical ethics. 1990.
3037-17 Knights Templar Eye Foundation, Springfield, IL, $15,000. For operating funds. 1990.
3037-18 Leukemia Society of America, Texas Gulf Coast Chapter, Houston, TX, $40,000. For operating funds. 1990.
3037-19 Lupus Foundation of America, Houston Chapter, Houston, TX, $15,000. For operating funds. 1990.
3037-20 March of Dimes Birth Defects Foundation, Houston, TX, $208,104. For operating funds. 1990.
3037-21 Methodist Hospital Foundation, Houston, TX, $1,000,000. Toward expansion and remodeling of Scurlock Tower. 1990.
3037-22 National Multiple Sclerosis Society, Southeast Texas Chapter, Houston, TX, $35,000. For operating funds. 1990.
3037-23 Planned Parenthood Center of Houston, Houston, TX, $50,000. For operating funds. 1990.
3037-24 Saint Joseph Hospital Foundation, Houston, TX, $15,000. For operating funds. 1990.
3037-25 Scott and White Memorial Hospital, Temple, TX, $50,000. For scholarships in nursing. 1990.
3037-26 Shriners Hospital for Crippled Children, Atlanta, GA, $500,000. Toward patient and employee educational programs. 1990.
3037-27 Shriners Hospital for Crippled Children, Galveston, TX, $1,000,000. Toward construction of new hospital for Burns Institute. 1990.
3037-28 Shriners Hospital for Crippled Children, Galveston, TX, $65,600. For fellowships in plastic surgery at Burns Institute. 1990.
3037-29 Shriners Hospital for Crippled Children, Houston, TX, $500,000. For operating funds for Orthopedic Unit. 1990.
3037-30 Straight, Dallas, TX, $25,000. For operating funds. 1990.
3037-31 Texas Society to Prevent Blindness, Houston, TX, $25,000. For operating funds. 1990.
3037-32 Texas Womans University, Denton, TX, $12,000. For Mary Gibbs Jones scholarships in nursing education. 1990.
3037-33 University of Texas Health Science Center, Houston, TX, $25,000. For JHJ fellowships in oral surgery. 1990.
3037-34 University of Texas Health Science Center, Houston, TX, $25,000. For residency program in orthopedics at Shriners Hospital for Crippled Children. 1990.
3037-35 University of Texas Health Science Center, Houston, TX, $16,000. For John A. Beck Fellowships Speech and Hearing Institute. 1990.
3037-36 University of Texas Medical Branch Hospitals, Galveston, TX, $1,500,000. For establishment of Jesse H. Jones Research Endowment in Medical Humanities. 1990.
3037-37 University of Texas System Cancer Center, M.D. Anderson Hospital and Tumor Institute, Houston, TX, $10,000. For Jesse H. Jones Fellowship in Cancer Education. 1990.
3037-38 Volunteer Services Council for Richmond State School, Richmond, TX, $221,264. Toward construction of Rehabilitation and Therapeutic Riding Center. 1990.

3038
Howell Corporate Giving Program
1010 Lamar Building, Suite 1800
Houston 77002 (713) 658-4000

Purpose and activities: Supports arts and culture, health and welfare, education, civic affairs, and community development.
Fields of interest: Arts, cultural programs, health, welfare, education, civic affairs, community development, general charitable giving.
Types of support: Continuing support, general purposes, operating budgets.
Limitations: Giving primarily in Houston and San Antonio, TX; also considers applications from other states/areas where company operates.
Application information: Application form not required.
Initial approach: Letter of inquiry
Copies of proposal: 1
Deadline(s): Applications accepted throughout the year
Board meeting date(s): Quarterly
Final notification: 6 weeks
Write: Paul W. Sunkhouser, Pres.
Administrators: Paul Sunkhouser, Pres.; Ann Hudson, Admin. Asst.

3039
The R. D. & Joan Dale Hubbard Foundation
(Formerly The R. Dee Hubbard Foundation)
301 Commerce, No. 3300
Fort Worth 76102 (817) 332-5006
Application address: P.O. Box 1679, Ruidoso Downs, NM 88346; Tel.: (505) 378-4142

Established in 1986 in CA.
Donor(s): R.D. Hubbard.
Foundation type: Independent
Financial data (yr. ended 12/31/90): Assets, $21,137,183 (M); expenditures, $1,045,103; qualifying distributions, $1,045,103, including $937,890 for grants (high: $50,000).
Purpose and activities: Support primarily for elementary, secondary, and higher education, early childhood education, business education, and building funds for schools; giving also for community funds, cancer research, museums and other cultural programs, and programs benefiting the disadvantaged, the handicapped, and Native Americans.
Fields of interest: Elementary education, secondary education, higher education, business education, community funds, cancer, cultural programs, disadvantaged, handicapped, Native Americans.
Types of support: Building funds, endowment funds, matching funds, professorships, scholarship funds.
Limitations: Giving primarily in TX, OK, KS, NM, and NE. No grants to individuals.
Publications: Program policy statement, annual report, application guidelines.
Application information: Application form not required.
Initial approach: Letter
Copies of proposal: 1
Deadline(s): None
Board meeting date(s): Varies
Write: Jim Stoddard

Officers: R.D. Hubbard, Pres.; Joan D. Hubbard, V.P.; Edward A. Burger, C.F.O.; Jennings J. Newcoms, Secy.
Number of staff: 1 full-time professional.
EIN: 330210158

3040
Huffington Foundation
P.O. Box 4337
Houston 77210

Established in 1987 in TX.
Donor(s): Terry L. Huffington, Michael Huffington, Roy M. Huffington.
Foundation type: Independent
Financial data (yr. ended 11/30/91): Assets, $16,972,320 (M); gifts received, $11,000,000; expenditures, $297,386; qualifying distributions, $255,500, including $255,500 for 2 grants (high: $250,000; low: $5,500).
Fields of interest: Medical education.
Types of support: Endowment funds.
Limitations: Giving primarily in TX. No grants to individuals.
Application information: Contributes only to a pre-selected organization. Applications not accepted.
Trustees: Michael Huffington, Phyliss Gough Huffington, Roy M. Huffington, Terry L. Huffington.
EIN: 766040840

3041
M. G. and Lillie A. Johnson Foundation, Inc. ▼
P.O. Box 2269
Victoria 77902 (512) 575-7970

Incorporated in 1958 in TX.
Donor(s): M.G. Johnson,‡ Lillie A. Johnson.‡
Foundation type: Independent
Financial data (yr. ended 11/30/91): Assets, $33,519,830 (M); gifts received, $1,180,100; expenditures, $1,910,462; qualifying distributions, $1,606,747, including $1,599,641 for 38 grants (high: $200,000; low: $3,000; average: $10,000-$100,000).
Purpose and activities: Emphasis on building funds for hospitals, higher educational institutions, social services, civic affairs, and health.
Fields of interest: Hospitals—building funds, education—building funds, social services, civic affairs, higher education, health services, community development, health.
Types of support: Building funds, equipment, land acquisition, matching funds, renovation projects, scholarship funds, capital campaigns.
Limitations: Giving limited to TX, especially the Gulf Coast area located between San Patricio and Wharton counties. No grants to individuals, or for general support, operating budgets, endowment funds, fellowships, research (except medical research), special projects, publications, or conferences; no loans.
Application information: Application form not required.
Initial approach: Proposal
Copies of proposal: 4
Deadline(s): Submit proposal 1 month before meetings; no set deadline

Board meeting date(s): Mar., July, and Oct.
Final notification: Varies
Write: Robert Halepeska, Exec. V.P.
Officers and Trustees:* Irving Moore, Jr.,* Pres.; Robert Halepeska, Exec. V.P.; Jack R. Morrison,* V.P.; Rev. M.H. Lehnhardt,* Secy.; M.H. Brock, Lloyd Rust, Munson Smith.
Number of staff: 1 full-time professional; 1 part-time support.
EIN: 746076961

3042
The Jonsson Foundation
5600 West Lovers Ln., Suite 323
Dallas 75209-4319 (214) 350-4626

Incorporated in 1955 in TX.
Donor(s): J.E. Jonsson, Margaret E. Jonsson.‡
Foundation type: Independent
Financial data (yr. ended 12/31/90): Assets, $3,984,098 (M); expenditures, $241,198; qualifying distributions, $203,305, including $199,000 for 15 grants (high: $100,000; low: $1,000; average: $1,000-$10,000).
Fields of interest: Health, education, cultural programs, community funds.
Types of support: General purposes, building funds, equipment, matching funds, capital campaigns.
Limitations: Giving primarily in the Dallas, TX, area. No grants to individuals, or for endowment funds, scholarships, or fellowships; no loans.
Publications: Application guidelines.
Application information: Funds largely committed. Application form not required.
Initial approach: Letter
Copies of proposal: 1
Deadline(s): None
Board meeting date(s): Feb., May, and Sept.
Final notification: At next meeting
Officers and Trustees:* Kenneth A. Jonsson,* Pres. and Treas.; Philip R. Jonsson,* V.P. and Treas.; Margaret J. Rogers,* V.P.; J.E. Jonsson.
Number of staff: 3 shared staff
EIN: 756012565

3043
The Kayser Foundation
Texas Commerce Bank Bldg.
712 Main St., Suite 1810
Houston 77002 (713) 222-7234

Incorporated in 1961 in TX.
Donor(s): Paul Kayser, Mrs. Paul Kayser.
Foundation type: Independent
Financial data (yr. ended 12/31/91): Assets, $3,677,681 (M); expenditures, $211,045; qualifying distributions, $165,676, including $140,200 for 82 grants (high: $70,000; low: $50).
Fields of interest: Medical research, ophthalmology, education, social services, youth.
Types of support: Research, special projects, building funds, annual campaigns, equipment.
Limitations: Giving primarily in TX. No grants to individuals.
Application information:
Initial approach: Letter
Deadline(s): None
Write: Henry O. Weaver, Pres.
Officers: Henry O. Weaver, Pres.; Bruce La Boon, V.P.; Charles Sapp, V.P.

EIN: 746050591

3044
Ben E. Keith Foundation Trust
c/o Team Bank, N.A.
P.O. Box 2050
Fort Worth 76113   (817) 884-4161

Trust established in 1951 in TX.
Foundation type: Independent
Financial data (yr. ended 06/30/91): Assets, $10,215,895 (M); expenditures, $720,140; qualifying distributions, $655,086, including $651,206 for 257 grants (high: $16,000; low: $250).
Purpose and activities: Giving for higher education and social service agencies; some support also for cultural programs and hospitals.
Fields of interest: Higher education, social services, cultural programs, hospitals.
Types of support: General purposes, operating budgets, continuing support, annual campaigns, seed money, emergency funds, deficit financing, building funds, equipment, land acquisition, endowment funds, matching funds, capital campaigns.
Limitations: Giving limited to TX. No grants to individuals, or for scholarships or fellowships; no loans.
Publications: 990-PF.
Application information:
   Initial approach: Letter
   Deadline(s): Sept.
   Board meeting date(s): Jan., Mar., June, and Oct.
   Write: Richard L. Mitchell, Secy.
Officers and Directors: John Beauchamp, Chair.; Richard L. Mitchell, Secy.; Howard Hallam, Robert Hallam, Troy LaGrone, Ronnie Wallace, Hugh Watson.
Advisory Board: Team Bank, N.A.
Number of staff: None.
EIN: 756013955

3045
Harris and Eliza Kempner Fund
P.O. Box 119
Galveston 77553-0119   (409) 765-6671

Established in 1946 in TX.
Donor(s): Various interests and members of the Kempner family.
Foundation type: Independent
Financial data (yr. ended 12/31/91): Assets, $28,092,568 (M); gifts received, $85,100; expenditures, $1,468,820; qualifying distributions, $1,324,282, including $973,780 for 115 grants (high: $125,000; low: $500; average: $1,000-$10,000), $75,565 for 164 employee matching gifts and $274,937 for 107 loans to individuals.
Purpose and activities: Emphasis on higher education, including medical education, programs for minorities, scholarship funds, student loans, and a matching gift program, health and medical services, including AIDS and cancer research and programs for the handicapped and mentally ill, international affairs and development, community funds, welfare, population studies, human rights, and community projects, programs supporting youth, women and Native Americans, Jewish organizations,

including welfare funds, libraries, and culture programs, including historic preservation, arts and dance, museums, theater, and fine arts. Giving also for the environment and conservation, literacy programs, and social services, including the homeless.
Fields of interest: Education, health, AIDS, community development, welfare, social services, women, youth, cultural programs, arts, libraries.
Types of support: General purposes, operating budgets, continuing support, seed money, emergency funds, building funds, equipment, scholarship funds, professorships, special projects, research, publications, conferences and seminars, student loans, capital campaigns, fellowships, lectureships, matching funds, renovation projects, annual campaigns.
Limitations: Giving primarily in Galveston, TX. No grants to individuals.
Publications: 990-PF, biennial report (including application guidelines).
Application information: Computerized solicitations not considered. Student loans will not be made by the fund for the 1992-93 academic year. Application form not required.
   Initial approach: Letter requesting guidelines
   Copies of proposal: 1
   Deadline(s): For grant program: Mar. 15, June 15, and Oct. 15; Dec. 1 for national/international requests in the areas of education, environment, population control, or Third World development
   Board meeting date(s): Usually in Apr., July, Dec., and as required
   Final notification: 2 weeks
   Write: Elaine Perachio, Exec. Dir.
Officers and Trustees: * Lyda Ann Quinn Thomas,* Chair.; Harris Kempner Weston,* Vice-Chair.; Robert Lee Kempner Lynch,* Secy.-Treas.; Arthur M. Alpert, John T. Currie, Ann O. Hamilton, Hetta T. Kempner, Barbara W. Sasser, Edward R. Thompson, Jr.
Number of staff: 1 part-time professional; 2 part-time support.
EIN: 746042458
Recent health grants:
3045-1 University of Texas Medical Branch Hospitals, Galveston, TX, $125,000. For Jeane B. Kempner fellowship program. 1991.
3045-2 University of Texas Medical Branch Hospitals, Galveston, TX, $50,000. For scholarships for minority medical and allied health students. 1991.
3045-3 University of Texas Medical Branch Hospitals, Galveston, TX, $37,500. For endowment centennial campaign for establishment of Dr. James E. Thompson Laboratory and scholarship endowment for allied health students. 1991.
3045-4 University of Texas Medical Branch Hospitals, Galveston, TX, $10,000. For project, Virtual Visual Environment Display (VIVED) for Medical Education in collaboration with NASA and GISD. 1991.

3046
Kimberly-Clark Foundation, Inc. ▼
P.O. Box 619100
Dallas 75261-9100   (214) 830-1200

Incorporated in 1952 in WI.
Donor(s): Kimberly-Clark Corp.

Foundation type: Company-sponsored
Financial data (yr. ended 12/31/90): Assets, $1,489,270 (M); gifts received, $2,747,075; expenditures, $1,868,904; qualifying distributions, $1,863,299, including $1,863,101 for 89 grants (high: $250,000; low: $100; average: $5,000-$20,000).
Purpose and activities: Emphasis on higher education, community funds, community development, social services, and cultural programs. The employee matching gift program was discontinued in 1986.
Fields of interest: Higher education, education, education—minorities, community funds, community development, social services, homeless, youth, health, cancer, drug abuse, cultural programs, performing arts, museums, engineering, conservation.
Types of support: Annual campaigns, building funds, continuing support, equipment, land acquisition, operating budgets, seed money, scholarship funds, general purposes, capital campaigns, program-related investments.
Limitations: Giving primarily in communities where the company has operations. No support for preschool, elementary, or secondary education, state-supported institutions, denominational religious organizations, or sports and athletics. No grants to individuals; no loans.
Publications: Annual report.
Application information: Application form not required.
   Initial approach: Proposal
   Copies of proposal: 1
   Deadline(s): None
   Board meeting date(s): Apr.
   Final notification: By year end
   Write: Colleen B. Berman, V.P.
Officers and Directors: * O. George Everbach,* Pres.; Colleen B. Berman, V.P.; Donald M. Crook, Secy.; W. Anthony Gamron,* Treas.; Brendan M. O'Neill, Darwin E. Smith.
Number of staff: 1 full-time professional; 1 full-time support.
EIN: 396044304
Recent health grants:
3046-1 American Diabetes Association, DC, $15,000. 1990.
3046-2 Arkansas Childrens Hospital, Little Rock, AR, $25,000. 1990.
3046-3 Metro Atlanta Recovery Residences, Clarkston, GA, $10,000. 1990.
3046-4 Susan G. Komen Foundation, Dallas, TX, $25,000. 1990.
3046-5 University of Texas System Cancer Center, Houston, TX, $250,000. For grant shared with M.D. Anderson Hospital and Tumor Institute. 1990.

3047
Carl B. and Florence E. King Foundation ▼
5956 Sherry Ln., Suite 620
Dallas 75225

Incorporated in 1966 in TX.
Donor(s): Carl B. King,‡ Florence E. King,‡ Dorothy E. King.
Foundation type: Independent
Financial data (yr. ended 12/31/90): Assets, $28,336,854 (M); expenditures, $2,438,420; qualifying distributions, $1,796,232, including $1,274,255 for 63 grants (high: $130,000; low:

$1,000; average: $2,000-$20,000) and $149,500 for grants to individuals (high: $4,000; low: $500; average: $1,000-$2,000).

Purpose and activities: Emphasis on higher and secondary education, youth and social service agencies, and cultural programs; scholarships and student loans limited to TX high school students and/or current college students; some support for hospitals and health agencies.

Fields of interest: Higher education, secondary education, youth, social services, cultural programs, health services, hospitals.

Types of support: Scholarship funds, special projects, student aid, student loans.

Limitations: Giving primarily in the Dallas, TX, area. No support for religious purposes.

Publications: Program policy statement, application guidelines.

Application information: Application forms required for scholarships only and available from the foundation and the Texas Interscholastic League; scholarships limited to TX high school students and/or current college students majoring in Math, Science, or English Education.

  Initial approach: Letter
  Copies of proposal: 1
  Deadline(s): None for organizations; students should contact Texas Interscholastic League
  Board meeting date(s): Quarterly
  Final notification: 6 weeks
  Write: Carl Yeckel, V.P.

Officers and Directors:* Dorothy E. King,* Pres.; Carl L. Yeckel,* V.P.; Thomas W. Vett,* Secy.-Treas.; M.E. Childs, Jack Phipps, Sam G. Winstead.

Number of staff: 4 full-time professional.

EIN: 756052203

3048
Robert J. Kleberg, Jr. and Helen C. Kleberg Foundation ▼
700 North St. Mary's St., Suite 1200
San Antonio 78205   (512) 271-3691

Incorporated in 1950 in TX.

Donor(s): Helen C. Kleberg,‡ Robert J. Kleberg, Jr.‡

Foundation type: Independent

Financial data (yr. ended 12/31/90): Assets, $107,088,578 (M); expenditures, $6,063,275; qualifying distributions, $4,517,408, including $4,468,684 for 48 grants (high: $750,000; low: $1,000; average: $10,000-$100,000).

Purpose and activities: Giving on a national basis for medical research, veterinary and animal sciences, wildlife research and preservation, health services, higher education, and the arts and humanities; support also for local community organizations.

Fields of interest: Health, medical research, biological sciences, health services, wildlife, higher education, arts.

Types of support: Building funds, equipment, research, conferences and seminars, matching funds, renovation projects.

Limitations: No support for community organizations outside TX, for non-tax-exempt organizations, or for organizations limited by race or religion. No grants to individuals, or for general purposes, endowments, deficit financing, ongoing operating expenses, overhead or indirect costs, scholarships, or fellowships; no loans.

Publications: Annual report, application guidelines.

Application information: Application form not required.

  Initial approach: Letter
  Copies of proposal: 1
  Deadline(s): None
  Board meeting date(s): Usually in June and Dec.
  Final notification: 6 months
  Write: Robert L. Washington, Grants Coord.

Officers and Directors:* Helen K. Groves,* Pres.; Helen C. Alexander,* V.P.; John D. Alexander, Jr.,* V.P. and Secy.; Emory G. Alexander,* V.P. and Treas.; Caroline R. Alexander, Dorothy D. Alexander, Henrietta K. Alexander.

Number of staff: 1 full-time professional.

EIN: 746044810

Recent health grants:

3048-1 American Society of Human Genetics, Bethesda, MD, $25,000. For 8th International Congress of Human Genetics. 1990.

3048-2 Baylor College of Medicine, Houston, TX, $420,000. For human genetics, N.M.R., and neurobiology research. 1990.

3048-3 Harlingen Community Emergency Care, Harlingen, TX, $10,000. For ambulance personnel training program. 1990.

3048-4 House Ear Institute, Los Angeles, CA, $50,000. For pediatric cochlear implant research. 1990.

3048-5 Louisiana State University, New Orleans, LA, $100,000. For hearing research laboratory. 1990.

3048-6 Medical College of Wisconsin, Milwaukee, WI, $75,000. For International Bone Marrow Transplant Registry. 1990.

3048-7 National Jewish Center for Immunology and Respiratory Medicine, Denver, CO, $10,000. For lupus erythamatosus research. 1990.

3048-8 Northeastern Ohio Universities College of Medicine, Rootstown, OH, $750,000. For medical research laboratory equipment. 1990.

3048-9 Oncology Nursing Foundation, Pittsburgh, PA, $50,000. For cancer nursing research and education. 1990.

3048-10 Planned Parenthood of San Antonio, San Antonio, TX, $20,000. For South Texas education project. 1990.

3048-11 Retina Research Foundation, Houston, TX, $45,000. For retinoblastoma research project. 1990.

3048-12 Salk Institute for Biological Studies, La Jolla, CA, $200,000. For brain hormone research projects. 1990.

3048-13 Santa Rosa Childrens Hospital Foundation, San Antonio, TX, $25,000. For neuroscience unit expansion. 1990.

3048-14 Southwest Foundation for Biomedical Research, San Antonio, TX, $90,000. For biomedical research symposium. 1990.

3048-15 University of California, San Francisco, CA, $100,000. For neuroscience fellowship program. 1990.

3048-16 University of Texas Health Science Center, Houston, TX, $29,934. For genetics research project in South Texas. 1990.

3048-17 University of Texas Health Science Center, San Antonio, TX, $45,000. For breast cancer research project. 1990.

3048-18 University of Texas Medical Branch Hospitals, Galveston, TX, $500,000. For tropical disease research center. 1990.

3048-19 University of Texas System Cancer Center, Houston, TX, $320,000. For cancer research and children's camp. 1990.

3048-20 Valley Baptist Medical Foundation, Harlingen, TX, $400,000. For computerized tomography scanner. 1990.

3048-21 Webb Waring Lung Institute, Denver, CO, $45,000. For tuberculosis immunity research. 1990.

3049
Mary Potishman Lard Trust
c/o Team Bank, N.A.
P.O. Box 2050
Fort Worth 76113

Trust established in 1968 in TX.

Donor(s): Mary P. Lard.‡

Foundation type: Independent

Financial data (yr. ended 12/31/90): Assets, $10,160,256 (M); gifts received, $19; expenditures, $539,404; qualifying distributions, $412,610, including $384,500 for 49 grants (high: $60,000; low: $500).

Fields of interest: Education, higher education, social services, youth, hospitals, medical research, cultural programs.

Limitations: Giving primarily in TX, with emphasis on Fort Worth. No grants to individuals.

Application information:

  Initial approach: Letter
  Deadline(s): None
  Board meeting date(s): Generally in June or July, and Dec.
  Final notification: Within 2 weeks of meeting
  Write: Bayard H. Friedman, Trustee

Trustees: Alan D. Friedman, Bayard H. Friedman, Walker C. Friedman.

Number of staff: 1 full-time professional.

EIN: 756210697

3050
LBJ Family Foundation
13809 Research Blvd., Suite 700
Austin 78750

Trust established in 1957 in TX.

Donor(s): Lyndon B. Johnson,‡ Mrs. Lyndon B. Johnson, Texas Broadcasting Corp.

Foundation type: Independent

Financial data (yr. ended 12/31/90): Assets, $2,862,973 (M); expenditures, $203,530; qualifying distributions, $187,524, including $185,417 for 137 grants (high: $35,000; low: $100; average: $500).

Purpose and activities: Emphasis on conservation and recreation; some support for higher and secondary education, educational television, hospitals, and cultural programs, including support of presidential libraries.

Fields of interest: Conservation, recreation, higher education, secondary education, media and communications, hospitals, cultural programs.

Types of support: Continuing support, general purposes, scholarship funds, special projects.

Limitations: Giving primarily in Austin, TX. No grants to individuals, or for endowment funds; no loans.

Application information: Application form not required.

  Initial approach: Letter

Copies of proposal: 1
Deadline(s): None
Board meeting date(s): June and Dec.
Write: John M. Barr, Mgr.
Officer: John M. Barr, Mgr.
Trustees: Claudia T. Johnson, Luci B. Johnson, Lynda J. Robb.
Number of staff: None.
EIN: 746045768

3051
Lightner Sams Foundation, Inc.
11811 Preston Rd., Suite 200
Dallas 75230   (214) 458-8813

Established in 1981 in TX.
Foundation type: Independent
Financial data (yr. ended 12/31/91): Assets, $16,050,191 (M); expenditures, $787,475; qualifying distributions, $686,500, including $648,633 for 64 grants (high: $167,183; low: $400; average: $5,000-$10,000).
Purpose and activities: Giving for the arts and cultural programs, including museums and the performing arts, and education; some support also for hospitals, health, youth organizations, Protestant religious organizations, community development, and social services; grants to a zoo and a playhouse.
Fields of interest: Arts, education, hospitals, health, youth, child welfare, Protestant giving, community development, social services, wildlife, physics.
Types of support: Annual campaigns, building funds, capital campaigns, equipment, operating budgets, renovation projects, research.
Limitations: Giving limited to Dallas, TX, and Jackson, WY. No grants to individuals.
Application information: Application form not required.
  Initial approach: Letter
  Copies of proposal: 1
  Deadline(s): Submit proposal 2 to 3 weeks prior
    to board meetings
  Board meeting date(s): Feb., May, Aug., and
    Nov.
  Final notification: As soon as possible after
    meetings
  Write: Donna Dunham
Trustees: Earl Sams Lightner, Larry Lightner, Robin Lightner, Sue B. Lightner.
Number of staff: 1 full-time professional.
EIN: 742139849

3052
The LTV Foundation ▼
c/o The LTV Corp.
P.O. Box 655003
Dallas 75265-5003   (214) 979-7726

Trust established in 1950 in OH.
Donor(s): Republic Steel Corp.
Foundation type: Company-sponsored
Financial data (yr. ended 12/31/90): Assets, $10,444,189 (M); expenditures, $1,064,952; qualifying distributions, $1,064,852, including $1,064,852 for 355 grants (high: $35,400; low: $100; average: $1,000-$5,000).
Purpose and activities: Giving largely for community funds, hospitals, higher and other education, youth agencies, health agencies, urban

renewal, and arts and cultural programs; employee-related scholarships through the National Merit Scholarship Corporation.
Fields of interest: Community funds, hospitals, health services, education, higher education, secondary education, elementary education, education—early childhood, engineering, science and technology, youth, child development, urban development, employment, family services, disadvantaged, homeless, arts, cultural programs, museums, general charitable giving.
Types of support: Operating budgets, annual campaigns, building funds, equipment, endowment funds, special projects, research, matching funds, capital campaigns, emergency funds, employee-related scholarships.
Limitations: Giving limited to areas of company operations, with emphasis on OH, TX, IL, IN, and NY. No support for religious purposes, fraternal or veterans' organizations, government agencies, or athletic teams. No grants to individuals, or for seed money, deficit financing, land acquisition, publications, conferences, or courtesy advertising; no loans.
Publications: Informational brochure (including application guidelines).
Application information: Application form not required.
  Initial approach: Proposal
  Copies of proposal: 1
  Deadline(s): None
  Board meeting date(s): Quarterly
  Final notification: 2 to 4 months
  Write: Brent Berryman, Exec. Dir.
Officer: Brent Berryman, Exec. Dir.
Trust Committee: Karl C. Caldabaugh, David H. Hoag, James F. Powers.
Trustee Bank: Ameritrust Co., N.A.
Number of staff: 1 part-time professional; 1 part-time support.
EIN: 346505330

3053
W. P. & Bulah Luse Foundation
P.O. Box 831041
Dallas 75283-1041
Application address: P.O. Box 830241, Dallas, TX 75283-0241; Tel.: (214) 508-1989

Established in 1947 in TX.
Foundation type: Independent
Financial data (yr. ended 12/31/90): Assets, $3,735,699 (M); gifts received, $1,093; expenditures, $390,656; qualifying distributions, $169,852, including $167,120 for 9 grants (high: $100,000; low: $5,000).
Purpose and activities: Giving limited to the "alleviation of poverty, education, and medical purposes."
Fields of interest: Social services, education, medical education, medical research, youth.
Limitations: Giving limited to TX. No grants to individuals.
Application information: Application form not required.
  Deadline(s): None
  Board meeting date(s): Annually at the end of
    the year
  Write: Bill Arrington, c/o NationsBank
Trustees: Jack Burrell, Jack Burrell, Jr., Louise Delarios, NationsBank.
EIN: 756007639

3054
Mary Kay Foundation
8787 Stemmons Freeway
P.O. Box 47033
Dallas 75247   (214) 630-8787

Incorporated in 1969 in TX.
Donor(s): Mary Kay Ash.
Foundation type: Independent
Financial data (yr. ended 06/30/91): Assets, $2,182,495 (M); expenditures, $226,497; qualifying distributions, $205,180, including $205,180 for 62 grants (high: $34,814; low: $300).
Fields of interest: Medical research, health, social services, public policy, performing arts.
Types of support: Research.
Limitations: Giving primarily in Dallas, TX.
Application information: Application form not required.
  Deadline(s): None
Trustees: Gerald M. Allen, Mary Kay Ash, Brad Glendening, Michael C. Lunceford, Richard R. Rogers.
EIN: 756081602

3055
Maxus Energy Corporate Contributions Program
717 North Harwood St.
Dallas 75201   (214) 953-2833

Financial data (yr. ended 12/31/90): Total giving, $255,000, including $210,000 for grants (high: $95,000; low: $100) and $45,000 for employee matching gifts.
Purpose and activities: Supports education, health and welfare, civic affairs, culture and the arts, and programs for women, youth, the homeless, and the disadvantaged.
Fields of interest: Education, health, welfare, civic affairs, cultural programs, arts, women, youth, performing arts, homeless.
Types of support: General purposes, matching funds, scholarship funds, annual campaigns, employee matching gifts, employee-related scholarships, special projects.
Limitations: Giving primarily in operating locations in Dallas and Amarillo, TX.
Publications: Program policy statement, application guidelines.
Application information: Public Relations staff handles giving. Application form not required.
  Initial approach: Letter or proposal
  Copies of proposal: 1
  Board meeting date(s): Varies
  Write: Linda T. Covington, Mgr., Communs.
Number of staff: 2 part-time professional; 1 part-time support.

3056
McAshan Foundation, Inc. ▼
(Formerly McAshan Educational and Charitable Trust)
Five Post Oak Park, Suite 1980
Houston 77027

Trust established in 1952 in TX; reorganized in Sept. 1989 under current name.
Donor(s): Susan C. McAshan, Susan Vaughn Clayton Trust No. 1.

Foundation type: Independent
Financial data (yr. ended 12/31/90): Assets, $37,437,109 (M); expenditures, $5,673,156; qualifying distributions, $5,525,417, including $5,471,676 for 74 grants (high: $1,000,000; low: $100; average: $5,000-$50,000).
Purpose and activities: Emphasis on education, the handicapped, population control, conservation, medical research, and the arts and music.
Fields of interest: Education, higher education, handicapped, family planning, conservation, arts, music.
Types of support: Scholarship funds, research.
Limitations: Giving primarily in TX, with emphasis on Houston.
Application information: Grants for scholarships to students specifically recommended under a scholarship program by a college or university.
Initial approach: Proposal
Officers and Trustees:* S.M. McAshan, Jr.,* Pres.; Susan C. McAshan,* V.P.; W.W. Vann, Secy.-Treas. and Exec. Dir.; Lucy Johnson Hadac, Susan Baker Powell.
EIN: 760285765
Recent health grants:
3056-1 Cannon Memorial Hospital, Banner Elk, NC, $96,000. 1990.
3056-2 Johns Hopkins University, School of Medicine, Baltimore, MD, $250,000. 1990.
3056-3 March of Dimes Birth Defects Foundation, Texas Gulf Coast Chapter, Houston, TX, $50,000. 1990.
3056-4 Planned Parenthood Association of Hidalgo County, McAllen, TX, $25,000. 1990.
3056-5 Planned Parenthood Federation of America, NYC, NY, $1,000,000. 1990.
3056-6 Planned Parenthood Federation, International, Western Hemisphere Region, NYC, NY, $35,000. 1990.
3056-7 Planned Parenthood of Greater Charlotte, Charlotte, NC, $11,000. 1990.
3056-8 Planned Parenthood of Houston and Southeast Texas, Houston, TX, $950,000. 1990.
3056-9 Population Crisis Committee, DC, $30,000. 1990.
3056-10 Population Institute, DC, $50,000. 1990.
3056-11 San Miguel Educational Foundation, San Miguel de Allende, Mexico, $99,000. 1990.
3056-12 Texas Heart Institute, Houston, TX, $110,000. 1990.
3056-13 Toe River Health District, Spruce Pine, NC, $25,000. 1990.

3057
McCombs Foundation, Inc.
9000 Tesoro, Suite 122
San Antonio 78217

Established in 1981 in TX.
Donor(s): Gary V. Woods, and members of the McCombs family.
Foundation type: Operating
Financial data (yr. ended 12/31/90): Assets, $66,457 (M); expenditures, $259,074; qualifying distributions, $259,074, including $258,650 for 53 grants (high: $100,000; low: $50).
Fields of interest: Science and technology, higher education, cultural programs, religion, civic affairs, social services, arts, medical research.

Limitations: Giving primarily in TX.
Application information: Application form not required.
Initial approach: Letter
Deadline(s): None
Write: Gary V. Woods, Secy.-Treas.
Officers: Billy J. McCombs, Pres.; Charline H. McCombs, V.P.; Gary V. Woods, Secy.-Treas.
EIN: 742204217

3058
The Eugene McDermott Foundation ▼
3808 Euclid Ave.
Dallas 75205   (214) 521-2924

Incorporated in 1972 in TX; The McDermott Foundation merged into above in 1977.
Donor(s): Eugene McDermott,‡ Mrs. Eugene McDermott.
Foundation type: Independent
Financial data (yr. ended 08/31/91): Assets, $39,654,499 (M); expenditures, $2,123,713; qualifying distributions, $2,036,542, including $2,000,800 for 90 grants (high: $500,000; low: $1,000; average: $1,000-$25,000).
Purpose and activities: Support primarily for museums and other cultural programs, higher and secondary education, health, and general community interests.
Fields of interest: Museums, cultural programs, historic preservation, education, higher education, secondary education, elementary education, education—early childhood, health, community development, child welfare, community funds.
Types of support: Building funds, equipment, operating budgets, scholarship funds.
Limitations: Giving primarily in Dallas, TX. No grants to individuals.
Application information: Application form not required.
Initial approach: Letter
Copies of proposal: 1
Deadline(s): None
Board meeting date(s): Quarterly
Final notification: Prior to Aug. 31
Write: Mrs. Eugene McDermott, Pres.
Officers and Trustees:* Mrs. Eugene McDermott,* Pres.; Charles Cullum,* V.P.; Mary McDermott Cook,* Secy.-Treas.; C.J. Thomsen.
Agent: NationsBank.
Number of staff: 2 part-time professional.
EIN: 237237919

3059
John P. McGovern Foundation ▼
6969 Brompton St.
Houston 77025   (713) 661-4808

Established in 1961 in TX.
Donor(s): John P. McGovern, M.D.
Foundation type: Independent
Financial data (yr. ended 08/31/90): Assets, $54,451,513 (M); gifts received, $1,717,274; expenditures, $2,189,175; qualifying distributions, $2,134,903, including $2,064,142 for 3 grants (high: $2,064,000; low: $42).
Purpose and activities: "To provide assistance to organizations engaged in teaching, training, research, and treatment, particularly relating to addiction (alcoholism, drug dependence, etc.),

family dynamics, and the behavioral sciences; to provide scholarship funds to institutions for deserving students to study and train in these areas; also support for health agencies, higher education, and worthy charities."
Fields of interest: Health, medical research, medical education, higher education, alcoholism, libraries, rehabilitation, drug abuse, nursing, general charitable giving.
Types of support: Research, scholarship funds, operating budgets, professorships, lectureships, endowment funds, building funds, conferences and seminars, continuing support, general purposes, matching funds, publications, emergency funds.
Limitations: Giving primarily in TX, with emphasis on Houston; giving also in the Southwest.
Application information: Grants primarily initiated by the foundation except for requests in the area of alcohol and/or drug addiction. Unsolicited grant requests are usually considered by the foundation. Application form not required.
Deadline(s): None
Board meeting date(s): Usually on or before Aug. 31
Officers: John P. McGovern, M.D., Pres.; Richard B. Davies, V.P.; Kathrine G. McGovern, Secy.-Treas.
Number of staff: 1 part-time professional; 6 part-time support.
EIN: 746053075

3060
McGovern Fund for the Behavioral Sciences ▼
(Formerly Texas Allergy Research Foundation)
6969 Brompton St.
Houston 77025   (713) 661-1444

Established in 1979 in TX.
Donor(s): John P. McGovern Foundation.
Foundation type: Independent
Financial data (yr. ended 11/30/90): Assets, $2,633,661 (M); gifts received, $2,064,500; expenditures, $2,090,426; qualifying distributions, $2,082,106, including $2,077,130 for 209 grants (high: $631,000; low: $100; average: $1,000-$10,000).
Purpose and activities: "To provide assistance to organizations engaged in teaching, training, research, and treatment, particularly relating to addiction (alcoholism, drug dependence, etc.), family dynamics, and the behavioral sciences; to provide scholarship funds to institutions for deserving students to study and train in these areas; also support for health agencies, higher education, and worthy charities."
Fields of interest: Medical research, alcoholism, medical education, rehabilitation, drug abuse, health, nursing, libraries, higher education, general charitable giving.
Types of support: Research, building funds, conferences and seminars, continuing support, emergency funds, endowment funds, general purposes, lectureships, matching funds, professorships, publications, scholarship funds.
Limitations: Giving primarily in TX, with emphasis on Houston; giving also in the Southwest.

Application information: Grants primarily initiated by the foundation except for requests in the area of alcohol and/or drug addiction.
Deadline(s): None
Board meeting date(s): Usually on or before Nov. 30
Officers and Directors: John P. McGovern,* Chair. and Pres.; Richard B. Davies,* V.P.; Kathrine G. McGovern,* Secy.-Treas.
Number of staff: 1 part-time professional; 6 part-time support.
EIN: 742086867

3061
Robert E. and Evelyn McKee Foundation
P.O. Box 220599
6006 North Mesa St., Suite 906
El Paso 79913   (915) 581-4025

Incorporated in 1952 in TX.
Donor(s): Robert E. McKee,‡ Evelyn McKee,‡ Robert E. McKee, Inc., The Zia Co.
Foundation type: Independent
Financial data (yr. ended 12/31/90): Assets, $4,475,982 (M); expenditures, $414,385; qualifying distributions, $331,867, including $331,867 for 99 grants (high: $50,000; low: $100).
Purpose and activities: Emphasis on local hospitals, community funds, and rehabilitation and the handicapped; grants also for religious organizations, higher and other education, youth agencies, child welfare, and medical research.
Fields of interest: Hospitals, community funds, rehabilitation, handicapped, religion, higher education, education, youth, child welfare, medical research.
Types of support: Operating budgets, continuing support, annual campaigns, seed money, emergency funds, building funds, equipment, scholarship funds, research.
Limitations: Giving primarily in TX, with emphasis on El Paso. No support for organizations limited by race or ethnic origin, other private foundations (except for a local community foundation), or religious organizations (except local Episcopal churches). No grants to individuals, or for endowment funds or deficit financing; no loans.
Publications: Annual report (including application guidelines), program policy statement, application guidelines.
Application information: Application form not required.
Initial approach: Proposal
Copies of proposal: 1
Deadline(s): Submit proposal preferably in Nov.; deadline Dec. 10
Board meeting date(s): June
Final notification: After Feb. 1
Write: Louis B. McKee, Pres.
Officers and Trustees: Louis B. McKee,* Pres. and Treas.; Frances McKee Hays,* V.P.; Margaret McKee Lund,* V.P.; C. David McKee,* V.P.; John S. McKee,* V.P.; Philip S. McKee,* V.P.; Robert L. Hazelton,* Secy.; Charlotte McKee Cohen, Leighton Green, Sharon Hays Herrera, C. Steven McKee, Louis B. McKee, Jr., Philip Russell McKee, Robert E. McKee III, Helen Lund Yancey.
Number of staff: 1 part-time professional; 1 full-time support.
EIN: 746036675

3062
Bruce McMillan, Jr. Foundation, Inc.
P.O. Box 9
Overton 75684   (214) 834-3148

Trust established in 1951 in TX.
Donor(s): V. Bruce McMillan, M.D.,‡ Mary Moore McMillan.‡
Foundation type: Independent
Financial data (yr. ended 06/30/91): Assets, $15,784,655 (M); expenditures, $895,486; qualifying distributions, $575,432, including $451,183 for 53 grants (high: $50,000; low: $500; average: $1,000-$40,000) and $63,919 for 94 grants to individuals (high: $1,500; low: $200).
Purpose and activities: Grants largely for higher education, including a scholarship program for graduates of eight specific high schools in the immediate Overton, TX, area; support also for health agencies, church support, social service and youth agencies, agricultural conservation, and medical research.
Fields of interest: Higher education, youth, health services, medical research, religion—Christian, agriculture, social services.
Types of support: Student aid, general purposes, scholarship funds, special projects.
Limitations: Giving limited to eastern TX.
Publications: Application guidelines.
Application information: Application form required.
Initial approach: Letter
Deadline(s): May 31 for scholarship interviews; June 15 for scholarship applications; and May 15 for other requests
Board meeting date(s): June and Oct.
Final notification: July 1 (for scholarships)
Write: Ralph Ward, Pres.
Officers and Directors: Reginald H. Field,* Chair.; Ralph Ward,* Pres. and Treas.; John L. Pope,* V.P.; Ralph Ward, Jr.,* Secy.; Drew R. Heard.
Number of staff: 2 full-time professional; 4 full-time support.
EIN: 750945924

3063
Adeline and George McQueen Foundation of 1960
c/o Team Bank, N.A.
P.O. Box 2050
Fort Worth 76113   (817) 884-4153

Trust established in 1960 in TX.
Foundation type: Independent
Financial data (yr. ended 06/30/91): Assets, $8,654,379 (M); expenditures, $815,303; qualifying distributions, $708,159, including $703,968 for 54 grants (high: $60,000; low: $3,468).
Purpose and activities: Emphasis on hospitals and youth agencies; support also for social service agencies, medical research, and a Protestant theological seminary.
Fields of interest: Hospitals, youth, social services, medical research, cultural programs, music.
Limitations: Giving primarily in TX. No grants to individuals.
Application information: Application form not required.
Initial approach: Proposal

Copies of proposal: 1
Deadline(s): None
Board meeting date(s): Nov.
Write: Jane Gallo
Trustee: Team Bank, N.A.
EIN: 756014459

3064
Meadows Foundation, Inc. ▼
Wilson Historic Block
2922 Swiss Ave.
Dallas 75204-5928   (214) 826-9431

Incorporated in 1948 in TX.
Donor(s): Algur Hurtle Meadows,‡ Virginia Meadows.‡
Foundation type: Independent
Financial data (yr. ended 12/31/90): Assets, $472,116,272 (M); expenditures, $20,437,815; qualifying distributions, $23,732,554, including $18,276,380 for 252 grants (high: $1,000,000; low: $3,300; average: $30,000-$60,000), $3,164,102 for loans and $3,300 for 1 in-kind gift.
Purpose and activities: Support for the arts, social services, health, education, and civic and cultural programs. Operates a historic preservation investment-related program using a cluster of Victorian homes as offices for nonprofit agencies.
Fields of interest: Arts, cultural programs, social services, welfare, health, health services, AIDS, nutrition, education, elementary education, secondary education, higher education, libraries, civic affairs, minorities, child welfare, conservation, wildlife, historic preservation, general charitable giving.
Types of support: Operating budgets, continuing support, seed money, emergency funds, deficit financing, building funds, equipment, land acquisition, matching funds, scholarship funds, professorships, internships, fellowships, special projects, research, publications, conferences and seminars, program-related investments, technical assistance, consulting services, renovation projects, capital campaigns, endowment funds, lectureships, general purposes.
Limitations: Giving limited to TX. No grants to individuals. In general, contributions are not made for annual fundraising appeals, media projects in initial planning stages, biomedical research projects, or for travel expenses for groups to perform or compete outside of TX.
Publications: Annual report (including application guidelines), program policy statement, application guidelines.
Application information: Application form not required.
Initial approach: Proposal
Copies of proposal: 1
Deadline(s): None
Board meeting date(s): Grants Review Committee meets monthly; full board meets 2 or 3 times a year to act on major grants
Final notification: 3 to 4 months
Write: Dr. Sally R. Lancaster, Exec. V.P.
Officers and Directors: Robert A. Meadows,* Chair. and V.P.; Curtis W. Meadows, Jr.,* Pres.; Sally R. Lancaster,* Exec. V.P.; G. Tomas Rhodus,* V.P. and Secy.; Robert E. Wise, V.P. and Treas.; Judy B. Culbertson, V.P.; Linda P. Evans,* V.P.; Eloise Meadows Rouse,* V.P.; Robert E. Weiss, V.P.; Evelyn Meadows Acton, John W. Broadfoot, Vela Meadows Broadfoot, J.W. Bullion, Eudine

Meadows Cheney, John A. Hammack, Harvey R. Mitchell, John H. Murrell, Evy Kay Ritzen, Dorothy C. Wilson.
Number of staff: 17 full-time professional; 1 part-time professional; 21 full-time support; 2 part-time support.
EIN: 756015322
Recent health grants:
3064-1 Ada Wilson Hospital of Physical Medicine and Rehabilitation, Corpus Christi, TX, $50,000. Toward facility improvements. 1991.
3064-2 American Red Cross, Blue Bonnet Chapter, Harker Height, TX, $10,000. For counseling and other assistance to persons affected by recent tragedy in Killeen. 1991.
3064-3 Bering Community Service Foundation, Houston, TX, $40,000. For equipment to enable Bering Dental Clinic to serve more persons with AIDS. 1991.
3064-4 Brown County Health Department, Brownwood, TX, $135,000. Toward facility purchase. 1991.
3064-5 Brownsville Community Health Clinic Corporation, Brownsville, TX, $16,500. Toward construction of administrative addition. 1991.
3064-6 Chaplaincy Ministries, Dallas, TX, $30,000. For Seminarian Project, providing chaplain services for patients at Medical City. 1991.
3064-7 Child Study Center, Fort Worth, TX, $150,000. Toward construction of second floor addition for expanded services to children with developmental and emotional disabilities. 1991.
3064-8 Childrens Defense Fund, Austin, TX, $50,000. To fund Guide for Local Assessment of Maternal and Child Health Systems, County by County Fact Book, and for general operating support. 1991.
3064-9 Dallas Child Guidance Clinic, Dallas, TX, $250,000. Toward construction of new facility. 1991.
3064-10 Elgin, City of, Elgin, TX, $38,000. Toward purchase of modular-type ambulance. 1991.
3064-11 Foundation for the Retarded, Houston, TX, $40,000. To purchase two passenger vans to service new residential facilities for trainable mentally retarded adults at Willow River Farms. 1991.
3064-12 HALO-Flight, Corpus Christi, TX, $120,000. For continuing operating subsidy for air ambulance service for South Texas. 1991.
3064-13 Hospice of Brazos County, Bryan, TX, $35,000. For operating reserve to bridge Medicare hospice reimbursement lag. 1991.
3064-14 Jeff Davis, County of, Fort Davis, TX, $40,000. Toward purchase of new vehicle for Volunteer Ambulance Service. 1991.
3064-15 New Horizons Ranch and Center, Goldthwaite, TX, $250,000. Toward construction, furnishing and equipping of Jeffrey Educational Complex. 1991.
3064-16 Planned Parenthood of Dallas and Northeast Texas, Dallas, TX, $50,000. To establish family planning clinic in Denton. 1991.
3064-17 Presbyterian Healthcare Foundation, Dallas, TX, $65,560. Toward emergency medical care study. 1991.

3064-18 Riceland Regional Mental Health Authority, Wharton, TX, $65,000. Toward renovations to substance abuse treatment facility. 1991.
3064-19 South Plains Health Provider Organization, Plainview, TX, $200,000. Toward purchase, renovation and equipping of building in Amarillo to be used as human services center for needy and homeless persons. 1991.
3064-20 Susan G. Komen Foundation, Dallas, TX, $23,500. To relocate information and referral service currently located at Baylor Medical Center and convert to volunteer staffing. 1991.
3064-21 Texas A & M University, College of Medicine, College Station, TX, $60,500. For research into effects of hyperbaric oxygen treatment on Post Polio Syndrome patients. 1991.
3064-22 Texas, State of, Office of the Governor, Austin, TX, $150,000. Toward task force to develop Texas Public Health Policy for reforming state's health care system. 1991.
3064-23 Turtle Creek Manor, Dallas, TX, $45,000. Toward expansion of job rehabilitation training to non-residential clients. 1991.
3064-24 Visiting Nurses Association of Brazoria County, Angleton, TX, $75,000. For first year's projected budget shortfall as Medicare-Certified Hospice Program is implemented. 1991.

3065
Mechia Foundation
P.O. Box 1310
Beaumont 77704

Established in 1978.
Donor(s): Ben J. Rogers.
Foundation type: Independent
Financial data (yr. ended 12/31/91): Assets, $235,675 (M); gifts received, $100,000; expenditures, $262,220; qualifying distributions, $262,200, including $262,184 for 131 grants (high: $20,000; low: $80).
Fields of interest: Cultural programs, higher education, health associations, hospitals, Jewish welfare, Jewish giving, Protestant giving, mental health.
Limitations: Giving primarily in Beaumont and Houston, TX. No grants to individuals.
Application information: Contributes only to pre-selected organizations. Applications not accepted.
  Board meeting date(s): June 15 and Dec. 15
Officers: Ben J. Rogers, Pres.; Julie Rogers, V.P.; Regina Rogers, Secy.-Treas.
Number of staff: 1
EIN: 741948840

3066
Alice Kleberg Reynolds Meyer Foundation
P.O. Box 6985
San Antonio 78209   (512) 820-0552

Established in 1978 in TX.
Donor(s): Alice K. Meyer.
Foundation type: Independent

Financial data (yr. ended 12/31/91): Assets, $4,116,869 (M); gifts received, $138,434; expenditures, $299,709; qualifying distributions, $286,000, including $286,000 for 15 grants (high: $208,000; low: $250; average: $250-$10,000).
Purpose and activities: Grants primarily for cultural organizations and medical research; support also for education.
Fields of interest: Cultural programs, fine arts, medical research, education.
Types of support: General purposes, building funds.
Limitations: Giving primarily in southcentral TX.
Application information: Application form not required.
  Initial approach: Proposal
  Copies of proposal: 1
  Deadline(s): None
  Board meeting date(s): Varies
  Write: Alice K. Meyer, Pres.
Officers: Alice K. Meyer, Pres. and Treas.; Vaughan B. Meyer, V.P.; Jesse H. Oppenheimer, Secy.
Number of staff: None.
EIN: 742020227

3067
Mitchell Energy and Development Corporate Contributions Program
2001 Timberloch Place
The Woodlands 77380   (713) 377-5500
Mailing address: P.O. Box 4000, The Woodlands, TX 77387

Purpose and activities: Supports education, including colleges, universities, engineering and business programs; health, welfare, social services, drug rehabilitation, historic preservation, literacy, medical research, museums, arts and humanities, youth services, and civic affairs.
Fields of interest: Education, engineering, business education, health, welfare, social services, arts, humanities, youth, civic affairs, drug abuse, historic preservation, literacy, medical research, museums.
Types of support: Annual campaigns, capital campaigns, research, employee-related scholarships, scholarship funds, special projects.
Limitations: Giving primarily in major operating locations. No grants to individuals, political organizations, mass mailed form letters, or telephone solicitations.
Application information: Application form not required.
  Initial approach: Submit letter and complete proposal including budget
  Deadline(s): Applications accepted throughout the year but best time to apply is after Feb. 1.
  Write: Minnie Adams, Corp. V.P.

3068
William A. and Elizabeth B. Moncrief Foundation
Ninth at Commerce
Fort Worth 76102   (817) 336-7232

Established in 1954.
Donor(s): W.A. Moncrief.‡
Foundation type: Independent

Financial data (yr. ended 09/30/91): Assets, $8,020,326 (M); expenditures, $221,101; qualifying distributions, $214,150, including $213,550 for 20 grants (high: $50,000; low: $250).
Fields of interest: Higher education, hospitals.
Types of support: General purposes, operating budgets.
Limitations: Giving primarily in TX.
Application information:
   Initial approach: Letter
   Deadline(s): None
   Write: William A. Moncrief, Jr., Pres.
Officers and Directors:* William A. Moncrief, Jr.,* Pres.; R.W. Moncrief,* V.P.; C.B. Moncrief,* Secy.-Treas.
EIN: 756036329

3069
The Moody Foundation ▼
704 Moody National Bank Bldg.
Galveston 77550   (409) 763-5333

Trust established in 1942 in TX.
Donor(s): William Lewis Moody, Jr.,‡ Libbie Shearn Moody.‡
Foundation type: Independent
Financial data (yr. ended 12/31/90): Assets, $400,587,000 (M); expenditures, $32,327,723; qualifying distributions, $28,413,723, including $28,413,723 for 75 grants (average: $10,000-$150,000).
Purpose and activities: Funds to be used for historic restoration projects, performing arts organizations, and cultural programs; promotion of health, science, and education; community and social services; and the field of religion.
Fields of interest: Historic preservation, performing arts, cultural programs, health services, community development, education, science and technology, social services, religion, AIDS.
Types of support: Seed money, emergency funds, building funds, equipment, consulting services, technical assistance, matching funds, professorships, special projects, research, publications, conferences and seminars, capital campaigns, land acquisition, renovation projects, student aid.
Limitations: Giving limited to TX. No grants to individuals (except for students covered by one scholarship program in Galveston County), or for operating budgets, except for start-up purposes, continuing support, annual campaigns, or deficit financing; no loans.
Publications: Annual report, application guidelines, 990-PF, financial statement.
Application information: Application format as outlined in guidelines required. Application form not required.
   Initial approach: Letter or telephone
   Copies of proposal: 1
   Deadline(s): 6 weeks prior to board meetings
   Board meeting date(s): Quarterly
   Final notification: 2 weeks after board meetings
   Write: Peter M. Moore, Grants Officer
Officer: Robert E. Baker, Exec. Admin. and Secy.
Trustees: Frances Moody Newman, Chair.; Robert L. Moody, Ross R. Moody.
Number of staff: 7 full-time professional; 6 full-time support.
EIN: 741403105

Recent health grants:
3069-1 Achievement Rewards for College Scientists (ARCS) Foundation, Lubbock, TX, $60,000. For matching grant for scholarships for students at undergraduate and graduate levels in fields of Natural Science, Medicine and Engineering. 1991.
3069-2 Candlelighters of Galveston, Galveston, TX, $14,000. Toward establishing sibling project as part of Rainbow Connection summer camp program for children with cancer to allow their siblings to share in camping experience. 1991.
3069-3 Cystic Fibrosis Foundation, Texas Gulf Coast Chapter, Houston, TX, $15,000. Toward 1991 Great Strides Walk to Cure Cystic Fibrosis project. 1991.
3069-4 Down Home Ranch, Elgin, TX, $29,325. Toward developing educational, vocational and therapeutic activities at residential working ranch facility being established for adults with Down's Syndrome, mental retardation and other developmental disabilities. 1991.
3069-5 Easter Seal Society for Children, Dallas, TX, $124,565. For start-up costs for furniture, supplies and equipment for new children's rehabilitation facility in Dallas and to upgrade and expand existing word processing software and hardware. 1991.
3069-6 Galveston, City of, Police Department, Galveston, TX, $50,000. For acquisition of computer hardware and software for Phase II of Police Information Network to more fully automate Police, Fire and EMS communications arms. 1991.
3069-7 Harbourview Care Center, League City, TX, $263,727. Toward additional costs of International Sleep and Respiration Symposium and toward program to assess psychological, cognitive and motor function of elderly individuals. 1991.
3069-8 Kick Drugs Out of America Foundation, Houston, TX, $126,000. Toward implementation of drug prevention/martial arts program for middle school level at two Houston inner-city schools and at Galveston's Central Middle School. 1991.
3069-9 Montrose Clinic, Houston, TX, $31,758. For establishment of HIV/AIDS Educational Outreach Program for deaf and hearing-impaired community of Houston/Galveston and surrounding areas. 1991.
3069-10 Telemedical Interactive Consultative Services, Austin, TX, $25,000. Toward equipment and program funds for Phase II of Texas Telemedicine Project which is addressing problems of delivery of medical services to rural Texas areas by medical support personnel via interactive video technology. 1991.
3069-11 Transitional Learning Center, Galveston, TX, $32,652,000. For endowment for this support organization of the Transitional Learning Community at Galveston, a head injury rehabilitation facility. 1991.
3069-12 Transitional Learning Community at Galveston, Galveston, TX, $16,158. For publication of book entitled A Functional Approach to Cognitive-Communicative Deficits After Traumatic Brain Injury. 1991.
3069-13 Transitional Learning Community at Galveston, Galveston Institute of Human

Communication/Speech Physiology Laboratory, Galveston, TX, $329,749. For clinical and research missions. 1991.

3070
The Morris Foundation
4850 Moss Hollow Court
Fort Worth 76109

Established in 1986 in TX.
Donor(s): Jack B. Morris, Linda C. Morris.
Foundation type: Independent
Financial data (yr. ended 12/31/90): Assets, $4,299,217 (M); gifts received, $189,900; expenditures, $231,813; qualifying distributions, $227,000, including $227,000 for 16 grants (high: $50,000; low: $500).
Purpose and activities: Giving primarily for child development, including educational programs; support also for a Methodist church, health, and social services, including family planning.
Fields of interest: Child development, child welfare, social services, women, family planning, health, volunteerism, education, Protestant giving.
Limitations: Giving primarily in Fort Worth, TX. No grants to individuals.
Application information: Contributes only to pre-selected organizations. Applications not accepted.
Trustees: Jack B. Morris, Linda C. Morris.
EIN: 752137184

3071
Morrison Trust
40 N.E. Loop 410, Suite 200
San Antonio 78216   (512) 342-8000

Foundation type: Independent
Financial data (yr. ended 09/30/91): Assets, $3,606,946 (M); expenditures, $259,088; qualifying distributions, $224,891, including $210,634 for 5 grants (high: $68,849; low: $24,375).
Purpose and activities: Giving primarily to support the treatment, research, and improvement of existing methods of treating and preventing human sickness, and the development of new methods of treatment within the fields of nutrition, blood chemistry, and radionics and electricity.
Fields of interest: Medical research, medical sciences, medical education, nutrition.
Types of support: Research.
Limitations: Giving primarily in TX, CA, and NM. No grants to individuals.
Application information:
   Initial approach: Proposal
   Deadline(s): July 1
   Write: W.T. Chumney, Jr., Mgr.
Officer: W.T. Chumney, Jr., Mgr.
Trustees: Richard W. Calvert, Charles E. Cheever, Jr., T.C. Frost, Jr.
EIN: 746013340

3072
Harry S. Moss Heart Trust ▼
c/o NationsBank
P.O. Box 831041
Dallas 75283-1041   (214) 508-2041

Trust established in 1973 in TX.
Donor(s): Harry S. Moss, Florence M. Moss.
Foundation type: Independent
Financial data (yr. ended 09/30/91): Assets, $26,924,192 (M); expenditures, $1,624,783; qualifying distributions, $1,352,348, including $1,325,000 for 5 grants (high: $850,000; low: $25,000; average: $25,000-$200,000).
Purpose and activities: Support for the prevention and cure of heart disease.
Fields of interest: Heart disease.
Types of support: Research, building funds, deficit financing, equipment.
Limitations: Giving limited to TX, with emphasis on Dallas County.
Application information: Application form not required.
Initial approach: Proposal
Copies of proposal: 1
Deadline(s): None
Board meeting date(s): As required
Final notification: 30 days
Write: Connie A. Rogers, Trust Officer, NationsBank
Trustees: Frank M. Ryburn, Jr., NationsBank.
Number of staff: None.
EIN: 756147501

3073
Kathryn Murfee Endowment
2200 Post Oak Blvd., Suite 320
Houston 77056   (713) 622-5855

Established in 1981 in TX.
Foundation type: Independent
Financial data (yr. ended 08/31/91): Assets, $3,719,696 (M); expenditures, $355,920; qualifying distributions, $235,400, including $235,000 for 11 grants (high: $80,000; low: $5,000).
Purpose and activities: Support primarily for medical research, higher education, Protestant and other religious organizations, and the arts.
Fields of interest: Religion, medical research, higher education, Protestant giving, fine arts.
Types of support: General purposes, research.
Limitations: Giving limited to TX, with emphasis on Houston. No grants to individuals.
Application information: Application form required.
Write: June R. Nabb, Trustee
Trustees: Dan R. Japhet, June R. Nabb, James V. Walzel.
EIN: 760007237

3074
Nation Foundation
P.O. Box 180849
Dallas 75218-0849

Established in 1961 in TX.
Donor(s): First Co., Oslin Nation, James H. Nation, Patricia Walsh.
Foundation type: Operating
Financial data (yr. ended 01/31/91): Assets, $4,066,649 (M); gifts received, $401,100; expenditures, $257,283; qualifying distributions, $254,850, including $254,850 for grants (high: $100,000; low: $500; average: $10,000).
Fields of interest: Hospitals, health services, Protestant giving, child welfare.

Limitations: Giving primarily in TX. No grants for scholarships.
Trustees: Freida Ashworth, James H. Nation, Oslin Nation.
EIN: 756036339

3075
The National Gypsum Company Foundation
2501 Cedar Springs Rd., No. 700
Dallas 75201-1433   (214) 969-3400

Trust established about 1952 in OH.
Donor(s): National Gypsum Co.
Foundation type: Company-sponsored
Financial data (yr. ended 12/31/90): Assets, $3,264,283 (M); expenditures, $190,441; qualifying distributions, $178,630, including $178,630 for 202 grants (high: $23,000; low: $50).
Fields of interest: Community funds, higher education, hospitals.
Limitations: Giving primarily in Dallas, TX.
Application information:
Initial approach: Letter
Deadline(s): None
Write: David F. Byrne, Chair.
Officer and Trustees:* David F. Byrne,* Chair.; R.O. Beasley, A.V. Cecil, Paul T. Even.
EIN: 346551614

3076
Navarro Community Foundation
512 Interfirst Bank Bldg.
P.O. Box 1035
Corsicana 75151   (903) 874-4301

Established in 1938 in TX.
Foundation type: Community
Financial data (yr. ended 12/31/91): Assets, $10,771,148 (M); expenditures, $717,851; qualifying distributions, $675,985, including $675,985 for 21 grants (high: $150,000; low: $500).
Purpose and activities: Support largely for public schools, higher education, community development, and a community fund; grants also for Protestant church support, child welfare, youth agencies, a hospital, a library, and cultural programs.
Fields of interest: Elementary education, secondary education, higher education, community development, community funds, Protestant giving, child welfare, youth, hospitals, libraries.
Types of support: Annual campaigns, seed money, building funds, scholarship funds, matching funds, general purposes, capital campaigns.
Limitations: Giving limited to Navarro County, TX. No grants to individuals, or for research, conferences, endowment funds, publications, or special projects; no loans.
Application information: Application form not required.
Initial approach: Proposal
Copies of proposal: 1
Deadline(s): Jan. 1, Apr. 1, July 1, and Oct. 1
Board meeting date(s): Jan., Apr., July, and Oct.
Write: W. Bruce Robinson, Exec. Secy.-Treas.

Officers and Trustees:* William Clarkson III,* Chair.; H.R. Stroube, Jr.,* 1st Vice-Chair.; W. Bruce Robinson,* Exec. Secy.-Treas.; O.L. Albritton, Jr., David M. Brown, C. David Campbell, M.D., Tom Eady, Embry Ferguson, Gioia Keeney, Mrs. Jack McFerran, Halsey M. Settle III, M.D., John B. Stroud.
Trustee Banks: Bank One, Corsicana, The Corsicana National Bank, NationsBank.
Number of staff: 1 full-time professional; 1 part-time professional.
EIN: 750800663

3077
The Kathryn O'Connor Foundation
One O'Connor Plaza, Suite 1100
Victoria 77901   (512) 578-6271

Incorporated in 1951 in TX.
Donor(s): Kathryn S. O'Connor,‡ Tom O'Connor, Jr., Dennis O'Connor, Mary O'Connor Braman.‡
Foundation type: Independent
Financial data (yr. ended 12/31/91): Assets, $6,258,972 (M); expenditures, $399,425; qualifying distributions, $360,120, including $360,120 for 16 grants (high: $100,000; low: $1,250; average: $10,000-$50,000).
Purpose and activities: Support for institutions for the advancement of religion, education, and the relief of poverty; grants also for hospitals. The foundation also operates and maintains a church.
Fields of interest: Religion—Christian, Catholic giving, religious schools, higher education, secondary education, hospitals, cancer, hospices, libraries.
Types of support: Operating budgets, continuing support, annual campaigns, building funds, general purposes.
Limitations: Giving limited to southern TX, especially Victoria and Refugio counties and the surrounding area. No grants to individuals, or for matching gifts; no loans.
Application information: Application form not required.
Initial approach: Letter
Deadline(s): None
Board meeting date(s): As required
Write: Dennis O'Connor, Pres.
Officers: Dennis O'Connor, Pres.; Tom O'Connor, Jr., V.P.; Venable B. Proctor, Secy.; Mary O'Connor Braman, Treas.
Number of staff: None.
EIN: 746039415

3078
O'Donnell Foundation ▼
1401 Elm St., Suite 3388
Dallas 75202   (214) 742-2111

Incorporated in 1957 in TX.
Donor(s): Peter O'Donnell, Jr., Edith Jones O'Donnell.
Foundation type: Independent
Financial data (yr. ended 11/30/90): Assets, $90,964,909 (M); gifts received, $2,001,500; expenditures, $7,646,396; qualifying distributions, $6,991,395, including $6,848,938 for 35 grants (high: $2,946,250; low: $350; average: $5,000-$250,000).
Purpose and activities: Giving primarily for science and engineering.

Fields of interest: Engineering, science and technology.
Limitations: Giving primarily in TX. No grants to individuals, or for scholarships.
Application information:
Initial approach: Letter with brief proposal
Deadline(s): None
Board meeting date(s): As required
Write: C.R. Bacon
Officers and Directors:* Peter O'Donnell, Jr.,* Pres.; Rita C. Clements,* V.P.; Edith Jones O'Donnell,* Secy.-Treas.; Duncan E. Boeckman, Philip O'B. Montgomery, Jr.
Number of staff: 1 full-time support.
EIN: 756023326
Recent health grants:
3078-1 Nexus, Dallas, TX, $50,000. For endowment. 1990.
3078-2 University of Texas Southwestern Medical Center, Dallas, TX, $2,946,250. For endowment. 1990.
3078-3 University of Texas Southwestern Medical Center, Dallas, TX, $100,000. For endowment. 1990.
3078-4 University of Texas Southwestern Medical Center, Dallas, TX, $100,000. For scholarships. 1990.

3079
Orange Memorial Hospital Corporation
P.O. Box 396
Orange 77630   (409) 882-2121

Foundation type: Independent
Financial data (yr. ended 12/31/90): Assets, $8,183,259 (M); expenditures, $684,415; qualifying distributions, $647,267, including $337,777 for 4 grants and $309,490 for 64 grants to individuals (high: $11,000; low: $889).
Purpose and activities: Awards scholarships to residents of Orange County, TX, pursuing medical degrees; support also for health associations.
Fields of interest: Medical education, health associations.
Types of support: Student aid, general purposes.
Limitations: Giving limited to Orange County, TX.
Application information: Application form required.
Deadline(s): Mar. 15
Write: Robert A. Walker, Board Member
Officers: Jim I. Graves, Pres.; John W. Magness, V.P.; Robert Cormier, Secy.; Harold Mills, Treas.
Board Members: Arthur J. Carruth, Fred Gregory, John Rogers, M.D., Robert A. Walker, James Wilson.
EIN: 741303719

3080
Overlake Foundation, Inc.
700 Preston Commons West
8117 Preston Rd.
Dallas 75225-6306   (214) 750-0722

Incorporated in 1981 in TX.
Donor(s): Mary Alice Fitzpatrick.
Foundation type: Independent
Financial data (yr. ended 11/30/91): Assets, $3,961,156 (M); expenditures, $233,032; qualifying distributions, $204,300, including $204,300 for 31 grants (high: $28,000; low: $500; average: $1,000-$10,000).

Fields of interest: Child welfare, health associations, drug abuse, agriculture, religion—Christian.
Limitations: Giving primarily in TX. No grants to individuals.
Application information:
Write: Donald J. Malouf, V.P.
Officers and Directors:* Rayford L. Keller,* Pres. and Treas.; Donald J. Malouf,* V.P. and Secy.; Michael Scott Anderson, Steve Craig Anderson.
EIN: 751793068

3081
B. B. Owen Trust
905 Custer Rd.
P.O. Box 830068
Richardson 75083   (214) 783-7170

Trust established in 1974 in TX.
Donor(s): B.B. Owen.‡
Foundation type: Independent
Financial data (yr. ended 09/30/91): Assets, $14,270,141 (M); expenditures, $1,364,414; qualifying distributions, $1,043,267, including $973,267 for 21 grants (high: $657,492; low: $50; average: $1,000-$50,000).
Fields of interest: Hospitals, Protestant welfare, Protestant giving, youth.
Types of support: Building funds, equipment, special projects, capital campaigns, operating budgets.
Limitations: Giving primarily in Dallas, TX. No grants to individuals.
Application information: Application form not required.
Initial approach: Letter
Deadline(s): None
Board meeting date(s): As necessary
Final notification: 3 to 4 months
Write: Monty J. Jackson, Trustee
Trustees: Spencer Carver, Monty J. Jackson, Wendell W. Judd.
Number of staff: 1 full-time professional.
EIN: 751385809

3082
Alvin and Lucy Owsley Foundation
3000 One Shell Plaza
Houston 77002-4995   (713) 229-1271

Trust established in 1950 in TX.
Donor(s): Alvin M. Owsley,‡ Lucy B. Owsley.
Foundation type: Independent
Financial data (yr. ended 12/31/90): Assets, $3,722,396 (M); expenditures, $187,755; qualifying distributions, $144,737, including $144,737 for 56 grants (high: $25,000; low: $25; average: $1,000-$2,000).
Fields of interest: Education, medical sciences, social services.
Types of support: Operating budgets, continuing support, annual campaigns, seed money, emergency funds, building funds, matching funds, scholarship funds.
Limitations: Giving limited to TX. No grants to individuals, or for endowment funds; no loans.
Application information: Application form not required.
Initial approach: Letter not exceeding 2 pages
Copies of proposal: 1

Deadline(s): Submit proposal preferably in months when board meets; no set deadline
Board meeting date(s): Mar., June, Sept., and Dec.
Final notification: 2 months
Write: Alvin Owsley, General Mgr.
Officer and Trustees:* Alvin M. Owsley, Jr.,* General Mgr.; Wendy Garrett, David T. Owsley, Lucy B. Owsley.
Number of staff: None.
EIN: 756047221

3083
Panhandle Eastern Pipe Line Corporate Giving Program
5400 Westheimer Court
Houston 77056   (713) 627-4900
Application address: P.O. Box 1642, Houston, TX 77251-1642

Purpose and activities: Giving for civic affairs, culture, education, health care, the handicapped/disabled and minority groups, legal advocacy and services, public broadcasting, United Way, welfare, and youth services.
Fields of interest: Civic affairs, arts, cultural programs, education, higher education, health, handicapped, minorities, legal services, media and communications, community funds, welfare, youth.
Types of support: Annual campaigns, building funds, capital campaigns, research.
Limitations: Giving primarily in Houston, Harris, and Fort Bend counties, TX.
Application information: Application form not required.
Deadline(s): Oct. 1 for inclusion in following year's budget
Board meeting date(s): Not formalized
Write: James W. Hart, Jr., V.P., Public Affairs
Number of staff: 1 part-time professional; 1 part-time support.

3084
Pardee Cancer Treatment Association of Greater Brazosport
127-C Circle Way
Lake Jackson 77566

Donor(s): Elsa Pardee Foundation.
Foundation type: Operating
Financial data (yr. ended 12/31/90): Assets, $192,679 (M); gifts received, $175,635; expenditures, $218,539; qualifying distributions, $218,539, including $206,930 for 137 grants to individuals.
Purpose and activities: A private operating foundation; grants for expenses involved in the treatment of cancer, including the services of doctors, the use of hospitals and clinics, and the purchase of prescription drugs and medical equipment.
Fields of interest: Cancer.
Types of support: Grants to individuals.
Limitations: Giving limited to Southern Brazoria County, TX.
Application information: Application form required.
Deadline(s): None
Write: Shirley Funk

Officers and Directors:* Everett Stovall,* Chair.; Charles P. Quirk, Jr.,* Treas.; and 10 additional directors.
Number of staff: 1 part-time professional.
EIN: 510169385

3085
Pearle Vision Foundation, Inc.
2534 Royal Ln.
Dallas 75229 (214) 277-5993
Application address: P.O. Box 227175, Dallas, TX 75222

Established in 1986 in CA.
Donor(s): Pearle, Inc.
Foundation type: Operating
Financial data (yr. ended 09/30/91): Assets, $769,948 (M); gifts received, $366,342; expenditures, $298,380; qualifying distributions, $289,685, including $88,696 for 26 grants (high: $30,000; low: $1,000) and $200,989 for 262 grants to individuals (high: $4,500; low: $50; average: $100-$3,500).
Purpose and activities: Support for vision-oriented giving, including examinations and surgery for needy individuals.
Fields of interest: Ophthalmology, welfare—indigent individuals, disadvantaged.
Types of support: Special projects.
Limitations: Giving primarily in the U.S. and Puerto Rico.
Application information: Application form required.
  Initial approach: Write for application form
  Copies of proposal: 1
  Deadline(s): Feb. 15, May 15, Aug. 15, and Nov. 15
  Board meeting date(s): Jan., Apr., July, and Oct.
  Final notification: Mid-Mar., mid-June, mid-Sept., and mid-Dec.
  Write: Cerise C. Blair, Admin.
Officers and Directors:* Joseph B. Neville,* Chair.; Dr. Kenneth D. Clanton,* V.P.; William A. Yost III, Secy.; Colin Heggie, Treas.; Robert S. Rosen, M.D., Exec. Dir.; Hedy Helsell, Richard Zaback.
Number of staff: 1 full-time professional.
EIN: 752173714

3086
J. C. Penney Corporate Giving Program
P.O. Box 659000
Dallas 75265-9000 (214) 591-1320

Financial data (yr. ended 01/31/91): Total giving, $20,600,000 for grants.
Purpose and activities: "JCPenny is committed to being a socially responsible business partner, both nationally and in the communities in which we do business. JCPenny recognizes a basic relationship between business and society. They are mutually dependent and need one another to exist. The Company has had a tradition of concern for community needs, because healthy communities benefit our business, and we have a moral obligation to be responsible citizens. The first social responsibility of a business is the fact that it exists--and so creates jobs, products and services necessary to society. The second social responsibility of a business is to prosper and grow. The third social responsibility of business is

accomplished through well-conceived, well-implemented involvement in community improvement efforts, including financial support for effective and efficient charitable and civic activities." Funding emphasis is given to: projects/organizations that serve a broad sector of the community; national projects that benefit local organizations across the country; organizations that provide direct services to their clients; and projects/organizations with a proven record of sucess. Priorities are Health and Welfare: United Way, Substance Abuse, Child Care; Education: Preschool, Primary and Secondary Education, Drop-out Prevention; Civic Betterment: Job training; Arts and Culture (lowest priority): Bringing the arts to the economically disadvantaged. Contributions to individual institutions of higher education are made primarily by local units or by matching gifts of employees. Contributions to hospitals and community-based organizations are made only by local units. Current giving entries represent national organizations or organizations in TX.
Fields of interest: Health, social services, civic affairs, higher education, cultural programs, arts, drug abuse, community funds, elementary education, education—early childhood, secondary education, volunteerism, youth, vocational education, education—minorities, education.
Types of support: Donated equipment, donated products, use of facilities, employee volunteer services.
Limitations: Giving limited to the fifty states of the U.S.A.
Publications: Corporate report, corporate giving report, application guidelines.
Application information: Corporate headquarters office only reviews requests from national organizations. Local units review local requests; there is a staff, corporate contributions, that only handles giving. Application form not required.
  Initial approach: Letter
  Copies of proposal: 1
  Deadline(s): None
  Write: David Lenz, V.P., J.C. Penney Fund and Mgr., Corp. Public Affairs and Robin Caldwell, Corp. Contribs. Mgr.
Number of staff: 2 full-time professional.

3087
Pennzoil Corporate Giving Program
Pennzoil Place
700 Milam
Houston 77002 (713) 546-4000
Mailing Address: P.O. Box 2967, Houston, TX 77252

Financial data (yr. ended 12/31/90): Total giving, $3,000,000 for grants.
Purpose and activities: Supports education, including colleges and universities, studies in accounting, geology and engineering; social betterment and welfare, including services for the handicapped and united funds; law and justice; health, including hospitals, clinics, rehabilitation centers and medical research; and civic affairs.
Fields of interest: Law and justice, medical research, education, higher education, social services, welfare, health, hospitals, cultural programs, performing arts, museums, libraries, civic affairs.

Types of support: Employee-related scholarships, employee matching gifts, general purposes, operating budgets, special projects.
Limitations: Giving primarily in Houston, TX and Shreveport, LA. No grants to individuals, or for scholarships, religious, fraternal or veterans' organizations, groups that discriminate on basis of race or religion, advertising or testimonials, or operating expenses of United Way recipients.
Publications: Informational brochure (including application guidelines).
Application information: Application form not required.
  Initial approach: Initial contact by brief letter or proposal
  Copies of proposal: 1
  Deadline(s): Best time to apply is July-Sept.
  Board meeting date(s): Quarterly
  Final notification: 4 weeks
  Write: Mickey Gentry, Mgr. Contribs., Community Relations and Special Projects
Contributions Committee: David Alderson, Sr. V.P., Fin.; Terry Hemeyer, Sr. V.P., Admin.; Mark Malinski, Sr. V.P., Acctg.; William Schell, Group V.P., Oil and Gas Operations; Robert Semrad, Group V.P., Sulphur; James Shaddix, Gen. Coun.
Number of staff: 1 full-time professional; 1 full-time support.

3088
The Joe and Lois Perkins Foundation
1212 City National Bldg.
P.O. Box 360
Wichita Falls 76307 (817) 723-7163

Incorporated in 1941 in TX.
Donor(s): J.J. Perkins.‡
Foundation type: Independent
Financial data (yr. ended 12/31/90): Assets, $12,451,122 (M); expenditures, $362,690; qualifying distributions, $255,853, including $255,853 for grants (high: $92,642).
Fields of interest: Hospitals, social services, religion—Christian, education, higher education.
Types of support: Operating budgets, building funds.
Limitations: Giving primarily in TX. No grants to individuals.
Application information: Contributes only to pre-selected organizations. Applications not accepted.
Officers and Directors:* Elizabeth P. Prothro,* Pres.; Charles N. Prothro,* V.P.; Mark H. Prothro,* V.P.; Glynn D. Huff, Secy.-Treas.; Charles V. Prothro, James E. Prothro, Joe N. Prothro, Herbert B. Story, Kathryn P. Yeager.
EIN: 756012450

3089
Perkins-Prothro Foundation
P.O. Box 360
Wichita Falls 76307 (817) 723-7163

Established in 1967.
Donor(s): Lois Perkins,‡ Charles N. Prothro, Elizabeth P. Prothro.
Foundation type: Independent
Financial data (yr. ended 06/30/91): Assets, $12,517,811 (M); gifts received, $394,450; expenditures, $710,334; qualifying distributions,

$664,081, including $661,876 for 11 grants (high: $394,450; low: $500).

Purpose and activities: Emphasis on higher education; support also for a hospice, health, and social services.

Fields of interest: Higher education, health, hospices, social services.

Limitations: Giving primarily in TX. No grants to individuals.

Application information: Unsolicited proposals rarely funded; most grantees are pre-selected.

Officers and Trustees:* Charles N. Prothro,* Pres.; Elizabeth P. Prothro,* V.P.; Joe N. Prothro,* V.P.; Kathryn Prothro Yeager,* V.P.; Glynn D. Huff, Secy.; Mark H. Prothro,* Treas.

EIN: 751247407

3090
The Mary L. Peyton Foundation
Bassett Tower, Suite 908
303 Texas Ave.
El Paso 79901-1456   (915) 533-9698

Incorporated in 1937 in TX.
Donor(s): Joe C. Peyton.‡
Foundation type: Operating
Financial data (yr. ended 05/31/91): Assets, $3,060,089 (M); gifts received, $85,909; expenditures, $310,619; qualifying distributions, $275,432, including $197,404 for 1,072 grants to individuals (high: $5,000; low: $8; average: $25-$2,000).
Purpose and activities: A private operating foundation; grants to provide health, welfare, and vocational educational benefits to those unable to obtain assistance elsewhere.
Fields of interest: Health, welfare—indigent individuals, vocational education.
Types of support: Grants to individuals, student aid.
Limitations: Giving limited to legal residents of El Paso County, TX. No support for groups or organizations. No grants for building or endowment funds, scholarships, fellowships, or matching gifts; no loans.
Application information: Application form required.
Initial approach: Letter
Copies of proposal: 1
Deadline(s): None
Board meeting date(s): 3rd Thursday of each month
Write: James M. Day, Exec. Admin.
Officers and Trustees:* Francis S. Ainsa,* Chair.; Mrs. Alfred Blumenthal,* Vice-Chair.; Mrs. R.F. Boverie, Freeman Harris, Mrs. William L. Massey, Ameritrust Texas, N.A.
Number of staff: 1 full-time professional; 1 full-time support; 1 part-time support.
EIN: 741276102

3091
The Powell Foundation
1001 Fannin, Suite 1420
Houston 77002   (713) 654-9700

Established in 1967 in TX.
Donor(s): Ben H. Powell, Jr.,‡ Kitty King Powell.
Foundation type: Independent
Financial data (yr. ended 12/31/91): Assets, $7,259,530 (M); expenditures, $337,489;

qualifying distributions, $337,489, including $322,830 for 76 grants (high: $110,000; low: $50; average: $50-$60,000).
Fields of interest: Education, educational associations, educational research, education—early childhood, higher education, legal education, education—minorities, cultural programs, social services, health, medical research, environment, general charitable giving.
Types of support: Scholarship funds, operating budgets.
Limitations: Giving primarily in Harris, Walker, and Travis counties, TX. No support for private foundations. No grants to individuals.
Publications: Informational brochure (including application guidelines).
Application information: Application form not required.
Initial approach: Letter
Copies of proposal: 1
Deadline(s): Varies
Board meeting date(s): Varies
Final notification: Positive replies only
Write: Ms. Nancy Powell Moore, Trustee
Officers and Trustees:* Kitty King Powell,* Chair.; Nancy Powell Moore,* Secy. and Mgr.; Antonia Scott Day, Ben H. Powell V.
Number of staff: 1 part-time professional.
EIN: 746104592

3092
The Prairie Foundation
303 West Wall, Suite 1901
Midland 79701-5116

Established in 1957 in TX.
Donor(s): David Fasken Special Trust.
Foundation type: Independent
Financial data (yr. ended 12/31/90): Assets, $2,109,005 (M); expenditures, $254,766; qualifying distributions, $254,746, including $254,746 for 25 grants (high: $100,000; low: $100).
Purpose and activities: Giving primarily for a hospital; support also for social service agencies, health organizations, education, and youth development organizations.
Fields of interest: Hospitals, social services, health, education, youth.
Limitations: Giving primarily in the San Francisco Bay Area, CA, and Midland, TX.
Application information: Application form not required.
Deadline(s): None
Write: Barbara T. Fasken, Pres.
Officers and Directors:* Barbara T. Fasken,* Pres.; Robert T. Dickson,* V.P.; Louis A. Bartha, Secy.-Treas.
EIN: 756012458

3093
RGK Foundation
2815 San Gabriel
Austin 78705-3594   (512) 474-9298

Incorporated in 1966 in TX.
Donor(s): George Kozmetsky, Ronya Kozmetsky.
Foundation type: Independent
Financial data (yr. ended 12/31/91): Assets, $29,671,537 (M); gifts received, $1,436,022; expenditures, $1,171,906; qualifying

distributions, $1,278,608, including $914,033 for 81 grants (high: $85,000; low: $500; average: $1,000-$10,000) and $14,763 for in-kind gifts.
Purpose and activities: Grants to higher educational institutions, with emphasis on medical and educational research; support also for business and economic issues.
Fields of interest: Higher education, medical research, educational research, business, economics.
Types of support: Matching funds, professorships, research, publications, conferences and seminars, special projects.
Limitations: No grants to individuals, or for deficit financing, building or endowment funds, operating budgets, or equipment; no loans.
Publications: Informational brochure (including application guidelines).
Application information: Proposals for medical research must follow NIH guidelines. Application form required.
Initial approach: Letter or telephone
Copies of proposal: 1
Deadline(s): Submit proposal before Dec.; no set deadline
Board meeting date(s): Annually
Final notification: 2 to 3 months
Write: Gregory A. Kozmetsky, Pres.
Officers and Trustees:* Ronya Kozmetsky,* Chair. and Secy.; Gregory Kozmetsky,* Pres. and Treas.; Nadya Kozmetsky Scott,* V.P.; Charles Hurwitz, Cynthia Kozmetsky, George Kozmetsky.
Number of staff: 1 full-time professional; 2 full-time support; 2 part-time support.
EIN: 746077587

3094
Sid W. Richardson Foundation ▼
309 Main St.
Fort Worth 76102   (817) 336-0494

Established in 1947 in TX.
Donor(s): Sid W. Richardson,‡ and associated companies.
Foundation type: Independent
Financial data (yr. ended 12/31/91): Assets, $245,920,328 (M); expenditures, $12,988,707; qualifying distributions, $12,030,702, including $10,942,707 for 96 grants (high: $2,200,000; low: $1,500; average: $2,000-$350,000) and $250,000 for program-related investments.
Purpose and activities: Giving primarily for education, health, the arts, and social service programs.
Fields of interest: Education, higher education, health, arts, performing arts, social services.
Types of support: Operating budgets, seed money, building funds, equipment, land acquisition, endowment funds, research, publications, conferences and seminars, matching funds, special projects, renovation projects, continuing support, general purposes.
Limitations: Giving limited to TX, with emphasis on Fort Worth for the arts and human services, and statewide for health and education. No support for religious organizations. No grants to individuals, or for scholarships or fellowships; no loans.
Publications: Annual report (including application guidelines).
Application information: Application form required.

Initial approach: Letter
Copies of proposal: 1
Deadline(s): Mar. 1, June 1, and Sept. 1
Board meeting date(s): Spring, summer, and fall
Final notification: Varies
Write: Valleau Wilkie, Jr., Exec. V.P.
Officers and Directors:* Perry R. Bass,* Pres.; Valleau Wilkie, Jr., Exec. V.P. and Exec. Dir.; Lee M. Bass,* V.P.; Nancy Lee Bass,* V.P.; Sid R. Bass,* V.P.; Jo Helen Rosacker, Secy. and Assoc. Dir.; M.E. Chappell,* Treas.
Number of staff: 4 full-time professional; 2 full-time support; 4 part-time support.
EIN: 756015828
Recent health grants:

3094-1 American Heart Association, Fort Worth Metropolitan Region, Fort Worth, TX, $100,000. Toward purchase of Volunteer Training and Education Center. 1990.

3094-2 Aransas County Emergency Medical Service, Rockport, TX, $40,000. Toward remounting and refurbishing ambulance. 1990.

3094-3 Baylor College of Medicine, Houston, TX, $300,000. For ocular research program, Studies in Ocular Bacterial and Fungal Infections, and to establish Diagnostic Ocular Microbiology Program. 1990.

3094-4 Because We Care, Fort Worth, TX, $155,000. For program in Fort Worth Public Schools. 1990.

3094-5 Child Study Center, Fort Worth, TX, $750,000. For expansion of facilities. 1990.

3094-6 Cook-Fort Worth Childrens Medical Center, Fort Worth, TX, $1,000,000. For completion of fifth floor of Medical Center. 1990.

3094-7 Dallas/Fort Worth Hospital Council Education and Research Foundation, Irving, TX, $17,489. For manpower program, specifically for second publication of Rising Star, brochure about allied health care professions for secondary school students. 1990.

3094-8 Gill Childrens Services, Fort Worth, TX, $150,000. For establishment of endowment fund and for general operating expenses for medical program for children who lack adequate medical care. 1990.

3094-9 Harris Methodist Health Systems, Fort Worth, TX, $1,029,000. For establishment of Outpatient Surgery Center at Harris Hospital-Fort Worth and for renovation of Polytechnic Community Health Clinic. 1990.

3094-10 Hutchinson County Hospital District, Borger, TX, $150,000. Toward purchase of equipment and for various hospital maintenance projects. 1990.

3094-11 Lena Pope Home, Fort Worth, TX, $100,000. Toward renovation of Mabee Ranch, residential drug abuse treatment facility. 1990.

3094-12 North Texas Easter Seal Rehabilitation Center, Wichita Falls, TX, $100,000. For construction of Center's new facility. 1990.

3094-13 Scott and White Memorial Hospital and Scott, Sherwood and Brindley Foundation, Temple, TX, $50,000. Toward renovation of Sid Richardson Auditorium. 1990.

3094-14 Stehlin Foundation for Cancer Research, Houston, TX, $300,000. For colon cancer research. 1990.

3094-15 Texas Society to Prevent Blindness, Fort Worth, TX, $12,000. For continued support for Glaucoma Screening Project. 1990.

3095
Rienzi Foundation, Inc.
2001 Kirby Dr., Suite 714
Houston 77019

Established in 1958 in TX.
Foundation type: Independent
Financial data (yr. ended 12/31/90): Assets, $3,254,932 (M); expenditures, $186,368; qualifying distributions, $173,400, including $173,400 for 181 grants (high: $10,000; low: $50).
Fields of interest: Cultural programs, social services, higher education, hospitals.
Limitations: Giving primarily in Houston, TX. No grants to individuals.
Application information: Contributes only to pre-selected organizations. Applications not accepted.
Officer: Evangeline Ehrensberger, Chief Administrator.
Directors: Carroll S. Masterson, Harris Masterson, Isla C. Reckling, Randa R. Roach, Bert F. Winston, Lynn David Winston.
EIN: 741484331

3096
Dora Roberts Foundation
c/o Team Bank, N.A.
P.O. Box 2050
Fort Worth 76113   (817) 884-4442

Trust established in 1948 in TX.
Donor(s): Dora Roberts.‡
Foundation type: Independent
Financial data (yr. ended 06/30/91): Assets, $24,119,759 (M); gifts received, $5,000; expenditures, $1,887,509; qualifying distributions, $1,600,640, including $1,593,103 for 23 grants (high: $500,000; low: $3,000; average: $25,000-$100,000).
Purpose and activities: Emphasis on higher education, social service and youth agencies, including a rehabilitation center, hospitals and health services, and Protestant church support.
Fields of interest: Higher education, social services, youth, rehabilitation, hospitals, health services, Protestant giving.
Types of support: General purposes.
Limitations: Giving limited to TX, with emphasis on Big Spring.
Application information:
Initial approach: Proposal
Deadline(s): Sept. 30
Board meeting date(s): Annually in Oct. or Nov.
Final notification: End of Dec.
Write: Rick Piersall, V.P. and Trust Officer, Team Bank, N.A.
Advisory Board: Ralph W. Caton, Chair.; Roger Canter, Mrs. Horace Garrett, Sue Garrett Partee, J.P. Taylor, R.H. Weaver.
Trustee: Team Bank, N.A.
Number of staff: None.
EIN: 756013899
Recent health grants:

3096-1 Big Bend Regional Medical Center, Big Spring, TX, $50,000. 1991.

3096-2 Dora Roberts Rehabilitation Center, Big Spring, TX, $136,030. 1991.

3096-3 Methodist Hospital, Lubbock, TX, $50,000. 1991.

3097
Summerfield G. Roberts Foundation
c/o NationsBank
P.O. Box 831041
Dallas 75283-1041
Application address: 8222 Douglas Ave., Dallas, TX 75225; Tel.: (214) 361-7363

Established in 1990 in TX.
Donor(s): Summerfield G. Roberts.‡
Foundation type: Independent
Financial data (yr. ended 03/31/91): Assets, $7,678,299 (M); gifts received, $3,993,615; expenditures, $274,435; qualifying distributions, $13,900.
Purpose and activities: Giving primarily through scholarship funds earmarked for the advanced study of business, commerce, banking, oil and gas, and other related subjects; or medical students and doctors performing medical research on diseases or disorders of the human body. Support also to educational institutions for the advancement of the study, research, and teaching of TX history.
Fields of interest: Business education, economics, energy, medical research, history, educational research.
Types of support: Scholarship funds.
Limitations: Giving limited to TX.
Application information: Scholarship application forms provided by educational institutions must be completed by prospective award recipients. The foundation does not make the final selection of individuals receiving support.
Deadline(s): None
Write: David Jackson, Trustee
Trustees: David Jackson, NationsBank.
EIN: 752341916

3098
Rockwell Fund, Inc. ▼
910 Travis St., Suite 2310
Houston 77002   (713) 659-7204
FAX: (713) 659-3446

Trust established in 1931; incorporated in 1949 in TX; absorbed Rockwell Brothers Endowment, Inc. in 1981.
Donor(s): Members of the James M. Rockwell family, Rockwell Bros. & Co., Rockwell Lumber Co.
Foundation type: Independent
Financial data (yr. ended 12/31/90): Assets, $55,838,610 (M); expenditures, $2,681,802; qualifying distributions, $2,494,806, including $2,337,650 for 153 grants (high: $50,000; low: $500; average: $5,000-$25,000).
Purpose and activities: Giving to causes of interest to the founders and donors, with emphasis on higher education, religious programs, hospitals, cultural programs, municipalities, and general welfare, and projects that fulfill the fund's philosophy of wanting to make its grants do as much good and touch the lives of as many people as possible.

Fields of interest: Arts, cultural programs, health services, child welfare, welfare, social services, civic affairs, religion—Christian, general charitable giving.
Types of support: Annual campaigns, seed money, general purposes, building funds, equipment, land acquisition, scholarship funds, lectureships, operating budgets, professorships, renovation projects, research, special projects, student aid.
Limitations: Giving primarily in TX, with emphasis on Houston. No grants to individuals; no loans; grants awarded on a year-to-year basis only; no future commitments; no multi-year grants.
Publications: Application guidelines.
Application information: Applicants should not submit more than 1 proposal per year. Application form required.
  Initial approach: Letter
  Copies of proposal: 1
  Deadline(s): Jan. 31, Apr. 30, July 31, Oct. 31
  Board meeting date(s): Quarterly
  Final notification: After each quarterly meeting
  Write: Joe M. Green, Jr., Pres., or Martha Vogt, Grant Coordinator
Officers and Trustees:* Joe M. Green, Jr.,* Pres.; R. Terry Bell,* V.P.; Helen N. Sterling,* Secy.-Treas.
Number of staff: 2 full-time professional; 1 part-time professional; 2 full-time support.
EIN: 746040258
Recent health grants:
3098-1 Alzheimers Disease and Related Disorders Association, Houston, TX, $10,000. For medical research in Texas Medical Center. 1990.
3098-2 Avondale House, Houston, TX, $20,000. For operating expenses and programs for autistic children. 1990.
3098-3 Baylor College of Medicine, Houston, TX, $30,000. For arthritis research, voice institute and teen clinic. 1990.
3098-4 Casa De Esperanza De Los Ninos, Houston, TX, $15,000. For AIDS Parent Care Program. 1990.
3098-5 Fourth Ward Clinic, Houston, TX, $15,000. For clinic services. 1990.
3098-6 Harris County Emergency Corps, Houston, TX, $10,000. For operating funds. 1990.
3098-7 Hermann Eye Center, Houston, TX, $20,000. For retinal pigment epithelian cell transplantation unit. 1990.
3098-8 Holly Hall, Houston, TX, $10,000. For operating expenses and remodeling of activities building. 1990.
3098-9 Houston Achievement Place, Houston, TX, $15,000. For therapeutic counseling services for youth. 1990.
3098-10 Institute for Rehabilitation and Research Foundation, Houston, TX, $25,000. For construction of new building. 1990.
3098-11 March of Dimes Birth Defects Foundation, Houston, TX, $30,000. For preterm birth prevention project. 1990.
3098-12 Marywood Maternity and Adoption Services, Austin, TX, $10,000. For renovation and building expansion. 1990.
3098-13 Mental Health Association of Houston and Harris County, Houston, TX, $10,000. For operating expenses and educational program. 1990.

3098-14 Methodist Hospital Foundation, Houston, TX, $26,000. For remodeling of mammography suite for new equipment. 1990.
3098-15 Planned Parenthood of Houston and Southeast Texas, Houston, TX, $10,000. For programs and services. 1990.
3098-16 Retina Research Foundation, Houston, TX, $10,000. For research programs. 1990.
3098-17 Saint Dominic Diocesan Center, Nursing Home, Houston, TX, $10,000. For nursing home patient care. 1990.
3098-18 Saint James House of Baytown, Baytown, TX, $10,000. For charitable assistance program for elderly. 1990.
3098-19 Saint Joseph Hospital Foundation, Houston, TX, $15,000. For Medtake beside computer systems. 1990.
3098-20 Saint Lukes Episcopal Hospital, Houston, TX, $20,000. For nursing scholarships. 1990.
3098-21 San Jose Clinic, Houston, TX, $10,000. For operating expenses. 1990.
3098-22 Scott and White Memorial Hospital, Temple, TX, $10,000. For nursing program. 1990.
3098-23 Texas Childrens Hospital, Houston, TX, $25,000. For discharge planning fund. 1990.
3098-24 United Cerebral Palsy of Texas Gulf Coast, Houston, TX, $10,000. For Lekotek Toy Library. 1990.
3098-25 University of Texas Health Science Center, Houston, TX, $15,000. For nursing scholarships. 1990.
3098-26 University of Texas M.D. Anderson Cancer Center, Houston, TX, $20,000. For scientific achievement fund for young scientists. 1990.
3098-27 Urban Affairs Corporation, Houston, TX, $15,000. For adolescent primary health care center programs. 1990.
3098-28 Volunteer Center of the Texas Gulf Coast, Houston, TX, $20,000. For project for youth volunteers in health. 1990.
3098-29 Volunteer Services Council for Richmond State School, Richmond, TX, $10,000. For therapeutic riding center for mentally retarded. 1990.
3098-30 Womens Christian Home, Houston, TX, $11,000. Toward salary for case manager. 1990.

3099
San Antonio Area Foundation ▼
530 McCullough, Suite 600
San Antonio 78215   (512) 225-2243
Mailing address: P.O. Box 120366, San Antonio, TX 78212-9566

Established in 1964 in TX.
Foundation type: Community
Financial data (yr. ended 09/30/91): Assets, $20,810,415 (M); gifts received, $2,106,303; expenditures, $1,795,039; qualifying distributions, $1,591,307, including $1,591,307 for 604 grants (high: $120,621; low: $50; average: $1,000-$10,000).
Purpose and activities: To provide an effective channel for private giving to meet educational, cultural, medical, research, social, religious, and civic needs at all levels of society.

Fields of interest: Education, cultural programs, health, civic affairs, social services, religion, medical research.
Types of support: Operating budgets, continuing support, annual campaigns, seed money, emergency funds, building funds, equipment, land acquisition, matching funds, scholarship funds, special projects, research, publications, conferences and seminars, student aid, general purposes, lectureships, professorships, renovation projects.
Limitations: Giving limited to TX, with emphasis on the Bexar County and San Antonio areas, except when otherwise specified by donor. No support for political or lobbying programs. No grants to individuals (except for designated scholarship funds), or for deficit financing, endowment funds, or salaries (except as part of a project); no loans.
Publications: Annual report, 990-PF, newsletter, application guidelines.
Application information: Application form required.
  Initial approach: Letter or telephone
  Copies of proposal: 15
  Deadline(s): Feb. 15
  Board meeting date(s): Annually and as required
  Final notification: 8 to 10 weeks
  Write: Candes P. Chumney, Exec. Dir.
Officer: Candes P. Chumney, Exec. Dir. and Secy.-Treas.
Distribution Committee: Al J. Notzon, Chair.; Mary Beth Williamson, Vice-Chair.; Clifton J. Bolner, Taylor Boone, Kenneth L. Farrimond, M.D., Richard E. Goldsmith, John B. Lahourcade, Pete R. Martinez, Aaronetta Pierce, Ed Polansky, Gaines Voigt, Jerome F. Weynand, Mollie Zachry.
Trustee Banks: Ameritrust Texas, N.A., Bank One, Texas, N.A., Broadway National Bank, Citizens State Bank, First City Texas-San Antonio, N.A., Frost National Bank, Groos Bank, Jefferson State Bank, Kelly Field National Bank, NationsBank, Texas Commerce Bank.
Number of staff: 2 full-time professional; 1 full-time support.
EIN: 746065414
Recent health grants:
3099-1 American Cancer Society, San Antonio, TX, $14,000. To establish facility to meet needs of underserved population in cancer education, early detection and prevention. 1990.
3099-2 Boys and Girls Clubs of San Antonio, San Antonio, TX, $10,070. For Smart Moves Program, to teach inner city children to say no to drugs, alcohol, early sexual activity and learn basic life skills. 1990.
3099-3 Daughters of Charity of Saint Vincent de Paul, San Antonio, TX, $15,000. To provide nutrition, medical care, child care and protection, dental care and basic necessities to children at risk of serious life-long impairment. 1990.
3099-4 Lutheran General Hospital, San Antonio, TX, $20,000. To purchase dedicated low-dose mammography system for early detection and diagnosis of breast cancer. 1990.
3099-5 Planned Parenthood of San Antonio, San Antonio, TX, $10,000. To purchase chemistry analyzer for in-house laboratory to process clients' blood tests. 1990.
3099-6 San Antonio Christian Dental Clinic, San Antonio, TX, $15,000. To provide dental care

to persons unable to pay for such services. 1990.

3099-7 University of Texas, San Antonio, TX, $13,750. For advanced brain imaging facility for medical research. 1990.

3099-8 University of Texas Health Science Center, Department of Ophthalmology, San Antonio, TX, $27,566. For biochemistry eye research laboratory. 1990.

3099-9 University of Texas Health Science Center, Department of Ophthalmology, San Antonio, TX, $22,813. For research in identifying patients with central retinal vein occlusion. 1990.

3099-10 University of Texas Health Science Center, Department of Ophthalmology, San Antonio, TX, $12,825. For pediatric ophthalmology, developmental eye biology and genetics laboratory. 1990.

3099-11 University of Texas Health Science Center, Department of Ophthalmology, San Antonio, TX, $11,197. For research to prevent clinical complications causing blindness following retinal reattachment surgery. 1990.

3100
Scurlock Foundation
700 Louisiana, Suite 3920
Houston 77002   (713) 236-1500

Incorporated in 1954 in TX.
Donor(s): E.C. Scurlock,‡ Scurlock Oil Co., D.E. Farnsworth,‡ W.C. Scurlock,‡ J.S. Blanton, and other members of the Blanton family.
Foundation type: Independent
Financial data (yr. ended 12/31/90): Assets, $7,943,049 (M); gifts received, $22,451; expenditures, $631,450; qualifying distributions, $610,761, including $609,300 for 108 grants (high: $49,600; low: $250).
Fields of interest: Education, secondary education, higher education, hospitals, health, Protestant giving, religion, social services, youth, cultural programs, arts, public affairs.
Types of support: Building funds, general purposes, annual campaigns, emergency funds, endowment funds, research, matching funds, continuing support.
Limitations: Giving primarily in TX. No grants to individuals, or for scholarships or fellowships; no loans.
Application information: Funds committed for approximately the next 2 years. Application form not required.
  Initial approach: Letter
  Copies of proposal: 1
  Deadline(s): None
  Board meeting date(s): Dec. and as required
  Write: J.S. Blanton, Pres.
Officers and Directors:* Laura Lee Blanton, Pres.; Eddy S. Blanton,* V.P.; Jack S. Blanton, Jr.,* V.P.; Elizabeth B. Wareing,* V.P.; Kenneth Fisher,* Secy.-Treas.
Number of staff: None.
EIN: 741488953

3101
Sarah M. & Charles E. Seay Charitable Trust
300 Crescent Court, Suite 1370
Dallas 75201

Established in 1983 in TX.
Donor(s): Charles E. Seay, Sarah M. Seay.
Foundation type: Independent
Financial data (yr. ended 05/31/91): Assets, $2,292,043 (M); gifts received, $107,566; expenditures, $1,101,391; qualifying distributions, $1,093,029, including $1,092,962 for 54 grants (high: $500,000; low: $15).
Fields of interest: Higher education, medical education, hospitals, medical research, religion—Christian, cultural programs, social services.
Types of support: Building funds, endowment funds, professorships.
Limitations: Giving primarily in TX, with emphasis on Dallas. No grants to individuals.
Application information: Contributes only to pre-selected organizations. Applications not accepted.
Trustees: Charles E. Seay, Charles E. Seay, Jr., Sarah M. Seay, Stephen M. Seay.
EIN: 751894505

3102
The M. L. Shanor Foundation
P.O. Box 7522
Wichita Falls 76307   (817) 761-2401

Donor(s): H. Campsey, J.D. Huffaker, N.T.P. Co.
Foundation type: Independent
Financial data (yr. ended 12/31/90): Assets, $2,181,115 (M); gifts received, $110,614; expenditures, $151,588; qualifying distributions, $145,538, including $7,050 for 4 grants (high: $6,000; low: $100) and $132,586 for 91 loans to individuals.
Purpose and activities: Scholarship loans to individuals; grants also to local charitable organizations, including higher education.
Fields of interest: Health, higher education.
Types of support: General purposes, student loans.
Limitations: Giving primarily in TX, with emphasis on Cherokee, Wichita, and Wilbarger counties.
Application information: Application form required for student loans.
  Deadline(s): Aug. 1 for student loans
  Write: Frank W. Jarratt, Secy.-Treas.
Officers and Directors:* J.B. Jarratt,* Pres.; Alvin L. Barnes,* V.P.; Mike Klappenbach,* V.P.; Frank W. Jarratt,* Secy.-Treas.; Ernestine Jarratt.
EIN: 756012834

3103
Charles S. and Ruth C. Sharp Foundation, Inc.
c/o Security Bank Bldg., No. 504
2626 Cole Ave.
Dallas 75204

Incorporated in 1965 in TX.
Donor(s): Charles S. Sharp, Ruth Collins Sharp.
Foundation type: Independent
Financial data (yr. ended 12/31/90): Assets, $3,412,401 (M); expenditures, $201,849;

qualifying distributions, $156,198, including $151,700 for 33 grants (high: $40,000; low: $100).
Fields of interest: Protestant giving, higher education, hospitals, youth.
Types of support: Operating budgets, general purposes.
Limitations: Giving primarily in Dallas, TX. No grants to individuals.
Application information: Contributes only to pre-selected organizations. Applications not accepted.
  Write: Ruth Collins Sharp, Pres.
Officers and Directors:* Ruth Collins Sharp,* Pres.; Margot Cryer,* Secy.-Treas.; Sally S. Jacobson, Susan S. McAdam, Charles S. Sharp, Jr.
EIN: 756045366

3104
Shell Oil Company Foundation ▼
(Formerly Shell Companies Foundation, Inc.)
Two Shell Plaza
P.O. Box 2099
Houston 77252   (713) 241-3616

Incorporated in 1953 in NY.
Donor(s): Shell Oil Co., and other participating companies.
Foundation type: Company-sponsored
Financial data (yr. ended 12/31/91): Assets, $7,563,736 (M); gifts received, $5,156,000; expenditures, $15,974,863; qualifying distributions, $15,405,611, including $13,670,125 for 1,247 grants (high: $200,000; low: $500; average: $5,000-$150,000) and $1,735,486 for 728 employee matching gifts.
Purpose and activities: Preferred areas of giving are education and community funds. About 56 percent of the budget channeled through a number of planned programs that provide student aid, faculty development, basic research grants, and departmental grants to some 700 colleges and universities (three-quarters of these schools participate in Shell Matching Gifts Program only), and to a few national educational organizations. Main interests in education are engineering, science, and business. Approximately 22 percent of the budget directed to United Way organizations in cities or towns where Shell employees reside. The remaining funds paid to a limited number of national organizations concerned with a broad range of needs and to a greater extent, to local organizations in communities where significant numbers of Shell employees reside.
Fields of interest: Education, arts, performing arts, health, civic affairs, public policy.
Types of support: Continuing support, employee matching gifts, fellowships, general purposes, operating budgets, professorships, publications, research, scholarship funds, special projects, employee-related scholarships, capital campaigns, student aid.
Limitations: Giving primarily in areas of company operations. No support for special requests of colleges, universities, and college fundraising associations, or hospital operating expenses. No grants to individuals, or for endowment funds, capital campaigns of national organizations, or development funds; no loans.
Publications: Corporate giving report (including application guidelines).

Application information: Scholarship programs administered through National Merit Scholarship Corp. Application form not required.

Initial approach: Letter

Copies of proposal: 1

Deadline(s): Submit proposal Jan. through Aug.; deadline Aug. 31

Board meeting date(s): Dec. and Mar.

Final notification: 1 month

Write: Doris J. O'Connor, Sr. V.P., or R.L. Kuhns, Secy.

Officers and Directors:* Frank H. Richardson,* Pres. and Exec. Comm. Chair.; Doris J. O'Connor,* Sr. V.P. and Member, Exec. Comm.; B.W. Levan,* V.P.; L.E. Sloan,* V.P.; R.L. Kuhns, Secy.; N.E. Gautier, Treas.; P.J. Carroll,* Member, Exec. Comm.; J.E. Little,* Member, Exec. Comm.; J.P. Parrish,* Member, Exec. Comm.; B.E. Bernard, R. Lopez, S.L. Miller, D.B. Richardson, L.L. Smith, C.W. Wilson.

Number of staff: 5 full-time professional; 3 full-time support.

EIN: 136066583

Recent health grants:

3104-1 American Council on Science and Health, NYC, NY, $10,000. 1990.

3104-2 American Heart Association, Houston Chapter, Houston, TX, $15,000. 1990.

3104-3 American Lung Association, San Jacinto Chapter, Houston, TX, $20,000. 1990.

3104-4 Arthritis Foundation, Atlanta, GA, $10,000. 1990.

3104-5 Baylor College of Medicine, Houston, TX, $200,000. For New Century Campaign. 1990.

3104-6 Crippled Childrens Hospital, New Orleans, LA, $20,000. 1990.

3104-7 Goleta Valley Community Hospital, Santa Barbara, CA, $10,000. 1990.

3104-8 Greater Bakersfield Memorial Hospital, Bakersfield, CA, $10,000. 1990.

3104-9 Houston Academy of Medicine, Houston, TX, $59,250. 1990.

3104-10 Institute for Evaluating Health Risks, San Francisco, CA, $10,000. 1990.

3104-11 Institute for Rehabilitation and Research, Houston, TX, $10,000. 1990.

3104-12 Island Hospital Medical Foundation, Anacortes, WA, $12,500. 1990.

3104-13 Johns Hopkins University, Division of Environmental Health and Engineering, Baltimore, MD, $10,000. For Shell Graduate Grants in Industrial Hygiene. 1990.

3104-14 M. D. Anderson Hospital and Tumor Institute, Houston, TX, $15,000. 1990.

3104-15 Methodist Hospital Foundation, Neurosensory Center, Houston, TX, $50,000. For capital campaign. 1990.

3104-16 National Council on the Aging, DC, $10,000. 1990.

3104-17 New York University, Institute of Environmental Medicine, NYC, NY, $10,000. For Shell Graduate Grants. 1990.

3104-18 Occupational Physicians Scholarship Fund, NYC, NY, $50,000. 1990.

3104-19 Texas Heart Institute, Houston, TX, $20,000. 1990.

3104-20 University of Alabama, Birmingham, AL, $10,000. For Shell Graduate Grants in Epidemiology. 1990.

3104-21 University of Alabama, University, AL, $75,000. For epidemiology - occupational environmental health studies. 1990.

3104-22 University of California, San Francisco, CA, $10,000. For Shell Graduate Grants in Occupational Medicine. 1990.

3104-23 University of Colorado Foundation, Denver, CO, $25,000. For Molecular Toxicology and Environmental Health Sciences program. 1990.

3104-24 University of Pittsburgh, Pittsburgh, PA, $10,000. For Shell Graduate Grants in Epidemiology. 1990.

3104-25 University of Texas Health Science Center, Medical School Department of Microbiology, Houston, TX, $20,000. 1990.

3104-26 University of Texas Health Science Center, Public Health School, Houston, TX, $15,000. For Residency Program in Occupational Medicine. 1990.

3104-27 Wood River Township Hospital, Wood River, IL, $40,000. 1990.

3104-28 Yeshiva University, Bronx, NY, $10,000. For Shell Graduate Grants in Neurosciences. 1990.

3105

Harold Simmons Foundation ▼

Three Lincoln Ctr.

5430 LBJ Freeway, Suite 1700

Dallas 75240-2697   (214) 233-1700

Incorporated in 1988 in TX.

Donor(s): NL Industries, Inc., and subsidiaries, Contran Corp.

Foundation type: Company-sponsored

Financial data (yr. ended 12/31/90): Assets, $6,612 (M); gifts received, $2,440,000; expenditures, $2,472,824; qualifying distributions, $2,467,076, including $2,413,238 for 179 grants (high: $270,033; low: $100; average: $1,000-$5,000) and $53,838 for employee matching gifts.

Purpose and activities: Grants for community programs and projects, health and social welfare agencies, culture and art, child development, youth, and education.

Fields of interest: Arts, cultural programs, community development, social services, minorities, housing, youth, child development, child welfare, health, literacy.

Types of support: Annual campaigns, building funds, continuing support, emergency funds, employee matching gifts, operating budgets, renovation projects, research, seed money, special projects.

Limitations: Giving limited to the Dallas, TX, area. No grants to individuals, or for endowment funds; no loans to individuals.

Publications: Application guidelines.

Application information: Application form not required.

Initial approach: Proposal

Copies of proposal: 1

Deadline(s): None

Board meeting date(s): As needed

Final notification: 3 months

Write: Lisa K. Simmons, Pres.

Officers and Directors:* Harold Simmons,* Chair.; Lisa K. Simmons,* Pres.; Steven L. Watson,* V.P. and Secy.; Eugene K. Anderson, Treas.; Keith A. Johnson, Controller.

Number of staff: 1 full-time professional; 1 full-time support.

EIN: 752222091

3106

Bob and Vivian Smith Foundation

1900 West Loop South, Suite 1050

Houston 77027   (713) 622-8611

Established about 1969.

Donor(s): R.E. Smith, Vivian L. Smith.‡

Foundation type: Independent

Financial data (yr. ended 12/31/90): Assets, $7,249,571 (M); expenditures, $364,126; qualifying distributions, $336,121, including $335,900 for 21 grants (high: $60,000; low: $2,500).

Purpose and activities: Emphasis on medical research and secondary education; support also for higher education.

Fields of interest: Medical research, secondary education, higher education.

Types of support: General purposes.

Limitations: Giving primarily in Houston, TX. No grants to individuals; no program-related investments.

Application information: Application form not required.

Initial approach: Proposal

Deadline(s): None

Write: Suzanne R. Benson, Secy.-Treas.

Officers and Trustees:* W.N. Finnegan III,* Pres.; Suzanne R. Benson, Secy.-Treas.; Bobby Smith Cohn, Sandra Smith Dompier.

EIN: 237029052

3107

Julia and Albert Smith Foundation

1360 Post Oak Blvd., Suite 2450

Houston 77056   (713) 871-8271

Established in 1986 in TX.

Donor(s): Albert J. Smith III, Gwendolyn Smith, Albert J. Smith, Jr., Julia C. Smith.

Foundation type: Independent

Financial data (yr. ended 11/30/91): Assets, $2,043,965 (M); expenditures, $79,714; qualifying distributions, $75,675, including $74,500 for 12 grants (high: $12,000; low: $2,000).

Purpose and activities: Support primarily for a medical research foundation, and for empowerment of battered women.

Fields of interest: Medical research, women, welfare, social services, arts, religious schools.

Types of support: General purposes, matching funds, seed money, research, student aid.

Limitations: Giving primarily in Houston, TX. No grants to individuals.

Application information: Contributes only to pre-selected organizations. Applications not accepted.

Write: Albert J. Smith, Jr., Secy.-Treas.

Officer: Julia C. Smith, Pres.; Albert J. Smith, Jr., Secy.-Treas.

Directors: Albert J. Smith III, William C. Smith, Julia Anne Stuckey.

EIN: 760207247

3108
Vivian L. Smith Foundation for Restorative Neurology
1900 West Loop South, Suite 1050
Houston 77027
Application address: One Baylor Plaza, Rm. 5821, Houston, TX 77030; Tel.: (713) 798-5168

Established in 1981 in TX.
Donor(s): Vivian L. Smith.‡
Foundation type: Operating
Financial data (yr. ended 06/30/91): Assets, $10,379,692 (M); gifts received, $2,500,000; expenditures, $1,571,711; qualifying distributions, $1,757,461, including $16,267 for 3 grants to individuals (high: $10,290; low: $970) and $1,541,947 for foundation-administered programs.
Purpose and activities: A private operating foundation; primary purpose to promote the development of and provide support for research in restorative neurology.
Fields of interest: Medical sciences, medical research.
Types of support: Research.
Limitations: Giving on a domestic and international basis.
Application information:
  Initial approach: Proposal
  Deadline(s): None
  Write: Dr. Milan Dimitrijevic, Research Dir.
Officers and Trustees:* R.A. Seale, Jr.,* Pres.; Suzanne R. Benson,* V.P.; W.N. Finnegan III,* V.P.; Ed McCraw, Secy.; Virgil E. Vickery, Treas.; Delmer Q. Bowman, Dee S. Osborne.
EIN: 742139770

3109
SnyderGeneral Corporate Giving Program
3219 McKinney Ave.
Dallas 75204-2418   (214) 754-0500

Purpose and activities: Supports health, welfare and the United Way.
Fields of interest: Health, welfare, community funds.
Types of support: In-kind gifts.
Limitations: No support for political campaigns or fraternal or religious organizations.
Application information:
  Initial approach: Initial contact by query letter describing project
  Deadline(s): Applications accepted throughout the year
  Final notification: 8 weeks
  Write: Bart L. Bailey, V.P., Administration
Number of staff: None.

3110
South Texas Charitable Foundation
P.O. Box 2549
Victoria 77902   (512) 573-4383

Established in 1981 in TX.
Donor(s): Maude O'Connor Williams.
Foundation type: Independent
Financial data (yr. ended 11/30/91): Assets, $13,616,898 (M); gifts received, $5,000,000; expenditures, $708,336; qualifying distributions, $708,100, including $708,100 for 20 grants (high: $240,000; low: $100).

Fields of interest: Hospitals, health associations, cancer, social services, religious welfare, Catholic giving.
Limitations: Giving primarily in TX. No grants to individuals.
Application information: Application form not required.
  Deadline(s): None
  Write: Rayford L. Keller, Secy.-Treas.
Officers: Maude O'Connor Williams, Pres.; Roger P. Williams, V.P.; Rayford L. Keller, Secy.-Treas.
EIN: 742148107

3111
Stemmons Foundation
1200 Tower East
2700 Stemmons Freeway
Dallas 75207   (214) 631-7910

Established in 1963 in TX.
Foundation type: Independent
Financial data (yr. ended 12/31/90): Assets, $3,544,601 (M); expenditures, $361,424; qualifying distributions, $359,144, including $328,099 for 60 grants (high: $100,000; low: $200).
Fields of interest: Medical research, higher education, education, health associations, cultural programs, youth.
Types of support: Scholarship funds.
Limitations: Giving primarily in Dallas, TX. No grants to individuals.
Application information:
  Initial approach: Proposal
  Write: Ann M. Roberts, Secy.-Treas.
Officers: John M. Stemmons, Sr., Pres.; Allison S. Simon, V.P.; Heinz K. Simon, V.P.; Ruth T. Stemmons, V.P.; John M. Stemmons, Jr., V.P.; Ann M. Roberts, Secy.-Treas.
EIN: 756039966

3112
Strake Foundation ▼
712 Main St., Suite 3300
Houston 77002-3210   (713) 546-2400

Trust established in 1952 in TX; incorporated in 1983.
Donor(s): George W. Strake, Sr.,‡ Susan K. Strake,‡ George W. Strake, Jr., Susan S. Dilworth,‡ Georganna S. Parsley.
Foundation type: Independent
Financial data (yr. ended 12/31/90): Assets, $22,733,775 (M); expenditures, $1,574,138; qualifying distributions, $1,485,230, including $1,398,800 for 230 grants (high: $100,000; low: $1,000; average: $2,000-$15,000).
Purpose and activities: Giving primarily to Roman Catholic-affiliated associations, including hospices and those serving the handicapped, with emphasis on programs for minorities and higher and secondary educational institutions; support also for the arts and social services, including programs for youth.
Fields of interest: Catholic giving, religion, hospitals, health, health services, hospices, handicapped, drug abuse, education, education—minorities, secondary education, higher education, literacy, cultural programs, museums, social services, youth, welfare, community funds, civic affairs.

Types of support: Operating budgets, continuing support, annual campaigns, special projects, research, matching funds, general purposes, capital campaigns.
Limitations: Giving primarily in TX, especially Houston; no grants outside the U.S. No support for elementary schools. No grants to individuals, or for deficit financing, consulting services, technical assistance, or publications; no loans.
Publications: Informational brochure (including application guidelines), application guidelines.
Application information: Application form not required.
  Initial approach: Brief written proposal
  Copies of proposal: 1
  Deadline(s): Submit proposal preferably by Apr. 1 or Oct. 1; deadline 1 month prior to board meetings
  Board meeting date(s): May and Nov.
  Final notification: 1 month after board meetings
  Write: George W. Strake, Jr., Pres.
Officers and Trustees:* George W. Strake, Jr.,* Pres. and Treas.; Georganna S. Parsley,* V.P. and Secy.; Willie J. Alexander, J.F. Niehaus, Sandra Parsley, Michele S. Sommerfield, Colleen D. Stroup, Linda D. Walsh, George O. Zenner, Jr.
Number of staff: 1 part-time professional; 1 full-time support; 1 part-time support.
EIN: 760041524
Recent health grants:
3112-1 American Cancer Society, Houston, TX, $10,000. For general support. 1990.
3112-2 Baylor College of Medicine, Houston, TX, $12,500. For general support. 1990.
3112-3 Baylor University Medical Center Foundation, Dallas, TX, $10,000. For general support. 1990.
3112-4 Capital Area Radiation and Research Foundation, Austin, TX, $12,500. For general support. 1990.
3112-5 Institute for Rehabilitation and Research Foundation, Houston, TX, $20,000. For general support. 1990.
3112-6 Memorial Hospital Foundation of Houston, Houston, TX, $15,000. For general support. 1990.
3112-7 Saint Joseph Hospital Foundation, Houston, TX, $100,000. For general support. 1990.
3112-8 Saint Lukes Episcopal Hospital, Houston, TX, $15,000. For general support. 1990.

3113
Eugene Straus Charitable Trust
c/o NationsBank
P.O. Box 830241
Dallas 75283   (214) 508-1965

Trust established in 1975 in TX.
Donor(s): Eugene Straus.‡
Foundation type: Independent
Financial data (yr. ended 08/31/91): Assets, $2,098,107 (M); expenditures, $116,327; qualifying distributions, $102,353, including $100,000 for 5 grants (high: $37,000; low: $13,000; average: $15,000).
Purpose and activities: For building construction or maintenance of permanent structures and improvements for local charitable, health and social service, and educational organizations.

Fields of interest: Adult education, child welfare, education—building funds, health services, rehabilitation, delinquency, drug abuse, housing.
Types of support: Building funds, renovation projects.
Limitations: Giving limited to Dallas County, TX. No grants to individuals, or for operating budgets, continuing support, annual campaigns, seed money, emergency funds, deficit financing, equipment, land acquisition, publications, conferences, endowment funds, research, scholarships, fellowships, or matching gifts; no loans.
Publications: Application guidelines.
Application information: Application form not required.
  Initial approach: Letter describing proposal for building maintenance or construction
  Copies of proposal: 2
  Deadline(s): Submit proposal preferably in July; deadline Aug. 1
  Board meeting date(s): Sept. 15
  Write: D.J. Kelly, V.P.-Trust, NationsBank
Trustee: NationsBank.
Number of staff: 1 part-time professional.
EIN: 756229249

3114
Roy and Christine Sturgis Charitable and Educational Trust ▼
c/o NationsBank of Texas, N.A.
P.O. Box 831041
Dallas 75283-1041

Established in 1981 in AR.
Donor(s): Christine Sturgis.‡
Foundation type: Independent
Financial data (yr. ended 09/30/91): Assets, $37,315,690 (M); expenditures, $2,719,263; qualifying distributions, $2,196,268, including $2,176,500 for 34 grants (high: $700,000; low: $1,000; average: $10,000-$75,000).
Purpose and activities: Support primarily for religious, charitable, scientific, literary, and educational organizations.
Fields of interest: Arts, education, libraries, health, medical research, hospitals, science and technology, social services, disadvantaged.
Types of support: Building funds, capital campaigns, endowment funds, general purposes, matching funds, operating budgets, research, special projects.
Limitations: Giving primarily in AR and TX. No grants to individuals; no loans.
Publications: Application guidelines.
Application information: No personal interviews granted.
  Initial approach: Letter or proposal
  Copies of proposal: 2
  Deadline(s): Mar. 1 or Sept. 1
  Board meeting date(s): Apr. and Oct.
  Final notification: May
  Write: Harry C. Mayer
Trustee Banks: NationsBank of Texas, N.A., First Trust Co. of Montana.
Number of staff: None.
EIN: 756331832

3115
Anne Burnett and Charles D. Tandy Foundation ▼
801 Cherry St., Suite 1400
Fort Worth 76102   (817) 877-3344

Established in 1978 in TX.
Donor(s): Anne Burnett Tandy,‡ Charles D. Tandy,‡ Ben Bird.
Foundation type: Independent
Financial data (yr. ended 12/31/91): Assets, $209,288,944 (M); expenditures, $8,408,897; qualifying distributions, $8,377,161, including $7,871,511 for 67 grants (high: $1,250,000; low: $3,000; average: $10,000-$100,000).
Purpose and activities: Support primarily for health care organizations; cultural institutions, including major museum projects; social service agencies; community affairs groups; and educational institutions; support also for youth agencies.
Fields of interest: Health, AIDS, arts, museums, social services, youth, civic affairs, education.
Types of support: Capital campaigns, general purposes, special projects, technical assistance, seed money.
Limitations: Giving primarily in the Fort Worth, TX, area. No grants to individuals, or for scholarships or fellowships.
Publications: Program policy statement, application guidelines, annual report (including application guidelines).
Application information: Application form required.
  Initial approach: Letter
  Copies of proposal: 1
  Deadline(s): None
  Board meeting date(s): Generally in Mar., June, and Nov.
  Final notification: 90 days
  Write: Thomas F. Beech, V.P.
Officers and Trustees:* Anne W. Marion,* Pres.; Edward R. Hudson, Jr.,* V.P. and Secy.; Benjamin J. Fortson,* V.P. and Treas.; Perry R. Bass,* V.P.; Thomas F. Beech, V.P.; John L. Marion.
Number of staff: 1 full-time professional; 1 full-time support.
EIN: 751638517
Recent health grants:
3115-1 AIDS Coordinating Council of Tarrant County, Fort Worth, TX, $26,225. For start-up support for operating expenses. 1990.
3115-2 Because We Care, Fort Worth, TX, $25,000. For expansion of substance abuse prevention and education program in Fort Worth Independent School District's middle schools. 1990.
3115-3 Child Study Center, Fort Worth, TX, $91,843. For operating expenses. 1990.
3115-4 Community Outreach Center, Fort Worth, TX, $56,000. For outreach and counseling to people with AIDS. 1990.
3115-5 Fort Worth Challenge, Fort Worth, TX, $25,000. For substance abuse prevention, education and treatment advocacy program. 1990.
3115-6 Memorial Sloan-Kettering Cancer Center, NYC, NY, $1,000,000. For capital campaign. 1990.
3115-7 National Community AIDS Partnership, DC, $50,000. For provision of matching funds and technical assistance to local community

foundation to develop AIDS grants programs. 1990.
3115-8 Planned Parenthood of North Texas, Fort Worth, TX, $54,000. For creation of working capital fund and development of market-oriented approach to new programs. 1990.
3115-9 United Way of Metropolitan Tarrant County, Fort Worth, TX, $75,000. For Arlington Human Service Center, neighborhood health clinic serving low-income people. 1990.
3115-10 Warm Place, Fort Worth, TX, $25,000. For start-up funds for counseling and support program for children and their families following death of sibling or parent. 1990.
3115-11 Womens Center of Tarrant County, Fort Worth, TX, $40,000. For Project Self-Sufficiency and Rape Crisis Center. 1990.

3116
The Community Foundation of Metropolitan Tarrant County
(Formerly The Community Trust of·Metropolitan Tarrant County)
Fort Worth Club Bldg.
306 West Seventh St., Suite 702
Fort Worth 76102   (817) 877-0702

Established in 1981 in TX as a program of the United Way; status changed to independent community foundation in 1989.
Foundation type: Community
Financial data (yr. ended 12/31/91): Assets, $18,039,348 (M); gifts received, $1,182,210; expenditures, $1,391,927; qualifying distributions, $1,121,250, including $964,015 for 231 grants (high: $47,790; low: $180; average: $500-$50,000) and $157,235 for 2 foundation-administered programs.
Purpose and activities: Support for community development, social services, education, youth, health, and arts and cultural programs; emphasis on one-time grants to new and innovative programs.
Fields of interest: Community development, social services, education, youth, health, AIDS, arts, cultural programs.
Types of support: General purposes, seed money, special projects, internships, renovation projects, scholarship funds.
Limitations: Giving primarily in Tarrant County, TX. No support for secular, religious, or fraternal organizations. No grants to individuals, or for annual or capital campaigns, deficit financing, endowment or emergency funds, matching grants, operating budgets, publications, research, continuing support, or conferences and seminars.
Publications: Application guidelines, annual report, informational brochure.
Application information: Application form not required.
  Initial approach: Letter requesting guidelines
  Copies of proposal: 1
  Deadline(s): Apr. 15 and Oct. 15
  Board meeting date(s): June and Dec.
  Final notification: June 30 and Dec. 31
  Write: James R. Holcomb, Pres.
Officers and Directors:* Leland Hodges,* Chair.; Louise Appleman,* Vice-Chair.; James R. Holcomb, Pres. and Exec. Dir.; Lynda Shropshire,* Secy.; Lloyd J. Weaver,* Treas.; R.G.

Alexander, Paul H. Brandt, Ronald Clinkscale, Tom Cravens, Robert W. Decker, Marty Leonard, Robert C. Mann, James R. Nichols, Robert S. Patterson, Bruce Petty, Earle A. Shields, Jr., Herman J. Smith, Vernell Sturns.
Number of staff: 1 full-time professional; 1 full-time support; 1 part-time support.
EIN: 752267767

3117
T. L. L. Temple Foundation ▼
109 Temple Blvd.
Lufkin 75901   (409) 639-5197

Trust established in 1962 in TX.
Donor(s): Georgie T. Munz,‡ Katherine S. Temple.‡
Foundation type: Independent
Financial data (yr. ended 11/30/91): Assets, $260,000,000 (M); gifts received, $100,000; expenditures, $11,850,000; qualifying distributions, $11,552,000, including $11,000,000 for 98 grants (high: $1,421,000; low: $500; average: $1,000-$55,000), $150,000 for 1 foundation-administered program and $300,000 for 1 program-related investment.
Purpose and activities: Support for education, health, and community and social services; support also for civic affairs and cultural programs.
Fields of interest: Education, higher education, adult education, education—early childhood, elementary education, hospitals, health services, mental health, rehabilitation, community development, social services, drug abuse, disadvantaged, hospices, civic affairs, cultural programs, animal welfare.
Types of support: Emergency funds, building funds, equipment, matching funds, scholarship funds, special projects, research, capital campaigns, general purposes.
Limitations: Giving primarily in counties in TX constituting the East Texas Pine Timber Belt. No support for private foundations, or religious organizations for religious purposes. No grants for deficit financing, or endowment funds; no loans.
Publications: Application guidelines, program policy statement, 990-PF.
Application information: Application form required.
  Initial approach: Letter
  Copies of proposal: 1
  Deadline(s): None
  Board meeting date(s): As required
  Final notification: 2 months
  Write: M.F. Buddy Zeagler, Deputy Exec. Dir.
Officers and Trustees:* Arthur Temple,* Chair.; Phillip M. Leach,* Exec. Dir.; M.F. Zeagler,* Deputy Exec. Dir.; Ward R. Burke, Arthur Temple III, W. Temple Webber, Jr.
Number of staff: 4 full-time professional; 2 full-time support.
EIN: 756037406

3118
Tenneco Corporate Contributions Program
P.O. Box 2511
Houston 77252-2511   (713) 757-3930

Financial data (yr. ended 12/31/90): Total giving, $7,772,900, including $5,560,123 for grants (high: $100,000; low: $1,000; average:

$1,000-$10,000), $212,777 for 959 employee matching gifts and $2,000,000 for in-kind gifts.
Purpose and activities: Supports education, health, welfare, united funds, youth groups, law and justice, urban affairs, hospitals, programs for the elderly, civic and public services, environmental issues, arts and humanities, museums, women's groups, libraries, performing arts, historic preservation and medical research. Other support includes in-kind donations, use of company facilities, and technical assistance. Emphasis on elementary and secondary education, including a Tenneco Presidential Scholarships Program for students at Jefferson Davis High School in Houston's inner city. The scholarship carries a maximum award of $4,000 for those ninth graders who are able to maintain a 2.5 grade point average and meet other academic requirements. To be eligible, students must also attend two summer enrichment sessions, which Tenneco helped develop under the sponsorship of a local philanthropic foundation and a local university.
Fields of interest: Higher education, health, welfare, youth, law and justice, urban development, hospitals, aged, civic affairs, environment, arts, humanities, museums, women, libraries, historic preservation, medical research, accounting, engineering, leadership development, literacy, public policy, science and technology, community development, conservation, disadvantaged, educational research, handicapped, education—minorities, cancer, elementary education, education—early childhood, educational associations, hospices, housing, homeless, hunger, secondary education, theater, United Kingdom.
Types of support: Building funds, capital campaigns, professorships, renovation projects, matching funds, fellowships, scholarship funds, employee matching gifts, in-kind gifts, internships, research, donated products, donated equipment, use of facilities, employee volunteer services.
Limitations: Giving primarily in areas of company operations in TX, WI, IL, VA, and CO; also in Canada and England. No grants to individuals, or for political, religious, fraternal or veterans' organizations.
Publications: Corporate report, informational brochure (including application guidelines).
Application information: Company has a staff than only handles contributions. Application form not required.
  Initial approach: Initial contact by letter on letterhead stationery; write to nearest company facility
  Copies of proposal: 1
  Deadline(s): Prior to Aug. 15 for consideration in next calendar year's budget
  Board meeting date(s): 2nd Tuesday in Jan. each year
  Final notification: 4 weeks after submission of application
  Write: Jo Ann Swinney, Dir., Community Affairs
Administrators: Connie Griffith, Sr. Contribs. Asst.; Ethel Samuels, Sr. Contribs. Coord.
Number of staff: 1 full-time professional; 1 full-time support.

3119
Texas Commerce Bank Foundation of Texas Commerce Bank - Houston, Inc.
c/o Texas Commerce Bank-Houston
P.O. Box 2558
Houston 77252-8050   (713) 236-4004

Incorporated in 1952 in TX.
Donor(s): Texas Commerce Bank-Houston.
Foundation type: Company-sponsored
Financial data (yr. ended 12/31/90): Assets, $512,461 (M); gifts received, $733,759; expenditures, $1,121,166; qualifying distributions, $1,062,436, including $1,032,022 for 249 grants (high: $380,000; low: $25) and $30,414 for 275 employee matching gifts.
Purpose and activities: Primary areas of interest include cultural programs, education, health services, housing, and civic affairs. Giving for a community fund and community development, museums and the performing arts, higher education, and health and medical research organizations; support also for social service agencies, including programs for minorities, child welfare, the homeless, and drug abuse.
Fields of interest: Community development, cultural programs, libraries, civic affairs, urban affairs, education, higher education, secondary education, elementary education, health services, cancer, family services, race relations, welfare, housing, conservation.
Types of support: Annual campaigns, building funds, continuing support, employee matching gifts, research, capital campaigns, in-kind gifts, endowment funds, renovation projects, equipment, operating budgets, special projects, conferences and seminars.
Limitations: Giving limited to Houston, TX. No grants to individuals.
Publications: Application guidelines.
Application information: Application form not required.
  Initial approach: Formal letter of request
  Copies of proposal: 1
  Deadline(s): 15th of each month
  Board meeting date(s): Last Thursday of each month
  Final notification: 15th of each month
  Write: D. Glenn Baird
Officers: Marshall Tyndall, Pres.; Shelby R. Rogers, Secy.; Beverly McCaskill, Treas.; Marc J. Shapiro, Member.
Number of staff: None.
EIN: 746036696

3120
Texas Instruments Foundation ▼
7839 Churchill Way
Dallas 75251   (214) 917-4505
Application address: P.O. Box 650311, M, S 3906, Dallas, TX 75265

Trust established in 1951 in TX; incorporated in 1964.
Donor(s): Texas Instruments, Inc., and wholly-owned subsidiaries.
Foundation type: Company-sponsored
Financial data (yr. ended 12/31/91): Assets, $12,217,801 (M); expenditures, $1,516,370; qualifying distributions, $1,516,370, including $1,162,844 for 53 grants (high: $178,594; low:

$500; average: $500-$178,594) and $353,526 for employee matching gifts.

Purpose and activities: Giving largely for community funds; grants also for higher and secondary education, including employee matching gifts, hospitals, youth agencies, and cultural programs; Founders' Prize awarded for outstanding achievement in the physical, health, or management sciences, or mathematics.

Fields of interest: Community funds, education, higher education, secondary education, education—early childhood, hospitals, youth, cultural programs, conservation.

Types of support: Employee matching gifts, building funds, research, continuing support, capital campaigns, renovation projects.

Limitations: Giving limited to plant site cities in TX: Attleboro, Austin, Dallas, Houston, Hunt Valley, Lubbock, Sherman, and Versailles. No grants to individuals (except for Founders' Prize award), or for company products or advertising; no loans.

Publications: Application guidelines.

Application information: Application for Founders' Prize by nomination only; application forms available from L.M. Rice, Jr., Pres. Application form not required.

Initial approach: Letter, 1 to 2 pages
Copies of proposal: 1
Deadline(s): Feb., May, Aug., and Nov.; Dec. 31 for Founders' Prize
Board meeting date(s): Mar., June, Sept., and Dec.
Final notification: 3 weeks after board meetings
Write: Ann Minnis, Grants Administrator

Officers and Directors:* Liston M. Rice, Jr.,* Pres.; William P. Weber,* V.P.; Joseph N. Richardson, Secy.; William A. Aylesworth, Treas.; Richard J. Agnich, Gerald W. Fronterhouse, Jerry R. Junkins, William B. Mitchell, Mark Shepherd, Jr.

Number of staff: 1 full-time professional; 1 part-time professional; 1 full-time support.

EIN: 756038519

3121
Transco Energy Corporate Giving Program
2800 Post Oak Boulevard
P.O. Box 1396
Houston 77251 (713) 439-2010

Financial data (yr. ended 12/31/89): Total giving, $1,171,610, including $1,143,451 for 259 grants (high: $216,845; low: $100) and $28,159 for 242 employee matching gifts.

Purpose and activities: Supports colleges and universities, and economic, elementary, minority, and business education, child welfare, engineering, heart disease, homeless, literacy, drug abuse programs, welfare, arts and culture, civic affairs, youth services, United Way and programs for the handicapped. Also gives in-kind donations.

Fields of interest: Education, museums, higher education, welfare, arts, cultural programs, civic affairs, youth, handicapped, business education, child welfare, education—early childhood, education—minorities, elementary education, engineering, fine arts, heart disease, homeless, literacy, theater, drug abuse, community development, child development, performing arts.

Types of support: Building funds, capital campaigns, employee matching gifts, general

purposes, research, operating budgets, special projects, employee-related scholarships, scholarship funds, in-kind gifts, donated equipment, use of facilities, employee volunteer services.

Limitations: Giving primarily in headquarters city and major operating areas in Houston and other parts of AL, LA, NC, NJ, PA, SC, TX, and VA. No support for religious, political, fraternal, or veterans' organizations. No grants to individuals.

Publications: Corporate report, informational brochure.

Application information: Company has a staff that only handles contributions. Application form not required.

Initial approach: Brief letter, proposal, or telephone call; Send requests to nearest company facility
Copies of proposal: 1
Deadline(s): None
Board meeting date(s): No set deadlines. Requests should be received by October 1st for funding at beginning of following year
Write: Beth Anne Clay, Mgr., Corp. Contribs.

Contributions Committee: G.L. Bellinger, R.M. Chiste, B.A. Clay, J.H. Lollar, D.F. Mackie, George S. Slocum, T.W. Spencer, D.E. Varne, J.P. Wise.

Number of staff: 1 full-time professional; 1 part-time support.

3122
The Trull Foundation
404 Fourth St.
Palacios 77465 (512) 972-5241

Trust established in 1967 in TX.

Donor(s): R.B. Trull, Florence M. Trull,‡ Gladys T. Brooking, Jean T. Herlin, Laura Shiflett, and others.

Foundation type: Independent

Financial data (yr. ended 12/31/90): Assets, $14,976,665 (M); expenditures, $894,397; qualifying distributions, $755,750, including $690,560 for 209 grants (high: $15,000; low: $60; average: $5,000).

Purpose and activities: Primary support for children's welfare organizations and for minorities; giving also for Protestant church support and welfare programs, denominational giving, elementary, secondary, and higher education with emphasis on religious schools, theological and legal education, and literacy programs, child development, and youth agencies; some support for Hispanic concerns, community development, assistance for immigrants, the homeless and disadvantaged, and the hungry, international relief activities, organizations promoting peace, ecology and the environment, population studies, AIDS research, museums, and the performing arts.

Fields of interest: Child welfare, minorities, Protestant welfare, welfare, elementary education, secondary education, higher education, youth, population studies, AIDS, aged.

Types of support: Operating budgets, continuing support, annual campaigns, seed money, equipment, professorships, internships, scholarship funds, special projects, publications, conferences and seminars, fellowships, consulting services, general purposes, renovation projects, technical assistance.

Limitations: Giving primarily in southern TX. No grants to individuals, and rarely for building or endowment funds; no loans.

Publications: Biennial report (including application guidelines).

Application information: Application form not required.

Initial approach: Letter
Copies of proposal: 1
Deadline(s): None
Board meeting date(s): Usually 3 to 5 times a year; contributions committee meets monthly and as required
Final notification: 6 weeks
Write: Colleen Claybourn, Exec. Dir.

Officers and Trustees:* R.B. Trull,* Chair.; J. Fred Huitt,* Vice-Chair.; Colleen Claybourn,* Secy.-Treas. and Exec. Dir.; Jean T. Herlin, Rose C. Lancaster.

Number of staff: 1 full-time professional; 1 full-time support.

EIN: 237423943

3123
Turner Charitable Foundation
811 Rusk, Suite 205
Houston 77002-2811 (713) 237-1117

Incorporated in 1956 in TX.

Donor(s): Isla Carroll Turner,‡ P.E. Turner.‡

Foundation type: Independent

Financial data (yr. ended 12/31/91): Assets, $17,719,391 (M); expenditures, $569,500; qualifying distributions, $475,000, including $475,000 for 63 grants (high: $75,000; low: $1,000; average: $1,000-$5,000).

Purpose and activities: Giving for higher and secondary education; social service and youth agencies; the elderly; fine and performing arts groups and other cultural programs; Catholic, Jewish, and Protestant church support and religious programs; hospitals; and health services including AIDS research; hospices; programs for women, children, minorities, the homeless, and the handicapped; urban and community development; civic and urban affairs; libraries; and conservation programs.

Fields of interest: Higher education, secondary education, youth, aged, arts, performing arts, Catholic giving, Jewish giving, Protestant giving, religious schools, hospitals, health services, AIDS, women, child welfare, minorities, handicapped, community development, libraries, conservation.

Types of support: Annual campaigns, building funds, capital campaigns, conferences and seminars, continuing support, emergency funds, endowment funds, equipment, fellowships, general purposes, land acquisition, lectureships, operating budgets, professorships, renovation projects, research, scholarship funds, matching funds, seed money, special projects.

Limitations: Giving limited to TX. No grants to individuals.

Application information: Application form not required.

Initial approach: Written request
Copies of proposal: 1
Deadline(s): Mar. 15
Board meeting date(s): Apr.
Final notification: None unless grant approved
Write: Eyvonne Moser, Asst. Secy.

Officers and Trustees:* T.R. Reckling III,* Pres.; Bert F. Winston, Jr.,* V.P.; Clyde J. Verheyden,* Secy.; Isla S. Reckling,* Treas.; Thomas E. Berry, Chaille W. Hawkins, Christiana R. McConn, James S. Reckling, T.R. "Cliffe" Reckling.
Number of staff: 1 full-time professional.
EIN: 741460482

3124
United Gas Pipe Line Corporate Giving Program
600 Travis
Houston 77002   (713) 229-4082
Application address: P.O. Box 1478, Houston, TX 77251-1478

Financial data (yr. ended 12/31/90): Total giving, $656,000, including $186,051 for grants, $426,949 for employee matching gifts and $43,000 for in-kind gifts.
Purpose and activities: Emphasis on health and human services, including United Way, drug abuse programs, and muscular dystrophy programs; support also for education, the arts, including music and theater, civic activities, and health. Funding is also given to local fire departments. In-kind contributions include printing and employee volunteerism.
Fields of interest: Education, health, humanities, arts, civic affairs, higher education, general charitable giving, music, theater.
Types of support: Employee matching gifts, general purposes, scholarship funds, in-kind gifts.
Limitations: Giving primarily in the Gulf Coast states: AL, FL, LA, MI and TX.
Application information: A formal proposal is required for major projects but a simple request is sufficient for requests under $500. Application form not required.
  Initial approach: Letter
  Deadline(s): Best time to apply is June
  Write: Jerrold Packler, Supervisor, Facilities Development
Number of staff: 3 part-time support.

3125
USAA Trust ▼
USAA Bldg., Special Payroll Svcs D-1-W
San Antonio 78288

Established in 1987 in TX.
Donor(s): United Services Automobile Assn., USAA Life Insurance Co.
Foundation type: Company-sponsored
Financial data (yr. ended 12/31/91): Assets, $2,846,258 (M); gifts received, $1,036,832; expenditures, $2,464,832; qualifying distributions, $2,455,000, including $2,455,000 for 6 grants (high: $2,000,000; low: $10,000).
Purpose and activities: Giving to universities, especially the U.S. Air Force, Naval, and other military academies, and for medical research.
Fields of interest: Higher education, military personnel, medical research.
Types of support: Endowment funds.
Limitations: Giving on a national basis. No grants to individuals.
Application information: Contributes only to pre-selected organizations. Applications not accepted.

Write: George H. Ensley and Chester A. Hammann, Trust Representatives
Trustee: Frost National Bank.
EIN: 746363461

3126
The Vale-Asche Foundation
910 River Oaks Bank Bldg.
2001 Kirby Dr., Suite 910
Houston 77019   (713) 520-7334

Incorporated in 1956 in DE.
Donor(s): Ruby Vale,‡ Fred B. Asche.‡
Foundation type: Independent
Financial data (yr. ended 11/30/91): Assets, $5,946,281 (M); expenditures, $277,980; qualifying distributions, $277,980, including $277,980 for 20 grants (high: $35,000; low: $1,500).
Purpose and activities: Grants for medical research, health care, child welfare, and aid to the aged and the handicapped; support also for secondary education and cultural programs, and projects that benefit the homeless.
Fields of interest: Medical research, health services, child welfare, aged, handicapped, cultural programs, secondary education, education, education—minorities, homeless, community development, drug abuse, AIDS, rehabilitation, hunger.
Types of support: Equipment, research, special projects.
Limitations: Giving primarily in Houston, TX. No grants to individuals, or for operating funds.
Application information: Request reviewed mid-Aug. through Oct. Application form not required.
  Initial approach: Letter
  Deadline(s): Aug. 15
  Board meeting date(s): Early Sept. and early Oct.
  Write: Mrs. Vale Asche Russell, Pres.
Officers and Trustees:* Mrs. Vale Asche Russell,* Pres.; Bettyann Asche Murray,* V.P.; William E. Blummer,* Secy.-Treas.; Asche Ackerman.
EIN: 516015320

3127
The Vaughn Foundation
P.O. Box 149036
Austin 78714-9036
Application address: 830 South Beckham, Tyler, TX 75701; Tel.: (903) 597-7652

Trust established in 1952 in TX.
Donor(s): Edgar H. Vaughn,‡ Lillie Mae Vaughn.‡
Foundation type: Independent
Financial data (yr. ended 12/31/90): Assets, $5,763,110 (M); expenditures, $331,069; qualifying distributions, $273,881, including $257,222 for 102 grants (high: $20,000; low: $25; average: $5-$50,000).
Fields of interest: Higher education, education, hospitals, health services, Protestant giving, child welfare.
Limitations: Giving primarily in the Southwest, with emphasis on Tyler, TX. No grants to individuals.
Application information: Application form not required.
  Initial approach: Letter

Copies of proposal: 1
Deadline(s): None
Write: Dr. Jim M. Vaughn, Dir.
Directors: James M. Vaughn, Jim M. Vaughn.
Trustee: Ameritrust Co., N.A.
Number of staff: 1 part-time support.
EIN: 756008953

3128
E. Paul and Helen Buck Waggoner Foundation, Inc.
P.O. Box 2130
Vernon 76384   (817) 552-2521

Incorporated in 1966 in TX.
Donor(s): E. Paul Waggoner,‡ Helen Buck Waggoner.‡
Foundation type: Independent
Financial data (yr. ended 04/30/91): Assets, $6,215,230 (M); expenditures, $260,890; qualifying distributions, $250,779, including $250,779 for 11 grants (high: $100,000; low: $432).
Purpose and activities: Giving for higher and secondary education, including agricultural research and scholarship funds; grants also for medical research and youth agencies.
Fields of interest: Higher education, secondary education, agriculture, medical research, youth.
Types of support: Building funds, scholarship funds, research.
Limitations: Giving primarily in TX.
Application information:
  Initial approach: Proposal
  Write: Gene W. Willingham, Dir.
Officers: Electra Waggoner Biggs, Pres.; Electra Biggs Winston, 1st V.P.; Helen Biggs Willingham, Secy.-Treas.
Directors: Gene W. Willingham, Charles F. Winston.
EIN: 751243683

3129
Marjorie T. Walthall Perpetual Charitable Trust
112 West Ridgewood Ct.
San Antonio 78212-2342   (512) 822-5433

Trust established in 1976 in TX.
Donor(s): Marjorie T. Walthall.
Foundation type: Independent
Financial data (yr. ended 12/31/90): Assets, $2,142,706 (M); expenditures, $147,997; qualifying distributions, $136,044, including $128,750 for 32 grants (high: $20,000; low: $1,000).
Purpose and activities: Emphasis on health, medical and nursing education, scientific research and similar activities; support also for an Episcopal church and animal welfare.
Fields of interest: Health, medical education, nursing, science and technology, medical research, Protestant giving, animal welfare.
Types of support: Scholarship funds, general purposes.
Limitations: Giving primarily in San Antonio, TX. No grants to individuals.
Application information:
  Initial approach: Letter
  Deadline(s): Oct. 1
  Write: Paul T. Walthall, Trustee

Trustees: Marjorie Walthall Fry, Paul T. Walthall, Wilson J. Walthall III.
EIN: 510170313

3130
Neva and Wesley West Foundation
P.O. Box 7
Houston 77001   (713) 850-7911

Trust established in 1956 in TX.
Donor(s): Wesley West,‡ Mrs. Wesley West.
Foundation type: Independent
Financial data (yr. ended 12/31/91): Assets, $18,475,422 (M); gifts received, $8,101,174; expenditures, $870,333; qualifying distributions, $830,000, including $830,000 for 9 grants (high: $250,000; low: $2,500).
Fields of interest: Education, higher education, health, medical research.
Types of support: General purposes, building funds, equipment, research, operating budgets.
Limitations: Giving primarily in TX. No grants to individuals, or for scholarships or fellowships; no loans.
Publications: Annual report.
Application information: Application form not required.
  Initial approach: Letter
  Copies of proposal: 1
  Deadline(s): Submit proposal in Nov.; deadline Dec. 1
  Board meeting date(s): Dec.
  Write: Marylene Weir
Trustees: W.H. Hodges, Betty Ann West Stedman, Stuart West Stedman, Mrs. Wesley West.
Number of staff: None.
EIN: 746039393
Recent health grants:
3130-1 Baylor College of Medicine, Department of Ophthalmology, Cullen Eye Institute, Houston, TX, $50,000. For research and education. 1990.
3130-2 Druid City Hospital Foundation, Tuscaloosa, AL, $40,000. For equipment purchase. 1990.
3130-3 Houston-Galveston Psychoanalytic Trust, Houston, TX, $75,000. For operating expenses. 1990.
3130-4 Methodist Hospital, Houston, TX, $25,000. For operating expenses. 1990.
3130-5 Retina Research Foundation, Houston, TX, $25,000. For research. 1990.
3130-6 Saint Joseph Hospital Foundation, Houston, TX, $25,000. For operating expenses. 1990.
3130-7 Texas Childrens Hospital, Houston, TX, $250,000. For capital campaign. 1990.

3131
J. M. West Texas Corporation
P.O. Box 491
Houston 77001

Incorporated in 1957 in TX.
Foundation type: Independent
Financial data (yr. ended 02/28/91): Assets, $5,737,312 (M); expenditures, $289,077; qualifying distributions, $256,300, including $252,500 for 18 grants (high: $37,500; low: $5,000).
Fields of interest: Higher education, secondary education, medical research, youth, arts.
Limitations: Giving primarily in TX, with some emphasis on Houston.
Application information:
  Initial approach: Letter
  Deadline(s): None
  Write: Coord. of Grants
Officers and Trustees:* William R. Lloyd, Jr.,* Pres.; William B. Blakemore II,* V.P.; Barbara Keyes, V.P.; John T. Trotter,* V.P.; Robert H. Parsley,* Secy.-Treas.; Margene West Lloyd.
EIN: 746040389

3132
Erle and Emma White Foundation
P.O. Box 4669
Wichita Falls 76308

Established in 1981 in TX.
Foundation type: Independent
Financial data (yr. ended 12/31/91): Assets, $4,071,472 (M); expenditures, $298,183; qualifying distributions, $286,006, including $271,300 for 42 grants (high: $40,000; low: $300).
Fields of interest: Protestant giving, social services, hospices, rehabilitation, higher education.
Limitations: Giving primarily in the Wichita Falls, TX, area. No grants to individuals.
Application information: Contributes only to pre-selected organizations. Applications not accepted.
Officers and Trustees:* Emma White,* Chair.; Marilyn Onstott,* Secy.-Treas.; Steve Onstott, Exec. Dir.; Carolyn Brown.
EIN: 751781596

3133
G. R. White Trust
c/o Team Bank, N.A.
P.O. Box 2050
Fort Worth 76113   (817) 884-4162

Established in 1965.
Donor(s): G.R. White.‡
Foundation type: Independent
Financial data (yr. ended 09/30/91): Assets, $6,943,700 (M); expenditures, $460,553; qualifying distributions, $363,746, including $360,523 for 41 grants (high: $75,000; low: $500).
Fields of interest: Hospitals, youth, higher education, legal education, religion—Christian, agriculture.
Types of support: General purposes, building funds, equipment, scholarship funds, professorships, student loans.
Limitations: Giving limited to TX. No grants to individuals.
Application information:
  Initial approach: Letter
  Deadline(s): Sept.
  Board meeting date(s): Annually, usually in the spring
  Final notification: Within 30 days
  Write: Joe T. Lenamon
Trustee: Team Bank, N.A.
Number of staff: None.
EIN: 756094930

3134
The Wills Foundation
P.O. Box 27534
Houston 77227-7534   (713) 965-9043
FAX: (713) 960-8111

Established in 1966 in TX and AR.
Donor(s): Fletcher S. Pratt,‡ Mrs. Fletcher S. Pratt.
Foundation type: Independent
Financial data (yr. ended 07/31/92): Assets, $3,732,841 (M); gifts received, $50,810; expenditures, $311,042; qualifying distributions, $311,042, including $309,040 for 10 grants (high: $40,000; low: $20,000).
Purpose and activities: Grants and post-doctoral fellowships only for research regarding hereditary diseases, particularly Huntington's Disease.
Fields of interest: Medical research.
Types of support: Research, fellowships.
Application information:
  Initial approach: Proposal
  Copies of proposal: 6
  Deadline(s): Pre-application letters must be received by Sept. 1 for Jan. 1 funding and Mar. 1 for July 1 funding
  Final notification: 30 days
  Write: Alice Evans Pratt, Pres.
Officers and Directors:* Charles Dillingham,* Chair.; Alice Evans Pratt,* Pres. and Treas.; Peter E. Pratt,* V.P.; St. Clare Pratt Seifert,* Secy.; John O. Heldenfels, Michael J. Murray, M.D.
Number of staff: 4 part-time professional; 2 part-time support.
EIN: 746078200

3135
The Pauline Sterne Wolff Memorial Foundation
c/o Texas Commerce Bank
P.O. Box 2558
Houston 77252   (713) 236-4407

Incorporated in 1922 in TX.
Foundation type: Independent
Financial data (yr. ended 12/31/90): Assets, $12,792,893 (M); expenditures, $841,765; qualifying distributions, $621,433, including $602,433 for 15 grants (high: $300,000; low: $2,500).
Purpose and activities: Giving primarily for Jewish welfare organizations, especially a home for the elderly; support also for medical education and research and hospitals.
Fields of interest: Jewish welfare, medical education, medical research, hospitals.
Limitations: Giving limited to TX, with emphasis on Harris County. No grants to individuals.
Application information:
  Initial approach: Letter
  Deadline(s): Dec. 1
  Write: Robert H. Richardson, Jr., Custodian, Texas Commerce Bank
Trustees: Jenard M. Gross, Regina J. Rogers, Marc J. Shapiro, Henry J.N. Taub, Henry J.N. Taub II.
EIN: 741110698

3136
B. M. Woltman Foundation
2200 West Loop South, Suite 810
Houston 77027
Application address: c/o Frederick Boden, Exec.
Dir., Lutheran Church-Missouri Synod, 7900
U.S. 290 East, Austin, TX 78724

Trust established in 1948 in TX.
Donor(s): B.M. Woltman,‡ Woltman Furniture
Co., and others.
Foundation type: Independent
Financial data (yr. ended 12/31/90): Assets,
$5,090,196 (M); gifts received, $1,252;
expenditures, $311,867; qualifying distributions,
$237,168, including $168,100 for 6 grants (high:
$121,000; low: $3,000) and $65,000 for 27
grants to individuals (high: $4,000; low: $600).
Purpose and activities: Giving only for Lutheran
church support, local church-related secondary
schools, hospitals, and higher education;
scholarships for students preparing for the
Lutheran ministry or for teaching in Lutheran
schools.
Fields of interest: Protestant giving, secondary
education, higher education, hospitals,
theological education.
Types of support: Student aid, general purposes.
Limitations: Giving limited to TX.
Application information: Application forms
provided for scholarships.
  Deadline(s): Before school term begins for
    scholarships
  Write: W.J. Woltman, Pres.
Officers and Trustees:* Richard D. Chandler, Jr.,*
Pres.; Carloss Morris,* Secy.-Treas.; Robert H.
McCanne, Mgr.; Rev. Donald G. Black, Rev. Louis
Pabor, Michael Richter, W.J. Woltman.
EIN: 741402184

3137
Lola Wright Foundation, Inc.
P.O. Box 1138
Georgetown 78627-1138   (512) 869-2574
Austin tel.: (512) 255-5353

Incorporated in 1954 in TX.
Donor(s): Johnie E. Wright.‡
Foundation type: Independent
Financial data (yr. ended 12/31/90): Assets,
$8,812,301 (M); expenditures, $1,122,002;
qualifying distributions, $1,001,578, including
$935,643 for 63 grants (high: $70,000; low:
$1,500; average: $1,500-$25,000).
Purpose and activities: Emphasis on social
services, including drug and alcohol abuse
programs, family services and planning,
organizations providing assistance to minorities,
the aged and youth; legal services; community
funds; and health services and hospitals,
including rehabilitation programs, AIDS research,
diseases of the heart, and organizations serving
the handicapped. Support also for the arts and
culture, including fine and performing arts; early
childhood, adult, higher and other education;
media and communications; and the
environment.

Fields of interest: Social services, family services,
minorities, aged, youth, community funds, health,
AIDS, arts, education, higher education.
Types of support: Matching funds, building funds,
equipment, endowment funds, continuing
support, renovation projects, research, special
projects.
Limitations: Giving limited to TX, primarily the
Austin area. No grants to individuals, or for
operating budgets.
Publications: Application guidelines, annual
report.
Application information: Application form not
required.
  Initial approach: Letter
  Copies of proposal: 9
  Deadline(s): Feb. 28 and Aug. 31
  Board meeting date(s): May and Nov.
  Final notification: May 15 and Nov. 15
  Write: Patrick H. O'Donnell, Pres.
Officers and Directors:* Patrick H. O'Donnell,*
Pres.; William Hilgers,* V.P.; Vivian E. Todd,*
Secy.-Treas.; Wilford Flowers, Linda Guererro,
James Meyers, Carole Rylander.
Number of staff: 1 part-time professional; 1
part-time support.
EIN: 746054717

3138
The Zachry Foundation
310 South St. Mary's St., Suite 2500
San Antonio 78205   (512) 554-4663
FAX: (512) 554-4605

Incorporated in 1960 in TX.
Donor(s): H.B. Zachry Co. International, H.B.
Zachry Co., H.B. Zachry, Sr.‡
Foundation type: Independent
Financial data (yr. ended 12/31/91): Assets,
$7,597,705 (M); gifts received, $700,000;
expenditures, $564,710; qualifying distributions,
$413,042, including $402,995 for 32 grants
(high: $64,000; low: $1,000).
Fields of interest: Education, arts, humanities,
health, science and technology.
Types of support: Capital campaigns, annual
campaigns, continuing support, internships,
research, scholarship funds, special projects,
matching funds.
Limitations: Giving limited to TX, with emphasis
on San Antonio. No grants to individuals.
Application information: Application form not
required.
  Initial approach: Letter
  Copies of proposal: 1
  Deadline(s): Feb. 15
  Board meeting date(s): 3 times per year
  Write: Pamela O'Connor, Exec. Dir.
Officers and Trustees:* J.P. Zachry,* Pres.; Murray
L. Johnston, Jr.,* Secy.; Charles Ebrom,* Treas.;
H.B. Zachry, Jr., Mollie S. Zachry.
Number of staff: 1 full-time professional.
EIN: 741485544

3139
The Zale Foundation
3102 Maple Ave., Suite 160
Dallas 75201   (214) 855-0627

Incorporated in 1951 in TX.
Donor(s): Members of the Zale and Lipshy
families.
Foundation type: Independent
Financial data (yr. ended 12/31/91): Assets,
$18,912,841 (M); gifts received, $346,300;
expenditures, $1,303,660; qualifying
distributions, $1,110,997, including $1,016,296
for 92 grants (high: $200,000; low: $100).
Purpose and activities: Primary areas of interest
include programs aiding the homeless and other
social services; support also for a university
medical center, Jewish religious and welfare
organizations, higher education, and hospitals.
Fields of interest: Jewish giving, Jewish welfare,
higher education, education, hospitals, social
services, disadvantaged, child welfare, homeless.
Types of support: Operating budgets, seed
money, professorships, technical assistance.
Limitations: No grants to individuals, or for
annual campaigns, emergency funds, deficit
financing, renovation projects, endowment funds,
conferences, study, films, publications, land
acquisition, matching gifts, or continuing support;
no loans. No grants for periods of more than 3 to
5 years.
Publications: Program policy statement,
application guidelines.
Application information: Application form not
required.
  Initial approach: Letter and proposal of not
    more than 2 or 3 pages
  Copies of proposal: 1
  Deadline(s): None
  Board meeting date(s): Semiannually
  Final notification: 3 months
  Write: Dr. Michael F. Romaine, Pres.
Officers and Trustees:* Donald Zale,* Chair.;
Michael F. Romaine,* Pres.; George Tobolowsky,
Secy.-Treas.; Leo Fields, Gloria Landsberg, Bruce
A. Lipshy, Abe Zale, David Zale.
Number of staff: 1 full-time professional; 1
full-time support.
EIN: 756037429

3140
William & Sylvia Zale Foundation
c/o Joe Bock
P.O. Box 223566
Dallas 75222   (214) 987-4688

Established in 1951 in TX.
Donor(s): Eugene Zale, Sylvia Zale, Lew D. Zale.
Foundation type: Independent
Financial data (yr. ended 08/31/90): Assets,
$3,716,931 (M); expenditures, $609,977;
qualifying distributions, $591,029, including
$591,029 for 47 grants (high: $50,000; low:
$100).
Fields of interest: Jewish giving, Jewish welfare,
hospitals, education.
Limitations: No grants to individuals, or for
scholarships, fellowships, or prizes; no loans.
Application information: Contributes only to
pre-selected organizations. Applications not
accepted.
Trustees: Eugene Zale, Lew D. Zale, Theodore
Zale.
EIN: 756037591

UTAH

3141
Ruth Eleanor Bamberger and John Ernest Bamberger Memorial Foundation
1201 Walker Bldg.
Salt Lake City 84111   (801) 364-2045

Incorporated in 1947 in UT.
Donor(s): Ernest Bamberger,‡ Eleanor F.
Bamberger.‡
Foundation type: Independent
Financial data (yr. ended 12/31/90): Assets,
$8,660,933 (M); expenditures, $425,062;
qualifying distributions, $405,511, including
$324,237 for 117 grants (high: $25,000; low:
$50) and $58,597 for 66 grants to individuals
(high: $2,997; low: $200).
Purpose and activities: Support for secondary
education, especially undergraduate scholarships
for student nurses, and for schools, hospitals and
health agencies, youth and child welfare agencies
and wildlife; occasional loans for medical
education.
Fields of interest: Secondary education, nursing,
hospitals, health services, youth, child welfare,
wildlife, medical education, general charitable
giving.
Types of support: Operating budgets, continuing
support, scholarship funds, equipment, student
aid, student loans, capital campaigns.
Limitations: Giving primarily in UT. No grants to
individuals (except for scholarships to local
students), or for endowment or building funds,
research, or matching gifts.
Application information: Interview required for
scholarship applicants. Application form not
required.
  Initial approach: Letter
  Copies of proposal: 1
  Deadline(s): None
  Board meeting date(s): Bimonthly beginning in
    Feb.
  Final notification: 2 months
  Write: William H. Olwell, Secy.-Treas.
Officer and Members:* William H. Olwell,*
Secy.-Treas.; Clifford L. Ashton, Clarence
Bamberger, Jr., Margaret Dooly Olwell, Roy W.
Simmons.
Number of staff: 1 part-time support.
EIN: 876116540

3142
Val A. Browning Charitable Foundation
P.O. Box 9936
Ogden 84409   (801) 626-9533
Application address: 1528 28th St., Ogden, UT
84401

Established in 1975 in UT.
Donor(s): Val A. Browning.
Foundation type: Independent
Financial data (yr. ended 12/31/90): Assets,
$5,502,662 (M); gifts received, $420,008;
expenditures, $550,839; qualifying distributions,
$520,140, including $519,700 for 13 grants
(high: $200,000; low: $100).

Purpose and activities: Support primarily for a
college and a historical center; some support for
health associations, social services, arts and
culture, and higher and other education.
Fields of interest: Higher education, hospitals,
health, social services, cultural programs, arts,
education, secondary education.
Types of support: Annual campaigns, building
funds, capital campaigns, continuing support,
endowment funds, special projects.
Limitations: Giving primarily in Ogden and Salt
Lake City, UT.
Application information: Application form not
required.
  Initial approach: Letter
  Copies of proposal: 1
  Deadline(s): Preferably by Sept. 30
  Write: Val A. Browning, Chair.
Directors: Val A. Browning, Chair.; Bruce
Browning, John Val Browning, Carol Dumke,
Judith B. Jones.
Trustee: First Security Bank of Utah, N.A.
EIN: 876167851

3143
Robert Harold Burton Private Foundation
c/o First Security Bank of Utah, N.A.
P.O. Box 30007
Salt Lake City 84130-0007   (801) 350-5562

Established in 1985 in UT.
Donor(s): Robert H. Burton.‡
Foundation type: Independent
Financial data (yr. ended 12/31/90): Assets,
$14,260,141 (M); gifts received, $50,450;
expenditures, $746,962; qualifying distributions,
$792,168, including $710,788 for 20 grants
(high: $112,455; low: $3,000).
Fields of interest: Health, hospitals, higher
education, secondary education, cultural
programs.
Types of support: Building funds, equipment.
Limitations: Giving primarily in Salt Lake County,
UT.
Application information: Application form not
required.
  Deadline(s): None
  Write: Patricia Richards, Admin.
Members: Richard Robert Burton, Chair.; Dan
Harold Burton, Judith B. Hoyle.
Trustee: First Security Bank of Utah, N.A.
EIN: 742425567

3144
Castle Foundation
c/o West One Trust Co.
P.O. Box 3058
Salt Lake City 84110-3058   (801) 534-6085

Established in 1953.
Foundation type: Independent
Financial data (yr. ended 06/30/91): Assets,
$2,161,685 (M); expenditures, $130,102;
qualifying distributions, $120,322, including
$111,600 for 50 grants (high: $9,000; low: $600).
Fields of interest: Arts, higher education,
secondary education, social services, child
welfare, hospitals.
Types of support: Scholarship funds, special
projects, equipment, operating budgets.

Limitations: Giving limited to UT, with emphasis
on Salt Lake City.
Application information: Application form
required.
  Initial approach: Letter
  Deadline(s): None
  Write: Gilbert M. Bean, Trust Officer, West One
    Trust Co.
Trustee: West One Trust Co.
EIN: 876117177

3145
Lawrence T. and Janet T. Dee Foundation
3905 Harrison Blvd., Suite W306
Ogden 84403   (801) 621-4863
Application address: c/o W. John Lamborn, First
Security Bank of Utah, N.A., P.O. Box 30007,
Salt Lake City, UT 84130

Established in 1971 in UT.
Donor(s): L.T. Dee,‡ Janet T. Dee.‡
Foundation type: Independent
Financial data (yr. ended 12/31/91): Assets,
$5,700,000 (L); expenditures, $270,000;
qualifying distributions, $248,000, including
$248,000 for 32 grants (high: $100,000; low:
$500; average: $1,000-$10,000).
Purpose and activities: Emphasis on health
services; support also for education, cultural
programs, including the fine and performing arts,
and social service agencies, including
rehabilitation programs, family services, and child
welfare and development.
Fields of interest: Health services, education,
higher education, cultural programs, fine arts,
performing arts, social services, rehabilitation,
family services, child welfare.
Types of support: Annual campaigns, building
funds, equipment, endowment funds, research,
scholarship funds, matching funds, special
projects.
Limitations: Giving primarily in UT. No grants to
individuals; no loans.
Publications: Application guidelines.
Application information: Application form not
required.
  Initial approach: Letter
  Copies of proposal: 3
  Deadline(s): Sept.
  Board meeting date(s): Mar., June, and Sept.
  Write: Thomas D. Dee II, Chair.
Officers: Thomas D. Dee II, Chair.; Thomas D.
Dee III, V.P.; David L. Dee, V.P.
Trustee: First Security Bank of Utah, N.A.
EIN: 876150803

3146
Dr. Ezekiel R. and Edna Wattis Dumke Foundation
448 South 400 East, No. 100
Salt Lake City 84111   (801) 328-3531

Incorporated in 1959 in UT.
Foundation type: Independent
Financial data (yr. ended 12/31/91): Assets,
$5,805,450 (M); expenditures, $304,449;
qualifying distributions, $249,278, including
$217,561 for 20 grants (high: $47,500; low:
$1,000).
Fields of interest: Cultural programs, health
services, youth, higher education, hospitals.

Types of support: Building funds, technical assistance, research, general purposes, equipment.
Limitations: Giving primarily in UT and ID. No grants to individuals.
Application information: Application form required.
Initial approach: Telephone or letter requesting application form
Copies of proposal: 4
Deadline(s): Feb. 1 and July 1
Board meeting date(s): Apr. and Sept.
Final notification: Within 6 weeks after board meeting
Officers and Directors: Ezekiel R. Dumke, Jr.,* Pres.; Martha Ann Dumke Healy,* V.P.; Edmund E. Dumke, Treas.; Valerie Dumke Rork, Claire Dumke Ryberg, Nancy Healy Schwanfelder.
Number of staff: None.
EIN: 876119783

3147
Willard L. Eccles Charitable Foundation
P.O. Box 45385
Salt Lake City 84145-0385 (801) 532-1500

Established in 1981 in UT.
Foundation type: Independent
Financial data (yr. ended 03/31/91): Assets, $25,742,174 (M); expenditures, $1,251,229; qualifying distributions, $1,146,899, including $1,097,032 for 28 grants (high: $125,000; low: $1,000; average: $10,000-$150,000).
Fields of interest: Health associations, health services, medical research, medical education.
Types of support: Equipment, research.
Limitations: Giving primarily in UT, with emphasis in the Ogden, UT, area. No grants to individuals, or for land acquisition, construction, building purposes, or to endow medical education positions.
Application information:
Initial approach: Letter
Deadline(s): Month preceeding meeting date
Board meeting date(s): Mar., June, and Oct.
Final notification: Following meeting
Write: Clark P. Giles, Secy.
Officers: Ruth P. Eccles, Chair.; Clark P. Giles, Secy.
Committee Members: Barbara E. Coit, William E. Coit, M.D., William H. Coit, Stephen E. Denkers, Stephen G. Denkers, Susan E. Denkers.
Trustee: First Security Bank of Utah, N.A.
Number of staff: None.
EIN: 942759395

3148
The George S. and Dolores Dore Eccles Foundation ▼
Deseret Bldg.
79 South Main St., 12th Fl.
Salt Lake City 84111 (801) 350-5336

Incorporated in 1958 in UT; absorbed Lillian Ethel Dufton Charitable Trust in 1981.
Donor(s): George S. Eccles.‡
Foundation type: Independent
Financial data (yr. ended 12/31/90): Assets, $104,619,694 (M); gifts received, $1,000,000; expenditures, $6,920,805; qualifying distributions, $6,519,277, including $6,437,792

for 122 grants (high: $700,000; low: $1,000; average: $10,000-$100,000).
Purpose and activities: Emphasis on higher education, hospitals and medical research, the performing and visual arts, and social service and youth agencies.
Fields of interest: Higher education, hospitals, medical research, performing arts, arts, fine arts, social services, youth, child welfare, economics.
Types of support: Annual campaigns, building funds, capital campaigns, equipment, general purposes, matching funds, professorships, program-related investments, research, scholarship funds.
Limitations: Giving primarily in the Intermountain area, particularly UT. No grants to individuals, or for endowment funds.
Application information: Application form required.
Initial approach: Letter
Copies of proposal: 3
Deadline(s): Two weeks prior to board meeting
Board meeting date(s): Quarterly
Final notification: Following meeting
Write: David P. Gandner, Chair., or Lisa Eccles
Officers and Directors: David P. Gardner,* Chair.; Spencer F. Eccles,* Pres.; Alonzo W. Watson, Jr.,* Secy.; Robert Graham, Treas.; Delores Dore Eccles.
Number of staff: 1
EIN: 876118245
Recent health grants:
3148-1 Alliance House, Salt Lake City, UT, $15,000. For general support. 1990.
3148-2 Arthritis Foundation, Utah Chapter, Salt Lake City, UT, $15,000. For rheumatology fellowship program. 1990.
3148-3 Autism Society of Utah, Salt Lake City, UT, $24,530. To purchase computer equipment. 1990.
3148-4 House Ear Institute, Los Angeles, CA, $50,000. For general support. 1990.
3148-5 National Society to Prevent Blindness, Salt Lake City, UT, $25,000. For general support. 1990.
3148-6 Planned Parenthood Association of Utah, Salt Lake City, UT, $15,000. For rural outreach programs. 1990.
3148-7 Primary Childrens Medical Center, Salt Lake City, UT, $333,333. For construction of new hospital. 1990.
3148-8 Saint Benedicts Foundation, Ogden, UT, $25,000. To purchase cancer treatment planning computer. 1990.
3148-9 University of Utah, Salt Lake City, UT, $300,000. For John A. Dixon Laser Institute. 1990.
3148-10 University of Utah, Institute of Human Genetics, Salt Lake City, UT, $700,000. 1990.
3148-11 University of Utah, School of Nursing, Salt Lake City, UT, $95,000. 1990.
3148-12 Weber State College, School of Allied Health Sciences, Ogden, UT, $50,000. To purchase equipment. 1990.

3149
Marriner S. Eccles Foundation ▼
701 Deseret Bldg.
79 South Main St.
Salt Lake City 84111 (801) 322-0116

Established in 1973 in Utah.

Donor(s): Marriner S. Eccles.‡
Foundation type: Independent
Financial data (yr. ended 03/31/91): Assets, $20,201,649 (M); expenditures, $1,240,650; qualifying distributions, $1,150,644, including $1,095,132 for 83 grants (high: $100,000; low: $1,500; average: $1,000-$10,000).
Purpose and activities: Giving primarily for higher education; health, hospitals, and medical research; arts and culture, including the performing arts, fine arts, and museums; and family and social services, including programs for rehabilitation, the aged, drug and alcohol abuse, welfare, youth, women, and the homeless.
Fields of interest: Medical research, hospitals, rehabilitation, mental health, alcoholism, drug abuse, cultural programs, arts, humanities, fine arts, performing arts, social services, family planning, family services, aged, women, youth, housing, higher education.
Types of support: Equipment, seed money, operating budgets, general purposes, scholarship funds, research, matching funds.
Limitations: Giving limited to UT. No grants to individuals, or for capital expenditures for construction of buildings.
Application information: Application form not required.
Initial approach: Proposal
Copies of proposal: 7
Deadline(s): None
Board meeting date(s): Quarterly, usually beginning in July
Final notification: Within a week after meeting
Write: Erma E. Hogan, Mgr.
Officers and Committee Members: Sara M. Eccles,* Chair.; Alonzo W. Watson, Jr.,* Secy.; John D. Eccles, Spencer F. Eccles, Harold J. Steele, Elmer D. Tucker.
Trustee: First Security Bank of Utah, N.A.
Number of staff: 1 full-time professional.
EIN: 237185855

3150
Emma Eccles Jones Foundation
c/o First Security Bank of Utah, N.A.
79 South Main St., Personal Trust, 3rd Fl.
Salt Lake City 84111
Application address: 400 Deseret Bldg., Salt Lake City, UT 84111; Tel.: (801) 532-1500

Established in 1972 in UT.
Foundation type: Independent
Financial data (yr. ended 08/31/91): Assets, $61,363,236 (M); gifts received, $4,145; expenditures, $309,940; qualifying distributions, $241,666, including $241,613 for grants.
Fields of interest: Medical research, health, family planning, social services, cultural programs.
Limitations: Giving primarily in UT.
Application information: Application form not required.
Deadline(s): None
Write: Clark P. Gilis
Trustee: First Security Bank of Utah, N.A.
EIN: 876155073

3151
Herbert I. and Elsa B. Michael Foundation
c/o West One Trust Co.
P.O. Box 3058
Salt Lake City 84111-3058

Established in 1950 in UT.
Donor(s): Elsa B. Michael.‡
Foundation type: Independent
Financial data (yr. ended 09/30/91): Assets, $4,616,076 (M); expenditures, $250,947; qualifying distributions, $223,783, including $203,500 for 59 grants (high: $11,500; low: $1,000).
Purpose and activities: Emphasis on cultural programs and higher and secondary education; support also for hospitals and social service agencies.
Fields of interest: Cultural programs, higher education, secondary education, hospitals, social services.
Limitations: Giving primarily in UT. No support for sectarian religious activities.
Application information:
  Initial approach: Proposal
  Deadline(s): None
  Write: Gilbert M. Bean, Trust Officer, West One Trust Co.
Trustees: William H. Adams, K. Jay Holdsworth, Hal Swanson, West One Trust Co.
Advisory Committee: Francis W. Douglas, Gordon Hall, Chase N. Peterson.
EIN: 876122556

3152
Questar Corporate Giving Program
180 East First South St.
P.O. Box 11150
Salt Lake City 84147   (801) 534-5435

Financial data (yr. ended 12/31/90): Total giving, $392,000, including $352,000 for grants and $40,000 for in-kind gifts.
Purpose and activities: Support for the aged, the disadvantaged, the handicapped, and the homeless; the arts and culture, including performing arts, and museums, child welfare and family services, education, hospital building funds, community development, health and health services, the humanities, and volunteerism.
Fields of interest: Aged, animal welfare, arts, child welfare, education, family services, general charitable giving, handicapped, health, health services, homeless, museums, community development, cultural programs, disadvantaged, hospitals—building funds, humanities, hunger, performing arts, volunteerism, business education, engineering.
Types of support: Building funds, scholarship funds, special projects, donated products, loaned talent, employee volunteer services, annual campaigns, in-kind gifts, loaned talent.
Limitations: Giving primarily in service and operating locations in UT and WY. No support for religious or fraternal organizations. No grants for group trips, exhibitions, or operating expenses.
Application information: Company has a staff that only handles giving. Application form not required.
  Initial approach: Letter; send to headquarters
  Copies of proposal: 1
  Board meeting date(s): Every 6-8 weeks

Write: Janice Bates, Dir. Commun. Affairs
Number of staff: 1 part-time professional; 1 part-time support.

3153
James LeVoy Sorenson Foundation
2511 South West Temple
Salt Lake City 84115   (801) 481-7300

Established in 1986.
Foundation type: Independent
Financial data (yr. ended 12/31/90): Assets, $386,757 (M); expenditures, $239,710; qualifying distributions, $236,110, including $235,486 for 14 grants (high: $110,000; low: $100).
Fields of interest: Social services, family planning, medical research, general charitable giving.
Types of support: Scholarship funds, general purposes.
Limitations: Giving primarily in Salt Lake City, UT. No grants to individuals.
Application information: Applications submitted early in the year have a better chance of funding. Application form not required.
  Initial approach: Letter
  Write: Christy Wright
Trustees: James LeVoy Sorenson, James Lee Sorenson.
EIN: 870440827

3154
Dr. W. C. Swanson Family Foundation
257 37th St.
Ogden 84405   (801) 399-5837

Established in 1978.
Donor(s): W.C. Swanson.‡
Foundation type: Independent
Financial data (yr. ended 12/31/90): Assets, $19,907,360 (M); gifts received, $23,701,184; expenditures, $159,501; qualifying distributions, $145,800, including $132,100 for 34 grants (high: $30,000; low: $400).
Fields of interest: Education, youth, homeless, hospitals, performing arts.
Types of support: Scholarship funds, building funds, operating budgets.
Limitations: Giving primarily in UT, with emphasis on Ogden. No grants to individuals.
Application information:
  Initial approach: Letter
  Deadline(s): None
  Write: Lew Costley, Trustee.
Officer: W. Charles Swanson, Mgr.
Trustee: Lew Costley.
EIN: 942478549

3155
Arthur L. Swim Foundation
1095 South 800 East, No. 4
Orem 84058

Established in 1942 in CA.
Foundation type: Independent
Financial data (yr. ended 12/31/90): Assets, $9,153,592 (M); expenditures, $740,725; qualifying distributions, $638,585, including $638,585 for 11 grants (high: $200,000; low: $85).

Purpose and activities: Giving primarily for education, with emphasis on medical education; support also for legal organizations.
Fields of interest: Education, medical education, law and justice.
Types of support: Equipment, capital campaigns, general purposes.
Limitations: Giving primarily in UT and CA. No grants to individuals.
Application information: Contributes only to pre-selected organizations. Applications not accepted.
Trustees: Marilyn S. Lenahan, Gaylord K. Swim, Katherine M. Swim, Roger C. Swim.
EIN: 826007432

3156
Thrasher Research Fund ▼
50 East North Temple St., 7th Fl.
Salt Lake City 84150   (801) 240-4753
FAX: (801) 240-1417

Established in 1977 in UT.
Donor(s): E.W. "Al" Thrasher.
Foundation type: Independent
Financial data (yr. ended 12/31/91): Assets, $34,664,235 (M); expenditures, $2,177,812; qualifying distributions, $1,952,452, including $1,952,452 for grants.
Purpose and activities: To promote both national and international child health research. The fund currently emphasizes practical and applied interventions that have the potential to improve the health of children throughout the world.
Fields of interest: Child welfare, medical sciences, nutrition, health, medical research.
Types of support: Research.
Limitations: Giving on a domestic and international basis. No support for studies in the areas of abortion, reproductive physiology, contraceptive technology, or sexually transmitted disease. No grants for conferences, workshops, or symposia. No support for general operations, construction or renovation of buildings or facilities, scholarships, or purchase of equipment; no loans.
Publications: Multi-year report (including application guidelines), informational brochure.
Application information: Application form required.
  Initial approach: Consultation by telephone or letter, followed by a 4-page prospectus. After initial prospectus review, applicant is notified whether a full proposal is requested. If so, an application kit is provided.
  Copies of proposal: 8
  Deadline(s): None
  Board meeting date(s): May and Nov.
  Final notification: 6-9 months
  Write: Robert M. Briem, Assoc. Dir.
Executive Committee: Glenn L. Pace, Chair.; E.W. "Al" Thrasher, Vice-Chair.; Victor L. Brown, Aileen H. Clyde, Isaac C. Ferguson, Addie Fuhriman, Harry L. Gibbons, Cecil O. Samuelson, Jr., Mary Ann Q. Wood.
Number of staff: 1 full-time professional; 2 part-time professional; 1 full-time support; 1 part-time support.
Recent health grants:
3156-1 Baylor College of Medicine, Department of Pediatrics, Houston, TX, $132,875. To investigate maternal energy balance as

determinant of lactation performance and resultant infant growth. Study will be conducted in Mexico. 1991.

3156-2 Institute for Research and Evaluation, Salt Lake City, UT, $103,485. To evaluate effectiveness of character/education/values program to determine its potential in teaching positive values and behavior to elementary school children, thus reducing risk behaviors and increasing healthy behaviors. 1991.

3156-3 Johns Hopkins University, School of Hygiene and Public Health, Department of International Health, Baltimore, MD,

$109,921. For research to determine efficacy of zinc supplemention in reducing diarrheal morbidity. Study will be conducted with permanent residents of Kal Kaji slum in New Delhi, India. 1991.

3156-4 Johns Hopkins University, School of Medicine, Baltimore, MD, $146,936. To determine child health benefits of linking vitamin A supplemention to Expanded Programme on Immunization. Project examines impact of vitamin A on immune responses, growth and hemtopiesis for clinical trial group of 280 children in Indonesia. 1991.

3156-5 University of California, Davis, CA, $152,188. For research to determine effects of introducing complementary foods on breast milk intake and maternal fertility in Honduras. 1991.

3156-6 Wageningen Agricultural University, Department of Human Nutrition, Wageningen, Netherlands, $81,600. To study impact of administration of iodine and iron supplements on mental and psychomotor performance and physical development of children in iodine-deficient district of Malawi. 1991.

VERMONT

3157
Lintilhac Foundation
100 Harbor Rd.
Shelburne 05482   (802) 985-4106

Established in 1975.
Donor(s): Claire Malcolm Lintilhac.‡
Foundation type: Independent
Financial data (yr. ended 12/31/90): Assets,
$6,683,243 (M); gifts received, $797,564;
expenditures, $694,952; qualifying distributions,
$632,814, including $632,814 for grants (high:
$166,667).
Purpose and activities: Support for medical
education programs at specified institutions in VT;
support also for health services, community
development, civic projects and educational
institutions.
Fields of interest: Medical education, education,
health services, community development, civic
affairs, family planning, family services,
environment, marine sciences.
Types of support: Annual campaigns, building
funds, capital campaigns, conferences and
seminars, continuing support, equipment, general
purposes, land acquisition, lectureships, matching
funds, professorships, renovation projects,
scholarship funds, seed money, special projects.
Limitations: Giving primarily in north central VT,
including Chittenden, Lamoille, and Washington
counties. No grants to individuals.
Publications: Annual report.
Application information: Application form not
required.
   Initial approach: Proposal
   Copies of proposal: 4
   Deadline(s): None
   Board meeting date(s): Quarterly
   Write: Crea S. Lintilhac, V.P.
Officers and Directors:* Philip M. Lintilhac,*
Pres.; Crea S. Lintilhac,* V.P. and Secy.; Raeman P.
Sopher,* Treas.
Number of staff: 1 full-time support; 1 part-time
support.
EIN: 510176851

3158
National Life Insurance Corporate
   ### Contributions Program
National Life Dr.
Montpelier 05604   (802) 229-3333

Financial data (yr. ended 12/31/90): Total giving,
$235,000, including $225,000 for 200 grants
(high: $15,000; low: $50) and $10,000 for 23
in-kind gifts.
Purpose and activities: Giving primarily for
health, including AIDS programs, and safety,

education and higher education, arts and culture
and civic, and community affairs; in-kind
contributions.
Fields of interest: AIDS, arts, cultural programs,
education, fine arts, higher education, safety,
women, performing arts, health.
Types of support: Annual campaigns, continuing
support, special projects, general purposes,
capital campaigns, operating budgets, in-kind
gifts, donated equipment, use of facilities, loaned
talent.
Limitations: Giving primarily in central VT; low
priority for programs outside of VT. No support for
political candidates, officeholders or parties,
fraternal, veterans', labor, or international
organizations, churches or religious groups,
groups on either side of controversial community
issues, and United Way member organizations
unless project is beyond the bounds of United
Way funding and meets other National Life
criteria. No grants to individuals.
Publications: Informational brochure (including
application guidelines).
Application information: Contributions are
handled by Communications Dept. Application
form not required.
   Initial approach: Letter; send to headquarters
   Copies of proposal: 1
   Final notification: 3 months
   Write: Jane W. Robb, Dir., Corp. Rels.
Number of staff: 2 part-time professional; 1
part-time support.

3159
Walter Scott Foundation
P.O. Box 1161
Wilmington 05363   (802) 464-5016
Additional mailing address: Three Grand Place,
Newtown, CT 06470; Tel.: (203) 426-4225

Incorporated in 1903 in NY.
Foundation type: Independent
Financial data (yr. ended 09/30/91): Assets,
$4,853,297 (M); expenditures, $288,874;
qualifying distributions, $236,664, including
$218,900 for 36 grants (high: $30,000; low:
$400; average: $2,000-$6,000).
Purpose and activities: Aid to institutions
concerned with handicapped children and adults.
Fields of interest: Child welfare, handicapped,
medical research.
Types of support: Operating budgets, continuing
support, annual campaigns, seed money, building
funds, equipment, endowment funds, research.
Limitations: Giving primarily in the New York,
NY, metropolitan area. No grants to individuals,
or for matching gifts; no loans.
Application information: Applications not
accepted.
   Board meeting date(s): Semiannually in the
      spring and early Sept.
   Write: Thorpe A. Nickerson, Pres.
Officers and Directors:* Thorpe A. Nickerson,*
Pres. and Secy.-Treas.; Jocelyn A. Nickerson, V.P.

and Exec. Dir.; Brett R. Nickerson,* V.P.; Lisa B.
Nickerson,* V.P.; Norman A. Hill.
Number of staff: None.
EIN: 135681161

3160
The Vermont Community Foundation
P.O. Box 30
Middlebury 05753   (802) 388-9955

Established in 1986 in VT.
Foundation type: Community
Financial data (yr. ended 12/31/89): Assets,
$2,934,855 (M); gifts received, $2,241,054;
expenditures, $218,526; qualifying distributions,
$85,150, including $85,150 for 36 grants.
Purpose and activities: Support for the arts and
humanities, education, health, public affairs and
community development, and social services.
The foundation is interested in projects which
increase citizens' commitment to community
needs, increase efficiency of nonprofit agencies,
eliminate duplication of services, develop
self-reliance, emphasize prevention as well as
treatment, and develop and disseminate seminal
research on VT.
Fields of interest: Arts, humanities, education,
health, public policy, community development,
social services.
Types of support: Conferences and seminars,
consulting services, exchange programs,
internships, program-related investments,
publications, renovation projects, research,
scholarship funds, fellowships, seed money,
student loans, technical assistance.
Limitations: Giving limited to VT. No support for
religious purposes. No grants for individual or for
annual campaigns, building funds, continuing
support, deficit financing, equipment and
materials, general endowments, land acquisition,
or operating budgets.
Publications: Informational brochure, application
guidelines, newsletter.
Application information: Application form not
required.
   Initial approach: Telephone, letter, or personal
      visit
   Deadline(s): May 1 and Nov. 1
   Board meeting date(s): 6 times per year
   Final notification: 2 months
   Write: Charlotte M. Stetson, Grants Mgr.
Officers and Directors:* Hilton A. Wick,* Chair.;
Robert S. Gillette,* Vice-Chair.; David G. Rahr,*
Secy. and Exec. Dir.; James B. Antell, Jonathan N.
Brownell, Richard M. Chapmen, Robert T.
Gannett, Luther F. Hackett, Frederick W. Lapham
III, Thomas P. Salmon, Barbara W. Snelling, Sarah
T. Soule, Louise R. Swainbank, R. Marshall Witten.
Number of staff: 1 full-time professional; 1
part-time support.
EIN: 222712160

VIRGINIA

3161
BDM International Corporate Giving Program
7915 Jones Branch Dr.
McLean 22102   (703) 848-5000

Purpose and activities: Support for culture, the humanities, music, education, business education, engineering, science and technology and general giving.
Fields of interest: Arts, business education, civic affairs, crime and law enforcement, cultural programs, education, educational associations, elementary education, engineering, fine arts, general charitable giving, health, health associations, heart disease, higher education, hospices, hospitals, humanities, military personnel, minorities, museums, music, performing arts, science and technology, secondary education, theater, transportation, volunteerism, welfare, women, youth.
Types of support: Annual campaigns, conferences and seminars, continuing support, general purposes, operating budgets, scholarship funds, special projects, seed money.
Limitations: Giving limited to areas of major offices. No grants for denominational or sectarian organizations.
Application information: Application form not required.
  Copies of proposal: 1
  Deadline(s): None
  Board meeting date(s): Periodic
  Write: Earle C. Williams, Pres. and C.E.O.
Administrators: George S. Newman, V.P., Govt. and Public Affairs; Paula Anderson, Secy.
Number of staff: 1 full-time professional.

3162
Beazley Foundation, Inc.
3720 Brighton St.
Portsmouth 23707-1788   (804) 393-1605

Incorporated in 1948 in VA.
Donor(s): Fred W. Beazley,‡ Marie C. Beazley,‡ Fred W. Beazley, Jr.‡
Foundation type: Independent
Financial data (yr. ended 12/31/91): Assets, $23,692,228 (M); expenditures, $1,260,027; qualifying distributions, $1,049,677, including $836,658 for 38 grants (high: $165,459; low: $50; average: $75-$80,000) and $16,678 for 2 foundation-administered programs.
Purpose and activities: "To further the causes of charity, education, and religion." Grants for operation of community and senior citizens centers and a dental clinic for the indigent. Support also for higher, secondary and medical education, youth agencies, community development, the aged, and other general charities, including health organizations and hospitals, the homeless, religion, recreation, and drug abuse prevention.
Fields of interest: Higher education, secondary education, medical education, community

development, youth, aged, health, homeless, drug abuse, general charitable giving.
Types of support: Capital campaigns, continuing support, scholarship funds.
Limitations: Giving primarily in the Hampton Roads area of VA. No grants to individuals.
Publications: Financial statement, application guidelines, program policy statement.
Application information: Application form not required.
  Initial approach: Proposal; request guidelines in writing
  Copies of proposal: 1
  Deadline(s): 15th of the month preceeding board meetings
  Board meeting date(s): Apr., July, Oct., and Jan.
  Write: Lawrence W. I'Anson, Jr., Pres.
Officers and Trustees:* Lawrence W. I'Anson, Jr.,* Pres.; Joseph J. Quadros, Jr.,* V.P. and Treas.; John T. Kavanaugh,* V.P.; W. Ashton Lewis,* Secy.; Jeanette C. Bridgeman, Treas.; Leroy T. Canoles, Jr., Mills E. Godwin, Jr., Mrs. Arnold B., McKinnon, P. Ward Robinetti, Jr.
Number of staff: 1 full-time professional; 6 full-time support; 2 part-time support.
EIN: 540550100

3163
Bell Atlantic Charitable Foundation ▼
1310 North Courthouse Rd., 10th Fl.
Arlington 22201   (703) 974-5440

Established in 1987 in PA.
Donor(s): Bell Atlantic Corp.
Foundation type: Company-sponsored
Financial data (yr. ended 12/31/90): Assets, $8,695,728 (M); gifts received, $5,100,000; expenditures, $2,166,044; qualifying distributions, $2,271,550, including $2,104,550 for 101 grants (high: $295,000; low: $1,000; average: $5,000-$25,000).
Purpose and activities: Giving for national and regional organizations, with two main areas of support: 1)general grants, including health and human services, arts and culture, and social and economic development and 2)education, including science and technology and literacy. In 1990, the foundation pledged funds to finance the Bell Atlantic/ALA Family Literacy Project, in conjunction with the Association for Library Service to Children and the Bell Atlantic/AAAS Science Institute.
Fields of interest: Health, arts, cultural programs, economics, education, higher education, secondary education, science and technology, literacy, libraries.
Limitations: Giving primarily in areas of company operations in DC, DE, MD, NJ, PA, VA, and WV. No support for hospitals, veterans' groups, labor organizations, sports programs, or for sectarian purposes of religious organizations. No grants to individuals, or for medical research, capital campaigns, fundraising events, or general endowment funds; no loans.
Publications: Program policy statement.
Application information: Application form not required.
  Initial approach: Letter or proposal
  Copies of proposal: 1
  Deadline(s): None
  Board meeting date(s): Three or four times a year

  Write: Ruth P. Caine, Dir.
Officers and Directors:* A. Gray Collins, Jr.,* Pres.; Carolyn S. Burger,* Secy.-Treas.; David Berry, James H. Brenneman, Hank Butta, William S. Ford, Bruce S. Gordon, William Harval, Joe Hulihan, John M. Kelleher, Del Lewis, Hugh Stallard.
Number of staff: 3
EIN: 232502809

3164
Bell Atlantic Corporate Contributions
1310 N. Court House Rd.
Arlington 22201   (202) 392-1564

Financial data (yr. ended 12/31/90): Total giving, $15,174,891, including $14,541,730 for grants and $633,161 for employee matching gifts.
Purpose and activities: Support for education, including higher and precollegiate education and science education, the arts, health and human services, including aid for the disabled, and economic and social development, and the United Way. Giving figures represent the Bell Atlantic Corporation and the seven operating companies.
Fields of interest: Education, arts, health, community funds, community development, social services.
Types of support: Matching funds, building funds, special projects.
Limitations: Giving primarily in company operating areas. No support for sectarian purposes, religious, veterans', or union organizations or political groups. No grants to individuals.
Application information:
  Initial approach: Letter; local organizations write to the nearest facility; regional or national organizations write to headquarters in VA
  Write: Ruth P. Caine, Dir., Corp. Contribs.

3165
Best Products Foundation
P.O. Box 26203
Richmond 23260
Application address: 1616 P St. N.W., Suite 100, Washington, DC 20036; Tel.: (202) 328-5188

Established in 1967 in VA.
Donor(s): Best Products Co.
Foundation type: Company-sponsored
Financial data (yr. ended 01/31/91): Assets, $1,175,601 (M); expenditures, $644,072; qualifying distributions, $622,378, including $466,484 for 333 grants (high: $150,000; low: $25; average: $100-$10,000).
Purpose and activities: Support primarily for higher, secondary, and elementary education, including educational programs for minorities and an employee matching gift program; museums and cultural programs; community and social welfare organizations, including youth agencies; and projects concerning reproductive rights.
Fields of interest: Higher education, secondary education, elementary education, education—minorities, vocational education,

museums, cultural programs, arts, community development, welfare, youth, family planning.
Types of support: Matching funds, special projects, employee matching gifts, seed money, emergency funds, scholarship funds.
Limitations: Giving primarily in areas of company operations. No support for religious institutions or government-supported organizations. No grants to individuals, or for publications, conferences, seminars, research, or building or endowment funds; no loans.
Publications: including application guidelines, 990-PF, informational brochure.
Application information: New proposals are not currently being accepted.
 Initial approach: Letter
 Copies of proposal: 1
 Deadline(s): 2 months before board meetings
 Board meeting date(s): Usually in Jan., Mar., June, Sept., and Nov.
 Final notification: 45 days after completion of screening process
 Write: Susan L. Butler, Exec. Dir.
Officers and Directors:* Frances A. Lewis,* Chair.; Sydney Lewis,* Pres.; Robert L. Burrus, Jr.,* Secy.; Susan L. Butler,* Treas. and Exec. Dir.
Number of staff: 1 full-time professional; 1 full-time support.
EIN: 237139981

3166
John Stewart Bryan Memorial Foundation, Inc.
P.O. Box 1234
Richmond 23209-1234   (804) 643-8363

Established in 1946 in VA.
Foundation type: Independent
Financial data (yr. ended 12/31/91): Assets, $2,501,390 (M); gifts received, $500; expenditures, $90,428; qualifying distributions, $81,423, including $81,423 for 44 grants (high: $21,000; low: $50).
Fields of interest: Community funds, higher education, religion—Christian, health.
Limitations: Giving primarily in VA. No grants to individuals.
Application information: Application form not required.
 Deadline(s): None
 Write: D. Tennant Bryan, Pres.
Officers and Directors:* D. Tennant Bryan,* Pres.; C.M. Trible,* V.P. and Secy.-Treas.; J. Stewart Bryan III, Mary Tennant Bryan, Florence Bryan Wishner.
EIN: 237425357

3167
Camp Foundation
P.O. Box 813
Franklin 23851   (804) 562-3439

Incorporated in 1942 in VA.
Donor(s): James L. Camp, P.D. Camp, and their families.
Foundation type: Independent
Financial data (yr. ended 12/31/91): Assets, $12,717,532 (M); expenditures, $739,670; qualifying distributions, $726,045, including $590,970 for 54 grants (high: $96,300; low: $1,000; average: $1,000-$20,000) and $76,000

for 28 grants to individuals (high: $4,000; low: $2,000; average: $2,000-$4,000).
Purpose and activities: "To provide or aid in providing in or near the town of Franklin, VA, ... parks, playgrounds, recreational facilities, libraries, hospitals, clinics, homes for the aged or needy, refuges for delinquent, dependent or neglected children, training schools, or other like institutions or activities." Grants also to select organizations statewide, with emphasis on youth agencies, safety programs, hospitals, mental illness, and nursing programs, higher and secondary education, including scholarships filed through high school principals, recreation, the environment, historic preservation, and cultural programs.
Fields of interest: Recreation, libraries, hospitals, health services, aged, youth, higher education, secondary education, civic affairs, cultural programs.
Types of support: Annual campaigns, seed money, emergency funds, building funds, equipment, land acquisition, matching funds, scholarship funds, student aid, research.
Limitations: Giving primarily in Franklin, Southampton County, Isle of Wight County, and Tidewater, VA, and northeastern NC.
Publications: Informational brochure, 990-PF.
Application information: Application form not required.
 Initial approach: Proposal
 Copies of proposal: 7
 Deadline(s): Submit proposal between June and Aug.; deadline Sept. 1; scholarship application deadlines Feb. 26 for filing with high school principals; Mar. 15 for principals to file with foundation
 Board meeting date(s): May and Dec.
 Final notification: 3 months
 Write: Harold S. Atkinson, Exec. Dir.
Officers and Directors:* Robert C. Ray,* Chair.; Sol W. Rawls, Jr.,* Pres.; James L. Camp,* V.P.; John M. Camp, Jr.,* Treas.; Harold S. Atkinson,* Exec. Dir.; John M. Camp III, W.M. Camp, Jr., Clifford A. Cutchins III, William W. Cutchins, Mills E. Godwin, Jr., John R. Marks, Paul Camp Marks, J. Edward Moyler, Jr., John D. Munford, Westbrook Parker, S. Waite Rawls, Jr., J.E. Ray III, Richard E. Ray, Toy D. Savage, Jr., W.H. Story.
Number of staff: 1 full-time professional; 1 full-time support; 1 part-time support.
EIN: 546052488

3168
The Beirne Carter Foundation
P.O. Box 26903
Richmond 23261   (804) 788-2964

Established in 1986 in VA.
Donor(s): Beirne B. Carter.‡
Foundation type: Independent
Financial data (yr. ended 12/31/90): Assets, $16,849,142 (M); gifts received, $17,838,652; expenditures, $190,582; qualifying distributions, $165,748, including $148,000 for 15 grants (high: $50,000; low: $1,000).
Fields of interest: Youth, cultural programs, history, health, ecology, education.
Limitations: Giving primarily in VA. No grants to individuals.
Publications: Informational brochure (including application guidelines).

Application information:
 Copies of proposal: 4
 Deadline(s): Mar. 1 and Sept. 1
 Board meeting date(s): Apr. and Oct.
 Final notification: After board meeting
 Write: J. Samuel Gillespie, Jr., Advisor
Number of staff: 2 shared staff
EIN: 541397827

3169
Caruthers Foundation, Inc.
333 South Glebe Rd., Suite 225
Arlington 22204   (703) 979-1331

Established in 1979.
Donor(s): Preston C. Caruthers.
Foundation type: Independent
Financial data (yr. ended 04/30/90): Assets, $39,153 (M); gifts received, $265,000; expenditures, $255,569; qualifying distributions, $255,569, including $255,500 for 18 grants (high: $200,000; low: $50).
Fields of interest: Hospitals, higher education, literacy, health, social services.
Types of support: General purposes.
Limitations: Giving primarily in VA.
Application information:
 Initial approach: Letter
 Deadline(s): Apr. 30
 Write: Dana J. Miller, Trustee
Trustees: Jeanne B. Caruthers, Lynn E. Caruthers, Preston C. Caruthers, Stephen P. Caruthers, Lisa N. Dawson, Dana J. Miller.
EIN: 510248560

3170
Central Fidelity Banks, Inc. Foundation
c/o Central Fidelity Bank
P.O. Box 27602
Richmond 23261

Established in 1980 in VA.
Donor(s): Central Fidelity Banks, Inc.
Foundation type: Company-sponsored
Financial data (yr. ended 12/31/90): Assets, $242,193 (M); gifts received, $950,500; expenditures, $814,607; qualifying distributions, $814,225, including $814,225 for 347 grants (high: $97,000; low: $75).
Purpose and activities: Giving for higher education, community funds, and cultural programs; support also for health and hospitals, youth agencies, and social services.
Fields of interest: Higher education, community funds, cultural programs, health, hospitals, youth, social services.
Limitations: Giving primarily in VA. No support for organizations that foster or encourage racial, religious, class, or other prejudices. No grants to individuals.
Application information:
 Initial approach: Letter
 Deadline(s): None
 Write: Charles Tysinger, Mgr.
Officer: Charles Tysinger, Mgr.
Directors: Lewis N. Miller, Jr., Carroll L. Saine.
EIN: 546173939

3171
Chesapeake Corporation Foundation
1021 East Cary St.
P.O. Box 2350
Richmond 23218-2350   (804) 697-1000

Established in 1955 in VA.
Donor(s): Chesapeake Corp.
Foundation type: Company-sponsored
Financial data (yr. ended 12/31/91): Assets, $1,200,177 (M); gifts received, $360,000; expenditures, $687,319; qualifying distributions, $676,101, including $608,884 for 120 grants (high: $63,157; low: $1,000) and $56,475 for 130 employee matching gifts.
Purpose and activities: Giving primarily for higher and other education, including an employee matching gift program for higher education, and scholarships for children of company employees; support also for community development, civic affairs, cultural programs, and health.
Fields of interest: Higher education, education, community development, civic affairs, cultural programs, health.
Types of support: Employee matching gifts, employee-related scholarships, capital campaigns, endowment funds.
Limitations: Giving primarily in areas of company operations. No support for athletic purposes. No grants to individuals.
Publications: Application guidelines.
Application information: Application form not required.
  Initial approach: Letter
  Board meeting date(s): Jan., June, and Oct.
  Write: Alvah H. Eubank, Jr., Secy.-Treas.
Officer: A.H. Eubank, Jr., Secy.-Treas.
Trustees: O.D. Dennis, T.G. Harris, G.P. Mueller, S.G. Olsson, W.T. Robinson.
Number of staff: 1 part-time professional; 1 part-time support.
EIN: 540605823

3172
Crestar Bank Charitable Trust
(Formerly United Virginia Charitable Trust)
c/o Crestar Bank, N.A.
P.O. Box 27385
Richmond 23261-7385
Application address: 919 East Main St., Richmond, VA 23219; Tel.: (804) 782-7906

Established in 1964.
Donor(s): Crestar Bank, N.A.
Foundation type: Company-sponsored
Financial data (yr. ended 12/31/91): Assets, $2,583,919 (M); expenditures, $642,760; qualifying distributions, $612,121, including $612,084 for 61 grants (high: $36,000; low: $100).
Fields of interest: Higher education, hospitals, cultural programs, arts, community funds, social services.
Types of support: General purposes, continuing support, annual campaigns, building funds, equipment, land acquisition, endowment funds, matching funds.
Limitations: Giving primarily in VA. No support for government-supported organizations, or for religious or national health agencies. No grants to

individuals, or for scholarships or fellowships; no loans.
Publications: Informational brochure, program policy statement, application guidelines.
Application information: Application form not required.
  Initial approach: Proposal
  Copies of proposal: 1
  Deadline(s): Large grant requests should be made by Oct. for consideration for the following year
  Board meeting date(s): Semiannually and as required
  Final notification: 1 to 6 months
  Write: J. Thomas Vaughan
Trustee: Crestar Bank, N.A.
Number of staff: 3
EIN: 546054608

3173
The Dalis Foundation
c/o Goodman & Co.
P.O. Box 3247
Norfolk 23514

Established in 1956.
Donor(s): M. Dan Dalis.‡
Foundation type: Independent
Financial data (yr. ended 05/31/91): Assets, $4,937,116 (M); expenditures, $229,221; qualifying distributions, $215,000, including $215,000 for 8 grants (high: $100,000; low: $1,000).
Purpose and activities: Emphasis on medical research, hospitals, and an international health services program; support also for libraries.
Fields of interest: Hospitals, medical research, health services, international relief, libraries.
Limitations: Giving primarily in Norfolk, VA.
Application information:
  Initial approach: Letter
  Write: Mrs. Joan D. Martone, Pres.
Officers: Joan Dalis Martone, Pres. and Treas.; Sandra W. Norment, V.P.
Number of staff: None.
EIN: 546046229

3174
Dominion Bankshares Charitable Trust
213 South Jefferson St.
Roanoke 24040   (703) 563-7000

Established in 1983 in VA.
Foundation type: Company-sponsored
Financial data (yr. ended 12/31/90): Assets, $2,513,000 (M); expenditures, $389,000; qualifying distributions, $389,000, including $389,000 for 76 grants (high: $15,000; low: $500).
Purpose and activities: Support for the arts, business education, civic affairs, and health and welfare.
Fields of interest: Arts, business education, civic affairs, health, welfare.
Types of support: Annual campaigns, building funds, capital campaigns, operating budgets, scholarship funds, student aid.
Limitations: Giving limited to VA.
Application information: Application form required.
  Initial approach: Proposal

  Copies of proposal: 1
  Deadline(s): None
  Final notification: When determined
  Write: Warner N. Dalhouse, Pres. and C.E.O., Dominion Bankshares Corp.
Number of staff: None.
EIN: 546205635

3175
Dominion Bankshares Corporate Giving Program
213 S. Jefferson St.
Roanoke 24040   (703) 563-7000

Financial data (yr. ended 12/31/90): Total giving, $730,000, including $641,534 for grants (high: $3,500; low: $25) and $88,466 for 278 employee matching gifts.
Purpose and activities: Main interests are arts, business education, health, and civic affairs; areas considered include fine arts, museums, and dance, health and hospitals, community development, and general welfare.
Fields of interest: Business education, community development, cultural programs, general charitable giving, higher education, hospitals, museums, arts, health, civic affairs, welfare.
Types of support: Employee matching gifts, equipment, special projects, annual campaigns, donated products, operating budgets, building funds, loaned talent, use of facilities, capital campaigns, matching funds, public relations services, scholarship funds.
Limitations: Giving primarily in headquarters city and all operating locations in VA, MD, TN, and DC.
Publications: Corporate report.
Application information: Include description of the project, project budget, a financial report, 501(c)(3) status letter, board member list and donor list; Trust department handles giving. Application form required.
  Initial approach: Proposal; Send request to headquarters
  Copies of proposal: 1
  Deadline(s): As submitted
  Board meeting date(s): As received
  Final notification: If turned down the company will send a rejection notice
  Write: Warner N. Dalhouse, Pres. and C.E.O.
Administrator: James W. Harkness, Exec. V.P.

3176
Andrew H. & Anne O. Easley Trust
(also known as The Easley Foundation)
c/o Trust Dept., Central Fidelity Bank
P.O. Box 700
Lynchburg 24505

Established in 1968 in VA.
Donor(s): Andrew H. Easley.‡
Foundation type: Independent
Financial data (yr. ended 06/30/91): Assets, $5,546,623 (M); expenditures, $315,548; qualifying distributions, $274,158, including $268,449 for 11 grants (high: $50,000; low: $2,000).
Fields of interest: Higher education, health, social services, cultural programs, historic preservation.
Limitations: Giving limited to the central VA, area, within a 30-mile radius of Lynchburg. No

support for religious organizations. No grants to individuals, or for research, deficit financing, seed money, annual campaigns, or conferences and seminars; no loans.
Publications: Application guidelines.
Application information: Application form not required.
> *Initial approach:* Proposal not exceeding 2 pages
> *Copies of proposal:* 6
> *Deadline(s):* Apr. 1 and Oct. 1
> *Board meeting date(s):* June and Dec.
> *Write:* Secy., The Easley Foundation
Trustee: Central Fidelity Bank.
Number of staff: None.
EIN: 546074720

3177
Ethyl Corporate Giving Program
330 South Fourth St.
P.O. Box 2189
Richmond 23217   (804) 788-5598

Financial data (yr. ended 12/31/90): Total giving, $3,300,000, including $3,145,000 for grants and $155,000 for employee matching gifts.
Purpose and activities: Support for education, arts and culture, civic affairs, community issues, and health and human services.
Fields of interest: Health, welfare, arts, cultural programs, civic affairs, community development, humanities, education.
Types of support: Employee matching gifts, general purposes, capital campaigns, endowment funds, scholarship funds, special projects, employee-related scholarships.
Limitations: Giving primarily in company headquarters and major operating areas. No support for fraternal or religious or community organizations located where company has no significant investments in terms of facilities or employees. No grants to individuals or for telephone or mass solicitations.
Publications: Application guidelines.
Application information: Application form not required.
> *Initial approach:* Letter; proposal
> *Copies of proposal:* 1
> *Deadline(s):* Applications accepted throughout the year
> *Board meeting date(s):* Executive committee meets annually to review consolidated budget proposals of company locations
> *Final notification:* Minimum 4 weeks required for full review and decision
> *Write:* A. Prescott Rowe, V.P., Corp. Communs.
Contributions Manager: Floyd D. Gottwald, Chair. and C.E.O.
Number of staff: 2 part-time professional; 1 part-time support.

3178
Fairchild Industries Foundation, Inc.
P.O. Box 10803
Chantilly 22021-9998   (703) 478-5800

Incorporated in 1953 in MD.
Donor(s): Fairchild Industries, Inc.
Foundation type: Company-sponsored
Financial data (yr. ended 12/31/91): Assets, $315,306 (M); gifts received, $376,900;

expenditures, $525,589; qualifying distributions, $525,458, including $506,766 for grants.
Purpose and activities: Giving primarily for higher education, including employee matching gifts, community funds, and civic affairs; support also for scholarships to children of employees and aid to needy employees or retired employees.
Fields of interest: Education, higher education, vocational education, community funds, civic affairs, arts, health, medical research, minorities, welfare.
Types of support: Operating budgets, continuing support, annual campaigns, emergency funds, general purposes, equipment, endowment funds, matching funds, scholarship funds, special projects, employee-related scholarships, research, fellowships, employee matching gifts.
Limitations: Giving primarily in areas of company operations.
Application information: Application form not required.
> *Initial approach:* Letter
> *Copies of proposal:* 1
> *Deadline(s):* None
> *Board meeting date(s):* Jan. or as required
> *Write:* John D. Jackson, Pres.
Officers and Trustees:* Jeffry J. Steiner, Chair.; John D. Jackson,* Pres.; Hazel S. Chilcote, V.P. and Secy.; Karen L. Schneckenburger, Treas.
Number of staff: 1 part-time professional.
EIN: 526043638

3179
Fitz-Gibbon Charitable Trust
P.O. Box 1377
Richmond 23211   (804) 780-2012

Established about 1983 in VA.
Donor(s): T. David Fitz-Gibbon.‡
Foundation type: Independent
Financial data (yr. ended 06/30/91): Assets, $2,504,600 (M); expenditures, $151,354; qualifying distributions, $119,100, including $119,100 for 23 grants (high: $20,000; low: $100).
Fields of interest: Higher education, secondary education, hospitals, social services, historic preservation.
Types of support: Endowment funds, professorships, scholarship funds.
Limitations: Giving primarily in VA. No grants to individuals.
Application information: Limited amount of funds available due to long-term commitments. Application form not required.
> *Initial approach:* Letter
> *Copies of proposal:* 1
> *Deadline(s):* July 1
> *Board meeting date(s):* Feb. and Aug.
> *Write:* Thomas Nelson Page Johnson, Jr., Chair.
Trustees: Thomas Nelson Page Johnson, Jr., Chair.; Thomas Nelson Page Johnson III, William M. Walsh, Jr.
Number of staff: None.
EIN: 521272224

3180
Frederick Foundation, Inc.
(Formerly Foundation Boys Academy)
3720 Brighton St.
Portsmouth 23707   (804) 393-1605

Established in 1986 in VA.
Donor(s): Fred W. Beazley,‡ Fred W. Beazley, Jr.,‡ Marie C. Beazley.‡
Foundation type: Independent
Financial data (yr. ended 12/31/90): Assets, $25,436,817 (M); expenditures, $1,367,419; qualifying distributions, $1,201,168, including $1,138,787 for 43 grants (high: $175,103; low: $1,000; average: $1,000-$175,103).
Purpose and activities: Support for education, including secondary, higher and medical education, health and hospitals, religion, social services, including substance abuse programs and the homeless, community development, recreation, youth, and other general charitable organizations.
Fields of interest: Secondary education, higher education, health, hospitals, religion, drug abuse, community development, recreation, youth, general charitable giving.
Types of support: Capital campaigns, continuing support, scholarship funds.
Limitations: Giving primarily in the Hampton Roads, VA, area. No grants to individuals.
Publications: Financial statement, application guidelines, program policy statement.
Application information: Guidelines available if requested in writing. Application form not required.
> *Initial approach:* Proposal
> *Copies of proposal:* 1
> *Deadline(s):* 15th of the month prior to board meetings
> *Board meeting date(s):* Apr., July, Oct., Jan.
> *Write:* Lawrence W. I'Anson, Jr., Pres.
Officers and Trustees:* Lawrence W. I'Anson, Jr.,* Pres.; John T. Kavanaugh,* V.P.; Joseph J. Quadros,* V.P.; Jeanette C. Bridgeman, Treas.; Leroy T. Canoles, Jr., Mills E. Godwin, Jr., W. Ashton Lewis.
Number of staff: 1 full-time professional; 2 full-time support; 1 part-time support.
EIN: 540604600
Recent health grants:
3180-1 Childrens Hospital of the Kings Daughters, Norfolk, VA, $25,000. 1990.
3180-2 Emily Green Home for the Aged, Norfolk, VA, $25,000. 1990.
3180-3 Maryview Hospital, Martha W. Davis Cancer Treatment Center, Portsmouth, VA, $50,000. 1990.
3180-4 Medical College of Hampton Roads Foundation, Norfolk, VA, $125,000. 1990.
3180-5 Navy Marine Coast Guard Residence Foundation, McLean, VA, $10,000. To build geriatric center. 1990.
3180-6 Planned Parenthood of Southeastern Virginia, Hampton, VA, $15,000. 1990.
3180-7 Portsmouth, City of, Department of Public Health, Portsmouth, VA, $175,103. 1990.

3181
The Freedom Forum ▼
(Formerly Gannett Foundation)
1101 Wilson Blvd.
Arlington 22209   (703) 528-0800

Incorporated in 1935 in NY.
Donor(s): Frank E. Gannett.‡
Foundation type: Independent

Financial data (yr. ended 12/31/90): Assets, $592,973,755 (M); gifts received, $2,500; expenditures, $33,192,523; qualifying distributions, $31,814,708, including $13,445,304 for 1,162 grants (high: $444,583; low: $500; average: $500-$25,000), $773,474 for 108 grants to individuals, $1,016,299 for 990 employee matching gifts and $4,503,253 for 2 foundation-administered programs.

Purpose and activities: "The foundation is dedicated primarily to supporting national, international and community programs that foster the First Amendment freedoms of press, speech, assembly, petition and religion and the free exercise thereof and for all peoples; secondarily to encouraging innovative programs and meeting needs to contribute to a better life in free society." Grants to nonprofit educational, charitable, civic, cultural, health, and social service institutions and organizations in areas served by daily newspapers, broadcast stations, outdoor advertising companies, and other properties of Gannett Company, Inc. in the U.S. and Canada. Primary national interests are support of journalism related programs and the advancement of philanthropy, volunteerism, and the promotion of adult literacy. The foundation also operates the Gannett Center for Media Studies, the nation's first institute for the advanced study of mass communication and technological change, located at Columbia University in NY, and the Paul Miller Washington Reporting Fellowships in Washington, DC.

Fields of interest: Journalism, media and communications, education, literacy, cultural programs, health, alcoholism, drug abuse, mental health, AIDS, social services, handicapped, homeless, housing, minorities, women, youth, civic affairs, volunteerism, community development.

Types of support: Operating budgets, continuing support, seed money, emergency funds, deficit financing, building funds, equipment, land acquisition, scholarship funds, employee-related scholarships, special projects, publications, conferences and seminars, general purposes, capital campaigns, matching funds, renovation projects, technical assistance, fellowships, employee matching gifts.

Limitations: Giving primarily in the U.S. and Canada. No support for national or regional organizations, medical or other research unrelated to journalism, literacy, philanthropy, or volunteerism; religious purposes; publications; video and film productions; fraternal and similar organizations; or for primary or secondary school programs, except for those helping exceptional or disadvantaged children and youth. No grants to individuals (except for employee-related scholarships, fellowships, and journalism-related research), or for annual campaigns (other than United Ways), or endowment funds; no loans.

Publications: Annual report, informational brochure (including application guidelines), newsletter, application guidelines.

Application information: Grant proposals from organizations in communities served by Gannett properties should be directed to the chief executive of the local property; executive committee of board approves grants monthly or as required. Journalism proposals should be directed to Gerald M. Sass, V.P./Education. Application form required.

Initial approach: Letter or proposal
Copies of proposal: 1
Deadline(s): Jan 31 for Journalism Scholarships
Board meeting date(s): 3 to 4 times a year, and as required; annual meeting in Apr. or May
Final notification: 3 to 4 months for positive responses
Write: Charles L. Overby, Pres.

Officers and Trustees:* Allen H. Neuharth, Chair.; Charles L. Overby,* Pres.; Gerald M. Sass, Sr. V.P.; Harvey S. Cotter, V.P. and Treas.; Calvin Mayne, V.P.-Administration; Tracy A. Quinn, V.P.-Communications; Pamela Y. Gallaway, V.P.-General Services; Christine Wells, V.P.-International Operations; Roderick C. Sandeen, V.P.-Publications; Jerry W. Friedheim, V.P.-Special Projects; Christy C. Bulkeley, V.P.; Everette E. Dennis, V.P.; Felix Gutierrez, V.P.; Paul K. McMasters, V.P.; Robert McCullough, Secy.; Martin F. Birmingham, Bernard R. Brody, M.D., Harry W. Brooks, Jr., John E. Heselden, Bette Bao Lord, Paul Miller, Dillard Munford, John C. Quinn, Frank H.T. Rhodes, Josefina A. Salas-Porras, John Seigenthaler, Dolph C. Simons, Jr.

Number of staff: 14 full-time professional; 2 part-time professional; 24 full-time support; 14 part-time support.

EIN: 166027020

3182
Gottwald Foundation
c/o Floyd D. Gottwald, Jr.
P.O. Box 2189
Richmond 23217   (804) 788-5738

Established in 1957.
Donor(s): Floyd D. Gottwald, Sr.,‡ Floyd D. Gottwald, Jr.
Foundation type: Independent
Financial data (yr. ended 12/31/91): Assets, $9,645,139 (M); expenditures, $522,803; qualifying distributions, $513,280, including $510,530 for 16 grants (high: $300,000; low: $100; average: $100-$200,000).
Purpose and activities: Emphasis on education, hospitals, the arts and cultural programs, and youth agencies; support also for a foundation benefiting a military institute.
Fields of interest: Education, hospitals, cultural programs, arts, youth.
Types of support: Operating budgets, capital campaigns, scholarship funds.
Limitations: Giving primarily in VA. No grants to individuals.
Application information: Contributes only to pre-selected organizations. Applications not accepted.
Write: Vernell B. Harris
Officers: Floyd D. Gottwald, Jr., Pres.; Anne C. Gottwald, V.P.; Bruce C. Gottwald, Secy.-Treas.
Number of staff: None.
EIN: 546040560

3183
Houff Foundation
P.O. Box 220
Weyers Cave 24486   (703) 234-9233

Donor(s): Cletus E. Houff, Houff Transfer, Inc.
Foundation type: Independent

Financial data (yr. ended 12/31/91): Assets, $2,119,581 (M); gifts received, $100,000; expenditures, $127,894; qualifying distributions, $124,500, including $124,500 for 19 grants (high: $50,000; low: $500).
Purpose and activities: Support primarily for higher education; support also for social services and health care.
Fields of interest: Higher education, social services, health.
Limitations: Giving primarily in Shenandoah Valley, VA, area. No grants to individuals.
Application information: Application form not required.
Deadline(s): None
Write: Dwight E. Houff, Secy.
Officers: Charlotte Houff, Pres.; Dwight E. Houff, Secy.
Directors: Douglas Z. Houff, Roxie Houff White.
EIN: 510236893

3184
Emily S. and Coleman A. Hunter Trust
c/o Crestar Bank, N.A.
P.O. Box 26548
Richmond 23261   (804) 782-5248

Established in 1985 in VA.
Donor(s): Coleman A. Hunter,‡ Emily S. Hunter.‡
Foundation type: Independent
Financial data (yr. ended 02/28/91): Assets, $4,013,170 (M); expenditures, $202,903; qualifying distributions, $164,323, including $164,286 for 52 grants (high: $3,528; low: $2,648).
Purpose and activities: Giving for hospitals and health associations, education, youth agencies, and a community fund.
Fields of interest: Hospitals, health associations, education, youth.
Types of support: General purposes.
Limitations: Giving limited to VA, with emphasis on Richmond. No grants to individuals.
Application information: Application form required.
Deadline(s): Dec. 15
Final notification: Feb. 1
Write: Bonnie B. Turner
Trustee: Crestar Bank, N.A.
EIN: 546219496

3185
James River Corporation Public Affairs Department
120 Tredegar Street
P.O. Box 2218
Richmond 23219   (804) 644-5411

Financial data (yr. ended 12/30/90): Total giving, $1,890,819 for grants.
Purpose and activities: James River's first social responsibility is "jobs first: the corporation can make the most effective social contribution by creating and maintaining secure, safe and productive jobs. The wealth these jobs create permeates the communities by way of the supplies and services purchased by the company and its employees, taxes paid and the enlightenment and philanthropy made possible. The second social responsibility of the company is to prosper and grow, and to contribute to the

health of society and provide a reasonable environment in which business can be conducted. As resources (cash and human) allow, it is James River's intent to demonstrate its civic responsibility through charitable contributions, business and professional memberships, community involvement and employee volunteerism in the communities where our employees live and work." Company supports education, economic development, health, the arts, and community development. Giving figure is for an eight month period from April (previously the end of the fiscal year) to December. The company's fiscal year now ends in December.
Fields of interest: Arts, education, community development, economics, health.
Types of support: Capital campaigns, employee matching gifts, general purposes, equipment, special projects, endowment funds, internships, employee volunteer services.
Limitations: Giving primarily in company operating areas; national organizations are generally not considered for support. No support for religious, fraternal, veterans', political, labor, or athletic organizations. No grants to individuals, or for telephone or mass mail solicitations.
Publications: Application guidelines.
Application information: Application form not required.
  Initial approach: Initial contact by query letter describing project
  Copies of proposal: 1
  Deadline(s): Applications accepted throughout the year; best time to apply is Mar.-Oct.
  Board meeting date(s): Nov.
  Final notification: 6-12 weeks
  Write: Stephen H. Garnett, V.P., Public Affairs
Number of staff: 1 part-time professional; 1 part-time support.

3186
Thomas F. and Kate Miller Jeffress Memorial Trust
c/o NationsBank, Trust Div.
P.O. Box 26903
Richmond 23261   (804) 788-2964

Established in 1981 in VA.
Donor(s): Robert M. Jeffress.‡
Foundation type: Independent
Financial data (yr. ended 06/30/91): Assets, $18,399,258 (M); gifts received, $2,081; expenditures, $1,301,720; qualifying distributions, $1,207,955, including $1,155,580 for 10 grants (high: $345,475; low: $8,424).
Purpose and activities: Grants to colleges and universities for research activities.
Fields of interest: Higher education, medical research, chemistry, physical sciences.
Types of support: Research.
Limitations: Giving limited to VA. No support for clinical research. No grants to individuals.
Publications: Informational brochure (including application guidelines).
Application information: Application form not required.
  Copies of proposal: 6
  Deadline(s): Mar. 1 and Sept. 1
  Board meeting date(s): May and Nov.
  Final notification: After meeting at which proposal has been considered

Write: Dr. J. Samuel Gillespie, Jr., Advisor
Trustee: NationsBank.
Advisor: J. Samuel Gillespie, Jr., M.D.
Allocations Committee: William L. Banks, William H. Barney, M.D., Malcolm M. Christian, Hugh K. Leary, William L. Pfost, Jr.
Number of staff: 2 shared staff
EIN: 546094925
Recent health grants:
3186-1 Eastern Virginia Medical School, Norfolk, VA, $104,089. 1991.

3187
W. Alton Jones Foundation, Inc. ▼
232 East High St.
Charlottesville 22902-5178   (804) 295-2134

Incorporated in 1944 in NY.
Donor(s): W. Alton Jones.‡
Foundation type: Independent
Financial data (yr. ended 12/31/90): Assets, $173,128,158 (M); expenditures, $17,076,092; qualifying distributions, $12,547,852, including $11,120,879 for grants (high: $550,000; average: $5,000-$500,000).
Purpose and activities: The goal of the foundation is to protect the earth's life-support systems from environmental harm and to eliminate the possibility of nuclear warfare.
Fields of interest: Peace, conservation, arms control, environment, ecology.
Types of support: Special projects, general purposes, research, conferences and seminars, seed money, matching funds, operating budgets.
Limitations: No support for conduit organizations. No grants to individuals, or for building construction or renovation, endowment funds, general support, basic research, scholarships, conferences, international exchanges, or fellowships.
Publications: Annual report, application guidelines, 990-PF, informational brochure (including application guidelines), newsletter.
Application information: Applicants must wait 1 year after a grant is approved or declined before submitting another application; applications accepted only for programs in environmental protection and arms control. Application form not required.
  Initial approach: Inquiry
  Copies of proposal: 1
  Deadline(s): None
  Board meeting date(s): Quarterly
  Final notification: Variable
  Write: J.P. Myers, Ph.D., Dir.
Officers and Directors:* Patricia Jones Edgerton,* Pres.; Bradford W. Edgerton,* V.P.; Diane Edgerton Miller,* Secy.; Bernard F. Curry,* Treas.
Trustees: James S. Bennett, James R. Cameron, William A. Edgerton, William A. McDonough, Scott McVay.
Number of staff: 8 full-time professional; 6 full-time support.
EIN: 136034219
Recent health grants:
3187-1 California Rural Legal Assistance Foundation, San Francisco, CA, $25,000. To educate California's farmworkers on hazards of exposure to pesticides. 1990.
3187-2 Industrial Mission of Puerto Rico, San Juan, PR, $10,000. To continue serving

low-income citizens who suffer from effects of industrial chemical pollution. 1990.
3187-3 Nuclear Safety Campaign, Seattle, WA, $25,000. To address issues of public health and safety, weapons production, environmental protection and government accountability of the Department of Energy. 1990.
3187-4 Physicians for Social Responsibility, DC, $200,000. To assess environmental and public health risks associated with nuclear weapons production, and to ensure that health professionals, local citizens, media and government officials are informed and motivated to participate vigorously in review of Department of Energy's plans to modernize complex. 1990.

3188
Lafarge Corporate Giving Program
1130 Sunrise Valley Dr., Suite 300
Reston 22091   (703) 264-3600
Mailing address: P.O. Box 4600, Reston, VA 22090

Purpose and activities: Support for child welfare, the homeless, the disadvantaged, community development, culture and the arts, medical research, Canadian issues, and United Way.
Fields of interest: Canada, child welfare, community development, cultural programs, disadvantaged, homeless, medical research, performing arts.
Types of support: Annual campaigns.
Limitations: Giving primarily in the Dallas, TX, area, and the Northeast and Midwest.
Publications: Informational brochure.
Application information: Application form not required.
  Initial approach: Letter
  Copies of proposal: 1
  Write: Katrina Farrell, Dir., Corp. Communs.
Staff Benedicte Barre, Asst. to Dir. of Corp. Communs.

3189
Lind Lawrence Foundation
c/o L.P. Martin and Co.
4132 Innslake Dr.
Glen Allen 23060-3307

Established in 1973 in VA.
Donor(s): Lind Lawrence.‡
Foundation type: Independent
Financial data (yr. ended 09/30/91): Assets, $6,124,075 (M); expenditures, $424,460; qualifying distributions, $349,123, including $347,000 for 11 grants (high: $145,000; low: $1,000).
Purpose and activities: Support primarily for neurosurgery research.
Fields of interest: Medical research.
Types of support: Operating budgets, research, building funds, capital campaigns.
Limitations: Giving primarily in Richmond, VA, and Los Angeles, CA.
Application information:
  Initial approach: Letter
  Deadline(s): July 31
  Write: Lee P. Martin, Jr., Trustee
Trustees: Fred J. Bernhardt, Jr., Lee P. Martin, Jr.

EIN: 237310359

3190
Little River Foundation
Whitewood Farm
The Plains 22171   (703) 253-5540

Established in 1972.
Donor(s): Ohrstrom Foundation.
Foundation type: Independent
Financial data (yr. ended 11/30/91): Assets,
$239,346 (M); gifts received, $296,500;
expenditures, $308,186; qualifying distributions,
$307,500, including $307,500 for 46 grants
(high: $100,000; low: $400; average:
$500-$100,000).
Purpose and activities: Support primarily for
hospitals, including AIDS and drug abuse
programs; education, including higher, secondary,
and early childhood institutions, building funds,
literacy programs, a veterinary school and clinic,
legal education, and international studies in
Africa; environmental conservation and
agriculture; legal services; religious organizations;
and community funds.
Fields of interest: Hospitals, AIDS, higher
education, secondary education, international
studies, animal welfare, conservation, agriculture,
legal services, religion—Christian.
Types of support: Building funds, conferences and
seminars, endowment funds, operating budgets,
research.
Limitations: Giving primarily in mid-Atlantic
states.
Application information: Application form not
required.
  Copies of proposal: 1
  Deadline(s): None
  Board meeting date(s): Sept.-Oct.
  Final notification: Nov.
  Write: Dale D. Hogoboom, Asst. Treas.
Officers: George L. Ohrstrom, Pres.; G.A.
Horkau, Jr., Secy.; Richard R. Ohrstorm, Treas.
Number of staff: 2 part-time support.
EIN: 237218919

3191
The Mars Foundation
6885 Elm St.
McLean 22101   (703) 821-4900

Incorporated in 1956 in IL.
Donor(s): Forrest E. Mars.
Foundation type: Independent
Financial data (yr. ended 12/31/91): Assets,
$4,898,035 (M); gifts received, $602,406;
expenditures, $886,700; qualifying distributions,
$834,784, including $819,000 for 133 grants
(high: $100,000; low: $1,000; average:
$2,000-$15,000).
Purpose and activities: Support for higher and
secondary education; conservation, ecology, and
wildlife preservation; fine arts groups; health
agencies, AIDS and cancer programs and other
medical research; youth organizations; hospices;
and the homeless.
Fields of interest: Higher education, secondary
education, fine arts, wildlife, conservation,
ecology, health services, medical research, AIDS,
cancer, homeless, hospices, youth.

Types of support: Continuing support, annual
campaigns, building funds, equipment,
endowment funds, research, matching funds.
Limitations: No grants to individuals, or for
scholarships; no loans.
Application information: Application form not
required.
  Initial approach: Proposal
  Copies of proposal: 1
  Deadline(s): 6 weeks prior to meeting
  Board meeting date(s): June and Dec.
  Final notification: 4 to 6 weeks after meeting
  Write: Roger G. Best, Secy.
Officers: Jacqueline M. Vogel, Pres.; Forrest E.
Mars, Jr., V.P..; John F. Mars, V.P.; Roger G. Best,
Secy.; William C. Turnbull, Treas.
Number of staff: 2
EIN: 546037592

3192
Massey Foundation ▼
P.O. Box 26765
Richmond 23261   (804) 788-1800

Established in 1958 in VA.
Donor(s): A.T. Massey Coal Co., Inc.
Foundation type: Company-sponsored
Financial data (yr. ended 11/30/91): Assets,
$36,276,226 (M); expenditures, $1,831,700;
qualifying distributions, $1,638,013, including
$1,637,600 for 72 grants (high: $330,000; low:
$1,000; average: $1,000-$25,000).
Purpose and activities: Giving primarily for
higher and secondary education; some support
for hospitals and health services, cultural
programs, and social services.
Fields of interest: Higher education, secondary
education, health services, hospitals, cultural
programs, social services.
Limitations: Giving primarily in VA, particularly
Richmond. No grants to individuals.
Application information:
  Initial approach: Letter
  Deadline(s): None
  Board meeting date(s): Annually
  Write: William E. Massey, Jr., Pres.
Officers and Directors:* William E. Massey, Jr.,*
Pres.; William Blair Massey,* V.P. and Secy.; E.
Morgan Massey,* Treas.
Number of staff: None.
EIN: 546049049

3193
Metropolitan Health Foundation, Inc.
700 West Grace St.
Richmond 23220   (804) 643-1958

Established in 1984 in VA.
Foundation type: Independent
Financial data (yr. ended 12/31/91): Assets,
$2,161,829 (M); expenditures, $140,549;
qualifying distributions, $106,097, including
$103,243 for 16 grants (high: $27,000; low:
$450).
Fields of interest: Health.
Types of support: General purposes.
Limitations: Giving primarily in the Richmond,
VA, area.
Application information:
  Initial approach: Letter
  Deadline(s): None

Write: Charles P. Winkler, M.D., Pres.
Officers: Raymond C. Hooker, Jr., M.D., Chair.;
Charles P. Winkler, M.D., Pres.; Charles P.
Cardwell III, M.D., V.P.; James Wood, Secy.-Treas.
Director: Malcolm E. Ritsch, Jr.
Number of staff: 1 part-time support.
EIN: 510186144

3194
Mobil Foundation, Inc. ▼
3225 Gallows Rd.
Fairfax 22037   (703) 846-3381

Incorporated in 1965 in NY.
Donor(s): Mobil Oil Corp.
Foundation type: Company-sponsored
Financial data (yr. ended 12/31/90): Assets,
$10,246,252 (M); gifts received, $9,913,500;
expenditures, $15,335,148; qualifying
distributions, $14,947,057, including $9,578,048
for 824 grants (high: $411,000; low: $100;
average: $1,000-$10,000) and $4,540,292 for
employee matching gifts.
Purpose and activities: Support for arts and
cultural programs, higher education, including
grants in fields relating to the petroleum and
chemical industries, a scholarship program for
children of employees, and an employee
matching gift program; support also for
community funds, civic affairs, social services,
health agencies, and hospitals.
Fields of interest: Cultural programs, arts, higher
education, physical sciences, community funds,
civic affairs, social services, hospitals, health
services.
Types of support: Employee-related scholarships,
employee matching gifts, research, exchange
programs, general purposes.
Limitations: Giving primarily in areas of company
operations in CA, CO, IL, LA, NJ, NY, TX, VA, and
WA. No support for local and national
organizations concerned with specific diseases or
religious or fraternal organizations. No grants to
individuals, or for building or endowment funds,
operating budgets, charity benefits, athletic
events, or advertising; no loans.
Publications: Financial statement, application
guidelines, grants list.
Application information: Application form not
required.
  Initial approach: Letter or proposal
  Copies of proposal: 1
  Deadline(s): None
  Board meeting date(s): Monthly
  Final notification: 6 to 8 weeks
  Write: Richard G. Mund, Secy.
Officers and Directors:* Ellen Z. McCloy,* Pres.;
Richard G. Mund, Secy. and Exec. Dir.; Anthony
L. Cavaliere, Treas.; H.K. Acord, John M. Baitseil,
Donald J. Bolger, G. Broadhead, Harold B. Olson,
Jr., Jerome F. Trautschold, Jr., John J. Wise.
Number of staff: 3 full-time professional; 8
full-time support.
EIN: 136177075
Recent health grants:
3194-1 American Health Foundation, NYC, NY,
$18,500. 1990.
3194-2 Brigham and Womens Hospital, Boston,
MA, $25,000. 1990.
3194-3 Children of Alcoholics Foundation, NYC,
NY, $25,000. 1990.

3194-4 Childrens National Medical Center, DC, $100,000. 1990.

3194-5 Columbia Presbyterian Medical Center Fund, NYC, NY, $50,000. 1990.

3194-6 D.A.R.E. America, Los Angeles, CA, $15,000. 1990.

3194-7 Duke University Medical Center, Durham, NC, $25,000. 1990.

3194-8 Fairfax Hospital Association Foundation, Falls Church, VA, $85,000. 1990.

3194-9 Foundation for Safety and Health, Chicago, IL, $30,000. 1990.

3194-10 Frederick Ferris Thompson Hospital, Canadaigua, NY, $20,000. 1990.

3194-11 Highland Hospital Foundation, Rochester, NY, $30,000. 1990.

3194-12 Media-Advertising Partnership for a Drug-Free America, NYC, NY, $100,000. 1990.

3194-13 Memorial Sloan-Kettering Cancer Center, NYC, NY, $10,000. 1990.

3194-14 Mercy Medical Airlift, Manassas, VA, $25,000. 1990.

3194-15 National Association on Drug Abuse Problems, NYC, NY, $12,000. 1990.

3194-16 National Foundation for Facial Reconstruction, NYC, NY, $15,000. 1990.

3194-17 New York Hospital-Cornell Medical Center Fund, NYC, NY, $75,000. 1990.

3194-18 New York University Medical Center, NYC, NY, $37,500. 1990.

3194-19 Rockefeller University, NYC, NY, $30,000. 1990.

3194-20 Saint Francis Hospital Foundation, Roslyn, NY, $50,000. 1990.

3194-21 Salk Institute for Biological Studies, La Jolla, CA, $15,000. 1990.

3194-22 Second Genesis, Bethesda, MD, $25,000. 1990.

3194-23 Society of New York Hospital, Cornell Medical Center, NYC, NY, $10,000. 1990.

3194-24 Straight, Hampton Roads, VA, $10,000. 1990.

3194-25 Torrance Memorial Hospital and Medical Center Health Care Foundation, Torrance, CA, $40,000. 1990.

3194-26 University of Texas M.D. Anderson Cancer Center, Houston, TX, $15,000. 1990.

3195

Marietta McNeil Morgan & Samuel Tate Morgan, Jr. Foundation
c/o NationsBank, Trust Dept.
P.O. Box 26903
Richmond 23261   (804) 788-2963

Trust established in 1967 in VA.
Donor(s): Marietta McNeil Morgan,‡ Samuel T. Morgan, Jr.‡
Foundation type: Independent
Financial data (yr. ended 06/30/91): Assets, $12,587,599 (M); expenditures, $672,533; qualifying distributions, $600,325, including $579,300 for 33 grants (high: $35,000; low: $5,000).
Purpose and activities: Grants of a capital nature only, with emphasis on promoting the cause of the church, fostering Christian education, and supporting agencies concerned with less fortunate local residents.
Fields of interest: Religion—Christian, higher education, secondary education, social services, hospitals.

Types of support: Building funds, equipment, matching funds.
Limitations: Giving limited to VA. No support for private foundations. No grants to individuals, or for any purposes except capital expenses; no loans.
Publications: Informational brochure (including application guidelines).
Application information: Application form not required.
  Initial approach: Letter
  Copies of proposal: 1
  Deadline(s): Submit proposal preferably in Feb., Mar., Sept. or Oct.; deadlines May 1 and Nov. 1
  Board meeting date(s): June and Dec.
  Final notification: 3 weeks after board meeting
  Write: Elizabeth D. Seaman, Advisor, NationsBank, Trust Dept.
Trustee: NationsBank.
Number of staff: 2 shared staff
EIN: 546069447

3196

The Norfolk Foundation ▼
1410 Nationsbank Center
Norfolk 23510   (804) 622-7951

Established in 1950 in VA by resolution and declaration of trust.
Foundation type: Community
Financial data (yr. ended 12/31/91): Assets, $41,684,848 (M); gifts received, $2,012,856; expenditures, $2,136,509; qualifying distributions, $1,817,907, including $1,493,807 for 38 grants (high: $291,500; low: $900; average: $25,000-$54,000) and $324,100 for 192 grants to individuals (high: $9,000; low: $300; average: $1,200-$2,000).
Purpose and activities: Support for hospitals, higher, medical, and other educational institutions, family and child welfare agencies, a community fund, programs for drug abuse, the aged, the homeless, and the handicapped, and cultural and civic programs; certain donor-designated scholarships restricted by residence in nearby localities and/or area colleges, and payable directly to the school.
Fields of interest: Education, higher education, libraries, medical education, hospitals, family services, youth, child welfare, drug abuse, rehabilitation, mental health, handicapped, homeless, health, aged, animal welfare, cultural programs, arts, community development, environment.
Types of support: Seed money, building funds, equipment, land acquisition, research, special projects, capital campaigns, student aid.
Limitations: Giving primarily in Norfolk, VA, and a 50-mile area from its boundaries. No support for national or international organizations, or religious organizations for religious purposes. No grants to individuals (except for donor-designated scholarships), or for operating budgets, endowment funds, or deficit financing; no loans.
Publications: Annual report, application guidelines, program policy statement, newsletter.
Application information: Application form not required.
  Initial approach: Letter or telephone
  Copies of proposal: 1

  Deadline(s): For scholarships only, Dec. 1 to Mar. 1
  Board meeting date(s): 4 times a year
  Final notification: 3 to 4 months
  Write: Lee C. Kitchin, Exec. Dir.
Officer: Lee C. Kitchin, Exec. Dir.
Distribution Committee: Charles F. Burroughs, Jr., Chair.; Toy D. Savage, Jr., Vice-Chair.; Jean C. Bruce, Joshua P. Darden, Jr., H.P. McNeal, H.B. Price III, Kurt M. Rosenbach.
Number of staff: 1 full-time professional; 3 part-time support.
EIN: 540722169
Recent health grants:
3196-1 Medical College of Hampton Roads, Norfolk, VA, $34,415. Toward mental health research. 1990.

3197

The Ohrstrom Foundation, Inc.
c/o Whitewood
The Plains 22171

Incorporated in 1953 in DE.
Donor(s): Members of the Ohrstrom family.
Foundation type: Independent
Financial data (yr. ended 05/31/91): Assets, $20,972,624 (M); expenditures, $843,917; qualifying distributions, $835,947, including $819,500 for 151 grants (high: $296,500; low: $500; average: $1,000-$10,000).
Purpose and activities: Emphasis on elementary, secondary, and higher education; support also for civic affairs, conservation, hospitals and medical research, and museums.
Fields of interest: Higher education, elementary education, secondary education, civic affairs, conservation, medical research, museums, alcoholism, environment, libraries.
Types of support: Operating budgets, continuing support, annual campaigns, seed money, emergency funds, building funds, equipment, land acquisition, endowment funds, matching funds.
Limitations: Giving primarily in VA and NY. No grants to individuals, or for deficit financing, scholarships, fellowships, research, special projects, publications, or conferences; no loans.
Application information: Contributes only to pre-selected organizations. Applications not accepted.
Officers and Trustees:* George L. Ohrstrom, Jr.,* V.P.; Ricard R. Ohrstrom, Jr.,* V.P.; Palma Cifu, Treas.; Magalen O. Bryant.
Number of staff: 1 part-time support.
EIN: 546039966

3198

Elis Olsson Memorial Foundation
c/o McGuire, Woods, Battle & Boothe
P.O. Box 397
Richmond 23203   (804) 644-4131
Application address: P.O. Box 311, West Point, VA 23181

Established in 1966 in VA.
Donor(s): Inga Olsson Nylander,‡ Signe Maria Olsson.‡
Foundation type: Independent
Financial data (yr. ended 12/31/91): Assets, $15,156,850 (M); expenditures, $712,729;

qualifying distributions, $664,452, including $626,050 for 111 grants (high: $100,000; low: $100).

Purpose and activities: Emphasis on education, including business and other higher educational institutions, elementary and secondary schools, and other education; support also for museums and the fine arts, medical and marine sciences, hospices, and Protestant church support.

Fields of interest: Higher education, business education, secondary education, elementary education, religious schools, arts, medical sciences, marine sciences, hospices, Protestant giving.

Types of support: Fellowships, professorships.

Limitations: Giving primarily in VA. No grants to individuals.

Application information:
 Initial approach: Letter
 Deadline(s): None
 Board meeting date(s): Oct. 1
 Write: Carle E. Davis, Secy.

Officers and Trustees:* Sture G. Olsson,* Pres.; Shirley C. Olsson,* V.P. and Treas.; Carle E. Davis,* Secy.

Number of staff: 1 part-time professional.

EIN: 546062436

3199
The Alison J. & Ella W. Parsons Foundation
2200 Dominion Tower
Norfolk 23510
Application address: 1700 Dominion Tower, Norfolk, VA 23510; Tel.: (806) 622-3366

Established in 1984 in VA.

Foundation type: Independent

Financial data (yr. ended 04/30/91): Assets, $5,077,438 (M); expenditures, $321,220; qualifying distributions, $276,000, including $276,000 for 12 grants (high: $50,000; low: $4,000).

Fields of interest: Higher education, civic affairs, social services, health, arts.

Types of support: Capital campaigns, professorships.

Limitations: Giving primarily in Norfolk, VA.

Application information:
 Initial approach: Letter
 Deadline(s): None
 Write: Marie Finch

Officers: William K. Butler II, Pres.; Howard L. Brantley, V.P.; Alan J. Hofheimer, Secy.-Treas.

Directors: Jane P. Batten, Robert C. Nusbaum.

EIN: 541253938

3200
Portsmouth Community Trust
P.O. Box 1394
Portsmouth 23705   (804) 397-5424

Established in 1965 in VA.

Foundation type: Community

Financial data (yr. ended 12/31/91): Assets, $1,106,784 (M); gifts received, $329,766; expenditures, $335,646; qualifying distributions, $310,358, including $310,358 for 74 grants (high: $25,000; low: $100; average: $100-$25,000).

Purpose and activities: Primary areas of interest include community development, community

funds, hospital building funds, religious organizations, and general charitable giving. Support also for museums, music, and other arts groups, libraries, public and civic affairs, recreational programs, seamen, medical education, education, including higher, secondary, adult education, and programs for minorities.

Fields of interest: Community development, community funds, hospitals—building funds, religion, general charitable giving, museums, arts, public affairs, civic affairs, community development, libraries, secondary education, higher education, adult education.

Types of support: Operating budgets, seed money, emergency funds, deficit financing, building funds, equipment, land acquisition, renovation projects, matching funds, scholarship funds, publications, conferences and seminars, capital campaigns, special projects.

Limitations: Giving limited to Portsmouth, VA, and the surrounding area. No grants to individuals.

Publications: Annual report, application guidelines, financial statement, grants list, informational brochure.

Application information: Application form required.
 Initial approach: Letter requesting application form
 Copies of proposal: 2
 Deadline(s): Feb. 28, May 1, Aug. 1, and Nov. 1
 Board meeting date(s): 1st Wednesday in Mar., June, Sept., and Dec.
 Write: Charles H. Leckrone, Exec. Dir.

Officers: W. Ashton Lewis, Chair.; Zelma Rivin, Vice-Chair.; Charles H. Leckrone, Exec. Dir.

Number of staff: 1 part-time professional.

EIN: 546062589

3201
Portsmouth General Hospital Foundation
P.O. Box 1053
Portsmouth 23705   (804) 398-4661

Established in 1987 in VA as the Seller's Trust through the sale of Portsmouth General Hospital, Inc. to Tidewater Health Care, Inc.; fully funded in 1988.

Foundation type: Independent

Financial data (yr. ended 06/30/91): Assets, $10,374,693 (M); expenditures, $1,190,692; qualifying distributions, $844,293, including $405,157 for 31 grants (high: $102,695; low: $50) and $18,750 for in-kind gifts.

Purpose and activities: "To promote and support innovative as well as established health care programs in the city of Portsmouth."

Fields of interest: Health, family services, family planning, health services, drug abuse.

Types of support: Matching funds, seed money, technical assistance, general purposes, equipment.

Limitations: Giving limited to Portsmouth, VA. No grants to individuals; or for scholarships or building funds.

Publications: Application guidelines, informational brochure (including application guidelines).

Application information: Application form not required.
 Initial approach: Letter of intent
 Copies of proposal: 1

Deadline(s): Jan. 31, Apr. 30, July 31, and Oct. 31
 Board meeting date(s): 1st Wednesday of Sept., Dec., Mar., and June
 Final notification: 2 weeks
 Write: Alan E. Gollihue, Exec. Dir.

Officer: Alan E. Gollihue, Exec. Dir.

Directors: J. Hunter Brantley, Jr., Ali A. Choudhury, Maury W. Cooke, Ernest F. Hardee, Douglas L. Johnson, Carl F. Medley, Jr., Sheila P. Pittman, Roger C. Reinhold, C. Edward Russell, Jr., Gordon E. Saffold, Theresa J. Saunders, David B. Stuart, Kevin Wilson.

Number of staff: 2 full-time professional.

EIN: 541463392

3202
Richard S. Reynolds Foundation ▼
Reynolds Metals Bldg.
P.O. Box 27003
Richmond 23261
Application address: David P. Reynolds, 6601 West Broad St., Richmond, VA 23230; Tel.: (804) 281-4801

Incorporated in 1965 in VA.

Donor(s): Julia L. Reynolds.‡

Foundation type: Independent

Financial data (yr. ended 06/30/91): Assets, $36,627,365 (M); gifts received, $64,877; expenditures, $1,710,108; qualifying distributions, $1,665,636, including $1,663,300 for 34 grants (high: $220,000; low: $1,000; average: $5,000-$50,000).

Purpose and activities: Support for higher and secondary education, health, hospitals, museums, cultural organizations, and human services.

Fields of interest: Higher education, secondary education, health, hospitals, museums.

Limitations: Giving primarily in VA. No grants to individuals.

Application information:
 Initial approach: Letter
 Deadline(s): None
 Write: David P. Reynolds, Pres.

Officers and Directors:* David P. Reynolds,* Pres.; Mrs. Glenn R. Martin,* V.P.; Richard S. Reynolds III,* Secy.; William G. Reynolds, Jr.,* Treas.

Number of staff: None.

EIN: 546037003

3203
Reynolds Metals Company Foundation
P.O. Box 27003
Richmond 23261-7003   (804) 281-2222

Established around 1978.

Donor(s): Reynolds Metals Co.

Foundation type: Company-sponsored

Financial data (yr. ended 12/31/91): Assets, $10,327,465 (M); gifts received, $2,475,000; expenditures, $874,817; qualifying distributions, $858,897, including $638,874 for 228 grants (high: $80,000; low: $35; average: $200-$75,000) and $219,140 for employee matching gifts.

Purpose and activities: Emphasis on higher education, including an employee matching gift program; support also for welfare, cultural

programs, hospitals and health associations, youth agencies, and civic affairs.
Fields of interest: Higher education, education, civic affairs, health associations, welfare, hospitals, youth, cultural programs.
Types of support: Employee matching gifts, building funds, scholarship funds, special projects.
Limitations: Giving primarily in areas of company operations, with emphasis on Richmond, VA.
Application information: Application form required.
  Initial approach: Letter
  Deadline(s): None
  Write: Janice H. Bailey, Admin.
Officers and Directors:* William O. Bourke,* Chair. and C.E.O.; D. Brickford Rider, Pres.; R. Bern Crowl,* Exec. V.P. and C.F.O.; Donald T. Cowles,* V.P., General Counsel, and Secy.; Julian H. Taylor, V.P. and Treas.; David C. Bilsing, V.P. and Controller; Henry S. Savedge, Jr., V.P., Finance; Joseph F. Awad,* V.P.; Douglas M. Jerrold, V.P.; John R. McGill,* V.P.; Yale M. Brandt, Richard G. Holder, Randolph N. Reynolds, W.G. Reynolds, Jr.
EIN: 541084698

3204
Greater Richmond Community Foundation
9211 Forest Hill Ave., Suite No. 109
Richmond 23235   (804) 330-7400

Established in 1968 in VA.
Foundation type: Community
Financial data (yr. ended 12/31/90): Assets, $7,363,241 (M); gifts received, $2,062,198; expenditures, $904,947; qualifying distributions, $744,727, including $662,716 for 103 grants (high: $50,000; low: $1,000; average: $1,000-$10,000) and $82,011 for 14 grants to individuals (high: $35,000; low: $8,000; average: $4,000-$5,000).
Fields of interest: Arts, cultural programs, education, community development, housing, child welfare, youth, AIDS, general charitable giving.
Types of support: Technical assistance, renovation projects, emergency funds, equipment, general purposes, matching funds, seed money, special projects.
Limitations: Giving limited to metropolitan Richmond, VA. No grants for annual campaigns, deficit financing, land acquisition, or building funds.
Publications: Annual report, application guidelines, financial statement, newsletter, informational brochure.
Application information: Application form required.
  Initial approach: Letter of intent
  Copies of proposal: 1
  Deadline(s): Dec. 5 and June 5
  Board meeting date(s): Quarterly
  Final notification: 90 days
  Write: Darcy S. Oman, Exec. Dir. and Secy.
Officers and Directors:* Wallace Stettinius,* Chair.; E. Bryson Powell,* Vice-Chair.; Paul H. Riley,* Vice-Chair.; Darcy S. Oman, Secy. and Exec. Dir.; Samuel A. Derieux,* Treas.; William L.S. Rowe,* General Counsel.
Number of staff: 2 full-time professional; 1 part-time professional.

EIN: 237009135

3205
Robins Foundation
c/o Central Fidelity Bank
P.O. Box 27602
Richmond 23261   (804) 697-6909

Established in 1957 in VA.
Foundation type: Independent
Financial data (yr. ended 12/31/91): Assets, $2,348,093 (M); expenditures, $110,080; qualifying distributions, $89,500, including $89,500 for 7 grants (high: $80,000; low: $500).
Fields of interest: Hospitals, youth, education, cultural programs, social services.
Application information:
  Initial approach: Letter
  Write: F.E. Deacon III, Secy.-Treas.
Officers and Directors:* E.C. Robins,* Pres.; E.B. Heilman,* V.P.; F.E. Deacon III,* Secy.-Treas.; A.R. Marchant, E.R. Porter, E.C. Robins, Jr., L.M. Robins.
Number of staff: None.
EIN: 540784484

3206
Edward W. and Betty Knight Scripps Foundation
Eagle Hill Farm HCR 1
P.O. Box 38
Charlottesville 22901   (804) 973-3345

Established in 1987 in VA.
Donor(s): The Scripps League Newspapers, Inc.
Foundation type: Company-sponsored
Financial data (yr. ended 04/30/91): Assets, $196,008 (M); gifts received, $251,597; expenditures, $253,608; qualifying distributions, $250,798, including $250,000 for 1 grant.
Fields of interest: Medical research.
Application information:
  Initial approach: Letter
  Board meeting date(s): May or June
  Write: Edward W. and Betty Knight Scripps, Dirs.
Officers and Directors:* Edward W. Scripps,* Pres. and Treas.; Betty Knight Scripps,* Secy.
EIN: 541426826

3207
Signet Banking Corporate Giving Program
Seven North 8th St.
P.O. Box 25970
Richmond 23260   (804) 747-2000

Financial data (yr. ended 12/31/90): Total giving, $1,956,191, including $1,895,610 for 528 grants (high: $200,000; low: $100; average: $3,700), $59,390 for 243 employee matching gifts and $1,191 for 70 in-kind gifts.
Purpose and activities: Support for the arts, health, education, community development, and civic affairs.
Fields of interest: Arts, community development, health, civic affairs, education.
Types of support: Donated products, use of facilities, public relations services, loaned talent, employee volunteer services, cause-related marketing, annual campaigns, employee

matching gifts, employee volunteer services, capital campaigns.
Limitations: Giving primarily in headquarters area and company locations.
Application information: Office of Corporate Secretary handles giving. Application form not required.
  Initial approach: Letter; Send requests to headquarters
  Copies of proposal: 1
  Deadline(s): Sept. 30 for next year's budget
  Board meeting date(s): Upon completion and approval of annual budget
  Write: Robert M. Freeman, Chair. and C.E.O.
Number of staff: 2 part-time professional; 1 part-time support.

3208
The Taylor Foundation
6969 Tidewater Dr.
Norfolk 23509

Trust established in 1951 in VA.
Donor(s): West India Fruit and Steamship Co., Inc., members of the Taylor family.
Foundation type: Independent
Financial data (yr. ended 12/31/90): Assets, $1,760,526 (M); expenditures, $222,791; qualifying distributions, $222,791, including $205,400 for 43 grants (high: $75,000; low: $500; average: $1,000)
Purpose and activities: Giving for hospitals, higher and secondary education, Protestant church support, social service agencies, and a sailors' retirement home.
Fields of interest: Hospitals, higher education, secondary education, Protestant giving, social services.
Types of support: Special projects.
Limitations: Giving primarily in NC, VA, and the Southeast. No grants to individuals.
Application information: Application form not required.
  Initial approach: Letter
  Deadline(s): Dec. 1
  Write: Robert T. Taylor, V.P.
Officers and Trustees:* Leslie M. Taylor,* Pres.; Robert T. Taylor,* V.P.; J. Lewis Rawls, Jr.,* Secy.; T.A. Bennett, Susan T. Kirkpatrick.
EIN: 540555235

3209
Theresa A. Thomas Memorial Foundation
c/o Sovran Ctr.
1111 East Main St., 21st Fl.
Richmond 23219
Application address: P.O. Box 1122, Richmond, VA 23208; Tel.: (804) 697-1200

Established in 1975.
Donor(s): George D. Thomas.‡
Foundation type: Independent
Financial data (yr. ended 08/31/91): Assets, $11,151,198 (M); expenditures, $9,261,660; qualifying distributions, $865,266, including $823,969 for 19 grants (high: $250,000; low: $2,000).
Purpose and activities: Giving for hospitals and health services, particularly for emergency rescue squads and medical training; support also for a college.

Fields of interest: Hospitals, health services, medical education, higher education.
Types of support: Operating budgets.
Limitations: Giving primarily in VA. No grants to individuals.
Application information:
  Initial approach: Letter
  Deadline(s): None
  Write: Charles L. Reed, Pres.
Officers and Directors:* Charles L. Reed,* Pres. and Treas.; James C. Roberts,* V.P.; Thomas P. Carr,* Secy.
Number of staff: None.
EIN: 510146629

3210
The Titmus Foundation, Inc.
P.O. Box 10
Sutherland 23885-0010   (804) 265-5834
Application address: 3522 Whippernock Farm Rd., Sutherland, VA 23885

Incorporated in 1945 in VA.
Donor(s): Edward Hutson Titmus, Sr.‡
Foundation type: Independent
Financial data (yr. ended 01/31/92): Assets, $12,606,197 (M); expenditures, $521,582; qualifying distributions, $500,147, including $480,767 for 159 grants (high: $28,825; low: $80; average: $80-$28,825).
Purpose and activities: Emphasis on Baptist church support and religious organizations, higher education, health, cancer research, and child welfare.
Fields of interest: Protestant giving, higher education, health, cancer, child welfare.
Types of support: Scholarship funds, building funds, matching funds, capital campaigns, land acquisition, emergency funds, professorships, research.
Limitations: Giving primarily in VA. No grants to individuals.
Application information: Application form not required.
  Initial approach: Proposal
  Deadline(s): None
  Board meeting date(s): July
  Write: Edward B. Titmus, Pres.
Officers: Edward B. Titmus, Pres. and Secy.; George M. Modlin, V.P.; John J. Whitt, Jr., V.P.; John O. Muldowney, Treas.
Number of staff: 1 full-time support.
EIN: 546051332

3211
The J. Edwin Treakle Foundation, Inc.
P.O. Box 1157
Gloucester 23061   (804) 693-0881

Incorporated in 1963 in VA.
Donor(s): J. Edwin Treakle.‡
Foundation type: Independent
Financial data (yr. ended 04/30/91): Assets, $4,369,686 (M); expenditures, $257,629; qualifying distributions, $208,067, including $166,000 for 43 grants (high: $23,000; low: $300).
Fields of interest: Protestant giving, youth, education, higher education, hospitals, community development, cultural programs, animal welfare, cancer.

Types of support: Annual campaigns, building funds, capital campaigns, continuing support, equipment, general purposes, scholarship funds.
Limitations: Giving primarily in VA. No grants to individuals.
Application information: Application form required.
  Copies of proposal: 1
  Deadline(s): Submit proposal between Jan. 1 and Apr. 30
  Board meeting date(s): Thursday after 2nd Monday in Feb., Apr., June, Aug., Oct., and Dec.
  Write: John Warren Cooke, Pres. and General Mgr.
Officers and Directors:* John W. Cooke,* Pres. and General Mgr.; Harry E. Dunn,* V.P. and Treas.; J. Kirkland Jarvis,* Secy.
Number of staff: 2 part-time professional; 2 part-time support.
EIN: 546051620

3212
Universal Leaf Foundation
Hamilton St. at Broad
P.O. Box 25099
Richmond 23260   (804) 359-9311

Established in 1975 in VA.
Donor(s): Universal Leaf Tobacco Co., Inc.
Foundation type: Company-sponsored
Financial data (yr. ended 06/30/91): Assets, $6,450,135 (M); gifts received, $4,949,278; expenditures, $380,611; qualifying distributions, $380,611, including $309,293 for 137 grants (high: $33,000; low: $50; average: $500-$1,000) and $70,262 for 202 employee matching gifts.
Purpose and activities: Emphasis on higher education, community funds, museums, youth agencies, health, medical research, the environment and animal welfare, civic affairs, public policy, the homeless, and the arts.
Fields of interest: Higher education, community funds, youth, health, medical research, museums, performing arts, fine arts, environment, conservation, wildlife, animal welfare, public policy, homeless, civic affairs.
Types of support: Annual campaigns, building funds, capital campaigns, emergency funds, employee matching gifts, operating budgets, renovation projects, research, technical assistance, internships, professorships, seed money.
Limitations: Giving primarily in VA.
Publications: Financial statement.
Application information: Application form not required.
  Initial approach: Letter of inquiry
  Deadline(s): None
  Final notification: 3 to 4 weeks
  Write: Nancy G. Powell, Mgr., Corp. Rels.
Officers and Directors:* Harry H. Harrell,* Pres. and C.E.O.; Wallace L. Chandler,* Vice-Chair.; T.R. Towers,* Vice-Chair.; O. Kemp Dozier, V.P. and Treas.; J.M. White, V.P.; F.V. Lowden III, Secy.
Number of staff: 1 full-time professional; 1 full-time support.
EIN: 510162337

3213
Virginia Electric & Power Company Corporate Giving Program
P.O. Box 26666
Richmond 23261   (804) 771-4417
Application address: 10 South Sixth Street, Richmond, VA 23261

Financial data (yr. ended 12/31/90): Total giving, $1,644,415, including $1,346,225 for grants, $143,745 for employee matching gifts and $154,445 for in-kind gifts.
Purpose and activities: Supports civic affairs, child welfare, higher education, race relations programs, science, youth, United Funds, environmental issues, hospitals, music, theater, the performing arts, museums, health, human services, and rescue and fire squads.
Fields of interest: Civic affairs, community development, environment, hospitals, music, science and technology, youth, theater, performing arts, museums, child welfare, higher education, race relations, safety, secondary education, higher education, medical education.
Types of support: General purposes, capital campaigns, employee matching gifts, building funds, in-kind gifts.
Limitations: Giving primarily in areas where the home offices and service areas are located. No support for tax-supported organizations or national health organizations.
Publications: Informational brochure (including application guidelines).
Application information: Application form required.
  Initial approach: Complete proposal with budget
  Copies of proposal: 1
  Deadline(s): Jan. is the best time to apply
  Final notification: 4 weeks
  Write: Thomas M. Hogg, Contribs. Admin.
Number of staff: 8 full-time professional; 1 full-time support.

3214
Washington Forrest Foundation
2300 South Ninth St.
Arlington 22204   (703) 920-3688

Incorporated in 1968 in VA.
Donor(s): Benjamin M. Smith.‡
Foundation type: Independent
Financial data (yr. ended 06/30/91): Assets, $7,376,137 (M); expenditures, $646,757; qualifying distributions, $350,242, including $313,864 for 82 grants (high: $35,000; low: $300; average: $500-$5,000).
Purpose and activities: Support for programs benefiting the Arlington, and northern VA community, with and emphasis on human services; support also for the arts, education, youth programs, health, and welfare.
Fields of interest: Arts, education, health, youth, welfare.
Types of support: General purposes, operating budgets, continuing support, annual campaigns, seed money, emergency funds, building funds, equipment, matching funds, special projects, capital campaigns, renovation projects, scholarship funds.
Limitations: Giving primarily in Arlington and northern VA. Generally, no support for public

colleges, national programs, or foreign programs. No grants to individuals, or for fellowships or multi-year pledges.
Publications: Program policy statement, application guidelines.
Application information: Application form required.
  Initial approach: Letter or telephone
  Copies of proposal: 1
  Deadline(s): Contact foundation
  Board meeting date(s): Contact foundation
  Final notification: 2 weeks
  Write: Lindsey Peete, Exec. Dir.
Officers and Directors:* Margaret S. Peete,* Pres.; Deborah Lucckese,* V.P.; Leslie Ariail,* Secy.; Benjamin M. Smith, Jr.,* Treas.
Number of staff: 1 part-time professional.
EIN: 237002944

3215
Wheat Foundation
Riverfront Plaza
901 East Byrd St.
Richmond 23219   (804) 782-3518

Established in 1959.
Donor(s): Wheat First Securities, Inc.
Foundation type: Company-sponsored
Financial data (yr. ended 03/31/91): Assets, $1,100,583 (M); gifts received, $351,621; expenditures, $391,614; qualifying distributions, $384,049, including $346,166 for 162 grants (high: $20,000; low: $250; average: $500-$100,000) and $36,770 for 159 employee matching gifts.
Fields of interest: Education, education—building funds, education—minorities, higher education, secondary education, hospitals, health services, science and technology, fine arts, museums, theater, cultural programs.
Types of support: Building funds, professorships, endowment funds, capital campaigns, renovation projects, scholarship funds, employee matching gifts.
Limitations: Giving primarily in VA, WV, NC, PA, OH, MD, DE, and Washington, DC. No grants to individuals, or for operating funds; no loans.
Application information: Application form not required.
  Initial approach: Telephone
  Copies of proposal: 1
  Deadline(s): None
  Board meeting date(s): Mar., June, Sept., and Dec.
  Final notification: Within 30 days following board meeting
  Write: William V. Daniel, Dir. and Treas.
Officers and Trustees:* John L. McElroy, Jr.,* Pres.; Howard T. Macrae, Jr., Secy.; William V. Daniel,* Treas.; Sharon L. Hobart, James C. Wheat, Jr., Marshall B. Wishnack.
Number of staff: None.
EIN: 546047119

WASHINGTON

3216
Airborne Freight Corporate Giving Program
c/o Corp. Giving Comm./Treas.
P.O. Box 662
Seattle 98111   (206) 285-4600

Purpose and activities: Support for culture and art, health and welfare, civic affairs, affirmative action, and business.
Fields of interest: Health, social services, cultural programs, arts, civic affairs, business.
Types of support: Annual campaigns, operating budgets, special projects, capital campaigns, continuing support.
Limitations: Giving primarily in WA.
Publications: Application guidelines.
Application information: Application form not required.
   Initial approach: Brief letter to headquarters
   Board meeting date(s): Corp. Contrib. Comm. meets quarterly
   Final notification: Within 2 weeks of meeting; denied requestors are not notified
   Write: Lanny H. Michael, V.P. or Francine Fay, Admin.
Number of staff: None.

3217
Paul G. Allen Foundation for Medical Research
1111 Third Ave. Bldg., Suite 3400
Seattle 98101-3299

Established in 1987 in WA; funded in 1989.
Donor(s): Paul G. Allen.
Foundation type: Independent
Financial data (yr. ended 12/31/90): Assets, $119,752 (M); expenditures, $301,040; qualifying distributions, $300,503, including $300,255 for 4 grants (high: $300,000; low: $30).
Fields of interest: Medical research, medical education, cancer.
Types of support: Research.
Limitations: No grants to individuals.
Application information: Application form not required.
   Initial approach: Proposal
   Deadline(s): None
   Write: Allen D. Israel, Asst. Secy.
Officers and Director:* Paul G. Allen,* Pres.; Bert Kolde, Secy.
EIN: 943082530

3218
Norman Archibald Charitable Foundation
c/o First Interstate Bank of Washington
P.O. Box 21927
Seattle 98111   (206) 292-3543

Established in 1976 in WA.
Donor(s): Norman Archibald.‡
Foundation type: Independent

Financial data (yr. ended 09/30/91): Assets, $6,970,429 (M); expenditures, $388,872; qualifying distributions, $337,918, including $301,200 for 96 grants (high: $15,000; low: $1,000).
Purpose and activities: Support primarily for youth and child development programs; support also for AIDS and other medical research, higher education and libraries, museums and the performing arts, social services for the aged and the handicapped, housing programs, and animal welfare and conservation.
Fields of interest: Youth, child welfare, social services, arts, libraries, higher education, environment, aged, AIDS, health.
Types of support: General purposes, seed money, building funds, equipment, land acquisition, conferences and seminars, program-related investments, publications, renovation projects, research, special projects.
Limitations: Giving primarily in the Puget Sound region of WA. No support for government entities or private foundations. No grants to individuals, or for deficit financing, endowment funds, scholarships, or fellowships; no loans.
Publications: Annual report, application guidelines.
Application information: Application form not required.
   Initial approach: Letter or telephone
   Copies of proposal: 3
   Deadline(s): None
   Board meeting date(s): 5 or 6 times per year as needed
   Write: Lawrence E. Miller, V.P. and Trust Officer, First Interstate Bank of Washington
Advisors: Durwood Alkire, J. Shan Mullin, Stuart H. Prestrud.
Trustee: First Interstate Bank of Washington.
Number of staff: None.
EIN: 911098014

3219
Benaroya Foundation
1001 4th Ave. Plaza, Suite 4700
Seattle 98154

Established in 1984 in WA.
Donor(s): Jack A. Benaroya, Larry R. Benaroya.
Foundation type: Independent
Financial data (yr. ended 11/30/90): Assets, $1,430,768 (M); gifts received, $682,500; expenditures, $543,692; qualifying distributions, $542,000, including $542,000 for 6 grants (high: $300,000; low: $5,000).
Purpose and activities: Support primarily for health, including medical research for diabetes and medical education; giving also for museums.
Fields of interest: Medical research, medical education, health, museums.
Types of support: Equipment.
Limitations: Giving primarily in Seattle, WA.
Application information:
   Initial approach: Proposal
   Deadline(s): None
   Write: Jack A. Benaroya, Pres.
Officers: Jack A. Benaroya, Pres.; Donna R. Benaroya, V.P.; Larry R. Benaroya, Secy.-Treas.
Directors: Alan G. Benaroya, Rebecca B. Benaroya, Sherry-Lee Benaroya.
EIN: 911280516

3220
Bishop Foundation
c/o Seafirst Bank, Charitable Trust Services
P.O. Box 24565, CSC-23
Seattle 98124   (206) 358-3388

Trust established in 1962 in WA.
Donor(s): E.K. Bishop,‡ Lillian F. Bishop.‡
Foundation type: Independent
Financial data (yr. ended 07/31/91): Assets, $2,593,400 (M); expenditures, $126,443; qualifying distributions, $102,756, including $90,193 for 1 grant.
Purpose and activities: Cure of diseases of the eye, the correction of faulty vision, the relief of needy sufferers from eye afflictions, and for use in related fields.
Fields of interest: Ophthalmology, medical research.
Types of support: Research.
Limitations: Giving primarily in WA. No grants to individuals.
Application information: Funds presently committed to the University of Washington School of Medicine. Applications not accepted.
   Board meeting date(s): Semiannually
   Write: Rod Johnson, Seafirst Bank
Directors: Charles H. Bagley, Winston D. Brown, John Hall, Carl D.F. Jensen, M.D., Walter Petersen, M.D.
Trustee: Seafirst Bank.
Number of staff: None.
EIN: 916027252

3221
Blue Mountain Area Foundation
11 South Second
P.O. Box 603
Walla Walla 99362   (509) 529-4371

Incorporated in 1984 in WA.
Foundation type: Community
Financial data (yr. ended 06/30/91): Assets, $2,688,305 (M); gifts received, $815,247; expenditures, $222,261; qualifying distributions, $127,201, including $91,018 for grants, $32,348 for 36 grants to individuals (high: $3,100; low: $300) and $3,835 for in-kind gifts.
Purpose and activities: Giving primarily for community projects, programs for organizations promoting welfare and education, social services, historical preservation, the arts, health, and animal welfare; support also for higher education through scholarship funds.
Fields of interest: Community development, education, social services, aged, family services, child welfare, arts, historic preservation, higher education, libraries, health, animal welfare.
Types of support: Scholarship funds, equipment, program-related investments, renovation projects, seed money, special projects, emergency funds.
Limitations: Giving limited to Walla Walla, Columbia, Garfield, Benton and Franklin counties, WA, and Umatilla County, OR.
Publications: Annual report, application guidelines, newsletter, informational brochure.
Application information: Application form not required.
   Initial approach: Letter
   Copies of proposal: 1
   Deadline(s): July 1
   Final notification: Oct.

Write: Eleanor S. Kane, Admin.

Officers and Trustees:* Gary Sirmon,* Pres.; Tom Baker,* V.P.; Thomas K. Baffney, Sharon Culley, Mark C. Graves, Barbara Hubbard, Eva M. Iverson, Vernon D. Kegley, Vernon Marll, Louis B. Perry, Wilbur Pribilsky, Mary Lou Tillay, Robert Zagelow.

Number of staff: 1 part-time professional.

EIN: 911250104

3222
The Boeing Company Corporate Giving Program

P.O. Box 3707, M/S 11/83
Seattle 98124-2207   (206) 655-6679

Financial data (yr. ended 12/31/90): Total giving, $23,670,333, including $17,845,169 for grants (high: $2,470,051; low: $200), $1,325,164 for employee matching gifts and $4,500,000 for in-kind gifts.

Purpose and activities: "The Boeing commitment to corporate citizenship is a basic part of our approach to doing business. We believe that the true quality of any company is measured not only by the quality of its products and services, but by the the strength of its partnership with the larger community. Boeing and its employees take great pride in our support for a wide range of educational, human service, civic, and cultural programs. In 1990, total gifts (company and employees) were more than $46 million. Boeing corporate gifts totaled $23.7 million. Our employees, through the Boeing Employees Good Neighbor Fund and gift matching programs, contributed $22.8 million. Employees also volunteered more than 1,000,000 hours of their own time to participate in hundreds of worthwhile projects."

Fields of interest: Arts, humanities, civic affairs, education, science and technology, social services, museums, performing arts, urban development, community development, delinquency, women, business, vocational education, aged, child welfare, drug abuse, community funds, handicapped, youth, education—early childhood, education—minorities, literacy, alcoholism, leadership development, rehabilitation, public affairs, volunteerism, hunger, housing, homeless, adult education, AIDS.

Types of support: Building funds, capital campaigns, employee matching gifts, equipment, fellowships, matching funds, professorships, renovation projects, research, scholarship funds, in-kind gifts, employee volunteer services, loaned talent, use of facilities, emergency funds, donated equipment, seed money, technical assistance, consulting services.

Limitations: Giving primarily in Wichita, KS; Philadelphia, PA; and Seattle, WA, and other operating locations; no support for programs whose beneficiaries are not in areas where Boeing employees live or work. No support for hospital or medical research organizations, political candidates, committees or organizations, or religious organizations or institutions. No grants to individuals; generally no support for endowments.

Publications: Corporate giving report (including application guidelines).

Application information: Company has a staff that only handles contributions. Application form not required.

Initial approach: Query letter to headquarters or nearest company facility
Copies of proposal: 1
Deadline(s): None, but few grants approved during fourth quarter
Board meeting date(s): No regular schedule
Final notification: 4-6 weeks; will send rejection letter
Write: Joe A. Taller, Mgr., Contribs. and Education Rels.

Administrator: Joe A. Taller, Corp. Dir., Contribs. and Educ. Rels.

Number of staff: 5 full-time professional; 3 full-time support; 1 part-time support.

3223
Burlington Resources Foundation ▼

999 Third Ave., 45th Fl.
Seattle 98104-4097   (206) 728-8625

Established in 1989.

Donor(s): Burlington Resources, Inc., and its subsidiaries.

Foundation type: Company-sponsored

Financial data (yr. ended 12/31/90): Assets, $5,028,371 (M); gifts received, $4,602,099; expenditures, $5,170,330; qualifying distributions, $5,147,793, including $5,147,793 for 334 grants (high: $1,000,000; low: $50; average: $5,000-$100,000).

Purpose and activities: Giving in the following areas: 1) Community funds and other federated organizations; 2) Educational institutions, both public and private, primarily at the college level, preferably directed toward the improvement of the quality of education; 3) Youth organizations; 4) Hospitals and medical facilities, including hospital building funds and equipment; 5) Cultural programs, including performing and visual arts, historical centers, and public and educational broadcasting; and 6) Human service agencies, including chemical dependency treatment and prevention, senior citizens, runaway youth, spouse and child abuse, offender programs, and women's programs.

Fields of interest: Community funds, education, higher education, youth, hospitals, cultural programs, social services, drug abuse, aged, women.

Types of support: Building funds, equipment.

Limitations: Giving primarily in areas of company operations. No support for religious groups for religious purposes, veterans' or fraternal service organizations, or national health organizations. No grants to individuals, or for endowment funds, fundraising events, or computers or computer-related projects.

Application information: Application form required.

Write: Donald K. North, Pres.

Officers and Directors:* Thomas H. O'Leary, Chair.; Donald K. North, Pres.; Christopher T. Bayley, V.P.; Leslie S. Leland, Secy.; H. Brent Austin, Treas.

EIN: 943096534

Recent health grants:

3223-1 Cancer Counseling, Houston, TX, $10,000. 1990.

3223-2 Crisis Pregnancy Center of King County, Seattle, WA, $12,500. 1990.

3223-3 Hope Heart Institute, Seattle, WA, $25,000. 1990.

3223-4 Texas Childrens Hospital, Houston, TX, $25,000. 1990.

3223-5 University of Texas System Cancer Center, Houston, TX, $150,000. 1990.

3223-6 Virginia Mason Medical Center, Seattle, WA, $25,000. 1990.

3224
Ben B. Cheney Foundation, Inc. ▼

1201 Pacific Ave., Suite 1600
Tacoma 98402   (206) 572-2442

Incorporated in 1955 in WA.

Donor(s): Ben B. Cheney,‡ Marian Cheney Olrogg.‡

Foundation type: Independent

Financial data (yr. ended 12/31/90): Assets, $22,433,926 (M); gifts received, $1,298,738; expenditures, $2,548,319; qualifying distributions, $2,387,744, including $2,143,670 for 138 grants (high: $100,000; low: $1,000; average: $1,500-$20,000).

Purpose and activities: Giving primarily for education; health and social services, including programs for the elderly, the disabled, and youth; community development, including recreational facilities; and museums and other cultural programs.

Fields of interest: Education, higher education, health, hospitals, social services, aged, handicapped, youth, community development, cultural programs, arts, museums.

Types of support: Seed money, building funds, equipment, general purposes, scholarship funds, special projects, emergency funds.

Limitations: Giving limited to WA and OR. No support for religious organizations for sectarian purposes. No grants to individuals, or for operating budgets, basic research, endowment funds, conferences or seminars, or book, film, or video production; no loans.

Publications: Informational brochure (including application guidelines).

Application information: Application form required.

Initial approach: Letter
Copies of proposal: 4
Deadline(s): 4 weeks prior to board meetings
Board meeting date(s): May, Sept., and Dec.
Final notification: Within 3 months
Write: Elgin E. Olrogg, V.P.

Officers and Trustees:* R. Gene Grant,* Pres.; John F. Hansler,* Secy.; Elgin E. Olrogg,* Treas. and Exec. Dir.; Bradbury F. Cheney.

Number of staff: 2 full-time professional; 1 full-time support.

EIN: 916053760

Recent health grants:

3224-1 American Cancer Society, Medford, OR, $19,570. To complete Cheney Conference Center, multimedia presentation room. 1990.

3224-2 Another Door to Learning of Tacoma, Tacoma, WA, $10,000. To provide testing and tutoring to learning-disabled children. 1990.

3224-3 Clallam-Jefferson Community Action Council, Port Townsend, WA, $10,000. To provide primary medical care for low-income families. 1990.

3224-4 Community Alcohol and Drug Service, Everett, PA, $10,000. To expand outpatient counseling program for teenagers. 1990.

3224-5 Community Health Center, Ashland, OR, $15,000. To expand primary medical care for low-income families. 1990.

3224-6 Evergreen Counseling Center, Aberdeen, WA, $10,000. To renovate offices and counseling rooms for expanding program. 1990.

3224-7 Good Samaritan Outreach Services, Puyallup, WA, $25,000. To establish respite center for Alzheimer patients. 1990.

3224-8 Greater Lakes Mental Health Foundation, Tacoma, WA, $17,000. To expand facilities for substance abuse treatment to mentally ill persons. 1990.

3224-9 Pierce County AIDS Foundation, Tacoma, WA, $18,000. To provide services for children affected by AIDS. 1990.

3224-10 Rogue Valley Medical Center, Medford, OR, $50,000. For equipment for Neonatal Intensive Care Unit. 1990.

3224-11 Rogue Valley Medical Center, Medford, OR, $25,000. To equip and furnish health education library. 1990.

3224-12 Ronald McDonald House, Seattle, WA, $25,000. For temporary medical housing. 1990.

3224-13 Saint Clare Hospital, Tacoma, WA, $50,000. To purchase operating table and surgical instruments. 1990.

3224-14 Tacoma General Hospital, Tacoma, WA, $150,000. To renovate inpatient regional cancer center. 1990.

3225
Comstock Foundation
819 Washington Trust Financial Ctr.
West 717 Sprague Ave.
Spokane 99204   (509) 747-1527

Established in 1950 in WA.
Donor(s): Josie Comstock Shadle.‡
Foundation type: Independent
Financial data (yr. ended 12/31/91): Assets, $13,282,182 (M); expenditures, $957,228; qualifying distributions, $876,904, including $876,028 for 72 grants (high: $147,600; low: $566; average: $300-$35,000).
Purpose and activities: Emphasis on capital grants to recreational facilities and other community development projects, social service agencies, aid to the disadvantaged and handicapped, child welfare, and youth agencies. Giving also for health organizations and hospitals, the arts, including music and the performing arts, civic affairs, vocational and higher education, transportation, drug abuse programs, crime and law enforcement, hunger programs, Native Americans, and religious organizations.
Fields of interest: Recreation, community development, social services, child welfare, youth, health, arts, civic affairs, higher education.
Types of support: Building funds, equipment, land acquisition, scholarship funds, research, general purposes, matching funds.
Limitations: Giving limited to WA, with a focus on the Spokane and Inland Empire areas. No grants to individuals, or for endowment funds or operating budgets; no loans. In general, no grants payable for reserve purposes, deficit financing,

publications, films, emergency funds, conferences, or travel.
Publications: Informational brochure, program policy statement, application guidelines.
Application information: Application form required.
  Initial approach: Proposal
  Copies of proposal: 1
  Deadline(s): None
  Board meeting date(s): Weekly
  Final notification: 10 days
  Write: Horton Herman, Trustee
Trustees: Harold W. Coffin, Horton Herman, Charles M. Leslie, Luke G. Williams.
Number of staff: 1 part-time support.
EIN: 911534637

3226
Fales Foundation Trust
c/o The Bank of California, N.A.
P.O. Box 3123
Seattle 98114

Established in 1985 in WA.
Foundation type: Independent
Financial data (yr. ended 01/31/91): Assets, $2,651,647 (M); expenditures, $229,247; qualifying distributions, $196,594, including $184,750 for 28 grants (high: $20,000; low: $500).
Fields of interest: Community development, health, cultural programs, arts.
Types of support: Operating budgets.
Limitations: Giving limited to WA. No grants to individuals.
Application information: Contributes only to pre-selected organizations. Applications not accepted.
Trustees: Ward L. Sax, The Bank of California, N.A.
EIN: 916087669

3227
The Foster Foundation
1201 Third Ave., Suite 2101
Seattle 98101

Established in 1984 in WA.
Donor(s): Evelyn W. Foster.
Foundation type: Independent
Financial data (yr. ended 12/31/91): Assets, $20,271,333 (M); expenditures, $1,338,248; qualifying distributions, $1,204,188, including $1,200,000 for 61 grants (high: $500,000; low: $1,000).
Fields of interest: Cultural programs, higher education, literacy, social services, housing, hunger, youth, child welfare, health.
Types of support: Seed money, building funds, equipment, research, matching funds, special projects, scholarship funds.
Limitations: Giving primarily in the Pacific Northwest and AK. No grants to individuals, or for fundraising, endowment funds, or unrestricted operating funds; no loans.
Application information:
  Initial approach: Letter
  Deadline(s): None
  Final notification: 3 months
  Write: Jill Goodsell, Administrator

Officer and Trustees:* Jill Goodsell,* Admin.; Evelyn W. Foster, Michael G. Foster, Thomas B. Foster.
EIN: 911265474

3228
Foundation Northwest
(Formerly Spokane Inland Northwest Community Foundation)
421 West Riverside Ave., No. 400
Spokane 99201-0403   (509) 624-2606

Incorporated in 1974 in WA.
Foundation type: Community
Financial data (yr. ended 06/30/92): Assets, $6,700,000 (M); gifts received, $450,000; expenditures, $835,997; qualifying distributions, $492,695, including $492,695 for 232 grants (high: $30,000; low: $500; average: $2,500-$7,500).
Purpose and activities: Giving for charitable and philanthropic purposes in the fields of the arts, the elderly, education and youth, civic improvement, historical restoration, rehabilitation, and social and health services.
Fields of interest: Arts, aged, education, youth, civic affairs, community development, historic preservation, social services, health services, rehabilitation.
Types of support: Special projects, seed money, technical assistance, general purposes, scholarship funds.
Limitations: Giving limited to the Inland Northwest (eastern WA and northern ID). No support for sectarian religious purposes. No grants to individuals, or for deficit financing, building funds, emergency funds, research, or matching grants; no loans.
Publications: Annual report, informational brochure (including application guidelines), newsletter, application guidelines.
Application information: Scholarship awards paid to educational institutions. Application form required.
  Initial approach: Letter or telephone requesting guidelines
  Copies of proposal: 3
  Deadline(s): Oct. 1 and Apr. 1 for grants; Mar. 1 for scholarships
  Board meeting date(s): Sept. through June
  Final notification: 3 months
  Write: Peter A. Jackson, Pres.
Officer: Peter A. Jackson, Pres.
Directors: Sue S. Flammia, Craig R. Soehren, and 23 additional trustees.
Number of staff: 2 full-time professional; 1 part-time support.
EIN: 910941053

3229
Gottfried & Mary Fuchs Foundation
c/o The Bank of California, N.A.
P.O. Box 1917
Tacoma 98401-1917   (206) 591-2548

Trust established in 1960 in WA.
Donor(s): Gottfried Fuchs,‡ Mary Fuchs.‡
Foundation type: Independent
Financial data (yr. ended 12/31/90): Assets, $11,694,288 (M); expenditures, $725,811; qualifying distributions, $554,402, including

$524,493 for 68 grants (high: $49,500; low: $500).

Purpose and activities: Priority of support for charitable, educational, scientific, literary or religious purposes not normally financed by tax funds; emphasis on child welfare and youth agencies, higher and secondary education, cultural programs, hospitals, and food programs. Prefers funding special capital or services projects rather than operating budgets.

Fields of interest: Child welfare, youth, education, higher education, secondary education, hospitals, cultural programs, drug abuse.

Types of support: Continuing support, annual campaigns, emergency funds, building funds, equipment, scholarship funds, research, operating budgets, matching funds, special projects, capital campaigns.

Limitations: Giving primarily in Tacoma, Pierce County, and the lower Puget Sound area of WA. No grants to individuals.

Publications: Application guidelines.

Application information: Application form required.

   Initial approach: Letter
   Copies of proposal: 5
   Deadline(s): 3 weeks prior to board meetings
   Board meeting date(s): Mar., June, Sept., and Dec.
   Write: Gayleene Berry, Asst. V.P. and Trust Officer, The Bank of California, N.A.

Trustee: The Bank of California, N.A.

Number of staff: 1 part-time professional.

EIN: 916022284

3230
Glaser Foundation, Inc.

P.O. Box 6548
Bellevue 98008-0548

Incorporated in 1952 in WA.

Donor(s): Paul F. Glaser.‡

Foundation type: Independent

Financial data (yr. ended 11/30/91): Assets, $6,864,474 (M); expenditures, $307,391; qualifying distributions, $303,320, including $278,192 for 36 grants (high: $150,000; low: $200; average: $3,000-$5,000).

Purpose and activities: Major focus on drug abuse; support also for direct-line service health agencies, and agencies serving children, youth, the handicapped, the aged, and the indigent; support also for some arts organizations.

Fields of interest: Drug abuse, child welfare, youth, handicapped, aged, disadvantaged, arts, education—minorities, medical education, health services.

Types of support: Matching funds, special projects, seed money.

Limitations: Giving primarily in the Puget Sound, WA, area. No grants to individuals, or for general purposes, building or endowment funds, scholarships, fellowships, publications, or conferences; no loans.

Publications: Application guidelines.

Application information: Application form required.

   Initial approach: Letter
   Copies of proposal: 2
   Deadline(s): None

Board meeting date(s): Jan., Mar., May, July, Sept., and Nov.

   Final notification: Last day in month of board meeting
   Write: Joanne Van Sickle

Officers and Directors:* Patrick F. Patrick,* Pres.; R. Thomas Olson,* V.P.; R.N. Brandenburg,* Secy.; Janet L. Politeo,* Treas.; R. William Carlstrom.

Number of staff: 1 part-time professional.

EIN: 916028694

3231
GTE Northwest Corporate Giving Program

1800 41 St.
Everett 98206   (206) 261-5321
Special address for applications: P.O. Box 1003 (5-COM), Everett, WA 98201

Financial data (yr. ended 12/31/90): Total giving, $788,000, including $650,000 for grants and $138,000 for in-kind gifts.

Purpose and activities: Main interests are K-12 education, substance abuse, and economic development; also support for historic preservation, museums, music, performing arts, theater, literacy, health and heart disease, hospitals, volunteerism, homeless, disadvantaged, hunger, and housing. Grants over $1,000 are made from the GTE Foundation and under $1,000 from the direct giving program.

Fields of interest: Business, business education, child welfare, community development, community funds, computer sciences, disadvantaged, drug abuse, education—building funds, family services, handicapped, health, heart disease, historic preservation, homeless, hospitals, hospitals—building funds, housing, hunger, literacy, museums, music, performing arts, public affairs, theater, women, youth, volunteerism, education, libraries, minorities, physical sciences, physics, mathematics, transportation.

Types of support: Annual campaigns, building funds, capital campaigns, equipment, fellowships, lectureships, matching funds, employee-related scholarships, technical assistance, employee matching gifts, donated equipment, publications, employee volunteer services, in-kind gifts, loaned talent, use of facilities.

Limitations: Giving limited to headquarters and company locations; no support for organizations which are outside of the GTE northwest serving area or do not significantly serve those areas.

Publications: Program policy statement, application guidelines, newsletter, corporate report.

Application information: Do not meet one-on-one with requestors, unless special information is required; Public Affairs office handles giving. Application form required.

   Initial approach: Request must be in writing; send requests to headquarters
   Copies of proposal: 1
   Deadline(s): June 1 of this year for consideration in budget for following year
   Board meeting date(s): Mid to late summer - with several additional levels of approval
   Final notification: Late 1st quarter of year grant is made
   Write: Marilyn Hoggarth, Community Affairs Mgr.

Administrator: Marilyn Hoggarth, Community Affairs Mgr.

Number of staff: 1 full-time professional.

3232
Robert G. Hemingway Foundation

c/o Seafirst Bank
P.O. Box 24565
Seattle 98124
Application address: 1301 Spring St., Unit 20J, Seattle, WA 98104

Foundation type: Independent

Financial data (yr. ended 04/30/91): Assets, $4,749,279 (M); expenditures, $210,495; qualifying distributions, $195,385, including $183,725 for 8 grants (high: $80,000; low: $1,000).

Fields of interest: Medical research, legal services, higher education.

Types of support: Scholarship funds, research, general purposes.

Limitations: Giving primarily in ID and WA. No grants to individuals.

Application information: Application form not required.

   Initial approach: Letter
   Deadline(s): Preferably before Mar. 1
   Write: Susan Hemingway, Admin. Dir.

Officer: Susan Hemingway, Admin. Dir.

Trustee: Seafirst Bank.

EIN: 876176774

3233
Florence B. Kilworth Charitable Foundation

c/o Puget Sound National Bank
P.O. Box 11500, MS 8262
Tacoma 98411-5052   (206) 593-3884

Established in 1977.

Foundation type: Independent

Financial data (yr. ended 12/31/91): Assets, $3,812,271 (M); expenditures, $204,519; qualifying distributions, $165,283, including $157,650 for 51 grants (high: $12,000; low: $500; average: $500-$12,000).

Fields of interest: Hospitals, medical research, medical education, education, recreation, arts, religion—missionary programs.

Types of support: Annual campaigns, building funds, capital campaigns, operating budgets, research, scholarship funds, special projects.

Limitations: Giving primarily in the Tacoma and Pierce counties, WA, area. No grants to individuals.

Application information: Application form not required.

   Initial approach: Letter
   Copies of proposal: 1
   Deadline(s): None
   Board meeting date(s): Month following end of calendar quarter
   Final notification: By letter
   Write: John D. Baker, V.P., Puget Sound National Bank

Trustees: Florence Morris, Puget Sound National Bank.

EIN: 916221495

3234
Leuthold Foundation, Inc.
1006 Old National Bank Bldg.
Spokane 99201   (509) 624-3944

Incorporated in 1948 in WA.
Donor(s): Members of the Leuthold family.
Foundation type: Independent
Financial data (yr. ended 06/30/91): Assets,
$6,991,013 (M); gifts received, $700;
expenditures, $472,750; qualifying distributions,
$361,273, including $323,345 for 72 grants
(high: $70,100; low: $100; average:
$75-$10,000).
Fields of interest: Youth, aged, hospitals, family
planning, elementary education, secondary
education, higher education, religious schools,
social services, performing arts.
Types of support: Operating budgets, continuing
support, annual campaigns, building funds,
matching funds, endowment funds, equipment,
general purposes, scholarship funds.
Limitations: Giving limited to Spokane County,
WA. No grants to individuals; no loans.
Publications: Application guidelines, program
policy statement.
Application information: Application form
required.
   Initial approach: Letter
   Copies of proposal: 1
   Deadline(s): Submit proposal preferably in May
     or Nov.; deadlines May 15 and Nov. 15
   Board meeting date(s): June and Dec.
   Final notification: 1 week after board meets
   Write: John H. Leuthold, Pres.
Officers and Trustees:* John H. Leuthold,* Pres.;
Betty B. Leuthold,* V.P.; O.M. Kimmel, Jr.,*
Secy.-Treas.; Caroline E. Leuthold, Allan H. Toole.
Number of staff: 1 part-time support.
EIN: 916028589

3235
Byron W. and Alice L. Lockwood
Foundation
8121 S.E. 44th St.
Mercer Island 98040   (206) 232-1881
Additional tel.: (206) 232-0131

Established in 1968 in WA.
Foundation type: Independent
Financial data (yr. ended 12/31/90): Assets,
$9,922,986 (M); expenditures, $602,952;
qualifying distributions, $494,876, including
$441,580 for 36 grants (high: $100,000; low:
$145).
Fields of interest: Health, health services,
hospitals—building funds, medical research,
cultural programs, museums, child welfare,
youth, social services, higher education.
Types of support: Professorships, general
purposes.
Limitations: Giving primarily in Seattle, WA.
Publications: 990-PF.
Application information: Application form not
required.
   Initial approach: Letter or proposal
   Copies of proposal: 1
   Deadline(s): Nov. 15
   Board meeting date(s): Nov.
   Final notification: Dec. 31 to Jan. 31
   Write: Sally Easterbrook

Officers and Trustees:* Paul R. Cressman,* Pres.;
James R. Palmer,* Secy.-Treas.; Paul R. Cressman,
Jr., Margaret Whiteman.
Number of staff: 1 part-time professional.
EIN: 910833426

3236
Matlock Foundation ▼
1201 Third Ave., Suite 4900
Seattle 98101-3009   (206) 224-5196

Incorporated in 1954 in WA.
Donor(s): Simpson Timber Co., Simpson Paper
Co., Pacific Western Extruded Plastics Co.
Foundation type: Company-sponsored
Financial data (yr. ended 12/31/90): Assets, $0
(M); gifts received, $2,225,033; expenditures,
$2,271,621; qualifying distributions, $2,269,560,
including $2,167,255 for 631 grants (high:
$66,667; low: $50; average: $500-$15,000) and
$102,305 for 167 employee matching gifts.
Purpose and activities: Allocates funds for giving
by Simpson Fund and Simpson Reed Fund to
community funds and for scholarships; giving
also for arts and cultural programs, other
education, social service and youth agencies, and
health services and hospitals.
Fields of interest: Community funds, education,
higher education, arts, cultural programs, youth,
social services, hospitals, health.
Types of support: Seed money, general purposes,
emergency funds, building funds, equipment,
land acquisition, employee matching gifts, annual
campaigns, capital campaigns, operating budgets,
special projects, renovation projects.
Limitations: Giving primarily in CA, IA, MI, NY,
OR, PA, TX, VT, and WA. No grants to
individuals, or for endowments; no loans.
Publications: Application guidelines.
Application information: Application form
required.
   Initial approach: Letter requesting application
     form
   Copies of proposal: 1
   Deadline(s): Submit application preferably 1
     month before fund committee meetings
   Board meeting date(s): March, June, and Nov.
   Final notification: 1 week following fund
     committee meeting
   Write: Lin L. Smith
Officers and Directors:* Joseph L. Leitzinger,*
Pres.; Colleen C. Musgrave, Secy.; J. Thurston
Roach, Treas.; John J. Fannon, Robert B.
Hutchinson, T.R. Ingham, Jr., Furman C. Moseley,
Susan R. Moseley, Eleanor H. Reed, William G.
Reed, Jr.
Number of staff: 5 part-time professional; 5
part-time support.
EIN: 916029303

3237
M. J. Murdock Charitable Trust ▼
703 Broadway, Suite 710
Vancouver 98660   (206) 694-8415
Mailing address: P.O. Box 1618, Vancouver, WA
98668; Tel.: (503) 285-4086

Trust established in 1975 in WA.
Donor(s): Melvin Jack Murdock.‡
Foundation type: Independent

Financial data (yr. ended 12/31/91): Assets,
$256,359,883 (M); expenditures, $16,906,971;
qualifying distributions, $10,227,298, including
$9,387,327 for 138 grants (high: $500,000; low:
$1,250; average: $20,000-$150,000).
Purpose and activities: Support primarily for
special projects or programs of private, nonprofit
charitable organizations aimed at the solution or
prevention of significant problems with
implications beyond the immediate geographical
area and which are able to thrive after initial
funding; support also for projects which address
critical problems for the Portland, OR/Vancouver,
WA, area. Desirable characteristics include
self-help, free enterprise concepts leading to
greater self-sufficiency and capability for
organizations and the people they serve, a
strategy for using up-front money including
assistance from other supporters, and evidence
that the problem-solving effort will make an
important difference. Giving primarily for higher
education; also provides seed money for selected
medical and scientific research programs which
have been identified as major priorities. Grants
usually for a limited time, one or two years.
Fields of interest: Higher education, social
services, science and technology, medical
research, physical sciences.
Types of support: Seed money, building funds,
equipment, research, special projects.
Limitations: Giving primarily in the Pacific
Northwest, (WA, OR, ID, MT, and AK); support
for community projects only in the Portland,
OR/Vancouver, WA, area. No support for
government programs; projects common to many
organizations without distinguishing merit;
sectarian or religious organizations whose
principal activities are for the benefit of their own
members; or agencies served by United Way of
Columbia-Willamette, except for approved
special projects. No grants to individuals, or for
annual campaigns, general support, continuing
support, deficit financing, endowment funds,
operating budgets, emergency funds,
scholarships, fellowships, or matching gifts; no
loans.
Publications: Annual report (including application
guidelines), informational brochure (including
application guidelines).
Application information: Submit original, plus 3
copies of non-research proposal; original, plus 9
copies of research or technical proposal.
Application form required.
   Initial approach: Letter or telephone
   Copies of proposal: 8
   Deadline(s): None
   Board meeting date(s): Monthly
   Final notification: 3 to 6 months
   Write: Ford A. Anderson II, Exec. Dir.
Officer: Ford A. Anderson II, Exec. Dir.
Trustees: James B. Castles, Walter P. Dyke,
Lynwood W. Swanson.
Number of staff: 4 full-time professional; 1
part-time professional; 5 full-time support; 1
part-time support.
EIN: 237456468
Recent health grants:
3237-1 Albany General Hospital Foundation,
   Albany, OR, $20,000. For critical care unit.
   1991.
3237-2 Easter Seal Society, Great Falls, MT,
   $42,650. For administrative systems update.

Grant shared with Goodwill Industries of Montana. 1991.

3237-3 I Am Third Foundation, Billings, MT, $18,000. For Billings Program expansion. 1991.

3237-4 Mountain States Health Corporation, Oregon Division, Salem, OR, $270,000. For community decisionmaking in rural hospital communities. 1991.

3237-5 Mountainview Memorial Hospital, White Sulphur Springs, MT, $55,500. For computerized health information system. 1991.

3237-6 National Center for Policy Analysis, Dallas, TX, $200,000. For new health care model. 1991.

3237-7 Oregon Health Sciences University Foundation, Portland, OR, $440,000. For synaptic membrane transporter studies. 1991.

3237-8 Oregon Health Sciences University Foundation, Portland, OR, $24,400. For Polyamine-Induced Organ Deterioration. 1991.

3237-9 Send International of Alaska, Glennallen, AK, $43,600. For Cross Roads Medical Center x-ray equipment. 1991.

3237-10 Silent Environment Educational Kamp (SEEK), Ellensburg, WA, $22,000. For sign language training for medical services providers. 1991.

3237-11 Sisters of the Holy Names of Jesus and Mary, Marylhurst, OR, $60,000. For nursing facility renovation. Grant made through United States Catholic Conference. 1991.

3237-12 Tualatin Valley Mental Health Center, Portland, OR, $100,000. For rehabilitation facilities expansion project. 1991.

3237-13 West Mont Home Health Services, Helena, MT, $25,000. For computer equipment. 1991.

3238
Murray Foundation
First Interstate Plaza, Suite 1750
Tacoma 98402   (206) 383-4911

Trust established in 1952 in WA.
Donor(s): L.T. Murray Trust.
Foundation type: Independent
Financial data (yr. ended 12/31/90): Assets, $3,300,000 (M); expenditures, $216,353; qualifying distributions, $158,400, including $158,400 for 29 grants (high: $30,000; low: $500).
Purpose and activities: Giving for higher and secondary education, hospitals, cultural programs, and community funds. Priority given to capital programs in the Puget Sound area.
Fields of interest: Higher education, secondary education, education, education—building funds, hospitals, cultural programs, community funds.
Types of support: Building funds, capital campaigns, endowment funds, matching funds, publications, scholarship funds, special projects.
Limitations: Giving restricted to Pierce County, WA. No grants to individuals, or for endowment funds, research, scholarships, or fellowships; no loans.
Publications: 990-PF, informational brochure (including application guidelines).
Application information: Application form not required.
  Initial approach: Letter
  Copies of proposal: 1

Board meeting date(s): Dec. and as required (3 to 4 times a year)
  Write: Lowell Anne Butson, Exec. Dir.
Officers and Directors:* Anne Murray Barbey,* Pres.; L.T. Murray, Jr.,* V.P.; Lowell Anne Butson,* Secy. and Exec. Dir.; Amy Lou Eckstrom,* Treas.; Steve Larson.
Number of staff: 1 part-time professional.
EIN: 510163345

3239
Nesholm Family Foundation
140 Lakeside Ave., Suite 230
Seattle 98122   (206) 324-3339

Established in 1987 in WA.
Donor(s): Elmer J. Nesholm.‡
Foundation type: Independent
Financial data (yr. ended 12/31/90): Assets, $11,599,424 (M); expenditures, $563,194; qualifying distributions, $507,004, including $470,815 for 48 grants (high: $35,000; low: $700).
Fields of interest: Education, health, performing arts.
Types of support: Special projects.
Limitations: Giving limited to Seattle, WA. No grants to individuals.
Publications: Program policy statement, application guidelines.
Application information:
  Initial approach: Proposal
  Copies of proposal: 5
  Deadline(s): None
  Write: Dian Kallmer
Officers and Directors:* John F. Nesholm,* Pres.; Laurel Nesholm, Exec. Dir.; Joseph M. Gaffney, Edgar K. Marcuse, M.D.
Number of staff: 1 part-time professional.
EIN: 943055422

3240
PACCAR Foundation ▼
c/o PACCAR, Inc.
P.O. Box 1518
Bellevue 98009   (206) 455-7400

Incorporated in 1951 in WA.
Donor(s): PACCAR, Inc.
Foundation type: Company-sponsored
Financial data (yr. ended 12/31/90): Assets, $7,162,574 (M); gifts received, $3,000,000; expenditures, $1,817,320; qualifying distributions, $1,747,621, including $1,693,917 for 103 grants (high: $343,050; low: $500; average: $2,000-$10,000) and $53,704 for employee matching gifts.
Purpose and activities: Support for civic organizations, community funds, higher educational institutions, cultural programs, youth agencies, and hospitals.
Fields of interest: Higher education, community funds, cultural programs, hospitals, youth, civic affairs.
Types of support: Employee matching gifts, annual campaigns, capital campaigns.
Limitations: Giving primarily in areas of company operations, particularly King County, WA. No grants to individuals, or for scholarships or fellowships.

Application information: Application form not required.
  Initial approach: Proposal
  Copies of proposal: 1
  Deadline(s): None
  Board meeting date(s): Quarterly; dates vary
  Final notification: 2 to 3 months
  Write: E.A. Carpenter, V.P.
Officers and Directors:* Charles M. Pigott,* Pres.; E.A. Carpenter, V.P. and Treas.; G. Glen Morie, Secy.; Joseph M. Dunn, J.M. Fluke, Jr., Harold J. Haynes, J.C. Pigott, John W. Pitts, James H. Wiborg, T.A. Wilson.
Number of staff: None.
EIN: 916030638
Recent health grants:
3240-1 AIDS Housing of Washington, Seattle, WA, $10,000. 1990.
3240-2 Overlake Hospital Foundation, Bellevue, WA, $20,000. 1990.

3241
Pacific First Financial Corporate Giving Program
1420 Fifth Ave., P.O. Box 91029
Seattle 98111   (206) 224-3000

Financial data (yr. ended 12/31/90): Total giving, $536,000, including $394,153 for grants and $141,847 for in-kind gifts.
Purpose and activities: Support for affordable low-income housing and shelters for the homeless, health and welfare, arts and culture, education, and the United Way. Funds are also contributed to the HOME (Housing Opportunities Made Easy) program.
Fields of interest: Homeless, housing, health, welfare, arts, cultural programs, education.
Types of support: Annual campaigns, building funds, capital campaigns, conferences and seminars, equipment, general purposes, lectureships, loans, renovation projects, research, special projects, scholarship funds, student loans.
Limitations: Giving primarily in the Northwest, primarily OR, CA, and WA.
Application information: Application form not required.
  Initial approach: Written application
  Copies of proposal: 1
  Deadline(s): Ongoing - however, 3rd quarter advantageous
  Board meeting date(s): 3rd Wednesday of each month
  Write: Michael K. Rogers, Sr. V.P., Public Affairs
Administrators: Michael K. Rogers, Sr. V.P.; Kathleen N. Heric, Asst. V.P.
Number of staff: 2 full-time professional.

3242
Pemco Foundation
325 Eastlake Ave. East
Seattle 98109   (206) 628-4000

Established in 1965 in WA.
Donor(s): Pemco Corp., Washington School Employees Credit Union, Evergreenbank.
Foundation type: Company-sponsored
Financial data (yr. ended 06/30/91): Assets, $173,058 (M); gifts received, $468,900; expenditures, $462,023; qualifying distributions, $462,023, including $373,677 for 144 grants

(high: $23,100; low: $20) and $88,250 for 201 grants to individuals (high: $1,400; low: $100).
Purpose and activities: Grants for social services, youth activities, education, and hospitals and medical research; also awards scholarships.
Fields of interest: Education, youth, social services, medical research, child welfare, hospitals.
Types of support: Research, student aid.
Limitations: Giving limited to WA residents for scholarships; organizational support mainly in Seattle.
Application information:
  Initial approach: For scholarships, letter from school principal stating academic qualifications
  Deadline(s): None
  Final notification: 2 months for scholarships
  Write: Stanley O. McNaughton, Secy.-Treas.
Officers and Trustees:* Astrid I. Merlino,* Pres.; Sandra Kurack,* V.P.; Stanley O. McNaughton,* Secy.-Treas.
EIN: 916072723

3243
Lorene M. Petrie Trust
c/o Bank of America
1301 Fifth Ave., T16-1
Seattle 98101
Application address: c/o Bank of America, P.O. Box 136, Yakima, WA 98907; Tel.: (509) 575-6722

Established in 1983 in WA.
Donor(s): Lorene Petrie.‡
Foundation type: Independent
Financial data (yr. ended 07/31/91): Assets, $2,220,406 (M); expenditures, $400,469; qualifying distributions, $383,995, including $372,733 for 8 grants (high: $100,000; low: $3,000).
Purpose and activities: Support primarily for medical centers; giving also for museums, arts councils, and higher education.
Fields of interest: Hospitals, museums, cultural programs, higher education.
Types of support: Capital campaigns.
Limitations: Giving limited to Yakima and Kittitas counties, WA.
Application information: Application form not required.
  Deadline(s): None
  Write: Doug McIntyre, V.P. and Mgr., Bank of America
Trustee: Bank of America.
EIN: 916256555

3244
Poncin Scholarship Fund
c/o Seafirst Bank, Charitable Services
P.O. Box 24565
Seattle 98124   (206) 358-3380

Trust established in 1966 in WA.
Donor(s): Cora May Poncin.‡
Foundation type: Independent
Financial data (yr. ended 12/31/91): Assets, $4,218,188 (M); expenditures, $172,247; qualifying distributions, $144,524, including $138,746 for 12 grants to individuals (average: $12,771).

Purpose and activities: Scholarships awarded to "people engaged in advanced medical research in connection with, or as a part of any recognized institution of learning within the state of Washington."
Fields of interest: Medical research.
Types of support: Research.
Limitations: Giving limited to WA.
Publications: Application guidelines.
Application information: Application must be approved by head of applicant's institution. Application form required.
  Initial approach: Proposal
  Copies of proposal: 1
  Deadline(s): May 1
  Board meeting date(s): Trust officers committee meets weekly
  Final notification: 8 weeks
  Write: Jennifer Sorensen, Trust Officer, Seafirst Bank
Trustee: Seafirst Bank.
Number of staff: None.
EIN: 916069573

3245
Puget Sound Power and Light Corporate Giving Program
P.O. Box 97034 OBC-9N
Bellevue 98009-9734   (206) 462-3799

Financial data (yr. ended 12/31/90): Total giving, $600,000 for grants.
Purpose and activities: "Puget Sound Power & Light Company and its employees actively promote the well being of communities we serve. One important, effective way we demonstrate this is through the company's contributions program, which helps support nonprofit organizations in the areas of health and human services, education, environment and conservation of natural resources, the arts and culture, and civic affairs." Priority is given to organizations that operate in the service area. Those headquartered outside must be of a regional or statewide nature and provide services to Puget customers. Requests are evaluated by the Contributions Committee, composed of company officers.
Fields of interest: Civic affairs, arts, education, health services, women, youth, social services, handicapped, employment, urban development, higher education, elementary education, humanities, music, museums, health, hospitals, medical research, engineering, environment, safety, volunteerism, performing arts, economics.
Types of support: Capital campaigns, conferences and seminars, employee matching gifts.
Limitations: Giving primarily in headquarters city and service area: nine counties in western WA. No support for churches or other religious organizations, except for programs which benefit the overall community and do not support a specific religious doctrine, fraternal, political, or labor organizations, organizations which are themselves strictly grant making bodies, or those that discriminate on the basis of race, color, religion, creed, age, sex, or national origin. No grants to individuals, or for mass mailings, tickets, goodwill advertising, endorsements, endowment funds, or travel; no support for the general funds of tax-supported educational institutions.
Publications: Informational brochure.

Application information: Application form required.
  Initial approach: Short letter; all requests must be in writing
  Copies of proposal: 1
  Deadline(s): Late summer and early fall
  Board meeting date(s): 3rd month of each quarter
  Write: Beverly DuFort, Corp. Contribs. Mgr.
Number of staff: 1

3246
Ray Foundation
1111 Third Ave., Suite 2770
Seattle 98101   (206) 292-9101

Established in 1962 in MT.
Donor(s): James C. Ray, Joan L. Ray.‡
Foundation type: Independent
Financial data (yr. ended 06/30/91): Assets, $11,682,559 (M); expenditures, $512,860; qualifying distributions, $474,344, including $410,868 for 16 grants (high: $150,000; low: $1,200).
Purpose and activities: Giving primarily for higher education, scientific research, youth agencies, mental health, and drug abuse prevention for children and adolescents; support also for a museum.
Fields of interest: Higher education, education—building funds, science and technology, youth, mental health, drug abuse, child welfare, fine arts.
Types of support: Operating budgets, continuing support, seed money, emergency funds, building funds, equipment, matching funds, special projects, research, publications, consulting services, technical assistance, general purposes.
Limitations: Giving primarily in AZ, OR, and WA. No grants to individuals, or for deficit financing; no loans.
Publications: Annual report, application guidelines.
Application information: Application form required.
  Initial approach: 1 page letter
  Copies of proposal: 1
  Deadline(s): None
  Board meeting date(s): Nov. and June
  Final notification: Immediately following board meetings
  Write: Shirley C. Brandenburg, Fdn. Admin.
Officers and Directors:* James C. Ray,* Pres.; Shirley C. Brandenburg,* Secy.-Treas.; John Stewart Darrell, Dennis O. Dugan.
Number of staff: 1 full-time professional.
EIN: 810288819
Recent health grants:
3246-1 University of California, Medical Education Associates, Los Angeles, CA, $50,000. 1991.

3247
SAFECO Corporate Giving Program
Community Relations
SAFECO Plaza
Seattle 98185   (206) 545-5015

Financial data (yr. ended 12/31/89): Total giving, $2,926,649, including $2,788,493 for 535 grants and $138,156 for 516 employee matching gifts.

Purpose and activities: Grants fall into three basic areas: corporate contributions, involvement grants, and matching gifts. Safeco takes a "hands-on approach to our communities because it allows us to affect, in a significant way, the environment in which we conduct our business". The Home Office Contributions Program gives in Seattle under the guidance of an employee committee made up of senior management. Public health is one area of great interest, including AIDS. For the Branch Contributions Program, employee committees in the branch offices consider requests from local nonprofits. In the Community Involvement Program, employees combine their volunteer time and the corporation's financial resources to undertake charitable projects. In 1989, 53 projects were completed for organizations such as Habitat for Humanity, Salvation Army, and YWCA. The Volunteer Involvement Program (VIP) matches Seattle Area employees with a nonprofit that needs their skills. The 12 Days of Christmas Program is a package of 12 different holiday projects for community groups. The Matching Gift Programs includes Your Gifts Plus which matches employees' cash gifts of $25 or more and Your Time Plus which donates $100 to a nonprofit for which an employee has volunteered 25 hours or more during a 12-month period. SAFECO also participates in the annual United Way Drive each year, raising employee dollars and making direct grants. Each branch has an employee committee to decide grants. At the home office in Seattle, corporate grant decisions and guidance for the overall community relations program come from a committee made up of senior management.
Fields of interest: Health, mental health, drug abuse, alcoholism, medical research, education, social services, aged, performing arts, arts, museums, libraries, civic affairs, community funds, AIDS, Canada, AIDS.
Types of support: Fellowships, employee matching gifts, matching funds, building funds, special projects, scholarship funds, employee volunteer services.
Limitations: Giving limited to areas where a significant number of employees live and work; branch offices in: Stone Mountain, GA; Hoffman Estates, IL; Cincinnati, OH; Richardson, TX; Denver, CO; Fountain Valley, San Ramon, Van Nuys, CA; Nashville, TN; Lake Oswego, OR; St. Louis, MO; Spokane, WA; and Mississaugain, Ontario. No support for national organizations, projects or programs operating outside the U.S. or Canada. No grants to individuals, or for endowment funds, loans and investments, general fundraising events and advertising associated with such events, or unrestricted operating funds for United Way agencies.
Application information:
Initial approach: Brief letter (no more than two pages) of inquiry describing organization, proposed program, amount requested, geographic area and people to be served, how project will be evaluated, and 501(c)(3)
Deadline(s): None
Board meeting date(s): All requests are evaluated either in SAFECO's Home Office or in the branch office closest to the requesting organizations
Final notification: 6 weeks
Write: Jill A. Ryan, Mgr., Comm. Rels.

Corp. Contribs. Comm.: Bruce Maines, Chair. and C.E.O.; Roger H. Eigsti, Pres. and C.O.O.; James W. Cannon, Exec. V.P.; Boh Dickey, Sr. V.P. and C.F.O.; Richard "Duke" Campbell II, V.P., Personnel; Roger Butz, M.D., V.P., Medical Dir.; Gordon Hamilton, V.P., Public Rels.; Jill A. Ryan, Asst. V.P., Public Rels.; Robert C. Alexander, Seattle Branch V.P.

3248
The Schack Family Trust Fund
1028 West Marine View Dr.
Everett 98201

Donor(s): James B. Schack, John B. Schack.
Foundation type: Independent
Financial data (yr. ended 12/31/91): Assets, $416,841 (M); gifts received, $150,000; expenditures, $226,754; qualifying distributions, $224,532, including $222,222 for 21 grants (high: $96,779; low: $500).
Fields of interest: General charitable giving, youth, fine arts, hospitals, religion, libraries.
Limitations: Giving limited to the Pacific Northwest, including Canada.
Application information:
Deadline(s): None
Write: John B. Schack, Pres.
Officers: John B. Schack, Pres.; James B. Schack, V.P.; Idamae Miles Schack, Secy.-Treas.
EIN: 911130805

3249
Seafirst Foundation ▼
P.O. Box 34661
Seattle 98124-1661   (206) 358-3443

Established in 1979 in WA.
Donor(s): Seafirst Corp.
Foundation type: Company-sponsored
Financial data (yr. ended 12/31/91): Assets, $207,525 (M); gifts received, $1,180,000; expenditures, $1,377,441; qualifying distributions, $1,382,476, including $1,377,441 for 56 grants (high: $630,000; low: $1,500; average: $2,500-$25,000).
Purpose and activities: Giving primarily for community development, including youth training and employment, higher and economic education, arts and culture, and to human service agencies through the United Way; multiple-year and capital grants sometimes considered but are limited in size and scope. All grants of more than one year are subject to review before funds are released for the subsequent year.
Fields of interest: Community development, youth, drug abuse, child development, child welfare, disadvantaged, family services, handicapped, homeless, housing, higher education, education, adult education, business education, educational associations, education—minorities, literacy, social services, arts, museums, performing arts, cultural programs, employment, economics, community funds, AIDS, health services.
Types of support: Building funds, general purposes, special projects, capital campaigns, operating budgets, renovation projects, annual campaigns, employee matching gifts, in-kind gifts.
Limitations: Giving limited to WA. No support for fraternal organizations or religious organizations

(unless the proposed project is non-denominational and does not promote religious advocacy), single-disease organizations, or primary or secondary schools. No grants to individuals, or for research, endowment funds, travel expenses, production of video tapes, publications, operating deficits, hospital operating funds, fundraising events, scholarships (except for Seafirst scholarship programs), or film.
Publications: Informational brochure (including application guidelines).
Application information: Application form required.
Initial approach: Letter (no more than 2 pages)
Copies of proposal: 1
Deadline(s): None, but requests received after Oct. 1 will be carried forward to the following Jan.
Board meeting date(s): Quarterly
Final notification: 4 to 6 weeks
Write: Nadine H. Troyer, V.P. and Secy.
Officers and Trustees:* James H. Williams, Pres.; Nadine Troyer,* V.P. and Secy.; Barbara Ells,* Treas.; Joan Enticknap, Hal Greene, Becki Johnson, Diane Mackey, Larry Ogg, Tim Turnpaugh.
Number of staff: 1 part-time professional; 1 part-time support.
EIN: 911094720

3250
The Seattle Foundation
425 Pike St., Suite 510
Seattle 98101   (206) 622-2294

Incorporated in 1946 in WA.
Foundation type: Community
Financial data (yr. ended 06/30/91): Assets, $37,704,110 (M); expenditures, $3,685,012; qualifying distributions, $3,685,012, including $3,685,012 for 390 grants (average: $5,000-$10,000).
Fields of interest: Education, health, welfare, cultural programs, community development.
Types of support: Building funds, equipment, renovation projects.
Limitations: Giving limited to Greater Puget Sound region of WA. No grants to individuals, or for scholarships, fellowships, endowment funds, research, operating budgets, general purposes, matching gifts, conferences, exhibits, film production, or publications; no loans.
Publications: Annual report, informational brochure, program policy statement, application guidelines.
Application information: Application form not required.
Initial approach: Write for guidelines
Copies of proposal: 1
Deadline(s): Feb. 1, May 1, Aug. 1, and Nov. 1
Board meeting date(s): Mar., June, Sept., and Dec.
Final notification: 6 weeks to 2 months
Write: Anne V. Farrell, Pres.
Officers and Trustees:* Elaine Monson,* Chair.; Kemper Freeman, Vice-Chair.; Brooks Ragen,* Vice-Chair.; Anne V. Farrell, Pres.; Jane C. Williams, V.P.; Susan Duffy, Secy.; James Ladd, Treas.; and 22 additional trustees.
Trustee Banks: The Bank of California, N.A., First Interstate Bank of Washington, R.B. Hooper and Co., Key Bank Co. of the Northwest, Laird Norton

Trust Co., Seafirst Bank, Bank of America, Sirach Capital Management, Inc., U.S. Bank of Washington, N.A., Washington Mutual Savings Bank.
Number of staff: 1 full-time professional; 3 part-time professional; 1 full-time support; 1 part-time support.
EIN: 916013536
Recent health grants:

3250-1 Childrens Hospital Foundation, Seattle, WA, $50,000. 1991.
3250-2 Community Health Centers of King County, Seattle, WA, $20,000. 1991.
3250-3 Community Health Centers of King County, Seattle, WA, $20,000. 1991.
3250-4 Forty-Fifth Street Community Health Clinic, Seattle, WA, $50,000. 1991.
3250-5 Forty-Fifth Street Community Health Clinic, Seattle, WA, $20,000. 1991.
3250-6 Fred Hutchinson Cancer Research Center, Seattle, WA, $70,000. 1991.
3250-7 Hospice of Seattle, Providence Home Care, Seattle, WA, $14,500. 1991.
3250-8 Overlake Hospital Foundation, Bellevue, WA, $15,000. 1991.
3250-9 Pike Market Medical Clinic, Seattle, WA, $10,000. 1991.
3250-10 Providence Foundation, Seattle, WA, $20,000. 1991.
3250-11 Puget Sound Neighborhood Health Centers, Seattle, WA, $25,000. 1991.
3250-12 Puget Sound Neighborhood Health Centers, Seattle, WA, $20,000. 1991.
3250-13 Seattle Counseling Service, Seattle, WA, $10,000. 1991.
3250-14 Seattle Institute/Biomedical and Clinical Research, Seattle, WA, $24,870. 1991.
3250-15 University of Washington, Seattle, WA, $ 40. For Fetal Alcohol Syndrome Research Program. 1991.
3250-16 University of Washington, Health Sciences Center, Seattle, WA, $15,000. 1991.
3250-17 University of Washington, Health Sciences Center, Seattle, WA, $12,750. 1991.
3250-18 University of Washington, Health Sciences Center, Seattle, WA, $10,000. 1991.
3250-19 University of Washington, Medical Center, Seattle, WA, $10,000. 1991.
3250-20 Virginia Mason Medical Center, Seattle, WA, $40,000. For grant shared with Virginia Mason Research Center. 1991.
3250-21 Virginia Mason Medical Foundation, Seattle, WA, $50,000. 1991.
3250-22 Virginia Mason Research Center, Seattle, WA, $30,000. 1991.

3251
Charles See Foundation
11100 N.E. Eighth St., Suite 610
Bellevue 98004   (206) 635-7250

Incorporated in 1960 in CA.
Donor(s): Charles B. See.
Foundation type: Independent
Financial data (yr. ended 12/31/91): Assets, $2,183,265 (M); expenditures, $124,808; qualifying distributions, $116,805, including $108,800 for 38 grants (high: $20,000; low: $100; average: $100-$20,000).
Purpose and activities: Emphasis on education and hospitals; giving also for mental health,

church support, conservation, cultural programs, and international affairs.
Fields of interest: Education, hospitals, mental health, religion, conservation, cultural programs, international affairs.
Limitations: Giving primarily in CA. No grants to individuals.
Publications: 990-PF.
Application information: Application form not required.
  Initial approach: Letter
  Copies of proposal: 1
  Deadline(s): Nov. 14
  Board meeting date(s): Around Dec. 1
  Write: Charles B. See, Pres.
Officers and Directors:* Charles B. See,* Pres.; Ann R. See,* V.P. and Secy.; Rhonda Logan,* Secy.; Harry A. See, Richard W. See.
Number of staff: None.
EIN: 956038358

3252
Skinner Foundation
1326 Fifth Ave., Suite 711
Seattle 98101   (206) 623-6480

Trust established in 1956 in WA.
Donor(s): Skinner Corp., Alpac Corp., NC Machinery.
Foundation type: Company-sponsored
Financial data (yr. ended 03/31/91): Assets, $5,351,315 (M); gifts received, $632,846; expenditures, $889,561; qualifying distributions, $889,561, including $805,005 for 291 grants (high: $50,000; low: $50; average: $1,000-$5,000) and $25,547 for 70 employee matching gifts.
Purpose and activities: "Giving for health and human services, culture and the arts, civic and community, and education. Within these categories, the focus is on children and families with special attention given to programs that provide preventive services."
Fields of interest: Civic affairs, cultural programs, arts, education, health, social services, environment, child development.
Types of support: Operating budgets, seed money, building funds, equipment, matching funds, technical assistance, employee matching gifts, capital campaigns, endowment funds, renovation projects, general purposes, special projects.
Limitations: Giving primarily in areas of company operations in WA, AK, HI, ID, and OR. No support for religious organizations for religious purposes. No grants to individuals, or for continuing support, operating funds for the United Way, deficit financing, fundraising events, or conferences; no loans.
Publications: Annual report, informational brochure (including application guidelines).
Application information: Application form required.
  Initial approach: Letter
  Copies of proposal: 10
  Deadline(s): Submit letter in May, July, Oct., or Jan.; deadline for application form 28 days before board meetings
  Board meeting date(s): May, Sept., Dec., and Mar.
  Final notification: 2 weeks
  Write: Sandra Fry, Foundation Dir.

Trustees: Catherine Eaton Skinner, Chair.; John S. Behnke, Sally Skinner Behnke, Shari Dunkelman Behnke, Arthur E. Nordhoff, Nancy Skinner Nordhoff, Sarah W.B. Nordhoff, David E. Skinner III, Kayla Skinner.
Number of staff: 1 full-time professional; 1 part-time support.
EIN: 916025144

3253
The Stewardship Foundation ▼
Tacoma Financial Ctr., Suite 1500
1145 Broadway Plaza
Tacoma 98402   (206) 272-8336
Application address: P.O. Box 1278, Tacoma, WA 98401

Trust established in 1962 in WA.
Donor(s): C. Davis Weyerhaeuser Irrevocable Trust.
Foundation type: Independent
Financial data (yr. ended 12/31/91): Assets, $72,690,398 (M); expenditures, $45,354,860; qualifying distributions, $3,668,388, including $3,657,388 for 288 grants (high: $340,000; low: $1,000; average: $5,000-$25,000) and $11,000 for loans.
Purpose and activities: At least 85 percent of funds paid for evangelical religious organizations whose ministries reach beyond the local community; grants primarily for Christian colleges, universities, and seminaries, international development organizations, foreign missions, and youth ministries; some support also for local social service agencies.
Fields of interest: Religious welfare, religion—missionary programs, theological education, Protestant giving, religion—Christian, religious schools, race relations, Africa, Southern Africa, social services, international development, Europe, education, welfare, media and communications, higher education, youth, women, arts.
Types of support: Annual campaigns, building funds, general purposes, continuing support, matching funds, operating budgets, publications, scholarship funds, special projects, capital campaigns.
Limitations: Giving internationally, nationally and in WA, especially in Tacoma and Pierce County. No support for churches; religious support only to Christian parachurch organizations. No grants to individuals, or for seed money, endowment funds, deficit financing, research, scholarships, or fellowships.
Publications: Biennial report, application guidelines.
Application information: Application form not required.
  Initial approach: Letter
  Copies of proposal: 1
  Deadline(s): None
  Board meeting date(s): Mar., June, Sept., and Dec.
  Final notification: 90 days
  Write: C. Davis Weyerhaeuser, Pres., or George S. Kovats, Exec. Dir.
Officers and Directors:* C. Davis Weyerhaeuser,* Pres. and Treas.; Annette B. Weyerhaeuser,* V.P.; James R. Hanson, Secy.; Charles L. Anderson, Louis A. Flora, Carl T. Fynboe, William T. Weyerhaeuser.

Number of staff: 1 full-time professional; 1 full-time support.
EIN: 916020515
Recent health grants:

3253-1 Chrestos Counseling Center, Tacoma, WA, $25,000. For building purchase. 1990.

3253-2 Chrestos Counseling Center, Tacoma, WA, $25,000. For unrestricted grant. 1990.

3253-3 Crisis Pregnancy Center/Pierce County, Tacoma, WA, $20,000. For unrestricted grant. 1990.

3253-4 Greater Lakes Mental Health Foundation, Tacoma, WA, $10,000. For youth suicide prevention program. 1990.

3253-5 I Am Third Foundation, Bozeman, MT, $10,000. For Eagle Mount cancer camp program. 1990.

3253-6 Mercy Medical Airlift, Manassas, VA, $34,000. For unrestricted grant. 1990.

3253-7 World Radio Missionary Fellowship, Opa Locka, FL, $20,000. For River Blindness research project. 1990.

3254
Estate of Joseph L. Stubblefield
P.O. Box 1757
Walla Walla 99362   (509) 527-3500

Trust established in 1902 in WA.
Donor(s): Joseph L. Stubblefield.‡
Foundation type: Independent
Financial data (yr. ended 12/31/90): Assets, $2,926,963 (M); expenditures, $150,498; qualifying distributions, $130,901, including $112,150 for 28 grants (high: $15,500; low: $100) and $14,718 for 40 grants to individuals (high: $2,000; low: $56).
Purpose and activities: Grants for indigent and elderly widows and orphans and organizations that assist such persons.
Fields of interest: Welfare—indigent individuals, aged, child welfare, higher education, social services, hospices.
Types of support: Grants to individuals, scholarship funds.
Limitations: Giving limited to WA and OR.
Application information: Application form not required.
  Initial approach: Letter
  Deadline(s): None
  Write: H.H. Hayner, Trustee
Trustees: H.H. Hayner, James K. Hayner, Robert O. Kenyon.
EIN: 916031350

3255
Greater Tacoma Community Foundation
P.O. Box 1995
Tacoma 98401-1995   (206) 383-5622

Incorporated in 1977 in WA.
Foundation type: Community
Financial data (yr. ended 05/31/92): Assets, $18,897,602 (M); gifts received, $3,845,203; expenditures, $3,261,374; qualifying distributions, $2,678,359, including $2,678,359 for grants (high: $15,000; low: $100; average: $100-$7,500).
Fields of interest: Education, cultural programs, health, social services, civic affairs, welfare—indigent individuals.

Types of support: Consulting services, technical assistance, emergency funds, seed money, building funds, equipment, matching funds, capital campaigns, loans, operating budgets, continuing support, scholarship funds, special projects, grants to individuals.
Limitations: Giving limited to Pierce County, WA. No support for religious, political, or lobbying activities. No grants for annual campaigns, scholarships, fellowships, or publications, unless specified by donor.
Publications: Annual report, informational brochure (including application guidelines), newsletter.
Application information: Application form required.
  Initial approach: Letter
  Copies of proposal: 2
  Deadline(s): Jan. 15, Apr. 15, and Sept. 15
  Board meeting date(s): 5 times yearly
  Final notification: Within 3 months
  Write: Margy McGroarty, Pres.
Officers and Trustees:* Ottie Ladd,* Chair.; Elizabeth A. Gingrich,* Vice-Chair.; Margy McGrouty,* Pres.; Dennis Seinfeld,* Secy.; Barbara Bingham,* Treas.; Lea Armstrong, Yolanda Bailey, Lowell Anne Butson, Mary W. Green, Lyle Quasim, Jeff Rounce, Janet Stanley, Raymond P. Tennison, Brewer B. Thompson, Kathryn Van Wagenen, Al Weaver.
Number of staff: 3 full-time professional; 1 part-time professional; 1 part-time support.
EIN: 911007459

3256
U.S. Bank Contributions Program
(Formerly U.S. Bank of Washington Contributions Program)
P.O. Box 720, WWH658
Seattle 98111-0720   (206) 344-2360

Financial data (yr. ended 12/31/90): Total giving, $1,091,137, including $903,710 for 333 grants (high: $30,000; low: $25; average: $15,000), $11,000 for employee matching gifts and $176,427 for 33 in-kind gifts.
Purpose and activities: Support for the arts and culture, including music, theater, fine and performing arts; child development and welfare; Also supports programs for the aged, the disadvantaged, families, the handicapped, substance abuse prevention, housing, education, hunger, minorities, women, and youth; capital campaign gifts are limited to 1 percent of total amount to be raised.
Fields of interest: Fine arts, arts, homeless, child welfare, child development, health, performing arts, health associations, theater, women, youth, medical research, education, handicapped, community development, drug abuse, family services, AIDS, community funds, cultural programs, elementary education, hunger, alcoholism, cancer, civic affairs, dance, education—minorities, higher education, housing, disadvantaged, minorities, secondary education, museums.
Types of support: Annual campaigns, capital campaigns, continuing support, emergency funds, employee matching gifts, equipment, general purposes, matching funds, donated products, operating budgets, donated land, in-kind gifts, loaned talent, professorships.

Limitations: Giving primarily in Adams, Benton, Clallam, Cowlitz, Franklin, Garfield, Grant, Grays Harbor, Island, Jefferson, King, Kitsap, Kittitas, Lincoln, Okanogan, Pierce, Skagit, Snohomish, Spokane, Thurston, Walla Walla, Whatcom, Whitman, and Yakima counties, WA. No grants to individuals, or to fund out-of-state travel, or to national organizations.
Publications: Corporate report.
Application information: Company has a staff that only handles contributions. Application form not required.
  Initial approach: Phone call or letter
  Copies of proposal: 1
  Deadline(s): None
  Board meeting date(s): Every 8 to 12 weeks
  Final notification: Phone call and/or letter following meeting
  Write: Molly W. Reed, V.P. and Mgr., Community Rels.
Number of staff: 2 full-time professional; 1 part-time support.

3257
Washington Mutual Savings Bank Foundation
c/o Washington Mutual Tower, P.O. Box 834
1201 Third Ave.
Seattle 98111   (206) 461-4663

Established in 1979 in WA.
Donor(s): Washington Mutual Savings Bank.
Foundation type: Company-sponsored
Financial data (yr. ended 12/31/90): Assets, $1,137,340 (M); gifts received, $774,372; expenditures, $642,450; qualifying distributions, $641,084, including $634,924 for 231 grants (high: $40,000; low: $25; average: $500-$40,000).
Purpose and activities: Emphasis is placed on housing/community reinvestment (developing affordable housing and preventing homelessness), education (educational initiatives serving as model programs serving at-risk youth and that support family involvement in educational achievement); and organizations emphasizing prevention-oriented strategies, strengthen families and have Washington Mutual employees involved are especially welcome. Funding is considered for elementary and secondary schools when the project has major community impact, will involve larger community participation, and has financial commitments for a cross-section of the community. The foundation will also consider loans to qualifying nonprofits for short-term housing acquisition bridge loans.
Fields of interest: Welfare, housing, youth, higher education, secondary education, elementary education, community development, urban development, health, performing arts.
Types of support: Operating budgets, matching funds, employee matching gifts, building funds, capital campaigns, loans, renovation projects, seed money, technical assistance, employee volunteer services, in-kind gifts, use of facilities.
Limitations: Giving primarily in WA, especially Seattle, Tacoma, and Spokane. No support for religious organizations for religious purposes, veterans' labor organizations, or organizations receiving funds from the United Way or Corporate Council for the Arts. No grants to individuals.

Publications: Annual report (including application guidelines), grants list, application guidelines, informational brochure (including application guidelines).
Application information: The foundation considers 1 request per organization per calendar year for generally not more than 3 consecutive years. Application form required.

Initial approach: Letter or telephone
Copies of proposal: 2
Deadline(s): Jan. 2, Apr. 2, July 2, and Oct. 2
Board meeting date(s): Quarterly
Final notification: Within 2 weeks of quarterly meeting
Write: Greg Tuke, Prog. Admin.
Officers and Directors:* Sally Skinner Behnke,* Pres.; Deloria Jones,* Secy.; Ernest Jurdana,* Treas.; Rev. Samuel B. McKinney, Lou H. Pepper, William G. Reed, Jr., Holt W. Webster.
Number of staff: 1 full-time professional; 2 part-time support.
EIN: 911070920

3258
Washington Water Power Corporate Giving Program
P.O. Box 3727
Spokane 99220   (509) 482-4561

Financial data (yr. ended 12/31/90): Total giving, $50,000 for in-kind gifts.
Purpose and activities: Emphasis on community development, education, particularly K-12, and youth.
Fields of interest: Community development, drug abuse, cultural programs, elementary education, environment, higher education, conservation, education, energy, health services, museums, volunteerism, women, youth, secondary education.
Types of support: Annual campaigns, continuing support, operating budgets, technical assistance, in-kind gifts, donated equipment, seed money, employee volunteer services, use of facilities, internships, cause-related marketing, emergency funds, public relations services.
Limitations: Giving limited to company service areas in eastern WA and northern ID. No grants for capital or endowment support.

Publications: Informational brochure (including application guidelines).
Application information: Public Relations (Community Affairs) office handles giving. Application form not required.

Initial approach: Letter or phone; Send requests to headquarters or nearest company facility
Copies of proposal: 1
Deadline(s): Quarterly
Final notification: 60-90 days
Write: Mr. J. Kent Adams, Comm. Affairs Coord.

3259
The Wharton Foundation, Inc.
12819 S.E. 38th, No. 11
Bellevue 98006   (206) 641-0589
Additional application addresses: 6199 North 20th St., Phoenix, AZ 85016 (for AZ and FL); 554 Lone Oak Dr., Thousand Oaks, CA 91362; and 633 West Hawthorne Blvd., Wheaton, IL 60187

Established in 1954 in MD.
Foundation type: Independent
Financial data (yr. ended 12/31/91): Assets, $3,748,747 (M); gifts received, $56,500; expenditures, $202,428; qualifying distributions, $198,844, including $187,457 for 70 grants (high: $35,000; low: $50; average: $1,000-$5,000).
Purpose and activities: To strengthen society by empowering and equipping its people, communities, and institutions, primarily through two major areas of interest: 1) Education - to provide and enhance educational programs, facilities, and institutions; and 2) Youth and families - to respond to the needs of children and youth who are at risk of not reaching their full potential. Priority consideration given to prevention and early intervention programs.
Fields of interest: Education, higher education, secondary education, social services, youth, family services, health, community development.
Types of support: Operating budgets, continuing support, annual campaigns, seed money, emergency funds, endowment funds, renovation projects, special projects, general purposes, research, scholarship funds.
Limitations: Giving primarily in metropolitan Phoenix, AZ; Ventura and Los Angeles counties,

CA; Indian River County, FL; metropolitan Chicago, IL; and WA. No grants to individuals, or for multi-year commitments; no loans.
Publications: Application guidelines.
Application information: Application form required.

Initial approach: Letter requesting application guidelines
Copies of proposal: 4
Deadline(s): Mar. 1 and Sept. 1
Board meeting date(s): May and Oct.
Final notification: May 30 and Oct. 31
Write: Martha Wharton, V.P.
Officers and Directors:* W.R. Wharton,* Pres.; M.W. Minnich,* V.P.; J.W. Pettitt,* V.P.; M.W. Wharton,* V.P.; Joseph B. Wharton III, Secy.-Treas.
Number of staff: None.
EIN: 366130748

3260
Wilkins Charitable Foundation
c/o Seafirst Bank
P.O. Box 24565
Seattle 98124-8824   (206) 358-3388

Established in 1986.
Donor(s): Catherine Wilkins.‡
Foundation type: Independent
Financial data (yr. ended 08/31/91): Assets, $2,450,470 (M); expenditures, $108,876; qualifying distributions, $108,876, including $93,628 for 18 grants (high: $10,000; low: $3,000; average: $3,000-$10,000).
Fields of interest: Health services, medical research, social services, education.
Limitations: Giving limited to Puget Sound, WA area. No grants to individuals, or for operating budgets or debt retirement.
Publications: Application guidelines.
Application information: Application form required.

Initial approach: Proposal
Copies of proposal: 3
Write: Rod Johnson, V.P. and Mgr., Seafirst Bank
Officers: Brian Comstock, Chair.; Bob Bunting, Vice-Chair.; Loy D. Smith, Secy.
Trustee: Seafirst Bank.
Number of staff: None.
EIN: 916277933

WEST VIRGINIA

3261
Beckley Area Foundation, Inc.
P.O. Box 1092
Beckley 25802-1575   (304) 253-3806

Established in 1985 in WV.
Donor(s): Dr. Thomas Walker Memorial Health Foundation.
Foundation type: Community
Financial data (yr. ended 03/31/92): Assets, $4,253,052 (M); gifts received, $843,905; expenditures, $304,098; qualifying distributions, $267,916, including $263,816 for 75 grants (high: $6,250; low: $100; average: $100-$6,250) and $4,100 for 12 grants to individuals (high: $1,000; low: $500; average: $100-$1,000).
Fields of interest: Education, social services, health, arts, recreation.
Types of support: Special projects.
Limitations: Giving primarily in the Beckley and Raleigh County, WV, area. No grants for operating budgets.
Publications: Annual report (including application guidelines), newsletter, occasional report, informational brochure, application guidelines.
Application information: Application form not required.
> *Initial approach:* Letter, no more than 2 pages
> *Copies of proposal:* 1
> *Deadline(s):* Dec. 31
> *Board meeting date(s):* Varies
> *Final notification:* Mar.
> *Write:* Charles K. Connor, Jr., Exec. Dir.
Officers and Directors:* Karen Gallagher,* Pres.; John Lilly, V.P.; Langhorne Abrams,* Secy.; Wayne Davis, Treas.; Charles K. Connor, Jr.,* Exec. Dir.; and 11 additional directors.
Number of staff: 1 part-time professional.
EIN: 311125238

3262
Carter Family Foundation
c/o Raleigh County National Bank
129 Main St.
Beckley 25801   (304) 256-7298

Established in 1981 in WV.
Donor(s): Bernard E. Carter,‡ Georgia Carter.‡
Foundation type: Independent
Financial data (yr. ended 06/30/91): Assets, $3,185,327 (M); gifts received, $18,296; expenditures, $168,080; qualifying distributions, $154,710, including $125,761 for 77 grants (high: $14,500; low: $500; average: $1,000-$2,000).
Purpose and activities: Emphasis on church support, social services, health, and education, including scholarship grants and loans to individuals to become teachers and teach for a period of time in WV.
Fields of interest: Religion—Christian, social services, health, education.
Types of support: Student aid, scholarship funds, special projects.

Limitations: Giving limited to WV, with priority given to Raleigh County residents for scholarships.
Application information: Application form not required.
> *Initial approach:* Letter and resume
> *Deadline(s):* None
> *Write:* Patrick Barbera, Trust Officer, Raleigh County National Bank
Trustee: Raleigh County National Bank.
EIN: 550606479

3263
Clay Foundation, Inc. ▼
1426 Kanawha Blvd., East
Charleston 25301   (304) 344-8656

Incorporated in 1986 in WV.
Donor(s): Charles M. Avampato, George Diab.
Foundation type: Independent
Financial data (yr. ended 10/31/91): Assets, $35,582,987 (M); expenditures, $4,808,662; qualifying distributions, $4,393,269, including $4,347,178 for 30 grants (high: $3,557,389; low: $595; average: $10,000-$50,000).
Purpose and activities: Giving in the following areas: 1) Aging, 2) Health Care, including research and education, 3) Vocational Education, and 4) Disadvantaged Youth and their families.
Fields of interest: Arts, cultural programs, higher education, community funds, aged, health, medical research, medical education, vocational education, disadvantaged, family services.
Types of support: Renovation projects, research.
Limitations: Giving limited to WV, with emphasis on the greater Kanawha Valley area. No support for religious purposes or private functions. No grants to individuals, or for operating expenses, deficit financing, or annual campaigns.
Application information: Application form not required.
> *Initial approach:* Letter (in triplicate)
> *Copies of proposal:* 6
> *Deadline(s):* No set deadline; 60 working days should be allowed for review of preliminary letter
> *Board meeting date(s):* Jan., Apr., July, and Oct.
> *Final notification:* 10 days after board meeting
> *Write:* Charles M. Avampato, Pres.
Officers and Directors:* Lyell B. Clay,* Chair.; Charles M. Avampato,* Pres.; Buckner W. Clay,* V.P.; Whitney Clay Diller,* Secy.; Hamilton G. Clay,* Treas.
Number of staff: 1
EIN: 550670193

3264
George D. Hott Memorial Foundation of Morgantown-Monongalia County, West Virginia
c/o First National Bank of Morgantown, Trust Dept.
201 High St.
Morgantown 26505-5414
Application address: c/o First National Bank of Morgantown, P.O. Box 895, Morgantown, WV 26507-0895; Tel.: (304) 291-7721

Established in 1980.
Donor(s): George D. Hott.‡
Foundation type: Operating

Financial data (yr. ended 12/31/90): Assets, $2,012,713 (M); expenditures, $133,785; qualifying distributions, $122,250, including $118,000 for 37 grants (high: $15,000; low: $500).
Purpose and activities: Giving primarily for human services, including welfare agencies, youth, and a community fund; support also for Methodist churches and programs and hospitals.
Fields of interest: Welfare, youth, community funds, Protestant giving, hospitals.
Types of support: Scholarship funds, endowment funds, equipment.
Limitations: Giving primarily in Morgantown, WV. No grants to individuals.
Application information: Application form required.
> *Deadline(s):* None
> *Write:* Daniel Ice, Trust Officer, First National Bank of Morgantown
Trustees: Jack Britton, Martin Piribek, Robert L. Shuman, First National Bank of Morgantown.
EIN: 556085230

3265
The Greater Kanawha Valley Foundation
1426 Kanawha Blvd., East
Charleston 25301   (304) 346-3620
Application address: P.O. Box 3041, Charleston, WV 25331

Established in 1962 in WV.
Foundation type: Community
Financial data (yr. ended 12/31/91): Assets, $39,889,431 (M); gifts received, $1,219,493; expenditures, $2,116,744; qualifying distributions, $2,096,338, including $1,433,159 for 390 grants (high: $18,000; low: $200; average: $200-$18,000), $408,904 for 250 grants to individuals (high: $8,000; low: $375; average: $375-$8,000) and $3,500 for 1 loan.
Purpose and activities: Support for higher and other education; social services, including child welfare and family services, women, and housing; health and the medical sciences, including research on AIDS, heart disease, and cancer; the fine and performing arts; ecology and the environment; and recreation and community development programs.
Fields of interest: Education, higher education, education—early childhood, social services, women, health, arts, ecology, libraries, youth.
Types of support: Operating budgets, continuing support, seed money, building funds, equipment, special projects, research, publications, conferences and seminars, technical assistance, annual campaigns, capital campaigns, general purposes, scholarship funds, matching funds.
Limitations: Giving limited to the Greater Kanawha Valley, WV, area, except scholarships which are limited to residents of WV; no loans. No grants for deficit financing, or general endowments.
Publications: Annual report (including application guidelines), informational brochure, application guidelines, financial statement.
Application information: Application form not required.
> *Initial approach:* Proposal
> *Copies of proposal:* 1
> *Deadline(s):* Deadlines change yearly, write or call for information

Board meeting date(s): Quarterly, usually in Apr., June, Sept., and Dec.
Final notification: Immediately after board action
Write: Betsy B. VonBlond, Exec. Dir.
Officers and Trustees:* G. Thomas Battle,* Chair.; Charles W. Loeb, Secy. and Advisory Committee member; Betsy B. VonBlond, Exec. Dir.; Elsie P. Carter, Deborah A. Faber, Brooks F. McCabe, Jr., Charles R. McElwee, Margaret C. Mills, William E. Mullett, K. Richard C. Sinclair, Louis S. Southworth II.
Advisory Committee: Frederick H. Belden, Jr., Elizabeth E. Chilton, William M. Davis, Willard H. Erwin, Jr., David C. Hardesty, Jr., Thomas N. McJunkin, Harry Moore, Mark H. Schaul, Dolly Sherwood, Olivia R. Singleton, Charles B. Stacy, L. Newton Thomas, Jr., Adeline J. Voorhees, Kartha G. Wehrle.
Trustee Banks: Charleston National Bank, National Bank of Commerce of Charleston, One Valley Bank, N.A., United National Bank.
Number of staff: 1 full-time professional; 2 full-time support.
EIN: 556024430

3266
Mark H. Kennedy Memorial Fund
c/o Security National Bank & Trust Co.
1114 Market St., P.O. Box 511
Wheeling 26003　　　　　(304) 233-0600

Established in 1986 in OH.
Donor(s): Mark H. Kennedy.‡
Foundation type: Independent
Financial data (yr. ended 04/30/92): Assets, $5,345,312 (M); expenditures, $244,465; qualifying distributions, $229,222, including $229,222 for 7 grants of $32,746 each.
Fields of interest: Social services, youth, environment, higher education, education—building funds, hospitals, community development.
Types of support: General purposes, building funds.
Limitations: Giving primarily in Wheeling and Bethany, WV, and Tampa, FL. No grants to individuals.
Publications: 990-PF.
Application information: Contributes only to pre-selected organizations. Applications not accepted.
Write: Dorothy L. Meigh, Sr. Trust Officer
Trustee: Security National Bank & Trust Co.
EIN: 550684352

3267
Bernard McDonough Foundation, Inc.
1000 Grand Central Mall
P.O. Box 1825
Parkersburg 26102　　　　　(304) 485-4494

Incorporated in 1961 in WV.
Donor(s): Bernard P. McDonough.‡
Foundation type: Independent
Financial data (yr. ended 12/31/90): Assets, $2,400,000 (M); expenditures, $301,000;

qualifying distributions, $290,000, including $290,000 for 38 grants (high: $100,000; low: $1,000; average: $1,000-$15,000).
Purpose and activities: Priority given to programs with no other source of funding. Support for higher and other education, including building funds; civic and public affairs, community funds, and leadership development programs; the humanities and cultural programs; and health and social service agencies, including rehabilitation programs for the handicapped and drug abuse, hospital building funds, and the elderly.
Fields of interest: Education, higher education, community funds, civic affairs, cultural programs, health, social services, drug abuse, handicapped, aged.
Types of support: Annual campaigns, building funds, capital campaigns, continuing support, emergency funds, equipment, general purposes, renovation projects, special projects.
Limitations: Giving primarily in WV. No support for religious organizations, or national health or welfare campaigns. No grants to individuals, or for personnel, operating expenses, or publications.
Application information: Application form not required.
Initial approach: Letter
Copies of proposal: 1
Deadline(s): Submit proposal preferably in Oct.; no deadline
Board meeting date(s): Dec.
Final notification: 1 to 2 weeks
Write: James T. Wakley, Pres.
Officers and Directors:* James T. Wakley,* Pres.; Mary Riccobene, V.P.; M. Norris, Secy.-Treas.; Carl L. Broughton, Robert E. Evans, Mark C. Kury, F.C. McCusker.
Number of staff: 1 part-time professional.
EIN: 556023693

3268
Parkersburg Community Foundation
1804 Market St.
P.O. Box 1762
Parkersburg 26102-1762　　　(304) 428-4438
Additional tel.: (304) 428-2584

Established in 1963 in WV.
Donor(s): Albert Wolfe, and members of the Wolfe family, Keystone Foundation.
Foundation type: Community
Financial data (yr. ended 06/30/92): Assets, $2,034,171 (M); gifts received, $313,080; expenditures, $128,023; qualifying distributions, $110,810, including $91,036 for 60 grants (high: $9,240; low: $200), $18,874 for 26 grants to individuals (high: $2,000; low: $70; average: $70-$2,000) and $900 for 2 in-kind gifts.
Purpose and activities: Support for programs leading toward the improvement or fulfillment of charitable, educational, cultural, health, and welfare activities, including direct human services and scholarships to individuals.
Fields of interest: Education, literacy, libraries, cultural programs, arts, social services, child development, handicapped, animal welfare, health, health services.

Types of support: Student aid, seed money, capital campaigns, deficit financing, scholarship funds.
Limitations: Giving limited to the Parkersburg, WV/Mid-Ohio Valley, area.
Publications: Annual report, program policy statement, informational brochure (including application guidelines).
Application information: Application form required.
Initial approach: Letter or telephone
Copies of proposal: 1
Deadline(s): Apr. 1
Board meeting date(s): 3rd Friday in Jan., Mar., May, Sept., and Nov.
Final notification: May; grants paid in June but will consider emergency grants at other times
Write: Edwin L.D. Dils, Exec. Dir.
Officers and Governors:* F. Richard Hall,* Chair.; Francis R. Hollendonner,* Vice-Chair.; Robert W. Burk, Jr.,* Secy.; Edwin L.D. Dils,* Exec. Dir.; and 10 additional members.
Trustee Banks: Commerce Bank, Commercial Banking & Trust Co., United National Bank, WesBanco Parkersburg.
Number of staff: None.
EIN: 556027764

3269
Hugh I. Shott, Jr. Foundation
c/o First National Bank of Bluefield
500 Federal St.
Bluefield 24701　　　　　(304) 325-8181

Established in 1985 in WV.
Donor(s): Hugh I. Shott, Jr.‡
Foundation type: Independent
Financial data (yr. ended 12/31/91): Assets, $23,272,138 (M); expenditures, $1,311,161; qualifying distributions, $1,192,778, including $1,110,343 for 11 grants (high: $300,000; low: $5,000).
Purpose and activities: Giving primarily for secondary and higher education, including business education and building funds for schools; support also for historic preservation, the arts, community development, and health, including ophthamology.
Fields of interest: Secondary education, higher education, business education, education—building funds, historic preservation, arts, community development, health, ophthalmology, general charitable giving.
Types of support: Annual campaigns, building funds, capital campaigns, matching funds.
Limitations: Giving limited to 9 counties within southwest VA and southern WV.
Application information: Application form not required.
Deadline(s): None
Write: Richard W. Wilkinson, Pres.
Officers: Richard W. Wilkinson, Pres.; Scott Shott, V.P.; John Shott, Secy.; B.K. Satterfield, Treas.
Director: L.R. Coulling, Jr.
Trustee: First National Bank of Bluefield.
Number of staff: 1 part-time professional.
EIN: 550650833

WISCONSIN

3270
Alexander Charitable Foundation, Inc.
One Port Plaza
Port Edwards 54469

Incorporated in 1955 in WI.
Donor(s): John E. Alexander.‡
Foundation type: Independent
Financial data (yr. ended 12/31/90): Assets,
$11,126,483 (M); gifts received, $200,000;
expenditures, $680,001; qualifying distributions,
$796,382, including $602,903 for 46 grants
(high: $339,701; low: $500).
Purpose and activities: Emphasis on community
centers, Protestant church support, and hospitals.
Fields of interest: Community development,
Protestant giving, hospitals, family services, social
services.
Limitations: Giving primarily in WI. No grants to
individuals.
Application information: Contributes only to
pre-selected charitable organizations.
Applications not accepted.
  Board meeting date(s): Quarterly
  Write: Samuel A. Casey, Treas.
Officers and Directors:* Gerard E. Veneman,*
Pres.; Charles R. Lester,* V.P.; Margaret Boyarski,
Secy.; Samuel A. Casey,* Treas.; Thomas J.
McCormick,* John E. Wright.
EIN: 396045140

3271
American Family Mutual Insurance Corporate Contributions
3099 East Washington Ave.
P.O. Box 7430
Madison 53783   (608) 249-2111

Financial data (yr. ended 12/31/90): Total giving,
$600,000 for grants.
Purpose and activities: Supports basic human
services, education, health care and safety, civic
affairs, youth groups, culture, and other general
charitable causes.
Fields of interest: Civic affairs, education, social
services, health, safety, youth, cultural programs.
Types of support: In-kind gifts, scholarship funds,
equipment, seed money, special projects.
Limitations: Giving primarily in headquarters city
and major operating locations in Eden Prairie,
MN, St. Joseph, MO, and Madison and
Milwaukee, WI.
Application information: Application form not
required.
  Initial approach: Submit 1-2 page letter
  Deadline(s): None
  Write: Gary Gibson, Community Rels. Liason
  or Patricia Barchus, Dir., Corp. Communs.
Number of staff: 1 full-time professional.

3272
Appleton Papers Corporate Giving Program
825 East Wisconsin Ave.
P.O. Box 359
Appleton 54912   (414) 734-9841

Financial data (yr. ended 12/31/90): Total giving,
$650,000, including $422,500 for grants (high:
$100,000; low: $50; average: $1,000-$5,000),
$162,500 for grants to individuals (high: $1,500;
low: $500; average: $500-$1,500), $32,500 for
employee matching gifts and $32,500 for in-kind
gifts.
Purpose and activities: Supports education,
including private colleges; health, including
health associations, AIDS programs, and drug
abuse; civic affairs; community funds; performing
arts; media and communications; youth; and
hospitals.
Fields of interest: Aged, education, higher
education, AIDS, child welfare, civic affairs,
community funds, conservation, drug abuse, fine
arts, general charitable giving, health associations,
hospices, hunger, performing arts, media and
communications, welfare, youth, hospitals.
Types of support: Annual campaigns, capital
campaigns, continuing support, operating
budgets, employee-related scholarships,
scholarship funds, special projects, employee
matching gifts, in-kind gifts.
Limitations: Giving primarily in operating
locations in MI, OH, PA, and WI.
Application information: Application form not
required.
  Initial approach: Phone call
  Board meeting date(s): Feb. and Dec.
  Write: Gordon Bond, Chair. and C.E.O.
Administrator: Dennis N. Hultgren, Dir.,
Environmental and Public Affairs.
Number of staff: 1 full-time professional; 1
full-time support.

3273
Banta Company Foundation, Inc.
100 Main St.
P.O. Box 8003
Menasha 54952-8003   (414) 722-7777

Incorporated in 1953 in WI.
Donor(s): Banta Corp.
Foundation type: Company-sponsored
Financial data (yr. ended 12/31/90): Assets,
$3,621 (M); gifts received, $210,000;
expenditures, $208,021; qualifying distributions,
$208,021, including $195,060 for 97 grants
(high: $10,000; low: $100; average:
$2,000-$3,000) and $12,918 for 37 employee
matching gifts.
Purpose and activities: Emphasis on higher
education and youth agencies; support also for
the performing arts and other cultural programs
and hospitals.
Fields of interest: Higher education, youth,
cultural programs, performing arts, hospitals.
Types of support: Operating budgets, continuing
support, annual campaigns, seed money,
emergency funds, deficit financing, building
funds, equipment, land acquisition, employee
matching gifts, matching funds, special projects.
Limitations: Giving limited to areas of company
operations including CA, IL, MN, MO, NC, NY,

VA, and WI. No grants to individuals, or for
scholarships, fellowships, or endowment funds;
no loans.
Application information: Application form not
required.
  Initial approach: Letter
  Copies of proposal: 1
  Deadline(s): Nov. 1
  Board meeting date(s): Apr., June, Sept., and
  Dec.
  Write: Dean E. Bergstrom, V.P.
Officers: Calvin W. Aurand, Jr., Pres.; Dean E.
Bergstrom, V.P. and Secy.-Treas.; Gerald A.
Henseler, V.P.; Margaret Banta Humleker, V.P.
Number of staff: None.
EIN: 396050779

3274
Alvin and Marion Birnschein Foundation, Inc.
c/o Lichstinn & Haensel
111 East Wisconsin Ave., No. 1940
Milwaukee 53202-4802   (414) 276-3400

Established in 1968 in WI.
Donor(s): Alvin Birnschein,‡ Marion Birnschein.‡
Foundation type: Independent
Financial data (yr. ended 12/31/90): Assets,
$2,644,833 (M); gifts received, $500;
expenditures, $174,521; qualifying distributions,
$174,521, including $165,100 for 22 grants
(high: $20,000; low: $3,000).
Fields of interest: Social services, child welfare,
higher education, cultural programs, hospitals,
nursing.
Types of support: General purposes, scholarship
funds.
Limitations: Giving primarily in the greater
Milwaukee, WI, area. No support for religious
purposes or primary or secondary schools. No
grants to individuals.
Publications: Informational brochure (including
application guidelines).
Application information: Application form
required.
  Initial approach: Letter requesting application
  form
  Copies of proposal: 1
  Deadline(s): Sept. 30
  Write: Peter C. Haensel, Pres.
Officers and Directors:* Peter C. Haensel,* Pres.;
Loraine E. Schuffler,* Secy.; Fred A. Erchul II.
Number of staff: 1 full-time professional; 1
part-time support.
EIN: 396126798

3275
The Lynde and Harry Bradley Foundation, Inc. ▼
777 East Wisconsin Ave., Suite 2285
Milwaukee 53202-5395   (414) 291-9915
FAX: (414) 291-9991

Incorporated in 1942 in WI as the Allen-Bradley
Foundation, Inc.; adopted present name in 1985.
Donor(s): Harry L. Bradley,‡ Caroline D.
Bradley,‡ Margaret B. Bradley,‡ Margaret Loock
Trust, Allen-Bradley Co.
Foundation type: Independent
Financial data (yr. ended 07/31/90): Assets,
$370,691,611 (M); expenditures, $29,136,489;

qualifying distributions, $27,020,936, including $25,535,549 for 409 grants (high: $750,000; low: $150; average: $25,000-$200,000).

Purpose and activities: Support locally for cultural programs, education, social services, medical programs, health agencies, and public policy. National support for research and education in domestic, international, and strategic public policy; grants also for higher education; in particular, activities that investigate and nurture the moral, cultural, intellectual, and economic institutions which form a free society.

Fields of interest: Education, higher education, public policy, public affairs, international affairs, foreign policy, economics, history, humanities, human rights, political science.

Types of support: Annual campaigns, capital campaigns, conferences and seminars, continuing support, equipment, fellowships, internships, lectureships, matching funds, operating budgets, professorships, publications, renovation projects, research, scholarship funds, special projects.

Limitations: No support for strictly denominational projects. No grants to individuals, or for endowment funds.

Publications: Multi-year report, informational brochure (including application guidelines).

Application information: Application form not required.

   Initial approach: Letter of inquiry
   Copies of proposal: 1
   Deadline(s): Mar. 15, July 15, Sept. 15, and Dec. 15
   Board meeting date(s): Feb., May, Sept., and Nov.
   Final notification: 3 to 5 months
   Write: Michael S. Joyce, Pres.

Officers and Directors:* I. Andrew Rader,* Chair.; Allen M. Taylor,* Vice-Chair.; Michael S. Joyce,* Pres.; Hillel G. Fradkin, V.P. for Prog.; Richard H. Lillie, M.D.,* V.P.; Wayne J. Roper,* Secy.; James D. Ericson,* Treas.; Sarah D. Barder, Reed Coleman, J. Clayburn La Force, Francis J. Shakespeare, David V. Uihlein, Jr.

Number of staff: 4 full-time professional; 1 part-time professional; 5 full-time support; 1 part-time support.

EIN: 396037928

Recent health grants:

3275-1 Cambridge Memorial Hospital, Cambridge, Canada, $86,941. For capital campaign. 1990.

3275-2 Georgetown University, Georgetown University Hospital, DC, $95,588. For continued support of pilot project for prevention of teenage pregnancy. 1990.

3275-3 Historic Sites Foundation, Baraboo, WI, $150,000. For 1990 Great Circus Parade. 1990.

3275-4 Historic Sites Foundation, Baraboo, WI, $25,000. For 1990 Great Circus Parade. 1990.

3275-5 Mayo Foundation, Rochester, MN, $300,000. For program to encourage cooperation between medical researchers and clinicians. 1990.

3275-6 University of Wisconsin, Medical School, Milwaukee, WI, $60,000. For research on teenage pregnancy and its medical implications. 1990.

3275-7 Wisconsin School of Professional Psychology, Milwaukee, WI, $30,000. For mental health clinic for low-income patients. 1990.

3276
Frank G. Brotz Family Foundation, Inc.
3518 Lakeshore Rd.
P.O. Box 551
Sheboygan 53083   (414) 458-2121

Incorporated in 1953 in WI.
Donor(s): Plastics Engineering Co., Inc.
Foundation type: Independent
Financial data (yr. ended 09/30/90): Assets, $11,092,478 (M); gifts received, $400,000; expenditures, $521,660; qualifying distributions, $502,504, including $502,475 for grants.
Fields of interest: Hospitals, higher education, youth, cultural programs, religion.
Types of support: Building funds.
Limitations: Giving primarily in WI. No grants to individuals.
Application information:
   Initial approach: Letter
   Deadline(s): None
   Board meeting date(s): Periodically
   Write: Grants Comm.
Officers and Trustees:* Ralph T. Brotz,* Pres.; Stuart W. Brotz,* V.P. and Treas.; Ralph R. Brotz,* Secy.; Roland M. Neumann.
EIN: 396060552

3277
Bucyrus-Erie Foundation, Inc.
(Formerly Becor Western Foundation, Inc.)
1100 Milwaukee Ave.
South Milwaukee 53172-0500 (414) 768-5005
Application address: P.O. Box 500, South Milwaukee, WI 53172

Incorporated in 1951 in WI.
Donor(s): Bucyrus-Erie Co.
Foundation type: Company-sponsored
Financial data (yr. ended 12/31/90): Assets, $10,097,845 (M); expenditures, $861,654; qualifying distributions, $798,505, including $771,361 for grants.
Purpose and activities: Grants for higher education, the arts, hospitals, and community funds; support also for social services and youth agencies.
Fields of interest: Higher education, arts, hospitals, community funds, youth, performing arts, social services.
Types of support: Operating budgets, continuing support, annual campaigns, building funds, equipment, endowment funds, employee matching gifts, employee-related scholarships, capital campaigns.
Limitations: Giving primarily in metropolitan Milwaukee. No grants to individuals (except scholarships for children of employees), or for research, special projects, seed money, emergency funds, deficit financing, land acquisition, matching or challenge grants, publications, or conferences; no loans.
Application information: Application form required for scholarships for children of employees.
   Initial approach: Letter
   Deadline(s): Dec. for scholarships
   Board meeting date(s): Feb. and Oct.
   Final notification: After next board meeting
   Write: D.L. Strawderman, Mgr. and Secy.

Officers and Directors:* W.B. Winter,* Pres.; N.J. Verville,* V.P. and Treas.; D.L. Strawderman,* Mgr. and Secy.; P.W. Cotter, D.E. Porter, B.H. Rupple.
Number of staff: 2 part-time support.
EIN: 396075537

3278
Emory T. Clark Family Foundation
1033 North Mayfair Rd., Suite 200
Wauwatosa 53226

Established in 1982 in WI.
Donor(s): Emory T. Clark.‡
Foundation type: Independent
Financial data (yr. ended 03/31/91): Assets, $5,924,404 (M); expenditures, $397,371; qualifying distributions, $355,064, including $349,000 for 7 grants (high: $99,000; low: $25,000).
Fields of interest: Education, higher education, hospitals, child welfare.
Types of support: Capital campaigns.
Limitations: Giving primarily in WI.
Publications: Informational brochure.
Application information: Application form not required.
   Initial approach: Proposal
   Deadline(s): July
   Board meeting date(s): Nov.
   Write: William J. Labadie, Dir.
Trustee: First Wisconsin Trust Co.
Number of staff: None.
EIN: 391410324

3279
Cleary Foundation, Inc.
1111 Cedar Rd.
La Crosse 54601-8401   (608) 783-7500

Established in 1982 in WI.
Donor(s): Russell G. Cleary, Gail K. Cleary.
Foundation type: Independent
Financial data (yr. ended 11/30/90): Assets, $2,175,684 (M); expenditures, $128,149; qualifying distributions, $128,149, including $115,159 for grants.
Fields of interest: General charitable giving, education, health.
Types of support: Endowment funds.
Limitations: Giving primarily in WI, MN, IL, and IA, especially the La Crosse, WI, area. No grants to individuals.
Application information: Application form not required.
   Initial approach: Letter
   Copies of proposal: 1
   Deadline(s): None
   Board meeting date(s): May, July, Sept., and Nov.
   Write: Russell G. Cleary, Pres.
Officers and Directors:* Russell G. Cleary,* Pres. and Treas.; Gail K. Cleary,* V.P. and Secy.; Kristine H. Cleary, Sandra G. Cleary, Lillian Hope Kumm.
Number of staff: 1
EIN: 391426785

3280
Consolidated Papers Foundation, Inc.
231 First Ave. North
P.O. Box 8050
Wisconsin Rapids 54495-8050 (715) 422-3368

Incorporated in 1951 in WI.
Donor(s): Consolidated Papers, Inc.
Foundation type: Company-sponsored
Financial data (yr. ended 12/31/91): Assets,
$28,620,358 (M); gifts received, $9,257,238;
expenditures, $1,072,515; qualifying
distributions, $1,042,108, including $992,916 for
119 grants (high: $123,000; low: $100; average:
$5,000-$10,000) and $49,192 for 634 employee
matching gifts.
Purpose and activities: Giving for local
community funds, and youth and social service
agencies in communities where Consolidated
Papers, Inc. conducts operations; higher
education grants generally limited to those in WI;
support also for the fine and performing arts and
other cultural programs.
Fields of interest: Community funds, youth, social
services, family planning, health services,
hospitals—building funds, education, higher
education, education—building funds, medical
education, secondary education, literacy,
engineering, cultural programs, fine arts, historic
preservation, performing arts, theater.
Types of support: Operating budgets, continuing
support, annual campaigns, seed money,
emergency funds, building funds, equipment,
endowment funds, employee matching gifts,
scholarship funds, employee-related scholarships,
capital campaigns, renovation projects,
professorships.
Limitations: Giving primarily in WI, usually near
areas of company operations. No grants to
individuals (except through scholarships), or for
deficit financing, research, or conferences; no
loans.
Application information: Application form not
required.
  Initial approach: Proposal
  Copies of proposal: 1
  Deadline(s): Mar. 31 and Sept. 30
  Board meeting date(s): May or June, and Nov.
    or Dec.
  Final notification: 3 months
  Write: Daniel P. Meyer, Pres.
Officers and Directors:* Daniel P. Meyer,* Pres.;
Donald L. Stein,* V.P.; Carl R. Lemke, Secy.; J.
Richard Matsch, Treas.; Lawrence H. Boling,
Patrick F. Brennan, Richard J. Kenney, George W.
Mead.
Number of staff: None.
EIN: 396040071

3281
Cremer Foundation, Inc.
P.O. Box 1
Madison 53701 (608) 837-5166
Additional tel.: (608) 837-2124

Established in 1965 in WI.
Foundation type: Independent
Financial data (yr. ended 12/31/90): Assets,
$2,179,974 (M); expenditures, $79,967;
qualifying distributions, $72,475, including
$72,475 for 16 grants (high: $11,500; low: $400).

Purpose and activities: Giving primarily to social
service agencies, especially those aiding troubled
youth, the homeless, the handicapped and senior
citizens.
Fields of interest: Youth, social services, child
welfare, alcoholism, child development, family
services, handicapped, medical sciences, aged.
Types of support: General purposes, matching
funds, scholarship funds, seed money.
Limitations: Giving limited to the northeast Dane
County, WI, area. Generally, no support for
religious-based programs. No grants to
individuals, or generally for deficit financing or
conferences or seminars.
Publications: Application guidelines.
Application information: Application form not
required.
  Initial approach: Letter or proposal
  Copies of proposal: 1
  Deadline(s): 1 month before meeting
  Board meeting date(s): Twice a year; usually in
    Mar. and Aug.
  Write: James A. Berkenstadt, Esq., Admin.
Officers and Directors:* J.T. Sykes,* Pres.; H.K.
George,* Secy.; H.L. Cremer,* Treas.; James A.
Berkenstadt,* Admin.; F.W. Haberman, H.B.
Klotzbach, R.R. Stroud.
Number of staff: None.
EIN: 396086822

3282
Patrick and Anna M. Cudahy Fund
P.O. Box 11978
Milwaukee 53211 (708) 866-0760

Incorporated in 1949 in WI.
Donor(s): Michael F. Cudahy.‡
Foundation type: Independent
Financial data (yr. ended 12/31/90): Assets,
$17,486,716 (M); expenditures, $1,363,906;
qualifying distributions, $1,132,379, including
$1,132,379 for 119 grants (high: $79,650; low:
$400; average: $5,000-$10,000).
Purpose and activities: Primary areas of interest
include the arts, education, youth, international
relief, and social services. Support for the
homeless, family services, and international
development programs focusing on Latin America
and Southern Africa; support also for national
programs concerned with environmental and
public interest issues, and cultural and civic affairs
programs.
Fields of interest: Social services, homeless,
youth, education, international development,
international relief, human rights, environment,
public policy, cultural programs, civic affairs.
Types of support: General purposes, operating
budgets, continuing support, annual campaigns,
seed money, building funds, equipment,
matching funds, technical assistance, special
projects, renovation projects.
Limitations: Giving primarily in WI and Chicago,
IL, for local programs and Latin America and
southern Africa for international (U.S.-based)
programs. No grants to individuals, or for
endowments; no loans.
Publications: Annual report, application
guidelines.
Application information: Application form not
required.
  Initial approach: Letter
  Copies of proposal: 1

  Deadline(s): 8 weeks prior to board meetings
  Board meeting date(s): Usually in Apr., June,
    Sept., and Dec.
  Final notification: 2 weeks after meetings
  Write: Sr. Judith Borchers, Exec. Dir.
Officers and Directors:* Richard D. Cudahy,
Chair.; Janet S. Cudahy,* Pres.; Louise A.
McMenamin, Secy.; Sr. Judith Borchers, Exec.
Dir.; James Bailey, Daniel Cudahy, Tia Cudahy,
Dudley J. Godfrey, Jr., Jean Holtz, Philip Lerman,
Wesley Scott, Annette Stoddard-Freeman.
Number of staff: 1 part-time professional; 1
part-time support.
EIN: 390991972
Recent health grants:
3282-1 Center for Public Representation,
  Madison, WI, $10,000. For AIDS Legal
  Services Project. 1990.
3282-2 Horizon House, Milwaukee, WI,
  $10,000. For capital support for drug treatment
  facility. 1990.
3282-3 Lad Lake, Dousman, WI, $10,000. For
  renovations of living facilities. 1990.
3282-4 Little Sisters of the Poor, Palatine, IL,
  $15,000. For renovations at Saint Joseph's
  Home for the Elderly. 1990.
3282-5 Maryknoll Sisters, Maryknoll, NY,
  $11,350. For AIDS control program in
  Tanzania. 1990.
3282-6 Maryknoll Sisters, Maryknoll, NY,
  $10,000. For health promotion in Chinandega,
  Nicaragua. 1990.
3282-7 Maryville City of Youth, Des Plaines, IL,
  $20,000. For care of newly born cocaine
  addicted babies. 1990.
3282-8 Penfield Childrens Center, Milwaukee,
  WI, $19,340. For Home Training Program.
  1990.
3282-9 SHARE Foundation, DC, $25,000. For
  health clinic in Calle Real, El Salvador. 1990.
3282-10 Southside Guadalupe Dental Clinic,
  Milwaukee, WI, $15,000. For dental care
  program for elderly Hispanics. 1990.
3282-11 Trinity Memorial Hospital, Cudahy, WI,
  $10,000. For capital campaign for new
  emergency department. 1990.

3283
CUNA Mutual Insurance Group
Charitable Foundation, Inc.
5910 Mineral Point Rd.
Madison 53705 (608) 231-7314

Incorporated in 1967 in WI.
Foundation type: Company-sponsored
Financial data (yr. ended 12/31/90): Assets,
$175,798 (M); gifts received, $526,237;
expenditures, $413,407; qualifying distributions,
$413,407, including $413,396 for 214 grants
(high: $162,000; low: $25).
Fields of interest: Community funds, higher
education, secondary education, cultural
programs, health, urban affairs, civic affairs.
Types of support: Operating budgets, continuing
support, annual campaigns, seed money,
emergency funds, employee matching gifts,
scholarship funds, fellowships, special projects,
research, capital campaigns, matching funds.
Limitations: Giving primarily in WI. No grants to
individuals, or for deficit financing, land
acquisition, endowment funds, or publications;
no loans.

Publications: Informational brochure (including application guidelines).
Application information: Application form required for requests over $500.
Initial approach: Proposal, letter, or telephone
Copies of proposal: 1
Deadline(s): None
Board meeting date(s): Feb., May, and Sept.
Final notification: 4 to 6 weeks
Write: Richard C. Radtke, Asst. Secy.
Officers: Rosemarie Shultz, Pres.; W.F. Broxterman, V.P.; Richard M. Heins, Secy.-Treas.
Number of staff: None.
EIN: 396105418

3284
Edward U. Demmer Foundation
c/o Bank One Wisconsin Trust Co., N.A.
P.O. Box 1308
Milwaukee 53201   (414) 765-2800

Trust established in 1963 in WI.
Donor(s): Edward U. Demmer.‡
Foundation type: Independent
Financial data (yr. ended 12/31/90): Assets, $1,983,201 (M); expenditures, $276,136; qualifying distributions, $256,123, including $249,500 for 37 grants (high: $40,000; low: $1,000).
Purpose and activities: Giving restricted to Protestant or non-sectarian institutions, with emphasis on projects related to children; support also for cultural institutions, health agencies, and hospitals.
Fields of interest: Protestant giving, youth, child welfare, cultural programs, hospitals, health.
Limitations: Giving primarily in WI. No grants to individuals.
Application information:
Initial approach: Proposal
Copies of proposal: 4
Deadline(s): None
Board meeting date(s): Mar., June, Sept., and Dec.
Write: Robert L. Hanley, Sr. V.P., Bank One Wisconsin Trust Co., N.A.
Trustees: Lawrence Demmer, Harrold J. McComas, Carl N. Otjen, Bank One Wisconsin Trust Co., N.A.
EIN: 396064898

3285
Ralph Evinrude Foundation, Inc.
c/o Quarles and Brady
411 East Wisconsin Ave.
Milwaukee 53202-4497   (414) 277-5000

Incorporated in 1959 in WI.
Donor(s): Ralph Evinrude.‡
Foundation type: Independent
Financial data (yr. ended 07/31/92): Assets, $2,299,552 (M); expenditures, $187,840; qualifying distributions, $168,820, including $168,820 for 70 grants (high: $6,000; low: $500; average: $1,000-$5,000).
Purpose and activities: Emphasis on education, health agencies, including mental health, and social services, including programs for the homeless, hunger, the handicapped, youth and child welfare, Catholic giving, and family services.

Fields of interest: Education, health, Catholic giving, social services, youth, family services, handicapped, employment, homeless.
Types of support: Annual campaigns, building funds, capital campaigns, equipment, general purposes, operating budgets, renovation projects, research.
Limitations: Giving primarily in Milwaukee, WI. No grants to individuals; no loans.
Application information: Application form not required.
Initial approach: Letter
Copies of proposal: 1
Deadline(s): Submit proposal preferably in Jan., Apr., July, or Oct.
Board meeting date(s): Quarterly in Feb., May, Aug., and Nov.
Final notification: Within 2 weeks after meeting
Write: Patrick W. Cotter, V.P.
Officers and Directors:* Thomas J. Donnelly,* Pres.; Patrick W. Cotter,* V.P. and Treas.; Theodore F. Zimmer,* Secy.
Number of staff: None.
EIN: 396040256

3286
A. Ward Ford Memorial Institute, Inc.
813 Second St.
Wausau 54401-4799   (715) 845-9287

Incorporated in 1984 in WI.
Donor(s): Caroline S. Mark, William B. Mark.‡
Foundation type: Independent
Financial data (yr. ended 06/30/90): Assets, $1,600,253 (M); gifts received, $1,700; expenditures, $258,503; qualifying distributions, $248,173, including $205,500 for 7 grants (high: $125,000; low: $12,000).
Purpose and activities: Giving primarily for scientific health care projects, including cardiology research with the use of laser equipment.
Fields of interest: Medical research, health, heart disease.
Types of support: Research, consulting services.
Publications: Financial statement, application guidelines.
Application information: Application form required.
Initial approach: Proposal
Copies of proposal: 3
Deadline(s): Mar. 31
Board meeting date(s): June and Sept.
Write: Sandra S. Robarge, Administrator
Officers and Trustees:* Caroline S. Mark,* Chair.; Ellet H. Drake,* Pres.; Konrad Tuchscherer,* V.P.; Sandra Robarge, Secy.-Treas.; James Lundberg, Richard Morehead, William Owen.
Number of staff: None.
EIN: 370983948

3287
Community Foundation for the Fox Valley Region, Inc.
P.O. Box 563
Appleton 54912   (414) 730-3773

Organized in 1986 in WI.
Foundation type: Community
Financial data (yr. ended 06/30/91): Assets, $8,332,960 (M); gifts received, $1,878,302;

expenditures, $761,175; qualifying distributions, $416,310, including $416,310 for 47 grants (high: $100,966; low: $250).
Purpose and activities: Primary areas of interest include social services and child care programs, community development, education, cultural programs, and health. Support also for civic affairs, AIDS research, alcohol and drug abuse, and medication and library services and information concerning diabetes.
Fields of interest: Social services, child welfare, community development, civic affairs, education, arts, cultural programs, health, AIDS, drug abuse, alcoholism, libraries.
Types of support: Seed money, general purposes, special projects, emergency funds.
Limitations: Giving limited to the Fox Valley, WI, area. No support for sectarian or religious purposes, or specific research or medical projects. No grants for operating expenses, annual fund drives, deficit financing, endowment funds, capital projects, or travel expenses.
Publications: Annual report (including application guidelines), informational brochure.
Application information: Application form required.
Initial approach: Letter or telephone
Copies of proposal: 4
Deadline(s): Jan. 15, Apr. 15, July 15, and Sept. 30
Board meeting date(s): Mar., June, Oct., and Jan.
Final notification: Mar., June, Oct., and Jan.
Write: Ruth C. Haviland, Exec. Dir., or Lynn VanLankvelt, Financial Admin.
Officers and Directors:* O.C. Boldt,* Chair.; Paul H. Groth,* Pres.; Jeffrey Reister,* V.P.; Larry L. Kath,* Secy.; Ruth C. Haviland, Exec. Dir.; F. John Barlow, and 44 additional directors.
Number of staff: 3 full-time professional; 1 part-time professional; 1 full-time support; 2 part-time support.
EIN: 391548450

3288
Evan and Marion Helfaer Foundation ▼
735 North Water St.
Milwaukee 53202   (414) 276-3600

Established in 1971 in WI.
Donor(s): Evan P. Helfaer.‡
Foundation type: Independent
Financial data (yr. ended 07/31/91): Assets, $15,954,522 (M); expenditures, $1,155,624; qualifying distributions, $1,058,221, including $987,225 for 142 grants (high: $100,000; low: $250; average: $1,000-$20,000).
Purpose and activities: Support for higher education, cultural programs, youth and social service agencies, and health.
Fields of interest: Cultural programs, higher education, social services, youth, health.
Types of support: Lectureships, professorships, building funds, research.
Limitations: Giving limited to WI. No grants to individuals.
Application information: Application form available, but not required or preferred.
Initial approach: Letter
Deadline(s): None
Board meeting date(s): Periodically
Final notification: Within 90 days after end of fiscal year

Write: Thomas L. Smallwood, Trustee
Trustees: Thomas L. Smallwood, Admin.; Jack F. Kellner, Marshall & Ilsley Trust Co.
Number of staff: 1
EIN: 396238856

3289
Glenn & Gertrude Humphrey Foundation, Inc.
1233 North Mayfair Rd., Suite 104
Wauwatosa 53226   (414) 774-8680

Established in 1972 in WI.
Foundation type: Independent
Financial data (yr. ended 12/31/90): Assets, $4,057,686 (M); expenditures, $800,363; qualifying distributions, $635,160, including $635,160 for 54 grants (high: $200,000; low: $60).
Fields of interest: Higher education, child development, youth, medical research, health services, health associations.
Types of support: Building funds, capital campaigns, scholarship funds, endowment funds, general purposes, operating budgets.
Limitations: Giving primarily in the greater Milwaukee, WI, area. No support for labor organizations or for religious purposes. No grants to individuals.
Application information: Application form required.
   Initial approach: Letter
   Deadline(s): Apr. 1 for spring board meeting, and Sept. 1 for fall board meeting
   Write: Loraine E. Schuffler, Pres.
Officers and Directors:* Gertrude Humphrey,* Chair.; Loraine E. Schuffler,* Pres.; Peter C. Haensel,* Secy.; Roy Gruber, Joseph Tierney.
EIN: 237207640

3290
Jeffris Family Foundation, Ltd.
445 North Jackson
P.O. Box 650
Janesville 53547-0650

Established in 1977.
Donor(s): Thomas M. Jeffris.
Foundation type: Independent
Financial data (yr. ended 12/31/90): Assets, $5,728,428 (M); expenditures, $90,250; qualifying distributions, $43,396, including $34,000 for grants.
Fields of interest: Hospitals.
Limitations: Giving primarily in IL. No grants to individuals.
Application information: Contributes only to pre-selected organizations. Applications not accepted.
Officers and Directors:* Thomas M. Jeffris,* Pres.; Charles R. Rydberg,* V.P.; Marion M. Schumacher,* Secy.-Treas.; Henry E. Fuldner.
EIN: 391281879

3291
S. C. Johnson & Son Corporate Contributions Program
1525 Howe St.
Racine 53403   (414) 631-2267

Purpose and activities: "We believe in contributing to the well-being of the countries and communities where we conduct business..." As we have in the past, we shall continue to support worthwhile programs in the local community and those which operate on the broader regional, national and international scene. The contributions program at SC Johnson Wax consists of the following three components: an annual corporate donation of at least 5 percent pre-tax profit dollars; corporate involvement in the communities where we do business; and community involvement by our employees. The corporation offers direct contributions of dollars and/or gifts of equipment, products or services. Support by the corporation, however, is directed to recipients who do not fall within the established guidelines of The Johnson's Wax Fund, Inc. Under these criteria, contributions are made to worthy causes in the following general areas: education (including scholarships), social welfare, culture and the arts, youth activities, health and medical concerns, preservation of the environment, international relations, emergency and disaster relief, and the disadvantaged.
Fields of interest: Community development, minorities, education, secondary education, health, civic affairs, cultural programs, youth.
Types of support: In-kind gifts, endowment funds, building funds, continuing support.
Limitations: No support for political causes, religious institutions for denominational purposes, or fraternal, labor, and veterans' organizations.
Application information: Application form not required.
   Initial approach: Letter or proposal
   Deadline(s): Two monthes prior to board meeting
   Board meeting date(s): Quarterly meetings
   Write: Reva Holmes, V.P. and Secy. Johnson Wax Fund

3292
Johnson Controls Foundation ▼
5757 North Green Bay Ave.
P.O. Box 591
Milwaukee 53201   (414) 228-2219

Trust established in 1952 in WI.
Donor(s): Johnson Controls, Inc.
Foundation type: Company-sponsored
Financial data (yr. ended 12/31/90): Assets, $16,679,236 (M); expenditures, $2,892,970; qualifying distributions, $2,776,357, including $2,668,291 for 1,089 grants (high: $225,000; low: $25; average: $100-$10,000) and $102,750 for 63 grants to individuals (high: $1,750; low: $500; average: $1,750).
Purpose and activities: Grants for higher education; health and hospitals; community funds; social services, including aid to the handicapped, care of children, and the aged; and civic, arts, and cultural organizations.
Fields of interest: Higher education, hospitals, health, AIDS, community funds, handicapped, aged, youth, child welfare, social services, performing arts, cultural programs, arts, civic affairs.
Types of support: Operating budgets, continuing support, annual campaigns, seed money, emergency funds, building funds, endowment funds, matching funds, employee-related scholarships, employee matching gifts.
Limitations: No support for religious purposes, public or private preschools, elementary or secondary schools, industrial groups or trade associations supported by industrial groups, foreign-based institutions, or fraternal, veterans', or labor groups. No grants to individuals (except employee-related scholarships), or for fundraising events, courtesy advertising, deficit financing, equipment, land acquisition, special projects, research, publications, conferences, or seminars; no loans.
Publications: Application guidelines.
Application information: Employee-related scholarship awards are paid directly to institutions and not to individuals. Application form not required.
   Initial approach: Letter
   Copies of proposal: 1
   Deadline(s): None
   Board meeting date(s): Usually Mar., June, and Sept.
   Final notification: Up to 120 days
   Write: Fred L. Brengel, Chair., Advisory Board
Advisory Board: James H. Keyes, R. Douglas Ziegler.
Trustee: First Wisconsin Trust Co.
Scholarship Selection Committee: Frederick E. Sperry, Norbert J. Tlachae, Marie Uihlein.
Number of staff: 1 full-time professional; 1 part-time professional; 4 part-time support.
EIN: 396036639
Recent health grants:
3292-1 American Cancer Society, Wisconsin Division, Milwaukee, WI, $10,000. 1990.
3292-2 Blood Center of Southeastern Wisconsin, Milwaukee, WI, $20,000. 1990.
3292-3 Catherine McAuley Health Center, Ann Arbor, MI, $10,000. 1990.
3292-4 Medical College of Wisconsin, Milwaukee, WI, $60,000. 1990.
3292-5 Medical College of Wisconsin, Milwaukee, WI, $10,000. 1990.
3292-6 Saint Francis Childrens Center, Milwaukee, WI, $25,000. 1990.
3292-7 Saint Joseph Hospital, Milwaukee, WI, $25,000. 1990.
3292-8 Saint Lukes Medical Center, Milwaukee, WI, $25,000. 1990.

3293
The Johnson's Wax Fund, Inc. ▼
1525 Howe St.
Racine 53403   (414) 631-2826

Incorporated in 1959 in WI.
Donor(s): S.C. Johnson & Son, Inc.
Foundation type: Company-sponsored
Financial data (yr. ended 06/30/92): Assets, $2,499,380 (M); gifts received, $3,321,393; expenditures, $2,554,891; qualifying distributions, $2,552,991, including $2,219,199 for 114 grants (high: $593,070; low: $25; average: $500-$100,000) and $214,993 for 715 employee matching gifts.
Purpose and activities: Scholarships for children of company employees through the Citizen's Scholarship Foundation of America; scholarships and fellowships in specific areas of interest, i.e., chemistry, biology, marketing, and business; grants to local colleges; support for local welfare,

cultural, and civic organizations; grants also for environmental protection, health, and education; seed funding for new programs which address high-priority human service needs.
Fields of interest: Chemistry, biology, business education, welfare, cultural programs, civic affairs, environment, health, education, higher education, education—minorities.
Types of support: Seed money, building funds, equipment, scholarship funds, exchange programs, fellowships, research, employee matching gifts, employee-related scholarships, capital campaigns.
Limitations: Giving primarily in WI and the Midwest in areas of company operations. No support for national health organizations or religious or social groups, organizations receiving support from the United Way, or veterans', labor, or fraternal organizations. No grants to individuals, or for operating budgets, emergency funds, deficit financing, demonstration projects, or conferences; no loans.
Publications: Informational brochure (including application guidelines), corporate giving report.
Application information: Application form not required.
  Initial approach: Letter and proposal
  Copies of proposal: 1
  Deadline(s): Dec. 15, April 15, Aug. 15
  Board meeting date(s): Feb., June, and Oct.
  Final notification: 3 to 4 months
  Write: Reva A. Holmes, V.P. and Secy.
Officers and Trustees:* Samuel C. Johnson,* Chair. and Pres.; Richard M. Carpenter,* Vice-Chair.; Reva A. Holmes, V.P. and Secy.; John M. Schroeder, Treas.; Darrel Campbell, Maria L. Campbell, James F. DiMarco, Roger H. Grothaus, Sue A. Helland.
Number of staff: 1 full-time professional; 1 part-time professional; 1 part-time support.
EIN: 396052089

3294
Herbert H. Kohl Charities, Inc.
825 North Jefferson St., Suite 250
Milwaukee 53202

Established in 1977 in WI.
Donor(s): Herbert H. Kohl, Mary Kohl.
Foundation type: Independent
Financial data (yr. ended 06/30/91): Assets, $6,125,352 (M); expenditures, $385,856; qualifying distributions, $339,544, including $331,509 for 513 grants (high: $100,000; low: $8).
Fields of interest: Health associations, medical research, education.
Limitations: Giving primarily in Milwaukee, WI. No grants to individuals.
Application information: Contributes only to pre-selected organizations. Applications not accepted.
Officers and Directors:* Herbert H. Kohl,* Pres.; Allen D. Kohl,* V.P.; Sidney A. Kohl,* Secy.; Delores K. Solovy,* Treas.
EIN: 391300476

3295
Kohler Corporate Giving Program
Public Affairs Dept. 019
444 Highland Dr.
Kohler 53044   (414) 457-4441

Purpose and activities: Education, arts, and community funds are major interests; also supports public broadcasting, civic and community programs, conservation, experimental programs, law and justice, drug abuse programs, and private colleges, economic education, business education, and economic development. In 1990, the company made in-kind grants to 85 organizations, cash grants to 230 organizations, and awarded 25 scholarships.
Fields of interest: Arts, business education, civic affairs, community development, community funds, conservation, education, environment, fine arts, higher education, history, housing, law and justice, performing arts, drug abuse, economics, education—building funds, heart disease, humanities, adult education, AIDS, citizenship, ecology, health, homeless, alcoholism, cancer, business, child development, health services, historic preservation, literacy, youth, media and communications.
Types of support: In-kind gifts, scholarship funds, seed money, matching funds, equipment, endowment funds, building funds, employee-related scholarships, donated equipment, donated products, use of facilities, loaned talent, employee volunteer services, internships, employee matching gifts.
Limitations: Giving primarily in headquarters city, and communities surrounding Brownwood, TX, Kohler, WI, and Spartanburg, SC, from which Kohler Co. draws its employees.
Publications: Informational brochure.
Application information: Public Affairs handles contributions. Application form not required.
  Initial approach: Letter of inquiry/proposal
  Copies of proposal: 1
  Deadline(s): Aug. 31
  Board meeting date(s): Decisions are made as needed
  Final notification: Contributions are made before Dec. 31
  Write: Peter J. Fetterer, Mgr., Media and Civic Services
Administrator: Peter J. Fetterer, Mgr., Media and Civic Services.
Number of staff: 1 full-time professional; 1 full-time support.

3296
Ladish Company Foundation
5481 South Packard Ave.
Cudahy 53110

Trust established in 1952 in WI.
Donor(s): Ladish Co.
Foundation type: Company-sponsored
Financial data (yr. ended 11/30/90): Assets, $12,029,517 (M); expenditures, $514,939; qualifying distributions, $505,395, including $505,395 for 106 grants (high: $47,500; low: $145; average: $2,000-$5,000).
Fields of interest: Community funds, youth, hospitals, medical research, higher education.

Types of support: General purposes, research, scholarship funds, endowment funds, annual campaigns.
Limitations: Giving primarily in WI. No grants to individuals.
Application information: Contributes only to pre-selected organizations. Applications not accepted.
  Write: Walter D. Aumann, Trustee
Trustees: Walter D. Aumann, Victor F. Braun, John H. Ladish, Henry P. McHale.
EIN: 396040489

3297
Herman W. Ladish Family Foundation, Inc.
c/o Ladish Malting Co.
790 North Jackson St., 2nd Fl.
Milwaukee 53202   (414) 271-4763
Additional address: P.O. Box 2044, Milwaukee, WI 53201

Incorporated in 1956 in WI.
Donor(s): Herman W. Ladish.‡
Foundation type: Independent
Financial data (yr. ended 06/30/91): Assets, $9,591,471 (M); expenditures, $860,802; qualifying distributions, $830,946, including $822,500 for 53 grants (high: $100,000; low: $2,000).
Fields of interest: Higher education, secondary education, medical research, health, hospitals, youth, cultural programs.
Limitations: Giving primarily in WI.
Application information: Application form not required.
  Deadline(s): None
  Board meeting date(s): Twice a year
  Write: John H. Ladish, Pres.
Officers and Directors:* John H. Ladish,* Pres.; Victor F. Braun,* V.P.; Robert T. Stollenwerk, Secy.-Treas.; Elwin J. Zarwell.
Number of staff: None.
EIN: 396063602

3298
Ladish Malting Company Foundation, Inc.
790 North Jackson St., 2nd Fl.
Milwaukee 53202   (414) 271-4763

Incorporated in 1957 in WI.
Donor(s): Ladish Malting Co.
Foundation type: Company-sponsored
Financial data (yr. ended 06/30/90): Assets, $2,938,941 (M); expenditures, $142,396; qualifying distributions, $141,135, including $137,750 for 14 grants (high: $30,000; low: $250).
Purpose and activities: Giving primarily to hospitals; grants also for youth and social service agencies, including a community fund.
Fields of interest: Hospitals, youth, social services, community funds.
Types of support: General purposes.
Limitations: Giving primarily in WI and ND.
Application information: Application form not required.
  Initial approach: Letter
  Deadline(s): None
  Write: John H. Ladish, Pres.

Officers and Directors:* John H. Ladish,* Pres. and Treas.; Victor F. Braun,* V.P.; Robert T. Stollenwerk,* Secy.
EIN: 396045284

3299
Lindsay Foundation, Inc.
c/o M & I Trust Co.
P.O. Box 2035
Milwaukee 53201-2035

Established in 1963 in WI.
Donor(s): Walter Lindsay.‡
Foundation type: Independent
Financial data (yr. ended 12/31/90): Assets, $2,476,329 (M); gifts received, $100,500; expenditures, $134,283; qualifying distributions, $110,200, including $110,000 for grants.
Fields of interest: Health services, hospitals, rehabilitation, social services, family services, aged, disadvantaged, handicapped, mental health, employment, vocational education, Protestant giving.
Types of support: Continuing support.
Limitations: Giving primarily in WI. No support for arts or education. No grants to individuals.
Application information:
  Write: Lorna L. Mayer, Pres.
Officer: Lorna L. Mayer, Pres.
Number of staff: None.
EIN: 396086904

3300
Marshall & Ilsley Bank Corporate Giving Program
770 North Water St.
Milwaukee 53202   (414) 765-7700

Purpose and activities: General charitable support.
Fields of interest: Social services, community funds, youth, aged, religious welfare, community development, education, higher education, secondary education, arts, music, museums, health, hospitals, medical research, media and communications, civic affairs, economics, environment.
Limitations: Giving primarily in the metropolitan Milwaukee, WI, area.
Application information:
  Initial approach: Letter
  Deadline(s): None
  Board meeting date(s): Once a month
  Write: Harold W. Reiter, V.P.

3301
Marshall & Ilsley Foundation, Inc.
(Formerly Marshall & Ilsley Bank Foundation, Inc.)
770 North Water St.
Milwaukee 53202   (414) 765-7835

Incorporated in 1958 in WI.
Donor(s): Marshall & Ilsley Bank.
Foundation type: Company-sponsored
Financial data (yr. ended 12/31/90): Assets, $3,738,310 (M); gifts received, $1,302,748; expenditures, $1,111,664; qualifying distributions, $1,104,273, including $1,086,273 for 93 grants (high: $166,250; low: $100; average:

$1,000-$20,000) and $18,000 for 12 grants to individuals (high: $3,000; low: $1,000).
Purpose and activities: Emphasis on higher education, including employee-related scholarships, social services, the arts, hospitals, and youth agencies.
Fields of interest: Higher education, arts, hospitals, youth, social services.
Types of support: Employee-related scholarships.
Limitations: Giving primarily in WI.
Application information: Scholarships only for children of permanent, full-time employees of the Marshall & Ilsley Corp. Application form not required.
  Initial approach: Letter
  Deadline(s): None
  Board meeting date(s): As necessary
  Final notification: Varies
  Write: Diane Sebion, Secy.
Officers and Directors:* John A. Puelicher,* Pres.; James B. Wigdale,* V.P.; Diane L. Sebion, Secy.; Wendell F. Bueche, Burleigh E. Jacobs, Jack F. Kellner, James O. Wright.
Number of staff: None.
EIN: 396043185

3302
Faye McBeath Foundation ▼
1020 North Broadway
Milwaukee 53202   (414) 272-2626

Trust established in 1964 in WI.
Donor(s): Faye McBeath.‡
Foundation type: Independent
Financial data (yr. ended 12/31/91): Assets, $13,881,252 (M); expenditures, $1,471,448; qualifying distributions, $1,304,470, including $1,304,470 for 55 grants (high: $50,000; low: $5,000; average: $12,000-$25,000).
Purpose and activities: To benefit the people of WI by providing homes and care for elderly persons; promoting education in medical science and public health; providing medical, nursing, and hospital care for the sick and disabled; promoting the welfare of children; and promoting research in civics and government directed towards improvement in the efficiency of local government.
Fields of interest: Aged, health services, hospitals, nursing, AIDS, alcoholism, cancer, nutrition, medical education, mental health, drug abuse, heart disease, disadvantaged, child development, elementary education, education—early childhood, education—minorities, handicapped, civic affairs, government, public policy.
Types of support: Seed money, building funds, equipment, special projects, matching funds, renovation projects, capital campaigns, continuing support, technical assistance, operating budgets.
Limitations: Giving limited to WI, with emphasis on the greater Milwaukee area. No support for specific medical or scientific research projects. No grants to individuals, or for annual campaigns, endowment funds, scholarships, or fellowships; grants rarely for emergency funds; no loans.
Publications: Annual report, program policy statement, application guidelines.
Application information: Application form required.
  Initial approach: 2 page preliminary application
  Copies of proposal: 1

Deadline(s): 1 month prior to board meetings
Board meeting date(s): At least bimonthly, beginning in Jan.
Final notification: 2 weeks after meetings
Write: Sarah M. Dean, Exec. Dir.
Officers and Trustees:* Bonnie R. Weigell,* Chair.; Thomas J. McCollow,* Vice-Chair.; William L. Randall,* Secy.; Sarah M. Dean, Exec. Dir.; Joan Hardy, Charles A. Krause, First Wisconsin Trust Co.
Number of staff: 1 part-time professional.
EIN: 396074450
Recent health grants:
3302-1 AIDS Resource Center of Wisconsin, Milwaukee, WI, $35,000. For demonstration project aimed at health promotion and early intervention for people who are HIV positive. 1991.
3302-2 Blood Center of Southeastern Wisconsin, Milwaukee, WI, $25,000. For capital campaign to raise funds for new research facility. 1991.
3302-3 Childrens Hospital of Wisconsin, Milwaukee, WI, $70,000. Toward research on behavioral and neurological effects of cocaine on babies who are exposed prior to birth. 1991.
3302-4 Counseling Center of Milwaukee, Milwaukee, WI, $10,000. For Pathfinders program providing frontline services to abused and neglected children and their families. 1991.
3302-5 Isaac Coggs Health Connection, Milwaukee, WI, $25,000. For renovation of Center which provides full array of medical services to Milwaukee's inner-city residents. 1991.
3302-6 Medical College of Wisconsin, Center for the Study of Bioethics, Wauwatosa, WI, $46,500. Toward nursing ethics leadership position. 1991.
3302-7 Mental Health Association in Milwaukee County, Milwaukee, WI, $50,000. Toward establishment of community based program of psychiatric rehabilitation which provides work oriented day programs, employment services, social, housing and psychiatric support to mentally ill. 1991.
3302-8 Milwaukee Hospice Home Care, Milwaukee, WI, $13,000. For nursing internship program for student nurses to familiarize them with Hospice nursing. 1991.
3302-9 Penfield Childrens Center, Milwaukee, WI, $30,000. For renovation and expansion of treatment center for disabled children. 1991.
3302-10 Planned Parenthood of Wisconsin, Milwaukee, WI, $12,000. For general operating support of programs. 1991.
3302-11 Rosalie Manor, Milwaukee, WI, $35,000. For First-Time Parenting Program, hospital-based outreach project which offers potentially high-risk parents child development and parenting assistance as well as community resource information. 1991.
3302-12 Sixteenth Street Community Health Center (H.O.P.E.), Milwaukee, WI, $20,000. For renovation and expansion of south side health clinic. 1991.
3302-13 Visiting Nurse Association of Milwaukee, Milwaukee, WI, $12,000. For operating support of Community Hospice Programs. 1991.

3303
Menasha Corporation Foundation
P.O. Box 367
Neenah 54957-0367   (414) 751-1000

Established in 1953 in WI.
Donor(s): Menasha Corp.
Foundation type: Company-sponsored
Financial data (yr. ended 12/31/91): Assets, $1,039,137 (M); gifts received, $287,350; expenditures, $460,341; qualifying distributions, $453,979, including $368,323 for grants (high: $20,000; low: $100; average: $50-$25,000), $58,967 for 42 grants to individuals (average: $2,000-$2,300) and $22,028 for 79 employee matching gifts.
Purpose and activities: Grants primarily for health, welfare, cultural, environmental, and higher educational organizations in areas of company operations; giving also for employee-related scholarships and an employee matching gift program.
Fields of interest: Health, cultural programs, higher education, social services, hospitals, community funds, environment.
Types of support: Employee matching gifts, employee-related scholarships.
Limitations: Giving primarily in areas of company operations.
Application information: Application form required.
    Initial approach: Proposal
    Copies of proposal: 1
    Deadline(s): Last day of month preceding board meeting
    Board meeting date(s): Quarterly
    Write: Richard D. Widmann, Pres.
Officers: Oliver C. Smith, Chair.; Richard D. Widmann, Pres.; Steven S. Kromholz, Secy.-Treas.
Number of staff: None.
EIN: 396047384

3304
Mielke Family Foundation, Inc.
P.O. Box 563
Appleton 54912   (414) 730-0770

Established in 1963 in WI.
Foundation type: Independent
Financial data (yr. ended 12/31/91): Assets, $5,503,155 (M); expenditures, $242,761; qualifying distributions, $231,143, including $227,901 for 61 grants (high: $75,000; low: $93; average: $93-$75,000).
Fields of interest: Health, education, arts.
Types of support: Endowment funds.
Limitations: Giving limited to the Appleton and Shawano, WI, areas.
Publications: Application guidelines.
Application information: Application form required.
    Initial approach: Letter
    Copies of proposal: 4
    Deadline(s): Apr. 15 and Oct. 15
    Board meeting date(s): May and Nov.
    Final notification: Distributions normally made in Dec.
Officers and Directors: Jeffrey Riester,* Pres.; Philip Keller,* V.P.; Warren Parsons,* Secy.-Treas.; Harold C. Adams, Paul H. Groth, John E. Mielke, Marion Nemetz.
Number of staff: None.

EIN: 396074258

3305
Miller Corporate Giving Program
3939 West Highland Blvd.
Milwaukee 53201   (414) 931-4540

Purpose and activities: Support for education, including business and minority education, alcohol abuse and community support. Different divisions have their own priorities.
Fields of interest: Alcoholism, business education, education—minorities, higher education.
Limitations: Giving primarily in 50-mile radius of plant city community or regional office. No support for capital campaigns. No grants for minors and individuals.
Application information:
    Initial approach: Applicants should write to the local Miller division
    Write: Janet Christiaansen, Community Relations Rep.
Administrators: Sue Rowe, Community Rels. Coord.; Janet Christiaansen, Commun. Rels. Rep.

3306
Milwaukee Foundation ▼
1020 North Broadway
Milwaukee 53202   (414) 272-5805

Established in 1915 in WI by declaration of trust.
Foundation type: Community
Financial data (yr. ended 12/31/90): Assets, $87,213,688 (M); gifts received, $7,412,242; expenditures, $6,464,563; qualifying distributions, $5,148,191, including $4,177,412 for 785 grants (high: $255,945; low: $100; average: $100-$255,945).
Purpose and activities: Present funds include many discretionary and some funds designated by the donors to benefit specific institutions or for special purposes, including educational institutions, the arts and cultural programs, social services, health care and hospitals; support also for community development, and conservation and historic preservation.
Fields of interest: Education, education—early childhood, higher education, arts, cultural programs, performing arts, social services, homeless, family services, aged, child welfare, youth, health, health services, AIDS, drug abuse, community development, urban development, historic preservation.
Types of support: Seed money, building funds, equipment, matching funds, scholarship funds, special projects, renovation projects, capital campaigns, conferences and seminars.
Limitations: Giving primarily in the Milwaukee, WI, area. No support for the general use of churches or for sectarian religious purposes, or for specific medical or scientific projects except from components of the foundation established for such purposes. No grants to individuals (except for established awards), or for operating budgets, continuing support, annual campaigns, endowment funds, or deficit financing.
Publications: Annual report, informational brochure (including application guidelines), grants list, newsletter, program policy statement.

Application information: Capital requests are reviewed at June and Dec. board meetings. Application form required.
    Initial approach: Proposal, telephone, or letter
    Copies of proposal: 1
    Deadline(s): Submit proposal preferably 10 weeks before board meetings; deadlines Jan. 2, Apr. 1, July 1, and Oct. 1
    Board meeting date(s): Mar., June, Sept., Dec., and as needed
    Final notification: 2 weeks after board meetings
    Write: Douglas M. Jansson, Exec. Dir.
Officer: David M.G. Huntington, Secy. and Exec. Dir.
Foundation Board: Orren J. Bradley, Chair.; Doris H. Chortek, Vice-Chair.; Harry F. Franke, John H. Hendee, Jr, Charles N. McNeer, Dennis Purtell, Brenton H. Rupple, Polly H. Van Dyke, Carl A. Weigell, Walter H. White, Jr.
Trustees: Bank One Wisconsin Trust Co., N.A., First Bank Milwaukee, First Wisconsin Trust Co., Marshall & Ilsley Trust Co.
Number of staff: 7 full-time professional; 5 full-time support; 1 part-time support.
EIN: 396036407
Recent health grants:
3306-1 Addiction Fighters, Milwaukee, WI, $15,000. For start-up funding of outpatient counseling and acupuncture program for low-income persons addicted to alcohol and other drugs. 1991.
3306-2 AIDS Resource Center of Wisconsin, Milwaukee, WI, $10,000. For second phase of facility renovations. 1991.
3306-3 AIDS Resource Center of Wisconsin, Milwaukee AIDS Project, Milwaukee, WI, $20,000. For collaborative effort with AIDS Coalition of Milwaukee to begin implementation of recommendations in Milwaukee metropolitan area plan for care and treatment of persons with HIV/AIDS. 1991.
3306-4 AIDS Resource Center of Wisconsin, Milwaukee AIDS Project, Milwaukee, WI, $15,000. For Milwaukee AIDS Outreach Consortium's street outreach program which seeks to educate high-risk target populations about AIDS/HIV in order to prevent or reduce spread of AIDS throughout Milwaukee community. 1991.
3306-5 Alliance for the Mentally Ill of Greater Milwaukee, Milwaukee, WI, $10,000. Toward development of program to help chronically mentally ill persons find affordable housing. 1991.
3306-6 Bethesda Lutheran Home, Watertown, WI, $10,000. Toward purchase and renovation of house to serve as group home for mentally retarded persons. 1991.
3306-7 Career Youth Development, Milwaukee, WI, $25,000. Toward construction of residential drug abuse treatment facility for inner city youth. 1991.
3306-8 Eisenhower Memorial Cerebral Palsy Work Center, Milwaukee, WI, $15,000. Toward remodeling of new facility for its sheltered workshop for persons with cerebral palsy. 1991.
3306-9 Isaac Coggs Health Connection, Milwaukee, WI, $25,000. To expand examining room and clinical service areas at Isaac Coggs Community Health Center. 1991.
3306-10 La Causa Day Care Center, Milwaukee, WI, $20,000. For further development of crisis

nursery program which provides shelter, child care and short term counseling for families with children under five years of age in crisis situations. 1991.

3306-11 Lake Area Club, Milwaukee, WI, $10,000. Toward purchase of equipment and furnishings for new facility for persons recovering from alcoholism. 1991.

3306-12 Marquette University, Milwaukee, WI, $10,000. Toward purchase of furnishings and equipment for Metcalfe Park Health Center, nurse-managed health care facility in Metcalfe Park neighborhood. 1991.

3306-13 Mental Health Association in Milwaukee County, Milwaukee, WI, $50,000. Toward purchase of facility which will house program based on Fountain House model of recreational and employment services for chronically mentally ill persons. 1991.

3306-14 Milwaukee Breast Cancer Awareness Project, Milwaukee, WI, $10,000. For breast cancer screening and outreach program for high-risk, low-income women. 1991.

3306-15 Penfield Childrens Center, Milwaukee, WI, $40,000. Toward expansion of facility serving children with multiple disabilities. 1991.

3306-16 Planned Parenthood of Wisconsin, Milwaukee, WI, $75,000. For family planning and counseling services primarily in inner-city clinics. 1991.

3306-17 Planning Council for Health and Human Services, Milwaukee, WI, $15,000. For second-year funding of Minority Health Initiative, collaborative project to plan for improvement of health status of Milwaukee area minority residents. 1991.

3306-18 Sixteenth Street Community Health Center (H.O.P.E.), Milwaukee, WI, $25,000. For second-year funding of Family Resource Center, program which targets new parents on Milwaukee's southside, integrating health and social services for mother and infant. 1991.

3306-19 Sixteenth Street Community Health Center (H.O.P.E.), Milwaukee, WI, $25,000. Toward expansion of facility. 1991.

3306-20 South Side Guadalupe Dental Clinic, Milwaukee, WI, $10,000. For creation of additional dental hygienist position. 1991.

3306-21 Transitional Living Services, Milwaukee, WI, $15,000. For rehabilitation of supervised apartments for mentally disabled persons. 1991.

3306-22 United Cerebral Palsy of Southeastern Wisconsin, Milwaukee, WI, $15,000. Toward renovation of facility. 1991.

3306-23 University of Wisconsin Foundation, School of Nursing, Milwaukee, WI, $20,000. For Milwaukee Teen Parent Child Health and Education Project, program designed to increase delivery of health services, improve parenting skills and offer support to teen and young adult mothers. 1991.

3307
Neenah Foundry Foundation, Inc.
2121 Brooks Ave.
Neenah 54956   (414) 725-7000

Incorporated in 1953 in WI.
Donor(s): Neenah Foundry Co.
Foundation type: Company-sponsored

Financial data (yr. ended 12/31/90): Assets, $4,256,405 (M); expenditures, $229,910; qualifying distributions, $225,825, including $225,825 for 56 grants (high: $33,700; low: $50).
Fields of interest: Higher education, secondary education, youth, health, social services.
Types of support: Program-related investments, general purposes, operating budgets.
Limitations: Giving primarily in WI. No grants to individuals.
Application information: Grants generally made only to pre-selected organizations. Applications not accepted.
    Write: Thomas R. Franklin, Secy.-Treas.
Officers: E.W. Aylward, Sr., Pres.; E.W. Aylward, Jr., V.P.; T.R. Franklin, Secy.-Treas.
Number of staff: None.
EIN: 396042143

3308
Northwestern Mutual Corporate Giving Program
720 E. Wisconsin Ave.
Milwaukee 53202   (414) 299-7021

Financial data (yr. ended 12/31/90): Total giving, $2,929,090, including $2,321,188 for 208 grants (high: $400,000; low: $500; average: $5,000-$10,000), $507,902 for 1,891 employee matching gifts and $100,000 for in-kind gifts.
Purpose and activities: Support for education, including public and private colleges, economic education, and elementary and secondary education; fine and performing arts, health, medical research; and civic and community programs, the United Way, minority programs, and urban programs. Company rarely considers national programs for funding. Types of support include: employee volunteer programs; use of facilities; and direct grants.
Fields of interest: Education, higher education, economics, elementary education, secondary education, arts, fine arts, health, medical research, civic affairs, community development, community funds, minorities, urban development, business education, child welfare, drug abuse, education—building funds, educational research, family services, handicapped, heart disease, hospitals—building funds, AIDS, cultural programs, homeless, alcoholism, education—minorities, housing, disadvantaged, health services, hospitals, insurance education, welfare—indigent individuals, literacy, medical education, museums, performing arts, social sciences, urban affairs.
Types of support: Employee matching gifts, annual campaigns, donated equipment, operating budgets, building funds, employee volunteer services, loaned talent, use of facilities, capital campaigns, internships, emergency funds, matching funds, public relations services.
Limitations: Giving limited to the southeastern part of WI.
Publications: Informational brochure (including application guidelines).
Application information: Application form not required.
    Initial approach: Letter; send to headquarters
    Deadline(s): Pre-September preferred
    Board meeting date(s): Nov.
    Final notification: Dec.

    Write: Robert O. Carboni, V.P.
Number of staff: 1 full-time professional; 1 full-time support.

3309
Oscar Mayer Corporate Giving Program
910 Mayer Ave.
Box 7188
Madison 53707   (608) 241-3311

Financial data (yr. ended 12/31/90): Total giving, $340,000, including $310,000 for 70 grants (high: $50,000; low: $500) and $30,000 for in-kind gifts.
Purpose and activities: Support for civic affairs, health and welfare, including drug abuse, hospital building funds, family services, hunger, youth, hospices, mental health, and education, including minority education; emphasis on projects benefiting employees and their families; 50 percent of support goes to United Way.
Fields of interest: Civic affairs, cultural programs, disadvantaged, drug abuse, education—minorities, family services, health, hospitals, hospitals—building funds, mental health, minorities, performing arts, welfare, hunger, youth, hospices.
Types of support: In-kind gifts, capital campaigns, special projects, program-related investments.
Limitations: Giving primarily in plant locations across the U.S.
Publications: Corporate report, application guidelines, informational brochure (including application guidelines).
Application information: Application form not required.
    Initial approach: Mail application along with appropriate information; send to nearest company facility; contributions handled in Human Resources Dept.
    Copies of proposal: 1
    Deadline(s): None
    Board meeting date(s): Mar. 15, June 15, Sept. 15, and Dec. 15
    Final notification: Immediately following quarterly board meetings
    Write: Lynette L. Byrnes, Community Affairs Administrator
Contributions Comm.: Kwame S. Salter, Chair.; Lynette L. Bynes, Community Affairs Administrator.
Number of staff: 2 full-time professional.

3310
Oshkosh Foundation
404 North Main St.
P.O. Box 1726
Oshkosh 54902   (414) 426-3993

Established in 1928 in WI by declaration of trust.
Donor(s): Combs Trust.
Foundation type: Community
Financial data (yr. ended 02/28/91): Assets, $9,250,652 (M); gifts received, $202,692; expenditures, $507,893; qualifying distributions, $435,372, including $319,826 for 66 grants (high: $59,250; low: $34) and $72,550 for 146 grants to individuals (high: $1,000; low: $300).
Purpose and activities: Emphasis on scholarships, hospitals, medical care of the indigent, community funds, and cultural programs.

Scholarships awarded for graduating Oshkosh high school seniors for a 4-year term only.
Fields of interest: Hospitals, welfare—indigent individuals, community funds, cultural programs, arts, theater, performing arts, music, education, recreation, general charitable giving.
Types of support: Continuing support, annual campaigns, emergency funds, building funds, equipment, student aid, grants to individuals, seed money, capital campaigns.
Limitations: Giving limited to Oshkosh, WI. No grants for endowments, matching gifts, seed money, deficit financing, special projects, research, publications, or conferences; no loans.
Publications: Annual report, application guidelines.
Application information: Applications not accepted unless residency requirements are met. Application form not required.
  Initial approach: Proposal
  Copies of proposal: 1
  Deadline(s): None
  Board meeting date(s): Monthly
  Final notification: 6 weeks
  Write: R. Andrew Swinney, Exec. Dir.
Officers and Foundation Committee: Gary Yakes, Pres.; Bob Pung, V.P.; Virginia Nelson, Secy.; Hibbard H. Engler, Marie Hoyer, Sheldon Lasky, Richard Rutledge.
Trustee: First Wisconsin National Bank of Oshkosh.
Number of staff: 1 full-time professional.
EIN: 396041638

3311
Oshkosh Truck Foundation, Inc.
P.O. Box 2566
2307 Oregon St.
Oshkosh 54901   (414) 235-9150

Incorporated in 1960 in WI.
Donor(s): Oshkosh Truck Corp.
Foundation type: Company-sponsored
Financial data (yr. ended 12/31/91): Assets, $27,445 (L); expenditures, $266,641; qualifying distributions, $266,641, including $250,000 for 79 grants (high: $25,000; low: $100; average: $2,800) and $16,641 for 21 grants to individuals (high: $850; low: $750; average: $750).
Purpose and activities: Primary areas of interest include local alcohol and drug abuse; support also for local youth and a community fund. Scholarships to children of company employees who attend local high schools.
Fields of interest: Youth, community funds, drug abuse, alcoholism.
Types of support: Operating budgets, continuing support, annual campaigns, emergency funds, building funds, equipment, employee-related scholarships.
Limitations: Giving primarily in the Oshkosh, Winnebago County, WI, area. No grants for seed money, deficit financing, land acquisition, special projects, research, publications, conferences, general endowments, or matching gifts; no loans.
Application information: Application form not required.
  Copies of proposal: 1
  Board meeting date(s): Mar., June, Sept., and Dec.
  Write: J. Peter Mosling, Jr., Pres.

Officers: J. Peter Mosling, Jr., Pres.; T.M. Dempsey, V.P.; Barbara E. Boycks, Secy.; F.S. Schulte, Treas.
Number of staff: None.
EIN: 396062129

3312
Jane and Lloyd Pettit Foundation, Inc. ▼
660 East Mason St.
Milwaukee 53202   (414) 271-5900

Incorporated in 1986 in WI.
Donor(s): Jane Bradley Pettit, Lloyd H. Pettit.
Foundation type: Independent
Financial data (yr. ended 06/30/90): Assets, $1,683 (M); gifts received, $6,546,150; expenditures, $6,432,707; qualifying distributions, $6,404,699, including $6,190,300 for 121 grants (high: $1,005,000; low: $200; average: $1,000-$50,000).
Purpose and activities: Giving for secondary and higher education, social services, including a community fund, recreation, and health and hospitals.
Fields of interest: Secondary education, higher education, recreation, social services, hospitals, health.
Limitations: Giving primarily in Milwaukee, WI. No grants to individuals.
Application information: Contributes only to pre-selected organizations. Applications not accepted.
  Write: Joseph E. Tierney, Jr., Secy.
Officers and Directors:* Jane Bradley Pettit, Pres. and Treas.; Lloyd H. Pettit,* V.P.; Joseph E. Tierney, Jr.,* Secy.
EIN: 391574123
Recent health grants:
3312-1 American Cancer Society, Milwaukee, WI, $30,000. 1990.
3312-2 American Heart Association, Milwaukee, WI, $10,000. 1990.
3312-3 Columbia Hospital, Milwaukee, WI, $32,000. 1990.
3312-4 Foundation for Mental Health, Springdale, AZ, $25,000. 1990.
3312-5 Make-A-Wish Foundation, Butler, WI, $10,000. 1990.
3312-6 Saint Joseph Hospital, Milwaukee, WI, $10,000. 1990.

3313
Pollybill Foundation, Inc.
111 East Kilbourn Ave., 19th Fl.
Milwaukee 53202   (414) 273-4390

Incorporated in 1960 in WI.
Donor(s): William D. Van Dyke, Polly H. Van Dyke.
Foundation type: Independent
Financial data (yr. ended 12/31/90): Assets, $1,279,104 (M); gifts received, $675,000; expenditures, $683,619; qualifying distributions, $683,619, including $673,200 for 24 grants (high: $150,000; low: $500).
Purpose and activities: Emphasis on private secondary education, higher education, the arts, conservation, health, and social services.
Fields of interest: Secondary education, higher education, arts, conservation, health, social services.

Limitations: Giving primarily in WI, especially Milwaukee.
Application information: Applications not accepted.
  Write: Paul F. Meissner, Dir.
Officers and Directors:* Polly H. Van Dyke,* Pres. and Treas.; William D. Van Dyke III,* Secy.; Leonard G. Campbell, Jr., Paul F. Meissner.
EIN: 396078550

3314
Gene & Ruth Posner Foundation, Inc.
152 West Wisconsin Ave., Rm. 404
Milwaukee 53203-2508   (414) 276-7440
FAX: (414) 276-8283

Established in 1963 in WI.
Donor(s): Gene Posner, Ruth Posner.
Foundation type: Independent
Financial data (yr. ended 12/31/90): Assets, $2,134,166 (M); expenditures, $106,315; qualifying distributions, $94,519, including $80,506 for 61 grants (high: $30,000; low: $20).
Purpose and activities: Primary areas of interest include crime and law enforcement, law and justice, health, and Jewish organizations.
Fields of interest: Jewish giving, health associations, health, higher education, cultural programs, arts, crime and law enforcement, law and justice, architecture, historic preservation.
Application information: Application form not required.
  Deadline(s): None
  Write: Jeffry A. Posner, V.P.
Officers: Gene Posner, Pres.; Jeffry A. Posner, V.P.; Ruth Posner, Secy.-Treas.
Directors: Fredrick Posner, Barbara Ward.
Number of staff: 1 part-time support.
EIN: 396050150

3315
Presto Foundation
3925 North Hastings Way
Eau Claire 54703   (715) 839-2119

Incorporated in 1952 in WI.
Donor(s): National Presto Industries, Inc.
Foundation type: Company-sponsored
Financial data (yr. ended 05/31/91): Assets, $16,150,312 (M); expenditures, $756,458; qualifying distributions, $702,161, including $617,790 for 126 grants (high: $100,000; low: $25) and $74,603 for 17 grants to individuals (high: $5,000; low: $1,053).
Purpose and activities: Giving for higher education, including scholarships for employees' children, educational television, local community funds, health, and social service agencies.
Fields of interest: Higher education, community funds, media and communications, health, social services.
Types of support: Employee-related scholarships.
Limitations: Giving primarily in northwestern WI; Eau Claire and Chippewa County preferred.
Application information:
  Initial approach: Letter
  Deadline(s): None
  Write: Norma Jaenke
Officers and Trustees:* Melvin S. Cohen,* Chair. and Pres.; R.J. Alexy,* V.P.; Walter Gold,* V.P.; William A. Nelson,* V.P.; Maryjo R. Cohen,*

Secy.-Treas.; Eileen Phillips Cohen, Donald Dickson, Kenneth Hansen, Richard Myhers.
EIN: 396045769

3316
Racine Community Foundation, Inc.
(Formerly Racine County Area Foundation, Inc.)
c/o Marge Kozina, Foundation Dir.
818 Sixth St., Suite 103
Racine 53403   (414) 632-8474
Application address: P.O. Box 444, Racine, WI 53401

Incorporated in 1975 in WI.
Foundation type: Community
Financial data (yr. ended 12/31/91): Assets, $3,580,385 (M); gifts received, $134,606; expenditures, $242,368; qualifying distributions, $160,689, including $153,610 for 60 grants (high: $19,211; low: $100) and $7,079 for grants to individuals.
Purpose and activities: Giving primarily in four areas: 1) improvement of community environment; 2) improvement of education, health, and community services; 3) encouragement and support of the fine arts and cultural activities; and 4) general support of agencies whose programs deal with basic community need. The foundation also awards scholarships to local area residents.
Fields of interest: Community development, health, social services, cultural programs, education, fine arts.
Types of support: Seed money, emergency funds, equipment, matching funds, student aid, conferences and seminars, operating budgets.
Limitations: Giving limited to Racine County, WI. No support for church or missionary groups unless for entire community benefit. No grants for capital expenditures, including building funds, endowment funds, research, travel, or publications; no continuing support after three years.
Publications: Annual report, application guidelines, informational brochure.
Application information: Application form required.
    Initial approach: Letter or telephone
    Copies of proposal: 10
    Deadline(s): Jan. 15, Apr. 15, July 15, and Oct. 15
    Board meeting date(s): Mar., June, Sept., and Dec.
    Final notification: By letter after meeting in which proposal was discussed
    Write: Sandra Kontra, V.P., Grants
Officers and Directors:* J. David Rowland,* Pres.; Mary M. Walker, 1st V.P.; Sandra L. Kontra,* 2nd V.P.; Stephen J. Smith,* Secy.; Clayton A. Meier,* Treas.; Marianne R. Cool,* Personnel Mgr.; Mary Jo Bichler, Gloria M. Bolm, Donald N. Botsford, William B. Boyd, William B. Danford, Ruth E. Foley, Ronald F. Goodspeed, Jane S. Gorton, Roy J. Josten, Richard L. Leuenberger, Serge E. Logan, James O. Parrish, Jay Price Ruffo, Mary Lou Schuler, C. Patricia Tolson.
Number of staff: 1 full-time professional; 2 part-time support.
EIN: 510188377

3317
The Oscar Rennebohm Foundation, Inc.
P.O. Box 5187
Madison 53705   (608) 274-1030

Incorporated in 1949 in WI.
Donor(s): Oscar Rennebohm.‡
Foundation type: Independent
Financial data (yr. ended 12/31/90): Assets, $24,755,202 (M); expenditures, $1,375,391; qualifying distributions, $1,264,400, including $1,264,400 for 16 grants (high: $359,500; low: $5,000).
Purpose and activities: Emphasis on higher education; support also for health and social service agencies.
Fields of interest: Higher education, medical education, health services, social services.
Types of support: Building funds, equipment, research.
Limitations: Giving primarily in WI.
Application information: Application form not required.
    Deadline(s): None
    Write: John L. Sonderegger, Secy.
Officers: Steven Skolaski, Pres. and Treas.; Mary F. Rennebohm, V.P.; John L. Sonderegger, Secy.
Directors: Frederick W. Jensen, Dennis G. Maki, William H. Young, Lenor Zeeh.
EIN: 396039252

3318
Rexnord Foundation Inc.
P.O. Box 2022
Milwaukee 53201-2022   (414) 643-3000

Incorporated in 1953 in WI.
Donor(s): Rexnord, Inc.
Foundation type: Company-sponsored
Financial data (yr. ended 10/31/90): Assets, $2,717,095 (M); expenditures, $337,374; qualifying distributions, $421,279, including $331,900 for grants.
Purpose and activities: Grants primarily for community funds, higher education (including an employee matching gift program), hospitals, cultural programs, and youth agencies.
Fields of interest: Community funds, higher education, hospitals, cultural programs, youth.
Types of support: Building funds, special projects, employee-related scholarships, employee matching gifts.
Limitations: Giving primarily in areas of company operations, with some emphasis on Milwaukee, WI. No support for religious organizations. No grants to individuals (except for employee-related scholarships), or for endowment funds.
Publications: Application guidelines.
Application information: Application form not required.
    Initial approach: Letter or proposal
    Copies of proposal: 1
    Deadline(s): Submit grant proposals preferably in Feb.-Mar. or June-July; deadline mid-May for scholarship applications only
    Board meeting date(s): 2 or 3 times a year
    Final notification: 6 months
    Write: Alice Lorenz, Foundation Administrator, or Barb Alcorn (for employee-related scholarships)
Officers and Directors:* Donald Taylor,* Pres.; John P. Calhoun,* V.P.; Charles R. Roy, Secy.; W.E.

Schauer, Jr.,* Treas.; F. Brengel, R.V. Krikorian, William C. Messinger, Gustave H. Moede, Jr., J. Swenson.
Number of staff: None.
EIN: 396042029

3319
Hamilton Roddis Foundation, Inc.
c/o Augusta D. Roddis
1108 East Fourth St.
Marshfield 54449

Incorporated in 1953 in WI.
Donor(s): Hamilton Roddis,‡ Augusta D. Roddis, Catherine P. Roddis, Roddis Plywood Corp.
Foundation type: Independent
Financial data (yr. ended 12/31/90): Assets, $3,398,712 (M); expenditures, $183,412; qualifying distributions, $159,051, including $157,000 for 43 grants (high: $19,000; low: $100).
Purpose and activities: Emphasis on Episcopal church support and religious education, social services, medical research, educational organizations, historic preservation, and local associations.
Fields of interest: Protestant giving, religious schools, social services, medical research, educational associations, historic preservation.
Limitations: Giving primarily in WI. No grants to individuals.
Application information: Contributes only to pre-selected organizations. Applications not accepted.
Officers: William H. Roddis II, Pres.; Mrs. Gordon P. Connor, V.P.; Augusta D. Roddis, Secy.-Treas.
EIN: 396077001

3320
Roehl Foundation, Inc.
P.O. Box 168
Oconomowoc 53066-0168   (414) 569-3000

Established in 1959.
Donor(s): Peter G. Roehl.
Foundation type: Independent
Financial data (yr. ended 06/30/90): Assets, $2,126,526 (M); expenditures, $126,026; qualifying distributions, $111,800, including $110,000 for 38 grants (high: $7,500; low: $200).
Purpose and activities: Giving for Lutheran churches and welfare organizations; support also for higher and secondary education, hospitals, and medical research.
Fields of interest: Protestant giving, Protestant welfare, higher education, secondary education, hospitals, medical research.
Limitations: Giving primarily in WI. No grants to individuals.
Application information:
    Initial approach: Proposal
    Deadline(s): None
    Write: Peter Roehl, V.P.
Officers: Ora C. Roehl, Pres.; Peter G. Roehl, V.P. and Treas.; Nathalia E. Christian, Secy.
Director: Janet L. Roehl.
EIN: 396048089

3321
Robert T. Rolfs Foundation, Inc.
735 South Main St.
West Bend 53095   (414) 335-1000

Established in 1981 in WI.
Donor(s): Amity Leather Products Co., Robert T. Rolfs.
Foundation type: Independent
Financial data (yr. ended 09/30/90): Assets, $4,308,225 (M); gifts received, $5,000; expenditures, $252,066; qualifying distributions, $243,575, including $243,575 for 22 grants (high: $90,000; low: $250).
Purpose and activities: Support primarily for social services, giving also for the arts and health.
Fields of interest: Social services, arts, health.
Limitations: Giving primarily in WI.
Application information: Application form not required.
Initial approach: Letter
Deadline(s): None
Write: Arthur P. Hoberg, V.P.
Officers: Robert T. Rolfs, Pres.; Arthur P. Hoberg, V.P.; John F. Rozek, Secy.-Treas.
EIN: 391390015

3322
Will Ross Memorial Foundation
c/o Bank One Wisconsin Trust Co., N.A.
P.O. Box 1308
Milwaukee 53201   (414) 765-2842

Foundation type: Independent
Financial data (yr. ended 12/31/90): Assets, $3,302,444 (M); gifts received, $11,618; expenditures, $380,357; qualifying distributions, $350,733, including $340,700 for 38 grants (high: $60,000; low: $200).
Fields of interest: Arts, social services, higher education, health.
Limitations: Giving only in Milwaukee, WI.
Application information: Application form not required.
Initial approach: Letter
Deadline(s): None
Board meeting date(s): End of calendar quarter
Write: Mary Ann LaBahn, Treas.
Officers and Directors:* Edmond C. Young,* Pres.; John D. Bryson, Jr.,* V.P.; Richard R. Teschner,* V.P.; David L. Kinnamon,* Secy.; Mary Ann W. LaBahn,* Treas.
EIN: 396044673

3323
Edward Rutledge Charity
404 North Bridge St.
Chippewa Falls 54729   (715) 723-6618
Mailing address: P.O. Box 758, Chippewa Falls, WI 54729

Incorporated in 1911 in WI.
Donor(s): Edward Rutledge.‡
Foundation type: Independent
Financial data (yr. ended 05/31/90): Assets, $2,905,550 (M); expenditures, $166,939; qualifying distributions, $154,045, including $49,609 for 43 grants (high: $7,500; low: $25; average: $25-$7,500), $48,649 for 34 grants to individuals and $21,711 for 235 loans to individuals.

Purpose and activities: To furnish relief and charity for worthy poor and to aid charitable associations or institutions.
Fields of interest: Welfare—indigent individuals, education, youth, disadvantaged, alcoholism, general charitable giving.
Types of support: Grants to individuals, student aid, special projects, operating budgets, student loans.
Limitations: Giving limited to Chippewa County, WI. No grants for endowment funds.
Application information: Application form required for scholarships and other grants to individuals. Application form required.
Initial approach: Letter
Copies of proposal: 1
Deadline(s): Scholarship applications must be submitted by July 1; no deadline for other grants
Board meeting date(s): Twice a week
Final notification: July for scholarships
Write: Gerald J. Naiberg, Pres.
Officers and Directors:* Gerald J. Naiberg,* Pres.; Richard H. Stafford,* V.P.; David Hancock,* Secy.-Treas.
Number of staff: 1 full-time professional; 1 full-time support.
EIN: 390806178

3324
Walter Schroeder Foundation, Inc. ▼
770 North Water St.
Milwaukee 53202   (414) 287-7177

Incorporated in 1963 in WI.
Donor(s): Walter Schroeder Trust.
Foundation type: Independent
Financial data (yr. ended 06/30/91): Assets, $6,783,674 (M); expenditures, $1,011,355; qualifying distributions, $980,700, including $980,700 for 60 grants (average: $1,000-$50,000).
Purpose and activities: Support for higher education, hospitals, community welfare, and youth agencies.
Fields of interest: Education, education—building funds, higher education, hospitals, welfare, disadvantaged, family services, youth, child development, social services, arts, conservation.
Types of support: Annual campaigns, building funds, capital campaigns, equipment.
Limitations: Giving primarily in Milwaukee County, WI.
Application information: Application form not required.
Initial approach: Letter
Copies of proposal: 1
Deadline(s): None
Board meeting date(s): May and Nov.
Final notification: Varies
Write: William T. Gaus, Administrator
Officers and Directors:* John A. Puelicher,* Pres.; William T. Gaus,* V.P.; Marjorie A. Vallier,* Secy.; Robert M. Hoffer, Ruthmarie M. Lawrenz.
Number of staff: None.
EIN: 396065789

3325
S. F. Shattuck Charitable Trust
c/o Bank One Wisconsin Trust Co., N.A.
P.O. Box 1308, Tax Section
Milwaukee 53201
Application address: c/o Bank One Wisconsin Trust Co., N.A., Neenah, WI; Tel.: (414) 727-3281

Established in 1951.
Foundation type: Independent
Financial data (yr. ended 10/31/90): Assets, $2,041,390 (M); expenditures, $111,721; qualifying distributions, $95,900, including $92,000 for 23 grants (high: $21,000; low: $250).
Fields of interest: Hospitals, medical education, higher education, secondary education, youth, social services.
Limitations: Giving primarily in Neenah, WI. No grants to individuals.
Application information: Contributes only to pre-selected organizations. Applications not accepted.
Write: Joe McGrane, Trust Officer, c/o Bank One Wisconsin Trust Co., N.A.
Trustee: Bank One Wisconsin Trust Co., N.A.
EIN: 396048820

3326
A. O. Smith Foundation, Inc.
P.O. Box 23965
Milwaukee 53223-0965   (414) 359-4100
Application address: P.O. Box 23975, Milwaukee, WI 53223-0975

Incorporated in 1951 in WI.
Donor(s): A.O. Smith Corp.
Foundation type: Company-sponsored
Financial data (yr. ended 06/30/90): Assets, $20,513 (M); gifts received, $600,000; expenditures, $598,810; qualifying distributions, $598,655, including $598,655 for grants.
Fields of interest: Higher education, social services, health services, hospitals, civic affairs, cultural programs, community funds.
Types of support: Continuing support, annual campaigns, building funds, scholarship funds, employee matching gifts.
Limitations: Giving primarily in areas of company operations in CA, IL, KY, NC, OH, SC, TN, WA, and WI. No grants to individuals.
Publications: Annual report, application guidelines.
Application information: Application form not required.
Initial approach: Letter, telephone, or proposal
Copies of proposal: 1
Deadline(s): None
Board meeting date(s): June and as required
Final notification: 3 months
Write: Edward J. O'Connor, Secy.
Officers and Directors:* L.B. Smith,* Pres.; T.I. Dolan,* V.P.; A.O. Smith,* V.P.; E.J. O'Connor,* Secy.
EIN: 396076924

3327
Souder Family Foundation, Inc.
c/o Henry E. Fuldner
980 North Water St.
Milwaukee 53202
Application address: c/o Northern First Bank of
Florida, 700 Brickell Ave., Miami, FL 33131

Established in 1986 in FL.
Foundation type: Independent
Financial data (yr. ended 12/31/90): Assets,
$2,024,295 (M); gifts received, $2,388;
expenditures, $85,843; qualifying distributions,
$66,494, including $57,642 for 20 grants (high:
$20,000; low: $281).
Fields of interest: Higher education, health.
Limitations: Giving primarily in WI and FL. No
grants to individuals.
Application information: Application form not
required.
  Deadline(s): None
Directors: Susanna Souder, William E. Souder, Jr.,
Paul Williams.
EIN: 361560019

3328
Stackner Family Foundation, Inc.
411 East Wisconsin Ave.
Milwaukee 53202-4497   (414) 277-5000

Incorporated in 1966 in WI.
Donor(s): John S. Stackner,‡ Irene M. Stackner.‡
Foundation type: Independent
Financial data (yr. ended 08/31/91): Assets,
$10,999,236 (M); expenditures, $1,022,177;
qualifying distributions, $906,000, including
$906,000 for 126 grants (high: $60,000; low:
$200; average: $1,000-$15,000).
Purpose and activities: Grants largely for higher,
secondary, and elementary education; support
also for social service and youth agencies,
including family services, the homeless and
hunger programs, child welfare, employment,
and minorities, medical research and health
agencies, including those serving the mentally ill
and the handicapped, environmental protection,
drug and alcohol abuse programs, and historic
preservation.
Fields of interest: Education, higher education,
secondary education, social services, youth, child
welfare, health, environment, drug abuse, historic
preservation.
Types of support: Operating budgets, continuing
support, annual campaigns, seed money, building
funds, equipment, matching funds, special
projects, research, capital campaigns.
Limitations: Giving limited to the greater
Milwaukee, WI, area. No grants to individuals, or
for deficit financing or fellowships; no loans.
Application information: Application form not
required.
  Initial approach: Letter
  Copies of proposal: 1
  Deadline(s): Dec. 15, Mar. 15, June 15, and
    Sept. 15
  Board meeting date(s): Jan., Apr., July, and Oct.
  Final notification: within 3 weeks after board
    meetings
  Write: Patrick W. Cotter, Exec. Dir.
Officers and Directors:* Patricia S. Treiber,* Pres.;
John A. Treiber,* V.P.; Patrick W. Cotter,* Secy. and
Exec. Dir.; David L. MacGregor,* Treas.

Number of staff: None.
EIN: 396097597

3329
Surgical Science Foundation for Research & Development
c/o First Wisconsin National Bank
One South Pinckney St.
Madison 53703-2808

Established in 1983 in WI.
Foundation type: Independent
Financial data (yr. ended 12/31/90): Assets,
$6,986,285 (M); gifts received, $375,000;
expenditures, $797,977; qualifying distributions,
$750,000, including $750,000 for grants.
Fields of interest: Medical education.
Limitations: No grants to individuals.
Application information: Contributes only to
pre-selected organizations. Applications not
accepted.
Trustees: Folkert Belzer, M.D., Herbert Berkoff,
M.D., David Dibbell, M.D., Andrew A. McBeath,
M.D., James R. Starling, M.D., David Uehling,
M.D., Charles E. Yale, M.D.
EIN: 930846339

3330
Time Insurance Foundation, Inc.
c/o Cathy Feierstein
501 West Michigan
Milwaukee 53203   (414) 299-7788

Established in 1973 in WI.
Donor(s): Time Insurance Co.
Foundation type: Company-sponsored
Financial data (yr. ended 12/31/91): Assets,
$1,607,154 (M); gifts received, $500,000;
expenditures, $298,309; qualifying distributions,
$297,159, including $296,949 for 123 grants
(high: $145,000; low: $20; average:
$100-$20,000).
Purpose and activities: Giving primarily to
epidemic health issues, substance abuse, and job
creation/economic development.
Fields of interest: AIDS, health services, drug
abuse, employment.
Types of support: Employee matching gifts,
employee-related scholarships, consulting
services, continuing support, matching funds,
special projects.
Limitations: Giving primarily in southeastern WI.
No support for labor or religious organizations, or
hospitals.
Publications: Application guidelines, financial
statement, informational brochure.
Application information: Application form
required.
  Initial approach: Letter requesting guidelines
  Copies of proposal: 1
  Board meeting date(s): Bimonthly
  Final notification: 10 days after board meeting
  Write: Donald G. Hamm, Jr., Pres.
Officers: Donald G. Hamm, Jr., Pres.; Catherine E.
Feierstein, V.P. and Secy.
Trustees: Jeanine H. Becker, Gwen A. Johnson,
Scott R. Siemon, Spencer N. Smith.
Number of staff: None.
EIN: 237346436

3331
U.S. Oil/Schmidt Family Foundation, Inc.
425 Washington St.
P.O. Box 25
Combined Locks 54113-1049

Established in 1984 in WI.
Donor(s): Raymond Schmidt, Arthur J. Schmidt,
William Schmidt.
Foundation type: Independent
Financial data (yr. ended 07/31/90): Assets,
$1,800,118 (M); gifts received, $7,187;
expenditures, $329,552; qualifying distributions,
$328,111, including $328,111 for 75 grants (high:
$100,000; low: $50).
Purpose and activities: Giving primarily for
Catholic organizations and churches; support also
for community funds, education, and hospitals.
Fields of interest: Catholic giving, religion,
community funds, education, hospitals, general
charitable giving.
Limitations: Giving primarily in WI. No grants to
individuals.
Application information: Contributes only to
pre-selected organizations. Applications not
accepted.
Officers and Directors:* Arthur J. Schmidt,* Pres.;
William Schmidt,* V.P.; Raymond Schmidt,*
Secy.; Paul Bachman, Thomas Schmidt.
EIN: 391540933

3332
Universal Foods Foundation, Inc.
433 East Michigan St.
Milwaukee 53202   (414) 271-6755

Incorporated in 1958 in WI.
Donor(s): Universal Foods Corp.
Foundation type: Company-sponsored
Financial data (yr. ended 09/30/90): Assets,
$7,725,969 (M); gifts received, $350,000;
expenditures, $781,668; qualifying distributions,
$733,977, including $733,977 for 263 grants
(high: $100,000; low: $25).
Purpose and activities: Giving largely for
community funds, social services and youth, arts
and culture, hospitals, food-related research,
higher education, and civic organizations.
Fields of interest: Community funds, hospitals,
higher education, civic affairs, nutrition, social
services, youth, arts, cultural programs.
Types of support: Employee matching gifts,
general purposes.
Limitations: No support for sectarian religious
organizations. No grants to individuals.
Application information: Contributes only to
pre-selected organizations. Applications not
accepted.
  Write: John E. Heinrich, V.P., Admin.
Officers: Guy A. Osborn, Pres.; John E. Heinrich,
V.P.; Kenneth Manning, V.P.; Dan E. McMullen,
Secy.-Treas.
Number of staff: 1 part-time professional; 1
part-time support.
EIN: 396044488

3333
Vilter Foundation, Inc.
2217 South First St.
Milwaukee 53207

Incorporated in 1961 in WI.
Donor(s): Vilter Manufacturing Co.
Foundation type: Company-sponsored
Financial data (yr. ended 07/31/90): Assets, $3,693,727 (M); gifts received, $1,000; expenditures, $195,163; qualifying distributions, $183,423, including $172,096 for 109 grants (high: $20,000; low: $100).
Purpose and activities: Giving for community funds, hospitals, religious welfare funds and church support, and higher and secondary education, including the promotion of education and research relating to the refrigeration and air conditioning industry.
Fields of interest: Community funds, denominational giving, hospitals, higher education, secondary education, religious welfare.
Limitations: Giving primarily in Milwaukee, WI.
Application information:
  Write: A.A. Silverman, Pres.
Officers: A.A. Silverman, Pres.; R.A. Hall, V.P.; K.E. Wegener, Secy.-Treas.
EIN: 390678640

3334
Wausau Area Community Foundation, Inc.
500 Third St., Suite 316
Wausau 54401   (715) 845-9555

Incorporated in 1987 in WI.
Foundation type: Community
Financial data (yr. ended 06/30/92): Assets, $2,986,336 (M); gifts received, $1,816,490; expenditures, $333,913; qualifying distributions, $226,749, including $226,749 for 111 grants (high: $78,737; low: $25; average: $200-$2,000).
Purpose and activities: ". . . to devote special emphasis to programs enriching area life in five distinct areas: education, the arts, health, social services, and the conservation and preservation of resources, including historical and cultural . . . ."
Fields of interest: Education, arts, social services, health, historic preservation, cultural programs.
Types of support: Scholarship funds, special projects, equipment.
Limitations: Giving limited to the Wausau, WI, area, including Marathon County. No grants to individuals, or for capital campaigns, endowments, or deficit financing.
Publications: Annual report, application guidelines, informational brochure, newsletter.
Application information: Application form required.
  Initial approach: Letter or telephone
  Copies of proposal: 2
  Deadline(s): Quarterly
  Board meeting date(s): Bimonthly
  Write: Jean C. Tehan, Exec. Dir.
Officers and Directors:* Dan O'Connor,* Chair.; Thomas A. Mack, Pres.; Caroline Mark,* V.P.; C. Duane Patterson,* Secy.; Robert Wolff,* Treas.; Jean C. Tehan, Exec. Dir.; A. Brenda Davis, B.A. Greenheck, John Michler, Ralph Mirman, Marion C. Viste, Leon J. Weinberger, Randy Westgate.
Number of staff: 1 full-time professional; 1 part-time professional; 2 part-time support.
EIN: 391577472

3335
Wausau Insurance Companies Corporate Giving Program
2000 Westwood Dr.
Box 8017
Wausau 54402-8017   (715) 845-5211

Financial data (yr. ended 12/31/90): Total giving, $630,000 for grants.
Purpose and activities: "Approved contributions should complement company objectives and provide potential benefit to the company, its employees, policyholders or the public." Support for education; health and welfare; civic and community organizations; culture and the arts, through community arts, literature, performing arts, music, theater, public TV/radio and museums. Also supports the United Way.
Fields of interest: Education, health, welfare, civic affairs, community development, cultural programs, arts, performing arts, music, theater, museums, community funds.
Types of support: Employee matching gifts, general purposes.
Limitations: Giving primarily in the city of Wausau, Marathon County, WI, and major operating locations. No support for religious, political or labor organizations, or organizations receiving funds from a local community fund. No grants for advertising, "token" contributions or administrative support.
Publications: Corporate giving report.
Application information: Funds have been committed for 1991.
  Initial approach: Letter or proposal
  Deadline(s): None
  Final notification: 6 weeks
  Write: Roger Drayna, Dir. Public Relations

3336
The Todd Wehr Foundation, Inc.
111 East Wisconsin Ave., Suite 2100
Milwaukee 53202   (414) 271-8210

Incorporated in 1953 in WI.
Donor(s): C. Frederic Wehr.‡
Foundation type: Independent
Financial data (yr. ended 12/31/90): Assets, $9,931,609 (M); expenditures, $614,404; qualifying distributions, $512,181, including $488,500 for 10 grants (high: $156,000; low: $10,000; average: $2,000-$750,000).
Purpose and activities: Support for higher education, including medical education, and community charitable institutions.
Fields of interest: Higher education, medical education, education.
Limitations: Giving limited to WI. No grants to individuals.
Application information: Application form not required.
  Initial approach: Letter
  Copies of proposal: 1
  Deadline(s): None
  Board meeting date(s): Quarterly
  Write: Ralph G. Schulz, Pres.
Officers and Directors:* Ralph G. Schulz,* Pres.; William J. Hardy,* V.P. and Treas.; M. James Termondt,* Secy.; Robert P. Harland, Winfred W. Wuesthoff.
Number of staff: 1 full-time professional.
EIN: 396043962

3337
Wisconsin Energy Corporation Foundation, Inc. ▼
(Formerly Wisconsin Electric System Foundation, Inc.)
231 West Michigan St.
Milwaukee 53201   (414) 221-2105

Incorporated in 1982 in WI.
Donor(s): Wisconsin Electric Power Co., Wisconsin Natural Gas Co.
Foundation type: Company-sponsored
Financial data (yr. ended 12/31/91): Assets, $28,743,400 (M); expenditures, $2,963,966; qualifying distributions, $2,916,848, including $2,767,339 for 1,383 grants (high: $500,000; low: $10; average: $500-$10,000) and $149,509 for 1,663 employee matching gifts.
Purpose and activities: Giving primarily for community funds, higher education, youth and social service agencies, cultural programs, hospitals and health organizations, community development, and civic affairs.
Fields of interest: Community funds, hospitals, health, higher education, community development, civic affairs, cultural programs, youth, social services.
Types of support: Employee matching gifts, general purposes.
Limitations: Giving primarily in service territories in southeastern WI.
Application information: Application form not required.
  Initial approach: Letter
  Copies of proposal: 1
  Deadline(s): None
  Board meeting date(s): As required
  Final notification: Usually 1 month
  Write: Jerry G. Remmel, Treas.
Officers and Directors:* Richard A. Abdoo,* Pres.; Jerry G. Remmel,* V.P. and Treas.; John H. Goetsch, Secy.; Charles S. McNeer.*
Number of staff: None.
EIN: 391433726

3338
Wisconsin Power and Light Foundation, Inc.
222 West Washington Ave.
Madison 53703   (608) 252-3181
Additional address: P.O. Box 192, Madison, WI 53701

Established in 1984 in WI.
Donor(s): Wisconsin Power and Light Co.
Foundation type: Company-sponsored
Financial data (yr. ended 12/31/91): Assets, $6,836,941 (M); gifts received, $1,000,000; expenditures, $1,006,422; qualifying distributions, $943,400, including $865,487 for grants, $20,000 for 4 grants to individuals of $5,000 each, $26,213 for 147 employee matching gifts and $31,700 for in-kind gifts.
Purpose and activities: Support for the fine and performing arts, including music, dance, theaters, and museums; family and social services, child welfare, and programs for minorities; citizenship, community development, and civic affairs; health, including hospital building funds, medical research, and hospices; and higher and other education, including business and minority programs, educational associations and building

funds, libraries, and literacy programs. The foundation provides employee-related scholarships administered through Citizens' Scholarship Foundation of America.

Fields of interest: Arts, cultural programs, welfare, family services, civic affairs, health, education—minorities, education, higher education, libraries.

Types of support: Annual campaigns, building funds, capital campaigns, continuing support, employee matching gifts, equipment, fellowships, operating budgets, scholarship funds, employee-related scholarships, seed money, renovation projects.

Limitations: Giving primarily in central and southcentral WI, in areas of company operations. No support for religious organizations. No grants to individuals.

Publications: Annual report, informational brochure (including application guidelines).

Application information: Application form not required.

Initial approach: Proposal
Copies of proposal: 1
Deadline(s): None
Board meeting date(s): Quarterly
Write: Donald R. Piepenburg, V.P.

Officers and Directors:* Anthony J. (Nino) Amato,* Pres.; Donald R. Piepenburg, V.P.; Edward M. Gleason, Secy.-Treas.; Joanne Acomb, Daniel Bartel, Willie Collins, Erroll B. Davis, Carl Diehls, Jules A. Nicolet, Linda Taplin-Canto.

Number of staff: 1 full-time professional; 1 part-time support.

EIN: 391444065

3339
Wisconsin Public Service Foundation, Inc.
700 North Adams St.
Green Bay 54301   (414) 433-1464
Application address: P.O. Box 19001, Green Bay, WI 54307
Scholarship application address: Wisconsin Public Service Foundation, Inc. Scholarship Program, College Scholarship Service, Sponsored Scholarships Program, CN 6730, Princeton, NJ 08541

Incorporated in 1964 in WI.
Donor(s): Wisconsin Public Service Corp.
Foundation type: Company-sponsored
Financial data (yr. ended 12/31/91): Assets, $8,787,000 (M); gifts received, $225,000; expenditures, $675,385; qualifying distributions, $626,404, including $515,465 for 146 grants (high: $66,500; low: $100; average: $100-$66,500) and $110,939 for grants to individuals (high: $2,000; low: $400; average: $400-$2,000).
Fields of interest: Higher education, health, cultural programs, arts, conservation.
Types of support: Operating budgets, building funds, equipment, student aid, employee-related scholarships.
Limitations: Giving limited to WI and upper MI. No grants for endowment funds.
Publications: Informational brochure, application guidelines, 990-PF.
Application information: Application form required for scholarships.
Initial approach: Letter
Copies of proposal: 1
Deadline(s): Dec. 15 for scholarships
Board meeting date(s): May and as required
Final notification: Feb.

Write: D.A. Bollom, Pres.
Officers: D.A. Bollom, Pres.; J.H. Liethen, V.P.; R.H. Knuth, Secy.; Daniel P. Bittner, Treas.
EIN: 396075016

3340
The Ziegler Foundation, Inc.
215 North Main St.
West Bend 53095-3317   (414) 334-5521

Incorporated in 1944 in WI.
Donor(s): Members of the Ziegler family.
Foundation type: Independent
Financial data (yr. ended 12/31/90): Assets, $5,470,593 (M); expenditures, $326,045; qualifying distributions, $318,245, including $312,500 for grants.
Purpose and activities: Support primarily for higher education, including a scholarship fund, church support, and youth agencies; support also for hospitals.
Fields of interest: Higher education, youth, hospitals.
Limitations: Giving primarily in the West Bend, WI, area. No grants to individuals.
Application information: Present plans preclude extensive consideration of unsolicited requests. Application form not required.
Initial approach: Letter
Deadline(s): None
Board meeting date(s): May and Nov.
Write: Bernard C. Ziegler, Pres.
Officers and Directors:* Bernard C. Ziegler,* Pres.; R. Douglas Ziegler,* V.P. and Secy.-Treas.; Harrold J. McComas,* V.P.
Number of staff: None.
EIN: 396044762

WYOMING

3341
The Goodstein Foundation
P.O. Box 1699
Casper 82602 (307) 237-0033

Incorporated in 1952 in CO.
Donor(s): J.M. Goodstein.
Foundation type: Independent
Financial data (yr. ended 06/30/91): Assets, $4,107,382 (M); expenditures, $577,940; qualifying distributions, $564,150, including $564,150 for 45 grants (high: $230,000; low: $100).
Fields of interest: Higher education, hospitals, Jewish giving.
Limitations: Giving primarily in CO and WY.
Application information:
  Initial approach: Letter
  Deadline(s): None
  Write: Charles L. Tangney, Pres.
Officers: Charles L. Tangney, Pres.; William H. Brown, V.P.
EIN: 836003815

3342
Paul Stock Foundation
P.O. Box 2020
Cody 82414 (307) 587-5275

Scholarship application address: 1239 Rumsey Ave., Cody, WY 82414

Incorporated in 1958 in WY.
Donor(s): Paul Stock,‡ Eloise J. Stock.
Foundation type: Independent
Financial data (yr. ended 12/31/91): Assets, $11,388,650 (M); expenditures, $734,267; qualifying distributions, $703,139, including $545,851 for 21 grants (high: $150,000; low: $500) and $131,563 for 87 grants to individuals (high: $3,000; low: $100).
Purpose and activities: Giving for higher education, including student aid to WY residents; grants also for museums and other arts groups, hospitals, child welfare, youth agencies, medical research, and community development.
Fields of interest: Higher education, arts, museums, hospitals, child welfare, youth, medical research, community development, general charitable giving.
Types of support: Student aid, annual campaigns, building funds, research.
Limitations: Giving primarily in WY; student aid limited to those who have resided in WY for one year or more.
Application information: Application form and instructions for educational grants only.
  Initial approach: Letter
  Deadline(s): June 30 and Nov. 30 for educational grants
  Board meeting date(s): July and Dec.
  Write: Charles G. Kepler, Pres.
Officers: Charles G. Kepler, Pres.; Esther C. Brumage, V.P.; Donald M. Robirds, Secy.-Treas.
Number of staff: 1 part-time professional.
EIN: 830185157

3343
William E. Weiss Foundation, Inc.
P.O. Box 1108
Jackson 83001 (307) 733-1680

Incorporated in 1955 in NY.
Donor(s): William E. Weiss, Jr.,‡ Helene K. Brown.‡
Foundation type: Independent
Financial data (yr. ended 03/31/91): Assets, $5,002,323 (M); expenditures, $169,665; qualifying distributions, $131,538, including $129,300 for 38 grants (high: $50,000; low: $300).
Fields of interest: Higher education, secondary education, historic preservation, arts, hospitals, health, health services, homeless, environment, Protestant giving.
Types of support: Building funds, special projects, continuing support.
Limitations: Giving limited to NY, WV, and WY. No grants to individuals.
Application information: Application form not required.
  Initial approach: Brief proposal
  Copies of proposal: 4
  Deadline(s): Submit proposal preferably in Nov.
  Board meeting date(s): Jan.
  Final notification: Mar.
  Write: Lulu Hughes, Secy.
Officers and Directors:* William D. Weiss,* Pres.; Daryl B. Uber,* V.P.; Lulu Hughes,* Secy.; P.W.T. Brown,* Treas.; Mary K. Weiss.
Number of staff: 1 part-time support.
EIN: 556016633

INDEX TO DONORS, OFFICERS, TRUSTEES

Aall, Sally Sample, 2194
Aarestad, Norman O., 389
Aaron, Roy H., 275
Abbamont, Thomas J., 2262
Abbey, G. Marshall, 787
Abbott, Robin B., 1923
Abbott Laboratories, 768
Abdoo, Richard A., 3337
Abegg, Edward, 978
Abel-Smith, Mary Mills, 507
Abeles, Charles C., 1117
Abell, Duane H., 2941
Abell, George T., 2941
Abell, Gladys H., 2941
Abell, W. Shepherdson, Jr., 1095
Abell Co., A.S., 1095
Abercrombie, Josephine E., 2942
Abercrombie, Michael G., 1110
Abercrombie, Ralph L., 2623
Abernathy, Bruce, 604
Abernathy, Sarah, 2397
Abess, Allan T., Jr., 623
Aboodi, Oded, 2231, 2278
Abraham, Alexander, 1795
Abraham, Anthony R., 567
Abraham, Henry L., 1141
Abraham, S. Daniel, 2311
Abraham, Thomas G., 567
Abrahamson, Lucille S., 288
Abramovitz, Charles, 2466
Abrams, Benjamin, 1730
Abrams, Langhorne, 3261
Abramson, Albert, 1096
Abramson, Clarence A., 1676
Abramson, Gary M., 1096
Abramson, Ronald D., 1096
Abrons, Alix, 1731
Abrons, Anne, 1731
Abrons, Anne S., 1731
Abrons, Henry, 1731
Abrons, Herbert L., 1731
Abrons, John, 1731
Abrons, Leslie, 1731
Abrons, Louis, 1731
Abrons, Peter, 1731
Abrons, Richard, 1731
Acers, Ebby Halliday, 2972
Achelis, Elizabeth, 1732
Acheson, George H., 1200
Achor, Robert L., 647
Ackerman, Asche, 3126
Ackerman, Barbara B., 2684
Ackerman, James H., 786
Ackerman, Lee James, 786
Ackerman, Loraine E., 786
Ackerman, Roger G., 1864
Ackerson, Robert L., 1066
Acklin, Robert G., 2442
Acmaro Securities Corp., The, 743
Acomb, Joanne, 3338
Acord, H.K., 3194
Acosta, Richard E., 1309
Acton, Evelyn Meadows, 3064
Acushnet Co., 1145
Adam, J. Marc, 1458, 1459

Adams, Alice E., 568
Adams, Buel T., 815
Adams, Caroline J., 1146
Adams, Charles E., 1146
Adams, Charles F., 1214
Adams, D. Nelson, 529, 1818
Adams, Daniel N., Jr., 1818
Adams, Edith M., 1215
Adams, Elizabeth Helms, 171
Adams, Eugene E., 709
Adams, Harold C., 3304
Adams, J.A., 1072
Adams, Jerry V., 2916
Adams, John, 1072
Adams, Nellie, 1072
Adams, Pamela D., 1873
Adams, Paul W., 489
Adams, Roy M., 926, 954
Adams, S.K., 901
Adams, Stewart E., 357
Adams, Tanzie D., 2451
Adams, W.L., 2852
Adams, Warren S. II, 678
Adams, William H., 3151
Addington, Leonard M., 1479
Addison, Francis G. III, 563
Addy, Frederick S., 775
Adel, Catherine, 39
Adelson, Andrew, 1790
Adler, Helen R., 405
Adler, Homer, 1072
Adler, James B., 541
Adler, John, 405
Adler, Louis, 1734
Adler, Marie, 143
Adler, Morton M., 405
Adler Realty Co., Louis, Inc., 1734
Admire, Jack G., 658
Admire, John G., 658
Admire, Ruth S., 658
Adolph's, Ltd., 281
Adolph's Food Products Manufacturing Co., 281
ADP Rental Co., 699
Aeroflex Corp., The, 1735
Aetna Life and Casualty Co., 406
Affiliated National Bank, 393
Affiliated Publications, Inc., 1160
Agan, Robert E., 1754
Agati, Giacomo, 1603
Agee, John H., 1472
Agger, David, 257
Agger, J.H., 2666
Agnich, Richard J., 3120
Agricola, Hugh W., 14
Agway, Inc., 1736
Ahern, Timothy P., 1861
Ahlheim, Norman R., 2158
Ahmanson, Caroline L., 96
Ahmanson, Howard F., 57
Ahmanson, Howard F., Jr., 57
Ahmanson, Robert H., 57
Ahmanson, William H., 57
Ahuja, Elias, 516
Aidinoff, M. Bernard, 1938

Aiken, Scott, 2455
Aikenhead, Kathleen, 166
Ainsa, Francis S., 3090
Ainsworth, Laine, 170
Air Products and Chemicals, Inc., 2666
Aitken Charitable Trust, Annie-Laurie, 1806
Ajinomoto U.S.A., Inc., 2728
Akel, Ferris G., 1880
Akins, Jeanne Ellen, 305
Akins, Waverly F., 2405
Akre, Charles T., 555
Akzo America, 1738
Alabama Power Co., 1
Alandt, Lynn F., 1324
Albers, C. Hugh, 825
Albert, Burton, 497
Alberts, Bruce, 151
Albright, Harry W., Jr., 1732, 1800
Albritton, O.L., Jr., 3076
Alcantar, Joe, Jr., 2996
Alco Standard Corp., 2667
Alcock, Nancy M., 450
Alcon Laboratories, Inc., 2944
Alcott, James A., 1431
Alda, Alan, 2224
Aldeen, Margaret, 770
Aldeen, Norris A., 770
Alden, George I., 1147
Alden, Priscilla, 1148
Aldercrest Development Corp., 1620
Alderson, Anne W., 2377
Alderson, David, 3087
Aldridge, Elizabeth A., 2631
Alegi, August P., 543
Alexander, Andrew M., 2945
Alexander, Anne, 1762
Alexander, Beatrice, 1379
Alexander, Caroline R., 3048
Alexander, Carolyn, 1047
Alexander, Dorothy D., 3048
Alexander, Emory G., 3048
Alexander, Eric P., 2945
Alexander, George W., 947
Alexander, Helen C., 3048
Alexander, Henrietta K., 3048
Alexander, Ilene S., 2945
Alexander, Joan, 2945
Alexander, John D., Jr., 3048
Alexander, John E., 3270
Alexander, Joseph, 1741
Alexander, Judith D., 1389
Alexander, Larry, 1569
Alexander, Norman E., 2261
Alexander, Quentin, 2560
Alexander, R.G., 3116
Alexander, Robert C., 3247
Alexander, Stanford, 2945
Alexander, Thomas S., 783
Alexander, W.R., 364
Alexander, William H., 2739
Alexander, Willie J., 3112
Alexy, R.J., 3315
Alfert, Arthur S., 1741
Alfiero, Sal H., 2089

Alford, John W., 2475
Alford, Kenneth M., 1869
Alford, L.E., 165
Alford, Wende A., 1863
Aliber, James A., 1380
Aljian, James D., 213
Alkire, Durwood, 3218
Allaire, Paul A., 500
Allan, Karen C., 2649
Allan, Richard, 2837
Allan, Ronald C., 2430
Allard, Robert A., 1604
Allardice, Edward, 1379
Allday, Doris Fondren, 3014
Allday, R. Edwin, 3014
Allegheny Ludlum Corp., 2670
Allen, Alexandra F., 1782
Allen, Alton C., 2984
Allen, Anne, 535
Allen, Avery, 2466
Allen, Charles, Jr., 1742
Allen, Charles C., Jr., 1546
Allen, Christine, 1782
Allen, David F., 1090
Allen, Douglas E., 1782
Allen, Douglas F., 1182
Allen, Douglas F., Mrs., 2296
Allen, Esther, 2426
Allen, Eugene, 2986
Allen, Gail E., 1299, 1338, 1369
Allen, Gerald M., 3054
Allen, Herbert, 1742
Allen, Herbert Anthony, 1742
Allen, Ivan, Jr., 743
Allen, Jack W., 730
Allen, Lee Barclay Patterson, Mrs., 730
Allen, Leigh B. III, 1494
Allen, Lew, Jr., 197
Allen, Lewis, Jr., 2984
Allen, Lloyd, 818
Allen, Lucy R., 1376
Allen, M. George, 1459
Allen, Marjorie P., 1363
Allen, Mayeta V., 58
Allen, Paul G., 3217
Allen, Phil N., 58
Allen, Philip D., 1782, 1886
Allen, Robert C., 2387
Allen, Roberta R., 1299
Allen, Shirley, 80
Allen, Suzanne Y., 580
Allen, W. George, 580
Allen, W. James, 1369
Allen, William J., 1299
Allen & Co., Inc., 1742
Allen-Bradley Co., 3275
Aller, Thomas L., 1016
Allied Bank of Texas, 3011
Allied-Signal, Inc., 1611
Allin, William B., 2899
Alling, James W., 899
Allinson, Millie Bluth, 2270
Allison, Diane M., 433
Allison, Dwight L., Jr., 1158
Allison, Ethelyn, 1707

Allison, J. Richard, Jr., 2888
Allison, Jerry, 2920
Allison, Jim, 3030
Allison, John A. IV, 2405
Allison, William W., 696
Allman, Edward L., 1631
Allman, Randall, 993
Allmon, Barbara, 1502
Allport, Roberta W., 2457
Allstate Insurance Co., 772
Allton, John D., 2576
Allyn, Charles S., Jr., 2431
Allyn, Compton, 2431
Allyn, Dawn N., 1744
Allyn, Elizabeth C., 2431
Allyn, Eric, 1744
Allyn, Janet J., 1744
Allyn, Lew F., 1744
Allyn, S.C., 2431
Allyn, Sonya, 1744
Allyn, William F., 1744
Allyn, William G., 1744
Allyn, William N., 1744
Alma Piston Co., 1390
Alpac Corp., 3252
Alpaugh, Lewis F., 1646
Alperin, Barry J., 2872
Alperin, Melvin, 2882
Alpern, Bernard E., 1745
Alpern, Edward M., 1745
Alpern, Lloyd J., 1745
Alperstein, Allan C., 1137
Alpert, Arthur M., 3045
Alpert, Benjamin, 1934
Alpert, Herb, 59
Alpert, Lani Hall, 59
Alsdorf, Marilyn, 939
Alster, Iris Berliner, 2365
Alta Mortgage Co., 177
Altamore, Ellen, 1313
Alter, Jeffrey, 423
Altermatt, Paul B., 445
Altman, Benjamin, 1746
Altman, Drew E., 194
Altman, Lawrence K., 2083
Altman, Michael S., 1460
Altman, Norman, 888
Alton, David, 1723
Altschul, Arthur G., 2146, 2171, 2339,
   2347
Altschul, Diana L., 2171
Altschul, Frank, 2171
Altschul, Helen G., 2171
Altschul, Jeanette Cohen, 1747
Altschul, Louis, 1747
Altschul, Stephen F., 2171
Altschuler, Richard A., 280
Altshuler, Ruth Sharp, 2972
Altshuler, Sharman B., 1677
Aluminum Co. of America, 2668
Alvarez, Aida, 2146
Alverdo, F. Javier, 285
Alworth, Marshall W., 1408
Amato, Anthony J. (Nino), 3338
Amaturo, Douglas Q., 569
Amaturo, Joseph C., 569
Amaturo, Lawrence V., 569
Amaturo, Lorna J., 569
Amaturo, Winifred, 569
Amaturo, Winifred L., 569
Amax, Inc., 1748
American and Efird Mills, Inc., 2385
American Bag & Paper Corp., 2765
American Bank & Trust Co., 2426
American Decal and Manufacturing
   Co., 839
American Express Co., 1750
American Fidelity Assurance Co., 2616
American Financial Corp., 2432
American Flange & Manufacturing Co.,
   Inc., 651
American Honda Motor Co., Inc., 60
American Hospital Supply Corp., 787

American Information Technologies, 774
American Insulated Wire Corp., 2066
American National Bank & Trust Co.,
   1475
American National Bank & Trust Co. of
   Chicago, 773, 820
American Natural Resources Co., 1302
American Petrofina, Inc., 3010
American Saw and Manufacturing Co.,
   1178
American Schlafhorst Co., 2367
American Telephone & Telegraph Co.,
   1762
American Trading and Production Corp.,
   1135
Americare Health Corp., 302
Ameritrust Co., N.A., 2447, 2456, 2457,
   2459, 2460, 2468, 2566, 2567,
   3052, 3127
Ameritrust Co. of Stark County, 2591
Ameritrust National Bank, 996
Ameritrust Texas, N.A., 3090, 3099
Ames, Aubin Z., 1705
Ames, Edward A., 1833
Ames, Eugenia, 2270
Ames, Gary A., 400
Ames, George J., 2118
Ames, Harriett, 2671
AMETEK, Inc., 2672
Amino, Toshi, 2504
Amiry, Reda, 2707
Amity Leather Products Co., 3321
Amoco Corp., 775
AMP, Inc., 2673
AmSouth Bank, N.A., 16, 18
Amsted Industries, Inc., 777
Amsterdam, Jack, 503, 2066
Amundson, W.R., 2429
Anacker, Josephine F., 1365
Andelman, David, 1264
Andersen, Arthur A., 778
Andersen, Arthur E. III, 778
Andersen, Arthur H., 2720
Andersen, Carol F., 1411
Andersen, Christine E., 1411
Andersen, Frank N., 1401
Andersen, Fred C., 1410, 1450
Andersen, Harold W., 1592
Andersen, Hugh J., 1411
Andersen, Jane K., 1411
Andersen, Joan N., 778
Andersen, Katherine B., 1410, 1411,
   1450
Andersen, Kathleen S., 2120
Andersen, Marilyn V., 1365
Andersen, Sarah J., 1411
Anderson, Andrew E., 2484
Anderson, Bruce J., 1510
Anderson, Carole Lewis, 2872
Anderson, Catherine M., 2527
Anderson, Charles L., 3253
Anderson, D. Kent, 3011
Anderson, David B., 868
Anderson, David G., 1057
Anderson, Dee, 659
Anderson, Dorothy, 2160
Anderson, Dudley N., 2861
Anderson, Elizabeth Milbank, 2120
Anderson, Eugene K., 3105
Anderson, Ford A. II, 3237
Anderson, Fred C., 2155
Anderson, George W., 1759
Anderson, Grenville, 2434
Anderson, Herbert T., 2116
Anderson, James C., 2308
Anderson, Joe M., 2899
Anderson, Joe M., Jr., 2888
Anderson, John W., 981
Anderson, John W. II, 1300
Anderson, Josephine, 2947
Anderson, Judy M., 711
Anderson, Katrina B., 1371
Anderson, Kenneth G., 665

Anderson, M.D., 2948
Anderson, Martha Goodnow, 1293
Anderson, Mary Lee, 369
Anderson, Maureen, 2194
Anderson, Michael Scott, 3080
Anderson, Patricia, 2208
Anderson, Paul M., 868
Anderson, Paula, 3161
Anderson, R. Wayne, 775
Anderson, R.E. Olds, 1371
Anderson, Ray, 463
Anderson, Richard B., 2452
Anderson, Roger E., 848
Anderson, Roy A., 348
Anderson, Stefan S., 983
Anderson, Steve Craig, 3080
Anderson, Thomas H., 2597
Anderson, Thomas P., 2907
Anderson, Wendell W., Jr., 1300, 1381
Anderson, Wilbur, 2437
Anderson, William G., 2434
Anderson, William J., 1021
Anderson, William P. V, 2434
Anderson, Wyndham, 2181
Andreas, Dorothy Inez, 779
Andreas, Dwayne O., 779
Andreas, Glenn A., 779
Andreas, Lowell W., 779, 782
Andreas, Michael D., 779
Andreoli, James M., 189
Andrew, Edith G., 780
Andrew, Edward J., 780
Andrews, Carol B., 497
Andrews, Christie F., 376
Andrews, Edward C., Jr., 1658, 1875
Andrews, H.D., 1493
Andrews, Matthew, Mrs., 2435
Andrews, Paul R., 433
Andrie, Barbara, 1365
Andrus, John E., 2302
Andrus, John E. III, 1451, 2302
Angel, Albert D., 1676
Angelbeck, Eleanor, 1525
Anglin, Paul V., 879
Angott, Thomas V., 1381
Anheuser-Busch, Inc., 1495, 1497
Anlyan, William G., 2386
Annenberg, Leonore A., 2675, 2676
Annenberg, Wallis, 2675, 2676
Annenberg, Walter H., 2671, 2675,
   2676, 2736, 2742, 2752, 2774, 2830
Annette, Kathleen R., 1418
Anolik, Alexander, 203
Ansley, Mildred B., 2910
Antell, James B., 3160
Anthony, Barbara Cox, 2463
Anthony, Eiland E., 2
Anthony, Frederick W., 2174
Anthony, June, 53
Anthony, Nancy B., 2633
Anthony, Otis, 624
Anthony, Ralph F., 2174
Anthony, Ray T., 2633
Anthony, Rebecca R., 266
Anthony, Ronald J., 1817
Antonelli, Edward A., 2134
Antrim, Janet M., 56
Aon Corp., 781
App, Robert G., 1376, 1401
Apparel Retail Corp., 1264
Appel, Gloria W., 2197
Appel, Wendy, 2248
Applebaum, Joseph, 570
Applebaum, Leila, 570
Applebaum, Stuart J., 1457
Appleby, Scott B., 531
Appleby, Thomas, 2061
Applegate, Timothy, 138
Applegate, William T., 1065
Appleman, Louise, 3116
Appleman, Nathan, 571
Apregan, Craig, 270
Apregan, George, 270

Aquilon, Nora, 1619
Arakas, Peter, 406
Aranow, Edward, 1731
Aranow, Judith, 1731
Aranow, Rita, 1731
Arbaugh, Eugene A., 1131
Arcadipane, Mildred, 1832
Archabal, Nina M., 1462
Archambault, Margaret M., 873
Archbold, Adrian, Mrs., 1756
Archer, Dennis W., Hon., 1381
Archer, Richard A., 297
Archer, Shreve, 782
Archer-Daniels-Midland Co., 782
Archibald, Norman, 3218
Archibald, R.W., 2632
Arel, Maurice L., 1607
Argyris, Marcia M., 232
Ariail, Leslie, 3214
Arias, Robert, 1931
Arizona Public Service Co., 26
Arkin, Norman A., 667
Arkwright, Richard T., 2287
Arledge, David A., 1302
Arlington, Harold L., 712
Armacost, Samuel H., 183
Armbruster, Timothy D., 1099, 1113
Armco Inc., 1614
Armington, Everett, 2436
Armour, Laurance H., 3022
Armour, Norton L., 1431
Armour, Vernon, 957
Armstrong, Arthur O., 252
Armstrong, Lea, 3255
Armstrong, Paul, 2039
Armstrong, Rose Ann, 2039
Armstrong, Whit, 13
Arnall, Ellis, 722
Arndt, Celestine Favrot, 3007
Arne, Marshall C., 823
Arnhart, James R., 2917
Arnof, Ian, 1082
Arnold, Anna Bing, 1595
Arnold, Florence, 685
Arnold, Frances A., 569
Arnold, Isaac, Jr., 2980
Arnold, R. Marks, 2405
Arnold, Robert O., 685
Arnold, Roland R., 3026
Arnold, Ross, 730
Arnold, Thomas C., 2423
Arnold B., Mrs., McKinnon, 3162
Arnstein, Leo H., 878
Aron, Jack R., 1758
Aron, Peter A., 1758
Aron, Robert, 1758
Aronson, Nancy P., 2183
Arrigoni, Peter R., 224
Arrison, Clement R., 2089
Arronson, Gertrude, 2678
Arthurs, Heidi D., 1884
Artis, Curtis R., 1762
as-Sayid, Farouk, 1799
ASARCO Inc., 1759
Asbury, Josephine W., 702
Asch, George, 2197
Asche, Fred B., 3126
Ash, Mary Kay, 3054
Ashe, Arthur, 1860
Ashe, Arthur R., Jr., 406
Ashe, Reid, 1048
Asher, Norman, 964
Asher, Thomas J., 731
Ashford, Theodore H., 1783
Ashkins, Robert J., 417
Ashland Oil, Inc., 1049
Ashley, Daniel J., 2320
Ashley, James W., 31
Ashmun, Candace McGee, 1637
Ashton, Clifford L., 3141
Ashworth, Freida, 3074
Aslin, Malcolm M., 1535
Aspinwall, Valerie, 1747

Asplundh, Barr E., 2679
Asplundh, Carl Hj., 2679
Asplundh, Edward K., 2679
Asplundh, Lester, 2679
Asplundh, Robert H., 2679
Astaire, Frederic, Jr., 92
Aston, James, 3013
Aston, James W., 3036
Astrove, Katherine A., 405
Atcheson, Elizabeth, 115
Atherton, Alexander S., 746
Atherton, Frank C., 746
Atherton, Juliette M., 746
Atkins, H. Kent, 2296
Atkins, Rosie, 695
Atkinson, Duane E., 66
Atkinson, George H., 66
Atkinson, Harold S., 692, 3167
Atkinson, Lavina M., 66
Atkinson, Mildred M., 66
Atkinson, Ray N., 66
Atlan Management Corp., 1763
Atlas, Martin, 535
Atlas, Sol G., 1778
Atlas Realty Co., 148
Atochem North America, 2721
Atteberry, William D., 2456
Atwater, Charles B., 1621
Atwater, H. Brewster, Jr., 1441, 1676
Atwater, Verne S., 2061
Atwood, Robert, 2392
Aubry, Julia Moon, 2302
Auchenpaugh, Faye V., 1095
Auchincloss, Lily vA., 2326
Auchincloss, Louis S., 2083
Auen, Joan, 80
Auen, Ronald, 80
Auer, Albert J., 175
Auerbach, Beatrice Fox, 410
Auerbach, Mollie, 1787
August, Bruce A., 2134
Auld, Richard, 2908
Aull, William E., 750
Ault, Frank H., 287
Ault, John D., 2604
Aumann, Walter D., 3296
Aurand, Calvin W., Jr., 3273
Austen, W. Gerald, 629
Austin, Donald G., Sr., 2438
Austin, Donald G., Jr., 2438
Austin, H. Brent, 3223
Austin, James W., 2438
Austin, Maurice, 2023
Austin, Richard C., 2438
Austin, Richard H., 1381
Austin, Stewart G., 2438
Austin, Thomas G., 2438
Austin, Winifred N., 2438
Autera, Michael E., 1809
Auto Specialties Manufacturing Co.,
1388
Auw, Pierre E., 129
Avampato, Charles M., 3263
Avansino, Kristen A., 1599
Avansino, Raymond C., Jr., 1599
Avery, Valeen T., 39
Avery, William, 2707
Averyt, Gayle O., 2888
Avon Products, Inc., 1764
Avondale Mills, 9
Awad, Joseph F., 3203
Ayaub, John J., 1375
Aycock, Linda, 1728
Ayers, Geneive S., 660
Ayers, Jule, 2837
Ayers, Margaret C., 1851
Aylesworth, William A., 3120
Aylmer, John F., 1222
Aylward, E.W., Sr., 3307
Aylward, E.W., Jr., 3307
Aymond, Charles H., 1347
Ayres, Frederic M., 1008
Ayres, Nancy, 1008

B.G. Wholesale, Inc., 1056
Babcock, Ann Kelsey, 144
Babcock, Betsy M., 2368
Babcock, Bruce M., 2368
Babcock, Carrol J., 817
Babcock, Charles H., 2368
Babcock, Gwendolyn Garland, 144
Babcock, John Carlile, 144
Babcock, Mary Reynolds, 2368, 2411
Babcock, Sarah Garland, 144
Babcock, Susan Hinman, 144
Baber, Wilbur H., Jr., 2984
Babicka, Jerry, 433
Babicka, Lynn P., 433
Babiuka, Lynn P., 1907
Babson, David F., Jr., 450
Babson, Donald P., 1151
Babson, Paul T., 1151
Babson, Susan A., 1151
Bache Halsey Stuart Shields, Inc., 2200
Bachhuber, R.A., 2562
Bachman, Paul, 3331
Bachmann, Louis, 1765
Bachner, Robert L., 2355
Backer, Murray, 1834
Bacon, Jody, 2430
Bacon, Robert L., 133
Badcock, Philip A., 717
Badgeley, Rose, 1766
Badman, Benjamin, Jr., 2837
Baechle, James J., 1815
Baehr, Dolpha, 1031
Baehr, L.W., 1031
Baer, J.A. II, 1539
Baer, Marion C., 1746
Baffney, Thomas K., 3221
Baggett, Fred W., 588
Bagley, Charles H., 3220
Bagley, Smith W., 2411
Bahl, John, 604
Bahle, Melvin C., 1510
Bahlman, Sarah Allyn, 2431
Bahrt, Fred R., 148, 149
Bailard, Tom, 269
Bailey, Andrew C., 1265
Bailey, Anita Lamb, 2659
Bailey, James, 3282
Bailey, Robert, 467
Bailey, Yolanda, 3255
Bain, Donald K., 369
Bair, Alberta M., 1582
Bair, Peggy, 309
Baird, Brian D., 1768
Baird, Bridget B., 1768
Baird, Bruce C., 1768
Baird, Cameron, 1767
Baird, Flora M., 1767
Baird, Frank B., Jr., 1767
Baird, Jane D., 1768
Baird, Nolan, 771
Baird, William C., 1767
Baisley, Susan J., 2337
Baitseil, John M., 3194
Baker, Ann, 620
Baker, Ann Cassidy, 2621
Baker, Anthony K., 1769
Baker, Berkley J., 327
Baker, Beverly, 1003
Baker, David S., 731
Baker, Dexter F., 2850
Baker, Doris G., 1413
Baker, George F., 1769
Baker, George F. III, 1769
Baker, James G., 479
Baker, John A., 704
Baker, John W., Jr., 965
Baker, Kane K., 1769
Baker, L.M., Jr., 2421
Baker, Laurel T., 678
Baker, Laurin M., 913
Baker, Louise A., 843
Baker, Marjorie Montgomery Ward, 971
Baker, Morris T., 1413

Baker, Morris T. III, 1413
Baker, Nancy W., 1413
Baker, R. Palmer, 1930
Baker, R.C., Sr., 67
Baker, Rebecca D., 68
Baker, Richard, 227
Baker, Richard W., 663
Baker, Robert E., 3069
Baker, Roger L., 1413
Baker, Russell S., Jr., 1130
Baker, Solomon R., 68
Baker, Tom, 3221
Baker, W.K., 673
Baker, W.O., 1334
Baker, William C., 2968
Baker, William M., 1413
Baker, William O., 1637
Baker Commodities, Inc., 189
Baker-Philbin, Mary, 1413
Bakken, Douglas A., 982
Balbach, Barbara, 1301
Balderston, Frederick, 257
Baldwin, Bennet M., 747
Baldwin, Ernest R., 82
Baldwin, Fred, 747
Baldwin, H. Furlong, 1100
Baldwin, J.J., 1622
Baldwin, John C., 749
Baldwin, Robert H.B., 1630
Baldwin, William P., 1298
Bales, Dane G., 1037
Balfour, Don, 713
Balgooyen, Warren, 2155
Balkas, Denise A., 1995
Ball, Anne F., 2480
Ball, Braden, 593
Ball, Edmund B., 982
Ball, Edmund F., 982
Ball, Frank C., 982
Ball, Frank E., 982
Ball, George A., 982, 983
Ball, Lucius L., 982
Ball, William A., 982
Ballantine, Robert W., 1347
Ballard, A.L., 165
Ballard, Bruce L., 2146
Ballard, Ernesta Drinker, 2803, 2808
Ballard, William C., Jr., 1057
Balter, Bernita B., 2690
Baltimore, David, 1124
Baltimore Gas and Electric Co., 1100
Bamberger, Clarence, Jr., 3141
Bamberger, Eleanor F., 3141
Bamberger, Ernest, 3141
BancOhio National Bank, 2460
BancOne Ohio Corp., 2456
Bancroft, Edith W., 2159
Bancroft, Thomas M., 2159
Bancroft, Thomas M., Jr., 2159
Banda, S.M., 2708
Bandier, Martin, 2305
Bandler, Ned W., 2323
Bangs, John K., 1704
Bangser, Michael R., 448
Bank, Helen S., 1101
Bank, Merrill L., 1101
Bank IV Kansas, N.A., 1032, 1040
Bank of America, 67, 96, 181, 266, 320,
329, 344, 3243, 3250
Bank of Boston, 1153, 1158, 1219, 1246
Bank of Boston Connecticut, 423, 470,
497
Bank of California, N.A., The, 2660,
3226, 3229, 3250
Bank of Delaware, 528, 2868
Bank of Hawaii, 748
Bank of Louisville, 1050
Bank of New York, The, 1848, 1871,
1971, 1976, 1988, 2085, 2146,
2164, 2210, 2251, 2277, 2333, 2346
Bank of Oklahoma, 2633
Bank of the West, 161
Bank of Western New York, N.A., 1817

Bank One Akron, N.A., 2430
Bank One of Alliance, 2591
Bank One Ohio Trust Co., N.A., 2460
Bank One Wisconsin Trust Co., N.A.,
3284, 3306, 3325
Bank One, Cleveland, N.A., 2457
Bank One, Corsicana, 3076
Bank One, Dayton, N.A., 2466, 2509,
2516
Bank One, Indianapolis, N.A., 996
Bank One, Mansfield, N.A., 2592
Bank One, Texas, N.A., 2981, 3099
Bank One, Youngstown, N.A., 2559
Bank South, N.A., 686
BankAmerica Corp., 70
Bankers Trust Co., 444, 1682, 2146
Banks, Henry H., 1294
Banks, William L., 3186
Bannan, Charles F., 261
Bannon, Robert D., 81
Banta Corp., 3273
Bapter, Lisa A., 1923
Bar Plate Manufacturing, 2816
Baranco, Juanita, 686
Baranoff, W., 1844
Barbato, Virginia M., 2547
Barber, George W., 3
Barber, George W., Jr., 3
Barber, Joseph, 716
Barber, Joseph H., 2832
Barber, Kathleen L., 2497
Barber, Martin S., 1673
Barbey, Anne Murray, 3238
Barbieri, Alexander F., 2759
Barbour, F.E., Mrs., 1757
Barbour, Fleming A., 670
Barclay, John W., 422
Barclays Bank of New York, N.A., 2146
Bard, C.R., Inc., 1773
Bard, Douglas, 1365
Barden, Don H., 1381
Barden, Glen A., 674
Barden Corp., The, 412
Barder, Sarah D., 3275
Bardes, Judith, 2770
Bardon, Ronald D., 2537
Bardwell, Stanley, 2196
Barger, A. Clifford, 1259
Barhydt, Dirck, 497
Barineau, E.C., 711
Bark, France de Sugny, 118
Barker, Donald J., 1166
Barker, Donald R., 71
Barker, John, 1704
Barker, Norman, Jr., 197
Barker, Patricia T., 492
Barker, Richard H., 68
Barker, Robert C., 451
Barker, William P., 2785
Barks, Herbert B., 2924
Barlow, F. John, 3287
Barnes, Alvin L., 3102
Barnes, Frances M. III, 1521
Barnes, Ronald R., 253
Barnes, W.M., 2819
Barnet, Saretta, 2035
Barnet, William H., 1740
Barnett, Carol Jenkins, 622
Barnett, Helaine, 2213
Barnett, Hoyt, 622
Barnett, Isabel, 1775
Barnett, James Joseph, 1775
Barnett, Kathleen M., 933
Barnett, Lawrence R., 1775
Barnett, Richard M., 1141
Barnett, Robert G., 1489
Barnett Banks Trust Co., N.A., 587, 608,
614, 680
Barney, William H., 3186
Baron, Jules M., 1946
Baron, Raymond S., 1946
Baron, Richard K., 1946
Barondes, Samuel H., 1453

Barone, Robert J., 1601, 1608
Barr, Donald, 1356
Barr, Harry C., 1250
Barr, John M., 3050
Barr, Maxine, 1356
Barre, Benedicte, 3188
Barrett, James S., 2902
Barrett, M. Patricia, 1576
Barrett, Richard W., 2609
Barrette, Raymond, 134
Barron, Blue, 1126
Barron, Janice E., 2358
Barrows, G.M., 1498
Barrows, Sidney, 862, 863
Barrozo, Tobin G., 1475
Barry, David W., 2377
Barsness, W.E. Bye, 1462
Barsotti, Priscilla Ann, 368
Bartel, Daniel, 3338
Bartelt, Sarah Caswell, 574
Barter, John W., 1611
Barth, Frederic C., 2715
Barth, J. Edward, 2633
Barth, Theodore H., 1776
Bartha, Louis A., 3092
Bartholdson, John R., 2779
Bartleson, Leslie Sheridan, 314
Bartlett, George W., 1365
Barton, Robert M., 80
Bartos, Adam, 2188
Bartos, Armand P., 2188
Bartos, Celeste G., 2188
Bartsch, Ruth, 1777
Baruch, Eduard, 412
Barun, Kenneth L., 894
Barwin, Thomas W., 1376
Bashful, Emmett W., 1082
Baskin, Philip, 2723
Basner, Ruth H., 2506
Bass, Anne T., 2952
Bass, Doris L., 2953
Bass, Harry W., Jr., 2953
Bass, Henry, 1718
Bass, Laura Hueter, 1726
Bass, Lawrence D., 1718
Bass, Lee M., 3094
Bass, Morton M., 1778
Bass, Nancy Lee, 3094
Bass, Perry R., 3094, 3115
Bass, Robert M., 2952
Bass, Sallie M., 1164
Bass, Sandra A., 1778
Bass, Sid R., 3094
Bass, Thomas E., 1243
Bassett, John P., 417
Bastian, H. Marvin, 1048
Bastien, Nellie J., 573
Batchelder, Anne Stuart, 921
Bateman, Maureen S., 1815
Bates, George E., 756
Bates, Jeanne M., 1526, 1527
Bato, Doris S., 1406
Batte, G.A., Jr., 2378
Batten, James K., 629
Batten, Jane P., 3199
Battle, G. Thomas, 3265
Baubonis, Patricia, 1960
Bauder, Lillian, 1380
Bauer, Charles, 469
Bauer, Evelyn M., 786
Bauer, M.R., 786
Bauer, Ray, 618
Bauervic-Wright, Rose, 1304, 1414
Baughman, James P., 439, 440
Baukol, Ronald O., 1458
Baum, Dale, 1299
Bauman, Morton, 159
Bauman, Paul, 1946
Bauman, R.P., 2852
Bauman, Steve, 50
Baumgardner, Anita A., 114
Baumgardner, Roberta A., 21
Baumgarten, H.J., 1683

Bavendick, Frank J., 2427
Bavernfeind, George G., 1057
Bavicchi, Ferris G., 1604
Baxter, Barbara J., 2435
Baxter, Delia B., 72
Baxter, George J., 666
Baxter, James G., 2724
Baxter, Laura S., 2435
Baxter Travenol Laboratories, Inc., 787
Bay Street Corp., 1491
BayBank Harvard Trust Co., 1164
Baybank Valley Trust Co., 1204
Bayless, Mary C., 113
Bayless, Romaine, 918
Bayley, Christopher T., 3223
Bayliss, Harry G., 1147
Bayrd, Blanche S., 1155
Bayrd, Frank A., 1155
Bazany, L.F., 1416
BE&K, Inc., 4
Beach, C. Randall, 1779
Beach, Clarence E., 2372
Beach, E.D., 2372
Beach, Ross, 1037
Beach, Thomas C., Jr., 1779
Beadle, Ann, 1094
Beal, Barry A., 2954
Beal, Carlton, 2954
Beal, Carlton E., Jr., 2954
Beal, David, 2394
Beal, Keleen, 2954
Beal, Spencer, 2954
Beale, Michelle, 696
Beall, Donald R., 2819
Beall, Kenneth S., Jr., 678
Beamer, William E., 263
Bean, Barbara, 2649
Bean, Elizabeth N., 1600
Bean, Elmo A., Rev., 2457
Bean, Michael A., 8
Bean, Norwin S., 1600
Bean, R.J., Jr., 2708
Bean, Roy H., 2437
Beane, Sydney, 977
Bear Stearns & Co., 2126
Beard, Anson, Jr., 2130
Beard, D. Paul, 2810
Beard, Marjorie J., 74
Beard, Nancy, 1728
Beardsley, George B., 373
Beardsley, Lehman F., 1004
Bearer, William S., 2346
Beargie, W.T., 2525
Bearn, Alexander G., 1120, 2083, 2348
Beasley, C.H., 2944
Beasley, Mary E., 2955
Beasley, R.O., 3075
Beasley, Theodore P., 2955
Beatrice, Dennis F., 194
Beatt, Bruce H., 430
Beattie, Art P., 1
Beattie, Catherine Hamrick, 2892
Beattie, Richard I., 1829, 2046
Beattie, William F., 364
Beatty, Helen D. Groome, 2681
Beatty, J. Guy, 2916
Beatty, J. Guy, Jr., 725
Beatus, E. Jack, 2316
Beaty, Harry N., 957
Beaty, Jack, 1212
Beaty, Julian B., Jr., 2052
Beauchamp, John, 3044
Beaudoin, Robert E., 497
Beaudoin, Roseann K., 2039
Beaumont, Dorothy, 302
Beaver, Howard O., Jr., 2697
Beaver, Thomas, Jr., 2697
Beaver, Thomas A., 2864
Beazley, Fred W., 3162, 3180
Beazley, Fred W., Jr., 3162, 3180
Beazley, Marie C., 3162, 3180
Bechdel, Donna, 1880
Bechdolt, William, 2755

Bechtel, R.P., 75
Bechtel, Riley P., 178
Bechtel, S.D., Jr., 178
Bechtel, Susan Peters, 178
Bechtel Power Corp., 75
Beck, Audrey Jones, 3037
Beck, Henry C., Jr., 2975
Beck, John C., 1780
Beck, Madeline C., 1780
Beck, Matthew B., 2515
Beck, Raymond, 2590
Beck, Richard A., 971
Beck, Robert N., 70
Beck, Susan K., 2515, 2516
Beck, T. Edmund, 1780
Beck, T.E., Jr., 1780
Becker, Frances, 1985
Becker, Jeanine H., 3330
Becker, Katrina H., 1774
Becker, Max, Jr., 1884
Becker, Robert A., 850
Becker, Thomas G., 2466
Beckham, Peggy, 2943
Beckman, Arnold O., 76
Beckman, Mabel M., 76
Beckwith, G. Nicholas, 2683
Bedell, Catherine, 2160
Bedell, George C., 594
Bedford, Edward T., 1781
Bedford, Ruth T., 1781
Beebe, Frederick S., 548
Beech, O.A., 1033
Beech, Thomas F., 3115
Beech Aircraft Corp., 1033
Beecher, Ward, 2441
Beecherl, John T., 2958
Beecherl, Julia T., 2958
Beecherl, Louis A., Jr., 2958, 2972
Beecherl, Louis A. III, 2958
Beecherl, William C., 2958
Beede, Russell S., 1281
Beekman, Robert, 2296
Beeler, Thomas J., 913
Beeman, Richard A., 2560
Beemer, K. Larry, 1337
Beer, Robert A., 414
Beers, William O., 1783
Beewwkes, Reinier III, 1259
Begin, William J., 1450
Behnke, Alvin, 822
Behnke, James R., 1442
Behnke, John S., 3252
Behnke, Sally Skinner, 3252, 3257
Behnke, Shari Dunkelman, 3252
Behr, Linda C., 1014
Behrenhausen, Richard A., 893
Behrman, Nancy, 1711
Beidler, Francis, 789
Beidler, Francis III, 789
Beimfohr, Edward G., 1633
Beinecke, Elizabeth G., 2199
Beinecke, Frederick W., 2199
Beinecke, John B., 2199
Beinecke, William S., 2199
Beir, Joan S., 1784
Beir, Robert L., 1784
Bekins, Jacqueline, 77
Bekins, Michael, 77
Bekins, Milo W., 77
Bekins, Milo W., Jr., 77
Bekins Co., The, 77
Belanger, Warren, 340
Belden, A.B., 2838
Belden, Frederick H., Jr., 3265
Belden, Henry S., 2503
Belden, William H., Jr., 2591
Belding Heminway Co., Inc., 1977
Belew, David, 2499
Belfer, Arthur B., 1785
Belfer, Robert A., 1785
Belfer Corp., 1785
Belic, Ellen Stone, 961
Belin, Daniel N., 57

Belin, J.C., 593
Belin, Oscar, 1037
Beling, Betty, 84
Beling, Willard A., 84
Belk, Claudia, 2369
Belk, John M., 2393
Belk, Judy, 212
Belk, Matthews, 2369
Belk, Thomas M., 2369
Belk Enterprises, 2369
Belk Mercantile Corps., The, 2369
Belk-Simpson Co., 2886
Bell, A.L. Loomis, Jr., 2296
Bell, Bradley J., 1399
Bell, Charles M., 1467
Bell, D.L., Jr., 508
Bell, Ford W., 1415
Bell, James Ford, 1415
Bell, L. Andrew III, 620
Bell, Peter D., 1850
Bell, R. Terry, 3098
Bell, Richard, 2639
Bell, Richard G., 470
Bell, Robert M., 2893
Bell, Samuel H., Jr., 1415
Bell, Stephen Helms, 171
Bell, Victor E., Jr., 2405
Bell, Walter A., 20
Bell Atlantic Corp., 3163
Bellairs, Robert J., Jr., 1306
Bellamah, Dale J., 1727
Bellet, Marilyn, 2841
Bellinger, G.L., 3121
Bellinger, Geraldine G., 1933
Bellini, J., 78
Bellini, Michael J., 78
Bellini, Patrick W., 78
Belloff, Mary Gretchen, 581
Bellor, Mary M., 548
Bellwood, Wesley E., 356
Belser, Clinch H., Jr., 2888
Belsky, Nancy Kaplan, 2022
Belsole, M. Palmer, Jr., 20
Belsom, Walter J., Jr., 1087
Belt, John L., 2633
Belton, Sharon Sayles, 1421
Belton, Steven L., 1462
Belvin, Christy H., 1600
Belz, Jack A., 2911
Belz, Martin, 2911
Belz, Martin S., 2911
Belz, Philip, 2911
Belz, Ron, 2911
Belz, Ronald A., 2911
Belzer, Alan, 1611
Belzer, Folkert, 3329
Belzer, Ruth K., 863
Bemis Co., Inc., 1416
Ben-Asher, David, 40
Ben-Ephraim Fund, Gershon, 1005
Benaroya, Alan G., 3219
Benaroya, Donna R., 3219
Benaroya, Jack A., 3219
Benaroya, Larry R., 3219
Benaroya, Rebecca B., 3219
Benaroya, Sherry-Lee, 3219
Benbough, Legler, 79
Bender, David W., 773
Bender, George A., 344
Bender, Richard A., 126
Bendheim, John M., 2078
Bendheim, Robert, 2078
Benedeck, Alan F., 772
Benedict, Peter B., 2302
Benedum, Michael Late, 2683
Benedum, Paul G., Jr., 2683
Benedum, Sarah N., 2683
Beneficial Corp., 504
Beneficial New Jersey, 504
Benenson, Charles, 2293
Benenson, Charles B., 1786
Benison, John E., 2141
Bennack, Frank A., Jr., 1980, 1981

Charles, Ellen MacNeille, 560
Charles, Gladys R., 2855
Charlestein, Gary, 2699
Charlestein, Morton, 2699
Charleston National Bank, 3265
Charlson, Beverly C., 1429
Charlson, Lynn L., 1429
Charlton, Earle P., Jr., 1167
Charlton, Earle P. II, 1167
Chase, Alfred E., 1168
Chase, Edith, 497
Chase, Lavania B., 1273
Chase, Leah, 1082
Chase Lincoln First Bank, N.A., 1883, 1898, 1995, 2161, 2307, 2350
Chase Manhattan Bank, N.A., The, 1777, 1838, 1882, 2146, 2198
Chase Manhattan Bank of Connecticut, 497
Chase/CT, 417
Chatlos, Alice E., 583
Chatlos, William F., 583
Chatlos, William J., 583
Chattem, Inc., 2924
Chavez, Luis, 2996
Chavis, Donna, 2160
Chazen, Jerome A., 1839, 1846
Chazen, Simona A., 1839
Cheatham, Celeste W., 1840
Cheatham, Owen Robertson, 1840
Cheever, Charles E., Jr., 3071
Chelberg, Bruce S., 975
Chellgren, Paul W., 1049
Chemical Bank, 1756, 1903, 1970, 1972, 2038, 2079, 2141, 2146, 2252, 2857
Cheney, Ben B., 3224
Cheney, Bradbury F., 3224
Cheney, Eudine Meadows, 3064
Chenoweth, Arthur I., 718
Chenoweth, B.M., Jr., 718
Chenoweth, Richard A., 2538
Chernofsky, Morris I., 1841
Cherrie, George E., Jr., 69
Cherry, James R., 2226
Cherry, Wendell, 1057
Chesapeake Corp., 3171
Chesebro, Marvin, Mrs., 139
Chew, David, 407
Chiara, Judith L., 2074
Chicago Board of Trade, 819
Chicago Bridge & Iron Co., 815
Chicago Title and Trust Co., 820, 822, 881
Chilcote, Hazel S., 3178
Child, John L., 214
Childress, Francis B., 584
Childress, Miranda Y., 584
Childress, Owens F., 43
Childs, Edward C., 422
Childs, Edward Calder, 1737
Childs, Hope S., 1737
Childs, James E., 422
Childs, John W., 422, 1737
Childs, M.E., 3047
Childs, Richard S., Jr., 422
Childs, Starling W., 422
Chiles, Earle A., 2650
Chiles, Earle M., 2650
Chiles, Virginia H., 2650
Chilton, Arthur L., 2966
Chilton, Elizabeth E., 3265
Chilton, Leonore, 2966
Chin, Carolyn, 1930
Ching, Gerry, Mrs., 755
Ching, Philip H., 753
Chinn, Louise, 2337
Chino, Tetsuo, 2504
Chirco, Anne Marie, 2710
Chisholm, A.F., 1843
Chisholm, Don, 1301
Chisholm, Margaret A., 1843
Chisholm, William H., 1959

Chisolm, Donald H., 1543
Chiste, R.M., 3121
Chisum, Clayton D., 2731
Chisum, Gloria Twine, 2803
Chittenden, William S., 1880
Chitty, Kay K., 2916
Choate, J.D., 772
Chole, Robert A., 280
Chong, Arthur, 232
Chopin, L. Frank, 605
Choppin, Purnell W., 1120
Choquette, Paul J., 2882
Chorob, I., 217
Choromanski, J.J., 1484
Chortek, Doris H., 3306
Choudhury, Ali A., 3201
Christ, Chris T., 1303, 1351
Christ, Peter J., 1303
Christensen, Henry III, 2111
Christensen, Leslie N., 873
Christenson, Bernard W., 2909
Christiaansen, Janet, 3305
Christian, Carolyn McKnight, 1426
Christian, Charles L., 2348
Christian, Malcolm M., 3186
Christian, Nathalia E., 3320
Christian, William, 356
Christiansen, Elva E., 1458, 1459
Christiansen, Paul J., 1631, 1713
Christie, Robert W., 1365
Christie, Warren A., 2315
Christman, Anne K., 2517
Christman, Thomas H., 2850
Christoffersen, Ralph, 2834
Christopher, Warren, 1829
Christopherson, Weston R., 930
Chrysler Corp., 1309
Chubb, Corinne A., 1719
Chubb, Hendon, 1719
Chubb, Percy III, 1719
Chubb, Sally, 1719
Chumney, Candes P., 3099
Chumney, W.T., Jr., 3071
Church, Andrew, 168
Churchill, Emma L.D., 1955
Churchman, Caroline A., 2689
Churchman, Deborah P., 2689
Churchman, John Alexander, 2689
Churchman, W. Morgan III, 2689
Ciani, Judith E., 257
Cifu, Palma, 3197
CIGNA Corp., 2701
Cincinnati Bell, Inc., 2455
Ciraulo, Jerry, 1640
Cisco, Thomas, 79
Cismoski, Jerome J., 841
Cisneros, Henry G., 2224
CIT Financial Corp., 1844
Citibank, N.A., 1769, 2146, 2258
Citizens Bank, 2882
Citizens Commercial Trust and Savings Bank, 266
Citizens Federal Savings and Loan Assn., 2466
Citizens Fidelity Bank & Trust Co., 1051
Citizens National Bank & Trust Co., 2739
Citizens National Bank of Greencastle, 2739
Citizens State Bank, 3099
Citizens Trust Co., 2878
City National Bank, 96
Cizik, Robert, 2977
Claeyssens, Ailene B., 354
Claeyssens, Pierre P., 354
Claiborne, Herbert A., Jr., 741
Claiborne, Liz, Inc., 1846
Clairol-Gelb Foundation, 2728
Clanton, B. Jae, 2882
Clanton, Kenneth D., Dr., 3085
Clapp, George H., 2703
Clapp, Joseph, 2490
CLARCOR, 823
Clare, David R., 1658

Clark, Alfred C., 1849
Clark, Amy Plant Statter, 2289
Clark, Andrew L., 1848
Clark, Arthur W., 2417
Clark, Charles F., Jr., 957
Clark, Claudie, Jr., 2916
Clark, Edna McConnell, 1850
Clark, Elizabeth G., 1106
Clark, Emory T., 3278
Clark, Florence B., 2638
Clark, Frank E., 1847
Clark, H. Ray, 2588
Clark, Hays, 1850
Clark, Henry B., Jr., 755
Clark, Irving, 1462
Clark, James McConnell, 1850
Clark, Jane Forbes II, 1849
Clark, John W., 1311
Clark, Mariana L., 1781
Clark, Marcella S., 2588
Clark, Mary Chichester duPont, 507
Clark, Mildred, 423
Clark, Nolan P., 2412
Clark, Noreen M., 1885
Clark, Robert Sterling, 1851
Clark, Roger A., 535
Clark, Stephen R., 1243, 1331, 1337
Clark, Sylvia, 2790
Clark, Theodore P., 375
Clark, W. Van Alan, 1850
Clark, W. Van Alan, Jr., 1218
Clark-Cannon, Bettye, 1365
Clarke, D.V., 656
Clarke, Glenn S., 1764
Clarke, Howard P., 1467
Clarke, Kay Knight, 1735
Clarke, Paul, 990
Clarke, Richard M., 1738
Clarke, Robert F., 754
Clarke, Susan S., 2124
Clarke, Witt, 2382
Clarkson, William III, 3076
Claud, Joseph, 2408
Clauser, Theodore, 850
Clauson, Bronwyn Baird, 1768
Clauss, Valerie, 2461
Claverle, Philip, 1082
Clay, B.A., 3121
Clay, Buckner W., 3263
Clay, Hamilton G., 3263
Clay, Lyell B., 3263
Claybourn, Colleen, 3122
Claypool, James, 1408
Clayton, Constance, 425
Clayton, Susan V., 2968
Clayton, William L., 2968
Clayton Trust No. 1, Susan Vaughn, 3056
Cleary, Gail K., 3279
Cleary, Kristine H., 3279
Cleary, Russell G., 3279
Cleary, Sandra G., 3279
Clem, George M., 1042
Clemans, Jerald G., 132
Clemens, Peter J. III, 25
Clement, Josephine D., 2411
Clement, Kathleen, 687
Clement, William A., Jr., 686
Clements, Keith R., 1410
Clements, Rita C., 3078
Cleveland, Barbara, 736
Cleveland, Harlan, 2115
Cleveland, T.C., Jr., 2887
Cleveland Electric Illuminating Co., The, 2452
Cleveland Research Institute, 2551
Cleveland-Cliffs, Inc., 2458
Cliff, Walter C., 1957
Clifford, Charles H., 206
Clifford, Ellinor B., 1169
Clifford, Frederic M., 1169
Clifford, Stewart H., 1169
Cline, Benjamin L., 1227
Cline, Platt C., 39

Clinkscale, Ronald, 3116
Clodfelter, Daniel G., 2411
Cloninger, Kermit, 2390
Clorox Co., 106
Close, Anne Springs, 2889, 2904
Close, David P., 560
Close, Derick S., 2889, 2904
Close, Elliott Springs, 2889, 2904
Close, H.W., Jr., 2889, 2904
Close, Katherine Anne, 2889, 2904
Close, Leroy Springs, 2889, 2904
Close, Pat, 2889, 2904
Cloud, Sanford, Jr., 406
Clougherty, Coleman, 2072
Clow, Samuel C., 2462
Clowes, Alexander W., 985
Clowes, Allen W., 985
Clowes, Edith W., 985
Clowes, George H.A., 985
Clowes, Jonathan J., 985
Clowes, Margaret J., 985
Clowes, Thomas J., 985
Clyde, Aileen H., 3156
Clymer, John H., 1216
Coates, Dudley W., 1069
Cobb, Catherine R., 1343
Cobb, Charles K., Jr., 1270
Cobb, G., 2973
Cobb, H. Hart, Jr., 739
Cobb, L.D., 3023
Cobb, Tyrus R., 695
Cobbin, W. Frank, Jr., 1762
Coble, Hugh K., 137
Coble, R. Larry, 2216
Coblentz, William K., 202
Coburn, Jean Crummer, 116
Coburn, Milton, 116
Coca-Cola Co., 696
Cocke, Dudley, 1364
Cocke, Frances F., 705
Cockerham, Sarah, 1072
Cockley, Hildreth, 987
Cockrell, Dula, Mrs., 2970
Cockrell, Ernest, Jr., 2970
Cockrell, Ernest H., 2970
Cockrell, Janet S., 2970
Cockrell, Virginia H., 2970
Codell, J.C., Jr., 1063
Codrington, George W., 2459
Coe, Charles R., Jr., 2630
Coe, Elizabeth Merrick, 2630
Coe, Ross, 2630
Coe, Ward I., 2630
Coen, C.S., 2704
Coen, Charles R., 2704
Coen, Earl, 2704
Coen, Mary, 2704
Coen Land Co., C.S., 2704
Coffey, Shelby III, 331
Coffey, William E., 1601
Coffin, Alice S., 422
Coffin, David L., 430
Coffin, Harold W., 3225
Cogan, James R., 1621, 2185
Cogan, Marshall S., 2322
Cogan, Robert E., 2552
Cogen, Harry C., 123
Coggeshall, Mary, 1719
Cogswell, Arnold, 1740
Cogswell, Leander A., 1602
Cogswell, Wilton III, 363
Cohen, Alan B., 1658
Cohen, Allie, 1294
Cohen, Amy Scheuer, 2250
Cohen, Barbara, 2741
Cohen, C., 99, 236
Cohen, Charlotte McKee, 3061
Cohen, Donald B., 652
Cohen, Eileen Phillips, 3315
Cohen, Eliahu, 2207
Cohen, Gerald, 2059
Cohen, Harold, 2250
Cohen, Herbert, 1787

Delaney, James M., 2457, 2583
Delano, Mignon Sherwood, 1313
Delany, Beatrice P., 1882
DeLapa, James P., 1305
Delarios, Louise, 3053
Delattre, Edwin J., 2815
Delbridge, Ed, 2917
Delchamps, Ann W., 20
deLima, Richard F., 1258
Delisle, Raymond C., 365
Delman, Neil M., 2163
Delmas, Gladys V.K., 462
DeLoache, Bond Davis, 2919
DeLoache, William, 2919
DeLoache, William R., Jr., 2919
Delouvrier, Judith, 2707
Delouvrier, Philippe, 2707
Delp, George C., 2712
DelSol, Lucy D., 591
Deluca, Anthony P., 2721
Demakes, Louis, 1197
Demakis, Charles, 1197
Demakis, Gregory C., 1197
Demakis, Paul C., 1197
Demakis, Thomas C., 1197
Demakis, Thomas L., 1197
Demas, William G., 926
Dembrow, Victor D., 667
DeMetz, Don J., Jr., 23
DeMeulenaere, Robert L., 1016
DeMichele, Robert H., 2216
Deming, Winifred, 79
Demmer, Edward U., 3284
Demmer, Lawrence, 3284
Demo, Bernelle, 2896
Demorest, Byron, 302
Demoulas, A.T., 1179
Demoulas, Telemachus A., 1179
Demoulas Super Markets, Inc., 1179
Dempsey, Hugh, 2734
Dempsey, James H., Jr., 2435, 2510
Dempsey, T.M., 3311
Dempsey, W., 2004
Denison, Harriet, 1566
Denit, Helen P., 537
Denius, Franklin W., 2962
Denkers, Stephen E., 3147
Denkers, Stephen G., 3147
Denkers, Susan E., 3147
Denman, Gilbert M., Jr., 2957, 3027
Denman, James E., 1817
Denman, Leroy G., Jr., 3027
Dennery, Moise, 1082
Dennett, Marie G., 429
Denning, Bernadine N., 1380
Dennis, Everette E., 3181
Dennis, O.D., 3171
Dennis, Richard J., 821
Dennis, Thomas A., 821
Denomme, Thomas G., 1309
Densmore, William P., 1295
Denson, Lawrence J., 1871
Dent, Frederick B., 1614
Dent, Gloria G., 1884
Dent, Harry M., 1884
Dent, Harry M. III, 1884
Denton, Joe D., 2972
Denworth, Raymond K., Jr., 2725
Denzer, T., 1646
dePalma, Robert A., 2819
DePaola, Michael, 869
Department of Health and Human
  Services, 1092
Deposit Guaranty National Bank, 1489
DePriest, Roy H., 2500
DeRedon, Margaret, 1603
DeRegt, Kenneth, 2130
Derham, Jessie T., 2409
DeRiemer, Charles, 1569
Derieux, Samuel A., 3204
Dern, James R., 1757
DeRoo, Curt, 1315
DeRoy, Helen L., 1314

Derrickson, Lloyd J., 542
Derry, William S., 2604
des Granges, Pauline, 94
deSaussure, Charlton, Jr., 2907
Desecktor, Lilian V., 2324
DeSimone, Livio D., 1458, 1459
DeSipio, George, 2253
Detan, D.P., 508
Detmer, Don Eugene, 1842
Detrick, Judson W., 359
Dettmer, Robert G., 2179
Deubel, George, 302
Deuble, Andrew H., 2468
Deuble, George H., 2468
Deuble, Stephen G., 2468
Deuble, Walter C., 2468
Deur, Grace J., 1337
Deussen, Helmut, 2367
Deutsch, Alex, 119
Deutsch, Carl, 119
Deutsch, Lawrence E., 281
Deutsch, Lester, 119
Deutsch Co., The, 119
DeVan, Charlotte S., 2829
DeVan, Lawrence S., 2829
DeVan, W. Todd, 2829
Devens, Charles, 1214
DeVlieg, Charles B., 1315
DeVlieg, Charles R., 1315
DeVlieg, Janet, 1315
DeVlieg, Julia, 1315
DeVlieg, Kathryn S., 1315
DeVlieg Machine Co., 1315
Devlin, J.R., 1046
Devlin, Thomas R., 1048
DeVore, Floyd, 1036
DeVore, Richard A., 1036, 1048
DeVore, William D., 1036
DeVos, Helen J., 1316
DeVos, Richard M., 1316
DeVries, Robert K., 1682
Dewey, Francis H. III, 1147
Dewey, Henry B., 1207
Dewey, Robert F., 1939
Dewey, Ballantine et al., 568
DeWind, Adrian W., 1885, 2145, 2213
Dewing, Merlin E., 1421
DeWoody, Beth Rudin, 2235, 2236
Dexter Corp., The, 430
Di San Faustino, Genevieve, 86
Diab, George, 3263
Diamond, Aaron, 1885
Diamond, Irene, 1885
Diamond, Richard E., 2151
Dibbell, David, 3329
diBuono, Anthony J., 1858
Dick, Edison, 833
Dick, John H., 833
Dickason, John H., 637
Dicke, Richard M., 1914
Dickes, Don D., 2595
Dickey, Boh, 3247
Dickey, Robert III, 2809
Dickie, Elizabeth R., 936
Dickinson, Dallas P., 372
Dickinson, Fairleigh, Jr., 1871
Dickinson, Pat, 2961
Dickoff, G.A., 1867
Dickson, Alan T., 2385
Dickson, Donald, 3315
Dickson, Margaret C., 715
Dickson, R. Stuart, 2385
Dickson, Raymond, 2984
Dickson, Robert T., 3092
Dickson, Rush S. III, 2385
Dickson, Stanley S., 1052
Dickson, Thomas W., 2385
Dickson, W.W., 2397
Diehls, Carl, 3338
Diener, Martha Stott, 2844
Dietrich, G. Phillip, 1313
Dietrich, Henry D., 2715
Dietrich, William B., 2715

Dietrich American Foundation, 2715
Dietrich Foundation, Daniel W., Inc.,
  2715
Dietz, Milton S., 1258
Dilatush, L., 27
DiLeo, Victor, 1706
Dilg, Joseph C., 2997
Dillard, Mary B., 2958
Diller, Whitney Clay, 3263
Dillingham, Charles, 3134
Dillion, Victoria B., 1231
Dillivan, Marilyn J., 1014
Dillon, C. Douglas, 1886
Dillon, Clarence, 1886
Dillon, Francis B., 63
Dillon, Margo, 834
Dillon, Monika, 2172
Dillon, Peter W., 834
Dillon, Robert D., Jr., 2280
Dils, Edwin L.D., 3268
Dilworth, Susan S., 3112
DiMarco, James F., 3293
DiMario, Joseph F., 2790
Dimeo, Thomas P., 2880
Dines, Allen, 591
Dines, Audrey K., 591
Dines, Sidney A., 591
Dingle, Jerry, 666
Dingledy, Thomas G., 994
Dingler, Ruth C., 374
Dingman, Michael D., 1601, 1975
Dinner, Joan Withers, 165
Dinner, Richard S., 324, 325
Dinovitz, Dino, 1499
Dinse, Ann G., 1713
Dinsmore, Gordon G., 1904
Dircks, Robert J., 1723
Director, Steven R., 511
Disharoon, L.B., 1100
Disher, J.W., 2403, 2419
Dishman, H.E., 2985
Dishman, Kate, 2985
Dishman Foundation, The, 2985
Disney, Roy E., 120
Disney Productions, Walt, 120
Dispatch Printing Co., The, 2610
Distanovich, Sophie, 2220
Dittus, Jay E., 868
Dixon, Edith Robb, 2858
Dixon, F. Eugene, Jr., 2858
Dixon, George Widener, 2858
Dixon, Martha B., 11
Dixon, Solon, 11
Dixon, Steward S., 957
Dixon, Thomas F., 1973
Dobbs, Stephen Mark, 224
Dobelman, Katherine B., 2959
Dobie, Robert A., 280
Dobkin, Kendel Kennedy, 626
Dobkin, Richard J., 1905
Dobson, Douglas R., 2840
Dobson, Jack, 1301
Dobson, John S., 1352
Dockry, K.A., 1759
Dodd, Marie, 686
Dodd, Ruth E., 113
Dodds, R. Harcourt, 2147
Dodge, Cleveland E., Jr., 38
Dodge, Geraldine R., 1630
Dodson, Clara May, 700
Dodson, David, 2368
Dodson, Sheila L., 1113
Doehla, Harry, 1181
Doerfler, Ronald J., 1826
Doering, Sarah C., 1165
Doermann, Humphrey, 1421
Doerr, Henry, 1418
Doerr, Howard P., 400
Doheny, Edward L., Mrs., 121
Doheny Foundation Corp., Carrie
  Estelle, 121
Doherty, J.B, 1683
Doherty, James P., Jr., 939

Doherty, Judie, 232
Dohrman, Pam, 760
Doino, David J., 2157
Doino, Rocco R., 2157
Dolan, James F., 529, 2746
Dolan, Miles, 390
Dolan, T.I., 3326
Doldo, John, Jr., 2158
Dole, Nancy, 1292
Doll, Henry C., 2547
Dollar Savings & Trust Co., The, 2517,
  2605, 2615
Dolle, Molly W., 355
Dombchick, Steven, 520
Dompier, Sandra Smith, 3106
Donahue, Donald J., 1966
Donahue, Frank R., Jr., 2680
Donahue, Robert A., 1653
Donahue, Susann Islami, 1653
Donaldson, Carl L., 711
Donaldson, Kenneth T., 2271
Donaldson, Matthew S., Jr., 2788
Donaldson, Oliver S., 1887
Donaldson, William H., 406
Donehue, Gerald F., 1186
Doniger, Marjorie, 1950
Donnelley, Dorothy Ranney, 835
Donnelley, Elliott R., 835
Donnelley, Gaylord, 835
Donnelley, James R., 1774
Donnelley, Strachan, 835
Donnelley-Morton, Laura, 835
Donnelly, Annelee, 2426
Donnelly, Susanne, 96
Donnelly, Thomas J., 3285
Donnelly, Jr., Robert, 618
Donner, Frederick H., 2759
Donner, William H., 2759
Donohue, Bernadine Murphy, 247
Donohue, Daniel J., 247
Donohue, Rosemary E., 247
Donovan, Ann Fuller, 1605
Donovan, John M., 1408
Donovan, Patrick J., 1475
Donovan, R. Scott, 1627
Donovan, R.G., Mrs., 659
Donovan, Thomas, 1600
Donovan, Thomas F., 2790
Donzelli, Robert H., 1905
Doody, J. Robert, 23
Doolittle, Tracy, 2005
Doolittle, William C., 240
Dooner, Marie E., 1670
Dopp, M., 60
Dor, Barbara, 1914
Dor, Benny, 1914
Doran, Gary, 1762
Dorann, Eileen, 1959
Dorf, Jerome, 864
Dorman, Gerald D., 2196
Dorn, Andrew W., Jr., 2157
Dorn, David F., 2731
Dorn, Frederick M., 2731
Dorn, John C., 2731
Dorn, Ruth H., 2731
Dornsife, David H., 170
Dornsife, Ester M., 170
Dornsife, Harold W., 170
Dorris, Thomas B., 789
Dorsey, Bob Rawls, 197
Dorsey, Peter, 1424
Dorskind, Albert A., 264
Dosberg, Paul P., 1889
Doss, Lawrence P., 1302, 1346
Doster, Gayl W., 994
Doucette, James W., 1057
Dougherty, James R., 2987
Dougherty, James R., Mrs., 2987
Dougherty, Mary Patricia, 2987
Dougherty, Stephen T., 2987
Douglas, Francis W., 3151
Douglas, Jean W., 2334

Douglas, Walter, 1380
Douglas, Walter E., 1381
Douglas, William A., 361
Douglass, Arthur, 2155
Douglass, Robert R., 1838
Doupe, David W., 2722
Douthat, Anne S., 1566
Douzinas, Nancy R., 2205
Dow, G. Lincoln, Jr., 1270
Dow, Melvin, 2945
Dowd, Hector G., 1927
Dowdle, James C., 893
Dower, Thomas W., 836
Dowling, Janet, 483
Dowling, Richard, 483
Downes, Lawrence M., 1685
Downs, Harry S., 695
Doyle, Frank P., 439, 440
Doyle, Kathy, 1871
Doyle, Terence N., 1422
Doyle, Thomas M., 611
Dozier, Graham P., 2421
Dozier, O. Kemp, 3212
Drackett, Jeanne H., 2609
Drackett, Roger, 2609
Draeger, Rosemary S., 2908
Draft, Shirley, 1440
Drake, Carl B., Jr., 1417
Drake, Ellet H., 3286
Drake, Philip M., 426
Drake, William F., Jr., 2667
Draper, E. Linn, Jr., 3023
Draper Corp., 1211
Dreby, Edwin C. III, 2825
Dreckshage, Ruth, 1538
Drees, Charles F., 3022
Drees, Donna, 1025
Dreibelbis, M.D., 1023
Dreitzer, Shirley, 1891
Dresdner, K. Philip, 2178
Dressel, Henry R., Jr., 729
Dresser, Joyce G., 1757
Dresser Industries, Inc., 2989
Drew, Helen Hall, 2840
Drexel Burnham Lambert, Inc., 2144
Drexler, Millard S., 142
Dreyfus, Jack, 1892
Dreyfus, Jack J., Jr., 1892
Dreyfus, John, 1892
Dreyfus, Louis, 1893
Dreyfus, Max, 1894
Dreyfus, Victoria, 1894
Driehaus, Margaret F., 837
Driehaus, Richard H., 837
Drinan, Robert F., 1688
Driscoll, Elizabeth S., 1486
Driscoll, George E., 954
Driscoll, Nancy, 292
Driscoll, W. John, 1462
Drown, Joseph W., 123
Drowota, Frank, 2910
Drowota, Frank F. III, 2925
Drucker, K.A., 2261
Drueding, Bernard J., Jr., 2717
Drueding, Frank, 2717
Drumm, Jean, 1006
Drummond, Gerard K., 2661
Drumwright, Elenita M., 2109
Drury, W. Roger, 1057
Drymalski, Raymond H., 912
Du Bain, Myron, 183
Dubes, Michael J., 1464
Dubin, Stephen V., 2724
Dubler, Robert, 2614
Duboc, Charles A., 1542, 1543
DuBois, Jennifer Land, 1267
DuBois, Philip, 1267
DuBois, Robert, 1718
Dubon, Manuel H., 2865
Dubose, Vivian N., 2631
Dubow, Isabella B., 555
Dubrow, Eli B., 124
Dubrow, Lowell H., 2732

Dubuque Packing Co., 1030
Duchossois, Craig J., 838
Duchossois, R. Bruce, 838
Duchossois, Richard L., 838
Duchossois Industries, Inc., 838
Ducournau, Jackson P., 1079
Dudley, Frances, 2900
Dudley, Henry A., Jr., 559
Dudley, R.W., 815
Dudley, Spottswood P., 559
Dudte, James, 2614
Duello, J. Donald, 1563
Dufek, Donald F., 2519
Duff, Patrick D., 2314
Duffy, John J., 1766, 2061
Duffy, Michael S., 913
Duffy, Susan, 3250
Dufour, Edith Libby, 1079
Dufrene, Phillip A., 1448
Dugan, Dennis O., 3246
Dugdale, J.W., Jr., 830
Duggan, Agnes B., 1052
Duggan, Patricia M., 2811
Duhme, Carol M., 1559
Duhme, Warren, 1559
Duke, Anthony Drexel, 1732, 1800
Duke, Barbara Foshay, 2119
Duke, David A., 1864
Duke, Doris, 2386
Duke, James Buchanan, 2386
Duke, Robin Chandler, 262
Duke Power Co., 2387
Dula, Julia W., 1895
Dulany, Peggy, 2224
Dulin, Eugenia B., 540
Dulin, Susan W., 85
Dull, Sandra V., 511
Dullea, Charles, Rev., 165
Dulude, Richard, 1864
Dumke, Carol, 3142
Dumke, Edmund E., 3146
Dumke, Ezekiel R., Jr., 3146
Dun & Bradstreet Group, The, 1896
Dunagan, J. Conrad, 2991
Dunagan, John C., 2991
Dunagan, Kathlyn C., 2991
Dunbar, C. Wendell, 1389
Dunbar, George R., 417
Dunbar, Leslie, 1364
Duncan, Anne S., 2992
Duncan, Brenda, 2992
Duncan, C.W., 2992
Duncan, C.W. III, 2992
Duncan, Charles W., Jr., 2992
Duncan, G. Cameron, 2984
Duncan, George T., 707
Duncan, Jeaneane, 2992
Duncan, John G., 370
Duncan, John H., 2992
Duncan, John H., Jr., 2992
Duncan, Mary Anne, 2992
Duncan, Nancy Young, 560
Dunckel, Jeanette M., 357
Duncombe, Harmon, 2125, 2326
Dunford, Betty P., 751
Dunford, Edsel D., 2603
Dunlap, Tully F., 642
Dunlop, J.A., 2536
Dunlop, Joy S., 428
Dunlop, Robert G., 2806
Dunn, Edward K., Jr., 1099, 1144
Dunn, Harry E., 3211
Dunn, John S., Sr., 2993
Dunn, John S., Jr., 2993
Dunn, Joseph M., 3240
Dunn, Milby Dow, 2993
Dunn, Richard, 95
Dunn, Richard C., 267
Dunn, Robert H., 212
Dunn, T.T., 1714
Dunnigan, Joseph J., 1349
Dunning, Richard E., 1337
Dunnington, Walter G., Jr., 2285

Dunwody, Atwood, 590, 670
Dunworth, Gerald J., Jr., 2174
duPont, A. Felix, Jr., 507
duPont, Caroline J., 507
duPont, Christopher T., 507
duPont, Edward B., 523, 530
duPont, Henry B. III, Mrs., 417
duPont, Irenee, 510
duPont, Irenee, Jr., 510
duPont, Jessie Ball, 593, 594
duPont, John E., 2718
duPont, Lammot Joseph, 525
duPont, Lydia Chichester, 507
duPont, Miren deA., 525
duPont, Pierre S., 523, 530
duPont, Pierre S. IV, 523
duPont, Richard C., Jr., Mrs., 507
duPont, Willis H., 525
duPont Trust, Margaret F., 525
Durand, H. Whitney, 2939
Durban, Barbara, 317
Durein, Ted, 65
Durgin, Diane, 712
Durgin, Eugene J., 1221
Durham, H.W., 2920
Durham, Thomas H., Jr., 2920
Durrett, William, 2616
Dutton, Uriel E., 2948
Duval, Albert F., 2722
Duval Spirits, Inc., 1085
Duvall, Paul F., 806
Dwier, Emma D., 2693
Dwight, George H.P., 2318
Dwyer, John J., 407, 2459
Dwyer, Maureen E., 557
Dybala, Richard L., 780
Dydo, Dale S., 1688
Dydo, Joan, 1688
Dyke, Walter P., 3237
Dykes, Martha M., 723
Dynamet Inc., 2719
Dyson, Anne E., 1897
Dyson, Charles H., 1897
Dyson, Harry, 2881
Dyson, Margaret M., 1897
Dyson, Robert R., 1897
Dyson-Kissner-Moran Corp., The, 1897

Eady, Tom, 3076
Eagle, Richard A., 632
Eagle-Tribune Publishing Co., 1266
Earl, J. Benjamin, 267
Early, Rexford C., 996
Early, W.B., 2654
Easley, Andrew H., 3176
Eason, J. Rod, 302
Eastham, Thomas, 1980, 1981
Eastman Kodak Co., 1898
Eaton, George, 2309
Eaton, Georgiana Goddard, 1183
Eaton, Joseph E., 1270
Eaton, Larry, 1459
Eaton Corp., 2470
Eaton Estate Trust, Hubert, 138
Eaton Foundation, 1249
Eberly, Tita, 2739
Ebert, Adrienne, 2389
Ebert, Lyda, 210
Ebert, Lyda G., 2389
Ebert, Robert H., 2120
Ebert, Robert O., 2389
Ebert, Viola R., 2389
Ebright, Mitchell, 189
Ebrom, Charles, 3138
Eby, Martin K., Jr., 1048
Eccles, Delores Dore, 3148
Eccles, E.V., 2852
Eccles, George S., 3148
Eccles, John D., 3149
Eccles, Marriner S., 3149
Eccles, Ruth P., 3147

Eccles, Sara M., 3149
Eccles, Spencer F., 335, 3148, 3149
Echement, John R., 2854
Echlin, Beryl G., 595
Echlin, John E., 595
Echols, Curtis E., 53
Echols, Harold, 53
Eckerd Corp., Jack, 596
Eckert, Constance L., 1448
Eckhart, James M., 2974
Eckley, Robert S., 959
Eckstrom, Amy Lou, 3238
Edder, Andrew J., 432
Eder, Arthur, 432
Eder, Sidney, 432
Eder Bros., Inc., 432
Edey, Helen, 2249
Edgar, Ann, Sr., 1822
Edgar, Carol, 999
Edgar, R. Allan, 2916
Edge, Robert E., 725
Edgerley, Edward, 1524
Edgerton, B.E., 1622
Edgerton, Bradford W., 3187
Edgerton, Patricia Jones, 3187
Edgerton, William A., 3187
Edison, Bernard, 1512, 1513
Edison, Charles, 1631
Edison, Harry, 1512
Edison, Irving, 1513
Edison, Marilyn, 1513
Edison, Peter A., 1513
Edlow, Kenneth, 2126
Edmiston, W. Allan, 267
Edmond, Lisette S., 1672
Edmonds, Clarence, 2930
Edmondson, J. Richard, 1809
Edmunds, Arthur J., 2809
Edmunds, R. Larry, 9
Edner, Leon E., 65
Edson, Catherine H., 3026
Edson, Thomas H., 3026
Edwards, A.B. Kirk, 2995
Edwards, Bennett M., Jr., 2414
Edwards, C. Rupert, 1381
Edwards, Edith W., 681
Edwards, Ernest J., 2668
Edwards, Frank G., 2637
Edwards, Gene, 3030
Edwards, James K., 1225
Edwards, James M., 2784
Edwards, Kathleen Bryan, 2373
Edwards, Morris D., 681
Edwards, O. Ralph, 768
Edwards, Ray, 1437
Edwards, Richard D., 2784
Edwards, Rodney J., 1436
Edwards, Rosalie, 1301
Edwards, William H., 1596
Eefting, Ilene B., 667
Effird, Tom D., 2391
Efird, Claire, 2886, 2900
Efroymson, Clarence W., 1005
Efroymson, Daniel R., 996, 1005
Efroymson, Lori, 1005
Efroymson, Robert A., 1005
Efroymson Fund, Gustave Aaron, 1005
Efroymson-Kahn, Shirley G., 1005
EG&G, Inc., 1184
Egan, Sean T., 497
Egan, Thomas J., 1082
Eggum, John, 934
Ehlers, Walter G., 1842
Ehrenfeld, David W., 433

Fitton, Richard J., 2499
Fitts, Harriet W., 1481
Fitz-Gibbon, T. David, 3179
Fitzgerald, A. Desmond, 1779
Fitzgerald, Anne, 431
Fitzgerald, Dennis M., 2329
Fitzgerald, Dennis W., 895
FitzGerald, Frances, 2224
Fitzgerald, Janet, 267
Fitzgerald, Jean E., 895
Fitzgerald, John A., 2113, 2114
Fitzgerald, Leslie Law, 633
Fitzmorris, Ann Wadsworth, 1068
Fitzpatrick, Carolyn, 659
Fitzpatrick, Jane P., 1205
Fitzpatrick, Jean R., 1287
Fitzpatrick, John H., 1205
Fitzpatrick, Mary Alice, 3080
Fitzpatrick, Nancy J., 1205
Fitzpatrick, R.R., 2562
Fitzsimmons, Hugh A., Jr., 3027
FitzSimons, John H., 1897
Fix, Duard, 380
Fizer, Don, 2093
Fjeld, Linda, 1432
Fjellman, Carl, 1713
Fjordbak, Edward M., 2972
Flad, Eleanor Beecher, 2441
Flad, Erle L., 2441
Flad, Ward Beecher, 2441
Flaherty, G.S., 814
Flammia, Sue S., 3228
Flanagan, Lewis, 1440
Flanagin, Neil, 947
Flanders, Graeme L., 1145
Flans, A., 237
Flanzer, Gloria M., 2123
Flather, Newell, 1173, 1265
Flatow, Frederick A., 467
Flaville, Victoria K., 2707
Flawn, Priscilla Pond, 2951
Fleck, Ernest R., 2427
Fleckenstein, Janie Holley, 1318
Fleet, Mary Anne, 366
Fleet Bank, N.A., 448, 470, 1245, 1296,
     1817, 1994, 2094, 2137, 2870
Fleet Bank of Maine, N.A., 1093
Fleet Bank of Massachusetts, N.A.,
     1158, 1168, 1223, 1254, 1295
Fleet National Bank, 2882
Fleet Norstar Investment Services, 1828
Fleischman, Charles D., 641
Fleischmann, Ruth H., 2350
Fleming, Larry D., 1048
Fleming, Nancy C., 2849
Fleming, Richard, 969
Fleming, Walter L., Jr., 2975
Flemm, John J., 1919
Fletcher, Allen W., 1285
Fletcher, Jesse C., 2943
Fletcher, Marion S., 1285
Fletcher, Mary F., 1295
Fletcher, Philip B., 1587
Fletcher, Warner S., 1147, 1285
Flick, Earl D., 56
Flick, James A., Jr., 2697
Flink, Richard A., 1773
Flinn, Irene, 30
Flinn, Robert S., 30
Flom, Joseph, 1689
Flood, Howard L., 2584
Flora, Louis A., 3253
Florence, Charlotte, 1190
Florence, David, 3013
Florence Trust, Fred F., The, 3013
Flores, Joseph D., 2358
Florie, Walter, Jr., 239
Flory, Lee J., 857
Flournoy, Houston, 192
Flow, Victor I., Jr., 2424
Flowers, Thomas I., 1999
Flowers, Wilford, 3137
Floyd, Kimberly, 2972

Flug, Laura Gurwin, 1969
Fluke, J.M., Jr., 3240
Fluor, J. Robert II, 137
Fluor Corp., 137
Flynn, Grayce B. Kerr, 2626
Flynn, James L., 1754, 1864
Flynn, Michael H., 417
Flynn, T.G., 75
Flynn, Thomas J., 1057
FMB Lumberman's Bank, 1365
FMC Corp., 842
Foellinger, Esther A., 989
Foellinger, Helene R., 989
Foerderer, Ethel Brown, 2726
Foerderer, Percival E., 2726
Foerderer Davis, Mignon, 2726
Foerstner, George C., 1018
Fogelson, David, 635
Fogerty, Arthur J., 1736
Fojtasek, Georgia R., 1347
Foley, Eileen D., 1604
Foley, Ruth E., 3316
Folger, John Dulin, 540
Folger, Kathrine Dulin, 540
Folger, Lee Merritt, 540
Folger, P., 229
Follis, R. Gwen, 229
Fondren, W.W., Sr., Mrs., 3014
Fondren, Walter W. III, 3014
Fonseca, Bruno, 2023
Fonseca, Caio, 2023
Fonseca, Elizabeth K., 2023
Fonseca, Isabel, 2023
Fonseca, Quina, 2023
Foorman, Barbara R., 1559
Foote, Robert L., 866
Foote, Susan Green, 1523
Forbes, Inc., 1920
Forbes, Christopher, 1920
Forbes, Greg, 1305
Forbes, Jay, 1728
Forbes, Malcolm S., Jr., 1920
Forbes, Margaret, 2408
Forchheimer, Leo, 1921
Forchheimer, Rudolph, 1921
Ford, Benson, 1324
Ford, Benson, Jr., 1324
Ford, Clara, 1191
Ford, David K., 2525
Ford, Edsel, 1922
Ford, Edsel B. II, 1327
Ford, Esther C., 1391
Ford, Frank, 601
Ford, Frank I., Jr., 64
Ford, Frederick B., 1391
Ford, Frederick S., Jr., 1391
Ford, Henry, 1922
Ford, Henry II, 1327
Ford, Horace C., 1391
Ford, James W., 1391
Ford, Jefferson L., Jr., 603
Ford, Joanne C., 905
Ford, Joseph F., 1191
Ford, Josephine F., 1325
Ford, Lana A., 1331
Ford, Martha F., 1326, 2480
Ford, Martha Firestone, 1326
Ford, Thomas P., 197
Ford, Walter B. II, 1325
Ford, William Clay, 1326
Ford, William Clay, Jr., 1381
Ford, William S., 3163
Ford, William S., Jr., 1684
Ford Foundation, The, 1930
Ford Motor Co., 1329
Fordyce, Anne B., 2056
Fordyce, James W., 2056
Foreman, Robert L., Jr., 744
Forest City Enterprises, Inc., 2482
Forest Lawn Co., 138
Forest Oil Corp., 2731
Forger, Alexander D., 2064
Forkner, Joanne S., 1655

Forlini, Rina, 2083
Forman, Willis M., 1475
Forrow, Brian D., 1611
Forsham, Peter H., 304
Forsyth, James G., 1544
Forsyth, John A., 1176
Forsyth, Marian E., 1176
Forsythe, John G., 1435
Forsythe, Peter W., 1850
Fort Wayne National Bank, 988, 1012
Fortin, Mary Alice, 605
Fortner, J.G., 1334
Fortson, Benjamin J., 3115
Fortunoff, Alan, 2096
Fortunoff of Westbury Corp., M., 2096
Forward, Charlotte H., 581
Fosbroke, Gerald E., 1165
Foster, Daniel H., 920
Foster, Debra L., 2384
Foster, Esther J., 1923
Foster, Evelyn W., 3227
Foster, Everett G., 2158
Foster, J.K., 2836
Foster, J.L., 2727
Foster, J.T., 2727
Foster, Jacqueline, 1923
Foster, Joseph C., 1923
Foster, Lawrence G., 1658
Foster, Lawrence T., 2597
Foster, M.J., 901
Foster, Michael G., 3227
Foster, Patricia, 152
Foster, Stephen A., 1875
Foster, T. Jack, Jr., 269
Foster, Terry N., 1301
Foster, Thomas B., 3227
Foster, W.R., 1410
Foster Industries, Inc., 2727
Foti, Samuel, 2140
Foundation Health Plan of Sacramento,
     302
Fountain, N. Jean, 1443
Fountain Industries Co., 1478
Four Wheels, Inc., 845
Fourcher, Myrna C., 2386
Fowler, Anderson, 1617
Fowler, Bill, 53
Fowler, Caleb L., 2701
Fowler, Candace L., 1552
Fowler, Helen M., 1318
Fowler, Lorraine A., 2128
Fowler, Robert III, 685
Fowles, Kirsten, 2201
Fox, Daniel M., 2120
Fox, David G., 2981
Fox, Emma R., 2483
Fox, Esther G., 2816
Fox, Jerry D., 997
Fox, Mary P., 1063
Fox, Raymond C., 275
Fox, Robert A., 2816
Fox, William J., 2212
Foy, Douglas I., 1241
Foy, Douglas J., 982, 983
Foy, Robert, 13
Fradkin, Hillel G., 3275
Fraedrich, David S., 2439
Frahm, Donald R., 455
Frampton, Betsy K., 546
Frampton, George T., Jr., 546
France, Annita A., 1112
France, George A., 2484
France, Jacob, 1112
France, Phyllis B., 1421
France Stone Co., The, 2484
Franchetti, Agnes M., 526
Franchetti, Anne Milliken, 526
Francis, H.D., 645
Francis, J. Scott, 1519
Francis, John B., 1519
Francis, Mary B., 1519
Francis, Mary Harris, 1519
Francis, Norman, 1082

Francis, Parker B., 1519
Francis, Parker B. III, 1519
Francke, Albert III, 2263
Frangos, Michael, 1197
Frank, Elaine S., 845
Frank, James S., 845
Frank, John V., 2538
Frank, Paul M., 2185
Frank, Roxanne Harris, 863
Frank, Ruby, 783
Frank, Stanley J., Jr., 2465
Frank, William H., 2212
Frank, Z., Inc., 845
Frank, Zollie S., 845
Franke, Harry F., 3306
Frankel, Elizabeth F., 1925
Frankel, G. David, 1925
Frankel, George, 1925
Frankel, Gerald, 846
Frankel, Gustav, 846
Frankel, Julius N., 846
Frankenheim, Samuel, 1195
Franklin, Barbara Hackman, 406
Franklin, Carl M., 313
Franklin, Carroll R., 543
Franklin, John, 707
Franklin, Leonard, 1891
Franklin, Mary O., 707
Franklin, Robert V., Jr., 2597
Franklin, T.R., 3307
Franklin, William P., 3006
Franks, Myron B., 1933
Frantzis, George, Sr., 497
Franz, Paul, 2772
Fraser, Helen T., 1192
Fraser, Howard H., 2489
Fraser, Richard M., 1192
Fraser, Thomas T., 2330
Fraser Foundation, Richard M. & Helen
     T., 1192
Frauenthal, Harold, 1365
Fray, John C.S., 1259
Frazee, John P., Jr., 817
Frazer, David R., 30
Frear, Mary D., 752
Frear, Walter F., 752
Freda-Chan, Patricia, 2005
Frederickson, Donald, 1124
Fredrick, Francis, 2833
Freeburg, Don, 95
Freed, Elizabeth Ann, 542
Freed, Frances W., 542
Freed, Gerald A., 542
Freedman, Margot E., 1901
Freeman, David F., 2249
Freeman, Elaine, 2902
Freeman, Houghton, 2288
Freeman, Kemper, 3250
Freeman, Lida, 2710
Freeman, Richard B., 701
Freeman, Richard F., 417
Freeman, Robert M., 2266
Freeman, Samuel, 1926
Freeman, Tara-Shelomith K., 2022
Frees, C. Norman, 3016
Frees, C. Norman, Jr., 3016
Frees, Shirley B., 3016
Freeth, Douglas, 1301
Frehse, Robert M., Jr., 1980, 1981
Freidenrich, John, 291
Freihofer, Charles C. III, 2124
Frelinghuysen, George L.K., 1636, 2183
Frelinghuysen, H.O.H., 1636
Frelinghuysen, Joseph S., Jr., 1684
Frelinghuysen, Peter, 1636, 1732, 1800
Fremer, Geraldine, 1822
Fremont National Bank & Trust Co.,
     1588
Fremont-Smith, Marion R., 1150
French, B.J., 1432
French, Ronald, Mrs., 1082
French, Taylor, 918
Frenette, Donald H., 1458, 1459

Frenkel, Barbara P., 1370
Frenkel, Dale P., 1370
Frenkel, Marvin A., 1370
Frenkel, Ronald E.P., 1370
Frenkel, Tom P., 1370
Frenza, James, 1301
Frenzer, Peter F., 2545
Frese, Arnold D., 1927
Frese, Ines, 1927
Freund, Hugh J., 2318
Frey, David G., 1332, 1340
Frey, Dorothy L., 356
Frey, Edward J., Sr., 1332
Frey, Edward J., Jr., 1332
Frey, Frances T., 1332
Frey, John H., 2712
Frey, John M., 1332
Frezel, Jerrold A., 2699
Frick, James W., 611
Frick, Merrill B., 986
Frick, Nancy J., 2476
Friday, William C., 2373
Fried, Mary, 40
Fried, Robert, 567
Friede, Barbara B., 134
Friedeman, William B., 972
Friedheim, Jerry W., 3181
Friedlaender, Helmut N., 2672
Friedlander, William A., 2456
Friedman, Alan D., 3049
Friedman, Arnold D., 1892
Friedman, Arthur N.K., 2594
Friedman, Bayard H., 3049
Friedman, Cheryl S., 2296
Friedman, D. Sylvan, 1119
Friedman, Darrell, 1113, 1141
Friedman, Harold E., 2483
Friedman, Louis F., 1119
Friedman, Phyliss C., 1119
Friedman, Robert A., 1865
Friedman, Robert S., 2234
Friedman, Sidney, 369
Friedman, Stephen, 1876
Friedman, Walker C., 3049
Friedman, Wilbur H., 1935
Friedman, William E., 2271
Friedman, William K., 1811
Friedsam, Michael, Col., 1746
Friedwald, William T., 2117
Friend, Eugene L., 202
Friend, Robert, 257
Friend, W.L., 75
Friend, William K., 2579
Friends' Fund, A., Inc., 606
Friese, George R., 2579
Frigon, Hank, 1527
Frist, Thomas F., 2910
Frist, Thomas F., Jr., 2925
Fritsche, W.F., Jr., 2708
Fritz, Bertha G., 1199
Fritz, William W., 1351
Froats, Laura B., 1323
Froderman, Carl M., 991
Froderman, Harvey, 991
Froehlich, Cecillie, 1984
Froelicher, F. Charles, 373
Frohlich, Ludwig W., 1928
Frohlich, William O., 1896
Frohman, Blanche P., 2486
Frohman, Daniel C., 2486
Frohman, Sidney, 2486
Frohring, Gertrude L., 2488
Frohring, Glenn H., 2488
Frohring, Lloyd W., 2488
Frohring, Maxine A., 2487
Frohring, Paul R., 2487
Frohring, William O., 2488
Froio, Anthony, 1209
Fromel, Robert A., 2001
Frommelt, Andrew E.R., Jr., 1700
Fronterhouse, Gerald W., 3036, 3120
Frost, Camilla C., 183
Frost, H.G., Jr., 47, 48

Frost, Louis B., 1972
Frost, Stevens L., 2185
Frost, T.C., Jr., 3071
Frost, Virginia C., 372
Frost National Bank, 3099, 3125
Frueauff, Charles A., 607
Frueauff, David, 607
Frueauff, Harry D., 607
Fruehauf, Angela, 1333
Fruehauf, Harvey C., Jr., 1333, 1599
Fry, J.C., 2391
Fry, Lloyd A., 848
Fry, Lloyd A., Jr., 848
Fry, Marjorie Walthall, 3129
Fry, May, 2646
Fryberger, Carol, 1408
Frye, C. Wesley, Jr., 2358
Frye, David B., 585
Fryling, Victor J., 1311
Fuchs, Gottfried, 3229
Fuchs, Mary, 3229
Fuegner, Robert C., 2620
Fuellgraf, Charles L., Jr., 2545
Fuges, Frederick L., 2825
Fuhriman, Addie, 3156
Fuhs, Wendy L., 806
Fuld, Florentine M., 1929
Fuld, James J., 2057
Fuld, Leonhard Felix, 1929
Fuldner, Henry E., 3290
Fullenwilder, W. Harry, 2380
Fuller, Alfred, 1167
Fuller, Alvan T., Sr., 1605
Fuller, Andrew P., 3018
Fuller, Charles A., Jr., 1565
Fuller, Cornell G., 2891
Fuller, Cynthia Q., 1715
Fuller, Ernest M., 1193
Fuller, George Freeman, 1193
Fuller, Jack, 893
Fuller, Joyce I., 1193
Fuller, Julia G., 21
Fuller, Mark W., 1193
Fuller, Orville, 2462
Fuller, Peter, 1605
Fuller, Peter D., Jr., 1605
Fuller, Russell E., 1193
Fuller, William M., 3018
Fullerton, Alma H., 2892
Fullerton, Harriet P., 282
Fullerton, James D., 282
Fullinwider, Jerome M., 2941
Fullmer, Joseph A., 383
Fulton Bank, 2739
Funding Exchange, Inc., 1859
Fung, Margaret, 2147
Funk, Elmer H., Jr., 2770
Funk, Eugene D. III, 849
Funk, Lafayette III, 849
Funk, Richard C., 849
Furay, Sally, Sr., 287
Furek, Robert, 425
Furek, Robert M., 451
Furey, J.J., 1622
Furia, Helen M., 610
Furlong, Brenda J., 1277
Furlong, Lawrence P., 2576
Furlong, R. Michael, 825
Furman, James M., 887
Furnas, Leto M., 850
Furnas, W.C., 850
Fusenot, Germaine, 139
Fuson, Esten, 991
Fusscas, Helen K., 462
Fusscas, J. Peter, 462
Futo, Kyle, 384
Fynboe, Carl T., 3253

G.P.D., Inc., 1390
Gaard, Thomas, 1028
Gabel, Ivan H., 2794

Gaberino, John A., Jr., 2645
Gaberman, Barry D., 1922
Gabier, Russell L., 1339
Gaddy, Charles W., 2405
Gaddy, Joe, 2414
Gaffney, Edward S., 2430
Gaffney, Frank J., 2730
Gaffney, John C., 184
Gaffney, Joseph M., 3239
Gaffney, Owen J., 1258
Gage, H.N., Jr., 1493
Gage, Joanne, 1951
Gailey, Jane E., 1884
Gaines, Curman L., 1475
Gaines, H. Clarke, 293
Gaiser, Mary Jewett, 190
Gaisman, Catherine V., 1931
Gaisman, Henry J., 1931
Gaither, Andrew C., 322
Gaither, James C., 164, 183
Galasso, August J., 1932
Galasso, Martin A., 1932
Galbraith, James R., 1596
Galbraith, William A., Jr., 2703
Galen, Albert J., 130
Galke, Heide, 84
Galkin, Arnold T., 2871
Galkin, Herbert S., 2871
Galkin, Ira S., 2871
Galkin, Irwin S., 2871
Gallagher, Daniel J., 1122
Gallagher, Edward, 2155
Gallagher, Karen, 3261
Gallagher, Lindsay R., 1122
Gallagher, Patrick S., 2173
Gallagher, Terence J., 2181
Gallagher Family Charitable Income
  Trust, Lewis P., 2489
Gallant, Murray, 2579
Gallantz, George G., 2057
Gallaway, Pamela Y., 3181
Gallegos, Herman, 288
Galler, Ida E., 2288
Galligan, Richard P., 1022
Gallo, Julio R., 140
Gallo, Robert J., 140
Gallo, Ronald V., 594
Galloway, Nina, 94
Galloway-May, Diane, 1922
Gallup, John G., 574
Galter, Dollie, 851
Galter, Jack, 851
Galudel, Robert, 1231
Galvin, Charles O., 959
Galvin, Christopher B., 852
Galvin, Mary G., 852
Galvin, Robert W., 852
Gambill, Malcolm W., 2740
Gamble, George F., 141
Gamble, Gerald L., 2620
Gamble, James N., 265
Gamble, Launce E., 141
Gamble, Mary S., 141
Gambrel, Amy H., 2464
Gamper, Albert R., Jr., 1844
Gamron, W. Anthony, 3046
Gancer, Donald C., 801
Gann, Ronald W., 720
Gannett, Frank E., 3181
Gannett, John D., 1211
Gannett, Robert T., 3160
Gannett, William B., 1211
Gannon, R.P., 1583
Gans, Carl W., 1409
Gant, Donald R., 1810
Gantz, Wilbur H., 787
Gap, Inc., The, 142
Garaventa, Mary, 143
Garaventa, Silvio, 143
Garber, Karlene Beal, 2954
Garcia, Daniel P., 2224
Garcia, Frieda, 1158
Garcia, Joseph, 624

Garcia, Nellie, 267
Garcia, Suzanne H., 1649
Garda, Annie Lewis, 2457
Garday, Louis J., 94
Gardiner, Nancy T., 2212
Gardner, David L., 2458
Gardner, David P., 3148
Gardner, Dorsey R., 1908
Gardner, George P., 1194
Gardner, George P., Jr., 1214
Gardner, James R., 2181
Gardner, John L., 1194
Gardner, Nina, 1144
Gardner, R.M., 597
Gardner, Robert G., 1194
Gardner, Stephen D., 2255
Gardner, William L., Jr., 2097
Garfield, Brian, 1638
Garfield, Elizabeth, 1638
Garfield, George, 1638
Garfield, Sarah B., 1295
Garfinkel, Barry H., 2146
Garlock, Edward, 135
Garner, James G., 608
Garner, John Michael, 608
Garnier, J.P., 2834
Garr, Carl R., 2697
Garran, Frank W., Jr., 1222
Garrett, Horace, Mrs., 3096
Garrett, J. Richard, 455
Garrett, Robert, 1095
Garrett, Wendy, 3082
Garrettson, Bettie P., 1774
Garrettson, John A., 1774
Garrison, Robert, 1365
Garrison, Theodore B., 2552
Garrity, J.P., 656
Garthwait, Robert W., Sr., 497
Gartland, John J., Jr., 2097
Garton, Deirdre Wilson, 2350
Gartzke, David G., 1467
Garvey, James S., 3019
Garvey, Richard F., 3019
Garvey, Shirley F., 3019
Garvey Foundation, 3019
Garwood, William L., Jr., 2968
Gary, Kathryn, 388
Gary, Nancy, 388
Gary, Samuel, 388
Gary Williams Co., 388
Gaskin, J.W., 2494
Gassaway, James M., 2735
Gassel, Virginia Stearns, 1281
Gates, Carol W., 2801
Gates, Charles, 373
Gates, Charles C., 373
Gates, Elmer, 2772
Gates, Freeman, 344
Gates, George A., 280
Gates, Hazel, 373
Gates, Hilliard, 989
Gates, John, 373
Gates, Moore, Jr., 1743
Gates, Philip C., 604
Gates, Richard D., 2573
Gatins, Martin, 728
Gauderer, Michael W.L., 2450
Gaugh, Richard A., 2790
Gaunt, Joseph A., 1617
Gaurreau, John C. II, 1069
Gaus, William T., 3324
Gautier, Agnes, 1984
Gautier, N.E., 3104
Gaviglio, James D., 1409
Gavin, Austin T., 121
Gavin, Stephen D., 96
Gaviser, Judy, 1432
Gay, Frank William, 1120
Gaydou, Danny R., 1323
Gayle, Gibson, Jr., 2948
Gaylord, Clifford W., 1521
Gaylord, Guilford W., 2064
Gaylord, Louis W., Jr., 2407

Griffith, Ruth Perry, 992
Griffith, Steve C., Jr., 2387
Griffith, W.C., Jr., 992
Griffith, Walter S., 992
Griffith, William C., 992
Griffith, William C. III, 992
Grigg, William H., 2387, 2393
Grimes, Susan H., 348
Grimes, Warren G., 2495
Grimm, Debra Mills, 640
Grimm, Ronald L., 2938
Grimsby, Hoover, 1447
Grisanti, Eugene P., 2004, 2125
Grisi, Jeanmarie C., 1829
Grissom, S.L., 884
Griswold, Benjamin H. IV, 1103
Griswold, Sally K., 2583
Grodin, Jay, 349
Groennings, Sven, 1751
Grogan, Robert, Mrs., 290
Groman, Arthur, 254
Gronewaldt, Alice Busch, 613
Gronner, Sam A., 1762
Groome, Harry, 2834
Groos Bank, 3099
Grosberg, Julius, 1338
Gross, Carl R., 2463
Gross, Gordon R., 1817
Gross, Howard, Mrs., 2462
Gross, Jenard M., 3135
Gross, Martin L., 1607
Gross, Ronald M., 456
Gross, Ronald N., 1428, 1455, 1488
Gross, Stella B., 161
Gross, Thomas R., 2496
Gross, Walter L., Jr., 2496
Grosse, Rose B., 808
Grossman, Harold I., 32
Grossman, Ryna Jean, 32
Groth, Paul H., 3287, 3304
Grothaus, Roger H., 3293
Groveman, Jan B., 2911
Groves, C.T., 1445
Groves, Frank M., 1445
Groves, Frank N., 1445
Groves, Helen K., 3048
Groves, Robert A., 1596
Groves & Sons Co., S.J., 1445
Grubb, Janet, 2533
Gruber, Barry, 1968
Gruber, Carl E., 1767
Gruber, Daryl, 1968
Gruber, Jon D., 162
Gruber, Linda W., 162
Gruber, Marilyn L., 1809
Gruber, Murray P., 1968
Gruber, Roy, 3289
Grubman, Stanley D., 1723
Grumhaus, Margaret A., 2438
Grun, Ann Kissel, 2086
Grundfest, Judy, 50
Grundy, Joseph R., 2735
Grunewald, Dale, 1025
Grunwald, Louise, 1734
Grzelak, Cynthia, 1301
GSC Enterprises, Inc., 858
GTE Corp., 444
Guaranty Bank & Trust, 369
Guaranty Trust Co. of Missouri, 1555
Gudger, Robert H., 500
Guenther, Paul, 2172
Guererro, Linda, 3137
Guerra, John C., Jr., 1762
Guerry, John P., 2916
Guerry, Zan, 2916
Guethle, Russ, 1524
Guggenheim, Charles, 1510
Guggenhime, Richard J., 206
Guggimio, Kathleen, 1727
Guidone, Rosemary L., 2197
Guiggio, John P., 1160
Guilford, Frank W., 623
Guilkey, Joan, 2376

Gulledge, Robert C., 2424
Gullen, David J., 30
Gulton, Edith, 1642
Gulton, Leslie K., 1642
Gumenick, Nathan S., 1115
Gumenick, Sophia, 1115
Gund, Ann L., 2497
Gund, Geoffrey, 2497
Gund, George, 2497
Gund, George III, 2497
Gund, Llura A., 2497
Gund, Louise L., 2611
Gunn, Colin, 2174
Gunther, D.J., 75
Gurash, John T., 348
Gurley, George Morris, 1806
Gurwin, Eric, 1969
Gurwin, Joseph, 1969
Gurwin, Rosalind, 1969
Gushee, Richard B., 1343
Gushing, N.V., 2536
Gustafson, Karl, 1726
Gustafson, Robert, 267
Gustin, Lester C., 1157
Guthman, Sandra P., 924
Gutierrez, Felix, 3181
Gutman, Agnes, 762
Gutman, Steven, 1986
Gutowicz, Leon, 217
Gutshall, James, 368
Gutterman, Gerald S., 2261
Gutterman, Jordan, 2056
Guttowsky, Lois K., 1362
Guyette, James M., 968
Guyton, Jean, 401
Guyton, S.P., 401
Guzman, Mariano, 99
Gwaltney, Nancy R., 21

Haake, Donald B., 72
Haake, Martha B., 72
Haake, Richard H., 72
Haas, Carole F., 2803
Haas, Chara C., 2803
Haas, David R., 2315
Haas, David W., 2803
Haas, Elise S., 163
Haas, Evelyn D., 164
Haas, Frederick R., 2803
Haas, Janet F., 2803
Haas, John C., 2803
Haas, Mary F., 3024
Haas, Otto, 2803
Haas, Paul R., 3024
Haas, Peter E., 163, 212, 288
Haas, Peter E., Jr., 163, 212
Haas, Phoebe W., 2803
Haas, Raymond P., 3024
Haas, Rene, 3024
Haas, Robert D., 164, 212, 1922
Haas, Thomas C., 2557
Haas, Thomas W., 2803
Haas, Walter A., 163
Haas, Walter A., Jr., 163, 164
Haas, Walter J., 163, 164
Haas, William D., 2803
Haas Charitable Trusts, Otto Haas &
   Phoebe W., 2803
Haber, Thomas R., 2396
Haberman, F.W., 3281
Habif, David V., 2123
Hachmann, Hans G., 2020
Hackel, M., 237
Hackerman, W., 1100
Hackett, Luther F., 3160
Hadac, Lucy Johnson, 3056
Haddock, Ronald W., 3010
Haensel, Peter C., 3274, 3289
Haerr, Donna, 918
Haeussler, Marilyn, 1299
Hafer, Fred D., 2864

Haft, Daniel Foster, 1923
Haft, Gloria G., 1107, 1108
Haft, Herbert H., 1107, 1108
Haft, Linda, 1107, 1108
Haft, Robert M., 1107, 1108
Haft, Wendy L., 1923
Hagan, Joseph, 1295
Hagedorn, William, 1970
Hager, Louis Busch, Jr., 613
Hager, Mary K., 2519
Hagerstrom, C. Richard, Jr., 2929
Haggar, Edmond R., Sr., 3025
Haggar, Joseph M., Sr., 3025
Haggar, Joseph M., Jr., 3025
Haggar, Rose M., 3025
Haggar Co., 3025
Haggerty, Betty Lee, 1680
Haggerty, Gretchen R., 2853
Haggerty, Robert Johns, 1959
Haggin, Margaret Voorhies, 1971
Hague, Thad, 2437
Hahn, Mary Louise, 2600
Hahn, Nick, 914
Hahn, T. Marshall, Jr., 712
Haight, Deborah, 2772
Haigney, John E., 454
Haines, Robert H., 2152
Hair, Charles M., 215
Hakim, Joseph E., 552
Hale, Elfreda, 165
Hale, Elwyn C., 165
Hale, M. Eugenie, 165
Halepeska, Robert, 3041
Haley, Beverly, 360
Halff, G.A.C., 3026
Halff, Hugh, Jr., 3026
Halff, Marie M., 3026
Hall, Adah F., 1166
Hall, Adele C., 1533
Hall, Andrew J., 2242
Hall, Charles T., 1933
Hall, Charles W., 2948, 2957
Hall, Daniel S., 631
Hall, David M., 1376
Hall, Donald J., 1525, 1527
Hall, E.A., 1525
Hall, Elizabeth, 850
Hall, Evelyn A., 2736
Hall, F. Richard, 3268
Hall, Gordon, 3151
Hall, Jesse C., 702
Hall, Jesse S., 703, 724
Hall, John, 3220
Hall, John F., 297
Hall, Joseph H., 1112
Hall, Joseph S., 1127
Hall, Joyce C., 1525
Hall, Lowell K., 1020
Hall, Lyle G., 2840
Hall, Lyle G., Jr., 2840
Hall, Margie, 1694
Hall, Mortimer W., 2252
Hall, R.A., 3333
Hall, R.B., 1525
Hall, Roderick C.M., 234
Hall, Serena Davis, 590
Hall, William A., 1525, 1527
Hallam, Howard, 3044
Hallam, Robert, 3044
Hallaq, Issa Y., 41
Halle, Edward A., 1138
Hallen, Philip B., 2723
Hallene, Alan M., 887
Hallinan, Cornelia I., 2528
Hallmark Cards, Inc., 1525, 1527
Hallock, David P., 1193
Hallock, Richard W., 2039
Hallock, Robert P., Jr., 1193
Hallowell, Barclay, 2770
Hallowell, Dorothy W., 2737
Hallowell, Howard T. III, 2737
Hallowell, Merritt W., 2737
Halls, Halsey, 1447

Halmond, John, 1365
Halper, Marice L., 1475
Halperin, Richard E., 2212
Halpern, C., 1085
Halpern, Charles R., 1870
Halprin, R., 2944
Halsell, Ewing, 3027
Halsell, Ewing, Mrs., 3027
Hamamoto, Howard, 752
Hamblett, Stephen, 2881
Hambrick, George W., Jr., 1752
Hamburg, Beatrix A., 1421, 1959, 1966,
   2213
Hamburg, David A., 1829
Hamby, Robert E., Jr., 2897
Hamilton, Ann O., 3045
Hamilton, Edward K., 406
Hamilton, Florence C., 2868
Hamilton, Florence P., 1528
Hamilton, Frank T., 2472
Hamilton, George E. III, 563
Hamilton, Gordon, 3247
Hamilton, Jack H., 327
Hamilton, James L. III, 2853
Hamilton, John D., 1828, 1933
Hamilton, Pamela J., 383
Hamilton, Peggy, 1330
Hamilton, Peter B., 993
Hamilton, Richard B., 768
Hamilton, Robert, 1528
Hamilton, Tullia Brown, 2460
Hamilton, William L., 224
Hamilton Bank, 2738, 2739
Hamje, Robert M., 2603
Hamm, Donald G., Jr., 3330
Hammack, John A., 3064
Hamman, George, 3028
Hamman, Henry R., 3028
Hamman, Mary Josephine, 3028
Hammer, Armand, 859
Hammer, Dru, 859
Hammer, Michael, 254
Hammer, Michael A., 859
Hammer, Roy A., 1173
Hammer, Thomas J., Jr., 286
Hammerly, Harry A., 1458, 1459
Hammes, Robert M., 785
Hammond, R.M., 2464
Hammonds, Risa, 710
Hammons, Royce, 2626
Hamolsky, Milton W., 2365
Hamolsky, Sandra Z., 2365
Hampton, Claudia H., 96
Hampton, Louis R., 2868
Hampton, Robert K., 2373
Hamrick, Charles F., 2892
Hamrick, John M., 2892
Hamrick, Wylie L., 2892
Hanavan, Claire F., 454
Hanavan, Taylor W., 454
Hancock, David, 3323
Hand, Avery, 2614
Hand, W. Brevard, 16
Hand, William Brevard, 19
Handelman, Donald E., 2093, 2283
Handelman, Joseph W., 2093, 2283
Handelman, Walter J., 2080
Handelman, William R., 2093, 2283
Handlan, Raymond L., 1763
Handleman, David, Sr., 1381
Handler, Leslie, 554
Hanes, Eldridge C., 2400
Hanes, Frank Borden, Sr., 2399
Hanes, Frank Borden, Jr., 2399
Hanes, Gordon, 2399
Hanes, James G. III, 2400
Hanes, R. Philip, Jr., 2399
Hankamer, Doris K., 3029
Hankamer, Earl Curtis, Jr., 3029
Hankins, Edward R., 33
Hankins, Ruth L., 33
Hanley, Daniel F., 1092
Hanley, Deborah, Sr., 493

Hanley, James A., 768
Hanley, John W., Sr., 615
Hanley, John W., Jr., 615
Hanley, Mary Jane, 615
Hanley, Mary Reel, 615
Hanley, Michael, 615
Hanley, Susan Jane, 615
Hanley, William Lee, Jr., 2011
Hanna, David, 28
Hannon, Patrick H., 166
Hannon, William Herbert, 95, 166
Hanrahan, Barbara D., 2158
Hanrahan, Clement E., 737
Hansen, A.G., 93
Hansen, Dane G., 1037
Hansen, Irving A., 1972
Hansen, Joanne B., 850
Hansen, Julia S., 1774
Hansen, Kenneth, 3315
Hansen, Richard W., 850
Hansen, Robert F., 2428
Hansen, Robert U., 379, 380, 387
Hansen, Rosalyn, 360
Hansler, John F., 3224
Hansmann, Ralph E., 2365
Hanson, James R., 3253
Hanson, Richard E., 1459
Hanson, Richard O., 1447
Hanson-Ristau, Josephine, 160
Hanssen, Marty Voelkel, 1122
Hanssen, Stephen A., 1122
Hapgood, Elaine P., 433, 1907
Harbaugh, Jane W., 2916
Harcourt, Ellen Knowles, 445
Hardee, Ernest F., 3201
Harden, Ercia E., 168
Harden, Eugene E., 168
Harden, Oleta J., 1685
Hardenbergh, Gabrielle, 1476
Hardenbergh, Ianthe B., 1476
Hardenbergh Charitable Annuity Trust,
  I., 1476
Harder, Henry U., 1630
Harder, William E., 1433
Hardesty, David C., Jr., 3265
Hardie, Eben, 1079
Hardin, P. Russell, 740, 741, 743
Harding, George Ann, 400
Harding, Louis, 1706
Hardinge Brothers, Inc., 1754
Hardison, James A., Jr., 2414
Hardware Supply, 2816
Hardwick Knitted Fabrics, Inc., 1255
Hardy, Donna, 1347
Hardy, Hubbard, 2971
Hardy, Joan, 3302
Hardy, Robert M., Jr., 1062
Hardy, William J., 3336
Hargrove, Joseph L., 1084
Harkless, Cathy, 2389
Harkness, Edward S., 1860
Harkness, Edward S., Mrs., 1860
Harkness, James W., 3175
Harkness, Stephen V., Mrs., 1860
Harkrider, Raymond, 922
Harl, Sidney W., 2173
Harland, John H., 715
Harland, Robert P., 3336
Harlem, Robert A., 2336
Harlow, James G., Jr., 2634
Harman, Nan M., 169
Harman, Reed L., 169
Harmon, Gail McGreevy, 565
Harner, G. William, 899
Harnett, Joseph D., 634
Harnois, L.P., 823
Harper, Charles M., 1587
Harper, Marianne S., 843
Harper, Philip S., 860
Harper, Philip S., Jr., 860
Harper-Wyman Co., 860
Harpole, Myron E., 297

Harrell, Harry H., 3212
Harrell, William A., 2466
Harriman, Gladys, 1973
Harriman, John, 463
Harriman, Mary W., 1974
Harriman, Pamela C., 1974
Harriman, Roland, 1973
Harrington, Donald D., 3030
Harrington, Earl W., Jr., 2868
Harrington, Francis A., 1201
Harrington, Francis A., Jr., 1201
Harrington, George, 1202
Harrington, George S., 525
Harrington, Jacquelyn H., 1201
Harrington, James H., 1201, 1295
Harrington, John L., 1298
Harrington, Sybil B., Mrs., 3030
Harris, Albert W., 820
Harris, Avery, 1919
Harris, Barbara L., 1643
Harris, Bette D., 862
Harris, Cameron M., 2401
Harris, Daniel, 1919
Harris, David, 818, 1698
Harris, Dorothy A., 197
Harris, E.B., 1122
Harris, Edward, 151
Harris, Edward C., 687
Harris, Freeman, 3090
Harris, George R., 1705
Harris, George W., 1643
Harris, Henry U., Jr., 1291
Harris, Henry U. III, 1291
Harris, Irving B., 863
Harris, J. Ira, 924
Harris, James, 2974
Harris, James J., 2401
Harris, Joan W., 863
Harris, John B., Jr., 1641
Harris, John H., 616
Harris, John Q., 41
Harris, John W., 2401
Harris, Katherine, 862
Harris, King W., 862
Harris, Lucile H., 616
Harris, Michael, 1919
Harris, Neison, 862, 863
Harris, Patricia B., 1347
Harris, Paul, 3013
Harris, Paul W., 3036
Harris, Robert C., 154
Harris, Robert Lynn, 3036
Harris, T. George, 2223
Harris, T.G., 3171
Harris, Walter I., 1643
Harris, William, 706
Harris, William W., 863
Harris Trust & Savings Bank, 794, 798,
  820, 846, 856, 943
Harrison, David B., 2145
Harrison, Edward E., 433
Harrison, Graham O., 1120
Harrison, Judy, 1890
Harrison, Lawrence M., 335
Harrison, Lois Cowles, 1866
Harrison, Nora Eccles Treadwell, 335
Harrison, Richard A., 335
Harrison, Ronald E., 2179
Harsco Corp., 2740
Hart, Barbara O., 622
Hart, Donald L., 2591
Hart, Frances Close, 2889, 2904
Hart, George D., 172
Hart, Jean E., 1475
Hart, John C., 2656
Hart, John M., 1143
Hart, Karen Schwartz, 2203
Hart, Margaret Stuart, 921
Hart, Roger, 2872
Hart, Tim, 1029
Hart, William D., Jr., 1982
Harte, Richard, Jr., 1291
Hartenstein, James L., 2461

Hartfield, Jay B., 1337
Hartford, George L., 1975
Hartford, John A., 1975
Hartford, Robert D., 90
Hartford, William, 2499
Hartford Fire Insurance Co., 455
Hartigan, Margaret D., 820
Hartigan, Mary, 836
Harting, Robert M., 2794
Hartle, Clifford G., 146
Hartley, Nedenia, 560
Hartley, Nedenia H., 2283
Hartley, Richard O., 1374
Hartloff, Paul W., Jr., 336
Hartman, Betty R., 934
Hartman, Daniel L., 2321
Hartmann, Virginia L., 1655
Hartmarx Corp., 864
Hartwell, David B., 1415
Hartz, Shelley A., 2726
Hartzell, G.W., 2500
Hartzell, Miriam H., 2500
Hartzell Industries, Inc., 2500
Harval, William, 3163
Harvey, Colleen C., 1409
Harvey, Constance, 2150
Harvey, Durwood C., 2924
Harvey, Elizabeth A., 106
Harvey, F. Barton, Jr., 1103
Harvey, Hal, 2115, 2150
Harvey, Herbert J., Jr., 1068
Harvey, James D., 2571
Harvey, James R., 334
Harvey, Joan, 2150
Harvey, Joseph, 2150
Harvey, Marion W., 1068
Harvey, Paul, 887
Harvey, Thomas E., 2120
Harvill, H. Doyle, 666
Hasbargen, Vernae, 1418
Hasbro, Inc., 2872, 2873
Hascoc, Andrew, 449
Hascoe, Lloyd, 449
Hascoe, Norman, 449
Hascoe, Stephanie, 449
Hascoe, Suzanne, 449
Haseltine, Art, 1505
Hashim, Carlisle V., 1122
Hashorva, Tanya, 2677
Haskell, Antoinette M., 561
Haskell, Coburn, 2501
Haskell, Mark, 2501
Haskell, Melville H., 2501
Haskell, Melville H., Jr., 2501
Haskell, Robert H., 561
Haskell, Schuyler A., 2501
Haskins, Ralph W., 1292
Haspel, Robert, Mrs., 1082
Hassel, Calvin, 2741
Hassel, Morris, 2741
Hassenfeld, Alan G., 2872, 2873
Hastings, Alfred B., Jr., 246
Hastings, Carl D., 198
Hastings, John T., Jr., 171
Hastings, Joseph V., 2084
Hatch, Francis W., 1235
Hatch, Francis W. III, 1677
Hatch, Margaret Milliken, 1976
Hatch, Rakia I., 1976
Hatch, Richard L., 1976
Hatch, Serena M., 1235
Hatcher, James A., 2463
Hatcher, Ruth, 1301
Hatfield, David L., 1349
Hatfield, Elizabeth, 2001
Hathaway, D.C., 2740
Hathaway, H. Grant, 1128
Hauben, Helen G., 635
Hauptfuhrer, Barbara D., 2808
Hauser, David L., 2387
Hauserman, Jacquita, 2451
Hauserman, Jacquita K., 2452
Hauslein, R.E., 2989

Hausman, Jack, 1977
Havens, Susan S., 2241
Haverty, J. Rhodes, 709
Haviland, David, 1994
Haviland, Ruth C., 3287
Hawaiian Electric Industries, Inc., 754
Hawaiian Trust Co., Ltd., 746, 750, 751,
  753, 757, 762
Hawkins, Chaille W., 3123
Hawkins, Harman, 1813
Hawkinson, Gary M., 2452
Hawley, Marion E., 2154
Hawn, Gates Helms, 1849
Hawn, Joe V., Jr., 3031
Hawn, Mildred, 3031
Hawn, W.A., Jr., 3031
Hawn, William Russell, 3031
Hawn, William Russell, Jr., 3031
Hay, John, 2093
Hayden, Charles, 1978
Hayden, J.P., Jr., 2590
Haydock, Francis B., Mrs., 1250
Hayes, Arthur H., Jr., 2083
Hayes, Betty Frost, 551
Hayes, Gerry, 1092
Hayes, J.K., 508
Hayes, Mariam C., 2378
Hayes, R.C., 2378
Hayes, Thomas A., 1547
Hayes, Tom, 1590
Haykin, Howard, 1855
Haykin, Marilyn, 1855
Hayling, Charles, 604
Hayner, H.H., 3254
Hayner, James K., 3254
Haynes, Harold J., 3240
Haynes, Larry N., 2917
Haynes, Maryann, 2706
Haynes, Noris R., Jr., 2932
Haynes, Thelma G., 1484
Hays, Frances McKee, 3061
Hays, Patricia A., 906
Hays, Preston, 701
Hays, Richard M., 2853
Hays, William H. III, Mrs., 529
Hayward, John T., 617
Hayward, Winifred M., 617
Haywood, Mary H., 2501
Haywood, T.C., 2378
Hazard, George, 1492
Hazeltine, Herbert S., 176
Hazelton, Robert L., 3061
Hazen, Joseph H., 1979
Hazen, Lita A., 2742
Head, Louise A., 2456
Head, R.J., 645
Head, Robert L., 911
Heafey, Edwin A., Jr., 125, 341
Heagney, L., 519
Heagney, Lawrence, 526
Healey, Harry W., 1161
Healy, Martha Ann Dumke, 3146
Healy, Patricia K., 976
Heard, Craig P., 1684
Heard, Drew R., 3062
Hearin, Robert M., Sr., 1491
Hearin, Robert M., Jr., 1491
Hearn, Ruby P., 1658
Hearn, Thomas A., 941
Hearst, George R., Jr., 1980, 1981
Hearst, John R., Jr., 1980, 1981
Hearst, Randolph A., 1980, 1981
Hearst, William R., Jr., 1980, 1981
Hearst, William Randolph, 1980, 1981
Heasley, Karen L., 2835
Heasley, Paul A., 2835
Heasley, Timothy, 2835
Heath, Charles K., 771
Heath, Harriet A., 771
Heath, John E.S., 771
Heaton, Mary Alice J., 1400
Hebert, C.J., 3023
Hebner, Paul C., 254

Hilton, Conrad N., 1596
Hilton, Eric M., 1596
Hilton, Steven M., 1596
Hiltz, Francie S., 2498
Hiltz, L. Thomas, 2498
Himmelman, Bonnie, 436
Hinchliff, James D., 936
Hinds, John A., 1762
Hinduja, G.P., 1206
Hinduja, P.P., 1206
Hinduja, Srichand P., 1206
Hinduja Trust, 1206
Hindy, James, 716
Hing, Gerald, 97
Hinkelman, L.G., 75
Hinks, Avis, 1366
Hinson, Robin L., 2393
Hipps, J.R., 729
Hipscher, Aaron, 1905
Hipwell, Arthur P., 1057
Hirsch, Philip J., 2025, 2122
Hirschey, Lee T., 2158
Hirschfeld, A. Barry, 361
Hirschfield, Ira S., 164
Hirschhorn, Barbara B., 1102, 1118
Hirschhorn, Daniel B., 1118
Hirschhorn, David, 1102, 1118
Hirschhorn, Michael J., 1118
Hirschl, Irma T., 1990
Hirshfield, Sylvia Weisz, 349
Hirt, F. William, 2722
Hiser, Harold R., Jr., 1702
Hitch, Harry M., 1743
Hitching, H. James, 2939
Hitchings, George H., 2377
Hitchner, Ruth, 2837
Hite, Betty, 383
Hitt, Wendy M., 2731
Hlavenka, Judith A., 492
Hoadley, Marilyn, 589
Hoag, David H., 3052
Hoag, George Grant, 175
Hoag, George Grant II, 175
Hoag, Grace E., 175
Hoag, Merritt E., 695
Hoag, Patty, 175
Hoar, Fred W., 139
Hobart, Sharon L., 3215
Hobbs, Emmert, 1119
Hobbs, F. Worth, 2668
Hobbs, Wilbur E., 2725
Hobby, Diana P., 3035
Hobby, Oveta Culp, 3035
Hobby, W.P., 3035
Hobby, William P., Jr., 3035
Hoben, John H., 1600
Hoberg, Arthur P., 3321
Hoblitzelle, Esther T., 3036
Hoblitzelle, Karl St. John, 3036
Hobson, Henry W., Jr., 2472
Hobstetter, Dorothy, 2520
Hochschild, Adam, 2052
Hock, Bernice, 1579
Hock, W. Fletcher, Jr., 1654
Hockaday, Irvine O., Jr., 1525, 1527
Hockenjos, G. Frederick, 1695
Hodes, Richard S., 624
Hodge, Eleanor D., 1177
Hodge, Lynn W., 2899
Hodges, Ashley W., 2422
Hodges, Gene R., 711
Hodges, Leland, 3116
Hodges, W.H., 3130
Hodgkinson, Marian A., 943
Hodgson, Morton S., Jr., 727
Hodsdon, Louise, 2329
Hoechst Celanese Corp., 1646
Hoechst Co., 2728
Hoechst-Roussel Pharmaceuticals, Inc., 1628
Hoelschen, Paul E., Jr., 771
Hoelzer, Alfred M., 2086
Hoenemeyer, Frank J., 1658, 1713

Hoernle, Adolph W., 1991
Hoerr, Edward, 918
Hoester, Robert G.H., 1521
Hoffberger, Judith R., 1135
Hoffenberg, Betty, 318
Hoffenberg, Marvin, 318
Hoffenberg, Peter H., 318
Hoffer, Robert M., 3324
Hoffius, Dirk C., 1340
Hoffman, Carol A., 184
Hoffman, Claire Giannini, 69
Hoffman, Effe K.D., 1208
Hoffman, Elaine S., 176
Hoffman, Eli, 1654
Hoffman, H. Leslie, 176
Hoffman, K., 398
Hoffman, Karen A., 57
Hoffman, Monica, 1936
Hoffman, Walter W., 215
Hoffmann, Michael J., 2583, 2600
Hoffmann-La Roche Inc., 1648
Hoffner, Charles C. III, 957
Hoffner, Roy C., 2425
Hofheimer, Alan J., 3199
Hofheimer, Carol Gerstley, 2698
Hofland, Brian F., 937
Hofman, Donald J., 2442
Hofmann, Kenneth H., 177
Hofmann, Lori, 177
Hofmann Co., 177
Hofmann-Sechrest, Lisa Ann, 177
Hogan, Bill, 1456
Hogan, Claude H., 342
Hogan, Dan III, 2633
Hogan, John E., Jr., 986
Hogan, Ronald P., 712
Hogancamp, Richard L., 1331
Hogen, Charles R., Jr., 1675, 1676
Hogg, Christopher, Sir, 1922
Hoggarth, Marilyn, 3231
Hoglund, W.E., 1336
Hoglund, William E., 1380
Hogness, John R., 1842
Hogue, William C., 407
Hohenlohe, Christian, 1791
Hohn, Harry G., 2148
Hokanson, Sandra, 1462
Hoke, Laurie, 2524
Hoke, M.N., Jr., 17
Holbert, James M., 2924
Holbrook, Alice Hager, 613
Holcomb, James R., 3116
Holcomb, Kent M., 2564
Holden, James S., 1345
Holden, Joseph M., 2461
Holden, Lynelle A., 1345
Holder, J.R., 2641
Holder, Richard G., 3203
Holderman, Pauline, 2622
Holding, Lewis R., 2405
Holdsworth, K. Jay, 3151
Holiday, Harry, Jr., 1614
Holifield, Marilyn, 587
Holland, Betty G., 708
Holland, Harold H., 1339
Holland, Hudson, Jr., 1346
Holland, J. Mack, Jr., 2391
Holland, J.P., 508
Holland, James W., 987
Holland, John, 739
Holland, William J., 708
Holleman, Matthew L. III, 1491
Holleman, Paul D., 359
Hollenbeck, Karen R., 1351
Hollenbeck, Susan L., 631
Hollendonner, Francis R., 3268
Hollern, John M., 1444
Hollern, Michael P., 1444
Hollern, Thomas R., 2615
Hollett, Byron P., 985
Holley, Barbara C., 1763
Holley, Danforth E., 1318
Holley, Earl, 1318

Holley, Earl, Mrs., 1318
Holley, Lisa C., 1318
Holley, Mark, 1318
Holley, Scott, 1318
Holley Carburetor Co., 1318
Holliman, Vonda, 1038
Holling, H.W., 814
Hollingsworth, Mildred, 619
Hollingsworth, Roger P., 2832
Hollingsworth, Susan Hunt, 2758
Hollington, Richard R., Jr., 33
Hollis, Howell, 718
Hollis, Jeffrey P., 2525
Hollis, Mark C., 622
Holloran, Thomas E., 1421
Holloway, Catherine, 642
Holloway, Henry S., 2545
Hollstadt, H.A., 1470
Holm, Herbert W., 581
Holman, David, 135
Holman, John W., Jr., 1651
Holmberg, Ronald K., 781
Holmberg, Ruth, 2916
Holmberg, Ruth S., 2300
Holmes, Cynthia, 1003
Holmes, Esther Smith, 181
Holmes, G. Burton, 2857
Holmes, Howdy, 1301
Holmes, John S., Jr., 2917
Holmes, Lee, 2646
Holmes, Reva A., 3293
Holmes, Robert, Jr., 1
Holmes, Robert W., Jr., 1265
Holmes, Ruth W., 2857
Holmes, Zan W., Jr., Rev., 2981
Holsapple, R.W., 2636
Holser, Linda M., 1348
Holst, Eugene R., 1029
Holstrom, Carleton A., 2751
Holstrom, Christina L., 2751
Holstrom, Marcia O., 2751
Holt, Buford, 1003
Holt, Melvin W., 2986
Holtz, Jean, 3282
Holtzman, Robert, 2353
Holzman, Steven D., 117
Homer, Arthur F., 1312
Homer, Ronald A., 1158
Homewood Holding Co., 1127
Honda of America Manufacturing, Inc., 2504
Hood, Charles H., 1210
Hood, Charles H. II, 1210
Hood, M. Gerald, 716
Hood, Mary Elizabeth, 1821
Hook, June C., 1054
Hook, Robert L., 1054
Hook Drugs, Inc., 994
Hooker, Janet A. Neff, 2752
Hooker, Raymond C., Jr., 3193
Hooker, Robert L., 1340
Hooks, Larry B., 708
Hoolihan, James, 1418
Hooper, Adrian S., 2753
Hooper, Bruce H., 2753
Hooper, Ralph W., 2753
Hooper, Ruth R., 771
Hooper, Thomas, 2753
Hooper and Co., R.B., 3250
Hoopes, Judith H., 511
Hoopes, Townsend W., 2688
Hootkin, Pamela N., 2186
Hooton, Paula, 3012
Hoover, H. Earl, 866
Hoover, Herbert, Jr., 179
Hoover, Herbert III, 179
Hoover, Herbert W., Jr., 2506
Hoover, Lawrence R., 2505
Hoover, Margaret W., 179
Hoover, Miriam W., 866
Hoover, Thomas H., 2591
Hoover, Thomas H., M.D., 2505
Hoover Foundation, The, 2506

Hope, J.R., 2852
Hopkins, Donald, 2874
Hopkins, John E., 1349
Hopkins, L. Nelson, Jr., 1884
Hoppel, T.H., 2004
Hopper, W. David, 2224
Hopping, K.H., 2525
Hopwood, John M., 2754
Hopwood, Mary S., 2754
Hopwood, William T., 2754
Horack, T.B., 2419
Horack, Thom B., 2403
Horan, John J., 1658, 1676
Hord, Juanita A., 780
Hord, Robert E., 780
Hord, Robert E., Jr., 780
Horiszny, Pamela, 1301
Horkau, G.A., Jr., 3190
Horn, Albert J., 269
Horn, Audrey, 3035
Horn, C. Flager, 323
Horn, Craig, 1401
Horn, Jerold, 918
Horn, Karen N., 2224
Horn, Nini Moore, 96
Hornblower & Weeks - Hemphill, Noyes, 1212
Horne, Mabel A., 1213
Horner, Matina, 1930
Horner, Matina S., 2213
Horning, Jackie A., 2508
Hornor, Townsend, 1222
Horowitz, Gedale B., 2242
Horr, Robert G., Jr., 2158
Horsehead Resources, 2755
Horton, Alice Kirby, 1661
Horton, Raymond D., 1851
Horvitz, Jane R., 2572
Horvitz, William D., 580
Horwitz, S.T., 1159
Hoskins, William K., 1511
Hospital Corp. of America, 2925
Hotchner, A.E., 471
Hotel Americana, 2316
Hott, George D., 3264
Houchens, Ervin G., 1056
Houchens, George Suel, 1056
Houchens Markets, Inc., 1056
Houck, James R., 2800
Houff, Charlotte, 3183
Houff, Cletus E., 3183
Houff, Douglas Z., 3183
Houff, Dwight E., 3183
Houff Transfer, Inc., 3183
Hough, Richard R., 1713
Houghton, James L., 2627
Houghton, James R., 1864
Houghton, Leroy B., 264
Housatonic Curtain Co., 1205
House, Helen Fasken, 3006
Houser, Frances C., 2445
Houston, Lawrence P., Jr., 2407
Houston Post Co., The, 3035
Hovereid, Maxine, 943
Hovey, Robert D., 1365
Howard, Edith Mason, 1994
Howard, Ernestine Broadhurst, 2621
Howard, Frances L., 1757
Howard, Horace, 1209
Howard, Jay M., 2007
Howard, Jerome L., 2993
Howard, John D., 150
Howard, William J., 2117
Howe, Emma B., 1447
Howe, James E., 1631
Howe, Linda M., 756
Howe, Mitchell B., 180
Howe, Mitchell B., Jr., 180
Howell, Arthur, 685
Howell, James S., 2393
Hower, Frank B., Jr., 1052
Howland, John, 290
Howley, John J., 599

Ittleson, Nancy S., 2008
Ivens, Barbara J., 1337
Iverson, Eva M., 3221
Iverson, F. Kenneth, 2393
Ives, H. Byron III, 2384
Ives, J. Atwood, 1195
Ivey, Harriet M., 538
Ivey, Ray N., 2708

Jacangelo, Nicholas, 2160
Jack, Joseph E., 580
Jackson, Alexander, 2127
Jackson, Andrew E., 1826
Jackson, Ann G., 187
Jackson, Charles, 36
Jackson, David, 3097
Jackson, Dorothy, 1779
Jackson, Edgar R., 264
Jackson, Eugene W., 2729
Jackson, J.F., 656
Jackson, J.W., Rev., 797
Jackson, Jack B., 2972
Jackson, Joe S., 275
Jackson, John D., 3178
Jackson, John E., 2548
Jackson, John N., 1417
Jackson, Maria C., 2653
Jackson, Marie Louis, 2729
Jackson, Monty J., 3081
Jackson, Palmer G., 187
Jackson, Peter, 187
Jackson, Peter A., 3228
Jackson, R.L., 901
Jackson, Sam, 217
Jackson, Stephen K., 712
Jackson Family Charitable Trust, Ann, The, 187
Jackson Mills, 2896
Jacob, Nancy, 1499
Jacobs, Burleigh E., 3301
Jacobs, J., 259
Jacobson, Allen F., 1458
Jacobson, Arthur L., 2009
Jacobson, Benjamin J., Jr., 2009
Jacobson, Charles W., 348
Jacobson, Jennifer, 1804
Jacobson, Leon O., 957
Jacobson, Lester E., 323
Jacobson, Malcolm B., 2698
Jacobson, Robert J., Sr., 2009
Jacobson, Robert J., Jr., 2009
Jacobson, Sally S., 3103
Jacobson, Sibyl C., 2117
Jacobson & Sons, Benjamin, 2009
Jacobus, Catherine H., 1791
Jacott, William E., 1408
Jacquette, F. Lee, 27
Jaffe, Edwin A., 2875
Jaffe, Ira J., 1407
Jaffe, Lola, 2875
Jaffe, Meyer, 2875
Jaffe, Miles, 1397
Jaffe, Robert, 2875
Jagow, Elmer, 2487
Jaicks, Frederick G., 868
Jaixen, Adla V., 1250
Jaixen, Charles B., 1250
Jalkut, Thomas P., 1260
Jallow, Raymond, 297
Jalonick, Mary M., 2981
James, George B., 212, 357
James, Jean Butz, 810
James, Patrick J., 1819
James, Ron, 400
Jameson, Ida M., 188
Jameson Corp., J.W., 188
Jamison, Zean, 2403, 2419
Jammal, Eleanor A., 2437
Janicki, Robert S., 768
Jannopoulo, Jerome A., 659
Jannotta, Edgar D., 796, 820

Janroe, Jane, 2639
Jansen, Arthur, 1997
Jansen, Raymond A., Jr., 446
Jansson, Douglas M., 2882
Januszewski, Edward, 469
Jao, C.S. Daisy, 1157
Japhet, Dan R., 3005, 3073
Jaqua, George R., 1654
Jaquith, Richard D., 930
Jaret, Ralph E., 659
Jarratt, Ernestine, 3102
Jarratt, Frank W., 3102
Jarratt, J.B., 3102
Jarrett, Jerry V., 2457, 2600
Jarvis, Charles H., 290
Jarvis, J. Kirkland, 3211
Jasinski, Gerald, 1366
Jath Oil Co., 2628
Jaudes, Robert C., 1538
Javier, Rey, 130
Jayswal, B.K., 78
Jeanmougin, David T., 2557
Jefferson Bank and Trust, 369
Jefferson Smurfit Corp., 1531
Jefferson State Bank, 3099
Jeffress, Robert M., 3186
Jeffries, McChesney H., 687
Jeffries, Yasmin Aga Khan, 1806
Jeffris, Thomas M., 3290
Jehan, Norman P., 2874
Jelden, Philip M., 304
Jelp Assocs., 2108
Jencks, Anne B., 1281
Jenison, William A., 1419
Jenkins, Charles H., Sr., 622
Jenkins, Charles H., Jr., 622
Jenkins, George P., 611
Jenkins, George W., 622
Jenkins, Howard, 622
Jenkins, John S., 1494
Jenkins, Paul R., 2683
Jenkins, Thomas M., 269, 2467
Jenkins, William R., 842
Jenks, John T., 628
Jenks, R. Murray, 628
Jennings, A. Drue, 1533
Jennings, Christina, 2762
Jennings, Evan D. II, 2762
Jennings, James, 1216
Jennings, Louis C., 2917
Jennings, Mary Hillman, 2762
Jennings-Byrd, Phyllis, 369
Jenrette, Richard H., 2224
Jensen, Carl D.F., 3220
Jensen, Debra J., 1027, 1028
Jensen, Frederick W., 3317
Jensen, Kathryn, 1418
Jenson, Thor, 1020
Jepsen, Sarah, 1762
Jepson, Hans G., 1758
Jernstedt, Dorothy, 170
Jerome, Frank, 189
Jerome, Joseph M., 2794
Jerome, Richard, 189
Jerrold, Douglas M., 3203
Jerue, Richard A., 1315
Jess, Mary Jo, 1408, 1418
Jesselson, Erica, 2010
Jesselson, Ludwig, 1921, 2010
Jesselson, Michael, 2010
Jessiman, Andrew G., 1250
Jessup, John B., 2312
Jewell, Robert, 1365
Jewett, George F., Jr., 190, 1486
Jewett, George Frederick, 190
Jewett, Lucille McIntyre, 190
Jewett, Robert K., 2984
Jewish Communal Fund, 2207
Jews, William, 1095
Jinks, G.C., Jr., 719

Jinks, G.C. III, 719
Jinks, H.L., 719
Jinks, Larry, 291, 629
JMK International, Inc., 876
Jobe, Warren Y., 711
Jochum, Emil, 2513
Joe, Margie, 2977
Joelson, Julius, 2012
Joelson, Stella, 2012
Johann, C.F., 874
John, Victor B., 2891
Johns, Richard J., 2857
Johns, Sheryl L., 3037
Johns, William M., 2624
Johnson, A.D., 870
Johnson, Alice, 713
Johnson, Allan, 2430
Johnson, Alvin, 146
Johnson, Becki, 3249
Johnson, Betty Wold, 2014
Johnson, Bruce R., 671
Johnson, C.E., 2641
Johnson, Carmella, 105
Johnson, Charleen L., 1238
Johnson, Charles B., 269
Johnson, Charles Ray, 1158
Johnson, Charlotte S., 1420
Johnson, Christopher, 191
Johnson, Christopher W., 2014
Johnson, Claudia H., 3050
Johnson, Curtis W., 1457
Johnson, Dale A., 1383
Johnson, David T., 733
Johnson, Deane F., 2315
Johnson, Diane T., 870
Johnson, Donald E., Jr., 1400
Johnson, Donald H., 1383
Johnson, Dorothy A., 1351
Johnson, Douglas L., 3201
Johnson, Douglas R., 1880
Johnson, Edward C. III, 1188
Johnson, Elizabeth Hill, 2655
Johnson, Elizabeth Ross, 2014
Johnson, Frank, 1419
Johnson, Frank M., 1401
Johnson, George, 686
Johnson, Geraldine W., 417
Johnson, Glen, 1145
Johnson, Glen M., 819
Johnson, Gwen A., 3330
Johnson, Hilda, 2428
Johnson, Howard B., 1221
Johnson, Howard Bates, 1221
Johnson, Howard D., 1221
Johnson, Howard Marshall, 3006
Johnson, Howard W., 2273
Johnson, Ivan, 1025
Johnson, J. Dorsey, Mrs., 1130
Johnson, J. Lee IV, 2965
Johnson, J. Phillip, 2426
Johnson, J.M. Hamlin, 2840
Johnson, James A., 538
Johnson, James D., 2337
Johnson, James D., Mrs., 2337
Johnson, Jerry R., 2893
Johnson, Judy, 32
Johnson, Kay, 1933
Johnson, Keith A., 3105
Johnson, Lawrence M., 748
Johnson, Lelia C., 362
Johnson, Lillie A., 3041
Johnson, Luci B., 3050
Johnson, Lyndon B., 3050
Johnson, Lyndon B., Mrs., 3050
Johnson, M.G., 3041
Johnson, Madeleine Rudin, 2236
Johnson, Marjory Hughes, 1996
Johnson, Mark L., 2965
Johnson, Mary W., 265
Johnson, Mayo, 1485
Johnson, Norman E., 823
Johnson, Patricia B., 1365
Johnson, Patricia Bates, 1221

Johnson, Paul A., 1357
Johnson, Peter J., 1408
Johnson, Richard S., 2157
Johnson, Robert H., 43
Johnson, Robert O., 681
Johnson, Robert W. IV, 2014
Johnson, Robert Wood, 1658
Johnson, Roland H., 2803
Johnson, Roni, 1006
Johnson, Samuel C., 3293
Johnson, Samuel S., 2655
Johnson, Stephen L., 136
Johnson, Thomas, 629
Johnson, Thomas Nelson Page, Jr., 3179
Johnson, Thomas Nelson Page III, 3179
Johnson, Tina, 622
Johnson, Tom, 2224
Johnson, Virginia, 1590
Johnson, Walter S., 191
Johnson, Walter W., Jr., 2506
Johnson, Wayne J., 870
Johnson, Wilma, 2900
Johnson & Johnson Baby Products, 2728
Johnson & Son, S.C., Inc., 3293
Johnson and Johnson, 1657
Johnson Controls, Inc., 3292
Johnson-Helm, Elizabeth K., 2655
Johnston, Fred, 604
Johnston, Fred E., 2462
Johnston, James M., 551
Johnston, Martha K., 1099
Johnston, Mary E., 255
Johnston, Murray L., Jr., 3138
Johnston, Penelope D., 1873
Johnston, Robert L., 1337
Johnston, Susan Kennedy, 1352
Johnston, Vivian G., Jr., 16
Johnstone, John W., Jr., 474
Johnstone, Phyllis Kimball, 2876
Johnstone, Shana B., 178
Jon F., Hanson, 1691
Jonas, Charles F., 220
Jones, Adrienne L., 2457
Jones, Amy F., 457
Jones, Anna Faith, 1158
Jones, B. Bryan III, 1490
Jones, B.L., 3006
Jones, Bernard B. II, 1490
Jones, Bernice, 47, 48
Jones, Betty Alyce, 1597
Jones, Caroline, 1724
Jones, Clarence, 1598
Jones, D. Paul, Jr., 8
Jones, D.L.E., 1683
Jones, Daisy Marquis, 2015
Jones, David A., 1057
Jones, Deloria, 3257
Jones, Donald R., 903
Jones, E. Bradley, 2458
Jones, Edward L., Jr., 2677
Jones, Edwin L., Jr., 2393
Jones, Fletcher, 192
Jones, Geoffrey, 1724
Jones, Gordon S., 11
Jones, Harvey, 48
Jones, Harvey, Mrs., 48
Jones, Heidi Hall, 896
Jones, Helen Jeane, 1597
Jones, J.W., 740
Jones, James H., 825
Jones, Jerry, 360
Jones, Jerry D., 895
Jones, Jesse H., 3037
Jones, Jesse H., Mrs., 3037
Jones, John E., 815
Jones, John M., 2549
Jones, Joseph A., 1182
Jones, Joseph L., 2697
Jones, Joseph W., 696, 743
Jones, Judith B., 3142
Jones, L.M., 2852
Jones, Larry D., 2524
Jones, Marilyn M., 1680

Langengerg, Donald N., 2273
Langer, Harry, 217
Langfitt, Thomas W., 2806
Langford, J. Beverly, 1372
Langford, Thomas Anderson, 2386
Lanier, Susan I., 717
Lanigan, Joanne, 797
Lanigar, Mary, 191
Lannert, Robert C., 906
Lansaw, Judy W., 2467
Lansford, Robert M., 2979
Lapatin, J.A., 2359
Lapham, Frederick W. III, 3160
LaPierre, Donald J., 1292
LaPlaca, Frank S., 656
Laporte, Cloyd, Jr., 1890
Lappin, W.R., 1037
Lard, Mary P., 3049
Larin Oil and Gas Co., 1466
Lark, J. Andrew, 1871
Larkin, Frank Y., 2154
Larkin, June Noble, 2154
LaRosa, William R., 617
Larry, Richard M., 2824
Larsen, Christopher, 2053
Larsen, Jonathan Z., 2053
Larsen, Robert R., 2053
Larsen, Roy E., 2053
Larson, Carl E., 2018
Larson, Donald W., 1458
Larson, Kristin, 1442, 1443
Larson, Marie, 912
Larson, Steve, 3238
LaRussa, Benny M., Jr., 6
LaSalle National Bank, 820
Lasdan, Mildred D., 2055
Lasdon, Gene S., 2054
Lasdon, J.S., 2054
Lasdon, Jacob S., 2055
Lasdon, Jeffrey S., 2054
Lasdon, M.S., 2054
Lasdon, Mildred D., 2054, 2055
Lasdon, Stanley S., 2054
Lasdon, W.S., 2054
Lasdon, William S., 2055
Laske, A.C., Jr., 2134
Laske, Arthur C., 2134
Lasker, Albert D., 2056
Lasker, Bernard J., 2057
Lasker, Mary W., 2056
Lasky, Sheldon, 3310
Lasser, Miles L., 2265
Lassiter, John W., 2369
Lassiter, Reynolds, 2368
Lasurdo, I. Jerry, 2331
Latham, John Brace, 416
Lathem, Edward, 122
Latimer, Ray, 2
Lattner, Forrest C., 631
Lattner, Forrest C., Mrs., 631
Lattner, Francis H., Mrs., 631
Latzer, Richard N., 334
Lauder, Estee, 2058
Lauder, Joseph H., 2058
Lauder, Leonard A., 2058
Lauder, Ronald S., 2058
Lauderbach, C. Ward, 1402
Lauderbach, William, 1299
Laughlin, Alexander M., 1975
Lauren, Charles B., 1970
Laurent, Carol, 1419
Lauricella, Francis E., Mrs., 1082
Laurie, Marilyn, 1762
Laventhol, David, 446
Laventhol, David L., 331
Laverack, Melissa, 1293
Lavezzo, Nellie, 63
Lavezzorio, Joan F., 891
Lavezzorio, Leonard M., 891
Lavezzorio, Tina, 891
LaViers, Barbara P., 1060
LaViers, Harry, 1060
LaViers, Harry, Jr., 1060

LaVoie, Rosemary, 1094
Law, Mary Jane, 633
Law, Robert O., 633
Law, Robert O. III, 633
Lawford, Patricia Kennedy, 552
Lawler, Oscar T., 247
Lawlor, Kieran J., 2146
Lawrence, Anne I., 2510
Lawrence, Barbara Childs, 1737
Lawrence, David, 587
Lawrence, Emily D., 1724
Lawrence, J. Vinton, 1737
Lawrence, James F., Mrs., 422
Lawrence, John E., 1206, 1214
Lawrence, John T., Jr., 2472
Lawrence, John T., Jr., Mrs., 2582
Lawrence, Kent, 786, 919
Lawrence, Larry E., 1033
Lawrence, Lind, 3189
Lawrence, Pauline, 2657
Lawrence, Ralph, 2920
Lawrence, Robert A., 1237, 1271
Lawrence, Robert J., 786, 919
Lawrence, Starling R., 422
Lawrence, Sull, 273
Lawrence, William J., Jr., 1349
Lawrence Aviation Industries, Inc., 2059
Lawrenz, Ruthmarie M., 3324
Laws, D.P., 2370
Lawson, Barbara B., 224
Lawson, Jay Bird, 2731
Lawton, Barbara P., 1521
Lay, Kenneth L., 3000
Laybourne, Everett B., 264
Layton, Thomas C., 153
Lazar, Helen B., 2060
Lazar, Jack, 2060
Lazar, William B., 2060
Lazarus, Charles, 1666
Lazarus, Cynthia A. Cecil, 2613
Lazarus, Leonard, 2279
Leach, Frances V., 2427
Leach, Phillip M., 3117
Leach, Thomas W., 2427
Leahy, Beverly H., 2402
Leahy, Charles E., 1301
Leahy, Michael S., 1369
Leahy, Richard A., 1249
Leamon, Joyce, 39
Lear, Frances, 1859
Lear, Lyn, 207
Lear, Norman, 207, 1859
Leary, Hugh K., 3186
Leather, Richard B., 1928
Leavens, Margaret R., 1667
Leavens, William B., Jr., 1667
Leavens, William B. III, 1667
Leavey, Dorothy E., 208
Leavey, Joseph James, 208
Leavey, Thomas E., 208
Leavitt, Michael D., 1295
Lebanon-Citizens National Bank, The, 2456
LeBein, Mary Ellen, 1852
LeBien, Alfred J.W., 1852
LeBien, Harry A., 1852
Leblang, Paul, 405
LeBlond, Daniel, 2456
LeBoeuf, Raymond W., 2812
LeBrun, Al, 383
LeBuhn, Robert, 1630
Lebworth, Carol G., 443
Leckart, Ida G., 1199
Leckrone, Charles H., 3200
Lederberg, Joshua, 1829, 2213
Lederer, Adrienne, 878
Lederer, Anne P., 879
Lederer, Francis L. II, 878
Lederman, Carol, 1711
Lederman, Constance M., 2123
Ledonne, Edmond V., 405
Lee, Carol Mon, 758
Lee, Charles R., 444

Lee, Francis Childress, 584
Lee, Homer W., 2608
Lee, Irene S., 557
Lee, J. Phillip, Mrs., 2189
Lee, J.R., 1441
Lee, James, 2047
Lee, James T., 2061
Lee, Joanne Brown, 1691
Lee, John Marshall, 417
Lee, Lewis S., Jr., 584
Lee, Mary Elizabeth, 720
Lee, Philip R., 194
Lee, Ray M., 720
Lee, Robert E., 369
Lee, Robert W., 2608
Lee, Thomas H., 2579
Lee, Wayne J., 1082
Lee, William S., 2387
Lee, William S. III, 2401
Lee, Yvonne A., 1337
Lee Enterprises, 1022
Leegant, Bernard, 1918
Leemhuis, Andrew J., 1484
Leeming, E. Janice, 1228
Lees, Wendy S., 355
Leeson, Joseph F., Jr., 2772
LeFevour, Suzanne A., 1422
Lefkowitz, Elise G., 544
Lefkowitz, Sidney M., Rabbi, 681
Lefkowitz, Stephen, 1930
Lefrak, Samuel J., 2062
Left, Peter, 1689
Leftwich, S.E., 817
LeGrand, Clay, 1015
Lehigh Valley Bank, 2772
Lehman, Alan G., 2674
Lehman, Edward, 361
Lehman, Elliot, 908
Lehman, Evelyn J., 1852
Lehman, Frances, 908
Lehman, Jane A., 2674
Lehman, Kenneth, 908
Lehman, Lucy, 908
Lehman, Paul, 908
Lehman, Ronna Stamm, 908
Lehmann, Otto W., 880
Lehner, Melk M., 2367
Lehnhardt, M.H., Rev., 3041
Lehr, Gustav J., 1563
Lehrman, Charlotte F., 554
Lehrman, Jacob J., 554
Lehrman, Robert, 554
Lehrman, Samuel, 545, 554
Leiblien, Frank, 323
Leibovitz, Morris P., 2063
Leibrock, Robert L., 2941
Leidy, John J., 1123
Leif, Carol Ann, 347
Leighner, William H., 2537
Leiman, Joan, 2147
Leinbach, Harold O., 2800
Leinbach, Peter, 2800
Leinbach, Richard O., 2800
Leith, Dean, Jr., 1994
Leitman, Nanetta L., 2055
Leitzinger, Joseph L., 3236
LeJeune, Michael L., 290
Leland, Leslie S., 3223
Lelash, Marie Keese, 463
Lelash, Richard, 463
Lemann, Thomas B., 1068, 1087
Lemke, Carl R., 3280
Lemon, Clinton, 2891
Lemons, Wishard, 2621
Lenahan, Helen Dent, 1884
Lenahan, Marilyn S., 3155
Lenczuk, Kimberly Duchossois, 838
Lenhart, Carole S., 574
Lenkowsky, Leslie, 1732, 1800
Lennon, A.P., 2521
Lennon, Fred A., 2521
Lennox, John W., 1563
LeNoir, Bertram E., Jr., 2924

Lenoir, James S., 1489
Lents, Max R., 197
Lentz, Hover T., 361
Leo, Diana, 2204
Leonard, Judith S., 1782
Leonard, Marty, 3116
Leonard, William J., 633
Leonardi, Alfredo, 272
Leongomez, Carol, 583
Leonhardt, Frederick H., 2064
Leontief, Wassily, 2281
Leopard, Jack, 1366
Lepak, Robert R., 1178
Leppen, Michael A., 866
Lerchen, Edward H., 1353
Lerman, Philip, 3282
Lerner, Bernice L., 2384
Lerner, I., 1648
Lerner, Morton S., 2384
Lesesne, Joab M., Jr., 2902
Lesher, Margaret W., 2773
Lesinski, Dean A., 1939
Lesley, J. Kenneth, 2375
Leslie, Charles M., 3225
Leslie, Diane C., 1008
Leslie, Gaylord E., 2604
Lesner, J., 99, 237, 238
Lesner, Jules, 236
Lessing, Fred W., 1991
Lessler, Edith, 318
Lester, Charles R., 3270
LeSuer, W.M., 2525
Letts, Christine W., 993
Leuenberger, Richard L., 3316
Leuthold, Betty B., 3234
Leuthold, Caroline E., 3234
Leuthold, John H., 3234
Levan, B.W., 3104
LeVan, John A., 372
Levas, Dimitri, 2088
Levee, Polly Annenberg, 2774
Leveen, Leonard, 1861
Leventhal, Walter, 2841
Lever Brothers Co., 2323, 2728
Levett, Edith, 1966
Levey, Norman James, 1379
Levey, Richard H., 1379
Levi, Arlo D., 1458, 1459
Levi, Constance M., 1452
Levi Strauss & Co., 212
Levie, Charles M., 881
Levie, Jerome M., 881
Levie, Maude M., 881
Levin, Elisabeth L., 2065
Levin, Jack I., 1471
Levin, John A., 2065
Levin, Lucile Lansing, 125
Levine, Al, 1678
Levine, George, 448
Levine, Hirschell E., 2260
Levine, Joel, 2597
Levine, Joseph, 1921
Levine, Rachmiel, 1628
Levine, Seymour, 1965
Levinson, Albert, 130
Levinson, Carl A., 2794
Levinson, Donald M., 2701
Levinson, Edward, 682
Levinson, Gerald, 2849
Levis, William E., 2453
Levison, S. Jarvin, 709
Leviton, Harold, 2066
Leviton, Louis, 349
Leviton, Shirley, 2066
Leviton Manufacturing Co., 2066
Levitt, Arthur, Jr., 2213, 2224, 2352
Levitt, Joe, 217
Levitt, Richard S., 1462
Levy, Andrew H., 2152
Levy, Austin T., 1225
Levy, David, 729
Levy, Edward C., Jr., 1355
Levy, Ellen White, 2109

Marohn, William D., 1399
Maroney, Eleanor S., 510
Marquardt, Laura, 1442
Marquet, Kay, 309
Marquis, Robert S., 2409
Marran, Elizabeth, 2029
Marran, Ethel K., 2029
Marran, Laura, 2029
Marriott, Alice S., 556
Marriott, J. Willard, 556
Marriott, J. Willard, Jr., 556
Marriott, Richard E., 556
Marriott Charitable Annuity Trust, J.
   Willard, 556
Marron, Donald B., 1875, 2172
Mars, B.S., 2727
Mars, Forrest E., 3191
Mars, Forrest E., Jr., 3191
Mars, John F., 3191
Marsella, Al, 68
Marsh, Charles Edward, 561
Marsh, Harold, 134
Marsh, Miles L., 1554
Marshal, Rose M., 1149
Marshall, Douglas B., Jr., 2980
Marshall, Gerald R., 2626
Marshall, Harriet McDaniel, 724
Marshall, John D., 2895
Marshall, John E. III, 1353
Marshall, Louise F., 36
Marshall, Ray, 1829
Marshall, Thomas C., 123
Marshall, Thomas O., 723
Marshall, William G., 2464
Marshall, William H., 985, 1155
Marshall & Ilsley Bank, 3301
Marshall & Ilsley Trust Co., 3288, 3306
Marsico, Louis J., Jr., 893
Marsilius, Newman M., Jr., 417
Martell, Saundra A., 1445
Martens, R.D., 1048
Martin, Ada La May, 889
Martin, Bert W., 889
Martin, C. Cecil, 1056
Martin, C. Virgil, 2115
Martin, Carmel C., Jr., 65
Martin, Carol E., 598
Martin, Casper, 1002
Martin, Elio L., 191
Martin, Elizabeth, 1002
Martin, Esther, 1002
Martin, Geraldine F., 1002
Martin, Gertrude Ann, 1671
Martin, Glen K., 280
Martin, Glenn R., Mrs., 3202
Martin, Ian A., 1442, 1443
Martin, Jack, 1329
Martin, Jennifer, 1002
Martin, John H., 1365
Martin, John R., 2569
Martin, Judith W., 2350
Martin, Lawrence G., 887
Martin, Lee, 1002
Martin, Lee P., Jr., 3189
Martin, Lois Lynn, 1056
Martin, Louis, 1303
Martin, Malcolm E., 413
Martin, Maurice H., 2939
Martin, Oscar T., 2581
Martin, Ralph H., 655
Martin, Robert Allan, 1671
Martin, Robert E., Jr., 2437
Martin, Roger L., 1384
Martin, Ross, 1002
Martin, Ruth, 1787
Martin, S. Walter, 695
Martin, Sylvia, 1671
Martin, Wayne S., 899
Martin, William T., 1757
Martin Marietta Corp., 1125
Martinez, Ignacio R., 106
Martinez, Nestor, 566
Martinez, Pete R., 3099

Martinez, William, 382
Martone, Joan Dalis, 3173
Martorella, Joseph, 2030
Maruhashi, M., 333
Marvin, Charles H. III, 2893
Marvin, Dennis H., 1311
Marx, Harry, 2091
Marx, Helen Schulman, 2091
Maryland National Bank, 1128
Mascotte, John P., 1525
Maslow, Carol, 2108
Mason, Elaine, 625
Mason, James K., 215
Mason, Katherine A., 1904
Mason, Paul W., 2965
Massaro, Marie F., 407
Massee, D. Lurton, Jr., 686
Massey, Doris J., 2781
Massey, E. Morgan, 3192
Massey, H.B., 2781
Massey, Jack C., 2930
Massey, James L., 2242
Massey, Joe B., 2781
Massey, William Blair, 3192
Massey, William E., Jr., 3192
Massey, William L., Mrs., 3090
Massey, William L. III, 2691
Massey Coal Co., A.T., Inc., 3192
Massey Rental, 2781
Massi, Frank, 1980, 1981
Master, El Roy P., 2761
Master, Helene L., 2761
Master, Joseph J., 601
Masterson, Carroll S., 3095
Masterson, Harris, 3095
Mastrangelo, Regina, 2021
Mastronardi, Carrie, 2092
Mastronardi, Charles A., 2092
Mastronardi, Margaret, 2092
Mastronardi, Nicholas D., 2092
Mastrota, Joan T., 451
Masuda, Hideki, 914
Masure, Morton, 281
Mather, Elizabeth Ring, 2528
Mather, Russell R., 2427
Mathers, G. Harold, 2093
Mathers, Leila Y., 2093
Matheson, Alline, 1774
Mathews, Jessica T., 2223
Mathey, Dean, 1621
Mathias, James H., 1784
Mathiasen, Karl, 1005
Mathieson, Andrew W., 2791
Mathis, Travis A., 2959
Mathison, William A., 1435
Mathson, Robert O., 1415
Matranga, Concetta, 2100
Matsch, J. Richard, 3280
Mattes, Joseph E., 2204
Matthews, B. Frank II, 2391
Matthews, Joe B., 2986
Matthews, John A., Jr., 2986
Matthews, Julia Jones, 2986
Matthews, Kade L., 2986
Matthews, L. White III, 2852
Matthews, Westina L., 2113, 2114
Matthews, William E. IV, 23
Matthies, Katherine, 466
Mattie, William A., 2560
Mattoon, Peter M., 2858
Matz, William, 2772
Mau, Richard R., 2819
Maudlin, John T., 709
Maulden, Jerry L., 45
Mauldin, Lyman H., 725
Mauldin, Vance, Mrs., 725
Maupin, Robert W., 1563
Maurer, Eleanor J., 2633
Maurer, Gilbert C., 1980, 1981
Maurer, Joseph, 212
Maurer, Mary Frances, 2628
Mauri Foods, 471
Mauritz, William W., 895

Mauze, Abby Rockefeller, 2223
Mavec, Ellen, 2586
Mawby, Russell G., 1351
Maxfield, Melinda, 226
Maxfield, Robert R., 226
Maxfield, Thomas O. III, 420
Maxon, Frank C., Jr., 2196
Maxwell, R. Blinn, 323
Maxwell, Robert E., 2683
May, Cordelia S., 2771
May, Gaylord, 1432
May, Irenee duPont, 523
May, Isabel, 612
May, L.H., 679
May, Peter, 612
May, Samuel D., 612
May, Thomas J., 1157
May, William F., 2242
May Department Stores Co., 1547
Mayberry, Sheila, 2618
Mayeda, Cynthia, 1433
Mayer, Allan C., 890
Mayer, Beatrice, 940
Mayer, Beatrice Cummings, 1870
Mayer, Elsa S., 890
Mayer, Harold F., 890
Mayer, Harold M., 890
Mayer, Helen Shumway, 2094
Mayer, Lorna L., 3299
Mayer, Louis B., 2095
Mayer, Oscar G., 890
Mayer, Oscar G., Sr., 890
Mayer, Paul, 2323
Mayer, R.D., 2614
Mayer, Robert N., 940, 1870
Mayerson, Manuel D., 2529
Mayerson, Philip, 1888
Mayerson, Rhoda, 2529
Mayher, John W., Jr., 717
Maynard, Ann, 1072
Maynard, Olivia T., 1323
Maynard, Robert C., 2224
Mayne, Calvin, 3181
Maynes, Judith A., 1762
Mayo, James O., 553
Mayrock, Elliot, 2096
Mayrock, Harry, 2096
Mayrock, Isidore, 2096
Mays, J.W., Inc., 2342
Maytag, Fred II, 1024
Maytag, Frederick L. III, 1024
Maytag, Kenneth P., 1024
Mazyck, Bernett, 2907
Mazza Trust, Louise T., 891
MCA, Inc., 227
McAdam, Susan S., 3103
McAdams, John R., 2898
McAdams, Rolla E., 1011
McAfee, John, 1652
McAfee, Robert E., 1092
McAlister, Consuela Cuneo, 829
McAlister, Fern Smith, 228
McAlister, Harold, 228
McAlister, Hobart S., 228
McAlister, Soni, 228
McAlister, Tim, 829
McAllister, Francis R., 1759
McAllister, Kenneth W., 2421
McAllister, Leo, 302
McAlonan, John A., 2530
McAree, Edward J., 2314
McAshan, S.M., Jr., 2968, 3056
McAshan, Susan C., 3056
McAvoy Trust, Agnes K., 801
McBean, Atholl, 229
McBean, Edith, 229
McBean, Peter, 229
McBeath, Andrew A., 3329
McBeath, Faye, 3302
McBride, Barbara, 1964
McBride, H.S. Graham, Mrs., 529
McBride, Hubert A., 2913, 2915
McBride, John H., 477

McCabe, Brooks F., Jr., 3265
McCabe, Eleonora W., 671
McCaffrey, Robert H., 1724
McCaffrey, William T., 1904
McCall, Arthur C., 2887
McCallie, Spencer III, 2916
McCallister, Alice, 445
McCamish, Henry F., Jr., 726
McCamish, Margaret P., 726
McCammon, David N., 1329, 1381
McCandliss, Len, 302
McCann, James J., 2097
McCann, Joseph F., 2179
McCanne, Robert H., 3136
McCannel, Dana D., 1481
McCannel, Laurie H., 1481
McCannel, Louise Walker, 1481
McCardle, M.A., 504
McCarter, C. Ted, 1553
McCarthy, C.V., 1622
McCarthy, Catherine, 2867
McCarthy, J. Thomas, 208
McCarthy, Jack, 1531
McCarthy, James A., 2098
McCarthy, James T., 230
McCarthy, Jane D., 230
McCarthy, John M., 2099
McCarthy, Kathleen Leavey, 208
McCarthy, Kristin L., 230
McCarthy, Louise Roblee, 1559
McCarthy, Lucy A., 2098
McCarthy, Marion P., 2098
McCarthy, Mary A., 2099
McCarthy, Mary E., 2315
McCarthy, Neil M., 2099
McCarthy, Peter F., 2098
McCarthy, Rachel K., 230
McCarthy, Robert H., 2098
McCarthy, Roblee, Jr., 1559
McCarthy, Stephen J., 2099
McCartin, William R., 1133
McCarty, Maclyn, 2348
McCarty, Marilu H., 707
McCashin, Helen B., 1781
McCaskey, Donald L., 2854
McCaskill, Beverly, 3119
McCasland, T.H., Jr., 2628
McCastlain, Hugh H., 46
McCaughan, Arthur R., 775
McClain, Marvin R., 267
McClarity, Harry C., 428
McClary, Donald F., 360
McClatchey, William, 686
McClenahan, Barry A., 2982
McClimon, Timothy J., 1762
McCloy, Ellen Z., 3194
McClung, James A., 842
McClung, Patrick L., 223
McClure, James J., Jr., 921
McClure, John V.N., 911
McColl, John A., 287
McCollow, Thomas J., 3302
McComas, Harrold J., 3284, 3340
McCombs, A. Parks, 2364
McCombs, Billy J., 3057
McCombs, Charline H., 3057
McConn, Christiana R., 3123
McConnell, B. Scott, 2100
McConnell, Leah F., 231
McConnell, Neil A., 2100
McConnell Trust III, Carl R., 231
McCormack, Elizabeth Jane, 887
McCormick, Anne, 2783
McCormick, Brooks, 892
McCormick, Charles Deering, 892
McCormick, J.L., 2429
McCormick, James H., 1331
McCormick, Mary, 1930
McCormick, Richard B., 1817
McCormick, Richard D., 400
McCormick, Robert R., 893
McCormick, Stephen, 849
McCormick, Thomas J., 3270

Menchette, James, 1960
Mendelsohn, Walter, 2025
Mendenhall, John R., 2772
Mendier, Donald, 2066
Mendik, Bernard H., 2110
Mendik, Susan, 2110
Mendoza, Roberto G., Jr., 2129
Menefee, Albert L., Jr., 2933
Menges, Carl B., 1966
Mengle, Glenn A., 2792
Menschel, David F., 2111
Menschel, Joyce F., 2111
Menschel, Richard L., 37, 1835, 1948
Menschel, Robert B., 1948, 2111
Menschel, Ronay, 1835
Menschel Foundation, The, 1835
Meoni, Ronald J., 2141
Mercader, George, 350
Mercantile Bank, N.A., 1532, 1550
Mercantile Bank of Springfield, 1565
Mercantile Bank of St. Louis, N.A., 1530
Mercantile Trust Co., 1550
Mercantile-Safe Deposit & Trust Co., 1098
Mercer, Bernard, 1025
Mercer, Henry D., Jr., 1927
Merchants National Bank & Trust Co., 992, 996
Merck, Adele Shook, 22
Merck, Albert W., 1676
Merck, Albert W., Jr., 1677
Merck, Antony M., 1677
Merck, Josephine A., 1677
Merck, Serena S., 1235
Merck, Wilhelm M., 1677
Merck & Co., Inc., 1676
Merck-Abeles, Anne, 1677
Mercy, Eugene, Jr., 2112
Mercy, Sue, 2112
Meredith Charitable Trust, Edna E., 1014
Meriden Trust & Safe Deposit Co., 458, 467
Meridian Bancorp, Inc., 2793
Meridian Bank, 2772
Meridian Trust Co., 2800, 2808
Merit Oil Co., 2794
Merkert, Eugene F., 1236
Merkert Enterprises, Inc., 1236
Merksamer, Geraldine F., 1925
Merlin, H. Stephen, 572, 726
Merlino, Astrid I., 3242
Merlo, Harry A., 2656
Merlotti, Frank H., 1384
Meroni, Denise, 1623
Merrell Dow Pharmaceuticals, Inc., 1511
Merriam, Robert, 1292
Merrick, Anne M., 1127
Merrick, Frank W., 2630
Merrick, Frank W., Mrs., 2630
Merrick, Jean D., 364
Merrick, Robert B., 2630
Merrick, Robert G., Sr., 1127
Merrick, Robert G. III, 1112, 1127
Merrick, Ward S., Jr., 2630
Merrill, Charles E., Sr., 1669
Merrill, Eleanor, 1104
Merrill, John S., 2
Merrill, Karen, 1763
Merrill, Philip, 1104
Merrill, Thomas, 168
Merrill Lynch Asset Management, Inc., 2989
Merrill Lynch, Pierce, Fenner & Smith, Inc., 2113
Merrin, Kenneth D., 1978
Merritt, Cynthia E., 1829
Merryman, Sam B., Jr., 181
Merryweather, Tom, 2430
Mertens, Gertrude H., 1650
Merthan, Claudia B., 361
Mertz, Richard J., 2115
Merves, Stanley, 2841
Mervis, M., 812

Mesalam, Russell D., 994
Meschke, John A., 118
Meserow, J. Tod, 941
Mesko, Carol, 2851
Messing, Andrew, 638
Messing, Gilbert, 638
Messing, Morris M., 638
Messinger, William C., 3318
Messner, R.T., 2798
Metcalf, Donna H., 1364
Metcalf, Karen, 2146
Metcalf, Stanley W., 2116
Methner, Cleland V., 1331
Metropolitan Life Insurance Co., 2117
Mettlen, Robert E., 2951
Mettler, Ruben F., 1676
Metzger, Henry L., 2503
Mewshaw, Linda, 2033
Meyer, Agnes E., 557
Meyer, Alex, 1018
Meyer, Alice K., 3066
Meyer, Arthur I., 644
Meyer, Baron de Hirsch, 639
Meyer, Bertram, 1678
Meyer, Carol R., 2324
Meyer, Charles G., Jr., 1851
Meyer, Daniel, 863
Meyer, Daniel P., 3280
Meyer, Eugene, 557
Meyer, Eva Chiles, 2650
Meyer, Fred G., 2657
Meyer, Gerald, 1900
Meyer, Henry L. III, 2442
Meyer, J.R., 2852
Meyer, John, 134
Meyer, John E., 18
Meyer, Lawrence A., 278
Meyer, Lyle L., 1531
Meyer, Phillipe, 2118
Meyer, Polly de Hirsch, 639
Meyer, Robert R., 18
Meyer, Roger F., 2771
Meyer, Ron J., 1456
Meyer, Roslyn M., 2123
Meyer, Russell W., Jr., 1035, 1048
Meyer, Vaughan B., 2984, 3066
Meyer, Vincent, 2118
Meyer, Virginia A.W., 476
Meyer Trust, M.L., 896
Meyers, Gail, 1982
Meyers, James, 3137
Meyers, Jerry K., 1384
Meyers, Mary Ann, 2675, 2676
Meyers, Robert M., 2141
Meyers, Warrin C., 2702
Meyerson, Ivan D., 232
Meyerson, Marvin, 937
Miami Corp., 831
Miami County National Bank and Trust, 1031
Michael, Elsa B., 3151
Michael, Max, Jr., 620
Michael, Sally, 1095
Michaels, William, 664
Michalis, Clarence F., 2083
Michaud, Sonja B., 1748
Michel, Bernice, 1314
Michel, Betsy S., 1655
Michel, Clifford L., 1655
Michelson, Gertrude G., 930, 2234
Michigan Avenue National Bank of Chicago, 932
Michigan National Bank, 1340
Michler, John, 3334
Mick, Roger E., 2925
Middlebrook, Stephen B., 406, 407
Middlebrooks, E.A., Jr., 665
Middleton, Henry B., Mrs., 2348
Midkiff, Robert R., 746, 750, 753
Mielke, John E., 3304
Mielnicki, Daniel D., 2025
Mihori, James S., 2495
Mike-Mayer, Maria, 2309

Mikkelsen, H.E., 125
Mikolaj, M.G., 2481, 2511
Mikusa, John, 806
Milano, Anthony V., 417
Milas, Lawrence W., 2274
Milbank, Albert G., 2109
Milbank, David M., 2109
Milbank, Dunlevy, 2119
Milbank, Jeremiah, 2011
Milbank, Jeremiah, Jr., 2011, 2120, 2263
Milbank, Jeremiah III, 2011
Milbank, Katharine S., 2011
Milbank, Samuel L., 2109, 2120
Milburn, Nancy S., 1259
Milby, Charles D., 3028
Miles, Inc., 1004
Miles, Mary L., 1616
Miles Inc., 2795
Milken, F., 236
Milken, L., 238
Milken, L.A., 236
Milken, L.J., 236
Milken, Lori A., 99, 237
Milken, Lowell, 236
Milken, Lowell J., 99
Milken, Michael, 236
Milken, Michael R., 99, 237
Milken, S., 99, 238
Milken, S.E., 236
Mill, Jean, 193
Millan, Jacqueline R., 2179
Millard, Kenneth E., 1381
Miller, Anne H., 2737
Miller, Arnold, 898
Miller, Buell, 1092
Miller, Burkett, 2939
Miller, Byron S., 828
Miller, C.G., 2603
Miller, Dana J., 3169
Miller, Diane Edgerton, 3187
Miller, Donn B., 96, 183
Miller, Duane, 978
Miller, Edward A., 322
Miller, Edward E., Jr., 2917
Miller, Edward J., 1381
Miller, Elaine G., 544
Miller, Eugene A., 1358
Miller, Frances Cameron, 2964
Miller, Francis C., 1024
Miller, Gary, 28
Miller, Gerald W., 2593
Miller, Harvey L., 898
Miller, Harvey S.S., 2677
Miller, J. Jefferson, 1138
Miller, Jack, 28
Miller, Jacqueline, 2888
Miller, James R., 1464
Miller, Jean, 763
Miller, Josepha S., 1138
Miller, Judith M., 2397
Miller, Kate W., 2560
Miller, Katharine K., 425
Miller, Kathryn B., 2122
Miller, Lester, 1506
Miller, Lewis N., Jr., 3170
Miller, Luther L., 2560
Miller, Mark A., 1305
Miller, Marlin M., Jr., 2697
Miller, Middleton, 835
Miller, Nancy, 232
Miller, P.G., 1100
Miller, Patricia Hillman, 2811
Miller, Paul, 3181
Miller, Paul F., Jr., 1922
Miller, Richard A., 2452
Miller, Robert C., 2193
Miller, Ruth, 654
Miller, Ruth C.H., 606
Miller, S.L., 3104
Miller, Sam, 2482
Miller, Shag, 1583
Miller, Talbot, 1792
Miller, Walter L., 2265

Millhouse, Barbara B., 2368
Milligan, Cynthia, 1590
Milligan, James H., 2638
Milligan, Lois Darlene, 2638
Milligan, Margaret L., 2638
Milligan, Michael J., 2638
Milligan, Nancy M., 1631
Milligan, Robert B., Jr., 489
Milliken, Agnes Gayley, 526
Milliken, Gerrish H., Jr., 526
Milliken, Minot K., 519
Milliken, Roger, 519, 526
Milliken, W. Dickerson, 175
Milliken, W.D., 43
Milliken, William G., 1922
Millikin, James, 899
Millipore Corp., 1238
Millner, Rita L., 875
Mills, Alice duPont, 507
Mills, Amelia Louise, 200
Mills, Anne Marie A., 1713
Mills, Basil, 240
Mills, Donald M., 1939
Mills, Frances Goll, 1360
Mills, Harold, 3079
Mills, John, 1728
Mills, John T., 2853
Mills, Kathryn, 640
Mills, Margaret C., 3265
Mills, Michael, 640
Mills, Phyllis J., 1833
Mills, Ralph E., 1062
Mills, Sharon, 2916
Mills, Suzanne B., 1354
Millsaps, Joe, 580
Millspaugh, Gordon A., Jr., 1719
Millstein, David J., 2796
Millstein, Jack H., Jr., 2796
Milne, Garth L., 903
Milone, Theresa A., 2313
Milstein, Edward L., 2123
Milstein, Howard P., 2123
Milstein, Irma P., 2123
Milstein, Paul, 2123
Milstein, Philip L., 2123
Milstein, Seymour, 2123
Milstein, Vivian, 2123
Milwaukee Golf Development Corp., 829
Minary, John S., 2173
Miner, Joshua L. IV, 1284
Miner, Phebe S., 1283, 1284
Mingenback, E.C., 1040
Mingst, Caryll S., 312
Minnema, John, 1654
Minnesota Mining & Manufacturing Co., 1459
Minnich, M.W., 3259
Minnick, B.R., 1563
Minnick, Walter, 2659
Minow, Martha L., 1959
Minow, Newton N., 1829
Minter, Steven A., 2457
Mirabella, Richard J., 2001
Mirick, John O., 1295
Mirman, Ralph, 3334
Miro, Jeffrey H., 1386
Mischi, J.E., 1336
Miscoll, James P., 69
Mitchell, A.S., 19
Mitchell, A.S., Mrs., 19
Mitchell, Carl, 256
Mitchell, David W., 291
Mitchell, Donald D., 1149
Mitchell, Elizabeth Seabury, 948
Mitchell, Greg, 2946
Mitchell, Harvey R., 3064
Mitchell, James A., 1409
Mitchell, James E., 2444
Mitchell, John C. II, 361
Mitchell, Joseph C., 2012, 2245
Mitchell, Lee H., 900
Mitchell, Lucy C., 1426

Mitchell, Margaret, 1460
Mitchell, Marjorie I., 900
Mitchell, Mary E., 988
Mitchell, Richard L., 3044
Mitchell, Wildey H., 1460
Mitchell, William, 13
Mitchell, William B., 3120
Mitchell Trust, Bernard A., 900
Mitsch, Ronald A., 1458, 1459
Mittelbusher, Richard L., 1554
Mittenthal, Stephen D., 27
Miyamoto, Richard T., 280
Miyashiro, Ruth E., 748
Mlodzinski, Marjorie R., 407
Mnuchin, Robert E., 2112
Mobil Oil Corp., 3194
Mobley, Chris, 580
Mobley, E.B., 3021
Mobley, Ernestine L. Finch, 2390
Mobley, Julia, 44
Mochan, Margaret, 1994
Model, Alan L., 2080
Model, Alice H., 2080
Modern Properties, Inc., 1943
Modlin, George M., 3210
Modugno, Patrick, 1596
Moede, Gustave H., Jr., 3318
Moelter, Helen, 1474
Moen, Timothy P., 773
Moench, Robert W., 2661
Moffat, Bill, 2649
Moffett, George M., 678
Moffett, George M. II, 678
Moffitt, Earle W., 414
Moffitt, F. Brower, 414
Mogy, Joel, 625
Mohr, T.H., 2767
Moldaw, Phyllis, 268
Moldaw, Stuart, 268
Molella, Salvador, 1832
Molen, Richard L., 2507
Moll, Curtis E., 2459, 2513
Moll, Darrell, 2513
Moll, Theo, 2513
Molloy, John F., 36
Molvar, Roger, 135
Monahan, Sherwood, 542
Monarch Machine Tool Co., 2536
Moncrief, C.B., 3068
Moncrief, R.W., 3068
Moncrief, W.A., 3068
Moncrief, William A., Jr., 3068
Monfort, Kenneth W., 384
Monheimer, Marc H., 87, 353
Monroe, J. Edgar, 1081
Monroe, J. Percy, Jr., 1081
Monroe, Jane "Coolie", 2417
Monroe, Mark, 979
Monroe, Robert J., 1081
Monson, Elaine, 3250
Monte, Constance, 2361
Montebello Trust, 2203
Monteiro, Manuel J., 1458
Monteith, Edgar W., 2959
Montera, Kaye C., 384
Montfort, Thierry, 2688
Montgomery, Deborah, 1419
Montgomery, Edward E., 2462
Montgomery, J.R., 2956
Montgomery, Mary Louise, 1222
Montgomery, Philip O'B., Jr., 3078
Montgomery, W. Barton, 2545
Montgoris, William J., 2126
Montrone, Michele M., 1608
Montrone, Paul M., 1601, 1608
Montrone, Sandra G., 1608
Monus, Michael I., 2594
Monus, Nathan H., 2594
Moody, Libbie Shearn, 3069
Moody, Robert L., 3069
Moody, Ross R., 3069
Moody, William Lewis, Jr., 3069
Moon, Frederick F. III, 2302

Moore, Betty I., 243
Moore, Carolyn N., 2127
Moore, Dan E., 1351
Moore, Edward S., Jr., 2127
Moore, Evelyn N., 2127
Moore, Gary L., 1673
Moore, George C., Mrs., 2296
Moore, Gordon E., 243
Moore, H.V., 2370
Moore, Harry, 3265
Moore, Harry C., 790
Moore, Irving, 3022
Moore, Irving, Jr., 3041
Moore, J.S., 2403, 2419
Moore, James D., 1048
Moore, John E., 1035
Moore, Joseph, 1694
Moore, Joseph A., 71
Moore, Kenneth G., 243
Moore, Kevin S., 1849
Moore, Lewis B., 2495
Moore, M.I., 2458
Moore, Martin L., Jr., 2802
Moore, Nancy Powell, 3091
Moore, R.D., 412
Moore, Randolph, 749
Moore, Sara Giles, 727
Moore, Starr, 727
Moore, Stephen A., 1208
Moore, Steven E., 243
Moore, Sue C., 2934
Moore, T. Jerald, 407
Moore, Taylor F., 372
Moore, Theresa A., 642
Moore, Virlyn B., Jr., 707
Moore, Wenda Weeks, 1351
Moore, William B., 975
Moore, William C., 3000
Moore, Winston C., 889
Moore-Hopkins, Fannie, 2524
Moores, Harry C., 2537
Moorhead, Thomas L., 2548
Moorman, Bette D., 1486
Moorman Manufacturing Co., 901
Moran, Gwyneth O., 2895
Moran, John A., 1897
Moran, John R., Jr., 364, 377
Morawetz, Cathleen Synge, 2273
Moreau, R.A., 823
Morehead, Richard, 3286
Morehouse, Dean H., 1331
Morency, Jeanne L., 2060
Moreno, Mary Lou, 2996
Moret, Marc, 2246
Moreton, Robert D., 2993
Morey, Joseph H., Jr., 1863
Morf, Claudia, 2179
Morf, Darrel A., 1018
Morgan, Axson Brown, 2915
Morgan, Bryan, 2915
Morgan, Burton D., 2538
Morgan, Charles A., 2468
Morgan, Charles O., 583
Morgan, Edward L., Jr., 455
Morgan, Frank J., 930
Morgan, Geraldine K., 494
Morgan, Glenn R., 864
Morgan, Helen F., 2482
Morgan, James A., 2573
Morgan, James F., Jr., 746
Morgan, John, 1552
Morgan, Marietta McNeil, 3195
Morgan, Paul S., 1207
Morgan, Roy E., 2837
Morgan, Roy T., 2879
Morgan, Samuel T., Jr., 3195
Morgan, Steve, 536
Morgan, Walter L., 524
Morgan Guaranty Trust Co. of New
  York, 529, 1714, 1801, 1938, 1958,
  2082, 2129, 2146, 2291
Morgan Stanley & Co., Inc., 2130
Morgenstein, Alvin, 536

Morgenstein, Gertrude, 536
Morgenstein, Melvin, 536
Morgenstern, Frank N., 2132
Morgenstern, Morris, 2132
Morgenthaler, Lindsay J., 2457
Morie, G. Glen, 3240
Morita, Akio, 2280
Morita, Masaaki, 2280
Moritz, Charles W., 1896
Morley, Burrows, Jr., 1362
Morley, Edward B., Jr., 1362
Morley, Jay D., 1362
Morley, Katharyn, 1362
Morley, Peter B., 1362
Morley, Ralph Chase, Sr., 1362
Morley, Ralph Chase, Sr., Mrs., 1362
Morley, Robert S., 1362
Morning, Ingrid, 2691
Morning, John, 426
Morning, Ober II, 2691
Morningstar, John M., 956
Morningstar, Leslie H., 956
Morningstar Irrevocable Trust, Katherine,
  956
Morrill, James A., 2826
Morrill, Richard L., 2308
Morris, Barbara Young, 787
Morris, Carloss, 3136
Morris, Florence, 3233
Morris, Irving, 520
Morris, Jack B., 3070
Morris, Jonathan B., 1809
Morris, Joseph W., 2639
Morris, Leland M., 2133
Morris, Lester, 1379
Morris, Linda C., 3070
Morris, Louis Fisk, 948
Morris, Margaret T., 37
Morris, Max, 590
Morris, Norman M., 2133
Morris, Robert E., 2133
Morris, Roland, 2716, 2775
Morris, Sally, 872
Morris, Thomas F., 915
Morris, William T., 2134, 2913
Morrison, Jack R., 3041
Morrison, Jacqueline A., 1758
Morrison, Jerri, 1616
Morrison, Philip, 2920
Morrissey, Thomas L., 1716
Morrow, G.E., 144
Morse, David S., 274
Morse, Everett, Jr., 1270
Morse, Peter C., 2011
Morse, Robert A., 406
Morse, Sarah D., 1177
Morse, Stephan A., 1621
Morse, Susan Lee, 274
Morse, Theresa J., 1216
Mortenson, Robert S., 1678
Mortimer, Kathleen L.H., 1974
Morton, Dean O., 262
Morton, Terry L., 1604
Morton, Vincent P., Jr., 1282
Mosbacher, Emil, Jr., 468, 1927
Mosbacher, Emil III, 468
Mosbacher, John D., 468
Mosbacher, Patricia, 468
Mosbacher, R. Bruce, 468
Moseley, Carlos, 1874, 1875
Moseley, Carlos D., 2245
Moseley, Frederick S. III, 1214
Moseley, Furman C., 3236
Moseley, James F., Jr., 620
Moseley, Kathleen C., 2153
Moseley, Susan R., 3236
Mosely, W. Kelly, 707
Moses, Henry L., 2135
Moses, Lucy G., 2135
Mosier, Frank E., 2452
Moskey, Stephen T., 407
Moskin, Morton, 1794
Mosley, Daniel L., 2173

Mosling, J. Peter, Jr., 3311
Moss, Diane, 2234
Moss, Florence M., 3072
Moss, Harry S., 3072
Moss, Morrie A., 254
Mostue, Emily C., 2649
Motley, John, 491
Motorola, Inc., 903
Motsinger, Jean K., 1105
Mott, C.S. Harding II, 1363
Mott, Charles Stewart, 1363
Mott, Kerry K., 197
Mott, Maryanne, 1363, 1364
Mott, Paul B., Jr., 1661
Mott, Peter T., 417
Mott, Ruth R., 1364, 2136
Mott, Stewart R., 2136
Mottaz, Rolla J., 1551
Moulding, Mary B., 676
Moulton, Franklin F., 343
Moulton, Hugh G., 2667
Mountcastle, Katharine B., 2368, 2411
Mountcastle, Katharine R., 2360
Mountcastle, Kenneth III, 2368
Mountcastle, Kenneth F., Jr., 2368
Mountcastle, Laura, 2368
Mountcastle, Mary, 2368, 2411
Moxley, Lucina B., 982
Moyers, Donald P., 2627
Moyler, J. Edward, Jr., 3167
Moynahan, John D., Jr., 2117
Moyse, Hollis, 979
MT Power Co., 1583
MTD Products, Inc., 2513
Muchnic, H.E., 1041
Muchnic, Helen Q., 1041
Mudd, John, 647
Mueller, G.P., 3171
Mueller, Gerd D., 2795
Mueller, Marvin, 1524
Mueller, Nancy Sue, 2042, 2043
Mueller, Stanley R., 2636
Muetzel, Martha J., 2178
Muhlenberg, Nicholas, 2864
Muhlfelder, Lewis, Mrs., 1740
Muir, Keith H., 1398
Muir, Martha M., 1398
Mulcahy, Betty Jane, 2498
Muldowney, John O., 3210
Mulholland, Richard G., 2001
Mulitz, Shelley G., 549
Mullan, C. Louise, 1129
Mullan, Charles A., 1129
Mullan, Thomas F., Sr., 1129
Mullan, Thomas F., Jr., 1129
Mullan, Thomas F. III, 1129
Mullane, D.A., 69
Mullane, Denis F., 425
Mullane, Donald A., 70
Mullarkey, Thomas F.X., 2162
Mullen, Catherine S., 385
Mullen, Donald, 2675, 2676
Mullen, John K., 385
Mullen, Lynda, 2224
Mullen, M.L., 2767
Mullen Co., J.K., The, 385
Muller, Frank, 244
Muller, George T., 1708
Muller, Henry, 1829
Muller, James, 244
Muller, John, 244
Muller, Sheila, 244
Muller, Tim, 244
Mullett, Heather M., 1611
Mullett, William E., 3265
Mulligan, Mary S., 2137
Mulligan, Terrence J., 787
Mulliken, David L., 205
Mullin, J. Shan, 3218
Mullins, Shelley, 2631
Mullins, T.C., 2323
Mullis, Harold H., 1063
Mulloney, Peter B., 2853

Mulreany, Robert H., 1975, 2216
Muma, Dorothy E., 2160
Muma, Edith N., 2160
Mund, Richard G., 3194
Munday, Heidi B., 933
Munder, Barbara A., 2104
Mundt, Ray B., 2667
Mundy, Donna T., 1094
Munford, Dillard, 3181
Munford, John D., 3167
Munger, Charles T., 83, 245, 312
Munger, Nancy B., 245
Munroe, George B., 38
Munyan, Winthrop R., 1851
Munz, Georgie T., 3117
Munzer, Rudy J., 192
Murakami, Edward S., 189
Murch, Creighton B., 2540
Murch, Maynard H., 2540
Murch, Maynard H. IV, 2540
Murch, Robert B., 2540
Murcott, Charles, 2138
Murcott, Constance, 2138
Murdock, Melvin Jack, 3237
Murdough, Joy P., 2541
Murdough, Thomas G., 2538
Murdough, Thomas G., Jr., 2541
Murdy, J.L., 2670
Murfree, Matt B. III, 2917
Murphey, Lluella Morey, 246
Murphy, Charles C., 585
Murphy, Charles E., 1975
Murphy, Charles E., Jr., 1975
Murphy, Christine, 2808
Murphy, Daniel T., 1381
Murphy, Darrell L., 2466
Murphy, Diana E., 1421
Murphy, Frank B., 2522
Murphy, Franklin D., 57
Murphy, Henry L., Jr., 1222
Murphy, J.J., 1583
Murphy, Jo, 3037
Murphy, John J., 2989
Murphy, John P., 2542
Murphy, John W., 30
Murphy, Lauren, 1159
Murphy, Marguerite M., 306
Murphy, Mark M., 1637
Murphy, Richard F., 1184
Murphy, Thomas E., 2519
Murphy, Thomas S., 1586, 1826
Murphy, Walter, 695
Murphy, William J., 2161
Murray, Archibald R., 2147
Murray, Bettyann Asche, 3126
Murray, Dennis, 1432
Murray, Haydn H., 1641, 1715
Murray, J. Terrance, 889
Murray, James F., 1838
Murray, James M., 2139
Murray, Jerri, 1224
Murray, John P., 2139
Murray, John P. III, 2139
Murray, L.T., Jr., 3238
Murray, Mary Beth Tietje, 2210
Murray, Michael J., 3134
Murray, Robert, 2660
Murray, Robert E., 1631
Murray, Shirley Foerderer, 2726
Murray, William E., 1887, 1926
Murray Trust, L.T., 3238
Murrell, John H., 3064
Murtagh, Robert J., 1801
Musen, Ken, 1760
Musgrave, Colleen C., 3236
Music, Rick E., 1049
Muskal, Joseph L., 951
Musolino, Joseph R., 2981
Musselman, Francis H., 2120
Musser, Clifton R., 374
Musser, Elizabeth W., 374
Musser, Marcie J., 374
Musser, Margaret K., 374
Musser, Robert W., 374

Musson, Irvin J., Jr., 2543
Musson, R.C., 2543
Muth, J.J., 815
Muth, Robert J., 1759
Mutual Life Insurance Co. of New York,
 The, 2140
Myerberg, Neal, 2351
Myers, Albert G., Jr., 2391
Myers, Albert G. III, 2391
Myers, Casey, 347
Myers, Charles F., Jr., 2386
Myers, Emilie W., 2863
Myers, Gertrude, 2641
Myers, Harmon L., 41
Myers, James A., 2434
Myers, Jerry, 1588
Myers, Joel H., 2367
Myers, June R., 655
Myers, Lynn Howe, 180
Myers, Mary, 2430
Myers, Paul D., 2434
Myers, Susan Hanley, 615
Myers, T. Cecil, 742
Myers, Wyckoff, 619
Myhers, Richard, 3315
Mylott, Colette, 2438
Myra, John E., 2428
Myran, Gundar, 1301
Myrin, Mabel Pew, 2806

N.T.P. Co., 3102
Nabb, Edward H., 1130
Nabb, June R., 3073
Nabers, Hugh Comers, Jr., 9
Nabisco Brands, Inc., 1682
Nabors, James D., 21
Nader, Ralph, 452
Nadolsky, David, 1366
Nagin, Lawrence M., 968
Nagle, Patricia Herold, 272
Nagy, Julia Ann, 1650
Naiberg, Gerald J., 3323
Naidoff, Stephanie W., 2803
Naiman, Ada, 550
Nakamura, Melvin M., 756
Nalbach, Kay C., 864
Nalco Chemical Co., 905
Nalle, Eleanor G., 2039
Nally, Joseph, 121
Nally, Joseph T., 261
Nalty, Donald J., 1070, 1083
Nance, Carlyle A., Jr., 2416
Nanon, Patricia, 2152
Napier Co., 2141
Napolitan, Tony, Jr., 174
Nardi, Nicholas J., 427
Nary, Gilbert R., 850
Nasby, David A., 1441
Nash, Frank E., 2650
Nash, Frederick C., 1403
Nash, Lucia S., 2586
Nasser, Muriel, 2245
Natale, Joseph S., 365
Nathan, Edgar J. III, 2324
Nathan, Edward A., 342, 357
Nathan, Robert R., 561
Nathans, Daniel, 1124
Nation, James H., 3074
Nation, Oslin, 3074
Nation, Robert F., 2740, 2768
National Bank of Commerce, 2914,
 2932
National Bank of Commerce of
 Charleston, 3265
National City Bank, 2430, 2454, 2457,
 2483, 2530, 2560
National City Bank, Akron, 2490
National Distributing Co., Inc., 699
National Electric Manufacturers Assn.,
 2070
National Gypsum Co., 3075

National Presto Industries, Inc., 3315
National Service Industries, Inc., 729
National Starch & Chemical Corp., 1683
NationsBank, 632, 636, 686, 689, 708,
 2400, 2403, 2419, 2424, 2891,
 2901, 2933, 2964, 2966, 2981,
 3013, 3034, 3053, 3058, 3072,
 3076, 3097, 3099, 3113, 3186, 3195
NationsBank of Texas, N.A., 3114
Nationwide Mutual Insurance Co., 2545
Naughton, John, 1869
Naughton, John A., 2645
Naughton, Marc G., 1039
Navistar International Transportation
 Corp., 906
NBD Bank, N.A., 1306, 1368, 1372,
 1404
NBD Grand Rapids, N.A., 1340
NC Machinery, 3252
NCNB Bank of Dallas, 2989
Neal, Stephen L., 2411
Neaves, Hope C., 2868
Nedley, R.E., 593
Nee, David M., 2008
Needleman, Harry, 1825
Neely, Grant F., 2785
Neely, Joseph F., 2424
Neely, W. Brock, 1299
Neenah Foundry Co., 3307
Neerhout, John, Jr., 75
Nees, Kenneth L., 2280
Neese, Alonzo A., Jr., 790
Neese, Elbert H., 790, 907
Neese, Gordon C., 790
Neese, Margaret K., 907
Neese-Malik, Laura, 790
Neeves, James P., 611
Neff, Peter G., 678
Neff, Robert C., 1684
Neff, W. Perry, 1794
Negri, Richard F., 365
Neidhard, Janet S., 2455
Neidorf, Murray, 207
Neier, Aryeh, 2166
Neill, A.K., 1583
Neilson, Phillipa Crowe, 558
Neish, Francis E., Jr., 2711
Nelson, Catherine B., 895
Nelson, Charles Stuart, 320
Nelson, Charlotte A., 2972
Nelson, Clarence J., 2712
Nelson, Clark, 229
Nelson, Clark A., 320
Nelson, David L., 3037
Nelson, E.L., 2562
Nelson, H. Alan, 2627
Nelson, H.J., 3037
Nelson, John M., 1295
Nelson, Kathryn, 1510
Nelson, Kent C., 737
Nelson, Larry W., 646
Nelson, Leonard B., 231
Nelson, Lynn I., 1409
Nelson, Maurice O., 978
Nelson, Patricia Johnson, 2655
Nelson, R., 2944
Nelson, Roy, 713
Nelson, Stuart K., 1790
Nelson, T.P., 1441
Nelson, Virginia, 3310
Nelson, William, 287
Nelson, William A., 3315
Nelson, William F., Jr., 1376, 1401
Nemchik, Rita, 1628
Nemer, Stanley, 1438
Nemetz, Marion, 3304
Nepomuceno, Javier J., 234
Neppl, Walter J., 1630
NERCO, Inc., 2661
Nesbeda, Lucy H., 1218, 1850
Nesbitt, Anne Wallace, 2940
Nesholm, Elmer J., 3239
Nesholm, John F., 3239

Nesholm, Laurel, 3239
Ness, Stanley, 1419
Nestor, Alexander R., 457, 459
Nethercutt, Dorothy S., 252
Nethercutt, Jack B., 252
Netley, Tom, 1159
Neu, Doris, 2143
Neu, Hugo, 2143
Neu, John L., 2143
Neu, Richard W., 2143
Neu & Sons, Hugo, Inc., 2143
Neuburg, Edward, 1760
Neuharth, Allen H., 3181
Neuhaus, David C., 1016
Neuhoff, Joe Boyd, 2981
Neumann, Roland M., 3276
Neuretuer, John, 1960
Neuwirth, Gloria S., 2321
Neville, Joseph B., 3085
Nevin, Elizabeth B., 1819
Nevoret, Chantal, 1366
New Castle Corp., 2273
New Connecticut Bank & Trust Co.,
 N.A., The, 488
New Discovery, Inc., 177
New England Medical Center Hospital,
 1092
New Haven Savings Bank, 470
New Jersey Resources Corp., 1685
New York Life Insurance Co., 2148
New York Post Corp., 2252
Newcomer, Arthur S., 2527
Newcoms, Jennings J., 3039
Newhall, H., 229
Newhouse, Donald E., 2151
Newhouse, Mitzi E., 2151
Newhouse, Samuel I., 2151
Newhouse, Samuel I., Jr., 2151
Newman, Bruce L., 820
Newman, David, 685
Newman, Douglas A., 2157
Newman, Elizabeth L., 2152
Newman, Eric P., 1512
Newman, Frances Moody, 3069
Newman, Frank H., 1005
Newman, George S., 3161
Newman, Howard A., 2152
Newman, J. Bonnie, 1607
Newman, Jerome A., 2152
Newman, Jon O., 448
Newman, Leland E., 1427
Newman, Louise K., 1609
Newman, Martha S., 446
Newman, Paul L., 471
Newman, Stephanie K., 2147
Newman, William C., 2152
News and Observer Publishing Co.,
 The, 2382
Newsweek, Inc., 548
Newton, Alice F., 1057
Ney, Lillian V., 1933
Neys, M. Alan, 98
Neys, Patricia M., 98
Ng, Henry, 2023
Nias, Henry, 641
NIBCO, Inc., 1002
Nichols, C. Walter III, 2153
Nichols, Claude E., 2739
Nichols, David H., 2153
Nichols, E. Marshall, Jr., 2680
Nichols, George, 1301
Nichols, James R., 1150, 1151, 1256,
 3116
Nichols, John D., 867
Nichols, Kate Cowles, 1866
Nichols, Linda, 2920
Nichols, Marguerite Sykes, 1732, 1800
Nichols, Wade H. III, 2212
Nicholson, Jan, 2733
Nicholson, Marion G., 2733
Nicholson, Norman C., Jr., 1250
Nicholson, Ruth, 2898
Nicholson, William B., 2733

Pierce, Aaronetta, 3099
Pierce, Harold Whitworth, 1256
Pierpont, Wilbur K., 1373
Pierson, Robert, 1123
Pierson, W. Michel, 1123
Pierson, Wayne G., 2657
Piet, William M., 979
Piette, James M., 733
Pifer, Erica, 433
Pigott, Charles M., 3240
Pigott, J.C., 3240
Pike, Robert W., 772
Pilcher, Helen Davis, 2803
Pildner, Henry, Jr., 2843
Pillsbury, Inc., 1443
Pincus, Lionel I., 2008
Pine, William C., 2651
Pineo, Charles C. III, 1413
Pineo, Linda Baker, 1413
Pingree, Sally E., 1633
Pinkard, Anne M., 1112, 1127
Pinkard, Robert M., 1112, 1127
Pinkard, Walter D., Jr., 1112, 1127
Pinson, Robert V., 2902
Pinzur, Laura F., 1745
Pioneer Bank & Trust Co., 1084
Piper, Virginia G., 922
Piper, William H., 1363
Pipkin, John, 1088
Pippin, Ronald G., 774
Piraneo, John A., 1684
Piribek, Martin, 3264
Pirozzoli, Cheryl, 131
Pisani, Bernard J., 2146
Pisetsky, Ingrid B., 2383
Piskor, Frank P., 2154
Pissocra, Ronald L., 2565
Pitluk, Marvin, 797
Pitman, Donne W., 2623
Pittinger, Vernon T., 1112, 1127
Pittman, J.E., 13
Pittman, Joe, 13
Pittman, Sheila P., 3201
Pitts, C.L., 690, 691
Pitts, John W., 3240
Pittsburgh National Bank, 2670, 2754,
    2782, 2797, 2809, 2810, 2819, 2860
Pitzman, Frederick, 1556
Pius, Alan P., 389
Pivnick, Isadore, 322
Pizzuti, Ann L., 2558
Pizzuti, Ronald A., 2558
Place, David E., 1174
Place, Linna, 1541
Plancher, Jill, 2259
Plastics Engineering Co., Inc., 3276
Platt, Adele Morse, 274
Platt, Helen B., 2030
Player, Willa B., 1363
Pleasants, C. Edward, Jr., 2424
Pletz, Francis G., 2593
Plitt, Henry G., 275
Plitt Southern Theatres, 275
Plotkin, Fred, 2254
Plotts, Diane J., 753
Plouff, Patricia, 1603
Plough, Abe, 2932
Plough Foundation, The, 1702
Plourde, Robert J., 68, 179
Plunkett, Paul E., 974
Plunkett, Paul M., 974
Pluta, Andrew, 2190
Pluta, Helen, 2190
Pluta, James, 2190
Pluta, John, 2190
Pluta, Peter, 2190
Pluta, Peter, Mrs., 2190
Pluta Manufacturing Corp., 2190
Podlich, William F., 96
Podlipny, Ann R., 1984
Pogue, Richard W., 2583
Pohl, David F., 1474
Pohle, Marianne L., 944

Poitras, James, 1257
Poitras, Patricia, 1257
Poitras, Patricia T., 1257
Pokross, David R., Sr., 1158
Polachek, Thomas A., 956
Polak, B. James, 287
Polak, Stanley J., 1186
Polakovic, Michael, 401
Polakovic, Teresa, 401
Polansky, Ed, 3099
Polaroid Corp., 1258
Polin, Jane L., 439, 440
Poling, Harold A., 1329
Polite, Lynn Getz, 31
Politeo, Janet L., 3230
Polk, Barbara J., 27
Polk, David D., 924
Polk, Eugene P., 35, 37, 1835
Polk, Harry, 924
Polk, Howard J., 924
Polk, Morris G., 924
Polk, Samuel H., 924
Polk, Samuel S., 2109
Polk, Sol, 924
Polk Bros., Inc., 924
Pollack, Anne, 2148
Pollack, Gerald J., 456
Pollack, James L., 839
Pollack, John V., 541
Pollack, Robert, 2147
Pollak, Henry II, 1690
Pollak, Jean deB., 1690
Pollak, Lucile R., 1690
Pollak, Maurice, 1690
Pollak, Thomas, 1690
Pollak, William, 1690
Pollard, Carl F., 1057
Pollay, Richard, 822
Pollicino, Joseph A., 1844
Pollin, Abe, 1132
Pollin, Irene S., 1132
Pollin, James, 1132
Pollin, Robert, 1132
Pollock, John P., 192
Pollock, Kathryn Challiss, 2559
Pollock, William B. II, 2559
Polsky, Cynthia Hazen, 1979
Polsky, Virginia Harris, 863
Pomerance, Rafe, 1364
Pomerantz, John J., 2191
Pomeroy, Katherine, 497
Poncin, Cora May, 3244
Pontikes, Kenneth N., 925
Pontikes, Nicholas K., 925
Pontikes, Victoria, 925
Poole, Cecil F., 164
Poole, Elisabeth S., 511
Poole, Margaret, 1305
Poole, Richard G., 2052
Pope, Anthony, 2192
Pope, Catherine, 2192
Pope, Elaine Klenk, 876
Pope, Fortune, 2192
Pope, Generoso, 2192
Pope, John C., 968
Pope, John L., 3062
Pope, Lois B., 2193
Pope, Robert G., 1569
Popoff, Jean U., 1338
Popovich, Jane H., 176
Popovich, John, 135
Popowcer, Leonard H., 844
Portenoy, Norman S., 1894
Portenoy, Winifred Riggs, 1894
Porter, D.E., 3277
Porter, E.R., 3205
Porter, John W., 1363
Porter, M., 2727
Porter, Robert C., 634
Porter, Victor B., 986
Portman, William, 2590
Poses, Fred M., 1611
Posey, Frances, 709

Posner, Fredrick, 3314
Posner, Gene, 3314
Posner, Jeffry A., 3314
Posner, Roy, 2076
Posner, Ruth, 3314
Posner, Steven, 2828
Posner, Victor, 2828
Post, Judith, 1919
Post, Leona, 1919
Post, Marjorie Merriweather, 559, 560
Post, Robert, 1919
Post, William J., 26
Post-Newsweek Stations, 548
Poston, Met R., 621
Poteat-Flores, Jennifer, 1389
Potenziani, A.F., 1727
Potenziani, Frank A., 1727
Potenziani, Martha M., 1727
Potenziani, William, 1727
Potter, Bruce W., 1460
Potter, Delcour, 2061
Potter, Helen A., 405
Potter, Justin, 2933
Potter, P.J., 2887
Potter, Peter, 92
Potter, Valere Blair, 2933
Poundstone, William N., 634
Poupore-Haats, Antoinette, 1467
Poussaint, Alvin, 2872
Powell, Amy L., 211
Powell, Arlene B., 2439
Powell, Ben H., Jr., 3091
Powell, Ben H. V, 3091
Powell, C.P., 2666
Powell, David G., 1611
Powell, E. Bryson, 3204
Powell, J. Key, 2888
Powell, James H., 2324
Powell, Jerry W., 8
Powell, Kitty King, 3091
Powell, M.C., 1079
Powell, Myrtis H., 561
Powell, Robert E., 868
Powell, Susan Baker, 3056
Powell, W.H., 1683
Powell, William, 2832
Powell, William R., 2615
Powelson, Leo, 978
Powers, Ed, 1145
Powers, James F., 3052
Powers, John A., 451, 1443
Powers, John G., 433
Powers, John P., 433, 1907
Powers, June M., 428
Powers, Whitney, 1754
PPG Industries, Inc., 2812
Prager, William W., 2301
Pramberg, John H., Jr., 1149
Prancan, Jane, 400
Pratt, Aileen Kelly, 1171
Pratt, Alice Evans, 3134
Pratt, Burt C., 510
Pratt, David W., 760
Pratt, Edwin H.B., 1171
Pratt, Fletcher S., 3134
Pratt, Fletcher S., Mrs., 3134
Pratt, G. Gerald, 2657
Pratt, Harold I., 1256
Pratt, Jeanette Gladys, 277
Pratt, Marsha, 1292
Pratt, Patricia R., 1164
Pratt, Peter E., 3134
Pratt, Richardson, Jr., 1851
Pray, Donald E., 2617
Prechter, Heinz, 1381
Prechter, Heinz C., 1405
Prechter, Waltraud, 1405
Prechter Charitable Lead Trust, Heinz
    C., 1405
Preece, William H.S., Jr., 903
Preiskel, Barbara Scott, 1922, 2146
Premier Bank, N.A., 1069, 1084
Premier Dental Products Co., 2699

Premier Medical Co., 2699
Prendergast, Larry, 1713
Prendergast, R.F., 803
Prentice-Hall, Inc., 2174
Prentiss, Elisabeth Severance, 2560
Prepouses, Nicholas T., 335
Presbyterian University Health Systems,
    Inc., 2763
Presbyterian/St. Lukes Health Care
    Corp., 364
Press, Frank, 2273
Prest, Eleanor, 2913
Preston, Carole, 550
Preston, E.G., 2429
Preston, James E., 1764
Preston, James Y., 2384
Preston, Jenny Childs, 1737
Preston, Lewis T., 2273
Preston, Ralph L., 172
Preston, Seymour S. III, 2721
Prestrud, Stuart H., 3218
Prewitt, Kenneth, 2224
Preyer, L. Richardson, 2216, 2368
Pribilsky, Wilbur, 3221
Price, Carol Swanson, 1528
Price, Charles H., 1999
Price, Charles H. II, 1528
Price, Clarence L., 214
Price, Craig, 290
Price, H.B. III, 3196
Price, Harold, 2197
Price, Harvey L., 348
Price, Hugh B., 2224
Price, Louis, 2197
Price, Pauline, 2197
Price, Richard, 1959
Price, Samuel P., 1828
Price, Sol, 348
Price, W. James, 1105
Pridham, Herbert H., 2615
Priebe, Kathie, 291
Priest, A. Earl, 2920
Prince, Frederick Henry IV, 927
Prince, Larry, 736
Prince, William Norman Wood, 927
Prince, William Wood, 927
Prindle, Bud, 292
Prindle, R. Leo, 2462
Priory, Sheila McNeil, 1660
Pritchard, Lee E., Mrs., 2372
Pritchett, Mebane M., 686
Pritzker, Daniel F., 928
Pritzker, James N., 928
Pritzker, Jay A., 928
Pritzker, John A., 928
Pritzker, Nicholas J., 928
Pritzker, Penny F., 928
Pritzker, Robert A., 928
Pritzker, Thomas J., 928
Pritzlaff, John C., Jr., 1551
Pritzlaff, Mary Olin, 1551
Probasco, S.L., Jr., 2916
Probert, Edward W., 1695
Probusco, Benjamin R., 2916
Prochnow, Robert G., 1754
Procknow, Donald E., 1691
Proctor, George H., 2
Proctor, James, 996
Proctor, Venable B., 3077
Proctor & Gamble Co., The, 2562
Project Four, Inc., 2594
Promboin, Gail R., 407
Propst, John L., 2809
Prothro, Caren H., 2981
Prothro, Charles N., 3088, 3089
Prothro, Charles V., 3088
Prothro, Elizabeth P., 3088, 3089
Prothro, James E., 3088
Prothro, Joe N., 3088, 3089
Prothro, Mark H., 3088, 3089
Prothrow-Stith, Deborah, 1216
Proudfoot, Allin, 797
Prout, Curtis, 1166, 1214

Prouty, Lewis I., 1260
Prouty, Olive Higgins, 1260
Prouty, Richard, 1260
Providence Journal Co., 2881
Provident Bank, 2456
Provident Investment Counsel, 2660
Provident National Bank, 2705, 2808, 2858
Prudential Insurance Co. of America, 1691
Prudential Property & Casualty Co., 1691
Pruis, John J., 982, 983
Pruitt, Terry, 1376
Prussian, Gordon, 924
Pryor, Millard H., Jr., 446
Puck, Robert J., 577
Puelicher, John A., 3301, 3324
Puget Sound National Bank, 3233
Pugh, Gordon A., 1069
Pullen, David E., 383
Pulliam, Larry, 2631
Pung, Bob, 3310
Purdum, Dennis R., 1905
Purdum, Robert L., 1614
Purks, W.K., 1493
Purmort, Paul W., Jr., 2604
Purnell, Edward, 2450
Purtell, Dennis, 3306
Purvis, G. Frank, 1082
Purvis, George A., 1337
Pusateri, Elizabeth, 2683
Puterbaugh, Jay Garfield, 2637
Puterbaugh, Leela Oliver, 2637
Putney, Freeman T., Jr., Mrs., 1740
Puzder, Andrew F., 196
Pyer, Sandra L., 125
Pyle, Edwin T., 1040
Pyne, Eben W., 611, 1749
Pyne, John, 1989
Pynn, Ward, 131
Pyramid Co., 1861
Pytte, Agnar, 436

Quadros, Joseph J., 3180
Quadros, Joseph J., Jr., 3162
Quaker Chemical Corp., 2815
Quaker Oats Co., The, 930
Qualls, Robert C., 3025
Quasim, Lyle, 3255
Queen, Harold A., 2755
Queenan, Charles L., Jr., 1908
Queener, Elizabeth, 2930
Quern, Arthur F., 840
Quick, Elizabeth L., 2378
Quick, Leslie C., Jr., 653
Quick, Patricia C., 2591
Quick, Regina A., 653
Quick, Robert F., 1782
Quickel, Kenneth E., Jr., 405
Quiley, W.G., 1334
Quill Corp., 898
Quillan, Debra J., 3019
Quilter, James F., 895
Quin, J. Marvin, 1049
Quinn, E.V., 803
Quinn, John C., 3181
Quinn, John P., 1684
Quinn, Tracy A., 3181
Quinones, Nathan, 1930
Quirk, Charles P., Jr., 3084
Quivey, M.B., 1593
Quivey, M.B., Mrs., 1593

R & B Machine Tool Co., 1373
R & T Liquidating Trust, 1165
Raattam, Henry, 587
Rabb, Harriet, 1005
Rabb, Harry W., 390
Rabb, Irving W., 1191

Rabb, Norman S., 1191
Rabb, Sidney R., 1261
Rabinowitch, Victor, 887
Rachmiel, George J., 1627
Radcliffe, G.G., 1100
Radecki, Martin, 1003
Rader, I. Andrew, 3275
Radin, H. Marcus, 278
Radin, Leta H., 278
RadiOhio, Inc., 2610
Radock, Michael, 1301
Radomski, Robyn L., 923
Rados, Alexander, 306
Radosh, Alice, 2147
Radov, Joseph, 935
Radov, Sylvia M., 935
Rafsky, Steven M., 1539
Ragen, Brooks, 3250
Ragen, Therse, 932
Ragen, Thomas, 932
Ragen, William, 932
Ragone, David V., 2458
Rahill, Richard E., 1864
Rahjes, Doyle D., 1037
Rahm, Susan B., 2684
Rahr, David G., 3160
Raiford, Donna, 2814
Raines, Franklin D., 538
Rainoff, Elizabeth, 2176
Raithel, M.L., 1625
Raizen, Charles S., 2202
Raizen, Nancy, 2202
Raizen, Patricia T., 2202
Raizen, Roy, 2202
Raleigh County National Bank, 3262
Raleigh Linen Service, Inc., 699
Ralston Purina Co., 1557
Ramer, Bruce M., 96
Ramo, Simon, 197
Ramsay, Patricia, 2115
Ramsey, Flora J., 187
Ramsey, Jack D., 2943
Ramsey, Lyle B., 429
Ramsey, Priscilla D., 429
Ramsey, Richard L., 429
Ramsland, Jane B., 2954
Ranalli, Robert J., 1762
Rand Realty and Development Co., 924
Randaccio, Sharon D., 1947
Randall, James A., 2893
Randall, William L., 3302
Randle, Kathryn A., 583
Randles, Robert H., 1740
Randolph, Walter R., Jr., 2912
Rankin, Alfred M., Jr., 2457
Rankin, Sarrah W., 23
Ranney, Clare, 702
Ranney, George A., Jr., 840, 887
Ranney, Phillip, 2614
Ransom, Dorothy, 1616
Raphael, Timothy, 2160
Rapoport, Bernard R., 2078
Rapoport, Daniel, 2204
Rapoport, Paul, 2204
Rapp, Joanne, 290
Rappleye, Richard K., 1363
Rasberry, W.C., Jr., 1084
Rash, Elsie, 239
Raskin, Cynthia, 961
Rasmussen, Arthur E., 840
Rasmussen, C. Peter, 1604
Rasmussen, C.A., Inc., 279
Rasmussen, Dean, 279
Rasmussen, Douglas J., 1381
Rasmussen, Larry, 279
Rasmussen, Laura R., 1486
Rasmussen, Vicki, 279
Rast, L. Edmund, 707
Ratcheson, Robert, 2450
Ratcliffe, G. Jackson, 453
Rathgeber, Susan, 469
Ratner, Albert, 2482
Ratner, Albert B., 654, 2600

Ratner, Audrey G., 879
Ratner, Charles, 2482
Ratner, Max, 2482
Ratner, Milton M., 1372
Ratner, Nathan, 654
Ratner, Stanley, 654
Ratowsky, Moses, 2311
Rauch, Louis J., 2205
Rauch, Philip J., 2205
Raudonat, Helen C., 1892
Rauenhorst, Gerald A., 1472
Rauenhorst, Henrietta, 1472
Rauenhorst Corp., 1472
Raun, Robert L., 1351
Ravitch, Richard, 194
Ravitz, Robert J., 1964
Rawle, Susan Stockard, 605
Rawlinson, Joseph E., 95, 166
Rawls, J. Lewis, Jr., 3208
Rawls, S. Waite, Jr., 3167
Rawls, Sol W., Jr., 3167
Ray, Donald E., 1539
Ray, George D., Jr., 721
Ray, Hilton T., 2982
Ray, J.E. III, 3167
Ray, James C., 3246
Ray, Joan L., 3246
Ray, Richard E., 3167
Ray, Richard L., 3004
Ray, Robert C., 3167
Raymond, R.O., 39
Rayson, E.H., 2931
Rea, William H., 2744, 2745, 2746
Read, Charles L., 1693
Reagan, Richard S., 2155
Reardon, Philip H., 1685
Reardon, Robert J., 1420
Reardon, Suzanne T., 1996
Rearwin, Kenneth R., 263
Reath, George, Jr., 2721
Reaves, Patricia, 1539
Reavis, Lincoln, 2586
Rebele, Rowland, 292
Recanati, Diane, 2207
Recanati, Michael A., 2170, 2207
Recanati, Raphael, 2170, 2207
Rechtschaffner, Steve, 923
Reckert, Peter, 2376
Reckler, Henry, 404
Reckling, Isla C., 3095
Reckling, Isla S., 3123
Reckling, James S., 3123
Reckling, T.R. III, 3123
Reckling, T.R. "Cliffe", 3123
Records, George J., 2633
Red Lion Inn, 1205
Red Wing Shoe Co., Inc., 1473
Redden, Roger, 1124
Reddy, Thomas, 1832
Redfearn, J. Michael, 2972
Redfield, Nell J., 1597
Redies, Robert D., 1373
Redmer, Evangeline, 1405
Redmond, Charles R., 331
Redstone, Sumner M., 1263
Redwine, Emily, 727
Reed, Anne E., 1633
Reed, Charles L., 3209
Reed, Cordell, 820
Reed, D. Creamer, 1048
Reed, Dorothy J., 1048
Reed, Dorothy W., 2434
Reed, Earl F., Jr., 2730
Reed, Eleanor H., 3236
Reed, Elizabeth C., 2446, 2501
Reed, Glenda C., 407
Reed, Ina N., 1484
Reed, Molly, 2663
Reed, Paul H., 2756
Reed, Philip D., 2208
Reed, Philip D., Jr., 2208
Reed, Thomas, 2157
Reed, Vincent E., 548

Reed, W. Brooks, 2444
Reed, William G., Jr., 3236, 3257
Reepmeyer, Lorraine M., 911
Reese, Eleanor Steele, 2291
Reese, Emmet P., 2291
Reese, J. Gilbert, 2475
Reeves, Helen F., 2565
Reeves, J.E., Jr., 1694
Reeves, J.Paul, 2893
Reeves, Jeneil, 1694
Reeves, Margaret H., 2565
Reeves, Margaret J., 2565
Reeves, Samuel J., 2565
Regan, Andrew W., 613
Regan, Douglas, 911
Regan, Joseph J., 889
Regenstein, Helen, 934
Regenstein, Joseph, 934
Regenstein, Joseph, Jr., 934
Rehr, Helen, 2147
Rehtmeyer, Calvin, 849
Reich, Lawrence A., 786
Reich, Theodore H., 2861
Reicher, Harry D., 2209
Reichert, Jack F., 806
Reichert, Rudolph, 1301
Reichman, Vivian C., 1747
Reid, Ala H., 1173, 1287
Reid, Jere K., 1728
Reilly, Elizabeth C., 1011
Reilly, John F., 660
Reilly, John H., Jr., 2289
Reilly, Marilyn L., 239
Reilly, Thomas E., Jr., 1011
Reilly Industries, Inc., 1011
Reimann, Ronald H., 2961
Reinberger, Clarence T., 2566
Reinberger, Louise F., 2566
Reinberger, Robert N., 2566
Reinberger, William C., 2566
Reinemund, Steven S., 2179
Reinhard, Mary Martha, Sister, 2452
Reinhardt, Hazel, 1431
Reinhart, Charles, 1301
Reinhart, James, 1603
Reinhart, M.H., 2696
Reinhold, John D., 2016
Reinhold, Paul E., 655
Reinhold, Paula Joy, 2016
Reinhold, Roger C., 3201
Reininga, Perry F., 2157
Reinis, Lois Barbara, 274
Reintjes, Robert J., 1519
Reisman, Evelyn R., 1264
Reisman, George C., 1264
Reisman, Howard, 1264
Reisman, Robert, 1264
Reiss, Barney, 1540
Reiss, Craig K., 1540
Reiss, Jacob L., 2210
Reiss, Robert R., 2210
Reiss, Theodore J., 2210
Reister, Jeffrey, 3287
Reister, Raymond A., 1476
Reitman, Robert S., 2599
Reitz, Ralph E., 1037
Reliance Electric Co., 2567
Relyea, Edna J., 293
Rembe, Toni, 342
Remmel, Jerry G., 3337
Renda, Joseph, 423
Rendelman, Patsy, 2413
Rendo, Elaine, 1603
Renfro, John F., 2894
Renfroe, Lowell E., 601
Rennebohm, Mary F., 3317
Rennebohm, Oscar, 3317
Renner, Daniel S., 2568
Renner, J. Robert, 2568
Renner, John W., 2568
Renner, Karen L., 2568
Renner, Mary A., 2568
Renner, R. Richard, 2568

Renner, Richard R., 2568
Renner, Robert R., 2568
Renner, Steven, 2568
Renner, Tami, 2568
Renner, Tara, 2568
Rennie, Robert, 2639
Reno, Robert H., 1606
Renshaw, John P., 269
Renzel, Ernest, Jr., 291
Republic National Bank of New York, 2146
Republic Steel Corp., 3052
Resnick, Martin, 2450
Resnick, Myron J., 772
Resnick, Sidney, 340
Resnik, Harold, 2203
Resseguier, Olga, 476
Reuben, Meredith Baum, 417
Reusing, Vincent P., 2117
Reuss, John F., 773
Reuss, L.E., 1336
Reuter, Carol J., 2148
Reuter, Irving J., 621
Reuter, Jeannett M., 621
Reuterfors, Robert E., 978
Revlon, Inc., 2212
Revson, Charles H., 2213
Revson, Charles H., Jr., 2213
Revson, John C., 2213
Rex, John, 2616
Rexnord, Inc., 3318
Reynolds, David P., 3202
Reynolds, Dorothy M., 1323
Reynolds, Julia L., 3202
Reynolds, Kate B., 2410
Reynolds, Nancy S., 2411
Reynolds, Pearl G., 1558
Reynolds, Randolph N., 3203
Reynolds, Richard C., 1658
Reynolds, Richard J., Jr., 2411
Reynolds, Richard S. III, 3202
Reynolds, Robert H., 1008
Reynolds, Rosemary T., 2643
Reynolds, Roy, 328
Reynolds, T.A., Jr., 2852
Reynolds, Thomas A., Jr., 1882, 1975
Reynolds, Thomas A., Jr., Mrs., 1882
Reynolds, Timothy T., 2643
Reynolds, W.G., Jr., 3203
Reynolds, Walter C., 2660
Reynolds, William, 700
Reynolds, William G., Jr., 3202
Reynolds, William N., 2411
Reynolds and Reynolds Co., The, 2569
Reynolds Metals Co., 3203
Rezich, George F., 2740
Reznicek, Bernard W., 1157
Rhame, Donald, 689
Rhea, S. Herbert, 2913
Rheingold, Susan S., 2575
Rhinehart, Mary, 383
Rhoades, Hazel T., 938
Rhoades, Otto L., 938
Rhoads, J.E., 1334
Rhoads, Jonathan E., 2788
Rhoads, Paul K., 865
Rhode Island Hospital Trust National Bank, The, 1228, 2866, 2876, 2882, 2885
Rhodebeck, Mildred T., 2214
Rhodes, Frank H.T., 2106, 3181
Rhodes, J.W. (Skip), Jr., 103
Rhodes, James, 1047
Rhodes-Bea, Winifred W., 346
Rhodus, G. Tomas, 3064
Rhoten, David, 2660
Ricci, A. Leo, 467
Ricci, Elaine L., 1224
Ricci, Joan D., 1633
Riccio, Ronald J., 1619
Riccobene, Mary, 3267
Rice, Ada, 939
Rice, Daniel F., 939

Rice, Harry F., 1249
Rice, Henry, 747
Rice, Liston M., Jr., 3120
Rice, Mary H., 1450
Rice, Nell M., 2886, 2900
Rice, Patricia E., 1249
Rich, David A., 2215
Rich, Harry E., 1503
Rich, Marsha E., 1269, 1282
Rich, William III, 1973, 1974, 2237
Rich, Zan McKenna, 2786
Rich Products Corp., 2215
Rich's, Inc., 731
Richard, Nancy, 1385
Richard, Oliver G. III, 1685
Richard, Shirley A., 26
Richard, Theodore Norman, Sr., 1777
Richards, Charles F., Jr., 511
Richards, Robert J., 1226
Richards, Walt, 1526
Richardson, D.B., 3104
Richardson, Dean E., 1381, 1386
Richardson, Douglas W., 2525, 2586
Richardson, Earl, 1113
Richardson, Elenora, 700
Richardson, Frank H., 3104
Richardson, Grace Jones, 2216
Richardson, H. Smith, Jr., 2216
Richardson, H.S., Sr., 2216
Richardson, Heather, 2216
Richardson, Joan, 153
Richardson, Joseph N., 3120
Richardson, Lundsford, Jr., 2216
Richardson, Nancy, 1559
Richardson, Peter L., 2216
Richardson, R. Randolph, 2216
Richardson, Roderick R., 2216
Richardson, Sarah Beinecke, 2199
Richardson, Sid W., 3094
Richardson, Stuart S., 2216
Richardson, Thomas R., 359
Richardson, William C., 194, 1113, 2806
Richenthal, Arthur, 2304
Richey, Kevin, 1483
Richey, S.W., 1483
Richie, Leroy C., 1309
Richman, Frederick, 100
Richman, Martin F., 2183
Richmond, Charles P., 1149
Richmond, Frederick W., 2217
Richmond, James M., 1332
Richter, Charles H., 1937
Richter, James A., 994
Richter, Michael, 3136
Rick, David F., 2761
Rickel, Janet, 1541
Rickman, Ronald L., 1022
Ricksen, John C., 74
Ricotta, Joseph J., 2157
Ridder, Kathleen Culman, 1417
Riddle, D. Raymond, 687
Riddle, Raymond D., 686
Rider, D. Brickford, 3203
Rider, Grace F., 3027
Ridings, Dorothy S., 1922
Ridler, Gregory L., 2441
Riecken, Henry W., 1959
Riecker, John E., 1389
Riecker, Margaret Ann, 1389
Riedel, Alan E., 2977
Riegel, John E., 514
Riegel, Richard E., Jr., 514
Riehl, Susan O., 1122
Rieman, Robert W., 576
Riemke, John W., 986
Rienhoff, William IV, 1103
Riesbeck, James E., 1864
Riester, Jeffrey, 3304
Riethman, R.B., 2536
Rifkind, Robert S., 2213
Rifkind, Simon H., 2352
Rigg, Douglas C., 1704
Rigg, Elizabeth Schultz, 1704

Rigg, Geoffrey B., 1704
Rigg, William L.S., 1704
Riggs, John A. III, 51
Riggs, Lew, 41
Riggs Tractor Co., J.A., Inc., 51
Rigler, Donald, 281
Rigler, James, 281
Rigler, Lloyd E., 281
Rihner, Sidney M., 1077
Riker, Bernard, 1313
Riley, David, 604
Riley, Emily L., 2707
Riley, Joseph H., 1106
Riley, Katherine M., 728
Riley, Mabel Louise, 1265
Riley, Michael J., 1022
Riley, Paul H., 3204
Riley, Richard W., 2386
Rimel, Rebecca W., 2806
Rincker, William, 1995
Rinella, Bernard B., 895
Rinfret, Pierre A., 806
Ring, Frank, 2218
Ring, Freeda, 2218
Ring, Leo, 2218
Ring, Michael, 2218
Ringel, Betsy, 557
Ringoen, Richard M., 982
Rinker, M.E., Sr., 656
Rinker Materials Corp., 656
Riordan, Richard, 99
Ripley, W.E., Jr., 679
Rippel, Eric R., 1695
Rippel, Julius S., 1695
Rippey, A. Gordon, 364
Rippy, Mary L., 1429
Rish, Stephen A., 2545
Rishel, Jane, 835
Risner, Ollie J., 2484
Ritchey, S. Donley, 125
Ritchie, H. Dean, 1048
Ritchie, Jane Olds, 185
Ritchie, Mabel M., 2570
Ritsch, Malcolm E., Jr., 3193
Ritter, Alan I., 2219
Ritter, David, 2219
Ritter, Gerald, 2220
Ritter, Irene, 2219
Ritter, Jerry E., 1495, 1497
Ritter, Lena, 2219
Ritter, Louis, 2219
Ritter, May Ellen, 2220
Ritter, Sidney, 2219
Ritter, Toby G., 2219
Ritz, Larry, 2908
Ritzen, Evy Kay, 3064
Riuituso, Louis F., 2685
Rivel, Robert, 2061
Rivel, Wesley, 2061
Rivera, Celestino, 2524
Rives, Claude G. III, 372, 1086
Rives, Howard P., 617
Rivin, Zelma, 3200
Rivitz, Jan, 1141
Rivlin, Alice, 557
Rizley, Robert S., 2639
Rizzo, James J., 2200
Rizzo, Joan N., 2153
Roach, J. Thurston, 3236
Roach, Kharis, 1000
Roach, Michele C., 583
Roach, Randa R., 3095
Roark, Alf, 2970
Robarge, Sandra, 3286
Robb, Lynda J., 3050
Robbins, Dick, 978
Robbins, Rebecca, 1828
Robbins, William C. III, 74
Roberts, Ann M., 3111
Roberts, Brooke, 2788
Roberts, Burnell F., 2466
Roberts, Charles S., 931
Roberts, Darrell C., 695

Roberts, David R., 581
Roberts, Dora, 3096
Roberts, Edith M., 385
Roberts, Eleanor T., 931
Roberts, Frank, 262
Roberts, George A., 327
Roberts, George R., 283
Roberts, James C., 3209
Roberts, James E., 996
Roberts, Jill A., 571
Roberts, John, 914
Roberts, John J., 2288
Roberts, Kenneth L., 2925
Roberts, Leanne B., 283
Roberts, Mary G., 1956
Roberts, Mary R., 931
Roberts, Ronald L., 1610
Roberts, Summerfield G., 3097
Roberts, Thomas H., 931
Roberts, Thomas H., Jr., 931
Roberts, Virgil, 96
Robertson, Charles S., 1770
Robertson, Donald, 1092
Robertson, E. Lorrie, 2447
Robertson, Heather M., 2283
Robertson, John L., 1770
Robertson, Julian H., Jr., 2314
Robertson, Marie H., 1770
Robertson, Oran B., 2657
Robertson, Oscar, 1752
Robertson, Wilhelmina Cullen, 2980
Robertson, William S., 1770
Robin, Howard W., 1788
Robinette, Douglas C., 2545
Robinetti, P. Ward, Jr., 3162
Robins, E.C., 3205
Robins, E.C., Jr., 3205
Robins, L.M., 3205
Robins, Marjorie M., 1559
Robinson, David K., 267
Robinson, E.B., Jr., 1489
Robinson, Edward O., 1063
Robinson, Elizabeth H., 2859
Robinson, J.D. III, 2852
Robinson, Jack A., 1381
Robinson, James D. III, 1750
Robinson, John R., 1783
Robinson, Joseph R., 1364
Robinson, Lecta Rae, 818
Robinson, Michael J., 867
Robinson, Michael J. III, 524
Robinson, Richard, 369, 2859
Robinson, Robert, 1003
Robinson, Robert A., 1818
Robinson, Rollen, 818
Robinson, Russell M. II, 2386
Robinson, S.W., 2798
Robinson, Sylvia B., 1783
Robinson, W. Bruce, 3076
Robinson, W.R., 815
Robinson, W.T., 3171
Robirds, Donald M., 3342
Roblee Trust, Florence, 1559
Robson, Leah K., 895
Roby, Katherine W., 2350
Rockefeller, David, 2223
Rockefeller, David, Jr., 1158, 2223
Rockefeller, Frederic L., 2869
Rockefeller, John D., Sr., 2224
Rockefeller, John D., Jr., 2223
Rockefeller, John D., 3rd, 2223
Rockefeller, L.S., 1334
Rockefeller, Laurance S., 2223, 2358
Rockefeller, Laurance S., Mrs., 2146
Rockefeller, Martha Baird, 2223
Rockefeller, Mary, 1799
Rockefeller, Mary F., 2358
Rockefeller, Nelson A., 2223
Rockefeller, Richard G., 2223
Rockefeller, Rodman C., 2223
Rockefeller, Steven C., 2223
Rockefeller, Winthrop, 2223
Rockefeller Foundation, The, 1842

Rockefeller Trust Co., 2146
Rockwell, George Peter, 2818
Rockwell, Lindsey J., 2820
Rockwell, Russell A., 2818
Rockwell, Virginia P., 369
Rockwell, Willard F., 2818
Rockwell, Willard F., Jr., 2818
Rockwell Bros. & Co., 3098
Rockwell International Corp., 2819
Rockwell Lumber Co., 3098
Roddis, Augusta D., 3319
Roddis, Catherine P., 3319
Roddis, Hamilton, 3319
Roddis, William H. II, 3319
Roddis Plywood Corp., 3319
Roddy, Fred M., 2884
Rodecker, Arthur, 1314
Rodenbeck, Fred, 2413
Rodes, Harold P., 1363
Rodes, Joe M., 1052
Rodgers, David A., 2438
Rodgers, Dorothy F., 2225
Rodgers, John H., 1604
Rodgers, Richard, 2225
Rodriguez, Javier G., 117
Rodriguez, V.C., 1071
Rodriquez, Lynne, 1760
Roedel, Paul R., 2697, 2864
Roehl, Janet L., 3320
Roehl, Ora C., 3320
Roehl, Peter G., 3320
Roesch, Charles, 2499
Roesch, John R., 994
Rogal, Alvin, 2763, 2809
Roge, Paul E., 768
Rogers, Ben J., 3065
Rogers, C.B., Jr., 704
Rogers, Charles B., 273
Rogers, Charles E., 2185
Rogers, Christopher W., 1283
Rogers, Dorothy K.G., 2040
Rogers, F. Patrick, 1822
Rogers, Florence L., 2412
Rogers, Fred M., 2785
Rogers, Irving E., 1266
Rogers, Irving E., Jr., 1266
Rogers, James B., 2785
Rogers, James H., 2785
Rogers, John, 3079
Rogers, Julie, 3065
Rogers, Julie L., 557
Rogers, Justin T., Jr., 2584
Rogers, Margaret J., 2981, 3042
Rogers, Martha B., 1266
Rogers, Mary Pickford, 273
Rogers, Mary Stuart, 284
Rogers, Michael K., 3241
Rogers, Milton, 600
Rogers, Nancy M., 2785
Rogers, Patricia, 2996
Rogers, Paul G., 1676
Rogers, Regina, 3065
Rogers, Regina J., 3135
Rogers, Richard R., 3054
Rogers, Robert, 1534
Rogers, Robert B., 1511
Rogers, Roy, 580
Rogers, Samuel S., 1283, 1284
Rogers, Shelby R., 3119
Rogers, William L., 2368
Rogers, William P., 535
Rogerson, Charles E. II, 1270
Rogerson, Thomas, 1270
Roggin, Gary, 1139
Rogut, Robert, 1626
Rohan, Helen, 2220
Rohlfing, Joan H., 746
Rohm, Robert F., Jr., 1999
Rohr, Loren, 2973
Roisman, Milton, 2557
Roland, Catherine D., 2
Rolen, Johnnie, 2630
Roletti, Marion, 566

Rolfs, Robert T., 3321
Rolfsen, Carl D., 989
Rolland, Kenneth S., 1959
Roller, D.E., 969
Rollins, Mary E., 1134
Romaine, Michael F., 3139
Romano, Sara C., 2120
Romans, John N., 1851
Romero, Gerri, 136
Romero, Isabel, 497
Romfh, Emily M., 642
Rones, Louis, 1934
Rones, Steven, 1934
Ronning, Maureen A., 1947
Rooks, Charles S., 2657
Roosevelt, James M., 2603
Roosevelt, Laura D., 2128
Root, Carol Jean, 895
Roper, Richard W., 1684
Roper, Wayne J., 3275
Rork, Valerie Dumke, 3146
Rosa, Karen, 1746
Rosacker, Jo Helen, 3094
Rosario, Rosaida Morales, 448
Rosati, James V., 2880
Rose, Billy, 2226
Rose, David, 1984
Rose, Elihu, 2227
Rose, Frederick P., 2025
Rose, John C., 426
Rose, Marian, 1984
Rose, Marshall A., 290
Rose, Milton C., 272, 1799
Rose, Nancy, 1293
Rose, Simon M.D., 1984
Rose, Susan, 2227
Rose, Suzanne R., 1078
Rose Charitable Foundation, Samuel
   and David, 2227
Rosen, Andrew M., 1503
Rosen, Leonard M., 2361
Rosen, Louis, 50
Rosen, Robert S., 3085
Rosenbach, Kurt M., 3196
Rosenberg, Abraham, 2228
Rosenberg, Albert J., 641
Rosenberg, Alexis, 2821
Rosenberg, Ann, 657
Rosenberg, Carol Kuyper, 1021
Rosenberg, Henry A., Jr., 1102, 1135
Rosenberg, James M., 2204
Rosenberg, Norman, 1658
Rosenberg, Richard, 70
Rosenberg, Ruth B., 1102
Rosenberg, Ruth Blaustein, 1135
Rosenberg, Sheli Z., 885
Rosenberg, Sonia, 2228
Rosenberg, Tina, 658
Rosenberg, William, 657
Rosenberg, William F., 641
Rosenberger, Henry, 2822
Rosenberry, Walter S. III, 1486
Rosenblatt, Bruce, 278
Rosenblatt, Roslyn, 2812
Rosenblum, Morris S., 2444
Rosendale, Robert D., 2882
Rosenfeld, George, 2483
Rosenfeld, Mark, 1347
Rosenfield, Bruce A., 2689
Rosengren, William R., 1435
Rosenkilde, Herbert C., 1628
Rosenstiel, Blanka A., 2229
Rosenstiel, Lewis S., 2229
Rosensweig, David, 490
Rosenthal, Alan, 1705
Rosenthal, Beth, 2108
Rosenthal, Betty M., 1064
Rosenthal, Doris, 2108
Rosenthal, Edward, 2108
Rosenthal, Harry, 405
Rosenthal, Hinda Gould, 484
Rosenthal, Leighton A., 2572
Rosenthal, Peter, 2108

Rosenthal, Richard L., 484
Rosenthal, Richard L., Jr., 484
Rosenthal, Warren W., 1064
Rosenwald, Nina, 2230
Rosenwald, William, 2230
Rosenzweig, Elias, 1946
Rosenzweig, Newton, 27
Rosenzweig, Richard, 923
Rosin, Axel G., 2249
Rosin, Katharine S., 2249
Rosner, Bernat, 1669
Ross, Alexander B., 1774
Ross, Charles F., 2604
Ross, David H., 2749, 2750
Ross, Dickinson C., 192
Ross, Dorothea Haus, 2232
Ross, E. Burke, Jr., 1684
Ross, J.G., 170
Ross, Malcolm S., 1305
Ross, Mary Caslin, 1732, 1800
Ross, Ralph, 340
Ross, Richard S., 1676
Ross, Robert T., 1822
Ross, Samuel D., 2768
Ross, Sarane H., 1774
Ross, Steven J., 2231
Ross, Stuart B., 500
Ross, T.L., 2378
Ross, William W., 1564
Rosse, James, 291
Rosser, Nancy Frees, 3016
Rossi, Ralph L., 494
Rossi, Walter T., 1433
Rossin, Ada E., 2719
Rossin, Peter C., 2719
Rossley, Paul R., 1234
Rostecki, Richard, 423
Roswell, Arthur E., 1102
Roswell, Elizabeth B., 1102
Rotan, Caroline, 3005
Roth, Abraham, 2822
Roth, Edythe M., 2822
Roth, Eugene D., 849
Roth, Joseph S., 1702
Roth, Majorie, 274
Roth, Michael, 2140
Roth, R.W., 2852
Roth, Robert, 1696
Roth, Robert G., 877
Roth, Robert W., 242
Roth, Roland P., 2822
Roth, Stanley, Sr., 1696
Roth, Stanley, Jr., 1696
Roth, Walter, 952
Rothberg, Jean C., 933
Rothberg, Lee Patrick, 933
Rothberg, Michael, 933
Rothberg, Samuel, 933
Rothblatt, Ben, 848
Rothchild, Kennon V., 1421
Rothmann, Bruce F., 2430
Rothschild, Hulda B., 940
Rothschild, Walter N., Jr., 1850, 2083
Rothstein, David, 1264
Rothstein, Edward, 1644
Rothstein, Joel D., 1825
Rothstein, Louis, 1747
Rothstein, Phyllis, 1747
Rothstein, Robert, 1644
Rothstein, William, 1747
Rothstein-Schwimmer, Susan, 1747
Rottenberg, Alan, 1287
Rottenberg, Alan W., 1278
Rottman, William A., 1331
Rottschafer, Mary Frey, 1332
Roulier, Jack, 29
Rounce, Jeff, 3255
Rountree, Robert B., 707
Roupe, Barbara Doyle, 291
Rouse, Eloise Meadows, 3064
Roush, Galen, 2490
Roush, Ruth C., 2490
Routh, Robert F., 829

Roux, Michel, 1640
Rovira, Luis D., 382
Rowan, Rita H., 2320
Rowe, George, Jr., 2125
Rowe, John J., 2553
Rowe, Joseph E., 2812
Rowe, Sue, 3305
Rowe, Thomas E., 134
Rowe, William L.S., 3204
Rowell, Harry B., Jr., 453
Rowen, Henry S., 2216
Rowland, Billy S., 2524
Rowland, Dorothy, 2951
Rowland, J. David, 3316
Roy, Barbara B., 1475
Roy, Charles R., 3318
Royal Brand Roofing, Inc., 1509
Royal Trust, May Mitchell, 1374
Royer, Robert L., 1052
Royfe, Ephram, 2741
Rozek, John F., 3321
Rozelle, Frank L., Jr., 705
Rozier, Nancy, 704
Ruane, William, 569
Ruane, William J., 1827
Rubbermaid, Inc., 2573
Ruben, Lawrence, 1785
Rubenstein, Anne C., 1268
Rubenstein, Jay, 1700
Rubenstein, Lawrence J., 1268
Rubin, Donald S., 2104
Rubin, Ephraim F., 2351
Rubin, Judith O., 2233
Rubin, Pearl W., 2015
Rubin, Robert E., 1829, 2233
Rubin, Steven I., 1745
Rubin, Sydney R., 2015
Rubinelli, Joseph O., 891
Rubinelli, Mary Jane, 891
Rubinovitz, Samuel, 1184
Ruby, Paul J., 98
Ruck, Harold, 2916
Rudd, Jean, 977
Rudder, Anne, 2201
Rudert, Eric W., 1331
Rudin, Eric C., 2236
Rudin, Jack, 2235, 2236
Rudin, Katherine L., 2236
Rudin, Lewis, 2235, 2236
Rudin, Samuel, 2236
Rudin, William, 2236
Rudner, Jocelyn P., 2932
Rudnick, Alford, 1286
Rue, C.J., 2658
Ruebhausen, Oscar M., 1966
Ruey, John S., 775
Ruffle, John F., 2129
Ruffner, Jay S., 30
Ruffo, Jay Price, 3316
Rukin, Barnett, 1697
Rukin, David, 1697
Rukin, Eleanore, 1697
Rumain, Jerry, 2204
Rumble, Marty Vaughan, 3025
Rumbough, J. Wright, Jr., 678
Rumbough, Stanley, 560
Rumbough, Stanley H., 2283
Ruml, Alvin, 1688
Rumore, Carol, 7
Rumple, Norman C., 1369
Rumsey, Charles C., 2237
Rumsey, Mary A.H., 2237
Rumsey, Mary M., 2237
Runk, Fred J., 2432
Runser, C. Allan, 2604
Runyan, Marion, 984
Ruocco, Roberta A., 2128
Rupp, Gerald E., 2330
Ruppert, Susan, 2631
Rupple, B.H., 3277
Rupple, Brenton H., 3306
Rush, Helen P., 2745
Rush, John, 44

Schmidt, B.C., 1334
Schmidt, Clifford, 2994
Schmidt, George P., 722
Schmidt, Jareen E., 2994
Schmidt, John G., 1009
Schmidt, Raymond, 3331
Schmidt, Thomas, 3331
Schmidt, William, 3331
Schmitt, Wolfgang R., 2573
Schmitz, Michael D., 806
Schmults, Edward, 444
Schmults, Edward C., 1850
Schnabel, Truman G., 2788
Schneckenburger, Karen L., 3178
Schneider, Al J., 1066
Schneider, David, 1653
Schneider, Frederic, 946
Schneider, Frederick W., 1692
Schneider, Gail, 1946
Schneider, Gene F., 573
Schneider, Henry, 2135
Schneider, Madeline M., 2116
Schneider, Melvin, 946
Schneider, Melvyn H., 954
Schneider, Phyllis, 946
Schneider, Richard, 946
Schneider, Ronald G., 1376
Schneider, Scott, 490
Schneider, Thelma E., 1066
Schnoes, Robert F., 773
Schnurmacher, Adolph, 2073, 2254
Schnurmacher, Charles M., 2254
Schnurmacher, Irwin, 2073
Schnurmacher, Rose, 2073
Schoenberg, Lawrence J., 1684
Schoendorf, Anthony, 2155
Schoenke, Richard W., 1457
Schoenwetter, L. James, 1458, 1459
Scholl, Jack E., 947
Scholl, Michael L., 947
Scholl, William H., 947
Scholl, William M., 947
Scholler, F.C., 2825
Scholz, Garrett A., 232
Schomer, Fred K., 1337
Schooler, Seward D., 2462
Schornack, John J., 1905
Schott, Harold C., 2498
Schott, Milton B., Jr., 2498
Schottenstein, Melvin L., 2613
Schrader, George, 2981
Schrafft, Bertha E., 1273
Schrafft, William E., 1273
Schramm, Carl J., Jr., 2120
Schrank, Edwin, 2430
Schrantz, John M., 2739
Schregel, Paul N., 2826
Schreiber, Elliot S., 2795
Schreier, Andrew M., 2203
Schreier, William, 2203
Schreyer, William A., 2113
Schroeder, Charles E., 831, 892
Schroeder, Clinton A., 1457
Schroeder, Diane, 428
Schroeder, John M., 3293
Schroeder, John P., 38
Schroeder, Lorraine D., 1011
Schroeder, Steven A., 1658
Schroeder Trust, Walter, 3324
Scholl, Maud Hill, 1462
Schroter, William, 622
Schroth, Virginia Cowles, 1866
Schubert, James, 302
Schuberth, Kenneth, 1144
Schuchardt, Daniel N., 842
Schueppert, George L., 815
Schuerman, Ken, 2618
Schuette, William, Jr., Mrs., 2296
Schuette, William D., 1338, 1369
Schuffler, Loraine E., 3274, 3289
Schuiteman, Norma A., 1331
Schuler, John A., 2697
Schuler, Mary Lou, 3316

Schullinger, John N., 1631
Schulman, Alvin H., 1855
Schulte, Anthony M., 2249
Schulte, F.S., 3311
Schultz, Clifford G. II, 660
Schultz, Eugene B., 1773
Schultz, Frederick H., 660
Schultz, Frederick H., Jr., 660
Schultz, George L., 1704
Schultz, John R., 660
Schultz, Mabel L., 1704
Schultz, Mae W., 660
Schultz, Margaret F., 1704
Schultz, Nancy R., 660
Schultz, Rhoda W., 86
Schulz, Ralph G., 3336
Schulze, A.R., 1441
Schulze, Peter Boyce, 1791
Schumacher, Jon L., 2221
Schumacher, Marion M., 3290
Schumacher, Robert A., 712
Schumann Foundation, Florence and
    John, 1705
Schunck, George J., 1861
Schutte, Thomas F., 2880
Schutte, Thomas P., 2880
Schuyler, Jean, 290
Schwab, Nelson, Jr., 2456
Schwanfelder, Nancy Healy, 3146
Schwanke, L.E., 1416
Schwartz, Alan, 1380, 2458
Schwartz, Alan E., 1381
Schwartz, Alan E., Mrs., 1346
Schwartz, Andy, 137
Schwartz, Arnold A., 1706
Schwartz, Bernard L., 527
Schwartz, Bernard W., 2008
Schwartz, David, 2255
Schwartz, Denise L., 1708
Schwartz, Eric A., 527
Schwartz, Henry L., 1812, 2203
Schwartz, Irene, 2255
Schwartz, Jane D., 2204
Schwartz, Julia D., 247
Schwartz, Linda, 2822
Schwartz, Lois F., 1675
Schwartz, Mandy, 716
Schwartz, Marie D., 2256
Schwartz, Michael L., 527
Schwartz, Rebecca, 2203
Schwartz, Renee G., 2150
Schwartz, Richard J., 2255
Schwartz, Robert A.D., 125
Schwartz, Rosalyn R., 527
Schwartz, Sheila, 2255
Schwartz, Stephen L., 1812, 2203
Schwartz Charitable Trust, Arnold, 2256
Schwarz, Bernard M., 434
Schwarz, Frederick A.O., Jr., 1930
Schwarz, Maurice L., 434
Schwarzman, Joseph, 2257
Schwarzman, Stephen A., 2257
Schwecherl, Robert, 529
Schweckendieck, Edith M., 2258
Schweid, Marjorie S., 2483
Schweiger, Patricia, 1587
Schweizer, Thomas, Jr., 1103
Schwerin, Suzanne, 1930
Scicutella, John V., 1838
SciMed, 674
Scinto, Robert D., 417
SCOA Industries, Inc., 2579
Scofield, Milton N., 2270
Scofield, William B., 1207
Scorsone, Vincent R., 2668
Scott, Andrew, 1449
Scott, David, 1329
Scott, Edgar, Jr., 2195
Scott, Frank L., 67
Scott, George A., 446
Scott, James R., 1462
Scott, Jo, 2920
Scott, Louis, 1292

Scott, Nadya Kozmetsky, 3093
Scott, Roderic M., 479
Scott, Ross G., 1331
Scott, Ruth H., 2221
Scott, Taylor, 1524
Scott, Wesley, 3282
Scott, William C., 2152
Scott Paper Co., 2826
Scovell, John Field, 2981
Scovil, Samuel K., 2458
Scovill, Elizabeth W., 1691
Scoville, Thomas W., 561
Scranton, William W., 2744
Screven, M.L., Jr., 19
Scribner, Edgar A., 1381
Scripps, Betty Knight, 3206
Scripps, Edward W., 3206
Scripps, Ellen Browning, 296
Scripps, Paul K., 296
Scripps, Robert Paine, 296
Scripps League Newspapers, Inc., The,
    3206
Scudder, Stevens, Clark, 2660
Scully, Arthur M., Jr., 2791
Scully, Jean T.J., 2086
Scully, Leonard T., 2086
Scurlock, E.C., 3100
Scurlock, W.C., 3100
Scurlock Oil Co., 3100
Seabury, B.J., 2872
Seabury, Charlene B., 948
Seabury, Charles Ward, 948
Seabury, David G., 948
Seabury, Louise Lovett, 948
Seafirst Bank, 321, 3220, 3232, 3244,
    3250, 3260
Seafirst Corp., 3249
Seager, Carol L., 1295
Seagram and Sons, Joseph E., Inc., 1811
Seale, R.A., Jr., 2998, 3108
Seaman, Avery H., 2876
Seaman, Carl, 1733
Seaman, Jeffrey, 2259
Seaman, Jordan, 1961
Seaman, Linda, 1733
Seaman, Lois, 2259
Seaman, Morton, 2259
Seamon, Dana, 1961
Searl, Alexander L., 511
Searle, Sally B., 944
Searle, William L., 944
Sears, Anna L., 2580
Sears, Lester M., 2580
Sears, Marvin L., 502
Sears, Ruth P., 2580
Seaver, Beatrice, 2260
Seaver, Blanche Ebert, 297
Seaver, Christopher, 297
Seaver, Frank R., 297
Seaver, Richard C., 297, 329
Seaver, Victoria, 297
Seay, Charles E., 3101
Seay, Charles E., Jr., 3101
Seay, Sarah M., 3101
Seay, Stephen M., 3101
Sebion, Diane L., 3301
Seccombe, James C., Jr., 381
Second National Bank of Saginaw,
    1307, 1319, 1360
Second National Bank of Warren, 2606
Security National Bank & Trust Co., 3266
Security Pacific Investment Mgrs., 290
Security Pacific National Bank, 321
Security Trust Co., N.A., 534, 537
Security Trust Company, N.A., 1113
Seder, J. Robert, 1295
See, Ann R., 3251
See, Charles B., 3251
See, Harry A., 3251
See, Jane R., 2568
See, Richard W., 3251
Seed, Harris W., 336
Seelboch, William, 2459

Seelenfreund, Alan, 232
Seely, Christopher W., 1650
SEG Trucking, 143
Segal, Bernard G., 2799
Segal, Martin E., 2234
Segall, Harold A., 2208
Segers, Ben, 2543
Segner, Edmund P. III, 3000
Sehn, Francis J., 1377
Sehn, James T., 1377
Seidel, Arnold, 195
Seidman, B. Thomas, 1378
Seidman, Esther L., 1378
Seidman, Frank E., 1378
Seidman, L. William, 1378
Seidman, Sarah B., 1378
Seifert, St. Clare Pratt, 3134
Seigenthaler, John, 3181
Seigle, John T., 87, 172
Seinfeld, Dennis, 3255
Seitel, Fraser P., 1838
Seitz, Collins J., 521
Seitz, Frederick, 2077
Sekera, Helen Mary, 2837
Selber, Irving H., 1518
Selby, Cecily B., 1752
Selby, John R., Jr., 2838
Self, James C., 2386, 2899
Self, James C., Jr., 2899
Self, Sally E., 2899
Self, W.M., 2899
Selfe, Jane B., 9
Seligman Trust Co., J. & W., 2146
Selinger, Maurice A., Jr., 1746
Selis, Pamela A., 2656
Sellars, Richard B., 1658
Sellers, Edna E., 129
Sellers, J.G., 2632
Sellers, Robert D., 112
Sellitti, W.J., 1668
Sellke, Dennis, 1456
Selsor, Della, 2581
Selvage, John R., 181
Selvidge, Glenn E., 3010
Selz, Fred, 50
Selznick, L. Jeffrey, 2095
Semans, Mary D.B.T., 2386
Semans, Truman T., 1103
Seminara, Joseph E., 1953
Semple, Louise Taft, 2582
Semrad, Robert, 3087
Seneker, Stanley A., 1329
Senger, Alan F., 2603
Senter, Allan Z., 500
Senturia, Brenda Baird, 1768
Sequa Corp., 2261
Seremet, Peter M., 451
Seretean, M.B., 2934
Seretean, Shirley, 2934
Sergio, Alexandrina M., 446
Servitex, Inc., 699
Servoss, Judith A., 400
Sessions, Moultrie, 13
Sessums, T. Terrell, 624
Setterstrom, William N., 911
Settle, Halsey M. III, 3076
Settles, Elizabeth J., 1303
Setzer, Debra, 661
Setzer, G. Cal, 300
Setzer, Hardie C., 300
Setzer, Leonard R., 661
Setzer, Mark, 300
Setzer, Sidney, 661
Seven-Up Bottling Co., 2017
Severson, Lawrence, 1474
Sevier, Sheila, 385
Sevlian, David, 2649
Sewell, Stace, 2994
Sexauer, James M., 2262
Sexauer, John A., 2262
Shack, Ruth, 587
Shaddix, James, 3087
Shade, T.L., 901

Southern Mills, 721
Southern National Bank, 2424
Southwestern Bell Corp., 1569
Southworth, Louis S. II, 3265
Sovern, Theodore E., 1303
Spaeth, Edmund B., Jr., 2803
Spaeth, Karl H., 2815
Spalding, Charles C., Jr., 751
Spalding, Hughes, Jr., 741
Spanier, David B., 2102
Spanier, Helen G., 2102
Spanier, Maury J., 2102
Spaniolo, James D., 629
Sparber, Norman H., 1946
Sparks, Fredda S., 1382
Sparks, Jack D., 1382
Sparks, Jack D., Jr., 1382
Sparks, Robert A., Jr., 1063
Sparks, W. Alvon, Jr., 543
Sparling, Alfred H., Jr., 1211
Sparrow, Marvin, 1278
Spartus Corp., 851
Speaks, Don, 686
Spear, Joel, Jr., 2674
Spears, Paul E., 2829
Spears, Richard W., 1049
Speas, Effie E., 1570, 1571
Speas, Victor E., 1570, 1571
Speas Co., 1570, 1571
Speegle, Christopher F., 806
Speer, Katie, 52
Speight, James T., Jr., 557
Speltz, Kate A., 1447
Spence, John, 2047
Spence, Lewis H., 1216
Spencer, A.N., 359
Spencer, D.B., 1071
Spencer, D.P., 1071
Spencer, Eben S., 1436
Spencer, Edson W., 1922
Spencer, Harriet S., 921
Spencer, Jacqueline E., 359
Spencer, Robert, 360
Spencer, T.W., 3121
Spencer, William L., 2393
Spencer, William M. III, 18
Spero, Joan E., 1750
Spero, Michael, 1825
Sperry, Frederick E., 3292
Spickard, Brian D., 711
Spiegal, Debra J., 267
Spiegel, Abraham, 109
Spiegel, Emily, 2282
Spiegel, Jerry, 2282
Spiegel, Lise, 2282
Spiegel, Thomas, 109
Spieler, Herber E., 1347
Spik, Rudolph, 2420
Spindler, George S., 775
Spitz, S. James, Jr., 2697
Spitzer, Anne, 2284
Spitzer, Bernard, 2284
Spivack, Marilyn Price, 1806
Spivak, Gloria H., 1842
Spliedt, William F., 1143
Spoto, Angelo P., Jr., 674
Spragins, Melchijah, 1144
Sprague, Caryll M., 312
Sprague, Charles C., 3036
Sprague, Norman F., Jr., 312
Sprague, Norman F. III, 312
Sprague, Seth, 2285
Sprague, William D., 2779
Sprain, Robert A., Jr., 6
Spratt, Anne D., 533
Sprinfield, James, 2932
Springer, Eric W., 2723
Springer, George, 469
Springer, Neil A., 906
Springs, Elliott W., 2904
Springs, Frances Ley, 2904
Spruell, Barbara H., 2128
SPS Technologies, Inc., 2838

Spurgeon, Carol, 84
Spurgeon, Edward D., 84
Spurgeon, Thomas E., 918
SPX Corp., 1383
St. Botolph Holding Co., 1272
St. Clair, D.W., 1668
St. Clair, James D., 1251
St. Clair, Margaret N., 1251
St. John, Bill D., 2989
St. Louis - San Francisco Railroad, 742
Staats, Elmer B., 2626
Stabler, Donald B., 2839
Stabler, Dorothy L., 2839
Stabler, W. Laird, Jr., Mrs., 530
Stabler Companies, Inc., 2839
Stachler, Robert G., 2456
Stack, Edward W., 1849
Stackner, Irene M., 3328
Stackner, John S., 3328
Stackpole, Harrison C., 2840
Stackpole, J. Hall, 2840
Stackpole, R. Dauer, 2840
Stacy, Charles B., 3265
Stacy, Mary, 3036
Stadler, Martin F., 1648
Staebell, Ron, 2908
Stafford, Richard H., 3323
Staggs, Vernon L., 2924
Stahl, Jack L., 696
Staley, Augustus Eugene, Jr., 958
Staley, R.W., 1514
Staley, Walter G., 1523
Staley, Walter G., Jr., 1523
Stallard, Hugh, 3163
Stamas, Stephen, 1966
Stamm, Robert J., 1726
Stanback, Fred J., Jr., 2413
Stanback, W.C., 2413
Standard Investment Co., 410
Standard Motor Products, Inc., 1917
Stanfill, Dennis, 348
Stanford, Henry King, 629
Stankard, Francis X., 1838
Stanley, Janet, 3255
Stanley Works, The, 488
Stanny, Norbert F., 1599
Stans, Maurice H., 76
Stanton, Robert J., 2645
Stanton, Ruth S., 1752
Stapleton, F. Eugene, 2761
Star Bank, N.A., Butler County, 2499
Star Bank, N.A., Cincinnati, 2456
Star-Telegram Employees Fund, 2965
Stark, Carlyn K., 194
Stark, Donald B., 57
Stark, Gertrud, 2207
Stark, H. Allan, 938
Stark, K.R., 2769
Stark, Richard A., 2064
Stark, Robert L., 1527
Stark, William B., 720
Starkins, Clifford E., 2195
Starling, James R., 3329
Starr, Cornelius V., 2288
Starr, Frederick B., 2416
Starr, S. Frederick, 2223
State Farm Insurance Cos., 959
State Street Bank & Trust Co., 1148,
    1158, 1280, 2005
Statter, Amy P., 2189
Stauber, Karl N., 1462
Stauffer, Beverly, 314
Stauffer, John, 313, 314
Stauffer, John H., 1047
Stawarky, Jack C., Jr., 417
Stayman, Joseph W., Jr., Mrs., 2408
Stearns, Artemas W., 1282
Stearns, Jean H., 1155
Stearns, Russell B., 1281
Stearns, Stewart W., 659
Stebman, Betty J., 1996
Stec, Cynthia M., 214
Stecher, Patsy Palmer, 574

Steckler, Allan, 2290
Steckler, Donald H., 2290
Steckler, Lois R., 2290
Steckler, Philip H., Jr., 1181, 2290
Steckler, Philip H. III, 2290
Stedman, Betty Ann West, 3130
Stedman, Stuart West, 3130
Steedman, Martin, 639
Steelcase, Inc., 1384
Steele, Elizabeth R., 315
Steele, Eugene W., 1458, 1459
Steele, Grace C., 315
Steele, Harold J., 3149
Steele, John H., 1658
Steele, Richard, 315
Steele, Theo, 283
Steenburg, Walter C., 1010
Steere, William C., Jr., 425
Stefanko, Robert, 2430
Steffes, Don C., 1040
Steger, C. Don, 2393
Steiber, Richard I., 417
Steimle, John, 1305
Stein, Allen A., 2292
Stein, Carey M., 864
Stein, Donald L., 3280
Stein, Elaine S., 2292
Stein, Eric, 1287
Stein, Helene, 1855
Stein, Jane, 1287
Stein, Jean L., 1798
Stein, Jean, 316
Stein, Joseph F., 2292
Stein, Kenneth L., 1942
Stein, Louis, 2841
Stein, Mary Ann, 1005
Stein, Melvin M., 2292
Stein, Nikki W., 924
Stein, Robert J., 1005
Stein, Roger H., 2292
Stein, Ronald J., 1758
Stein, Sidney, 1855
Stein, Stuart M., 2292
Stein Family Trust, Doris Jones, 316
Stein, Stein & Engel, 2841
Steinberg, Edward L., 2311
Steinberg, Harold, 2293
Steinbright, Edith C., 2677
Steinbright, Marilyn Lee, 2677
Steiner, Jeffry J., 3178
Steiner, Lisa A., 2348
Steinfeldt, O.J., 1463
Steinfeldt, S.J., 1463
Steinhardt, Michael, 2264
Steinhauer, Bruce W., 1358
Steinkraus, Eric M., 502
Steinkraus, Helen Z., 502
Steinman, Beverly R., 2842
Steinman, James Hale, 2842
Steinman, John Frederick, 2843
Steinman, Lewis, 2235
Steinman, Shirley W., 2843
Steinmann, David P., 2230
Steinschneider, Jean M., 454
Steitz, Joan A., 422
Stekas, Lynn, 2140
Stella, Ethel, 2155
Stella, Frank D., 1381
Stella Louise, Sister, 937
Stemen, Milton E., 1373
Stemmler, Edward J., 2770
Stemmons, John M., 3036
Stemmons, John M., Sr., 3111
Stemmons, John M., Jr., 3111
Stemmons, Ruth T., 3111
Stempel, Ernest E., 2288
Stempel, R.C., 1334
Stempel, Robert C., 1336
Stender, Bruce, 1418
Stensrud, Richard, 1524
Step, Eugene L., 999
Stepanian, Ira, 1153
Stepanian, Tania W., 115
Stephan, Edmund A., 848

Stephan, John S., 70
Stephanoff, Kathryn, 2850
Stephans, Joan R., 2719
Stephans, Peter N., 2719
Stephen, Josephine L., 266
Stephens, Ann C., 110
Stephens, Deborah, 1371
Stephens, Dianne E., 29
Stephens, Donald R., 1065
Stephens, John, 2972
Stephens, K.F., 398
Stephens, Louis C., Jr., 2386
Stephens, Lowell F., 1489
Stephens, Martha Roby, 1866
Stephens, Susan A., 110
Stephenson, H. Howard, 748
Stephenson, John W., 693
Stephenson, Rex, 363
Stephenson, Thomas E., 138
Sterkel, Justine, 2592
Sterling, Helen N., 3098
Sterling, Mary K., 38
Stern, Alfred R., 1860
Stern, Bernard, 2295
Stern, D. Fink, 1689
Stern, Edward A., 2429
Stern, Irene, 2295
Stern, Irvin, 960
Stern, Jean L., 1798
Stern, John, 2280
Stern, Judith M., 1698
Stern, Julian N., 146
Stern, Lynn, 443
Stern, Peter, 1690
Stern, Ray, 2295
Stern, Robert A., 1798
Stern, Roy, 2295
Stern, S. Sidney, 318
Stern, Sam, 2429
Stern, Steven, 2295
Stern, William, 2429
Stern Trust, Anna S., 317
Sterne, Charles S., 392
Sterne, Dorothy Elder, 392
Sterne, Edwin L., 700
Stetler, Gerald, 1315
Stetson, E. William III, 2216
Stettinius, Wallace, 3204
Stevens, Abbot, 1283
Stevens, Charles F., 1453
Stevens, Clara R., 2620
Stevens, Dorothy W., 1635
Stevens, E.W. Dann, 1955
Stevens, H. Allen, 1155
Stevens, John T., 2905
Stevens, Mike, 1456
Stevens, Nathaniel, 1284
Stevens, Richard L., 1297
Stevens, Robert T., Jr., 1635
Stevens, Rosemary A., 2120
Stevens, Sylvia L., 1250
Stevens, Whitney, 1635
Stevenson, John R., 2106
Stevenson, Kenneth, 2539
Stevenson, Ruth Carter, 2965
Steves, David, 659
Stewart, Cheryl, 1094
Stewart, Dorothy I., 266
Stewart, Elizabeth T., 2397
Stewart, Isabel C., 2368
Stewart, J. Benham, 689
Stewart, J. Benton, 624
Stewart, James G., 2701
Stewart, James H., Jr., 2982
Stewart, Mary E., 563
Stewart, Patricia Carry, 1850
Stewart, Vicky, 918
Stiles, Leslie H., 1429
Stiles, Meredith N., Jr., 1992
Stilley, John, 39
Stillwater, Ann, 2568
Stine, Charles E., 242
Stine, Lynn B., 791

Van Roden, John, 2779
Van Ryn, John, 619
Van Sant, R.W., 2779
Van Schaick, Nellie Kellogg, 42
Van Schoonhoven, William L., 1817
Van Sickle, Jean, 1596
Van Wagenen, Kathryn, 3255
Van Wyck, Bronson, 44
Vance, Douglas, 80
Vance, Katherine R., 350
Vance, Robert C., 495
Vance-Lewis, Sheilah, 2808
Vander Dussen, Neil, 2280
Vanderbilt, Hugh B., 496
Vanderbilt, Robert T., Jr., 496
Vanderlinde, Elizabeth Schultz, 1704
VanderVeer, Joseph B., 2770
Vann, W.W., 2968, 3056
Vanneck, Barbara Bailey, 2328
Vanneck, John, 2328
Vanneck, John B., 2328
Vanneck, William P., 2328
Vanneste, Donald, 646
Varet, Elizabeth R., 2230
Vargas, Sandra, 1457
Varnau, Mark A., 994
Varne, D.E., 3121
Vaughan, Ben F. III, 2987
Vaughan, Genevieve, 2987
Vaughan, J. Robert, 95
Vaughan, Peter, 2808
Vaughan, Rosemary Haggar, 3025
Vaughn, Edgar H., 3127
Vaughn, J. Robert, 166
Vaughn, James M., 3127
Vaughn, Jim M., 3127
Vaughn, Lillie Mae, 3127
Vaun, William S., 1966
Veale, Francis R., 2832
Veitch, Christopher, 260
Veitch, Stephen W., 260
Veith, Frank, 2086
Velasquez, Arthur R., 820
Velay, Christophe, 2330
Velto, Alex C., 2158
Veneman, Gerard E., 3270
Venghiattis, Burdine, 2968
Verenes, George, 445
Vergin, Brian, 1418
Verhagen, Timothy J., 1039
Verheyden, Clyde J., 3123
Verity, C. William, Jr., 197
Verity, Jonathan G., 2515
Vermeulen, Bertram W., 1331
Vernam, Claude, 963
Vernon, Gerald B., 1587
Vernon, Miles Hodsdon, 2329
Verrant, James J., 1611
Verrecchia, Alfred J., 2873
Verret, Paul A., 1417, 1452, 1475
Verville, N.J., 3277
Vesey, Jeanne, 290
Vestner, Eliot N., 1153
Vetlesen, Maude Monell, 2125
Vetrovec, Pauline, 188
Vett, Thomas W., 3047
Veysey, M.C., 2494
Viall, Richmond, Jr., 2880
Viall, William A., 2878
Vickers, Thomas, 993
Vickery, Virgil E., 3108
Victor, Edward G., 99
Victor, Lois B., 2794
Victory Memorial Park Foundation, 1616
Video Indiana, Inc., 2610
Vidinha, Antone, 758
Vidinha, Edene, 758
Viederman, Stephen, 2160
Viener, John D., 2268
Viermetz, Kurt F., 2129
Vietor, Anna Glen, 1752
Vietor, Lynn A., 181
Vietor, Vera P., 181

Viets, Robert, 918
Vignos, Edith Ingalls, 2510
Vigorito, Thomas, 41
Villanueva, Daniel, 96
Villemaire, Roland, 2449
Vilmure, Richard, 244
Vilter Manufacturing Co., 3333
Vinal, Pamela K., 2041
Vincent, Richard, 2070
Vinovich, William, 981
Vinson, C. Roger, 600
Vinson, Frank B., Jr., 19
Vinyl Building Products, Inc., 2816
Virciglio, Paul T., 1376
Visceglia, Diego R., 1720
Visceglia, John B., 1720
Visceglia, Vincent, 1720
Visser, Jacqueline, 1995
Viste, Marion C., 3334
Vitanza, Michelle, 2706
Vititoe, William P., 1346
Vittachi, V. Tarzie, 1688
Vitti, Linda, 2197
Viviano, J.P., 2748
Vladeck, Bruce C., 194
Vlasic, James J., 1394
Vlasic, Joseph, 1394
Vlasic, Michael A., 1394
Vlasic, Richard R., 1394
Vlasic, Robert J., 1394
Vlasic, William J., 1394
Voelkel, Alice K., 1122
Voelkel, Mary M., 1122
Voelker, Larry, 2579
Vogel, Jacqueline M., 3191
Vogelstein, Deborah H., 1118
Vogler, John J., 2331
Vogler, Laura B., 2331
Vogt, Phyllis P., 1554
Vogt, Theodore, 2549
Voigt, Gaines, 3099
Voigt, Judith, 659
Volk, Harry J., 348
Volk, Max, 217
Volk, Norman H., 1975
Vollmer, Alberto F., 1721
Vollmer, Alberto J., 1722
Vollmer, Christine de, 1722
Vollmer, Gustavo A., 1721
Vollmer, Gustavo J., 1721
Vollmer Foundation, Inc., 1722
Volpi, W.M., 2323
von Arx, Carol R., 1559
von Auersperg, Alexander, 1806
von Bernuth, C.W., 2852
Von Essen, H. Clyde, 69
von Furstenberg, Cecil Blaffer, 2957
Von Herrman, Pieter, 2070
von Hess, Louise Steinman, 2842
von Kalinowski, Julian O., 197
Von Mehren, Joan, 1164
VonBlond, Betsy B., 3265
Vonckx, Paul N., Jr., 497
Voorhees, Adeline J., 3265
Voorhis, Caspar J., 2001
Voran, Reed D., 982, 983
Vorhees, Charles A., 805
Vorhees, Charles M., 805
Vossler, Robert P., 319
Vouras, Peter, Jr., 467
Vout, Murray C., 65
Voute, Mary Jane, 2332
Voute, William J., 2332
Vowles, Joan Hoover, 179
Vulcan Materials Co., 25

Wachenfeld, William T., 1978
Wachenheim, Edgar III, 1888, 2188, 2335
Wachenheim, Edward III, 2147
Wachenheim, Sue W., 2335

Wachovia Bank & Trust Co., N.A., 2370, 2390, 2410, 2416, 2421, 2424
Wachovia Bank of Georgia, N.A., 687, 744
Wachovia Bank of North Carolina, N.A., 2399
Wachtell, Esther, 96
Wachter, James P., 2427
Wackenreuter, Richard J., 407
Wada, Yori, 322
Waddell, Chauncey L., 1996
Waddell, Chauncey L., Mrs., 1996
Waddell, J.S., 823
Waddell, Oliver W., 2590
Waddell, Theodore H., 1996
Wade, Charles B., Jr., 2386
Wade, Jeptha H., 2458
Wadleigh, Theodore, 1602
Wadsworth, Erminia, 1068
Wadsworth, Homer C., 2583
Waffle House, Inc., 713
Wagar, James L., 1831
Wagele, James S., 70
Wageman, Richard M., 1419
Waggoner, E. Paul, 3128
Waggoner, Helen Buck, 3128
Wagner, Ann, 206
Wagner, David J., 1340
Wagner, David L., 2683
Wagner, Harold A., 2666
Wagner, Jeffry, 2565
Wagner, Lawrence M., 2749, 2811
Wagner, Martin S., 500
Wagner, Thomas J., 2701
Wagniere, Daniel C., 2246
Wagnon, Kenneth J., 1048
Wahlert, David, 1030
Wahlert, Donna, 1030
Wahlert, H.W., 1030
Wahlert, James, 1030
Wahlert, R.C., 1030
Wahlert, R.C. II, 1030
Wahlert, R.H., 1030
Wahlstrom, Agnes S., 671
Wahlstrom, Magnus, 671
Waid, John B., 1070
Waidner, Robert A., 634
Wainwright, Carroll L., Jr., 2146, 2154
Wajnert, Thomas C., 1762
Wakefield, Thomas H., 592
Wakley, James T., 3267
Wal-Mart Stores, Inc., 54
Walcott, Lee E., 57
Wald, Bernard, 2044
Walda, Julie Inskeep, 997
Waldbauer, Robert T., 2331
Waldbaum, Inc., 672
Waldbaum, Bernice, 672
Waldbaum, Ira, 672
Waldbaum, Julia, 672
Waldbaum, Mimi S., 1592
Waldman, Eric W., 1931
Waldron, Joan, 1782
Waldsmith, Dinah, 1276
Wales, Alice A., 1880
Wales, Darwin R., 2047
Walker, Abigail M., 1481
Walker, Amy C., 1481
Walker, Archie D., 1481
Walker, Archie D., Jr., 1481
Walker, Archie D. III, 1481
Walker, B.J., 2392
Walker, Berta, 1481
Walker, Bertha H., 1481
Walker, Billy J., 620
Walker, Earl E., 1577
Walker, Elaine B., 1481
Walker, Geraldine M., 1347
Walker, Gloria M., 1494
Walker, Harry W., 692
Walker, Harry W. II, 2697
Walker, Harvey L., 2962
Walker, Janice C., 2386

Walker, K. Grahame, 430
Walker, Kenneth G., 1597
Walker, Mallory, 538
Walker, Mary M., 3316
Walker, Myrtle E., 1577
Walker, Pat, 1505
Walker, Patricia, 1481
Walker, Richard F., 364
Walker, Robert A., 3079
Walker, W. Evelyn, 2779
Walker, W.E., Jr., 1494
Walker, W.E. III, 1494
Walker, Walter W., 1481
Walker, William, 48
Walker Memorial Health Foundation, Thomas, Dr., 3261
Walker Stores, W.E., Inc., 1494
Wall, Barbara, 196
Wall, Hugh III, 2518
Wallace, Ann Fowler, 1173
Wallace, Arthur, 2005
Wallace, Bruce, 2462
Wallace, Charles F., 1637
Wallace, David F., 1401
Wallace, David W., 501
Wallace, Elizabeth Bullard, 2940
Wallace, Henry A., 2334
Wallace, Henry B., 2334
Wallace, J. Bransford, Jr., 2940
Wallace, Jean W., 501
Wallace, Paul G., 981
Wallace, Robert B., 2334
Wallace, Ronnie, 3044
Wallace, Sarah R., 2475
Wallach, Diane Gates, 373
Wallach, Ira D., 2335
Wallach, James G., 2335
Wallach, Judith, 1891
Wallach, Kate B., 2335
Wallach, Kenneth L., 2335
Wallach, Mary K., 2335
Wallach, Miriam G., 2335
Wallach, Peggy, 1690
Wallach, Susan S., 2335
Wallin, Franklin W., 2115
Wallin, Maxine H., 1482
Wallin, Winston R., 1482
Wallingford, L.W., 508
Wallis, Jeff, 2337
Wallman, Susan A., 2104
Walsh, Edward F., Jr., 1955
Walsh, Edward T., Jr., 2226
Walsh, Frank E., Jr., 1673, 1699
Walsh, G.M., 807
Walsh, James S., 1297
Walsh, Jeffrey R., 1699
Walsh, John F., 1712
Walsh, John N., Jr., 1869
Walsh, Linda D., 3112
Walsh, Mary D., 1699
Walsh, Mason, Jr., 2791
Walsh, Michael, 2332
Walsh, Michael W., 2770
Walsh, Nancy S., 2262
Walsh, Patricia, 3074
Walsh, William M., Jr., 3179
Walsky, Lawrence A., 2864
Walter, G.K., 777
Walter, Henry G., Jr., 2125, 2326
Walter, James W., 673
Walter, Joseph J., Rev., 1822
Walter, Robert A., 673
Walter Corp., Jim, 673
Walters, John A., 2944
Walters, Sumner J., 2604
Walthall, Marjorie T., 3129
Walthall, Paul T., 3129
Walthall, Wilson J. III, 3129
Walther, Jules G., 1623
Walton, James M., 2745, 2823, 2824
Walton, Jon D., 2670
Walton, Jonathan T., 1351, 1381
Walton, Richard E., 451

Walton, S. Robson, 54
Walzel, James V., 3073
Ward, Adelaide C., 1578
Ward, Barbara, 3314
Ward, Bob D., 3011
Ward, Carl, 601
Ward, Carl G., 2417
Ward, George B.P., Jr., 1128
Ward, J., 2973
Ward, Judy C., 368
Ward, Lester L., Jr., 397
Ward, Louis L., 1578
Ward, Ralph, 3062
Ward, Ralph, Jr., 3062
Ward, Scott H., 1578
Ward, Terry, 1499
Ward, Terry W., 3005
Ward, Thomas W., 2573
Warden, Bert M., 889
Warden, William G. III, 2848
Warden, Winifred M., 889
Wardlaw, Edna Raine, 738
Wardlaw, Gertrude, 738
Wardlaw, William C., Jr., 738
Wardlaw, William C. III, 738
Ware, Carl, 696
Ware, John H. III, 2801
Ware, John H. IV, 2801
Ware, Marian S., 2801
Ware, Paul W., 2801
Wareck, Barbara, 470
Wareing, Elizabeth B., 3100
Wargo, Bruce W., 981
Warhall, Dolores, 1603
Waring, Bayard D., 1251
Waring, Lloyd B., 1251
Warner, Donald T., 561
Warner, Douglas, 2129
Warner, Glen W., 2437
Warner, Joseph C., 662
Warner, Meryl, 662
Warner, Philip G., 3037
Warner, Robert S., 343
Warner, Rose, 1483
Warner, Steve, 2756
Warner, Theodore K., Jr., 2759
Warner, William S., 417
Warner Communications, Inc., 2315
Warner-Lambert Co., 1723
Warren, Clifford M., 1904
Warren, Gina, 1762
Warren, Joan B., 1381
Warren, Karen M., 104
Warren, Natalie O., 2645
Warren, Peter F., Jr., 1125
Warren, Rupert, 2018
Warren, W.K., Jr., 2644, 2645
Warren, Wilbert W., 2439
Warren, William A., 2603
Warren, William K., 2644, 2645
Warren, William K., Mrs., 2645
Warriner, Jane Cunningham, 1010
Warrington, John W., 2553
Warsh, Herman E., 1364
Wasch, Susan Beck, 1780
Washington, Paul M., 2803
Washington, Valora, 1351
Washington Magazine, Inc., 1104
Washington Mutual Savings Bank, 3250, 3257
Washington Post Co., The, 548
Washington School Employees Credit Union, 3242
Washington Trust Co., The, 2882
Washingtonian, 1104
Wasie, Donald A., 1484
Wasie, Marie F., 1484
Wasie, Stanley L., 1484
Wassenberg, Charles F., 2604
Wasserman, Edith, 347
Wasserman, George, 564
Wasserman, Lew R., 316, 347
Wasserman, Lynne, 347

Watanabe, Jeffrey, 754
Watanabe, Ruth K., 96
Water, Robert N., 67
Waters, Nathan H., Jr., 2739
Watkins, Carol Frees, 3016
Watkins, John C.A., 2881
Watrous, Helen C., 387
Watson, Alonzo W., Jr., 335, 3148, 3149
Watson, Bernard C., 2803
Watson, Charles H., 993
Watson, Eliza Jane, 1651
Watson, Greg, 2160
Watson, Hugh, 3044
Watson, James, 1124
Watson, K.H., 656
Watson, Maurice T., 287
Watson, P.K., 1493
Watson, Roslyn M., 1216
Watson, Stephen E., 1433
Watson, Steven L., 3105
Watson, Walter E., 2605
Watson Clinic, 674
Watts, Russell E., 1155
Watts, Vinson A., 1063
Waugh, Richard W., 1028
Wawro, Judith S., 448
Way, Janice H., 1712
Wayne County National Bank, 2485
WBNS TV, Inc., 2610
Wean, Gordon B., 2606
Wean, Raymond J., 2606
Wean, Raymond J., Jr., 2606
Wean, Raymond J. III, 2606
Wearn, Wilson C., 2906
Weatherford, T.L., 2370
Weatherstone, Dennis, 1676, 2129
Weatherwax, David E., 2708
Weaver, Al, 3255
Weaver, E.H., 2422
Weaver, Edith H., 2422
Weaver, George B., Jr., 2157
Weaver, George E., 937
Weaver, H.M., 2422
Weaver, Henry O., 3043
Weaver, James D., 2963
Weaver, James R., 518
Weaver, Jean J., 255
Weaver, Lloyd J., 3116
Weaver, Michele D., 2422
Weaver, R.H., 3096
Weaver, Sharyn A., 2963
Weaver, Terrance R., 775
Weaver, Thomas C., 1145
Weaver, Thomas M., 2942
Weaver, W.H., 2422
Weaver, Warren W., 1504
Webb, Del E., 43
Webb, Francis M., 1579
Webb, Lewis, Jr., 80
Webb, Louis A., 266
Webb, Marion L., 266
Webb, Pearl M., 1579
Webb, Thomas K., Jr., 2157
Webber, Barbara, 1728
Webber, Eloise, 1346
Webber, Pamela L., 739
Webber, Richard, 1346
Webber, W. Temple, Jr., 3117
Webber, Warren, 918
Webber Charitable Fund, Richard H. and Eloise Jenks, The, 1346
Webber Foundation, Eloise and Richard, 1346
Weber, Charlotte C., 2776
Weber, Clement C., 2427
Weber, John C., 2776
Weber, Nancy W., 637
Weber, Thomas L., 1050
Weber, William P., 3120
Webster, Curtis M., 1672
Webster, Cynthia F., 2481
Webster, Edwin S., 1291
Webster, Elizabeth McGraw, 1672

Webster, Holt W., 3257
Webster, June Norcross, 2155
Webster, Marjorie K., 976
Webster, Martin H., 200
Webster, Wendy W., 125
Wechsler, Alan, 662
Wechsler, Irving A., 2762
Weckbaugh, Anne H., 385
Weckbaugh, Eleanore Mullen, 401
Weckbaugh, John K., 385
Weckbaugh, Walter S., 385
Wedum, John A., 1485
Wedum, Mary Beth, 1485
Wedum, Maynard C., 1485
Weeden, Curtis G., 1657
Weeks, John F., Jr., 1607
Weeks, Joshua J., 1221
Weeks, W.E., 2644
Weeks, William H., 1221
Wege, Peter M., 1384, 1396
Wege, Peter M. II, 1396
Wegener, Clenard, 2646
Wegener, Herman H., 2646
Wegener, K.E., 3333
Wegener, Kenneth, 2646
Wegener, Raymond Lee, 2646
Wegener, Willis B., 2646
Wegmeyer, Carolynne, 1366
Wegner, Karl, 2908
Wehling, R.L., 2562
Wehmeier, Helge H., 2795
Wehr, C. Frederic, 3336
Wehrle, Kartha G., 3265
Weiffenbach, B., 2515
Weigell, Bonnie R., 3302
Weigell, Carl A., 3306
Weiksner, Sandra S., 436
Weil, Andrew L., 2762
Weiler, Alan G., 2187
Weiler, Elaine, 2187
Weiler-Arnow Investment Co., The, 2187
Weiller, Margaret S., 731
Weinberg, Carol, 935
Weinberg, Daniel C., 935
Weinberg, David A., 935
Weinberg, Jean H., 2339
Weinberg, John L., 2339, 2347
Weinberg, John S., 2339
Weinberg, Martin S., 1064
Weinberg, Peter A., 2340
Weinberg, Samuel, 2333
Weinberg, Sidney J., Jr., 1850, 2340
Weinberg, Sue Ann, 2339
Weinberg, Sydney H., 2340
Weinberger, Leon J., 3334
Weiner, Leonard H., 1314
Weingart, Ben, 348
Weingart, Stella, 348
Weingarten, Charles, 2675
Weingarten, Gregory, 2675, 2676
Weingarten, Lauren, 2675
Weingarten, Seth, 2293
Weinman, Charles H., 839
Weinstein, Andrea, 1172
Weinstein, Ira J., 2254
Weinstein, Joe, 2342
Weinstein, Linda S., 2221
Weintraub, Hortense, 675
Weintraub, Joseph, 675
Weintraub, Michael, 675
Weintraub, Robert M., 1741
Weir, J. Roy, 2449
Weir, Susan, 232
Weisbrod, Mary E., 2854
Weisel, H.C., Jr., 2767
Weisglass, Celeste C., 1840
Weisglass, Stephen S., 1840
Weisheit, Bowen P., 1121
Weisheit, Bowen P., Jr., 1121
Weisman, Frances R., 2219
Weiss, Arthur, 1407
Weiss, C.C., 434
Weiss, Catherine, 1650

Weiss, Cathy M., 2803
Weiss, Donald P., 1084
Weiss, Eve, 2872
Weiss, Jill Paulette, 432
Weiss, Mary K., 3343
Weiss, Richard M., 432
Weiss, Rickie, 2524
Weiss, Robert E., 3064
Weiss, Solomon M., 2278
Weiss, Stephen, 1652
Weiss, William D., 3343
Weiss, William E., Jr., 3343
Weiss, William L., 774, 930
Weissfeld, Joachim A., 2878
Weissinger, Walter C., Jr., 2148
Weissman, Robert E., 1896
Weitzel, John, 1427
Welch, Henry W., Mrs., 2408
Welch, Karen, 1047
Welch, Robert F., 2165
Welch, Tom, 2954
Welch, W. Perry, 2348
Welch & Forbes, 1183
Welch Allyn, Inc., 1744
Welder, Paul E., 2899
Welker, Ann, 1559
Welker, Norris J., 2637
Weller, Leroy A., 290
Welles, Barbara C., 389
Wellin, Nancy Brown, 2959
Wellington, Elizabeth D., 2343
Wellington, Herbert C., 2198
Wellington, Herbert G., 2343
Wellington, Herbert G., Jr., 2343
Wellington, Patricia B., 2343
Wellington, R.H., 777
Wellington, Thomas D., 2343
Wellman, Barclay O., 2265
Wells, Christine, 3181
Wells, D.K., 648
Wells, Frank G., 120
Wells, Fred W., 1292
Wells, H.K., 1100
Wells, Kappy J., 2136
Wells, L.A., 648
Wells, M.W., Jr., 648
Wells, Preston A., Jr., 676
Wells, William, 2157
Wells Annuity Trust, Ruth L., 2855
Wells Fargo Bank, N.A., 58, 77, 91, 96, 145, 181, 204, 225, 289, 298
Wells Marital Trust, Frank, 2855
Welsh, Gloria, 292
Welsh, Matthew E., 996, 1975
Wenco, Inc. of North Carolina, 2654
Wenco, Inc. of Ohio, 2654
Wendel, Donald C., 2476
Wendel, Edith, 217
Wendel, Larry L., 2604
Wendt, Margaret L., 2344
Wendt, Nancy, 2654
Wendt, R.C., 2654
Wendt, R.L., 2654
Wenger, Consuelo S., 1397
Wenger, Diane, 1397
Wenger, Henry Penn, 1397
Wennberg, John, 1092
Wentworth, Elizabeth B., 1306
Wentz, Sydney F., 1658
Wenzell, Alan T., 2120
Werbelow, David A., 266
Werblow, Nina W., 2345
Werderger, David, 224
Werderman, Del V., 43, 175
Werner, Christine, 1749
Werner, R. Budd, 1383
Werner, S.R., 2490
Werner, Vanda N., 386
Wertheim, Herbert A., 677
Wertheim, Nicole J., 677
Wertheimer, Thomas, 227
Wertlieb, Robert Barry, 554
Wertz, Ronald W., 2749, 2750, 2811

Willis, Ralph N., 1144
Willison, Bruce, 135
Willison, Robert E., 2771
Willits, Harris L., 1724
Willits, Itto A., 1724
Willits, John F., 1724
Willmore, Richard H., 987
Wills, Kenneth, 1490
Willson, George C. III, 1523
Wilmington Trust Co., 519
Wilsen, Carlotta, 2201
Wilsey, Alfred, 257
Wilson, Alfred G., 1403
Wilson, Betty, 1003
Wilson, Blenda J., 1860
Wilson, C.W., 3104
Wilson, Courtenay, 620
Wilson, Donald M., 1705
Wilson, Dorothy B., 2938
Wilson, Dorothy C., 3064
Wilson, Faye, 154
Wilson, Frances W., Mrs., 742
Wilson, Fred B., 742
Wilson, G. Dale, 2604
Wilson, Herbert J., 1345
Wilson, Howard O., 318
Wilson, Isabel Brown, 2959
Wilson, James, 3079
Wilson, James B., 954
Wilson, James Q., 2216
Wilson, Janet C., 2350
Wilson, Jess C., Jr., 192
Wilson, John, 2130
Wilson, John A., 291
Wilson, John J., 2982
Wilson, Joseph C., 2350
Wilson, Joseph R., 2350
Wilson, Josephine D., 2929
Wilson, Justin P., 2933
Wilson, Karen, 1152
Wilson, Katherine M., 2350
Wilson, Kevin, 3201
Wilson, Lee Anne, 2639
Wilson, Lula C., 1404
Wilson, Malcolm, 1832, 1849
Wilson, Marvin N., 3004
Wilson, Matilda R., 1403
Wilson, Michael G., 89
Wilson, Penelope P., 2180
Wilson, Peter, 1510
Wilson, Richard A., 113
Wilson, Rita P., 772
Wilson, Robert A., 2181, 2898
Wilson, Robert F., 1134
Wilson, Sam A., Mrs., 2951
Wilson, Sandra, 2005
Wilson, Sandra H., 624
Wilson, Spence, 2913
Wilson, T.A., 3240
Wilson, Thomas, 1144
Wilson, William III, 269
Wilson, William C., 2938
Wiltse, Leon L., 239
Wimmer, James A., 2755
Winant, Rivington R., 1959
Winchcole, Dorothy C., 1106
Winchester, David P., 939
Windels, Paul, Jr., 433
Winder, Patricia S., 2829
Windle, Janice W., 2996
Windscheffel, Steve, 1043
Windship, William B., 1793
Windsor, Francis, 1419
Windsor, Robert G., 367
Winestone, Ted M., 2928
Wingfield, W.T., 742
Winikow, Linda, 2167
Winkelman, Stanley J., 1381
Winkelmann, Hermann, 1644
Winkler, Charles P., 3193
Winmill, Mark C., 2310
Winn, William R., 1217
Winn, Willis J., 2788

Winn-Dixie Stores, Inc., 679
Winslow, Alicia B., 1819
Winslow, Enid, 2019
Winslow, Julia D., 1725
Winslow, William P., 1303
Winstead, Sam G., 3047
Winston, Bert F., 3095
Winston, Bert F., Jr., 3123
Winston, Charles F., 3128
Winston, Electra Biggs, 3128
Winston, Harry, 2353
Winston, Hathily J., 191
Winston, Lynn David, 3095
Winston, Melinda, 267
Winston, Norman K., 2352
Winston, Ronald, 2353
Winston, Samuel, 797
Winston Foundation, N.K., Inc., The, 2352
Winter, Arthur, 960
Winter, Dorothy G., 960
Winter, Herbert, 217
Winter, Irwin W., 2186
Winter, Stanley, 960
Winter, W.B., 3277
Winters, Mary-Francis, 2221
Winters, Robert C., 1691
Winthrop, John, 1812
Winthrop, Robert, 2354
Wirkkala, Brian M., 2661
Wirtanen, Donald G., 1467
Wirth, Wren Winslow, 1725
Wirtz, Arthur M., Mrs., 972
Wisconsin Electric Power Co., 3337
Wisconsin Natural Gas Co., 3337
Wisconsin Power and Light Co., 3338
Wisconsin Public Service Corp., 3339
Wise, Anderson, 2158
Wise, J.P., 3121
Wise, John J., 3194
Wise, Robert E., 1874, 3064
Wiseman, Ellen E., 2473
Wishart, Alfred W., Jr., 2744, 2745, 2809
Wishart, Steve W., 1464
Wishnack, Marshall B., 3215
Wishner, Florence Bryan, 3166
Wishnia, Steve, 2932
Wishnick, William, 2355
Wismer, Stephen H., 1175
Witcher, Robert C., Rt. Rev., 2031
Witco Chemical Corp., 2355
Witham, Richard N., 1365
Witherspoon, Douglas C., 947
Witherspoon, Jere W., 2386
Withington, Nathan N., 1212
Witten, R. Marshall, 3160
Witunski, Michael, 1549
Witz, Carol A., 1121
Witz, Herbert E., 1121
Wlochowski, Jane E., 493
Wo, David C., 761
Wo, James C., 761
Wo, Juanita C., 761
Wo, Julia C., 761
Wo, Richard C., 761
Wo, Robert C., 761
Wo & Sons, C.S., Inc., 761
Wochok, Taras M., 2718
Wogsland, James, 918
Wohlert, Roger, 1569
Wohlgemuth, Alexander, 2356
Wohlgemuth, Esther, 2356
Wohlgemuth, Morton, 2356
Wohlgemuth, Robert, 2356
Wohlstetter, Charles, 2226
Wojtak, Barry R., 768
Woldenberg, Dorothy, 1085
Woldenberg, Malcolm, 1085
Wolf, Austin K., 417
Wolf, Diane, 1752
Wolf, Elaine, 404
Wolf, Flora Barth, 2808
Wolf, Jamie G.R., 484

Wolf, John M., Sr., 2025
Wolf, Leon M., 1075
Wolf, Lester K., 2802
Wolf, May H., 1074, 1075
Wolf, Melvin, 404
Wolf, Milton A., 2600
Wolf, Richard L., 2018
Wolf, Robert, 2150
Wolf, Rosalie J., 2204
Wolf, Stephen M., 968
Wolfe, Albert, 3268
Wolfe, J.W., 2460
Wolfe, Joan M., 2084
Wolfe, John F., 2610
Wolfe, John W., 2610
Wolfe, Judson A., 2084
Wolfe, Kenneth L., 2748
Wolfe, Laurence A., 348
Wolfe, Mary, 2597
Wolfe, Merle, 2937
Wolfe, William C., Jr., 2610
Wolfen, Werner, 59
Wolfensohn, Elaine, 1804
Wolfensohn, James D., 1120, 1804
Wolff, Benno F., 863
Wolff, John M., 1581
Wolff, John M. III, 1581
Wolff, Robert, 3334
Wolff, Rosalie S., 2279
Wolfson, Cecil, 681
Wolfson, Florence M., 681
Wolfson, Gary L., 681
Wolfson, Louis E., 681, 1294
Wolfson, Merle, 2741
Wolfson, Nathan, 681
Wolfson, Sam W., 681
Wolfson, Saul, 681
Wolfson, Stephen P., 681
Wollen, Carolyn S., 1793
Wollenberg, H.L., 353
Wollenberg, J. Roger, 353
Wollenberg, Richard P., 353
Wollowick, Burton, 682
Wollowick, Gladys, 682
Wollowick, Herbert, 682
Wollowick, Isidore, 682
Wollowick, Janet Amy, 682
Wollowick, Patricia, 682
Wolters, Kate Pew, 1384
Woltman, B.M., 3136
Woltman, W.J., 3136
Woltman Furniture Co., 3136
Womack, C. Suzanne, 1000
Wommack, William W., 2590
Wondergem, Casey, 1340
Wong, Merrily F., 286
Wonsiewicz, Bud, 400
Wood, Anthony C., 2023
Wood, Barbara M.J., 939
Wood, C.O. III, 2863
Wood, Cynthia S., 354
Wood, David S., 2863
Wood, J. Warren III, 1658
Wood, James, 3193
Wood, John M., Jr., 1273
Wood, Mary Ann Q., 3156
Wood, Miriam M., 2863
Wood, Richard D., 999
Wood, Robert A., 1523
Wood, Susannah C.L., 1737
Wood, William, 850
Wood, William P., 2735, 2844
Woodard, Milton P., 581
Woodard, Mitchell R., 372
Woodbury, David K., 1295
Woodd-Cahusac, Sidney A., 450
Wooden, Ruth A., 1850
Woodman, George, 2444
Woodruff, D. Stratton, Jr., 2770
Woodruff, J. Barnett, 718
Woodruff, Robert W., 743
Woodrum, Robert L., 1749
Woods, Charles, 232

Woods, David F., 574
Woods, Earl C., Rev., 1068
Woods, Edward, 1347
Woods, Frank H., 977
Woods, Gary V., 3057
Woods, J.A., 2359
Woods, Laura-Lee Whittier, 351
Woods, Nelle C., 977
Woods, Thomas C. III, 977, 1590
Woodside, Blair C., Jr., 2506
Woodson, James L., 2425
Woodson, Margaret C., 2425
Woodson, Mary Holt W., 2425
Woodson, Paul B., Jr., 2425
Woodson, Robert W., 693
Woodward, Ann Eden, 2359
Woodward, Catherine M., 403
Woodward, Helen W., 346
Woodward, Joanne, 471
Woodward, Paul E., 403
Woodward, Richmond B., 1200
Woodward Governor Co., 978
Woolcott, James, 621
Woolf, Geraldine H., 1086
Woolf, Harry, 2224
Woolf, William C., 1086
Woolley, Donna P., 2660
Woolsey, J.B., 2931
Woolsey, Roy B., 173
Worfel, C. Christopher, 1340, 1357
Workman, James, Rev., 1161
Worley, Kenneth, 1524
Worthen Bank and Trust Co., N.A., 51
Wortz, Peggy Fouke, 96
Wrap-On Co., Inc., 941
Wrather, Christopher C., 355
Wray, Gilda G., 1978
Wright, Arnold W., Jr., 2701
Wright, Arthur M., 867
Wright, Barbara P., 262
Wright, Bernard, 899
Wright, Charles K., 732
Wright, David M., 1296
Wright, Donald F., 331
Wright, Gary, 1510
Wright, Grace A., 2158
Wright, Hasbrouck S., 2769
Wright, Irving S., 1871
Wright, J., 2869
Wright, James O., 3301
Wright, John E., 3270
Wright, Johnie E., 3137
Wright, Kernan, 2604
Wright, Lawrence A., 66
Wright, Linda, 2663
Wright, Marshall, 2470
Wright, Nancy L., 1667
Wright, Patricia D., 775
Wright, R.E., 2708
Wright, Robert G., 2265, 2542
Wright, S.H., 1131
Wright, Shirley A., 1295
Wright, Spencer D. III, 2726
Wright, W.F., Jr., 2970
Wright, W.R., 590
Wright, William B., 1621
Wright, William L., 1999
Wrightson, J. Wallace, 573
Wrightson, Lois I., 1156
Wrigley, R. Alexander, Mrs., 1381
Wrigley, William, 979
Wrigley, William, Jr., 979
Wrigley Jr. Co., Wm., 979
Wriston, Kathryn D., 1975
Wrzesinski, Susan, 1347
Wuester, William O., 1715
Wuesthoff, Winfred W., 3336
Wuliger, E. Jeffrey, 2612
Wuliger, Ernest M., 2612
Wuliger, Gregory, 2612
Wuliger, Timothy F., 2612
Wurtele, C. Angus, 1421
Wyatt, Grady E., Jr., 2897

GEOGRAPHIC INDEX

Foundations and corporate giving programs in boldface type make grants on a national, regional, or international basis; the others generally limit giving to the city or state in which they are located. For local funders with a history of giving in another state, consult the "see-also" references at the end of each state section.

ALABAMA

Alexander City: Russell 21
Andalusia: Andalusia 2, Dixon 11
Bessemer: Hill 14
Birmingham: Alabama 1, Barber 3, BE&K 4, **Bolden 5,** Bruno 6, Bruno 7, Central 8, Daniel 10, Meyer 18, Shook 22, Sonat 23, Stockham 24, Vulcan 25
Brewton: McMillan 17
Enterprise: Gibson 13
Mobile: Dravo 12, May 16, Mitchell 19, Mobile 20
Montgomery: Lowder 15
Sylacauga: Comer 9

see also 103, 419, 596, 645, 693, 702, 717, 739, 741, 763, 777, 903, 1262, 1308, 1309, 1384, 1458, 1634, 2005, 2602, 2817, 2826, 3121, 3124, 3185

ALASKA

see 103, 763, 2826, 3227, 3237, 3252

ARIZONA

Flagstaff: Raymond 39
Phoenix: A.P.S. 26, Arizona 27, Bank 28, First 29, Flinn 30, Grossman 32, Phelps 38
Prescott: **Kieckhefer 35,** Morris 37
Scottsdale: Globe 31, Hankins 33
Tucson: Hermundslie 34, Marshall 36, Southern 40, Tucson 41, **Van Schaick 42**
Wickenburg: Webb 43

see also 103, 400, 420, 581, 763, 903, 922, 1240, 1456, 1458, 1548, 1581, 1599, 1751, 1837, 1948, 2214, 2494, 2654, 2926, 3246, 3259

ARKANSAS

Arkadelphia: Sturgis 53
Bentonville: Wal-Mart 54
Harrison: McKesson 49
Little Rock: Arkansas 44, Arkansas 45, Arkla 46, Ottenheimer 50, Riggs 51
Malvern: Sturgis 52
Springdale: Jones 47, Jones 48

see also 103, 160, 212, 763, 913, 1337, 1399, 1458, 1563, 1569, 1574, 1624, 1634, 2005, 2433, 2445, 2626, 2627, 2852, 2913, 2926, 2935, 3114, 3185

CALIFORNIA

Anaheim: Karcher 196
Aptos: Solari 308
Arcadia: Berger 80
Bakersfield: Arkelian 64
Berkeley: Langendorf 206
Beverly Hills: Ahmanson 57, Brotman 90, Factor 128, Goldsmith 157, Grancell 159, Great 160, Hanover 167, Kantor 195, **Konheim 201,** Lincy 213, Litton 214, Pickford 273, Smith 306, Stein 316, Western 350, Wrather 355
Borrego Springs: Burnand 93
Buena Park: Jerome 189
Burbank: Burns 95, Disney 120, Gold 155, Rigler-Lawrence 281, Thornton 330
Carmel: McMahan 233, Segal 299
Clayton: Schlinger 294
Commerce: Strauss 319
Compton: Familian 130
Concord: Garaventa 143, Hofmann 177, Tosco 332
Corona del Mar: Hewitt 173
Cupertino: Apple 62
Davis: **Research 280**
Downey: Pacific 261
El Segundo: Aerospace 56, Computer 111
Eureka: Humboldt 181
Fresno: Peters 270, Radin 278
Gardena: Nissan 250
Glendale: Bireley 82, Forest 138, Itakura 186
Hollywood: Fusenot 139
Irvine: Fluor 137, Irvine 184
La Jolla: Copley 114, Dr. Seuss 122, Parker 263, Stern 317
Laguna Beach: Oser 256
Larkspur: Marin 224
Long Beach: Fairfield 129, Miller 239, Norris 253
Los Altos: **Packard 262**
Los Altos Hills: **Moore 243**
Los Angeles: Alpert 59, Baker 68, Barker 71, Booth 83, Boswell 85, Broccoli 89, California 96, **Carsey 100,** Cedars-Sinai 101, City 104, Cohen 107, Coldwell 108, Columbia 109, Crummer 116, Day 117, Doheny 121, Drown 123, Early 124, **Eisenberg 126,** Farmers 132, First 135, Geffen 147, Goldwyn 158, Hoag 175, Irmas 182, Jones 192, **Keck 197,** Keck 198, Kirchgessner 200, **Lear 207,** Leavey 208, **Lebus 209,** Leonardt 211, Lodzer 217, Mann 222, McAlister 228, Munger 245, Murphy 247, Norman 251, Occidental 254, Ostern 258, Parsons 264, Platt 274, **Plitt 275,** Pointer 276, Seaver 297, Southern 310, Sprague 312, Stauffer 314, Stuart 320, Teledyne 327, Thomas 329, Times 331, Union 338, Union 339, Van Nuys 344, Wasserman 347, Weingart 348, Weisz 349

Menlo Park: **Compton 110,** Johnson 191, **Kaiser 194,** Lucas 219
Modesto: Bright 88, Gallo 140, Rogers 284
Monterey: AT&T 65, Monterey 240, Monterey 241
Moraga: Beaver 74
Napa: Gasser 146
Newark: PCS 268
Newport Beach: Beckman 76, Steele 315, Thagard 328
Novato: Fireman's 134
Oakland: Clorox 105, Clorox 106, East 125, Hedco 170, Skaggs 304
Orange: Baker 67, Gerard 152, Wynn 356
Oxnard: Livingston 215, Swift 323
Pacific Palisades: Stern 318
Pacifica: Callison 97
Palo Alto: Hewlett-Packard 174, Syntex 326, Varian 345
Palos Verdes Estates: **Harman 169,** Van Nuys 343
Pasadena: Baxter 72, Beynon 81, Connell 113, Essick 127, Garland 144, Hoffman 176, Hoover 179, Howe 180, MacKenzie 221, Murphey 246, Pasadena 265, Pasadena 266, Patron 267, Rincon 282, Simon 303, Smith 305, Stauffer 313
Pico Rivera: Ziegler 358
Playa del Rey: Hannon 166
Rancho Cordova: Sierra 302
Redding: McConnell 231
Redlands: **Pfeiffer 272**
Ross: Gruber 162
Sacramento: Arata 63, Sacramento 286, Setzer 300
Salinas: Harden 168
San Diego: Benbough 79, Burnham 94, Joslyn 193, Lane 205, Masserini 225, McCarthy 230, Pratt 277, San Diego 287, Scripps 296
San Francisco: Allen 58, Bank 69, **BankAmerica 70,** Bechtel 75, Bekins 77, Bothin 86, Brenner 87, Brunetti 91, Campini 98, Chevron 103, Crocker 115, de Dampierre 118, First 136, Gamble 141, Gap 143, Garnier 145, Gellert 148, Gellert 149, Gellert 150, Gerbode 153, Gilmore 154, Goldman 156, Haas 163, Haas 164, Hale 165, Herbst 172, Hogan 178, Irvine 183, Irwin 185, Jewett 190, Koret 202, Kovshar 203, Laffin 204, Levi 212, Lurie 220, Margoes 223, McBean 229, McKesson 232, McMicking 234, Montgomery 242, Osher 257, Oxnard 260, Roberts 283, San Francisco 288, Sanguinetti 289, Schwab 295, Seebe 298, Shaklee 301, Southern 311, Stuart 321, Stulsaft 322, Swig 324, Swig 325, Transamerica 334, U.S. 337, van Loben Sels 342, Wilbur 352, Wollenberg 353, Zellerbach 357
San Jose: Center 102, Gross 161, Santa Clara 291, Valley 340
San Leandro: Bellini 78, Treadwell 335
San Mateo: Bay 73, Peninsula 269, Petersen 271

COLORADO

CONNECTICUT

DELAWARE

DISTRICT OF COLUMBIA

FLORIDA

GEORGIA

Atlanta: Anncox 684, Arnold 685, Atlanta 686, Atlanta 687, Camp 692, Campbell 693, Center 694, Coca-Cola 696, Cox 698, Davis 699, Dodson 700, Dunn 701, Elkin 702, English 703, Equifax 704, Exposition 705, Franklin 707, Gage 708, Georgia 709, Georgia 710, Georgia 711, Georgia-Pacific 712, Glancy 714, Harland 715, Health 716, Lee 720, Lipscomb 721, Livingston 722, Marshall 723, Marshall 724, Mauldin 725, McCamish 726, Moore 727, Murphy 728, National 729, Patterson-Barclay 730, Rich 731, Shallenberger 732, Spalding 734, Tomlinson 735, Tull 736, UPS 737, Wardlaw 738, Whitehead 740, Whitehead 741, Woodruff 743, Woodward 744
Colquitt: Jinks 719
Columbus: Bradley-Turner 688, Illges 717, Illges 718
Decatur: Wilson 742
Forest Park: Cobb 695
La Grange: Callaway 690, Callaway 691
Macon: Burke 689
Norcross: GFF 713
Savannah: South 733
Thomaston: Community 697
West Point: West Point 739

see also 103, 212, 419, 456, 488, 531, 596, 628, 645, 660, 763, 864, 905, 913, 1348, 1372, 1458, 1493, 1526, 1634, 1641, 1676, 1708, 1751, 1764, 1837, 1872, 2154, 2242, 2243, 2323, 2392, 2401, 2449, 2463, 2474, 2548, 2713, 2817, 2893, 2895, 2926, 2934, 3185, 3247

HAWAII

Honolulu: Alexander 745, Atherton 746, Baldwin 747, Bancorp 748, Castle 750, Cooke 751, Frear 752, Hawaii 753, Hawaiian 754, McInerny 755, PRI 756, Scott 757, Vidinha 758, Wilcox 759, Wilcox 760, Wo 761, Zimmerman 762
Kailua: Castle 749

see also 103, 136, 153, 185, 763, 1374, 1555, 2194, 2994, 3252

IDAHO

Boise: Boise 763, Cunningham 764, Daugherty 765, West 766
Sun Valley: Whiting 767

see also 174, 190, 400, 1462, 1599, 1672, 2291, 2494, 2852, 3146, 3185, 3228, 3232, 3237, 3252, 3258

ILLINOIS

Arlington Heights: McGraw 895
Aurora: Aurora 783, Northern 910
Barrington: Andersen 778
Batavia: Furnas 850
Bloomington: Funk 849, State 959
Centralia: Centralia 818
Chicago: Allen-Heath 771, American 773, Ameritech 774, Amoco 775, Amsted 776, Amsted 777, AON 781, Bauer 786, Beidler 789, Bersted 792, Bersted 793, Best 794, Blair 796, Blum 798, Blum-Kovler 799, Boothroyd 801, Borwell 802, Bowyer 803, Brach 805, Buehler 808, Butz 810, Caestecker 811, Carylon 812, Centel 816, Centel 817, Chicago 819, Chicago 820, Chicago 821, Chicago 822, CNA 824, Coleman 825, Commonwealth 826, Cox 827, Crown 828, Davee 830, Deering 831, Donnelley 835, Driehaus 837, Eisenberg 839, Field 840, FMC 842, Fraida 844, Frankel 846, Fry 848, Galter 851, GATX 853, Geraldi-Norton 854, Getz 855, Goldenberg 856, GSC 858, Hammer 859, Harris 861, Harris 863, Hartmarx 864, Hermann 865, Inland 870, Johnson 870, Keeney 871, Kelly 872, Kemper 873, Knowles 877, Lederer 878, Lederer 879, Lehmann 880, Levie 881, Lewis 882, Lumpkin 884, Lurie 885, MacArthur 887, Manilow 888, Martin 889, Mayer 890, Mazza 891, McCormick

892, McCormick 893, Mitchell 900, Morton 902, Navistar 906, Northern 911, Offield 912, Opler 915, Payne 916, Peoples 917, Perkins 919, Pilot 921, Piper 922, Playboy 923, Polk 924, Prentice 926, Prince 927, Pritzker 928, Quaker 929, Quaker 930, R.F. 931, Ragen 932, Regenstein 934, Replogle 936, Retirement 937, Rhoades 938, Rothschild 940, Ryan 942, Salerno 943, Sang 945, Schneider 946, Scholl 947, Seabury 948, Sears 950, Shapiro 951, Shaw 952, Simpson 953, Siragusa 954, Smail 955, Special 956, Sprague 957, Stern 960, Stone 961, Stone 962, Susman 964, Thompson 965, Thorson 966, Trans 967, United 968, USG 969, Ward 971, Washington 972, Winona 976, Woods 977, Wrigley 979
Decatur: Andreas 779, Archer-Daniels-Midland 782, Millikin 899, Staley 958
Deerfield: Baxter 787, Baxter 788, Walgreen 970
DeKalb: DeKalb 832
Des Plaines: Blowitz-Ridgeway 797, Frank 845
Elmhurst: Duchossois 838
Evergreen Park: Dower 836, First 841
Glen Ellyn: Klenk 876
Glencoe: Hoover 866
Glenview: Illinois 867, Logan 883, Rice 939, Yacktman 980
Gurnee: Petersen 920
Hinsdale: Bere 791, Harper 860
Lake Forest: Brach 804, Buchanan 807, Dick 833
Libertyville: Forest 843
Lincolnshire: Milbro 898
Lombard: MidCon 897
Long Grove: Kemper 874
Mattoon: Bock 800
Melrose Park: Alberto-Culver 769, Jewel 869
Naperville: Nalco 904, Nalco 905
Niles: Cuneo 829, MacArthur 886
North Chicago: Abbott 768
Northbrook: Allstate 772, Harris 862, Salwil 944
Northfield: White 974
Oak Brook: Axia 784, Buntrock 809, CBI 815, McDonald's 894, Russell 941, Waste 973
Oakbrook Terrace: Meyer-Ceco 896
Orland Park: Andrew 780
Peoria: Bielfeldt 795, Caterpillar 813, Caterpillar 814, Peoria 918, Redhill 933
Quincy: Moorman 901
Rockford: Aldeen 770, Barber-Colman 785, CLARCOR 823, Sundstrand 963, Woodward 978
Rolling Meadows: Whitman 975
Roscoe: Beloit 790, Neese 907
Rosemont: Pontikes 925
Schaumburg: Galvin 852, Motorola 903, OMRON 914
Skokie: Brunswick 806, Grainger 857, Searle 949
Springfield: Franklin 847
St. Charles: Norris 909
Sterling: Dillon 834
Waukegan: OMC 913
Wilmette: New Prospect 908
Winnetka: Klein 875, Relations 935

see also 31, 105, 114, 137, 220, 250, 362, 396, 420, 612, 625, 676, 763, 994, 1019, 1022, 1029, 1219, 1297, 1308, 1322, 1348, 1397, 1433, 1435, 1458, 1466, 1526, 1562, 1563, 1624, 1701, 1708, 1751, 1764, 1774, 1830, 1837, 1882, 1954, 2104, 2242, 2243, 2445, 2449, 2474, 2709, 2838, 2852, 2895, 2926, 2991, 3052, 3118, 3185, 3194, 3247, 3259, 3273, 3279, 3282, 3290, 3326

INDIANA

Columbus: Custer 987, Heritage 993
Elkhart: Martin 1002, Miles 1004
Fort Wayne: Cole 986, English-Bonter-Mitchell 988, Foellinger 989, Fort 990, Journal-Gazette 997, Lincoln 1000, Magee-O'Connor 1001, Schust 1012, Zollner 1013
Hammond: Northern 1007
Indianapolis: Clowes 985, Griffith 992, Hook 994, INB 995, Indianapolis 996, Lilly 998, Lilly 999, Metropolitan 1003, Moriah 1005, Noyes 1008, Reilly 1011

Muncie: Ball 982, Ball 983, Muncie 1006
South Bend: Clark 984, Oliver 1010
Terre Haute: Froderman 991, Oakley 1009
Valparaiso: Anderson 981

see also 763, 774, 776, 777, 823, 864, 868, 869, 873, 885, 906, 913, 937, 1055, 1308, 1309, 1322, 1337, 1348, 1358, 1399, 1563, 1624, 1774, 1830, 1872, 2323, 2415, 2445, 2474, 2533, 2544, 2602, 2668, 2669, 2670, 2709, 2713, 2817, 3052, 3185

IOWA

Belle Plaine: Mansfield 1023
Cedar Rapids: Cedar 1016, Hall 1018
Davenport: Iowa 1019, Lee 1022, Quad 1029
Des Moines: Bohen 1014, Employers 1017, Mid-Iowa 1025, Pioneer 1026, Principal 1027, Principal 1028
Dubuque: Wahlert 1030
Mason City: Kinney-Lindstrom 1020
Muscatine: Carver 1015
Newton: Maytag 1024
Pella: Kuyper 1021

see also 136, 326, 400, 850, 869, 873, 874, 903, 937, 1348, 1458, 1462, 1563, 1589, 1872, 2445, 2602, 2654, 2668, 3185, 3236, 3279

KANSAS

Atchison: Muchnic 1041
Kansas City: Breidenthal 1034
Lawrence: Rice 1042
Logan: Hansen 1037
McPherson: Mingenback 1040
Mission Woods: Marley 1039
Overland Park: Smith 1044
Paola: Baehr 1031
Smith Center: Sarver 1043
Topeka: Topeka 1047
Westwood: Sprint 1045, Sprint 1046
Wichita: Bank 1032, Beech 1033, Cessna 1035, DeVore 1036, Koch 1038, Wichita 1048

see also 46, 316, 631, 763, 777, 874, 1466, 1500, 1501, 1502, 1522, 1525, 1526, 1534, 1535, 1541, 1553, 1563, 1567, 1569, 1571, 1574, 1578, 2626, 2627, 2628, 2852, 2926, 3019, 3039, 3222

KENTUCKY

Bowling Green: Houchens 1056
Frankfort: Mills 1062
Irvine: LaViers 1060
Lexington: Long 1061, Robinson 1063, Young 1067
Louisville: Bank 1050, Brennan 1051, Brown 1052, Capital 1053, Cooke 1054, Courier-Journal 1055, Humana 1057, Kentucky 1059, Rosenthal 1064, Rural 1065, Schneider 1066
Newport: Juilfs 1058
Russell: Ashland 1049

see also 105, 142, 212, 421, 509, 702, 937, 1287, 1317, 1348, 1458, 1563, 1971, 2291, 2389, 2409, 2433, 2455, 2474, 2544, 2654, 2713, 2817, 2864, 2918, 2926, 2937, 3185, 3326

LOUISIANA

Alexandria: Coughlin-Saunders 1072
Baton Rouge: Baton 1069
Jennings: Zigler 1088
Metairie: LaNasa-Greco 1077
New Orleans: Azby 1068, Booth-Bricker 1070, Brown 1071, Freeport-McMoRan 1073, Heymann 1074, Heymann-Wolf 1075, Keller 1076, Latter 1078, Libby-Dufour 1079, Lupin 1080, Monroe 1081, New Orleans 1082, Schlieder 1083, Woldenberg 1085, Zemurray 1087
Shreveport: Shreveport-Bossier 1084, Woolf 1086

see also 46, 103, 492, 596, 741, 905, 1563, 1612, 1758, 2005, 2445, 2708, 2852, 2926, 3023, 3087, 3121, 3124, 3185, 3194

MAINE

Augusta: Central 1090
Ellsworth: Maine 1091
Manchester: Maine 1092
Portland: Casco 1089, Shaw's 1093, UNUM 1094

see also 419, 518, 526, 739, 1153, 1173, 1210, 1218, 1234, 1243, 1249, 1272, 1604, 1736, 1793, 1813, 2005, 2094, 2797, 2826, 2870, 2879, 3185

MARYLAND

Accokeek: Higginson 1117
Baltimore: Abell 1095, Aegon 1097, Baltimore 1099, Baltimore 1100, Blaustein 1102, Brown 1103, Capital 1104, First 1111, France 1112, Goldseker 1113, Gross 1114, Hirschhorn 1118, Kelly 1121, Knott 1122, Leidy 1123, Life 1124, Mechanic 1126, Merrick 1127, MNC 1128, Rollins-Luetkemeyer 1134, Rosenberg 1135, Signet 1140, Straus 1141, USF&G 1142, USF&G 1143, Wilson 1144
Bethesda: Clark-Winchcole 1106, Davis 1109, Martin 1125
Chevy Chase: **Hughes 1120,** Pollin 1132
Columbia: Rouse 1136
Gaithersburg: Casey 1105
Hunt Valley: PHH 1131, Procter 1133
Landover: Crown 1107, Dart 1108, Hechinger 1116
Linthicum: Baldwin 1098, Nathan 1130, Schoeneman-Weiler 1138
Lutherville: Mullan 1129
North Bethesda: Abramson 1096
Potomac: Shapiro 1139
Salisbury: Eastern 1110
Silver Spring: **Gumenick 1115**
Timonium: Bank 1101
Towson: Hobbs 1119, Rymland 1137

see also 103, 142, 505, 507, 509, 536, 537, 545, 557, 776, 777, 823, 1736, 1837, 2205, 2323, 2474, 2494, 2555, 2709, 2713, 2780, 2789, 2817, 2835, 2859, 3163, 3175, 3215

MASSACHUSETTS

Bedford: Millipore 1238
Belmont: Pappas 1247, Pappas 1248
Beverly: **New England 1241**
Boston: Adams 1146, Alden 1148, Ashton 1150, Babson 1151, Bank 1152, Bank 1153, BayBanks 1154, Birmingham 1156, Boston 1157, Boston 1158, Boston 1159, Boston 1160, **Cabot 1162,** Cabot-Saltonstall 1163, Cambridge 1165, Campbell 1166, Charlton 1167, Chase 1168, Clifford 1169, **Conservation 1170,** Cove 1171, Cox 1173, Cox 1174, Eaton 1183, Fidelity 1188, Fraser 1192, Gardner 1194, Goldberg 1198, Harrington 1202, Hinduja 1206, Hoffman 1208, Hood 1210, Hornblower 1212, Horne 1213, Humane 1214, Hurdle 1215, Hyams 1216, Jackson 1219, John 1220, King 1223, Levy 1225, **Little 1228,** Marks 1232, **Merck 1235,** Middlecott 1237, New England 1243, New England 1244, Noonan 1245, Old 1246, Peabody 1249, Peabody 1250, Peabody 1251, Perpetual 1254, Pierce 1256, Porter 1259, Prouty 1260, Rabb 1261, Redstone 1263, Reisman 1264, Riley 1265, Rubenstein 1268, Sailors' 1270, Saltonstall 1271, Sawyer 1272, Schrafft 1273, Shapiro 1275, Shawmut 1276, Sheraton 1277, Sherman 1278, State 1280, Stoneman 1287, Stratford 1288, Thompson 1289, Tupancy-Harris 1290, Webster 1291, Wolfson 1294
Brockton: Home 1209
Brookline: Cowan 1172, Florence 1190, Gorin 1199
Burlington: Heydt 1204
Cambridge: Cambridge 1164, Lotus 1229, Polaroid 1258, Rowland 1267
Canton: Merkert 1236
Chestnut Hill: Ford 1191, General 1195, General 1196, Smith 1279
Concord: Stearns 1281
Dalton: Crane 1175
Dedham: Yawkey 1298
East Longmeadow: Davis 1178
Fairhaven: Acushnet 1145
Framingham: Feldberg 1187, Perini 1252, Perini 1253, Williams 1293
Groton: NEBS 1240
Holliston: Poitras 1257
Hopedale: Hopedale 1211
Hyannis: Kelley 1222
Lawrence: Rogers 1266
Lexington: Raytheon 1262
Lowell: Fay 1186
Lynn: Eastern 1182, Gerondelis 1197
Malden: Lipsky 1227
Marion: Island 1218
Maynard: Digital 1180
Melrose: Bayrd 1155
Methuen: Russell 1269, Stearns 1282
Needham: **Linnell 1226**
Newburyport: Arakelian 1149
North Andover: Stevens 1283, Stevens 1284
Quincy: Brooks 1161, **Grass 1200**
Readville: Shapiro 1274
South Weymouth: Johnson 1221
Springfield: Massachusetts 1233, Monarch 1239, Wells 1292
Stockbridge: High 1205
Sudbury: Henderson 1203
Tewksbury: Demoulas 1179
Wakefield: M/A-Com 1231
Waltham: First 1189
Wareham: Stone 1286
Wellesley: **EG&G 1184, Iacocca 1217**
Westborough: New England 1242
Woburn: Cummings 1176, Lechmere 1224
Worcester: Alden 1147, Daniels 1177, Doehla 1181, Ellsworth 1185, Fuller 1193, Harrington 1201, Hoche-Scofield 1207, Luce 1230, McEvoy 1234, Persky 1255, Stoddard 1285, Worcester 1295, Wright 1296, Wyman-Gordon 1297

see also 111, 174, 210, 250, 297, 362, 472, 481, 490, 501, 502, 529, 574, 742, 831, 985, 1087, 1092, 1093, 1456, 1458, 1605, 1612, 1624, 1634, 1655, 1736, 1745, 1751, 1755, 1776, 1813, 1837, 1848, 1887, 1908, 1948, 1951, 1956, 1978, 2043, 2072, 2094, 2103, 2104, 2162, 2178, 2205, 2242, 2243, 2257, 2283, 2285, 2299, 2326, 2449, 2494, 2555, 2602, 2709, 2758, 2817, 2864, 2867, 2869, 2870, 2875, 2879, 2884, 3185

MICHIGAN

Alpena: Northeast 1366
Ann Arbor: Ann Arbor 1301, Great 1342, Kennedy 1352, Towsley 1389
Battle Creek: Battle 1303, Kellogg 1350, **Kellogg 1351**
Benton Harbor: Whirlpool 1399
Birmingham: Zuckerman 1407
Bloomfield Hills: DeVlieg 1315, Taubman 1386, Vlasic 1394, Westerman 1398, Wilson 1404
Dearborn: Ford 1328, Ford 1329, Sehn 1377
Detroit: Anderson 1300, ANR 1302, DeRoy 1314, Farwell 1320, Federal-Mogul 1321, Ford 1324, Ford 1325, Ford 1326, Ford 1327, **General 1334,** General 1335, General 1336, Herrick 1343, Hess 1344, Hudson-Webber 1346, Levy 1355, McGregor 1358, Pagel 1368, Ratner 1372, Shiffman 1379, Skillman 1380, Southeastern 1381, Tracy 1390, Wenger 1397, Wilson 1403, Zimmerman 1406
Farmington Hills: Michigan 1359, Sage 1375, Thomas 1387
Flint: Bishop 1306, Flint 1323, **Mott 1363, Mott 1364,** Whiting 1400
Fremont: Fremont 1331, Gerber 1337
Grand Haven: Loutit 1357

Grand Rapids: DeVos 1316, Frey 1332, Grand 1340, **Seidman 1378,** Steelcase 1384, Wege 1396
Grosse Pointe: Stewart 1385
Grosse Pointe Farms: Lincoln 1356
Harper Woods: **Triford 1391**
Highland Park: Chrysler 1308, Chrysler 1309
Holland: Padnos 1367
Huntington Woods: Prentis 1370
Jackson: Consumers 1310, Consumers 1311, Jackson 1347
Kalamazoo: Dalton 1312, DeLano 1313, First 1322, Gilmore 1339, Kalamazoo 1349, Upjohn 1392, Upjohn 1393
Lansing: Granger 1341, Lansing 1354, Ransom 1371
Midland: **Allen 1299,** Dow 1317, Gerstacker 1338, Pardee 1369, Royal 1374
Monroe: Monroe 1361
Muskegon: Muskegon 1365, SPX 1383
Romeo: Four 1330
Saginaw: Boutell 1307, Eddy 1319, Mills 1360, Morley 1362, Saginaw 1376, Wickes 1401, Wickson-Link 1402
Saline: Redies 1373
Southgate: World 1405
St. Clair Shores: Earl-Beth 1318, Fruehauf 1333
St. Joseph: Berrien 1305, Sparks 1382, Tiscornia 1388
Troy: Bauervic-Paisley 1304, Holden 1345, K Mart 1348, Kresge 1353, Volkswagen 1395

see also 111, 136, 419, 488, 714, 774, 776, 823, 864, 869, 871, 876, 885, 905, 912, 913, 937, 1297, 1433, 1458, 1577, 1612, 1872, 2458, 2474, 2602, 2709, 2815, 2817, 2838, 3124, 3236, 3272, 3339

MINNESOTA

Bayport: Andersen 1410, Andersen 1411, MAHADH 1450
Duluth: Alworth 1408, Eddy 1436, Mitchell 1460, Ordean 1467
Eden Prairie: Sundet 1478, Wedum 1485
Edina: Caring 1425, Wallin 1482
Excelsior: **Charlson 1429**
Fergus Falls: Otter 1468
Grand Rapids: Blandin 1418
Mahtomedi: O'Brien 1465
Minneapolis: American 1409, Anderson 1412, Baker 1413, Bemis 1416, Cargill 1423, Cargill 1424, Carolyn 1426, Chadwick 1428, Cowles 1430, Cowles 1431, Dain 1432, Dayton 1433, Fingerhut 1438, **Fiterman 1439,** General 1441, Grand 1442, Grand 1443, Greystone 1444, Groves 1445, Honeywell 1446, Howe 1447, Marbrook 1451, **McKnight 1453,** McKnight 1454, Meadowood 1455, Medtronic 1456, Minneapolis 1457, Northern 1461, Numero-Steinfeldt 1463, NWNL 1464, Pax 1469, Phillips 1471, Rauenhorst 1472, Thorpe 1479, Walker 1481, Wasie 1484, Whitney 1487, **Wood-Rill 1488**
Minnetonka: Bell 1415
Red Wing: Red 1473
St. Cloud: Central 1427
St. Louis Park: Tonka 1480
St. Paul: Bauervic 1414, Bigelow 1417, Blue 1419, Bremer 1420, Bush 1421, Butler 1422, Ecolab 1434, Ecolab 1435, Edwards 1437, Fuller 1440, Hubbard 1448, Lang 1449, Mardag 1452, Minnesota 1458, Minnesota 1459, Northwest 1462, O'Shaughnessy 1466, Pentair 1470, Saint 1475, St. Croix 1476, St. Paul 1477, Warner 1483, **Weyerhaeuser 1486**
Stillwater: Rivers 1474

see also 46, 84, 297, 400, 419, 646, 1691, 1751, 1993, 2053, 2426, 2427, 2429, 2458, 3271, 3273, 3279

MISSISSIPPI

Columbus: Phillips 1492
Jackson: Deposit 1489, Feild 1490, Hearin 1491, Walker 1494
Vicksburg: Vicksburg 1493

see also 46, 212, 596, 741, 1399, 1458, 1563, 1843, 2005, 2826, 2913

MISSOURI
Birch Tree: Shaw 1562
Chesterfield: Sachs 1560
Clayton: Brown 1503, Pettus 1555, Stupp 1573, Wolff 1581
Columbia: Shelter 1563
Joplin: Craig 1509
Kansas City: Barrows 1498, Bloch 1499, Bloch 1500, Block 1501, Block 1502, Commerce 1504, Cowden 1507, Dow 1511, Enright 1516, Farmland 1517, Feld 1518, **Francis 1519,** Goppert 1522, Hall 1525, Hallmark 1526, Hallmark 1527, Hamilton 1528, Kansas 1533, Kauffman 1534, Kemper 1535, Kemper 1536, Kemper 1537, Long 1541, Loose 1542, Loose 1543, Lowenstein 1545, Oppenstein 1552, Patton 1553, Reynolds 1558, Smith 1566, Sosland 1567, Speas 1570, Speas 1571, Sunderland 1574, Tension 1575, Ward 1578
Mexico: Green 1523
Sedalia: Ilgenfritz 1529
Springfield: Community 1505, Slusher 1565
St. Louis: Anheuser-Busch 1495, Anheuser-Busch 1496, Anheuser-Busch 1497, Contico 1506, CPI 1508, Danforth 1510, Edison 1512, Edison 1513, Emerson 1514, Emerson 1515, Fullbright 1520, Gaylord 1521, Group 1524, Interco 1530, Jefferson 1531, Jordan 1532, Laclede 1538, Leader 1539, Lichtenstein 1540, Love 1544, **Mallinckrodt 1546,** May 1547, McDonnell 1548, **McDonnell 1549,** Mercantile 1550, Olin 1551, Pet 1554, Pitzman 1556, Ralston 1557, Roblee 1559, Schnuck 1561, Shoenberg 1564, Souers 1568, Southwestern 1569, Stupp 1572, Union 1576, Walker 1577, **Webb 1579,** Whitaker 1580

see also 105, 316, 326, 421, 565, 631, 777, 913, 937, 994, 1034, 1240, 1308, 1309, 1612, 1680, 1993, 2104, 2323, 2474, 2626, 2627, 2643, 2852, 2926, 2991, 3247, 3271, 3273

MONTANA
Billings: Bair 1582, Sample 1584
Butte: MPCo/Entech 1583

see also 396, 400, 419, 605, 1022, 1462, 2489, 3237

NEBRASKA
Chappell: Buckley 1585
Fremont: Keene 1588
Lincoln: Lincoln 1590, **McDonald 1591**
Omaha: Buffett 1586, ConAgra 1587, Kiewit 1589, Omaha 1592, Storz 1594
Scottsbluff: Quivey-Bay 1593

see also 46, 317, 400, 482, 676, 777, 823, 919, 977, 1022, 1350, 1458, 1563, 1574, 1701, 1751, 2852, 2856, 3000, 3019, 3039

NEVADA
Las Vegas: Bing 1595
Reno: **Hilton 1596,** Redfield 1597, Stearns-Blodgett 1598, Wiegand 1599

see also 43, 191, 212, 2852, 2926

NEW HAMPSHIRE
Concord: Bean 1600, Eastman 1603, Jameson 1606, New Hampshire 1607, Smith 1609
Hampton: Chatham 1601, **Penates 1608**
Manchester: Cogswell 1602
Portsmouth: Foundation 1604

Rye Beach: Fuller 1605
Salem: **Trust 1610**

see also 1093, 1153, 1173, 1210, 1224, 1240, 1243, 1249, 1262, 1266, 1272, 1291, 1736, 1813, 2094, 2104, 2817, 2870, 2879, 2926

NEW JERSEY
Annandale: Rippel 1695
Basking Ridge: **Crum 1627**
Bayonne: **Vollmer 1722**
Bernardsville: Jockey 1655
Bridgewater: **Diabetes 1628,** National 1683, Thomas 1712
Camden: Campbell 1622
Chatham: Hyde 1651
Cherry Hill: Subaru 1708
Clifton: Kramer 1664, Schultz 1704
Collingswood: Maneely 1670
Cranbury: Hoyt 1649
Cranford: Brennan 1619, Meyer 1678
Cresskill: Magowan 1669
Denville: Pate 1688
East Orange: Edison 1631
Edison: Midlantic 1679, Visceglia-Summit 1720
Englewood Cliffs: CPC 1624, **Crane 1625,** Lipton 1668
Far Hills: Engelhard 1633, Frelinghuysen 1636
Florham Park: Islami 1653
Fort Lee: La Sala 1665
Gladstone: Brady 1617
Hackensack: Creamer 1626
Haledon: Brawer 1618
Iselin: Englehard 1634
Jersey City: Merck 1677
Kinnelon: **Vollmer 1721**
Lakewood: Havens 1644
Lebanon: Harris 1643
Livingston: Taub 1710
Madison: Schering-Plough 1701, Schering-Plough 1702
Mahwah: Rukin 1697
Millburn: Read 1693
Montclair: Schumann 1705, Victoria 1719
Montvale: Mercedes-Benz 1674
Moorestown: Snyder 1707
Morris Plains: Warner-Lambert 1723
Morristown: Allied-Signal 1611, Dodge 1630, Kirby 1661, MCJ 1673, New Jersey 1684, Sandy 1699
Murray Hill: Willits 1724
New Brunswick: Fund 1637, Johnson 1656, Johnson 1657, Rutgers 1698
New Vernon: Klipstein 1663
Newark: Mutual 1680, Ohl 1686, Prudential 1691, Public 1692, Sutcliffe 1709, Upton 1716, Van Houten 1717
North Bergen: Capita 1623
North Haledon: Schamach 1700
North Plainfield: **Fanwood 1635**
Nutley: Hoffmann-La Roche 1647, Hoffmann-La Roche 1648
Oakhurst: Terner 1711
Old Bridge: Brunetti 1620
Paramus: **Gulton 1642,** Lazarus 1666
Parsippany: Armco 1614, General 1639, Nabisco 1681, Nabisco 1682
Princeton: American 1613, **Bonner 1615,** Borden 1616, Bunbury 1621, Garfield 1638, **Johnson 1658,** Kerney 1660, McGraw 1672, Winslow 1725
Rahway: Merck 1675
Roseland: Dickinson 1629, **Schimmel 1703**
Rumson: **Huber 1650**
Saddle River: Martin 1671
Secaucus: Petrie 1689
Somers Point: **Innovating 1652**
Somerville: Hoechst 1645, Hoechst 1646
Summit: **Reeves 1694**
Teaneck: **Grand 1640**
Tenafly: Kennedy 1659
Teterboro: Klatskin 1662
Union: Elizabethtown 1632
Upper Saddle River: **Roth 1696**
Wall: New Jersey 1685
Warren: Grassmann 1641, Schwartz 1706, Union 1715

Wayne: American 1612, Union 1714
West Caldwell: Orenstein 1687
West Long Branch: Pollak 1690
West Orange: Leavens 1667, Turrell 1713
West Paterson: **Jaqua 1654**
Westwood: Van Pelt 1718
Whitehouse Station: Merck 1676

see also 103, 136, 137, 174, 250, 428, 504, 509, 536, 542, 596, 618, 635, 874, 905, 1116, 1118, 1348, 1435, 1736, 1773, 1813, 1831, 1846, 1848, 1862, 1865, 1871, 1886, 1934, 1960, 1970, 1978, 2004, 2031, 2072, 2096, 2103, 2104, 2114, 2140, 2164, 2167, 2174, 2210, 2310, 2323, 2433, 2449, 2555, 2602, 2709, 2713, 2751, 2775, 2780, 2803, 2817, 2826, 2856, 3121, 3163, 3190, 3194

NEW MEXICO
Albuquerque: Albuquerque 1726, **Bellamah 1727**
Carlsbad: Carlsbad 1728
Hobbs: Maddox 1729

see also 103, 212, 260, 359, 400, 1262, 2626, 2627, 3039, 3071

NEW YORK
Albany: Albany 1739, Albany's 1740, **Kirby 2033,** Klock 2037, Mohawk-Hudson 2124
Armonk: IBM 2002, **Laerdal 2050**
Auburn: Metcalf 2116
Bayside: Vogler 2331
Bedford: Joyce 2017
Binghamton: Decker 1880, Hoyt 1995
Bronxville: McGraw 2103, Voute 2332
Brooklyn: Parshelsky 2175, Ritter 2220, St. Giles 2287, **Winkler 2351**
Buffalo: Baird 1768, Buffalo 1816, Buffalo 1817, Cornell 1863, Cummings 1869, Goldome 1947, Goode 1952, Goodyear 1955, Graphic 1960, Julia 2018, Knox 2040, Mark 2089, National 2142, Rich 2215, Wendt 2344
Canajoharie: Arkell 1757
Carmel: Weinstein 2342
Chappaqua: Hettinger 1987
Cobleskill: Galasso 1932
Cold Spring Harbor: Kennedy 2029
Corning: Corning 1864
Cortland: **McDonald 2101**
Dunkirk: Northern 2157
Endicott: Kresge 2047
Garden City: McCarthy 2099
Glen Cove: Murcott 2138
Glen Head: Barker 1774
Great Neck: Bass 1778, Ferkauf 1914, Gruber 1968, Gurwin 1969, Seaman 2259, Ushkow 2325, Weinstein 2341
Hartsdale: Gaisman 1931
Hobart: O'Connor 2161
Horseheads: Anderson 1754
Hudson: **Potts 2196**
Huntington: **Porter 2195**
Jamestown: Carnahan-Jackson 1828, Gebbie 1933, Hultquist 1999, Sheldon 2265
Jericho: Alpern 1745, Boxer 1805
Johnstown: Knox 2039
Lewiston: Dent 1884
Little Neck: Leviton 2066
Long Island City: Fife 1917, Schweckendieck 2258
Manhasset: **Glenn 1941, Patrina 2176**
Middle Granville: Beach 1779
Mill Neck: **Smithers 2276**
Millbrook: Millbrook 2121
Millerton: Kramer 2045
Mineola: Flemm 1919
Mount Kisco: Icahn 2003, Kohlberg 2041, Mathers 2093
New Hyde Park: Brown 1814
New Rochelle: **Kaufmann 2026**
New York: Abrams 1730, Abrons 1731, Achelis 1732, **Ada 1733,** Adler 1734, **Aeroflex 1735,** AKC 1737,

Akzo **1738,** Alexander 1741, Allen 1742, Allen 1743, Altman 1746, Altschul 1747, Amax 1748, AmBase 1749, **American 1750,** American 1751, **American 1752,** American 1753, Aquidneck 1755, **Archbold 1756,** Aron 1758, ASARCO 1759, **ASDA 1760,** AT&T 1761, **AT&T 1762, Atlantic 1763,** Avon 1764, Bachmann 1765, Badgeley 1766, **Baker 1769,** Banbury 1770, Bank 1771, Bankers 1772, Bard 1773, Barth 1776, **Bartsch 1777, Beck 1780, Bedminster 1782,** Beir 1784, Belfer 1785, Benenson 1786, Berkowitz 1787, **Berlex 1788, Bernhard 1789,** Bernstein 1790, **Biddle 1791,** Bilotti 1792, Bingham 1793, **Blackmer 1794,** Bleibtreu 1795, Blinken 1796, Bluhdorn 1797, Bobst 1799, Bodman 1800, Booth 1801, Borden 1802, Botwinick-Wolfensohn 1804, Brain 1806, Branta 1807, Bristol-Myers 1808, Bristol-Myers 1809, Brody 1810, Bronfman 1811, **Brookdale 1812,** Brooks 1813, BT 1815, **Bugher 1818, Burnham 1819,** Burns 1820, Burns 1821, **Butler 1822,** Calder 1823, Canno 1824, **Cantor 1825,** Capital 1826, Carmel 1827, **Carnegie 1829,** Carter-Wallace 1831, Carvel 1832, Cary 1833, Chait 1834, Charina 1835, Chase 1837, **Chase 1838,** Cheatham 1840, Chernow 1841, **China 1842,** Chisholm 1843, CIT 1844, Citicorp/Citibank 1845, Claiborne 1846, Clark 1847, Clark 1848, Clark 1849, **Clark 1850,** Clark 1851, Clemente 1852, Coleman 1853, Coleman 1854, Coles 1855, Colgate-Palmolive 1856, **Collins 1857,** Coltec 1858, Common 1859, Commonwealth 1860, Cooperman 1862, Corzine 1865, Cowles 1866, Crane 1867, Cullman 1868, **Cummings 1870,** Cummings 1871, **Dammann 1873, Dana 1874, Dana 1875, Day 1876, de Rothschild 1877,** Dean 1878, DeCamp 1879, Delacorte 1881, Delany 1882, Diamond 1885, Dillon 1886, Donaldson 1887, **Dorot 1888,** Dover 1890, Dreitzer 1891, Dreyfus 1892, Dreyfus 1893, Dreyfus 1894, **Dula 1895,** Dun 1896, Dyson 1897, Edouard 1900, **Eisner 1901, Ellworth 1902,** Enders 1903, **Equitable 1904,** Ernst 1905, **Ettinger 1907,** Evans 1908, Evans 1909, Fahey 1910, Falk 1911, Feil 1912, Feuerstein 1915, **Fife 1916, Fish 1918,** Forbes 1920, Forchheimer 1921, **Ford 1922,** Foster 1923, Foundation 1924, **Frankel 1925, Freeman 1926,** Frese 1927, Frohlich 1928, **Fuld 1929,** Fund 1930, Geist 1934, **Gelb 1935,** Gerschel 1936, Gerschel 1937, Gibbs 1938, Gilman 1940, Goldie-Anna 1942, Golding 1943, Goldman 1944, Goldman 1945, Goldman 1946, Goldsmith 1948, Goldstein 1949, Goldstein 1950, Goodman 1953, Goodstein 1954, Gordon/Rousmaniere/Roberts 1956, **Gould 1957, Grant 1958,** Grant 1959, Grateful 1961, Green 1962, Greenberg 1963, Greene 1964, Greene 1965, Greenwall 1966, Griffis 1967, Hagedorn 1970, Haggin 1971, **Hansen 1972,** Harriman 1973, Harriman 1974, **Hartford 1975,** Hatch 1976, Hausman 1977, Hayden 1978, Hazen 1979, **Hearst 1980, Hearst 1981,** Heckscher 1982, Heijmans 1983, Heineman 1984, Helmsley 1985, Hess 1986, Heyward 1988, Hilson 1989, Hirschl 1990, Hopkins 1992, Hughes 1996, Hugoton 1997, Hunt 2000, Hutchins 2001, IFF 2004, Iroquois 2006, **Ittleson 2008,** Jacobson 2009, Jesselson 2010, JM 2011, Joelson 2012, Johnson 2013, Johnson 2014, Jurodin 2019, **Kade 2020,** Kalikow 2021, Kaplan 2022, Kaplan 2023, Katz 2024, Kaufmann 2025, Kekst 2027, Kellogg 2028, Kidder 2030, Killough 2031, Kimmelman 2032, Klau 2034, Klein 2035, Klingenstein 2036, Klosk 2038, Kopf 2042, Kopf 2043, Kramer 2044, Kravis 2046, Krim 2048, L and L 2049, Lang 2051, Langeloth 2052, Larsen 2053, Lasdon 2054, Lasdon 2055, **Lasker 2056, Lasker 2057,** Lauder 2058, Lazar 2060, Lee 2061, Leibovitz 2063, Leonhardt 2064, Levin 2065, Levy 2067, Lewis 2068, Lieb 2069, **Lighting 2070,** Link 2072, Lippman 2073, Loeb 2074, Loewenberg 2075, Loews 2076, Lounsbery 2077, Lowenstein 2078, Luce 2079, **MacDonald 2081, MacKall 2082, Macy 2083,** Mailman 2084, Manley 2085, **Manning 2086,** Manufacturers 2087, **Mapplethorpe 2088,** Marks 2090, **Marx 2091,** Mastronardi 2092, Mayer 2095, McConnell 2100, McGonagle 2102, McGraw-Hill 2104, Mellam 2105, Mellon 2106, Melly 2107, Memton 2109, Mendik 2110, Menschel 2111, Mercy 2112, Merrill 2113, Merrill 2114, **Mertz-Gilmore 2115,** Metropolitan 2117, Meyer 2118, Milbank 2119, **Milbank 2120,** Miller 2122, Milstein 2123, Monell 2125, Monterey 2126, Moore 2127, Morgan 2128, Morgan 2129, Morgan 2130, Morgan 2131, Morris 2134, Moses 2135, **Mott 2136,** Murray 2139, Mutual 2140, Napier 2141, Neu 2143, New Street 2144, **New World 2145,** New York 2146, New York 2147, **New York 2148,** New York 2149, **New-Land 2150,** Newhouse 2151, Nichols 2153, Noble 2154, **Norcross 2155,** North 2156, Norwood 2159, **Noyes 2160,** O'Herron 2162, O'Toole 2164, Oestreicher 2165, Open 2166, Orentreich 2168, Osborn 2169, OSG 2170, Overbrook 2171, PaineWebber 2172, Paley 2173, Palisades 2174, Peierls 2177, Penick 2178, Perkins 2180, Pfizer 2181, Pfizer 2182, Pforzheimer 2183, Philip 2184, Phillips 2185, **Phillips 2186,** Pines 2187, **Pinewood 2188,** Plant 2189, Pomerantz 2191, Pope 2192, Pope 2193, Port 2194, Price 2197, **Pritschard 2198,** Prospect 2199, Prudential-Bache 2200, Quantum 2201, Ramapo 2203, Rapoport 2204, Recanati 2207, Reed 2208, Reicher 2209, Reiss 2210, Republic 2211, **Revlon 2212,** Revson 2213, Rhodebeck 2214, **Richardson 2216,** Ring 2218, Ritter 2219, **Rockefeller 2223, Rockefeller 2224,** Rodgers 2225, Rose 2226, Rose 2227, Rosenberg 2228, Rosenstiel 2229, Rosenwald 2230, Ross 2231, Rubin 2233, Rubinstein 2234, Rudin 2235, Rudin 2236, **Rumsey 2237,** Sacerdote 2238, Sackler 2239, Saks 2240, Salomon 2241, Salomon 2242, Salomon 2243, Saltz 2244, Samuels 2245, **Sandoz 2246,** Saul 2247, Schaffer 2248, Scherman 2249, Scheuer 2250, Schieffelin 2251, Schiff 2252, Schmeelk 2253, Schnurmacher 2254, Schwartz 2255, Schwartz 2256, Schwarzman 2257, Seaver 2260, Sequa 2261, Sharp 2263, Sheinberg 2264, Silfen 2266, Silver 2267, Singer 2268, Sinsheimer 2269, Slaner 2270, Slaughter 2271, Slifka 2272, **Sloan 2273,** Smith 2274, SO 2278, Solow 2279, **Sony 2280, Soros 2281,** Spiegel 2282, Spitzer 2284, Sprague 2285, Spunk 2286, Starr 2288, **Statter 2289,** Steckler 2290, Steele-Reese 2291, Steinberg 2293, Sterling 2294, Stern 2295, Stony 2296, Stott 2297, Stuart 2299, Sulzberger 2300, Summerfield 2301, **Surdna 2302,** Sussman 2303, Swanson 2304, Swid 2305, **Tai 2306, Teagle 2308,** Thanksgiving 2310, **Thompson 2311,** Thorne 2312, Thorne 2313, Tiger 2314, Time 2315, Tisch 2316, Tishman 2317, **Tortuga 2318,** Trimble 2320, Turner 2321, '21' 2322, Unilever 2323, Unterberg 2324, van Ameringen 2326, van Ameringen 2327, **Vanneck-Bailey 2328,** Vidda 2330, Wakefield 2333, Wallach 2335, Washington 2337, Weill-Caulier 2338, Weinberg 2339, **Weinberg 2340,** Wellington 2343, Werblow 2345, Westvaco 2346, Whitehead 2347, **Whitney 2348,** Wiley 2349, Winston 2352, Winston 2353, **Winthrop 2354,** Wishnick 2355, Wohlgemuth 2356, Woodland 2357, Woodstock 2358, Woodward 2359, **Youths' 2360,** Zarkin 2361, **Zenkel 2362, Ziff 2363,** Zimmermann 2364, **Zlinkoff 2365,** Zuckerberg 2366
North Merrick: Lindner 2071
North Tarrytown: Vernon 2329
North Tonawanda: Joy 2016
Norwich: Totman 2319
Nyack: **Chazen 1839**
Old Westbury: Bostwick 1803
Oneonta: Hulbert 1998, Warren 2336
Ossining: Horncrest 1993
Pearl River: Orange 2167
Pleasantville: Reader's 2206
Port Chester: Straus 2298
Port Jefferson Station: Lawrence 2059
Poughkeepsie: McCann 2097
Pound Ridge: Blum 1798
Pulaski: Snow 2277
Purchase: **Essel 1906,** International 2005, PepsiCo 2179, Spiritus 2283
Rego Park: Lefrak 2062

Rochester: Chase 1836, Curtice-Burns/Pro-Fac 1872, Delavan 1883, Dosberg 1889, Eastman 1898, Eastman 1899, Jones 2015, Mayer 2094, Mulligan 2137, Pluta 2190, Rochester 2221, Rochester 2222, **Ross 2232,** Taylor 2307, Wilson 2350
Rockville Centre: Morgenstern 2132
Rye: Barnett 1775, Beinecke 1783
Scarsdale: Bedford 1781, Fein 1913, Raizen 2202, **Sexauer 2262,** Stein 2292
Schenectady: Golub 1951, Smith 2275
Skaneateles: Allyn 1744
Syracuse: Agway 1736, Carrier 1830, Congel-Pyramid 1861, Gifford 1939
Tarrytown: Wallace 2334
Troy: Howard 1994, McCarthy 2098
Wantagh: **Richmond 2217**
Watertown: Northern 2158
Westbury: Mayrock 2096, O'Sullivan 2163, Rauch 2205
White Plains: Israel 2007, Macdonald 2080, Memorial 2108, Morris 2133, Newman 2152, Texaco 2309
Williamsville: Baird 1767
Yonkers: Hoernle 1991

see also 101, 105, 136, 142, 147, 167, 227, 260, 281, 316, 416, 419, 421, 428, 434, 443, 449, 468, 473, 482, 483, 487, 490, 492, 494, 496, 501, 502, 503, 504, 509, 519, 526, 529, 547, 570, 571, 589, 612, 613, 635, 641, 650, 652, 653, 662, 672, 684, 864, 874, 875, 913, 923, 933, 960, 980, 1102, 1114, 1116, 1118, 1132, 1206, 1221, 1224, 1289, 1291, 1308, 1309, 1337, 1348, 1397, 1559, 1569, 1599, 1612, 1620, 1636, 1647, 1648, 1649, 1651, 1659, 1661, 1664, 1665, 1666, 1669, 1670, 1671, 1673, 1687, 1689, 1690, 1693, 1695, 1699, 1711, 1718, 2374, 2449, 2555, 2642, 2668, 2669, 2670, 2671, 2676, 2708, 2709, 2713, 2736, 2742, 2746, 2751, 2752, 2774, 2817, 2826, 2830, 2864, 2867, 2870, 3007, 3008, 3052, 3159, 3190, 3194, 3197, 3236, 3273, 3343

NORTH CAROLINA

Asheville: Western 2423
Chapel Hill: Thomas 2415
Charlotte: American 2367, Belk 2369, Dalton 2381, Dickson 2385, Duke 2386, Duke 2387, Ebert 2389, First 2392, Foundation 2393, Hanes 2400, Hemby 2402, Lance 2403, O'Herron 2406, Provident 2409, Smith 2414, United 2418, Van Every 2419
Concord: Cannon 2378
Durham: **Nickel 2404**
Fayetteville: Rogers 2412
Gastonia: First 2391
Greensboro: Bryan 2373, Burlington 2374, Burlington 2375, Greensboro 2398, Volvo 2420, Weaver 2422
Greenville: Perkins 2407
Lenoir: Broyhill 2372
Mount Airy: Gilmer-Smith 2394
Raleigh: Carolina 2379, Daniels 2382, Daniels 2383, Durham 2388, North Carolina 2405
Research Triangle Park: Burroughs 2376, **Burroughs 2377,** Glaxo 2395, **Glaxo 2396,** Triangle 2417
Salisbury: **Deichman-Lerner 2384,** Salisbury 2413, Woodson 2425
Southern Pines: Cooke 2380
Tryon: Polk 2408
Wilson: Glenn 2397
Winston-Salem: **Babcock 2368,** Blue 2370, Brenner 2371, Finch 2390, Hanes 2399, Harris 2401, Reynolds 2410, Reynolds 2411, Thomasville 2416, Wachovia 2421, Winston-Salem 2424

see also 212, 419, 551, 576, 592, 596, 608, 621, 630, 645, 692, 693, 702, 739, 741, 913, 1116, 1287, 1317, 1337, 1384, 1526, 1559, 1624, 1647, 1751, 1820, 1869, 2445, 2595, 2654, 2713, 2817, 2856, 2889, 2892, 2926, 3121, 3167, 3208, 3215, 3273, 3326

NORTH DAKOTA

Bismarck: Leach 2427
Fargo: Fargo-Moorhead 2426, Stern 2429
Grand Forks: Myra 2428

see also 400, 1022, 1420, 1421, 1461, 1462, 1468, 3298

OHIO

Akron: Akron 2430, Bridgestone/Firestone 2445, Corbin 2461, **Firestone 2480,** GAR 2490, Goodyear 2492, McAlonan 2530, Morgan 2538, Musson 2543, Ritchie 2570, Sisler 2584
Ashtabula: Ashtabula 2437
Aurora: **Austin 2438**
Bryan: **Markey 2527**
Canton: Calhoun 2448, Hoover 2506, Miller 2535, Stark 2591, Timken 2595
Cincinnati: American 2432, Anderson 2434, Campeau 2449, Cincinnati 2455, Cincinnati 2456, Dater 2465, Emery 2472, Fifth 2479, Gould 2493, Gross 2496, Jarson 2512, Kroger 2519, Mayerson 2529, Merrell 2533, Nippert 2546, Ohio 2553, Penn 2555, Procter 2561, Procter 2562, Russell 2574, Schiff 2575, Schmidlapp 2577, Schmidlapp 2578, Semple 2582, Star 2590, Wodecroft 2609
Cleveland: American 2433, Andrews 2435, Bicknell 2442, Britton 2446, BP 2443, Bruening 2447, Case 2450, Centerior 2451, Chisholm 2454, Cleveland 2457, Cleveland-Cliffs 2458, Codrington 2459, Deuble 2468, East 2469, Eaton 2470, **Elisha-Bolton 2471,** Ferro 2477, Ferro 2478, Firman 2481, Forest 2482, Fox 2483, Frohring 2487, Frohring 2488, Gallagher 2489, Gund 2497, H.C.S. 2498, Haskell 2501, **Heed 2502,** Humphrey 2508, Ireland 2511, Jochum-Moll 2513, Kangesser 2514, Lincoln 2523, Mather 2528, Murch 2540, Murphy 2542, National 2544, O'Neill 2550, O'Neill 2551, Ohio 2552, Parker-Hannifin 2554, **Perkins 2556,** Prentiss 2560, Reinberger 2566, Reliance 2567, Renner 2568, Rosenthal 2572, Sears 2580, Sherwick 2583, Smith 2585, Smith 2586, Society 2589, Tippit 2596, Treu-Mart 2600, TRW 2602, TRW 2603, White 2607, Women's 2611, Wuliger 2612
Cleveland Heights: Medusa 2532
Columbus: **Armington 2436,** Baird 2439, Battelle 2440, Columbus 2460, English 2473, Evans 2474, Moores 2537, Nationwide 2545, O'Bleness 2549, Pizzuti 2558, SCOA 2579, Wildermuth 2608, Wolfe 2610, Yassenoff 2613
Coshocton: Coshocton 2462
Dayton: Allyn 2431, Cox 2463, Dayton 2466, Dayton 2467, Huffy 2507, Iddings 2509, Kettering 2515, Kettering 2516, Kramer 2518, Kuntz 2520, Mead 2531, Philips 2557, Reynolds 2569
Dover: Reeves 2565
Eastlake: Gould 2494
Elyria: Miller 2534, Nord 2547
Fairlawn: GenCorp 2491
Hamilton: Hamilton 2499
Independence: Centerior 2452
Lancaster: Fairfield 2476
Lorain: Lorain 2524
Loudonville: Young 2614
Mansfield: Sterkel 2592
Marysville: Honda 2504
Maumee: Trinova 2601
Mayfield Heights: Progressive 2563
Mentor: RB&W 2564
Mount Vernon: Mount Vernon 2539
Newark: Evans 2475, Licking 2522
North Canton: Hoover 2505
Norwalk: Schlink 2576
Orrville: Smucker 2587, Smucker 2588
Pepper Pike: Tranzonic 2598, Tranzonic 2599
Piqua: Hartzell-Norris 2500
Sandusky: Frohman 2486
Shaker Heights: Ingalls 2510
Sharon Center: Hillier 2503
Sidney: Monarch 2536
Solon: Lennon 2521

Springfield: Selsor 2581
Toledo: Charities 2453, France 2484, M/B 2526, Ritter 2571, Stranahan 2593, Toledo 2597
Twinsburg: Murdough 2541
Urbana: Grimes 2495
Van Wert: Van Wert 2604
Warren: Wean 2606
Westlake: Nordson 2548
Wickliffe: Lubrizol 2525
Wooster: Frick 2485, Rubbermaid 2573
Youngstown: Beecher 2441, Bremer 2444, Crandall 2464, Kilcawley 2517, Pollock 2559, Tamarkin 2594, Watson 2605, Youngstown 2615

see also 33, 136, 250, 255, 419, 482, 488, 509, 774, 776, 874, 905, 906, 994, 1049, 1058, 1116, 1308, 1309, 1338, 1342, 1348, 1358, 1399, 1612, 1736, 1764, 1837, 2389, 2420, 2654, 2668, 2708, 2709, 2714, 2838, 2860, 2989, 3052, 3215, 3247, 3272, 3326

OKLAHOMA

Ardmore: Goddard 2624, Merrick 2630, **Noble 2631**
Bartlesville: Phillips 2636
Duncan: McCasland 2628
McAlester: Puterbaugh 2637
Norman: Sarkeys 2639
Oklahoma City: American 2616, Boatmen's 2618, Brand 2620, Johnson 2625, Kerr 2626, McGee 2629, Oklahoma 2633, Oklahoma 2634, Oklahoma 2635, Rapp 2638, Scrivner 2640, Share 2641, Wegener 2646
Tulsa: Bernsen 2617, Bovaird 2619, Broadhurst 2621, Campbell 2622, Chapman 2623, Mabee 2627, Occidental 2632, Taubman 2642, Titus 2643, Warren 2644, Warren 2645, Williams 2647, Zarrow 2648

see also 46, 596, 1528, 1548, 1563, 2427, 2445, 2555, 2669, 2670, 2708, 2729, 2852, 2934, 2949, 2983, 3019, 3039

OREGON

Klamath Falls: Jeld-Wen 2654
Lake Oswego: OCRI 2659
Medford: Carpenter 2649
Portland: Chiles 2650, Collins 2651, Collins 2652, Jackson 2653, Louisiana-Pacific 2656, Meyer 2657, Northwest 2658, Oregon 2660, PacifiCorp 2661, Tucker 2662, U.S. 2663, Wheeler 2664
Redmond: Johnson 2655

see also 71, 154, 174, 250, 398, 400, 419, 488, 766, 864, 913, 1022, 1317, 1462, 1599, 1708, 2005, 2852, 3221, 3224, 3227, 3236, 3237, 3241, 3246, 3247, 3252, 3254

PENNSYLVANIA

Allentown: Air 2665, Air 2666, Kift-Thomas 2767, Lehigh 2772, Mack 2780, Pennsylvania 2804, Trexler 2850
Bethlehem: Union 2851, Union 2852
Bradford: **Glendorn 2731**
Bristol: Grundy 2735
Bryn Mawr: McLean 2787, Smith 2831
Camp Hill: Harsco 2740, Kunkel 2769
Chalfont: Byers 2692
Chambersburg: Wood 2863
Coatesville: Lukens 2779
Conshohocken: Quaker 2815
Coraopolis: Massey 2781
Devon: Hooper 2753
Doylestown: Holstrom 2751
DuBois: Mengle 2792
Elkins Park: RAF 2816
Erie: Erie 2722, Lord 2777
Farrell: Sharon 2828
Forty Fort: Sordoni 2837

Gladwyne: Drueding 2717
Greensburg: Greensburg 2734
Gwynedd: J.D.B. 2760
Hanover: Sheppard 2829
Harrisburg: AMP 2673, Harrisburg 2739, Kline 2768, McCormick 2783, Stabler 2839
Haverford: Merit 2794
Havertown: Smith 2832
Hershey: Hershey 2747, Hershey 2748
Huntingdon Valley: Roth 2822
Jeannette: Millstein 2796
Johnstown: Crown 2713
King of Prussia: Berry 2685
Lafayette Hill: Widener 2858
Lancaster: Hamilton 2738, Steinman 2842, Steinman 2843
Latrobe: **Kennametal 2766,** McFeely-Rogers 2785, McKenna 2786
Lebanon: Caplan 2695
McKeesport: Crawford 2711, Murphy 2798
Mechanicsburg: Wells 2855, **Whitaker 2857**
Media: Measey 2788
New Castle: Hoyt 2756
New Holland: Crels 2712
Newtown: SPS 2838
Norristown: Arcadia 2677, Charlestein 2699
Norwood: Boiron 2688
Oil City: Justus 2764, Lesher 2773
Oley: **Butz 2691**
Oxford: Oxford 2801
Palmerton: Horsehead 2755
Paoli: AMETEK 2672, **duPont 2718**
Philadelphia: Arronson 2678, Beatty 2681, Bell 2682, Betz 2686, Buck 2689, Cameron 2693, **Carpenter 2696, Cassett 2698,** CIGNA 2700, CIGNA 2701, Colket 2705, Colonial 2706, Consolidated 2709, Craig-Dalsimer 2710, Dietrich 2715, Dolfinger-McMahon 2716, Elf 2721, Farber 2724, Fels 2725, Foerderer 2726, Foundation 2728, Goldman 2732, Hallowell 2737, Hassel 2741, Independence 2759, Kardon 2765, Kynett 2770, Lindback 2775, Live 2776, Meridian 2793, Oberkotter 2799, Penn 2803, **Peterson 2805, Pew 2806,** Philadelphia 2807, Philadelphia 2808, Provident 2813, Provident 2814, Rosenberg 2821, Scholler 2825, Scott 2826, SmithKline 2833, SmithKline 2834, Stein 2841, **Stott 2844,** Strauss 2845, **Strawbridge 2846, Tabas 2849,** Widgeon 2859
Phoenixville: West 2856
Pittsburgh: Alcoa 2668, Allegheny 2669, Allegheny 2670, Anathan 2674, Benedum 2683, Berkman 2684, Bloch 2687, Buncher 2690, Campbell 2694, Clapp 2703, Consolidated 2708, Cyclops 2714, Eden 2720, **Falk 2723,** Foster 2727, Gibson 2730, Grable 2733, Heinz 2743, Heinz 2744, Heinz 2745, Heinz 2746, Hillman 2749, Hillman 2750, Hopwood 2754, Hulme 2757, Hunt 2758, Jennings 2762, Jewish 2763, Laurel 2771, Love 2778, McCandless 2782, McCune 2784, Mellon 2789, Mellon 2790, Mellon 2791, Miles 2795, Mudge 2797, Patterson 2802, Pittsburgh 2809, Pittsburgh 2810, Polk 2811, PPG 2812, Rockwell 2818, Rockwell 2819, Rockwell 2820, Scaife 2823, **Scaife 2824,** Snee-Reinhardt 2835, Snyder 2836, **USX 2853,** Weisbrod 2854, Williams 2860, Wilson 2862
Plymouth Meeting: Claneil 2702
Radnor: Simon 2830
Reading: Carpenter 2697, Oberlaender 2800
Scranton: Scranton 2827
Shiremanstown: Rite 2817
St. Davids: Ames 2671, Annenberg 2675, Annenberg 2676, Hall 2736, Hazen 2742, Hooker 2752, Levee 2774
St. Marys: Stackpole-Hall 2840
Valley Forge: Alco 2667
Washington: Coen 2704, Dynamet 2719
Wayne: Strawbridge 2847
West Conshohocken: Connelly 2707
Williamsport: Williamsport-Lycoming 2861
Willow Grove: Asplundh 2679, Fourjay 2729
Wyndmoor: Barra 2680
Wynnewood: Superior-Pacific 2848

Wyomissing: Janssen 2761, Wyomissing 2864

---

see also 137, 174, 473, 488, 505, 507, 509, 518, 523, 524, 526, 777, 823, 916, 1049, 1116, 1132, 1348, 1350, 1622, 1624, 1639, 1661, 1670, 1676, 1691, 1699, 1736, 1751, 1813, 1872, 1889, 1951, 1960, 2025, 2051, 2104, 2134, 2142, 2167, 2193, 2247, 2266, 2326, 2374, 2474, 2507, 2555, 2595, 2606, 2922, 2989, 3121, 3121, 3163, 3190, 3215, 3222, 3236, 3272

PUERTO RICO

Hato Rey: Puerto Rico 2865

---

see also 326, 1229, 1348, 1701, 2838

RHODE ISLAND

Cranston: Cranston 2869, Hodges 2874
Pawtucket: **Hasbro 2872,** Hasbro 2873
Providence: **Allendale 2866,** Chace 2867, Champlin 2868, Fleet/Norstar 2870, Galkin 2871, Jaffe 2875, Johnstone 2876, Koffler 2877, Littlefield 2878, Morgan 2879, Old 2880, Providence 2881, Rhode Island 2882, Rhode Island 2883, Roddy 2884, Textron 2885

---

see also 488, 501, 631, 927, 1153, 1173, 1210, 1218, 1224, 1225, 1243, 1249, 1262, 1272, 1276, 1624, 1634, 1751, 1813, 2066, 2094, 2199, 2205, 2299

SOUTH CAROLINA

Charleston: Trident 2907
Columbia: Burgiss 2887, Central 2888, Colonial 2890, Fuller 2891, Symmes 2906
Fort Mill: Spring 2903
Gaffney: Fullerton 2892
Graniteville: Gregg-Graniteville 2893
Greenville: Belk-Simpson 2886, Piedmont 2897, Sargent 2898, Simpson 2900, Smith 2901
Greenwood: Self 2899
Inman: Inman-Riverdale 2894
Kershaw: Stevens 2905
Lancaster: Close 2889, Springs 2904
Salem: McDonnell 2895
Spartanburg: Moore 2896, Spartanburg 2902

---

see also 137, 419, 488, 596, 645, 693, 700, 702, 733, 739, 741, 800, 835, 913, 1116, 1337, 1634, 1898, 2005, 2369, 2375, 2379, 2386, 2387, 2392, 2393, 2403, 2406, 2419, 2595, 2780, 3121, 3295, 3326

SOUTH DAKOTA

Pierre: South Dakota 2909
Sioux Falls: Sioux Falls 2908

---

see also 400, 1421, 1461, 1462, 1468, 2654

TENNESSEE

Brentwood: Massey 2930
Bristol: Massengill-DeFriece 2929
Chattanooga: Benwood 2912, Chattanooga 2916, Hamico 2924, Hurlbut 2927, Tonya 2939
Knoxville: Cole 2918, Melrose 2931, Stokely 2936, Thompson 2937, Toms 2938
Memphis: Belz 2911, Briggs 2913, Brinkley 2914, Brown 2915, Durham 2920, First 2921, Goldsmith 2923, Lowenstein 2928, Plough 2932, Snider 2935
Murfreesboro: Christy-Houston 2917
Nashville: Ansley 2910, Davis 2919, Genesco 2922, HCA 2925, Hospital 2926, Potter 2933, Wallace 2940
Soddy-Daisy: Seretean 2934

---

see also 212, 250, 488, 494, 540, 568, 596, 693, 702, 741, 913, 965, 1262, 1337, 1350, 1399, 1563, 1701, 1702, 1830, 1898, 2005, 2300, 2409, 2433, 2449, 2474, 2602, 2668, 2713, 3175, 3247, 3326

TEXAS

Abilene: Abilene 2943, Dodge 2986
Amarillo: Amarillo 2946, Anderson 2947, Harrington 3030
Austin: Austin 2951, Cain 2962, LBJ 3050, RGK 3093, Vaughn 3127
Beaumont: Dishman 2985, Gulf 3023, Mechia 3065
Beeville: Dougherty 2987
Corpus Christi: Coastal 2969, Haas 3024
Corsicana: Navarro 3076
Dallas: Bass 2953, Beasley 2955, Bosque 2958, Chilton 2966, Collins 2971, Communities 2972, Constantin 2975, Cox 2978, Dallas 2981, Dr. Pepper 2988, Dresser 2989, Dresser 2990, Enserch 3001, Feldman 3008, Fikes 3009, FINA 3010, Florence 3013, Green 3020, Haggar 3025, Hawn 3031, Hillcrest 3034, Hoblitzelle 3036, Jonsson 3042, Kimberly-Clark 3046, King 3047, Lightner 3051, LTV 3052, Luse 3053, Mary Kay 3054, Maxus 3055, McDermott 3058, Meadows 3064, Moss 3072, Nation 3074, National 3075, O'Donnell 3078, Overlake 3080, **Pearle 3085,** Penney 3086, Roberts 3097, Seay 3101, Sharp 3103, Simmons 3105, SnyderGeneral 3109, Stemmons 3111, Straus 3113, Sturgis 3114, Texas 3120, **Zale 3139,** Zale 3140
El Paso: Cimarron 2967, El Paso 2996, McKee 3061, Peyton 3090
Fort Worth: **Alcon 2944,** Bass 2952, Bryce 2960, Burlington 2961, Carter 2965, Crump 2979, Davis 2983, Edwards 2994, Fuller 3018, Garvey 3019, Hubbard 3039, Keith 3044, Lard 3049, McQueen 3063, Moncrief 3068, Morris 3070, Richardson 3094, Roberts 3096, Tandy 3115, Tarrant 3116, White 3133
Galveston: Kempner 3045, Moody 3069
Georgetown: Wright 3137
Graham: Bertha 2956
Hallettsville: Dickson 2984
Houston: Abercrombie 2942, Alexander 2945, Anderson 2948, Apache 2949, Blaffer 2957, Brown 2959, Cain 2963, Cameron 2964, Clayton 2968, Cockrell 2970, Community 2973, Compaq 2974, Cooley 2976, Cooper 2977, Cullen 2980, Duncan 2992, Dunn 2993, Elkins 2997, Elkins 2998, Ellwood 2999, Enron 3000, Exxon 3002, Farish 3005, Favrot 3007, First 3011, Fish 3012, Fondren 3014, Frees 3016, Hamman 3028, Hankamer 3029, Herzstein 3033, Hobby 3035, Houston 3037, Howell 3038, Huffington 3040, Kayser 3043, McAshan 3056, McGovern 3059, McGovern 3060, Murfee 3073, Owsley 3082, Panhandle 3083, Pennzoil 3087, Powell 3091, Rienzi 3095, Rockwell 3098, Scurlock 3100, Shell 3104, Smith 3106, Smith 3107, **Smith 3108,** Strake 3112, Tenneco 3118, Texas 3119, Transco 3121, Turner 3123, United 3124, Vale-Asche 3126, West 3130, West 3131, **Wills 3134,** Wolff 3135, Woltman 3136
Irving: Associates 2950, Exxon 3003
Kilgore: Griffin 3021
Lake Jackson: Pardee 3084
Lufkin: Henderson 3032, Temple 3117
Midland: Abell-Hanger 2941, Beal 2954, Davidson 2982, Fasken 3006, Prairie 3092
Monahans: Dunagan 2991
Orange: Orange 3079
Overton: McMillan 3062
Palacios: Trull 3122
Post: Franklin 3015
Richardson: Owen 3081
Roanoke: Edwards 2995
San Antonio: Frost 3017, Halff 3026, Halsell 3027, **Kleberg 3048,** McCombs 3057, Meyer 3066, Morrison 3071, San Antonio 3099, **USAA 3125,** Walthall 3129, Zachry 3138
The Woodlands: Mitchell 3067
Tyler: Fair 3004

Vernon: Waggoner 3128
Victoria: Johnson 3041, O'Connor 3077, South 3110
Wharton: Gulf 3022
Wichita Falls: Perkins 3088, Perkins-Prothro 3089, Shanor 3102, White 3132

---

see also 23, 46, 55, 137, 212, 250, 260, 396, 419, 492, 509, 596, 739, 876, 903, 905, 913, 1308, 1433, 1435, 1466, 1526, 1548, 1559, 1569, 1583, 1701, 1729, 1837, 1898, 2000, 2005, 2242, 2243, 2433, 2445, 2449, 2474, 2525, 2555, 2563, 2602, 2624, 2626, 2627, 2628, 2632, 2636, 2668, 2797, 2852, 3188, 3194, 3236, 3247, 3295

UTAH

Ogden: Browning 3142, Dee 3145, Swanson 3154
Orem: Swim 3155
Salt Lake City: Bamberger 3141, Burton 3143, Castle 3144, Dumke 3146, Eccles 3147, Eccles 3148, Eccles 3149, Jones 3150, Michael 3151, Questar 3152, Sorenson 3153, **Thrasher 3156**

---

see also 82, 84, 174, 335, 400, 766, 1116, 1599, 1837, 2274, 2420, 2433, 2852

VERMONT

Middlebury: Vermont 3160
Montpelier: National 3158
Shelburne: Lintilhac 3157
Wilmington: Scott 3159

---

see also 488, 1153, 1173, 1210, 1243, 1249, 1272, 1289, 1713, 1813, 1951, 2094, 2162, 2319, 2358, 2879, 3236

VIRGINIA

Arlington: Bell 3163, Bell 3164, Caruthers 3169, **Freedom 3181,** Washington 3214
Chantilly: Fairchild 3178
Charlottesville: **Jones 3187, Scripps 3206**
Fairfax: Mobil 3194
Franklin: Camp 3167
Glen Allen: Lawrence 3189
Gloucester: Treakle 3211
Lynchburg: Easley 3176
McLean: BDM 3161, **Mars 3191**
Norfolk: Dalis 3173, Norfolk 3196, Parsons 3199, Taylor 3208
Portsmouth: Beazley 3162, Frederick 3180, Portsmouth 3200, Portsmouth 3201
Reston: Lafarge 3188
Richmond: Best 3165, Bryan 3166, Carter 3168, Central 3170, Chesapeake 3171, Crestar 3172, Ethyl 3177, Fitz-Gibbon 3179, Gottwald 3182, Hunter 3184, James 3185, Jeffress 3186, Massey 3192, Metropolitan 3193, Morgan 3195, Olsson 3198, Reynolds 3202, Reynolds 3203, Richmond 3204, Robins 3205, Signet 3207, Thomas 3209, Universal 3212, Virginia 3213, Wheat 3215
Roanoke: Dominion 3174, Dominion 3175
Sutherland: Titmus 3210
The Plains: Little 3190, Ohrstrom 3197
Weyers Cave: Houff 3183

---

see also 111, 212, 250, 509, 557, 594, 663, 692, 741, 777, 1109, 1116, 1117, 1624, 1661, 1676, 1908, 2375, 2409, 2420, 2445, 2563, 2602, 2708, 2713, 2859, 2929, 2937, 3118, 3121, 3269, 3273

WASHINGTON

Bellevue: Glaser 3230, PACCAR 3240, Puget 3245, See 3251, Wharton 3259
Everett: GTE 3231, **Schack 3248**
Mercer Island: Lockwood 3235
Seattle: Airborne 3216, **Allen 3217,** Archibald 3218, Benaroya 3219, Bishop 3220, Boeing 3222,

---

Burlington 3223, Fales 3226, Foster 3227, Hemingway 3232, Matlock 3236, Nesholm 3239, Pacific 3241, Pemco 3242, Petrie 3243, Poncin 3244, Ray 3246, SAFECO 3247, Seafirst 3249, Seattle 3250, Skinner 3252, U.S. 3256, Washington 3257, Wilkins 3260
Spokane: Comstock 3225, Foundation 3228, Leuthold 3234, Washington 3258
Tacoma: Cheney 3224, Fuchs 3229, Kilworth 3233, Murray 3238, **Stewardship 3253,** Tacoma 3255
Vancouver: Murdock 3237
Walla Walla: Blue 3221, Stubblefield 3254

see also 105, 160, 174, 190, 321, 353, 400, 419, 456, 494, 766, 864, 1462, 1872, 2440, 2654, 2655, 2658, 2826, 2852, 2961, 3194, 3326

WEST VIRGINIA

Beckley: Beckley 3261, Carter 3262
Bluefield: Shott 3269
Charleston: Clay 3263, Kanawha 3265
Morgantown: Hott 3264
Parkersburg: McDonough 3267, Parkersburg 3268
Wheeling: Kennedy 3266

see also 492, 1049, 2474, 2568, 2683, 2708, 2709, 2713, 2835, 2860, 3163, 3215, 3343

WISCONSIN

Appleton: Appleton 3272, Fox 3287, Mielke 3304
Chippewa Falls: Rutledge 3323
Combined Locks: U.S. 3331
Cudahy: Ladish 3296
Eau Claire: Presto 3315
Green Bay: Wisconsin 3339
Janesville: Jeffris 3290
Kohler: Kohler 3295
La Crosse: Cleary 3279
Madison: American 3271, Cremer 3281, CUNA 3283, Oscar 3309, Rennebohm 3317, Surgical 3329, Wisconsin 3338
Marshfield: Roddis 3319
Menasha: Banta 3273
Milwaukee: Birnschein 3274, **Bradley 3275,** Cudahy 3282, Demmer 3284, Evinrude 3285, Helfaer 3288, **Johnson 3292,** Kohl 3294, Ladish 3297, Ladish 3298, Lindsay 3299, Marshall 3300, Marshall 3301, McBeath 3302, Miller 3305, Milwaukee 3306, Northwestern 3308, Pettit 3312, Pollybill 3313, **Posner 3314,** Rexnord 3318, Ross 3322, Schroeder 3324, Shattuck 3325, Smith 3326, Souder 3327,

Stackner 3328, Time 3330, Universal 3332, Vilter 3333, Wehr 3336, Wisconsin 3337
Neenah: Menasha 3303, Neenah 3307
Oconomowoc: Roehl 3320
Oshkosh: Oshkosh 3310, Oshkosh 3311
Port Edwards: Alexander 3270
Racine: Johnson 3291, Johnson's 3293, Racine 3316
Sheboygan: Brotz 3276
South Milwaukee: Bucyrus-Erie 3277
Wausau: **Ford 3286,** Wausau 3334, Wausau 3335
Wauwatosa: Clark 3278, Humphrey 3289
West Bend: Rolfs 3321, Ziegler 3340
Wisconsin Rapids: Consolidated 3280

see also 105, 774, 776, 790, 811, 873, 874, 890, 906, 907, 913, 937, 978, 1022, 1240, 1337, 1411, 1420, 1435, 1450, 1624, 1993, 2210, 2507, 2826, 2989, 3118

WYOMING

Casper: Goodstein 3341
Cody: Stock 3342
Jackson: Weiss 3343

see also 377, 396, 400, 1589, 1820, 2949, 3051, 3152

TYPES OF SUPPORT INDEX

Foundations in boldface type make grants on a national or regional basis; the others generally limit giving to the city or state in which they are located.

Annual campaigns: any organized effort by a nonprofit to secure gifts on an annual basis; also called annual appeals.

Building funds: money raised for construction of buildings; may be part of an organization's capital campaign.

Capital campaigns: a campaign, usually extending over a period of years, to raise substantial funds for enduring purposes, such as building or endowment funds.

Conferences and seminars: a grant to cover the expenses of holding a conference.

Consulting services: professional staff support provided by the foundation to a nonprofit to consult on a project of mutual interest or to evaluate services (not a cash grant).

Continuing support: a grant that is renewed on a regular basis.

Deficit financing: also known as debt reduction. A grant to reduce the recipient organization's indebtedness; frequently refers to mortgage payments.

Emergency funds: a one-time grant to cover immediate short-term funding needs on an emergency basis.

Employee matching gifts: a contribution to a charitable organization by a corporate employee which is matched by a similar contribution from the employer. Many corporations support employee matching gift programs in higher education to stimulate their employees to give to the college or university of their choice. In addition, many foundations support matching gift programs for their officers and directors.

Employee-related scholarships: a scholarship program funded by a company-sponsored foundation usually for children of employees; programs are frequently administered by the National Merit Scholarship Corporation which is responsible for selection of scholars.

Endowment funds: a bequest or gift intended to be kept permanently and invested to provide income for continued support of an organization.

Equipment: a grant to purchase equipment, furnishings, or other materials.

Exchange programs: usually refers to funds for educational exchange programs for foreign students.

Fellowships: usually indicates funds awarded to educational institutions to support fellowship programs. A few foundations award fellowships directly to individuals.

General purposes: a grant made to further the general purpose or work of an organization, rather than for a specific purpose or project; also called unrestricted grants.

Grants to individuals: awards made directly by the foundation to individuals rather than to nonprofit organizations; includes aid to the needy. (See also 'Fellowships' and 'Student aid.')

In-kind gifts: a contribution of equipment, supplies, or other property as distinct from a monetary grant. Some organizations may also donate space or staff time as an in-kind contribution.

Internships: usually indicates funds awarded to an institution or organization to support an internship program rather than a grant to an individual.

Land acquisition: a grant to purchase real estate property.

Lectureships: usually indicates a grant to an educational institution to support a lectureship program.

Loans: temporary award of funds which usually must be repaid. (See also 'Program-related investments' and 'Student loans.')

Matching funds: a grant which is made to match funds provided by another donor. (See also 'Employee matching gifts.')

Operating budgets: a grant to cover the day-to-day personnel, administrative, and other expenses for an existing program or organization.

Professorships: usually indicates a grant to an educational institution to endow a professorship or chair.

Program-related investments: a loan made by a private foundation to profit-making or nonprofit organizations for a project related to the foundation's stated purpose and interests. Program-related investments are often made from a revolving fund; the foundation generally expects to receive its money back with interest which will then provide additional funds for loans to other organizations.

Publications: a grant to fund reports or other publications issued by a nonprofit resulting from research or projects of interest to the foundation.

Renovation projects: grants for renovating, remodeling, or rehabilitating property.

Research: usually indicates funds awarded to institutions to cover costs of investigations and clinical trials. Research grants for individuals are usually referred to as fellowships.

Scholarship funds: usually indicates a grant to an educational institution or organization to support a scholarship program, mainly for students at the undergraduate level. (See also 'Employee-related scholarships'; for scholarships paid to individuals, see 'Student aid.')

Seed money: a grant or contribution used to start a new project or organization. Seed grants may cover salaries and other operating expenses of a new project. Also known as 'start-up funds.'

Special projects: grants to support specific projects or programs as opposed to general purpose grants.

Student aid: assistance awarded directly to individuals in the form of educational grants or scholarships. (See also 'Employee-related scholarships.')

Student loans: assistance awarded directly to individuals in the form of educational loans.

Technical assistance: operational or management assistance given to nonprofit organizations; may include fundraising assistance, budgeting and financial planning, program planning, legal advice, marketing, and other aids to management. Assistance may be offered directly by a foundation staff member or in the form of a grant to pay for the services of an outside consultant.

Annual campaigns

Alabama: Bruno 6, Central 8, Sonat 23, Vulcan 25
Arizona: Bank 28, First 29, **Kieckhefer 35,** Phelps 38
Arkansas: Arkla 46, McKesson 49
California: Aerospace 56, **American 60,** Baker 67, **BankAmerica 70,** Beckman 76, Boswell 85, Brenner 87, **Carsey 100, Compton 110,** Copley 114, Disney 120, **Eisenberg 126,** Farmers 132, Fireman's 134, First 135, Fluor 137, Fusenot 139, Gamble 141, Gellert 148, Gellert 149, Gilmore 154, Goldsmith 157, Goldwyn 158, Gruber 162, **Kerr 199,** Lockheed 216, Mann 222, MCA 227, Montgomery 242, Ottenstein 259, Parker 263, Pratt 277, Rincon 282, **S.G. 285,** Stauffer 314, Stern 318, Syntex 326, Times 331, Tosco 332, Transamerica 334, Union 339, Varian 345, Wilbur 352, Wood-Claeyssens 354
Colorado: Boettcher 361, Colorado 363, Duncan 370, Hughes 378, Norgren 386, Rabb 390
Connecticut: **Aetna 406,** Bulkley 418, Culpeper 427, Dexter 430, Echlin 431, Eder 432, **General 439,** Hubbell 453, ITT 455, ITT 456, Kaman 460, Meriden 467, Obernauer 473, Olin 474, Panwy 476, Saunders 486, Stanley 488, **Xerox 500,** Ziegler 502
Delaware: Beneficial 504, Columbia 508, Delmarva 512, DuPont 513, ICI 517, Laffey-McHugh 521, Longwood 523, Lovett 524, Welfare 530
District of Columbia: Bloedorn 533, **Fannie 538,** First 539, Freed 542, Kiplinger 553, Wasserman 564, Westport 565
Florida: Briggs 578, Dade 587, Davis 589, Eckerd 596, Friends' 606, **Frueauff 607,** Grace 611, Phipps 649, Reinhold 655, TECO 668, Winn-Dixie 679
Georgia: Callaway 690, Callaway 691, Coca-Cola 696, Equifax 704, Exposition 705, Gage 708, Georgia 710, Georgia 711, Glancy 714, Harland 715, Illges 717, Jinks 719, Lee 720, Livingston 722, Marshall 723, Murphy 728, Patterson-Barclay 730, Rich 731, South 733, Wilson 742
Hawaii: Atherton 746, Castle 749, Cooke 751, Hawaiian 754
Idaho: West 766
Illinois: **Allen-Heath 771,** American 773, Amoco 775, Blair 796, Brach 805, CBI 815, CLARCOR 823, Crown 828, DeKalb 832, Dillon 834, Furnas 850, Harris 862, Harris 863, Hartmarx 864, Hermann 865, Illinois 867, Kemper 874, Lehmann 880, McGraw 895, Nalco 905, Northern 911, OMC 913, Perkins 919, Quaker 930, R.F. 931, **Salwil 944,** Sears 950, Thorson 966, United 968, USG 969, Walgreen 970, Waste 973, White 974, Woodward 978
Indiana: Ball 982, Foellinger 989, INB 995, Indianapolis 996, Lilly 999, Miles 1004, Oliver 1010, Zollner 1013

Iowa: Bohen 1014, Employers 1017, Hall 1018, Iowa 1019, Maytag 1024, Principal 1027, Principal 1028, Wahlert 1030
Kansas: Beech 1033, Cessna 1035, DeVore 1036, Koch 1038, Marley 1039, Sprint 1045, Sprint 1046, Topeka 1047
Kentucky: Bank 1050, Brown 1052, Cooke 1054, Juilfs 1058, Kentucky 1059, LaViers 1060, Long 1061
Louisiana: Freeport-McMoRan 1073, Monroe 1081
Maine: Central 1090, Shaw's 1093
Maryland: Aegon 1097, Baltimore 1100, Brown 1103, First 1111, Kelly 1121, PHH 1131, Procter 1133, Rouse 1136, Signet 1140, USF&G 1143
Massachusetts: Acushnet 1145, Bank 1153, Bayrd 1155, Boston 1157, **Cabot 1162,** Chase 1168, Clifford 1169, Cove 1171, Cox 1174, Daniels 1177, Davis 1178, Ellsworth 1185, Fuller 1193, General 1196, Goldberg 1198, Gorin 1199, High 1205, Hoffman 1208, Hopedale 1211, **Little 1228,** Pappas 1248, Poitras 1257, Polaroid 1258, Rubenstein 1268, Russell 1269, Schrafft 1273, Sheraton 1277, Smith 1279, State 1280, Stearns 1281, Stearns 1282, Stoddard 1285, Stone 1286, Stoneman 1287, Thompson 1289, Wyman-Gordon 1297
Michigan: Bishop 1306, Chrysler 1309, Consumers 1310, Flint 1323, Ford 1329, General 1336, Gerber 1337, Gerstacker 1338, Granger 1341, Holden 1345, Hudson-Webber 1346, Lansing 1354, Loutit 1357, McGregor 1358, Morley 1362, Pagel 1368, **Seidman 1378,** Tiscornia 1388, Towsley 1389, **Triford 1391,** Whirlpool 1399, Wickson-Link 1402, Wilson 1404
Minnesota: Andersen 1411, Baker 1413, Bemis 1416, Butler 1422, Cargill 1423, Cowles 1430, Dain 1432, Dayton 1433, Fingerhut 1438, Grand 1443, Greystone 1444, Groves 1445, MAHADH 1450, Marbrook 1451, Medtronic 1456, Minnesota 1459, O'Brien 1465, O'Shaughnessy 1466, Otter 1468, Pentair 1470, Red 1473, St. Paul 1477, Tonka 1480, Walker 1481, Whitney 1487
Mississippi: Deposit 1489, Walker 1494
Missouri: Block 1501, Block 1502, Brown 1503, Commerce 1504, CPI 1508, Edison 1512, Farmland 1517, Goppert 1522, Hallmark 1526, Hallmark 1527, Laclede 1538, Olin 1551, Pettus 1555, Pitzman 1556, Reynolds 1558, Schnuck 1561, Shaw 1562, Shoenberg 1564, Sunderland 1574, Union 1576, Ward 1578, **Webb 1579**
New Hampshire: Fuller 1605
New Jersey: Allied-Signal 1611, Brawer 1618, **Crum 1627, Fanwood 1635, Huber 1650,** Johnson 1656, Johnson 1657, Kirby 1661, Maneely 1670, McGraw 1672, Mercedes-Benz 1674, Prudential 1691, Schering-Plough 1702, Subaru 1708, Thomas 1712, Union 1714, Warner-Lambert 1723
New York: Abrons 1731, Achelis 1732, Agway 1736, AKC 1737, Albany 1739, Alexander 1741, **American 1750, American 1752,** Aron 1758, **AT&T**

1762, Badgeley 1766, Banbury 1770, Barker 1774, **Bernhard 1789,** Blinken 1796, Bodman 1800, Booth 1801, Botwinick-Wolfensohn 1804, Bristol-Myers 1809, Carter-Wallace 1831, Charina 1835, Chase 1836, **Chase 1838,** Claiborne 1846, Clark 1849, Colgate-Palmolive 1856, Cornell 1863, Cowles 1866, Crane 1867, Cummings 1869, **Cummings 1870,** Curtice-Burns/Pro-Fac 1872, **Dammann 1873,** Dillon 1886, Dun 1896, Eastman 1899, Evans 1909, Foster 1923, **Freeman 1926,** Gebbie 1933, Gifford 1939, Goldome 1947, Goldstein 1949, Goodstein 1954, Graphic 1960, Hagedorn 1970, Harriman 1974, Hultquist 1999, Icahn 2003, International 2005, Kaplan 2022, Klau 2034, Lang 2051, Larsen 2053, Lasdon 2054, Lee 2061, Macdonald 2080, Manufacturers 2087, McCann 2097, McConnell 2100, **McDonald 2101,** McGonagle 2102, McGraw-Hill 2104, Memton 2109, Metcalf 2116, Moore 2127, Morgan 2128, Morgan 2129, Moses 2135, National 2142, **New-Land 2150,** Nichols 2153, Northern 2158, Norwood 2159, O'Connor 2161, O'Toole 2164, Orange 2167, Paley 2173, Palisades 2174, Pfizer 2181, **Phillips 2186,** Price 2197, Quantum 2201, Rochester 2222, Salomon 2241, Salomon 2243, Sheldon 2265, **Sony 2280,** Stuart 2299, Sulzberger 2300, Thorne 2313, '21' 2322, Weinberg 2339, Whitehead 2347, Wiley 2349, Wilson 2350, Wishnick 2355, Woodland 2357, **Zenkel 2362,** Ziff 2363
North Carolina: Belk 2369, Burlington 2375, Burroughs 2376, Cannon 2378, Daniels 2382, Duke 2386, Finch 2390, Hanes 2399, Hanes 2400, Reynolds 2410, Smith 2414, Thomas 2415, Thomasville 2416, Volvo 2420, Wachovia 2421
North Dakota: Stern 2429
Ohio: Anderson 2434, Andrews 2435, **Armington 2436,** Battelle 2440, Beecher 2441, Bridgestone/Firestone 2445, Britton 2446, Centerior 2451, Centerior 2452, Cincinnati 2455, Cleveland-Cliffs 2458, Codrington 2459, Dater 2465, Dayton 2467, Deuble 2468, East 2469, Eaton 2470, Evans 2474, Ferro 2478, Fifth 2479, Firman 2481, Forest 2482, France 2484, Frohring 2488, GenCorp 2491, Gould 2494, Haskell 2501, Hillier 2503, Hoover 2505, Huffy 2507, Humphrey 2508, Iddings 2509, Kangesser 2514, Kettering 2515, Kilcawley 2517, Kroger 2519, Lubrizol 2525, Mather 2528, Medusa 2532, Moores 2537, Murch 2540, Murdough 2541, Murphy 2542, Nationwide 2545, Nippert 2546, Nordson 2548, O'Neill 2551, Pollock 2559, Procter 2561, Procter 2562, RB&W 2564, Reinberger 2566, Reynolds 2569, Rubbermaid 2573, Sears 2580, Selsor 2581, Smith 2586, Society 2589, Trinova 2601, Watson 2605, Wodecroft 2609, Wolfe 2610, Youngstown 2615

Building funds

Marbrook 1451, McKnight 1454, Northern 1461, NWNL 1464, Pentair 1470, Red 1473, Saint 1475, St. Paul 1477, Thorpe 1479, Tonka 1480
Mississippi: Deposit 1489, Walker 1494
Missouri: Anheuser-Busch 1495, Anheuser-Busch 1497, Bloch 1500, Block 1501, Block 1502, Commerce 1504, Cowden 1507, CPI 1508, Farmland 1517, Feld 1518, **Francis 1519,** Goppert 1522, Green 1523, Hall 1525, Hallmark 1526, Hallmark 1527, Long 1541, McDonnell 1548, Pet 1554, Ralston 1557, Roblee 1559, Shoenberg 1564, Speas 1570, Stupp 1573, Union 1576, Ward 1578, Wolff 1581
Montana: MPCo/Entech 1583, Sample 1584
Nebraska: Keene 1588, Kiewit 1589
New Hampshire: Smith 1609
New Jersey: American 1612, Armco 1614, Borden 1616, Brennan 1619, Campbell 1622, CPC 1624, **Crum 1627,** Frelinghuysen 1636, Grassmann 1641, Hoechst 1645, Hoechst 1646, Hyde 1651, Kramer 1664, Leavens 1667, Mutual 1680, Nabisco 1682, Ohl 1686, Public 1692, Schering-Plough 1702, Thomas 1712, Union 1714, Union 1715, Van Houten 1717, Van Pelt 1718
New Mexico: **Bellamah 1727**
New York: Achelis 1732, AKC 1737, Albany 1739, Albany's 1740, Alexander 1741, Aron 1758, **AT&T 1762,** Avon 1764, Baird 1767, Banbury 1770, Bank 1771, Bankers 1772, **Bernhard 1789,** Bingham 1793, Bodman 1800, Booth 1801, Botwinick-Wolfensohn 1804, BT 1815, Buffalo 1816, Carnahan-Jackson 1828, Carrier 1830, Carter-Wallace 1831, Charina 1835, Chase 1836, Chase 1837, Citicorp/Citibank 1845, Clark 1849, Cornell 1863, Cowles 1866, Cummings 1869, **Cummings 1870,** Curtice-Burns/Pro-Fac 1872, Decker 1880, Evans 1909, Gebbie 1933, Goldsmith 1948, Goldstein 1949, Goodyear 1955, Graphic 1960, Hagedorn 1970, Harriman 1974, Hayden 1978, Hoyt 1995, Hultquist 1999, International 2005, Jones 2015, Kaplan 2022, Kaufmann 2025, Klau 2034, Kresge 2047, Larsen 2053, McCarthy 2099, Memton 2109, Merrill 2113, Merrill 2114, Metcalf 2116, Milbank 2119, Millbrook 2121, Morgan 2128, Morgan 2129, Moses 2135, National 2142, New York 2149, **Norcross 2155,** Northern 2158, Norwood 2159, O'Sullivan 2163, Pfizer 2181, Quantum 2201, Republic 2211, Ritter 2219, Rochester 2222, Sequa 2261, Sheldon 2265, Stuart 2299, Sulzberger 2300, Thorne 2313, '21' 2322, Whitehead 2347, Wiley 2349, Woodland 2357
North Carolina: Burroughs 2376, Carolina 2379, Daniels 2382, Duke 2386, Duke 2387, Durham 2388, First 2391, First 2392, Hanes 2399, Harris 2401, Reynolds 2410, Smith 2414, Wachovia 2421
North Dakota: Fargo-Moorhead 2426, Leach 2427
Ohio: Allyn 2431, American 2433, Anderson 2434, Andrews 2435, Battelle 2440, Beecher 2441, BP 2443, Bridgestone/Firestone 2445, Bruening 2447, Centerior 2451, Centerior 2452, Cincinnati 2455, Cincinnati 2456, Cleveland-Cliffs 2458, Codrington 2459, Columbus 2460, Coshocton 2462, Dayton 2466, Dayton 2467, East 2469, Evans 2474, Ferro 2478, Fifth 2479, Frohman 2486, Gallagher 2489, Huffy 2507, Iddings 2509, Ingalls 2510, Kangesser 2514, Kettering 2515, Kilcawley 2517, Kramer 2518, Kroger 2519, Lubrizol 2525, Mayerson 2529, Moores 2537, Mount Vernon 2539, Murch 2540, Murphy 2542, Nationwide 2545, Nippert 2546, Nordson 2548, Ohio 2552, Ohio 2553, Procter 2561, Reinberger 2566, Reliance 2567, Reynolds 2569, Ritchie 2570, Russell 2574, Schmidlapp 2578, Sears 2580, Selsor 2581, Sherwick 2583, Sisler 2584, Society 2589, Stark 2591, Timken 2595, Watson 2605, Wodecroft 2609
Oklahoma: Boatmen's 2618, Mabee 2627, Phillips 2636, Rapp 2638, Sarkeys 2639, Scrivner 2640
Oregon: Jackson 2653, Louisiana-Pacific 2656, Northwest 2658, Tucker 2662, U.S. 2663
Pennsylvania: Air 2665, Air 2666, Alcoa 2668, Allegheny 2670, Arcadia 2677, Beatty 2681, Bell 2682, Benedum 2683, Berkman 2684, Connelly 2707, Consolidated 2708, Crown 2713, Cyclops

2714, Dietrich 2715, Eden 2720, Erie 2722, Fourjay 2729, **Glendorn 2731,** Grable 2733, Greensburg 2734, Heinz 2743, Heinz 2744, Heinz 2745, Hershey 2747, Hershey 2748, Hillman 2749, Hillman 2750, Holstrom 2751, Horsehead 2755, Hoyt 2756, Hulme 2757, Jennings 2762, Kline 2768, Lehigh 2772, Lindback 2775, Love 2778, McCune 2784, McFeely-Rogers 2785, McKenna 2786, McLean 2787, Mellon 2789, Mellon 2790, Mengle 2792, Meridian 2793, Millstein 2796, Murphy 2798, Oberlaender 2800, Patterson 2802, Penn 2803, Philadelphia 2807, Polk 2811, PPG 2812, Provident 2814, Rockwell 2818, Sordoni 2837, SPS 2838, Stackpole-Hall 2840, Steinman 2842, Steinman 2843, Trexler 2850, Union 2851, Union 2852, **USX 2853,** Weisbrod 2854, Wells 2855, West 2856, Williams 2860, Wyomissing 2864
Rhode Island: Champlin 2868, Fleet/Norstar 2870, Hasbro 2873, Littlefield 2878, Old 2880, Providence 2881, Rhode Island 2882, Textron 2885
South Carolina: Colonial 2890, Gregg-Graniteville 2893, Smith 2901
Tennessee: Ansley 2910, Chattanooga 2916, Genesco 2922, HCA 2925, Massengill-DeFriece 2929, Plough 2932
Texas: Abell-Hanger 2941, Austin 2951, Beasley 2955, Bosque 2958, Brown 2959, Cain 2962, Carter 2965, Cimarron 2967, Cockrell 2970, Communities 2972, Community 2973, Constantin 2975, Cooper 2977, Dallas 2981, Dougherty 2987, Elkins 2998, Enron 3000, Exxon 3002, Exxon 3003, Fikes 3009, Garvey 3019, Green 3020, Gulf 3022, Haas 3024, Hoblitzelle 3036, Houston 3037, Johnson 3041, Jonsson 3042, Keith 3044, Kempner 3045, Kimberly-Clark 3046, Lightner 3051, LTV 3052, Meadows 3064, Mitchell 3067, Moody 3069, Navarro 3076, Owen 3081, Panhandle 3083, Shell 3104, Strake 3112, Sturgis 3114, Tandy 3115, Temple 3117, Tenneco 3118, Texas 3119, Texas 3120, Transco 3121, Turner 3123, Zachry 3138
Utah: Bamberger 3141, Browning 3142, Eccles 3148, Swim 3155
Vermont: Lintilhac 3157, National 3158
Virginia: Beazley 3162, Chesapeake 3171, Dominion 3174, Dominion 3175, Ethyl 3177, Frederick 3180, **Freedom 3181,** Gottwald 3182, James 3185, Lawrence 3189, Norfolk 3196, Parsons 3199, Portsmouth 3200, Signet 3207, Titmus 3210, Treakle 3211, Universal 3212, Virginia 3213, Washington 3214, Wheat 3215
Washington: Airborne 3216, Boeing 3222, Fuchs 3229, GTE 3231, Kilworth 3233, Matlock 3236, Murray 3238, PACCAR 3240, Pacific 3241, Petrie 3243, Puget 3245, Seafirst 3249, Skinner 3252, **Stewardship 3253,** Tacoma 3255, U.S. 3256, Washington 3257
West Virginia: Kanawha 3265, McDonough 3267, Parkersburg 3268, Shott 3269
Wisconsin: Appleton 3272, **Bradley 3275,** Bucyrus-Erie 3277, Clark 3278, Consolidated 3280, CUNA 3283, Evinrude 3285, Humphrey 3289, Johnson's 3293, McBeath 3302, Milwaukee 3306, Northwestern 3308, Oscar 3309, Oshkosh 3310, Schroeder 3324, Stackner 3328, Wisconsin 3338

Conferences and seminars

Alabama: Gibson 13
Arizona: **Kieckhefer 35**
Arkansas: Arkla 46
California: Beckman 76, **Kaiser 194,** Milken 236, Milken 238, Nissan 250, Ostern 258, Peninsula 269, Sacramento 286, Santa Cruz 292, van Loben Sels 342
Colorado: Comprecare 365, **Frost 372,** True 398
Connecticut: ASEA 409, Bodenwein 415, Bridgeport 417, Ensworth 435, New Britain 469, Olin 474, Palmer 475, Rosenthal 484, Waterbury 497, **Xerox 500**
Delaware: Delmarva 512, DuPont 513, **Good 516**

District of Columbia: **Fannie 538,** Kennedy 552, **Pettus-Crowe 558,** Post 560
Florida: Bush 581, Davis 589, Friends' 606, Palm 644, Winn-Dixie 679
Georgia: Georgia 710, Georgia 711, Glancy 714, Lee 720, Livingston 722, South 733
Hawaii: Cooke 751, Frear 752, Hawaii 753
Illinois: Ameritech 774, Coleman 825, Fry 848, Harris 863, Kemper 874, Quaker 930, Scholl 947, **Sears 950,** Stern 960, Waste 973
Indiana: Ball 982, Foellinger 989, Fort 990, Heritage 993, Metropolitan 1003
Kansas: Koch 1038
Kentucky: Brown 1052, Long 1061
Louisiana: Shreveport-Bossier 1084
Maine: Central 1090, Maine 1091
Maryland: Abell 1095, Eastern 1110, Higginson 1117
Massachusetts: Alden 1147, Campbell 1166, **Merck 1235,** Stevens 1284
Michigan: Ann Arbor 1301, Battle 1303, Berrien 1305, Consumers 1310, Ford 1329, Gerber 1337, Lansing 1354, **Mott 1363, Mott 1364,** Muskegon 1365, Northeast 1366
Minnesota: Bremer 1420, Central 1427, Eddy 1436, Greystone 1444, Marbrook 1451, Otter 1468, Saint 1475, Walker 1481, Wedum 1485
Missouri: Community 1505, Green 1523, Group 1524, Laclede 1538, **McDonnell 1549,** Oppenstein 1552, Reynolds 1558, Southwestern 1569
Nebraska: Omaha 1592
New Hampshire: Bean 1600, Eastman 1603
New Jersey: American 1612, Dodge 1630, Fund 1637, Johnson 1657, Pate 1688, Prudential 1691
New Mexico: Carlsbad 1728
New York: Agway 1736, Alexander 1741, **Archbold 1756, Berlex 1788,** Bristol-Myers 1808, **Brookdale 1812,** Buffalo 1817, **Carnegie 1829, China 1842,** Curtice-Burns/Pro-Fac 1872, **Ford 1922,** Graphic 1960, **Hartford 1975,** Jones 2015, Klingenstein 2036, Lang 2051, Larsen 2053, McCann 2097, McConnell 2100, National 2142, **New World 2145,** New York 2146, New York 2149, Northern 2158, O'Connor 2161, Pfizer 2181, **Potts 2196,** Quantum 2201, Ramapo 2203, Rapoport 2204, Rauch 2205, Rochester 2221, **Rockefeller 2223, Rockefeller 2224, Sloan 2273, Smithers 2276, Soros 2281,** Stony 2296, Sulzberger 2300, Wiley 2349, Wilson 2350, Wishnick 2355
North Carolina: Burroughs 2376, Daniels 2383, Duke 2386, Reynolds 2411, Rogers 2412
North Dakota: Fargo-Moorhead 2426, Stern 2429
Ohio: Battelle 2440, Dayton 2466, Deuble 2468, East 2469, Gund 2497, Hamilton 2499, Iddings 2509, Pollock 2559, Stark 2591, Youngstown 2615
Oklahoma: Phillips 2636
Oregon: Johnson 2655
Pennsylvania: Alcoa 2668, Benedum 2683, Consolidated 2708, Dolfinger-McMahon 2716, Erie 2722, **Falk 2723,** Fels 2725, Grundy 2735, Heinz 2743, Hershey 2748, Kynett 2770, Laurel 2771, McLean 2787, **Pew 2806, Scaife 2824,** Scranton 2827
Puerto Rico: Puerto Rico 2865
Rhode Island: Rhode Island 2882
South Carolina: Central 2888, Close 2889, Colonial 2890, Spartanburg 2902
Tennessee: Benwood 2912, Chattanooga 2916, Durham 2920, HCA 2925
Texas: Abilene 2943, **Alcon 2944,** Austin 2951, Dougherty 2987, Kempner 3045, **Kleberg 3048,** McGovern 3059, McGovern 3060, Meadows 3064, Moody 3069, RGK 3093, Richardson 3094, San Antonio 3099, Texas 3119, Trull 3122, Turner 3123
Vermont: Lintilhac 3157, Vermont 3160
Virginia: BDM 3161, **Freedom 3181, Jones 3187,** Little 3190, Portsmouth 3200
Washington: Archibald 3218, Pacific 3241, Puget 3245
West Virginia: Kanawha 3265
Wisconsin: **Bradley 3275,** Milwaukee 3306, Racine 3316

Consulting services

California: AT&T 65, **Compton 110,** Gerbode 153, Koret 202, Monterey 240, **Packard 262,** Peninsula 269, Sacramento 286, Santa Clara 291, Santa Cruz 292, Sierra 302
Colorado: **Frost 372,** United 399
Connecticut: Bodenwein 415, Bridgeport 417, New Haven 470, Palmer 475, Waterbury 497, **Xerox 500**
District of Columbia: Kennedy 552
Florida: Bush 581, Jacksonville 620
Georgia: Lee 720, Rich 731
Hawaii: Hawaii 753
Illinois: Northern 911
Indiana: Foellinger 989, Fort 990, Heritage 993
Kentucky: Courier-Journal 1055
Maryland: Baltimore 1099, Eastern 1110
Massachusetts: Stevens 1284
Michigan: Fremont 1331, Grand 1340, Hudson-Webber 1346, Jackson 1347, Lansing 1354, Mills 1360, Muskegon 1365
Minnesota: Dayton 1433, Northwest 1462, Saint 1475
Missouri: Danforth 1510, Long 1541, Oppenstein 1552
New Hampshire: Bean 1600, Eastman 1603, New Hampshire 1607
New Jersey: Prudential 1691, Union 1714, Victoria 1719
New Mexico: Albuquerque 1726, Carlsbad 1728
New York: Abrons 1731, Buffalo 1817, **Clark 1850,** Cummings 1869, **Cummings 1870,** Cummings 1871, **Ford 1922,** Fund 1930, Hoyt 1995, Joy 2016, Larsen 2053, New Street 2144, New York 2146, Rochester 2221, **Rockefeller 2223,** Sulzberger 2300
North Carolina: Burlington 2374, Duke 2386
North Dakota: Fargo-Moorhead 2426
Ohio: **Armington 2436,** Cleveland 2457, Dater 2465, Dayton 2466, Huffy 2507, Iddings 2509, Nord 2547, Stark 2591
Pennsylvania: Benedum 2683, Crown 2713, **Falk 2723,** McLean 2787, Philadelphia 2808, Scott 2826, Scranton 2827
Puerto Rico: Puerto Rico 2865
Rhode Island: Rhode Island 2882
South Carolina: Spartanburg 2902
Texas: Abilene 2943, Amarillo 2946, Austin 2951, Meadows 3064, Moody 3069, Trull 3122
Vermont: Vermont 3160
Washington: Boeing 3222, Ray 3246, Tacoma 3255
Wisconsin: **Ford 3286,** Time 3330

Continuing support

Alabama: Vulcan 25
Arizona: Arizona 27, First 29, **Kieckhefer 35,** Phelps 38, Raymond 39
California: **American 60, Atkinson 66,** Baker 67, **BankAmerica 70,** Beaver 74, Boswell 85, Chevron 103, **Compton 110,** Disney 120, **Eisenberg 126,** Factor 128, Fireman's 134, First 135, Fusenot 139, Gamble 141, Gellert 148, Gellert 149, Gellert 150, Gilmore 154, Goldsmith 157, Gross 161, Gruber 162, Haas 163, Hoover 179, Howe 180, Humboldt 181, Joslyn 193, **Kerr 199,** Kirchgessner 200, Koret 202, Litton 214, Livingston 215, Lockheed 216, Margoes 223, Marin 224, McKesson 232, Monterey 240, Murphy 247, Nissan 250, Norris 253, Oser 256, Parker 263, Patron 267, Peninsula 269, Pratt 277, Santa Cruz 292, Skaggs 304, Stauffer 314, Steele 316, Stein 316, Syntex 326, Times 331, Transamerica 334, Union 339, Wilbur 352, Wood-Claeyssens 354, Zellerbach 357
Colorado: Bancroft 359, Colorado 363, Duncan 370, El Pomar 372, Gates 373, Hughes 378, Kitzmiller-Bales 380, Sterne-Elder 392, US 400
Connecticut: Bridgeport 417, Connecticut 425, Culpeper 427, Eder 432, **Educational 433,** EIS 434, Ensworth 435, **General 439,** Gimbel 443, GTE 444, ITT 456, New Haven 470, Northeast 472, Olin 474, Panwy 476, People's 478, Rosenthal 484, Stanley 488, Ziegler 502
Delaware: Beneficial 504, Columbia 508, Kent-Lucas 518, **Schwartz 527**

District of Columbia: Bloedorn 533, Cafritz 535, First 539, Foundation 541, Freed 542, Gelman 544, Giant 545, Johnston 551, Kiplinger 553, Marriott 556, Meyer 557, **Pettus-Crowe 558,** Post 560, Stewart 563, Wasserman 564, Westport 565
Florida: Beveridge 574, Briggs 578, Bush 581, Dade 587, Davis 589, **Davis 590,** Eckerd 596, Friends' 606, **Frueauff 607,** Grace 611, Greenburg-May 612, Lowe 635, Nias 641, Phipps 649, Tampa 666, Wahlstrom 671, Winn-Dixie 679, Winter 680
Georgia: Callaway 690, Equifax 704, Georgia 710, Glancy 714, Health 716, Lee 720, Livingston 722, Murphy 728, Patterson-Barclay 730, Rich 731, **UPS 737,** Wilson 742
Hawaii: Atherton 746, Castle 749, McInerny 755, Wilcox 759, Wilcox 760
Illinois: Abbott 768, American 773, Amoco 775, Amsted 777, Andreas 779, Beidler 789, Blair 796, Blowitz-Ridgeway 797, Brunswick 806, Butz 810, CBI 815, Chicago 820, **Chicago 821,** Chicago 822, CLARCOR 823, Crown 828, DeKalb 832, Dillon 834, FMC 842, Grainger 857, Illinois 867, Kemper 873, Kemper 874, McGraw 895, **Meyer-Ceco 896,** Motorola 903, Nalco 905, New Prospect 908, Northern 911, OMC 913, OMRON 914, Perkins 919, Polk 924, Prince 927, Quaker 930, R.F. 931, Replogle 936, Stern 960, Thorson 966, USG 969, Waste 973, White 974, Woods 977, Woodward 978
Indiana: Anderson 981, Clowes 985, Cole 986, Griffith 992, Heritage 993, Martin 1002, Miles 1004, **Moriah 1005,** Oliver 1010
Iowa: Employers 1017, Iowa 1019, Maytag 1024, Principal 1027, Principal 1028, Wahlert 1030
Kansas: Beech 1033, DeVore 1036, Hansen 1037, Koch 1038, Marley 1039, Smith 1044, Sprint 1045, Topeka 1047
Kentucky: Bank 1050, Cooke 1054, Courier-Journal 1055, Robinson 1063
Maine: Central 1090
Maryland: Brown 1103, Higginson 1117, Rouse 1136, Signet 1140, USF&G 1142, USF&G 1143
Massachusetts: Acushnet 1145, Boston 1157, **Cabot 1162,** Campbell 1166, Cove 1171, Cox 1174, Daniels 1177, Davis 1178, Ellsworth 1185, Fuller 1193, Goldberg 1198, Henderson 1203, High 1205, Hoche-Scofield 1207, Hoffman 1208, Hyams 1216, Levy 1225, **Little 1228,** Old 1246, Pappas 1248, Poitras 1257, Polaroid 1258, Porter 1259, Schrafft 1273, Sheraton 1277, State 1280, Stevens 1283, Stevens 1284, Stoddard 1285, Wyman-Gordon 1297
Michigan: Bishop 1306, Chrysler 1308, Chrysler 1309, Dalton 1312, Flint 1323, Ford 1329, Four 1330, General 1336, Gerber 1337, Gerstacker 1338, Holden 1345, Hudson-Webber 1346, McGregor 1358, Mills 1360, Morley 1362, **Mott 1363, Mott 1364,** Muskegon 1365, Northeast 1366, Pagel 1368, Tiscornia 1388, Towsley 1389, Whirlpool 1399, Wilson 1404
Minnesota: Bemis 1416, Bigelow 1417, Bremer 1420, Bush 1421, Butler 1422, Cargill 1423, Cargill 1424, Cowles 1430, Dain 1432, Dayton 1433, Eddy 1436, Fingerhut 1438, Greystone 1444, Marbrook 1451, Medtronic 1456, Minneapolis 1457, Northern 1461, O'Brien 1465, O'Shaughnessy 1466, Ordean 1467, Otter 1468, Pentair 1470, Red 1473, St. Paul 1477, Wasie 1484, Whitney 1487
Missouri: Anheuser-Busch 1497, Block 1501, Block 1502, Brown 1503, Commerce 1504, CPI 1508, Farmland 1517, Feld 1518, Goppert 1522, Hallmark 1526, Hallmark 1527, Jordan 1532, Leader 1539, Pettus 1555, Pitzman 1556, Reynolds 1558, Shaw 1562, Shoenberg 1564, Sunderland 1574, Union 1576, **Webb 1579**
Montana: MPCo/Entech 1583
Nebraska: Omaha 1592
Nevada: **Hilton 1596**
New Hampshire: Fuller 1605
New Jersey: Allied-Signal 1611, Armco 1614, **Bonner 1615,** Brawer 1618, **Crum 1627,** Dodge 1630, Edison 1631, Engelhard 1633, Fund 1637, Hoechst 1646, Johnson 1656, Johnson 1657, Kirby 1661, Leavens 1667, McGraw 1672, Prudential 1691,

Schering-Plough 1702, Schultz 1704, Snyder 1707, Subaru 1708, Union 1714, Van Pelt 1718, Victoria 1719, **Vollmer 1721,** Warner-Lambert 1723, Winslow 1725
New Mexico: Carlsbad 1728
New York: Abrons 1731, Agway 1736, AKC 1737, Albany's 1740, Amax 1748, **Archbold 1756,** ASARCO 1759, Avon 1764, Badgeley 1766, Banbury 1770, Bank 1771, Barker 1774, Booth 1801, Botwinick-Wolfensohn 1804, BT 1815, **Butler 1822,** Carnahan-Jackson 1828, **Carnegie 1829,** Cary 1833, Chase 1836, Chase 1837, **Chase 1838,** Citicorp/Citibank 1845, Clark 1849, **Clark 1850,** Cornell 1863, Cowles 1866, Crane 1867, Curtice-Burns/Pro-Fac 1872, **Dammann 1873,** Diamond 1885, Dun 1896, Dyson 1897, Eastman 1898, Eastman 1899, **Eisner 1901, Equitable 1904,** Evans 1909, Ferkauf 1914, **Ford 1922, Freeman 1926,** Gebbie 1933, Goldman 1946, Goldome 1947, Goodstein 1954, **Grant 1958,** Graphic 1960, Griffis 1967, **Hartford 1975,** Hoyt 1995, Hughes 1996, International 2005, Joyce 2017, Kaplan 2022, Kaplan 2023, Klingenstein 2036, Krim 2048, Lang 2051, Langeloth 2052, Lasdon 2054, **Lasker 2056,** Lee 2061, Leonhardt 2064, Macdonald 2080, Manufacturers 2087, Mark 2089, Mayer 2095, McCann 2097, **McDonald 2101,** McGraw-Hill 2104, Mellon 2106, Merrill 2113, **Mertz-Gilmore 2115,** Metcalf 2116, Metropolitan 2117, Moore 2127, Morgan 2130, Moses 2135, Mulligan 2137, New York 2147, **New-Land 2150,** Nichols 2153, Noble 2154, Norwood 2159, **Noyes 2160,** O'Connor 2161, O'Toole 2164, Paley 2173, Palisades 2174, Pfizer 2181, Philip 2184, Phillips 2185, **Phillips 2186,** Price 2197, Quantum 2201, Rapoport 2204, Reader's 2206, Rochester 2222, **Rockefeller 2223,** Rubinstein 2234, Salomon 2243, Samuels 2245, Scherman 2249, Schieffelin 2251, Sequa 2261, **Sony 2280,** Starr 2288, Stony 2296, Sulzberger 2300, **Surdna 2302, Teagle 2308,** Thorne 2313, Tisch 2316, **Vanneck-Bailey 2328,** Weinstein 2342, Wilson 2350
North Carolina: Bryan 2373, Daniels 2382, Duke 2386, Finch 2390, Reynolds 2410, Reynolds 2411, Smith 2414, Thomas 2415, Winston-Salem 2424
North Dakota: Fargo-Moorhead 2426, Leach 2427, Stern 2429
Ohio: Allyn 2431, **Armington 2436,** Bicknell 2442, Bridgestone/Firestone 2445, Britton 2446, Centerior 2452, Codrington 2459, Columbus 2460, Coshocton 2462, Dater 2465, Deuble 2468, **Elisha-Bolton 2471,** Evans 2474, Fairfield 2476, Fifth 2479, France 2484, Frohring 2488, Gund 2497, Haskell 2501, Huffy 2507, Humphrey 2508, Iddings 2509, Kangesser 2514, Kettering 2515, Lubrizol 2525, Medusa 2532, Mount Vernon 2539, Murphy 2542, Nationwide 2545, Nord 2547, Nordson 2548, Ohio 2552, Pollock 2559, Prentiss 2560, Procter 2562, Reeves 2565, Reinberger 2566, Reliance 2567, Sears 2580, Smith 2586, Society 2589, Trinova 2601, Watson 2605, Wean 2606, White 2607, Wolfe 2610, Youngstown 2615
Oklahoma: Bernsen 2617, Broadhurst 2621, Goddard 2624, Oklahoma 2633, Oklahoma 2634, Phillips 2636, Scrivner 2640
Oregon: Jackson 2653, Johnson 2655, Louisiana-Pacific 2656, U.S. 2663
Pennsylvania: Air 2666, Alcoa 2668, Allegheny 2669, Allegheny 2670, Arcadia 2677, Berkman 2684, Consolidated 2708, Consolidated 2709, Elf 2721, **Falk 2723,** Fels 2725, Goldman 2732, Grable 2733, Harsco 2740, Heinz 2743, Hershey 2748, Hillman 2749, Hillman 2750, Hoyt 2756, Justus 2764, **Kennametal 2766,** Kline 2768, Lukens 2779, Mellon 2790, Mellon 2791, Merit 2794, Murphy 2798, Oberlaender 2800, Patterson 2802, **Pew 2806,** Philadelphia 2808, Pittsburgh 2810, PPG 2812, Provident 2814, Rockwell 2818, **Scaife 2824,** Scott 2826, Smith 2831, Sordoni 2837, SPS 2838, Stabler 2839, **Stott 2844,** Strawbridge 2847, Trexler 2850, Union 2852, **USX 2853,** Wyomissing 2864
Puerto Rico: Puerto Rico 2865

Deficit financing

Emergency funds

Employee matching gifts

Employee-related scholarships

Endowment funds

Maryland: Abell 1095, Aegon 1097, Baltimore 1099, Brown 1103, Kelly 1121, Knott 1122, Procter 1133, Rouse 1136, USF&G 1143

Massachusetts: Alden 1147, Bank 1152, Bank 1153, Bayrd 1155, Boston 1157, Boston 1160, **Cabot 1162,** Daniels 1177, Fidelity 1188, Fuller 1193, Goldberg 1198, Hornblower 1212, **Iacocca 1217,** John 1220, Merkert 1236, Pappas 1248, Peabody 1249, Perini 1253, Rubenstein 1268, Schrafft 1273, State 1280, Stevens 1283, Stevens 1284, Stone 1286, Webster 1291

Michigan: Berrien 1305, Consumers 1310, Flint 1323, Gerber 1337, Gerstacker 1338, Gilmore 1339, Muskegon 1365, **Seidman 1378,** Southeastern 1381, Towsley 1389, Upjohn 1392, Whirlpool 1399, Wilson 1403

Minnesota: Bell 1415, Bush 1421, Butler 1422, Cowles 1430, Ecolab 1434, Grand 1442, MAHADH 1450, Marbrook 1451, O'Brien 1465, O'Shaughnessy 1466, Otter 1468, Pentair 1470, St. Paul 1477

Mississippi: Vicksburg 1493

Missouri: Commerce 1504, Goppert 1522, Green 1523, Ralston 1557, Roblee 1559, Shaw 1562, Sosland 1567, Stupp 1573, Sunderland 1574, Union 1576, Ward 1578, Whitaker 1580

Nebraska: Keene 1588

Nevada: **Hilton 1596,** Redfield 1597

New Jersey: Brunetti 1620, **Fanwood 1635,** Grassmann 1641, Klatskin 1662, Kramer 1664, Schering-Plough 1702, Union 1714, Union 1715

New York: Achelis 1732, Agway 1736, Alexander 1741, **AT&T 1762,** Banbury 1770, Booth 1801, Brooks 1813, Buffalo 1817, Carter-Wallace 1831, Charina 1835, Chase 1836, **China 1842,** Corzine 1865, Cowles 1866, Cummings 1871, Curtice-Burns/Pro-Fac 1872, **Dammann 1873,** Dillon 1886, Dosberg 1889, Dyson 1897, **Fish 1918,** Forbes 1920, **Ford 1922,** Goldsmith 1948, **Hearst 1980, Hearst 1981,** Larsen 2053, Leonhardt 2064, Link 2072, Macdonald 2080, Mayer 2095, Mayrock 2096, McGonagle 2102, Mellon 2106, Memton 2109, Merrill 2113, Metcalf 2116, Milbank 2119, Monell 2125, Moore 2127, Morgan 2129, Moses 2135, Mulligan 2137, Nichols 2153, Noble 2154, Norwood 2159, O'Connor 2161, O'Sullivan 2163, Pfizer 2181, Pforzheimer 2183, Philip 2184, Phillips 2185, Price 2197, Quantum 2201, Ritter 2219, **Ross 2232,** Schweckendieck 2258, Slaner 2270, **Sony 2280,** Starr 2288, Steele-Reese 2291, Stuart 2299, Sulzberger 2300, Summerfield 2301, Thorne 2313, van Ameringen 2326, Vidda 2330, Weinstein 2342, Wiley 2349, Wilson 2350, Wishnick 2355, Woodland 2357

North Carolina: Bryan 2373, Daniels 2382, Duke 2386, First 2392, Hanes 2399, Hanes 2400, Smith 2414, Wachovia 2421

North Dakota: Leach 2427

Ohio: American 2432, Andrews 2435, Bridgestone/Firestone 2445, Britton 2446, Crandall 2464, Dayton 2466, Deuble 2468, Evans 2474, Gallagher 2489, GAR 2490, H.C.S. 2498, Haskell 2501, Humphrey 2508, Ingalls 2510, Kettering 2515, Mather 2528, Morgan 2538, Murch 2540, Nippert 2546, O'Neill 2551, Pollock 2559, Prentiss 2560, Reinberger 2566, Reynolds 2569, Semple 2582, Sisler 2584, Timken 2595

Oklahoma: American 2616, **Noble 2631,** Puterbaugh 2637, Rapp 2638, Sarkeys 2639, Scrivner 2640, Warren 2645

Oregon: Collins 2652, Jackson 2653

Pennsylvania: AMETEK 2672, Arcadia 2677, Arronson 2678, Berkman 2684, Connelly 2707, Eden 2720, Heinz 2743, Hershey 2748, Hillman 2749, Holstrom 2751, Hopwood 2754, Hunt 2758, Independence 2759, Jennings 2762, **Kennametal 2766,** Lindback 2775, Lord 2777, McCune 2784, McFeely-Rogers 2785, McKenna 2786, McLean 2787, Murphy 2798, Rockwell 2818, Sheppard 2829, Sordoni 2837, Stabler 2839

South Carolina: Close 2889, Colonial 2890, Gregg-Graniteville 2893, McDonnell 2895, Smith 2901, Springs 2904

South Dakota: South Dakota 2909

Tennessee: Hamico 2924, Plough 2932

Texas: Abell-Hanger 2941, Brown 2959, Cain 2962, Cockrell 2970, Cooley 2976, Davidson 2982, Dougherty 2987, Dunn 2993, Elkins 2998, Fair 3004, Fikes 3009, Franklin 3015, Gulf 3022, Houston 3037, Hubbard 3039, Huffington 3040, Keith 3044, LTV 3052, McGovern 3059, McGovern 3060, Meadows 3064, Richardson 3094, Scurlock 3100, Seay 3101, Sturgis 3114, Texas 3119, Turner 3123, **USAA 3125,** Wright 3137

Utah: Browning 3142, Dee 3145

Vermont: Scott 3159

Virginia: Chesapeake 3171, Crestar 3172, Ethyl 3177, Fairchild 3178, Fitz-Gibbon 3179, James 3185, Little 3190, **Mars 3191,** Ohrstrom 3197, Wheat 3215

Washington: Leuthold 3234, Murray 3238, Skinner 3252, Wharton 3259

West Virginia: Hott 3264

Wisconsin: Bucyrus-Erie 3277, Cleary 3279, Consolidated 3280, Humphrey 3289, Johnson 3291, **Johnson 3292,** Kohler 3295, Ladish 3296, Mielke 3304

Equipment

Alabama: Andalusia 2, Dixon 11, Gibson 13, Hill 14, Meyer 18

Arizona: Arizona 27, First 29, **Kieckhefer 35**

Arkansas: Arkla 46

California: Ahmanson 57, AT&T 65, Baker 67, Barker 71, Beckman 76, Bothin 86, Copley 114, de Dampierre 118, Fairfield 129, Fireman's 134, Fusenot 139, Gamble 141, Gellert 148, Gellert 149, Gellert 150, Genentech 151, Haas 163, Hale 165, Harden 168, Hedco 170, Hewlett-Packard 174, Hogan 178, Humboldt 181, Irvine 183, Irwin 185, Jewett 190, Jones 192, **Keck 197, Kerr 199,** Kirchgessner 200, Marin 224, MCA 227, McConnell 231, McKesson 232, Mericos 235, Monterey 240, Murphey 246, Norris 253, Occidental 254, **Packard 262,** Parker 263, Parsons 264, Pasadena 266, Patron 267, Peninsula 269, Pratt 277, Sacramento 286, San Diego 287, Santa Barbara 290, Santa Cruz 292, Sonoma 309, Stauffer 313, Stauffer 314, Steele 315, Stein 316, Stern 318, Stulsaft 322, Times 331, Treadwell 335, Tuohy 336, Union 339, Van Nuys 343, Weingart 348

Colorado: Boettcher 361, Colorado 363, Duncan 370, El Pomar 371, **Frost 372,** Gates 373, Heginbotham 375, Hughes 378, Joslin-Needham 379, Kitzmiller-Bales 380, Lowe 382, Norgren 386, Petteys 387, Schramm 391, Stone 393, Swan 395, True 398, Wolf 404

Connecticut: Bodenwein 415, Culpeper 427, Hartford 446, Hartford 448, ITT 456, New Haven 470, Northeast 472, Olin 474, Palmer 475, Panwy 476, Patterson 477, People's 478, Union 492, Waterbury 497

Delaware: Beneficial 504, Crystal 510, DuPont 513, ICI 517, Laffey-McHugh 521, Longwood 523, Marmot 525, **Schwartz 527,** Welfare 530

District of Columbia: **Fannie 538,** Freed 542, Graham 548, **Marpat 555,** Stewart 563, Westport 565

Florida: Beveridge 574, Briggs 578, Broward 580, Bush 581, Catlin 582, Chatlos 583, Conn 585, Dade 587, **Davis 590,** duPont 594, Falk 599, Fish 601, Friends' 606, **Frueauff 607,** Grace 611, Hersh 618, Jones 624, Kennedy 626, Lost 634, Lowe 635, Palm 644, Phipps 649, Sarasota 659, Wahlstrom 671, Whitehall 678, Winn-Dixie 679, Wolfson 681

Georgia: Atlanta 686, Atlanta 687, Callaway 690, Callaway 691, Dodson 700, English 703, Exposition 705, Georgia 711, Glancy 714, Harland 715, Illges 717, Lee 720, Marshall 724, Murphy 728, Rich 731, South 733, **UPS 737,** Whitehead 740, Wilson 742, Woodruff 743, Woodward 744

Hawaii: Alexander 745, Atherton 746, Castle 749, Castle 750, Cooke 751, Frear 752, Hawaii 753, McInerny 755, PRI 756, Vidinha 758, Wilcox 759

Idaho: Cunningham 764, Daugherty 765

Illinois: Amoco 775, Aurora 783, Barber-Colman 785, Beloit 790, Brach 805, Buehler 808, Butz 810, Chicago 820, **Chicago 821,** CLARCOR 823, Crown 828, Cuneo 829, DeKalb 832, Dillon 834, Field 840, FMC 842, Fry 848, Furnas 850, Grainger 857, Harris 863, Hermann 865, Kemper 873, Kemper 874, Klenk 876, McGraw 895, Moorman 901, Nalco 905, OMC 913, Payne 916, Peoria 918, Perkins 919, Playboy 923, Polk 924, Quaker 930, R.F. 931, Regenstein 934, Scholl 947, **Sears 950,** Siragusa 954, Stern 960, Sundstrand 963, Thompson 965, USG 969, Walgreen 970, Washington 972, Waste 973, Woodward 978

Indiana: Ball 983, Cole 986, Foellinger 989, Fort 990, Froderman 991, Heritage 993, INB 995, Indianapolis 996, Martin 1002, Metropolitan 1003, Muncie 1006, Oliver 1010, Zollner 1013

Iowa: Employers 1017, Hall 1018, Maytag 1024, Mid-Iowa 1025, Wahlert 1030

Kansas: Baehr 1031, Bank 1032, DeVore 1036, Hansen 1037, Koch 1038, Marley 1039, Mingenback 1040, Rice 1042

Kentucky: Brown 1052, Cooke 1054, Courier-Journal 1055, Robinson 1063

Louisiana: Baton 1069, Coughlin-Saunders 1072, Monroe 1081, New Orleans 1082, Schlieder 1083, Shreveport-Bossier 1084, Zigler 1088

Maine: Central 1090

Maryland: Abell 1095, Davis 1109, Eastern 1110, Higginson 1117, Kelly 1121, Knott 1122, PHH 1131, Procter 1133, USF&G 1143

Massachusetts: Alden 1147, Bank 1153, Bayrd 1155, Boston 1158, Brooks 1161, Cambridge 1164, Campbell 1166, Chase 1168, Daniels 1177, Ellsworth 1185, Harrington 1201, Heydt 1204, High 1205, Kelley 1222, Levy 1225, **Little 1228,** Old 1246, Peabody 1249, Polaroid 1258, Raytheon 1262, Riley 1265, Rubenstein 1268, Russell 1269, State 1280, Stearns 1282, Stevens 1283, Stevens 1284, Stoddard 1285, Stone 1286, Stoneman 1287, Thompson 1289, Worcester 1295, Wyman-Gordon 1297

Michigan: Ann Arbor 1301, Battle 1303, Bishop 1306, Chrysler 1308, Consumers 1310, Dalton 1312, Eddy 1319, Ford 1329, Fremont 1331, General 1335, General 1336, Gerber 1337, Gerstacker 1338, Gilmore 1339, Grand 1340, Herrick 1343, Holden 1345, Hudson-Webber 1346, Jackson 1347, Kalamazoo 1349, Kellogg 1350, Kennedy 1352, Kresge 1353, Lansing 1354, Loutit 1357, McGregor 1358, Mills 1360, Morley 1362, Muskegon 1365, Northeast 1366, Ratner 1372, Redies 1373, Royal 1374, Saginaw 1376, **Seidman 1378,** Tiscornia 1388, Wege 1396, Whirlpool 1399, Wickes 1401, Wickson-Link 1402, Wilson 1403, Wilson 1404

Minnesota: Bigelow 1417, Bremer 1420, Cargill 1423, Grand 1442, Greystone 1444, Marbrook 1451, Mardag 1452, McKnight 1454, Minneapolis 1457, NWNL 1464, O'Brien 1465, O'Shaughnessy 1466, Ordean 1467, Otter 1468, Phillips 1471, Saint 1475, Thorpe 1479

Missouri: Anheuser-Busch 1495, Block 1501, Block 1502, Brown 1503, Cowden 1507, Goppert 1522, Green 1523, Hall 1525, Hallmark 1526, Hallmark 1527, Laclede 1538, Pet 1554, Reynolds 1558, Roblee 1559, Shaw 1562, Speas 1570, Speas 1571, Sunderland 1574, Union 1576, **Webb 1579**

Montana: MPCo/Entech 1583

Nebraska: Kiewit 1589, Omaha 1592

Nevada: **Hilton 1596,** Redfield 1597, Wiegand 1599

New Hampshire: Bean 1600

New Jersey: Allied-Signal 1611, **Crum 1627,** Edison 1631, Englehard 1634, Frelinghuysen 1636, Grassmann 1641, Hoechst 1645, Hyde 1651, Johnson 1656, Kerney 1660, Kirby 1661, Merck 1676, Ohl 1686, Pollak 1690, Prudential 1691, Rippel 1695, Schamach 1700, Schering-Plough 1702, Snyder 1707, Turrell 1713, Union 1714, Union 1715, Van Houten 1717, Van Pelt 1718, Warner-Lambert 1723

New Mexico: **Bellamah 1727,** Carlsbad 1728, Maddox 1729

Exchange programs

Fellowships

NATIONAL GUIDE TO FUNDING IN HEALTH

General purposes

Alabama: Central 8, Lowder 15, Mobile 20, Russell 21, Sonat 23, Vulcan 25

Arizona: Arizona 27, Bank 28, First 29, Globe 31, Morris 37

Arkansas: Arkansas 44

California: Aerospace 56, **American 60,** American 61, Arata 63, **Atkinson 66,** Baker 67, **BankAmerica 70,** Bay 73, Beaver 74, Bechtel 75, Benbough 79, Beynon 81, Boswell 85, Broccoli 89, Callison 97, **Carsey 100,** Chevron 103, Clorox 106, **Compton 110,** Computer 111, Crocker 115, Day 117, de Dampierre 118, Disney 120, Doheny 121, Drown 123, Factor 128, Familian 130, Farmers 132, First 135, Fluor 137, Fusenot 139, Gap 142, Gellert 148, Gellert 149, Gellert 150, Gerard 152, Gilmore 154, Great 160, Gross 161, Haas 164, Harden 168, Hewlett-Packard 174, Hoffman 176, Hogan 178, Irmas 182, Irwin 185, Jackson 187, Jameson 188, Jewett 190, Johnson 191, Karcher 196, Kirchgessner 200, Koret 202, Leavey 208, Leonardt 211, Levi 212, Lockheed 216, Lurie 220, MCA 227, McConnell 231, Milken 236, Milken 238, Miller 239, Monterey 240, Montgomery 242, Murphey 246, Murphy 247, National 248, Nissan 250, Norris 253, Occidental 254, Osher 257, **Packard 262,** Parker 263, Peninsula 269, Pickford 273, Platt 274, **Plitt 275,** Pratt 277, **S.G. 285,** San Diego 287, Santa Cruz 292, Sattler 293, Schlinger 294, Shaklee 301, Simon 303, Skaggs 304, Smith 306, Sonoma 309, Southern 310, Stauffer 313, Stauffer 314, Steele 315, Stein 316, Teledyne 327, Times 331, Tosco 332, Treadwell 335, U.S. 337, Union 339, Valley 340, Valley 341, Van Nuys 343, Weisz 349, Wollenberg 353, Wood-Claeyssens 354

Colorado: Bancroft 359, Boettcher 361, Coors 366, Coors 367, El Pomar 371, Gates 373, **General 374,** Joslin-Needham 379, Lowe 382, Manville 383, Monfort 384, Norgren 386, Schramm 391, Stone 393, Swan 395, Taylor 396, Thatcher 397, True 398, US 400, Weckbaugh 401, Wolf 404

Connecticut: Auerbach 410, Barden 412, Bridgeport 417, Champion 419, Chesebrough-Pond's 421, **Culpeper 426,** Culpeper 427, **Educational 433, General 439,** Gilman 442, Harcourt 445, Hartford 446, Herzog 450, **Hoffman 452, Lelash 463,** Loctite 464, Meriden 467, Northeast 472, Olin 474, Panwy 476, People's 478, Phoenix 481, Rosenthal 484, Satter 485, Saunders 486, Sosnoff 487, Stone 489, Travelers 491, Union 492, UST 494, **Xerox 500,** Young 501, Ziegler 502

Delaware: Amsterdam 503, Columbia 509, Delaware 511, Delmarva 512, DuPont 513, ICI 517, Kent-Lucas 518, Kingsley 519, Kutz 520, Laffey-McHugh 521, Lovett 524, Milliken 526, **Vale 528**

District of Columbia: Appleby 531, Bernstein 532, Cafritz 535, **Fannie 538,** Folger 540, Foundation 541, Freed 542, GEICO 543, Giant 545, Glen 546, Gottesman 547, Kennedy 552, Meyer 557, Post 560, Ross 562, Wasserman 564, Westport 565

Florida: Blair 576, Catlin 582, Dade 587, **Davis 590,** Dunspaugh-Dalton 592, duPont 594, Falk 599, Friends' 606, **Frueauff 607,** Goodwin 610, Gronewaldt 613, Janirve 621, Kennedy 626, **Knight 629,** Lauffer 632, Lost 634, Lowe 635, Palm 644, Phillips 648, Ratner 654, Rinker 656, **Rosenberg 657,** Rosenberg 658, Schultz 660, Storer 664, Swisher 665, Wells 676, Winter 680, Wollowick 682

Georgia: Atlanta 687, Callaway 690, Callaway 691, Dodson 700, Equifax 704, Exposition 705, Franklin 707, Gage 708, Georgia 709, Georgia 710, Glancy 714, Jinks 719, Lee 720, Marshall 723, Murphy 728, Patterson-Barclay 730, South 733, Wilson 742, Woodruff 743

Hawaii: Bancorp 748, Castle 749, Castle 750, Vidinha 758, Wilcox 759

Idaho: Boise 763

Illinois: Alberto-Culver 769, Aldeen 770, American 773, Amoco 775, Amsted 776, Bauer 786, Bere 791, Bersted 792, Blair 796, Blum-Kovler 799, Bock 800, Brach 805, Brunswick 806, CBI 815,

Centralia 818, Chicago 819, Chicago 820, Coleman 825, Crown 828, Cuneo 829, Davee 830, Deering 831, DeKalb 832, Dillon 834, Donnelley 835, Driehaus 837, Duchossois 838, FMC 842, Frank 845, GATX 853, Geraldi-Norton 854, Grainger 857, GSC 858, Harris 862, Harris 863, Hartmarx 864, Hermann 865, Inland 868, Johnson 870, Kemper 874, Klenk 876, Lewis 882, MacArthur 887, Mayer 890, McCormick 892, McCormick 893, Moorman 901, Motorola 903, Nalco 905, Neese 907, New Prospect 908, Northern 911, Payne 916, Peoples 917, Perkins 919, Petersen 920, Playboy 923, Polk 924, Prentice 926, Prince 927, Quaker 930, Redhill 933, Rice 939, **Salwil 944,** Seabury 948, Siragusa 954, Smail 955, Special 956, Stone 962, Susman 964, Thompson 965, USG 969, Walgreen 970, White 974, Woods 977

Indiana: Ball 983, Clark 984, Cole 986, Foellinger 989, Hook 994, INB 995, Indianapolis 996, Lilly 999, Martin 1002, **Moriah 1005,** Muncie 1006, Northern 1007, Oakley 1009, Reilly 1011, Zollner 1013

Iowa: Iowa 1019, Mansfield 1023, Mid-Iowa 1025, Pioneer 1026, Principal 1027, Principal 1028

Kansas: DeVore 1036, Hansen 1037, Koch 1038, Sarver 1043, Sprint 1046, Topeka 1047

Kentucky: Capital 1053, Cooke 1054, Houchens 1056, Long 1061, Rosenthal 1064, Schneider 1066

Louisiana: Freeport-McMoRan 1073, Zigler 1088

Maine: Maine 1091

Maryland: Abell 1095, Abramson 1096, Aegon 1097, Baldwin 1098, Baltimore 1099, Baltimore 1100, Blaustein 1102, Brown 1103, Capital 1104, Casey 1105, Clark-Winchcole 1106, Crown 1107, Dart 1108, Davis 1109, First 1111, France 1112, Hechinger 1116, Higginson 1117, Hobbs 1119, Knott 1122, Leidy 1123, Martin 1125, Merrick 1127, Rollins-Luetkemeyer 1134, Rouse 1136, Shapiro 1139, Signet 1140

Massachusetts: Adams 1146, Boston 1157, Boston 1159, Brooks 1161, **Cabot 1162,** Cambridge 1164, Chase 1168, Cove 1171, Cox 1174, Crane 1175, Daniels 1177, Davis 1178, Eaton 1183, **EG&G 1184,** Ellsworth 1185, Fuller 1193, General 1195, General 1196, Goldberg 1198, Harrington 1201, Henderson 1203, Hinduja 1206, Hoffman 1208, Hopedale 1211, Hornblower 1212, Hyams 1216, Island 1218, John 1220, Johnson 1221, Lechmere 1224, Levy 1225, Lipsky 1227, Millipore 1238, New England 1242, Old 1246, Perini 1252, Polaroid 1258, Rowland 1267, Rubenstein 1268, Russell 1269, Schrafft 1273, Sheraton 1277, Smith 1279, State 1280, Stearns 1281, Stearns 1282, Stevens 1284, Stoddard 1285, Stone 1286, Worcester 1295, Wright 1296, Wyman-Gordon 1297

Michigan: ANR 1302, Consumers 1310, Dalton 1312, DeVlieg 1315, DeVos 1316, Dow 1317, Flint 1323, Ford 1328, Ford 1329, Fremont 1331, Fruehauf 1333, General 1335, Gerstacker 1338, Herrick 1343, Hess 1344, Holden 1345, Hudson-Webber 1346, K Mart 1348, Kalamazoo 1349, McGregor 1358, Michigan 1359, **Mott 1363, Mott 1364,** Pagel 1368, Ratner 1372, Sage 1375, Sehn 1377, **Seidman 1378,** Skillman 1380, Sparks 1382, SPX 1383, Steelcase 1384, Tracy 1390, **Triford 1391,** Upjohn 1393, Vlasic 1394, Whiting 1400, Wilson 1403, Zuckerman 1407

Minnesota: Andersen 1411, Baker 1413, Bell 1415, Cargill 1424, Carolyn 1426, Chadwick 1428, Dain 1432, Dayton 1433, Edwards 1437, Fingerhut 1438, Lang 1449, MAHADH 1450, Mardag 1452, McKnight 1454, Meadowood 1455, Minneapolis 1457, Minnesota 1458, Northern 1461, NWNL 1464, O'Shaughnessy 1466, Phillips 1471, Red 1473, Rivers 1474, St. Croix 1476, Sundet 1478, Thorpe 1479, Wasie 1484, **Wood-Rill 1488**

Mississippi: Walker 1494

Missouri: Barrows 1498, Block 1501, Block 1502, Brown 1503, Commerce 1504, CPI 1508, Enright 1516, Goppert 1522, Hall 1525, Hallmark 1526, Hallmark 1527, Kansas 1533, Kemper 1535,

Laclede 1538, McDonnell 1548, Olin 1551, Oppenstein 1552, Pet 1554, Pettus 1555, Pitzman 1556, Ralston 1557, Slusher 1565, Speas 1571, Union 1576, Ward 1578, Whitaker 1580, Wolff 1581

Montana: Bair 1582, MPCo/Entech 1583

Nebraska: Buckley 1585, Buffett 1586, Keene 1588, Kiewit 1589

New Hampshire: Bean 1600, Chatham 1601, Jameson 1606, New Hampshire 1607

New Jersey: American 1612, Armco 1614, Borden 1616, Brennan 1619, Bunbury 1621, CPC 1624, **Crum 1627,** Engelhard 1633, Frelinghuysen 1636, Fund 1637, General 1639, Hoffmann-La Roche 1647, Johnson 1656, Johnson 1657, Kirby 1661, Klatskin 1662, Kramer 1664, Leavens 1667, Mercedes-Benz 1674, Mutual 1680, Prudential 1691, Schering-Plough 1702, Schultz 1704, Snyder 1707, Subaru 1708, Turrell 1713, Upton 1716, Van Pelt 1718, Victoria 1719, **Vollmer 1721, Vollmer 1722,** Willits 1724

New Mexico: **Bellamah 1727,** Maddox 1729

New York: Abrons 1731, Achelis 1732, **Ada 1733,** AKC 1737, Albany's 1740, Alexander 1741, Amax 1748, **American 1750,** American 1751, American 1753, Anderson 1754, **Archbold 1756,** Aron 1758, **ASDA 1760,** Avon 1764, Badgeley 1766, Baird 1767, **Baker 1769,** Bank 1771, Bankers 1772, Bard 1773, **Bedminster 1782,** Beinecke 1783, **Bernhard 1789, Biddle 1791,** Bingham 1793, Blinken 1796, Bluhdorn 1797, Bodman 1800, Booth 1801, Botwinick-Wolfensohn 1804, Boxer 1805, Bristol-Myers 1809, Bronfman 1811, BT 1815, Buffalo 1817, **Butler 1822,** Calder 1823, Canno 1824, Carnahan-Jackson 1828, **Carnegie 1829,** Carrier 1830, Carter-Wallace 1831, Cary 1833, Chase 1836, Chase 1837, **Chase 1838,** Chisholm 1843, CIT 1844, Citicorp/Citibank 1845, Clark 1849, Common 1859, Cooperman 1862, Corzine 1865, Cowles 1866, Crane 1867, **Cummings 1870,** Curtice-Burns/Pro-Fac 1872, **Dammann 1873, Dana 1875, de Rothschild 1877,** Delany 1882, Diamond 1885, Dillon 1886, Dun 1896, Edouard 1900, **Equitable 1904,** Evans 1908, Evans 1909, Fahey 1910, **Fife 1916,** Forbes 1920, **Ford 1922, Freeman 1926,** Fund 1930, Galasso 1932, Gebbie 1933, Goldsmith 1948, Goodstein 1954, **Grant 1958,** Greene 1964, Gruber 1968, Hagedorn 1970, Harriman 1974, **Hearst 1980, Hearst 1981,** Hettinger 1987, Heyward 1988, Horncrest 1993, Hoyt 1995, Hughes 1996, Hunt 2000, Hutchins 2001, Icahn 2003, Iroquois 2006, Israel 2007, Julia 2018, Kaplan 2022, Kaplan 2023, Kaufmann 2025, Killough 2031, Kimmelman 2032, Klau 2034, Klingenstein 2036, Knox 2040, Kramer 2045, Kravis 2046, Larsen 2053, Leonhardt 2064, Lowenstein 2078, Manufacturers 2087, Mathers 2093, McConnell 2100, **McDonald 2101,** McGraw-Hill 2104, Memton 2109, Merrill 2113, Merrill 2114, **Mertz-Gilmore 2115,** Metcalf 2116, Metropolitan 2117, Meyer 2118, Milbank 2119, Millbrook 2121, Monell 2125, Morgan 2128, Morgan 2129, Morgan 2130, Morgenstern 2132, Moses 2135, **Mott 2136,** Murray 2139, Neu 2143, New Street 2144, New York 2147, **New York 2148, New-Land 2150,** Noble 2154, Northern 2157, O'Connor 2161, O'Toole 2164, Orange 2167, Overbrook 2171, Paley 2173, Palisades 2174, Philip 2184, Pope 2192, Port 2194, **Pritchard 2198,** Prospect 2199, Prudential-Bache 2200, Quantum 2201, Rapoport 2204, Reader's 2206, Rhodebeck 2214, Ritter 2219, **Rockefeller 2223,** Rosenstiel 2229, Rosenwald 2230, Rubinstein 2234, Salomon 2241, Salomon 2243, Scherman 2249, Schwartz 2255, Schwartz 2256, Schweckendieck 2258, Sequa 2261, Sheinberg 2264, Sheldon 2265, Slaner 2270, Solow 2279, **Sony 2280,** Spitzer 2284, Sprague 2285, Spunk 2286, St. Giles 2287, Starr 2288, Steele-Reese 2291, Stein 2292, Sterling 2294, Stuart 2299, Sulzberger 2300, **Surdna 2302, Tai 2306, Teagle 2308, Thompson 2311,** Thorne 2313, '21' 2322, Vidda 2330, **Weinberg 2340,** Weinstein 2342,

Grants to individuals

In-kind gifts

Internships

Texas: Cain 2962, Exxon 3002, Meadows 3064, Tarrant 3116, Tenneco 3118, Trull 3122, Zachry 3138
Vermont: Vermont 3160
Virginia: James 3185, Universal 3212
Washington: Washington 3258
Wisconsin: **Bradley 3275,** Kohler 3295, Northwestern 3308

Land acquisition

Alabama: Meyer 18, Sonat 23
Arizona: **Kieckhefer 35,** Morris 37
California: Ahmanson 57, Copley 114, First 135, Fusenot 139, Haas 163, Hedco 170, Irwin 185, Jewett 190, **Kerr 199,** Marin 224, Monterey 240, **Packard 262,** Parker 263, Pratt 277, Santa Barbara 290, Stern 318, Tuohy 336
Colorado: Boettcher 361, El Pomar 371, Gates 373
Connecticut: Hartford 446, Hartford 448, ITT 456, Olin 474
Delaware: Crystal 510, Laffey-McHugh 521, Longwood 523
District of Columbia: Freed 542
Florida: Beveridge 574, Briggs 578, Bush 581, Chatlos 583, Dade 587, **Davis 590,** Falk 599, Friends' 606, Kennedy 626, Phipps 649
Georgia: Atlanta 686, Atlanta 687, Callaway 690, Campbell 693, Equifax 704, Glancy 714, Lee 720, South 733, Whitehead 740, Wilson 742, Woodruff 743
Hawaii: Castle 750
Illinois: Chicago 820, DeKalb 832, Dillon 834, Field 840, Nalco 905, Quaker 930
Indiana: Cole 986, Foellinger 989, Fort 990, Heritage 993, Lilly 999
Iowa: Hall 1018, Maytag 1024
Kentucky: Brown 1052, Rosenthal 1064
Maryland: Abell 1095, Knott 1122, Procter 1133
Massachusetts: Alden 1147, Boston 1158, **Cabot 1162,** Cox 1174, Daniels 1177, Davis 1178, Ellsworth 1185, Heydt 1204, Riley 1265, State 1280, Stevens 1284, Stoddard 1285, Thompson 1289, Wyman-Gordon 1297
Michigan: Battle 1303, Bishop 1306, Dalton 1312, General 1336, Gerstacker 1338, Gilmore 1339, Grand 1340, Herrick 1343, Jackson 1347, Kresge 1353, Loutit 1357, Mills 1360, Northeast 1366
Minnesota: Bigelow 1417, Greystone 1444, Marbrook 1451, Wedum 1485
Missouri: Block 1501, Block 1502, Brown 1503, Cowden 1507, Reynolds 1558, Sunderland 1574
Nebraska: Kiewit 1589
New Hampshire: Bean 1600
New Jersey: Grassmann 1641, Hyde 1651, Turrell 1713, Union 1715, Victoria 1719
New York: Achelis 1732, Barker 1774, Bodman 1800, Buffalo 1817, Cary 1833, Cornell 1863, Cummings 1869, Goodyear 1955, **Grant 1958,** Hayden 1978, Heckscher 1982, Jones 2015, Kaplan 2023, Kaufmann 2025, Lang 2051, Larsen 2053, Macdonald 2080, McCann 2097, Moore 2127, **Norcross 2155,** Northern 2158, O'Connor 2161, **Sony 2280,** Thorne 2313
North Carolina: Daniels 2382, Hanes 2399, Hanes 2400
Ohio: Ashtabula 2437, Columbus 2460, Dayton 2466, Frohring 2488, Gund 2497, Iddings 2509, Kettering 2515, Nippert 2546, Pollock 2559, Procter 2562, Russell 2574, Schmidlapp 2578, Sears 2580, Star 2590, Stark 2591, Timken 2595
Oklahoma: Goddard 2624, Phillips 2636
Oregon: Jeld-Wen 2654, Oregon 2660, Tucker 2662
Pennsylvania: Cyclops 2714, Elf 2721, Grundy 2735, Hillman 2749, J.D.B. 2760, Justus 2764, Kline 2768, Laurel 2771, Lehigh 2772, McKenna 2786, McLean 2787, Mellon 2791, Patterson 2802, Penn 2803, Pittsburgh 2810, Sheppard 2829, Smith 2831, **Stott 2844,** Trexler 2850, Wells 2855
Rhode Island: Champlin 2868, Old 2880, Rhode Island 2882
South Carolina: Close 2889, Colonial 2890
Tennessee: Benwood 2912, HCA 2925, Toms 2938, Tonya 2939

Texas: Amarillo 2946, Austin 2951, Carter 2965, Communities 2972, Constantin 2975, Cullen 2980, Dougherty 2987, Fikes 3009, Frees 3016, Halsell 3027, Hillcrest 3034, Hoblitzelle 3036, Houston 3037, Johnson 3041, Keith 3044, Kimberly-Clark 3046, Meadows 3064, Moody 3069, Richardson 3094, Rockwell 3098, San Antonio 3099, Turner 3123
Vermont: Lintilhac 3157
Virginia: Camp 3167, Crestar 3172, **Freedom 3181,** Norfolk 3196, Ohrstrom 3197, Portsmouth 3200, Titmus 3210
Washington: Archibald 3218, Comstock 3225, Matlock 3236
Wisconsin: Banta 3273

Lectureships

Alabama: Gibson 13, Sonat 23
California: Peninsula 269
Connecticut: GTE 444
District of Columbia: Westport 565
Florida: **Davis 590**
Georgia: Lee 720, Livingston 722
Kansas: Koch 1038, Sarver 1043
Maryland: Higginson 1117
Massachusetts: **Grass 1200**
Minnesota: Eddy 1436, Phillips 1471, Red 1473
Missouri: Group 1524, Kansas 1533, Oppenstein 1552, Southwestern 1569
Nebraska: Keene 1588
New York: Agway 1736, Alexander 1741, **Berlex 1788,** Carnahan-Jackson 1828, **Cummings 1870,** Ernst 1905, Graphic 1960, Larsen 2053, Sterling 2294, Sulzberger 2300, Wiley 2349
North Carolina: Burroughs 2376, **Burroughs 2377**
North Dakota: Stern 2429
Oregon: Collins 2652, Johnson 2655
Pennsylvania: Kline 2768, Laurel 2771, Miles 2795
South Carolina: Spartanburg 2902
Texas: **Alcon 2944,** Crump 2979, Green 3020, Kempner 3045, McGovern 3059, McGovern 3060, Meadows 3064, Rockwell 3098, San Antonio 3099, Turner 3123
Vermont: Lintilhac 3157
Washington: GTE 3231, Pacific 3241
Wisconsin: **Bradley 3275,** Helfaer 3288

Loans

California: Gerbode 153, Marin 224, **Packard 262, Plitt 275,** San Francisco 288, Santa Clara 291, Sierra 302, van Loben Sels 342
Connecticut: Connecticut 424, Connecticut 425, Hartford 448, New Haven 470, Panwy 476, People's 478
District of Columbia: Post 560
Florida: Bush 581, Jacksonville 620
Illinois: Chicago 820, Playboy 923
Indiana: Heritage 993
Kentucky: Houchens 1056
Louisiana: Coughlin-Saunders 1072
Maryland: Straus 1141
Massachusetts: Polaroid 1258
Michigan: Grand 1340, Jackson 1347, **Mott 1363,** Muskegon 1365
Minnesota: Bremer 1420, Minneapolis 1457, Ordean 1467
New Hampshire: Bean 1600, New Hampshire 1607
New Jersey: Snyder 1707
New Mexico: Albuquerque 1726
New York: Fund 1930, Gebbie 1933, **Hartford 1975,** Hoyt 1995, **New World 2145,** New York 2146, O'Connor 2161
Ohio: Cincinnati 2456, Deuble 2468, National 2544, Nord 2547, Stark 2591
Oklahoma: Broadhurst 2621
Pennsylvania: Williamsport-Lycoming 2861
South Carolina: Central 2888
Texas: Crump 2979
Washington: Pacific 3241, Tacoma 3255, Washington 3257

Matching funds

Alabama: Dravo 12, Hill 14, Sonat 23
Arizona: A.P.S. 26, Arizona 27, **Kieckhefer 35**
Arkansas: McKesson 49, Wal-Mart 54
California: Ahmanson 57, **American 60,** American 61, AT&T 65, **BankAmerica 70,** Beckman 76, California 96, Clorox 106, **Compton 110,** Confidence 112, Crocker 115, Drown 123, Fairfield 129, Fireman's 134, First 135, Great 160, Haas 163, Harden 168, Hedco 170, Hofmann 177, Hoover 179, Humboldt 181, Jewett 190, **Kaiser 194,** Kirchgessner 200, Levi 212, Livingston 215, Lurie 220, Margoes 223, Marin 224, McCarthy 230, McKesson 232, Mericos 235, Miller 239, Monterey 240, Murphey 246, National 248, Norris 253, Ostern 258, Oxnard 260, **Packard 262,** Parker 263, Parsons 264, Pasadena 266, Peninsula 269, **Pfeiffer 272,** Pratt 277, Rincon 282, **S.G. 285,** San Diego 287, Santa Barbara 290, Santa Clara 291, Santa Cruz 292, Seaver 297, Shaklee 301, Sierra 302, Sonoma 309, Southern 310, Stauffer 313, Steele 315, Stein 316, Stern 318, Stulsaft 322, Swift 323, Syntex 326, Transamerica 334, Tuohy 336, U.S. 337, Valley 340, Valley 341, van Loben Sels 342, Varian 345, W.W.W. 346, Weingart 348, Whittier 351
Colorado: Boettcher 361, Denver 369, **Frost 372,** Gates 373, Hill 377, Kitzmiller-Bales 380, Norgren 386, US 400
Connecticut: **Aetna 406,** Bodenwein 415, Champion 419, Connecticut 425, Culpeper 427, **Educational 433,** Ensworth 435, Hartford 446, Hartford 448, ITT 456, New Britain 469, New Haven 470, Olin 474, Palmer 475, Patterson 477, Rosenthal 484, Saunders 486, Stanley 488, United 493, Waterbury 497
Delaware: Columbia 509, DuPont 513, ICI 517, Laffey-McHugh 521, Marmot 525, Welfare 530
District of Columbia: Cafritz 535, **Fannie 538,** Glen 546, Graham 548, Kiplinger 553, Lehrman 554, Meyer 557, Post 560, **Public 561,** Ross 562, Stewart 563
Florida: Beveridge 574, Broward 580, Bush 581, Chatlos 583, Conn 585, Dade 587, **Davis 590,** duPont 594, Falk 599, Friends' 606, **Frueauff 607,** Grace 611, Jacksonville 620, Jones 624, Kennedy 626, **Knight 629,** Lost 634, Lowe 635, **Markey 637,** Palm 644, Phipps 649, Rosenberg 658, Storer 664, Swisher 665, TECO 668, Wahlstrom 671, Winn-Dixie 679
Georgia: Atlanta 686, Callaway 690, Callaway 691, Campbell 693, Jinks 719, Lee 720, **UPS 737**
Hawaii: Atherton 746, Cooke 751, Frear 752, Hawaiian 754, McInerny 755, PRI 756, Wilcox 759
Idaho: Daugherty 765
Illinois: Alberto-Culver 769, Aurora 783, Beloit 790, Chicago 820, **Chicago 821,** Coleman 825, Crown 828, Cuneo 829, DeKalb 832, Dillon 834, Fry 848, Furnas 850, GATX 853, Kemper 874, MacArthur 887, McCormick 893, McDonald's 894, McGraw 895, New Prospect 908, Northern 911, Quaker 930, Replogle 936, Retirement 937, Siragusa 954, Stern 960, USG 969, Waste 973, Woods 977
Indiana: Ball 982, Clark 984, Cole 986, Foellinger 989, Fort 990, Heritage 993, INB 995, Lilly 999, Martin 1002, Metropolitan 1003, **Moriah 1005,** Northern 1007, Noyes 1008, Oliver 1010
Iowa: Hall 1018, Maytag 1024, Mid-Iowa 1025, Pioneer 1026
Kansas: Baehr 1031, Beech 1033, Koch 1038, Topeka 1047
Kentucky: Brown 1052, Capital 1053, Robinson 1063
Louisiana: Baton 1069, Freeport-McMoRan 1073, New Orleans 1082, Shreveport-Bossier 1084, Zigler 1088
Maine: Central 1090, Maine 1091, UNUM 1094
Maryland: Abell 1095, Baltimore 1099, Capital 1104, Eastern 1110, Goldseker 1113, Higginson 1117, Kelly 1121, Knott 1122, Procter 1133
Massachusetts: Alden 1147, Bank 1153, Boston 1158, Brooks 1161, Cowan 1172, Daniels 1177, Digital 1180, General 1195, General 1196, Heydt 1204, High 1205, Hyams 1216, John 1220, Kelley 1222, **Little 1228, New England 1241,** New England

Operating budgets

NATIONAL GUIDE TO FUNDING IN HEALTH

Merck 1235, Monarch 1239, Old 1246, Peabody 1251, Perpetual 1254, Polaroid 1258, Raytheon 1262, Schrafft 1273, Shawmut 1276, State 1280, Stevens 1283, Stevens 1284, Webster 1291, Worcester 1295, Wyman-Gordon 1297

Michigan: Anderson 1300, ANR 1302, Bauervic-Paisley 1304, Bishop 1306, Chrysler 1308, Chrysler 1309, Consumers 1311, Dalton 1312, Fremont 1331, General 1335, General 1336, Gilmore 1339, Great 1342, Holden 1345, Hudson-Webber 1346, Kennedy 1352, McGregor 1358, Mills 1360, Morley 1362, **Mott 1363, Mott 1364,** Muskegon 1365, Sage 1375, Skillman 1380, Taubman 1386, Whirlpool 1399, Wickes 1401, Wickson-Link 1402, Wilson 1403, Wilson 1404, World 1405

Minnesota: American 1409, Andersen 1411, Baker 1413, Bremer 1420, Cargill 1423, Cargill 1424, Dain 1432, Dayton 1433, Ecolab 1434, Ecolab 1435, Fingerhut 1438, General 1441, Grand 1443, Greystone 1444, Honeywell 1446, Hubbard 1448, MAHADH 1450, Marbrook 1451, McKnight 1454, Medtronic 1456, Minneapolis 1457, Minnesota 1458, Minnesota 1459, Northern 1461, O'Brien 1465, Ordean 1467, Phillips 1471, St. Croix 1476, Thorpe 1479, Walker 1481, Wasie 1484

Mississippi: Deposit 1489

Missouri: Block 1501, Block 1502, Brown 1503, CPI 1508, Feld 1518, Hallmark 1526, Hallmark 1527, Ilgenfritz 1529, Jordan 1532, Laclede 1538, Long 1541, Oppenstein 1552, Pet 1554, Slusher 1565, Speas 1570, Speas 1571, Stupp 1573, Sunderland 1574, Union 1576, **Webb 1579,** Wolff 1581

Nevada: **Hilton 1596**

New Hampshire: Eastman 1603, Fuller 1605

New Jersey: Allied-Signal 1611, American 1612, Borden 1616, CPC 1624, **Crum 1627,** Dodge 1630, Edison 1631, Engelhard 1633, **Fanwood 1635,** General 1639, Hoechst 1645, Hoechst 1646, Hoffmann-La Roche 1647, **Huber 1650,** Johnson 1656, Johnson 1657, Kirby 1661, Maneely 1670, McGraw 1672, MCJ 1673, Mutual 1680, Prudential 1691, Schering-Plough 1702, Schultz 1704, Schumann 1705, Snyder 1707, Subaru 1708, Turrell 1713, Union 1714, Victoria 1719, Warner-Lambert 1723

New Mexico: Carlsbad 1728

New York: Abrons 1731, Achelis 1732, Alexander 1741, **AT&T 1762,** Avon 1764, Bank 1771, Bankers 1772, Barker 1774, Blum 1798, Bodman 1800, BT 1815, Buffalo 1816, Buffalo 1817, Calder 1823, Cary 1833, Chase 1837, **Chase 1838,** Claiborne 1846, Clark 1849, Coltec 1858, Common 1859, Cornell 1863, Cowles 1866, Curtice-Burns/Pro-Fac 1872, Delavan 1883, Diamond 1885, Dillon 1886, **Dula 1895,** Dun 1896, Eastman 1898, Eastman 1899, Evans 1909, **Freeman 1926,** Gibbs 1938, Gifford 1939, Goldome 1947, Goldsmith 1948, **Grant 1958,** Griffis 1967, Hagedorn 1970, Harriman 1974, **Hartford 1975,** Hoyt 1995, Hunt 2000, International 2005, Jones 2015, Joy 2016, Killough 2031, Klingenstein 2036, Kresge 2047, Lang 2051, Macdonald 2080, McGraw-Hill 2104, Merrill 2113, **Mertz-Gilmore 2115,** Metcalf 2116, Metropolitan 2117, Moore 2127, Morgan 2128, Morgan 2129, Morgan 2130, Moses 2135, New Street 2144, New York 2147, **New York 2148,** New York 2149, **New-Land 2150,** Norwood 2159, Palisades 2174, Pfizer 2181, Philip 2184, Phillips 2185, **Phillips 2186,** Price 2197, Prospect 2199, Rapoport 2204, Republic 2211, Rubinstein 2234, Salomon 2243, Scherman 2249, **Smithers 2276, Sony 2280,** Sprague 2285, Steele-Reese 2291, Sterling 2294, Sulzberger 2300, Thorne 2313, Unilever 2323, van Ameringen 2326, Vidda 2330, Weinberg 2339, Wilson 2350

North Carolina: **Babcock 2368,** Belk 2369, Bryan 2373, Duke 2386, Finch 2390, First 2392, **Glaxo 2396,** Lance 2403, Provident 2409, Reynolds 2410, Reynolds 2411, Rogers 2412, Wachovia 2421

North Dakota: Fargo-Moorhead 2426, Leach 2427, Stern 2429

Ohio: American 2432, American 2433, **Armington 2436,** BP 2443, Britton 2446, Centerior 2452, Cincinnati 2455, Dayton 2467, Eaton 2470, Evans 2475, Ferro 2478, Frohman 2486, Frohring 2488, Gallagher 2489, Gund 2497, H.C.S. 2498, Haskell 2501, Hoover 2505, Huffy 2507, Humphrey 2508, Iddings 2509, Kangesser 2514, Kettering 2515, Kramer 2518, Kroger 2519, Lubrizol 2525, Morgan 2538, Murphy 2542, Nationwide 2545, Nippert 2546, Nord 2547, Nordson 2548, Pollock 2559, Prentiss 2560, Reinberger 2566, Reynolds 2569, Ritter 2571, Sears 2580, Sisler 2584, Smith 2586, Society 2589, Star 2590, Tamarkin 2594, TRW 2603, White 2607, Wolfe 2610

Oklahoma: American 2616, Boatmen's 2618, Goddard 2624, Occidental 2632, Oklahoma 2633, Oklahoma 2634, Phillips 2636, Titus 2643, Warren 2645, Wegener 2646, Zarrow 2648

Oregon: Carpenter 2649, Johnson 2655, Meyer 2657, Oregon 2660, Tucker 2662

Pennsylvania: Air 2665, Air 2666, Alcoa 2668, Arcadia 2677, Benedum 2683, Berkman 2684, CIGNA 2701, Connelly 2707, Consolidated 2708, Crawford 2711, Crels 2712, Dietrich 2715, Dolfinger-McMahon 2716, Elf 2721, Goldman 2732, Grable 2733, Grundy 2735, Hallowell 2737, Harsco 2740, Heinz 2743, Hershey 2748, Hillman 2750, Hooper 2753, Hulme 2757, Justus 2764, Laurel 2771, McFeely-Rogers 2785, McKenna 2786, Mellon 2789, Mellon 2790, Mellon 2791, Mengle 2792, Merit 2794, Miles 2795, Oberkotter 2799, Patterson 2802, **Pew 2806,** Philadelphia 2807, Philadelphia 2808, Pittsburgh 2810, PPG 2812, Provident 2814, Rockwell 2818, Rockwell 2819, Rockwell 2820, Scaife 2823, **Scaife 2824,** Smith 2831, Smith 2832, SmithKline 2834, Snyder 2836, SPS 2838, Stabler 2839, **Stott 2844,** Strawbridge 2847, Trexler 2850, **USX 2853,** Wyomissing 2864

Puerto Rico: Puerto Rico 2865

Rhode Island: Cranston 2869, Providence 2881, Rhode Island 2882

South Carolina: Colonial 2890, Springs 2904, Trident 2907

Tennessee: Cole 2918, First 2921, HCA 2925, Lowenstein 2928, Massengill-DeFriece 2929, Plough 2932, Potter 2933

Texas: Abell-Hanger 2941, Abercrombie 2942, Abilene 2943, Alexander 2945, Apache 2949, Beasley 2955, Bertha 2956, Brown 2959, Cain 2962, Cain 2963, Cimarron 2967, Clayton 2968, Cockrell 2970, Cooley 2976, Cooper 2977, Dickson 2984, Dougherty 2987, Edwards 2994, Edwards 2995, Ellwood 2999, Enron 3000, Exxon 3002, Fasken 3006, Favrot 3007, Fikes 3009, Fish 3012, Green 3020, Griffin 3021, Gulf 3022, Gulf 3023, Haas 3024, Haggar 3025, Halsell 3027, Houston 3037, Howell 3038, Keith 3044, Kempner 3045, Kimberly-Clark 3046, Lightner 3051, LTV 3052, McDermott 3058, McGovern 3059, McKee 3061, Meadows 3064, Moncrief 3068, O'Connor 3077, Owen 3081, Owsley 3082, Pennzoil 3087, Perkins 3088, Powell 3091, Richardson 3094, Rockwell 3098, San Antonio 3099, Sharp 3103, Shell 3104, Simmons 3105, Strake 3112, Sturgis 3114, Texas 3119, Transco 3121, Trull 3122, Turner 3123, West 3130, **Zale 3139**

Utah: Bamberger 3141, Castle 3144, Eccles 3149, Swanson 3154

Vermont: National 3158, Scott 3159

Virginia: BDM 3161, Dominion 3174, Dominion 3175, Fairchild 3178, **Freedom 3181,** Gottwald 3182, **Jones 3187,** Lawrence 3189, Little 3190, Ohrstrom 3197, Portsmouth 3200, Thomas 3209, Universal 3212, Washington 3214

Washington: Airborne 3216, Fales 3226, Fuchs 3229, Kilworth 3233, Leuthold 3234, Matlock 3236, Ray 3246, Seafirst 3249, Skinner 3252, **Stewardship 3253,** Tacoma 3255, U.S. 3256, Washington 3257, Washington 3258, Wharton 3259

West Virginia: Kanawha 3265

Wisconsin: Appleton 3272, Banta 3273, **Bradley 3275,** Bucyrus-Erie 3277, Consolidated 3280, Cudahy

3282, CUNA 3283, Evinrude 3285, Humphrey 3289, **Johnson 3292,** McBeath 3302, Neenah 3307, Northwestern 3308, Oshkosh 3311, Racine 3316, Rutledge 3323, Stackner 3328, Wisconsin 3338, Wisconsin 3339

Professorships

Alabama: Hill 14, Lowder 15, Sonat 23
California: Baxter 72, Beckman 76, Haas 163, Jones 192, **Keck 197,** Kirchgessner 200, Norris 253, Stauffer 313, Treadwell 335, Valley 341
Colorado: **Frost 372**
Connecticut: **Educational 433,** Patterson 477, **Xerox 500**
Delaware: **Good 516**
District of Columbia: Bloedorn 533
Florida: **Davis 590,** duPont 594, **Knight 629, Rosenberg 657**
Georgia: Georgia 710, Harland 715, Lee 720, South 733, Tull 736, **UPS 737**
Hawaii: Hawaiian 754
Illinois: Bauer 786, Coleman 825, Crown 828, Hartmarx 864, Perkins 919
Indiana: Ball 982
Iowa: Employers 1017
Kentucky: Ashland 1049, Brown 1052, Cooke 1054
Louisiana: Coughlin-Saunders 1072
Massachusetts: Acushnet 1145, Alden 1147, Daniels 1177, Harrington 1202, **Iacocca 1217,** Pappas 1248, Rowland 1267, Rubenstein 1268, Stoddard 1285
Michigan: Muskegon 1365
Minnesota: Cargill 1423, Eddy 1436, Marbrook 1451, Phillips 1471
Missouri: Anheuser-Busch 1495, Commerce 1504, Edison 1512
New Jersey: Hoechst 1645, Schering-Plough 1702, Warner-Lambert 1723
New York: Amax 1748, **American 1752, Bernhard 1789,** Bronfman 1811, Buffalo 1817, Cowles 1866, Cummings 1871, Curtice-Burns/Pro-Fac 1872, Ernst 1905, **Ford 1922,** Griffis 1967, Kaufmann 2025, Lang 2051, Larsen 2053, Leonhardt 2064, Moses 2135, Palisades 2174, Pfizer 2181, Pforzheimer 2183, Philip 2184, Starr 2288, Steele-Reese 2291, Sterling 2294, Sulzberger 2300, Weinberg 2339
North Carolina: Burlington 2375, Burroughs 2376, **Burroughs 2377,** Duke 2386, Smith 2414
North Dakota: Stern 2429
Ohio: Cleveland-Cliffs 2458, Humphrey 2508, Renner 2568, TRW 2603, Wolfe 2610
Oklahoma: Oklahoma 2634, Phillips 2636, Puterbaugh 2637, Sarkeys 2639
Oregon: Johnson 2655
Pennsylvania: Heinz 2743, Hillman 2749, Independence 2759, McCune 2784, Miles 2795, Rockwell 2819, Stabler 2839
Puerto Rico: Puerto Rico 2865
South Carolina: Close 2889, Springs 2904
Tennessee: Benwood 2912, HCA 2925, Plough 2932, Toms 2938
Texas: Austin 2951, Brown 2959, Cain 2962, Carter 2965, Cockrell 2970, Cullen 2980, Dunagan 2991, Fikes 3009, Green 3020, Houston 3037, Hubbard 3039, Kempner 3045, McGovern 3059, McGovern 3060, Meadows 3064, Moody 3069, RGK 3093, Rockwell 3098, San Antonio 3099, Seay 3101, Shell 3104, Tenneco 3118, Trull 3122, Turner 3123, White 3133, **Zale 3139**
Utah: Eccles 3148
Vermont: Lintilhac 3157
Virginia: Fitz-Gibbon 3179, Olsson 3198, Parsons 3199, Titmus 3210, Universal 3212, Wheat 3215
Washington: Boeing 3222, Lockwood 3235, U.S. 3256
Wisconsin: **Bradley 3275,** Consolidated 3280, Helfaer 3288

Program-related investments

Alabama: Sonat 23
Arizona: Arizona 27

Publications

Renovation projects

Ohio: Ashtabula 2437, Beecher 2441, Bruening 2447, Centerior 2452, Cincinnati 2456, Cleveland 2457, Columbus 2460, Coshocton 2462, Dayton 2466, Fifth 2479, Iddings 2509, Murch 2540, Murphy 2542, Nippert 2546, Ohio 2553, Prentiss 2560, Reinberger 2566, Russell 2574, Sisler 2584, Watson 2605, Yassenoff 2613, Youngstown 2615

Oklahoma: Broadhurst 2621, Mabee 2627, McGee 2629, Occidental 2632, Phillips 2636

Oregon: Johnson 2655, Meyer 2657, Oregon 2660

Pennsylvania: Air 2666, Alcoa 2668, Arcadia 2677, Beatty 2681, Byers 2692, Connelly 2707, Consolidated 2708, Elf 2721, Grundy 2735, Heinz 2744, Heinz 2745, Hillman 2749, Hillman 2750, Horsehead 2755, Jennings 2762, Justus 2764, Kline 2768, Lehigh 2772, McCune 2784, McLean 2787, Mellon 2791, Murphy 2798, Oberlaender 2800, Penn 2803, **Pew 2806,** Pittsburgh 2809, Polk 2811, Scranton 2827, Smith 2831, Snee-Reinhardt 2835, Stackpole-Hall 2840, **Stott 2844,** Trexler 2850, Union 2851, Union 2852, **USX 2853,** Wells 2855, Widener 2858, Williams 2860

Puerto Rico: Puerto Rico 2865

Rhode Island: Champlin 2868, Fleet/Norstar 2870, Littlefield 2878, Old 2880, Rhode Island 2882

South Carolina: Close 2889, Gregg-Graniteville 2893, Self 2899, Spartanburg 2902, Trident 2907

South Dakota: Sioux Falls 2908

Tennessee: Benwood 2912, Chattanooga 2916, HCA 2925

Texas: Abilene 2943, Austin 2951, Brown 2959, Cain 2963, Carter 2965, Constantin 2975, Cullen 2980, Dallas 2981, Dougherty 2987, Ellwood 2999, Enron 3000, Exxon 3003, Haas 3024, Harrington 3030, Hillcrest 3034, Hoblitzelle 3036, Houston 3037, Johnson 3041, Kempner 3045, **Kleberg 3048,** Lightner 3051, Meadows 3064, Moody 3069, Richardson 3094, Rockwell 3098, San Antonio 3099, Simmons 3105, Straus 3113, Tarrant 3116, Tenneco 3118, Texas 3119, Texas 3120, Trull 3122, Turner 3123, Wright 3137

Vermont: Lintilhac 3157, Vermont 3160

Virginia: **Freedom 3181,** Portsmouth 3200, Richmond 3204, Universal 3212, Washington 3214, Wheat 3215

Washington: Archibald 3218, Blue 3221, Boeing 3222, Matlock 3236, Pacific 3241, Seafirst 3249, Seattle 3250, Skinner 3252, Washington 3257, Wharton 3259

West Virginia: Clay 3263, McDonough 3267

Wisconsin: **Bradley 3275,** Consolidated 3280, Cudahy 3282, Evinrude 3285, McBeath 3302, Milwaukee 3306, Wisconsin 3338

Research

Alabama: Dixon 11, Hill 14, Lowder 15, Meyer 18, Shook 22, Sonat 23, Vulcan 25

Arizona: Arizona 27, Flinn 30, Hermundslie 34, **Kieckhefer 35**

Arkansas: Arkansas 44

California: Allen 58, Baker 67, Bank 69, Baxter 72, Beckman 76, **Carsey 100,** Chevron 103, City 104, de Dampierre 118, Early 124, **Eisenberg 126,** Factor 128, Femino 133, Fusenot 139, Gellert 148, Gellert 149, Gellert 150, Genentech 151, Gerard 152, Goldwyn 158, Hofmann 177, Hoover 179, Howe 180, Irwin 185, Jameson 188, Jewett 190, Johnson 191, **Kaiser 194, Keck 197,** Kirchgessner 200, Lucas 219, Margoes 223, Masserini 225, **Maxfield 226,** McCarthy 230, Milken 236, Milken 238, Monterey 240, National 248, Norris 253, Ostern 258, Oxnard 260, **Packard 262,** Parker 263, Parsons 264, Pasadena 266, Patron 267, **Pfeiffer 272,** Platt 274, Pratt 277, **Research 280,** Schlinger 294, Seaver 297, Simon 303, Stein 316, Stern 317, Stern 318, Stulsaft 322, Swift 323, Treadwell 335, Valley 341, van Loben Sels 342, Van Nuys 343, Wasserman 347, Western 350

Colorado: Comprecare 365, Duncan 370, **Frost 372,** General 374, Hughes 378, Swan 395, Taylor 396, True 398, Williams 403

Connecticut: **Adler 405,** ASEA 409, Bodenwein 415, Chesebrough-Pond's 421, Childs 422, **Culpeper 426, Educational 433, General 439, General 440,** Hascoe 449, Herzog 450, Huisking 454, ITT 456, Olin 474, Palmer 475, Patterson 477, Rosenthal 484, Stanley 488, Tow 490, Travelers 491, United 493, Waterbury 497, Whitehead 498, Xerox 499, **Xerox 500,** Young 501, Ziegler 502

Delaware: Amsterdam 503, Beneficial 504, Columbia 509, Delmarva 512, DuPont 513, **Lalor 522,** Longwood 523, Marmot 525, **Schwartz 527, Vale 528**

District of Columbia: **Fannie 538,** Foundation 541, Kennedy 552, Lehrman 554, Post 560, Ross 562, Wasserman 564, Westport 565

Florida: Abbey 566, Amaturo 569, Appleman 571, Briggs 578, Dade 587, **Davis 590,** duPont 594, Falk 599, Greenburg-May 612, **Hayward 617, Markey 637,** Mills 640, Phipps 649, Ratner 654, **Rosenberg 657,** Simon 662, Storer 664, Wahlstrom 671, Wells 676, Wertheim 677, Whitehall 678, Winn-Dixie 679

Georgia: Equifax 704, **Foundation 706,** Georgia 709, Georgia 710, Georgia 711, Glancy 714, Lee 720, Rich 731, **UPS 737**

Hawaii: Atherton 746, Castle 749, Cooke 751, Hawaii 753, Hawaiian 754

Idaho: Boise 763

Illinois: Abbott 768, Ameritech 774, Bauer 786, Blowitz-Ridgeway 797, Boothroyd 801, Brach 805, Buehler 808, Butz 810, CBI 815, Chicago 820, Coleman 825, Crown 828, Fry 848, Geraldi-Norton 854, Grainger 857, GSC 858, Harris 863, Johnson 870, Kemper 873, Klenk 876, MacArthur 887, McGraw 895, OMC 913, Perkins 919, Petersen 920, Redhill 933, Regenstein 934, Relations 935, Retirement 937, Rothschild 940, Scholl 947, Siragusa 954, Sprague 957, United 968, USG 969, Washington 972, Waste 973, Woods 977

Indiana: Ball 982, Clowes 985, Fort 990, Heritage 993, Miles 1004, Northern 1007, Oliver 1010

Iowa: Carver 1015, Maytag 1024, Pioneer 1026

Kansas: Baehr 1031, Bank 1032, Rice 1042

Kentucky: Brown 1052

Louisiana: Baton 1069, Booth-Bricker 1070, Brown 1071, Freeport-McMoRan 1073, Monroe 1081, Schlieder 1083, Shreveport-Bossier 1084, Zigler 1088

Maine: Central 1090

Maryland: Davis 1109, Higginson 1117, **Hughes 1120,** Life 1124, Procter 1133, Signet 1140

Massachusetts: Alden 1147, Alden 1148, Bayrd 1155, Boston 1157, Boston 1160, **Cabot 1162,** Campbell 1166, **Conservation 1170,** Cox 1174, Digital 1180, Fuller 1193, General 1195, **Grass 1200,** Hinduja 1206, Hood 1210, **Iacocca 1217,** Island 1218, John 1220, Kelley 1222, King 1223, Levy 1225, **Merck 1235,** Merkert 1236, **New England 1241,** Pappas 1248, Peabody 1249, Peabody 1250, Poitras 1257, Rowland 1267, Smith 1279, Stoddard 1285, Stone 1286, Webster 1291

Michigan: Ann Arbor 1301, Berrien 1305, Bishop 1306, Dalton 1312, Ford 1329, General 1336, Gerstacker 1338, Herrick 1343, Holden 1345, Jackson 1347, Kennedy 1352, Lansing 1354, Lincoln 1356, Morley 1362, Muskegon 1365, Pardee 1369, Ratner 1372, Royal 1374, Sage 1375, Whirlpool 1399, Wilson 1403, Zuckerman 1407

Minnesota: Chadwick 1428, **Charlson 1429,** Eddy 1436, Fingerhut 1438, Greystone 1444, Lang 1449, Marbrook 1451, Mardag 1452, **McKnight 1453,** Minnesota 1458, Minnesota 1459, Northwest 1462, O'Brien 1465, O'Shaughnessy 1466, Phillips 1471, Red 1473, Saint 1475, Thorpe 1479, Walker 1481

Missouri: Group 1524, Loose 1543, **Mallinckrodt 1546,** McDonnell 1548, **McDonnell 1549,** Olin 1551, Patton 1553, Reynolds 1558, Shelter 1563, Southwestern 1569, Speas 1570, Speas 1571, Stupp 1573, Union 1576, **Webb 1579,** Whitaker 1580, Wolff 1581

Nebraska: Lincoln 1590

New Hampshire: Fuller 1605

New Jersey: American 1612, Brunetti 1620, Capita 1623, **Diabetes 1628,** Dodge 1630, Edison 1631, Fund 1637, Hoechst 1645, Hoechst 1646, Hoffmann-La Roche 1648, Hyde 1651, Johnson 1656, Johnson 1657, **Johnson 1658,** Kirby 1661, Klatskin 1662, Lipton 1668, Maneely 1670, Mercedes-Benz 1674, Merck 1675, Ohl 1686, Public 1692, Rippel 1695, Schamach 1700, Schultz 1704, Sutcliffe 1709, Union 1714, Upton 1716, Victoria 1719, **Vollmer 1721,** Warner-Lambert 1723

New Mexico: Albuquerque 1726, **Bellamah 1727**

New York: Abrons 1731, Achelis 1732, **Ada 1733,** Alexander 1741, Allyn 1744, Alpern 1745, Amax 1748, **American 1752,** Aron 1758, **ASDA 1760, AT&T 1762,** Badgeley 1766, Baird 1767, Banbury 1770, Berkowitz 1787, Blum 1798, Bodman 1800, Bostwick 1803, Botwinick-Wolfensohn 1804, Bristol-Myers 1808, Bristol-Myers 1809, **Brookdale 1812,** Buffalo 1816, Buffalo 1817, **Bugher 1818, Burnham 1819, Carnegie 1829, China 1842,** Citicorp/Citibank 1845, **Clark 1850,** Commonwealth 1860, Cummings 1869, Cummings 1871, Curtice-Burns/Pro-Fac 1872, **Dana 1874,** DeCamp 1879, Diamond 1885, Dillon 1886, Dosberg 1889, Dreyfus 1892, Dreyfus 1894, Dyson 1897, Eastman 1899, Edouard 1900, **Essel 1906,** Evans 1909, Ferkauf 1914, **Ford 1922,** Gerschel 1937, Gibbs 1938, Gifford 1939, **Glenn 1941,** Goode 1952, Goodyear 1955, Grant 1959, Graphic 1960, Grateful 1961, Greenwall 1966, Griffis 1967, Gruber 1968, **Hartford 1975,** Heyward 1988, Hirschl 1990, Hughes 1996, Hugoton 1997, IFF 2004, International 2005, **Ittleson 2008,** JM 2011, Julia 2018, Kaplan 2022, **Kaufmann 2026,** Kekst 2027, Killough 2031, Klingenstein 2036, Krim 2048, **Laerdal 2050,** Larsen 2053, Lasdon 2054, Lee 2061, Leonhardt 2064, **Lighting 2070,** Loewenberg 2075, Lounsbery 2077, Lowenstein 2078, Macdonald 2080, **Manning 2086, Mapplethorpe 2088,** Mathers 2093, Mayer 2095, McConnell 2100, McGonagle 2102, McGraw-Hill 2104, Mellon 2106, Merrill 2113, Metropolitan 2117, Meyer 2118, **Milbank 2120,** Milstein 2123, Monell 2125, Moore 2127, Moses 2135, Mulligan 2137, Murray 2139, New York 2146, New York 2149, **New-Land 2150,** Nichols 2153, Northern 2158, O'Connor 2161, O'Toole 2164, Open 2166, Palisades 2174, Pfizer 2181, Philip 2184, **Phillips 2186, Potts 2196,** Price 2197, Quantum 2201, Ramapo 2203, Rauch 2205, Revson 2213, **Richardson 2216,** Ritter 2219, **Rockefeller 2223, Rockefeller 2224,** Rose 2226, **Ross 2232,** Rubinstein 2234, Salomon 2241, Saltz 2244, Samuels 2245, Sinsheimer 2269, Slaughter 2271, **Sloan 2273,** Smith 2274, **Smithers 2276,** Snow 2277, **Soros 2281,** Spunk 2286, St. Giles 2287, Starr 2288, Stein 2292, Stony 2296, Stuart 2299, Texaco 2309, Thorne 2313, Tisch 2316, Totman 2319, Turner 2321, van Ameringen 2326, **Vanneck-Bailey 2328,** Vernon 2329, Vidda 2330, Vogler 2331, Wallace 2334, Weinberg 2339, Wilson 2350, Winston 2353, Wishnick 2355

North Carolina: **Burroughs 2377,** Carolina 2379, Daniels 2383, Duke 2386, Hanes 2400, **Nickel 2404,** Rogers 2412, Wachovia 2421, Winston-Salem 2424

North Dakota: Stern 2429

Ohio: Akron 2430, **Armington 2436,** BP 2443, Bridgestone/Firestone 2445, Cleveland-Cliffs 2458, Codrington 2459, Dayton 2466, France 2484, GAR 2490, Gould 2494, Gund 2497, Humphrey 2508, Ingalls 2510, Kettering 2515, Lubrizol 2525, Morgan 2538, Murphy 2542, Pollock 2559, Prentiss 2560, Procter 2561, Reinberger 2566, Sears 2580, Stark 2591, Treu-Mart 2600, TRW 2603, White 2607, Women's 2611, Youngstown 2615

Oklahoma: American 2616, Goddard 2624, **Noble 2631,** Oklahoma 2633, Phillips 2636, Sarkeys 2639, Taubman 2642

Oregon: Carpenter 2649, Collins 2651, Collins 2652, Jackson 2653, Johnson 2655, Meyer 2657

Scholarship funds

2497, H.C.S. 2498, Hamilton 2499, Haskell 2501, Hillier 2503, Honda 2504, Hoover 2505, Huffy 2507, Iddings 2509, Licking 2522, Lorain 2524, Lubrizol 2525, Moores 2537, Mount Vernon 2539, Murch 2540, Nationwide 2545, Nippert 2546, Philips 2557, Reinberger 2566, Renner 2568, Ritchie 2570, Semple 2582, Stark 2591, TRW 2603, Wolfe 2610, Young 2614

Oklahoma: Bovaird 2619, Broadhurst 2621, McCasland 2628, Oklahoma 2633, Oklahoma 2634, Phillips 2636, Puterbaugh 2637, Rapp 2638, Sarkeys 2639, Scrivner 2640, Share 2641

Oregon: Carpenter 2649, Collins 2652, Jeld-Wen 2654, Johnson 2655, Oregon 2660, Tucker 2662, U.S. 2663

Pennsylvania: Alcoa 2668, Allegheny 2670, AMETEK 2672, Arcadia 2677, Arronson 2670, Berkman 2684, Carpenter 2697, CIGNA 2701, Connelly 2707, Crawford 2711, Crown 2713, Cyclops 2714, Dolfinger-McMahon 2716, Eden 2720, Fourjay 2729, Goldman 2732, Greensburg 2734, Harrisburg 2739, Hazen 2742, Heinz 2743, Hershey 2748, Hooper 2753, Independence 2759, Kline 2768, Lindback 2775, McCune 2784, McFeely-Rogers 2785, McKenna 2786, McLean 2787, Measey 2788, Oberlaender 2800, Pennsylvania 2804, Philadelphia 2807, PPG 2812, Quaker 2815, Rockwell 2818, Rockwell 2819, Scranton 2827, Smith 2831, Stabler 2839, Union 2852, **USX 2853**

Rhode Island: Champlin 2868, Cranston 2869, Fleet/Norstar 2870, Rhode Island 2882

South Carolina: Central 2888, Colonial 2890, Fullerton 2892, Smith 2901, Spartanburg 2902, Trident 2907

South Dakota: Sioux Falls 2908

Tennessee: Benwood 2912, Chattanooga 2916, Durham 2920, Lowenstein 2928, Potter 2933

Texas: Abell-Hanger 2941, Abilene 2943, **Alcon 2944,** Amarillo 2946, Bass 2953, Bertha 2956, Cain 2962, Cain 2963, Clayton 2968, Coastal 2969, Cockrell 2970, Community 2973, Crump 2979, Davidson 2982, Dougherty 2987, Dunagan 2991, Ellwood 2999, Exxon 3003, Fair 3004, Feldman 3008, Fikes 3009, FINA 3010, First 3011, Franklin 3015, Green 3020, Haas 3024, Hamman 3028, Harrington 3030, Houston 3037, Hubbard 3039, Johnson 3041, Kempner 3045, Kimberly-Clark 3046, King 3047, LBJ 3050, Maxus 3055, McAshan 3056, McDermott 3058, McGovern 3059, McGovern 3060, McKee 3061, McMillan 3062, Meadows 3064, Mitchell 3067, Navarro 3076, Owsley 3082, Powell 3091, Roberts 3097, Rockwell 3098, San Antonio 3099, Shell 3104, Stemmons 3111, Tarrant 3116, Temple 3117, Tenneco 3118, Transco 3121, Trull 3122, Turner 3123, United 3124, Waggoner 3128, Walthall 3129, White 3133, Zachry 3138

Utah: Bamberger 3141, Castle 3144, Dee 3145, Eccles 3148, Eccles 3149, Questar 3152, Sorenson 3153, Swanson 3154

Vermont: Lintilhac 3157, Vermont 3160

Virginia: BDM 3161, Beazley 3162, Best 3165, Camp 3167, Dominion 3174, Dominion 3175, Ethyl 3177, Fairchild 3178, Fitz-Gibbon 3179, Frederick 3180, **Freedom 3181,** Gottwald 3182, Portsmouth 3200, Reynolds 3203, Titmus 3210, Treakle 3211, Washington 3214, Wheat 3215

Washington: Blue 3221, Boeing 3222, Cheney 3224, Comstock 3225, Foster 3227, Foundation 3228, Fuchs 3229, Hemingway 3232, Kilworth 3233, Leuthold 3234, Murray 3238, Pacific 3241, SAFECO 3247, **Stewardship 3253,** Stubblefield 3254, Tacoma 3255, Wharton 3259

West Virginia: Carter 3262, Hott 3264, Kanawha 3265, Parkersburg 3268

Wisconsin: American 3271, Appleton 3272, Birnschein 3274, **Bradley 3275,** Consolidated 3280, Cremer 3281, CUNA 3283, Humphrey 3289, Johnson's 3293, Kohler 3295, Ladish 3296, Milwaukee 3306, Smith 3326, Wausau 3334, Wisconsin 3338

Seed money

Alabama: Hill 14, Sonat 23, Vulcan 25

Arizona: Arizona 27, First 29, Flinn 30

Arkansas: Arkansas 44

California: **American 60, Atkinson 66,** Beckman 76, California 96, **Compton 110,** Confidence 112, Crocker 115, Drown 123, Fusenot 139, Gamble 141, Goldman 156, Goldwyn 158, Gross 161, Haas 163, Haas 164, Harden 168, Hoover 179, Irvine 183, Jewett 190, Johnson 191, **Kaiser 194, Keck 197,** Kirchgessner 200, Koret 202, Levi 212, Litton 214, Marin 224, **Maxfield 226,** McCarthy 230, McKesson 232, Miller 239, Monterey 240, Norman 251, Norris 253, **Packard 262,** Parker 263, Parsons 264, Patron 267, Peninsula 269, **Pfeiffer 272,** Sacramento 286, San Diego 287, San Francisco 288, Santa Clara 291, Santa Cruz 292, Sierra 302, Sonoma 309, Stern 318, Stuart 321, Stulsaft 322, Times 331, Tuohy 336, van Loben Sels 342, Varian 345, Weingart 348

Colorado: Boettcher 361, Colorado 363, Colorado 364, Comprecare 365, Coors 367, Denver 369, Duncan 370, **Frost 372, General 374,** Hughes 378, Lowe 382, Piton 388, True 398, US 400

Connecticut: **Adler 405,** Bodenwein 415, Bridgeport 417, Connecticut 425, **Culpeper 428,** Eder 432, **Educational 433,** Ensworth 435, **General 439,** Hartford 446, Hartford 448, ITT 456, New Britain 469, New Haven 470, Olin 474, Palmer 475, Panwy 476, Patterson 477, People's 478, Phoenix 481, Stanley 488, Stone 489, Travelers 491, Waterbury 497, **Xerox 500**

Delaware: Beneficial 504, Crystal 510, Delaware 511, DuPont 513, Kutz 520, Laffey-McHugh 521

District of Columbia: Cafritz 535, **Fannie 538,** Foundation 541, Glen 546, Graham 548, Kennedy 552, Meyer 557, **Pettus-Crowe 558, Public 561,** Stewart 563, Wasserman 564

Florida: Beveridge 574, Broward 580, Bush 581, Conn 585, Dade 587, duPont 594, Falk 599, Fish 601, Jacksonville 620, **Knight 629,** Lost 634, Palm 644, Phipps 649, **Rosenberg 657,** Rosenberg 658, Sarasota 659, Tampa 666, Wahlstrom 671, Whitehall 678

Georgia: Atlanta 686, Atlanta 687, Equifax 704, Georgia 709, Georgia 710, Georgia 711, Glancy 714, Illges 717, Lee 720, Murphy 728, South 733, Tull 736, **UPS 737,** Whitehead 740, Wilson 742

Hawaii: Atherton 746, Baldwin 747, Castle 749, Castle 750, Cooke 751, Frear 752, Hawaii 753, McInerny 755, Wilcox 759, Wilcox 760

Illinois: Amoco 775, Aurora 783, Barber-Colman 785, **Baxter 787,** Beloit 790, Chicago 820, **Chicago 821,** Coleman 825, DeKalb 832, Dillon 834, Fry 848, GATX 853, Harris 863, Hermann 865, Illinois 867, **MacArthur 886,** McDonald's 894, McGraw 895, Nalco 905, New Prospect 908, Northern 911, OMC 913, Peoria 918, Playboy 923, Prince 927, Retirement 937, Rothschild 940, **Sears 950,** Stern 960, Waste 973, Woods 977, Woodward 978

Indiana: Ball 982, Cole 986, Foellinger 989, Fort 990, Heritage 993, INB 995, Indianapolis 996, Martin 1002, Metropolitan 1003, Miles 1004, **Moriah 1005,** Oliver 1010

Iowa: Carver 1015, Hall 1018, Maytag 1024, Wahlert 1030

Kansas: Baehr 1031, Beech 1033, DeVore 1036, Koch 1038, Topeka 1047

Kentucky: Courier-Journal 1055

Louisiana: Baton 1069, New Orleans 1082, Shreveport-Bossier 1084

Maine: Maine 1091, UNUM 1094

Maryland: Abell 1095, Baltimore 1099, Eastern 1110, Goldseker 1113, Higginson 1117, Knott 1122, PHH 1131, Procter 1133, Rouse 1136, Straus 1141

Massachusetts: Acushnet 1145, Adams 1146, Alden 1147, Alden 1148, Birmingham 1156, Boston 1158, Boston 1159, **Cabot 1162,** Cambridge 1164, Campbell 1166, Cove 1171, Cowan 1172, Cox 1173, Davis 1178, Ellsworth 1185, Fuller 1193, General 1196, Heydt 1204, Hoche-Scofield 1207, Kelley 1222, Levy 1225, Lotus 1229, **New England 1241,** Old 1246, Polaroid 1258, Porter 1259, Riley

1265, Smith 1279, Stevens 1283, Stevens 1284, Stoddard 1285, Stoneman 1287, Worcester 1295, Wyman-Gordon 1297

Michigan: Ann Arbor 1301, Battle 1303, Berrien 1305, Bishop 1306, Consumers 1310, Dalton 1312, Dow 1317, Earl-Beth 1318, Four 1330, Fremont 1331, Frey 1332, General 1336, Gerstacker 1338, Gilmore 1339, Grand 1340, Hudson-Webber 1346, Jackson 1347, Kalamazoo 1349, **Kellogg 1351,** Kennedy 1352, Lansing 1354, Loutit 1357, Mills 1360, Morley 1362, **Mott 1363, Mott 1364,** Muskegon 1365, Northeast 1366, Saginaw 1376, Skillman 1380, Southeastern 1381, Tiscornia 1388, Upjohn 1393, Wilson 1404

Minnesota: Bigelow 1417, Blandin 1418, Bremer 1420, Bush 1421, Central 1427, Dain 1432, Grand 1443, Greystone 1444, Honeywell 1446, Howe 1447, Marbrook 1451, Mardag 1452, McKnight 1454, Medtronic 1456, Minneapolis 1457, Northwest 1462, O'Brien 1465, Red 1473, Saint 1475, Wedum 1485, **Weyerhaeuser 1486**

Missouri: Block 1501, Block 1502, Commerce 1504, Community 1505, Cowden 1507, Green 1523, Group 1524, Hall 1525, Hallmark 1526, Hallmark 1527, Kansas 1533, McDonnell 1548, Oppenstein 1552, Reynolds 1558, Roblee 1559, Slusher 1565, Southwestern 1569, Speas 1570, Speas 1571, Sunderland 1574, **Webb 1579**

Nebraska: Keene 1588, Kiewit 1589, Lincoln 1590, Omaha 1592

Nevada: **Hilton 1596**

New Hampshire: Bean 1600, Foundation 1604, New Hampshire 1607

New Jersey: Allied-Signal 1611, Armco 1614, Borden 1616, **Crum 1627,** Dodge 1630, Edison 1631, Fund 1637, Hoffmann-La Roche 1647, **Huber 1650, Innovating 1652,** Johnson 1657, **Johnson 1658,** Kirby 1661, Merck 1676, Merck 1677, New Jersey 1684, Ohl 1686, Pollak 1690, Prudential 1691, Public 1692, Rutgers 1698, Schering-Plough 1702, Schultz 1704, Schumann 1705, Snyder 1707, Turrell 1713, Union 1714, Van Houten 1717, Van Pelt 1718, Warner-Lambert 1723

New Mexico: Albuquerque 1726, Carlsbad 1728, Maddox 1729

New York: Abrons 1731, Agway 1736, Albany's 1740, **American 1750,** American 1751, Banbury 1770, Booth 1801, Botwinick-Wolfensohn 1804, **Brookdale 1812,** Buffalo 1817, Carnahan-Jackson 1828, **Carnegie 1829,** Charina 1835, Chase 1836, **Chase 1838,** Clark 1849, **Clark 1850,** Cornell 1863, Corning 1864, Cowles 1866, Cummings 1869, Cummings 1871, **Dammann 1873,** DeCamp 1879, Decker 1880, Eastman 1899, **Fish 1918, Ford 1922, Freeman 1926,** Fund 1930, Gebbie 1933, Gifford 1939, Goldsmith 1948, Goodyear 1955, **Grant 1958,** Graphic 1960, Griffis 1967, Hayden 1978, Heckscher 1982, Horncrest 1993, Hoyt 1995, Hughes 1996, Hunt 2000, International 2005, **Ittleson 2008,** JM 2011, Jones 2015, Kaplan 2022, Kaplan 2023, Klingenstein 2036, Lang 2051, Larsen 2053, Lindner 2071, Lounsbery 2077, Lowenstein 2078, Macdonald 2080, Mayer 2095, McCann 2097, McGonagle 2102, **Mertz-Gilmore 2115,** Metropolitan 2117, Mohawk-Hudson 2124, Moore 2127, Morgan 2128, Morgan 2129, **New World 2145,** New York 2146, New York 2147, New York 2149, **New-Land 2150, Norcross 2155,** Northern 2158, Norwood 2159, **Noyes 2160,** O'Connor 2161, Palisades 2174, Pfizer 2181, Pforzheimer 2183, **Potts 2196,** Prospect 2199, Ramapo 2203, Rapoport 2204, Rauch 2205, **Richardson 2216, Richmond 2217,** Rochester 2221, **Rockefeller 2223, Rockefeller 2224,** Rosenstiel 2229, **Ross 2232,** Rubinstein 2234, Samuels 2245, Scherman 2249, **Sloan 2273,** Snow 2277, **Sony 2280,** Sprague 2285, Sulzberger 2300, **Surdna 2302, Teagle 2308,** Thorne 2313, van Ameringen 2326, Vogler 2331, Washington 2337, Wilson 2350

North Carolina: **Babcock 2368,** Bryan 2373, Burroughs 2376, Daniels 2382, Duke 2386, First 2392, Foundation 2393, Glaxo 2395, **Glaxo 2396,**

Special projects

New Hampshire: Bean 1600, Eastman 1603, Foundation 1604, Fuller 1605, New Hampshire 1607, Smith 1609, **Trust 1610**

New Jersey: American 1612, Armco 1614, Borden 1616, CPC 1624, Dodge 1630, Edison 1631, Engelhard 1633, Fund 1637, General 1639, Hoechst 1646, Hoffmann-La Roche 1647, **Huber 1650,** Hyde 1651, **Innovating 1652,** Johnson 1656, Johnson 1657, **Johnson 1658,** Kirby 1661, Leavens 1667, Merck 1675, Merck 1676, Merck 1677, Mutual 1680, New Jersey 1684, Ohl 1686, Pollak 1690, Prudential 1691, Rippel 1695, Schering-Plough 1702, Schultz 1704, Schumann 1705, Snyder 1707, Subaru 1708, Sutcliffe 1709, Turrell 1713, Union 1714, Van Houten 1717, Victoria 1719

New Mexico: Albuquerque 1726, **Bellamah 1727,** Carlsbad 1728, Maddox 1729

New York: Abrons 1731, Albany's 1740, Alexander 1741, Altman 1746, **American 1750,** American 1751, American 1753, Aron 1758, **AT&T 1762,** Avon 1764, Badgeley 1766, Barker 1774, Berkowitz 1787, Bluhdorn 1797, Blum 1798, Botwinick-Wolfensohn 1804, **Brookdale 1812,** Buffalo 1817, **Butler 1822,** Calder 1823, Carnahan-Jackson 1828, **Carnegie 1829,** Cary 1833, Chase 1836, Chase 1837, **Chase 1838, China 1842,** Citicorp/Citibank 1845, Claiborne 1846, Clark 1849, **Clark 1850,** Commonwealth 1860, Corning 1864, Cowles 1866, **Cummings 1870,** Cummings 1871, Curtice-Burns/Pro-Fac 1872, **Dammann 1873, Dana 1874,** DeCamp 1879, Decker 1880, Diamond 1885, Dillon 1886, Dreyfus 1894, Dyson 1897, **Equitable 1904, Ford 1922, Fuld 1929,** Fund 1930, Goodyear 1955, **Grant 1958,** Grant 1959, Graphic 1960, Greenwall 1966, **Hartford 1975,** Hayden 1978, **Hearst 1980, Hearst 1981,** Heckscher 1982, Heineman 1984, Howard 1994, Hoyt 1995, Hughes 1996, Hugoton 1997, Hunt 2000, International 2005, **Ittleson 2008,** JM 2011, Jones 2015, Joy 2016, Kaplan 2023, Killough 2031, Klingenstein 2036, Kresge 2047, Lang 2051, Larsen 2053, Lazar 2060, Lee 2061, Lindner 2071, Lowenstein 2078, Macdonald 2080, **MacDonald 2081, Macy 2083, Mapplethorpe 2088,** Mayer 2095, McConnell 2100, Mellon 2106, Memton 2109, Merrill 2113, **Mertz-Gilmore 2115,** Metropolitan 2117, Milbank 2119, Mohawk-Hudson 2124, Moore 2127, Morgan 2128, Morgan 2129, Mutual 2140, **New World 2145,** New York 2146, New York 2147, **New York 2148,** New York 2149, **New-Land 2150,** Noble 2154, **Norcross 2155,** Northern 2157, Northern 2158, **Noyes 2160,** O'Connor 2161, O'Toole 2164, Orange 2167, Palisades 2174, **Patrina 2176,** Pfizer 2181, Pforzheimer 2183, Philip 2184, **Phillips 2186, Potts 2196,** Price 2197, Prospect 2199, Quantum 2201, Ramapo 2203, Rapoport 2204, Rauch 2205, Republic 2211, Revson 2213, Rhodebeck 2214, **Richardson 2216, Richmond 2217,** Rochester 2221, **Rockefeller 2223, Rockefeller 2224,** Rose 2226, **Ross 2232,** Salomon 2243, Samuels 2245, Scherman 2249, **Sloan 2273, Smithers 2276, Soros 2281,** Sprague 2285, Sterling 2294, Stony 2296, Stuart 2299, Sulzberger 2300, **Surdna 2302, Teagle 2308,** Texaco 2309, Thorne 2313, van Ameringen 2326, Vidda 2330, Vogler 2331, Washington 2337, Wilson 2350

North Carolina: **Babcock 2368,** Broyhill 2372, Bryan 2373, Burroughs 2376, **Burroughs 2377,** Carolina 2379, Daniels 2382, Duke 2386, Finch 2390, First 2392, Glaxo 2395, Greensboro 2398, Hanes 2399, Hanes 2400, Harris 2401, Reynolds 2410, Reynolds 2411, Rogers 2413, Salisbury 2413, Smith 2414, Triangle 2417, Wachovia 2421, Western 2423, Winston-Salem 2424

North Dakota: Fargo-Moorhead 2426, Leach 2427, Stern 2429

Ohio: Akron 2430, American 2432, **Armington 2436,** Bicknell 2442, BP 2443, Bridgestone/Firestone 2445, Campeau 2449, Centerior 2452, Cincinnati 2456, Cleveland 2457, Codrington 2459,

Columbus 2460, Coshocton 2462, Dater 2465, Dayton 2466, Eaton 2470, **Elisha-Bolton 2471,** Fifth 2479, Fox 2483, Gund 2497, Hamilton 2499, Haskell 2501, Hillier 2503, Huffy 2507, Iddings 2509, Ingalls 2510, Kettering 2515, Lorain 2524, Mayerson 2529, Morgan 2538, Murphy 2542, Nationwide 2545, Nippert 2546, Nord 2547, Ohio 2552, Pollock 2559, Prentiss 2560, Progressive 2563, Reeves 2565, Reinberger 2566, Reynolds 2569, Russell 2574, Schmidlapp 2577, Sherwick 2583, Sisler 2584, Stark 2591, Stranahan 2593, Tamarkin 2594, Taubman 2597, Treu-Mart 2600, TRW 2603, Watson 2605, Women's 2611, Yassenoff 2613, Youngstown 2615

Oklahoma: Oklahoma 2633, Puterbaugh 2637, Sarkeys 2639, Taubman 2642, Warren 2645, Wegener 2646

Oregon: Collins 2651, Collins 2652, Jeld-Wen 2654, Johnson 2655, Meyer 2657, OCRI 2659, Oregon 2660, Tucker 2662, U.S. 2663

Pennsylvania: Air 2665, Air 2666, Alcoa 2668, Allegheny 2670, Annenberg 2675, Arcadia 2677, Barra 2680, Bell 2682, Benedum 2683, Berkman 2684, Carpenter 2697, CIGNA 2701, Connelly 2707, Consolidated 2708, Crown 2713, Dietrich 2715, Dolfinger-McMahon 2716, **Falk 2723,** Fels 2725, Goldman 2732, Grable 2733, Greensburg 2734, Grundy 2735, Harrisburg 2739, Heinz 2743, Heinz 2744, Heinz 2745, Heinz 2746, Hershey 2747, Hillman 2749, Hillman 2750, Hooper 2753, Hopwood 2754, Horsehead 2755, Jennings 2762, Jewish 2763, Kynett 2770, Laurel 2771, Lehigh 2772, Lord 2777, McCune 2784, McKenna 2786, McLean 2787, Mellon 2790, Miles 2795, Millstein 2796, Oberlaender 2800, Penn 2803, Pennsylvania 2804, **Pew 2806,** Philadelphia 2808, Pittsburgh 2809, PPG 2812, Provident 2814, Scaife 2823, **Scaife 2824,** Scott 2826, Scranton 2827, Smith 2831, Smith 2832, SmithKline 2834, Snee-Reinhardt 2835, Sordoni 2837, SPS 2838, Stackpole-Hall 2840, **Stott 2844,** Union 2851, Union 2852, **USX 2853,** Wells 2855, **Whitaker 2857,** Widener 2858, Williamsport-Lycoming 2861

Rhode Island: **Hasbro 2872,** Old 2880, Rhode Island 2882, Textron 2885

South Carolina: Central 2888, Fullerton 2892, Gregg-Graniteville 2893, Self 2899, Springs 2904, Trident 2907

South Dakota: Sioux Falls 2908

Tennessee: Chattanooga 2916, Davis 2919, Durham 2920, First 2921, HCA 2925, Massengill-DeFriece 2929, Potter 2933

Texas: Abell-Hanger 2941, Amarillo 2946, Apache 2949, Brown 2959, Carter 2965, Coastal 2969, Cockrell 2970, Communities 2972, Cooley 2976, Cooper 2977, Dallas 2981, Dunagan 2991, El Paso 2996, Elkins 2998, Exxon 3002, Exxon 3003, Fair 3004, Feldman 3008, Fikes 3009, Florence 3013, Frees 3016, Green 3020, Gulf 3022, Haas 3024, Haggar 3025, Hillcrest 3034, Hoblitzelle 3036, Houston 3037, Kayser 3043, Kempner 3045, King 3047, LBJ 3050, LTV 3052, Maxus 3055, McMillan 3062, Meadows 3064, Mitchell 3067, Moody 3069, Owen 3081, **Pearle 3085,** Pennzoil 3087, RGK 3093, Richardson 3094, Rockwell 3098, San Antonio 3099, Shell 3104, Simmons 3105, Strake 3112, Sturgis 3114, Tandy 3115, Tarrant 3116, Temple 3117, Texas 3119, Transco 3121, Trull 3122, Turner 3123, Vale-Asche 3126, Wright 3137, Zachry 3138

Utah: Browning 3142, Castle 3144, Dee 3145, Questar 3152

Vermont: Lintilhac 3157, National 3158

Virginia: BDM 3161, Bell 3164, Best 3165, Dominion 3175, Ethyl 3177, Fairchild 3178, **Freedom 3181,** James 3185, **Jones 3187,** Norfolk 3196, Portsmouth 3200, Reynolds 3203, Richmond 3204, Taylor 3208, Washington 3214

Washington: Airborne 3216, Archibald 3218, Blue 3221, Cheney 3224, Foster 3227, Foundation 3228, Fuchs 3229, Glaser 3230, Kilworth 3233, Matlock 3236, Murdock 3237, Murray 3238, Nesholm 3239, Pacific 3241, Ray 3246, SAFECO

3247, Seafirst 3249, Skinner 3252, **Stewardship 3253,** Tacoma 3255, Wharton 3259

West Virginia: Beckley 3261, Carter 3262, Kanawha 3265, McDonough 3267

Wisconsin: American 3271, Appleton 3272, Banta 3273, **Bradley 3275,** Cudahy 3282, CUNA 3283, Fox 3287, McBeath 3302, Milwaukee 3306, Oscar 3309, Rexnord 3318, Rutledge 3323, Stackner 3328, Time 3330, Wausau 3334

Wyoming: Weiss 3343

Student aid

Alabama: Andalusia 2, Gibson 13

Arizona: Tucson 41

Arkansas: Arkansas 44, Jones 48, Sturgis 53, Wal-Mart 54

California: **Atkinson 66,** Confidence 112, Humboldt 181, Peninsula 269, Sacramento 286, Sonoma 309

Colorado: Coulter 368, Piton 388, Thatcher 397

Connecticut: Meriden 467, Waterbury 497

Delaware: Kutz 520

Florida: Chatlos 583, Fort 604, Olliff 643, Palm 644, Rinker 656, **Watson 674,** Winter 680

Georgia: Callaway 691, Cobb 695, GFF 713

Hawaii: Atherton 746, Hawaii 753, Scott 757, Zimmerman 762

Illinois: Aurora 783, Caestecker 811, Centralia 818, Furnas 850, Levie 881, Polk 924, Special 956

Indiana: Cole 986, Miles 1004

Iowa: Quad 1029

Kansas: Hansen 1037, Topeka 1047

Louisiana: Brown 1071, Zigler 1088

Maine: Central 1090, Maine 1091

Massachusetts: Kelley 1222, M/A-Com 1231, Williams 1293, Worcester 1295

Michigan: Fremont 1331, Gilmore 1339, Grand 1340, Muskegon 1365

Minnesota: Alworth 1408, Blandin 1418, Eddy 1436, Wedum 1485

Missouri: Fullbright 1520, Ilgenfritz 1529, Shelter 1563, Walker 1577

Montana: Bair 1582

Nebraska: Kiewit 1589

New Hampshire: Foundation 1604, New Hampshire 1607

New Jersey: Snyder 1707, Sutcliffe 1709

New Mexico: Carlsbad 1728

New York: Buffalo 1817, Chase 1836, **Chazen 1839,** Clark 1849, Galasso 1932, Golub 1951, National 2142, Northern 2158, Open 2166, Pforzheimer 2183, Rochester 2221, Salomon 2243, **Soros 2281,** Starr 2288, Stony 2296, **Tai 2306**

North Carolina: Duke 2387, First 2391, Winston-Salem 2424

Ohio: Coshocton 2462, **Elisha-Bolton 2471,** Licking 2522, Lorain 2524, Ritter 2571, Stark 2591, Van Wert 2604

Oklahoma: Johnson 2625

Pennsylvania: Goldman 2732, Hassel 2741, Hoyt 2756, Lesher 2773, Mack 2780, Roth 2822

Rhode Island: Hodges 2874

South Carolina: Fuller 2891, Moore 2896, Springs 2904, Trident 2907

Tennessee: Chattanooga 2916

Texas: Amarillo 2946, Community 2973, Fasken 3006, Franklin 3015, Haas 3024, Hamman 3028, King 3047, McMillan 3062, Moody 3069, Orange 3079, Peyton 3090, Rockwell 3098, San Antonio 3099, Shell 3104, Smith 3107, Woltman 3136

Utah: Bamberger 3141

Virginia: Camp 3167, Dominion 3174, Norfolk 3196

Washington: Pemco 3242

West Virginia: Carter 3262, Parkersburg 3268

Wisconsin: Oshkosh 3310, Racine 3316, Rutledge 3323, Wisconsin 3339

Wyoming: Stock 3342

Student loans

Arizona: Tucson 41

Arkansas: Arkansas 44

California: Great 160, Santa Barbara 290, Weingart 348

Florida: Fellows 600, Lauffer 632
Illinois: Waste 973
Kentucky: Rural 1065
Massachusetts: Hopedale 1211
Michigan: Eddy 1319
Mississippi: Feild 1490
Missouri: Speas 1570
New Hampshire: New Hampshire 1607
New Jersey: Snyder 1707
New Mexico: Carlsbad 1728, Maddox 1729
New York: Quantum 2201
North Carolina: Winston-Salem 2424
Ohio: Stark 2591, Youngstown 2615
Oklahoma: Johnson 2625
Oregon: U.S. 2663
Pennsylvania: Gibson 2730
South Carolina: Close 2889, Springs 2904
Tennessee: Davis 2919
Texas: Franklin 3015, Kempner 3045, King 3047, Shanor 3102, White 3133
Utah: Bamberger 3141
Vermont: Vermont 3160
Washington: Pacific 3241
Wisconsin: Rutledge 3323

Technical assistance

Alabama: Hill 14, Sonat 23
Arizona: Arizona 27
California: **Atkinson 66,** California 96, Clorox 106, Fireman's 134, First 135, First 136, Fluor 137, Gerbode 153, Haas 164, Harden 168, Irvine 183, Jewett 190, Johnson 191, **Kaiser 194,** Kirchgessner 200, Levi 212, Marin 224, Monterey 240, **Packard 262,** Peninsula 269, **S.G. 285,** Sacramento 286, San Diego 287, San Francisco 288, Santa Barbara 290, Santa Clara 291, Santa Cruz 292, Sierra 302, Sonoma 309, Southern 310, Zellerbach 357
Colorado: Colorado 364, Denver 369, **Frost 372,** Piton 388, US 400

Connecticut: Bridgeport 417, Connecticut 425, Hartford 446, Hartford 448, New Haven 470, Northeast 472, Travelers 491, Waterbury 497
Delaware: Delaware 511, DuPont 513
District of Columbia: **Fannie 538,** Foundation 541, Kennedy 552, Meyer 557, Wasserman 564
Florida: Beveridge 574, Bush 581, Dade 587, **Davis 590,** duPont 594, Jacksonville 620, Palm 644, Whitehall 678
Georgia: Atlanta 686, Georgia 710, Lee 720, Rich 731
Hawaii: Hawaii 753
Illinois: Barber-Colman 785, Bersted 792, Chicago 820, Crown 828, Field 840, McCormick 893, Northern 911, Peoples 917, Playboy 923, Polk 924, Prince 927, USG 969, Woods 977
Indiana: Ball 982, Fort 990, Heritage 993, INB 995, Metropolitan 1003, **Moriah 1005**
Louisiana: New Orleans 1082
Maine: Central 1090, Maine 1091
Maryland: Baltimore 1099, Goldseker 1113
Massachusetts: Boston 1158, **Conservation 1170,** Fidelity 1188, Hyams 1216, Raytheon 1262, Riley 1265, State 1280, Stevens 1283, Stevens 1284, Worcester 1295
Michigan: Ford 1328, General 1336, Grand 1340, Jackson 1347, Kalamazoo 1349, **Mott 1363,** Saginaw 1376
Minnesota: Blandin 1418, Bremer 1420, Central 1427, Dayton 1433, Ecolab 1435, Eddy 1436, Grand 1443, McKnight 1454, Minneapolis 1457, Northwest 1462, Saint 1475, St. Paul 1477
Missouri: Danforth 1510, Hallmark 1526, Hallmark 1527, Southwestern 1569, Union 1576
Nebraska: Omaha 1592
Nevada: **Hilton 1596**
New Hampshire: Eastman 1603, Foundation 1604, New Hampshire 1607
New Jersey: Hoffmann-La Roche 1647, Hyde 1651, Johnson 1656, Johnson 1657, Mutual 1680, New Jersey 1684, Prudential 1691, Subaru 1708, Victoria 1719
New Mexico: Albuquerque 1726, Carlsbad 1728

New York: Abrons 1731, American 1753, **AT&T 1762,** Avon 1764, Buffalo 1817, **China 1842,** Citicorp/Citibank 1845, **Clark 1850, Ford 1922,** Fund 1930, Graphic 1960, Hayden 1978, Hoyt 1995, Hunt 2000, **Ittleson 2008,** JM 2011, Jones 2015, Kaplan 2023, **Mertz-Gilmore 2115,** Morgan 2128, Morgan 2129, New Street 2144, **New World 2145,** New York 2146, New York 2147, O'Connor 2161, Orange 2167, Pfizer 2181, Rochester 2221, **Rockefeller 2223, Rockefeller 2224, Ross 2232,** Scherman 2249, Sulzberger 2300, **Surdna 2302**
North Carolina: Bryan 2373, Duke 2386, Reynolds 2411, Western 2423
North Dakota: Fargo-Moorhead 2426
Ohio: Cincinnati 2456, Cleveland 2457, Columbus 2460, Dayton 2466, East 2469, Humphrey 2508, Lorain 2524, Mayerson 2529, Nord 2547, Sherwick 2583, Stark 2591
Oregon: Carpenter 2649, Meyer 2657, Oregon 2660
Pennsylvania: AMETEK 2672, Benedum 2683, Berkman 2684, **Falk 2723,** Fels 2725, Heinz 2743, Heinz 2745, Mack 2780, Mellon 2790, Penn 2803, **Pew 2806,** Philadelphia 2808, Pittsburgh 2809, Scott 2826
Puerto Rico: Puerto Rico 2865
Rhode Island: Rhode Island 2882, Textron 2885
South Carolina: Self 2899, Trident 2907
South Dakota: Sioux Falls 2908
Tennessee: Durham 2920, First 2921
Texas: Abilene 2943, Amarillo 2946, Austin 2951, Communities 2972, El Paso 2996, Halsell 3027, Meadows 3064, Moody 3069, Tandy 3115, Trull 3122, **Zale 3139**
Utah: Dumke 3146
Vermont: Vermont 3160
Virginia: **Freedom 3181,** Portsmouth 3201, Richmond 3204, Universal 3212
Washington: Boeing 3222, Foundation 3228, GTE 3231, Ray 3246, Skinner 3252, Tacoma 3255, Washington 3257, Washington 3258
West Virginia: Kanawha 3265
Wisconsin: Cudahy 3282, McBeath 3302

INDEX TO FOUNDATIONS AND CORPORATE GIVING PROGRAMS BY SUBJECT

Foundations and corporate giving programs in boldface type make grants on a national, regional, or international basis; the others generally limit giving to the city or state in which they are located. For a subject index to the individual grants in this volume, see the Index to Grants by Subject.

AIDS	Health services	Mental health
Alcoholism	Heart disease	Nursing
Cancer	Hospices	Ophthalmology
Dentistry	Hospitals	Pharmacy
Dermatology	Hospitals—building funds	Psychiatry
Drug abuse	Leprosy	Psychology
Family planning	Medical education	Rehabilitation
Health	Medical research	Schistosomiasis
Health associations	Medical sciences	Speech pathology

AIDS

Alabama: Sonat 23
Arizona: Arizona 27, First 29
Arkansas: Arkla 46
California: Alpert 59, **American 60, Apple 62, Atkinson 66,** Brotman 90, California 96, Campini 98, Chevron 103, Cohen 107, **Compton 110,** First 136, Gap 142, Geffen 147, Gilmore 154, Haas 164, Hale 165, Irvine 183, **Kaiser 194,** Koret 202, Laffin 204, Langendorf 206, LEF 210, Levi 212, Lockheed 216, Lurie 220, MCA 227, McCarthy 230, Milken 237, **National 248,** Parker 263, Parsons 264, PCS 268, Platt 274, Pointer 276, Rigler-Lawrence 281, San Diego 287, San Francisco 288, Santa Clara 291, Schwab 295, Sierra 302, Swig 324, Swig 325, Syntex 326, Times 331, **Toyota 333,** Transamerica 334, U.S. 337, van Loben Sels 342, Zellerbach 357
Colorado: Denver 369, US 400, Weckbaugh 401
Connecticut: **Aetna 406,** Bodenwein 415, Bridgeport 417, Champion 419, Connecticut 424, Connecticut 425, Ensworth 435, **General 439,** Hartford 448, ITT 455, New Haven 470, Northeast 472, Palmer 475, Phoenix 481, Travelers 491, Waterbury 497
District of Columbia: Bernstein 532, Cafritz 535, **Fannie 538,** Foundation 541, Freed 542, Glen 546, Himmelfarb 550, **Kennedy 552,** Meyer 557, **Pettus-Crowe 558**
Florida: Dade 587, Davis 589, Schultz 660
Georgia: Atlanta 686, Exposition 705, Georgia 710, Moore 727, **UPS 737**
Hawaii: Frear 752, McInerny 755, Wilcox 759

Illinois: Chicago 820, **Chicago 821,** Field 840, Forest 843, Fry 848, GATX 853, Kemper 874, Logan 883, **MacArthur 887,** New Prospect 908, Payne 916, Playboy 923, **Walgreen 970**
Indiana: Foellinger 989, Fort 990, Lincoln 1000, Metropolitan 1003
Iowa: **Bohen 1014,** Principal 1027, Principal 1028
Kentucky: Capital 1053
Louisiana: Woldenberg 1085
Maine: UNUM 1094
Maryland: Higginson 1117
Massachusetts: Bank 1153, Boston 1158, **Digital 1180,** Eastern 1182, General 1196, John 1220, Lotus 1229, **Monarch 1239,** Polaroid 1258, **Williams 1293,** Worcester 1295
Michigan: Chrysler 1308, Flint 1323, Ford 1329, Grand 1340, **Kresge 1353, Mott 1363,** Steelcase 1384
Minnesota: American 1409, Andersen 1411, Bell 1415, **Grand 1443,** Howe 1447, Mardag 1452, McKnight 1454, Minneapolis 1457, **NWNL 1464,** Ordean 1467, Pax 1469, Thorpe 1479, Whitney 1487
Missouri: Block 1501, Block 1502, Feld 1518, Hallmark 1526, Hallmark 1527, Kansas 1533, **May 1547,** Oppenstein 1552, Roblee 1559, Speas 1570
New Hampshire: Foundation 1604
New Jersey: Fund 1637, Hoffmann-La Roche 1648, **Johnson 1658,** Kirby 1661, McGraw 1672, **Merck 1675,** Mutual 1680, New Jersey 1684, Prudential 1691, Snyder 1707, Victoria 1719
New York: **Ada 1733,** Albany's 1740, Alexander 1741, Altman 1746, **American 1750,** American 1751, **ASDA 1760, AT&T 1762,** Badgeley 1766, Bluhdorn

1797, Blum 1798, Bodman 1800, **Bristol-Myers 1808, Bristol-Myers 1809, Bronfman 1811,** Buffalo 1817, **Chase 1838,** Chernow 1841, **Citicorp/Citibank 1845,** Claiborne 1846, Clark 1849, Cowles 1866, Cummings 1871, **DeCamp 1879,** Diamond 1885, **Edouard 1900, Equitable 1904, Ford 1922,** Fund 1930, Gilman 1940, Goldsmith 1948, Goode 1952, Graphic 1960, Grateful 1961, Hagedorn 1970, Heckscher 1982, Howard 1994, Hoyt 1995, Hughes 1996, Hunt 2000, **Ittleson 2008, Johnson 2014,** Joy 2016, Kaplan 2022, Klau 2034, Krim 2048, **MacDonald 2081, Mapplethorpe 2088, Merrill 2113,** Metropolitan 2117, Mohawk-Hudson 2124, **Monell 2125,** Morgan 2129, Morgan 2131, Moses 2135, Mutual 2140, **New World 2145,** New York 2146, New York 2147, **New York 2148, Philip 2184,** Rapoport 2204, Republic 2211, **Revlon 2212,** Revson 2213, **Richmond 2217,** Rochester 2221, **Rockefeller 2223,** Rubinstein 2234, **Saks 2240,** Samuels 2245, Schiff 2252, Spunk 2286, **Starr 2288,** Sterling 2294, Sussman 2303, Turner 2321, van Ameringen 2327, Wallach 2335, Wendt 2344, Wiley 2349, **Zenkel 2362, Ziff 2363**
North Carolina: Burroughs 2376, Daniels 2382, Reynolds 2410
Ohio: Cleveland 2457, Codrington 2459, Columbus 2460, Gund 2497, Sherwick 2583
Oklahoma: American 2616, Sarkeys 2639
Pennsylvania: Connelly 2707, Dietrich 2715, Dolfinger-McMahon 2716, Fels 2725, Heinz 2745,

Jewish 2763, **Pew 2806,** Philadelphia 2808,
Pittsburgh 2809, Smith 2831
Puerto Rico: Puerto Rico 2865
Rhode Island: **Hasbro 2872,** Rhode Island 2882
South Carolina: Colonial 2890, Trident 2907
Texas: Cain 2963, Dougherty 2987, Fikes 3009,
Hoblitzelle 3036, Kempner 3045, Meadows 3064,
Moody 3069, Tandy 3115, Tarrant 3116, Trull 3122,
Turner 3123, Vale-Asche 3126, Wright 3137
Vermont: National 3158
Virginia: **Freedom 3181,** Little 3190, **Mars 3191,**
Richmond 3204
Washington: Archibald 3218, Boeing 3222, SAFECO
3247, Seafirst 3249, U.S. 3256
Wisconsin: Appleton 3272, Fox 3287, **Johnson 3292,**
Kohler 3295, McBeath 3302, Milwaukee 3306,
Northwestern 3308, Time 3330

Alcoholism

Alabama: Sonat 23
Arkansas: **Wal-Mart 54**
California: Aerospace 56, Beynon 81, **Farmers 132,**
First 136, Lockheed 216, Montgomery 242,
National 248, Patron 267, **S.G. 285,** San Diego
287, Sierra 302, Stauffer 314, Swift 323,
Transamerica 334, Wynn 356
Colorado: Comprecare 365
Connecticut: Bulkley 418, ITT 455, UST 494
Florida: Conn 585, **Hanley 615**
Illinois: Driehaus 837, Illinois 867, **Walgreen 970**
Indiana: Foellinger 989
Kentucky: Courier-Journal 1055
Massachusetts: Hyams 1216, Stearns 1281
Michigan: Chrysler 1308
Minnesota: **Minnesota 1459,** Walker 1481, Wedum
1485, Whitney 1487
Missouri: **Anheuser-Busch 1496,** Community 1505,
Kauffman 1534, Speas 1570
New Jersey: **Johnson 1658, Mercedes-Benz 1674,**
Victoria 1719, Winslow 1725
New York: Badgeley 1766, Baird 1767, Banbury 1770,
Beck 1780, Graphic 1960, **JM 2011,** Joy 2016,
Metropolitan 2117, Monell 2125, Smithers 2276,
Ziff 2363
North Carolina: Reynolds 2410
North Dakota: Stern 2429
Ohio: Andrews 2435, Coshocton 2462, Hamilton
2499, M/B 2526, National 2544, Nordson 2548,
Van Wert 2604, **Women's 2611**
Pennsylvania: Justus 2764, **Scaife 2823**
South Carolina: Colonial 2890
Tennessee: Ansley 2910, Davis 2919, Genesco 2922
Texas: Coastal 2969, Fasken 3006, Henderson 3032,
Hoblitzelle 3036, McGovern 3059, McGovern
3060
Utah: Eccles 3149
Virginia: **Freedom 3181,** Ohrstrom 3197
Washington: Boeing 3222, SAFECO 3247, U.S. 3256
Wisconsin: Cremer 3281, Fox 3287, Kohler 3295,
McBeath 3302, **Miller 3305,** Northwestern 3308,
Oshkosh 3311, Rutledge 3323

Cancer

Alabama: **Bolden 5,** Bruno 6, Lowder 15, May 16
Arizona: Grossman 32
Arkansas: Ottenheimer 50
California: Bireley 82, Brunetti 91, Burnham 94,
Campini 98, **Carsey 100,** Early 124, **Farber 131,**
First 136, Hoffman 176, Kovshar 203, Lane 205,
Lucas 219, **Maxfield 226,** Milken 236, Milken 237,
Milken 238, Norris 253, Oxnard 260, Sattler 293,
Sierra 302, Stauffer 314, Thornton 330
Colorado: **Manville 383,** Monfort 384, Presbyterian
389, Schramm 391, White 402
Connecticut: **Adler 405,** Bulkley 418, **Childs 422,**
Pfriem 480, Satter 485, Tow 490
Delaware: Bernard 505, **Delmarva 512, Vale 528**
District of Columbia: Folger 540, Himmelfarb 550,
Lehrman 554, Stewart 563

Florida: Goodwin 610, Greenburg-May 612, Groover
614, Kennedy 626, Meyer 639, **Rosenberg 657,**
Weintraub 675
Georgia: Burke 689, Elkin 702
Illinois: Blair 796, Coleman 825, Duchossois 838,
Russell 941, Sprague 957, Stern 960, Thompson
965, **Walgreen 970**
Iowa: Hall 1018, Maytag 1024
Kansas: Sarver 1043
Kentucky: Courier-Journal 1055, Mills 1062
Massachusetts: Hoffman 1208, Perini 1252, Perini
1253, Rubenstein 1268, Smith 1279, **Williams 1293**
Michigan: **General 1334, General 1336, Levy 1355,**
Michigan 1359, Pardee 1369, Prentis 1370, Royal
1374, Whiting 1400, Zuckerman 1407
Minnesota: Howe 1447, Otter 1468
Missouri: Barrows 1498, **Bloch 1499,** Craig 1509,
McDonnell 1549, Shelter 1563, Slusher 1565,
Speas 1570
Nevada: Wiegand 1599
New Jersey: Lazarus 1666, **Mercedes-Benz 1674,**
Rippel 1695, Sutcliffe 1709
New York: Alexander 1741, **Allen 1743,** Alpern 1745,
Aquidneck 1755, Badgeley 1766, Banbury 1770,
Berkowitz 1787, **Biddle 1791,** Bilotti 1792,
Bristol-Myers 1808, CIT 1844, Clark 1848,
Cummings 1871, **de Rothschild 1877,** Donaldson
1887, Geist 1934, Goldsmith 1948, **Goldstein**
1949, Goode 1952, **Hansen 1972,** Hausman 1977,
Hettinger 1987, **Heyward 1988,** IFF 2004, Kaplan
2022, Lauder 2058, Mayer 2094, McConnell 2100,
McGonagle 2102, Milbank 2119, Nichols 2153,
Pfizer 2182, Rose 2227, **Saltz 2244,** Samuels 2245,
Schweckendieck 2258, **Solow 2279,** Steckler 2290,
Tiger 2314
North Carolina: Reynolds 2410
North Dakota: Stern 2429
Ohio: Gould 2493, Stranahan 2593
Oklahoma: **Noble 2631,** Warren 2644
Oregon: Collins 2652
Pennsylvania: AMETEK 2672, Betz 2686, Lesher 2773,
Smith 2831, Snee-Reinhardt 2835, **Strawbridge**
2846
South Carolina: Colonial 2890
Tennessee: Davis 2919, Hurlbut 2927, Thompson
2937, Toms 2938
Texas: Crump 2979, Dunn 2993, Edwards 2995, Fair
3004, Franklin 3015, Garvey 3019, Halff 3026,
Hankamer 3029, Harrington 3030, Hillcrest 3034,
Hubbard 3039, **Kimberly-Clark 3046,** O'Connor
3077, Pardee 3084, South 3110, Tenneco 3118,
Texas 3119
Virginia: **Mars 3191,** Titmus 3210, Treakle 3211
Washington: **Allen 3217,** U.S. 3256
Wisconsin: Kohler 3295, McBeath 3302

Dentistry

Arizona: **Van Schaick 42**
Florida: Fort 604
Georgia: Cobb 695
Minnesota: Minnesota 1458
Missouri: Lichtenstein 1540, Speas 1570
New Jersey: **Johnson 1658**
Pennsylvania: Measey 2788
Texas: Hillcrest 3034

Dermatology

California: Bireley 82
Connecticut: **Herzog 450**
New York: **American 1752, Archbold 1756**
Pennsylvania: **Foundation 2728**

Drug abuse

Alabama: BE&K 4, **Vulcan 25**
Arizona: First 29
Arkansas: Arkla 46, **Wal-Mart 54**
California: Aerospace 56, Beynon 81, Copley 114,
Drown 123, Fireman's 134, First 136, Gellert 148,
Gellert 149, Goldsmith 157, Howe 180, Irmas 182,
Johnson 191, **Kaiser 194,** Lockheed 216,

Montgomery 242, **National 248,** Osher 257,
Pasadena 266, Patron 267, **S.G. 285,** San Diego
287, Sierra 302, Southern 310, Stauffer 314, Swift
323, Tosco 332, Transamerica 334, Wynn 356
Colorado: Boettcher 361
Connecticut: Bridgeport 417, ITT 455, **Olin 474,** RORD
483, **Xerox 500**
Delaware: Kutz 520
District of Columbia: Cafritz 535, Foundation 541,
Kennedy 552, Post 559
Florida: Banyan 572, Conn 585, Falk 599, **Hanley 615,**
Lost 634, Phillips 648, TECO 668
Georgia: Georgia 710, Rich 731
Illinois: Bersted 793, Field 840, Forest 843, GATX 853,
Kemper 874, Northern 911, **Walgreen 970**
Indiana: Foellinger 989, INB 995
Iowa: Hall 1018, Mid-Iowa 1025
Kansas: **Sprint 1046,** Topeka 1047
Kentucky: Courier-Journal 1055, Kentucky 1059
Louisiana: Zigler 1088
Massachusetts: Boston 1159, Eastern 1182, Humane
1214, Hyams 1216, Kelley 1222, Lechmere 1224,
Linnell 1226, New England 1244, Pappas 1248,
Peabody 1249
Michigan: Chrysler 1308, Dalton 1312, Granger 1341,
Jackson 1347, **Michigan 1359, Monroe 1361,**
Royal 1374, Skillman 1380
Minnesota: Butler 1422, Minnesota 1458, **Minnesota**
1459, Rauenhorst 1472, Whitney 1487
Missouri: Feld 1518, Hallmark 1527, Kauffman 1534,
Pitzman 1556, Speas 1570
Nevada: **Hilton 1596**
New Hampshire: Fuller 1605
New Jersey: CPC 1624, Hyde 1651, **Innovating 1652,**
Johnson 1656, Johnson 1658, McGraw 1672,
Mercedes-Benz 1674, Public 1692, Schultz 1704,
Subaru 1708, **Union 1714,** Victoria 1719
New Mexico: Maddox 1729
New York: Achelis 1732, **American 1750,** Bodman
1800, Carnahan-Jackson 1828, **Carnegie 1829,**
Crane 1867, Curtice-Burns/Pro-Fac 1872, Dreyfus
1893, Graphic 1960, Hayden 1978, Heckscher
1982, **JM 2011,** Joy 2016, Kresge 2047, Leibovitz
2063, **Metropolitan 2117,** Mohawk-Hudson 2124,
New York 2146, Norwood 2159, **Pfizer 2182,**
Republic 2211, Rhodebeck 2214, Rubinstein 2234,
Saks 2240, Salomon 2243, Samuels 2245,
Steele-Reese 2291, Sterling 2294, **Ziff 2363**
North Carolina: **Dalton 2381,** Glenn 2397, North
Carolina 2405, Reynolds 2410, Wachovia 2421,
Winston-Salem 2424
Ohio: Fairfield 2476, Forest 2482, Hamilton 2499,
Huffy 2507, **Kroger 2519, Mead 2531,** National
2544, **Procter 2561,** Van Wert 2604, White 2607
Oregon: Carpenter 2649, Jackson 2653, Johnson 2655
Pennsylvania: **Air 2665, Air 2666,** Jewish 2763, **Pew**
2806, Scaife 2823, Snee-Reinhardt 2835, Union
2852, Williamsport-Lycoming 2861
South Carolina: Central 2888, Colonial 2890
Tennessee: Davis 2919, Genesco 2922, Plough 2932
Texas: Abell-Hanger 2941, Coastal 2969, Cullen 2980,
Exxon 3002, Fasken 3006, Fikes 3009, Frees 3016,
Halff 3026, Henderson 3032, Hillcrest 3034,
Kimberly-Clark 3046, McGovern 3059, McGovern
3060, Mitchell 3067, Overlake 3080, **Penney**
3086, Strake 3112, Straus 3113, Temple 3117,
Transco 3121, Vale-Asche 3126
Utah: Eccles 3149
Virginia: Beazley 3162, Frederick 3180, **Freedom**
3181, Norfolk 3196, Portsmouth 3201
Washington: Boeing 3222, **Burlington 3223,** Fuchs
3229, Glaser 3230, GTE 3231, Ray 3246, SAFECO
3247, Seafirst 3249, U.S. 3256, Washington 3258
West Virginia: McDonough 3267
Wisconsin: Appleton 3272, Fox 3287, Kohler 3295,
McBeath 3302, Milwaukee 3306, Northwestern
3308, **Oscar 3309,** Oshkosh 3311, Stackner 3328,
Time 3330

Family planning

Arizona: Morris 37

Health

Health associations

North Carolina: O'Herron 2406, Reynolds 2410
Ohio: Gould 2493, Hoover 2506
Pennsylvania: Kynett 2770, Lesher 2773, Smith 2831
South Carolina: Colonial 2890
Texas: Fair 3004, Moss 3072, Transco 3121
Virginia: **BDM 3161**
Washington: GTE 3231
Wisconsin: **Ford 3286,** Kohler 3295, McBeath 3302, Northwestern 3308

Hospices

California: Aerospace 56, AT&T 65, Copley 114, Goldsmith 157, McMahan 233, Mericos 235, **National 248, Petersen 271,** Pratt 277, Santa Clara 291, Segal 299
Colorado: El Pomar 371
Connecticut: Bulkley 418, Chapin 420, **Echlin 431, Olin 474, Rosenthal 484,** Union 492
Delaware: Crystal 510
District of Columbia: Appleby 531, Cafritz 535, Ross 562, Stewart 563
Florida: Beveridge 574, Davis 589, **Davis 590,** Eckerd 596, Rosenberg 658
Georgia: Georgia 710
Illinois: **Barber-Colman 785,** Beloit 790, Bock 800, CLARCOR 823, Furnas 850, GATX 853, Johnson 870, Logan 883, **Walgreen 970**
Kansas: Sarver 1043
Louisiana: Monroe 1081
Maryland: Rouse 1136
Massachusetts: Birmingham 1156, Cowan 1172, Eastern 1182, Perini 1253, Polaroid 1258, Raytheon 1262
Michigan: Gerber 1337, Royal 1374
Minnesota: **Honeywell 1446,** Otter 1468
Missouri: Hallmark 1526, Pettus 1555, Shaw 1562, Speas 1570
New Jersey: Schultz 1704
New York: Albany's 1740, Dreyfus 1893, **Grant 1958, Kirby 2033,** Langeloth 2052, **Marx 2091,** Mutual 2140, **Quantum 2201,** Samuels 2245, Steele-Reese 2291
North Carolina: Duke 2387, Polk 2408, Rogers 2412, Salisbury 2413
North Dakota: Stern 2429
Ohio: Kramer 2518, **Mead 2531**
Oregon: Collins 2651
Pennsylvania: Arronson 2678, Millstein 2796, **Union 2851,** Wells 2855
Tennessee: Christy-Houston 2917
Texas: Dishman 2985, Frees 3016, O'Connor 3077, Perkins-Prothro 3089, Strake 3112, Temple 3117, Tenneco 3118, White 3132
Virginia: **BDM 3161, Mars 3191,** Olsson 3198
Washington: Stubblefield 3254
Wisconsin: Appleton 3272, **Oscar 3309**

Hospitals

Alabama: Alabama 1, Hill 14, McMillan 17, Meyer 18, Mitchell 19, Russell 21, Shook 22, Stockham 24, **Vulcan 25**
Arizona: A.P.S. 26, Bank 28, Globe 31, Hankins 33, Raymond 39
Arkansas: Arkla 46, Jones 47, Jones 48, Ottenheimer 50, Riggs 51, Stallaway 52, Sturgis 53
California: Arata 63, **Baker 67, BankAmerica 70,** Barker 71, Bekins 77, Bellini 78, Berger 80, Beynon 81, Bireley 82, Booth 83, Borchard 84, Boswell 85, Brenner 87, **Broccoli 89,** Brunetti 91, Burnand 93, Burns 95, Callison 97, Cedars-Sinai 101, Center 102, City 104, Clorox 106, Connell 113, Copley 114, Crummer 116, Day 117, de Dampierre 118, Deutsch 119, Disney 120, Doheny 121, Essick 127, Factor 128, Fairfield 129, First 135, Forest 138, Fusenot 139, Gamble 141, Garland 144, Gasser 146, Gellert 148, Gellert 149, Gellert 150, Gerard 152, Goldsmith 157, Grancell 159, Gross 161, Haas 164, Hannon 166, Harden 168, **Harman 169, Helms 171,** Herbst 172, Hewlett-Packard 174, Hoag 175, Hogan 178, Howe 180, Irmas 182, Irwin 185, Jackson 187, Jameson 188, Jerome 189,

Jones 192, Joslyn 193, **Keck 198, Kerr 199, Konheim 201,** Leavey 208, **Lebus 209,** Leonardt 211, Livingston 215, Lockheed 216, **Lodzer 217,** Lurie 220, McAlister 228, McBean 229, Miller 239, **Moore 243,** Muller 244, Munger 245, Murphey 246, Murphy 247, Norris 253, **Occidental 254,** Oser 256, Pacific 261, Parsons 264, **Pasadena 265,** Pasadena 266, Peters 270, Pickford 273, Platt 274, **Plitt 275,** Radin 278, Rogers 284, Sanguinetti 289, Setzer 300, Sierra 302, Smith 305, Smith 306, Smith-Walker 307, **Southern 311,** Sprague 312, Stauffer 313, Stauffer 314, Steele 315, Stein 316, Strauss 319, Stuart 320, **Teledyne 327,** Thagard 328, Thomas 329, Tosco 332, Tuohy 336, Union 339, Valley 341, Van Nuys 343, Van Nuys 344, W.W.W. 346, Wasserman 347, Weingart 348, Weisz 349, Western 350, Whittier 351, Wilbur 352, Wood-Claeyssens 354, Ziegler 358
Colorado: Bancroft 359, Bloedorn 360, Carroll 362, Comprecare 365, Denver 369, Duncan 370, El Pomar 371, **Frost 372,** Heginbotham 375, Hill 377, Hughes 378, Joslin-Needham 379, Kitzmiller-Bales 380, Mullen 385, Norgren 386, Petteys 387, Rabb 390, Schramm 391, Sterne-Elder 392, Taylor 396, White 402, Williams 403, Wolf 404
Connecticut: **Aetna 407, American 408,** Auerbach 410, Barden 412, Bennett 413, Brace 416, Champion 419, Chapin 420, Culpeper 427, Dell 428, **Dennett 429, Echlin 431,** Eder 432, EIS 434, **General 441,** Gilman 442, Gimbel 443, **GTE 444,** Hartford 448, **Herzog 450,** Heublein 451, **Hoffman 452,** Hubbell 453, **Huisking 454,** Jost 459, **Krieble 462,** Long 465, Matthies 466, Meriden 467, Mosbacher 468, New Haven 470, **Newman's 471, Olin 474, Panwy 476,** Patterson 477, People's 478, Pfriem 480, Saunders 486, Sosnoff 487, Tow 490, Vance 495, Vanderbilt 496, Young 501
Delaware: Beneficial 504, **Birch 506,** Columbia 509, Crystal 510, **Delmarva 512, DuPont 513,** Ederic 514, **Gerard 515, Good 516,** Kent-Lucas 518, Kingsley 519, Laffey-McHugh 521, Longwood 523, Lovett 524, Marmot 525, Milliken 526, **Schwartz 527,** Weezie 529, Welfare 530
District of Columbia: Appleby 531, Bloedorn 533, Brownley 534, Cohen 536, **First 539,** Folger 540, **GEICO 543,** Gottesman 547, Gudelsky 549, Post 560, Ross 562
Florida: **Abraham 567,** Adams 568, Amaturo 569, Applebaum 570, Appleman 571, Bastien 573, Beveridge 574, Bickerton 575, Blank 577, Broad 579, Bush 581, Catlin 582, **Chatlos 583,** Childress 584, Davis 589, Dunspaugh-Dalton 592, duPont 594, **Echlin 595,** Eckerd 596, Ellis 598, Falk 599, **Fish 601,** Ford 603, Fortin 605, **Frueauff 607, Gerson 609, Grace 611,** Greenburg-May 612, Gronewaldt 613, Groover 614, Hersh 618, Hollingsworth 619, Janirve 621, Jennings 623, Keating 625, Kimmel 627, Kirbo 628, Krueger 630, Lattner 631, Law 633, Lowe 635, Meyer 639, Nias 641, Oak 642, Olliff 643, **Psychists 651,** Pyramid 652, Quick 653, Ratner 654, Reinhold 655, Rinker 656, Setzer 661, Simon 662, Speer 663, Storer 664, Swisher 665, **Taylor 667,** Toppel 669, United States 670, Wahlstrom 671, Waldbaum 672, Walter 673, Weintraub 675, **Winn-Dixie 679,** Wolfson 681, Wollowick 682, Yablick 683
Georgia: Atlanta 687, Callaway 690, Camp 692, Center 694, Community 697, Davis 699, Dodson 700, Franklin 707, Gage 708, Georgia 710, Georgia-Pacific 712, Glancy 714, Health 716, Illges 718, Jinks 719, Lee 720, Lipscomb 721, Livingston 722, Marshall 723, Murphy 728, Patterson-Barclay 730, Rich 731, Shallenberger 732, Spalding 734, Tomlinson 735, Wardlaw 738, West Point 739, Woodward 744
Hawaii: Bancorp 748, Castle 749, Vidinha 758
Idaho: Cunningham 764, Daugherty 765, West 766, **Whiting 767**
Illinois: **Abbott 768,** Aldeen 770, **Allen-Heath 771,** American 773, Andersen 778, **Andreas 779,** Andrew 780, **AON 781, Archer-Daniels-Midland 782,** Aurora 783, Bauer 786, Bere 791, Bersted 793, Best 794, Blair 796, Blum 798, Blum-Kovler

799, Boothroyd 801, Borwell 802, Bowyer 803, Buchanan 807, Buehler 808, Buntrock 809, Caestecker 811, **Carylon 812,** CBI 815, Centralia 818, Chicago 819, Chicago 822, CLARCOR 823, Commonwealth 826, Cuneo 829, Davee 830, Deering 831, Dick 833, Dillon 834, Dower 836, Eisenberg 839, First 841, **FMC 842,** Frank 845, Frankel 846, Fry 848, Funk 849, Furnas 850, **Galter 851,** Galvin 852, Geraldi-Norton 854, Goldenberg 856, Grainger 857, Hoover 866, Illinois 867, Inland 868, Johnson 870, Keeney 871, Kelly 872, Kemper 874, Klein 875, Klenk 876, **Lewis 882,** Logan 883, Lumpkin 884, Manilow 888, Martin 889, Mayer 890, Mazza 891, McCormick 892, **Meyer-Ceco 896,** Millikin 899, Moorman 901, **Morton 902,** Motorola 903, **Nalco 904,** Neese 907, **Norris 909,** Offield 912, OMC 913, Opler 915, Payne 916, Peoples 917, Perkins 919, Petersen 920, Piper 922, Prince 927, **Pritzker 928,** Quaker 930, R.F. 931, Ragen 932, Redhill 933, Rice 939, Russell 941, Salerno 943, **Salwil 944,** Sang 945, **Schneider 946, Scholl 947,** Seabury 948, Shapiro 951, **Shaw 952, Simpson 953,** Smail 955, **Special 956,** Sprague 957, Staley 958, Stone 962, **Sundstrand 963,** Susman 964, Thorson 966, **USG 969,** Ward 971, White 974, Winona 976, Yacktman 980
Indiana: Anderson 981, Cole 986, Custer 987, English-Bonter-Mitchell 988, Griffith 992, Heritage 993, INB 995, Journal-Gazette 997, Miles 1004, **Northern 1007,** Noyes 1008, Oakley 1009, Oliver 1010, **Reilly 1011,** Schust 1012, Zollner 1013
Iowa: Employers 1017, Hall 1018, Kuyper 1021, Lee 1022
Kansas: Baehr 1031, Bank 1032, Beech 1033, Breidenthal 1034, Cessna 1035, Hansen 1037, **Marley 1039,** Mingenback 1040, Sarver 1043, Smith 1044
Kentucky: Brennan 1051, Juilfs 1058, **Long 1061,** Mills 1062, Robinson 1063, Rosenthal 1064
Louisiana: Booth-Bricker 1070, Brown 1071, Freeport-McMoRan 1073, Heymann 1074, Heymann-Wolf 1075, Keller 1076, Latter 1078, Libby-Dufour 1079, Monroe 1081, Zemurray 1087
Maine: Central 1090, Shaw's 1093
Maryland: **Aegon 1097,** Baldwin 1098, Baltimore 1100, Brown 1103, Capital 1104, Clark-Winchcole 1106, Crown 1107, Davis 1109, First 1111, Gross 1114, **Gumenick 1115,** Knott 1122, Leidy 1123, Mechanic 1126, Mullan 1129, Nathan 1130, Procter 1133, Rollins-Luetkemeyer 1134, Rymland 1137, Shapiro 1139, USF&G 1142, USF&G 1143, Wilson 1144
Massachusetts: Acushnet 1145, Alden 1148, Arakelian 1149, Ashton 1150, Bank 1152, BayBanks 1154, Boston 1157, Boston 1159, Boston 1160, Cabot-Saltonstall 1163, Charlton 1167, Chase 1168, Clifford 1169, Cove 1171, Cox 1174, Cummings 1176, Davis 1178, **Demoulas 1179, Digital 1180,** Eastern 1182, Ellsworth 1185, Fay 1186, Feldberg 1187, First 1189, Ford 1191, Fraser 1192, Fuller 1193, Gardner 1194, General 1196, Gerondelis 1197, Gorin 1199, Harrington 1201, **Henderson 1203,** Hinduja 1206, Hoffman 1208, Home 1209, Hopedale 1211, Hornblower 1212, Hurdle 1215, Jackson 1219, John 1220, Johnson 1221, Kelley 1222, Levy 1225, Lipsky 1227, **Little 1228,** Luce 1230, M/A-Com 1231, McEvoy 1234, Merkert 1236, **Middlecott 1237, Millipore 1238, New England 1242,** New England 1243, Noonan 1245, Pappas 1248, Peabody 1249, Peabody 1251, Perini 1252, Perini 1253, Perpetual 1254, Persky 1255, Poitras 1257, Prouty 1260, Rabb 1261, Raytheon 1262, Redstone 1263, Reisman 1264, Rogers 1266, Rubenstein 1268, Russell 1269, Saltonstall 1271, Sawyer 1272, Schrafft 1273, Shapiro 1274, **Shapiro 1275,** Sheraton 1277, Sherman 1278, Stearns 1282, Stevens 1284, Stone 1286, Stoneman 1287, Tupancy-Harris 1290, Webster 1291, Wells 1292, Wright 1296, Wyman-Gordon 1297, Yawkey 1298
Michigan: **Allen 1299,** Anderson 1300, Battle 1303, **Bauervic-Paisley 1304,** Bishop 1306, Boutell 1307, DeRoy 1314, DeVlieg 1315, Dow 1317, Earl-Beth

1318, Eddy 1319, Ford 1324, Ford 1325, Ford 1326, Ford 1327, Ford 1329, Fremont 1331, Fruehauf 1333, **General 1336,** Gerber 1337, Gerstacker 1338, Herrick 1343, Hess 1344, Holden 1345, Hudson-Webber 1346, Kellogg 1350, Lincoln 1356, Mills 1360, Morley 1362, Pagel 1368, Ransom 1371, Ratner 1372, Redies 1373, Royal 1374, Sage 1375, Shiffman 1379, Thomas 1387, Tracy 1390, **Triford 1391,** Wege 1396, Wenger 1397, Wickes 1401, Wilson 1403, World 1405, Zimmerman 1406

Minnesota: **Andersen 1410,** Anderson 1412, Baker 1413, **Bemis 1416,** Blue 1419, Chadwick 1428, Edwards 1437, Hubbard 1448, Lang 1449, Meadowood 1455, Lilly 1460, Phillips 1471, Rivers 1474, St. Croix 1476, **Tonka 1480**

Mississippi: Deposit 1489, Feild 1490, Hearin 1491

Missouri: Anheuser-Busch 1495, Bloch 1500, Brown 1503, Commerce 1504, Cowden 1507, CPI 1508, Craig 1509, Edison 1512, Edison 1513, **Emerson 1514, Emerson 1515,** Enright 1516, Gaylord 1521, Goppert 1522, Hamilton 1528, Interco 1530, Jefferson 1531, Judon 1532, Lichtenstein 1540, **May 1547,** Mercantile 1550, Sachs 1560, Schnuck 1561, Shaw 1562, Shoenberg 1564, Slusher 1565, Souers 1568, Speas 1570, Speas 1571, Stupp 1572, Stupp 1573, Sunderland 1574, Union 1576, **Webb 1579,** Wolff 1581

Montana: Bair 1582, MPCo/Entech 1583, Sample 1584

Nebraska: Buckley 1585, Storz 1594

Nevada: **Bing 1595,** Wiegand 1599

New Hampshire: Cogswell 1602, Jameson 1606

New Jersey: **Armco 1614, Bonner 1615,** Brady 1617, **Brawer 1618,** Brunetti 1620, Campbell 1622, CPC 1624, **Crane 1625,** Creamer 1626, **Crum 1627,** Dickinson 1629, **Edison 1631,** Elizabethtown 1632, Frelinghuysen 1636, General 1639, Harris 1643, Havens 1644, **Hoechst 1646,** Hoyt 1649, Hyde 1651, **Jaqua 1654,** Jockey 1655, **Johnson 1656, Johnson 1657, Johnson 1658,** Kerney 1660, Klatskin 1662, Kramer 1664, La Sala 1665, Lazarus 1666, Leavens 1667, **Lipton 1668,** Magowan 1669, Martin 1671, McGraw 1672, MCJ 1673, **Mercedes-Benz 1674,** Merck 1676, **Merck 1677,** Meyer 1678, Midlantic 1679, Mutual 1680, **Nabisco 1682, National 1683,** New Jersey 1685, Ohl 1686, Petrie 1689, **Public 1692,** Read 1693, **Reeves 1694,** Rippel 1695, **Roth 1696, Rukin 1697,** Schamach 1700, Schering-Plough 1701, Schering-Plough 1702, **Schimmel 1703,** Schwartz 1706, Taub 1710, Terner 1711, Thomas 1712, **Union 1714,** Union 1715, Upton 1716, Van Houten 1717, Van Pelt 1718, Visceglia-Summit 1720, **Warner-Lambert 1723,** Willits 1724

New Mexico: **Bellamah 1727,** Carlsbad 1728

New York: Abrams 1730, Abrons 1731, Achelis 1732, Adler 1734, **Aeroflex 1735,** Albany 1739, Albany's 1740, Allen 1742, Allyn 1744, Altman 1746, **AmBase 1749,** Anderson 1754, **Archbold 1756,** Arkell 1757, Aron 1758, **ASARCO 1759, AT&T 1761,** Avon 1764, Bachmann 1765, Badgeley 1766, Baird 1767, **Baker 1769,** Barth 1776, **Bartsch 1777,** Beach 1779, Bedford 1781, **Bedminster 1782,** Beir 1784, Berkowitz 1787, **Bernhard 1789, Biddle 1791,** Bilotti 1792, **Blackmer 1794,** Bleibtreu 1795, Blinken 1796, Bluhdorn 1797, Bodman 1800, Bostwick 1803, Boxer 1805, Branta 1807, Brody 1810, Brooks 1813, Buffalo 1817, **Burnham 1819,** Burns 1820, Burns 1821, Canno 1824, **Cantor 1825, Capital 1826,** Carnahan-Jackson 1828, Carrier 1830, Carter-Wallace 1831, **Carvel 1832,** Chait 1834, Charina 1835, Clemente 1852, Coleman 1853, **Colgate-Palmolive 1856, Coltec 1858, Common 1859, Commonwealth 1860,** Congel-Pyramid 1861, **Crane 1867, Cullman 1868,** Cummings 1869, **Dammann 1873, Day 1876, de Rothschild 1877, DeCamp 1879,** Delany 1882, Dent 1884, Dillon 1886, Donaldson 1887, Dreyfus 1893, **Dreyfus 1894, Dula 1895, Edouard 1900, Eisner 1901,** Enders 1903, Evans 1908, Fahey 1910, Feil 1912, Ferkauf 1914, Fife 1917, **Fish 1918, Forbes 1920,** Forchheimer 1921, Foster 1923, Frese 1927,

Frohlich 1928, Gaisman 1931, Gebbie 1933, **Gelb 1935,** Gibbs 1938, Gifford 1939, Goldie-Anna 1942, Golding 1943, Goldman 1944, Goldman 1945, Goldome 1947, Goldsmith 1948, Goldstein 1950, Goode 1952, Goodman 1953, Goodstein 1954, Goodyear 1955, Gordon/Rousmaniere/Roberts 1956, **Grant 1958,** Graphic 1960, Green 1962, Greene 1964, Greene 1965, Gurwin 1969, Hagedorn 1970, Haggin 1971, **Harriman 1973,** Harriman 1974, Hatch 1976, Hausman 1977, Hazen 1979, Heckscher 1982, Heijmans 1983, **Helmsley 1985, Hess 1986,** Hettinger 1987, Hilson 1989, Hoernle 1991, Hopkins 1992, Hugoton 1997, Hulbert 1998, Hultquist 1999, Hutchins 2001, Icahn 2003, IFF 2004, Iroquois 2006, Israel 2007, Joelson 2012, Jones 2015, Joyce 2017, Julia 2018, Jurodin 2019, Kalikow 2021, Katz 2024, **Kaufmann 2026, Kellogg 2028,** Kennedy 2029, Kidder 2030, Killough 2031, Klein 2035, Klock 2037, **Knox 2039,** Knox 2040, Kohlberg 2041, Kopf 2042, Kopf 2043, Kramer 2045, L and L 2049, Lang 2051, Langeloth 2052, Larsen 2053, Lasdon 2055, **Lasker 2057,** Lauder 2058, Lawrence 2059, Lazar 2060, Lee 2061, Levin 2065, Leviton 2066, Lewis 2068, Lieb 2069, Lindner 2071, Link 2072, Lippman 2073, Loeb 2074, Luce 2079, Macdonald 2080, **MacDonald 2081, Mailman 2084,** Manley 2085, Manufacturers 2087, Mark 2089, Marks 2090, Mastronardi 2092, Mayer 2094, Mayrock 2096, McCann 2097, McCarthy 2098, **McCarthy 2099,** McConnell 2100, **McDonald 2101,** McGonagle 2102, McGraw 2103, Mellam 2105, Memorial 2108, Mendik 2110, **Menschel 2111,** Mercy 2112, Metcalf 2116, Milbank 2119, Millbrook 2121, Miller 2122, Mohawk-Hudson 2124, **Monell 2125, Monterey 2126,** Moore 2127, Morgan 2129, Morgan 2130, Morgan 2131, Morgenstern 2132, Morris 2133, Morris 2134, Moses 2135, Mulligan 2137, Murcott 2138, Napier 2141, Neu 2143, **New York 2148, Newhouse 2151,** Newman 2152, Nichols 2153, Northern 2157, Norwood 2159, O'Connor 2161, O'Herron 2162, O'Sullivan 2163, O'Toole 2164, Oestreicher 2165, Orange 2167, Orentreich 2168, Osborn 2169, OSG 2170, Overbrook 2171, PaineWebber 2172, Paley 2173, Palisades 2174, Parshelsky 2175, Penick 2178, **Perkins 2180, Pfizer 2182, Pforzheimer 2183,** Phillips 2185, **Phillips 2186, Pines 2187, Pinewood 2188,** Plant 2189, Pluta 2190, Pope 2192, Pope 2193, **Porter 2195,** Price 2197, **Pritschard 2198, Quantum 2201,** Reicher 2209, Reiss 2210, Rich 2215, Ritter 2220, Rodgers 2225, Rosenberg 2228, Rosenwald 2230, Ross 2231, Rubin 2233, Rudin 2236, **Rumsey 2237,** Sacerdote 2238, **Sackler 2239, Saks 2240,** Salomon 2241, Salomon 2243, Samuels 2245, Saul 2247, Schiff 2252, Schmeelk 2253, Schnurmacher 2254, Schwartz 2255, Schwartz 2256, Schwarzman 2257, Seaman 2259, Seaver 2260, Sequa 2261, **Sexauer 2262,** Sharp 2263, Sheinberg 2264, Sheldon 2265, Silver 2267, Singer 2268, Slaughter 2271, Slifka 2272, Smith 2275, SO 2278, **Sony 2280,** Spiegel 2282, Sprague 2285, **St. Giles 2287, Starr 2288, Statter 2289,** Steckler 2290, Steinberg 2293, Sterling 2294, Stern 2295, Stony 2296, Stott 2297, Straus 2298, Stuart 2299, Sulzberger 2300, **Summerfield 2301,** Swanson 2304, Swid 2305, Taylor 2307, **Texaco 2309,** Thanksgiving 2310, Thorne 2312, Thorne 2313, Time 2315, Trimble 2320, Unterberg 2324, Ushkow 2325, **Vanneck-Bailey 2328,** Vidda 2330, Voute 2332, Wakefield 2333, Warren 2336, Weinberg 2339, **Weinberg 2340,** Weinstein 2341, Weinstein 2342, Wendt 2344, Werblow 2345, **Westvaco 2346, Winkler 2351,** Winston 2352, Winston 2353, **Wishnick 2355,** Wohlgemuth 2356, **Woodland 2357,** Woodward 2359, Zarkin 2361, Zuckerberg 2366

North Carolina: American 2367, Belk 2369, **Blue 2370,** Brenner 2371, Burlington 2375, Cannon 2378, Dickson 2385, Duke 2386, Ebert 2389, Finch 2390, First 2391, Harris 2401, Hemby 2402,

Provident 2409, Smith 2414, Thomasville 2416, **United 2418,** Wachovia 2421, Woodson 2425

North Dakota: Leach 2427

Ohio: Allyn 2431, American 2432, Anderson 2434, **Austin 2438,** Baird 2439, Beecher 2441, **BP 2443,** Bridgestone/Firestone 2445, Britton 2446, Calhoun 2448, Centerior 2452, Charities 2453, Chisholm 2454, Cincinnati 2455, Cleveland 2457, Cleveland-Cliffs 2458, Codrington 2459, Corbin 2461, Coshocton 2462, Cox 2463, Crandall 2464, Dater 2465, Dayton 2466, Double 2468, East 2469, Emery 2472, Evans 2474, Fairfield 2476, Ferro 2478, Fifth 2479, **Firestone 2480,** Firman 2481, Fox 2483, Frick 2485, Frohman 2486, Gallagher 2489, GAR 2490, Gould 2494, Grimes 2495, Gross 2496, Hartzell-Norris 2500, Humphrey 2508, Ireland 2511, Jochum-Moll 2513, Kettering 2516, Kramer 2518, Kuntz 2520, Lennon 2521, Lincoln 2523, Lubrizol 2525, M/B 2526, **Markey 2527,** Mather 2528, McAlonan 2530, Miller 2535, Monarch 2536, Moores 2537, Murch 2540, Murdough 2541, O'Bleness 2549, Ohio 2553, **Parker-Hannifin 2554, Perkins 2556,** Phillips 2557, Pollock 2559, Prentiss 2560, Reeves 2565, **Reliance 2567,** Renner 2568, Ritchie 2570, Ritter 2571, Rosenthal 2572, Schiff 2575, Schlink 2576, Schmidlapp 2578, **SCOA 2579,** Selsor 2581, Smith 2585, Smucker 2588, Society 2589, Star 2590, Stark 2591, Tamarkin 2594, Timken 2595, Trinova 2601, TRW 2602, TRW 2603, Watson 2605, Wean 2606, White 2607, Wodecroft 2609, Wolfe 2610, Wuliger 2612, Yassenoff 2613, Youngstown 2615

Oklahoma: Campbell 2622, Goddard 2624, Mabee 2627, McCasland 2628, Merrick 2630, Oklahoma 2634, Rapp 2638, Share 2641, Taubman 2642, Titus 2643, Warren 2644, Wegener 2646

Oregon: Johnson 2655, Tucker 2662

Pennsylvania: **Alco 2667,** Alcoa 2668, Allegheny 2669, Allegheny 2670, **AMETEK 2672,** AMP 2673, Anathan 2674, Arcadia 2677, Arronson 2678, Beatty 2681, Berry 2685, Betz 2686, Buck 2689, **Butz 2691,** Byers 2692, Cameron 2693, Campbell 2694, Caplan 2695, Carpenter 2697, **Cassett 2698,** Clapp 2703, Coen 2704, Colket 2705, Connelly 2707, Crawford 2711, Crels 2712, Cyclops 2714, **duPont 2718,** Eden 2720, Elf 2721, Farber 2724, Foster 2727, Fourjay 2729, Gibson 2730, Goldman 2732, Grundy 2735, Hall 2736, Hallowell 2737, Hamilton 2738, **Harsco 2740,** Hassel 2741, Hazen 2742, **Heinz 2743,** Hillman 2750, Holstrom 2751, Hopwood 2754, Horsehead 2755, Hoyt 2756, Hunt 2758, J.D.B. 2760, Janssen 2761, Jennings 2762, Jewish 2763, Kardon 2765, **Kennametal 2766,** Kline 2768, Kynett 2770, Levee 2774, Lindback 2775, **Live 2776,** Love 2778, Mack 2780, Massey 2781, McCandless 2782, McCormick 2783, McFeely-Rogers 2785, McLean 2787, Mellon 2790, Mengle 2792, Millstein 2796, Oberlaender 2800, Oxford 2801, Patterson 2802, Pennsylvania 2804, Philadelphia 2808, Pittsburgh 2810, Quaker 2815, Rockwell 2818, Rosenberg 2821, Scholler 2825, **Sharon 2828,** Simon 2830, Smith 2831, Smith 2832, Stabler 2839, Steinman 2843, Strauss 2845, **Strawbridge 2846,** Strawbridge 2847, Superior-Pacific 2849, Trexler 2850, **Union 2851,** Union 2852, Weisbrod 2854, Wells 2855, West 2856, Widgeon 2859, Williams 2860, Williamsport-Lycoming 2861, **Wilson 2862,** Wood 2863

Rhode Island: Chace 2867, Champlin 2868, Cranston 2869, Fleet/Norstar 2870, Galkin 2871, **Hasbro 2872,** Hodges 2874, Jaffe 2875, Johnstone 2876, Koffler 2877, Morgan 2879, Providence 2881, Roddy 2884, **Textron 2885**

South Carolina: Belk-Simpson 2886, Burgiss 2887, Colonial 2890, Fullerton 2892, McDonnell 2895, Piedmont 2897, Sargent 2898, **Spring 2903,** Springs 2904, Symmes 2906

Tennessee: Brinkley 2914, Brown 2915, Christy-Houston 2917, Lowenstein 2928, Melrose 2931, Seretean 2934, Stokely 2936, Thompson 2937, Tonya 2939, Wallace 2940

Texas: Anderson 2947, Bass 2952, Bass 2953, Beal 2954, Beasley 2955, Bertha 2956, Bryce 2960, Burlington 2961, Cain 2962, Carter 2965, Chilton 2966, Clayton 2968, Cockrell 2970, Collins 2971, Communities 2972, Cullen 2980, Davidson 2982, Davis 2983, Dickson 2984, **Dr. Pepper 2988,** Dresser 2989, **Dresser 2990,** Duncan 2992, Dunn 2993, Edwards 2995, Elkins 2997, Elkins 2998, Ellwood 2999, Fair 3004, Feldman 3008, FINA 3010, Fish 3012, Franklin 3015, Frees 3016, Fuller 3018, Garvey 3019, Green 3020, Griffin 3021, Haggar 3025, Hamman 3028, Harrington 3030, Hawn 3031, Hillcrest 3034, Hobby 3035, Hoblitzelle 3036, Keith 3044, King 3047, Lard 3049, LBJ 3050, Lightner 3051, LTV 3052, McKee 3061, McQueen 3063, Mechia 3065, Moncrief 3068, Nation 3074, National 3075, Navarro 3076, O'Connor 3077, Owen 3081, Pennzoil 3087, Perkins 3088, Prairie 3092, Rienzi 3095, Roberts 3096, Scurlock 3100, Seay 3101, Sharp 3103, South 3110, Strake 3112, Sturgis 3114, Temple 3117, Tenneco 3118, Texas 3120, Turner 3123, Vaughn 3127, White 3133, Wolff 3135, Woltman 3136, **Zale 3139, Zale 3140**
Utah: Bamberger 3141, Browning 3142, Burton 3143, Castle 3144, Dumke 3146, Eccles 3148, Eccles 3149, Michael 3151, Swanson 3154
Virginia: **BDM 3161,** Camp 3167, Caruthers 3169, Central 3170, Crestar 3172, Dalis 3173, Dominion 3175, Fitz-Gibbon 3179, Frederick 3180, Gottwald 3182, Hunter 3184, Little 3190, Massey 3192, Mobil 3194, Morgan 3195, Norfolk 3196, Reynolds 3202, **Reynolds 3203, Robins 3205,** Taylor 3208, Thomas 3209, Treakle 3211, Virginia 3213, Wheat 3215
Washington: **Burlington 3223,** Cheney 3224, Fuchs 3229, GTE 3231, Kilworth 3233, Leuthold 3234, Matlock 3236, Murray 3238, PACCAR 3240, Pemco 3242, Petrie 3243, Puget 3245, **Schack 3248,** See 3251
West Virginia: Hott 3264, Kennedy 3266
Wisconsin: Alexander 3270, Appleton 3272, Banta 3273, Birnschein 3274, Brotz 3276, Bucyrus-Erie 3277, Clark 3278, Demmer 3284, Jeffris 3290, **Johnson 3292,** Ladish 3296, Ladish 3297, Ladish 3298, Lindsay 3299, Marshall 3300, Marshall 3301, McBeath 3302, **Menasha 3303,** Northwestern 3308, **Oscar 3309,** Oshkosh 3310, Pettit 3312, Rexnord 3318, Roehl 3320, Schroeder 3324, Shattuck 3325, Smith 3326, U.S. 3331, **Universal 3332,** Vilter 3333, Wisconsin 3337, Ziegler 3340
Wyoming: Goodstein 3341, Stock 3342, Weiss 3343

Hospitals—building funds

Arkansas: Arkla 46, **McKesson 49**
California: **Baker 67,** Lockheed 216, Norman/Nethercutt 252, Stauffer 313, Tosco 332, Weingart 348
Connecticut: Champion 419, ITT 456, Northeast 472, People's 478, Stanley 488
Delaware: Columbia 509, Longwood 523
District of Columbia: **First 539**
Florida: Beveridge 574, Eckerd 596, Wolfson 681
Georgia: Georgia 710
Idaho: West 766
Illinois: Beloit 790, Navistar 906, Neese 907, **State 959**
Indiana: INB 995, **Northern 1007**
Iowa: Hall 1018
Louisiana: Freeport-McMoRan 1073
Maryland: Baltimore 1100, Brown 1103, PHH 1131
Massachusetts: BayBanks 1154, Bayrd 1155, Eastern 1182, Peabody 1249, Peabody 1251, Smith 1279
Michigan: Hudson-Webber 1346, **Michigan 1359**
Minnesota: Otter 1468
Missouri: Shaw 1562
New Jersey: Grassmann 1641, **Hoechst 1645, Mercedes-Benz 1674, Public 1692,** Schering-Plough 1702, Van Houten 1717, Van Pelt 1718
New York: **Albany 1739,** Bankers 1772, **Chazen 1839,** National 2142, **Quantum 2201,** Samuels 2245

North Carolina: First 2392, Salisbury 2413, Volvo 2420
Ohio: Cincinnati 2455, Cleveland-Cliffs 2458, East 2469, **Eaton 2470,** Hoover 2505, Kangesser 2514, **RB&W 2564,** Timken 2595
Oklahoma: **Oklahoma 2635**
Pennsylvania: **AMETEK 2672,** Crown 2713, McFeely-Rogers 2785, Murphy 2798, **Union 2851**
Tennessee: Christy-Houston 2917
Texas: Franklin 3015, Johnson 3041
Utah: Questar 3152
Virginia: Portsmouth 3200
Washington: GTE 3231, Lockwood 3235
Wisconsin: Consolidated 3280, Northwestern 3308, **Oscar 3309**

Leprosy

California: Sierra 302
Connecticut: **Xerox 500**
New York: **Butler 1822**

Medical education

Alabama: Andalusia 2, Gibson 13
Arizona: Flinn 30, Morris 37, Raymond 39, Tucson 41, **Van Schaick 42**
Arkansas: Jones 48
California: Bireley 82, **Femino 133,** Genentech 151, Irvine 184, **Kaiser 194,** MacKenzie 221, **National 248,** Norman 251, Stein 316, Western 350, Wollenberg 353
Colorado: **Frost 372,** Williams 403
Connecticut: **Berbecker 414, Clark 423, Culpeper 426, Educational 433,** Jones 458, Mosbacher 468, Sosnoff 487, **Stone 489**
Delaware: Amsterdam 503, **Good 516**
District of Columbia: Bloedorn 533
Florida: Abbey 566, Einstein 597, Fellows 600, Fort 604, Kennedy 626, Lauffer 632, Lost 634, Lowe 635, Nias 641, Oak 642, **Watson 674**
Georgia: Cobb 695, **Foundation 706,** Georgia 709, Health 716, Whitehead 741
Hawaii: Zimmerman 762
Illinois: **Abbott 768,** Bauer 786, Boothroyd 801, Galvin 852, Levie 881, Prentice 926, **Pritzker 928,** Regenstein 934, Rice 939, **Scholl 947,** Washington 972
Indiana: Ball 982, Froderman 991, Hook 994
Iowa: Mansfield 1023, Mid-Iowa 1025, Principal 1027, Principal 1028, Quad 1029
Kentucky: Cooke 1054, Rural 1065
Maryland: **Aegon 1097, Gumenick 1115, Hughes 1120,** Pollin 1132
Massachusetts: Adams 1146, Ford 1191, Gerondelis 1197, Peabody 1251, **Porter 1259, Wolfson 1294**
Michigan: Gerber 1337, Holden 1345, Lincoln 1356, Towsley 1389, Upjohn 1392, Zuckerman 1407
Minnesota: Alworth 1408, **Charlson 1429,** O'Brien 1465
Mississippi: Vicksburg 1493
Missouri: Dow 1511, Edison 1512, Fullbright 1520, **Mallinckrodt 1546, Olin 1551,** Patton 1553, Speas 1570, Speas 1571, Whitaker 1580
Nevada: Wiegand 1599
New Hampshire: Foundation 1604
New Jersey: **Hoechst 1646,** Hyde 1651, Islami 1653, **Johnson 1657, Johnson 1658,** Merck 1676, Schering-Plough 1702, Sutcliffe 1709, Van Houten 1717, **Warner-Lambert 1723**
New Mexico: Carlsbad 1728
New York: Allyn 1744, Arkell 1757, Aron 1758, Beinecke 1783, Boxer 1805, **Bronfman 1811, China 1842, Collins 1857, Commonwealth 1860,** Cummings 1869, **DeCamp 1879, Dorot 1888,** Dosberg 1889, Dyson 1897, **Ernst 1905,** Falk 1911, Feil 1912, Forchheimer 1921, **Frankel 1925, Freeman 1926,** Goodstein 1954, Graphic 1960, **Hansen 1972,** Hirschl 1990, Horncrest 1993, IFF 2004, Kimmelman 2032, Klosk 2038, Kramer 2044, Lee 2061, Lewis 2068, **Lighting 2070, Macy 2083,** McGonagle 2102, **Metropolitan 2117,** Moses 2135, **New York 2148, Pfizer 2182, Potts 2196,** Price 2197, Recanati 2207, **Ritter 2219,**

Rosenwald 2230, Rudin 2235, **Sackler 2239, Sandoz 2246,** Sterling 2294, Stony 2296, Straus 2298, **Tai 2306,** van Ameringen 2326, Weill-Caulier 2338, Winston 2352, **Zimmermann 2364, Zlinkoff 2365**
North Carolina: Burroughs 2376, **Burroughs 2377, Deichman-Lerner 2384,** Gilmer-Smith 2394, Glenn 2397, Polk 2408
Ohio: Bremer 2444, Cox 2463, Firman 2481, France 2484, Nippert 2546, Renner 2568, Schlink 2576
Oregon: Collins 2652, Johnson 2655
Pennsylvania: Annenberg 2676, Crown 2713, Foerderer 2726, Goldman 2732, Greensburg 2734, Kynett 2770, Lindback 2775, Measey 2788, **SmithKline 2834**
South Carolina: Smith 2901, Springs 2904, Stevens 2905
Tennessee: Potter 2933, Snider 2935
Texas: Abercrombie 2942, **Alcon 2944,** Alexander 2945, Cain 2962, Clayton 2968, Collins 2971, Community 2973, Cooley 2976, Elkins 2998, Ellwood 2999, Fikes 3009, Franklin 3015, Gulf 3022, Herzstein 3033, Hoblitzelle 3036, Huffington 3040, Luse 3053, McGovern 3059, McGovern 3060, Morrison 3071, Orange 3079, Seay 3101, Walthall 3129, Wolff 3135
Utah: Bamberger 3141, Eccles 3147, Swim 3155
Vermont: Lintilhac 3157
Virginia: Beazley 3162, Norfolk 3196, Thomas 3209, Virginia 3213
Washington: **Allen 3217,** Benaroya 3219, Glaser 3230, Kilworth 3233
West Virginia: Clay 3263
Wisconsin: Consolidated 3280, McBeath 3302, Northwestern 3308, Rennebohm 3317, Shattuck 3325, **Surgical 3329,** Wehr 3336

Medical research

Alabama: Barber 3, Dixon 11, Shook 22
Arizona: Flinn 30, **Hermundslie 34, Kieckhefer 35,** Marshall 36, Morris 37, Southern 40, Webb 43
Arkansas: Ottenheimer 50
California: Allen 58, **Baker 67,** Baker 68, Bank 69, Baxter 72, Beckman 76, Bellini 78, Bireley 82, Brotman 90, Burns 95, Campini 98, **Capital 99,** City 104, Columbia 109, **Confidence 112,** Doheny 121, Dr. Seuss 122, **Eisenberg 126,** Factor 128, Familian 130, **Farber 131, Femino 133,** Gallo 140, Garaventa 143, Garnier 145, Geffen 147, Gellert 148, Gellert 149, Goldsmith 157, Goldwyn 158, Hannon 166, Hanover 167, Hedco 170, Hewitt 173, Hoag 175, Hofmann 177, **Hoover 179,** Howe 180, Irvine 184, Irwin 185, Itakura 186, Jameson 188, Jerome 189, Jewett 190, Kantor 195, **Keck 197,** Kirchgessner 200, Laffin 204, Leavey 208, Lincy 213, Lucas 219, **Mann 222,** Masserini 225, **Maxfield 226,** McCarthy 230, Mericos 235, Milken 236, Milken 237, Milken 238, **National 248,** National 249, Norris 253, **Ostern 258,** Oxnard 260, Pacific 261, Parker 263, Pasadena 266, PCS 268, **Pfeiffer 272,** Platt 274, **Plitt 275,** Pointer 276, Rasmussen 279, **Research 280,** Rigler-Lawrence 281, Rincon 282, Rogers 284, Scripps 296, Seebe 298, **Simon 303,** Smith 305, Stauffer 314, Stein 316, Stern 317, Thagard 328, Thomas 329, Thornton 330, Treadwell 335, **Union 338,** Valley 340, Valley 341, W.W.W. 346, Wasserman 347, Western 350, Whittier 351, Wynn 356
Colorado: Coulter 368, Lowe 382, **Stuart-James 394,** Swan 395, Taylor 396
Connecticut: **Adler 405, Childs 422, Culpeper 426, Educational 433, Fairchild 436,** Hascoe 449, **Herzog 450, Lelash 463,** Obernauer 473, Patterson 477, **Perkin 479, Rosenthal 484,** UST 494, **Whitehead 498**
Delaware: Amsterdam 503, Beneficial 504, Columbia 509, **Good 516,** Schwartz 527
District of Columbia: Bloedorn 533, Gelman 544, Himmelfarb 550, **Kennedy 552,** Lehrman 554, Ross 562
Florida: **Abraham 567,** Applebaum 570, Bickerton 575, **Davis 588, duPont 593,** Einstein 597, Ford 603,

Garner 608, Greenburg-May 612, Groover 614, **Harris 616, Hayward 617,** Kennedy 626, Lowe 635, **Markey 637, Messing 638,** Parsons 645, Paulucci 646, Pearce 647, Quick 653, **Rosenberg 657,** Simon 662, Tampa 666, TECO 668, Wells 676, Wertheim 677, Wollowick 682

Georgia: Anncox 684, Center 694, Dodson 700, **Foundation 706,** Georgia 709, Glancy 714, Livingston 722, Mauldin 725, South 733

Illinois: **Abbott 768, Amoco 775,** Blum-Kovler 799, Boothroyd 801, Butz 810, CBI 815, Centel 817, Eisenberg 839, Getz 855, Goldenberg 856, GSC 858, **Hammer 859, Harper 860,** Harris 862, Johnson 870, Klenk 876, **Knowles 877,** Lederer 878, Milbro 898, Mitchell 900, Perkins 919, **Pontikes 925,** Redhill 933, Regenstein 934, Relations 935, Retirement 937, **Schneider 946, Searle 949, Shaw 952,** Siragusa 954, Sprague 957, **Trans 967, Waste 973**

Indiana: Lincoln 1000

Iowa: Carver 1015, Principal 1027, Principal 1028

Kansas: Muchnic 1041

Kentucky: Humana 1057, LaViers 1060, **Long 1061**

Louisiana: Lupin 1080, Schlieder 1083, Woolf 1086, Zemurray 1087

Maine: Maine 1092

Maryland: Abramson 1096, **Aegon 1097,** Casey 1105, Dart 1108, **Gumenick 1115, Hughes 1120, Life 1124,** Wilson 1144

Massachusetts: Alden 1148, Campbell 1166, Clifford 1169, Cox 1174, General 1195, General 1196, **Grass 1200,** Harrington 1201, Hood 1210, Humane 1214, **Iacocca 1217,** King 1223, Levy 1225, Marks 1232, McEvoy 1234, **Merck 1235,** Merkert 1236, Peabody 1249, Peabody 1250, Pierce 1257, Poitras 1257, Rowland 1267, Rubenstein 1268, Saltonstall 1271, Smith 1279, Tupancy-Harris 1290, Webster 1291

Michigan: Farwell 1320, Ford 1325, Ford 1326, **Ford 1328,** Gerber 1337, Holden 1345, Kennedy 1352, **Pardee 1369,** Prentis 1370, Ratner 1372, **Seidman 1378,** Stewart 1385, Taubman 1386, Towsley 1389, Upjohn 1393

Minnesota: **Andersen 1410,** Baker 1413, **Bauervic 1414,** Chadwick 1428, **Charlson 1429,** Eddy 1436, Fingerhut 1438, **Fiterman 1439, Grand 1442,** Greystone 1444, Groves 1445, Howe 1447, **McKnight 1453, Minnesota 1459,** O'Brien 1465, O'Shaughnessy 1466, Phillips 1471, Sundet 1478, Thorpe 1479

Mississippi: Vicksburg 1493, Walker 1494

Missouri: Contico 1506, Dow 1511, Edison 1512, **Emerson 1515, Francis 1519,** Love 1544, **Mallinckrodt 1546, McDonnell 1549, Olin 1551,** Patton 1553, Reynolds 1558, Shaw 1562, Shoenberg 1564, Smith 1566, Speas 1570, Speas 1571, Stupp 1573, Whitaker 1580

Nevada: Redfield 1597, Wiegand 1599

New Hampshire: Fuller 1605, **Penates 1608**

New Jersey: Bonner 1615, Brunetti 1620, **Capita 1623,** CPC 1624, **Diabetes 1628, Edison 1631,** Garfield 1638, **Gulton 1642,** Havens 1644, Hoffmann-La Roche 1647, Hoffmann-La Roche 1648, Hoyt 1649, Hyde 1651, **Johnson 1656, Johnson 1657,** Klatskin 1662, Kramer 1664, Lazarus 1666, Martin 1671, **Mercedes-Benz 1674, Merck 1675, Merck 1677, Nabisco 1681,** Ohl 1686, Orenstein 1687, **Reeves 1694,** Rippel 1695, Schamach 1700, Schering-Plough 1701, Schultz 1704, Sutcliffe 1709, **Warner-Lambert 1723**

New York: **Ada 1733,** Allen 1742, **Allen 1743,** Allyn 1744, Alpern 1745, Altschul 1747, **American 1752,** Aron 1758, **ASDA 1760,** Badgeley 1766, Baird 1767, Banbury 1770, Bard 1773, Barnett 1775, **Beck 1780, Berlex 1788,** Bernstein 1790, **Biddle 1791,** Bingham 1793, Bluhdorn 1797, **Bobst 1799,** Bodman 1800, Bostwick 1803, Botwinick-Wolfensohn 1804, **Brain 1806, Bristol-Myers 1808, Bristol-Myers 1809, Brookdale 1812, Bugher 1818, Burnham 1819,** Carmel 1827, Chait 1834, **Cheatham 1840,** Chernow 1841, **China 1842, Clark 1850,** Coles 1855, Cummings 1869, Cummings 1871, **Dana**

1874, de Rothschild 1877, **DeCamp 1879,** Dent 1884, Diamond 1885, Dillon 1886, Donaldson 1887, Dreyfus 1892, Dreyfus 1893, **Dreyfus 1894,** Dyson 1897, **Eisner 1901, Essel 1906,** Evans 1909, Fahey 1910, Ferkauf 1914, **Fife 1916,** Foster 1923, **Frankel 1925, Freeman 1926,** Frohlich 1928, Gaisman 1931, Gebbie 1933, Geist 1934, Gerschel 1936, Gerschel 1937, Gifford 1939, **Glenn 1941,** Goldie-Anna 1942, Goldman 1944, Goode 1952, Grateful 1961, Greenberg 1963, Greenwall 1966, Gruber 1968, Hagedorn 1970, **Hansen 1972, Heineman 1984, Helmsley 1985,** Hilson 1989, Hirschl 1990, Hugoton 1997, IFF 2004, Iroquois 2006, Jacobson 2009, **Johnson 2014,** Julia 2018, Kaplan 2022, **Kaufmann 2026,** Kekst 2027, Kimmelman 2032, Klein 2035, **Klingenstein 2036,** Kohlberg 2041, Krim 2048, **Laerdal 2050,** Lang 2051, **Lasker 2056, Lasker 2057,** Lauder 2058, Leonhardt 2064, **Lighting 2070,** Link 2072, Loewenberg 2075, **Lounsbery 2077,** Lowenstein 2078, **Manning 2086, Mapplethorpe 2088, Mathers 2093, Mayer 2095,** McGonagle 2102, McGraw 2103, **Meyer 2118,** Milbank 2119, Miller 2122, Milstein 2123, **Monell 2125,** Morris 2133, **Murray 2139, North 2156,** O'Sullivan 2163, Orentreich 2168, Osborn 2169, Overbrook 2171, Palisades 2174, **Peierls 2177,** Phillips 2185, **Pomerantz 2191,** Port 2194, **Potts 2196, Raizen 2202, Ramapo 2203,** Revson 2213, Rose 2226, **Ross 2232,** Rubinstein 2234, **Sackler 2239, Saltz 2244, Sandoz 2246,** Schnurmacher 2254, Schwartz 2256, Sharp 2263, Silfen 2266, Singer 2268, Sinsheimer 2269, Slaughter 2271, Snow 2277, SO 2278, Spiritus 2283, Spitzer 2284, Spunk 2286, Stein 2292, Stony 2296, Straus 2298, Swanson 2304, **Thompson 2311,** Totman 2319, Turner 2321, '21' 2322, Vernon 2329, Wakefield 2333, Weinberg 2339, Wellington 2343, **Whitney 2348,** Wilson 2350, Winston 2353, **Winthrop 2354, Zenkel 2362, Zlinkoff 2365**

North Carolina: Burroughs 2376, **Burroughs 2377,** Lance 2403, Smith 2414, Van Every 2419

Ohio: **Armington 2436,** Case 2450, Honda 2504, Ingalls 2510, **Kettering 2515,** National 2544, O'Neill 2550, Pizzuti 2558, Prentiss 2560, Reinberger 2566, Schlink 2576, Wolfe 2610

Oklahoma: Broadhurst 2621, Merrick 2630, **Noble 2631,** Puterbaugh 2637, Rapp 2638, Scrivner 2640, Taubman 2642, Warren 2644, Warren 2645, Zarrow 2648

Oregon: Chiles 2650, Collins 2652, Wheeler 2664

Pennsylvania: Allegheny 2670, Ames 2671, **AMETEK 2672,** Annenberg 2676, Arronson 2678, Berry 2685, **Boiron 2688,** Buncher 2690, **Butz 2691, Cassett 2698,** Craig-Dalsimer 2710, Dynamet 2719, Foerderer 2726, **Glendorn 2731,** Hall 2736, Hazen 2742, **Heinz 2743,** Heinz 2746, Hooker 2752, Kline 2768, Kynett 2770, Laurel 2771, Lesher 2773, Levee 2774, Lindback 2775, **Live 2776,** Massey 2781, Millstein 2796, Mudge 2797, **Oberkotter 2799, Peterson 2805,** Polk 2811, RAF 2816, Rockwell 2820, Roth 2822, **Sharon 2828,** Smith 2831, **SmithKline 2834, Stott 2844, Strawbridge 2846,** Strawbridge 2847, **Tabas 2849,** Weisbrod 2854, **Whitaker 2857,** Widener 2858

Rhode Island: Littlefield 2878, Roddy 2884

South Carolina: Fuller 2891

Tennessee: Ansley 2910, Cole 2918, Davis 2919, Massey 2930, Potter 2933

Texas: **Alcon 2944,** Alexander 2945, Austin 2951, Blaffer 2957, Bosque 2958, Cain 2962, Cimarron 2967, Clayton 2968, Collins 2971, Cooley 2976, Cox 2978, Crump 2979, Cullen 2980, Davidson 2982, Dickson 2984, Dunn 2993, Edwards 2994, Elkins 2997, Elkins 2998, Ellwood 2999, Farish 3005, Feldman 3008, Fikes 3009, FINA 3010, Fish 3012, Florence 3013, Gulf 3022, Halsell 3027, Hamman 3028, Hankamer 3029, Harrington 3030, Hawn 3031, Herzstein 3033, Hillcrest 3034, Kayser 3043, **Kleberg 3048,** Lard 3049, Luse 3053, Mary Kay 3054, McCombs 3057, McGovern 3059, McGovern 3060, McKee 3061, McMillan 3062, McQueen 3063, Meyer 3066, Mitchell 3067,

Morrison 3071, Murfee 3073, Pennzoil 3087, Powell 3091, **RGK 3093,** Roberts 3097, San Antonio 3099, Seay 3101, Smith 3106, Smith 3107, **Smith 3108,** Stemmons 3111, Sturgis 3114, Tenneco 3118, **USAA 3125,** Vale-Asche 3126, Waggoner 3128, Walthall 3129, West 3130, West 3131, **Wills 3134,** Wolff 3135

Utah: Eccles 3147, Eccles 3148, Eccles 3149, Jones 3150, Sorenson 3153, **Thrasher 3156**

Vermont: Scott 3159

Virginia: Dalis 3173, **Fairchild 3178,** Jeffress 3186, Lafarge 3188, Lawrence 3189, **Mars 3191,** Ohrstrom 3197, **Scripps 3206,** Universal 3212

Washington: **Allen 3217,** Benaroya 3219, Bishop 3220, Hemingway 3232, Kilworth 3233, Lockwood 3235, Murdock 3237, Pemco 3242, Poncin 3244, Puget 3245, SAFECO 3247, U.S. 3256, Wilkins 3260

West Virginia: Clay 3263

Wisconsin: **Ford 3286,** Humphrey 3289, Kohl 3294, Ladish 3296, Ladish 3297, Marshall 3300, Northwestern 3308, Roddis 3319, Roehl 3320

Wyoming: Stock 3342

Medical sciences

Alabama: Andalusia 2

California: Ahmanson 57, Booth 83, Bright 88, **Confidence 112,** Connell 113, **Farber 131,** Genentech 151, Hofmann 177, Irvine 184, Montgomery 242, **National 248,** Oser 256, Sierra 302, **Simon 303,** Swift 323, Valley 341, **Varian 345**

Connecticut: **Culpeper 426, Educational 433,** Jones 457, **Perkin 479,** Pfriem 480, **Rosenthal 484, Stone 489**

Florida: Bastien 573, **Davis 590,** Fellows 600

Georgia: Arnold 685, Georgia 709

Illinois: **Fraida 844,** Geraldi-Norton 854, Kemper 874, OMRON 914, Rothschild 940

Iowa: Quad 1029

Louisiana: Azby 1068

Maine: Maine 1092

Maryland: **Hughes 1120**

Massachusetts: **Grass 1200,** Humane 1214, **Porter 1259**

Michigan: **Upjohn 1393**

Minnesota: Alworth 1408, **Bauervic 1414, Wood-Rill 1488**

Missouri: Feld 1518

New Hampshire: **Trust 1610**

New Jersey: **Engelhard 1633, Hoechst 1646,** Islami 1653, **Johnson 1657,** Kirby 1661, Merck 1676, **Vollmer 1722**

New York: Alexander 1741, **Archbold 1756,** Cummings 1869, Gebbie 1933, Gilman 1940, **Goldstein 1949, Heineman 1984, Kade 2020, Lasdon 2054, Lasker 2056, Macy 2083, Marx 2091,** McConnell 2100, McGonagle 2102, Nichols 2153, **Open 2166, PepsiCo 2179,** Price 2197, Ring 2218, Smith 2274, Sterling 2294, Wendt 2344, Winston 2353

North Carolina: **Burroughs 2377**

Ohio: Kangesser 2514, Renner 2568

Oklahoma: Bernsen 2617, Taubman 2642

Oregon: Collins 2652, Johnson 2655, **Louisiana-Pacific 2656**

Pennsylvania: Annenberg 2676, Bloch 2687, McKenna 2786, Mellon 2791, Miles 2795, **Pew 2806,** Smith 2831, **SmithKline 2834,** Whitaker 2857

South Carolina: Simpson 2900

Texas: Ellwood 2999, Morrison 3071, Owsley 3082, **Smith 3108**

Utah: Thrasher 3156

Virginia: Olsson 3198

Wisconsin: Cremer 3281

Mental health

Alabama: Dixon 11, Hill 14, McMillan 17

Arizona: Arizona 27, Morris 37

Arkansas: Arkla 46

California: **Baker 67,** Baker 68, Harden 168, Lockheed 216, Margoes 223, **National 248,** Pasadena 266, Patron 267, **Plitt 275,** Roberts 283, Sanguinetti

289, Santa Clara 291, Sierra 302, **Simon 303,** Swift 323, Zellerbach 357
Colorado: Comprecare 365, Presbyterian 389
Connecticut: Pfriem 480
Delaware: **Delmarva 512**
District of Columbia: **First 539,** Freed 542, Giant 545, Meyer 557
Florida: Banyan 572, Beveridge 574, **Frueauff 607,** Keating 625
Illinois: Bersted 792, Blowitz-Ridgeway 797, Field 840, GATX 853, Inland 868, **MacArthur 887,** Northern 911, Retirement 937, **Scholl 947,** Stern 960, **Walgreen 970**
Indiana: INB 995, Indianapolis 996, Metropolitan 1003, **Northern 1007**
Iowa: Hall 1018, Iowa 1019, Mid-Iowa 1025
Kansas: Baehr 1031
Kentucky: Courier-Journal 1055, **Long 1061**
Maryland: Nathan 1130, Pollin 1132
Massachusetts: Boston 1159, Cambridge 1164, Cummings 1176, Doehla 1181, Harrington 1202, Poitras 1257
Michigan: Consumers 1310, Dalton 1312, Kennedy 1352
Minnesota: Edwards 1437, Minnesota 1458, Otter 1468, Wasie 1484
Missouri: CPI 1508, Roblee 1559, Speas 1570, Speas 1571
New Jersey: CPC 1624, **Gulton 1642,** Hyde 1651, **Innovating 1652, Johnson 1658,** McGraw 1672, **Merck 1677**
New Mexico: Carlsbad 1728
New York: Barker 1774, Carmel 1827, Cummings 1871, **Essel 1906,** Goldman 1946, Grant 1959, Graphic 1960, Green 1962, IFF 2004, **Ittleson 2008,** Mohawk-Hudson 2124, **Monell 2125, New-Land 2150,** Orange 2167, Parshelsky 2175, Price 2197, Rhodebeck 2214, **Ritter 2219,** van Ameringen 2326, van Ameringen 2327, Wendt 2344
North Carolina: **Dalton 2381,** Volvo 2420
Ohio: Columbus 2460, Iddings 2509, Morgan 2538, Nordson 2548
Oklahoma: Taubman 2642, Zarrow 2648
Pennsylvania: **Falk 2723, Peterson 2805, Pew 2806,** Stackpole-Hall 2840, Steinman 2843, **USX 2853**
South Carolina: Colonial 2890
Tennessee: Durham 2920
Texas: Alexander 2945, Ellwood 2999, Fasken 3006, Fikes 3009, Frees 3016, Gulf 3022, Mechia 3065, Temple 3117
Utah: Eccles 3149
Virginia: **Freedom 3181,** Norfolk 3196
Washington: Ray 3246, SAFECO 3247, See 3251
Wisconsin: Lindsay 3299, McBeath 3302, **Oscar 3309**

Nursing

Alabama: Andalusia 2, Gibson 13
Arkansas: Jones 48
California: **National 248**
Colorado: Coulter 368
Connecticut: Bulkley 418, Jones 458, Pfriem 480
District of Columbia: Johnston 551
Florida: **Chatlos 583,** Fellows 600, Fort 604
Georgia: Whitehead 741
Hawaii: Zimmerman 762

Illinois: **Abbott 768,** Levie 881, Piper 922, **Scholl 947,** Washington 972
Indiana: Anderson 981, INB 995
Michigan: Gerber 1337, Royal 1374
Minnesota: Alworth 1408
Mississippi: Vicksburg 1493
New Hampshire: Foundation 1604
New Jersey: **Johnson 1657, Johnson 1658,** Snyder 1707, Sutcliffe 1709, Van Houten 1717
New York: **China 1842, Commonwealth 1860,** Diamond 1885, **Fuld 1929,** Hugoton 1997, **Macy 2083,** Penick 2178, **Pforzheimer 2183,** Rudin 2235, **Teagle 2308**
North Carolina: Burroughs 2376, Rogers 2412
Ohio: **Elisha-Bolton 2471,** Ireland 2511, Mount Vernon 2539, Murphy 2542, Schlink 2576, Schmidlapp 2577
Oregon: Collins 2652
Pennsylvania: Allegheny 2670, Fourjay 2729, **Independence 2759,** Roth 2822
South Carolina: Colonial 2890
Tennessee: Christy-Houston 2917
Texas: Abell-Hanger 2941, Clayton 2968, Franklin 3015, Frees 3016, McGovern 3059, McGovern 3060, Walthall 3129
Utah: Bamberger 3141
Wisconsin: Birnschein 3274, McBeath 3302

Ophthalmology

California: Doheny 121
Connecticut: Ziegler 502
Florida: Wollowick 682
Michigan: Royal 1374
Minnesota: St. Paul 1477
Nevada: Stearns-Blodgett 1598, Wiegand 1599
New Jersey: Merck 1676
New York: **Clark 1850,** Gaisman 1931, **MacKall 2082**
Ohio: **Heed 2502,** Kangesser 2514, Wildermuth 2608
Pennsylvania: Campbell 2694
Texas: **Alcon 2944,** Cullen 2980, Kayser 3043, **Pearle 3085**
Washington: Bishop 3220
West Virginia: Shott 3269

Pharmacy

California: Long 218, **Pfeiffer 272,** Syntex 326
Colorado: El Pomar 371
Florida: Eckerd 596
Hawaii: Zimmerman 762
Illinois: **Abbott 768, Walgreen 970**
Indiana: Hook 994, Lilly 999
Minnesota: Alworth 1408
New Jersey: **Johnson 1657,** Merck 1676, **Warner-Lambert 1723**
New York: Sterling 2294
North Carolina: Burroughs 2376, **Burroughs 2377**
Pennsylvania: West 2856

Psychiatry

Alabama: Hill 14
California: Fairfield 129, Schlinger 294, **Simon 303**
Illinois: Blowitz-Ridgeway 797, Lederer 879
Massachusetts: Harrington 1202
New York: **Essel 1906,** Grant 1959, van Ameringen 2326

North Carolina: Daniels 2383
Oklahoma: Taubman 2642
Pennsylvania: **Falk 2723,** Steinman 2843

Psychology

California: **National 248,** Swift 323
Hawaii: Scott 757
Illinois: Lederer 879
New York: Grant 1959, McConnell 2100, van Ameringen 2326
North Carolina: Daniels 2383
Pennsylvania: **Peterson 2805**

Rehabilitation

California: Fireman's 134, Herbst 172, Montgomery 242, **National 248,** Sanguinetti 289, Swift 323, Wrather 355
Colorado: Boettcher 361, Colorado 363
Connecticut: Gimbel 443, **Kaman 460,** Pfriem 480
Florida: Conn 585, Kennedy 626, Lost 634
Georgia: Georgia 710
Hawaii: McInerny 755
Illinois: **Allstate 772,** CNA 824, Coleman 825, Field 840, Galvin 852, GATX 853, Harris 862, Inland 868, Lehmann 880, **MacArthur 887, Morton 902, Nalco 904,** OMRON 914, Prince 927, Rhoades 938, **Walgreen 970**
Indiana: Indianapolis 996, Martin 1002
Kentucky: Courier-Journal 1055
Massachusetts: Boston 1158, Eaton 1183
Michigan: Fremont 1331, Pagel 1368
Minnesota: **Minnesota 1459,** Ordean 1467
Missouri: Hallmark 1526, Hallmark 1527, Ilgenfritz 1529, Long 1541, Speas 1570
New Jersey: Petrie 1689, Victoria 1719
New York: Albany's 1740, Barker 1774, Bodman 1800, Charina 1835, Cummings 1871, **Fish 1918,** Goldsmith 1948, Graphic 1960, **JM 2011,** Mohawk-Hudson 2124, Moses 2135, **Pfizer 2182, Potts 2196,** Price 2197, Rosenstiel 2229, **Ross 2232**
Ohio: **Mead 2531,** Musson 2543, Sterkel 2592
Pennsylvania: Allegheny 2669, Allegheny 2670, Gibson 2730, Hulme 2757, Rosenberg 2821, **Union 2851,** Union 2852, **USX 2853**
Texas: Austin 2951, Constantin 2975, Davis 2983, **Exxon 3002,** Fasken 3006, Haas 3024, Hillcrest 3034, Hoblitzelle 3036, McGovern 3059, McGovern 3060, McKee 3061, Roberts 3096, Straus 3113, Temple 3117, Vale-Asche 3126, White 3132
Utah: Dee 3145, Eccles 3149
Virginia: Norfolk 3196
Washington: Boeing 3222, Foundation 3228
Wisconsin: Lindsay 3299

Schistosomiasis

New York: **Clark 1850**

Speech pathology

Kentucky: Courier-Journal 1055
Minnesota: Eddy 1436
Missouri: Shoenberg 1564
Oklahoma: Johnson 2625

INDEX TO GRANTS BY SUBJECT

For each subject term, grants are listed first by foundation entry number, then by grant number within the foundation entry. For a general subject index to the purposes and activities of the grantmakers in this volume, see the Index to Foundations and Corporate Giving Programs by Subject.

NATIONAL GUIDE TO FUNDING IN HEALTH

302-6, 302-11, 302-18, 316-3, 321-7, 321-14,
406-18, 557-12, 561-1, 561-26, 561-28, 709-7,
1153-8, 1160-4, 1173-15, 1216-14, 1249-4,
1265-2, 1280-1, 1420-7, 1658-6, 1658-9, 1658-33,
1658-81, 1658-87, 1658-124, 1658-126,
1658-130, 1658-137, 1658-148, 1658-173,
1658-177, 1658-215, 1658-237, 1658-238,
1658-293, 1658-295, 1684-7, 1746-12, 1746-27,
1750-6, 1762-8, 1800-2, 1879-14, 1885-37,
1885-64, 1922-13, 2011-14, 2023-2, 2076-1,
2146-19, 2146-35, 2146-72, 2171-5, 2235-27,
2316-4, 2497-31, 2806-67, 3250-15, 3282-7
Drug/alcohol abusers, health—specific diseases 18-1,
142-1, 194-42, 253-15, 290-11, 302-3, 316-3,
336-3, 406-18, 406-32, 455-4, 535-16, 561-1,
561-28, 772-2, 893-27, 1160-2, 1216-14, 1339-2,
1343-6, 1399-2, 1497-1, 1497-2, 1552-3, 1633-13,
1661-34, 1684-7, 1713-10, 1713-11, 1719-4,
1750-6, 1762-8, 1801-2, 1885-37, 1885-48,
1885-71, 1922-13, 1973-6, 2011-5, 2011-14,
2023-2, 2076-1, 2093-39, 2115-6, 2125-14,
2125-20, 2146-35, 2146-81, 2171-5, 2223-1,
2223-3, 2285-1, 2316-4, 2326-7, 2344-1, 2410-2,
2447-2, 2456-3, 2809-11, 2857-1, 3037-15
Drug/alcohol abusers, housing/shelter 455-4, 1265-4,
1981-23
Drug/alcohol abusers, human services—multipurpose
321-7, 321-8, 321-14, 357-4, 357-8, 361-10,
455-4, 511-4, 535-16, 1095-2, 1173-15, 1218-4,
1280-1, 1332-11, 1340-12, 1420-7, 1421-9,
1746-27, 1778-5, 1800-2, 1800-10, 1800-14,
1815-6, 1870-28, 1980-2, 1980-36, 2011-16,
2146-72, 2223-1, 2236-16, 2411-8, 2411-10,
2424-12, 2447-2, 2547-4, 2660-19, 2725-7,
2806-67, 2823-11, 3282-7
Drug/alcohol abusers, medical research 321-25,
709-7, 1441-20, 1447-12, 1691-33, 1885-61,
1885-76, 1885-91, 2249-6, 3250-15, 3302-3
Drug/alcohol abusers, mental health/substance abuse
18-1, 57-1, 57-7, 57-22, 96-2, 123-9, 123-12,
123-22, 142-3, 163-1, 163-9, 164-3, 183-33,
190-7, 191-5, 194-40, 202-2, 224-13, 224-14,
257-2, 257-5, 262-30, 287-11, 288-12, 288-19,
290-11, 290-12, 302-3, 302-6, 302-11, 336-3,
336-4, 348-7, 348-9, 348-11, 351-6, 357-4, 357-8,
361-5, 361-10, 369-1, 372-2, 406-33, 444-4,
444-7, 446-4, 448-13, 455-4, 455-6, 470-6, 500-7,
510-2, 511-4, 535-26, 535-32, 535-35, 541-1,
556-22, 557-3, 557-13, 561-8, 561-26, 561-28,
561-33, 594-10, 629-6, 629-8, 629-9, 629-10,
629-11, 686-7, 690-6, 690-8, 709-7, 737-5, 746-1,
746-2, 749-3, 750-1, 752-1, 755-1, 755-2, 755-3,
755-4, 755-5, 759-1, 772-2, 772-6, 820-15,
820-16, 820-19, 848-7, 848-11, 891-5, 891-6,
893-18, 893-27, 937-33, 947-23, 947-48, 977-2,
977-6, 988-9, 989-1, 989-4, 990-1, 996-7, 996-8,
1038-1, 1095-2, 1105-9, 1153-3, 1158-6, 1158-24,
1160-2, 1218-4, 1218-5, 1218-9, 1218-12, 1249-2,
1309-14, 1323-2, 1332-1, 1332-11, 1336-5,
1339-2, 1351-162, 1353-3, 1358-6, 1380-19,
1381-12, 1384-7, 1384-8, 1389-6, 1410-3, 1411-5,
1417-6, 1417-11, 1418-5, 1420-2, 1420-3, 1420-7,
1420-8, 1420-10, 1420-11, 1420-14, 1421-9,
1421-10, 1421-14, 1421-17, 1421-20, 1421-27,
1424-2, 1426-4, 1441-4, 1441-20, 1447-3, 1447-8,
1447-12, 1452-2, 1452-5, 1457-2, 1459-3,
1475-11, 1475-12, 1475-15, 1475-17, 1497-12,
1533-5, 1533-6, 1552-2, 1552-3, 1552-4, 1599-2,
1616-1, 1616-3, 1630-9, 1651-2, 1658-6, 1658-9,
1658-17, 1658-33, 1658-81, 1658-87, 1658-124,
1658-126, 1658-130, 1658-137, 1658-148,
1658-173, 1658-177, 1658-189, 1658-215,
1658-237, 1658-238, 1658-293, 1658-295,
1661-26, 1661-28, 1713-3, 1713-7, 1713-10,
1719-2, 1719-8, 1729-2, 1732-3, 1746-8, 1746-28,
1750-16, 1778-5, 1800-2, 1800-9, 1800-10,
1815-5, 1815-6, 1823-12, 1826-4, 1829-6,
1849-13, 1849-14, 1850-21, 1860-10, 1870-28,
1870-30, 1870-33, 1885-5, 1885-10, 1885-11,
1885-16, 1885-48, 1885-64, 1885-70, 1885-71,
1885-77, 1885-91, 1922-13, 1922-26, 1922-61,
1933-2, 1959-14, 1978-2, 1978-4, 1978-5, 1978-6,
1980-2, 1980-21, 1980-31, 1980-35, 1980-36,

1981-23, 1981-44, 1982-2, 2011-5, 2011-8,
2011-14, 2011-16, 2011-17, 2011-21, 2011-22,
2052-28, 2093-39, 2113-2, 2115-16, 2117-3,
2117-7, 2117-8, 2117-9, 2117-11, 2117-12,
2117-15, 2117-16, 2117-18, 2117-25, 2117-28,
2117-29, 2117-30, 2117-31, 2117-32, 2146-12,
2146-19, 2146-26, 2146-62, 2146-72, 2147-4,
2214-3, 2223-1, 2224-28, 2224-116, 2224-139,
2234-12, 2235-27, 2236-15, 2236-44, 2245-19,
2288-27, 2288-30, 2326-7, 2344-1, 2347-1,
2373-7, 2410-1, 2410-2, 2410-7, 2410-14,
2410-15, 2410-30, 2410-35, 2410-67, 2410-74,
2411-8, 2411-10, 2424-1, 2424-11, 2424-12,
2430-4, 2449-5, 2456-3, 2456-5, 2457-24,
2457-25, 2460-3, 2460-13, 2497-31, 2545-4,
2547-5, 2552-3, 2615-1, 2627-3, 2631-9, 2636-1,
2639-4, 2651-1, 2660-19, 2668-9, 2668-25,
2675-12, 2683-16, 2696-2, 2720-1, 2720-9,
2722-1, 2722-4, 2725-7, 2743-11, 2743-22,
2744-6, 2749-4, 2762-9, 2784-6, 2791-2, 2791-4,
2791-8, 2803-1, 2809-6, 2810-2, 2812-5, 2823-1,
2823-3, 2823-5, 2823-9, 2823-11, 2824-2, 2826-3,
2826-10, 2852-11, 2853-4, 2853-5, 2857-1,
2868-8, 2868-18, 2868-24, 2882-21, 2882-27,
2882-28, 2941-14, 2941-15, 2948-10, 2961-2,
2965-3, 2965-11, 2974-1, 2975-2, 2975-4, 2975-6,
3005-21, 3014-3, 3034-3, 3034-6, 3034-18,
3036-4, 3036-5, 3037-15, 3037-30, 3046-3,
3064-18, 3078-1, 3094-11, 3115-5, 3194-15,
3194-22, 3194-24, 3224-4, 3224-8, 3302-3,
3306-1, 3306-7, 3306-11
Drug/alcohol abusers, public affairs/government
348-11, 886-1
Drug/alcohol abusers, recreation/sports/athletics
191-5, 1332-1, 1351-162, 2430-4, 2651-1
Drug/alcohol abusers, religion 224-13, 535-16,
2011-17
Drug/alcohol abusers, social sciences 321-25, 937-33,
1038-2, 2011-16, 2224-116, 2224-139
Drug/alcohol abusers, youth development 2011-8,
2011-22
Ear & throat disease 2077-6
Ear & throat disease, deaf 389-3, 2683-14
Ear & throat disease, economically disadvantaged
57-24
Ear & throat disease, equipment 57-24
Ear & throat disease, faculty/staff development 2683-14
Ear & throat disease, fellowships 389-3
Ear & throat research 2799-13
Ear & throat research, aging 937-28
Ear & throat research, building/renovation 3048-5
Ear & throat research, children & youth 3005-15,
3048-4
Ear & throat research, computer systems/equipment
1599-5
Ear & throat research, deaf 57-20, 121-2, 237-21,
265-3, 281-3, 318-3, 937-28, 1038-3, 1596-8,
1599-5, 1599-6, 1611-6, 1973-3, 1980-14, 2125-6,
2134-4, 2377-13, 2799-7, 2993-2, 3005-15,
3048-4, 3148-4
Ear & throat research, endowments 1980-14
Ear & throat research, equipment 1599-6
Ear & throat research, fellowships 1980-14, 2377-13,
3037-35
Eastern Europe, education 1657-31
Eastern Europe, health—general 1922-73, 1922-105
Eastern Europe, international affairs/development
2106-5
Eastern Europe, social sciences 2106-5
Eating disorders 213-2
Eating disorders, children & youth 1622-7
Eating disorders, Native Americans 1622-7
Eating disorders, seed money 96-16
Eating disorders, women 96-16
Economic development 1922-37
Economic development, blacks 1351-128
Economic development, children & youth 1351-121,
2683-10
Economic development, curriculum development
1363-10, 2273-2
Economic development, economically disadvantaged
1363-10, 1922-72, 2224-114, 2683-10
Economic development, fellowships 1351-66, 1351-67

Economic development, men 1351-128
Economic development, minorities 1363-10, 2224-114
Economic development, People with AIDS (PWA)
887-30
Economic development, research 288-73, 887-34,
2224-114, 2273-2, 2683-10
Economic development, rural areas 887-34, 1351-66,
1351-67, 1351-118, 1351-121, 1922-72
Economic development, seed money 288-72, 1363-10
Economic development, technical aid 887-30, 1095-1
Economic development, urban/community
development 887-30, 1095-1, 1363-10, 2224-114
Economic development, women 887-30, 887-34,
1363-10, 1922-72, 1922-94, 2683-10
Economic development, youth 1351-118
Economically disadvantaged, arts/culture/humanities
1462-1, 1897-1, 1922-27, 2146-84, 2224-123
Economically disadvantaged, civil rights 937-15,
1447-16, 1462-1, 1922-2
Economically disadvantaged, community
improvement/development 887-33, 1363-10,
1457-12, 1922-72, 2224-114, 2224-116, 2234-7,
2683-10
Economically disadvantaged, crime/courts/legal
services 194-44, 288-2, 288-10, 321-30, 937-26,
1363-14, 1421-11, 1719-5, 1801-2, 1885-60,
2115-11, 2146-16, 2146-56, 2146-57, 2224-139,
2657-11
Economically disadvantaged, education 194-1, 194-7,
194-8, 194-24, 194-27, 194-61, 194-75, 264-1,
288-17, 302-5, 302-12, 321-30, 561-89, 848-14,
848-19, 1158-21, 1160-7, 1173-16, 1332-6,
1351-30, 1351-37, 1351-225, 1363-3, 1363-14,
1363-15, 1363-25, 1421-1, 1447-5, 1447-6,
1447-16, 1467-2, 1467-4, 1622-12, 1713-17,
1885-38, 1885-78, 1885-79, 1959-10, 2236-24,
2368-3, 2377-29, 2657-10, 2806-101, 2806-117,
3069-8
Economically disadvantaged, employment 887-33,
1158-21, 1158-30, 1295-3, 1363-5, 1363-10,
1363-25, 1851-4, 2224-114, 2368-3, 2657-10
Economically disadvantaged, environment 288-20,
561-12, 561-15, 561-37, 561-113, 3187-2
Economically disadvantaged, food/nutrition/agriculture
194-1, 194-8, 194-26, 264-16, 288-32, 557-11,
561-12, 561-119, 1160-7, 1173-16, 1658-69,
1691-6, 1980-38, 2213-1, 2368-2, 2410-73,
2840-1, 3156-3, 3156-4, 3156-5, 3156-6
Economically disadvantaged, health—general 57-24,
57-31, 96-4, 96-6, 96-9, 96-14, 96-15, 183-5,
183-6, 183-7, 183-8, 183-9, 183-10, 183-11,
183-14, 183-15, 183-16, 183-18, 183-19, 183-20,
183-22, 183-29, 183-30, 183-31, 183-32, 183-33,
183-35, 183-36, 183-38, 183-39, 183-43, 183-44,
183-46, 183-47, 183-48, 183-49, 183-50, 183-52,
191-3, 194-1, 194-3, 194-4, 194-6, 194-7, 194-8,
194-9, 194-14, 194-17, 194-18, 194-20, 194-22,
194-24, 194-26, 194-36, 194-42, 194-44, 194-45,
194-46, 194-53, 194-61, 194-62, 194-66, 194-68,
194-70, 194-73, 194-74, 224-7, 224-15, 237-12,
237-13, 237-29, 237-41, 253-5, 253-20, 262-10,
262-18, 262-19, 262-35, 262-45, 262-50, 262-56,
264-1, 264-4, 264-11, 264-18, 264-19, 287-30,
288-4, 288-17, 288-20, 288-28, 288-30, 288-31,
288-37, 288-41, 288-43, 288-44, 288-46, 288-52,
288-60, 288-62, 288-65, 288-79, 292-1, 302-1,
302-2, 302-4, 302-5, 302-6, 302-8, 302-9, 302-10,
302-11, 302-12, 302-13, 302-15, 302-16, 302-17,
302-18, 302-19, 316-17, 318-5, 318-12, 321-14,
321-29, 321-30, 348-18, 364-15, 364-18, 364-27,
364-29, 364-41, 371-2, 389-10, 406-8, 425-2,
440-2, 444-18, 448-3, 448-4, 455-3, 491-11,
535-9, 535-24, 535-25, 535-36, 535-38, 548-7,
548-8, 557-6, 557-11, 557-19, 561-12, 561-15,
561-18, 561-20, 561-21, 561-31, 561-37,
561-51, 561-54, 561-64, 561-70, 561-72, 561-85,
561-89, 561-91, 561-108, 561-113, 561-119,
583-26, 594-4, 629-5, 629-19, 709-3, 743-4,
755-6, 787-4, 820-7, 840-1, 848-8, 848-9, 848-14,
848-15, 848-19, 848-23, 887-21, 887-33, 891-4,
911-1, 937-5, 937-12, 937-15, 937-26, 947-18,
1095-4, 1106-1, 1106-5, 1106-11, 1106-15,
1106-17, 1106-20, 1158-21, 1158-28, 1160-7,

1173-7, 1173-18, 1332-5, 1332-9, 1340-10,
1343-16, 1351-9, 1351-29, 1351-30, 1351-35,
1351-37, 1351-41, 1351-53, 1351-62, 1351-70,
1351-79, 1351-116, 1351-148, 1351-175,
1351-190, 1351-217, 1351-225, 1358-10, 1363-6,
1363-8, 1363-10, 1363-15, 1363-25, 1380-7,
1380-16, 1380-21, 1380-27, 1381-7, 1384-10,
1417-4, 1417-8, 1420-7, 1421-3, 1421-12, 1441-5,
1441-15, 1441-16, 1447-1, 1447-9, 1447-16,
1457-3, 1462-1, 1462-3, 1462-5, 1467-2, 1467-3,
1467-5, 1475-22, 1475-27, 1552-1, 1616-4,
1657-5, 1658-8, 1658-48, 1658-69, 1658-91,
1658-133, 1658-155, 1658-249, 1658-305,
1684-4, 1684-6, 1691-6, 1691-29, 1691-31,
1691-32, 1732-4, 1800-12, 1809-40, 1823-9,
1829-42, 1838-4, 1850-18, 1851-1, 1851-8,
1870-2, 1870-7, 1870-9, 1870-11, 1870-13,
1870-14, 1870-15, 1870-17, 1870-18, 1870-23,
1885-13, 1885-17, 1885-42, 1885-78, 1885-79,
1897-1, 1922-1, 1922-2, 1922-4, 1922-6, 1922-7,
1922-9, 1922-11, 1922-17, 1922-22, 1922-23,
1922-27, 1922-34, 1922-35, 1922-41, 1922-43,
1922-44, 1922-55, 1922-60, 1922-67, 1922-79,
1922-81, 1922-85, 1922-98, 1922-103, 1959-4,
1959-16, 1959-18, 1959-34, 1980-8, 1980-10,
1980-46, 1981-18, 1981-37, 2000-3, 2011-3,
2146-17, 2146-20, 2146-24, 2146-60, 2146-84,
2154-4, 2212-1, 2213-1, 2224-114, 2234-3,
2234-7, 2234-9, 2234-14, 2302-2, 2368-2, 2368-3,
2386-3, 2386-5, 2386-7, 2386-8, 2386-12,
2386-13, 2386-15, 2386-21, 2386-22, 2386-23,
2386-24, 2386-27, 2386-33, 2386-36, 2386-40,
2386-42, 2386-43, 2386-45, 2386-47, 2386-51,
2386-58, 2386-65, 2386-67, 2386-69, 2386-70,
2386-72, 2386-74, 2386-76, 2386-77, 2386-79,
2386-82, 2386-83, 2386-84, 2386-86, 2386-90,
2386-91, 2386-94, 2386-96, 2386-100, 2386-104,
2386-106, 2386-108, 2386-111, 2386-113,
2386-115, 2386-116, 2386-117, 2386-118,
2386-119, 2386-120, 2386-121, 2386-125,
2386-128, 2386-130, 2386-131, 2386-134,
2386-135, 2386-136, 2386-137, 2386-138,
2386-140, 2386-141, 2386-143, 2386-146,
2386-149, 2386-151, 2386-154, 2386-155,
2386-156, 2386-159, 2386-160, 2386-164,
2386-166, 2386-167, 2386-170, 2386-171,
2386-173, 2386-174, 2386-175, 2386-177,
2410-5, 2410-10, 2410-12, 2410-29, 2410-31,
2410-39, 2410-48, 2410-61, 2410-71, 2410-73,
2424-4, 2447-7, 2457-13, 2457-19, 2460-1,
2460-9, 2460-16, 2490-10, 2497-29, 2516-1,
2603-11, 2627-1, 2639-2, 2651-4, 2651-5, 2657-3,
2660-10, 2660-11, 2683-10, 2683-11, 2683-12,
2683-17, 2701-4, 2701-5, 2722-6, 2744-7, 2744-8,
2744-11, 2744-14, 2744-15, 2744-16, 2806-4,
2806-33, 2806-38, 2806-51, 2806-117, 2806-129,
2806-130, 2806-132, 2831-2, 2831-5, 2831-8,
2831-9, 2831-15, 2831-23, 2831-26, 2899-2,
2925-11, 2932-4, 2996-1, 2996-4, 2996-12,
3005-5, 3034-7, 3034-15, 3034-20, 3064-16,
3094-8, 3099-6, 3115-9, 3156-3, 3156-4, 3156-5,
3156-6, 3187-2, 3224-3, 3224-5, 3302-5, 3302-11,
3306-9, 3306-14, 3306-16, 3306-17
Economically disadvantaged, health—specific diseases
57-24, 123-38, 194-42, 224-7, 288-5, 288-11,
288-17, 288-30, 288-31, 288-44, 288-47, 288-52,
288-79, 369-9, 561-9, 561-72, 583-5, 594-1,
709-4, 740-5, 1158-30, 1684-4, 1684-6, 1719-4,
1801-2, 1823-9, 1851-8, 1885-60, 1897-3,
1980-19, 1980-38, 2000-3, 2115-11, 2146-8,
2146-16, 2146-17, 2146-20, 2146-24, 2146-36,
2146-56, 2146-57, 2146-64, 2234-9, 2236-41,
2386-136, 2410-10, 2410-27, 2410-71, 2760-1,
2806-1, 2806-4, 3306-14
Economically disadvantaged, housing/shelter 194-23,
389-10, 561-67, 1380-21, 1457-12, 2146-2,
2146-36, 2791-18, 2840-1
Economically disadvantaged, human
services—multipurpose 191-3, 194-9, 194-23,
194-62, 194-74, 288-5, 288-10, 288-30, 288-60,
302-1, 321-2, 321-14, 535-9, 557-11, 561-54,
561-67, 561-70, 561-72, 561-89, 737-8, 848-23,
1158-30, 1332-6, 1351-23, 1351-41, 1351-53,

1351-217, 1351-225, 1363-8, 1363-14, 1363-15,
1363-22, 1380-7, 1420-3, 1441-15, 1447-1,
1447-2, 1454-4, 1457-12, 1462-4, 1467-5,
1475-27, 1658-48, 1658-69, 1691-32, 1719-5,
1746-1, 1850-2, 1851-4, 1897-3, 1922-39,
1922-40, 1922-63, 1922-71, 1922-77, 1922-101,
1946-19, 1959-10, 1959-16, 1980-19, 2011-3,
2146-60, 2146-83, 2213-1, 2236-41, 2326-8,
2410-31, 2410-39, 2460-9, 2490-10, 2657-11,
2683-10, 2683-17, 2791-18, 2806-1, 2806-22,
2806-33, 2806-131, 2806-132, 3064-19, 3094-8,
3098-18, 3099-2, 3302-11
Economically disadvantaged, international
affairs/development 561-85, 1002-2, 1380-27
Economically disadvantaged, medical research 96-15,
194-70, 1981-2, 2386-136, 3156-1, 3156-3,
3156-4, 3156-5, 3156-6
Economically disadvantaged, mental health/substance
abuse 123-22, 164-3, 183-33, 194-23, 194-68,
194-75, 208-4, 288-10, 288-13, 288-17, 302-6,
302-11, 321-2, 535-23, 737-8, 820-19, 1351-23,
1363-5, 1363-14, 1420-3, 1420-7, 1421-11,
1447-5, 1454-4, 1457-12, 1651-19, 1658-48,
1719-5, 1719-8, 1746-28, 1870-18, 1946-19,
2146-2, 2224-116, 2224-123, 2224-139, 2326-6,
2326-8, 2326-10, 2386-107, 2460-8, 2460-10,
2657-11, 2744-6, 2791-18, 3005-9, 3014-3,
3034-6, 3069-8, 3099-2, 3275-7, 3306-1
Economically disadvantaged, philanthropy/voluntarism
1850-2
Economically disadvantaged, public affairs/government
262-19, 1343-16, 1462-5, 1851-4, 2213-1
Economically disadvantaged, recreation/sports/athletics
208-4
Economically disadvantaged, religion 288-5
Economically disadvantaged, social sciences 194-17,
262-35, 937-12, 1173-16, 1922-1, 1922-22,
1922-34, 1959-10, 1959-18, 1959-34, 2224-116,
2224-139
Economically disadvantaged, youth development
183-16, 302-15, 1363-5, 1363-25
Economics & finance 1676-67, 1676-68
Economics & finance, children & youth 1829-22,
1959-9
Economics & finance, curriculum development 2273-2
Economics & finance, drug/alcohol abusers 1038-2
Economics & finance, girls & young women 2224-108
Economics & finance, research 1038-2, 1658-68,
1829-22, 1959-9, 2224-108, 2224-165, 2273-2
Ecuador, education 1351-19, 1351-132
Ecuador, environment 2224-76
Ecuador, food/nutrition/agriculture 2224-76
Ecuador, health—general 262-13, 262-58, 1351-19,
1351-132, 2224-76
Ecuador, international affairs/development 2224-76
Education 1351-14, 1351-15, 1418-4, 2146-3
Education, adult 1158-21, 1922-94
Education, adult—literacy & basic skills 96-2, 1433-7,
1829-47, 2657-10
Education, Africa 1829-1
Education, aging 288-17, 937-39, 1363-25, 1630-23
Education, Argentina 1351-133, 1351-134, 1351-153,
1351-173
Education, association 1676-10, 1676-11
Education, blacks 1351-119, 1351-149, 1630-15,
2411-12
Education, Botswana 1351-100, 1351-186
Education, boys & young men 1389-10, 1897-7,
1980-26, 2490-1
Education, Brazil 561-6, 1351-28, 1351-42, 1351-44,
1351-45, 1351-46, 1351-47, 1351-48, 1351-49,
1351-55, 1351-73, 1351-141, 1351-147,
1351-203, 1351-204, 1351-205
Education, building/renovation 57-26, 197-2, 232-3,
262-36, 367-2, 696-9, 737-4, 740-13, 1353-24,
1421-7, 1800-5, 1978-4, 1978-8, 1978-11,
1980-26, 1980-32, 2631-10, 3037-38, 3064-15
Education, Canada 1630-4, 1860-12, 1860-37,
1929-93, 1929-124, 1929-130, 2224-96
Education, capital campaigns 715-5, 1800-4, 1800-5,
2199-6
Education, Caribbean 2806-8
Education, Central America 1351-24, 2806-8

Education, child development 191-2, 1510-1, 1823-8,
2882-26
Education, children & youth 57-23, 57-26, 57-27,
70-3, 96-7, 123-17, 123-20, 191-2, 194-1, 194-8,
194-24, 194-61, 194-75, 197-2, 208-5, 224-10,
232-3, 232-4, 237-15, 237-19, 262-42, 264-1,
264-12, 288-54, 318-2, 321-1, 321-5, 321-9,
321-12, 321-19, 321-31, 361-12, 364-13, 364-14,
367-2, 369-11, 373-5, 448-9, 448-11, 491-6,
491-14, 535-7, 535-27, 535-31, 557-4, 557-15,
561-6, 594-3, 629-14, 696-9, 715-5, 737-4,
740-13, 848-13, 989-3, 1173-5, 1173-8, 1332-3,
1332-6, 1351-17, 1351-58, 1351-81, 1351-140,
1351-225, 1353-24, 1363-15, 1420-9, 1421-1,
1441-1, 1447-5, 1447-6, 1510-1, 1510-2, 1533-1,
1569-2, 1630-15, 1630-16, 1630-17, 1630-24,
1658-189, 1658-203, 1658-206, 1673-4, 1673-5,
1713-5, 1713-15, 1713-17, 1750-17, 1800-4,
1800-7, 1800-16, 1823-8, 1823-16, 1829-7,
1870-19, 1885-12, 1885-40, 1885-45, 1885-52,
1922-45, 1959-25, 1978-5, 1978-11, 1980-32,
2000-2, 2011-22, 2146-1, 2146-4, 2224-185,
2236-24, 2236-48, 2245-5, 2245-8, 2288-16,
2288-25, 2368-4, 2368-6, 2457-2, 2460-3,
2460-15, 2675-3, 2675-11, 2677-6, 2809-8,
2882-16, 2882-26, 2959-6, 2965-8, 3014-4,
3064-15, 3069-8, 3094-4, 3115-2, 3224-2, 3292-6
Education, Chile 1351-7, 1351-55, 1922-20
Education, China 1351-171, 1351-172, 1842-2,
1842-3, 1842-4, 1842-6, 1842-7, 1842-9, 1842-10,
1842-11, 1842-12, 1842-13, 1842-14, 1842-15,
1842-16, 1842-18, 1842-19, 1842-20, 1842-21,
1842-22
Education, Colombia 1351-129, 1351-130, 1351-181
Education, community/cooperative 1351-61
Education, computer systems/equipment 594-3, 2902-2
Education, conferences/seminars 232-2, 321-19,
1363-4, 1363-14, 1885-45, 1885-53, 2411-12,
2631-11
Education, continuing 1630-23
Education, Costa Rica 1351-24, 1351-180
Education, crime/abuse victims 535-17, 535-27,
1630-23
Education, curriculum development 321-13, 364-4,
491-6, 848-13, 1351-17, 1630-17, 1870-19
Education, deaf 686-2, 740-6, 2631-10, 2902-2
Education, developing countries 440-3, 1316-2,
1657-32, 1829-16, 1885-30, 2224-47, 2224-96
Education, disabled 1421-1, 2199-6
Education, drug/alcohol abusers 96-2, 1280-7, 1447-3,
1658-189, 1978-4, 1978-5, 2011-8, 2011-22,
2460-3
Education, early childhood 194-61, 364-13, 364-14,
491-14, 535-27, 1332-6, 1351-81, 1351-225,
1447-5, 1447-6, 1630-17, 1713-15, 1885-12,
1885-40, 2245-5, 2368-4, 2368-6, 2460-15
Education, Eastern Europe 1657-31
Education, economically disadvantaged 194-1, 194-8,
194-24, 194-27, 194-61, 194-75, 264-1, 288-17,
561-89, 1158-21, 1332-6, 1351-225, 1363-5,
1363-14, 1363-15, 1363-25, 1421-1, 1447-5,
1447-6, 1713-17, 2236-24, 2657-10, 3069-8
Education, Ecuador 1351-19, 1351-132
Education, Egypt 440-3
Education, elementary/secondary 57-23, 96-7, 123-20,
191-4, 194-1, 194-8, 194-13, 194-24, 194-75,
208-5, 224-10, 232-2, 237-19, 262-42, 264-1,
288-54, 304-6, 318-2, 321-1, 321-5, 321-12,
321-13, 321-18, 321-19, 321-26, 361-12, 364-4,
364-11, 364-12, 369-11, 373-5, 448-9, 491-6,
535-7, 535-31, 548-3, 557-4, 557-15, 561-6,
696-3, 848-13, 911-2, 947-68, 1173-5, 1216-20,
1351-17, 1351-58, 1380-13, 1380-14, 1420-9,
1421-1, 1447-3, 1510-1, 1510-3, 1510-4, 1533-1,
1630-15, 1630-16, 1630-24, 1658-203, 1658-206,
1673-4, 1684-17, 1800-7, 1800-16, 1823-18,
1829-7, 1870-19, 1885-45, 1885-52, 1885-53,
1922-45, 1978-5, 2000-2, 2000-6, 2011-6, 2011-8,
2011-22, 2117-4, 2146-1, 2146-4, 2146-50,
2146-67, 2146-101, 2236-24, 2236-48, 2288-1,
2411-11, 2457-2, 2460-3, 2657-1, 2809-8, 2959-6,
2965-8, 3014-4, 3069-8, 3094-4, 3115-2
Education, emergency funds 224-1

NATIONAL GUIDE TO FUNDING IN HEALTH

2386-128, 2386-130, 2386-131, 2386-134,
2386-135, 2386-136, 2386-137, 2386-138,
2386-140, 2386-141, 2386-143, 2386-146,
2386-149, 2386-151, 2386-155, 2386-159,
2386-160, 2386-164, 2386-166, 2386-167,
2386-171, 2386-173, 2386-174, 2386-175,
2386-177, 2410-31, 2490-10, 2831-5, 2831-8,
2831-9, 2831-15, 2831-23, 2831-26, 3302-11
Hospital (general), endowments 106-2, 336-1, 947-24,
1173-10, 1661-32, 1732-5, 1746-4, 1746-21,
1800-13, 1981-12, 2606-2, 2720-17, 2784-10,
3045-3
Hospital (general), equipment 57-39, 80-3, 192-2,
290-4, 290-8, 290-10, 313-2, 313-3, 313-4, 361-4,
371-5, 371-12, 583-12, 607-3, 607-8, 607-17,
607-18, 750-2, 840-4, 947-61, 947-62, 1160-3,
1331-3, 1343-12, 1343-23, 1401-2, 1599-3,
1599-4, 1599-7, 1599-8, 1599-9, 1599-10,
1599-11, 1599-12, 1599-13, 1599-14, 1599-16,
1599-17, 1616-5, 1651-8, 1651-13, 1695-4,
1695-10, 1695-12, 1817-7, 1946-8, 1980-47,
2199-12, 2199-13, 2236-43, 2245-2, 2288-15,
2378-9, 2386-17, 2386-18, 2386-48, 2386-50,
2386-66, 2386-68, 2386-73, 2386-88, 2386-89,
2386-126, 2386-132, 2386-136, 2386-139,
2386-172, 2410-31, 2410-65, 2490-9, 2560-14,
2627-7, 2627-13, 2639-5, 2651-8, 2657-9,
2720-13, 2784-1, 2852-15, 2852-16, 2852-18,
2868-2, 2868-4, 2868-7, 2868-10, 2868-14,
2868-15, 2868-22, 2868-25, 3048-20, 3094-10,
3130-2, 3224-13, 3237-9
Hospital (general), faculty/staff development 2011-12,
2725-6
Hospital (general), fellowships 787-10, 1799-3, 3045-1
Hospital (general), film/video/radio 590-5
Hospital (general), FL 556-24, 587-3, 587-10, 589-5,
620-7, 620-8, 631-10, 635-2, 988-5, 1731-4,
1882-18, 1882-19, 2125-8, 2134-14, 2668-13,
2762-8, 2806-94
Hospital (general), GA 686-8, 688-2, 688-4, 740-1,
1657-16, 2893-3
Hospital (general), HI 444-11, 749-2, 749-4
Hospital (general), homeless 629-23, 2212-1, 2236-6
Hospital (general), IA 1658-259
Hospital (general), IL 556-13, 772-3, 772-7, 772-8,
772-26, 787-5, 828-6, 828-7, 828-11, 828-12,
834-2, 867-4, 893-7, 893-12, 893-20, 927-2,
927-5, 927-10, 927-11, 927-12, 939-4,
939-5, 939-7, 939-8, 947-45, 1057-6, 1657-8,
1658-143, 1762-22, 1860-34, 1882-1, 1882-26,
1882-27, 1882-28, 1882-29, 1882-30, 3104-27
Hospital (general), immigrants/refugees 787-1
Hospital (general), IN 981-8, 988-4, 988-7, 988-8,
999-7, 999-14, 1658-58
Hospital (general), KS 631-16, 2309-18
Hospital (general), KY 1049-5
Hospital (general), LA 556-26
Hospital (general), land acquisition 3014-11
Hospital (general), Lebanon 440-1, 1799-2
Hospital (general), MA 194-56, 444-8, 444-9, 444-14,
444-15, 556-11, 1153-9, 1153-11, 1153-12,
1153-13, 1179-1, 1179-2, 1179-4, 1179-7, 1193-3,
1249-1, 1249-7, 1249-11, 1249-12, 1273-7,
1288-4, 1615-3, 1633-1, 1633-7, 1633-9, 1633-12,
1633-15, 1658-30, 1658-233, 1676-28, 1702-8,
1809-27, 1809-35, 1860-6, 1860-7, 1874-4,
1874-5, 1874-6, 1874-12, 1874-13, 1874-14,
1874-15, 1874-16, 1874-17, 1874-18, 1874-19,
1874-20, 1874-21, 1874-22, 1874-23, 1874-33,
1948-26, 1948-29, 1986-5, 2146-63, 2171-2,
2171-7, 2212-3
Hospital (general), MD 556-20, 1102-3, 1106-19,
1112-1, 1112-3, 1112-6, 1125-1, 1127-1, 1127-3,
1127-6, 1128-1, 1128-2, 1128-3, 1128-4, 1128-5,
1128-8, 1128-9, 1128-10, 1128-11, 1128-13,
1141-1, 1622-4, 1622-10, 1658-132, 1676-26,
2346-2
Hospital (general), ME 1249-9, 1976-5, 2826-7
Hospital (general), mentally disabled 1467-6,
1658-134, 2386-35, 2560-20
Hospital (general), Mexico 2743-2
Hospital (general), MI 556-2, 556-6, 1316-1, 1323-6,
1329-15, 1331-5, 1343-11, 1343-18, 1381-1,

1381-6, 1381-10, 1381-11, 1882-20, 1882-21,
2562-6, 2826-6, 2977-4, 3292-3
Hospital (general), minorities 1658-153, 2236-6,
2236-7
Hospital (general), MN 556-12, 981-6, 1410-5,
1410-6, 1410-7, 1411-9, 1457-1, 1475-19,
1596-10, 1615-5, 1633-8, 1658-1, 1658-104,
1658-107, 1676-30, 1676-31, 1676-32, 2470-1,
3275-5
Hospital (general), MO 556-21, 1497-4, 1497-9,
1532-2, 1569-7, 1569-8
Hospital (general), MT 396-2, 1633-11, 1658-151,
1658-214
Hospital (general), NC 1331-2, 1676-18, 1869-5,
2179-2, 2203-1, 2378-7, 2386-2, 2386-55,
2386-57, 2386-152, 2386-157, 2393-3, 2393-7,
2393-8, 3056-1, 3194-7
Hospital (general), ND 1658-213, 1980-48
Hospital (general), Netherlands 2146-90
Hospital (general), NH 1153-7, 1607-6, 1676-17,
1762-5
Hospital (general), NJ 1657-9, 1657-17, 1657-18,
1657-20, 1657-22, 1657-23, 1657-24, 1657-27,
1657-30, 1657-39, 1658-170, 1661-29, 1661-38,
1676-22, 1676-38, 1676-39, 1676-51, 1676-62,
1699-2, 1699-3, 1702-4, 1702-10, 1702-13,
1702-18, 1702-19, 1723-7, 1723-15, 1723-21,
1723-22, 1723-29, 1762-16, 1762-27, 1762-30,
1879-19, 1886-2, 1946-22, 2001-5, 2001-9,
2179-4, 2212-2, 2216-5, 2668-1, 2808-21
Hospital (general), Norway 2146-75
Hospital (general), NV 213-14, 213-16, 213-17
Hospital (general), NY 213-11, 237-26, 237-31, 316-5,
436-2, 583-34, 589-4, 737-3, 1038-7, 1102-2,
1633-14, 1633-17, 1661-43, 1676-43, 1723-16,
1723-20, 1731-6, 1731-9, 1746-22, 1750-14,
1762-3, 1778-15, 1778-17, 1809-10, 1809-31,
1809-43, 1813-4, 1815-7, 1826-6, 1826-7, 1838-3,
1838-5, 1849-7, 1849-8, 1869-6, 1874-27,
1874-30, 1874-34, 1879-25, 1898-4, 1909-2,
1940-1, 1948-20, 1948-24, 1948-25, 1948-32,
1948-39, 1948-41, 1956-2, 1957-1, 1957-3,
1973-4, 1973-7, 1973-8, 1976-2, 1976-6, 1976-9,
1982-7, 1982-8, 1985-2, 1985-4, 1986-3, 1986-8,
2001-1, 2001-4, 2001-7, 2001-8, 2001-12,
2001-13, 2001-14, 2001-15, 2001-16, 2001-17,
2003-3, 2005-1, 2041-2, 2046-2, 2051-1, 2052-2,
2052-6, 2052-11, 2052-13, 2052-14, 2052-16,
2052-17, 2052-18, 2052-19, 2052-20, 2052-23,
2052-24, 2052-25, 2052-26, 2052-27, 2052-29,
2077-10, 2078-6, 2078-8, 2115-18, 2124-2,
2125-15, 2125-28, 2129-18, 2129-25, 2134-3,
2134-12, 2135-5, 2135-6, 2151-6, 2154-1, 2179-3,
2183-1, 2203-6, 2203-8, 2216-4, 2250-2, 2250-3,
2265-1, 2285-2, 2285-3, 2309-2, 2309-17,
2309-23, 2316-5, 2316-6, 2316-7, 2316-10,
2346-1, 2562-4, 2675-10, 2799-12, 3194-5,
3194-10, 3194-11, 3194-17, 3194-18, 3194-20,
3194-23
Hospital (general), OH 265-1, 556-4, 556-10,
1658-239, 1898-11, 2466-3, 2490-3, 2521-5,
2560-5, 2560-19, 2603-8, 2603-10, 2606-4,
2610-2, 2615-6, 2615-7, 2615-9, 2708-5
Hospital (general), OK 1569-10, 1569-16, 2633-2,
2633-3
Hospital (general), OR 1658-198, 2650-3, 2660-7,
2660-8, 2660-9, 2660-17, 2661-6, 3237-4
Hospital (general), PA 556-19, 988-6, 1658-192,
1661-51, 1762-21, 1948-6, 1975-14, 2288-5,
2668-2, 2668-10, 2668-26, 2668-32, 2675-1,
2677-7, 2677-13, 2677-14, 2707-3, 2707-5,
2722-5, 2748-7, 2748-8, 2748-9, 2762-12,
2762-14, 2791-10, 2801-3, 2808-18, 2808-31,
2810-3, 2810-5, 2810-8, 2837-1, 2977-2
Hospital (general), People with AIDS (PWA) 1691-9,
2146-6, 2701-6
Hospital (general), physically disabled 208-13
Hospital (general), PR 2743-13
Hospital (general), professorships 396-5, 947-24,
2521-8
Hospital (general), publication 1658-167, 1658-234,
1975-3, 2386-61

Hospital (general), research 194-17, 208-2, 426-3,
1346-4, 1658-31, 1658-41, 1658-66, 1658-80,
1658-120, 1658-131, 1658-166, 1658-167,
1658-197, 1658-234, 1658-243, 1658-305,
1860-8, 1860-28, 1860-37, 1975-11, 2093-29,
2146-11, 2245-9, 2386-63, 2645-4, 2806-54
Hospital (general), RI 631-20, 2882-15, 2882-22
Hospital (general), SC 23-3, 1723-28, 1898-9,
1898-10, 2386-20, 2636-5, 2889-2, 2904-2
Hospital (general), scholarships 80-3, 316-21, 1147-2,
1179-5, 1235-6, 2235-19, 3045-3
Hospital (general), seed money 1695-12, 2146-58,
2386-11, 2386-25, 2386-35, 2386-38, 2386-49,
2386-75, 2386-78, 2386-87, 2386-123, 2386-147,
2386-158, 2784-8
Hospital (general), single parents 3302-11
Hospital (general), student aid 3009-17
Hospital (general), technical aid 1658-80, 1658-116,
1658-175, 1658-221, 1975-3, 2236-33
Hospital (general), TN 737-14, 737-19, 1658-297
Hospital (general), TX 450-8, 583-2, 737-11, 1309-2,
1569-1, 1569-6, 1569-18, 1762-15, 2093-11,
2668-3, 2668-27, 2696-7, 2946-1, 2948-9,
2948-12, 2948-13, 2948-16, 2948-19, 2959-11,
2965-7, 2972-5, 2972-23, 2972-27, 2972-36,
2975-7, 2975-8, 2989-2, 2989-4, 3030-1, 3030-5,
3037-24, 3046-5, 3096-1, 3096-3, 3104-14,
3112-3, 3112-6, 3112-7, 3112-8, 3130-4, 3130-6
Hospital (general), UT 1658-109, 1658-283, 2661-4,
2661-5, 2852-21
Hospital (general), VA 1976-10, 3194-8
Hospital (general), VT 1658-61, 1658-298
Hospital (general), WA 556-17, 2668-16, 3104-12,
3223-6, 3240-2, 3250-8, 3250-10, 3250-19,
3250-20, 3250-21
Hospital (general), WI 947-60, 1410-9, 1411-7,
1475-16, 1658-216, 2819-5, 2819-10, 2989-3,
3292-7, 3292-8, 3312-3, 3312-6
Hospital (general), women 741-79, 1358-4, 1691-9,
2386-9, 2386-29, 2386-39, 2386-48, 2386-99,
2386-102, 2386-139, 2725-6, 3098-14, 3302-11
Hospital (general), WV 2812-13
Hospital (general), youth 2386-35, 3275-2
Hospital (psychiatric) 1879-25
Hospital (psychiatric), building/renovation 629-2,
715-4, 740-11, 2457-3, 2852-9
Hospital (psychiatric), capital campaigns 740-11
Hospital (psychiatric), children & youth 740-11,
2457-3, 2852-9
Hospital (psychiatric), equipment 2657-8
Hospital (psychiatric), faculty/staff development 696-5
Hospital (psychiatric), mentally disabled 629-2, 688-1,
696-5, 715-4, 740-11, 1158-5, 1173-1, 2410-60,
2457-3, 2657-8, 2808-11, 2852-9
Hospital (psychiatric), research 1769-7
Hospital (psychiatric), seed money 2657-8
Hospital (specialty), aging 1363-13, 2245-7, 2386-114
Hospital (specialty), blind 2627-4, 2743-10, 2762-4
Hospital (specialty), building/renovation 1-1, 57-9,
313-1, 348-3, 369-3, 629-3, 693-2, 746-3, 752-3,
840-2, 840-6, 1336-1, 1353-5, 1353-8, 1353-9,
1353-10, 1353-12, 1353-16, 1353-23, 1353-31,
1651-6, 1651-9, 1879-4, 2386-114, 2386-142,
2449-4, 2490-2, 2627-5, 2631-4, 2631-5, 2720-6,
2720-16, 2743-10, 2743-25, 2749-3, 2852-17,
2853-3, 2963-5, 2970-5, 2980-7, 3009-8, 3037-27,
3048-13, 3064-1, 3094-6, 3148-7
Hospital (specialty), CA 175-1, 253-16, 318-7, 1601-5
Hospital (specialty), capital campaigns 23-1, 137-1,
164-5, 400-20, 693-2, 840-6, 1601-2, 1601-3,
1849-5, 1981-9, 2288-14, 2449-2, 2449-4, 2745-3,
2791-11, 2809-15, 3004-1, 3115-6, 3130-7
Hospital (specialty), children & youth 1-1, 18-3, 23-1,
47-1, 47-2, 57-9, 80-4, 95-1, 137-1, 164-5, 208-3,
247-1, 253-7, 253-19, 262-11, 288-24, 288-48,
291-3, 313-1, 348-3, 364-2, 367-1, 369-3, 400-20,
440-5, 444-1, 455-1, 551-7, 556-3, 556-16, 587-4,
587-8, 590-2, 607-1, 620-5, 629-3, 631-18, 664-6,
686-9, 693-2, 742-3, 742-5, 820-12, 828-8, 840-2,
867-1, 911-1, 927-7, 947-67, 981-4, 1057-4,
1106-11, 1112-7, 1127-7, 1153-6, 1162-10, 1249-3,
1273-1, 1288-2, 1329-5, 1329-6, 1336-1, 1343-7,
1346-2, 1353-5, 1353-8, 1353-9, 1353-10,

821-8, 887-4, 937-24, 1235-3, 1351-56, 1351-62, 1351-83, 1351-146, 1351-209, 1497-6, 1684-14, 1684-16, 1829-31, 1829-45, 1851-9, 1870-9, 1879-37, 1885-39, 1975-4, 2115-19, 2224-201, 2288-23, 2386-60, 2410-20, 2447-6, 2806-65, 2808-14, 2980-5, 3048-6, 3064-8, 3064-20, 3094-7, 3237-5

Medicine/medical care, internships 1351-120, 1351-189

Medicine/medical care, land acquisition 290-3

Medicine/medical care, management/technical aid 164-8, 194-35, 194-64, 302-11, 374-7, 374-8, 561-68, 561-74, 887-9, 887-29, 887-30, 937-27, 1162-3, 1351-3, 1351-11, 1351-24, 1351-28, 1351-36, 1351-38, 1351-57, 1351-63, 1351-126, 1351-170, 1351-177, 1351-178, 1351-181, 1351-182, 1351-185, 1351-188, 1351-197, 1351-200, 1351-210, 1351-211, 1351-224, 1363-24, 1421-25, 1658-85, 1719-9, 1829-29, 1842-12, 1860-29, 1885-46, 1922-15, 1922-21, 1922-54, 1922-96, 1922-97, 1922-100, 1980-24, 2129-25, 2146-70, 2146-77, 2199-7, 2224-4, 2224-83, 2236-33

Medicine/medical care, men 1351-128, 2154-15, 3009-3

Medicine/medical care, mentally disabled 194-16, 302-7, 351-7, 371-13, 937-21, 937-38, 1235-5, 1235-10, 1235-16, 1235-17, 1235-19, 1658-35, 1658-114, 1980-15, 1981-33, 2560-16, 2744-10, 2745-2, 2806-96, 2809-13, 3037-38, 3069-11, 3098-29, 3224-7

Medicine/medical care, migrant workers 1351-126, 1684-8

Medicine/medical care, minorities 194-15, 194-18, 194-64, 194-70, 288-17, 374-6, 561-72, 561-74, 937-12, 1351-62, 1363-16, 1684-4, 1826-1, 1870-9, 1885-46, 2011-10, 2147-1, 2236-7, 2745-5

Medicine/medical care, Native Americans 106-3, 400-24, 977-5, 1351-91

Medicine/medical care, offenders/ex-offenders 302-3, 561-5, 1684-13

Medicine/medical care, outpatient care 70-11, 123-20, 142-1, 194-14, 194-52, 194-53, 194-61, 224-7, 224-15, 237-1, 237-12, 262-10, 269-2, 290-3, 316-3, 318-6, 406-18, 448-8, 511-2, 561-21, 561-89, 594-11, 690-5, 820-18, 848-9, 848-19, 927-20, 1095-4, 1106-5, 1112-2, 1127-2, 1128-6, 1158-2, 1158-3, 1216-3, 1351-7, 1351-8, 1351-19, 1351-20, 1351-25, 1351-29, 1351-35, 1351-38, 1351-42, 1351-44, 1351-45, 1351-46, 1351-47, 1351-48, 1351-49, 1351-53, 1351-65, 1351-68, 1351-77, 1351-78, 1351-92, 1351-93, 1351-94, 1351-95, 1351-96, 1351-97, 1351-98, 1351-99, 1351-100, 1351-102, 1351-103, 1351-106, 1351-108, 1351-109, 1351-110, 1351-111, 1351-112, 1351-113, 1351-114, 1351-122, 1351-124, 1351-127, 1351-129, 1351-130, 1351-131, 1351-132, 1351-133, 1351-134, 1351-135, 1351-141, 1351-152, 1351-153, 1351-156, 1351-157, 1351-172, 1351-173, 1351-178, 1351-189, 1351-196, 1351-201, 1351-203, 1351-204, 1351-205, 1351-208, 1351-210, 1351-213, 1351-214, 1351-215, 1353-13, 1353-18, 1353-25, 1384-15, 1417-1, 1417-7, 1447-14, 1454-3, 1457-4, 1457-8, 1467-5, 1475-5, 1475-10, 1657-6, 1657-35, 1658-51, 1658-93, 1658-200, 1691-21, 1695-12, 1732-4, 1746-6, 1746-26, 1750-6, 1762-8, 1800-12, 1809-11, 1829-27, 1838-4, 1885-17, 1885-37, 1885-78, 1885-79, 1980-20, 1980-23, 1982-3, 2001-2, 2015-3, 2023-2, 2052-5, 2052-8, 2076-1, 2129-6, 2135-3, 2146-15, 2146-35, 2146-70, 2171-5, 2224-4, 2224-104, 2224-215, 2245-10, 2316-4, 2386-81, 2386-109, 2386-136, 2410-32, 2410-63, 2410-69, 2410-70, 2410-71, 2460-16, 2490-8, 2560-16, 2660-10, 2720-11, 2743-1, 2744-16, 2745-1, 2806-4, 2806-127, 2809-2, 2812-2, 2826-8, 2977-3, 3005-11, 3094-9, 3099-3, 3224-3, 3282-9

Medicine/medical care, patient services 57-25, 80-5, 156-4, 177-1, 213-13, 224-9, 232-6, 237-38, 288-16, 288-17, 288-30, 288-31, 288-44, 288-52, 288-79, 316-9, 321-24, 369-8, 396-1, 500-13,

574-3, 631-17, 715-2, 772-14, 772-24, 772-25, 947-38, 982-1, 999-4, 1052-3, 1106-2, 1329-11, 1331-4, 1332-7, 1353-11, 1384-2, 1651-11, 1661-15, 1684-12, 1746-9, 1746-16, 1746-18, 1778-8, 1778-16, 1823-1, 1826-12, 1849-4, 1870-5, 1879-9, 1879-10, 1882-2, 1897-1, 1948-17, 1980-13, 1980-33, 1982-9, 1986-4, 2125-11, 2236-7, 2236-42, 2245-3, 2250-4, 2288-10, 2308-2, 2308-3, 2410-36, 2410-47, 2631-7, 2677-11, 2743-18, 2784-9, 2791-5, 2823-7, 2840-2, 2925-9, 2925-10, 2948-7, 2996-3, 2996-6, 2996-10, 2996-11, 3064-6, 3224-7, 3224-12, 3312-5

Medicine/medical care, People with AIDS (PWA) 142-1, 194-30, 224-7, 287-3, 302-3, 316-3, 406-18, 448-7, 561-1, 561-2, 561-74, 821-8, 887-30, 1684-3, 1684-5, 1684-7, 1684-8, 1684-12, 1684-13, 1684-14, 1684-16, 1684-19, 1746-26, 1750-6, 1762-8, 1885-18, 1885-37, 1922-64, 2023-2, 2076-1, 2115-4, 2115-14, 2115-15, 2115-19, 2129-4, 2146-15, 2146-35, 2146-69, 2147-7, 2171-5, 2236-42, 2316-4, 2373-6, 2373-11, 3302-1

Medicine/medical care, performance/productions 1684-17, 1885-37

Medicine/medical care, physically disabled 125-2, 237-23, 253-8, 335-1, 371-13, 396-1, 433-6, 561-52, 583-9, 629-26, 686-10, 715-12, 742-6, 1532-4, 1599-20, 1800-15, 1946-9, 1978-7, 1980-6, 1981-48, 2011-4, 2011-10, 2134-11, 2457-11, 2603-4, 2612-3, 2615-3, 2615-4, 2631-18, 2660-6, 2808-15, 2852-25, 2941-22, 2948-6, 2961-3, 3037-2, 3037-27, 3037-28, 3064-1, 3094-12, 3098-24, 3104-11

Medicine/medical care, professorships 1879-27

Medicine/medical care, public education 110-9, 183-18, 183-24, 208-2, 224-11, 288-52, 288-53, 302-3, 361-7, 364-1, 373-2, 374-6, 374-9, 389-9, 406-4, 439-1, 561-2, 561-5, 561-93, 561-118, 814-2, 848-2, 893-24, 937-7, 937-8, 937-32, 988-2, 1128-7, 1158-12, 1173-4, 1351-75, 1351-91, 1351-120, 1351-125, 1351-128, 1351-202, 1497-3, 1630-13, 1658-300, 1684-3, 1684-4, 1684-5, 1684-6, 1684-7, 1684-8, 1684-9, 1684-12, 1684-13, 1684-14, 1684-16, 1684-17, 1684-19, 1684-20, 1719-7, 1723-18, 1799-1, 1809-32, 1829-1, 1870-14, 1885-75, 1922-54, 1922-66, 1946-3, 1980-29, 1980-46, 1981-8, 2117-6, 2146-73, 2154-16, 2179-1, 2199-9, 2236-36, 2288-4, 2373-11, 2386-101, 2386-170, 2562-1, 2683-19, 2683-21, 2748-1, 2824-1, 2899-3, 2972-19, 3009-3, 3048-10, 3104-1, 3194-9, 3302-1

Medicine/medical care, public policy 183-18, 183-24, 194-4, 194-10, 194-12, 194-16, 194-19, 194-28, 194-29, 194-32, 194-34, 194-36, 194-38, 194-39, 194-45, 194-47, 194-50, 194-51, 194-53, 194-54, 194-59, 194-64, 194-68, 194-69, 194-72, 262-19, 321-26, 364-33, 364-34, 406-19, 439-3, 561-43, 561-57, 561-93, 787-4, 787-6, 820-6, 848-15, 887-15, 927-6, 937-2, 937-9, 937-12, 937-14, 937-15, 937-21, 937-26, 1173-4, 1173-7, 1309-3, 1351-2, 1351-50, 1351-145, 1351-190, 1363-8, 1456-2, 1611-4, 1630-6, 1630-18, 1637-1, 1657-13, 1658-81, 1658-82, 1658-84, 1658-94, 1658-146, 1658-158, 1658-161, 1658-242, 1658-255, 1658-256, 1658-269, 1676-67, 1676-68, 1691-15, 1691-29, 1829-14, 1829-17, 1851-1, 1851-2, 1860-18, 1860-29, 1860-37, 1860-38, 1870-23, 1922-20, 1922-64, 1959-15, 1959-16, 1959-33, 1975-7, 1975-8, 2000-5, 2011-2, 2011-9, 2011-13, 2011-20, 2146-19, 2146-82, 2213-1, 2224-80, 2224-81, 2236-8, 2410-20, 2410-61, 2668-12, 2806-14, 2806-38, 2806-39, 2806-47, 2806-82, 2806-107, 2808-8, 2809-18, 2925-16, 3064-22

Medicine/medical care, publication 57-2, 164-2, 194-18, 194-29, 194-59, 194-69, 374-6, 561-5, 937-2, 937-12, 1351-192, 1658-14, 1658-56, 1658-72, 1658-81, 1658-127, 1658-138, 1658-167, 1658-194, 1658-234, 1658-272, 1658-292, 1684-20, 1719-9, 1829-14, 1851-2, 1870-5, 1922-64, 1959-15, 1959-33, 2011-20,

2224-201, 2447-6, 2806-65, 2925-19, 3064-8, 3069-12, 3094-7

Medicine/medical care, rehabilitation 70-2, 99-5, 125-2, 177-5, 212-7, 236-1, 237-23, 253-8, 265-10, 290-7, 335-1, 336-2, 367-7, 369-2, 371-13, 406-15, 433-6, 444-2, 500-1, 510-1, 523-3, 535-25, 561-52, 583-9, 583-33, 587-6, 631-11, 686-10, 690-3, 690-4, 696-6, 715-12, 742-6, 746-3, 749-6, 751-1, 752-3, 774-3, 814-1, 840-7, 887-31, 891-7, 893-6, 893-10, 927-14, 927-15, 927-16, 927-17, 927-18, 939-6, 947-16, 947-17, 947-22, 947-41, 947-57, 981-10, 999-6, 1106-7, 1106-14, 1162-10, 1218-13, 1235-5, 1235-10, 1235-16, 1235-17, 1235-19, 1265-1, 1309-6, 1329-7, 1336-9, 1343-3, 1351-26, 1353-6, 1353-28, 1358-5, 1381-8, 1447-4, 1523-1, 1532-4, 1599-20, 1611-20, 1651-7, 1658-114, 1661-20, 1661-52, 1732-2, 1762-13, 1800-6, 1800-15, 1849-6, 1879-5, 1879-11, 1882-25, 1898-1, 1922-91, 1946-6, 1946-9, 1946-11, 1946-12, 1948-5, 1959-7, 1978-7, 1980-6, 1980-15, 1980-25, 1981-13, 1981-19, 1981-33, 1981-48, 2011-4, 2011-10, 2011-18, 2052-3, 2052-22, 2078-5, 2125-13, 2134-11, 2146-84, 2171-3, 2181-2, 2288-21, 2288-22, 2430-2, 2457-11, 2490-5, 2490-7, 2545-9, 2547-1, 2547-6, 2603-4, 2612-3, 2615-2, 2615-3, 2615-4, 2627-2, 2631-18, 2660-3, 2660-6, 2666-1, 2668-8, 2668-11, 2668-23, 2668-24, 2677-4, 2696-1, 2720-6, 2720-7, 2720-8, 2720-16, 2743-9, 2743-12, 2743-25, 2745-3, 2749-3, 2762-3, 2762-5, 2784-4, 2791-11, 2803-5, 2806-28, 2806-60, 2806-96, 2806-97, 2808-4, 2808-6, 2808-15, 2809-15, 2810-4, 2810-7, 2812-4, 2812-6, 2831-16, 2852-15, 2852-25, 2853-3, 2853-6, 2857-16, 2868-19, 2893-2, 2912-5, 2912-6, 2941-22, 2948-6, 2961-3, 2965-5, 2972-15, 2980-4, 3030-2, 3037-2, 3037-38, 3064-1, 3069-5, 3069-11, 3069-12, 3094-12, 3096-2, 3098-10, 3098-24, 3098-29, 3104-11, 3112-5, 3237-2, 3237-3, 3302-9, 3306-15

Medicine/medical care, research 30-5, 183-24, 194-4, 194-15, 194-16, 194-18, 194-28, 194-30, 194-32, 194-34, 194-36, 194-38, 194-39, 194-48, 194-55, 194-68, 194-70, 208-2, 262-10, 262-19, 302-3, 302-19, 321-24, 321-26, 321-29, 348-17, 364-5, 364-13, 373-1, 561-43, 561-93, 583-3, 774-3, 787-4, 787-5, 787-6, 848-15, 887-15, 887-23, 887-34, 937-9, 937-12, 937-14, 937-15, 937-26, 937-34, 937-35, 937-38, 937-42, 947-57, 1057-6, 1235-5, 1235-10, 1235-16, 1235-17, 1235-19, 1343-3, 1343-16, 1351-123, 1351-184, 1351-192, 1363-8, 1456-2, 1607-2, 1658-7, 1658-14, 1658-29, 1658-31, 1658-35, 1658-41, 1658-56, 1658-66, 1658-67, 1658-68, 1658-72, 1658-80, 1658-82, 1658-91, 1658-96, 1658-97, 1658-98, 1658-100, 1658-120, 1658-127, 1658-131, 1658-133, 1658-138, 1658-141, 1658-163, 1658-166, 1658-167, 1658-194, 1658-197, 1658-234, 1658-240, 1658-243, 1658-246, 1658-249, 1658-256, 1658-266, 1658-272, 1658-277, 1658-284, 1658-291, 1658-302, 1658-305, 1658-314, 1676-29, 1691-15, 1691-29, 1829-1, 1829-14, 1829-15, 1829-18, 1829-30, 1829-33, 1842-9, 1850-6, 1851-1, 1860-1, 1860-2, 1860-8, 1860-12, 1860-18, 1860-19, 1860-20, 1860-21, 1860-28, 1860-29, 1860-31, 1860-32, 1860-34, 1860-37, 1860-40, 1879-2, 1885-75, 1922-20, 1922-28, 1922-64, 1922-70, 1922-95, 1922-97, 1922-105, 1959-15, 1959-33, 1975-4, 1975-5, 1975-6, 1975-7, 1975-10, 1975-12, 2011-2, 2011-4, 2011-9, 2083-8, 2083-12, 2146-22, 2146-76, 2146-82, 2154-11, 2154-15, 2199-1, 2224-104, 2245-9, 2273-1, 2288-23, 2308-2, 2377-8, 2377-30, 2386-63, 2410-61, 2410-62, 2457-15, 2744-10, 2745-2, 2745-5, 2806-2, 2806-37, 2806-39, 2806-47, 2806-76, 2806-87, 2806-107, 2806-117, 2806-138, 2809-13, 2812-1, 2889-2, 2925-16, 2925-19, 3037-36, 3048-9, 3112-4

Medicine/medical care, scholarships 125-1, 426-8, 426-10, 426-11, 1719-9, 2743-17, 3037-16

NATIONAL GUIDE TO FUNDING IN HEALTH

INDEX OF FOUNDATIONS AND CORPORATE
GIVING PROGRAMS

McKenna Foundation, Inc., Katherine Mabis, PA, 2786
McKesson Foundation, Inc., CA, 232
McKesson Service Merchandising, AR, 49
McKnight Endowment Fund for Neuroscience, The, MN, 1453
McKnight Foundation, The, MN, 1454
McLean Contributionship, The, PA, 2787
McMahan Foundation, Catherine L. & Robert O., The, CA, 233
McMicking Foundation, CA, 234
McMillan Foundation, D. W., AL, 17
McMillan, Jr. Foundation, Inc., Bruce, TX, 3062
McQueen Foundation of 1960, Adeline and George, TX, 3063
Mead Corporate Giving Program, The, OH, 2531
Meadowood Foundation, MN, 1455
Meadows Foundation, Inc., TX, 3064
Measey Foundation, Benjamin and Mary Siddons, The, PA, 2788
Mechanic Foundation, Inc., Morris A., The, MD, 1126
Mechia Foundation, TX, 3065
Medtronic Foundation, The, MN, 1456
Medusa Corporate Giving Program, OH, 2532
Mellam Family Foundation, NY, 2105
Mellon Bank Corporate Giving Program, PA, 2789
Mellon Bank Foundation, PA, 2790
Mellon Foundation, Andrew W., The, NY, 2106
Mellon Foundation, Richard King, PA, 2791
Melly Foundation, L. Thomas, NY, 2107
Melrose Foundation, Inc., TN, 2931
Memorial Fund, Inc., NY, 2108
Memton Fund, Inc., The, NY, 2109
Menasha Corporation Foundation, WI, 3303
Mendik Foundation, The, NY, 2110
Mengle Foundation, Glenn and Ruth, PA, 2792
Menschel Foundation, Robert and Joyce, The, NY, 2111
Mercantile Trust Company Charitable Trust, MO, 1550
Mercedes-Benz of North America, NJ, 1674
Merck & Company Corporate Giving Program, NJ, 1675
Merck Company Foundation, The, NJ, 1676
Merck Family Fund, NJ, 1677
Merck Fund, John, The, MA, 1235
Mercy, Jr. Foundation, Sue and Eugene, The, NY, 2112
Mericos Foundation, CA, 235
Meriden Foundation, The, CT, 467
Meridian Foundation, PA, 2793
Merit Gasoline Foundation, The, PA, 2794
Merkert Foundation, E. F., The, MA, 1236
Merrell Dow Pharmaceuticals Corporate Giving Program, OH, 2533
Merrick Foundation, The, OK, 2630
Merrick Foundation, Inc., Robert G. and Anne M., MD, 1127
Merrill Lynch & Company Foundation, Inc., NY, 2113
Merrill Lynch & Company, Inc. Corporate Contributions Program, NY, 2114
Mertz-Gilmore Foundation, Joyce, NY, 2115
Messing Foundation, Morris M. and Helen F., The, FL, 638
Metcalf Foundation, Inc., Stanley W., NY, 2116
Metropolitan Health Council of Indianapolis, Inc., The, IN, 1003
Metropolitan Health Foundation, Inc., VA, 3193
Metropolitan Life Foundation, NY, 2117
Meyer Charitable Trust, Fred see 2657
Meyer Foundation, The, NY, 2118
Meyer Foundation, Alice Kleberg Reynolds, TX, 3066
Meyer Foundation, Baron de Hirsch, The, FL, 639
Meyer Foundation, Eugene and Agnes E., DC, 557
Meyer Foundation, Robert R., AL, 18
Meyer Memorial Foundation, Inc., Aaron and Rachel, NJ, 1678
Meyer Memorial Trust, OR, 2657
Meyer-Ceco Foundation, The, IL, 896
Michael Foundation, Herbert I. and Elsa B., UT, 3151
Michigan National Corporate Contributions Program, MI, 1359
Microwave Associates Communities Foundation see 1231
Mid-Iowa Health Foundation, IA, 1025
MidCon Corporate Giving Program, IL, 897
Middlecott Foundation, MA, 1237
Midlantic Corporate Giving Program, NJ, 1679

Mielke Family Foundation, Inc., WI, 3304
Milbank Foundation, Inc., Dunlevy, The, NY, 2119
Milbank Memorial Fund, NY, 2120
Milbro Charitable Foundation, IL, 898
Miles Foundation, IN, 1004
Miles Inc. Foundation, PA, 2795
Miles Laboratories Foundation see 1004
Milken Family Foundation, The see 99
Milken Family Foundation, The, CA, 236
Milken Family Medical Foundation, CA, 237
Milken Foundation, L. and S., CA, 238
Millbrook Tribute Garden, Inc., NY, 2121
Miller Charitable Trust, Lewis N., OH, 2534
Miller Corporate Giving Program, WI, 3305
Miller Foundation, Earl B. & Loraine H., CA, 239
Miller Fund, Inc., Kathryn & Gilbert, NY, 2122
Miller Memorial Trust, George Lee, OH, 2535
Milliken Foundation, Agnes G., The, DE, 526
Millikin Trust, James, IL, 899
Millipore Foundation, The, MA, 1238
Mills Charitable Foundation, Henry L. & Kathryn, FL, 640
Mills Foundation, Ralph E., KY, 1062
Mills Fund, Frances Goll, MI, 1360
Millstein Charitable Foundation, The, PA, 2796
Milstein Family Foundation, Inc., NY, 2123
Milwaukee Foundation, WI, 3306
Mingenback Foundation, Inc., Julia J., The, KS, 1040
Minneapolis Foundation, The, MN, 1457
Minnesota Mining and Manufacturing Company Contributions Program, MN, 1458
Minnesota Mining and Manufacturing Foundation, Inc., MN, 1459
Mitchell Energy and Development Corporate Contributions Program, TX, 3067
Mitchell Family Foundation, Bernard & Marjorie, IL, 900
Mitchell Family Foundation, Wildey H., MN, 1460
Mitchell Foundation, Inc., The, AL, 19
MNC Financial Foundation, Inc., MD, 1128
Mobil Foundation, Inc., VA, 3194
Mobile Community Foundation, The, AL, 20
Mohawk-Hudson Community Foundation, Inc., NY, 2124
Monarch Capital Corporate Giving Program, MA, 1239
Monarch Machine Tool Company Foundation, OH, 2536
Moncrief Foundation, William A. and Elizabeth B., TX, 3068
Monell Foundation, Ambrose, The, NY, 2125
Monfort Charitable Foundation, CO, 384
Monroe Auto Equipment Company Giving Program, MI, 1361
Monroe Foundation (1976), J. Edgar, LA, 1081
Monterey County, Community Foundation for, CA, 240
Monterey Fund, Inc., NY, 2126
Monterey Peninsula Golf Foundation, CA, 241
Montgomery Street Foundation, CA, 242
MONY Financial Services Foundation see 2140
Moody Foundation, The, TX, 3069
Moore Family Foundation, CA, 243
Moore Foundation, Alfred, SC, 2896
Moore Foundation, Inc., Edward S., NY, 2127
Moore Memorial Foundation, Inc., James Starr, GA, 727
Moores Foundation, Harry C., The, OH, 2537
Moorman Company Fund, IL, 901
Morgan and Company Corporate Giving Program, J. P., NY, 2128
Morgan Foundation, Inc., Burton D., OH, 2538
Morgan Foundation, Inc., Roy T., The, RI, 2879
Morgan Guaranty Trust Company of New York Charitable Trust, NY, 2129
Morgan Stanley Foundation, NY, 2130
Morgan Stanley Group Corporate Giving Program, NY, 2131
Morgan, Jr. Foundation, Marietta McNeil Morgan & Samuel Tate, VA, 3195
Morgenstern Foundation, Morris, NY, 2132
Moriah Fund, IN, 1005
Morley Brothers Foundation, MI, 1362
Morris Foundation, The, TX, 3070
Morris Foundation, Margaret T., AZ, 37
Morris Foundation, Inc., Norman M., NY, 2133

Morris Foundation, Inc., William T., The, NY, 2134
Morrison Trust, TX, 3071
Morton International Corporate Giving Program, IL, 902
Mosbacher, Jr. Foundation, Inc., Emil, CT, 468
Moses Fund, Inc., Henry and Lucy, NY, 2135
Moss Heart Trust, Harry S., TX, 3072
Motorola Foundation, IL, 903
Mott Charitable Trust, Stewart R., NY, 2136
Mott Charitable Trust/Spectemur Agendo, Stewart R. see 2136
Mott Foundation, Charles Stewart, MI, 1363
Mott Fund, Ruth, MI, 1364
Mount Vernon Community Trust, The, OH, 2539
Mountain Bell Foundation see 400
MPCo/Entech Foundation, Inc., MT, 1583
Muchnic Foundation, KS, 1041
Mudge Foundation, PA, 2797
Mullan Foundation, Inc., Thomas F. and Clementine L., The, MD, 1129
Mullen Benevolent Corporation, John K. and Catherine S., The see 385
Mullen Foundation, J. K., The, CO, 385
Muller Foundation, CA, 244
Muller, Sr. Foundation, Frank see 244
Mulligan Charitable Trust, Mary S., NY, 2137
Muncie and Delaware County, Inc., Community Foundation of, The, IN, 1006
Munger Foundation, Alfred C., CA, 245
Murch Foundation, The, OH, 2540
Murcott Charitable Trust, Charles & Constance, NY, 2138
Murdock Charitable Trust, M. J., WA, 3237
Murdough Foundation, The, OH, 2541
Murdough Foundation, Thomas G. & Joy P. see 2541
Murfee Endowment, Kathryn, TX, 3073
Murphey Foundation, Lluella Morey, CA, 246
Murphy Company Foundation, G. C., PA, 2798
Murphy Foundation, Dan, CA, 247
Murphy Foundation, John P., OH, 2542
Murphy Foundation, Katherine John, GA, 728
Murray Foundation, WA, 3238
Murray Foundation for Eye Research, Inc., The, NY, 2139
Murray, Jr. Foundation, Inc., John P. see 2139
Muskegon County Community Foundation, Inc., MI, 1365
Musson Charitable Foundation, R. C. and Katharine M., OH, 2543
Mutual Benefit Life Insurance Company Giving Program, NJ, 1680
Mutual Of New York Foundation, NY, 2140
Myers-Ti-Caro Foundation, Inc. see 2391
Myra Foundation, ND, 2428

Nabisco Brands Corporate Giving Program, NJ, 1681
Nabisco Foundation, NJ, 1682
Nalco Chemical Company Giving Program, IL, 904
Nalco Foundation, The, IL, 905
Napier Foundation, The, NY, 2141
Nathan Foundation, Inc., MD, 1130
Nation Foundation, TX, 3074
National Biscuit Company Foundation Trust, The see 1682
National Central Foundation, The see 2738
National City Corporate Giving Program, OH, 2544
National Fuel Gas Corporate Giving Program, NY, 2142
National Gypsum Company Foundation, The, TX, 3075
National Life Insurance Corporate Contributions Program, VT, 3158
National Medical Enterprises Corporate Giving Program, CA, 248
National Semiconductor Corporate Giving Program, CA, 249
National Service Foundation, GA, 729
National Starch and Chemical Foundation, Inc., NJ, 1683
Nationwide Insurance Foundation, OH, 2545
Navarro Community Foundation, TX, 3076
Navistar Foundation, IL, 906
NEBS Corporate Giving Program, MA, 1240
Neenah Foundry Foundation, Inc., WI, 3307
Neese Family Foundation, Inc., The, IL, 907